Published by

The Dallas Morning News

2 0 0 0 - 2 0 0 1
TEXAS ALMANAC

TABLE OF CONTENTS

Mary G. Ramos, Editor
Robert Plocheck, Associate Editor
Steve Chambers, Cover Design

The
Difference Between

THEN

J.J. Haverty opened his first furniture store in Atlanta in **1885**...a **25 x 75 foot** showroom! He succeeded by offering fine home furnishings, fairly priced, along with **"special terms for responsible people"**! Mr Haverty understood the **value of a dollar** and knew that **proper treatment of his customers** would be the cornerstone of Haverty Furniture's success.

Haverty's downtown Dallas store in the late 1930s and an early ad from The Dallas Morning News

Today, Haverty's is **still family-owned** but there are **100 showrooms** throughout the United States...and most are **50,000 sq. ft.!** We still offer the **finest quality home furnishings** at the **best price** possible along with a variety of **credit options**. And 114 years later, our top priority remains a **dedication** to providing premium **service** to our customers.

NOW

Our new Coppell showroom and today's advertising.

HAVERTYS℠
MAKES IT HOME

Texas

The Lone Star State

On this and the following page we present a demographic and geographic profile of the second-largest, second-most-populous state in the United States. Look in the index for more detailed information on each subject.

The Government

Capital: Austin
Government: Bicameral Legislature
28th State to enter the Union: Dec. 29, 1845
Present Constitution adopted: 1876
State motto: Friendship (1930)
State symbols:
  Flower: Bluebonnet (1901)
  Bird: Mockingbird (1927)
  Tree: Pecan (1919)
  Song: "Texas, Our Texas" (1929)

Origin of name: Texas, or Tejas, was the Spanish pronunciation of a Caddo Indian word meaning "friends" or "allies."

Nickname: Texas is called the Lone Star State because of the design of the state flag: a broad vertical blue stripe at left centered by a single white star, with horizontal bars of white (uppermost) and red on the right.

The People

Population (1990 U.S. Census) 16,986,510
Population (Jan. 1998 State Data Center estimate) 19,598,471
Population (July 1998 U.S. Bureau of the Census estimate) 19,760,000

Ethnicity (1990) (Please see explanation of categories on p. 130):
  White 12,775,000
  Black 2,022,000
  Asian 319,000
  American Indian 66,000
  Other 1,804,780

  Hispanic 4,340,000

Population density (1997) . . . . 74.2 per sq. mi.

Voting-age Pop., 1996. 13,622,000
(1998 Statistical Abstract of the United States, Bureau of the Census)

On an average day in Texas in 1997:

The **population** increased by 524.
There were **915** resident live **births**.
There were **391** resident **deaths**.
There were **501 marriages**.
There were **255 divorces**.
  (1997 Texas Vital Statistics, Texas Dept. of Health)

Ten largest cities:
  Houston (Harris Co.) 1,841,064
  San Antonio (Bexar Co.) 1,123,626
  Dallas (Dallas Co.) 1,085,614
  Austin (Travis Co.) 608,053
  El Paso (El Paso Co.) 600,277
  Fort Worth (Tarrant Co.) 489,277
  Arlington (Tarrant Co.) 301,991
  Corpus Christi (Nueces Co.) 276,712
  Plano (Collin Co.) 198,186
  Garland (Dallas Co.) 193,475
(Texas State Data Center estimates, Jan. 1, 1998)

Number of counties. 254
Number of incorporated cities 1,194
Number of cities of 100,000 pop. or more. 23
Number of cities of 50,000 pop. or more. 47
Number of cities of 10,000 pop. or more. 209

The Natural Environment

Area (total) . . . . 267,277 sq. miles
  (171,057,280 acres)
Land area . . . . 261,914 sq. miles
  (167,624,960 acres)
Water area . . . . 5,363 sq. miles
  (3,432,320 acres)
Forested area . . . . 22.032 million acres
State forests . . . . 5 (7,519 acres)
National forests . . . . 4 (637,386 acres)

Geographic center: About 15 miles northeast of Brady in northern McCulloch County.
Highest point: Guadalupe Peak (8,749 ft.) in Culberson County in far West Texas.
Lowest point: Gulf of Mexico (sea level).

Normal average annual precipitation range:
  From 58.3 inches at Orange, on the Gulf Coast, to 8.8 inches at El Paso, in West Texas.
111-year average precipitation . . . . **28.14"**

Record highest temperature:
  Seymour, August 12, 1936. . . . . 120°F
  Monahans, June 28, 1994. . . . . 120°F
Record lowest temperature:
  Tulia, Feb. 12, 1899. -23°F
  Seminole, Feb. 8, 1933 . . . . -23°F

Business

Gross State Product:
  In current dollars (1996) . . . . $551.8 billion
  In chained dollars (1992) . . . . $502.9 billion

Per Capita Personal Income (1997) $23,656

Civilian Labor Force (average, 1996) 9,748,000
(1998 Statistical Abstract of the United States)

Principal products:

  Manufactures: Chemicals and allied products, petroleum and coal products, food and kindred products, transportation equipment.

  Farm products: Cattle, cotton, dairy products, nursery and greenhouse.

  Minerals: Petroleum, natural gas, natural gas liquids.

Finance (as of 12/31/97):
  Number of insured commercial banks 839
  Total deposits . . . . $191.8 billion

Agriculture (1997):
  Number of farms 205,000
  Land in farms (acres) 129,000,000
  Cropland (acres, 1992) 28,261,000
  Pastureland (acres, 1992). 16,710,000
  Rangeland (acres, 1992). 94,155,000
(1998 Statistical Abstract of the United States)

Texas' Rank Among the United States

Texas' rank among the United States in selected categories are given below. Others categories are covered in other chapters in the book; i.e. Agriculture, Business and Transportation, Science and Health.
Source (unless otherwise noted): U.S. Bureau of the Census.

Ten Most Populous States, 1998

Rank		Pop. est. 1998	Pop./sq. mile of land area
1.	California	32,667,000	206.9
2.	**Texas**	**19,760,000**	**74.2**
3.	New York	18,175,000	384.1
4.	Florida	14,916,000	271.7
5.	Illinois	12,045,000	214.0
6.	Pennsylvania	12,001,000	268.2
7.	Ohio	11,209,000	273.2
8.	Michigan	9,817,000	172.0
9.	New Jersey	8,115,000	1,085.4
10.	Georgia	7,642,000	129.3
	(United States	270,299,000	75.7)

Ten Fastest-Growing States, 1997

Rank	State	Population change 1990-1997
1.	Nevada	39.5 %
2.	Arizona	24.3 %
3.	Idaho	20.2 %
4.	Utah	19.5 %
5.	Colorado	18.2 %
6.	Georgia	15.6 %
7.	Washington	15.3 %
8.	**Texas**	**14.4 %**
9.	New Mexico	14.2 %
10.	Oregon	14.1 %

States with Highest Birth Rates, 1996

Rank	State	Births per 1,000 pop.
1.	Utah	20.7
2.	Arizona	18.0
3.	**Texas**	**17.1**
4.	California	16.9
5.	Alaska	16.7
6.	Nevada	16.2
7.	Idaho	16.0
8.	New Mexico	15.9
9.	Georgia	15.6
	Illinois	15.6
	(United States	14.8)

States with Most Vehicles, 1996

Rank	State	Vehicles	Lic. drivers
1.	California	25,214,000	20,249,000
2.	**Texas**	**13,487,000**	**12,568,000**
3.	Florida	10,889,000	11,400,000
4.	New York	10,636,000	10,484,000
5.	Ohio	9,770,000	7,853,000
6.	Illinois	8,817,000	7,610,000
7.	Pennsylvania	8,640,000	8,221,000
8.	Michigan	8,010,000	6,717,000
9.	Georgia	6,283,000	4,966,000
10.	New Jersey	5,822,000	5,486,000

Source: Federal Highway Admin., Highway Statistics, annual, and Selected Highway Statistics and Charts, annual.

Miscellaneous Categories

Category	Number	Rank
Gross State Product, 1996	$551.8 billion	3
Per Capita Personal Income, 1997	$23,656	28
Violent Crime Rate per 100,000 Pop., 1996	.644	13
Child Abuse Cases Reported, 1996	99,780	4
Public School Teachers' Avg. Salaries, 1996	$33,038	35
Educational Attainment (25 years old +), 1997:		
High school graduate	78.5%	40
Bachelor's degree or higher	22.4%	24

Category	Number	Rank
Social Security Recipients, 1996	2,498,000	4
Persons Below Poverty Level, 1996	3,180,000	2
Percent below poverty level, 1996	16.6	11
Persons Without Health Insurance, 1996:		
Persons without health insurance	4,680,000	2
Percent without health insurance	24.3	1
AIDS cases reported, 1997	4,718	4
Hazardous Waste Sites, 1997	27	14
Toxic Chemical Releases, 1995	188,296	1

States with Most Farms, 1997

Rank	State	No. of farms
1.	Texas	205,000
2.	Missouri	102,000
3.	Iowa	98,000
4.	Kentucky	88,000
5.	Minnesota	87,000
6	California	84,000
7.	Tennessee	80,000
8.	Wisconsin	79,000
9.	Illinois	76,000
10.	Ohio	73,000
	Oklahoma	73,000

States with Most Land in Farms, 1997

Rank	State	Farm acreage
1.	Texas	129,000,000
2.	Montana	60,000,000
3.	Kansas	48,000,000
4.	Nebraska	47,000,000
5.	New Mexico	44,000,000
	South Dakota	44,000,000
7.	North Dakota	40,000,000
8.	Arizona	35,000,000
	Wyoming	35,000,000
10.	Oklahoma	34,000,000

State Flags and Symbols

United States, 1845-1861; 1865-Present

Republic, 1836-1845; State, 1845-Present

Spain,
1519-1685
1690-1821

Mexico,
1821-1836

France,
1685-1690

Confederacy,
1861-1865

Texas often is called the **Lone Star State** because of its state flag with a single star. This was also the **flag of the Republic of Texas**. The following information about historic Texas flags, the current flag and other Texas symbols may be supplemented by information available from the **Texas State Library**, Austin.

Six Flags of Texas

Six different flags have flown over Texas during eight changes of sovereignty. The accepted sequence of these flags follows:

Spanish — 1519-1685.
French — 1685-1690.
Spanish — 1690-1821.
Mexican — 1821-1836.
Republic of Texas — 1836-1845.
United States — 1845-1861.
Confederate States — 1861-1865.
United States — 1865 to the present.

Evolution of the Lone Star Flag

The Convention at Washington-on-the-Brazos in March 1836 allegedly adopted a flag for the Republic that was designed by Lorenzo de Zavala. The design of de Zavala's flag is unknown, but the convention journals state that a "Rainbow and star of five points above the western horizon; and a star of six points sinking below" was added to de Zavala's flag. There was a suggestion that the letters "T E X A S" be placed around the star in the flag, but there is no evidence that the Convention ever approved a final flag design. Probably because of

the hasty dispersion of the Convention and loss of part of the Convention notes, nothing further was done with the Convention's proposals for a national flag. A so-called "Zavala flag" is sometimes flown in Texas today that consists of a blue field with a white five-pointed star in the center and letters "T E X A S" between the star points, but there is no historical evidence to support this flag's design.

The **first official flag of the Republic,** known as **David G. Burnet's flag,** was adopted on Dec. 10, 1836, as the national standard, "the conformation of which shall be an azure ground with a large golden star central."

The Lone Star Flag

On Jan. 25, 1839, President Mirabeau B. Lamar approved the adoption by Congress of a new national flag. This flag consisted of "a blue perpendicular stripe of the width of one-third of the whole length of the flag, with a white star of five points in the center thereof, and two horizontal stripes of equal breadth, the upper stripe white, the lower red, of the length of two-thirds of the whole flag." This is the **Lone Star Flag,** which later became the state flag. Although Senator William H. Wharton proposed the adoption of the Lone Star Flag in 1844, no one knows who actually designed the flag. The legislature in 1879 inadvertently repealed the law establishing the state flag, but the legislature adopted a new law in 1933 that legally re-established the flag's design. The state flag's colors represent the same virtues as they do in the national flag: Red means bravery; white,

State Seal

(See information and description on next page.)

purity; and blue, loyalty.

The Texas Flag Code was first adopted in 1933 and completely revised in 1993. The following is a summary of the rules concerning the proper display of the state flag:

Flown out-of-doors, the Texas flag should not be flown earlier than sunrise nor later than sunset unless properly illuminated. It should not be left out in inclement weather unless a weatherproof flag is used. It should be flown with the white stripe uppermost except in case of distress. When the flag is displayed against a wall, the blue field should be at the flag's own right (observer's left). When the flag is displayed vertically, the blue stripe should be uppermost and the white stripe should be to the state flag's right (observer's left). The state flag should be flown on all state holidays and on special occasions of historical significance, and it should fly at every school on regular school days.

If the state and national flags are both carried in a procession, the national flag should be on the marching right (observer's left) and state flag should be on the national flag's left (observer's right). If the state and national flags are displayed from crossed staffs, the state flag should be on the national flag's left (observer's right) and behind the national flag's staff. No flag other than the national flag should be placed above or, if on the same level, to the state flag's right (observer's left). The state flag should be underneath the national flag when the two are flown from the same halyard. When flown from adjacent flagpoles, the national flag and the state flag should be of approximately the same size and on flagpoles of equal height, and the national flag should be on the flag's own right (observer's left). The state flag should neither be flown above the flags of other U.S. states, nations and international organizations on the same flagpole, nor be flown from a higher adjacent flagpole.

The state flag should never be used for any utilitarian or strictly decorative purpose. No advertising should be placed upon the flag or flagstaff, and no picture of the flag should be used in an advertisement. When the state flag is in such condition that it is no longer a suitable emblem for display, it should be destroyed, preferably by burning.

Pledge to the Texas Flag

A pledge to the Texas flag was adopted by the 43rd Legislature. It contained a phrase, "Flag of 1836," which inadvertently referred to the David G. Burnet flag instead of the Lone Star Flag adopted in 1839. In 1965, the 59th Legislature changed the pledge to its current form:

"Honor the Texas flag;
I pledge allegiance to thee,
Texas, one and indivisible."

A person reciting the pledge to the state flag should face the flag, place the right hand over the heart and remove any easily removable hat. The pledge to the Texas flag may be recited at all public and private meetings at which the pledge of allegiance to the national flag is recited and at state historical events and celebrations. The pledge to the Texas flag should be recited after the pledge of allegiance to the United States flag if both are recited.

State Song

The state song of Texas is **"Texas, Our Texas."** The music was written by the late William J. Marsh (who died Feb. 1, 1971, in Fort Worth at age 90), and the words by Marsh and Gladys Yoakum Wright, also of Fort Worth. It was the winner of a state song contest sponsored by the legislature and was adopted in 1929. The wording has been changed once: Shortly after Alaska became a state in Jan. 1959, the word "Largest" in the third line was changed by Mr. Marsh to "Boldest." The text follows:

Texas, Our Texas

Texas, our Texas! all hail the mighty State!
Texas, our Texas! So wonderful, so great!
Boldest and grandest, Withstanding ev'ry test;
O Empire wide and glorious, You stand supremely blest.

Chorus
God bless you, Texas!
And keep you brave and strong,
That you may grow in power and worth,
Thro' out the ages long.

Refrain
Texas, O Texas! Your freeborn Single Star,
Sends out its radiance To nations near and far.
Emblem of freedom! It sets our hearts aglow,
With thoughts of San Jacinto And glorious Alamo.

Texas, dear Texas! From tyrant grip now free,
Shines forth in splendor Your Star of Destiny!
Mother of Heroes! We come your children true,
Proclaiming our allegiance, Our Faith, Our Love for you.

State Motto

The state motto of Texas is **"Friendship."** The word, Texas, or Tejas, was the Spanish pronunciation of a Caddo Indian word meaning "friends" or "allies." (Acts of 1930, fourth called session of the 41st Legislature, p. 105.)

State Citizenship Designation — The people of Texas usually call themselves **Texans.** However, **Texian** was generally used in the early period of the state's history.

State Seal

The design of the obverse (front) of the Great Seal of the State of Texas consists of "a star of five points, encircled by olive and live oak branches, and the words, 'The State of Texas'." (State Constitution, Art. IV, Sec. 19.) This design is a slight modification of the Great Seal of the Republic of Texas, adopted by the Congress of the Republic, Dec. 10, 1836, and readopted with modifications in 1839. An official design for the reverse (back) of the seal was adopted by the 57th Legislature in 1961, but there were discrepancies between the written description and the artistic rendering that was adopted at the same time. To resolve the problems, the 72nd Legislature in 1991 adopted an official design "... the design for the reverse side of the Great Seal of Texas shall consist of a shield, the lower half of which is divided into two parts; on the shield's lower left is a depiction of the cannon of the Battle of Gonzales; on the shield's lower right is a depiction of Vince's Bridge; on the upper half of the shield is a depiction of the Alamo; the shield is circled by live oak and olive branches, and the unfurled flags of the Kingdom of France, the Kingdom of Spain, the United Mexican States, the Republic of Texas, the Confederate States of America, and the United States of America; above the shield is emblazoned the motto, "REMEMBER THE ALAMO", and beneath the shield are the words, "TEXAS ONE AND INDIVISIBLE"; over the entire shield, centered between the flags, is a white five-pointed star ..." Since the description of the design of the reverse of the seal was contained in a concurrent resolution rather than a bill, the design is not a matter of law but can be considered the intent of the Legislature. (CR 159, 72nd Legislature, May 1991).

Other Symbols

State Tree — The **pecan** is the state tree of Texas. The sentiment that led to its official adoption probably grew out of the request of Gov. James Stephen Hogg that a pecan tree be planted at his grave. (Acts of 1919, 36th Legislature, regular session, p. 155; also Acts of 1927, 40th Legislature, p. 234.)

State Flower — The state flower of Texas is the **bluebonnet**, also called **buffalo clover, wolf flower** and *el conejo* (the rabbit). The bluebonnet was adopted as the state flower, on request of the Society of Colonial Dames in Texas, by the 27th Legislature, 1901. (See acts of regular session, p. 232.) The original resolution designated *Lupinus subcarnosus* as the state flower, but a resolution (HCR 44) signed March 8, 1971, by Gov. Preston Smith provided legal status as the state flower of Texas for "*Lupinus Texensis* and any other variety of bluebonnet."

State Bird — The **mockingbird** (*Mimus polyglottos*) is the state bird of Texas, adopted by the Legislature at the request of the Texas Federation of Women's Clubs. (Acts of 1927, 40th Legislature, regular session, p. 486.)

State Air Force — The **Confederate Air Force**, based in Midland at the Midland International Airport, was proclaimed the state air force of Texas by the 71st Legislature in 1989.

State Dinosaur — The **Brachiosaur Sauropod, Pleurocoelus,** was designated the state dinosaur by the 75th Legislature in 1997.

State Dish — **Chili** was proclaimed the Texas state dish by the 65th Texas Legislature in 1977.

State Fiber and Fabric - **Cotton** was designated the state fiber and fabric by the 75th Legislature in 1997.

State Fish — The **Guadalupe bass,** a member of the genus *Micropterus* within the sunfish family, was named the state fish of Texas by the 71st Legislature in 1989. It is one of a group of fish collectively known as black bass.

State Folk Dance — The **square dance** was designated the state folk dance by the 72nd Legislature in 1991.

State Fruit — The **Texas red grapefruit** was designated the state fruit by the 73rd Legislature in 1993.

State Gem — **Texas blue topaz,** the state gem of Texas, is found in the Llano uplift area, especially west to northwest of Mason. It was designated by the 61st Legislature in 1969.

State Grass — **Sideoats grama** (*Bouteloua curtipendula*), a native grass found on many different soils, was designated by the 62nd Legislature as the state grass of Texas in 1971.

State Insect — The **Monarch butterfly** (*Danaus plexippus*) was designated the state insect by the 74th Legislature in 1995.

State Mammals — The **armadillo** was designated the state **small mammal**; the **longhorn** was designated the state **large mammal**; and the **Mexican free-tailed bat** was designated the state **flying mammal** by the 74th Legislature in 1995.

State Musical Instrument - The **guitar** was named the state musical instrument of Texas by the 75th Legislature in 1997.

State Native Pepper - The **chiltepin** was named the state native pepper of Texas by the 75th Legislature in 1997.

State Pepper — The **jalapeño pepper** was designated the state pepper by the 74th Legislature in 1995.

State Plant — The **prickly pear cactus** was designated the state plant by the 74th Legislature in 1995.

State Reptile — The **Texas horned lizard** was named the state reptile by the 73rd Legislature in 1993.

State Seashell — The **lightning whelk** (*Busycon perversum pulleyi*) was named as the official state seashell by the 70th Legislature in 1987. One of the few shells that open on the left side, the lightning whelk is named for its colored stripes. It is found only on the Gulf Coast.

State Ship — The battleship **Texas** was designated the state ship by the 74th Legislature in 1995.

State Shrub — The crape myrtle (*Lagerstroemia indica*) was designated the official state shrub by the 75th Legislature in 1997.

State Sport — **Rodeo** was named the state sport of Texas by the 75th Legislature in 1997.

State Stone — **Petrified palmwood**, found in Texas principally in counties near the Texas Gulf Coast, was designated the state stone by the 61st Legislature in March 1969.

State Vegetable — The **Texas sweet onion** was designated the state vegetable by the 75th Legislature in 1997. ☆

Dallas! ★
THE TEXAS STAR

#1 VISITOR DESTINATION IN TEXAS

Toll Free:
1-800-C-DALLAS
Let us assist you with customized information and or/send you a complete Visitor Information packet.

FREE PUBLICATIONS
•*Dallas By Day/Dallas By Night*
•*Dallas Official Visitors Guide*
•*Dallas Quarterly Calendar of Events*
•*50 Free Things To Do In Dallas*
•*Dallas Illustrated Map*

INTERNET/WEB ACCESS
For Sights and Attractions, Arts and Culture, Sports, Outdoor Activities, Entertainment Districts, Accommodations, Calendar of Events, Dining, Shopping and much more contact us at our website:
www.dallascvb.com

VISITOR INFORMATION CENTER
Historic courthouse is home to touch-screen computer kiosks, Internet access stations and a multi-lingual staff.
Telephone: 214-571-1300
E-mail: info@dallascvb.com

MAILING ADDRESS
Dallas Convention & Visitors Bureau
1201 Elm Street, Suite 2000 • Dallas, Texas 75270
Phone: 214-571-1000 • Fax: 214-712-1917
24 Hour Events Hotline: 214-571-1301

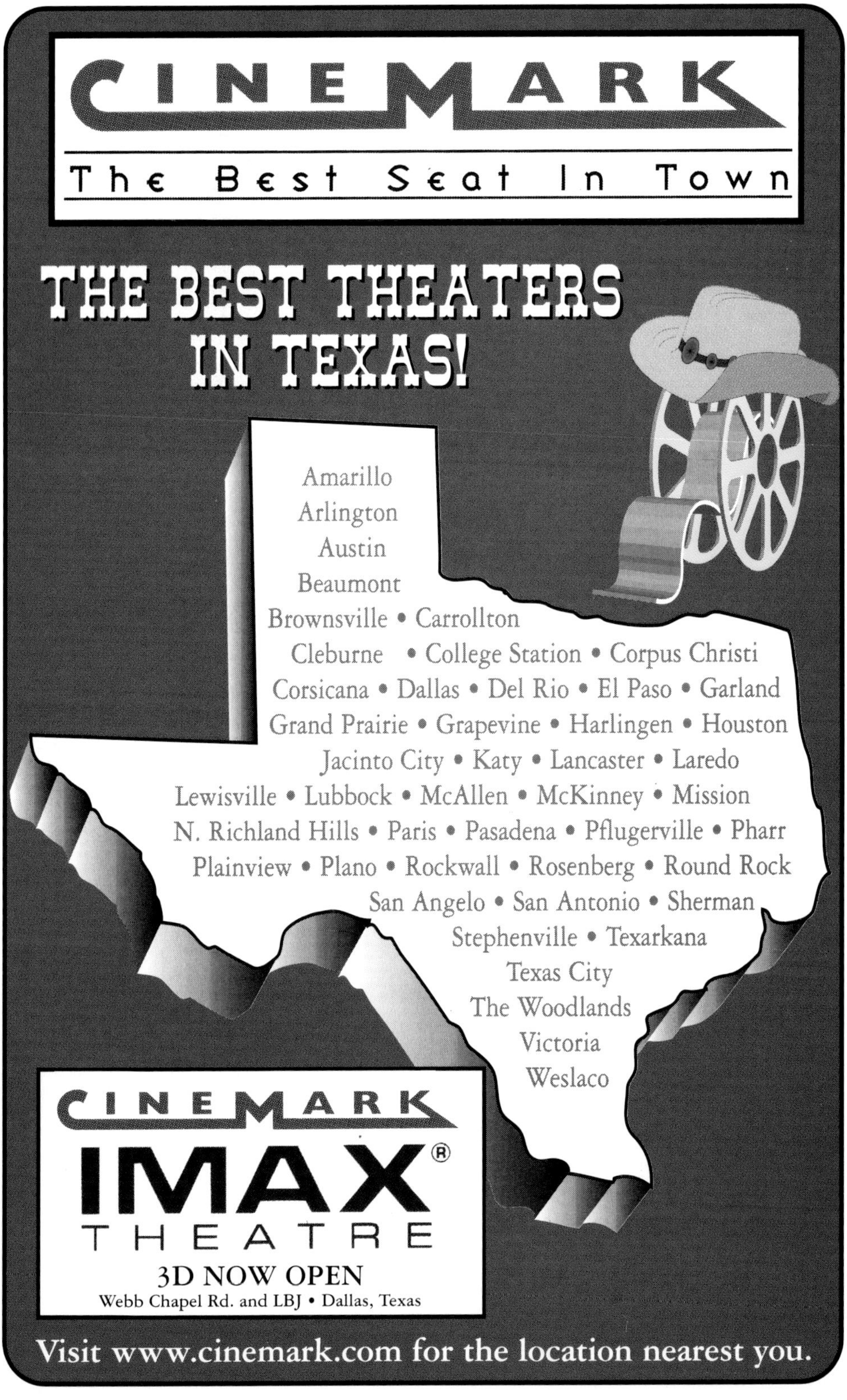
CINEMARK
The Best Seat In Town
THE BEST THEATERS IN TEXAS!
Amarillo
Arlington
Austin
Beaumont
Brownsville • Carrollton
Cleburne • College Station • Corpus Christi
Corsicana • Dallas • Del Rio • El Paso • Garland
Grand Prairie • Grapevine • Harlingen • Houston
Jacinto City • Katy • Lancaster • Laredo
Lewisville • Lubbock • McAllen • McKinney • Mission
N. Richland Hills • Paris • Pasadena • Pflugerville • Pharr
Plainview • Plano • Rockwall • Rosenberg • Round Rock
San Angelo • San Antonio • Sherman
Stephenville • Texarkana
Texas City
The Woodlands
Victoria
Weslaco
CINEMARK
IMAX®
THEATRE
3D NOW OPEN
Webb Chapel Rd. and LBJ • Dallas, Texas
Visit www.cinemark.com for the location nearest you.

Enjoy.

Thanks for drinking responsibly.

www.beeresponsible.com

Ben E. Keith Beers
Fort Worth, TX.

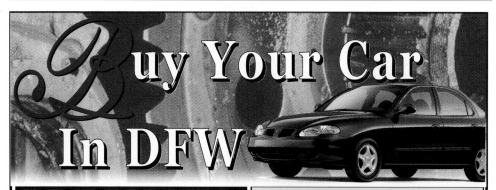

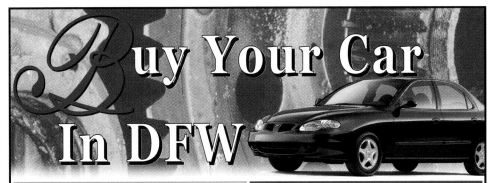

ENDING A CENTURY
BEGINNING AN ERA

The Texas Rangers: From Horses to Helicopters
by Mike Cox

Sealed in a stone-covered concrete vault next to a bronze statue of Republic of Texas-era Ranger George B. Erath that stands in front of the Texas Ranger Hall of Fame and Museum in Waco is a 36 by 24-inch steel time capsule containing the musings and memorabilia of various active and retired 20th-century Rangers.

The capsule was sealed in place on May 28, 1998, and dedicated on June 6 during ceremonies marking the 175th anniversary of the Rangers. But when the argon gas-filled capsule is opened in 2098, future historians will not find the answer to one nagging question: Just when did the Texas Rangers really begin?

Three unidentified Texas Rangers were photographed while on a scouting expedition (ca. 1892). Photo courtesy Texas Ranger Hall of Fame and Museum.

The 1998 ceremony, attended by Gov. George W. Bush, was based on the popular — and majority — belief that the Rangers came into being in the summer of 1823, when Texas colonizer Stephen F. Austin penned a document on the back of a proclamation by the Baron de Bastrop. Austin did not date what he wrote, but the piece of paper he was using bore, on the other side, the date of August 4. What the empresario set down on that paper was that he would ". . . employ ten men . . . to act as rangers for the common defense . . . The wages I will give said ten men is fifteen dollars a month payable in property . . ."

Other historians, most notably Dr. Malcolm D. McLean, editor of the multivolume *Papers Concerning Robertson's Colony in Texas*, hold that the Rangers were not formally constituted until mid-June 1835, when Robert M. Coleman led a company of mounted riflemen against a party of Tonkawa Indians in present-day Limestone County. Another school of thought is that the Rangers were not an official entity until Nov. 24, 1835, when the provisional government of Texas — on the verge of rebellion against Mexico — passed an ordinance creating a "Corps of Rangers" consisting of three companies.

No matter what their date of origin, the history of the Texas Rangers is a vital and colorful part of the history of Texas.

Specifically, as Texas was settled, the Rangers evolved from a paramilitary force primarily concerned with Indian fighting to a civil law enforcement organization. Sometimes the Rangers were government employees, sometimes they were unpaid volunteers. As tenacious as the enemies they faced, a lack of funding was a constant obstacle for the Rangers until well into the 20th century.

The early Rangers furnished their own clothing, weapons and horses. In return, those who were not volunteers earned a little money and a lot of fame.

For nearly half a century, if their beginning is accepted as 1823, Rangers chose their own officers. Even after the state got around to designating officers as well as furnishing its Rangers weapons and food, quality leadership sometimes was lacking. Partisan politics interfered with their effectiveness at various periods in their history and sometimes the Rangers were overly prone to shoot first and ask questions later. But history bears out that the Rangers were right more than they were wrong and prevailed more often than they did not.

John (Jack) Coffee Hays, a young surveyor from Tennessee, was the first Ranger captain to gain fame for his exploits. As a Ranger in the 1840s, he played a major role in establishing the Ranger reputation — a mixture of fearlessness and innovative fighting techniques. His Rangers learned from the Comanches, adding something the Indians did not have — five-shot revolvers. (The six-shooter would come later, thanks to one of Hays' Rangers, Samuel Walker. Walker suggested various improvements to pistol designer Sam Colt, including the addition of another round.) With revolvers in their hands as they faced the fierce Comanches, the Rangers had the frontier equivalent of nuclear weapons.

Within a year of Texas' admission as the 28th state of the Union, the United States and Mexico were at war. Several companies of Rangers were mustered into federal service. While they were under the command of the U.S. military, they served as scouts and guerrilla fighters. By war's end they had earned a nickname on the south side of the river: "Los Diablos Tejanos" — the Texas Devils.

The Ranger reputation for effectiveness was firmly established by 1848, thanks to Capt. Hays and others and the newspaper coverage of their role in the Mexican War.

"Four newly raised ranging companies, have all been organized, and taken their several stations on our frontier," the Victoria *Advocate* reported on Nov. 16, 1848. "We are much pleased. We know they are true men; and they know exactly what they are about. With many of them Indian and Mexican fighting has been their trade for years. That they may be permanently retained in the service on our frontier is extremely desir-

Texas Ranger Bigfoot Wallace, who was born in Virginia in 1817. Photo courtesy Texas Ranger Hall of Fame and Museum.

able; and we cannot permit ourselves to doubt but such will be the case."

Despite the sentiment expressed by that anonymous scribe, permanence eluded the Rangers for nearly another quarter of a century. The state funded and organized Ranger companies only when necessary.

Twice during the 1850s, Indian depredations along the frontier forced the state to fund Ranger operations. Several companies, including one led by the legendary William Alexander Anderson Wallace — better known simply as Bigfoot — joined the U.S. Army in an Indian campaign in the summer of 1850.

As more settlers came, planting their homes and their crops on lands that were the Indians' traditional living and hunting areas, need for a standing Ranger organization grew.

By the mid-1850s, protection from Indians — or the lack of protection — was a major political issue. The Indian situation in Texas cost Sam Houston the only statewide election he ever lost. Houston was defeated in the 1857 gubernatorial election by Hardin R. Runnels, who promised action against the Indians. On Jan. 27, 1858, the newly-inaugurated governor signed a bill appropriating $70,000 to fund a force of Rangers. Commissioned as Senior Captain was John Salmon "RIP" (for Rest In Peace) Ford.

Ford recruited 100 Rangers and soon mounted a major campaign against the Plains Indians, who had persisted in their raiding. On May 12, 1858, Ford and his Rangers attacked a Comanche village on the Canadian River in what is now Oklahoma, killing at least 76 Indians, including their chief Iron Jacket.

The Canadian River campaign was a significant event in Ranger history because it marked the point at which the people of Texas, and their political leadership, understood that they could not rely on a thinly-stretched U.S. military for protection. Texas needed a permanent Ranger force. But by the late 1850s, more serious political problems were afoot. Any hope of a standing Ranger force disappeared in the gathering clouds of war.

During the Civil War, men who for whatever reason choose not to fight Yankees stayed in Texas and scouted the frontier for Indians, deserters and Union sympathizers. They were not called Rangers, but that's what they were in function.

Rangers during Reconstruction achieved mixed results. The state fielded 14 Ranger companies in 1870-71 and 41 local companies of minutemen, but the effort at frontier protection failed for lack of funding. The effort was to have been funded by the sale of bonds, but no one wanted to buy the state's paper. A company under German-born Captain H.J. Richarz did some suc-

cessful Indian fighting in South Texas, but another company experienced a whiskey-fueled mutiny.

The first Ranger historian was Wilburn H. King, a Confederate veteran and former legislator who served as Adjutant General from 1881 to 1891. Six years after leaving the Adjutant General's Department, King contributed a history of the Rangers to Dallas writer Dudley G. Wooten's *A Comprehensive History of Texas*. In flowery Victorian language, King assessed the early-day Rangers:

"No gaudy trappings, no gay equipments, had any place in the necessary outfit of a Ranger, and no fifes nor drums, no brass bands, and no silken banners nor fluttering pennons accompanied these stern men on their swift and silent rides on the trail of the foe . . . This remarkable organization was the outgrowth of the times and admirably suited to the circumstances and conditions under which it was developed."

An organization even more "admirably suited to the circumstances and conditions" of Texas was created by the Legislature in 1874: the Frontier Battalion. Six companies of 75 men each under the overall command of Major John B. Jones, a Civil War veteran from Corsicana, were in the field by that summer.

Under Jones, the Frontier Battalion achieved results in a state that had been plagued by Indians and outlaws. More than 40 parties of Indians raided on the frontier of the state during the battalion's first six months. By September 1875, no Indian raids were reported anywhere in the battalion's area of operations, a hunk of Texas 100 miles wide stretching 400 miles from the Red River to the Rio Grande. By their count, the Rangers killed a minimum of 27 Indians, though they believed many additional wounded raiders later died.

"We have had in all," Jones reported to Adjutant General William Steele, "nineteen engagements with Indians [and] pursued about forty bands that we could not overtake. In a majority of instances we met them coming in, or found their trail, followed them in and prevented them from doing mischief."

The Rangers also were preventing mischief on the part of certain citizens and newly-arrived visitors who thought they could get away with cattle theft or murder along the sparsely-settled frontier.

"Have broken up several organizations of outlaws and fugitives from justice," Jones continued in his report. "Have had six fights with them. Have arrested and turned over to the civil authorities about 110 fugitives from justice, and recovered . . . fifteen or twenty thousand dollars worth of cattle and horses and returned them to the rightful owners."

Two years after Jones submitted his first biennial report, one piece of mischief prevented by the Rangers was a bank robbery planned by Sam Bass and his gang for Round Rock, a flourishing little railroad town 18 miles north of Austin.

"We are at Georgetown on our way to Round Rock to rob the bank, the railroad or to get killed," an informant who was a peripheral member of Bass' gang wrote Jones on July 17, 1878, "so for God's sake be there to prevent it."

Jones sent three men, the only Rangers he had in Austin, rushing to Round Rock. To back them up, he ordered Company E, then camped near San Saba, to ride for Williamson County. The following day, July 18,

Jones and a Travis County deputy sheriff who was a former Ranger took the train from Austin to Round Rock to join the trio of Rangers who had ridden in earlier. The full company that Jones wanted in Round Rock was still en route.

The Bass gang was not as large as Jones thought. Other than Bass, there was Seab Barnes, Frank Jackson and Jim Murphy, Jones' informant. On July 19, Bass, Barnes and Jackson rode into town to check out the bank and study possible getaway routes. While they were at it, they stopped by a store to buy some tobacco.

Outside the store, Bass and his fellow outlaws were confronted by Williamson County Sheriff's deputy Ahijah W. "Caige" Grimes, who had noticed they were packing pistols. As the deputy moved to disarm Bass, the outlaw pulled his revolver and fired five shots. Grimes fell dead. A general gunbattle ensued as the Travis County deputy who had accompanied Jones to Round Rock, Maurice Moore, returned the outlaw's fire. Soon Jones and the Rangers came running to the scene and began firing on the Bass gang as they rode out of town. One Ranger dropped Barnes and another wounded Bass. Aided by Jackson, he disappeared into the brush outside town.

Ten minutes after the shooting, Company E reached Round Rock and began searching for Bass and Jackson. The next day, the Rangers found the mortally wounded Bass, sitting against a tree. They took him to town, where he died on Sunday, July 20. Jackson was never heard of again.

John Wesley Hardin, another noted outlaw, managed to survive his confrontation with the Rangers. Hardin, reputed to have killed 31 men, was taken into custody near Pensacola, Fla., in 1877 by Ranger Lt. John B. Armstrong. Hardin, wanted for the murder of a Comanche County sheriff's deputy, was returned to Texas. He served a lengthy prison sentence, but in 1896, not long after his release from the penitentiary in Huntsville, he was shot to death in El Paso.

Armstrong learned his rangering while serving in South Texas under Leander H. McNelly, another individualist captain who added to the Ranger legend. McNelly's men were not members of the Frontier Battalion. They had been commissioned under a different statute as members of a Special Force intended to focus on the Texas-Mexican border. But again, like the men of the Frontier Battalion, they were Rangers in function if not title. McNelly's Rangers left graves of outlaws and Mexican bandits all across South Texas, once piling up 12 bodies of "adjudicated" cattle thieves in Brownsville as a reminder to anyone else inclined to take livestock not belonging to them.

Even Alex Sweet, whose satirical weekly humor magazine, *Texas Siftings,* enjoyed a large national circulation, treated the Rangers with fair reverence. In an 1882 article he wrote: "The rangers have done more to suppress lawlessness, to capture criminals, and to prevent Mexican and Indian raids on the frontier, than any other agency employed by either the State or national government."

Successful as they generally were, Frontier Battalion Rangers were not as autonomous as their legend suggests. They still had to follow orders. In the spring of 1885, Capt. J.T. Gillespie was forced to issue an order reminding his men in Company E where they could and

could not wear their pistols. Sidearms were for Ranger business only, he said. "Visiting houses of prostitution with your arms is forbidden unless in company with some city or county officer," the captain wrote. "Complaint . . . has been made that members of Company E while visiting said houses of prostitution have rudely displayed their pistols to the annoyance of all present."

"Though organized originally for the protection of the frontier only," King wrote in 1897, "the healthful and beneficial effects of their work became so marked as to attract attention everywhere . . . "

Ranger work was not always "healthful" — particularly for felons — but their services always were in demand. They fought their last Indians in January 1881 in the mountains of far West Texas, but after that there were feuds to settle, barbed-wire fence cutters to stop, killers and robbers to catch, and lynch mobs to suppress. During the fence-cutting crisis in the mid-1880s, Ranger Ira Aten proposed an innovative solution: eliminate fence cutters by rigging fences with bombs triggered to explode if the fence wire was cut. Headquarters in Austin ignored the suggestion, but it is reflective of 19th-century Ranger thinking.

By the end of that century, at least 62 Rangers had died in the line of duty from Indian arrows or outlaw bullets.

At the beginning of the 20th century, what threatened to kill off the Rangers was not the criminals they encountered but lawyers. Defense attorneys began challenging the legality of Ranger arrests by pointing out that the 1874 law that created the Frontier Battalion provided that only "officers" could take someone into custody. Gov. J.D. Sayers requested an opinion from Attorney General Thomas S. Smith. On May 26, 1900, Smith interpreted the meaning of "officer" as someone in command, not a peace officer or police officer. Until corrective legislation could be passed, Ranger privates suddenly were little more than armed guards, powerless to make an arrest. Only their supervisors — of which there were four for the whole state — could take someone into custody.

That lawyers had the luxury of drawing such a fine point of law showed that the frontier had indeed faded. The Frontier Battalion ceased to exist as of July 8, 1901, when new legislation went into effect. The new law authorized a Ranger force of only four companies of no more than 20 men each.

Five years into the new century, the Rangers still had their Wild West-era reputation, but they were evolving into detectives. On Sept. 26, 1905, a woman and her four children were found murdered on a farm near Edna in Jackson County. Local officers soon arrested Monk Gibson, a black man who had worked for the husband and father of the victims. Rangers and state troops were called out to protect the suspect from a lynch mob. Gibson escaped from jail, was recaptured in San Antonio and stood trial. But the jury hung.

Ranger Captain W.D. "Bill" McDonald reopened the investigation at the request of the prosecutors. A key piece of evidence, three bloody fingerprints with a dot beneath them, had been found on a board in the home of the victims. McDonald developed a second suspect in the murder. The Ranger made an imprint of the man's hand holding a knife, and it matched perfectly with the print found at the crime scene. With evidence developed by the Ranger, Gibson was convicted and hanged as well as Felix Powell, the second suspect, whose bloody hand print had cleared the case.

The Jackson County case was an example of modern crime-fighting. When Revolution broke out in Mexico five years later, the job facing the Rangers was more in keeping with their heritage. The revolution that began in 1910 marked the beginning of a decade of fighting and political instability. Bloodshed soon seeped across the shallow Rio Grande as Mexicans began raiding into Texas seeking supplies, weapons and horses. Others, inclined to banditry for less political reasons, took advantage of the situation as well.

"I instruct you and your men to keep them [Mexican raiders] off of Texas territory if possible," Gov. Oscar B. Colquitt wrote Ranger Capt. John R. Hughes in El Paso, "and if they invade the State let them understand they do so at the risk of their lives."

Frank Hamer is shown in 1906, shortly after he became a Ranger. Photo courtesy Texas Ranger Hall of Fame and Museum.

Before it was over, many lives were risked and lost, mostly those of Mexicans and Mexican-Americans. Though more than a score of Anglos were killed along the border by Mexican bandits, the number of deaths along the border attributed to Texas Rangers and vigilante groups varied from a minimum of 300 to 5,000.

Representative José T. Canales of Brownsville spearheaded a Legislative investigation of the Rangers in 1919. After hearing testimony of misdeeds ranging from the shooting of prisoners to drunkenness, the Legislature passed on March 31 a bill that reduced the number of Rangers. The measure also raised Rangers' pay, in an effort to attract higher-quality men. A procedure for handling citizen complaints against Rangers also was established.

The Canales hearings marked a turning point in Ranger history, and so did the development of the automobile. During the second decade of the 20th century, Rangers responding to reports of bandit raids sometimes rode horses and sometimes they piled into automobiles. Automobiles need gasoline, not corn or oats. The emergence of the automobile, coupled with World War I, fueled Texas' oil boom. Beginning in 1917 and continuing through the early 1930s, the job description of a Ranger included town taming. Several times during the 1920s, Gov. Dan Moody found it necessary to invoke martial law in oil-boom towns, such as Mexia and Borger. Other cities, such as Burkburnett, Desdemona, Kilgore, Ranger (named for a Ranger camp located there in the 1870s) and Wink, escaped martial law but still required the presence of Rangers.

Two captains and eight Ranger privates were sent to the Hutchinson County town of Borger on April 7, 1927. "A thorough-going clean-up was put underway," the Adjutant General reported. "The liquor traffic was broken up, many stills being seized and destroyed, and several thousand gallons of whiskey being captured and

poured out. Two hundred and three gambling slot machines were seized and destroyed . . . and in a period of twenty-four hours . . . no less than 1200 prostitutes left the town of Borger."

Rangers also were sent to handle labor troubles in Denison and Galveston. In a practice that would continue into the 1960s, Rangers were, in effect, state-employed strike breakers.

Two well-known Ranger captains, Frank Hamer and Tom Hickman, took on an assignment from Governor Moody in 1927 that would become much more common for the Rangers in future decades: investigating political corruption. The two captains made a bribery case against two members of the Legislature who were collecting cash to kill a bill one of them had introduced. In addition to the criminal charges against them, both representatives were expelled by the House.

Five years later, however, it was the Rangers getting the boot from the state. In 1932, the Rangers publicly supported incumbent Gov. Ross Sterling in his race against Miriam A. "Ma" Ferguson. She was the wife of Jim Ferguson, who as governor was impeached, convicted and removed from office in 1917. Mrs. Ferguson won the election. Those Rangers who did not resign prior to her inauguration were fired the moment she took office.

Among those who left was Capt. Hamer. Two years later, though carrying a commission as a Highway Patrolman and not a Ranger, he got national headlines when he and former Ranger Manny Gault tracked down the outlaws Bonnie Parker and Clyde Barrow in Louisiana. The couple, wanted for the murder of two Texas Highway Patrolmen and other slayings, died in a barrage of gunfire when they drove into a trap Hamer had set for them.

Today's Texas Rangers can trace their heritage to a recommendation from a Chicago-based consulting firm, Griffenhagen and Associates. Hired by the Legislature in 1933 to assess the state of law enforcement in Texas, the consultants found it was not much to brag about. Crime was rampant and the means of fighting it, at the state level, was underfunded, undermanned, disorganized and lacking any modern scientific backup. The recommendation of the firm: Remove the Rangers from the Adjutant General's Department and merge them with the young Highway Patrol to form a new agency called the Department of Public Safety.

Members of the 44th Texas Legislature, after conducting a committee meeting on the matter, agreed with the suggestion and passed a bill providing for the new state law-enforcement agency in 1935. University of Texas history professor Dr. Walter Prescott Webb predicted the new department would be the end of the Texas Rangers.

"It is safe to say that as time goes on," Webb wrote in his 1935 work *The Texas Rangers: A Century of Frontier Defense*, "the functions of the un-uniformed

Texas Rangers will gradually slip away . . . "

While Webb and others worried that the Rangers had been legislated to boot hill, many Texas sheriffs fretted that the new DPS would usurp their authority as the chief law-enforcement officers of their counties. As it developed, those viewpoints were wrong. The Rangers survived and the state's 254 sheriffs lost none of their authority.

With an appropriation of $450,000, the Department of Public Safety officially came into being on Aug. 10, 1935.

"When we build a good department," Commission Chairman Albert Sidney Johnson said at the Public Safety Commission's October 6, 1935, meeting in Austin, "you will all probably consider this the day that it got started . . . We plan to be one force, one Department of Public Safety. I do not wish you to get the idea that we are going to do away with the Highway Patrol or the Rangers . . . The Ranger Force is the finest thing in the world, however, in the last few years they have suffered terribly . . . through politics."

By the late 1930s, the DPS had a state-of-the-art crime lab in operation at its headquarters at Camp Mabry in Austin. The hiring of Rangers was made less political, and, for the first time ever, the state furnished formal training.

Following America's entrance into World War II after the Japanese attack on Pearl Harbor, in addition to their other duties, the Rangers took on a new role. They traveled the state training air-raid wardens and helping local officials organize civil-defense measures. That activity was news only in Texas, but on Aug. 19, 1942, the Rangers made headlines around the world when the Associated Press reported that "Many French officials and some diplomats were excited today by mistaken reports that 'Texas Rangers' had landed in Dieppe with Allied commandoes." The source of the confusion was a report from London that American Army Rangers had participated in the action.

In the 1950s, Rangers helped Attorney General Will Wilson clean up illegal gambling in Galveston. Capt. R.A. "Bob" Crowder added to the Ranger mystique in 1955 when he single-handedly quelled a melee at the Rusk State Hospital for the Criminally Insane. When Texas schools were desegregated following the Supreme Court's 1954 Brown vs. Board of Education decisions, Rangers stood by at several schools, keeping the transition for the most part peaceful.

The Rangers found themselves in a different sort of situation involving ethnic minorities in 1967: the Starr County farmworkers strike. Rangers under Capt. A.Y. Allee came to Starr County after a railroad trestle was burned in an incident believed related to the strike. The Rangers made mass arrests under the state's anti-picketing laws and were accused of brutality. For the second time in 50 years, the Rangers became the subject of hearings by lawmakers — this time the U.S. Congress. Congressional subcommittees in June 1967 and December 1968 found that Rangers had used excessive force during the strike. Allee also was named in a class-action lawsuit filed by the farmworkers. The case went all the way to the U.S. Supreme Court, where it was affirmed in 1974. But by that time, Allee had retired from the Rangers.

By the late 1980s, the makeup of the Rangers had

Ranger Sgt. Christine Nix, stationed with Company F in Waco, is one of two women Rangers (as of mid-1999). Dallas Morning News file photo.

changed dramatically since the days of Allee. Lee Roy Young Jr., a 15-year DPS veteran, became the first black Texas Ranger in modern times* on Sept. 1, 1988. By the first quarter of 1999, there were six black Rangers, including one captain, and 14 Hispanic Rangers.

In the old days, the only requirements for rangering were that a man be a good shot and a good horseman. These days, a Ranger does not even have to be a man. The first female Rangers were appointed in August 1993. As of 1999, the 107-member Ranger force included two females. Though sex is no longer a barrier, a Ranger applicant must have at least eight years of law-enforcement experience, including at least four years with the DPS. For acceptance into the DPS, a person must have at least 60 hours of college education or equivalencies. It is not unusual for 150 to 200 DPS officers to apply for only a handful of Ranger openings, and some Rangers have been interviewed numerous times before being accepted.

New Rangers — as were their early-day counterparts — are still expected to be good shots, but they receive additional training in fingerprint-recovery technique, photography, blood-splatter interpretation, investigative hypnosis, and numerous other skills aimed at assisting them in handling criminal investigations.

Each Ranger is issued a laptop computer, a digital camera, a video camera, a full-size and microcassette recorder, a cellular telephone and evidence-collection kits, along with more traditional crime-fighting weapons, including a .357 caliber Sig Sauer P226 semi-automatic pistol (or a .45 caliber Colt semi-automatic), a Ruger Mini-14 rifle, a 12-gauge shotgun, gas mask, body armor, helmet and baton. For prisoners they have handcuffs and leg irons.

Despite all the modern equipment available to them, one Ranger tradition continued at the turn of the 21th century: They still do not wear uniforms. Clothing choice is up to each Ranger, though white hats, Western-style clothing and boots are their unofficial "uniform." For tactical situations, each Ranger does have a set of black military-style combat fatigues. The shoulder bears an embroidered patch.

The Rangers are divided into six companies, A through F. Each company is commanded by a captain and a lieutenant. The six field captains report to headquarters in Austin, where Senior Captain Bruce Casteel is Commander of the Rangers. Assistant Commander is Capt. Gene Powell.

In the 1990s, Rangers continued to do what they had done for generations: investigate felony crimes, be available for riot-suppression duty, protect prisoners in high-profile criminal cases and execute court orders. In addition, Rangers handle complicated white-collar crime investigations, public-integrity cases and computer crimes.

On Oct. 16, 1991, the Rangers were called on to investigate the worst mass slaying by gunfire in American history. During the noon hour that day, George Hennard crashed his pickup truck into a crowded Luby's Cafeteria in Killeen. He got out of the truck and calmly began killing people. Before he died from a self-inflicted gunshot, he had killed 22 people. Working with the Killeen Police Department, the Rangers conducted an exhaustive investigation of the case. They found Hennard had acted alone, his motivations — truly known by no one but him — were open to conjecture.

Rangers assisted the FBI during the Feb. 28-April 19, 1993, Branch Davidian stand-off at Mt. Carmel, 10 miles east of Waco in McLennan County. After the self-styled messiah David Koresh's compound burned on the final day of the siege, leaving him and nearly 80 of his followers dead, the U.S. Attorney's Office requested that the Rangers conduct the crime-scene investigation. The undertaking was the most complex in the history of the Rangers. A third of the Ranger service was on the scene for nearly three weeks, collecting more than 2,000 pieces of evidence. For the first time in Ranger history, a computer system was set up at the crime scene for use in cataloging the evidence, which ranged from thousands of fired and unexpended rounds of ammunition to scores of charred firearms and other items.

Four years later, a separatist movement in 1997 drew the Rangers into a drama that was a virtual re-enactment of their history. On April 27 that year, two men and a woman — all camouflaged and carrying semi-automatic weapons — stormed a private residence in the Davis Mountains subdivision southwest of Fort Davis. Following hours of negotiations with Rangers and FBI agents, the three suspects released their two hostages and retreated up a winding mountain road to the "Embassy" of the so-called "Republic of Texas." During the seven-day Republic of Texas stand-off in Jeff Davis County, Rangers scouted the area in helicopters and on horseback.

In addition to the incident in Fort Davis, Rangers undertook 5,205 investigations in fiscal 1997-1998. Because Texas is so big, they traveled more than 2 million miles, a figure which includes flights in DPS aircraft to other states to return wanted fugitives or to interview witnesses. The work the Rangers did in 1997-1998 led to 829 felony and 130 misdemeanor arrests. Ranger investigations during the fiscal year resulted in 860 convictions, including 4 death sentences and 57 life sentences. In addition, $21.4 million in stolen property was recovered.

On Thanksgiving Day 1998, a convicted killer named Martin Gurule became the first Death Row inmate to escape from the Texas prison system since the Depression era. The Rangers participated in a large-scale manhunt and on Dec. 3, Gurule was found drowned in a creek only a mile from the prison from which he escaped a week earlier. Though Gurule was no longer a problem to society, Gov. George W. Bush and others wanted to know how he could have escaped from a maximum-security facility in the first place. The governor, as his predecessors had been doing for generations, turned to the Rangers.

"I'm upset about it," he said of the highly-publicized escape. "I've asked the Texas Rangers to step in and answer the question for me and for Texas."

A spokeswoman for the Texas Rangers Hall of Fame and Museum library says that in the 19th century, blacks were thought to have worked as teamsters with the Rangers and black Seminoles served as scouts. Researchers are attempting to document this part of Ranger history.

Mike Cox, an Austin-based historian and Chief of Media Relations for the Texas Department of Public Safety, has written three books on the Texas Rangers. ☆

History Highlight: Texas Capital Once a Steamboat

For 11 days in April 1836, the capital of Texas was the steamboat *Cayuga*.

The 80-ton side-wheeler had been hauling cargo on the Brazos River during 1834 and 1835. After their victory at the Alamo on March 6, 1836, Mexican Gen. Antonio López de Santa Anna and his troops began moving toward Harrisburg (today it's a part of Houston), pursuing the Texas rebels. In early April, David G. Burnet, the interim president of the new republic, impressed the *Cayuga* into public service to transport provisions to the Texas army. On April 15, Burnet and his cabinet boarded the *Cayuga* just ahead of the advancing Mexican army. The steamboat made stops at Lynch's Ferry and New Washington, in the vicinity of today's Morgan's Point in Harris County, then proceeded to Anahuac and Galveston with the officials, who conducted the republic's business as they went. The officials went ashore at Galveston on April 26, then moved to a succession of locations before finally settling in January 1839 in the new capital at Waterloo, which soon was renamed Austin. ☆

Oil and Texas:
A Cultural History

By Mary G. Ramos, editor, Texas Almanac

For Texans, the 20th century did not begin on January 1, 1901, as it did for everyone else. It began nine days later, on Jan. 10, when, spurting drilling pipe, mud, gas and oil, the Lucas No. 1 well blew in at Spindletop near Beaumont. The gusher spewed oil more than 100 feet into the air until it was capped nine days later. With that dramatic fanfare, Texas' economy was wrenched from its rural, agricultural roots and flung headlong into the petroleum and industrial age.

In the last two decades of the 19th century, railroads had made sweeping changes in the lives of many of Texas' mostly rural, mostly agrarian citizens and forever altered the face of the state. Settlements formed around temporary railroad-workers' camps. Speculators created brand-new towns out of virgin prairie beside the gleaming rails. And existing communities that were bypassed by the tracks often curled up their municipal toes and died unless they were willing to pick up businesses, homes and churches and move to the rails.

The arrival of railroad transportation expanded Texas farmers' and ranchers' markets by

Spindletop blew in on Jan. 10, 1901, changing almost all Texans' lives in the process. Dallas Morning News file photo.

providing faster and cheaper shipping of products. Cattle raisers were no longer forced to trail their herds long miles to railheads in the Midwest. In their classic Texas history text, "Texas, the Lone Star State," Rupert Richardson, Ernest Wallace and Adrian Anderson summarized it this way: " . . . railroads were the key to progress and prosperity at the end of the 19th century."

When oil came gushing into Texas early in the 20th century, the changes were even more profound. Petroleum began to displace agriculture as the principal fuel driving the economy of the state, and Texans' lives were even more drastically affected than they had been by railroads.

The impact of oil on Texas and Texans is often analyzed in terms of corporate development, personal or corporate wealth, or the overall economy of the state and politics. Oil also dramatically affected the lives of those who owned the land from which oil was produced, or who were directly involved in oil exploration, extraction and processing. The discoveries of oil fields led to the founding and flourishing of numerous Texas towns, to the establishment of companies that have become

multinational conglomerates, and to the amassing of vast personal fortunes.

Conversely, the playing out of pumped-out oil fields led to the death of any number of those once-flourishing towns. Betting fortunes on what turned out to be dusters resulted in the bankruptcies of companies and individuals.

However, Texas oil has affected the lives of millions of Texans not directly involved in the oil business — Texans who receive neither a paycheck nor a royalty check based on petroleum. Oil has profoundly changed the culture of the state, and it continues to affect most Texans' lives in ways that may not be obvious to the casual observer.

Early Oil Discoveries

The presence of natural oil seeps in Texas had been known for hundreds of years before Europeans arrived in the area. Indians in Texas are said to have told European explorers that the substance had medicinal uses. In July 1543, the remnants of Spanish explorer Hernando de Soto's expedition, led by Luis de Moscoso Alvarado, were forced ashore along the Texas coast between Sabine Pass and High Island. Moscoso reported that the group found oil floating on the surface of the water and used it to caulk their boats.

Texas' first producing oil well was drilled by Lyne T. Barret at Melrose in Nacogdoches County in 1866. The following year, a well was brought in at nearby Oil Springs by Amory Reily Starr and Peyton F. Edwards. Other wells followed, making Nacogdoches County the site of Texas' first commercial oil field, first pipeline and first effort to refine crude. Several thousand barrels of oil were produced, but the price of oil was not high enough to justify further efforts at development.

While drilling for water in 1886, Bexar County rancher George Dullnig found a small quantity of oil, but he did not attempt commercial production.

City crews in Corsicana were also drilling for water in 1894, when they made the first economically significant oil discovery in Texas. That well was abandoned because the drillers needed to find water, not oil. But several producing oil wells were drilled in 1895 by Joseph S. Cullinan, who later helped found the Texas Company, which became Texaco. The first well-

equipped refinery in Texas was built at this field, and despite the early efforts at Nacogdoches, it is usually called Texas' first refinery.

Spindletop

The oil discovery that jump-started Texas' transformation into a major petroleum producer and industrial power was Spindletop. Exploration in the area of the upper Gulf Coast near Beaumont had begun in 1892. After drilling several dry holes, Louisiana mining engineer and oil prospector Capt. Anthony F. Lucas drilled the discovery well of the Spindletop field. Initially, the Lucas No. 1 produced more than an estimated 75,000 barrels of oil a day. Peak annual production was 17.5 million barrels in 1902.

Spindletop, which was also the first salt-dome oil discovery, triggered a flood of speculation in the area, resulting in several other significant discoveries. The boom included an influx of hundreds of eager wildcatters — including former Governor James Stephen Hogg — lusting after a piece of the action, as well as thousands of workers looking for jobs. Right behind them came a tidal wave of related service, supply and manufacturing firms, such as refineries, pipelines and oil-field equipment manufacturers and dealers. It was California's fabled Gold Rush of 50 years earlier repeated on the Texas Gulf Coast with rotary drill bits and derricks instead of pick axes and gold pans.

The boom turned into a feeding frenzy of human sharks: scores of speculators sniffing out a quick buck; scam artists peddling worthless leases; and prostitutes, gamblers and liquor dealers, all looking for a chunk of the workers' paychecks.

Within three years, several additional major fields were developed within a 150-mile radius of Spindletop; Sour Lake, Batson and Humble were among them.

Companies were soon established to develop the Gulf Coast oil fields. Many of them became the industry giants of today: Gulf Oil; Sun Oil Company; Magnolia Petroleum Company; the Texas Company; and Humble Oil, which later affiliated with Standard Oil of New Jersey and became Esso, then today's Exxon. Refineries, pipelines and export facilities became the nucleus of the major industrial region that began to form along the Texas coast around Port Arthur and Beaumont.

The *New Handbook of Texas* summarizes the effect of Spindletop in this way: "The discovery of the Spindletop oil field had an almost incalculable effect on world history, as well as Texas history. Eager to find similar deposits, investors spent billions of dollars throughout the Lone Star State in search of oil and natural gas. The cheap fuel they found helped to revolutionize American transportation and industry."

Texas oil production was 836,039 barrels in 1900. In 1902, Spindletop alone produced more than 17 million barrels, or 94 percent of the state's production. As a result of the glut, oil prices dropped to an all-time low 3 cents a barrel, while water in some boom towns sold for 5 cents a cup.

Oil in North Texas

Between 1902 and 1910, oil fever spread through North Central Texas, with finds at Brownwood, Petrolia and Wichita Falls.

Water-well drillers on the W.T. Waggoner Ranch in Wichita County in 1911 found oil instead, creating the Electra field. In 1917, the Ranger field was discovered in Eastland County by W.K. Gordon, general manager of the T&P Coal Company's mines at nearby Thurber. Ironically, the wealth of oil at Ranger, and elsewhere in the state, encouraged railroads to switch their locomotives from coal to oil and helped kill the coal-mining town of Thurber.

Oil was found west of Burkburnett in Wichita County in 1912, followed by another oil field in the town itself in 1918. The feverish activity that followed inspired the 1940 movie "Boom Town," starring Clark Gable, Spencer Tracy, Claudette Colbert and Hedy Lamarr.

The boom-town phenomenon became common across the state: The infrastructures of small farming communities near oil discoveries were inadequate to the demands of the population explosions. They hadn't sufficient lodging or eating establishments for the sudden influx. Newcomers were forced to live in hastily erected shacks, tents or even their cars or trucks. Since some of those drawn to oil fields by dreams of riches brought their families, schools became overcrowded. There were lines at cafes, at post-office counters, everywhere.

Unexpectedly heavy traffic on the often-unpaved streets created massive clouds of dust during dry weather — dust that invaded every corner and settled on every surface. In wet weather, the streets became vehicle-swallowing mudholes.

During the 1920s, there were discoveries near Mexia in Limestone County and more in Navarro County.

Oil was discovered in the Panhandle starting in 1921, and major fields were developed all across the state during the next decade — East Texas, west-central Texas and additional fields in the Gulf Coast.

Biggest of Them All — East Texas

In October 1930, the Daisy Bradford No. 3 well blew in near Turnertown and Joinerville in Rusk County, opening the East Texas field, the biggest field of all. Veteran wildcatter C.M. (Dad) Joiner drilled the well on land long rejected by major companies' geologists as not worthy of their efforts. The biggest leasing campaign in history ensued, and the activity spread to include Kilgore, Longview and many points north. Overproduction soon followed, as oil derricks sprouted thick as bamboo all over the field. With no well-spacing regulations and no limits on production, the price of oil nosedived again.

On Aug. 17, 1931, Gov. Ross S. Sterling ordered the National Guard into the East Texas field, which he placed under martial law. This drastic action was taken after the Texas Railroad Commission had been enjoined from enforcing production restrictions. After more than two years of legal battles, most East Texas operators accepted proration, the system of regulation still utilized.

By the time the East Texas field was developed, Texas' economy was powered not by agriculture, but by petroleum.

Oil's Ripple Effects

Gradually, the oil glut began to affect ordinary Texans.

Downtown Kilgore, at the height of the East Texas oil boom, is jammed with automobiles. Dallas Morning News file photo.

Soon after Spindletop, the availability of an ocean of cheap oil encouraged its use as fuel for transportation and manufacturing. After railroads converted from coal to oil, steamships followed, led by those operating in the Gulf of Mexico and the Caribbean.

As automobiles became more common, roads began to be paved across the state.

Mechanization of farm work increased quickly, enabling farmers to produce more food with fewer people. Manufacturing plants developed in the formerly agricultural state, using cheap oil as fuel.

Texas' population scales, heavily weighted toward the rural before Spindletop, started to balance, and by 1940, the population was almost even: 55 percent rural and 45 percent urban. World War II tipped the scales, however, when wartime jobs at manufacturing plants in the cities lured large numbers of people from farms and small towns. Most never returned.

This displacement of farming families was exacerbated by the absorbtion of many family farms into large corporate operations. Increasing numbers of migrants from other states and foreign countries also settled principally in urban centers. By 1980, the state was four-fifths urban.

As of Jan. 1, 1997, State Data Center population estimates indicate that of the state's population (19,598,471), more than one-third was concentrated in the three largest counties: Harris (3,178,995), Dallas (2,032,171) and Bexar (1,342.934).

State Government Tax on Oil Production

Another change brought about by the discovery of oil was the enrichment of the state treasury after the legislature authorized an oil-production tax in 1905. The first full year the tax was collected, the public coffers swelled by $101,403. By 1919, the revenue from the oil-production tax was more than $1 million; by 1929, it was almost $6 million. In 1996, the last year for which we had figures at press time, it was just short of $376 million for the fiscal year.

Oil Benefits to Texas Higher Education

Many thousands of students attending Texas universities have benefited from oil. The boon that they have enjoyed began with Mirabeau B. Lamar, known as the "Father of Texas Education." During his tenure as presi-

dent of the Republic of Texas, he urged the Texas Congress to appropriate public domain to support education. In 1839, the Congress set aside 50 leagues (221,400 acres) of land for the endowment of a university. (Land was also set aside in a separate endowment for public elementary and secondary schools.) In 1858, the university endowment was increased to 1 million acres, with the stipulation that the endowment be good agricultural land.

However, the writers of the Constitution of 1876 evidently felt there was no need to appropriate arable land for an as-yet-nonexistent university. The first million acres in the endowment were located in Schleicher, Crockett, Terrell, Pecos, Upton, Reagan and Irion counties in arid far-west Texas.

When the University of Texas opened in 1883, the legislature added a second million acres in Andrews, Crane, Culberson, Dawson, Ector, El Paso, Gaines, Hudspeth, Loving, Martin, Ward and Winkler counties. The fledgling university was backed by an endowment of a vast amount of land of extremely dubious value.

Around the turn of the century, the University's Bureau of Economic Geology began exploring the possibility of finding oil and gas on University Lands. In 1916, although most other geologists disagreed, the University's Dr. Johan A. Udden reported that oil could be found lying atop an underground fold of rock that was believed to run from the Marathon area through Pecos County and into Upton and Reagan counties.

Udden's theory led to the first major oil discovery in the West Texas Permian Basin. The Santa Rita No. 1, discovery well of the Big Lake Field, blew in on May 28, 1923, in Reagan County. It was drilled on University Lands by Frank Pickerell and Carl G. Cromwell of Texon Oil and Land Company.

Within a year, there were 17 producing wells in the Big Lake Field, and the University of Texas was on its way to becoming a very wealthy school.

The Santa Rita continued to produce oil until it was finally plugged in 1990.

The University of Texas had built few permanent, substantial buildings before the Santa Rita began producing. Most of the campus was covered by shacks, which housed classrooms, labs, gymnasiums and other campus facilities. When the oil money started flowing, however, it triggered a building boom that produced many of the structures that are still used by the University.

In 1931, the legislature split the net income of the Permanent University Fund, with two-thirds going to the University of Texas and one-third to Texas A&M University.

The income was further split in 1984, when the legislature voted to include all the institutions in the University of Texas System, not just the main university at Austin, and the entire Texas A&M University System.

The Permanent University Fund, which receives all revenue from oil, gas, sulfur and water royalties; increases in investments; rent payments on mineral leases; and sales of university lands, is one of the largest university endowments in the world. The mineral income on University Lands from 1923 through fiscal 1998 has been $3.146 billion. Investment return in the same period has been $8.163 billion.

The net income from interest and dividends from those investments plus the revenue from grazing leases on University Lands comprise the Available University Fund. The total amount of money paid to the universities from the AUF from 1923 through fiscal 1998 was $4.792 billion. These distributions help pay for construction bonds and contribute to the education and general revenues. As of August 31, 1998, the market value of the PUF was more than $6.517 billion.

Oil Benefits to Public Schools

Texas public schools have benefited from oil, as well. In 1839, the Congress of the Republic appropriated from the public

The circulation desk in the grand main-building library at the University of Texas is shown in this 1943 photo. This and other impressive buildings on the University campus were made possible by the discovery of oil on University Lands beginning in 1923. Dallas Morning News file photo.

domain three leagues of land (one league is about 4,400 acres) to each county for public schools. The following year, they increased each county's allotment by one league. Public-school land grants from this source totaled more than 4 million acres.

To encourage construction of railroads, the legislature in 1854 granted lands to railroad companies; the amount of land was based on the miles of track that each company laid. The legislature also required the railroads to allot alternate sections of their land grants to the public schools.

Finally, in the Constitution of 1876, the Texas legislature granted half the unappropriated public domain to the public schools, which amount included the alternate sections of the railroad grants. More than 42 million acres were earmarked for public schools by this provision.

The Permanent School Fund was established under rules similar to those guiding the Permanent University Fund. While most of the money in the Permanent School Fund has come from land sales, the fund retained mineral rights on more than 7 million acres of school lands. The land-sales moneys have been augmented by mineral royalties. The investment fund at the end of fiscal year 1997 totalled just under $15.5 billion. Interest drawn from the Permanent School Fund is paid into the Available School Fund, from which it is paid to the public-school districts based on average daily attendance. The total amount paid in fiscal 1997 by the PSF to the ASF from all sources was almost $692.7 million. Of that total, a bit less than $3 million could probably be attributed to oil-related sources.

Philanthropy from Black Gold

Thousands of Texans have been touched by Texas' black gold through the philanthropy of people who have made fortunes from its discovery, production and processing.

Institutions all over the state in many different fields — health research and hospitals, education, social services, fine arts, and engineering and technology research — have benefited from the wealth and generosity of petroleum millionaires. Ordinary Texans have reaped the rewards of such gifts through the programs of those institutions.

There have been far too many petroleum philanthro-

pists to list them all in this article. A representative few, however, will suggest the great good that has been done for the residents of Texas by people who pumped their money out from under Texas dirt.

Eclectic Givers

Some philanthropists have donated to electic arrays of programs and institutions:

Algur Meadows, major stockholder and chairman of the board of General American Oil Company for many years, established the Meadows Foundation in 1948. The foundation has given generously — and continues to donate — to a wide range of programs throughout Texas, primarily in the health, education, visual arts, social services and historic-preservation areas. Meadows himself endowed a museum of Spanish art at Southern Methodist University, and he willed much of his private art collection to the Dallas Museum of Art.

Hugh Roy Cullen, called "King of the Wildcatters" and who made major oil discoveries in the Houston area, gave large gifts to the University of Houston, the Texas Medical Center, and the Gonzales Warm Springs Foundation (originally a hospital specializing in the treatment of victims of pediatric polio). He also made significant contributions to Houston arts organizations, the Boy Scouts and the YMCA. He established the Cullen Foundation in 1947 to direct contributions to a variety of charities.

Also founded in 1947 was the Sid W. Richardson Foundation. Richardson was an independent oil producer with headquarters in Fort Worth. His foundation's gifts have been primarily in support of health, medicine, education and the Sid Richardson Collection of Western Art, open free to the public in its own Fort Worth museum. His great-nephews, the Bass brothers of Fort Worth — Ed, Sid, Robert and Lee — and their parents Perry and Nancy Lee, carry on the family tradition. The most recent and most visible Bass contribution is the Bass Performance Hall in Fort Worth, opened in May 1998.

Walter William Fondren got his start in oil in the Corsicana field before the turn of the century, later becoming one of the founders of Humble Oil. Major gifts from the Fondren Foundation have gone to health and educational facilities, including Rice University, Southern Methodist University, Southwestern University, Methodist Hospital of Houston and the Methodist

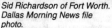

Sid Richardson of Fort Worth. Dallas Morning News file photo.

Dominique de Menil, Houston arts patron. Dallas Morning News file photo.

Home for Orphans at Waco.

Robert Everett Smith, in the oil-field supplies business as well as drilling in the East Texas field, gave to a variety of causes in the fields of health and medicine, social services, education and the arts, including the Houston Symphony, the Houston Museum of Fine Arts, the Harris County Association for the Blind, Methodist Hospital of Houston, Southern Methodist University and Southwestern University.

Supporters of Fine Arts and Literature

Several oil millionaires have supported mainly the fine arts and literature:

Everette Lee DeGolyer of Dallas was active in petroleum exploration and production and in technological development, largely through Amerada, Texas Instruments and Texas Eastern Transmission. He and his wife supported the Dallas Symphony Orchestra and other Dallas-area musical groups. DeGolyer was also a collector of rare books; he donated 89,000 volumes of his personal collection to university libraries. He was one of the main financial backers of Texas Country Day School in Dallas, which became St. Mark's School of Texas. In 1942, DeGolyer rescued the *Saturday Review*, the greatly respected national literary magazine, from a serious financial crisis. DeGolyer had become friends with Norman Cousins, who was named editor at the height of the crisis. DeGolyer became publisher and subsidized the magazine until it regained its economic feet.

Dominique Schlumberger de Menil, whose father was founder of Schlumberger, the multinational oil-exploration engineering firm, and her husband John de Menil, an executive in the company, collected more than 10,000 works of art. In 1954, they formed The Menil Foundation in Houston to oversee the Menil Collection, a museum that showcases their art collection.

Nina Cullinan and Sarah Campbell Blaffer, daughters of early oil entrepreneurs, have generously supported many fine-arts organizations — Cullinan primarily in the Houston area, and Blaffer across the state.

Nina Cullinan's father, Joseph S. Cullinan, developed the Corsicana field and built Texas' first commercial oil refinery there, was a founder of Magnolia Petroleum and helped organize the Texas Company. Nina Cullinan was a supporter of many Houston arts entities, among them the Houston Symphony, Houston Ballet, Houston Museum of Fine Arts and other art museums, as well as health and parks organizations.

Sarah Campbell Blaffer, daughter of another of the founders of the Texas Company and wife of one of the founders of Humble Oil, acquired an extensive art collection. She donated many original works to the Houston Museum of Fine Arts, and she established the Sarah Campbell Blaffer Foundation to send art exhibits on tours across the state.

Local Philanthropy

Some philanthropists have preferred to keep their charity mostly close to home:

Popularly known as "Uncle Gash," J.G. Hardin gave to Texas educational institutions, but he also provided funds for many community needs around Wichita County, where he had made his fortune in the Burkburnett oil boom. He donated land for playgrounds and contributed to several church buildings, to retiring public-school bonds and for a new electric-power plant. Hardin provided funds to establish Hardin Junior College, the forerunner of Midwestern State University, in Wichita Falls. Other colleges that benefited from Hardin's generosity included Baylor Female College (now Mary Hardin-Baylor) in Belton, Simmons College (now Hardin-Simmons University) in Abilene, Abilene Christian College (now Abilene Christian University) and Howard Payne College (now Howard Payne University) in Brownwood. He also sent more than two dozen young people through college and threw a financial lifeline to half a dozen colleges during the Depression.

Edgar Byram Davis made a fortune in the shoe business in Massachusetts, then made another in rubber plantations, all by shortly after the turn of the century. With his brother as partner, Davis found oil in the Luling field in Caldwell County in the early 1920s. He built a golf course, several athletic clubhouses and various other facilities for the citizens of Luling. He also established a demonstration farm to help improve agricultural production in the area. He gave away so much money that he was almost broke when he died.

Ruth Legett Jones, an Abilene native, and her husband Percy acquired vast amounts of land in west-central Texas on which oil was discovered. The foundation she established gave funds primarily to organizations in the Abilene area, including Hardin-Simmons University, McMurry College, Abilene Christian University, West Texas Rehabilitation Center and Hendrick Medical Center. The foundation also built parks and swimming pools and helped finance college educations for many black Abilene students, as well as supporting ecological, medical and historical research.

George T. Abell of Midland was a self-taught geologist who made a fortune as an independent oil producer. Through their Abell-Hanger Foundation, established in 1954, he and his wife Gladys were major supporters of Midland-area organizations concerned with higher education, youth activities, cultural programs, health services and social welfare.

Albert and Mamie George established the George Foundation in 1945 to direct their contributions in similar fields in their home county of Fort Bend. Much of their fortune came from oil and gas fields that were discovered on their ranch in the 1920s and 1930s.

Although Amon G. Carter of Fort Worth was primarily a newspaper publisher, the Amon G. Carter Foundation he established in 1945 was funded by the sale of oil interests. The most public of the foundation's responsibilities is the Amon Carter Museum of Western Art, which opened in 1961. Its collection was built around a nucleus of Carter's extensive holdings of art by Frederic Remington and Charles M. Russell. Also benefiting from foundation funds are other charities in Fort Worth and Tarrant County in the fields of the arts, education, health care, social and human services, and programs for youth and the elderly.

Much of Jake and Nancy Hamon's generosity has gone to Dallas-area charities. Hamon got his start in the East Texas oil field. Together the Hamons were major supporters of the arts in Dallas, and Nancy Hamon has continued the tradition since her husband's death in 1985. In the last decade alone, she has made major contributions to the Dallas Zoo for a gorilla habitat, to Southern Methodist University for an arts library, to the University of Texas Southwestern Medical Center for several medical-research facilities and to the Dallas Museum of Art for a major building addition. The Dallas Theater Center and the Dallas Symphony, among others, have also received gifts.

Don Harrington, an Amarillo oilman, and his wife Sybil supported many charities in the Panhandle. Through the Don and Sybil Harrington Foundation, founded in 1951, they generously gave to hospitals and health-care agencies, cultural programs, higher education, youth agencies, social services and civic affairs. Among their major beneficiaries were the Don and Sybil Harrington Cancer Center; the Panhandle-Plains Historical Museum at Canyon; a science museum in Amarillo; and the Harrington Library Consortium, a computerized network of libraries of the city of Amarillo, Amarillo College, Texas Tech Medical School, West Texas A&M University and many small Panhandle towns. Mrs. Harrington also was the largest individual donor to New York's Metropolitan Opera in the company's history.

Supporter of History

Although Governor James Hogg did not live long enough to see oil discovered on family property near West Columbia in the 1920s, his children did. His daughter Ima established the Hogg Foundation for Mental Health at The University of Texas. She also gave her Houston mansion, Bayou Bend, and its collection of early American art and antiques to the Houston Museum of Fine Arts. She presented the restored Hogg family home near West Columbia to the state of Texas; it is now the Varner-Hogg Plantation State Historical Park. She also restored the Winedale Inn, a 19th-century stagecoach stop near Round Top, and gave it to the University of Texas. It is now the focus of the Winedale Historical Center, which is used for the study of Texas history.

Gifts For Scientific Research

Tom Slick Jr., whose father drilled the discovery well for a large Oklahoma oil field in 1912, carried on the family's involvement in oil exploration and production. The younger Slick had a lifelong interest in science and engineering. In 1947, he established the Southwest Research Institute in San Antonio. The SwRI does leading-edge research for corporations and the government in a wide range of areas — from materials and techniques for constructing stronger bridges to more effective methods for disposing of nuclear waste to making

biocidal paints that prevent the growth of mold and mildew. (See related article in the Science and Health section.)

Supporter of Environmental Protection

Robert Hughes Welder, a cattleman and wildlife conservationist, provided in his will for the establishment of the Rob and Bessie Welder Wildlife Foundation and Refuge. Although Welder was primarily a cattleman, the foundation is supported by income from oil and gas leases. The 7,800-acre refuge, formally dedicated in 1961, is eight miles northeast of Sinton in San Patricio County. Teacher-training programs are offered at the refuge, and the foundation grants fellowships and other aids to graduate students and researchers.

Jake Hamon of Dallas. Dallas Morning News file photo.

Texas Oil's Cultural Influence

Today, oil is no longer the predominant engine driving Texas' economy. However, in the century since Spindletop roared to life on the Texas Gulf Coast, oil has touched the lives of many Texans, and it continues to provide benefits to residents of the Lone Star State, as well as to people throughout the country. ☆

The author wishes to thank historians Roger M. Olien, Ph.D., J. Conrad Dunagan Chair in Regional and Business History, University of Texas of the Permian Basin, and Diana Davids Olien, Ph.D., Senior Lecturer in History, University of Texas of the Permian Basin, for their help in presenting this material accurately. Any errors are the author's own.

For Further Reading

Barnhill, J. Herschel, *From Surplus to Substitution: Energy in Texas*, American Press, Boston, 1983.

Berry, Margaret C., *The University of Texas: A Pictorial Account of Its First Century*; University of Texas Press, Austin and London, 1980.

Crawford, Mary G., "A History of West Texas," **Texas Almanac 1990-1991**; *The Dallas Morning News*, Dallas, 1989.

House, Boyce, *Were You in Ranger?*; Tardy Publishing Company, Inc., Dallas, 1935.

Jordan, Terry G., with John L. Bean Jr. and William M. Holmes; *Texas: A Geography*; Westview Press, Boulder and London, 1984.

McComb, David G., *Houston: A History*; University of Texas Press, Austin, 1981.

Presley, James, *Saga of Wealth; The Rise of the Texas Oilmen*; Texas Monthly Press, Austin, 1983 (orig. pub. by Putnam, New York, c. 1978).

Texas State Historical Association, *The New Handbook of Texas*; TSHA, Austin, 1996.

Weaver, Bobby D., "**Black Gold: Oil Development in Texas**," **Texas: A Sesquicentennial Celebration**, Donald W. Whisenhunt, ed.; Eakin Press, Austin, 1984.

A Brief Sketch of Texas History

This brief, two-part sketch of Texas' past, from prehistoric times to 1920, is based on "A Concise History of Texas" by former Texas Almanac editor Mike Kingston. Mr. Kingston's history was published in the 1986-87 sesquicentennial edition of the Texas Almanac. Robert Plocheck, associate editor of the Texas Almanac, prepared this excerpt.

Texas: Prehistory to Annexation

Prehistoric Texas

Early Texans are believed to have been descendants of Asian groups that migrated across the Bering Strait during the Ice Ages of the past 50,000 years.

At intermittent periods, enough water accumulated in massive glaciers worldwide to lower the sea level several hundred feet. During these periods, the Bering Strait became a 1,300-mile-wide land bridge between North America and Asia.

These early adventurers worked their way southward for thousands of years, eventually getting as far as Tierra del Fuego in South America 10,000 years ago.

Biologically they were completely modern homo sapiens. No evidence has been found to indicate that any evolutionary change occurred in the New World.

Four basic stages reflecting cultural advancement of early inhabitants are used by archaeologists in classifying evidence. These stages are the Paleo-Indian (20,000 to 7,000 years ago), Archaic (7,000 years ago to about the time of Christ), Woodland (time of Christ to 800-1,000 years ago), and Neo-American or Late Prehistoric (800-1,000 years ago until European contact).

Not all early people advanced through all these stages in Texas. Much cultural change occurred in adaptation to changes in climate. The Caddo tribes of East Texas, for example, reached the Neo-American stage before the Spanish and French explorers made contact in the 1500s and 1600s.

Others, such as the Karankawas of the Gulf Coast, advanced no further than the Archaic stage of civilization at the same time. Still others advanced and then regressed in the face of a changing climate.

The earliest confirmed evidence indicates that humans were in Texas between 10,000 and 13,000 years ago.

Paleo-Indians were successful big-game hunters. Artifacts from this period are found across the state but not in great number, indicating that they were a small, nomadic population.

As Texas' climate changed at the end of the Ice Age about 7,000 years ago, inhabitants adapted. Apparently the state experienced an extended period of warming and drying, and the population increased.

These Texans began to harvest fruits and nuts and, to exploit rivers for food, as indicated by the fresh-water mussel shells in ancient garbage heaps.

The Woodland stage is distinguished by the development of settled societies, with crops and local wild plants providing much of their diet. The bow and arrow came into use, and the first pottery is associated with this period.

Pre-Caddoan tribes in East Texas had formed villages and were building distinctive mounds for burials and for ritual.

The Neo-American period is best exemplified by the highly-civilized Caddoes, who had a complex culture with well-defined social stratification. They were fully agricultural and participated in trade over a wide area of North America.

The Spanish Explorations

Spain's exploration of North America was one of the first acts of a vigorous nation that was emerging from centuries of campaigns to oust the Islamic Moors from the Iberian Peninsula.

In early 1492, the Spanish forces retook the province of Granada, completing the *reconquista* or reconquest. Later in the year, the Catholic royals of the united country, Ferdinand and Isabella, took a major stride toward shaping world history by commissioning Christopher Columbus for the voyage that was to bring Europeans to America.

As early as **1519,** Capt. Alonso Alvarez de Pineda, in the service of the governor of Jamaica, mapped the coast of Texas.

The first recorded exploration of today's Texas was made in the **1530s** by Alvar Núñez Cabeza de Vaca, along with two other Spaniards and a Moorish slave named Estevanico. They were members of an expedition commanded by Panfilo de Narváez that left Cuba in 1528 to explore what is now the southeastern United States. Ill-fated from the beginning, many members of the expedition lost their lives, and others, including Cabeza de Vaca, were shipwrecked on the Texas coast. Eventually the band wandered into Mexico in 1536.

In **1540,** Francisco Vázquez de Coronado was commissioned to lead an exploration of the American Southwest. The quest took him to the land of the Pueblo Indians in what is now New Mexico. Native Americans, who had learned it was best to keep Europeans away from their homes, would suggest vast riches could be found in other areas. So Coronado pursued a fruitless search for gold and silver across the **High Plains of Texas**, Oklahoma and Kansas.

While Coronado was investigating Texas from the west, Luis Moscoso de Alvarado approached from the east. He assumed leadership of Hernando de Soto's expedition when the commander died on the banks of the Mississippi River. In **1542,** Moscoso's group ventured as far west as **Central Texas** before returning to the Mississippi.

Forty years passed after the Coronado and Moscoso expeditions before Fray Agustín Rodríguez, a Franciscan missionary, and Francisco Sánchez Chamuscado, a soldier, led an expedition into Texas and New Mexico.

Following the Río Conchos in Mexico to its confluence with the Rio Grande near present-day **Presidio** and then turning northwestward up the great river's valley, the explorers passed through the El Paso area in **1581.**

Juan de Oñate was granted the right to develop this area populated by Pueblo Indians in 1598. He blazed a trail across the desert from Santa Barbara, Chihuahua, to intersect the Rio Grande at the Pass of the North. For the next 200 years, this was the supply route from the interior of Mexico that served the northern colonies.

Texas was attractive to the Spanish in the 1600s. Small expeditions found trade possibilities, and missionaries ventured into the territory. Frays Juan de Salas and Diego López responded to a request by the Jumano Indians for religious instruction in **1629**, and for a brief time priests lived with the Indians near present-day **San Angelo.**

The first permanent settlement in Texas was established in **1681-82** after New Mexico's Indians rebelled and drove Spanish settlers southward. The colonists retreated to the **El Paso** area, where the missions of Corpus Christi de la Isleta and Nuestra Señora del Socorro — each named for a community in New Mexico — were established. Ysleta pueblo originally was located on the south side of the Rio Grande, but as the river changed course, it ended up on the north bank. Now part of El Paso, the community is considered the oldest European settlement in Texas.

French Exploration

In 1682, **René Robert Cavelier, Sieur de La Salle**, explored the Mississippi River to its mouth at the Gulf of Mexico. La Salle claimed the vast territory drained by the river for France.

Two years later, La Salle returned to the New World with four ships and enough colonists to establish his country's claim. Guided by erroneous maps, this second expedition overshot the mouth of the Mississippi by 400 miles and ended up on the Texas coast. Though short of supplies because of the loss of two of the ships, the French colonists established Fort Saint Louis on Garcitas Creek several miles inland from Lavaca Bay.

In 1687, La Salle and a group of soldiers began an overland trip to find French outposts on the Mississippi. Somewhere west of the Trinity River, the explorer was murdered by some of his men. His grave has never been found. (A more detailed account of La Salle's expedition can be found in the 1998-1999 Texas Almanac.)

In 1689, Spanish authorities sent **Capt. Alonso de León**, governor of Coahuila (which at various times included Texas in its jurisdiction), into Texas to confront the French. He headed eastward from present-day Eagle Pass and found the tattered remnants of Fort Saint Louis.

Indians had destroyed the settlement and killed many colonists. De León continued tracking survivors of the ill-fated colony into East Texas.

Spanish Rule

Father **Damián Massanet** accompanied de León on this journey. The priest was fascinated with tales about the "Tejas" Indians of the region.

Tejas meant friendly, but at the time the term was considered a tribal name. Actually these Indians were members of the Caddo Confederacy that controlled parts of our present states: Texas, Louisiana, Arkansas and Oklahoma.

The Caddo religion acknowledged one supreme god, and when a Tejas chief asked Father Massanet to stay and instruct his people in his faith, the Spaniards promised to return and establish a mission.

The pledge was redeemed in **1690** when the mission San Francisco de los Tejas was founded near present-day Weches in Houston County.

Twin disasters struck this missionary effort. Spanish government officials quickly lost interest when the French threat at colonization diminished. And as was the case with many New World Indians who had no resistance to European diseases, the Tejas soon were felled by an epidemic. The Indians blamed the new religion and resisted conversion. The mission languished, and it was hard to supply from other Spanish outposts in northern Mexico. In 1693, the Spanish officials closed the mission effort in **East Texas**.

Although Spain had not made a determined effort to settle Texas, great changes were coming to the territory.

Spain introduced horses into the Southwest. By the late 1600s, Comanches were using the horses to expand their range southward across the plains, displacing Apaches.

In the 1720s, the Apaches moved onto the lower Texas Plains, usurping the traditional hunting grounds of the Jumanos and others. The nomadic Coahuiltecan bands were particularly hard hit.

In 1709, Fray Antonio de San Buenaventura y Olivares had made an initial request to establish a mission at San Pedro Springs (today's San Antonio) to minister to the Coahuiltecans. The request was denied. However, new fears of French movement into East Texas changed that.

Another Franciscan, **Father Francisco Hidalgo**, who had earlier served at the missions in East Texas returned to them when he and **Father Antonio Margil de Jesús** accompanied **Capt. Diego Ramón** on an expedition to the area in 1716. In that year, the mission of San Francisco de los Neches was established near the site of the old San Francisco de los Tejas mission. Nuestra Señora de Guadalupe was located at the present-day site of Nacogdoches, and Nuestra Señora de los Dolores was placed near present-day San Augustine.

The East Texas missions did little better on the second try, and supplying the frontier missions remained difficult. It became apparent that a way station between northern Mexico and East Texas was needed.

In **1718,** Spanish officials consented to Fray Olivares' request to found a mission at San Pedro Springs. That mission, called **San Antonio de Valero**, was later to be known as the **Alamo**. Because the Indians of the region often did not get along with each other, other missions were established to serve each group.

These missions flourished and each became an early ranching center. But the large herds of cattle and horses attracted trouble. The San Antonio missions began to face the wrath of the Apaches. The mission system, which attempted to convert the Indians to Christianity and to "civilize" them, was partially successful in subduing minor tribes but not larger tribes like the Apaches.

The Spanish realized that more stable colonization efforts must be made. Indians from Mexico, such as the Tlascalans who fought with Cortés against the Aztecs, were brought into Texas to serve as examples of "good" Indians for the wayward natives.

In **1731,** Spanish colonists from the Canary Islands were brought to Texas and founded the Villa of San Fernando de Béxar, the first civil jurisdiction in the province and today's **San Antonio.**

In the late 1730s, Spanish officials became concerned over the vulnerability of the large area between

the Sierra Madre Oriental and the Gulf Coast in northern Mexico. The area was unsettled, a haven for runaway Indian slaves and marauders, and it was a wide-open pathway for the English or French from the Gulf to the rich silver mines in Durango.

For seven years the search for the right colonizer went on before José de Escandón was selected in 1746. A professional military man and successful administrator, Escandón earned a high reputation by subduing Indians in central Mexico. On receiving the assignment, he launched a broad land survey of the area running from the mountains to the Gulf and from the Río Pánuco in Tamaulipas, Mexico, to the Nueces River in Texas.

In 1747, he began placing colonists in settlements throughout the area. Tomás Sánchez received a land grant on the Rio Grande in **1755** from which **Laredo** developed. And other small Texas communities along the river sprang up as a result of Escandón's well-executed plan. Many old Hispanic families in Texas hold title of their land based on grants in this period.

In the following decades, a few other Spanish colonists settled around the old missions and frontier forts. Antonio Gil Ybarbo led one group that settled **Nacogdoches** in the **1760s and 1770s.**

The Demise of Spain

Spain's final 60 years of control of the province of Texas were marked with a few successes and a multitude of failures, all of which could be attributed to a breakdown in the administrative system.

Charles III, the fourth of the Bourbon line of kings, took the Spanish throne in 1759. He launched a series of reforms in the New World. The king's choice of administrators was excellent. In 1765, José de Gálvez was dispatched to New Spain (an area that then included all of modern Mexico and much of today's American West) with instructions to improve both the economy and the defense.

Gálvez initially toured parts of the vast region, gaining first-hand insight into the practical problems of the colony. There were many that could be traced to Spain's basic concepts of colonial government. Texas, in particular, suffered from the mercantilist economic system that attempted to funnel all colonial trade through ports in Mexico.

But administrative reforms by Gálvez and his nephew, Bernardo Gálvez, namesake of Galveston, were to be followed by ill-advised policies by successors.

Problems with the Comanches, Apaches and "Norteños," as the Spanish called some tribes, continued to plague the province, too.

About the same time, Spain undertook the administration of Louisiana Territory. One of the terms of the cession by France was that the region would enjoy certain trading privileges denied to other Spanish dependencies. So although Texas and Louisiana were neighbors, trade between the two provinces was banned.

The crown further complicated matters by placing the administration of Louisiana under authorities in Cuba, while Texas remained under the authorities in Mexico City.

The death of Charles III in 1788 and the beginning of the French Revolution a year later weakened Spain's hold on the New World dominions. Charles IV was not as good a sovereign as his predecessor, and his choice of

ministers was poor. The quality of frontier administrators declined, and relations with Indians soured further.

Charles IV's major blunder, however, was to side with French royalty during the revolution, earning Spain the enmity of Napoleon Bonaparte. Spain also allied with England in an effort to thwart Napoleon, and in this losing cause, the Spanish were forced to cede Louisiana back to France.

In 1803, Napoleon broke a promise to retain the territory and sold it to the United States. Spain's problems in the New World thereby took on an altogether different dimension. Now, Anglo-Americans cast longing eyes on the vast undeveloped territory of Texas.

With certain exceptions for royalists who left the American colonies during the revolution, Spain had maintained a strict prohibition against Anglo or other non-Spanish settlers in their New World territories. But they were unprepared to police the eastern border of Texas after removing the presidios in the 1760s. What had been a provincial line became virtually overnight an international boundary, and an ill-defined one at that.

American Immigrants

Around **1800**, **Anglo-Americans** began to probe the Spanish frontier. Some settled in East Texas and others crossed the Red River and were tolerated by authorities.

Others, however, were thought to have nefarious designs. Philip Nolan was the first of the American filibusters to test Spanish resolve. Several times he entered Texas to capture wild horses to sell in the United States.

But in 1801, the Spanish perceived an attempted insurrection by Nolan and his followers. He was killed in a battle near present-day Waco, and his company was taken captive to work in the mines in northern Mexico.

Spanish officials were beginning to realize that the economic potential of Texas must be developed if the Anglo-Americans were to be neutralized.

But Spain's centuries-long role in the history of Texas was almost over.

Resistance to Spanish rule had developed in the New World colonies. Liberal ideas from the American and French revolutions had grown popular, despite the crown's attempts to prevent their dissemination.

In Spain, three sovereigns — the Charles IV, Napoleon's brother Joseph Bonaparte, and Ferdinand VII — claimed the throne, often issuing different edicts simultaneously. Since the time of Philip II, Spain had been a tightly centralized monarchy with the crown making most decisions. Now, chaos reigned in the colonies.

As Spain's grip on the New World slipped between 1790 and 1820, Texas was almost forgotten, an internal province of little importance. Colonization was ignored; the Spanish government had larger problems in Europe and in Mexico.

Spain's mercantile economic policy penalized colonists in the area, charging them high prices for trade goods and paying low prices for products sent to markets in the interior of New Spain. As a result, settlers from central Mexico had no incentives to come to Texas. Indeed, men of ambition in the province often prospered by turning to illegal trade with Louisiana or to smuggling. On the positive side, however, Indians of the province had been mollified through annual gifts and by developing a dependence on Spain for trade goods.

Ranching flourished. In **1795,** a census found **69**

families living on 45 ranches in the **San Antonio** area. A census in **1803** indicated that there were **100,000 head of cattle** in Texas. But aside from a few additional families in Nacogdoches and La Bahía (near present-day Goliad), the province was thinly populated.

The largest group of early immigrants from the United States was not Anglo, but Indian.

As early as **1818, Cherokees** of the southeastern United States came to Texas, settling north of Nacogdoches on lands between the Trinity and Sabine rivers. The Cherokees had been among the first U.S. Indians to accept the federal government's offers of resettlement. As American pioneers entered the newly-acquired lands of Georgia, Alabama and other areas of the Southeast, the Indians were systematically removed, through legal means or otherwise.

Some of the displaced groups settled on land provided in Arkansas Territory, but others, such as the Cherokees, came to Texas. These Cherokees were among the "Five Civilized Tribes" that had adopted agriculture and many Anglo customs in an unsuccessful attempt to get along with their new neighbors. Alabama and Coushatta tribes had exercised squatters' rights in present Sabine County in the early 1800s, and soon after the Cherokees arrived, groups of Shawnee, Delaware and Kickapoo Indians came from the United States.

A **second wave of Anglo** immigrants began to arrive in Texas, larger than the first and of a different character. These Anglos were not so interested in agricultural opportunities as in other schemes to quickly recoup their fortunes.

Spain recognized the danger represented by the unregulated colonization by Americans. The Spanish Cortes' colonization law of 1813 attempted to build a buffer between the eastern frontier and northern Mexico. Special permission was required for Americans to settle within 52 miles of the international boundary, although this prohibition often was ignored.

As initially envisioned, Americans would be allowed to settle the interior of Texas. Colonists from Europe and Mexico would be placed along the eastern frontier to limit contact between the Americans and the United States. Spanish officials felt that the Americans already in Texas illegally would be stable if given a stake in the province through land ownership.

Moses Austin, a former Spanish subject in the vast Louisiana Territory, applied for the first empresario grant from the Spanish government. With the intercession of Baron de Bastrop, a friend of Austin's from Missouri Territory, the request was approved in January **1821.**

Austin agreed to settle **300 families** on land bounded by the Brazos and Colorado rivers on the east and west, by El Camino Real (the old military road running from San Antonio to Nacogdoches) on the north and by the Gulf Coast.

But Austin died in June 1821, leaving the work to his son, **Stephen F. Austin**. Problems began as soon as the first authorized colonists arrived in Texas the following December when it was learned that Mexico had gained independence from Spain.

Mexico, 1821-1836

Mexico's war for independence, 1810-1821, was savage and bloody in the interior provinces, and Texas suffered as well.

In early 1812, Mexican revolutionary José Bernardo Gutiérrez de Lara traveled to Natchitoches, La., where, with the help of U.S. agents, an expedition was organized. **Augustus W. Magee**, a West Point graduate, commanded the troop, which entered Texas in August 1812. This "Republican Army of the North" easily took Nacogdoches, where it gathered recruits.

Stephen F. Austin

After withstanding a siege at La Bahía, the army took San Antonio and proclaimed the First Republic of Texas in April 1813. A few months later, the republican forces were bloodily subdued at the Battle of Medina River.

Royalist Gen. Joaquín de Arredondo executed a staggering number of more than 300 republicans, including some Americans, at San Antonio, and a young lieutenant, **Antonio López de Santa Anna**, was recognized for valor under fire.

When the war finally ended in Mexico in 1821, little more had been achieved than separation from Spain.

Sensing that liberal reforms in Spain would reduce the authority of royalists in the New World, Mexican conservatives had led the revolt against the mother country. They also achieved early victories in the debate over the form of government the newly independent Mexico should adopt.

An independent Mexico was torn between advocates of centralist and federalist forms of government.

The former royalists won the opening debates, settling Emperor Agustín de Iturbide on the new Mexican throne. But he was overthrown and the Constitution of 1824, a federalist document, was adopted.

The Mexican election of 1828 was a turning point in the history of the country when the legally-elected administration of Manuel Gómez Pedraza was overthrown by supporters of Vicente Guerrero, who in turn was ousted by his own vice president Anastasio Bustamante. Mexico's most chaotic political period followed. Between 1833 and 1855, the Mexican presidency changed hands 36 times.

Texas, 1821-1833

Mexico's **land policy**, like Spain's, differed from the U.S. approach. Whereas the United States sold land directly to settlers or to speculators who dealt with the pioneers, the Mexicans retained tight control of the property transfer until predetermined agreements for development were fulfilled.

But a 4,428-acre *sitio* — a square league — and a 177-acre *labor* could be obtained for only surveying costs and administrative fees as low as $50. The empresario was rewarded with grants of large tracts of land, but only when he fulfilled his quota of families to be brought to the colonies.

Considering the prices the U.S. government charged, Texas' land was indeed a bargain and a major attraction to those Americans looking for a new start.

More than 25 empresarios were commissioned to settle colonists. Empresarios included **Green DeWitt** and **Martín de León**, who in 1824 founded the city of Guadalupe Victoria (present-day Victoria).

By 1830, Texas boasted an estimated population of 15,000, with Anglo-Americans outnumbering Hispanics by a margin of four to one.

Stephen F. Austin was easily the most successful empresario. After his initial success, Austin was authorized in 1825 to bring 900 more families to Texas, and in 1831, he and his partner, **Samuel Williams**, received another concession to bring 800 Mexican and European families.

Through Austin's efforts, 1,540 land titles were issued to settlers.

In the early years of colonization, the settlers busied themselves clearing land, planting crops, building homes and fending off Indian attacks. Many were successful in establishing a subsistence economy.

One weakness of the Mexican colonial policy was that it did not provide the factors for a market economy. Although towns were established, credit, banks and good roads were not provided by the government.

Ports were established at Galveston and Matagorda bays after Mexican independence, but the colonists felt they needed more, particularly one at the mouth of the Brazos. And foreign ships were barred from coastwise trade, which posed a particular hardship since Mexico had few merchant ships.

To settle in Texas, pioneers had to become Mexican citizens and to embrace Roman Catholicism. Most of the Americans were Protestants, if they adhered to any religion, and they were fiercely defensive of the right to **religious freedom** enjoyed in the United States.

Although no more than one-fourth of the Americans ever swore allegiance to the Catholic Church, the requirement was a long-standing irritation.

Slavery, too, was a point of contention. Mexico prohibited the introduction of slavery after December 1827. Nevertheless, several efforts were made to evade the government policy. Austin got the state legislature to recognize labor contracts under which slaves were technically free but bound themselves to their masters for life. Often entire families were covered by a single contract. While many early Anglo colonists were not slaveholders, they were Southerners, and the ownership of slaves was a cultural institution that they supported. The problem was never settled during the colonial period despite the tensions it generated.

Most of the early Anglo-American colonists in Texas intended to fulfill their pledge to become good Mexican citizens. But the political turmoil following the 1828 presidential election raised doubts in the Americans' minds about the ability of Mexico to make representative government function properly.

On a tour of the state in 1827 and 1828, Gen. Manuel Mier y Terán noted that the Texans "carried their constitutions in their pockets." And he feared the Americans' desire for more rights and liberties than the government was prepared to offer would lead to rebellion.

Unrest increased in Texas when Gen. Mier y Terán began reinforcing existing garrisons and establishing new ones.

But a major factor in the discontent of Americans came with the **decree of April 6, 1830**, when the Mexican government in essence banned further American immigration into Texas and tried to control slavery.

Austin protested that the prohibition against American immigration would not stop the flow of Anglos into Texas; it would stop only the stable, prosperous Americans from coming.

Austin's predictions were fulfilled. Illegal immigrants continued to come. By 1836, the estimated number of people in Texas had reached 35,000.

Prelude to Revolution

In the midst of all the turmoil, Texas was prospering. By 1834, some 7,000 bales of cotton with a value of $315,000 were shipped to New Orleans. In the middle of the decade, Texas exports, including cotton and beaver, otter and deer skins, amounted to $500,000.

Trade ratios were out of balance, however, because $630,000 in manufactured goods were imported. And, there was little currency in Texas. Ninety percent of the business transactions were conducted in barter or credit.

In 1833 and 1834, the **Coahuila y Texas** legislature was diligently trying to respond to the complaints of the Texas colonists. The English language was recognized for official purposes. Religious toleration was approved. The court system was revised, providing Texas with an appellate court and trial by jury.

In Mexico City, however, a different scenario was developing. **Santa Anna** assumed supreme authority in April 1834 and began dismantling the federalist government. Among the most offensive changes dictated by Santa Anna was the reduction of the state militias to one man per each 500 population. The intent was to eliminate possible armed opposition to the emerging centralist government.

But liberals in the state of Zacatecas in central Mexico rebelled. Santa Anna's response was particularly brutal, as he tried to make an example of the rebels. Troops were allowed to sack the state capital after the victory over the insurgents.

Trouble also was brewing closer to the Texans.

In March 1833, the Coahuila y Texas legislature moved the state capital from Saltillo to Monclova. The Monclova legislature in 1834 gave the governor authority to sell 400 sitios — or 1.77 million acres of land — to finance the government and to provide for protection. A year later the lawmakers criticized Santa Anna's reputation on federalism. Seeing a chance to regain lost prestige, Saltillo declared for Santa Anna and set up an opposition government. In the spring of 1835, Santa Anna sent his brother-in-law, Martín Perfecto de Cos, to break up the state government at Monclova.

Texans were appalled by the breakdown in state government, coming on the heels of so many assurances that the political situation was to improve.

Texas politics were polarizing. A "war party" advocated breaking away from Mexico altogether, while a "peace party" urged calm and riding out the political storm. Most of the settlers, however, aligned with neither group.

In January 1835, Santa Anna sent a detachment of soldiers to Anahuac to reinforce the customs office, but duties were being charged irregularly at various ports on the coast. William B. Travis, in an act not supported by all colonists, led a contingent of armed colonists against the Mexican soldiers, who withdrew without a fight.

Although some members of the peace party wrote Mexican Gen. **Martín Perfecto de Cos**, stationed at Matamoros, apologizing for the action, he was not compromising. Cos demanded that the group be arrested and turned over to him. The Texans refused.

The committees of correspondence, organized at the Convention of 1832 (which had asked that Texas be separated from Coahuila), began organizing another meeting. Because the term "convention" aroused visions of revolution in the eyes of Mexican officials, the gathering at Washington-on-the-Brazos in October 1835 was called a "consultation." But with the breakdown of the state government and with Santa Anna's repeal of the Constitution of 1824, the American settlers felt well within their rights to provide a new framework with which to govern Texas.

Fresh from brutally putting down the rebellion in Zacatecas, Santa Anna turned his attention to Texas. Gen. Cos was determined to regarrison the state, and the settlers were equally adamant about keeping soldiers out.

Col. **Domingo de Ugartechea**, headquartered at San Antonio, became concerned about armed rebellion when he heard of the incident at Anahuac. He recalled a six-pound cannon that had been given DeWitt colonists to fight Indians.

Ugartechea ordered Cpl. Casimira de León with five men to Gonzales to retrieve the weapon. No problems were expected, but officials at Gonzales refused to surrender the weapon. When the Mexicans reinforced Cpl. de León's men, a call was sent out for volunteers to help the Gonzales officials. Dozens responded.

On Oct. 2, 1835, the Texans challenged the Mexicans with a **"come-and-take-it" flag** over the cannon. After a brief skirmish, the Mexicans withdrew, but the first rounds in the Texas Revolution had been fired.

Winning Independence

As 1836 opened, Texans felt in control of their destiny and secure in their land and their liberties. The Mexican army had been driven from their soil.

But tragedy loomed. Easy victories over government forces at Anahuac, Nacogdoches, Goliad, Gonzales and San Antonio in the fall of 1835 had given them a false sense of security. That independent mood was their undoing, for no government worthy of the name coordinated the defense of Texas. Consequently, as the Mexican counterattack developed, no one was in charge. Sam Houston was titular commander-in-chief of the Texas forces, but he had little authority.

Some even thought the Mexicans would not try to re-enter Texas. Few Texans counted on the energy and determination of Santa Anna, the dictator of Mexico.

The status of the strongholds along the San Antonio River was of concern to Houston. In mid-January, Houston sent **James Bowie** to San Antonio to determine if the Alamo was defensible. If not, Bowie had orders to destroy it and withdraw the men and artillery to Gonzales and Copano.

On Feb. 8, David Crockett of Tennessee, bringing 12 men with him, arrived to aid the revolutionaries.

On Feb. 12, 1836, Santa Anna's main force crossed

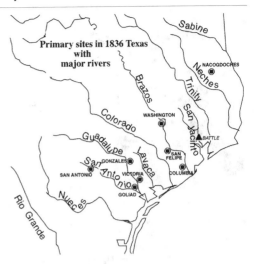

the Rio Grande headed for San Antonio. The Mexican battle plan has been debated. But Mexico's national pride had been bruised by the series of defeats the nation's army had suffered in 1835, capped by Gen. Cos's ouster from San Antonio in December.

On Feb. 11, the Consultation's "governor of the government" **Henry Smith**, sent **William B. Travis** to San Antonio. Immediately a split in command at the **Alamo** garrison arose. Most were American volunteers who looked to the Houston-appointed Bowie as their leader. Travis had only a handful of Texas army regulars. So Bowie and Travis agreed to share the command of 150 men.

Arriving at the Alamo on Feb. 23, Santa Anna left no doubt regarding his attitude toward the defenders. He hoisted a blood-red flag, the traditional Mexican symbol of no quarter, no surrender, no mercy. Travis and Bowie defiantly answered the display with a cannon shot.

Immediately the Mexicans began surrounding the Alamo and bombarding it. Throughout the first night and nights to come, Santa Anna kept up a continual din to destroy the defenders' morale.

On Feb. 24, Bowie became ill and relinquished his share of command to Travis. Although the Mexican bombardment of the Alamo continued, none of the defenders was killed. In fact, they conducted several successful forays outside the fortress to burn buildings that were providing cover for the Mexican gunners and to gather firewood.

Messengers also successfully moved through the Mexican lines at will, and 32 reinforcements from Gonzales made it into the Alamo without a loss on March 1.

Historians disagree over which flag flew over the defenders of the Alamo.

Mexican sources have said that Santa Anna was outraged when he saw flying over the fortress a Mexican tricolor, identical to the ones carried by his troops except with the numbers "1 8 2 4" emblazoned upon it. Some Texas historians have accepted this version because the defenders of the Alamo could not have known that Texas' independence had been declared on March 2. To the knowledge of the Alamo's defenders, the last official

David Crockett

position taken by Texas was in support of the Constitution of 1824, which the flag symbolized. But the only flag found after the battle, according to historian Walter Lord, was one flown by the **New Orleans Greys**.

By March 5, Santa Anna had 4,000 men in camp, a force he felt sufficient to subdue the Alamo.

Historians disagree on the date, but the story goes that on March 3 or 5, Travis called his command together and explained the bleak outlook. He then asked those willing to die for freedom to stay and fight; those not willing could try to get through enemy lines to safety. Even the sick Jim Bowie vowed to stay. Only Louis (Moses) Rose, a veteran of Napoleon's retreat from Moscow slipped out of the Alamo that night.

At dawn March 6, Santa Anna's forces attacked. When the fighting stopped between 8:30 and 9 a.m., all the defenders were dead. Only a few women, children and black slaves survived the assault. **Davy Crockett**'s fate is still debated. Mexican officer Enrique de la Peña held that Crockett was captured with a few other defenders and was executed by Santa Anna.

Santa Anna's victory came at the cost of almost one-third his forces killed or wounded. Their deaths in such number set back Santa Anna's timetable. The fall of the Alamo also brutally shook Texans out of their lethargy.

Sam Houston, finally given command of the entire Texas army, left the convention at **Washington-on-the-Brazos** on the day of the fall of the Alamo.

On March 11, he arrived at Gonzales to begin organizing the troops. Two days later, **Susanna Dickinson**, the wife of one of the victims of the Alamo, and two slaves arrived at Houston's position at Gonzales with the news of the fall of the San Antonio fortress.

Houston then ordered **James Fannin** to abandon the old presidio **La Bahía** at Goliad and to retreat to Victoria. Fannin had arrived at the fort in late January with more than 400 men. As a former West Pointer, he had a background in military planning, but Fannin had refused Travis' pleas for help, and after receiving Houston's orders, Fannin waited for scouting parties to return.

Finally, on March 19, he left, but too late. Forward elements of Gen. José de Urrea's troops caught Fannin's command on an open prairie. After a brief skirmish Fannin surrendered.

Santa Anna was furious when Gen. Urrea appealed for clemency for the captives. The Mexican leader issued orders for their execution. On March 27, a Palm Sunday, most of the prisoners were divided into groups and marched out of Goliad, thinking they were being transferred to other facilities. When the executions began, many escaped. But about 350 were killed.

On March 17, Houston reached the Colorado near the present city of La Grange and began receiving reinforcements. Within a week, the small force of several hundred had become almost respectable, with 1,200-1,400 men in camp.

At the time Houston reached the Colorado, the convention at Washington-on-the-Brazos was completing work. **David Burnet**, a New Jersey native, was named interim president of the new Texas government, and **Lorenzo de Zavala**, a Yucatán native, was named vice president.

On March 27, Houston moved his men to San Felipe on the Brazos. The Texas army was impatient for a fight, and there was talk in the ranks that, if action did not develop soon, a new commander should be elected.

As the army marched farther back toward the San Jacinto River, two Mexican couriers were captured and gave Houston the information he had hoped for. Santa Anna in his haste had led the small Mexican force in front of Houston. Now the Texans had an opportunity to win the war.

Throughout the revolt, Houston's intelligence system had operated efficiently. Scouts, commanded by **Erastus "Deaf" Smith**, kept the Texans informed of Mexican troop movements. **Hendrick Arnold**, a free black, was a valuable spy, posing as a runaway slave to enter Mexican camps to gain information.

Early on April 21, Gen. Cos reinforced Santa Anna's troops with more than 500 men. The new arrivals, who had marched all night, disrupted the camp's routine for a time, but soon all the soldiers and officers settled down for a midday rest.

About 3 p.m., Houston ordered his men to parade and the battle was launched at 4:30 p.m.

A company of Mexican-Texans, commanded by **Juan Seguín**, had served as the rear guard for Houston's army through much of the retreat across Texas and had fought many skirmishes with the Mexican army in the process.

Perhaps fearing the Mexican-Texans would be mistaken for Santa Anna's soldiers, Houston had assigned the company to guard duty as the battle approached. But after the men protested, they fought in the battle of San Jacinto.

Historians disagree widely on the number of troops on each side. Houston probably had about 900 while Santa Anna had between 1,100 and 1,300.

But the Texans had the decided psychological advantage. Two thirds of the fledgling Republic's army were "old Texans" who had family and land to defend. They had an investment of years of toil in building their homes. And they were eager to avenge the massacre of men at the Alamo and Goliad.

In less than 20 minutes they set the Mexican army to rout. More than 600 Mexicans were killed and hundreds more wounded or captured. Only nine of the Texans died in the fight.

It was not until the following day that Santa Anna was captured. One Texan noticed that a grubby soldier his patrol found in the high grass had a silk shirt under his filthy jacket. Although denying he was an officer, he was taken back to camp, where he was acknowledged with cries of "El Presidente" by other prisoners.

Santa Anna introduced himself when taken to the wounded Houston.

President Burnet took charge of Santa Anna, and on May 14 the dictator signed **two treaties at Velasco**, a public document and a secret one. The public agreement declared that hostilities would cease, that the Mexican army would withdraw to south of the Rio Grande, that prisoners would be released and that Santa Anna would be shipped to Veracruz as soon as possible.

In the secret treaty, Santa Anna agreed to recognize Texas' independence, to give diplomatic recognition, to negotiate a commercial treaty and to set the **Rio Grande** as the new Republic's boundary.

Republic of Texas, 1836-1845

Sam Houston was easily the most dominant figure through the nearly 10-year history of the Republic of Texas. While he was roundly criticized for the retreat across Texas during the revolution, the victory at San Jacinto endeared him to most of the new nation's inhabitants.

Houston handily defeated Henry Smith and Stephen F. Austin in the election called in September 1836 by the interim government, and he was inaugurated as president on Oct. 22.

In the same September election, voters overwhelmingly approved a proposal to request annexation to the United States.

The first cabinet appointed by the new president represented an attempt to heal old political wounds. Austin was named secretary of state and Smith was secretary of the treasury. But Texas suffered a major tragedy in late December 1836 when Austin, the acknowledged **"Father of Texas,"** died of pneumonia.

A host of problems faced the new government. Santa Anna was still in custody, and public opinion favored his execution. Texas' leadership wisely kept Santa Anna alive, first to keep from giving the Mexicans an emotional rallying point for launching another invasion. Second, the Texas leaders hoped that the dictator would keep his promise to work for recognition of Texas.

Santa Anna was released in November 1836 and made his way to Washington, D.C. Houston hoped the dictator could persuade U.S. President **Andrew Jackson** to recognize Texas. Jackson refused to see Santa Anna, who returned to Mexico, where he had fallen from power.

Another major challenge was the Texas army. The new commander, Felix Huston, favored an invasion of Mexico, and the troops, made up now mostly of American volunteers who came to Texas after the battle of San Jacinto, were rebellious and ready to fight.

President Houston tried to replace Felix Huston with **Albert Sidney Johnston**, but Huston seriously wounded Johnston in a duel. In May 1837, Huston was asked to the capital in Columbia to discuss the invasion. While Huston was away from the troops, Houston sent **Thomas J. Rusk**, the secretary of war, to furlough the army without pay — but with generous land grants. Only 600 men were retained in the army.

The Republic's other problems were less tractable. The economy needed attention, Indians still were a threat, Mexico remained warlike, foreign relations had to be developed, and relations with the United States had to be solidified.

The greatest disappointment in Houston's first term was the failure to have the Republic annexed to the United States. Henry Morfit, President Jackson's agent, toured the new Republic in the summer of 1836. Although impressed, Morfit reported that Texas' best

chance at continued independence lay in the "stupidity of the rulers of Mexico and the financial embarrassment of the Mexican government." He recommended that annexation be delayed.

Houston's foreign policy achieved initial success when **J. Pinckney Henderson** negotiated a trade treaty with Great Britain. Although the agreement was short of outright diplomatic recognition, it was progress. In the next few years, France, Belgium, The Netherlands and some German states recognized the new Republic.

Under the constitution, Houston's first term lasted only two years, and he could not succeed himself. His successor, **Mirabeau B. Lamar**, had grand visions and was a spendthrift. Houston's first term cost Texas only about $500,000, while President Lamar and the Congress spent $5 million in the next three years.

Early in 1839, Lamar gained recognition as the **"Father of Education"** in Texas when the Congress granted each of the existing 23 counties three leagues of land to be used for education. Fifty leagues of land were set aside for a university.

Despite the lip service paid to education, the government did not have the money for several years to set up a school system. Most education during the Republic was provided by private schools and churches.

Lamar's Indian policies differed greatly from those under Houston. Houston had lived with Cherokees as a youth, was adopted as a member of a tribe and advocated Indian rights long before coming to Texas. Lamar reflected more the frontier attitude toward American Indians. His first experience in public life was as secretary to Gov. George Troup of Georgia, who successfully opposed the federal government's policy of assimilation of Indians at the time. Indians were simply removed from Georgia.

Texans' first tried to negotiate the Cherokees' removal from the region, but in July 1839, the Indians were forcibly ejected from Texas at the **Battle of the Neches River** in Van Zandt County. Houston's close friend, the aging Cherokee chief **Philip Bowles**, was killed in the battle while Houston was visiting former President Jackson in Tennessee. The Cherokees moved on to Arkansas and Indian Territory.

Houston was returned to the presidency of the Republic in 1841. His second administration was even more frugal than his first; soon income almost matched expenditures.

Houston re-entered negotiations with the Indians in Central Texas in an attempt to quell the raids on settlements. A number of trading posts were opened along the frontier to pacify the Indians.

War fever reached a high pitch in Texas in 1842, and Houston grew increasingly unpopular because he would not launch an offensive war against Mexico.

In March 1842, Gen. **Rafael Vásquez** staged guerrilla raids on San Antonio, Victoria and Goliad, but quickly left the Republic.

A force of 3,500 Texas volunteers gathered at San Antonio demanding that Mexico be punished. Houston urged calm, but the clamor increased when Mexican **Gen. Adrian Woll** captured San Antonio in September. He raised the Mexican flag and declared the reconquest of Texas.

Ranger Capt. **Jack Hays** was camped nearby. Within days 600 volunteers had joined him, eager to drive the Mexican invaders from Texas soil. Gen. Woll withdrew after the **Battle of Salado**.

Alexander Somervell was ordered by Houston to follow with 700 troops and harass the Mexican army. He reached Laredo in December and found no Mexican troops. Somervell crossed the Rio Grande to find military targets. A few days later, the commander returned home, but 300 soldiers decided to continue the raid under the command of William S. Fisher. On Christmas day, this group attacked the village of **Mier**, only to be defeated by a Mexican force that outnumbered them 10-to-1.

After attempting mass escape, the survivors of the Mier expedition were marched to Mexico City where Santa Anna, again in political power, ordered their execution. When officers refused to carry out the order, it was amended to require execution of one of every 10 Texans. The prisoners drew beans to determine who would be shot; bearers of **black beans** were executed. Texans again were outraged by the treatment of prisoners, but the war fever soon subsided.

As Houston completed his second term, the United States was becoming more interested in annexation. Texas had seriously flirted with Great Britain and France, and the Americans did not want a rival republic with close foreign ties on the North American continent. Houston orchestrated the early stages of the final steps toward annexation. It was left to his successor, **Anson Jones**, to complete the process.

The Republic of Texas' main claim to fame is simply endurance. Its settlers, unlike other Americans who had military help, had cleared a large region of Indians by themselves, had established farms and communities and had persevered through extreme economic hardship.

Adroit political leadership had gained the Republic recognition from many foreign countries. Although dreams of empire may have dimmed, Texans had established an identity on a major portion of the North American continent. The frontier had been pushed to a line running from Corpus Christi through San Antonio and Austin to the Red River.

The U.S. presidential campaign of 1844 was to make Texas a part of the Union. ☆

Texas: Annexation to 1920

Annexation

Annexation to the United States was far from automatic for Texas once independence from Mexico was gained in 1836. Sam Houston noted that Texas "was more coy than forward" as negotiations reached a climax in 1845.

William H. Wharton was Texas' first representative in Washington. His instructions were to gain diplomatic recognition of the new Republic's independence.

After some squabbles, the U.S. Congress appropriated funds for a minister to Texas, and President Andrew Jackson recognized the new country in one of his last acts in office in March 1837.

Texas President **Mirabeau B. Lamar** (1838-41) opposed annexation. He held visions of empire in which Texas would rival the United States for supremacy on the North American continent.

During his administration, Great Britain began a close relationship with Texas and made strenuous efforts to get Mexico to recognize the Republic. This relationship between Great Britain and Texas raised fears in the United States that Britain might attempt to make Texas part of its empire.

Southerners feared for the future of slavery in Texas, which had renounced the importation of slaves as a concession to get a trade treaty with Great Britain, and American newspapers noted that trade with Texas had suffered after the Republic received recognition from European countries.

In Houston's second term in the Texas presidency, he instructed **Isaac Van Zandt**, his minister in Washington, to renew the annexation negotiations. Although U.S. President **John Tyler** and his cabinet were eager to annex Texas, they were worried about ratification in the U.S. Senate. The annexation question was put off.

In January 1844, Houston again gave Van Zandt instructions to propose annexation talks. This time the United States agreed to Houston's standing stipulation that, for serious negotiations to take place, the United States must provide military protection to Texas. U.S. naval forces were ordered to the Gulf of Mexico and U.S. troops were positioned on the southwest border close to Texas.

On April 11, 1844, Texas and the United States signed a treaty for annexation. Texas would enter the Union as a territory, not a state, under terms of the treaty. The United States would assume Texas' debt up to $10 million and would negotiate Texas' southwestern boundary with Mexico.

On June 8, 1844, the U.S. Senate rejected the treaty with a vote of 35-16, with much of the opposition coming from the slavery abolition wing of the Whig Party.

But **westward expansion** became a major issue in the U.S. presidential election that year. James K. Polk, the Democratic nominee, was a supporter of expansion, and the party's platform called for adding Oregon and Texas to the Union.

After Polk won the election in November, President Tyler declared that the people had spoken on the issue of annexation, and he resubmitted the matter to Congress. Several bills were introduced in the U.S. House of Representatives containing various proposals.

In **February 1845**, the U.S. Congress approved a resolution that would bring Texas into the Union as a state. Texas would cede its public property, such as forts and custom houses, to the United States, but it could keep its public lands and must retain its public debt. The region could be divided into four new states in addition to the original Texas. And the United States would negotiate the Rio Grande boundary claim.

British officials asked the Texas government to delay consideration of the U.S. offer for 90 days to attempt to get Mexico to recognize the Republic. The delay did no good: Texans' minds were made up.

President Anson Jones, who succeeded Houston in 1844, called a convention to write a **state constitution** in Austin on July 4, 1845.

Mexico finally recognized Texas' independence, but

the recognition was rejected. **Texas voters overwhelmingly accepted the U.S. proposal** and approved the new constitution in a referendum.

On **Dec. 29, 1845**, the U.S. Congress accepted the state constitution, and Texas became a part of the United States.

1845-1860

The entry of Texas into the Union touched off the **War with Mexico**, a war that some historians now think was planned by President James K. Polk to obtain the vast American Southwest.

Gen. **Zachary Taylor** was sent to Corpus Christi, just above the Nueces River, in July 1845. In February 1846, right after Texas formally entered the Union, the general was ordered to move troops into the disputed area south of the Nueces to the mouth of the Rio Grande. Mexican officials protested the move, claiming the status of the territory was under negotiation.

After Gen. Taylor refused to leave, Mexican President **Mariano Paredes** declared the opening of a defensive war against the United States on April 24, 1846.

After initial encounters at **Palo Alto** and **Resaca de la Palma**, both a few miles north of today's **Brownsville**, the war was fought south of the Rio Grande.

President Polk devised a plan to raise 50,000 volunteers from every section of the United States to fight the war. About 5,000 Texans saw action in Mexico.

Steamboats provided an important supply link for U.S. forces along the Rio Grande. Historical figures such as **Richard King**, founder of the legendary King Ranch, and **Mifflin Kenedy**, another rancher and businessman, first came to the **Lower Rio Grande Valley** as steamboat operators during the war.

Much farther up the Rio Grande, the war was hardly noticed. U.S. forces moved south from Santa Fe, which had been secured in December 1846. After a minor skirmish with Mexican forces north of El Paso, the U.S. military established American jurisdiction in this part of Texas.

Gen. **Winfield Scott** brought the war to a close in March 1847 with the capture of Mexico City.

When the **Treaty of Guadalupe Hidalgo** was signed on Feb. 2, 1848, the United States had acquired the American Southwest for development. And in Texas, the Rio Grande became an international boundary.

Germans, rather than Anglos, were the first whites to push the Texas frontier into west Central Texas after annexation. **John O. Meusebach** became leader of the German immigration movement in Texas, and he led a wagon train of some 120 settlers to the site of **Fredericksburg** in May 1846.

Germans also migrated to the major cities, such as San Antonio and Galveston, and by 1850 there were more people of German birth or parentage in Texas than there were Mexican-Texans.

The estimated population of 150,000 at annexation grew to 212,592, including 58,161 slaves, in the first U.S. census count in Texas in 1850.

As the state's population grew, the regions developed distinct population characteristics. The southeast and eastern sections attracted immigrants from the Lower South, the principal slaveholding states. Major plantations developed in these areas.

North Texas got more Upper Southerners and Mid-westerners. These immigrants were mostly small farmers and few owned slaves.

Mexican-Texans had difficulty with Anglo immigrants. The **"cart war"** broke out in 1857. Mexican teamsters controlled the transportation of goods from the Gulf coast to San Antonio and could charge lower rates than their competition.

A campaign of terror was launched by Anglo haulers, especially around Goliad, in an attempt to drive the Mexican-Texans out of business. Intervention by the U.S. and Mexican governments finally brought the situation under control, but it stands as an example of the attitudes held by Anglo-Texans toward Mexican-Texans.

Cotton was by far the state's largest money crop, but corn, sweet potatoes, wheat and sugar also were produced. **Saw milling** and grain milling became the major industries, employing 40 percent of the manufacturing workers.

Land disputes and the public-debt issue were settled with the **Compromise of 1850**. Texas gave up claims to territory extending to Santa Fe and beyond in exchange for $10 million from the federal government. That sum was used to pay off the debt of the Republic.

Personalities, especially Sam Houston, dominated elections during early statehood, but, for most Texans, politics were unimportant. Voter turnouts were low in the 1850s until the movement toward secession gained strength.

Secession

Texas' population almost tripled in the decade between 1850 and 1860, when 604,215 people were counted, including 182,921 slaves.

Many of these new settlers came from the Lower South, a region familiar with slavery. Although three-quarters of the Texas population and two-thirds of the farmers did not own slaves, slaveowners controlled 60 to 70 percent of the wealth of the state and dominated politics.

In 1850, 41 percent of the state's officeholders were from the slaveholding class; a decade later, more than 50 percent of the officeholders had slaves.

In addition to the political power of the slaveholders, they also provided role models for new immigrants to the state. After these newcomers got their first land, they saw slave ownership as another step up the economic ladder, whether they owned slaves or not. Slave ownership was an economic goal.

This attitude prevailed even in areas of Texas where slaveholding was not widespread or even practical.

These factors were the wind that fanned the flames of the secessionist movement throughout the late 1850s.

The appearance of the **Know-Nothing Party**, which based its platform on a pro-American, anti-immigrant foundation, began to move Texas toward party politics. Because of the large number of foreign-born settlers, the party attracted many Anglo voters.

In 1854, the Know-Nothings elected candidates to city offices in San Antonio, and a year later, the mayor of Galveston was elected with the party's backing. Also in 1855, the Know-Nothings elected 20 representatives and five senators to the Legislature.

The successes spurred the **Democrats** to serious party organization for the first time. In 1857, **Hardin Runnels** was nominated for governor at the Democratic

E.J. Davis

convention held in Waco.

Sam Houston sought the governorship as an independent, but he also got Know-Nothing backing. Democrats were organized, however, and Houston was dealt the only election defeat in his political career.

Runnels was a strong states'-rights Democrat who irritated many Texans during his administration by advocating reopening the slave trade. His popularity on the frontier also dropped when Indian raids became more severe.

Most Texans still were ambivalent about secession. The Union was seen as a protector of physical and economic stability. No threats to person or property were perceived in remaining attached to the United States.

In 1859, Houston again challenged Runnels, basing his campaign on Unionism. Combined with Houston's personal popularity, his position on the secession issue apparently satisfied most voters, for they gave him a solid victory over the more radical Runnels. In addition, Unionists **A.J. Hamilton** and **John H. Reagan** won the state's two congressional seats. Texans gave the states'-rights Democrats a sound whipping at the polls.

Within a few months, however, events were to change radically the political atmosphere of the state. On the frontier, the army could not control Indian raids, and with the later refusal of a Republican-controlled Congress to provide essential aid in fighting Indians, the federal government fell into disrepute.

Secessionists played on the growing distrust. Then in the summer of 1860, a series of fires in the cities around the state aroused fears that an abolitionist plot was afoot and that a slave uprising might be at hand — a traditional concern in a slaveholding society.

Vigilantes lynched blacks and Northerners across Texas, and a siege mentality developed.

When **Abraham Lincoln** was elected president (he was not on the ballot in Texas), secessionists went to work in earnest.

Pleas were made to Gov. Houston to call the Legislature into session to consider secession. Houston refused, hoping the passions would cool. They did not. Finally, **Oran M. Roberts** and other secessionist leaders issued a call to the counties to hold elections and send delegates to a convention in Austin. Ninety-two of 122 counties responded, and on Jan. 28, 1861, the meeting convened.

Only eight delegates voted against secession, while 166 supported it. An election was called for Feb. 23, 1861, and the ensuing campaign was marked by intolerance and violence. Opponents of secession were often intimidated — except the governor, who courageously stumped the state opposing withdrawal from the Union. Houston also argued that if Texas did secede it should revert to its status as an independent republic and not join the Confederacy.

Only one-fourth of the state's population had been in Texas during the days of independence, and the argument carried no weight. On election day, 76 percent of 61,000 voters favored secession.

President Lincoln, who took office within a couple of weeks, reportedly sent the Texas governor a letter offering 50,000 federal troops to keep Texas in the Union. But after a meeting with other Unionists, Houston declined the offer. "I love Texas too well to bring strife and bloodshed upon her," the governor declared.

On March 16, Houston refused to take an oath of loyalty to the Confederacy and was replaced in office by Lt. Gov. **Edward Clark**.

Civil War

Texas did not suffer the devastation of its Southern colleagues in the Civil War. On but a few occasions did Union troops occupy territory in Texas, except in the El Paso area.

The state's cotton was important to the Confederate war effort because it could be transported from Gulf ports when other Southern shipping lanes were blockaded.

Some goods became difficult to buy, but unlike other states of the Confederacy, Texas still received consumer goods because of the trade that was carried on through Mexico during the war.

Although accurate figures are not available, historians estimate that between 70,000 and 90,000 Texans fought for the South, and between 2,000 and 3,000, including some former slaves, saw service in the Union army.

Texans became disenchanted with the Confederate government early in the war. State taxes were levied for the first time since the Compromise of 1850, and by war's end, the Confederacy had collected more than $37 million from the state.

But most of the complaints about the government centered on Brig. Gen. **Paul O. Hebert**, the Confederate commander of the Department of Texas.

In April 1862, Gen. Hebert declared martial law without notifying state officials. Opposition to the South's new conscription law, which exempted persons owning more than 15 slaves among other categories of exemptions, prompted the action.

In November 1862, the commander prohibited the export of cotton except under government control, and this proved a disastrous policy.

The final blow came when Gen. Hebert failed to defend **Galveston** and it fell into Union hands in the fall of 1862.

Maj. Gen. **John B. Magruder**, who replaced Hebert, was much more popular. The new commander's first actions were to combat the Union offensive against Texas ports. Sabine Pass had been closed in September 1862 by the Union blockade, and Galveston was in Northern hands.

On Jan. 1, 1863, Magruder retook Galveston with the help of two steamboats lined with cotton bales. Sharpshooters aboard proved devastating in battles against the Union fleet. Three weeks later, Magruder used two other cotton-clad steamboats to break the Union blockade of Sabine Pass, and two of the state's major ports were reopened.

Late in 1863, the Union launched a major offensive against the Texas coast that was partly successful. On

Sept. 8, however, Lt. **Dick Dowling** and 42 men fought off a 1,500-man Union invasion force at **Sabine Pass**. In a brief battle, Dowling's command sank two Union gunboats and put the other invasion ships to flight.

Federal forces were more successful at the mouth of the Rio Grande. On Nov. 1, 1863, 7,000 Union troops landed at **Brazos Santiago**, and five days later, Union forces entered Brownsville.

Texas Unionists led by **E.J. Davis** were active in the Valley, moving as far upriver as Rio Grande City. Confederate Col. **John S. "Rip" Ford**, commanding state troops, finally pushed the Union soldiers out of Brownsville in July 1864, reopening the important port for the Confederacy.

Most Texans never saw a Union soldier during the war. The only ones they might have seen were in the **prisoner-of-war camps**. The largest, **Camp Ford**, near Tyler, housed 5,000 prisoners. Others operated in Kerr County and at Hempstead.

As the war dragged on, the mood of Texans changed. Those on the homefront began to feel they were sacrificing loved ones and suffering hardship so cotton speculators could profit.

Public order broke down as refugees flocked to Texas. And slaves from other states were sent to Texas for safekeeping. When the war ended, there were an estimated 400,000 slaves in Texas, more than double the number counted in the 1860 census.

Morale was low in Texas in early 1865. Soldiers at Galveston and Houston began to mutiny. At Austin, Confederate soldiers raided the state treasury in March and found only $5,000 in specie. Units broke up, and the army simply dissolved before Gen. **Robert E. Lee** surrendered at **Appomattox** in April 1865.

The last battle of the Civil War was fought at **Palmito Ranch** near Brownsville on May 11, 1865. After the Confederate unit's victory, it learned of the South's defeat.

Reconstruction

On June 19, 1865, **Gen. Gordon Granger**, under the command of Gen. Philip M. Sheridan, arrived in Galveston with 1,800 federal troops to begin the Union occupation of Texas. Gen. Granger proclaimed the emancipation of the slaves.

A.J. Hamilton, a Unionist and former congressman from Texas, was named provisional governor by President Andrew Johnson.

Texas was in turmoil. Thousands of the state's men had died in the conflict. Indian raids had caused as much damage as the skirmishes with the Union army, causing the frontier to recede up to 100 miles eastward in some areas.

Even worse, confusion reigned. No one knew what to expect from the conquering forces.

Gen. Granger dispatched troops to the population centers of the state to restore civil authority. But only a handful of the 50,000 federal troops that came to Texas was stationed in the interior. Most were sent to the Rio Grande as a show of force against the French forces in Mexico, and clandestine aid was supplied to Mexican President Benito Juarez in his fight against the French and Mexican royalists.

The **frontier forts**, most of which were built during the early 1850s by the federal government to protect western settlements, had been abandoned by the U.S. Army after secession. These were not remanned, and a prohibition against a militia denied settlers a means of self-defense against Indian raids.

Thousands of freed black slaves migrated to the cities, where they felt the federal soldiers would provide protection. Still others traveled the countryside, seeking family members and loved ones from whom they had been separated during the war.

The **Freedman's Bureau**, authorized by Congress in March 1865, began operation in September 1865 under Gen. E.M. Gregory. It had the responsibility to provide education, relief aid, labor supervision and judicial protection for the newly freed slaves.

The bureau was most successful in opening schools for blacks. Education was a priority because 95 percent of the freed slaves were illiterate.

The agency also was partially successful in getting blacks back to work on plantations under reasonable labor contracts.

Some plantation owners harbored hopes that they would be paid for their property loss when the slaves were freed. In some cases, the slaves were not released from plantations for up to a year.

To add to the confusion, some former slaves had the false notion that the federal government was going to parcel out the plantation lands to them. These blacks simply bided their time, waiting for the division of land.

Under pressure from President Johnson, Gov. Hamilton called for an election of delegates to a **constitutional convention** in January 1866. Hamilton told the gathering what was expected: Former slaves were to be given civil rights; the secession ordinance had to be repealed; Civil War debt had to be repudiated; and slavery was to be abolished with ratification of the Thirteenth Amendment.

Many delegates to the convention were former secessionists, and there was little support for compromise.

J.W. Throckmorton, a Unionist and one of eight men who had opposed secession in the convention of 1861, was elected chairman of the convention. But a coalition of conservative Unionists and Democrats controlled the meeting. As a consequence, Texas took limited steps toward appeasing the victorious North.

Slavery was abolished, and blacks were given some civil rights. But they still could not vote and were barred from testifying in trials against whites.

No action was taken on the Thirteenth Amendment because, the argument went, the amendment already had been ratified.

Otherwise, the constitution that was written followed closely the constitution of 1845. President Johnson in August 1866 accepted the new constitution and declared insurrection over in Texas, the last of the states of the Confederacy so accepted under **Presidential Reconstruction**.

Throckmorton was elected governor in June, along with other state and local officials. However, Texans had not learned a lesson from the war.

When the Legislature met, a series of laws limiting the rights of blacks were passed. In labor disputes, for example, the employers were to be the final arbitrators. The codes also bound an entire family's labor, not just the head of the household, to an employer.

James Stephen Hogg   Norris Wright Cuney

Funding for black education would be limited to what could be provided by black taxpayers. Since few blacks owned land or had jobs, that provision effectively denied education to black children. The thrust of the laws and the attitude of the legislators was clear, however: Blacks simply were not to be considered full citizens.

Many of the laws later were overturned by the Freedman's Bureau or military authorities when, in March 1867, Congress began a **Reconstruction plan** of its own. The Southern states were declared to have no legal government and the former Confederacy was divided into districts to be administrated by the military until satisfactory Reconstruction was effected. Texas and Louisiana made up the Fifth Military District under the command of Gen. Philip H. Sheridan.

Gov. Throckmorton clashed often with Gen. Sheridan. The governor thought the state had gone far enough in establishing rights for the newly freed slaves and other matters. Finally in August 1867, Throckmorton and other state officials were removed from office by Sheridan because they were considered an "impediment to the reconstruction." **E.M. Pease**, the former two-term governor and a Unionist, was named provisional governor by the military authorities.

A **new constitutional convention** was called by Gen. Winfield S. Hancock, who replaced Sheridan in November 1867. For the first time, blacks were allowed to participate in the elections that selected delegates. A total of 59,633 whites and 49,497 blacks registered. The elected delegates met on June 1, 1868. Deliberations got bogged down on partisan political matters, however, and the convention spent $200,000, an astronomical sum for the time.

This constitution of 1869, as it came to be known, granted full rights of citizenship to blacks, created a system of education, delegated broad powers to the governor and generally reflected the views of the state's Unionists.

Gov. Pease, disgusted with the convention and with military authorities, resigned in September 1869. Texas had no chief executive until January 1870, when the newly-elected **E.J. Davis** took office.

Meeting in February 1870, the Legislature created a **state militia** under the governor's control; created a **state police force**, also controlled by the governor; postponed the 1870 general election to 1872; enabled the governor to appoint more than 8,500 local officeholders; and granted subsidized **bonds for railroad construc-**

tion at a rate of $10,000 a mile.

For the first time, a **system of public education** was created. The law required compulsory attendance at school for four months a year, set aside one-quarter of the state's annual revenue for education and levied a poll tax to support education. Schools also were to be integrated, which enraged many white Texans.

The Davis administration was the most unpopular in Texas' history. In fairness, historians have noted that Davis did not feel that whites could be trusted to assure the rights of the newly freed blacks.

Violence was rampant in Texas. One study found that between the close of the Civil War and mid-1868, 1,035 people were murdered in Texas, including 486 blacks, mostly victims of white violence.

Gov. Davis argued that he needed broad police powers to restore order. Despite their unpopularity, the state police and militia — blacks made up 40 percent of the police and a majority of the militia — brought the lawlessness under control in many areas.

Democrats, aided by moderate Republicans, regained control of the Legislature in the 1872 elections, and, in 1873, the lawmakers set about stripping the governor of many of his powers.

The political turmoil ended with the gubernatorial election of 1873, when **Richard Coke** easily defeated Davis. Davis tried to get federal authorities to keep him in office, but President Grant refused to intervene.

In January of 1874, Democrats were in control of state government again. The end of Reconstruction concluded the turbulent Civil War era, although the attitudes that developed during the period lasted well into the 20th century.

Capital and Labor

A **constitutional convention** was called in 1875 to rewrite the 1869 constitution, a hated vestige of Radical Republican rule.

Every avenue to cutting spending at any level of government was explored. Salaries of public officials were slashed. The number of offices was reduced. Judgeships, along with most other offices, were made elective rather than appointive.

The state road program was curtailed, and the immigration bureau was eliminated.

Perhaps the worst change was the destruction of the statewide school system. The new charter created a "community system" without a power of taxation, and schools were segregated by race.

Despite the basic reactionary character, the new constitution also was visionary. Following the lead of several other states, the Democrats declared railroads to be common carriers and subject to regulation.

To meet the dual challenge of lawlessness and Indian insurrection, Gov. Coke in 1874 re-established the **Texas Rangers**.

While cowboys and cattle drives are romantic subjects for movies on the Texas of this period, the fact is that the simple cotton farmer was the backbone of the state's economy.

But neither the farmer nor the cattleman prospered throughout the last quarter of the 19th century. At the root of their problems was federal monetary policy and the lingering effects of the Civil War.

Although the issuance of paper money had brought about a business boom in the Union during the war, inflation also increased. Silver was demonetized in 1873. Congress passed the Specie Resumption Act in 1875 that returned the nation to the gold standard in 1879.

Almost immediately a contraction in currency began. Between 1873 and 1891, the amount of national bank notes in circulation declined from $339 million to $168 million.

The reduction in the money supply was devastating in the defeated South. Land values plummeted. In 1870, Texas land was valued at an average of $2.62 an acre, compared with the national average of $18.26 an acre.

With the money supply declining and the national economy growing, farm prices dropped. In 1870, a bushel of wheat brought $1. In the 1890s, wheat was 60 cents a bushel. Except for a brief spurt in the early 1880s, cattle prices followed those of crops.

Between 1880 and 1890, the number of farms in Texas doubled, but the number of tenants tripled. By 1900, almost half the state's farmers were tenants.

The much-criticized crop-lien system was developed following the war to meet credit needs of the small farmers. Merchants would extend credit to farmers through the year in exchange for liens on their crops. But the result of the crop-lien system, particularly when small farmers did not have enough acreage to operate efficiently, was a state of continual debt and despair.

The work ethic held that a man would benefit from his toil. When this apparently failed, farmers looked to the monetary system and the railroads as the causes. Their discontent hence became the source of the agrarian revolt that developed in the 1880s and 1890s.

The entry of the Texas & Pacific and the Missouri-Kansas-Texas **railroads** from the northeast changed trade patterns in the state.

Since the days of the Republic, trade generally had flowed to Gulf ports, primarily Galveston. Jefferson in Northeast Texas served as a gateway to the Mississippi River, but it never carried the volume of trade that was common at Galveston.

The earliest railroad systems in the state also were centered around Houston and Galveston, again directing trade southward. With the T&P and Katy lines, North Texas had direct access to markets in St. Louis and the East.

Problems developed with the railroads, however. In 1882, Jay Gould and Collis P. Huntington, owner of the Southern Pacific, entered into a secret agreement that amounted to creation of a monopoly of rail service in Texas. They agreed to stop competitive track extensions; to divide under a pooling arrangement freight moving from New Orleans and El Paso; to purchase all competing railroads in Texas; and to share the track between Sierra Blanca and El Paso.

The Legislature made weak attempts to regulate railroads, as provided by the state constitution. Gould thwarted an attempt to create a commission to regulate the railroads in 1881 with a visit to the state during the Legislature's debate.

The railroad tycoon subdued the lawmakers' interest with thinly disguised threats that capital would abandon Texas if the state interfered with railroad business.

As the 19th century closed, Texas remained an agricultural state. But the industrial base was growing. Between 1870 and 1900, the per capita value of manu-

factured goods in the United States rose from $109 to $171. In Texas, these per capita values increased from $14 to $39, but manufacturing values in Texas industry still were only one-half of annual agricultural values.

In 1886, a new breed of Texas politician appeared. **James Stephen Hogg** was not a Confederate veteran, and he was not tied to party policies of the past.

As a reform-minded attorney general, Hogg had actively enforced the state's few railroad regulatory laws. With farmers' support, Hogg was elected governor in 1890, and at the same time, a debate on the constitutionality of a **railroad commission** was settled when voters amended the constitution to provide for one.

The reform mood of the state was evident. Voters returned only 22 of the 106 members of the Texas House in 1890.

Despite his reputation as a reformer, Hogg accepted the growing use of **Jim Crow laws** to limit blacks' access to public services. In 1891, the Legislature responded to public demands and required railroads to provide separate accommodations for blacks and whites.

The stage was being set for one of the major political campaigns in Texas history, however. Farmers did not think that Hogg had gone far enough in his reform program, and they were distressed that Hogg had not appointed a farmer to the railroad commission. Many began to look elsewhere for the solutions to their problems. The **People's Party** in Texas was formed in August 1891.

The 1892 general election was one of the most spirited in the state's history. Gov. Hogg's supporters shut conservative Democrats out of the convention in Houston, so the conservatives bolted and nominated railroad attorney George Clark for governor.

The People's Party, or **Populists**, for the first time had a presidential candidate, James Weaver, and a gubernatorial candidate, T.L. Nugent.

Texas Republicans also broke ranks. The party's strength centered in the black vote. After the death of former Gov. E.J. Davis in 1883, **Norris Wright Cuney**, a black, was party leader. Cuney was considered one of the most astute politicians of the period, and he controlled federal patronage.

White Republicans revolted against the black leadership, and these "Lily-whites" nominated **Andrew Jackson Houston**, son of Sam Houston, for governor.

Black Republicans recognized that, alone, their strength was limited, and throughout the latter part of the 19th century, they practiced fusion politics, backing candidates of third parties when they deemed it appropriate. Cuney led the Republicans into a coalition with the conservative Democrats in 1892, backing George Clark.

The election also marked the first time major Democratic candidates courted the black vote. Gov. Hogg's supporters organized black voter clubs, and the governor got about half of the black vote.

Black farmers were in a quandary. Their financial problems were the same as those small farmers who backed the Populists.

White Populists varied in their sympathy with the racial concerns of blacks. On the local level, some whites showed sympathy with black concerns about education, voting and law enforcement. Black farmers also were reluctant to abandon the Republican Party because it was their only political base in Texas.

Hogg was re-elected in 1892 with a 43 percent plurality in a field of five candidates.

Populists continued to run well in state races until 1898. Historians have placed the beginning of the party's demise in the 1896 presidential election in which national Populists fused with the Democrats and supported **William Jennings Bryan**.

Although the Populist philosophy lived on, the party declined in importance after 1898. Farmers remained active in politics, but most returned to the Democratic Party, which usurped many of the Populists' issues.

Oil

Seldom can a people's history be profoundly changed by a single event on a single day. But Texas' entrance into the industrial age can be linked directly to the discovery of oil at **Spindletop**, three miles from **Beaumont**, on Jan. 10, 1901.

From that day, Texas' progress from a rural, agricultural state to a modern industrial giant was steady. (Please see **"The Impact of Oil on Texas and Texans: A Cultural History,"** starting on page 29.)

1900-1920

One of the greatest natural disasters ever to strike the state occurred on Sept. 8, 1900, when a **hurricane devastated Galveston**, killing 6,000 people. (For a more detailed account, see "After the Great Storm" in the 1998-1999 *Texas Almanac*). In rebuilding from that disaster, Galveston's civic leaders fashioned the **commission form of municipal government**.

Amarillo later refined the system into the **council-manager organization** that is widely used today.

The great Galveston storm also reinforced arguments by Houston's leadership that an inland port should be built for protection against such tragedies and disruptions of trade. The **Houston Ship Channel** was soon a reality.

The reform spirit in government was not dead after the departure of Jim Hogg. In 1901, the Legislature prohibited the issuing of railroad passes to public officials. More than 270,000 passes were issued to officials that year, and farmers claimed that the free rides increased their freight rates and influenced public policy as well.

In 1903, state Sen. **A.W. Terrell** got a major **election-reform law** approved, a measure that was further modified two years later. A **primary system** was established to replace a hodgepodge of practices for nominating candidates that had led to charges of irregularities after each election.

Also in the reform spirit, the Legislature in 1903 prohibited abuse of **child labor** and set minimum ages at which children could work in certain industries. The action preceded federal child-labor laws by 13 years.

However, the state, for the first time, imposed the **poll tax** as a requirement for voting. Historians differ on whether the levy was designed to keep blacks or poor whites — or both — from voting. Certainly the poll tax cut election turnouts. Black voter participation dropped from about 100,000 in the 1890s to an estimated 5,000 in 1906.

The Democratic State Executive Committee also recommended that county committees limit participation in primaries to whites only, and most accepted the suggestion.

The election of **Thomas M. Campbell** as governor in 1906 marked the start of a progressive period in Texas politics. Interest revived in controlling corporate influence.

Under Campbell, the state's **antitrust laws** were strengthened and a **pure food and drug bill** was passed. Life insurance companies were required to invest in Texas 75 percent of their reserves on policies in the state. Less than one percent of the reserves had been invested prior to the law.

Some companies left Texas. But the law was beneficial in the capital-starved economy. In 1904, voters amended the constitution to allow the state to charter **banks** for the first time, and this eased some of the farmers' credit problems. In 1909, the Legislature approved a bank-deposit insurance plan that predated the federal program.

With corporate influence under acceptable control, attention turned to the issue of prohibition of alcohol. Progressives and prohibitionists joined forces against the conservative establishment to exert a major influence in state government for the next two decades.

Prohibitionists had long been active in Texas. They had the **local-option clause** written into the Constitution of 1876, which allowed counties or their subdivisions to be voted dry. But in 1887, a prohibition amendment to the state constitution had been defeated by a two-to-one margin, and public attention had turned to other problems.

In the early 20th century, the prohibition movement gathered strength. Most of Texas already was dry because of local option. When voters rejected a prohibition amendment by a slim margin in 1911, the state had 167 dry counties and 82 wet or partially wet counties. The heavily populated counties, however, were wet. Prohibition continued to be a major issue.

Problems along the U.S.-Mexico border escalated in 1911 as the decade-long **Mexican Revolution** broke out. Soon the revolutionaries controlled some northern Mexican states, including Chihuahua. Juarez and El Paso were major contact points. El Paso residents could stand on rooftops to observe the fighting between revolutionaries and government troops. Some Americans were killed.

After pleas to the federal government got no action, Gov. Oscar Colquitt sent state militia and Texas Rangers into the Valley in 1913 to protect Texans after Matamoros fell to the rebels. Unfortunately, the Rangers killed many innocent Mexican-Texans during the operation. In addition to problems caused by the fighting and raids, thousands of Mexican refugees flooded Texas border towns to escape the violence of the revolution.

In 1914, **James E. Ferguson** entered Texas politics and for the next three decades, "Farmer Jim" was one of the most dominating and colorful figures on the political stage. Ferguson, a banker from Temple, skirted the prohibition issue by pledging to veto any legislation pertaining to alcoholic beverages.

His strength was among farmers, however. Sixty-two percent of Texas' farmers were tenants, and Ferguson pledged to back legislation to limit tenant rents. Ferguson also was a dynamic orator. He easily won the primary and beat out three opponents in the general election.

Ferguson's first administration was successful. The Legislature passed the law limiting tenants' rents, although it was poorly enforced, and aid to rural schools was improved.

In 1915, the border problems heated up. A Mexican national was arrested in the Lower Rio Grande Valley carrying a document outlining plans for Mexican-Americans, Indians, Japanese and blacks in Texas and the Southwest to eliminate all Anglo males over age 16 and create a new republic. The document, whose author was never determined, started a bloodbath in the Valley. Mexican soldiers participated in raids across the Rio Grande, and Gov. Ferguson sent in the Texas Rangers.

Historians differ on the number of people who were killed, but a safe assessment would be hundreds. Gov. Ferguson and Mexican President Venustiano Carranza met at Nuevo Laredo in November 1915 in an attempt to improve relations. The raids continued.

Pancho Villa raided Columbus, N.M., in early 1916; two small Texas villages in the Big Bend, Glenn Springs and Boquillas, also were attacked. In July, President **Woodrow Wilson** determined that the hostilities were critical and activated the National Guard.

Soon 1,000 U.S. troops were stationed along the border. **Fort Bliss** in El Paso housed 60,000 men, and **Fort Duncan** near Eagle Pass was home to 16,000 more.

With the exception of Gen. John J. Pershing's pursuit of Villa into Northern Mexico, few U.S. troops crossed into Mexico. But the service along the border gave soldiers basic training that was put to use when the United States entered World War I in 1917.

Ferguson was easily re-elected in 1916, and he worked well with the Legislature the following year. But after the Legislature adjourned, the governor got into a dispute with the board of regents of the **University of Texas**. The disagreement culminated in the governor's vetoing all appropriations for the school.

As the controversy swirled, the Travis County grand jury indicted Ferguson for misappropriation of funds and for embezzlement. In July 1917, Speaker of the Texas House F.O. Fuller called a special session of the Legislature to consider **impeachment** of the governor.

The Texas House voted 21 articles of impeachment, and the Senate in August 1917 convicted Ferguson on 10 of the charges. The Senate's judgment not only removed Ferguson from office, but also barred him from seeking office again. Ferguson resigned the day before the Senate rendered the decision in an attempt to avoid the prohibition against seeking further office.

Texas participated actively in **World War I**. Almost 200,000 young Texans, including 31,000 blacks, volunteered for military service, and 450 Texas women served in the nurses' corps. Five thousand lost their lives overseas, either fighting or in the **influenza pandemic** that swept the globe.

Texas also was a major training ground during the conflict, with 250,000 soldiers getting basic training in the state.

On the negative side, the war frenzy opened a period of intolerance and nativism in the state. German-Texans were suspect because of their ancestry. A law was passed to prohibit speaking against the war effort. Per-

William P. Hobby

James E. Ferguson

sons who failed to participate in patriotic activities often were punished. Gov. William P. Hobby even vetoed the appropriation for the German department at the University of Texas.

Ferguson's removal from office was a devastating blow to the anti-prohibitionists. Word that the former governor had received a $156,000 loan from members of the brewers' association while in office provided ammunition for the progressives.

In February 1918, a special session of the Legislature prohibited saloons within a 10-mile radius of military posts and ratified the national prohibition amendment, which had been introduced in Congress by Texas Sen. **Morris Sheppard**.

Women also were given the **right to vote in state primaries** at the same session.

Although national prohibition was to become effective in early 1920, the Legislature presented a prohibition amendment to voters in May 1919, and it was approved, bringing prohibition to Texas earlier than to the rest of the nation. At the same time, a woman suffrage amendment, which would have granted women the right to vote in all elections, was defeated.

Although World War I ended in November 1918, it brought many changes to Texas. Rising prices during the war had increased the militancy of labor unions.

Blacks also became more militant after the war. Discrimination against black soldiers led in 1917 to a riot in Houston in which several people were killed.

With the election of Mexican President Alvaro Obregón in 1920, the fighting along the border subsided.

In 1919, state Rep. J.T. Canales of Brownsville initiated an investigation of the **Texas Rangers'** role in the border problems. As a result of the study, the Rangers' manpower was reduced from 1,000 members to 76, and stringent limitations were placed on the agency's activities. Standards for members of the force also were upgraded. (Please see **"Texas Rangers: Horses to Helicopters,"** beginning on page 23.)

By 1920, although still a rural state, the face of Texas was changing. Nearly one-third of the population was in the cities. ☆

Photo credit: Photo of Norris Wright Cuney, page 50, is from the Texas Collection, The Center for American History, The University of Texas at Austin: CN 01074A.

Environment

Extending from sea level at the Gulf of Mexico to over 8,000 feet in the Guadalupe Mountains of far West Texas and from the semitropical Lower Rio Grande Valley to the High Plains of the Panhandle, Texas has a natural environment best described as "varied." This section discusses the physical features, geology, soils, water, vegetation and wildlife that are found in the Lone Star State.

The Physical State of Texas

Area of Texas

Texas occupies about 7 percent of the total water and land area of the United States. **Second in size** among the states, Texas, according to the 1996 Statistical Abstract of the United States, has a land and water area of 267,277 square miles as compared with Alaska's 615,230 square miles. California, third largest state, has 158,869 square miles. Texas is as large as all of New England, New York, Pennsylvania, Ohio and North Carolina combined.

The **state's area** consists of 261,914 square miles of land and 5,363 square miles of water.

The area given here differs from that given by the State Land Office in the chapter on State Government.

Length and Breadth

The **longest straight-line distance** in a general north-south direction is 801 miles from the northwest corner of the Panhandle to the extreme southern tip of Texas on the Rio Grande below Brownsville. The greatest east-west distance is 773 miles from the extreme eastward bend in the Sabine River in Newton County to the extreme western bulge of the Rio Grande just above El Paso.

The **geographic center** of Texas is southwest of Mercury in the northern portion of McCulloch County.

Texas' Boundary Lines

The boundary of Texas by segments, including only larger river bends and only the great arc of the coastline, is as follows:

Boundary	Miles
Rio Grande	889.0
Coastline	367.0
Sabine River, Lake and Pass	180.0
*Sabine River to Red River	106.5
Red River	480.0
*East Panhandle line	133.6
*North Panhandle line	167.0
*West Panhandle line	310.2
*Along 32nd parallel	209.0
Total	2,842.3

Following the smaller meanderings of the rivers and the tidewater coastline, the following are the boundary measurements:

Rio Grande	1,254
Coastline (tidewater)	624
Sabine River, Lake and Pass	292
Red River	726
*The five unchanged line segments above	926
Total (including segments marked *)	3,822

Latitude and Longitude

The extremes of latitude and longitude are as follows: From Latitude 25° 50' N. at the extreme southern turn of the Rio Grande on the south line of Cameron County to Latitude 36° 30' N. along the north line of the Panhandle, and from Longitude 93° 31' W. at the extreme eastern point on the Sabine River on the east line of Newton County to Longitude 106° 38' W. on the extreme westward point on the Rio Grande above El Paso.

Texas' Highs and Lows

The highest point in the state is **Guadalupe Peak** at **8,749 feet** above sea level. Its twin, **El Capitan**, stands at **8,085** feet and also is located in Culberson county near the New Mexico state line. Both are in the Guadalupe Mountains National Park, which includes scenic McKittrick Canyon. These elevations and the others in this article have been determined by the U. S. Geological Survey, unless otherwise noted.

The named peaks above 8,000 feet and the counties in which they are located are listed below. These elevations may differ from those in earlier editions of the Almanac because of the more accurate measuring methods currently being used by the USGS.

Named Peaks in Texas Above 8,000 Feet

Name, County	Elevation
Guadalupe Peak, Culberson	8,749
Bush Mountain, Culberson	8,631
Shumard Peak, Culberson	8,615
Bartlett Peak, Culberson	8,508
Mount Livermore (Baldy Peak), Jeff Davis	8,378
Hunter Peak (Pine Top Mtn.), Culberson	8,368
El Capitan, Culberson	8,085

Fort Davis in Jeff Davis County is the **highest town** of any size in Texas at 5,050 feet, and the county has the **highest average elevation.** The **highest state highway point** also is in the county at **McDonald Observatory** at the end of a tap from State Highway 118 on **Mount Locke.** The observatory stands at 6,781 feet, as determined by the Texas Department of Transportation.

The **highest railway point** is Paisano Pass, 14 miles east of Marfa on the Southern Pacific in Presidio County.

Sea level is the **lowest elevation** determined in Texas, and it can be found in all the coastal counties. No point in the state has been found by the geological survey to be below sea level. ☆

Physical Regions

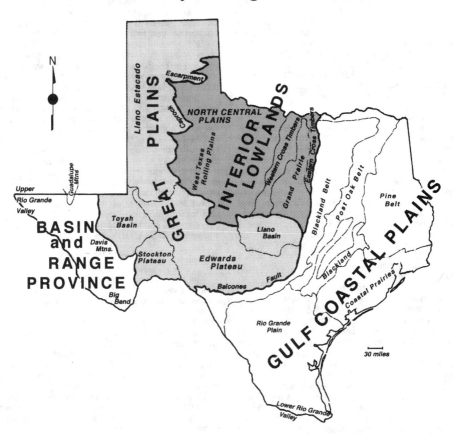

A special thanks to Dr. William M. Holmes, chairman of the Department of Geography at the University of North Texas, for his review of this section.

The principal physical regions of Texas are usually listed as follows (see also **Vegetational Areas** and **Soils**.):

The Gulf Coastal Plains

Texas' Gulf Coastal Plains are the western extension of the coastal plain extending from the Atlantic to beyond the Rio Grande. Its characteristic rolling to hilly surface covered with a heavy growth of pine and hardwoods extends into East Texas. In the increasingly arid west, however, its forests become secondary in nature, consisting largely of post oaks and, farther west, prairies and brushlands.

The interior limit of the Gulf Coastal Plains in Texas is the line of the **Balcones Fault and Escarpment.** This geologic fault or shearing of underground strata extends eastward from a point on the Rio Grande near Del Rio. It extends to the northwestern part of Bexar County where it turns northeastward and extends through Comal, Hays and Travis counties, intersecting the Colorado River immediately above Austin. The fault line is a single, definite geologic feature, accompanied by a line of southward- and eastward-facing hills.

The resemblance of the hills to balconies when viewed from the plain below accounts for the Spanish name, *balcones.*

North of Waco, features of the fault zone are sufficiently inconspicuous that the interior boundary of the Coastal Plain follows the traditional geologic contact

between upper and lower Cretaceous rocks. This contact is along the western edge of the **Eastern Cross Timbers.**

This fault line is usually accepted as the boundary between lowland and upland Texas. Below the fault line the surface is characteristically coastal plains. Above the Balcones Fault the surface is characteristically interior rolling plains.

Pine Belt or "Piney Woods"

The Pine Belt, called the "Piney Woods," extends into Texas from the east 75 to 125 miles. From north to south it extends from the Red River to within about 25 miles of the Gulf Coast. Interspersed among the pines are some hardwood timbers, usually in valleys of rivers and creeks. This area is the source of practically all of Texas' large commercial timber production (see "Forest Resources" in index). It was settled early in Texas' history and is an older farming area of the state.

This area's soils and climate are adaptable to production of a variety of fruit and vegetable crops. Cattle raising is widespread, accompanied by the development of pastures planted to improved grasses. Lumber production is the principal industry. There is a large iron-and-steel industry near Daingerfield in Morris County based on nearby iron deposits. Iron deposits are also worked in Rusk and one or two other counties.

A great oil field discovered in Gregg, Rusk and Smith counties in 1931 has done more than anything else to contribute to the economic growth of the area. This area has a variety of clays, lignite and other minerals as potentials for development.

Post Oak Belt

The main Post Oak Belt of Texas is wedged between the Pine Belt on the east, Blacklands on the west, and the Coastal Prairies on the south, covering a considerable area in East Central Texas. Principal industry is diversified farming and livestock raising. Throughout, it is spotty in character, with some insular areas of blackland soil and some that closely resemble those of the Pine Belt. There is a small isolated area of pines in Bastrop County known as the **"Lost Pines."** The Post Oak Belt has lignite, commercial clays and some other minerals.

Blackland Belt

The Blackland Belt stretches from the Rio Grande to the Red River, lying just below the line of the **Balcones Fault,** and varying in width from 15 to 70 miles. It is narrowest below the segment of the Balcones Fault from the Rio Grande to Bexar County and gradually widens as it runs northeast to the Red River. Its rolling prairie, easily turned by the plow, developed rapidly as a farming area until the 1930s and was the principal cotton-producing area of Texas. Now, however, other Texas irrigated, mechanized areas lead in farming. Because of the early growth, the Blackland Belt is still the most thickly populated area in the state and contains within it and along its border more of the state's large and middle-sized cities than any other area. Primarily because of this concentration of population, this belt has the most diversified manufacturing industry of the state.

Coastal Prairies

The Texas Coastal Prairies extend westward along the coast from the Sabine River, reaching inland 30 to 60 miles. Between the Sabine and Galveston Bay, the line of demarcation between the prairies and the Pine Belt forests to the north is very distinct. The Coastal Prairie extends along the Gulf from the Sabine to the Lower Rio Grande Valley. The eastern half is covered with a heavy growth of grass; the western half, which is more arid, is covered with short grass and, in some places, with small timber and brush. The soil is heavy clay. Grass supports the densest cattle population in Texas, and cattle ranching is the principal agricultural industry. Rice is a major crop, grown under irrigation from wells and rivers. Cotton, grain sorghum and truck crops are grown.

Coastal Prairie areas have seen the greatest industrial development in Texas history since World War II. Chief concentration has been from Orange and Beaumont to Houston, and much of the development has been in petro-chemicals.

Corpus Christi, in the Coastal Bend, and Brownsville, in the Lower Rio Grande Valley, have seaports and agricultural and industrial sections. Cotton, grain, vegetables and citrus fruits are the principal crops. Cattle production is significant, with the famed King Ranch and other large ranches located here.

Lower Rio Grande Valley

The deep alluvial soils and distinctive economy cause the Lower Rio Grande Valley to be classified as a subregion of the Gulf Coastal Plain. The Lower Valley, as it is called locally, is Texas' greatest citrus-winter vegetable area because of the normal absence of freezing weather and the rich delta soils of the Rio Grande. Despite occasional damaging freezes, as in 1951 and 1961, the Lower Valley ranks high among the nation's fruit-and-truck regions. Much of the acreage is irrigated, although dryland farming also is practiced.

Rio Grande Plain

This may be roughly defined as lying south of San Antonio between the Rio Grande and the Gulf Coast. The Rio Grande Plain shows characteristics of both the Texas Gulf Coastal Plain and the North Mexico Plains because there is similarity of topography, climate and plant life all the way from the Balcones Escarpment in Texas to the Sierra Madre Oriental in Mexico, which runs past Monter-

rey about 160 miles south of Laredo.

The Rio Grande Plain is partly prairie, but much of it is covered with a dense growth of **prickly pear, cactus, mesquite, dwarf oak, catclaw, guajillo, huisache, blackbrush, cenizo** and other wild shrubs. This country is devoted primarily to raising cattle, sheep and goats. The Texas Angora goat and mohair industry centers in this area and on the **Edwards Plateau,** which borders it on the north. San Antonio and Laredo are its chief commercial centers, with San Antonio dominating trade.

There is some farming, and the **Winter Garden,** centering in Dimmit and Zavala counties north of Laredo, is irrigated from wells and streams to produce vegetables in late winter and early spring. Primarily, however, the central and western part of the Rio Grande Plain is devoted to livestock raising. The rainfall is less than 25 inches annually and the hot summers bring heavy evaporation, so that cultivation without irrigation is limited. Over a large area in the central and western parts of the Rio Grande Plain, the growth of **small oaks, mesquite, prickly pear (Opuntia) cactus** and a variety of wild shrubs is very dense and it is often called the **Brush Country.** It is also referred to as the **chaparral** and the **monte.** (Monte is a Spanish word, one meaning of which is dense brush.)

Interior Lowlands

North Central Plains

The North Central Plains of Texas are a southwestern extension into Texas of the interior lowlands that extend northward to the Canadian border, paralleling the Great Plains to the West. The North Central Plains of Texas extend from the Blackland Belt on the east to the Caprock Escarpment on the west. From north to south they extend from the Red River to the Colorado.

West Texas Rolling Plains

The West Texas Rolling Plains, approximately the western two-thirds of the North Central Plains in Texas, rise from east to west in altitude from about 750 feet to 2,000 feet at the base of the **Caprock Escarpment.** Annual rainfall ranges from about 30 inches on the east to 20 on the west. Temperature varies rather widely between summer's heat and winter's cold.

This area still has a large cattle-raising industry with many of the state's largest ranches. However, there is much level, cultivable land.

Grand Prairie

Near the eastern edge of the North Central Plains is the Grand Prairie, extending south from the Red River in an irregular band through Cooke, Montague, Wise, Denton, Tarrant, Parker, Hood, Johnson, Bosque, Coryell and some adjacent counties. It is a limestone-based area, usually treeless except along the numerous streams, and adapted primarily to livestock raising and staple-crop growing. Sometimes called the Fort Worth Prairie, it has an agricultural economy and largely rural population, with no large cities except Fort Worth on its eastern boundary.

Eastern and Western Cross Timbers

Hanging over the top of the Grand Prairie and dropping down on each side are the Eastern and Western Cross Timbers. The two southward-extending bands are connected by a narrow strip along the Red River. The Eastern Cross Timbers extend southward from the Red River through eastern Denton County and along the Dallas-Tarrant County boundary, then through Johnson County to the Brazos River and into Hill County. The much larger Western Cross Timbers extend from the Red River south through Clay, Montague, Jack, Wise, Parker, Palo Pinto, Hood, Erath, Eastland, Comanche, Brown and Mills counties to the Colorado River, where they meet the Edwards Plateau. Their soils are adapted to fruit and vegetable crops, which reach considerable commercial production in some areas in Parker, Erath, Eastland and Comanche counties.

Great Plains

The Great Plains which lie to the east of the base of the Rocky Mountains extend into Northwest Texas. This area, which is a vast, flat, high plain covered with thick layers of alluvial material, is known as the **Staked Plains** or the Spanish equivalent, **Llano Estacado**.

Historians differ as to the origin of this name. Some think that it came from the fact that the Coronado expedition, crossing the trackless sea of grass, staked its route so that it would be guided on its return trip. Others think that the "estacado" refers to the palisaded appearance of the Caprock in many places, especially the west-facing escarpment in New Mexico.

The **Caprock Escarpment** is the dividing line between the High Plains and the Lower Rolling Plains of West Texas. Like the Balcones Escarpment, the Caprock Escarpment is a striking physical feature, rising abruptly 200, 500 and in some places almost 1,000 feet above the plains. Unlike the **Balcones Escarpment**, the Caprock was caused by surface erosion. Where rivers issue from the eastern face of the Caprock, there frequently are notable canyons, such as the **Palo Duro Canyon** on the **Prairie Dog Town Fork (main channel) of the Red River** and the breaks along the Canadian as it crosses the Panhandle north of Amarillo.

Along the eastern edge of the Panhandle there is a gradual descent of the earth's surface from high to low plains, but at the Red River the Caprock Escarpment becomes a striking surface feature. It continues as an east-facing wall south through Briscoe, Floyd, Motley, Dickens, Crosby, Garza and Borden counties, gradually decreasing in elevation. South of Borden County the escarpment is less obvious, and the boundary between the High Plains and the Edwards Plateau occurs where the alluvial cover of the High Plains disappears.

Stretching over the largest level plain of its kind in the United States, the **High Plains** rise gradually from about 2,700 feet on the east to more than 4,000 in spots along the New Mexico border.

Chiefly because of climate and the resultant agriculture, subdivisions are called the North Plains and South Plains. The North Plains, from Hale County north, has primarily wheat and grain sorghum farming, but with significant ranching and petroleum developments. Amarillo is the largest city, with Plainview on the south and Borger on the north as important commercial centers. The South Plains, also a leading grain sorghum region, leads Texas in cotton production. Lubbock is the principal city, and Lubbock County is one of the state's largest cotton producers. Irrigation from underground reservoirs, centered around Lubbock and Plainview, waters much of the crop acreage.

Edwards Plateau

Geographers usually consider that the Great Plains at the foot of the Rocky Mountains actually continue southward from the High Plains of Northwest Texas to the Rio Grande and the Balcones Escarpment. This southern and lower extension of the Great Plains in Texas is known as the Edwards Plateau.

It lies between the Rio Grande and the Colorado River. Its southeastern border is the **Balcones Escarpment** from the Rio Grande at Del Rio eastward to San Antonio and thence to Austin on the Colorado. Its upper boundary is the Pecos River, though the **Stockton Plateau** is geologically and topographically classed with the Edwards Plateau. The Edwards Plateau varies from about 750 feet high at its southern and eastern borders to about 2,700 feet in places. Almost the entire surface is a thin, limestone-based soil covered with a medium to thick growth of **cedar, small oak** and **mesquite** with a varying growth of **prickly pear.** Grass for cattle, weeds for sheep and tree foliage for the browsing goats support three industries — cattle, goat and sheep raising — upon which the area's economy depends. It is the **nation's leading Angora goat**

and mohair producing region and one of the nation's leading sheep and wool areas. A few crops are grown.

Toyah Basin

To the northwest of the Edwards and Stockton plateaus is the Toyah Basin, a broad, flat remnant of an old sea floor that occupied the region as recently as Quaternary time. Located in the Pecos River Valley, this region, in relatively recent time, has become important for many agricultural products as a result of irrigation. Additional economic activity is afforded by local oil fields.

The Hill Country

The Hill Country is a popular name for an area of hills and spring-fed streams along the edge of the **Balcones Escarpment.** Notable large springs include **Barton Springs** at Austin, **San Marcos Springs** at San Marcos, **Comal Springs** at New Braunfels, several springs at San Antonio, and a number of others.

The Llano Basin

The Llano Basin lies at the junction of the Colorado and Llano rivers in Burnet and Llano counties. Earlier this was known as the **"Central Mineral Region,"** because of the evidence there of a large number of minerals.

On the Colorado River in this area, a succession of dams impounds two large and five small reservoirs. Uppermost is **Lake Buchanan,** one of the large reservoirs, between Burnet and Llano counties. Below it in the western part of Travis County is **Lake Travis.** Between these two large reservoirs are three smaller ones, **Inks, L. B. Johnson** (formerly Granite Shoals) and **Marble Falls** reservoirs, used primarily for maintaining heads to produce electric power from the overflow from Lake Buchanan. **Lake Austin** is just above the city of Austin. Still another small lake, **Town Lake,** is formed by a low-water dam in Austin. The recreational area around these lakes is called the **Highland Lakes Country.** This is an interesting area with Precambrian and Paleozoic rocks found on the surface.

Basin and Range Province

The Basin and Range province, with its center in Nevada, surrounds the Colorado Plateau on the west and south and enters far West Texas from southern New Mexico. It consists of broad interior drainage, basins interspersed with scattered fault-block mountain ranges. Although this is the only part of Texas regarded as mountainous, these should not be confused with the Rockies. Of all the independent ranges in West Texas, only the Davis Mountains resemble the Rockies and there is much debate about this.

Texas west of the Edwards Plateau, bounded on the north by New Mexico and on the south by the Rio Grande, is distinctive in its physical and economic conditions. Traversed from north to south by an eastern range of the Rockies, it contains all of **Texas' true mountains** and also is very interesting geologically.

Highest of the Trans-Pecos Mountains is the **Guadalupe Range,** which enters the state from New Mexico. It comes to an abrupt end about 20 miles south of the boundary line, where are situated **Guadalupe Peak,** (8,749 feet, highest in Texas) and **El Capitan** (8,085 feet). El Capitan, because of perspective, appears to the observer on the plain below to be higher than Guadalupe. Lying just west of the Guadalupe range and extending to the **Hueco Mountains** a short distance east of El Paso is the **Diablo Plateau** or basin. It has no drainage outlet to the sea. The runoff from the scant rain that falls on its surface drains into a series of salt lakes that lie just west of the Guadalupe Mountains. These lakes are entirely dry during periods of low rainfall, exposing bottoms of solid salt, and for years they were a source of **commercial salt.**

Davis Mountains

The Davis Mountains are principally in Jeff Davis County. The highest peak, **Mount Livermore,** (8,378 feet) is **one of the highest in Texas;** there are several others more than 7,000 feet high. These mountains intercept the moisture-bearing winds and receive more precipitation than elsewhere in the Trans-Pecos, so they have more vegetation than the other Trans-Pecos mountains. Noteworthy are the **San Solomon Springs** at the northern base of these mountains.

Big Bend

South of the Davis Mountains lies the Big Bend country, so called because it is encompassed on three sides by a great southward swing of the Rio Grande. It is a mountainous country of scant rainfall and sparse population. Its principal mountains, the **Chisos,** rise to 7,825 feet in **Mount Emory.** Along the Rio Grande are the **Santa Elena, Mariscal and Boquillas canyons** with rim elevations of 3,500 to 3,775 feet. They are among the noteworthy canyons of the North American continent. Because of its remarkable topography and plant and animal life, the

southern part of this region along the Rio Grande is home to the **Big Bend National Park,** with headquarters in a deep valley in the Chisos Mountains. It is a favorite recreation area.

Upper Rio Grande Valley

The Upper Rio Grande (El Paso) Valley is a narrow strip of irrigated land running down the river from El Paso for a distance of 75 miles or more. In this area are the historic towns and missions of **Ysleta, Socorro and San Elizario, oldest in Texas.** Cotton is the chief product of the valley, much of it long-staple variety. This limited area has a dense urban and rural population, in marked contrast to the territory surrounding it. ☆

For Further Reading:
"Texas: A Geography," by Terry G. Jordan with John L. Bean Jr. and William M. Holmes; Westview Press, Boulder and London, 1984.

Geology of Texas

Source: Bureau of Economic Geology, The University of Texas at Austin.

History in the Rocks

Mountains, seas, coastal plains, rocky plateaus, high plains, forests — all this physiographic variety in Texas is controlled by the varied rocks and structures that underlie and crop out in Texas. The fascinating geologic history of Texas is recorded in the rocks — both those exposed at the surface and those penetrated by holes drilled in search of oil and natural gas. The rocks reveal a dynamic, ever-changing earth — ancient mountains, seas, volcanoes, earthquake belts, rivers, hurricanes and winds. Today, the volcanoes and great earthquake belts are no longer active, but rivers and streams, wind and rain, and the slow, inexorable alterations of rocks at or near the surface continue to change the face of Texas. The geologic history of Texas, as documented by the rocks, began more than a billion years ago. Its legacy is the mineral wealth and varied land forms of modern Texas.

Geologic Time Travel

The story preserved in the rocks requires an understanding of the origin of the strata and how they have been deformed. **Stratigraphy** is the study of the composition, sequence and origin of the rocks: what the rocks are made of, how they were formed and the order in which the layers were formed. Structural geology reveals the architecture of the rocks: the locations of the mountains, volcanoes, sedimentary basins and earthquake belts. Above is a map showing where rocks of various geologic ages are visible on the surface of Texas today.

History concerns events through time, but geologic time is such a grandiose concept that most of us find it difficult to comprehend. So, geologists have named the various chapters of earth history.

Precambrian Eon

Precambrian rocks, more than 600 million years old, are exposed at the surface in the Llano Uplift of Central Texas and in scattered outcrops in West Texas, around and north of Van Horn and near El Paso. These rocks, some more than a billion years old, include complexly deformed rocks that were originally formed by cooling from a liquid state as well as rocks that were altered from pre-existing rocks.

Precambrian rocks, often called the "basement complex," are thought to form the foundation of continental masses. Precambrian rocks underlie all of Texas. The outcrop in Central Texas is only the exposed part of the **Texas Craton,** which is primarily buried by younger rocks. (A craton is a stable, almost immovable portion of the earth's crust that forms the nuclear mass of a continent.)

Paleozoic Era

During the early part of the Paleozoic Era (approximately 600 million to 350 million years ago), broad, relatively shallow seas repeatedly inundated the Texas Craton and much of

North and West Texas. The evidence for these events is found exposed around the Llano Uplift and in far West Texas near Van Horn and El Paso, and also in the subsurface throughout most of West and North Texas. The evidence includes early Paleozoic rocks — sandstones, shales and limestones, similar to sediments that form in seas today — and the fossils of animals, similar to modern crustaceans — the brachiopods, clams, snails and related organisms that live in modern marine environments.

By **late Paleozoic** (approximately 350 million to 240 million years ago), the Texas Craton was bordered on the east and south by a long, deep marine basin called the Ouachita Trough. Sediments slowly accumulated in this trough until late in the Paleozoic Era. Plate-tectonic theory postulates that the collision of the North American Plate (upon which the Texas Craton is located) with the European and African-South American plates uplifted the thick sediments that had accumulated in the trough to form the Ouachita Mountains. At that time, the Ouachitas extended across Texas. Today, the Texas portion of the old mountain range is entirely buried by younger rocks, and all that remains at the surface of the once-majestic Ouachita Mountain chain is exposed only in southeastern Oklahoma and southwestern Arkansas.

During the **Pennsylvanian Period,** however, the Ouachita Mountains bordered the eastern margin of shallow inland seas that covered most of West Texas. Rivers flowed westward from the mountains to the sea bringing sediment to form deltas along an ever-changing coastline. The sediments were then reworked by the waves and currents of the inland sea. Today, these fluvial, delta and shallow marine deposits compose the late Paleozoic rocks that crop out and underlie the surface of North Central Texas.

Broad marine shelves divided the West Texas seas into several sub-basins, or deeper areas, that received more sediments than accumulated on the limestone shelves. Limestone reefs rimmed the deeper basins. Today, these reef limestones are important **oil reservoirs in West Texas.** These seas gradually withdrew from Texas, and by the late **Permian Period,** all that was left in West Texas were shallow basins and wide tidal flats in which salt, gypsum and red muds accumulated in a hot, arid land. Strata deposited during the Permian Period are exposed today along the edge of the Panhandle, as far east as Wichita Falls and south to Concho County, and in the Trans-Pecos.

Mesozoic Era

Approximately 240 million years ago, the major geologic events in Texas shifted from West Texas to East and Southeast Texas. The European and African-South American plates, which had collided with the North American plate to form the Ouachita Mountains, began to separate from North America. A series of faulted basins, or rifts, extending from Mexico to Nova Scotia were formed. These rifted basins received sediments

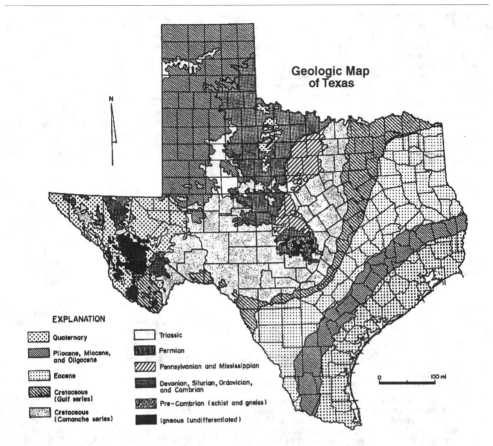

Geologic Map
of Texas

N

EXPLANATION

Quaternary

Pliocene, Miocene,
and Oligocene

Eocene

Cretaceous
(Gulf series)

Cretaceous
(Comanche series)

Triassic

Permian

Pennsylvanian and Mississippian

Devonian, Silurian, Ordovician,
and Cambrian

Pre-Cambrian (schist and gneiss)

Igneous (undifferentiated)

0   100 mi

from adjacent uplifts. As Europe and the southern continents continued to drift away from North America, the Texas basins were eventually buried beneath thick deposits of marine salt within the newly formed East Texas and Gulf Coast basins. **Jurassic** and **Cretaceous** rocks in East and Southeast Texas document a sequence of broad limestone shelves at the edge of the developing Gulf of Mexico. From time to time, the shelves were buried beneath deltaic sandstones and shales, which built the northwestern margin of the widening Gulf of Mexico to the south and southeast. As the underlying salt was buried more deeply by dense sediments, the salt became unstable and moved toward areas of least pressure. As the salt moved, it arched or pierced overlying sediments forming, in some cases, columns known as **"salt domes."** In some cases, these salt domes moved to the surface; others remain beneath a sedimentary overburden. This mobile salt formed numerous structures that would later serve to trap oil and natural gas.

By the early **Cretaceous** (approximately 140 million years ago), the shallow **Mesozoic seas** covered a large part of Texas, eventually extending west to the Trans-Pecos area and north almost to the present-day state boundaries. Today, the limestones deposited in those seas are exposed in the walls of the magnificent **canyons of the Rio Grande** in the Big Bend National Park area and in the canyons and headwaters of streams that drain the Edwards Plateau, as well as in Central Texas from San Antonio to Dallas.

Animals of many types lived in the shallow Mesozoic seas, tidal pools and coastal swamps. Today these lower Cretaceous rocks are some of the most fossiliferous in the state. Tracks of **dinosaurs** occur in several localities, and remains of **terrestrial, aquatic and flying reptiles** have been collected from Cretaceous rocks in many parts of Texas.

During most of the late Cretaceous, much of Texas lay beneath **marine waters** that were deeper than those of the

early Cretaceous seas, except where rivers, deltas and shallow marine shelves existed. River delta and strandline sandstones are the reservoir rocks for the most prolific oil field in Texas. When discovered in 1930, this East Texas oil field contained recoverable reserves estimated at 5.6 billion barrels. The chalky rock that we now call the "Austin Chalk" was deposited when the Texas seas became deeper. Today, the chalk (and other Upper Cretaceous rocks) crops out in a wide band that extends from near Eagle Pass on the Rio Grande, east to San Antonio, north to Dallas and eastward to the Texarkana area. The Austin Chalk and other upper Cretaceous rocks dip southeastward beneath the East Texas and Gulf Coast basins. The late Cretaceous was the time of the last major seaway across Texas, because mountains were forming in the western United States that influenced areas as far away as Texas.

A **chain of volcanoes** formed beneath the late Cretaceous seas in an area roughly parallel to and south and east of the old, buried Ouachita Mountains. The eruptions of these volcanoes were primarily on the sea floor and great clouds of steam and ash likely accompanied them. Between eruptions, invertebrate marine animals built reefs on the shallow volcanic cones. Pilot Knob, located southeast of Austin, is one of these old volcanoes that is now exposed at the surface.

Cenozoic Era

At the dawn of the Cenozoic Era, approximately 65 million years ago, the northern and northwestern margins of the East Texas Basin were sites of deltas fed by rivers. These streams flowed eastward, draining areas to the north and west. Although there were minor incursions of the seas, the Cenozoic rocks principally document extensive seaward building by broad deltas, marshy lagoons, sandy barrier islands and embayments. Thick vegetation covered the levees and areas between the streams. Coastal plains were taking shape, under the same processes still at work today.

The Mesozoic marine salt became buried by thick sediments in the coastal plain area. The salt began to form ridges and domes in the Houston and Rio Grande areas. The heavy load of sand, silt and mud deposited by the deltas eventually caused some areas of the coast to subside and form large fault systems, essentially parallel to the coast. Many of these coastal faults moved slowly and probably generated little earthquake activity. However, movement along the Balcones and Luling-Mexia-Talco zones, a **complex system of faults** along the western and northern edge of the basins, likely generated large earthquakes millions of years ago.

Predecessors of modern animals roamed the Texas Cenozoic coastal plains and woodlands. Bones and teeth of **horses, camels, sloths, giant armadillos, mammoths, mastodons, bats, rats, large cats** and other modern or extinct mammals have been excavated from coastal plain deposits. Vegetation in the area included varieties of plants and trees both similar and dissimilar to modern ones. **Fossil palmwood,** the Texas "**state stone,**" is found in sediments of early Cenozoic age.

The Cenozoic Era in Trans-Pecos Texas was entirely different. There, **extensive volcanic eruptions** formed great calderas and produced copious lava flows. These eruptions ejected great clouds of volcanic ash and rock particles into the air — many times the amount of material ejected by the 1980 eruption of Mount St. Helens. Ash from the eruptions drifted eastward and is found in many of the sand-and-siltstones of the Gulf Coastal Plains. **Lava** flowed over the older Paleozoic and Mesozoic rocks, and igneous intrusions melted their way upward into the crustal rocks. These volcanic and intrusive igneous rocks are well exposed in the arid areas of the Trans-Pecos today.

In the Texas Panhandle, streams originating in the recently elevated southern Rocky Mountains brought floods of gravel and sand into Texas. As the braided streams crisscrossed the area, they formed great **alluvial fans.** These fans, which were deposited on the older **Paleozoic** and **Mesozoic** rocks, occur from northwestern Texas into Nebraska. Between 1 million and 2 million years ago, the streams of the Texas Panhandle were isolated from their Rocky Mountain source, and the eastern edge of this sheet of alluvial material began to retreat westward, forming the **Caprock** of the modern High Plains of Texas.

During the latter part of the Cenozoic Era, a great **Ice Age** descended upon the northern part of the North American continent. For more than 2 million years, there were successive advances and retreats of the thick sheets of glacial ice. Four periods of extensive glaciation were separated by warmer interglacial periods. Although the glaciers never reached as far south as Texas, the state's climate and sea level underwent major changes with each period of glacial advance and retreat. Sea level during times of glacial advance was 300 to 450 feet lower than during the warmer interglacial periods because so much sea water was captured in the ice sheets. The climate was both more humid and cooler than today, and the major Texas rivers carried more water and more sand and gravel to the sea. These deposits underlie the outer 50 miles or more of the Gulf Coastal Plain.

Approximately 3,000 years ago, sea level reached its modern position. The rivers, deltas, lagoons, beaches and barrier islands that we know as coastal Texas have formed since that time. ☆

Oil and natural gas, as well as nonfuel minerals, are important to the Texas economy. For a more detailed discussion, look for "Minerals" in the index.

Soil Conservation and Use

Source: *Natural Resources Conservation Service, U. S. Department of Agriculture, Temple, Texas.*

Soil is one of Texas' most important natural resources. The soils of Texas are complex because of the wide diversity of climate, vegetation, geology and landscapes. More than 1,200 different kinds of soil are recognized in the state. Each soil has a specific set of properties that affect its use in some way. The location of each soil and information about its use is in soil survey reports available for most counties. Contact the **Natural Resources Conservation Service** for more information: 101 S. Main St., Temple 76501-7682; phone: 254-742-9850.

The vast expanse of Texas soils encouraged wasteful use of soil and water throughout much of the state's history. About 21 percent of all land area in Texas has been classified as "prime farmland." Settlers were attracted by these rich soils and the abundant water of the eastern half of the region, used them to build an agriculture and agribusiness of vast proportions, then found their abuse had created critical problems.

In the 1930s, interest in soil and water conservation began to mount. In 1935, the Soil Conservation Service, now called the **Natural Resources Conservation Service,** was created in the U. S. Department of Agriculture. In 1939, the **Texas Soil Conservation Law** made it possible for landowners to organize local soil and water conservation districts.

As of April 1997, the state had 214 conservation districts, which manage the conservation functions within the district. A subdivision of state government, each district is governed by a board of five elected landowners. Technical assistance in planning and applying conservation work is provided through the USDA, Natural Resources Conservation Service. State funds for districts are administered through the **Texas State Soil and Water Conservation Board.**

The 1992 National Resources Inventory showed that land use in Texas consisted of about 56 percent rangeland, 17 percent cropland, 10 percent pastureland, 6 percent forestland, 5 percent urban land, 2 percent federal land and 4 percent miscellaneous land. The Inventory also revealed that wind and water erosion removed about 326 million tons of soil annually from Texas cropland.

Soil Subdivisions

Most authorities divide Texas into 19 major subdivisions, called **Major Land Resource Areas,** that have similar or related soils, vegetation, topography, climate and land uses. Brief descriptions of these subdivisions follow.

1. Trans-Pecos Soils

The 18.7 million acres of the Trans-Pecos, mostly west of the Pecos River, are diverse plains and valleys intermixed with mountains. Surface drainage is slow to rapid. This arid region is used mainly as rangeland. A small amount of irrigated cropland is on the more fertile soils along the Rio Grande and the Pecos River. Vineyards are a more recent use of these soils, as is the disposal of large volumes of municipal wastes.

Upland soils are mostly well-drained, light reddish-brown to brown clay loams, clays and sands (some have a large amount of gypsum or other salts). Many areas have shallow soils and rock outcrops, and sizable areas have deep sands. **Bottomland soils** are deep, well-drained, dark grayish-brown to reddish-brown silt loams, loams, clay loams and clays. Lack of soil moisture and wind erosion are the major soil-management problems. Only irrigated crops can be grown on these soils, and most areas lack an adequate source of good water.

2. High Plains Soils

The High Plains area comprises a vast high plateau of more than 19.4 million acres in northwestern Texas. It lies in the southern part of the Great Plains province that includes large similar areas in Oklahoma and New Mexico. The flat, nearly level treeless plain has few streams to cause local relief. However, several major rivers originate in the High Plains or cross the area. The largest is the **Canadian River,** which has cut a deep valley across the Panhandle section.

Playas, small intermittent lakes scattered through the area, lie up to 20 feet below the surrounding plains. A 1965 survey counted more than 19,000 playas in 44 counties, occupying some 340,000 acres. They receive most of the runoff from rains, but only 10 to 40 percent of this water percolates back to the aquifer.

Upland soils are mostly well-drained, deep, neutral to alkaline clay loams and sandy loams in shades of brown or red. Sandy soils are in the southern part. Many soils have large amounts of lime at various depths and some are shallow over caliche. Soils of bottomlands are minor in extent.

The area is used mostly for cropland, but significant areas of rangeland are in the southwestern and extreme northern parts. The soils are moderately productive, and the flat surface encourages irrigation and mechanization. Limited soil moisture, constant danger of wind erosion and irrigation water management are the major soil-management problems, but the region is Texas' leading producer of three important crops: **cotton, grain sorghums and wheat**.

3. Rolling Plains Soils

The Rolling Plains include 21.7 million acres east of the High Plains in northwestern Texas. The area lies west of the North Central Prairies and extends from the edge of the Edwards Plateau in Tom Green County northward into Oklahoma. The landscape is nearly level to strongly rolling, and surface drainage is moderate to rapid. Outcrops of red beds geologic materials and associated reddish soils led to use of the name "Red Plains" by some. Limestone underlies the soils in the southeastern part. The eastern part contains large areas of badlands.

Upland soils are mostly deep, pale-brown through reddish-brown to dark grayish-brown, neutral to alkaline sandy loams, clay loams and clays; some are deep sands. Many soils have a large amount of lime in the lower part, and a few others are saline; some are shallow and stony. **Bottomland soils** are mostly reddish-brown and sandy to clayey; some are saline.

This area is used mostly for rangeland, but cotton, grain sorghums and wheat are important crops. The major soil-management problems are brush control, wind erosion, low fertility and lack of soil mosture. Salt spots are a concern in some areas.

4. North Central Prairie Soils

The North Central Prairie occupies about 7 million acres in North Central Texas. Adjacent to this area on the north is the rather small (less than 1 million acres) Rolling Red Prairies area, which extends into Oklahoma and is included here because the soils and land use are similar. This area lies between the Western Cross Timbers and the Rolling Plains. It is dominantly grassland intermixed with small wooded areas. The landscape is undulating with slow to rapid surface drainage.

Upland soils are mostly deep, well-drained, brown or reddish-brown, slightly acid soils over neutral to alkaline, clayey subsoils. Some soils are shallow or moderately deep to shale. Bottomland soils are mostly well-drained, dark-brown or gray loams and clays.

This area is used mostly as rangeland, but wheat, grain sorghums and other crops are grown on the better soils. Brush control, wind and water erosion and limited soil moisture are the major soil-management concerns.

5. Edwards Plateau Soils

The 22.7 million acres of the Edwards Plateau are in southwest Texas east of the Trans-Pecos and west of the Blackland Prairie. Uplands are nearly level to undulating except near large stream valleys where the landscape is hilly with deep canyons and steep slopes. Surface drainage is rapid.

Upland soils are mostly shallow, very stony or gravelly, dark alkaline clays and clay loams underlain by limestone. Lighter-colored soils are on the steep sideslopes and deep, less-stony soils are in the valleys. Bottomland soils are mostly deep, dark-gray or brown, alkaline loams and clays.

Raising beef cattle is the main enterprise in this region, but it is also the center of Texas' and the nation's mohair and wool production. The area is a major deer habitat; hunting leases produce income. Cropland is mostly in the valleys on the deeper soils and is used mainly for growing forage crops and hay. The major soil-management concerns are brush control, large stones, low fertility, excess lime and limited soil moisture.

6. Central Basin Soils

The Central Basin, also known as the **Llano Basin**, occupies a relatively small area in Central Texas. It includes parts or all of Llano, Mason, Gillespie and adjoining counties. The total area is about 1.6 million acres of undulating to hilly landscape.

Upland soils are mostly shallow, reddish-brown to brown, mostly gravelly and stony, neutral to slightly acid sandy loams over granite, limestone, gneiss and schist bedrock. Large boulders are on the soil surface in some areas. Deeper, less stony sandy-loam soils are in the valleys. Bottomland soils are minor areas of deep, dark-gray or brown loams and clays.

Ranching is the main enterprise, with some farms producing peaches, grain sorghum and wheat. The area provides excellent deer habitat, and hunting leases are a major source of income. Brush control, large stones and limited soil moisture are soil-management concerns.

7. Northern Rio Grande Plain Soils

The Northern Rio Grande Plain comprises about 6.3 million acres in an area of Southern Texas extending from Uvalde to Beeville. The landscape is nearly level to rolling, mostly brush-covered plains with slow to rapid surface drainage.

The major upland soils are deep, reddish-brown or dark grayish-brown, neutral to alkaline loams and clays. Bottomland soils are mostly dark-colored loams.

The area is mostly rangeland with significant areas of cropland. Grain sorghums, cotton, corn and small grains are the major crops. Crops are irrigated in the western part, especially in the Winter Garden area, where vegetables such as spinach, carrots and cabbage are grown. Much of the area is good deer and dove habitat; hunting leases are a major source of income. Brush control, soil fertility, and irrigation-water management are the major soil-management concerns.

8. Western Rio Grande Plain Soils

The Western Rio Grande Plain comprises about 5.3 million acres in an area of southwestern Texas from Del Rio to Rio Grande City. The landscape is nearly level to undulating except near the Rio Grande where it is hilly. Surface drainage is slow to rapid.

The major soils are mostly deep, brown or gray alkaline clays and loams. Some are saline.

Most of the soils are used for rangeland. Irrigated grain sorghums and vegetables are grown along the Rio Grande. Hunting leases are a major source of income. Brush control and limited soil moisture are the major soil-management problems.

9. Central Rio Grande Plain Soils

The Central Rio Grande Plain comprises about 5.9 million acres in an area of Southern Texas from Live Oak County to Hidalgo County. It Includes the South Texas Sand Sheet, an area of deep, sandy soils and active sand dunes. The landscape is nearly level to gently undulating. Surface drainage is slow to rapid.

Upland soils are mostly deep, light-colored, neutral to alkaline sands and loams. Many are saline or sodic. Bottomland soils are of minor extent.

Most of the area is used for raising beef cattle. A few areas, mostly in the northeast, are used for growing grain sorghums, cotton and small grains. Hunting leases are a major source of income. Brush control is the major soil-management problem on rangeland; wind erosion and limited soil moisture are major concerns on cropland.

10. Lower Rio Grande Valley Soils

The Lower Rio Grande Valley comprises about 2.1 million acres in extreme southern Texas. The landscape is level to gently sloping with slow surface drainage.

Upland soils are mostly deep, grayish-brown, neutral to alkaline loams; coastal areas are mostly gray, silty clay loam and silty clay; some are saline. Bottomland soils are minor in extent.

Most of the soils are used for growing irrigated vegetables and citrus, along with cotton, grain sorghums and sugar cane. Some areas are used for growing beef cattle. Irrigation water management and wind erosion are the major soil-management problems on cropland; brush control is the major problem on rangeland.

11. Western Cross Timbers Soils

The Western Cross Timbers area comprises about 2.6 million acres. It includes the wooded section west of the Grand Prairie and extends from the Red River southward to the north edge of Brown County. The landscape is undulating and is dissected by many drainageways including the Brazos and Red rivers. Surface drainage is rapid.

Upland soils are mostly deep, grayish-brown, slightly acid loams with loamy and clayey subsoils. Bottomland soils along the major rivers are deep, reddish-brown, neutral to alkaline silt loams and clays.

The area is used mostly for grazing beef and dairy cattle on native range and improved pastures. Crops are peanuts, grain sorghums, small grains, peaches, pecans and vegetables. The major soil-management problem on grazing lands is brush control. Waste management on dairy farms is a more recent concern. Wind and water erosion are the major problems on cropland.

12. Eastern Cross Timbers Soils

The Eastern Cross Timbers area comprises about 1 million acres in a long narrow strip of wooded land that separates the northern parts of the Blackland Prairie and Grand Prairie and extends from the Red River southward to Hill County. The landscape is gently undulating to rolling and is dissected by many streams, including the Red and Trinity rivers. Sandstone-capped hills are prominent in some areas. Surface runoff is moderate to rapid.

The upland soils are mostly deep, light-colored, slightly acid sandy loams and loamy sands with reddish loamy or clayey subsoils. Bottomland soils are reddish-brown to dark gray, slightly acid to alkaline loams or gray clays.

Grassland consisting of native range and improved pastures is the major land use. Peanuts, grain sorghums, small grains, peaches, pecans and vegetables are grown in some areas. Brush control, water erosion and low fertility are the major concerns in soil management.

13. Grand Prairie Soils

The Grand Prairie comprises about 6.3 million acres in North Central Texas. It extends from the Red River to about the Colorado River between the Eastern and Western Cross Timbers in the northern part and just west of the Blackland Prairie in the southern part. The landscape is undulating to hilly and is dissected by many streams including the Red, Trinity and Brazos rivers. Surface drainage is rapid.

Upland soils are mostly dark-gray, alkaline clays; some are shallow over limestone and some are stony. Some areas have light-colored loamy soils over chalky limestone. Bottomland soils along the Red and Brazos rivers are reddish silt loams and clays. Other bottomlands have dark-gray loams and clays.

Land use is a mixture of rangeland, pastureland and cropland. The area is mainly used for growing beef cattle. Some small grain, grain sorghums, corn and hay are grown. Brush control and water erosion are the major management concerns.

14. Blackland Prairie Soils

The Blackland Prairies consist of about 12.6 million acres of east-central Texas extending southwesterly from the Red River to Bexar County. There are smaller areas to the southeast. The landscape is undulating with few scattered wooded areas that are mostly in the bottomlands. Surface drainage is moderate to rapid.

Both upland and bottomland soils are deep, dark-gray to black alkaline clays. Some soils in the western part are shallow to moderately deep over chalk. Some soils on the eastern edge are neutral to slightly acid, grayish clays and loams over mottled clay subsoils (sometimes called graylands). Blackland soils are known as "cracking clays" because of the large, deep cracks that form in dry weather. This high shrink-swell property can cause serious damage to foundations, highways and other structures and is a safety hazard in pits and trenches.

Land use is divided about equally between cropland and grassland. Cotton, grain sorghums, corn, wheat, oats and hay are grown. Grassland is mostly improved pastures, with native range on the shallower and steeper soils. Water erosion, cotton root rot, soil tilth and brush control are the major management problems.

15. Claypan Area Soils

The Claypan Area consists of about 6.1 million acres in east-central Texas just east of the Blackland Prairie. The landscape is a gently undulating to rolling, moderately dissected woodland also known as the Post Oak Belt or Post Oak Savannah. Surface drainage is moderate.

Upland soils commonly have a thin, light-colored, acid sandy loam surface layer over dense, mottled red, yellow and gray claypan subsoils. Some deep, sandy soils with less clayey subsoils exist. Bottomlands are deep, highly fertile, reddish-brown to dark-gray loamy to clayey soils.

Land use is mainly rangeland. Some areas are in improved pastures. Most cropland is in bottomlands that are protected from flooding. Major crops are cotton, grain sorghums, corn, hay and forage crops, most of which are irrigated. Brush control on rangeland and irrigation water management on cropland are the major management problems. Water erosion is a serious problem on the highly erosive claypan soils, especially where they are overgrazed.

16. East Texas Timberland Soils

The East Texas Timberlands area comprises about 16.1 million acres of the forested eastern part of the state. The landscape is gently undulating to hilly and well dissected by many streams. Surface drainage is moderate to rapid.

This area has many kinds of upland soils but most are deep, light-colored, acid sands and loams over loamy and clayey subsoils. Deep sands are in scattered areas and red clays are in areas of "redlands." Bottomland soils are mostly brown to dark-gray, acid loams and some clays.

The land is used mostly for growing commercial pine timber and for woodland grazing. Improved pastures are scattered throughout and are used for grazing beef and dairy cattle and for hay production. Some commercial hardwoods are in the bottomlands. Woodland management problems include seedling survival, invasion of hardwoods in pine stands, effects of logging on water quality and control of the southern pine beetle. Lime and fertilizers are necessary for productive cropland and pastures.

17. Coast Prairie Soils

The Coast Prairie includes about 8.7 million acres near the Gulf Coast in southeast Texas. It ranges from 30 to 80 miles in width and parallels the coast from the Sabine River in Orange County to Baffin Bay in Kleberg County. The landscape is level to gently undulating with slow surface drainage.

Upland soils are mostly deep, dark-gray, neutral to slightly acid clay loams and clays. Lighter-colored and more-sandy soils are in a strip on the northwestern edge; some soils in the southern part are alkaline; some are saline and sodic. Bottomland soils are mostly deep, dark-colored clays and loams along small streams but are greatly varied along the rivers.

Land use is mainly grazing lands and cropland. Some hardwood timber is in the bottomlands. Many areas are also managed for wetland wildlife habitat. The nearly level topography and productive soils encourage farming. Rice, grain sorghums, cotton, corn and hay are the main crops. Brush management on grasslands and removal of excess water on cropland are the major management concerns.

18. Coast Saline Prairies Soils

The Coast Saline Prairies area includes about 3.2 million acres along a narrow strip of wet lowlands adjacent to the coast; it includes the barrier islands that extend from Mexico to Louisiana. The surface is at or only a few feet above sea level with many areas of salt-water marsh. Surface drainage is very slow.

The soils are mostly deep, dark-colored clays and loams; many are saline and sodic. Light-colored sandy soils are on the barrier islands. The water table is at or near the surface of most soils.

Cattle grazing is the chief economic use of the various salt-tolerant cordgrasses and sedges. Many areas are managed for wetland wildlife. Recreation is popular on the barrier islands. Providing fresh water and access to grazing areas are the major management concerns.

19. Flatwoods Soils

The Flatwoods area includes about 2.5 million acres of woodland in humid southeast Texas just north of the Coast Prairie and extending into Louisiana. The landscape is level to gently undulating. Surface drainage is slow.

Upland soils are mostly deep, light-colored, acid loams with gray, loamy or clayey subsoils. Bottomland soils are deep, dark-colored, acid clays and loams. The water table is near the surface at least part of the year.

The land is mainly used for forest; cattle are grazed in some areas. Woodland management problems include seedling survival, invasion of hardwoods in pine stands, effects of logging on water quality and control of the southern pine beetle. ☆

Water Resources

Beginning in September 1993, regulation of water quality of water resources of the state were placed in the jurisdiction of the **Texas Natural Resource Conservation Commission**. In addition, the **Texas Water Development Board** is responsible for the development of Texas water resources and the financing of facilities, such as dams, that are part of that development. The TWDB furnished the information for this section of the Texas Almanac.

Texas, through its river authorities, municipalities, water districts and state-level agencies, exercises the dominant role in development of municipal and industrial water supplies. Approximately 80 percent of the money invested in the state's water projects has been provided by Texas entities of government.

To develop a comprehensive statewide water plan, the 75th Texas Legislature, in 1997, required the TWDB to divide the state into 16 regional water-planning areas. Each area's Regional Water Planning Group (RWPG), whose membership includes representatives from 11 interest groups, will adopt a water plan addressing conservation of water supplies, meeting future water needs and responding to future droughts, by Sept. 1, 2000. The TWDB is charged with incorporating these into a comprehensive state water plan by Sept. 1, 2001.

For more information, see the TWDB Web page at www.twdb.state.tx.us.

Ground-water Supplies and Use

Texas has historically relied on its wealth of fresh to slightly saline water that underlies more than 81 percent of the state. Fifty-six percent of the more than 13.5 million acre-feet of water currently being used in Texas is derived from underground sources that occupy nine major and 20 minor aquifers. Approximately 75 percent of the ground water produced is used for irrigating agricultural crops, especially in the Panhandle region. Ground water also supplies about 41 percent of the state's municipal needs.

Major Aquifers (see map on next page):

Ogallala - The Ogallala aquifer extends under 46 counties of the Texas Panhandle and is the southernmost extension of the largest aquifer (High Plains aquifer) in North America. The Ogallala Formation of late Miocene to early Pliocene age consists of heterogeneous sequences of coarse-grained sand and gravel in the lower part, grading upward into clay, silt and fine sand. In Texas, the Panhandle is the most extensive region irrigated with ground water. Approximately 95 percent of the water pumped from the Ogallala is used for irrigation. Water-level declines are occurring in part of the region because of extensive pumping that far exceeds recharge. Water-conservation measures by both agricultural and municipal users are being promoted in the area. A new computer model of the northern portion of the Ogallala aquifer is being developed by the University of Texas Bureau of Economic Geology, and several agencies are investigating playa recharge and agricultural re-use projects.

Gulf Coast Aquifer - The Gulf Coast aquifer forms an irregularly shaped belt that parallels the Texas coastline and extends through 54 counties from the Rio Grande northeastward to the Louisiana border. The aquifer system is composed of the water-bearing units of the **Catahoula, Oakville, Fleming, Goliad, Willis, Lissie, Bentley, Montgomery** and **Beaumont formations**. This system has been divided into three major water-producing components referred to as the **Chicot, Evangeline**, and **Jasper** aquifers. Municipal uses account for about 51 percent and irrigation accounts for about 36 percent of the total pumpage from the aquifer. Water quality is generally good northeast of the San Antonio River basin, but deteriorates to the southwest. Years of heavy pumpage have caused significant water-level declines in portions of the aquifer. Some of these declines have resulted in significant **land-surface subsidence,** particularly in the Houston-Galveston area.

Edwards (Balcones Fault Zone) - The Edwards (BFZ) aquifer forms a narrow belt extending through nine counties from a ground-water divide in Kinney County through the San Antonio area northeastward to the Leon River in Bell County. A poorly defined ground-water divide in Hays County hydrologically separates the aquifer into the San Antonio and Austin regions. Water in the aquifer occurs in fractures, honeycomb zones and solution channels in the Edwards and associated limestone formations of Cretaceous age. More than 50 percent of aquifer pumpage is for municipal use, while irrigation is the principal use in the western segment. San Antonio is one of the largest cities in the world that relies solely on a single ground-water source for its municipal supply. The aquifer also feeds several well-known recreational springs and underlies some of the most environmentally sensitive areas in the state.

In 1993, the Edwards Aquifer Authority was created by the legislature to regulate aquifer pumpage for the benefit of all users: agricultural, municipal and environmental. The authority's jurisdiction extends from Uvalde County through a portion of Hays County. Barton Springs-Edwards Aquifer Conservation District provides aquifer management for the remaining portion of Hays and southern Travis counties. The EAA has an active program to educate the public on water conservation and also operates several active groundwater recharge sites. The San Antonio River Authority also has a number of flood-control structures that effectively recharge the aquifer.

Conservation districts are promoting the use of more-efficient irrigation techniques, and market-based, voluntary transfers of unused agricultural water rights to municipal uses are becoming more common.

Carrizo-Wilcox - Extending from the Rio Grande in South Texas northeastward into Arkansas and Louisiana, the Carrizo-Wilcox aquifer provides water to all or parts of 60 counties. The Wilcox Group and overlying Carrizo Sand form a hydrologically connected system of sand locally interbedded with clay, silt, lignite and gravel. Throughout most of its extent in Texas, the aquifer yields fresh to slightly saline water, which is used primarily for irrigation in the **Winter Garden District** of South Texas and for public supply and industrial use in Central and Northeast Texas. Because of excessive pumping, the water level in the aquifer has been significantly lowered, particularly in the artesian portion of the Winter Garden District of Atascosa, Frio and Zavala counties and in municipal and industrial areas located in Angelina and Smith counties.

Trinity Group - The Trinity aquifer consists of basal Cretaceous-age Trinity Group formations that extend from the Red River in North Texas to the Hill Country of Central Texas. Formations comprising the aquifer include the **Twin Mountains, Glen Rose** and **Paluxy**. Where the Glen Rose thins or is absent, the Twin Mountains and Paluxy formations coalesce to form the **Antlers Formation**. In the southern extent, the Trinity includes the Glen Rose and underlying Travis Peak formations. Water from the Antlers portion of the Trinity is used mainly for irrigation in the outcrop area of North and Central Texas. Elsewhere, water from the Trinity is used primarily for municipal and domestic supply. Extensive development of the Trinity aquifer in the Dallas-Fort Worth and Waco areas has historically resulted in water-level declines of several hundred feet.

Edwards-Trinity (Plateau) - This aquifer underlies the **Edwards Plateau**, extending from the Hill Country of Central Texas westward to the Trans-Pecos region. The aquifer

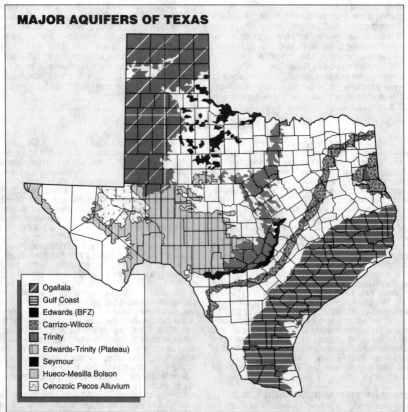

MAJOR AQUIFERS OF TEXAS

Legend:
- Ogallala
- Gulf Coast
- Edwards (BFZ)
- Carrizo-Wilcox
- Trinity
- Edwards-Trinity (Plateau)
- Seymour
- Hueco-Mesilla Bolson
- Cenozoic Pecos Alluvium

The Dallas Morning News

consists of sandstone and limestone formations of the Trinity Group formations, and limestones and dolomites of the Edwards and associated limestone formations. Groundwater movement in the aquifer is generally toward the southeast. Near the edge of the plateau, flow is toward the main streams, where the water issues from springs. Irrigation, mainly in the northwestern portion of the region, accounted for approximately 79 percent of the total aquifer use in 1994 and has resulted in significant water-level declines in Glasscock and Reagan counties. Elsewhere, the aquifer supplies fresh but hard water for municipal, domestic and livestock use.

Seymour - This aquifer consists of isolated areas of alluvium found in parts of 22 north-central and Panhandle counties in the upper Red River and Brazos River basins. Eastward-flowing streams during the Quaternary Period deposited discontinuous beds of poorly sorted gravel, sand, silt and clay that were later dissected by erosion, resulting in the isolated remnants of the formation. Individual accumulations vary greatly in thickness, but most of the Seymour is less than 100 feet. The lower, more permeable part of the aquifer produces the greatest amount of ground water. Irrigation pumpage accounted for 93 percent of the total use from the aquifer in 1994. Water quality generally ranges from fresh to slightly saline. However, the salinity has increased in many heavily pumped areas to the point where the water has become unsuitable for domestic and municipal use. Natural salt pollution in the upper reaches of the Red and Brazos River basins precludes the full utilization of these water resources.

Hueco-Mesilla Bolson - These aquifers are located in El Paso and Hudspeth counties in far western Texas and occur in Quaternary basin-fill deposits that extend northward into New Mexico and westward into Mexico. The Hueco Bolson, located on the eastern side of the Franklin Mountains, consists of up to 9,000 feet of clay, silt, sand and gravel and is the principal source of drinking water for both El Paso and Juarez. Located west of the Franklin

Mountains, the Mesilla Bolson reaches up to 2,000 feet in thickness and contains three separate water-producing zones. Ground-water depletion of the Hueco Bolson has become a serious problem. Historical large-scale ground-water withdrawals, especially for the municipal uses of El Paso and Juarez, have caused major water-level declines and significantly changed the direction of flow, causing a deterioration of the chemical quality of the ground water in the aquifer.

Cenozoic Pecos Alluvium - Located in the upper Pecos River Valley of West Texas, this aquifer is the principal source of water for irrigation in Reeves and northwestern Pecos counties and for industrial uses, power supply and municipal use elsewhere. Consisting of up to 1,500 feet of alluvial fill, the aquifer occupies two hydrologically separate basins: the Pecos Trough in the west and the Monument Draw Trough in the east. Water from the aquifer is generally hard and contains dissolved-solids concentrations ranging from less than 300 to more than 5,000 parts per million. Water-level declines in excess of 200 feet have historically occurred in Reeves and Pecos counties, but have moderated since the mid-1970s with the decrease in irrigation pumpage.

Major Rivers

Some **11,247 named Texas streams** are identified in the **U.S. Geological Survey Geographic Names Information System.** Their combined length is about 80,000 miles, and they drain 263,513 square miles within Texas. **Thirteen major rivers** are described below, starting with the southernmost and moving northward:

Rio Grande

The Pueblo Indians called this river **P'osoge,** "river of great water." In 1582, Antonio de Espejo of Nueva Vizcaya, Mexico, followed the course of the **Río Conchos** to its confluence with a great river, which Espejo named **Río del**

Principal Rivers

Canadian
Red
Sabine
Neches
Pecos
Brazos
Trinity
San Jacinto
Colorado
Guadalupe
Lavaca
San Antonio
Nueces
Rio Grande

Norte (River of the North). The name **Rio Grande** was first given the stream apparently by the explorer **Juan de Oñate,** who arrived on its banks near present-day El Paso in 1598.

Thereafter the names were often consolidated, as **Río Grande del Norte.** It was shown also on early Spanish maps as **Río San Buenaventura** and **Río Ganapetuan.** In its lower course it early acquired the name **Río Bravo,** which is its name on most Mexican maps. At times it has also been known as **Río Turbio,** probably because of its muddy appearance during its frequent rises. Some people erroneously call this watercourse the **Rio Grande River.**

From source to mouth, the Rio Grande drops 12,000 feet to sea level as a snow-fed mountain torrent, desert stream and meandering coastal river. Along its banks and in its valley Indian civilizations developed, and Europeans made some of their first North American settlements.

This river rises in Colorado, flows the north-south length of New Mexico and **forms the boundary of Texas and international U.S.-Mexican boundary for 889 to 1,254 river miles,** depending upon method of measurement. (See **Texas Boundary Line.)** The length of the Rio Grande, as of other rivers, depends on method of measurement and varies yearly as its course changes. Latest **International Boundary and Water Commission** figure is 1,896 miles, which is considerably below the 2,200-mile figure often used. Depending upon methods of measurement, the Rio Grande is the fourth- or fifth-longest North American river, exceeded only by the Missouri-Mississippi, McKenzie-Peace, St. Lawrence and possibly Yukon. Since all of these except the Missouri-Mississippi are partly in Canada, the Rio Grande is the **second-longest river entirely within or bordering the United States.** It is **Texas' longest river.**

The snow-fed flow of the Rio Grande is used for **irrigation** in Colorado below the San Juan Mountains, where the river rises at the Continental Divide. Turning south, it flows through a canyon in northern New Mexico and again irrigates a broad valley of central New Mexico. This is the oldest irrigated area of the United States, where Spanish missionaries encouraged Indian irrigation in the 1600s.

Southern New Mexico impounds Rio Grande waters in Elephant Butte Reservoir for irrigation of 150 miles of valley above and below El Paso. Here is the **oldest irrigated area in Texas** and one of the oldest in the United States. Extensive irrigation practically exhausts the water supply. In this valley are situated the **three oldest towns in Texas — Ysleta, Socorro** and **San Elizario.** At the lower end of the El Paso irrigated valley, the upper Rio Grande virtually ends except in seasons of above-normal flow.

It starts as a perennially flowing stream again where the Río Conchos of Mexico flows into it at Presidio-Ojinaga. Through the **Big Bend** the Rio Grande flows through three successive **canyons,** the **Santa Elena,** the **Mariscal** and the **Boquillas.** The Santa Elena has a river bed elevation of 2,145 feet and a canyon-rim elevation of 3,661. Corresponding figures for Mariscal are 1,925 and 3,625, and for Boquillas, 1,850 and 3,490. The river here flows around the base of the **Chisos Mountains.** For about 100 miles the river is the southern boundary of **Big Bend National Park.** Below the Big Bend, the Rio Grande gradually emerges from mountains onto the Coastal Plains. A 191.2-mile strip on the American shore from Big Bend National Park downstream to the Terrell-Val Verde County line, has federal designation as the **Rio Grande Wild and Scenic River.**

At the confluence of the Rio Grande and the Devils River, the United States and Mexico have built **Amistad Dam,** to impound 3,383,900 acre-feet of water, of which Texas' share is 56.2 percent. **Falcon Reservoir,** also an international project, impounds 2,667,600 acre-feet of water, of which Texas' share in Zapata and Starr counties is 58.6 percent. The Rio Grande, where it joins the Gulf of Mexico, has created a fertile delta called the **Lower Rio Grande Valley,** a major vegetable- and fruit-growing area.

The Rio Grande drains over 40,000 square miles of Texas. Principal tributaries flowing from the Texas side of the Rio Grande are the **Pecos** and **Devils** rivers. On the Mexican side are the **Río Conchos,** the **Río Salado** and the **Río San Juan.** About three-fourths of the water running into the Rio Grande below El Paso comes from the Mexican side.

Nueces River

The Nueces River rises in Edwards County and flows 315 miles to Nueces Bay on the Gulf near Corpus Christi. Draining 17,000 square miles, it is a beautiful, **spring-fed stream** flowing through **canyons** until it issues from the **Balcones Escarpment** onto the Coastal Plain in northern Uvalde County. Alonso de León, in 1689, gave it its name. (Nueces, plural of nuez, means nuts in Spanish.) Much earlier, Cabeza de Vaca had referred to a **Río de las Nueces** in this region, probably the same stream. Its original Indian name seems to have been **Chotilapacquen.** Crossing Texas in 1691, Terán de los Rios named the river **San Diego.** The Nueces was the boundary line between the Spanish provinces of Texas and Nuevo Santander. After the Revolution of 1836, both Texas and Mexico claimed the territory between the Nueces and the Rio Grande, a dispute which was settled by the **Treaty of Guadalupe Hidalgo** in 1848, which fixed the international boundary at the Rio Grande. Nueces runoff is about 620,000 acre-feet a year in its lower course. Principal water conservation projects are **Lake Corpus Christi** and **Choke Canyon Reservoir.** Principal tributaries of the Nueces are the **Frio** and the **Atascosa.**

San Antonio River

The San Antonio River has its source in **large springs** within and near the city limits of San Antonio. It flows 180 miles across the Coastal Plain to a junction with the **Guadalupe** near the Gulf Coast. Its channel through San Antonio has been developed into a parkway known as the River Walk. Its principal tributaries are the **Medina River** and **Cibolo Creek,** both spring-fed streams and this, with its spring origin, gives it a remarkably steady flow of clear water. This stream was first named the **León** by Alonso de León in 1689. De León was not naming the stream for himself, but called it "lion" because its channel was filled with a rampaging flood.

Because of its limited and arid drainage area (4,200 square miles) the average runoff of the San Antonio River is relatively small, about 350,000 acre-feet annually near its mouth, but its flow, because of its springs, is one of the steadiest of Texas rivers.

Guadalupe River

The Guadalupe rises in its north and south prongs in

the west-central part of Kerr County. A **spring-fed stream,** it flows eastward through the **Hill Country** until it issues from the **Balcones Escarpment** near New Braunfels. It then crosses the Coastal Plain to San Antonio Bay. Its total length is about 250 miles, and its drainage area is about 6,000 square miles. Its principal tributaries are the **San Marcos**, another spring-fed stream, which joins it in Gonzales County; the San Antonio, which joins it just above its mouth on San Antonio Bay; and the Comal, which joins it at New Braunfels. The **Comal River** has its source in large springs within the city limits of New Braunfels and flows only about 2.5 miles to the Guadalupe. It is the **shortest river in Texas** and also the **shortest river in the United States** carrying an equivalent amount of water.

There has been power development on the Guadalupe near Gonzales and Cuero for many years, and there is also power generation at **Canyon Lake.** Because of its springs, and its considerable drainage area, the Guadalupe has an annual runoff of more than 1 million acre-feet in its lower course.

The name Guadalupe is derived from **Nuestra Señora de Guadalupe,** the name given the stream by Alonso de León.

Lavaca River

The Lavaca is considered a primary stream in the Texas Basin because it flows directly into the Gulf, through Lavaca Bay. Without a spring-water source and with only a small watershed, including that of its principal tributary, the **Navidad,** its flow is intermittent. The Spanish called it the Lavaca (cow) River because of the numerous bison they found. It is the principal stream running to the Gulf between the Guadalupe and the Colorado. The principal lake on the **Navidad** is **Lake Texana.** Runoff averages about 600,000 acre-feet yearly into the Gulf.

Colorado River

Measured by length and drainage area, the Colorado is the **largest river wholly in Texas.** (The drainage basin of the Brazos River extends into New Mexico.) Rising in Dawson County, the Colorado flows about 600 miles to Matagorda Bay on the Gulf. Its drainage area is 39,900 square miles. Its runoff reaches a volume of more than 2 million acre-feet near the Gulf. Its name is a Spanish word meaning **"reddish."** There is evidence that Spanish explorers originally named the muddy Brazos "Colorado," but Spanish mapmakers later transposed the two names.

The river flows through a rolling, mostly prairie terrain to the vicinity of San Saba County, where it enters the rugged **Hill Country** and **Burnet-Llano Basin.** It passes through a picturesque series of **canyons** until it issues from the **Balcones Escarpment** at Austin and flows across the Coastal Plain to the Gulf. In this area **the most remarkable series of reservoirs in Texas** has been built. There are two large reservoirs, **Lake Buchanan** in Burnet and Llano counties and **Lake Travis** in Travis County. Between these, in Burnet County, are three smaller reservoirs: **Inks, Johnson** (formerly **Granite Shoals**) and **Marble Falls,** built to aid power production from water running over the Buchanan Lake spillway. Below Lake Travis is the older **Lake Austin,** largely filled with silt, whose dam is used to produce power from waters flowing down from the lakes above. **Town Lake** is in the city of Austin. This area is known as the **Highland Lakes Country.**

As early as the 1820s, Anglo-Americans settled on the banks of the lower Colorado, and in 1839 the **Capital Commission of the Republic of Texas** chose the picturesque area where the river flows from the **Balcones Escarpment** as the site of a new capital of the Republic — now **Austin,** capital of the state. The early colonists encouraged navigation along the lower channel with some success, and boats occasionally ventured as far upstream as Austin. However, a **natural log "raft"** in the channel near the Gulf blocked river traffic. Conservation and utilization of the waters of the Colorado are under jurisdiction of three agencies created by the state Legislature, the **Lower, Central** and **Upper Colorado River Authorities.**

The principal tributaries of the Colorado are the several prongs of the **Concho River** on its upper course, the **Pecan Bayou** (farthest west **"bayou"** in the United States) and the **Llano, San Saba** and **Pedernales** rivers. All except the Pecan Bayou flow into the Colorado from the **Edwards Plateau** and are spring-fed, perennially flowing. In the numerous mussels found along these streams occasional **pearls** have been found. The Middle Concho was designated on early Spanish maps as **Río de las Perlas.**

Brazos River

The Brazos is the largest river between the Rio Grande and the Red River and is **third in size** of all rivers in Texas. It rises in three upper forks, the **Double Mountain, Salt** and **Clear forks** of the Brazos. The Brazos River proper is considered as beginning where the Double Mountain and Salt Forks flow together in Stonewall County. The Clear Fork joins this main stream in Young County, just above **Possum Kingdom Lake.** The Brazos crosses most of the main physiographic regions of Texas — High Plains, West Texas Lower Rolling Plains, Western Cross Timbers, Grand Prairie and Gulf Coastal Plain.

The total length from the source of its longest upper prong, the Double Mountain Fork, to the mouth of the main stream at the Gulf, was reported to be 923.2 miles in a 1970 study by the Army Corps of Engineers. The drainage area is about 42,800 square miles. It flows directly into the Gulf near Freeport. Its annual runoff at places along its lower channel exceeds 5 million acre-feet.

The original name of this river was **Brazos de Dios,** meaning "Arms of God." There are several legends as to why. One is that the Coronado expedition, wandering on the trackless **Llano Estacado,** exhausted its water and was threatened with death from thirst. Arriving at the bank of the river they gave it the name of Brazos de Dios in thankfulness. Another is that a ship exhausted its water supply and its crew was saved when they found the mouth of the Brazos. Still another story is that miners on the San Saba were forced by drouth to seek water near present-day Waco and in gratitude called it Brazos de Dios.

Much early Anglo-American colonization of Texas took place in the Brazos Valley. Along its channel were **San Felipe de Austin,** capital of Austin's colony, **Washington-on-the-Brazos,** where Texans declared independence, and other historic settlements. There was some **navigation of the lower channel** of the Brazos in this period. Near its mouth it intersects the **Gulf Intracoastal Waterway,** which provides connection with the commerce on the Mississippi.

Most of the Brazos Valley lies within the boundaries of the **Brazos River Authority,** which conducts a multipurpose program for development. A large reservoir on the Brazos is **Whitney Lake** (622,800 acre-feet capacity) on the main channel, where it is the boundary line between Hill and Bosque counties. Another large reservoir is **Possum Kingdom Lake** in Palo Pinto, Stephens, Young and Jack counties. **Waco Lake** on the Bosque and **Belton Lake** on the Leon are among the principal reservoirs on its tributaries. In addition to its three upper forks, other chief tributaries are the **Paluxy, Little** and **Navasota** rivers.

San Jacinto River

A short river with a drainage basin of 3,976 square miles and nearly 2 million acre-feet runoff, the San Jacinto runs directly to the Gulf through Galveston Bay. It is formed by the junction of its East and West forks in the northeastern part of Harris County. Its total length, including the East Fork, is about 85 miles. There are two stories of the origin of its name. One is that when early explorers discovered it, its channel was choked with hyacinth ("**jacinto**" is the Spanish word for hyacinth). The other is that it was discovered on Aug. 17, St. Hyacinth's Day. Through the lower course of the San Jacinto and its tributary, **Buffalo Bayou,** runs the **Houston Ship Channel** connecting the Port of Houston with the Gulf. On the shore of the San Jacinto was fought the **Battle of San Jacinto,** April 21, 1836, in which Texas won its independence from Mexico. The **San Jacinto State Park and monument** commemorate the battle. **Lake Conroe** is on the **West Fork,** and **Lake Houston** is located at the junction of the West Fork and the **East Fork.**

Trinity River

The Trinity rises in its East Fork, Elm Fork, West Fork and Clear Fork in Grayson, Montague, Archer and Parker counties, respectively. The main stream begins with the junction of the Elm and West forks at Dallas. Its length is

550 river miles, and its drainage area is 17,969 square miles. Because of moderate to heavy rainfall over its drainage area, it has a flow of 5,800,000 acre-feet near its mouth on the Gulf, exceeded only by the Neches, Red and Sabine River basins.

The Trinity derives its name from the Spanish **"Trinidad."** Alonso de León named it **La Santísima Trinidad** (the Most Holy Trinity).

Navigation was developed along its lower course with several riverport towns, such as **Sebastopol** in Trinity County. For many years there has been a basin-wide movement for navigation, conservation and utilization of its water. The **Trinity River Authority** is a state agency and the **Trinity Improvement Association** is a publicly supported nonprofit organization advocating its development.

The Trinity has in its valley **more large cities, greater population and more industrial development** than any other river basin in Texas. On the Lower Coastal Plain there is large use of its waters for **rice irrigation**. Largest reservoir on the Elm Fork is **Lewisville Lake** (formerly **Garza-Little Elm** and **Lake Dallas**). There are four reservoirs above Fort Worth — **Lake Worth, Eagle Mountain** and **Bridgeport** on the West Fork and **Benbrook Lake** on the Clear Fork. **Lavon Lake** in southeast Collin County and **Lake Ray Hubbard** in Collin, Dallas, Kaufman and Rockwall counties are on the East Fork. **Livingston Lake** is in Polk, San Jacinto, Trinity and Walker counties. The three major reservoirs below the Dallas-Fort Worth area are **Cedar Creek Reservoir** and **Richland-Chambers Reservoir**.

Neches River

The Neches is in East Texas, with total length of about 416 miles and drainage area of 10,011 square miles. Abundant rainfall over its entire basin gives it a flow near the Gulf of about 6 million acre-feet a year. The river takes its name from the **Neches Indians** that the early Spanish explorers found living along its banks. Principal tributary of the Neches, and comparable with the Neches in length and flow above their confluence, is the **Angelina River**, so named from **Angelina (Little Angel)**, a Hainai Indian girl who converted to Christianity and played an important role in the early development of this region.

Both the Neches and the Angelina run most of their courses in the **Piney Woods** and there was much settlement along them as early as the 1820s. **Sam Rayburn (McGee Bend) Reservoir**, near Jasper on the Angelina River, was completed and dedicated in 1965.

Reservoirs located on the Neches River include **Lake Palestine** in the upper portion of the basin and **B. A. Steinhagen Lake** located at the junction of the Neches and the Angelina rivers.

Sabine River

The Sabine River is formed by three forks rising in Collin and Hunt counties. From its sources to its mouth on **Sabine Lake**, it flows approximately 360 miles and drains 9,733 square miles. Sabine comes from the **Spanish word for cypress**, as does the name of the **Sabinal River**, which flows into the Frio in Southwest Texas. The Sabine has the largest water discharge (6.8 million acre-feet) at its mouth of any Texas river. Throughout most of Texas history the lower Sabine has been the **eastern Texas boundary line,** though for a while there was doubt as to whether the Sabine or the Arroyo Hondo, east of the Sabine in Louisiana, was the boundary. For a number of years the outlaw-infested **neutral ground** lay between them. There was also a **boundary dispute** in which it was alleged that the Neches was really the Sabine and, therefore, the boundary.

Travelers over the part of the **Camino Real** known as the **Old San Antonio Road,** crossed the Sabine at the famous **Gaines Ferry,** and there were famous crossings for the **Atascosito Road** and other travel and trade routes of that day.

Two of Texas' larger man-made reservoirs have been created by dams constructed on the Sabine River. The first of these is **Lake Tawakoni**, in Hunt, Rains and Van Zandt counties, with a capacity of 936,200 acre-feet. **Toledo Bend Reservoir** impounds 4,472,900 acre-feet of water on the Sabine in Newton, Panola, Sabine and Shelby counties. This is a joint project of Texas and Louisiana, through the **Sabine River Authority**.

Red River

The Red River (1,360 miles) is **exceeded in length only by the Rio Grande** among rivers associated with Texas. Its original source is water in Curry County, New Mexico, near the Texas boundary, forming a definite channel as it crosses Deaf Smith County, Texas, in tributaries that flow into **Prairie Dog Town Fork of the Red River.** These waters carve the spectacular **Palo Duro Canyon** of the High Plains before the Red River leaves the **Caprock Escarpment,** flowing eastward.

Where the Red River crosses the 100th meridian, the river becomes the **Texas-Oklahoma boundary** and is soon joined by the Salt Fork to form the main channel. Its length across the Panhandle is about 200 miles and, from the Panhandle east, it is the Texas-Oklahoma boundary line for 440 miles and thereafter the **Texas-Arkansas boundary** for 40 miles before it flows into Arkansas, where it swings south to flow through Louisiana. The Red River is a part of the **Mississippi drainage basin,** and at one time it emptied all of its water into the Mississippi. In recent years, however, part of its water, especially at flood stage, has flowed to the Gulf via the **Atchafalaya**.

The Red River takes its name from the red color of the current. This caused every explorer who came to its banks to call it "red" regardless of the language he spoke — **Río Rojo** or **Río Roxo** in Spanish, **Rivière Rouge** in French and **Red River** in English. The Spanish and French names were often found on maps until the middle of the last century when the English came to be generally accepted. At an early date, the river became the axis for French advance from Louisiana northwestward as far as present-day Montague County. There was consistent **early navigation** of the river from its mouth on the Mississippi to Shreveport, above which navigation was blocked by a **natural log raft**. A number of important gateways into Texas from the North were established along the stream such as **Pecan Point** and **Jonesborough** in Red River County, **Colbert's Ferry** and **Preston** in Grayson County and, later, **Doan's Store Crossing** in Wilbarger County. The river was a menace to the early traveler because of both its variable current and its **quicksands**, which brought disaster to many a trail-herd cow as well as ox team and covered wagon.

The largest water conservation project on the Red River is **Texoma Lake**, which is the **largest lake** lying wholly or partly in Texas and the **tenth-largest reservoir (in capacity) in the United States.** Its capacity is 5,382,000 acre feet. Texas' share is 2,722,000.

Red River water's high content of salt and other minerals limits its usefulness along its upper reaches. Ten **salt springs** and tributaries in Texas and Oklahoma contribute most of these minerals.

The uppermost tributary of the Red River in Texas is **Tierra Blanca Creek**, which rises in Curry County, N.M., and flows easterly across Deaf Smith and Randall counties to become the **Prairie Dog Town Fork** a few miles east of Canyon. Other principal tributaries in Texas are the **Pease** and the **Wichita** in North Central Texas and the **Sulphur** in Northeast Texas, which flows into the Red River after it has crossed the boundary line into Arkansas. The last major tributary in Northeast Texas is **Cypress Creek**, which flows into Louisiana before joining with the Red River. Major reservoirs on the Northeast Texas tributaries are **Wright Patman Lake, Lake O' the Pines** and **Caddo Lake**. From Oklahoma the principal tributary is the **Washita**. The **Ouachita**, a river with the same pronunciation of its name, though spelled differently, is the principal tributary to its lower course.

Canadian River

The Canadian River heads near **Raton Pass** in northern New Mexico near the Colorado boundary line and flows into Texas on the west line of Oldham County. It crosses the Texas Panhandle into Oklahoma and there flows into the Arkansas. Most of its course across the Panhandle is in a deep gorge. A tributary dips into Texas' northern Panhandle and then flows to a confluence with the main channel in Oklahoma. One of several theories as to how the Canadian got its name is that some early explorers thought it flowed into Canada. **Lake Meredith**, formed by Sanford Dam on the Canadian, provides water for 11 Panhandle cities.

Because of the **deep gorge** and the **quicksand** at many places, the Canadian has been a peculiarly difficult stream to bridge. It is known especially in its lower course in Oklahoma as outstanding among the streams of the country for great amount of quicksand in its channel. ☆

Lakes and Reservoirs

The large increase in the number of reservoirs in Texas during the past half-century has greatly improved water conservation and supplies. As late as 1913, Texas had only eight major reservoirs with a total storage capacity of 376,000 acre-feet. Most of this capacity was in Medina Lake, with 254,000 acre-feet capacity, created by a dam completed in May 1913. (An acre-foot is the amount of water necessary to cover an acre of surface area with water one foot deep.)

By 1920, Texas had 11 major reservoirs with combined storage capacity of 449,710 acre-feet. The state water agency reported 32 reservoirs and 1,284,520 acre-feet capacity in 1930. By 1950, this number had increased to 66 with 9,623,870 acre-feet capacity and to 168 with total capacity of 53,302,400 acre-feet in 1980. By January 1998, Texas had 203 major reservoirs (those with a normal capacity of 5,000 acre-feet or larger) existing or under construction, with a total conservation surface area of 1,678,708 acres and a conservation storage capacity of 43,017,613 acre-feet.

According to the U.S. Statistical Abstract of 1996, Texas has **4,959 square miles of inland water,** ranking it first in the 48 contiguous states, followed by Minnesota, with 4,780 sq. mi.; Florida, 4,683; and Louisiana, 4,153. There are about **6,736 reservoirs** in Texas with a normal storage capacity of 10 acre-feet or larger.

The following table lists reservoirs in Texas having **more than 5,000 acre-feet capacity**. With few exceptions, the listed reservoirs are those that were completed by Jan. 1, 1997, and in use. An asterisk (*) indicates those that are under construction.

Conservation storage capacity is used in the table below; the surface area used is that area at conservation elevation only. (Different methods of computing capacity area used; detailed information may be obtained from the Texas Water Development Board, Austin; U.S. Army Corps of Engineers; or local sources.) Also, it should be noted that boundary reservoir capacities include water designated for Texas use and non-Texas water, as well.

In the list below, information is given in the following order: (1) Name of lake or reservoir; (2) county or counties in which located; (3) river or creek on which located; (4) location with respect to some city or town; (5) purpose of reservoir; (6) owner of reservoir. Some of these items, when not listed, are not available. For the larger lakes and reservoirs, the dam impounding water to form the lake bears the same name, unless otherwise indicated. Abbreviations in the list below are as follows: L., lake; R., river; Co., county; Cr., creek; (C) conservation; (FC) flood control; (R) recreation; (P) power; (M) municipal; (D) domestic; (Ir.) irrigation; (In.) industry; (Mi.) mining, including oil production; (FH) fish hatchery; USAE, United States Army Corps of Engineers; WC&ID, Water Control and Improvement District; WID, Water Improvement District; USBR, United States Bureau of Reclamation.

Lakes and Reservoirs	Conservation Surface Area (Acres)	Conservation Storage Capacity (Acre-Ft.)
Abilene L. — Taylor Co.; Elm Cr.; 6 mi. NW Tuscola; (M-In.-R); City of Abilene	595	7,900
Alan Henry Reservoir — Garza Co.; Double Mountain Fork Brazos River, 10 mi. E Justiceburg; (M-In.-Ir.); City of Lubbock	3,504	115,937
Alcoa L. — Milam Co.; Sandy Cr.; 7 mi. SW Rockdale; (In.-R); Aluminum Co. of America	880	14,750
Amistad Reservoir — Val Verde Co.; Rio Grande, dam between Del Rio and confluence of Rio Grande and Devils River; an international project of the U.S. and Mexico; 12 mi. NWDel Rio; (C-R-Ir.-P-FC); International Boundary and Water Com. (Texas' share of conservation capacity is 56.2 percent.) (Formerly **Diablo R.**)	64,900	3,383,900
Amon G. Carter, L. — Montague Co.; Big Sandy Cr.; 6 mi. S Bowie; (M-In.); City of Bowie	1,540	20,050
Anahuac L. — Chambers Co.; Turtle Bayou; near Anahuac; (Ir.-In.-Mi.); Chambers-Liberty Counties Navigation District.	5,300	35,300
Anzalduas Channel Dam — Hidalgo Co.; Rio Grande; 11 mi. upstream from Hidalgo; (Ir.-FC); United States and Mexico	—	8,400
Aquilla L. — Hill Co.; Aquilla Cr.; 10.2 mi. W of Hillsboro; (FC-M-Ir.-In.-R); USAE-Brazos R. Auth.	3,266	45,670
Arlington L. — Tarrant Co.; Village Cr.; 7 mi. W Arlington; (M-In.); City of Arlington	1,939	38,740
Arrowhead, L. — Clay Co.; Little Wichita R.; 13 mi. SE Wichita Falls; (M); City of Wichita Falls	16,200	262,100
Athens, L. — Henderson Co.; 8 mi. E Athens; (M-FC-R); Athens Mun. Water Authority {formerly **Flat Creek Reservoir**)	1,799	29,440
Aubrey R. — (see **Ray Roberts L.**)	—	—
Austin, L. — Travis Co.; Colorado R.; W Austin city limits; (M-In.-P); City of Austin, leased to LCRA (impounded by **Tom Miller Dam**)	1,830	21,000
Ballinger L. — Runnels Co.; Valley Creek; 5 mi. W Ballinger; (M); City of Ballinger (also known as **Moonen Lake**)	—	6,850
Balmorhea, L. — Reeves Co.; Sandia Cr.; 3 mi. SE Balmorhea; (Ir.); Reeves Co. WID No. 1.	573	6,350
Bardwell L. — Ellis Co.; Waxahachie Cr.; 3 mi. SE Bardwell; (FC-C-R); USAE	3,570	53,580
Barney M. Davis Cooling Reservoir — Nueces Co.; off-channel storage reservoir of Laguna Madre arm of Gulf; 14 mi. SE Corpus Christi; (In.); Central Power & Light Co.	1,100	6,600
Bastrop, L. — Bastrop Co.; Spicer Cr.; 3 mi. NE Bastrop; (In.); LCRA	906	16,590
Baylor Creek L. — Childress Co.; 10 mi. NW Childress; (M-R); City of Childress	610	9,220
Belton L. — Bell-Coryell counties; Leon R.; 3 mi. N. Belton; (M-FC-In.-Ir.); USAE-Brazos R. Auth.	12,385	434,500
Benbrook L. — Tarrant Co.; Clear Fk. Trinity R.; 10 mi. SW Fort Worth; (FC-R); USAE	3,635	85,650
Big Brown Creek Reservoir — Freestone Co. (see **Fairfield L.**)	—	—
Big Hill Reservoir — Jefferson Co. (see **J. D. Murphree Area Impoundments**)	—	—
Bivins L. — Randall Co.; Palo Duro Cr.; 8 mi. NW Canyon; (M); Amarillo (also known as **Amarillo City Lake**); City of Amarillo	379	5,120
Blackburn Crossing L. — (see **Lake Palestine**)		
Bonham, L. — Fannin Co.; Timber Cr.; 5 mi. NE Bonham; (M); Bonham Mun. Water Auth.	1,020	12,000
Bowie L. — (see **Amon G. Carter, L.**)		
Brady Creek Reservoir — McCulloch Co.; Brady Cr.; 3 mi. W Brady; (M-In.); City of Brady	2,020	29,110

Brandy Branch Reservoir — Harrison Co.; Brandy Br.; 10 mi. SW Marshall; (In.); Southwestern Electric Power Co.	1,240	29,500
Brazoria Reservoir — Brazoria Co.; off-channel reservoir; 1 mi. NE Brazoria; (In.); Dow Chemical Co. .	1,865	21,970
Bridgeport, L. — Wise-Jack counties; W. Fk. of Trinity R.; 4 mi. W Bridgeport; (M-In.-FC-R); Tarrant Co. WC&ID Dist. No. 1	13,000	386,420
Brownwood, L. — Brown Co.; Pecan Bayou; 8 mi. N Brownwood; (M-In.-Ir.); Brown Co. WC&ID No. 1.	7,298	131,430
Brushy Creek Reservoir — (see **Valley L.**)	—	—
Bryan Utilities L. — Brazos Co.; unnamed stream; 6 mi. NW Bryan; (R-In.); City of Bryan	829	15,227
Buchanan, L. — Burnet-Llano-San Saba counties; Colorado R.; 13 mi. W Burnet; (M-Ir.-Mi-P); LCRA . .	23,060	955,200
Buffalo Springs L. — Lubbock Co.; Double Mtn.Fk. Brazos R.; 9 mi. SE Lubbock; (M-In.-R); Lubbock Co. WC & ID No. 1; (impounded by **W. G. McMillan Sr. Dam**)	200	4,200
Caddo L. — Harrison-Marion counties, Texas and Caddo Parish, La. An original natural lake, whose surface and capacity were increased by construction of dam on Cypress Creek near Mooringsport, La.	25,400	59,800
Calaveras L. — Bexar Co.; Calaveras Cr.; 15 mi. SE San Antonio; (In.); Pub. Svc. Bd. of San Antonio . .	3,450	61,800
Camp Creek L. — Robertson Co.; 13 mi. E Franklin; (R); Camp Creek Water Co.	750	8,550
Canyon L. — Comal Co.; Guadalupe R.; 12 mi. NW New Braunfels; (M-In.-P-FC); Guadalupe-Blanco R. Authority & USAE	8,240	385,600
Casa Blanca L. — Webb Co.; Chacon Cr.; 3 mi. NE Laredo; (R); Webb County (impounded by **Country Club Dam**)	1,656	20,000
Cedar Bayou Cooling Reservoir — Chambers Co.; Cedar Bayou; 15 mi. SW Anahuac; (In.); Houston Lighting & Power Co.	2,600	20,000
Cedar Creek Reservoir — Henderson-Kaufman counties; Cedar Cr.; 3 mi. NE Trinidad; (also called **Joe B. Hogsett, L.**); (M-R); Tarrant Co. WC&ID No. 1	32,623	637,050
Cedar Creek Reservoir — Fayette Co.; Cedar Cr.; 8.5 mi. E. La Grange; (In.); LCRA	2,420	71,400
Champion Creek Reservoir — Mitchell Co.; 7 mi. S. Colorado City; (M-In.); Texas Electric Service Co..	1,560	41,600
Chapman L., Jim — (formerly Cooper Lake) Delta-Hopkins counties; Sulphur R.; 3 mi.SE Cooper; (FC-M-R); USAE.	19,305	310,000
Cherokee L. — Gregg-Rusk counties; Cherokee Bayou; 12 mi. SE Longview; (M-In.-R); Cherokee Water Co.	3,083	37,340
Choke Canyon Reservoir — Live Oak-McMullen counties; Frio R.; 4 mi. W Three Rivers; (M-In.-R-FC); City of Corpus Christi-USBR	25,989	695,262
Cisco, L. — Eastland Co.; Sandy Cr.; 4 mi. N. Cisco; (M); City of Cisco (impounded by **Williamson Dam**)	445	8,800
Cleburne, L. Pat — Johnson Co.; Nolan R.; 4 mi. S. Cleburne; (M); City of Cleburne	1,558	25,730
Clyde, L. — Callahan Co.; N. Prong Pecan Bayou; 6 mi. S. Clyde; (M); City of Clyde and USDA Soil Conservation Service	449	5,748
Coffee Mill L. — Fannin Co.; Coffee Mill Cr.; 12 mi. NW Honey Grove; (R); U.S. Forest Service	650	8,000
Coleman L. — Coleman Co.; Jim Ned Cr.; 14 mi. N. Coleman; (M-In.); City of Coleman	2,000	40,000
Coleto Creek Reservoir — Goliad-Victoria counties; Coleto Cr.; 12 mi. SW Victoria; (In); Guadalupe-Blanco River Auth.	3,100	35,080
Colorado City, L. — Mitchell Co.; Morgan Cr.; 4 mi. SW Colorado City; (M-In.-P); Texas Electric Service Co.	1,612	30,800
Conroe, L. — Montgomery-Walker counties; W. Fk. San Jacinto R.; 7 mi. NW Conroe; (M-In.-Mi.); San Jacinto River Authority, City of Houston and Texas Water Dev. Bd.	20,118	416,188
Cooper L. — (see **Chapman Lake, Jim**)		
Corpus Christi, L. — Live Oak-San Patricio-Jim Wells counties; Nueces R.; 4 mi. SW Mathis; (P-M-In.-Ir.-Mi.-R.); Lower Nueces River WSD (impounded by **Wesley E. Seale Dam**)	19,336	269,900
Crook, L. — Lamar Co.; Pine Cr.; 5 Mi. N. Paris; (M); City of Paris	1,226	9,964
Cypress Springs, L. — Franklin Co.; Big Cypress Cr.; 8 mi. SE Mount Vernon; (In-M); Franklin Co. WD and Texas Water Development Board (formerly **Franklin Co. L.**); impounded by **Franklin Co. Dam**) .	2,461	67,690
Dallas, L. — (see **Lewisville L.**)	—	—
Dam B Reservoir — (see **Steinhagen L., B.A.**)		
Daniel, L. — Stephens Co.; Gunsolus Cr.; 7 mi. S Breckenridge; (M-In.); City of Breckenridge; (impounded by **Gunsolus Creek Dam**)	924	9,515
Davis L. — Knox Co.; Double Dutchman Cr.; 5 mi. SE Benjamin; (Ir); League Ranch	585	5,395
Decker, L.— (see **Walter E. Long L.**)		
DeCordova Bend Reservoir — (see **Granbury Lake**)		
Delta Lake Res. Units 1 and 2 — Hidalgo Co.; Rio Grande (off channel); 4 mi. N. Monte Alto; (Ir.); Hidalgo-Willacy counties WC&ID No. 1 (formerly **Monte Alto Reservoir**).	2,371	25,000
Diablo Reservoir — (see **Amistad Reservoir**)	—	—
Diversion, L. — Archer-Baylor counties; Wichita R.; 14 mi. W Holliday; (M-In.); City of Wichita Falls and Wichita Co. WID No. 2	3,419	40,000
Dunlap, L. — Guadalupe Co.; Guadalupe R.; 9 mi. NW Seguin; (P); Guadalupe-Blanco R. Auth.; (impounded by **TP-1 Dam**)	410	3,550
Eagle L. — Colorado Co.; Colorado R. (off channel); in Eagle Lake; (Ir); Lakeside Irrigation Co.	1,200	9,600
Eagle Mountain Lake — Tarrant-Wise counties; W. Fk. Trinity R.; 14 mi. NW Fort Worth; (M-In.-Ir.); Tarrant Co. WC&ID No. 1	9,200	190,300
East L. — (see **Victor Braunig Lake**)	—	—
Eddleman L. — (see **Graham Lake**)	—	—
Edinburg L. — (see **Retama Reservoir**)		
Electra City L. — Wilbarger Co.; Camp Cr. and Beaver Cr.; 7 mi. SW Electra; (In.-M); City of Electra	660	8,055
Ellison Creek Reservoir — Morris Co.; Ellison Cr.; 8 mi. S. Daingerfield; (P-In.); Lone Star Steel	1,516	24,700
Fairfield L. — Freestone Co.; Big Brown Cr.; 11 mi. NE Fairfield; (In.); TP&L, Texas Elec. Service Co., DP&L and Industrial Generating Co. (formerly **Big Brown Creek Reservoir**).	2,350	50,600
Falcon Reservoir — Starr-Zapata counties; Rio Grande; (International—U.S.-Mexico); 3 mi. W Falcon Heights; (M-In.-Ir.-FC-P-R); International Boundary and Water Com.; (Texas' share of total conservation capacity is 58.6 per cent).	87,210	2,667,600
Farmers Creek Reservoir — Montague Co.; 8 mi. NE Nocona; (M-In.-Mi.) N Montague County Water Supply District (also known as **Lake Nocona**)	1,470	25,400
Ferrell's Bridge Dam Reservoir — (see **Lake O' the Pines**)	—	—
Flat Creek Reservoir — (see **Athens, Lake**)		

Forest Grove Reservoir — Henderson Co.; Caney Cr.; 7 mi. NW Athens; (In.); Texas Utilities Services, Inc., Agent	1,502	20,038
Forney Reservoir — (see **Ray Hubbard, Lake**)	—	—
Fort Phantom Hill, Lake — Jones Co.; Elm Cr.; 5 mi. S. Nugent; (M-R); City of Abilene	4,213	70,030
Franklin County L. — (see **Cypress Springs, Lake**)	—	—
Galveston County Industrial Water Reservoir — Galveston Co.; off-channel storage Dickinson Bayou; 16 mi. S La Porte; (In.-M.); Galveston Co. Water Auth.	812	7,308
Garza-Little Elm — (see **Lewisville L.**)		
Georgetown, L. — Williamson Co.; N. Fk. San Gabriel R.; 3.5 mi. W Georgetown; (FC-M-In.); USAE (formerly **North Fork L.**)	1,297	37,010
Gibbons Creek Reservoir — Grimes Co.; Gibbons Cr.; 9.5 mi NW Anderson; (In.); Texas Mun. Power Agency	2,490	26,824
Gladewater, L. — Upshur Co.; Glade Cr.; in Gladewater; (M-R); City of Gladewater	800	6,950
Graham L. — Young Co.; Flint and Salt Creeks; 2 mi. NW Graham; (M-In.); City of Graham	2,444	45,260
Granbury L. — Hood-Parker counties; Brazos R.; 8 mi. SE Granbury; (M-In.-Ir.-P); Brazos River Authority (impounded by **DeCordova Bend Dam**)	8,310	135,683
Granger L. — Williamson Co.; San Gabriel R.; 10 mi. NE Taylor; (FC-M-In.); USAE (formerly **Laneport L.**)	4,009	54,280
Granite Shoals L. — (see **Johnson L., Lyndon B.**)	—	—
Grapevine L. — Tarrant-Denton counties; Denton Cr.; 2 mi. NE Grapevine; (M-FC-In.-R.); USAE.	7,380	187,700
Greenbelt L. — Donley Co.; Salt Fk. Red R.; 5 mi. N Clarendon; (M-In.); Greenbelt M&I Water Auth.	1,990	58,200
H-4 Reservoir — Gonzales Co.; Guadalupe R.; 4.5 mi. SE Belmont; (P); Guadalupe- Blanco R. Auth. (also called **Guadalupe Reservoir H-4**)	696	5,200
Halbert, L. — Navarro Co.; Elm Cr.; 4 mi. SE Corsicana; (M-In-R); City of Corsicana	650	7,420
Harris Reservoir — Brazoria Co.; off-channel between Brazos R. and Oyster Cr.; 8 mi. NW Angleton; (In.); Dow Chemical Co.	1,663	12,000
Hawkins, L. — Wood Co.; Little Sandy Cr.; 3 mi. NW Hawkins; (FC-R); Wood County; (impounded by **Wood Co. Dam No. 3**)	776	11,570
Holbrook L. — Wood Co.; Keys Cr.; 4 mi. NW Mineola; (FC-R); Wood County; (impounded by **Wood Co. Dam No. 2**)	653	7,770
Honea Reservoir — (see **Conroe, Lake**)	—	—
Hords Creek L. — Coleman Co.; Hords Cr.; 5 mi. NW Valera; (M-FC); City of Coleman and USAE	510	8,600
Houston, L. — Harris Co.; San Jacinto R.; 4 mi. N Sheldon; (M-In.-Ir.-Mi.-R); City of Houston; (impounded by **Lake Houston Dam**)	11,854	128,863
Houston County L. — Houston Co.; Little Elkhart Cr.; 10 mi. NW Crockett; (M-In.); Houston Co. WC&ID No. 1	1,282	19,500
Hubbard Creek Reservoir — Stephens Co.; 6 mi. NW Breckenridge; (M-In.-Mi.); West Central Texas Mun. Water Authority	14,922	318,070
Imperial Reservoir — Reeves-Pecos counties; Pecos R.; 35 mi. N Fort Stockton; (Ir.); Pecos County WC&ID No. 2	1,530	6,000
Inks L. — Burnet-Llano counties; Colorado R.; 12 mi. W Burnet; (M-Ir.-Mi.-P); LCRA	803	17,540
Iron Bridge Dam L. — (see **Tawakoni, Lake**)	—	—
Jacksonville, L. — Cherokee Co.; Gum Cr.; 5 mi. SW Jacksonville; (M-R); City of Jacksonville; (impounded by **Buckner Dam**)	1,320	30,500
J. B. Thomas, L. — Scurry-Borden counties; Colorado R.; 16 mi. SW Snyder; (M- In.-R); Colorado River Mun. Water Dist.; (impounded by **Colorado R. Dam**)	7,820	202,300
J. D. Murphree Wildlife Management Area Impoundments — Jefferson Co.; off-channel reservoirs between Big Hill and Taylor Bayous; at Port Acres; (FH-R); TP&WD (formerly **Big Hill Reservoir**)	6,881	13,500
Jim Chapman Lake (see **Chapman Lake, Jim**)		
Joe B. Hogsett, L. — (see **Cedar Creek Reservoir**)	—	—
Joe Pool Reservoir — Dallas- Tarrant-Ellis counties; Mountain Cr.; 14 mi. SW Dallas; (FC-M-R); USAE-Trinity River Auth. (formerly **Lakeview Lake**)	7,470	176,900
Johnson Creek Reservoir — Marion Co.; 13 mi. NW Jefferson; (In.); Southwestern Electric Co.	650	10,100
Kemp, L. — Baylor Co.; Wichita R.; 6 mi. N Mabelle; (M-P-Ir.); City of Wichita Falls; Wichita Co. WID 2.	16,540	319,600
Kemp Diversion Dam — (see **Diversion Lake**)	—	—
Kickapoo, L. — Archer Co.; N. Fk. Little Wichita R.; 10 mi. NW Archer City; (M); City of Wichita Falls	6,200	106,000
Kiowa, L. — Cooke Co.; Indian Cr.; 8 mi. SE Gainesville; (R); Lake Kiowa, Inc.	560	7,000
Kirby L. — Taylor Co.; Cedar Cr.; 5 mi. S Abilene; (M); City of Abilene	740	7,620
Kurth, L. — Angelina Co.; off-channel reservoir; 8 mi. N Lufkin; (In.); Southland Paper Mills, Inc.	726	14,769
Lake Creek L. — McLennan Co.; Manos Cr.; 4 mi. SW Riesel; (In.); Texas P&L Co.	550	8,400
Lake Fork Reservoir — Wood-Rains counties; Lake Fork Cr.; 5 mi. W Quitman; (M-In.); SRA	27,690	635,200
Lake O' the Pines — Marion-Upshur-Harrison-Morris-Camp counties; Cypress Cr.; 9 mi. W Jefferson; (FC-C-R-In.-M); USAE (impounded by **Ferrell's Bridge Dam**)	18,700	252,000
Lakeview L. — (see **Joe Pool Reservoir**)	—	—
Lampasas Reservoir — (see **Stillhouse Hollow Reservoir**)	—	—
Laneport L. — (see **Granger Lake**)	—	—
Lavon L. (Enlargement) — Collin Co.; East Fk. Trinity R.; 2 mi. W Lavon; (M-FC-In.); USAE	21,400	443,800
Leon, Lake — Eastland Co.; Leon R.; 7 mi. S Ranger; (M-In.); Eastland Co. Water Supply Dist.	1,590	26,420
Lewis Creek Reservoir — Montgomery Co.; Lewis Cr.; 10 mi. NW Conroe; (In.); Gulf States Util. Co.	1,010	16,400
Lewisville L. — Denton Co.; Elm Fk. Trinity R.; 2 mi. NE Lewisville; (M-FC-In.-R); USAE; (also called **Lake Dallas** and **Garza-Little Elm**)	23,280	464,500
Limestone, L. — Leon-Limestone-Robertson cos.; Navasota R.; 7 mi. NW Marquez; (M-In.-Ir.); BRA	13,379	215,748
Livingston L. — Polk-San Jacinto-Trinity-Walker counties; Trinity R.; 6 mi. SW Livingston; (M-In.-Ir.); City of Houston and Trinity River Authority	82,600	1,750,000
Loma Alta Lake — Cameron Co.; off-channel Rio Grande; 8 mi. NE Brownsville; (M-In.); Brownsville Navigation Dist.	2,490	26,500
Lone Star Reservoir — (see **Ellison Creek R.**)		
Lost Creek Reservoir — Jack Co.; Lost Cr.; 4 mi. NE Jacksboro; (M); City of Jacksboro	360	11,960
Lyndon B. Johnson L. — Burnet-Llano counties; (formerly Granite Shoals L.); Colorado R.; 5 mi. SW Marble Falls; (P); LCRA; (impounded by **Alvin Wirtz Dam**)	6,375	138,500
McGee Bend Reservoir — (see **Sam Rayburn Reservoir**)	—	—

McQueeney, L. — Guadalupe Co.; Guadalupe R.; 5 mi. W Seguin; (P); Guadalupe-Blanco R. Authority; (impounded by **Abbott Dam**)	396	5,000
Mackenzie Reservoir — Briscoe Co.; Tule Cr.; 9 mi. NW Silverton; (M); Mackenzie Mun. Water Auth.	910	46,250
Marble Falls L. — Burnet County; Colorado R.; (impounded by Max Starcke Dam); 1.25 mi. SE Marble Falls; (P); LCRA	780	8,760
Martin L. — Rusk-Panola counties; Martin Cr.; 17 mi. NE Henderson; (P); Texas Util. Service Co., Inc.	5,020	77,620
Medina L. — Medina-Bandera counties; Medina R.; 8 mi. W Rio Medina; (Ir.); Bexar- Medina-Atascosa Co. WID No. 1	6,066	254,843
Meredith, L. — Moore-Potter-Hutchinson counties; Canadian R.; 10 mi. NW Borger; (M-In.- FC-R); cooperative project for municipal water supply by Amarillo, Lubbock and other High Plains cities. Canadian R. Municipal Water Authority-USBR; (impounded by **Sanford Dam**)	16,411	779,560
Mexia, L. — Limestone Co.; Navasota R.; 7 mi. SW Mexia; (M-In); Bistone Mun. Water Dist.; (impounded by **Bistone Dam**)	1,048	4,806
Millers Creek Reservoir — Baylor Co.; Millers Cr.; 9 mi. SE Goree; (M); North Central Texas Mun. Water Auth. and Texas Water Development Board	2,268	27,888
Mineral Wells L. — Parker Co.; Rock Cr.; 4 mi. E Mineral Wells; (M); Palo Pinto Co. Mun. WD No. 1.	646	6,760
Mitchell County Reservoir — Mitchell Co.; Beals Creek; (Mi.-In.); Colorado River MWD	1,463	27,266
Monte Alto Reservoir — (see **Delta Lake Res. Units 1 and 2**)	—	—
Monticello Reservoir — Titus Co.; Blundell Cr.; 2.5 mi. E. Monticello; (In.); Industrial Generating Co.	2,001	34,740
Moonen L. — Runnels Co. (see **Ballinger L.**)		
Moss L., Hubert H. — Cooke Co.; Fish Cr.; 10 mi. NW Gainesville; (M-In.); City of Gainesville	1,125	23,210
Mountain Creek L. — Dallas Co.; Mountain Cr.; 4 mi. SE Grand Prairie; (In.); Dallas P&L Co.	2,710	22,840
Mud Creek Dam L. — (see **Tyler Lake, East**)	—	—
Murphree, J. D. Area Impoundments — (see **J. D. Murphree**)	—	—
Murvaul L. — Panola Co.; Murvaul Bayou; 10 mi. W Carthage; (M-In.-R); Panola Co. Fresh Water Supply Dist. No. 1	3,820	45,815
Mustang Lake East & **Mustang Lake West** — Brazoria co.; Mustang Bayou; 6 mi. S Alvin; (Ir.-In.-R); Chocolate Bayou Land & Water Co.	—	6,451
Nacogdoches, L. — Nacogdoches Co.; Bayo Loco Cr.; 10 mi. W Nacogdoches; (M); City of Nacogdoches	2,212	39,521
Nasworthy, L. — Tom Green Co.; S Concho Cr.; 6 mi. SW San Angelo; (M-In.-Ir); City of San Angelo.	1,380	9,615
Natural Dam L. — Howard Co.; Sulphur Springs Draw; 8 mi. W Big Spring; (FC); Wilkinson Ranch & Colorado River MWD	—	32,000
Navarro Mills L. — Navarro-Hill counties; Richland Cr.; 16 mi. SW Corsicana; (M-FC); USAE	5,070	60,900
Nocona L. — (see **Farmers Creek Reservoir**)	—	—
North Fk. Buffalo Creek Reservoir — Wichita Co.; 5 mi. NW Iowa Park; (M); Wichita Co. WC&ID No.3	1,500	15,400
North Fork L. — (see **L. Georgetown**)	—	—
North L. — Dallas Co.; S. Fork Grapevine Cr.; 2 mi. SE Coppell; (In.); Dallas P&L Co.	800	17,000
Oak Creek Reservoir — Coke Co.; 5 mi. SE Blackwell; (M-In.); City of Sweetwater	2,375	39,360
O. C. Fisher L. — Tom Green Co.; N. Concho R.; 3 mi. NW San Angelo; (M-FC-C- Ir.-R-In.-Mi); USAE —Upper Colo. River Auth. (formerly **San Angelo L.**)	5,440	119,200
O. H. Ivie Reservoir — Coleman-Concho-Runnels counties; 24 mi. SE Ballinger; (M-In.), Colorado R. Mun. Water Dist. (formerly **Stacy Reservoir**)	19,150	554,340
Palestine, L. — Anderson-Cherokee-Henderson-Smith counties; Neches R.; 4 mi. E Frankston; (M-In.-R); Upper Neches R. MWA (impounded by **Blackburn Crossing Dam**)	25,560	411,300
Palmetto Bend Reservoir — (see **Texana, L.**)	—	—
Palo Duro Reservoir — Hansford Co.; Palo Duro Cr.; 12 mi. N Spearman; (M-R); Palo Duro River Auth.	2,410	60,900
Palo Pinto, L. — Palo Pinto Co.; 15 mi. SW Mineral Wells; (M-In.); Palo Pinto Co. Muni. Water Dist. 1	2,661	42,200
Panola L. — (see **Murvaul L.**)	—	—
Pat Mayse L. — Lamar Co.; Sanders Cr.; 2 mi. SW Arthur City; (M-In.-FC); USAE	5,993	124,500
Pinkston Reservoir — Shelby Co.; Sandy Cr.; 12.5 mi. SW Center; (M); City of Center; (formerly **Sandy Creek Reservoir**)	523	7,380
Possum Kingdom L. — Palo Pinto-Young-Stephens-Jack counties; Brazos R.; 11 mi. SW Graford; (M-In.-Ir.-Mi.-P-R); Brazos R. Authority; (impounded by **Morris Sheppard Dam**)	17,624	551,818
Proctor L. — Comanche Co.; Leon R.; 9 mi. NE Comanche; (M-In.-Ir.-FC); USAE- Brazos River Auth.	4,761	55,590
Quitman, L. — Wood Co.; Dry Cr.; 4 mi. N Quitman; (FC-R); Wood County (impounded by **Wood Co. Dam No.1**)	814	7,440
Randell, L. — Grayson Co.; Shawnee Cr.; 4 mi. NW Denison; (M); City of Denison	311	6,290
Raw Water Lake — Calhoun Co. (See **Cox Lake**)		
Ray Hubbard, L. — Collin-Dallas-Kaufman-Rockwall counties; (formerly **Forney Reservoir**); E. Fk. Trinity R.; 15 mi. E Dallas; (M); City of Dallas	22,745	490,000
Ray Roberts L. — Denton-Cooke-Grayson counties; Elm Fk. Trinity R.; 11 mi. NE Denton; (FC-M-D); City of Denton, Dallas, USAE; (also known as **Aubrey Reservoir**)	29,350	799,600
Recycle Lake — Calhoun Co. (see **Cox Lake**)		
Red Bluff Reservoir — Loving-Reeves counties, Texas; and Eddy Co., N.M.; Pecos R.; 5 mi. N Orla; (Ir.-P); Red Bluff Water Power Control District	11,700	307,000
Red Draw L. — Howard Co.; Red Draw; 5 mi. E Bi Spring; (Mi.-In.); Colorado River MWD	374	8,538
Resacas — Cameron-Hidalgo-Willacy counties; Rio Grande; these reservoirs are primarily for storage of water during periods of normal or above-normal flow in the river for use when the river's water volume is low. Some of these are old loops and bends in the river that have been isolated by the river's changing its channel. They are known by the Spanish ame of resacas. Also a number of reservoirs have been constructed and connected with the main channel of the river by ditches through which the reservoirs are filled either by gravity flow or by pumping. This is reserve irrigation water for use during periods of low flow in the river channel. Most of these reservoirs are near the main channel of the river, but some of them are 20 or 25 miles distant.	—	
Retama Reservoir — Hidalgo Co.; Off-Channel Rio Grande; 5 mi. N Edinburg; (Ir.); Santa Cruz ID #15; (also known as **Edinburg Lake**)	—	5,000
Richland-Chambers Reservoir — Freestone-Navarro counties; Richland Cr.; 20 mi. SE Corsicana; (M); Tarrant Co. WCID No. 1	41,356	1,103,816
Rita Blanca L. — Hartley Co.; Rita Blanca Cr.; 2 mi. S Dalhart; (R) City of Dalhart	524	12,100
River Crest L. — Red River County; off-channel reservoir; 7 mi. SE Bogata; (In.); Texas P&L	555	7,000

Robert Lee Reservoir — (see **Spence Reservoir**)	—	—
Salt Creek L. — (see **Graham L.**)	—	—
Sam Rayburn Reservoir — Jasper-Angelina-Sabine-Nacogdoches-San Augustine counties; Angelina R.; (formerly **McGee Bend Reservoir**); (FC-P-M-In.-Ir.-R); USAE.	114,500	2,876,300
San Angelo L. — (see **O. C. Fisher L.**)	—	—
San Bernard Reservoirs #1, #2, #3 — Brazoria Co.; Off-Channel San Bernard R.; 3 mi. N Sweeney; (In.); Phillips 66 Co.	—	8,610
Sandlin, L. Bob — Titus-Wood-Camp-Franklin counties; Big Cypress Cr.; 5 mi. SW Mount Pleasant; (In.-M-R); Titus Co. FWSD No. 1 (impounded by **Fort Sherman Dam**)	9,004	192,350
Sandow L. — (see **Alcoa Lake**)	—	—
Sandy Creek Reservoir — (see **Pinkston Reservoir**)	—	—
Sanford Reservoir — (see **Meredith, Lake**)	—	—
Santa Rosa L. — Wilbarger Co.; Beaver Cr.; 15 mi. S Vernon; (Mi.); W. T. Waggoner Estate	1,500	11,570
Sheldon Reservoir — Harris Co.; Carpenters Bayou; 2 mi. SW Sheldon; (R-FH); TP&WD.	1,700	5,420
Smithers L. — Fort Bend Co.; Dry Creek; 10 mi. SE Richmond; (In.); Houston Lighting & Power Co.	2,480	18,700
Somerville L. — Burleson-Washington counties; Yegua Cr.; 2 mi. S Somerville; (M-In.-Ir.- FC); USAE-Brazos River Authority	11,456	155,062
Southland Paper Mills Reservoir — (see **Kurth, Lake**)	—	—
South Texas Project Reservoir — Matagorda Co.; off-channel Colorado R.; 16 mi. S Bay City; (In.); Houston Lighting & Power	7,000	187,000
Spence Reservoir, E. V. — Coke Co.; Colorado R.; 2 mi. W. Robert Lee; (M-In.-Mi.); Colorado R. Mun. Water Dist.; (impounded by **Robert Lee Dam**)	14,950	484,800
Squaw Creek Reservoir — Somervell-Hood counties; Squaw Cr.; 4.5 mi. N Glen Rose; (In.); Texas Utilities Services, Inc.	3,296	151,030
Stacy Reservoir — (see **O. H. Ivie Reservoir**)	—	—
Stamford, L. — Haskell Co.; Paint Cr.; 10 mi. SE Haskell; (M-In.); City of Stamford	4,690	52,700
Steinhagen L., B. A. — (Also called **Town Bluff Reservoir** and **Dam B. Reservoir**); Tyler-Jasper counties; Neches R.; 1/2 mi. N Town Bluff; (FC-R-C); (impounded by **Town Bluff Dam**)	13,700	94,200
Stillhouse Hollow L. — Bell Co.; Lampasas R.; 5 mi. SW Belton; (M-In.-Ir.-FC); USAE-BRA; (sometimes called **Lampasas Reservoir**)	6,429	226,060
Striker Creek Reservoir — Rusk-Cherokee counties; Striker Cr.; 18 mi. SW Henderson; (M -In.); Angelina-Nacogdoches WC&ID No. 1	1,920	16,930
Sulphur Springs L. — Hopkins Co.; White Oak Cr.; 2 mi. N Sulphur Springs; (M); Sulphur Springs WD; (impounded by **Lake Sulphur Springs Dam**; formerly called **White Oak Creek Reservoir**)	1,910	17,710
Swauano Creek Reservoir — (see **Welsh Reservoir**)	—	—
Tawakoni, L. — Rains-Van Zandt-Hunt counties; Sabine R.; 9 mi. NE Wills Point; (M-In.-Ir-R); Sabine River Authority; (impounded by **Iron Bridge Dam**)	37,879	888,130
Terrell City L., New — Kaufman Co.; Muddy Cedar Cr.; 6 mi. E Terrell; (M-R); City of Terrell	830	8,580
Texana, L. — Jackson Co.; Navidad R. and Sandy Cr.; 6.8 mi. SE Edna; (M-Ir); USBR, Lavaca-Navidad R. Auth., Texas Water Dev. Bd.; (formerly **Palmetto Bend Reservoir**)	11,000	157,900
Texarkana L. — (see **Wright Patman Lake**)	—	—
Texoma L. — Grayson-Cooke cos., Texas; Bryan-Marshall-Love cos., Okla.; impounded by **Denison Dam** on Red R. short distance below confluence of Red and Washita Rivers; (P-FC-C-R); USAE (Texas' share of capacity is 2,722,000 acre-feet)	89,000	5,382,000
Thomas L. — (see **J. B. Thomas L.**)	—	—
Toledo Bend Reservoir — Newton-Panola-Sabine-Shelby counties; Sabine R.; 14 mi. NE Burkeville; (M-In.-Ir.-PR); Sabine River Authority (Texas' share of capacity is half amount shown)	181,600	4,472,900
Town Bluff Reservoir — (see **Steinhagen, Lake B. A.**)	—	—
Tradinghouse Creek Reservoir — McLennan Co.; Tradinghouse Cr.; 9 mi. E Waco; (In.); Texas P&L	2,010	35,124
Travis, L. — Travis-Burnet counties; Colorado R.; 13 mi. NW Austin; (M-In.-Ir.- Mi.-P-FC-R); LCRA: (impounded by **Mansfield Dam**)	18,930	1,144,100
Trinidad L. — Henderson Co.; off-channel reservoir Trinity R.; 2 mi. S. Trinidad; (P); Texas P&L Co.	740	7,450
Truscott Brine L. — Knox Co.; Bluff Cr.; 26 mi. NNW Knox City; (Chlorine Control); Red River Auth.	2,978	107,000
Turtle Bayou Reservoir — (see **Anahuac Lake**)	—	—
Twin Buttes Reservoir — Tom Green Co.; Concho R.; 8 mi. SW San Angelo; (M-In. -FC-Ir.-R.); City of San Angelo-USBR-Tom Green Co. WC&ID No. 1	9,080	177,800
Twin Oaks Reservoir — Robertson Co.; Duck Cr.; 12 mi. N. Franklin; (In); Texas P&L	2,300	30,319
Tyler L. — Smith Co.; Prairie and Mud Crs.; 12 mi. SE Tyler; (M-In); City of Tyler; impounded by **Whitehouse** and **Mud Creek dams**)	4,800	73,260
Upper Nueces Reservoir — Zavala Co.; Nueces R.; 6 mi. N Crystal City; (Ir.); Zavala-Dimmit Co. WID No. 1	316	7,590
Valley Acres Reservoir — Hidalgo Co.; off-channel Rio Grande; 7 mi. N Mercedes; (Ir-M-FC); Valley Acres Water Dist.	906	7,840
Valley L. — Fannin-Grayson counties; 2.5 mi. N Savoy; (P); TP&L; (formerly **Brushy Creek Reservoir**)	1,080	16,400
Victor Braunig L. — Bexar Co.; Arroyo Seco; 15 mi. SE San Antonio; (In.); Pub. Svc. Bd./San Antonio	1,350	26,500
Waco L. — McLennan Co.; Bosque R.; 2 mi. W Waco; (M-FC-C-R); City of Waco- USAE-BRA	7,194	144,546
***Wallisville L.** — Liberty-Chambers counties; Trinity R.; 2 mi. S Wallisville; (M-In.-Ir.); USAE	19,700	58,000
Walter E. Long L. — Travis Co.; Decker Cr.; 9 mi. E of capital, Austin; (M-In.-R); City of Austin (formerly **Decker Lake**)	1,269	33,940
Waxahachie L. — Ellis Co.; S Prong Waxahachie Cr.; 4 mi. SE Waxahachie; (M-In); Ellis County WC&ID No. 1; (impounded by **S. Prong Dam**)	690	13,500
Weatherford L. — Parker Co.; Clear Fork Trinity River; 7 mi. E Weatherford; (M-In.); City of Weatherford	1,158	18,650
Welsh Reservoir — Titus Co.; Swauano Cr.; 11 mi. SE Mount Pleasant; (R-In.); Southwestern Electric Power Co.; (formerly **Swauano Creek Reservoir**)	1,365	23,587
White Oak Creek Reservoir — (see **Sulphur Springs Lake**)	—	—
White River L. — Crosby Co.; 16 mi. SE Crosbyton; (M-In.-Mi.); White River Municipal Water Dist.	1,642	29,880
White Rock L. — Dallas Co.; White Rock Cr.; within NE Dallas city limits; (R); City of Dallas	1,088	9,004
Whitney L. — Hill-Bosque-Johnson counties; Brazos R.; 5.5 mi. SW Whitney; (FC-P); USAE.	23,560	622,800
Wichita, L. — Wichita Co.; Holliday Cr.; 6 mi. SW Wichita Falls; (M-P-R); City of Wichita Falls	2,200	9,000
Winnsboro, L. — Wood Co.; Big Sandy Cr.; 6 mi. SW Winnsboro; (FC-R); Wood County; (impounded by **Wood Co. Dam No. 4**)	806	8,100
Winters L. — Runnels Co.; Elm Cr.; 4.5 mi. E Winters; (M); City of Winters.	640	8,370
Worth, L. — Tarrant Co.; W. Fk. Trinity R.; in NW Fort Worth; (M); City of Fort Worth	3,560	38,130
Wright Patman L. — Bowie-Cass-Morris-Titus-Red River counties; Sulphur R.; 8 mi. SW Texarkana; (FC-M); USAE; (formerly **Texarkana Lake**)	18,944	110,900

Texas Plant Life

(Editor's note: This article was updated for The Texas Almanac by **Stephan L. Hatch**, Curator, S.M. Tracy Herbarium and Professor, Dept. of Rangeland Ecology and Management, Texas A&M University.)

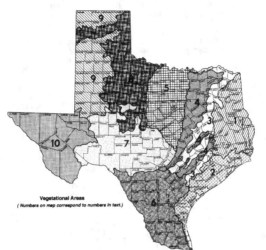

Vegetational Areas
(Numbers on map correspond to numbers in text.)

Difference in amount and frequency of rainfall, in soils and in frost-free days gives Texas a great variety of vegetation. From the forests of East Texas to the deserts of West Texas, from the grassy plains of North Texas to the semi-arid brushlands of South Texas, plant species change continuously.

More than 100 million acres of Texas are devoted to providing grazing for domestic and wild animals. This is the **largest single use for land in the state.** More than 80 percent of the acreage is devoted to range in the Edwards Plateau, Cross Timbers and Prairies, South Texas Plains and Trans-Pecos Mountains and Basins.

Sideoats grama, which occurs on more different soils in Texas than any other native grass, was officially designated as the **state grass of Texas** by the Texas Legislature in 1971.

The **10 principal plant life areas** of Texas, starting in the east, are:

1. Piney Woods. Most of this area of some 16 million acres ranges from about 50 to 700 feet above sea level and receives 40 to 56 inches of rain yearly. Many rivers, creeks and bayous drain the region. Nearly all of Texas' commercial timber comes from this area. There are three native species of pine, the principal timber.: longleaf, shortleaf and loblolly. An introduced species, the **slash pine,** is also widely grown. Hardwoods include **oaks, elm, hickory, magnolia, sweet and black gum, tupelo** and others.

The area is interspersed with **native and improved grasslands.** Cattle are the primary grazing animals. **Deer** and **quail** are abundant in properly managed localities. Primary forage plants, under proper grazing management, include species of the **bluestems, rossettegrass, panicums, paspalums, blackseed needlegrass, Canada and Virginia wildryes, purpletop, broadleaf and spike woodoats, switchcane, lovegrasses, indiangrass** and numerous **legume** species.

Highly disturbed areas have understory and overstory of undesirable woody plants that suppress growth of pine and desirable grasses. The primary forage grasses have been reduced and the grasslands have been invaded by **three-awns, annual grasses, weeds, broomsedge bluestem, red lovegrass** and shrubby woody species.

2. Gulf Prairies and Marshes. The Gulf Prairies and Marshes cover approximately 10 million acres. There are two subunits: (a) The marsh and salt grasses immediately at tidewater, and (b) a little farther inland, a strip of bluestems and tall grasses, with some gramas in the western part. Many of these grasses make excellent grazing. **Oaks, elm** and other hardwoods grow to some extent, especially along streams, and the area has some **post oak** and brushy extensions along its borders. Much of the Gulf Prairies is fertile farmland. The area is well suited for cattle.

Principal grasses of the Gulf Prairies are **tall bunchgrasses,** including **big bluestem, little bluestem, seacoast bluestem, indiangrass, eastern gamagrass, Texas wintergrass, switchgrass** and **gulf cordgrass.** Seashore **saltgrass** occurs on moist saline sites. Heavy grazing has changed the range vegetation in many cases so that the predominant grasses are the less desirable **broomsedge bluestem, smutgrass, threeawns, tumblegrass** and many other inferior grasses. The other plants that have invaded the productive grasslands include **oak underbrush, Macartney rose, huisache, mesquite, prickly pear, ragweed, bitter sneezeweed, broomweed** and others.

Vegetation of the Gulf Marshes consists primarily of sedges, bullrush, flatsedges, beakrush and other rushes, smooth cordgrass, marshhay cordgrass, marsh millet and maidencane. The marshes are grazed best during winter.

3. Post Oak Savannah. This secondary forest region, also called the **Post Oak Belt,** covers some 7 million acres. It is immediately west of the primary forest region, with less annual rainfall and a little higher elevation. Principal trees are **post oak, blackjack oak** and **elm. Pecans, walnuts** and other kinds of water-demanding trees grow along streams. The southwestern extension of this belt is often poorly defined, with large areas of prairie.

The upland soils are **sandy and sandy loam,** while the bottomlands are **sandy loams and clays.**

The original vegetation consisted mainly of **little bluestem, big bluestem, indiangrass, switchgrass, purpletop, silver bluestem, Texas wintergrass, spike woodoats, longleaf woodoats, post oak** and **blackjack oak.** The area is still largely native or improved grasslands, with small farms located throughout. Intensive grazing has contributed to dense stands of a woody understory of **yaupon, greenbriar** and **oak** brush. **Mesquite** has become a serious problem. Good forage plants have been replaced by such plants as **splitbeard bluestem, red lovegrass, broomsedge bluestem, broomweed, bullnettle** and **western ragweed.**

4. Blackland Prairies. This area of about 12 million acres, while called a "prairie," has much timber along the streams, including a variety of **oaks, pecan, elm, horseapple (bois d'arc)** and **mesquite.** In its native state it was largely a grassy plain — the first native grassland in the westward extension of the Southern Forest Region.

Most of this fertile area has been cultivated, and only small acreages of meadowland remain in original vegetation. In heavily grazed pastures, the tall bunchgrass has been replaced by **buffalograss, Texas grama** and other less productive grasses. **Mesquite, lotebush** and other woody plants have invaded the grasslands.

The original grass vegetation includes **big and little bluestem, indiangrass, switchgrass, sideoats grama, hairy grama, tall dropseed, Texas wintergrass** and **buffalograss.** Non-grass vegetation is largely legumes and composites.

5. Cross Timbers and Prairies. Approximately 15 million acres of alternating woodlands, often called the **Western Cross Timbers,** and prairies constitute this region. Sharp changes in the vegetational cover are associated with different soils and topography, but the grass composition is rather uniform.

The prairie-type grasses are **big bluestem, little bluestem, indiangrass, switchgrass, Canada wildrye, sideoats grama, hairy grama, tall grama, tall dropseed, Texas wintergrass, blue grama** and **buffalograss.**

On the Cross Timbers soils, the grasses are composed of **big bluestem, little bluestem, hooded windmillgrass, sand lovegrass, indiangrass, switchgrass** and many species of legumes. The woody vegetation includes **shinnery, blackjack, post** and **live oaks.**

The entire area has been invaded heavily by woody brush plants of **oaks, mesquite, juniper** and other unpalatable plants that furnish little forage for livestock.

6. South Texas Plains. South of San Antonio, between the coast and the Rio Grande, are some 21 million acres of subtropical dryland vegetation, consisting of small trees, shrubs, cactus, weeds and grasses. The area is noteworthy for extensive brushlands, known as the **brush country,** or the

Spanish equivalents of **chaparral** or **monte**. Principal plants are **mesquite, small live oak, post oak, prickly pear (Opuntia) cactus, catclaw, blackbrush, whitebrush, guajillo, huisache, cenizo** and others which often grow very densely. The original vegetation was mainly perennial warm-season **bunchgrasses** in **post oak, live oak** and **mesquite savannahs**. Other brush species form dense thickets on the ridges and along streams. Long-continued grazing has contributed to the dense cover of brush. Most of the desirable grasses have persisted under the protection of brush and cacti.

There are distinct differences in the original plant communities on various soils. Dominant grasses on the sandy loam soils are **seacoast bluestem, bristlegrass, paspalum, windmillgrass, silver bluestem, big sandbur** and **tanglehead**. Dominant grasses on the clay and clay loams are **silver bluestem, Arizona cottontop, buffalograss, common curlymesquite, bristlegrass, pappusgrass, gramas, plains lovegrass, Texas cupgrass, vinemesquite**, other **panicums** and **Texas wintergrass**. Low saline areas are characterized by **gulf cordgrass, seashore saltgrass, alkali sacaton** and **switchgrass**. In the post oak and live oak savannahs, the grasses are mainly **seacoast bluestem, indiangrass, switchgrass, crinkleawn, paspalums** and **panicums**. Today much of the area has been reseeded to **buffelgrass**.

7. Edwards Plateau. These 25 million acres are rolling to mountainous, with woodlands in the eastern part and grassy prairies in the west. There is a good deal of brushy growth in the central and eastern parts. The combination of grasses, weeds and small trees is ideal for **cattle, sheep, goats, deer and wild turkey.**

This limestone-based area is characterized by the large number of **springfed, perennially flowing streams** which originate in its interior and flow across the **Balcones Escarpment**, which bounds it on the south and east. The soils are shallow, ranging from sands to clays and are calcareous in reaction. This area is predominantly rangeland, with cultivation confined to the deeper soils.

In the east-central portion is the well-marked **Central Basin** centering in Mason, Llano and Burnet counties, with a mixture of granitic and sandy soils. The western portion of the area comprises the semi-arid **Stockton Plateau**.

Noteworthy is the growth of **cypress** along the perennially flowing streams. Separated by many miles from cypress growth of the moist Southern Forest Belt, they constitute one of Texas' several **"islands"** of vegetation. These trees, which grow to stately proportions, were commercialized in the past.

The principal grasses of the clay soils are **cane bluestem, silver bluestem, little bluestem, sideoats grama, hairy grama, indiangrass, common curlymesquite, buffalograss, fall witchgrass, plains lovegrass, wildryes** and **Texas wintergrass.**

The rocky areas support tall or mid-grasses with an overstory of **live oak, shinnery oak, cedar and mesquite**. The heavy clay soils have a mixture of **tobosagrass, buffalograss, sideoats grama** and **mesquite.**

Throughout the Edwards Plateau, **live oak, shinnery oak, mesquite** and **cedar** dominate the woody vegetation. Woody plants have invaded to the degree that they should be controlled before range forage plants can re-establish.

8. Rolling Plains. This is a region of approximately 24 million acres of alternating woodlands and prairies. The area is half **mesquite woodland** and half **prairie**. Mesquite trees have steadily invaded and increased in the grasslands for many years, despite constant control efforts.

Soils range from coarse sands along outwash terraces adjacent to streams to tight or compact clays on redbed clays and shales. Rough broken lands on steep slopes are found in the western portion. About two-thirds of the area is rangeland, but cultivation is important in certain localities.

The original vegetation includes **big, little, sand and silver bluestems, Texas wintergrass, indiangrass, switchgrass, sideoats and blue gramas, wildryes, tobosagrass** and **buffalograss** on the clay soils.

The sandy soils support **tall bunchgrasses, mainly sand bluestem. Sand shinnery oak, sand sagebrush** and **mesquite** are the dominant woody plants.

Continued heavy grazing contributes to the increase in woody plants, low-value grasses such as **red grama, red lovegrass, tumblegrass, gummy lovegrass, Texas grama, sand dropseed, sandbur, western ragweed, croton** and many other weeds. **Yucca** is a problem plant on certain rangelands.

9. High Plains. The High Plains, some 19 million treeless acres, are an extension of the Great Plains to the north. The level nature and porous soils prevent drainage over wide areas. The relatively light rainfall flows into the numerous shallow **"playa" lakes** or sinks into the ground to feed the great **underground aquifer** that is the source of water for the countless wells that irrigate the surface of the plains. A large part of this area is under irrigated farming, but native grassland remains in about one-half of the High Plains.

Blue grama and **buffalograss** comprise the principal vegetation on the clay and clay loam "hardland" soils. Important grasses on the sandy loam "sandy land" soils are **little bluestem, western wheatgrass, indiangrass, switchgrass** and **sand reedgrass**. Sand shinnery oak, sand sagebrush, mesquite and yucca are conspicuous invading brushy plants.

10. Trans-Pecos, Mountains and Basins. With as little as eight inches of annual rainfall, long hot summers and usually cloudless skies to encourage evaporation, this 18-million-acre area produces only drouth-resistant vegetation without irrigation. Grass is usually short and sparse. The principal vegetation consists of **lechuguilla, ocotillo, yucca, cenizo** and other arid land plants. In the more arid areas, **yeso, chino and tobosagrass** prevail. There is some **mesquite**. The vegetation includes **creosote-tarbush, desert shrub, black grama, grama grassland, yucca and juniper savannahs, pine oak forest and saline flats.**

The mountains are 3,000 to 8,751 feet in elevation and support **piñon pine, juniper** and some **ponderosa pine** and other forest vegetation on a few of the higher slopes.

The grass vegetation, especially on the higher mountain slopes, includes many **southwestern and Rocky Mountain species** not present elsewhere in Texas. On the desert flats, **black grama, burrograss and fluffgrass** are frequent. More productive sites have numerous species of **grama, muhly, Arizona cottontop, dropseed** and **perennial threeawn grasses**. At the higher elevations, **plains bristlegrass, little bluestem, Texas bluestem, sideoats grama, chino grama, blue grama, piñon ricegrass, wolftail** and several species of **needlegrass** are frequent.

The common invaders on all depleted ranges are **woody plants, burrograss, fluffgrass, hairy erioneuron, ear muhly, sand muhly, red grama, broom snakeweed, croton, cacti** and several poisonous plants. ☆

For Further Reading
Hatch, S. L., K. N. Gandhi and L. E. Brown, **Checklist of the Vascular Plants of Texas**; MP1655, Texas Agricultural Experiment Station, College Station, 1990.

Texas Forest Resources

Source: Texas Forest Service, The Texas A&M University System, College Station, TX 77843- 2136. On the Web agcomwww.tamu.edu/agcom/news/TFShome/tfs.html

Texas' forest resources are abundant and diverse. Trees cover roughly 13 percent of the state's land area. The 22 million acres of forests and woodlands in Texas is an area larger than the states of Massachusetts, Connecticut, New Hampshire, Rhode Island and Vermont combined. The principal forest and woodlands regions are: the East Texas pine-hardwood region, often called the Piney Woods; the Post Oak Belt, which lies immediately west of the pine-hardwood forest; the Eastern and Western Cross Timbers areas of North Central Texas; the Cedar Brakes of Central Texas; the mountain forests of West Texas; and the coastal forests of the southern Gulf Coast.

The East Texas Piney Woods

Although Texas' forests and woodlands are extensive, detailed forest resource data is available for only the 43-county East Texas timber region. The Piney Woods, which form the western edge of the southern pine region, extending from Bowie and Red River counties in Northeast Texas to Jefferson, Harris and Waller counties in southeast Texas, contain 11.9 million acres of forest and produce nearly all of the state's commercial timber. Following is a summary of the findings of the most recent Forest Survey of East Texas, conducted in 1992 by the USDA Forest Service Southern Forest Experiment Station.

Timberland Acreage and Ownership

Nearly all (11.8 of 11.9 million acres) of the East Texas forest is classified as "timberland," which is suitable for production of timber products and not reserved as parks or wilderness areas. In contrast to the trends in several other Southern states, Texas timberland acreage increased by 2 percent between 1986 and 1992. Seventy-four percent of the new timberland acres came from agricultural lands, such as idle farmland and pasture, which was either intentionally planted with trees or naturally reverted to forest.

Sixty-one percent of East Texas timberland is owned by approximately 150,000 farmers, private individuals, families, partnerships and non-wood-using corporations. Thirty-two percent is owned by forest-products companies, and 7 percent is owned by the government. The following table shows acreage of timberland by ownership:

Ownership Class	Thous. Acres
Non-industrial Private:	
Farmer	1,161.8
Corporate	954.3
Individual	5,106.9
Forest Industry	3,767.4
Public:	
National Forest	576.7
Misc. Federal	91.8
State	68.1
County & Municipal	46.8
Total	**11,773.8**

There are distinct regional differences in ownership patterns. Most forest-industry land is found south of Nacogdoches County, and timberland in some counties, such as Polk and Hardin, is as much as 75 percent owned by the forest-products industry. North of Nacogdoches, the nonindustrial private landowner predominates, and industry owns a much smaller percent of the timberland.

Forest Types

Six major forest types are found in the East Texas Piney Woods. Two pine-forest types are most common. The loblolly-shortleaf and longleaf-slash forest types are dominated by the four species of southern yellow pine. In these forests, pine trees make up at least 50 percent of the trees.

Oak-hickory is the second most common forest type. These are upland hardwood forests in which oaks or hickories make up at least 50 percent of the trees, and pine species are less than 25 percent. Oak-pine is a mixed-forest type in which more than 50 percent of the trees are hardwoods, but pines make up 25 to 49 percent of the trees.

Two forest types, oak-gum-cypress and elm-ash-cottonwood, are bottomland types which are commonly found along creeks, river bottoms, swamps and other wet areas. The oak-gum-cypress forests are typically made up of many species including blackgum, sweetgum, oaks and southern cypress. The elm-ash-cottonwood bottomland forests are dominated by those trees but also contain many other species, such as willows, sycamore and maple. The following table shows the breakdown in acreage by forest type:

Forest Type Group	Thous. Acres
Southern Pine:	
Loblolly-shortleaf	4,063.7
Longleaf-slash	232.9
Oak-pine	2,503.8
Oak-hickory	3,146.9
Bottomland Hardwood:	
Oak-gum-cypress	1,755.8
Elm-ash-cottonwood	71.0
Total	**11,773.8**

Southern pine plantations, established by tree planting and usually managed intensively to maximize timber production, are an increasingly important source of wood fiber. Texas forests include 1.8 million acres of pine plantations, 72 percent of which are on forest-industry-owned land, 22 percent on nonindustrial private, and 6 percent on public land. Plantation acreage increased 48 percent between 1986 and 1992. Genetically superior tree seedlings, produced at industry and Texas Forest Service nurs-

eries, are usually planted to improve survival and growth.

Timber Volume and Number of Trees

Texas timberland contains 12.9 billion cubic feet of timber "growing-stock" volume. This is enough wood fiber to produce 200 billion copies of National Geographic. The inventory of softwood remained steady at 7.9 billion cubic feet, while the hardwood inventory increased nearly 12 percent to 5.1 billion cubic feet between 1986 and 1992.

There are an estimated 6.9 billion live trees in East Texas, according to the 1992 survey. This includes 2 billion softwoods, 4.1 billion hardwoods, and .7 billion trees of noncommercial species. The predominant species are loblolly and shortleaf pine; 1.9 billion trees of these two species are found in East Texas.

Timber Growth and Removals

Between 1986 and 1992, an annual average of 691.6 million cubic feet of timber was removed from the inventory either through harvest or land-use changes. Meanwhile, 728.6 million cubic feet were added to the inventory through growth each year, resulting in a net increase in timber inventory in East Texas.

For pine, however, slightly more is being cut than is being grown. An average 530.5 million cubic feet were removed during those years, while 522.9 million feet were added by growth. For hardwoods, 161.1 million feet were removed, while 205.7 million cubic feet were added by growth.

Other Tree Regions

Compared to commercially important East Texas, relatively little data are available for the other tree regions of Texas. However, these areas are environmentally important with benefits of wildlife habitat, improved water quality, recreation and aesthetics. A brief description of these areas — the Post Oak Belt, the Eastern and Western Cross Timbers, the Cedar Brakes, the Mountain Forests and the Coastal Forests — can be found in the descriptions of Texas' vegetation regions preceding this article.

Economic Impact of Timber in Texas

Timber is a major contributor to the state's economy. The forest-products industry in Texas produces lumber, plywood, oriented-strand board, poles, railroad crossties, wood furniture, pulp, paper and paperboard, and a host of other products from the timber grown in Texas forests. Consider these Texas forest-industry facts:

• Texas is one of the top producers of forest products in the nation. In 1997, it was the source of 4 percent of lumber, 11 percent of structural panels, and 3 percent of paper and paperboard produced in the United States.

• In 1997, timber ranked first in East Texas and fifth statewide in the value of agricultural production after beef, cotton, poultry and milk. The delivered value of the timber harvest was $1.01 billion.

• In 1997, the forest-products industry in Texas produced and sold goods valued at $9.2 billion, 50 percent of which came from the paper sector.

• In 1997, the forest industry directly employed 97,300 people: 45,000 in lumber and wood-products industries, 19,500 in the furniture industry and 29,800 in the paper industry.

• Forest industries pay $1.6 billion in wages and salaries each year.

The 1997 Timber Harvest

Total Removals

Total removals in East Texas, including both pine and hardwood, rose 2.8 percent from 1996. The total volume removed from the 43-county region was 763.6 million cubic feet in 1997, compared to 742.5 million in 1996. Included in total removals is the harvest of timber for industrial use and an estimate of the logging residue and other timber removals.

By species group, removals comprised 617.3 million cubic feet of pine and 146.3 million cubic feet of hardwood. Hardwood removals increased by 2.9 percent, while removals from the softwood inventory were 2.8 percent over 1996.

Eighty-nine percent of timber removed, including 90

percent of pine and 81 percent of hardwood, was used in the manufacture of wood products. This portion of total removals, called the industrial roundwood harvest, totaled 557.5 and 118.4 million cubic feet for pine and hardwood, respectively. The pine roundwood harvest was up 2.6 percent, while harvest of hardwood for industrial use climbed by 1.6 percent from 1996. The combined harvest was up 2.4 percent to 675.9 million cubic feet. Top producing counties included Angelina, Cherokee, Jasper, Newton and Tyler counties.

Total Harvest Value

Stumpage value of the timber harvest increased 0.1 percent from 1996 to $667.8 million. Pine timber accounted for 94 percent of that total. The value of the timber harvest delivered to the first point of processing (mill or intermediate woodyard) was $1,009.9 million in 1997, down 0.4 percent from the previous year. Pine comprised 89 percent of the total delivered value.

The harvest of **sawlogs** for production of lumber and ties was down 7.1 percent to 1,372.7 million board feet and comprised 33 percent of the 1997 timber harvest. Timber cut for the production of **structural panels and hardwood veneer** represented 29 percent of the timber harvest in 1997. The harvest for these products was down 9 percent to 198.3 million cubic feet. Pine represents over 99 percent of the volume in this product category. Counties producing more than 10 million cubic feet included Angelina, Jasper, Newton, Polk and Tyler.

Harvest of timber for manufacture of **pulp and paper products** rose 26.4 percent between 1996 and 1997. The pulpwood harvest totaled 3.1 million cords. Pine production was up 32.5 percent to 2.2 million cords; the hardwood pulpwood harvest increased 14.1 percent 0.9 thousand cords. Roundwood pulpwood harvest constituted 38 percent of the timber harvest. Angelina, Cass, Cherokee, Newton and Polk counties were top producers.

Mill residues are another source of wood fiber for paper manufacturing. In 1997, Texas produced 2.62 million cords of mill residue, including 1.96 million cords of pine residues and 0.66 million cords of hardwood, an increase of 0.9 percent. Total pulpwood production, including roundwood and residues, was 5.76 million cords, up 13.4 percent from 1996. Forty-five percent was residue, down from 51 percent in 1996.

Import-Export Trends

Texas was a net exporter of timber products from surrounding states in 1997. Net import of roundwood was 6.9 million cubic feet, or about 1 percent of industrial wood production. Exports of roundwood from Texas were 85.5 million cubic feet, while imports totaled 78.6 million cubic feet. In 1997, 87 percent of the timber harvested in the state was consumed by Texas mills. The remainder was processed in Arkansas, Louisiana and Oklahoma.

Lumber and Ties: Texas sawmills produced 1,477 million board feet of lumber and ties in 1997, an increase of 3.7 percent. Production of pine lumber rose 5.5 percent to 1,316.8 million board feet. Hardwood lumber production decreased by 8.5 percent to 160.6 million board feet.

Texas Lumber Production, 1992-1997

Year	*Lumber Production		Tie Production	
	Pine	Hardwood	Pine	Hardwood
	(thousand board feet)		(thousand pieces)	
1992	1,092,738	138,874	13	498
1993	1,244,373	171,976	69	725
1994	1,340,882	195,693	66	739
1995	1,139,462	159,831	66	502
1996	1,248,627	175.570	66	576
1997	1,316,762	160,553	65	481

*Includes tie volumes.

Structural Panel Products: Production of structural panels at Texas' seven plywood and six oriented-strand board mills increased in 1997. Production rose 5.2 percent

to 3,200.3 million square feet (3/8-inch basis).

Texas Structural Panel Production, 1992-1997

Year	Pine (Thd. sq. ft.*)	Year	Pine (Thd. sq. ft.*)
1992	2,557,103	1995	2,721,487
1993	2,754,949	1996	3,042,736
1994	2,632,833	1997	3,200,317

*3/8-inch basis

Paper Products: Paper production at Texas' seven pulp and paper mills totaled 2.66 million tons, down 10 percent from 1996, because of weakness in the Asian market and overcapacity. Paper production decreased 4.2 percent to 1.12 million tons, while output of paperboard was 1.54 million tons, down 18.1 percent. Market pulp production was up 1.3 percent to 173.7 thousand tons.

Texas Pulpwood Production, 1992-1997

Year	Roundwood		Chips & Sawdust		Total Pulpwood Production
	Pine	Hardwood	Pine	Hardwood	
	(Thousand cords)				
1992	1,861	1,038	1,769	605	5,273
1993	1,636	1,099	1,782	674	5,191
1994	1,574	1,213	1,924	795	5,506
1995	1,879	1,218	1,685	651	5,433
1996	1,666	816	1,876	721	5,079
1997	2,207	931	1,962	657	5,757

Growth and Removals

Removals of pine timber continued to exceed estimated net annual growth in 1997. The removal of 617.3 million cubic feet exceeded estimated growth of 577.9 million cubic feet by 7 percent. Pine removals have exceed growth in 17 of the last 20 years.

Hardwood removals totaled 146.3 million cubic feet compared to 227.1 million cubic feet of estimated growth, indicating that only 64 percent of growth was removed during the year.

During the winter 1996/spring 1997 tree-planting season, trees were planted on 126,236 acres. Nonindustrial private owners received $894,514 in assistance for reforestation and timber-stand improvement through federal and industry cost-share programs. Federal programs provided $409,272 in funds, complemented by $485,242 provided by the Texas Reforestation Foundation and industry cost-share program. On nonindustrial private lands, tree planting reached 47,010 acres, 31 percent higher than 1996.

Future of Texas' Forest Resources

Because of recent reductions of timber harvests from the vast federal forests of the Pacific Northwest brought about by environmental pressures, most analysts believe that the forest-products industry will continue to expand in the South. Demand for wood products continues to grow both domestically and globally. No other region of the United States has as much potential to fill the void left by the decline of timber harvest in the Pacific Northwest.

However, the South's ability to increase its supply of timber will be a limiting factor for long-term industry growth in the region. The major problem is increasing timber supplies to meet wood needs in the future without over-harvesting our forests.

The forest-products industry in Texas is doing a credible job in replanting after harvest by maintaining their own tree nurseries, growing and planting 133 million tree seedlings every year. In fact, projections show that timber growth on industry lands may increase by as much as 30 percent as a result of intensive timber-management practices and genetically improved tree seedlings.

However, nonindustrial private forest landowners (NIPF's) are currently replanting only one acre for every nine acres harvested. Thousands of acres in NIPF ownership have been cut-over repeatedly and are not producing the amount of timber they could. Through improved forest management on less productive NIPF forests, and conversion of marginal crop and pastureland to forest, it is estimated that East Texas pine growth could be increased by as much as 40 percent. This would support significant growth of the forest-products industry and provide additional timber income to landowners, while providing environmental benefits such as cleaner air and water, reduced erosion and more wildlife habitat.

Forest Fires

During 1997, Texas Forest Service fire crews battled only 650 fires in East Texas that burned an estimated 8,446 acres, the second-lowest fire and acreage totals since the agency began keeping wildfire records in 1922.

In 1998, a record-setting drought contributed to a fire siege across the state. The TFS mobilized additional personnel and equipment to strategic locations across the state for fire prevention and rapid response. Across the state, a total of 10,155 fires burned 422,096 acres during the 1998 fire siege. The combined TFS and interagency resources battled 2,794 fires that seared 197,502 acres. Rapid response limited property losses to less than $5 million, and saved more than $250 million worth of property.

Forest Pests

In the South, southern pine beetles kill more timber annually than forest fires. The Texas Forest Service coordinates all beetle-control activity in Texas, which includes detecting infestations from the air, notifying landowners,

and assisting them in controlling the infestations. The TFS has developed a system, now used in 12 states across the South, for predicting beetle activity each year. The predictions are posted on the TFS Web page (http://txforestservice.tamu.edu).

Extensive mortality of oaks in the Hill Country of Central Texas is creating increasing public concern. The vascular wilt disease, "oak wilt," is the major cause. A suppression project, which offers affected landowners professional assistance and cost sharing, is administered by the Texas Forest Service.

The TFS oversees a cooperative project to provide research and technical assistance to co-op members for control of a variety of forest pests including cone and seed insects, regeneration insects, and Texas leaf-cutting ants.

Urban Forests

Because an estimated 80 percent of Texans live in cities with more than 100,000 population, urban trees and forests play an important part in the lives of many. Trees mitigate the urban heat island effect through shading and evaporative cooling. They also purify the air by absorbing pollutants, slowing the chemical reactions that produce harmful ozone, and filtering dust. Urban forests reduce stormwater runoff and soil erosion and buffer against noise, glare and strong winds, while providing habitat for urban wildlife. Environmental benefits from a single tree may be worth more than $275 each year. Emotional and psychological benefits of urban trees raise the value even higher. ☆

Total Timber Production and Value by County in Texas, 1997

County	Pine	Hardwood	Total	Stumpage Value	Delivered Value
	Cubic feet			Thousand dollars	
Anderson	8,181,428	7,296,578	15,478,006	$ 9,134	$ 17,876
Angelina	30,807,305	4,864,608	35,671,913	38,633	56,220
Bowie	5,532,747	5,680,830	11,213,576	9,419	15,423
Camp	1,072,900	948,972	2,021,873	1,429	2,543
Cass	16,825,833	10,048,739	26,874,572	18,896	33,592
Chambers	271,907	256,180	528,087	475	754
Cherokee	21,308,615	9,860,734	31,169,349	20,885	38,017
Franklin	354,138	784,724	1,138,862	888	1,515
Gregg	3,684,911	1,730,148	5,415,059	6,483	9,120
Grimes	3,538,840	4,254	3,543,094	5,098	6,677
Hardin	20,527,621	3,102,963	23,630,584	22,144	34,214
Harris	5,331,109	676,771	6,007,880	8,221	10,972
Harrison	16,160,018	5,051,457	21,211,475	19,843	30,752
Houston	16,045,847	1,800,267	17,846,114	19,842	28,562
Jasper	30,771,537	2,476,191	33,247,729	38,024	54,103
Jefferson	1,145,778	428,109	1,573,888	1,370	2,195
Leon	463,635	5,271	468,906	672	882
Liberty	15,571,014	8,403,003	23,974,017	22,298	34,769
Marion	9,826,412	5,107,590	14,934,002	10,770	18,894
Montgomery	25,127,421	3,723,082	28,850,503	38,722	52,059
Morris	8,868,341	2,200,657	11,068,998	13,453	18,758
Nacogdoches	21,535,534	3,134,022	24,669,556	24,201	36,661
Newton	34,259,133	1,687,172	35,946,305	32,870	51,208
Orange	6,151,460	901,906	7,053,366	6,803	10,379
Panola	15,130,759	2,570,121	17,700,880	16,773	25,793
Polk	48,319,506	4,052,492	52,371,998	43,900	71,154
Red River	6,783,553	4,377,029	11,160,581	8,830	14,825
Rusk	15,559,610	4,335,396	19,895,006	22,343	32,126
Sabine	16,714,504	1,655,690	18,370,194	23,747	32,312
San Augustine	21,506,022	2,336,867	23,842,889	27,395	38,929
San Jacinto	13,405,584	1,427,719	14,833,302	14,501	21,981
Shelby	22,773,319	3,592,925	26,366,244	25,882	39,202
Smith	5,100,935	2,659,171	7,760,106	6,621	10,724
Titus	1,075,485	1,369,225	2,444,710	2,097	3,405
Trinity	22,324,507	718,384	23,042,891	22,688	34,234
Tyler	33,169,676	2,994,335	36,164,011	37,221	55,216
Upshur	6,435,236	2,845,821	9,281,058	8,591	13,401
Walker	16,206,452	494,115	16,700,567	23,401	30,934
Waller	665,273	—	665,273	987	1,280
Wood	3,635,581	2,198,002	5,833,583	3,790	7,017
Other Counties	5,302,434	636,872	5,939,306	8,486	11,162
Totals	**557,471,919**	**118,438,391**	**675,910,311**	**$ 667,824**	**$ 1,009,839**

State Forests

Texas has five state forests, all of which are used primarily for demonstration and research:

The first state forest, now known as the **E.O. Siecke State Forest** in Newton County, was purchased by the state in 1924. It contains 1,722 acres of pine land. An additional 100 acres was obtained by a 99-year lease in 1946.

The **W. Goodrich Jones State Forest**, south of Conroe in Montgomery County, containing 1,725 acres, was purchased in 1926. A 20-acre adjunct was given to the state in 1969.

The **I.D. Fairchild State Forest**, Texas' largest, is located west of Rusk in Cherokee County. This forest was transferred from the state prison system in 1925. An additional 536 acres were added to the original 2,360 acres in 1963 from the Texas State Hospitals and Special Schools, for a total acreage of 2,896.

The 626-acre **John Henry Kirby State Forest** was donated by the late lumberman, John Henry Kirby, in 1929, and later donors. Revenue from this forest is given to the Association of Former Students of Texas A&M University for student-loan purposes.

The 520-acre **Paul N. Masterson Memorial Forest** in Jasper County was donated in the fall of 1984 by Mrs. Leonora O'Neal Masterson of Beaumont in honor of her husband, an active member of the Texas Forestry Association and a tree farmer. ☆

National Forests and Grasslands in Texas

Source: National Forest Service, Lufkin and Albuquerque, NM.

There are four national forests and all or part of five national grasslands in Texas. These federally owned lands are administered by the **U.S. Department of Agriculture-Forest Service**. The national forests cover 637,386 acres in parts of 12 Texas counties. The national grasslands cover a total of 117,394 acres in six Texas counties. Two of these grasslands extend into Oklahoma, as well.

Supervision of the East Texas forests and North Texas grasslands is by the Forest Supervisor of the division known as the **National Forests and Grasslands in Texas** (701 N. 1st St., Lufkin 75901; 409-639-8501). The three **National Grasslands in West Texas** (Black Kettle, McClellan Creek and Rita Blanca) are administered by the Forest Supervisor in Albuquerque, New Mexico, as units of the Cibola National Forest. The forests and grasslands are locally administered by district rangers.

The following list gives the name of the forest or grassland, the administrative district(s) for each, the acreage in each county and the total acreage:

Angelina National Forest - Angelina Ranger District (Lufkin) - Angelina County, 58,539 acres; Jasper, 21,013; Nacogdoches, 9,238; San Augustine, 64,389. Total, 153,179.

Davy Crockett National Forest - Davy Crockett District (Crockett) - Houston County, 93,238 acres; Trinity, 67,329. Total, 160,567.

Sabine National Forest - Sabine District (Hemphill) - Jasper County, 64 acres; Newton, 1,781; Sabine, 95,457; San Augustine, 4,317; Shelby, 59,037. Total, 160,656.

Sam Houston National Forest - Sam Houston District (New Waverly) - Montgomery County, 47,801 acres; San Jacinto, 60,639; Walker, 54,544. Total, 162,984.

Black Kettle National Grassland - Lake Marvin District Ranger in Cheyenne, Okla. - Hemphill County, 576 acres; Roger Mills County, Okla., 31,000 acres. Total, 31,576.

Lyndon B. Johnson and Caddo National Grasslands - District Ranger at Decatur - Fannin County, 17,873 acres; Montague , 61 acres; Wise, 20,252. Total, 38,186.

McClellan Creek National Grassland - District Ranger at Cheyenne, Okla. - Gray County, 1,449 acres. Total, 1,449.

Rita Blanca National Grassland — District Ranger at Clayton, New Mex. — Dallam County, 77,183 acres; Cimarron County, Okla., 15,639 acres. Total, 92,822.

Establishment of National Forests and Grasslands

National Forests in Texas were established by invitation of the Texas Legislature by an Act of 1933, authorizing the purchase of lands in Texas for the establishment of national forests. President Franklin D. Roosevelt proclaimed these purchases on Oct. 15, 1936. The **National Grasslands** were originally submarginal Dust Bowl project lands, purchased by the federal government primarily under the Bankhead-Jones Farm Tenant Act (1937). Today they are well covered with grasses and native shrubs.

Uses of National Forests and Grasslands

The forests are managed for multiple uses, including production and sales of timber and minerals and programs involving recreation, fish and wildlife, soil and water. The grasslands are administered for uses including range, watershed, recreation and wildlife.

Timber Production

More than 521,000 acres of the National Forests in Texas are suitable for timber production. Sales of sawtimber, pulpwood and other forest products are made at regular intervals. The estimated net growth is over 200 million board feet per year and is valued at $25 million. About one-third of this growth is removed by cutting. The balance is left to grow.

Cattle Grazing

Permits to graze cattle on national forests and national grasslands are granted to the public for an annual fee. Approximately 1,000 head of cattle are grazed on national forests, and 1,163 head of cattle are grazed on the Caddo-Lyndon B. Johnson National Grasslands annually. On the Rita Blanca NG, 5,425 cattle are grazed each year, most of them in Texas.

Hunting and Fishing

State hunting and fishing laws and regulations apply to all national-forest land. Game-law enforcement is carried out by the Texas Parks and Wildlife. The Angelina, Sabine, Neches and San Jacinto rivers, Sam Rayburn and Toledo Bend reservoirs, Lake Conroe and many small streams provide a wide variety of fishing opportunities. Hunting is not permitted on the McClellan Creek N.G. nor the Lake Marvin Unit of the Black Kettle N.G.

Recreation Facilities

An estimated 3 million people visited the recreational areas in the National Forests and Grasslands in Texas in 1997, primarily for picnicking, swimming, fishing, camping, boating and nature enjoyment. These areas are listed in the Recreation section of the Texas Almanac. ☆

Texas' Threatened and Endangered Species

Endangered species are those which the Texas Parks and Wildlife Department (TPW) has named as being at risk of statewide extinction. Threatened species are those which are likely to become endangered in the future. The following species of Texas flora and fauna are either endangered or threatened as of Jan. 8, 1999, according to the TPW. This list varies slightly from the federal list. Any questions about protected species should be directed to the Endangered Resources Branch, Texas Parks and Wildlife, 4200 Smith School Road, Austin 78744; (800) 792-1112; www.tpwd.state.tx.us/nature/endang/endang.htm

Endangered Species

Mammals: Greater long-nosed bat; black-footed ferret; jaguarundi; West Indian manatee; ocelot; black right, blue, finback and sperm whales; gray and red wolves.

Birds: Whooping crane; Eskimo curlew; peregrine, American peregrine and northern aplomado falcons; southwestern willow flycatcher; brown pelican; Attwater's greater prairie chicken; interior least tern; black-capped vireo; ivory-billed and red-cockaded woodpecker; Bachman's and golden-cheeked warblers.

Reptiles: Atlantic hawksbill, leatherback and Kemp's ridley sea turtles.

Amphibians: Texas blind salamander; Houston toad.

Fishes: Fountain darter; Big Bend, Clear Creek, Pecos and San Marcos gambusias; Rio Grande silvery minnow; Comanche Springs and Leon Springs pupfishes.

Mollusks: Ouachita rock pocketbook.

Vascular Plants: Black lace, Nellie cory, Sneed pincushion, star and Tobusch fishhook cactus; Davis' green pitaya; little aguja pondweed; Texas wild-rice; Navasota ladies'-tresses; Texas ayenia; Johnston's frankenia; Walker's manioc; Texas snowbells; South Texas ambrosia; white bladderpod; Terlingua Creek cat's-eye; ashy dogweed; Texas trailing phlox; Texas poppy-mallow; Texas prairie dawn; slender rush-pea; large-fruited sand verbena.

Threatened Species

Mammals: Rafinesque's big-eared, southern yellow and spotted bats; black and Louisiana black bears; white-nosed coati; Atlantic spotted and rough-toothed dolphins; jaguar; margay; Palo Duro mouse; Coues' rice and Texas kangaroo rats; dwarf sperm, false killer, Gervais' beaked, goose-beaked, killer, pygmy killer, pygmy sperm and short-finned pilot whales.

Birds: Rose-throated becard; bald eagle; reddish egret; Arctic peregrine falcon; common black, gray, white-tailed and zone-tailed hawks; white-faced ibis; swallow-tailed kite; Mexican spotted owl; cactus ferruginous pygmy-owl; tropical parula; piping plover; Bachman's,

The endangered jaguarundi. Photo by Robert W. Parvin, courtesy the Nature Conservancy of Texas.

Texas Botteri's and Arizona Botteri's sparrows; wood stork; sooty tern; northern beardless tyrannulet.

Reptiles: Speckled racer; Big Bend blackhead, black-striped, Brazos water, Concho water, indigo, Louisiana pine, northern cat-eyed, smooth green, Texas scarlet, northern scarlet and Texas lyre snakes and timber (cane-brake) rattlesnake; Texas tortoise; alligator snapping and Chihuahuan mud turtles; loggerhead and green sea turtles; reticulated gecko; mountain short-horned, reticulate collared and Texas horned lizards.

Amphibians: Black-spotted newt; Blanco blind, Cascade Caverns, Comal blind and San Marcos salamanders; South Texas siren (large form); Mexican burrowing toad; Mexican treefrog; white-lipped and sheep frogs.

Fishes: Toothless and widemouth blindcats; Rio Grande chub; creek chubsucker; blackside and Rio Grande darters; blotched gambusia; river and blackfin gobies; Devil's River minnow; paddlefish; opossum pipefish; Conchos and Pecos pupfishes; bluehead, bluntnose, Chihuahua and proserpine shiners; Mexican stoneroller; shovelnose sturgeon; blue sucker.

Vascular Plants: Bunched cory, Chisos Mountains hedgehog and Lloyd's mariposa cactus; Hinckley's oak; McKittrick pennyroyal. ☆

Nature Conservancy Protects Natural Heritage

The Nature Conservancy of Texas (TNCT) is a private, nonprofit organization using scientific research and a cooperative, community-based approach to protect the unique diversity of animals and plants native to the state. Active in Texas since 1966, TNCT now owns or manages more than 100,000 acres of ecologically significant conservation lands in Texas. Other lands once acquired by the conservancy are now managed as state or national parks or wildlife refuges.

The Nature Conservancy of Texas preserves listed below welcome visitors, but please call the number listed for each property in advance of your visit.

Chihuahua Woods Preserve: In the Lower Rio Grande Valley near Mission, this preserve is an example of vanishing Tamaulipan thornbrush habitat that supports the Valley's famed variety of unusual bird life, including green jay, great kiskadee, chachalaca, Altamira oriole, peregrine falcon and hook-billed kite. Also found here is a rare assemblage of cactus plants of various species growing packed together like barnacles on a rock. Open during daylight hours. Call 956-580-4241.

Roy E. Larsen Sandyland Sanctuary: In the Piney Woods of East Texas, longleaf pines that once covered the southeastern United States now make one of their last stands on Village Creek near Silsbee. The more than

5,000-acre preserve supports 722 native plant species, including the endangered Texas trailing phlox, and a wide array of birds and animals. Open during daylight hours. Call 409-385-0445.

Eckert James River Bat Cave, in the heart of the Hill Country near Mason, houses a summer colony of an estimated 6 million female Mexican free-tailed bats, who migrate here in early summer to give birth to their "pups." Visitors can learn about the bats from a bat steward, then watch the creatures' spectacular emergence from their cave at dusk. The preserve is open Thursdays through Sundays, 6 to 9 p.m., mid-May to mid-October. Call 915-347-5970 during bat season, or 512-263-8878.

Lennox Woods is 366 acres of pristine old-growth forest of loblolly and shortleaf pines and several species of oaks. A vital refuge for several species whose habitat is being destroyed elsewhere, this preserve in Red River County in far northeast Texas is a unique window into the forests of the past. A self-guiding nature trail provides information on plant communities. Open during daylight hours. Call 903-568-4139.

For more information on the organization: PO Box 1440, San Antonio 78295; 210-224-8774; on the Web: www. tnc.org/texas. ☆

Texas Wildlife

Source: Texas Parks and Wildlife, Austin

Texas has many native animals and birds, plus species introduced on game preserves.

More than **540 species of birds** — about three fourths of all different species found in the United States — have been identified in Texas.

Some **142 species of animals,** including some that today are extremely rare, are found in Texas; a list of plant and animal species designated as threatened or endangered by federal or state natural resource officials is found on the preceding page.

Through efforts of the **Texas Parks and Wildlife,** several nonprofit organizations, and many individual landowners involved in conservation, our wildlife should be a permanent resource.

A few of the leading native animals of Texas are described here. Information is provided by the **Nongame and Urban Program**, Texas Parks and Wildlife.

Mammals

Armadillo — The **nine-banded armadillo** *(Dasypus novemcinctus)* is one of Texas' most interesting mammals. It has migrated north and east and is now common as far north and east as Oklahoma and Mississippi. There has been limited commercialization of the armadillo's shell in the manufacture of curios.

Badger — The **badger** *(Taxidea taxus)* is found throughout West Texas, but in greatly reduced numbers since wholesale eradication of the prairie dog on which the badger preyed. It is a predator, but its pelt is valuable. The range of the badger includes the Texas Panhandle and South Texas, where it is common.

Bat — Thirty-two species of these winged mammals have been found in Texas, more than in any other state in the United States. Of these, 27 species are known residents, though they are seldom seen by the casual observer. The **Mexican free-tailed bat** *(Tadarida brasiliensis)* and the **cave myotis** *(Myotis velifer)* constitute most of the cave-dwelling bats of Southwest and West Texas. They have some economic value for their deposits of nitrogen-rich **guano.** Some commercial guano has been produced from **James River Bat Cave**, Mason County; **Beaver Creek Cavern**, Burnet County; and from large deposits in other caves including **Devil's Sinkhole** in Edwards County, **Blowout Cave** in Blanco County and **Bandera Bat Cave**, Bandera County. The largest concentration of bats in the world is found at **Bracken Cave** in Comal County. The **big brown bat** *(Eptesicus fuscus)*, the **red bat** *(Lasiurus borealis)* and the **evening bat** *(Nycticeius humeralis)* are found in East and Southeast Texas. The evening and big brown bats are forest and woodland dwelling mammals. Most of the rarer species of Texas bats have been found along the Rio Grande and in the Trans-Pecos. Bats can be observed at dusk near a water source, and many species may also be found foraging on insects attracted to street lights. Everywhere bats occur, they are the main predators of night-flying insects, including mosquitoes and many crop pests.

Bear — The **black bear** *(Ursus americanus)* was formerly common throughout most of the state. It is now surviving in the inaccessible river bottoms of eastern Texas and in portions of the Trans-Pecos with potential habitat.

Beaver — Two subspecies of beaver are found in Texas, the **Mexican beaver** *(Castor canadensis mexicanus)* ranging along the Rio Grande and Devils River and the **Texas beaver** *(Castor canadensis texensis)* which has been brought back from the verge of extinction to abundance through restocking.

Bighorn — (See **Sheep.**)

Bison — The largest of native terrestrial wild mammals of North America, the **American bison** *(Bison bison)*, commonly called **buffalo**, is found today on a few ranches and in zoos. Deliberate slaughter of this majestic animal for hides and to eliminate the Plains Indians' main food source reached a peak about 1875, and the bison was almost eradicated by 1885. Estimates of the number of buffalo killed vary, but as many as 200,000 hides were sold in Fort Worth at a single two-day sale. Except for the interest of the late **Col. Charles Goodnight** and a few other foresighted men, the bison might be extinct.

Cat — The **jaguar** *(Felis onca)* is probably now extinct in Texas and, along with the **ocelot, jaguarundi** and **margay**, is listed as rare and endangered by both federal and state wildlife agencies. The **cougar** *(Felis concolor)*, which is also known as **mountain lion, puma, panther** and **Mexican cougar**, is found in many areas of the state, including the broken country of the Edwards Plateau, the Trans-Pecos Mountains and the South Texas brush country. The former panther of the East Texas forest, which was closely related, may be extinct in Texas but still exists in a few areas of Southeastern U.S. The **ocelot** *(Felis pardalis)*, also known as the **leopard cat**, is found usually along the border. The **red-and-gray cat**, or **jaguarundi** *(Felis yagouaroundi Geoffroy)* is found in extreme South Texas. The **margay** *(Felis wiedii)* was reported in 1884 near Eagle Pass. There is currently a margay breeding program underway at a wildlife center near Glen Rose with the goal of eventually re-establishing the small cat in the wild. The **bobcat** *(Felis rufus)* is found over the state in large numbers. The **feral housecat** may have impact on game birds in many parts of Texas.

Chipmunk — The **gray-footed chipmunk** *(Tamias canipes)* is found at high altitudes in the Guadalupe and Sierra Diablo ranges of the Trans-Pecos (see also **Ground Squirrel,** with which it is often confused in public reference).

Coati — The **coati** *(Nasua narica)*, a relative of the raccoon, is occasionally found in southern Texas. It inhabits woodland areas and feeds both on the ground and in trees. The coati, which is on the list of threatened species, is also found occasionally in Big Bend National Park. There is a captive-breeding project for the coati at a wildlife center near Glen Rose in Somervell County.

Coyote — The **coyote** *(Canis latrans)*, great in number, is the most destructive Texas predator of livestock. On the other hand, it is probably the most valuable predator in the balance of nature. It is a protection to crops and range lands by its control of rodents, rabbits, etc. It is found throughout the state, but is most numerous in the brush country of southwest Texas.

Deer — The **white-tailed deer** *(Odocoileus virginianus)* is an important Texas game animal. Its number in Texas is estimated at 3 million. It thrives best in the wooded and broken areas of the Edwards Plateau and south of San Antonio where it often competes for feed with domestic and exotic animals. Texas Parks and Wildlife has had success in **transplanting deer**. In East Texas, the timbered sections of North Central Texas, and even in the thinly populated areas of Northwest Texas, the white-tailed deer population has increased greatly. The **mule deer** *(Odocoileus heminous)* is found principally in the Trans-Pecos and in smaller numbers in the less thickly settled parts of the Staked Plains. It has increased in number in recent years. The little **Del Carmen deer** (white-tailed subspecies) is found in limited numbers in the high valleys of the Chisos Mountains in the Big Bend. The **American elk** *(Cervus canadensis)*, though not the original subspecies found in Texas, has been introduced into the Guadalupe and Davis mountains.

Ferret — The **black-footed ferret** *(Mustela nigripes)* was formerly found widely ranging through the West Texas country of the prairie dog on which it preyed. It is now considered extinct in Texas. It is of the same genus as the weasel and the mink.

Fox — Most common is the **gray fox** (*Urocyon cinere-oargenteus*) found in the forested area of East Texas and throughout most of the state where there is cover, notably in the broken parts of the Edwards Plateau and the rough country at the foot of the Staked Plains. The **kit** or **Swift fox** (*Vulpes velox*) is found in the plains country of Northwest Texas. A second species of **kit fox** (*Vulpes macrotis*) is found in the Trans-Pecos and is fairly numerous in some localities. The **red fox** (*Vulpes vulpes*) is not a native but was introduced for sport.

Gopher — Six species of pocket gophers occur in Texas. The **Botta's pocket gopher** (*Thomomys bottae*) is found in West Texas south of the High Plains, notably along the Rio Grande. The **plains pocket gopher** (*Geomys bursarius*) is found in the Panhandle and throughout North Central and East Texas. The **desert pocket gopher** (*Geomys arenarius*) and the **yellow-faced pocket gopher** (*Pappogeomys castanops*) are found in the Trans-Pecos. The **Texas pocket gopher** (*Geomys personatus*) is found in the sandy soils of the lower coastal region.

Ground Squirrel — Five or more species of ground squirrel live in Texas, mostly in the western part of the state. The **rock squirrel** (*Spermophilus variegatus*) is found throughout the Edwards Plateau and Trans-Pecos. The **Mexican ground squirrel** (*Spermophilus mexicanus*) is found in the Mexican border country from Brownsville to the Davis Mountains. The **spotted ground squirrel** (*Spermophilus spilosoma*) is found generally in favorable localities throughout the western half of the state. The **thirteen-lined ground squirrel** (*Spermophilus tridecemlineatus*) is found in the Panhandle and in a narrow strip from Red River to the Gulf between Dallas and Corpus Christi. The **Texas antelope squirrel** (*Ammospermophilus interpres*) is found along the Rio Grande from El Paso to Val Verde County.

Javelina — The **javelina** or **collared peccary** (*Tayassu tajacu*) is found in South and Southwest Texas. It is fairly numerous. Its meat is edible if properly prepared, and there is limited use of its hide for the manufacture of gloves and other leather articles. A scrappy animal, it is the subject of many tall tales.

Mink — The **mink** (*Mustela vison*) is found in East Texas and along the Coastal Belt, usually in forested river bottoms. It yields a considerable fur crop. It is akin to the otter and weasel. **Mink farming**, partly with native and partly with introduced species, is found on a limited scale, usually in East Texas.

Mole — The **mole** (*Scalopus aquaticus*) is found generally throughout the eastern half of the state.

Muskrat — There are three subspecies of muskrat in Texas: the **muskrat** (*Ondatra zibethica rivalicia*), which is found in Southeast Texas near Beaumont where it is commercially produced on muskrat ranges; the **Pecos River muskrat** (*Ondatra zibethica ripensis*) of Western Texas; and the **Great Plains muskrat** (*Ondatra zibethica cinnamonia*) of the Panhandle region. The muskrat is one of the most valuable of Texas' fur-bearing animals. Production of pelts comes largely from the coastal area near Beaumont.

Nutria — This introduced species (*Myocastor coypus*) is found in Texas, except the Panhandle and extreme western portions. The fur is not highly valued and, since nutria are in competition with muskrats, their spread is discouraged. They are used widely in Texas as a cure-all for ponds choked with vegetation.

Opossum — A **marsupial,** the **Virginia opossum** (*Didelphis virginiana*) is found in nearly all parts of the state. The opossum has economic value for its pelt, and its meat is considered a delicacy by some. It is one of the chief contributors to the Texas fur crop.

Otter — A few **river otter** (*Lutra canadensis*) are found along East Texas rivers and coastal marshes. Although it is a prized fur-bearing animal, there is no evidence that the river otter can be considered either rare or endangered. The species is numerous in Liberty County where biologists have determined that its numbers have increased in recent years. While excess populations of this species, like other forms of wildlife, can be harvested with no danger to the species, loss of habitat through encroaching civilization presents the most formidable threat to its continued existence.

The coyote is found throughout the state, but is most prevalent in the brush country of southwest Texas. Dallas Morning News file photo.

Porcupine — The **yellow-haired porcupine** (*Erethizon dorsatum*) is found in the higher mountain ranges of the Trans-Pecos and in the western Edwards Plateau. It has recently moved into the eastern portion of the Panhandle along the Caprock.

Prairie Dog — Until recent years probably no sight was so universal in West Texas as the **black-tailed prairie dog** (*Cynomys ludovicianus*) and its burrow. Naturalists estimated its population in the hundreds of millions. Its destruction of range grasses, plus its peculiar susceptibility to eradication (usually by the introduction of the fumes of carbon disulphide into its burrow) have caused a great reduction of its numbers over its past range. However, it is making a comeback. Prairie dog towns often covered many acres with thickly spaced burrows or prairie dog holes. It is being propagated in several public zoos, notably in the **prairie dog town in Mackenzie Park** at Lubbock. It has been honored in Texas by the naming of the **Prairie Dog Town Fork** of the Red River, along one segment of which is located the beautiful **Palo Duro Canyon**.

Pronghorn — The **Pronghorn** (*Antilocapra americana*) is primarily a plains animal. It almost became extinct, but a continuous closed season and a sound management program raised its numbers. There have been limited open seasons since 1944. Specifically, these animals inhabit the plains and basin regions of Brewster, Presidio, Jeff Davis, Culberson and Hudspeth counties. They have also sufficiently increased in numbers in the Permian Basin and Panhandle to permit open seasons in recent years.

Rabbit — The **black-tailed jack rabbit** (*Lepus californicus*) is found throughout Texas except in the East Texas forest area. It breeds rapidly, and its long hind legs make it one of the world's faster-running animals. The **Eastern cottontail** (*Sylvilagus floridanus*) is found throughout Texas except in Trans-Pecos region. The **desert cottontail** (*Sylvilagus auduboni*) is found in South and West Texas, usually on the open range. The **swamp rabbit** (*Sylvilagus aquaticus*) is found in East Texas and the coastal area.

Raccoon — The **raccoon** (*Procyon lotor*) is found throughout Texas, especially along streams and in urban settings.

Rats and Mice — There are 40 or 50 species of rats and mice in Texas of varying characteristics, habitats and economic destructiveness. The **Norway rat** (*Rattus norvegicus*) and the **black rat** (*Rattus rattus*) are probably the most common and the most destructive. Some of the species are native, and others, notably the Norway rat, are invaders. The **common house mouse** (*Mus musculis*) is estimated in the hundreds of millions annually. The rare **Guadalupe Mountain vole** (*Microtus mexicanus guadalupensis*) is found only in the Guadalupe Mountains National Park and just over the border into New Mexico.

Ringtail — The **ringtail** (*Bassariscus astutus*) is found generally in wooded areas west of the Trinity and in the broken sections of the Edwards Plateau. It is a valuable fur-bearing mammal.

Sheep — The **barbary,** or **Aoudad, sheep** *(Ammotragus lervia),* first introduced to the Palo Duro Canyon area in 1957-58, have become firmly established. Barbary sheep have been introduced into many areas of Texas, but are designated as game animals in only eight counties of the Panhandle surrounding Palo Duro Canyon. Efforts are now under way by the Texas Parks and Wildlife to establish the **desert bighorn** *(Ovis canadensis)* in range they formerly occupied. Currently 300 bighorns are free-ranging in West Texas.

Shrew — Three species are found in Texas, the **northern short-tailed shrew** *(Blarina brevicauda),* the **least shrew** *(Cryptotis parva)* and the **desert shrew** *(Notiosorex crawfordi).* The first-mentioned is rarer, occurring in the Big Thicket. The least shrew is found generally in South Central and East Texas. The **gray shrew** is found in very limited numbers in the semiarid areas of West Texas and along the border.

Skunk — There are six species of skunk in Texas. The **Eastern spotted skunk** *(Spilogale putorius)* is found throughout North Texas. A small skunk, it is often erroneously called civet cat. This skunk also is found in East Texas and the Gulf area. The **Western spotted skunk** *(Spilogale gracilis)* is found in the central, western and southern parts of the state. The **long-tailed,** or **broad-striped skunk** *(Mephitis mephitis)* is found in many parts of the state, usually along streams or in wooded areas. The **hooded skunk** *(Mephitis macroura)* is found in limited numbers in the Trans-Pecos mountains. The Gulf Coast **hog-nosed skunk** *(Conepatus leuconotus),* found in the Brownsville area, ranges southward into Mexico. The **mountain hog-nosed skunk** *(Conepatus mesoleucus)* is found in sparsely timbered areas of Edwards Plateau, Central Texas, Trans-Pecos.

Squirrel — The **fox squirrel** *(Sciurus niger)* is found throughout East, Central and West Central Texas. The **gray,** or **cat, squirrel** *(Sciurus carolinensis)* is found generally in the eastern third of the state. The **flying squirrel** *(Glaucomys volans)* is widely distributed in the Piney Woods and the East Texas Post Oak Belt.

Weasel — The **brindled** or **long-tailed weasel** *(Mustela frenata),* akin to the mink, is found in the Panhandle-Plains and South Texas.

Wolf — The **red wolf** *(Canis rufus)* was once found over a wide range in Eastern and Central Texas. It is now considered extirpated from the wild, with the only known remnants of the population now in captive propagation. The **gray wolf** *(Canis lupus)* once had a wide range over Central, Southern and Western Texas. It has been reduced almost to extinction. The **red wolf** and **gray wolf** are listed on the federal and state rare and endangered species lists. The few gray wolves which may be encountered in Texas are believed to be occasional individuals crossing over from Mexico.

Reptiles and Arachnids

Most of the more than **100 species and subspecies of snakes** found in Texas are beneficial, as also are other reptiles. There are **16 poisonous species and subspecies.**

Poisonous reptiles include **three species of copperheads** (southern, broad-banded and Trans-Pecos); one kind of **cottonmouth** (western); **11 kinds of rattlesnakes** (canebrake, western massasauga, desert massasauga, western pigmy, western diamondback, timber, banded rock, mottled rock, northern blacktailed, Mojave and prairie); and the **Texas coral snake.**

Also noteworthy are the **horned lizard,** also called **horned toad,** which is on the list of **threatened species;** the **vinegarone,** a type of whip scorpion; **tarantula,** a hairy spider; and **alligator.** ☆

National Wildlife Refuges

Source: U.S. Fish and Wildlife Service, U.S. Department of the Interior.

Texas has more than 463,000 acres in **17 national wildlife refuges.** Included in this acreage are two conservation easement refuges, which may be visited at different times of the year for bird watching and wildlife viewing, as well as hunting and fishing. Their descriptions follow. Write or call before visiting to check on facilities and to be sure the refuge is open to visitors when you plan to go. Addresses and phone numbers are given at the ends of the descriptions of the refuges. On the Web: http://sturgeon.irm.r2.fws.gov/u2/refuges/texas

Anahuac: The more than 34,000 acres of this refuge are located along the upper Gulf Coast in Chambers County. **Fresh and saltwater marshes** and miles of beautiful, sweeping **coastal prairie** provide wintering habitat for large flocks of **geese** and other **waterfowl. Roseate spoonbills, white ibis** and **yellow rails** are among the other birds frequenting the refuge. Other species include **alligator, muskrat** and **bobcat.** Fishing, bird watching and hunting are available. Office: Box 278, Anahuac 77514; 409-267-3337.

Aransas: This refuge comprises 70,504 acres on Blackjack Peninsula and three satellite units. The three mainland units consist of **oak woodlands, fresh and saltwater marshes** and **coastal grasslands.** Besides providing wintering grounds for the endangered **whooping crane,** the refuge is home to many species of waterfowl and other migratory birds. This refuge has reported the **largest number of bird species** of any refuge in the country — more than 390. Refuge is open daily sunrise to sunset. Interpretive center is open daily 8:30 a.m.-4:30 p.m. Other facilities include a 40-foot observation tower at the edge of a whooping crane marsh, a paved auto-tour

loop and walking trails. Office: Box 100, Austwell 77950; 512-286-3559.

Attwater Prairie Chicken: Established in 1972 in Colorado County to preserve habitat for the endangered **Attwater's prairie chicken,** the refuge comprises more than 8,000 acres of **native tallgrass prairie,** potholes, sandy knolls and some wooded areas. An auto-tour route is available year-round, and 350 acres of marsh are accessible for birding. Refuge open sunrise to sunset. Office: Box 519, Eagle Lake 77434; 409-234-3021.

Balcones Canyonlands: This 14,144-acre refuge was dedicated in 1992. Located in the **Hill Country** northwest of Austin, it was established to protect the nesting habitat of two endangered birds: **black-capped vireo** and **golden-cheeked warbler.** Eventually, the refuge will encompass 46,000 acres of **oak-juniper woodlands** and other habitats. Hunting available. Office: 10711 Burnet Rd., #201, Austin 78758; 512-339-9432.

Big Boggy: This refuge occupies 4,526 acres of **coastal prairie** and **salt marsh** along East Matagorda Bay for the benefit of wintering **waterfowl,** attracting thousands of **ducks and geese** to its ponds and potholes. **The refuge is generally closed,** and visitors are encouraged to visit nearby **San Bernard or Brazoria refuges.** Waterfowl hunting is permitted in season. Office: 1212 N. Velasco, #200, Angleton 77515; 409-849-7771.

Brazoria: The 43,388 acres of this refuge, located along the Gulf Coast in Brazoria County, serve as haven for wintering waterfowl and a wide variety of other migratory birds. The refuge also supports many **marsh** and **water birds,** from **roseate spoonbills** and **great blue herons** to **white ibis** and **sandhill cranes.** Brazoria Refuge is within the **Freeport Christmas Bird Count** circle, which frequently achieves the highest number of species seen in a 24-hour period. Open daily 8 a.m.-4 p.m., Sept.-May, when visitors can drive through the refuge to observe coastal wildlife. From June 1 through Aug. 31, refuge is open the first full weekend each month and intermittently throughout the week. Hunting and fishing also available. Call for details. Office: 1212 N. Velasco, #200, Angleton 77515; 409-849-7771.

Buffalo Lake: Comprising 7,664 acres in the Central Flyway in Randall County in the Panhandle, this refuge contains some of the best remaining shortgrass prairie in the United States. Buffalo Lake is now dry; a marsh area is artifically maintained for the numerous birds, reptiles and mammals. Available activities include picnicking, auto tour, birding, photography and hiking. Office: Box 179, Umbarger 79091; 806-499-3382.

Hagerman: Hagerman National Wildlife Refuge lies on the Big Mineral arm of Texoma Lake in Grayson County. The 3,000 acres of **marsh** and water and 8,000 acres of **farmland, grassland** and **woodlands** provide a feeding and resting place for migrating **waterfowl.** Bird watching, fishing and hunting are available. Office: Rt. 3, Box 123, Sherman 75090-9564; 903-786-2826.

Laguna Atascosa: Established in 1946 as southern-most waterfowl refuge in the **Central Flyway,** this refuge contains more than 45,000 acres fronting on the **Laguna Madre** in the Lower Rio Grande Valley. Open **lagoons, coastal prairies, salt flats and brushlands** support a wide diversity of wildlife. The United States' largest concentration of **redhead ducks** winters here, along with many other species of **waterfowl** and **shorebirds. White-tailed deer, javelina and armadillo** can be found, along with endangered **ocelot.** Bird watching and nature study are popular, with an abundance of migratory birds in the winter and many **Mexican birds** present year-round. Camping and fishing are permitted within Adolph Thomae Jr. County Park. Hunting also available. Office: Box 450, Rio Hondo 78583; 956-748-3607.

Lower Rio Grande Valley: The U.S. Fish and Wildlife Service has acquired approximately half the planned acreage in the Lower Rio Grande Valley for this refuge, which will eventually include 132,500 acres within Cameron, Hidalgo, Starr and Willacy counties. The refuge will include 11 different habitat types, including **sabal palm forest, tidal flats, coastal brushland, mid-delta thorn forest, woodland potholes and basins, upland thorn scrub, flood forest, barretal, riparian woodland** and **Chihuahuan thorn forest.** More than 400 species of birds and 265 butterfly species have been found there, as well as four of the five cats that occur within the United States: **jaguarundi, ocelot, bobcat** and **mountain lion.** Office: Santa Ana/Lower Rio Grande Valley National Wildlife Refuges, Rt. 2, Box 202A, Alamo 78516; 210-787-3079.

Matagorda Island: Matagorda Island is jointly owned and managed by the U.S. Fish and Wildlife Service and the State of Texas. The 56,668-acre island is a natural accreting barrier island located offshore between Port O'Connor and Fulton. The island is home to a variety of migratory and resident wildlife, including 18 state or federally listed **endangered species.** More than **50 whooping cranes** winter on the island. Matagorda has the first nesting **aplomado falcons** outside the Rio Grande Valley in the United states in more than 50 years. It also supports **white-tailed deer, American alligators** and **Texas horned lizards.** Activities include salt-water fishing, hunting (in season), birding, picnicking and historical interpretation. Boat access only. For information on visiting, contact Texas Parks and Wildlife, PO Box 117, Port O'Connor, 77982. For information on the Refuge, contact Matagorda Island NWR, Box 100, Austwell 77950; 512-286-3559.

McFaddin: Purchased in 1980, this refuge's 55,000 acres are of great importance to wintering populations of

Alligators can be spotted at Laguna Atascosa NWR, as well as many of Texas' other coastal refuges. Dallas Morning News file photo.

migratory waterfowl. One of the densest populations of **alligators** in Texas is found here. Activities on the refuge include wildlife observation, hunting, fishing and crabbing. Access best by boat; limited roadways. Office: Box 609, Sabine Pass 77655; 409-971-2909.

Muleshoe: Oldest of national refuges in Texas, Muleshoe provides winter habitat for **waterfowl** and the continent's largest wintering population of **sandhill cranes.** Comprising 5,809 acres in the High Plains of Bailey County, the refuge contains three **playa lakes, marsh areas, caliche outcroppings** and **native grasslands.** A nature trail, campground and picnic area are available. Office: Box 549, Muleshoe 79347; 806-946-3341.

San Bernard: Located on the Gulf of Mexico near Freeport, this refuge's 27,414 acres attract **migrating waterfowl,** including thousands of **white-fronted and Canada geese and several duck species,** which spend the winter on the refuge. Habitats, consisting of **coastal prairies, salt/mud flats** and saltwater and freshwater ponds and potholes, also attract yellow rails, roseate spoonbills, reddish egrets and American bitterns. Visitors enjoy auto and hiking trails, photography, bird watching, fishing, and waterfowl hunting in season. Contact refuge office for details. Office: Rte. 1, Box 1335, Brazoria 77422; 409-964-3639.

Santa Ana: Established in 1943, Santa Ana is located on the north bank of the Rio Grande in Hidalgo County. Santa Ana's 2,088 acres of **subtropical forest** and **native brushland** are at an **ecological crossroads** of subtropical, Gulf Coast, Great Plains and Chihuahuan desert habitats. Santa Ana attracts birders from across the United States who can view many species of **Mexican birds** as they reach the northern edge of their ranges in South Texas. Also found at Santa Ana are **ocelot** and **jaguarundi,** endangered members of the cat family. Visitors enjoy a tram or auto drive, bicycling and hiking trails. Office: Rt. 2, Box 202A, Alamo 78516; 956-787-3079.

Texas Point: Texas Point's 8,900 acres are located on the Upper Gulf Coast, 12 miles east of McFaddin NWR, where they serve a large wintering population of **waterfowl** as well as migratory birds. The endangered **southern bald eagle** and **peregrine falcon** may occasionally be seen during peak fall and spring migrations. **Alligators** are commonly observed during the spring, summer and fall months. Activities include wildlife observation, hunting, fishing and crabbing. Access to the refuge is by boat and on foot only. Office: Box 609, Sabine Pass 77655; 409-971-2909.

Trinity River: Established in 1994 to protect remnant bottomland hardwood forests and associated wetlands, this refuge, located in northern Liberty County off State Highway 787 approximately 15 miles east of Cleveland, provides habitat for wintering, migrating and breeding waterfowl and a variety of other wetland-dependent wildlife. Approximately 4,547 acres of the proposed 20,000-acre refuge have been purchased. The refuge is currently closed to the public, but conservation groups may tour with prior arrangements. Office: Box 10015, Liberty 77575; 409-336-9786. ✩

Texas Wildlife Management Areas

Source: Texas Parks and Wildlife Department

Texas Parks and Wildlife (TPW) is currently responsible for managing 50 wildlife management areas (WMAs) totaling approximately three quarters of a million acres. Of these, 32 WMAs are owned in fee title, while 19 are managed under license agreements with other agencies.

Wildlife management areas are used principally for hunting, but many are also used for research, fishing, wildlife viewing, hiking, camping, bicycling and horseback riding, when those activities are compatible with the primary goals for which the WMA was established.

Access to WMAs at times designated for public use is provided by various permits, depending on the activity performed. Hunting permits include Special ($50 or $100), Regular daily ($10), or Annual ($40). A Limited Public Use Permit ($10) allows access for such activities as birdwatching, hiking, camping or picnicking and on some WMAs under the Texas Conservation Passport (Gold $50, Silver $25). The Gold Passport also allows entry to state parks.

For further information, write to Texas Parks and Wildlife, 4200 Smith School Rd., Austin 78744; 1-800-792-1112 or 512-389-8900. On the Web: www.tpwd.state.tx.us.

A brief description of the WMAs is given below. On most WMAs, restrooms and drinking water are not provided; check with the TPW at the contacts above before you go.

WMA (Acreage)	COUNTY	Day Use Only	Hunting	Fishing	Camping	Wildlife Viewing	Hiking	Interpretive Trail	Auto Tour	Bicycling	Horseback Riding	Comments
Candy Abshier (207)	CHAMBERS	★				★						Excellent birding spring and fall
Alabama Creek (14,561)	TRINITY		★	★	★	★	★		★	★	★	In Davy Crockett National Forest
Alazan Bayou (1,973)	NACOGDOCHES	★	★	★		★					★	
Angelina-Neches/Dam B (16,360)	JASPER/TYLER		★	★	★	★	★		★	★		
Aquilla (9,700)	HILL	★	★	★		★	★					
Atkinson Island (150)	HARRIS	★				★						
Bannister (25,695)	SAN AUGUSTINE		★	★	★	★	★		★	★	★	In San Augustine National Forest
Big Lake Bottom (3,176)	ANDERSON	★	★	★		★	★				★	900 acres available to public
Black Gap (105,708)	BREWSTER		★	★	★	★	★		★	★	★	Primitive camping only
Walter Buck (2,155)	KIMBLE	★	★			★	★		★	★		
Caddo National Grasslands (16,150)	FANNIN		★	★	★	★	★			★		
Caddo Lake State Park & WMA (6,929)	MARION/HARRISON		★	★	★	★	★		★	★	★	
Cedar Creek Islands (160)	HENDERSON	★		★		★						Access by boat only
Chaparral (15,200)	LA SALLE/DIMMIT		★		★	★	★		★			
Cooper (14,480)	DELTA/HOPKINS	★	★	★		★	★					
James E. Daughtrey (4,000)	LIVE OAK/MCMULLEN	★	★		★	★	★					Primitive camping for hunters
Elephant Mountain (23,147)	BREWSTER		★		★	★	★		★			Primitive camping only
Gus Engling (10,958)	ANDERSON		★		★	★	★		★			Seasonal closings
Granger (11,116)	WILLIAMSON	★	★	★	★	★	★		★	★		Primitive camping only
Guadalupe Delta (6,000)	REFUGIO	★	★	★		★	★		★	★		Freshwater marsh
Tony Houseman (3,313)	ORANGE		★	★	★	★	★					
Sam Houston Natl Forest (161,154)	SAN JACINTO/WALKER/		★	★	★	★	★		★	★	★	Also Montgomery County
Gene Howe (5,821)	HEMPHILL		★	★	★	★	★	★	★	★	★	Riding March - August only
Keechi Creek (1,500)	LEON		★									
Kerr (6,493)	KERR		★			★			★	★		
Las Palomas:												
Lower Rio Grande Valley Units (5,886)	CAMERON/HIDALGO	★	★			★	★					Also Starr & Willacy counties
Ocotillo Unit (2,082)	PRESIDIO		★	★	★	★	★		★	★		
Lower Neches (7,998)	ORANGE	★	★	★		★	★					
Mad Island (7,281)	MATAGORDA	★				★						
Mason Mountain (5,301)	MASON		★									
Matador (28,183)	COTTLE		★	★	★	★	★		★	★	★	
Matagorda Island (43,900)	CALHOUN		★	★	★	★	★					(See also Matagorda NWR)
Pat Mayse (8,925)	LAMAR	★	★	★	★	★	★		★	★		
Moore Plantation (27,547)	SABINE/JASPER		★	★	★	★	★		★	★	★	In Sabine National Forest
J.D. Murphree (24,366)	JEFFERSON	★	★	★		★						Access by boat only
The Nature Center (85)	SMITH	★				★		★				Primarily for public-school groups
North Toldeo Bend (3,650)	SHELBY		★	★	★	★	★			★		
M.O. Neasloney (100)	GONZALES	★			★	★	★					
Old Sabine Bottom (5,167)	SMITH	★	★	★		★	★		★	★	★	
Old Tunnel (11)	KENDALL	★				★						Bat-viewing June-October
Peach Point (10,311)	BRAZORIA		★			★	★	★				Excellent birding spring and fall
Playa Lakes (1,096 in 3 units)	CASTRO/DONLEY	★	★			★	★					
Ray Roberts (41,220)	COOKE/DENTON	★	★	★		★	★					Also Grayson Co.
Redhead Pond (37)	NUECES	★				★						
Richland Creek (13,796)	FREESTONE/NAVARRO		★	★	★	★	★		★	★	★	
Sierra Diablo (11,625)	CULBERSON		★									Restricted access
Somerville (3,180)	BURLESON/LEE	★	★	★		★				★		
Tawakoni (1,562)	HUNT/VAN ZANDT		★	★	★	★	★				★	
Welder Flats (1,480)	CALHOUN			★								Boat access only
White Oak Creek (25,700)	BOWIE/CASS/MORRIS	★	★			★	★					Also Titus Co.
D.R. Wintermann (246)	WHARTON					★						Restricted access

Weather

Source (unless otherwise noted): John F. Griffiths, Texas State Climatologist, and graduate assistants Richard K. Scott and Chris Gordon, Texas A&M University, College Station.

Weather Highlights 1997

January 7-8: After record-high temperatures for several Texas cities on the 4th, much of Texas experienced below-freezing temperatures in addition to snow and ice. On the 7th, Red River Co. received two inches of snow, parts of the Hill Country were covered with a half inch of ice, with two to five inches of snow mixed with sleet falling on the Dallas/Fort Worth area. Many schools and businesses closed on the 8th as snow, sleet and rain blanketed portions of the state from Central Texas to the Permian Basin.

January 27: Heavy thunderstorms along the Gulf Coast spawned a tornado in Pasadena (Harris Co.) that caused $10 million in damage, but no injuries or deaths.

February 12: An intense cold front collided with Gulf moisture, resulting in copious amounts of rainfall and very heavy snow. Lubbock received one to six inches of snow, with isolated reports of up to 10 inches. Inundating rains fell at Beaumont/Port Arthur (2.57"), Houston (3.08"), Lufkin (2.86"), Tyler (2.04") and Waco (3.28"). Nearly six inches of rain fell in Pearland (Brazoria Co.), just south of Houston, and a tornado was spotted in Galveston (no injuries or damage).

March 2: Straight-line winds up to 100 mph were reported in rural northern Texas associated with a potent cold front that traversed the state. Many injuries were reported, and two people were killed in Bazette (Navarro Co.) when they were pinned beneath their mobile home. Heavy rain fell at Dallas/Fort Worth International Airport (0.77"), Waco (1.53"), College Station (1.22"), Lufkin (1.24") and Texarkana (0.93"). Counties hardest hit by these storms included Kaufman, Van Zandt, Henderson, Mills, Falls and Bell.

April 25: The Panhandle was blanketed by heavy snowfall; some regions of Parmer County received up to eight inches. Amarillo's 6.4" set a new record for snowfall during a 24-hour period in April. At the same time, Galveston was being drenched with more than five inches of rain. The combination of heavy rainfall and exceptionally high tides (due to strong easterly winds) caused flooding of many streets and residences.

May 27: Tragedy struck the Central Texas town of Jarrell as a half-mile wide F5 tornado (the most destructive on the Fujita scale) tore through, killing 27 people and leaving almost nothing to salvage. The intense thunderstorms that cut across the region also produced 125 mph winds that uprooted trees and downed power lines in San Antonio, cutting power to nearly 100,000 people. In all, 11 tornadoes were reported in McLennan, Bell, Williamson and Travis counties, five of which resulted in damage and injuries. Cedar Park and the northwestern part of Austin, where three more lives were lost, were among the areas hit by other twisters. Baseball-sized hail was reported in Limestone and Freestone counties later in the evening.

June 21-22: Twenty counties in Central Texas were hit by heavy rains and flooding. Three people in Bandera County and one person in Brown County lost their lives as water from rising rivers and lakes covered portions of the Hill Country. West of San Antonio 18 to 20 inches of rain fell in Ban-

Divisions of counties for climatic data

dera, Kerr and Kendall counties. In D'Hanis, 10.50" fell on the 22nd, while other towns in south-central Texas received five to six inches of rain on both the 21st and the 22nd.

September 21-23: A cool front collided with warm, moist air from the Gulf of Mexico, producing copious rainfall in southeast Texas. Palacios (11"), Friendswood (5.6") and Santa Fe (7.8") were among the cities receiving the greatest 24-hour totals, with Santa Fe's precipitation measured more than 12 inches for the three-day period.

October: Abundant Gulf moisture brought in by persistent winds into southern and coastal regions of Texas was the source of heavy rains in those areas. Victoria (360 percent), Corpus Christi (398 percent) and Brownsville (470 percent) all experienced total monthly precipitation amounts which were more than triple the normal values.

1997 Weather Extremes

Lowest Temp.: Follett, Lipscomb Co., Jan. 14 . . . . - 2° F
Highest Temp.: Castolon, Brewster Co., June 4 . . . . . 113° F
24-hour Precip.: Sisterdale, Kendall Co., June 22 . . . . 10.80"
Monthly Precip.: Chapman Ranch, Nueces Co., Oct. . . 22.51"
Least Annual Precip.: El Paso, El Paso Co. . . . . 8.53"
Greatest Annual Precip.: Houston, Harris Co. . . . . 66.81"

Weather Summary - 1997

Near-normal temperatures in **January and February** were followed by above-average temperatures across all regions in **March**. The spring months of **April, May and**

Average Temperatures 1997

	High Plains	Low Plains	North Central	East Texas	Trans-Pecos	Edwards Plateau	South Central	Upper Coast	South Texas	Lower Valley
Jan.	35.7	41.2	44.1	45.5	44.1	45.2	50.8	51.9	52.6	56.9
Feb.	39.1	44.8	48.8	50.4	47.9	48.6	54.8	56.4	57.6	62.7
Mar.	51.3	56.1	58.0	60.0	58.7	59.8	64.5	65.7	67.5	69.9
April	51.1	56.4	59.5	60.0	60.2	60.5	64.6	65.0	67.3	69.7
May	64.6	67.9	69.6	70.2	72.7	71.3	74.1	74.3	76.9	77.7
June	72.9	76.1	77.7	77.4	78.7	77.9	80.1	80.8	82.5	83.2
July	79.1	82.4	83.7	83.2	81.9	83.3	84.6	84.5	87.1	86.1
Aug.	76.8	81.0	82.4	81.1	80.8	83.5	85.0	84.4	88.0	86.8
Sep.	72.5	77.0	79.5	77.9	77.5	79.5	81.4	80.6	83.7	83.3
Oct.	59.4	64.3	67.0	66.1	64.9	67.1	70.6	70.6	72.5	75.0
Nov.	44.6	49.1	51.8	52.1	53.1	53.8	58.0	58.4	60.8	66.0
Dec.	35.9	41.2	44.9	45.7	43.2	45.5	51.9	52.6	54.2	59.5
Ann.	56.9	61.5	63.9	64.1	63.6	64.7	68.4	68.8	70.9	73.1

Precipitation 1997
(Inches)

	High Plains	Low Plains	North Central	East Texas	Trans-Pecos	Edwards Plateau	South Central	Upper Coast	South Texas	Lower Valley
Jan.	0.50	0.37	1.03	3.45	0.23	0.81	2.13	4.50	0.45	0.73
Feb.	1.13	3.66	7.30	8.49	1.30	3.95	2.72	4.95	1.23	0.73
Mar.	0.05	0.40	2.90	4.65	0.46	2.62	4.27	8.06	2.25	6.50
April	5.72	6.05	5.87	7.20	1.27	3.94	5.67	7.97	4.25	4.02
May	2.88	3.05	4.04	3.64	1.39	3.17	5.52	6.23	4.61	2.95
June	3.13	5.19	4.95	4.91	1.98	6.83	6.57	3.39	5.34	1.60
July	2.31	1.39	1.19	1.78	1.91	0.50	0.63	2.24	0.45	0.05
Aug.	3.14	3.05	2.49	5.10	1.72	1.14	1.26	2.12	0.72	0.42
Sep.	2.01	2.29	0.85	2.26	1.23	1.31	3.72	8.66	2.26	3.23
Oct.	1.10	2.01	4.33	5.33	0.46	2.08	8.51	7.83	3.82	8.39
Nov.	0.65	0.75	2.05	4.38	0.62	1.25	3.33	4.02	1.84	1.13
Dec.	1.88	2.67	5.82	5.39	1.29	1.82	2.19	4.32	0.62	0.47
Ann.	24.50	30.88	42.82	56.58	13.86	29.42	46.52	64.29	27.84	30.22

A subdivision in Jarrell was destroyed by this F5 tornado on the afternoon of May 27, 1997. An outbreak of several tornadoes killed 27 people and injured many more in three Central Texas counties. AP file photo.

June brought below-average temperatures, with April averaging nearly six degrees cooler across the entire state. **July** temperatures were slightly above normal, and **August** was split roughly north and south, with the northern portions of Texas just under their average and the south a little above average. **September** brought above-average temperatures for all 10 climate regions (+2.5°), while near-normal temperatures returned in **October**. The year ended on a cool note with both **November** and **December** bringing cooler-than-average temperatures for all regions of the state. Except for **January**, the first half of 1997 was wetter than usual, while most regions in the second half of the year had below-average precipitation. Exceptions were the southern and coastal regions in **October** and most of the state in **December**, when eight of the 10 regions recorded above-average rainfall.

January's temperatures, within one degree of average for all regions, were accompanied by less-than-average rainfall. The Southern and Low Rolling Plains regions received only 41 percent and 47 percent of their monthly averages, respectively, while the High Plains and Upper Coast had slightly more rainfall than usual. **February** had only slight temperature anomalies, but higher-than-normal precipitation for all but the Southern and Lower Valley divisions. The largest surpluses were in the Trans-Pecos (288 percent), Edwards Plateau (397 percent), Low Rolling Plains (333 percent), North Central (324 percent) and the East Region (246 percent).

March brought warmer-than-normal temperatures to all climatic regions, ranging from 1.5°F above normal in the Lower Valley to 3.7°F above normal in the Upper Coast. March was the first of four consecutive months of above-average rainfall for nearly the entire state. Only the High Plains and the Low Rolling Plains had precipitation deficits in March, while the Upper Coast and Southern regions had approximately three times their usual rainfall. The Lower Valley averaged 6.5", 10 times their normal. Excess rainfall continued into April, with all regions averaging more than twice

their usual totals. These rain events kept temperature averages down for the state in **April**, ranging from 4.4°F below normal for the Upper Coast to 7.4°F below normal for the High Plains.

This pattern of above-average rain and below-average temperatures continued into **May** and **June**, although less extreme. May temperatures were generally only one to three degrees below normal, and June temperatures were about one to two degrees below normal. Unlike April, there were several regions that had precipitation deficits in May and June. The Low Rolling Plains and parts of northern and eastern Texas recorded less-than-average rainfall in May, and the Upper Coast and the Lower Valley had slightly more than half their usual rain for the month of June.

July, August and **September** were drier and warmer than normal for most of Texas. The southern half of the state showed the most temperature excesses in July and August, with typical averages of one to two degrees above the mean, while in August, the entire state was two to three degrees warmer than usual. Rainfall amounts in July ranged from 71 percent of normal in the Low Rolling Plains to only 5 percent in the Lower Valley; no region in the southern half averaged more than half of their usual rainfall. For southern parts of Texas, the lack of sufficient rain continued into August and September, while the northern regions received above average rain in August.

October brought much-needed rain to South Texas, where some locations hadn't received significant amounts since spring. Northern and western Texas recorded little rain in October and **November**, but **December** brought more than three times the usual amount to the High Plains, the Low Rolling Plains and the North Central regions. Temperatures were below normal for regions in both November and December. November anomalies were three to four degrees below normal for most of the state, while in December temperatures were one to three degrees cooler than normal.

Weather Highlights - 1998

January 4-7: An Arctic cold front moved across the northwestern half of north Texas as an upper-level disturbance moved into the Southern Plains. Widespread rain and thunderstorms developed across the area. More than four inches of rain fell between Dallas and Bonham, and another four inches fell from Temple to Fairfield. Flash flooding resulted, as the soil was already saturated from the unusually wet December 1997. Many roads were flooded and vehicles became stranded in the rising waters. At Irving (Dallas Co.), a boy drowned in fast-moving flood waters after he jumped off a bridge into a swollen stream. The front remained stationary through the 7th, and each rain event triggered another period of flash flooding. A three-day total of seven inches was reported from Arlington to Bonham, and five to 10 inches fell in a band through Temple, Waco, Corsicana and Tyler. This was the third-wettest January for the Dallas/Fort Worth area and the second-wettest in the Waco area.

February 10: In Medina County, hail propelled by winds estimated at over 80 mph broke windows and destroyed vegetation across the southeast corner of the county shortly after sunrise. Hail piled up to three feet deep in some locations, and piles were still visible at noon when the National

Average Temperatures 1998

	High Plains	Low Plains	North Central	East Texas	Trans-Pecos	Edwards Plateau	South Central	Upper Coast	South Texas	Lower Valley
Jan.	41.5	45.4	48.7	50.4	49.2	51.7	58.1	58.3	61.1	65.5
Feb.	43.0	46.6	50.2	51.0	49.6	52.0	56.9	57.1	60.7	64.6
Mar.	45.3	50.2	53.7	55.2	55.5	56.5	60.8	61.0	64.6	67.9
April	55.2	60.2	62.5	62.6	63.0	65.5	67.4	67.6	72.0	72.9
May	71.5	76.7	77.0	76.3	76.9	79.3	79.5	78.8	83.3	81.6
June	78.7	83.9	83.9	84.2	84.1	84.5	86.2	84.7	89.4	87.7
July	82.6	87.8	88.7	88.3	83.9	87.1	87.5	86.1	89.6	87.8
Aug.	77.3	82.7	85.2	84.9	79.6	81.6	84.8	84.7	86.2	87.5
Sep.	75.8	80.6	81.5	80.9	77.8	78.7	81.9	82.4	82.9	83.1
Oct.	62.5	67.5	68.9	68.4	68.1	68.7	72.7	73.7	74.1	77.0
Nov.	50.4	55.0	57.7	58.5	57.8	59.1	64.6	65.5	66.6	71.5
Dec.	39.6	43.3	46.9	49.5	47.3	48.3	55.0	56.4	57.1	61.5
Ann.	60.3	65.0	67.1	67.5	66.1	67.8	71.3	71.4	74.0	75.7

Precipitation 1998

(Inches)

	High Plains	Low Plains	North Central	East Texas	Trans-Pecos	Edwards Plateau	South Central	Upper Coast	South Texas	Lower Valley
Jan.	0.16	0.85	4.16	6.96	0.07	1.09	1.87	6.37	0.99	0.26
Feb.	1.25	1.80	3.48	5.34	0.18	1.85	4.63	5.22	2.98	3.24
Mar.	2.12	2.86	4.13	3.34	0.28	2.59	2.20	2.44	1.65	0.85
April	0.60	0.40	1.26	1.75	0.01	0.23	0.70	0.83	0.15	0.09
May	0.84	1.43	1.39	1.09	0.19	0.91	0.25	0.05	0.02	0.00
June	0.38	1.31	1.74	1.04	0.56	1.89	0.94	3.26	0.74	0.11
July	2.02	0.87	1.12	1.30	1.56	0.73	1.17	1.76	0.40	0.28
Aug.	2.35	1.36	1.77	3.61	2.23	7.75	6.28	5.97	5.26	0.93
Sep.	0.31	0.26	3.18	7.94	0.43	1.60	6.78	13.49	4.12	9.61
Oct.	4.32	2.66	5.44	7.67	2.11	3.25	12.89	7.94	5.54	5.56
Nov.	1.15	1.55	4.13	6.71	0.65	2.58	5.24	6.50	2.46	3.42
Dec.	0.42	0.47	3.55	5.35	0.33	0.95	1.80	3.30	0.34	0.49
Ann.	15.92	15.82	35.35	52.10	8.60	25.42	44.75	57.13	24.65	24.84

Weather Service survey team arrived. Over 1,000 windows were broken out of homes and cars in Devine, 12 homes were reported to have major damage, and nearly 1,300 others suffered minor damage. Tornadoes were reported in Wilson and Frio counties, as well as straight winds of nearly 100 mph. As these storms moved eastward, high winds downed nearly 103,000 acres of trees in Sabine and Angelina National Forests, with damage estimated at $150 million.

April-September: A drought gripped most of Texas from the early spring into the late summer, when the hurricane season brought welcome rains. Both San Antonio and Midland endured the driest April on record, with monthly rainfall totals of 0.05" and 0.00," respectively. In May, the average precipitation for the first-order stations was only 10% of normal. By June, according to the Palmer Drought Severity Index, most stations were experiencing severe drought, and the East division was experiencing extreme drought. Many temperature records were set for May, June and July, and for the entire state in general, July 1998 was the second-warmest July on record. On July 6, Waco and Dallas/Fort Worth began a streak of 29 consecutive 100-degree days, and College Station's 30-day streak broke the record of 26 set in 1917. From April through July, San Antonio, College Station, Lubbock and Houston all set records for the lowest amount of precipitation during that four-month period. The drought continued into August and September for the northern portions of the state, while the southern and coastal regions received much-needed rains. With 56 days of 100 degrees or better, Dallas/Fort Worth recorded their second-warmest summer, and Brownsville's summer was their hottest on record, eclipsing the 1980 summer.

May: An unusual atmospheric phenomenon began affecting Texas during the latter half of May. A dense, smoky haze drifting north from Mexican forest fires entered South Texas on the 12th. Over the next two weeks, the entire state was affected by limited visibility and health cautions. At some locations, concentrations of particulate matter exceeded three times the accepted limit defined by the Environmental Protection Agency. The concurrent dry spell resulted in very little rain to wash the pollutants from the air. This lack of rainfall, a persistent high-pressure dome and a low-level temperature inversion all helped trap the smoke and haze near the surface, allowing the contaminants to linger for an extended period of time.

June: The continued hot and dry conditions were partly to blame for numerous wildfires across the state. The Texas Emergency Response Division reported that wildfires burned 143,000 acres of land through the end of June, while the Texas Forest Service estimated that more than 200,000 acres were affected by fires during this time period. A total of 3,042 fires were reported throughout May and June, mostly in East and Central Texas.

August 22-25: Tropical Storm Charley made landfall on the middle Texas coast near Port Aransas during the morning of the 22nd. It was accompanied by welcome moisture, but it also caused local flash flooding. Rain totaling 17.03 inches fell in Del Rio on the 23rd, setting a record for a one-day period. Southern Kimble and northern Edwards County in the northwest Hill Country received three to six inches of rain on this same day. Thirteen people lost their lives in flash floods in Real and Val Verde counties, while more than 200 people were injured in these and other counties in the Hill Country.

September 11-15: Southeastern Texas received more than four inches of rainfall as Tropical Storm Frances made landfall between Corpus Christi and Victoria on Friday morning, the 11th. As it drifted northward towards Victoria, it dumped three to seven inches of rain in De Witt and Lavaca counties. Rainfall totals of more than 10 inches were common in the coastal counties south and east of Houston. Two swimmers drowned in the heavy surf on Galveston Island, and a surfer drowned at Surfside in Brazoria County while surfing the large waves.

October 17-19: One of the most disastrous floods in Texas history brought tragedy and devastation to many parts of South Central Texas. A very slow-moving upper level trough of low pressure, a cold front, and a continuous stream of moisture at both low and upper levels set the stage for record breaking rainfall and river levels that caused the deaths of 31 people. Rainfall amounts ranged from 15 to 22 inches in Bexar, Kendall, Comal, and Hays counties, with some reports as high as 31 inches. Damage and destruction

The home of Richard and Angie Navarro floats through the town of Cuero as floodwaters of the Guadalupe River rise on Oct. 19, 1998. AP file photo.

to livestock and agriculture, roads and bridges, and both public property and buildings approached $1 billion. Thousands to tens of thousands of livestock were killed, nearly 3000 homes were destroyed, and another 8000 homes were damaged. Nearly 1000 mobile homes were destroyed, and another 3000 were damaged. Besides the 31 deaths, many hundreds of others were injured in what will surely remembered as one of the greatest floods in Texas history.

1998 Weather Extremes

Lowest Temp.: Dalhart, Hartley Co., December 23 . . . . . - 2° F
Stratford, Sherman Co., December 22 . . - 2° F
Highest Temp.: Boquillas Ranger Station, Brewster
County, June 4 .117°F
Red Bluff Dam, Reeves Co., June 22 . . .117°F
24-hour Precip: San Marcos, Hays Co., October 17. . . 15.78"
Monthly Precip.: New Braunfels, Comal Co., October . 26.75"
Least Annual Precip.: Midland Int'l Airport, Midland Co.. 4.21"
Greatest Annual Precip.: Sam Rayburn Dam, Jasper
County . . . . .62.96"

Weather Summary - 1998

The main weather issues of 1996 were the drought conditions across Texas, which affected everyone in different ways. Farmers and ranchers were especially hit hard, being forced to sell cattle and watch crops wither in the dry soil. Along with the extremely dry conditions, anomalously warm temperatures, especially in February, May, June and July broke many records statewide and caused 1996 to be warmer than normal across Texas.

The year began on a very dry note. **January** precipitation was almost non-existent in the southern portion of the state, and minimal elsewhere. Mean monthly temperatures were 1 to 2 degrees F above normal over most of Texas.

The beginning of **February** was very cold across most of the state, but this was not characteristic of the remainder of the month. After the first week, when snow and ice were reported as far south as Waco, temperatures began and continued to rise throughout the month; 80s, 90s and 100s were observed over most of the Lone Star State near the latter part of February. In most places, mean monthly temperatures were greater than 4°F above normal, while all regions received less than half of the normal monthly precipitation throughout the state.

The hot trend reversed during **March and April** as temperature anomalies were as far below normal in March as they had been above normal in February. Relatively no relief from the dry conditions occurred during March as all regions in Texas again received significantly below-normal precipitation. April did provide above-normal precipitation for extreme West and East Texas, but other locations were not as lucky. The Panhandle suffered most during April; Amarillo and Lubbock received zero percent and 11 percent of their normal monthly precipitation, respectively.

Extreme heat, even more anomalous than February, returned to Texas during **May**. West Texas observed monthly temperatures greater than 8 degrees F above normal. In other regions of the state, except near the Texas coast, where the water modifies temperature extremes, anomalies of 6 and 7 degrees F above normal were experienced. Drought conditions continued to worsen throughout May. The Southern Panhandle was the only location in Texas to receive greater than 70 percent of the normal monthly precipitation.

Temperatures remained 2 to 3 degrees F above normal for **June and July**. The intense heat, in combination with the continued devastating lack of rainfall throughout Texas, drew down lakes and reservoirs to minuscule levels. The Palmer Drought Severity Index indicated much of Central and Eastern Texas as being in an "Extreme Drought" while a "Severe Drought" was being experienced in the Panhandle, the Rio Grande Valley and the Texas Coast.

August brought much-needed relief to the state as all locations reported above-normal precipitation. Rain amounts were as much as 400 percent above normal across Central Texas and at least 200 percent above normal in many other regions. The break from dry conditions was caused mainly by

the remnants of Hurricane Dolly, which caused numerous showers and thunderstorms to occur. During this welcome relief, monthly temperatures were slightly below normal.

As quickly as hopes of escaping the drought were excited in August, they were destroyed in both **September and October**. Except for a tongue of moisture between Dallas and San Angelo, rainfall departures once again reached devastating values in October: 25 percent of normal rainfall was typical for most of Texas.

A line extending across Midland and Waco separated below-normal temperatures to the north from above-normal temperatures to the south in **November**. Except for extreme West and South Texas, precipitation amounts were well above normal across the state. But as learned a few months earlier, Mother Nature can play with our emotions. **December** returned Texas to well-below-normal rainfall conditions, ending a year Texans will not soon forget and hope not to experience again. ☆

Destructive Weather

Source: This list of exceptionally destructive weather in Texas since 1766 was compiled from ESSA-Weather Bureau information.

Sept. 4, 1766: Hurricane. Galveston Bay. A Spanish mission destroyed.

Sept. 12, 1818: Hurricane. Galveston Island. Salt water flowed four feet deep. Only six buildings remained habitable. Of the six vessels and two barges in the harbor, even the two not seriously damaged were reduced to dismasted hulks. Pirate **Jean Lafitte** moved to one hulk so his **Red House** might serve as a hospital.

Aug. 6, 1844: Hurricane. Mouth of Rio Grande. All houses destroyed at the mouth of the river and at **Brazos Santiago**, eight miles north; 70 lives lost.

Sept. 19, 1854: Hurricane. After striking near **Matagorda**, the hurricane moved inland northwestward over **Colum-**

bus. The main impact fell in **Matagorda and Lavaca bays**. Almost all buildings in Matagorda were destroyed. Four lives were lost in the town; more lives were lost on the peninsula.

Oct. 3, 1867: Hurricane. This hurricane moved inland **south of Galveston**, but raked the entire Texas coast **from the Rio Grande to the Sabine. Bagdad and Clarksville**, towns at the mouth of the Rio Grande, were destroyed. Much of Galveston was flooded and property damage there was estimated at $1 million.

Sept. 16, 1875: Hurricane. Struck **Indianola**, Calhoun County. Three-fourths of town swept away; 176 lives lost. Flooding from the bay caused nearly all destruction.

Aug. 13, 1880: Hurricane. Center struck **Matamoros,**

Meteorological Data

Source: NOAA, Environmental Data Service, Local Climatological Data.

Additional data for these locations are listed in the table of Texas temperature, freeze, growing season, and precipitation records, by counties.

City	Temperature						Precipitation						Relative Humidity		Wind		Sun
	Record High	Month & Year	Record Low	Month & Year	No. Days Max. 90° and Above	No. Days Min. 32° and Below	Maximum in 24 Hours	Month & Year	Snowfall (Mean Annual)	Max. Snowfall in 24 Hours	Month & Year	6:00 a.m., CST	Noon, CST	Speed, MPH (Mean Annual)	Highest MPH	Month & Year	Percent Possible Sunshine
Abilene	110	7/1978	-9	1/1947	96.6	53.6	6.70	9/1961	4.9	7.5	1/1973	74	51	12.1	54	5/1996	70
Amarillo	108	6/1990	-14	2/1951	63.8	110.7	6.75	5/1951	14.9	13.5	2/1971	73	46	13.6	58	9/1979	73
Austin	109	‡7/1954	-2	1/1949	105.0	21.1	7.22	10/1960	1.1	7.0	1/1944	83	56	9.2	52	9/1987	60
Brownsville	106	3/1984	16	12/1989	117.3	2.2	12.19	9/1967	**	0.0	—	89	60	11.5	51	9/1996	60
Corpus Christi	104	7/1939	13	12/1989	101.9	6.6	8.92	8/1980	0.1	1.1	2/1973	90	62	12.0	55	8/1980	62
Dallas-Fort Worth	113	6/1980	-1	12/1989	96.2	40.9	5.91	10/1959	3.2	12.1	1/1964	82	56	10.9	73	8/1959	64
Del Rio	112	6/1988	10	12/1989	124.2	17.3	7.60	10/1984	0.9	8.6	1/1985	79	54	9.9	60	8/1970	70
El Paso	114	7/1994	-8	1/1962	104.0	65.0	2.63	7/1968	5.4	16.8	12/1987	35	28	8.9	64	1/1996	83
Galveston	101	7/1932	8	2/1999	12.2	3.6	14.35	7/1900	0.2	15.4	2/1995	83	72	11.0	*100	9/1900	62
†Houston	107	8/1980	7	12/1989	94.2	21.2	10.36	5/1989	0.4	2.0	1/1973	90	59	7.8	51	8/1983	56
Lubbock	114	6/1994	-16	1/1963	78.6	94.6	5.82	10/1983	10.5	16.3	1/1983	74	47	12.4	70	3/1952	72
Midland-Odessa	116	6/1994	-11	2/1985	96.2	64.7	5.99	7/1961	4.1	6.8	1/1974	74	43	11.0	67	2/1960	74
Prt. Arthur-Beaumont	107	8/1962	12	12/1989	81.2	16.3	17.16	9/1980	0.4	4.4	2/1960	91	64	9.8	55	6/1986	58
San Angelo	111	‡7/1960	-4	12/1989	106.8	53.9	6.25	9/1980	3.3	7.4	1/1978	78	49	10.4	75	4/1969	73
San Antonio	108	8/1986	0	1/1949	110.8	22.7	7.28	9/1973	0.8	13.2	1/1985	83	55	9.3	48	7/1979	60
Victoria	107	8/1962	9	12/1989	102.7	12.1	9.30	6/1977	0.2	2.1	1/1985	89	60	10.0	99	7/1963	62
Waco	112	8/1969	-5	1/1949	108.5	35.2	7.18	5/1953	1.5	7.0	1/1949	83	57	11.3	69	6/1961	63
Wichita Falls	117	6-80	-8	2/1985	105.9	68.1	6.22	9/1980	6.0	8.1	1/1985	82	51	11.7	60	6/1954	68
§Shreveport, LA	107	8/1962	3	1/1962	89.4	37.3	7.17	4/1953	1.3	5.6	1/1982	87	58	8.4	52	4/1975	63

*100 mph recorded at 6:15 p.m. Sept. 8 just before the anemometer blew away. Maximum velocity was estimated to be 120 mph from the northeast between 7:30 p.m. and 8:30 p.m.

†The official Houston station was moved from near downtown to Intercontinental Airport, located 12 miles north of the old station.

‡ Also recorded on earlier dates, months or years.

§This station is included because it is near the boundary line and its data can be considered representative of the eastern border of Texas.

**Trace, an amount too small to measure.

Mexico; lower Texas coast affected.

Oct. 12-13, 1880: Hurricane. Brownsville. City nearly destroyed, many lives lost.

Aug. 23-24, 1882: Torrential rains caused **flooding** on the **North and South Concho and Bosque rivers** (South Concho reported 45 feet above normal level), destroying **Benficklen**, then county seat of Tom Green County, leaving only the courthouse and the jail. More than 50 persons were reported drowned in **Tom Green and Erath counties**, with property damage at $200,000 and 10,000 to 15,000 head of livestock lost.

Aug. 19-21, 1886: Hurricane. Indianola. Every house destroyed or damaged. Indianola never rebuilt.

Oct. 12, 1886: Hurricane. Sabine, Jefferson County. Hurricane passed over Sabine. The inundation extended 20 miles inland and nearly every house in the vicinity was moved from its foundation; 150 persons were drowned.

April 28, 1893: Tornado. Cisco, Eastland County; 23 killed, 93 injured; damage $400,000.

May 15, 1896: Tornadoes, Sherman, Grayson County; **Justin**, Denton County; **Gribble Springs**, Cooke County; 76 killed; damage $225,000.

Sept. 12, 1897: Hurricane. Many houses in **Port Arthur** were demolished; 13 killed, damage $150,000.

May 1, 1898: Tornado. Mobeetie, Wheeler County. Four killed, several injured; damage $35,000.

June 27-July 1, 1899: Rainstorm. A storm, centered over the **Brazos River watershed**, precipitated an average of 17 inches over an area of 7,000 square miles. At **Hearne** the gage overflowed at 24 inches, and there was an estimated total rainfall of 30 inches. At **Turnersville**, Coryell County, 33 inches were recorded in three days. This rain caused the **worst Brazos River flood on record**. Between 30 and 35 lives were lost. Property damage was estimated at $9 million.

April 5-8, 1900: Rainstorm. This storm began in two centers, over **Val Verde County** on the Rio Grande, and over **Swisher County** on the High Plains, and converged in the vicinity of **Travis County**, causing disastrous floods in the **Colorado, Brazos and Guadalupe rivers**. McDonald Dam on the Colorado River at Austin crumbled suddenly. A wall of water swept through the city taking at least 23 lives. Damage was estimated at $1,250,000.

Sept. 8-9, 1900: Hurricane. Galveston. The Great Galveston Storm was the **worst natural disaster in U.S. history** in terms of human life. Loss of life at Galveston has been estimated at 6,000 to 8,000, but the exact number has never been exactly determined. The island was completely inundated; not a single structure escaped damage. Most of the loss of life was due to drowning by storm tides that reached 15 feet or more. The anemometer blew away when the wind reached 100 miles per hour at 6:15 p.m. on the 8th. Wind reached an estimated maximum velocity of 120 miles per hour between 7:30 and 8:30 p.m. Property damage has been estimated at $30 to $40 million.

May 18, 1902: Tornado. Goliad. This tornado cut a 250-year-wide path straight through town, turning 150 buildings into rubble. Several churches were destroyed, one of which was holding services; all 40 worshippers were either killed or injured. This tornado killed 114, injured 230, and caused an estimated $200,000 in damages.

April 26, 1906: Tornado. Bellevue, Clay County, demolished; considerable damage done at **Stoneburg**, seven miles east; 17 killed, 20 injured; damage $300,000.

May 6, 1907: Tornado. North of Sulphur Springs, Hopkins County; five killed, 19 injured.

May 13, 1908: Tornado. Linden, Cass County. Four killed, seven injured; damage $75,000.

May 22-25, 1908: Rainstorm; unique because it originated on the Pacific Coast. It moved first into **North Texas** and southern Oklahoma and thence to **Central Texas**, precipitating as much as 10 inches. Heaviest floods were in the upper Trinity basin, but flooding was general as far south as the Nueces. Property damage exceeded $5 million and 11 lives were lost in the Dallas vicinity.

March 23, 1909: Tornado. Slidell, Wise County; 11 killed, 10 injured; damage $30,000.

May 30, 1909: Tornado. Zephyr, Brown County; 28 killed, many injured; damage $90,000.

July 21, 1909: Hurricane. Velasco, Brazoria County. One-half of town destroyed, 41 lives lost; damage $2,000,000.

Dec. 1-5, 1913: Rainstorm. This caused the **second major Brazos River flood**, and caused more deaths than the storm of 1899. It formed over **Central Texas** and spread both southwest and northeast with precipitation of 15 inches at **San Marcos** and 11 inches at **Kaufman**. Floods caused loss of 177

Texas Annual Average Precipitation, 1888-1998

Year	Inches	Year	Inches
1888	38.61	1944	33.38
1889	34.52	1945	29.37
1890	31.52	1946	33.25
1891	27.49	1947	23.73
1892	26.91	1948	20.70
1893	18.66	1949	34.09
1894	25.37	1950	24.98
1895	30.12	1951	20.74
1896	24.94	1952	22.41
1897	24.94	1953	23.64
1898	25.97	1954	18.01
1899	26.34	1955	22.75
1900	38.54	1956	15.52
1901	20.31	1957	37.01
1902	30.83	1958	30.78
1903	30.16	1959	30.33
1904	27.65	1960	31.90
1905	37.89	1961	28.90
1906	28.90	1962	24.32
1907	30.87	1963	19.75
1908	30.10	1964	23.75
1909	21.50	1965	26.82
1910	19.59	1966	26.93
1911	26.47	1967	25.47
1912	23.89	1968	33.20
1913	32.85	1969	29.82
1914	34.66	1970	23.87
1915	29.33	1971	28.39
1916	22.51	1972	27.06
*1917	14.80	1973	35.44
1918	26.28	1974	32.27
1919	41.95	1975	27.30
1920	31.39	1976	30.71
1921	26.19	1977	22.75
1922	29.88	1978	25.87
1923	36.63	1979	31.39
1924	21.36	1980	24.45
1925	23.66	1981	32.69
1926	33.06	1982	26.97
1927	25.41	1983	25.85
1928	26.54	1984	26.19
1929	28.34	1985	30.05
1930	27.12	1986	34.14
1931	27.43	1987	30.56
1932	32.69	1988	21.13
1933	23.11	1989	25.59
1934	23.04	1990	31.77
1935	34.58	1991	37.94
1936	28.57	1992	34.16
1937	25.16	1993	27.60
1938	24.98	1994	29.65
1939	23.24	1995	27.62
1940	32.09	1996	24.71
**1941	40.94	1997	34.90
1942	30.35	1998	28.52
1943	32.41		

111-year average: 28.14"
*Driest year
** Wettest year
Source: Office of the State Climatologist

lives and $8,541,000 damage.

April 20-26, 1915: Rainstorm. Originated over Central Texas and spread into North and East Texas with precipitation up to 17 inches, causing floods in **Trinity, Brazos, Colorado, and Guadalupe rivers.** More than 40 lives lost and $2,330,000 damage.

Aug. 16-19, 1915: Hurricane. Galveston. Peak wind gusts of 120 miles recorded at Galveston; tide ranged 9.5 to 14.3 feet above mean sea level in the city, and up to 16.1 feet near the causeway. Business section flooded with 5 to 6 feet of water. At least 275 lives lost, damage $56 million. A new seawall prevented a repetition of the 1900 disaster.

Aug. 18, 1916: Hurricane. Corpus Christi. Maximum wind speed 100 miles per hour. 20 Lives lost; damage $1,600,000.

Jan. 10-12, 1918: Blizzard. This was the most severe since that of February, 1899; it was accompanied by zero degree temperature in **North Texas** and temperatures from 7 to 12 below freezing along the **lower coast.**

April 9, 1919: Tornado. Leonard, Ector and Ravenna in Fannin County; 20 killed, 45 injured; damage $125,000.

April 9, 1919: Tornado. Henderson, Van Zandt, Wood, Camp, and Red River counties, 42 killed, 150 injured; damage $450,000.

May 7, 1919: Windstorms. Starr, Hidalgo, Willacy and Cameron counties. Violent thunderstorms with high winds, hail and rain occurred near **Rio Grande City** and the coast, killing 10 persons. Damage to property and crops was $500,000. Seven were killed at **Mission.**

Sept. 14, 1919: Hurricane. Near **Corpus Christi.** Center moved inland south of Corpus Christi; tides 16 feet above normal in that area and 8.8 feet above normal at **Galveston.** Extreme wind at Corpus Christi measured at 110 miles per hour;

284 lives lost; damage $20,272,000.

April 13, 1921: Tornado. Melissa, Collin County, and **Petty,** Lamar County. Melissa was practically destroyed; 12 killed, 80 injured; damage $500,000.

April 15, 1921: Tornado. Wood, Cass and Bowie counties; 10 killed, 50 injured; damage $85,000.

Sept. 8-10, 1921: Rainstorm. Probably the **greatest rainstorm in Texas history,** it entered Mexico as a hurricane from the Gulf. Torrential rains fell as the storm moved northeasterly across Texas. **Record floods** occurred in **Bexar, Travis, Williamson, Bell and Milam counties,** killing 215 persons, with property losses over $19 million. Five to nine feet of water stood in downtown **San Antonio.** A total of 23.98 inches was measured at the U.S. Weather Bureau station at **Taylor** during a period of 35 hours, with a 24-hour maximum of 23.11 on September 9-10. The **greatest rainfall recorded in United States history during 18 consecutive hours fell at Thrall,** Williamson County, 36.40 inches fell on Sept. 9.

April 8, 1922: Tornado. Rowena, Runnels County. Seven killed, 52 injured; damage $55,000.

April 8, 1922: Tornado. Oplin, Callahan County. Five killed, 30 injured; damage $15,000.

April 23-28, 1922: Rainstorm. An exceptional storm that entered Texas from the west and moved from the **Panhandle** to **North Central and East Texas.** Rains up to 12.6 inches over Parker, Tarrant, and Dallas counties caused severe floods in the Upper Trinity at **Fort Worth;** 11 lives were lost; damage was estimated at $1 million.

May 4, 1922: Tornado. Austin, Travis County; 12 killed, 50 injured; damage $500,000.

Texas is Tornado Capital

An **average of 139 tornadoes** have touched Texas soil each year during the 40-year period 1959-1998. The annual total varies considerably, and certain areas are struck more often than others. Tornadoes occur with **greatest frequency** in the Red River Valley.

Tornadoes may occur in any month and at any hour of the day, but they occur with greatest frequency during the late spring and early summer months, and between the hours of 4:00 p.m. and 8:00 p.m. In the period 1959-1998, nearly 64 percent of all Texas tornadoes occurred within the three-month period of April, May and June. Nearly one-third of the total occurred in May.

Partly because of the state's size, **more tornadoes have been recorded in Texas than in any other state.** Between 1959 and 1998, 5,569 funnel clouds reached the ground, thus becoming tornadoes. In the density of tornadoes, Texas ranks eleventh among the 50 states, with an average of 5.2 tornadoes per 10,000 square miles per year during this period.

The **greatest outbreak of tornadoes on record in Texas** was associated with Hurricane Beulah in September 1967. Within a five-day period, Sept. 19-23, 115 known tornadoes, all in Texas, were spawned by this great hurricane. Sixty-seven occurred on Sept. 20, a **Texas record for a single day.**

In September 1967, Hurricane Beulah produced 124 tornadoes, a **Texas record for a single month.** The **greatest number in Texas in a single year** was 232, also in 1967. The second-highest number in a single year was in 1995, when 223 tornadoes occurred in Texas. In 1982, 123 tornadoes occurred in May, making it the **worst outbreak of spring tornadoes** in Texas.

The table at right, compiled by Environmental Data Service, National Oceanic and Atmospheric Administration, lists tornado occurrences in Texas, by months, for the period 1959-1998.

Number of Tornadoes In Texas, 1959-1998

Source: Office of State Climatologist

Year	Jan.	Feb.	March	April	May	June	July	Aug.	Sept.	Oct.	Nov.	Dec.	Annual
1959	0	0	8	4	32	14	10	3	4	5	6	0	86
1960	4	1	0	8	29	14	3	4	2	11	1	0	77
1961	0	1	21	15	24	30	9	2	12	0	10	0	124
1962	0	4	12	9	25	56	12	15	7	2	0	1	143
1963	0	0	3	9	19	24	8	4	6	4	5	0	82
1964	0	1	6	12	15	11	9	7	3	1	3	0	78
1965	2	5	3	7	43	24	2	9	4	6	0	3	108
1966	0	4	1	21	22	15	3	8	3	0	0	0	77
1967	0	2	11	17	34	22	10	5	124	2	0	5	232
1968	2	1	3	13	47	21	4	8	5	8	11	16	139
1969	0	1	1	16	65	16	6	7	6	8	1	0	127
1970	1	3	5	23	23	9	5	20	9	20	0	3	121
1971	0	20	10	24	27	33	7	20	7	16	4	23	191
1972	1	0	19	13	43	12	19	13	8	9	7	0	144
1973	14	1	29	25	21	24	4	8	5	3	9	4	147
1974	2	1	8	19	18	26	3	9	6	22	2	0	116
1975	5	2	9	12	50	18	10	3	3	3	1	1	117
1976	1	1	8	53	63	11	16	6	13	4	0	0	176
1977	0	0	3	34	50	4	5	5	12	0	6	4	123
1978	0	0	0	34	65	10	13	6	6	1	2	0	137
1979	1	2	24	33	39	14	12	10	4	15	3	0	157
1980	0	2	7	26	44	21	2	34	10	5	0	2	153
1981	0	7	7	9	71	26	5	20	5	23	3	0	176
1982	0	0	6	27	123	36	4	0	3	0	3	1	203
1983	5	7	24	1	62	35	4	22	5	0	7	14	186
1984	0	13	9	18	19	19	0	4	1	5	2	5	95
1985	0	0	5	41	28	5	3	1	1	3	1	2	90
1986	0	12	4	21	50	24	3	5	4	7	1	0	131
1987	1	1	7	0	54	19	11	3	8	0	16	4	124
1988	0	0	0	11	7	7	6	2	42	4	10	0	89
1989	3	0	5	3	70	63	0	6	3	6	1	0	160
1990	3	3	4	56	62	20	5	2	3	0	0	0	158
1991	20	5	2	39	72	36	1	2	3	8	4	0	192
1992	0	5	13	22	43	66	4	4	4	7	21	0	189
1993	1	4	5	17	39	4	4	0	12	23	8	0	117
1994	0	1	1	48	88	2	1	4	3	9	8	0	165
1995	6	0	13	36	66	75	11	3	2	1	0	10	223
1996	7	1	2	21	33	9	3	8	33	8	4	1	130
1997	0	6	7	31	59	50	2	2	1	16	3	0	177
1998	24	15	4	9	11	6	3	5	3	28	1	0	109
Total	103	132	309	847	1,755	931	242	299	395	293	164	99	5,569

May 14, 1923: Tornado. Howard and Mitchell counties; 23 killed, 100 injured; damage $50,000.

April 12, 1927: Tornado. Edwards, Real and Uvalde counties; 74 killed, 205 injured; damage $1,230,000. Most of damage was in **Rocksprings** where 72 deaths occurred and town was practically destroyed.

May 9, 1927: Tornado. **Garland**; eleven killed; damage

Texas Droughts, 1892-1998

The following tables show the **duration and extent of Texas droughts by climatic division, 1892-1998**. For this purpose, droughts are arbitrarily defined as when the division has less than 75 percent of the 1931-1960 average precipitation. The 1931-1960 average precipitation in inches is shown at the bottom of the table for each division. The short table at bottom right shows the frequency of droughts in each area and the total years of droughts in the area.

Year	High Plains	Low Rolling Plains	North Central	East Texas	Trans-Pecos	Edwards Plateau	South Central	Upper Coast	Southern	Lower Valley
1892	...	...	...	...	68	...	...	73	...	...
1893	...	...	67	70	...	49	56	64	53	59
1894	...	...	...	68	...	...	...	...	...	...
1897	...	...	...	...	...	73	...	72	...	...
1898	...	...	...	...	...	...	...	69	...	51
1901	...	71	70	...	...	60	62	70	44	...
1902	...	...	...	...	...	...	...	65	...	73
1907	...	...	...	...	...	...	...	...	...	65
1909	...	...	72	68	67	74	70	...	...	...
1910	59	59	64	69	43	65	69	74	59	...
1911	...	...	...	...	...	...	...	...	...	70
1916	...	73	...	74	70	...	73	69	...	...
1917	58	50	63	59	44	46	42	50	32	48
1920	...	...	...	...	...	...	...	...	...	71
1921	...	...	...	...	...	72	...	...	...	73
1922	...	...	...	...	68	...	...	...	...	...
1924	...	...	73	73	...	71	...	72	...	...
1925	...	...	72	...	...	...	...	72	...	...
1927	...	...	...	...	...	...	...	74	...	74
1933	72	...	...	...	62	68	...	...	...	...
1934	66	...	...	...	46	69	...	...	...	...
1937	...	...	...	...	...	...	...	72	...	...
1939	...	...	...	...	...	69	...	...	...	72
1943	...	...	72	...	...	...	...	...	...	...
1948	...	...	73	74	62	...	71	67	...	...
1950	...	...	...	...	...	...	68	...	74	64
1951	...	...	...	...	61	53	...	...	...	...
1952	68	66	...	...	73	...	...	...	56	70
1953	69	...	...	...	49	73	...	...	...	...
1954	70	71	68	73	...	50	50	57	71	...
1956	51	57	61	68	44	43	55	62	53	53
1962	...	...	...	...	...	68	...	...	67	65
1963	...	...	63	68	...	65	61	73	...	...
1964	74	...	...	69	...	...	...	...	...	63
1970	65	63	...	...	...	72	...	...	...	...
1988	...	...	...	...	...	67	62	67	68	...
1989	...	...	...	...	...	72	...	...	66	64
1990	...	...	...	...	...	...	...	...	...	73
1994	...	...	...	...	68	...	...	...	...	...
1996	...	...	...	...	...	...	71	...	60	70
1998	...	69	...	...	71	...	...	...	...	...

Normal Annual Rainfall by Region

Listed below is the normal annual rainfall in inches for four 30-year periods in each geographical division. The normals for each division are given in the same order as the divisions which appear in the table above.

Period	Normal Rainfall in Inches									
	High Plains	Low Rolling Plains	North Central	East Texas	Trans-Pecos	Edwards Plateau	South Central	Upper Coast	Southern	Lower Valley
1931-1960	18.51	22.99	32.93	45.96	12.03	25.91	33.24	46.19	22.33	24.27
1941-1970	18.59	23.18	32.94	45.37	11.57	23.94	33.03	46.43	21.95	23.44
1951-1980	17.73	22.80	32.14	44.65	11.65	23.52	34.03	45.93	22.91	24.73
1961-1990	18.88	23.77	33.99	45.67	13.01	24.00	34.49	47.63	23.47	25.31

$100,000.

May 9, 1927: Tornado. **Nevada**, Collin County; **Wolfe City**, Hunt County; and **Tigertown**, Lamar County; 28 killed, over 200 injured; damage $900,000.

Jan. 4, 1929: Tornado. Near **Bay City**, Matagorda County. Five killed, 14 injured.

April 24, 1929: Tornado. **Slocum**, Anderson County; seven killed, 20 injured; damage $200,000.

May 24-31, 1929: Rainstorm. Beginning over **Caldwell County**, a storm spread over much of **Central and Coastal Texas** with maximum rainfall of 12.9 inches, causing **floods in Colorado, Guadalupe, Brazos, Trinity, Neches and Sabine rivers**. Much damage at **Houston** from overflow of bayous. Damage estimated at $6 million.

May 6, 1930: Tornado. **Bynum, Irene and Mertens** in Hill County; **Ennis**, Ellis County; and **Frost**, Navarro County; 41 killed; damage $2,100,000.

May 6, 1930: Tornado. **Kenedy and Runge** in Karnes County; **Nordheim**, DeWitt County; 36 killed, 34 injured; damage $127,000.

June 30-July 2, 1932: Rainstorm. Torrential rains fell over the upper watersheds of the **Nueces and Guadalupe rivers**, causing destructive floods. Seven persons drowned; property losses exceeded $500,000.

Aug. 13, 1932: Hurricane. Near **Freeport**, Brazoria County. Wind speed at **East Columbia** estimated at 100 miles per hour; 40 lives lost, 200 injured; damage $7,500,000.

March 30, 1933: Tornado. **Angelina, Nacogdoches and San Augustine counties**; 10 killed, 56 injured; damage $200,000.

April 26, 1933: Tornado. **Bowie County** near Texarkana. Five killed, 38 injured; damage $14,000.

July 22-25, 1933: Tropical Storm. One of the greatest U.S. storms in area and general rainfall. The storm reached the vicinity of **Freeport** late on July 22 and moved very slowly overland across eastern Texas, July 22-25. The storm center moved into northern Louisiana on the 25th. Rainfall averaged 12.50 inches over an area of about 25,000 square miles. Twenty inches or more fell in a small area of eastern Texas and western Louisiana surrounding Logansport, La. The 4-day total at Logansport was 22.30 inches. Property damage was estimated at $1,114,790.

July 30, 1933: Tornado. **Oak Cliff section of Dallas**, Dallas County. Five killed, 30 injured; damage $500,000.

Sept. 4-5, 1933: Hurricane. Near **Brownsville**. Center passed inland a short distance north of Brownsville, where an extreme wind of 106 miles per hour was measured before the anemometer blew away. Peak wind gusts were estimated at 120 to 125 miles per hour. 40 known dead, 500 injured; damage $16,903,100. About 90 percent of the citrus crop in the **Lower Rio Grande Valley** was destroyed.

July 25, 1934: Hurricane. Near **Seadrift**, Calhoun County, 19 lives lost, many minor injuries; damage $4.5 million. About 85 percent of damage was in crops.

Sept. 15-18, 1936: Rainstorm. Excessive rains over the **North Concho and Middle Concho rivers** caused a sharp rise

Drought Frequency

This table shows the number of years of drought and the number of separate droughts. For example, the **High Plains** has had 10 drought years, consisting of five 1-year droughts, one 2-year drought and one 3-year drought, a total of 7 droughts.

Years	High Plains	Low Rolling Plains	North Central	East Texas	Trans-Pecos	Edwards Plateau	South Central	Upper Coast	Southern	Lower Valley
1	5	7	8	6	7	7	12	9	10	14
2	1	1	2	2	4	5	2	2	3	2
3	1	...	...	...	1	...	...	...	...	...
Total Droughts	7	8	10	8	12	12	14	11	13	14
Dr'ght Yrs.	10	9	12	10	18	17	16	13	16	18

in the Concho River, which overflowed **San Angelo**. Much of the business district and 500 homes were flooded. Four persons drowned and property losses estimated at $5 million. Four-day storm rainfall at San Angelo measured 25.19 inches, of which 11.75 inches fell on the 15th.

June 10, 1938: Tornado. Clyde, Callahan County; 14 killed, 9 injured; damage $85,000.

Sept. 23, 1941: Hurricane. Near **Matagorda**. Center moved inland near Matagorda, and passed over **Houston** about midnight. Extremely high tides along coast in the **Matagorda to Galveston** area. Heaviest property and crop losses were in counties from Matagorda County to the Sabine River. Four lives lost. Damage was $6,503,300.

April 28, 1942: Tornado. Crowell, Foard County; 11 killed, 250 injured; damage $1,500,000.

Aug. 30, 1942: Hurricane. Matagorda Bay. Highest wind estimated 115 miles per hour at **Seadrift**. Tide at **Matagorda**,14.7 feet. Storm moved west-north-westward and finally diminished over the **Edwards Plateau**; eight lives lost, property damage estimated at $11.5 million, and crop damage estimated at $15 million.

May 10, 1943: Tornado. Laird Hill, Rusk County, and **Kilgore**, Gregg County. Four killed, 25 injured; damage $1 million.

July 27, 1943: Hurricane. Near **Galveston**. Center moved inland across **Bolivar Peninsula and Trinity Bay.** A wind gust of 104 miles per hour was recorded at **Texas City**; 19 lives lost; damage estimated at $16,550,000.

Aug. 26-27, 1945: Hurricane. Aransas-San Antonio Bay area. At **Port O'Connor**, the wind reached 105 miles per hour when the cups were torn from the anemometer. Peak gusts of 135 miles per hour were estimated at Seadrift, Port O'Connor and Port Lavaca; three killed, 25 injured; damage $20,133,000.

Jan. 4, 1946: Tornado. Near **Lufkin**, Angelina County and **Nacogdoches**, Nacogdoches County; 13 killed, 250 injured; damage $2,050,000.

Jan. 4, 1946: Tornado. Near **Palestine**, Anderson County; 15 killed, 60 injured; damage $500,000.

May 18, 1946: Tornado. Clay, Montague and Denton counties. Four killed, damage $112,000.

April 9, 1947: Tornado. White Deer, Carson County; **Glazier**, Hemphill County; and **Higgins**, Lipscomb County; 68 killed, 201 injured; damage $1,550,000. Glazier completely destroyed. **One of the largest tornadoes on record.** Width of path, 1 miles at Higgins; length of path, 221 miles across portions of Texas, Oklahoma and Kansas. This tornado also struck

Woodward, Okla.

May 3, 1948: Tornado. McKinney, Collin County; three killed, 43 injured; $2 million damage.

May 15, 1949: Tornado. Amarillo and vicinity; six killed, 83 injured. Total damage from tornado, wind and hail, $5,310,000. Total destruction over one-block by three-block area in southern part of city; airport and 45 airplanes damaged; 28 railroad boxcars blown off track.

Sept. 8-10, 1952: Rainstorm. Heavy rains over the **Colorado and Guadalupe River watersheds** in southwestern Texas caused major flooding. From 23 to 26 inches fell between **Kerrville, Blanco and Boerne**. Highest stages ever known occurred in the **Pedernales River**; five lives lost, three injured; 17 homes destroyed, 454 damaged. Property loss several million dollars.

March 13, 1953: Tornado. Jud and O'Brien, Haskell County; and **Knox City**, Knox County; 17 killed, 25 injured; damage $600,000.

May 11, 1953: Tornado. Near **San Angelo**, Tom Green County; eleven killed, 159 injured; damage $3,239,000.

May 11, 1953: Tornado. Waco, McLennan County; 114 killed, 597 injured; damage $41,150,000. **One of two most disastrous tornadoes;** 150 homes destroyed, 900 homes damaged; 185 other buildings destroyed; 500 other buildings damaged.

April 2, 1957: Tornado. Dallas, Dallas County; 10 killed, 200 injured; damage $4 million. Moving through Oak Cliff and West Dallas, it damaged 574 buildings, largely homes.

April-May, 1957: Torrential Rains. Excessive flooding occurred throughout the area **east of the Pecos River to the Sabine River** during the last 10 days of April; 17 lives were lost, and several hundred homes were destroyed. During May, more than 4,000 persons were evacuated from unprotected lowlands on the **West Fork of the Trinity above Fort Worth** and along creeks in Fort Worth. Twenty-nine houses at **Christoval** were damaged or destroyed and 83 houses and furnishings at San Angelo were damaged. Five persons were drowned in floods in **South Central Texas**.

May 15, 1957: Tornado. Silverton, Briscoe County; 21 killed, 80 injured; damage $500,000.

June 27, 1957: Hurricane Audrey. Center crossed the Gulf coast near the Texas-Louisiana line. **Orange** was in the western portion of the eye between 9 and 10 a.m. In Texas, nine lives were lost, 450 persons injured; property damage was $8 million. Damage was extensive in **Jefferson and Orange counties**, with less in **Chambers and Galveston counties**. Maximum wind reported in Texas, 85 m.p.h. at **Sabine Pass**,

Extreme Weather Records in Texas

NOAA Environmental Data Service lists the following recorded extremes of weather in Texas:

Temperature

Lowest - Tulia, February 12, 1899	-23°F
Seminole, February 8, 1933	-23°F
Highest - Seymour, August 12, 1936	120°F
Monahans, June 28, 1994	120°F
Coldest Winter	1898-1899

Snowfall

Greatest seasonal - Romero, 1923-1924	65.0 in.
Greatest monthly - Hale Center, Feb. 1956	36.0 in.
Greatest single storm - Hale Center, Feb. 2-5, 1956	33.0 in.
Greatest in 24 Hours - Plainview, Feb. 3-4, 1956	24.0 in.
Maximum depth on ground - Hale Center, Feb. 5, 1956	33.0 in.

Rainfall

Wettest year - entire state	1941...42.62 in.
Driest year - entire state	1917...14.30 in.
Greatest annual - Clarksville	1873..109.38 in.
Least annual - Wink	1956....1.76 in.
†Greatest in 24 hours - Thrall, Sept. 9-10 , 1921	38.20. in

†The greatest 24-hour rainfall ever recorded in Texas at an official observing site occurred at Albany, Shackelford County, on Aug. 4, 1978 - 29.05 inches.

Wind Velocity

Highest sustained wind (fastest mile)
*Matagorda - Sept. 11, 1961 ...... SE, 145 mph
*Port Lavaca - Sept. 11, 1961....... NE, 145 mph
Highest peak gust (instantaneous velocity)
*Aransas Pass - Aug. 3, 1970 .....SW, 180 mph
*Robstown - Aug. 3, 1970 (est.) .. WSW, 180 mph

*These velocities occurred during hurricanes. Theoretically, much higher velocities are possible within the vortex of a tor-

nado, but no measurement with an anemometer has ever been made. The U.S. Weather Bureau's experimental Doppler radar equipment, a device which permits direct measurement of the high speeds in a spinning tornado funnel, received its first big test in the Wichita Falls tornado of April 2, 1958. This was the first tornado tracked by the Doppler radar, and for the first time in history, rotating winds up to 280 mph were clocked.

with gusts to 100 m.p.h.

Oct. 28, 1960: Rainstorm. Rains of 7-10 inches fell in **South Central Texas**; 11 died from drowning in flash floods. In **Austin** about 300 families were driven from their homes. Damage in Austin was estimated at $2.5 million.

Sept. 8-14, 1961: Hurricane Carla. Port O'Connor; maximum wind gust at **Port Lavaca** estimated at 175 miles per hour. Highest tide was 18.5 feet at Port Lavaca. Most damage was to **coastal counties between Corpus Christi and Port Arthur** and inland **Jackson, Harris and Wharton counties.** In Texas, 34 persons died; seven in a **tornado** that swept across **Galveston Island**; 465 persons were injured. Property and crop damage conservatively estimated at $300 million. The evacuation of an estimated 250,000 persons kept loss of life low. **Hurricane Carla was the largest hurricane of record.**

Sept. 7, 1962: Rainstorm. Fort Worth. Rains fell over the Big Fossil and Denton Creek watersheds ranging up to 11 inches of fall in three hours. Extensive damage from flash flooding occurred in **Richland Hills and Haltom City.**

Sept. 16-20, 1963: Hurricane Cindy. Rains of 15 to 23.5 inches fell in portions of **Jefferson, Newton and Orange counties** when Hurricane Cindy became stationary west of **Port Arthur.** Flooding from the excessive rainfall resulted in total property damage of $11,600,000 and agricultural losses of $500,000.

April 3, 1964: Tornado. Wichita Falls. Seven killed, 111 injured; damage $15 million; 225 homes destroyed, 50 with major damage, and 200 with minor damage. Sixteen other buildings received major damage.

Sept. 21-23, 1964: Rainstorm. Collin, Dallas and Tarrant counties. Rains of more than 12 inches fell during the first eight hours of the 21st. Flash flooding of tributaries of the Trinity River and smaller creeks and streams resulted in two drownings and an estimated $3 million property damage. Flooding of homes occurred in all sections of **McKinney.** In **Fort Worth**, there was considerable damage to residences along Big Fossil and White Rock creeks. Expensive homes in **North Dallas** were heavily damaged.

Jan. 25, 1965: Dust Storm. West Texas. The worst dust storm since February 1956 developed on the **southern High Plains.** Winds, gusting up to 75 miles per hour at **Lubbock**, sent dust billowing to 31,000 feet in the area **from the Texas-New Mexico border eastward to a line from Tulia to Abilene.** Ground visibility was reduced to about 100 yards in many sections. The worst hit was the **Muleshoe, Seminole, Plains, Morton** area on the South Plains. The rain gage at Reese Air Force Base, Lubbock, contained 3 inches of fine sand.

June 2, 1965: Tornado. Hale Center, Hale County. Four killed, 76 injured; damage $8 million.

June 11, 1965: Rainstorm. Sanderson, Terrell County. Torrential rains of up to eight inches in two hours near Sanderson caused a major flash flood that swept through the town. As a result, 26 persons drowned and property losses were estimated at $2,715,000.

April 22-29, 1966: Flooding. Northeast Texas. Twenty to 26 inches of rain fell in portions of Wood, Smith, Morris, Upshur, Gregg, Marion and Harrison counties. Nineteen persons drowned in the rampaging rivers and creeks that swept away bridges, roads and dams, and caused an estimated $12 million damage.

April 28, 1966: Flash flooding. Dallas County. Flash flooding from torrential rains in Dallas County resulted in 14 persons drowned and property losses estimated at $15 million.

Sept. 18-23, 1967: Hurricane Beulah. Near **Brownsville.** The **third largest hurricane of record**, Hurricane Beulah moved inland near the mouth of the Rio Grande on the 20th. Wind gusts of 136 miles per hour were reported during Beulah's passage. Rains 10 to 20 inches over much of the area **south of San Antonio** resulted in record-breaking floods. An unofficial gaging station at Falfurrias registered the highest accumulated rainfall, 36 inches. The resultant stream overflow and surface runoff inundated 1.4 million acres. Beulah spawned 115 tornadoes, all in Texas, the **greatest number of tornadoes on record for any hurricane.** Hurricane Beulah caused 13 deaths and 37 injuries, of which five deaths and 34 injuries were attrib-

uted to tornadoes. Property losses were estimated at $100 million and crop losses at $50 million.

April 18, 1970: Tornado. Near **Clarendon**, Donley County. Seventeen killed, 42 injured; damage $2,100,000. Fourteen persons were killed at a resort community at Green Belt Reservoir, 7 miles north of Clarendon.

May 11, 1970: Tornado. Lubbock, Lubbock County. Twenty-six killed, 500 injured; damage $135 million. Fifteen square miles, almost one-quarter of the city of Lubbock, suffered damage.

Aug. 3-5, 1970: Hurricane Celia. Corpus Christi. Hurricane Celia was a unique but severe storm. Measured in dollars, it was **the costliest in the state's history to that time.** Sustained wind speeds reached 130 miles per hour, but it was great bursts of kinetic energy of short duration that appeared to cause the severe damage. Wind gusts of 161 miles per hour were measured at the **Corpus Christi** National Weather Service Office. At **Aransas Pass**, peak wind gusts were estimated as high as 180 miles per hour, after the wind equipment had been blown away. Celia caused 11 deaths in Texas, at least 466 injuries, and total property and crop damage in Texas estimated at $453,773,000. Hurricane Celia crossed the Texas coastline midway between Corpus Christi and Aransas Pass about 3:30 p.m. CST on Aug. 3. Hardest hit was the metropolitan area of **Corpus Christi**, including **Robstown, Aransas Pass, Port Aransas** and small towns on the north side of Corpus Christi Bay.

Feb. 20-22, 1971: Blizzard. Panhandle. Paralyzing blizzard, worst since March 22-25, 1957, storm transformed Panhandle into one vast snowfield as six to 26 inches of snow were whipped by 40 to 60 miles per hour winds in drifts up to 12 feet high. At **Follett**, three-day snowfall was 26 inches. Three persons killed; property and livestock losses were $3.1 million.

Sept. 9-13, 1971: Hurricane Fern. Coastal Bend. Ten to 26 inches of rain resulted in some of worst flooding since Hurricane Beulah in 1967. Two persons killed; losses were $30,231,000.

May 11-12, 1972: Rainstorm. South Central Texas. Seventeen drowned at **New Braunfels**, one at **McQueeney.** New Braunfels and **Seguin** hardest hit. Property damage $17.5 million.

June 12-13, 1973: Rainstorm. Southeastern Texas. Ten drowned. Over $50 million in property and crop damage. From 10-15 inches of rain recorded.

Nov. 23-24, 1974: Flash Flooding. Central Texas. Over $1 million in property damage. Thirteen people killed, ten in **Travis County.**

Jan. 31-Feb. 1, 1975: Flooding. Nacogdoches County. Widespread heavy rain caused flash flooding here, resulting in three deaths; damage over $5.5 million.

May 23, 1975: Rainstorm. Austin area. Heavy rains, high winds and hail resulted in over $5 million property damage; 40 people injured. Four deaths were caused by drowning.

June 15, 1976: Rainstorm. Harris County. Rains in excess of 13 inches caused damage estimated at near $25 million. Eight deaths were storm-related, including three drownings.

Aug. 1-4, 1978: Heavy Rains, Flooding. Edwards Plateau, Low Rolling Plains. Remnants of **Tropical Storm Amelia** caused some of the worst flooding of this century. As much as 30 inches of rain fell near **Albany** in Shackelford County, where six drownings were reported. **Bandera, Kerr, Kendall and Gillespie counties** were hit hard, as 27 people drowned and the damage total was at least $50 million.

Dec. 30-31, 1978: Ice Storm. North Central Texas. Possibly the **worst ice storm in 30 years** hit Dallas County particularly hard. Damage estimates reached $14 million, and six deaths were storm-related.

April 10, 1979: The worst single tornado in Texas' history hit **Wichita Falls.** Earlier on the same day, **several tornadoes** hit farther west. The destruction in Wichita Falls resulted in 42 dead, 1,740 injured, over 3,000 homes destroyed and damage of approximately $400 million. An estimated 20,000 persons were left homeless by this storm. In all, the tornadoes on April 10 killed 53 people, injured 1,812 and caused over $500 million damages.

May 3, 1979: Thunderstorms. Dallas County was hit by a wave of the most destructive thunderstorms in many years; 37 injuries and $5 million in damages resulted.

July 24-25, 1979: Tropical storm Claudette caused over $750 million in property and crop damages, but fortunately only few injuries. Near **Alvin**, 43 inches of rain fell, a new state record for 24 hours.

Aug. 24, 1979: One of the worst **hailstorms** in **West Texas** in the past 100 years; $200 million in crops, mostly cotton, destroyed.

Sept. 18-20, 1979: Coastal flooding from heavy rain, 18 inches in 24 hours at **Aransas Pass**, and 13 inches at **Rockport**.

Aug. 9-11, 1980: Hurricane Allen hit **South Texas** and left three dead, causing $650 million-$750 million in property and crop damages. Over 250,000 coastal residents had to be evacuated. The worst damage occurred along **Padre Island** and in **Corpus Christi**. Over 20 inches of rain fell in **extreme South Texas**, and 29 tornadoes occurred; one of the worst hurricane-related outbreaks.

Summer 1980: One of the hottest summers in Texas history.

Sept. 5-8, 1980: Hurricane Danielle brought **rain and flooding** to both **Southeast and Central Texas**. Seventeen inches of rain fell at **Port Arthur**, and 25 inches near **Junction**.

May 8, 1981: The most destructive thunderstorm ever in the United States occurred in **Tarrant, Dallas and surrounding counties. Hail** damage was estimated at $200 million.

May 24-25, 1981: Severe flooding in **Austin** claimed 13 lives, injured about 100 and caused $40 million in damages. Up to 5.5 inches of rain fell in one hour just west of the city.

Oct. 11-14, 1981: Record rains in North Central Texas caused by the remains of **Pacific Hurricane Norma**. Over 20 inches fell in some locations.

April 2, 1982: A tornado outbreak in Northeast Texas. The most severe tornado struck **Paris**; 10 people were killed, 170 injured and 1,000 left homeless. Over $50 million in damages resulted. A total of 7 tornadoes that day left 11 dead and 174 injured.

May 25, 1982: Golf ball-sized **hail** in **Monahans** did $8 million in damages.

May, 1982: Texas recorded **123 tornadoes**, the most ever in May, and one less than the most recorded in any single month in the state. One death and 23 injuries occurred.

Sept. 11, 1982: Tropical Storm Chris. The year's only tropical storm in Texas hit the coast near **Port Arthur** with 55 mph winds. Rainfall was minimal.

Dec. 24, 1982: Rains of up to 15 inches occurred in **Southeast Texas.**

Dec. 1982: Heavy snow. El Paso recorded 18.2 inches of snow, the most in any month there.

Aug. 15-21, 1983: Hurricane Alicia was the first hurricane to make landfall in the continental U.S. in three years (Aug. 18), and **one of the costliest in Texas history** ($3 billion). Alicia caused widespread damage to a large section of **Southeast Texas**, including coastal areas near **Galveston** and the entire **Houston** area. Alicia spawned 22 tornadoes, and highest winds were estimated near 130 mph. In all, 18 people in South Texas were killed and 1,800 injured as a result of the tropical storm.

Jan. 12-13, 1985: A record-breaking snowstorm struck **West and South Central Texas** with up to 15 inches of snow that fell at many locations **between San Antonio and the Rio Grande**. San Antonio recorded 13.2 inches of snow for Jan. 12 (the greatest in a day) and 13.5 inches for the two-day total. **Eagle Pass** reported 14.5 inches of snow.

June 26, 1986: Hurricane Bonnie made landfall between **High Island and Sabine Pass** around 3:45 a.m. The highest wind measured in the area was a gust to 97 m.p.h., which was recorded at the **Sea Rim State Park.** As much as 13 inches of rain fell in **Ace** in southern Polk County. There were several reports of funnel clouds, but no confirmed tornadoes. While the

storm caused no major structural damage, there was widespread minor damage. Numerous injuries were reported.

May 22, 1987: A strong, **multiple-vortex tornado** struck the town of **Saragosa** (Reeves Co.), essentially wiping it off the map. Of the town's 183 inhabitants, 30 were killed and 121 were injured. Eight-five percent of the town's structures were completely destroyed, while total damage topped $1.3 million.

Sept. 16-18, 1988: Hurricane Gilbert stuck 125 miles south of **Brownsville**, Cameron County, bringing tides of three to six feet above average, rainfalls of six inches to 10 inches and at least 29 tornadoes. Total damage associated with Gilbert in Texas was estimated at $3 million-$5 million. The only death attributed to the storm was a woman who was killed by a tornado spawned by remnants of Gilbert in the **San Antonio** area.

Dec. 18-31, 1991: Flooding, entire state. The month of December was one of the wettest in Texas since records began in 1888. Rainfall amounts, from the Hill Country into North Central Texas totaled 12 to 16 inches over the four-day period of Dec. 18-21. Eleven people died as a result of the flooding, and more than $50 million dollars in damages were incurred.

June 20-22, 1993: Tropical Storm Arlene made landfall 5 miles south of **Corpus Christi**; all of eastern Texas was inundated by the remains. **Henderson** (Rusk Co.) received 14,83 inches of rain, and widespread areas reported greater than 7 inches. One person was killed; damage, mostly as a result of tidal flooding, was estimated at $22 million.

October 15-19, 1994: Extreme amounts of rainfall, up to 28.90 inches over a 4-day period, fell throughout southeastern part of the state. Seventeen lives were lost, most of them victims of flash flooding. Many rivers reached record flood levels during this period. **Houston** was cut off from many other parts of the state, as numerous roads, including Interstate 10, were under water. Damage was estimated to be near $700 million; 26 counties were declared disaster areas.

May 5, 1995: A **thunderstorm** moved across the **Dallas/Fort Worth** area with 70 mph wind gusts and rainfall rates of almost three inches in 30 minutes (five inches in one hour). Twenty people lost their lives as a result of this storm, 109 people were injured by large hail and, with more than $2 billion in damage, the National Oceanic and Atmospheric Administration dubbed it the **"costliest thunderstorm event in history."**

May 28, 1995: A **supercell thunderstorm** produced extreme winds and giant hail in **San Angelo**, injuring at least 80 people and causing about $120 million in damage. Sixty-one homes were destroyed, and more than 9,000 were slightly damaged. In some areas, hail was six inches deep, with drifts to two feet.

February 21, 1996: Anomalously **high temperatures** were reported over the **entire state**, breaking records in nearly every region of the state. Temperatures near 100°F shattered previous records by as many as 10°F as Texans experienced heat more characteristic of mid-summer than winter.

May 10, 1996: Hail up to five inches in diameter fell in **Howard County**, causing injuries to 48 people and $30 million worth of property damage.

May 27, 1997: A half-mile-wide **F5 tornado** struck **Jarrell** (Williamson Co.), leveling the Double Creek subdivision, claiming 27 lives, injuring 12 others, and causing more than $40 million in damage.

March-May, 1998: According to the Climate Prediction Center, this three-month period ranks as the **seventh driest** for a region including Texas, Oklahoma, Arkansas, Louisiana and Mississippi. May 1998 has been ranked as both the **warmest and the driest May** that this region has ever seen.

August 22-25, 1998: Tropical Storm Charley brought torrential rains and flash floods to the Hill Country. Thirteen people lost their lives and more than 200 were injured.

October 17-19, 1998: A **massive and devastating flood** set all-time records for rainfall and river levels, resulted in the deaths of 25 people, injured more than 2,000 others, and caused more than $500 million damage from the **Hill Country to the counties surrounding San Antonio to the south and east.** ☆

Texas Temperature, Freeze, Growing Season and Precipitation Records by Counties

Data in the table below are from the office of the **State Climatologist for Texas**, College Station. Because of the small change in averages, data are revised only at intervals of 10 years. Data below are the latest compilations, as of Jan. 1, 1993. Table shows temperature, freeze, growing season and precipitation for each county in Texas. Data for counties where a National Weather Service Station has not been maintained long enough to establish a reliable mean are interpolated from isoline charts prepared from mean values from stations with long-established records. **Mean maximum temperature for July** is computed from the sum of the daily maxima. **Mean minimum January** is computed from the sum of the daily minima. For stations where precipitation "Length of Record" are designated with an "N," data are based on the 30-year normal period 1961-90. Stations which have a specified precipitation "Length of Record" are based on data mainly from the period 1931-1993.

County and Station	Temp Length of Record (Yr.)	July Mean Max. (F.)	January Mean Min. (F.)	Highest Record (F.)	Lowest Record (F.)	Freeze Last in Spring Mo.	Day	First in Fall Mo.	Day	Growing Season Days	Precip Length of Record (Yr.)	Jan	Feb	Mar	Apr	May	June	July	Aug	Sep	Oct	Nov	Dec	Annual
Anderson, Palestine	29	94	36	114	-6	Mar.	8	Nov.	27	264	29	3.1	3.2	3.9	3.9	4.8	4.5	2.3	2.3	3.6	4.4	3.9	3.6	43.3
Andrews, Andrews	N	94	29	113	0	Apr.	6	Nov.	5	213	29	0.4	0.5	0.6	0.9	1.6	2.0	2.5	1.9	2.5	1.5	0.6	0.6	15.4
Angelina, Lufkin	N	93	37	108	-2	Mar.	14	Nov.	13	244	N	3.7	2.8	3.2	3.3	4.9	2.6	2.6	2.4	4.0	3.5	3.1	2.3	38.9
Aransas, Rockport	N	91	44	103	9	Feb.	7	Dec.	16	312	N	2.7	2.4	1.4	2.1	4.2	4.7	3.2	3.1	6.2	4.0	2.1	2.7	36.9
Archer, Archer	27	98	29	114	-10	Mar.	31	Nov.	6	220	27	1.0	1.7	2.0	2.6	4.3	3.0	1.7	2.5	4.3	2.9	1.8	1.3	29.3
Armstrong, Claude	28	92	20	108	-7	Apr.	6	Nov.	5	213	N	0.4	0.6	1.1	1.1	3.0	3.7	2.9	3.1	2.4	1.7	0.8	0.4	21.2
Atascosa, Poteet	N	96	38	110	-1	Feb.	25	Dec.	2	282	N	1.4	1.7	1.2	2.5	4.0	3.2	1.8	2.6	3.6	2.9	1.8	1.4	28.0
Austin, Sealy	N	94	39	110	1	Feb.	27	Dec.	5	282	N	3.0	2.9	2.2	2.7	4.8	4.4	2.3	3.2	4.6	3.9	3.6	3.0	40.4
Bailey, Muleshoe	N	92	19	112	-21	Apr.	22	Oct.	20	181	N	0.4	0.5	0.6	0.9	1.9	2.6	2.9	3.2	2.2	1.4	0.8	0.5	16.8
Bandera, Medina*	15	94	31	109	5	Mar.	26	Nov.	16	235	15	1.7	1.8	1.7	3.3	4.5	2.9	2.8	4.7	4.5	3.7	2.3	1.2	35.1
Bastrop, Smithville	N	95	35	111	6	Mar.	7	Nov.	30	268	N	2.6	2.5	2.2	2.9	5.1	3.9	2.1	2.3	4.7	4.0	3.2	2.6	38.3
Baylor, Seymour	N	97	26	116	-14	Apr.	3	Nov.	3	214	N	0.9	1.5	1.6	2.2	3.6	3.4	2.4	2.4	4.1	2.7	1.3	1.2	27.3
Bee, Beeville	N	94	41	109	9	Feb.	22	Dec.	4	285	N	2.0	1.9	1.2	2.3	3.6	3.8	2.8	2.9	4.8	3.1	2.0	1.6	32.1
Bell, Temple	N	95	35	112	-4	Mar.	9	Nov.	24	260	N	1.9	2.7	2.5	2.5	4.2	3.6	2.0	2.3	3.8	3.3	2.9	1.6	34.9
Bexar, San Antonio	27	95	38	108	0	Mar.	6	Nov.	26	265	27	1.7	1.8	1.5	2.8	4.5	4.2	2.2	2.5	3.4	3.2	2.3	1.4	31.0
Blanco, Blanco	N	94	33	109	-6	Mar.	26	Nov.	15	234	N	1.8	1.5	0.4	2.2	4.2	3.8	2.2	2.3	3.9	3.2	2.3	2.0	34.2
Borden, Gail	N	94	31	113	-1	Apr.	6	Nov.	6	214	N	0.5	0.4	1.5	0.5	1.2	2.2	2.7	3.0	3.3	1.5	0.6	0.5	16.9
Bosque, Lake Whitney*	27	97	33	111	-3	Mar.	23	Nov.	21	243	27	1.9	2.4	1.5	4.1	4.4	3.5	1.6	2.3	3.2	2.7	2.8	2.0	31.6
Bowie, Texarkana*	18	93	35	101	-6	Mar.	21	Nov.	11	235	18	3.6	3.3	3.3	5.1	5.2	4.2	3.5	3.2	3.6	4.0	4.7	4.1	45.3
Brazoria, Angleton	N	92	41	105	10	Mar.	5	Nov.	28	268	N	4.5	3.5	2.6	5.1	4.8	6.3	5.2	5.1	7.3	4.0	4.7	4.1	56.4
Brazos, College Station	N	94	39	110	-3	Mar.	1	Nov.	30	274	N	2.7	2.6	2.6	3.4	4.8	3.7	2.3	2.4	4.9	3.8	3.2	2.8	39.1
Brewster, Alpine	N	89	30	106	-2	Apr.	1	Nov.	8	223	N	0.5	0.5	0.4	0.5	1.6	2.3	2.7	2.6	3.3	1.5	0.6	0.5	16.9
Brewster, Chisos Basin	N	85	30	103	-3	Mar.	31	Nov.	9	223	N	0.6	0.6	0.4	0.6	1.2	2.3	3.1	3.6	3.3	1.9	0.6	0.5	19.2
Briscoe, Silverton	29	91	20	109	-9	Apr.	7	Nov.	5	214	29	0.4	0.7	1.1	1.3	2.8	4.2	2.2	3.0	2.7	1.6	0.9	0.5	21.4
Brooks, Falfurrias	N	97	43	110	-6	Feb.	10	Dec.	10	303	N	1.3	1.6	0.5	0.7	2.6	3.4	2.2	2.5	4.9	2.7	1.2	1.1	25.9
Brown, Brownwood	N	97	37	111	-3	Mar.	22	Nov.	19	242	N	1.3	1.7	1.9	2.6	3.6	3.4	1.7	2.2	3.2	2.9	1.6	1.1	27.3
Burleson, Somerville*	16	94	32	105	-4	Mar.	1	Dec.	1	275	16	2.7	2.5	2.4	3.9	5.1	3.6	2.2	2.1	3.2	2.9	3.1	2.8	39.1
Burnet, Burnet	N	96	36	108	-3	Mar.	29	Nov.	14	230	N	1.7	2.0	1.9	3.0	4.8	3.4	1.9	2.0	4.9	3.5	3.4	2.1	31.2
Caldwell, Luling	N	96	36	110	11	Feb.	27	Nov.	29	275	N	2.2	2.2	2.0	3.0	4.8	4.4	1.7	2.2	4.4	3.5	3.1	1.9	35.3
Calhoun, Port O'Connor	N	90	46	110	11	Feb.	19	Dec.	16	300	N	3.1	2.7	1.6	1.7	4.0	3.7	3.7	3.3	6.1	3.5	3.1	2.4	39.4
Callahan, Putnam	27	96	32	107	-8	Mar.	28	Nov.	11	228	27	1.6	1.4	1.7	2.0	4.0	2.6	1.8	2.1	3.1	2.8	1.7	1.9	25.2
Cameron, Brownsville	N	93	50	106	16	Feb.	4	Dec.	4	341	N	1.6	1.1	0.5	1.6	3.0	2.7	1.8	2.8	6.0	2.8	1.5	1.3	26.6
Camp, Pittsburg*	27	94	32	109	-3	Mar.	19	Nov.	14	238	27	2.9	3.3	3.8	5.4	4.8	3.4	2.7	2.2	4.0	3.2	4.0	3.5	43.3
Carson, Panhandle	29	93	22	109	-10	Apr.	21	Oct.	25	191	29	0.5	0.8	1.1	1.3	2.6	3.7	2.3	3.1	2.3	1.7	0.9	0.5	20.8
Cass, Linden	22	93	31	103	8	Mar.	17	Nov.	11	237	22	3.3	3.9	4.9	5.0	4.5	4.8	2.9	2.8	3.2	3.6	4.9	4.5	48.3
Castro, Dimmitt	22	91	19	107	-8	Apr.	19	Oct.	25	193	22	0.4	0.6	0.8	0.8	2.3	3.0	2.3	2.8	2.4	1.5	0.7	0.5	18.0
Chambers, Anahuac	29	92	41	110	8	Mar.	6	Nov.	20	261	29	4.0	2.9	3.0	3.6	4.8	5.8	4.5	4.5	6.2	3.8	4.4	4.2	51.7

County and Station	Temp. Length of Record (Yr.)	Mean Max. July (F.)	Mean Min. January (F.)	Record Highest (F.)	Record Lowest (F.)	Last in Spring (Mo.)	Last in Spring (Day)	First in Fall (Mo.)	First in Fall (Day)	Growing Season (Days)	Precip. Length of Record (Yr.)	January (In.)	February (In.)	March (In.)	April (In.)	May (In.)	June (In.)	July (In.)	August (In.)	September (In.)	October (In.)	November (In.)	December (In.)	Annual (In.)
Cherokee, Rusk	N	93	35	107	7	Mar.	8	Nov.	21	258	N	3.7	3.5	3.6	4.1	4.0	5.1	4.0	2.9	2.2	2.2	4.2	4.2	46.1
Childress, Childress	N	96	26	117	-7	Apr.	3	Nov.	3	217	N	0.5	0.9	1.2	1.5	3.0	3.0	1.9	2.6	2.8	2.8	2.0	0.7	20.7
Clay, Henrietta	27	97	26	116	-8	Mar.	27	Nov.	14	232	N	1.3	2.0	2.5	3.0	4.3	3.9	2.6	3.3	4.2	3.1	1.7	1.7	31.9
Cochran, Morton	28	91	22	110	-12	Apr.	18	Oct.	24	189	N	0.4	0.6	0.6	0.9	1.8	2.7	2.4	2.0	3.0	1.7	0.5	0.5	18.6
Coke, Robert Lee	N	96	32	111	-2	Mar.	31	Nov.	11	226	N	0.8	1.2	1.1	1.8	3.3	2.8	2.0	2.5	3.8	2.8	1.6	0.9	23.2
Coleman, Coleman	N	96	32	114	-4	Mar.	26	Nov.	16	235	N	1.2	1.5	1.6	2.4	4.1	3.3	2.0	2.4	3.0	2.8	1.6	1.2	28.0
Collin, McKinney	N	95	26	118	-7	Mar.	26	Nov.	11	230	N	2.0	2.8	3.5	3.9	5.8	4.0	2.4	2.1	4.6	3.4	1.0	2.3	40.0
Collingsworth, Wellington	28	97	26	113	-6	Apr.	5	Nov.	3	212	N	0.5	0.8	1.3	1.7	3.9	3.2	2.0	2.1	3.0	2.0	1.0	0.6	21.5
Colorado, Columbus	N	95	37	108	4	Mar.	1	Dec.	6	280	N	3.3	2.8	2.5	3.2	5.5	4.1	2.9	2.9	5.0	3.2	3.6	2.9	41.8
Comal, New Braunfels	27	95	37	110	8	Mar.	12	Nov.	25	261	N	1.9	2.2	1.8	2.6	5.0	3.4	2.0	2.5	4.1	3.5	2.0	1.3	34.3
Comanche, Proctor Reservoir	N	95	31	110	-8	Mar.	27	Nov.	20	238	N	1.6	1.9	2.1	3.1	4.6	4.1	2.0	1.9	3.9	3.0	1.3	1.1	30.4
Concho, Paint Rock	N	98	27	108	-1	Mar.	29	Nov.	12	228	27	1.0	1.3	2.1	3.1	3.4	2.9	1.9	2.1	4.0	2.6	2.4	1.8	24.8
Cooke, Gainesville	N	95	33	111	-6	Mar.	27	Nov.	8	226	N	1.7	2.3	2.4	3.2	4.7	3.5	2.0	2.4	4.5	4.0	2.3	1.8	35.8
Coryell, Gatesville	N	96	25	112	-7	Mar.	25	Nov.	21	241	N	2.0	2.3	3.3	3.1	3.5	3.4	3.1	2.5	3.7	3.1	1.7	0.8	32.9
Cottle, Paducah	28	96	31	112	2	Apr.	2	Nov.	7	219	N	0.7	1.0	1.2	1.5	3.2	1.7	1.8	1.9	3.1	2.1	0.7	0.6	22.3
Crane, Crane	N	97	30	118	-7	Mar.	31	Nov.	11	225	N	0.5	0.6	0.4	0.9	2.6	2.0	1.5	2.1	3.0	1.6	1.0	0.6	14.8
Crockett, Ozona	N	94	23	115	4	Mar.	26	Nov.	14	233	28	0.7	0.9	0.9	1.5	2.3	3.0	2.0	2.1	3.3	2.2	1.0	0.7	19.2
Crosby, Crosbyton	N	93	28	109	-6	Apr.	10	Nov.	2	206	N	0.5	0.9	0.9	1.3	2.9	1.4	2.3	3.1	3.6	2.1	2.1	0.7	22.6
Culberson, Van Horn	N	94	19	113	-7	Apr.	7	Nov.	10	224	N	0.4	0.3	0.2	0.1	0.6	0.7	2.1	2.5	2.7	1.3	0.7	0.4	13.1
Dallam, Dalhart	N	92	19	112	-21	Apr.	23	Oct.	18	178	N	0.5	0.4	0.8	1.1	2.6	3.1	3.1	3.1	1.9	1.0	0.7	0.7	17.9
Dallas, Dallas	N	96	35	113	1	Mar.	23	Nov.	13	235	28	1.8	2.3	3.2	3.9	5.0	3.5	2.4	2.3	3.6	3.9	2.4	1.9	36.1
Dawson, Lamesa	N	96	25	114	-12	Apr.	8	Nov.	6	210	N	0.4	0.6	0.8	1.0	2.3	2.8	1.9	1.9	3.5	1.8	0.7	0.5	16.2
De Witt, Yoakum	N	95	39	110	12	Mar.	3	Nov.	29	270	N	2.4	2.3	2.0	3.3	4.3	4.5	2.9	3.0	4.1	3.2	3.0	2.0	37.0
Deaf Smith, Hereford	N	90	20	108	-17	Apr.	16	Oct.	28	195	N	0.4	0.6	0.8	1.0	1.9	3.0	1.9	3.1	2.1	1.4	0.8	0.5	17.2
Delta, Cooper*	15	94	30	110	-1	Mar.	25	Nov.	13	233	N	2.7	2.4	3.6	4.8	5.3	3.9	2.8	3.1	4.5	3.6	3.3	3.4	42.7
Denton, Denton	28	94	30	113	-3	Mar.	27	Nov.	8	217	N	1.8	0.6	3.0	3.7	5.0	5.0	2.8	2.2	4.8	3.6	2.4	2.1	37.3
Dickens, Dickens*	N	94	29	110	10	Apr.	4	Nov.	7	226	N	0.9	0.8	1.1	1.8	3.3	2.6	2.0	2.3	3.3	4.0	0.7	0.9	21.7
Dimmit, Carrizo Springs	27	99	21	114	0	Feb.	19	Dec.	6	290	N	0.9	1.3	1.2	1.5	4.2	1.3	1.3	2.5	2.9	1.8	1.0	0.6	22.0
Donley, Clarendon	27	94	41	112	-11	Apr.	16	Nov.	1	206	15	0.5	1.7	0.8	1.7	1.9	3.7	1.3	2.1	2.7	2.6	1.0	0.9	20.7
Duval, Freer	N	96	29	109	-12	Mar.	16	Nov.	11	298	N	1.3	1.7	1.2	1.7	3.1	3.1	2.5	1.6	4.1	1.7	1.4	1.3	24.8
Eastland, Rising Star	N	95	28	109	0	Feb.	27	Nov.	11	299	N	1.5	1.5	2.1	2.7	3.5	3.8	2.1	1.6	3.5	2.8	1.3	1.3	29.7
Ector, Penwell	28	95	34	110	-8	Apr.	3	Nov.	6	217	N	0.3	0.6	0.5	0.8	0.3	0.7	1.5	2.0	2.5	1.2	0.7	0.5	13.1
Edwards, Carta Valley	N	96	34	109	-4	Mar.	16	Nov.	21	250	27	0.7	1.2	0.9	0.9	1.5	2.5	1.6	2.8	3.0	2.4	1.1	0.6	22.0
El Paso, El Paso	27	94	31	114	-7	Mar.	9	Nov.	12	248	27	0.4	0.5	0.3	0.2	0.3	0.7	1.5	2.8	1.7	0.8	0.4	0.6	8.8
Ellis, Waxahachie	N	96	36	114	-4	Mar.	20	Nov.	21	246	27	1.9	2.8	3.1	3.8	5.1	3.1	2.0	2.1	3.9	3.8	2.7	2.4	36.8
Erath, Dublin	N	96	29	110	3	Mar.	27	Nov.	18	238	N	1.7	2.1	2.3	3.3	4.7	3.4	2.2	2.0	3.6	3.3	2.1	2.5	32.9
Falls, Marlin	N	96	40	112	3	Mar.	13	Nov.	25	257	N	2.1	3.1	3.0	3.3	5.2	2.0	2.0	2.8	3.6	3.8	3.2	2.7	36.8
Fannin, Bonham	N	94	30	114	-9	Mar.	27	Nov.	10	228	N	2.1	2.4	3.9	3.8	6.1	4.5	3.1	2.3	4.9	4.1	3.4	2.3	44.0
Fayette, Flatonia	28	94	22	110	6	Mar.	2	Nov.	4	277	18	2.5	2.5	2.0	3.0	4.8	4.3	1.9	2.5	5.0	3.2	3.2	2.3	37.1
Fisher, Rotan	N	96	24	110	-1	Apr.	2	Nov.	6	218	N	0.7	1.1	1.1	1.9	3.8	3.6	2.1	2.6	3.8	2.4	1.2	0.7	24.3
Floyd, Floydada	N	96	41	116	9	Apr.	7	Nov.	6	213	N	0.4	0.7	1.0	1.2	2.8	2.7	2.2	2.6	3.0	1.7	0.9	1.0	20.5
Foard, Crowell*	N	92	33	111	-6	Apr.	2	Nov.	7	219	N	0.9	1.1	1.3	1.2	2.4	2.5	3.7	4.1	3.1	2.7	1.2	0.5	23.9
Fort Bend, Sugar Land	18	93	36	106	9	Feb.	14	Dec.	7	296	N	3.3	2.8	2.7	2.8	4.6	4.9	3.4	2.5	5.6	3.5	4.0	3.3	45.3
Franklin, Mount Vernon*	29	93	38	105	-1	Mar.	23	Nov.	12	234	29	2.8	3.3	4.3	4.4	4.7	4.1	2.0	2.3	4.9	3.9	3.7	4.8	46.8
Freestone, Fairfield	N	95	36	109	9	Mar.	11	Nov.	29	263	N	2.5	3.1	3.2	3.2	4.9	3.5	2.0	2.3	4.0	4.1	3.6	3.6	39.8
Frio, Pearsall	N	97	38	111	9	Feb.	23	Dec.	2	291	N	1.2	1.3	1.0	2.2	3.6	3.3	1.6	2.5	3.0	3.1	1.5	1.1	25.4

County and Station	Temperature — Length of Record (Yr.)	July Mean Max. (F.)	January Mean Min. (F.)	Record Highest (F.)	Record Lowest (F.)	Last in Spring Mo.	Last in Spring Day	First in Fall Mo.	First in Fall Day	Growing Season (Days)	Precip — Length of Record (Yr.)	January (In.)	February (In.)	March (In.)	April (In.)	May (In.)	June (In.)	July (In.)	August (In.)	September (In.)	October (In.)	November (In.)	December (In.)	Annual (In.)
Gaines, Seminole	N	94	25	114	-9	Apr.	8	Nov.	4	210	N	0.5	0.7	0.7	0.9	2.0	2.6	2.5	2.3	2.5	1.4	0.8	0.6	17.5
Galveston, Galveston	N	87	47	101	8	Jan.	24	Dec.	25	335	N	3.3	2.3	2.2	2.4	3.6	4.4	4.0	4.5	5.9	2.8	3.4	3.5	42.3
Garza, Post	28	94	27	115	-1	Apr.	5	Nov.	7	216	N	0.6	0.8	0.9	1.2	2.7	3.1	2.1	2.8	2.9	2.0	0.9	0.7	20.9
Gillespie, Fredericksburg	N	93	35	109	-5	Apr.	2	Nov.	6	219	N	1.3	1.4	1.4	2.5	4.2	3.6	2.2	2.7	3.3	3.6	1.9	1.3	30.0
Glasscock, Garden City	26	94	25	114	0	Apr.	2	Nov.	10	222	N	0.6	0.7	0.7	1.2	2.2	2.0	2.0	2.0	3.3	1.8	0.8	0.6	18.0
Goliad, Goliad	N	95	43	112	7	Feb.	24	Dec.	6	285	N	2.1	2.1	1.4	2.8	4.1	4.5	3.2	3.4	5.0	3.6	2.3	2.0	36.5
Gonzales, Nixon	N	95	40	113	3	Feb.	28	Dec.	1	276	N	2.2	2.1	1.6	3.2	4.0	3.5	1.9	2.3	4.6	3.2	2.4	1.7	32.4
Gray, Pampa	N	92	21	111	-12	Apr.	15	Oct.	27	195	N	0.5	0.9	1.4	1.3	2.9	3.6	2.4	2.6	2.4	1.5	1.0	0.5	21.0
Grayson, Sherman	N	92	30	110	-2	Mar.	27	Nov.	9	227	N	1.9	2.6	3.4	3.9	5.8	4.2	1.9	2.1	5.1	4.2	3.1	2.0	40.4
Gregg, Longview	N	93	33	110	-7	Mar.	16	Nov.	15	247	N	3.5	3.7	4.1	4.5	5.1	4.4	2.9	2.9	3.9	3.7	4.3	4.3	47.0
Grimes, Anderson*	9	96	40	108	4	Mar.	1	Dec.	4	278	N	3.1	3.3	2.8	4.3	4.3	3.4	2.4	2.8	4.1	3.7	3.4	3.4	40.4
Guadalupe, Seguin*	N	96	40	110	0	Mar.	6	Nov.	28	267	N	1.8	2.5	1.8	3.3	3.4	3.5	1.8	2.3	4.1	3.4	2.1	1.7	31.4
Hale, Plainview	N	92	24	111	-7	Apr.	10	Nov.	6	211	N	0.5	0.8	0.8	1.1	3.0	3.5	2.4	2.3	2.5	1.7	0.8	0.6	19.8
Hall, Memphis	N	96	32	117	-7	Apr.	4.	Nov.	6	213	N	0.5	0.7	1.3	1.7	3.5	3.1	1.7	2.5	2.4	1.6	0.9	0.6	20.5
Hamilton, Hico	N	96	32	111	-11	Mar.	27	Nov.	11	239	N	1.9	2.4	2.4	3.0	4.6	3.2	2.1	2.5	3.4	3.3	2.2	1.5	31.8
Hansford, Spearman	N	95	21	109	-22	Apr.	22	Oct.	25	186	N	0.4	0.7	1.3	1.1	2.9	3.0	2.9	2.4	2.1	1.2	1.0	0.5	19.4
Hardeman, Quanah	13	97	23	119	-15	Mar.	31	Nov.	7	221	N	0.8	1.0	1.5	1.7	3.5	2.4	2.4	2.5	3.6	2.4	1.2	0.9	24.5
Hardin, Evadale	22	93	37	102	12	Feb.	14	Dec.	14	246	N	4.8	3.9	4.0	3.8	5.4	5.8	4.7	4.0	5.3	4.0	4.9	5.1	55.7
Harris, Houston	N	92	43	107	7	Feb.	14	Dec.	11	300	N	3.3	3.3	2.9	3.2	4.6	4.4	3.0	3.5	4.3	4.3	3.8	3.5	46.1
Harrison, Marshall	N	93	32	110	7	Mar.	16	Nov.	17	245	N	3.8	4.0	4.0	4.4	4.9	4.4	3.0	2.5	3.8	3.9	4.3	4.5	47.7
Hartley, Channing*	13	92	21	108	-9	Apr.	22	Oct.	19	180	N	0.4	0.5	0.7	1.1	2.2	1.9	2.4	2.8	1.2	1.2	0.7	0.2	16.1
Haskell, Haskell	N	96	27	115	-6	Mar.	28	Nov.	16	232	N	0.9	1.4	1.4	2.2	3.6	3.0	2.1	2.9	3.7	2.6	1.3	1.1	26.1
Hays, San Marcos	N	95	36	110	-6	Mar.	14	Nov.	23	254	N	2.0	2.3	1.8	2.8	5.0	4.2	2.1	2.3	3.7	3.1	3.1	2.1	34.6
Hemphill, Canadian	N	96	22	112	-14	Apr.	9	Oct.	30	204	N	0.3	0.8	1.3	1.4	3.4	3.1	1.9	2.6	3.8	1.4	0.9	0.5	20.1
Henderson, Athens	N	95	35	110	-2	Mar.	11	Nov.	26	260	N	2.5	3.1	3.6	3.7	5.2	3.6	1.9	1.8	3.8	4.0	3.7	3.3	39.7
Hidalgo, McAllen	N	96	49	110	17	Feb.	7	Dec.	8	327	39	1.4	1.3	0.6	1.3	2.8	2.7	1.7	2.2	4.4	2.6	1.0	1.1	23.4
Hill, Hillsboro	N	95	34	113	-1	Mar.	13	Nov.	28	250	N	1.9	2.6	3.0	3.0	4.8	3.9	2.2	3.1	3.3	3.7	2.5	2.3	35.1
Hockley, Levelland	28	92	22	115	-16	Apr.	15	Oct.	28	196	N	0.4	0.7	0.6	0.9	2.0	2.6	2.5	1.8	2.9	1.7	0.7	0.6	19.3
Hood, Granbury*	N	97	33	110	-6	Mar.	26	Nov.	13	232	N	1.9	2.0	1.7	3.9	4.9	3.4	1.8	2.3	2.9	3.2	2.1	1.5	30.9
Hopkins, Sulphur Springs	N	94	30	110	-4	Mar.	23	Nov.	16	238	N	2.5	3.3	4.1	4.7	5.5	4.1	3.0	2.3	3.4	4.6	4.0	3.5	46.0
Houston, Crockett	N	93	34	110	0	Mar.	6	Nov.	26	265	N	3.5	2.9	3.2	4.1	4.4	3.7	3.0	2.2	4.4	3.9	3.8	3.5	42.4
Howard, Big Spring	N	94	28	114	21	Apr.	4	Nov.	7	217	N	0.6	0.8	0.8	1.3	2.8	2.3	1.7	2.0	3.9	1.6	0.8	0.6	19.2
Hudspeth, Cornudas Ser.	N	95	25	109	-13	Apr.	27	Nov.	11	231	N	0.4	0.3	0.2	0.2	0.5	1.1	1.5	2.0	1.9	0.9	0.4	0.4	10.0
Hunt, Greenville	N	94	29	108	-3	Mar.	13	Nov.	13	237	N	2.2	3.0	3.8	3.9	5.7	3.7	2.7	2.2	3.1	4.1	3.3	2.6	41.6
Hutchinson, Borger	27	94	23	107	-12	Apr.	20	Oct.	24	187	N	0.5	0.9	1.3	1.3	2.8	3.4	3.4	2.5	2.0	1.3	0.8	0.5	20.3
Irion, Mertzon	N	95	32	113	-7	Apr.	4	Oct.	27	232	N	0.7	1.3	1.0	1.6	3.1	2.3	1.5	2.5	3.1	2.0	1.2	0.9	21.1
Jack, Jacksboro	N	94	29	113	-7	Apr.	1	Nov.	5	218	N	1.3	1.6	2.1	2.8	4.7	4.6	2.5	2.2	3.8	3.2	2.0	1.5	30.7
Jackson, Edna*	8	94	42	105	17	Feb.	19	Nov.	6	290	26	4.4	2.8	1.7	2.8	5.1	5.3	3.8	3.6	5.7	3.9	2.8	2.5	40.9
Jasper, Jasper	22	93	36	106	17	Mar.	18	Nov.	13	230	N	4.4	4.4	4.4	3.7	5.6	5.3	3.9	3.4	3.5	3.6	4.6	5.3	52.7
Jeff Davis, Mount Locke	N	82	30	104	-10	Mar.	–	Nov.	16	–	N	0.5	0.5	0.4	0.5	1.5	2.6	3.8	4.3	3.5	1.7	0.7	0.6	20.8
Jefferson, Port Arthur	N	92	42	107	12	Feb.	11	Dec.	15	250	N	4.8	3.4	3.2	3.5	5.7	5.6	3.9	5.3	6.3	4.3	4.9	5.3	57.2
Jim Hogg, Hebbronville	N	97	42	109	12	Feb.	15	Dec.	4	303	N	1.1	1.3	0.7	1.7	3.4	2.9	1.5	3.6	4.9	1.9	1.2	0.9	22.7
Jim Wells, Alice	N	96	43	111	-5	Feb.	18	Dec.	14	289	N	1.3	1.6	0.8	1.6	3.2	3.5	2.5	2.7	5.1	2.7	2.1	1.1	27.8
Johnson, Cleburne	N	97	33	114	-12	Mar.	25	Nov.	13	233	N	1.9	2.2	2.9	3.6	5.4	2.9	2.0	2.1	3.3	3.3	1.8	1.8	34.0
Jones, Anson	N	96	31	114	-12	Mar.	31	Nov.	9.	223	N	1.0	1.4	1.3	2.2	3.4	2.9	2.0	2.6	4.3	2.4	1.3	1.1	25.8
Karnes, Kenedy*	18	97	41	112	7	Feb.	24	Dec.	2	281	N	2.3	2.4	1.1	2.2	4.0	4.2	1.2	3.0	5.3	3.6	2.0	1.8	33.2

County and Station	Temp. Length of Record (Yr.)	July Mean Max. (°F.)	January Min. Mean (°F.)	Record Highest (°F.)	Record Lowest (°F.)	Last in Spring Mo.	Last in Spring Day	First in Fall Mo.	First in Fall Day	Growing Season Days	Precip. Length of Record (Yr.)	Jan. (in.)	Feb. (in.)	Mar. (in.)	Apr. (in.)	May (in.)	June (in.)	July (in.)	Aug. (in.)	Sept. (in.)	Oct. (in.)	Nov. (in.)	Dec. (in.)	Annual (in.)
Kaufman, Kaufman	N	95	32	112	-3	Mar.	18	Nov.	21	248	N	2.4	3.0	3.2	3.8	5.0	3.1	2.6	1.8	3.8	3.9	3.3	3.0	38.9
Kendall, Boerne	N	93	33	107	-4	Mar.	25	Nov.	11	236	N	1.7	2.1	2.1	3.1	4.1	3.8	2.2	2.9	3.6	3.6	2.7	1.8	34.2
Kenedy, Armstrong*	14	95	45	110	14	Feb.	2	Dec.	18	319	14	1.2	1.7	0.5	1.3	4.4	3.4	2.1	3.2	6.4	2.9	1.3	1.3	29.7
Kent, Jayton	18	96	25	116	-5	Apr.	4	Nov.	6	216	18	0.7	1.0	1.1	1.6	3.0	2.9	1.8	2.7	2.1	2.1	0.9	0.8	21.8
Kerr, Kerrville*	N	94	32	110	-7	Apr.	6	Nov.	6	216	N	1.6	2.0	2.0	3.1	3.8	2.6	1.7	2.7	4.0	3.6	1.6	1.6	29.8
Kimble, Junction	N	96	31	110	-11	Apr.	3	Nov.	3	213	N	1.0	1.6	1.2	2.1	3.6	2.8	1.7	2.5	2.8	2.4	1.2	1.1	23.8
King, Guthrie	27	98	24	109	-10	Apr.	3	Nov.	3	219	45	0.9	1.3	1.1	1.6	3.5	3.1	1.9	2.7	3.7	2.4	1.1	0.7	23.8
Kinney, Brackettville	23	95	36	109	10	Mar.	4	Nov.	26	270	N	0.8	1.3	0.9	2.3	2.6	3.1	1.6	2.9	3.7	2.4	1.2	0.8	21.7
Kleberg, Kingsville	N	95	45	108	9	Feb.	5	Dec.	16	314	N	1.5	1.8	0.9	1.6	3.4	4.0	2.2	2.9	4.3	2.7	1.4	1.0	27.6
Knox, Munday	N	98	28	117	7	Apr.	3	Nov.	6	217	N	1.1	1.1	1.6	2.1	3.7	3.0	2.0	2.6	3.9	2.8	1.3	1.0	26.2
La Salle, Fowlerton	N	94	38	112	9	Feb.	20	Nov.	14	288	N	1.1	1.1	0.8	1.8	3.2	2.2	1.5	2.4	3.0	3.0	1.2	1.0	22.5
Lamar, Paris	N	99	30	111	-14	Mar.	25	Nov.	14	235	N	2.2	3.2	4.2	4.0	5.9	3.9	3.6	2.7	4.8	4.6	3.9	3.3	46.1
Lamb, Littlefield	N	91	22	112	-12	Apr.	16	Oct.	27	194	N	0.6	0.6	0.6	1.0	2.3	3.3	1.8	2.5	2.5	1.6	0.7	0.5	18.7
Lampasas, Lampasas	N	95	30	111	-5	Apr.	1	Nov.	6	223	N	1.5	2.4	2.1	2.7	4.1	2.9	2.5	2.8	5.1	3.3	2.0	1.7	29.6
Lavaca, Hallettsville	N	95	41	104	5	Mar.	1	Dec.	6	280	N	2.8	2.5	2.2	3.0	5.3	4.4	2.5	2.7	4.2	3.2	3.3	2.4	39.1
Lee, Lexington	28	94	36	111	-3	Mar.	6	Nov.	29	273	28	2.5	2.5	2.4	2.9	4.8	3.8	1.7	2.0	4.5	3.8	3.0	2.3	35.6
Leon, Centerville	N	93	34	107	-7	Mar.	3	Nov.	19	270	N	3.1	3.6	3.1	3.5	4.4	3.5	2.5	2.0	5.7	4.1	3.2	3.1	40.5
Liberty, Liberty	N	95	39	110	-12	Mar.	15	Nov.	26	261	N	3.8	3.6	3.2	3.6	5.4	6.1	4.5	4.0	4.7	4.0	5.2	4.8	54.1
Limestone, Mexia	N	95	33	110	-6	Mar.	10	Nov.	29	255	N	2.5	3.0	3.4	3.5	4.9	3.5	1.9	3.1	4.1	4.1	3.4	3.2	40.3
Lipscomb, Follett	N	93	20	109	-14	Apr.	20	Dec.	6	202	N	0.5	1.0	1.9	1.9	3.5	3.4	2.3	2.3	1.4	1.4	1.2	0.7	22.8
Live Oak, George West*	N	96	41	109	-16	Feb.	6	Dec.	6	289	N	1.7	1.6	0.8	2.5	3.8	2.8	1.5	2.9	4.7	3.1	2.7	1.4	27.6
Llano, Llano	N	96	28	113	-5	Mar.	29	Nov.	13	229	N	1.2	1.8	1.6	2.1	3.8	2.8	1.8	2.4	3.1	2.7	1.8	1.2	26.4
Loving, Mentone*	N	92	25	114	-2	Apr.	3	Nov.	8	222	N	0.3	0.3	0.3	0.2	1.1	0.9	1.8	1.4	2.7	1.0	0.3	0.3	9.1
Lubbock, Lubbock	N	92	24	111	-8	Apr.	9	Nov.	6	208	N	0.4	0.7	0.9	1.0	2.4	3.0	2.4	2.5	1.0	1.9	0.8	0.7	18.7
Lynn, Tahoka	N	95	38	111	5	Apr.	5	Nov.	9	217	N	0.5	0.8	0.9	1.4	2.7	3.9	2.5	2.6	1.8	1.8	0.8	0.7	19.7
Madison, Madisonville	N	91	32	110	-10	Mar.	5	Dec.	2	272	N	3.0	2.8	3.2	3.5	5.0	4.6	2.3	2.6	4.5	4.1	3.7	3.0	41.6
Marion, Jefferson*	N	98	30	109	-5	Mar.	18	Nov.	6	236	N	3.9	3.5	3.9	5.3	4.6	3.4	3.1	2.5	3.6	2.0	3.8	4.1	44.7
Martin, Lenorah*	N	95	31	109	-2	Apr.	5	Nov.	6	215	N	0.6	0.6	0.8	1.2	2.3	1.6	2.4	1.7	1.6	1.6	0.8	0.6	17.2
Mason, Mason	N	95	45	109	-11	Apr.	3	Nov.	6	217	N	1.1	2.4	1.5	2.1	3.7	3.3	1.9	2.6	3.2	3.1	1.6	1.1	26.8
Matagorda, Matagorda	N	91	38	102	-7	Feb.	17	Dec.	10	296	N	3.6	2.6	1.9	2.6	3.4	3.0	4.0	3.3	6.9	3.9	3.9	2.7	44.7
Maverick, Eagle Pass	N	94	30	115	10	Feb.	21	Dec.	3	285	N	0.7	0.7	0.7	1.9	3.4	2.9	1.7	2.2	2.8	2.4	1.0	0.8	21.5
McCulloch, Brady	N	95	34	110	-7	Mar.	31	Nov.	12	226	N	1.1	1.8	1.4	2.1	3.6	2.9	2.3	2.5	3.6	2.4	1.5	1.1	26.1
McLennan, Waco	N	97	40	112	-11	Mar.	16	Nov.	24	253	N	3.2	2.6	2.3	3.2	4.6	3.3	2.0	2.0	3.5	3.4	2.4	1.9	32.0
McMullen, Tilden	N	98	37	109	-18	Feb.	19	Dec.	7	291	N	1.3	1.6	0.9	1.8	3.0	2.9	1.7	2.0	3.5	2.0	1.4	1.0	23.4
Medina, Hondo	N	94	30	112	-5	Mar.	6	Nov.	24	263	N	1.4	1.7	1.4	2.6	3.8	3.0	2.4	2.7	3.1	2.0	1.5	1.4	27.3
Menard, Menard	28	95	34	110	-4	Mar.	31	Nov.	6	220	24	1.4	1.5	1.9	0.7	2.8	1.4	1.6	1.9	2.5	1.4	1.2	0.9	24.3
Midland, Midland	N	95	29	116	-11	Apr.	13	Nov.	6	218	24	0.5	0.6	0.5	0.7	2.2	2.9	1.9	1.7	1.9	1.3	0.7	0.5	15.2
Milam, Cameron	N	97	38	112	-7	Mar.	31	Nov.	24	256	N	2.2	2.6	2.2	3.3	4.7	3.4	2.0	2.1	4.2	3.2	3.0	2.3	34.2
Mills, Goldthwaite	N	96	34	109	-7	Apr.	4	Nov.	16	229	N	1.4	2.0	1.9	1.9	3.7	2.2	1.7	2.3	3.1	2.1	1.0	0.7	19.8
Mitchell, Colorado City*	24	96	38	112	-11	Apr.	27	Nov.	5	230	25	0.6	0.7	1.0	3.8	2.9	2.8	2.4	3.6	3.7	1.7	2.3	1.6	32.9
Montague, Bowie	N	94	34	115	-18	Mar.	1	Nov.	11	217	N	3.6	3.5	2.6	1.9	4.8	3.4	2.8	3.6	5.0	3.7	4.2	4.0	47.3
Montgomery, Conroe	N	92	38	110	(—)	Mar.	11	Nov.	26	270	N	3.2	3.2	2.9	2.9	5.4	4.5	4.0	2.4	4.1	3.1	0.8	0.4	47.3
Moore, Dumas	N	92	20	107	-5	Apr.	26	Oct.	22	185	N	0.4	0.7	1.0	1.1	2.7	2.4	2.4	3.0	1.1	1.1	1.0	0.5	17.4
Morris, Daingerfield	N	95	35	109	-5	Mar.	30	Nov.	12	236	N	2.9	3.5	4.4	4.8	4.7	3.6	2.8	2.4	3.2	3.9	4.5	4.1	44.6
Motley, Matador	N	95	26	116	(—)	Apr.	21	Nov.	7	218	N	0.8	0.8	1.1	1.3	2.8	3.4	2.1	2.4	3.0	2.0	1.0	0.7	21.2
Nacogdoches, Nacogdoches*	N	94	36	110	0	Mar.	16	Nov.	12	243	N	4.2	3.9	3.7	4.8	5.5	3.9	3.9	2.5	3.8	3.3	3.8	4.7	47.5

County and Station	Temperature					Average Freeze Dates				Growing Season Days	Length of Record Yr.	Normal Total Precipitation												
	Length of Record Yr.	July Mean Max. F.	January Mean Min. F.	Record Highest F.	Record Lowest F.	Last in Spring Mo.	Day	First in Fall Mo.	Day			January In.	February In.	March In.	April In.	May In.	June In.	July In.	August In.	September In.	October In.	November In.	December In.	Annual In.
Navarro, Corsicana	27	94	33	113	-5	Mar.	10	Nov.	19	253	27	2.2	2.8	3.1	3.6	5.8	3.1	2.1	1.9	3.4	4.2	2.9	2.9	37.9
Newton, Kirbyville Forest Service*	N	93	40	107	7	Mar.	24	Nov.	9	228	N	4.8	4.3	3.7	4.6	5.3	4.6	5.3	3.7	5.1	3.8	4.7	6.0	56.0
Nolan, Roscoe	N	94	30	113	-11	Apr.	2	Nov.	9	221	N	1.0	1.2	1.3	1.8	2.9	2.9	2.0	3.3	4.3	2.6	1.2	0.9	24.4
Nueces, Corpus Christi	26	93	45	104	13	Feb.	9	Dec.	15	309	26	1.7	2.0	0.9	1.7	3.3	3.4	2.4	3.3	5.5	3.0	1.6	1.3	30.1
Ochiltree, Perryton	N	94	17	110	-8	Apr.	18	Oct.	26	191	N	0.4	0.7	0.9	1.3	3.3	3.3	2.8	2.5	1.8	1.1	1.1	1.3	19.5
Oldham, Vega*	27	91	19	108	-17	Apr.	19	Oct.	21	186	27	0.5	0.6	0.8	1.1	2.4	2.8	2.8	2.5	2.0	1.2	0.7	0.5	17.4
Orange, Orange	N	96	39	104	10	Mar.	16	Nov.	11	240	N	5.2	3.9	3.5	3.4	5.4	5.6	5.6	4.7	6.2	4.3	4.7	5.5	58.3
Palo Pinto, Mineral Wells	N	94	30	114	3	Mar.	31	Nov.	7	221	N	1.6	2.0	2.6	3.2	4.5	3.5	2.2	2.7	3.4	3.5	1.9	1.4	32.2
Panola, Carthage	N	94	33	108	1	Mar.	16	Nov.	11	240	N	4.0	3.7	3.8	3.2	4.9	4.4	3.2	2.4	4.1	3.9	4.7	4.6	48.0
Parker, Weatherford	28	96	28	119	-10	Mar.	29	Nov.	9	225	28	1.6	2.2	2.7	3.3	4.5	3.6	2.3	2.4	3.5	3.3	2.0	1.6	32.9
Parmer, Friona	N	90	21	108	-15	Apr.	20	Oct.	20	183	N	0.5	0.6	0.4	0.7	1.9	2.8	2.1	1.8	3.3	1.3	0.7	0.5	16.8
Pecos, Fort Stockton	N	95	30	117	1	Mar.	31	Nov.	10	224	N	0.5	0.5	0.4	0.7	1.5	1.6	1.3	3.1	2.8	1.6	0.6	0.6	13.9
Polk, Livingston	N	94	35	111	3	Mar.	11	Nov.	16	250	N	4.0	3.4	3.8	3.6	5.5	4.7	3.6	2.9	4.5	3.5	4.3	4.7	48.7
Potter, Amarillo	N	92	21	108	-14	Apr.	17	Oct.	24	190	N	0.5	0.6	1.0	1.0	2.5	3.7	2.6	2.9	2.0	1.4	0.7	0.4	19.6
Presidio, Marfa	N	90	26	106	-2	Apr.	20	Oct.	13	238	N	0.4	0.4	0.3	0.6	1.2	2.1	2.6	3.1	2.9	1.6	0.4	0.5	15.9
Presidio, Presidio	29	102	34	117	4	Mar.	20	Nov.	18	242	22	0.4	0.4	0.2	0.3	0.6	1.7	1.7	2.9	2.0	1.0	0.4	0.5	10.8
Rains, Emory	N	94	31	110	-5	Mar.	21	Nov.	21	195	N	2.6	3.4	3.7	4.1	5.7	3.9	2.5	2.1	3.7	4.2	3.6	3.3	42.9
Randall, Canyon	27	92	23	107	-14	Apr.	15	Oct.	27	236	27	0.4	0.6	0.9	1.0	2.4	3.5	2.2	1.7	2.0	1.6	0.6	0.4	18.9
Reagan, Big Lake	19	94	28	109	1	Apr.	28	Nov.	12	234	19	0.6	0.9	0.9	1.5	2.4	1.8	2.0	3.5	3.2	2.2	1.0	0.8	19.2
Real, Prade Ranch	N	92	29	107	0	Mar.	26	Nov.	17	226	N	1.2	1.5	0.9	2.3	3.3	3.0	2.6	2.4	2.0	2.1	1.1	1.1	25.7
Red River, Clarksville	N	96	28	109	-5	Mar.	23	Nov.	12	226	N	2.3	3.2	4.5	4.3	5.5	3.9	2.9	2.0	3.9	4.5	4.2	3.7	44.9
Reeves, Balmorhea	N	99	29	112	-9	Apr.	2	Nov.	11	304	N	0.5	0.5	0.4	0.6	1.4	1.3	1.8	2.5	3.0	1.3	0.7	0.5	14.3
Reeves, Pecos	N	94	27	118	-9	Apr.	1	Nov.	12	192	27	0.4	0.5	1.3	0.4	1.0	1.2	1.2	2.5	1.1	1.6	0.5	0.5	11.0
Refugio, Refugio	29	93	43	106	8	Feb.	14	Dec.	15	268	N	2.2	2.3	1.6	2.3	4.1	4.4	3.6	3.1	6.7	3.9	2.1	1.7	38.0
Roberts, Miami	26	95	20	111	-15	Apr.	16	Oct.	25	236	26	0.5	1.0	1.6	1.6	3.3	2.9	2.0	3.1	2.4	1.6	1.1	0.5	21.6
Robertson, Franklin	N	96	37	110	-1	Mar.	6	Nov.	29	228	25	2.7	2.8	3.1	3.6	4.5	2.9	2.4	3.1	4.3	2.9	2.9	2.8	37.5
Rockwall, Rockwall*	N	96	33	118	-7	Mar.	23	Nov.	14	250	N	2.1	2.4	3.1	2.7	5.2	3.1	1.5	2.1	3.8	4.0	2.5	2.4	36.9
Runnels, Ballinger	N	93	30	114	-9	Mar.	30	Nov.	13	236	N	1.0	1.3	1.2	4.7	3.4	2.6	2.8	2.1	3.3	3.3	1.3	1.0	23.3
Rusk, Henderson	6	93	33	108	-1	Mar.	11	Nov.	16	238	19	3.6	3.6	3.8	1.9	5.1	4.3	4.0	3.5	3.6	4.0	4.3	3.9	45.6
Sabine, Hemphill*	24	93	36	104	8	Mar.	21	Nov.	12	261	24	5.2	5.2	5.7	4.0	5.1	4.5	3.4	3.5	3.8	4.5	4.0	4.5	52.5
San Augustine, Broaddus	N	93	35	106	9	Mar.	19	Nov.	12	303	25	4.5	3.2	3.9	4.8	4.8	4.6	3.4	3.1	4.3	3.8	4.3	5.0	48.6
San Jacinto, Coldspring	27	94	36	105	3	Mar.	5	Nov.	12	227	N	3.7	3.3	3.9	3.8	5.5	5.5	3.1	3.1	5.7	3.8	4.1	4.7	48.3
San Patricio, Sinton	N	92	43	107	11	Feb.	14	Dec.	14	229	N	2.0	2.2	1.2	2.1	4.1	5.5	3.4	2.1	6.1	3.8	1.8	1.4	35.0
San Saba, San Saba	15	96	32	107	-1	Apr.	1	Nov.	14	214	N	1.1	0.9	1.0	1.7	3.6	2.8	1.6	2.5	3.1	2.1	2.0	1.2	26.3
Schleicher, Eldorado*	N	93	28	112	3	Mar.	28	Nov.	12	224	N	0.7	0.8	1.0	1.7	2.5	1.9	1.6	3.0	3.1	2.4	0.9	0.6	19.0
Scurry, Snyder	N	93	25	107	-10	Apr.	4	Nov.	4	240	N	0.6	1.6	1.7	2.6	3.2	2.9	2.0	3.5	3.5	2.8	1.2	1.3	22.2
Shackelford, Albany	N	97	31	115	-8	Mar.	30	Nov.	12	182	N	1.2	1.6	1.6	4.0	4.0	3.0	1.9	2.5	3.9	2.8	4.2	4.7	28.6
Shelby, Center	N	93	33	110	0	Mar.	17	Nov.	12	259	N	4.3	4.0	4.1	4.6	5.3	4.4	3.3	3.5	4.5	4.5	4.2	4.7	50.2
Sherman, Stratford	N	94	18	108	-19	Apr.	23	Oct.	22	236	24	0.3	0.5	0.9	1.2	2.7	3.3	2.7	1.8	2.0	0.9	3.8	3.7	17.2
Smith, Tyler*	27	92	33	108	0	Mar.	7	Nov.	21	314	N	3.0	3.3	4.9	4.9	4.9	3.7	2.8	3.5	4.5	3.4	2.0	1.8	43.1
Somervell, Glen Rose	N	98	30	110	-15	Mar.	25	Nov.	7	222	N	1.7	2.1	3.5	3.2	5.3	3.7	2.2	1.8	5.2	2.1	1.0	1.0	33.3
Starr, Rio Grande City	N	99	43	115	10	Feb.	16	Dec.	16	314	N	1.0	1.1	2.7	1.5	2.8	2.5	1.4	1.9	3.8	2.4	0.6	0.6	22.3
Stephens, Breckenridge	27	97	28	111	-7	Apr.	1	Nov.	7	222	27	1.4	1.5	0.5	2.6	3.6	3.0	2.0	2.1	3.6	1.7	1.1	1.3	27.6
Sterling, Sterling City	27	96	29	112	-7	Apr.	1	Nov.	11	224	27	0.8	0.9	0.9	1.4	2.9	2.4	1.6	2.3	3.8	2.4	1.3	0.8	20.3
Stonewall, Aspermont	29	97	27	117	-2	Mar.	31	Nov.	10	220	29	0.8	1.1	1.3	1.9	3.2	3.0	1.7	2.7	3.6	2.4	1.3	0.8	23.3
Sutton, Sonora	N	96	30	109	-8	Mar.	26	Nov.	16	235	N	0.8	1.2	1.0	1.9	2.6	2.2	2.1	2.7	3.4	2.7	1.2	0.7	22.4

County and Station	Temperature – Length of Record (Yr.)	July Mean Max. (F.)	January Mean Min. (F.)	Record Highest (F.)	Record Lowest (F.)	Freeze – Last in Spring		Freeze – First in Fall		Growing Season (Days)	Freeze – Length of Record (Yr.)	Jan. (In.)	Feb. (In.)	Mar. (In.)	Apr. (In.)	May (In.)	June (In.)	July (In.)	Aug. (In.)	Sept. (In.)	Oct. (In.)	Nov. (In.)	Dec. (In.)	Annual (In.)
						Mo.	Day	Mo.	Day															
Swisher, Tulia	N	91	22	110	-10	Apr.	10	Nov.	1	205	N	0.5	0.7	0.9	1.0	2.4	3.9	2.0	2.6	2.5	1.5	0.8	0.6	19.4
Tarrant, Fort Worth*	N	96	35	108	-4	Mar.	26	Nov.	11	230	29	2.0	2.2	2.5	3.6	4.6	3.0	1.8	1.7	2.5	2.6	2.5	2.4	31.3
Taylor, Abilene	N	95	31	110	-9	Mar.	31	Nov.	11	225	N	1.0	1.2	1.4	1.4	3.0	2.9	2.1	2.8	3.2	2.5	1.5	1.0	24.4
Terrell, Sanderson	28	92	29	110	-2	Mar.	21	Nov.	13	237	N	0.3	0.6	0.4	1.0	1.6	1.8	1.3	1.8	2.7	1.8	0.7	0.5	14.3
Terry, Brownfield	N	93	24	111	-8	Apr.	10	Nov.	2	206	N	0.5	0.7	0.8	0.9	2.7	3.0	2.4	2.4	2.6	1.7	0.7	0.6	19.0
Throckmorton, Throckmorton	N	96	27	114	-11	Mar.	31	Nov.	6	220	N	1.0	1.5	1.6	1.6	3.5	3.1	2.0	2.6	4.2	2.2	1.4	1.3	27.1
Titus, Mount Pleasant	N	94	29	111	-12	Mar.	23	Nov.	12	233	N	2.8	3.7	4.4	4.3	5.1	4.3	3.4	2.4	3.9	4.2	4.5	3.9	46.8
Tom Green, San Angelo	N	96	31	111	-4	Mar.	25	Nov.	15	235	N	0.8	1.1	0.9	1.7	3.0	2.3	1.1	1.9	3.4	2.4	1.1	0.8	20.5
Travis, Austin	23	94	39	109	-2	Mar.	3	Nov.	28	270	23	1.7	2.2	1.9	3.4	4.8	3.7	2.0	2.1	3.3	3.4	2.4	1.9	31.9
Trinity, Groveton	N	93	36	108	1	Mar.	6	Nov.	21	260	N	3.6	3.2	3.6	3.9	4.8	4.5	2.0	3.4	4.1	3.4	3.9	4.1	44.9
Tyler, Warren	N	93	38	106	6	Mar.	17	Nov.	16	241	N	4.5	4.0	3.9	3.9	6.0	5.8	3.8	2.3	4.5	4.0	4.8	5.8	54.3
Upshur, Gilmer	N	95	30	109	-4	Mar.	16	Nov.	16	245	N	2.9	3.7	4.3	4.3	4.6	4.6	2.8	1.6	4.0	3.8	4.0	4.0	45.2
Upton, McCamey	N	96	31	113	-2	Mar.	26	Nov.	12	232	N	0.4	0.6	0.4	0.9	1.7	1.5	1.0	2.7	2.8	2.2	0.7	0.6	14.3
Uvalde, Uvalde	N	96	36	111	6	Mar.	10	Nov.	21	255	N	1.1	1.4	2.3	2.3	3.3	2.1	1.9	1.5	2.8	3.0	1.3	1.1	24.8
Val Verde, Del Rio	N	95	39	112	10	Feb.	12	Dec.	9	300	N	0.6	1.0	0.7	0.9	2.0	2.1	1.9	1.5	2.8	2.2	0.9	0.6	18.2
Van Zandt, Wills Point	N	94	32	113	-2	Mar.	16	Nov.	21	250	N	2.7	3.2	3.6	4.7	5.4	4.2	2.2	3.0	3.9	4.2	3.6	3.3	43.0
Victoria, Victoria	15	94	43	107	9	Feb.	19	Dec.	6	290	23	2.2	2.5	1.6	2.4	4.5	4.5	3.3	3.0	5.6	3.5	2.5	2.0	37.4
Walker, Huntsville	N	95	38	107	13	Mar.	7	Nov.	27	265	N	3.6	3.1	3.1	3.5	5.2	4.9	2.4	3.3	5.0	3.6	4.2	3.8	45.0
Waller, Hempstead*	N	96	38	120	-9	Feb.	28	Dec.	4	283	N	2.8	2.9	2.1	3.9	4.7	3.6	2.0	2.4	4.6	4.0	3.2	3.0	38.2
Ward, Monahans	27	96	27	110	1	Apr.	1	Nov.	10	223	N	0.4	0.6	0.4	0.7	1.8	1.4	1.4	1.4	2.4	1.4	0.6	0.5	12.7
Washington, Brenham	N	99	41	108	13	Mar.	3	Dec.	4	277	N	3.1	2.9	2.8	3.3	5.2	4.3	2.0	2.5	4.8	3.6	3.9	3.2	41.4
Webb, Laredo	27	92	43	113	7	Feb.	5	Dec.	26	322	N	0.8	1.0	0.5	1.6	2.7	3.1	1.4	2.6	3.3	2.9	1.1	0.9	21.4
Wharton, Danevang	N	95	22	117	-8	Feb.	7	Dec.	1	266	14	2.8	2.9	2.6	2.5	4.9	4.7	3.6	3.6	5.9	3.9	3.1	2.7	42.3
Wheeler, Shamrock	N	97	28	119	-9	Apr.	27	Nov.	26	208	N	1.0	1.2	1.5	3.0	3.5	3.4	2.0	2.5	2.8	1.8	1.0	0.5	22.1
Wichita, Wichita Falls	N	97	25	107	14	Mar.	31	Nov.	11	229	N	0.9	1.2	1.8	2.3	4.1	3.5	3.6	2.5	3.8	2.7	1.5	1.3	28.9
Wilbarger, Vernon	N	96	46	112	-5	Mar.	6	Nov.	7	221	N	1.5	1.6	0.8	1.5	3.8	2.9	2.0	3.1	5.8	2.6	1.3	0.8	25.7
Willacy, Raymondville	N	96	34	108	7	Feb.	6	Dec.	11	331	N	1.5	1.6	0.8	1.5	3.13	3.3	2.0	2.3	4.2	2.2	1.3	1.2	27.6
Williamson, Taylor	28	96	36	117	-14	Mar.	11	Nov.	24	258	14	2.0	2.5	1.2	2.9	4.7	3.6	1.7	2.0	3.6	3.6	2.7	2.1	34.4
Wilson, Floresville	N	97	28	115	-8	Mar.	3	Dec.	1	280	N	1.9	1.9	1.2	2.4	3.4	2.9	2.0	2.3	3.6	1.5	2.7	1.6	29.4
Winkler, Wink	N	99	30	107	2	Mar.	31	Nov.	8	219	N	0.3	0.4	0.4	0.7	1.0	1.9	1.7	1.4	2.3	1.3	0.6	0.4	12.6
Wise, Bridgeport	14	94	31	111	-12	Mar.	17	Nov.	6	220	N	1.5	3.0	1.9	3.1	5.3	3.5	2.3	2.0	3.6	3.3	2.0	1.5	32.6
Wood, Mineola*	N	94	22	111	-8	Mar.	15	Nov.	18	246	N	3.1	3.0	4.0	2.8	4.9	2.4	2.6	2.5	4.8	3.3	3.0	3.6	45.0
Yoakum, Plains	N	91	26	111	-12	Apr.	15	Oct.	31	199	N	0.4	0.7	0.6	1.0	2.1	2.4	2.1	2.3	2.6	1.3	0.7	0.7	17.7
Young, Graham	N	96	43	112	2	Apr.	2	Nov.	4	216	12	1.3	1.6	1.6	1.4	4.5	3.4	1.6	1.7	4.2	1.6	1.9	1.4	30.6
Zapata, Zapata	27	99	42	112	16	Feb.	14	Dec.	15	304	N	0.8	1.1	0.6	1.4	2.4	2.5	1.6	1.7	4.3	1.6	1.0	0.9	19.7
Zavala, Crystal City	N	97	42	109	11	Feb.	24	Dec.	1	280	N	0.9	1.2	0.8	1.8	2.9	2.8	1.6	1.9	2.7	2.5	1.1	0.8	21.0

Astronomical Calendar For 2000 and 2001

The subsequent calendars were calculated principally from data in the U.S. Naval Observatory's Internet site (http://aa.usno.navy.mil/AA/data/), and from its publication, **Astronomical Phenomena** for **2000** and **2001**.

Times listed here are **Central Standard Time**, except for the period from 2:00 a.m. on the first Sunday in April until 2:00 a.m. on the last Sunday in October, when **Daylight Saving Time,** which is one hour later than Central Standard Time, is in effect.

All of Texas is in the Central Time Zone, except El Paso and Hudspeth counties and the northwest corner of Culberson County, which observe **Mountain Time** (see accompanying map). Mountain Time is one hour earlier than Central Time.

All times are figured for the intersection of 99° 20' west longitude and 31° 08' north latitude, which is the location of Brady, McCulloch County. This point is about 22 miles south-southwest of the **approximate geographical center of the state**.

To get the time of sunrise or sunset, moonrise or moonset for any point in Texas, apply the following rule: Add four minutes to the time given in this calendar for each degree of longitude that the place lies west of the 99th meridian; subtract four minutes for each degree of longitude the place lies east of the 99th meridian.

At times there will be considerable variation for distances north and south of the line of 31° 08' north latitude, but the rule for calculating it is complicated. The formula given above will get sufficiently close results. An accompanying map shows the intersection for which all times given here are calculated, with some major Texas cities and their longitudes. These make it convenient to calculate time at any given point.

The Naval Observatory's Web site (address above) will allow you to determine more exactly the rise and set times of the Sun and the Moon at your location on a given date or for an entire year.

Planetary Configurations and Phenomena

The phenomena and planetary configurations of heavens for 2000 and 2001 are given in the center column of the calendar on pages 103-108. Below is an explanation of the symbols used in those tables:

⊙ The Sun	● The Earth	⛢ Uranus
☾ The Moon	♂ Mars	♆ Neptune
☿ Mercury	♃ Jupiter	♇ Pluto
♀ Venus	♄ Saturn	

Aspects

☌ This symbol appearing between the symbols for heavenly bodies means they are "in conjunction," that is, having the same longitude as applies to the sky and appearing near each other.

☍ This symbol means that the two heavenly bodies are in "opposition," or differ by 180 degrees of longitude.

Common Astronomical Terms

★ **Aphelion** — Point at which a planet's orbit is farthest from the sun.

★ **Perihelion** — Point at which a planet's orbit is nearest the sun.

★ **Apogee** — That point of the moon's orbit farthest from the earth.

★ **Perigee** — That point of the moon's orbit nearest the earth.

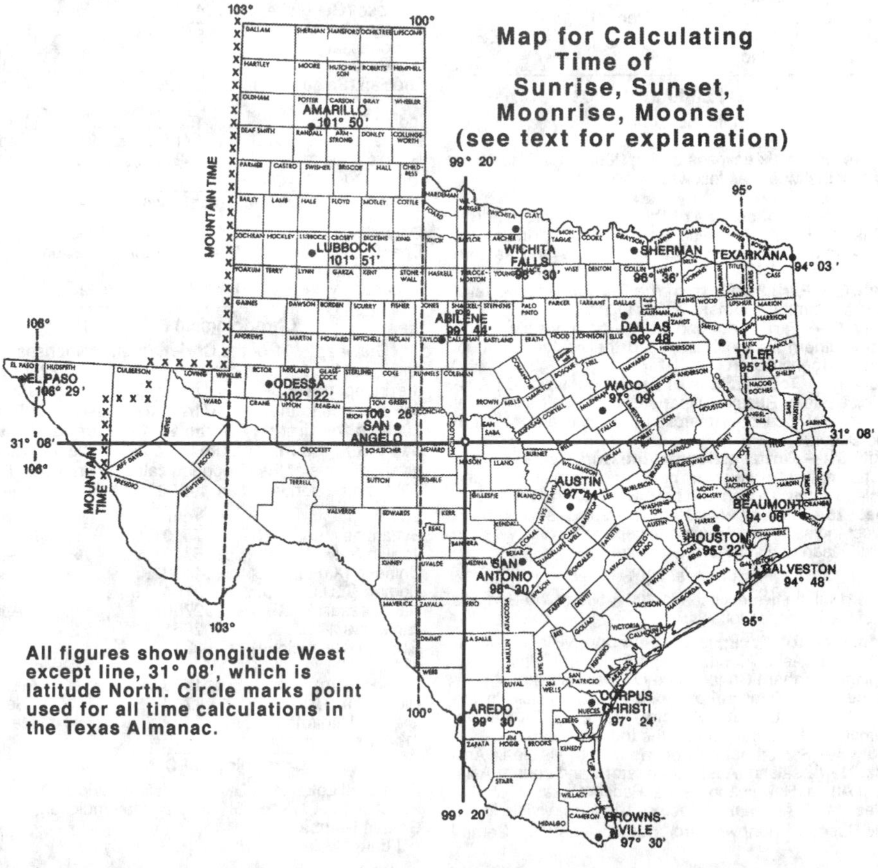
103°
100°
99° 20'
95°
106°
31° 08'
MOUNTAIN TIME
AMARILLO 101° 50'
LUBBOCK 101° 51'
WICHITA FALLS 98° 30'
SHERMAN 96° 36'
TEXARKANA 94° 03'
ABILENE 99° 44'
DALLAS 96° 48'
TYLER 95° 18'
EL PASO 106° 29'
ODESSA 102° 22'
SAN ANGELO 100° 26'
WACO 97° 09'
AUSTIN 97° 44'
BEAUMONT 94° 06'
HOUSTON 95° 22'
GALVESTON 94° 48'
SAN ANTONIO 98° 30'
CORPUS CHRISTI 97° 24'
LAREDO 99° 30'
BROWNSVILLE 97° 30'

Map for Calculating Time of Sunrise, Sunset, Moonrise, Moonset (see text for explanation)

All figures show longitude West except line, 31° 08', which is latitude North. Circle marks point used for all time calculations in the Texas Almanac.

★ **Aspect** — Apparent situation of a planet with respect to another body.

The Seasons, 2000 and 2001

2000

The seasons of 2000 begin as follows: **Spring,** March 20, 1:35 a.m. (CST); **Summer,** June 20, 8:48 p.m. (CDT); **Fall,** Sept. 22, 12:27 p.m. (CDT); **Winter,** Dec. 21, 7:37 a.m. (CST).

2001

The seasons of 2001 begin as follows: **Spring,** March 20, 7:31 a.m. (CST); **Summer,** June 21, 2:38 a.m. (CDT); **Fall,** Sept. 22, 6:04 p.m. (CDT); **Winter,** Dec. 21, 1:21 p.m. (CST).

Morning and Evening Stars, 2000 and 2001

Morning Stars, 2000

Venus — Jan. 1 - May 5
Jupiter — May 22 - Nov. 28
Saturn — May 29 - Nov. 19
Mars — Aug. 20 - Dec. 31

Evening Stars, 2000

Saturn — Jan. 1 - April 23; Nov. 19 - Dec. 31
Jupiter — Jan. 1 - April 24; Nov. 28 - Dec. 31
Mars — Jan. 1 - May 8
Venus — July 18 - Dec. 31

Morning Stars, 2001

Mars — Jan. 1 - June 13
Venus — April 4 - Dec. 3
Saturn — June 13 - Dec. 3
Jupiter — June 29 - Dec. 31

Evening Stars, 2001

Venus — Jan. 1 - March 26
Saturn — Jan. 1 - May 7; Dec. 3 - Dec. 31
Jupiter — Jan. 1 - May 31
Mars — June 13 - Dec. 31

Eclipses, 2000 and 2001

Eclipses, 2000

There will be six eclipses during 2000, four of the Sun and two of the Moon, as follows:

Jan. 21 — Total eclipse of the Moon, visible in northern Russia, Europe including British Isles, northwestern Africa, Atlantic Ocean, Arctic, the Americas and eastern Pacific Ocean.

Feb. 5 — Partial eclipse of the Sun, visible in Antarctica and the central southern Indian Ocean.

July 1 — Partial eclipse of the Sun, visible in central southern Pacific Ocean and the southern part of Chile and Argentina.

July 16 — Total eclipse of the Moon, visible in Australasia, eastern Russia, Japan, China, southeast Asia, India, Indian Ocean, Antarctica, Hawaii and eastern Pacific Ocean.

July 31 — Partial eclipse of the Sun, visible in western and northern Russia, northern Scandinavia and Greenland, Arctic Ocean and northwest North America.

Dec. 25 — Partial eclipse of the Sun, visible in Mexico, West Indies, North America except northwest, western Atlantic Ocean and southern Greenland.

Eclipses, 2001

There will be five eclipses in 2001, two of the Sun and three of the Moon, as follows:

Jan. 9 — Total eclipse of the Moon, visible in western Australia, Asia, Africa, Europe including British Isles, Greenland, northern Canada and northern Alaska.

June 21 — Total eclipse of the Sun, visible in the south Atlantic Ocean, Angola, Zambia, Zimbabwe, Mozambique, Madagascar and the Indian Ocean.

July 5— Partial eclipse of the Moon, visible in Antarctica, New Zealand, Australia, eastern and central Asia, eastern Africa, Hawaii and central Pacific Ocean.

Dec. 14 — Annular eclipse of the Sun, visible in the Pacific Ocean, northwestern South America, Central America, United States and western and southern Canada.

Dec. 30 — Penumbral eclipse of the Moon, visible in Australasia, Asia except southwest, northern Europe, Greenland, the Americas and the Pacific Ocean.

Major Meteor Showers, 2000 and 2001

Note: These dates are not firm. Listen to your local news and weather broadcasts several days before the listed dates to determine peak observation days and hours.

Meteor dates provided by R.L Hawkes, Mount Allison University, Canada.

Meteor Shower	Peak Day 2000	Peak Day 2001
Quadrantids	Jan. 3	Jan. 3
Perseids	Aug. 11	Aug. 12
Orionids	Oct. 21	Oct. 21
Leonids	Nov. 16	Nov. 17
Geminids	Dec. 13	Dec. 14

Chronological Eras and Cycles, 2000 and 2001

Chronological Eras, 2000

The year 2000 of the **Christian** era comprises the latter part of the 224th and the beginning of the 225th year of the independence of the United States of America, and corresponds to the year 6713 of the Julian period. **Dec. 31, 2000, is the last day of the 20th century and the last day of the 2nd millennium.** All dates in the list below are given in terms of the Gregorian calendar, in which Jan. 14, 2000, corresponds to Jan. 1, 2000, Julian calendar.

Era	Year	Begins
Byzantine	7509	Sept. 14
Jewish (A.M.)*	5761	Sept. 29
Chinese (Geng-chen)	4637	Feb. 5
Roman (A.U.C.)	2753	Jan. 14
Nabonassar	2749	April 23
Japanese	2660	Jan. 1
Grecian (Seleucidae)	2312	Sept. 14 or Oct. 14
Indian (Saka)*	1922	March 21
Diocletian	1717	Sept. 11
Islamic (Hegira)*	1421	April 5

Year begins at sunset.

Chronological Cycles, 2000

Dominical Letter	BA	Julian Period	6713
Epact	24	Roman Indiction	8
Golden Number or			
Lunar Cycle	VI	Solar Cycle	21

Chronological Eras, 2001

The year 2001 of the **Christian** era comprises the latter part of the 225th and the beginning of the 226th year of the independence of the United States of America, and corresponds to the year 6714 of the Julian period. **Jan. 1, 2001, is the first day of the 21st century and the first day of the 3rd millennium.** All dates in the list below are given in terms of the Gregorian calendar, in which Jan. 14, 2001, corresponds to Jan. 1, 2001, of the Julian calendar:

Era	Year	Begins
Byzantine	7510	Sept. 14
Jewish (A.M.)*	5762	Sept. 17
Chinese (Xin-si)	4638	Jan. 24
Roman (A.U.C.)	2754	Jan. 14
Nabonassar	2750	April 23
Japanese	2661	Jan. 1
Grecian (Seleucidae)	2313	Sept. 14 or Oct. 14
Indian (Saka)	1923	March 22
Diocletian	1718	Sept. 11
Islamic (Hegira)*	1422	March 25

Year begins at sunset.

Chronological Cycles, 2001

Dominical Letter	G	Julian Period	6714
Epact	5	Roman Indiction	9
Golden Number or			
Lunar Cycle	VII	Solar Cycle	22

Calendar for 2000

Times are **Central Standard Time**, except from April 2 to Oct. 29, during which **Daylight Saving Time** is observed. **Boldface times for moonrise and moonset** indicate p.m. Times are figured for the point **99° 20' West and 31° 08' North,** the approximate center of the state. **See page 101 for explanation of how to get the approximate time at any other Texas point.** (On the Web: http://aa.usno.navy.mil/AA/data/) **Dec. 31, 2000, is the end of the 20th century and of the 2nd millennium**. Please note: Not all **eclipses** are visible in United States. For visibility, see listing p. 102.

1st Month — January 2000 — 31 Days

Moon's Phases — New, Jan. 6, 12:14 p.m.; First Qtr., Jan. 14, 7:34 a.m.; Full, Jan. 20, 10:40 p.m.; Last Qtr., Jan. 28, 1:57 a.m.

Day of Year	Day of Month	Day of Week	Planetary Configurations and Phenomena	*Hour of Sunrise	*Hour of Sunset	*Hour of Moonrise	*Hour of Moonset
1	1	Sa.		7:36	5:46	3:06	**2:30**
2	2	Su.	♀ ☌ ☾; ● at perihelion	7:36	5:47	4:00	**3:06**
3	3	Mo.		7:36	5:47	4:53	**3:44**
4	4	Tu.	☾ at apogee	7:36	5:48	5:46	**4:26**
5	5	We.		7:37	5:49	6:37	**5:11**
6	6	Th.		7:37	5:50	7:27	**6:00**
7	7	Fr.		7:37	5:50	8:14	**6:52**
8	8	Sa.	♆ ☌ ☾; ♅ ☌ ☾	7:37	5:51	8:57	**7:46**
9	9	Su.		7:37	5:52	9:38	**8:41**
10	10	Mo.	♂ ☌ ☾	7:37	5:53	10:16	**9:38**
11	11	Tu.		7:37	5:54	10:52	**10:35**
12	12	We.	♄ stationary	7:37	5:55	11:26	**11:33**
13	13	Th.		7:37	5:55	**12:01**	. . .
14	14	Fr.	♃ ☌ ☾	7:37	5:56	**12:37**	12:32
15	15	Sa.	♄ ☌ ☾; ☿ superior	7:36	5:57	**1:15**	1:34
16	16	Su.		7:36	5:58	**1:58**	2:38
17	17	Mo.		7:36	5:59	**2:46**	3:44
18	18	Tu.		7:36	6:00	**3:40**	4:51
19	19	We.	☾ at perigee	7:36	6:01	**4:40**	5:58
20	20	Th.		7:35	6:02	**5:46**	7:01
21	21	Fr.	Eclipse ☾	7:35	6:02	**6:53**	7:58
22	22	Sa.		7:35	6:03	**8:00**	8:48
23	23	Su.		7:34	6:04	**9:05**	9:33
24	24	Mo.	♆ ☌ ☉	7:34	6:05	**10:07**	10:12
25	25	Tu.		7:33	6:06	**11:06**	10:49
26	26	We.		7:33	6:07	. . .	11:23
27	27	Th.		7:33	6:08	12:03	11:56
28	28	Fr.		7:32	6:09	12:58	**12:30**
29	29	Sa.		7:32	6:10	1:53	**1:05**
30	30	Su.		7:31	6:10	2:47	**1:43**
31	31	Mo.	☾ at apogee	7:30	6:11	3:40	**2:23**

2nd Month — February 2000 — 29 Days

Moon's Phases — New, Feb. 5, 7:03 a.m.; First Qtr., Feb. 12, 5:21 p.m.; Full, Feb. 19, 10:27 a.m.; Last Qtr., Feb. 26, 9:53 p.m.

Day of Year	Day of Month	Day of Week	Planetary Configurations and Phenomena	*Hour of Sunrise	*Hour of Sunset	*Hour of Moonrise	*Hour of Moonset
32	1	Tu.		7:30	6:12	4:31	**3:07**
33	2	We.	♀ ☌ ☾	7:29	6:13	5:22	**3:55**
34	3	Th.		7:29	6:14	6:10	**4:46**
35	4	Fr.		7:28	6:15	6:55	**5:40**
36	5	Sa.	Partial eclipse ☉	7:27	6:16	7:37	**6:35**
37	6	Su.	♅ ☌ ☉; ☿ ☌ ☾	7:26	6:17	8:16	**7:32**
38	7	Mo.		7:26	6:18	8:53	**8:30**
39	8	Tu.	♂ ☌ ☾	7:25	6:18	9:28	**9:28**
40	9	We.		7:24	6:19	10:03	**10:27**
41	10	Th.	♃ ☌ ☾	7:23	6:20	10:38	**11:27**
42	11	Fr.	♄ ☌ ☾	7:22	6:21	11:15	. . .
43	12	Sa.		7:22	6:22	11:55	12:29
44	13	Su.		7:21	6:23	**12:39**	1:32
45	14	Mo.	☿ greatest elongation E.	7:20	6:24	**1:29**	2:37
46	15	Tu.		7:19	6:24	**2:24**	3:42
47	16	We.	☾ at perigee	7:18	6:25	**3:25**	4:44
48	17	Th.		7:17	6:26	**4:31**	5:42
49	18	Fr.		7:16	6:27	**5:37**	6:35
50	19	Sa.		7:15	6:28	**6:44**	7:22
51	20	Su.	☿ stationary	7:14	6:28	**7:48**	8:04
52	21	Mo.		7:13	6:29	**8:49**	8:42
53	22	Tu.	♀ ☌ ♆	7:12	6:30	**9:49**	9:18
54	23	We.		7:11	6:31	**10:46**	9:53
55	24	Th.		7:10	6:32	**11:42**	10:27
56	25	Fr.		7:09	6:32	. . .	11:02
57	26	Sa.		7:08	6:33	12:37	11:39
58	27	Su.		7:07	6:34	1:31	**12:19**
59	28	Mo.	☾ at apogee	7:06	6:35	2:24	**1:01**
60	29	Tu.		7:05	6:35	3:15	**1:48**

*See text before January calendar for explanation.

3rd Month — March 2000 — 31 Days

Moon's Phases — New, March 5, 11:17 p.m.; First Qtr., March 13, 12:59 a.m.; Full, March 19, 10:44 p.m.; Last Qtr., March 27, 6:21 p.m.

Day of Year	Day of Month	Day of Week	Planetary Configurations and Phenomena	*Hour of Sunrise	*Hour of Sunset	*Hour of Moonrise	*Hour of Moonset
61	1	We.	☿ inferior	7:04	6:36	4:04	**2:37**
62	2	Th.	♆ ☌ ☾	7:02	6:37	4:50	**3:30**
63	3	Fr.	♀ ☌ ♅; ♅ ☌ ☾; ♀ ☌ ☾	7:01	6:37	5:33	**4:25**
64	4	Sa.		7:00	6:38	6:14	**5:22**
65	5	Su.		6:59	6:39	6:52	**6:21**
66	6	Mo.		6:58	6:40	7:28	**7:20**
67	7	Tu.		6:57	6:40	8:03	**8:19**
68	8	We.	♂ ☌ ☾	6:55	6:41	8:39	**9:20**
69	9	Th.	♃ ☌ ☾	6:54	6:42	9:16	**10:23**
70	10	Fr.	♄ ☌ ☾	6:53	6:42	9:55	**11:26**
71	11	Sa.		6:52	6:43	10:37	. . .
72	12	Su.		6:51	6:44	11:25	12:30
73	13	Mo.	☿ stationary	6:49	6:44	**12:17**	1:34
74	14	Tu.	☿ ☌ ♀; ☾ at perigee	6:48	6:45	**1:15**	2:36
75	15	We.		6:47	6:46	**2:17**	3:34
76	16	Th.	♇ stationary	6:46	6:46	**3:22**	4:27
77	17	Fr.		6:44	6:47	**4:26**	5:15
78	18	Sa.		6:43	6:48	**5:30**	5:57
79	19	Su.		6:42	6:48	**6:32**	6:37
80	20	Mo.	Spring begins.	6:41	6:49	**7:33**	7:13
81	21	Tu.		6:39	6:50	**8:32**	7:48
82	22	We.		6:38	6:50	**9:29**	8:23
83	23	Th.		6:37	6:51	**10:26**	8:58
84	24	Fr.		6:36	6:52	**11:21**	9:34
85	25	Sa.		6:34	6:52	. . .	10:13
86	26	Su.		6:33	6:53	12:15	10:55
87	27	Mo.	☾ at apogee	6:32	6:54	1:07	11:40
88	28	Tu.	☿ greatest elongation W.	6:31	6:54	1:57	**12:28**
89	29	We.		6:29	6:55	2:44	**1:19**
90	30	Th.	♆ ☌ ☾	6:28	6:56	3:28	**2:13**
91	31	Fr.	♅ ☌ ☾	6:27	6:56	4:09	**3:09**

4th Month — April 2000 — 30 Days

Moon's Phases - New, April 4, 1:12 p.m.; First Qtr., April 11, 8:30 a.m.; Full, April 18, 12:41 p.m.; Last Qtr., April 26, 2:30 p.m.

Day of Year	Day of Month	Day of Week	Planetary Configurations and Phenomena	*Hour of Sunrise	*Hour of Sunset	*Hour of Moonrise	*Hour of Moonset
92	1	Sa.		6:26	6:57	4:48	**4:07**
93	†2	Su.	☿ ☌ ☾	7:24	7:58	6:25	**6:06**
94	3	Mo.	♀ ☌ ☾	7:23	7:58	7:01	**7:06**
95	4	Tu.		7:22	7:59	7:36	**8:08**
96	5	We.		7:21	7:59	8:13	**9:11**
97	6	Th.	♂, ♃ and ♄ ☌ ☾; ♂ ☌ ♃	7:19	8:00	8:52	**10:16**
98	7	Fr.		7:18	8:01	9:34	**11:22**
99	8	Sa.	☾ at perigee	7:17	8:01	10:21	. . .
100	9	Su.		7:16	8:02	11:13	12:28
101	10	Mo.		7:15	8:03	**12:10**	1:31
102	11	Tu.		7:14	8:03	**1:10**	2:31
103	12	We.		7:12	8:04	**2:13**	3:25
104	13	Th.		7:11	8:05	**3:17**	4:13
105	14	Fr.		7:10	8:05	**4:20**	4:56
106	15	Sa.		7:09	8:06	**5:21**	5:35
107	16	Su.	♂ ☌ ♄	7:08	8:07	**6:21**	6:12
108	17	Mo.		7:07	8:07	**7:20**	6:46
109	18	Tu.		7:06	8:08	**8:17**	7:20
110	19	We.		7:04	8:09	**9:14**	7:55
111	20	Th.		7:03	8:09	**10:10**	8:30
112	21	Fr.		7:02	8:10	**11:05**	9:08
113	22	Sa.		7:01	8:11	**11:59**	9:49
114	23	Su.		7:00	8:11	. . .	10:33
115	24	Mo.	☾ at apogee	6:59	8:12	12:50	11:20
116	25	Tu.		6:58	8:13	1:38	**12:10**
117	26	We.	♆ ☌ ☾	6:57	8:13	2:23	**1:02**
118	27	Th.	♅ ☌ ☾	6:56	8:14	3:05	**1:57**
119	28	Fr.	☿ ☌ ♀	6:55	8:15	3:44	**2:53**
120	29	Sa.		6:54	8:15	4:21	**3:50**
121	30	Su.		6:53	8:16	4:56	**4:49**

†Daylight Saving Time begins at 2:00 a.m.

Calendar for 2000 (Cont'd.)

5th Month — May 2000 — 31 Days

Moon's Phases — New, May 3, 11:12 p.m.; First Qtr., May 10, 3:00 p.m.; Full, May 18, 2:34 a.m., Last Qtr., May 26, 6:55 a.m.

Day of Year	Day of Month	Day of Week	Planetary Configurations and Phenomena	*Hour of Sunrise	*Hour of Sunset	*Hour of Moonrise	*Hour of Moonset
122	1	Mo.		6:52	8:17	5:32	**5:50**
123	2	Tu.		6:51	8:17	6:08	**6:53**
124	3	We.		6:51	8:18	6:46	**7:59**
125	4	Th.		6:50	8:19	7:27	**9:06**
126	5	Fr.	♂ ☌ ☾	6:49	8:19	8:13	**10:14**
127	6	Sa.	☾ at perigee	6:48	8:20	9:04	**11:21**
128	7	Su.	♃ ☌ ☉	6:47	8:21	10:01	. . .
129	8	Mo.	♆ stationary; ☿ superior	6:46	8:22	11:02	12:24
130	9	Tu.		6:46	8:22	**12:06**	1:22
131	10	We.	♄ ☌ ☉	6:45	8:23	**1:10**	2:13
132	11	Th.		6:44	8:24	**2:13**	2:57
133	12	Fr.		6:43	8:24	**3:15**	3:37
134	13	Sa.		6:43	8:25	**4:14**	4:14
135	14	Su.		6:42	8:26	**5:12**	4:48
136	15	Mo.		6:41	8:26	**6:09**	5:21
137	16	Tu.		6:41	8:27	**7:06**	5:55
138	17	We.		6:40	8:28	**8:02**	6:29
139	18	Th.		6:40	8:28	**8:57**	7:06
140	19	Fr.	☿ ☌ ♂	6:39	8:29	**9:52**	7:45
141	20	Sa.		6:39	8:30	**10:44**	8:28
142	21	Su.	☾ at apogee	6:38	8:30	**11:33**	9:14
143	22	Mo.		6:38	8:31	. . .	10:03
144	23	Tu.	♆ ☌ ☾	6:37	8:31	12:20	10:54
145	24	We.		6:37	8:32	1:02	11:47
146	25	Th.	♅ ☌ ☾; ♅ stationary	6:36	8:33	1:42	**12:42**
147	26	Fr.		6:36	8:33	2:19	**1:38**
148	27	Sa.		6:35	8:34	2:54	**2:35**
149	28	Su.		6:35	8:34	3:28	**3:33**
150	29	Mo.		6:35	8:35	4:03	**4:34**
151	30	Tu.		6:35	8:36	4:39	**5:37**
152	31	We.	♃ ☌ ♄; ♄ ☌ ☾	6:34	8:36	5:18	**6:44**

6th Month — June 2000 — 30 Days

Moon's Phases — New, June 2, 7:14 a.m.; First Qtr., June 8, 10:29 p.m.; Full, June 16, 5:27 p.m.; Last Qtr., June 24, 8:00 p.m.

Day of Year	Day of Month	Day of Week	Planetary Configurations and Phenomena	*Hour of Sunrise	*Hour of Sunset	*Hour of Moonrise	*Hour of Moonset
153	1	Th.	♃ ☌ ☾; ♇ ☍	6:34	8:37	6:01	**7:52**
154	2	Fr.		6:34	8:37	6:50	**9:02**
155	3	Sa.	☾ at perigee; ☿ ☌ ☾	6:34	8:38	7:45	**10:09**
156	4	Su.		6:33	8:38	8:47	**11:11**
157	5	Mo.		6:33	8:39	9:52	. . .
158	6	Tu.		6:33	8:39	10:59	12:07
159	7	We.		6:33	8:40	**12:05**	12:56
160	8	Th.		6:33	8:40	**1:08**	1:38
161	9	Fr.	☿ greatest elongation E.	6:33	8:41	**2:09**	2:16
162	10	Sa.		6:33	8:41	**3:08**	2:51
163	11	Su.	♀ superior	6:33	8:41	**4:05**	3:24
164	12	Mo.		6:33	8:42	**5:01**	3:57
165	13	Tu.		6:33	8:42	**5:56**	4:31
166	14	We.		6:33	8:42	**6:52**	5:06
167	15	Th.		6:33	8:43	**7:46**	5:44
168	16	Fr.		6:33	8:43	**8:39**	6:25
169	17	Sa.		6:33	8:43	**9:30**	7:10
170	18	Su.	☾ at apogee	6:33	8:44	**10:17**	7:58
171	19	Mo.		6:34	8:44	**11:01**	8:48
172	20	Tu.	Summer begins; ♆ ☌ ☾	6:34	8:44	**11:42**	9:41
173	21	We.	♅ ☌ ☾	6:34	8:44	. . .	10:35
174	22	Th.	☿ stationary	6:34	8:45	12:19	11:30
175	23	Fr.		6:35	8:45	12:54	**12:26**
176	24	Sa.		6:35	8:45	1:28	**1:22**
177	25	Su.		6:35	8:45	2:01	**2:20**
178	26	Mo.		6:35	8:45	2:35	**3:20**
179	27	Tu.		6:36	8:45	3:11	**4:23**
180	28	We.	♄ ☌ ☾; ♃ ☌ ☾	6:36	8:45	3:51	**5:29**
181	29	Th.		6:36	8:45	4:36	**6:38**
182	30	Fr.		6:37	8:45	5:28	**7:46**

*See text before January calendar for explanation.

7th Month — July 2000 — 31 Days

Moon's Phases — New, July 1, 2:20 p.m.; First Qtr., July 8, 7:53 a.m.; Full, July 16, 8:55 a.m.; Last Qtr., July 24, 6:02 a.m.; New, July 30, 9:25 p.m.

Day of Year	Day of Month	Day of Week	Planetary Configurations and Phenomena	*Hour of Sunrise	*Hour of Sunset	*Hour of Moonrise	*Hour of Moonset
183	1	Sa.	♂ ☌ ☉; ☾ at perigee	6:37	8:45	6:26	**8:52**
184	2	Su.		6:38	8:45	7:31	**9:53**
185	3	Mo.	● at aphelion	6:38	8:45	8:39	**10:47**
186	4	Tu.		6:39	8:45	9:48	**11:33**
187	5	We.		6:39	8:45	10:55	. . .
188	6	Th.	☿ inferior	6:39	8:45	11:59	12:14
189	7	Fr.		6:40	8:45	**1:00**	12:52
190	8	Sa.		6:40	8:44	**1:58**	1:26
191	9	Su.		6:41	8:44	**2:55**	2:00
192	10	Mo.		6:41	8:44	**3:51**	2:33
193	11	Tu.		6:42	8:44	**4:47**	3:08
194	12	We.		6:43	8:43	**5:41**	3:45
195	13	Th.		6:43	8:43	**6:34**	4:24
196	14	Fr.		6:44	8:43	**7:26**	5:08
197	15	Sa.	☾ at apogee	6:44	8:42	**8:14**	5:54
198	16	Su.	Eclipse ☾	6:45	8:42	**9:00**	6:44
199	17	Mo.	☿ stationary; ♆ ☌ ☾	6:45	8:41	**9:42**	7:36
200	18	Tu.	♅ ☌ ☾	6:46	8:41	**10:20**	8:30
201	19	We.		6:47	8:40	**10:56**	9:25
202	20	Th.		6:47	8:40	**11:30**	10:20
203	21	Fr.		6:48	8:39	. . .	11:16
204	22	Sa.		6:48	8:39	12:02	**12:12**
205	23	Su.		6:49	8:38	12:35	**1:10**
206	24	Mo.		6:50	8:38	1:10	**2:10**
207	25	Tu.		6:50	8:37	1:46	**3:13**
208	26	We.	♄ ☌ ☾; ♃ ☌ ☾	6:51	8:37	2:27	**4:18**
209	27	Th.	☿ greatest elongation W.	6:51	8:36	3:14	**5:25**
210	28	Fr.		6:52	8:35	4:08	**6:31**
211	29	Sa.	☿ ☌ ☾	6:53	8:34	5:09	**7:34**
212	30	Su.	☾ at perigee	6:53	8:34	6:15	**8:31**
213	31	Mo.	Partial eclipse ☉	6:54	8:33	7:24	**9:22**

8th Month — August 2000 — 31 Days

Moon's Phases — First Qtr., Aug. 6, 8:02 p.m.; Full, Aug. 15, 12:13 a.m.; Last Qtr., Aug. 22, 1:51 p.m.; New, Aug. 29, 5:19 a.m.

Day of Year	Day of Month	Day of Week	Planetary Configurations and Phenomena	*Hour of Sunrise	*Hour of Sunset	*Hour of Moonrise	*Hour of Moonset
214	1	Tu.		6:55	8:32	8:34	**10:07**
215	2	We.		6:55	8:31	9:41	**10:47**
216	3	Th.		6:56	8:31	10:46	**11:24**
217	4	Fr.		6:56	8:30	11:47	**11:59**
218	5	Sa.		6:57	8:29	**12:46**	. . .
219	6	Su.		6:58	8:28	**1:44**	12:33
220	7	Mo.		6:58	8:27	**2:40**	1:08
221	8	Tu.		6:59	8:26	**3:35**	1:44
222	9	We.		7:00	8:25	**4:29**	2:23
223	10	Th.	☿ ☌ ♂	7:00	8:24	**5:21**	3:05
224	11	Fr.	♅ ☍; ☾ at apogee	7:01	8:23	**6:11**	3:51
225	12	Sa.		7:02	8:22	**6:57**	4:40
226	13	Su.	♆ ☌ ☾	7:02	8:21	**7:41**	5:31
227	14	Mo.	♅ ☌ ☾	7:03	8:20	**8:20**	6:25
228	15	Tu.		7:03	8:19	**8:57**	7:20
229	16	We.		7:04	8:18	**9:32**	8:15
230	17	Th.		7:05	8:17	**10:05**	9:11
231	18	Fr.		7:05	8:16	**10:38**	10:08
232	19	Sa.		7:06	8:15	**11:11**	11:05
233	20	Su.		7:06	8:14	**11:46**	**12:03**
234	21	Mo.	☿ superior	7:07	8:13	. . .	**1:04**
235	22	Tu.	♄ ☌ ☾; ♇ stationary	7:08	8:12	12:25	**2:07**
236	23	We.	♃ ☌ ☾	7:08	8:11	1:08	**3:11**
237	24	Th.		7:09	8:10	1:57	**4:15**
238	25	Fr.		7:09	8:08	2:53	**5:18**
239	26	Sa.		7:10	8:07	3:55	**6:16**
240	27	Su.	☾ at perigee; ♂ ☌ ☾	7:11	8:06	5:02	**7:09**
241	28	Mo.		7:11	8:05	6:11	**7:57**
242	29	Tu.		7:12	8:04	7:19	**8:39**
243	30	We.	♀ ☌ ☾	7:12	8:03	8:26	**9:18**
244	31	Th.		7:13	8:01	9:30	**9:54**

Calendar for 2000 (Cont'd.)

9th Month — September 2000 — 30 Days

Moon's Phases — First Qtr., Sept. 5, 11:27 a.m.; Full, Sept. 13, 2:37 p.m.; Last Qtr., Sept. 20, 8:28 p.m.; New, Sept. 27, 2:53 p.m.

Year	Month	Week	Planetary Configurations and Phenomena	Sunrise	Sunset	Moonrise	Moonset
245	1	Fr.		7:14	8:00	10:32	10:29
246	2	Sa.		7:14	7:59	11:31	11:04
247	3	Su.		7:15	7:58	12:30	11:41
248	4	Mo.		7:15	7:56	1:27	...
249	5	Tu.		7:16	7:55	2:22	12:20
250	6	We.		7:17	7:54	3:15	1:01
251	7	Th.		7:17	7:53	4:06	1:46
252	8	Fr.	☾ at apogee	7:18	7:51	4:54	2:33
253	9	Sa.	♆ ☌ ☾	7:18	7:50	5:38	3:24
254	10	Su.	♅ ☌ ☾	7:19	7:49	6:19	4:17
255	11	Mo.		7:19	7:48	6:57	5:12
256	12	Tu.	♄ stationary	7:20	7:46	7:32	6:08
257	13	We.		7:21	7:45	8:06	7:04
258	14	Th.		7:21	7:44	8:39	8:01
259	15	Fr.		7:22	7:42	9:12	8:59
260	16	Sa.		7:22	7:41	9:47	9:58
261	17	Su.		7:23	7:40	10:25	10:58
262	18	Mo.	♄ ☌ ☾	7:23	7:38	11:06	12:01
263	19	Tu.	♃ ☌ ☾	7:24	7:37	11:52	1:04
264	20	We.		7:25	7:36	...	2:07
265	21	Th.		7:25	7:35	12:45	3:09
266	22	Fr.	Fall begins.	7:26	7:33	1:43	4:07
267	23	Sa.		7:26	7:32	2:47	5:01
268	24	Su.	☾ at perigee	7:27	7:31	3:53	5:49
269	25	Mo.	♂ ☌ ☾	7:28	7:29	5:00	6:32
270	26	Tu.		7:28	7:28	6:06	7:11
271	27	We.		7:29	7:27	7:11	7:48
272	28	Th.		7:29	7:26	8:14	8:24
273	29	Fr.	☿ and ♀ ☌ ☾; ♃ stationary	7:30	7:24	9:15	8:59
274	30	Sa.		7:31	7:23	10:15	9:36

10th Month — October 2000 — 31 Days

Moon's Phases — First Qtr., Oct. 5, 5:59 a.m.; Full, Oct. 13, 3:53 a.m.; Last Qtr., Oct. 20, 2:59 a.m.; New, Oct. 27, 2:58 a.m.

Year	Month	Week	Planetary Configurations and Phenomena	Sunrise	Sunset	Moonrise	Moonset
275	1	Su.		7:31	7:22	11:14	10:14
276	2	Mo.		7:32	7:21	12:11	10:55
277	3	Tu.		7:32	7:19	1:06	11:39
278	4	We.		7:33	7:18	1:59	...
279	5	Th.		7:34	7:17	2:48	12:25
280	6	Fr.	☾ at apogee	7:34	7:16	3:34	1:15
281	7	Sa.	♆ ☌ ☾	7:35	7:14	4:16	2:08
282	8	Su.	♅ ☌ ☾	7:36	7:13	4:54	3:02
283	9	Mo.		7:36	7:12	5:30	3:57
284	10	Tu.		7:37	7:11	6:05	4:53
285	11	We.		7:38	7:10	6:38	5:50
286	12	Th.		7:38	7:09	7:12	6:48
287	13	Fr.		7:39	7:07	7:46	7:48
288	14	Sa.		7:40	7:06	8:23	8:49
289	15	Su.	♆ stationary	7:40	7:05	9:04	9:52
290	16	Mo.	♄ ☌ ☾; ♃ ☌ ☾	7:41	7:04	9:49	10:57
291	17	Tu.		7:42	7:03	10:41	12:02
292	18	We.	☿ stationary	7:42	7:02	11:37	1:05
293	19	Th.	☾ at perigee	7:43	7:01	...	2:04
294	20	Fr.		7:44	7:00	12:39	2:58
295	21	Sa.		7:45	6:59	1:43	3:46
296	22	Su.		7:45	6:58	2:49	4:30
297	23	Mo.		7:46	6:57	3:53	5:09
298	24	Tu.	♂ ☌ ☾	7:47	6:56	4:57	5:46
299	25	We.		7:48	6:55	5:59	6:21
300	26	Th.	♅ stationary	7:48	6:54	7:01	6:55
301	27	Fr.		7:49	6:53	8:01	7:31
302	28	Sa.		7:50	6:52	9:00	8:08
303	†29	Su.	☿ inferior	6:51	5:51	8:59	7:48
304	30	Mo.	♀ ☌ ☾	6:52	5:50	9:56	8:31
305	31	Tu.		6:52	5:49	10:50	9:17

11th Month — November 2000 — 30 Days

Moon's Phases — First Qtr., Nov. 4, 1:27 a.m.; Full, Nov. 11, 3:15 p.m.; Last Qtr., Nov. 18, 9:24 a.m.; New, Nov. 25, 5:11 p.m.

Year	Month	Week	Planetary Configurations and Phenomena	Sunrise	Sunset	Moonrise	Moonset
306	1	We.		6:53	5:48	11:41	10:06
307	2	Th.	☾ at apogee	6:54	5:48	12:28	10:57
308	3	Fr.	♆ ☌ ☾	6:55	5:47	1:12	11:51
309	4	Sa.	♅ ☌ ☾	6:56	5:46	1:51	...
310	5	Su.		6:56	5:45	2:28	12:45
311	6	Mo.		6:57	5:44	3:02	1:43
312	7	Tu.	☿ stationary	6:58	5:44	3:36	2:36
313	8	We.		6:59	5:43	4:09	3:33
314	9	Th.		7:00	5:42	4:42	4:32
315	10	Fr.		7:01	5:42	5:18	5:33
316	11	Sa.		7:01	5:41	5:58	6:37
317	12	Su.	♄ ☌ ☾; ♃ ☌ ☾	7:02	5:41	6:42	7:42
318	13	Mo.		7:03	5:40	7:33	8:49
319	14	Tu.	☾ at perigee	7:04	5:39	8:29	9:55
320	15	We.	☿ greatest elongation W.	7:05	5:39	9:31	10:58
321	16	Th.		7:06	5:38	10:36	11:55
322	17	Fr.		7:07	5:38	11:42	12:46
323	18	Sa.		7:07	5:38	...	1:31
324	19	Su.	♄ ☍	7:08	5:37	12:46	2:11
325	20	Mo.		7:09	5:37	1:50	2:47
326	21	Tu.	♂ ☌ ☾	7:10	5:36	2:51	3:22
327	22	We.		7:11	5:36	3:51	3:55
328	23	Th.		7:12	5:36	4:51	4:30
329	24	Fr.	☿ ☌ ☾	7:13	5:36	5:49	5:05
330	25	Sa.		7:13	5:36	6:48	5:44
331	26	Su.		7:14	5:35	7:45	6:25
332	27	Mo.	♃ ☍	7:15	5:35	8:41	7:10
333	28	Tu.		7:16	5:35	9:34	7:58
334	29	We.	♀ ☌ ☾	7:17	5:35	10:23	8:49
335	30	Th.	♆ ☌ ☾; ☾ at apogee	7:18	5:35	11:08	9:41

12th Month — December 2000 — 31 Days

Moon's Phases — First Qtr., Dec. 3, 9:55 p.m.; Full, Dec. 11, 3:03 a.m.; Last Qtr., Dec.17, 6:41 p.m.; New, Dec. 25, 11:22 a.m.

Year	Month	Week	Planetary Configurations and Phenomena	Sunrise	Sunset	Moonrise	Moonset
336	1	Fr.	♅ ☌ ☾	7:18	5:35	11:49	10:35
337	2	Sa.		7:19	5:35	12:26	11:29
338	3	Su.		7:20	5:35	1:01	...
339	4	Mo.	♇ ☌ ☉	7:21	5:35	1:34	12:24
340	5	Tu.		7:22	5:35	2:06	1:19
341	6	We.		7:22	5:35	2:38	2:16
342	7	Th.		7:23	5:35	3:12	3:14
343	8	Fr.		7:24	5:35	3:49	4:16
344	9	Sa.	♄ ☌ ☾	7:25	5:35	4:31	5:20
345	10	Su.	♃ ☌ ☾	7:25	5:35	5:19	6:27
346	11	Mo.	♀ ☌ ♆	7:26	5:36	6:14	7:36
347	12	Tu.	☾ at perigee	7:27	5:36	7:15	8:43
348	13	We.		7:27	5:36	8:22	9:45
349	14	Th.		7:28	5:37	9:30	10:41
350	15	Fr.		7:29	5:37	10:37	11:29
351	16	Sa.		7:29	5:37	11:43	12:12
352	17	Su.		7:30	5:38	...	12:50
353	18	Mo.		7:30	5:38	12:45	1:25
354	19	Tu.		7:31	5:39	1:46	1:58
355	20	We.	♂ ☌ ☾	7:31	5:39	2:45	2:32
356	21	Th.	Winter begins.	7:32	5:40	3:43	3:06
357	22	Fr.		7:32	5:40	4:41	3:43
358	23	Sa.	♀ ☌ ♅	7:33	5:41	5:38	4:22
359	24	Su.		7:33	5:41	6:34	5:06
360	25	Mo.	Partial eclipse ☉	7:34	5:42	7:27	5:52
361	26	Tu.		7:34	5:42	8:18	6:42
362	27	We.		7:35	5:43	9:05	7:34
363	28	Th.	♆ ☌ ☾; ☾ at apogee	7:35	5:44	9:47	8:27
364	29	Fr.	♀ ☌ ☾; ♅ ☌ ☾	7:35	5:44	10:26	9:21
365	30	Sa.		7:35	5:45	11:01	10:16
366	31	Su.		7:36	5:46	11:34	11:10

*See text before January calendar for explanation.
† Daylight Saving Time ends at 2:00 a.m.

Calendar for 2001

Times are **Central Standard Time**, except from April 1 to Oct. 28, during which **Daylight Saving Time** is observed. **Boldface times for moonrise and moonset** indicate p.m. Times are figured for the point **99° 20' West and 31° 08' North,** the approximate center of the state. **See page 101 for explanation of how to get the approximate time at any other Texas point.** (On the Web: http://aa.usno.navy.mil/AA/data/) **January 1, 2001, is the beginning of the 21st century and of the 3rd millennium.** Please note: Not all **eclipses** are visible in United States. For visibility, see listing p. 102.

1st Month — **January 2001** — **31 Days**

Moon's Phases — First Qtr., Jan. 2, 4:31 p.m.; Full, Jan. 9, 2:24 p.m.; Last Qtr., Jan. 16, 6:35 a.m.; New, Jan. 24, 7:07 a.m.

Day of			Planetary Configurations and Phenomena	*Hour of			
Year	Month	Week		Sunrise	Sunset	Moon-rise	Moon-set
1	1	Mo.		7:36	5:46	**12:06**	. . .
2	2	Tu.		7:36	5:47	**12:37**	12:04
3	3	We.		7:36	5:48	**1:09**	1:00
4	4	Th.	● at perihelion	7:36	5:49	**1:43**	1:58
5	5	Fr.	♄ ☌ ☾	7:37	5:49	**2:21**	2:59
6	6	Sa.	♃ ☌ ☾	7:37	5:50	**3:04**	4:03
7	7	Su.		7:37	5:51	**3:55**	5:10
8	8	Mo.		7:37	5:52	**4:53**	6:18
9	9	Tu.	Eclipse ☾	7:37	5:53	**5:58**	7:24
10	10	We.	☾ at perigee	7:37	5:53	**7:08**	8:25
11	11	Th.		7:37	5:54	**8:18**	9:19
12	12	Fr.		7:37	5:55	**9:28**	10:06
13	13	Sa.	☿ ☌ ♆	7:37	5:56	**10:34**	10:47
14	14	Su.		7:36	5:57	**11:37**	11:25
15	15	Mo.		7:36	5:58	. . .	**12:00**
16	16	Tu.		7:36	5:59	12:38	**12:34**
17	17	We.	♂ ☌ ☾	7:36	6:00	1:38	**1:08**
18	18	Th.		7:36	6:00	2:36	**1:44**
19	19	Fr.		7:35	6:01	3:33	**2:22**
20	20	Sa.		7:35	6:02	4:29	**3:04**
21	21	Su.		7:35	6:03	5:23	**3:49**
22	22	Mo.	☿ ☌ ♅	7:34	6:04	6:14	**4:38**
23	23	Tu.		7:34	6:05	7:02	**5:29**
24	24	We.	☾ at apogee	7:34	6:06	7:46	**6:22**
25	25	Th.	♃ and ♄ stationary	7:33	6:07	8:26	**7:16**
26	26	Fr.		7:33	6:08	9:02	**8:10**
27	27	Sa.		7:32	6:08	9:36	**9:04**
28	28	Su.	♀ ☌ ☾	7:32	6:09	10:07	**9:58**
29	29	Mo.		7:31	6:10	10:38	**10:53**
30	30	Tu.		7:31	6:11	11:09	**11:49**
31	31	We.		7:30	6:12	11:41	. . .

2nd Month — **February 2001** — **28 Days**

Moon's Phases — First Qtr., Feb. 1, 8:02 a.m.; Full, Feb. 8, 1:12 a.m.; Last Qtr., Feb. 14, 9:23 p.m.; New, Feb. 23, 2:21 a.m.

Day of			Planetary Configurations and Phenomena	*Hour of			
Year	Month	Week		Sunrise	Sunset	Moon-rise	Moon-set
32	1	Th.		7:29	6:13	**12:16**	12:47
33	2	Fr.	♃ ☌ ☾; ♄ ☌ ☾	7:29	6:14	**12:55**	1:47
34	3	Sa.	☿ stationary	7:28	6:15	**1:40**	2:50
35	4	Su.		7:27	6:16	**2:33**	3:56
36	5	Mo.		7:27	6:16	**3:33**	5:01
37	6	Tu.		7:26	6:17	**4:40**	6:03
38	7	We.	☾ at perigee	7:25	6:18	**5:51**	7:01
39	8	Th.		7:24	6:19	**7:02**	7:52
40	9	Fr.	♅ ☌ ☉	7:24	6:20	**8:13**	8:38
41	10	Sa.		7:23	6:21	**9:20**	9:18
42	11	Su.		7:22	6:22	**10:24**	9:56
43	12	Mo.	☿ inferior	7:21	6:22	**11:27**	10:31
44	13	Tu.		7:20	6:23	. . .	11:07
45	14	We.		7:19	6:24	12:27	11:43
46	15	Th.	♂ ☌ ☾	7:18	6:25	1:26	**12:21**
47	16	Fr.		7:17	6:26	2:23	**1:02**
48	17	Sa.		7:16	6:27	3:18	**1:46**
49	18	Su.		7:15	6:27	4:10	**2:34**
50	19	Mo.		7:14	6:28	4:59	**3:24**
51	20	Tu.	☾ at apogee; ♆ ☌ ☾	7:13	6:29	5:44	**4:17**
52	21	We.	♀ greatest brilliancy	7:12	6:30	6:25	**5:11**
53	22	Th.		7:11	6:31	7:03	**6:05**
54	23	Fr.		7:10	6:31	7:37	**6:59**
55	24	Sa.	☿ stationary	7:09	6:32	8:10	**7:54**
56	25	Su.		7:08	6:33	8:41	**8:49**
57	26	Mo.	♀ ☌ ☾	7:07	6:34	9:11	**9:44**
58	27	Tu.		7:06	6:34	9:43	**10:41**
59	28	We.		7:05	6:35	10:16	**11:40**

*See text before January calendar for explanation.

3rd Month — **March 2001** — **31 Days**

Moon's Phases — First Qtr., March 2, 8:03 p.m.; Full, March 9, 11:23 a.m.; Last Qtr., March 16, 2:45 p.m.; New, March 24, 7:21 p.m.

Day of			Planetary Configurations and Phenomena	*Hour of			
Year	Month	Week		Sunrise	Sunset	Moon-rise	Moon-set
60	1	Th.	♄ ☌ ☾	7:04	6:36	10:53	. . .
61	2	Fr.	♃ ☌ ☾	7:03	6:37	11:35	12:40
62	3	Sa.		7:02	6:37	**12:22**	1:43
63	4	Su.		7:00	6:38	**1:17**	2:46
64	5	Mo.		6:59	6:39	**2:19**	3:48
65	6	Tu.		6:58	6:39	**3:26**	4:45
66	7	We.	♀ stationary	6:57	6:40	**4:36**	5:38
67	8	Th.	☾ at perigee	6:56	6:41	**5:46**	6:25
68	9	Fr.		6:54	6:42	**6:56**	7:08
69	10	Sa.	☿ ☌ ♅	6:53	6:42	**8:03**	7:47
70	11	Su.	☿ greatest elongation W.	6:52	6:43	**9:08**	8:24
71	12	Mo.		6:51	6:44	**10:11**	9:01
72	13	Tu.		6:50	6:44	**11:13**	9:38
73	14	We.		6:48	6:45	. . .	10:16
74	15	Th.	♂ ☌ ☾	6:47	6:46	12:13	10:57
75	16	Fr.		6:46	6:46	1:10	11:41
76	17	Sa.		6:45	6:47	2:05	**12:28**
77	18	Su.	♇ stationary	6:43	6:48	2:55	**1:18**
78	19	Mo.		6:42	6:48	3:42	**2:10**
79	20	Tu.	Spring begins. ♆ ☌ ☾	6:41	6:49	4:24	**3:04**
80	21	We.	♅ ☌ ☾	6:40	6:50	5:03	**3:58**
81	22	Th.	☿ ☌ ☾	6:38	6:50	5:38	**4:53**
82	23	Fr.		6:37	6:51	6:11	**5:47**
83	24	Sa.		6:36	6:52	6:43	**6:43**
84	25	Su.		6:35	6:52	7:13	**7:39**
85	26	Mo.		6:33	6:53	7:45	**8:36**
86	27	Tu.		6:32	6:54	8:18	**9:34**
87	28	We.	♄ ☌ h	6:31	6:54	8:54	**10:35**
88	29	Th.	♃ ☌ ☾; ♀ inferior	6:30	6:55	9:33	**11:37**
89	30	Fr.		6:28	6:55	10:19	. . .
90	31	Sa.		6:27	6:56	11:10	12:39

4th Month — **April 2001** — **30 Days**

Moon's Phases - First Qtr., April 1, 5:49 a.m.; Full, April 7, 10:22 p.m.; Last Qtr., April 15, 10:31 a.m.; New, April 23, 10:26 a.m; First Qtr., April 30, 12:03 p.m.

Day of			Planetary Configurations and Phenomena	*Hour of			
Year	Month	Week		Sunrise	Sunset	Moon-rise	Moon-set
91	†1	Su.		7:26	7:57	**12:08**	1:40
92	2	Mo.		7:25	7:57	**2:11**	3:38
93	3	Tu.		7:23	7:58	**3:18**	4:31
94	4	We.		7:22	7:59	**4:26**	5:18
95	5	Th.	☾ at perigee	7:21	7:59	**5:34**	6:01
96	6	Fr.	☿ ☌ ♀	7:20	8:00	**6:41**	6:40
97	7	Sa.		7:19	8:01	**7:47**	7:18
98	8	Su.		7:17	8:01	**8:52**	7:54
99	9	Mo.		7:16	8:02	**9:55**	8:30
100	10	Tu.		7:15	8:03	**10:57**	9:08
101	11	We.		7:14	8:03	**11:58**	9:49
102	12	Th.	♂ ☌ ☾	7:13	8:04	. . .	10:32
103	13	Fr.		7:11	8:04	12:55	11:19
104	14	Sa.		7:10	8:05	1:48	**12:09**
105	15	Su.		7:09	8:06	2:37	**1:01**
106	16	Mo.	♆ ☌ ☾	7:08	8:06	3:22	**1:55**
107	17	Tu.	☾ at apogee; ♀ stationary	7:07	8:07	4:02	**2:49**
108	18	We.		7:06	8:08	4:38	**3:43**
109	19	Th.		7:05	8:08	5:11	**4:38**
110	20	Fr.	♀ ☌ ☾	7:04	8:09	5:43	**5:33**
111	21	Sa.		7:03	8:10	6:14	**6:29**
112	22	Su.		7:01	8:10	6:45	**7:26**
113	23	Mo.	☿ superior	7:00	8:11	7:18	**8:26**
114	24	Tu.		6:59	8:12	7:53	**9:27**
115	25	We.	♄ ☌ ☾	6:58	8:12	8:32	**10:30**
116	26	Th.	♃ ☌ ☾	6:57	8:13	9:16	**11:33**
117	27	Fr.		6:56	8:14	10:06	. . .
118	28	Sa.		6:55	8:15	11:02	12:36
119	29	Su.		6:54	8:15	**12:04**	1:35
120	30	Mo.		6:54	8:16	**1:09**	2:28

†Daylight Saving Time begins at 2:00 a.m.

Calendar for 2001 (Cont'd.)

5th Month **May 2001** **31 Days**

Moon's Phases — Full, May 7, 8:53 a.m.; Last Qtr., May 15, 5:11 a.m.; New, May 22, 9:46 p.m., First Qtr., May 29, 5:09 p.m.

Day of			Planetary Configurations and Phenomena	*Hour of			
Year	Month	Week		Sunrise	Sunset	Moon-rise	Moon-set
121	1	Tu.	☾ at perigee	6:53	8:17	**2:16**	3:17
122	2	We.		6:52	8:17	**3:22**	4:00
123	3	Th.		6:51	8:18	**4:27**	4:39
124	4	Fr.	♀ greatest brilliancy	6:50	8:19	**5:32**	5:15
125	5	Sa.		6:49	8:19	**6:35**	5:50
126	6	Su.		6:48	8:20	**7:38**	6:26
127	7	Mo.	☿ ☌ ♄	6:47	8:21	**8:41**	7:03
128	8	Tu.		6:47	8:21	**9:43**	7:42
129	9	We.		6:46	8:22	**10:42**	8:24
130	10	Th.	♂ ☌ ☾; ♆ stationary	6:45	8:23	**11:38**	9:09
131	11	Fr.	♂ stationary	6:44	8:23	. . .	9:59
132	12	Sa.		6:44	8:24	12:30	10:51
133	13	Su.	♆ ☌ ☾	6:43	8:25	1:17	11:44
134	14	Mo.	☾ at apogee	6:42	8:25	1:59	**12:39**
135	15	Tu.	♅ ☌ ☾	6:42	8:26	2:37	**1:33**
136	16	We.	☿ ☌ ♃	6:41	8:27	3:11	**2:28**
137	17	Th.		6:40	8:27	3:43	**3:22**
138	18	Fr.		6:40	8:28	4:14	**4:17**
139	19	Sa.	♀ ☌ ☾	6:39	8:29	4:44	**5:14**
140	20	Su.		6:39	8:29	5:16	**6:12**
141	21	Mo.	☿ greatest elongation E.	6:38	8:30	5:50	**7:13**
142	22	Tu.		6:38	8:31	6:27	**8:16**
143	23	We.		6:37	8:31	7:10	**9:21**
144	24	Th.	♃ ☌ ☾; ☿ ☌ ☾	6:37	8:32	7:58	**10:26**
145	25	Fr.	♄ ☌ ☉	6:36	8:32	8:54	**11:28**
146	26	Sa.		6:36	8:33	9:55	. . .
147	27	Su.	☾ at perigee	6:36	8:34	11:01	12:25
148	28	Mo.		6:35	8:34	**12:08**	1:16
149	29	Tu.	♅ stationary	6:35	8:35	**1:15**	2:01
150	30	We.		6:35	8:35	**2:20**	2:41
151	31	Th.		6:34	8:36	**3:23**	3:17

6th Month **June 2001** **30 Days**

Moon's Phases — Full, June 5, 8:39 p.m.; Last Qtr., June 13, 10:28 p.m.; New, June 21, 6:58 a.m.; First Qtr., June 27, 10:28 p.m.

Day of			Planetary Configurations and Phenomena	*Hour of			
Year	Month	Week		Sunrise	Sunset	Moon-rise	Moon-set
152	1	Fr.		6:34	8:37	**4:26**	3:52
153	2	Sa.		6:34	8:37	**5:27**	4:26
154	3	Su.		6:34	8:38	**6:29**	5:01
155	4	Mo.	☿ stationary; ♇ ☍	6:33	8:38	**7:30**	5:38
156	5	Tu.		6:33	8:39	**8:30**	6:18
157	6	We.	♂ ☌ ☾	6:33	8:39	**9:28**	7:02
158	7	Th.		6:33	8:40	**10:22**	7:50
159	8	Fr.	♀ greatest elongation W.	6:33	8:40	**11:11**	8:41
160	9	Sa.		6:33	8:40	**11:55**	9:34
161	10	Su.	♆ ☌ ☾; ☾ at apogee	6:33	8:41	. . .	10:29
162	11	Mo.		6:33	8:41	12:35	11:23
163	12	Tu.		6:33	8:42	1:10	**12:18**
164	13	We.	♂ ☍	6:33	8:42	1:43	**1:12**
165	14	Th.	♃ ☌ ☉	6:33	8:42	2:14	**2:06**
166	15	Fr.		6:33	8:43	2:44	**3:01**
167	16	Sa.	☿ inferior	6:33	8:43	3:14	**3:57**
168	17	Su.	♀ ☌ ☾	6:33	8:43	3:46	**4:56**
169	18	Mo.		6:33	8:44	4:21	**5:58**
170	19	Tu.	♄ ☌ ☾	6:34	8:44	5:01	**7:03**
171	20	We.		6:34	8:44	5:47	**8:09**
172	21	Th.	Summer begins.	6:34	8:44	6:40	**9:14**
173	22	Fr.		6:34	8:45	7:41	**10:15**
174	23	Sa.	☾ at perigee	6:34	8:45	8:47	**11:10**
175	24	Su.		6:35	8:45	9:56	**11:58**
176	25	Mo.		6:35	8:45	11:05	. . .
177	26	Tu.		6:35	8:45	**12:12**	12:41
178	27	We.		6:36	8:45	**1:17**	1:19
179	28	Th.	☿ stationary	6:36	8:45	**2:20**	1:54
180	29	Fr.		6:36	8:45	**3:21**	2:28
181	30	Sa.		6:37	8:45	**4:22**	3:03

*See text before January calendar for explanation.

7th Month **July 2001** **31 Days**

Moon's Phases — Full, July 5, 10:04 a.m.; Last Qtr., July 13, 1:45 p.m.; New, July 20, 2:44 p.m.; First Qtr., July 27, 5:08 a.m.

Day of			Planetary Configurations and Phenomena	*Hour of			
Year	Month	Week		Sunrise	Sunset	Moon-rise	Moon-set
182	1	Su.		6:37	8:45	**5:22**	3:38
183	2	Mo.		6:38	8:45	**6:22**	4:17
184	3	Tu.	♂ ☌ ☾	6:38	8:45	**7:20**	4:59
185	4	We.	● at aphelion	6:38	8:45	**8:15**	5:44
186	5	Th.	Eclipse ☾	6:39	8:45	**9:05**	6:34
187	6	Fr.		6:39	8:45	**9:51**	7:26
188	7	Sa.	♆ ☌ ☾	6:40	8:45	**10:33**	8:20
189	8	Su.	♅ ☌ ☾	6:40	8:44	**11:10**	9:15
190	9	Mo.	☾ at apogee	6:41	8:44	**11:43**	10:10
191	10	Tu.		6:41	8:44	. . .	11:04
192	11	We.		6:42	8:44	12:14	11:57
193	12	Th.	☿ ☌ ♃	6:42	8:43	12:44	**12:51**
194	13	Fr.		6:43	8:43	1:14	**1:46**
195	14	Sa.		6:43	8:43	1:44	**2:42**
196	15	Su.	♀ ☌ ♄	6:44	8:42	2:17	**3:41**
197	16	Mo.		6:45	8:42	2:53	**4:43**
198	17	Tu.	♄ ☌ ☾; ♀ ☌ ☾	6:45	8:42	3:35	**5:48**
199	18	We.	♃ ☌ ☾	6:46	8:41	4:24	**6:54**
200	19	Th.	☿ ☌ ☾; ♂ stationary	6:46	8:41	5:21	**7:57**
201	20	Fr.		6:47	8:40	6:26	**8:56**
202	21	Sa.	☾ at perigee	6:48	8:40	7:35	**9:49**
203	22	Su.		6:48	8:39	8:47	**10:36**
204	23	Mo.		6:49	8:39	9:57	**11:17**
205	24	Tu.		6:49	8:38	11:05	**11:54**
206	25	We.		6:50	8:37	**12:11**	. . .
207	26	Th.		6:51	8:37	**1:14**	12:29
208	27	Fr.		6:51	8:36	**2:16**	1:04
209	28	Sa.		6:52	8:35	**3:17**	1:40
210	29	Su.		6:53	8:35	**4:16**	2:17
211	30	Mo.	♆ ☍; ♂ ☌ ☾	6:53	8:34	**5:14**	2:58
212	31	Tu.		6:54	8:33	**6:10**	3:42

8th Month **August 2001** **31 Days**

Moon's Phases — Full, Aug. 4, 12:56 a.m.; Last Qtr., Aug. 12, 2:53 a.m.; New, Aug. 18, 9:55 p.m.; First Qtr., Aug. 25, 2:55 p.m.

Day of			Planetary Configurations and Phenomena	*Hour of			
Year	Month	Week		Sunrise	Sunset	Moon-rise	Moon-set
213	1	We.		6:54	8:32	**7:02**	4:30
214	2	Th.		6:55	8:32	**7:49**	5:21
215	3	Fr.	♆ ☌ ☾	6:56	8:31	**8:32**	6:15
216	4	Sa.	♅ ☌ ☾	6:56	8:30	**9:10**	7:09
217	5	Su.	☾ at apogee; ♀ ☌ ♃	6:57	8:29	**9:44**	8:04
218	6	Mo.		6:58	8:28	**10:16**	8:58
219	7	Tu.		6:58	8:27	**10:46**	9:51
220	8	We.		6:59	8:27	**11:15**	10:45
221	9	Th.		6:59	8:26	**11:45**	11:39
222	10	Fr.		7.00	8:25	. . .	**12:33**
223	11	Sa.		7:01	8:24	12:16	**1:30**
224	12	Su.		7:01	8:23	12:50	**2:29**
225	13	Mo.	♄ ☌ ☾	7:02	8:22	1:28	**3:31**
226	14	Tu.		7:03	8:21	2:12	**4:34**
227	15	We.	♃ ☌ ☾; ♅ ☍	7:03	8:20	3:04	**5:38**
228	16	Th.	♀ ☌ ☾	7:04	8:19	4:04	**6:38**
229	17	Fr.		7:04	8:18	5:10	**7:34**
230	18	Sa.		7:05	8:17	6:22	**8:24**
231	19	Su.	☾ at perigee	7:06	8:15	7:34	**9:08**
232	20	Mo.		7:06	8:14	8:45	**9:49**
233	21	Tu.		7:07	8:13	9:54	**10:26**
234	22	We.		7:08	8:12	11:00	**11:02**
235	23	Th.		7:08	8:11	**12:05**	**11:38**
236	24	Fr.		7:09	8:10	**1:08**	. . .
237	25	Sa.	♇ stationary	7:09	8:09	**2:10**	12:16
238	26	Su.		7:10	8:08	**3:09**	12:56
239	27	Mo.	♂ ☌ ☾	7:11	8:06	**4:06**	1:40
240	28	Tu.		7:11	8:05	**4:59**	2:27
241	29	We.		7:12	8:04	**5:47**	3:17
242	30	Th.	♆ ☌ ☾	7:12	8:03	**6:31**	4:10
243	31	Fr.		7:13	8:02	**7:10**	5:04

Calendar for 2001 (Cont'd.)

9th Month — September 2001 — 30 Days

Moon's Phases — Full, Sept. 2, 4:43 p.m.; Last Qtr., Sept. 10, 1:59 p.m.; New, Sept. 17, 5:27 a.m.; First Qtr., Sept. 24, 2:31 a.m.

Day of Year	Day of Month	Day of Week	Planetary Configurations and Phenomena	*Hour of Sunrise	Sunset	Moon-rise	Moon-set
244	1	Sa.	♅ ☌ ☾; ☾ at apogee	7:14	8:00	**7:46**	5:59
245	2	Su.		7:14	7:59	**8:18**	6:53
246	3	Mo.		7:15	7:58	**8:49**	7:47
247	4	Tu.		7:15	7:57	**9:18**	8:40
248	5	We.		7:16	7:55	**9:47**	9:34
249	6	Th.		7:16	7:54	**10:17**	10:28
250	7	Fr.		7:17	7:53	**10:50**	11:24
251	8	Sa.		7:18	7:52	**11:26**	**12:22**
252	9	Su.		7:18	7:50	...	**1:21**
253	10	Mo.	♄ ☌ ☾	7:19	7:49	12:06	**2:22**
254	11	Tu.		7:19	7:48	12:54	**3:24**
255	12	We.	♃ ☌ ☾	7:20	7:47	1:48	**4:24**
256	13	Th.		7:20	7:45	2:50	**5:20**
257	14	Fr.		7:21	7:44	3:57	**6:12**
258	15	Sa.	♀ ☌ ☾	7:22	7:43	5:08	**6:58**
259	16	Su.	☾ at perigee	7:22	7:41	6:19	**7:39**
260	17	Mo.		7:23	7:40	7:30	**8:18**
261	18	Tu.	☿ ☌ ☾	7:23	7:39	8:39	**8:55**
262	19	We.		7:24	7:38	9:46	**9:32**
263	20	Th.		7:25	7:36	10:52	**10:10**
264	21	Fr.		7:25	7:35	11:57	**10:51**
265	22	Sa.	Fall begins.	7:26	7:34	**12:59**	**11:34**
266	23	Su.		7:26	7:32	**1:59**	...
267	24	Mo.	♂ ☌ ☾	7:27	7:31	**2:54**	12:21
268	25	Tu.		7:27	7:30	**3:45**	1:11
269	26	We.	♄ stationary	7:28	7:29	**4:30**	2:04
270	27	Th.	♆ ☌ ☾	7:29	7:27	**5:11**	2:58
271	28	Fr.	♅ ☌ ☾	7:29	7:26	**5:47**	3:52
272	29	Sa.	☾ at apogee	7:30	7:25	**6:20**	4:47
273	30	Su.		7:31	7:23	**6:51**	5:41

10th Month — October 2001 — 31 Days

Moon's Phases — Full, Oct. 2, 8:49 a.m.; Last Qtr., Oct. 9, 11:20 p.m.; New, Oct. 16, 2:23 p.m.; First Qtr., Oct. 23, 9:58 p.m.; Full, Oct. 31, 11:41 p.m.

Day of Year	Day of Month	Day of Week	Planetary Configurations and Phenomena	*Hour of Sunrise	Sunset	Moon-rise	Moon-set
274	1	Mo.	☿ stationary	7:31	7:22	**7:21**	6:35
275	2	Tu.		7:32	7:21	**7:50**	7:29
276	3	We.		7:32	7:20	**8:20**	8:24
277	4	Th.		7:33	7:18	**8:51**	9:19
278	5	Fr.		7:34	7:17	**9:26**	10:17
279	6	Sa.		7:34	7:16	**10:05**	11:16
280	7	Su.	♄ ☌ ☾	7:35	7:15	**10:50**	**12:16**
281	8	Mo.		7:36	7:14	**11:41**	**1:17**
282	9	Tu.	♃ ☌ ☾	7:36	7:12	...	**2:16**
283	10	We.		7:37	7:11	12:38	**3:12**
284	11	Th.		7:38	7:10	1:42	**4:04**
285	12	Fr.		7:38	7:09	2:49	**4:50**
286	13	Sa.	☿ inferior	7:39	7:08	3:58	**5:32**
287	14	Su.	☾ at perigee; ♀ ☌ ☾	7:40	7:07	5:07	**6:11**
288	15	Mo.		7:40	7:05	6:15	**6:48**
289	16	Tu.		7:41	7:04	7:23	**7:25**
290	17	We.	♆ stationary	7:42	7:03	8:31	**8:02**
291	18	Th.		7:42	7:02	9:37	**8:42**
292	19	Fr.		7:43	7:01	10:42	**9:25**
293	20	Sa.		7:44	7:00	11:45	**10:11**
294	21	Su.		7:45	6:59	**12:44**	**11:01**
295	22	Mo.	☿ stationary	7:45	6:58	**1:38**	**11:54**
296	23	Tu.	♂ ☌ ☾	7:46	6:57	**2:27**	...
297	24	We.	♆ ☌ ☾	7:47	6:56	**3:09**	12:49
298	25	Th.	♅ ☌ ☾	7:47	6:55	**3:47**	1:44
299	26	Fr.	☾ at apogee	7:48	6:54	**4:22**	2:39
300	27	Sa.		7:49	6:53	**4:53**	3:33
301	†28	Su.		6:50	5:52	**4:23**	3:27
302	29	Mo.		6:51	5:51	**4:52**	4:21
303	30	Tu.	♅ stationary	6:51	5:50	**5:21**	5:16
304	31	We.		6:52	5:49	**5:52**	6:12

*See text before January calendar for explanation.
† Daylight Saving Time ends at 2:00 a.m.

11th Month — November 2001 — 30 Days

Moon's Phases — Last Qtr., Nov. 8, 6:21 a.m.; New, Nov. 15, 12:40 a.m.; First Qtr., Nov. 22, 5:21 p.m.; Full, Nov. 30, 2:49 p.m.

Day of Year	Day of Month	Day of Week	Planetary Configurations and Phenomena	*Hour of Sunrise	Sunset	Moon-rise	Moon-set
305	1	Th.		6:53	5:49	**6:26**	7:09
306	2	Fr.	♃ stationary	6:54	5:48	**7:04**	8:09
307	3	Sa.	♄ ☌ ☾	6:55	5:47	**7:47**	9:10
308	4	Su.	♂ ☌ ♆	6:55	5:46	**8:37**	10:12
309	5	Mo.		6:56	5:45	**9:32**	11:12
310	6	Tu.	♃ ☌ ☾	6:57	5:45	**10:34**	**12:09**
311	7	We.		6:58	5:44	**11:39**	**1:02**
312	8	Th.		6:59	5:43	...	**1:48**
313	9	Fr.		7:00	5:43	12:46	**2:30**
314	10	Sa.		7:00	5:42	1:52	**3:09**
315	11	Su.	☾ at perigee	7:01	5:41	2:59	**3:45**
316	12	Mo.		7:02	5:41	4:05	**4:20**
317	13	Tu.		7:03	5:40	5:11	**4:56**
318	14	We.		7:04	5:40	6:16	**5:34**
319	15	Th.		7:05	5:39	7:22	**6:15**
320	16	Fr.		7:05	5:39	8:27	**7:00**
321	17	Sa.		7:06	5:38	9:29	**7:49**
322	18	Su.		7:07	5:38	10:27	**8:42**
323	19	Mo.		7:08	5:37	11:19	**9:37**
324	20	Tu.	♆ ☌ ☾	7:09	5:37	**12:05**	**10:33**
325	21	We.	♂ ☌ ☾; ♅ ☌ ☾	7:10	5:37	**12:45**	**11:29**
326	22	Th.		7:11	5:36	**1:21**	...
327	23	Fr.	☾ at apogee	7:12	5:36	**1:53**	12:24
328	24	Sa.		7:12	5:36	**2:23**	1:18
329	25	Su.		7:13	5:35	**2:52**	2:11
330	26	Mo.	♂ ☌ ♅	7:14	5:35	**3:21**	3:05
331	27	Tu.		7:15	5:35	**3:51**	4:00
332	28	We.		7:16	5:35	**4:24**	4:57
333	29	Th.		7:17	5:35	**5:00**	5:56
334	30	Fr.	♄ ☌ ☾	7:17	5:35	**5:42**	6:58

12th Month — December 2001 — 31 Days

Moon's Phases — Last Qtr., Dec. 7, 1:49 p.m.; New, Dec. 14, 2:47 p.m.; First Qtr., Dec. 22, 2:56 p.m.; Full, Dec. 30, 4:40 a.m.

Day of Year	Day of Month	Day of Week	Planetary Configurations and Phenomena	*Hour of Sunrise	Sunset	Moon-rise	Moon-set
335	1	Sa.		7:18	5:35	**6:30**	8:01
336	2	Su.		7:19	5:35	**7:25**	9:04
337	3	Mo.	♃ ☌ ☾; ♄ ☍	7:20	5:35	**8:26**	10:04
338	4	Tu.	☿ superior	7:21	5:35	**9:31**	10:59
339	5	We.		7:21	5:35	**10:38**	11:48
340	6	Th.	☾ at perigee; ♇ ☌ ☉	7:22	5:35	**11:45**	**12:31**
341	7	Fr.		7:23	5:35	...	**1:10**
342	8	Sa.		7:24	5:35	12:50	**1:46**
343	9	Su.		7:24	5:35	1:55	**2:20**
344	10	Mo.		7:25	5:35	2:59	**2:55**
345	11	Tu.		7:26	5:36	4:03	**3:30**
346	12	We.		7:26	5:36	5:07	**4:09**
347	13	Th.		7:27	5:36	6:11	**4:51**
348	14	Fr.	Eclipse ☉	7:28	5:36	7:13	**5:38**
349	15	Sa.		7:28	5:37	8:13	**6:29**
350	16	Su.		7:29	5:37	9:08	**7:24**
351	17	Mo.		7:30	5:38	9:58	**8:20**
352	18	Tu.	♆ ☌ ☾	7:30	5:38	10:41	**9:17**
353	19	We.	♅ ☌ ☾	7:31	5:38	11:19	**10:13**
354	20	Th.	♂ ☌ ☾	7:31	5:39	11:53	**11:07**
355	21	Fr.	Winter begins.	7:32	5:39	**12:23**	...
356	22	Sa.		7:32	5:40	**12:53**	12:01
357	23	Su.		7:33	5:40	**1:21**	12:54
358	24	Mo.		7:33	5:41	**1:50**	1:48
359	25	Tu.		7:34	5:42	**2:21**	2:43
360	26	We.		7:34	5:42	**2:55**	3:40
361	27	Th.		7:34	5:43	**3:34**	4:40
362	28	Fr.	♄ ☌ ☾	7:35	5:43	**4:19**	5:43
363	29	Sa.		7:35	5:44	**5:11**	6:47
364	30	Su.	Eclipse ☾; ♃ ☌ ☾	7:35	5:45	**6:11**	7:50
365	31	Mo.		7:36	5:45	**7:17**	8:49

Recreation

Information about recreational opportunities in state and national parks and forests and at U.S. Army Corps of Engineers Lakes, a representative list of festivals and celebrations in individual towns and communities across the state, as well as information on hunting and fishing opportunities and regulations is found in the following pages. Information about hunting, fishing and other recreation on State Wildlife Management Areas and National Wildlife Refuges can be found in the Environment section. Recreation and special events in each county are also mentioned in the Counties chapter.

Texas' State Parks

Texas' expanding system of state parks offers contrasting attractions — mountains and canyons, arid deserts and lush forests, spring-fed streams, sandy dunes, saltwater surf and fascinating historic sites.

The state park information below was provided by **Texas Parks and Wildlife** (TPW). Additional information and brochures on individual parks are available from the TPW's Austin headquarters, 4200 Smith School Rd., Austin 78744; 1-800-792-1112; Web: www.tpwd.state.tx.us/park/.

The TPW's **Central Reservation Center** can take reservations for almost all parks that accept reservations. Exceptions are Indian Lodge and the Texas State Railroad and facilities not operated by the TPW. Call the center during the usual business hours at 512-389-8900. The TDD line is 512-389-8915.

The **Gold Conservation Passport**, currently costing $50 per year, allows free entrance for member and all passengers in member's vehicle to state parks, as well as other benefits. For further information, contact TPW at numbers or address above.

Texas State Parklands Passport is a windshield decal granting free or discounted entrance to state parks for senior citizens and disabled veterans. Available at state parks with proper identification. Details can be obtained at numbers or address above.

The following information is a brief glimpse of what each park has to offer. Refer to the chart on pages 114-115 for a more complete list of available activities and facilities. Fees for entrance range from $1 to $5 per person. There are also fees for tours and some activities. For up-to-date information, call the information number listed above before you go. Road abbreviations used in this list are: IH - interstate highway, US - U.S. Highway, TX - state highway, FM - farm-to-market road, RM - ranch-to-market road, PR - park road.

List of State Parks

Abilene State Park, 16 miles southwest of Abilene on FM 89 and PR 32 in Taylor County, consists of 529.4 acres that were deeded by the City of Abilene in 1933. A part of the **official Texas longhorn herd** and a bison are located in the park. Large groves of pecan trees that once shaded bands of Comanches now shade visitors at picnic tables. Activities include camping, hiking, nature study and fishing. In addition to **Lake Abilene, Buffalo Gap,** the original Taylor County seat (1878) and one of the early frontier settlements, is nearby. Buffalo Gap was on the **Western,** or **Goodnight-Loving, Trail,** over which pioneer Texas cattlemen drove herds to railheads in Kansas.

Acton State Historical Park is a .01-acre cemetery plot in Hood County where **Davy Crockett's** second wife, Elizabeth, was buried in 1860. It is 4.5 miles east of Granbury on US 377 to FM 167 south, then 2.4 miles south on FM 167 to Acton. Nearby attractions include Cleburne, Dinosaur Valley and Lake Whitney state parks.

Adm. Nimitz Museum and Historical Center is 7 acres in downtown Fredericksburg. First established as a state agency in 1969 by Texas Legislature; transferred to TPW in 1981. Named for **Adm. Chester W. Nimitz** of World War II fame, it includes the **Pacific War Museum** in the **Nimitz Steamboat Hotel;** the **Japanese Garden of Peace,** donated by the people of Japan; the **History Walk of the Pacific War,** featuring planes, boats and other equipment from World War II; and other special exhibits.

Nearby is **Kerrville State Park**.

Atlanta State Park is 1,475 acres located 11 miles northwest of Atlanta on FM 1154 in Cass County; adjacent to **Wright Patman Dam and Reservoir.** Land acquired from the U.S. Army in 1954 by license to 2004 with option to renew to 2054. Camping, biking and hiking in pine forests, as well as water activities, such as boating, fishing, lake swimming. Nearby are historic town of **Jefferson and Caddo Lake and Daingerfield state parks.**

Balmorhea State Park is 45.9 acres four miles southwest of Balmorhea on TX 17 between Balmorhea and Toyahvale in Reeves County. Deeded in 1934-35 by private owners and Reeves Co. Water Imp. Dist. No. 1 and built by the Civilian Conservation Corps (CCC). Swimming pool fed by artesian **San Solomon Springs;** also provides water to **pupfish refuge** in park. Activities include swimming, picnicking, camping, scuba and skin diving. Motel rooms available at **San Solomon Springs Courts.** Nearby are city of Pecos, **Fort Davis National Historic Site, Davis Mountains State Park and McDonald Observatory.**

Barton Warnock Environmental Education Center consists of 99.2 acres in Brewster County. Originally built by the Lajitas Foundation in 1982 as the Lajitas Museum Desert Gardens, the TPW purchased it in 1990 and renamed it for Texas botanist Dr. Barton Warnock. The center is also the eastern entrance station to **Big Bend Ranch State Park** (below). Self-guiding botanical and museum tours. Bus tours of Big Bend Ranch State Park operate from center. On FM 170 one mile east of Lajitas.

Bastrop State Park is 3,503.7 acres one mile east of Bastrop on TX 21 or from TX 71. The park was acquired by deeds from the City of Bastrop and private owners in 1933-35; additional acreage acquired in 1979. Site of famous **"Lost Pines,"** isolated region of loblolly pine and hardwoods. **Swimming pool, cabins and lodge** are among facilities. Fishing, backpacking, picnicking, canoeing, bicycling, hiking. Golf course adjacent to park. **State capitol** at Austin 30 miles away; 13-mile drive through forest leads to **Buescher State Park.**

Battleship Texas State Historic Site (see **San Jacinto Battleground State Historic Site and Battleship Texas**)

Bentsen-Rio Grande Valley State Park, a scenic park, is along the Rio Grande five miles southwest of Mission off FM 2062 in Hidalgo County. The 587.7 acres of **subtropical resaca woodlands and brushlands** were acquired from private owners in 1944. Park is excellent base from which to tour **Lower Rio Grande Valley** of Texas and adjacent **Mexico;** most attractions within an hour's drive. Hiking trails provide chance to study unique plants and animals of park. Many birds unique to southern United States found here, including **pauraque, groove-billed ani, green kingfisher, rose-throated becard and tropical parula.** Park also one of last natural refuges in Texas for **ocelot** and **jaguarundi.** Trees include **cedar elm, anaqua, ebony and Mexican ash.** Nearby are **Santa Ana National Wildlife Refuge** and **Sabal Palm Sanctuary.**

Big Bend Ranch State Park, 279,640.58 acres of **Chihuahuan Desert wilderness** in Brewster and Presidio counties, was purchased from private owners in 1988. The purchase more than doubled the size of the state park system, which comprised at that time 220,000 acres. Eastern entrance at Barton Warnock Environmental Education Center one mile east of Lajitas on FM 170; western entrance is at **Fort Leaton State Historical Park** four miles east of Presidio on FM 170. The area includes **extinct volcanoes,** several **waterfalls,** two **mountain ranges,** at least **11 rare species of plants and animals,**

and **90 major archaeological sites**. There is little development. Vehicular access limited; some wilderness backpacking and hiking access. Scheduled **bus tours** depart from **Barton Warnock Environmental Educational Center** (see above); call for schedule. Picnicking, fishing and swimming allowed in designated areas. Part of **state longhorn cattle herd** is in park.

Big Spring State Park is 382 acres located on FM 700 within the city limits of Big Spring in Howard County. Both city and park were named for a natural spring that was replaced by an artificial one. The park was deeded by the City of Big Spring in 1934 and 1935. Drive to top of **Scenic Mountain** provides panoramic view of surrounding country and look at **prairie dog colony**. The "big spring," nearby in a city park, provided watering place for herds of bison, antelope and wild horses. Used extensively also as campsite for early Indians, explorers and settlers.

Blanco State Park is 104.6 acres along the Blanco River four blocks south of Blanco's town square in Blanco County. The land was deeded by private owners in 1933. Park area was used as campsite by early explorers and settlers. Fishing for **winter rainbow trout, perch, catfish and bass. LBJ Ranch** and **LBJ State Historical Park, Pedernales Falls** and **Guadalupe River** state parks are nearby.

Boca Chica State Park is 1,054.46 acres of open beach located at the mouth of the Rio Grande in southeastern Cameron County. Park was acquired in May 1994. From US 77/83 at Olmito, take FM 511 12 miles to TX 4, then 17 miles east to park. Picnicking, wading, swimming, birding, camping, fishing allowed. No facilities provided.

Bonham State Park is a 261-acre park located two miles southeast of Bonham on TX 78, then two miles southeast on FM 271 in Fannin County. It includes a 65-acre lake, **rolling prairies and woodlands**. The land was acquired in 1933 and 1934 from the city of Bonham. Swimming beach, camping, mountain-bike trail, lighted fishing pier, boating, boat rentals. **Sam Rayburn Memorial Library** in Bonham. **Sam Rayburn Home** and **Valley Lake** nearby.

Brazos Bend State Park in Fort Bend County, seven miles west of Rosharon off FM 1462 on FM 762, approximately 28 miles south of Houston. The 4,897-acre park was purchased from private owners in 1976-77. **George Observatory. Observation platform** for spotting and photographing the **270 species of birds and 23 species of mammals** that frequent the park. Interpretive and educational programs every weekend. Backpacking, camping, hiking, biking, fishing.

Buescher State Park, a scenic area, is 1,016.7 acres 2 miles northwest of Smithville off TX 71 then FM 153 in Bastrop County. Acquired between 1933 and 1936, about one-third deeded by private owner; heirs donated a third; balance from City of Smithville. **El Camino Real** once ran near park, connecting **San Antonio de Béxar** with **Spanish missions in East Texas.** Parkland was part of **Stephen F. Austin's colonial grant.** Some **250 species of birds** can be seen. **Camping, fishing, hiking.** Scenic park road connects with **Bastrop State Park** through **Lost Pines** area.

Caddo Lake State Park, north of Karnack one mile off TX 43 to FM 2198 in Harrison County, consists of 8,017.2 acres (including adjoining wildlife management area) along **Cypress Bayou,** which runs into Caddo Lake. A scenic area, it was acquired from private owners in 1933-37. Nearby Karnack is childhood home of Mrs. Lyndon B. Johnson. Close by is old city of **Jefferson,** famous as commercial center of Northeast Texas during last half of 19th century. Caddo Indian legend attributes formation of Caddo Lake to **earthquake.** Lake originally only natural lake of any size in state; dam added in 1914 for flood control; new dam replaced old one in 1971. **Cypress trees, American lotus** and **lily pads,** as well as **71 species of fish,** predominate in lake. **Nutria, beaver, mink, squirrel, armadillo, alligator** and **turtle** abound. Activities include camping, hiking, swimming, fishing, boating. Screened shelters, cabins.

Caddoan Mounds State Historical Park in Cherokee County six miles southwest of Alto on TX 21. Total of 93.8 acres acquired in 1975 by condemnation. Open for day

The spring-fed pool at Balmorhea State Park has a natural bottom and crystal-clear water. Dallas Morning News file photo.

visits only, park offers exhibits and interpretive trails through reconstructed **Caddo dwellings and ceremonial areas,** including two temple mounds, a burial mound and a village area typical of people who lived in region for 500 years beginning about A.D. 800. Nearby are **Jim Hogg State Historical Park, Mission Tejas State Historical Park** and **Texas State Railroad.**

Caprock Canyons State Park, 3.5 miles north of Quitaque off RM 1065 and TX 86 in Briscoe, Floyd and Hall counties, has 15,160.6 acres. Purchased in 1975. Scenic escarpment's **canyons** provided camping areas for **Indians of Folsom culture** more than 10,000 years ago. **Mesquite and cacti in the badlands** give way to tall grasses, cottonwood and plum thickets in the bottomlands. Wildlife includes **aoudad sheep, coyote, bobcat, porcupine, ringtail** and **fox.** Activities include scenic drive, camping, hiking, mountain-bike riding, rock climbing, horse riding and horse camping. A 64.25-mile trailway (hike, bike and equestrian trail) extends from South Plains to Estelline.

Casa Navarro State Historical Park, on .7 acre at corner of S. Laredo and W. Nueva streets in downtown San Antonio, was acquired by donation from San Antonio Conservation Society Foundation in 1975. Has furnished **Navarro House** three-building complex built about 1848, home of the statesman, rancher and Texas patriot **José Antonio Navarro.** Guided tours; exhibits. Open Wednesday through Sunday.

Cedar Hill State Park, an urban park on 1,826 acres 15 miles southwest of Dallas via US 67 and FM 1382 on **Joe Pool Reservoir,** was acquired in 1982 and opened in 1992. Camping mostly in wooded areas; reservations recommended. Fishing from two lighted jetties and a perch pond for children. Swimming, boating, bicycling and picnicking. Vegetation includes several sections of **tall-grass prairie.** Penn Farm Agricultural Center has reconstructed buildings of the **19th-century Penn Farm** and exhibits; self-guided tours.

Choke Canyon State Park consists of two units, South Shore and Calliham, located on 26,000-acre **Choke Canyon Reservoir.** Park acquired in 1981 in a 50-year agreement among Bureau of Reclamation, City of Corpus Christi and Nueces River Authority. Thickets of **mesquite** and **blackbrush acacia** predominate, supporting populations of **javelina, coyote, skunk** and **alligator,** as well as the **crested caracara.** The 385-acre South Shore Unit is located 3.5 miles west of Three Rivers on TX 72 in Live Oak County; the 1,100-acre Calliham Unit is located 12 miles west of Three Rivers, on TX 72, in McMullen County. Both units offer camping, picnicking, boating, fishing, lake swimming, and baseball and volleyball areas. The Calliham Unit also has a hiking trail, wildlife educational center, screened shelters, rentable **gym and kitchen. Sports complex** includes swimming pool and tennis, volleyball, shuffleboard and basketball courts. Equestrian camping area.

Cleburne State Park is a 528.8-acre park located 10 miles southwest of Cleburne via US 67 and PR 21 in Johnson County with 116-acre spring-fed lake; acquired from the City of Cleburne, Johnson County and private owners in 1935 and 1936. **Oak, elm, mesquite, cedar** and **redbud** cover white rocky hills. Bluebonnets in spring. Activities include camping, picnicking, lake swimming, boating, fishing. Nearby are Fossil Rim Wildlife Center and **dinosaur tracks** in Paluxy River at **Dinosaur Valley State Park**.

Colorado Bend State Park, a 5,328.3-acre facility, is located 28 miles west of Lampasas in Lampasas and San Saba counties. Access is from Lampasas to Bend on FM 580 west, then follow signs (access road subject to flooding). Park site was purchased partly in 1984, with balance acquired in 1987. Primitive camping, river fishing, hiking, biking and picnicking; guided tours to Gorman Falls. Rare and endangered species here include **golden-cheeked warbler, black-capped vireo** and **bald eagle.**

Confederate Reunion Grounds State Historical Park, located in Limestone County on the Navasota River, is 77.1 acres in size. Acquired 1983 by deed from Joseph E. Johnston Camp No. 94 CSA. Entrance is 6 miles south of Mexia on TX 14, then 2.5 miles west on FM 2705. **Historic buildings,** two **scenic footbridges** span creek; hiking trail. Nearby are **Fort Parker State Park** and **Old Fort Parker State Historical Park**.

Cooper Lake State Park, comprises 3,026 acres three miles southeast of Cooper in Delta and Hopkins counties acquired in 1991 by 25-year lease from Corps of Engineers. Two units, Doctors Creek and South Sulphur, adjoin 19,300-surface-acre Cooper Lake. Fishing, boating, camping, picnicking, swimming. Screened shelters and cabins. Access to Doctors Creek Unit is via TX 24 east from Commerce to Cooper, then east on TX 154 to FM 1529 to park. To South Sulphur Unit, take IH 30 to Exit 122 west of Sulphur Springs to TX 19, then TX 71, then FM 3505.

Copano Bay State Fishing Pier, a 5.9-acre park, is located 5 miles north of Rockport on TX 35 in Aransas County. Acquired by transfer of jurisdiction from state highway department in 1967. Picnicking, saltwater fishing, boating and swimming. Operated by leased concession.

Copper Breaks State Park, 12 miles south of Quanah on TX 6 in Hardeman County, was acquired by purchase from private owner in 1970. Park features rugged scenic beauty on 1,898.8 acres, a 70-acre lake, **grass-covered mesas** and juniper breaks. Nearby **medicine mounds** were important ceremonial sites of Comanche Indians. Nearby **Pease River** was site of 1860 battle in which **Cynthia Ann Parker** was recovered from Comanches. Part of **state longhorn herd** lives at park. Abundant wildlife. Nature, hiking and equestrian trails; natural and historical exhibits; summer programs; horseback riding; camping, equestrian camping.

Daingerfield State Park, off TX 49 and PR 17 southeast of Daingerfield in Morris County, is a 550.9-acre recreational area that includes an 80-surface-acre lake; deeded in 1935 by private owners. This area is center of iron industry in Texas; nearby is Lone Star Steel Co. In spring, **dogwood, redbuds** and **wisteria** bloom; in fall, brilliant foliage of **sweetgum, oaks** and **maples** contrast with dark green pines. Campsites, lodge and cabins.

Davis Mountains State Park is 2,708.9 acres in Jeff Davis County, 4 miles northwest of Fort Davis via TX 118 and PR 3. The scenic area was deeded in 1933-1937 by private owners. **First European, Antonio de Espejo,** came to area in 1583. Extremes of altitude produce both **plains grasslands and piñon-juniper-oak woodlands. Montezuma quail,** rare in Texas, visit park. Scenic drives, camping and hiking. **Indian Lodge,** built by the Civilian Conservation Corps during the early 1930s, has 39 rooms, restaurant and swimming pool (reservations: 915-426-3254). Four-mile hiking trail leads to **Fort Davis National Historic Site.** Other nearby points of interest include **McDonald Observatory** and 74-mile scenic loop through **Davis Mountains.** Nearby are scenic **Limpia, Madera, Musquiz** and **Keesey** canyons; **Camino del Rio;** ghost town of **Shafter; Big Bend National Park; Big Bend Ranch State Park; Fort Davis National Historic Site;** and **Fort Leaton State Historical Park.**

Devil's River State Natural Area comprises 19,988.6 acres in Val Verde County, 22 miles off US 277, about 65 miles north of Del Rio on graded road. It is an **ecological and archaeological crossroads.** Ecologically, it is in a transitional area between the **Edwards Plateau, the Trans-Pecos desert and the South Texas brush country.** Archaeological studies suggest occupation and/or use by cultures from both east and west. Camping, hiking. Canyon and pictograph-site tours by prearrangement only. Park accessible by reservation only. **Dolan Falls,** owned by The Nature Conservancy of Texas and open only to its members, is nearby.

Devil's Sinkhole State Natural Area, comprising 1,859.7 acres about 6 miles northeast of Rocksprings in Edwards County, is a **vertical cavern.** The sinkhole, discovered by Anglo settlers in 1867, is a registered **National Natural Landmark;** was acquired in 1985. The cavern opening is about 40 by 60 feet, with a vertical drop of about 140 feet. Access limited pending development. Bats can be viewed in summer leaving cave at dusk; no access to cave itself. Access to the park is made by contacting **Kickapoo Cavern State Park** to arrange a tour.

Dinosaur Valley State Park, located off US 67 just south of Glen Rose in Somervell County, is a 1,524.72-acre scenic park. Land was acquired from private owners in 1969 and 1973. **Dinosaur tracks** in bed of Paluxy River and two full-scale dinosaur models, originally created for New York World's Fair in 1964-65, on display. Part of state **longhorn herd** is in park. Camping, picnicking, hiking, mountain biking, river swimming, fishing.

Eisenhower Birthplace State Historical Park is 6 acres off US 75 at 208 E. Day, Denison, Grayson County. The property was acquired in 1958 from the Eisenhower Birthplace Foundation. Restoration of home of Pres. Dwight David Eisenhower includes furnishings of period and some personal effects of Gen. Eisenhower, including a crank-type telephone with personal greetings from **"Ike."** Guided tour; call for days and hours available. Park open Monday-Saturday, except Thanksgiving, Christmas Day and New Year's Day. Town of Denison established on **Butterfield Overland Mail** Route in 1858.

Eisenhower State Park, 423.1 acres five miles northwest of Denison via US 75 to TX 91N to FM 1310 on the shores of **Lake Texoma** in Grayson County, was acquired by an Army lease in 1954. Named for the **34th U.S. president, Dwight David Eisenhower.** First Anglo settlers came to area in 1835 and 1836; **Fort Johnson** was established in area in 1840; **Colbert's Ferry** established on Red River in 1853 and operated until 1931. Remnants of **tallgrass prairie** exist. Hiking, camping, picnicking, fishing, swimming.

Enchanted Rock State Natural Area is 1,643.5 acres on Big Sandy Creek 18 miles north of Fredericksburg on RM 965 on the line between Gillespie and Llano counties. Acquired in 1978 by The Nature Conservancy of Texas; state acquired from TNCT in 1984. Enchanted Rock is huge **pink granite boulder** rising 425 feet above ground and covering 640 acres. It is **second-largest batholith** (underground rock formation uncovered by erosion) in the United States. Indians believed **ghost fires** flickered at top and were awed by weird creaking and groaning, which geologists say resulted from rock's heating and expanding by day, cooling and contracting at night. Enchanted Rock is a **National Natural Landmark** and is on the **National Register of Historic Places.** Activities include hiking, geological study, camping, **rock climbing** and star gazing.

Fairfield Lake State Park is 1,460 acres adjacent to Lake Fairfield, 6 miles northeast of the city of Fairfield off FM 2570 and FM 3285 in Freestone County. It was leased from Texas Utilities in 1971-72. Surrounding, predominantly oak, woods offer sanctuary for many species of birds and wildlife. Extensive schedule of tours, seminars and other activities.

Falcon State Park is 572.6 acres located 15 miles north of Roma off US 83 and FM 2098 at southern end of Falcon Reservoir in Starr and Zapata counties. Park leased from International Boundary and Water Commission in 1949. Gently rolling hills covered by **mesquite, huisache, wild olive, ebony, cactus.** Excellent **birding** and **fishing.** Nearby are **Mexico, Fort Ringgold** in Rio Grande City and historic city of **Roma. Bentsen-Rio Grande Valley State Park** is 65 miles away.

Fannin Battleground State Historical Park, 9 miles east of Goliad in Goliad County off US 59 to PR 27. The

13.6-acre park site was acquired by the state in 1914; transferred to TPW by legislative enactment in 1965. At this site on March 20, 1836, **Col. J. W. Fannin** surrendered to Mexican **Gen. José Urrea** after **Battle of Coleto;** 342 massacred and 28 escaped near what is now **Goliad State Historical Park.** Near Fannin site is **Gen. Zaragoza's Birthplace** and partially restored **Mission Nuestra Señora del Espíritu Santo de Zúñiga.** (See also **Goliad State Historical Park** in this list.)

Fanthorp Inn State Historical Park includes a historic double-pen cedar-log dogtrot house and 1.4 acres in Anderson, county seat of Grimes County on TX 90. Acquired by purchase in 1977 from a Fanthorp descendant and opened to the public in 1987. Inn records report visits from many prominent civic and military leaders, including **Sam Houston, Anson Jones, Ulysses S. Grant** and generals **Robert E. Lee** and **Stonewall Jackson.** Originally built in 1834, it has been restored to its 1850 use a family home and travelers' hotel. Tours available Friday, Saturday, Sunday. Call TPW for stagecoach-ride schedule. No dining or overnight facilities.

Fort Griffin State Historical Park is 506.2 acres 15 miles north of Albany off US 283 in Shackelford County. The state was deeded the land by the county in 1935. Portion of **state longhorn herd** resides in park. On bluff overlooking townsite of **Fort Griffin** and **Clear Fork of Brazos River** valley are partially restored ruins of **Old Fort Griffin,** restored bakery, replicas of enlisted men's huts. Fort constructed in 1867, deactivated 1881. Camping, hiking. Nearby are **Albany** with restored courthouse square, **Abilene and Possum Kingdom State Park.** Albany annually holds **"Fandangle"** musical show in commemoration of frontier times.

Fort Lancaster State Historical Park, 81.6-acres located about 8 miles east of Sheffield on IH 10 then US 290 and paved access road in Crockett County. Acquired in 1968 by deed from Crockett County; Henry Meadows donated 41 acres in 1975. **Fort Lancaster** established Aug. 20, 1855, to guard San Antonio-El Paso Road and protect movement of supplies and immigrants from Indian hostilities. Site of part of Camel Corps experiment. Fort abandoned March 19, 1861, after Texas seceded from Union. Exhibits on history, natural history and archaeology; nature trail, picnicking. Day use only. Call for days and hours.

Fort Leaton State Historical Park, 4 miles southeast of Presidio in Presidio County on FM 170, was acquired in 1967 from private owners. Consists of 23.4 acres, 5 of which are on site of **pioneer trading post.** In 1848, **Ben Leaton** built fortified adobe trading post known as Fort Leaton near present Presidio. Ben Leaton died in 1851. Guided tours; exhibits trace history, natural history and archaeological history of area. Serves as western entrance to **Big Bend Ranch State Park.** Day use only.

Fort McKavett State Historical Park, 79.5 acres acquired from 1967 through the mid-1970s from Fort McKavett Restoration, Inc., Menard County and private individuals, is located 23 miles west of Menard off US 190 and RM 864. Originally called **Camp San Saba,** the fort was built by War Department in 1852 to protect frontier settlers and travelers on Upper El Paso Road from Indians. Camp later renamed for **Capt. Henry McKavett,** killed at Battle of Monterrey, Sept. 21, 1846. A **Buffalo Soldier** post. Fort abandoned March 1859; reoccupied April 1, 1868. After Indian hostilities toward white settlers waned, fort no longer needed; abandoned June 30, 1883. Once called by Gen. Wm. T. Sherman, "the prettiest post in Texas." More than 25 restored buildings, ruins of many others. Interpretive exhibits. Day use only.

Fort Parker State Park includes 1,458.8 acres, including 758.78 land acres and 700-acre lake between Mexia and Groesbeck off TX 14 in Limestone County. Named for the former private fort built near present park in 1836, the site was acquired from private owners and the City of Mexia 1935-1937. Boating, fishing, swimming, canoeing, camping, picnicking. Nearby is **Old Fort Parker State Historical Park.**

Fort Richardson State Historical Park, located one-half mile south of Jacksboro off US 281 in Jack County, contains 402.2 acres. Acquired in 1968 from City of Jacksboro. Fort founded in 1867, northernmost of line of federal forts established after Civil War for protection from Indians; originally named **Fort Jacksboro.** In April 1867, fort was moved to its present location from 20 miles farther south; on Nov. 19, 1867, made permanent post at Jacksboro and named for **Israel Richardson,** who was fatally wounded at Battle of Antietam. Expeditions sent from Fort Richardson arrested Indians responsible for **Salt Creek Massacre** in 1871 and fought Comanches in **Palo Duro Canyon.** Fort abandoned in May 1878. Park contains seven restored buildings and two replicas. Interpretive center, picnicking, camping, fishing; 10-mile trailway.

Franklin Mountains State Park, created by an act of the legislature in 1979 to protect the mountain range as a wilderness preserve and acquired by TPW in 1981, comprises 24,049.6 acres within El Paso city limits. **Largest urban park in the nation.** It includes virtually an entire **Chihuahuan Desert mountain range,** with an elevation of 7,192 feet at the summit. Located completely within the city limits of El Paso, the park is habitat for many Chihuahuan Desert plants including **sotol, lechuguilla, ocotillo, cholla** and **barrel cactus,** as well as **mule deer, fox** and an occasional **cougar.** Pedestrian access for day-use activities such as hiking, nature study and picnicking is permitted. Has multi-use trails. Camping, mountain biking, hiking, picnicking, rock-climbing.

Fulton Mansion State Historic Structure is 3.5 miles north of Rockport off TX 35 in Aransas County. The 2.3 acre-property was acquired by purchase from private owner in 1976. Three-story wooden structure, built in 1874-1877, was home of **George W. Fulton,** prominent in South Texas for economic and commercial influence; mansion derives significance from its innovative construction and Victorian design. Call ahead for days and hours of guided tours; structure open Wednesday-Sunday.

Galveston Island State Park, located approximately 6 miles southwest of Galveston on FM 3005, is a 2,013.1-acre site acquired in 1969 from private owners. Camping, birding, nature study and fishing amid **sand dunes and grassland.** Musical productions in **amphitheater** during summer.

Garner State Park is 1,419.8 acres of recreational facilities on US 83 on the Frio River in Uvalde County 9 miles south of Leakey. Named for **John Nance Garner,** U.S. Vice President, 1933-1941, the park was deeded in 1934-36 by private owners. Camping, hiking, picnicking, river recreation, miniature golf, biking, boat rentals. Cabins available. Nearby is **John Nance "Cactus Jack" Garner Museum** in Uvalde. Nearby also are ruins of historic **Mission Nuestra Señora de la Candelaria del Cañon,** founded in 1749; **Camp Sabinal** (a U.S. Cavalry post and later Texas Ranger camp) established 1856; **Fort Inge,** established 1849.

Goliad State Historical Park is 188.3 acres one-fourth mile south of Goliad on US 183 and 77A, along the San Antonio River in Goliad County. The land was deeded to state in 1931 by the City and County of Goliad; transferred to TPW 1949. Nearby are the sites of several battles in the Texas fight for independence from Mexico. The park includes a replica of **Mission Nuestra Señora del Espíritu Santo de Zúñiga,** originally established 1722 and settled at its present site in 1749. Park unit includes **Gen. Ignacio Zaragoza's Birthplace,** which is located near **Presidio la Bahía.** He was Mexican national hero who led troops against French at historic **Battle of Puebla** on May 5, 1862. Park also contains ruins of **Nuestra Señora del Rosario** mission, established 1754, located four miles west of Goliad on US 59. Camping, picnicking, historical exhibits, nature trail. Other nearby points of historical interest: restored **Nuestra Señora de Loreto de la Bahía** presidio, established 1722 and settled on site in 1749; it is located short distance south on US 183. Memorial shaft marking common burial site of **Fannin** and victims of **Goliad massacre** (1836) is near **Presidio la Bahía.** (See also **Fannin Battleground State Historical Park,** above.)

Goose Island State Park, 321.4 acres 10 miles northeast of Rockport on TX 35 and PR 13 on St. Charles and Aransas bays in Aransas County, was deeded by private

Parks text continues on page 116.

☆ Texas State Parks ☆

Park/†Type of Park/Special Features	Nearest Town	Day Use Only	Historic Site/Museum	Exhibit/Interpretive Center	Restrooms	Showers	Trailer Dump Stn.	††Camping	Screened Shelters	Cabins	Group Facilities	Nature Trail	Hiking Trail	Picnicking	Boat Ramp	Fishing	Swimming	Water Skiing	Miscellaneous
Abilene SP	BUFFALO GAP				★	★	★	19	★		BG	★	★			☆	★		L
Acton SHP (Grave of Davy Crockett's wife)	GRANBURY	★	★																
Admiral Nimitz Museum SHP	FREDERICKSBURG	★	★	★	★						★								
Atlanta SP	ATLANTA				★	★	★	25			DG	★	★	★	★	☆	☆	☆	
Balmorhea SP (San Solomon Springs Courts)	BALMORHEA			★	★	★	★	20			DG			★			★		I
Barton Warnock Environmental Education Ctr.	LAJITAS	★		★	★														
Bastrop SP	BASTROP				★	★	★	13		★	BG	★		☆			☆	★	G
Battleship Texas HS (At San Jacinto Battleground)	DEER PARK	★	★	★															
Bentsen-Rio Grande Valley SP	MISSION				★	★	★	16			BG	★	★	★	★	☆			
Big Bend Ranch SP Complex	PRESIDIO				★	★	★	1			NG	★	★	★		☆	☆		B1, L
Big Spring SP	BIG SPRING				★	★		2			BG	★	★						
Blanco SP	BLANCO				★	★	★	25	★		DG	★	★			☆	☆		
Boca Chica SP (Open Beach)	BROWNSVILLE							1						☆		☆	☆		
Bonham SP	BONHAM				★	★	★	20			BG		★	★	★	★	☆		B1
Brazos Bend SP (George Observatory)	RICHMOND			★	★	★	★	4	★		DG	★	★	★		★			B1, B2
Buescher SP	SMITHVILLE				★	★	★	20	★		BG	★	★				☆	☆	
Caddo Lake SP	KARNACK				★	★	★	21	★	★	BG	★	★	★	★	★	☆	☆	
Caddoan Mounds SHP	ALTO	★	★	★	★							★							
Caprock Canyons SP and Trailway	QUITAQUE			★	★	★	★	11			BG	★	★	★	★	★	☆		B1, E, R
Casa Navarro SHP	SAN ANTONIO	★	★	★	★														
Cedar Hill SP	CEDAR HILL				★	★	★	17			DG		★	★	★	★	☆	☆	B1
Choke Canyon SP, Calliham Unit	CALLIHAM				★	★	★	13	★		BG	★		★	★	★	★	☆	
Choke Canyon SP, South Shore Unit	THREE RIVERS				★	★	★	19			DG		★	★	★	★	☆	☆	B1
Cleburne SP	CLEBURNE				★	★	★	25	★		BG	★	★	★	★	★	☆	☆	
Colorado Bend SP (Cave Tours)	BEND				★			1				★	★	★	★	★			B1
Confederate Reunion Grounds SHP	MEXIA	★		★	★			1			BG			★		☆			
Cooper Lake SP (Doctors Creek Unit)	COOPER				★	★	★	4	★		DG	★	★	★	★	★	★	☆	
Cooper Lake SP (South Sulphur Unit)	SULPHUR SPRINGS				★	★	★	23	★	★	DG	★	★	★	★	★	★	★	B1, E
Copano Bay SFP ▲	FULTON				★									★	★				
Copper Breaks SP	QUANAH			★	★	★	★	15			BG	★	★		★	★	☆		B1, E, L
Daingerfield SP	DAINGERFIELD				★	★	★	21		★	BG	★	★	★	★	★	☆		
Davis Mountains SP (Indian Lodge)	FORT DAVIS				★	★	★	22			BG	★	★						
Devils River SNA (Use by reservation only)	DEL RIO				★			1			BG								B1
Devil's Sinkhole SNA	ROCKSPRINGS	(No access to cavern. Tours of SNA by special request only.)																	
Dinosaur Valley SP (Dinosaur Footprints)	GLEN ROSE			★	★	★	★	18			DG	★	★	★		☆	☆		B1, E, L
Eisenhower SP (Marina)	DENISON				★	★	★	21	★		BG	★	★	★	★	★	☆	☆	B1
Eisenhower Birthplace SHP	DENISON	★	★	★	★														B1
Enchanted Rock SNA	FREDERICKSBURG			★	★	★		12			DG	★	★	★					R
Fairfield Lake SP	FAIRFIELD				★	★	★	14			DG	★	★	★	★	★	☆	☆	B1
Falcon SP (Airstrip)	ZAPATA				★	★	★	21	★		BG	★		★	★	☆	☆	☆	B1
Fannin Battleground SHP	GOLIAD	★	★	★	★						DG			★					
Fanthorp Inn SHP	ANDERSON	★	★	★	★									★					
Fort Griffin SHP	ALBANY	★	★	★	★	★		15			BG	★	★	★		☆			L
Fort Lancaster SHP	OZONA	★	★	★	★									☆					
Fort Leaton SHP	PRESIDIO	★	★	★	★									★					
Fort McKavett SHP	FORT McKAVETT	★	★	★	★							★		★					
Fort Parker SP	MEXIA				★	★	★	20	★		BG	★	★	★	★	★	☆		B1
Fort Richardson SHP (Lost Creek Trailway)	JACKSBORO		★	★	★	★	★	17	★		DG	★		★		☆			
Franklin Mountains SP	EL PASO	★			★			6					★	★					B1, E, R
Fulton Mansion SHP	FULTON	★	★	★	★														
Galveston Island SP (Summer Theater)	GALVESTON				★	★	★	4				★		★		☆	☆		B1
Garner SP	CONCAN				★	★	★	20	★	★	BG	★		★		☆	☆		B2
Goliad SHP	GOLIAD	★		★	★	★	★	14	★		DG	★	★	★		☆	★		
Goose Island SP	ROCKPORT				★	★	★	20			BG			★	★	★	☆		
Governor Hogg Shrine SHP	QUITMAN	★	★	★	★						DG	★		★					
Guadalupe River SP/Honey Creek SNA	BOERNE				★	★	★	20				★	★			☆	☆		
Hill Country SNA	BANDERA							10			NG	★				☆	☆		B1, E
Hueco Tanks SHP (Indian Pictographs)	EL PASO		★	★	★	★	★	20			BG	★	★	★					R
Huntsville SP	HUNTSVILLE				★	★	★	20			DG	★	★	★	★	★	☆		B1, B2
Inks Lake SP	BURNET				★	★	★	13	★		BG	★	★	★	★	★	☆	☆	G
Jim Hogg SHP	RUSK	★	★	★	★							★		★					
Kerrville-Schreiner SP	KERRVILLE				★	★	★	14	★		BG	★	★	★	★	★	☆		B1

†Types of Parks

SP	State Park
SHP	State Historical Park
SNA	State Natural Area
SFP	State Fishing Pier

††Type(s) of Camping

1-Primitive; 2-Developed (no utilities); 3-Water at or near site; 4-Water and Electricity; 5-Water, Electricity, Sewage; 6-Equestrian; 7-1 & 2; 8-1, 2 & 4; 9-1, 2, 3 & 4; 10-1, 2 & 6; 11-1, 2, 3, 4 & 6; 12-1 & 3; 13-1, 3 & 4; 14-1, 3, 4 & 5; 15-1, 3, 4 & 6; 16-1, 3 & 5; 17-1 & 4; 18-1, 4 & 6; 19-2, 3 & 4; 20-3 & 4; 21-3, 4 & 5; 22-3, 4, 5 & 6; 23-3, 4 & 6; 24-3 & 5; 25-4 & 5.

☆ Texas State Parks ☆

Park/†Type of Park/Special Features	NEAREST TOWN	Day Use Only	Historic Site/Museum	Exhibit/Interpretive Center	Restrooms	Showers	Trailer Dump Stn.	††Camping	Screened Shelters	Cabins	Group Facilities	Nature Trail	Hiking Trail	Picnicking	Boat Ramp	Fishing	Swimming	Water Skiing	Miscellaneous
Kickapoo Cavern SP (Use by reservation only)	BRACKETTVILLE							1			NG								B1
Lake Arrowhead SP	WICHITA FALLS				★	★	★	15			DG	★		★	★	★	☆	☆	E
Lake Bob Sandlin SP	MOUNT PLEASANT				★	★	★	13	★		DG		★	★	★	★	☆		B1
Lake Brownwood SP	BROWNWOOD				★	★	★	21	★	★	BG	★	★	★	★	★	★	☆	
Lake Casa Blanca International SP	LAREDO				★	★	★	20			BG			★	★	☆	★	☆	B1
Lake Colorado City SP	COLORADO CITY				★	★	★	20			BG			★	★	★	☆	☆	
Lake Corpus Christi SP	MATHIS				★	★	★	21	★		DG	★		★	★	★	☆	☆	
Lake Houston SP	NEW CANEY				★	★		3			BG	★	★	★					B1
Lake Livingston SP	LIVINGSTON				★	★	★	20	★		DG	★	★	★	★	★	☆	☆	B1, B2, E
Lake Mineral Wells SP and Trailway	MINERAL WELLS				★	★	★	15	★		DG	★	★	★	★	★	☆		B1, E, R
Lake Rita Blanca SP	DALHART	★												★					B1, E
Lake Somerville SP and Trailway	SOMERVILLE			★	★	★	★	15			BG	★	★	★	★	★	☆	☆	B1, E
Lake Tawakoni SP	WILLS POINT	(Opening pending at press time)																	
Lake Texana SP	EDNA			★	★	★	★	20			DG	★		★	★	★	☆	☆	
Lake Whitney SP (Airstrip)	WHITNEY				★	★	★	21	★		BG	★		★	★	★	☆	☆	B1
Landmark Inn SHP (Hotel Rooms)	CASTROVILLE	★	★	★							DG	★		★			☆		I
Lipantitlan SHP	SAN PATRICIO	★										★							
Lockhart SP	LOCKHART				★	★		25			BG			★			★		G
Longhorn Cavern SP (Cavern Tours) ▲	BURNET	★	★	★								★	★	★					
Lost Maples SNA	VANDERPOOL			★	★	★	★	17				★	★	★			☆	☆	
Lubbock Lake Landmark SHP	LUBBOCK	★	★	★	★						DG	★	★						
Lyndon B. Johnson SHP	STONEWALL	★	★	★	★						DG	★		★			☆	★	L
Magoffin Home SHP	EL PASO	★	★	★	★														
Martin Creek Lake SP	TATUM				★	★	★	17	★	★	DG		★	★	★	★	☆	☆	B1
Martin Dies Jr. SP	JASPER				★	★	★	20	★		BG	★		★	★	★	☆	☆	B1
Matagorda Island SP (Boat or Air Access Only)	PORT O'CONNOR		★	★	☆	☆		1			NG	★		☆	☆	☆	☆		B1
McKinney Falls SP	AUSTIN	★		★	★	★	★	19	★		BG	★	★	★			☆	☆	B1, B2
Meridian SP	MERIDIAN				★	★	★	19	★		BG	★	★	★	★	★	☆	☆	
Mission Tejas SHP	WECHES		★		★	★	★	21			BG	★	★	★			☆		
Monahans Sandhills SP	MONAHANS			★	★	★	★	20			DG	★		★					E
Monument Hill/Kreische Brewery SHP	LA GRANGE	★	★	★	★							★		★					
Mother Neff SP	MOODY				★	★	★	13			BG	★	★	★			☆		
Mustang Island SP	PORT ARANSAS				★	★	★	17						★			☆	☆	B1
Old Fort Parker SHP	GROESBECK		★	★	★			3				★		★					
Palmetto SP	LULING				★	★	★	21			DG	★	★	★		★	☆		
Palo Duro Canyon SP (Summer Drama: "Texas")	CANYON			★	★	★	★	11		★		★	★	★		★			B1, E, L
Pedernales Falls SP	JOHNSON CITY				★	★	★	12			NG	★	★	★			☆	☆	B1, E
Port Isabel Lighthouse SHP	PORT ISABEL	★	★		★														
Port Lavaca SFP ▲	PORT LAVACA				★										★	★			
Possum Kingdom SP	CADDO				★	★	★	13		★		★	★	★	★	★	☆	☆	
Purtis Creek SP	EUSTACE				★	★	★	17				★	★	★	★	★	☆		P
Ray Roberts Lake SP	DENTON				★	★	★	19			BG	★	★	★	★	★	☆	☆	B1, B2, E
Rusk/Palestine SP (Texas State RR Terminals)	RUSK/PALESTINE				★	★	★	21			DG	★		★	★	★			
Sabine Pass Battleground SHP	SABINE PASS		★		★			17						★	★	☆			
Sam Bell Maxey House SHP	PARIS	★	★	★	★														
San Angelo SP	SAN ANGELO				★	★		11			BG	★	★	★	★	★	☆	☆	B1, E, L
San Jacinto Battleground SHP (Battleship Texas)	HOUSTON	★	★	★	★						DG	★		★			☆		
San José Mission SHP ▲	SAN ANTONIO	(See San Antonio Missions National Park)																	
San Marcos SP (John J. Stokes) (No facilities)	SAN MARCOS	★						(No development)									☆		
Sea Rim SP	PORT ARTHUR			★	★	★	★	13				★		★	★	☆	★		B1
Sebastopol SHP	SEGUIN	★	★	★								★							
Seminole Canyon SHP (Indian Pictographs)	LANGTRY	★		★	★	★	★	20				★	★	★					B1
Sheldon Lake SP	HOUSTON											★	☆	★	★				
South Llano River SP	JUNCTION			★	★	★	★	13				★	★	★			☆	☆	B1
Starr Family SHP	MARSHALL	★	★	★	★														
Stephen F. Austin SP	SAN FELIPE				★	★	★	21	★		DG	★	★	★			☆		G
Texas State Railroad SHP (Contact Park for Schedule)	PALESTINE/RUSK	★	★	★	★														
Tyler SP	TYLER				★	★	★	14	★		BG	★	★	★	★	★	☆		B1
Varner-Hogg Plantation SHP (Guided Tours)	WEST COLUMBIA	★	★	★	★							★	★	★			☆		
Village Creek SP	LUMBERTON				★	★	★	13			BG	★	★	★	★	★	☆	☆	B1
Washington-on-the-Brazos SHP (Anson Jones Home)	WASHINGTON	★	★	★	★						DG	★	★						

Facilities

▲ Facilities not operated by Parks & Wildlife.
★ Facilities or services available for activity.
☆ Facilities or services not provided.

Miscellaneous Codes

B1	Mountain Biking	G	Golf
B2	Surfaced Bike Trail	I	Hotel-Type Facilities
BG	Both Day & Night Group Facilities	L	Texas Longhorn Herd
DG	Day-Use Group Facilities	NG	Overnight Group Facilities
E	Equestrian Trails	R	Rock Climbing

owners in 1931-1935 plus an additional seven acres donated in the early 1990s by Sun Oil Co. Located here is "Big Tree" estimated to be more than 1,000 years old and listed as the **state champion coastal live oak.** Water activities, picnicking and camping, plus excellent birding. Rare and endangered **whooping cranes** can be viewed during winter just across St. Charles Bay in **Aransas National Wildlife Refuge.**

Gov. Hogg Shrine State Historical Park is a 26.7-acre tract on TX 37 about six blocks south of the Wood County Courthouse in Quitman. Named for **James Stephen Hogg, first native-born governor of Texas,** the park includes museums housing items which belonged to the Hogg and Stinson families. Seventeen acres deeded by the Wood County Old Settlers Reunion Association in 1946; 4.74 acres gift of Miss Ima Hogg in 1970; 3 acres purchased. **Gov. James Stephen Hogg Memorial Shrine** created in 1941. Three museums: Gov. Hogg's wedding held in **Stinson Home; Honeymoon Cottage; Miss Ima Hogg Museum** houses both park headquarters and display of representative history of entire Northeast Texas area.

Guadalupe River State Park comprises 1,938.7 acres on cypress-shaded Guadalupe River in Kendall and Comal counties, 13 miles east of Boerne on TX 46. Acquired by deed from private owners in 1974. Park has four miles of river frontage with several **white-water rapids** and is located in middle of 9-mile stretch of **Guadalupe River** noted for canoeing, tubing. Picnicking, camping, nature study. Trees include **sycamore, elm, basswood, pecan, walnut, persimmon, willow** and **hackberry.** (see also **Honey Creek State Natural Area,** below).

Hill Country State Natural Area in Bandera and Medina counties, 9 miles west of Bandera on RM 1077. The 5,369.8-acre site acquired by gift from Merrick Bar-O-Ranch and purchase in 1976. Park is located in typical Texas Hill Country on West Verde Creek and contains several **spring-fed streams.** Primitive and equestrian camping, hiking, horseback riding, mountain biking. Group lodge. Access from TX 173 and TX 1077.

Honey Creek State Natural Area consists of 2,293.7 acres adjacent to **Guadalupe River State Park** (above). Entrance is in the park. Acquired from The Nature Conservancy of Texas in 1985 with an addition from private individual in 1988. Diverse plant life includes agarita, Texas persimmon and Ashe juniper in hills, and cedar elm, Spanish oak, pecan, walnut and Mexican buckeye in bottomlands. Abundant wildlife includes ringtail, leopard frog, green kingfisher, golden-cheeked warbler and canyon wren. Open Saturdays only for **guided naturalist tours;** call for details.

Hueco Tanks State Historical Park, located 32 miles northeast of El Paso in El Paso County on RM 2775 just north of US 62-180, was obtained from the county in 1969, with additional 121 acres purchased in 1970. Featured in this 860.3-acre park are large **natural rock basins** that provided water for archaic hunters, Plains Indians, Butterfield Overland Mail coach horses and passengers, and other travelers in this arid region. In park are **Indian pictographs, old ranch house** and relocated **ruins of stage station. Rock** climbing, picnicking, camping. Guided tours. Wildlife includes **gray fox, bobcat, prairie falcons, golden eagles.**

Huntsville State Park is 2,083.2-acre recreational area off IH 45 and PR 40 six miles southeast of Huntsville in Walker County, acquired by deeds from private owners in 1937. Heavily wooded park adjoins **Sam Houston National Forest** and encloses **Lake Raven.** Hiking, camping, fishing, biking, pedal boats, canoeing. At nearby Huntsville are the **Sam Houston's old homestead (Steamboat House),** containing some of his personal effects, and **his grave.** Approximately 50 miles away is **Alabama-Coushatta Indian Reservation** in Polk County.

Inks Lake State Park is 1,201.7 acres of recreational facilities along Inks Lake, 9 miles west of Burnet on the Colorado River off TX 29 on PR 4 in Burnet County. Acquired by deeds from the Lower Colorado River Authority and private owners in 1940. Camping, hiking, fishing, swimming, boating, 9 holes of golf. Nearby are **Longhorn Cavern State Park, LBJ Ranch, LBJ State Historical**

Park, Pedernales Falls State Park and **Enchanted Rock State Natural Area. Granite Mountain** and quarry at nearby Marble Falls furnished red granite for **Texas state capitol. Deer, turkey** and other wildlife abundant. **Buchanan Dam,** largest multi-arch dam in world, located 4 miles from park.

More Travel Information

Call the **Texas Department of Transportation's** toll-free number: **1-800-888-8TEX** for:

• The **Texas State Travel Guide,** a free 288-page, full-color publication with a wealth of information about attractions, activities, history and historic sites.

• The official **Texas state highway map.**

On the Internet: **www.traveltex.com**

Jim Hogg State Historical Park is 178.4 acres of East Texas Piney Woods off US 84 and PR 50 two miles northeast of Rusk in Cherokee County. A memorial to the state's **first native-born governor, James Stephen Hogg,** the property was deeded by the city of Rusk in 1941. Scale replica of birthplace; museum; family cemetery. Day use only.

Kerrville-Schreiner State Park is a 517.2-acre area 3 miles southeast of Kerrville off TX 173 and PR 19 along the Guadalupe River in Kerr County. Land deeded by City of Kerrville in 1934. Trees include **redbud, sumac, buckeye, pecan, mesquite.** Birding, camping, fishing, picnicking, cycling. Near park is site of **Camp Verde,** active 1855-1869, which was a base for an army experiment using of **camels** to haul equipment. **Bandera Pass,** 12 miles south of Kerrville, noted gap in chain of mountains through which passed camel caravans, wagon trains, Spanish conquistadores, immigrant trains. In nearby **Fredericksburg** is atmosphere of old country of Germany and famous **Nimitz Hotel** (see **Admiral Nimitz Museum Historical Park).**

Kickapoo Cavern State Park is located about 22 miles north of Brackettville on RM 674 on the Kinney/Edwards county line in the southern Edwards Plateau. The 6,368.4-acre park contains **15 known caves,** two of which are large enough to be significant: **Kickapoo Cavern,** about 1/4 mile in length, has impressive formations, and **Green Cave,** slightly longer, supports a nursery colony of **Brazilian freetail bats** in summer. Birds include rare species such as **black-capped vireo, varied bunting** and **Montezuma quail.** Reptiles and amphibians include **barking frog, mottled rock rattlesnake** and **Texas alligator lizard.** Tours of Kickapoo and observation of bats available only by special arrangement. Group lodge; primitive camping; hiking and mountain-biking trails. Open only by reservation.

Kreische Brewery State Historical Park (see Monument Hill and Kreische Brewery State Historical Parks)

Lake Arrowhead State Park consists of 524 acres in Clay County, about 6 miles south of Wichita Falls on US 281 to FM 1954, then 8 miles to park. Acquired in 1970 from the City of Wichita Falls. **Lake Arrowhead** is a reservoir on the Little Wichita River with 106 miles of shoreline. The land surrounding the lake is generally semiarid, gently rolling prairie, much of which has been invaded by mesquite in recent decades. Fishing, camping, lake swimming, picnicking, horseback-riding area.

Lake Bastrop South Shore Park, 773 acres 2 miles northeast of Bastrop off TX 21 and CR 352 in Bastrop County, was made possible through a lease agreement with the Lower Colorado River Authority in 1989. Lake Bastrop is a cooling pond for Sim Gideon Power Plant. Picnicking, camping, swimming, boating and fishing. Near **Bastrop** and **Buescher** state parks.

Lake Bob Sandlin State Park, on the wooded shoreline of 9,400-acre Lake Bob Sandlin, is located 12 miles southwest of Mount Pleasant off FM 21 in Titus County. Activities in the 639.8-acre park include picnicking, camping, mountain biking, hiking, swimming, fishing and boating. **Oak, hickory, dogwood, redbud, maple** and **pine** produce spectacular fall color. Reservoir stocked with

largemouth bass, catfish and **crappie.**

Lake Brownwood State Park in Brown County is 537.5 acres acquired from Brown County Water Improvement District No. 1 in 1934. Park reached from TX 279 to PR 15, 16 miles northwest of Brownwood on Lake Brownwood near **geographical center of Texas.** Water sports, hiking, camping. Cabins available.

Lake Casa Blanca International State Park, located one mile east of Laredo off US 59 on Loop 20, was formerly operated by the City of Laredo and Webb County and was acquired by TPW in 1990. Park includes 371 acres on Lake Casa Blanca. **Recreation hall** can be reserved. Camping, picnicking, fishing, ball fields, playgrounds, amphitheater, tennis courts and county-operated golf course.

Lake Colorado City State Park, 500 acres leased for 99 years from a utility company. It is located in Mitchell County 11 miles southwest of Colorado City off IH 20 on FM 2836. Water sports, picnicking, camping, hiking. Park of state longhorn herd can be seen in park.

Lake Corpus Christi State Park, a 288 land-acre park located in San Patricio, Jim Wells and Live Oak counties four miles southwest of Mathis off TX 359 and FM 1068, was leased from City of Corpus Christi in 1934. Lake noted for **catfish, sunfish, bass** and **crappie.** Camping, picnicking, birding, water sports. Nearby are **Padre Island National Seashore; Mustang Island, Choke Canyon, Goliad and Goose Island** state parks; **Aransas National Wildlife Refuge,** and **Fulton Mansion State Historical Park.**

Lake Houston State Park is situated at the confluence of Caney Creek and the East Fork of the San Jacinto River. The 4,919.5-acre site, purchased from Champion Paper Company in 1981, is northeast of Houston in Harris and Montgomery counties. Camping, birding, hiking, biking, horseback riding.

Lake Livingston State Park, in Polk County, about five miles southwest of Livingston on US 59, FM 3126 and PR 65, contains 635.5 acres along Lake Livingston. Acquired by deed from private landowners in 1971. Near ghost town of **Swartwout,** steamboat landing on Trinity River in 1830s and 1840s. Camping, picnicking, swimming pool, fishing, bicycling.

Lake Mineral Wells State Park, located 4 miles east of Mineral Wells on US 180 in Parker County, consists of 3,282.5 acres encompassing Lake Mineral Wells. In 1975, the City of Mineral Wells donated 1,057 land acres and the lake to TPW; the U.S. Government transferred additional land from Fort Wolters army post. Popular for **rock-climbing/rappelling.** Swimming, fishing, boating, camping; Lake Mineral Wells State Trailway (hiking, bicycling, equestrian trail).

Lake Rita Blanca State Park, the **northernmost state park** in Texas, is located just south of Dalhart off US 385/87 and FM 281 in Hartley County. Consisting of about 1,668.4 acres, the park was acquired in 1990 through a 101-year lease with Dallam and Hartley counties. Important wintering area for migratory waterfowl, particularly ducks and geese. Other wildlife include scaled quail; bald eagles; mule deer; and swift, gray and red fox. Approved activities are hiking, horseback riding and bicycling on the 9 miles of trails. Day-use only.

Lake Somerville State Park, northwest of Brenham in Lee and Burleson counties, was leased from the federal government in 1969. **Birch Creek Unit** (2,365 acres reached from TX 60 and PR 57) and **Nails Creek Unit** (3,155 acres reached from US 290 and FM 180), are connected by a 14-mile trailway system, with equestrian and primitive camp sites, rest benches, shelters and drinking water. Also camping, birding, picnicking, volleyball and water sports. Somerville Wildlife Management Area is nearby.

Lake Tawakoni State Park is a 376.3-acre park in Hunt County along the shore of its namesake reservoir. It was acquired in 1984 through a 50-year lease agreement with the Sabine River Authority. At press time, opening is tentatively set for mid-1999. Development plans include a swimming beach, half-mile trail, picnic sites, boat ramp and campsites. A 40-acre tallgrass prairie will be managed and enhanced in the post-oak woodlands. The park is reached

Pedernales State Park, near Johnson City in the Hill Country, offers swimming and tubing in the clear waters of the Pedernales River. Dallas Morning News file photo.

from IH 20 on TX 47 north to FM 2475 about 20 miles past Wills Point.

Lake Texana State Park is 575 acres, 6.5 miles east of Edna on TX 111, half-way between Houston and Corpus Christi in Jackson County, with camping, boating, fishing and picnicking facilities. It was acquired by a 50-year lease agreement with the Bureau of Reclamation in 1977. **Oak/pecan woodlands.** Camping, picnicking, hiking, birding. **Alligators** found in park coves.

Lake Whitney State Park is 955 acres along the east shore of Lake Whitney west of Hillsboro via TX 22 and FM 1244 in Hill County. Acquired in 1954 by a Department of the Army lease, effective through 2003. Located near ruins of **Towash,** early Texas settlement inundated by the lake. Towash Village named for chief of Hainai Indians. Park noted for **bluebonnets** in spring. Camping, hiking, birding, picnicking, water activities.

Landmark Inn State Historical Park, 4.7 acres in Castroville, about 15 miles west of San Antonio, was acquired through donation by Miss Ruth Lawler in 1974. Castroville, settled in the 1840s by Alsatian farmers, is called **Little Alsace of Texas.** Landmark Inn built about 1844 as residence and store for **Cesar Monod,** mayor of Castroville 1851-1864. Special workshops, tours and events held at inn; grounds may be rented for receptions, family reunions and weddings. **Overnight lodging;** no phones; some rooms air-conditioned.

Lipantitlan State Historical Park is 5 acres 9 miles east of Orange Grove in Nueces County off Texas 359, FM 624 and FM 70. The property was deeded by private owners in 1937. Fort constructed here in 1833 by Mexican government fell to Texas forces in 1835. Only facilities are picnic tables. **Lake Corpus Christi State Park** is nearby.

Lockhart State Park is 263.7 acres 4 miles south of Lockhart via US 183, FM 20 and PR 10 in Caldwell County. The land was deeded by private owners between 1934 and 1937. Camping, picnicking, hiking, fishing, **9-hole golf course.** After Comanche raid at Linnville, **Battle of Plum Creek** (1840) was fought in area.

Longhorn Cavern State Park, off US 281 and PR 4 about 6 miles west and 6 miles south of Burnet in Burnet County, is 639 acres dedicated as a natural landmark in 1971. It was acquired in 1932-1937 from private owners. The cave has been used as a shelter since prehistoric times. Among legends about the cave is that the outlaw **Sam Bass** hid stolen money there. Confederates made gunpowder in the cave during the Civil War. **Nature trail;**

The 570-foot tall San Jacinto Monument is shown in an early photo. Dallas News file photo.

guided tours of cave; picnicking, hiking. Cavern operated by concession agreement. **Inks Lake State Park** and **Lyndon B. Johnson Ranch** located nearby.

Lost Maples State Natural Area consists of 2,174.2 scenic acres on the Sabinal River in Bandera and Real counties, 5 miles north of Vanderpool on RM 187. Acquired by purchase from private owners in 1973-1974. Outstanding example of Edwards Plateau flora and fauna, features isolated stand of uncommon **Uvalde big-tooth maple**. Rare **golden-cheeked warbler**, **black-capped vireo** and **green kingfisher** nest and feed in park. Fall foliage can be spectacular (late Oct.-early Nov.). Hiking trails, camping, fishing, picnicking, birding.

Lubbock Lake Landmark State Historical Park is a 336.6-acre **archaeological site** and botanical and zoological preserve in **Yellowhouse Draw** on the northwest edge of the city of Lubbock near intersection of Loop 289 and Clovis Road (US 84). The site was leased from the City of Lubbock for 50 years in 1986. **Only known site in North America containing deposits related to all cultures known to have existed on the Southern Plains for the last 11,500 years.** Site is **State Archeological Landmark**, **National Historic Landmark** and is on the **National Register of Historic Places.** Interpretive center, guided and self-guiding tours of on-going excavation; hiking, fishing, camping, swimming. Day use only.

Lyndon B. Johnson State Historical Park, off US 290 in Gillespie County 14 miles west of Johnson City near Stonewall, contains 717.9 acres. Acquired in 1965 with private donations. **Home of Lyndon B. Johnson** located north bank of **Pedernales River** across Ranch Road 1 from park; portion of **official Texas longhorn herd** maintained at park. Wildlife exhibit includes **turkey, deer** and **bison. Living-history demonstrations** at restored **Sauer-Beckmann house.** Reconstruction of **Johnson birthplace** is open to public. Historic structures, swimming pool, tennis courts, baseball field, picnicking. Park is day-use only. Nearby is family cemetery where former president and relatives are buried. In Johnson City is **boyhood home of President Johnson.** (See also **National Parks.)**

Magoffin Home State Historical Park, in El Paso, is a 19-room territorial-style adobe on a 1.5-acre site. Purchased by the state and City of El Paso in 1976, it is operated by TPW. Home was built in 1875 by pioneer El Pasoan **Joseph Magoffin.** Furnished with original family artifacts. Guided tours; call for schedule.

Martin Creek Lake State Park, 286.9 acres, is located 4 miles south of Tatum off TX 43 and CR 2183 in Rusk County. It was deeded to the TPW by Texas Utilities in 1976. Water activities; also cabins, camping, picnicking. Roadbed of **Trammel's Trace,** old Indian trail that became major route for settlers moving to Texas from Arkansas, can be seen. **Hardwood and pine** forest shelters abundant wildlife including **swamp rabbits, gophers, nutria** and numerous species of land birds and waterfowl.

Martin Dies Jr. State Park, until 1965 the **Dam B State Park,** is 705 acres in Jasper and Tyler counties on B. A. Steinhagen Reservoir between Woodville and Jasper via US 190. Land leased for 50 years from Corps of Engineers in 1964. Located at edge of **Big Thicket.** Plant and animal life varied and abundant. Winter **bald eagle census** conducted at reservoir. Camping, hiking, mountain biking, water activities. Wildscape/herb garden. Park is approximately 30 miles from **Alabama and Coushatta Indian Reservation.**

Matagorda Island State Park and Wildlife Management Area is separated from the mainland by San Antonio and Espíritu Santo bays. Matagorda Island is one of the

barrier islands that border the Gulf and protect the mainland from the great tides and strong wave action of the open ocean. About 43,893 acres of park and WMA are managed by the TPW. The park occupies abut 7,325 acres of the total. **La Salle** had a camp on the island in 1684. **Lighthouse** was constructed in 1852. Nineteen endangered or threatened species are found here, including **whooping crane, peregrine falcon, brown pelican** and **Ridley sea turtle.** More than **300 species of birds** use island during spring and fall migrations. Camping, birding; scheduled tours. Access only by boat; passenger **ferry** operates from Port O'Connor Thursday-Saturday.

McKinney Falls State Park is 744.4 acres 13 miles southeast of the state capitol in Austin off US 183. Acquired in 1970 by gift from private owners. Named for Thomas F. McKinney, **one of Stephen F. Austin's first 300 colonists,** who built his home here in the mid-1800s on Onion Creek. Ruins of his homestead can be viewed. Hiking, biking, camping, picnicking, fishing, guided tours.

Meridian State Park in Bosque County is a 505.4-acre park. The heavily wooded land was acquired from private owners in 1933-1935. **Texan-Santa Fe** expedition of 1841 passed through Bosque County near present site of park on Bee Creek. **Endangered golden-cheeked warbler** nests here. Camping, picnicking, hiking, fishing, lake swimming, birding, bicycling.

Mission Tejas State Historical Park is a 363.5-acre park in Houston County. Situated 12 miles west of Alto in Weches via TX 21 and PR 44, the park was acquired from the Texas Forest Service in 1957. In the park is a replica of **Mission San Francisco de los Tejas,** the first mission in East Texas (1690). It was abandoned, then re-established 1716; abandoned again 1719; re-established again 1721; abandoned for last time in 1730 and moved to San Antonio. Also in park is restored **Rice Family Log Home,** built about 1828. Camping, hiking, fishing, picnicking.

Monahans Sandhills State Park consists of 3,840 acres of sand dunes, some up to 70 feet high, in Ward and Winkler counties 5 miles northeast of Monahans on IH 20 to PR 41. Land leased by state from private foundation until 2056. Dunes used as meeting place by raiding Indians. Camping, hiking, picnicking, **sand-surfing.** Scheduled tours. **Odessa meteor crater** is nearby, as is **Balmorhea State Park.**

Monument Hill State Historical Park and **Kreische Brewery State Historical Park** are operated as one park unit. Monument Hill consists of 4 acres one mile south of La Grange on US 77 to Spur Road 92 in Fayette County. Monument and tomb area acquired by state in 1907; additional acreage acquired from the Archbishop of San Antonio in 1956. Brewery and home purchased from private owners in 1977. Monument is dedicated to **Capt. Nicholas Dawson** and his men, who fought at **Salado Creek** in 1842, in Mexican **Gen. Woll's** invasion of Texas, and to the men of the **"black bean lottery"** (1843) of the **Mier Expedition.** Remains were brought to **Monument Hill** for reburial in 1848. Kreische Complex linked to Monument Hill through interpretive trail. **Kreische Brewery State Historical Park** includes Kreische Brewery and stone-and-wood house built between 1850-1855 on Colorado River. One of **first commercial breweries** in state, it closed in 1884. Smokehouse and barn also in complex. Guided tours of brewery and house; call for schedule.

Mother Neff State Park was the **first official state park** in Texas. It originated with 6 acres donated by Mrs. I. E. Neff, mother of **Pat M. Neff,** Governor of Texas from 1921 to 1925. Gov. Neff and Frank Smith donated remainder in 1934. The park, located 8 miles west of Moody on FM 106 and TX 236, now contains 259 acres along the Leon River in Coryell County. Heavily wooded. Camping, picnicking, fishing, hiking.

Mustang Island State Park, 3,954 acres on Gulf of Mexico in Nueces County, 14 miles south of Port Aransas on TX 361, was acquired from private owners in 1972. Mustang Island is a barrier island with a complicated ecosystem, dependent upon the sand dune. The foundation plants of the dunes are **sea oats, beach panic grass** and **soilbind morning glory.** Beach camping; sun, sand and water activities. Excellent birding. **Padre Island National Seashore** 14 miles south.

Old Fort Parker State Historical Park, a 37.5-acre park between Groesbeck and Mexia off TX 14 in Limestone County, was deeded by private owners in 1936. In the park is a replica of **Fort Parker** stockade, a family fort built in 1834, and the site of abduction of **Cynthia Ann Parker** on May 19, 1836, by Comanche and Kiowa Indians. Visitors can explore cabins and blockhouses. Park operated by City of Groesbeck. Nearby is recreational **Fort Parker State Park.**

Palmetto State Park, a scenic park, is 270.3 acres 8 miles southeast of Luling on US 183 and PR 11 along the San Marcos River in Gonzales County. Land deeded in 1934-1937 by private owners and City of Gonzales. Named for **tropical dwarf palmetto** found there. Diverse plant and animal life; excellent birding. Also picnicking, fishing, hiking, swimming. Nearby **Gonzales** and **Ottine** important in early Texas history. Gonzales settled 1825 as center of **Green DeWitt's colonies.**

Palo Duro Canyon State Park consists of 16,402.1 acres 12 miles east of Canyon on TX 217 in Armstrong and Randall counties. The land was deeded by private owners in 1933 and is the scene of the annual summer production of the drama, **"Texas."** Spectacular **scenic canyon** one million years old exposes rocks spanning about 200 million years of geological time. **Coronado** may have visited canyon in 1541. Canyon officially discovered by **Capt. R. B. Marcy** in 1852. Scene of decisive battle in 1874 between Comanche and Kiowa Indians and U.S. Army troops under **Gen. Ranald Mackenzie.** Also scene of ranching enterprise started by **Charles Goodnight** in 1876. Part of **state longhorn herd** is kept here. Camping, horseback and hiking trails, horse rentals.

Pedernales Falls State Park, 5,211.7 acres in Blanco County about 9 miles east of Johnson City on FM 2766 along Pedernales River, was acquired from private owners in 1970. Typical **Edwards Plateau** terrain, with **live oaks, deer, turkey** and **stone hills.** Camping, picnicking, hiking, swimming, tubing. Falls main scenic attraction.

Port Isabel Lighthouse State Historical Park consists of 0.9 acre in Port Isabel, Cameron County. Acquired by purchase from private owners in 1950, site includes **lighthouse** constructed in 1852; visitors can climb to top. Park is near sites of Civil War battle of **Palmito Ranch** (1865), and Mexican War battles of **Palo Alto** and **Resaca de la Palma (1846).** Operated by City of Port Isabel.

Port Lavaca State Fishing Pier, a 10.8-acre recreational area on Lavaca Bay in Calhoun County, was acquired by transfer of authority from state highway department in 1963. The 3,200-foot fishing pier was created from former causeway. **Port Lavaca City Park,** at base of pier, offers a boat ramp and picnicking facilities. Operated by City of Port Lavaca.

Possum Kingdom State Park, west of Mineral Wells via US 180 to Caddo then north on PR 33 in Palo Pinto County, is 1,528.7 acres adjacent to **Possum Kingdom Lake,** in **Palo Pinto Mountains** and **Brazos River Valley.** Rugged canyons home to **deer,** other wildlife. Acquired from the Brazos River Authority in 1940. Camping, picnicking, swimming, fishing, boating. Cabins available.

Purtis Creek State Park is 1,582.4 acres in Henderson and Van Zandt counties 3.5 miles north of Eustace on FM 316. Acquired in 1977 from private owners. Fishing, camping, hiking and picnicking.

Ray Roberts Lake State Park (Isle du Bois Unit), consists of 2,263 acres on the south side of Ray Roberts Lake on FM 455 in Denton County. **Johnson Branch Unit** contains 1,514 acres on north side of lake in Denton and Cooke counties 7 miles east of IH 30 on FM 3002. Land acquired in 1984 by lease from secretary of Army. Abundant and varied plant and animal life. Fishing, camping, picnicking, swimming, hiking, biking; tours of 19-century farm buildings at Johnson Branch.

Rusk/Palestine State Park, a total of 136 acres, includes Rusk unit, adjacent to **Texas State Railroad Rusk Depot** off US 84 in Cherokee County, and Palestine unit, off US 84 adjacent to **Texas State Railroad Palestine Depot.** Fishing, picnicking, camping, tennis courts, playground. **Train rides** in restored passenger cars (see also **Texas State Railroad State Historical Park).**

Sabine Pass Battleground State Historical Park in Jefferson County 1.5 miles south of Sabine Pass on Dowlen Road, contains 57.6 acres acquired from Kountze County Trust in 1972. Lt. **Richard W. Dowling,** with small Confederate force, repelled an attempted 1863 invasion of Texas by Union gunboats. **Monument, World War II ammunition bunkers.** Boating, fishing, picnicking, camping.

Sam Bell Maxey House State Historical Park, at the corner of So. Church and Washington streets in Paris, Lamar County, was donated by City of Paris in 1976. Consists of .4 acre with 1868 Victorian Italianate-style frame house, plus outbuildings. Most of furnishings accumulated by Maxey family. Maxey served in Mexican and Civil wars and was two-term U.S. Senator. House is on the **National Register of Historic Places.** Open for tours Friday through Sunday.

San Angelo State Park, on **O.C. Fisher Reservoir** adjacent to the city of San Angelo in Tom Green County, contains 7,667 acres of land, most of which will remain undeveloped. Leased from U.S. Corps of Engineers in 1995. Access is from US 87 or 67, then FM 2288. Area gives evidence of **11,000 years of human occupation.** Highly diversified plant and animal life. Activities include boating, fishing, swimming, hiking, mountain biking, horseback riding, camping, picnicking. Park of state longhorn herd in park. Nearby is **Fort Concho.**

San Jacinto Battleground State Historical Park and **Battleship Texas State Historic Site** are located 20 miles east of downtown Houston off TX 225 East to TX 134 to PR 1836 in east Harris County. The park is 1,120.6 acres with 570-foot-tall monument erected in 1936-1939 in honor of Texans who defeated Mexican **Gen. Antonio López de Santa Anna** on April 21, 1836, to win Texas' independence from Mexico. The park is original site of Texan's camp acquired in 1883. Subsequent acquisitions made in 1897, 1899 and 1985. Park transferred to TPW in 1965. Park registered as **National Historic Landmark.** Elevator ride to observation tower near top of monument; museum. Monument known as **tallest masonry structure in the world.** Interpretive trail around battleground. Adjacent to park is the **U.S.S. Texas,** commissioned in 1914. The battleship, the only survivor of the dreadnought class and the only surviving veteran of two world wars, was donated to people of Texas by U.S. Navy. Ship was moored in the Houston Ship Channel at the **San Jacinto Battleground** on San Jacinto Day, 1948. Extensive repairs were done 1988-1990. Some renovation is ongoing, but ship is open for tours. Ship closed Christmas Eve and Christmas Day.

San José Mission is operated as part of **San Antonio Missions National Historical Park** (see page 122).

San Marcos River State Park (John J. Stokes), also known as Thompson's Island, is a 5.5-acre site donated by John H. Stokes Sr. and operated by the City of San Marcos. Provides access to river for fishing, canoeing and boating. No facilities; no development; day use only.

Sea Rim State Park in Jefferson County, 20 miles south of Port Arthur, off TX 87, contains 4,141.1 acres of marshland and 5.2 miles of **Gulf beach** shoreline, acquired from private owners in 1972. It is prime wintering area for **waterfowl.** Wetlands also shelter such wildlife as river otter, nutria, alligator, mink, muskrat. Camping, fishing, swimming; wildlife observation; nature trail; boating. **Airboat tours of marsh.** Near **McFaddin National Wildlife Refuge.**

Sebastopol State Historical Park at 704 Zorn Street in Seguin, Guadalupe County, was acquired by purchase in 1976 from Seguin Conservation Society; approximately 2.2 acres. Built about 1856 by **Col. Joshua W. Young** of **limecrete,** concrete made from local gravel and lime, the Greek Revival-style house was restored to its 1880 appearance by the TPW and opened to the public in 1989. House on National Register of Historic Places. Tours available Friday through Monday or by appointment. Also of interest in the area is historic **Seguin,** founded 1838.

Seminole Canyon State Historical Park in Val Verde County, 9 miles west of Comstock off US 90, contains 2,172.5 acres; acquired by purchase from private owners 1973-1977. **Fate Bell Shelter** in canyon contains several important **prehistoric Indian pictographs**. Historic interpretive center. Tours of rock-art sites Wednesday-Sunday; also hiking, mountain biking, camping.

Sheldon Lake State Park and Wildlife Management Area, 2,503 acres in Harris County on Carpenter's Bayou, lies on Garrett Road 20 miles east of Beltway 8. Acquired by purchase in 1952 from the City of Houston. Freshwater marsh habitat. Activities include nature study, birding and fishing. Wildscape gardens of native plants.

South Llano River State Park, 5 miles south of Junction in Kimble County off US 377, is a 2,656-acre site. Land donated to the TPW by private owner in 1977. Wooded bottomland along the winding South Llano River is **largest and oldest winter roosting site for the Rio Grande turkey** in Central Texas. Roosting area closed to visitors October-March. Other animals include **wood ducks, javelina, fox, beaver, bobcat** and **armadillo.** Camping, picnicking, tubing, swimming and fishing, hiking, mountain biking.

Starr Family State Historical Park, 3.1 acres at 407 W. Travis in Marshall, Harrison County. Greek Revival-style mansion, **Maplecroft**, built 1870-1871, was home to five generations of Starr family, powerful and economically influential Texans. Acquired by gift in 1976; additional land donated in 1982. House on National Register of Historic Places. Tours Friday-Sunday or by appointment. Special events during year.

Stephen F. Austin State Historical Park is 663.3 acres along the Brazos River in San Felipe, Austin County, named for the **"Father of Texas."** The area was deeded by the San Felipe de Austin Corporation and the San Felipe Park Association in 1940. Site of township of **San Felipe** was seat of government where conventions of 1832 and 1833 and Consultation of 1835 held. These led to **Texas Declaration of Independence.** San Felipe was home of **Stephen F. Austin** and other famous early Texans; home of Texas' **first Anglo newspaper (the Texas Gazette)** founded in 1829; postal system of Texas originated here; beginning of **Texas Rangers.** Area called **"Cradle of Texas Liberty."** Museum. Camping, picnicking, golf.

Texas State Railroad State Historical Park, in Anderson and Cherokee counties between the cities of Palestine and Rusk, adjacent to US 84, contains 499 acres. Acquired by Legislative Act in 1971. Trains run seasonal schedules on 25.5 miles of track. Call for information and reservations: In Texas 1-800-442-8951; outside 903-683-2561. Railroad built by the State of Texas to support the **state-owned iron works** at Rusk. Begun in 1896, and built largely by inmates from the state prison system, the railroad was gradually extended until it reached Palestine in 1909 and established regular rail service between the towns. (See also **Rusk/Palestine State Park**.)

Tyler State Park is 985.5 acres 2 miles north of IH 20 on FM 14 north of Tyler in Smith County. Includes 64-acre lake. The land was deeded by private owners in 1934-1935. Heavily wooded. Camping, hiking, fishing, boating, lake swimming. Nearby Tyler called **rose capital of world, with Tyler Rose Garden and annual Tyler Rose Festival. Also in Tyler are Caldwell Children's Zoo** and **Goodman Museum.**

Varner-Hogg Plantation State Historical Park is 65 acres in Brazoria County two miles north of West Columbia on FM 2852. Land originally owned by Martin Varner, a member of Stephen F. Austin's **"Old Three Hundred"** colony; later was home of Texas governor **James Stephen Hogg**. Property was deeded to the state in 1957 by Miss Ima Hogg, Gov. Hogg's daughter. **First rum distillery** in Texas established in 1829 by Varner. Mansion tours Wednesday-Sunday. Also picnicking.

Village Creek State Park, comprising 1,003.86 heavily forested acres, is located in Lumberton, Hardin County, 10 miles north of Beaumont off US 69 and FM 3513. Acquired in 1979, the park contains abundant flora and fauna typical of the Big Thicket area. The **200 species of birds** found there include wood ducks, egrets and herons. Activities include fishing, camping, canoeing, swimming, hiking and picnicking. Nearby is the **Big Thicket National Preserve.**

Washington-on-the-Brazos State Historical Park consists of 293.1 acres 7 miles southwest of Navasota in Washington County on TX 105 and FM 1155. Land acquired by deed from private owners in 1916, 1976 and 1996. Park includes the site of the signing on March 2, 1836, of the **Texas Declaration of Independence** from Mexico, as well as the site of the later **signing of the Constitution of the Republic of Texas**. In 1842 and 1845, the land included the **capitol of the Republic**. Daily tours of Barrington, restored **home of Anson Jones, last president of the Republic of Texas. Star of the Republic Museum**. Activities include picnicking and birding.

Future Parks

The following parks were in the development stage when this Texas Almanac went to press: **Bright Leaf SP,** Austin; **Chinati Mountains SNA,** Presidio; **Davis Hill SP,** Cleveland; **Eagle Mountain Lake SP,** Fort Worth; **Fort Boggy SP,** Centerville; **Government Canyon SNA,** San Antonio (late 2000-early 2001). ☆

National Parks, Historical Sites, Recreation Areas in Texas

Below are listed the facilities in and the activities that can be enjoyed at the two national parks, a national seashore, a biological preserve, several historic sites, memorials and recreation areas in Texas. They are under supervision of the **U.S. Department of Interior.** On the Web: www.nps.gov/parklists/tx.html. In addition, the recreational opportunities in the national forests and national grasslands in Texas, under the jurisdiction of the **U.S. Department of Agriculture,** are listed at the end of the article.

Alibates Flint Quarries National Monument consists of 1,079 acres in Potter County. For more than 10,000 years, **pre-Columbian Indians** dug agatized limestone from the quarries to make projectile points, knives, scrapers and other tools. The area is presently undeveloped. You may visit the flint quarries on guided walking tours with a park ranger. Tours are at 10:00 a.m. and 2:00 p.m. from Memorial Day to Labor Day. Off-season tours can be arranged by writing to Lake Meredith National Recreation Area, Box 1460, Fritch 79036, or by calling 806-857-3151; e-mail: LAMR_Interpretation@nps.gov.

Amistad National Recreation Area is located on the U.S. side of **Amistad Reservoir**, an international reservoir on the Texas-Mexico border. The 57,292-acre park's attractions include boating, water skiing, swimming, fishing, camping and archaeological sites. At Panther and Parida caves, accessible only by boat, visitors can see 4000-year-old prehistoric pictographs. The area is one of the densest concentrations of Archaic rock art in North America — more than 300 sites. Commercial campgrounds, motels and restaurants nearby. Marinas located at Diablo East and Rough Canyon. Open year round. ANRA, HCR 3, Box 5-J, Del Rio 78840; 830-775-7591; e-mail: Amis_Interpretation@nps.gov.

Big Bend National Park, established in 1944, has spectacular **mountain and desert scenery,** a variety of **unusual geological structures.** Located in the great bend of the Rio Grande, the 801,000-acre park, which is part of the **international boundary** between the United States and Mexico, was designated a U.S. Biosphere Reserve in 1976. Hiking, birding and float trips are popular. Numerous campsites are located in park, and the **Chisos Mountain Lodge** has accommodations for approximately 345 guests. Write for reservations to

National Park Concessions, Inc., Big Bend National Park, Texas 79834. Park open year round; facilities most crowded during spring break. PO Box 129, Big Bend National Park 79834; 915-477-2251; e-mail: BIBEInformation@nps.gov.

Big Thicket National Preserve, established in 1974, consists of 86,000 acres of diverse flora and fauna, often nicknamed the **"biological crossroads of North America."** The preserve has been designated an **"International Biosphere Reserve"** by the United Nations Educational, Scientific and Cultural Organization (UNESCO). The visitor information station is located on FM 420, seven miles north of Kountze; phone 409-246-2337. Open daily from 9 a.m. to 5 p.m. Naturalist activities are available by reservation only; reservations are made through the station. **Nine trails,** ranging in length from one-half mile to 18 miles, visit a variety of forest communities. The two shortest trails are handicapped accessible. Trails are open year round, but flooding may occur after heavy rains. Horses permitted on the **Big Sandy Horse Trail** only. Boating and canoeing are popular on preserve corridor units. Park headquarters are located at 3785 Milam, Beaumont 77701; 409-246-2337.

Chamizal National Memorial, established in 1963 and opened to the public in 1973, stands as a monument to Mexican-American friendship and goodwill. The memorial, on 52 acres, commemorates the peaceful settlement on Aug. 29, 1963, of a 99-year-old boundary dispute between the United States and Mexico. Chamizal uses the visual and performing arts as a medium of interchange, helping peple better understand not only other cultures but their own, as well. It hosts a variety of programs throughout the year, including: the **Border Folk Festival** (first weekend in September) musical event; the **Siglo de Oro** drama festival (early March); the **Oñate Historical Festival** celebrating the First Thanksgiving (April); and **Music Under the Stars** (Sundays, June-August). The park has a 1.8-mile trail and picnic areas. Phone: 915-532-7273.

Fort Davis National Historic Site in Jeff Davis County was a key post in the West Texas defense system, guarding immigrants and tradesmen on the San Antonio-El Paso road. Fort Davis was manned by black troops, called **"Buffalo Soldiers"** because of their fierce service in the Indian Wars. **Henry O. Flipper, the first black graduate of West Point,** served at Fort Davis in the early 1880s. The 460-acre historic site is located on the north edge of the town of Fort Davis in the **Davis Mountains,** the second-highest mountain range in the state. The site includes a museum, an auditorium with daily audio-visual programs, restored and refurnished buildings, picnic area and hiking trails. Open year round except Christmas Day. PO Box 1456, Fort Davis 79734; 915-426-3224.

Guadalupe Mountains National Park, established in 1972, includes 86,416 acres in Hudspeth and Culberson counties. The Park contains one of the most extensive **fossil reefs** on record. Deep **canyons** cut through this reef and provide a rare opportunity for geological study. Special points of interest are **McKittrick Canyon,** a fragile riparian environment, and **Guadalupe Peak,** the highest in Texas. Camping, hiking on 80 miles of trails, Frijole Ranch Museum, summer amphitheater programs. Orientation, free information and natural history exhibits available at Visitor Center. Open year round. Lodging at Van Horn, Texas, and White's City or Carlsbad, NM. HC 60, Box 400, Salt Flat 79847; 915-828-3251; e-mail GUMO_SUPERINTENDENT@NPS.GOV.

Lake Meredith National Recreation Area, 30 miles northeast of Amarillo, centers on a reservoir on the Canadian River, in Moore, Hutchinson and Potter counties. The 44,977-acre park is popular for water-based activities. Boat ramps, picnic areas, unimproved campsites. Commercial lodging and trailer hookups available in nearby towns. Open year round. PO Box 1460, Fritch 79036; 806-

Mountain and desert scenery can both be found in Big Bend National Park in far West Texas. Photo courtesy National Park Service.

857-3151; e-mail: LAMR_Interpretation@nps.gov.

Lyndon B. Johnson National Historical Park includes two separate districts 14 miles apart. The **Johnson City District** comprises the **boyhood home of the 36th President of United States** and the **Johnson Settlement,** where his grandparents resided during the late 1800s. The **LBJ Ranch District** can be visited only by taking the National Park Service bus tour starting at the LBJ State Historical Park. The tour includes the reconstructed **LBJ Birthplace,** old school, family cemetery, show barn and a view of the Texas White House. Site in Blanco and Gillespie counties was established in 1969, and contains 1,572 acres, 551 of which are federal. Open year round except Christmas Day and New Year's Day. No camping on site; commercial campgrounds, motels in area. PO Box 329, Johnson City 78636; 830-868-7128.

Padre Island National Seashore consists of a 67.5-mile stretch of a barrier island along the Gulf Coast; noted for white-sand beaches, excellent fishing and abundant bird and marine life. Contains 133,000 acres in Kleberg, Willacy and Kenedy counties. Open year round. One paved campground (fee charged) located north of Malaquite Beach; unpaved (primitive) campground area south on beach. Five miles of beach are accessible by regular vehicles; 55 miles are accessible only by 4x4 vehicles. Off-road vehicles prohibited. Camping permitted in two designated areas. Commercial lodging available on the island outside the National Seashore boundaries. PO Box 181300, Corpus Christi 78480; 361-949-8068.

Palo Alto Battlefield National Historic Site, Brownsville, preserves the site of the **first major battle in the Mexican-American War.** Fought on May 8, 1846, it is recognized for the innovative use of light or "flying" artillery. Participating in the battle were three future presidents: **General Zachary Taylor and Ulysses S. Grant** on the U.S. side, and **Gen. Mariano Arista** on the Mexican. Historical markers are located at the junction of Farm-to-Market roads 1847 and 511. Access to the site is currently limited. Exhibits at the park's interim visitor center, at 1623 Central Blvd., Ste. 213 in Brownsville (78520), interpret the battle as well as the causes and consequences of the war. Phone 956-541-2785.

Rio Grande Wild and Scenic River is a 196-mile strip on the American shore of the Rio Grande in the **Chihuahuan Desert,** beginning in Big Bend National Park and continuing downstream to the Terrell-Val Verde County line. There are federal facilities in Big Bend National Park only. Contact Big Bend National Park (above) for more information.

San Antonio Missions National Historical Park preserves four Spanish Colonial Missions — **Concepción, San José, San Juan and Espada** — as well as the Espada dam and aqueduct, which are two of the best-preserved remains in the United States of the **Spanish Colonial irrigation system**, and Rancho de las Cabras, the colonial ranch of Mission Espada. All were crucial elements to Spanish settlement on the Texas frontier. When Franciscan attempts to establish a chain of missions in East Texas in the late 1600s failed, the Spanish Crown ordered three missions transferred to the San Antonio River valley in 1731. The missions are located within the city limits of San Antonio, while Rancho de las Cabras is located 25 miles south in Wilson County near Floresville. The four missions, which are still in use as active parishes, are open to the public from 9 a.m. to 5 p.m. daily except Thanksgiving, Christmas and New Year's. Public roadways connect the sites; a hike-bike trail is being developed. The Rancho de las Cabras site is closed to the public pending development. The visitor center for the mission complex is at San José. For more information, write to 2202 Roosevelt Ave., San Antonio 78210; 210-534-8833 or 210-932-1001 (Visitor Center).

Recreational Facilities, Corps of Engineers Lakes, 1998

Source: Southwestern Division, Corps of Engineers, Dallas

Reservoir	Swim Areas	Boat Ramps	Picnic Sites	Camp Sites	Rental Units	Visitor Hours, 1998
Addicks*	0	0	721	0	0	5,859,200
Aquilla	0	2	0	0	0	202,900
Bardwell	2	7	29	174	0	953,800
Barker*	0	0	50	0	0	2,036,200
Belton	5	21	435	245	10	10,749,400
Benbrook	1	17	115	178	0	6,829,200
Canyon	5	23	411	468	44	4,679,800
Cooper	2	5	98	177	30	1,903,000
Georgetown	1	3	118	234	0	3,838,100
Granger	2	5	125	133	0	1,134,800
Grapevine	4	17	140	178	0	4,203,900
Hords Creek	2	8	15	140	0	2,247,800
Joe Pool	3	7	315	556	0	4,672,100
Lake O' the Pines	8	34	197	525	0	6,720,400
Lavon	3	22	302	265	0	6,232,000
Lewisville	8	25	324	572	0	12,953,100
Navarro Mills	3	6	16	267	0	4,068,100
O.C. Fisher	0	17	90	61	0	2,349,200
Pat Mayse**	6	11	14	317	0	1,248,200
Proctor	0	6	44	215	0	2,563,800
Ray Roberts	2	9	278	326	0	21,974,400
Sam Rayburn	4	31	30	775	98	17,489,300
Somerville	2	12	229	827	22	15,316,200
Stillhouse Hollow	3	5	91	62	0	2,379,500
Texoma**†	3	25	173	904	237	80,541,100
Town Bluff	1	13	126	359	0	4,186,300
Truscott Brine	0	1	3	0	0	15,700
Waco	7	9	112	253	0	3,300,100
Wallisville*	0	0	0	0	0	173,600
Whitney	5	30	40	701	0	6,392,900
Wright Patman	4	22	209	601	0	13,248,700
Totals	**83**	**393**	**4,850**	**9,513**	**441**	**250,642,800**

All above lakes managed by the Fort Worth District, U.S. Army Corps of Engineers, with the following exceptions:
*Managed by Galveston District, USACE.
**Managed by Tulsa District, USACE.
†Figures for facilities on Texas side of lake. Visitation is for entire lake.

Recreation on the National Forests

An estimated 3 million people visit the National Forests in Texas for recreation annually. These visitors use established recreation areas primarily for hiking, picnicking, swimming, fishing, camping, boating and nature enjoyment. Some of these areas are:

Angelina NF: Bouton Lake, 7 miles southeast of Zavalla off Texas Highway 63, has a 9-acre natural lake with facilities for camping, picnicking and fishing. **Boykin Springs,** 15 miles southeast of Zavalla, has a 6-acre lake and facilities for hiking, swimming, picnicking, fishing and camping. **Caney Creek,** on Sam Rayburn Reservoir 10 miles southeast of Zavalla off FM 2743, also has an amphitheaser. **Sandy Creek,** 17 miles east of Zavalla on Sam Rayburn, offers fishing, sailing and picnicking.

The **Saw Mill Trail** is 5 miles long and goes from Bouton Lake to Boykin Springs Recreation Area in the **Angelina National Forest.**

Davy Crockett NF: Ratcliff Lake, 25 miles west of Lufkin on Highway 7, includes a 45-acre lake and facilities for picnicking, hiking, swimming, boating, fishing, camping. There is also an amphitheater.

The **4Cs National Recreation Trail** is 19 miles long and goes from Ratcliff Recreation Area to the Neches Bluff overlook. The **Piney Creek Horse Trail,** 50 miles long, can be entered approximately three miles south of Kennard off Forest Service Road 525. There is a 30-unit horse camp at this location, but it does not have drinking water available.

Sabine NF: Indian Mounds Recreation Area, accessible via FM 83 and FM 3382, a total of 12 miles east of Hemphill, has camping facilities and a boat-launch ramp. **Lakeview,** on Toledo Bend Reservoir 10 miles from Yellowpine, and offering hiking, boating and fishing, can be reached via TX 87, FM 2928 and FSR 120. **Ragtown,** 25 miles southeast of Center and accessible by TX 87 and TX 139, CR 3184 and FSR 132, is also on Toledo Bend and has facilities for hiking, camping and boating. **Red Hills Lake,** 3 miles north of Milam on TX 87, has facilities for hiking, fishing, swimming, camping and picnicking. **Willow Oak Recreation Area,** on Toledo Bend 14 miles south of Hemphill off TX 87, offers fishing, picnicking and camping and boating.

Trail Between the Lakes is 26 miles long from Lakeview Recreation Area on Toledo Bend to US 96 near Sam Rayburn Reservoir.

Sam Houston NF: Double Lake, 3 miles south of Coldspring on FM 2025, has facilities for picnicking, camping, swimming and fishing. **Stubblefield Lake,** 15 miles west-northwest of New Waverly off TX 1375 on the shores of Lake Conroe, has facilities for camping, hiking, picnicking and fishing.

The **Lone Star Hiking Trail,** approximately 140 miles long, is located on Sam Houston National Forest in Montgomery, Walker and San Jacinto counties.

Recreation on the National Grasslands

East and North Texas: Lake Davy Crockett Recreation Area, 11 miles north of Honey Grove on FM 100, has a boat-launch ramp and camping sites on a 450-acre lake. **Coffee Mill Lake Recreation Area** has camping and picnic facilities on a 750-acre lake. This area is 4 miles west of Lake Davy Crockett Recreation Area. **Black Creek Lake Picnic Area** is located 8 miles southeast of Alvord. It has camping and picnic facilities and a boat-launch ramp on a 30-acre lake.

West Texas: Lake McClellan in Gray County and **Lake Marvin,** which is part of the **Black Kettle National Grassland** in Hemphill County, receive over 28,000 recreation visitors annually. These areas provide camping, picnicking, fishing and boating facilities. Concessionaires operate facilities at Lake McClellan, and a nominal fee is charged for use of the areas. At the **Rita Blanca National Grassland,** about 4,500 visitors a year enjoy picnicking and hunting. ☆

Fairs, Festivals and Special Events

Fairs, festivals and other special events provide year-round recreation in Texas. Some are of national interest, while many attract visitors from across the state. In addition to those listed here, the recreational paragraphs in the Counties chapter list numerous events. Information was furnished by the event sponsors. You can find more events on the Web at: www.traveltex.com/events.asp.

Albany - Fort Griffin Fandangle; June; PO Box 155 (76430-0155); www.albanytexas.com.

Alvarado - Pioneers and Old Settlers Reunion; Aug.; PO Box 217 (76009-0217).

Amarillo - Tri-State Fair; Sept.; PO Box 31087 (79120-1087).

Angleton - Brazoria County Fair; Oct.; PO Box 818 (77516-0818).

Arlington - Texas Scottish Festival; June; PO Box 171193 (76003-1193); www.texasscottishfestival.com.

Athens - Black-Eyed Pea Fall Harvest; Oct.; PO Box 2600 (75751-2600); www.athenscc.org.

Athens - Old Fiddlers Reunion; May; PO Box 1441 (75751-1441).

Austin - Austin-Travis County Livestock Show; March; PO Box 9876 (78766-9876); www.austinrodeo.com.

Austin - Laguna Gloria Fiesta; May; PO Box 5705 (78763-5705); www.citysearch.com/aus/fiesta.

Beaumont - South Texas State Fair; Oct.; PO Box 3207 (77704-3207).

Big Spring - Howard County Fair; Sept.; PO Box 2356 (79720-2356).

Boerne - Berges Feset; June; PO Box 748 (78006-0748).

Brackettville - Western Horse Races and Barbecue; Sept.; PO Box 528 (78832-0528).

Brenham - Washington County Fair; Sept.; PO Box 1257 (77834-1257).

Brownsville - Charro Days Fiesta; Feb.; PO Box 3247 (78523-3247).

Burton - Burton Cotton Gin Festival; April; PO Box 98 (77835-0098).

Caldwell - Burleson County Fair; Sept.; PO Box 634 (77836-0634).

Canyon - "TEXAS" Historical Musical Drama; June-Aug.; PO Box 268 (79015-0268); www.texasmusicaldrama.com.

Clifton - Norse Smorgasbord; Nov.; RR 2 Box 40 (76634-9606).

Clute - Great Texas Mosquito Festival; July; PO Box 997 (77531-0997).

Columbus - Springtime Festival & Magnolia Homes Tour; May; PO Box 817 (78934-0817).

Conroe - Montgomery County Fair; March; PO Box 869 (77305-0869); www.mcfa.org.

Corpus Christi - Bayfest; Sept.; PO Box 1858 (78403-1858); www.interconnect.net/bayfest.

Corpus Christi - Buccaneer Days; April-May; 402 S. Shoreline Dr. (78401-2814); www.buccaneer.org.

Dalhart - XIT Rodeo & Reunion; Aug.; PO Box 966 (79022-0966); www.dalharttx.com.

Dallas - State Fair of Texas; Sept.-Oct.; PO Box 150009 (75315-0009); www.texfair.com.

De Leon - De Leon Peach & Melon Festival; Aug.; PO Box 44 (76444-0044).

Denton - North Texas State Fair and Rodeo; Aug.; PO Box 1695 (76202-1695).

Ennis - National Polka Festival; May; PO Box 1237 (75120-1237); www.visitennis.org.

Fairfield - Freestone County Fair; June; PO Box 196 (75840-0196).

Flatonia - Czhilispiel; Oct.; PO Box 651 (78941-0651); http://flatonia.fais.net.

Fort Worth - Pioneer Days; Sept.; 131 E. Exchange Ave. Ste. 100B (76106-8200); www.fortworthstockyards.org.

Fort Worth - Southwestern Exposition & Livestock Show; Jan.-Feb.; PO Box 150 (76101-0150); www.fwssr.com.

Fredericksburg - Easter Fires Pageant; March-April; PO Box 526 (78624-0526).

Fredericksburg - Night in Old Fredericksburg; July; 106 N. Adams (78624-4204); www.fredericksburg-texas.com.

Fredericksburg - Oktoberfest; Oct.; PO Box 222 (78624-0222).

Freer - Freer Rattlesnake Roundup; April; PO Box 717 (78357-0717); www.angelfire.com/tx/freerrattlesnake.

Galveston - Dickens on The Strand; Dec.; 2016 Strand (77550-1661); www.galvestonhistory.org.

Galveston - Galveston Historic Homes Tour; May; 2016 Strand (77550-1661); www.galvestonhistory.org.

Georgetown - Georgetown Mayfair; May; 703 N. Llano; Fredericksburg (78624).

Gilmer - East Texas Yamboree; Oct.; PO Box 854 (75644-0854); www.upshurcounty.com.

Grand Prairie - National Championship Pow-Wow; Sept.; 2602 Mayfield Rd (75052-7299); wwwtradersvillage.com/events.html.

Hallettsville - Hallettsville Kolache Fest; Sept.; PO Box 313 (77964-0313); www.hallettsville.com.

Helotes - Helotes Cornyval; May; PO Box 376 (78023-0376); www.cornyval.com.

Hidalgo - Border Fest; March; 611 E. Coma (78557-2512).

Hondo - Medina County Fair; Sept.; PO Box 4 (78861-0004).

Houston - Houston Livestock Show & Rodeo; Feb.-March; PO Box 20070 (77225-0070); www.hlsr.com.

Hughes Springs - Wildflower Trails of Texas; April; PO Box 805 (75656-0805).

Huntsville - Walker County Fair; March-April; PO Box 1817 (77342-1817).

Kerrville - Kerr County Fair; Oct.; PO Box 842 (78029-0842); www.ktc.com/personal/kcfa.

Kerrville - Kerrville Folk Festival; May-June; PO Box 1466 (78029-1466); www.kerrville-music.com.

Kerrville - Texas State Arts & Crafts Fair; May; PO Box 1527 (78029-1527); www.tacef.org.

Killeen - Central Texas Exposition; March-April; PO Box 878 (76541-0878).

La Grange - Fayette County Country Fair; Sept.; PO Box 544 (78945-0544).

Lamesa - Dawson County Fair; Aug.; PO Box 1268 (79331-1268).

Laredo - Washington's Birthday Celebration; Feb.; 1819 E. Hillside Rd. (78041-3383); www.wbcaldo.com.

Longview - Gregg County Fair & Expo.; Sept.; PO Box 1124 (75606-1124).

Lubbock - Panhandle-South Plains Fair; Sept.; PO Box 208 (79408-0208).

Lufkin - Texas Forest Festival; Sept.; PO Box 1606 (75902-1606); www.chamber.angelina.tx.us.

Luling - Luling Watermelon Thump; June; PO Box 710 (78648-0710); www.bcsnet.net/lulingcc.

Mercedes - Rio Grande Valley Livestock Show; March; PO Box 867 (78570-0867).

Mesquite - Mesquite Balloon Festival; July; 703 N. Llano; Fredericksburg (78624).

Mesquite - Mesquite Championship Rodeo; April-Sept.; 1818 Rodeo Dr. (75149); www.mesquiterodeo.com.

Mount Pleasant - Titus County Fair; Sept.; PO Box 1232 (75456-1232).

Nederland - Nederland Heritage Festival; March; PO Box 1176 (77627-1176).

New Braunfels - Comal County Fair; Sept.; PO Box 310223 (78131-0223).

Odessa - Permian Basin Fair & Exposition; Sept.; PO Box 4812 (79760-4812).

Palestine - Dogwood Trails Festival; March-April; PO Box 2828 (75802-2828).

Paris - Red River Valley Fair; Aug.; 570 E. Center St. (75460-2680).

Pasadena - Pasadena Livestock Show & Rodeo; Oct.; PO Box 565 (77501-0565); www.pasadenarodeo.com.

Plantersville - Texas Renaissance Festival; Oct.-Nov.; Rt. 2 Box 650 (77363-1505); www.texrenfest.com.

Port Arthur - CavOILcade; Oct.; PO Box 2336 (77643-2336); www.portarthurtexas.com.

Poteet - Poteet Strawberry Festival; April; PO Box 227 (78065-0227); www.strawberryfestival.com.

Praha - Prazska Pout; Aug.; PO Box 651; Flatonia (78941-0651); http://flatonia.fais.net.
Refugio - Refugio County Fair & Rodeo; March; PO Box 88 (78377-0088).
Rio Grande City - Starr County Fair; Feb.-March; PO Box 841 (78582-0841).
Rosenberg - Fort Bend County Fair; Sept.-Oct.; PO Box 428 (77471-0428); www.fortbend.net/county-fair.
Salado - Gathering of the Clans; Nov.; PO Box 36 (76571-0036).
San Angelo - San Angelo Stock Show & Rodeo; March; 200 W. 43rd (76903-1675).
San Antonio - Fiesta San Antonio; April; 122 Heiman (78205-3311); www.fiesta-sa.org.
San Antonio - Texas Folklife Festival; Aug.; 801 S. Bowie St. (78205-3296); www.texancultures.utsa.edu.
Sanderson - Cinco de Mayo Celebration; May; PO Box 297 (79848-0297).
Sanderson - Independence Day Celebration; July; Terrell County Courthouse (79848).
Sanderson - Prickly Pear Pachanga; Oct.; Terrell County Courthouse (79848).
Santa Fe - Galveston County Fair & Rodeo; April; PO Box 889 (77510-0889).
Seguin - Guadalupe Agriculture & Livestock Fair; Oct.; PO Box 334 (78155-0334).
Shamrock - St. Patricks Day Celebration; March; PO Box

588 (79079-0588).
Stamford - Texas Cowboy Reunion; July; PO Box 928 (79553-0928).
Sulphur Springs - Hopkins County Fall Festival; Sept.; PO Box 177 (75483-0177).
Sweetwater - Rattlesnake Roundup; March; PO Box 416 (79556-0416); http://camalott.com/~sweetwater.
Texarkana - Four States Fair; Sept.; PO Box 1915; Texarkana AR (75504-1915); www.fourstatesfair.com.
Tyler - East Texas State Fair; Sept.-Oct.; 2112 W. Front St. (75702-6828); www.statefair.tyler.com.
Tyler - Texas Rose Festival; Oct.; PO Box 8224 (75711-8224).
Waco - Brazos River Festival & Cotton Palace Pageant; April; 810 S. 4th St. (76706-1036).
Waco - Heart O' Texas Fair & Rodeo; Oct.; PO Box 7581 (76714-7581); www.hotfair.com
Waxahachie - Scarborough Faire; April-June; PO Box 538 (75168-0538); www.scarboroughrenfest.com.
Weatherford - Parker County Peach Festival; July; PO Box 310 (76086-0310).
Wharton - Wharton County Youth Fair & Expo.; April; PO Box 167; Glen Flora (77443-0167); www.wcnet.net/wcyf.
Woodville - Tyler County Dogwood Festival; March-April; PO Box 2151 (75979-2151).
Yorktown - Western Days; Oct.; PO Box 488 (78164-0488). ☆

Texas Tourism Facts, 1997

Texas' 160 million visitors ranked second in the nation behind California (248 million) and ahead of Florida (158 million). The **length of time visitors spent in Texas**, measured in "person-days" (one person-day being one person staying in the state for one day), was estimated at 347 million person-days in 1997. Texas ranked third in person-days, behind California (533 million) and Florida (500 million).

Business travel accounted for 32 percent of travel to Texas, while **leisure travel** accounted for 67 percent. Texans traveling within the state accounted for 61.6 percent of the travelers, and they spent an average of $75 per person per day. Non-Texans spent an average of $111 per person each day.

Texas regions preferred as destinations by non-Texan travelers were **Metroplex** (30.4 percent), **South** (21.4 percent) and **Gulf Coast** (20.6 percent). These three accounted for 72 percent of non-Texan person-days.

The **states generating the largest numbers of non-Texan travelers** were Oklahoma (16 percent), Louisiana (10 percent), California (9 percent), Illinois (5 percent), New Mexico (4 percent), Florida (4 percent) and Arkansas (3 percent). ☆

Source: "1997 Report of Travel to Texas," July 1998. Research conducted by D.K. Shifflet & Associates, Ltd. for the Texas Department of Economic Development.

Hunting and Fishing Licenses

A **hunting license** is required of Texas residents and nonresidents of Texas who hunt any bird or animal. Hunting licenses and stamps are valid during the period September 1 through the following August 31 of each year, except lifetime licenses and licenses issued for a specific number of days. A hunting license (except the nonresident special hunting license and non-resident 5-day special hunting license) is valid for taking all legal species of wildlife in Texas including **deer, turkey, javelina, antelope, aoudad (sheep)** and all **small game and migratory game birds.**

Special licenses and tags are required for taking **alligators**, and a **trapper's license** is required to hunt **fur-bearing animals.**

All **sport fishing licenses and stamps** are valid only during the period September 1 through August 31, except lifetime licenses and licenses issued for a specific number of days. In addition to sports hunting and fishing licenses, **hunting/fishing stamps** are required for special hunting/fishing privileges.

Detailed information concerning licenses, stamps, seasons, regulations and related information can be obtained from **Texas Parks and Wildlife, 4200 Smith School Road, Austin 78744; (800) 792-1112 or 512-389-4800.** On the Web, information from TPW on hunting:

www.tpwd.state.tx.us/hunt/hunt.htm; on fishing: www.tpwd.state.tx.us/fish/fish.htm.

The Texas Parks and Wildlife reported revenue of $60.3 million from sales of all licenses during fiscal 1998; 3.2 million licenses were sold.

During the 1996-1997 license year, there were 333,819 **white-tailed deer** killed, 21,917 **wild turkey** in the fall and 45,594 in the spring, 3,743 **mule deer**, and 14,276 **javelina.**

The **U.S. Fish and Wildlife Service, Division of Federal Aid**, reports that Texas had the third-largest number of paid **hunting license holders** in 1997, with 942,359. They purchased a total of 1,246,420 licenses, tags, permits and stamps, at a gross cost to hunters of $23,570,980. Pennsylvania led the way with 1,091,568 hunters purchasing a total of 2,602,094 licenses, tags, permits and stamps. Michigan was second, with 952,584 hunters purchasing a total of 2,600,134 licenses, tags, permits and stamps.

Comparing **fishing-license holders** during 1997 shows Texas third, with 1,434,447 anglers at a cost of $32,817,539. California led with 2,218,894 paid fishing-license holders, and Minnesota was second, with 1,499,317 anglers. ☆

Freshwater and Saltwater Fish and Fishing

Freshwater Fish and Fishing

In Texas, **247 species of freshwater fish** are found. This includes 78 species that are found in areas with low salinity and can be found in rivers entering the Gulf of Mexico. Also included in that total are 18 species that are not native, but were introduced into the state.

The estimated **number of freshwater recreational anglers** is 2.14 million, with annual expenditures of $1.9 billion annually. Catch-and-release fishing has emerged on the Texas scene as the conservation theme of anglers who desire continued quality fishing.

The **most popular fish** for recreational fishing are largemouth bass; catfish; crappie; and striped, white and hybrid striped bass.

The **Texas Parks and Wildlife** (TPW) operates field stations, fish hatcheries and research facilities to support the conservation and management of fishery resources.

TPW has continued its programs of stocking fish in public waters to increase angling opportunities. The hatcheries operated by TPW raise largemouth and smallmouth bass, as well as catfish, striped and hybrid striped bass, crappie, sunfish and paddlefish.

Texas Freshwater Fisheries Center

The Texas Freshwater Fisheries Center in Athens, about 75 miles southeast of Dallas, is an $18 million hatchery, research laboratory, aquarium and educational center, where visitors can learn about the underwater life in Texas' freshwater streams, ponds and lakes.

The 24,000-square-foot hatchery and research facility concentrates on genetic research and the production of 5 to 6 million Florida largemouth bass for restocking Texas rivers and reservoirs.

The interactive Cox Visitors Center includes aquarium displays of fish in their natural environment. Visitors get an "eye-to-eye" view of three authentically-designed Texas freshwater habitats: a Hill Country stream, an East Texas pond and a reservoir. A marsh exhibit features live American alligators.

Through touch-screen computer exhibits, visitors can learn more about fish habitat and life cycles and the importance of catch-and-release fishing. Films, seminars and demonstrations are also offered.

A casting pond stocked with rainbow trout in the winter and catfish in the summer provides a place for children to learn how to bait a hook, cast a line and land a fish. The center also has an active schedule of special programs and events.

The center is a cooperative effort of Texas Parks and Wildlife, the U.S. Fish and Wildlife Service, the City of Athens and private organizations.

The Texas Freshwater Fisheries Center is open Tuesday through Saturday, 9:00 a.m. to 4:00 p.m., and Sunday, 1:00 to 4:00 p.m. It is closed on Monday. Admission is charged. The Center is located four-and-a-half miles east of Athens on FM 2495 at Lake Athens. Address: 5550 Flat Creek Road, Athens 75751, or call 903-676-2277.

Saltwater Fish and Fishing

There are approximately 1 million saltwater anglers in Texas (6 years old and older) who have a nearly $772.5 million economic impact annually.

The most popular saltwater sport fish in Texas waters are: Atlantic croaker, black drum, gafftopsail catfish, groupers, king mackerel, red drum, red snapper, sand seatrout, sharks, sheepshead, southern flounder, spotted seatrout, tarpon and yellowfin tuna (winter time on headboats).

Sea Center Texas

Sea Center Texas is a $13 million marine hatchery, aquarium and educational center located in Lake Jackson, Brazoria County. The center opened in March 1996, featuring interpretive displays and several huge aquariums, where saltwater fish are on display, including Gordon the grouper and several sharks.

The red-drum (redfish) hatchery, said to be the largest in the world, produces 20 million fingerlings per year for stocking in Texas coastal waters. Although established primarily as a red drum and spotted seatrout hatchery, Sea Center will also serve as a testing ground for production of other marine species, such as flounder and Atlantic croaker.

A half-acre youth fishing pond introduces youngsters to saltwater fishing through scheduled activities. The pond is handicapped accessible and is stocked with a variety of marine fish.

Sea Center Texas is a joint venture of Texas Parks and Wildlife; Dow Chemical Company, Texas Operations; and the Coastal Conservation Association. For more information on Sea Center Texas, call 409-292-0100. ☆

Commercial Fisheries

Total coastwide landings in 1997 were more than 81.5 million pounds, valued at more than $188 million. Shrimp accounted for 75 percent of the weight and 88 percent of the value of all seafood landed during calendar year 1997. The approximately 15,000 saltwater commercial fishermen in Texas in 1997 made an economic impact of more than $576 million.

Commercial Landings, 1997

Finfish	Pounds	Value
Drum, Black	2,775,800	$2,362,900
Flounder	135,700	236,800
Sheepshead	65,300	31,900
Snapper	1,930,600	3,296,200
Other	1,621,100	2,378,400
Total Finfish	**6,528,400**	**$8,306,300**
Shellfish		
Shrimp (Heads On):		
Brown and Pink	40,583,800	$109,542,400
White	19,013,300	53,056,700
Other	5,006,000	2,862,700
Crabs, Blue	5,739,000	3,670,700
Oyster, Eastern	4,579,100	11,200,200
Other	118,700	89,300
Total Shellfish	**75,039,700**	**$180,422,000**
Grand Total	**81,568,200**	**$188,728,400**

Source: Trends in Texas Commercial Fishery Landings, 1972-1997, Texas Parks and Wildlife Department Coastal Fisheries Div., Management Data Series No. 158, Austin, 1998.

Texan Bobby Jo Morrow won three gold medals in track at the 1956 Summer Olympic Games (see related article at right).

Texas Olympic Medalists

Below are listed Texans who have won medals in modern Olympic Games, Pan American Games or U.S. Olympic Festivals. Information included is: the athlete's name; * a code letter indicating whether they were born in Texas and were living in Texas when they competed (T); born in Texas, but not living in Texas when they competed (B); and not born in Texas, but living in Texas when they competed (L); sport; the year and the games** in which a medal or medals were won (SOG=Summer Olympic Games, WOG=Winter Olympic Games, PAG=Pan American Games, USOC=U.S. Olympic Festival); and the types of medals (G=Gold, S=Silver, B=Bronze). If the athlete won more than one of the same kind of medal in any one Games, the number is noted before the letter code; i.e., 2G indicates that the athlete won two gold medals in the games indicated. The symbol (†) following the medal code indicates that the athlete participated in preliminary contests only; the medal was awarded because of membership on a winning team. Years in which the athlete participated in the Games but did not win a medal are not included because of space limitations.

Abbreviations used in the Sport column are: Mod. Penta.=Modern Pentathlon; Fig. Skating=Figure Skating; Sp'd Skating=Speed Skating; Tm Handball=Team Handball; Track=all track and field events except those noted separately.

Source: United States Olympic Committee

Olympian	*	Sport	Games**	Medal
Acuff, Amy Lynn	B	Track	1995 USOF	S
Allen, Chad	T	Baseball	1996 SOG	B
Anderson, Terence M.	L	Shooting	1995 PAG	2G
			1994 USOF	S
			1983 PAG	2G
			1979 PAG	S
Anti, Michael E.	L	Shooting	1991 PAG	4G, B
Arnette, Jay Hoyland	T	Basketball	1960 SOG	G
Austin, Charles	T	Track	1996 SOG	G
Baker, Walter Thane	L	Track	1956 SOG	G, S, B
			1952 SOG	S
Baptiste, Kirk	T	Track	1984 SOG	S
Bassham, Lanny Robert	B	Shooting	1976 SOG	G
			1975 PAG	2G, S, B
			1972 SOG	S
			1971 PAG	G
Bates, Michael D.	B	Track	1992 SOG	B
Beck, Robert Lee	L	Mod. Penta.	1971 PAG	G
			1963 PAG	2G
			1960 SOG	2B
Berube, Ryan Thomas	L	Swimming	1996 SOG	G
			1995 PAG	G
Bleamaster, Leslie F.	L	Mod. Penta.	1959 PAG	G, B
Bourland, Elizabeth Jagush	L	Shooting	1995 PAG	2G, 2S
			1995 USOF	G
			1991 PAG	G
Brown, Earlene Dennis	B	Track	1960 SOG	B
			1959 PAG	2G
Buckner, William Quinn	L	Basketball	1976 SOG	G
Buford-Bailey, Tonja	L	Track	1996 SOG	B
			1995 PAG	S
			1991 PAG	B
Burrell, Leroy Russel	L	Track	1992 SOG	G
Cain, Sharon D.	B	Tm Handball	1995 PAG	G
			1995 USOF	G
Carter, Michael D.	T	Shotput	1984 SOG	S
Chowen, Wesley John	L	Cycling	1967 PAG	B
Cline, Nancy Lieberman	L	Basketball	1979 PAG	S
			1976 SOG	S
			1975 PAG	G
Coffman, Robert E.	T	Decathlon	1979 PAG	G
Corbelli, Laurie Flachmeier	L	Volleyball	1984 SOG	S
			1983 PAG	S
Cross-Battle, Tara	T	Volleyball	1995 PAG	S
			1992 SOG	B
Davis, Clarissa G.	T	Basketball	1992 SOG	B
			1987 PAG	G
Davis, Jack Wells	B	Track	1956 SOG	S
			1955 PAG	G
			1952 SOG	S
Davis, Josh Clark	T	Swimming	1996 SOG	3G
			1995 PAG	3G, B
Donie, Scott R.	L	Diving	1995 USOF	B
			1992 SOG	S

Olympian	*	Sport	Games**	Medal
Drexler, Clyde	L	Basketball	1992 SOG	G
Dunn, Robert W.(Bobby)	L	Tm Handball	1995 USOF	B
Dyer, Kimberly Sue	L	Shooting	1983 PAG	2G
Ethridge, Mary (Kamie)	B	Basketball	1988 SOG	G
			1987 PAG	G
Everist, Kirk F.	B	Water Polo	1995 PAG	G
			1991 PAG	S
Farmer-Patrick, Sandra	L	Track	1992 SOG	S
Ferguson, Kent M.	L	Diving	1995 USOF	G
			1991 PAG	G
Finn-Burrell, Michelle Bonae	L	Track	1995 USOF	G
			1992 SOG	G
			1987 PAG	G
Forbes, James Ricardo	L	Basketball	1972 SOG	S
Ford, Gilbert (Gib)	B	Basketball	1956 SOG	G
Foreman, George	T	Boxing	1968 SOG	G
Forney, Kathy Howard	B	Gymnastics	1975 PAG	G, S
Glenesk, Dean William	L	Mod. Penta.	1984 SOG	S
Gonzáles, Paul G. Jr.	B	Boxing	1984 SOG	G
			1983 PAG	S
Guidry, Carlette D.	T	Track	1996 SOG	G †
			1992 SOG	G
Harkrider, Kiplan P.	T	Baseball	1996 SOG	B
Hartwell, Erin Wesley	L	Cycling	1996 SOG	S
			1995 PAG	S
			1992 SOG	B
			1991 PAG	S
Heath, Michael Steward	B	Swimming	1984 SOG	2G, S
Hedgepeth, Whitney L.	L	Swimming	1996 SOG	G, 2S
			1987 PAG	G, S
Henry, James Edward	B	Diving	1968 SOG	B
Henry, Mark Jerrold	B	Weightlifting	1995 PAG	G,S,B
Hill, Denean E.	B	Track	1992 SOG	S
			1988 SOG	S
			1987 PAG	G, B
			1984 SOG	G
Hill, Grant Henry	B	Basketball	1996 SOG	G
			1991 PAG	B
Homfeld, Conrad E.	B	Equestrian	1984 SOG	G, S
Hooper, Clarence D.	T	Shotput	1952 SOG	S
Howard, Plimon Davis	L	RollerHockey	1991 PAG	B
			1987 PAG	B
Howard, Sherri Francis	B	Track	1988 SOG	S
			1984 SOG	G
Huckaby, Karl Roy	T	RollerHockey	1991 PAG	B
Huckaby, Keith Wayne	L	RollerHockey	1991 PAG	B
			1987 PAG	B
Jackson, Lucious Brown	T	Basketball	1964 SOG	G
			1963 PAG	G
Jackson, Zina Garrison	L	Tennis	1988 SOG	G, B
Johnson, Michael	T	Track	1996 SOG	2G
			1992 SOG	G
Johnson, Rafer Lewis	B	Decathlon	1960 SOG	G
			1956 SOG	S
			1955 PAG	Medal
Jones, David Winston	T	RollerHockey	1991 PAG	B
			1987 PAG	S
Keeler, Kathryn Elliott	B	Rowing	1984 SOG	G

Olympian	*	Sport	Games**	Medal
Kern, Douglas James	L	Sailing	1992 SOG	S
King, Judith Brown	L	Track	1987 PAG	G
			1984 SOG	S
			1983 PAG	2G
Kleine, Megan	B	Swimming	1992 SOG	G †
Kolius, John Waldrip	T	Sailing	1976 SOG	S
Langkop, DorothyFraney	L	Sp'd Skating	1932 WOG	B
Lewis, Fred(Carl)Carlton	L	Track	1996 SOG	G
			1995 USOF	G
			1992 SOG	2G
			1988 SOG	2G, S
			1987 PAG	2G
			1984 SOG	4G
			1979 PAG	B
Lienhard, William Barner	B	Basketball	1952 SOG	G
Lipinski, Tara K.	L	Fig. Skating	1998 WOG	G
Losey, Robert G. (Greg)	L	Mod. Penta.	1995 USOF	S
			1984 SOG	S
Macklin, Kim Rhodenbaugh	L	Swimming	1983 PAG	G, 2B
Magers, Rose Mary	B	Volleyball	1984 SOG	S
			1983 PAG	S
Marino-Bradford, Cathy	B	Canoe/Kayak	1987 PAG	S
Marsh, Michael L.	L	Track	1996 SOG	S
			1992 SOG	2G
Matson, James Randel	T	Shotput	1968 SOG	G
			1976 PAG	G
			1964 SOG	S
Matson, Ollie G.	B	Track	1952 SOG	S, B
McKenzie, Kim	B	Track	1984 SOG	B
			1983 PAG	S
McNally, John Tsuyshi	L	Shooting	1995 PAG	G
			1994 USOF	G
			1991 PAG	2G
			1987 PAG	S, B
			1983 PAG	G
			1979 PAG	2S
Merten, Kenneth Owen	L	Swimming	1967 PAG	2 B
			1963 PAG	S
Mills, Ronald P.	T	Swimming	1968 SOG	B
Moceanu, Dominique H.	L	Gymnastics	1996 SOG	G
Montgomery, James P.	L	Swimming	1976 SOG	3G, B
Moore, James Warren	L	Mod. Penta.	1964 SOG	S
			1963 PAG	G, B
Morrow, Bobby Joe	T	Track	1956 SOG	3G
Neal, McClinton Earl	T	Track	1991 PAG	S
Neel, Ernest W.	T	Shooting	1979 PAG	G, B
Neilson-Bell, Sandy	L	Swimming	1972 SOG	3G
			1971 PAG	2G, S
Newhouse, Frederick V.	B	Track	1976 SOG	G, S
			1971 PAG	G, S
Nightingale, Conrad K.	L	Track	1967 PAG	S
Nolen, Marilyn McReavy	B	Volleyball	1967 PAG	G
O'Hara, Michael Futch	B	Volleyball	1963 PAG	S
			1959 PAG	G
Olajuwon, Hakeem A.	L	Basketball	1996 SOG	G
Orrange, Elexa Diana	T	Track	1995 USOF	G
Paddock, Charles W.	B	Track	1924 SOG	G
			1920 SOG	2G, S
Patrick, David	L	Track	1987 PAG	B
Pesthy, Paul Karoly	L	Fencing	1983 PAG	B
			1979 PAG	G, S
			1975 PAG	G, B
			1967 PAG	G, B
			1964 SOG	S
Postma, Joan Spillane	L	Swimming	1960 SOG	G
			1959 PAG	G, 2B
Potter, Cynthia Ann	B	Diving	1976 SOG	B
			1975 PAG	B
Raglin, Johnny Wayne	T	RollerHockey	1991 PAG	B
Rambo, John Barnett	B	Track	1964 SOG	B
Richards, Robert E.	L	Track	1956 SOG	G
			1955 PAG	G, S
			1952 SOG	G
			1951 PAG	G
			1948 SOG	B
Ritter, Louise Dorothy	L	Track	1988 SOG	G
			1979 PAG	G
Robertson, Alvin Cyrrale	L	Basketball	1984 SOG	G
Robinson, David M.	L	Basketball	1996 SOG	G
			1992 SOG	G
			1988 SOG	B
			1987 PAG	S
Robinson, Robert J.	B	Basketball	1948 SOG	G
Robinzine, Kevin B.	L	Track	1988 SOG	G
			1987 PAG	G
Ross, David III	L	Shooting	1975 PAG	2G
			1971 PAG	G
			1967 PAG	G
Russell, John William	L	Equestrian	1952 SOG	B
Schneider, Jill Rankin	T	Basketball	1979 PAG	S
Schneider, Marcus B.	B	Rowing	1996 SOG	B
Scoggin, Mathew Aaron	L	Diving	1987 PAG	S
Shelley, Charles (Lee)	B	Fencing	1987 PAG	S
			1979 PAG	G
Sherrard, Cherrie Mae	B	Track	1967 PAG	G
Shurtz, Sewall	B	Fencing	1955 PAG	2S
Smith, Dean	T	Track	1952 SOG	G
Smith, Lamont	L	Track	1996 SOG	G
Smith, Owen Guinn	B	Track	1948 SOG	G
Smith, Tommie C.	B	Track	1968 SOG	G
Southern, Silas Edward	T	Track	1959 PAG	S
			1956 SOG	S
Stack, Chelle	L	Gymnastics	1991 PAG	2G, S
Stapleton, William J.	L	Swimming	1987 PAG	2G
Sterkle, Jill Ann	L	Swimming	1988 SOG	2 B
			1983 PAG	G
			1979 PAG	3G, S
			1976 SOG	G
			1975 PAG	G, S
Stokes, Herman Ray	B	Track	1959 PAG	S
Stoll, Richard Milton	L	Mod. Penta.	1963 PAG	G, S
Stulce, Michael S.	T	Shotput	1992 SOG	G
Stull, Robert Ernest	L	Fencing	1987 PAG	S
Swoopes, Sheryl Denise	T	Basketball	1996 SOG	G
Thomas, Kurt B.	L	Gymnastics	1975 PAG	2S,2B
Tisdale, Wayman L.	B	Basketball	1984 SOG	G
			1983 PAG	G
Turner, Rebecca Ann	L	Gymnastics	1995 PAG	S
Valdez, Jesse	B	Boxing	1972 SOG	B
			1967 PAG	B
Van, Allen	L	Ice Hockey	1952 WOG	S
Van Os, George (Chip) Jr.	T	Tm Handball	1995 USOF	B
Walker, Laura Anne	L	Swimming	1988 SOG	B
Walton-Floyd, Delisa A.	L	Track	1987 PAG	S
Washington, Jacqueline	T	Track	1983 PAG	G, S
Wells, Rhoshii S.	B	Boxing	1996 SOG	B
			1995 USOF	B
Wells, Wayne A.	B	Wrestling	1972 SOG	G
			1971 PAG	S
Whitfield, Malvin G.	B	Track	1952 SOG	G, S
			1951 PAG	3G
			1948 SOG	2G, B
Williams, Christa L.	B	Softball	1996 SOG	G
			1995 USOF	B
Wilson, Craig Martin	B	Water Polo	1991 PAG	S
			1988 SOG	S
			1987 PAG	G
			1984 SOG	S
			1983 PAG	G
Wolfe, Rowland "Flip"	T	Gymnastics	1932 SOG	G
Wooley, James Ralph	B	Judo	1975 PAG	B
Wrightson, Bernard C.	B	Diving	1968 SOG	G
			1967 PAG	G
Young, Earl Verdelle	L	Track	1963 PAG	2G
			1960 SOG	G
Zaharias, Mildred (Babe) Didrikson	T	Track	1932 SOG	2G, S
Zmeskal, Kim	B	Gymnastics	1992 SOG	B

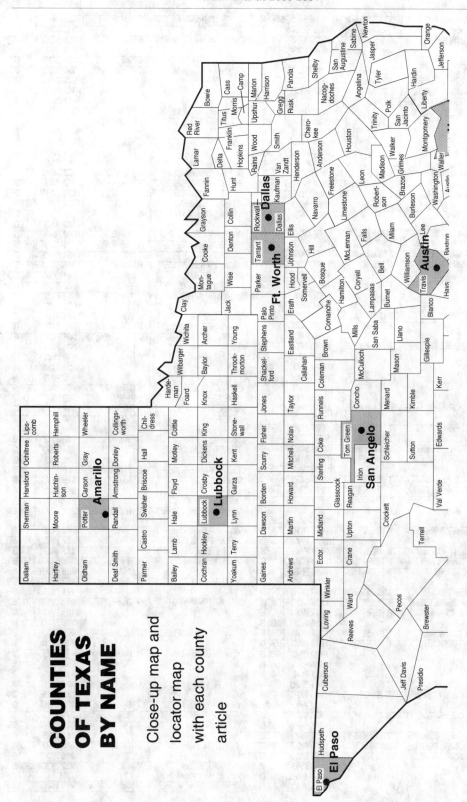

COUNTIES
OF TEXAS
BY NAME

Close-up map and
locator map
with each county
article

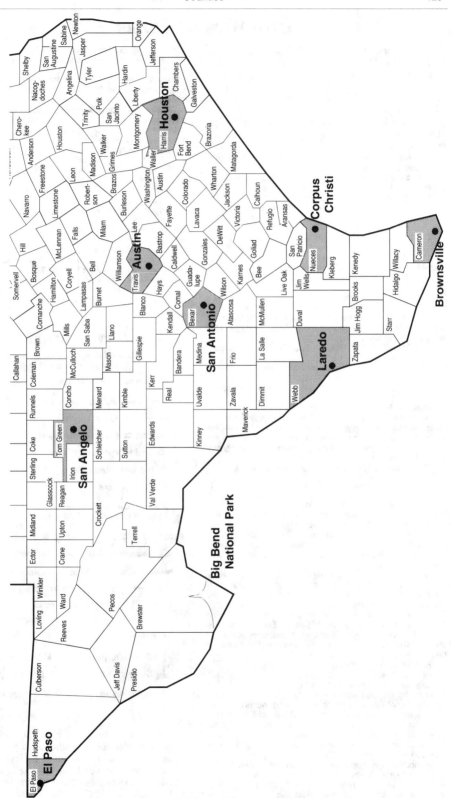

Counties of Texas

These pages describe Texas' 254 counties and hundreds of towns. Descriptions are based on reports from chambers of commerce, the Texas Agricultural Extension Service, federal and state agencies, the New Handbook of Texas and other sources. Consult the index for other county information.

County maps are based on those of the Texas Department of Transportation and are copyrighted, 1999, as are the entire contents.

Physical Features: Descriptions are from U.S. Geological Survey and local sources.

Economy: From information provided by local chambers of commerce and county agricultural extension agents.

History: From Texas statutes, Fulmore's History and Geography of Texas as Told in County Names, WPA Historical Records Survey, Texas Centennial Commission Report and the New Handbook of Texas.

Ethnicity, 1990: Based on the U.S. Bureau of the Census count of 1990. In many cases the county percentages will total more than 100 for this reason: In the forms used by the bureau, residents are asked to classify themselves according to race as "White"; "Black"; "American Indian, Eskimo and Aleut"; "Asian and Pacific Islander"; or "Other."

In another question the bureau asks respondents to mark their ethnic background, such as Mexican, Cuban, Puerto Rican, to be classified by the bureau as "Hispanic". Hispanic people can be of any race, thus their numbers are also included in one of the basic racial categories.

Vital Statistics, 1997: From the Texas Department of Health Annual Report, 1997.

Recreation: From information provided by local chambers of commerce and county agents. Attempts were made to note activities unique to the area or that point to ethnic or cultural heritage.

Minerals: From agricultural agents.

Agriculture: Condensed from information provided to the Texas Almanac by county agricultural agents in 1998. **Market value** of agricultural products sold and rankings are from the 1997 Census of Agriculture of the U.S. Department of Agriculture for that year.

Cities: The county seat and principal cities are listed.

Sources of Data List

Population: The estimate of county population from the State Data Center of the Texas Department of Commerce for 1998. The figures are prepared by the Department of Rural Sociology, Texas A&M University. The following line gives the percentage of increase or decrease from the 1990 census count.

Area: Total area in squrare miles, including water surfaces.

Land Area: The land area in square miles as determined by the census bureau, 1990.

Altitude (ft.): From the U.S. Geological Survey. Not all of the surface of Texas has been precisely surveyed for elevation; in some cases data are from the Texas Railroad Comission or the Texas Department of Transportation.

Climate: Provided by the National Oceanic and Atmospheric Administration state climatologist, College Station. Data are revised at 10-year intervals. Listed are the latest compilations, as of Jan. 1, 1993, and pertain to a particular site within the county (usually the county seat). The data include:

Rainfall (annual in inches).

January mean minimum temperature.

July mean maximum temperature.

Growing season (days).

Workforce/Wages: Prepared by the Texas Workforce Commission, Austin, in cooperation with the Bureau of Labor Statistics of the U.S. Department of Labor, for fourth quarter 1997 through third quarter 1998. The data are computed from reports by all establishments subject to the Texas Unemployment Compensation Act.

(Agricultural employers are subject to the act if they employ as many as three workers for 20 weeks or pay cash wages of $6,250 in a quarter. Employers who pay $1,000 in wages in a quarter for domestic services are subject also. Still not mandato-

rily covered are self-employed, unpaid family workers, and those employed by churches and some small nonprofit organizations.)

Federal workers are not included in annual wages and average weekly wage. The data include (with state, lowest and highest county):

Civilian labor force. Texas, 8,939,000; Loving Co., 85; Harris Co., 1,766,119.

Unemployed: (Percentage of workforce): Texas, 4.9; Hartley Co., 1.5; Presidio Co., 30.6.

Annual Wages: Texas, $263,165,927,007; Loving Co. $1,377,260; Harris Co., $63,355,297,784.

Average Weekly Wage: Texas, $591.64; Real Co., $276.01; Carson Co., $791.99.

Federal Wages: Texas, $7,726,348,523; Loving Co., $13,567; Bexar Co., $1,408,335,166.

Agriculture Net Cash Return: From sales, government payments, other farm-related income and Commodity Credit Corporation loans. The source for this is the 1997 U.S. Census of Agriculture.

Property Values: The appraised gross market value of real and personal property in each county appraisal district in 1997 as reported to the State Property Tax Board.

Retail Sales: Preliminary figures for 1998 as reported to the state Comptroller of Public Accounts. The figures are subject to change in the comptroller's final report.

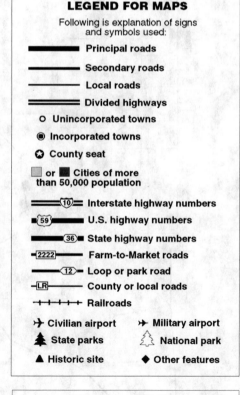

LEGEND FOR MAPS

Following is explanation of signs and symbols used:

━━━━ **Principal roads**

──── **Secondary roads**

──── **Local roads**

═══ **Divided highways**

○ **Unincorporated towns**

◉ **Incorporated towns**

✪ **County seat**

▦ or ▮ **Cities of more than 50,000 population**

═⟨10⟩═ **Interstate highway numbers**

⟨59⟩ **U.S. highway numbers**

⟨36⟩ **State highway numbers**

▬2222▬ **Farm-to-Market roads**

⟨12⟩ **Loop or park road**

─LR─ **County or local roads**

+++++ **Railroads**

✈ **Civilian airport**   ✈ **Military airport**

▲ **State parks**   🌲 **National park**

▲ **Historic site**   ◆ **Other features**

A small outline map of Texas counties accompanies each county article. The county is shaded to help locate it within the context of the state. A larger map of Texas with the counties named appears on pages 128 and 129.

Anderson County

Physical Features: Forested, hilly East Texas county, slopes to Trinity and Neches rivers; sandy, clay, black soils; pines, hardwoods.

Economy: Manufacturing, distribution, agribusiness, tourism; hunting and fishing leases; prison units.

History: Comanche, Waco, other tribes. Anglo-American settlers arrived in 1830s. Antebellum slaveholding area. County created from Houston County in 1846; named for K.L. Anderson, last vice president of the Republic of Texas.

Ethnicity, 1990: White, 33,354 (69.5%); Black, 11,143 (23.2%); American Indian, 129 (0.3%); Asian, 125 (0.3%); Other, 3,273 (6.8%).
Hispanic, 3,953 (8.2%).

Vital Statistics, 1997: Births, 624; deaths, 569; marriages, 495; divorces, 270.

Recreation: Fishing, hunting, streams, lakes; dogwood trails; historic sites; railroad park; museum. Tourist information at 1890 depot.

Minerals: Oil and gas.

Agriculture: Cattle, hay, truck vegetables, melons, pecans, peaches. Market value $24.3 million. Timber sold.

PALESTINE (18,725), county seat; wholesale meats, auto parts, clothing, metal, wood products; transportation and agribusiness center; scientific balloon station; historic bakery; library; vocational-technical facilities; hospitals; community college; hot pepper festival in October.

Other towns include: **Cayuga** (200); **Elkhart** (1,140); **Frankston** (1,245); **Montalba** (110); **Neches** (175); and **Tennessee Colony** (300) site of state prisons.

Population	53,424
Change fm '90	11.2
Area (sq. mi.)	1,078.0
Land Area (sq. mi.)	1,070.9
Altitude (ft.)	198-725
Rainfall (in.)	43.3
Jan. mean min.	36
July mean max.	94
Growing season (days)	264
Civ. Labor	20,740
Unemployed	5.8
Annual Wages	$425,985,931
Av. Weekly Wage	$455.80
Fed. Wages	$5,040,632
Ag. Net Cash Return	-$1,557,000
Prop. Value	$1,780,437,522
Retail Sales	$3,286,059,042

MILES 0 2 4 6 8

🏢 STATE PRISONS

▲ PILGRIM CHURCH

🏞 ENGELING WILDLIFE MANAGEMENT AREA

🌲 TEXAS STATE RAILROAD STATE HISTORICAL PARK

Railroad Abbreviations

AGC	Alamo Gulf Coast Railway Co.
ATK	AMTRAK
ANR	Angelina & Neches River Railroad Co.
AUNW	Austin & Northwestern Railroad Co.
ATCX	Austin & Texas Central Railroad
BLR	Blacklands Railroad
BNSF	Burlington Northern & Santa Fe Railroad Co.
BOP	Border Pacific Railroad Co.
BRG	Brownsville & Rio Grande Int'l Railroad Co.
CCTA	Corpus Christi Terminal Assoc.
DART	Dallas Area Rapid Transit
DGNO	Dallas, Garland & Northeastern Railroad
FAPR	Floydada & Plainview Railroad Co.
FWWR	Fort Worth & Western Railroad Company
GCSR	Gulf, Colorado & San Saba RailwayCorp.
GRR	Georgetown Railroad Co.
GVSR	Galveston Railroad, L.P.
KCS	Kansas City Southern Railway Co., The
KRR	Kiamichi Railroad Company, Inc.
LHRR	Longhorn Railway Company
LSR	Lone Star Railroad, Inc.
MCSA	Moscow, Camden & San Augustine RR Co.
PCN	Point Comfort & Northern Railway Company

PNR	Panhandle Northern Railroad Company
PTRA	Port Terminal Railroad Association
PVS	Pecos Valley Southern Railway Co., Inc.
RSS	Rockdale, Sandow & Southern Railroad Co.
RV	Rio Valley Railroad
SO	South Orient Railroad Company, LTD
SRN	Sabine River & Northern Railroad Company
SSC	Southern Switching Co. (Lone Star Railroad)
SW	Southwestern Railroad
TCT	Texas City Terminal Railway Co.
TEXC	Texas Central Railroad Co.
TIBR	Timber Rock Railroad, Inc.
TM	The Texas Mexican Railway Company
TN	Texas & Northern Railway Co.
TNER	Texas Northeastern Railroad
TNMR	Texas and New Mexico Railroad
TSE	Texas South-Eastern Railroad Company
TXGN	Texas, Gonzales & Northern Railway Co.
TXNW	Texas North Western Railway Co.
TXR	Texas Rock Crusher Railway Co.
TXTC	Texas Transportation Company
TXTX	Econo-Rail Corp. (Port of Beaumont)
UP	Union Pacific Railroad Company
WTJR	Wichita, Tillman & Jackson Railway Co.
WTLR	West Texas & Lubbock Railroad Co. Inc.

Andrews County

Physical Features: South Plains, drain to playas; grass, mesquite, shin oak; red clay, sandy soils.

Economy: Oil; agribusiness.

History: Apache, Comanche area until U.S. Army campaigns of 1875. Ranching developed around 1900. Oil boom in 1940s. County created 1876 from Bexar Territory; organized 1910; named for Texas Revolutionary soldier Richard Andrews.

Ethnicity, 1990: White, 10,834 (75.6%); Black, 274 (1.9%); American Indian, 82 (0.6%); Asian, 154 (1.1%); Other, 2,994 (20.9%).

Hispanic, 4,552 (31.7%).

Vital Statistics, 1997: Births, 230; deaths, 112; marriages, 145; divorces, 75.

Recreation: Prairie dog town; museum; camper facilities.

Minerals: Oil and gas.

Agriculture: Cattle; cotton, sorghums contribute; grains, corn, hay raised; significant irrigation. Market value $9.3 million.

ANDREWS (10,491) county seat; amphitheatre; hospital, mental health center; parks.

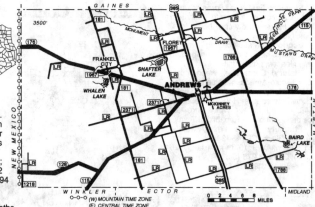

Population	**14,731**
Change fm '90	2.7
Area (sq. mi.)	1,501.0
Land Area (sq. mi.)	1,500.7
Altitude (ft.)	2,900-3,500
Rainfall (in.)	15.4
Jan. mean min.	29
July mean max.	94
Growing season (days)	213

Civ. Labor	5,606
Unemployed	7.9
Annual Wages	$121,034,638
Av. Weekly Wage	$514.92
Fed. Wages	$971,924
Ag. Net Cash Return	$2,013,000
Prop. Value	$1,642,378,424
Retail Sales	$75,690,074

Angelina County

Physical Features: Rolling, hilly East Texas county; black, red, gray soils; Angelina National Forest.

Economy: Timber; manufacturers of oil-field pumping units, iron and steel castings, truck trailers, mobile homes, horse stables; government/services; newsprint, other paper products, wood products, commercial printing; concrete products; cabinet works.

History: Caddoan area. First land deed to Vicente Micheli 1801. Anglo-American setters arrived in 1820s. County created 1846 from Nacodoches County; named for legendary Indian maiden Angelina.

Ethnicity, 1990: White, 54,752 (78.3%); Black, 10,731 (15.4%); American Indian, 153 (0.2%); Asian, 295 (0.4%); Other, 3,953 (5.7%).

Hispanic, 6,072 (8.7%).

Vital Statistics, 1997: Births,1,277; deaths, 751; marriages, 857; divorces, 468.

Recreation: Sam Rayburn Reservoir; national, state forests, parks; locomotive exhibit; Forest Festival, bike ride in fall.

Minerals: Limited output of natural gas and oil.

Agriculture: Poultry, beef, horses, hay, melons, peaches, pecans. Market value $15.9 million. A leading timber-producing county, $58 million in 1997.

LUFKIN (34,425) county seat; manufacturing; Angelina College; hospitals; U.S., Texas Forest centers; zoo; Museum of East Texas, civic center.

Other towns include: **Burke** (402); **Diboll** (5,608); **Hudson** (3,061); **Huntington** (2,156); **Keltys** (800); **Pollok** (300); **Zavalla** (864).

Population	**79,270**
Change from '90	13.4
Area (sq. mi.)	864.4
Land Area (sq. mi.)	801.6
Altitude (ft.)	139-406
Rainfall (in.)	38.9
Jan. mean min.	37
July mean max.	93
Growing season (days)	244
Civ. Labor	36,010
Unemployed	5.7
Annual Wages	$824,900,228
Av. Weekly Wage	$457.64
Fed. Wages	$16,466,509
Ag. Net Cash Return	-$1,156,000
Prop. Value	$2,506,644,266
Retail Sales	$710,236,057

For explanation of sources, abbreviations and symbols, see p. 130.

Aransas County

Physical Features: Coastal plains; sandy loam, coastal clays; bays, inlets; mesquites, oaks.

Economy: Tourism, fishing and shrimping; oil production; refining; shipbuilding, offshore equipment fabricated; carbon plant.

History: Karankawa, Coahuiltecan area. Settlement by Irish and Mexicans began in 1829. County created 1871 from Refugio County; named for Rio Nuestra Señora de Aranzazu, derived from a Spanish palace.

Ethnicity, 1990: White, 15,282 (85.4%); Black, 319 (1.8%); American Indian, 111 (0.6%); Asian, 589 (3.3%); Other, 1,591 (8.9%). Hispanic, 3,588 (20.1%).

Vital Statistics, 1997: Births, 212; deaths, 223; marriages, 320; divorces, 112.

Recreation: Fishing, hunting, tourist facilities; Fulton Mansion; state marine lab; Texas Maritime Museum; bird sanctuaries (a nationally known birding hotspot); Rockport Art Center.

Minerals: Oil and gas, also oystershell and sand.

Agriculture: Cow-calf operations; major crops are cotton, sorghum, corn. Market value $304,000. Fishing; redfish hatchery.

ROCKPORT (6,494) county seat; fishing; tourism, retirement and weekend residences; library; clinics; carbon-black plant; Del Mar College program.

Aransas Pass (7,901) deepwater port on Intracoastal Waterway; oil production, refining; industrial plants; tourism; hospital. **Fulton** (848).

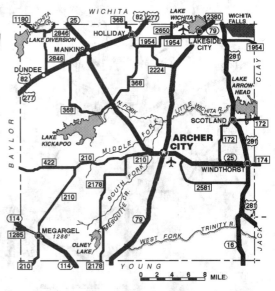

Population 21,111	
Change fm '90 .... 18.0	
Area (sq. mi.) 527.9	
Land Area (sq. mi.) 252.0	Unemployed 6.1
Altitude (ft.) .... sea level-25	Annual Wages $110,159,208
Rainfall (in.) 36.9	Av. Weekly Wage $396.43
Jan. mean min. 44	Fed. Wages $1,049,592
July mean max. 91	Ag. Net Cash Return .. -$261,000
Growing season (days) 312	Prop. Value $976,435,261
Civ. Labor 9,712	Retail Sales $187,648,361

Archer County

Physical Features: North Central county, rolling to hilly, drained by Wichita, Trinity River forks; black, red loams, sandy soils; mesquites, post oaks.

Economy: Cattle; oil services. Part of Wichita Falls metropolitan area.

History: Caddo, Comanche, Kiowas and other tribes in area until 1875; Anglo-American settlement developed soon afterward. County created from Fannin Land District, 1858; organized 1880. Named for Dr. B.T. Archer, Republic commissioner to United States.

Ethnicity, 1990: White, 7,789 (97.7%); Black, 11 (0.1%); American Indian, 36 (0.5%); Asian, 4 (0.1%); Other, 133 (1.7%). Hispanic, 189 (2.4%).

Vital Statistics, 1997: Births, 100; deaths, 61; marriages, 47; divorces, 44.

Recreation: Lakes; hunting of dove, quail, deer, feral hog, coyote.

Minerals: Oil and natural gas.

Agriculture: Dairy, cow/calf, stocker cattle; swine; poultry; wheat, cotton. Market value $53.4 million.

ARCHER CITY (1,993) county seat; cattle, oil field service center; museum; book center; some manufacturing.

Other towns include: **Holliday** (1,564) Mayfest in spring; **Lakeside City** (1,048); **Megargel** (264); **Scotland** (555); **Windthorst** (395), biannual German sausage festival (also in Scotland). Part of **Wichita Falls**.

Population.................................. 8,688	Rainfall (in.) 29.3	Annual Wages................... $33,360,840
Change fm '90 .... 9.0	Jan. mean min............................... 29	Av. Weekly Wage.................. $383.49
Area (sq. mi.) 925.7	July mean max. 98	Fed. Wages.......................... $891,917
Land Area (sq. mi.).................... 909.8	Growing season (days) 220	Ag. Net Cash Return........ $13,151,000
Altitude (ft.) 900-1,286	Civ. Labor..................................... 4,179	Prop. Value....................... $515,388,961
	Unemployed..................................... 3.4	Retail Sales..................... $34,317,355

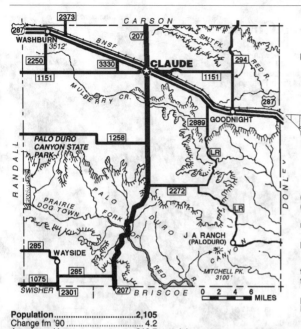

Armstrong County

Physical Features: Partly on High Plains, broken by Palo Duro Canyon. Chocolate loam, gray soils.

Economy: Agribusiness, tourism.

History: Apache, then Comanche territory until U.S. Army campaigns of 1874-75. Anglo-Americans began ranching soon afterward. County created from Bexar District, 1876; organized 1890; name honors pioneer Texas family.

Ethnicity, 1990: White, 1,976 (97.8%); Black, 0 (0.0%); American Indian, 10 (0.5%); Asian, 7 (0.3%); Other, 28 (1.4%). Hispanic, 55 (2.7%).

Vital Statistics, 1997: Births, 21; deaths, 33; marriages, 20; divorces, 9.

Recreation: Caprock Roundup in July, state park; Goodnight Ranch Home.

Minerals: Sand, gravel.

Agriculture: Stocker cattle, cow-calf operations; wheat, sorghum, cotton and hay; some irrigation. Market value $27.9 million.

CLAUDE (1,227) county seat; farm, ranch supplies; glass company; medical center; Caprock Roundup.

Other towns include: **Wayside** (35).

Population	2,105		
Change fm '90	4.2		
Area (sq. mi.)	913.7	July mean max.	92	Av. Weekly Wage	$407.89
Land Area (sq. mi.)	909.8	Growing season (days)	213	Fed. Wages	$268,467
Altitude (ft.)	2,300-3,512	Civ. Labor	905	Ag. Net Cash Return	$7,901,000
Rainfall (in.)	21.2	Unemployed	2.0	Prop. Value	$153,751,960
Jan. mean min.	20	Annual Wages	$7,835,502	Retail Sales	$5,202,329

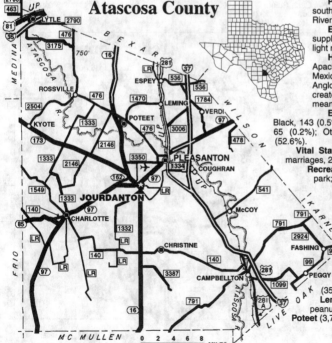

Atascosa County

Physical Features: On grassy prairie south of San Antonio, drained by Atascosa River, tributaries; mesquites, other brush.

Economy: Peanut dryer/shellers; oil-well supplies; government/services; coal plant; light manufacturing, shipping.

History: Coahuiltecan Indians; later Apaches, Comanches in area. Families from Mexico established ranches in mid-1700s. Anglo-Americans arrived in 1840s. County created from Bexar District, 1856. Atascosa means boggy in Spanish.

Ethnicity, 1990: White, 25,019 (81.9%); Black, 143 (0.5%); American Indian, 109 (0.4%); Asian, 65 (0.2%); Other, 5,197 (17.0%). Hispanic, 16,064 (52.6%).

Vital Statistics 1997: Births, 549; deaths, 259; marriages, 259; divorces, 100.

Recreation: Quail, deer hunting; museum; river park; theater group; Kactus Kick in May.

Minerals: Lignite, oil, gas.

Agriculture: Beef cattle; strawberries, peanuts, corn, milo, watermelons, wheat, winery. 25,000 acres irrigated. Market value $46.2 million.

JOURDANTON (3,875) county seat; hospital.

PLEASANTON (8,930) trading center; hospital; cowboy homecoming in August.

Other towns include: **Campbellton** (350); **Charlotte** (1,640); **Christine** (492); **Leming** (268); **Lytle** (2,608) greenhouse, peanuts processed; **McCoy** (30); **Peggy** (22); **Poteet** (3,735) strawberry "capital," festival in April.

Population	35,089		
Change frm '90	14.9	Rainfall (in.)	28.0	Unemployed	4.7
Area (sq. mi.)	1,232.7	Jan. mean min.	38	Annual Wages	$179,412,504
Land Area (sq. mi.)	1,232.2	July mean max.	96	Av. Weekly Wage	$422.80
Altitude (ft.)	200-750	Growing season (days)	282	Fed. Wages	$1,888,871
		Civ. Labor	16,855	Ag. Net Cash Return	$6,525,000
				Prop. Value	$1,312,233,932
				Retail Sales	$245,176,498

Austin County

Physical Features: Southeast county; level to hilly, drained by San Bernard, Brazos rivers; black prairie to sandy upland soils.

Economy: Agribusiness; steel, other manufacturing; tourism, government/services; commuting to Houston.

History: Tonkawa Indians; reduced by diseases. Birthplace of Anglo-American colonization, 1821, and German mother colony at Industry, 1831. County created 1837; named for Stephen F. Austin, father of Texas.

Ethnicity, 1990: White, 16,244 (81.9%); Black, 2,608 (13.2%); American Indian, 46 (0.2%); Asian, 26 (0.1%); Other, 908 (4.6%). Hispanic, 2,073 (10.5%).

Vital Statistics, 1997: Births, 306; deaths, 227; marriages, 177; divorces, 90.

Recreation: Fishing, hunting; state park, Pioneer Trail; Country Livin' festival; Lone Star Raceway Park.

Minerals: Oil and natural gas.

Agriculture: Beef production. Also, hay, cotton, grain sorghum, corn, pecans. Market value $24.5 million.

BELLVILLE (3,715) county seat; varied manufacturing; hospital; oil.

SEALY (5,723) oil-field and military vehicle manufacturing, varied industries; polka fest.

Other towns include: **Bleiblerville** (71); **Cat Spring** (76); **Frydek** (150) Grotto celebration in April; **Industry** (475); **Kenney** (200); **New Ulm** (650); **San Felipe** (819) colonial capital of Texas; **Wallis** (1,311).

Population	22,823
Change fm '90	15.1
Area (sq. mi.)	656.3
Land Area (sq. mi.)	652.7
Altitude (ft.)	96-400

Rainfall (in.)	40.4
Jan. mean min.	39
July mean max.	94
Growing season (days)	282
Civ. Labor	12,213
Unemployed	3.3

Annual Wages	$202,160,873
Av. Weekly Wage	$508.78
Fed. Wages	$4,117,025
Ag. Net Cash Return	$1,029,000
Prop. Value	$1,637,403,120
Retail Sales	$224,958,514

Bailey County

Physical Features: High Plains county, sandy loam soils; mesquite brush; drains to draws forming upper watershed of Brazos River, playas.

Economy: Farm supply manufacturing; electric generating plant; food-processing plants; muffler manufacturing.

History: Settlement began after 1900. County created from Bexar 1876, organized 1917. Named for Alamo hero Peter J. Bailey.

Ethnicity, 1990: White, 6,537 (92.5%); Black, 124 (1.8%); American Indian, 10 (0.1%); Asian, 12 (0.2%); Other, 381 (5.4%). Hispanic, 2,740 (38.8%).

Vital Statistics, 1997: Births, 123; deaths, 65; marriages, 97; divorces, 19.

Recreation: Muleshoe National Wildlife Refuge; "Old Pete," the national mule memorial; outdoor drama; historical building park; museum; motorcycle rally; pheasant hunting.

Minerals: Insignificant.

Agriculture: Feedlot, dairy cattle; cotton, wheat, sorghum, corn, vegetables; 100,000 acres irrigated. Market value $171.7 million.

MULESHOE (4,362) county seat; agribusiness center; feed-corn milling; hospital; livestock show.

Other towns include: **Bula** (35); **Enochs** (80); **Maple** (75).

Population	6,769
Change fm '90	- 4.2
Area (sq. mi.)	827.3
Land Area (sq. mi.)	826.7
Altitude (ft.)	3,700-4,085
Rainfall (in.)	16.8

Jan. mean min.	19
July mean max.	92
Growing season (days)	181
Civ. Labor	3,661
Unemployed	6.1
Annual Wages	$44,803,980

Av. Weekly Wage	$364.12
Fed. Wages	$1,102,195
Ag. Net Cash Return	$19,927,000
Prop. Value	$338,429,282
Retail Sales	$56,295,289

For explanation of sources, abbreviations and symbols, see p. 130.

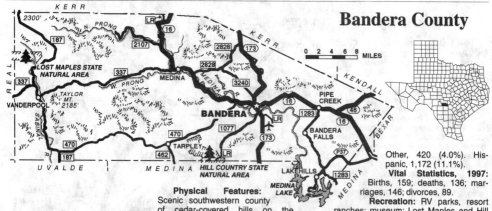

Bandera County

Population 14,712
Change fm '90 ....39.3
Area (sq. mi.) 797.5
Land Area (sq. mi.) 791.8
Altitude (ft.) 1,064-2,300
Rainfall (in.) 35.1
Jan. mean min. 31
July mean max. 94
Growing season (days) 235
Civ. Labor 6,344
Unemployed 3.6
Annual Wages $38,912,958
Av. Weekly Wage $340.14
Fed. Wages $635,985
Ag. Net Cash Return.... -$1,349,000
Prop. Value $1,077,170,303
Retail Sales $59,760,898

Physical Features: Scenic southwestern county of cedar-covered hills on the Edwards Plateau; Medina, Sabinal Rivers; limestone, sandy soils; species of oaks, walnuts, native cherry and Uvalde maple.

Economy: Tourism, hunting, fishing, ranching supplies, marketing, forest products.

History: Apache, then Comanche territory. White settlement began in early 1850s, including Mormons and Poles. County created from Bexar, Uvalde counties, 1856; named for Bandera (flag) Mountains.

Ethnicity, 1990: White, 10,027 (94.9%); Black, 23 (0.2%); American Indian, 66 (0.6%); Asian, 26 (0.2%); Other, 420 (4.0%). Hispanic, 1,172 (11.1%).

Vital Statistics, 1997: Births, 159; deaths, 136; marriages, 146; divorces, 89.

Recreation: RV parks, resort ranches; museum; Lost Maples and Hill Country State Natural Areas; race track; Fun-tier Days on Memorial Day weekend; apple festival in July, Cajun festival in September; Medina Lake.

Agriculture: Beef cattle, horses, poultry, sheep, goats; apples, greenhouse crops, pecans. Market value $4.7 million.

BANDERA (1,296) county seat; "cowboy capital of the world"; cedar mill, shingle factory; purse factory; spurs, bits manufactured.

Other towns include: **Medina** (515) apple growing; **Pipe Creek** (NA); **Tarpley** (30); **Vanderpool** (20).

Also, the community of **Lakehills** (3,032) on Medina Lake.

Bastrop County

Physical Features: Rolling; alluvial, sandy, loam soils; varied timber, Lost Pines; bisected by Colorado River.

Economy: Government/services; tourism; agribusiness; computer equipment; commuters to Austin.

History: Tonkawa Indian area; Comanches also present. Spanish fort established 1804. County created 1836; named for Baron de Bastrop, who aided Moses Austin and colonists who settled in 1827.

Ethnicity: White, 29,607 (77.4%); Black, 4,512 (11.8%); American Indian, 181 (0.5%); Asian, 129 (0.3%); Other, 3,834 (10.0%). Hispanic, 6,933 (18.1%).

Vital Statistics, 1997: Births, 764; deaths, 381; marriages, 443; divorces, 314.

Recreation: Fishing, hunting; state parks; Lake Bastrop; historic sites, homes; museum; railroad park; natural science center.

Minerals: Clay, oil, gas and lignite.

Agriculture: Hay; beef cattle; turfgrasses; horses, goats; pecans. Market value $27.9 million. Pine for lumber, oak for firewood.

BASTROP (5,855) county seat; government/services, tourism, oil-well supply, some manufacturing; medical clinic; University of Texas cancer research center; federal prison; Cajun fest in October.

Elgin (5,999) computer manufacturing, sausage plants, brick plant; horse, cattle breeding; medical research; library; Western Days in July, Hogeye festival in October.

Smithville (4,076) rail maintenance, light manufacturing, environmental science park; hospital, model recycling center; jamboree in April.

Other towns include: **Cedar Creek** (200); **McDade** (345) watermelon festival in July; **Paige** (275); **Red Rock** (125); **Rosanky** (250).

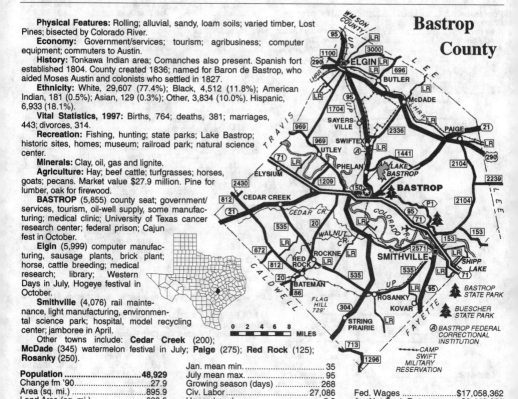

Population 48,929
Change fm '90 ....27.9
Area (sq. mi.) 895.9
Land Area (sq. mi.) 888.5
Altitude (ft.) 300-729
Rainfall (in.) 38.3
Jan. mean min. 35
July mean max. 95
Growing season (days) 268
Civ. Labor 27,086
Unemployed 3.0
Annual Wages $179,454,684
Av. Weekly Wage $397.32
Fed. Wages $17,058,362
Ag. Net Cash Return..........-$2,140,000
Prop. Value $1,791,338,674
Retail Sales...................$423,288,036

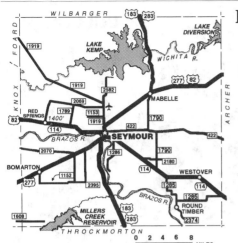

Baylor County

Physical Features: North Central county; level to hilly; drains to Brazos, Wichita rivers; sandy, loam, red soils; grassy, mesquites, cedars.

Economy: Agribusiness; retail/service; health services.

History: Comanches, with Wichitas and other tribes; removed in 1874-75. Anglo-Americans settled in the 1870s. County created from Fannin County 1858; organized 1879. Named for H.W. Baylor, Texas Ranger surgeon.

Ethnicity, 1990: White, 3,962 (90.4%); Black, 180 (4.1%); American Indian, 9 (0.2%); Asian, 13 (0.3%); Other, 221 (5.0%). Hispanic, 334 (7.6%).

Vital Statistics, 1997: Births, 42; deaths, 64; marriages, 29; divorces, 18.

Recreation: Lakes; hunting; park, pavilions; settlers reunion, fish day in spring, autumn leaves festival in October.

Minerals: Oil, gas produced.

Agriculture: Cattle, cow-calf operations; wheat, cotton, grain sorghum, hay. Market value $38 million.

SEYMOUR (3,079) county seat; agribusiness; hospital; dove hunters' breakfast in September.

Population	4,326
Change fm '90	-1.3
Area (sq. mi.)	901.0
Land Area (sq. mi.)	870.8
Altitude (ft.)	1,053-1,400
Rainfall (in.)	27.3
Jan. mean min.	26
July mean max.	97

Growing season (days)	214		
Civ. Labor	1,811	Fed. Wages	$705,409
Unemployed	5.6	Ag. Net Cash Return	$5,917,000
Annual Wages	$21,563,809	Prop. Value	$251,463,001
Av. Weekly Wage	$336.70	Retail Sales	$30,203,727

Bee County

Physical Features: South Coastal Plain, level to rolling; black clay, sandy, loam soils; brushy.

Economy: Oil supplies, agribusiness; small feedlots; state prison installations.

History: Karankawa, Apache, Pawnee territory. First Spanish land grant, 1789. Irish settlers arrived 1826-29. County created from Karnes, Live Oak, Goliad, Refugio, San Patricio, 1857; organized 1858; named for Gen. Barnard Bee.

Ethnicity, 1990: White, 19,443 (77.4%); Black, 727 (2.9%); American Indian, 103 (0.4%); Asian, 231 (0.9%); Other, 4,631 (18.4%). Hispanic, 12,909 (51.4%).

Vital Statistics, 1997: Births, 416; deaths, 243; marriages, 213; divorces, 116.

Recreation: Hunting, camping; historical sites; Western week in November.

Minerals: Oil, gas produced.

Agriculture: Cow-calf production, feedlot, horses raised; grain sorghums, corn, wheat and cotton. Market value $27.7 million.

BEEVILLE (14,284) county seat; prison units, training academy; Bee County College; hospital; Cinco de Mayo, Diez y Seis festivals.

Other towns include: **Mineral** (50); **Normanna** (75); **Pawnee** (249); **Pettus** (400); **Skidmore** (500); **Tuleta** (98); **Tynan** (200).

Population	27,659
Change fm '90	10.0
Area (sq. mi.)	880.3
Land Area (sq. mi.)	880.2
Altitude (ft.)	87-500
Rainfall (in.)	32.1
Jan. mean min.	41
July mean max.	94

Growing season (days)	285		
Civ. Labor	11,108		
Unemployed	5.8		
Annual Wages	$184,952,903		
Av. Weekly Wage	$407.96		
Fed. Wages	$1,687,768		
Ag. Net Cash Return	$6,741,000		
Prop. Value	$793,848,300		
Retail Sales	$159,448,728		

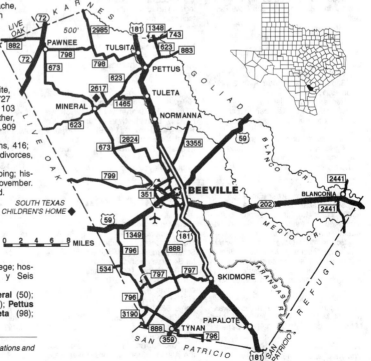

For explanation of sources, abbreviations and symbols, see p. 130.

Bell County

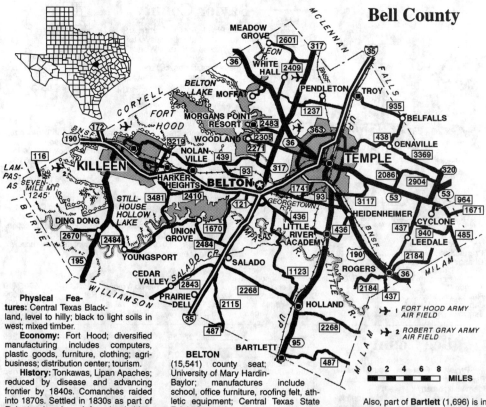

Physical Features: Central Texas Blackland, level to hilly; black to light soils in west; mixed timber.

Economy: Fort Hood; diversified manufacturing includes computers, plastic goods, furniture, clothing; agribusiness; distribution center; tourism.

History: Tonkawas, Lipan Apaches; reduced by disease and advancing frontier by 1840s. Comanches raided into 1870s. Settled in 1830s as part of Robertson's colony. A few slaveholders in 1850s. County created from Milam County in 1850; named for Gov. P.H. Bell.

Ethnicity, 1990: White, 136,066 (71.2%); Black, 36,095 (18.9%); American Indian, 944 (0.5%); Asian, 5,531 (2.9%); Other, 12,452 (6.5%). Hispanic, 24,995 (13.1%).

Vital Statistics, 1997: Births, 5,103; deaths, 1,459; marriages, 3,429; divorces, 1,896.

Recreation: Fishing, hunting; lakes; historic sites; exposition center; Salado gathering of Scottish clans in November.

Minerals: Stone, sand, gravel.

Agriculture: Cattle, corn, turkeys; sorghums, wheat, cotton. Market value $51.5 million. Firewood, cedar posts.

BELTON (15,541) county seat; University of Mary Hardin-Baylor; manufactures include school, office furniture, roofing felt, athletic equipment; Central Texas State Fair in September.

KILLEEN (84,488) Fort Hood; colleges; varied manufacturing; convention facilities; medical center, psychiatric center.

TEMPLE (51,476) rail, market, distribution center; diversified industries; convention center; junior college; medical centers, VA hospital; early-day tractor, engine show.

Other towns include: **Harker Heights** (17,243) Founder's Day in October; **Heidenheimer** (144); **Holland** (1,334) corn festival in June; **Little River-Academy** (1,678); **Morgan's Point Resort** (2,425); **Nolanville** (2,619); **Pendelton** (60); **Rogers** (1,198); **Salado** (1,385) arts fairs in August, May; civic center; **Troy** (1,462).

Also, part of **Bartlett** (1,696) is in Bell County.

Fort Hood has a population of 38,259.

Population	226,952
Change fm '90	18.8
Area (sq. mi.)	1,087.1
Land Area (sq. mi.)	1,059.0
Altitude (ft.)	400-1,245
Rainfall (in.)	34.9
Jan. mean min.	35
July mean max.	95
Growing season (days)	260
Civ. Labor	92,764
Unemployed	4.3
Annual Wages	$1,732,729,589
Av. Weekly Wage	$435.21
Fed. Wages	$194,606,819
Ag. Net Cash Return	$9,535,000
Prop. Value	$6,237,822,017
Retail Sales	$3,233,043,231

Physical Features: On edge of Balcones Escarpment, Coastal Plain; heavy black to thin limestone soils; spring-fed streams; underground water; mesquite, other brush.

Economy: Government center with large federal payroll, five military bases; tourism second-largest industry; developing high-tech industrial park, research center; education center with 14 colleges.

History: Coahuiltecan Indian area; also Lipan Apaches and Tonkawas present. Mission San Antonio de Valero (Alamo) founded in 1718. Canary

For explanation of sources, abbreviations and symbols, see p. 130.

Bexar County

Islanders arrived in 1731. Anglo-American settlers began arriving in late 1820s. County created 1836 from Spanish municipality named for Duke de Bexar; a colonial capital of Texas.

Ethnicity, 1990: White, 878,736 (74.1%); Black, 84,670 (7.1%); American Indian, 4,265 (0.4%); Asian, 15,429 (1.3%); Other, 202,294 (17.1%). Hispanic, 589,180 (49.7%).

Vital Statistics, 1997: Births, 22,952; deaths, 9,561; marriages, 5,597; divorces, 6,293.

Recreation: Historic sites include the Alamo, other missions; River Walk;

Seaworld; El Mercado (market), La Villita; Tower of the Americas; Brackenridge Park; zoo; symphony orchestra; HemisFair Plaza; Fiesta Texas; Institute of Texan Cultures; parks, museums; hunting, fishing.

Minerals: Cement, stone, oil, gas, sand and gravel, lime, clays.

Agriculture: Nursery, greenhouse crops; cattle; corn, sorghums, vegetables, hay, some irrigation. Market value $68.3 million.

Education: Fourteen colleges including Our Lady of the Lake, St. Mary's University, Trinity University and the University of Texas at San Antonio.

SAN ANTONIO (1,123,626) county

Bexar County

(continued)

Population	1,342,934
Change fm '90	13.3
Area (sq. mi.)	1,256.7
Land Area (sq. mi.)	1,246.9
Altitude (ft.)	486-1,892
Rainfall (in.)	31.0

Jan. mean min.	38
July mean max.	95
Growing season (days)	265
Civ. Labor	665,621
Unemployed	3.8
Annual Wages	$15,183,292,991
Av. Weekly Wage	$505.29
Fed. Wages	$1,408,335,166
Ag. Net Cash Return	$14,968,000
Prop. Value	$42,597,779,375
Retail Sales	$14,984,909,321

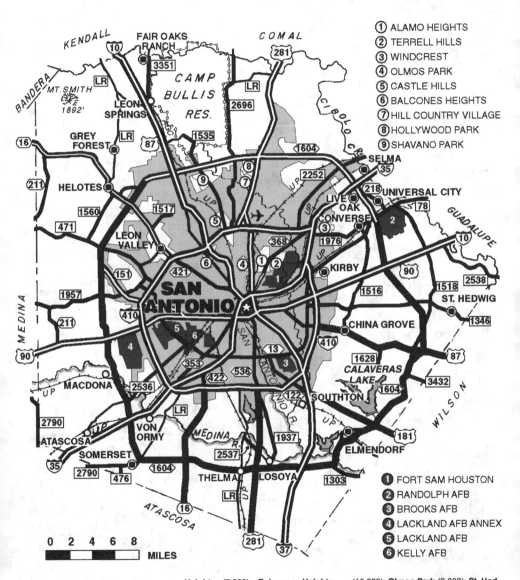

1. ALAMO HEIGHTS
2. TERRELL HILLS
3. WINDCREST
4. OLMOS PARK
5. CASTLE HILLS
6. BALCONES HEIGHTS
7. HILL COUNTRY VILLAGE
8. HOLLYWOOD PARK
9. SHAVANO PARK

1. FORT SAM HOUSTON
2. RANDOLPH AFB
3. BROOKS AFB
4. LACKLAND AFB ANNEX
5. LACKLAND AFB
6. KELLY AFB

(continued)

seat; Texas' second largest city; varied manufacturing with emphasis on high-tech industries; other products include construction equipment, concrete and dairy products; industrial warehousing. Other towns include: **Alamo** **Heights** (7,338); **Balcones Heights** (3,275); **Castle Hills** (4,329); **China Grove** (1,230); **Converse** (10,664); **Elmendorf** (1,053); **Fair Oaks Ranch** (3,734); **Grey Forest** (532) **Helotes** (2,003); **Hill Country Village** (1,298); **Hollywood Park** (3,116); **Kirby** (9,167); **Leon Valley** (10,404); **Live Oak** (10,839); **Olmos Park** (2,302); **St. Hedwig** (1,882); **Selma** (700); **Shavano Park** (2,102); **Somerset** (1,530); **Terrell Hills** (5,108); **Universal City** (14,914); **Windcrest** (5,846).

For explanation of sources, abbreviations and symbols, see p. 130.

Blanco County

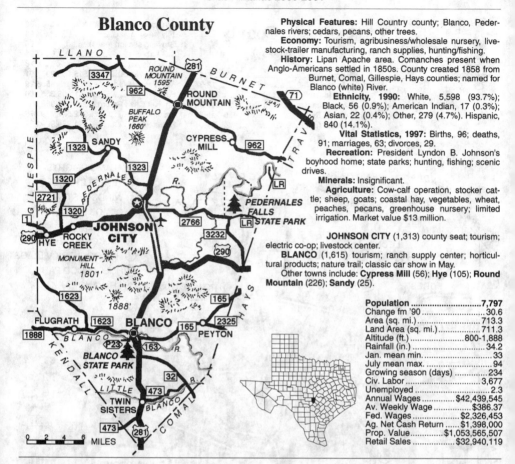

Physical Features: Hill Country county; Blanco, Pedernales rivers; cedars, pecans, other trees.

Economy: Tourism, agribusiness/wholesale nursery, livestock-trailer manufacturing, ranch supplies, hunting/fishing.

History: Lipan Apache area. Comanches present when Anglo-Americans settled in 1850s. County created 1858 from Burnet, Comal, Gillespie, Hays counties; named for Blanco (white) River.

Ethnicity, 1990: White, 5,598 (93.7%); Black, 56 (0.9%); American Indian, 17 (0.3%); Asian, 22 (0.4%); Other, 279 (4.7%). Hispanic, 840 (14.1%).

Vital Statistics, 1997: Births, 96; deaths, 91; marriages, 63; divorces, 29.

Recreation: President Lyndon B. Johnson's boyhood home; state parks; hunting, fishing; scenic drives.

Minerals: Insignificant.

Agriculture: Cow-calf operation, stocker cattle; sheep, goats; coastal hay, vegetables, wheat, peaches, pecans, greenhouse nursery; limited irrigation. Market value $13 million.

JOHNSON CITY (1,313) county seat; tourism; electric co-op; livestock center.

BLANCO (1,615) tourism; ranch supply center; horticultural products; nature trail; classic car show in May.

Other towns include: **Cypress Mill** (56); **Hye** (105); **Round Mountain** (226); **Sandy** (25).

Population	7,797
Change fm '90	30.6
Area (sq. mi.)	713.3
Land Area (sq. mi.)	711.3
Altitude (ft.)	800-1,888
Rainfall (in.)	34.2
Jan. mean min.	33
July mean max.	94
Growing season (days)	234
Civ. Labor	3,677
Unemployed	2.3
Annual Wages	$42,439,545
Av. Weekly Wage	$386.37
Fed. Wages	$2,326,453
Ag. Net Cash Return	$1,398,000
Prop. Value	$1,053,565,507
Retail Sales	$32,940,119

Borden County

Physical Features: West Texas county of rolling surface, broken by Caprock Escarpment; drains to Colorado River; sandy loam, clay soils.

Economy: Oil, agribusiness.

History: Comanche area. Anglo-Americans settled in 1870s. County created 1876 from Bexar District, organized 1891; named for Gail Borden, patriot, inventor, editor.

Ethnicity, 1990: White, 769 (96.2%); Black, 2 (0.3%); American Indian, 10 (1.3%); Asian, 0 (0.0%); Other, 18 (2.3%). Hispanic, 120 (15.0%).

Vital Statistics, 1997: Births, 4; deaths, 2; marriages, 2; divorces, 4.

Recreation: Fishing, hunting; Lake J.B. Thomas; museum; Coyote Opry in September.

Minerals: Oil, gas, caliche, sand, gravel.

Agriculture: Beef cattle, cotton; also, horses, milo, oats, pecans; some irrigation for cotton. Market value $12.4 million.

GAIL (189) county seat; museum; antique shop, ambulance service; "star" construction atop Gail Mountain.

For explanation of sources, abbreviations and symbols, see p. 130.

Population	758
Change fm '90	-5.1
Area (sq. mi.)	906.0
Land Area (sq. mi.)	898.9
Altitude (ft.)	2,258-3,000
Rainfall (in.)	16.9
Jan. mean min.	31
July mean max.	94
Growing season (days)	214
Civ. Labor	394
Unemployed	2.0
Annual Wages	$2,721,954
Av. Weekly Wage	$424.59
Fed. Wages	$83,528
Ag. Net Cash Return	$4,449,000
Prop. Value	$339,898,787
Retail Sales	$159,675

Bosque County

Physical Features: North Central county; hilly, broken by Bosque, Brazos rivers; limestone to alluvial soils; cedars, oaks, mesquites.

Economy: Agribusiness, government/services, tourism, small industries.

History: Tonkawa, Waco and Tawakoni Indians. Settlers from England and Norway arrived in 1850s. County created 1854 from Milam District, McLennan County; named for Bosque (woods) River.

Vital Statistics, 1997: Births, 203; deaths, 273; marriages, 104; divorces, 90.

Ethnicity, 1990: White, 14,173 (93.7%); Black, 319 (2.1%); American Indian, 26 (0.2%); Asian, 41 (0.3%); Other, 566 (3.7%). Hispanic, 1,430 (9.5%).

Recreation: Lake, state park, museum at Clifton, conservatory of fine art; fishing, hunting; scenic routes, Norwegian smorgasbord at Norse in November.

Minerals: Limestone.

Agriculture: Cattle, hunting, wheat and oats, forages, turkeys, dairy farms, feed grains. Market value $41.4 million.

MERIDIAN (1,414) county seat; distribution center; varied manufacturing.

CLIFTON (3,577) tourism; trade center; light manufacturing; hospital.

Other towns include: **Cranfills Gap** (303); **Iredell** (357); **Kopperl** (225); **Laguna Park** (550); **Morgan** (547); **Valley Mills** (1,107); **Walnut Springs** (825).

Population......16,346	Rainfall (in.) 31.6	Annual Wages......$69,774,952
Change fm '90 ......8.1	Jan. mean min. 33	Av. Weekly Wage......$380.04
Area (sq. mi.)......1,002.6	July mean max. 97	Fed. Wages......$2,403,073
Land Area (sq. mi.)......989.3	Growing season (days) 243	Ag. Net Cash Return......$4,338,000
Altitude (ft.) 450-1,250	Civ. Labor......6,548	Prop. Value $932,171,466
	Unemployed 4.4	Retail Sales $61,036,767

Bowie County

Physical Features: Forested hills at northeast corner of state; clay, sandy, alluvial soils; drained by Red and Sulphur rivers.

Economy: Government/services; agribusiness; manufacturing, paper mill.

History: Caddo area, abandoned in 1790s after trouble with Osage tribe. Anglo-Americans began arriving 1815-20. County created 1840 from Red River County; named for Alamo hero James Bowie.

Ethnicity, 1990: White, 62,878 (77.0%); Black, 17,798 (21.8%); American Indian, 412 (0.5%); Asian, 262 (0.3%); Other, 315 (0.4%). Hispanic, 1,334 (1.6%).

Vital Statistics, 1997: Births, 1,124; deaths, 890; marriages, 672; divorces, 540.

Recreation: Lakes, Crystal Springs beach; hunting, fishing, historic sites; Four-States Fair in September, Red Neck Day in July.

Minerals: Oil, gas, sand, gravel.

Agriculture: Beef, dairy cattle, poultry; soybeans, wheat, corn, milo, wholesale nursery, peanuts, fruit, truck crops. Market value $40.2 million. Pine timber, hardwoods, pulpwood harvested.

BOSTON (200) county seat (but courthouse now located in New Boston).

TEXARKANA (33,234 in Texas, 22,918 in Arkansas) distribution, manufacturing, hospitals; tourism; colleges; federal correctional unit; Quadrangle Festival in September, Perot Theatre.

New Boston (5,049) site of courthouse; steel manufactured; agribusiness; lumber mill; state prison unit; Pioneer Days in August.

Other towns include: **De Kalb** (1,865); **Hooks** (2,826); **Leary** (432); **Maud** (1,024); **Nash** (2,316); **Red Lick** (NC); **Redwater** (844); **Simms** (240); **Wake Village** (5,105).

① LEARY
② RED LICK

◆ FEDERAL CORRECTIONAL INSTITUTION

Population......82,854	
Change fm '90 ......1.5	
Area (sq. mi.) 922.7	
Land Area (sq. mi.) 887.9	
Altitude (ft.) 200-437	
Rainfall (in.) 45.3	
Jan. mean min. 35	
July mean max. 93	
Growing season (days)......235	
Civ. Labor 39,553	
Unemployed 8.2	
Annual Wages $787,161,400	
Av. Weekly Wage $448.87	
Fed. Wages $136,240,676	
Ag. Net Cash Return $4,130,000	
Prop. Value......$2,699,108,558	
Retail Sales $925,911,831	

Brazoria County

Physical Features: Flat Coastal Plain, coastal soils, drained by Brazos and San Bernard rivers.

Economy: Petroleum and chemical industry; fishing; tourism; agribusiness. Part of Houston metropolitan area.

History: Karankawa area. Part of Austin's "Old Three Hundred" colony of families arriving in early 1820s. County created 1836 from Municipality of Brazoria; name derived from Brazos River.

Ethnicity, 1990: White, 154,875 (80.8%); Black, 15,981 (8.3%); American Indian, 812 (0.4%); Asian, 1,961 (1.0%); Other, 18,078 (9.4%). Hispanic, 33,797 (17.6%).

Vital Statistics, 1997: Births, 3,548; deaths, 1,509; marriages, 1,698; divorces, 1,289.

Recreation: Water sports; fishing, hunting; historic sites; state and county parks; replica of the first capitol of the Republic of Texas at West Columbia.

Minerals: Oil, gas, sand, gravel.

Agriculture: Cattle, hay, rice, soybeans, sorghum, nursery, corn, cotton, aquaculture. 20,000 acres of rice irrigated. Market value $42.6 million.

ANGLETON (22,524) county seat; banking, distribution center for oil, chemical, agricultural area; fish-processing plant; hospital.

BRAZOSPORT (60,519) is a community of nine cities; chemical complex; deepwater seaport; commercial fishing; tourism; college; hospital; Brazosport cities include: **Brazoria** (3,164) No-Name Festival in May; **Clute** (10,215), **Freeport** (13,753), **Jones Creek** (2,256), **Lake Jackson** (26,291), **Oyster Creek** (1,083), **Quintana** (65), **Richwood** (2,955), **Surfside Beach** (737).

ALVIN (20,715) petrochemical processing; agribusiness; rail, trucking; junior college; hospital; Rice & Crawfest in March; Nolan Ryan museum.

PEARLAND (29,686) commuting to Houston, NASA; community college.

Other towns include: **Bailey's Prairie** (718); **Bonney** (470); **Brookside Village** (1,961); **Damon** (375); **Danbury** (1,785); **Danciger** (357); **Hillcrest Village** (852); **Holiday Lakes** (1,302); **Iowa Colony** (816); **Liverpool** (490); **Manvel** (4,868); **Old Ocean** (915); **Rosharon** (435); **Sweeny** (3,603) petrochemical industries, hospital, Pride Day in May; **West Columbia** (5,260) tortilla factory, chemical companies; historic sites, San Jacinto Festival.

Population	227,523
Change fm '90	18.7
Area (sq. mi.)	1,597.4
Land Area (sq. mi.)	1,386.9
Altitude (ft.)	sea level-146
Rainfall (in.)	56.4
Jan. mean min.	41
July mean max.	92
Growing season (days)	268
Civ. Labor	106,083
Unemployed	6.1
Annual Wages	$2,352,362,792
Av. Weekly Wage	$624.09
Fed. Wages	$17,380,321
Ag. Net Cash Return	$4,444,000
Prop. Value	$13,288,982,660
Retail Sales	$1,716,002,587

For explanation of sources, abbreviations and symbols, see p.130.

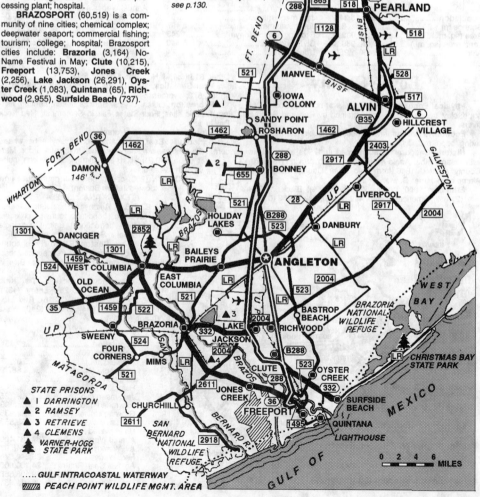

STATE PRISONS
▲ 1 DARRINGTON
▲ 2 RAMSEY
▲ 3 RETRIEVE
▲ 4 CLEMENS
🌲 VARNER-HOGG STATE PARK

..... GULF INTRACOASTAL WATERWAY
▨▨▨ PEACH POINT WILDLIFE MGMT. AREA

Brazos County

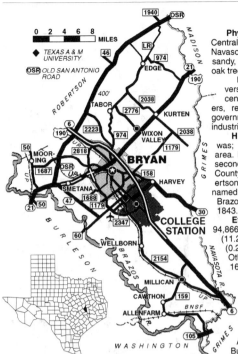

Physical Features: South Central county between Brazos, Navasota rivers; rich bottom soils, sandy, clays on rolling uplands; oak trees.

Economy: Texas A&M University; market and medical center; agribusiness; computers, research and development; government/services; winery; industrial parks; tourism.

History: Bidais and Tonkawas; Comanches hunted in area. Part of Stephen F. Austin's second colony, late 1820s. County created 1841 from Robertson, Washington counties and named Navasota; renamed for Brazos River in 1842, organized 1843.

Ethnicity, 1990: White, 94,866 (77.8%); Black, 13,672 (11.2%); American Indian, 274 (0.2%); Asian, 4,313 (3.5%); Other, 8,737 (7.2%). Hispanic, 16,713 (13.7%).

Vital Statistics, 1997: Births, 1,995; deaths, 613; marriages, 1,431; divorces, 436.

Recreation: Fishing, hunting; raceway; many events related to Texas A&M activities; George Bush Presidential Library and Museum.

Minerals: Sand and gravel, lignite, gas, oil.

Agriculture: Cattle, eggs; cotton, hay, corn, sorghum; horses. Market value $41.2 million.

BRYAN (62,685) county seat; defense electronics, other varied manufacturing; agribusiness center; hospital, psychiatric facilities; Blinn College extension.

COLLEGE STATION (64,119) home of Texas A&M University, varied high-tech manufacturing; research; hospitals.

Other towns include: **Kurten** (150); **Millican** (157); **Wellborn** (100); **Wixon Valley** (244).

Population	140,025
Change fm '90	14.9
Area (sq. mi.)	590.3
Land Area (sq. mi.)	585.8
Altitude (ft.)	197-400
Rainfall (in.)	39.1
Jan. mean min.	39
July mean max.	94
Growing season (days)	274
Civ. Labor	73,988
Unemployed	1.7
Annual Wages	$1,546,858,086
Av. Weekly Wage	$414.97
Fed. Wages	$41,620,681
Ag. Net Cash Return	$5,371,000
Prop. Value	$4,613,210,290
Retail Sales	$1,482,682,817

Brewster County

Physical Features: Largest county, with area slightly less than that of Connecticut plus Rhode Island; mountains, canyons, distinctive geology, plant life, animals.

Economy: Sul Ross State University; ranching; tourism; government/services; retirement developments; hunting leases.

History: Pueblo culture had begun when Spanish explored in 1500s. Mescalero Apaches in Chisos; Comanches raided in area. Ranching developed in northern part 1880s; Mexican agricultural communites along river. County created 1887 from Presidio County; named for Henry P. Brewster, Republic secretary of war.

Ethnicity, 1990: White, 8,300 (95.6%); Black, 85 (1.0%); American Indian, 20 (0.2%); Asian, 52 (0.6%); Other, 224 (2.6%). Hispanic, 3,702 (42.6%).

Vital Statistics, 1997: Births, 108; deaths, 85; marriages, 83; divorces, 0.

Recreation: Big Bend National Park; ghost towns; scenic drives; museum; rockhound areas; November chili cookoff at Terlingua; cavalry post at Lajitas; hunting.

Minerals: Bentonite.

Agriculture: Cattle, horses, hunting, sheep, goats; pecans, apples, other fruit. Market value $9 million.

ALPINE (5,962) county seat; ranch trade center; tourism; Sul Ross State University; hospital; varied manufacturing. **Marathon** (850) ranching center, tourism, Fall Purple Sage quilt show. Also, **Big Bend National Park** (194) and **Terlingua** (35).

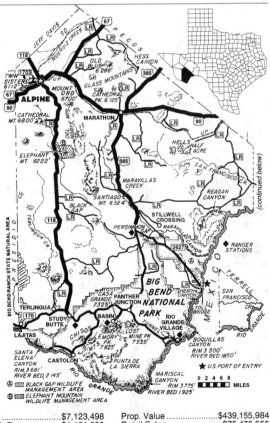

Population	9,265
Change fm '90	7.1
Area (sq. mi.)	6,193.1
Land Area (sq. mi.)	6,193.0
Altitude (ft.)	1,700-7,825
Rainfall (in.)	16.9
Jan. mean min.	30
July mean max.	89
Growing season (days)	223
Civ. Labor	5,121
Unemployed	2.5
Annual Wages	$67,461,851
Av. Weekly Wage	$353.72

Fed. Wages	$7,123,498
Ag. Net Cash Return	$1,131,000

Prop. Value	$439,155,984
Retail Sales	$75,476,555

144 Texas Almanac 2000-2001

Briscoe County

Physical Features: Partly on High Plains, broken by Caprock Escarpment, fork of Red River; sandy, loam soils.

Economy: Agribusiness.

History: Apaches, displaced by Comanches around 1700. Ranchers settled in 1880s. County created from Bexar District, 1876, organized 1892; named for Andrew Briscoe, Republic of Texas soldier.

Ethnicity, 1990: White, 1,559 (79.1%); Black, 68 (3.5%); American Indian, 5 (0.3%); Asian, 0 (0.0%); Other, 339 (17.2%). Hispanic, 367 (18.6%).

Vital Statistics, 1997: Births, 22; deaths, 28; marriages, 11; divorces, 2.

Recreation: Hunting, fishing; scenic drives; museum; state park, Mackenzie Reservoir.

Minerals: Insignificant.

Agriculture: Cotton, wheat, cow/calf, stocker cattle, sorghum, peanuts, corn, hay. Approximately 65 percent of cropland irrigated. Market value $22.6 million.

SILVERTON (764) county seat; agribusiness center; irrigation supplies manufactured; clinics.

Quitaque (470) trade center.

Population	1,919
Change fm '90	-2.6
Area (sq. mi.)	901.6
Land Area (sq. mi.)	900.3
Altitude (ft.)	2,100-3,350
Rainfall (in.)	21.4

Jan. mean min.	20
July mean max.	91
Growing season (days)	214
Civ. Labor	971
Unemployed	3.9

Annual Wages	$8,595,657
Av. Weekly Wage	$353.65
Fed. Wages	$405,660
Ag. Net Cash Return	$6,237,000
Prop. Value	$106,846,505
Retail Sales	$5,951,260

Brooks County

Physical Features: On Rio Grande plain near Gulf; level to rolling; brushy; light to dark sandy loam soils.

Economy: Oil, gas, cattle, hunting leases.

History: Coahuiltecan Indians. Spanish land grants date to around 1800. County created from Hidalgo, Starr, Zapata counties, 1911. Named for J.A. Brooks, Texas Ranger and legislator.

Ethnicity, 1990: White, 6,748 (82.3%); Black, 3 (0.0%); American Indian, 13 (0.2%); Asian, 10 (0.1%); Other, 1,430 (17.4%). Hispanic, 7,338 (89.4%).

Vital Statistics, 1997: Births, 146; deaths, 81; marriages, 74; divorces, 7.

Recreation: Hunting, fishing; Heritage Museum, Don Pedrito Shrine; fiestas, May and October.

Minerals: Oil, gas production.

Agriculture: Beef cow-calf operations, stocker; crops include watermelons, grain sorghums, hay. Market value $8.7 million.

FALFURRIAS (5,823) county seat; agricultural market center, government/services; oil & gas production; hospital; museum, library.

Other towns include: **Encino** (110).

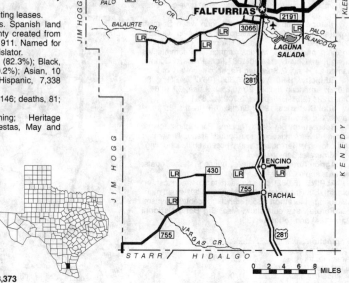

Population	8,373
Change fm '90	2.1
Area (sq. mi.)	943.6
Land Area (sq. mi.)	943.3
Altitude (ft.)	46-400
Rainfall (in.)	25.9
Jan. mean min.	43
July mean max.	97

Growing season (days)	303
Civ. Labor	2,885
Unemployed	9.6
Annual Wages	$33,158,102
Av. Weekly Wage	$327.79
Fed. Wages	$5,808,868

Ag. Net Cash Return	-$1,712,000
Prop. Value	$626,232,890
Retail Sales	$49,538,299

For explanation of sources, abbreviations and symbols, see p. 130.

Brown County

Physical Features: Rolling, hilly; drains to Colorado River; varied soils, timber.

Economy: Manufacturing plants, distribution center; government/services; agribusiness.

History: Apaches; displaced by Comanches who were removed by U.S. Army in 1874-75. Anglo-Americans first settled in mid-1850s. County created 1856 from Comanche, Travis counties, organized in 1857. Named for frontiersman Henry S. Brown.

Ethnicity, 1990: White, 30,267 (88.1%); Black, 1,552 (4.5%); American Indian, 131 (0.4%); Asian, 88 (0.3%); Other, 2,333 (6.8%). Hispanic, 3,799 (11.1%).

Vital Statistics, 1997: Births, 482; deaths, 463; marriages, 387; divorces, 142.

Recreation: State park; museum; fishing, hunting.

Minerals: Oil, gas, paving materials, gravel, clays.

Agriculture: Cattle, dairies, poultry, hay, peanuts, pecans, hogs, wheat. Market value $32.9 million.

BROWNWOOD (19,303) county seat; manufacturing, retail trade; distribution center; Howard Payne University, MacArthur Academy of Freedom; state substance abuse treatment center; state 4-H Club center; hospital; PecanFest in October.

Other towns include: **Bangs** (1,572); **Blanket** (443); **Brookesmith** (61); **Early** (2,619); **May** (285); **Zephyr** (198).

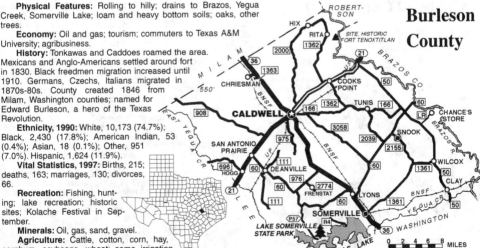

Population	37,175
Change fm '90	8.2
Area (sq. mi.)	956.9
Land Area (sq. mi.)	945.0
Altitude (ft.)	1,300-1,894
Rainfall (in.)	27.3
Jan. mean min.	33
July mean max.	97
Growing season (days)	242
Civ. Labor	16,724
Unemployed	4.9
Annual Wages	$263,196,041

Av. Weekly Wage | $434.31
Fed. Wages | $3,955,390

Ag. Net Cash Return | $3,698,000
Prop. Value | $1,323,235,130
Retail Sales | $328,311,220

Burleson County

Physical Features: Rolling to hilly; drains to Brazos, Yegua Creek, Somerville Lake; loam and heavy bottom soils; oaks, other trees.

Economy: Oil and gas; tourism; commuters to Texas A&M University; agribusiness.

History: Tonkawas and Caddoes roamed the area. Mexicans and Anglo-Americans settled around fort in 1830. Black freedmen migration increased until 1910. Germans, Czechs, Italians migrated in 1870s-80s. County created 1846 from Milam, Washington counties; named for Edward Burleson, a hero of the Texas Revolution.

Ethnicity, 1990: White, 10,173 (74.7%); Black, 2,430 (17.8%); American Indian, 53 (0.4%); Asian, 18 (0.1%); Other, 951 (7.0%). Hispanic, 1,624 (11.9%).

Vital Statistics, 1997: Births, 215; deaths, 163; marriages, 130; divorces, 66.

Recreation: Fishing, hunting; lake recreation; historic sites; Kolache Festival in September.

Minerals: Oil, gas, sand, gravel.

Agriculture: Cattle, cotton, corn, hay, sorghum, soybeans, wheat; some irrigation. Market value $27.4 million.

CALDWELL (3,820) county seat; agribusiness, oil & gas; manufacturing; tourism; hospitals, museum.

Somerville (1,660) tourism, railroad center, some manufacturing.

Other towns include: **Chriesman** (30); **Clay** (61); **Deanville** (130); **Lyons** (360); **Snook** (525).

Population	15,253
Change fm '90	11.9
Area (sq. mi.)	677.8
Land Area (sq. mi.)	665.6
Altitude (ft.)	200-550
Rainfall (in.)	39.1
Jan. mean min.	37
July mean max.	94
Growing season (days)	275

Civ. Labor	7,011
Unemployed	4.2
Annual Wages	$68,595,421
Av. Weekly Wage	$402.13
Fed. Wages	$1,695,525
Ag. Net Cash Return	-$2,265,000
Prop. Value	$931,279,520
Retail Sales	$94,417,739

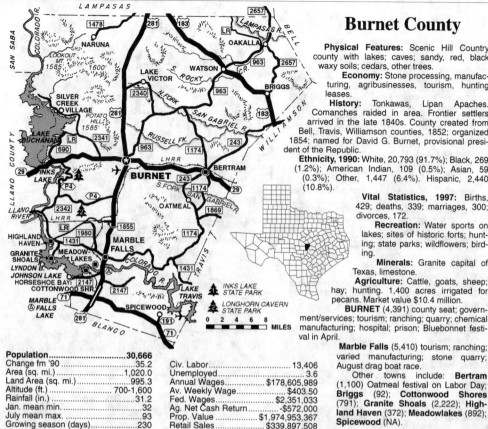

Burnet County

Physical Features: Scenic Hill Country county with lakes; caves; sandy, red, black waxy soils; cedars, other trees.

Economy: Stone processing, manufacturing, agribusinesses, tourism, hunting leases.

History: Tonkawas, Lipan Apaches. Comanches raided in area. Frontier settlers arrived in the late 1840s. County created from Bell, Travis, Williamson counties, 1852; organized 1854; named for David G. Burnet, provisional president of the Republic.

Ethnicity, 1990: White, 20,793 (91.7%); Black, 269 (1.2%); American Indian, 109 (0.5%); Asian, 59 (0.3%); Other, 1,447 (6.4%). Hispanic, 2,440 (10.8%).

Vital Statistics, 1997: Births, 429; deaths, 339; marriages, 300; divorces, 172.

Recreation: Water sports on lakes; sites of historic forts; hunting; state parks; wildflowers; birding.

Minerals: Granite capital of Texas, limestone.

Agriculture: Cattle, goats, sheep; hay; hunting. 1,400 acres irrigated for pecans. Market value $10.4 million.

BURNET (4,391) county seat; government/services; tourism; ranching; quarry; chemical manufacturing; hospital; prison; Bluebonnet festival in April.

Marble Falls (5,410) tourism; ranching; varied manufacturing; stone quarry; August drag boat race.

Other towns include: **Bertram** (1,100) Oatmeal festival on Labor Day; **Briggs** (92); **Cottonwood Shores** (791); **Granite Shoals** (2,222); **Highland Haven** (372); **Meadowlakes** (892); **Spicewood** (NA).

Population	30,666
Change fm '90	35.2
Area (sq. mi.)	1,020.0
Land Area (sq. mi.)	995.3
Altitude (ft.)	700-1,600
Rainfall (in.)	31.2
Jan. mean min.	32
July mean max.	93
Growing season (days)	230
Civ. Labor	13,406
Unemployed	3.6
Annual Wages	$178,605,989
Av. Weekly Wage	$403.50
Fed. Wages	$2,351,033
Ag. Net Cash Return	-$572,000
Prop. Value	$1,974,953,367
Retail Sales	$339,897,508

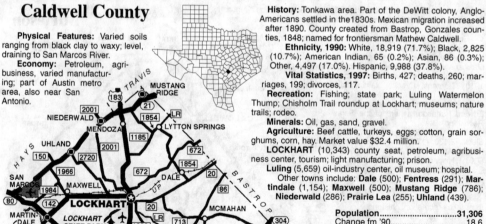

Caldwell County

Physical Features: Varied soils ranging from black clay to waxy; level, draining to San Marcos River.

Economy: Petroleum, agribusiness, varied manufacturing; part of Austin metro area, also near San Antonio.

History: Tonkawa area. Part of the DeWitt colony, Anglo-Americans settled in the 1830s. Mexican migration increased after 1890. County created from Bastrop, Gonzales counties, 1848; named for frontiersman Mathew Caldwell.

Ethnicity, 1990: White, 18,919 (71.7%); Black, 2,825 (10.7%); American Indian, 65 (0.2%); Asian, 86 (0.3%); Other, 4,497 (17.0%). Hispanic, 9,988 (37.8%).

Vital Statistics, 1997: Births, 427; deaths, 260; marriages, 199; divorces, 117.

Recreation: Fishing; state park; Luling Watermelon Thump; Chisholm Trail roundup at Lockhart; museums; nature trails; rodeo.

Minerals: Oil, gas, sand, gravel.

Agriculture: Beef cattle, turkeys, eggs; cotton, grain sorghums, corn, hay. Market value $32.4 million.

LOCKHART (10,343) county seat; petroleum, agribusiness center, tourism; light manufacturing; prison.

Luling (5,659) oil-industry center, oil museum; hospital.

Other towns include: **Dale** (500); **Fentress** (291); **Martindale** (1,154); **Maxwell** (500); **Mustang Ridge** (786); **Niederwald** (286); **Prairie Lea** (255); **Uhland** (439).

Population	31,306
Change fm '90	18.6
Area (sq. mi.)	547.3
Land Area (sq. mi.)	545.8
Altitude (ft.)	350-705
Rainfall (in.)	35.3
Jan. mean min.	36
July mean max.	96
Growing season (days)	275
Civ. Labor	16,063
Unemployed	3.7
Annual Wages	$121,104,020
Av. Weekly Wage	$371.01
Fed. Wages	$1,948,622
Ag. Net Cash Return	-$763,000
Prop. Value	$931,431,107
Retail Sales	$173,934,149

Calhoun County

Physical Features: Sandy, broken by bays; partly on Matagorda Island.

Economy: Aluminum manufacturing, plastics plant, marine construction, agribusinesses; petroleum; tourism; fish processing.

History: Karankawa area. Empresario Martín De León brought 41 families in 1825. County created from Jackson, Matagorda, Victoria counties, 1846. Named for John C. Calhoun, U.S. statesman.

Ethnicity, 1990: White, 14,819 (77.8%); Black, 556 (2.9%); American Indian, 35 (0.2%); Asian, 556 (2.9%); Other, 3,087 (16.2%). Hispanic, 6,893 (36.2%).

Vital Statistics, 1997: Births, 354; deaths, 168; marriages, 213; divorces, 103.

Recreation: Beaches, fishing, water sports, duck, goose hunting; historic sites, county park; La Salle Days in April.

Minerals: Oil, gas.

Agriculture: Cotton, cattle, corn, grain sorghum. Market value $20.5 million. Commercial fishing.

PORT LAVACA (12,137) county seat; commercial seafood operations; offshore drilling operations; tourist center; some manufacturing; convention center; hospital.

Other towns include: **Long Mott** (76); **Point Comfort** (1,116) aluminum, plastic plants, deepwater port; **Port O'Connor**, (1,184), tourist center; seafood processing; manufacturing; **Seadrift** (1,557).

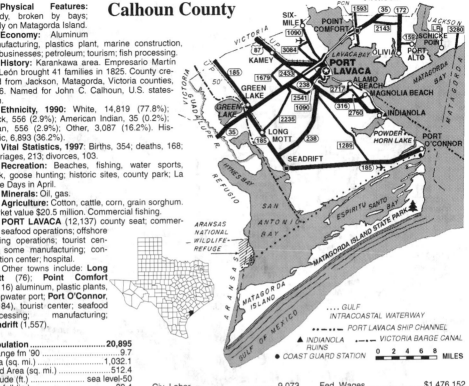

Population	20,895	
Change fm '90	9.7	
Area (sq. mi.)	1,032.1	
Land Area (sq. mi.)	512.4	
Altitude (ft.)	sea level-50	
Rainfall (in.)	39.4	
Jan. mean min.	46	
July mean max.	90	
Growing season (days)	300	

Civ. Labor	9,073	
Unemployed	7.0	
Annual Wages	$384,620,710	
Av. Weekly Wage	$715.92	

Fed. Wages	$1,476,152
Ag. Net Cash Return	$5,652,000
Prop. Value	$3,420,395,057
Retail Sales	$132,594,016

Callahan County

Physical Features: West Texas county on divide between Brazos, Colorado rivers; level to rolling.

Economy: Feed and fertilizer business; many residents commute to Abilene; 200,000 acres in hunting leases.

History: Comanche territory until 1870s. Anglo-American settlement began around 1860. County created 1858 from Bexar, Bosque, Travis counties; organized 1877. Named for Texas Ranger J.H. Callahan.

Ethnicity, 1990: White, 11,482 (96.8%); Black, 2 (0.0%); American Indian, 44 (0.4%); Asian, 40 (0.3%); Other, 291 (2.5%). Hispanic, 489 (4.1%).

Vital Statistics, 1997: Births, 148; deaths, 127; marriages, 64; divorces, 83.

Recreation: Hunting; museum; lake; Hunters' Supper at deer season.

Minerals: Oil and gas.

Agriculture: Cattle; wheat, dairy, hay, peanuts, sorghum; goats, horses. Market value $21 million.

BAIRD (1,870) county seat; ranching; antique shops; some manufacturing; shipping; hospital.

Clyde (3,449) manufacturing.

Other towns include: **Cross Plains** (1,070) government/services, agriculture, home of creator of Conan the Barbarian; **Putnam** (116).

Population	12,853
Change fm '90	8.4
Area (sq. mi.)	901.2
Land Area (sq. mi.)	898.7

Altitude (ft.)	1,400-2,204
Rainfall (in.)	25.2
Jan. mean min.	32
July mean max.	96
Growing season (days)	228
Civ. Labor	5,817
Unemployed	4.1

Annual Wages	$35,848,897
Av. Weekly Wage	$386.35
Fed. Wages	$1,009,732
Ag. Net Cash Return	$2,864,000
Prop. Value	$586,167,198
Retail Sales	$33,199,384

For explanation of sources, abbreviations and symbols, see p. 130.

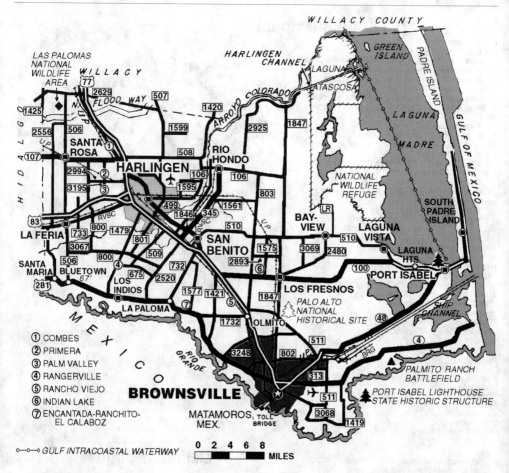

WILLACY COUNTY

LAS PALOMAS NATIONAL WILDLIFE AREA

HARLINGEN CHANNEL

GREEN ISLAND

PADRE ISLAND

GULF OF MEXICO

LAGUNA MADRE

NATIONAL WILDLIFE REFUGE

SOUTH PADRE ISLAND

LAGUNA VISTA

LAGUNA HTS.

PORT ISABEL

SANTA ROSA

HARLINGEN

RIO HONDO

BAY-VIEW

LA FERIA

SAN BENITO

SANTA MARIA BLUETOWN

LOS INDIOS

LOS FRESNOS

PALO ALTO NATIONAL HISTORICAL SITE

SHIP CHANNEL

LA PALOMA

OLMITO

PALMITO RANCH BATTLEFIELD

PORT ISABEL LIGHTHOUSE STATE HISTORIC STRUCTURE

BROWNSVILLE

MATAMOROS, MEX. TOLL BRIDGE

M E X I C O

RIO GRANDE

① COMBES
② PRIMERA
③ PALM VALLEY
④ RANGERVILLE
⑤ RANCHO VIEJO
⑥ INDIAN LAKE
⑦ ENCANTADA-RANCHITO-EL CALABOZ

o—o—o GULF INTRACOASTAL WATERWAY

0 2 4 6 8 MILES

Cameron County

Physical Features: Southernmost county in rich Rio Grande Valley soils; flat landscape; semitropical climate.

Economy: Agribusiness; tourism; seafood processing; shipping, manufacturing; government/services.

History: Coahuiltecan Indian area. Spanish land grants date to 1781. County created from Nueces County, 1848; named for Capt. Ewen Cameron of Mier Expedition.

Ethnicity, 1990: White, 214,424 (82.4%); Black, 825 (0.3%); American Indian, 413 (0.2%); Asian, 750 (0.3%); Other, 43,708 (16.8%). Hispanic, 212,995 (81.9%).

Vital Statistics, 1997: Births, 7,639; deaths, 1,904; marriages, 3,323; divorces, 706.

Recreation: South Padre Island: year-round resort; fishing, hunting, water sports; historical sites; gateway to Mexico, state parks; wildlife refuge; recreational vehicle center; Birding Festival in mid-November.

Minerals: Natural gas, oil.

Agriculture: Cotton top crop with grain sorghums, vegetables, and sugar cane raised; wholesale nursery plants raised; small feedlot and cow-calf operations; 200,000 acres irrigated, mostly cotton and grain sorghums. Market value $79.4 million.

BROWNSVILLE (136,187) county seat; varied industries, shipping, college, hospitals, crippled children health center; Gladys Porter Zoo; University of Texas at Brownsville.

Harlingen (56,657) government/services; hospitals; garment, apparel industries; agribusiness, college; Riofest in April.

San Benito (23,557) varied manufacturing, bottling; tourism; hospital; recreation facilities.

Other towns include: **Bayview** (300); **Combes** (2,650); **Indian Lake** (501); **La Feria** (5,736); **Laguna Vista** (1,591); **Los Fresnos** (2,920); **Los Indios** (206); **Lozano** (200); **Olmito** (200); **Palm Valley** (1,315).

Also, **Port Isabel** (5,217) tourist center, fishing, Shrimp Cook-Off on Columbus Day, lighthouse; **Primera** (2,816); **Rancho Viejo** (1,125); **Rangerville** (334); **Rio Hondo** (2,429); **Santa Maria** (210); **Santa Rosa** (2,901); **South Padre Island** (2,260).

Population	**318,737**
Change fm '90	22.5
Area (sq. mi.)	1,276.3
Land Area (sq. mi.)	905.6
Altitude (ft.)	sea level-67
Rainfall (in.)	26.6
Jan. mean min.	50
July mean max.	93
Growing season (days)	341
Civ. Labor	127,817
Unemployed	12.6
Annual Wages	$1,950,017,267
Av. Weekly Wage	$388.24
Fed. Wages	$94,828,554
Ag. Net Cash Return	$20,171,000
Prop. Value	$6,791,580,759
Retail Sales	$2,260,678,990

For explanation of sources, abbreviations and symbols, see p. 130.

Camp County

Physical Features: East Texas county with forested hills; drains to Cypress Creek on north; Lake O' the Pines, Lake Bob Sandlin; third smallest county in Texas.

Economy: Agribusiness, chicken processing; timber industries; light manufacturing; retirement center.

History: Caddo area. Anglo-American settlers arrived in late 1830s. Antebellum slaveholding area. County created from Upshur County 1874; named for jurist J.L. Camp.

Ethnicity, 1990: White, 7,130 (72.0%); Black, 2,360 (23.8%); American Indian, 35 (0.4%); Asian, 5 (0.1%); Other, 374 (3.8%). Hispanic, 501 (5.1%).

Vital Statistics, 1997: Births, 185; deaths, 142; marriages, 106; divorces, 46.

Recreation: Water sports, fishing on lakes; Chick Fest in April.

Minerals: Oil, gas, clays, coal.

Agriculture: Poultry and products important; beef, dairy cattle, horses; peaches, hay, blueberries, vegetables. Market value $150.7 million. Forestry.

PITTSBURG (4,454) county seat; agribusiness; timber; tourism; food processing; light manufacturing; community college; Prayer Tower.

Other towns include: **Leesburg** (115) and **Rocky Mound** (60).

Population	10,850
Change fm '90	9.6
Area (sq. mi.)	203.1
Land Area (sq. mi.)	197.5
Altitude (ft.)	277-538
Rainfall (in.)	43.3
Jan. mean min.	32
July mean max.	94
Growing season (days)	238
Civ. Labor	5,548
Unemployed	8.1
Annual Wages	$78,986,858
Av. Weekly Wage	$386.45
Fed. Wages	$1,065,142
Ag. Net Cash Return	$11,754,000
Prop. Value	$429,363,303
Retail Sales	$77,372,786

Carson County

Physical Features: In center of Panhandle on level, some broken land; loam soils.

Economy: Pantex nuclear weapons assembly/disassembly facility (U.S. Department of Energy), commuting to Amarillo, petrochemical plants; agribusiness.

History: Apaches, displaced by Comanches. Anglo-American ranchers settled in 1880s. German, Polish farmers arrived around 1910. County created from Bexar District, 1876; organized 1888. Named for Republic secretary of state S.P. Carson.

Ethnicity, 1990: White, 6,315 (96.0%); Black, 11 (0.2%); American Indian, 44 (0.7%); Asian, 9 (0.1%); Other, 197 (3.0%). Hispanic, 354 (5.4%).

Vital Statistics, 1997: Births, 69; deaths, 64; marriages, 50; divorces, 32.

Recreation: Museum, sausage festivals.

Minerals: Oil, gas production.

Agriculture: Wheat, cattle, sorghum, corn, soybeans; row, sprinkler irrigation. Market value $72.5 million.

PANHANDLE (2,275) county seat; agribusiness, petroleum center; government/services; Veterans Day celebration.

Other towns include: **Groom** (641), **Skellytown** (694), **White Deer** (1,231).

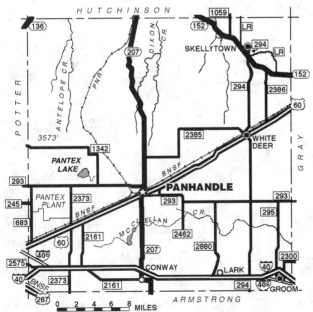

Population	6,688
Change fm '90	1.7
Area (sq. mi.)	924.1
Land Area (sq. mi.)	923.2
Altitude (ft.)	3,000-3,573
Rainfall (in.)	20.8
Jan. mean min.	22
July mean max.	93
Growing season (days)	191
Civ. Labor	3,136
Unemployed	3.9
Annual Wages	$212,565,047
Av. Weekly Wage	$791.99
Fed. Wages	$12,163,363
Ag. Net Cash Return	$13,816,000
Prop. Value	$795,067,960
Retail Sales	$22,478,601

For explanation of sources, abbreviations and symbols, see p. 130.

Cass County

Population	31,206
Change fm '90	4.1
Area (sq. mi.)	960.3
Land Area (sq. mi.)	937.5
Altitude (ft.)	200-600
Rainfall (in.)	48.3
Jan. mean min.	31
July mean max.	93
Growing season (days)	237
Civ. Labor	15,572

Unemployed	8.7
Annual Wages	$212,565,047
Av. Weekly Wage	$456.22
Fed. Wages	$2,278,214
Ag. Net Cash Return	$4,316,000
Prop. Value	$1,476,650,481
Retail Sales	$202,898,593

Physical Features: Forested Northeast county rolling to hilly; drained by Cypress Bayou, Sulphur River.

Economy: Government/services; timber; agribusiness; paper production.

History: Caddoes, displaced by other tribes in 1790s. Anglo-Americans arrived in 1830s. Antebellum slaveholding area. County created 1846 from Bowie County; named for U.S. Sen. Lewis Cass.

Ethnicity, 1990: White, 23,651 (78.9%); Black, 6,057 (20.2%); American Indian, 105 (0.4%); Asian, 25 (0.1%); Other, 144 (0.5%). Hispanic, 373 (1.2%).

Vital Statistics, 1997: Births, 371; deaths, 430; marriages, 223; divorces, 176.

Recreation: Fishing, hunting, water sports; state, county parks; lake, wildflower trails.

Minerals: Oil, iron ore.

Agriculture: Poultry, cattle; nursery; forage; watermelons. Market value $22.7 million. Timber important.

LINDEN (2,389) county seat, wood-treating plants, timber, oldest courthouse still in use as courthouse, hospital.

ATLANTA (6,219) varied manufacturing, timber, cattle, two hospitals.

Other towns include: **Avinger** (509); **Bivins** (195); **Bloomburg** (388); **Domino** (108); **Douglassville** (213); **Hughes Springs** (2,104) varied manufacturing, warehousing; **Kildare** (49); **Marietta** (184); **McLeod** (230); **Queen City** (1,995).

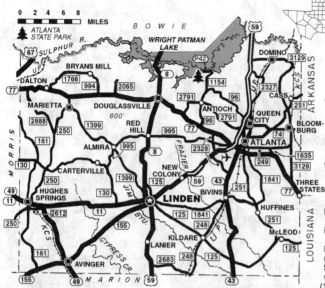

Castro County

Physical Features: Flat northwest county, drains to creeks, draws and playas; underground water.

Economy: Agribusiness.

History: Apaches, displaced by Comanches in 1720s. Anglo-American ranchers began settling in 1880s. Germans settled after 1900. Mexican migration increased after 1950. County created 1876 from Bexar, organized 1891. Named for Henri Castro, Texas colonizer.

Ethnicity, 1990: White, 5,526 (60.9%); Black, 261 (2.9%); American Indian, 10 (0.1%); Asian, 15 (0.2%); Other, 3,258 (35.9%). Hispanic, 4,187 (46.2%).

Vital Statistics, 1997: Births, 139; deaths, 62; marriages, 46; divorces, 29.

Recreation: Pheasant hunting; Harvest Days celebrated in August; Italian POW camp site.

Minerals: Not significant.

Agriculture: Fed, stocker cattle; corn, cotton, wheat, sheep. Market value $668.4 million; ranked first in state, 19th in nation.

DIMMITT (4,309) county seat; agribusiness center; library, geriatric-care facility; Fiestas Patrias in September.

Other towns include: **Hart** (1,230), **Nazareth** (330), **Summerfield** (60).

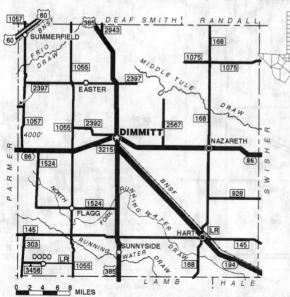

Population	8,678
Change fm '90	-4.3
Area (sq. mi.)	899.3
Land Area (sq. mi.)	898.4
Altitude (ft.)	3,600-4,000
Rainfall (in.)	18.0
Jan. mean min.	19
July mean max.	91
Growing season (days)	193
Civ. Labor	4,276
Unemployed	4.5
Annual Wages	$50,816,791
Av. Weekly Wage	$389.79
Fed. Wages	$876,297
Ag. Net Cash Return	$137,523,000
Prop. Value	$479,600,025
Retail Sales	$47,551,796

For explanation of sources, abbreviations and symbols, see p. 130.

Chambers County

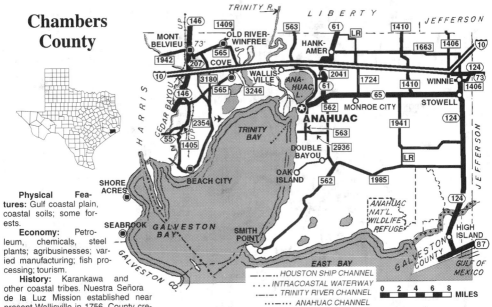

Physical Features:
Gulf coastal plain, coastal soils; some forests.

Economy: Petroleum, chemicals, steel plants; agribusinesses; varied manufacturing; fish processing; tourism.

History: Karankawa and other coastal tribes. Nuestra Señora de la Luz Mission established near present Wallisville in 1756. County created 1858 from Liberty, Jefferson counties. Named for Gen. T. J. Chambers, surveyor.

Ethnicity, 1990: White, 16,725 (83.3%); Black, 2,550 (12.7%); American Indian, 53 (0.3%); Asian, 116 (0.6%); Other, 644 (3.2%). Hispanic, 1,195 (5.9%).

Vital Statistics, 1997: Births, 306; deaths, 152; marriages, 156; divorces, 135.

Recreation: Fishing, hunting; water sports; camping; county parks; wildlife refuge; historic sites; Wallisville Heritage Park; Texas Rice Festival, Texas Gatorfest in September.

Minerals: Oil, gas, salt, clays, sand and gravel.

Agriculture: Rice, soybeans; cattle; nursery; significant irrigation. Market value $15.7 million. Timber important.

ANAHUAC (2,220) county seat; canal connects with Houston Ship Channel; agribusiness; hospital.

Winnie (2,653) fertilizer manufacturing; wholesale greenhouse; medical center; depot museum.

Other towns include: **Beach City** (1,195), **Cove** (528), **Hankamer** (525), **Monroe City** (90), **Mont Belvieu** (1,824), **Old River-Winfree** (1,512), **Stowell** (1,814) and **Wallisville** (460).

Population	25,401
Change fm '90	26.4
Area (sq. mi.)	868.5
Land Area (sq. mi.)	599.4
Altitude (ft.)	sea level-73
Rainfall (in.)	51.7
Jan. mean min.	41
July mean max.	92
Growing season (days)	261
Civ. Labor	11,930
Unemployed	4.2
Annual Wages	$210,251,582
Av. Weekly Wage	$632.56
Fed. Wages	$1,958,478
Ag. Net Cash Return	$1,908,000
Prop. Value	$3,479,175,130
Retail Sales	$445,181,059

Ships line up in Galveston Bay to enter the Houston Ship Channel. AP/The Dallas Morning News file photo.

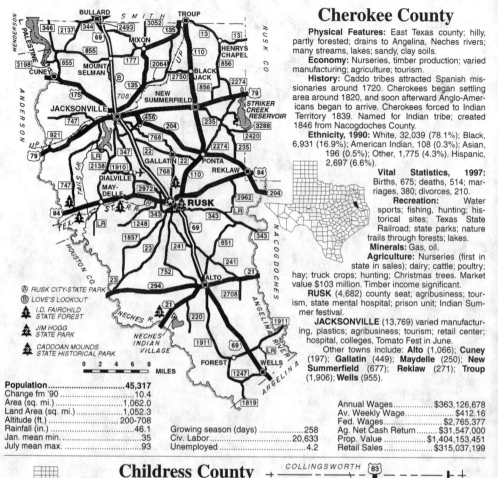

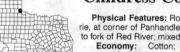

Cherokee County

Physical Features: East Texas county; hilly, partly forested; drains to Angelina, Neches rivers; many streams, lakes; sandy, clay soils.

Economy: Nurseries, timber production; varied manufacturing; agriculture; tourism.

History: Caddo tribes attracted Spanish missionaries around 1720. Cherokees began settling area around 1820, and soon afterward Anglo-Americans began to arrive. Cherokees forced to Indian Territory 1839. Named for Indian tribe; created 1846 from Nacogdoches County.

Ethnicity, 1990: White, 32,039 (78.1%); Black, 6,931 (16.9%); American Indian, 108 (0.3%); Asian, 196 (0.5%); Other, 1,775 (4.3%). Hispanic, 2,697 (6.6%).

Vital Statistics, 1997: Births, 675; deaths, 514; marriages, 380; divorces, 210.

Recreation: Water sports; fishing, hunting; historical sites; Texas State Railroad; state parks; nature trails through forests; lakes.

Minerals: Gas, oil.

Agriculture: Nurseries (first in state in sales); dairy; cattle; poultry; hay; truck crops; hunting; Christmas trees. Market value $103 million. Timber income significant.

RUSK (4,682) county seat; agribusiness; tourism, state mental hospital; prison unit; Indian Summer festival.

JACKSONVILLE (13,769) varied manufacturing, plastics; agribusiness; tourism; retail center; hospital, colleges, Tomato Fest in June.

Other towns include: **Alto** (1,066); **Cuney** (197); **Gallatin** (449); **Maydelle** (250); **New Summerfield** (677); **Reklaw** (271); **Troup** (1,906); **Wells** (955).

Population	45,317
Change fm '90	10.4
Area (sq. mi.)	1,062.0
Land Area (sq. mi.)	1,052.3
Altitude (ft.)	200-708
Rainfall (in.)	46.1
Jan. mean min.	35
July mean max.	93
Growing season (days)	258
Civ. Labor	20,633
Unemployed	4.2

Annual Wages	$363,126,678
Av. Weekly Wage	$412.16
Fed. Wages	$2,765,377
Ag. Net Cash Return	$31,547,000
Prop. Value	$1,404,153,451
Retail Sales	$315,037,199

Map legend:
- (A) RUSK CITY-STATE PARK
- (B) LOVE'S LOOKOUT
- I.D. FAIRCHILD STATE FOREST
- JIM HOGG STATE PARK
- CADDOAN MOUNDS STATE HISTORICAL PARK

Childress County

Physical Features: Rolling prairie, at corner of Panhandle, draining to fork of Red River; mixed soils.

Economy: Cotton; government/services; tourism.

History: Apaches, displaced by Comanches. Ranchers arrived around 1880. County created 1876 from Bexar, Young districts; organized 1887; named for author of Texas Declaration of Independence, George C. Childress.

Ethnicity, 1990: White, 4,969 (83.5%); Black, 321 (5.4%); American Indian, 26 (0.4%); Asian, 17 (0.3%); Other, 620 (10.4%). Hispanic, 853 (14.3%).

Vital Statistics, 1997: Births, 93; deaths, 108; marriages, 80; divorces, 26.

Recreation: Recreation on lakes and creek, fishing, hunting of deer, turkey, wild hog, quail, dove; parks; county museum.

Agriculture: Cotton, beef cattle, wheat, hay, sorghum, hunting; 10 percent irrigated. Market value $19.3 million.

CHILDRESS (4,971) county seat; varied manufacturing, hospital, high school all-star football game; settlers reunion; prison unit. Other towns include: **Tell** (63).

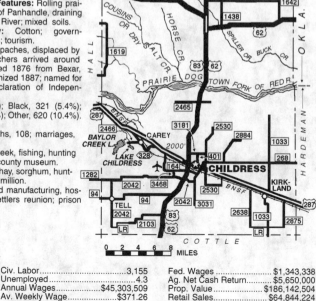

Population	7,411
Change fm '90	24.5
Area (sq. mi.)	713.5
Land Area (sq. mi.)	710.4
Altitude (ft.)	1,600-2,000
Rainfall (in.)	20.7
Jan. mean min.	26
July mean max.	96
Growing season (days)	217
Civ. Labor	3,155
Unemployed	4.3
Annual Wages	$45,303,509
Av. Weekly Wage	$371.26

Fed. Wages	$1,343,338
Ag. Net Cash Return	$5,650,000
Prop. Value	$186,142,504
Retail Sales	$64,844,224

Clay County

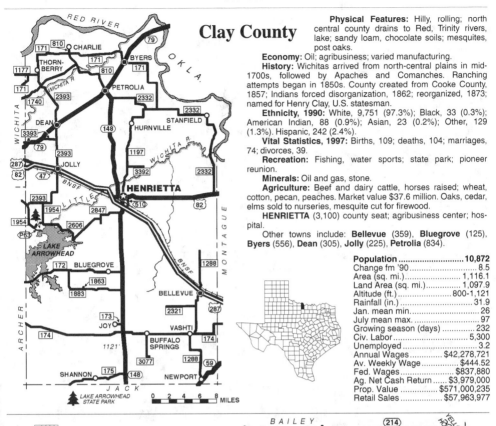

Physical Features: Hilly, rolling; north central county drains to Red, Trinity rivers, lake; sandy loam, chocolate soils; mesquites, post oaks.

Economy: Oil; agribusiness; varied manufacturing.

History: Wichitas arrived from north-central plains in mid-1700s, followed by Apaches and Comanches. Ranching attempts began in 1850s. County created from Cooke County, 1857; Indians forced disorganization, 1862; reorganized, 1873; named for Henry Clay, U.S. statesman.

Ethnicity, 1990: White, 9,751 (97.3%); Black, 33 (0.3%); American Indian, 88 (0.9%); Asian, 23 (0.2%); Other, 129 (1.3%). Hispanic, 242 (2.4%).

Vital Statistics, 1997: Births, 109; deaths, 104; marriages, 74; divorces, 39.

Recreation: Fishing, water sports; state park; pioneer reunion.

Minerals: Oil and gas, stone.

Agriculture: Beef and dairy cattle, horses raised; wheat, cotton, pecan, peaches. Market value $37.6 million. Oaks, cedar, elms sold to nurseries, mesquite cut for firewood.

HENRIETTA (3,100) county seat; agribusiness center; hospital.

Other towns include: **Bellevue** (359), **Bluegrove** (125), **Byers** (556), **Dean** (305), **Jolly** (225), **Petrolia** (834).

Population	**10,872**
Change fm '90	8.5
Area (sq. mi.)	1,116.1
Land Area (sq. mi.)	1,097.9
Altitude (ft.)	800-1,121
Rainfall (in.)	31.9
Jan. mean min.	26
July mean max.	97
Growing season (days)	232
Civ. Labor	5,300
Unemployed	3.2
Annual Wages	$42,278,721
Av. Weekly Wage	$444.52
Fed. Wages	$837,880
Ag. Net Cash Return	$3,979,000
Prop. Value	$571,000,235
Retail Sales	$57,963,977

Cochran County

Physical Features: South Plains bordering New Mexico with small lakes (playas); underground water; loam, sandy loam soils.

Economy: Agribusiness, government/services, oil.

History: Hunting area for various Indian tribes. Ranches operated in 1880s but population in 1900 was still only 25. Farming began in 1920s. County created from Bexar, Young districts, 1876; organized 1924; named for Robert Cochran, who died at the Alamo.

Ethnicity 1990: White, 2,997 (68.5%); Black, 234 (5.3%); American Indian, 13 (0.3%); Asian, 1 (0.0%); Other, 1,132 (25.9%). Hispanic, 1,857 (42.4%).

Vital Statistics, 1997: Births, 42; deaths, 39; marriages, 29; divorces, 24.

Recreation: Rodeo; Last Frontier days in July; museum.

Minerals: Oil, gas.

Agriculture: Cotton, sorghum, wheat, peanuts, sunflowers (first in state in acres). Crops 60 percent irrigated. Cattle, swine, sheep. Market value $51.3 million.

MORTON (2,421) county seat; oil, farm center, meat packing; light manufacture; hospital.

Other towns include: **Bledsoe** (125), **Whiteface** (466).

Population	**4,050**
Change fm '90	-7.5
Area (sq. mi.)	775.2
Land Area (sq. mi.)	775.2

For explanation of sources, abbreviations and symbols, see p. 130.

Altitude (ft.)	3,600-4,000
Rainfall (in.)	18.6
Jan. temp. min.	22
July temp. max.	91
Growing season (days)	189
Civ. Labor	1,501
Unemployed	5.6

Annual Wages	$20,687,193
Av. Weekly Wage	$387.56
Fed. Wages	$561,406
Ag. Net Cash Return	$17,974,000
Prop. Value	$533,886,650
Retail Sales	$22,761,649

Coke County

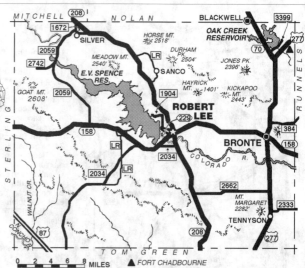

Physical Features: West Texas prairie, hills, Colorado River valley; sandy loam, red soils; reservoir.

Economy: Oil-well supplies, agribusiness, tourism.

History: From 1700 to 1870s, Comanches roamed the area. Ranches began operating after the Civil War. County created 1889 from Tom Green County; named for Gov. Richard Coke.

Ethnicity, 1990: White, 3,222 (94.1%); Black, 6 (0.2%); American Indian, 17 (0.5%); Asian, 2 (0.1%); Other, 177 (5.2%). Hispanic, 422 (12.3%).

Vital Statistics, 1997: Births, 30; deaths, 60; marriages, 21; divorces, 17.

Recreation: Hunting, fishing; lakes; historic sites, county museum; Ole Coke County Pageant, July 4.

Minerals: Oil, gas, sand, gravel.

Agriculture: Cattle; sheep, goats; small grain; some irrigation for hay. Market value $8 million.

ROBERT LEE (1,297) county seat; petroleum center, ranching.

Bronte (950) ranching, oil.

Other towns include: **Blackwell** (381), **Silver** (60) and **Tennyson** (35).

Population	3,586
Change fm '90	4.7
Area (sq. mi.)	927.9
Land Area (sq. mi.)	898.9
Altitude (ft.)	1,700-2,608
Rainfall (in.)	23.2
Jan. mean min.	28
July mean max.	96
Growing season (days)	226
Civ. Labor	1,492
Unemployed	3.4
Annual Wages	$20,106,638
Av. Weekly Wage	$392.79
Fed. Wages	$437,308
Ag. Net Cash Return	- $3,355,000
Prop. Value	$317,707,850
Retail Sales	$25,841,133

Coleman County

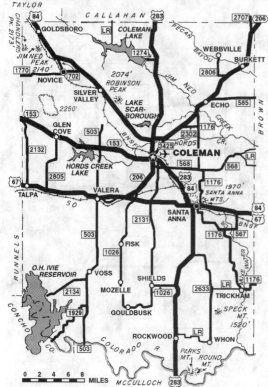

Physical Features: Hilly, rolling; drains to Colorado River, Pecan Bayou; lakes; mesquite, oaks.

Economy: Agribusiness, petroleum, tile plant, varied manufacturing.

History: Presence of Apaches and Comanches brought military outpost, Camp Colorado, before the Civil War. Settlers arrived after organization. County created 1858 from Brown, Travis counties; organized 1864; named for Houston's aide, R.M. Coleman.

Ethnicity, 1990: White, 8,995 (92.6%); Black, 246 (2.5%); American Indian, 29 (0.3%); Asian, 7 (0.1%); Other, 433 (4.5%). Hispanic, 1,139 (11.7%).

Vital Statistics, 1997: Births, 116; deaths, 175; marriages, 99; divorces, 52.

Recreation: Fishing, hunting; water sports; city park, historic sites; lakes; Santa Anna Peak.

Minerals: Oil, gas, stone, clays.

Agriculture: Cattle, wheat, sheep, hay, grain sorghum, goats, oats, cotton. Market value $20.8 million. Mesquite for firewood and furniture.

COLEMAN (5,379) county seat; clay tile, furniture, other manufacturing; agribusiness center; hospital, museum, Fiesta de la Paloma in October.

Santa Anna (1,233) agribusiness; some manufacturing; tourism.

Other towns include: **Burkett** (30), **Goldsboro** (30), **Gouldbusk** (70), **Novice** (194), **Rockwood** (80), **Talpa** (127), **Valera** (80), **Voss** (20) and **Whon** (15).

Population	9,951
Change fm '90	2.5
Area (sq. mi.)	1,281.5
Land Area (sq. mi.)	1,272.9
Altitude (ft.)	1,400-2,250
Rainfall (in.)	28.0
Jan. mean min.	32
July mean max.	96
Growing season (days)	235
Civ. Labor	3,566
Unemployed	10.0
Annual Wages	$40,699,306
Av. Weekly Wage	$325.94
Fed. Wages	$1,367,234
Ag. Net Cash Return	$538,000
Prop. Value	$460,213,589
Retail Sales	$53,898,305

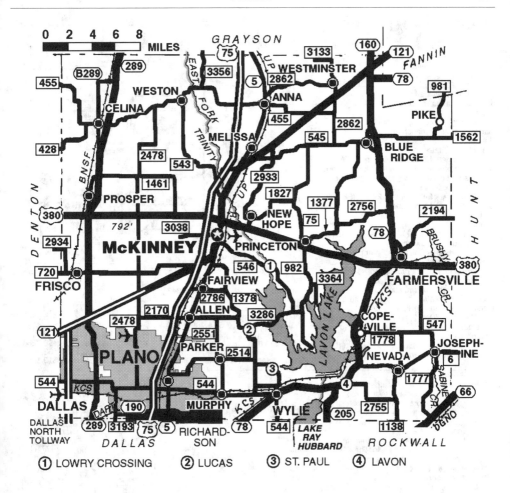

0 2 4 6 8 MILES

① LOWRY CROSSING   ② LUCAS   ③ ST. PAUL   ④ LAVON

Collin County

Physical Features: North Texas county with heavy, black clay soil; level to rolling; drains to Trinity, Lavon Lake.

Economy: Varied manufacturing plants, agribusinesses, retail and wholesale center; government/services; many residents work in Dallas.

History: Caddo area until 1850s. Settlers of Peters colony arrived in early 1840s. County created from Fannin County 1846. Named for pioneer settler Collin McKinney.

Ethnicity, 1990: White, 235,290 (89.1%); Black, 10,925 (4.1%); American Indian, 1,112 (0.4%); Asian, 7,480 (2.8%); Other, 9,229 (3.5%). Hispanic, 18,158 (6.9%).

Vital Statistics, 1997: Births, 6,814; deaths, 1,451; marriages, 3,664; divorces, 1,878.

Recreation: Fishing, water sports; historic sites; old homes restoration, tours; natural science museum; hot-air balloon festival.

Minerals: Limited stone production.

Agriculture: Cattle; greenhouse; wheat, grain sorghum, corn, hay, cotton; horses, sheep. Market value $34 million.

For explanation of sources, abbreviations and symbols, see p. 130.

McKINNEY (34,979) county seat; agribusiness, trade center; varied industry; hospital; museums.

PLANO (198,186) telecommunications; manufacturing; newspaper printing; medical services, research center; community college; commercial and financial center; hospitals.

Other towns include: **Allen** (32,501); **Anna** (1,159); **Blue Ridge** (608); **Celina** (2,127); **Copeville** (106); **Fairview** (3,010); **Farmersville** (3,607) agribusiness, light industries; **Frisco**

(17,798) technical, areospace industry, community college.

Also, **Josephine** (723); **Lavon** (437); **Lowry Crossing** (1,165); **Lucas** (3,472); **Melissa** (898); **Murphy** (2,553); **Nevada** (674); **New Hope** (592); **Parker** (1,698); **Princeton** (3,355); **Prosper** (1,465); **St. Paul** (613); **Westminster** (572); **Weston** (507); **Wylie** (11,760).

Population	**416,620**
Change fm '90	57.8
Area (sq. mi.)	885.8
Land Area (sq. mi.)	847.7
Altitude (ft.)	434-792
Rainfall (in.)	40.0
Jan. mean min.	32
July mean max.	95
Growing season (days)	230
Civ. Labor	251,999
Unemployed	2.1
Annual Wages	$5,031,901,615
Av. Weekly Wage	$701.65
Fed. Wages	$31,397,694
Ag. Net Cash Return	$2,942,000
Prop. Value	$28,245,617,651
Retail Sales	$6,147,852,367

Collingsworth County

Physical Features: Panhandle county of rolling, broken terrain, draining to Red River forks; sandy and loam soils.

Economy: Chiefly agribusiness, varied manufacturing.

History: Apaches, displaced by Comanches. Ranchers from England arrived in late 1870s. County created 1876, from Bexar and Young districts, organized 1890. Named for Republic of Texas' first chief justice, James Collinsworth (name misspelled in law).

Ethnicity, 1990: White, 2,977 (83.3%); Black, 230 (6.4%); American Indian, 32 (0.9%); Asian, 3 (0.1%); Other, 331 (9.3%). Hispanic, 561 (15.7%).

Vital Statistics, 1997: Births, 38; deaths, 51; marriages, 48; divorces, 7.

Recreation: Children's camp, county museum, peanut festival; pioneer park.

Minerals: Gas, oil production.

Agriculture: Peanuts (second in state in acreage), cotton, wheat, alfalfa; cow-calf operation, stocker cattle; 18,000 acres irrigated. Market value $30.6 million.

WELLINGTON (2,316) county seat; peanut-processing plants, varied manufacturing; agriculture; hospital.

Other towns include: **Dodson** (104), **Quail** (92), **Samnorwood** (110).

Population	3,343
Change fm '90	-6.4
Area (sq. mi.)	919.4
Land Area (sq. mi.)	918.8
Altitude (ft.)	1,789-2,600
Rainfall (in.)	21.5
Jan. mean min.	26
July mean max.	97
Growing season (days)	212
Civ. Labor	1,557
Unemployed	1.7
Annual Wages	$15,835,016
Av. Weekly Wage	$350.36
Fed. Wages	$715,172
Ag. Net Cash Return	$8,726,000
Prop. Value	$153,052,900
Retail Sales	$10,589,745

Colorado County

Physical Features: South central county in three soil areas; level to rolling; bisected by Colorado River; oaks.

Economy: Agribusiness; oil-field services and equipment manufacturing; plants process minerals.

History: Karankawa and other tribes. Anglo settlers among Stephen F. Austin's Old Three Hundred families. First German settlers arrived around 1840. Antebellum slaveholding area. County created 1836, organized 1837; named for river.

Ethnicity, 1990: White, 13,352 (72.6%); Black, 3,118 (17.0%); American Indian, 30 (0.2%); Asian, 16 (0.1%); Other, 1,867 (10.2%). Hispanic, 2,833 (15.4%).

Vital Statistics, 1997: Births, 263; deaths, 261; marriages, 143; divorces, 82.

Recreation: Hunting, historic sites; prairie chicken refuge; opera house in Columbus.

Minerals: Gas, oil, uranium.

Agriculture: Rice (second in state in acres, sales), cattle, nursery, corn, poultry, hay, sorghum; significant irrigation for rice. Market value $53.3 million. Cedar, pine marketed.

COLUMBUS (3,827) county seat; agribusiness center; oil-field servicing; tourism; hospital; historical sites, homes, walking tour.

Eagle Lake (3,826) rice drying center, wildflower celebration; goose hunting; hospital.

Weimar (2,238) feed mill, light industry, sausage company; hospital; "Gedenke" celebration in May.

Other towns include: **Alleyton** (165), **Altair** (30), **Freisburg** (75), **Garwood** (975), **Glidden** (255), **Nada** (165), **Oakland** (80), **Rock Island** (160), **Sheridan** (225).

Population	19,612
Change fm '90	6.7
Area (sq. mi.)	973.6
Land Area (sq. mi.)	963.0
Altitude (ft.)	150-450
Rainfall (in.)	41.8
Jan. mean min.	37
July mean max.	95
Growing season (days)	280
Civ. Labor	8,135
Unemployed	3.9
Annual Wages	$120,995,523
Av. Weekly Wage	$390.60
Fed. Wages	$2,042,551
Ag. Net Cash Return	$11,426,000
Prop. Value	$1,341,015,104
Retail Sales	$188,913,150

Inner-tubers fill the Guadalupe River near New Braunfels. AP/The Dallas Morning News file photo.

Comal County

Population	**72,354**
Change fm '90	39.6
Area (sq. mi.)	574.5
Land Area (sq. mi.)	561.5
Altitude (ft.)	600-1,473
Rainfall (in.)	34.3
Jan. mean min.	37
July mean max.	95
Growing season (days)	261
Civ. Labor	37,250
Unemployed	2.7
Annual Wages	$554,071,989
Av. Weekly Wage	$417.86
Fed. Wages	$7,320,872
Ag. Net Cash Return	-$1,355,000
Prop. Value	$4,469,242,733
Retail Sales	$2,153,627,653

Physical Features: Scenic Southwest county of hills. Eighty percent above Balcones Escarpment. Spring-fed streams; 2.5-mile-long Comal River, Guadalupe River; Canyon Lake.

Economy: Varied manufacturing; tourism; government/services; county in San Antonio metropolitan area.

History: Tonkawa, Waco Indians. A pioneer German settlement 1845. Mexican migration peaked during Mexican Revolution. County created from Bexar, Gonzales, Travis counties and organized in 1846; named for river, a name for Spanish earthenware or metal pan used for cooking tortillas.

Ethnicity, 1990: White, 46,821 (90.3%); Black, 443 (0.9%); American Indian, 148 (0.3%); Asian, 164 (0.3%); Other, 4,256 (8.2%). Hispanic, 11,864 (22.9%).

Vital Statistics, 1997: Births, 959; deaths, 660; marriages, 728; divorces, 276.

Recreation: Fishing, hunting; historic sites, Hummel museum; scenic drives; lake facilities; Prince Solms Park, other county parks; Landa Park with 76 species of trees; Gruene historic area; caverns; river resorts; river tubing; Schlitterbahn water park; Wurstfest in October-November.

Minerals: Stone, lime, sand and gravel.

Agriculture: Cattle, sheep, goats, hogs; nursery, hay, corn, sorghum, wheat. Market value $5.2 million.

NEW BRAUNFELS (35,663) county seat; manufacturing; retail, distribution; one of the most picturesque cities in Texas, making it a tourist center; Conservation Plaza; rose garden; hospital; library; mental health and retardation center. **Gruene** is now part of New Braunfels.

Other towns include: **Bulverde** (500), **Fair Oaks Ranch** (3,734), **Fischer** (20), **Garden Ridge** (2,206), **Schertz** (15,364), **Spring Branch** (200), and the retirement community around **Canyon Lake** (12,988).

◆ *NATURAL BRIDGE CAVERNS*

🌲 *GUADALUPE RIVER STATE PARK*

▨ *HONEY CREEK STATE NATURAL AREA*

0 2 4 6 8 MILES

For explanation of sources, abbreviations and symbols, see p. 130.

Comanche County

Physical Features: West central county with rolling, hilly terrain; sandy, loam, waxy soils; drains to Leon River, Proctor Lake; pecans, oaks, mesquites, cedars.

Economy: Dairies, other agribusiness; Peanut- and pecan-shelling plants; food processing; manufacturing.

History: Comanche area. Anglo-American settlers arrived in 1854 on land granted earlier to Stephen F. Austin and Samuel May Williams. County created 1856 from Bosque, Coryell counties; named for Indian tribe.

Ethnicity, 1990: White, 12,297 (91.9%); Black, 16 (0.1%); American Indian, 51 (0.4%); Asian, 8 (0.1%); Other, 1,009 (7.5%). Hispanic, 2,205 (16.5%).

Vital Statistics, 1997: Births, 167; deaths, 192; marriages, 90; divorces, 62.

Recreation: Hunting, fishing, water sports; museum, parks, community center, museums; Comanche Pow-Wow in September, rodeo in July.

Minerals: Limited gas, oil, stone, clay.

Agriculture: Dairy (third in state in sales), cattle, swine, sheep, goats; peanuts, hay, pecans, fruit; 38,000 acres irrigated. Market value $94.2 million.

COMANCHE (4,675) county seat; plants process feed, food; varied manufacturing; agribusiness; hospital; Ranger College branch; library; state's oldest courthouse, "Old Cora," on display on town square.

De Leon (2,370) marketing center for peanuts, pecans.

Other towns include: **Energy** (65), **Gustine** (499), **Hasse** (43), **Proctor** (220), and **Sidney** (196).

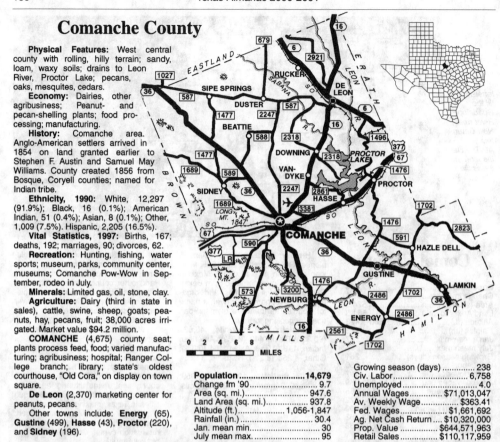

Population	14,679
Change fm '90	9.7
Area (sq. mi.)	947.6
Land Area (sq. mi.)	937.8
Altitude (ft.)	1,056-1,847
Rainfall (in.)	30.4
Jan. mean min.	30
July mean max.	95

Growing season (days)	238
Civ. Labor	6,758
Unemployed	4.0
Annual Wages	$71,013,047
Av. Weekly Wage	$363.41
Fed. Wages	$1,661,692
Ag. Net Cash Return	$10,320,000
Prop. Value	$644,571,963
Retail Sales	$110,117,959

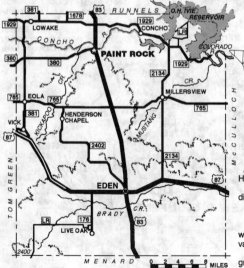

Concho County

Physical Features: West central county on Edwards Plateau, rough, broken to south; level in north; sandy, loam and dark soils; drains to creeks and Colorado River.

Economy: Agribusinesses.

History: Athabascan-speaking Plains Indians, then Jumanos in 1600s, absorbed by Lipan Apaches 1700s. Comanches raided after 1800. Anglo-Americans began ranching around 1850; farming after the Civil War. Mexican-Americans employed on sheep ranches 1920s-30s. County created from Bexar District, 1858, organized 1879; named for river.

Ethnicity, 1990: White, 2,718 (89.3%); Black, 16 (0.5%); American Indian, 5 (0.2%); Asian, 5 (0.2%); Other, 300 (9.9%). Hispanic, 1,194 (39.2%).

Vital Statistics, 1997: Births, 26; deaths, 55; marriages, 13; divorces, 12.

Recreation: Famed for 1,500 Indian pictographs; reservoir.

Minerals: Oil, gas, stone.

Agriculture: Sheep (fifth in state in inventory); cattle, goats; wheat, feed grains; 10,000 acres irrigated for cotton. Market value $19.8 million.

PAINT ROCK (204) county seat; named for Indian pictographs nearby; farming, ranching center.

EDEN (1,675) steel fabrication, detention center; hospital; fall fest.

Other towns include: **Eola** (218), **Lowake** (40) and **Millersview** (75).

Population	3,096
Change fm '90	1.7
Area (sq. mi.)	993.7
Land Area (sq. mi.)	991.5
Altitude (ft.)	1,500-2,400
Rainfall (in.)	24.8
Jan. mean min.	31
July mean max.	98
Growing season (days)	228

Civ. Labor	1,548
Unemployed	2.8
Annual Wages	$15,998,747
Av. Weekly Wage	$337.62
Fed. Wages	$791,113
Ag. Net Cash Return	$3,323,000
Prop. Value	$309,053,543
Retail Sales	$16,120,254

For explanation of sources, abbreviations and symbols, see p. 130.

Cooke County

Physical Features: North central county; drains to Red, Trinity rivers, lakes; sandy, red, loam soils.

Economy: Agribusiness, oil industries, varied manufacturing.

History: Frontier between Caddoes and Comanches. Anglo-Americans arrived in late 1840s. Germans settled western part around 1890. County created 1848 from Fannin County; named for Capt. W.G. Cooke of the Texas Revolution.

Ethnicity, 1990: White, 28,375 (92.2%); Black, 1,169 (3.8%); American Indian, 232 (0.8%); Asian, 131 (0.4%); Other, 870 (2.8%). Hispanic, 1,408 (4.6%).

Vital Statistics, 1997: Births, 465; deaths, 349; marriages, 713; divorces, 211.

Recreation: Water sports; hunting, fishing; zoo; museum; park.

Minerals: Oil, gravel.

Agriculture: Beef, dairy operations, wheat, sorghum, corn, oats, horses. Market value $37.3 million.

GAINESVILLE (15,486) county seat; aircraft, steel fabrication, tourism; agribusiness center; zoo, Victorian homes, walking tours; hospital; community college, state school; Camp Sweeney for diabetic children.

Muenster (1,536) dairy center, food processing, oil, varied manufacturing; hospital, Germanfest.

Other towns include: **Callisburg** (442), **Era** (200), **Lindsay** (798), **Myra** (300), **Oak Ridge** (244), **Rosston** (75), **Valley View** (799) and the residential community around **Lake Kiowa** (1,850).

Population	34,200
Change fm '90	11.1
Area (sq. mi.)	898.7
Land Area (sq. mi.)	873.8
Altitude (ft.)	617-1,200
Rainfall (in.)	35.8
Jan. mean min.	27
July mean max.	95
Growing season (days)	226
Civ. Labor	16,777
Unemployed	3.3
Annual Wages	$252,766,849
Av. Weekly Wage	$412.43
Fed. Wages	$2,503,191
Ag. Net Cash Return	$3,725,000
Prop. Value	$1,494,488,703
Retail Sales	$382,678,826

Coryell County

Physical Features: Leon Valley in center, remainder rolling, hilly.

Economy: Fort Hood, agribusiness, state prisons, plastics and other manufacturing.

History: Tonkawa area, later various other tribes. Anglo-Americans settled around Fort Gates in late 1840s. Permanent establishment of Fort Hood in 1950 changed cultural geography. County created from Bell County 1854; named for local pioneer James Coryell.

Ethnicity, 1990: White, 45,078 (70.2%); Black, 13,592 (21.2%); American Indian, 461 (0.7%); Asian, 1,670 (2.6%); Other, 3,412 (5.3%). Hispanic, 6,243 (9.7%).

Vital Statistics, 1997: Births, 929; deaths, 313; marriages, 478; divorces, 486.

Recreation: state park; hunting; nearby lakes and Leon River, bluebonnet area. Historic homes; log jail; Shivaree in June.

Minerals: Small stone, sand and gravel production.

Agriculture: Cattle, sheep, goats, hogs, horses; wheat, corn, maize. Market value $28 million.

GATESVILLE (12,340) county seat; varied manufacturing; prisons; hospital; refurbished courthouse; museum; antique shows; branch Central Texas College.

COPPERAS COVE (30,708) business center for Fort Hood; industrial filters, other manufacturing; hospital; Central Texas College; Rabbit Fest in May.

Other towns include: **Evant** (453), **Flat** (210), **Jonesboro** (200), **Leon Junction** (25), **Mound** (75), **Oglesby** (490), **Purmela** (61), **South Mountain** (333).

Population	76,197
Change fm '90	18.6
Area (sq. mi.)	1,056.7
Land Area (sq. mi.)	1,051.9
Altitude (ft.)	600-1,500
Rainfall (in.)	32.9
Jan. mean min.	33
July mean max.	96
Growing season (days)	241
Civ. Labor	22,160
Unemployed	4.2
Annual Wages	$242,293,952
Av. Weekly Wage	$398.53
Fed. Wages	$10,160,518
Ag. Net Cash Return	$2,042,000
Prop. Value	$1,304,903,517
Retail Sales	$296,642,655

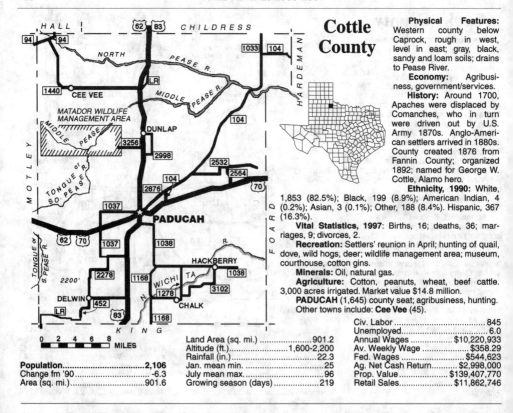

Cottle County

Physical Features: Western county below Caprock, rough in west; level in east; gray, black, sandy and loam soils; drains to Pease River.

Economy: Agribusiness, government/services.

History: Around 1700, Apaches were displaced by Comanches, who in turn were driven out by U.S. Army 1870s. Anglo-American settlers arrived in 1880s. County created 1876 from Fannin County; organized 1892; named for George W. Cottle, Alamo hero.

Ethnicity, 1990: White, 1,853 (82.5%); Black, 199 (8.9%); American Indian, 4 (0.2%); Asian, 3 (0.1%); Other, 188 (8.4%). Hispanic, 367 (16.3%).

Vital Statistics, 1997: Births, 16; deaths, 36; marriages, 9; divorces, 2.

Recreation: Settlers' reunion in April; hunting of quail, dove, wild hogs, deer; wildlife management area; museum, courthouse, cotton gins.

Minerals: Oil, natural gas.

Agriculture: Cotton, peanuts, wheat, beef cattle. 3,000 acres irrigated. Market value $14.8 million.

PADUCAH (1,645) county seat; agribusiness, hunting. Other towns include: **Cee Vee** (45).

Population	2,106
Change fm '90	-6.3
Area (sq. mi.)	901.6
Land Area (sq. mi.)	901.2
Altitude (ft.)	1,600-2,200
Rainfall (in.)	22.3
Jan. mean min.	25
July mean max.	96
Growing season (days)	219
Civ. Labor	845
Unemployed	6.0
Annual Wages	$10,220,933
Av. Weekly Wage	$358.29
Fed. Wages	$544,623
Ag. Net Cash Return	$2,998,000
Prop. Value	$139,407,770
Retail Sales	$11,862,746

Crane County

Physical Features: Rolling prairie, Pecos Valley, some hills; sandy, loam soils; Juan Cordona Lake.

Economy: Oil-based economy.

History: Lipan Apache area. Ranching developed in 1890s. Oil discovered in 1926. County created from Tom Green County 1887, organized 1927; named for Baylor University president W. C. Crane.

Ethnicity, 1990: White, 3,097 (66.6%); Black, 130 (2.8%); American Indian, 11 (0.2%); Asian, 10 (0.2%); Other, 1,404 (30.2%). Hispanic, 1,577 (33.9%).

Vital Statistics, 1997: Births, 53; deaths, 34; marriages, 34; divorces, 13.

Recreation: Sites of pioneer trails and historic Horsehead Crossing on Pecos River; county stock show in January; camping park.

Minerals: Among leaders in oil, gas production.

Agriculture: Cattle ranching. Market value $2.1 million.

CRANE (3,408) county seat; oil-well servicing, production; foundry; steel, surfboard manufacturing; hospital.

Population	4,583
Change fm '90	-1.5
Area (sq. mi.)	785.6
Land Area (sq. mi.)	785.6
Altitude (ft.)	2,300-2,902
Rainfall (in.)	14.8
Jan. mean min.	31
July mean max.	97
Growing season (days)	225
Civ. Labor	2,296
Unemployed	5.7
Annual Wages	$46,961,392
Av. Weekly Wage	$513.72
Fed. Wages	$229,290
Ag. Net Cash Return	$518,000
Prop. Value	$917,598,930
Retail Sales	$21,990,503

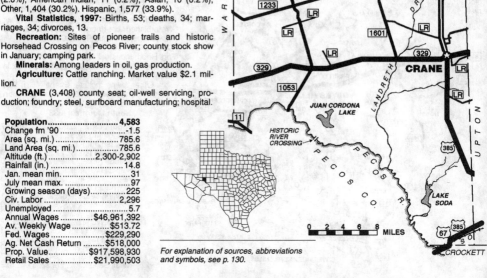

For explanation of sources, abbreviations and symbols, see p. 130.

Crockett County

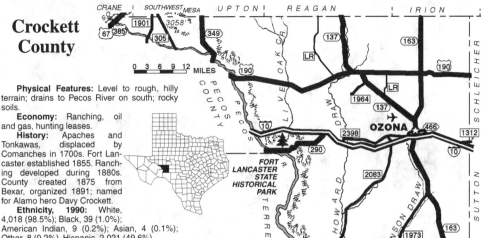

Physical Features: Level to rough, hilly terrain; drains to Pecos River on south; rocky soils.

Economy: Ranching, oil and gas, hunting leases.

History: Apaches and Tonkawas, displaced by Comanches in 1700s. Fort Lancaster established 1855. Ranching developed during 1880s. County created 1875 from Bexar, organized 1891; named for Alamo hero Davy Crockett.

Ethnicity, 1990: White, 4,018 (98.5%); Black, 39 (1.0%); American Indian, 9 (0.2%); Asian, 4 (0.1%); Other, 8 (0.2%). Hispanic, 2,021 (49.6%).

Vital Statistics, 1997: Births, 70; deaths, 33; marriages, 45; divorces, 17.

Recreation: Hunting; historic sites, state park; museum; Davy Crockett statue in park; Deerfest and Wild Game dinner in December; world championship goat roping in June.

Minerals: Oil, gas production.

Agriculture: Sheep (first in state in inventory), Spanish and Angora goats; income also from beef cattle. Market value $15.2 million.

OZONA (3,534) county seat; trade center for ranching; hunting leases; tourism.

Population	4,711
Change fm '90	15.5
Area (sq. mi.)	2,807.6
Land Area (sq. mi.)	2,807.6
Altitude (ft.)	1,700-3,058
Rainfall (in.)	19.2
Jan. mean min.	30
July mean max.	94
Growing season (days)	233
Civ. Labor	2,074
Unemployed	4.9
Annual Wages	$31,872,465
Av. Weekly Wage	$394.33
Fed. Wages	$221,205
Ag. Net Cash Return	$1,310,000
Prop. Value	$956,827,761
Retail Sales	$28,630,370

Crosby County

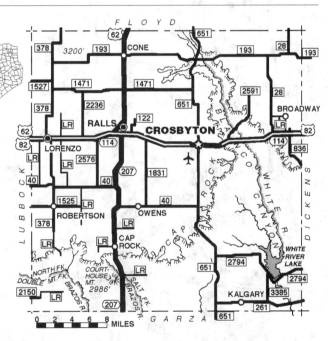

Phyical Features: Flat, rich soil above Caprock, broken below; drains into Brazos River forks and playas.

Economy: Agribusiness, tourism, food processing; commuters to Lubbock.

History: Comanches, driven out by U.S. Army in 1870s; ranching developed soon afterward. Quaker colony founded in 1879. County created from Bexar District 1876, organized 1886; named for Texas Land Commissioner Stephen Crosby.

Ethnicity, 1990: White, 5,784 (79.2%); Black, 321 (4.4%); American Indian, 13 (0.2%); Asian, 8 (0.1%); Other, 1,178 (16.1%). Hispanic, 3,111 (42.6%).

Vital Statistics, 1997: Births, 119; deaths, 102; marriages, 52; divorces, 33.

Recreation: Lake; Silver Falls Park; outdoor theater in August.

Minerals: Sand, gravel, oil, gas.

Agriculture: Cotton, beef cattle; sorghum, hay and sunflowers; about 130,000 acres irrigated. Market value $74.3 million.

CROSBYTON (2,034) county seat; agribusiness center; Pioneer Museum, hospital.

Other towns include: **Ralls** (1,951) government/services, agribusiness; museum of Indian artifacts; Cotton Boll Fest in September; **Lorenzo** (1,269).

For explanation of sources, abbreviations and symbols, see p. 130.

Population	7,028
Change fm '90	-3.8
Area (sq. mi.)	901.6
Land Area (sq. mi.)	899.6
Altitude (ft.)	2,300-3,200
Rainfall (in.)	22.6
Jan. mean min.	23
July mean max.	93
Growing season (days)	206
Civ. Labor	3,026
Unemployed	7.7
Annual Wages	$36,067,831
Av. Weekly Wage	$369.00
Fed. Wages	$718,089
Ag. Net Cash Return	$25,592,000
Prop. Value	$295,930,869
Retail Sales	$70,375,651

The Guadalupe Mountains jut into Culberson County from southern New Mexico. NYT/The Dallas Morning News file photo.

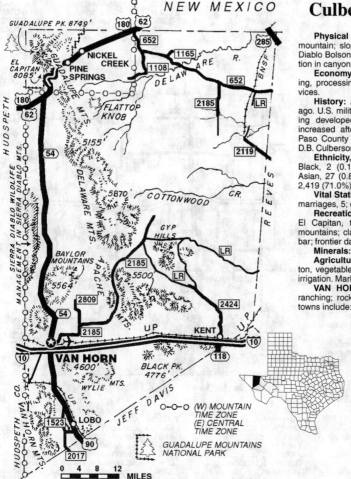

Culberson County

Physical Features: Contains Texas' highest mountain; slopes toward Pecos Valley on east, Diablo Bolson on west; salt lakes; unique vegetation in canyons.

Economy: Agribusiness; tourism; talc mining, processing; oil production; government/services.

History: Apaches arrived about 600 years ago. U.S. military frontier after Civil War. Ranching developed after 1880. Mexican migration increased after 1920. County created from El Paso County 1911, organized 1912; named for D.B. Culberson, Texas congressman.

Ethnicity, 1990: White, 2,400 (70.4%); Black, 2 (0.1%); American Indian, 16 (0.5%); Asian, 27 (0.8%); Other, 962 (28.2%). Hispanic, 2,419 (71.0%).

Vital Statistics, 1997: Births, 36; deaths, 18; marriages, 5; divorces, 11.

Recreation: National park; Guadalupe and El Capitan, twin peaks; scenic canyons and mountains; classic car museum, antique saloon bar; frontier days in June, big buck tournament.

Minerals: Sulfur, talc, marble.

Agriculture: Beef cattle; crops include cotton, vegetables, melons, pecans; 4,000 acres in irrigation. Market value $6 million.

VAN HORN (2,834) county seat; tourism; ranching; rock crushing; hospital; airport. Other towns include: **Kent** (60).

Population	3,302
Change fm '90	-3.1
Area (sq. mi.)	3,812.8
Land Area (sq. mi.)	3,812.7
Altitude (ft.)	3,000-8,749
Rainfall (in.)	13.1
Jan. mean min.	28
July mean max.	94
Growing season (days)	224
Civ. Labor	1,219
Unemployed	8.6
Annual Wages	$23,948,332
Av. Weekly Wage	$434.11
Fed. Wages	$2,181,992
Ag. Net Cash Return	$801,000
Prop. Value	$290,546,940
Retail Sales	$41,858,898

Dallam County

Physical Features: Prairie, broken by creeks; playas; sandy, loam soils; Rita Blanca National Grassland.

Economy: Agribusiness, tourism, small manufacturing.

History: Earliest Plains Apaches; displaced by Comanches and Kiowas. Ranching developed in late 19th century. Farming began after 1900. County created from Bexar District, 1876, organized 1891. Named for lawyer-editor James W. Dallam.

Ethnicity, 1990: White, 4,600 (84.2%); Black, 112 (2.1%); American Indian, 43 (0.8%); Asian, 14 (0.3%); Other, 692 (12.7%). Hispanic, 1,151 (21.1%).

Vital Statistics, 1997: Births, 98; deaths, 65; marriages, 72; divorces, 44.

Recreation: Interstate Fair in September; XIT Museum; XIT Rodeo in August; hunting, wildlife; grasslands; La Rita Theater in June-August.

Minerals: Petroleum.

Agriculture: Cattle; hogs (first in state in sales, inventory); corn, wheat, grain sorghum, sugar beets, potatoes, sunflowers, beans; substantial irrigation. Market value $357 million.

DALHART (6,734, partly in Hartley County) county seat; government/services; agribusiness center for parts of Texas, New Mexico, Oklahoma; railroad; some manufacturing; hospital; prison.

Other towns include: **Kerrick** (60) and **Texline** (438).

Population	5,891
Change fm '90	7.9
Area (sq. mi.)	1,505.3
Land Area (sq. mi.)	1,504.8
Altitude (ft.)	3,700-4,700
Rainfall (in.)	17.9
Jan. mean min.	19
July mean max.	92
Growing season (days)	178
Civ. Labor	3,488
Unemployed	3.5
Annual Wages	$70,934,665
Av. Weekly Wage	$417.25
Fed. Wages	$1,064,157
Ag. Net Cash Return	$35,813,000
Prop. Value	$545,063,648
Retail Sales	$67,513,660

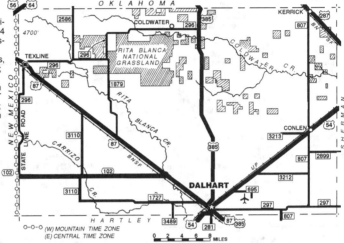

o-o-o (W) MOUNTAIN TIME ZONE
(E) CENTRAL TIME ZONE

Physical Features: Mostly flat, heavy blackland soils, sandy clays in west; drains to Trinity River.

Economy: A national center for telecommunications, transportation, electronics manufacturing, data processing, conventions and trade shows; foreign-trade zone located at D/FW International Airport, U.S. Customs port of entry; government/services.

History: Caddoan area. Anglo-Americans began arriving in 1840. Antebellum slaveholding area. County created 1846 from Nacogdoches, Rob-

Dallas County

ertson counties; named for U.S. Vice President George Mifflin Dallas.

Ethnicity, 1990: White, 1,241,455 (67.0%); Black, 369,597 (19.9%); American Indian, 9,437 (0.5%); Asian, 52,238 (2.8%); Other, 180,083 (9.7%). Hispanic, 315,630 (17.0%).

Vital Statistics, 1997: Births, 38,682; deaths, 13,390; marriages, 18,244; divorces, 10,950.

Recreation: One of the state's top

tourist destinations and one of the nation's most popular convention centers.

State Fair, museums, zoo, West End shopping and tourist district, historical sites, including Sixth Floor museum in the old Texas School Book Depository, site of the assassination of President Kennedy.

Other important attractions include the Morton H. Meyerson Symphony Center; performing arts; professional

(continued)

Dallas County

(continued)

sports; Texas broadcast museum; lakes; theme and amusement parks.

Agriculture: Horticultural crops; wheat, hay, corn; horses (15th in state in value of sales), cattle. Market value $22.3 million.

Education: Southern Methodist University, University of Dallas, Dallas Baptist University, University of Texas at Dallas, University of Texas Southwestern Medical Center and many other education centers.

DALLAS (1,085,614) county seat; center of state's largest consolidated metropolitan area and third-largest city in Texas; D/FW International Airport is one of the world's busiest; headquarters for the U.S. Army and Air Force Exchange Service; Federal Reserve Bank; a leader in fashions and in computer operations; Infomart, a large computer-sales complex; many hotels in downtown area offer adequate accomodations for most conventions.

Garland (193,475) varied manufacturing, community college branch, hospital, performing arts center.

For explanation of sources, abbreviations and symbols, see p. 130.

Irving (175,983) Texas Stadium, home of the Dallas Cowboys; headquarters for the Boy Scouts of America; varied light manufacturing, food processing; distribution center; North Lake College; hospitals.

Other large cities include: **Addison** (11,722) general aviation airport; **Balch Springs** (18,418); **Carrollton** (100,950) residential community, distribution center; **Cedar Hill** (28,100) residential community, Northwood University; **Cockrell Hill** (4,136); **Coppell** (27,625) distribution, varied manufacturing; office center; **DeSoto** (35,615) residential community, light industry and distribution, hospitals.

Also, **Duncanville** (36,364) varied manufacturing, residential community; **Farmers Branch** (26,227) distribution center, varied manufacturing, Brookhaven College, hospital; **Glenn Heights** (5,553); **Grand Prairie** (113,672) manufacturing, distribution center, hospital,

Joe Pool Reservoir, Indian pow-wow in September, Lone Star horse-racing track; **Highland Park** (9,454); **Hutchins** (3,326) varied manufacturing; **Lancaster** (27,147) residential, industrial, distribution, agricultural center, Cedar Valley College, airport, hospital.

Also, **Mesquite** (114,699) residential city with varied industries, hospitals; championship rodeo, Samuell Farm; **Richardson** (90,798) telecommunications, software development, Richland College, hospital, Owens Spring Creek Farm; **Rowlett** (38,203) hospital, farmers market; **Sachse** (7,508); **Seagoville** (9,987) rural/suburban setting, federal prison; **Sunnyvale** (2,767); **University Park** (22,872); **Wilmer** (2,590).

Population	2,032,171
Change fm '90	9.7
Area (sq. mi.)	908.7
Land Area (sq. mi.)	879.9
Altitude (ft.)	382-750
Rainfall (in.)	36.1
Jan. mean min.	35
July mean max.	96
Growing season (days)	235
Civ. Labor	1,212,879
Unemployed	3.6
Annual Wages	$54,360,760
Av. Weekly Wage	$732.02
Fed. Wages	$1,253,245,553
Ag. Net Cash Return	$4,249,000
Prop. Value	$108,381,479,855
Retail Sales	$38,436,330,507

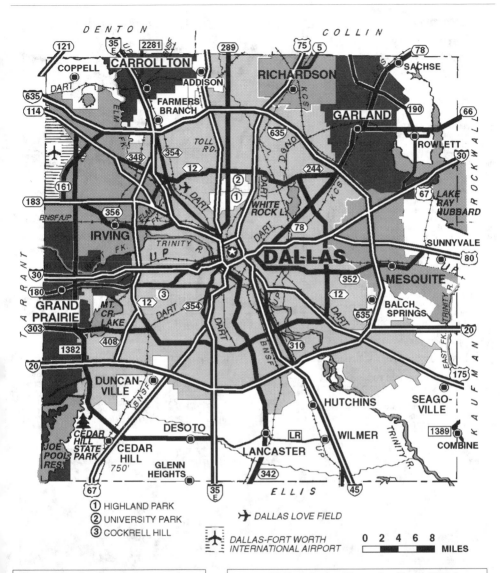

① HIGHLAND PARK
② UNIVERSITY PARK
③ COCKRELL HILL

✈ DALLAS LOVE FIELD

✈ DALLAS-FORT WORTH
INTERNATIONAL AIRPORT

0 2 4 6 8 MILES

Top Media Markets in U.S.

1. New York
2. Los Angeles
3. Chicago
4. Philadelphia
5. San Francisco
6. Boston
7. Washington
8. **Dallas/Fort Worth**
9. Detroit
10. Atlanta
11. **Houston**

Source: National Assn. of Broadcasters, 1998

U.S. Metro Populations 1996

Rank	Pop. Estimate
1. New York	19.94 million
2. Los Angeles	15.50 million
3. Chicago	8.60 million
4. Washington/Baltimore	7.17 million
5. San Francisco	6.61 million
6. Philadelphia	5.97 million
7. Boston	5.56 million
8. Detroit	5.28 million
9. **Dallas/Fort Worth**	**4.56 million**
10. **Houston**	**4.25 million**

Source: U.S. Bureau of the Census

Dawson County

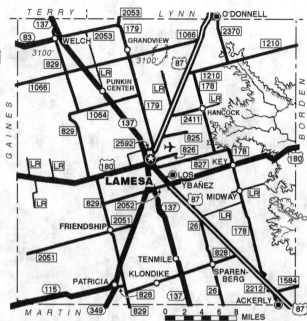

Physical Features: South High Plains county in West Texas, broken on the east; loam and sandy soils.

Economy: Agriculture; farm, gin equipment manufacturing; peanut plant; government/services.

History: Comanche, Kiowa area. Ranching developed in 1880s. Farming began after 1900. Hispanic population increased after 1940. County created from Bexar District, 1876, organized 1905; named for Nicholas M. Dawson, San Jacinto veteran.

Ethnicity, 1990: White, 9,789 (68.2%); Black, 622 (4.3%); American Indian, 23 (0.2%); Asian, 19 (0.1%); Other, 3,896 (27.2%). Hispanic, 6,120 (42.7%).

Vital Statistics, 1997: Births, 191; deaths, 144; marriages, 121; divorces, 64.

Recreation: Parks; museum; campground; May Fun Fest; July 4 celebration.

Minerals: Oil, natural gas.

Agriculture: A major cotton-producing county; also sorghums, peanuts; beef cattle; 63,000 acres irrigated. Market value $89.6 million.

LAMESA (10,773) county seat; agribusiness; food processing, oil-field services; some manufacturing; computerized cotton-classing office; hospital; campus of Howard College; prison unit.

Other towns include: **Los Ybañez** (88) and **Welch** (110). **Ackerly** (261, partly in Martin County). Part of **O'Donnell** (1,155).

Population	**14,911**
Change fm '90	3.9
Area (sq. mi.)	902.1
Land Area (sq. mi.)	902.1
Altitude (ft.)	2,600-3,100
Rainfall (in.)	16.2
Jan. mean min.	25
July mean max.	95
Growing season (days)	210

Civ. Labor	5,993
Unemployed	6.2
Annual Wages	$99,924,638
Av. Weekly Wage	$390.93
Fed. Wages	$2,071,601
Ag. Net Cash Return	$28,157,000
Prop. Value	$848,181,168
Retail Sales	$90,684,502

On the High Plains of the Texas Panhandle, a farmer putting in wheat seeds. AP/The Dallas Morning News file photo.

Deaf Smith County

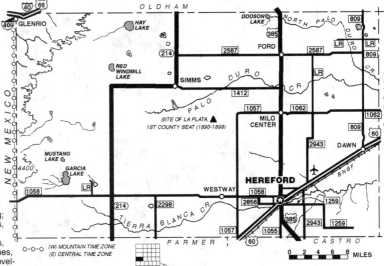

Physical Features: Panhandle High Plains county, partly broken; chocolate and sandy loam soils; drains to Palo Duro and Tierra Blanca creeks.

Economy: Meat packers; offset printing; other varied industries, mostly agribusiness.

History: Apaches, displaced by Comanches, Kiowas. Ranching developed after U.S. Army drove out Indians 1874-75. Farming began after 1900. Hispanic settlement increased after 1950. County created 1876, from Bexar District; organized 1890. Named for famed scout in Texas Revolution, Erastus (Deaf) Smith.

Ethnicity, 1990: White, 14,522 (75.8%); Black, 307 (1.6%); American Indian, 49 (0.3%); Asian, 39 (0.2%); Other, 4,236 (22.1%). Hispanic, 9,356 (48.8%).

Vital Statistics, 1997: Births, 396; deaths, 157; marriages, 191; divorces, 77.

Recreation: Museum, tours, POW camp chapel; Cinco de Mayo, Pioneer Day in May.

Minerals: Not significant.

Agriculture: A leading farm county; large cattle feedlot operations; crops are wheat, sorghum, corn, cotton, onions, beets, other vegetables, sunflowers; 205,000 acres irrigated. Market value $656.6 million; second in state.

HEREFORD (14,562) county seat; agribusinesses, food processing; varied manufacturing; hospital.

Other towns include: **Dawn** (52).

Population	19,193
Change fm '90	0.2
Area (sq. mi.)	1,498.3
Land Area (sq. mi.)	1,497.4
Altitude (ft.)	3,700-4,400
Rainfall (in.)	17.2
Jan. mean min.	20
July mean max.	90
Growing season (days)	195
Civ. Labor	8,097
Unemployed	7.5
Annual Wages	$127,234,191
Av. Weekly Wage	$418.17
Fed. Wages	$2,229,172
Ag. Net Cash Return	$80,288,000
Prop. Value	$743,329,609
Retail Sales	$136,987,180

Delta County

Physical Features: Northeast county between two forks of Sulphur River; lake; black, sandy loam soils.

Economy: Agribusiness; tourism; manufacturing.

History: Caddo area, but disease, other tribes caused displacement around 1790.

Anglo-Americans arrived in 1820s. County created from Lamar, Hopkins counties 1870. Greek letter delta origin of name, because of shape of the county.

Ethnicity, 1990: White, 4,388 (90.3%); Black, 404 (8.3%); American Indian, 41 (0.8%); Asian, 7 (0.1%); Other, 17 (0.4%). Hispanic, 67 (1.4%).

Vital Statistics, 1997: Births, 54; deaths, 82; marriages, 40; divorces, 14.

Recreation: Fishing, hunting; lakes, state park; Mayfest.

Minerals: Not significant.

Agriculture: Beef, dairy cattle; crops include hay, soybeans, corn, sorghum, cotton, wheat. Market value $11.6 million.

COOPER (2,227) county seat; industrial park, some manufacturing; agribusiness; museum; Chiggerfest in October.

Other towns include: **Ben Franklin** (75), **Enloe** (113), **Klondike** (135), **Lake Creek** (60) and **Pecan Gap** (260).

Population	5,137
Change fm '90	5.8
Area (sq. mi.)	277.8
Land Area (sq. mi.)	277.2
Altitude (ft.)	350-536
Rainfall (in.)	42.7
Jan. mean min.	30
July mean max.	94
Growing season (days)	233
Civ. Labor	2,503
Unemployed	4.0
Annual Wages	$22,539,093
Av. Weekly Wage	$406.29
Fed. Wages	$782,404
Ag. Net Cash Return	$1,942,000
Prop. Value	$158,836,185
Retail Sales	$13,765,357

For explanation of sources, abbreviations and symbols, see p. 130.

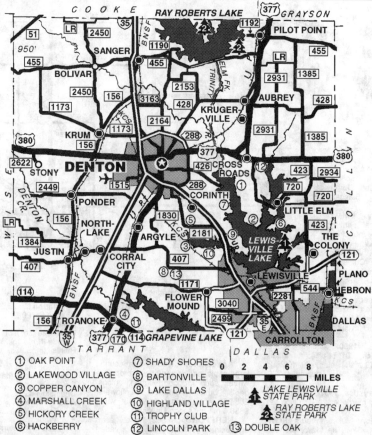

① OAK POINT   ⑦ SHADY SHORES
② LAKEWOOD VILLAGE   ⑧ BARTONVILLE
③ COPPER CANYON   ⑨ LAKE DALLAS
④ MARSHALL CREEK   ⑩ HIGHLAND VILLAGE
⑤ HICKORY CREEK   ⑪ TROPHY CLUB
⑥ HACKBERRY   ⑫ LINCOLN PARK   ⑬ DOUBLE OAK

LAKE LEWISVILLE STATE PARK
RAY ROBERTS LAKE STATE PARK

Denton County

Physical Features: North Texas county; partly hilly, draining to Elm Fork of Trinity River, two lakes; Blackland and Grand Prairie soils and terrain.

Economy: Varied industries; colleges; tourism; government/services; part of Dallas-Fort Worth metropolitan area.

History: Land grant from Texas Congress 1841 for Peters colony. County created out of Fannin County 1846; named for John B. Denton, pioneer Methodist minister.

Ethnicity, 1990: White, 241,982 (88.5%); Black, 13,569 (5.0%); American Indian, 1,416 (0.5%); Asian, 6,870 (2.5%); Other, 9,688 (3.5%). Hispanic, 19,013 (7.0%).

Vital Statistics, 1997: Births, 5,914; deaths, 1,442; marriages, 3,249; divorces, 1,832.

Recreation: Water sports at Lewisville, Grapevine lakes, seven U.S. Corps of Engineers parks; Ray Roberts lake; universities' cultural, athletic activities, including "Texas Women; A Celebration of History'" exhibit at TWU library; State D.A.R. Museum "First Ladies of Texas" collection of gowns and memorabilia; Little Chapel in the Woods; Denton Jazzfest in April.

Minerals: Salt, sand, gravel.

Education: University of North Texas and Texas Woman's University.

For explanation of sources, abbreviations and symbols, see p. 130.

Agriculture: Horses (first in state in sales), eggs, nurseries, turf, cattle; hay and wheat are the top crops; sorghum, peanuts also grown. Market value $53.5 million.

DENTON (78,028) county seat; University of North Texas, Texas Woman's University, Denton State School (for the retarded); plants manufacture a variety of products; hospitals.

LEWISVILLE (67,180) retail center, electronics and varied industries including missile manufacturing; Lewisville Lake, hospital; Western Festival in September.

CARROLLTON (100,950, partly in Dallas, Collin counties).

Other towns include: **The Colony** (28,956) on eastern shore of Lewisville Lake, tourism, IBM offices, chili cook-off in June, Las Vegas Night in April; **Flower Mound** (40,291) residential community.

Also, **Argyle** (2,164); **Aubrey** (1,413); **Bartonville** (1,248); **Copper Canyon** (1,439); **Corinth** (6,267); **Corral City** (60); **Cross Roads** (487); **Double Oak** (2,224); **Hackberry** (269); **Hebron** (1,512); **Hickory Creek** (2,312); **Highland Village** (11,561); **Justin** (1,747); **Krugerville** (1,049); **Krum** (2,236); **Lake Dallas** (5,090) light manufacturing, marina.

Also, **Lakewood Village** (229); **Lincoln Park** (448); **Little Elm** (1,739); **Marshall Creek** (489); **Northlake** (369); **Oak Point** (1,123); **Pilot Point** (3,363) light manufacturing, agribusinesses, near Lake Ray Roberts, pioneer days in June; **Ponder** (547); **Roanoke** (2,477); **Sanger** (4,491) lake recreation enterprises; **Shady Shores** (1,496); **Trophy Club** (5,179).

Population	**382,389**
Change fm '90	39.8
Area (sq. mi.)	957.6
Land Area (sq. mi.)	888.5
Altitude (ft.)	450-950
Rainfall (in.)	37.3
Jan. mean min.	30
July mean max.	94
Growing season (days)	226
Civ. Labor	232,418
Unemployed	2.0
Annual Wages	$2,761,675,299
Av. Weekly Wage	$518.03
Fed. Wages	$44,489,889
Ag. Net Cash Return	$3,236,000
Prop. Value	$19,370,251,634
Retail Sales	$4,055,466,251

DeWitt County

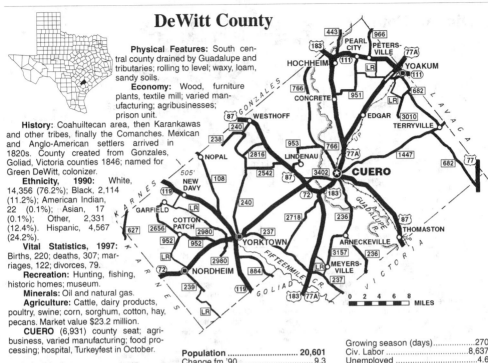

Physical Features: South central county drained by Guadalupe and tributaries; rolling to level; waxy, loam, sandy soils.

Economy: Wood, furniture plants, textile mill; varied manufacturing; agribusinesses; prison unit.

History: Coahuiltecan area, then Karankawas and other tribes, finally the Comanches. Mexican and Anglo-American settlers arrived in 1820s. County created from Gonzales, Goliad, Victoria counties 1846; named for Green DeWitt, colonizer.

Ethnicity, 1990: White, 14,356 (76.2%); Black, 2,114 (11.2%); American Indian, 22 (0.1%); Asian, 17 (0.1%); Other, 2,331 (12.4%). Hispanic, 4,567 (24.2%).

Vital Statistics, 1997: Births, 220; deaths, 307; marriages, 122; divorces, 79.

Recreation: Hunting, fishing, historic homes; museum.

Minerals: Oil and natural gas.

Agriculture: Cattle, dairy products, poultry, swine; corn, sorghum, cotton, hay, pecans. Market value $23.2 million.

CUERO (6,931) county seat; agribusiness, varied manufacturing; food processing; hospital, Turkeyfest in October.

Yorktown (2,328) hospital; museum; oil-well servicing.

Other towns include: **Hochheim** (70), **Meyersville** (110), **Nordheim** (340), **Thomaston** (45), **Westhoff** (410) and **Yoakum** (6,364).

Population	20,601
Change fm '90	9.3
Area (sq. mi.)	910.4
Land Area (sq. mi.)	909.3
Altitude (ft.)	100-505
Rainfall (in.)	37.0
Jan. mean min.	39
July mean max.	95

Growing season (days)	270
Civ. Labor	8,637
Unemployed	4.6
Annual Wages	$134,115,639
Av. Weekly Wage	$395.92
Fed. Wages	$1,555,125
Ag. Net Cash Return	$1,604,000
Prop. Value	$1,018,739,904
Retail Sales	$114,769,605

Dickens County

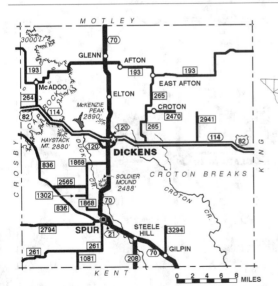

Physical Features: West Texas county; broken land, Caprock in northwest; sandy, chocolate, red soils; drains to Croton, Duck creeks.

Economy: Services/prison unit, agribusiness, hunting leases.

History: Comanches driven out by U.S. Army 1874-75. Ranching and some farming began in late 1880s. County created 1876, from Bexar District; organized 1891; named for Alamo hero who is variously listed as James R. Demkins or Dimpkins and J. Dickens.

Ethnicity, 1990: White, 2,193 (85.3%); Black, 113 (4.4%); American Indian, 13 (0.5%); Asian, 1 (0.0%);Other, 251 (9.8%). Hispanic, 479 (18.6%).

Vital Statistics, 1997: Births, 25; deaths, 45; marriages, 18; divorces, 19.

Recreation: Hunting, fishing; Soldiers Mound site, Dickens Springs; downtown Spur.

Agriculture: Cattle, cotton, horses, hay, wheat, sorghum; goats also raised; alfalfa, pecans, peanuts; some irrigation. Market value $14 million. Hunting leases important.

DICKENS (288) county seat, market for ranching country.

SPUR (1,119) agribusiness and shipping center, homecoming in October; state prison.

Other towns include: **Afton** (15) and **McAdoo** (75).

Population	2,314
Change fm '90	-10.0
Area (sq. mi.)	905.2
Land Area (sq. mi.)	904.3
Altitude (ft.)	1,800-3,000
Rainfall (in.)	20.7
Jan. mean min.	26
July mean max.	95
Growing season (days)	217

Civ. Labor	1,071
Unemployed	4.7
Annual Wages	$12,718,392
Av. Weekly Wage	$370.44
Fed. Wages	$494,032
Ag. Net Cash Return	$3,247,000
Prop. Value	$164,653,660
Retail Sales	$9,957,889

Dimmit County

Physical Features: Southwest county; level to rolling; much brush; sandy, loam, red soils; drained by Nueces River.

Economy: Agribusiness; petroleum products; varied manufacturing; tourism; government/services.

History: Coahuiltecan area, later Comanches. John Townsend, a black man from Nacogdoches, led first attempt at settlement before the Civil War. Texas Rangers forced Indians out in 1877. Mexican migration increased after 1910. County created 1858 from Bexar, Maverick, Uvalde, Webb counties; organized 1880. Named for Philip Dimitt of Texas Revolution; law misspelled name.

Ethnicity, 1990: White, 7,599 (72.8%); Black, 60 (0.6%); American Indian, 16 (0.2%); Asian, 12 (0.1%); Other, 2,746 (26.3%). Hispanic, 8,688 (83.3%).

Vital Statistics, 1997: Births, 197; deaths, 88; marriages, 76; divorces, 6.

Recreation: Hunting, fishing, campsites; winter haven for tourists.

Minerals: Oil, gas production.

Agriculture: Among leading irrigated vegetable-growing counties; cattle, poultry raised; nursery, hay, pecans. Market value $19.9 million.

CARRIZO SPRINGS (5,842) county seat; agribusiness center, feedlot, food processing; oil, gas processing; hunting center; hospitals.

Other towns include: **Asherton** (1,658), **Big Wells** (829) and **Catarina** (45).

Population	10,875
Change fm '90	4.2
Area (sq. mi.)	1,334.5

Land Area (sq. mi.)	1,331.0
Altitude (ft.)	400-871
Rainfall (in.)	21.7
Jan. mean min.	41
July mean max.	99
Growing season (days)	290
Civ. Labor	3,677
Unemployed	16.3
Annual Wages	$43,826,806
Av. Weekly Wage	$342.66
Fed. Wages	$4,789,793
Ag. Net Cash Return	-$361,000
Prop. Value	$491,407,056
Retail Sales	$49,029,041

Donley County

Physical Features: Northwest county bisected by Red River Salt Fork; rolling to level; clay, loam, sandy soils.

Economy: Agribusiness; distribution; varied manufacturing.

History: Apaches displaced by Kiowas and Comanches, who were driven out in 1874-75 by U.S. Army. Methodist colony from New York settled in 1878. County created in 1876, organized 1882, out of Bexar District; named for Texas Supreme Court Justice S.P. Donley.

Ethnicity, 1990: White, 3,522 (95.3%); Black, 127 (3.4%); American Indian, 13 (0.4%); Asian, 2 (0.1%); Other, 32 (0.9%). Hispanic, 139 (3.8%).

Vital Statistics, 1997: Births, 43; deaths, 63; marriages, 22; divorces, 13.

Recreation: Lake, hunting, fishing, camping, water sports; Col. Goodnight Chuckwagon cook-off, late September.

Minerals: Small amount of natural gas.

Agriculture: Cattle top revenue source; cotton, peanuts, alfalfa, hay; 10,000 acres irrigated. Market value $92 million.

CLARENDON (2,089) county seat; junior college; Saints Roost museum; library; agribusiness; tourism; medical center.

Other towns include: **Hedley** (420), **Howardwick** (221) and **Lelia Lake** (125).

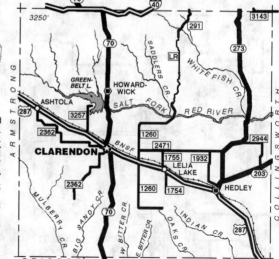

Population	3,765
Change fm '90	1.9
Area (sq. mi.)	933.0
Land Area (sq. mi.)	929.8
Altitude (ft.)	2,200-3,250
Rainfall (in.)	22.0
Jan. mean min.	21
July mean max.	94
Growing season (days)	206

Civ. Labor	1,506
Unemployed	5.2
Annual Wages	$15,844,998
Av. Weekly Wage	$343.38
Fed. Wages	$707,989
Ag. Net Cash Return	$10,675,000
Prop. Value	$218,770,158
Retail Sales	$15,618,220

For explanation of sources, abbreviations and symbols, see p. 130.

Duval County

Physical Features: Southwestern county; level to hilly, brushy in most areas; varied soils.

Economy: Ranching; petroleum; tourism; government/services.

History: Coahuiltecans, displaced by Comanche bands. Mexican settlement began in 1812. County created from Live Oak, Nueces, Starr counties, 1858, organized 1876; named for Burr H. Duval, a victim of Goliad massacre.

Ethnicity, 1990: White, 10,183 (78.8%); Black, 12 (0.1%); American Indian, 12 (0.1%); Asian, 17 (0.1%); Other, 2,694 (20.9%). Hispanic, 11,267 (87.2%).

Vital Statistics, 1997: Births, 207; deaths, 122; marriages, 87; divorces, 53.

Recreation: Hunting, tourist crossroads, rattlesnake roundup.

Minerals: Production of oil, gas, salt, uranium, sand and gravel.

Agriculture: Most income from beef cattle; grains, cotton, vegetables, hay, dairy. Market value $12.9 million.

SAN DIEGO (5,134, partly in Jim Wells County) county seat; ranching, oil field, tourist center; hospital.

Freer (3,483) center of oil and livestock-raising; rattlesnake roundup in April.

Benavides (1,918) serves truck farming area.

Other towns include: **Concepcion** (25) and **Realitos** (250).

Population	13,971
Change fm '90	8.2
Area (sq. mi.)	1,795.7
Land Area (sq. mi.)	1,792.9
Altitude (ft.)	150-833
Rainfall (in.)	24.8
Jan. mean min.	41
July mean max.	96
Growing season (days)	298

Civ. Labor	5,069
Unemployed	12.5
Annual Wages	$72,946,308
Av. Weekly Wage	$410.12
Fed. Wages	$3,487,292
Ag. Net Cash Return	-$1,267,000

Prop. Value	$769,309,514
Retail Sales	$37,064,280

Eastland County

Physical Features: West central county; hilly, rolling; sandy, loam soils; drains to Leon River forks.

Economy: Agribusinesses; education; petroleum industries; varied manufacturing.

History: Plains Indian area. Frank Sánchez among first settlers in 1850s. County created from Bosque, Coryell, Travis counties, 1858, organized 1873; named for W.M. Eastland, Mier Expedition casualty.

Ethnicity, 1990: White, 17,474 (94.5%); Black, 397 (2.1%); American Indian, 52 (0.3%); Asian, 37 (0.2%); Other, 528 (2.9%). Hispanic, 1,404 (7.6%).

Vital Statistics, 1997: Births, 209; deaths, 272; marriages, 172; divorces, 78.

Recreation: Lakes, water sports; fishing, hunting; festivals; historic sites and displays.

Minerals: Oil, gas, gravel and sand.

Agriculture: Beef and goats, forages, peanuts, melons. 20,000 acres irrigated. Market value $25.9 million.

EASTLAND (3,669) county seat; plants make various goods; agribusiness; printing; mental health center; hospital.

CISCO (4,120) agribusiness; plants clothing, windows, molding; Conrad Hilton's first hotel renovated, museum; junior college; hospital; folklife festival; Kendrick Religous Diorama.

RANGER (2,743) oil center, varied manufacturing; junior college; hospital.

Other towns include: **Carbon** (289) livestock equipment manufacturing; **Desdemona** (180); **Gorman** (1,373) peanut processing, agribusiness, hospital; **Olden** (110), and **Rising Star** (860) cap manufacturing, plant nursery; Octoberfest.

Population	19,025
Change fm '90	2.9
Area (sq. mi.)	931.8
Land Area (sq. mi.)	926.1
Altitude (ft.)	1,000-1,882
Rainfall (in.)	29.7
Jan. mean min.	29
July mean max.	94
Growing season (days)	299
Civ. Labor	8,948
Unemployed	4.9
Annual Wages	$126,521,465

Av. Weekly Wage	$386.62
Fed. Wages	$2,166,164
Ag. Net Cash Return	$1,723,000
Prop. Value	$665,083,722
Retail Sales	$133,449,305

For explanation of sources, abbreviations and symbols, see p. 130.

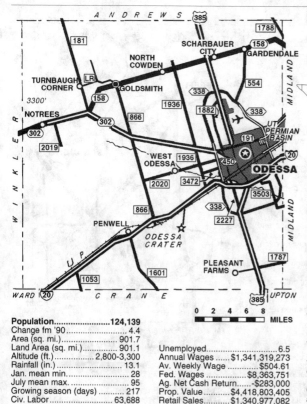

Ector County

Physical Features: West Texas county; level to rolling, some sand dunes; meteor crater; desert vegetation.

Economy: Center for Permian Basin oil field operations; rubber and plastics.

History: First settlers in late 1880s. Oil boom in 1926. County created from Tom Green County, 1887; organized 1891; named for jurist M.D. Ector.

Ethnicity, 1990: White, 91,309 (76.8%); Black, 5,557 (4.7%); American Indian, 647 (0.5%); Asian, 662 (0.6%); Other, 20,759 (17.5%). Hispanic, 37,315 (31.4%).

Vital Statistics, 1997: Births, 2,264; deaths, 955; marriages, 1,212; divorces, 789.

Recreation: Globe Theatre replica; presidential museum; art institute; second-largest U.S. meteor crater; antique auto museum; jazz festival in May, oil show in October .

Minerals: More than 2 billion barrels of oil produced since 1926; gas, cement, stone.

Agriculture: Beef cattle, horses are chief producers; pecans, hay raised; poultry; minor irrigation. Market value $3.4 million.

Education: University of Texas of Permian Basin; Texas Tech University Health Science Center; Odessa (junior) College.

ODESSA (95,384) county seat; oil field services, supplies; petrochemical complex; hosptial; cultural center; fair and expo in September.

Other towns include: **Gardendale** (1,174), **Goldsmith** (301), **Notrees** (338), **Penwell** (74), and **West Odessa** (18,612).

Population....................**124,139**	
Change fm '90 .... 4.4	
Area (sq. mi.)........................ 901.7	
Land Area (sq. mi.)............... 901.1	
Altitude (ft.)................. 2,800-3,300	
Rainfall (in.).......................... 13.1	
Jan. mean min......................... 28	
July mean max. 95	
Growing season (days) 217	
Civ. Labor........................... 63,688	

Unemployed............................6.5	
Annual Wages $1,341,319,273	
Av. Weekly Wage $504.61	
Fed. Wages $8,363,751	
Ag. Net Cash Return......-$283,000	
Prop. Value $4,418,803,405	
Retail Sales..........$1,340,977,082	

Edwards County

Physical Features: Rolling, hilly; caves; spring-fed streams; rocky, thin soils; drained by Llano, Nueces rivers; varied timber.

Economy: Ranching; hunting leases; tourism; oil, gas production.

History: Apache area. First land sold in 1876. County created from Bexar District, 1858; organized 1883; named for Nacogdoches empresario Hayden Edwards.

Ethnicity, 1990: White, 2,114 (93.3%); Black, 0 (0.0%); American Indian, 4 (0.2%); Asian, 4 (0.2%); Other, 144 (6.4%). Hispanic, 1,182 (52.2%).

Vital Statistics, 1997: Births, 20; deaths, 23; marriages, 12; divorces, 8.

Recreation: Hunting, fishing; scenic drives; state park.

Minerals: Gas.

Agriculture: Center for mohair-wool production; Angora goats, sheep, cattle; some pecans. Market value $9 million. Cedar for oil.

ROCKSPRINGS (1,552) county seat; ranching, tourism, Top of the World Festival, July 4.

Other towns include: **Barksdale** (1,081) and **Carta Valley** (12).

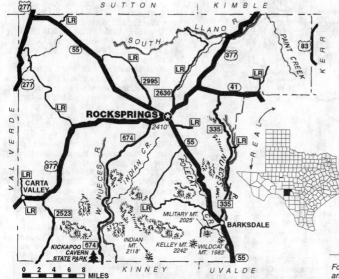

Population **2,965**	
Change fm '90 ....30.8	
Area (sq. mi.)......................2,120.0	
Land Area (sq. mi.)..............2,119.9	
Altitude (ft.) 1,507-2,410	
Rainfall (in.) 22.0	
Jan. mean min. 35	
July mean max. 95	
Growing season (days)..............250	
Civ. Labor 838	
Unemployed 7.2	
Annual Wages...............$6,412,907	
Av. Weekly Wage.............. $327.21	
Fed. Wages...................... $875,103	
Ag. Net Cash Return ....-$283,000	
Prop. Value $337,317,059	
Retail Sales $9,287,072	

For explanation of sources, abbreviations and symbols, see p. 130.

Ellis County

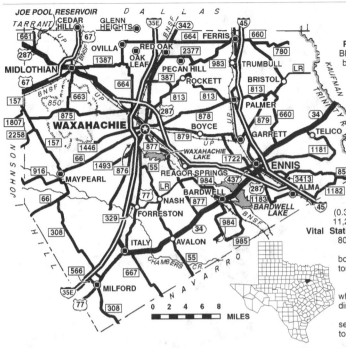

Physical Features: North Texas Blackland soils; level to rolling; Chambers Creek, Trinity River.

Economy: Varied manufacturing; agribusiness; many residents work in Dallas.

History: Tonkawa area. Part of Peters colony settled in 1843. County created 1849, organized 1850, from Navarro County. Named for Richard Ellis, president of convention that declared Texas' independence.

Ethnicity, 1990: White, 69,049 (81.1%); Black, 8,525 (10.0%); American Indian, 370 (0.4%); Asian, 214 (0.3%); Other, 7,009 (8.2%). Hispanic, 11,243 (13.2%).

Vital Statistics, 1997: Births, 1,590; deaths, 802; marriages, 1,014; divorces, 515.

Recreation: Medieval-theme Scarborough Faire; Gingerbread Trail homes tour, fall festival; lakes, fishing, hunting.

Minerals: Cement, oil, gas.

Agriculture: Cattle; hay, cotton, wheat; dairies; corn, milo, grass, bedding plants. Market value $40.4 million.

WAXAHACHIE (20,961) county seat; manufacturing; movie production; tourism; hospital; colleges.

Ennis (15,538) agribusiness; manufacturing; bluebonnet trails, National Polka Festival; tourism; hospital.

Midlothian (6,532) trade zone, cement plant, steel manufacturing; other factories; fall festival.

Other towns include: **Alma** (271); **Avalon** (130); **Bardwell** (450); **Cedar Hill** (28,100); **Ferris** (2,387); **Forreston** (200); **Garrett** (452); **Glenn Heights** (5,553); **Italy** (2,080); **Maypearl** (923); **Milford** (893); **Oak Leaf** (1,226); **Ovilla** (2,753); **Palmer** (1,903); **Pecan Hill** (681); **Red Oak** (4,519) manufacturing, Founders Day in September, and **Telico** (95).

Population	102,200
Change fm '90	20.0
Area (sq. mi.)	951.6
Land Area (sq. mi.)	940.0
Altitude (ft.)	300-850
Rainfall (in.)	36.8
Jan. mean min.	34
July mean max.	96
Growing season (days)	246
Civ. Labor	53,701
Unemployed	3.6

Annual Wages	$757,771,877
Av. Weekly Wage	$479.42
Fed. Wages	$7,379,835
Ag. Net Cash Return..	$7,781,000
Prop. Value	$4,135,229,400
Retail Sales	$673,283,675

For explanation of sources, abbreviations and symbols, see p. 130.

The Ellis County courthouse in Waxahachie. The Dallas Morning News file photo.

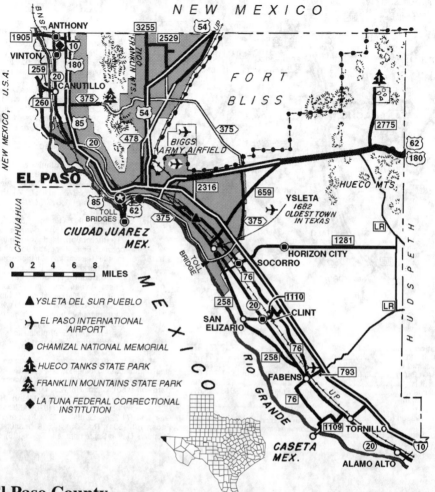

El Paso County

Physical Features: Westernmost county in fertile Rio Grande Valley; 7,000-foot mountains; desert vegetation except where irrigated.

Economy: Government, military are major economic factors; wholesale, retail distribution center; education; tourism; maquiladora plants, varied manufacturers; ore smelting, refining, cotton, food processing.

History: Various Indian tribes inhabited the valley before Spanish civilization arrived in late 1650s. Spanish and Tigua and Piro tribes fleeing Santa Fe uprising of 1680 sought refuge at Ysleta and Socorro. County created from Bexar District, 1849; organized 1850; named for historic pass (Paso del Norte), lowest all-weather pass through Rocky Mountains.

Ethnicity, 1990: White, 452,512 (76.5%); Black, 22,110 (3.7%); American Indian, 2,590 (0.4%); Asian, 6,485 (1.1%); Other, 107,913 (18.2%). Hispanic, 411,619 (69.6%).

Vital Statistics, 1997: Births, 14,473; deaths, 3,765; marriages, 6,965; divorces, 1,675.

Recreation: Gateway to Mexico;

Chamizal Museum; major tourist center; December Sun Carnival with football game; state parks, missions and other historic sites.

Minerals: Production of cement, stone, sand and gravel.

Agriculture: Dairy products (fourth in state in value of sales); cattle; cotton, pecans, onions, forage, peppers also raised; 50,000 acres irrigated, mostly cotton. Market value $76.7 million.

Education: University of Texas at El Paso; UT School of Nursing at El Paso; Texas Tech University Health Science Center; El Paso Community College.

EL PASO (600,277) county seat; fourth-largest Texas city, largest U.S. city on Mexican border.

A center for government operations. Federal installations include Fort Bliss, William Beaumont General Hospital, La Tuna correctional institution, and headquarters of the U.S. Army Air Defense Command;

Manufactured products include clothing, electronics, auto equipment, plastics; trade and distribution; refining;

processing of ore, oil, food, cotton, and other farm products.

Hospitals; museums; convention center; theater, symphony orchestra.

Other towns include: **Anthony** (3,731); **Canutillo** (5,134); **Clint** (1,138); **Fabens** (5,934); **Horizon City** (3,234); **San Elizario** (4,770); **Socorro** (29,131); **Sparks** (1,470); **Tornillo** (241); **Vinton** (807); **Westway** (2,707) and **Ysleta**, oldest town in Texas (now within El Paso).

Population	**688,626**
Change fm '90	16.4
Area (sq. mi.)	1,014.6
Land Area (sq. mi.)	1,013.1
Altitude (ft.)	3,582-7,192
Rainfall (in.)	8.8
Jan. mean min.	29
July mean max.	96
Growing season (days)	248
Civ. Labor	289,499
Unemployed	10.2
Annual Wages	$5,342,088,039
Av. Weekly Wage	$436.80
Fed. Wages	$366,523,262
Ag. Net Cash Return	$19,939,000
Prop. Value	$18,382,340,822
Retail Sales	$5,515,712,759

Erath County

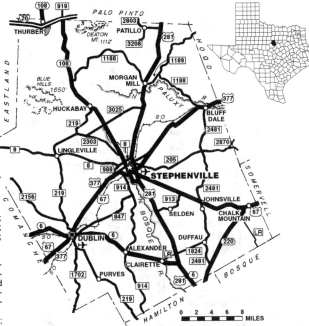

Physical Features: West central county on Rolling Plains; clay loam, sandy soils; drains to Bosque, Paluxy Rivers.

Economy: Agricultural, industrial and educational enterprises.

History: Caddo and Anadarko Indians moved to Oklahoma in 1860. Anglo-American settlement began 1854-55. County created from Bosque, Coryell counties 1856; named for George B. Erath, Texas Revolution figure.

Ethnicity, 1990: White, 26,413 (94.4%); Black, 195 (0.7%); American Indian, 94 (0.3%); Asian, 115 (0.4%); Other, 1,174 (4.2%). Hispanic, 2,458 (8.8%).

Vital Statistics, 1997: Births, 445; deaths, 298; marriages, 324; divorces, 169.

Recreation: Old courthouse; log cabins; museums; nearby lakes, Bosque River Park; Tarleton State University with fine arts center; Dairy Fest in June.

Minerals: Gas, oil.

Agriculture: Leading county in milk production; beef cattle, horses raised; horticulture industry, especially tree growing and greenhouses; peanuts, hay, silage; some irrigation, mostly peanuts and silage crops. Market value $232.9 million.

STEPHENVILLE (15,589) county seat; Tarleton State University; various manufacturing plants; hospital, mental health center; Texas A&M research and extension center.

Dublin (3,658) agribusiness; food processing; tourism; library; St. Patrick's celebration; old Dr Pepper plant.

Other towns include: **Bluff Dale** (123); **Lingleville** (100); **Morgan Mill** (206); **Thurber** (8) former coal-mining town.

Population	31,680
Change fm '90	13.2
Area (sq. mi.)	1,089.8
Land Area (sq. mi.)	1,086.4
Altitude (ft.)	900-1,650
Rainfall (in.)	32.9
Jan. mean min.	31
July mean max.	94

Growing season (days)	238
Civ. Labor	16,447
Unemployed	2.9
Annual Wages	$244,329,994
Av. Weekly Wage	$388.48
Fed. Wages	$3,231,193
Ag. Net Cash Return	$42,627,000
Prop. Value	$1,349,819,149
Retail Sales	$305,868,748

Falls County

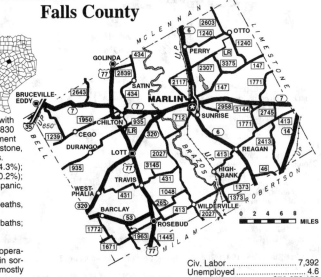

Physical Features: East central county on rolling prairie; bisected by Brazos; blackland, red, sandy loam soils; mineral springs.

Economy: Government/services, agribusiness, varied manufacturing.

History: Wacos, Tawokanis, Anadarkos in conflict with Comanches. Cherokees alone in area 1830 until 1835 when Anglo-American settlement began. County created 1850 from Limestone, Milam counties; named for Brazos River falls.

Ethnicity, 1990: White, 11,390 (64.3%); Black, 4,810 (27.2%); American Indian, 41 (0.2%); Asian, 21 (0.1%); Other, 1,450 (8.2%). Hispanic, 2,072 (11.7%).

Vital Statistics, 1997: Births, 235; deaths, 261; marriages, 106; divorces, 62.

Recreation: Fishing, camping, mineral baths; Highland Mansion and Falls on the Brazos.

Minerals: Rock, sand, oil.

Agriculture: Stocker cattle, cow-calf operations, goats, sheep, swine raised; corn, grain sorghum, oats, wheat, soybeans; 5,000 acres, mostly cotton, irrigated. Market value $52.3 million.

MARLIN (6,647) county seat; veterans hospital, prison, hospital; agribusiness, small industries; mineral water and spas; tourism; Festival Days in May.

Other towns include: **Chilton** (274); **Golinda** (404); **Lott** (877); **Otto** (48); **Perry** (76); **Reagan** (208); **Rosebud** (1,522) feed, fertilizer processing, clothing manufactured; **Satin** (86).

Population	18,331
Change fm '90	3.5
Area (sq. mi.)	773.8
Land Area (sq. mi.)	769.1
Altitude (ft.)	300-650
Rainfall (in.)	36.8
Jan. mean min.	36
July mean max.	96
Growing season (days)	257

Civ. Labor	7,392
Unemployed	4.6
Annual Wages	$76,670,158
Av. Weekly Wage	$393.96
Fed. Wages	$1,565,770
Ag. Net Cash Return	$5,954,000
Prop. Value	$677,542,890
Retail Sales	$72,421,633

For explanation of sources, abbreviations and symbols, see p. 130.

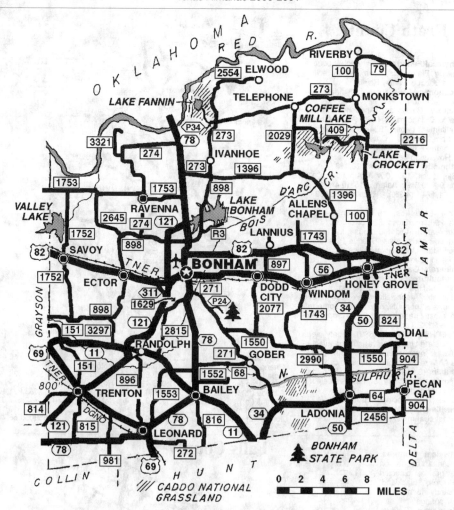

Fannin County

Physical Features: North Texas county of rolling prairie, drained by Red River, Bois d'Arc Creek; mostly blackland soils; national grassland.

Economy: Agribusiness; government/services; distribution; meat packing; tourism.

History: Caddoes who joined with Cherokees. Anglo-American settlement began in 1836. County created from Red River County, 1837, organized 1838; named for James W. Fannin, a victim of Goliad massacre.

Ethnicity, 1990: White, 22,722 (91.6%); Black, 1,633 (6.6%); American Indian, 182 (0.7%); Asian, 54 (0.2%); Other, 213 (0.9%). Hispanic, 485 (2.0%).

Vital Statistics, 1997: Births, 361; deaths, 419; marriages, 242; divorces, 133.

Recreation: Water activities on lakes; hunting; state park; Ivanhoe Winery; Sam Rayburn home, memorial library.

Minerals: Not significant; some sand produced.

Agriculture: Cattle, soybeans, wheat, nursery, corn; also poultry, horses, goats, hogs; hay, sorghum, turf grass; 2,500 acres irrigated, mainly peanuts. Market value $39.2 million.

BONHAM (7,073) county seat; varied manufacturing; veterans hospital and private hospital; state jail; Bois D'Arc Festival in May.

Other towns include: **Bailey** (219); **Dodd City** (432); **Ector** (539); **Gober** (146); **Honey Grove** (1,828) agribusiness center, varied manufacturing, tourism, historic buildings, Davy Crockett Day in October; **Ivanhoe** (110); **Ladonia** (710) restored historical downtown, varied manufacturing; **Leonard** (1,870) varied manufacturing; **Randolph** (70); **Ravenna** (239); **Savoy** (947); **Telephone** (210); **Trenton** (717); **Windom** (311).

Population	28,015
Change fm '90	12.9
Area (sq. mi.)	899.1
Land Area (sq. mi.)	891.6
Altitude (ft.)	450-800
Rainfall (in.)	44.0
Jan. mean min.	29
July mean max.	94
Growing season (days)	228
Civ. Labor	12,477
Unemployed	4.8
Annual Wages	$161,899,614
Av. Weekly Wage	$422.19
Fed. Wages	$23,536,134
Ag. Net Cash Returns	$2,580,000
Prop. Value	$974,738,348
Retail Sales	$183,297,139

For explanation of sources, abbreviations and symbols, see p. 130.

Fayette County

Physical Features: Southeast county bisected by Colorado River; rolling to level; sandy loam, black waxy soils.

Economy: Agribusiness; tourism; production of electricity; mineral production; small manufacturing.

History: Lipan Apaches and Tonkawas. Austin's colonists arrived in 1822. Germans and Czechs began arriving in 1840s. County created from Bastrop, Colorado counties, 1837; organized, 1838; named for hero of American Revolution, Marquis de Lafayette.

Ethnicity, 1990: White, 17,323 (86.2%); Black, 1,686 (8.4%); American Indian, 29 (0.1%); Asian, 15 (0.1%); Other, 1,042 (5.2%). Hispanic, 1,702 (8.5%).

Vital Statistics, 1997: Births, 263; deaths, 294; marriages, 140; divorces, 64.

Recreation: Monument Hill State Park, Faison Home Museum, brewery, other historic sites including "Painted Churches"; hunting, fishing, lake; German and Czech ethnic foods; Prazska Pout in August.

Minerals: Oil, gas, sand, gravel.

Agriculture: Poultry; beef, dairy cows; corn, sorghum, peanuts, hay, pecans. Market value $59.7 million. Some firewood sold.

LA GRANGE (4,145) county seat; electric-power generation; varied manufacturing; food processing; retail trade center; tourism; hospital, Texas Independence Day celebration.

Schulenburg (2,855) varied manufacturing; food processing; Bluebonnet Festival.

Round Top (88) music center, and **Winedale** (41), historic restorations including Winedale Inn.

Other towns include: **Carmine** (215); **Ellinger** (200); **Fayetteville** (314); **Flatonia** (1,372) farm market, Czhilispiel in October; **Ledbetter** (76); **Muldoon** (98); **Plum** (95); **Warda** (98); **Warrenton** (65); **West Point** (205), and **Winchester** (50).

Population.............................. 21,768
Change fm '90 .... 8.3
Area (sq. mi.)............................... 959.8

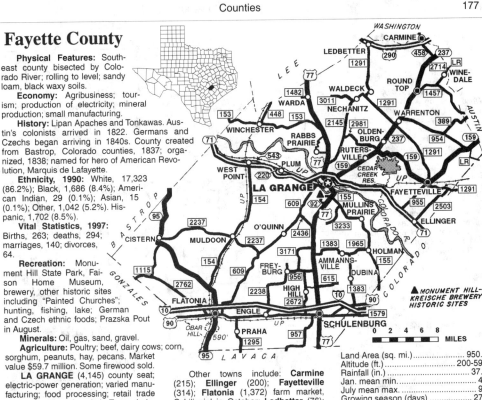

Land Area (sq. mi.)...................... 950.1
Altitude (ft.)............................. 200-590
Rainfall (in.)................................. 37.1
Jan. mean min. 40
July mean max. 95
Growing season (days) 277
Civ. Labor................................. 10,398
Unemployed 2.8
Annual Wages................ $170,020,661
Av. Weekly Wage................... $417.89
Fed. Wages $2,501,967
Ag. Net Cash Return .... -$5,704,000
Prop. Value................. $1,778,995,118
Retail Sales $262,595,878

Fisher County

Physical Features: West central county on rolling prairie; mesquite; red, sandy loam soils; drains to forks of Brazos River.

Economy: Agribusiness; electric co-op; oil; gypsum.

History: Lipan Apaches, disrupted by Comanches and other tribes around 1700. Ranching began in 1876. County created from Bexar District, 1876; organized 1886; named for S.R. Fisher, Republic of Texas secretary of navy.

Ethnicity, 1990: White, 4,445 (91.8%); Black, 190 (3.9%); American Indian, 19 (0.4%); Asian, 0 (0.0%); Other, 188 (3.9%). Hispanic, 997 (20.6%).

Vital Statistics, 1997: Births, 45; deaths, 82; marriages, 38; divorces, 22.

Recreation: Quail, dove, turkey hunting; wildlife viewing; fair, rodeo in August.

Minerals: Gypsum, oil.

Agriculture: Cotton, hay, wheat, sorghum; irrigation for cotton, alfalfa. Cattle, horses, sheep, goats. Market value $30.8 million.

ROBY (574) county seat; agribusiness, cotton gin; hospital between Roby and Rotan.

ROTAN (1,757) gypsum plant; oil mill; agribusinesses.

Other towns include: **McCaulley** (96) and **Sylvester** (79). Part of **Hamlin** (2,429).

Population 4,464
Change fm '90 .... -7.8
Area (sq. mi.) 901.7
Land Area (sq. mi.) 901.2
Altitude (ft.) 1,723-2,400
Rainfall (in.).............................. 24.3

Jan. mean min................................ 30
July mean max............................... 96
Growing season (days) 218
Civ. Labor................................. 1,808
Unemployed 4.4

Annual Wages.................. $20,114,399
Av. Weekly Wage................... $394.37
Fed. Wages $887,656
Ag. Net Cash Return.......... $5,294,000
Prop. Value $307,142,355
Retail Sales..................... $10,788,587

Floyd County

Physical Features:
Flat High Plains, broken by Caprock on east, by White River on south; many playas; red, black loam soils.

Economy: Cotton; livestock feedlots; farm machinery and oil-field manufacturing; metal products; printing.

History: Plains Apaches and later Comanches. First white settlers arrived in 1884. County created from Bexar District, 1876; organized 1890. Named for Dolphin Ward Floyd, who died at Alamo.

Ethnicity, 1990: White, 5,523 (65.0%); Black, 320 (3.8%); American Indian, 16 (0.2%); Asian, 15 (0.2%); Other, 2,623 (30.9%). Hispanic, 3,381 (39.8%).

Vital Statistics, 1997: Births, 139; deaths, 74; marriages, 58; divorces, 37.

Recreation: Hunting, fishing; Blanco Canyon; Pumpkin Days; museum.

Minerals: Not significant.

Agriculture: Cotton, wheat, sorghum, corn; beef cattle; 260,000 acres irrigated. Market value $130.7 million.

FLOYDADA (3,759) county seat; some manufacturing; meat, vegetable processing; distribution center; Old Settlers Reunion; Texas A&M engineering extension.

Lockney (2,048) agriculture center; manufacturing; hospital.

Other towns include: **Aiken** (57), **Dougherty** (109), and **South Plains** (92).

Population	**8,140**
Change fm '90	-4.2
Area (sq. mi.)	992.5

Land Area (sq. mi.)	992.3
Altitude (ft.)	2,574-3,316
Rainfall (in.)	20.5
Jan. mean min.	22
July mean max.	92
Growing season (days)	213
Civ. Labor	3,421

Unemployed	8.3
Annual Wages	$41,605,712
Av. Weekly Wage	$359.15
Fed. Wages	$1,269,528
Ag. Net Cash Return	$22,214,000
Prop. Value	$346,058,940
Retail Sales	$45,117,453

Foard County

Physical Features: Northwest county drains to North Wichita, Pease rivers; sandy, loam soils, rolling surface.

Economy: Agribusiness, clothes manufacturing, government/service.

History: Comanches, Kiowas ranged the area until driven away in 1870s. Ranching began in 1880. County created out of Cottle, Hardeman, King, Knox counties, 1891; named for Maj. Robert L. Foard of Confederate army.

Ethnicity, 1990: White, 1,552 (86.5%); Black, 88 (4.9%); American Indian, 11 (0.6%); Asian, 4 (0.2%); Other, 139 (7.7%). Hispanic, 233 (13.0%).

Vital Statistics, 1997: Births, 17; deaths, 22; marriages, 6; divorces, 4.

Recreation: Three museums, wild hog cookoff in November.

Minerals: Oil, gas.

Agriculture: Wheat, cotton, alfalfa; cow-calf operations, stockers; irrigation for alfalfa. Market value $11 million.

CROWELL (1,213) county seat; agriculture center; manufacturing.

Population	**1,852**
Change fm '90	3.2
Area (sq. mi.)	707.7
Land Area (sq. mi.)	706.7
Altitude (ft.)	1,300-1,830
Rainfall (in.)	23.9
Jan. mean min.	24
July mean max.	97
Growing season (days)	219
Civ. Labor	859
Unemployed	4.1
Annual Wages	$6,396,056
Av. Weekly Wage	$293.08
Fed. Wages	$379,555
Ag. Net Cash Return	$2,125,000
Prop. Value	$113,822,636
Retail Sales	$5,152,889

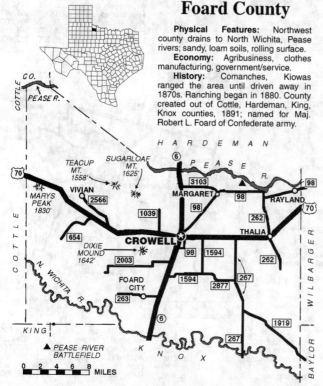

For explanation of sources, abbreviations and symbols, see p. 130.

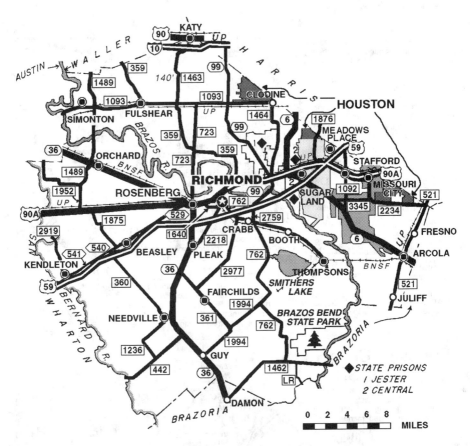

Fort Bend County

Physical Features: On Gulf Coastal Plain; drained by Brazos, San Bernard rivers; level to rolling; rich alluvial soils.

Economy: Agribusiness, petrochemicals, sulfur, sugar refinery; government/service; many residents work in Houston; part of Houston metropolitan area.

History: Karankawas retreated to Mexico by 1850s. Named for river bend where some of Austin's colonists settled 1824. Antebellum plantations made it one of six Texas counties with black majority in 1850. County created 1837 from Austin County; organized 1838.

Ethnicity, 1990: White, 141,125 (62.6%); Black, 46,593 (20.7%); American Indian, 525 (0.2%); Asian, 14,328 (6.4%); Other, 22,850 (10.1%). Hispanic, 43,892 (19.5%).

Vital Statistics, 1997: Births, 4,450; deaths, 1,271; marriages, 1,865; divorces, 1,202.

Recreation: Many historic sites, museum, memorials; state park with George Observatory; fishing, waterfowl hunting.

Minerals: Oil, gas, sulphur, salt, clays, sand and gravel.

Agriculture: Nursery crops (second in state in value of sales); cotton, sorghum, hay, soybeans; cattle, horses; irrigation for rice. Market value $76.4 million.

RICHMOND (14,196) county seat; foundry; Richmond State School (for mentally retarded).

SUGAR LAND (68,716) sugar refinery, prison units.

MISSOURI CITY (58,002, partly in Harris County).

ROSENBERG (29,588) varied industry; annual Czech festival; Wharton County Junior College campus.

Other towns include: **Arcola** (898); **Beasley** (639); **Fairchilds** (500); **Fresno** (4,499); **Fulshear** (809); **Guy** (60); **Katy** (11,175, partly in Harris, Waller counties); **Kendleton** (701); **Meadows Place** (6,730).

Also, **Needville** (3,205); **Orchard** (532); **Pleak** (1,050); **Simonton** (1,005); **Stafford** (15,302); **Thompsons** (248).

Population	**324,189**
Change fm '90	43.8
Area (sq. mi.)	886.0
Land Area (sq. mi.)	875.0
Altitude (ft.)	46-140
Rainfall (in.)	45.3
Jan. mean min.	41
July mean max.	93
Growing season (days)	296
Civ. Labor	176,288
Unemployed	2.9
Annual Wages	$2,662,081,283
Av. Weekly Wage	$636.95
Fed. Wages	$16,965,923
Ag. Net Cash Return	$22,952,000
Prop. Value	$15,278,973,204
Retail Sales	$2,414,002,058

For explanation of sources, abbreviations and symbols, see p. 130.

Franklin County

Physical Features: Small Northeast county with many wooded hills; drained by numerous streams; alluvial to sandy clay soils; two lakes.

Economy: Agribusiness; tourism, retirement center; oil.

History: Caddoes abandoned the area in 1790s because of disease and other tribes. White settlement began in 1830s. County created 1875 from Titus County; named for jurist B.C. Franklin.

Ethnicity, 1990: White, 7,139 (91.5%); Black, 349 (4.5%); American Indian, 47 (0.6%); Asian, 18 (0.2%); Other, 249 (3.2%). Hispanic, 357 (4.6%).

Vital Statistics, 1997: Births, 87; deaths, 103; marriages, 59; divorces, 47.

Recreation: Fishing, water sports; Countryfest in October; historic homes.

Minerals: Oil, gas and lignite.

Agriculture: Among top counties in dairy and broiler production; hay is principal crop; blueberries, peaches, Christmas trees, soybeans sorghum, wheat; beef cattle raised. Market value $49.2 million.

MOUNT VERNON (2,416) county seat; distribution center, manufacturing; tourism; dairies, blueberries; hospital.

Other towns include: **Scroggins** (125), and **Winnsboro** (3,223, mostly in Wood County) commercial center.

Population	**8,747**
Change fm '90	12.1
Area (sq. mi.)	294.7
Land Area (sq. mi.)	285.7
Altitude (ft.)	300-600
Rainfall (in.)	46.8
Jan. mean min.	33
July mean max.	93
Growing season (days)	234
Civ. Labor	4,450
Unemployed	4.4
Annual Wages	$49,948,798
Av. Weekly Wage	$396.90
Fed. Wages	$457,753
Ag. Net Cash Return	$3,838,000
Prop. Value	$574,761,075
Retail Sales	$51,181,790

Freestone County

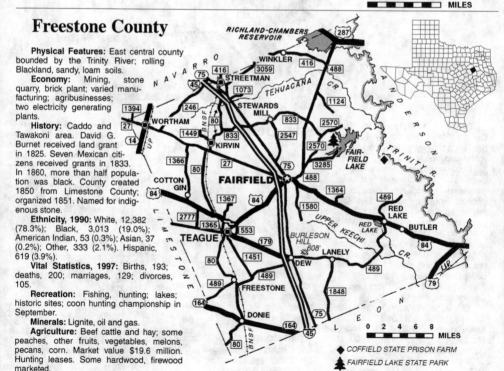

◆ COFFIELD STATE PRISON FARM

🌲 FAIRFIELD LAKE STATE PARK

Physical Features: East central county bounded by the Trinity River; rolling Blackland, sandy, loam soils.

Economy: Mining, stone quarry, brick plant; varied manufacturing; agribusinesses; two electricity generating plants.

History: Caddo and Tawakoni area. David G. Burnet received land grant in 1825. Seven Mexican citizens received grants in 1833. In 1860, more than half population was black. County created 1850 from Limestone County; organized 1851. Named for indigenous stone.

Ethnicity, 1990: White, 12,382 (78.3%); Black, 3,013 (19.0%); American Indian, 53 (0.3%); Asian, 37 (0.2%); Other, 333 (2.1%). Hispanic, 619 (3.9%).

Vital Statistics, 1997: Births, 193; deaths, 200; marriages, 129; divorces, 105.

Recreation: Fishing, hunting; lakes; historic sites; coon hunting championship in September.

Minerals: Lignite, oil and gas.

Agriculture: Beef cattle and hay; some peaches, other fruits, vegetables, melons, pecans, corn. Market value $19.6 million. Hunting leases. Some hardwood, firewood marketed.

FAIRFIELD (3,312) county seat; lignite mining; GTE telephone operations; trade center; hospital, museum; peach festival on July 4 weekend.

TEAGUE (3,678) nursing homes; oil; manufacturing, railroad museum; prison unit.

Other towns include: **Donie** (206), **Kirvin** (129), **Streetman** (276), **Wortham** (953).

Population	17,872
Change fm '90	13.0
Area (sq. mi.)	892.1
Land Area (sq. mi.)	885.3
Altitude (ft.)	209-608
Rainfall (in.)	39.8
Jan. mean min.	36
July mean max.	95
Growing season (days)	263
Civ. Labor	7,298
Unemployed	5.8
Annual Wages	$100,033,053
Av. Weekly Wage	$443.58
Fed. Wages	$1,203,959
Ag. Net Cash Return	-$2,824,000
Prop. Value	$1,329,327,046
Retail Sales	$120,595,084

Frio County

Physical Features: South Texas county of rolling terrain with much brush; bisected by Frio River; sandy, red sandy loam soils.

Economy: Agribusiness; oilfield services.

History: Coahuiltecans; many taken into San Antonio missions. Comanche hunters kept settlers out until after the Civil War. Mexican citizens recruited for labor after 1900. County created 1871 from Atascosa, Bexar, Uvalde counties; named for Frio (cold) River.

Ethnicity, 1990: White, 9,119 (67.7%); Black, 183 (1.4%); American Indian, 23 (0.2%); Asian, 38 (0.3%); Other, 4,109 (30.5%). Hispanic, 9,749 (72.4%).

Vital Statistics, 1997: Births, 292; deaths, 132; marriages, 110; divorces, 47.

Recreation: Hunting; Big Foot Wallace Museum; Winter Garden area; potato festival.

Minerals: Oil, natural gas, stone.

Agriculture: A leading peanut-producing county; other crops potatoes, spinach, cucumbers, watermelons; cattle, hogs, goats raised. Market value $68 million.

PEARSALL (7,821) county seat; agriculture center; oil, gas; food processing, shipping; old jail museum; hospital; Pioneer days in April.

Dilley (2,977) shipping center for melons, peanuts.

Other towns include: **Bigfoot** (75), **Derby** (50), and **Moore** (230).

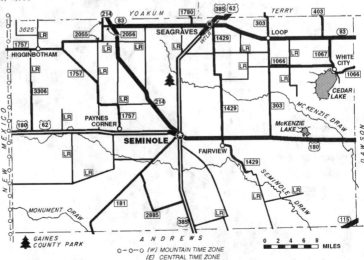

Population	15,719
Change fm '90	16.7
Area (sq. mi.)	1,134.3
Land Area (sq. mi.)	1,133.1
Altitude (ft.)	400-763
Rainfall (in.)	25.4
Jan. mean min.	38
July mean max.	97

Growing season (days)	291
Civ. Labor	6,446
Unemployed	8.9
Annual Wages	$78,078,072
Av. Weekly Wage	$358.72
Fed. Wages	$929,549
Ag. Net Cash Return	$20,495,000
Prop. Value	$594,424,417
Retail Sales	$66,783,456

Gaines County

Physical Features: On South Plains, drains to draws; playas; underground water.

Economy: Oil and gas production, agribusiness.

History: Comanche country until U.S. Army campaigns of 1875. Ranchers arrived in 1880s; farming began around 1900. County created from Bexar District, 1876; organized 1905; named for James Gaines, signer of Texas Declaration of Independence.

Ethnicity, 1990: White, 10,378 (73.5%); Black, 334 (2.4%); American Indian, 38 (0.3%); Asian, 15 (0.1%); Other, 3,358 (23.8%). Hispanic, 4,608 (32.6%).

Vital Statistics, 1997: Births, 240; deaths, 108; marriages, 202; divorces, 68.

Recreation: Cedar Lake one of largest alkali lakes on Texas plains; Ag and Oil Day in September.

Minerals: One of leading oil-producing counties; gas.

Agriculture: Cotton (first in state in value of sales), peanuts; small grains, vegetables raised; cattle, sheep, hogs; substantial irrigation. Market value $218.3 million.

SEMINOLE (6,497) county seat; market center; hospital.

Seagraves (2,269) market for three-county area; manufacturing, distribution.

Other towns include: **Loop** (315).

Population	14,251
Change fm '90	0.9
Area (sq. mi.)	1,502.8
Land Area (sq. mi.)	1,502.4
Altitude (ft.)	3,000-3,625
Rainfall (in.)	17.5
Jan. mean min.	25
July mean max.	94
Growing season (days)	210
Civ. Labor	6,996
Unemployed	5.0
Annual Wages	$100,177,427
Av. Weekly Wage	$429.61
Fed. Wages	$1,281,268
Ag. Net Cash Return	$52,322,000
Prop. Value	$2,850,045,245
Retail Sales	$103,934,531

For explanation of sources, abbreviations and symbols, see p. 130.

Galveston County

Physical Features: Partly island, partly coastal; flat, artificial drainage; sandy, loam, clay soils; broken by bays.

Economy: Port activities dominate economy; insurance and finance center; petrochemical plants; varied manufacturing; tourism; medical education center; oceanographic research center; ship building; commercial fishing.

History: Karankawa and other tribes roamed the area until 1850. French, Spanish and American settlement began in 1815 and reached 1,000 by 1817. County created from Brazoria County 1838; organized 1839; named for Spanish governor of Louisiana Count Bernardo de Galvez.

Ethnicity, 1990: White, 164,210 (75.5%); Black, 38,154 (17.6%); American Indian, 752 (0.3%); Asian, 3,569 (1.6%); Other, 10,714 (4.9%). Hispanic, 30,962 (14.2%).

Vital Statistics, 1997: Births, 3,565; deaths, 1,976; marriages, 1,933; divorces, 1,111.

Recreation: One of Texas' most historic cities; popular tourist and convention center; fishing, surfing, boating, sailing and other water sports; state park; Historical District tour in spring includes homes, sites; Mardi Gras celebration; Rosenberg Library; museums, drama *Lone Star* presented in outdoor amphitheater in summer; restored sail-

For explanation of sources, abbreviations and symbols, see p. 130.

ing ship, "Elissa," railroad museum; Dickens on the Strand in early December.

Minerals: Production of oil, gas, clays, sand and gravel.

Agriculture: Cattle, aquaculture, nursery crops, rice, hay; horses raised; some soybeans. Market value $6.8 million.

GALVESTON (64,493) county seat; tourist center; shipyard; other industries; insurance; port container facility; University of Texas Medical Branch; National Maritime Research Center; Texas A&M University at Galveston; Galveston College; hospitals.

Texas City (42,110) refining, petrochemical plants; shipping; College of the Mainland; hospital; dike; Shrimp Boil in August.

Other towns include: **Bacliff** (6,047); **Bayou Vista** (1,595); **Clear**

Lake Shores (1,336); **Crystal Beach** (787) on Bolivar Peninsula, seafood industry; Fort Travis Seashore Park, shorebird sanctuary; crab festival in May.

Also, **Dickinson** (17,578) manufacturing, commuters; strawberry festival in May; **Friendswood** (30,247); **Gilchrist** (750); **High Island** (500); **Hitchcock** (6,482) residential community, tourism, fishing and shrimping, Good Ole Days in August, WWII blimp base.

Also, **Jamaica Beach** (757); **Kemah** (1,519) fishing; **La Marque** (14,367) refining, greyhound racing, Grill-off in March; **League City** (43,601); **Port Bolivar** (1,200); **San Leon** (3,977); **Santa Fe** (10,238); **Village of Tiki Island** (737).

Population	**242,253**
Change fm '90	11.4
Area (sq. mi.)	876.3
Land Area (sq. mi.)	398.7
Altitude (ft.)	sea level-35
Rainfall (in.)	42.3
Jan. mean min.	47
July mean max.	87
Growing season (days)	335
Civ. Labor	124,475
Unemployed	6.6
Annual Wages	$2,398,597,430
Av. Weekly Wage	$530.13
Fed. Wages	$43,241,691
Ag. Net Cash Return	-$366,000
Prop. Value	$18,065,353,799
Retail Sales	$1,824,430,388

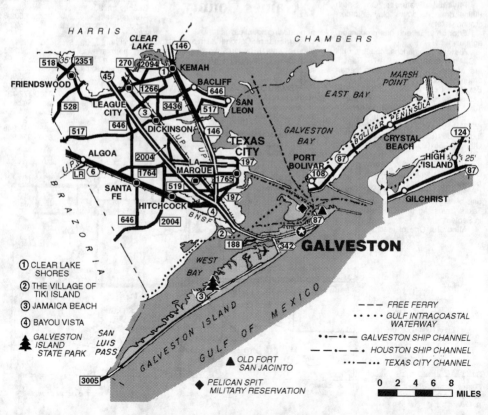

① CLEAR LAKE SHORES
② THE VILLAGE OF TIKI ISLAND
③ JAMAICA BEACH
④ BAYOU VISTA
🌲 GALVESTON ISLAND STATE PARK

▲ OLD FORT SAN JACINTO
♦ PELICAN SPIT MILITARY RESERVATION

– – – FREE FERRY
• • • • • GULF INTRACOASTAL WATERWAY
•—••—•• GALVESTON SHIP CHANNEL
—•—•— HOUSTON SHIP CHANNEL
•••—•••— TEXAS CITY CHANNEL

0 2 4 6 8 MILES

Garza County

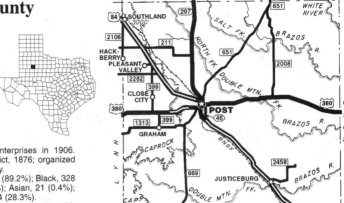

Physical Features: On edge of Caprock; rough, broken land, with playas, gullies, canyons, Brazos River forks; sandy, loam, clay soils.

Economy: Cotton, oil, tourism.

History: Kiowas and Comanches yielded to U.S. Army in 1875. Ranching began in 1870s, farming in the 1890s. C.W. Post, the cereal millionaire, established enterprises in 1906. County created from Bexar District, 1876; organized 1907; named for early Texas family.

Ethnicity, 1990: White, 4,588 (89.2%); Black, 328 (6.4%); American Indian, 9 (0.2%); Asian, 21 (0.4%); Other, 197 (3.8%). Hispanic, 1,454 (28.3%).

Vital Statistics, 1997: Births, 76; deaths, 58; marriages, 45; divorces, 22.

Recreation: Post Stampede in August, scenic areas; Post-Garza Museum.

Minerals: Oil.

Agriculture: Cotton is major cash crop, hay; beef cattle, horses; 4,000 acres irrigated. Market value $14.8 million.

POST (3,622) county seat; founded by C.W. Post; oil, agribusiness center; hospital.

Other towns include: **Justiceburg** (76).

Population	4,987
Change fm '90	-3.0
Area (sq. mi.)	896.2
Land Area (sq. mi.)	895.6
Altitude (ft.)	2,176-3,000
Rainfall (in.)	20.9
Jan. mean min.	27
July mean max.	94
Growing season (days)	216
Civ. Labor	2,060
Unemployed	7.1
Annual Wages	$23,845,463
Av. Weekly Wage	$365.66
Fed. Wages	$649,694
Ag. Net Cash Return	$3,668,000
Prop. Value	$471,641,960
Retail Sales	$24,992,846

Gillespie County

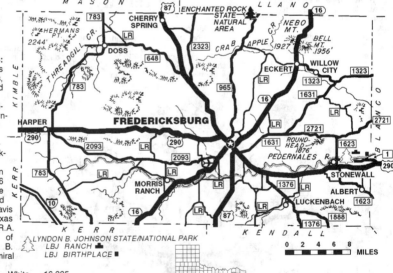

Physical Features: Picturesque Edwards Plateau area with hills, broken by spring-fed streams.

Economy: Agribusiness; tourism; government/services; food processing; hunting leases; small manufacturing; granite for markers.

History: German settlement founded 1846 in heart of Comanche country. County created 1848 from Bexar, Travis counties; named for Texas Ranger Capt. R.A. Gillespie. Birthplace of President Lyndon B. Johnson and Fleet Admiral Chester W. Nimitz.

Ethnicity, 1990: White, 16,325 (94.9%); Black, 34 (0.2%); American Indian, 60 (0.3%); Asian, 27 (0.2%); Other, 758 (4.4%). Hispanic, 2,426 (14.1%).

Vital Statistics, 1997: Births, 209; deaths, 278; marriages, 171; divorces, 99.

Recreation: Among leading deer-hunting areas; fishing; numerous historic sites and tourist attractions include LBJ Ranch, Nimitz Hotel; Pioneer Museum Complex, Enchanted Rock.

Minerals: Sand, gravel, gypsum, limestone rock.

Agriculture: Most income from beef cattle, turkeys, sheep and goats; a leading peach-producing county; hay, grain sorghum, oats, wheat, grapes also raised.

Market value $29.3 million. Hunting leases.

FREDERICKSBURG (8,550) county seat; government/services; varied manufacturing; wine production; food processing; museum; tourist attractions; hospital; Easter Fires.

Other towns include: **Doss** (75); **Harper** (383) ranching, deer hunting; Dachshund Hounds Downs race and Trades Day in October; **Luckenbach** (25); **Stonewall** (245) agribusiness, wineries, tourism, Peach Jamboree in June, and **Willow City** (75).

Population	20,386
Change fm '90	18.5
Area (sq. mi.)	1,061.5
Land Area (sq. mi.)	1,061.2
Altitude (ft.)	1,400-2,244
Rainfall (in.)	30.0
Jan. mean min.	35
July mean max.	93
Growing season (days)	219
Civ. Labor	10,267
Unemployed	1.8
Annual Wages	$131,743,233
Av. Weekly Wage	$361.85
Fed. Wages	$3,750,127
Ag. Net Cash Return	$911,000
Prop. Value	$1,784,878,612
Retail Sales	$219,178,657

Glasscock County

Physical Features: Western county on rolling plains, broken by small streams; sandy, loam soils.

Economy: Farming, ranching, hunting leases, oil and gas.

History: Hunting area for Kickapoos and Lipan Apaches. Anglo-American sheep ranchers and Mexican-American shepherds or *pastores* moved into the area in 1880s. County created 1887, from Tom Green County; organized, 1893; named for Texas pioneer George W. Glasscock.

Ethnicity, 1990: White, 1,156 (79.9%); Black, 0 (0.0%); American Indian, 2 (0.1%); Asian, 0 (0.0%); Other, 289 (20.0%). Hispanic, 424 (29.3%).

Vital Statistics, 1997: Births, 13; deaths, 4; marriages, 7; divorces, 3.

Recreation: Hunting of deer, quail, turkey; St. Lawrence Fall Festival.

Minerals: Oil, gas.

Agriculture: Cotton, extensive irrigation; cattle, sheep, goats, swine raised. Market value $23.7 million.

GARDEN CITY (293), county seat; serves sparsely settled ranching, oil area.

Population		
Population		1,341
Change fm '90		-7.3
Area (sq. mi.)		900.9
Land Area (sq. mi.)		900.8
Altitude (ft.)		2,495-2,727
Rainfall (in.)		18.0
Jan. mean min.		25
July mean max.		94
Growing season (days)		222
Civ. Labor		654
Unemployed		2.3
Annual Wages		$7,258,048
Av. Weekly Wage		$391.77
Fed. Wages		$147,091
Ag. Net Cash Return		$4,397,000
Prop. Value		$471,574,860
Retail Sales		$2,293,438

Goliad County

Physical Features: South Texas county; rolling, brushy; bisected by San Antonio River; sandy, loam, alluvial soils.

Economy: Primarily based on oil; agribusiness; tourism, electricity-generating plant.

History: Karankawas, Comanches and other tribes in area in historic period. La Bahía mission established 1749. County created 1836 from Spanish municipality; organized 1837; name is anagram of (H)idalgo. Birthplace of Gen. Zaragoza, hero of Battle of Puebla (Mexico).

Ethnicity, 1990: White, 4,953 (82.8%); Black, 407 (6.8%); American Indian, 19 (0.3%); Asian, 5 (0.1%); Other, 596 (10.0%). Hispanic, 2,145 (35.9%).

Vital Statistics, 1997: Births, 71; deaths, 77; marriages, 37; divorces, 21.

Recreation: Missions, restored Presidio La Bahía, Fannin Battleground; Gen. Ignacio Zaragoza statue; Old Market House museum; lake, fishing, hunting, camping.

Minerals: Production of oil, gas.

Agriculture: Beef cattle, stocker operations and fed cattle are top revenue producers; corn, grain sorghums, hay; minor irrigation for pasture, fruit trees. Market value $12.4 million.

GOLIAD (2,204) county seat; one of state's oldest towns; tourism; oil; agriculture; Christmas in Goliad.

Other towns include: **Berclair** (253), **Fannin** (359) and **Weesatche** (411).

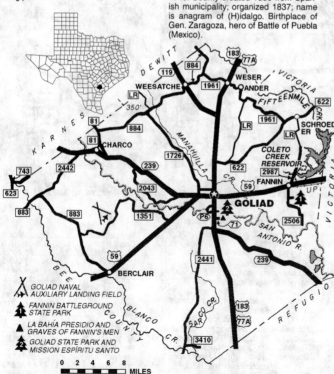

Population		
Population		6,578
Change fm '90		10.0
Area (sq. mi.)		859.3
Land Area (sq. mi.)		853.6
Altitude (ft.)		50-350
Rainfall (in.)		36.5
Jan. mean min.		43
July mean max.		95
Growing season (days)		285
Civ. Labor		2,702
Unemployed		3.8
Annual Wages		$26,179,901
Av. Weekly Wage		$404.12
Fed. Wages		$591,238
Ag. Net Cash Return		$329,000
Prop. Value		$668,170,100
Retail Sales		$28,589,942

For explanation of sources, abbreviations and symbols, see p. 130.

Gonzales County

Physical Features: South Texas county; rolling, rich bottom soils along Guadalupe River and its tributaries; some sandy areas; many oaks, pecans.

Economy: Agribusiness.

History: Coahuiltecan area. Among first Anglo-American settlements; the De-Witt colony late 1820s. County created 1836; organized 1837; named for Coahuila y Texas Gov. Rafael Gonzales.

Ethnicity, 1990: White, 13,025 (75.7%); Black, 1,716 (10.0%); American Indian, 46 (0.3%); Asian, 23 (0.1%); Other, 2,395 (13.9%). Hispanic, 6,142 (35.7%).

Vital Statistics, 1997: Births, 234; deaths, 191; marriages, 143; divorces, 68.

Recreation: Historic sites, 86 officially recognized homes or historical markers; Pioneer Village Living History Center; state park; museums, Independence Park.

Minerals: Gas, oil, clay, gravel.

Agriculture: Major poultry county (first in turkeys sold); cattle, hogs; corn, hay, sorghum, peanuts, wheat. Market value $294.4 million.

GONZALES (6,512) county seat; first shot in Texas Revolution fired here; shipping, processing center; manufacturing; hospitals; "Come and Take It" festival.

Other towns include: **Bebe** (52); **Belmont** (60); **Cost** (62); **Harwood** (112); **Leesville** (150); **Nixon** (2,034, partly in Wilson County) Feather Fest; **Ottine** (90), crippled children's hospital, Gonzales Warm Springs Foundation Hospital; **Smiley** (507) Settlers Set-To; **Waelder** (821) Guacamole Fest; **Wrightsboro** (76).

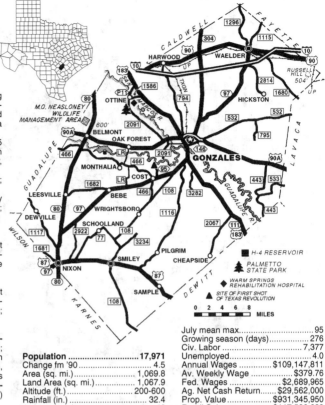

Population	17,971
Change fm '90	4.5
Area (sq. mi.)	1,069.8
Land Area (sq. mi.)	1,067.9
Altitude (ft.)	200-600
Rainfall (in.)	32.4
Jan. mean min.	40

July mean max.	95
Growing season (days)	276
Civ. Labor	7,377
Unemployed	4.0
Annual Wages	$109,147,811
Av. Weekly Wage	$379.76
Fed. Wages	$2,689,965
Ag. Net Cash Return	$29,562,000
Prop. Value	$931,345,950
Retail Sales	$117,590,682

Gray County

Physical Features: Panhandle High Plains, broken by Red River forks, tributaries; sandy loam, waxy soils.

Economy: Petroleum, agriculture, feedlot operations, chemical plant, other manufacturing.

History: Apaches, displaced by Comanches and Kiowas. Ranching began in late 1870s. Farmers arrived around 1900. Oil discovered 1926. County created 1876, from Bexar District; organized 1902; named for Peter W. Gray, member of first Legislature.

Ethnicity, 1990: White, 21,566 (90.0%); Black, 899 (3.8%); American Indian, 216 (0.9%); Asian, 115 (0.5%); Other, 1,171 (4.9%). Hispanic, 1,895 (7.9%).

Vital Statistics, 1997: Births, 302; deaths, 290; marriages, 224; divorces, 160.

Recreation: Water sports, Lake McClellan and grassland; White Deer Land Museum; barbed-wire museum, Chautauqua on Labor Day.

Minerals: Production of oil, gas.

Agriculture: Cattle, wheat, sorghum, hay, corn, soybeans. Market value $85.2 million.

PAMPA (19,808) county seat; petroleum and agriculture; chemical plant; hospital; college; prison unit.

Other towns include: **Alanreed** (48); **Lefors** (715); **McLean** (828) commercial center for southern part of county.

Population	24,883
Change fm '90	3.8
Area (sq. mi.)	929.2
Land Area (sq. mi.)	928.3
Altitude (ft.)	2,500-3,300

Rainfall (in.)	21.0
Jan. mean min.	21
July mean max.	92
Growing season (days)	195
Civ. Labor	10,583
Unemployed	4.8

Annual Wages	$257,789,951
Av. Weekly Wage	$560.88
Fed. Wages	$2,614,493
Ag. Net Cash Return	$8,279,000
Prop. Value	$1,125,178,064
Retail Sales	$230,872,710

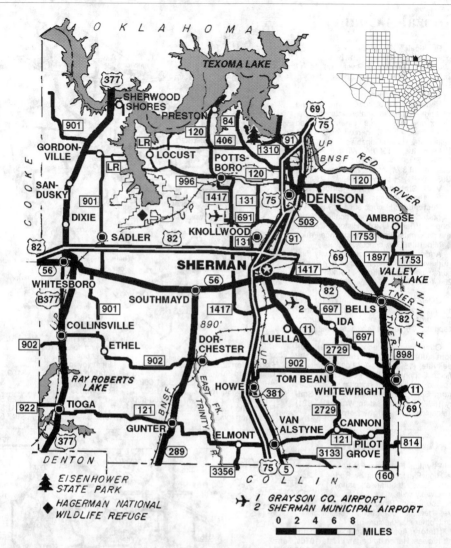

EISENHOWER STATE PARK

HAGERMAN NATIONAL WILDLIFE REFUGE

✈ 1 GRAYSON CO. AIRPORT
2 SHERMAN MUNICIPAL AIRPORT

0 2 4 6 8 MILES

Physical Features: North Texas county; level, some low hills; sandy loam, blackland soils; drains to Red River and tributaries of Trinity River.

Economy: A manufacturing, distribution and trade center for northern Texas and southern Oklahoma; tourism; agribusiness.

History: Caddo and Tonkawa area. Preston Bend trading post established 1836-37. Peters colony settlers arrived in 1840s. County created 1846 from Fannin County; named for Republic Atty. Gen. Peter S. Grayson.

Altitude, 1990: White, 85,553 (90.0%); Black, 6,565 (6.9%); American Indian, 1,046 (1.1%); Asian, 412 (0.4%); Other, 1,445 (1.5%). Hispanic, 2,795 (2.9%).

Vital Statistics, 1997: Births, 1,445; deaths, 1,174; marriages, 1,043; divorces, 708.

Recreation: Lakes; fishing; water sports; state park; cultural activities; wildlife refuge; Pioneer Village; railroad museum.

Grayson County

Minerals: Sand, gravel.

Agriculture: Cattle, horses, hogs, sheep, goats; wheat, sorghum, corn, soybeans, peanuts. 3,000 acres irrigated. Market value $35.5 million.

Education: Austin College in Sherman and Grayson County College located between Sherman and Denison.

SHERMAN (34,395) county seat; varied manufacturing; processors, distributors for major companies; Austin College; hospitals.

DENISON (22,425) Tourism, hospital, food processing; transportation center; Eisenhower birthplace; Main Street Fall festival.

Other towns include: **Bells** (1,006); **Collinsville** (1,248); **Dorchester** (167); **Gordonville** (165); **Gunter** (950); **Howe** (2,350) distribution; varied manufacturing, Founders' Day in May; **Knollwood**

(304); **Pottsboro** (1,578); **Sadler** (380); **Southmayd** (849); **Tioga** (688); **Tom Bean** (946); **Van Alstyne** (2,423) window screen, electronics, saddle, tack manufacturing; **Whitesboro** (3,445) agribusiness, tourism, Peanut Festival; **Whitewright** (1,777, partly in Fannin County), meat company, government/services.

Population	104,202
Change fm '90	9.7
Area (sq. mi.)	979.1
Land Area (sq. mi.)	933.7
Altitude (ft.)	500-890
Rainfall (in.)	40.4
Jan. mean min.	30
July mean max.	95
Growing season (days)	227
Civ. Labor	50,607
Unemployed	4.8
Annual Wages	$1,123,768,476
Av. Weekly Wage	$508.61
Fed. Wages	$13,155,309
Ag. Net Cash Return	$260,000
Prop. Value	$3,825,989,656
Retail Sales	$1,070,938,599

Physical Features: A populous, leading petroleum county, heart of the famed East Texas oil field; bisected by the Sabine River; hilly, timbered; with sandy, clay, alluvial soils.

Economy: Oil but with significant other manufacturing; tourism, conventions; agribusiness and lignite coal production.

History: Caddoes; later Cherokees, who were driven out in 1838 by President Lamar. First land grants issued in 1835 by Republic of Mexico. County created and organized in 1873 from Rusk, Upshur counties; named for Confederate Gen. John Gregg. In U.S. censuses 1880-1910, blacks were more numerous than whites. Oil discovered in 1931.

Ethnicity, 1990: White, 81,883 (78.0%); Black, 19,937 (19.0%); American Indian, 478 (0.5%); Asian, 491 (0.5%); Other, 2,159 (2.1%). Hispanic, 3,775 (3.6%).

Vital Statistics, 1997: Births, 1,748; deaths, 1,131; marriages, 1,540; divorces, 600.

Gregg County

Recreation: Water activities on lakes; hunting; varied cultural events; the East Texas Oil Museum, Glory Days in Kilgore in May, Depot Fest and Loblolly Festival in October.

Minerals: Leading oil-producing county with more than 3 billion barrels produced since 1931; also, sand, gravel and natural gas.

Agriculture: Cattle, horses, hay,

nursery crops. Market value $2.8 million. Timber sales.

LONGVIEW (75,973) county seat; manufacturing, brewery, distribution center; hospitals; LeTourneau University; convention center; balloon race in July.

Kilgore (11,723, partly in Rusk County), oil center; manufacturing; hospital; Kilgore College (junior college); East Texas Treatment Center; Shakespeare festival in summer; Celtic Heritage festival in April.

Gladewater (6,258) manufacturing, antique center, oil; Gusher Days in April, Christmas Tyme in Gusherville on Thanksgiving weekend; airport.

Other towns include: **Clarksville City** (909); **Easton** (485); **Judson** (650); **Lakeport** (891); **Liberty City** (1,730); **Warren City** (345); **White Oak** (5,712), petroleum, commuting to Longview; Roughneck Days in April.

For explanation of sources, abbreviations and symbols, see p. 130.

Population	112,848
Change fm '90	7.5
Area (sq. mi.)	276.3
Land Area (sq. mi.)	274.1
Altitude (ft.)	280-500
Rainfall (in.)	47.0
Jan. mean min.	33
July mean max.	93
Growing season (days)	247
Civ. Labor	60,119
Unemployed	6.9
Annual Wages	$1,512,184,261
Av. Weekly Wage	$474.79
Fed. Wages	$16,541,636
Ag. Net Cash Return	-$625,000
Prop. Value	$5,668,182,583
Retail Sales	$1,694,075,110

Grimes County

Physical Features: Rich bottom soils along Brazos, Navasota rivers; remainder hilly, partly forested.

Economy: Varied manufacturing; agribusiness; tourism.

History: Bidais (customs similar to the Caddoes) lived peacefully with Anglo-American settlers who arrived in 1820s, but tribe was removed to Indian Territory. Planter agriculture reflected in 1860 census, which listed 77 persons owning 20 or more slaves. County created from Montgomery County 1846; named for Jesse Grimes, who signed Texas Declaration of Independence.

Ethnicity, 1990: White, 12,879 (68.4%); Black, 4,614 (24.5%); American Indian, 52 (0.3%); Asian, 30 (0.2%); Other, 1,253 (6.7%). Hispanic, 2,657 (14.1%).

Vital Statistics, 1997: Births, 294; deaths, 198; marriages, 158; divorces, 73.

Recreation: Hunting, fishing; Gibbons Creek Reservoir; historic sites; fall Renaissance Festival at Plantersville.

Minerals: Lignite coal.

Agriculture: Cattle, forage, dairy, poultry, horses; peaches, pecans, berries; honey sales significant (first in state in value of sales). Market value $23.3 million. Some timber sold, Christmas tree farms.

ANDERSON (370) county seat; rural center; Fanthorp Inn historical site; Go-Texan weekend in February.

NAVASOTA (7,036) agribusiness center for parts of three counties; varied manufacturing; food, wood processing; hospital; La Salle statue; blues festival in May.

Other towns include: **Bedias** (301); **Iola** (331); **Plantersville** (212); **Richards** (296); **Roans Prairie** (56); **Shiro** (205); **Todd Mission** (69).

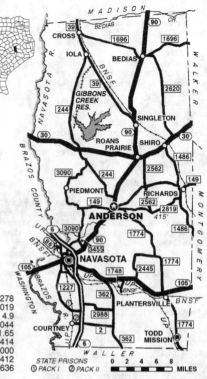

STATE PRISONS
① PACK I   ② PACK II

Population	22,057
Change fm '90	17.1
Area (sq. mi.)	801.2
Land Area (sq. mi.)	793.8
Altitude (ft.)	150-415
Rainfall (in.)	40.4
Jan. mean min.	40
July mean max.	96
Growing season (days)	278
Civ. Labor	9,019
Unemployed	4.9
Annual Wages	$179,479,044
Av. Weekly Wage	$521.65
Fed. Wages	$1,523,414
Ag. Net Cash Return	$63,000
Prop. Value	$1,326,348,412
Retail Sales	$350,046,636

Guadalupe County

Physical Features: South central county bisected by Guadalupe River; level to rolling surface; sandy, loam, blackland soils.

Economy: Varied manufacturing; many residents work in San Antonio (county in San Antonio metropolitan area), agribusiness, tourism.

History: Karankawas, Comanches, other tribes until 1850s. Spanish land grant in 1806 to José de la Baume. DeWitt colonists arrived in 1827. County created 1846 from Bexar, Gonzales counties; named for river.

Ethnicity, 1990: White, 52,948 (81.6%); Black, 3,665 (5.6%); American Indian, 235 (0.4%); Asian, 465 (0.7%); Other, 7,560 (11.7%). Hispanic, 19,246 (29.7%).

Vital Statistics, 1997: Births, 1,046; deaths, 639; marriages, 559; divorces, 386.

Recreation: Fishing, hunting, river floating; historic sites; Freedom Fiesta in July, historic festival in April.

Minerals: Oil, gas, sand and gravel, clays.

Agriculture: Cattle, poultry, nursery crops, dairy products, hogs; grain sorghum, hay, wheat, corn, pecans, peanuts, peaches. Market value $31.4 million.

SEGUIN (21,754) county seat; varied manufacturing; hospital, museum; Texas Lutheran University.

Other towns include: **Cibolo** (1,974), **Geronimo** (400), **Kingsbury** (200), **Marion** (1,083), **McQueeney** (2,318), **New Berlin** (220), **Schertz** (15,364), **Selma** (700), **Staples** (350).

Population	75,906
Change fm '90	17.0
Area (sq. mi.)	714.2
Land Area (sq. mi.)	711.2
Altitude (ft.)	350-850
Rainfall (in.)	31.4
Jan. mean min.	40
July mean max.	96
Growing season (days)	267
Civ. Labor	41,398
Unemployed	2.6
Annual Wages	$494,819,103
Av. Weekly Wage	$458.01
Fed. Wages	$7,156,074
Ag. Net Cash Return	$1,186,000
Prop. Value	$3,270,504,505
Retail Sales	$508,520,694

Hale County

Physical Features: High Plains; fertile sandy, loam soils; many playas; large underground water supply.

Economy: Agribusiness, food-processing plants; manufacturing; government/services.

History: Comanche hunters driven out by U.S. Army in 1875. Ranching began in 1880s. First motor-driven irrigation well drilled in 1911. County created from Bexar District, 1876; organized 1888; named for Lt. J.C. Hale, who died at San Jacinto.

Ethnicity, 1990: White, 23,823 (68.7%); Black, 1,852 (5.3%); American Indian, 148 (0.4%); Asian, 136 (0.4%); Other, 8,712 (25.1%). Hispanic, 14,428 (41.6%).

Vital Statistics, 1997: Births, 642; deaths, 288; marriages, 282; divorces, 188.

Recreation: Llano Estacado Museum; art gallery, antique stores; Cinco de Mayo and Dies y Seis fiestas in Plainview.

Minerals: Production of oil, gas.

Agriculture: Cattle, cotton, hogs, sheep. Other crops, corn, sorghum, wheat, soybeans. Market value $239.6 million.

PLAINVIEW (22,125) county seat; packing plants, distribution center; food processing, other industries; Wayland Baptist University; hospital, mental health center; state prisons.

Hale Center (2,071) farming trade center, hospital, wildlife museum.

Other towns include: **Abernathy** (2,703, partly in Lubbock County), **Cotton Center** (205), **Edmonson** (124), **Petersburg** (1,266), **Seth Ward** (1,633).

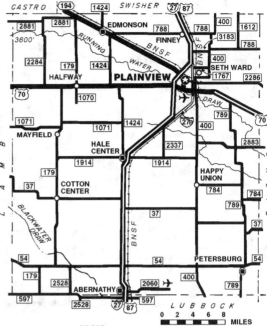

Population	35,997
Change fm '90	3.8
Area (sq. mi.)	1,004.8
Land Area (sq. mi.)	1,004.7
Altitude (ft.)	3,315-3,600
Rainfall (in.)	19.8
Jan. mean min.	24
July mean max.	92
Growing season (days)	211

Civ. Labor	17,098
Unemployed	6.1
Annual Wages	$311,760,633
Av. Weekly Wage	$417.00
Fed. Wages	$5,123,632
Ag. Net Cash Return	$73,664,000
Prop. Value	$1,343,174,634
Retail Sales	$2,162,469,262

Hall County

Physical Features: Rolling to hilly, broken by Red River forks, tributaries; red and black sandy loam.

Economy: Grain, cotton processing; farm, ranch supplies, marketing for large rural area.

History: Apaches displaced by Comanches, who were removed to Indian Territory in 1875. Ranching began in 1880s. Farming expanded after 1910. County created 1876 from Bexar, Young districts; organized 1890; named for Republic of Texas secretary of war W.D.C. Hall.

Ethnicity, 1990: White, 2,908 (74.5%); Black, 303 (7.8%); American Indian, 15 (0.4%); Asian, 7 (0.2%); Other, 672 (17.2%). Hispanic, 727 (18.6%).

Vital Statistics, 1997: Births, 57; deaths, 66; marriages, 36; divorces, 18.

Recreation: Fishing, hunting; museum.

Minerals: Not significant.

Agriculture: Most income from crops including cotton, peanuts; also beef cattle, hogs; some irrigation. Market value $23.6 million.

MEMPHIS (2,431) county seat; foundry; cotton gins; food processing; manufacturing; hospital.

Other towns include: **Estelline** (193), **Lakeview** (232), **Turkey** (551) Bob Wills Day in April.

For explanation of sources, abbreviations and symbols, see p. 130.

Population	3,937
Change fm '90	0.8
Area (sq. mi.)	904.0
Land Area (sq. mi.)	903.1
Altitude (ft.)	1,799-2,400
Rainfall (in.)	20.5
Jan. mean min.	24
July mean max.	96
Growing season (days)	213

Civ. Labor	1,677
Unemployed	7.6
Annual Wages	$15,424,880
Av. Weekly Wage	$308.01
Fed. Wages	$943,208
Ag. Net Cash Return	$7,797,000
Prop. Value	$166,751,274
Retail Sales	$16,096,151

Hamilton County

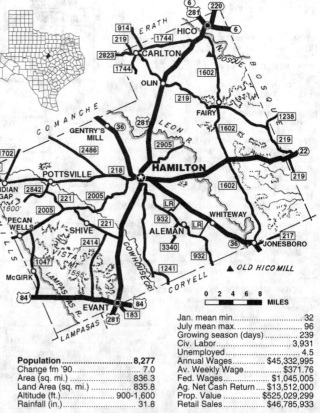

Physical Features: Hilly north central county broken by scenic valleys; loam soils.

Economy: Agribusiness; varied manufacturing; hunting leases; tourism; many residents work outside county.

History: Waco and Tawakoni Indian area. Anglo-American settlers arrived in mid-1850s. County created 1842; then re-created, organized 1858, from Bosque, Comanche, Lampasas counties; named for South Carolina Gov. James Hamilton, who aided Texas Revolution and Republic.

Ethnicity, 1990: White, 7,389 (95.6%); Black, 2 (0.0%); American Indian, 21 (0.3%); Asian, 24 (0.3%); Other, 297 (3.8%). Hispanic, 403 (5.2%).

Vital Statistics, 1997: Births, 120; deaths, 139; marriages, 67; divorces, 39.

Recreation: Deer, quail, duck hunting; dove festival on Labor Day; July arts and crafts show.

Minerals: Limited oil, gas.

Agriculture: Dairies, beef cattle top revenue sources. Hay, sorghum, wheat, oats; rangeland. Market value $52.4 million.

HAMILTON (2,995) county seat; dairies, hunting, antique shops, historical homes; varied manufacturing; hospital; library.

Hico (1,469) farm center, Old Settlers Reunion in summer.

Other towns include: **Carlton** (70), **Evant** (453, partly in Coryell County), **Pottsville** (100).

Population	**8,277**
Change fm '90	7.0
Area (sq. mi.)	836.3
Land Area (sq. mi.)	835.8
Altitude (ft.)	900-1,600
Rainfall (in.)	31.8
Jan. mean min.	32
July mean max.	96
Growing season (days)	239
Civ. Labor	3,931
Unemployed	4.5
Annual Wages	$45,332,995
Av. Weekly Wage	$371.76
Fed. Wages	$1,045,005
Ag. Net Cash Return	$13,512,000
Prop. Value	$525,029,299
Retail Sales	$46,785,933

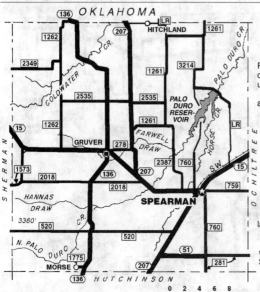

Hansford County

Physical Features: High Plains, many playas, creeks, draws; sandy, loam, black soils; underground water.

Economy: Agribusinesses; mineral operations.

History: Apaches, pushed out by Comanches around 1700. U.S. Army removed Comanches in 1874-75 and ranching began soon afterward. Farmers, including some from Norway, moved in around 1900. County created 1876, from Bexar, Young districts; organized 1889; named for jurist J.M. Hansford.

Ethnicity, 1990: White, 4,821 (82.4%); Black, 0 (0.0%); American Indian, 23 (0.4%); Asian, 14 (0.2%); Other, 990 (16.9%). Hispanic, 1,174 (20.1%).

Vital Statistics, 1997: Births, 78; deaths, 56; marriages, 44; divorces, 12.

Recreation: Stationmasters House Museum; hunting; lake activities.

Minerals: Production of gas, oil.

Agriculture: Large cattle-feeding operations; corn, wheat, sorghum; hogs. Substantial irrigation. Market value $346.2 million.

SPEARMAN (3,043) county seat; feedlots; grain marketing, storage center; gas processing; hospital; windmill collection. Other towns include: **Gruver** (1,104) farm-ranch market, natural gas production; Fourth of July barbecue; **Morse** (150).

Population	**5,572**
Change fm '90	-4.7
Area (sq. mi.)	920.4
Land Area (sq. mi.)	919.9
Altitude (ft.)	2,800-3,360
Rainfall (in.)	19.4
Jan. mean min.	21
July mean max.	95
Growing season (days)	186
Civ. Labor	2,485
Unemployed	2.6
Annual Wages	$49,350,464
Av. Weekly Wage	$471.51
Fed. Wages	$654,963
Ag. Net Cash Return	$35,655,000
Prop. Value	$710,320,360
Retail Sales	$32,321,792

Hardeman County

Physical Features: Rolling, broken area on divide between Pease, Red rivers' forks; sandy loam soils.

Economy: Agribusiness; some manufacturing, tourism.

History: Apaches, later the semi-sedentary Wichitas and Comanche hunters. Ranching began in late 1870s. Farming expanded after 1900. County created 1858 from Fannin County; re-created 1876, organized 1884; named for pioneer brothers Bailey and T.J. Hardeman.

Ethnicity, 1990: White, 4,427 (83.8%); Black, 321 (6.1%); American Indian, 26 (0.5%); Asian, 16 (0.3%); Other, 493 (9.3%). Hispanic, 589 (11.1%).

Vital Statistics, 1997: Births, 61; deaths, 77; marriages, 39; divorces, 30.

Recreation: state park; lake activities; Medicine Mound aborigine gathering site; Quanah Parker monument; old railroad depot.

Minerals: Oil, gypsum.

Agriculture: Wheat, cattle, cotton are top revenue producers; pumpkins; some cotton irrigated. Market value $15.9 million.

QUANAH (3,200) county seat; agribusiness; cotton oil mill; manufacturing; hospital; historical sites; Copper Breaks Fun Day on Memorial Day.

Other towns include: **Chillicothe** (784) farm market center.

Population................................. 5,006		
Change fm '90 ....-5.2	July mean max. 97	Av. Weekly Wage..................$396.90
Area (sq. mi.)............................. 697.0	Growing season (days) 221	Fed. Wages.........................$770,030
Land Area (sq. mi.) 695.4	Civ. Labor.................................. 2,009	Ag. Net Cash Return.........$3,735,000
Altitude (ft.) 1,287-1,749	Unemployed 6.0	Prop. Value $330,892,130
Rainfall (in.) 24.5	Annual Wages $29,847,674	Retail Sales....................$20,267,648
Jan. mean min. 23		

Hardin County

Physical Features: Southeast county; timbered; many streams; sandy, loam soils; Big Thicket covers much of area.

Economy: Paper manufacturing; wood processing; minerals; food processing; county in Beaumont-Port Arthur-Orange metropolitan area.

History: Lorenzo de Zavala received first land grant in 1829. Anglo-American settlers arrived in 1830. County created 1858 from Jefferson, Liberty counties. Named for Texas Revolutionary leader William Hardin.

Ethnicity, 1990: White, 37,485 (90.7%); Black, 3,485 (8.4%); American Indian, 123 (0.3%); Asian, 58 (0.1%); Other, 169 (0.4%). Hispanic, 679 (1.6%).

Vital Statistics, 1997: Births, 630; deaths, 443; marriages, 510; divorces, 338.

Recreation: Big Thicket with rare plant, animal life; national preserve; Red Cloud Water Park; hunting, fishing; state park.

Minerals: Oil, gas, sand, gravel.

Agriculture: Beef cattle, hay, blueberries and rice; market value $2.9 million. Timber provides most income; more than 85 percent of county forested. Hunting leases.

KOUNTZE (2,711) county seat; sawmill; some manufacturing; tourism; library.

SILSBEE (6,865) trade, manufacturing center; oil, gas processing; Christmas in the Big Thicket festival; hospital.

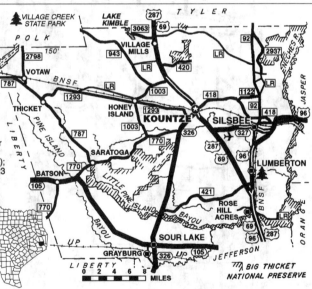

LUMBERTON (7,820) construction company; government/services; tourism, Village Creek Festival in April.

Other towns include: **Batson** (140); **Grayburg** (326); **Rose Hill Acres** (568); **Saratoga** (1,000) Big Thicket Museum; **Sour Lake** (1,755) oil, lumbering; Old Timer's Day in September; **Thicket** (306); **Village Mills** (1,700); **Votaw** (160).

Population................................47,553
Change fm '90 ....15.1
Area (sq. mi.) 897.3

Land Area (sq. mi.)..................... 894.4	
Altitude (ft.)............................... 25-150	
Rainfall (in.)................................. 55.7	
Jan. mean min. 37	
July mean max. 93	
Growing season (days) 246	
Civ. Labor................................ 23,377	
Unemployed................................... 6.4	
Annual Wages $225,322,229	
Av. Weekly Wage................. $421.89	
Fed. Wages.................... $2,437,500	
Ag. Net Cash Return .... -$1,103,000	
Prop. Value $1,729,506,750	
Retail Sales.................. $337,527,382	

For explanation of sources, abbreviations and symbols, see p. 130.

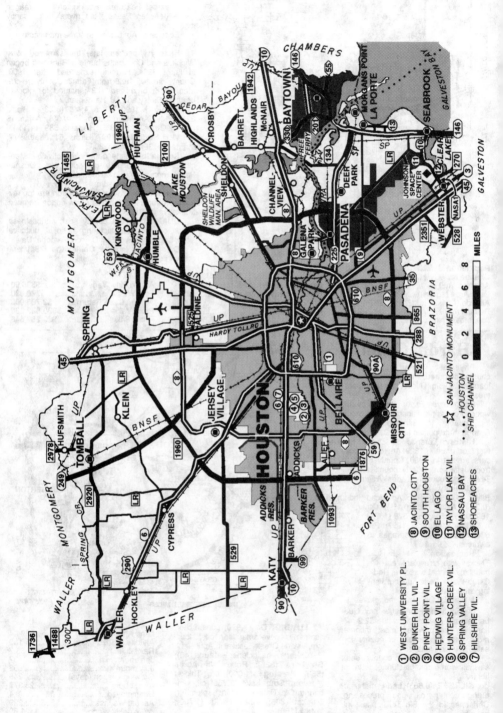

① WEST UNIVERSITY PL.
② BUNKER HILL VIL.
③ PINEY POINT VIL.
④ HEDWIG VILLAGE
⑤ HUNTERS CREEK VIL.
⑥ SPRING VALLEY
⑦ HILSHIRE VIL.

⑧ JACINTO CITY
⑨ SOUTH HOUSTON
⑩ EL LAGO
⑪ TAYLOR LAKE VIL.
⑫ NASSAU BAY
⑬ SHOREACRES

SAN JACINTO MONUMENT

☆ HOUSTON SHIP CHANNEL

Physical Features: Largest county in eastern half of state; level; typically coastal surface and soils; many bayous, lakes, canals for artificial drainage; partly forested.

Economy: Highly industrialized county with largest population; more than 55 foreign governments maintain offices in Houston; corporate management center; nation's largest concentration of petrochemical plants; largest U.S wheat-exporting port, among top U.S. ports in the value of foreign trade and total tonnage.

Petroleum refining, chemicals, food, fabricated metal products, nonelectrical machinery, primary metals, scientific instruments; paper and allied products, printing and publishing; center for energy, space and medical research; center of international business.

History: Orcoquiza villages visited by Spanish authorities in 1746. Pioneer settlers arrived by boat from Louisiana in 1822. Antebellum planters brought black slaves. Mexican migration increased after Mexican Revolution. County created 1836, organized 1837; named for John R. Harris, founder of Harrisburg (now part of Houston) in 1824.

Ethnicity, 1990: White, 1,824,137 (64.7%); Black, 541,180 (19.2%); American Indian, 8,044 (0.3%); Asian, 110,848 (3.9%); Other, 333,990 (11.9%). Hispanic, 644,935 (22.9%).

Vital Statistics, 1997: Births, 59,167; deaths, 18,944; marriages, 34,752; divorces, 16,170.

Recreation: Professional baseball, basketball; rodeo and other activities; Jones Hall for the Performing Arts, Nina Vance Alley Theatre, Houston Theatre Center, Convention Center, the Summit, a 17,000-seat sports and entertainment center; Astroworld and WaterWorld amusement parks near the Astrodome.

Sam Houston Park, with restored early Houston homes, church, stores; Museum of Fine Arts, Contemporary Arts Museum, Rice Museum; Wortham Theater for performing arts; museum of natural science, planetarium, zoo in Hermann Park.

San Jacinto Battleground, Battleship Texas; Johnson Space Center; annual livestock show.

Fishing, boating, other freshwater and saltwater activities.

Minerals: Among leading oil, gas, petrochemical areas; production of petroleum, cement, natural gas, liquids, salt, lime, sulfur, sand and gravel, clays, stone.

Harris County

Agriculture: Nursery crops, cattle, rice, horses (fourth in state in numbers sold, inventory), hay. Also, vegetables, corn. Irrigation for rice. Market value $43.3 million. Substantial income from forest products.

Education: Houston is a major center of higher education, with more than 140,000 students enrolled in 28 colleges and universities in the county. Among these are Rice University, the University of Houston, Texas Southern University, University of St. Thomas, Houston Baptist University.

Medical schools include University of St. Thomas and Houston Baptist University Schools of Nursing, University of Texas Health Science Center, Baylor College of Medicine, Institute of Religion and Human Development, Texas Chiropractic College, Texas Woman's University-Houston Center.

HOUSTON (1,841,064) county seat; largest Texas city; fourth largest in nation.

Ranks first in manufacture of petroleum equipment, agricultural chemicals, fertilizers, pesticides, oil and gas pipeline transmission; a leading scientific center; ranks high in manufacture of machinery, fabricated metals; a major distribution, shipping center; engineering and research center; food processing and textile mills.

Plants make apparel, lumber and wood products; furniture, paper, chemical, petroleum and coal products; publishing center; one of the nation's largest public school systems; prominent corporate center, with more than 200 firms relocating corporate headquarters, divisions or subsidiaries to county since 1970; Go Texan Days in February.

Pasadena (133,675) residential city with large industrial area manufacturing petrochemicals and other petroleum-related products; civic center; San Jacinto College, Texas Chiropractic College; four hospitals; historical museum; Strawberry Festival.

Baytown (68,731) refining, petrochemical center; Lee College; hospitals; historical homes; youth fair in April.

Bellaire (14,490) residential city with several major office buildings.

The **Clear Lake Area**, which includes **El Lago** (3,601); **Nassau Bay** (4,762); **Seabrook** (8,919); **Taylor Lake Village** (4,034) Johnson Space Center, University of Houston-Clear Lake; Bayport Industrial Complex includes Port of Bayport; 12 major marinas; two hospitals; **Webster** (5,570).

Other towns include: **Aldine** (12,465); **Bunker Hill Village** (3,912); **Channelview** (27,866); **Crosby** (1,929); **Deer Park** (30,396) ship-channel industries, fall festival; hospital; **Galena Park** (10,269); **Hedwig Village** (3,123); **Highlands** (7,737); **Hilshire Village** (740); **Hockley** (300); **Humble** (15,452) oilfield equipment manufactured, retail center, hospital; **Hunters Creek Village** (4,224); **Jacinto City** (9,783); **Jersey Village** (5,659).

Also, **Katy** (11,175, partly in Fort Bend, Waller counties) varied manufacturing, hospital; rice harvest festival in October, G.I. Joe museum; **La Porte** (32,822) varied manufacturing; Sylvan Beach Festival in April; Galveston Bay; **Missouri City** (58,002, mostly in Fort Bend County); **Morgan's Point** (387); **Piney Point Village** (3,662); **Sheldon** (2,011); **Shoreacres** (1,583); **South Houston** (15,266).

Also, **Southside Place** (1,358); **Spring** (36,018); **Spring Valley** (3,841); **Tomball** (7,346) computers, retail center; hospital; sports medical center; museum, junior college, parks; **West University Place** (13,093).

Addicks, **Alief** and **Kingwood** are now within the city limits of Houston.

Population	3,178,995
Change fm '90	12.8
Area (sq. mi.)	1,777.8
Land Area (sq. mi.)	1,729.0
Altitude (ft.)	sea level-300
Rainfall (in.)	46.1
Jan. mean min.	43
July mean max.	92
Growing season (days)	300
Civ. Labor	1,766,119
Unemployed	4.2
Annual Wages	$63,355,297,784
Av. Weekly Wage	$705.62
Fed. Wages	$1,192,089,544
Ag. Net Cash Return	$12,290,000
Prop. Value	$144,306,426,710
Retail Sales	$42,744,358,635

For explanation of sources, abbreviations and symbols, see p. 130.

Harrison County

Physical Features: East Texas county; hilly, rolling; over half forested; Sabine River; Caddo Lake.

Economy: Oil, gas processing; lumbering; pottery, other varied manufacturing.

History: Agriculturist Caddo Indians whose numbers were reduced by disease. Anglo-Americans arrived in 1830s. In 1850, the county had more slaves than any other in the state. County created 1839 from Shelby County; organized 1842. Named for eloquent advocate of Texas Revolution, Jonas Harrison.

Ethnicity, 1990: White, 40,387 (70.3%); Black, 16,038 (27.9%); American Indian, 192 (0.3%); Asian, 144 (0.3%); Other, 722 (1.3%). Hispanic, 1,278 (2.2%).

Vital Statistics, 1997: Births, 735; deaths, 602; marriages, 582; divorces, 226.

Recreation: Fishing, other water activities on Caddo and other lakes; hunting; plantation homes, historic sites; Stagecoach Days in May; Old Courthouse Museum; Old World Store; state park, performing arts; Fire Ant festival in October.

Minerals: Oil, gas, lignite coal, clays, sand and gravel.

Agriculture: Cattle, hay. Also, poultry, horses, hogs; nursery plants. Market value $12 million. Hunting leases important. Substantial timber industry.

MARSHALL (25,066) county seat; petroleum, lumber processing; varied manufacturing; Wonderland of Lights in December; civic center; historic sites; hospital; Wiley College; East Texas Baptist University.

Other towns include: **Elysian Fields** (300); **Hallsville** (2,821) Western Days in October, museum; **Harleton** (260); **Jonesville** (28); **Karnack** (775); **Nesbitt** (390); **Scottsville** (288); **Uncertain** (219); **Waskom** (1,871) oil, gas; ranching; Armadillo Daze in April; **Woodlawn** (370). Also, part of **Longview**.

Population	60,609
Change fm '90	5.4
Area (sq. mi.)	915.1
Land Area (sq. mi.)	898.8
Altitude (ft.)	168-545
Rainfall (in.)	47.7
Jan. mean min.	32
July mean max.	93
Growing season (days)	245
Civ. Labor	28,383
Unemployed	7.5
Annual Wages	$587,137,190
Av. Weekly Wage	$534.74
Fed. Wages	$5,019,934
Ag. Net Cash Return	-$1,826,000
Prop. Value	$3,113,292,705
Retail Sales	$402,742,940

Hartley County

Physical Features: Panhandle High Plains; drains to Canadian River tributaries, playas; sandy, loam, chocolate soils; lake.

Economy: Agriculture, gas production; varied manufacturing.

History: Apaches, pushed out by Comanches around 1700. U.S. Army removed Indians in 1875. *Pastores* (Hispanic sheepmen) in area until 1880s. Cattle ranching began in 1880s. Farming expanded after 1900. County created 1876 from Bexar, Young districts; organized 1891; named for Texas pioneers O.C. and R.K. Hartley.

Ethnicity, 1990: White, 3,510 (96.6%); Black, 9 (0.2%); American Indian, 30 (0.8%); Asian, 7 (0.2%); Other, 78 (2.1%). Hispanic, 201 (5.5%).

Vital Statistics, 1997: Births, 60; deaths, 22; marriages, 19; divorces, 21.

Recreation: Rita Blanca Lake activities; ranch museum; local events; XIT Rodeo and Reunion at Dalhart.

Minerals: Natural gas.

Agriculture: Cattle, corn, wheat, sorghum, hay; 120,000 acres irrigated; blue corn, pop corn. Market value $350 million.

CHANNING (285) county seat.

DALHART (6,734, mostly in Dallam County), feedlots; feed, meat processing; other industries. Also, **Hartley** (319).

Population	5,022
Change fm '90	38.2
Area (sq. mi.)	1,463.3
Land Area (sq. mi.)	1,462.4
Altitude (ft.)	3,400-4,470
Rainfall (in.)	16.1
Jan. mean min.	21
July mean max.	92
Growing season (days)	180
Civ. Labor	2,883
Unemployed	1.5
Annual Wages	$19,588,433
Av. Weekly Wage	$403.77
Fed. Wages	$403,684
Ag. Net Cash Return	$69,107,000
Prop. Value	$523,544,550
Retail Sales	$11,598,803

Haskell County

Physical Features: West central county; rolling; broken areas; drained by Brazos tributaries; lake; sandy loam, gray, black soils.

Economy: Agribusiness, oilfield operations.

History: Apaches until 1700, then Comanche area. Ranching began in late 1870s after Indians removed. Farming expanded after 1900. County created 1858, from Milam, Fannin counties; re-created 1876; organized 1885; named for Goliad victim C.R. Haskell.

Ethnicity,1990: White, 5,481 (80.4%); Black, 244 (3.6%); American Indian, 17 (0.2%); Asian, 16 (0.2%); Other, 1,062 (15.6%). Hispanic, 1,312 (19.2%).

Vital Statistics, 1997: Births, 55; deaths, 105; marriages, 67; divorces, 30.

Recreation: Lake Stamford activities; bass tournament, arts & crafts show; hunting of deer, geese, wild hog.

Minerals: Oil and gas.

Agriculture: Wheat, cotton, peanuts; 28,000 acres irrigated. Beef cattle raised. Market value $39.7 million.

HASKELL (3,075) county seat; farming center; hospital; city park; Wild Horse Prairie Days in June.

Other towns include: **O'Brien** (163), **Rochester** (496), **Rule** (720), **Sagerton** (115), **Weinert** (246). Also, **Stamford** (3,213, mostly in Jones County),

Population **6,417**
Change fm '90 .... -5.9

Area (sq. mi.)	910.2
Land Area (sq. mi.)	903.0
Altitude (ft.)	1,400-1,681
Rainfall (in.)	26.1
Jan. mean min.	27
July mean max.	96
Growing season (days)	232

0 2 4 6 8
▬▬▬▬▬ MILES

Civ. Labor	2,633
Unemployed	4.1
Annual Wages	$30,231,722
Av. Weekly Wage	$351.88
Fed. Wages	$1,289,423
Ag. Net Cash Return	$9,006,000
Prop. Value	$360,092,940
Retail Sales	$53,218,395

Hays County

Physical Features: Hilly in west, blackland in east; on edge of Balcones Escarpment.

Economy: Education, tourism, retirement area, some manufacturing; part of Austin metropolitan area.

History: Tonkawa area, also Apache and Comanche presence. Spanish authorities attempted first permanent settlement in 1807. Mexican land grants in early 1830s to Juan Martín Veramendi, Juan Vicente Campos and Thomas Jefferson Chambers. County created 1843 from Travis County; named for Capt. Jack Hays, famous Texas Ranger.

Ethnicity, 1990: White, 55,360 (84.4%); Black, 2,220 (3.4%); American Indian, 230 (0.4%); Asian, 427 (0.7%); Other, 7,377 (11.2%). Hispanic, 18,249 (27.8%).

Vital Statistics, 1997: Births, 1,205; deaths, 440; marriages, 760; divorces, 314.

Recreation: Fishing, hunting; college cultural, athletic events; Cypress Creek and Blanco River resorts, guest ranches; Wonder World park.

Minerals: Sand and gravel, cement produced.

Agriculture: Beef cattle, goats, exotic wildlife; greenhouse nurseries; hay, corn, sorghum, wheat and cotton. Market value $10.8 million.

SAN MARCOS (38,394) county seat; Southwest Texas State University, San Marcos Baptist Academy, Gary Job Corps Training Center; government/services; distribution center; two outlet malls; hospital, sports medicine, physical therapy center; Scheib Center for mentally handicapped; Dies y Seis Lowrider Festival, Water Safari in June.

Other towns include: **Bear Creek** (400); **Buda** (2,152); **Driftwood** (21); **Dripping Springs** (1,181); **Hays** (307); **Kyle** (2,922); **Mountain City** (430); **Niederwald** (286, partly in Caldwell County); **Uhland** (439); **Wimberley** (2,812) tourism, retirement community, artists, concert series; Country Pie Social and Fair in April; **Woodcreek** (1,305).

Population	**86,475**
Change fm '90	31.8
Area (sq. mi.)	679.8
Land Area (sq. mi.)	677.9
Altitude (ft.)	550-1,501
Rainfall (in.)	34.6
Jan. mean min.	36
July mean max.	95
Growing season (days)	254
Civ. Labor	50,488
Unemployed	2.7
Annual Wages	$656,357,801
Av. Weekly Wage	$404.08
Fed. Wages	$5,041,483
Ag. Net Cash Return	-$1,452,000
Prop. Value	$3,982,165,945
Retail Sales	$858,664,128

0 2 4 6 8
▬▬▬▬▬ MILES

For explanation of sources, abbreviations and symbols, see p. 130.

Hemphill County

Physical Features: Panhandle county; sloping surface, broken by Canadian, Washita rivers; sandy, red, dark soils.

Economy: Petroleum production and refining, livestock production.

History: Apaches, who were pushed out by Comanches, Kiowas. Tribes removed to Indian Territory in 1875. Ranching began in late 1870s. Farmers began to arrive after 1900. County created from Bexar, Young districts, 1876; organized 1887; named for Republic of Texas Justice John Hemphill.

Ethnicity, 1990: White, 3,503 (94.2%); Black, 7 (0.2%); American Indian, 22 (0.6%); Asian, 5 (0.1%); Other, 183 (4.9%). Hispanic, 412 (11.1%).

Vital Statistics, 1997: Births, 27; deaths, 39; marriages, 45; divorces, 18.

Recreation: Lake Marvin activities; fall foliage tours; hunting, fishing; Buffalo Wallow Indian Battleground, wildlife management area; 4th of July rodeo.

Minerals: Oil, natural gas.

Agriculture: Fed beef, stocker cattle top revenue sources; crops include wheat, sorghum, hay, improved pastures; some irrigation. Market value $103.9 million.

CANADIAN (2,398) county seat; oil, gas production; feedlot; hospital.

Population.....................3,628
Change fm '90 ....-2.5

Area (sq. mi.)	912.0	Civ. Labor	1,896
Land Area (sq. mi.)	909.7	Unemployed	2.8
Altitude (ft.)	2,185-3,000	Annual Wages	$38,419,816
Rainfall (in.)	20.1	Av. Weekly Wage	$519.26
Jan. mean min.	22	Fed. Wages	$655,203
July mean max.	96	Ag. Net Cash Return	$28,759,000
Growing season (days)	204	Prop. Value	$768,869,272
		Retail Sales	$20,814,296

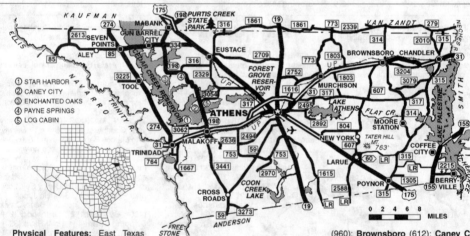

Physical Features: East Texas county bounded by Neches, Trinity rivers; hilly, rolling; one-third forested; sandy, loam, clay soils; commercial timber; Cedar Creek, other lakes.

Economy: Agibusiness, retail trade; varied manufacturing; minerals; recreation; tourism.

History: Caddo area. Cherokee, other tribes migrated into the area in 1819-20 ahead of white settlement. Cherokees forced into Indian Territory in 1839. Anglo-American settlers arrived in 1840s. County created 1846 from Nacogdoches, Houston counties and named for Gov. J. Pinckney Henderson.

Ethnicity, 1990: White, 52,216 (89.2%); Black, 4,755 (8.1%); American Indian, 181 (0.3%); Asian, 141 (0.2%); Other, 1,250 (2.1%). Hispanic, 2,368 (4.0%).

Vital Statistics, 1997: Births, 928; deaths, 835; marriages, 597; divorces, 162.

Recreation: Cedar Creek Reser-

Henderson County

voir, Lake Palestine, and other lakes; Purtis Creek State Park; hunting, fishing; Black-eyed Pea Jamboree, fiddlers' reunion.

Minerals: Oil, gas, clays, lignite, sulphur, sand and gravel.

Agriculture: Cattle, greenhouse/nurseries, forages, horses, dairies, vegetables, melons. Market value $29.5 million. Hardwood timber marketed.

ATHENS (12,405) county seat; agribusiness center; varied manufacturing; tourism; state fish hatchery and museum; hospital, mental health/mental retardation center; Trinity Valley Community College.

Gun Barrel City (4,484) recreation, retirement, retail center.

Malakoff (2,311) brick factory, varied industry, Lakefest.

Other towns include: **Berryville**

(960); **Brownsboro** (612); **Caney City** (214); **Chandler** (2,023); **Coffee City** (256); **Enchanted Oaks** (328); **Eustace** (863); **Larue** (160); **Log Cabin** (600); **Moore Station** (322); **Murchison** (624); **Payne Springs** (794); **Poynor** (282); **Seven Points** (861); **Star Harbor** (410); **Tool** (2,064), and **Trinidad** (1,191).

Population 68,962
Change fm '90 ....17.8
Area (sq. mi.) 949.0
Land Area (sq. mi.) 874.4
Altitude (ft.) 256-763
Rainfall (in.) 39.7
Jan. mean min. 35
July mean max. 95
Growing season (days)...................260
Civ. Labor 29,794
Unemployed 4.1
Annual Wages $309,093,964
Av. Weekly Wage $406.97
Fed. Wages $3,281,629
Ag. Net Cash Return $618,000
Prop. Value $2,833,919,301
Retail Sales $523,432,848

Hidalgo County

Physical Features: Rich alluvial soils along Rio Grande; sandy, loam soils in north; semitropical vegetation.

Economy: Food processing, shipping; other agribusinesses; tourism; mineral operations.

History: Coahuiltecan and Karankawa area. Comanches forced Apaches southward into valley in 1700s; Comanches arrived in valley in 1800s. Spanish settlement occurred 1750-1800. County created 1852 from Cameron, Starr counties; named for leader of Mexico's independence movement, Father Miguel Hidalgo y Costillo.

Ethnicity, 1990: White, 286,858 (74.8%); Black, 806 (0.2%); American Indian, 668 (0.2%); Asian, 1,088 (0.3%); Other, 94,125 (24.5%). Hispanic, 326,972 (85.2%).

Vital Statistics, 1997: Births, 13,074; deaths, 2,680; marriages, 5,190; divorces, 224.

Recreation: Winter resort, retirement area; fishing, hunting; gateway to Mexico; historical sites; Bentsen-Rio Grande Valley State Park; museums; All-Valley Winter Vegetable Show at Pharr.

Minerals: Oil, gas, stone, sand and gravel.

Agriculture: Ninety percent of farm cash receipts from crops (first in state in market value), principally from sugar cane, grain, vegetables, citrus, cotton; livestock includes cattle; 270,000 acres irrigated. Market value $197.2 million.

EDINBURG (41,996) county seat; vegetable processing, packing; petroleum operations; clothing; tourism; planetarium; the University of Texas-Pan American; hospital; mental health center; museum; Fiesta Hidalgo in February.

McALLEN (104,791) food processing, packing, shipping; foreign trade zone; agriculture; tourism; varied manufacturing; new air terminal; community college; cancer center.

Mission (41,085) citrus groves, with Citrus Fiesta in January; agricultural processing and distribution; hospital; community college.

Pharr (41,839) agriculture, trading center; trucking; tourism; old clock, juke box museums; folklife festival in February.

Other towns include: **Alamo** (11,899) live steam museum; **Alton** (3,519); **Donna** (15,282) citrus center, varied manufacturing; lamb, sheep show; **Edcouch** (4,070); **Elsa** (6,332); **Hargill** (1,349); **Hidalgo** (5,563); La

Blanca (150); **La Joya** (4,002); **La Villa** (1,930); **Linn** (450); **Los Ebanos** (100).

Also, **Mercedes** (15,051) "boot capital," citrus, vegetable center; food processing; tourism; recreation vehicle show in January; **Monte Alto** (1,769); **Palmhurst** (445); **Palmview** (2,696); **Peñitas** (1,398); **Progreso** (3,273); **Progreso Lakes** (221); **San Juan** (22,844); **Sullivan City** (3,010); **Weslaco** (27,449) Bicultural Museum.

Population	**518,878**
Change fm '90	35.3
Area (sq. mi.)	1,582.7
Land Area (sq. mi.)	1,569.1
Altitude (ft.)	28-350
Rainfall (in.)	23.4
Jan. mean min.	49
July mean max.	96
Growing season (days)	327
Civ. Labor	195,240
Unemployed	17.7
Annual Wages	$2,836,175,076
Av. Weekly Wage	$385.48
Fed. Wages	$116,023,588
Ag. Net Cash Return	$46,064,000
Prop. Value	$11,385,528,197
Retail Sales	$3,951,439,351

Hill County

Physical Features: North central county; level to rolling; blackland soils, some sandy loams; drains to Brazos; lakes.

Economy: Agribusiness, varied manufacturing, tourism.

History: Waco and Tawakoni area, later Comanches. Believed to be Indian "council spot," without evidence of raids and a place of safe passage. Anglo-

Americans of the Robertson colony arrived in early 1830s. County created from Navarro County 1853; named for G.W. Hill, Republic of Texas official.

Ethnicity, 1990: White, 23,669 (87.2%); Black, 2,520 (9.3%); American Indian, 80 (0.3%); Asian, 38 (0.1%); Other, 839 (3.1%). Hispanic, 2,230 (8.2%).

Vital Statistics, 1997: Births, 403; deaths, 407; marriages, 302; divorces, 154.

Recreation: Lake activities; excursion boat on Whitney; Confederate Museum, Audie Murphy Gun Museum, historic structures; art festival; motorcycle track.

Minerals: Limestone, gas, oil.

Agriculture: Cattle, nursery crops, sorghum, dairies, wheat, hay, turkeys, cotton. Market value $57.7 million. Some firewood marketed.

HILLSBORO (7,801) county seat; retail, outlet center; tourism; manufacturing, agribusiness; antique malls; Hill College; hospital; crafts fair; restored courthouse.

Whitney (1,618) tourist center; hospital, varied manufacturing.

Other towns include: **Abbott** (369); **Aquilla** (169); **Blum** (444); **Brandon** (80); **Bynum** (213); **Carl's Corner** (124); **Covington** (303); **Hubbard** (1,681); **Irene** (160); **Itasca** (1,616); **Malone** (335); **Mertens** (113); **Mount Calm** (331); **Penelope** (246).

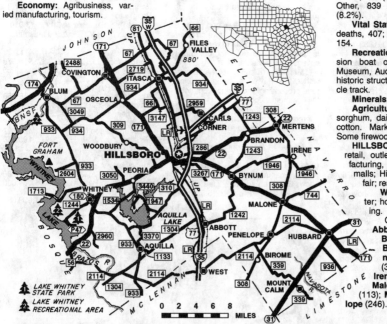

Population	30,060			
Change fm '90	10.7		Annual Wages	$168,032,681
Area (sq. mi.)	985.6	Jan. mean min.	34	Av. Weekly Wage	$377.16
Land Area (sq. mi.)	962.4	July mean max.	95	Fed. Wages	$2,972,666
Altitude (ft.)	450-880	Growing season (days)	250	Ag. Net Cash Return	$1,136,000
Rainfall (in.)	35.1	Civ. Labor	15,851	Prop. Value	$1,164,086,641
		Unemployed	4.0	Retail Sales	$333,101,684

Hockley County

Physical Features: West Texas High Plains, numerous playas, drains to Yellow House Draw; loam, sandy loam soils.

Economy: Extensive oil, gas production and services; manufacturing; varied agribusiness.

History: Comanches displaced Apaches in early 1700s. Large ranches of 1880s brought few residents. Homesteaders arrived after 1900. County created 1876, from Bexar, Young districts; organized 1921. Named for Republic of Texas secretary of war Gen. G.W. Hockley.

Ethnicity, 1990: White, 18,937 (78.3%); Black, 1,023 (4.2%); American Indian, 86 (0.4%); Asian, 33 (0.1%); Other, 4,120 (17.0%). Hispanic, 7,650 (31.6%).

Vital Statistics, 1997: Births, 324; deaths, 212; marriages, 215; divorces, 140.

Recreation: Early Settlers' Day in July; Marigolds Arts, Crafts Festival in November.

Minerals: Oil, gas, stone; one of leading oil counties with more than 1 billion barrels produced.

Agriculture: Cotton, grain sorghum are top crops; cattle, hogs raised; substantial irrigation. Market value $89.3 million.

LEVELLAND (13,938) county seat; oil, cotton, cattle center; government/services; hospital; South Plains College; Hot Burrito & Bluegrass Music Festival in July.

Other towns include: **Anton** (1,254); **Opdyke West** (132); **Pep** (35); **Ropesville** (574); **Smyer** (439); **Sundown** (1,732); **Whitharral** (175).

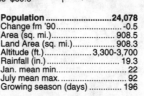

Population	24,078			
Change fm '90	-0.5		Civ. Labor	11,068
Area (sq. mi.)	908.5		Unemployed	6.3
Land Area (sq. mi.)	908.3		Annual Wages	$181,160,901
Altitude (ft.)	3,300-3,700		Av. Weekly Wage	$413.2
Rainfall (in.)	19.3		Fed. Wages	$2,004,54
Jan. mean min.	22		Ag. Net Cash Return	$24,175,00
July mean max.	92		Prop. Value	$2,299,713,04
Growing season (days)	196		Retail Sales	$182,866,01

Hood County

Physical Features: Hilly; broken by Paluxy, Brazos rivers; sandy loam soils.

Economy: Tourism; agribusiness; nuclear power plant.

History: Lipan Apache and Comanche area. Anglo-American settlers arrived in late 1840s. County created, organized 1866 from Johnson County; named for Confederate Gen. John B. Hood.

Ethnicity, 1990: White, 28,054 (96.8%); Black, 52 (0.2%); American Indian, 154 (0.5%); Asian, 177 (0.6%); Other, 544 (1.9%). Hispanic, 1,353 (4.7%).

Vital Statistics, 1997: Births, 407; deaths, 440; marriages, 327; divorces, 216.

Recreation: Lakes, fishing, scenic areas; summer theater; state park; site of grave of Elizabeth Crockett, wife of Davy; Gen. Granbury's Bean & Rib cookoff in March.

Minerals: Oil, gas, stone.

Agriculture: Cattle, nursery crops, hay, peanuts, pecans; some irrigation. Market value $18.3 million.

GRANBURY (5,711) county seat; tourism; agribusiness; historic downtown area; opera house; hospital; Civil War re-enactment in fall.

Other towns include: **Acton** (1,129), **Cresson** (208), **Lipan** (438), **Paluxy** (76), **Tolar** (602).

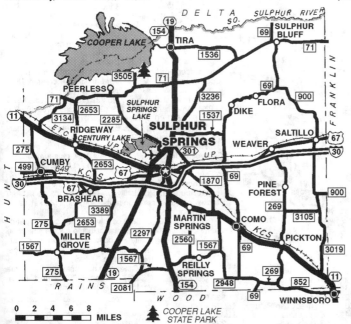

Population	34,661		
Change fm '90	19.6	Civ. Labor	16,676
Area (sq. mi.)	436.7	Unemployed	4.3
Land Area (sq. mi.)	421.6	Annual Wages	$176,102,630
Altitude (ft.)	600-1,230	Av. Weekly Wage	$404.05
Rainfall (in.)	30.9	Fed. Wages	$2,884,060
Jan. mean min.	33	Ag. Net Cash Return	$1,601,000
July mean max.	97	Prop. Value	$1,768,788,011
Growing season (days)	232	Retail Sales	$302,203,516

Hopkins County

Physical Features: Northeast Texas county of varied timber, including pines; drains north to South Sulphur River; Cooper Lake; light, sandy to heavier black soils.

Economy: Dairies, large milk-processing plants; agribusiness; varied manufacturing.

History: Caddo area, displaced by Cherokees, who in turn were forced out by President Lamar in 1839. First Anglo-American settlement in 1837. County created 1846 from Lamar, Nacogdoches counties; named for pioneer Hopkins family.

Ethnicity, 1990: White, 25,381 (88.0%); Black, 2,476 (8.6%); American Indian, 126 (0.4%); Asian, 70 (0.2%); Other, 780 (2.7%). Hispanic, 1,407 (4.9%).

Vital Statistics, 1997: Births, 382; deaths, 413; marriages, 335; divorces, 201.

Recreation: Fishing, hunting; lake activities; stew contest in September; dairy museum; dairy festival in June.

Minerals: Lignite coal.

Agriculture: Leading dairy county (second in state in value of sales); also cattle, horses, poultry; hay (first in state in acreage), sweet potatoes, wheat; some irrigation. Market value $127.1 million. Firewood and hardwood lumber marketed.

SULPHUR SPRINGS (14,977) county seat; dairy farming center; food processing, distribution; varied manufacturing; tourism; hospital; library, heritage park; music box gallery; civic center.

Other towns include: **Brashear** (280), **Como** (627), **Cumby** (683), **Dike** (170), **Pickton** (90), **Saltillo** (200), **Sulphur Bluff** (280), **Tira** (288).

Population	31,184
Change fm '90	8.2
Area (sq. mi.)	792.7
Land Area (sq. mi.)	784.8
Altitude (ft.)	350-649
Rainfall (in.)	46.0
Jan. mean min.	30
July mean max.	94
Growing season (days)	238
Civ. Labor	15,882
Unemployed	5.2
Annual Wages	$286,840,024
Av. Weekly Wage	$492.53
Fed. Wages	$3,531,347
Ag. Net Cash Return	$26,441,000
Prop. Value	$1,231,285,901
Retail Sales	$375,902,911

For explanation of sources, abbreviations and symbols, see p. 130.

Houston County

Physical Features: East Texas county over half forested; rolling terrain, draining to Neches, Trinity rivers; commercial timber production.

Economy: Livestock, timber, government/services, manufacturing, tourism.

History: Caddo group attracted mission San Francisco de los Tejas, 1690. Spanish town of Bucareli established in 1774. Both lasted only a few years. Anglo-American settlers arrived in 1820s. County created 1837 from Nacogdoches County by Republic; named for Sam Houston. Cotton plantations before the Civil War had many slaves.

Ethnicity, 1990: White, 14,373 (67.2%); Black, 6,326 (29.6%); American Indian, 32 (0.1%); Asian, 49 (0.2%); Other, 595 (2.8%). Hispanic, 965 (4.5%).

Vital Statistics, 1997: Births, 271; deaths, 342; marriages, 153; divorces, 77.

Recreation: Fishing, hunting; national forest; Mission Tejas State Park; 75 historical markers; Houston County Lake.

Minerals: Oil, gas, sand, gravel.

Agriculture: Cattle, poultry, hay, watermelons, cotton. Market value $27.3 million. Timber principal income source.

CROCKETT (7,138), county seat; wood and plastic products; Crockett State School; fifth oldest town in Texas, historic sites; fiddlers festival, coon hunters finals.

Other towns include: **Grapeland** (1,696); **Kennard** (385); **Latexo** (327); **Lovelady** (654) Lovefest in February; **Ratcliff** (106).

Population................................22,125	July mean max. 93	Av. Weekly Wage....................$482.45
Change fm '90 .... 3.5	Growing season (days) 265	Fed. Wages.........................$3,127,492
Area (sq. mi.)............................ 1,236.8	Civ. Labor....................................8,824	Ag. Net Cash Return.............$604,000
Land Area (sq. mi.)................. 1,231.0	Unemployed 4.1	Prop. Value $1,034,814,232
Altitude (ft.) 160-552	Annual Wages...............$174,970,993	Retail Sales...................$133,483,706
Rainfall (in.) 42.4		
Jan. mean min. 34		

Howard County

Physical Features: On edge of Llano Estacado; sandy loam soils.

Economy: Government/services; agribusiness; oil, gas; varied manufacturing, including clothing.

History: Pawnee and Comanche area. Anglo-American settlement began in 1870. Oil boom in mid-1920s. County named for V.E. Howard, legislator; created 1876 from Bexar, Young districts organized 1882.

Ethnicity, 1990: White, 25,282 (78.2%); Black, 1,225 (3.8%); American Indian, 179 (0.6%); Asian, 162 (0.5%); Other, 5,495 (17.0%). Hispanic, 8,607 (26.6%).

Vital Statistics, 1997: Births, 455; deaths, 398; marriages, 304; divorces, 72.

Recreation: Lakes; state park; campground in Comanche Trail Park; Native Plant Trail; museum; historical sites; West Texas agricultural expo in March; Cranefest in February.

Minerals: Oil, gas, sand, gravel and stone.

Agriculture: Principally dry-land cotton; also, beef, stocker cattle, horses, peanuts, sorghum. Market value $31.5 million.

BIG SPRING (23,389) county seat; agriculture, petrochemicals produced; hospitals, including a state institution and Veterans Administration hospital; federal prison; varied manufacturing; Howard College; railroad plaza.

Other towns include: **Coahoma** (1,321), **Forsan** (292), **Knott** (685), **Vealmoor** (179), **Vincent** (500).

Population................................ 33,003	Civ. Labor 14,378	
Change fm '90 ....2.0	Unemployed 4.9	
Area (sq. mi.) 904.2	Annual Wages $267,127,959	
Land Area (sq. mi.)...................... 902.9	Av. Weekly Wage $437.83	
Altitude (ft.)....................... 2,200-2,776	Fed. Wages..........................$33,667,389	
Rainfall (in.) 19.2	Ag. Net Cash Return $8,782,000	
Jan. mean min................................. 28	Prop. Value.................$1,342,464,288	
July mean max. 94	Retail Sales $268,213,045	
Growing season (days) 217		

For explanation of sources, abbreviations and symbols, see p. 130.

Hudspeth County

Physical Features: Plateau, basin terrain, draining to salt lakes; Rio Grande; mostly rocky, alkaline, clay soils and sandy loam soils, except alluvial along Rio Grande; desert, mountain vegetation. Fertile agricultural valleys.

Economy: Agribusiness, mining, tourism, hunting leases.

History: Mescalero Apache area. Fort Quitman established in 1858 to protect routes to west. Railroad in 1881 brought Anglo-American settlers. Political turmoil in Mexico (1912-29) brought more settlers from Mexico. County named for Texas political leader Claude B. Hudspeth; created 1917 from El Paso County.

Ethnicity, 1990: White, 2,345 (80.4%); Black, 15 (0.5%); American Indian, 9 (0.3%); Asian, 2 (0.1%); Other, 544 (18.7%). Hispanic, 1,935 (66.4%).

Vital Statistics, 1997: Births, 31; deaths, 23; marriages, 19; divorces, 1.

Recreation: Scenic drives; fort ruins; hot springs; salt basin; white sands; hunting; part of Guadalupe Mountains National Park, containing unique plant life, canyons.

Minerals: Talc, stone, gypsum.

Agriculture: Most income from cotton, vegetables, hay, alfalfa; beef cattle raised; 35,000 acres irrigated. Market value $24.9 million.

SIERRA BLANCA (700) county seat; ranching center; tourist stop on interstate highway; 4th of July fair, livestock show in January.

DELL CITY (780) feedlots; vegetable packing; gypsum processing; clinic; trade center; airport; some of largest water wells in state. Other towns include: **Fort Hancock** (400) and **Salt Flat** (35).

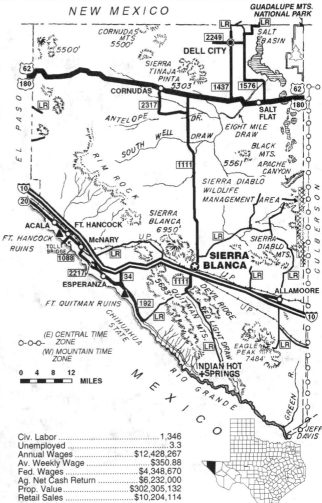

Population.........................3,475	Civ. Labor 1,346
Change fm '90 ....19.2	Unemployed 3.3
Area (sq. mi.)....................4,572.2	Annual Wages $12,428,267
Land Area (sq. mi.)............4,571.3	Av. Weekly Wage $350.88
Altitude (ft.)...............3,200-7,484	Fed. Wages $4,348,670
Rainfall (in.) 10.0	Ag. Net Cash Return ...$6,232,000
Jan. mean min. 25	Prop. Value.............$302,305,132
July mean max. 95	Retail Sales $10,204,114
Growing season (days) 231	

A pronghorn buck poses against a high desert backdrop in Hudspeth County. The Dallas Morning News file photo.

Hunt County

Physical Features: North Texas county; level to rolling surface; Sabine, Sulphur rivers; Lake Tawakoni; mostly heavy Blackland soil, some loam, sandy loams.

Economy: Education, varied manufacturing, agribusiness; several Fortune 500 companies in county; many residents employed in Dallas area.

History: Kiowa Indians who left soon after Anglo-American settlers arrived in 1839. County named for Memucan Hunt, Republic secretary of navy; created 1846 from Fannin, Nacogdoches counties.

Ethnicity, 1990: White, 55,705 (86.6%); Black, 6,802 (10.6%); American Indian, 266 (0.4%); Asian, 351 (0.5%); Other, 1,219 (1.9%). Hispanic, 2,876 (4.5%).

Vital Statistics, 1997: Births, 1,030; deaths, 761; marriages, 691; divorces, 450.

Recreation: Lake sports; Texas A&M University-Commerce events; museum; Audie Murphy exhibit.

Minerals: Sand and white rock, gas, oil.

Agriculture: Cattle, forage, greenhouse crops, top revenue sources; horses, wheat, oats, cotton, grain sorghum. Market value $24 million. Some firewood sold.

GREENVILLE (25,238) county seat; aircraft electronics; plastics distribution; varied manufacturing; hospitals; branch of Paris Junior College; Cotton Jubilee in October, cotton museum.

Commerce (7,123) Texas A&M University-Commerce; varied manufacturing; tourism; Bois d'Arc Bash in September; hospital.

Other towns include: **Caddo Mills** (1,156); **Campbell** (819); **Celeste** (896); **Hawk Cove** (NA); **Lone Oak** (614);

Merit (215); **Neylandville** (116); **Quinlan** (1,616); **West Tawakoni** (1,168) tourist center, light industry, catfish tournament, Lakefest; **Wolfe City** (1,600).

Population	71,039
Change fm '90	10.4
Area (sq. mi.)	882.0
Land Area (sq. mi.)	841.2
Altitude (ft.)	437-692
Rainfall (in.)	41.6
Jan. mean min.	29
July mean max.	94
Growing season (days)	237
Civ. Labor	35,977
Unemployed	3.9
Annual Wages	$625,212,312
Av. Weekly Wage	$486.74
Fed. Wages	$13,242,841
Ag. Net Cash Return	$35,000
Prop. Value	$2,128,661,904
Retail Sales	$554,643,401

For explanation of sources, abbreviations and symbols, see p. 130.

Hutchinson County

Physical Features: High Plain, broken by Canadian River and tributaries, Lake Meredith; fertile valleys along streams.

Economy: Oil, gas, petrochemicals; agribusiness; varied manufacturing; tourism.

History: Antelope Creek Indian area. Later Comanches were driven out in U.S. cavalry campaigns of 1874-75. Adobe Walls site of two Indian attacks, 1864 and 1874. Ranching began in late 1870s. Oil boom in early 1920s. County created 1876 from Bexar Territory; organized 1901; named for pioneer jurist Anderson Hutchinson.

Ethnicity, 1990: White, 22,661 (88.2%); Black, 677 (2.6%); American Indian, 362 (1.4%); Asian, 105 (0.4%); Other, 1,884 (7.3%). Hispanic, 2,509 (9.8%).

Vital Statistics, 1997: Births, 338; deaths, 252; marriages, 222; divorces, 147.

Recreation: Lake activities; fishing, camping; Adobe Walls, historic Indian battle site; fish fry in June.

Minerals: Gas, oil, sand, gravel.

Agriculture: Cattle, corn, wheat, grain sorghum; about 45,000 acres irrigated. Market value $42.9 million.

STINNETT (2,298) county seat; petroleum refining; farm center.

BORGER (15,359) petroleum refining, petrochemicals, carbon-black production, oilfield servicing; varied manufacturing; retail center; Frank Phillips College; hospital.

Other cities include: **Fritch** (2,474), **Sanford** (245).

Population	25,614
Change fm '90	-0.3
Area (sq. mi.)	894.9
Land Area (sq. mi.)	887.4
Altitude (ft.)	2,700-3,350
Rainfall (in.)	20.3
Jan. mean min.	23
July mean max.	93
Growing season (days)	187

Civ. Labor	9,620
Unemployed	5.8
Annual Wages	$278,411,193
Av. Weekly Wage	$575.51
Fed. Wages	$2,425,970
Ag. Net Cash Return	$9,077,000
Prop. Value	$1,445,709,671
Retail Sales	$164,997,268

Irion County

Physical Features: West Texas county with hilly surface, broken by Middle Concho, tributaries; clay, sandy soils.

Economy: Ranching; oil, gas production.

History: Tonkawa Indian area. Anglo-American settlement begin in late 1870s. County named for Republic leader R.A. Irion; created 1889 from Tom Green County.

Ethnicity, 1990: White, 1,609 (98.8%); Black, 2 (0.1%); American Indian, 1 (0.1%); Asian, 0 (0.0%); Other, 17 (1.0%). Hispanic, 385 (23.6%).

Vital Statistics, 1997: Births 11; deaths, 14; marriages, 14; divorces, 3.

Recreation: Hunting; historic sites, including Dove Creek battlefield and stagecoach stops, old Sherwood courthouse built 1900.

Minerals: Oil, gas.

Agriculture: Beef cattle, sheep, goats; wheat, cotton, hay. Market value $5.9 million.

MERTZON (657) county seat; farm center; wool warehousing.

Other towns include: **Barnhart** (160).

Population	1,525
Change fm '90	-6.4
Area (sq. mi.)	1,051.6
Land Area (sq. mi.)	1,051.6
Altitude (ft.)	2,000-2,725
Rainfall (in.)	21.1

Jan. mean min.	32
July mean max.	95
Growing season (days)	232
Civ. Labor	754
Unemployed	2.9

Annual Wages	$10,976,203
Av. Weekly Wage	$502.61
Fed. Wages	$122,768
Ag. Net Cash Return	$594,000
Prop. Value	$311,741,460
Retail Sales	$2,624,129

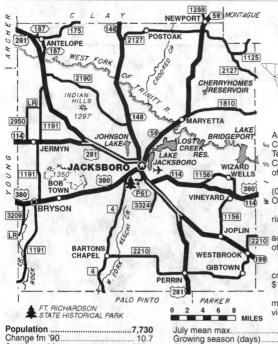

Jack County

Physical Features: Rolling Cross Timbers, broken by West Fork of the Trinity, other streams; sandy, dark brown, loam soils; lakes.

Economy: Petroleum production, oil-field services, livestock, manufacturing, tourism.

History: Caddo and Comanche borderland. Anglo-American settlers arrived in 1855, part of Peters Colony. County named for brothers P.C. and W.H. Jack, leaders in Texas' independence effort; created 1856 from Cooke County; organized 1857 with Mesquiteville (orginal name of Jacksboro) as county seat.

Ethnicity,1990: White, 6,748 (96.7%); Black, 51 (0.7%); American Indian, 18 (0.3%); Asian, 10 (0.1%); Other, 154 (2.2%). Hispanic, 232 (3.3%).

Vital Statistics, 1997: Births, 92; deaths, 78; marriages, 70; divorces, 48.

Recreation: Hunting, wildlife leases; fishing; Lake activities; Fort Richardson State Historical Park, museum, other historic sites; rattlesnake roundup in March.

Minerals: Oil, gas.

Agriculture: Cattle, hay, wheat, small grains, nursery crops; also, horses, sheep, goats, swine. Market value $16.9 million. Firewood sold.

JACKSBORO (3,637) county seat; agribusiness; manufacturing; tourism; petroleum production and services; hospital; hospice; library; Old Mesquiteville Festival in fall.

Other towns include: **Bryson** (579), **Jermyn** (75), **Perrin** (300).

Population	7,730
Change fm '90	10.7
Area (sq. mi.)	920.1
Land Area (sq. mi.)	917.4
Altitude (ft.)	836-1,350
Rainfall (in.)	30.7
Jan. mean min.	29
July mean max.	95
Growing season (days)	218
Civ. Labor	3,451
Unemployed	3.4
Annual Wages	$40,794,284
Av. Weekly Wage	$419.08
Fed. Wages	$574,073
Ag. Net Cash Return	$94,000
Prop. Value	$578,280,610
Retail Sales	$25,949,909

Physical Features: Southeastern county of prairie and motts of trees; loam, clay, black soils; drains to creek, rivers, bays.

Jackson County

Economy: Petroleum production and operation; metal fabrication and tooling, sheet-metal works, plastics manufacturing; agribusinesses; lake recreation.

History: Karankawa area. Six of Austin's Old Three Hundred families (1820s) settled in area. Lipan Apaches and Kiowas arrived in early 1830s. Mexican municipality, created 1835, became original county the following year; named for U.S. President Andrew Jackson. Oil discovered in 1934.

Ethnicity, 1990: White, 10,857 (83.3%); Black, 1,218 (9.3%); American Indian, 41 (0.3%); Asian, 12 (0.1%); Other, 911 (7.0%). Hispanic, 2,772 (21.3%).

Vital Statistics, 1997: Births, 92; deaths, 78; marriages, 96; divorces, 67.

Recreation: Hunting, fishing; historic sites; Texana Museum; Lake Texana, Brackenridge Plantation campground, state park; county fair, rodeo in October.

Minerals: Oil and natural gas.

Agriculture: Rice, beef cattle and cotton; also, sorghums, corn, soybeans, wheat, pecans; almost 22,000 acres of rice irrigated. Market value $47.3 million.

EDNA (6,437) county seat; oil; gas; tourism; agriculture; varied manufacturing; hospitals; bicycle event in November.

Other towns include: **Francitas** (143), **Ganado** (1,984), **LaSalle** (103), **La Ward** (188), **Lolita** (453), **Vanderbilt** (618).

Population	14,684
Change fm '90	12.6
Area (sq. mi.)	857.0
Land Area (sq. mi.)	829.5
Altitude (ft.)	sea level-150
Rainfall (in.)	40.9
Jan. mean min.	42
July mean max.	94
Growing season (days)	290
Civ. Labor	8,618
Unemployed	3.6
Annual Wages	$122,505,927
Av. Weekly Wage	$447.20
Fed. Wages	$1,211,902
Ag. Net Cash Return	$8,635,000
Prop. Value	$1,568,354,710
Retail Sales	$124,121,075

Jasper County

Physical Features: East Texas county; hilly to level; national forests; lakes; Neches River.

Economy: Timber industries; oil; tourism; fishing; agriculture.

History: Caddo and Atakapa Indian area. Land grants to John R. Bevil and Lorenzo de Zavala in 1829. County created 1836, organized 1837, from Mexican municipality; named for Sgt. William Jasper of American Revolution.

Ethnicity, 1990: White, 24,750 (79.6%); Black, 5,868 (18.9%); American Indian, 76 (0.2%); Asian, 38 (0.1%); Other, 370 (1.2%). Hispanic, 594 (1.9%).

Vital Statistics, 1997: Births, 528; deaths, 408; marriages, 349; divorces, 228.

Recreation: Lake activities; hunting; state park; azalea trail.

Minerals: Oil, gas produced.

Agriculture: Cattle, hogs, poultry, major revenue source; vegetables, fruit, pecans. Market value $3.5 million. Timber is major income producer.

JASPER (8,547) county seat; wood industries; plywood mill, sawmills; tourism; oil, gas production; hospital; fall fest.

Other towns include: **Browndell** (233), **Buna** (2,437), **Evadale** (1,788), **Kirbyville** (1,937), **Magnolia Springs** (80), **Sam Rayburn** (600).

Population...................................34,261
Change fm '90.............................. 10.2
Area (sq. mi.)............................. 969.6
Land Area (sq. mi.)..................... 937.5
Altitude (ft.)............................. 25-550
Rainfall (in.)............................. 52.7
Jan. mean min............................. 36
July mean max............................. 93
Growing season (days) 230
Civ. Labor................................ 14,669

Unemployed............................... 11.4
Annual Wages............... $273,334,497
Av. Weekly Wage.................. $490.23
Fed. Wages....................... $3,272,995
Ag. Net Cash Return .... -$1,562,000
Prop. Value $2,088,263,238
Retail Sales $323,060,972

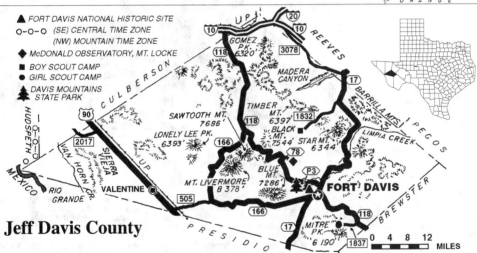

Jeff Davis County

▲ FORT DAVIS NATIONAL HISTORIC SITE

O–O–O (SE) CENTRAL TIME ZONE
(NW) MOUNTAIN TIME ZONE

◆ McDONALD OBSERVATORY, MT. LOCKE

■ BOY SCOUT CAMP

● GIRL SCOUT CAMP

▲ DAVIS MOUNTAINS STATE PARK

Physical Features: Highest average elevation in Texas; peaks (Mt. Livermore, 8,378 ft.), canyons, plateaus; intermountain wash, clay, loam soils; cedars, oaks in highlands.

Economy: Tourism; greenhouse nurseries; ranching; small businesses; government/services; hunting leases.

History: Mescalero Apaches in area when Antonio de Espejo explored in 1583. U.S. Army established Fort Davis in 1854 to protect routes to west. Civilian settlers followed, including Manuel Músquiz, a political refugee from Mexico. County named for Jefferson Davis, U.S. war secretary, Confederate president; created 1887 from Presidio County.

Ethnicity, 1990: White, 1,671 (85.9%); Black, 7 (0.4%); American Indian, 12 (0.6%); Asian, 4 (0.2%); Other, 252 (12.9%). Hispanic, 770 (39.6%).

Vital Statistics, 1997: Births, 17; deaths, 15; marriages, 16; divorces, 1.

Recreation: Scenic drives including scenic loop along Limpia Creek, Mt. Livermore, Blue Mountain; hunting; Fort Davis National Historic Site (with Restoration Festival on Columbus Day weekend); state park; McDonald Observatory; solar power park; Hummingbird Roundup in July; Chihuahuan Desert Research Institute.

Minerals: Not significant.

Agriculture: Greenhouse nuseries; beef cattle; horses, hunting, sheep and goats; wine grapes, apples, pecans. Market value $9.3 million.

FORT DAVIS (1,179), county seat; ranch center; trade, tourism; government; manufacturing of hats, candles; Christian music festival on Memorial Day weekend. Other town, **Valentine** (267).

Population.............................2,014
Change fm '90.............................3.5
Area (sq. mi.) 2,264.6
Land Area (sq. mi.) 2,264.6
Altitude (ft.)................... 3,500-8,378
Rainfall (in.)...........................20.8
Jan. mean min. 30
July mean max............................82
Growing season (days) 209
Civ. Labor...........................1,552
Unemployed................................2.2
Annual Wages..........$20,279,257
Av. Weekly Wage...............$331.81
Fed. Wages.....................$846,905
Ag. Net Cash Funds..........$877,000
Prop. Value $241,342,002
Retail Sales.................$8,034,553

For explanation of sources, abbreviations and symbols, see p. 130.

Jefferson County

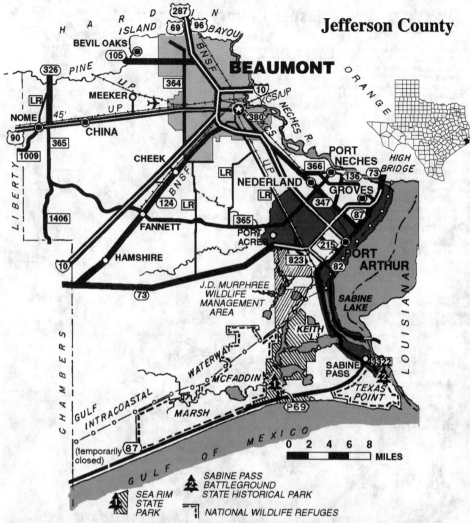

Physical Features: Gulf Coast grassy plain, with timber in northwest; beach sands, sandy loams, black clay soils; drains to Neches River, Gulf of Mexico.

Economy: Government/services; petrochemical, other chemical plants; shipbuilding; steel mill; port activity; oilfield supplies; .

History: Atakapas and Orcoquizas, whose numbers were reduced by epidemics or migration before Anglo-American settlers arrived in 1820s. Cajuns arrived in 1840s; Europeans in 1850s. Antebellum slaveholding area. County created 1836 from Mexican municipality; organized 1837; named for U.S. President Thomas Jefferson.

Ethnicity, 1990: White, 154,273 (64.4%); Black, 74,412 (31.1%); American Indian, 578 (0.2%); Asian, 5,145 (2.1%); Other, 4,989 (2.1%). Hispanic, 12,629 (5.3%).

Vital Statistics, 1997: Births, 3,409; deaths, 2,590; marriages, 2,665; divorces, 1,246.

Recreation: Beaches, fresh and saltwater fishing; duck, goose hunting; water activities; Dick Dowling Monument and Park; Spindletop site, museums; saltwater lake; wildlife refuge; Lamar University events; historic sites; South Texas Fair.

Minerals: Large producer of oil, gas, sulfur, salt, sand and gravel.

Agriculture: Rice, soybeans; crawfish; beef cattle; hay; considerable rice irrigated. Market value $25.9 million. Timber sales significant.

BEAUMONT (115,967) county seat; government/services; petrochemical production; shipbuilding; port activities; rice milling; Lamar University; hospital; Main Street on the Neches.

Port Arthur (58,582) oil, chemical activities; shrimping and crawfishing; shipping; offshore marine; tourism; hospital; prison. Chinese New Year Tet, Janis Joplin Birthday Bash in January. **Sabine Pass** and **Port Acres** are now within the city limits of Port Arthur.

Other towns include: **Bevil Oaks** (1,550); **China** (1,225); **Fannett** (105); **Groves** (16,727) some manufacturing, government/service, hospital, pecan festival; **Hamshire** (350).

Also, **Nederland** (17,844) marine manufacturing; tourism; Windmill and French museums; hospital; Tex Ritter memorial and park, heritage festival (city founded by Dutch immigrants in 1898); **Nome** (447); **Port Neches** (13,016) chemical and synthetic rubber industry, manufacturing, river-front festival at Christmas.

Population	248,481
Change fm '90	3.8
Area (sq. mi.)	1,111.2
Land Area (sq. mi.)	903.6
Altitude (ft.)	sea level-45
Rainfall (in.)	57.2
Jan. mean min.	42
July mean max.	92
Growing season (days)	250
Civ. Labor	118,597
Unemployed	6.7
Annual Wages	$3,525,202,449
Av. Weekly Wage	$571.96
Fed. Wages	$94,865,447
Ag. Net Cash Return	$3,336,000
Prop. Value	$13,083,622,602
Retail Sales	$2,497,134,799

Physical Features: South Texas county on rolling plain, with heavy brush cover; white blow sand and sandy loam; hilly, broken.

Economy: Oil, cattle operations.

History: Coahuiltecan area, then Lipan Apache. Spanish land grant in 1805 to Xavier Vela. County named for Gov. James Stephen Hogg; created, organized 1913 from Brooks, Duval counties.

Ethnicity, 1990: White, 4,375 (85.6%); Black, 4 (0.1%); American Indian, 12 (0.2%); Asian, 4 (0.1%); Other, 714 (14.0%). Hispanic, 4,659 (91.2%).

Vital Statistics, 1997: Births, 71; deaths, 41; marriages, 38; divorces, 1.

Recreation: White-tailed deer and bobwhite hunting.

Minerals: Oil and gas.

Agriculture: Cattle, hay, milk goats; some irrigation. Market value $6.5 million.

HEBBRONVILLE (4,098) county seat; ranching, oil-field center. Other towns include: **Guerra** (75).

Population	4,825
Change fm '90	-5.6
Area (sq. mi.)	1,136.2
Land Area (sq. mi.)	1,136.2
Altitude (ft.)	249-886
Rainfall (in.)	22.7
Jan. mean min.	42
July mean max.	97
Growing season (days)	303
Civ. Labor	2,197
Unemployed	9.9
Annual Wages	$26,088,055
Av. Weekly Wage	$367.19
Fed. Wages	$4,131,329
Ag. Net Cash Return	$1,147,000
Prop. Value	$412,432,264
Retail Sales	$39,672,018

Jim Hogg County

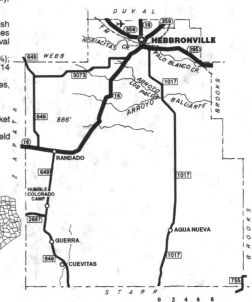

Jim Wells County

Population	39,846
Change fm '90	5.8
Area (sq. mi.)	868.2
Land Area (sq. mi.)	864.7
Altitude (ft.)	50-400
Rainfall (in.)	27.8
Jan. mean min.	43
July mean max.	96
Growing season (days)	289
Civ. Labor	17,198
Unemployed	8.7
Annual Wages	$274,026,558
Av. Weekly Wage	$406.90
Fed. Wages	$3,667,557
Ag. Net Cash Return	$5,399,000
Prop. Value	$1,004,635,703
Retail Sales	$263,015,270

Physical Features: South Coastal Plains; level to rolling; sandy to dark soils; grassy with mesquite brush.

Economy: Oil, gas production, sorghum and cattle.

History: Coahuiltecans, driven out by Lipan Apaches in 1775. Tomás Sánchez established settlement in 1754. Anglo-American settlement in 1878. County created 1911 from Nueces County; organized 1912; named for developer J.B. Wells Jr.

Ethnicity, 1990: White, 28,504 (75.6%); Black, 218 (0.6%); American Indian, 82 (0.2%); Asian, 103 (0.3%); Other, 8,772 (23.3%). Hispanic, 27,201 (72.2%).

Vital Statistics, 1997: Births, 662; deaths, 317; marriages, 265; divorces, 99.

Recreation: Hunting; fiestas.

Minerals: Oil, gas, caliche.

Agriculture: Cattle, dairy products, goats; grain sorghum, wheat, corn, cotton; some irrigation for coastal Bermuda, vegetables. Market value $35.6 million.

ALICE (20,230) county seat; oil-field service center; agri-business; government/services; hospital; Fiesta Bandana (from original name of city) in May; Bee County College extension.

Other towns include: **Orange Grove** (1,338); **Premont** (2,934) wildflower tour, youth rodeo; **Sandia** (215). Also part of **San Diego** (5,134).

For explanation of sources, abbreviations and symbols, see p. 130.

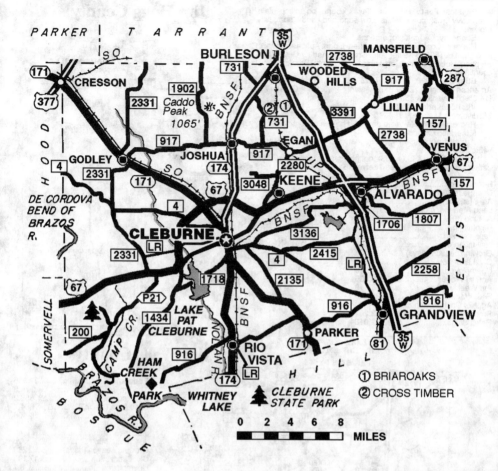

① BRIAROAKS
② CROSS TIMBER

CLEBURNE STATE PARK

0 2 4 6 8 MILES

Johnson County

Physical Features: North central county drained by tributaries of Trinity, Brazos rivers; lake; hilly, rolling, many soil types.

Economy: Agribusiness; railroad shops; manufacturing; distribution; lake activities; many residents employed in Fort Worth; part of Fort Worth-Arlington metropolitan area.

History: No permanent Indian villages existed in area. Anglo-American settlers arrived in 1840s. County named for Col. M.T. Johnson of Mexican War, Confederacy; created, organized 1854 out of Ellis, Hill, Navarro counties.

Ethnicity, 1990: White, 90,328 (93.0%); Black, 2,521 (2.6%); American Indian, 419 (0.4%); Asian, 447 (0.5%); Other, 3,450 (3.6%). Hispanic, 7,457 (7.7%).

Vital Statistics, 1997: Births, 1,665; deaths, 936; marriages, 1,087; divorces, 589.

Recreation: Bird, deer hunting; water activities on Lake Pat Cleburne; state park; museum.

Minerals: Limestone, sand and gravel.

Agriculture: A leading dairy county; cattle, horses (first in state in number sold), hogs; crops include hay, sorghum, wheat, corn. Market value $48.1 million.

CLEBURNE (24,277) county seat; dairy center; rail-shipping terminal; varied manufacturing; hospital; Layland Museum; Hill College, Cleburne campus.

BURLESON (20,500, part in Tarrant County) agriculture, retail center; hospital.

Other towns include: **Alvarado** (3,447) County Pioneer Days; **Briaroaks** (656); **Cross Timber** (289); **Godley** (642); **Grandview** (1,368); **Joshua** (4,665) many residents work in Fort Worth; **Keene** (4,764) Southwestern Adventist University; **Lillian** (105); **Rio Vista** (716), and **Venus** (1,283).

Population 114,916
Change fm '90 ....18.3
Area (sq. mi.) 734.3
Land Area (sq. mi.) 729.4
Altitude (ft.) 600-1,065
Rainfall (in.) 34.0
Jan. mean min. 33
July mean max. 97
Growing season (days)..................233
Civ. Labor 59,186
Unemployed 3.5
Annual Wages $654,214,331
Av. Weekly Wage $431.49
Fed. Wages $8,150,947
Ag. Net Cash Return $4,208,000
Prop. Value..................$3,649,855,488
Retail Sales $762,796,642

For explanation of sources, abbreviations and symbols, see p. 130.

Jones County

Physical Features: West Texas Rolling Plains; drained by Brazos River fork, tributaries; Lake Fort Phantom Hill.

Economy: Agribusiness; government/services; varied manufacturing.

History: Comanches and other tribes hunted in area. Military presence began in 1851. Ranching established in 1870s. County named for the last president of the Republic, Anson Jones; created 1858 from Bexar, Bosque counties; re-created 1876; organized 1881.

Ethnicity, 1990: White, 13,786 (83.6%); Black, 666 (4.0%); American Indian, 47 (0.3%); Asian, 31 (0.2%); Other, 1,960 (11.9%). Hispanic, 2,786 (16.9%).

Vital Statistics, 1997: Births, 162; deaths, 202; marriages, 87; divorces, 78.

Recreation: Lake activities; Fort Phantom Hill site, museum; Cowboys Christmas Ball; Cowboy Reunion on July 4 weekend; old courthouse, opera house, museum, art show.

Minerals: Oil, gas, sand and gravel, stone.

Agriculture: Cotton, wheat, sesame and peanuts; cattle. some 10,000 acres irrigated for peanuts and hay. Market value $39 million.

ANSON (2,576) county seat; farming center; boat-trailer factory, Western clothing manufacturing; hospital; historic buildings.

STAMFORD (3,213) trade center for three counties.

HAMLIN (2,429) trade center for farm and oil, gas area; government/services; feed mills; hospital; historical festival in June.

Other towns include: **Avoca** (121), **Hawley** (633), **Lueders** (360).

Part of **Abilene** extends into the county.

Population	17,962
Change fm '90	8.9
Area (sq. mi.)	937.1
Land Area (sq. mi.)	931.1
Altitude (ft.)	1,500-1,950
Rainfall (in.)	25.8
Jan. mean min.	31
July mean max.	96
Growing season (days)	223
Civ. Labor	10,327
Unemployed	3.4
Annual Wages	$111,418,410
Av. Weekly Wage	$416.21
Fed. Wages	$3,582,758
Ag. Net Cash Return	$5,971,000
Prop. Value	$579,185,508
Retail Sales	$120,148,557

Karnes County

Physical Features: Sandy loam, dark clay, alluvial soils in rolling terrain; traversed by San Antonio River; mesquite, oak trees.

Economy: Government/services; agribusiness, mineral production, tourism; commuting to San Antonio.

History: Coahuiltecan Indian area. Spanish ranching began around 1750. Anglo-Americans arrived in 1840s; Polish in 1850s. County created 1854 from Bexar, Goliad, San Patricio counties; named for Texas Revolutionary figure Henry W. Karnes.

Ethnicity, 1990: White, 9,548 (76.7%); Black, 362 (2.9%); American Indian, 35 (0.3%); Asian, 14 (0.1%); Other, 2,496 (20.0%). Hispanic, 5,916 (47.5%).

Vital Statistics, 1997: Births, 166; deaths, 179; marriages, 80; divorces, 22.

Recreation: Panna Maria, nation's oldest Polish settlement, founded Dec. 24, 1854; Old Helena restored courthouse, museum; bird hunting.

Minerals: Oil, gas, stone.

Agriculture: Cattle, poultry, hogs, goats, rabbits; hay, corn, sorghum, wheat, sunflowers. Market value 15.9 million.

KARNES CITY (2,859) county seat; agribusiness; tourism; processing center; oil-field servicing; varied manufacturing; hospital; library.; Lonesome Dove Festival.

KENEDY (6,205) farm and oil center, dove and quail hunting leases, prison; Bluebonnet Days in April.

Other towns include: **Falls City** (511) ranching, sausage making, library, city park on river; **Gillett** (120); **Hobson** (135); **Panna Maria** (96); **Runge** (1,133) farm center.

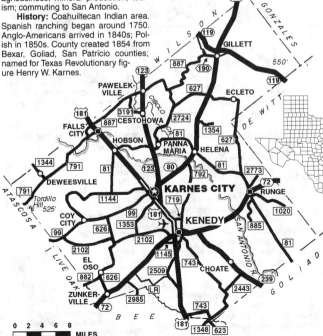

Population	14,392
Change fm '90	15.6
Area (sq. mi.)	753.5
Land Area (sq. mi.)	750.3
Altitude (ft.)	180-550
Rainfall (in.)	33.2
Jan. mean min.	41
July mean max.	97
Growing season (days)	281
Civ. Labor	6,266
Unemployed	4.1
Annual Wages	$84,943,997
Av. Weekly Wage	$397.05
Fed. Wages	$1,261,723
Ag. Net Cash Return	-$1,584,000
Prop. Value	$614,729,500
Retail Sales	$63,386,045

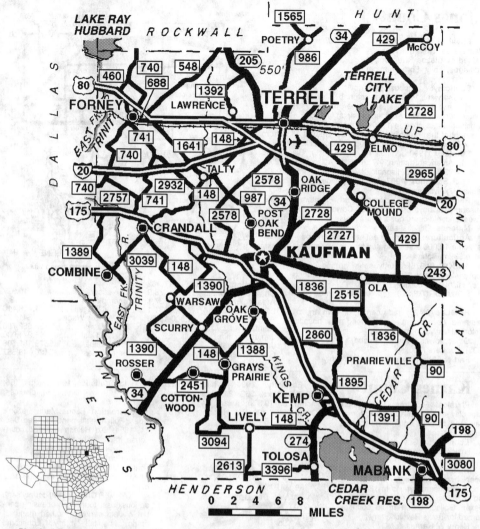

Kaufman County

Physical Features: North Blackland prairie, draining to Trinity River, Cedar Creek and Lake.

Economy: varied manufacturing; trade center; government/services; antique center; commuting to Dallas.

History: Caddo and Cherokee Indians; removed by 1840 when Anglo-American settlement began. County created from Henderson County and organized, 1848; named for member of Texas and U.S. congresses D.S. Kaufman.

Ethnicity, 1990: White, 42,810 (82.0%); Black, 7,295 (14.0%); American Indian, 198 (0.4%); Asian, 229 (0.4%); Other, 1,688 (3.2%). Hispanic, 3,340 (6.4%).

Vital Statistics, 1997: Births, 870; deaths, 553; marriages, 680; divorces, 322.

Recreation: Lake activities; Porter Farm near Terrell is site of origin of U.S.-Texas Agricultural Extension program; antique centers near Forney; historic homes at Terrell.

Minerals: Oil, gas, stone, sand.

Agriculture: Nursery crops; beef cattle, horses, goats, hogs, sheep; wheat, hay, sorghum, oats, cotton, peaches. Market value $29 million.

KAUFMAN (7,042) county seat; varied manufacturing; commuters to Dallas; hospital; Summerfest in June.

TERRELL (14,039) agribusiness, varied manufacturing; outlet center; private hospital, state hospital; community college, Southwestern Christian College.

Other towns include: **Crandall** (2,298); **Combine** (1,858, partly in Dallas County); **Cottonwood** (204); **Elmo** (90); **Forney** (5,106) antiques,

light manufacturing, historic homes; **Grays Prairie** (391); **Kemp** (1,414); **Mabank** (2,012, partly in Henderson County) tourism; manufacturing, retail trade; **Oak Grove** (738); **Oak Ridge** (349); **Post Oak Bend** (374); **Rosser** (460); **Scurry** (315).

Population	**63,583**
Change fm '90	21.8
Area (sq. mi.)	806.8
Land Area (sq. mi.)	786.1
Altitude (ft.)	300-550
Rainfall (in.)	38.9
Jan. mean min.	32
July mean max.	95
Growing season (days)	248
Civ. Labor	32,206
Unemployed	4.3
Annual Wages	$426,788,405
Av. Weekly Wage	$436.01
Fed. Wages	$5,629,001
Ag. Net Cash Return	-$5,689,000
Prop. Value	$2,419,796,663
Retail Sales	$616,416,443

For explanation of sources, abbreviations and symbols, see p. 130.

Kendall County

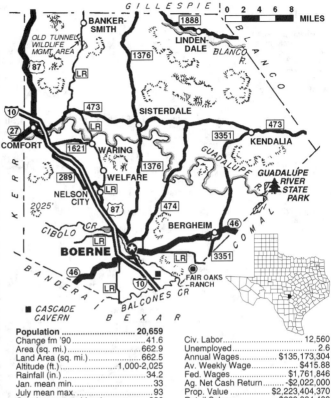

Physical Features: Hill Country, plateau, with springfed streams; caves; scenic drives.

Economy: Commuters to San Antonio, tourism, agribusiness, some manufacturing.

History: Lipan Apaches, Kiowas and Comanches in area when German settlers arrived in 1840s. County created from Blanco, Kerr counties 1862; named for pioneer journalist-sheepman and early contributor to Texas Almanac, George W. Kendall.

Ethnicity, 1990: White, 13,682 (93.8%); Black, 58 (0.4%); American Indian, 71 (0.5%); Asian, 38 (0.3%); Other, 740 (5.1%). Hispanic, 2,392 (16.4%).

Vital Statistics, 1997: Births, 285; deaths, 203; marriages, 234; divorces, 85.

Recreation: Hunting, fishing, state park; tourist center; Cascade Caverns; historic sites.

Minerals: Natural gas.

Agriculture: Cattle, sheep, Angora goats, Spanish goats raised; small grains. Market value $6.5 million.

BOERNE (5,899) county seat; commuting to San Antonio; tourism; antiques; some manufacturing; Berges Fest on Father's Day weekend; village band concerts in summer.

Other towns include: **Bergheim** (NA); **Comfort** (1,941) ranching, tourism, has state's only Civil War monument honoring Unionists; **Kendalia** (76); **Sisterdale** (63); **Waring** (73).

Population	20,659
Change fm '90	41.6
Area (sq. mi.)	662.9
Land Area (sq. mi.)	662.5
Altitude (ft.)	1,000-2,025
Rainfall (in.)	34.2
Jan. mean min.	33
July mean max.	93
Growing season (days)	236

Civ. Labor	12,560
Unemployed	2.6
Annual Wages	$135,173,304
Av. Weekly Wage	$415.88
Fed. Wages	$1,761,846
Ag. Net Cash Return	-$2,022,000
Prop. Value	$2,223,404,370
Retail Sales	$389,884,488

Kenedy County

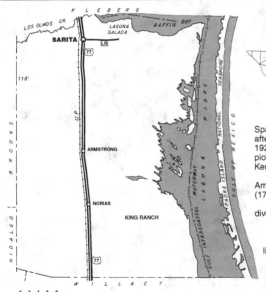

Physical Features: Gulf coastal county; flat, sandy terrain; some loam soils; motts of live oaks.

Economy: Oil, ranching; hunting leases a factor.

History: Coahuiltecan Indians who assimilated or were driven out by Lipan Apaches. Spanish ranching began in 1790s. Anglo-Americans arrived after Mexican War. Among last counties created, organized 1921, from Cameron, Hidalgo, Willacy counties; named for pioneer steamboat operator and cattleman, Capt. Mifflin Kenedy.

Ethnicity, 1990: White, 378 (82.2%); Black, 0 (0.0%); American Indian, 0 (0.0%); Asian, 0 (0.0%); Other, 82 (17.8%). Hispanic, 362 (78.7%).

Vital Statistics, 1997: Births, 10; deaths, 3; marriages, 2; divorces, 1.

Recreation: Hunting a major enterprise; fishing.

Minerals: Oil, gas.

Agriculture: Beef cattle, horses. Market value $6.8 million. Hunting leases.

SARITA (250) county seat; cattle-shipping point; ranch headquarters; gas processing; one of state's least populous counties. Also, **Armstrong** (20).

Population	422
Change fm '90	-8.3
Area (sq. mi.)	1,945.5
Land Area (sq. mi.)	1,456.9
Altitude (ft.)	sea level-118

Rainfall (in.)	29.7
Jan. mean min.	45
July mean max.	95
Growing season (days)	319
Civ. Labor	227
Unemployed	3.5

Annual Wages	$6,631,065
Av. Weekly Wage	$417.51
Fed. Wages	$51,168
Ag. Net Cash Return	-$1,554,000
Prop. Value	$420,349,970
Retail Sales	$96,203

Kent County

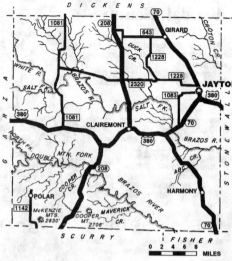

Physical Features: West central county of rolling, broken terrain; drains to Salt and Double Mountain forks of Brazos River; sandy, loam soils.

Economy: Agribusiness, oil-field operations, hunting leases.

History: Comanches driven out by U.S. Army in 1870s. Ranching developed in 1880s. County created 1876 from Bexar, Young territories; organized 1892. Name honors Andrew Kent, one of 32 volunteers from Gonzales who died at the Alamo.

Ethnicity, 1990: White, 902 (89.3%); Black, 6 (0.6%); American Indian, 1 (0.1%); Asian, 0 (0.0%); Other, 101 (10.0%). Hispanic, 120 (11.9%).

Vital Statistics, 1997: Births, 11; deaths, 16; marriages, 4; divorces, 5.

Recreation: Hunting; scenic croton breaks and salt flat.

Minerals: Oil, gas.

Agriculture: Cattle, sheep, goats; cotton, wheat, sorghum. Market value $7.3 million.

JAYTON (573) county seat; oil-field services; farming center; fun fest in August.

Other towns include: **Girard** (125).

Population.....................942	Jan. mean min.....................25	Av. Weekly Wage...............$373.47
Change fm '90 ....-6.7	July mean max.....................96	Fed. Wages..................$265,514
Area (sq. mi.).....................902.8	Growing season (days) 216	Ag. Net Cash Return..........$1,537,000
Land Area (sq. mi.).............. 902.4	Civ. Labor.....................453	Prop. Value $767,125,269
Altitude (ft.).....................1,823-2,830	Unemployed 3.3	Retail Sales.....................$11,332,637
Rainfall (in.) 21.8	Annual Wages.................$5,259,475	

Kerr County

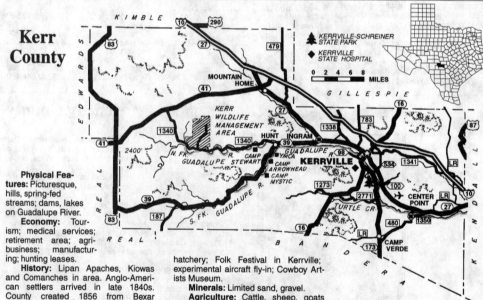

Physical Features: Picturesque, hills, spring-fed streams; dams, lakes on Guadalupe River.

Economy: Tourism; medical services; retirement area; agribusiness; manufacturing; hunting leases.

History: Lipan Apaches, Kiowas and Comanches in area. Anglo-American settlers arrived in late 1840s. County created 1856 from Bexar County; named for member of Austin's Colony, James Kerr.

Ethnicity, 1990: White, 32,842 (90.5%); Black, 805 (2.2%); American Indian, 128 (0.4%); Asian, 141 (0.4%); Other, 2,388 (6.6%). Hispanic, 5,994 (16.5%).

Vital Statistics, 1997: Births, 479; deaths, 579; marriages, 373; divorces, 207.

Recreation: Popular area for tourists, hunters, fishermen; private and youth camps; dude ranches; state park; Point theater; wildlife management area; hatchery; Folk Festival in Kerrville; experimental aircraft fly-in; Cowboy Artists Museum.

Minerals: Limited sand, gravel.

Agriculture: Cattle, sheep, goats for wool, mohair; crops include apples, hay, pecans; Spanish goats on increase. Market value $7.2 million.

KERRVILLE (21,706) county seat; tourist center; youth camps; agribusiness; aircraft and parts and varied manufacturing; Schreiner College; Kerrville State Hospital; Veterans Administration Medical Center; retirement center; retail trade; state arts, crafts show in May-June; experimental aircraft fly-in during October.

Other towns include: **Camp Verde** (41); **Center Point** (1,250); **Hunt** (708), youth camps; **Ingram** (1,615) camps, cabins; **Mountain Home** (96).

For explanation of sources, abbreviations and symbols, see p. 130.

Population 43,238	
Change fm '90.....................19.1	
Area (sq. mi.).....................1,107.6	
Land Area (sq. mi.).....................1,106.3	
Altitude (ft.).....................1,450-2,400	
Rainfall (in.).....................29.8	
Jan. mean min.....................32	
July mean max.....................94	
Growing season (days) 216	
Civ. Labor.....................17,417	
Unemployed 2.6	
Annual Wages.............$292,200,176	
Av. Weekly Wage................$401.70	
Fed. Wages.................$28,796,893	
Ag. Net Cash Return.....-$2,009,000	
Prop. Value $2,076,564,725	
Retail Sales...............$456,254,443	

Kimble County

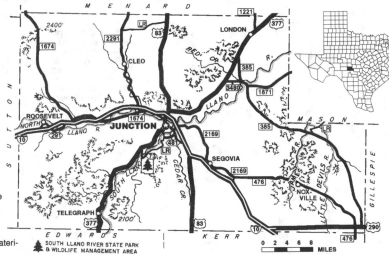

Physical Features: Picturesque southwestern county; rugged, broken by numerous streams; drains to Llano River; sandy, gray, chocolate loam soils.

Economy: Livestock production, large goat market, wool, mohair; tourism, hunting, fishing; cedar oil and wood products sold; metal building materials manufactured.

History: Apache, Kiowas and Comanche stronghold until 1870s. Military outposts protected first Anglo-American settlers in 1850s. County created from Bexar County 1858; organized 1876. Named for George C. Kimble, a Gonzales volunteer who died at the Alamo.

Ethnicity, 1990: White, 3,654 (88.6%); Black, 2 (0.0%); American Indian, 5 (0.1%); Asian, 10 (0.2%); Other, 451 (10.9%). Hispanic, 772 (18.7%).

Vital Statistics, 1997: Births, 48; deaths, 54; marriages, 28; divorces, 23.

Recreation: Hunting, fishing in spring-fed streams; among leading deer counties; state park; Kimble Kounty Kow Kick on Labor Day.

Minerals: Limited sand, gravel.

Agriculture: Cattle, Angora and Spanish goats, sheep, are primary products; pecans, hay also raised; some irrigation for grasses. Market value $7.2 million. Hunting leases important. Firewood, cedar sold.

JUNCTION (2,672) county seat; tourism; varied manufacturing; livestock production; two museums; Texas Tech University center; hospital; library; gun and knife show.

Other towns include: **London** (180); **Roosevelt** (14); **Telegraph** (3).

Population **4,269**
Change fm '90 ....3.6
Area (sq. mi.)..........................1,250.9
Land Area (sq. mi.).................1,250.8
Altitude (ft.)...................... 1,500-2,400
Rainfall (in.)...............................23.8
Jan. mean min................................31
July mean max. 96
Growing season (days) 213
Civ. Labor....................................2,358
Unemployed 2.4
Annual Wages $30,842,616
Av. Weekly Wage.................$381.14
Fed. Wages $527,645
Ag. Net Cash Return .... -$1,452,000
Prop. Value....................$461,738,168
Retail Sales $50,375,218

Fishermen on the South Llano River in theTexas Hill Country. The Dallas Morning News file photo.

King County

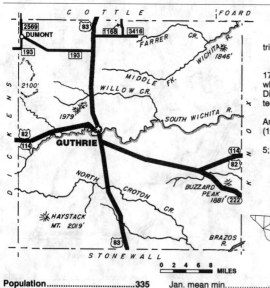

Physical Features: Hilly, broken by Wichita, Brazos tributaries; extensive grassland; dark loam to red soils.

Economy: Minerals, ranching.

History: Apache area until Comanches moved in about 1700. Comanches removed by U.S. Army in 1874-75 after which ranching began. County created 1876 from Bexar District; organized 1891; named for William P. King, a volunteer from Gonzales who died at the Alamo.

Ethnicity, 1990: White, 317 (89.5%); Black, 0 (0.0%); American Indian, 0 (0.0%); Asian, 0 (0.0%); Other, 37 (10.5%). Hispanic, 53 (15.0%).

Vital Statistics, 1997: Births, 1; deaths, 1; marriages, 5; divorces, 1.

Recreation: Four Sixes, other large ranches cover most of county.

Minerals: Oil, gas.

Agriculture: Cow-calf, stocker cattle operations, horses; cotton, wheat, sorghum, hay. Market value $6.6 million.

GUTHRIE (160) county seat; ranch-supply center; community center complex; museum, library.

Other town: **Dumont** (85).

Population	335	
Change fm '90	-5.4	
Area (sq. mi.)	913.3	
Land Area (sq. mi.)	912.3	
Altitude (ft.)	1,500-2,100	
Rainfall (in.)	23.8	
Jan. mean min.	24	
July mean max.	98	
Growing season (days)	219	
Civ. Labor	120	
Unemployed	7.5	
Annual Wages	$3,299,820	
Av. Weekly Wage	$454.14	
Fed. Wages	$149,400	
Ag. Net Cash Return	$797,000	
Prop. Value	$230,764,416	
Retail Sales	$1,384,151	

Kinney County

Physical Features: Hilly, broken by Rio Grande tributaries; Anacacho Mountains; Nueces Canyon.

Economy: Agribusinesses, tourism, government/services, hunting leases.

History: Coahuiltecans, Apaches, Comanches in area. Spanish Franciscans established settlement in late 1700s. English empresarios John Beales and James Grant established English-speaking colony in 1834. Black Seminoles served as army scouts in 1870s. County created from Bexar County 1850; organized 1874; named for H.L. Kinney, founder of Corpus Christi.

Ethnicity, 1990: White, 2,746 (88.0%); Black, 57 (1.8%); American Indian, 26 (0.8%); Asian, 9 (0.3%); Other, 281 (9.0%). Hispanic, 1,570 (50.3%).

Vital Statistics, 1997: Births, 35; deaths, 40; marriages, 17; divorces, 10.

Recreation: Hunting; replica of Alamo; old Fort Clark Springs; new state park; Seminole Days.

Minerals: Not significant.

Agriculture: Cattle, meat goats, Angora goats; hay, pecans, wheat, cotton. Market value $6.1 million.

BRACKETTVILLE (1,858) county seat; agriculture, tourism; museum; cowboy cauldron.

Other towns include: **Fort Clark Springs** (1,070); **Spofford** (66).

Population	3,358	
Change fm '90	7.7	
Area (sq. mi.)	1,365.3	
Land Area (sq. mi.)	1,363.5	
Altitude (ft.)	850-2,000	
Rainfall (in.)	21.7	
Jan. mean min.	36	
July mean max.	95	
Growing season (days)	270	
Civ. Labor	1,115	
Unemployed	9.8	
Annual Wages	$8,655,485	
Av. Weekly Wage	$313.03	
Fed. Wages	$3,465,366	
Ag. Net Cash Return	-$6,000	
Prop. Value	$300,767,515	
Retail Sales	$7,653,799	

For explanation of sources, abbreviations and symbols, see p. 130.

Kleberg County

Physical Features: Coastal plain, broken by bays; sandy, loam, clay soils; tree motts.
Economy: Naval air station; ranch operation; chemicals and plastics; Texas A&M University-Kingsville.
History: Coahuiltecan and Karankawa area. Spanish land grants date to 1750s. In 1853 Richard King purchased Santa Gertrudis land grant. County created 1913 from Nueces County; named for San Jacinto veteran and rancher Robert Kleberg.
Ethnicity, 1990: White, 20,650 (68.2%); Black, 998 (3.3%); American Indian, 81 (0.3%); Asian, 414 (1.4%); Other, 8,131 (26.9%). Hispanic, 18,529 (61.2%).

Vital Statistics, 1997: Births, 529; deaths, 222; marriages, 275; divorces, 135.
Recreation: Fishing, hunting, water sports, park on Baffin Bay; wildlife sanctuary; winter bird watching; university events, museum; King Ranch headquarters, tours; La Posada celebration in November.
Minerals: Oil, gas.
Agriculture: Beef cattle, cotton, grain sorghum. Market value $44.3 million. Hunting leases.
KINGSVILLE (26,541) county seat; oil, gas center; agribusiness; areospace, military training; tourism; chemical plant; university, Coastal Bend College branch; hospital. Other towns include: **Riviera** (1,064).

Population	31,232
Change fm '90	3.2
Area (sq. mi.)	1,090.4
Land Area (sq. mi.)	871.1
Altitude (ft.)	sea level-151
Rainfall (in.)	27.6
Jan. mean min.	45
July mean max.	95
Growing season (days)	314
Civ. Labor	13,296
Unemployed	6.7
Annual Wages	$196,506,196
Av. Weekly Wage	$375.89
Fed. Wages	$25,808,619
Ag. Net Cash Return	$2,711,000
Prop. Value	$1,269,524,984
Retail Sales	$224,651,309

Knox County

Physical Features: Eroded breaks on West Texas Rolling Plains; Brazos, Wichita rivers; sandy, loam soils.
Economy: Agribusiness, government/services.
History: Indian conscripts used during Spanish period to mine copper deposits along the Brazos. Ranching, farming developed in 1880s. German colony settled in 1895. County created from Bexar, Young territories 1858; re-created 1876; organized 1886; named for U.S. Secretary of War Henry Knox.
Ethnicity, 1990: White, 3,765 (77.8%); Black, 338 (7.0%); American Indian, 7 (0.1%); Asian, 5 (0.1%); Other, 722 (14.9%). Hispanic, 1,088 (22.5%).
Vital Statistics, 1997: Births, 46; deaths, 62; marriages, 24; divorces, 12.
Recreation: Lake activities, fishing; hunting; Knox City watermelon festival in July.
Minerals: Oil, gas.
Agriculture: Stocker cattle, cow/calf, horses, goats; wheat, cotton, sorghum, hay, melons. Cotton irrigated. Market value $49 million.
BENJAMIN (230) county seat; ranching, farm center.

MUNDAY (1,461) portable buildings, other manufacturing; Texas A&M Vegetable Research Station; vegetable festival.
KNOX CITY (1,406) agribusiness, petroleum center; USDA Plant Materials Research Center; home of seedless watermelon; hospital.
Other towns include: **Goree** (425); **Rhineland** (100); **Truscott** (50); **Vera** (50).

Population	4,553
Change fm '90	-5.9
Area (sq. mi.)	855.4
Land Area (sq. mi.)	854.2
Altitude (ft.)	1,300-1,700
Rainfall (in.)	26.2
Jan. mean min.	28
July mean max.	98
Growing season (days)	217
Civ. Labor	2,123
Unemployed	5.2
Annual Wages	$27,525,439
Av. Weekly Wage	$383.38
Fed. Wages	$2,441,034
Ag. Net Cash Return	$8,089,000
Prop. Value	$216,559,185
Retail Sales	$18,527,722

Lamar County

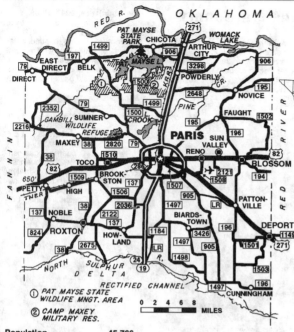

Physical Features: North Texas county on divide between Red, Sulphur rivers; soils chiefly blackland, except along Red; pines, hardwoods.

Economy: Varied manufacturing; agribusiness; tourism; government/services.

History: Caddo Indian area. First Anglo-American settlers arrived about 1815. County created 1840 from Red River County; organized 1841; named for second president of Republic, Mirabeau B. Lamar.

Ethnicity, 1990: White, 36,814 (83.8%); Black, 6,397 (14.6%); American Indian, 406 (0.9%); Asian, 153 (0.3%); Other, 179 (0.4%). Hispanic, 475 (1.1%).

Vital Statistics, 1997: Births, 613; deaths, 572; marriages, 521; divorces, 367.

Recreation: Lake activities; Gambill goose refuge; hunting, fishing; state park; Sam Bell Maxey Home; State Sen. A.M. Aikin Archives; other museums; fiddlers contest.

Minerals: Negligible.

Agriculture: Beef, hay, soybeans, dairy, wheat, corn, sorghum, cotton, peanuts, turfgrass. Market value $35.4 million. Firewood marketed.

PARIS (26,241) county seat; varied manufacturing; food processing; government/services; hospitals; junior college; Tour de Paris bicycle rally in July.

Other towns include: **Arthur City** (200), **Blossom** (1,687), **Brookston** (70), **Chicota** (125), **Cunningham** (110), **Deport** (852, partly in Red River County), **Pattonville** (180), **Petty** (100), **Powderly** (185), **Reno** (2,491), **Roxton** (704), **Sumner** (80), **Sun Valley** (84), **Toco** (133).

Population........................... 45,766	
Change fm '90 .... 4.1	Clv. Labor........................... 20,745
Area (sq. mi.)........................ 932.4	Unemployed............................. 7.1
Land Area (sq. mi.)............... 917.1	Annual Wages........ $474,828,859
Altitude (ft.)...................350-650	Av. Weekly Wage............ $471.08
Rainfall (in.) 46.1	Fed. Wages................ $5,572,078
Jan. mean min. 30	Ag. Net Cash Return ... $2,739,000
July mean max. 94	Prop. Value $1,995,693,290
Growing season (days)............ 235	Retail Sales $504,229,785

Lamb County

Physical Features: Rich, red, brown soils on West Texas High Plains; some hills; drains to upper Brazos River tributaries; numerous playas.

Economy: Agribusiness; distribution center; denim textiles.

History: Apaches, displaced by Comanches around 1700. U.S. Army pushed Comanches into Indian Territory in 1875. Ranching began in 1880s; farming after 1900. County created 1876 from Bexar District; organized 1908; named for Lt. G.A. Lamb, who died in battle of San Jacinto.

Ethnicity, 1990: White, 13,036 (86.5%); Black, 822 (5.5%); American Indian, 88 (0.6%); Asian, 25 (0.2%); Other, 1,101 (7.3%). Hispanic, 5,509 (36.6%).

Vital Statistics, 1997: Births, 244; deaths, 165; marriages, 109; divorces, 54.

Recreation: Pioneer celebration in August.

Minerals: Oil, stone, gas.

Agriculture: Fed cattle; cotton, corn, wheat, grain sorghum, vegetables, soybeans, hay; sheep. 385,000 acres irrigated. Market value $253.5 million.

LITTLEFIELD (6,381) county seat; tourism; agribusiness; varied manufacturing; hospital; Denim Festival on Labor Day.

Olton (2,118) agribusiness, commercial center in northwest part of county; Sandhills Celebration in summer.

Other towns include: **Amherst** (747); **Earth** (1,382) farming center, manufacturing, feed lot, supplies; **Fieldton** (126); **Spade** (174); **Springlake** (145); **Sudan** (972) farming center, Pioneer Day in fall.

Population 15,207	
Change fm '90 .... 0.9	Clv. Labor 6,535
Area (sq. mi.)..................... 1,017.7	Unemployed 6.8
Land Area (sq. mi.)............ 1,016.3	Annual Wages $96,639,750
Altitude (ft.)...............3,400-3,849	Av. Weekly Wage $415.28
Rainfall (in.) 18.7	Fed. Wages................ $1,563,770
Jan. mean min. 22	Ag. Net Cash Return $43,439,000
July mean max. 91	Prop. Value............. $1,080,633,729
Growing season (days) 194	Retail Sales $63,095,040

Lampasas County

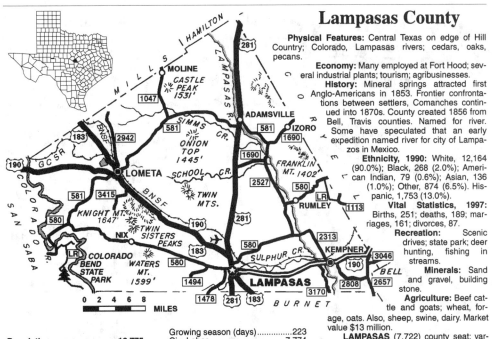

Physical Features: Central Texas on edge of Hill Country; Colorado, Lampasas rivers; cedars, oaks, pecans.

Economy: Many employed at Fort Hood; several industrial plants; tourism; agribusinesses.

History: Mineral springs attracted first Anglo-Americans in 1853. Frontier confrontations between settlers, Comanches continued into 1870s. County created 1856 from Bell, Travis counties. Named for river. Some have speculated that an early expedition named river for city of Lampazos in Mexico.

Ethnicity, 1990: White, 12,164 (90.0%); Black, 268 (2.0%); American Indian, 79 (0.6%); Asian, 136 (1.0%); Other, 874 (6.5%). Hispanic, 1,753 (13.0%).

Vital Statistics, 1997: Births, 251; deaths, 189; marriages, 161; divorces, 87.

Recreation: Scenic drives; state park; deer hunting, fishing in streams.

Minerals: Sand and gravel, building stone.

Agriculture: Beef cattle and goats; wheat, forage, oats. Also, sheep, swine, dairy. Market value $13 million.

Population 16,775	Growing season (days)..............223
Change fm '90 ....24.1	Civ. Labor 7,774
Area (sq. mi.)...........................713.9	Unemployed................................4.4
Land Area (sq. mi.)..................712.1	Annual Wages $68,002,055
Altitude (ft.)........................800-1,647	Av. Weekly Wage $356.61
Rainfall (in.) 29.6	Fed. Wages $1,599,385
Jan. mean min..............................30	Ag. Net Cash Return........ -$436,000
July mean max. 95	Prop. Value $747,552,657
	Retail Sales..................$86,598,205

LAMPASAS (7,722) county seat; varied manufacturing; government/services; ranching, hunting center; historic downtown; hospital; Spring Ho in July.

Other towns include: **Adamsville** (41); **Izoro** (17); **Kempner** (400); **Lometa** (750) market and shipping point; Diamondback Jubilee in March.

La Salle County

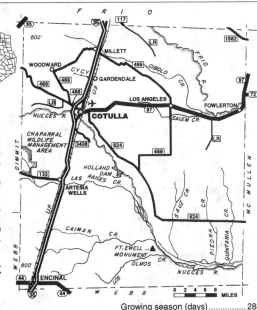

Physical Features: Southwestern county on brushy plain, broken by Nueces, Frio rivers and their tributaries; chocolate, dark gray, sandy loam soils.

Economy: Agribusiness, hunting leases; tourism; government services.

History: Coahuiltecans, squeezed out by migrating Apaches. U.S. military outpost in 1850s; settlers of Mexican descent established nearby village. Anglo-American ranching developed in 1870s. County created from Bexar County 1858; organized 1880; named for Robert Cavelier Sieur de la Salle, French explorer who died in Texas.

Ethnicity, 1990: White, 3,567 (67.9%); Black, 53 (1.0%); American Indian, 9 (0.2%); Asian, 10 (0.2%); Other, 1,615 (30.7%). Hispanic, 4,068 (77.4%).

Vital Statistics, 1997: Births, 92; deaths, 48; marriages, 33; divorces, 3.

Recreation: Nature trails; Cotulla school where Lyndon B. Johnson taught; wildlife management area; deer, bird, javelina hunting; wild hog cookoff in March; fishing.

Minerals: Oil, gas.

Agriculture: Beef cattle and peanuts; also, watermelons, grain sorghum, corn, meat goats. Market value $18.7 million.

COTULLA (4,411) county seat; livestock, state prison; hunting center; Brush Country museum; Cinco de Mayo celebration.

Other towns include: **Artesia Wells** (35), **Encinal** (655), **Fowlerton** (50).

For explanation of sources, abbreviations and symbols, see p. 130.

Population 6,120	Growing season (days) 288
Change fm '90 ....16.5	Civ. Labor 2,997
Area (sq. mi.) 1,494.2	Unemployed................................. 8.7
Land Area (sq. mi.) 1,489.0	Annual Wages $22,826,671
Altitude (ft.).........................250-600	Av. Weekly Wage $351.97
Rainfall (in.)...............................22.5	Fed. Wages $2,718,837
Jan. mean min. 38	Ag. Net Cash Return............-$5,000
July mean max.............................99	Prop. Value $388,151,947
	Retail Sales..................$24,586,522

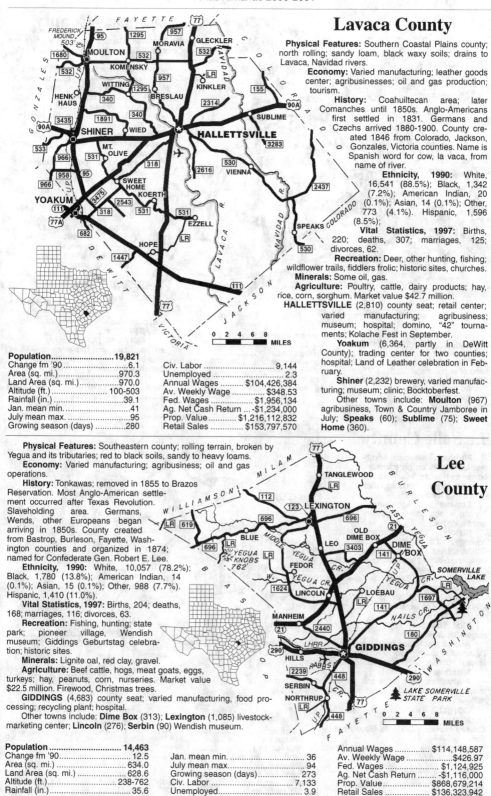

Lavaca County

Physical Features: Southern Coastal Plains county; north rolling; sandy loam, black waxy soils; drains to Lavaca, Navidad rivers.

Economy: Varied manufacturing; leather goods center; agribusinesses; oil and gas production; tourism.

History: Coahuiltecan area; later Comanches until 1850s. Anglo-Americans first settled in 1831. Germans and Czechs arrived 1880-1900. County created 1846 from Colorado, Jackson, Gonzales, Victoria counties. Name is Spanish word for cow, la vaca, from name of river.

Ethnicity, 1990: White, 16,541 (88.5%); Black, 1,342 (7.2%); American Indian, 20 (0.1%); Asian, 14 (0.1%); Other, 773 (4.1%). Hispanic, 1,596 (8.5%).

Vital Statistics, 1997: Births, 220; deaths, 307; marriages, 125; divorces, 62.

Recreation: Deer, other hunting, fishing; wildflower trails, fiddlers frolic; historic sites, churches.

Minerals: Some oil, gas.

Agriculture: Poultry, cattle, dairy products; hay, rice, corn, sorghum. Market value $42.7 million.

HALLETTSVILLE (2,810) county seat; retail center; varied manufacturing; agribusiness; museum; hospital; domino, "42" tournaments; Kolache Fest in September.

Yoakum (6,364, partly in DeWitt County); trading center for two counties; hospital; Land of Leather celebration in February.

Shiner (2,232) brewery, varied manufacturing; museum; clinic; Bocktoberfest.

Other towns include: **Moulton** (967) agribusiness, Town & Country Jamboree in July; **Speaks** (60); **Sublime** (75); **Sweet Home** (360).

Population.........................19,821	Civ. Labor 9,144	
Change fm '90 ....6.1	Unemployed 2.3	
Area (sq. mi.)..........................970.3	Annual Wages $104,426,384	
Land Area (sq. mi.)................970.0	Av. Weekly Wage $348.53	
Altitude (ft.) 100-503	Fed. Wages $1,956,134	
Rainfall (in.) 39.1	Ag. Net Cash Return ... -$1,234,000	
Jan. mean min. 41	Prop. Value $1,216,112,832	
July mean max. 95	Retail Sales $153,797,570	
Growing season (days) 280		

Lee County

Physical Features: Southeastern county; rolling terrain, broken by Yegua and its tributaries; red to black soils, sandy to heavy loams.

Economy: Varied manufacturing; agribusiness; oil and gas operations.

History: Tonkawas; removed in 1855 to Brazos Reservation. Most Anglo-American settlement occurred after Texas Revolution. Slaveholding area. Germans, Wends, other Europeans began arriving in 1850s. County created from Bastrop, Burleson, Fayette, Washington counties and organized in 1874; named for Confederate Gen. Robert E. Lee.

Ethnicity, 1990: White, 10,057 (78.2%); Black, 1,780 (13.8%); American Indian, 14 (0.1%); Asian, 15 (0.1%); Other, 988 (7.7%). Hispanic, 1,410 (11.0%).

Vital Statistics, 1997: Births, 204; deaths, 168; marriages, 116; divorces, 63.

Recreation: Fishing, hunting; state park; pioneer village, Wendish museum; Giddings Geburtstag celebration; historic sites.

Minerals: Lignite oal, red clay, gravel.

Agriculture: Beef cattle, hogs, meat goats, eggs, turkeys; hay, peanuts, corn, nurseries. Market value $22.5 million. Firewood, Christmas trees.

GIDDINGS (4,683) county seat; varied manufacturing, food processing; recycling plant; hospital.

Other towns include: **Dime Box** (313); **Lexington** (1,085) livestock-marketing center; **Lincoln** (276); **Serbin** (90) Wendish museum.

Population 14,463	Jan. mean min. 36	Annual Wages $114,148,587
Change fm '90................................ 12.5	July mean max................................. 94	Av. Weekly Wage $426.97
Area (sq. mi.) 634.0	Growing season (days)................. 273	Fed. Wages $1,124,925
Land Area (sq. mi.) 628.6	Civ. Labor 7,133	Ag. Net Cash Return .... -$1,116,000
Altitude (ft.)................................ 238-762	Unemployed.................................... 3.9	Prop. Value $868,679,214
Rainfall (in.)................................ 35.6		Retail Sales $136,323,942

Leon County

Physical Features: East central county; hilly, rolling, almost half covered by timber; drains to Navasota, Trinity rivers and tributaries; sandy, dark, alluvial soils.

Economy: Oil, gas production; agribusiness.

History: Bidais band, absorbed into Kickapoos and other groups. Permanent settlement by Anglo-Americans occurred after Texas Revolution; Germans in 1870s. County created 1846 from Robertson County; named for founder of Victoria, Martin de Leon.

Ethnicity, 1990: White, 10,730 (84.7%); Black, 1,615 (12.8%); American Indian, 39(0.3%); Asian, 8 (0.1%); Other, 273 (2.2%). Hispanic, 509 (4.0%).

Vital Statistics, 1997: Births, 178; deaths, 210; marriages, 101; divorces, 74.

Recreation: Hilltop Lakes resort area; sites of Camino Real, Fort Boggy; deer hunting.

Minerals: Oil, gas, iron ore, lignite.

Agriculture: A leading county in cow-calf production; hogs, poultry raised; hay, watermelons, vegetables, small grains; Christmas trees. Market value $27.1 million. Hardwoods, pine marketed value $10 million.

CENTERVILLE (947) county seat; farm center; hunting; tourism; oil, gas; timber.

Buffalo (2,098) farm center; clinic; library; stampede in September.

Other towns include: **Flynn** (81); **Hilltop Lakes** (300), resort, retirement center; **Jewett** (828) electricity-generating plant; civic center, fall frolic; **Leona** (235) candle factory; **Marquez** (293); **Normangee** (737) city park; **Oakwood** (644).

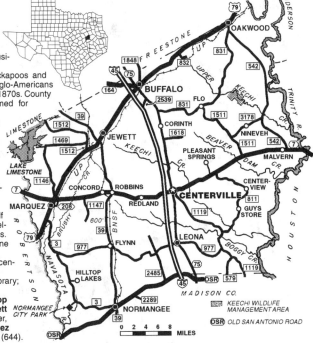

Population 14,174	July mean max................................ 95	Ag. Net Cash Return.......... -$1,073,000
Change fm '90 .... 11.9	Growing season (days)................. 270	Prop. Value $1,398,789,972
Area (sq. mi.) 1,080.4	Civ. Labor 5,857	Retail Sales...................... $81,716,063
Land Area (sq. mi.) 1,072.1	Unemployed.................................... 6.9	
Altitude (ft.) 150-600	Annual Wages $111,971,786	*For explanation of sources, abbreviations*
Rainfall (in.)...................................... 40.5	Av. Weekly Wage $558.76	*and symbols, see p. 130.*
Jan. mean min. 34	Fed. Wages $1,378,950	

The church of the Wendish community in Serbin in Lee County. The Dallas Morning News file photo.

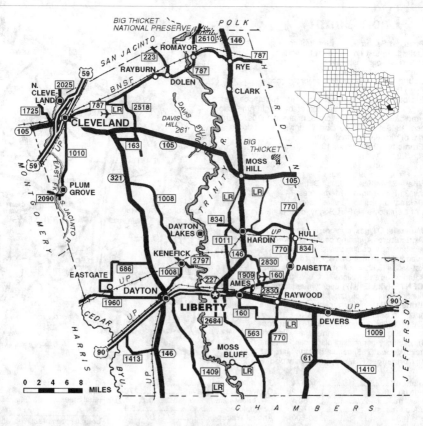

Liberty County

Physical Features: Coastal Plain county east of Houston; 60 percent in pine, hardwood timber; bisected by Trinity River; sandy, loam, black soils; Big Thicket.

Economy: Agribusiness; chemical plants; varied manufacturing; tourism; forest industries; many residents work in Houston; part of Houston metropolitan area.

History: Karankawa area until 1740s. Nuestra Señora de la Luz Mission established in 1746 and Atascosito settlement developed. Settlers from Louisiana began arriving in 1810s. County named for Spanish municipality, Libertad; created 1836, organized 1837.

Ethnicity, 1990: White, 44,014 (83.5%); Black, 6,911 (13.1%); American Indian, 181 (0.3%); Asian, 124 (0.2%); Other, 1,496 (2.8%). Hispanic, 2,880 (5.5%).

Vital Statistics, 1995: Births, 1,012; deaths, 614; marriages, 636; divorces, 327.

Recreation: Big Thicket; hunting, fishing; historic sites; Trinity Valley exposition; Liberty Opry.

Minerals: Oil, gas, sulphur, sand and gravel.

Agriculture: Rice is principal crop; soybeans (first in state in acreage); sorghum; cow-calf operations; nursery crops. Market value $23.7 million. Some lumbering.

LIBERTY (9,334) county seat; petroleum-related industry; agribusiness; library; museum; regional historical resource depository; Liberty Bell; hospital; state prisons.

Cleveland (8,407) forest products processed, shipped; tourism; library; museum; hospital.

Dayton (6,085) rice, oil center.

Other towns include: **Ames** (1,292); **Daisetta** (1,046); **Dayton Lakes** (239);

Devers (373); **Hardin** (616); **Hull** (1,800); **Kenefick** (910); **North Cleveland** (208); **Plum Grove** (600); **Raywood** (231); **Romayor** (96); **Rye** (76).

Population	**65,844**
Change fm '90	24.9
Area (sq. mi.)	1,176.3
Land Area (sq. mi.)	1,159.8
Altitude (ft.)	23-261
Rainfall (in.)	54.1
Jan. mean min.	39
July mean max.	93
Growing season (days)	261
Civ. Labor	28,788
Unemployed	6.5
Annual Wages	$358,893,776
Av. Weekly Wage	$447.91
Fed. Wages	$4,206,565
Ag. Net Cash Returns	$1,753,000
Prop. Value	$2,352,934,046
Retail Sales	$1,104,778,065

For explanation of sources, abbreviations and symbols, see p. 130.

Limestone County

Physical Features: East central county on divide between Brazos and Trinity rivers; borders Blacklands, level to rolling; drained by Navasota and tributaries.

Economy: Varied manufacturing; agribusiness; tourism; mineral operations.

History: Tawakoni (Tehuacana) and Waco area, later Comanche raiders. First Anglo-Americans arrived in 1833. Antebellum slaveholding area. County created from Robertson County and organized 1846; named for indigenous rock.

Ethnicity, 1990: White, 15,695 (74.9%); Black, 4,156 (19.8%); American Indian, 41(0.2%); Asian, 50 (0.2%); Other, 1,004 (4.8%). Hispanic, 1,459 (7.0%).

Vital Statistics, 1997: Births, 264; deaths, 317; marriages, 216; divorces, 128.

Recreation: Fishing, lake activities; Fort Parker; Confederate Reunion Grounds; historic sites; museum; hunting; Christmas at the Fort.

Minerals: Lignite, crushed rock, sand, oil, gas.

Agriculture: Cow-calf, stocker cattle operations; dairies, horses, goats, sheep, some exotic animals; crops include hay, corn, cotton, wheat, peaches. Market value $25.8 million.

GROESBECK (3,803) county seat, agribusiness, tourism, hunting, mining, prison, power generating, hospital.

MEXIA (6,935) agribusiness, grocery distribution, state school, hospital.

Other towns include: **Coolidge** (750), **Kosse** (558), **Prairie Hill** (150), **Tehuacana** (341), **Thornton** (609).

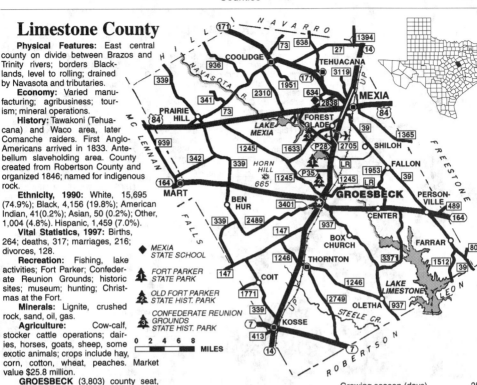

Population	21,527
Change fm '90	2.8
Area (sq. mi.)	933.1
Land Area (sq. mi.)	908.9
Altitude (ft.)	363-665
Rainfall (in.)	40.3
Jan. mean min.	33
July mean max.	95

Growing season (days)	255
Civ. Labor	9,147
Unemployed	5.2
Annual Wages	$151,866,881
Av. Weekly Wage	$403.44
Fed. Wages	$2,016,348
Ag. Net Cash Return	-$692,000
Prop. Value	$1,607,157,735
Retail Sales	$150,684,633

Lipscomb County

Physical Features: High Plain, broken in east; drains to tributaries of Canadian, Wolf Creek; sandy loam, black soils.

Economy: Agribusinesses; government/services; oil, gas operations.

History: Apaches, later Kiowas and Comanches who were driven into Indian Territory in 1875. Ranching began in late 1870s. County created 1876 from Bexar District; organized 1887; named for A.S. Lipscomb, Republic of Texas leader.

Ethnicity, 1990: White, 3,092 (98.4%); Black, 1 (0.0%); American Indian, 34 (1.1%); Asian, 13 (0.4%); Other, 3 (0.1%). Hispanic, 379 (12.1%).

Vital Statistics, 1997: Births, 40; deaths, 37; marriages, 45; divorces, 9.

Recreation: Will Rogers Day; Darrouzett festival; Wolf Creek museum.

Minerals: Oil, natural gas.

Agriculture: Stocker, cow-calf, registered cattle; wheat, sorghum, corn, soybean; 19,000 acres irrigated. Market value $45.3 million.

LIPSCOMB (50), county seat; livestock center.

Booker (1,255, part in Ochiltree County) trade center.

Other towns include: **Darrouzett** (365), **Follett** (458); **Higgins** (479).

Population	3,263
Change fm '90	3.8
Area (sq. mi.)	932.2
Land Area (sq. mi.)	932.2
Altitude (ft.)	2,300-2,837
Rainfall (in.)	22.8

Jan. mean min.	20
July mean max.	93
Growing season (days)	202
Civ. Labor	1,617
Unemployed	2.5

Annual Wages	$23,258,180
Av. Weekly Wage	$456.63
Fed. Wages	$745,013
Ag. Net Cash Value	$6,550,000
Prop. Value	$415,527,700
Retail Sales	$8,500,658

Live Oak County

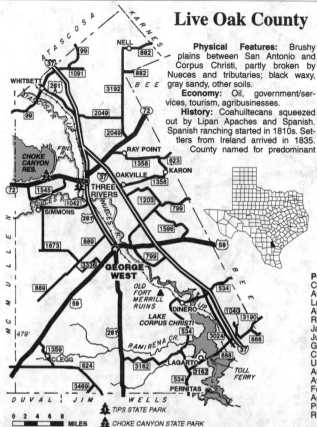

Physical Features: Brushy plains between San Antonio and Corpus Christi, partly broken by Nueces and tributaries; black waxy, gray sandy, other soils.

Economy: Oil, government/services, tourism, agribusinesses.

History: Coahuiltecans squeezed out by Lipan Apaches and Spanish. Spanish ranching started in 1810s. Settlers from Ireland arrived in 1835. County named for predominant tree; created, organized 1856 from Nueces, San Patricio counties.

Ethnicity, 1990: White, 8,316 (87.0%); Black, 10 (0.1%); American Indian, 36 (0.4%); Asian, 31 (0.3%); Other, 1,163 (12.2%).

Hispanic, 3,324 (34.8%).

Vital Statistics, 1997: Births, 104; deaths, 120; marriages, 71; divorces, 65.

Recreation: Lakes; water activities; state parks; hunting; historic sites.

Minerals: Oil, gas, sand, gravel.

Agriculture: Cow-calf operations; hogs; corn, grain sorghum; cotton; some irrigation for hay, coastal Bermuda pastures. Market value $11.8 million.

GEORGE WEST (2,718) county seat, agribusiness, petroleum refineries, Storyfest in November.

Three Rivers (1,988) agribusinesses, refineries, federal prison.

Other towns include: **Dinero** (344), **Oakville** (260), **Pernitas Point** (180), **Whitsett** (200).

Population	10,159
Change fm '90	6.3
Area (sq. mi.)	1,078.8
Land Area (sq. mi.)	1,036.4
Altitude (ft.)	94-479
Rainfall (in.)	27.6
Jan. mean min.	41
July mean max.	95
Growing season (days)	289
Civ. Labor	4,487
Unemployed	4.4
Annual Wages	$56,620,070
Av. Weekly Wage	$436.97
Fed. Wages	$15,387,063
Ag. Net Cash Return	-$2,934,000
Prop. Value	$977,769,340
Retail Sales	$82,548,470

Hikers make their way up Enchanted Rock. The Dallas Morning News file photo.

Llano County

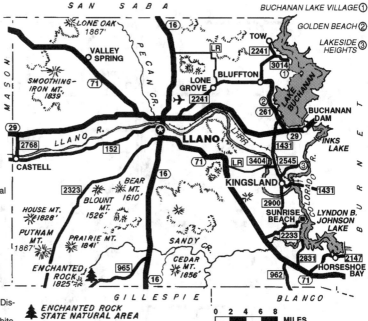

Physical Features: Central county drains to Colorado, Llano rivers; rolling to hilly; Highland lakes.

Economy: Tourism, retirement; ranch trading center; vineyards; granite mined.

History: Tonkawas, later Comanches. Anglo-American and German settlers arrived in 1840s. County name is Spanish for plains; created, organized 1856 from Bexar District, Gillespie County.

Ethnicity, 1990: White, 11,386 (97.9%); Black, 22 (0.2%); American Indian, 39 (0.3%); Asian, 20 (0.2%); Other, 164 (1.4%). Hispanic, 453 (3.9%);

Vital Statistics, 1997: Births, 130; deaths, 246; marriages, 88; divorces, 70.

Recreation: Leading deer-hunting county; fishing; lake activities; major tourist area; Enchanted Rock; bluebonnet festival; hang gliding.

Minerals: Granite, vermiculite, llanite.

Agriculture: Beef cattle, turkeys, hogs, sheep, goats; hay; peanuts and oats. Market value $9.8 million.

LLANO (3,302) county seat; varied manufacturing; hunting center; government/services; hospital; livestock trading; historic district; museum.

Kingsland (3,099) tourism, retirement community, fishing and water sports; metal fabrication; wood work; library.

Other towns include: **Bluffton** (75), **Buchanan Dam** (1,205), **Castell** (72), **Horseshoe Bay** (1,759, partly in Burnet County), **Sunrise Beach** (567), **Tow** (305), **Valley Spring** (50).

Population	13,260
Change fm '90	14.0
Area (sq. mi.)	966.1
Land Area (sq. mi.)	934.9
Altitude (ft.)	825-1,867
Rainfall (in.)	26.4
Jan. mean min.	31
July mean max.	96
Growing season (days)	229
Civ. Labor	5,282
Unemployed	3.4
Annual Wages	$73,832,560
Av. Weekly Wage	$383.91
Fed. Wages	$1,206,189
Ag. Net Cash Return	-$755,000
Prop. Value	$1,556,193,475
Retail Sales	$86,870,071

Loving County

Physical Features: Western county of dry, rolling prairies; slopes to Pecos River; Red Bluff Reservoir; sandy, loam, clay soils.

Economy: Petroleum operations; cattle.

History: Land developers began operations in late 19th century. Oil discovered in 1925. County created 1887 from Tom Green; organized 1931, last county organized. Named for Oliver Loving, trail driver. Loving is Texas' least populous county.

Ethnicity, 1990: White, 93 (86.9%); Black, 0 (0.0%); American Indian, 0 (0.0%); Asian, 0 (0.0%); Other, 14 (13.1%). Hispanic, 14 (13.1%).

Vital Statistics, 1997: Births, 0; deaths, 0; marriages, 2; divorces, 0.

Recreation: NA.

Minerals: Oil, gas.

Agriculture: Some cattle. Market value $880,000.

MENTONE (95) county seat, oilfield supply center; only town.

For explanation of sources, abbreviations and symbols, see p. 130.

Population	95
Change fm '90	-11.2
Area (sq. mi.)	676.8
Land Area (sq. mi.)	673.1
Altitude (ft.)	2,685-3,311
Rainfall (in.)	9.1
Jan. mean min.	28
July mean max.	96
Growing season (days)	222
Civ. Labor	85
Unemployed	10.6
Annual Wages	$1,377,260
Av. Weekly Wage	$771.90
Fed. Wages	$13,567
Ag. Net Cash Return	NA
Prop. Value	$128,559,403
Retail Sales	$41,909

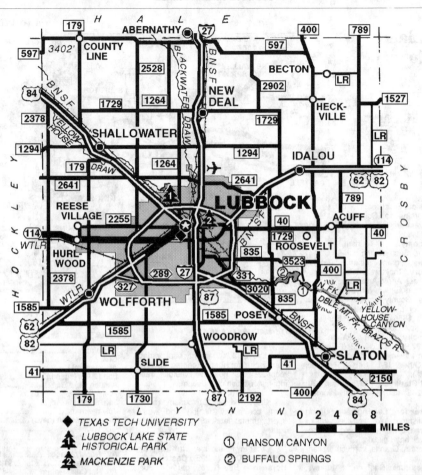

◆ TEXAS TECH UNIVERSITY
🌲 LUBBOCK LAKE STATE
    HISTORICAL PARK
🌲 MACKENZIE PARK

① RANSOM CANYON
② BUFFALO SPRINGS

0 2 4 6 8 MILES

Lubbock County

Physical Features: High Plains of West Texas, broken by 1,500 playas, upper Brazos River tributaries; rich soils with underground water.

Economy: Among world's largest cottonseed processing centers; a leading agribusiness center; cattle feedlots; manufacturing; higher education center; medical center; government/services.

History: Evidence of human habitation for 12,000 years. In historic period, Apache Indians, followed by Comanche hunters. Sheep raisers from Midwest arrived in late 1870s. Cotton farms brought in Mexican laborers in 1940s-60s. County named for Col. Tom S. Lubbock, an organizer of Confederate Terry's Rangers; county created 1876 from Bexar District; organized 1891.

Ethnicity, 1990: White, 176,037 (79.1%); Black, 17,154 (7.7%); American Indian, 686 (0.3%); Asian, 2,722 (1.2%); Other, 26,037 (11.7%). Hispanic, 51,011 (22.9%).

Vital Statistics, 1997: Births, 3,653; deaths, 1,835; marriages, 2,130; divorces, 1,231.

Recreation: Lubbock Lake State Historical Park and archaeological site; Texas Tech events; civic center, Buddy Holly statue and Walk of Fame, planetarium; Ranching Heritage Center; Pan-handle-South Plains Fair; Buffalo Springs Lake.

Minerals: Oil, gas, stone, sand and gravel.

Agriculture: Cotton (first in state in acreage). Fed beef, cow-calf operations; poultry, eggs; hogs. Other crops, nursery, grain sorghum, wheat, sunflowers, soybeans, hay, vegetables; more than 230,000 acres irrigated, mostly cotton. Market value $133.7 million.

Education: Texas Tech University with law and medical schools; Lubbock Christian University; South Plains College branch; Wayland Baptist University off-campus center.

LUBBOCK (192,732) county seat; center for large agricultural area; manufacturing includes electronics, earth-moving equipment, food containers, fire-protection equipment, clothing, other products; distribution center for South Plains; feedlots; psychiatric hospital; museum; hospitals, government/services, state school for retarded; wind power center.

Other towns include: **Buffalo Springs** (446); **Idalou** (2,056); **New Deal** (721); **Ransom Canyon** (904); **Shallowater** (2,045); **Slaton** (6,100) agribusiness, government/services, varied manufacturing, sausagefest in October; **Wolfforth** (2,492).

Population	231,841
Change fm '90	4.1
Area (sq. mi.)	900.6
Land Area (sq. mi.)	899.6
Altitude (ft.)	2,900-3,402
Rainfall (in.)	18.7
Jan. mean min.	25
July mean max.	92
Growing season (days)	208
Civ. Labor	123,409
Unemployed	3.4
Annual Wages	$2,656,258,126
Av. Weekly Wage	$461.49
Fed. Wages	$54,205,496
Ag. Net Cash Return	$19,104,000
Prop. Value	$7,370,275,279
Retail Sales	$3,047,312,211

For explanation of sources, abbreviations and symbols, see p. 130.

Lynn County

Physical Features: South High Plains, broken by Caprock Escarpment, playas, draws; sandy loam, black, gray soils.

Economy: Agribusiness.

History: Apaches, ousted by Comanches who were removed to Indian Territory in 1875. Ranching began in 1880s. Farming developed after 1900. County created 1876 from Bexar District; organized 1903; named for Alamo victim W. Lynn.

Ethnicity,1990: White, 5,214 (77.2%); Black, 223 (3.3%); American Indian, 22 (0.3%); Asian, 11 (0.2%); Other, 1,288 (19.1%). Hispanic, 2,819 (41.7%).

Vital Statistics, 1997: Births, 88; deaths, 58; marriages, 52; divorces, 20.

Recreation: Pioneer museum in Tahoka; Dan Blocker museum in O'Donnell.

Minerals: Oil, natural gas, stone.

Agriculture: Cotton produces largest income; peanuts, grain sorghums, cattle raised; 80,000 acres of cotton irrigated. Market value $71.4 million.

TAHOKA (2,687) county seat; agribusiness center; cotton compress; some manufacturing; hospital; Harvest Festival.

O'Donnell (1,155, partly in Dawson County), commercial center.

Other towns include: **New Home** (206); **Wilson** (565).

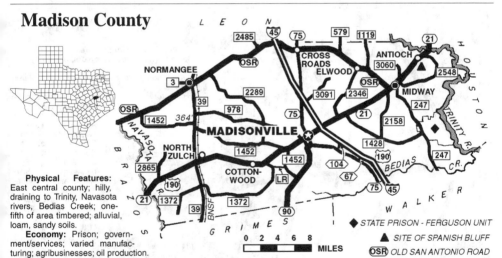

Population.................................**6,587**	
Change fm '90.............................-2.5	
Area (sq. mi.)..............................893.4	
Land Area (sq. mi.).....................891.9	
Altitude (ft.).....................2,800-3,300	

Rainfall (in.)..................................19.7	
Jan. mean min.................................24	
July mean max................................92	
Growing season (days)................217	
Civ. Labor..................................3,068	
Unemployed....................................4.8	

Annual Wages.................$33,672,830	
Av. Weekly Wage.................$385.41	
Fed. Wages.......................$875,317	
Ag. Net Cash Return........$25,578,000	
Prop. Value $360,645,160	
Retail Sales.................$34,894,547	

Madison County

Physical Features: East central county; hilly, draining to Trinity, Navasota rivers, Bedias Creek; one-fifth of area timbered; alluvial, loam, sandy soils.

Economy: Prison; government/services; varied manufacturing; agribusinesses; oil production.

History: Caddo and Bidai Indian area; Kickapoos migrated from east. Spanish settlements established in 1774 and 1805. Anglo-Americans arrived in 1829. Census of 1860 showed 30 percent of population was black. County named for U.S. President James Madison; created from Grimes, Leon, Walker counties 1853; organized 1854.

Ethnicity, 1990: White, 7,984 (73.0%); Black, 2,575 (23.6%); American Indian, 67 (0.6%); Asian, 13 (0.1%); Other, 292 (2.7%). Hispanic, 1,178 (10.8%).

Vital Statistics, 1997: Births, 142; deaths, 140; marriages, 99; divorces, 34.

Recreation: Fishing, hunting; Spanish Bluff where survivors of Battle of Medina were executed; other historic sites.

Minerals: sand, oil.

Agriculture: Nursery crops, cattle, horses, poultry raised; forage for livestock. Market value $42.7 million.

MADISONVILLE (4,243) county seat; farm-trade center; varied manufacturing; hospital, library; Spring Fling in April.

Other towns, **Midway** (333); **Normangee** (737, mostly in Leon County); **North Zulch** (150).

◆ STATE PRISON - FERGUSON UNIT
▲ SITE OF SPANISH BLUFF
(OSR) OLD SAN ANTONIO ROAD

Population **12,324**	
Change fm '90 ....12.7	
Area (sq. mi.)...............................472.3	
Land Area (sq. mi.)....................469.7	
Altitude (ft.).........................150-364	
Rainfall (in.) 41.6	
Jan. mean min................................38	
July mean max. 96	
Growing season (days)..................272	
Civ. Labor...................................4,200	
Unemployed 3.5	
Annual Wages.................$77,376,028	
Av. Weekly Wage $397.24	
Fed. Wages $787,346	
Ag. Net Cash Return $3,608,000	
Prop. Value.................$597,030,776	
Retail Sales $67,098,607	

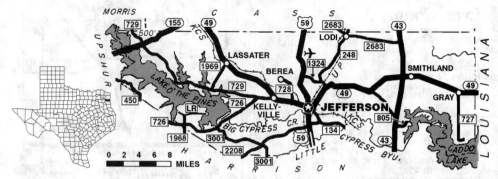

Physical Features: Northeastern county; hilly, three-quarters forested with pines, hardwoods; drains to Caddo Lake, Lake O' the Pines, Cypress Bayou.

Economy: Tourism; timber; food processing.

History: Caddoes forced out in 1790s. Kickapoo in area when settlers arrived from Deep South around 1840. Antebellum slaveholding area. County created 1860 from Cass County; named for Gen. Francis Marion of American Revolution.

Ethnicity, 1990: White, 6,792 (68.0%); Black, 3,100 (31.0%); American Indian, 44 (0.4%); Asian, 7 (0.1%); Other, 41 (0.4%). Hispanic, 147 (1.5%).

Vital Statistics, 1997: Births, 136; deaths, 169; marriages, 81; divorces, 72.

Recreation: Lake activities; hunting; Excelsior Hotel; 84 medallions on historic sites including Jay Gould railroad car; museum; Mardi Gras; historical pilgrimage in May, founder's day in October.

Minerals: Iron ore.

Agriculture: Beef cattle, hay, goats. Market value $2 million. Forestry is most important industry.

JEFFERSON (2,578) county seat; tourism; board plant; agriculture center; timber; museums, library; historical sites.

Other towns include: **Lodi** (164).

Marion County

Population	**10,697**
Change fm '90	7.1
Area (sq. mi.)	420.3
Land Area (sq. mi.)	381.2
Altitude (ft.)	168-500
Rainfall (in.)	44.7
Jan. mean min.	32
July mean max.	94
Growing season (days)	236
Civ. Labor	3,792
Unemployed	10.2
Annual Wages	$36,382,473
Av. Weekly Wage	$367.72
Fed. Wages	$1,181,392
Ag. Net Cash Return	$113,000
Prop. Value	$479,261,039
Retail Sales	$48,334,985

Martin County

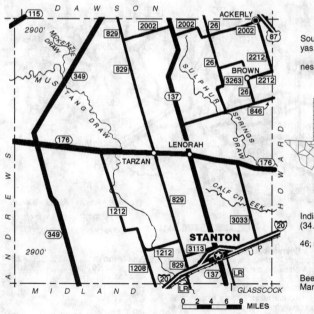

Physical Features: Western county on South Plains; sandy, loam soils, broken by playas, creeks.

Economy: Petroleum production, agribusiness.

History: Apaches, ousted by Comanches who in turn were forced out by U.S. Army 1875. Farming began in 1881. County created from Bexar District 1876; organized 1884; named for Wylie Martin, senator of Republic of Texas.

Ethnicity, 1990: White, 3,159 (63.7%); Black, 89 (1.8%); American Indian, 11 (0.2%); Asian, 8 (0.2%); Other, 1,689 (34.1%). Hispanic, 1,960 (39.5%).

Vital Statistics, 1997: Births, 80; deaths, 46; marriages, 41; divorces, 15.

Recreation: Museum, settlers reunion.

Minerals: Oil, gas.

Agriculture: Cotton, milo, sorghum, oats; Beef cattle, meat goats, horses, sheep raised. Market value $39.9 million.

STANTON (2,605) county seat; farm, ranch, oil, center; varied manufacturing; electric co-op; hospital, restored convent, other historic buildings; old sorehead days three times a year.

Other towns include: **Ackerly** (261, partly in Dawson County); **Lenorah** (70); **Tarzan** (80).

Population	**5,156**
Change fm '90	4.0
Area (sq. mi.)	915.6
Land Area (sq. mi.)	914.9
Altitude (ft.)	2,500-2,900
Rainfall (in.)	17.2
Jan. mean min.	30
July mean max.	94
Growing season (days)	215
Civ. Labor	1,693
Unemployed	5.4
Annual Wages	$28,364,506
Av. Weekly Wage	$462.65
Fed. Wages	$683,596
Ag. Net Cash Return	$14,659,000
Prop. Value	$569,297,752
Retail Sales	$33,367,595

For explanation of sources, abbreviations and symbols, see p. 130.

Mason County

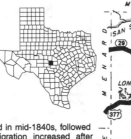

Physical Features: Southwestern county; hilly, draining to Llano, San Saba rivers and tributaries; limestone, red soils; varied timber.

Economy: Ranching; hunting; tourism; soft-drink bottling.

History: Lipan Apaches, driven south by Comanches around 1790. German settlers arrived in mid-1840s, followed by Anglo-Americans. Mexican immigration increased after 1930. County created from Bexar, Gillespie counties 1858; named for Mexican War victim U.S. Army Lt. G.T. Mason.

Ethnicity, 1990: White, 3,084 (90.1%); Black, 6 (0.2%); American Indian, 13 (0.4%); Asian, 4 (0.1%); Other, 316 (9.2%). Hispanic, 671 (19.6%).

Vital Statistics, 1997: Births, 35; deaths, 57; marriages, 35; divorces, 19.

Recreation: Outstanding deer, turkey hunting, river fishing; camping; historic homes of stone; Fort Mason, where Robert E. Lee served; wildflower drives in spring.

Minerals: Topaz, granite.

Agriculture: Cattle, peanuts, hay, sheep, goats. Market value $19.6 million. Hunting leases important.

MASON (2,167) county seat; ranching center; camping; tourism; museum; historical district, homes, rock fences built by German settlers; wild game dinner in November.

Other towns include: **Art** (18), **Fredonia** (50), **Pontotoc** (125).

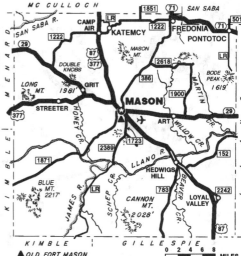

▲ OLD FORT MASON

Population		3,679
Change fm '90		7.5
Area (sq. mi.)		932.2
Land Area (sq. mi.)		932.1
Altitude (ft.)		1,200-2,217
Rainfall (in.)		26.8
Jan. mean min.		31
July mean max.		95
Growing season (days)		217
Civ. Labor		1,460
Unemployed		3.0
Annual Wages		$14,081,486
Av. Weekly Wage		$318.91
Fed. Wages		$436,033
Ag. Net Cash Return		$1,478,000
Prop. Value		$504,162,008
Retail Sales		$17,105,973

Matagorda County

▲ MATAGORDA PENINSULA STATE PARK

0 2 4 6 8 MILES

Physical Features: Gulf Coast county; flat, broken by bays; contains part of Matagorda Island; many different soils; drains to Colorado River, creeks, coast.

Economy: Petroleum operations, petrochemicals, agribusiness; varied manufacturing; tourism significant.

History: Karankawa Indian area, Tonkawas later. Anglo-Americans arrived in 1822. Mexican immigration increased after 1920. An original county, created 1836 from Spanish municipality, named for canebrake; organized 1837; settled by Austin colonists.

Ethnicity, 1990: White, 26,622 (72.1%); Black, 5,106 (13.8%); American Indian, 88 (0.2%); Asian, 842 (2.3%); Other, 4,270 (11.6%). Hispanic, 9,088 (24.6%).

Vital Statistics, 1997: Births, 620; deaths, 347; marriages, 340; divorces, 193.

Recreation: Fishing, water sports, hunting; state park; historic sites, museums; rice festival.

Minerals: Gas, oil, salt.

Agriculture: Major rice-growing area, cotton, turfgrass, grains, soybeans; cow-calf operations, purebred cattle; 35,000 acres irrigated for rice. Market value $58 million.

BAY CITY (18,624) county seat; petrochemicals; oil, gas processing; nuclear power plant; commercial fishing.

Palacios (4,472) tourism; seafood industry; hospital; Marine Education Center; Bay Festival Labor Day; public fishing piers.

Other towns include: **Blessing** (571), historic sites; **Cedar Lane** (55); **Collegeport** (85); **Elmaton** (140); **Markham** (1,412); **Matagorda** (710); **Midfield** (70); **Pledger** (159); **Sargent** (300), retirement community, fishing, birding, commercial fishing; **Van Vleck** (1,817); **Wadsworth** (160).

Population		38,378
Change fm '90		3.9
Area (sq. mi.)		1,612.2
Land Area (sq. mi.)		1,114.5
Altitude (ft.)		sea level-70
Rainfall (in.)		44.7
Jan. mean min.		45
July mean max.		91
Growing season (days)		296
Civ. Labor		16,997
Unemployed		11.7
Annual Wages		$369,296,897
Av. Weekly Wage		$577.42
Fed. Wages		$3,338,175
Ag. Net Cash Return		NA
Prop. Value		$4,132,209,461
Retail Sales		$242,852,613

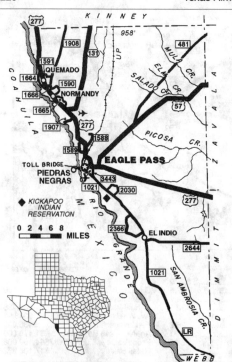

Maverick County

Physical Features: Southwestern county on Rio Grande; broken, rolling surface, with dense brush; clay, sandy, alluvial soils.

Economy: Oil; government/services; agribusinesses; feedlots; tourism.

History: Coahuiltecan Indian area; later Comanches in area. Spanish ranching began in 1760s. First Anglo-Americans arrived in 1834. County named for Sam A. Maverick, whose name is now a synonym for unbranded cattle; created 1856 from Kinney County; organized 1871.

Ethnicity, 1990: White, 23,748 (65.3%); Black, 32 (0.1%); American Indian, 714 (2.0%); Asian, 71 (0.2%); Other, 11,813 (32.5%). Hispanic, 34,024 (93.5%).

Vital Statistics, 1997: Births, 1,035; deaths, 250; marriages, 605; divorces, 103.

Recreation: Tourist gateway to Mexico; white-tailed deer, bird hunting; fishing; historic sites.

Minerals: Oil, gas, sand, gravel.

Agriculture: Cattle feedlots; pecans, vegetables, sorghum, wheat; goats, sheep. Some irrigation from Rio Grande. Market value $19.6 million.

EAGLE PASS (26,767) county seat; varied manufacturing; tourism center; rail, highway entry point to Piedras Negras, Mex.; hospital.

Other towns include: **El Indio** (148); **Quemado** (426).

Population	45,763
Change fm '90	25.8
Area (sq. mi.)	1,291.7
Land Area (sq. mi.)	1,280.2
Altitude (ft.)	600-958
Rainfall (in.)	21.5
Jan. mean min.	38
July mean max.	98
Growing season (days)	285
Civ. Labor	17,942
Unemployed	26.5
Annual Wages	$181,879,607
Av. Weekly Wage	$351.72
Fed. Wages	$20,452,605
Ag. Net Cash Return	$2,498,000
Prop. Value	$943,258,934
Retail Sales	$313,082,463

McCulloch County

Physical Features: Central county; hilly and rolling; drains to Colorado, Brady Creek and Lake, San Saba River; black loams to sandy soils.

Economy: Agribusiness; manufacturing; tourism; hunting leases.

History: Apache area. First Anglo-American settlers arrived in late 1850s, but Comanche raids delayed further settlement until 1870s. County created from Bexar District 1856; organized 1876; named for San Jacinto veteran Gen. Ben McCulloch.

Ethnicity, 1990: White, 7,855 (89.5%); Black, 166 (1.9%); American Indian, 14 (0.2%); Asian, 8 (0.1%); Other, 735 (8.4%). Hispanic, 2,317 (26.4%).

Vital Statistics, 1997: Births, 119; deaths, 127; marriages, 86; divorces, 47.

Recreation: Hunting; lake activities; museum, restored Santa Fe depot, goat cookoff, muzzle-loading rifle association state championship; rodeos; golf, tennis tournaments.

Minerals: Sand, gravel, gas and oil.

Agriculture: Beef cattle provide most income; wheat, sheep, goats, hay, cotton, sorghum, hogs, dairy cattle; some irrigation for peanuts. Market value $18 million.

BRADY (5,962) county seat; ranching, tourism; mohair, wool processed; oil-field equipment, other manufacturing; hospital; Central Texas College extension; July Jubilee.

Other towns: **Doole** (74), **Lohn** (149), **Melvin** (169), **Pear Valley** (37), **Rochelle** (163) and **Voca** (56).

For explanation of sources, abbreviations and symbols, see p. 130.

Population	8,704
Change fm '90	-0.8
Area (sq. mi.)	1,073.3
Land Area (sq. mi.)	1,069.4
Altitude (ft.)	1,300-2,021
Rainfall (in.)	26.1
Jan. mean min.	30
July mean max.	95
Growing season (days)	226
Civ. Labor	3,653
Unemployed	6.7
Annual Wages	$51,196,283
Av. Weekly Wage	$367.54
Fed. Wages	$983,884
Ag. Net Cash Return	$1,303,000
Prop. Value	$494,939,700
Retail Sales	$72,622,913

McLennan County

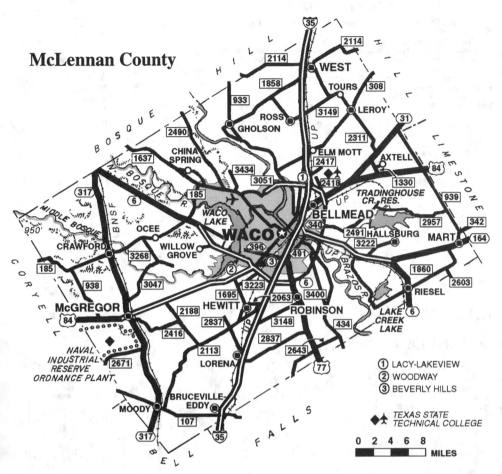

① LACY-LAKEVIEW
② WOODWAY
③ BEVERLY HILLS

◆✈ TEXAS STATE
TECHNICAL COLLEGE

0 2 4 6 8
▬▬▭▬▭ MILES

Physical Features: Central Texas county of mostly Blackland prairie, but rolling hills in west; drains to Bosque, Brazos rivers and Lake Waco; heavy, loam, sandy soils.

Economy: A leading distribution, government center for Central Texas; diversified manufacturing; agribusiness; education.

History: Tonkawas, Wichitas and Wacos in area. Anglo-American settlers arrived in 1840s. Indians removed to Brazos reservations in 1854. County created from Milam County in 1850; named for settler, Neil McLennan Sr.

Ethnicity, 1990: White, 146,100 (77.3%); Black, 29,520 (15.6%); American Indian, 563 (0.3%); Asian, 1,384 (0.7%); Other, 11,556 (6.1%). Hispanic, 23,643 (12.5%).

Vital Statistics, 1997: Births, 3,089; deaths, 1,929; marriages, 2,036; divorces, 1,163.

Recreation: Varied metropolitan activies; Fort Fisher Park with camping facilities; Texas Ranger Hall of Fame; Texas Sports Hall of Fame; Dr Pepper Museum; Cameron Park; Brazos River festival; zoo; historic sites, homes; museums; libraries, art center; symphony; civic theater; Baylor University events; Heart o' Texas Fair.

Minerals: Sand and gravel, limestone, oil, gas.

Agriculture: Corn, wheat, hay, grain sorghums, soybeans; beef cattle, also dairy cows; nursery crops; poultry. Market value $92.9 million.

Education: Baylor University; community college; Texas State Technical College.

WACO (110,024) county seat; varied manufacturing; tourism center, conventions; agribusiness; hospitals; Veterans Administration regional office, hospital.

Hewitt (10,718) iron works, other manufacturing; hamburger cookoff.

West (2,841) famous for Czech foods; varied manufacturing; Westfest.

Other towns include: **Axtell** (300); **Bellmead** (8,403); **Beverly Hills**

(2,133); **Bruceville-Eddy** (1,337, partly in Falls County); **China Spring** (1,000); **Crawford** (680); **Elm Mott** (190); **Gholson** (754); **Hallsburg** (542); **Lacy-Lakeview** (4,431); **Leroy** (344); **Lorena** (1,650); **Mart** (2,006) agricultural center, some manufacturing, museum; **McGregor** (4,834) varied manufacturing; private telephone museum; Frontier Founders Day in September; **Moody** (1,401); **Riesel** (902); **Robinson** (8,112); **Ross** (220); **Woodway** (9,471).

Population	204,265
Change fm '90	8.0
Area (sq. mi.)	1,060.2
Land Area (sq. mi.)	1,041.9
Altitude (ft.)	350-950
Rainfall (in.)	32.0
Jan. mean min.	34
July mean max.	97
Growing season (days)	253
Civ. Labor	100,966
Unemployed	4.3
Annual Wages	$2,189,399,917
Av. Weekly Wage	$467.80
Fed. Wages	$185,954,027
Ag. Net Cash Return	$1,142,000
Prop. Value	$5,949,753,208
Retail Sales	$2,169,467,437

For explanation of sources, abbreviations and symbols, see p. 130.

McMullen County

Physical Features: Southern county of brushy plain, sloping to Frio, Nueces rivers and tributaries; saline clay soils.

Economy: Livestock, hunting leases, hay.

History: Coahuiltecans, squeezed out by Lipan Apaches and other tribes. Anglo-American settlers arrived in 1858. Sheep ranching of 1870s attracted Mexican laborers. County created from Atascosa, Bexar, Live Oak counties 1858; organized 1862, reorganized 1877; named for Nueces River pioneer-empresario John McMullen.

Ethnicity, 1990: White, 713 (87.3%); Black, 0 (0.0%); American Indian, 3 (0.4%); Asian, 0 (0.0%); Other, 101 (12.4%). Hispanic, 320 (39.2%).

Vital Statistics, 1997: Births, 11; deaths, 9; marriages, 5; divorces, 4.

Recreation: Deer hunting; lake activities, state park; Labor Day rodeo; Dogtown Day cook-off in October.

Minerals: Gas, oil, lignite coal, zeolite-kaline.

Agriculture: Beef cattle; hay. Market value $5.6 million.

TILDEN (450), county seat; kitty-litter production; natural gas processing; ranch center; tourism.

Other towns include: **Calliham** (200).

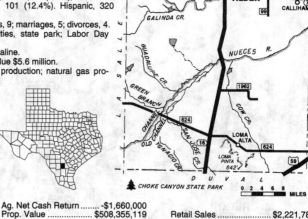

Population	763
Change fm '90	-6.6
Area (sq. mi.)	1,142.6
Land Area (sq. mi.)	1,113.1
Altitude (ft.)	200-642
Rainfall (in.)	23.4
Jan. mean min.	40
July mean max.	98
Growing season (days)	291
Civ. Labor	269
Unemployed	4.5
Annual Wages	$5,638,361
Av. Weekly Wage	$502.44
Fed. Wages	$141,151

Ag. Net Cash Return .... -$1,660,000
Prop. Value $508,355,119

Retail Sales $2,221,787

Medina County

Physical Features: Southwestern county with scenic hills in north; south has fertile valleys, rolling surface; Medina River, Lake.

Economy: Agribusinesses; tourism; varied manufacturing; commuters to San Antonio; government/services.

History: Lipan Apaches and Comanches. Settled by Alsatians led by Henri Castro in 1844. Mexican immigration increased after 1900. County created 1848 from Bexar; named for river, probably for Spanish engineer Pedro Medina.

Ethnicity, 1990: White, 23,608 (86.4%); Black, 92 (0.3%); American Indian, 119 (0.4%); Asian, 68 (0.2%); Other, 3,425 (12.5%). Hispanic, 12,134 (44.4%).

Vital Statistics, 1997: Births, 529; deaths, 312; marriages, 206; divorces, 138.

Recreation: A leading deer area; scenic drives; camping, fishing; historic buildings, museum; market trail days most months.

Minerals: Oil, gas, clay, sand, gravel.

Agriculture: Most income from cattle; crops include corn, grains, peanuts, hay, vegetables; 40,000 acres irrigated. Market value $59.9 million.

HONDO (8,047) county seat; Air Force screening center; aerospace industry; agribusiness; varied manufacturing; hunting leases; hospital; prisons.

Castroville (2,838) farm center; tourism; government/services; commuting to San Antonio; Landmark Inn; St. Louis Day celebration in August.

Devine (5,130) commuters to San Antonio, shipping for truck crop-livestock; fall festival in October.

Other towns include: **D'Hanis** (548); **La Coste** (1,440); **Mico** (98); **Natalia** (1,420); **Riomedina** (53); **Yancey** (202). And, **Lytle** (2,608) which lies partly in Atascosa and Bexar counties.

Population	35,894
Change fm '90	31.4
Area (sq. mi.)	1,334.5
Land Area (sq. mi.)	1,327.9
Altitude (ft.)	635-1,995
Rainfall (in.)	27.3
Jan. mean min.	37
July mean max.	94
Growing season (days)	263
Civ. Labor	15,704
Unemployed	4.7
Annual Wages	$159,958,744
Av. Weekly Wage	$391.49
Fed. Wages	$1,984,208
Ag. Net Cash Return	$6,036,000
Prop. Value	$1,551,460,599
Retail Sales	$260,266,514

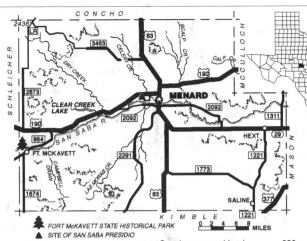

FORT McKAVETT STATE HISTORICAL PARK
SITE OF SAN SABA PRESIDIO

0 2 4 6 8 MILES

Menard County

Physical Features: West central county of rolling topography, draining to San Saba River and tributaries; limestone soils.

Economy: Agribusiness; tourism; oil, gas production.

History: Apaches, followed by Comanches in 18th century. Mission Santa Cruz de San Sabá established in 1757. A few Anglo-American and German settlers arrived in 1840s. County created from Bexar County in 1858, organized, 1871; named for Galveston's founder, Michel B. Menard.

Ethnicity, 1990: White, 2,076 (92.2%); Black, 7 (0.3%); American Indian, 5 (0.2%); Asian, 0 (0.0%); Other, 164 (7.3%). Hispanic, 726 (32.2%).

Vital Statistics, 1997: Births, 23; deaths, 35; marriages, 21; divorces, 4.

Recreation: Hunting, fishing; historic sites, including Spanish presidio, mission, state park; museum; Jim Bowie days in June.

Minerals: Oil, gas.

Agriculture: Sheep, goats, cattle; pecans, wheat, alfalfa, peaches, melons, grapes. Market value $12.9 million.

MENARD (1,660) county seat; hunting, ranching center, hospital. Other towns include: **Fort McKavett** (15); **Hext** (73).

Population.............................. 2,360	Growing season (days) 220
Change fm '90............................4.8	Civ. Labor..............................1,102
Area (sq. mi.)...........................902.2	Unemployed...............................4.0
Land Area (sq. mi.)..................902.0	Annual Wages.............. $10,034,635
Altitude (ft.)................... 1,690-2,436	Av. Weekly Wage............... $313.26
Rainfall (in.) 24.3	Fed. Wages...................... $242,930
Jan. mean min. 30	Ag. Net Cash Return......... $613,000
July mean max. 95	Prop. Value................ $224,866,350
	Retail Sales $10,050,263

Midland County

Physical Features: Flat western county, broken by draws; sandy, loam soils with native grasses.

Economy: Among leading petroleum-producing counties; distribution, administrative center for oil industry; varied manufacturing; government/services.

History: Comanches in area in 19th century. Sheep ranching developed in 1880s. Permian Basin oil boom began in 1920s. County created from Tom Green County 1885; name came from midway location on railroad between El Paso and Fort Worth. Chihuahua Trail and Emigrant Road were pioneer trails that crossed county.

Ethnicity, 1990: White, 86,977 (81.6%); Black, 8,281 (7.8%); American Indian, 414 (0.4%); Asian, 888 (0.8%); Other, 10,051 (9.4%). Hispanic, 22,780 (21.4%).

Vital Statistics, 1997: Births, 1,922; deaths, 821; marriages, 1,026; divorces, 606.

Recreation: Permian Basin Petroleum Museum, Library, Hall of Fame; Museum of Southwest; Confederate Air Force and Museum; community theater; metropolitan events; Cinco de Mayo International soccer tournament.

Minerals: Oil, natural gas.

Agriculture: Beef cattle, horses, sheep and goats; cotton, hay, pecans; 20,000 acres irrigated. Market value $18.7 million.

MIDLAND (99,734) county seat; petroleum, petrochemical center; varied manufacturing; livestock sale center; hospitals; cultural activities; junior college; Celebration of the Arts in May; Texas League baseball.

Odessa city limits extend into Midland County.

MIDLAND AIRPORT
MIDLAND INTERNATIONAL AIRPORT

0 2 4 6 8 MILES

Population.............................. 119,576	Rainfall (in.) 15.2
Change fm '90 ....12.2	Jan. mean min...................................29
Area (sq. mi.) 902.2	July mean max...................................95
Land Area (sq. mi.) 900.3	Growing season (days) 218
Altitude (ft.) 2,600-2,985	Civ. Labor.................................64,291
	Unemployed.......................................4.2
	Annual Wages............. $1,608,055,646
	Av. Weekly Wage $574.06
	Fed. Wages...................... $25,695,399
	Ag. Net Cash Return $4,368,000
	Prop. Value................. $4,650,999,684
	Retail Sales $1,421,135,149

For explanation of sources, abbreviations and symbols, see p. 130.

Milam County

Physical Features: East central county of partly level Blackland; southeast rolling to Post Oak Belt; Brazos, Little rivers.

Economy: Aluminum manufacturing; other varied manufacturing; lignite mining; agribusiness.

History: Lipan Apaches, Tonkawas and Comanches in area. Mission San Francisco Xavier established in 1746. Anglo-American settlers arrived in 1834. County created 1836 from municipality named for Ben Milam, a leader who died at the battle for San Antonio in December 1835; organized 1837.

Ethnicity, 1990: White, 18,603 (81.1%); Black, 2,940 (12.8%); American Indian, 69 (0.3%); Asian, 37 (0.2%); Other, 1,297 (5.7%). Hispanic 3,456 (15.1%).

Vital Statistics, 1997: Births, 329; deaths, 295; marriages, 175; divorces, 88.

Recreation: Fishing, hunting; historic sites include Fort Sullivan, Indian battlegrounds, mission site; museum in old jail at Cameron.

Minerals: Large lignite deposits; limited oil, natural gas production.

Agriculture: Poultry, cattle; hay, corn, sorghum, wheat, cotton, melons, peanuts. Market value $62.6 million.

CAMERON (6,128) county seat; government/services; manufacturing; hospital; library; Festival Cameron in March.

Rockdale (5,658) aluminum plant, utility company; agribusiness; hospital; Jubilee Days in June.

Other towns include: **Ben Arnold** (148); **Buckholts** (383); **Burlington** (140); **Davilla** (200); **Gause** (400); **Maysfield** (140); **Milano** (498); **Thorndale** (1,360, partly in Williamson County) market center.

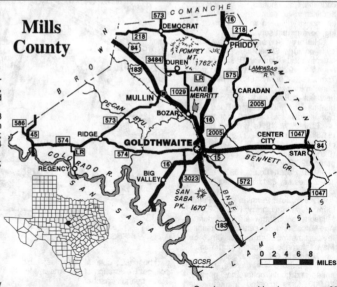

Population	**25,139**
Change fm '90	9.6
Area (sq. mi.)	1,021.6
Land Area (sq. mi.)	1,016.8
Altitude (ft.)	250-648
Rainfall (in.)	34.2
Jan. mean min.	38

July mean max.	95
Growing season (days)	256
Civ. Labor	9,533
Unemployed	4.6
Annual Wages	$176,037,061
Av. Weekly Wage	$514.99
Fed. Wages	$2,108,328
Ag. Net Cash Return	$4,564,000
Prop. Value	$1,274,050,463
Retail Sales	$135,413,741

Mills County

Physical Features: West central county of hills, plateau draining to Colorado River; sandy, loam soils.

Economy: Agribusiness, hunting leases.

History: Apache-Comanche area of conflict. Anglo-Americans and a few Germans settled in 1850s. County created 1887 from Brown, Comanche, Hamilton, Lampasas counties; named for pioneer jurist John T. Mills.

Ethnicity, 1990: White, 4,238 (93.5%); Black, 10 (0.2%); American Indian, 4 (0.1%); Asian, 1 (0.0%); Other, 278 (6.1%). Hispanic, 484 (10.7%).

Vital Statistics, 1997: Births, 57; deaths, 74; marriages, 24; divorces, 23.

Recreation: Fishing; deer, dove and turkey hunting; historic suspension bridge; fiddlers' contest; rangeland recreation.

Minerals: Not significant.

Agriculture: Beef cattle; sheep, goats also raised; grain sorghum, hay, dairies; some irrigation for pecans, Bermuda grass pasture. Market value $22.9 million.

GOLDTHWAITE (1,877) county seat; agribusiness; livestock center; light manufacturing; hospital; bike rally, old timers rodeo.

Other towns include: **Mullin** (244); **Priddy** (215); **Star** (85).

For explanation of sources, abbreviations and symbols, see p. 130.

Population	**5,366**
Change fm '90	18.4
Area (sq. mi.)	749.8
Land Area (sq. mi.)	748.2
Altitude (ft.)	1,200-1,762
Rainfall (in.)	27.6
Jan. mean min.	34
July mean max.	95

Growing season (days)	230
Civ. Labor	2,299
Unemployed	3.2
Annual Wages	$26,249,812
Av. Weekly Wage	$352.76
Fed. Wages	$659,424
Ag. Net Cash Return	$2,551,000
Prop. Value	$340,846,024
Retail Sales	$30,835,394

Mitchell County

Physical Features: Rolling, draining to Colorado and tributaries; sandy, red, dark soils; Lake Colorado City and Champion Creek Reservoir.

Economy: Government/services; agribusiness, oil, some manufacturing.

History: Jumano Indians in area; Comanches arrived about 1780. Anglo-American settlers arrived in late 1870s after Comanches forced into Indian Territory. County created 1876 from Bexar District; organized 1881; named for pioneer brothers Asa and Eli Mitchell.

Ethnicity, 1990: White, 6,317 (78.8%); Black, 363 (4.5%); American Indian, 14 (0.2%); Asian, 5 (0.1%); Other, 1,317 (16.4%). Hispanic, 2,389 (29.8%).

Vital Statistics, 1997: Births, 92; deaths, 116; marriages, 64; divorces, 44.

Recreation: Lake activities; state park; museum; hunting; railhead arts, crafts show, Colorado City playhouse.

Minerals: Oil.

Agriculture: Cotton principal crop, grains also produced. Cattle, sheep, goats, hogs raised. Market value $20.3 million.

COLORADO CITY (6,030) county seat; prisons; varied manufacturing; tourism; electric service center; hospital.

Other towns include: **Loraine** (687) and **Westbrook** (235), trade centers.

Population **8,962**	Rainfall (in.).................................... 19.8	Annual Wages $50,819,884
Change fm '90.............................. 11.8	Jan. mean min. 30	Av. Weekly Wage $406.82
Area (sq. mi.) 915.9	July mean max................................. 97	Fed. Wages $865,289
Land Area (sq. mi.) 910.1	Growing season (days).................. 217	Ag. Net Cash Return $6,262,000
Altitude (ft.).........................2,000-2,574	Civ. Labor 3,469	Prop. Value....................$503,384,966
	Unemployed 7.8	Retail Sales $42,505,847

Montague County

Physical Features: Rolling, draining to tributaries of Trinity, Red rivers; sandy loams, red, black soils; Farmers Creek Reservoir, Lake Amon G. Carter.

Economy: Agribusiness; oil production; varied manufacturing; government/services.

History: Kiowas and Wichitas who allied with Comanches. Anglo-American settlements developed in 1850s. County created from Cooke County 1857, organized 1858; named for pioneer Daniel Montague.

Ethnicity, 1990: White, 16,834 (97.5%); Black, 5 (0.0%); American Indian, 72 (0.4%); Asian, 13 (0.1%); Other, 350 (2.0%). Hispanic, 548 (3.2%).

Vital Statistics, 1997: Births, 227; deaths, 308; marriages, 164; divorces, 107.

Recreation: Lake activities; quail, turkey, deer hunting; scenic drives; museums; historical sites; Chisholm Trail Days, Jim Bowie Days in June; cattleman's roundup.

Minerals: Oil, rock, limestone.

Agriculture: Beef, dairy cattle; hay, wheat, grasses, pecans, peaches, melons. Some irrigation for peanuts, fruits. Market value $29.6 million.

MONTAGUE (400), county seat.

BOWIE, (5,350) varied manufacturing, livestock, hospital, library; fall bash; second Monday trade day.

NOCONA (3,171) boots, athletic goods manufacturing; hospital; Fun Day each May.

Other towns include: **Forestburg** (50); **Saint Jo** (1,130) farm center; Pioneer Days on last weekend in May; **Ringgold** (100); **Sunset** (375).

Population...............................**18,191**	Jan. mean min. 31	Av. Weekly Wage $373.21
Change fm '90.............................. 5.3	July mean max.................................96	Fed. Wages $2,229,445
Area (sq. mi.)............................. 938.4	Growing season (days)..................229	Ag. Net Cash Return $3,265,000
Land Area (sq. mi.)..................... 930.7	Civ. Labor 7,401	Prop. Value...................$779,872,857
Altitude (ft.)..........................750-1,318	Unemployed....................................4.6	Retail Sales $127,124,685
Rainfall (in.).............................. 32.9	Annual Wages $84,250,257	

Montgomery County

Physical Features: Rolling, three-fourths timbered; Sam Houston National Forest; loam, sandy, alluvial soils.

Economy: Many residents work in Houston; lumber, oil production; government/services; part of Houston metropolitan area.

History: Orcoquisacs and Bidais, removed from area by 1850s. Anglo-Americans arrived in 1820s as part of Austin's colony. County created 1837 from Washington County; named for Richard Montgomery, American Revolution general.

Ethnicity, 1990: White, 166,107 (91.2%); Black, 7,763 (4.3%); American Indian, 687 (0.4%); Asian, 1,232 (0.7%); Other, 6,412 (3.5%). Hispanic, 13,237 (7.3%).

Vital Statistics, 1997: Births, 3,860; deaths, 1,716; marriages, 2,191; divorces, 1,236.

Recreation: Hunting, fishing; Lake Conroe activities; national and state forests; hiking, boating, horseback riding; historic sites.

Minerals: Natural gas.

Agriculture: Greenhouse crops, cattle, horses, hay, poultry, goats. Christmas trees (first in state in harvested acres) and berries. Market value $15.7 million. Timber is primary industry.

CONROE (43,617) county seat; retail/wholesale center; government/services; manufacturing; commuters to Houston; hospital; community college; Cajun Catfish festival in October.

The Woodlands (41,628) residential planned community.

Other towns include: **Cut and Shoot** (1,220); **Dobbin** (170); **Magnolia** (1,283); **Montgomery** (499) historic buildings, antique stores; **New Caney** (2,771); **Patton Village** (1,498); **Pinehurst** (4,807); **Porter** (2,146); **Roman Forest** (1,378); **Splendora** (975); **Willis** (3,979); **Woodbranch** (1,750); **Woodloch** (329).

Population	259,999
Change fm '90	42.7
Area (sq. mi.)	1,076.8
Land Area (sq. mi.)	1,044.3
Altitude (ft.)	50-415
Rainfall (in.)	47.3
Jan. mean min.	38
July mean max.	94
Growing season (days)	270
Civ. Labor	133,646
Unemployed	3.4
Annual Wages	$1,788,106,965
Av. Weekly Wage	$523.44
Fed. Wages	$19,644,438
Ag. Net Cash Return	-$1,141,000
Prop. Value	$10,947,855,497
Retail Sales	$2,761,859,123

For explanation of sources, abbreviations and symbols, see p. 130.

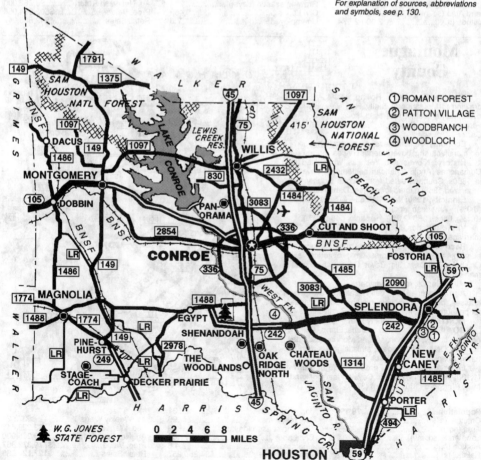

① ROMAN FOREST
② PATTON VILLAGE
③ WOODBRANCH
④ WOODLOCH

W. G. JONES STATE FOREST

0 2 4 6 8 MILES

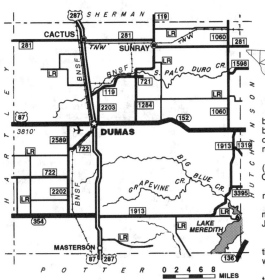

Moore County

Physical Features: Northern Panhandle county; flat to rolling, broken by creeks; sandy loams; lake.

Economy: Extensive petroleum operations; major natural gas producing county; varied agribusiness.

History: Comanches, removed to Indian Territory in 1874-75; ranching began soon afterward. Farming developed after 1910. Oil boom in 1920s. County created 1876 from Bexar District; organized 1892; named for Republic of Texas navy commander E.W. Moore.

Ethnicity, 1990: White, 12,789 (71.6%); Black, 95 (0.5%); American Indian, 123 (0.7%); Asian, 282 (1.6%); Other, 4,576 (25.6%). Hispanic, 5,693 (31.9%).

Vital Statistics, 1997: Births, 402; deaths, 139; marriages, 184; divorces, 104.

Recreation: Lake Meredith activities; historical museum; arts center; free overnight RV park; dogie days in June.

Minerals: Natural gas, oil, helium.

Agriculture: Fed beef, stocker cattle, cow/calf operations; about 130,000 acres irrigated for corn, sorghums, wheat. Market value $294.2 million.

DUMAS (13,764) county seat; tourist, retail trade center; varied agribusiness; hospital, hospice, retirement complex. Other towns include: **Cactus** (1,957), **Sunray** (1,848).

Population		19,595
Change fm '90		9.7
Area (sq. mi.)		909.6
Land Area (sq. mi.)		899.7
Altitude (ft.)		2,900-3,810
Rainfall (in.)		17.4
Jan. mean min.		20
July mean max.		92
Growing season (days)		185
Civ. Labor		9,281
Unemployed		3.1
Annual Wages		$205,862,278
Av. Weekly Wage		$469.36
Fed. Wages		$2,995,464
Ag. Net Cash Return		$23,338,000
Prop. Value		$1,504,558,860
Retail Sales		$129,306,710

Morris County

Physical Features: East Texas county of forested hills; drains to streams, lakes.

Economy: Steel manufacturing, agriculture, timber, government/services.

History: Caddo Indians until 1790s. Kickapoo and other tribes in area 1820s-30s. Anglo-American settlement began in mid-1830s. Antebellum slaveholding area. County named for legislator-jurist W.W. Morris; created from Titus County and organized in 1875.

Ethnicity, 1990: White, 9,770 (74.0%); Black, 3,227 (24.4%); American Indian, 70 (0.5%); Asian, 18 (0.1%); Other, 115 (0.9%). Hispanic, 239 (1.8%).

Vital Statistics, 1997: Births, 179; deaths, 162; marriages, 158; divorces, 67.

Recreation: Activities on Lake O' the Pines, small lakes; fishing, hunting; state park; old courthouse museum in Daingerfield.

Minerals: Iron ore.

Agriculture: Beef cattle, broiler production; hay. Market value $14.6 million. Timber industry significant.

DAINGERFIELD (2,764) county seat; varied manufacturing; library; Northeast Texas Community College; Captain Daingerfield Day in October.

Other towns include: **Cason** (173); **Lone Star** (1,646) oil-field equipment manufactured, catfish farming, Starfest in September; **Naples** (1,464) trailer manufacturing, livestock, watermelon festival in July; **Omaha** (979).

Population		13,467
Change fm '90		2.0
Area (sq. mi.)		258.6
Land Area (sq. mi.)		254.5
Altitude (ft.)		228-598
Rainfall (in.)		44.6
Jan. mean min.		35
July mean max.		95
Growing season (days)		236
Civ. Labor		6,612
Unemployed		12.9
Annual Wages		$156,716,697
Av. Weekly Wage		$584.08
Fed. Wages		$980,438
Ag. Net Cash Return		-$291,000
Prop. Value		$641,273,312
Retail Sales		$51,011,420

For explanation of sources, abbreviations and symbols, see p. 130.

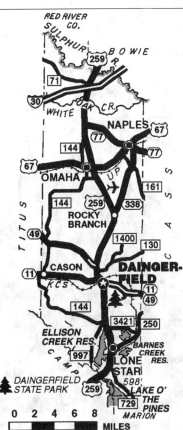

Motley County

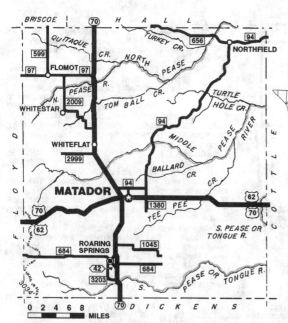

Physical Features: Western county just below Caprock; rough terrain, broken by Pease tributaries; sandy to red clay soils.

Economy: Government/services; ranching; cotton; hunting.

History: Comanches, removed to Indian Territory by U.S. Army in 1874-75. Ranching began in late 1870s. County created out of Bexar District 1876; organized 1891; named for Dr. J.W. Mottley, signer of Texas Declaration of Independence (name misspelled in statute).

Ethnicity, 1990: White, 1,362 (88.9%); Black, 68 (4.4%); American Indian, 5 (0.3%); Asian, 4 (0.3%); Other, 93 (6.1%). Hispanic, 136 (8.9%).

Vital Statistics, 1997: Births, 22; deaths, 25; marriages, 7; divorces, 4.

Recreation: Quail, dove, turkey, deer hunting; Matador Ranch headquarters; spring-fed pool at Roaring Springs; settlers reunion in August.

Minerals: Minimal.

Agriculture: Beef cattle, cotton, peanuts, hunting leases. Also vegetables, wheat, hay produced. Extensive irrigation. Market value $18.6 million.

MATADOR (673) county seat; farm trade center; pony express days in June.

Other towns include: **Flomot** (181); **Roaring Springs** (213).

Population **1,327**	Growing season (days) 218	Fed. Wages...................... $327,978
Change fm '90.........................-13.4	Civ. Labor................................ 598	Ag. Net Cash Return...... $5,064,000
Area (sq. mi.)......................... 989.8	Unemployed............................. 4.2	Prop. Value $120,928,404
Land Area (sq. mi.)................. 989.4	Annual Wages............... $6,208,031	Retail Sales................... $5,243,894
Altitude (ft.).................. 1,900-3,034	Av. Weekly Wage............... $357.74	
Rainfall (in.)............................ 21.2		
Jan. mean min............................ 26		
July mean max. 95		

A logcutter harvests a pine tree in East Texas. The Dallas Morning News file photo.

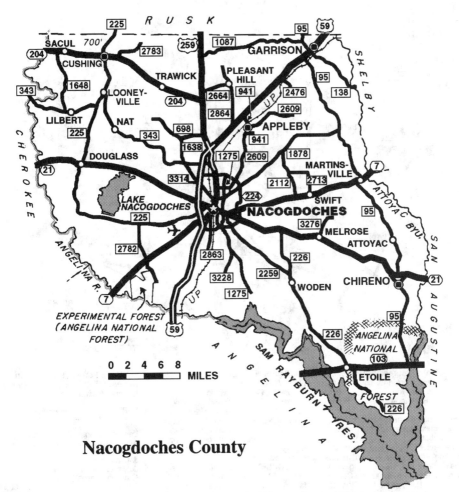

Nacogdoches County

Physical Features: East Texas county on divide between streams; hilly; two-thirds forested; red, gray, sandy soils; Sam Rayburn Reservoir.

Economy: Agribusiness; timber; manufacturing; education; tourism.

History: Caddo tribes, joined by displaced Cherokees in 1820s. Indians moved west of Brazos by 1840. Spanish missions established in 1716. Spanish settlers in mid-1700s. Anglo-Americans arrived in 1820s. Original county of Republic 1836, organized 1837.

Ethnicity, 1990: White, 43,772 (79.9%); Black, 9,020 (16.5%); American Indian, 144 (0.3%); Asian, 311 (0.6%); Other, 1,506 (2.8%). Hispanic, 2,788 (5.1%).

Vital Statistics, 1997: Births, 809; deaths, 575; marriages, 533; divorces, 139.

Recreation: Lake, river activities; Stephen F. Austin University events; Angelina National Forest; historic sites; major tourist attractions include the Old Stone Fort, pioneer homes, museums; Piney Woods Fair, Blueberry Festival in June.

Minerals: First Texas oil found here, 1866; gas, oil, clay, stone.

Agriculture: A leading poultry-producing county; extensive dairy operations; beef cattle raised. Market value $166.9 million. Substantial timber sold.

NACOGDOCHES (32,973) county seat; varied manufacturing; lumber mills, wood products; trade center; hospitals; Stephen F. Austin University.

Other towns include: **Appleby** (550), **Chireno** (502), **Cushing** (658), **Douglass** (75), **Etoile** (70), **Garrison** (1,050), **Martinsville** (126), **Sacul** (170), **Woden** (70).

Population	59,717
Change fm '90	9.1
Area (sq. mi.)	981.3
Land Area (sq. mi.)	946.8
Altitude (ft.)	164-700
Rainfall (in.)	47.5
Jan. mean min.	36
July mean max.	94
Growing season (days)	243
Civ. Labor	26,624
Unemployed	4.4
Annual Wages	$447,423,386
Av. Weekly Wage	$414.59
Fed. Wages	$7,035,454
Ag. Net Cash Return	$10,850,000
Prop. Value	$2,012,691,283
Retail Sales	$535,331,511

For explanation of sources, abbreviations and symbols, see p. 130.

Navarro County

Physical Features: North central county of level Blackland, some rolling; drains to creeks, Trinity River; Navarro Mills Lake, Richland-Chambers Reservoir.

Economy: Diversified manufacturing; agribusinesses; oil-field operations, distribution.

History: Kickapoo and Comanche area. Anglo-Americans settled in late 1830s. Antebellum slaveholding area. County created from Robertson County, organized in 1846; named for Republic of Texas leader Jose Antonio Navarro.

Ethnicity, 1990: White, 30,322 (75.9%); Black, 7,574 (19.0%); American Indian, 127 (0.3%); Asian, 271 (0.7%); Other, 1,632 (4.1%). Hispanic, 2,891 (7.2%).

Vital Statistics, 1997: Births, 619; deaths, 507; marriages, 426; divorces, 255.

Recreation: Lake activities; Pioneer Village; historic buildings; youth exposition, Derrick Days in April.

Minerals: Longest continuous Texas oil flow; more than 200 million barrels produced since 1895; natural gas, sand and gravel also produced.

Agriculture: Beef cattle; cotton, hay, grain sorghum, wheat, herbs, corn. Market value $33.6 million.

CORSICANA (24,450) county seat; major distribution center; varied manufacturing; agribusiness; hospital; Navarro College; Texas Youth Commission facility.

Other towns include: **Angus** (440); **Barry** (198); **Blooming Grove** (881); **Chatfield** (40); **Dawson** (783); **Emhouse** (242); **Eureka** (290); **Frost** (617); **Goodlow** (390); **Kerens** (1,693) some manufacturing; **Mildred** (214); **Mustang** (47); **Navarro** (258); **Oak Val-** **ley** (448); **Powell** (116); **Purdon** (133); **Retreat** (355); **Rice** (650, partly in Ellis County); **Richland** (323).

Population	**43,082**
Change frm'90	7.9
Area (sq. mi.)	1,086.2
Land Area (sq. mi.)	1,071.2
Altitude (ft.)	250-600
Rainfall (in.)	37.9
Jan. mean min.	33
July mean max.	94
Growing season (days)	253
Civ. Labor	20,960
Unemployed	5.2
Annual Wages	$349,995,559
Av. Weekly Wage	$429.23
Fed. Wages	$4,728,487
Ag. Net Cash Return	$2,340,000
Prop. Value	$1,539,211,501
Retail Sales	$351,062,311

For explanation of sources, abbreviations and symbols, see p. 130.

Counties

Newton County

Physical Features: East Texas county of densely forested hills, valleys; spring-fed streams; Toledo Bend Reservoir; Sabine River; mostly sandy soils.

Economy: Forestry, government/services, tourism.

History: Caddo Indian area. Displaced Coushattas moved across area from South. Anglo-American settlement established in 1830s. Antebellum slaveholding area. County created 1846 from Jasper County; named for American Revolutionary soldier John Newton.

Ethnicity, 1990: White, 10,402 (76.7%); Black, 3,039 (22.4%); American Indian, 44 (0.3%); Asian, 11 (0.1%); Other, 73 (0.5%). Hispanic, 153 (1.1%).

Vital Statistics, 1997: Births, 178; deaths, 130; marriages, 139; divorces, 90.

Recreation: Toledo Bend Reservoir; water sports; fishing, hunting; birding; tourism; state forest; Azalea Canyons. Belgrade, site of early town.

Minerals: Oil, gas.

Agriculture: Cattle, hay, nursery crops, vegetables, goats, hogs. Market value $1.4 million. Hunting leases. Major forestry area.

NEWTON (1,925) county seat; lumber manufacturing; plywood mill; private prison unit; tourist center; genealogical library; Wild Azalea festival in March.

Deweyville (1,376) commercial center for forestry, farming area.

Other towns include: **Bon Wier** (475); **Burkeville** (515); **Call** (170); **Wiergate** (461).

Population	14,436
Change fm '90	6.4
Area (sq. mi.)	939.5
Land Area (sq. mi.)	932.8
Altitude (ft.)	23-510
Rainfall (in.)	56
Jan. mean min.	40
July mean max.	93
Growing season (days)	228
Civ. Labor	5,831
Unemployed	12.1
Annual Wages	$45,867,871
Av. Weekly Wage	$396.91
Fed. Wages	$715,971
Ag. Net Cash Return	-$507,000
Prop. Value	$869,258,334
Retail Sales	$87,026,528

Nolan County

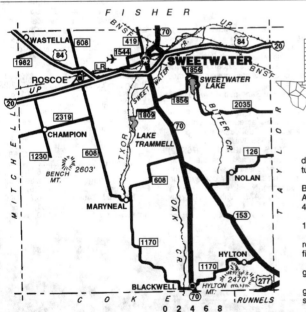

Physical Features: On divide between Brazos, Colorado watersheds; mostly red sandy loams, some waxy, sandy soils; lakes.

Economy: Varied manufacturing; ranching; oil and gas production.

History: Anglo-American settlement began in late 1870s. County created from Bexar, Young districts 1876; organized 1881; named for adventurer Philip Nolan, who was killed near Waco.

Ethnicity, 1990: White, 12,942 (78.0%); Black, 775 (4.7%); American Indian, 46 (0.3%); Asian, 18 (0.1%); Other, 2,813 (17.0%). Hispanic, 4,246 (25.6%).

Vital Statistics, 1997: Births, 237; deaths, 193; marriages, 130; divorces, 89.

Recreation: Lakes; hunting; rattlesnake roundup; pioneer museum; national junior rodeo finals in summer.

Minerals: Oil, gas, gypsum, limestone, and gravel.

Agriculture: Beef cattle, sheep, Angora goats, horses; cotton is the principal crop, wheat, sorghum also raised. Market value $32.4 million.

SWEETWATER (11,733) county seat; gypsum plant; varied manufacturing; hospital; Texas State Technical College.

Other towns include: **Blackwell** (381, partly in Coke County), Oak Creek Reservoir; **Maryneal** (61); **Nolan** (47); **Roscoe** (1,363).

For explanation of sources, abbreviations and symbols, see p. 130.

Population	16,625
Change fm '90	0.2
Area (sq. mi.)	913.9
Land Area (sq. mi.)	912.1
Altitude (ft.)	1,990-2,603
Rainfall (in.)	24.4
Jan. mean min.	30
July mean max.	94
Growing season (days)	221
Civ. Labor	7,371
Unemployed	6.7
Annual Wages	$127,720,733
Av. Weekly Wage	$415.02
Fed. Wages	$1,840,924
Ag. Net Cash Return	$8,231,000
Prop. Value	$818,136,308
Retail Sales	$153,708,693

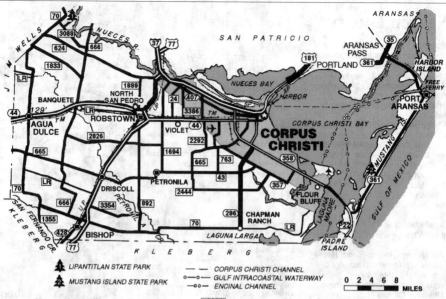

Nueces County

Physical Features: Southern Gulf Coast county; flat, rich soils, broken by bays, Nueces River, Petronila Creek; includes Mustang Island, north tip of Padre Island.

Economy: Diversified economy includes petroleum processing and production; deepwater port facilities; agriculture; tourism, conventions; coastal shipping; manufacturing; military complex.

History: Coahuiltecan, Karankawa and other tribes who succumbed to disease or fled by 1840s. Spanish settlers arrived in 1760s. Settlers from Ireland arrived around 1830. County name is Spanish for nuts; county named for river; created 1846 out of San Patricio County.

Ethnicity, 1990: White, 220,168 (75.6%); Black, 12,691 (4.4%); American Indian, 1,175 (0.4%); Asian, 2,483 (0.9%); Other, 54,628 (18.8%). Hispanic, 152,051 (52.2%).

Vital Statistics, 1997: Births, 5,397; deaths, 2,418; marriages, 2,616; divorces, 1,637.

Recreation: Major resort area; fishing, water sports; Padre Island National Seashore; Mustang Island State Park; Lipantitlan State Historical Park; Art Museum of South Texas, Corpus Christi Museum of Science and History; Texas State Aquarium; various metropolitan events; greyhound race track.

Minerals: Sand and gravel, oil and gas.

Agriculture: Grain sorghum (first in state in sales, acreage); cotton, corn, nursery crops. Beef cattle, hogs, goats. Market value $66.3 million.

CORPUS CHRISTI (276,712) county seat; varied manufacturing; petroleum processing; seaport; hospitals; museums; recreation centers; tourist destination; Naval Air Station; Army depot; Texas A&M University-Corpus Christi; Del Mar College; Buccaneer Days; replicas of Columbus' ships on display, U.S.S. Lexington museum.

Port Aransas (2,699) tourism, sea research institute, fishing accomodations, fisheries management, deep sea roundup, birding facility.

Robstown (13,094) market center for oil, farm area; Cottonfest in October; Fiesta Mexicana in March.

Other towns include: **Agua Dulce** (831); **Banquete** (449); **Bishop** (3,398) petrochemical, pharmaceutical manufacturing, fall carnival; **Chapman Ranch** (100); **Driscoll** (739); **Petronila** (162). **Flour Bluff** is now part of Corpus Christi.

Population	**312,081**
Change fm '90	7.2
Area (sq. mi.)	1,166.4
Land Area (sq. mi.)	835.9
Altitude (ft.)	sea level-129
Rainfall (in.)	30.1
Jan. mean min.	45
July mean max.	93
Growing season (days)	309
Civ. Labor	147,689
Unemployed	6.7
Annual Wages	$3,448,301,342
Av. Weekly Wage	$492.52
Fed. Wages	$235,677,094
Ag. Net Cash Return	$16,783,000
Prop. Value	$12,261,340,849
Retail Sales	$3,170,169,638

A sailor tries to right the boat on Corpus Christi Bay. AP/The Dallas Morning News file photo.

Ochiltree County

Physical Features: Panhandle county bordering Oklahoma; level, broken by creeks; deep loam, clay soils.

Economy: Oil; agribusiness, center of large feedlot operations, hunting leases.

History: Apaches, pushed out by Comanches in late 1700s. Comanches removed to Indian Territory in 1874-75. Ranching developed in 1880s; farming after 1900. County created from Bexar District 1876, organized 1889; named for Republic of Texas leader W.B. Ochiltree.

Ethnicity, 1990: White, 8,023 (87.9%); Black, 2 (0.0%); American Indian, 105 (1.2%); Asian, 8 (0.1%); Other, 990 (10.8%). Hispanic, 1,641 (18.0%).

Vital Statistics, 1997: Births, 124; deaths, 71; marriages, 130; divorces, 45.

Recreation: Wolf Creek park; Wheatheart of the Nation celebration in August; Museum of the Plains; Indian "Buried City" site; pheasant hunting, also deer and dove.

Minerals: Oil, natural gas, caliche.

Agriculture: Cattle, hogs; wheat (first in state in acreage), grain sorghum, corn, soybeans, hay; 80,000 acres irrigated. Market value $104 million.

PERRYTON (7,756) county seat; cattle feeding; grain center; hospital; convention center.

Other towns include: **Farnsworth** (130); **Waka** (65). Also, **Booker** (1,255, mostly in Lipscomb County).

Population	9,254
Change fm '90	1.4
Area (sq. mi.)	918.1
Land Area (sq. mi.)	917.6
Altitude (ft.)	2,642-3,105
Rainfall (in.)	19.5
Jan. mean min.	17
July mean max.	94
Growing season (days)	191
Civ. Labor	4,877
Unemployed	3.2
Annual Wages	$97,121,618
Av. Weekly Wage	$469.20
Fed. Wages	$1,199,051
Ag. Net Cash Return	$12,660,000
Prop. Value	$546,021,331
Retail Sales	$70,933,316

Oldham County

Physical Features: Northwestern Panhandle county; level, broken by Canadian River and tributaries.

Economy: Ranching center.

History: Apaches; followed later by Comanches, Kiowas. U.S. Army removed Indians in 1875. Anglo ranchers and Spanish *pastores* (sheep men) from New Mexico were in area in 1870s. County created 1876 from Bexar District; organized 1880; named for editor-Confederate senator W.S. Oldham.*

Ethnicity, 1990: White, 2,112 (92.7%); Black, 9 (0.4%); American Indian, 29 (1.3%); Asian, 18 (0.8%); Other, 110 (4.8%). Hispanic, 200 (8.8%).

Vital Statistics, 1997: Births, 22; deaths, 19; marriages, 20; divorces, 5.

Recreation: Old Tascosa with Boot Hill Cemetery nearby, pioneer town; County Roundup in August; midway point on old Route 66.

Minerals: Sand and gravel, oil, natural gas, stone.

Agriculture: Beef cattle; crops include wheat, grain sorghum. Market value $88.5 million.

VEGA (925) county seat; ranch trade center.

Other towns: **Adrian** (228); **Wildorado** (180). Cal Farley's Boys Ranch.

Population	2,376
Change fm '90	4.3
Area (sq. mi.)	1,501.4
Land Area (sq. mi.)	1,500.7
Altitude (ft.)	3,200-4,300
Rainfall (in.)	17.4
Jan. mean min.	19
July mean max.	91
Growing season (days)	186
Civ. Labor	1,085
Unemployed	3.4
Annual Wages	$18,223,722
Av. Weekly Wage	$409.70
Fed. Wages	$207,034
Ag. Net Cash Return	$9,377,000
Prop. Value	$219,083,570
Retail Sales	$8,906,016

For explanation of sources, abbreviations and symbols, see p. 130.

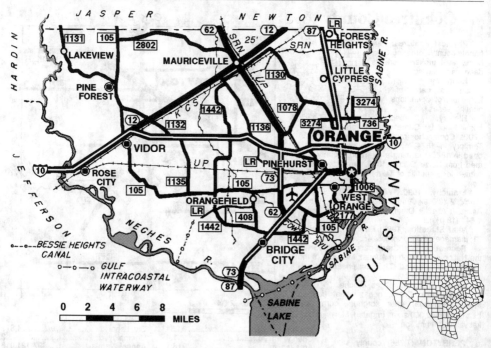

Physical Features: In southeast-
ern corner of the state; bounded by
Sabine, Neches rivers, Sabine Lake;
coastal soils; two-thirds timbered.
  Economy: Petrochemicals; ship-
ping; agribusinesses; tourism; lumber
processing; county part of Beaumont-
Port Arthur metropolitan area.
  History: Atakapan Indian area.
French traders in area by 1720. Anglo-
American settlement began in 1820s.
County created from Jefferson County
in 1852; named for early orange grove.
  Ethnicity, 1990: White, 72,607
(90.2%); Black, 6,768 (8.4%); American
Indian, 189 (0.2%); Asian, 484 (0.6%);
Other, 461 (0.6%). Hispanic, 1,933
(2.4%).
  Vital Statistics, 1997: Births,
1,175; deaths, 802; marriages, 729;
divorces, 499.
  Recreation: Fishing, hunting; water
sports; county park; museums; histori-
cal homes; crawfish festivals in spring.

Orange County

  Minerals: Salt, oil, gas, clays, sand
and gravel.
  Agriculture: Cattle, Christmas
trees and rice are top revenue sources;
honey a significant revenue producer;
vegetables, poultry. Market value $3.3
million. Hunting leases. Timber important.
  ORANGE (19,024) county seat;
seaport; petrochemical plants; varied
manufacturing; food, timber processing; shipping; hospital, theater, museums; Lamar University branch; gumbo
festival in May.
  Bridge City (8,336) varied manufacturing; ship repair yard; steel fabrication; fish farming; government/services;
library; tall bridge and newer suspension bridge over Neches; stop for Monarch butterfly in fall during its migration
to Mexico.

  Vidor (11,312) steel processing;
railroad-car refinishing; library.

  Other towns include: Mauriceville
(2,223); Pine Forest (779); Pinehurst
(2,605); Rose City (647); West Orange
(4,625).

Population	84,194
Change fm '90	4.6
Area (sq. mi.)	379.5
Land Area (sq. mi.)	356.4
Altitude (ft.)	sea level-25
Rainfall (in.)	58.3
Jan. mean min.	39
July mean max.	91
Growing season (days)	240
Civ. Labor	42,068
Unemployed	9.0
Annual Wages	$737,157,474
Av. Weekly Wage	$568.82
Fed. Wages	$4,918,651
Ag. Net Cash Return	$288,000
Prop. Value	$3,933,692,290
Retail Sales	$634,063,449

Physical Features: North central
county west of Fort Worth; broken, hilly,
wooded in parts; Possum Kingdom
Lake, Lake Palo Pinto; sandy, gray,
black soils.
  Economy: Varied manufacturing;
tourism; petroleum; agribusiness.
  History: Anglo-American ranchers
arrived in 1850s. Conflicts began settlers and numerous Indian tribes who
had sought refuge on Brazos resulted in
Texas Rangers removing Indians in
1856. County created 1856 from
Bosque, Navarro counties; organized
1857; named for creek (in Spanish
name means painted stick).
  Ethnicity, 1990: White, 22,810
(91.0%); Black, 792 (3.2%); American
Indian, 87 (0.3%); Asian, 171 (0.7%);

Palo Pinto County

Other, 1,195 (4.8%). Hispanic, 2,301
(9.2%).
  Vital Statistics, 1997: Births, 375;
deaths, 342; marriages, 259; divorces,
166.
  Recreation: Lake activities; hunting, fishing, water sports; state park.
  Minerals: Oil, gas, clays, sand and
gravel.
  Agriculture: Cattle, dairy products, nursery crops, hay, wheat. Market
value $15 million. Cedar fence posts
marketed.
  PALO PINTO (411) county seat; old

settlers reunion; government center.
  MINERAL WELLS (15,367) varied
manufacturing; tourism; agriculture;
hospital; Weatherford College extension; Crazy Water Festival in June; state
park east of city in Parker County.
  Other towns include: Gordon (465);
Graford (610) retirement and recreation
area; Mardi Gras along the Brazos;
Mingus (239), Santo (445), Strawn
(706).

(Map on next page.)

For explanation of sources, abbreviations
and symbols, see p. 130.

Palo Pinto County

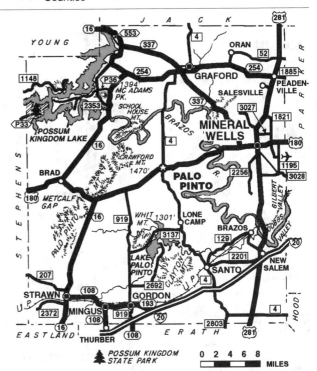

Population	26,520
Change fm '90	5.8
Area (sq. mi.)	985.4
Land Area (sq. mi.)	953.0
Altitude (ft.)	782-1,470
Rainfall (in.)	32.2
Jan. mean min.	30
July mean max.	96
Growing season (days)	221
Civ. Labor	12,491
Unemployed	5.4
Annual Wages	$173,159,583
Av. Weekly Wage	$396.62
Fed. Wages	$2,249,945
Ag. Net Cash Return	$3,000
Prop. Value	$1,138,460,943
Retail Sales	$235,625,735

POSSUM KINGDOM STATE PARK   0 2 4 6 8 MILES

Panola County

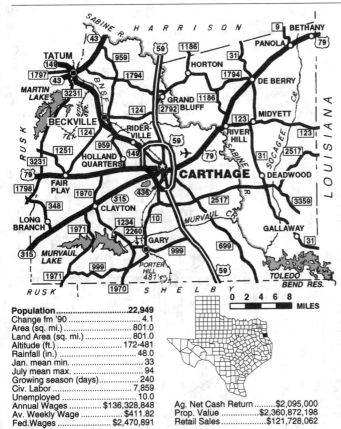

Physical Features: East Texas county; sixty percent forested, rolling plain; broken by Sabine, Murvaul Creek and Lake, Toledo Bend Reservoir.

Economy: Gas processing; oil-field operation; agribusinesses; varied manufacturing; forest industries.

History: Caddo area. Anglo-American settlement established in 1833. Antebellum slaveholding area. County name is Indian word for cotton; created from Harrison, Shelby counties 1846.

Ethnicity, 1990: White, 17,702 (80.3%); Black, 4,057 (18.4%); American Indian, 57 (0.3%); Asian, 23 (0.1%); Other, 196 (0.9%). Hispanic, 477 (2.2%).

Vital Statistics, 1997: Births, 289; deaths, 236; marriages, 197; divorces, 77.

Recreation: Lake fishing, other water activities; hunting; scenic drives; Jim Reeves memorial; historic sites, homes; museum.

Minerals: Oil, gas, lignite.

Agriculture: A leading broiler-producing county; beef cattle, dairies, hay, truck crops, silage; market value $45.9 million. Timber sales significant.

CARTHAGE (6,605) county seat; petroleum processing; poultry; sawmills; hospital; junior college.

Other towns include: **Beckville** (799), **Clayton** (79), **DeBerry** (191), **Gary** (285), **Long Branch** (181), **Panola** (296). Also, **Tatum** (1,368, mostly in Rusk County).

Population	22,949
Change fm '90	4.1
Area (sq. mi.)	801.0
Land Area (sq. mi.)	801.0
Altitude (ft.)	172-481
Rainfall (in.)	48.0
Jan. mean min.	33
July mean max.	94
Growing season (days)	240
Civ. Labor	7,859
Unemployed	10.0
Annual Wages	$136,328,848
Av. Weekly Wage	$411.82
Fed.Wages	$2,470,891
Ag. Net Cash Return	$2,095,000
Prop. Value	$2,360,872,198
Retail Sales	$121,728,062

For explanation of sources, abbreviations and symbols, see p. 130.

Parker County

Physical Features: Hilly, broken by Brazos, Trinity tributaries, lakes; varied soils.

Economy: Agribusiness; varied manufacturing; government/services; many residents work in Fort Worth; county part of Fort Worth-Arlington metropolitan area.

History: Comanche and Kiowa area in late 1840s when Anglo-American settlers arrived. County named for pioneer legislator Isaac Parker; created 1855 from Bosque, Navarro counties.

Ethnicity, 1990: White, 62,267 (96.1%); Black, 589 (0.9%); American Indian, 367 (0.6%); Asian, 231 (0.4%); Other, 1,331 (2.1%). Hispanic, 2,697 (4.2%).

Vital Statistics, 1997: Births, 938; deaths, 580; marriages, 768; divorces, 428.

Recreation: Water sports; state park; nature trails; hunting; horse racing at Trinity Meadows; peach festival in July and frontier days; first Monday trade days monthly.

Minerals: Natural gas, oil, stone, sand and gravel, clays.

Agriculture: Cattle, horticultural plants, horses (second in sate in inventory), dairies, peaches, peanuts, pecans. Market value $43.8 million.

WEATHERFORD (18,171) county seat; varied manufacturing; commuting; agribusiness center; hospital; Weatherford College.

Other towns include: **Aledo** (1,476); **Annetta** (867), **Annetta North** (346) and **Annetta South** (541); **Cool** (277); **Dennis** (90); **Hudson Oaks** (1,196); **Millsap** (644); **Peaster** (102); **Poolville** (520); **Reno** (2,772); **Sanctuary** (293);

① ANNETTA SOUTH
② ANNETTA
③ ANNETTA NORTH

0 2 4 6 8 MILES

Springtown (2,022) government/services, manufacturing; **Whitt** (38); **Willow Park** (2,864). Also, **Azle** (10,478) and **Briar** (4,700) mostly in Tarrant County, and part of **Mineral Wells.**

Population 77,525
Change fm '90 .... 19.7
Area (sq. mi.) 910.0
Land Area (sq. mi.) 903.6

Altitude (ft.) 700-1,275
Rainfall (in.) 32.9
Jan. mean min. 28
July mean max. 96
Growing season (days) 225
Civ. Labor 40,359
Unemployed 2.9
Annual Wages $354,490,813
Av. Weekly Wage $418.86
Fed. Wages $5,805,198
Ag. Net Cash Return $945,000
Prop. Value $3,100,441,884
Retail Sales $783,905,684

Parmer County

Population 10,258
Change fm '90............................... 4.0
Area (sq. mi.) 885.2
Land Area (sq. mi.) 881.7
Altitude (ft.) 3,850-4,400
Rainfall (in.) 16.8
Jan. mean min. 21
July mean max. 90
Growing season (days) 183
Civ. Labor 4,364
Unemployed 3.1
Total Wages $104,133,720
Av. Weekly Wage $426.78
Fed. Wages $2,450,068
Ag. Net Cash Return $76,497,000
Prop. Value $506,808,497
Retail Sales $50,037,256

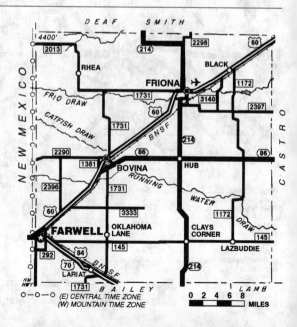

Physical Features: Western High Plains, broken by draws, playas; sandy, clay, loam soils.

Economy: Cattle feeding; grain elevators; meat-packing plant; other agribusiness.

History: Apaches, pushed out in late 1700s by Comanches, Kiowas. U.S. Army removed Indians in 1874-75. Anglo-Americans arrived in 1880s. Mexican migration increased after 1950. County named for Republic figure Martin Parmer; created from Bexar District 1876, organized 1907.

(Map on preceding page.)

Parmer County

Ethnicity, 1990: White, 8,980 (91.0%); Black, 123 (1.2%); American Indian, 29 (0.3%); Asian, 24 (0.2%); Other, 707 (7.2%). Hispanic, 4,096 (41.5%).

Vital Statistics, 1997: Births, 178; deaths, 101; marriages, 79; divorces, 52.

Recreation: Hunting, Border Town Days in July.

Minerals: Not significant.

Agriculture: Among leading counties in total farm income. Beef cattle; crops include wheat, corn, cotton, grain sorghum, alfalfa; apples and potatoes also raised; 190,000 acres irrigated. Market value $550.9 million.

FARWELL (1,452) county seat; agribusiness center; grain storage; plants make farm equipment.

FRIONA (3,834) feedlots, meat packing, grain elevators, hospital; Maize Days in September.

Other towns include: **Bovina** (1,783) farm trade center; **Lazbuddie** (248).

Pecos County

Physical Features: Second largest county; high, broken plateau in West Texas; draining to Pecos and tributaries; sandy, clay, loam soils.

Economy: Agribusiness center; oil, gas chief factors; tourism; government/services.

History: Comanches in area when military outpost established in 1859. Settlement began after Civil War. County created from Presidio 1871; organized 1872; named for Pecos River, name origin uncertain.

Ethnicity, 1990: White, 9,449 (64.4%); Black, 62 (0.4%); American Indian, 45 (0.3%); Asian, 31 (0.2%); Other, 5,088 (34.7%). Hispanic, 8,331 (56.8%).

Vital Statistics, 1997: Births, 210; deaths, 110; marriages, 112; divorces, 49.

Recreation: Old Fort Stockton, Annie Riggs Museum, stagecoach stop; scenic drives; Dinosaur Track Roadside Park; cattle-trail sites; archaeological museum with oil, ranch-heritage collections; Cinco de Mayo.

Minerals: Natural gas, oil.

Agriculture: Most income from vegetables, pecans, cotton, hay, vineyard; 30,000 acres irrigated. Cattle, goats, sheep, horses. Market value $40.2 million. Aquaculture firm producing shrimp.

FORT STOCKTON (8,644) county seat; distribution center for petroleum industry; government/services; agriculture; tourism; varied manufacturing; winery; hospital; historical tours; prison units.

Iraan (1,219) oil, gas center, tourism; ranching, meat processing, hospital, birthplace of Alley Oop comic strip; chili, brisket cookoff.

Other towns include: **Coyanosa** (270); **Girvin** (30); **Imperial** (350), center for irrigated farming; **Sheffield** (600), oil, gas center.

Population	15,574
Change fm '90	6.1
Area (sq. mi.)	4,765.0
Land Area (sq. mi.)	4,764.0
Altitude (ft.)	2,168-5,200
Rainfall (in.)	13.9
Jan. mean min.	30
July mean max.	95
Growing season (days)	224
Civ. Labor	6,618
Unemployed	6.9
Annual Wages	$108,134,085
Av. Weekly Wage	$416.95
Fed. Wages	$1,760,032
Ag. Net Cash Return	$13,097,000
Prop. Value	$2,941,439,185
Retail Sales	$104,554,911

For explanation of sources, abbreviations and symbols, see p. 130.

Polk County

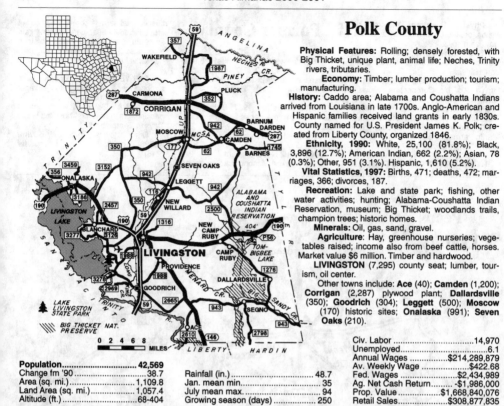

Physical Features: Rolling; densely forested, with Big Thicket, unique plant, animal life; Neches, Trinity rivers, tributaries.

Economy: Timber; lumber production; tourism; manufacturing.

History: Caddo area; Alabama and Coushatta Indians arrived from Louisiana in late 1700s. Anglo-American and Hispanic families received land grants in early 1830s. County named for U.S. President James K. Polk; created from Liberty County, organized 1846.

Ethnicity, 1990: White, 25,100 (81.8%); Black, 3,896 (12.7%); American Indian, 662 (2.2%); Asian, 78 (0.3%); Other, 951 (3.1%). Hispanic, 1,610 (5.2%).

Vital Statistics, 1997: Births, 471; deaths, 472; marriages, 366; divorces, 187.

Recreation: Lake and state park; fishing, other water activities; hunting; Alabama-Coushatta Indian Reservation, museum; Big Thicket; woodlands trails, champion trees; historic homes.

Minerals: Oil, gas, sand, gravel.

Agriculture: Hay, greenhouse nurseries; vegetables raised; income also from beef cattle, horses. Market value $6 million. Timber and hardwood.

LIVINGSTON (7,295) county seat; lumber, tourism, oil center.

Other towns include: **Ace** (40); **Camden** (1,200); **Corrigan** (2,287) plywood plant; **Dallardsville** (350); **Goodrich** (304); **Leggett** (500); **Moscow** (170) historic sites; **Onalaska** (991); **Seven Oaks** (210).

Population	42,569
Change fm '90	38.7
Area (sq. mi.)	1,109.8
Land Area (sq. mi.)	1,057.4
Altitude (ft.)	68-404
Rainfall (in.)	48.7
Jan. mean min.	35
July mean max.	94
Growing season (days)	250
Civ. Labor	14,970
Unemployed	6.1
Annual Wages	$214,289,879
Av. Weekly Wage	$422.68
Fed. Wages	$2,434,989
Ag. Net Cash Return	-$1,986,000
Prop. Value	$1,668,840,076
Retail Sales	$308,877,835

Potter County

Physical Features: Panhandle county; mostly level, part rolling; broken by Canadian River and tributaries; sandy, sandy loam, chocolate loam, clay soils; Lake Meredith.

Economy: Transportation, distribution hub for large area; feedlot operations, agri-businesses; tourism; government/services; petrochemicals; gas processing; .

History: Apaches, pushed out by Comanches in 1700s. Comanches removed to Indian Territory in 1874-75. Ranching began in late 1870s. Oil boom in 1920s. County named for Robert Potter, Republic leader; created 1876 from Bexar District; organized 1887.

Ethnicity, 1990: White, 73,884 (75.5%); Black, 8,673 (8.9%); American Indian, 901 (0.9%); Asian, 2,570 (2.6%); Other, 11,846 (12.1%). Hispanic, 19,246 (19.7%).

Vital Statistics, 1997: Births, 2,025; deaths, 1,169; marriages, 1,738; divorces, 487.

Recreation: Metropolitan activities, events; lake activities; Alibates Flint Quarries National Monument; hunting, fishing; Tri-State Fair.

Minerals: Natural gas, oil, helium.

Agriculture: Beef cattle; wheat, sorghums, corn are chief crops. Market value $18.6 million.

AMARILLO (172,289, part in Randall County) county seat; hub for northern Panhandle oil, ranching; distribution, marketing center; tourism; varied manufacturing; food processing; hospitals; museum; varied cultural, recreational events; junior college, Texas Tech medical, engineering schools; Texas State

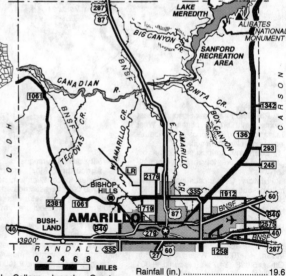

Technical College branch; Quarter Horse Heritage Center; *Texas* drama, cowboy breakfasts during summer.

Other towns include: **Bishop Hills** (250) and **Bushland** (130).

Population	109,577
Change fm '90	12.0
Area (sq. mi.)	922.0
Land Area (sq. mi.)	909.4
Altitude (ft.)	2,915-3,900
Rainfall (in.)	19.6
Jan. mean min.	21
July mean max.	92
Growing season (days)	190
Civ. Labor	55,389
Unemployed	5.6
Annual Wages	$1,765,700,724
Av. Weekly Wage	$469.49
Fed. Wages	$83,291,440
Ag. Net Cash Return	$1,725,000
Prop. Value	$4,191,154,305
Retail Sales	$1,923,367,375

Presidio County

Physical Features: Rugged, some of Texas' tallest mountains; scenic drives; clays, loams, sandy loams on uplands; intermountain wash; timber sparse; Capote Falls, state's highest.

Economy: Ranching; government/services; hunting leases; tourism.

History: Area around Presidio believed to be oldest continuously cultivated farmland in Texas, since 1500 B.C. Jumanos, Apaches and Comanches in area when Spanish arrived in 1680s. Anglo-Americans arrived in 1840s. County created 1850 from Bexar District; organized 1875; named for Spanish Presidio del Norte (fort of the north).

Ethnicity, 1990: White, 5,624 (84.7%); Black, 6 (0.1%); American Indian, 16 (0.2%); Asian, 16 (0.2%); Other, 975 (14.7%). Hispanic, 5,417 (81.6%).

Vital Statistics, 1997: Births, 127; deaths, 49; marriages, 69; divorces, 7.

Recreation: Mild climate and scenic surroundings; hunting; scenic drives along Rio Grande, in mountains; ghost towns, mysterious Marfa Lights; Fort D.A. Russell; Big Bend Ranch State Natural Area; hot springs.

Minerals: Sand and gravel.

Agriculture: Cattle, onions, hay, melons; bees, honey; horses. 5,500 acres irrigated near Rio Grande. Market value $13.6 million.

MARFA (2,639) county seat; ranching supply, Border Patrol sector headquarters; tourist center; gateway to mountainous area; Old Timers Roping in April.

PRESIDIO (3,794) international bridge to Ojinaga, Mex., gateway to Mexico's West Coast by rail; Fort Leaton State Park; Onion Festival in May.

Other towns include: **Redford** (80); **Shafter** (26) old mining town.

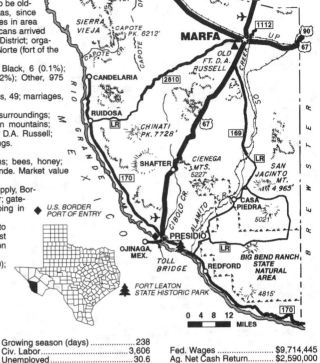

Population	7,588
Change fm '90	14.3
Area (sq. mi.)	3,856.4
Land Area (sq. mi.)	3,855.8
Altitude (ft.)	2,400-7,728
Rainfall (in.) Marfa	15.9
Rainfall (in.) Presidio	10.8
Jan. mean min. Marfa	26
Jan. mean min. Presidio	34
July mean max. Marfa	90
July mean max. Presidio	102

Growing season (days)	238	Fed. Wages	$9,714,445
Civ. Labor	3,606	Ag. Net Cash Return	$2,590,000
Unemployed	30.6	Prop. Value	$281,656,506
Annual Wages	$21,981,763	Retail Sales	$28,227,169
Av. Weekly Wage	$350.86		

Rains County

Physical Features: Northeastern county; rolling; partly Blackland, sandy loams, sandy soils; Sabine River, Lake Tawakoni.

Economy: Oil, tourism, agribusinesses, some manufacturing.

History: Caddo area. In 1700s, Tawakoni Indians entered the area. Anglo-Americans arrived in 1840s. County, county seat named for Emory Rains, Republic leader; created 1870 from Hopkins, Hunt and Wood counties.

Ethnicity, 1990: White, 6,310 (94.0%); Black, 286 (4.3%); American Indian, 29 (0.4%); Asian, 8 (0.1%); Other, 82 (1.2%). Hispanic, 158 (2.4%).

Vital Statistics, 1997: Births, 83; deaths, 86; marriages, 134; divorces, 50.

Recreation: Lake Tawakoni and Lake Fork Reservoir activities; Eagle Fest in January.

Minerals: Gas, oil.

Agriculture: Beef, dairy cattle, horses; crops are vegetables, hay, small grains. Market value $15.8 million.

EMORY (1,034) county seat; local trade, tourism; some manufacturing.

Other towns include: **East Tawakoni** (746) and **Point** (799).

For explanation of sources, abbreviations and symbols, see p. 130.

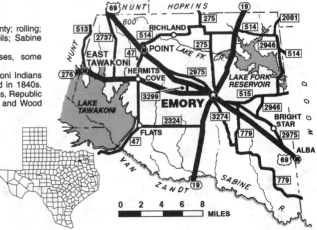

Population	7,603
Change fm '90	13.2
Area (sq. mi.)	258.8
Land Area (sq. mi.)	232.1
Altitude (ft.)	345-600
Rainfall (in.)	42.9
Jan. mean min.	31
July mean max.	94

Growing season (days)	242
Civ. Labor	3,732
Unemployed	4.4
Annual Wages	$21,981,763
Av. Weekly Wage	$350.86
Fed. Wages	$542,520
Ag. Net Cash Return	$3,900,000
Prop. Value	$300,021,842
Retail Sales	$40,256,565

Randall County

Physical Features: Northwestern county; level, but broken by scenic Palo Duro Canyon, Buffalo Lake; silty clay, loam soils.

Economy: Agribusinesses; education; some manufacturing; tourism; part of Amarillo metropolitan area.

History: Comanche Indians removed in mid-1870s; ranching began soon afterward. County created 1876 from Bexar District; organized 1889; named for Confederate Gen. Horace Randal (name misspelled in statute).

Ethnicity, 1990: White, 84,633 (94.4%); Black, 1,115 (1.2%); American Indian, 454 (0.5%); Asian, 646 (0.7%); Other, 2,825 (3.2%). Hispanic, 6,144 (6.9%).

Vital Statistics, 1997: Births, 1,344; deaths, 634; marriages, 312; divorces, 635.

Recreation: Palo Duro Canyon State Park, with *Texas* drama a tourist attraction each summer; Panhandle-Plains Historical Museum; West Texas A&M University events; aoudad sheep, migratory waterfowl hunting in season; Buffalo Lake National Wildlife Refuge.

Minerals: Not significant.

Agriculture: Wheat, corn, sorghum, hay, sugar beets; 61,000 acres irrigated. Beef, dairy cattle, horses. Market value $202.9 million.

CANYON (13,219) county seat; West Texas A&M University, major economic factor; commuting to Amarillo; ranching, farm center; light manufacturing; gateway to state park.

Other towns include: **Lake Tanglewood** (764); **Palisades** (350); **Timbercreek Canyon** (378); **Umbarger** (327). A significant part of **Amarillo** (172,289) lies in the county.

Population	101,076
Change fm '90	12.7
Area (sq. mi.)	922.4
Land Area (sq. mi.)	914.5
Altitude (ft.)	2,700-3,900
Rainfall (in.)	18.9
Jan. mean min.	23
July mean max.	92
Growing season (days)	195

Civ. Labor	57,543
Unemployed	1.6
Annual Wages	$442,793,145
Av. Weekly Wage	$458.87
Fed. Wages	$1,791,236
Ag. Net Cash Return	$15,080,000
Prop. Value	$3,708,369,133
Retail Sales	$671,840,224

Reagan County

Physical Features: Western county; level to hilly, broken by draws, Big Lake; sandy, loam, clay soils.

Economy: Oil production; natural gas; ranching.

History: Comanches in area until mid-1870s. Ranching began in 1880s. Hispanic migration increased after 1950. County named for Sen. John H. Reagan, first chairman, Texas Railroad Commission; county created 1903 from Tom Green County.

Ethnicity, 1990: White, 3,550 (78.6%); Black, 127 (2.8%); American Indian, 7 (0.2%); Asian, 1 (0.0%); Other, 829 (18.4%). Hispanic, 1,941 (43.0%).

Vital Statistics, 1997: Births, 73; deaths, 33; marriages, 41; divorces, 14.

Recreation: Texon reunion; rodeo; site of 1923 discovery well Santa Rita No. 1 on University of Texas land.

Minerals: Gas, oil.

Agriculture: Cotton, cattle, sheep, goats, sheep; cotton, grains principal crops; 36,000 acres irrigated. Market value $12.5 million.

BIG LAKE (3,481) county seat; center for oil activities, farming, ranching; hospital; Blue Grass Festival in April.

Population	4,229
Change fm '90	-6.3
Area (sq. mi.)	1,176.0
Land Area (sq. mi.)	1,175.4
Altitude (ft.)	2,400-2,953
Rainfall (in.)	19.2
Jan. mean min.	28

July mean max.	94
Growing season (days)	229
Civ. Labor	1,991
Unemployed	6.3
Annual Wages	$29,490,663
Av. Weekly Wage	$457.44

Fed. Wages	$472,886
Ag. Net Cash Return	$2,488,000
Prop. Value	$495,282,630
Retail Sales	$29,610,275

Real County

Physical Features: Hill Country, spring-fed streams, scenic canyons; Frio, Nueces rivers; cedars, pecans, walnuts, many live oaks.

Economy: Tourism, hunting leases; ranch supplies; cedar sales; popular area for artists, recreational "second homes."

History: Tonkawa area; Lipan Apaches arrived in early 1700s; later, Comanche hunters in area. Spanish mission established 1762. Anglo-Americans arrived in 1850s. County created 1913 from Bandera, Edwards, Kerr counties; named for legislator-ranchman Julius Real.

Ethnicity, 1990: White, 2,064 (85.6%); Black, 0 (0.0%); American Indian, 23 (1.0%); Asian, 0 (0.0%); Other, 325 (13.5%). Hispanic, 574 (23.8%).

Vital Statistics, 1997: Births, 31; deaths, 52; marriages, 23; divorces, 17.

Recreation: Tourist, hunting center; many deer killed each season; fishing; camping; scenic drives; state natural area.

Minerals: Not significant.

Agriculture: Beef cattle, sheep, goats produce most income; hay, grain sorghums. Market value $2.5 million. Cedar posts processed.

LEAKEY (408) county seat; center for ranching, tourism; cedar-oil mill; medical facilities; July Jubilee.

CAMP WOOD (795) San Lorenzo de la Santa Cruz mission site; settlers reunion in August; a tourist, ranching hub for parts of three counties.

Other towns include: **Rio Frio** (50).

Population..................................... 2,629	Rainfall (in.)................................... 25.7	Annual Wages $8,569,439
Change fm '90 .... 9.0	Jan. mean min. 29	Av. Weekly Wage $276.01
Area (sq. mi.)................................ 700.0	July mean max. 92	Fed. Wages $182,267
Land Area (sq. mi.)....................... 700.0	Growing season (days) 236	Ag. Net Cash Return......... -$1,975,000
Altitude (ft.) 1,450-2,381	Civ. Labor..................................... 1,223	Prop. Value $305,955,394
	Unemployed.................................... 4.1	Retail Sales....................... $8,912,238

Red River County

Physical Features: On Red-Sulphur rivers' divide; 39 different soil types; half timbered.

Economy: Agribusinesses; lumbering; manufacturing.

History: Caddo Indians abandoned area in 1790s. One of the oldest counties; settlers were moving in from the United States in 1810s. Kickapoo and other tribes arrived in 1820s. Antebellum slaveholding area. County created 1836 as original county of the Republic; organized 1837; named for Red River, its northern boundary.

Ethnicity, 1990: White, 11,203 (78.2%); Black, 2,872 (20.1%); American Indian, 75 (0.5%); Asian, 14 (0.1%); Other, 153 (1.1%). Hispanic, 273 (1.9%).

Vital Statistics, 1997: Births, 169; deaths, 207; marriages, 106; divorces, 76.

Recreation: Historical sites include pioneer homes, birthplace of John Nance Garner; water activities; hunting of deer, turkey, duck, small game.

Minerals: Small oil flow.

Agriculture: Cattle; soybeans, corn, wheat, cotton are principal crops. Market value $39.4 million. Timber sales substantial.

CLARKSVILLE (4,323) county seat; varied manufacturing; hospital; library; century-old courthouse; Historical Society bazaar in October.

Other towns include: **Annona** (358); **Avery** (479); **Bagwell** (150); **Bogata** (1,307) serves farming area; **Detroit** (799) commercial center in west.

	Annual Wages $67,049,260
	Av. Weekly Wage $349.63
	Fed. Wages $1,436,286
	Ag. Net Cash Return......... $3,596,000
	Prop. Value.................... $571,326,730
	Retail Sales.................... $67,063,683

Population...............................14,496	Rainfall (in.)................................... 44.9	
Change fm '90 .... 1.3	Jan. mean min................................... 28	
Area (sq. mi.)............................ 1,057.6	July mean max................................... 92	
Land Area (sq. mi.) 1,050.2	Growing season (days) 234	
Altitude (ft.) 287-525	Civ. Labor..................................... 5,995	

For explanation of sources, abbreviations and symbols, see p. 130.

Reeves County

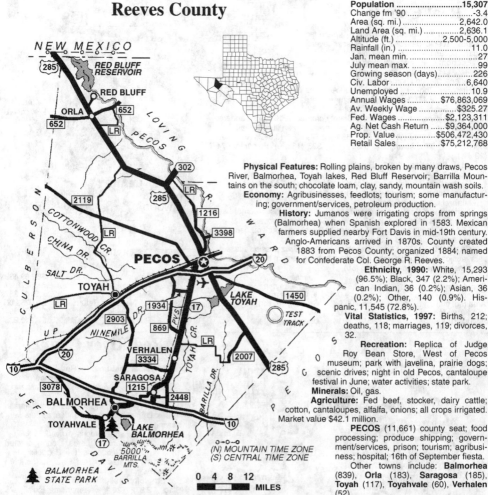

Population	15,307
Change fm '90	-3.4
Area (sq. mi.)	2,642.0
Land Area (sq. mi.)	2,636.1
Altitude (ft.)	2,500-5,000
Rainfall (in.)	11.0
Jan. mean min.	27
July mean max.	99
Growing season (days)	226
Civ. Labor	6,640
Unemployed	10.9
Annual Wages	$76,863,069
Av. Weekly Wage	$325.27
Fed. Wages	$2,123,311
Ag. Net Cash Return	$9,364,000
Prop. Value	$506,472,430
Retail Sales	$75,212,768

Physical Features: Rolling plains, broken by many draws, Pecos River, Balmorhea, Toyah lakes, Red Bluff Reservoir; Barrilla Mountains on the south; chocolate loam, clay, sandy, mountain wash soils.

Economy: Agribusinesses, feedlots; tourism; some manufacturing; government/services, petroleum production.

History: Jumanos were irrigating crops from springs (Balmorhea) when Spanish explored in 1583. Mexican farmers supplied nearby Fort Davis in mid-19th century. Anglo-Americans arrived in 1870s. County created 1883 from Pecos County; organized 1884; named for Confederate Col. George R. Reeves.

Ethnicity, 1990: White, 15,293 (96.5%); Black, 347 (2.2%); American Indian, 36 (0.2%); Asian, 36 (0.2%); Other, 140 (0.9%). Hispanic, 11,545 (72.8%).

Vital Statistics, 1997: Births, 212; deaths, 118; marriages, 119; divorces, 32.

Recreation: Replica of Judge Roy Bean Store, West of Pecos museum; park with javelina, prairie dogs; scenic drives; night in old Pecos, cantaloupe festival in June; water activities; state park.

Minerals: Oil, gas.

Agriculture: Fed beef, stocker, dairy cattle; cotton, cantaloupes, alfalfa, onions; all crops irrigated. Market value $42.1 million.

PECOS (11,661) county seat; food processing; produce shipping; government/services, prison; tourism; agribusiness; hospital; 16th of September fiesta.

Other towns include: **Balmorhea** (839), **Orla** (183), **Saragosa** (185), **Toyah** (117), **Toyahvale** (60), **Verhalen** (52).

The Pecos River flows through West Texas and defines an area known as the Trans-Pecos. Here in Pecos County is the Horse-head Crossing, a famous cattle-trail crossing. The Dallas Morning New file photo.

Refugio County

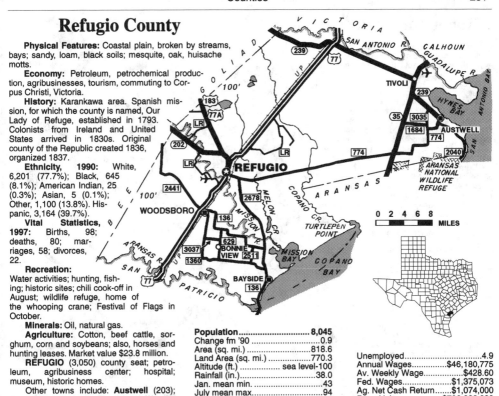

Physical Features: Coastal plain, broken by streams, bays; sandy, loam, black soils; mesquite, oak, huisache motts.

Economy: Petroleum, petrochemical production, agribusinesses, tourism, commuting to Corpus Christi, Victoria.

History: Karankawa area. Spanish mission, for which the county is named, Our Lady of Refuge, established in 1793. Colonists from Ireland and United States arrived in 1830s. Original county of the Republic created 1836, organized 1837.

Ethnicity, 1990: White, 6,201 (77.7%); Black, 645 (8.1%); American Indian, 25 (0.3%); Asian, 5 (0.1%); Other, 1,100 (13.8%). Hispanic, 3,164 (39.7%).

Vital Statistics, 1997: Births, 98; deaths, 80; marriages, 58; divorces, 22.

Recreation: Water activities; hunting, fishing; historic sites; chili cook-off in August; wildlife refuge, home of the whooping crane; Festival of Flags in October.

Minerals: Oil, natural gas.

Agriculture: Cotton, beef cattle, sorghum, corn and soybeans; also, horses and hunting leases. Market value $23.8 million.

REFUGIO (3,050) county seat; petroleum, agribusiness center; hospital; museum, historic homes.

Other towns include: **Austwell** (203); **Bayside** (451) resorts; **Tivoli** (550); **Woodsboro** (1,848) commercial center.

Population	8,045
Change fm '90	0.9
Area (sq. mi.)	818.6
Land Area (sq. mi.)	770.3
Altitude (ft.)	sea level-100
Rainfall (in.)	38.0
Jan. mean min.	43
July mean max.	94
Growing season (days)	304
Civ. Labor	2,950

Unemployed	4.9
Annual Wages	$46,180,775
Av. Weekly Wage	$428.60
Fed. Wages	$1,375,073
Ag. Net Cash Return	$1,074,000
Prop. Value	$706,023,380
Retail Sales	$47,315,147

Roberts County

Physical Features: Rolling, broken by Canadian and tributaries; Red Deer Creek; black, sandy loam, alluvial soils.

Economy: Agribusinesses; oil-field operations.

History: Apaches; pushed out by Comanches who were removed in 1874-75 by U.S. Army. Ranching began in late 1870s. County created 1876 from Bexar District; organized 1889; named for Texas leaders John S. Roberts and Gov. O.M. Roberts.

Ethnicity, 1990: White, 1,002 (97.8%); Black, 0 (0.0%); American Indian, 1 (0.1%); Asian, 2 (0.2%); Other, 20 (2.0%). Hispanic, 34 (3.3%).

Vital Statistics, 1997: Births, 3; deaths, 9; marriages, 4; divorces, 4.

Recreation: National cow-calling contest; scenic drives; museum.

Minerals: Production of gas, oil.

Agriculture: Beef cattle top producer; wheat, sorghum, corn, soybeans, hay; 6,000 acres irrigated. Market value $14 million.

MIAMI (531) county seat; ranching, oil center; some manufacturing.

Population	884
Change fm '90	-13.8
Area (sq. mi.)	924.1
Land Area (sq. mi.)	924.1
Altitude (ft.)	2,400-3,250
Rainfall (in.)	21.6
Jan. mean min.	20

July mean max.	93
Growing season (days)	192
Civ. Labor	514
Unemployed	3.7
Annual Wages	$3,989,030
Av. Weekly Wage	$399.80
Fed. Wages	$277,608

Ag. Net Cash Return	$2,295,000
Prop. Value	$270,319,415
Retail Sales	$1,791,991

For explanation of sources, abbreviations and symbols, see p. 130.

Robertson County

Physical Features: Rolling in north and east, draining to bottoms along Brazos, Navasota rivers; sandy soils, heavy in bottoms.

Economy: Agribusiness; small manufacturing; power-generating plant.

History: Tawakoni, Waco, Comanche and other tribes. Anglo-Americans arrived in 1820s. Antebellum slaveholding area. County created 1837, organized 1838, subdivided into many others later; named for pioneer Sterling Clack Robertson.

Ethnicity, 1990: White, 10,047 (64.8%); Black, 4,259 (27.5%); American Indian, 36 (0.2%); Asian, 15 (0.1%); Other, 1,154 (7.4%). Hispanic, 1,904 (12.3%).

Vital Statistics, 1997: Births, 243; deaths, 195; marriages, 94; divorces, 40.

Recreation: Hunting, fishing; historic sites; historic-homes tour; dogwood trails, wildlife preserves.

Minerals: Gas, oil, lignite coal.

Agriculture: Most revenue from beef cattle, cotton, hay, corn; 20,000 acres of cropland irrigated. Market value $31.5 million.

FRANKLIN (1,502) county seat; farm-trade center, power plants.

HEARNE (5,118) some manufacturing; sunflower festival in September.

Other towns include: **Bremond** (1,146) Polish Days in July; **Calvert** (1,498) agriculture, tourism, antiques, tour of homes in April; **Mumford** (170); **New Baden** (150); **Wheelock** (225).

Population	15,555
Change fm '90	0.3
Area (sq. mi.)	865.7
Land Area (sq. mi.)	854.6
Altitude (ft.)	250-550
Rainfall (in.)	37.5
Jan. mean min.	37
July mean max.	95

Growing season (days)	268
Civ. Labor	6,207
Unemployed	5.1
Annual Wages	$77,502,490

Av. Weekly Wage	$431.33
Fed. Wages	$1,458,169
Ag. Net Cash Return	$650,000
Prop. Value	$1,314,975,890
Retail Sales	$61,065,513

Rockwall County

Physical Features: Rolling prairie, mostly Blackland soil; Lake Ray Hubbard. Texas' smallest county.

Economy: Industrial employment in local plants and in Dallas; in Dallas metropolitan area; tourist and residential development around Lake Ray Hubbard.

History: Caddo area. Cherokees arrived in 1820s. Anglo-American settlers arrived in 1840s. County created 1873 from Kaufman; named for wall-like rock formation.

Ethnicity, 1990: White, 23,991 (93.7%); Black, 855 (3.3%); American Indian, 102 (0.4%); Asian, 164 (0.6%); Other, 492 (1.9%). Hispanic, 1,500 (5.9%).

Vital Statistics, 1997: Births, 563; deaths, 232; marriages, 1,615; divorces, 190.

Recreation: Lake activities; proximity to Dallas; unusual rock outcrop.

Minerals: Not significant.

Agriculture: Small grains, cattle, horticulture, horses, cotton. Market value $3.7 million.

ROCKWALL (15,235) county seat; varied manufacturing; hospital; youth fair in April.

Other towns include: **Fate** (461); **Heath** (3,340); **McLendon-Chisholm** (975) chili cookoff in October; **Mobile City** (207); **Royse City** (3,105) varied manufacturing, agribusiness, Funfest in October, North Texas Speedway. Part of **Rowlett** (38,203).

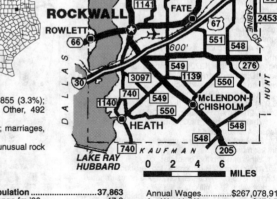

Population	37,863
Change fm '90	47.9
Area (sq. mi.)	148.6
Land Area (sq. mi.)	128.8
Altitude (ft.)	450-600
Rainfall (in.)	36.9
Jan. mean min.	33
July mean max.	96
Growing season (days)	236
Civ. Labor	21,116
Unemployed	2.1

Annual Wages	$267,078,912
Av. Weekly Wage	$474.71
Fed. Wages	$2,313,969
Ag. Net Cash Return	-$882,000
Prop. Value	$2,024,202,929
Retail Sales	$376,455,238

For explanation of sources, abbreviations and symbols, see p. 130.

Runnels County

Physical Features: West central county; level to rolling; bisected by Colorado and tributaries; sandy loam, black waxy soils.

Economy: Agribusiness; oil activity; manufacturing; government/services.

History: Spanish explorers found Jumanos in area in 1650s; later, Apaches and Comanches driven out in 1870s by U.S. military. First Anglo-Americans arrived in 1850s; Germans, Czechs around 1900. County named for planter-legislator H.G. Runnels; created 1858 from Bexar, Travis counties; organized 1880.

Ethnicity, 1990: White, 10,438 (92.4%); Black, 183 (1.6%); American Indian, 16 (0.1%); Asian, 16 (0.1%); Other, 641 (5.7%). Hispanic, 2,740 (24.3%).

Vital Statistics, 1997: Births, 166; deaths, 150; marriages, 86; divorces, 48.

Recreation: Deer and turkey hunting; O.H. Ivie Reservoir; fishing; historical markers in county.

Minerals: Oil, gas, sand, gravel.

Agriculture: Cattle, cotton, wheat, sorghum, dairy products, sheep. Market value $27.4 million.

BALLINGER (4,129) county seat; varied manufacturing; oil-field services; meat processing; fertilizer produced; Carnegie Library; hospital; Western Texas College extension; the Cross, 100-ft. tall atop hill south of city; Festival of Ethnic Cultures in April.

Other towns include: **Miles** (913); **Norton** (76); **Rowena** (466); **Wingate** (216); **Winters** (2,944) manufacturing, museum; hospital.

Population.................................. 11,672	Rainfall (in.).................................... 23.3	Annual Wages $73,290,538
Change fm '90.................................3.3	Jan. mean min.................................. 30	Av. Weekly Wage $368.74
Area (sq. mi.)........................... 1,057.2	July mean max................................. 95	Fed. Wages $1,492,431
Land Area (sq. mi.)................... 1,054.5	Growing season (days) 228	Ag. Net Cash Return............$4,384,000
Altitude (ft.)......................... 1,600-2,301	Civ. Labor.................................. 5,160	Prop. Value....................$494,457,877
	Unemployed.................................... 4.7	Retail Sales.....................$70,881,643

Rusk County

Physical Features: East Texas county on Sabine-Angelina divide; varied deep, sandy soils; over half in pines, hardwoods; lakes.

Economy: Oil, lumbering, agribusiness, government/services, tourism.

History: Caddo area. Cherokees settled in 1820s; removed in 1839. First Anglo-Americans arrived in 1829. Antebellum slaveholding area. County named for Republic, state leader Thomas J. Rusk; created from Nacogdoches County 1843.

Ethnicity, 1990: White, 33,730 (77.1%); Black, 8,984 (20.5%); American Indian, 150 (0.3%); Asian, 51 (0.1%); Other, 820 (1.9%). Hispanic, 1,736 (4.0%).

Vital Statistics, 1997: Births, 536; deaths, 557; marriages, 379; divorces, 262.

Recreation: Water sports, state park; historic homes, sites; scenic drives; marked site of East Texas Field discovery oil well; syrup festival in November.

Minerals: A leading oil county; over 1.5 billion barrels produced since 1930; natural gas, lignite, clays also produced.

Agriculture: Beef cattle top producer; dairy products, poultry, horses raised; crops include vegetables, nursery plants, hay and watermelons. Market value $29 million. Timber income substantial.

HENDERSON (11,892) county seat; center for agribusiness, oil activities; varied manufacturing; hospital; state jail.

Other towns include: **Joinerville** (140); **Laird Hill** (405); **Laneville** (200); **Minden** (350); **Mount Enterprise** (528); **New London** (1,022) site of 1937 school explosion that killed 293 students and faculty; **Overton** (2,154) oil, lumbering center, petroleum processing, A&M research center, blue grass festival in July, prison unit; **Price** (275); **Reklaw** (271); **Selman City** (271); **Tatum** (1,368, partly in Panola County). Part of **Kilgore** (11,723).

Population............................. 45,571	Civ. Labor 20,550	
Change fm '90............................. 4.2	Unemployed..............................6.0	
Area (sq. mi.).............................. 938.6	Annual Wages $325,463,351	
Land Area (sq. mi.)................... 923.6	Av. Weekly Wage $507.33	
Altitude (ft.).......................... 280-662	Fed. Wages $3,578,251	
Rainfall (in.).............................. 45.6	Ag. Net Cash Return....$2,680,000	
Jan. mean min. 33	Prop. Value...............$2,104,123,200	
July mean max. 93	Retail Sales...............$243,343,231	
Growing season (days) 250		

Sabine County

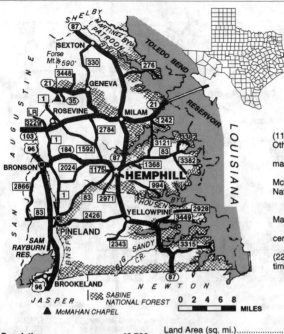

Physical Features: Eighty percent forested; 114,498 acres in national forest; Sabine River, Toledo Bend Reservoir on east; Sam Rayburn Reservoir on southwest.

Economy: Timber industries; government/ services; tourism; agriculture.

History: Caddo area. Spanish land grants in 1790s brought first Spanish and Anglo settlers. An original county, created 1836; organized 1837. Name means cypress in Spanish.

Ethnicity, 1990: White, 8,394 (87.6%); Black, 1,117 (11.7%); American Indian, 10 (0.1%); Asian, 12 (0.1%); Other, 53 (0.6%). Hispanic, 111 (1.2%).

Vital Statistics, 1997: Births, 103; deaths, 157; marriages, 86; divorces, 26.

Recreation: Lake activities; campsites; marinas; McMahan's Chapel, pioneer Protestant church; Sabine National Forest; hunting.

Minerals: Glauconite.

Agriculture: Poultry, cattle; vegetables, fruit raised. Market value $10.9 million. Significant timber industry.

HEMPHILL (1,327) county seat; timber, livestock center; tourism; hospital.

Other towns include: **Bronson** (377); **Brookeland** (220); **Geneva** (100); **Milam** (177); **Pineland** (1,265) timber processing.

July mean max.	93
Growing season (days)	236
Civ. Labor	4,018
Unemployed	9.1
Annual Wages	$54,373,126
Av. Weekly Wage	$437.06
Fed. Wages	$2,190,759
Ag. Net Cash Return	$545,000
Prop. Value	$430,948,954
Retail Sales	$43,021,069

Population	10,720	Land Area (sq. mi.)	490.3
Change fm '90	11.8	Altitude (ft.)	164-590
Area (sq. mi.)	576.5	Rainfall (in.)	52.5
		Jan. mean min.	36

San Augustine County

Physical Features: Hilly East Texas county, 80 percent forested with 66,799 acres in Angelina National Forest, 4,317 in Sabine National Forest; Sam Rayburn Reservoir; varied soils, sandy to black alluvial.

Economy: Lumbering; shipping; varied manufacturing.

History: Presence of Caddoes attracted Spanish mission in 1717. First Anglos and Indians from U.S. southern states arrived around 1800. Antebellum slaveholding area. County created and named for Mexican municipality in 1836; an original county; organized 1837.

Ethnicity, 1990: White, 5,663 (70.8%); Black, 2,244 (28.1%); American Indian, 15 (0.2%); Asian, 6 (0.1%); Other, 71 (0.9%). Hispanic, 138 (1.7%).

Vital Statistics, 1997: Births, 117; deaths, 127; marriages, 95; divorces, 21.

Recreation: Lake activities; pine fest, annual tour of homes in April, sassafras festival in October; many historic homes; tourist facilities in national forests.

Minerals: Small amount of oil.

Agriculture: Poultry, cattle, horses; watermelons, peas, corn, truck crops. Market value $25.1 million. Timber sales significant.

SAN AUGUSTINE (2,365) county seat; tourism; livestock center; varied manufacturing; Deep East Texas Electric Cooperative; lumbering; hospital; Tour of Homes.

Other towns include: **Broaddus** (210).

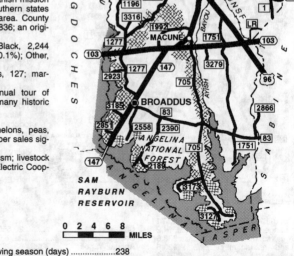

Population	8,276
Change fm '90	3.5
Area (sq. mi.)	592.2
Land Area (sq. mi.)	527.9
Altitude (ft.)	164-550
Rainfall (in.)	48.6
Jan. mean min.	35
July mean max.	93

For explanation of sources, abbreviations and symbols, see p. 130.

Growing season (days)	238		
Civ. Labor	3,398	Fed. Wages	$975,977
Unemployed	7.2	Ag. Net Cash Return	$351,000
Annual Wages	$36,048,348	Prop. Value	$349,921,261
Av. Weekly Wage	$351.99	Retail Sales	$36,624,209

San Jacinto County

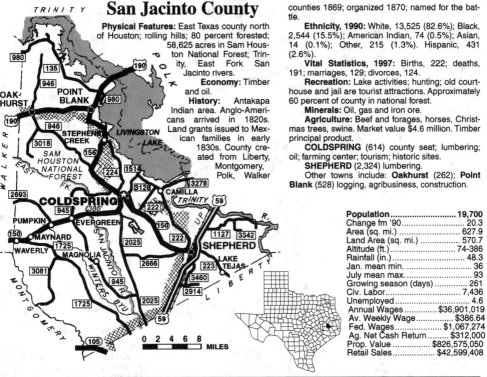

Physical Features: East Texas county north of Houston; rolling hills; 80 percent forested; 58,625 acres in Sam Houston National Forest; Trinity, East Fork San Jacinto rivers.

Economy: Timber and oil.

History: Antakapa Indian area. Anglo-Americans arrived in 1820s. Land grants issued to Mexican families in early 1830s. County created from Liberty, Montgomery, Polk, Walker

counties 1869; organized 1870; named for the battle.

Ethnicity, 1990: White, 13,525 (82.6%); Black, 2,544 (15.5%); American Indian, 74 (0.5%); Asian, 14 (0.1%); Other, 215 (1.3%). Hispanic, 431 (2.6%).

Vital Statistics, 1997: Births, 222; deaths, 191; marriages, 129; divorces, 124.

Recreation: Lake activities; hunting; old courthouse and jail are tourist attractions. Approximately 60 percent of county in national forest.

Minerals: Oil, gas and iron ore.

Agriculture: Beef and forages, horses, Christmas trees, swine. Market value $4.6 million. Timber principal product.

COLDSPRING (614) county seat; lumbering; oil; farming center; tourism; historic sites.

SHEPHERD (2,324) lumbering.

Other towns include: **Oakhurst** (262); **Point Blank** (528) logging, agribusiness, construction.

Population	19,700
Change fm '90	20.3
Area (sq. mi.)	627.9
Land Area (sq. mi.)	570.7
Altitude (ft.)	74-386
Rainfall (in.)	48.3
Jan. mean min.	36
July mean max.	93
Growing season (days)	261
Civ. Labor	7,436
Unemployed	4.6
Annual Wages	$36,901,019
Av. Weekly Wage	$386.64
Fed. Wages	$1,067,274
Ag. Net Cash Return	$312,000
Prop. Value	$826,575,050
Retail Sales	$42,599,408

San Patricio County

Population	67,205
Change fm '90	14.4
Area (sq. mi.)	707.0
Land Area (sq. mi.)	691.8
Altitude (ft.)	sea level-200
Rainfall (in.)	35.0
Jan. mean min.	43
July mean max.	94
Growing season (days)	303
Civ. Labor	29,482
Unemployed	6.9
Annual Wages	$363,904,997
Av. Weekly Wage	$491.84
Fed. Wages	$13,318,682
Ag. Net Cash Return	$14,767,000
Prop. Value	$2,556,369,132
Retail Sales	$370,101,651

Physical Features: Grassy, coastal prairie draining to Aransas, Nueces rivers, and to bays; sandy loam, clay, black loam soils; lake.

Economy: Oil, petrochemicals; agribusiness; manufacturing; tourism; naval base; in Corpus Christi metropolitan area.

History: Karankawa area. Mexican sheep herders in area before colonization. Settled by Irish families in 1830 (name is Spanish for St. Patrick). Created, named for municipality 1836; organized 1837, reorganized 1847.

Ethnicity, 1990: White, 44,834 (76.3%); Black, 968 (1.6%); American Indian, 219 (0.4%); Asian, 163 (0.3%); Other, 12,565 (21.4%). Hispanic, 29,809 (50.7%).

Vital Statistics, 1997: Births, 1,145; deaths, 504; marriages 361; divorces, 286.

Recreation: Water activities; hunting; Corpus Christi Bay; state park; Welder Wildlife Foundation and Park; shrimporee; birdwatching.

Minerals: Production of oil, gas, stone, clays, caliche.

Agriculture: Cotton, grain sorghum, beef cattle, corn. Market value $74.3 million. Fisheries income significant.

SINTON (6,856) county seat; oil, agribusiness; tourism; Go Texan Days in October.

ARANSAS PASS (7,901) shrimping, tourist center; offshore oil-well servicing; aluminum, chemical plants; hospitals.

PORTLAND (14,324) petrochemicals; many residents work in Corpus Christi, naval bases; Indian Point pier; Windfest in April.

Other towns include: **Edroy** (200); **Gregory** (2,606); **Ingleside** (7,664) naval base, chemical and manufacturing plants, ship repair, hospital, birding, Navy Days in May; **Ingleside-on-the-Bay** (526); **Lake City** (503); **Lakeside** (331); **Mathis** (5,734); **Odem** (2,661); **San Patricio** (457); **Taft** (3,755) manufacturing, processing; drug rehabilitation center, hospital; Christmas parade.

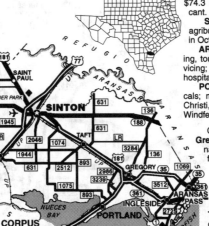

San Saba County

Physical Features: West central county; hilly, rolling; bisected by San Saba River; Colorado River on east; black, gray sandy loam, alluvial soils.

Economy: Agribusiness; stone processing; tourism; hunting leases; government/services.

History: Apaches and Comanches in area when Spanish explored. Anglo-American settlers arrived in 1850s. County created from Bexar 1856; named for river.

Ethnicity, 1990: White, 4,944 (91.5%); Black, 14 (0.3%); American Indian, 8 (0.1%); Asian, 1 (0.0%); Other, 434 (8.0%). Hispanic, 998 (18.5%).

Vital Statistics, 1997: Births, 55; deaths, 83; marriages, 36; divorces, 27.

Recreation: State park; deer hunting; historic sites; log cabin museum; fishing; scenic drives; wildflower trail; Gorman Falls; pecan festival.

Minerals: Limited stone production.

Agriculture: Cattle, poultry, sheep, goats; crops include pecans, wheat, hay, peanuts. Market value $25.1 million.

SAN SABA (2,915) county seat; claims title "Pecan Capital of the World"; stone processing; varied manufacturing; state prison unit; hospital, cow camp cookoff in May.

Other towns include: **Bend** (115); **Cherokee** (175); **Richland Springs** (323).

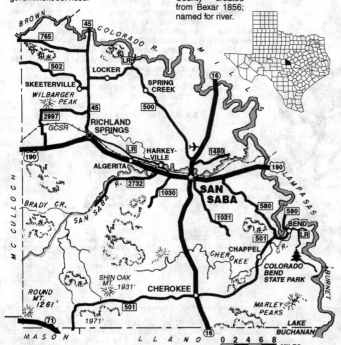

Population	5,535
Change fm '90	2.5
Area (sq. mi.)	1,138.2
Land Area (sq. mi.)	1,134.5
Altitude (ft.)	1,100-1,971
Rainfall (in.)	26.3
Jan. mean min.	32
July mean max.	96
Growing season (days)	227
Civ. Labor	2,531
Unemployed	4.3
Annual Wages	$33,201,030
Av. Weekly Wage	$341.03
Fed. Wages	$856,123
Ag. Net Cash Return	$1,613,000
Prop. Value	$504,689,353
Retail Sales	$27,158,240

Schleicher County

Physical Features: Southwestern county on edge of Edwards Plateau, broken by Devils, Concho, San Saba tributaries; part hilly; black soils.

Economy: Oil, ranching; hunting.

History: Jumanos in area in 1630s.

Later, Apaches and Comanches; removed in 1870s. Ranching began in 1870s. Census of 1890 showed third of population from Mexico. County named for Gustav Schleicher, founder of German colony; county created from Crockett 1887, organized 1901.

Ethnicity, 1990: White, 2,078 (69.5%); Black, 27 (0.9%); American Indian, 3 (0.1%); Asian, 1 (0.0%); Other, 881 (29.5%). Hispanic, 1,062 (35.5%).

Vital Statistics, 1997: Births, 38; deaths, 34; marriages, 21; divorces, 12.

Recreation: Hunting; livestock show in January, youth, open rodeos; mountain bike events; playhouse "Way off Broadway".

Minerals: Oil, natural gas.

Agriculture: Sheep, cattle, Angora and meat goats; crops include cotton, milo, hay, small grains. Market value $11.7 million. Hunting leases important.

ELDORADO (2,228) county seat; oil activities; center for livestock, woolen mill, mohair marketing; government/services, medical center.

Population	3,372
Change fm '90	12.8
Area (sq. mi.)	1,310.7
Land Area (sq. mi.)	1,310.7
Altitude (ft.)	2,100-2,600
Rainfall (in.)	19.0
Jan. mean min.	28
July mean max.	93
Growing season (days)	229
Civ. Labor	1,521
Unemployed	4.6
Annual Wages	$18,376,609
Av. Weekly Wage	$417.69
Fed. Wages	$356,701
Ag. Net Cash Return	$1,109,000
Prop. Value	$329,061,060
Retail Sales	$9,222,089

For explanation of sources, abbreviations and symbols, see p. 130.

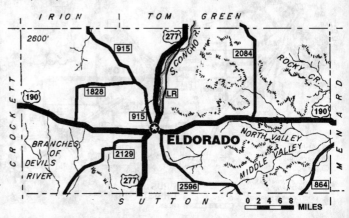

Scurry County

Physical Features: Plains county below Caprock, some hills; drained by Colorado, Brazos tributaries; lake; sandy, loam soils.

Economy: Oil production; textiles, agribusinesses, manufacturing; tourism.

History: Apaches; displaced later by Comanches who were relocated to Indian Territory in 1875. Ranching began in late 1870s. County created from Bexar 1876; organized 1884; named for Confederate Gen. W.R. Scurry.

Ethnicity, 1990: White, 14,113 (75.7%); Black, 879 (4.7%); American Indian, 62 (0.3%); Asian, 35 (0.2%); Other, 3,545 (19.0%). Hispanic, 4,454 (23.9%).

Vital Statistics, 1997: Births, 197; deaths, 157; marriages, 127; divorces, 99.

Recreation: Lake J.B. Thomas water recreation; Towle Memorial Park; museums, community theater, White Buffalo festival in October.

Minerals: Leading oil-producing county; also gas.

Agriculture: Cotton, grain sorghums, wheat, oats. Livestock includes cow/calf and stocker cattle and sheep, goats. Market value $24.3 million.

SNYDER (11,865) county seat; textiles, cotton, oil center; varied manufacturing; Western Texas (Jr.) College; hospital; prison; walking trail; Western swing days in June.

Other towns include: **Dunn** (75); **Fluvanna** (180); **Hermleigh** (200); **Ira** (250).

Population	18,720
Change fm '90	0.5
Area (sq. mi.)	907.6
Land Area (sq. mi.)	902.6
Altitude (ft.)	2,000-2,822
Rainfall (in.)	22.2
Jan. mean min.	25
July mean max.	93
Growing season (days)	214

Civ. Labor	8,232
Unemployed	5.3
Annual Wages	$164,255,186
Av. Weekly Wage	$455.14
Fed. Wages	$1,744,424
Ag. Net Cash Return	$4,852,000
Prop. Value	$812,668,198
Retail Sales	$147,192,634

Shackelford County

Physical Features: Rolling, hilly, drained by tributaries of Brazos; sandy and chocolate loam soils; lake.

Economy: Oil and ranching; some manufacturing.

History: Apaches; driven out by Comanches. First Anglo-American settlers arrived soon after establishment of military outpost in 1850s. County created from Bosque County 1858; organized 1874; named for Dr. Jack Shackelford (sometimes referred to as John), Texas Revolutionary hero.

Ethnicity, 1990: White, 3,125 (94.2%); Black, 12 (0.4%); American Indian, 9 (0.3%); Asian, 2 (0.1%); Other, 168 (5.1%). Hispanic, 272 (8.2%).

Vital Statistics, 1997: Births, 31; deaths, 36; marriages, 28; divorces, 15.

Recreation: Fort Griffin State Park, June Fandangle musical about area history; courthouse historical district; lake activities, hunting.

Minerals: Oil, natural gas.

Agriculture: Cattle, wheat, cotton, dairy products, hay, poultry. Market value $11.3 million. Mesquite firewood sold.

ALBANY (2,003) county seat; tourism; oil, agriculture center; quarter-horse breeding; hospital; historical district, Old Jail art center.

Other town: **Moran** (285).

Population	3,416
Change fm '90	3.0
Area (sq. mi.)	915.5
Land Area (sq. mi.)	914.0
Altitude (ft.)	1,200-2,000
Rainfall (in.)	28.6

Jan. mean min.	31
July mean max.	97
Growing season (days)	224
Civ. Labor	1,414
Unemployed	5.7
Annual Wages	$18,245,035

Av. Weekly Wage	$397.52
Fed. Wages	$401,698
Ag. Net Cash Return	$1,201,000
Prop. Value	$301,873,371
Retail Sales	$12,121,082

Shelby County

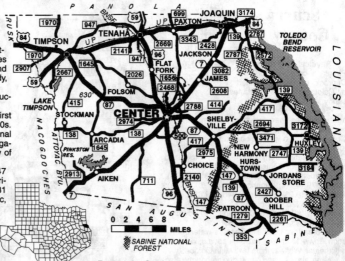

Physical Features: East Texas county; partly hills, much bottomland; well-timbered, 67,762 acres in national forest; Attoyac Bayou and Toledo Bend, other streams; sandy, clay, alluvial soils.

Economy: Broiler, egg production; cattle; timber; tourism.

History: Caddo Indian area. First Anglo-Americans settled in 1810s. Antebellum slaveholding area. Original county of Republic, created 1836; organized 1837; named for Isaac Shelby of American Revolution.

Ethnicity, 1990: White, 17,047 (77.4%); Black, 4,727 (21.5%); American Indian, 36 (0.2%); Asian, 31 (0.1%); Other, 193 (0.9%). Hispanic, 539 (2.4%).

Vital Statistics, 1997: Births, 353; deaths, 348; marriages, 216; divorces, 127.

Recreation: Toledo Bend Reservoir activities; Sabine National Forest; hunting, fishing; camping; historic sites; antique show, wolf hunt.

Minerals: Natural gas, oil.

Agriculture: A leader in broiler (first in state in inventory), egg production; cattle; hay, vegetables, watermelons. Market value $181.2 million. Timber sales significant.

CENTER (5,112) county seat; poultry, lumber processing; tourism; hospital; Shelby College Center; Poul-try Festival in October; fall fox hunt.

Other towns: Arcadia (20); **Huxley** (376); **Joaquin** (948); **Shelbyville** (215); **Tenaha** (1,113); **Timpson** (1,030) timber, poultry, livestock; Frontier Days in July.

Population	**23,265**
Change fm '90	5.6
Area (sq. mi.)	834.5
Land Area (sq. mi.)	794.2

Altitude (ft.)	174-630
Rainfall (in.)	50.2
Jan. mean min.	33
July mean max.	94
Growing season (days)	240
Civ. Labor	9,328
Unemployed	6.5
Annual Wages	$145,537,349
Av. Weekly Wage	$380.70
Fed. Wages	$2,932,533
Ag. Net Cash Return	$10,261,000
Prop. Value	$765,357,591
Retail Sales	$171,749,283

Sherman County

Physical Features: A northernmost Panhandle county; level, broken by creeks, playas; sandy to dark loam soils; underground water.

Economy: Agribusiness.

History: Apaches; pushed out by Comanches in 1700s. Comanches removed to Indian Territory in 1875. Ranching began around 1880; farming after 1900. County named for Texas Gen. Sidney Sherman; created from Bexar District 1876; organized 1889.

Ethnicity, 1990: White, 2,816 (98.5%); Black, 4 (0.1%); American Indian, 12 (0.4%); Asian, 7 (0.2%); Other, 19 (0.7%). Hispanic, 538 (18.8%).

Vital Statistics, 1997: Births, 51; deaths, 26; marriages, 26; divorces, 4.

Recreation: Depot museum; jamboree in September; pheasant hunting.

Minerals: Natural gas, oil.

Agriculture: Beef and stocker cattle important; wheat, corn, grain sorghum; swine; 145,000 acres irrigated. Market value $295 million.

STRATFORD (1,912) county seat; agribusiness center; feedlot operations; industrial authority; some manufacturing.

Texhoma (311 in Texas, pop. 746 in Oklahoma) other principal town.

Population	**3,083**
Change fm '90	7.9
Area (sq. mi.)	923.2
Land Area (sq. mi.)	923.1
Altitude (ft.)	3,200-3,800
Rainfall (in.)	17.2
Jan. mean min.	18
July mean max.	92
Growing season (days)	182
Civ. Labor	1,404
Unemployed	1.9
Annual Wages	$18,414,097
Av. Weekly Wage	$401.95
Fed. Wages	$477,151
Ag. Net Cash Return	$53,951,000
Prop. Value	$503,416,991
Retail Sales	$11,938,134

For explanation of sources, abbreviations and symbols, see p. 130.

Smith County

Physical Features: Populous East Texas county of rolling hills, many timbered; Sabine, Neches, other streams; Tyler, Palestine lakes; alluvial, gray, sandy loam, clay soils.

Economy: Agribusiness; petroleum production; distribution center; tourism; medical facilities; education; government/services.

History: Caddoes of area reduced by disease and other tribes in 1790s. Cherokees settled in 1820s; removed in 1839. In late 1820s, first Anglo-American settlers arrived. Antebellum slave-holding area. County named for Texas Revolutionary Gen. James Smith; county created 1846 from Nacogdoches.

Ethnicity, 1990: White, 113,676 (75.1%); Black, 31,572 (20.9%); American Indian, 520 (0.3%); Asian, 638 (0.4%); Other, 4,903 (3.2%). Hispanic, 8,986 (5.9%).

Vital Statistics, 1997: Births, 2,498; deaths, 1,661; marriages, 1,849; divorces, 992.

Recreation: Activities on Palestine, Tyler lakes and others; famed Rose Garden; Texas Rose Festival in October; Azalea Trail; state park; Goodman Museum; Juneteenth celebration, East Texas Fair in Sept./Oct.; collegiate events.

Minerals: Oil, gas, clays, sand and gravel, stone.

Agriculture: Horticultural crops and roses; cattle; dairy products; hay, watermelons, fruits, pecans. Market value $38.4 million. Timber sales substantial; some sawlogs, pulpwood produced.

TYLER (82,509) county seat; claims title, "Rose Capital of the Nation"; administrative center for oil production; varied manufacturing; University of Texas at Tyler, Tyler Junior College; Texas College, University of Texas Health Center; hospitals, nursing school.

Other towns include: **Arp** (977) Strawberry Festival in April; **Bullard** (1,250, part in Cherokee County); **Flint** (700); **Lindale** (2,677) rose distribution, food processing; Country Fest in October, youth rodeo in August; **New Chapel Hill** (471); **Noonday** (558) Sweet Onion Festival in June; **Troup** (1,906, part in Cherokee County); **Whitehouse** (5,064) commuters to Tyler, government/services, Yesteryear festival in June; **Winona** (604). Part of **Overton** (2,154, mostly in Rusk County).

Population	166,275
Change fm '90	9.9
Area (sq. mi.)	949.4
Land Area (sq. mi.)	928.5
Altitude (ft.)	300-631
Rainfall (in.)	43.1
Jan. mean min.	33
July mean max.	94
Growing season (days)	259
Civ. Labor	89,982
Unemployed	5.1
Annual Wages	$2,113,414,147
Av. Weekly Wage	$519.95
Fed. Wages	$39,484,433
Ag. Net Cash Return	$6,535,000
Prop. Value	$6,820,586,070
Retail Sales	$2,248,379,329

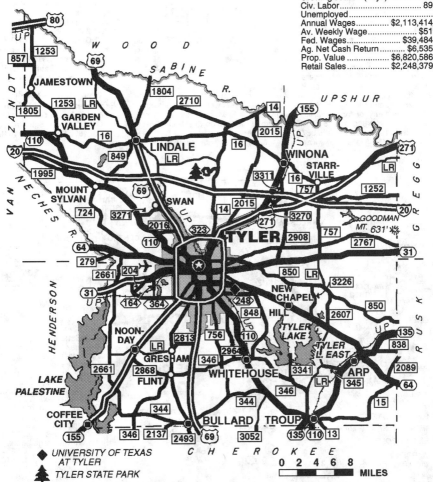

Somervell County

Physical Features: Hilly terrain southwest of Fort Worth; Brazos, Paluxy rivers; gray, dark, alluvial soils; second smallest county.

Economy: Nuclear power plant; tourism, agribusiness.

History: Wichita, Tonkawa area; Comanches later. Anglo-Americans arrived in 1850s. County created as Somerville County 1875 from Hood, Bosque. Spelling changed 1876; named for Republic of Texas Gen. Alexander Somervell.

Ethnicity, 1990: White, 4,849 (90.5%); Black, 10 (0.2%); American Indian, 34 (0.6%); Asian, 22 (0.4%); Other, 445 (8.3%). Hispanic, 749 (14.0%).

Vital Statistics, 1997: Births, 84; deaths, 62; marriages, 76; divorces, 34.

Recreation: Fishing, hunting; unique geological formations; state park; Glen Rose Big Rocks Park; Fossil Rim Wildlife Center; nature trails, museum; exposition center; Celtic festival in April; Passion Play at amphitheatre June-October.

Minerals: Sand, gravel, silica.

Agriculture: Cattle, hay, small grains, goats. Market value $2.2 million.

GLEN ROSE (2,258) county seat; tourism, farm trade center; hospital, nuclear power plant.

Other towns include: **Nemo** (56); **Rainbow** (76).

Population	**5,930**
Change fm '90	10.6
Area (sq. mi.)	191.8
Land Area (sq. mi.)	187.2
Altitude (ft.)	600-1,200
Rainfall (in.)	33.3
Jan. mean min.	30
July mean max.	98
Growing season (days)	236
Civ. Labor	1,978
Unemployed	7.6
Annual Wages	$124,795,677
Av. Weekly Wage	$704.40
Fed. Wages	$408,728
Ag. Net Cash Return	-$224,000
Prop. Value	$7,844,126,348
Retail Sales	$33,821,034

Starr County

Physical Features: Rolling, some hills; dense brush; clay, loam, sandy soils, alluvial on Rio Grande; Falcon Reservoir.

Economy: Vegetable packing, shipping, other agribusiness; oil processing; tourism; government/services.

History: Coahuiltecan Indian area. Settlers from Spanish villages that were established in 1749 on south bank began to move across river soon afterward. County named for Dr. J.H. Starr, secretary of treasury of the Republic; county created from Nueces 1848.

Ethnicity, 1990: White, 25,067 (61.9%); Black, 25 (0.1%); American Indian, 31 (0.1%); Asian, 25 (0.1%); Other, 15,370 (37.9%). Hispanic, 39,390 (97.2%).

Vital Statistics, 1997: Births, 1,382; deaths, 232; marriages, 635; divorces, 16.

Recreation: Falcon Reservoir activities; deer, white-wing dove hunting; access to Mexico; historic houses; grotto at Rio Grande City; Roma Fest in November.

Minerals: Oil, gas, sand, gravel.

Agriculture: Beef and fed cattle; vegetables, cotton, sorghum; 18,000 acres irrigated for vegetables. Market value $50.6 million.

RIO GRANDE CITY (12,358) county seat; agriculture center; food processing; exports to Mexico; hospital.

ROMA-Los Saenz (11,128) agriculture center; La Purísima Concepción Visita.

Other towns include: **Delmita** (50); **Escobares** (2,205); **Falcon Heights** (400); **La Casita-Garciasville** (1,534); **La Grulla** (1,844); **Salineno** (175); **San Isidro** (160); **Santa Elena** (64).

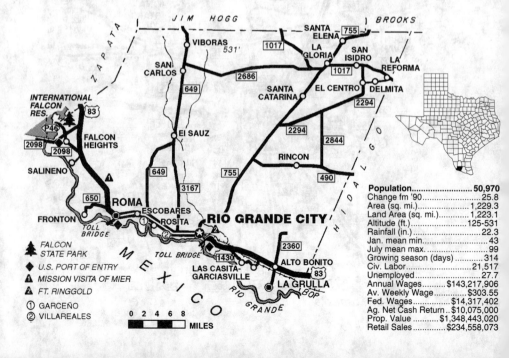

Population	**50,970**
Change fm '90	25.8
Area (sq. mi.)	1,229.3
Land Area (sq. mi.)	1,223.1
Altitude (ft.)	125-531
Rainfall (in.)	22.3
Jan. mean min.	43
July mean max.	99
Growing season (days)	314
Civ. Labor	21,517
Unemployed	27.7
Annual Wages	$143,217,906
Av. Weekly Wage	$303.55
Fed. Wages	$14,317,402
Ag. Net Cash Return	$10,075,000
Prop. Value	$1,348,443,020
Retail Sales	$234,558,073

Stephens County

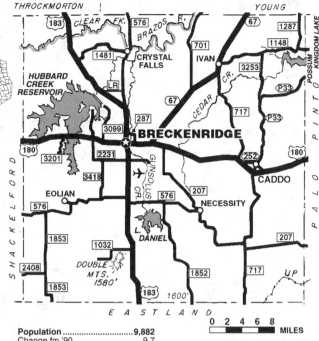

Physical Features: West central county; broken, hilly; Hubbard Creek Reservoir, Possum Kingdom, Daniel lakes; Brazos River; loam, sandy soils.

Economy: Oil, agribusinesses, recreation, some manufacturing.

History: Comanches, Tonkawas in area when Anglo-American settlement began in 1850s. County created as Buchanan 1858 from Bosque; renamed 1861 for Confederate Vice President Alexander H. Stephens; organized 1876.

Ethnicity, 1990: White, 8,187 (90.9%); Black, 252 (2.8%); American Indian, 30 (0.3%); Asian, 28 (0.3%); Other, 513 (5.7%). Hispanic, 767 (8.5%).

Vital Statistics, 1997: Births, 142; deaths, 124; marriages, 120; divorces, 58.

Recreation: Lakes activities; hunting; campsites; historical points; Swenson Museum; Sandefer Oil Museum; aviation museum; drag boat races in June.

Minerals: Oil, natural gas, stone.

Agriculture: Beef cattle, hogs, goats, sheep; wheat, oats, hay, peanuts, grain sorghums, cotton, pecans. Market value $8 million.

BRECKENRIDGE (5,808) county seat; oil; agriculture center; mobil home, aircraft parts manufacturing; petrochemical production; hospital; prison unit; arts center, library.

Other towns include: **Caddo** (64), gateway to Possum Kingdom State Park.

Population	9,882
Change fm '90	9.7
Area (sq. mi.)	921.5
Land Area (sq. mi.)	894.7
Altitude (ft.)	995-1,600
Rainfall (in.)	27.6
Jan. mean min.	28
July mean max.	97
Growing season (days)	222
Civ. Labor	4,213

Unemployed	4.6
Annual Wages	$69,693,755
Av. Weekly Wage	$406.48
Fed. Wages	$837,635
Ag. Net Cash Return	$193,000
Prop. Value	$549,591,300
Retail Sales	$69,607,328

Sterling County

Physical Features: Central prairie, surrounded by hills, broken by Concho River and tributaries; sandy to black soils.

Economy: Ranching, hunting leases, oil.

History: Ranching began in late 1870s after Comanches, Kickapoos and other tribes removed by U.S. Army. County named for buffalo hunter W.S. Sterling; created 1891 from Tom Green County.

Ethnicity, 1990: White, 1,244 (86.5%); Black, 0 (0.0%); American Indian, 9 (0.6%); Asian, 0 (0.0%); Other, 185 (12.9%). Hispanic, 366 (25.5%).

Vital Statistics, 1997: Births, 20; deaths, 12; marriages, 11; divorces, 6.

Recreation: Hunting of deer, quail, turkey, dove; junior livestock show in January.

Minerals: Oil, natural gas.

Agriculture: Beef cattle, sheep and goats; wheat, hay; about 1,000 acres irrigated. Market value $8.5 million.

STERLING CITY (1,053) county seat; farm, ranch trade center; oil-field services.

Population	1,397
Change fm '90	-2.9
Area (sq. mi.)	923.5
Land Area (sq. mi.)	923.4
Altitude (ft.)	2,100-2,700
Rainfall (in.)	20.3
Jan. mean min.	29
July mean max.	96
Growing season (days)	224
Civ. Labor	693
Unemployed	3.3
Annual Wages	$11,279,849
Av. Weekly Wage	$425.92
Fed. Wages	$151,614
Ag. Net Cash Return	$1,084,000
Prop. Value	$330,745,370
Retail Sales	$6,338,391

For explanation of sources, abbreviations and symbols, see p. 130.

Stonewall County

Physical Features: Western county on rolling plains below Caprock, bisected by Brazos forks; sandy loam, sandy, other soils; some hills.

Economy: Agribusiness, light fabrication, government/services.

History: Anglo-American ranchers arrived in 1870s after Comanches and other tribes removed by U.S. Army. German farmers settled after 1900. County named for Confederate Gen. T.J. (Stonewall) Jackson; created from Bexar 1876, organized 1888.

Ethnicity, 1990: White, 1,898 (94.3%); Black, 89 (4.4%); American Indian, 2 (0.1%); Asian, 7 (0.3%); Other, 17 (0.8%). Hispanic, 237 (11.8%).

Vital Statistics, 1997: Births, 20; deaths, 27; marriages, 14; divorces, 12.

Recreation: Deer, quail, feral hog, turkey hunting; rodeos in June, September; livestock show.

Minerals: Gypsum, gravel, oil.

Agriculture: Beef cattle, wheat, cotton, peanuts, hay. Also, grain sorghum, meat goats and swine. Market value $10.6 million.

ASPERMONT (1,006) county seat; oil field, ranching center; light fabrication; hospital; springfest; livestock show in February.

Other towns include: **Old Glory** (125), farming center; **Peacock** (125); **Swenson** (185).

Population	1,800
Change fm '90	-10.6
Area (sq. mi.)	920.2
Land Area (sq. mi.)	918.7
Altitude (ft.)	1,500-2,500

Rainfall (in.)	23.3
Jan. mean min.	27
July mean max.	97
Growing season (days)	220
Civ. Labor	783

Unemployed	6.3
Annual Wages	$12,031,527
Av. Weekly Wage	$390.95
Fed. Wages	$336,049
Ag. Net Cash Return	$2,352,000
Prop. Value	$250,332,219
Retail Sales	$10,611,798

Population	4,458
Change fm '90	7.8
Area (sq. mi.)	1,454.4
Land Area (sq. mi.)	1,453.9
Altitude (ft.)	1,900-2,500
Rainfall (in.)	22.4
Jan. mean min.	30
July mean max.	96
Growing season (days)	235
Civ. Labor	2,252
Unemployed	4.4
Annual Wages	$45,114,530
Av. Weekly Wage	$466.16
Fed. Wages	$388,876
Ag. Net Cash Return	$174,000
Prop. Value	$595,082,480
Retail Sales	$27,992,694

Sutton County

Physical Features: Southwestern county; level in west, rugged terrain in east, broken by tributaries of Devils, Llano rivers; black, red loam soils.

Economy: Oil and gas; agribusiness; hunting; tourism.

History: Lipan Apaches drove out Tonkawas in 1600s. Comanches, military outpost and disease forced Apaches south. Anglo-Americans settled in 1870s. Mexican immigration increased after 1890. County created from Crockett 1887; organized 1890;

named for Confederate officer Col. John S. Sutton.

Ethnicity, 1990: White, 3,125 (75.6%); Black, 2 (0.0%); American Indian, 16 (0.4%); Asian, 6 (0.1%); Other, 986 (23.8%). Hispanic, 1,866 (45.1%).

Vital Statistics, 1995: Births, 62; deaths, 32; marriages, 33; divorces, 16.

Recreation: Hunting; Meirs Museum; Caverns of Sonora; goat cookoff; Cinco de Mayo.

Minerals: Oil, natural gas.

Agriculture: Cattle, sheep, meat goats, Angora goats, cashmere goats, mohair. Exotic wildlife. Wheat raised for grazing, hay; minor irrigation. Market value $9.2 million. Hunting leases important.

SONORA (2,983) county seat; oil, gas production; ranching; tourism; hospital; wool, mohair show in June.

For explanation of sources, abbreviations and symbols, see p. 130.

Swisher County

Physical Features: High Plains county; level, broken by Tule Canyon and Creek; playas; large underground water supply; rich soils.

Economy: Feedlots, grain storage, other agribusinesses; varied manufacturing; tourism; prison unit.

History: Apaches; displaced by Comanches around 1700. U.S. Army removed Comanches in 1874. Ranching began in late 1870s. Farming developed after 1900. County named for J.G. Swisher of Texas Revolution; county created from Bexar, Young territories 1876; organized 1890.

Ethnicity, 1990: White, 5,702 (70.1%); Black, 340 (4.2%); American Indian, 26 (0.3%); Asian, 17 (0.2%); Other, 2,048 (25.2%). Hispanic, 2,496 (30.7%).

Vital Statistics, 1997: Births, 123; deaths, 80; marriages, 45; divorces, 30.

Recreation: Tule Lake activities; museum; county picnic in July.

Minerals: Not significant.

Agriculture: A major agricultural county. Stocker cattle, feed lots. Cotton, corn, wheat, sorghum raised. Some 150,000 acres irrigated. Market value $364.1 million.

TULIA (4,975) county seat; farming center; government/services; food processing; hospital; library, museum; prison; Sidewalk Chalk artfest in May.

Other towns include: **Happy** (629, part in Randall County), **Kress** (724).

Population 8,432	Growing season (days)..............205
Change fm '90 .... 3.7	Civ. Labor 3,598
Area (sq. mi.)......................... 900.6	Unemployed 3.9
Land Area (sq. mi.)................. 900.5	Annual Wages $45,704,182
Altitude (ft.)....................3,100-3,700	Av. Weekly Wage $379.98
Rainfall (in.)............................ 19.4	Fed. Wages $1,457,744
Jan. mean min........................... 22	Ag. Net Cash Return $54,568,000
July mean max. 91	Prop. Value $368,974,540
	Retail Sales................$43,046,743

Tarrant County

Physical Features: Part Blackland, level to rolling; drains to Trinity; Worth, Grapevine, Eagle Mountain, Benbrook lakes.

Economy: Tourism; planes, helicopters, foods, mobile homes, electronic equipment, chemicals, plastics among products of more than 1,000 factories; large federal expenditure; D/FW International Airport; economy closely associated with Dallas urban area.

History: Caddoes in area. Comanches, other tribes arrived about 1700. Anglo-Americans settled in 1840s. Named for Gen. Edward H. Tarrant, who helped drive Indians from area. County created 1849 from Navarro County; organized 1850.

Ethnicity, 1990: White, 917,501 (78.4%); Black, 140,740 (12.0%); American Indian, 5,551 (0.5%); Asian, 29,705 (2.5%); Other, 76,606 (6.5%). Hispanic, 139,879 (12.0%).

Vital Statistics, 1997: Births, 22,605; deaths, 8,917; marriages, 12,440; divorces, 7,372.

Recreation: Scott Theatre; Amon G. Carter Museum; Kimbell Art Museum; Fort Worth Art Museum; Museum of Science and History; Casa Manana; Botanic Gardens; Fort Worth Zoo; Log Cabin Village; Six Flags Over Texas at Arlington; Southwestern Exposition, Stock Show; Convention Center; Stockyards Historical District; Texas Rangers major league baseball at Arlington, other athletic events.

Minerals: Production of cement, sand, gravel, stone, gas.

Agriculture: Beef cattle primarily; some sheep, goats, dairies; hay, wheat, grain sorghum, corn, horticulture. Market value $20.9 million. Firewood marketed.

Education: Texas Christian University, University of Texas at Arlington, Texas Wesleyan University, Southwestern Baptist Theological Seminary and several other academic centers including a junior college system (three campuses).

FORT WORTH (489,277) county seat; a major mercantile, commercial and financial center; wholesale trade center for much of West Texas; airplane, helicopter and other plants.

A cultural center with renowned art museums; many conventions held in downtown center; agribusiness center for wide area with grain-storage and feed-mill operations; adjacent to D/FW International Airport; hospitals).

ARLINGTON (301,991) industrial and distribution center for automobiles, food products, electronic components, aircraft and parts, rubber and plastic products; medical center, hospitals. A tourist center with Six Flags Over Texas, the Texas Rangers baseball team, numerous restaurants; educational facilities; Scottish Highland games in June.

(Map on following page.)

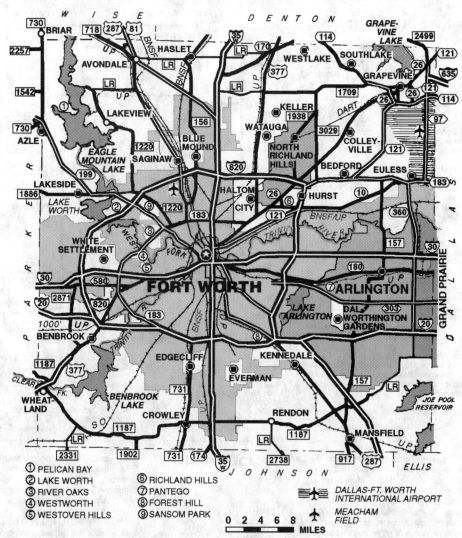

① PELICAN BAY
② LAKE WORTH
③ RIVER OAKS
④ WESTWORTH
⑤ WESTOVER HILLS
⑥ RICHLAND HILLS
⑦ PANTEGO
⑧ FOREST HILL
⑨ SANSOM PARK

✈ DALLAS-FT. WORTH INTERNATIONAL AIRPORT

✈ MEACHAM FIELD

0 2 4 6 8 ✈
MILES

Tarrant County (continued)

Other towns include: **Hurst** (39,274); **Euless** (46,632); **Bedford** (48,813); **North Richland Hills** (54,688).

Azle (10,478) varied industries, Jumpin' Jack Jamboree in October; **Benbrook** (22,902) varied manufacturing; hospitals; **Blue Mound** (2,502); **Colleyville** (18,812) major residential development, some retail, manufacturing; **Crowley** (7,478, partly in Johnson County), varied manufacturing, government/services; hospital; **Dalworthington Gardens** (2,139); **Edgecliff** (2,845); **Everman** (6,490); **Forest Hill** (12,282).

Also, **Grapevine** (38,528, partly in Denton County), varied manufacturing; near D/FW International Airport; tourist center; **Haltom City** (36,177) light manufacturing, food processing, medical center; **Haslet** (999, partly in Denton County); **Keller** (21,580) Bear Creek Park, Wild West Fest.

Also, **Kennedale** (4,865) printing manufacturing; **Lakeside** (1,004); **Lake Worth** (5,032); **Mansfield** (22,679, partly in Johnson County) varied manufacturing; hospital; Frontier Days, hometown celebration in fall; **Pantego** (2,684); **Pelican Bay** (1,499); **Rendon** (8,854); **Richland Hills** (8,730).

Also, **River Oaks** (7,179); **Saginaw** (10,578); **Sansom Park** (4,093); **Southlake** (13,440) retail, IBM marketing/education center; **Watauga** (22,682); **Westlake** (231, partly in Denton County); **Westover Hills** (720); **Westworth Village** (2,485); **White Settlement** (15,994) near aircraft manufacturing, museum, historical sites; hospital; industrial park. Part of **Grand Prairie**.

Population	1,340,037
Change fm '90	14.5
Area (sq. mi.)	897.5
Land Area (sq. mi.)	863.5
Altitude (ft.)	450-1,000
Rainfall (in.)	31.3
Jan. mean min.	35
July mean max.	96
Growing season (days)	230
Civ. Labor	763,211
Unemployed	3.3
Annual Wages	$20,146,624,919
Av. Weekly Wage	$607.61
Fed. Wages	$664,327,448
Ag. Net Cash Return	$448,000
Prop. Value	$62,007,345,357
Retail Sales	$16,879,818,372

Taylor County

Physical Features: Prairies, with Callahan Divide, draining to Colorado tributaries, Brazos forks; Lakes Abilene, Kirby; mostly loam soils.

Economy: Dyess Air Force Base, feedlots, agribusinesses, diversified manufacturing and education; government/services.

History: Comanches in area about 1700. Anglo-American settlers arrived in the 1870s. Named for Alamo heroes Edward, James and George Taylor, brothers; county created from Bexar, Travis 1858; organized 1878.

Ethnicity, 1990: White, 100,237 (83.8%); Black, 7,547 (6.3%); American Indian, 450 (0.4%); Asian, 1,449 (1.2%); Other, 9,972 (8.3%). Hispanic, 17,511 (14.6%).

Vital Statistics, 1997: Births, 2,027; deaths, 1,068; marriages, 1,390; divorces, 891.

Recreation: Abilene State Park; lake activities; Nelson Park Zoo; Texas Cowboy Reunion, West Texas Fair; Buffalo Gap historical tour and art festival; rodeo, college events.

Minerals: Oil, natural gas, stone, caliche, clays, sand and gravel.

Agriculture: Wheat; cattle, fed, cow/calf, and stocker; cotton; milo. Market value $52.9 million.

Education: Abilene Christian University, Hardin-Simmons University, McMurry University, Cisco Junior College branch.

ABILENE (117,111, part in Jones County) county seat; distribution center; plants make a variety of products; meat, dairy processing; oil-field service center; hospitals; Abilene State School; West Texas

Rehabilitation Center; Fort Phantom Hill (in Jones County).

Other communities include: **Buffalo Gap** (520) historic sites; **Impact** (23); **Lawn** (370); **Merkel** (2,557) agribusiness center, clothing manufacturing, oil-field services; **Ovalo** (225); **Potosi** (1,501); **Trent** (318); **Tuscola** (634); **Tye** (1,211).

Population	127,877
Change fm '90	6.9
Area (sq. mi.)	919.3
Land Area (sq. mi.)	915.7
Altitude (ft.)	1,670-2,500
Rainfall (in.)	24.4
Jan. mean min.	31
July mean max.	95
Growing season (days)	225
Civ. Labor	61,603
Unemployed	3.5
Annual Wages	$1,165,861,547
Av. Weekly Wage	$421.97
Fed. Wages	$44,434,397
Ag. Net Cash Return	$6,129,000
Prop. Value	$4,311,823,623
Retail Sales	$1,452,165,905

For explanation of sources, abbreviations and symbols, see p. 130.

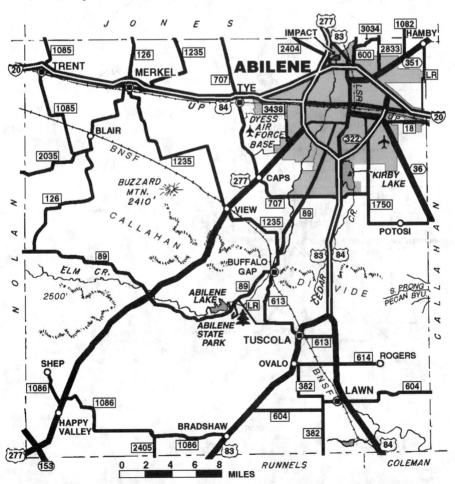

Terrell County

Physical Features: Trans-Pecos southwestern county; semi-mountainous, many canyons; rocky, limestone soils.

Economy: Ranching; some tourism; oil and natural gas exploration; hunting leases.

History: Coahuiltecans, Jumanos and other tribes left many pictographs in area caves. Sheep ranching began in 1880s. Named for Confederate Gen. A.W. Terrell; county created 1905 from Pecos County.

Ethnicity, 1990: White, 1,189 (84.3%); Black, 1 (0.1%); American Indian, 5 (0.4%); Asian, 2 (0.1%); Other, 213 (15.1%). Hispanic, 751 (53.3%).

Vital Statistics, 1997: Births, 12; deaths, 13; marriages, 4; divorces, 1.

Recreation: Hunting, especially white-tailed, mule deer; lower canyons of Rio Grande accessible by boat; varied wildlife; Cinco de Mayo, Prickly Pear Pachanga in October.

Minerals: Gas, oil, limestone.

Agriculture: Sheep, wool; Angora goats, mohair; beef cattle. Also, pecans and Bermuda grass. Market value $4.6 million.

SANDERSON (876) county seat; ranching, petroleum operations center. Other town: **Dryden** (13).

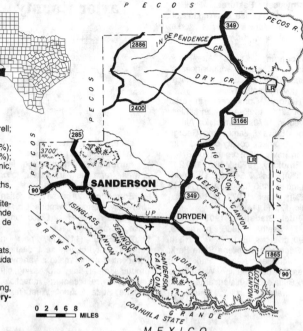

Population 1,163		
Change fm '90 ....-17.5		
Area (sq. mi.) 2,357.9	July mean max. 92	Av. Weekly Wage $357.77
Land Area (sq. mi.) 2,357.9	Growing season (days) 237	Fed. Wages $551,000
Altitude (ft.) 1,400-3,700	Civ. Labor 476	Ag. Net Cash Return $347,000
Rainfall (in.)................................14.3	Unemployed 5.0	Prop. Value $344,235,736
Jan. mean min. 29	Annual Wages $4,532,568	Retail Sales $2,754,989

Terry County

Physical Features: Western county on South Plains, broken by draws, playas; sandy, sandy loam, loam soils.

Economy: Agribusiness, petroleum, government/services, trade.

History: Comanches removed in 1870s by U.S. Army. Ranching developed in 1890s; farming after 1900. Oil discovered in 1940. County named for head of famed Texas Ranger troop, Col. B.F. Terry. County created from Bexar District 1876; organized 1904.

Ethnicity, 1990: White, 10,202 (77.2%); Black, 449 (3.4%); American Indian, 38 (0.3%); Asian, 28 (0.2%); Other, 2,501 (18.9%). Hispanic, 5,194 (39.3%).

Vital Statistics, 1997: Births, 196; deaths, 119; marriages, 185; divorces, 80.

Recreation: Museum; harvest festival in October; brisket and bean cook-off in April.

Minerals: Oil, gas, caliche.

Agriculture: Cotton is principal crop; peanuts, sorghum, watermelon, wheat, cucumbers; half of cropland irrigated. Beef cattle, swine, sheep, goats and horses. Market value $92.3 million.

BROWNFIELD (9,193) county seat; oil-field services; agribusiness; minerals processed; hospital; prison.

Other towns include: **Meadow** (613); **Tokio** (60); **Wellman** (257).

Population 13,295		
Change fm '90..............................0.6	Growing season (days)...............206	
Area (sq. mi.) 890.8	Civ. Labor 5,527	
Land Area (sq. mi.).................889.9	Unemployed................................7.6	
Altitude (ft.).......................3,100-3,600	Annual Wages $88,558,889	
Rainfall (in.) 19.0	Av. Weekly Wage $424.17	
Jan. mean min............................24	Fed. Wages $1,289,112	Prop. Value $653,002,663
July mean max. 93	Ag. Net Cash Return.....$26,596,000	Retail Sales $98,844,258

Throckmorton County

Physical Features: North Central county southwest of Wichita Falls; rolling, between Brazos forks; red to black soils.

Economy: Oil, agri-business, hunting leases.

History: Site of Comanche Indian Reservation 1854-59. Ranching developed after Civil War. County named for Dr. W.E. Throckmorton, father of Gov. J.W. Throckmorton; county created from Fannin 1858; organized 1879.

Ethnicity, 1990: White, 1,778 (94.6%); Black, 0 (0.0%); American Indian, 4 (0.2%); Asian, 8 (0.4%); Other, 90 (4.8%). Hispanic, 136 (7.2%).

Vital Statistics, 1997: Births, 16; deaths, 23; marriages, 16; divorces, 4.

Recreation: Hunting, fishing; historic sites include Camp Cooper, site of former Comanche reservation; restored ranch home, Miller's Creek Reservoir; Pioneer Day in June.

Minerals: Natural gas, oil.

Agriculture: Beef cattle; crops include wheat, oats, cotton, hay, sorghum. Market value $20.5 million. Mesquite firewood sold.

THROCKMORTON (902) county seat; varied manufacturing; oil-field services; hospital.

Other towns include: **Elbert** (150), **Woodson** (205).

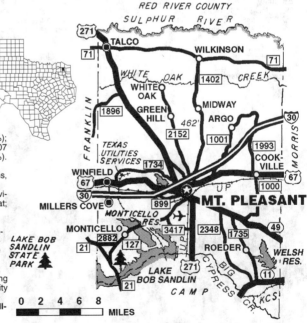

Population	1,626	Jan. mean min.	27	Av. Weekly Wage	$331.89
Change fm '90	-13.5	July mean max.	96	Fed. Wages	$396,248
Area (sq. mi.)	915.5	Growing season (days)	220	Ag. Net Cash Return	$2,659,000
Land Area (sq. mi.)	912.4	Civ. Labor	736	Prop. Value	$218,732,558
Altitude (ft.)	1,140-1,710	Unemployed	2.7	Retail Sales	$5,018,116
Rainfall (in.)	27.1	Annual Wages	$7,715,225		

Titus County

Physical Features: East Texas county; hilly, timbered; drains to Big Cypress Creek, Sulphur River.

Economy: Agribusinesses, varied manufacturing; lignite mining and power generation; tourism.

History: Caddo area. Cherokees and other tribes settled in 1820s. Anglo-American settlers arrived in 1840s. Named for pioneer settler A.J. Titus; county created from Bowie, Red River counties 1846.

Ethnicity, 1990: White, 18,664 (77.7%); Black, 3,229 (13.4%); American Indian, 107 (0.4%); Asian, 27 (0.1%); Other, 1,982 (8.3%). Hispanic, 2,556 (10.6%).

Vital Statistics, 1997: Births, 500; deaths, 287; marriages, 299; divorces, 57.

Recreation: Fishing, hunting; lake activities; state park; railroad museum; riverboat; flower gardens.

Minerals: Oil, gas, lignite.

Agriculture: Poultry, among leading counties in broilers; cattle. Crops include hay, watermelons, grain sorghum, corn. Market value $41.4 million.

MOUNT PLEASANT (13,595) county seat; tourism; varied manufacturing; food-processing plants; hospital; Northeast Texas Community College; WranglerFest in October.

Other towns include: **Cookville** (105), **Millers Cove** (94), **Talco** (597), **Winfield** (368).

Population	26,199	July mean max.	94	Ag. Net Cash Return	$1,167,000
Change fm '90	9.1	Growing season (days)	233	Prop. Value	$1,788,841,806
Area (sq. mi.)	425.6	Civ. Labor	12,834	Retail Sales	$320,050,887
Land Area (sq. mi.)	410.6	Unemployed	6.5		
Altitude (ft.)	300-462	Annual Wages	$341,916,910		
Rainfall (in.)	46.8	Av. Weekly Wage	$456.35	*For explanation of sources, abbreviations*	
Jan. mean min.	29	Fed. Wages	$4,984,288	*and symbols, see p. 130.*	

Tom Green County

- ↟ GOODFELLOW
  AIR FORCE BASE
- ◆ AGRICULTURE RESEARCH &
  WILDLIFE MANAGEMENT AREA

0 2 4 6 8
|———|———| MILES

Physical Features: West central county of plains, rolling hills, broken by Concho forks; loams in basin, stony hillsides; lakes.

Economy: "Sheep and Wool Capital"; varied agribusinesses, manufacturing; trade center for area, education center, medical center; government/services.

History: Jumano Indians attracted Spanish missionaries around 1630. Comanches controlled area when U.S. military established outposts in 1850s. Anglo-American settlement occurred after Civil War. County created from Bexar District 1874, named for Gen. Tom Green of Texas Revolution; organized 1875; 12 other counties created from this original area.

Ethnicity, 1990: White, 79,533 (80.8%); Black, 4,136 (4.2%); American Indian, 373 (0.4%); Asian, 998 (1.0%); Other, 13,418 (13.6%). Hispanic, 25,501 (25.9%).

Vital Statistics, 1997: Births, 1,542; deaths, 955; marriages, 1,121; divorces, 687.

Recreation: Water sports; hunting;

Fort Concho Museum; urban, collegiate activities; roping fiesta, June Fiesta del Concho; March rodeo; minor league hockey team.

Minerals: Oil, natural gas.

Agriculture: Cattle; cotton; sheep (first in number of sheep sold); goats; dairy products. Also, sorghum, wheat, swine, horses. About 30,000 acres irrigated. Market value $85.9 million.

SAN ANGELO (90,935) county seat; manufacturing of medical devices, denim jeans; distribution center; varied agribusiness; oil and gas; hospitals; Angelo State University, A&M extension center.

Other towns include: **Carlsbad** (100); **Christoval** (216); **Knickerbocker** (50); **Mereta** (75); **Vancourt**

(125); **Veribest** (40); **Wall** (200); **Water Valley** (120).

Population	**105,578**
Change fm '90	7.2
Area (sq. mi.)	1,540.5
Land Area (sq. mi.)	1,522.2
Altitude (ft.)	1,700-2,600
Rainfall (in.)	20.5
Jan. mean min.	31
July mean max.	96
Growing season (days)	235
Civ. Labor	52,439
Unemployed	4.1
Annual Wages	$980,915,476
Av. Weekly Wage	$439.10
Fed. Wages	$46,381,661
Ag. Net Cash Return	$18,235,000
Prop. Value	$3,188,069,673
Retail Sales	$1,011,631,404

San Angelo has built walkways along the Concho River. The Dallas Morning News file photo.

Physical Features: Central county of scenic hills, broken by Colorado River and lakes; cedars, pecans, other trees; diverse soils, mineral deposits.

Economy: Education, state government, tourism, research and industry; conventions.

History: Tonkawa and Lipan Apache area; Comanches, Kiowas arrived about 1700. Spanish missions from East Texas temporarily relocated near Barton Springs in 1730 before removing to San Antonio. Anglo-Americans arrived in early 1830s. County created 1840, when Austin became Republic's capital, from Bastrop County; organized 1843; named for Alamo commander Col. William B. Travis; many other counties created from its original area.

Ethnicity, 1990: White, 422,749 (73.3%); Black, 63,173 (11.0%); American Indian, 2,089 (0.4%); Asian, 16,497 (2.9%); Other, 71,899 (12.5%). Hispanic, 121,689 (21.1%).

Vital Statistics, 1997: Births, 11,934; deaths, 3,736; marriages, 6,895; divorces, 3,429.

Recreation: Colorado River lakes; hunting, fishing;

Travis County

McKinney Falls State Park; Austin Aqua Festival; collegiate, metropolitan, governmental events; official buildings and historic sites; museums; Sixth St. restoration area; scenic drives; city parks.

Minerals: Production of lime, stone, sand, gravel, oil and gas.

Agriculture: Cattle, nursery crops, hogs; sorghum, corn, cotton, small grains, pecans. Market value $16.4 million.

Education: University of Texas main campus; St. Edward's University, Maryhill College, Concordia Lutheran College, Huston-Tillotson College, Austin Community College, Episcopal and Presbyterian seminaries; state schools and institutions for blind, deaf, mental illnesses.

AUSTIN (608,053) county seat and state capital; state and federal payrolls; IRS center; a leading convention, tourist city; Lyndon B. Johnson Library; research, high-tech industries; hospitals, including state institutions; popular retirement area.

Other towns include: **Bee Cave**

(309); **Briarcliff** (376); **Creedmoor** (224); **Del Valle** (2,476); **Jonestown** (1,314); **Lago Vista** (2,526); **Lakeway** (5,494); **Manchaca** (2,259); **Manor** (1,230); **McNeil** (70); **Mustang Ridge** (786); **Pflugerville** (11,263) high-tech industries, agriculture, government/services, Deutchenfest in May; **Rollingwood** (1,632); **San Leanna** (385); **Sunset Valley** (376); **Village of the Hills** (1,100); **West Lake Hills** (2,809).

Population	**699,981**
Change fm '90	21.4
Area (sq. mi.)	1,022.1
Land Area (sq. mi.)	989.4
Altitude (ft.)	400-1,330
Rainfall (in.)	31.9
Jan. mean min.	39
July mean max.	95
Growing season (days)	270
Civ. Labor	454,920
Unemployed	2.8
Annual Wages	$17,462,219,113
Av. Weekly Wage	$654.25
Fed. Wages	$339,479,519
Ag. Net Cash Return	$1,661,000
Prop. Value	$41,168,920,176
Retail Sales	$10,750,285,133

For explanation of sources, abbreviations and symbols, see p. 130.

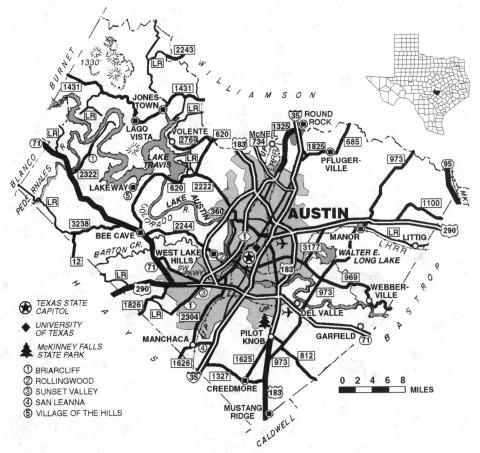

TEXAS STATE CAPITOL

UNIVERSITY OF TEXAS

McKINNEY FALLS STATE PARK

① BRIARCLIFF
② ROLLINGWOOD
③ SUNSET VALLEY
④ SAN LEANNA
⑤ VILLAGE OF THE HILLS

Trinity County

Physical Features: Heavily forested East Texas county of hills, between Neches and Trinity (Livingston Lake) rivers; rich alluvial soils, sandy upland; 67,910 acres in national forest.

Economy: Forestry, tourism, cattle; government/services.

History: Caddoes, reduced by disease in late 1700s. Kickapoo, Alabama, Coushatta in area when Anglo-Americans settled in 1840s. Named for river; county created 1850 out of Houston County.

Ethnicity, 1990: White, 9,619 (84.0%); Black, 1,645 (14.4%); American Indian, 24 (0.2%); Asian, 21 (0.2%); Other, 136 (1.2%). Hispanic, 272 (2.4%).

Vital Statistics, 1997: Births, 167; deaths, 184; marriages, 123; divorces, 51.

Recreation: Lake activities; fishing, hiking, hunting; Davy Crockett National Forest; historic sites; Timber Festival in March; Scottish festival at Thanksgiving.

Minerals: Limited oil, gas, lignite, sand and gravel.

Agriculture: Beef cattle, horses, hogs, meat goats; crops include hay, vegetables. Market value $6.1 million. Timber sales significant.

GROVETON (1,172) county seat; gateway to national forest recreation areas; lumber center; petroleum processing.

TRINITY (2,887) steel fabrication; forest-industries center; government/services; hospital; near Livingston Lake.

Other towns include: **Apple Springs** (185); **Centralia** (53); **Pennington** (67); **Sebastopol** (120) historic town; **Woodlake** (98).

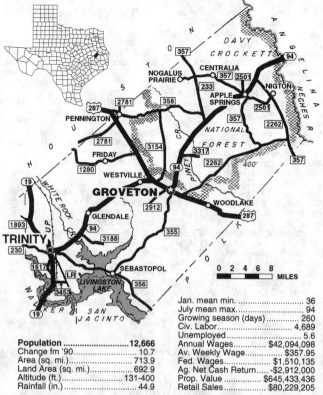

Jan. mean min.	36
July mean max.	94
Growing season (days)	260
Civ. Labor.	4,689
Unemployed.	5.6
Annual Wages.	$42,094,098
Av. Weekly Wage.	$357.95
Fed. Wages.	$1,510,135
Ag. Net Cash Return.	-$2,912,000
Prop. Value	$645,433,436
Retail Sales	$80,229,205

Population	**12,666**
Change fm '90	10.7
Area (sq. mi.)	713.9
Land Area (sq. mi.)	692.9
Altitude (ft.)	131-400
Rainfall (in.)	44.9

Tyler County

Physical Features: Hilly East Texas county; densely timbered; drains to Neches River; B.A. Steinhagen Lake; Big Thicket is unique plant and animal area.

Economy: Lumbering; government/services, some manufacturing; tourism, hunting leases.

History: Caddoan area. Cherokees, Alabama and Coushatta pushed into area from U.S. South in 1820s. Anglo-Americans settled in 1830s. Named for U.S. President John Tyler; county created 1846 from Liberty.

Ethnicity, 1990: White, 14,550 (87.4%); Black, 1,994 (12.0%); American Indian, 46 (0.3%); Asian, 12 (0.1%); Other, 44 (0.3%). Hispanic, 177 (1.1%).

Vital Statistics, 1997: Births, 206; deaths, 248; marriages, 162; divorces, 128.

Recreation: Big Thicket National Preserve; Heritage Village; lake activities; Allan Shivers Museum; state forest; historic sites; dogwood festival; rodeo, frontier frolics in September; gospel music fest in June.

Minerals: Oil, natural gas.

Agriculture: Cattle, hay, nursery crops, blueberries, horses. Market value $3.1 million. Timber sales significant.

WOODVILLE (4,033) county seat; lumber, cattle market; varied manufacturing; tourism; hospital; prison unit.

Other towns include: **Chester** (342) **Colmesneil** (629), **Doucette** (131), **Fred** (239), **Hillister** (200), **Spurger** (472), **Warren** (304).

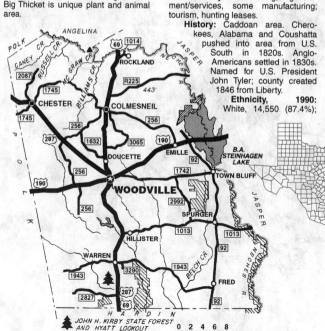

Population	**19,799**
Change fm '90	18.9
Area (sq. mi.)	935.7
Land Area (sq. mi.)	923.0
Altitude (ft.)	50-443
Rainfall (in.)	54.3
Jan. mean min.	38
July mean max.	93
Growing season (days)	241
Civ. Labor.	6,342
Unemployed.	8.4
Annual Wages.	$71,092,735
Av. Weekly Wage.	$378.66
Fed. Wages.	$1,566,093
Ag. Net Cash Return.	-$1,296,000
Prop. Value	$881,598,433
Retail Sales	$99,568,810

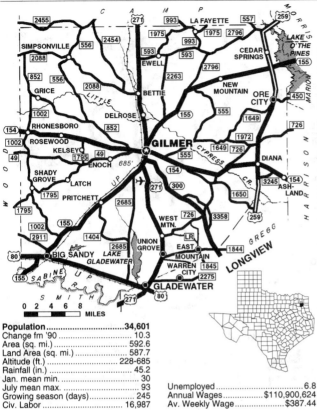

Upshur County

Physical Features: East Texas county; rolling to hilly, over half forested; drains to Sabine River, Little Cypress Creek, Lake O' the Pines, Lake Gladewater.

Economy: Manufacturing, agribusinesses, government/services, petroleum products and lumber mill; many residents work at area plants.

History: Caddoes; reduced by epidemics in 1700s. Cherokees in area in 1820s. Anglo-American settlement in mid-1830s. County created from Harrison, Nacogdoches counties 1846; named for U.S. Secretary of State A.P. Upshur.

Ethnicity, 1990: White, 27,076 (86.3%); Black, 3,881 (12.4%); American Indian, 121 (0.4%); Asian, 29 (0.1%); Other, 263 (0.8%). Hispanic, 641 (2.0%).

Vital Statistics, 1997: Births, 429; deaths, 405; marriages, 276; divorces, 256.

Recreation: Scenic trails; hunting, fishing; rose festival, pecan festival, East Texas Yamboree in October.

Minerals: Oil, gas, sand, gravel.

Agriculture: Poultry (among leading broiler counties), dairies, beef cattle; vegetable crops, hay, peaches raised. Market value $30.9 million. Timber a major product.

GILMER (5,376) county seat; varied manufacturing; timber, ceramics produced; vegetable processing; medical center; civic center.

Other towns include: **Big Sandy** (1,294); **Diana** (585); **East Mountain** (927); **Ore City** (1,039); **Union Grove** (303).

Population	34,601
Change fm '90	10.3
Area (sq. mi.)	592.6
Land Area (sq. mi.)	587.7
Altitude (ft.)	228-685
Rainfall (in.)	45.2
Jan. mean min.	30
July mean max.	93
Growing season (days)	245
Civ. Labor	16,987
Unemployed	6.8
Annual Wages	$110,900,624
Av. Weekly Wage	$387.44
Fed. Wages	$1,865,949
Ag. Net Cash Return	$335,000
Prop. Value	$1,393,557,484
Retail Sales	$184,601,465

Upton County

Physical Features: Western county; north flat, south rolling, hilly; limestone, sandy loam soils, drains to creeks.

Economy: Oil, electric power plant, cotton, ranching.

History: Apache and Comanche area until tribes removed by U.S. Army in 1870s. Sheep and cattle ranching developed in 1880s. Oil discovered in 1925. County created in 1887 from Tom Green County; organized 1910; name honors brothers John and William Upton, Confederate colonels.

Ethnicity, 1990: White, 3,487 (78.4%); Black, 94 (2.1%); American Indian, 20 (0.4%); Asian, 2 (0.0%); Other, 844 (19.0%). Hispanic, 1,666 (37.5%).

Vital Statistics, 1997: Births, 59; deaths, 21; marriages, 24; divorces, 10.

Recreation: Historic sites, Mendoza Trail Museum; scenic areas; chili cookoff in October, Christmas bazaar.

Minerals: Oil, natural gas.

Agriculture: Cotton; cattle; pecans, mostly irrigated; sheep, goats, Barbados sheep. Market value $7.7 million.

RANKIN (899) county seat, oil, ranching; Barbados cookoff on Memorial Day weekend.

McCAMEY (2,227) oil, ranching; hospital; pecan show. Other town: **Midkiff** (98).

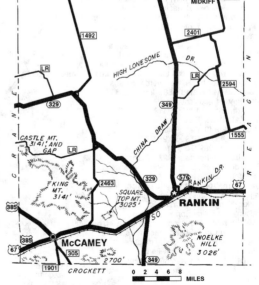

Population	4,030
Change fm '90	-9.4
Area (sq. mi.)	1,241.8
Land Area (sq. mi.)	1,241.8
Altitude (ft.)	2,400-3,141
Rainfall (in.)	14.3
Jan. mean min.	31
July mean max.	95
Growing season (days)	232
Civ. Labor	1,596
Unemployed	6.0
Annual Wages	$33,355,393
Av. Weekly Wage	$517.72
Fed. Wages	$203,246
Ag. Net Cash Return	$1,503,000
Prop. Value	$792,391,479
Retail Sales	$14,555,366

For explanation of sources, abbreviations and symbols, see p. 130.

Uvalde County

Physical Features: Edwards Plateau, rolling hills below escarpment; spring-fed Sabinal, Frio, Leona, Nueces rivers; cypress, cedar, other trees; unique maple groves.

Economy: Agribusinesses; light manufacturing; tourism; hunting leases.

History: Spanish mission Nuestra Señora de la Candelaria founded in 1762 for Lipan Apaches near present-day Montell; Comanches harassed mission. U.S. military outpost established in 1849. County created from Bexar 1850; re-created, organized 1856; named for 1778 governor of Coahuila, Juan de Ugalde, with name Anglicized.

Ethnicity, 1990: White, 15,078 (64.6%); Black, 47 (0.2%); American Indian, 49 (0.2%); Asian, 70 (0.3%); Other, 8,096 (34.7%). Hispanic, 14,104 (60.4%).

Vital Statistics, 1997: Births, 427; deaths, 239; marriages, 226; divorces, 98.

Recreation: Deer, turkey hunting area; Garner State Park; water activities on rivers; John Nance Garner Museum; Uvalde Memorial Park; scenic trails; historic sites; recreational homes.

Minerals: Asphalt, stone, sand and gravel.

Agriculture: Beef cattle, vegetables, corn, cotton, grain sorghum; sheep, goats; hay, wheat. Substantial irrigation. Market value $68.5 million.

UVALDE (16,051) county seat; varied manufacturing; vegetable, wool, mohair processing; junior college; A&M research center; hospital.

Sabinal (1,704) farm, ranch center; gateway to Frio and Sabinal canyons; tourist, retirement area.

Other towns include: **Concan** (225); **Knippa** (360); **Utopia** (360), resort.

Population	**25,071**
Change fm '90	7.4
Area (sq. mi.)	1,558.6
Land Area (sq. mi.)	1,556.6
Altitude (ft.)	699-2,000

Rainfall (in.)	24.8
Jan. mean min.	36
July mean max.	96
Growing season (days)	255
Civ. Labor	11,401
Unemployed	10.1
Annual Wages	$169,990,767
Av. Weekly Wage	$353.27
Fed. Wages	$5,898,842
Ag. Net Cash Return	$14,423,000
Prop. Value	$1,306,602,485
Retail Sales	$214,635,033

Val Verde County

Physical Features: Southwestern county bordering Mexico, rolling, hilly; brushy; Devils, Pecos rivers, Amistad Reservoir; limestone, alluvial soils.

Economy: Agribusiness; tourism; area trade center; large military, other federal expenditures; hunting leases.

History: Apaches, Coahuiltecans, Jumanos present when Spanish explored area 1535. Comanches arrived later. U.S. military outposts established in 1850s to protect settlers. Only county named for Civil War battle; Val Verde means green valley. Created 1885 from Crockett, Kinney, Pecos counties.

Ethnicity, 1990: White, 26,694 (68.9%); Black, 757 (2.0%); American Indian, 126 (0.3%); Asian, 244 (0.6%); Other, 10,900 (28.2%). Hispanic, 27,299 (70.5%).

Vital Statistics, 1997: Births, 913; deaths, 272; marriages, 495; divorces, 163.

Recreation: Gateway to Mexico; deer hunting, fishing; Amistad lake activities; two state parks; Langtry restoration of Judge Roy Bean's saloon; San Felipe Springs; winery.

Minerals: Production sand and gravel, gas, oil.

Agriculture: Sheep (first in state in value of sales), Angora goats, cattle, meat goats; minor irrigation. Market value $19.5 million.

DEL RIO (34,167) county seat; government/services, including federal agencies and military; tourism and trade with Mexico; varied manufacturing, twin plants; hospital; extension colleges; Fiesta de Amistad in October.

Laughlin Air Force Base (2,952).

Other towns include: **Comstock** (375); **Langtry** (145).

Population	**42,813**
Change fm '90	10.6
Area (sq. mi.)	3,232.6
Land Area (sq. mi.)	3,170.7
Altitude (ft.)	900-2,300
Rainfall (in.)	18.2
Jan. mean min.	39
July mean max.	96
Growing season (days)	300

Civ. Labor	17,725
Unemployed	9.6
Annual Wages	$207,874,603
Av. Weekly Wage	$354.10
Fed. Wages	$58,485,993
Ag. Net Cash Return	-$293,000
Prop. Value	$1,005,716,508
Retail Sales	$323,274,701

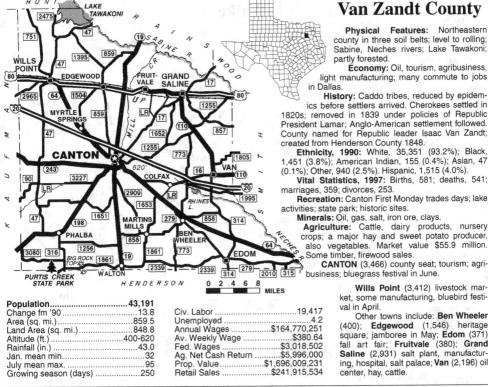

Van Zandt County

Physical Features: Northeastern county in three soil belts; level to rolling; Sabine, Neches rivers; Lake Tawakoni; partly forested.

Economy: Oil, tourism, agribusiness, light manufacturing; many commute to jobs in Dallas.

History: Caddo tribes, reduced by epidemics before settlers arrived. Cherokees settled in 1820s; removed in 1839 under policies of Republic President Lamar; Anglo-American settlement followed. County named for Republic leader Isaac Van Zandt; created from Henderson County 1848.

Ethnicity, 1990: White, 35,351 (93.2%); Black, 1,451 (3.8%); American Indian, 155 (0.4%); Asian, 47 (0.1%); Other, 940 (2.5%). Hispanic, 1,515 (4.0%).

Vital Statistics, 1997: Births, 581; deaths, 541; marriages, 359; divorces, 253.

Recreation: Canton First Monday trades days; lake activities; state park; historic sites.

Minerals: Oil, gas, salt, iron ore, clays.

Agriculture: Cattle, dairy products, nursery crops; a major hay and sweet potato producer, also vegetables. Market value $55.9 million. Some timber, firewood sales.

CANTON (3,466) county seat; tourism; agribusiness; bluegrass festival in June.

Wills Point (3,412) livestock market, some manufacturing, bluebird festival in April.

Other towns include: **Ben Wheeler** (400); **Edgewood** (1,546) heritage square; jamboree in May; **Edom** (371) fall art fair; **Fruitvale** (380); **Grand Saline** (2,931) salt plant, manufacturing, hospital, salt palace; **Van** (2,196) oil center, hay, cattle.

Population	43,191
Change fm '90	13.8
Area (sq. mi.)	859.5
Land Area (sq. mi.)	848.8
Altitude (ft.)	400-620
Rainfall (in.)	43.0
Jan. mean min.	32
July mean max.	95
Growing season (days)	250
Civ. Labor	19,417
Unemployed	4.2
Annual Wages	$164,770,251
Av. Weekly Wage	$380.64
Fed. Wages	$3,018,502
Ag. Net Cash Return	$5,996,000
Prop. Value	$1,696,009,231
Retail Sales	$241,915,534

Victoria County

Physical Features: South Central county of rolling prairies, intersected by many streams; sandy loams, clays, alluvial soils.

Economy: Petrochemical plants, government services, oil, manufacturing, agribusiness, tourism.

History: Karankawas, other tribes in area when Spanish explored in 1528. Comanches, Tawakonis arrived later. French Fort St. Louis on Garcitas Creek 1685-87. Spanish ranching developed in 1750s. Anglo-Americans arrived after 1836. An original county, created 1836 from Mexican municipality named for President Guadalupe Victoria of Mexico.

Ethnicity, 1990: White, 59,251 (79.7%); Black, 4,906 (6.6%); American Indian, 208 (0.3%); Asian, 257 (0.3%); Other, 9,739 (13.1%). Hispanic, 25,372 (34.1%).

Vital Statistics, 1997: Births, 1,297; deaths, 663; marriages, 806; divorces, 371.

Recreation: Fishing, hunting; saltwater activities; historic homes, sites; riverside park, Coleto Creek Reservoir and park; recreational park; zoo; Czech Heritage Festival in October.

Minerals: Oil, gas, sand, gravel.

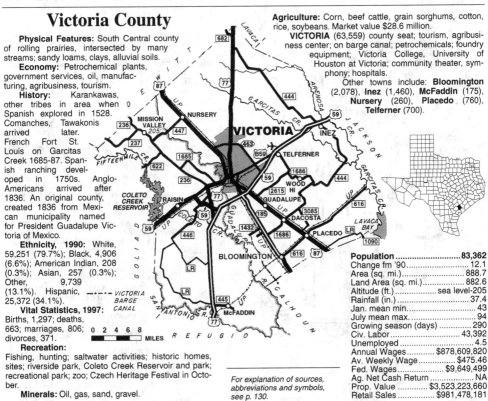

Agriculture: Corn, beef cattle, grain sorghums, cotton, rice, soybeans. Market value $28.6 million.

VICTORIA (63,559) county seat; tourism, agribusiness center; on barge canal; petrochemicals; foundry equipment; Victoria College, University of Houston at Victoria; community theater, symphony; hospitals.

Other towns include: **Bloomington** (2,078), **Inez** (1,460), **McFaddin** (175), **Nursery** (260), **Placedo** (760), **Telferner** (700).

Population	83,362
Change fm '90	12.1
Area (sq. mi.)	888.7
Land Area (sq. mi.)	882.6
Altitude (ft.)	sea level-205
Rainfall (in.)	37.4
Jan. mean min.	43
July mean max.	94
Growing season (days)	290
Civ. Labor	43,392
Unemployed	4.5
Annual Wages	$878,609,820
Av. Weekly Wage	$475.46
Fed. Wages	$9,649,499
Ag. Net Cash Return	NA
Prop. Value	$3,523,223,660
Retail Sales	$981,478,181

For explanation of sources, abbreviations and symbols, see p. 130.

Physical Features: Southeastern county north of Houston of rolling hills; more than 70 percent forested; national forest; San Jacinto, Trinity rivers.

Economy: State employment in prison system, education; tourism; timber; beef cattle.

History: Coahuiltecans, Bidais in area when Spanish explored around 1690. Later, area became trading ground for many Indian tribes. Anglo-Americans settled in 1830s. Antebellum slaveholding area. County created 1846 from Montgomery County; first named for U.S. Secretary of Treasury R.J. Walker; renamed 1863 for Texas Ranger Capt. S.H. Walker.

Ethnicity, 1990: White, 34,946 (68.6%); Black, 12,334 (24.2%); American Indian, 187 (0.4%); Asian, 323 (0.6%); Other, 3,127 (6.1%). Hispanic, 5,493 (10.8%).

Vital Statistics, 1997: Births, 598; deaths, 447; marriages, 491; divorces, 214.

Recreation: Fishing, hunting; lake activities; Sam Houston Museum, homes, grave; prison museum; other historic sites; state park; Sam Houston National Forest; Cinco de Mayo celebration, Sam Houston folk festival in April.

Minerals: Clays, natural gas, oil, sand and gravel, stone.

Agriculture: Cattle, nursery plants, poultry, cotton, hay. Market value $10.9 million. Timber sales substantial; Christmas trees.

HUNTSVILLE (35,222) county seat; Texas Department of Criminal Justice headquarters, prisons; Sam Houston State University, forest products; museum; varied manufacturing; hospital.

Other towns include: **Dodge** (150), **New Waverly** (1,070), **Riverside** (522).

Walker County

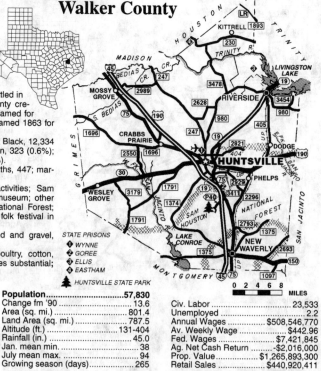

STATE PRISONS
◊ WYNNE
◊ GOREE
◊ ELLIS
◊ EASTHAM

🌲 HUNTSVILLE STATE PARK

Population	57,830
Change fm '90	13.6
Area (sq. mi.)	801.4
Land Area (sq. mi.)	787.5
Altitude (ft.)	131-404
Rainfall (in.)	45.0
Jan. mean min.	38
July mean max.	94
Growing season (days)	265

Civ. Labor	23,533
Unemployed	2.2
Annual Wages	$508,546,770
Av. Weekly Wage	$442.96
Fed. Wages	$7,421,845
Ag. Net Cash Return	-$2,016,000
Prop. Value	$1,265,893,300
Retail Sales	$440,920,411

Waller County

Physical Features: Southeastern county near Houston on rolling prairie; drains to Brazos; alluvial soils; about 20 percent forested.

Economy: Agribusiness, manufacturing, education, county part of Houston metropolitan area; oil.

History: Bidais Indians reduced to about 100 when Anglo-Americans settled in 1820s. Antebellum slaveholding area. County named for Edwin Waller, Republic leader; created 1873 from Austin, Grimes counties.

Ethnicity, 1990: White, 12,987 (55.5%); Black, 8,796 (37.6%); American Indian, 28 (0.1%); Asian, 69 (0.3%); Other, 1,510 (6.5%). Hispanic, 2,592 (11.1%).

Vital Statistics, 1997: Births, 457; deaths, 237; marriages, 267; divorces, 119.

Recreation: Fishing, hunting; historic sites; museum.

Minerals: Oil, gas, sand, gravel.

Agriculture: Cattle, rice, nursery crops, aquaculture, corn; also, hogs, poultry, horses, goats; hay, watermelons. 10,000 acres irrigated. Market value $29.1 million. Some timber marketed.

HEMPSTEAD (4,173) county seat; varied manufacturing; commuting to Houston; agribusiness center, large vegetable market; watermelon fest in July.

Prairie View (4,427) home of Prairie View A&M University.

Other towns include: **Brookshire** (3,968), **Pattison** (423), **Pine Island** (699), **Waller** (1,997, partly in Harris County). Also, **Katy** (11,175, partly in Harris and Fort Bend Counties).

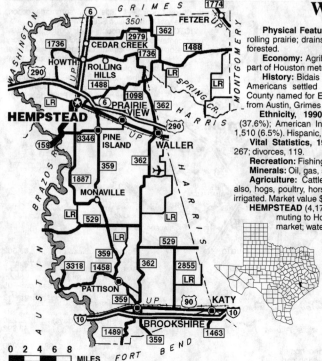

Population	29,183
Change fm '90	24.8
Area (sq. mi.)	518.4

Land Area (sq. mi.)	513.6
Altitude (ft.)	100-350
Rainfall (in.)	38.2

Jan. mean min.	38
July mean max.	95
Growing season (days)	283
Civ. Labor	12,599
Unemployed	4.3
Annual Wages	$202,893,234
Av. Weekly Wage	$436.22
Fed. Wages	$1,851,585
Ag. Net Cash Return	-$322,000
Prop. Value	$7,193,493,030
Retail Sales	$487,717,818

Ward County

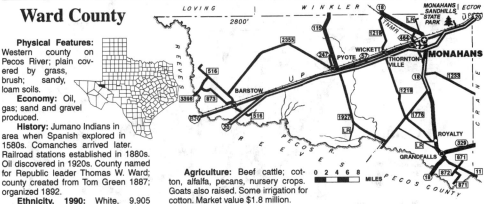

Physical Features: Western county on Pecos River; plain covered by grass, brush; sandy, loam soils.

Economy: Oil, gas; sand and gravel produced.

History: Jumano Indians in area when Spanish explored in 1580s. Comanches arrived later. Railroad stations established in 1880s. Oil discovered in 1920s. County named for Republic leader Thomas W. Ward; county created from Tom Green 1887; organized 1892.

Ethnicity, 1990: White, 9,905 (75.5%); Black, 457 (3.5%); American Indian, 75 (0.6%); Asian, 25 (0.2%); Other, 2,653 (20.2%). Hispanic, 4,830 (36.8%).

Vital Statistics, 1997: Births, 174; deaths, 112; marriages, 105; divorces, 81.

Recreation: Sandhills state park; museum; Pyote Rattlesnake museum; Million Barrel museum; county park; stagecoach festival in August.

Minerals: Oil, gas, caliche, sand, gravel.

Agriculture: Beef cattle; cotton, alfalfa, pecans, nursery crops. Goats also raised. Some irrigation for cotton. Market value $1.8 million.

MONAHANS (7,641) county seat; center for oil, gas; sand, gravel; agribusiness; tourism; hospital; fajita festival in May.

Other towns: **Barstow** (567); **Grandfalls** (627); **Pyote** (408) West Texas Children's Home; **Royalty** (29); **Thorntonville** (770); **Wickett** (527).

Population **12,761**
Change fm '90 .... -2.7
Area (sq. mi.) 835.7
Land Area (sq. mi.) 835.6

Altitude (ft.) 2,400-2,800
Rainfall (in.) 12.7
Jan. mean min. 27
July mean max. 96
Growing season (days) 223
Civ. Labor 4,715
Unemployed 7.9
Annual Wages $92,902,198
Av. Weekly Wage $470.96
Fed. Wages $977,111
Ag. Net Cash Return $335,000
Prop. Value $819,287,428
Retail Sales $75,382,388

Washington County

Physical Features: Southeastern county in Brazos valley; rolling prairie of sandy loam, alluvial soils.

Economy: Agribusinesses, oil, tourism; manufacturing; government/services.

History: Coahuiltecan tribes and Tonkawas in area when Anglo-American settlers arrived in 1821. Antebellum slaveholding area. Germans arrived around 1870. County named for George Washington; an original county, created 1836, organized 1837.

Ethnicity, 1990: White, 19,782 (75.6%); Black, 5,463 (20.9%); American Indian, 46 (0.2%); Asian, 186 (0.7%); Other, 677 (2.6%). Hispanic, 1,158 (4.4%).

Vital Statistics, 1997: Births, 361; deaths, 336; marriages, 233; divorces, 113.

Recreation: Many historic sites; Washington-on-the-Brazos State Park; Texas Baptist Historical Museum; Star of Republic Museum; Somerville Lake; fishing, hunting; antique rose nursery, spring fling.

Minerals: Oil, gas and stone.

For explanation of sources, abbreviations and symbols, see p. 130.

Agriculture: Beef cattle, poultry, dairy products, hogs, horses; hay, corn, sorghum, cotton, small grains, nursery crops. Market value $26.1 million.

BRENHAM (13,796) county seat; cotton processing; varied manufacturing including ceramics, mattresses, computers, Blue Bell creamery; wholesale distribution center; tourism; Blinn College, Brenham State School; Maifest.

Other towns include: **Burton** (326) national landmark cotton gin; **Chappell Hill** (600) historic homes; **Washington** (265), site of signing of Texas Declaration of Independence.

Population **30,030**
Change fm '90 .... 14.8
Area (sq. mi.) 621.3
Land Area (sq. mi.) 609.3
Altitude (ft.) 150-505
Rainfall (in.) 41.4
Jan. mean min. 41
July mean max. 96
Growing season (days) 277
Civ. Labor 14,882
Unemployed 2.5
Annual Wages $289,908,740
Av. Weekly Wage $432.61
Fed. Wages $2,483,821
Ag. Net Cash Return ...... -$778,000
Prop. Value $1,798,941,040
Retail Sales $262,294,506

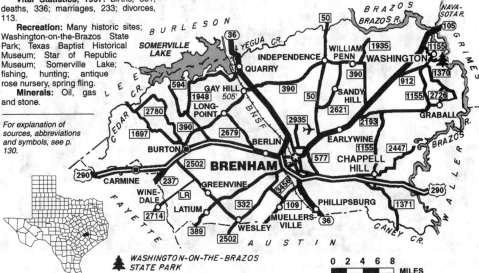

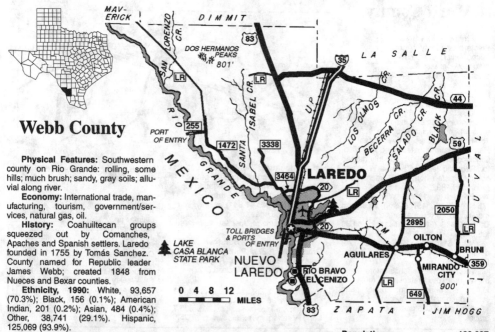

Webb County

Physical Features: Southwestern county on Rio Grande: rolling, some hills; much brush; sandy, gray soils; alluvial along river.

Economy: International trade, manufacturing, tourism, government/services, natural gas, oil.

History: Coahuiltecan groups squeezed out by Comanches, Apaches and Spanish settlers. Laredo founded in 1755 by Tomás Sanchez. County named for Republic leader James Webb; created 1848 from Nueces and Bexar counties.

Ethnicity, 1990: White, 93,657 (70.3%); Black, 156 (0.1%); American Indian, 201 (0.2%); Asian, 484 (0.4%); Other, 38,741 (29.1%). Hispanic, 125,069 (93.9%).

Vital Statistics, 1997: Births, 5,143; deaths, 905; marriages, 2,195; divorces, 402.

Recreation: Major tourist gateway to Mexico; top hunting, fishing; Lake Casa Blanca State Park, water recreation; art festival; Washington's Birthday celebration; historic sites; museum; Fort McIntosh.

Minerals: Natural gas, oil, coal, caliche, stone, sand and gravel.

Agriculture: Cattle, vegetables, horses, hay, nursery crops, melons, goats. About 4,500 acres irrigated. Market value $28.2 million. Mesquite sold.

LAREDO (175,400) county seat; international trade; retail; tourism; manufacturing; meat packing; rail; highway gateway to Mexico; agribusiness; junior college, Texas A&M International University; hospitals; "El Grito" on Sept. 15.

Other towns include: **Bruni** (581); **El Cenizo** (1,775); **Mirando City** (707); **Oilton** (585); **Rio Bravo** (4,131).

For explanation of sources, abbreviations and symbols, see p. 130.

Population	189,037
Change fm '90	41.9
Area (sq. mi.)	3,375.6
Land Area (sq. mi.)	3,357.0
Altitude (ft.)	300-900
Rainfall (in.)	21.4
Jan. mean min.	43
July mean max.	99
Growing season (days)	322
Civ. Labor	72,969
Unemployed	9.2
Annual Wages	$1,319,590,362
Av. Weekly Wage	$412.14
Fed. Wages	$87,340,768
Ag. Net Cash Return	-$346,000
Prop. Value	$5,861,543,552
Retail Sales	$1,800,683,411

Trucks line up as they wait at the border crossing in Laredo. The Dallas Morning News file photo.

Wharton County

Physical Features: Southeastern county near Houston on prairie; bisected by Colorado River; alluvial, black, sandy loam soils.

Economy: Oil, sulphur, other minerals; agribusiness, hunting leases, varied manufacturing.

History: Karankawas in area until 1840s. Anglo-American colonists settled in 1823. Czechs, Germans arrived in 1880s. Mexican migration increased after 1950. County named for John A. and William H. Wharton, brothers active in the Texas Revolution; created 1846 from Jackson, Matagorda counties.

Ethnicity, 1990: White, 29,127 (72.9%); Black, 6,308 (15.8%); American Indian, 38 (0.1%); Asian, 131 (0.3%); Other, 4,351 (10.9%). Hispanic, 10,103 (25.3%).

Vital Statistics, 1997: Births, 582; deaths, 380; marriages, 282; divorces, 151.

Recreation: Waterfowl hunting, fishing, big-game, birding; art and historical museums; riverfront park in Wharton; historic sites; WhartonFest on Colorado.

Population	41,289
Change fm '90	3.3
Area (sq. mi.)	1,094.5
Land Area (sq. mi.)	1,090.2
Altitude (ft.)	50-150
Rainfall (in.)	42.3
Jan. mean min.	41
July mean max.	92
Growing season (days)	266
Civ. Labor	18,966
Unemployed	5.6
Annual Wages	$312,619,565
Av. Weekly Wage	$416.41
Fed. Wages	$3,584,791
Ag. Net Cash Return	NA
Prop. Value	$1,920,999,622
Retail Sales	$358,768,061

Minerals: Oil, gas.

Agriculture: Leading rice-producing county; other crops are cotton, milo, corn, grain sorghum, soybeans; about 130,000 acres irrigated, mostly rice. Also, eggs, turfgrass, beef cattle. Market value $133.6 million.

WHARTON (9,926) county seat; mineral, produce processing; hospitals; Wharton County Junior College.

EL CAMPO (10,665) rice processing, aluminum processing, manufacturing, storage; plastic, styrofoam processing; wholesale nursery; hospital; polka expo on weekend before Thanksgiving.

Other towns include: **Boling-lago** (1,175); **Danevang** (61); **East Bernard** (1,718) agribusiness, varied manufacturing; **Egypt** (26); **Glen Flora** (210); **Hungerford** (178); **Lane City** (111); **Lissie** (70); **Louise** (310); **Pierce** (49).

Wheeler County

Physical Features: Panhandle county adjoining Oklahoma. Plain, on edge of Caprock; Red River, Sweetwater Creek; some canyons; red sandy loam, black clay soils.

Economy: Oil, agribusinesses, tourism.

History: Apaches, displaced by Kiowas, Comanches around 1700. Military outpost established in 1875 after Indians forced into Oklahoma. Ranching began in late 1870s. Oil boom in 1920s. County named for pioneer jurist R.T. Wheeler; county created from Bexar, Young districts 1876; organized 1879.

Ethnicity, 1990: White, 5,424 (92.3%); Black, 154 (2.6%); American Indian, 42 (0.7%); Asian, 23 (0.4%); Other, 236 (4.0%). Hispanic, 378 (6.4%).

Vital Statistics, 1997: Births, 48; deaths, 78; marriages, 132; divorces, 29.

Recreation: Pioneer West museum at Shamrock; historic sites; Old Mobeetie trading post, Fort Elliott; ostrich depot.

Minerals: Oil, natural gas.

Agriculture: Fed beef, cow-calf and stocker cattle, swine, horses; crops include wheat, grain sorghum, cotton. Market value $80.7 million.

WHEELER (1,339) county seat; agribusiness; petroleum center; tourism; slaughter plant; library.

SHAMROCK (2,228) tourism; agribusiness; hospital; library; St. Patrick's Day event; Octoberfest.

Other towns include: **Allison** (135); **Briscoe** (135); **Mobeetie** (171).

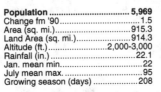

Population	5,969
Change fm '90	1.5
Area (sq. mi.)	915.3
Land Area (sq. mi.)	914.3
Altitude (ft.)	2,000-3,000
Rainfall (in.)	22.1
Jan. mean min.	22
July mean max.	95
Growing season (days)	208
Civ. Labor	2,792
Unemployed	3.4
Annual Wages	$34,604,444
Av. Weekly Wage	$355.52
Fed. Wages	$874,512
Ag. Net Cash Return	$45,126,000
Prop. Value	$569,945,180
Retail Sales	$34,382,445

Wichita County

Physical Features: North central county in prairie bordering Oklahoma; drained by Red, Wichita rivers; lakes; sandy, loam soils.

Economy: Retail trade center for large area; air base; government, manufacturing, oil, medical services and agribusiness.

History: Wichitas and other Caddoan tribes in area in 1700s; Comanches, Apaches also present until 1850s. Ango-American settlement increased after 1870. County named for Indian tribe; created from Young Territory 1858; organized 1882.

Ethnicity, 1990: White, 102,427 (83.7%); Black, 11,221 (9.2%); American Indian, 903 (0.7%); Asian, 1,851 (1.5%); Other, 5,976 (4.9%). Hispanic, 10,555 (8.6%).

Vital Statistics, 1997: Births, 1,876; deaths, 1,196; marriages, 2,478; divorces, 806.

Recreation: Metropolitan events; museums; historic Kell House; Oil Bowl football game in August; collegiate activities; water sports on lakes.

Minerals: Oil, natural gas, sand, gravel, stone.

Agriculture: Stocker, cow-calf production important; wheat, cotton; 2,500 acres irrigated for cotton and coastal Bermuda. Market value $21.9 million.

WICHITA FALLS (98,161) county seat; distribution center for large area in Texas, Oklahoma; varied manufacturing; oil-field services; hospitals; Midwestern State University, vocational-technical training center; Wichita Falls State Hospital; hiking trails, major bicycle race in summer; **Sheppard Air Force Base.**

Other cities include: **Burkburnett** (10,875) some manufacturing; **Electra** (3,270); **Iowa Park** (6,864) some manufacturing, clinic; **Kamay** (642); **Pleasant Valley** (431).

Population	**127,975**
Change fm '90	4.6
Area (sq. mi.)	632.9
Land Area (sq. mi.)	627.7
Altitude (ft.)	954-1,225
Rainfall (in.)	28.9
Jan. mean min.	28
July mean max.	97
Growing season (days)	229
Civ. Labor	61,817
Unemployed	4.8
Annual Wages	$1,223,545,854
Av. Weekly Wage	$436.73
Fed. Wages	$74,092,509
Ag. Net Cash Return	$2,358,000
Prop. Value	$4,295,580,647
Retail Sales	$1,203,738,790

For explanation of sources, abbreviations and symbols, see p. 130.

Wilbarger County

Physical Features: Gently rolling prairie draining to Red, Pease rivers, tributaries; sandy, loam, waxy soils; Santa Rosa Lake.

Economy: Government/services, agribusinesses.

History: Anglo-American settlement developed after removal of Comanches into Indian Territory in 1875. County named for pioneers Josiah and Mathias Wilbarger; created from Bexar District 1858; organized 1881.

Ethnicity, 1990: White, 12,010 (79.4%); Black, 1,349 (8.9%); American Indian, 80 (0.5%); Asian, 82 (0.5%); Other, 1,600 (10.6%). Hispanic, 2,185 (14.5%).

Vital Statistics, 1997: Births, 187; deaths, 169; marriages, 340; divorces, 51.

Recreation: Doan's Crossing, on route of cattle drives; other historic sites; Red River Valley Museum; Santa Rosa roundup in May; hunting, fishing.

Minerals: Oil, natural gas.

Agriculture: Wheat, alfalfa, beef cattle, cotton, peanuts, watermelons; 25,000 acres irrigated. Market value $33.2 million.

VERNON (12,012) county seat; government/services; agribusiness; varied manufacturing; electricity-generating plant; junior college; mental health center, hospitals; prison; downtown antiques, crafts mall.

Other towns include: **Harrold** (320); **Lockett** (200); A&M extension center; **Odell** (131); **Oklaunion** (138).

Population	15,349
Change fm '90	1.5
Area (sq. mi.)	978.1
Land Area (sq. mi.)	971.1
Altitude (ft.)	1,099-1,400
Rainfall (in.)	25.7
Jan. mean min.	25
July mean max.	97
Growing season (days)	221
Civ. Labor	7,096
Unemployed	3.4
Annual Wages	$128,610,433
Av. Weekly Wage	$403.35
Fed. Wages	$2,848,305
Ag. Net Cash Return	$3,662,000
Prop. Value	$853,426,794
Retail Sales	$99,748,034

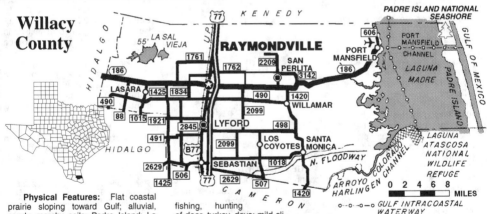

Willacy County

Physical Features: Flat coastal prairie sloping toward Gulf; alluvial, sandy, marshy soils; Padre Island; La Sal Vieja, salt lake; wildlife refuge.

Economy: Oil, agribusinesses; tourism; shipping.

History: Coahuiltecan area when Spanish explored in 1500s. Spanish ranching began in 1790s. County named for Texas legislator John G. Willacy; created 1911 from Cameron, Hidalgo counties; reorganized 1921.

Ethnicity, 1990: White, 13,820 (78.1%); Black, 79 (0.4%); American Indian, 29 (0.2%); Asian, 13 (0.1%); Other, 3,764 (21.3%). Hispanic, 14,937 (84.4%).

Vital Statistics, 1997: Births, 404; deaths, 116; marriages, 141; divorces, 60.

Recreation: Fresh and saltwater fishing, hunting of deer, turkey, dove; mild climate attracts many winter tourists; Port Mansfield fishing tournament.

Minerals: Oil, natural gas.

Agriculture: Cotton, sorghum, corn, vegetables, sugar cane; 20 percent of cropland irrigated. Livestock includes cattle, horses, goats, hogs. Market value $49.5 million.

RAYMONDVILLE (9,247) county seat; agribusiness, oil center; clothing manufacturing; food processing, shipping; tourist center; museum; hospital; enterprise zone; prison unit.

Other towns include: **Lasara** (100); **Lyford** (1,992); **Port Mansfield** (731), popular fishing port; shrimp processing; fishing tournament in late July; **San Perlita** (602); **Sebastian** (1,732).

Population	19,217
Change fm '90	8.5
Area (sq. mi.)	784.2
Land Area (sq. mi.)	596.7
Altitude (ft.)	sea level-55
Rainfall (in.)	27.6
Jan. mean min.	46
July mean max.	96
Growing season (days)	331
Civ. Labor	7,352
Unemployed	21.0
Annual Wages	$69,164,746
Av. Weekly Wage	$354.51
Fed. Wages	$1,278,510
Ag. Net Cash Return	$11,752,000
Prop. Value	$790,785,807
Retail Sales	$65,161,627

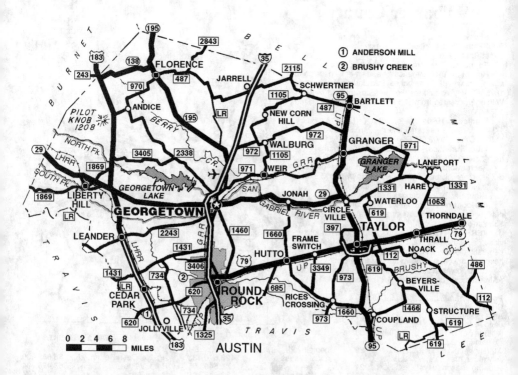

① ANDERSON MILL
② BRUSHY CREEK

Williamson County

Physical Features: Central county near Austin. Level to rolling; mostly Blackland soil, some loam, sand; drained by San Gabriel River and tributaries.

Economy: Agribusinesses, varied manufacturing, education center, government/services; the county is part of Austin metropolitan area.

History: Tonkawa area; later, other tribes. Comanches raided until 1860s. Anglo-American settlement began in late 1830s. County named for Robert M. Williamson, pioneer leader; created from Milam and organized in 1848.

Ethnicity, 1990: White, 121,914 (87.4%); Black, 6,861 (4.9%); American Indian, 508 (0.4%); Asian, 1,846 (1.3%); Other, 8,422 (6.0%). Hispanic, 20,004 (14.3%).

Vital Statistics, 1997: Births, 3,411; deaths, 1,025; marriages, 1,827; divorces, 883.

Recreation: Lake recreation; Inner Space Cavern; historic sites; deer hunting, fishing; Gov. Dan Moody Museum at Taylor; San Gabriel Park; old settlers park; walking tours, rattlesnake sacking, barbecue cookoff, frontier days in summer.

Minerals: Building stone, sand and gravel.

Agriculture: Beef cattle, sorghum, cotton, corn, wheat. Market value $48.1 million.

GEORGETOWN (26,576) county seat; agribusiness, manufacturing, education, tourism, mining; hospital; Southwestern University; Mayfair; Christmas Stroll.

ROUND ROCK (53,427, partly in Travis County) varied manufacturing; tourism and distribution center; hospital; Texas Baptist Children's Home.

Taylor (14,722) agribusiness, publishing center; varied manufacturing including cottonseed and meat processing; hospital; Temple Junior College extension.

Other towns include: **Bartlett** (1,696, partly in Bell County) first rural electrification in nation in 1933, clinic; library; **Brushy Creek** (8,011); **Cedar Park** (13,659) varied manufacturing, Cedar Chopper festival in June; **Coupland** (135), **Florence** (1,171).

Also, **Granger** (1,472); **Hutto** (827); **Jarrell** (410); **Jollyville** (20,718); **Leander** (6,598); **Liberty Hill** (1,500), artisans center; **Schwertner** (150); **Thrall** (796); **Walburg** (250); **Weir** (300).

Also, the residential community of **Anderson Mill** (12,959), which extends from Travis County.

Population	**212,893**
Change fm '90	52.6
Area (sq. mi.)	1,136.4
Land Area (sq. mi.)	1,124.4
Altitude (ft.)	400-1,208
Rainfall (in.)	34.4
Jan. mean min.	34
July mean max.	96
Growing season (days)	258
Civ. Labor	133,173
Unemployed	1.9
Annual Wages	$1,345,009,404
Av. Weekly Wage	$476.42
Fed. Wages	$13,315,140
Ag. Net Cash Return	$5,772,000
Prop. Value	$13,761,089,554
Retail Sales	$2,115,471,756

For explanation of sources, abbreviations and symbols, see p. 130.

Wilson County

Physical Features: South central county on rolling plains; mostly sandy soils, some heavier; San Antonio River, Cibolo Creek.

Economy: Agribusiness; some residents employed in San Antonio; part of San Antonio metropolitan area.

History: Coahuiltecan Indians in area when Spanish began ranching around 1750. Anglo-American settlers arrived in 1840s. German, Polish settled in 1850s. County created from Bexar, Karnes counties 1860; named for James C. Wilson, member of the Mier Expedition.

Ethnicity, 1990: White, 19,652 (86.8%); Black, 242 (1.1%); American Indian, 45 (0.2%); Asian, 22 (0.1%); Other, 2,689 (11.9%). Hispanic, 8,054 (35.6%).

Vital Statistics, 1997: Births, 379; deaths, 237; marriages, 177; divorces, 118.

Recreation: Mission ranch ruins, historic homes; Stockdale watermelon festival; Floresville peanut festival in October.

Minerals: Oil, gas, clays.

Agriculture: Cattle, dairy products, hogs, poultry; peanuts, sorghum, corn, small grains, vegetables, watermelons, fruit. Market value $46 million.

FLORESVILLE (6,718) county seat; agribusiness center; hospital; Hertiage Days in spring; annual Pony Express ride.

Other towns include: **La Vernia** (1,051); **Pandora** (125); **Poth** (2,140); **Stockdale** (1,507) food processing; medical center; recreation facilities; **Sutherland Springs** (362).

▲ RANCHO DE LAS CABRAS RUINS

Population	29,378
Change fm '90	29.7
Area (sq. mi.)	808.5
Land Area (sq. mi.)	807.2
Altitude (ft.)	300-781
Rainfall (in.)	29.4
Jan. mean min.	36
July mean max.	96
Growing season (days)	280
Civ. Labor	14,870
Unemployed	3.0
Annual Wages	$80,384,351
Av. Weekly Wage	$343.43
Fed. Wages	$1,700,803
Ag. Net Cash Return	$1,494,000
Prop. Value	$1,118,223,956
Retail Sales	$94,162,593

Winkler County

Physical Features: Western county adjoining New Mexico on plains, partly sandy hills.

Economy: Oil, natural gas; ranching; prison.

History: Apache area until arrival of Comanches in 1700s. Anglo-Americans began ranching in 1880s. Oil discovered 1926. Mexican migration increased after 1960. County named for Confederate Col. C.M. Winkler; created from Tom Green 1887; organized 1910.

Ethnicity, 1990: White, 6,184 (71.7%); Black, 167 (1.9%); American Indian, 48 (0.6%); Asian, 9 (0.1%); Other, 2,218 (25.7%). Hispanic, 3,172 (36.8%).

Vital Statistics, 1997: Births, 115; deaths, 69; marriages, 63; divorces, 18.

Recreation: Sandhills Park; museum; zoo; wooden oil derrick; Roy Orbison Festival in June at Wink; Wink Sink, large sinkhole.

Minerals: A leading petroleum-producing county; gas.

Agriculture: Beef cattle, meat goats, horses, forage. Market value $1.8 million.

KERMIT (6,553) the county seat, and **Wink** (1,165) oil, gas, ranching; hospital.

N & W - MOUNTAIN TIME ZONE
S & E - CENTRAL TIME ZONE

Population	8,355
Change fm '90	-3.1
Area (sq. mi.)	841.2
Land Area (sq. mi.)	841.1
Altitude (ft.)	2,671-3,300
Rainfall (in.)	12.6
Jan. mean min.	28

July mean max.	97
Growing season (days)	219
Civ. Labor	3,184
Unemployed	9.0
Annual Wages	$55,101,618

Av. Weekly Wage	$468.44
Fed. Wages	$452,295
Ag. Net Cash Return	$445,000
Prop. Value	$754,034,070
Retail Sales	$37,347,506

Wise County

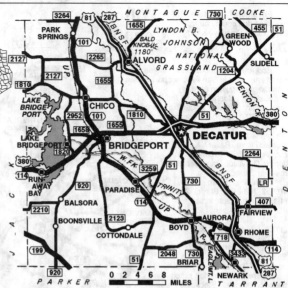

Physical Features: North central county of rolling prairie, some oaks; clay, loam, sandy soils; lakes.

Economy: Agribusiness, petroleum, recreation, hunting leases; many residents work in Fort Worth.

History: Caddo Indian groups. Delaware tribe present when Anglo-Americans arrived in 1850s. County created 1856 from Cooke County; named for Virginian, U.S. Sen. Henry A. Wise, who favored annexation of Texas.

Ethnicity, 1990: White, 32,550 (93.9%); Black, 390 (1.1%); American Indian, 210 (0.6%); Asian, 83 (0.2%); Other, 1,446 (4.2%). Hispanic, 2,663 (7.7%).

Vital Statistics, 1997: Births, 607; deaths, 395; marriages, 389; divorces, 255.

Recreation: Lake activities; hunting; exotic deer preserve; historical sites; Lyndon B. Johnson National Grasslands; Chisholm trail days in June, antique auto swap meet; Butterfield stage days in July; heritage museum, old courthouse.

Minerals: Gas, oil, sand, gravel.

Agriculture: Beef cattle, dairy operations, horses, sheep, goats; crops include hay, wheat, peanuts and pecans. Market value $34.3 million.

DECATUR (4,858) county seat; petroleum center; dairying; cattle marketing; some manufacturing; hospital.

BRIDGEPORT (4,093) trade center for lake resort; oil, gas production; timeshare housing; artistic community; manufacturing.

Other towns include: **Alvord** (1,056); **Aurora** (846); **Boyd** (1,249); **Briar** (4,700); **Chico** (964); **Fairview** (269); **Greenwood** (76); **Lake Bridgeport** (416); **Newark** (896); **Paradise** (275); **Rhome** (768); **Runaway Bay** (922); **Slidell** (175).

Population	42,206
Change fm '90	21.7
Area (sq. mi.)	922.7
Land Area (sq. mi.)	904.7
Altitude (ft.)	649-1,180
Rainfall (in.)	32.6
Jan. mean min.	30
July mean max.	99
Growing season (days)	220
Civ. Labor	23,092
Unemployed	3.2
Annual Wages	$264,173,620
Av. Weekly Wage	$468.44
Fed. Wages	$2,993,941
Ag. Net Cash Return	NA
Prop. Value	$1,990,755,882
Retail Sales	$335,051,893

Wood County

Physical Features: Hilly northeastern county almost half forested; sandy to alluvial soils; drained by Sabine and tributaries; many lakes.

Economy: Oil, natural gas, agribusiness, tourism.

History: Caddo Indians; reduced by disease. Anglo-American settlement developed in 1840s. County created from Van Zandt County 1850; named for Gov. George T. Wood.

Ethnicity, 1990: White, 26,363 (89.7%); Black, 2,402 (8.2%); American Indian, 109 (0.4%); Asian, 40 (0.1%); Other, 466 (1.6%). Hispanic, 788 (2.7%).

Vital Statistics, 1997: Births, 425; deaths, 482; marriages, 269; divorces, 224.

Recreation: Autumn trails; lake activities; hunting; Gov. Hogg Shrine State Park and museum; historic sites; scenic drives; Mineola May Days; railroad heritage days; autumn trails.

Minerals: Natural gas, oil, sand, gravel.

Agriculture: Dairy, beef cattle, poultry, hay, nurseries, sweet potatoes. Market value $74.6 million. Timber production.

QUITMAN (1,849) county seat; tourism; food processing; some manufacturing; hospital.

MINEOLA (4,756) farm, railroad center, Amtrak stop; food processing; some manufacturing; museum.

Winnsboro (3,223, partly in Franklin County) gas and oil, dairies, tourism; hospital.

Other towns include: **Alba** (538, partly in Rains County); **Golden** (156); **Hawkins** (1,422) oil, Jarvis Christian College; Oil festival in October; **Yantis** (307).

GOV. HOGG SHRINE STATE PARK

Population	33,380
Change fm '90	13.6
Area (sq. mi.)	695.7
Land Area (sq. mi.)	650.3
Altitude (ft.)	299-630
Rainfall (in.)	45.0
Jan. mean min.	31
July mean max.	94
Growing season (days)	246
Civ. Labor	13,431
Unemployed	5.7
Annual Wages	$159,116,414
Av. Weekly Wage	$392.35
Fed. Wages	$2,706,232
Ag. Net Cash Return	$12,877,000
Prop. Value	$1,635,217,471
Retail Sales	$227,079,113

Yoakum County

Physical Features: Western county is level to rolling; playas, draws; sandy, loam, chocolate soils.

Economy: Oil, agriculture.

History: Comanche hunting area. Anglo-Americans began ranching in 1890s. Oil discovered 1936. Mexican migration increased in 1950s. County named for Henderson Yoakum, pioneer historian; created from Bexar District 1876; organized 1907.

Ethnicity, 1990: White, 6,300 (71.7%); Black, 86 (1.0%); American Indian, 31 (0.4%); Asian, 11 (0.1%); Other, 2,358 (26.8%). Hispanic, 3,217 (36.6%).

Vital Statistics, 1997: Births, 126; deaths, 61; marriages, 66; divorces, 44.

Recreation: Tsa Mo Ga Museum at Plains; Roughneck rodeo and farmboy jamboree in May; settlers reunion in August.

Minerals: Oil, natural gas.

Agriculture: Cotton, peanuts, watermelons, sorghum, wheat, chili peppers; substantial irrigation. Cattle, horses, swine, goats raised. Market value $52.2 million.

PLAINS (1,380) county seat; oil, agribusiness center.

DENVER CITY (5,009) center for oil, agriculture activities in two counties; hospital, library.

Population	8,519
Change fm '90	-3.0
Area (sq. mi.)	799.8
Land Area (sq. mi.)	799.8
Altitude (ft.)	3,490-3,891
Rainfall (in.)	17.7
Jan. mean min.	22
July mean max.	91

Growing season (days)	199
Civ. Labor	3,531
Unemployed	7.3
Annual Wages	$78,047,588
Av. Weekly Wage	$494.69

Fed. Wages	$605,769
Ag. Net Cash Return	$16,177,000
Prop. Value	$1,785,837,070
Retail Sales	$55,689,944

o—o—o (W) MOUNTAIN TIME ZONE
(E) CENTRAL TIME ZONE

0 2 4 6 8 MILES

Young County

Physical Features: Hilly, broken; drained by Brazos and tributaries; Possum Kingdom Lake, Lake Graham.

Economy: Oil, agribusiness, tourism; hunting leases.

History: U.S. military outpost established 1851. Site of Brazos Indian Reservation 1854-59 with Caddoes, Wacos, other tribes. Anglo-American settlers arrived in 1850s. County named for early Texan, Col. W.C. Young; created 1856 from Bosque, Fannin counties; reorganized 1874.

Ethnicity, 1990: White, 17,023 (93.9%); Black, 268 (1.5%); American Indian, 62 (0.3%); Asian, 49 (0.3%); Other, 724 (4.0%). Hispanic, 1,164 (6.4%).

Vital Statistics, 1997: Births, 229; deaths, 261; marriages, 185; divorces, 105.

Recreation: Lake activities; hunting; Fort Belknap restoration; marker at oak tree in Graham where ranchers formed forerunner of Texas and Southwestern Cattle Raisers Association; vintage auto club spring tour; western heritage festival in fall.

Minerals: Oil, gas, sand, gravel.

Agriculture: Beef cattle; wheat chief crop, also hay, cotton, pecans, nursery plants. Market value $23.2 million.

GRAHAM (8,896) county seat; oil, agribusiness, manufacturing, tourism, hunting; hospital, mental health clinic; Ranger Junior College extension; Possum Fest in September.

Other towns include: **Eliasville** (150); **Loving** (300); **Newcastle** (559); **Olney** (3,348) agribusiness center, manufacturing, hospital; Music at the Gazebo in summer; one-arm dove hunt in September; **South Bend** (140).

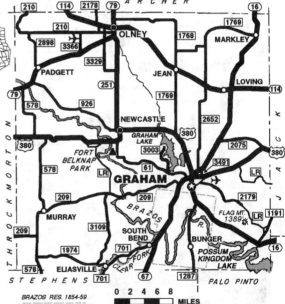

BRAZOS RES. 1854-59

0 2 4 6 8 MILES

Population	17,822
Change fm '90	-1.7
Area (sq. mi.)	930.8
Land Area (sq. mi.)	922.4
Altitude (ft.)	995-1,389
Rainfall (in.)	30.6
Jan. mean min.	26
July mean max.	96
Growing season (days)	216
Civ. Labor	8,190

Unemployed	6.3
Annual Wages	$140,982,105
Av. Weekly Wage	$439.85
Fed. Wages	$1,592,487
Ag. Net Cash Return	$1,340,000
Prop. Value	$725,396,310
Retail Sales	$132,612,837

For explanation of sources, abbreviations and symbols, see p. 130.

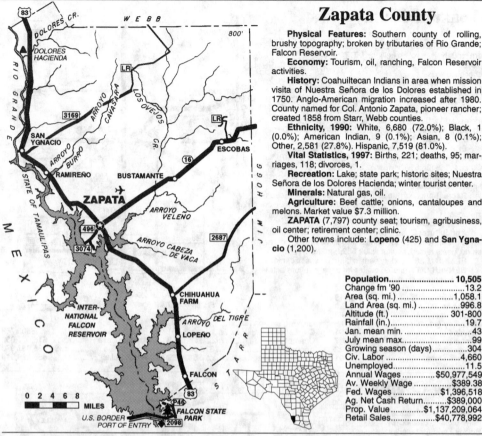

Zapata County

Physical Features: Southern county of rolling, brushy topography; broken by tributaries of Rio Grande; Falcon Reservoir.

Economy: Tourism, oil, ranching, Falcon Reservoir activities.

History: Coahuiltecan Indians in area when mission visita of Nuestra Señora de los Dolores established in 1750. Anglo-American migration increased after 1980. County named for Col. Antonio Zapata, pioneer rancher; created 1858 from Starr, Webb counties.

Ethnicity, 1990: White, 6,680 (72.0%); Black, 1 (0.0%); American Indian, 9 (0.1%); Asian, 8 (0.1%); Other, 2,581 (27.8%). Hispanic, 7,519 (81.0%).

Vital Statistics, 1997: Births, 221; deaths, 95; marriages, 118; divorces, 1.

Recreation: Lake; state park; historic sites; Nuestra Señora de los Dolores Hacienda; winter tourist center.

Minerals: Natural gas, oil.

Agriculture: Beef cattle; onions, cantaloupes and melons. Market value $7.3 million.

ZAPATA (7,797) county seat; tourism, agribusiness, oil center; retirement center; clinic.

Other towns include: **Lopeno** (425) and **San Ygnacio** (1,200).

Population	10,505
Change fm '90	13.2
Area (sq. mi.)	1,058.1
Land Area (sq. mi.)	996.8
Altitude (ft.)	301-800
Rainfall (in.)	19.7
Jan. mean min.	43
July mean max.	99
Growing season (days)	304
Civ. Labor	4,660
Unemployed	11.5
Annual Wages	$50,977,549
Av. Weekly Wage	$389.38
Fed. Wages	$1,396,518
Ag. Net Cash Return	$389,000
Prop. Value	$1,137,209,064
Retail Sales	$40,778,992

Zavala County

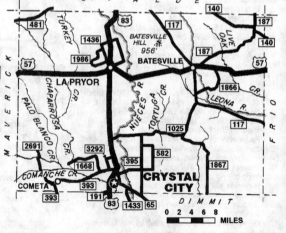

Physical Features: Southwestern county near Mexican border of rolling plains broken by much brush; Nueces, Leona, other streams.

Economy: Agribusiness, leading county in Winter Garden truck-farming area; oil, gas, government/services.

History: Coahuiltecan area; Apaches, Comanches arrived later. Ranching developed in late 1860s. County created from Maverick, Uvalde counties 1858; organized 1884; named for Texas Revolutionary leader Lorenzo de Zavala.

Ethnicity, 1990: White, 6,443 (53.0%); Black, 296 (2.4%); American Indian, 16 (0.1%); Asian, 3 (0.0%); Other, 5,404 (44.4%). Hispanic, 10,875 (89.4%).

Vital Statistics, 1997: Births, 210; deaths, 91; marriages, 60; divorces, 15.

Recreation: Hunting, fishing; spinach festival in November.

Minerals: Oil, natural gas.

Agriculture: Cattle, vegetables, corn, pecans, grain sorghum; cotton, hay; goats, sheep. About 40,000 acres irrigated. Market value $45.4 million. Hunting leases important.

CRYSTAL CITY (8,088) county seat; agribusiness; food processing; oilfield services; site of Japanese detention center. Home of Popeye statue.

Other towns include: **Batesville** (1,275) and **La Pryor** (1,230).

Population	11,771	Av. Weekly Wage	$294.98
Change fm '90	-3.2	Fed. Wages	$387,105
Area (sq. mi.)	1,301.7	Ag. Net Cash Return	$13,325,000
Land Area (sq. mi.)	1,298.6	Prop. Value	$392,280,552
Altitude (ft.)	540-956	Retail Sales	$25,884,374
Rainfall (in.)	21.0		
Jan. mean min.	42		
July mean max.	97		
Growing season (days)	280		
Civ. Labor	4,264		
Unemployed	22.2		
Annual Wages	$42,057,042		

For explanation of sources, explanations and symbols, see p. 130.

Twenty Million Texans and Growing

The following article was written by Steve H. Murdock, Md. Nazrul Hoque and Beverly Pecotte

As Texas enters the 21st century it will have more than 20 million persons. According to the most recent estimates available from the U.S. Bureau of the Census, Texas' population was nearly 19.8 million as of July 1, 1998.

If its 1990 to 1998 rate of growth continues it will have obtained its 20 millionth person by early 1999 and is likely to have more than 20.3 million persons at the time of the 2000 census (April 1, 2000). This will result in a 1990 to 2000 increase of more than 3.3 million persons, making it the largest numerical increase in Texas' population in any decade in history.

Already by 1998, Texas' population had increased to 19,759,614 persons, an increase of 2,773,249 persons from the revised April 1, 1990 census count of 16,986,335. This numerical increase was second in size only to that in California (see Table 1), and the 16.3 percent increase in Texas' population was the eighth largest in percentage terms among the 50 states and the largest among those states with populations of 8 million or more.

Texas' numerical increase of nearly 2.8 million from 1990 to 1998 was roughly equivalent to adding another city of Houston plus another city of Dallas to Texas' population in just over 8 years (from April 1, 1990 to July 1, 1998).

Texas' growth has also been unique among the largest states in the fact that its growth has resulted from increases in both of the major components of population change — natural increase and migration (both immigration from countries other than the United States and domestic migration from other states in the United States).

Thus, 56.7 percent of the 1990 to 1998 increase in the Texas population was a result of natural increase

Table 1: Population Increase 1990-98

State	Numerical change	Percent change
California	2,880,693	9.7
Texas	**2,773,279**	**16.3**
Florida	1,977,909	15.3
Georgia	1,164,058	18.0
Arizona	1,003,292	27.4
North Carolina	914,045	13.8
Washington	822,594	16.9
Colorado	676,498	20.5
Illinois	614,724	5.4
Virginia	602,148	9.7
U.S. population, Jan. 1, 1999	**271,645,214**	

Source: U.S. Burearu of the Census

(more births than deaths), 23.6 percent was due to international immigration from other countries, and 19.7 percent of its increase was from domestic migration to Texas from other states in the United States (see Table 2).

By comparison, California has experienced immigration of more than 2 million persons and New York more than one million and both states have experienced negative domestic migration, meaning that more of their residents have left these states to go to other states in the United States than have entered them from other states.

Texas' growth in the 1990s has thus shown a substantial increase that reflects a relatively balanced form of growth. In addition, the fact that the relatively slow changing natural increase component alone adds roughly 190,000 persons to Texas' population each year makes continued growth likely.

Patterns of Growth

As with any pattern of change, that in Texas varies across the regions, metropolitan areas, counties and cities of the state. Given space limitations, we can only highlight some of the patterns of change across these areas in Texas.

In addition, because data are not available for all geographical subunits in Texas for 1998, these data are limited to the period from 1990 to 1997 and are based on data obtained from the Texas State Data Center in

Table 2: Texas Growth by Component of Change

	State Population	Annual Change	Natural Increase	Percent of Total	International Immigration	Percent of Total	Net Domestic Migration	Percent of Total
1990	16,986,335	--	--	--	--	--	--	
1991	17,348,540	362,205	238,977	66.0	73,185	20.2	50,043	13.8
1992	17,661,971	313,431	192,839	61.5	71,516	22.9	48,907	15.6
1993	18,009,031	347,060	189,635	54.6	77,516	22.4	79,909	23.0
1994	18,347,571	338,540	185,657	54.8	74,658	22.1	78,225	23.1
1995	18,694,223	346,652	186,527	53.8	73,510	21.2	86,615	25.0
1996	19,032,987	338,764	185,329	54.7	88,439	26.1	64,996	19.2
1997	19,385,699	352,712	198,882	56.4	96,498	27.3	57,332	16.3
1998	19,759,614	373,915	194,943	52.1	100,175	26.8	78,797	21.1
Total	--	2,773,279	1,572,789	56.7	655,666	23.6	544,824	19.7

Source: Estimated from U.S. census figures by State Data Center

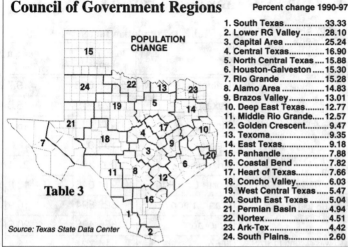

Council of Government Regions

POPULATION CHANGE

Table 3

Source: Texas State Data Center

Percent change 1990-97

1. South Texas 33.33
2. Lower RG Valley 28.10
3. Capital Area 25.24
4. Central Texas 16.90
5. North Central Texas 15.88
6. Houston-Galveston 15.30
7. Rio Grande 15.28
8. Alamo Area 14.83
9. Brazos Valley 13.01
10. Deep East Texas 12.77
11. Middle Rio Grande 12.57
12. Golden Crescent 9.47
13. Texoma 9.35
14. East Texas 9.18
15. Panhandle 7.88
16. Coastal Bend 7.82
17. Heart of Texas 7.66
18. Concho Valley 6.03
19. West Central Texas 5.47
20. South East Texas 5.04
21. Permian Basin 4.94
22. Nortex 4.51
23. Ark-Tex 4.42
24. South Plains 2.60

those for the COG regions of the state with those metropolitan areas along the Texas-Mexico border and the central corridor of Texas plus those in the Houston area showing the most substantial numerical and percentage increases.

Laredo showed the largest percentage increase from 1990 to 1997, 38.8 percent (see Table 4), followed by McAllen-Edinburg-Mission with 33.3 percent, Austin-San Marcos with 25.8 percent, and Brownsville-Harlingen-San Benito at 21.7 percent.

On the other hand, the slowest growth occurred in such East Texas and Panhandle areas as Texarkana, Lubbock, Beaumont-Port Arthur, Wichita Falls and Abilene, all of which increased by less than 7 percent. It is evident, however, that the metropolitan areas of the state are the major growth centers.

the Department of Rural Sociology at Texas A&M University. In this discussion we examine data for council of government regions, metropolitan areas, counties and places in Texas.

Regional and Metropolitan Patterns

The Council of Government (COG) regions and metropolitan areas of Texas reflect both the overall growth in the state and the diversity of that growth by area of the state.

All 24 council of government regions have experienced growth during the 1990s (see Table 3) with the North Central Texas area showing the largest numerical increase (652,757 persons from 1990 to 1997), followed by the Houston-Galveston region (with 596,074) and the Capital Area region (with 232,054). These areas plus the Alamo Area also had the largest populations in the state, with all having populations over one million persons.

The North Central Texas region had nearly 4.8 million persons by 1997, the Houston-Galveston area nearly 4.5 million, the Alamo Area 1.7 million, and the Capital Area more than 1.1 million persons.

Slowest numerical growth occurred in the Concho Valley (8,585), South Plains (9,424), and Nortex (9,539) areas each of which increased by less than 10,000 persons.

In percentage terms, three areas have shown the most rapid growth in the 1990s. These are the South Texas, Lower Rio Grande, and Capital Area regions all of which have increased by more than 25 percent.

Four others including the Central Texas, North Central Texas, Houston-Galveston and Rio Grande regions each increased by more than 15 percent.

The smallest increases occurred in the South Plains, Ark-Tex, Nortex, and Permian Basin regions, which have each increased by less than 5 percent. Overall these patterns of growth point to two major corridors of growth in Texas — one along the Texas and Mexico border and a second in the center of Texas (running from Dallas-Fort Worth to San Antonio) with extensive growth also occurring in the Houston-Galveston area.

Texas' metropolitan areas show similar patterns to

Metropolitan suburban counties increased by 28.3 percent from 1990 to 1997, metropolitan central city counties by 12.8 percent, nonmetropolitan adjacent counties by 9.8 percent, and nonmetropolitan nonadjacent areas by 6.8 percent. Overall, 89.8 percent of the state's net increase from 1990 to 1997 occurred in its metropolitan (suburban and central city) areas, which contained 84.2 percent of the total population of the state in 1990.

Change in Counties and Places

Texas' growth has been generally pervasive among its counties and cities, but substantial differences in rates of growth are also evident.

Although data for all Texas' counties and places cannot be presented here due to space limitations, several generalizations regarding growth in Texas' counties and places are examined.

Overall, 207 of Texas' 254 counties have shown population increases from 1990 to 1997, but counties with the largest percentage increases have tended to be located in the areas around the state's large cities, while more rural counties, particularly those in areas with economies based on such extractive industries as agriculture and gas and oil, have tended to show patterns of slow growth or decline.

Numerical increases in population in the 1990s tend to reflect the overall size of counties with Harris showing the largest numerical increase in the 1990-97 period (339,774), followed by Dallas (168,277), Bexar (149,328), Tarrant (158,629), Travis (117,110) and El Paso (92,047).

However, the rapid growth in the suburban and Texas-Mexico border areas is also evident in the fact that four smaller counties, Hidalgo (with an increase of 127,779), Collin (an increase of 137,407), Denton (an increase of 97,993) and Fort Bend (an increase of 91,265) showed similar patterns of numerical increases

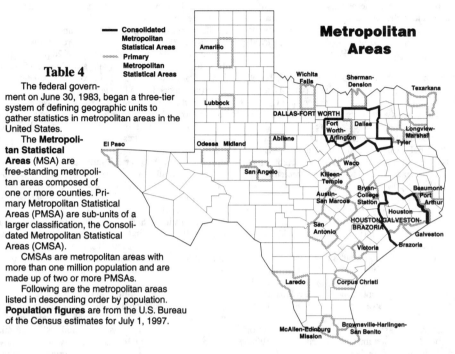

Table 4

The federal government on June 30, 1983, began a three-tier system of defining geographic units to gather statistics in metropolitan areas in the United States.

The **Metropolitan Statistical Areas** (MSA) are free-standing metropolitan areas composed of one or more counties. Primary Metropolitan Statistical Areas (PMSA) are sub-units of a larger classification, the Consolidated Metropolitan Statistical Areas (CMSA).

CMSAs are metropolitan areas with more than one million population and are made up of two or more PMSAs.

Following are the metropolitan areas listed in descending order by population. **Population figures** are from the U.S. Bureau of the Census estimates for July 1, 1997.

Consolidated Metropolitan Statistical Areas (CMSA)

Dallas-Fort Worth (Dallas and Fort Worth-Arlington PMSAs)	4,683,991
Houston (Houston, Galveston and Brazoria PMSAs)	4,313,697

Metropolitan Statistical Areas (MSA) and Primary Metropolitan Statistical Areas (PMSA)

		Percent change 1990-97
Level A — Population 1,000,000 or More:		
1. **Houston** PMSA (Chambers, Fort Bend, Harris, Liberty, Montgomery and Waller counties)	3,846,654	15.8
2. **Dallas** PMSA(Collin, Dallas, Denton, Ellis, Henderson, Hunt, Kaufman,Rockwall counties)	3,131,795	17.0
3. **Fort Worth-Arlington** PMSA (Hood, Johnson, Parker and Tarrant counties)	1,552,193	14.1
4. **San Antonio** MSA (Bexar, Comal, Guadalupe and Wilson counties)	1,509,482	13.9
5. **Austin-San Marcos** MSA (Bastrop, Caldwell, Hays, Travis and Williamson counties)	1,064,325	25.8
Level B — Population 250,000 to 1,000,000		
6. **El Paso** MSA (El Paso County)	683,657	15.6
7. **McAllen-Edinburg-Mission** MSA (Hidalgo County)	511,324	33.3
8. **Beaumont-Port Arthur** MSA (Hardin, Jefferson and Orange counties)	379,427	5.0
9. **Corpus Christi** MSA (Nueces and San Patricio counties)	378,292	8.1
10. **Brownsville-Harlingen-San Benito** MSA (Cameron County)	316,542	21.7
11. **Killeen-Temple** MSA (Bell and Coryell counties)	300,940	17.9
Level C — Population 100,000 to 250,000		
12. **Odessa-Midland** MSA (Ector and Midland County)	242,429	7.5
13. **Galveston-Texas City** PMSA (Galveston County)	242,133	11.4
14. **Lubbock** MSA (Lubbock County)	232,458	4.4
15. **Brazoria** PMSA (Brazoria County)	224,910	17.3
16. **Amarillo** MSA (Potter and Randall counties)	210,145	12.1
17. **Longview-Marshall** MSA (Gregg, Harrison and Upshur counties)	207,659	7.2
18. **Waco** MSA (McLennan County)	203,788	7.8
19. **Laredo** MSA (Webb County)	184,980	38.8
20. **Tyler** MSA (Smith County)	165,705	9.5
21. **Wichita Falls** MSA (Archer and Wichita counties)	137,889	5.8
22. **Bryan-College Station** MSA (Brazos County)	139,352	14.4
23. **Abilene** MSA (Taylor County)	127,909	6.9
24. **Texarkana** MSA (Bowie County, TX, and Miller County, AR)	123,276	2.4
25. **San Angelo** MSA (Tom Green County)	105,416	7.1
26. **Sherman-Denison** MSA (Grayson County)	102,998	8.4
Level D — Population Under 100,000		
27. **Victoria** MSA (Victoria County)	82,580	11.1

to the state's most populous counties.

In percentage terms, the highest rates of growth in the counties clearly reflect suburban patterns of growth with Collin increasing by 52 percent from 1990 to 1997, Williamson increasing by 48.4 percent, Rockwall increasing by 43 percent, and Fort Bend by 40.5 percent.

Of the counties showing population decline, Terrell (with a decline of 15.3 percent), Roberts (with a decline of 14.1 percent), Motley (with a decline of 11.2 percent) and Loving (with a decline of 11.2 percent) showed the largest percentage decreases.

Similar patterns of generally pervasive growth but with substantial variation across the state are evident when data for cities are examined. Of the 1,280 cities for which the Texas State Data Center completes estimates, 1,154 or 90.1 percent experienced population growth from 1990 to 1997.

Growth was more pervasive among larger than smaller places, however.

All but one (1.1 percent) of the 93 cities with a population greater than 25,000 showed population increases from 1990 to 1997, but 8.8 percent of the 113 places with 1997 populations of 10,001 to 25,000, 9.7 percent of those 124 places with populations of 5,001 to 10,000, and 10.3 percent of the 950 places with populations of 5,000 or fewer people showed population decline.

Numerical increases generally reflected the size of the city, but the largest numerical increase in the 1990-97 period was in the second largest city of San Antonio (an increase of 175,857), followed by Houston (160,283), Austin (108,738), El Paso (80,611) and Dallas (69,988).

The only other place to increase by 60,000 or more was Plano, which had a population of 127,885 in 1990 but increased by 64,540 from 1990 to 1997. In percentage terms, Plano's increase of 50.5 percent from 1990 to 1997 was the largest percentage increase for any city with 100,000 or more population in 1990 while increases of 100 percent or more occurred in areas reflecting the Texas-Mexico and suburban locations noted above.

Thus, the largest percentage increase was in Frisco (168.9 percent), followed by Flower Mound (145.7 per-

cent), Cedar Park (145.4 percent), Sugar Land (122.5 percent), Pflugerville (117.3 percent) and San Juan (103.0 percent).

The largest percentage declines among places with at least 1,000 persons in 1990 were in rural areas including Sanderson (with a decline of 20 percent from 1990 to 1997), Aspermont (with a decline of 15.3 percent), Stamford (with a decline of 14.1 percent) and Spur (with a decline of 12.9 percent).

As with Texas' counties, its towns have generally shown growth but, in some parts of Texas, maintaining population has been more difficult, particularly for small, rural communities.

Projected Population

Texas' population is expected to continue to show extensive growth. Data suggest that Texas' population will nearly double by 2030 (increasing by 99.6 percent from 1990 to 2030).

The data in the tables below show that Texas' population will be older and increasingly racially and ethnically diverse. By 2030, 16.8 percent of Texas' population is projected to be 65 years of age or older with 46.2 percent of the population being Hispanic.

Summary

The 1990s have brought unprecedented population growth to Texas, bringing it into the 21st century with more than 20 million persons compared with just 3 million at the beginning of the 20th century.

This growth has been pervasive across its regions, metropolitan areas, counties and cities. Although areas of more limited population growth, and even population decline, exist in Texas, Texas' growth, fueled in large part by natural increase, is likely to continue.

In fact, by the end of the third decade of the new century, Texas is projected to have a population of nearly 34 million.

Texas' demographic future, like its past, is likely to be one of continued expansion and growth.

Dr. Murdock is professor and head of the Department of Rural Sociology at Texas A&M University and chief demographer of the Texas State Data Center. Dr. Hogue is an associate research scientist in the department. Ms. Pecotte is a research associate.

Projected Percentage by Ethnicity

Year	Anglo	Hispanic	Black	Other
1990	60.7	25.5	11.7	2.1
2000	54.5	31.0	11.4	3.1
2010	48.4	36.3	10.9	4.4
2020	42.3	41.4	10.3	6.0
2030	36.4	46.2	9.5	7.9

Source: State Data Center

Projected Percentage by Age Group in 2030

Age	Anglo	Hispanic	Black	Other	Total
- 18	18.2	27.4	25.9	13.8	22.8
18-24	7.5	10.4	10.4	6.3	9.1
25-44	25.7	30.3	28.7	22.4	27.8
45-64	25.0	21.5	21.8	29.9	23.5
65+	23.6	10.4	13.2	27.6	16.8

Source: State Data Center

Population 1990 and 1998

Towns that no longer exist or town names no longer in use are in italics.

For further information about these places turn to page 356 and the list of names beginning on page 357.

Population: Numbers in **parentheses** are from the 1990 count by the U.S. Bureau of the Census. The figures include revisions after the original publication.

The U.S. census counts only incorporated cities and some unincorporated towns called Census Designated Places (CDPs). CDPs in the following list have a double dagger symbol (‡). Cities that have incorporated since 1990 have "NC" (Not Counted).

Population figures to the right for those same cities are State Data Center estimates of Jan. 1, 1998. Names of the incorporated places are in capital letters, e.g., "ABBOTT."

The population figure given for all other towns is an estimate received from local officials through a Texas Almanac survey. In some cases, we could not obtain a population estimate; these places show "NA" (Not Available) in place of a population figure.

Location: The county in which the town is/was located follows the name of town. If more than one county is listed, the town is principally in the first-named county, e.g., "AMARILLO, Potter-Randall."

Businesses: The number following the county name indicates the number of business that have been given a credit rating by Dun & Bradstreet as of March 1999. For example, "ABBOTT, Hill, 36" means that Abbott in Hill County had 36 businesses.

County seats: County seats are marked with a section mark (§).

Post Offices: Places with post offices, as of Jan. 1995, are marked with an asterisk (*) e.g., "*Ace".

Town /County .... Pop. 1998	Town/County .... Pop. 1998	Town/County ....Pop. 1998
Abbie, Jones	*Ada, Montgomery*	*Agua Negra, Atascosa*
Abbieville, Denton	*Adair, Fisher*	**Agua Nueva, Jim Hogg** 20
Abbington, Childress	*Adair, Swisher*	*Ague, Walker*
***ABBOTT, Hill, 36 (314)** 369	*Adalia, Caldwell*	**Aguilares, Webb**...............37
Abe, Houston	*Adams, Fort Bend*	*Aid, Grimes*
Abell, Carson	*Adams[ville], Panola*	*Aiken, Bell*
Abell City, Pecos	*Adams, Pecos*	***Aiken, Floyd, 4** 57
Abercrombie, Travis	*Adams, Schleicher*	**Aiken, Shelby**.................75
Aberdeen, Collingsworth	*Adams Bayou, Orange*	**Aikin Grove, Red River** 26
Aberdeen, Henderson	**Adams Gardens, Cameron**...... 200	*Air, Mason*
Aberdeen, Smith	*Adams Hill, Bexar*	*Air Hall, Bell*
Aberfoyle, Hunt 35	*Adams Spring, Falls*	*Airline, Harris*
***ABERNATHY, Hale-Lubbock,**	**Adams Store, Panola** ....NA	**Airport City, Bexar**...........106
175 (2,720) 2,703	*Adamston, Brazoria*	**Airville, Bell** 10
§*ABILENE, Taylor-Jones,	**Adamsville, Lampasas**......... 41	*Ajax, Panola*
5,720 (106,707)........ 117,111	*Addicks, Harris*	*Aken, Shelby*
Ables, Hudspeth	**Addielou, Red River** 31	*Akin, Sabine*
Ables Springs, Hudspeth	*Addingtonville, Karnes*	*Akers, Schleicher*
Ables Springs, Kaufman........ NA	***ADDISON, Dallas, 1,557**	*Akron, Smith*
Abner, Kaufman............... NA	(8,783). 11,722	*Alabama, Callahan*
Abner, Rusk	*Add-Ran, Hood*	*Alabama, Houston*
Abney, Cameron	**Addran, Hopkins**..............NA	*Alabama, Trinity*
Abney's Farm, Denton	**Adell, Parker** ....NA	*Alabama Creek, Trinity*
Abney's Farm, Falls	*Ad Hall, Milam*	**Alabama-Coushatta Indian**
Abra, Collingsworth	*Adieu, Jack*	**Reservation, Polk** 478
‡ Abram-Perezville, Hidalgo	*Adina, Lee*	*Alameda, Eastland*
(3,999) 5,021	***Adkins, Bexar, 159.** 241	*Alamita, Karnes*
Acacia, Cameron	*Adkins' Store, Grimes*	*Alamito, Presidio*
Academy, Bell	**Admiral, Callahan**............. 18	*Alamo, Cass*
Acala, Hudspeth 25	*Adobe, Hutchinson*	***ALAMO, Hidalgo, 351**
Acampo, Shackelford	**Adobes, Presidio** ....NA	(8,210) 11,899
***Ace, Polk, 4**...................40	*Adobe Walls, Hutchinson*	*Alamo, Wharton*
***ACKERLY, Dawson-Martin, 53**	*Adora [City], Montague*	**Alamo Alto, El Paso**............25
(243)....................261	*Adora, Titus*	**Alamo Beach, Calhoun** .... NA
Acker's Ferry, Henderson	***ADRIAN, Oldham, 28 (220)** 228	***ALAMO HEIGHTS, Bexar**
Acme, Hardeman 14	*Adrian, Orange*	(6,502) 7,338
Acme, Henderson	*Adsul, Newton*	*Alamo Mills, Cass*
Acme, Hudspeth	*Adullam, Mason*	*Alamositas, Oldham*
Acme, Van Zandt	**Advance, Parker** ....NA	***Alanreed, Gray, 8** 48
Acol, Angelina	*Ady, Potter*	*Alarm Creek, Erath*
Acol, Polk	*Affie, Wheeler*	**Alazan, Nacogdoches** .... NA
Acol, Tyler	*Afra, Scurry*	***ALBA, Wood-Rains, 102 (489)** ...538
Acomb, McLennan	*Africa, Liberty*	*Albade, Caldwell*
Acona, Guadalupe	***Afton, Dickens, 11**............. 15	**§*ALBANY, Shackelford, 184**
Acorn, Robertson	*Afton, Fisher*	(1,962) 2,003
Acrey, Erath	*Afton, Lubbock*	*Albert, Angelina*
Acton, Hood............... 1,129	*Agatite, Hardeman*	**Albert, Gillespie, 4**.............25
Acuff, Lubbock.................30	*Agee, Hamilton*	**Albion, Red River**..............50
Acworth, Red River.............52	**Agnes, Parker** ....NA	*Albritten, Cherokee*
Ada, Camp	*Agricola, Parker*	*Albuquerque, Wilson*
Ada, Lampasas	***AGUA DULCE, Nueces, 26 (794). 831**	*Alcedo, Angelina*

Alcino, Floyd
Alco, Angelina
Alcorn, Washington
Alcott, Falls
Alderbranch, Anderson..........5
Aldie, Yoakum
‡ Aldine, Harris (11,133) 12,465
Aldine, Uvalde
Aldridge, Jasper
Aldridge's, Nacogdoches
Aleck, Tyler
*ALEDO, Parker, 280 (1,169) ... 1,476
Aleman, Hamilton 60
Aleo, Collin
Alethia, Montgomery........... NA
Alexander, Erath 40
Alexander Spur, Orange
Alexander's, Fayette
Alexanders Store, Shelby .... NA
Aley, Henderson................20
Alfalfa, El Paso
Alfalfa, Ochiltree
Alford, Sabine
Alfred, Henderson
Alfred, Jim Wells 10
Alfred, Nueces
Alfred, Shelby
Algana, Coryell
Algereta, Menard
Algeria, Travis
Algerita, San Saba, 5 48
Algoa, Galveston..............135
Algoma, Stephens
Alguna, San Patricio
Alhambra, Hutchinson
§*ALICE, Jim Wells, 1,115
  (19,788)............... 20,230
Alief, Harris
Allah, Hunt
Allamoore, Hudspeth 25
Allard, Erath
Allardale, Newton
Allarton, Newton
Allcorn's, Washington
*ALLEN, Collin, 1,282
  (19,315) 32,501
Allendale, Montgomery......... NA
Allendale, Wichita
Allenfarm, Brazos 30
Allenhurst, Matagorda 50
Allen's Chapel, Fannin 41
Allen's Creek, Austin
Allen's Gin, Angelina
Allen's Grove, Grayson
Allen's Mills, Milam
Allen's Point, Fannin 76
Allentown, Angelina
Allentown, Ward
Allenville, Milam
Alley, Hale
Alleys Mill, Marion
*Alleyton, Colorado, 18 165
Alliance, Hunt
Alliance Hall, Navarro
Alligator, Brazos
Alligator Head, Calhoun
*Allison, Wheeler, 19 135
Allison, Williamson
Allison, Wise.................. NA
Allisonville, Tyler
Allis School, Lavaca
Allmon, Floyd..................24
Allred, Yoakum 90
Alluvia, Stonewall
Alma, Clay
ALMA, Ellis (205)..............271
Alma, Houston
Alma, Rusk

Almeda, Harris
Almedes, Anderson
Almira, Cass 30
Almon, Llano
Almond Grove, Red River
Almont, Bowie
Alon, Limestone
Alp, Montague
Alpha, Bowie
Alpha, Coke
Alpha, Dallas
Alpha, Hutchinson
§*ALPINE, Brewster, 470
  (5,622)..................5,962
Alredge, Angelina
Alsa, Van Zandt 30
Alsdorf, Ellis
Alsobrooks, Tyler
Alsonia, Hidalgo
Alston's [Store], Ellis
*Altair, Colorado, 11 30
Alta Loma, Galveston
Alta Mesa, Dallas
Alta Mira, Grimes
Altavista, Jim Hogg
Althea, Bell
Altman, Erath
Altman, Moore
*ALTO, Cherokee, 113 (1,027)...1,066
Alto Bonito, Starr 170
Altoga, Collin.................. 367
Alton, Denton
*ALTON, Hidalgo (3,069) 3,519
Altonia, San Augustine
Alto Springs, Falls
Altuda, Brewster
Altura, El Paso
Alum, Wilson..................NA
Alum Creek, Bastrop ....NA
Alum Wells, Houston
*ALVARADO, Johnson, 334
  (2,918)..................3,447
Alverde, Lampasas
*ALVIN, Brazoria, 1,300
  (19,220)...............20,715
Alvin, Henderson
Alvis, Ellis
*ALVORD, Wise, 78 (865) 1,056
Alwoodco, Ellis
Amanda, Kinney
Amanda, McLennan
Amarada, Brown
§*AMARILLO, Potter-Randall,
  9,416 (157,571).........172,289
Ambia, Lamar 20
Ambrose, Grayson 90
Amelbulk, Jefferson
Amelia, Jefferson
Ames, Coryell 10
AMES, Liberty (989) 1,292
Ameus, Cherokee
Amherst, Lamar ....NA
*AMHERST, Lamb, 49 (742) 747
Amicus, Marion
Amigo Station, Smith
Amistad, Val Verde
Amity, Comanche
Ammann's, Kendall
Ammannsville, Fayette.......... 42
Amo, Montague
Amonda, McLennan
Amphion, Atascosa 26
Ample, Haskell
Amsterdam, Brazoria 193
Amy, Delta
Anacacho, Kinney
Anacostia, Panola
Anadarco, Rusk

Anadarko, Rusk................30
§*ANAHUAC, Chambers, 198
  (1,993)..................2,220
Anaqua, Victoria
Anarene, Archer
Ancaster, La Salle
Anchor, Brazoria
Anchorage, Atascosa
Ander, Goliad
Ander-Weser-Kilgore, Goliad 322
§*ANDERSON, Grimes, 79
  (NC) 370
‡ Anderson Mill, Williamson-
  Travis (9,468)........... 12,959
Andersonville, Williamson
*Andice, Williamson, 61 .... NA
§*ANDREWS, Andrews, 626
  (10,678)...............10,491
Andrews, Wood
Angel City, Goliad
Angeles, Reeves
Angelina, Angelina
Angelita, San Patricio
Angle, Walker
Angler, Wood
§*ANGLETON, Brazoria,
  1,073 (17,140)........... 22,524
Anglin's, Anderson
Anglo American, Bowie
Angoria, Palo Pinto
ANGUS, Navarro (363).........440
Anhalt, Comal
Anita, Palo Pinto
Ann Eliza, Grayson
*ANNA, Collin, 87 (904) 1,159
Annadale, Callahan
Annarose, Live Oak
Annaville, Nueces
ANNETTA, Parker (672).........867
ANNETTA NORTH, Parker
  (265) 346
ANNETTA SOUTH, Parker
  (413) 541
Anneville, Wise
Annie, Bowie
*ANNONA, Red River, 19 (329) ...358
§*ANSON, Jones, 183 (2,644) .. 2,576
Antelope, Culberson
Antelope [Antelope Springs],Foard
Antelope, Jack, 4 65
Antelope Flats, Briscoe......... NA
Antelope Gap, Lampasas
Antelope Gap, Wise
Antelope Mesa, Carson
*ANTHONY, El Paso, 112
  (3,328).................3,731
Anthony, Fannin
Anti, Cass
Antioch, Cass..................45
Antioch, Delta.................25
Antioch, Houston
Antioch, Johnson
Antioch, Lavaca
Antioch, Lee
Antioch, Madison...............15
Antioch, Navarro
Antioch, Panola 121
Antioch, Shelby .... NA
Antioch, Smith .... NA
Antioch, Stonewall
Antiquity, Anderson
Antlers, Fannin
*ANTON, Hockley, 70 (1,212)... 1,254
Apache Shores, Travis.......... NA
Apex, San Saba
Apolonia, Grimes
Apperson's, Bowie
APPLEBY, Nacogdoches (449)...550

Bedi, Grimes
*Bedias, Grimes, 37 301
BEE CAVE[s], Travis (241) 309
Beech[wood], Shelby
Beech Creek, Tyler
Beech [Beach] Grove, Jasper
Bee Creek, Ellis
Bee House [Bee], Coryell 40
§*BEEVILLE, Bee, 823
   (13,547). 14,284
Behring Store, Guadalupe
Behrnville, Williamson. 30
Belcherville [Belcher], Montague . .34
Belden, Morris
Belding, Pecos
Belen, El Paso
Belen, Mitchell
Belfalls, Bell 20
Belgrade, Newton . . . . NA
Belk, Lamar 55
Belknap, Young
Bell, Montgomery
Belladonna, Bastrop
Bellah, Baylor
*BELLAIRE, Harris, 1,115
   (13,844). 14,490
Bell Bottom, Waller
Bell Branch, Ellis 20
Bellco, Wheeler
Belle Branch, Atascosa
Belle Plain[e], Callahan
Belle Plain, Moore
Belle Point, Navarro
Belleview, Rusk
Belleville, Gonzales
*BELLEVUE, Clay, 42 (333) 359
Bell Fountain, Panola
*BELLMEAD, McLennan, 190
   (8,336). 8,403
Bello, DeWitt
Bellona, Falls
*BELLS, Grayson, 80 (962) 1,006
Bell's Ferry, Jasper
Bell's Landing, Brazoria
Bell Springs, Hill
§*BELLVILLE, Austin, 448
   (3,378) 3,715
Bellville, Zapata
Bellwood, Smith
Belmena, Milam 15
*Belmont, Gonzales, 6 60
Belott, Houston 101
§*BELTON, Bell, 934
   (12,463). 15,541
Belt's, Tyler
Belt's Store, Navarro
Belvey, Borden
Belzora, Smith
Ben, Wood
Benada, DeWitt
*Ben Arnold, Milam, 13 148
*BENAVIDES, Duval, 54
   (1,788) 1,918
Benavides Hill, Webb
*Ben Bolt, Jim Wells, 7 110
*BENBROOK, Tarrant
   (19,564) 22,902
Benchley, Brazos
Benchley, Robertson, 32 110
Bencini, Newton
*Bend, San Saba, 8 115
Bender, Harris
Bendetsen, Liberty
Bendy's Landing, Tyler
Ben Ficklen, Tom Green
Benford, Polk
*Ben Franklin, Delta, 8 75
Ben Hur, Limestone 100

Benina, San Augustine
§*BENJAMIN, Knox, 23 (225) 230
Benner, Gillespie
Bennett, Llano
Bennett, Parker 40
Bennett, Red River
Bennett, Sabine
Bennett, San Saba
Bennett, Yoakum
Bennette['s Mills], Montgomery
Bennett's, Houston
Bennett's Bridge, Brazoria
Bennett's Ferry, Brazoria
Bennett Station, Frio
Bennie, Moore
Bennview, Jackson
Benoit, Runnels 22
Benonine, Wheeler
Benson, Hunt
Benton, Atascosa
Bentonville, Fannin
Bentonville, Jim Wells 15
Benvanue, Clay
Benville, Eastland
Benwest, Jackson
*Ben Wheeler, Van Zandt, 119 . . . 400
Benz, Bexar
Benzine, Jackson
*Berclair, Goliad, 12 253
Berea, Bell
Berea, Houston 41
Berea, Marion 74
Berger, Bell
*Bergheim, Kendall, 13 . . . . .NA
Bergs, Bexar
Berg's Mill, Bexar
Bering, Polk
Berlin, Erath
Berlin, Washington . . . . .NA
Berlin, Wilbarger
Bermuda, Chambers
Bermuda, Shelby
Bermuda, Webb
Bernardo [Prairie], Colorado. 155
Bernard Station, Wharton
Bernecker, Fisher
Bernhardsville, Guadalupe
Bernice, Andrews
Bernstein, Hansford
Berrien, Smith
Berryhill, Shackelford. 5
Berry's Creek, Williamson 50
BERRYVILLE, Henderson (749). . 960
Bertie, Hardeman
*BERTRAM, Burnet, 107 (849) . .1,100
Berwick, Jack
Bess, Delta
Bessemer, Llano
Bessie, Cameron
Bessie, Gaines
Bessmay, Jasper. . . . . .NA
Best, Hays
Best, Reagan, 5 2
Beth, Collin
Beth, Palo Pinto
Bethany, Collin
Bethany, Fayette
Bethany, Panola 50
Bethany, Tyler
Bethard, Dallas
Bethel, Anderson 50
Bethel, Brazos
Bethel, Ellis 25
Bethel, Henderson 25
Bethel, Hopkins
Bethel, Runnels. 12
Bethel, San Saba
Bethel, Tarrant

Bethel, Wheeler
Bethelder, Brazoria
Bethesda, Grayson
Bethesda, Titus
Bethlehem, Hill
Bethlehem [Old Bethlehem],
   Upshur 75
Betner, Lamar
Bettie, Upshur 110
Bettina, Llano
Betts, Bastrop
Betts, Grimes
Beulah, Angelina
Beulah, Hamilton
Beulah, Johnson
Beulah, Limestone. 12
Beulah, Moore
Beulah, Palo Pinto
Beulah, Wilbarger
Beverly, Briscoe
Beverly, Coryell
Beverly, Llano
Beverly, McLennan
Beverly, Swisher
Beverly Hill, Collin
*BEVERLY HILLS, McLennan
   (2,048) 2,133
BEVIL OAKS, Jefferson
   (1,350). 1,550
Bevilport, Jasper . . . . NA
Bevil Settlement, Jasper
Bexar, Bexar
Beyersville, Williamson. 75
Biardstown, Lamar 75
Bibb, Comanche
Bibles, Hardeman
Biddle, Scurry
Biegel, Fayette
Bigbend, Brewster
*Big Bend National Park,
   Brewster, 7 194
Bigby Corner, Glasscock
Big Creek, Burleson . . . . NA
Big Creek, Fort Bend
Big Creek, Hutchinson
Big Creek, Jasper
Big Creek, Liberty
Big Creek, San Jacinto
Big Cut, Panola
Big Cypress, Camp
Big Cypress, Harris
Big Dollar, Wood
*Bigfoot, Frio, 16 75
Big Four, Hunt
Biggers, Collin
Biggs, Panola
Biggs, Shelby
*Biggs Field, El Paso 4,226
Big Hill, Gonzales
Big Hill, Limestone 9
§*BIG LAKE, Reagan, 195
   (3,672) 3,481
Big Lump, Milam
Big Motte, Jackson
Big Oaks, Marion
Big Paint, Real
Big Ridge, Liberty
Big Rock, Van Zandt
Big Sandy, Polk
*BIG SANDY, Upshur, 180
   (1,185) 1,294
§*BIG SPRING, Howard,
   1,307 (23,093) 23,389
Big Spring, Polk
Big Square, Castro 3
Big Thicket, Liberty . . . . NA
Big Valley, Comanche
Big Valley, Mills 35

Bonnie View, Refugio 135
Bono, Johnson
Bonton, Kendall
Bonus, Wharton...............42
*Bon Wier, Newton, 19.........475
Booker, Bowie
*BOOKER, Lipscomb-Ochiltree,
   92 (1,236) 1,255
Booker, Panola
Bookout, Scurry
Boom, Castro
Boon, Blanco
Boone, Hale
Boone, Walker
Boone, Williamson
Boone Prairie, Robertson
Booner, Hidalgo
Boonesboro[ugh], Uvalde
Boone's Rock, Floyd
Booneville, Hopkins
Boons Ferry, Tyler
Boonsville, Wise 52
Boonville, Brazos
Boory, Cameron
Booth, Fort Bend, 130 .... NA
Booth, Walker
Boot Hill, Oldham
Booth Spur, Floyd
Bootleg, Deaf Smith
Booton, Caldwell
Boquillas, Brewster
Boquillas Hot Springs, Brewster
Boracho, Culberson
Borden[ville, Station], Colorado ...60
Borden's, Fort Bend
Bordentown, Fort Bend
Borders [Chapel, Hill], Taylor
Bordersville, Harris
Boren, Panola
Borens Mills, San Augustine
*BORGER, Hutchinson, 834
   (15,675)................ 15,359
Borrego, Bexar
Borrillo, Pecos
Bosque, Bosque
Bosqueville, McLennan........200
Boss, Tarrant
Bossier, Fisher
Bostick, Smith
Bostick's Crossing, Austin
§*Boston, Bowie, 48 200
Boston, Houston
Boston Ranch, Oldham
Boswell, Walker
Botha, Gonzales
Bottle Springs, Bowie
Bottom, Bell
Botts, Gonzales
Boudreaux Estates, Harris
Boulevard Junction, Cameron
Bourland, Floyd
*BOVINA, Parmer, 84 (1,549) ... 1,783
Bovine, Lavaca
Bovine Bend, Austin
Bowden, Red River
Bowen, Erath
Bowers, Milam .... NA
Bowers, Polk .... NA
Bowers, Scurry
Bowers City, Gray 26
Bowery, Leon
*BOWIE, Montague, 557
   (4,990) 5,350
Bowie Hill, Cass
Bowlder, Mills
Bowles, Uvalde
Bowling, Leon
Bowling, McLennan

Bowman, Archer 200
Bowman, Taylor
Bowman's Springs, Tarrant
Bowser, San Saba........... 20
Bowser Bend, San Saba
Box, Lamar
Box Church, Limestone 45
Box Creek, Cherokee
Boxelder, Red River 258
Box Quarter, Robertson
Boxville, Lavaca
Boxwood, Upshur.............. 20
Boy, Montgomery
Boyce, Ellis 75
Boyd, Fannin................ 40
*BOYD, Wise, 188 (1,041) 1,249
Boyds Chapel, Jones
Boyd's Mill, Wise
Boydston, Donley
Boydston, Gray
Boyle, Bastrop
Boyles, Falls
Boynton, Comanche
*Boys' Ranch, Oldham, 18 435
Boyt, Jefferson
Boz, Ellis
Bozar, Mills 9
Bracewell, Polk
Brachfield, Rusk.............. 40
Brack, Hutchinson
Bracken, Comal............... 76
Brackenridge, Karnes
Brackenville, Milam
§*BRACKETTVILLE, Kinney, 105
   (1,740) 1,858
Bracy Island, Waller
Bracy's Ferry, Waller
Brad, Palo Pinto 16
Bradburn, Hunt
Braden, Colorado
Bradfield, Kaufman
Bradford, Anderson 30
Bradley, Angelina
Bradley, Houston
Bradley, Johnson
Bradley, Sherman
Bradleys Corner, Wichita
Bradshaw, Rusk
Bradshaw, Taylor, 18........... 61
Bradville, Waller
§*BRADY, McCulloch, 409
   (5,946) 5,962
Brady, Shelby ....NA
Bragg, Hardin
Bragg, Navarro
Brambleton, Tarrant
Branch, Collin................ 447
Branchville, Milam 200
Brand, Scurry
Brandenburg, Harris
Brandenburg, Stonewall
Brandon, Hill, 3 80
Brand Rock, Frio
Brannon's Store, Parker
*Branom, Hopkins..............NA
Branon, Lavaca
Bransford['s Store], Tarrant
Brantley, Montgomery
Branton, Eastland
*Brashear, Hopkins, 26......... 280
Bratton, Harris
Bravo, Bastrop
Bravo, Hartley
Bray, Donley
Bray, Navarro
Bray, Stephens
Brazlime, Hill
*BRAZORIA, Brazoria, 349

(2,717) 3,164
Brazos, Palo Pinto.............97
Brazos Agency, Young
Brazos Point, Bosque .... NA
Brazosport, Brazoria....... 59,971
Brazos Santiago, Cameron
Breaker, Angelina
Breckenridge, Medina
§*BRECKENRIDGE, Stephens,
   578 (5,665) 5,808
Breckenridge Springs, Panola
Breckinridge, Dallas
Breckwalker, Stephens
Bremen, Callahan
*BREMOND, Robertson, 68
   (1,110)...................1,146
§*BRENHAM, Washington,
   1,315 (11,952)........... 13,796
Brenner, Guadalupe
Bresford, Garza
Breslau, Lavaca...............65
Brethern Farm, Brooks
Brewer's Station, Taylor
Brewster, Brown
Brewster's Bluff, Panola
Briar, Archer
‡ Briar, Tarrant-Wise-Parker
   (3,899)................. 4,700
Briar Branch, Medina
*BRIARCLIFF, Travis (335).......376
BRIAROAKS, Johnson (535).....656
Briary, Milam ....NA
Brice, Hall....................37
Brick, Liberty
Bridge, Kaufman
*BRIDGE CITY, Orange, 334
   (8,010)................. 8,336
*BRIDGEPORT, Wise, 477
   (3,581)................. 4,093
Bridges, Polk
Bridges Chapel, Titus 90
Bridgetown, Wichita
Bridgevalley, Fayette
Briggs, Bexar
*Briggs, Burnet, 7..............92
Briggs, Dallas
Bright, Navarro
Brighton, Harris
Brighton, Nueces
Bright Star, Hopkins
Bright Star, Rains.............592
Bright Star, Van Zandt
Brigman, Hill
Brinker, Hopkins .... NA
Briquette, Milam
*Briscoe, Wheeler, 17..........135
Bristol, Ellis 94
Bristol City, Collin
Bristow, Hamilton
Bristow, Llano
Bristow, Montgomery
Bristow, Nacogdoches
Bristow's Ferry, Panola
Brit, Anderson
Britamer, Baylor
Brite [Ranch], Presidio
Britt, Leon
Britt, Scurry
Brittain, Shelby
Britton, Ellis
Britton, Tarrant
Brizendine Mills, Williamson
*BROADDUS, San Augustine,
   53 (212)..................210
Broadmoor, McCulloch
Broadview, Lubbock
Broadway, Armstrong
Broadway, Crosby 20

*Burkett, Coleman, 16 30
Burkett, Stephens
*Burkeville, Newton, 57 515
Burkland, Williamson
Burks, Cass
Burks, La Salle
Burl, Guadalupe
Burleigh, Austin. 69
Burleson['s], Bastrop
*BURLESON, Johnson-Tarrant,
   1,432 (16,113). 20,500
Burleson, Lampasas
Burleson's Springs,Williamson
*Burlington, Milam, 11 140
Burlington, Montague
Burnam, Callahan
Burnam [Burnham], Ellis
Burnell, Karnes
Burnell Switch, Bee
§*BURNET, Burnet, 456
   (3,423) 4,391
Burney's Bridge, Navarro
Burns, Bowie 400
Burns, Van Zandt
Burns City [Burns], Cooke. 60
Burn's Ford, Burnet
Burnside, Ochiltree
Burns Mill, Panola
Burns Siding, Rusk
Burns Station, DeWitt
Burr, Tarrant
Burr, Wharton
Burrantown, Houston 70
Burris' Prairie, Angelina
Burrough, Austin
Burroughsville, Victoria
Burrow, Hunt . . . . NA
Burt, Comal
*BURTON, Washington, 81
   (311) 326
Burton Springs, Jack
Burtonsville, Shelby
Busby, Fisher
Busco, Harris
Bush, Anderson
Bush, Bowie
Bush, Coryell
Bush, Jones
*Bushland [Bush], Potter, 27 130
Bush's Store, Waller
Bustamante, Zapata, 1. 15
Buster's, Washington
Busterville, Hockley. 6
Busyton, Hamilton
Bute, Henderson
Butler, Bastrop. . . . . NA
Butler, Freestone 67
Butler's, Bee
Buttercup, Williamson
Butter Krust, Travis
Buttermilk Station, Brazoria
Buttfield, Jefferson
Buzzard Roost, Llano
Byerly's Gin, Jasper
*BYERS, Clay, 24 (510) 556
Byfield's Store, Llano
*BYNUM, Hill, 13 (192). 213
Byran, Duval
Byrd, Ellis. 15
Byrd, Houston
Byrds, Brown . . . . NA
Byrd's Store, Brown
Byrdtown, Lamar . . . . NA
Byrne, Tom Green
Byron [Switch], Anderson
Byron, Ellis
Byspot, San Jacinto
Byzone, Hunt

C

Cabell, Fort Bend
Cabeza, DeWitt
Cabot Kingsmill, Gray
*CACTUS, Moore, 33 (1,529) . . .1,957
Cactus, Webb
Cactus Flat, Fisher
Cactus Hill, Wise
Caddell, San Augustine
*Caddo, Stephens, 11 40
Caddo Camp, Hunt
Caddo Grove, Johnson
*CADDO MILLS, Hunt, 96
   (1,068) 1,156
Caddo Peak, Callahan
Caddo Peak, Johnson
Caddo Villa, Hunt
Cade Chapel [Cade], Navarro. 25
Cade Lake, Burleson . . . . .NA
Cadiz, Bee 15
Caesar, Bee
Caesar, Kleberg
Cage, San Patricio
Cain, Dallas
Cain, Lee
Cain City, Gillespie . . . . .NA
Cairo [Springs], Jasper
Cairo, Leon
Caison's, Rusk
Calallen, Nueces
Calaveras, Wilson 100
Calcote, San Augustine
Caldren, Bailey
§*CALDWELL, Burleson, 382
   (3,181) 3,820
Caldwell, Lubbock
Caldwell's Hill, Gillespie
Caldwell's Store, Bastrop
Caldwell's Store, Leon
Caleb, Johnson
Caledonia, Rusk 75
Calef, Tarrant
Calera, Hill
Caleta, Polk
Calf Creek, McCulloch 23
Calgando, Palo Pinto
Calgary, San Augustine
Calhoun, Calhoun
Calhoun, Colorado
Calhoun, Dallas
Calhoun, Gregg
Calhoun, Rusk
Calhoun School, DeWitt
Calhoun's Ferry, Houston
Caliche, San Patricio
California, Jones
California Store, Hidalgo
Calina[Callina],, Limestone. 10
*Call, Newton, 19. 170
Calla, Brazos
Callaghan, Webb
Callahan, Callahan
Callahan, Webb
Callan, Menard
Call Field, Wichita
Callie, Montgomery
*Calliham, McMullen, 6. 200
CALLISBURG, Cooke (344) 442
Call Junction, Jasper 50
Calloway, Upshur
Calloway's Gin, Wood
*CALVERT, Robertson, 68
   (1,536) 1,498
Calvert Junction, Robertson
Calvin, Bastrop
Calvin, Red River
Calvin City, Nueces
Camada Ranch, Jim Wells

Camanche [Comanche] Peak, Hood
Camanche Springs, Blanco
Cambridge, Clay
Camden, Comanche
Camden, Falls
*Camden, Polk, 8 1,200
Camden, Rusk
Camel, Houston
Cameo, Guadalupe
§*CAMERON, Milam, 381
   (5,635). 6,128
Cameron, Travis
‡ Cameron Park, Cameron
   (3,802) 4,738
Camey Spur, Denton
Camilla, San Jacinto 200
Camp Air, Mason 15
Camp Allison, Sutton
Camp Barkley, Taylor
*CAMPBELL, Hunt, 87 (683) 819
Campbell, Navarro
Campbell's Retreat, Refugio
*Campbellton, Atascosa, 12 350
Camp Charlotte, Irion
Camp Colorado, Coleman
Camp Concordia, El Paso
Camp Cooper, Throckmorton
Camp Creek, Bell
Camp Creek, Johnson
Camp Creek Lake, Robertson . . .350
Camp Dallas, Denton
Camp Ford, Smith
Camp Henderson, Johnson
Camp Hudson, Val Verde
Camp Hulen, Matagorda
Camp Lucille, Denton
Camp Maxey, Lamar
Camp Melbourne, Crockett
Camp Melvin, Crockett
Camp Nancy, Angelina
Campo Alto, Hidalgo . . . . .NA
Camp on San Pedro, Val Verde
Camp Providence, Polk
Camp Rice, Hudspeth
Camp Ruby, Polk 35
Camps, Gregg
Camp San Saba, McCulloch 36
Camp San Saba, Menard
Camp Scenic, Kerr
Camp Seale, Polk. . . . . NA
Camp Springs, Scurry. 10
Camp Stockton, Pecos
‡ Camp Swift, Bastrop
   (2,681). 3,516
Camp Switch, Gregg 70
Campti, Shelby. . . . . NA
*Camp Verde, Kerr, 18 41
Camp Willow, Guadalupe . . . . . . .NA
*CAMP WOOD, Real, 52 (679) 795
Camp Worth, San Augustine. . . . . NA
Cana, Bandera
Canaan, Grayson
Canaan, Harrison
Canaan, Limestone
Canada Verde, Wilson 23
§*CANADIAN, Hemphill, 276
   (2,417). 2,398
Canary, Leon . . . . NA
Canary, Madison
Canary, Polk
Canby, Angelina
Candelaria, Presidio 55
Candish, Bee
Candish, Bee
Candon, Tarrant
Cane Branch, Leon
Cane Island, Harris
Caney, Matagorda 300

CANEY CITY, Henderson (170)...214
Caney Creek, Newton
Caney Head, Hardin
Caney Station, Montgomery
Cann, Hemphill
Cannel, Webb
Cannett, Orange
Cannon, Grayson...............50
Cannon Switch, Camp
Cannonville, Hays
Canton, Smith
§*CANTON, Van Zandt, 626
  (2,949)..................3,466
Cantrell, Anderson
Cantu, Hidalgo...............NA
‡*Canutillo, El Paso, 223
  (4,442)..................5,134
Canyon, Lubbock...............40
§*CANYON [City], Randall, 644
  (11,365)................13,219
Canyon City, Comal...........100
‡*Canyon Lake, Comal
  (9,975)................12,988
Canyon Valley, Crosby..........NA
Capiote, Gonzales
Capitola, Fisher...............NA
Capitola, Mason
Caplen, Galveston..............30
Caples, DeWitt
Capps, Moore
Capps Corner, Montague.......NA
Cap Rock, Crosby.............25
Caprock, Ector
Caps, Taylor..................100
Caps Sides, Taylor
Capt's Mill, Hays
Caput, Gaines
Car[r], Mitchell
Cara Blanca, Baylor
Caradan, Mills, 3..............20
Carancahua, Jackson..........301
Caranchua, Jackson
Carbody, Bosque
*CARBON, Eastland, 31 (255)...289
Carbon, Webb
Carbondale, Bowie.............30
Carbondale, Young
Carbonville, Uvalde
Cardiff, Bastrop
Cardiff, Waller
Cardova, Guadalupe
Carew, Van Zandt
*Carey, Childress, 12..........60
Cargray, Carson
Cariker, Panola
Carl, Navarro
Carl, Travis...................NA
Carleton, Cass
Carley, Robertson
Carlisle, Rusk
Carlisle, Trinity...............68
Carlos [Ranch[o], Victoria
Carlos, Grimes...............NA
Carlos City, Aransas
Carlota, Hidalgo
*Carlsbad, Tom Green, 17.......100
CARL'S CORNER, Hill (94)......124
Carlson, Travis................61
*Carlton, Hamilton, 10..........70
Carmean, Fayette
Carmel, Bexar
Carmel, Pecos
Carmel, Walker
*CARMINE, Fayette, 38 (192).....215
Carmona, Polk.................50
Carnell, Refugio
Carnes, Hardeman
Carney, Haskell

Caro, Nacogdoches...........113
Carolina, Falls
Carolina, San Jacinto
Carolina, Walker
Caron, Live Oak
Carp, Falls
Carpenter, Bexar
Carpenter, Wilson.............NA
Carpenters Bluff, Grayson
Carr, Titus
Carr, Victoria
Carriage, Cooke
Carricitos, Cameron...........25
Carrizo, Hudspeth
Carrizo, Zapata
§*CARRIZO SPRINGS, Dimmit,
  270 (5,745)..............5,842
Carroll, Bastrop
Carroll, Hardin
Carroll, Smith................60
Carroll, Stephens
Carroll Springs, Anderson.......20
Carrolla, Jasper
Carroll's Prairie, Hopkins
Carroll's Store, Shelby
Carroll Switch, Tyler
*CARROLLTON, Denton-Dallas-
  Collin, 5,075 (82,169).....100,950
Carrollton, Hopkins
Carr's, Hill
Carruth, Caldwell
Carsner, Victoria
Carson, Fannin................22
Carson, Midland
Carson City, Carson
*Carswell Base, Tarrant........3,162
*Carta Valley, Edwards..........12
Carter, Denton
Carter[sville], Parker
Carter, Polk
Carter, Stephens
Carter Lake, Brazos...........NA
Carter's Flat, Edwards
Carter's Prairie, Washington
Carter's Station, Liberty
Carterville, Cass..............39
Carterville, Harrison
§*CARTHAGE, Panola, 666
  (6,496)..................6,605
Cartwright, Kaufman..........NA
Cartwright, Wood..............61
Caruth, Dallas
Carver, Leon.................NA
Carver Park, Bexar...........NA
Casa Piedra, Presidio..........NA
Casco, Dickens
Case's [Mills], Travis
Casey, Bell
Casey, El Paso...............115
Casey, Harris
Casey, Jeff Davis
Caseyville, Young
Cash, Goliad
Cash, Hunt...................56
*Cason, Morris, 8.............173
Cass, Cass....................60
Cassie, Burnet...............446
Cassin, Bexar.................NA
*Castell, Llano, 9.............72
Castine, Karnes
Castle, DeWitt
Castle Heights, McLennan
*CASTLE HILLS, Bexar (4,198).4,329
Castolon, Brewster.............8
Castor, Mills
*CASTROVILLE, Medina, 229
  (2,159)..................2,838
Cataline, Hemphill

*Catarina, Dimmit, 5...........45
Cat Claw, Callahan
Catfish, Henderson
Cathedral, Brewster
Cathrans Store, Lamar
Cathron's Store, Lamar
Catlett's Creek, Wise
Cato, McLennan
Caton[ville], Red River
*Cat Spring, Austin, 36.........76
Cat Town, Llano
Cavan, Sterling
Cavazos, Cameron............201
Cave, Bosque
Cave Creek, Gillespie.........NA
Cave Springs, Bosque
Cave Springs, Harrison
Caviness, Lamar..............80
Cavins Mill, Newton
Cavitt, Coryell
Cawthon, Brazos..............75
Cawthon, Grimes
Cayote, Bosque...............75
*Cayuga, Anderson, 8..........200
Caywood, Brazos
Cecil, Walker
Cedar, Fayette
Cedar, Kaufman
Cedar Bayou, Harris-Chambers.1,287
Cedar Bayou, Liberty
Cedar Bluff, Harris
Cedar Brakes, Brazoria
Cedar Creek, Anderson
*Cedar Creek, Bastrop, 131.....200
Cedar Creek, Waller...........NA
Cedar Creek, Washington
Cedar Creek Park, Hill
Cedarfield, Grayson
Cedar Fork, Kaufman
Cedar Grove, Brazoria
Cedar Grove, Kaufman
*CEDAR HILL, Dallas-Ellis, 851
  (19,988)...............28,100
Cedar Hill, Floyd..............36
Cedar Island, Limestone
Cedar Knob, Bell
Cedar Knob, Palo Pinto
Cedar Lake, Brazoria
Cedar Lake, Gaines
Cedar Lake, Matagorda........160
*Cedar Lane, Matagorda, 7......55
Cedar Mills, Grayson
*CEDAR PARK, Williamson-
  Travis, 912 (5,161).......13,659
Cedar Point, Brown
Cedar Point, Collin
Cedar Point, Erath
Cedar Point, Falls
Cedar Point, Llano............NA
Cedar Shores, Bosque.........170
Cedar Spring, Washington
Cedar Springs, Falls...........90
Cedar Springs, Upshur........100
Cedar Station, Liberty
Cedarton, Brown
Cedarvale, Kaufman..........NA
Cedar Valley, Bell.............4
Cedar Valley, Hays
Cedar Valley, Travis...........70
Cedar Yard, Shelby
*Cee Vee, Cottle, 4............45
Cego, Falls...................42
Cele, Travis..................NA
*CELESTE, Hunt, 64 (733)......896
Celeste, Montague
*CELINA, Collin, 168 (1,737)...2,127
Celotex, Fisher
Celynda, Lee

Coshatte Bluff, Polk
Cosner, Denton
*Cost, Gonzales, 21 62
Coth, Montague
Cotland, Newton
Cottage, Angelina
Cottage, Henderson
Cottage Hill, Bexar
Cottage Hill, Titus
Cottage Home, Grimes
Cottle, Cottle
Cotton, Grimes
Cotton Center, Fannin 5
*Cotton Center, Hale, 18 205
Cottondale, Wise . . . . NA
Cotton Flat, Midland
Cotton Gin, Freestone. 28
Cotton Mill Spur, Grayson
Cotton Patch, DeWitt. 11
Cotton Plant, Lamar
Cotton Plant, Rusk
Cotton Plant, Stephens
Cottonwood, Brazos . . . . NA
Cottonwood [Springs], Callahan . . .65
Cottonwood, Dickens
Cottonwood, Erath. 23
Cottonwood, Falls
Cottonwood, Fayette
Cottonwood, Foard
Cottonwood, Jack
COTTONWOOD, Kaufman, 2
   (156) 204
Cottonwood, Madison 40
Cottonwood, McLennan 150
Cottonwood, Nolan
Cottonwood, Somervell. 24
Cottonwood, Travis
Cottonwood, Wilbarger
Cottonwood Flat, Scurry
COTTONWOOD SHORES, Burnet
   (548) 791
Cottonwood Springs, Young
§*COTULLA, La Salle, 154
   (3,694) 4,411
Couch, Dallas
Couch, Karnes 10
Couch, Roberts
Couchman, Freestone
Cougar, Parker
Coughran, Atascosa 20
Country Campus, Walker
County Line, Anderson
County Line, Austin
County Line, Coke
Countyline, Cooke
County Line, Lubbock. 30
County Line, Rains 40
County Line, Runnels
County Line, Sterling
*Coupland, Williamson, 37 135
Coursey, Lamar
Courtland, Cass
Courtland, Shelby
Courtney, Grimes. 55
Courtney, Martin
Cousinville, Knox
COVE, Chambers (402) 528
Cove, Coryell
Cove, Palo Pinto
Cove, San Patricio
Cove City, Fort Bend
Cove City, Orange
Cove Springs, Cherokee 40
Covey, Frio
*COVINGTON, Hill, 38 (238). 303
Cowan, Bee
Cowan, Erath
Cow Bayou, McLennan

Cow Bayou, Orange
Cowboy, McCulloch
Cow Creek, Burnet
Cow Creek, Erath 14
Cow Creek, Newton
Cowen, Bowie
Cowen, Wise
Cowhill, Hunt
Cow Prairie, Van Zandt
Cow Spur, Garza
Cox, Lamar
Cox, Milam
Cox, Titus
Cox, Upshur 30
Coxburgh, Lamar
Coxey, Montgomery
Cox Point, Calhoun
Cox's, Lamar
Cox's Colony, Crosby
Cox's Gin, Van Zandt
Cox's Mill, Coryell
Cox's Switch, Montgomery
Coxton, Jack
Coxville, Bastrop
Coxville, Hill
Coxville, Travis . . . . .NA
Coy, Mills
*Coyanosa, Pecos, 15. 270
Coy City, Karnes, 17 30
Coymack, Falls
Coyote, Knox
Cozart, Panola
Crab Apple, Gillespie
Crabb, Fort Bend 125
Crabbs Prairie, Walker . . . . .NA
Cracker's Neck, Chambers
Craddock, Gaines
Craft, Cherokee. 21
Craft, Ellis
Crafton, Wise. 20
Craig, Rusk . . . . .NA
Craig, Victoria
Craig's, Lamar
Crain, DeWitt
Crain, Maverick
Crain, Zavala
*CRANDALL, Kaufman, 82
   (1,652) 2,298
§*CRANE, Crane, 203
   (3,533) 3,408
Crane's [Crain's] Mill, Comal
*CRANFILLS GAP, Bosque, 35
   (269). 303
Cranz, Gonzales
Crasco, Colorado
Cravens [Mill], Red River
Cravenville, Bee
Crawfish, Floyd
Crawfish, Hale
*CRAWFORD, McLennan, 73
   (631) 680
Crawford, Titus
Cream, Parker
Creamer, Comanche
Cream Level [or Liel], Parker
Creamlevel, Van Zandt
Creath, Houston 20
Creath, Houston
Crecy, Trinity 15
Creech, San Augustine
Creechville, Ellis. 15
Creed, Cooke
*CREEDMOOR, Travis, 6 (194) . . . 224
Creek, Houston
Crenshaw, Falls
Creole, Lavaca
Crescent, Titus
Crescent Heights, Henderson 35

Crescent Lake, Leon
Crescent Village, Refugio
Cresco, Hale
Cresco, Palo Pinto
*Cresson, Hood-Johnson, 34 208
Cresswell, Ochiltree
Crestonio, Duval
Crestwood, Llano. . . . . NA
Crestwood, Marion
Creswell [Criswell], Houston
Crete, Trinity
Crews, Runnels 40
Crews Church, Gregg
Crewville, McCulloch
Crim, Rusk
Crimea, Hill
Crims Chapel, Rusk
Cring, Harris
Crisp, Ellis
Crisp, Hopkins
Crockett, Bandera
§*CROCKETT, Houston, 515
   (7,024) 7,138
Crockett's Bluff, Smith-Van Zandt
Crockettsville, Panola
Croft's Mills, Harris
Cronin, Anderson
Cronje, Bell
‡*Crosby, Harris, 575 (1,811). . . 1,929
§*CROSBYTON, Crosby, 116
   (2,026) 2,034
Crosbyville [Crosby's Landing], Brazoria
Cross, Grimes 49
Cross, McMullen 60
Cross Creek, Travis
Cross Cut, Brown. . . . . NA
Crossett, Upton
Cross Gin, Cooke
Crossland, Gray
Crossland, Young
‡ Cross Mountain, Bexar
   (1,112) 1,278
Cross Out, Brown
*CROSS PLAINS, Callahan, 122
   (1,063) 1,070
Cross Roads, Anderson
Cross Roads, Bastrop
Crossroads, Cass 40
Cross Roads, Comanche
Crossroads, Delta 10
CROSS ROADS, Denton (361). . . .487
Crossroads, Grayson
Crossroads, Harrison 100
Cross Roads, Henderson 135
Crossroads, Hopkins. . . . . NA
Crossroads, Jackson
Cross Roads, Madison 75
Cross Roads, Milam 35
Crossroads, Montgomery
Cross Roads, Nacogdoches
Crossroads, Nacogdoches
Cross Roads, Navarro
Cross Roads, Robertson
Cross Roads, Rusk . . . . NA
Cross Roads, Wheeler
Cross Roads, Williamson
CROSS TIMBER, Johnson (NC) . .289
Crossville, Bell
Crossville, Cooke
Crothers, McCulloch
Crotan, Stonewall
Croton, Dickens 5
Crouch, Atascosa
Crow, Cass
Crow, Wood. 5
§*CROWELL [City], Foard, 102
   (1,230) 1,213
*CROWLEY, Tarrant-Johnson,

Debard's, Smith
Debbie, Wood
*DeBerry, Panola, 36 191
Decatur, Collin
§*DECATUR, Wise, 643
(4,245) 4,858
Decker, Nolan
Decker, Travis
Decker Prairie, Montgomery . . . . . NA
Deckman, Dallas
Deco, Harris
Decorah, Hunt
DeCordova, Hood
Decoy, Nacogdoches
Dee, Jones
Dee, Randall
Deep Creek, Baylor
Deep Creek, Callahan
Deep Creek, McCulloch
Deep Lake, Hall
Deepwater, Harris
Deer Creek, Clay
Deer Creek, Falls
Deer Creek, Mason
Deer Haven, Llano . . . . NA
*DEER PARK, Harris, 923
(27,424) 30,396
Deerton, Mason
Deeville, Lamar
Defense, Bowie
Defo, Van Zandt
De Graffenreid, Henderson
De Gress, Jack
*DE KALB, Bowie, 171 (1,976) . 1,865
Deland, McCulloch
Delaware, Brown
Delaware, Cooke
Delaware Bend, Cooke
Delba, Fannin
*DE LEON, Comanche, 269
(2,190) 2,370
Delfina, Hidalgo
Delgado, Brown
Delhi, Bosque
Delhi, Caldwell 300
Delia, Limestone 20
Delight, Kerr
Delk, Jones
Dell, Bosque
Della Plain, Floyd
*DELL CITY, Hudspeth, 42
(569) 780
Dellwood, Webb
Delma, Newton
Del Mar, Cameron
Delmar, Eastland
Del Mar Hills, Webb
Delmer, Cherokee
*Delmita, Starr, 5 50
Delong, Tom Green
Delphi, Taylor
Delphine, Jefferson
Delphine, Parker
Delray, Panola 40
§*DEL RIO, Val Verde, 1,306
(30,705) 34,167
Delrose, Upshur. 35
Delta, Hamilton
*Del Valle, Travis, 205 2,476
Delvin, Floyd
Delwau, Travis
Delwin, Cottle. 12
Demarco, Burnet
Demi-John Island, Brazoria 18
Demings Bridge, Matagorda
Democrat, Comanche
Democrat, Mills 8
Dempsey, Cass

Denhawken, Wilson 46
*DENISON, Grayson, 1,350
(21,505) 22,425
Denman Crossroads, Van Zandt . .NA
Denmark, Anderson
Denning, San Augustine 361
*Dennis, Parker, 7 90
Dennis Chapel, Hopkins
Denny, Dallas
Denny, Falls
Denrock, Dallam
Denson Springs, Anderson 100
Dent, Hunt
Denton, Callahan 6
§*DENTON, Denton, 3,606
(66,270) 78,028
Denton, Franklin
Denton Community, Callahan
Denton Creek, Denton
Denton Creek, Montague
Dentonio, Dimmit
Denver, Montague
*DENVER CITY, Yoakum, 305
(5,156) 5,009
Denworth, Gray
*DEPORT, Lamar-Red River, 41
(746) 852
Derby, Frio, 4 50
Derden, Hill
Dermott, Scurry
Dernal, Victoria
*Desdemona [Desdimonia],
Eastland, 21. 180
Desert, Collin 25
*DESOTO, Dallas, 1,437
(30,544) 35,615
Dessau, Travis. . . . . .NA
Detmold, Milam . . . . .NA
*DETROIT, Red River, 59 (706). . . 799
Dety, Leon
Devenport, Hunt
*DEVERS, Liberty, 29 (318) 373
DeVilbiss Ranch, Frio
Devillia, Angelina
Devil's Drag, Jackson
Devil's Pocket, Wharton
Devil's River, Val Verde
*DEVINE, Medina, 276 (3,928) . .5,130
Dew, Freestone 71
Dewalt, Fort Bend, 159 . . . . .NA
Dewdrop, Liberty
DeWees, Wilson 35
Deweesville, Karnes. 12
Dewet, Gonzales
Dewey, Comanche
Dewey, Hunt
Dewey, Liberty
Dewey, Montague
Dewey, Rusk
‡*Deweyville, Newton, 46
(1,218) 1,376
Dewville, Gonzales 15
Dexter, Cooke 18
Dextra, Nacogdoches. . . . . .NA
*D'Hanis, Medina, 36. 548
Dial, Fannin 76
Dial, Hutchinson
Dialville, Cherokee, 8 200
Diamond City, Lamar
*Diana, Upshur, 86 585
Diantha, Foard
Diaz, Cameron
Diaz, Hidalgo
*DIBOLL, Angelina, 187
(4,341). 5,608
Dice, Bell
Dicey, Parker . . . . .NA
Dick, Jack

§*DICKENS, Dickens, 24 (322) . . .288
Dickey, Leon
*DICKINSON, Galveston, 776
(9,497). 17,578
Dickson, Hunt
Dickworsham, Clay
Dido, Tarrant
Dido, Walker
Dierlam, Calhoun
Dies, Hardin
Dies, Tyler. . . . . NA
Dietz, Guadalupe
*Dike, Hopkins, 16 170
Dillard, Erath
Dillard, Floyd
Dillard's, Falls
*DILLEY, Frio, 110 (2,632) 2,977
Dillingham Prairie, Jack
Dillon, Hopkins
Dilworth, Gonzales 15
Dilworth, Red River 22
*Dime Box, Lee, 38. 313
§*DIMMITT, Castro, 335
(4,408). 4,309
Dimple, Red River 60
*Dinero, Live Oak, 7 344
Ding Dong, Bell 22
Dingler, Comanche
Dinkins, Brazos
Dinsmore, Nolan
Dinsmore, Wharton
Direct, Lamar 70
Dirgin, Rusk 12
Discus, Culberson
Dittlinger, Comal
Ditto, Atascosa
Divide, Coke
Divide, Guadalupe
Divide, Hopkins . . . . NA
Divot, Frio
Dix, Martin
Dixico, Harris
Dixie, Brooks
Dixie, Edwards
Dixie, Grayson 17
Dixie, Jackson
Dixie, Lamar
Dixie, Panola
Dixie, San Jacinto
Dixon, Hunt. 31
Dixon-Hopewell, Houston 49
Dixon Prairie, Bastrop
Dixson, Cooke
Doak Springs, Lee 50
Doans [Crossing, Store], Wilbarger
. 20
*Dobbin, Montgomery, 10 170
Dobbs City, Dickens
Dobrowolski, Atascosa 10
Dobskyville, Goliad
Dobyville, Burnet
Dock, Polk
Dock, Scurry
Dock, Tyler
Dockum Ranch, Dickens
Dodd, Castro 15
Dodd, Webb
*DODD CITY, Fannin, 19 (350). . . .432
Dodd City, Travis
Dodd's Store, Williamson
Doddville, Lee
Dode, Crosby
Dode, Floyd
*Dodge [Station], Walker, 12. 150
*DODSON, Collingsworth, 7
(113). 104
Dodson, Tarrant
Dodson Prairie, Palo Pinto 18

Dodson[ville], Houston
Dodson's Store, Coryell
Dodsonville, Collingsworth
Dog Ridge, Bell 125
Dog Town, Falls
Dogwood, Tyler
Dogwood City, Smith 800
Dogwood Grove, San Augustine
Doke, Llano
Dolan, Angelina
Dolce, Shelby
Dolchburg, Maverick
Dolen, Liberty . . . . NA
Dolive, San Jacinto
Dollarhide, Andrews
Dollarhide, Atascosa
Dolman, Stonewall
Dolores, Kinney
Dolores, Webb
Dolph, Grimes
Dome, Mitchell
‡ **Dominion, Bexar (1,196)** 1,427
DOMINO, Cass (101) 108
Donahoe, Bell
Donald, Denton
Donald, Johnson
Donelton, Hunt
*Donie, Freestone, 23 206
Donley, Donley
*DONNA, Hidalgo, 418
   (12,652) 15,282
Donnell, Wilbarger
Donnell's Mill, Young
Donnybrook Place, Harris
Donovan, Angelina
Don Tol, Wharton
*Doole, McCulloch, 6 74
Dooley, Limestone
Dora, Nolan
DORCHESTER, Grayson, 15
   (137) 167
Dorman, Wharton
Dorne, Liberty
Dorras, Fisher
Dorras, Stonewall 30
Dorr Junction, Nacogdoches
Dorsey, Montague
Dorsey, Titus
Dorso, Val Verde
*Doss, Cass . . . . NA
Doss, Clay
Doss, Gillespie, 10 75
Dot, Anderson
Dot, Falls .17
Dothan, Eastland 20
Dothan, Hall
Dotson, Panola 40
Doty, Orange
Double Bayou, Chambers 400
Double Diamond Estates,
   Hutchinson-Moore 175
Double Header, Bell
Double Horn, Burnet
Double Mountain, Stonewall
*DOUBLE OAK, Denton
   (1,664) 2,224
Double Oak, Denton
Double Springs, Tarrant
*Doucette, Tyler, 6 131
*Dougherty, Floyd, 5 109
Dougherty, Rains 342
Douglas, Smith . . . . NA
*Douglass, Nacogdoches, 23 75
Douglass, Red River
*DOUGLASSVILLE, Cass, 22
   (192) .213
Douro, Ector

Dove, Tarrant
Dover, Navarro
Dovie, Wise
Dow, Brazoria
Dow, Gray
Dowco, Smith
Dowden, Polk
Dowell, Fisher
Dowlin, Lamar
Dowling, Jefferson
Downing, Comanche 30
Downs, McLennan
Downsville, McLennan 150
Dowson Springs, Anderson
Doxey, Travis
Doxie, Houston
Doyle, Limestone 50
Doyle, Limestone
Dozier, Collingsworth 30
Draco, Runnels
Draco, Williamson
Draco, Wise
Dragoo, Burnet
Drake, Liberty
Drane, Navarro 16
Draper, Bowie
Draper, Dickens
Draper, Jack
Drasco, Runnels 20
Draw, Lynn 39
Dreamland, Starr
Drefoos, Hemphill
Dreka, Shelby . . . . .NA
Dreka, Swisher
Drennan, Sterling
Drennen's Store, Coryell
Dresden, Navarro 25
Dresser, Bell
Dressy, Callahan
Drew, Kaufman
Drews Landing, Polk
Dreyer, Gonzales 20
*Driftwood, Hays, 59 21
*DRIPPING SPRINGS, Hays, 386
   (1,033) 1,181
Driscoll, Jim Wells
*DRISCOLL, Nueces, 20 (688) . . . 739
Driskill, Travis
Driver's Store, Cass
Drop, Denton
Drum, Terrell
Drummond, Cottle
Drummond, Young
Drumright, Glasscock
Drury, San Jacinto
Drusilla, Wood
Druso, Houston
Dryburg, Jasper
Dry Creek, Parker
*Dryden, Terrell, 2 13
Dryer, Gonzales
Dry Medio, Bee
Dry Valley, Montague
Dubina, Fayette 44
*DUBLIN, Erath, 388 (3,190) 3,658
Dubois, Aransas
Dubois, Refugio
Dubose, Duval
Dubwright, Taylor
Duck Creek, Dallas
Dudeville, Milam
Dudley, Callahan 25
Dudley Place, Grayson
Duff, Foard
Duff, Shelby
Duffau, Erath, 5 76
Duffau Wells, Erath
Duff Prairie, Stephens

Duff's Settlement, Austin
Dugan's Chapel, Grayson
Dugansville [Dugan's Store], Grayson
Dugger, Guadalupe 20
Dugout, Fisher
Dugout, McCulloch
Duke, Fort Bend
Duke, Panola
Dulaney, Hunt
Duley, Jones
Dulin, Brown
Dull['s Ranch], La Salle
§***DUMAS, Moore, 765**
   (12,871) 13,764
Dumont, Harris
*Dumont, King-Dickens, 4 85
Dump, Collin
Dump, Limestone
Dunagan, Angelina
Dunbar, Rains 40
Dunbar, Trinity
Duncan, Hartley
Duncan, Jasper
Duncan, Smith
Duncan, Wharton
Duncan Switch, Dallas
Duncan's Woods, Orange
*DUNCANVILLE [Duncan Switch],
   Dallas, 1,612 (35,008) 36,364
Dundee, Archer 12
Dunkin, Angelina
Dunlap, Brazos
Dunlap, Cottle 10
Dunlap, Travis 80
Dunlay, Medina, 33 119
Dunlay, Travis
*Dunn, Scurry, 2 75
Dunn's, Coryell
Dunn's, Robertson
Dunnville, Tarrant
Dunstan, Bastrop
Duplex, Fannin 25
DuPont, Denton
Dupree, Hays
Dupree, Wood
Dura, Brazoria
Duraglas, McLennan
Durango, Falls 54
Durant, Angelina
Durant, Robertson
Durant, Van Zandt
Durban, Atascosa
Duren, Mills 15
Durham, Borden
Durie, Bell
Duroc, Brazoria
Durst, Angelina
Durst's, Leon
Duster, Comanche 25
Dutch, Smith
Dutch Colony, Cottle
Dutchman, Motley
Dutchtown, DeWitt
Dutch Waterhole, Travis
Duval, Duval
Duval, Travis . . . . NA
Duval, Winkler
Duxbury, Montague
Dwire, San Augustine
Dye, Cooke
Dye [Mound], Montague 200
Dyer, Fort Bend
Dyer, Hunt
Dyer, Limestone
Dyersdale, Harris
*Dyess Air Force Base, Taylor, 6
  4,676
Dyess Grove, Bell

Elm, Collingsworth
Elm, Karnes
Elm, Rains
*Elmaton, Matagorda, 11 140
Elm Creek, Bell
Elm Creek, Hunt
Elm Creek, Taylor
Elmdale, Taylor 30
*ELMENDORF, Bexar, 114
   (568) 1,053
Elmer, Guadalupe
Elm Flat, Navarro
Elm Grove, Burnet
Elm Grove, Caldwell
Elm Grove, Cherokee 50
Elm Grove, Dallas
Elmgrove, Erath
Elm Grove, Fayette
Elm Grove, Fort Bend
Elm Grove, Johnson
Elm Grove, Limestone
Elm Grove, San Saba 15
Elm Grove, Van Zandt
Elm Grove, Wharton . . . . NA
Elm Grove Camp, Guadalupe 150
Elm Hill, Navarro
Elmina, Walker
*Elm Mott, McLennan, 105 190
Elm Mound, Gonzales
Elmo, Bandera
*Elmo, Kaufman, 14 90
Elmo, Limestone
Elmont, Grayson 15
Elmore, Hall
Elm Ridge, Milam 25
Elms, Bexar
Elmtown, Anderson 5
Elmview, Grayson
Elmwood, Anderson
Eloise, Falls 29
El Oso, Karnes 35
El Par, Jim Wells
§*EL PASO, El Paso, 18,378
   (515,342) 600,277
El Pleasant, Austin
Elrod, Anderson
Elrod, McLennan
Elroy, Travis 125
*ELSA, Hidalgo, 144 (5,242) . . . 6,332
El Sal de Rey, Hidalgo
El Sauz, Hidalgo
El Sauz, Starr, 34 50
El Sauz, Willacy
Elser, Montague
El Sordo, Jim Hogg
Elstone, Medina
El Tacalote, Jim Wells 100
Elton, Dickens 1
El Toro, Jackson 126
Elva, Ellis
Elva, Uvalde
El Vista, Jefferson
Elwood, Fannin 31
Elwood, Jefferson
Elwood, Madison 50
Ely, Bell
Ely, Fannin
Ely, McLennan
*Elysian Fields, Harrison, 27 300
Elysium, Angelina
Elysium, Bastrop . . . . NA
Emberson, Lamar 80
Emblem, Hopkins 52
Embree, Dallas
Embrey, Menard
Embryfield, San Jacinto
Emelia, Fort Bend
Emerald [Grove], Crockett

Emerald Bay, Smith 616
Emerson, Collin
Emerson, Terrell
*EMHOUSE, Navarro (195) 242
Emille[e], Tyler . . . . .NA
Emmett, Navarro 100
Eminence, Chambers
Emma, Crosby
Emmaus, Cherokee
Emmett, Navarro
Emmett, Red River
Emmit, Polk
§*EMORY, Rains, 198 (963) 1,034
Empire, Collin
Emporia, Angelina
Enal, Angelina
‡ Encantada-Ranchito El Calaboz,
   Cameron (1,143) 1,417
Enchanted Forest, Montgomery . .NA
ENCHANTED OAKS, Henderson
   (290) 328
Encina, Uvalde
*ENCINAL, La Salle, 18 (620) 655
*Encino, Brooks, 21 110
*Energy, Comanche, 2 65
Engelwood, Robertson
England, Baylor
Engle, Fayette 106
Englehart, Colorado
Engleman, Collin
English, Brazoria
English, Red River 92
*Enloe, Delta, 8 113
*ENNIS [Station], Ellis, 815
   (13,869) 15,538
Ennis, Scurry
Enoch, Clay
Enoch, Upshur 25
*Enochs, Bailey, 5 80
Enon, Rusk
Enon, Tarrant
Enon, Upshur
Enos, Waller
Enright, Brazos . . . . .NA
Ensign, Ellis
Enso, Comanche
Enterprise, Liberty
Enterprise [Station], Medina
Enterprise, Red River
Enterprise, Van Zandt 90
Entre, Montgomery
*Eola, Concho, 15 218
Eolian, Stephens 9
Ephesus, Leon
Ephraim, Hall
Epperson, Marion
Epperson's Ferry, Bowie
Eppler, Bastrop
Epworth, Hale
Equestria, Johnson
*Era, Cooke, 17 200
Erambert's Mill, Marion
Erath, Erath
Erath, McLennan
Ericksdahl, Jones 35
Erie, Polk
Erin, Jasper 40
Erin, Jasper
Ermis, Gonzales
Erna, Mason
Erna, Menard
Ernest, Travis
Ernies Acres, Brazoria . . . . .NA
Ernst, Atascosa
Erskine, Concho
Erudia, Collin
Erwin, Grimes . . . . .NA
Esbon, Llano

Escarbada, Deaf Smith
‡ Escobares, Starr (1,705) 2,205
Escobas, Zapata 3
Escom Hill, Trinity
Eshman, Erath
Eskota, Fisher
Esoes, Cameron
Esparanza, Smith
Esperanza, Hudspeth 75
Esperanza, Montgomery
Esperanza Ranch, Hidalgo
Esperson, Liberty
Espey, Atascosa 55
Espuela, Dickens
Esser Crossing, Comal
Esseville, Live Oak
Essie, Jones
Estacad[d]o, Crosby
Estacado, Lubbock 80
Estelle, Dallas
Estelle, Tarrant
*ESTELLINE, Hall, 9 (194) 193
Estes, Aransas 50
Estes, Harrison
Estill's Station, Tarrant
Ethel, Grayson 40
Ethel, Wharton
Etholen, Hudspeth
Etna, Smith
*Etoile, Nacogdoches, 24 70
Etta, Baylor
Etta, Bowie
Etta, Harris
Etta, Red River
Etter, Moore
Ettowa, Gonzales
Ettra, Lamar
Eudor, Sterling
Eudora, Angelina
Eufaula, Hill
Eula, Callahan 125
Eula, Kaufman
Eulalie, Rusk
*EULESS, Tarrant, 1,696
   (38,149) 46,632
Eulogy, Bosque 45
Eunice, Leon . . . . NA
Eunice, Swisher
Eunice, Titus
Eunice, Walker
Eura, Kerr
Eureka, Franklin 18
Eureka, Kaufman
EUREKA, Navarro (242) 290
Eureka, Stephens . . . . NA
Eureka, Tarrant
Eureka Mills, Harris
Eureka Mills, Williamson
*EUSTACE, Henderson, 98
   (662) .863
Eutaw, Limestone
Eutaw, Robertson
Eva, Caldwell
Eva, Jim Wells
Eva, Leon
Eva, San Augustine
‡*Evadale, Jasper, 40 (1,422) . . 1,788
Evan, Cameron
Evana, Wood
Evans, Hardeman
Evans, Hardin
Evans, Williamson
Evans Cross Roads, Bosque
Evans Point, Hopkins
Evansville, Leon
*EVANT, Coryell-Hamilton, 48
   (444) .453
Evelena, Dawson

Four Way, Moore
Fouts, Liberty
Fowler, Bosque
Fowler's Gin, Bell
Fowler's Store, Hopkins
Fowler's Store, Tarrant
*Fowlerton, La Salle, 6. 50
Fowlkes, Wichita
Fox, Dallas
Fox, Eastland
Fox, Gonzales
Fox, Harrison
Fox, Henderson
Fox, Hunt
Fox, Liberty
Fox, Parker
Fox Nation, Live Oak
Foy, Collin
Fraimville, Burleson
Frame, Clay
Frame Switch, Williamson. 20
Frances, Henderson
Frances, Zavala
Francis, Dallas
Francis, Orange
Francisco, Medina
*Francitas, Jackson, 3 143
Franco, Parker
Frank, Fannin
Frankel City, Andrews 2
Frankell, Stephens. . . . . .NA
Frankford, Collin
Frankford, Dallas
Frankfort, Anderson
Frankfort, Guadalupe
Franklin, El Paso
Franklin, Lamar
§*FRANKLIN, Robertson, 125,
   (1,336) 1,502
Franklin Center, Scurry
Franklin Settlement, McMullen
Franklinville, Anderson
*FRANKSTON, Anderson, 216,
   (1,127) 1,245
Frankston, Jefferson
Frankville, Leon
Fraser, Hill
Frazer, Hopkins
Frean, Lamar
*Fred, Tyler, 9 239
§*FREDERICKSBURG, Gillespie,
   1,134 (6,934) 8,550
Fredonia, Gregg
*Fredonia, Mason, 22. 50
Free, Polk
Free, Terrell
Freedmen's Colony, Blanco
Freedom, McLennan
Freedom, Rains 60
Freeland, Johnson
Freeman, Brown
Freeman, Panola
Freeman, Polk
Freeman's Store, Nacogdoches
Freemound, Cooke
Freeneytown, Rusk . . . . NA
*FREEPORT, Brazoria, 742,
   (11,389) 13,753
Freeport, Brazoria
Freeport, Hale
*FREER, Duval, 189 (3,271) 3,483
Free State, Van Zandt
Freestone, Freestone 35
Freheit, Comal . . . . NA
Frels, Fort Bend
Frels, Colorado
Freisburg[h], Colorado 75
Fremont, Parker

French, Callahan
French, Denton
French, Falls
French, Marion
French, Navarro
Frenstat, Burleson . . . . .NA
Fresenius, Hardin
Fresnal, Cameron
Fresnito, Maverick
*Fresno, Collingsworth . . . . .NA
‡ Fresno, Fort Bend, 94
   (3,182). 4,499
Freyburg, Fayette 45
Friar, Rusk
Friday, Trinity. 99
Friday, Trinity
Frieden, Washington
Friendly, Van Zandt . . . . .NA
Friendship, Dawson 5
Friendship, Denton
Friendship, Falls
Friendship, Franklin
Friendship, Hardin
Friendship, Harrison
Friendship, Jack
Friendship, Jasper
Friendship, Lamb
Friendship, Leon. . . . . .NA
Friendship, Milam
Friendship, Smith 200
Friendship, Trinity
Friendship, Upshur 25
Friendship, Williamson. 48
Friendship Village, Bowie 200
*FRIENDSWOOD, Galveston-
   Harris, 1,475 (22,814) 30,247
Frier, Guadalupe
Frijole, Culberson
Frio, Castro 15
Frio [City, Town], Frio
Frio, McMullen
Frio, Parmer
*FRIONA, Parmer, 228
   (3,688) 3,834
Frio Water Hole, Real
*FRISCO [City], Collin-Denton,
   783, (6,138) 17,798
Frisco, Lamar
Frisco, Sherman
Frisco Junction, Newton
*FRITCH, Hutchinson-Moore, 169,
   (2,335) 2,474
Fritze, Nacogdoches
Fritzvann, Trinity
Frog, Kaufman . . . . .NA
Frognot, Collin . . . . .NA
Fromme, Travis
Fromme's Store, Guadalupe
Front, Panola. . . . . .NA
Frontera, El Paso
Fronton, Cameron
Fronton, Starr 110
Frosa, Limestone
*FROST, Navarro, 41 (579) 617
Frost, Navarro
Fruit, Smith
Fruitdale, Dallas
Fruitland, Fort Bend
Fruitland, Montague 20
*FRUITVALE, Van Zandt, 31,
   (349) 380
Fry, Brown
Fryar, McLennan
Fryar, Red River
Frydek, Austin. 150
Frye['s Ranch], Wheeler
Frys Gap, Cherokee
Fuch's Mill, Blanco

Fulbright, Red River 150
Fulda, Baylor
Fuller, Wheeler
Fuller, Wichita
Fuller Springs, Angelina
Fullerton, Andrews
Fullerton, Liberty
Fullerville, Scurry
*FULSHEAR, Fort Bend, 79
   (557) .809
Fulsher, Fort Bend
*FULTON, Aransas, 79 (763) 848
Fulton, Lamar
Fulton, Van Zandt
Fulton, Wharton
Funston, Jefferson
Funston, Jones 26
Funston, Mason
Funston, Taylor
Fuqua, Grimes
Fuqua, Liberty
Furguson, Hale
Furman, Panola
Furrh, Panola 40
Fussell, Rusk

G

Gable, Navarro
Gabriel Mills, Williamson
Gabriel River, Williamson
Gadsden, Lamar
Gadston, Lamar . . . . NA
Gafford, Hopkins . . . . NA
Gage, Grayson
Gageby [Valley], Hemphill
Gageby, Wheeler
Gage's, Bastrop
Gage's, Rusk
Gagne, Shelby
§*Gail, Borden, 10 189
Gail, Concho
Gaines Ferry, Sabine
Gainesmore, Matagorda
§*GAINESVILLE, Cooke, 1,305,
   (14,256) 15,486
Gainesville, Llano
Gainey, Fort Bend
Gale, Borden
Galena, Smith. . . . . NA
*GALENA PARK, Harris, 222,
   (10,033) 10,269
Galesville [Gailsville], Kaufman
Galilee, Smith. 150
Galilee, Walker
Gallagher, Shelby
Gallagher's Ranch, Medina
Gallalia, Harrison
*GALLATIN, Cherokee, 6 (368) . . .449
Galle, Guadalupe. 130
Gallina, Presidio
Gallinas, Atascosa
Galloway, Jefferson
Galloway, Panola 71
Galloway [Gallaway], Cass
§*GALVESTON, Galveston, 2,641,
   (59,067) 64,493
Galvez, Jim Wells
Gamble, Ellis
Gamma, Coke
Gamma, Parker
*GANADO, Jackson, 141
   (1,701) 1,984
Ganahl, Kerr
Gander Slue, Guadalupe
Gandy, Burnet
Gandy, Jackson
Gandy[bend], Lavaca
Gange, Jasper

Gannon, Fisher
Gano, Van Zandt
Gano, Williamson
Gansel, McCulloch
Gantt, Lamar
Gap, Comanche
Garceño, Starr 100
Garcia, Deaf Smith
Garcias, Starr 200
Garciasville, Starr (See La
    Casita-Garciasville)
Garcias, Zapata
Garcias Ranch, Starr
Garciasville, Starr
Garcitas, Victoria
§*Garden City, Glasscock, 120 . . .293
Gardendale, Bexar . . . . NA
‡*Gardendale, Ector, 63
    (1,103) 1,174
Gardendale, La Salle 40
Gardendale, Nueces
Garden Oaks, Harris
GARDEN RIDGE, Comal (1,450)
    2,206
Gardentown, Harris
Garden Valley, Childress
Garden Valley, Smith 150
Gardner, Milam
Gardner, Roberts
Gardner's Saline, Smith
Garfield, Bastrop
Garfield, DeWitt 16
‡ Garfield, Travis (1,336) 1,494
Garland, Bowie. 125
*GARLAND, Dallas-Collin-
    Rockwall, 7,266 (180,650)
    193,475
Garlock, Grayson
Garner, Frio
Garner, Lavaca
Garner, Parker 196
Garner's, Jefferson
Garner State Park, Uvalde. 50
GARRETT[Junction], Ellis (340) . . .452
Garretts Bluff, Lamar 20
Garrett's Mills, McLennan
Garrett's Store, Marion
*GARRISON, Nacogdoches, 108,
    (883) 1,050
Garry, Henderson
Garth, Harris
Garthright, Calhoun
Garvin, Wise
Garvinsville, Red River
*Garwood, Colorado, 63 975
Gary, Montgomery
*GARY, Panola, 41 (271) 285
Garza, Denton
Garza's, Bexar
Garza's Crossing, Bexar
Gasca, San Jacinto
Gasco, Dallas
Gasoline, Briscoe
Gas Plant, Terrell
Gaston, Dallas
Gaston, Fort Bend
Gaston, Rusk
Gastonia, Kaufman 30
Gates, Coryell
Gates, Dallas
Gates Valley, Atascosa
§*GATESVILLE, Coryell, 540,
    (11,492) 12,340
Gatling, Stonewall
Gaujoco, La Salle
Gaultville, McCulloch
*Gause, Milam, 15 400
Gavett, Morris

Gavilan, Terrell
Gay, San Augustine
Gay Assembly, Marion
Gay Hill, Fayette
Gay Hill, Milam
Gay Hill, Washington 145
Gayle Estates, Brazoria 102
Gaylord, Lipscomb
Gay's Mill, Hopkins
Gazelle, Hall
Gear's Tanyard, Red River
Gee's Store, Anderson
Gem, Collin
Gem [City], Hemphill
Gemmer&Tanner, Colorado
Gene, Colorado
Gene, Gonzales
Geneva, Polk
*Geneva, Sabine, 3 100
Geneva, San Jacinto
Geneva Station, McLennan
Geneview, Stonewall 6
Genoa, Harris
Gentry, Harris
Gentry, Potter
Gentry, Stephens
Gentry, Wise
Gentrys Mill [Gentry], Hamilton . . . 17
George, Madison
George's Creek, Somervell 66
Georgetown, Grayson
Georgetown, Van Zandt
§*GEORGETOWN, Williamson,
    1,540 (14,842) 26,576
§*GEORGE WEST, Live Oak,
    228 (2,586) 2,718
Georgia [Georgiaville],, Lamar . . . .NA
Georgia Camp, Houston
Georgia Colony, Hays
Gerald, Denton
Gerald, McLennan
Geraldine, Archer
German Cove, Goliad
Germania, Midland
Germantown, Goliad
Germantown, Hamilton
Germany, Houston 43
Germany, Navarro
Gerome, Henderson
*Geronimo, Guadalupe, 17. 400
Gerron, Bell
Gertie, Red River
Gertie, Tarrant
Gertrude[s], Jack
Gertrude, Wise
Gethsemane, Marion
Gewhitt, Hutchinson
Gholson, Brown
GHOLSON, McLennan, (692) 754
Ghost Hill, Ellis
Gibbons Creek, Grimes
Gibbs, Dallas
Gibbs, Smith
Gibbs, Sterling
Gibson, Kimble
Gibson, Lamar
Gibsontown, Rusk
Gibtown, Jack . . . . .NA
§*GIDDINGS, Lee, 551
    (4,093) 4,683
Giesecke's Store, Burnet
Giesinger, Grimes
Gifco, Ellis
Gifford, Dallas
Gilaloo, Ochiltree
Gilbert, Angelina
Gilbert, Eastland
Gilbert, McLennan

Gilbert, Wichita
Gilburg, Jefferson
*Gilchrist, Galveston, 25 750
Gilead, Callahan
Giles, Donley
Gilesburg, Travis
Gilford, Shelby
Gilking, Stephens
Gill, Callahan
Gill, Harrison
Gilleland Creek, Travis
*Gillett, Karnes, 9. 120
Gilley, Burleson
Gilliam, Webb
Gilliamsville, Coryell
Gilliamsville, Lampasas
Gilliland, Callahan
Gilliland, Knox 25
Gilliland, Parker
Gillis, Morris
Gilmer, Orange
§*GILMER, Upshur, 626
    (4,824) 5,376
Gilmerville, Jasper
Gilmore, Carson
Gilmore, Erath
Gilmore, Tarrant
Gilpin, Childress
Gilpin, Dickens. 3
Gilpin, McLennan
Gilpin, Motley
Gilpin, Titus
Gindale, Bell
Giner, Rains
Ginger, Rains 96
Ginsite, Cottle
Gipaw, Hall
*Girard, Kent, 5. 125
Girlstown USA, Cochran. 95
*Girvin, Pecos, 2. 30
Gish, Harris
Gist, Hill
Gist, Jasper . . . . NA
Gist, Jones
Givens, Lamar 135
Givensville, Bastrop
Glade, Polk
Glade, Tarrant
Glade Branch, Franklin
Glade Creek, Hopkins
*GLADEWATER, Gregg-Upshur,
    472, (6,027) 6,258
Gladewater, Titus
Gladish, Waller
Gladstell, Liberty
Gladstone, Walker
Gladys, Jefferson
Gladys, Montague
Glasgow, Gray
Glasgow, Wilbarger
Glass, Bastrop
Glass, Robertson
Glass, Somervell . . . . NA
Glasscock, Bastrop
Glaze City, Gonzales 10
Glazier, Hemphill 48
Gleam, Lee
Glecker, Lavaca . . . . NA
Glen Cove, Coleman 40
Glen, Chambers
Glen, Parker
Glen, Smith
Glenbelto, Bastrop
Glencoe, Ellis
Glencoe, Houston
Glencross, Donley
Glendale, Dallas
Glendale, Trinity 175

Glenfawn, Rusk 16
*Glen Flora, Wharton, 19 210
Glen Flora Place, Wharton
Glenham, Bastrop
Glenn, Dickens. 7
Glenn, Hutchinson
Glenn, Liberty
GLENN HEIGHTS, Dallas-Ellis
  (4,564) 5,553
Glenn Springs, Brewster
Glen Oaks, Kerr
Glenpark, Yoakum
Glenrio, Deaf Smith 5
§*GLEN ROSE, Somervell, 283,
  (1,949) 2,258
Glen Spring, Brewster
Glenwood, Upshur. 150
*Glidden, Colorado, 1 255
Globe, Lamar . . . . NA
Glory, Lamar. 30
Glover, Leon
Gluck, Potter
Gnarled Oaks, Washington
Goather's, Erath
Goather's, Hood
Goatneck, Johnson
*Gober, Fannin, 4 146
*GODLEY, Johnson, 120 (569) . . .642
Goforth, Hays
Golan, Jones
Golconda, Palo Pinto
Gold, Gillespie
Gold Dollar, Hopkins
*Golden, Wood, 28 156
Golden Acres, Harris
Golden Beach, Llano . . . . NA
Golden Drain, Rusk
Golden Pond, Stonewall
Goldenrod, Colorado
Goldenrod, Lavaca
Goldenrod, Wharton
Golden Vale, Panola
Goldfinch, Frio 35
Gold Hill, Hopkins
*Goldsboro, Coleman, 1 30
*GOLDSMITH, Ector, 34 (297) 301
§*GOLDTHWAITE, Mills, 188
  (1,658) 1,877
§*GOLIAD, Goliad, 189
  (1,946) 2,204
GOLINDA [Golindo], Falls-
  McLennan (347) 404
Golly, DeWitt. 41
Gomez, Terry 16
§*GONZALES, Gonzales, 522
  (6,527) 6,512
Goober Hill, Shelby . . . . NA
Gooch's Mill Shop, Hamilton
Good, Hays
Good Creek, Foard
Good Exchange, Cass
*Goodfellow Air Force Base,
  Tom Green, 7 345
Good Hope, Franklin
Good Hope, Lavaca
Good Hope, Val Verde
Goodland, Bailey 10
Goodland, Robertson
Goodlett, Hardeman 80
GOODLOW, Navarro (319) 390
Good Luck, Uvalde
Goodman, Bastrop
Goodman's Crossing, Nacogdoches
Good Neighbor, Hopkins. . . . . NA
Goodnight, Armstrong 18
Goodnight, Navarro 25
*GOODRICH, Polk, 63 (239). 304
Goodson, Smith

Goodsonville, Anderson
Goodsprings [Good Springs], Rusk 40
Goodville, Falls
Goodwill, Burleson . . . . .NA
Goodwin, Comal
Goodwin, San Augustine . . . . . . .NA
Goolesboro, Titus
Goose Creek, Harris
Gorbett, Dallas
Gorbit, Dallas
Gordon, Lynn
*GORDON, Palo Pinto, 42 (465) . . 465
Gordon Coal Mines, Palo Pinto
Gordon Junction, Palo Pinto
*Gordonville, Grayson, 44 165
Gore, Anderson
*GOREE, Knox, 16 (412) 425
Gorey, Mills
Gorgona, Montague
*GORMAN, Eastland, 92
  (1,290) 1,373
Gose City, Archer
Goshen, Henderson
Goshen, Walker . . . . .NA
Gospel Ridge, Grayson
Gossett, Kaufman
Gossett, Kaufman
Gossett Switch, Henderson
Gossip, Johnson
Gotcher's, Bastrop
Gotier's, Bastrop
Goucher's, Bastrop
Gouge Eye, Gray
Gough, Delta
Gould, Bell
Gould, Cherokee. 20
Gould, Rusk
*Gouldbusk, Coleman, 13. 70
Gould City, Callahan
Gouldsborough, Titus
Gourdneck, Panola 30
Gourdneck, Rusk
Gover, Grayson
Government Wells, Duval
Gower, Williamson
Gozar, Reeves
Graball, Washington . . . . .NA
Grace, King 20
Grace Hill, Polk
Graceland, Llano
Graceton, Upshur 100
Grady, Fisher
Grady, Liberty
Grady, Marion
Grady, Smith
Grady's Mill, Ellis
Gradyville, Ellis
Gradyville, Navarro
Graeb, Guadalupe
*GRAFORD, Palo Pinto, 121
  (561) 610
Graham, Garza 139
Graham, Jasper. . . . . .NA
Graham, Wood
§*GRAHAM, Young, 837
  (8,986) 8,896
Graham Prairie, Hunt
Graham's Mills, Shelby
Granada, Hutchinson
Granada, Pecos
§*GRANBURY, Hood, 1,627,
  (4,045) 5,711
Granby, Hunt
Granda, Mason
Grand [Grant's] Bluff, Jasper
Grand Bluff, Orange
Grand Bluff, Panola 97
Grand Cane, Liberty

*GRANDFALLS, Ward, 25 (583). . .627
Grand Lake, Montgomery
Grand Prairie, Bastrop
*GRAND PRAIRIE, Dallas-Tarrant-
  Ellis, 4,048 (99,606) 113,672
Grand Ranche, Palo Pinto
*GRAND SALINE, Van Zandt, 265,
  (2,630) 2,931
Grandview, Dawson. 12
Grandview, Gray 13
*GRANDVIEW, Johnson, 207
  (1,245). 1,368
Grand Vista, Armstrong
Grange, Newton
Grange Hall, Harrison
*GRANGER, Williamson, 77
  (1,190). 1,472
*Grangerland, Montgomery . . . . . NA
Grangerville, Hemphill
Granite [Mountain], Burnet
*GRANITE SHOALS, Burnet
  (1,378). 2,222
GRANJENO, Hidalgo . . . . NA
Gran Sabana, Burnet
Grant, Burleson
Grant, Eastland
Grant, Marion
Grantville, Red River
Granville, Angelina
Grape Creek, Gillespie
Grape Creek, Tom Green . . . . NA
*GRAPELAND, Houston, 157
  (1,450) 1,696
Grapetown, Gillespie . . . . NA
Grapetown, Gillespie
Grapetown, Kendall
Grapevine, Dickens
Grapevine, Houston
*GRAPEVINE [Prairie], Tarrant-
  Dallas-Denton, 2,408 (29,198)
  38,528
Graphite, Llano
Grassbur, DeWitt
Grassdale, Travis
Grassland, Lynn. 61
Grassmyer's [Grassmeyer's], Fayette
Grassyville, Bastrop 50
Grassyville, Lee
Gratis, Orange
Gravel, Cottle
Gravel, Floyd
Gravel Hill, Sabine
Gravel Spur, Cooke
Gravis, Duval
Gravis, Williamson
Gravity, Brown
Gray, Eastland
Gray, Marion . . . . NA
Grayback, Wilbarger 25
Graybill, Cameron
Graybill, Collin
GRAYBURG, Hardin, 6 (257) 326
Grayco, Grayson
Graydale, Stonewall
Graydon, Chambers
Grayflat, Stonewall
Gray Hill, Washington
Gray Rock, Franklin
Gray's Gin, Dallas
GRAYS PRAIRIE, Kaufman
  (286) 391
Grayton, Hudspeth
Graytown, Bexar
Graytown, Wilson. 64
Greasy Neck, Hall
Great Falls, Ward
Greathouse, Jack
Green, Karnes 35

Green, Kaufman
Greenbrier, Smith
Green DeWitt, DeWitt
Green Grove, Lavaca
Green Hill, Titus 150
Green Lake, Calhoun. 51
Green Lake, Edwards
Greenock, Bosque
Greenpond, Hopkins . . . . NA
Greens Creek, Erath 75
Greenview, Hopkins. . . . . NA
Green's, Liberty
Green's [Greenville], Polk
Greens Bayou, Harris
Green's Bluff, Orange
Greensborough, Panola
Greens Creek, Erath
Green's Point, Hunt
Green's Store, Cass
Green Valley, Denton
Green Valley, Jones
Greenview, Hopkins
§*GREENVILLE, Hunt, 1,410,
     (23,071) 25,238
Greenvine, Washington. 35
Greenwade's Mills, Hill
Greenway, Bexar . . . . NA
Greenway, Johnson
Greenwood, Hopkins. 35
Greenwood, Midland 2,000
Greenwood, Nacogdoches
Greenwood, Red River 20
*Greenwood, Wise, 7 76
Greer, McLennan
Greer's, Brazos
Greeson, Henderson
Gregg, Travis
Greggton, Gregg
*GREGORY, San Patricio, 53,
     (2,458) 2,606
Grenada, Deaf Smith
Grenada, Jefferson
Gresham, Smith. 100
Greta, Refugio
*GREY FOREST, Bexar (425) 532
Gribble, Dallas
Gribble Springs, Denton
Grice, Upshur. 20
Griffhill, Denton
Griffin, Cherokee
Griffing Park, Jefferson
Griffin Store, Rusk
Griffinsville, Bosque
Griffith, Cochran 12
Griffith, Ellis 10
Grigsby [Bluff], Jefferson
Grigsby, Shelby 45
Grimes, Nolan
Grimes [Bluff], Tyler
Grimes' Gin, Navarro
Grimes Prairie, Grimes
Grimes Switch, Grimes
Grimesville, Grimes
Grimshaw, Young
Grindale, Bell
Grindstone, Parker
Grisham, Castro
Grit, Mason. 30
Grit, Medina
Grit, Rains
Groce's Retreat, Grimes
Groceville, Montgomery
Groesbeck, Hardeman
§*GROESBECK [Groesbeeck],
     Limestone, 244, (3,360) 3,803
Grogan, Ochiltree
*GROOM, Carson, 71 (613) 641
Groos, Fayette

Groschkeville, Harris
Grossville, Mason. . . . . .NA
Grosvenor, Brown
Grotto, Hopkins
Grove, Collin
Grove, Jack
Grove, Lamar
Grove Controls, Harrison
Groveland, Jack
Grover, Bell
Grover, Coke
Grover, Comanche
Grover, Guadalupe
Grover, Hays
Grover, Montgomery
Grover, Navarro
Grover, Panola
Grover, Shelby
Grover, Williamson
Grove Ranch, Williamson
*GROVES, Jefferson, 505
     (16,744) 16,727
Grovesville, Lubbock
§*GROVETON, Trinity, 135
     (1,071) 1,172
Grow, Jones
Grow, King. 70
Gruenau, DeWitt 18
Gruene, Comal
Gruhlkey, Oldham
Grulla, Starr (see La Grulla)
Grundyville, Lampasas
*GRUVER, Hansford, 131
     (1,172). 1,104
Guadalupe, Guadalupe
Guadalupe, Kendall
Guadalupe, Victoria 106
Guadalupe, Zapata
Guadalupe Ranch, Hidalgo
Guadalupe Station, Culberson . . . 80
Guadalupe Valley, Comal
Guadalupe Victoria, Victoria
Guadelupe, Victoria
Guajillo, Duval
Guda, Falls
Gude, Limestone
Gudger, Stephens
Guelph, Polk
*Guerra, Jim Hogg, 1 75
Guerrero, Maverick
Guest, Stonewall
Guest's Station, Runnels
Guffey, Jefferson
Guide, Ellis
Guilford, DeWitt
Guion, Taylor 18
Gulf, Austin
Gulf, Matagorda
Gulf Camp, Ward
Gulf Dial, Hutchinson
Gulf Hill, Matagorda
Gulf Park, Brazoria
Gulf Prairie, Brazoria
Gum, Wise
Gum Branch, Hamilton
Gum Island, Harris
Gum Spring, Comal
Gum Spring, Smith
Gum Springs, Burnet
Gum Springs, Cass. 50
Gum Springs, Harrison
Gumwood, Smith
*GUN BARREL CITY, Henderson,
     (3,526) 4,484
Gunn, Gonzales
Gunsight, Stephens 6
*GUNTER, Grayson, 45 (898) 950
Gurley, Falls

Gus, Burleson . . . . NA
Gusher, Hardin
Gussettville, Live Oak
*GUSTINE, Comanche, 39 (430) . .499
Guthrie, Jack
§*Guthrie, King, 16. 160
*Guy, Fort Bend, 29 60
Guy, Van Zandt
Guyler, Montgomery
Guys Store, Leon. . . . . NA
Gwynn, Schleicher
Gyp, Collingsworth
Gyp, Fisher
Gypmine, Brooks
Gypsum, Hardeman
Gypsum, Hudspeth

H

Habermacher, Harris
Haby, Medina
Hacienda, Uvalde
Hacienda Glorieta, Crosby
Haciendito, Presidio . . . . NA
Hackberry, Collin
Hackberry, Cottle 30
HACKBERRY, Denton, (200) 269
Hackberry, Edwards. 3
Hackberry, Garza-Lynn . . . . NA
Hackberry, Lavaca . . . . NA
Hackberry Bluff, Collin
Hackberry Grove, Grayson
Hackberry [Hackberry Grove], Cottle
Hackney's Mill, Montgomery
Hadley's Prairie, Grimes
Hagansport, Franklin. 40
Hager, Hopkins
Hagerman, Grayson
Hagerville, Houston. 70
Hagler's Store, Montague
Hague, McLennan
Hahn, Wharton
Haiduk, Atascosa
Hail, Fannin 30
Hailesburgh, Houston
Hailville, Houston
Haines, Tarrant
Hainesville, Wood 74
Hajek, Baylor
Halamicek's Store, Fayette
Halbert, Shelby
*HALE CENTER, Hale, 135
     (2,067) 2,071
Hale City, Hale
Halesboro[ugh], Red River
Hale's Store, Runnels
Hale Station, Dallas
Haley, Jack
Haley's Mill, Erath
Haley's Mill, Hood
Haley Springs, Jack
Halfmoon, Lavaca
Halfway, Hale 58
Halfway, Hill
Half Way, Hunt
Halfway, Shelby
Halfway House, Archer
Halfway House, Ochiltree
Half-Way House, Parker
Halifax, Polk
Hall, Marion
Hall, San Saba 15
Halladay, Liberty
§*HALLETTSVILLE [Hallett's],
     Lavaca, 382, (2,718) 2,810
Hallmark Prairie, Bastrop
Halls Bayou, Brazoria
Halls Bluff, Houston 67
HALLSBURG, McLennan (450). . .542

Halls Store, Panola .... NA
*HALLSVILLE, Harrison, 184,
  (2,288) 2,821
Halltown, San Augustine
Halsell, Clay
Halsted, Fayette 26
*HALTOM CITY, Tarrant
  (32,856) 36,177
Haltom's, Montgomery
Ham, Henderson
Haman's, Lamar
Hamblin's, Harris
Hamburg, Red River
Hamburg, Travis
Hamburg, Van Zandt
Hamby, Taylor 100
Hamco, Coryell
Hamilton, Franklin
§*HAMILTON, Hamilton, 320
  (2,937) 2,995
Hamilton['s], Shelby
Hamiltonburg, Live Oak
Hamilton Dam, Llano
Hamilton Pool, Travis
Hamilton Valley, Burnet
Hamlet[t], Angelina
Hamlin, Frio
*HAMLIN, Jones-Fisher, 171
  (2,791) 2,429
Hammels Branch, Hill
Hammer, Uvalde
Hammer's Station, Uvalde
Hammock, Polk
Hammond, Robertson 44
Hamon, Gonzales 15
Hampton, Coryell
Hampton, Hamilton
Hampton, Nacogdoches .... NA
Hampton, Palo Pinto
Hampton, Tyler
Hamrick, Coleman
Ham's Creek, Johnson
*Hamshire, Jefferson, 52 350
Hancock, Collin
Hancock, Comal .... NA
Hancock, Dawson 30
Hancock, Houston
Hancock['s], Limestone
Hander, Falls
Handley, Tarrant
Handville, Randall
Handy, Jack
Handy, Milam .... NA
Handy, Nolan
Handy Stop, Kendall
Haney, Hunt
Haney, Randall
Hanger, Grayson
*Hankamer, Chambers, 22 525
Hanks, Anderson
Hanks, Titus
Hanna, Wise
Hanna Valley, Mills
Hannaville, Mills
Hanner, Polk
Hannibal, Erath .... NA
Hanover, Goliad
Hanover, Hill
Hanover, Milam 27
Hanrahan, Grimes
Hansford, Hansford
Hanson, Fort Bend
Hanson Mill, Shelby
Hanson's, Rusk
Hans' Settlement, Bandera
Happiness, Newton
Happle, La Salle
*HAPPY, Swisher-Randall, 74

  (588) 629
Happy Hill, Johnson ....NA
Happy Hollow, Burnet
Happy Hollow, Swisher
Happy Hollow, Uvalde
Happy Land, Nolan
Happy Union, Hale 15
Happy Valley, Taylor 10
Haralson Lakes, Tyler ....NA
Harbin, Erath 21
Harbor City, San Patricio
Harborview, Brazoria ....NA
Hardeman's, Nacogdoches
Hardin, Coleman
Hardin, Hardin
*HARDIN, Liberty, 33 (563)...... 616
Hardin's [Harden's] Store, Leon
Hardman's, Anderson
Hardwick, Hudspeth
Hardy, Harris
Hardy, Montague 6
Hardys Chapel, Navarro
Hare, Williamson.............. 70
*Hargill, Hidalgo, 10 1,349
Hargrave, Roberts
Hargrove, Somervell
HARKER HEIGHTS, Bell, 102
  (12,932) 17,243
Harkeyville, San Saba.......... 12
Harland, Robertson
Harlanville, Falls
Harlem [Switch], Fort Bend
*Harleton, Harrison, 51......... 260
*HARLINGEN, Cameron, 2,739
  (48,746) 56,657
Harlow, Eastland
Harlow, Hunt ....NA
Harman, Coryell
Harmaston, Harris
Harmon, Lamar 35
Harmon, Waller
Harmony, Floyd............... 42
Harmony [Grove], Gonzales
Harmony, Grimes 12
Harmony, Hutchinson
Harmony, Kent................. 7
Harmony, Limestone
Harmony, Nacogdoches.........NA
Harmony, Panola
Harmony Hill, Rusk
Harp['s Store], Montague
*Harper, Gillespie, 70 383
Harpersville, Stephens.........NA
Harrell, Hunt
Harrells, Newton
Harrellton, Lamar
Harriet[t], Tom Green
Harrington, Nacogdoches
Harris, Edwards
Harris, Hudspeth
Harris, Terry
Harrisburg[h], Harris
Harrisburg, Jasper
Harris Chapel, Panola.......... 180
Harris Chapel, Rusk
Harris Creek, McLennan
Harris Ferry, Red River
Harrison, McLennan 100
Harrisonia, Montague
Harriss Valley, La Salle
Harrisville, Bell
*Harrold, Wilbarger, 18 320
Harrys, Dallas
*HART, Castro, 100 (1,221).....1,230
Hart, Marion
Hartburg, Newton 275
Hart Camp, Lamb 8
Hartex, Archer

Hartland, Brooks
*Hartley, Hartley, 40 319
Hartley, Montgomery
Hartman, Bowie
Hart's, Bee
Harts Bluff, Red River
Hart Spur, Tarrant
Harts Ranch, Atascosa
Hartsville, Austin
Hartsville, Callahan
Hartville Settlement, Bee
Hartzo, Marion
Harvard Switch, Camp..........48
Harvester, Waller
Harvey, Brazos 310
Harvey's Mill, Red River
Harwell, Kaufman
Harwell Point, Burnet..........88
*Harwood, Gonzales, 27 112
Hash Knife, Taylor
Hasima, Brazoria
§*HASKELL, Haskell, 266
  (3,362) 3,075
Haskins Mill, Leon
Haslam, Shelby 101
*HASLET, Tarrant-Denton, 86
  (795) 999
*Hasse, Comanche, 1 43
Hassell, Anderson
Hassett, Polk
Hastings, Brazoria
Hastings, Kendall
Hastings, Titus
Hatch, Kaufman
Hatchel, Runnels 25
Hatchton, Gaines
Hathaway, Hardin
Hatti, Cooke
Hattie, Taylor
Hatton, Polk
Hatton, Van Zandt
Haught's Store, Dallas
Haulk, Wilbarger
Hauser, Hidalgo
Hausier City, Archer
Hatchetville, Hopkins ....NA
Havana, Cass
Havana, Hidalgo...............NA
Haven, Cochran
Hawcreek, Fayette
Hawdon, Fort Bend
Haw Grove, Cass
HAWK COVE, Hunt.............NA
Hawkeye, Bastrop
Hawkeye, Denton
Hawkins, Denton
*HAWKINS [Store], Wood, 178
  (1,309)................. 1,422
Hawkins Springs, Ellis
Hawkinsville, Matagorda
Hawkinsville, Tarrant
Hawks Store, Anderson
Hawley, Hunt
*HAWLEY, Jones, 77 (606).......633
Haws, Dallas
Hawthorn, Lee
Hawthorne, Shelby ....NA
Hawthorne, Walker.............NA
Hay, Deaf Smith
Hay, Eastland
Hayden, Van Zandt
Hayes, Jefferson
Hayes, Oldham
Hayes, Robertson
Hayflat, Loving
Hayflat, Winkler
Haymond, Brewster
Haynes, Lamar

Haynesburgh, Hood
Haynesville, Wichita 60
Haynie Flat, Travis-Burnet....... NA
Haynie's Chapel, Bastrop
Haynie's Chapel, Travis
Hayrick, Coke
*HAYS, Hays (251) 307
Hays City, Hays
Haysland, Panola
Hays Station, Panola
Hayter, Tarrant
Hayward, Nacogdoches
Haywood, Jasper
Haywood, Panola
Hazel, Hardeman
Hazel, Montgomery
Hazle [Hazel] Dell, Comanche.... NA
Heacker, Harris
Head of California, Fisher
Head of Elm, Montague
Heads Prairie, Robertson
Headsville, Robertson.......... NA
Heald, Wheeler
Heard, Uvalde
*HEARNE, Robertson, 253
   (5,132) 5,118
Heath, Fayette
Heath, Kaufman
*HEATH, Rockwall (2,108)..... 3,340
Heaton, DeWitt
Heaton, Gray
‡§*Hebbronville, Jim Hogg, 210
   (4,465) 4,098
Hebert, Hardin
Hebert, Jefferson
HEBRON, Denton (1,128) 1,512
Hebron, Jefferson
Heckler, Hill
Heckville, Lubbock .... NA
*HEDLEY, Donley, 27 (391) 420
Hedwigs Hill, Mason 10
HEDWIG VILLAGE, Harris
   (2,616) 3,123
Heelstring, Ellis
Hefner, Knox...................5
Hegar, Walker
Hegar ['s Store], Waller.......... NA
Heidelberg, Hidalgo............ NA
*Heidenheimer, Bell, 8.........144
Heilbrun, Bowie
Helbig, Jefferson
Helena, Karnes.................35
Helinora, Fort Bend
Hellandville, Ellis
Hellemans, Bexar
Helmic, Trinity.................86
Helms, Colorado
*HELOTES, Bexar, 316
   (1,535)................ 2,003
Help, Bosque
Hembrie, Crockett
Hemming, Cooke
§*HEMPHILL, Sabine, 222
   (1,182) 1,327
§*HEMPSTEAD, Waller, 347
   (3,556) 4,173
Henderson, Comal
§*HENDERSON, Rusk, 976,
   (11,139) 11,892
Henderson Chapel, Concho ..... NA
Hendersonville, Anderson
Hendricks, Hunt............... NA
Hendricks, Rusk
Henkhaus, Lavaca .... NA
Henly, Hays...................55
Hennen, Gillespie
Hennessey, Harris
Henning, Nacogdoches

§*HENRIETTA, Clay, 227
   (2,896)...................3,100
Henry, Bastrop
Henry, Ellis
Henry, Swisher
Henry County Settlement, Polk
Henry's Chapel, Cherokee....... 75
Hensley, Jack
Henson's Creek, Coryell
Henze, Edwards
Herbert, Fort Bend
Herbert, Mitchell
Hereford, Calhoun
§*HEREFORD, Deaf Smith, 856,
   (14,745) 14,562
Herg, Hardeman
Heritage, Hill
Herman, Wise
Hermans, Fort Bend
Hermia, Kerr
Hermis, Gonzales
Hermitage, Cass
Hermits Cove, Rains............ 40
*Hermleigh, Scurry, 46 200
Hermon, Shelby
Hermosa, Reeves
Hermoson, McLennan
Herndon, Nolan
Hero, Mills
Heron, Montgomery
Herring, Anderson
Herring, Bell
Herrington, Angelina
Herrington, Brazos
Herron City, Young
Hersfeld, Mason
Herty, Angelina 605
Herwig, Blanco
Hesse, Webb
Hester, Hardin
Hester, Navarro 35
Hesterville, DeWitt
Hetty, Hunt
Heugh, Johnson
Hewett's Store, Cooke
*HEWITT, McLennan, 344
   (8,983) 10,718
Hewitt, Titus
Hewsville, Smith
*Hext, Menard, 4 (76848)........ 73
Hey, Mason
Heyser, Randall
Hiawatha, Newton
Hickey, Panola
Hickey's Store, Panola
Hickman, Collin
Hickmuntown, Travis
Hickok, Atascosa
Hickory, Denton
Hickory, Llano
Hickory Creek, Cooke
HICKORY CREEK, Denton
   (1,893) 2,312
Hickory Creek, Fannin
Hickory Creek, Houston......... 31
Hickory Creek, Hunt ....NA
Hickory Creek, Limestone
Hickory Forrest, Guadalupe..... 300
Hickory Grove, Limestone
Hickory Grove, Smith
Hickory Grove, Travis
Hickory Grove, Van Zandt
Hickory Hill, Cass
Hickory Hollow, Hunt ....NA
Hickory Plains, Wise
Hickory Ridge, Sabine
Hicks, Lee
Hicks, Shackelford

Hicks, Tarrant
Hicksbaugh, Tyler .... NA
Hickson, Coryell
Hickston, Gonzales .... NA
Hicksville, Tyler
*HICO, Hamilton, 149 (1,342)... 1,469
*HIDALGO, Hidalgo, 298 (3,292)
   5,563
Hidalgo Park, Hidalgo
Hide Away, Brazoria............69
Hide-A-Way Lake, Smith 3,800
Hidesville, Lavaca
Hidetown, Scurry
Hidetown, Wheeler
Higginbotham, Gaines.......... NA
Higgins, Jefferson
*HIGGINS, Lipscomb, 34 (464) ...479
Higgins Gap, Lampasas
High, Lamar 55
Highbank, Falls 68
High Bridge, Val Verde
High Grove, Bastrop
High Hill, Fayette 116
*High Island, Galveston, 21......500
Highland, Collin
Highland, Erath 60
Highland, McLennan
Highland, Montgomery
Highland, Randall
Highland, Scurry
Highland, Smith .... NA
Highland, Young
Highland Addition, Parker....... NA
Highland Bayou, Galveston ... 1,209
HIGHLAND HAVEN, Burnet
   (NC)......................372
HIGHLAND PARK, Dallas
   (8,739) 9,454
‡*Highlands, Harris, 289
   (6,632)................. 7,737
HIGHLAND VILLAGE, Denton,
   (7,027) 11,561
High Lonesome, Reagan
High Point, Collin
High Point, Grimes
High Prairie, Houston
Highsmith's, Bastrop
Hight, Stephens
Hightop, Cottle
Hightower, Liberty 30
Hightown, Polk................ NA
High Valley, San Saba
Highway, Dallas
Highway, Grayson
Highway Village, Nueces
Hiland, Dallas
Hilburn, Castro
Hilburn, Eastland
Hilda, Guadalupe
Hilda, Mason
Hilger, Fannin
Hill, Bastrop
Hill, Callahan
Hill, Travis
Hillard, Carson
Hillard, Dallas
Hill City, Hood
Hillcoat, Kinney
HILL COUNTRY VILLAGE, Bexar,
   (1,038)................. 1,298
Hill Creek, Bosque
Hillcrest, Colorado.............25
Hillcrest, Floyd
Hillcrest, Hunt
Hillcrest, Wichita
HILLCREST VILLAGE, Brazoria
   (695) 852
Hill Dale, Hopkins

Hillebrand, Colorado
Hillendahl, Harris
Hillger, Bastrop
Hilliard's, Shelby
*Hillister, Tyler, 13. 200
Hillje, Wharton 51
Hills, Lee. 20
Hillsboro, Guadalupe
§*HILLSBORO [ugh], Hill, 600
 (7,072) 7,801
Hillsborough, Bexar
Hillsdale, Nolan
Hill's Ferry, Clay
Hillside, Culberson
Hillside, McLennan
Hills Prairie, Bastrop 50
Hillspur, Lee
Hilltop, Coryell
Hilltop, Gillespie
Hill Top, Milam
*Hilltop Lakes, Leon 300
Hilltown, Denton
Hillville, Hunt
Hilo, Stephens
HILSHIRE VILLAGE, Harris (665).. 740
Hilton, Grayson
Himmons, Erath
Himmons, Hood
Hinckley, Hunt
Hinckley, Lamar 40
Hinde, Crockett
Hindenburg, Atascosa
Hindes, Atascosa. 14
Hindman, Dawson
Hinds' [Hines], Brazoria
Hiner, Parker
Hines, Ellis
Hines, Johnson . . . . NA
Hines, Taylor
Hines, Walker
Hinkles Ferry, Brazoria 35
Hippie Ridge, Wise. . . . . NA
Hiram, Kaufman. 34
Hirams' [Hiroms'], Polk
*HITCHCOCK, Galveston, 246,
 (5,868) 6,482
Hitchland, Hansford. 27
Hitson [Hittson], Fisher
Hitson's Crossing, Palo Pinto
Hitt, Dallam
Hix, Burleson 35
Hixon Switch, Austin
Hoard, Wood. 45
Hoban, Reeves
Hobart, Eastland
Hobart, Llano
Hobbs, Delta
Hobbs, Fisher. 91
Hobbs Spur, Bell
Hobby, Fort Bend
Hobby's Mills, Cass
*Hobson, Karnes, 16 135
Hobson, Van Zandt
*Hochheim, DeWitt, 2. 70
Hochkird, Williamson
*Hockley, Harris, 141 300
Hodge, Burnet
Hodge [Junction], Tarrant
Hodges, Jones. 150
Hodges' [Mills], Kendall
Hodge's Bend, Fort Bend
Hodgins, Pecos
Hodgson, Bowie
Hoefer, Colorado
Hoen, McLennan
Hogan Acres, Johnson . . . . NA
Hogansville, Rains. 200
Hog Creek, Bosque

Hog Creek, Comanche
Hog Creek, McLennan
Hog Eye, Bastrop
Hog Eye, Gregg
Hogeye, Hunt
Hogeye, Jack
Hogeye, Travis
Hogg, Borden
Hogg, Burleson . . . . .NA
Hogg, Coke
Hogg, Ellis
Hogg, Kaufman
Hogg, Leon
Hogg, Robertson
Hogtown, Eastland
Hog Valley, Brown
Hokah, Red River
Holbrook, Bowie
Holcomb Store, Cherokee
Holden, Limestone
Holden Springs, Van Zandt
Holder, Brown
Holder's Gin, Bastrop
Holford Prairie, Denton
Holiday Beach, Aransas. 1,000
HOLIDAY LAKES, Brazoria
 (1,039) 1,302
Holiday Shores, Brazoria . . . . . . .NA
Holik, Waller
Holiness [University], Hunt
*HOLLAND, Bell, 76 (1,118) 1,334
Hollandale, Grimes
Holland Hill, San Saba
Holland Quarters, Panola. 40
Hollebeke, Andrews
*HOLLIDAY, Archer, 71 (1,475). .1,564
Holliman, Milam
Hollimon, Colorado
Hollis, Madison
Hollister, Tyler
Hollomon, Tyler
Holloways Store, Walker
Hollub, Victoria
Holly, Houston. 112
Holly Acres, Angelina
Holly Beach, Cameron . . . . .NA
Holly Grove, Polk 20
Holly Spring[s], Wood
Holly Springs, Jasper. 50
Holly Springs, Newton
Holly Springs, Robertson
Hollywood, Atascosa
*HOLLYWOOD PARK, Bexar
 (2,870) 3,116
Holman, Fayette 116
Holmes, Caldwell
Holmes, Foard
Holmes', Jasper
Holmes, Panola
Holt, Mason
Holt, San Saba
Holton, Randall
Home, Red River
Home, Titus
Home, Walker
Homer, Angelina 360
Homestead, Floyd
‡ Homestead Meadows, El Paso
 (4,978) 5,929
Homewood, Leon
Hondo, Gillespie
Hondo, Llano
§*HONDO, Medina, 343
 (6,018). 8,047
Hondo Cañon, Bandera
Honea, Montgomery
Honest, Delta
Honey Creek, Bandera

Honey Creek, Comal
Honey Creek, Hamilton
Honey Creek, Llano
Honey Creek, Mason
*HONEY GROVE, Fannin, 130,
 (1,681) 1,828
Honey Island, Hardin. 401
Honey Springs, Dallas
Hood, Borden
Hood, Cooke. 20
Hoodville, Marion
Hooker, Hunt
Hooker, Stonewall
Hooker Ridge, Rains 250
Hookers, Rains
Hooker's, Tyler
*HOOKS, Bowie, 135 (2,684) . . . 2,826
Hooks, Hidalgo
Hooks' Ferry, Red River
Hooks Switch, Hardin
Hooleyan, Hardeman
Hoop and Holler, Liberty
Hooper[ville], Brown
Hoot, Bowie
Hootsville, Cass
Hoover['s Valley], Burnet
Hoover, Gray. 5
Hoover, Guadalupe
Hoover, Lamar . . . . NA
Hoover's Gin, Hunt
Hoover's Valley, Burnet
Hoovers Valley, Llano
Hope, Cooke
Hope, Lavaca 45
Hope, Ochiltree
Hope Church, Falls
Hopewell, Burnet
Hopewell, Camp
Hopewell, Franklin. 35
Hopewell, Houston 22
Hopewell, Lamar
Hopewell, Leon
Hopewell, Madison
Hopewell, Montgomery
Hopewell, Navarro
Hopewell, Red River 150
Hopewell, Smith
Hopewell, Somervell
Hopewell, Williamson
Hopkins, Hemphill
Hopkins Store, Walker
Hopkinsville, DeWitt
Hopkinsville, Gonzales
Horace, Hutchinson
Hord, Milam
Hord's Ridge, Dallas
Horger, Jasper
HORIZON CITY, El Paso
 (2,308). 3,234
Hornbeck, Sabine
Horn Hill [Horn], Limestone
Horn Hill, Montague
Hornsby Bend [Hornsby's], Travis . .20
Horseshoe, Erath
‡*Horseshoe Bay, Llano-Burnet,
 (1,546) 1,759
Horse Shoe Bend, Cooke
Hortense, Polk 20
Horton, Delta 25
Horton, Jasper
Horton, Panola . . . . NA
Hortonsville, Karnes
Hortonville, Red River
Hoskins, Brazoria
Hoskins Junction, Brazoria
Hostyn, Fayette
Hot, Shelby
Hot Springs, Brewster

Hot Wells, Hudspeth
Houmont Park, Harris
House, Fort Bend
House's Ranch, Coke
Houseville, Harris
Housh, Palo Pinto
Housley, Dallas
§*HOUSTON, Harris-Fort Bend-
 Montgomery, 111,714
 (1,668,261) 1,841,064
Houston Creek, Ellis
Houston Heights, Harris
Houston Terminals, Harris
Hovey, Brewster
Hovey, Pecos
Howard, Archer
Howard, Bell
Howard, Ellis
Howard, Wichita
Howard Lake, Frio
Howards, Newton
Howardsville, Bosque
Howard Valley, Jack
HOWARDWICK, Donley (211) 221
*HOWE, Grayson, 106 (2,173) . . 2,350
Howell, Jasper
Howell's Store, Wise
Howellville, Harris
Howerton's Ranch, Kinney
Howe Settlement, Ellis
Howland, Lamar. 90
Howth [Station], Waller. 65
Hoxie, Cass
Hoxie, Palo Pinto
Hoxie, Williamson 50
Hoya, Nacogdoches
Hoyt, Wood
Hoyte, Milam. 20
Hranice, Lee
H.S. Ranch, Mitchell
Huaca, Hays
Hub, Parmer 25
Hubbard, Bowie 269
Hubbard, Coryell
*HUBBARD [City], Hill, 99
 (1,589). 1,681
Huber, Shelby. . . . . NA
Hubert, San Patricio
Hucal, Somervell
Huckabay, Erath. 150
Hud[d], Scurry
Huddleston, Montague
HUDSON, Angelina (2,374) 3,061
Hudson, Carson
Hudson, Harris
Hudson, Panola
Hudson, Red River
Hudson Bend, Travis . . . . NA
HUDSON OAKS, Parker (711) . . 1,196
Hudsons Chapel, Cherokee
Hudsonville, Fannin
Hudsonville, Henderson
Huelster, Jeff Davis
Huff, Archer
Huff, Wichita
Huff, Williamson
Huffines [Huffins], Cass 140
*Huffman, Harris, 253 250
Huff Valley, Wise
*Hufsmith, Harris 250
Huggins, Clay
Hughes', Cass
Hughes, Newton
Hughes, Tom Green
Hughes, Victoria
*HUGHES SPRINGS, Cass-Morris,
 169 (1,938) 2,104
Hughes' Store, Mills

Hughey, Gregg
Hughlett, Armstrong
Hugo, Bell
Hugo, Hays
Hulda, Gillespie
Hulin, Denton
*Hull, Liberty, 41 1,800
Hulldale, Schleicher
Hull's Store, Panola
Hulltown, Shackelford
Hulsey, Hopkins
Hulver, Hall
*HUMBLE, Harris, 4,043
 (12,060) 15,452
Humble, Harris
Humble, Wilbarger
Humble Camp, Refugio
Humble Colorado Camp, Jim
 Hogg. .NA
Humble Government Wells Camp,
 Duval
Humboldt, Hunt
Humbra, Motley
Hume, Cherokee
Hume, Travis
Humline, Bee
Humphrey, Hunt
*Hungerford, Wharton, 32. 178
Hunt, Hunt
*Hunt, Kerr, 68 708
Hunter, Comal 30
Hunter, Grayson
Hunter's, Fort Bend
Hunter's, Harris
Hunter's Store, Taylor
HUNTERS CREEK VILLAGE,
 Harris (3,954). 4,224
Hunters Retreat, Montgomery
Huntersville, Travis
*HUNTINGTON, Angelina, 165
 (1,794) 2,156
Huntley, Orange
Huntoon, Ochiltree
Hunts Store, Leon
§*HUNTSVILLE, Walker, 1,493
 (27,925) 35,222
Hurley, Bailey
Hurley, Wood 30
Hurley Station, Ellis
Hurlwood, Lubbock 115
Hurnville, Clay. 15
Huron, Hill
Hurst, Shelby
*HURST, Tarrant, 2,230
 (33,574) 39,274
Hurst, Tarrant
Hurstland, McLennan
Hurstown, Shelby . . . . .NA
Hurst Springs [Hurst], Coryell 8
Hustler, Eastland
Hutcherson, Wilbarger
Hutcheson, Walker
Hutchings City, Runnels
Hutchingsville, Titus
*HUTCHINS, Dallas, 145
 (2,719) 3,326
Hutchison's Ranch, Kinney
Hutson, Brown
*HUTTO, Williamson, 140 (630) . . 827
Hutton, Archer
Hutton, DeWitt
Hutto's Grove, Polk
HUXLEY, Shelby (335) 376
Hyatt, Tyler
Hydesport, Mills
Hydro, Eastland
*Hye, Blanco, 6 105
Hylton, Nolan. 6

Hyman, Mitchell
Hynds City, Montague
Hynesville, Refugio

I

Iago, Wharton. 56
Iatan, Mitchell
Iberis, Taylor
Ibex, Shackelford
Ida, Andrews
Ida, Gaines
Ida, Grayson. 30
Ida, Harris
Ida, Scurry
Idaho, Collingsworth
Idaho, Dawson
Idalia, Newton
*IDALOU, Lubbock, 138
 (2,074) 2,056
Ideal, Hutchinson
Ideal, Sherman
Idlewild, Bexar
Idlewild, Dallas
Igie, Hopkins
Ike, Ellis 10
Ike, Live Oak
Ila, King
Ilah, Polk
Ilka, Guadalupe
Illinois Bend, Montague 30
Illinois Colony, Clay
Illinois Torpedo Company, Eastland
Ima, Red River
Immermere, Erath
Imogene, Atascosa
IMPACT, Taylor (25) 23
Imperial, Fort Bend
*Imperial, Pecos, 26 350
Imperial Valley, Travis. . . . . NA
Inadale, Scurry. 8
Inari, Refugio
Independence, Terrell
Independence, Washington 140
Independent, Leon
Index, Bowie
Index, Van Zandt
Index, Wheeler
India, Ellis. 12
India, Polk
Indianapolis, Mason
Indianapolis, Menard
Indian Creek, Brown
Indian Creek, Smith 300
Indian Creek, Tarrant
Indian Gap, Hamilton. 36
Indian Grove, Grayson
Indian Harbor Estates, Hood . . 2,620
Indian Hill, Newton. . . . . NA
Indian Hills, Llano . . . . NA
INDIAN LAKE, Cameron (390). . . .501
Indian Lake, Newton . . . . NA
Indian Lodge, Bosque
Indian Mound, Young
Indianola, Calhoun. 200
Indian Point, Calhoun
Indian Rock, Upshur 45
Indian Spring, Polk
Indian Springs, Polk 250
Indio [Ranch], Maverick
Indio, Presidio . . . . NA
Indio, Zavala
Indpark, Brazos
*INDUSTRY, Austin, 55 (NC) 475
‡*Inez, Victoria, 56 (1,371) 1,460
Inge, Uvalde
Ingemal, Dimmit
Ingersoll, Bowie
Ingerton, Hutchinson

§*JOHNSON CITY, Blanco, 150,
  (932) 1,313
Johnson Creek, Marion
Johnson Mines, Erath
Johnson's Chapel, Stonewall
Johnson's Institute, Hays
Johnson's Mill, Erath
Johnson's Point, Kaufman
Johnsons Station, Tarrant
Johnsonton, Van Zandt
Johnstone, Val Verde
Johnston Store, Nacogdoches. . . NA
Johnstown, Travis
Johnsue, Waller
Johnsville, Erath .... .25
Johntown, Red River.......... .175
John Tucker, Erath
Joiel, Winkler
Joiner, Fayette
*Joinerville, Rusk, 4........... .140
Joliet, Caldwell. .... NA
JOLLY, Clay, (201) .... .225
‡ Jollyville, Williamson-Travis
  (15,206) 20,718
Jolo, Henderson
Jonah, Williamson, 3 .... .60
Jones', Fayette
Jones, Hood
Jones [Mill, Valley], Mills
Jones', Panola
Jones, Van Zandt .... NA
*Jonesboro, Coryell-Hamilton, 28
  .... .200
Jonesboro, Hamilton
Jonesboro[ugh], Red River
Jones Chapel, Cass
Jones City, Kinney
JONES CREEK, Brazoria.
  (2,160) 2,256
Jones Creek, Wharton
Jonesdale, Wichita
Jones' Gin, Bell
Jones Gin, Kaufman
Jones Mill, Coryell
Jones Mound, Frio
Jones Prairie, Milam .... .35
Jones Prairie, Polk
Jones' Ranch, Jim Hogg
Jones Store, Grimes
*JONESTOWN, Travis (1,250) . . 1,314
Jonestown, Travis
Jonesville, Angelina
Jonesville, Dallas
*Jonesville, Harrison, 17........ .28
Joplin, Jack .... NA
Joppa, Burnet .... .34
Jordan, Bastrop
Jordan, Brazoria
Jordan, Collin
Jordan, Concho
Jordan, Walker
Jordan Springs, Brown
Jordan's Saline, Van Zandt
Jordans Store, Shelby.......... NA
Joseph, Waller
*JOSEPHINE, Collin-Hunt, 15
  (503) 723
Joseway, Kendall
*JOSHUA, Johnson, 309
  (3,821) 4,665
Josie, Tyler
Josselet, Haskell .... NA
Josserand, Trinity .... .29
Jot-Em-Down, Hunt-Delta........10
§*JOURDANTON, Atascosa,
  186, (3,220) 3,875
Joy, Clay .... .100
Joy, Smith

Joyce, Harris
Joyce, Webb
Joy's Store, Kerr
Jozye, Madison
Juanita, Loving
Juan Saenz, Nueces
Jud, Haskell.................. 40
Jude, Oldham
Judkins, Ector
*Judson, Gregg, 9............ 650
Julia, Borden
Julia, Nueces
Julia, Wilbarger
Julian, Houston
Julia Pens, Victoria
Julietta, Floyd
Juliff, Fort Bend .... .NA
Julliard, Potter
Jumbo, Cass
Jumbo, Castro................. 3
Jumbo, Panola .... .NA
Junction, Coleman
§*JUNCTION, Kimble, 231
  (2,654) 2,672
Junior, Guadalupe
Junker's Cove, Harris
Juno, Val Verde 10
Jupiter, Coke
Jury, Bowie
*Justiceburg, Garza, 2 76
*JUSTIN [Justine], Denton, 190
  (1,234) 1,747

                K

Ka, Dallas
Kadane Corner, Wichita
Kaffir, Schleicher
Kaffir, Swisher
Kaleta, San Patricio
Kalgary, Crosby................ 70
*Kamay, Wichita, 9............ 642
Kamey, Calhoun ....NA
Kanawha, Red River 149
Kane, Hidalgo
Kane, Mitchell
Kane, Scurry
Karen, Montgomery
Karlshaven, Calhoun
*Karnack, Harrison, 68 775
§*KARNES CITY, Karnes, 157,
  (2,916) 2,859
Karney, Gonzales
Karney, Lavaca
Karon, Live Oak 25
Kasoga, Knox
Kasota, Armstrong
Kate, Delta
Katemcy, Mason, 2 90
Katherine, Kenedy
Kathleen, Brown
Katula, Nolan
*KATY, Harris-Waller-Fort Bend,
  2,626 (8,004) 11,175
§*KAUFMAN, Kaufman, 479
  (5,251) 7,042
Kaufman Estates, Kaufman..... 240
Kay, Trinity
Kayare, Cameron
Kayser's Prairie, Trinity
Kayville, Falls
Keahey, Liberty
Keck, Gonzales
Keechi, Jack
*Keechi, Leon 67
Keefer, Montgomery
Keeler, Johnson
Keenan, Montgomery
*KEENE, Johnson, 111

  (3,944) 4,764
Keeney's [Ranch], San Saba
Keeran, Victoria
Keeter, Wise .... NA
Keisler, Montgomery
Keith, Franklin
Keith, Grimes................. NA
Keith Lake, Jefferson .... NA
Keithton Switch, Jasper
Kelat, Navarro
Keliehor, Williamson
*KELLER, Tarrant, 866
  (13,683). 21,580
Kellers Corner, Cameron........123
Kellerville, Wheeler .... .50
Kellerville, Williamson
Kelley's, Walker
Kellner, Waller
Kellogg, Hunt .... NA
Kellum's Springs, Grimes
Kelly, Carson
Kelly, Collin. .... NA
*Kelly Air Force Base, Bexar. . . 2,363
Kelly Store, San Jacinto
Kellyville [Kelleyville], Marion. . . . NA
Kelm, Navarro
Kelow, Walker
Kelsay, Starr
Kelsey, Upshur................. .50
Kelso, Deaf Smith
Kelsoville, Bell
Kelton, Wheeler .... .20
*Keltys, Angelina .... .800
*KEMAH, Galveston, 330
  (1,094)................... 1,519
*KEMP, Kaufman, 397 (1,184) . . 1,414
Kemp City, Wichita
Kemper City, Victoria........... .16
*KEMPNER, Lampasas, 65
  (NC) .... .400
Kemp Newby, Wichita
Ken, Hidalgo
*Kendalia, Kendall, 10 .... .76
Kendall, Grayson
*KENDLETON, Fort Bend, 13
  (496) .... .701
Kendrick's, San Augustine
*KENEDY, Karnes, 254
  (3,763) 6,205
Kenedy, Karnes
Kenedy Junction, Karnes
KENEFICK, Liberty (435).......910
Kenelm, Henderson
Kenerly, Jasper
*KENNARD, Houston, 37 (341) . . .385
Kennebunk, Hale
*KENNEDALE, Tarrant, 383
  (4,098)................... 4,865
Kenner, Matagorda
Kenneth, Walker
*Kenney [Kenneyville], Austin, 4 . .200
Keno, Liberty
Kenser, Hunt................. NA
Kensing, Delta .... .35
Kent, Bosque
*Kent, Culberson, 16 .... .60
Kent['s Hill, Store], Houston
Kenton, Bastrop
Kentuck, Live Oak
Kentucky Town, Grayson 20
Kerby, Hill
*KERENS, Navarro, 102
  (1,702)................... 1,693
§*KERMIT, Winkler, 308
  (6,875) 6,553
Kern, Polk
Kern, Collin
Kerr, Williamson

Latex, Harrison. 75
Latex, Panola
*LATEXO, Houston, 12 (289). 327
Lathrop, Oldham
Laticia, Harris
La Tina, Cameron. 519
Latium, Washington. 30
Lato, Shelby
Lattington, Bee
La Tuna, El Paso
Laubach, Guadalupe. 20
‡*Laughlin Air Force Base,
   Val Verde (2,556). 2,952
La Union, Cameron 20
Laura, Harris
Laura, Johnson
Laura, Knox
Laurel, Newton. 125
Laurel, Webb
Laureles, Cameron 20
Laurel Hill, Newton
Laurelia, Polk
Lautz, Sherman
Lavaca, Calhoun
Lavacca, Jackson
Lavada, Franklin
Lavada, Johnson
La Valley, Hudspeth
Lavender, Limestone. . . . . NA
Laverne, Crockett
*LA VERNIA, Wilson, 148 (639) . 1,051
La Verte, Jasper
La Vierne, Runnels
*LA VILLA, Hidalgo, 18
   (1,388) 1,930
La Villa de los Jacallas, Refugio
*LAVON, Collin, 14 (303) 437
Law, Brazos . . . . NA
*LA WARD, Jackson, 11 (162) 188
Lawhon's Mills, Newton
*LAWN, Taylor, 23 (358) 370
Lawn City, Kaufman
Lawndale, Kaufman
Lawrence, Kaufman (231) 283
Lawrence Chapel, Williamson
Lawson, Dallas
Lawson, Wharton
Lawsonville, Rusk . . . . NA
Lawther, Dallas
Lay, Angelina
Layden's Ridge, Kaufman
Laytonia, Brazoria
Lazare, Cottle
Lazare, Hardeman
Lazarus, Archer
*Lazbuddie, Parmer, 18 248
Leachville, Milam
Leaday, Coleman
League, Crosby
League, Ellis
*LEAGUE CITY, Galveston,
   1,381 (30,159) 43,601
Leagueville, Henderson 32
Leah, Tyler
Leake's, Ellis
§*LEAKEY, Real, 93 (399) 408
Leal, Bexar
*LEANDER, Williamson-Travis,
   786, (3,398) 6,598
*LEARY, Bowie (395) 432
Leavitt, Haskell
Lebanon, Bee
Lebanon, Collin
Lebanon, Ellis
Lecomteville, Bexar
*Ledbetter, Fayette, 24. 76
Ledbetter, Lee
Ledford, Caldwell

Ledger, Karnes
Lee, Bell
Lee, Carson
Lee, Comanche
Lee, Hamilton
Lee, Hill
Lee, Van Zandt
Leedale, Bell 16
Leeray, Stephens
Lees [Store], Glasscock
*Leesburg, Camp, 29 115
Leesburg, Gonzales
Lees Mill, Newton
Lee Spring, Smith . . . . .NA
*Leesville, Gonzales, 12. 150
Leeton, Jasper
Leevan, Fayette
Lefman, Wharton
LeForest, Garza
*LEFORS, Gray, 21 (656). 715
Legard's Ranch, Jeff Davis
*Leggett, Polk, 19 500
Leggs Store, Nacogdoches
Legion, Kerr
Legion, Llano
Lehigh, Wilbarger
Lehman, Bastrop
Lehman, Cochran 8
Lehmann's Ranch, Maverick
Lehmberg, Llano
Leida, Edwards
Leigh, Harrison 100
Leila, Red River
Leisure Acres, Coryell 25
Lela, Wheeler. 135
Lelan, Montague
Leland, Ellis
Leland, McLennan
Lelavale, Hardin
*Lelia Lake, Donley, 8 125
*Leming, Atascosa, 10 268
Lemit, Shelby
Lemley, Parker
Lemo, Harrison
Lemons Gap, Taylor
Lemonville, Orange
Len, Fisher
Lena, Fayette
Lena, Henderson
Lenley's, Montgomery
Leno, Falls
Lenoir, Lamar
Lenor, San Augustine
Lenora, Harris
*Lenorah, Martin, 19 70
Lenore, Frio
Lenore, Jones
Lenox, Brewster
Lenoxville, Bowie
Lent, Taylor
Lenz, Colorado
Lenz, Karnes 20
Leo, Cooke 20
Leo, Lee 10
Leon, Leon
Leona, Frio
*LEONA, Leon, 19 (178) 235
Leona Mills, Leon
*LEONARD, Fannin, 109
   (1,744) 1,870
Leona Schroder, Nueces 40
Leonidas, Montgomery . . . . .NA
*Leon Junction, Coryell 25
Leon Springs, Bexar. 137
*LEON VALLEY, Bexar
   (9,581) 10,404
Leonville, Coryell
Lera, Nacogdoches

Leroy, Llano
*LEROY, McLennan, 19 (292). 344
Leroy, McLennan
Lesley, Hall 45
Leslie, Waller
Leslieville, Montgomery
Lester, Hunt
Leta, Hopkins
Letot, Dallas
Leubner, Williamson
Levada, Brown
§*LEVELLAND, Hockley, 820,
   (13,986) 13,938
Leverett's Chapel, Rusk 450
Levi, McLennan 50
Levin, Grimes
Levin, Pecos
Levinson, Culberson
Levita, Coryell, 1 70
Lewalt, Stephens
Lewis, Anderson
Lewis, Cass
Lewis, Henderson
Lewis', Houston
Lewis Ferry, Jasper
*LEWISVILLE, Denton-Dallas,
   4,291 (46,521) 67,180
Lewis' Wharf, Jackson
Lexington, Denton
*LEXINGTON, Lee, 102 (953). . . 1,085
Leyendecker, Webb
Libby, Nacogdoches
Liberty, Coleman
Liberty, Ellis
Liberty, Falls
Liberty, Freestone
Liberty, Hamilton
Liberty, Hopkins. . . . . NA
Liberty, Hopkins
§*LIBERTY, Liberty, 638
   (7,690) 9,334
Liberty, Lubbock 10
Liberty, Milam. 40
Liberty, Newton . . . . NA
Liberty, Rusk
Liberty, Van Zandt
Liberty Chapel, Johnson. . . . . NA
‡ Liberty City, Gregg (1,607) . . . 1,730
Liberty Grove, Collin
Liberty Grove, Dallas
Liberty Grove, Delta
Liberty Grove, Hill
Liberty Hill, Bowie
Liberty Hill, Hays
Liberty Hill, Houston 73
Liberty Hill, Milam 25
Liberty Hill, Rusk
*LIBERTY HILL, Williamson, 148,
   (NC) 1,500
Liberty Point, Wise
Liberty Springs, Collin
Lick, Fannin
Lick Skillet, Fayette
Lickskillet, Grayson
Lieb, Hutchinson
Liendo, Waller
Lieu, Collin
Liggett, Dallas
Light, Dimmit
Light, Howard
Light, Scurry
Lightfoot, Lampasas
Lightner, Concho
Ligon, Cochran
Ligonville, Guadalupe
Lilac, Milam
Lilbert, Nacogdoches . . . . NA
Liles, Rusk

Lilla, Lavaca
Lillard, Hardin
Lilley, Morris
*Lillian, Johnson, 14 105
Lillie, Collingsworth
Lillie, Newton
Lilly, Camp
Lilly, Hunt
Lilly, Wilbarger
Lilly Grove, Nacogdoches
Lily Island, Polk
Lima, Bandera
Lime City, Coryell
Limestone, Limestone
Limpia, Jeff Davis
Limpia Cañon, Jeff Davis
Lin, Young
Linberg, Tarrant
*Lincoln, Lee, 22 276
Lincoln, San Jacinto
Lincoln City, Harris
LINCOLN PARK, Denton (287) . . .448
Lincoln Park, Grayson
*LINDALE, Smith, 500 (2,428) . . 2,677
Lindeman, DeWitt
§*LINDEN, Cass, 166 (2,375) . . . 2,389
Lindenau, DeWitt 50
Lindendale, Kendall . . . . NA
Lindley, Comanche
*LINDSAY, Cooke, 32 (610) 798
Lindsay Gardens, Hidalgo
Lindsey, Henderson
Lindsey, Smith
Line, Hopkins
Line Creek, McLennan
Liner, Swisher
Lineville, Panola
*Lingleville, Erath, 8. 100
Lingo, Hill
Lingo, Stonewall
Link, Limestone
Link, Mitchell
Link, Scurry
Linksville, Jones
*Linn, Hidalgo, 16. 450
Linn Flat, Nacogdoches . . . . NA
Linnie, Fisher
Lint, Collin
Linus, Panola
Linwood, Cherokee 40
Linwood, Shelby
Lipan, Atascosa
*LIPAN, Hood, 83 (354) 438
Lipan, Tom Green
§*Lipscomb, Lipscomb, 10 50
Lisbon, Dallas
Lisle, Young
*Lissie, Wharton, 6. 70
Littig, Travis 37
Little Brazos, Robertson
Little Chicago, DeWitt
Little Cow Creek, Newton
Little Cypress, Orange 1,050
*LITTLE ELM, Denton, 137
(1,255). 1,739
§*LITTLEFIELD, Lamb, 363
(6,489) 6,381
Little Flock, Leon
Little Georgia, Brazos
Littleglade, Limestone
Little Hope, Wood. 25
Little Lost Valley, Jack
Little Midland, Burnet 32
Little Mineral, Grayson
Little New York, Gonzales 20
Little River, Milam
*LITTLE RIVER-ACADEMY, Bell,
53 (1,390) 1,678

Littleton's Springs, Parker
Littletonville, Parker
Littleville, Hamilton
Litwalton, Garza
Lively, Kaufman . . . . .NA
Live Oak, Bell
*LIVE OAK, Bexar (10,023). . . .10,839
Live Oak, Blanco
Live Oak, Bosque
Liveoak, Brazoria
Live Oak, Caldwell
Live Oak, Concho . . . . .NA
Live Oak, Crockett
Live Oak, DeWitt
Live Oak, Falls
Liveoak, Newton
Live Oak Bend, Matagorda
Live Oak Hill, Fayette
Live Oak Point, Aransas
Live Oaks, Bastrop
Live Oak Springs, Travis
*LIVERPOOL, Brazoria, 23
(396) 490
§*LIVINGSTON, Polk, 1,025
(5,019). 7,295
Livonia, Newton
Llano, Armstrong
§*LLANO, Llano, 321 (2,962) . . .3,302
Llano Grande, Hidalgo
Lloyd, Brown
Lloyd, Denton
Lloyd, Falls
Lloyd Mountain, Scurry
Lo, Limestone
Lobo, Culberson 40
Lochridge, Brazoria . . . . .NA
Lock, Smith
Locke Hill, Bexar
Locker, San Saba 16
Locker Spur, Reeves
Locket, Navarro
Lockett, Jones
Lockett, Marion
Lockett, Wilbarger. 200
Lockettville, Hockley 20
§*LOCKHART, Caldwell, 480,
(9,205) 10,343
Locklin, Rusk
*LOCKNEY, Floyd, 143
(2,207) 2,048
Loco, Childress
Locus, Hall
Locus, Limestone
Locust, Grayson 118
*Lodi, Marion, 3. 164
Lodi, Wilson
Lodwick, Marion
Loeb, Hardin
Loebau, Lee. 20
Loftin, Smith
Logan, Brazoria
Logan, Panola 40
LOG CABIN, Henderson (487) . . . 600
Logco, Karnes
Loggins, Cameron
Logsdon, Andrews
Logsdon, Gaines
Logtown, Newton
Logville, San Augustine
*Lohn, McCulloch, 18 149
Loire, Atascosa
Loire, Wilson 50
Lois, Cooke 20
Lois, Harris
Lolaville, Collin
*Lolita, Jackson, 25. 453
Loma, San Patricio
Loma, Walker

Loma Alta, McMullen. 100
Loma Alta, Val Verde 30
Loma Vista, [Luma Vista], Zavala
Lomax, Harris
Lomax, Howard 3,554
*LOMETA, Lampasas, 60 (625) . . .750
Lomita, Bee
*London, Kimble, 7 180
London, Rusk. . . . . NA
Londonderry, Harris
Londy, Van Zandt
Lone Camp, Palo Pinto 110
Lone Cedar, Ellis 18
Lone Cottonwood, Hunt
Lone Elm, Kaufman . . . . NA
Lone Elm, Kaufman
Lone Grove, Falls
Lone Grove, Llano 50
Lone Hand, San Saba
Lone Mill, Sterling
Lone Mountain, Upshur
Lone Oak, Bexar . . . . NA
Lone Oak, Colorado. 50
Lone Oak, Erath . . . . NA
*LONE OAK, Hunt, 91 (521) 614
Lone Oak, Montgomery
Lone Oak, Navarro
Lone Pine, Houston 81
Lonepine, Milam
Lonesome Dove, Tarrant
Lone Spring, Lamar
Lone Star, Bell
Lone Star, Burnet
Lone Star, Cherokee 20
Lonestar, Collingsworth
Lone Star, Floyd. 42
Lone Star, Franklin
Lone Star, Hopkins
Lone Star, Kaufman. . . . . NA
Lone Star, Lamar . . . . NA
Lone Star, Llano
*LONE STAR, Morris, 87
(1,615) 1,646
Lone Star, Titus
Lone Tree, Collin
Lone Willow, Johnson
Longbranch, Eastland
*Long Branch, Panola, 8 181
Long Bridge, Polk
Longfellow, Pecos
Long Hollow, Jack
Long Hollow, Leon. . . . . NA
Long King, Polk
Long Lake, Anderson 15
Long Leaf, San Augustine
*Long Mott, Calhoun, 5 76
Long Mount, Mason
Long Mountain, Llano
Long Mountain, Mason
Longoria, Brooks
Longorio, Jones
Long Point, Fort Bend
Longpoint[Long Point], Washington
. 80
Long Prairie, Fayette
Long Station, Hardin
Longstreet, Houston
Longstreet, Montgomery
§*LONGVIEW, Gregg-Harrison-
Upshur, 4,987 (70,311). 75,973
Longview, Midland
Longwood, Lipscomb
Longwood, Sabine
Longworth, Fisher, 2 65
Lon Hill, Nueces
Lon Hill's Town, Cameron
Lonnie, Childress
Lonsboro, Hidalgo

Lookout, Bexar
Lookout, Leon
Lookout, Mills
Look Out Point, Aransas
Lookout Station, Lamar
Looneyville, Nacogdoches . . . . . . NA
Loop, Clay
*Loop, Gaines, 31 315
Loop, Gaines
*Lopeno[Lopena], Zapata, 3 425
Loper, Henderson
‡ Lopezville, Hidalgo (2,827). . . 3,631
Lora, Roberts
*LORAINE, Mitchell, 27 (731) 687
Lord, Harris
Lord, Ochiltree
*LORENA, McLennan, 218
    (1,158) 1,650
*LORENZO, Crosby, 76 (1,208) . 1,269
Loring, Cooke
Los Angeles, La Salle 20
Los Barreras, Starr 75
Los Coyotes, Willacy 4
Los Dinero, Mills
*Los Ebanos, Hidalgo, 4 100
Los Escondidos, Burnet 30
*LOS FRESNOS, Cameron,
    210 (2,473) 2,920
Los Fresnos, Presidio
*LOS INDIOS, Cameron, 8 (NC). . .206
Los Machos, Jim Wells
Los Nogales, Guadalupe
Los Ojuelos, Webb
Los Olmos, Brooks
Losoya, Bexar 322
Los Saenz, Starr
Loss Creek, Coleman . . . . NA
Lost, Montague
Lost Creek, Jack
‡ Lost Creek, Travis (4,095). . . . 4,414
Lost Prairie, Bell
Lost Prairie, Limestone 2
Lost Prairie, Limestone
Lostprong, Wharton
LOS YBANEZ, Dawson (83) 88
*LOTT, Falls, 81 (775) 877
Lott, Washington
Lotta, Harrison
Lotta, Kaufman
Lotta, Parker
Lottie, Wood
Lotus, Harris
Lou, Dawson
Louetta, Harris
Louis, Limestone
*Louise, Wharton, 83 310
Louisiana Settlement, Polk
Louisville, Bowie
Louisville, Fort Bend
Louisville, Limestone
Lourwood, Lipscomb
Love, Goliad
Love Branch, Eastland
Lovelace, Hill 12
*LOVELADY, Houston, 62 (587). . .654
*Loving, Young, 18 300
Loving's Valley, Palo Pinto
Low, Wood
*Lowake, Concho, 5 40
Lowell, DeWitt
Lowell, Erath
Lowell, Guadalupe
Lower Medio, Bee
Lower Mott, Calhoun
Lower Station, Grayson
Lower Taylor Bayou, Jefferson
Lowery, Grimes
Lowery, Nacogdoches

Lowesville, Guadalupe
Lowman, Lamar . . . . .NA
Low Pin Oak, Lee
Lowry, Collin
Lowry, Panola
LOWRY CROSSING, Collin (895)
   1,165
Loyal Valley, Mason 50
Loyola, Martin
Loyola Beach, Kleberg 125
*Lozano, Cameron, 5 200
Lozier, Terrell
Luanna, Cass
Lubbock, Hardeman
§*LUBBOCK, Lubbock, 10,754
    (186,206) 192,732
Lucas, Atascosa
LUCAS, Collin (2,205) 3,472
Lucas, Milam
Lucas City, Atascosa
Lucas Spring, Bexar
Luce, Trinity
Lucern, Hansford
Lucero, Brooks
Lucile, Lampasas
Luck, Collin
Luckenbach, Gillespie 25
Luckey, Coryell
Lucknow, Nacogdoches
Lucky, Montague
Lucky, Polk
Lucy, Victoria
*LUEDERS, Jones-Shackelford,
    28 (365) 360
Luella, Grayson (559) 698
§*LUFKIN, Angelina, 2,620
    (30,206) 34,425
Luke, Atascosa
Luke Wilson, Archer
Lula, Culberson
Lula, Real
*LULING, Caldwell, 340
    (4,661) 5,659
Lull, Hidalgo . . . . .NA
Lumber, Marion
*LUMBERTON, Hardin, 482
    (6,640) 7,820
Lumkins, Ellis 20
Lumpkin, Smith
Lums Chapel, Lamb 6
Lunarville, Jack
Lund, Travis
Lundy, Houston
Lunette, Eastland
Luray, Houston
Lusk, McLennan
Lusk, Throckmorton 10
Luster, Van Zandt
Lutes, Henderson
Luther, Howard 335
Luther, Lamar
Luther, Limestone
Lutie, Collingsworth 35
Luvial, Colorado
Luxello, Bexar
Luzon, Van Zandt
Lydia, Red River 109
Lyford, Navarro
*LYFORD, Willacy, 75 (1,674) . . .1,992
Lyle, Rusk
Lyman, Motley
Lynch, Hopkins
Lynch, Rains
Lynchburg[h], [Lynch's Ferry], Harris
Lynchs Creek, Lampasas
Lyndale, Smith
Lynn, King
Lynn Grove, Grimes . . . . .NA

Lynnell, Sterling
Lynox, Bowie
Lyon, Grayson
*Lyons, Burleson, 16 360
Lyons [Lyonsville], Fayette
Lyra, Palo Pinto
Lyric, Liberty
Lystra, Jones
*LYTLE, Atascosa-Medina-
    Bexar, 136 (2,255). 2,608
Lytle, Tarrant
Lytle, Taylor
Lytle Cove, Taylor
Lytton Springs, Caldwell 500

M

*MABANK, Kaufman-Henderson,
    696 (1,739) 2,012
Mabel, Bexar
Mabel, Fisher
Mabel, Lipscomb
Mabeldean, Clay
Mabelle, Baylor 9
Mabry, Harris
Mabry, Red River 60
Macaroni Station, Jackson
MacBain, Motley
*Macdona, Bexar, 6 297
Mace, Lampasas
Macedonia, Bowie
Macedonia, Harrison
Macedonia, Liberty
Macedonia, Walker
Macedonia, Waller
Macey, Brazos . . . . NA
MacGrath, Tom Green
Machos, La Salle
Machovec, Moore
Macie, Kinney
Mack, Polk
Mack, Wilbarger
Mackay, Wharton
Mackie, Ellis
Mackville, Collin
Macomb, Grayson
Macon, Franklin 21
Macon, Harrison
Macrod, Cameron
Macune, San Augustine 100
Mada, Milam
Madden, Hudspeth
Madera Springs, Jeff Davis
Madero, Hidalgo . . . . NA
Madison, Orange
Madison, Swisher
§*MADISONVILLE, Madison,
    346 (3,569) 4,243
Madras, Red River 61
Mae, Jim Wells . . . . NA
Magasco, Sabine
Magenta, Oldham
Maggie, Montgomery
Magic City, Wheeler
Magill, Milam
Maginnis, Bowie
Maglab, Dallas
Magnesium, Brazoria
Magnet, Wharton 42
Magnet, Wharton
Magnolia, Anderson
Magnolia, Borden
Magnolia, Montgomery
*MAGNOLIA, Montgomery, 699,
    (940) 1,283
Magnolia, San Jacinto 330
Magnolia, Wilbarger
Magnolia Beach, Calhoun . . . . NA
Magnolia Gardens, Harris

Magnolia Mills, Sabine
*Magnolia Springs, Jasper, 2 80
Magoffinsville, El Paso
Magoun, Lipscomb
Magpetco, Jefferson
Maguire, Robertson
Magwalt, Winkler
Maha, Travis .... **NA**
Mahala, Live Oak
Mahl, Nacogdoches .... **NA**
Mahomet, Burnet 47
Mahon, Panola
Mahoney, Hopkins .... **NA**
Mahoney, Hopkins
Mainz, Kendall
Mainzer, Dallas
Maize, Scurry
Major, Limestone
Majors, Franklin 13
*MALAKOFF, Henderson, 199
  (2,038) 2,311
Malcom, Smith
Malden, Armstrong
Mallard, Montague 12
Mallard Prairie, Henderson
Mallett, Sherman
Mallie, Hudspeth
*MALONE, Hill, 27 (306) 335
Maloney [Malony], Ellis
Malta, Bowie 297
Malta, King
Malvado, Terrell
Malvern, Fort Bend
Malvern, Leon .... **NA**
Mambrino, Hood 74
Mammoth, Lipscomb
Mamre, Atascosa
Mance, Henderson
Manchac, Hays
Manchac [Manchac House], Travis
*Manchaca, Travis, 166 .... **2,259**
Manchester, Red River 185
Manchester Mills, Tarrant
Manda, Travis
Manestee, Tom Green
Mangold, Archer
Mangum, Eastland 15
Mangus Corner, Bexar .... **NA**
Manheim, Lee 40
Manila, Crosby
Manila, Grimes
Mankin, Henderson 20
Mankins, Archer 10
Manle, Young
Mann, Navarro
Mann, Reeves
Manning, Angelina
Manning, Bexar
Mann's Crossing, Bexar
Manoah, Ward
*MANOR, Travis, 187 (1,041) ... **1,230**
*MANSFIELD, Tarrant-Johnson-
  Ellis, 1,123 (15,615) **22,679**
Mansker Lake, Eastland
Manson, Anderson
Manson, Jackson
Mantha, Camp
Manton, Angelina
Manton's, Fayette
Mantu, Harris
Mantua, Collin
*MANVEL, Brazoria, 240
  (3,733) 4,868
Mapes, Wood
*Maple[Maple Wilson], Bailey, 10 ...75
Maple, Collin
Maples, Wichita
Maple, Red River 30

Maple Spring [Maple], **Titus** 25
Maple Springs, Red River
Maple Springs, Titus
Mapleton, Houston **32**
Mara, Tarrant
Marak[sville], Milam
*Marathon, Brewster, 42 .... **850**
*MARBLE FALLS, Burnet, 931,
  (4,007) 5,410
Marble Hill, Burnet
Marble Mountain, Brewster
Marcelina, Karnes
March, Rusk
Marco, McCulloch
Marcy, Haskell
Marekville, Bell
Marekville, Calhoun
Marella [Store], Collingsworth
Marengo, Menard
§*MARFA, Presidio, 150
  (2,424) 2,639
Margaret, Coke
Margaret, Foard **51**
Margie, Leon
Marianna, Polk
Marianna, Victoria
Marie, Runnels **12**
Marienfeld, Martin
Marietta, Anderson
*MARIETTA, Cass, 30 (161) **184**
Marietta, Crosby
Marietta, Van Zandt
Marilee, Collin
Marilla, Collingsworth
Marine, Tarrant
Marion, Angelina
Marion, Brazoria
*MARION, Guadalupe, 128
  (984) 1,083
Marion Ferry Park, Angelina
Mariscal, Brewster
Marith, Dallas
Marjorie, Milam
Mark, McCulloch
Markbelt, Brazoria
Market, Polk
‡*Markham, Matagorda, 31
  (1,206) 1,412
Markley, Young **50**
Markout, Kaufman **80**
Marks, Frio
Marley, Fayette
Marley Springs, Burnet
§*MARLIN, Falls, 288 (6,386) ...6,647
Marlow, Anderson
Marlow, Fort Bend
Marlow, Milam **45**
Marlow's Mill, Anderson
Marmaduke, Jack
Marmion, Brazoria
*MARQUEZ, Leon, 45 (270) **293**
Marr, Polk
Mars, Van Zandt .... **NA**
Marsh, Bowie
Marsh, Polk
Marsh, Potter
§*MARSHALL, Harrison, 1,518,
  (23,682) 25,066
*MARSHALL CREEK, Denton,
  (315) 489
Marshall Ford [Dam], Travis ...... **NA**
Marshall Northeast, Harrison ...1,500
Marshall's Store, Jack
Marston, Polk **25**
Marstonville, Polk
*MART, McLennan, 118 (2,004)
 2,006
Martin, Angelina

Martin, Coryell
Martin, Hill
Martin, Lamar
Martin, Red River
Martinburg, Camp
*MARTINDALE, Caldwell, 35,
  (904) 1,154
Martinez, Bexar .... **NA**
Martin Lake Junction, Panola
Martin Prairie, Grimes
Martinsburgh, Blanco
Martinsburgh, Gillespie
Martins Gap, Hamilton
Martins Mills, Van Zandt 125
Martin Springs, Grayson
Martin Springs, Hopkins 115
*Martinsville[Martin's Mill, City],
  Nacogdoches, 6 126
Marvel Wells, Milam
Marville, Panola
Marvin, Lamar .... **NA**
Marvin, McLennan
Marvin, Robertson
Marvin [Chapel], Van Zandt
Marx, Limestone
Mary, Jim Wells
Mary, Montague
Maryetta, Jack 7
*Maryneal, Nolan, 7 61
Marys Creek, Baylor
Mary's Creek, Parker
Mary's Creek, Tarrant
Marysee, Liberty
Marystown [Marysville], Johnson
Marysville, Cooke 15
Maryville, Bee
§*MASON, Mason, 220
  (2,041) 2,167
Masons, Reeves
Mason's Ranch, Terry
Massey, Hill
Massey Lake, Anderson .... **NA**
Massie, San Augustine
Massie, Trinity
Masters', Houston
Masters, Throckmorton
Masterson, Brazoria
Masterson, Moore, 5 15
Masterson, Potter
Masterville, McLennan
Maston, Comanche
§*MATADOR, Motley, 64 (790) 673
Matador, Motley
*Matagorda, Matagorda, 39 710
Matalfos, Coke
Matejowsky, Washington
Mather Mills, Williamson
*MATHIS, San Patricio, 289
  (5,423) 5,734
Matilda, Jackson
Matile, Hardin
Matinburg, Camp
Matlock, Dallam
Matson, Hill
Matthews, Colorado 25
Mattie, Stonewall
Mattox [Mill], Newton
*MAUD, Bowie, 58 (1,049) **1,024**
Maud, Knox
Maud, Parker
Maud, Wise
Maudlowe, Refugio
‡*Mauriceville, Orange, 99
  (2,046) 2,223
Maurin, Gonzales
Maverick, Medina
Maverick, Runnels 31
Maxbury, Stephens

(1,390) 1,414
*Merit[t], Hunt, 8 215
Merito, Hidalgo
Meritt's, Jasper
*MERKEL, Taylor, 224 (2,469) . . 2,557
Merle, Burleson . . . . NA
Merret, Red River
Merriam, Eastland 14
Merrick, Martin
Merrilltown, Travis
Merrimac, Wood
Merriman, Eastland
Merrivale, Bosque
Merry Flat, Wheeler
*MERTENS, Hill, 6 (104). 113
§*MERTZON, Irion, 69 (778). 657
Merv, Henderson
Mesa, El Paso. 50
Mesa, Grimes
Mesa, Randall
Mescalero Park, Randall
Mesquital, San Patricio
Mesquite, Borden
*MESQUITE, Dallas, 4,675
(101,484) 114,699
Mesquite Acres Island, San
Patricio . . . . NA
Mesquite Flat, Coryell
Mesquiteville, Jack
Metcalf Gap, Palo Pinto. 6
Meteor, Floyd
Methodist Colony, Donley
Mettina, Falls
Metz, Denton
Metz, Ector
Metz, Gonzales
Mewshaw, Cherokee
*MEXIA, Limestone, 469
(6,933). 6,935
Mexico, Hunt . . . . NA
Mexline, Cochran
Meyer City, Mills
*Meyersville, DeWitt, 12. 110
§*MIAMI, Roberts, 63 (675) 531
Mica, Hudspeth
Micars, Caldwell
Michelle, Angelina
Michies, Dawson
Mickey, Floyd
*Mico, Medina, 10. 98
Micolithic, Culberson
Micomber, Floyd
Mid, Haskell
Midcity, Lamar . . . . NA
Middle Bayou, Harris
Middle Bosque, McLennan
Middle Caddo, Hunt
Middle Gabriel, Burnet
Middleton, Leon 26
Middletown, Blanco
Middletown, Goliad
Middletown, Kendall
Middle Valley, Schleicher
Middle Water, Hartley
*Midfield, Matagorda, 1 70
Midkiff, Midland
*Midkiff, Upton, 29 98
§*MIDLAND, Midland, 6,893
(89,443). 99,734
Midlin, Denton
Midline, Montgomery
*MIDLOTHIAN, Ellis, 558
(5,040). 6,532
Midway, Bell 122
Midway, Bexar . . . . NA
Midway, Bosque
Midway, Dawson 20
Midway, Dickens

Midway, Fannin 7
Midway, Franklin
Midway, Hamilton
Midway, Henderson
Midway, Hill
Midway, Howard
Midway, Jim Wells. . . . . .NA
Midway, Johnson
Midway, Jones
Midway, Lavaca. . . . . .NA
Midway, Limestone. 9
Midway, Lubbock
*MIDWAY, Madison, 24 (274). 333
Midway, Midland
Midway, Montgomery . . . . .NA
Midway, Newton
Midway, Nueces
Midway, Polk . . . . .NA
Midway, Red River 40
Midway, San Patricio
Midway, Scurry
Midway, Smith. . . . . .NA
Midway, Titus. 110
Midway, Tom Green
Midway, Upshur. 20
Midway, Van Zandt 31
Midway Center, Grayson
Midwest, Wheeler
Midyett, Panola . . . . .NA
Mifflin, Donley
Mifflin, Kenedy
Miguel, Frio
Miguiel, Frio
Mikado, Wood
Mikeska, Live Oak. 10
‡ Mila Doce, Hidalgo (2,089) . . .2,671
Milam, Falls
Milam, Milam
*Milam, Sabine, 29 177
*MILANO, Milam, 41 (408). 498
Milburn, McCulloch. 8
Milby, Travis
MILDRED, Navarro (173). 214
Miles, Gonzales
*MILES [Station], Runnels, 87
(793) 913
*MILFORD, Ellis, 35 (711) 893
Millay, Denton
Mill Creek, Bowie
Mill Creek, Guadalupe
Mill Creek, Red River
Mill Creek, San Jacinto
Mill Creek, Waller . . . . .NA
Mill Creek, Washington. 40
Milledge, San Jacinto
Miller [Station], Bell
Miller, Dallas
Miller [Schoolhouse], Rusk
Miller Grove, Camp. . . . . .NA
Miller Grove, Hopkins. 115
Miller's, Fayette
Miller's, Lamar
Miller's, Panola
MILLER'S COVE, Titus (75) 94
Miller's Farm, Lavaca
*Millersview, Concho, 12 75
Millerton, Milam
Millerton, San Augustine
Millerville, Erath
Millett, La Salle 40
Millett's [Ranch], Baylor
Millheim, Austin 150
Millheim Station, Austin
*MILLICAN, Brazos, 6 (NC). 157
Milligan, Collin
Milliken, Runnels
Millino, Colorado
Mills, Dallas

Mills, Grayson
*MILLSAP, Parker, 78 (485) 644
Mills Bennett, Webb
Millseat, Hays
Mills Store, Brown
Millsville, San Patricio. . . . . NA
Millville, Gillespie
Millville, Rusk
Millwood, Collin
Milner, Cass
Milo, Baylor
Milo, Briscoe
Milo, Wood
Milo Center, Deaf Smith. 5
Milred, Navarro
Milton, Lamar. 80
Milton, Red River
Milton, Shelby
Milton, Tyler
Milvid, Liberty
Milvid, Montgomery
Mims, Brazoria. . . . . NA
Mims [Store], Marion
Mims, Rusk
Mims Chapel, Marion. . . . . NA
Mina, Bastrop
Mina, Eastland
Mina, Hunt
Mina, Wise
*Minden, Rusk, 6 350
Mindiette, Duval
Minear, Gonzales
*MINEOLA, Wood, 506 (4,321). . 4,756
Minera, Webb
*Mineral [City], Bee, 2 50
Mineral Heights, Hunt
Mineral Springs, Gray
Mineral Springs, Kendall
*MINERAL WELLS, Palo Pinto-
Parker, 949 (14,935) 15,367
Minerva, Foard
Minerva, Milam, 57 60
Minerva, Travis
Mingo, Denton
Mings Chapel, Upshur. 50
*MINGUS, Palo Pinto, 21 (215) . . .239
Mink, Montgomery
Minnie, Jackson
Minnis, Wilbarger
Minnocks, Montgomery
Minor, Mills
Minter, Lamar 78
Minter[s], Tarrant
Minters, Kerr
Minterville, Howard
Minton, Lamar
Mirage, Deaf Smith
Miranda, Tarrant
*Mirando City, Webb, 16. 707
Miriam, Liberty
Mirror, Floyd
*MISSION, Hidalgo, 1,609
(28,653). 41,085
Mission, Moore
‡ Mission Bend, Fort Bend
(24,945). 30,175
Mission Valley, Comal
Mission Valley, Victoria 225
Missoula, Fort Bend
*MISSOURI CITY, Fort Bend-
Harris, 1,422 (36,176). 58,002
Mitchell, Cameron
Mitchell, Eastland 46
Mitchell, Lipscomb
Mitchell, Swisher
Mitchell Hill, Tyler. . . . . NA
Mitchell Pens, Victoria
Mitchell's, Cooke

Mitchells, Madison
Mitchell's Valley, Limestone
Mittie, Cherokee
Mitto, Anderson
Mitzpah, Anderson
Mixon, Cherokee 50
Mixon, Lavaca
Moab, Lee
Mobberly, Red River
*MOBEETIE, Wheeler, 21 (154) . . .171
Mobile, Crockett
Mobile, Tyler
MOBILE CITY, Rockwall (NC) 207
Moccasin, Coryell
Mode, Floyd
Modera, Bandera
Modern, Jim Wells . . . . NA
Modeville, Wise
Modisett, Angelina
Modoc, Henderson
Mofeta, Terrell
Moffat, Bell 150
Moffett, Angelina 100
Moglia, Webb
Mogul, Tom Green
Mohair, Blanco
Mohat, Colorado
Mohegan, Hunt
Moistown, Cameron. 25
Moline, Lampasas 12
Mollie, Red River
§*MONAHANS [Well, Monahan],
    Ward-Winkler, 473 (8,101) . . . 7,641
Monaville, Waller 180
Moncass, Cass
Monico, Van Zandt
Monington, Anderson
Monkeyville, Hays
Monkstown, Fannin 35
Monodale, Williamson
Monroe, Dallas
Monroe, Lubbock
Monroe, Rusk. 96
*Monroe City, Chambers 90
Monserate, Lavaca
Mont, Lavaca 30
Montadale, Williamson
§*Montague, Montague, 32 400
Montague Village, Coryell 1,410
*Montalba, Anderson, 34. 110
Montana, Uvalde
*MONT BELVIEU, Chambers-
    Liberty, 112 (1,323). 1,824
*Monte Alto, Hidalgo 1,769
Monte C[h]risto, Hidalgo
Monte Cristo, Hidalgo
Monte Grande, Cameron. 97
Montell, Uvalde 20
Monteola, Bee
Monterey, Angelina
Monterey, Hill
Monterey [Old, Point Monterey], Marion
Monterey, Red River
Monterey Station, Marion
Montero, McLennan
Monte Robles Park, Bexar . . . . . . NA
Monterrey, Lubbock
Montezuma, Bailey
Montezuma, Colorado
Montfort, Navarro
*MONTGOMERY, Montgomery,
    682 (356). 499
Monthalia, Gonzales 65
Monticello, Titus. 20
Montopolis, Travis
Montoya, El Paso
Mont Truby, Jones
Montvale, Hamilton

Montvale, Lampasas
Montvale, Sterling
Montville, Washington
Moody, Bell
*MOODY, McLennan, 140
    (1,329) 1,401
Moody's Cross Roads, Leon
Moody Store, Lubbock
Moon, Baylor
Moon Chapel, Sterling
Mooney, Harris
Moonshine Colony, Baylor
Moonshine Hill, Harris
Moore, Brazos. . . . . .NA
Moore, Clay
*Moore [Hollow, Station], Frio, 15
    230
Moore Chapel, Fannin
Mooredale, Fort Bend
Moore Hill, Polk. . . . . .NA
Moores' [Mooresville], Bowie
Moore's Crossing, Travis 25
Moores' Landing, Bowie
MOORE STATION, Henderson
    (256) 322
Mooresville, Wood
Mooreville, Falls 96
Moorhead, Val Verde
Mooring, Brazos 80
Moorman, Comanche
Morales, Jackson 72
Morales De Lavaca, Jackson
Moran, Dallas
*MORAN, Shackelford, 22 (285). . 285
Morard, Liberty
Moravia, Lavaca 165
Morceville, El Paso
Moreland, Collin
Moreland, Navarro
Morey, Jefferson
Morg, Stephens
*MORGAN, Bosque, 29 (451) 547
Morgan, Ellis
Morgan, Lynn
Morgan, Robertson
Morgan, Williamson
Morgan, Young
Morgan Center, Wichita
Morgan Creek, Burnet 76
Morganlea, Robertson
*Morgan Mill, Erath, 11 206
MORGAN'S POINT, Harris
    (341) 387
MORGAN'S POINT RESORT,
    Bell (1,766). 2,425
Morgan Springs, Parker
Morgan's Store, Shelby
Morganville, Polk
Morince, Van Zandt
Morita, Howard
Morman, Falls
Mormon Grove, Grayson
Mormon Mills, Burnet
Mornack, Bosque
Moro, Tarrant
Moro [Mount Moro], Taylor
Morrill, Cherokee
Morris, Borden
Morris, Dallas
Morris, DeWitt
Morris, Howard
Morris Ferry, Jasper
*Morrison, Fort Bend
Morrison's Chapel, Leon
Morris Ranch, Gillespie . . . . .NA
Morristown {Morris}, Morris
*Morse, Hansford, 23 150
Mortimer, Milam

§*MORTON, Cochran, 164
    (2,597) 2,421
Morton, Grayson
Morton, Harrison 75
Morton, Lipscomb
Morton Valley, Eastland. 46
Moscow, Falls
*Moscow, Polk, 17 170
Mosel, Gillespie
Moseley, Henderson
Mosely, Red River
Moses, Stephens
Moses Bluff, Angelina
Moseville, Cameron
Mosheim, Bosque, 13 75
Mosley, Montgomery
Mosquito Prairie, Lee
Moss, Medina
Moss, Smith
Moss Bluff, Liberty 65
Moss Hill, Liberty. 49
Mossville, Cooke
Mosswood, Montgomery. . . . . NA
Mossy Grove, Walker. . . . . NA
Mostyn, Montgomery. . . . . NA
Mote's Mill, Delta
Motley, Rusk
Mott, Angelina
Mottomosa, Atascosa
Mott Springs, Shelby
*MOULTON, Lavaca, 96 (923) 967
Moulton Institute, Lavaca
*Mound, Coryell, 3 75
Mound, Dickens
Mound, Gonzales
Mound City, Anderson-Houston. . NA
Mound City, Red River
Mound Prairie, Anderson
Mound Prairie, Lamar
Mount, Hamilton
MOUNTAIN CITY, Hays (377). 430
Mountain Community, Coryell . . .300
Mountain Creek, Dallas
Mountain Creek, Tarrant
Mountain Home, Bell
*Mountain Home, Kerr, 35 96
Mountain Peak, Ellis 20
Mountain Spring, Cooke
Mountain Springs, Cooke 100
Mountain Springs, Hill
Mountain Top, Eastland. 22
Mountain Valley, Comal
Mountain View, Blanco
Mountain View, Travis 393
Mount Airy, Erath
Mount Bethel, Panola 62
Mount Blanco, Crosby. . . . . NA
*MOUNT CALM, Hill, 14 (303) 331
Mount Calm, Limestone
Mount Carmel, Smith
Mount Eden, Gonzales
*MOUNT ENTERPRISE, Rusk,
    83 (501) 528
Mount Gainor, Hays
Mount Haven, Cherokee 30
Mount Hecla, Jack
Mount Hermon, Shelby 56
Mount Holland, Hardin
Mount Hope, San Jacinto
Mount Hope, Tyler
Mount Houston, Harris
Mount Huling, Nacogdoches
Mount Jordan, Jasper
Mount Joy, Delta
Mount Juliet, Travis
Mount Margaret, Coke
Mount Mitchell, Morris
Mount Mourne, Panola

Mount Olive, Lavaca .... NA
Mount Olive, Mills
Mount Olive, Shelby
Mount Olivet, McLennan
Mount Pesrea, DeWitt
Mount Pisgah, Hopkins
Mount Pleasant, Bastrop
Mount Pleasant, Freestone
Mount Pleasant, Grimes
Mount Pleasant, San Saba
§*MOUNT PLEASANT, Titus,
  1,003 (12,291) 13,595
Mount Pleasant, Wharton
Mount Prairie, Freestone
Mount Rose, Falls 26
Mount Rose, Polk
Mount Scopus, Atascosa
Mount Selman, Cherokee 200
Mount Sharp, Hays
Mount Sterling, Nacogdoches
Mount Sylvan, Smith 181
Mount Union, Jasper .... NA
§*MOUNT VERNON, Franklin,
  262 (2,219) 2,416
Mount Vernon, Gonzales
Mount Vernon, Houston 43
Mount Vernon, Lamar
Mount Vernon, Limestone
Mount Vernon, Washington
Mount Zion, Coryell
Mount Zion, Montgomery
Mount Zion, Rockwall
Mount Zora, Haskell
Moursund, Victoria
Mouth of Pedernales, Travis
Mowatt, Bastrop
Moyer, Childress
Mozart, Crockett
Mozelle, Cochran
Mozelle, Coleman .... NA
Mozo, Williamson
Muckymuck, Travis
Mud, Travis
Mud Creek, Smith
Muddig, Hunt .... NA
Mud Spring, Denton
Mud Town, Hill
Mudville, Brazos .... NA
Muela, Maverick
Muela, Zavala
Muellersville, Washington 40
*MUENSTER, Cooke, 217
  (1,387) 1,536
Muerto, Cameron
Mulberry, Fannin 17
Mulberry, Fayette
Mulberry, Red River
Mulberry Flats, Armstrong
Mulberry Grove, Rusk
*Muldoon, Fayette, 11 98
Mule Creek, Gonzales
§*MULESHOE, Bailey, 433
  (4,571) 4,362
Mulford, Orange
Mulkey, Hill
*MULLIN, Mills, 41 (194) 244
Mullin, Tom Green
Mullins, Falls
Mullins Prairie, Fayette 52
Mulvey, Polk
*Mumford, Robertson, 7 170
Muncy, Floyd
*MUNDAY, Knox, 124 (1,600) ... 1,461
Munger, Limestone 5
Mungerville, Dawson 25
Munn, Eastland
Munson, Rockwall
Munz, Cass

*MURCHISON, Henderson, 79
  (510) 624
Murchison's Prairie, Houston
Murdo, Oldham
Murdocks Landing, Kenedy
Muriel, Tarrant
Murlock, Hansford
MURPHY, Collin (1,547) 2,553
Murphy, Medina
Murphy's Store [Gin, Mill], Burnet
Murphyville, Brewster
Murray, Cameron ....NA
Murray, Dallam
Murray, Medina
Murray, Panola
Murray, Young 45
Murval [Murvaul], Rusk
Murvaul, Panola 110
Murvaul, Panola
Muse, Wise
Musgrove, Wood ....NA
Music, Frio
Muskegon, Orange
Muskete, Navarro
Musquis, Jeff Davis
Mustang, Bosque
Mustang, Denton ....NA
Mustang, Lavaca
Mustang, Limestone
MUSTANG, Navarro (35) 47
Mustang, Van Zandt
Mustang, Washington
Mustang, Wharton
Mustang Branch, Dallas
Mustang Creek, Johnson
Mustang Island, Nueces
Mustang Mott, DeWitt 20
Mustang Prairie, Falls
Mustang Prairie, Houston
Mustang Prairie, Walker
MUSTANG RIDGE, Caldwell-
  Travis-Bastrop (576) 786
Mustang Settlement, Jackson
Mutt and Jeff, Wood
Myers, Burleson
Myers, Collingsworth
Myers' Mill, Bell
Mykawa, Harris
*Myra, Cooke, 5 300
Myricks [Ferry], Shelby
Myrtle, Clay
Myrtle [Turf], Harris
Myrtle, Marion
Myrtle Springs, Anderson
Myrtle Springs, Bowie
Myrtle Springs, Van Zandt 131

N

Naaman, Dallas
Nabors, Haskell
Nabors, Jones
Nacalina, Angelina
Nacalina, Nacogdoches ....NA
Naches, Houston
§*NACOGDOCHES, Nacogdoches,
  2,073 (30,872) 32,973
*Nada, Colorado, 24 165
Nagiller, Potter
Nag Park, Cherokee
Nailton, Lipscomb
Naizerville, Williamson
Nall, Howard
Nalley['s Store], McLennan
Nalyon, Bandera
Nameless, Travis
Nan, Fort Bend
Nancy, Angelina
Nancy, Colorado

Nanhattie, Coke
Nanhattie, Sterling
Napier, Bastrop
Napier, San Jacinto
*NAPLES, Morris, 78 (1,508) ... 1,464
Narcisso, Cottle
Naruna, Burnet................45
*NASH, Bowie, 109 (2,162) 2,316
Nash, Ellis....................25
Nashland, Jefferson
Nash's Foundry, Marion
Nash's Mill, Gonzales
Nashville [-on-the-Brazos,
  New Nashville], Milam
Nashville, Shelby
Nassau, Fayette
NASSAU BAY, Harris (4,320)... 4,762
Nat, Nacogdoches 25
Natali, Fort Bend
*NATALIA, Medina, 55 (1,216) .. 1,420
Natalie, Dawson
Natalie, Palo Pinto
Natches, Tyler
Nathan, Johnson
Nathan, Trinity
Nathen, Caldwell
Nations, Pecos
Naught, Henderson
Navarro, Atascosa
Navarro, Guadalupe
Navarro [Crossing], Leon
NAVARRO, Navarro (193).......258
Navarro County Town, Ellis
Navarro Mills, Navarro..........50
*NAVASOTA, Grimes, 529
  (6,296) 7,036
Navasota [Navasotto], Robertson
Navidad, Fayette
Navidad, Jackson 227
Navidad, Jackson
Navo, Denton 35
Nay, Hunt
Naylor [Springs], Donley
*NAZARETH, Castro, 50 (293)....330
Neal, Hill
Neal, Madison
Neale, McLennan
Neals, Upshur
Neals Valley, Ellis
Neason, Grimes
Nebo, Denton
Nebo, Gillespie
Nebo, Hall
Nebo, Parker
Nebo, Smith
Nebraska, Cameron
Necessity, Stephens 10
Nechanitz, Fayette 21
Neche, Houston
*Neches [ville], Anderson,
  18...........................175
Neches Saline, Smith
Ned, Taylor
*NEDERLAND, Jefferson, 1,031
  (16,192) 17,844
Nedra, Wharton
Need, Lamar
Needmore, Bailey...............45
Needmore, Bowie
Needmore, Delta
Needmore, Nacogdoches
Needmore, Terry...............14
*NEEDVILLE, Fort Bend, 222
  (2,199) 3,205
Neelie, Live Oak
Neely, Nolan
Neely, San Augustine
Neely Ward, Cochran............5

Neese's Store, Fayette
Neff, Erath
Neff, Stonewall
Negley, Red River 136
Neill's Creek, Bosque
Neill's Creek, Hamilton
Neinda, Jones 21
Nell, Henderson
Nell, Live Oak.................60
Nelleva, Brazos ....NA
Nelson, Ellis
Nelson, Kerr
Nelsonberg, Bexar
Nelson City, Kendall ....NA
Nelsonville, Austin.............110
Nelta, Hopkins 36
*Nemo, Somervell, 9 56
Nena, Ellis
Neola, Hunt
Neosho, Henderson
Neri, Hood
NESBITT, Harrison (327).......390
Nesbitt, Robertson ....NA
Nesmith, Brewster
Nesterville, Wichita
Nestorville, Navarro
Nettaville, La Salle
Nettie, Polk
Neugent, Hill
Neusser, Williamson
Neut, Fannin
Neuville, Shelby................43
Neva, Stonewall
*NEVADA, Collin, 51 (456).......674
Neville, Gonzales
New Anhalt, Lee
*NEWARK, Wise-Tarrant, 68
  (651) 896
New Artesia, Atascosa
*New Baden, Robertson, 9 150
NEW BERLIN, Guadalupe
  (188) 220
New Bern, Williamson
New Bethel, Jefferson ....NA
New Bielau, Colorado 75
New Birmingham, Cherokee
New Birthright, Hopkins ....NA
New Blox, Jasper..............NA
New Bolivar, Denton
*NEW BOSTON, Bowie, 307
  (5,057)...................5,049
New Brandenberg, Stonewall
§*NEW BRAUNFELS, Comal-
  Guadalupe, 2,907 (27,334)
 35,663
New Bremen, Austin 75
Newburg, Comanche............35
Newburg, Parker
Newby, Leon...................40
New California, Zavala
New Camp, Nacogdoches
New Camp Ruby, Polk..........NA
*New Caney, Montgomery, 386
 2,771
New Carlisle, Rusk
*NEWCASTLE, Young, 16 (505)...559
New Center, Blanco
*NEW CHAPEL HILL, Smith
  (439) 471
New Cincinnati, Walker
New Clarkson, Milam...........NA
New Colony, Bell 4
New Colony, Cass 65
New Columbia, Newton
Newcomb, Shackelford
New Corn Hill, Williamson.......NA
New Danville, Rusk
New Davy, DeWitt..............20

*NEW DEAL, Lubbock, 26 (521)..721
New Diana, Upshur
New Emmaus, Cherokee
New Epworth, Hale
New Era, Bowie
New Fountain, Medina ....NA
*Newgulf, Wharton, 4 ....NA
New Hagensport, Franklin
New Harmony, Shelby ....NA
New Harmony, Smith 350
New Harp, Montague 8
New Henrietta, Clay
New Home, Hays
New Home, Limestone
*NEW HOME, Lynn, 26 (175) 206
New Hope, Angelina
New Hope, Cherokee 50
NEW HOPE, Collin (523).......592
New Hope, Coryell
New Hope, Dallas
New Hope, Franklin
New Hope, Freestone
New Hope, Jones 9
New Hope, Liberty
New Hope, Limestone
New Hope, Mitchell
New Hope, Polk
New Hope, Runnels
New Hope, Rusk
New Hope, San Augustine.......75
New Hope, Smith 75
New Hope, Wood...............15
New Hope City, Jack
New Knoxville, Kimble
New Leon, Comanche
Newlin, Hall 31
New Loco, Collingsworth
*NEW LONDON, Rusk, 39
  (926).....................1,022
New Loven, Dallas
New Lynn, Lynn 18
New Mainz, Colorado
Newman, El Paso 60
Newman['s Ranch], Fisher
Newmanville, Jones
New Martindale, Caldwell
New Mesquite, Collin
New Mobeetie, Wheeler
New Moore, Lynn 10
New Mountain, Upshur.........20
New Philadelphia, Wharton
New Pittsburg, Blanco
New Pleasant Grove, Lamar
New Pleasanton, Atascosa
Newport, Clay-Jack.............70
Newport, San Jacinto
Newport, Walker
New Prague, Fayette
New Prospect, Denton
New Prospect, Houston
New Prospect, Rusk
New Salem, Leon
New Salem, Palo Pinto..........89
New Salem, Rusk 55
New Serbin, Lee
Newsom, Jones
Newsome, Bailey
Newsome, Camp...............100
New Sour Lake, Hardin
*NEW SUMMERFIELD,
  Cherokee, 41 (521) 677
New Sweden, McCulloch
New Sweden, Travis 60
Newt, Fannin
New Taiton, Wharton
§*NEWTON, Newton, 187
  (1,885)....................1,925
Newton [Court House], Newton

Newtonville, Gonzales
Newtonville, Jasper
Newtown, Wichita
*New Ulm, Austin, 67...........650
New Vineyard, Jack
New Washington, Harris
*NEW WAVERLY, Walker, 132
  (936)....................1,070
New Wehdem, Austin...........100
New Willard, Polk..............160
New York, Henderson 15
Neyland, Hardin
Neyland, Hunt
NEYLANDVILLE, Hunt (94)......116
Nibletts Bluff, Newton
Niblock, McCulloch
Nicholas, Robertson
Nichols, Bell
Nichols, Karnes
Nichol[a]sville, McLennan
Nickel, Gonzales
Nickel Creek, Culberson 16
Nickelville, Collin
Nickleberry, Cass
Nickleville, Wise...............NA
Nicks, Red River
NIEDERWALD, Hays-Caldwell
  (233).....................286
Nigh, Colorado
Nigton, Trinity.................87
Niland, Lamar
Nilar, Floyd
Nile, Milam
Niles, Lee
Niles City, Tarrant
Nimrod, Eastland...............85
Nina, Castro
Nina, Wise
Nine, McCulloch
Nineveh, Leon 101
Nip and Tuck, Rusk
Nisbet, Swisher
Nivac, Nacogdoches
Nix, Lampasas 6
*NIXON [ville], Gonzales-Wilson,
  85 (1,995) 2,034
Nixon, Guadalupe
Nix's Ranch, Crockett
Noack, Williamson.............60
Nob Hill, Llano ....NA
Nobility, Fannin 21
Noble, Hardin
Noble, Lamar 40
Noble, Lamar
Noble, Potter
Nockenut, Wilson..............10
*NOCONA, Montague, 334
  (2,870)..................3,171
Nod, Cooke
Nodena, Titus
Noelette, Carson
Noell, Dallas
Noelton, Carson
Nogal, Ochiltree
Nogalus Prairie[Nogallis Prairie,
  Nogalus], Trinity 109
Nola, Cooke
*Nolan, Nolan, 4 47
Nolands River [n's River], Johnson
Nolanville, Bell
Nolan Valley, Bell
*NOLANVILLE, Bell, 60
  (1,834)..................2,619
Nolanville, Grimes
Noleda, Duval
Nolia, Sabine
Nolte, Guadalupe..............25
Noma, Nueces

Odesco, Panola
§*ODESSA, Ector-Midland, 5,782
   (89,699) 95,384
Odessa, Wise
Odlaw, Kinney
*O'DONNELL, Lynn-Dawson, 91
   (1,102) 1,155
Odum's Town, Angelina
Oenaville, Bell, 50 120
O'Farrell [O'Ferrall], Cass. 20
Ogan, Erath
Ogarita, Travis
Ogburn, Smith
Ogburn, Wood 10
Ogden, Comal
Ogden, Cottle
Ogden, Falls
Ogden, Tyler
Ogg, Randall
Ogle[s], Lampasas
*OGLESBY, Coryell, 21 (452). 490
Ogletree, Coryell
O'Hair, Johnson
O'Hair's Hill, Burnet
Ohio, Cameron
Ohio, Hamilton
Oil Center, Eastland
Oil City, Clay
Oil City, Hutchinson
Oil City, Young
Oildom, Wichita
Oilla, Orange
Oil Spring, Taylor
*Oilton, Webb, 7 585
Ojo de Agua, Hidalgo
Ojuelos, Webb
Okay, Bell
Oklahoma [Oklohoma], Cooke
Oklahoma, Montgomery . . . . NA
Oklahoma Flat, Hockley 8
Oklahoma Lane, Parmer 25
*Oklaunion, Wilbarger, 9 138
Okra, Eastland 20
Ola, Dallas
Ola, Kaufman 50
Ola, Taylor
Olcott, Harris
Old Aiken, Bell
Old Boston, Bowie. 100
Old Bowling, Leon. 20
Old Canton, Smith
Old Carolina, Walker
Old Center, Panola. 83
Old Decatur, Collin
Old Diana, Upshur
Old Dime Box, Lee. 200
Old Emma, Crosby
*Olden, Eastland, 10 110
Oldenburg, Fayette 30
Oldenburg, Fayette
Oldenburg, Smith
Olden Switch, Eastland
Old Evergreen, Lee
Old Ferry, Travis
Old Franklin, Robertson
Old Frio Town, Frio
Old Gay Hill, Washington
*Old Glory, Stonewall, 8. 125
Old Glover, Houston
Old Graball, Milam
Oldham, Houston
Oldham, Tyler. . . . . NA
Old Hardin, Hardin
Old Hope, Polk
Old Howard, Bell
Old Larissa, Cherokee
Old Midway, Leon. . . . . NA
Old Milsap, Parker

Old Minden, Rusk
Old Mobettie, Wheeler
Old Moulton, Lavaca
*Old Ocean, Brazoria, 22 915
Old Philadelphia, Nacogdoches
Old Red Rock, Bastrop
Old River Lake, Chambers
Old River Lake, Liberty
OLD RIVER-WINFREE, Chambers
   (1,233) 1,512
Old Round Rock, Williamson
Olds, Kinney
Olds, Ochiltree
Old Sabinetown, Sabine
Old Salem, Bowie 50
Old Salem, Newton . . . . .NA
Old San Antonio, Jim Hogg
Old Snake River, Liberty
Old Spanish Trail Acres, Harris
Old Springfield, Limestone
Old Sutherland, Wilson
Old Tarrant, Hopkins
Old Tascosa, Oldham
Old Towash, Hill
Old Union, Bowie 238
Old Union, Limestone. 25
Old Union, Tarrant
Old Warren, Fannin
Old Waverly, San Jacinto
Old Waverly, Walker
Oletha, Limestone. 53
Olfen, Runnels 50
Olga, Nolan
Olga, Swisher
Olin, Hamilton 12
Olio, Fisher
Oliphint, Walker
Olive, Hardin
Olive, Hays
Olive Branch, McLennan
Olive Branch, Parker
Oliver, Denton
Oliver, Limestone
Oliver, Montague
Olivera, Hunt
Oliverea, Hunt
Oliver Springs, Comanche
Olivia, Calhoun 215
Ollie, Polk 5
Ollis, Falls
*Olmito, Cameron, 53 200
Olmos, Bee
*Olmos [Olmus], Guadalupe 75
Olmos, Maverick
Olmos, Starr
*OLMOS PARK, Bexar
   (2,161) 2,302
*OLNEY, Young, 248 (3,519) 3,348
*OLTON, Lamb, 147 (2,116) 2,118
Olympus, Childress
Oma, Fisher
*OMAHA, Morris, 59 (833) 979
Omega, Gregg
Omen, Smith 150
Onaga, Denton
*ONALASKA, Polk, 157 (728) 991
Ondee, Hamilton
Oneal, Morris
Oneida, Orange
Oneida, Potter
Oneta, Leon
Onie, Floyd
Onion, Ellis
Onion, Jones
Onion Creek, Ellis
‡ Onion Creek, Travis (1,544). . .1,599
Onslow, Edwards
Ontario, Gray

Ontario, Oldham
Onward, Taylor
Opah, Red River
Opal, Wise
Opdyke, Hockley 20
OPDYKE WEST, Hockley (100) . . .132
Opelika, Henderson
Ophelia, Caldwell
Ophir, Cooke
Ophir, Lubbock
Oplin, Callahan. 75
O'Quinn, Fayette 25
Ora, Angelina
Oral, Hays
Oran, Palo Pinto. 61
Oran, Roberts
§*ORANGE, Orange, 1,541
   (19,370) 19,024
Orangedale, Bee 35
*Orangefield, Orange, 31. 725
Orange Grove, Harris
*ORANGE GROVE, Jim Wells,
   116 (1,175) 1,338
Orange Hill, Austin
Orangeville, Fannin
*ORCHARD, Fort Bend, 19
   (373) 532
Orchard, Guadalupe
Ore, Morris
O'Rear's Mill, Cass
*ORE CITY, Upshur, 108
   (898) 1,039
Oregon City, Baylor
Orelia, Frio
Oriana, Stonewall
Orient, Knox
Orient, Stonewall
Orient, Tom Green 40
Orient, Wichita
Orio, Van Zandt
Oriole, Houston
Orion, Hunt
Orizaba, Fayette
*Orla, Reeves, 2 183
Orland, Stephens
Orleans, Hunt
Orlena, Cooke
Orme, Ellis
Orme, Tarrant
Ormel, Tarrant
Ornaville, Bell
Orozimbo, Brazoria
Orphans Home, Dallas
Orr, Dallas
Orr, Johnson
Orr, Harris
Orrs [Orrville], Marion
Orsack, Lavaca
Orth, Young
Orvil, Webb
Osage, Colorado
Osage, Coryell, 7 30
Osborne, Brewster
Osborne, Montgomery
Osborne, Wheeler
Osborne, Wilbarger
Osburnville, Eastland
Oscar, Bell 40
Oscar, Bexar
Oscar, Kaufman
Osceola, Hill. 90
Oslo, Hansford
Oso, Coke
Oso, Fayette
Ossaba, Grayson
Ossey, Tarrant
Ostella, Hall
Oswego, Travis

Otey, Brazoria. 318
Otho, Shelby
Otis, Bastrop
Otis, Red River
Otis, Van Zandt
Otis Chalk, Howard 79
Otley, Frio
Otta, Lubbock
Otta [Springs] [Ottie Springs], Cottle
Ottillie, Armstrong
*Ottine, Gonzales, 3. 90
*Otto, Falls, 9 48
Otto, Gonzales
Otto, Hardin
Otwell, Ellis
Ouida, Moore
Oval, Nacogdoches
*Ovalo, Taylor, 23 225
Overall, Coleman
Overby, Karnes
*OVERTON, Rusk-Smith, 178
   (2,105). 2,154
Ovid, Jack
OVILLA, Ellis-Dallas (2,027) . . . 2,753
Owego, Pecos
Owens, Brown . . . . NA
Owens, Crosby. 40
Owensburg, Bowie
Owensville, Robertson . . . . NA
Owentown, Smith. 100
Owenville, Sutton
Owl, Camp
Owl, Wise
Owl Creek, Bell 45
Owl Creek, Burnet
Owlet Green, Van Zandt
Oxford, Llano
Oxford [City], Milam
Oxford, Palo Pinto
Oxidine, Falls
Oxien, Runnels
OYSTER CREEK, Brazoria
   (912) 1,083
Oyster Creek, Brazoria
Oyster Point, Nueces
Ozark, Lamar
Ozarking, Ward
Ozias, Angelina
‡§*Ozona, Crockett, 230
   (3,181). 3,534
Ozro, Ellis

P

Pace, Webb
Pace's Chapel, Anderson
Pace's Ferry, Jasper
Pacific, La Salle
Pacio, Delta 15
Pacita, Lubbock
Pack Saddle, Llano
Pacono, Camp
Paddock, Lamar
Padgett, Young. 28
Padreco, Cherokee
§*PADUCAH, Cottle, 98
   (1,788) 1,645
Page, Panola
Pagoda, Trinity
*Paige [Station], Bastrop, 37 275
Paint Creek, Edwards
Paint Creek, Haskell
Painted Comanche, Jeff Davis
§*PAINT ROCK, Concho, 33
   (227) .204
Paisano, Presidio
Palace, Van Zandt
Palace Hill, Dallas
*PALACIOS, Matagorda, 228

   (4,418) 4,472
Palafox [Palafax], Webb
Palangana, Duval
Palava, Fisher
Palaxy, Erath
§*PALESTINE, Anderson, 1,258
   (18,042) 18,725
PALISADES, Randall (NC) 350
Palito Blanco, Jim Wells. 35
*PALMER, Ellis, 74 (1,659) 1,903
Palmer's, San Jacinto
Palmetal, Cameron
Palmetto, San Jacinto
Palm Harbor, Aransas 125
PALMHURST, Hidalgo (326). 445
Palm Park, Bexar. . . . . .NA
PALM VALLEY, Cameron
   (1,199). 1,315
PALMVIEW, Hidalgo (1,818) 2,696
Palo, Llano
Palo Alto, Bell
Palo Alto, Gonzales
Palo Alto, Nueces 15
Palo Alto Park, Bexar . . . . .NA
Palo Blanco, Zavala
Palo Curo Creek, Hansford
Paloduro, Armstrong 10
Palo Gacho, San Augustine
Paloma, Edwards
Paloma, Maverick
Palomas, San Patricio
§*Palo Pinto, Palo Pinto, 41 411
Paluxy, Erath
*Paluxy, Hood, 3 76
§*PAMPA, Gray, 1,194
   (19,959) 19,808
Pamplin's Creek, Tyler
Pancake, Coryell 11
Panchita, Hidalgo
Pancho, El Paso
Pandale, Val Verde. 20
*Pandora, Wilson. 125
§*PANHANDLE [City], Carson,
   185 (2,353) 2,275
Pankey, Grimes
Pansy, Crosby
Pansy, Navarro
Pansy [Mills], Crosby
PANTEGO, Tarrant (2,371) 2,684
Panter [Branch], Hood
Pantex, Carson
Pantex, Hutchinson
Panther, Edwards
Panther Chapel, Franklin
Panther Creek, Kendall
Panther Junction, Brewster 112
Papalote [Papalota], Bee 70
*PARADISE [Prairie], Wise, 82
   (NC). 275
Pardo, Cameron
§*PARIS, Lamar, 1,744
   (24,799). 26,241
Parita, Bexar . . . . .NA
Park, Bowie
Park, Fayette 47
Park Community, Navarro 160
Parkdale, Bell
Parker, Bowie
Parker, Burleson
Parker, Clay
PARKER, Collin (1,213) 1,698
Parker, Johnson 21
Parker['s Station], Parker

Parker Gin, Collin
Parkers, Jasper
Parker's Bluff, Anderson
Parker's Mills, Houston
Parker's Point, Brazoria
Parker's Point, Limestone
Parker's Shop, Parker
Parkersville, Anderson
Parker's Voting Box, Lamar
Parkerton, Lamar
Parkhurst, Wise
Parkinson, Gaines
Parks, Williamson
Parks Bluff, Red River
Parks Camp, Stephens . . . . NA
Parksdale, Hutchinson
Park Springs, Wise. . . . . NA
Parkview Estates, Guadalupe. . . .500
Parmerton, Parmer
Parmley, Montague
Parnell, Hall
Parnell, Roberts
Parrott, Castro
Parry's, Panola
Parryville, Wood
Parsell's Ranch, Roberts
Parsley Hill, Wilbarger 40
Parsons, Parker
Parson's Seminary, Travis
Parvin, Denton 44
*PASADENA, Harris, 3,915
   (119,604). 133,675
Pascal, Comanche
Paschall, Wise
Pasche, Concho
Paso Real, Willacy
Paso Station, Houston
Pastura, Jones
Patella, Walker
Patillo, Erath. 10
Patman, Cass
Patman Switch, Cass. 40
Patmos, Hopkins
Pato, Webb
Paton, Carson
Patonia, Polk . . . . NA
Patricia, Dawson 60
Patrick, McLennan. . . . . NA
Patricks Ferry, San Jacinto
Patrole, Reeves
Patroon, Shelby, 6 55
Pattengill, Cass
Patterson, Uvalde
Patterson['s Station], Waller
Patterson Settlement, Uvalde
Pattie, Grayson
Pattillos, Orange
*PATTISON, Waller, 25 (327) 423
Patton, Comanche
Patton, Galveston
Patton, McLennan
Pattonfield, Upshur 20
Patton's Mill, Hill
Patton's Port, Smith
PATTON VILLAGE, Montgomery
   (1,155) 1,498
*Pattonville, Lamar, 17. 180
Paul, Midland
Pauldie, Cameron
Pauli, Montgomery
Paulina, Jack
Pauline, Collin
Pauline, Hardeman
Pauline, Henderson
Pauline, Ochiltree
Paulineville [Paulinasville], Hardin
Paul's, Bexar
Pauls Store, Shelby

Paul Wheeler, Jefferson
Pavo, Kinney
Pawelekville, Karnes 105
*Pawnee, Bee, 9 249
Paxton, Shelby 161
Payne, Brown
Payne [Gap], Mills
Payne, Navarro
Payne, Shelby
Paynes, Fort Bend
Paynes Corner, Gaines . . . . NA
PAYNE['s] SPRINGS, Henderson
  (606) 794
Paynes Store, Hunt
Payton, Blanco
Peacevale, Hutchinson
Peacevale, Roberts
Peach, Wood
Peach Creek, Brazos . . . . NA
Peach Creek, Gonzales
Peach Creek, Wharton
Peach Tree, Jasper
Peach Tree Village, Tyler
Peacock, Stonewall, 1 125
Peadenville, Palo Pinto 15
Peak, Castro
Peak, San Patricio
Pealoreville, Foard
Pearl, Collingsworth
Pearl, Coryell 125
Pearl, Orange
Pearl, Swisher
*PEARLAND, Brazoria-Harris,
  1,709 (18,927) 29,686
Pearl City, DeWitt 4
Pearl City, Ellis
Pear Ridge, Jefferson
§*PEARSALL, Frio, 308
  (6,924) 7,821
Pearson, Medina . . . . NA
Pearson, Montague
Pearsons Chapel, Houston 95
Pearson's Ranch, Sterling
*Pear Valley, McCulloch, 1 37
Pearville, Houston
Peary Place, Nueces
Pease [Pease River City], Foard
*Peaster[ville],, Parker, 4 102
Peatown, Gregg
Peavey, Angelina
Pebble, Kerr
Pebble Mound, Burnet
Pecan, Callahan
Pecan [Branch], Delta
Pecan, Fayette
‡ Pecan Acres, Wise-Tarrant
  (1,587) 1,890
Pecan Creek, Tom Green . . . . NA
*PECAN GAP, Delta-Fannin, 14
  (245) 260
Pecan Grove, Collin . . . . NA
Pecan Grove, Coryell
‡ Pecan Grove, Fort Bend
  (9,502) 13,063
Pecan Grove, Gonzales
Pecan Grove, Jefferson
Pecan Grove, San Saba
PECAN HILL, Ellis (564) 681
Pecan Hill, Fort Bend
Pecan Plantation, Hood 3,456
Pecan Point, Red River
Pecan Wells, Hamilton 7
Peck, Harris
§*PECOS, Reeves, 442
  (12,069) 11,661
Pecos High Bridge, Val Verde
Pecos Springs, Pecos
Pecos Station, Crockett

Pecosa, Maverick
Pedeco, Liberty
Peden, Tarrant
Pedigo, Tyler
Pedro, Coke
Peede [Peede's Mill], Kaufman
Peek, Stonewall
Peeler, Dallas
Peeler, Leon
Peel Junction, Montgomery
Peeltown, Kaufman . . . . .NA
Peerless, Hopkins . . . . .NA
Peerless Spur, Brazoria
Peeryville, Kaufman
Pegasus, Midland
*Peggy, Atascosa, 3 22
Pegoda, Trinity
Peirce Junction, Harris
Pelham, Navarro 75
Pelican, Liberty
PELICAN BAY, Tarrant (1,271) . .1,499
Pella, Wise
Pelly, Harris
Pen, Shackelford
Pen Oak, Liberty
Peña Station, Jim Hogg
Pencilville, Frio
Pendell, Bosque
*Pendleton[ville, Pendleton Station],
  Bell, 9 60
Pendleton, Sabine
*PENELOPE, Hill, 14 (210) 246
Penfield, Travis
Peniel, Hunt
*PEÑITAS, Hidalgo, 17 (1,077) . .1,398
Penitas, Jim Wells
Penland, Grayson
Penn, Hopkins
Penn City, Harris
*Pennington, Trinity-Houston, 11. . 67
Penn's, Harris
Penrose, Shackelford
*Penwell, Ector, 12 74
Peoria, Hill 81
*Pep, Hockley, 7. 35
Pepper, Rusk
Perch, Falls
Perch Hill, Wise
Percilla, Houston 95
Percy, Mills
Perdenales [Pedernales], Travis
Perdido, Goliad
Perdiz, Presidio
Perezville, Hidalgo
Perico, Dallam
Perkins, Cass
Perkins, Dallas
Perkins, Lamar
Perley, Cochran
Perley, Henderson
Permian, Reeves
PERNITAS POINT, Live Oak-
  Jim Wells (174) 180
Peron, Wood
*Perrin, Jack, 24 300
*Perry, Falls, 3 76
Perry, McLennan
Perry Landing, Brazoria
Perryman, Liberty
Perryman's, Waller
Perryman's Crossing, Guadalupe
Perry's Landing, Brazoria
Perry's Point, Chambers
§*PERRYTON, Ochiltree, 590
  (7,619) 7,756
Perryville, Bastrop
Perryville, Wood 52
Pershing, Polk

Pershing, Travis
Persimmon Grove, Kaufman
Personville, Freestone
Personville, Limestone 50
Pert, Anderson 20
Peru, DeWitt
Peru, La Salle
Peruna, Coryell
Pescadito, Webb
Pesch, Washington
Pete, Nolan
Peters, Austin 95
Petersburg, Floyd
*PETERSBURG, Hale, 72
  (1,292) 1,266
Petersburg[h], Lavaca
Petersburg, Red River
Peters Colony, Dallas
Peter's Prairie, Red River 40
Petersville, Cherokee
Petersville, DeWitt 38
Petersville, Fayette
Petersville, Polk
Petroleum, Jim Hogg
*PETROLIA, Clay, 29 (762). 834
PETRONILA, Nueces (155) 162
Petteway, Robertson 25
Pettit, Comanche
Pettibone, Milam 25
Pettit, Hockley 26
Pettit's, Houston
*Pettus [City], Bee, 28. 400
*Petty, Lamar, 6. 100
Petty, Lynn 24
Petty's Chapel, Navarro. 25
Petzel's Camp, Crosby
Peveto, Orange
Pewitt, Morris
Peyton, Blanco. 30
Peyton, Falls
Peyton, Williamson
*PFLUGERVILLE, Travis, 853
  (4,444) 11,263
Phair, Brazoria
Phalba, Van Zandt 58
Phanton Hill, Jones
*PHARR, Hidalgo, 1,187
  (32,921) 41,839
Pheasant, Matagorda
Phelan, Bastrop . . . . NA
Phelps, Walker 98
Phelps, Walker
Phenix, Pecos
Philadelphia, Wood
Phillips, Hutchinson
Phillips, Montgomery
Phillips, Wharton
Phillipsburg[h], Washington 40
Phillipsburgh, Robertson
Phillips Camp, Hansford
Phillips Ranch, Llano
Phillips Station, Washington
Phillips Store, Ellis
Phillips Store, Wood
Phoenix, Polk
Phosopolis, Waller
Pickens, Henderson 20
Pickett, Liberty
Pickett, Navarro 30
Pickett, Wise
Pickettville, Stephens
*Pickton, Hopkins, 29 90
Pickwick, Palo Pinto
Pidcock Ranch, Coryell
Pidcoe, Coryell
Pidcoke, Coryell. 30
Piedmont, Grimes 46
Piedmont, Upshur 20

Prospect, Clay
Prospect, Lee
Prospect, McLennan
Prospect, Rains 40
Prospect Hill, Wood
*PROSPER, Collin, 95 (1,018) . . 1,465
Prosperity, Falls
Prosser, Angelina
Providence, Angelina
Providence, Floyd 85
Providence, Polk 350
Providence, Van Zandt
Providence Camp, Polk
Providence Hill, Hardin
Provident City, Colorado
Pruitt, Cass. 25
Pruitt, Van Zandt . . . . NA
Pryor, Fort Bend
Pryor, Navarro
Pueblo, Baylor
Pueblo, Callahan 1
Pueblo, Eastland 46
Pueblo, McCulloch
Pueblo Nuevo, Webb 377
Puente, Potter
Puente Piedra, Live Oak
Puerto Rico, Hidalgo 91
Pugh, Parker
Pulaski, Panola
Pulliam, Tom Green
Pulliam, Uvalde
Pulliam, Zavala
Pullin, Karnes
Pullman, Potter 31
Pull Tight, Bee
Pull Tight, Erath
Pull Tight, Hood
Pull Tight, Van Zandt
Pulltype, Newton
Pulteville, Cooke
Pulvo, Presidio
Pumphrey, Runnels 15
Pumpkin, San Jacinto 150
Pumps, Harrison
Pumpville, Val Verde 21
Punchard's, Austin
Punkin Center, Dawson. 30
Punkin Center, Eastland 12
Punkin Center, Hardeman
*Purdon, Navarro, 21 133
Purgatory [Springs], Hays
Purley, Franklin 81
*Purmela, Coryell, 8. 61
Pursley, Navarro. 40
Purves, Erath 50
*PUTNAM, Callahan, 7 (103) 116
Putnam, Llano
Putnam's Store, Caldwell
Puxico, Van Zandt
Pyland, Marion
Pylas, Rusk
Pyle's Prairie, Kaufman
*PYOTE, Ward, 14 (348) 408
Pyramid, Nolan
Pyron, Scurry

Q

*Quail, Collingsworth, 7 92
Quail Creek, San Jacinto 50
Quail Valley, Anderson
Quality, Harris
Qualls, Clay
§*QUANAH, Hardeman, 223
(3,413) 3,200
Quanto, Bee
Quaro, DeWitt
Quarry, Washington. . . . . NA
Quarterway, Hale 12

Quarton, Moore
Quebec, Presidio
*QUEEN CITY, Cass, 106
(1,748) 1,995
Queen[s] Peak, Montague
*Quemado, Maverick, 18. 426
Quemado, Maverick
Quemado Spur, Maverick
Quicksand, Johnson
Quicksand, Newton . . . . .NA
Quihi, Medina 104
Quillin's Store, Hill
Quinan, Wharton
Quincy, Bee
Quincy, Harrison
Quinif, Milam
*QUINLAN, Hunt, 353 (1,360) . . .1,616
Quintana, Bexar
*QUINTANA, Brazoria (51) 65
*QUITAQUE, Briscoe, 45 (513) . . . 470
Quitaque, Floyd
§*QUITMAN, Wood, 356
(1,684). 1,849
Quito, Leon
Quito, Ward

R

Rabb, Nueces 20
Rabbit Creek, Rusk
Rabbit Hill, Navarro
Rabbs Prairie [Rabb], Fayette. 36
Rabke, DeWitt
Raccoon Bend, Austin 400
Race Track, Delta
Rachal, Brooks 36
Rachal, San Patricio
Radford, Karnes
Radio Junction, Lampasas
Radium, Jones 10
Rafael, Cameron
Ragland, Lamar
Ragley, Marion
Ragley, Panola
Ragtown, Garza
Ragtown, Lamar 25
Ragtown, Wise
Rail, Hamilton
Rainbow, Newton
*Rainbow, Somervell, 15 76
Rainey's Creek, Coryell
Rains, Rains
Rainsville, Shelby
Raisin, Victoria 50
Rake Pocket, Rusk
Raleigh, Navarro 40
*RALLS, Crosby, 106 (2,172) . . .1,951
Ralls, Randall
Ralph, Lamar
Ralph, Randall
Ralston, El Paso
Ramage, Guadalupe
Ramal, Kinney
Rambert, Marion
Rambo, Archer
Rambo, Cass
Ramirena, Live Oak
Ramirena, San Patricio
Ramireno, Zapata 25
Ramireno, Zapata
Ramirez, Duval 40
Ramirez, Jim Hogg
Ramirito, Jim Hogg
Ramona, Hidalgo
Ramsdell, Wheeler
Ramsey, Colorado
Ramsey, Loving
Ramsey, Shelby
Ramseyville, Colorado

Ranch, Crane
Ranch Branch, Mason
Ranchito, Cameron
Ranchland, Wilbarger
Rancho, Gonzales
Rancho Alegre, Jim Wells 1,950
Rancho Davis, Starr
Rancho de la Parita, Jim Wells . . . NA
Rancho San Luis, Hidalgo
RANCHO VIEJO, Cameron
(885) 1,125
Rand, Kaufman . . . . NA
Randado, Jim Hogg. 15
Randalia, Walker
Randall, Grayson
Randall, Smith
Randal's Store, Palo Pinto
Randal's Store, Stephens
Randol['s Mill], Tarrant
*Randolph, Fannin, 2 70
Randolph, Houston
*Randolph Air Force Base, Bexar,
47. .3,015
Randolphsville, San Jacinto
Randon, Fort Bend
Rane, Eastland
Raney, Hunt
Range Creek, Grayson
Rangel, Duval
*RANGER, Eastland, 163
(2,803). 2,743
Ranger Camp Valley, Eastland
RANGERVILLE, Cameron
(280) 334
Ranier, Coryell
Rankin, Ellis. 12
§*RANKIN, Upton, 48 (1,011). 899
Rankin's, San Jacinto
Ransom, San Augustine
RANSOM CANYON, Lubbock, 25,
(763) 904
Rast, Van Zandt
Rat, Burnet
Ratama, Frio
*Ratcliff, Houston, 7. 106
Ratcliff, Starr
Ratcliff's, Tyler
Rath City, Stonewall
Rather, Shelby
Rathjen Farm, Wheeler
Ratibor, Bell 10
Ratler, Mills
Ratliff's Store, Lamar
Rattan, Delta. 10
*RAVENNA, Fannin, 28 (199). 239
Ravenwood, Brazos. . . . . .NA
Rawlings, Coke
Rawlins, Dallas
Rawls, Brazoria
Ray, Ellis
Ray, Grayson
Rayburn, Liberty 30
Rayford, Montgomery
Raylake, Angelina
Rayland, Foard. 30
Ray Lee, Stephens
Raymer, Colorado
Raymer Junction, Colorado
Raymond, Brazos
Raymond, Carson
Raymond, Clay
Raymond, Leon
§*RAYMONDVILLE, Willacy,
322 (8,880) 9,247
Rayner, Stonewall
Ray Point, Live Oak 200
Ray School, Parker
Rayville, Parker

*RIO BRAVO, Webb (2,987). . . . 4,131
Rio del Sol, Cameron
*Rio Frio, Real, 12 50
‡§*Rio Grande City[Riogrande],
Starr, 461 (9,891) 12,358
Rio Grande Station, El Paso
Rio Grande Village, Brewster 9
*RIO HONDO, Cameron, 112
(1,793). 2,429
*Riomedina, Medina, 11. 53
Rio Pecos, Crane
Rios, Duval. 100
*RIO VISTA, Johnson, 65 (541) . . .716
Rip, Montague
Ripley, Lubbock
Ripley, San Saba
Ripley, Titus
*RISING STAR, Eastland, 94,
(859) .860
Rising Sun, Jones
Rising Sun, Shackelford
Rita, Burleson 50
Rita Santa, Reagan
Ritchen, Uvalde
Ritchie, McLennan
Rite-Care, Shelby
Ritter, Panola
River, Liberty
River, Zavala
Rivera, Ellis
River Acres, Tyler
River Bend, Newton. . . . . NA
River Bend, Palo Pinto
Riverbottom, San Jacinto
Riverbrook, Montgomery . . . . NA
Riverby, Fannin 15
River Crest, Red River
River Crest Estates, Angelina . . .250
Riverdale, Goliad
Riverdale, Kent
River Fork, Nacogdoches
River Hill, Panola . . . . NA
Riverland, Clay
River Oaks, Brazos . . . . NA
RIVER OAKS, Tarrant
(6,580). 7,179
River Plantation, Montgomery . . . NA
Rivers End, Brazoria . . . . NA
River Side, Bee
Riverside, Caldwell
Riverside, Collingsworth
*RIVERSIDE, Walker, 32 (451) 522
River.Terrace, Harris
Riverton, Reeves
River View, Red River
Riverwood, Montgomery. . . . . NA
Rives, Fisher
*Riviera, Kleberg, 58 1,064
Riviera Beach, Kleberg 125
Roa, Garza
Roach, Austin
Roach, Cass. 50
Roach Prairie, Austin
Roadville, Anderson
Roadville, Houston
Roane, Navarro 120
*ROANOKE, Denton, 608
(1,616) 2,477
*Roans Prairie, Grimes, 5 56
*ROARING SPRINGS, Motley, 22
(264) .213
Roark, Karnes
Robberson, Starr
Robbins, Carson
Robbins, Leon 20
Robbins Ferry, Houston
Robbinsville, Red River
Roberta, Limestone

§*ROBERT LEE, Coke, 90
(1,276) 1,297
Roberts, Hunt
Roberts, Parker
Robertson, Crosby 35
Robertson, Hill
Robertson, Jasper
Robertson Mills, Van Zandt
ROBINSON, McLennan
(7,111) 8,112
Robinson, Montgomery
Robinson Arms Landing,Reeves
Robinson's, Bee
Robinson's Mills, Tarrant
Robison, Van Zandt
*ROBSTOWN, Nueces, 589
(12,849) 13,094
§*ROBY, Fisher, 71 (616). 574
Rochelle, Bowie
*Rochelle, McCulloch, 27 163
*ROCHESTER, Haskell, 35
(458) 496
Rock, Dallas
Rock Bluff, Burnet 40
Rock Creek, Briscoe
Rock Creek, Grayson
Rock Creek, Johnson
Rock Creek, McLennan 25
Rock Creek, Parker
Rock Creek, Somervell. 36
Rock Crossing, Wilbarger
Rock Crusher, Coleman
*ROCKDALE, Milam, 314
(5,235) 5,658
Rock Dam, Falls
Rockett, Ellis 124
Rockett, Hamilton
Rockey, Blanco
Rockey Well, Fort Bend
Rock Falls, Erath
Rockford, Lamar . . . . .NA
Rock Harbor, Hood. 522
Rock Hill, Collin
Rock Hill, Stephens
Rock Hill, Wood
Rockhouse, Austin 30
Rock House, Culberson
Rockhouse, Fayette
Rock House, Williamson
Rockingham, Tyler
*Rock Island, Colorado, 8. 160
Rock Island, Marion
Rock Island, Waller
Rock Island, Washington
Rock Lake, Oldham
Rockland, Tyler 105
Rockne, Bastrop 400
Rockne, Bastrop
§*ROCKPORT, Aransas, 836
(4,753) 6,494
Rock Shoals, San Saba
Rock Springs, Cass
§*ROCKSPRINGS, Edwards,
63 (1,339) 1,552
Rockville, Henderson
§*ROCKWALL, Rockwall, 1,395
(10,486) 15,235
*Rockwood, Coleman. 80
Rocky [Falls], Erath
Rocky, Lee
Rocky Branch, Morris. 135
Rocky Cedar Creek, Kaufman
Rocky Creek, Blanco 20
Rocky Hill, Angelina
Rocky Hill, Falls
Rocky Mills, Lavaca
ROCKY MOUND, Camp (53). 60
Rocky Mound, Young

Rocky Point, Burnet. 102
Rocky Point, Rains
Rocky Valley, Burnet
Rockyville, San Jacinto
Roda, Limestone
Roddy, McLennan
Roddy, Van Zandt. . . . . NA
Rodet, Mitchell
Rodgers, Bell
Rodney [Calm], Navarro. 15
Roebuck, Camp
Roebuck, Leon
Roeder, Titus 110
Roeder's Mill, Austin
Roeville, Brazoria
Roganville, Jasper. 100
Rogatton, Young
*ROGERS, Bell, 70 (1,131). 1,198
Rogers[town], Ochiltree
Rogers, Taylor 151
Rogers Ferry, Red River
Rogers Hill, McLennan . . . . NA
Rogers Hill, Travis
Rogerslacy, Hidalgo
Rogers Mill, Bowie
Rogers Plantation, Brazos . . . . . . NA
Rogers Prairie, Leon
Rogersville, Bastrop
Rogersville, Parker
Rogersville, Waller
Rohde, Atascosa
Roland, Clay
Roland, Collin
Roland, Sabine
Rolla, Collingsworth
Rolling Hills, Potter 1,000
Rolling Hills, Waller . . . . NA
Rolling Hills Shores, Hood 421
Rolling Meadows, Gregg (291) . . .362
ROLLINGWOOD, Travis
(1,388) 1,632
Rolyat, Bowie
*ROMA-Los Saenz, Starr, 218
(8,059) 11,128
ROMAN FOREST, Montgomery
(1,033). 1,378
*Romayor, Liberty, 8. 96
Rome, Milam
Romero, Hartley
Romney, Eastland 12
Ronda, Wilbarger
Rook, Rusk
*Roosevelt, Kimble, 4 14
Roosevelt, Lubbock. 3,500
Roosevelt Heights, Dallas
Rooster Springs, Hays
Roosterville, Shelby
*ROPESVILLE, Hockley, 53
(494) 574
Ropesville, Nueces
Rosalie, Red River. 100
*Rosanky, Bastrop, 21. 250
Rosborough, Bowie
Rosborough Springs, Harrison
*ROSCOE, Nolan, 79 (1,446) . . . 1,363
Rose, Hamilton
Rose, Jackson
Rose, Lee
*ROSEBUD, Falls, 112
(1,638). 1,522
ROSE CITY, Orange (572) 647
Rosedale, Falls
Rosedale, Hardin
Rosedale, Jefferson
Rose Hill, Dallas
Rose Hill, Harris
Rose Hill, San Jacinto. 30
ROSE HILL ACRES, Hardin

Sardis, Rusk
Sardis, Shelby
Sargent, Dallas
*Sargent, Matagorda 300
§*Sarita, Kenedy, 6. 250
Saron, Trinity 5
Sartartia, Fort Bend
Sartor, Guadalupe
Sash, Fannin
Saspamco, Wilson 443
Sasseville, DeWitt
Satan's Flat, Mitchell
*Satin, Falls, 6 86
Satren, Sherman
Satsuma, Harris
Satterfeild, Stephens
Sattler, Comal. 30
Satuit, McCulloch
Saturn, Gonzales 15
Sauer, Milam
Sauls, Cass
Saul's Mills, Williamson
Saunders, Anderson
Saunders, Bexar
Saunders, Trinity
Sauney Stand, Washington. . . . . . NA
Sava, Van Zandt
Savage, Crosby . . . . NA
Savage, Hidalgo
Savannah [Springs], Red River
Savilla, Foard
*SAVOY, Fannin, 49 (877). 947
Sawmill, Bastrop
Saxet, Shelby
Saxie, Dallas
Sayers, Bexar . . . . NA
Sayersville [Sayers], Bastrop . . . . NA
Sayles Cross Roads, Camp
Scallorn, Bastrop
Scallorn, Mills
Scalp Creek, Menard
Scatter Branch, Hunt. . . . . NA
Scenic Brook, Travis . . . . NA
Scenic Hills, Guadalupe 170
‡ Scenic Oaks, Bexar (2,352) . . 2,730
Scharbauer City, Ector 20
Schattel, Frio
Schendelville, Fort Bend
*SCHERTZ, Guadalupe-Comal-
  Bexar, 479 (10,597). 15,364
Schicke Point, Calhoun. 70
Schiller, Kendall
Schindler, Austin
Schkade, Lee
Schleicher, Callahan
Schleicher's Bend, San Saba
Schley, Smith
Schneider, Orange
Schoenau, Austin
School, Guadalupe
School Creek, Lampasas
Schooler's Store, Terry
Schoolerville, Hamilton
School Hill, Erath. 22
Schoolland, Gonzales . . . . NA
School Land, Navarro
Schraeder, Red River
Schreiner, Kerr
Schroeder, Goliad 347
*SCHULENBURG, Fayette,
  251 (2,455) 2,855
Schull, Bell
Schumansville, Guadalupe. 650
Schussler, Gillespie
City, Polk. 500
*Schwertner, Williamson, 6 150
Science Hall, Hays
Science Hall, Jasper . . . . NA

‡ Scissors, Hidalgo (1,513) 1,933
Scobee, Burnet
Scofield, Burleson
Scooba, Rusk
*SCOTLAND, Archer-Clay, 20
  (490). 555
Scott, Lamar
Scott, Panola
Scott, Van Zandt
Scottdale, Dallas
Scott's, Rusk
Scott's Mills, Cass
*SCOTTSVILLE, Harrison, 14
  (283) 288
Scottsville, Henderson
Scoville, Harris
Scranton, Eastland 40
Scrap, Red River
Scrappin Valley, Newton. . . . . .NA
Scratch Eye, Harrison
*Scroggins, Franklin, 60 125
Scroggins, Wood
Scroungeout, Anderson
Scruggs, Wise
Scurlock, Goliad
*Scurry, Kaufman, 76 315
Scyene, Dallas
Scyene Switch, Dallas
Sea, Grayson
Sea, Houston
Seaborn, Baylor
Seabreeze, Chambers
*SEABROOK, Harris-Galveston,
  809 (6,685). 8,919
*SEADRIFT, Calhoun, 60
  (1,277). 1,557
Seago, Duval
*SEAGOVILLE, Dallas-Kaufman,
  442 (8,969). 9,987
*SEAGRAVES, Gaines, 101
  (2,398) 2,269
Seale, Robertson 60
Seale's Chapel, Karnes
*SEALY, Austin, 491 (4,541) 5,723
Sealy's, Falls
Seaman, Liberty
Sears, Scurry
Searsville, Bosque
Searsville, McLennan
Seaton, Bell 60
Seattle, Coryell
Seawillow, Caldwell 100
‡*Sebastian, Willacy, 17 (1,598) . 1,732
Sebastopol, Trinity 120
Sebree, Jack
Sebrick, Stephens
Seclusion, Lavaca
Seco, Collin
Seco, Medina
Seco Mines, Maverick. . . . . .NA
Second Corinth, Waller
Second Creek, Lipscomb
Secrect Springs, Clay
Security, Montgomery 24
Sedalia, Collin. 25
Sedan, Gonzales
Sedwick, Shackelford
Seefeld, Dimmit
Seeligson, Jim Wells
Seger, Robertson
Seglar, Bexar
Segno, Polk. 120
Segovia, Kimble, 1 12
§*SEGUIN, Guadalupe, 1,501
  (18,692). 21,754
Sejita, Duval 22
Selden, Erath. 71
Self, San Saba

Self's, Brown
Selfs, Fannin 30
Selkirk Island, Matagorda
Sellers, Collin
Sellers, Harris
SELMA, Bexar-Guadalupe-Comal,
  (520) .700
Selman, McCulloch
*Selman City, Rusk, 12 271
Selmer, Hansford
Seltser, Tarrant
Selvin, Houston
Seminary Hill, Tarrant
§*SEMINOLE, Gaines, 508
  (6,342) 6,497
Sempronius, Austin. 15
Senate, Jack
Seneca, Coryell
Seneca, Tyler
Senior, Bexar . . . . NA
Senterfitt, Lampasas
Sequoyah, Trinity
Serbin, Lee 90
‡ Serenada, Williamson
  (3,242). 4,365
Service, Ellis
Servsand, Atascosa
Seth, Hardin
‡ Seth Ward, Hale (1,402) 1,633
Settlement, Hall
Settlers Village, Harris
Seven D, Reagan
Seven Leagues, Smith
Seven Oaks, Hemphill
SEVEN OAKS, Polk (171) 210
Seven Pines, Gregg-Upshur 50
Seven Points, Collin
SEVEN POINTS, Henderson-
  Kaufman (723) 861
Seven Sisters, Duval 60
77 Ranch, Crockett
Sevier, Hill
Sevilla, Brown
Sewell, Young
Sexton, Sabine. 27
Sexton, Van Zandt
Sexton City, Rusk. . . . . NA
Seymore, Hopkins . . . . NA
§*SEYMOUR, Baylor, 275
  (3,185). 3,079
Seymour Colony, Baylor
Shackelford, Henderson
Shackelford, Lipscomb
Shack Town, Dawson
Shadeland, Lipscomb
Shadeville, Henderson
Shadowland, Red River
Shady, Baylor
Shady, Smith
Shady Grove, Burnet. 64
Shady Grove, Cherokee 30
Shady Grove, Dallas
Shady Grove, Franklin
Grove, Houston 83
Shady Grove, Limestone
Shady Grove, Panola. . . . . NA
Shady Grove, Polk
Shady Grove, Smith. 250
Shady Grove, Upshur 40
Shady Oaks, Brazoria
Shady Oaks, Henderson 100
SHADY SHORES, Denton
  (1,045) 1,496
Shaeffer, Duval
*Shafter, Presidio. 26
Shafter Lake, Andrews
Shahan's Prairie, Collin
Shale, Hill

*SHALLOWATER, Lubbock, 120
(1,708)................. 2,045
Shamrock, Castro
*SHAMROCK, Wheeler, 209
(2,286)................. 2,228
Shangri La, Burnet 58
Shankleville, Newton........... NA
Shannon, Clay 23
Shannon['s], Montgomery
Sharon, Bandera
Sharon, Hardin
Sharon, Panola
Sharon, Scurry
Sharon, Wood
Sharp, Milam 75
Sharpsburg[h], San Patricio
Sharpstown, Harris
Sharpville, San Augustine
Sharyland, Hidalgo
Shaufler, Nolan
Shavano [Valley], Bexar
SHAVANO PARK, Bexar
(1,708). 2,102
Shaw, Bowie
Shaw['s Farm], Bowie
Shaw, Kaufman
Shaw, Robertson
Shaw, Terrell
Shawnee, Angelina
Shawnee, Concho
Shawnee, Red River
Shawnee Creek, Angelina
Shawnee Prairie, Angelina 20
Shawnee Town, Rusk
Shaws Bend, Colorado 100
Shaw's Ranch, Callahan
Shawville, Coke
Shea, Webb
Shealey, Brazos
Shed, Panola
Sheeks, Liberty
Sheerin, Moore
Sheffield, Cass
*Sheffield, Pecos, 26 600
Sheid, McLennan
Shelby, Austin 175
*Shelbyville, Shelby, 50........215
‡ Sheldon, Harris (1,653)...... 2,011
Shell Camp, Gregg
Shell Rock, Tarrant
Shelton's, Lamar
Shelton's Store, Shelby
SHENANDOAH, Montgomery
(1,718).................. 2,302
Shep, Taylor 60
*SHEPHERD, San Jacinto, 136
(1,812) 2,324
Shepherds Valley, Walker
*Sheppard Air Force Base,
Wichita, 22 3,825
Shepton, Collin
*Sheridan, Colorado, 26 225
Sheridan, Houston
Sherley, Hopkins
Sherlock, Lipscomb
§*SHERMAN, Grayson, 2,134
(31,584)................ 34,395
Sherry, Red River..............15
Sherwood, Irion 150
Sherwood Shores, Bell 600
Sherwood Shores, Burnet.......870
Sherwood Shores, Grayson ... 1,590
Shields, Coleman..............13
Shields Gin, Milam
Shilo, Clay
Shiloah, Denton
Shiloh, Bastrop .... NA
Shiloh, Dallas

Shiloh, Denton
Shiloh, DeWitt
Shiloh, Erath
Shiloh, Houston
Shiloh, Hunt
Shiloh, Lavaca................NA
Shiloh, Leon ....NA
Shiloh, Limestone............ 250
Shiloh, Madison
Shiloh, Rusk
Shiloh, Travis
Shiloh, Williamson
Shiloh Academy, Lamar
Shimek, Colorado
*SHINER, Lavaca, 210
(2,074) 2,232
Shinnery, Collingsworth
Shinnery Lake, Stonewall
Shinoak, Eastland
Ship, Montague
Shire, Rusk 200
Shirley, Hopkins ....NA
Shirley Creek, Nacogdoches.....NA
*Shiro, Grimes, 8.............. 205
Shive, Hamilton................ 61
Shockeys Prairie, Lamar
Shoe-Bar Ranch, Hall
Shoe String, Harrison
Sholar, Shelby
Shooks Bluff, Cherokee
SHOREACRES, Harris-
Chambers, (1,316).........1,583
Short, Shelby.................NA
Short Pone, Rusk
Shoup, Jasper
Shovel Mountain, Burnet 98
*Sidney, Comanche, 19........ 196
Shult's Store, Fayette
Shumla, Val Verde
Siam, Leon
Siam, Terry
Sid, Hays
Sidney, Comanche
Sidney, Marion
Sid Richardson, Ector
Sieper's, Austin
Siep Springs, Comanche
§*Sierra Blanca, Hudspeth, 38... 700
Siesta, Atascosa
Siesta Dara, Medina
Signal Hill, Hutchinson
Signal Peak, Culberson
Sigsbee, Coryell
Sikes, Hunt
Silas, Shelby ....NA
Silesia, Bexar
Siloam, Bowie 50
Siloam, Comanche
Siloam, Williamson
*SILSBEE, Hardin, 627
(6,368)..................6,865
*Silver, Coke, 7 60
Silver City, Bell
Silver City, Fannin
Silver City, Milam 25
Silver City, Montgomery........NA
Silver City, Navarro 100
Silver City, Red River 25
Silver Creek Village, Burnet..... 250
Silver Glade, Cooke
Silver Hill, Polk
Silver Hills, Comal ....NA
Silver Lake, Cochran
Silver Lake, Van Zandt 42
Silver Pines, Smith ....NA
§*SILVERTON, Briscoe, 89
(779)................... 764
Silver Valley, Coleman 20

Simmons, Live Oak 65
Simmons, Marion
Simmons Bottom, Liberty....... NA
Simmonsville, Bell
*Simms, Bowie, 28.............240
Simms, Deaf Smith 10
Simms, Mills
Simon, Webb
Simonds, Dallas
*SIMONTON, Fort Bend, 48
(717) 1,005
Simpkins Prairie, Wood
Simpson, Webb
Simpson's, Nacogdoches
Simpson's, Shelby
Simpson's Bend, Llano
Simpson's Ranch, Taylor
Simpsonville, Coryell
Simpsonville, Matagorda.........10
Simpsonville, Upshur 100
Sims, Brazos .... NA
Sims, Ellis
Simsboro, Freestone........... NA
Sims Creek, Lampasas
Simtrott, Hunt
Sinclair, Jones
Sinclair City, Smith .... NA
Sinco, Harris
Sines, Liberty
Singer's Store, Lubbock
Singletary Sites, Newton........ NA
Singleton, Grimes, 1 44
Singleton's, Ellis
§*SINTON, San Patricio, 332
(5,549)................. 6,856
Sion, Walker .... NA
Sipe Springs, Comanche 75
Sipe Springs, Milam
Sisk, Erath
*Sisterdale, Kendall, 12..........63
Sister Grove, Collin
Sivells Bend, Cooke 50
Sixmile, Calhoun .... NA
Six Mile, Hopkins
Sixmile, Llano
Six-Shooter Junction, Cameron
Six Shooter Junction, Karnes
Skeen, Lynn
Skeeterville, San Saba 10
*SKELLYTOWN [Skellyville], Carson,
24 (664)..................694
Skellyville, Travis .... NA
*Skidmore [Station], Bee, 46 500
Skiles, Karnes
Skinner Springs, Clay
Skippers Gap, Erath
Skull Creek, Colorado
Skunk Hill, Nueces
Sky Harbor, Hood............. 687
Sky Lakes, Walker
Slabtown, Lamar .... NA
Slack's Wells, Fayette
Slade's Camp, Jasper
Slapfoot, Dallas
Slap Out, Hill
Slater, Coryell
Slate Shoals, Lamar........... NA
*SLATON, Lubbock, 320
(6,078).................. 6,100
Slaughter, Midland
Slaughtersville, Lampasas
Slay, Ellis
Slayden, Gonzales..............15
Slayden, Lampasas
Slayden, Llano
Slayton, Harris
Sleepy Hollow, Montgomery.....NA
Slick Hill, Comanche

Slide, Lubbock................44
*Slidell, Wise, 8.................175
Sligo, Yoakum
Slinkerts, Cameron
Sloan, Navarro
Sloan, Navarro
Sloan, San Saba...............30
Slocum, Anderson, 1...........250
Slocum, Hood
Slover, Parker
Slutter, Colorado
Sm oot, Travis
Smackover, Andrews
Smada, Fort Bend
Smada, Lee
Small, Hudspeth
Small, Van Zandt
Small, Williamson
Smead, McLennan
Smeltertown, El Paso
Smetana, Brazos...............80
Smilax, Wood
*SMILEY [Lake], Gonzales, 32
    (463) 507
Smith, Bell
Smith, Kaufman
Smith, Upshur
Smith Creek, Clay
Smithdale, Childress
Smithers Lake, Fort Bend
Smith[s] Ferry, Tyler
Smithfield, Polk
Smithfield, Tarrant
Smith Grove, Houston
Smithland, Marion.............179
Smithland, Marion
Smithland, Milam
Smith Oaks, Grayson
Smith Point, Chambers........150
Smiths Bend, Bosque.......... NA
Smiths Bluff, Jefferson........ NA
Smith's Landing, Marion
Smithson Valley, Comal.........15
Smith's Ranch, Culberson
Smith's Ranch, Hudspeth
Smith's Store, Cass
Smithton, Montague
*SMITHVILLE, Bastrop, 245
    (3,196)................. 4,076
Smithville, Bosque
Smithwick [Mills], Burnet........52
Smithwick's, Travis
Smitty, Henderson
Smoothing Iron, Lavaca
Smoots, Denton
*SMYER, Hockley, 28 (442)......439
Smyrna, Cass.................215
Smyrna, Harrison
Smyrna, Nacogdoches
Smyrna, Rains.................25
Smyrna, Rusk
Smyth, Uvalde
Smyth's Bluff, Jefferson
Snake Prairie, Bastrop
Snap, Panola
Snead, Burnet
Sneed, Mills
Sneed, Travis
Sneedville, Cottle
Sneedville, San Augustine
Snell's [Store], Newton
Snider Springs, Van Zandt
Snipe, Brazoria
*SNOOK, Burleson, 32 (489).....525
Snow, Leon
Snowball, Walker
Snow Hill, Collin...............20
Snow Hill, Morris

Snow Hill, Titus
Snow Hill, Upshur..............75
Snowsville, Hamilton
Snowtown, San Jacinto
Snuff City, Smith
Snuff Ridge, Liberty............NA
Snug Harbor, Brazoria.........193
Snyder, Bowie
Snyder, Hale
§*SNYDER, Scurry, 734
    (12,195)............... 11,865
Soash, Howard
Soco, Victoria
SOCORRO, El Paso (22,995)..29,131
Soda, Polk
Soda Springs, Caldwell
Sodom, Hunt
Sodom, Wood
Sodville, San Patricio
Soldier Mound, Dickens........ 12
Soldiers' Camp, Medina
Solino, Hidalgo
Solitude, Brazoria
Solitude, El Paso
Solms, Comal 40
Solon, Wilbarger
Somerset, Atascosa
*SOMERSET, Bexar, 80
    (1,144) 1,530
Somerset, Williamson
*SOMERVILLE, Burleson, 123
    (1,542) 1,660
Sommer, Cottle
Sommers Mill, Bell.............. 6
Soncy, Potter
§*SONORA, Sutton, 279
    (2,751)..................2,983
Soon-over, Hopkins
Sorghumville, Houston
Sorgo, Bandera
Sorrella, Wharton
Sorrels Creek, Comal
Sotol, Kinney
Sotol, Val Verde
Souleman, Archer
Soules Chapel, Upshur
Soumethun, Dallas
*SOUR LAKE, Hardin, 120
    (1,547) 1,755
Sour Lake, Jefferson
Sour Lake Spring, Hardin
Sour Spring, Caldwell
Sour Spring, Caldwell
Southard, Donley
Southbank, Wichita
*South Bend, Young, 5 140
South Bosque, McLennan...... 500
South Brice, Hall.............. 15
South Camp, King.............. 20
South Concho, Tom Green
Southdown, Brazoria..........2,427
South Franklin, Franklin........30
South Gabriel, Burnet
South Gabriel, Williamson
South Gale, Grayson
South Grape Creek, Kendall
South Groveton, Trinity
South Hanlon, Stephens
South Haven, Howard
*SOUTH HOUSTON, Harris, 636
    (14,207) 15,266
South Jericho, Shelby
*SOUTHLAKE, Tarrant-Denton,
    461 (7,082)...............13,440
Southland, Garza, 2 157
South Laredo, Webb
South Leon, Comanche
South LIberty, Liberty

*SOUTHMAYD, Grayson, 10
    (643) 849
Southmost, Cameron
SOUTH MOUNTAIN, Coryell
    (301) 333
South Nolan, Bell
*SOUTH PADRE ISLAND,
    Cameron, 243 (1,677)....... 2,260
*South Plains, Floyd, 6 92
South Plains, Martin
Southpoint, Cameron
South Prairie, Stephens
South Purmela, Coryell...........3
Southridge Estates, Guadalupe ..125
South Riverside, Gonzales
Southsan, Bexar
South San Antonio, Bexar
South San Pedro, Nueces.....1,912
South Shore, Bell................40
SOUTHSIDE PLACE, Harris
    (1,392)...................1,358
South Sulphur, Hunt 60
South Texarkana, Bowie 370
South Texarkana, Cass
Southton, Bexar...............113
South Vernon, Wilbarger
Souz Creek, La Salle
Sowell, Nolan
Sowells Bluff, Fannin
Sowers, Dallas
*Spade, Lamb, 10...............174
Spade, Mitchell
Spanish Camp, Wharton
Spanish Fort, Montague 50
Spanish Trail, Hood 478
Sparenberg, Dawson............20
Sparks, Bell..................30
‡ Sparks, El Paso (1,276) 1,470
Sparks Colony, Aransas
Sparksville, Leon
Sparta, Bell
Sparta, Palo Pinto
Spat, Montague
Spaulding, Hidalgo
Speakeville, Lavaca
*Speaks, Lavaca................60
Spear, Brazos
§*SPEARMAN, Hansford, 314
    (3,197)...................3,043
Spears Chapel, Newton
Specht Store, Bexar............20
Speckville, Menard
Speed, Van Zandt
Speedwell, Hale
Speegleville, McLennan 111
Speer, Wood
Speer's Mill, Denton
Spence, Harris
Spencer, Hunt
Spencer, Montague
Spencer, Parker
Spencer, Red River
Spencer's Ranch, Presidio
Sperry, Grayson
*Spicewood, Burnet, 199........ NA
Spicewood Springs, Travis ...... NA
Spider Mountain, Burnet.........42
Spidletop, Jefferson
Spiers', Fayette
Spil[l]man's Island, Harris
Spillers Rancho, McCulloch
Spillers Store, Leon............ NA
Spivey, Rusk
Spivey, Shelby
Splawn, Milam
*SPLENDORA, Montgomery,
    165 (745)..................975
SPOFFORD, Kinney, 1 (68) 66

Storrs[ville], Limestone
Story, Hill
Stout, Wood 86
Stovall, Johnson
Stove Foundry, Tarrant
Stover, Terrell
Stover's Cross Roads, Kaufman
Stoverville, Denton
‡*Stowell, Chambers, 24
　(1,419) 1,814
Straddle, Chambers
Strain, Hardin
Strang, Harris
Stranger, Falls 27
§*STRATFORD, Sherman, 178
　(1,781) 1,912
Stratton[burg], Brazoria
Stratton, DeWitt 25
Stratton Ridge, Brazoria
Strawberry, Smith
Strawbridge, Terrell
*STRAWN, Palo Pinto, 30 (709). . .706
Straw's, Shelby
Straws Mill, Coryell
Streeter, Mason, 2 100
*STREETMAN, Freestone-
　Navarro, 46 (260) 276
Streets, Harris
Streichville, Williamson
Strickland Crossing, Sabine
Strickling['s Grove], Burnet
Striker Creek, Cherokee
String, Bell
Stringer, Cherokee
String Prairie, Bastrop 125
String Prairie, Lee
Stringtown, Bell
Stringtown, Coryell
Stringtown, Hays
Stringtown, Hunt . . . . NA
Stringtown, Newton . . . . NA
Strip, Hale
Strobel, Brewster
Strobel, Hamilton
Stroman, Gonzales
Strong, Anderson
Strong, Shelby . . . . NA
Strong's Bluff, Orange
Stroud, Hardeman
Stroud's, Limestone
Structure, Williamson 60
Strumberg, Bexar
Stryker, Polk
Stuart, Falls
Stuart Place, Cameron 990
Stubblefield, Houston 15
Stubblefield, Johnson
Stubblefield's, Polk
Stubbs, Kaufman . . . . NA
Study Butte, Brewster 160
Stuebner, Harris
Stump, Henderson
Stumpville, Houston
Sturdivant, Palo Pinto
Sturgeon, Cooke 10
Sturgis, San Augustine
Styx, Kaufman . . . . NA
Sublett, Tarrant
*Sublime, Lavaca, 5 75
*SUDAN, Lamb, 81 (983) 972
Sudduth, Burnet
Sue, Atascosa
Sue, Navarro
Sueville, Wise
Suez, Comanche
Sugar Hill, Panola
Sugar Hill, Titus
*SUGAR LAND, Fort Bend,

2,605 (24,549) 68,716
Sugarland Junction, Fort Bend
Sugar Loaf, Coryell
Sugar Mill, Brazoria 523
Sugar Valley, Matagorda 35
Sullivan [Siding], Guadalupe
Sullivan, Johnson
‡*Sullivan City, Hidalgo, 27
　(2,371) 3,010
Sullivan's Bluff, Houston
Sulphur [Station], Bowie
Sulphur, Franklin
*Sulphur Bluff, Hopkins, 6 280
Sulphur Docks, Brazoria
Sulphuria, Culberson
Sulphur Spring, Karnes
Sulphur Springs, Angelina
Sulphur Springs, Cherokee
Sulphur Springs, Grimes
Sulphur Springs, Hood
§*SULPHUR SPRINGS, Hopkins,
　1,148 (14,062) 14,977
Sulphur Springs, Rusk
Sulphur Springs, Trinity
Suman, Robertson
Sumatra, Montgomery
Summerall, Henderson
*Summerfield, Castro, 5 60
Summer Grove, Rusk
Summer Grove, Smith
Summer Hill, Henderson
Summers, Bell
Summers' Mills, Bell
Summerville, Gonzales . . . . .NA
Summerville, Travis
Summit, Burnet
Summit, Grayson
Summit, Medina
Summit, Motley
Summit, Tyler
*Sumner, Lamar, 51 80
Sumpter, Trinity
Sumptner, Angelina
Sun, Bosque
Sun, Jefferson
Sunbeam, Grayson
Sunday Creek, Erath
Sunday School Creek, Falls
*SUNDOWN, Hockley, 100
　(1,759) 1,732
Sunflower Flat, Stonewall
Suniland, Live Oak
Sunny Lane, Burnet
Sunnyside, Castro 80
Sunnyside, Waller 120
Sunnyside, Wilson 300
SUNNYVALE, Dallas (2,228) 2,767
Sun Oil Camp, Starr
*SUNRAY, Moore, 124 (1,729). . .1,848
Sunrise, Falls 845
*SUNRISE BEACH, Llano (497) . . 567
Sunset, Dawson
Sunset, Hardin
*SUNSET, Montague, 29 (NC). . . . 300
Sunset, Wise
Sunset Heights, Harris
Sunset Oaks, Burnet 148
Sunset Station, Harris
SUNSET VALLEY, Travis (327) . . . 376
Sunshine, Houston
Sunshine, Nueces
SUN VALLEY, Lamar (60) 84
Sunview, Marion
Superior, Brazoria
Surfside, Brazoria
SURFSIDE BEACH, Brazoria,
　(611) 737
Surveyville, Newton

*Sutherland Springs, Wilson,
　10 362
Sutton, Gray
Sutton['s Station], Robertson
Swain, Bastrop
Swain, Young
Swallow, Hidalgo
Swamp City, Gregg 8
Swan[n], Smith 150
Swan Lake, Jackson
Swanntown, Red River
Swannville, San Augustine
Swanson, Falls
Swanville, Red River
Swartwout, Polk
Swearingen, Collingsworth . . . . . . NA
Swearingen, Cottle
Swearingen's, Austin
Sweden, Duval
Swedonia, Fisher
*SWEENY, Brazoria, 179
　(3,297) 3,603
Sweeten, Panola
Sweet Farms, Williamson
Sweet Home, Guadalupe 80
*Sweet Home, Lavaca, 13 360
Sweet Home, Lee 30
Sweet Oak, Leon
Sweet Union, Cherokee 40
Sweetwater, Comanche
§*SWEETWATER, Nolan, 700
　(11,967) 11,733
Sweetwater, Wheeler
Swenson, Stonewall 185
Swift, Nacogdoches 125
Swiftex, Bastrop . . . . NA
Swindall, Van Zandt
Swindells, Baylor
Swinney Switch, Live Oak
Swinneytown, Smith
Swinson, Travis
Swiss Alp, Fayette 46
Switch, Navarro
Sycamore, Burnet
Sycamore, Wise
Sylvan, Fayette
Sylvan, Lamar 68
Sylvania, Tarrant
*Sylvester, Fisher, 9 79
Sylvester, Trinity
Sylvia, Hunt
Syracuse, Harris

T
Tabasco, Hidalgo
Tabor, Brazos 150
Tabor, Brewster
Tacitus, Haskell
Tacoma, Panola
Tacubaya, Brooks
Tadella, Bell
Tadlock, Tarrant
Tadmor, Houston 67
*TAFT, San Patricio, 186
　(3,222) 3,755
‡ Taft Southwest, San Patricio
　(2,012) 2,401
Tage, Montague
Taggart, Swisher
§*TAHOKA, Lynn, 186 (2,868) . . 2,687
Tait, Colorado
Tait, Wharton
Taiton, Wharton 24
Talbot, Navarro
*TALCO, Titus, 37 (592) 597
Talledgea, Cherokee
Talley, Grayson
Talltimber, Sabine

Tallys, Harrison
Talma, Comanche
Talmage, Wilbarger
Talo, Smith
*Talpa, Coleman, 17 127
Talty, Kaufman 32
Tama, Coryell
Tam Anne, Castro
Tamar, Bowie
Tamaulipas, Blanco
Tamberg, Fayette
Tamega, Burnet
Tamina, Montgomery . . . . NA
Tampareka, Foard
Tampico, Hall
Tanglewood, Lee, 2 48
‡ Tanglewood Forest, Travis
   (2,941) 3,254
Tankersley, Tom Green
Tank Hollow, Atascosa
Tanks, Cottle
Tannahill, Tarrant
Tanner, Eastland
Taopi, Fisher
Taos, Navarro
Taos, Shackelford
Tap, Dickens
Tarbutton, Atascosa
Tar Heel Flat, Collin
Tarkington['s] Prairie, Liberty . . . . NA
*Tarpley, Bandera, 12 30
Tarpon, Nueces
Tarrant, Hopkins
Tarrant, Tarrant
Tarver, Culberson
*Tarzan, Martin, 18 80
Tascosa, Oldham . . . . NA
Tascosa Hills, Potter 90
Tasso, Rusk
Tata, Sherman
Tate, Rusk
Tate, Travis
Tate Springs, Tarrant
Tatsie, Robertson
*TATUM, Rusk-Panola, 92
   (1,289) 1,368
Tavener, Fort Bend
Tax, Leon
Taylor, Red River
*TAYLOR[sville], Williamson, 599
   (11,472) 14,722
TAYLOR LAKE VILLAGE,
   Harris (3,352) 4,034
Taylor's Bayou, Jefferson
Taylors Creek, Lampasas
Taylor's Gin, Burnet
Taylorsville, Caldwell 20
Taylorsville, Wise
Taylor Town, Lamar 40
Taz, Ochiltree
Taza, Hudspeth
Tazewell, Hopkins . . . . NA
T.C. Junction, Bowie
Teacup, Kimble
*TEAGUE, Freestone, 185
   (3,268) 3,678
Teas, Gonzales
Teaselville, Smith 150
Tebo, Sabine
Tebo, Taylor
Tech, Lubbock
Teci, Wheeler
Teck, Travis
Teco, Clay
Tecula, Cherokee
Tecumseh, Callahan
Teddy, Montgomery
Teddy, San Jacinto

Tee Pee City, Motley
Teferville, Coke
Tegaco, Refugio
*TEHUACANA, Limestone, 10
   (322) 341
Tejon, Cameron
Teka, McLennan
*Telegraph, Kimble, 3 3
Telegraph Mills, Houston
*Telephone, Fannin, 19 210
*Telferner, Victoria, 20 700
*Telico, Ellis 95
*Tell, Childress, 8 63
Tell, Cottle
Tell, Hall
Tell, Stonewall
Tellico, Ellis
Tell Tale Flat, Childress
Temco, Jasper
Tempest, Erath
*TEMPLE, Bell, 2,486
   (46,150) 51,476
Temple Junction, Polk
Temple Springs, Jasper . . . . .NA
Templeton, Cameron
Templeton, Ellis
Tenaha, Bexar
*TENAHA, Shelby, 75 (1,072) . . .1,113
Tenark, Cass
Teneryville, Gregg
Ten Mile, Dallas
Tenmile, Dawson 30
Ten Mile, Henderson
Ten Mile, Mason
Tennessee, Shelby . . . . .NA
*Tennessee Colony, Anderson, 34
   300
Tennessee Valley, Bell
Tennessee Valley, Cottle
*Tennyson, Coke 35
Tenoxtitlan, Burleson
Tenrag, Hopkins
Teresita, Milam
*Terlingua, Brewster, 44 35
Terminal, Midland
Terrace, Bexar . . . . .NA
Terrace, Grayson
*TERRELL, Kaufman, 943
   (12,490) 14,039
TERRELL HILLS, Bexar
   (4,592) 5,108
Terrell Wells, Bexar
Terrels, Brazos
Terry, Milam
Terry, Orange
Terry [Station], Orange
Terry Chapel, Falls 30
Terryville, DeWitt 40
Tesco, Nolan
Tesla, Houston
Tesnus, Brewster
Tessie, Pecos
Teville, Mitchell
Tevis Bluff, Jefferson
Tewockony Springs, Limestone
Texaco, Fayette
Texana, Jackson
Texand, McLennan
*TEXARKANA (Texas portion only),
   Bowie, 2,846 (31,658) 33,234
   [1990, including Arkansas portion]
   (54,287) 56,152
*TEXAS CITY, Galveston, 1,374
   (40,822) 42,110
Texas Elf Co. Settlement, Gray
Texas Iron Works, Marion
Texas National, Montgomery . . . . .NA
Tex-Harvey, Martin

TEXHOMA, Sherman (291) 311
Texhoma City, Archer
Texico, Parmer
Texla, Harrison
Texla, Orange
*TEXLINE, Dallam, 60 (425) 438
Texon, Reagan, 1 12
Texroy, Hutchinson
Thackwell, Smith
Thalia, Foard 104
Tharp, Montgomery
Thayer, Hidalgo
THE COLONY, Denton
   (22,113) 28,956
Thedford, Smith 65
The Ditch, Lipscomb
The Divide, Kerr 250
The Flat, Taylor
The Grove, Coryell 65
The Knobbs, Lee
Thelma, Bexar 45
Thelma, Limestone . . . . NA
The Motts, Nueces
Theny, Comanche
Theo, Falls
Theodocia, Hopkins
Theodore, Grayson
Theodore, Winkler
Theon, Williamson 20
The Point, Live Oak
Thermo, Hopkins . . . . NA
The Rock, Marion
The Survey, Newton
The Switch, Mills
Theta, Hunt
The Valley, Guadalupe
‡*The Woodlands, Montgomery,
   1,091 (29,205) 41,628
*Thicket, Hardin, 9 306
Thomas, Upshur 100
Thicket, Polk
Thomas, Burnet
Thomas, Denton
Thomas, Moore
Thomas, Panola
Thomas, Upshur
*Thomaston, DeWitt, 4 45
Thomasville, Bell
Thom Hill, Comal
Thompson, Austin
Thompson, Harris
Thompson Chapel, Fort Bend
Thompson Switch, Fort Bend
Thompson Switch, Harris
*THOMPSONS, Fort Bend, 15
   (174) .248
Thompsonville, Gonzales 30
Thompsonville, Harris
Thompsonville, Jim Hogg . . . . NA
Thomson, Collin
Thornberry, Clay 60
*THORNDALE, Milam-Williamson,
   85 (1,092) 1,360
*THORNTON, Limestone, 36
   (540) .609
THORNTONVILLE, Ward (693) . . .770
Thorp['s] Spring, Hood 184
Thorpe, Schleicher
Thorpeville, Dallas
Thors, Nacogdoches
*THRALL, Williamson, 29 (550) . . .796
Thrash, Nacogdoches
Thrasher, Victoria
Three Leagues, Martin
Three Oaks, Wilson 150
Three Points, Travis
*THREE RIVERS, Live Oak, 153
   (1,889) 1,988

Three States, Cass 45
Three Way, Erath ....NA
Thrift, Wichita
Thrifty, Brown................NA
§*THROCKMORTON, Throckmorton,
  97 (1,036) 902
Thulemeyer's, Fayette
Thurber, Erath 8
Thurber Junction, Palo Pinto
Thurman, Hardin
Thurman, Panola
Thurman, Shelby
Thurman, Young
Thurst[on], Terrell
Tib, Collin
Tibb, Collin
Tibbie, Polk
Tickey, Collin
Ticklefoot, Grimes
Tidwell, Hunt ....NA
Tidwell, Limestone
Tidwell, Williamson
Tidwell Creek, Hunt
Tidwell Prairie, Robertson ......NA
Tie City, Bastrop
Tierra Alta, Schleicher
Tierra Blanca, Hidalgo
Tiffin, Eastland
Tige, Hopkins
Tiger, Kaufman
Tiger Mill, Burnet
Tiger Prairie, Limestone
Tigertown, Lamar..............NA
Tigertown, Washington
Tigg, Bastrop
Tight Wad, Ellis
Tigua, El Paso
TIKI ISLAND VILLAGE,
  Galveston (537) 737
§*Tilden, McMullen, 40 450
Tilecrete, Smith
Tillis Prairie, Montgomery
Tilmon['s Mill], Caldwell 117
Tilton, Montague
Timber, Montgomery
Timber Creek, Hunt
TIMBERCREEK CANYON,
  Randall (277) 378
Timber Lake, Burnet
‡ Timberwood, Bexar (2,578) .. 3,108
Time, Houston
Time, Sabine
Timesville, Leon...............NA
Timm City, Lipscomb
Timme's Store, Austin
Timmons', Panola
Timm's Store, Guadalupe
Timo, Hidalgo
Timothy, Hidalgo
Timothy, Navarro
*TIMPSON, Shelby, 122
  (1,029)...................1,030
Tinaja, Presidio
Tince, Henderson
Tindel, Henderson
Tinimax, Cherokee
Tinnen's, Robertson
Tinney Creek, Caldwell
Tinnin, Lamar
Tinnin's, Lamar
Tin Top, Matagorda
Tin Top, Parker 31
Tin Top, Polk
Tio, Frio
Tiocano, Cameron
*TIOGA, Grayson, 48 (625) 688
Tippett's Crossing, Wood
TIRA, Hopkins (237)...........288

Titley, Brewster
Tittle, Hill
Titus, Titus
*Tivoli, Refugio, 25 550
Tivy, Kerr
Tivydale, Gillespie
Toadsuck, Grayson
Tobacco Patch, Polk............NA
Tobey, Atascosa
Tobin, El Paso
Tobin, Erath
Toccoa, Leon
TOCO, Lamar (127)............ 133
Todd, Grayson
Todd, Grimes
Todd, Milam
Todd, Montague
Todd, Newton
Todd City, Anderson........... 10
TODD MISSION, Grimes (54) 69
Todd's [Mill], Shelby
Toddville, Upshur
Togo, Bastrop
Tokeen, Runnels
Tokio, McLennan.............. 250
*Tokio, Terry, 6................. 24
Toksana, Wichita
*TOLAR, Hood, 63 (523) 602
Tolbert, Wilbarger 30
Toledo, Fayette
Toledo, Newton
Toledo Village, Newton..........NA
Tolette [Tollette], Lamar..........NA
Toliver, Nacogdoches
Tollett's Prairie, Lamar
Toll Town, Denton
Tolosa, Henderson
Tolosa, Kaufman.............. 58
Toluca, Hidalgo
Tom, Sterling
Tom, Wichita
Tomaha, Red River
Tomato, Callahan
*TOMBALL, Harris-Montgomery,
  1,387 (6,370) 7,346
*TOM BEAN, Grayson, 44 (827) .. 946
Tomburnett, Wichita
Tom Campell, Hunt
Tomday, Shelby
Tomday, Shelby
Tom Gill, Hidalgo
Tomlinson Hill, Falls............ 64
Tommie, Lavaca
Tompkins Store, Williamson
Tona, Kaufman
Tonk, Young
Tonkawa Springs, Williamson
Tonk Creek, McLennan
Tony, Hunt
TOOL, Henderson (1,712)......2,064
Toombs, Runnels
Toomey, Shelby
Topaz, Erath
Topeka Junction, Lavaca
Topp, Hopkins
Topsey, Coryell 20
Torbert, Hudspeth
Torcer, Hudspeth
Tordia, Atascosa
Tordilla, Atascosa
Tordilla Mound, Atascosa
Torian, Jim Wells
*Tornillo, El Paso, 35........... 241
Toro, Callahan
Toronto, Brewster
Torpedo, Comanche
Torrecillas, Webb
Torres, Val Verde

Tosca, Blanco
Tosca, Gillespie
Toto, Parker
Tours, McLennan..............100
*Tow [Valley], Llano, 33.........305
Towash, Hill
Towles, Van Zandt
Tower Lake, Wilson 100
Towers, Panola
Town Bluff, Tyler................26
Townley, Walker
Townsend, Fayette
Townsend, San Augustine ......NA
Townsen Mills, Lampasas
Towns' Mill, Williamson
Townsville, Williamson
‡ Town West, Fort Bend
  (6,166)..................8,512
Towson, Red River
*TOYAH, Reeves, 9 (115) 117
*Toyahvale, Reeves, 6 60
Tracy, Milam
Tradinghouse Creek, McLennan
Traildust, Denton
Tram, Jasper
Trammells, Fort Bend
Traprock, Uvalde
Traver, Terrell
Travis, Austin
Travis, Falls, 1.................48
Travis Peak, Travis
Trawick, Nacogdoches 100
Treasure Island, Guadalupe 600
Tredway, Borden
*TRENT, Taylor, 32 (319)........318
*TRENTON, Fannin, 57 (655).....717
Trevat [Trevathan], Trinity
Trevino, Duval
Trexler, Bowie
Triangle, Falls
Tribune, Grayson
Trickham, Coleman 12
Trigg, Stephens
Trimmier, Bell.................90
*TRINIDAD, Henderson, 68
  (1,056)..................1,191
Trinidad, Kaufman
Trinidad, Madison
*TRINITY, Trinity, 318 (2,648) ... 2,887
Trinity City, Dallas
Trinity Mills, Dallas
Trinity River Spur, Liberty
Trinity Switch, Henderson
Trinto, Kaufman
Trion, Palo Pinto
Trip, Dallas
Triplett, Wise
Trixie, Gaines
TROPHY CLUB, Denton
  (3,922) 5,179
Trot, Polk
Trotti, Newton
Trouble, Washington
Troup, Cass
Troup, Cherokee
Troup, Smith
*TROUP, Smith-Cherokee, 231
  (1,659)..................1,906
Trout, Lamar
Trout Creek, Newton ....NA
*TROY, Bell, 90 (1,395)........ 1,462
Troy, Comanche
Troy, Freestone
Truby, Jones..................26
Truce, Jack
True, Young
Truebsal, Washington
Trueheart, Ward

Truit's Store, Shelby
Truitt, Runnels
Trukton, Rusk................**NA**
Truman, Dallas
Trumble, Moore
Trumbull, Ellis.................**65**
*****Truscott, Knox, 8**.............**50**
Trygillo, Oldham
Tryon, Hardin
Tubbes, Nacogdoches
Tubbs Corner, Crane
Tucker [Station], Anderson......**304**
Tucker, McCulloch
Tucker's Mills, Limestone
Tucumcari, Williamson
Tudor, Eastland
Tuff, Bandera
Tulane, Orange
Tularosa, Kinney
*****Tuleta, Bee, 15.**................**98**
§*TULIA, Swisher, 356
  (4,703)..................**4,975**
Tulip, Fannin..................**10**
Tulip, Newton
Tulosa, Nueces
Tulsa, Bee
Tulsa, Lamb
Tulsa, Winkler
Tulsita, Bee.....................**25**
Tulsy, Brazoria
Tuna, La Salle
Tundra, Van Zandt..............**34**
Tunis, Burleson...............**150**
Tunnell's [Camp, Chapel], Van Zandt
Tupelo, Navarro...............**NA**
Turcotte, Kenedy
*****TURKEY [Roost], Hall, 32 (507)**..**551**
Turkey, Wharton
Turkey Creek, Cass
Turkey Creek, Hunt
Turkey Creek, San Jacinto
Turkey Creek, Uvalde
Turkey Creek, Washington
Turkey Creek, Williamson
Turlington, Freestone..........**27**
Turnbaugh Corner, Ector.......**NA**
Turner, Clay
Turner's Point, Kaufman
Turnersville, Coryell..........**155**
Turnersville, Travis.............**90**
Turnertown, Jefferson
Turnertown, Rusk..............**76**
Turney, Cherokee
Turney's Store, Travis
Turpentine, Jasper
Turtle, Kerr
Turtle Bayou, Chambers........**42**
Turtle Bayou, Liberty
Turtle Cove, Brazoria...........**50**
Tuscaloosa, Titus
Tuscaloosa, Walker
*****TUSCOLA, Taylor, 88 (620)**.....**634**
Tusculum, Kendall
Tuttle's Store, Fayette
Tuxedo, Jones.................**42**
25 Mile Post, Montgomery
Twichell, Ochiltree
Twin Buttes, Hall
Twin Creek, Bexar............**NA**
Twin Creek, Webb
Twin Groceries, Hopkins
Twin Mountain, Hamilton
Twin Oak, Falls
Twin Ranch & Farm, Lubbock
Twin Sisters, Blanco..........**78**
Twist, Hartley
Twist, Swisher
Twist Junction, Dallam

Twitty, Wheeler, 4 12
Twohig, La Salle
*****TYE, Taylor, 53 (1,088)**........**1,211**
§*TYLER, Smith, 6,178
  (75,450)................**82,509**
Tyler Bluff, Cooke
Tyler's Prairie, Trinity
Tyler Springs, Wise
*****Tynan, Bee, 19**...............**200**
Tyner, Blanco
Type, Bastrop
Type, Williamson...............**40**
Tyro, Parker
Tyro, San Saba
Tyson, Hill

U

Ubell, Fannin
Udston, Houston
Ufnau, Comal
UHLAND, Caldwell-Hays (368)...**439**
Ula, Foard
Ulmer, Grimes
Ultzville, Bexar
*****Umbarger, Randall, 19**........**327**
Una, Marion
Una, Robertson
UNCERTAIN, Harrison (194).....**219**
Underwood, Hale
Uneva, Henderson
Union, Brazos.................**NA**
Union, Dawson
Union, Eastland
Union, Falls
Union, Hopkins
Union, Jasper
Union, Lubbock
Union, San Augustine..........**NA**
Union, Scurry.................**20**
Union, Terry..................**55**
Union [Hill], Washington
Union, Wilson.................**22**
Union Bluff, Hill
Union Bower, Dallas
Union Bridge, Titus
Union Center, Eastland.........**NA**
Union Flat, Childress
Union Flat, Navarro
Union Grove, Bell..............**4**
Union Grove, Brown
Union Grove, Erath............**12**
Union Grove, Kaufman
Union Grove, McLennan
UNION GROVE, Upshur (271)...**303**
Union Hall, Swisher
Union High, Navarro...........**30**
Union Hill, Kaufman
Union Hill, McLennan
Union Hill, Walker
Union Hill, Van Zandt
Union Point, Jack
Union Valley, Hunt.............**25**
Unionville, Cass
Unit, Waller
Unitia, Delta
Unity, Collingsworth
Unity, Colorado
Unity, Lamar..................**NA**
*****UNIVERSAL CITY, Bexar, 582**
  (13,057).................**14,914**
University Community, Cottle
UNIVERSITY PARK, Dallas
  (22,259).................**22,872**
Uno, Stonewall
Upland, Upton
Upper Cuero Creek Settlement, DeWitt
Upper Hondo, Medina
Upper Medio, Bee

Upper Meyersville, DeWitt........**33**
Upper Mott, Calhoun
Upper Quihi, Medina
Upper Yorktown, DeWitt
Upshaw, Nacogdoches.........**NA**
Upson, Maverick
Upton, Bastrop.................**25**
Urban, Dallas
Urbana, San Jacinto...........**25**
Uriah, Coryell
U.S. Factory, Lamar
Utica, Smith
Utley, Bastrop..................**50**
*****Utopia, Uvalde, 55.**............**360**
§*UVALDE, Uvalde, 833
  (14,729).................**16,051**
Uvalde Junction, Uvalde
Uz, Montague

V

Vaca, Callahan
Vahlsing, San Patricio
Vair, Trinity
Valda, Polk
Valdasta, Collin
Valdesta, Collin
Vale, Runnels
*****VALENTINE, Jeff Davis, 6**
  (217)....................**267**
Valenzuela, Webb
*****Valera, Coleman, 9**............**80**
Valletta Ranch, Denton
Valley, Grayson
Valley, Guadalupe
Valley Creek, Fannin...........**12**
Valley Farm, Reeves
Valley Farms, Navarro
Valley Grove, Erath
Valley Grove, Rusk.............**NA**
Valley Grove, Young
Valley Hi, Bexar.............**3,000**
Valley Home, Brown
Valley Junction, Robertson
*****VALLEY MILLS, Bosque-**
  McLennan, 101 (1,085).......**1,107**
Valley Park, Lipscomb
Valley Pass, Bell
Valley Ridge, Brazos...........**NA**
*****Valley Spring, Llano, 8**........**50**
Valley Springs, Hill
*****VALLEY VIEW, Cooke, 107**
  (640)....................**799**
Valley View, Cottle............**23**
Valley View, DeWitt
Valley View, McLennan
Valley View, Mitchell
Valley View, Rockwall
Valley View, Runnels...........**22**
Valley View, Upshur...........**75**
Valley View, Wichita..........**200**
Valley View, Williamson
Valley Wells, Dimmit...........**25**
Valmont, Bexar
Valparaiso, Calhoun
Valparaiso, Hopkins
Valton, Hopkins
Val Verde, Denton
Val Verde, Hidalgo............**NA**
Val Verde, Milam................**25**
Van, Leon
*****VAN, Van Zandt, 172 (1,854)**...**2,196**
*****VAN ALSTYNE, Grayson, 189**
  (2,090).................**2,423**
Van Camp, Young
Vance, Colorado
Vance, Real....................**20**
Vance, Taylor
*****Vancourt, Tom Green, 12**......**125**

Vandalia, Red River 35
Vandenburg, Medina
*Vanderbilt, Jackson, 18 618
*Vanderpool, Bandera, 10 20
Vanderpool, Bandera
Vandersville, Collin
Vandyke, Comanche 20
Vanetia, Leon
§*VAN HORN, Culberson, 149
   (2,930) 2,834
Vannoy's, Rusk
Van Pelt, Brazoria
Van Raub, Bexar . . . . NA
Van Sickle, Hunt. . . . . NA
Van Slyke, Cooke
Van Syckles, Cameron
‡*Van Vleck, Matagorda, 60
   (1,534) 1,817
Varela, Limestone
Varina, Haskell
Varisco, Brazos
Vasco, Delta 20
Vashti, Clay. 80
Vashtie, Bosque
Vattman, Kleberg 125
Vaughan['s Store], Bosque
Vaughan, Hill 70
Vaughan's Mill, Trinity
Veach, San Augustine . . . . NA
*Vealmoor, Howard 179
Veals, Morris
Veals Station, Parker
§*VEGA, Oldham, 90 (840) 925
Vela, Hidalgo
Velasco, Brazoria
Veldt, Kaufman
Velehrad, Lavaca
Velma, San Saba
Velma, Sherman
Velpo, San Jacinto
Venable, San Augustine
Venadito, Cameron
Venetia, Leon
Venice, Coke
Venice, Nacogdoches
Ventura, Montgomery
*VENUS, Johnson-Ennis, 72
   (977) 1,283
Vera, Gray
*Vera, Knox. 50
Vera, Tyler
Verand, Schleicher
Verbena, Garza
Vercal, Anderson
Verde Mills, Bexar . . . . NA
Verdi, Atascosa 110
Verdina, Medina
*Verhalen, Reeves 52
Verhelle, DeWitt
*Veribest, Tom Green, 6 40
Vermont Ranch, Schleicher
Vern, Liberty
Verna[ville], Collin
Vernal, McLennan
Vernon, Gonzales
Vernon, Panola
§*VERNON, Wilbarger, 696
   (12,001) 12,012
Verona, Collin
Vesper, La Salle
Vesrue, Winkler
Vessey, Red River 14
Vesta, Sabine
Vesta, Shackelford
Veto, Gillespie
Veto, Jack
Viboras, Starr. 22
Vick, Concho 20

Vickery, Callahan
Vickery, Dallas
Vicksburg, Montgomery . . . . .NA
Vicksburgh, Caldwell
Victor, Erath
Victor, Harris
Victoria, Limestone. 25
Victoria, Stonewall
§*VICTORIA, Victoria, 3,400
   (55,076) 63,559
Victoria Peak, Montague
Victoria Ranch, Oldham
Victory City, Bowie 250
Vida, Tyler
Vidauri, Refugio
Vidette, Liberty
Vidor, Montgomery
*VIDOR, Orange, 645
   (10,935) 11,312
Vienna, Lavaca 40
Viesca, Falls
View, Comal
View [City], Taylor 75
Viewpoint, Lamar . . . . .NA
Vigo, Callahan
Vigo, Concho
Vigo Park [Vigo], Swisher, 1 31
Vilas, Bell
Vilas, Houston
Vilas, Panola
Villa, Hudspeth
Villa, Mills
Villa Cavazos, Cameron
Village Creek, Hardin
*Village Mills, Hardin, 33. 1,700
VILLAGE OF THE HILLS, Travis,
   (NC) .1,100
Villa Nueva, Cameron 402
Villa Nueva, Hidalgo
Villa Nueva, Nueces
Villareales, Starr 100
Villas, Bell
Villegas, Webb
Vilott, Cooke
Vina, Clay
Vincent, Howard 500
Vinegarone, Val Verde. . . . . .NA
Vine Green, Washington
Vine Grove, Washington
Vineland, Collin
Viney, Collin
Vineyard, Jack. 37
Vineyard, Jack
Vineyard, Morris
Vinson, Howard
Vinson, Travis
VINTON, El Paso (605) 807
Viola, Cass
Viola, Milam
Viola, Nueces
Violet, Nueces 160
Virgie, Montgomery
Virgile, Johnson
Virginia, Armstrong
Virginia, Dallas
Virginia City, Bailey
Virginia Mills, Montague
Visco, Mitchell
Vista, Dickens
Vista, Hamilton
Vista, Mitchell
Vista, Nolan
Vistula, Houston 21
Viterbo, Jefferson
Vivian, Foard . . . . .NA
Vivian, Marion
Vix, Kerr
Vliets, Mitchell

*Voca, McCulloch, 7 56
Voelkle, Grayson
Volente, Travis . . . . NA
Volga, Houston. 300
Vollmer, Harris
Volney, Delta
Volney, Robertson
Volo, Bell
*Von Ormy, Bexar, 123 . . . . NA
Vontress, Haskell . . . . NA
*Voss, Coleman, 2 20
Voss, Coryell
Vossville, Fort Bend
*Votaw, Hardin, 3 160
Votaw, Live Oak
*Voth, Jefferson . . . . NA
Voxpopuli, Colorado
Vsetin, Lavaca . . . . NA
Vysehrad, Lavaca . . . . NA

W
§*WACO, McLennan, 6,384
   (103,590) 110,024
Wade, Guadalupe
Wade Mill, San Augustine
Wade's, Fayette
Wade's Chapel, Parker
Wade's City, Jim Wells
Wadeville, Navarro
Wadsworth, Hale
*Wadsworth, Matagorda, 19 160
*WAELDER, Gonzales, 25 (745) . .821
Waggoner, Wichita
Wagner, Hartley
Wagner, Hunt . . . . NA
Wagram, Mason
Waildville, Montague
Waintown, Denton
Wainwright, Navarro
Waite, Hidalgo
*Waka, Ochiltree, 3. 65
Wake, Crosby . . . . NA
Wakefield, Howard
Wakefield, Polk. 25
Wakefield's, Denton
Waketon, Denton
*WAKE VILLAGE, Bowie
   (4,761) 5,105
*Walburg, Williamson, 13. 250
Walch, San Jacinto
Walcott, Martin
Waldeck, Fayette 35
Walden, Jefferson
Walden, Montgomery . . . . NA
Waldo, McLennan
Waldrip, McCulloch 15
Waldrop's Gin, Stonewall
Wales, Lamar
Walhalla, Comal
Walhalla, Fayette 37
Walk, Lampasas
Walker, Howard
Walker, Parker
Walker, Walker
Walker's, Rusk
Walkers Mill, Harrison
Walker's Store, McLennan
Walker Station, Red River
Walkerton, Williamson
*Wall, Tom Green, 15 200
Wallace, Bandera
Wallace, Parker
Wallace, Travis
Wallace, Uvalde
Wallace, Van Zandt. . . . . NA
Wallace Chapel, Upshur
Wallace Creek, San Saba
Wallace Mill, Shelby

Westbrook, Jack . . . . NA
Westbrook, Jasper
Westbrook, Johnson
*WESTBROOK, Mitchell, 16
(237) 235
Westbrook, Webb
Westbrook Mill, Newton
Westbury [Westberry], Jefferson
West Carisle, Lubbock
*WEST COLUMBIA, Brazoria,
298 (4,372) 5,260
Westcott, San Jacinto 25
West Eden, Wise
Western Lake, Parker . . . . NA
Westerville, Palo Pinto
Westfield, Harris
Westfork, Archer
West Falls, Falls
West Fork, Wise
*Westhoff, DeWitt, 25. 410
West Junction, Harris
WESTLAKE, Tarrant-Denton
(185) 231
*WEST LAKE HILLS, Travis,
(2,542) 2,809
Westland, Tarrant
West Liberty, Liberty
West Mesquite, Dallas
West Mineola, Wood 20
*WESTMINSTER [Westminister],
Collin, 8 (388). 572
West Mountain, Upshur. 445
West Nona, Hardin
West Nueces, Kinney
West Oaks, Travis. . . . . NA
‡ West Odessa, Ector
(16,568) 18,612
*WESTON, Collin, 11 (362) 507
*WEST ORANGE, Orange
(4,187) 4,625
West Oso, Nueces
Westover, Baylor 18
WESTOVER HILLS, Tarrant
(672) .720
West Park, Harris
Westphalia, Falls 186
*West Point, Fayette, 21. 205
West Point, Hamilton
West Point, Hays
West Point, Lynn . . . . NA
West Port Arthur, Jefferson
Westprong, Uvalde
West St. Paul, San Patricio
Westside, Morris
West Sinton, San Patricio . . . . NA
West Sweden, McCulloch
WEST TAWAKONI, Hunt (932) . . 1,168
West Tempe, Polk
WEST UNIVERSITY PLACE,
Harris (12,920) 13,093
West Vernon, Wilbarger
Westville, Trinity. 46
Westway, Deaf Smith. 15
West Waco, McLennan
‡ Westway, El Paso (2,381) 2,707
WESTWORTH VILLAGE,
Tarrant (2,350) 2,485
West Yegua, Lee
Wetmore, Bexar, 4 . . . . NA
Wetsel, Collin
Whaley, Bowie
§*WHARTON, Wharton, 619
(9,011) 9,926
Whatley, Marion
Wheat, Scurry
Wheatland, Dallas
Wheatland, Hardeman
Wheatland, Parker

Wheatland, Tarrant 175
Wheatland, Wilbarger
Wheat Valley, Wilbarger
Wheatville, Morris
Wheeler, Potter
§*WHEELER, Wheeler, 136
(1,393). 1,339
Wheeler, Wheeler
Wheeler's Hill, Trinity
Wheeler Springs, Houston. . . . . . .NA
Wheeler's Store, Travis
Wheeler's Switch, Polk
*Wheelock, Robertson, 11 225
Wherry['s], Rusk
Whig, Carson
Whistler, Kinney
Whistleville, Llano
Whit, Harris
White, El Paso
White, Milam
White, Uvalde
White City, Chambers
White City, Gaines . . . . .NA
White City, San Augustine 20
White City, Wilbarger 40
White City, Wise
White Cottage, Shelby
Whited, Gray
*WHITE DEER, Carson, 68
(1,125) 1,231
*WHITEFACE, Cochran, 40
(512) 466
Whitefish, Donley
White Flat, Fisher
White Flat, Knox
Whiteflat, Motley 3
White Hall, Bell 45
White Hall, Cass
White Hall, Coryell
White Hall, Grimes . . . . .NA
White Hall, Jackson . . . . .NA
Whitehall, Kaufman . . . . .NA
Whitehead, Hunt . . . . .NA
*WHITEHOUSE, Smith, 349
(4,018) 5,064
Whiteland, McCulloch
White League, Ellis
White Mound, Coryell
White Mound, Grayson
*WHITE OAK, Gregg, 191
(5,136) 5,712
White Oak, Harris
White Oak, Hopkins
Whiteoak, Hopkins
Whiteoak, Marion
White Oak, Titus 100
White Oak Junction, Hopkins . . . .NA
White Point, San Patricio
White River, Crosby 35
White Rock, Dallas
White Rock, Grayson
White Rock, Hill
White Rock, Hunt 73
White Rock, Red River 85
White Rock, Robertson 80
White Rock, San Augustine 60
Whites, Robertson
White's, Sabine
*WHITESBORO[gh], Grayson,
257 (3,209) 3,445
Whitesboro, Hamilton
White's Colony, Grayson
*WHITE SETTLEMENT, Tarrant,
(15,472) 15,994
Whitesides, Washington
Whiteside's Prairie, Fayette
Whitesmine, Uvalde
Whites Ranch, Chambers

White's Store, Chambers
White's Switch, Fort Bend
Whitestar, Motley 5
Whitestone, Motley
White Stone, Williamson
White Sulphur Springs, Cass
White Sulphur Springs, Grimes
Whitesville, Houston
White's Wells, Hill
Whitetail, Williamson
White Water Springs, Wheeler
Whiteway, Hamilton 10
*WHITEWRIGHT, Grayson-
Fannin, 143 (1,713). 1,777
Whitfield, Swisher
Whitfield's, Waller
Whitham, Jones
*Whitharral, Hockley, 13 175
Whiting's Farm, Washington
Whitley, Briscoe
Whitman[s], Washington 25
*WHITNEY, Hill, 324 (1,626) 1,618
*Whitsett, Live Oak, 9 200
Whitson, Coryell 30
*Whitt, Parker, 3 38
Whittaker, Burleson
Whittenburg, Hutchinson
*Whitton, Van Zandt. . . . . NA
Whittville, Comanche
Whitworth, Kaufman
Whizzerville, Caldwell
*Whon, Coleman 15
Whybark, Bowie
Whynot, Hunt
Wichita [City], Clay
Wichita Colony, Baylor
§*WICHITA FALLS, Wichita-Archer,
5,268 (96,259) 98,161
Wicker, Brazos. . . . . NA
Wickes Spur, Brazoria
*WICKETT, Ward, 28 (560) 527
Wied, Lavaca 65
Wiedeville, Washington. . . . . NA
Wieland, Hunt. . . . . NA
*Wiergate, Newton, 11 461
Wigfall, Houston
Wiggins, Cass
Wiggins, Houston
Wiggins, Rusk
Wigginsville, Montgomery . . . . . . NA
Wight, Val Verde
Wightman, Newton
Wihan, Newton
Wilbarger, Bastrop
Wilbarger, Wilbarger
Wilborn, Donley
Wilbourn, Walker
Wilburton, Montgomery
Wilco, Hartley
Wilcox, Burleson 40
Wilcox, Gray 5
Wilda, Liberty
Wildcat, Eastland
Wildcat, Henderson
Wild Cat Bluff, Anderson
Wilder's Gin, Williamson
Wilderville, Falls. 45
Wildhorse, Culberson
Wild Horse Prairie, Wise
Wild Hurst, Cherokee
*Wildorado, Oldham, 30. 180
‡ Wild Peach, Brazoria
(2,440) 2,705
Wild Plum Valley, Williamson
Wildwood, Bexar . . . . NA
Wiles, Stephens
Wilford, Stonewall
Wilhite, Lamar

Wilkie, Burnet
Wilkins, Upshur 75
Wilkinson, Titus 150
Wilkinson's [Valley], Bell
Willaluce, Shelby
Willamar, Willacy 15
Willard, Jones
Willard, Trinity
Willa Walla, Montague
Willett, Cottle
William Penn, Washington 100
William Routt, Fort Bend
Williams, Brown
Williams, Hardeman
Williams, Hardin
Williams, Jefferson
Williams', Lamar
Williams, Liberty . . . . **NA**
Williamsburg[h]**, Lavaca** . . . . **NA**
Williams Creek, Gillespie
Williamson Settlement, Orange . .175
Williams Ranch, Mills
Williams Ranch, Montague
Williams Settlement, Rusk
Williams' Store, Guadalupe
Willingham, Smith
Willingham Store, Martin
*WILLIS, Montgomery, 592
   (2,764) 3,979
Willman, Bastrop
Willow, Harris
Willow, Travis
Willow Bar, Colorado
*Willow City, Gillespie, 8 75
Willow Creek, Howard
Willow Creek, Mason
Willow Creek, Robertson
Willow Dale, Comanche
Willow Grove, McLennan 100
Willow Grove, Shelby
Willow Hole, Madison
WILLOW PARK, Parker
   (2,328) 2,864
Willow Point, Wise
Willow Pond, Ellis
Willow Pond, Palo Pinto
Willow Prairie, Travis
Willow Spring, Travis
Willow Springs, Bell
Willow Springs, Fayette 35
Willow Springs, McLennan
Willow Springs, Milam
Willow Springs, Rains 50
Willow Springs, San Jacinto
Willow Springs, Travis
Wills', Van Zandt
*WILLS POINT, Van Zandt, 406
   (2,986) 3,412
Willton, Williamson
*WILMER, Dallas, 57 (2,479) . . 2,590
Wilmerding, Navarro
Wilmeth, Runnels 25
Wilmoth, Angelina
Wilmoth, Montgomery
Wilna, Bastrop
Wilsey, Parmer
Wilson, Collingsworth
Wilson, Comanche
Wilson, Cooke
Wilson, Cottle
Wilson, Falls 42
Wilson, Kaufman . . . . **NA**
Wilson, Limestone
*WILSON, Lynn, 45 (568) 565
Wilson, Navarro
Wilson's, Tyler
Wilson Springs, Shelby
Wilson Springs, Williamson

Wilson's Switch, Collin
Wilton, Cass
Wilton, Ellis
Wilton, Tarrant
Wilton, Wilbarger
‡*Wimberley, Hays, 637
   (2,403) 2,812
Wimberly, Fort Bend
Win Town, Panola
Winchell, Brown . . . .**NA**
*Winchester, Fayette, 2 50
*WINDCREST, Bexar (5,331) . . .5,846
‡ Windemere, Travis (3,207) 3,536
Windham, Callahan
Windmill Town, Taylor
Windom, Angelina
*WINDOM, Fannin, 16 (269) 311
Windom, Hutchinson
Windsor, Cooke
Windsor, Kendall
Windsor, McLennan . . . .**NA**
*WINDTHORST, Archer-Clay, 68
   (367) 395
Winedale, Fayette 41
Winedale, Washington
Winfield, Bastrop
*WINFIELD, Titus, 16 (345) 368
Winfree, Chambers
*Wingate, Runnels, 15 216
*WINK, Winkler, 41 (1,189) 1,165
Winkler, Navarro-Freestone, 1 26
Winkler City, Winkler
Winn, Robertson
‡*Winnie, Chambers, 249
   (2,238) 2,653
Winningkoff, Collin
*WINNSBORO[ugh]**, Wood-Franklin,**
   448 (2,904) 3,223
Winnton, Gonzales
*WINONA, Smith, 75 (457) 604
Winscott, Tarrant
Winston, Dallas
Winston, Mitchell
Winston, Scurry
Winterfield, Hopkins . . . .**NA**
Winter Garden, Dimmit
Winter Haven, Dimmit. 112
*WINTERS, Runnels, 178
   (2,905) 2,944
Wire, Trinity
Wise, Liberty
Wise, Van Zandt 29
Wise, Webb
Wison Station, Jack
Witcher, Milam
Witco, Reagan
Witting[Wittinghouse], Lavaca. 90
WIXON VALLEY, Brazos (229) . . . 244
Wizard Wells, Jack 69
*Woden, Nacogdoches, 13 70
Wofford, DeWitt
Wokaty, Milam . . . .**NA**
Wolcott, Brown
Wolf Creek, Ochiltree
Wolf Creek, Tyler
*WOLFE CITY, Hunt, 101
   (1,505) 1,600
Wolfe's, Bee
*WOLFFORTH, Lubbock, 177
   (1,941) 2,492
Wolf Hollow, Leon
Wolfpen, Hopkins
Wolf Point, Calhoun
Wolf Point, Jefferson
Wolf's Crossing, Burnet
Wolf's Mill, Hunt
Womack, Bosque 25
Womack, Colorado

Womble, Collin
Wonderland Forest, San Jacinto . .40
Wonders, Nacogdoches
Wood, Robertson
Woodal Farm, Milam . . . . **NA**
Woodall, Harrison
Woodbine, Cooke. 250
Woodborough, Grayson
WOODBRANCH, Montgomery
   (1,312) 1,750
Woodbury, Grayson
Woodbury, Hill 40
Wood City, Bastrop
WOODCREEK, Hays (889) 1,305
Wood Creek, Montgomery . . . . . . **NA**
Wooded Hills, Johnson 310
Woodhaven, Montgomery . . . .**NA**
Wood Hi, Victoria 35
Wood Hollow, Montgomery . . . . . . **NA**
Woodlake, Brazos . . . . **NA**
Woodlake, Grayson
*Woodlake, Trinity, 4 98
Woodland, Bell . . . . **NA**
Woodland, Brazoria
Woodland, Hopkins
Woodland, Limestone
Woodland, Red River. 128
Woodland, Robertson
Woodland Park, Nueces
*Woodlawn, Harrison, 10 370
Woodlawn, Jasper
Woodlawn, Montgomery . . . . **NA**
WOODLOCH, Montgomery
   (291) .329
Woodmyer, Newton
Wood Port, Jackson
Woodport, Victoria
Woodridge, Orange 1,000
Woodridge Park, Bexar . . . . **NA**
Woodrow, Fort Bend
Woodrow, Hardin
Woodrow, Lubbock 85
Woodruff, Jefferson
Woods, Navarro
Woods, Panola. 65
*WOODSBORO, Refugio, 86
   (1,731) 1,848
Wood's Creek, Polk
*WOODSON, Throckmorton,
   27 (262) 205
Wood's Prairie, Fayette
Wood Springs, Smith. 200
Woodstock, Bowie
Woodstock, Parker
Woodswitch, Grimes
Woodswitch, Montague
Wood Valley, Limestone
Woodville, Cherokee 20
Woodville, Parker
§*WOODVILLE, Tyler, 363
   (2,636) 4,033
Woodward, Kinney
Woodward, La Salle 10
WOODWAY, McLennan
   (8,695) 9,471
Woody, Loving
Wooland, Tom Green
Woosley, Rains. 47
Wooster, Harris
Wootan [Wooten] Wells, Robertson
Wooten's, Rusk
Wooters, Houston
Worbaino, Orange
Word, Shelby
Worley, Parker
Worleys, Baylor
Worsham, Reeves
Worsham [Springs], Wilbarger

*WORTHAM, Freestone, 56
  (1,020)......................953
Worthing, Lavaca...............55
Worthy, Uvalde
Wragg's Hill, Rusk
Wren, Washington
Wright, Hale
Wright, Swisher
Wright City, Smith.............172
Wright's, Jasper
Wright's Bend, Colorado
*Wrightsboro, Gonzales, 1 76
Wrightsville, Lamar
Wrightsville, Red River
Wurst, Comal
Wursten, Fayette
Wyatt [Switch], Ellis
Wyattsville, Williamson
‡ Wyldwood, Bastrop (1,764) .. 2,338
*WYLIE, Collin-Rockwall-Dallas,
  684 (8,716) 11,760
Wylie, Franklin
Wylie, Taylor
Wylieville, Erath
Wylma, Shelby
Wyly, Gaines
Wynema, Foard
Wynne, Castro
Wynne, Swisher
Wynne, Van Zandt 175
Wynton, Hunt
Wyser[']s Bluff, Walker

X
X-ray, Erath

Y
Yager, Blanco
Yakima, Grayson
Yakimo, Collin
Yale, Franklin
Yale Seminary, Henderson
Yam, Walker
Yampareka, Foard
*Yancey, Medina, 14...........202
Yancey, Panola
Yancy, Hunt
Yancy, Smith
Yandell, Tom Green
*YANTIS [Mill], Wood, 108 (210)...307
Yantis' Store, Brown
Yarboro, Grimes
Yarbroville, Limestone

Yard, Anderson 18
Yarrellton [Yaralton], Milam.......35
Yaterville, Hill
Yates, Hill
Yates [Crossing], Kimble
Yates Prairie, Delta
Yegua, Lee
Yegua, Lee
Yellow Bank, Lavaca
Yellow House, Lamb
Yellow House Cañon, Crosby
Yellow Mound, Eastland
Yellowpine, Sabine 74
Yell, Hays
Yell Settlement, Hays
Yero, Walker
Yescas, Cameron
Yesner, Hopkins
Yewpon, Bastrop
*YOAKUM, Lavaca-DeWitt, 359
  (5,611) 6,364
Yoca, Gaines
York, Wharton
York Creek [Valley], Guadalupe
*YORKTOWN, DeWitt, 175
  (2,207) 2,328
Youens, Montgomery
Yougeen, Bee
Young, Freestone 27
Younger, Navarro
Youngsboro, Smith
Youngsport, Bell 40
Youngs Settlement , Bastrop
Young's Store, Fayette
Younkin, Webb
Yowell, Delta 15
Yowell, Hunt...................NA
Ysleta del Sur Pueblo, El Paso .. 292
Yturria, Willacy
Yucca, Uvalde
Yuma, Brazos
Yuno, Angelina

Z
Zabcikville, Bell...............38
Zack, Brazos
Zana, San Augustine
Zandt, Kaufman
Zanzenburg, Kerr
Zapalaca, Fayette
‡§*Zapata, Zapata, 267
  (7,119).................7,797

Zapp['s Store], Fayette
Zaragosa, Starr
Zareda, Sterling
Zavala, Smith
*ZAVALLA, Angelina, 65 (701)....864
Zavalla, Jasper
Zavalla, Zavala
Zedlar's Mills [Zedler's Mills], Gonzales
Zeevee, Hill
Zeirath, Jasper
Zelda, Leon
Zella, McMullen
Zelma, Stephens
Zelo, Jones
Zenith, Swisher
Zeno, Smith
*Zephyr, Brown, 22.............198
Zig Zag, Medina
Zim, Montague
Zimerman, Pecos
Zimmerscheidt, Colorado........50
Zink's Settlement, Kendall
Zinnia, Montague
Zint, Gonzales
Zion, Denton
Zion[sville], Washington
Zion Grove, Rusk..............NA
Zion Hill, Guadalupe 30
Zion Hill, Jasper...............NA
Zipp City, Dallas
Zipperlandville, Falls...........22
Zippville, Guadalupe...........110
Zita, Randall
Zither, Montgomery
Zoar, Gonzales
Zobel's, DeWitt
Zorn, Guadalupe 60
Zourette, Brown
Zourette, Comanche
Zuber, Panola
Zuehl, Guadalupe.............150
Zulch, Madison
Zulime, Presidio
Zulu, Hansford
Zummo, Jefferson
Zuniga, Nolan
Zunkerville, Karnes 15
Zury, Cottle
Zybach, Hemphill
Zybach, Wheeler

Sources for town names in italics

Sources used by the Texas Almanac in compiling these two lists of early Texas communities and/or previous names of existing towns and cities:

— *Texas Post Offices by County*, John J. Germann and Myron R. Janzen, 1986, unpublished.

— *The New Handbook of Texas*, six volumes, Austin, The Texas State Historical Association, 1996.

— *Geographic Names Information System*, U.S. Geological Survey.

— Texas Department of Transportation.

— Local officials who were asked periodically to provide information on the existence and population of smaller, unincorporated towns and communities.

In presenting the names, variation in spelling or slight variation in names follow in brackets [] the current town names.

Not all names associated with one place are included in each reference in the list by counties, but are included with the present name or the last known name of the place.

Some places no longer exist as towns because they have been taken in or annexed by cities. However, they are recognized now as areas or neighborhoods of the larger city.

It is not always clear that one community evolved into another. In some cases there may have been years, even decades, in which no town existed in a particular place and a new town was established later at that location.

In some cases, a town name is listed twice in one county because it is believed these were different communities existing at different times or at different locations.

Towns and cities recognized as currently existing are in roman type. — RP

Town Names: Past and Present

Listed by counties are the towns of Texas, old and new.

Existing towns are in roman type. Incorporated cities are in capital letters.

Defunct places/earlier names are in italic type.

In parenthesis or brackets are earlier or later names or variations associated with that location. Due to space limitations, not all names associated with one place are listed in each reference but are included with the present name or the last known name of the place.

For example, **Beaver Valley** in **Anderson County** was a name associated with the present location of **Montalba**. The Montalba entry includes a list of all names associated with that location.

Anderson Co.
Alderbranch *[Alder Branch]*
Almedes *(Salmon)*
Anglin's
Antiquity
Ayers *(Frankston)*
Barton
Beaver
Beaver Valley (Montalba)
Bethel *(Gee's Store)*
Blackfoot *(Gore)*
Black Rock (Montalba)
Bois d'Arc
Bradford *(Hawks Store)*
Brit *(Dott)*
Broom City
Brownsville *(Ioni)*
Broyles Chapel
Brushy Creek *(Cely's Store, Hendersonville)*
Bush (Denson Springs)
Byron *[Switch]* (Salmon)
Cantrell
Carroll Springs
Cayuga
Cedar Creek
Cely's Store (Brushy Creek)
Comanche Crossing *(Magnolia)*
Cooks Store
County Line *(Strong)*
Cronin
Cross Roads *(Slocum)*
Crystal Lake
Deanwright
Denmark
Denson Springs *(Bush)*
Dott *(Brit)*
Dowson Springs (Massey Lake)
ELKHART
Elkheart
Elmtown *(Elmwood)*
Elmwood (Elmtown)
Elrod *(Mound Prairie)*
Fitzgerald
Fort Houston
Fosterville
Frankfort *(Frankston)*
Franklinville (Massey Lake)
FRANKSTON *(Ayers, Frankfort)*
Gee's Store *(Bethel)*
Goodsonville *(Saunders)*
Gore *(Blackfoot)*
Hanks
Hardman's
Hassell
Hawks Store *(Bradford)*
Hendersonville (Brushy Creek)
Herring
Ioni *(Brownsville)*
Jarvis
Kickapoo
Kossuth
Lewis
Long Lake *(Monington)*
Magnolia *(Comanche Crossing)*
Manson
Marietta
Marlow *(Still's Creek)*
Marlow's Mill
Massey Lake *(Dowson Springs, Franklinville)*
Mitto *(Still's Creek)*
Mizpah
Monington (Long Lake)
Montalba *(Beaver Valley, Black Rock, Pace's Chapel)*
Mound City, Anderson-Houston
Mound Prairie *(Elrod, Plenitude)*
Myrtle Springs
Neches *[Nechesville]*
Pace's Chapel (Montalba)
PALESTINE
Parker's Bluff *(Parkersville)*
Parkersville *(Parker's Bluff)*
Pert
Plenitude *(Mound Prairie)*
Prairie Point (Tucker)
Prewitt's Tan Yard
Price
Quail Valley
Redtown
Roadville
Salmon *(Almedes, Byron)*
Sand Spring
Saunders *(Goodsonville)*
Scroungeout
Slocum *(Cross Roads)*
Springfield
Steelboro
Still's Creek *(Marlow)*
Still's Creek *(Mitto)*
Strong *(County Line)*
Tennessee Colony
Todd City
Tucker *[Station]* *(Prairie Point)*
Vercal
Wells Creek
Wild Cat Bluff
Yard

Andrews Co.
ANDREWS

Bernice (Shafter Lake)
China Pond *(Hollebeke)*
Dollarhide
Florey *(Smackover)*
Frankel City *(Fullerton)*
Fullerton *(Frankel City)*
Hollebeke *(China Pond)*
Ida *(Logsdon)*
Logsdon *(Ida)*
McKinney Acres
Shafter Lake *(Bernice)*
Smackover *(Florey)*

Angelina Co.
Acol
Albert *(Lay)*
Alcedo *(Gilbert)*
Alco
Allen's Gin *(Allentown)*
Allentown *(Allen's Gin, Modisett)*
Alredge *(Durant)*
Angelina *(Cottage)*
Angelina *(Durst, Michelle)*
Angelina *(Homer)*
Ard
Baber
Baker
Bald Hill
Barge *(Yuno)*
Beulah *(Lay)*
Biloxi *(Hamlet)*
Blackburn
Blix
Bodan *(Pollok)*
Bonner's Mills
Bonnersville *(Clawson)*
Bradley
Breaker *(Ora)*
Buck Creek
BURKE *(Rhodes)*
Burris' Prairie
Camp Nancy *(Nancy)*
Canby *(Durant)*
Central
Chambers *(Jake)*
Chancey
Cheeseland *(Cheesland)*
Cheesland *(Cheeseland)*
Clawson *(Bonnersville)*
Cochranville *(Ora)*
Cottage *(Angelina)*
Dana *(Eudora)*
Davisville
Devillia *(Hamlet)*
DIBOLL
Dolan
Donovan
Dunagan
Dunkin *(Enal, Nancy, Win-*
dom)
Durant *(Alredge, Canby, Odum's Town)*
Durst *(Angelina, Michelle)*
Elysium
Emporia
Enal *(Dunkin, Windom)*
Eudora *(Dana)*
Ewing
Fairview
Farrell
Flournoy *(Shawnee Prairie)*
Fort Stanley Creek
Fort Teran *(Fort Turan)*
Fort Turan *(Fort Teran)*
Fuller Springs
Gilbert *(Alcedo)*
Granville
Hamlet[t] *(Biloxi, Devillia)*
Herrington *(Sumpter)*
Herty
Holly Acres
Homer *(Angelina)*
HUDSON
HUNTINGTON
Ivy
Jake *(Chambers)*
Jonesville
Keltys
Koury
Krub
Kurth
Lay *(Albert, Beulah, Renfro Prairie)*
LUFKIN
Manning
Manton
Marion *(McNeill's Landing, Moses Bluff)*
Marion Ferry Park
Martin
McNeill's Landing *(Marion)*
McNeil Switch *(Platt)*
Michelle *(Angelina)*
Modisett *(Allen's Gin, Allentown)*
Moffett
Monterey
Moses Bluff *(Marion)*
Mott *(New Hope)*
Nacalina
Nancy *(Camp Nancy, Dunkin)*
New Hope *(Mott)*
Odell
Odum's Town *(Durant)*
Ora *(Breaker, Cochranville)*

Ozias (Retrieve)
Peavey
Platt (McNeil Switch)
Pleasure Point
Pollok (Bodan)
Popher
Prestidge
Prosser
Providence
Raylake
Red (Redtown)
Redland
Redtown (Red)
Renfro Prairie (Lay)
Retrieve (Ozias, Shawnee)
Rhodes (Burke)
River Crest Estates
Rocky Hill
Rutland
Shawnee (Retrieve)
Shawnee Creek (Yuno)
Shawnee Prairie (Flourney)
Sulphur Springs (Yuno)
Sumptner (Herrington)
Wilmoth
Windom (Dunkin, Enal)
Yuno (Barge, Sulphur Springs)
ZAVALLA [Zavalla Prairie]

Aransas Co.
Aransas (Live Oak Point)
Aransas (Saint Joseph's, Sport)
Aransas City (Fulton)
ARANSAS PASS [Aransas Harbor]
Aransas Pass (Rockport)
Aransas Pass Light House
Carlos City
Copano Village
Dubois
Estes
Falkner (Saint Charles)
FULTON (Aransas City)
Holiday Beach
Key Allegro
Kosmos
Lamar (Look Out Point)
Live Oak Point (Aransas)
Live Oak Point (Rockport)
Look Out Point (Lamar)
Palm Harbor
ROCKPORT (Aransas Pass, Live Oak Point)
Saint Charles (Falkner)
Saint Joseph's (Aransas, Sport)
Sparks Colony
Sport (Aransas, Saint Joseph's)

Archer Co.
Anarene
ARCHER CITY [Archer]
Atwood (Briar, Rambo)
Baxter (Fleerton)
Black Flat
Bowman
Briar (Atwood, Rambo)
Cimarron Springs
Cobb

Dads Corner
Dundee
Fleerton (Baxter)
Four Corners
Geraldine
Gose City (Texhoma City)
Halfway House (Souleman)
Hartex
Hausler City
HOLLIDAY
Howard
Huff
Hutton (McCormick)
LAKESIDE CITY
Lazarus (Mankins)
Luke Wilson
Mangold (Mankins)
Mankins (Lazarus, Mangold)
McCormick (Hutton)
MEGARGEL
Needmore Store (Westfork)
North Olney
North Star
Rambo (Atwood, Briar)
Riman
SCOTLAND
Souleman (Halfway House)
Texhoma City (Gose City)
Westfork (Needmore Store)
WINDTHORST

Armstrong Co.
Bissell (Broadway, Mulberry Flats)
Broadway (Bissell)
CLAUDE
Cornelia (Virginia)
Fairview
Goodnight
Grand Vista (Paloduro)
Hughlett (Llano)
J A Ranch (Paloduro)
Kasota
Lake View (Ottilie)
Llano (Hughlett)
Malden
Mulberry Flats (Bissell)
Ottilie (Lake View)
Paloduro (Grand Vista, J A Ranch)
Virginia (Cornelia)
Washburn
Wayside

Atascosa Co.
Agua Negra (Ditto)
Amphion (Navarro)
Anchorage
Arp
Belle Branch
Benton
Black Hill
Bonito (Pleasanton)
Campbellton
CHARLOTTE
CHRISTINE (New Artesia)
Coughran [Ranch]
Crouch (Crown)
Crown (Crouch)

Davis[Davistown]
Ditto (Agua Negra)
Dobrowolski
Dollarhide
Durban (Siesta)
Ernst
Espey
Fashing (Hickok, Hindenburg)
Gallinas (Leming)
Gates Valley
Haiduk
Harts Ranch (Tordilla)
Hickok (Fashing)
Hindenburg (Fashing)
Hindes
Hollywood (Peggy)
Imogene (New Pleasanton)
Iuka (Lucy)
JOURDANTON
Kyote (Mamre)
Laguna
Lammburg
La Parita
Leming (Gallinas, Prospect)
Lipan (Tordilla)
Loire (Lucas)
Lucas (Loire)
Lucas City (Verdi)
Lucy (Iuka)
Luke
LYTLE [Station]
Mamre (Kyote)
McCoy
Mottomosa
Mount Scopus (Tobey)
Navarro (Amphion)
New Artesia (Christine)
New Pleasanton (Imogene)
North Pleasanton
Peggy (Hollywood)
PLEASANTON (Bonito)
POTEET
Prospect (Leming)
Rohde
Rossville
Siesta (Durban)
Servsand
Somerset
Sue (Tank Hollow)
Tank Hollow (Sue)
Tarbutton
Tobey (Mount Scopus)
Tordia (Tordilla)
Tordilla (Harts Ranch, Lipan, Tordia)
Tordilla Mound
Verdi (Lucas City)

Austin Co.
Allen's Creek
Beard
BELLVILLE
Bleiblerville
Bostick's Crossing (Swearington's)
Bovine Bend
Broomtown
Buckhorn
Burleigh (Timme's Store)
Burrough (EllPleasant)

Cat Spring
Centre Hill
Cleveland
Cochran
Cook's Ferry
County Line
Dante
Duff's Settlement (New Ulm)
Ellis
EllPleasant (Burrough)
El Pleasant
Frydek
Gulf
Hartsville
Hixon Switch
INDUSTRY (Sieper's)
Kenney [Kenneyville] (Thompson)
Ladig
McDowell
Millheim
Millheim Station (Peters)
Nelsonville
New Bremen
New Ulm (Duff's Settlement)
New Wehdem (Wehdem)
Orange Hill
Peters (Millheim Station)
Piney
Post Oak Point
Punchard's
Raccoon Bend
Rexville
Roach [Prairie]
Roeder's Mill (Shelby)
Rockhouse (Schoenau)
SAN FELIPE [de Austin]
Schindler
Schoenau (Rockhouse)
Schoenau
SEALY
Sempronius
Shelby (Roeder's Mill)
Sieper's (Industry)
Swearingen's
Swearingen's (Bostick's Crossing)
Thompson (Kenney)
Timme's Store (Burleigh)
Travis
WALLIS [Wallis Station]
Wehdem (New Wehdem)
Welcome
Wesley

Bailey Co.
Baileyboro
Bula (Newsome)
Caldren (Hurley)
Circleback [Circle Back]
Enochs
Fairview
Goodland
Hurley (Caldren)
Janes
Maple [Maple Wilson]
Montezuma (Virginia City)
MULESHOE
Needmore
Newsome (Bula)
Progress
Stegall

Virginia City (Montezuma)

Bandera Co.
BANDERA
Bandera Falls
Bluewater
Bluff (Wallace)
Cana (Nalyon)
Crockett (Tuff)
Eagle Rock (Nalyon)
Elmo (Powers)
Fagan (Honey Creek)
Hans' Settlement (Modera)
Hondo Cañon (Tarpley)
Honey Creek (Fagan)
Lakehills
Lima
Medina [Medina City]
Modera (Hans' Settlement)
Nalyon (Cana, Eagle Rock, Vanderpool)
Pipe Creek
Polly (Privilege)
Powers [Ranch] (Elmo)
Privilege (Polly)
Sharon
Sorgo
Tarpley (Hondo Cañon)
Tuff (Crockett)
Vanderpool
Vanderpool (Nalyon)
Wallace (Bluff)

Bastrop Co.
Alum Creek (Cope's Store)
Bart [Barton]
Barton's Creek
BASTROP *(Mina)*
Bateman [Bateman Spur], *(Cross Roads)*
Belladonna
Betts (Henry)
Bishop Spur (Glenbelto)
Boyle
Bravo
Brushy Creek (String Prairie)
Burleson['s]
Butler
Caldwell's Store (Kenton)
Calvin
Camp Swift
Cardiff
Carroll
Cedar Creek
Circle D-KC Estates
Coldwater (Otis, Winfield)
Cold Water (Eppler)
Colorado
Como (Upton)
Cope's Store (Alum Creek)
Coxville [Cox's Store]
Cross Roads (Bateman)
Cunninghams
Dixon Prairie
Dunstan (Glenham)
Eagle Branch (Rosanky)
Eblin's
ELGIN *(Glasscock, Hogeye)*
Elysium (Garfield)
Eppler (Cold Water)
Flower Hill
Gage's (Mount Pleasant)

Garfield (Elysium, *Haynie's Chapel*)
Givensville
Glass (Holder's Gin)
Glasscock (Elgin)
Glenbelto (Bishop Spur)
Glenham (Dunstan)
Goodman (Miller)
Gotier's (Gotcher's, *Goucher's*)
Gotcher's (Gotier's)
Goucher's (Gotier's)
Grand Prairie (Young's *Settlement*)
Grassyville
Hallmark Prairie (Jeddo)
Haynie's Chapel (Garfield)
Hawkeye
Henry (Betts)
High Grove
Highsmith's (Rosanky)
Hill
Hillger (Sand)
Hills Prairie (Jenkins Prairie, McDonald's Store)
Hog Eye (Elgin)
Hog Eye (Youngs *Settlement*)
Holder's Gin (Glass)
Jeddo (Hallmark Prairie)
Jenkins Prairie (Hills *Prairie*)
Jordan
Kenton (Caldwell's Store)
Kovar (Stasny)
Lasher
Lehman
Live Oaks (Walnut Creek)
McDade (Tie City)
McDonald's Store (Hills Prairie)
McDuff (Wood City)
Miller (Goodman)
Mina (Bastrop)
Mount Pleasant (Gage's)
Mowatt
Napier (Swain)
Old Red Rock
Otis (Coldwater, Winfield)
Paige [Paige Station]
Perryville (Young's *Settlement*)
Phelan
Pleasant Grove
Pontotoc (Sand Fly)
Potter's Shop
Red Rock (Wilna)
Ridgeway
Rockne
Rockne (String Prairie)
Rogersville (Utley)
Rosanky [Rosankie] *(Eagle Branch, Highsmith's, Snake Prairie)*
Sacred Heart
Sand (Hillger)
Sand Fly (Pontotoc)
Sandy
Sayersville [Sayers]
Saw Mill (Yewpon)
Scallorn
Shiloh
SMITHVILLE

Snake Prairie (Rosanky)
Stacks
Stasny (Kovar)
String Prairie *(Brushy Creek, Rockne)*
Swain (Napier)
Swiftex
Tie City (McDade)
Togo
Trigg
Type
Upton (Como)
Utley (*Rogersville, Wilbarger*)
Walnut Creek (Live Oaks)
Watterson (Live Oaks)
Wilbarger (Utley)
Willman
Wilna (Red Rock)
Wood City (McDuff)
Winfield (Coldwater, Otis)
Wyldwood
Yewpon (Saw Mill)
Young''s Settlement (Grand Prairie, Hogeye, Perryville)

Baylor Co.
Arkansas Colony
Bellah
Bomarton
Britamer
Cara Blanca
Coffee Creek (Moon)
Deep Creek (Saint Bernard)
England
Etta
Fancher
Fulda
Grace (Pueblo)
Hajek
Mabelle
Marys Creek
Millett's [Miillett's Ranch]
Milo (Seaborn)
Moon (Coffee Creek)
Moonshine Colony
Oregon City (Seymour)
Pueblo (Grace)
Red Springs
Rendham
Round Timber
Saint Bernard (Deep Creek)
Seaborn (Milo)
SEYMOUR *(Oregon City)*
Seymour Colony
Shady
Swindells
Westover
Wichita Colony
Worleys

Bee Co.
Aransas (Skidmore)
BEEVILLE *(Maryville)*
Beeville (Medio Hill)
Blanconia *(Dark Corners, Kymo, Lower Medio, Pull Tight)*
Burnell Switch
Butler's (Monteola)
Cadiz *(Lapara, Lebanon)*

Caesar (Wolfe's)
Candish
Candlish (Cummingsville, Medio Hill, Robinson's, Upper Medio)
Clareville *(Lomita)*
Colbay Settlement (Normanna)
Cowan
Cravenville (Papalote)
Cummingsville (Candlish)
Darby
Dark Corners (Blanconia)
Dry Medio (Pettus)
Hart's (Papalote)
Hartville Settlement (Papalote)
Humline
Kymo (Blanconia)
Lapara (Cadiz)
Lattington (Skidmore)
Lebanon (Cadiz)
Lomita (Clareville)
Lower Medio (Blanconia)
Maryville (Beeville)
Medio Hill (Beeville)
Medio Hill (Candlish)
Mennonite Colony (Normanna)
Mineral [Mineral City]
Monteola (Butler's)
Normanna *(Colbay Settlement, Mennonite Colony, Norwegian Colony, Walton)*
Norwegian Colony (Normanna)
Oaks
Olmos
Orangedale
Papalote [Papalota, Popolote] *(Cravenville, Hart's, Hartville Settlement, Steenville)*
Pawnee
Pettus [Pettus City] *(Dry Medio)*
Poesta
Pull Tight (Blanconia)
Quincy
Quanto
River Side (Skidmore)
Robinson's (Candlish)
Roundtree
San Domingo
Skidmore [Skidmore Station] *(Aransas, Lattington, River Side)*
Steenville (Papalote)
Tuleta
Tulsa (Tulsita)
Tulsita (Tulsa)
Tynan
Upper Medio (Candlish)
Walton (Normanna)
Wolfe's (Caesar)
Yougeen

Bell Co.
Academy (Little River-Academy)
Agathos (Herring)
Aiken
Air Hall

Airville
Althea (Fowler's Gin)
Armstrong
Ayres Retreat
Bacon
BARTLETT
Bean Hill
Belfalls
BELTON (Nolansville)
Berea (Perryview)
Berger
Birdsdale
Bland (Kirkwood, Pokerville)
Bluff (Parkdale, Volo)
Bottom
Brookhaven
Buckhorn
Burgess (Reeds Lake)
Camp Creek (Cyclone)
Casey (Meeks)
Cedar Knob (Tadella)
Cedar Valley
Clark (Hugo)
Content
Coppage
Charter Oak
Cronje (Agathos, Herring)
Crossville
Cyclone (Camp Creek)
Dice
Ding Dong
Dog Ridge
Donahoe
Double Header
Dresser
Durie (Kolls)
Dyess Grove
Echo (Miller)
Edgeworth
Elm Creek (Troy)
Ely (Okay)
Farm Town (Oenaville)
Finks
Finland
Forest Hill
Fort Griffin
Fort Hood
Fowler's Gin (Althea)
Gerron
Gindale (Grindale)
Gould
Grindale (Gindale)
Grover (Vilas)
HARKER HEIGHTS
Harrisville
Heidenheimer
Herring (Agathos, Cronje)
Hobbs Spur
HOLLAND
Howard
Hugo (Clark)
Joe Lee
Jones' Gin (Oscar)
Kelsoville
KILLEEN (Palo Alto)
Kirkwood (Bland, Pokerville)
Knobs (Rogers)
Kolls (Durie)
Krauseland
Lee (Ocker)
Leedale

LITTLE RIVER-ACADEMY
Live Oak (Valley Pass)
Lone Star
Lost Prairie (Seaton)
Marekville
Maxdale
McMillin
Meadow Grove
Medo (Myers' Mill)
Meeks (Casey)
Midway
Miller [Miller Station] (Echo)
Moffat
Moody
MORGAN'S POINT RESORT
Mountain Home
Myers' Mill (Medo)
New Colony
Nichols
Nolansville (Belton, Walnut Springs)
Noland Valley (Nolanville)
NOLANVILLE (Noland Valley, Warren)
Ocker['s Store] (Lee)
Oenaville (Farm Town)
Okay (Ely)
Old Aiken
Old Howard
Ornaville
Oscar (Jones' Gin)
Owl Creek
Palo Alto (Killeen)
Parkdale (Bluff, Volo)
Pendleton [Station, Pendletonville]
Perryview (Berea)
Pokerville (Bland, Kirkwood)
Prairie Dell
Ratibor
Red Ranger
Reeds Lake (Burgess)
Rodgers (Rogers)
ROGERS [Rogers Station] (Knobs, Rodgers)
Salado
Sampson
Schull
Seaton (Lost Prairie)
Sherwood Shores
Silver City
Simmonsville
Smith
Sommers Mill
South Nolan
South Shore
Sparks
Sparta
Stampede
String
Stringtown
Summers
Summers' Mills
Tadella (Cedar Knob)
TEMPLE
Tennessee Valley (Thomasville)
Thomasville [Thomas Hill] (Tennessee Valley)
Trimmier

TROY (Elm Creek)
Union Grove
Valley Pass (Live Oak)
Vilas (Grover)
Villas
Volo (Bluff, Parkdale)
Walnut Springs (Belton, Nolansville)
Warren (Noland Valley, Nolanville)
White Hall
Wilkinson's [Valley]
Willow Springs
Woodland
Youngsport
Zabcikville

Bexar Co.
Adams Hill
Adkins
Airport City
ALAMO HEIGHTS
Atascosa (Strumberg)
BALCONES HEIGHTS
Beckman
Benz
Bergs
Berg's Mill
Bexar (Center Point)
Béxar (San Antonio)
Boldtville
Borrego
Briggs (Seglar)
Brooks Air Force Base
Bulverde (Piper's Settlement)
Carmel
Carpenter
Carver Park
Cassin, Bexar
CASTLE HILLS
Center Point (Bexar)
CHINA GROVE
Cibolo (Selma)
CONVERSE
Cottage Hill (St. Hedwig)
Cross Mountain
Culebra
Dominion
Earle
ELMENDORF
Elms (Silesia)
Evergreen (Oakley)
FAIR OAKS RANCH
Fort Sam Houston (Warwick)
Gardendale
Garza's
Garza's Crossing (Medinaville)
Graytown
Greenway
GREY FOREST
Hellemans
HELOTES
HILL COUNTRY VILLAGE
Hillsborough (Selma)
HOLLYWOOD PARK
Idlewild (Ivanhoe)
Ivanhoe (Idlewild)
Kelly Air Force Base
Kinley's
KIRBY
Lackland Air Force Base

Landa (Luxello)
Leal
Lecomteville (Losoya)
Leon Springs
LEON VALLEY
LIVE OAK
Locke Hill
Lone Oak
Lookout (Salado Creek)
Losoya (Lecomteville)
Lucas Spring (San Lucas Springs)
Luxello (Landa)
Mabel (Von Ormy)
Macdona
Mangus Corne
Manning (Oak Island)
Mann's Crossing (Von Ormy)
Martinez (St. Hedwig)
Medina Base
Medina Station (Von Ormy)
Medinaville (Garza's Crossing)
Midway
Monte Robles Park
Nelsonberg (Oscar)
North San Antonio Hills
Oak Creek
Oak Island (Manning)
Oakley (Evergreen)
Oak Moss
Oak Village
OLMOS PARK
Oscar (Nelsonberg)
Palm Park
Palo Alto Park
Parita
Paul's (Silesia)
Piper's Settlement (Bulverde)
Pleasant Oaks
Quintana (Von Ormy)
Randolph Air Force Base
Royal View
ST. HEDWIG (Cottage Hill, Martinez)
St. John's Mission (San Juan)
Salado Creek (Lookout)
SAN ANTONIO (Béxar, San Fernando de Béxar)
San Fernando de Béxar (San Antonio)
San Geronimo
San Jose (Terrell Wells)
San Juan (St. John's Mission)
San Lucas Springs (Lucas Spring)
Saunders (Sayers)
Sayers (Saunders)
Scenic Oaks
Seglar (Briggs)
SELMA (Cibolo, Hillsborough)
Senior (Stone Gin)
Shavano [Valley]
SHAVANO PARK
Silesia (Elms, Paul's)
SOMERSET
South San Antonio (Southsan)

Southsan (South San
Antonio)
Southton
Specht Store
Stone Gin (Senior)
Strumberg (Atascosa)
Tenaha
Terrace
TERRELL HILLS
Terrell Wells (San Jose)
Thelma (Watsonville)
Timberwood
Twin Creek
UNIVERSAL CITY
Ultzville
Valley Hi
Valmont
Van Raub
Verde Mills
Von Ormy (Mabel, Mann's
Crossing, Medina
Station, Quintana)
Warwick (Fort Sam
Houston
Watsonville (Thelma)
Wetmore
Wildwood
WINDCREST
Woodridge Park

Blanco Co.
Bird Town (Round
Mountain)
BLANCO (New Pittsburg)
Blowout (Comanche
Spring)
Board House
Boon (New Center)
Camanche Springs
Comanche Spring
(Blowout)
Cypress Mill (Fuch's Mill)
Flugrath (Live Oak)
Freedmen's Colony
(Peyton)
Fuch's Mill (Cypress Mill)
Herwig (Yager)
Hye (Martinsburgh,
Rockey)
JOHNSON CITY
Krueger's Store (Twin
Sisters)
Live Oak (Flugrath)
Martinsburgh (Hye)
Middletown (Twin Sisters)
Mohair (Post Oak)
Mountain View
New Center (Boon)
New Pittsburg[h] (Blanco)
Payton (Peyton)
Peyton (Payton, Freed-
men's Colony)
Pleasant Valley
Poe
Post Oak (Mohair)
Rockey (Hye)
Rocky Creek
Roughrock
ROUND MOUNTAIN (Bird
Town)
Round Valley
Sandy
Tamaulipas
Tosca

Twin Sisters (Krueger's
Store, Middletown)
Tyner
Westbrook
Yager (Herwig)

Borden Co.
Belvey
Bob (Julia)
Champ (Julia)
Durham (Magnolia)
Gail (Gale, Hogg)
Gale (Gail)
Hogg (Gail)
Hood (Julia)
Jack (Julia)
Julia (Bob, Champ, Hood,
Jack)
Kingsmere
Magnolia (Durham)
Mesquite
Morris
Plains
Tredway

Bosque Co.
Bosque
Brazos Point (Day)
Carbody
Cave [Springs] (Dell)
Cayote (Evans Cross
Roads)
Cedar Shores
Chase
Clifftown (Clifton)
Clifstone
CLIFTON (Clifftown)
CRANFILLS GAP
Coon Creek
Cyrus (Smith[s] Bend)
Day (Brazos Point)
Delhi (Eulogy, Smithville)
Dell (Cave, Cave Springs)
Eulogy (Delhi, Smithville)
Evans Cross Roads
(Cayote)
Fairview (Merrivale)
Flag Pond
Footout (Rural)
Fowler (Steiner)
Greenock
Griffinsville
Help (Spring Creek,
Vashtie)
Hill Creek
Hog Creek
Howardsville (Live Oak,
Mosheim)
Indian Lodge
IREDELL
Kent
Kimball
Kopperl
Laguna Park
Lakeside Village
Lakewood Harbor
Live Oak (Howardsville,
Mosheim)
MERIDIAN
Merrivale (Fairview)
Midway
MORGAN (Steele's Creek)
Mornack (Womack)
Mosheim (Howardsville,

Live Oak)
Mustang
Neill's Creek (Searsville)
Norman Hill
Norse (Norse Grove,
Norway)
Norse Grove (Norse)
Norway (Norse)
Norway Hills [Norway Mills]
Pendell
Pikesville
Poesville
Powell Dale
Roswell (Smith[s] Bend)
Rural (Footout)
Russell's Gap
Searsville (Neill's Creek)
Smith[s] Bend (Cyrus,
Roswell)
Smithville (Delhi, Eulogy)
Spring Creek (Help,
Vashtie)
Steele's Creek (Morgan)
Steiner (Fowler)
Sun
VALLEY MILLS
Vashtie (Help, Spring
Creek)
Vaughan [Vaughan's
Store]
WALNUT SPRINGS
[Walnut]
Womack (Mornack)

Bowie Co.
Almont (Shaw's Farm)
Alpha (Oak Grove)
Anglo American
Annie
Apperson's (Epperson's
Ferry)
Arkadelphia
Ball Hill (College Hill)
Bassett
Beaver Dams
Booker (Etta, Ruth)
Boston
Bottle Springs (Siloam)
Brownstown (Darden)
Buchanan
Bush
Bunker Hill (Corley)
Burns
Carbondale
Chancey
College Hill (Ball Hill)
Corley (Bunker Hill)
Cowen (Spring Hill)
Dalby Springs
Daniels Chapel
Darden (Brownstown, Fin-
lay)
Defense
DE KALB
Draper
Eli
Epperson's Ferry
(Apperson's)
Etta (Booker, Ruth)
Eylau (Fleming Station)
Finlay (Darden)
Fleming Station (Eylau)
Friendship Village
Garland

Hartman
Heilbrun
Hodgson
Holbrook
HOOKS
Hoot
Hubbard
Index
Ingersoll (Redwater)
Jetie
Jury
Kingsville [King's Store]
Knight (Pope)
Lane
Lane's (Louisville)
LEARY
Lenoxville
Liberty Hill
Louisville (Lane's)
Lynox
Macedonia
Maginnis (McGinnis,
Rogers Mill)
Malta
Marsh (Spring Hill)
MAUD
McCowen [Ferry]
McGinnis (Maginnis)
Mill Creek
Moores' [Mooresville]
Moores' Landing
Myrtle Springs
Myrtle Springs (Rochelle)
NASH (Park, Parker, T.C.
Junction)
Needmore (Ward Creek)
NEW BOSTON
New Era (Siloam)
North Texarkana
Oak Grove (Alpha, Rolyat)
Old Boston
Old Salem
Old Union
Owensburg
Park (Nash)
Parker (Nash)
Pinkham
Pleasant Grove
Poer
Pope (Knight)
Powell Grove
Red Bank
Red Cut Heights
RED LICK
Red Springs
REDWATER (Ingersoll)
Rochelle (Myrtle Springs)
Rogers Mill (Maginnis)
Rolyat (Oak Grove)
Rosborough (Wamba)
Ruth (Booker, Etta)
Shaw
Shaw['s Farm] (Almont)
Siloam (Bottle Springs,
New Era)
Simms
South Texarkana
Spring Hill (Cowen, Marsh)
Snyder (Whybark)
Sulphur [Station]
Tamar (Wamba)
T.C. Junction (Nash)
TEXARKANA

Trexler
Victory City
WAKE VILLAGE
Wamba *(Rosborough, Tamar)*
Ward Creek *(Needmore)*
Weaver's [Wever's]
Whaley
Whybark *(Snyder)*
Woodstock

Brazoria Co.
Adamston (Sweeny)
ALVIN
Amsterdam
Anchor *(Chenango Junction)*
ANGLETON
Ashland *(Manvel)*
BAILEY'S PRAIRIE
Ballowe *(Bennett's Bridge)*
Bar-X
Bastrop Beach
Bell's Landing *(East Columbia)*
Bennett's Bridge *(Ballowe)*
Bennett's Ferry
Bethelder *(Rawls)*
Bolivar
Bond *(El Bernardo)*
BONNEY *(Custer Station)*
BRAZORIA
Brazosport
BROOKSIDE VILLAGE
Brown's
Bryan Beach
Bryan Mound
Buffalo Camp
Buttermilk Station *(Rosharon)*
Cedar Brakes *(Danciger)*
Cedar Grove
Cedar Lake *(Dura, Duroc)*
Chenango
Chenango Junction *(Anchor)*
Chocolate Bayou *(Rowan[ville])*
Chance's Prairie *(Old Ocean)*
Churchill *[Churchill Bridge]*
Clemens
CLUTE
Columbia *(East Columbia)*
Columbia Lakes
Crosbyville *[Crosby's Landing] (Perry's Landing)*
Custer Station *(Bonney)*
Damon *[Damon City, Damon's Mound]*
DANBURY
Danciger *(Cedar Brakes)*
Demi-John Island
Dow
Dura *(Cedar Lake)*
Duroc *(Cedar Lake)*
East Columbia *(Bell's Landing, Columbia, Marion)*
Edmunds *(Retrieve, Snipe)*
El Bernardo *(Bond, Marmion, San Bernardo)*
English

Ernies Acres
Floral Park *(Liveoak)*
Four Corners
Four Corners
Freeport
FREEPORT
Gayle Estates
Gulf Park *(Jones Creek)*
Gulf Prairie *(Perry's Landing)*
Halls Bayou
Harborview
Hasima
Hastings
Hide Away
HILLCREST VILLAGE
Hinds' *[Hines]*
Hinkles Ferry
HOLIDAY LAKES
Holiday Shores
Hoskins *(Phair)*
Hoskins Junction
IOWA COLONY
JONES CREEK *(Gulf Park)*
Jordan *(Stratton)*
Kiber
Lake Alaska
LAKE JACKSON
Lakeside
Las Playas
Laytonia
Liveoak *(Floral Park)*
LIVERPOOL
Lochridge
Logan *(Adamston, Sweeny)*
Magnesium
MANVEL *(Ashland, Pomona)*
Marion *(East Columbia)*
Markbelt
Marmion *(El Bernardo)*
Masterson *(Rosharon)*
McBeth
McNeel
Mims
Oak Bend
Oakland
Oak Manor
Old Ocean *(Chance's Prairie)*
Orozimbo
Otey *(Ramsey)*
Oyster Creek
Oyster Creek *(Solitude)*
OYSTER CREEK
Parker's Point
PEARLAND
Peerless Spur
Perry Landing
Perry's Landing *(Crosbyville, Gulf Prairie)*
Phair *(Hoskins)*
Pomona *(Manvel)*
Port-Au-Prince
QUINTANA *[Quintanna] (Velasco)*
Ramsey *(Otey)*
Rawls *(Bethelder)*
Retrieve *(Edmunds, Snipe)*
Rhodes
RICHWOOD

Rivers End
Roeville
Rosharon *(Buttermilk Station, Masterson)*
Ross
Rowan[ville] (Chocolate Bayou)
Roweville
San Bernardo *(El Bernardo)*
Sandy Point
San Luis
Shady Oaks
Snipe *(Edmunds, Retrieve)*
Snug Harbor
Solitude *(Oyster Creek)*
Southdown
Stratton[burg] *(Jordan, Woodland)*
Stratton Ridge
Sulphur Docks
Superior
Surfside
SURFSIDE BEACH
Sugar Mill
SWEENY *(Adamston, Logan)*
Tulsy
Turtle Cove
Van Pelt
Velasco
Velasco (Quintana)
WEST COLUMBIA
Wickes Spur
Wild Peach, Brazoria
Woodland *(Stratton)*

Brazos Co.
Allenfarm *(Alligator, Ella)*
Alligator *(Allenfarm)*
Barron *(Harvey)*
Benchley
Bethel *(Harvey)*
Boonville *(Bryan)*
Brushy Creek
BRYAN *[Bryan City] (Boonville)*
Bryan Junction *(Stone City)*
Calla
Carter Lake
Cawthon
Caywood
COLLEGE STATION
Cottonwood
Curds Prairie *(Locust Grove)*
Dallam
Dinkins *(Dunlap)*
Dunlap *(Dinkins)*
Edge
Ella *(Allenfarm)*
Enright
Fairview
Forest Lake
Fountain
Greer's
Harvey *(Barron, Bethel)*
Herrington
Indpark
Irishtown *(Red Top)*
Jackson *(Tabor)*
Kings Highway
Koppe

Kosarek
Kurten *(Raymond)*
Lake Placid
Law
Little Georgia *(Reliance, Shealey)*
Locust Grove *(Curds Prairie)*
Macey
MILLICAN
Moore
Mooring *(Mudville, Steeles Station, Steeles Store)*
Mudville *(Mooring)*
Nelleva
Peach Creek
Ravenwood
Raymond *(Kurten)*
Red Top *(Irishtown)*
Reliance *(Little Georgia, Shealey)*
River Oaks
Rogers Plantation
Rosprim
Royder
Rye
Shealey *(Little Georgia, Reliance)*
Sims
Smetana *(Sramek)*
Spear
Sramek *(Smetana)*
Steel
Steeles Station *(Mooring)*
Steeles Store *(Mooring)*
Steep Hollow
Stone City *(Bryan Junction)*
Tabor *(Jackson)*
Terrels
Union
Valley Ridge
Varisco
Weddington
Wellborn *[Wellborn's Station]*
Wicker
WIXON VALLEY
Woodlake
Yuma
Zack

Brewster Co.
ALPINE *(Murphyville, Osborne)*
Altuda
Basin
Bigbend *(Big Bend National Park)*
Big Bend National Park *(Bigbend)*
Boquillas *(San Vicente)*
Boquillas Hot Springs *(Hot Springs)*
Castolon *(Santa Helena)*
Cathedral *(Marble Mountain)*
Chisos Basin
Chisos Mines *(Terlingua)*
Glenn Springs *(McKinney Springs)*
Glen Spring
Haymond *(McLeary)*
Hot Springs *(Boquillas Hot*

Wilkie
Wolf's Crossing

Caldwell Co.
Adalia
Albade (Lytton Springs)
Black Ankle *(Polk)*
Booton (Mendoza)
Brownsboro
Burditt Well
Carruth *(Clanton)*
Cibolo (Seawillow)
Clanton *(Carruth)*
Clark's Chapel *(Ledford)*
Clear Fork
Dale
Delhi *(Iron Mountain)*
Elandel
Elm Grove (Taylorsville)
Eva (Tilmon)
Fentress *(Jersey, Riverside)*
Holmes
Iron Mountain (Delhi)
Jersey (Fentress)
Joliet
Lamb's Shop *(Ophelia)*
Larremore
Live Oak (Uhland)
Ledford *(Clark's Chapel)*
LOCKHART *(Plum Creek)*
LULING *(Plum Creek)*
Lytton Springs *(Albade)*
MARTINDALE
Maxwell *(Nathen, New Martindale)*
McMahan (*Tinney Creek, Whizzerville)*
McNeil
Mendoza *(Booton)*
Micars
MUSTANG RIDGE
Nathen (Maxwell)
New Martindale (Maxwell)
NIEDERWALD
Ophelia *(Lamb's Shop)*
Plum Creek (Lockhart)
Plum Creek (Luling)
Polk *(Black Ankle)*
Prairie Lea
Putnam's Store (Tilmon)
Reedville
Rest *(St. Clair)*
Reynolds Spur
Riverside (Fentress)
Saint John Colony
Seawillow *(Cibolo)*
Soda Springs (Sour Spring)
Sour Spring *(Soda Springs)*
Sour Spring *(Sour Well)*
St. Clair *(Rest)*
Stairtown
Taylorsville *(Elm Grove)*
Tilmon *[Tilmon's Mill]* (Eva, Putnam's Store)
Tinney Creek (McMahan)
UHLAND *(Live Oak)*
Vicksburgh
Whizzerville (McMahan)

Calhoun Co.
Alamo Beach

Alligator Head (Port O'Connor)
Calhoun
Clarks
Cox Point
Dierlam (Seadrift)
Garthright
Green Lake
Hereford *(Wolf Point)*
Indianola *(Indian Point, Karlshaven, Powderhorn)*
Indian Point (Indianola)
Kamey *(McKamey)*
Karlshaven (Indianola)
La Salle
Lavaca (Port Lavaca)
Long Mott *(Upper Mott)*
Lower Mott (Seadrift)
Magnolia Beach
Marekville *(Sixmile)*
McKamey (Kamey)
North Seadrift
Olivia
POINT COMFORT
Port Alto
Portilla
Port Labaca (Port Lavaca)
PORT LAVACA *(Lavaca, Port Labaca)*
Port O'Connor *(Alligator Head)*
Powderhorn (Indianola)
Royal (Sixmile)
Saluria
Schicke Point
SEADRIFT *(Dierlam, Lower Mott)*
Sixmile *(Marekville, Royal)*
Upper Mott (Long Mott)
Valparaiso
Wolf Point (Hereford)

Callahan Co.
Admiral *(Buchen's Store, Buchenville)*
Alabama (Oplin)
Annadale
Atwell *(Flag Springs)*
BAIRD *(Vickery)*
Belle Plain[e] *(Callahan)*
Bremen (Putnam)
Buchen's Store (Admiral)
Buchenville (Admiral)
Burnam
Caddo Peak
Callahan *(Belle Plain[e])*
Callahan *(Deep Creek)*
Cat Claw (Putnam)
Chautaugua
Chautauqua *(Vigo)*
Cherry *(Rowden)*
CLYDE
Cottonwood *[Cottonwood Springs]*
CROSS PLAINS *(Lamson, Schleicher)*
Deep Creek *(Callahan)*
Denton *[Denton Community]*
Dressy
Dudley
Eagle Cove *(Prew's Place)*
East Caddo

Eula *(Pecan)*
Flag Springs (Atwell)
French *(Spring Gap)*
Gilead *(Rough Creek)*
Gill *(Rough Creek)*
Gilliland *(Toro)*
Gould City
Hartsville *(Knobview)*
Hill *(Toro)*
Jayell
Knobview (Hartsville)
Lamson (Cross Plains)
Land (Pueblo)
Oplin *(Alabama)*
Pecan (Eula)
Prew's Place *(Eagle Cove)*
Pueblo *(Land)*
PUTNAM *(Bremen, Cat Claw)*
Rough Creek *(Gilead, Gill)*
Rowden *(Cherry)*
Schleicher (Cross Plains)
Shaw's Ranch
Spring Gap *(French, Tomato)*
Tecumseh *(Windham)*
Tomato *(Spring Gap)*
Toro *(Gilliland, Hill, Vaca)*
Vaca *(Toro)*
Vickery *(Baird)*
Vigo *(Chautauqua)*
Windham *(Tecumseh)*

Cameron Co.
Abney
Acacia
Adams Gardens
Arroyo
Arroyo Bonito
Arroyo City
Avondale
Bagdad
Barreda *(Russelltown)*
Bayside (Laguna Heights)
BAYVIEW
Bessie (San Benito)
Blalack
Bluetown
Boca Chica
Boca Del Rio (Clarksville)
Boory
Boulevard Junction
Brazos Santiago
BROWNSVILLE
Buena Vista
Cameron Park
Carricitos *(Moistown)*
Cavazos
Clarksville (Boca Del Rio)
COMBES *(Templeton)*
Del Mar
Diaz (San Benito)
El Calaboz
El Ebano (Santa Maria)
Encantada-Ranchito El Calaboz
Esoes
Evan
Fermina
Fernado
Fresnal
Fronton (Port Isabel)
Graybill
HARLINGEN *(Lon Hill's*

Town, Six-Shooter Junction)
Holly Beach
INDIAN LAKE
Isabel (Port Isabel)
Jim Rogers
Kayare
Kellers Corner
Kipfer
Kopernik Shores
Lacoma
LA FERIA
La Gloria
Lago
Laguna Heights *(Bayside)*
LAGUNA VISTA
La Leona
Landrum Station
Lantana
La Paloma
La Paloma Junction
Las Rusias
Las Yescas *[Rancho]* *(Preceno Rancho, Yescas)*
La Tina
La Union
Laureles
Loggins
Lon Hill's Town (Harlingen)
LOS FRESNOS *(Moseville)*
LOS INDIOS
Lozano
Macrod
Mitchell
Moistown (Carricitos)
Monte Grande
Moseville (Los Fresnos)
Muerto *(San Julian)*
Murray
Nebraska
Ohio
Olmito
Palmetal
PALM VALLEY
Pardo
Pauldie
Place
Point Isabel (Port Isabel)
Port Brownsville
PORT ISABEL *(Fronton, Isabel, Point Isabel)*
Preceno Rancho (Las Yescas)
PRIMERA
Rafael
Ranchito
RANCHO VIEJO
RANGERVILLE
RIO HONDO
Rio del Sol
Rosita
Russelltown (Barreda)
SAN BENITO *(Bessie, Diaz)*
San Julian (Muerto)
San Pedro
San Vicente
Santa Elena
Santa Maria *(El Ebano)*
Santa Rita
SANTA ROSA
Santander

Six-Shooter Junction
(Harlingen)
Slinkerts
Southmost
SOUTH PADRE ISLAND
Southpoint
Stuart Place
Tejon
Templeton (Combes)
Tiocano
Van Syckles
Venadito [El Venadito]
Villa Cavazos
Villa Nueva
Yescas (Las Yescas)

Camp Co.
Ada
Big Cypress
Cannon Switch (Pine)
Center Point
Ebenezer
Fairview (Martinburg)
Felton (Mantha)
Harvard Switch
Hopewell
Leesburg
Lilly (Matinburg)
Mantha (Felton)
Matinburg (Lilly)
Martinburg (Fairview)
Miller Grove
Newsome
Oby (Owl)
Owl (Oby)
Pacono (Sayles Cross
Roads)
Pine (Cannon Switch,
Pine Tree)
Pine Tree (Pine)
PITTSBURG
ROCKY MOUND
Roebuck
Sayles Cross Roads
(Pacono)

Carson Co.
Abell
Antelope Mesa
Cargray
Carson City (Panhandle)
Conway (Kelly, Raymond)
Cuyler
Deal
Farish
Gilmore
GROOM
Hillard
Hudson (Lee)
Kelly (Conway)
Lark (Robbins)
Lee (Hudson)
McBride
Noelette (Noelton)
Noelton (Noelette)
PANHANDLE [Panhandle
City] (Carson City)
Pantex
Paton (White Deer)
Pomeroy
Raymond (Conway)
Robbins (Lark)
Roxana
Royal

SKELLYTOWN [Skellyville]
Whig (White Deer)
WHITE DEER (Paton,
Whig)
Yarnall

Cass Co.
Alamo (Domino)
Alamo Mills (Domino)
Almira (Round Mountain)
Anti (Antioch)
Antioch (Anti)
Atlanta (Lanark)
ATLANTA (Scott's Mills)
AVINGER (Hickory Hill)
Axine (Lewis)
Banckers
Baugus Springs
Bear Creekchr
Bivens (Bivins)
Bivins (Bivens, Hoxie,
Wayne)
BLOOMBURG
Bowie Hill
Bryans Mill (Wilton)
Burks (Jaybart)
Carleton (Dempsey)
Carterville
Cass (Rock Springs,
Sheffield)
Centre
Chalybeate Springs
(Hughes Springs)
Cobb [Mill] (Viola)
Collinsburg (Lanier)
Cornett (Perkins, Troupe)
Courtland
Crossroads
Crow (Fant)
Culberson (Lacy)
Curtright (Munz)
Cusseta
Dalton
Dempsey (Carleton)
DOMINO (Alamo, Alamo
Mills)
Doss
DOUGLASSVILLE
Driver's Store (White Hall)
Fairview
Fant (Crow)
Fite (Patman)
Flynn
Forest Home (Lanark)
Forest Home (Springdale)
Galloway [Gallaway]
(Milner)
Good Exchange (McLeod)
Green's Store (Jaybart)
Gum Springs
Havana
Haw Grove
Hermitage
Hickory Hill (Avinger)
Hobby's Mills (Jumbo)
Hootsville
Hoxie (Bivins)
Huffines [Huffins]
HUGHES SPRINGS
(Chalybeate Springs)
Hughes'
Jaybart (Burks, Green's
Store)

Jennings Lake
Jones Chapel
Jumbo (Hobby's Mills)
Kildare
King's Farm [King's Store]
Lacy (Culberson)
Lanark (Atlanta, Forest
Home)
Lanier (Collinsburg)
Lewis (Axine)
LINDEN
Luanna
MARIETTA (Oak Ridge)
McLeod (Good Exchange)
Milner (Galloway)
Moncass
Munz (Curtright, White
Sulphur Springs)
New Colony
Nickleberry
Oak Ridge (Marietta)
O'Farrell [O'Ferrall]
O'Rear's Mill (Roach)
Patman (Fite, Turkey
Creek)
Patman Switch
Pattengill
Perkins (Cornett)
Pruitt
QUEEN CITY
Rambo
Red Hill
Roach (O'Rear's Mill)
Rock Springs (Cass)
Round Mountain (Almira)
Salem
Sardis
Sauls
Scott's Mills (Atlanta)
Sheffield (Cass)
Smith's Store (Viola)
Smyrna
South Texarkana
Springdale (Forest Home)
Tenark
Three States
Troupe (Cornett)
Turkey Creek (Patman)
Unionville
Viola (Cobb [Mill], Smith's
Store)
Warren Springs
Wayne (Bivins)
White Hall (Driver's Store)
White Sulphur Springs
(Munz)
Wiggins
Wilton (Bryans Mill)

Castro Co.
Arney (Renfro)
Big Square
Boom (Summerfield)
Cleo
DIMMITT
Dodd
Easter
Flagg
Frio
Grisham
HART (Nina)
Hilburn
Jumbo

NAZARETH (Shamrock)
Nina (Hart)
Parrott (Platteville)
Peak
Platteville (Parrott)
Red Barn
Renfro (Arney)
Roy
Shamrock (Nazareth)
Summerfield (Boom)
Sunnyside
Tam Anne
Wynne

Chambers Co.
ANAHUAC (Chambersea,
Chambersia, Perry's
Point, Round Point)
Bancroft
Barber's Hill (Mont Belvieu)
BEACH CITY
Bermuda (Glen)
Cedar Bayou
COVE (Old River Lake)
Chambersea (Anahuac)
Chambersia (Anahuac)
Cracker's Neck
Double Bayou
Eagle (Eagle Nest, Glen)
Eagle Nest (Eagle)
Eminence
Figridge
Four Corners
Glen (Eagle, Bermuda)
Graydon (Nugent)
Hankamer
John's
Lake Charlotte
Monroe City (White City)
MONT BELVIEU (Barber's
Hill)
Nugent (Graydon)
Oak Island
Old River Lake (Cove)
OLD RIVER-WINFREE
(Straddle)
Perry's Point (Anahuac)
Pine Ridge
Round Point (Anahuac)
Seabreeze
Smith Point
Stowell
Straddle (Old River)
Turtle Bayou (White's
Store)
Wallis Hill (Wallisville)
Wallisville (Wallis Hill)
White City (Monroe City)
Whites Ranch
White's Store (Turtle
Bayou)
Winfree (Old River-Win-
free)
Winnie

Cherokee Co.
Albritten
ALTO
Ameus (Emmaus)
Atoy
Beans Creek
Black Jack
Box Creek
Broughton

Brunswick
Bulah
BULLARD
Central High
Circle
Concord
Cooks Fort
Cove Springs
Craft
CUNEY
Delmer
Dialville
Elm Grove
Emmaus (Ameus)
Fastrill
Forest
Frys Gap
GALLATIN
Gould
Griffin
Henry's Chapel
Holcomb Store
Hudsons Chapel
Hume
Ironton
JACKSONVILLE
Java
Knoxville
Lacys Fort
Larissa (Old Larissa)
Linwood
Lone Star
Maydelle
McCrossin
Mewshaw
Mittie
Mixon
Morrill
Mount Haven
Mount Selman
Nag Park
New Birmingham
New Emmaus [Emmaus]
New Hope
NEW SUMMERFIELD
North Rusk
Norvall
Oakland
Old Larissa (Larissa)
Padreco
Petersville
Pierces Chapel
Pine Grove
Pinetown
Pomona
Ponta
Prices
Redlawn
Reese
REKLAW
RUSK
Salem
Shady Grove
Shooks Bluff
Striker Creek
Stringer
Sulphur Springs
Sweet Union
Talledgea
Tecula
Tinimax
TROUP
Turney

Weeping Mary
WELLS
Wild Hurst
Woodville

Childress Co.
Abbington
Arlie (Loco)
Baylor Lake
Carey
CHILDRESS
Garden Valley
Gilpin
Kirkland
Kola
Loco (Arlie)
Lonnie
Moyer
Olympus
Smithdale
Tell (Tell Tale Flat)
Tell Tale Flat (Tell)
Union Flat

Clay Co.
Alma (Vina)
Bear Hill (Newport)
Beaver Creek
BELLEVUE (Skinner Springs)
Benvanue
Big Wichita [Valley] (Charlie)
Bluegrove
Buffalo Springs
BYERS
Cambridge (New Henrietta, Pinhead)
Charlie (Big Wichita [Valley])
Circle City (Halsell)
Dan (Dean)
DEAN (Dan, Mabledean)
Deer Creek (Shilo)
Dickworsham
Doss
Eden (Thornberry)
Edwards
Enoch (Joy)
Fannintown (Joy)
Flat Rock Spring
Frame
Halsell (Circle City)
HENRIETTA
Hill's Ferry
Huggins
Hurnville (Iowa Point, Parker)
Illinois Colony (Thornberry)
Iowa Point (Hurnville)
JOLLY
Joy (Enoch, Fannintown)
Kola
Lake Arrowhead
Lodge [Creek]
Loop
Mabledean (Dean)
Moore (Watson)
Myrtle
New Henrietta (Cambridge)
Newport (Bear Hill)
Oil City (Petrolia)
Parker (Hurnville)

PETROLIA (Oil City)
Pinhead (Cambridge)
Prospect (Richards, Star Ridge)
Qualls
Raymond
Richards (Prospect)
Riverland
Roland (Smith Creek)
Rosson
Secret Springs
Shannon (Stampede)
Shilo (Deer Creek)
Skinner Springs (Bellevue)
Smith Creek (Roland)
Stampede (Shannon)
Stanfield [Ranch]
Star Ridge (Prospect)
Teco
Thornberry (Illinois Colony)
Turner (Vashti)
Vashti (Turner)
Vina (Alma)
Watson (Moore)
Wichita [City]

Cochran Co.
Bledsoe
Cochran (Mexline)
Edwards (Silver Lake)
Famuliner
Girlstown USA
Griffith (Oasis)
Haven
Lehman
Ligon
Mexline (Cochran)
MORTON
Mozelle
Neely Ward
Oasis (Griffith)
Perley
Silver Lake (Edwards)
Star Route
WHITEFACE

Coke Co.
Alpha (Hogg)
BLACKWELL
Bliss (County Line)
Bronco (Bronte)
BRONTE (Bronco, Oso)
County Line (Bliss)
Divide
Edith
Fort Chadbourne
Gamma
Grover (Silver)
Hayrick
Hogg (Alpha)
House's Ranch (Venice)
Jupiter (Margaret, Mount Margaret)
Margaret (Jupiter)
Matalfos (Teferville)
Mount Margaret (Jupiter)
Nanhattie
Oso (Bronte)
Pedro
Rawlings
ROBERT LEE
Sanco
Shawville
Silver (Grover)
Stokes

Teferville (Matalfos)
Tennyson
Venice (House's Ranch)

Coleman Co.
Buffalo
Burkett
Camp Colorado
Centennial
COLEMAN
Echo
Fisk
Glen Cove
Goldsboro
Gouldbusk
Hamrick
Hardin
Junction
Leaday
Liberty
Loss Creek
Mozelle
NOVICE
Obregon
Overall
Rock Crusher
Rockwood
SANTA ANNA
Shields
Silver Valley
Talpa
Trickham
Valera
Voss
Webbville
Whon

Collin Co.
Aleo
ALLEN
Altoga
ANNA
Ardath (Gem, Land, Stiff, Tickey, Viney)
Arnold
Beth
Bethany
Beverly Hill
Biggers (Lowry Crossing)
Bishop (East Fork, Lowry)
Black Hill (Tar Heel Flat)
Bloomdale
BLUE RIDGE
Branch
Bristol City (Fayburg(h)
Buckner (McKinney)
Callis
Cedar Point (Hancock)
CELINA
Chambersville
Chambliss (Stoney Point)
Clearlake
Climax
Collin
Connor (Sellers)
Copeville
Culleoka
Currey
Danville
Decatur (Maxwell)
Desert
Donna
Dump (St. Paul)
East Fork (Bishop)

Eden (Hancock)
Emerson (Frisco)
Empire
Engleman
Erudia
FAIRVIEW
FARMERSVILLE *(Sugar Hill)*
Fayburg(h) *(Bristol City)*
Fisher's Gin *(Foncine)*
Fitzhugh *(Grove)*
Foncine *(Fisher's Gin)*
Foot *(Luck)*
Forest Grove *(Grove)*
Foy
Frankford *(Pauline)*
FRISCO *[Frisco City]*
   (Emerson)
Frognot
Gem *(Ardath)*
Graybill *(Verna)*
Grove *(Fitzhugh, Forest Grove)*
Hackberry *(Vineland)*
Hackberry Bluff
Hancock *(Cedar Point, Eden)*
Hickman
Highland
High Point
Jordan *(Josephine)*
JOSEPHINE *(Jordan)*
Kelly
Kerr *(Vineland)*
Knox
Lake Mills *(Mackville)*
Land *(Ardath)*
LAVON *(Thomson)*
Lebanon *(Shahan's Prairie)*
Liberty Grove
Liberty Springs *(Roland)*
Lieu
Lint
Lolaville
Lone Tree
Lowry *(Bishop)*
LOWRY CROSSING
   (Biggers)
LUCAS *(St. Jo)*
Luck *(Foot)*
Mackville *(Lake Mills)*
Mantua
Maple
Marilee
Maxwell *(Decatur)*
Maxwell's Branch *(Murphy)*
McGarrah's
McKINNEY *(Buckner)*
MELISSA
Milligan
Millwood
Moreland
MURPHY *(Maxwell's Branch, Old Decatur)*
NEVADA
NEW HOPE
New Mesquite
Nickelville *(Wylie)*
Old Decatur *(Murphy)*
PARKER *(Parker Gin)*
Parker Gin *(Parker)*
Pauline *(Frankford)*

Pecan Grove
Pike
*PLANO
Price
PRINCETON *(Wilson's Switch)*
PROSPER *(Richland)*
Renner
Rhea Mills
Rhymer
Richards *(Tib)*
*RICHARDSON
Richland *(Prosper)*
Rock Hill
Roland *(Liberty Springs, Rowland Springs)*
Roseland
Rowland Springs *(Roland)*
Rowlett's Creek
ROYSE CITY
SACHSE
St. Jo *(Lucas)*
ST. PAUL *(Dump)*
Seco
Sedalia
Sellers *(Connor)*
Seven Points *(Westminster)*
Shahan's Prairie *(Lebanon)*
Shepton
Sister Grove
Snow Hill
Spring Creek
Stiff *[Stiff's Creek] (Ardath)*
Stoney Point *(Chambliss)*
Sugar Hill *(Farmersville)*
Tar Heel Flat *(Black Hill)*
Thomson *(Lavon)*
Tib *(Richards)*
Tibb
Tickey *(Ardath)*
Valdasta *(Vandersville)*
Valdesta
Vandersville *(Valdasta)*
Verna[ville] *(Graybill)*
Verona *(Womble)*
Vineland *(Hackberry, Kerr)*
Viney *(Ardath)*
Walnut Grove
WESTMINSTER *[Westminster] (Seven Points)*
WESTON
Wetsel
Winningkoff
Wilson's Switch *(Princeton)*
Womble *(Verona)*
WYLIE *(Nickelville)*
Yakimo

Collingsworth Co.
Aberdeen
Abra *(Lonestar, Unity)*
Clifford
Club Lake
Collingsworth *(Elm, Gyp)*
DODSON *[Dodsonville]*
Dozier
Elm *(Collingsworth)*
Fresno *(Myers)*
Gyp *(Collingsworth)*
Idaho *(Quail)*
Lonestar *(Abra)*

Lillie
Lutie *(Pleasant Valley)*
Marella *[Store]*
Marilla
Myers *(Fresno)*
New Loco
Pearl
Pleasant Valley *(Lutie)*
Plymouth *(Riverside)*
Quail *(Idaho, Wilson)*
Ring
Riverside *(Plymouth)*
Rolla
Samnorwood
Shinnery
Swearingen
Unity *(Abra)*
WELLINGTON
Wilson *(Quail)*

Colorado Co.
Alleyton
Altair *(Stafford's Ranch)*
Aren
Barnard *(Eagle Lake)*
Beason's *(Columbus)*
Bernardo *[Prairie] (Braden)*
Blue Roan
Boedecker Junction
Borden *[Borden Station, Bordenville]*
Braden *(Bernardo)*
Calhoun
Cheetham *(Sheridan)*
Chesterville
COLUMBUS *(Beason's [Ferry], Montezuma)*
Content
Crasco *(Rock Island)*
Cuba
Cummins' Creek *[Cummings' Creek] (Frels)*
Dar Junction
EAGLE LAKE *(Barnard)*
Eldridge *(Faber)*
Ellinger
Englehart
Faber *(Eldridge)*
Flower Hill
Frels *(Cummins' Creek)*
Frelsburg(h)
Garwood
Gemmer&Tanner
Gene
Glidden
Goldenrod *(Provident City)*
Helms
Hillcrest
Hillebrand
Hoefer
Hollimon
Jackson Station *(Weimar)*
Jayray
Kesler's Bluffs
Klimek
Laban
Lafitte
Lakeside
Lenz *(Nada)*
Lone Oak
Luvial *(Wright's Bend)*
Matthews
Mentz *(New Mainz, San*

Barnard)*
Millino *(Prairie Cottage)*
Mohat
Montezuma *(Columbus)*
Nada *(Lenz)*
Nancy
New Bielau
New Mainz *(Mentz)*
Nigh *(Ramsey)*
Oak Grove
Oakland *(Prairie Point)*
Osage
Pisek *(Sandy Point)*
Prairie Cottage
Prairie Point *(Oakland)*
Provident City *(Goldenrod)*
Raymer
Raymer Junction
Ramsey *(Nigh)*
Ramseyville
Riceland
Ricks
Ridge
Rock Island *(Crasco)*
San Barnard *(Mentz)*
Sandy Point *(Pisek)*
Shaws Bend
Sheridan *(Cheetham)*
Shimek
Skull Creek
Slutter
Stafford's Ranch *(Altair)*
Stallings
Tait
Unity
Vance
Voxpopuli *(Willow Bar)*
WEIMAR *(Jackson Station)*
Willow Bar *(Voxpopuli)*
Womack
Wright's Bend *(Luvial)*
Zimmerscheid

Comal Co.
Anhalt *(Krause Settlement, Ufnau)*
Austin Hill *(View)*
Bracken *(Davenport)*
BULVERDE
Burt
Canyon City
Canyon Lake
Comal
Comal Ranche
Corbyn
Crane's *[Crain's] Mill (Gum Spring)*
Danville *(Eight Mile Creek)*
Davenport *(Bracken)*
Dittlinger
Eight Mile Creek *(Danville)*
Esser Crossing *(Wesson)*
FAIR OAKS RANCH
Fischer *[Fischer Store]*
Four Mile Creek *(Solms)*
Freheit
GARDEN RIDGE
Guadalupe Valley *(Wesson)*
Goodwin *(Thom Hill)*
Gruene
Gum Spring *(Crain's Mill)*
Hancock *(Sorrels Creek)*

Henderson Crossing
(Wesson)
Honey Creek
Hunter
Krause Settlement (Anhalt)
Mission Valley
Mountain Valley (Sattler)
NEW BRAUNFELS
Oak Cliff Acres
Ogden
Royal Forest
Sattler (Mountain Valley,
Walhalla)
SCHERTZ
Silver Hills
Smithson Valley
Solms (Four Mile Creek)
Sorrels Creek (Hancock)
Spring Branch
Startzville
Stonetown
Thom Hill (Goodwin)
Ufnau (Anhalt)
View (Austin Hill)
Walhalla (Sattler)
Wesson (Esser Crossing,
Guadalupe Valley, Hend-
erson Crossing)
Wurst

Comanche Co.
Amity
Ararat (Pisgah)
Beattie (Dewey, Oakflatt)
Bibb
Big Valley (Sabana Creek)
Board Church (Dingler)
Boynton
Camden (Comyn)
COMANCHE
Comyn (Camden, Grover,
Theny)
Cora (Fleming, Troy)
Creamer
Cross Roads
Dawning (Downing)
DE LEON
Democrat
Dewey (Beattie)
Dingler (Board Church)
Downing (Dawning)
Duster (Patton)
Edey (Hasse)
Energy (Slick Hill)
Enso
Evergreen (Gustine)
Fairview
Flat Creek (Oliver Springs)
Fleming (Cora, Pettit)
Fork Valley (Talma)
Gap
Grover (Comyn)
GUSTINE (Evergreen)
Hasse (Edey)
Hazle Dell [Hazel Dell]
Hog Creek (Jakehamon)
Jakehamon (Hog Creek)
Jimmie's Creek (Sidney)
Lamkin [Lamkinsville]
Lee (Newburg)
Lindley (Shrum)
Maston (Zourette)
Mercer's Gap

Moorman
Newburg (Lee, New Leon,
South Leon)
New Leon (Newburg)
Oakflatt (Beattie)
Oliver Springs (Flat Creek)
Pascal
Patton (Duster)
Pisgah (Ararat)
Pettit (Fleming)
Proctor [Procter]
Resley's Creek
Round Mountain (Sidney)
Rowland
Rucker
Sabana Creek (Big Valley)
Salt Spring
Sand Hill
Shrum (Lindley)
Sidney (Jimmie's Creek,
Round Mountain)
Siep Springs (Sipe
Springs)
Siloam
Sipe Springs (Siep
Springs)
Slick Hill (Energy)
South Leon (Newburg)
Stag Creek
Suez
Sweetwater
Talma (Fork Valley)
Theny (Comyn)
Torpedo
Troy (Cora)
Vandyke
Ware
Watson
Whittville
Willow Dale
Wilson
Zourette (Maston)

Concho Co.
Comanche
Concho
EDEN
Eola (Jordan)
Erskine (Kickapoo
Springs)
Gail (Vick)
Henderson Chapel
Jordan (Eola)
Kickapoo Springs
(Erskine)
Lightner
Live Oak (Ruth)
Lowake (Shawnee)
Millersview
PAINT ROCK
Pasche
Ruth (Live Oak)
Shawnee (Lowake)
Vick [Vick's Station] (Gail)
Vigo
Welview

Cooke Co.
Arcade (Burns City)
Ardell (Countyline)
Baker
Balm (Oklahoma)
Barlow (Copperas Bluff)
Baum

Bloomfield
Bulcher (Chio, Saddler's
Bend)
Burns City [Burns]
(Arcade, Mountain
Spring)
CALLISBURG(h)
Carriage
Centennial City (Custer
City)
Childress (Myra)
Chio (Bulcher)
Clear Creek (Rich Valley)
Coesfield (Horse Shoe
Bend)
Coleville (Walnut Bend)
Copperas Bluff (Barlow)
Countyline (Ardell)
Creed (Myra)
Cross Gin (Hewett's Store)
Crossville (Warren)
Custer City (Centennial
City)
Davenport (Hatti)
Delaware [Bend] (Orlena)
Dexter
Dixson (Woodbine)
Dye
Early (Van Slyke)
Era
Fair Plains
Fish Creek (McCrawville,
Mossville)
Fisherburgh
Freemound (Nod)
GAINESVILLE
Gravel Spur
Hatti (Davenport)
Hemming
Hewett's Store (Cross Gin)
Hickory Creek (Walnut
Bend)
Hood
Hope
Horse Shoe Bend
(Coesfield)
Lake Kiowa
Leo
LINDSAY
Lois (Nola, Wilson)
Loring (Nox, Obal)
Marysville
McCrawville (Fish Creek)
Mitchell's (Woodbine)
Mossville (Fish Creek)
Mountain Spring (Burns
City)
Mountain Springs
[Mountain Spring]
MUENSTER
Myra (Childress, Creed)
Nod (Freemound)
Nola (Lois)
Nox (Loring)
OAK RIDGE
Oak Valley
Obal (Loring)
Oklahoma [Oklohoma]
(Balm)
Orlena (Delaware)
Ophir
Prairie Grove
Prairie Point

Pulteville (Reed)
Reed (Pulteville)
Rich Valley (Clear Creek)
Rosston
Saddler's Bend (Bulcher)
Silver Glade (Vilott)
Sivells Bend
Sturgeon
Tyler Bluff
VALLEY VIEW
Van Slyke (Early)
Vilott (Silver Glade)
Walnut Bend (Coleville,
Hickory Creek)
Warren (Crossville)
Windsor
Wilson (Lois)
Woodbine (Dixson,
Mitchell's)

Coryell Co.
Algana (Topsey)
Ames
Aristo (Henson's Creek,
Luckey)
Arnett (Voss)
Ater (Sardis)
Bain (Harman)
Bee House [Bee]
Beverly
Big Valley Ranchettes
Boaz (Dunn's House)
Boaz (Eliga)
Bobbville (Pancake)
Buchanan Springs
(Turnersville)
Bush (Pancake)
Cavitt
Cold Springs
COPPERAS [Coperas]
COVE (Ogletree)
Coryell City [Coryell]
(Rainey's Creek)
Cove (Evant)
Cox's Mill (Straw[']s Mill)
Davenport (Slater)
Dodson's Store (Jink)
Drennen's Store (Purmela)
Dunn's House (Boaz)
Eagle Springs (Station
Creek)
Eliga (Boaz, Elijah)
Elijah (Eliga)
EVANT (Cove, Langford
Cove)
Ewing
Farmers Spring (Ruth)
Flat (Mesquite Flat)
Forest Hill Estates
Fort Gates
Fort Hood
Gates (Gatesville)
GATESVILLE (Gates)
Gilliamsville (Izoro)
Hamco (Ireland)
Hampton
Harman (Bain)
Henson's Creek (Aristo)
Hickson
Hilltop (Oglesby)
Hubbard
Hurst Springs [Hurst]
Ireland (Hamco, Lanham)

Izoro (Gilliamsville)
Jink (Dodson's Store)
Jonesboro[ugh] (Jones Mill)
Jones Mill (Jonesboro)
King (New Hope, Stringtown)
Langford Cove (Evant)
Lanham (Ireland)
Leisure Acres
Leon Junction
Leonville
Levita (Simpsonville)
Lime City
Luckey (Aristo)
Martin (Slater)
Meadow Brook (Slater)
Mesquite Flat (Flat)
Moccasin
Montague Village
Mound (White Mound)
Mountain Community
Mount Zion (Pancake)
New Hope (King)
North Fort Hood
Oak Grove (The Grove)
OGLESBY (Hilltop)
Ogletree (Copperas Cove)
Osage
Pancake (Bobbville, Bush, Mount Zion)
Pearl (Wayback)
Pecan Grove
Peruna
Pidcock Ranch (Pidcoke)
Pidcoe (Pidcoke)
Pidcoke (Pidcock Ranch, Pidcoe)
Prairie Mills (Whitson)
Purmela (Drennen's Store)
Ranier
Rainey's Creek (Coryell City)
Ross Valley (Seneca)
Ruth (Farmers Spring)
Sardis (Ater)
Seattle (Sigsbee)
Seneca (Ross Valley)
Sigsbee (Seattle)
Simpsonville (Levita)
Slater (Davenport, Martin, Meadow Brook)
SOUTH MOUNTAIN
South Purmela
Station Creek (Eagle Springs)
Straw['[]s Mill (Cox's Mill)
Stringtown (King)
Sugar Loaf
Tama
The Grove (Oak Grove)
Topsey (Algana)
Turnersville (Buchanan Springs)
Uriah
Voss (Arnett)
Wayback (Pearl)
White Hall
White Mound (Mound)
Whitson (Prairie Mills)

Cottle Co.
Baker

Bala
Blanche (Wilson)
Buck Creek (Ginsite, Ryan, Willett)
Cee Vee
Chalk (Dutch Colony, Richards)
Cline's Corner (Coleyville)
Coleyville (Cline's Corner)
Cordel (Delwin)
Cottle (Zury)
Delwin (Cordel, Drummond)
Drummond (Delwin)
Dunlap
Dutch Colony (Chalk)
Ginsite (Buck Creek)
Gravel
Hackberry [Grove] (Stewart)
Hackberry (Tanks)
Hightop (Plainview)
Jacobs
Lazare
May (Paducah)
Narcisso
Ogden
Otta [Springs, Ottie Springs]
PADUCAH (May)
Plainview (Hightop)
Pleasant Hill (Tanks)
Ryan (Buck Creek)
Richards (Chalk)
Salt Creek
Sneedville
Sommer
Stewart (Hackberry)
Swearingen
Tanks (Hackberry, Pleasant Hill, Tennessee Valley)
Tell [Tell-Tale Flat]
Tennessee Valley (Tanks)
University Community
Valley View
Willett (Buck Creek)
Wilson (Blanche)
Zury (Cottle)

Crane Co.
CRANE
Edruvera
Ranch
Rio Pecos
Tubbs Corner

Crockett Co.
77 Ranch (Hembrie)
Bonita (Hinde)
Camp Melbourne (Camp Melvin)
Camp Melvin (Camp Melbourne, Connelley's Crossing, Ficklin, Pecos Station, Pontoon Bridge)
Connelley's Crossing (Camp Melvin)
Emerald [Grove] (Laverne)
Ficklin (Camp Melvin)
Fort Lancaster [Camp Lancaster] (Mobile)
Hembrie (Nix's Ranch, 77 Ranch)

Hinde (Bonita)
Laverne (Emerald)
Live Oak
Mobile (Fort Lancaster)
Mozart
Nix's Ranch (Hembrie)
Ozona
Pecos Station (Camp Melvin)
Pontoon Bridge (Camp Melvin)

Crosby Co.
Broadway
Canyon Valley
Cap Rock
Cone
Cox's Colony (Estacado)
CROSBYTON (Petzel's Camp)
Dode
Emma
Estacad[d]o (Cox's Colony, Marietta)
Fairview
Falcon (Springdale, Yellow House Cañon)
Farme
Hacienda Glorieta (Mount Blanco)
Kalgary (Spur, Watson)
League
LORENZO
Manila (Wake)
Marietta (Estacado)
Mount Blanco (Hacienda Glorieta)
Old Emma
Owens
Pansy (Wake)
Pansy [Mills]
Petzel's Camp (Crosbyton)
RALLS
Robertson
Savage
Springdale (Falcon)
Spur (Kalgary)
Wake (Manila, Pansy)
Watson (Kalgary)
White River
Yellow House Cañon (Falcon)

Culberson Co.
Antelope (Kent)
Boracho
Collado
Danube
Daugherty (Figure 2 Ranch)
Discus
Fay
Figure 2 Ranch (Daugherty)
Frijole (Pine Springs)
Guadalupe Station
Hillside
Kent (Antelope)
Levinson
Lobo
Lula (Tarver)
Micolithic
Nickel Creek
Pine Springs (Frijole,

Smith's Ranch, Springhill)
Plateau
Rock House
Rustler Springs
Signal Peak
Smith's Ranch (Pine Springs)
Springhill (Pine Springs)
State Line
Sulphuria
Tarver (Lula)
VAN HORN
Wildhorse

Dallam Co.
Bolin
Chamberlin
Coldwater
Coloney
Conlen (Murray)
Corlena
DALHART (Denrock, Twist Junction)
Denrock (Dalhart)
Farwell Park (Perico)
Hitt
Irwin
Kerrick
Matlock
Murray (Conlen)
Perico (Farwell Park)
TEXLINE
Twist Junction (Dalhart)
Ware

Dallas Co.
ADDISON (Noell)
Alpha (Moran)
Alta Mesa
Arcadia Park
Armo
Arnold (Orphans Home)
Atkins
Audelia (Jackson School House)
Bachman
BALCH SPRINGS
Barker's Store (Wheatland)
Bear Creek
Beckley Heights
Bethard
Bobwyn
Breckinridge (Richardson)
Briggs
Brouchard
Browder
Buckingham
Buck&Breck
Bug Eye
Burbank Gardens
Cain (Gray's Gin)
Calhoun (Fisher Station)
CARROLLTON
Caruth (Oasis)
CEDAR HILL
Cement
Centerville
Chaha (Francis)
Charleston
Cheisa
China Grove (Rowlett)
Ciel (Mount Harrison, Rawlins)

Clint (Trip)
Cloudy
COCKRELL HILL
COMBINE
COPPELL (Gibbs, Orr)
Couch
Curtis
DALLAS (Peters Colony)
Dal Nor
Dalrock
Dalworth Park
Davis' Mills (Rowlett)
DESOTO (Jeddo)
Deckman (Grand Prairie)
Denny
Duck Creek
Duck Creek (Garland)
DUNCANVILLE [Duncan Switch]
Eagle Ford
East Dallas (Gaston)
Elam [Station]
Elm Grove
Embree (Garland)
Estelle
Exall
Fair Park
FARMERS BRANCH (Mustang Branch)
Field City
Finley (Mills)
Fisher Station (Calhoun)
Five Mile
Florence Hill
Fox
Francis (Chaha)
Frankford
Fruitdale
GARLAND (Duck Creek, Embree)
Gasco
Gaston (East Dallas)
Gates
Gibbs (Coppell)
Gifford
GLENN HEIGHTS
Glendale
Gorbett (Irving)
Gorbit (Irving)
GRAND PRAIRIE (Deckman)
Gray's Gin (Cain)
Gribble
Hale Station
Harrys
Haught's Store (Lawson)
Haws
HIGHLAND PARK
Highway
Hiland
Hillard
Honey Springs
Hord's Ridge (Oak Cliff)
Housley
HUTCHINS
Idlewild
Inwood
IRVING (Gorbett, Gorbit, Kit)
Jackson School House (Audelia)
Jeddo (DeSoto)
Jim Town

Joe's Branch
Jonesville
Ka
Kingsley
Kit (Irving)
Kleberg [Kleburg[h]
Knight Spur
Lake June
Lakeview
LANCASTER (Pleasant Run)
La Reunion (Reunion)
Lawson (Haught's Store, Slapfoot)
Lawther
Letot
Liberty Grove
Liggett
Lisbon (Virginia)
Locust Shade
Maglab
Mainzer
Marith
McNairy (Winston)
Meaders
MESQUITE
Miller
Mills (Finley)
Monroe
Moran (Alpha)
Morris (Rowlett)
Mountain Creek
Mount Harrison (Rawlins)
Mustang Branch (Farmers Branch)
Naaman
New Hope
New Loven
Norwood
Noell (Addison)
Oak Cliff (Hord's Ridge)
Oasis (Caruth)
Ola
Orphans Home (Arnold, Scyene Switch)
Orr (Coppell)
Palace Hill
Peeler
Perkins
Peters Colony (Dallas)
Pleasant Grove
Pleasant Mound
Pleasant Run (Lancaster)
Pleasant Valley
Prairie Creek (Scyene)
Prairie Valley (Wilmer)
Preston Hollow
Rawlins (Ciel, Mount Harrison)
Reinhardt
Reunion (La Reunion)
RICHARDSON (Breckin-ridge)
Rock
Roosevelt Heights
Rose Hill
Roselawn
ROWLETT (China Grove, Davis' Mills, Morris)
Rylie
SACHSE (Saxie)
Sand Branch
Sargent

Saxie (Sachse)
Scottdale
Scyene (Prairie Creek)
Scyene Switch (Orphans Home)
SEAGOVILLE
Shady Grove
Shiloh
Simonds
Slapfoot (Lawson)
Soumethun
Sowers
Sprowls (Wheatland)
Stargas
Starlong
Stewart
SUNNYVALE
Ten Mile
Thorpeville
Trinity City
Trinity Mills
Trip (Clint, Tripp)
Truman
Union Bower
UNIVERSITY PARK
Urban
Vickery
Virginia (Lisbon)
West Mesquite
Wheatland (Barker's Store, Sprowls)
White Rock
WILMER (Prairie Valley)
Winston (McNairy)
Zipp City

Dawson Co.
ACKERLY
Arvana
Central (Idaho)
Chicago (Stemmons)
Evelena
Friendship
Grandview
Hancock
Hindman
Idaho (Central)
Key
Klondike
LAMESA
LOS YBANEZ
Lou (Red)
Michies (Wayside)
Midway
Mungerville
Natalie (Patricia)
Nueve
O'DONNELL
Patricia (Natalie)
Pride
Punkin Center
Red (Lou)
Sand (Sunset)
Shack Town (Welch)
Sparenberg
Stemmons (Chicago)
Sunset (Sand)
Tenmile
Union
Wayside (Michies)
Welch (Shack Town)

Deaf Smith Co.
Ayr

Blue Water (Hereford)
Bootleg
Dawn (Hay)
Dean
Escarbada
Ford
Garcia
Glenrio
Grenada (La Plata)
Hay (Dawn)
HEREFORD (Blue Water)
Joel
Kelso
La Plata (Grenada)
Milo Center
Mirage
Simms
Westway

Delta Co.
Amy (Hobbs)
Antioch
Barton (Volney)
Ben Franklin
Bess (Gough)
Charleston
Clem
COOPER (Yates Prairie)
Crossroads
Cuba (Pacio)
East Delta
Enloe
Gough (Bess)
Hobbs (Amy)
Honest
Horton
Jot-Em-Down
Kate (Klondike)
Kensing
Klondike (Kate, Pleasant Grove)
Lake Creek (Odd's Creek)
Liberty Grove
Mote's Mill (Pacio)
Mount Joy
Needmore (Pecan)
Odd's Creek (Lake Creek)
Pacio (Cuba, Mote's Mill)
Pecan [Branch] (Need-more)
PECAN GAP
Pleasant Grove (Klondike)
Post Oak
Prattville
Price
Race Track
Rattan
Unitia
Vasco
Volney (Barton)
Yates Prairie (Cooper)
Yowell

Denton Co.
Abbieville
Abney's Farm (Charlton)
Alton
ARGYLE (Waintown)
Armide
AUBREY (Onaga)
Barksdale (Hebron)
BARTONVILLE (Chinn's Chapel, Double Oak)

Bartonville (Shilo[a]h)
Bates (Hawkins, Zion)
Bolivar *(Clear Creek, New Prospect)*
Bugtown
Camey Spur [Camey]
Camp Dallas
Camp Lucille
CARROLLTON
Carter
Charlton (Abney's Farm)
Chinn's Chapel (Bartonville)
Clear Creek (Bolivar)
Cooper Creek
COPPER CANYON
CORINTH *(Shiloh)*
CORRAL CITY
Cosner
CROSS ROADS
Davenport's Mill (Roanoke)
Davy
DENTON
Denton Creek
Denton Creek
Donald (Shilo[a]h)
DOUBLE OAK
Double Oak (Shilo[a]h)
Drop (Oliver)
DuPont
Elizabeth
Elizabethtown
Fiddlers Green
FLOWER MOUND
French (Lake Dallas)
Friendship
Garza (Lake Dallas)
Gerald (Ponder)
Green Valley (Toll Town)
Gribble Springs
Griffhill
Griggs (Hebron)
HACKBERRY
Hawkeye
Hawkins (Bates, Zion)
HEBRON *(Barksdale, Griggs, Shepton)*
Hickory (Meadville)
HICKORY CREEK
HIGHLAND VILLAGE
Hilltown (Little Elm)
Holford Prairie (Lewisville)
Hulin (Sanger)
Jagoe
JUSTIN [Justine]
King's Crossing (Little Elm)
Knob Hill
KRUGERVILLE
KRUM
LAKE DALLAS *(Garza, French)*
LAKEWOOD VILLAGE
*LEWISVILLE *(Holford Prairie)*
Lexington
LINCOLN PARK
LITTLE ELM *(Hilltown, King's Crossing)*
Lloyd
MARSHALL CREEK
Mayhill

Meadville (Hickory)
Metz
Midlin (Roanoke)
Millay
Mingo
Mud Spring
Mustang
Navo *(Salt Branch)*
Nebo
New Bolivar (Sanger)
New Prospect (Bolivar)
NORTHLAKE
OAK POINT
Oliver (Drop)
Onaga (Aubrey)
Parvin *(Rue)*
Pilot Knob
PILOT POINT
Pinckneyville
PONDER *(Gerald)*
Rector
Renner
ROANOKE *(Davenport's Mill, Midlin)*
Rue (Parvin)
Salt Branch (Navo)
SANGER *(Hulin, New Bolivar)*
SHADY SHORES
Shepton (Hebron)
Shilo[a]h *(Bartonville, Donald, Double Oak)*
Shiloh (Corinth)
Smoots
Speer's Mill
Steward's Creek
Stewart's Creek
Stewartsville
Stonewall (Stony)
Stony (Stonewall)
Stoverville
THE COLONY
Thomas
Toll Town (Green Valley)
Traildust
TROPHY CLUB
Val Verde
Valletta Ranch
Wakefield's (Waketon)
Waketon (Wakefield's)
Waintown (Argyle)
Zion (Bates, Hawkins)

DeWitt Co.
Arneckeville
Bello (Westhoff)
Benada
Blair's (Cuero)
Brown
Brushy (Peru)
Buchel
Burns Station (Verhelle)
Cabeza
Calhoun School (Green DeWitt)
Caples
Castle
Cheapside
Chisholm's Ferry (Clinton)
Clinton (Chisholm's Ferry)
Coletto (Zobel's)
Colletto (Rabke)
Concrete

Conroy (Yoakum)
Cook's Mill (Terryville)
Cotton Patch
CUERO *(Blair's, Quaro)*
Crain (Stratton)
Davy
Dutchtown (Hochheim)
Edgar
Foresville
Garfield
Golly
Grassbur (Hutton)
Green DeWitt (Calhoun School)
Gruenau
Guilford
Heaton
Hesterville
Hochheim *(Dutchtown)*
Hopkinsville
Hutton (Grassbur)
Irish Creek
Kokernot
Kubala Store
Langley
Lindeman (Lindenau)
Lindenau *(Lindeman, Wofford)*
Little Chicago
Live Oak
Lowell
Meyersville
Morris
Mount Pesrea
Mustang Mott
New Davy
Nopal *(Sasseville)*
NORDHEIM *(Welden Switch)*
Pearl City
Peru *(Brushy)*
Petersville
Pierpont Place
Price's Creek
Quaro (Cuero)
Rabke (Colletto)
Sasseville (Nopal)
Shiloh
Steen
Stratton *(Crain)*
Terryville (Cook's Mill)
Thomaston
Upper Cuero Creek Settlement
Upper Meyersville
Upper Yorktown
Valley View
Verhelle *(Burns Station)*
Welden Switch (Nordheim)
Westhoff *(Bello)*
Wofford (Lindenau)
YOAKUM *(Conroy)*
YORKTOWN
Zobel's (Coletto)

Dickens Co.
Afton *(Cottonwood, Grapevine)*
Casco (Draper)
Corners (Dumont)
Cottonwood (Afton)
Croton *(Noview)*
Beckton

DICKENS
Dobbs City (Glenn)
Dockum Ranch
Draper *(Casco, Vista)*
Dumont *(Corners)*
East Afton
Elton *(Midway)*
Espuela
Gilpin *(Poet)*
Glenn *(Dobbs City)*
Grapevine (Afton)
McAdoo *(Prairie View)*
Midway (Elton)
Mound (Soldier(s) Mound)
Noview (Croton)
Poet (Gilpin)
Prairie View (McAdoo)
Soldier Mound *(Mound)*
SPUR
Spur *(Tap)*
Steele Hill
Tap *(Spur, Warren)*
Vista *(Draper)*
Warren *(Tap)*

Dimmit Co.
ASHERTON
BIG WELLS
Brundage
CARRIZO SPRINGS
Catarina
Dentonio
El Jardin
Ingemal
Las Vegas
Light
Nopal
Seefeld
Valley Wells
Winter Garden
Winter Haven

Donley Co.
Ashtola *(Southard)*
Boydston
Bray
CLARENDON *(Methodist Colony, Saints' Roost)*
Donley *(Rowe)*
Giles
Glencross
HEDLEY
HOWARDWICK
Jericho
Lake Creek (Naylor)
Lelia Lake
Methodist Colony (Clarendon)
Mifflin (Wilborn)
Naylor [Naylor Springs] (Lake Creek)
Rowe (Donley)
Saints' Roost (Clarendon)
Southard (Ashtola)
Whitefish
Wilborn (Mifflin)

Duval Co.
BENAVIDES
Bess (Mindiette, Shaeffer)
Borjas
Byran
Chapa (Ramirez)
Concepcion

Copita
Crestonio (Melvine)
Cruz Calle
Dubose
Duval (Noleda)
Ella (Mazatlan)
FREER (Government
  Wells, Rosita Valley)
Government Wells (Freer)
Gravis
Guajillo
Humble Government
  Wells Camp
La Rosita (Rosita)
Mazatlan (Ella)
Melvine (Crestonio)
Mindiette (Bess)
Noleda (Duval, Piedras
  Pintas)
Norway
Palangana
Piedras Pintas (Noleda)
Ramirez (Chapa)
Rangel
Realitos
Reyes (Seago)
Rios
Rosita (La Rosita, Trevino)
Rosita Valley (Freer)
SAN DIEGO
San Jose
Santa Cruz
Seago (Reyes)
Sejita
Seven Sisters
Shaeffer (Bess)
Sweden
Trevino (Rosita)

Eastland Co.
Alameda (Chauncey,
  Mansker Lake)
Benville (Hay)
Bluff Branch
Branton (Union Center)
Bull Creek (Tiffin)
Bullock
CARBON
Chaney
Chauncey (Alameda)
Chuckville
CISCO (Red Gap)
Clarkridge (Hilburn, Oil
  Center, Wildcat)
Clifford (Hobart)
Comer (Kokomo)
Coperas [Creek] (Rising
  Star)
Corinth
Curtis (Nimrod)
Delmar (Dothan)
Desdemona [Desdimonia]
  (Hogtown)
Dothan (Delmar)
EASTLAND
Edhobby
Flannagan's Ranch
  (Merriman)
Flatwoods
Fox (Rustler)
Gilbert (Lunette)
GORMAN (Rane,
  Shinoak)

Grant (Olden)
Gray
Harlow (Lamont)
Hay (Benville)
Hilburn (Clarkridge)
Hobart (Clifford, Love
  Branch)
Hogtown (Desdemona)
Hustler (Rustler)
Hydro
Illinois Torpedo Company
Jewell
Kokomo (Comer)
Lake Cisco
Lake Leon
Lackawanna
Lamont (Harlow, Pleasant
  Valley)
Lee (Mina)
Longbranch (Romney)
Love Branch (Hobart)
Lunette (Gilbert)
Mangum
Mansker Lake (Alameda)
McGough Springs
  (McGue Springs)
McGue Springs
  (McGough Springs)
McLennan
McMinn
Merriam
Merriman (Flannagan's
  Ranch)
Mina (Lee)
Mitchell
Morton Valley
Mountain Top
Munn (Nimrod)
Nimrod (Curtis, Munn)
Oil Center (Clarkridge)
Oakridge
Okra
Olden (Grant, Olden
  Switch, Silver Pass)
Olden Switch (Olden)
Osburnville (Rising Star)
Pioneer
Pisgah
Pleasant Grove
Pleasant Hill
Pleasant Valley (Lamont)
Pueblo
Punkin Center
Rane (Gorman)
RANGER (Ranger Camp
  Valley)
Ranger Camp Valley
  (Ranger)
Red Gap (Cisco)
RISING STAR (Coperas
  [Creek], Osburnville)
Romney (Longbranch)
Round Mountain (Staff)
Rustler (Fox, Hustler)
Sabanno
Salem
Scranton
Shinoak (Gorman)
Silver Pass (Olden)
Staff (Round Mountain)
Tanner
Tiffin (Bull Creek)
Tudor

Union
Union Center (Branton)
Wildcat (Clarkridge)
Yellow Mound

Ector Co.
Arcade
Badger (Penwell)
Caprock (Notrees)
Douro
Gardendale
GOLDSMITH
Judkins
Metz
North Cowden
Notrees (Caprock)
ODESSA
Penwell (Badger)
Pleasant Farms
Prairie Home
Scharbauer City
Sid Richardson
Turnbaugh Corner
West Odessa

Edwards Co.
Barksdale (Dixie)
Beach
Bins
Carta Valley (Carter's Flat)
Carter's Flat (Carta Valley)
Cheyenne
Cortelyou (Pothole City)
Dixie (Barksdale)
Ellis (Kickapoo Springs)
Green Lake
Hackberry (Paloma)
Harris
Henze
Kickapoo Springs (Ellis)
Kirby
Leida
Nueces Cañon (Panther)
Onslow
Paloma (Hackberry)
Paint Creek (Reynolds)
Panther (Nueces Cañon)
Pothole City (Cortelyou)
Reynolds (Paint Creek)
ROCKSPRINGS

Ellis Co.
ALMA (Willow Pond)
Alvis (Gamble)
Alsdorf (Faulkner)
Alston's [Store] (Astonia)
Alwoodco
Armaglas
Astonia (Alston's [Store])
Auburn (Autumn)
Autumn (Auburn)
Avalon
Baldridge
Ballie (Phillips Store)
BARDWELL
Barker (Midlothian)
Bee Creek (Tight Wad)
Bell Branch
Bethel
Bluff Grove (Ike)
Boyce
Boz (Sims)
Bristol (Heelstring)
Britton (Hellandville)

Brocksville (Heelstring)
Brooksville
Burnam [Burnham]
  (Ensign)
Byrd (Byron, Gradyville,
  Onion)
Byron (Byrd)
CEDAR HILL
Center Point
Chambers Creek
  (Forreston)
Charles Barker (Mid-
  lothian)
Clemma (Trumbull)
Craft
Creechville
Crisp (Hines)
Cummins' Creek (Ensign)
Elva
ENNIS [Ennis Station]
Ensign (Burnam,
  Cummins' Creek)
Eyrie (Maypearl)
Faulkner (Alsdorf)
FERRIS
Five Points
Forrest (Forreston)
Forreston (Chambers
  Creek, Forrest, Howe
  Settlement)
Gamble (Alvis, Knox)
GARRETT [Junction]
  (Guide)
Ghost Hill (Trumbull)
Gifco
Glencoe (Leake's)
GLENN HEIGHTS
Grady's Mill
Gradyville (Byrd)
Griffith
Guide (Garrett)
Hawkins Springs
  (Midlothian)
Heelstring (Bristol,
  Brocksville)
Hellandville (Britton)
Henry
Hines (Crisp)
Hogg (Pluto)
Houston Creek (Italy)
Howard (League, White
  League)
Howe Settlement
  (Forreston)
Hurley Station (Sardis)
Ike (Bluff Grove)
India (Morgan)
ITALY (Houston Creek)
Knox (Gamble)
Kus (Ozro)
League (Howard)
Leake's (Glencoe)
Lebanon (Midlothian)
Leland (Price's Cross
  Roads, Spunkie's Ridge)
Liberty (Rockett)
Lone Cedar
Lone Elm
Lumkins
Mackie (Trumbull)
Maloney [Malony]
May (Ozro)
MAYPEARL (Eyrie, Pearl

City)
McCullough
MIDLOTHIAN *(Barker, Charles Barker, Hawkins Springs, Lebanon)*
MILFORD
Morgan *(India)*
Mountain Peak *(Singleton's)*
Nash
Navarro County Town *(Red Oak)*
Neals Valley
Nelson
Nena
Oak *[Branch]*
Oak Grove
OAK LEAF
Onion *(Byrd)*
Onion Creek
Orme *(Slay)*
Otwell
OVILLA
Ozro *(Kus, May)*
PALMER
Pearl City *(Maypearl)*
PECAN HILL
Phillips Store *(Ballie)*
Plum Grove
Pluto *(Hogg)*
Possum Trot *(Red Oak)*
Price's Cross Roads *(Leland)*
Rankin
Ray *(Reagor Springs)*
Reager's *(Reagor Springs)*
Reagor Springs *(Ray, Reager's)*
Red Bank
RED OAK *(Navarro County Town, Possum Trot)*
RICE
Rivera
Rockett *(Liberty)*
Sandlake
Saralvo *(Sardis)*
Sardis *(Hurley Station, Saralvo)*
Service
Sims *(Boz)*
Singleton's *(Mountain Peak)*
Slay *(Orme)*
Spunkie's Ridge *(Leland)*
Sterrett
Telico
Tellico
Templeton
Tight Wad *(Bee Creek)*
Trumbull *(Clemma, Ghost Hill, Mackie)*
Walnut Springs
Ward Spur
WAXAHACHIE
White League *(Howard)*
Wilton
Willow Pond *(Alma)*
Wyatt *[Switch]*

El Paso Co.
Altura
Alamo Alto
Alfalfa

ANTHONY
Ascarate
Ashley
Belen *(McCombs)*
Biggs Field
Buford
Bunsen
Camp Concordia *(Fort Bliss)*
Canutillo
Casey
CLINT *(Collinsburgh)*
Cockrell
Collinsburgh *(Clint)*
Concordia *(El Paso)*
Cuadrilla
East El Paso
EL PASO *(Concordia, Franklin, Magoffinsville)*
Elizario *(San Elizario)*
Fabens
Fleig
Fort Bliss *(Camp Concordia, Post of El Paso)*
Franklin *(El Paso)*
Frontera
Homestead Meadows
HORIZON CITY
Isleta *(Ysleta)*
La Isla
La Tuna
Magoffinsville *(El Paso)*
McCombs *(Belen)*
Mesa
Montoya
Morceville *(Vinton)*
Newman
Pancho
Planeport
Polvo
Post of El Paso *(Fort Bliss)*
Ralston
Rio Grande Station *(Solitude)*
San Elceario *(San Elizario)*
San Elizario *(Elizario, San Elceario)*
San Jose
San Ysidro
Smeltertown
SOCORRO
Solitude *(Rio Grande Station)*
Sparks
Tigua
Tobin
Tornillo
VINTON *(Morceville)*
Westway
White
Ysleta del Sur Pueblo

Erath Co.
Acrey *(Truitt)*
Alarm Creek
Alexander
Allard *(Salt Spring)*
Altman *(Gilmore)*
Armstrong
Atkinson
Berlin
Birch *(Lowell)*
Bishop *(Harbin)*

Bluff Dale *(Bluff Spring)*
Bluff Spring *(Bluff Dale)*
Bowen *(Topaz)*
Bunyan
Cedar Point *(Cowan)*
Cedar Point *(Elmgrove)*
Chalk Mountain
Clairette *(Mayfield)*
Colbert *(Cole, Pizarro)*
Cole *(Colbert)*
Cottonwood
Cowan *(Cedar Point)*
Cow Creek
De Alva *(Hannibal)*
Dillard
DUBLIN
Duffau
Duffau Wells
Edna Hil
Elmgrove *(Cedar Point, Flinn)*
Erath
Eshman
Exray *(X-ray)*
Field Schoolhouse
Flat Creek *(Victor)*
Flat Woods *(Huckabay)*
Flinn *(Elmgrove)*
Gilmore *(Altman)*
Goather's *(Paluxy)*
Greens Creek *(Horseshoe)*
Haley's Mill *(Paluxy)*
Hannibal *(De Alva)*
Harbin *(Bishop)*
Harper's Mill
Highland
Himmons *(Paluxy)*
Horseshoe *(Green's Creek)*
Huckabay *(Flat Woods)*
Immermere
Johnson Mines *(Thurber)*
Johnson's Mill *(Patillo)*
Johnsville
John Tucker
Lingleville
Lone Oak
Lowell *(Birch)*
Mayfield *(Clairette)*
Millerville
Morgan Mill
Mount Airy
Neff
Ogan
Palaxy
Paluxy *(Goather's, Haley's Mill, Himmons, Pull Tight)*
Patillo *(Johnson's Mill)*
Pigeon
Pizarro *(Colbert)*
Pull Tight *(Paluxy)*
Purves
Rock Falls *(Sisk)*
Rocky *[Rocky Falls]*
Salem
Salt Spring *(Allard)*
Sapoak *(Sunday Creek)*
School Hill
Selden
Shiloh
Sisk *(Rock Falls)*

Skippers Gap
STEPHENVILLE
Sunday Creek *(Sapoak)*
Tempest
Three Way
Thurber *(Johnson Mines)*
Tobin
Topaz *(Bowen)*
Truitt *(Acrey)*
Union Grove
Valley Grove
Victor *(Flat Creek)*
Wenona
Wylieville
X-ray *(Exray)*

Falls Co.
Abney's Farm *(Chilton)*
Adams Spring *(Marlin)*
Alcott *(Noon)*
Alto *[Alta] Springs (Sealy's)*
Barclay
Bellona
Blaine *(Knox)*
Blevins *(Chek)*
Blue Ridge *(Stranger)*
Boyles *(Highbank)*
BRUCEVILLE-EDDY
Bucksnort *(Marlin)*
Camden *(Live Oak)*
Carolina *(Deer Creek)*
Carp *(Theo)*
Cedar Point *(Satin)*
Cedar Springs *[Creek] ([Sarahville de] Viesca)*
Cego *(Leno, Pleasant Valley)*
Chek *(Blevins)*
Chilton *(Abney's Farm)*
Cottonwood
Coymack
Crenshaw *(Sunday School Grove)*
Deer Creek *(Carolina)*
Denny *(Mustang Prairie)*
Dillard's
Dog Town *(Jena)*
Dot
Durango *(Moscow, West Falls)*
Eloise
Falls of Brazos
Fertile Hill
French *(North Prairie)*
Friendship *(Theo)*
GOLINDA *[Golindo]*
Goodville
Guda *(Gurley)*
Gurley *(Guda)*
Hander *(Stamp)*
Harlanville
Highbank *(Boyles)*
Hope Church
Jackwood *(Stanley, Wedemeyer)*
Jena *(Dog Town)*
Kayville *(Stranger)*
Knox *(Blaine)*
Laguna *(Satin)*
Landrum
Lang *(Travis)*
Leno *(Cego)*

Liberty (Stranger)
Live Oak (Camden, Oakley, Rupee)
Lloyd
Lone Grove (Travis)
LOTT
MARLIN (Adams Spring, Bucksnort)
McClanahan
Mettina
Milam
Moore[s]ville
Morman (Rosebud)
Moscow (Durango)
Mount Rose
Mullins (Rosebud)
Mustang Prairie (Denny)
Noon (Alcott)
North Prairie (French, Swanson)
Oakley (Live Oak)
Ogden
Ollis
Otto
Oxidine
Perch
Perry (Peyton)
Peyton (Perry)
Pleasant Grove
Pleasant Valley (Cego)
Pool's Crossing (Rosebud)
Prosperity
Reagan
Rock Dam
Rocky Hill
ROSEBUD (Morman, Mullins, Pool's Crossing)
Rosedale
Rupee (Live Oak)
Saint Paul
Sarahville de Viesca (Cedar Springs)
Satin (Cedar Point, Laguna)
Sealy's (Alto Springs)
Stamp (Hander)
Stanley (Jackwood)
Stranger (Blue Ridge, Kayville, Liberty, Union)
Stuart
Sunday School Grove (Crenshaw)
Sunrise
Swanson (North Prairie)
Terry Chapel
Theo (Carp, Friendship)
Tomlinson Hill
Travis (Lang, Lone Grove)
Triangle
Twin Oak
Union (Stranger)
Viesca (Cedar Springs)
Wedemeyer
West Falls (Durango)
Westphalia
Wilderville
Wilson
Zipperlandville

Fannin Co.
Allen's Chapel
Allen's Point
Anthony
Antlers

Bagby
BAILEY
Bartley Woods
Bentonville
Blackmonk
BONHAM
Boyd
Bug Tussle
Carson
Cotton Center
Cunninghams Store
Delba
Dial
DODD CITY
Duplex
ECTOR
Edhube
Elwood
Ely
Fort Kitchen
Fort Warren
Frank
Gober
Hail
Hickory Creek
Hilger
HONEY GROVE
Hudsonville
Ivanhoe
LADONIA
Lake Crockett Estates
Lamasco
Lannius
LEONARD
Lick
Midway
Monkstown
Moore Chapel
Mulberry
Neut (Newt)
Newt (Neut)
Nobility
Nunelee
Oak Ridge
Old Warren
Orangeville
PECAN GAP
Randolph
RAVENNA
Ridings
Riverby
Sash
Savage
SAVOY
Selfs
Silver City
Sowells Bluff
Telephone
TRENTON
Tulip
Ubell
Valley Creek
WINDOM

Fayette Co.
Alexander's (Fayetteville)
Ammannsville
Baker's Store (Toledo)
Bethany
Biegel
Black Jack [Springs]
Bluff
Blum Hill (High Hill)
Bridgevalley

Buckner
Carmean (Carmine)
CARMINE (Carmean, Sylvan)
Cedar
Cistern (Cockrell's Hill, Whiteside's Prairie)
Cockrell's Hill (Cistern)
Colony (Young's Store)
Colorado City (Electra, Manton's)
Content
Cottonwood (Walhalla)
Cunningham's
Dubina (East Navidad)
East Navidad (Dubina)
Electra (Colorado City)
Elm Grove
Ellinger (Live Oak Hill)
Engle
FAYETTEVILLE (Alexander's, Lick Skillet)
FLATONIA
Florida (Round Top)
Freyburg (Thulemeyer's)
Gay Hill
Grassmyer's [Grassmeyer's]
Groos (Nassau)
Halamicek's Store (Roznov)
Halsted
Hawcreek
Heath (Slack's Wells)
High Hill (Blum Hill, Oldenburg, Wursten)
Holman (Pecan)
Hostyn
Ingram's Prairie (Miller's)
Joiner
Jones'
Kirtley (Primm)
LA GRANGE
Ledbetter
Leevan
Lenas
Lick Skillet (Fayetteville)
Live Oak Hill (Ellinger)
Long Prairie
Lyons [Lyonsville] (Navidad)
Manton's (Colorado City)
Marley
Miller's (Ingram's Prairie)
Mulberry (Praha)
Muldoon (Oso)
Mullins Prairie
Nassau (Groos)
Navidad (Lyons)
Nechanitz
Neese's Store (Warrenton)
New Prague
Oldenburg
Oldenburg (High Hill)
O'Barr's
O'Quinn
Orizaba
Oso
Oso (Muldoon)
Park
Pecan (Holman)
Petersville (Roznov)
Pin Oak (Tuttle's Store)

Plum [Plum Grove]
Praha (Mulberry)
Primm (Kirtley)
Rabbs Prairie [Rabb]
Reaganville
Rek Hill
Richers
Rockhouse (Willow Spring[s])
Ross Prairie
Rossville (Round Prairie)
Round Prairie (Rossville)
ROUND TOP (Florida, Shults' Store, Townsend)
Roznov (Halamicek's Store, Petersville)
Rutersville
SCHULENBURG
Shult's Store (Round Top)
Slack's Wells (Heath)
Spiers'
Stellar
Swiss Alp
Sylvan (Carmine)
Tamberg
Texaco
Thulemeyer's (Freyburg)
Toledo (Baker's Store)
Townsend (Round Top)
Tuttle's Store (Pin Oak)
Wade's
Waldeck
Walhalla (Cottonwood)
Warda
Warrenton (Neese's Store)
Wessels
West Point (Wood's Prairie)
Whiteside's Prairie (Cistern)
Willow Spring[s] (Rockhouse, Zapp)
Winchester
Winedale
Wood's Prairie (West Point)
Wursten (High Hill)
Young's Store (Colony)
Zapalaca
Zapp['s Store] (Willow Spring[s])

Fisher Co.
Adair (Rico)
Afton (Dugout, Oma)
Bernecker
Bossier (Hobbs)
Buffalo (Hobbs)
Busby
Cactus Flat (Dorras)
Capitola
Celotex
Center
Center Hill (Palava)
Center Point (Palava)
Claytonville
Dorras (Cactus Flat)
Dowell
Dugout (Afton)
Eskota
Fisher (North Roby)
Gannon
Grady (Gyp, Mabel)

Gyp (Grady)
HAMLIN
Head of California (Swedonia)
Hitson [Hittson]
Hobbs (Bossier, Buffalo, Red Town)
Jamesville (North Roby)
Len
Linnie
Longworth
Mabel (Grady)
McCaulley (Olio, Taopi)
Newman[s Ranch]
North Roby (Fisher, Jamesville)
Olio (McCaulley)
Oma (Afton)
Palava (Center Hill, Center Point)
Red Town (Hobbs)
Reynolds Siding
Rico (Adair)
Rives
ROBY
ROTAN[do] (White Flat)
Rotando (Rotan)
Round Top
Royston
Rud's Ranch
Sand Spur
Sardis
Steele
Swedonia (Head of California)
Sylvester
Taopi (McCaulley)
White Flat (Rotan)

Floyd Co.
Aiken (Floco)
Alcino (Dillard)
Allmon
Baker
Ball
Barwise
Boone's Rock (Meteor)
Booth Spur
Bourland
Cedar Hill
Cereal
Cochran's Peak (Starkey)
Crawfish
Curlew
Della Plain
Delvin (Starkey)
Dillard (Alcino)
Dode
Dougherty
Edgin
Fairmont
Fairview
Floco (Aiken)
Flomot
Floyd
FLOYDADA [Floyd City]
Gravel
Harmony
Hillcrest
Homestead
Jo Bailey
Johnfarris
Julietta

Lakeview
LOCKNEY
Lone Star
Mayshaw
McCoy
Meteor (Boone's Rock, Mode)
Mickey (Sandhill)
Micomber
Mirror
Mode (Meteor)
Muncy
Nilar
Onie
Petersburg
Providence
Quitaque
Sandhill (Mickey)
South Plains
Starkey (Cochran's Peak, Delvin)
Sterley

Foard Co.
Antelope (Rayland)
CROWELL [Crowell City]
Cottonwood (Wynema)
Diantha (Minerva)
Duff
Foard City
Good Creek (Vivian)
Holmes (Rayland)
Knott (Margaret)
Margaret (Knott, Pease [River City])
Minerva (Diantha)
Pealoreville (Vivian)
Pease (Margaret)
Rayland (Antelope [Springs], Holmes)
Sand Rock
Savilla
Tampareka (Yampareka)
Thalia (Rex)
Rex (Thalia)
Ula
Vivian (Good Creek, Pealoreville)
Wynema (Cottonwood)
Yampareka (Tampareka)

Fort Bend Co.
Adams (Smada)
ARCOLA (Juliff)
Bassett&Blakeley's Store (Kendleton)
BEASLEY (Dyer)
Big Creek
Blue Ridge State Farm (Hobby)
Booth
Borden's (Louisville)
Bordentown (Louisville)
Cabell
Claudine (Clodine)
Clear Lake
Clear Lake Station (Duke)
Cleveland (Foster)
Clodine (Claudine)
Coalson (Smada)
Cove City (Foster)
Crabb
Damon Junction
Damon's Mills (Needville)

Dewalt
Duke (Clear Lake Station, Fenn Lake)
Dyer (Beasley)
Elm Grove (Juliff)
Emelia
FAIRCHILDS (Kneitz)
Fayetteville
Fenn Lake (Duke)
First Colony
Flewellen
Foster (Cleveland, Cove City)
Fort Bend (Pittsville)
Four Corners
Frells
Fresno (Malvern, Riceton)
Fruitland (Orchard)
FULSHEAR
Fulsher (Katy)
Gainey
Gaston (White's Switch)
Guy (Missoula)
Harlem [Switch]
Hanson (San Bernard, Spring Vale)
Hawdon
Helinora (Thompsons)
Herbert
Hermans
Hobby (Blue Ridge State Farm)
Hodge's Bend (Sugar Land)
House
Hunter's (Rockey Well)
Imperial (Sartartia)
Juliff (Arcola, Elm Grove)
KATY (Fulsher, Wimberly)
KENDLETON (Bassett &Blakeley's Store)
Kneitz (Fairchilds)
Long Point
Louisville (Borden's, Bordentown)
Malvern (Fresno)
Marlow
Mayfair Park
McHattie
MEADOWS PLACE
Mission Bend
Missoula (Guy)
MISSOURI CITY
Mooredale
Morrison (Tavener)
Nan
Natali (Tavener)
NEEDVILLE (Damon's Mills, Schendelville)
ORCHARD (Fruitland)
Paynes
Pecan Grove
Pecan Hill
Pillot
Pittsville (Fort Bend)
PLEAK
Powell Point
Pryor
Randon
Riceton (Fresno)
RICHMOND
Rockey Well (Hunter's)
ROSENBERG

San Bernard (Hanson)
Sartartia (Imperial)
Schendelville (Needville)
SIMONTON
Spring Vale (Hanson)
Smada (Adams, Coalson)
Smithers Lake
STAFFORD [Stafford's Point, Staffordville]
SUGAR LAND (Hodge's Bend)
Sugarland Junction
Tavener (Morrison, Natali)
Thompson Chapel
THOMPSONS (Helinora, Thompson Switch, Vossville)
Thompson Switch (Thompsons)
Town West
Trammells
Vossville (Thompson's)
White's Switch (Gaston)
William Routt
Wimberly (Katy)
Woodrow

Franklin Co.
Center Grove
Clearwater
Clopton
Cypress
Daphne
Denton
Eureka
Fairview
Flora Bluff
Friendship
Glade Branch
Good Hope
Gray Rock
Hagansport
Hamilton
Hopewell
Keith
Kinney Point
Lakeview
Lavada
Lone Star
Macon
Majors
Midway
MOUNT VERNON
New Hagensport
New Hope
Panther Chapel
Pleasant Hill
Prairie Grove
Purley
Scroggins
Shady Grove
South Franklin
Spring Place
Sulphur
WINNSBORO
Wylie
Yale

Freestone Co.
Avant (Dew)
Bonnerville
Butler
Cotton Gin
Couchman

Dew *(Avant [Prairie])*
Donie
FAIRFIELD *(Mount Pleasant, Mount Prairie)*
Fair Oaks
Freestone
Israel
KIRVIN
Lanely *[Laneley]*
Liberty
Mount Pleasant (Fairfield)
Mount Prairie (Fairfield)
New Hope
Personville
Pine Bluff (Troy)
Plum Creek
Postoak
Red Lake
Saint Elmo
Simsboro
Stewards Mill
Stonewall
STREETMAN
TEAGUE
Troy (Pine Bluff)
Turlington
Winkler
WORTHAM
Young

Frio Co.
Beatrice *(Brand Rock)*
Bennett Station (Derby)
Bigfoot
Bishop Hollow *(Ireland)*
Brand Rock *(Beatrice)*
Coal *(Music)*
Covey *(Ratama)*
Darlington (Dilley)
DeVilbiss Ranch *(Orelia)*
Derby *(Bennett Station, Lenore)*
DILLEY *(Darlington, Ford)*
Divot *(King's Store, Kingsville, Leona)*
Ford (Dilley)
Frio *[City, Town]*
Garner *(Goldfinch)*
Goldfinch *(Garner, Key Stone)*
Hamlin
Howard Lake *(Miguel)*
Ireland *(Bishop Hollow, Pencilville)*
Jensen
Jones Mound *(Music)*
Key Stone (Goldfinch)
King's Store *(Divot)*
Kingsville (Divot)
Lenore (Derby)
Leona (Divot)
Marks
Melon *[Mellon]*
Miguel *(Howard Lake, Miguiel)*
Miguiel *(Miguel)*
Moore *[Hollow, Station]*
Music *(Coal, Jones Mound)*
Old Frio Town (Frio)
Orelia *(DeVilbiss Ranch)*
Otley

PEARSALL
Pencilville *(Ireland)*
Ratama *(Covey)*
Reep
Schattel
Tio

Gaines Co.
Ashmore *(Loop)*
Bessie
Blue Goose (Loop)
Blythe *(Seagraves)*
Caput
Cedar Lake (Loop)
Craddock
Eclipse
Fairview
Hatchton
Higginbotham
Ida *(Logsdon)*
Logsdon *(Ida, Wyly)*
Loop *(Ashmore)*
Loop *(Blue Goose, Cedar Lake, Stanley)*
Parkinson
Paynes Corner
SEAGRAVES *(Blythe)*
SEMINOLE
Stanley *(Loop)*
Trixie
Wasson
White City
Wyly *(Logsdon)*
Yoca

Galveston Co.
Algoa
Alta Loma *(Santa Fe)*
Arcadia
Bacliff
BAYOU VISTA
Bay View
Caplen
CLEAR LAKE SHORES
Crystal Beach
DICKINSON
FRIENDSWOOD
GALVESTON
Gilchrist
High Island
Highland Bayou
HITCHCOCK
JAMAICA BEACH
KEMAH
LA MARQUE
LEAGUE CITY
Ocean Shore
Patton
Port Bolivar
San Leon
SANTA FE *(Alta Loma)*
TEXAS CITY
TIKI ISLAND, VILLAGE OF

Garza Co.
Augustus
Bresford *(Southland)*
Buenos
Close City *(Ragtown)*
Cow Spur
Davies *(Southland)*
Graham
Hackberry
Justiceburg *(LeForest)*

LeForest *(Justiceburg)*
Litwalton
Pleasant Valley
POST *[Post City]*
Ragtown *(Close City)*
Roa *(Verbena)*
Southland *(Bresford, Davies)*
Verbena *(Roa)*

Gillespie Co.
Albert *(Martinsburgh, Williams Creek)*
Bankersmith *(Grapetown)*
Benner *(Mosel)*
Blumenthal
Cain Cit
Caldwell's Hill *(Gold)*
Cave Creek
Cherry Spring
Christel
Crab Apple
Dearing *(Schussler)*
Doss *[Valley]*
Eckert *(Nebo)*
FREDERICKSBURG
Gold *(Caldwell's Hill, Rheingold)*
Grape Creek
Grapetown *(Bankersmith)*
Grapetown (Luckenbach)
Harper
Hennen (Morris Ranch)
Hilltop
Hondo
Hulda *(Tosca)*
Lange['s Mill]
Luckenbach *(Grapetown)*
Martinsburgh (Albert)
Millville (Stonewall)
Morris Ranch *(Hennen)*
Mosel *(Benner)*
Nebo *(Eckert)*
Rheingold *(Gold)*
Schussler *(Dearing)*
Spring Creek *(Spring Garden)*
Spring Garden *(Spring Creek)*
Squaw Creek
Stonewall *(Millville)*
Tivydale
Tosca *(Hulda)*
Veto
Williams Creek (Albert)
Willow City *[Willow]*

Glasscock Co.
Bigby Corner
Drumright
Garden City
Konohasset
Lees *[Store]*
Saint Lawrence

Goliad Co.
Ander *(Hanover)*
Ander-Weser-Kilgore
Angel City
Berclair
Cash *(Sarco Creek)*
Centerville *(Cologne)*
Charco
Clip

Coleto Creek
Cologne *(Centerville, Ira, Perdido)*
Cooksville *(Weser)*
Cummingsville
Dobskyville
Fannin *(Perdido)*
Fannin[g]'s Defeat
German Cove (Schroeder)
Germantown (Schroeder)
GOLIAD *(La Bahia)*
Hanover *(Ander)*
Ira *(Cologne)*
Kilgore
La Bahia (Goliad)
La Bahia *(Love)*
Love *(La Bahia)*
McNamara
Melo
Middletown *(Weesatche)*
Perdido *(Fannin)*
Perdido *(Cologne)*
Riverdale
Sarco
Sarco Creek *(Cash)*
Schroeder *(German Cove, Germantown)*
Scurlock
Weesatche *(Middletown, Wesatch)*
Wesatch *(Weesatche)*
Weser *(Cooksville)*

Gonzales Co.
Arkansas *(Walsh)*
Bartek
Bebe *(Stroman)*
Belleville *(Belmont)*
Belmont *(Belleville, Centreville)*
Big Hill
Botha *(Dewet)*
Botts
Brown Hill
Capiote *(Leesville)*
Centreville *(Belmont)*
Cheapside
China Grove
Clabbertown *(Round Lake, Zint)*
Cordova
Cost *(Oso)*
Cranz *(Thompsonville)*
Dewet *(Botha, Fox, Metz, Zedlar's [Zedler's] Mill[s])*
Dewville
Dilworth
Dreyer *(Dryer)*
Dryer *(Dreyer)*
Elm Mound *(Sedan)*
Ermis *(Hermis)*
Ettowa *(Saturn)*
Fox *(Dewet)*
Gene *(Walsh)*
Glaze City
GONZALES
Gunn
Hamon *(Mount Vernon, South Riverside, Vernon)*
Harmony *[Harmony Grove]*
Harwood
Hermis *(Ermis)*
Hickston *(Mount Eden)*

Hopkinsville
Janice
Karney (Pilgrim)
Keck
Kokernot
Lakeland
Leesburg (Leesville)
Leesville (Capiote, Lees-
   burg)
Little New York
Maurin
McClure's Hill
McGee Mill (Saturn)
Metz (Dewet)
Miles (Nopal)
Minear (Neville)
Mound (Sedan)
Monthalia (Potts Mill)
Mount Eden (Hickston)
Mount Vernon (Hamon)
Mule Creek
Nash's Mill (Saturn)
Neville (Minear)
Newtonville
Nickel
NIXON [Nixonville]
Nopal (Miles, Teas)
Oak Forest
Oso (Cost)
Ottine (Otto)
Otto (Ottine)
Palo Alto
Peach Creek
Pecan Grove
Pilgrim (Karney)
Pilgrim's Lake
Possum Trot (Saturn)
Potts Mill (Monthalia)
Prickly Pear (Saturn)
Princeville
Rancho
Round Lake (Clabbertown,
   Zint)
Salt Stream
Sample
Sandies
Sandy Fork
Saturn (Ettowa, McGee
   Mill, Nash's Mill, Possum
   Trot, Prickly Pear)
Schoolland
Sedan (Elm Mound,
   Mound)
Slayden
SMILEY [Smiley Lake]
South Riverside (Hamon)
Stieren
Stroman (Bebe)
Summerville
Teas (Nopal)
Thompsonville (Cranz)
Vernon (Hamon)
WAELDER
Walsh (Arkansas, Gene)
Wells
Winnton
Wrightsboro
Zedlar's Mill (Dewet)
Zint (Clabbertown, Round
   Lake)
Zoar

Gray Co.
Alanreed (Gouge Eye,

Prairie Dog Town,
   Springtown)
Back
Bowers City
Boydston
Cabot Kingsmill
Coltexo
Crossland (Dow)
Denworth (Northfork)
Dow (Crossland)
Ecla (Kings Mill)
Eldridge (Elfin Grove)
Elfco (Texas Elf Co. Settle-
   ment)
Elfin Grove (Eldridge)
Glasgow (Pampa)
Gouge Eye (Alanreed)
Grandview
Heaton
Hoover
Kings Mill (Ecla)
Lacus (Laketon)
Laketon (Lacus)
LEFORS (Vera)
McLEAN
Meldavis
Mineral Springs
Northfork (Denworth)
Ontario (Pampa)
PAMPA (Glasgow,
   Ontario, Sutton)
Prairie Dog Town (Alan-
   reed)
Springtown (Alanreed)
Standish
Stanolind Camp
Sutton (Pampa)
Texas Elf Co. Settlement
   (Elfco)
Vera (Lefors)
Wesco
Whited
Wilcox

Grayson Co.
Allen's Grove (Pilot Grove)
Ambrose
Ann Eliza (Kentucky Town)
Bailey Junction (Bells)
Bain (Tribune)
Basin Springs
Bell Plain (Bells)
BELLS (Bailey Junction,
   Bell Plain, Gospel
   Ridge)
Bethesda
Blanton's Gin (Bliss)
Bliss (Blanton's Gin)
Boddie
Bona
Bug Tussle (Day)
Canaan
Cannon
Carpenters Bluff (Key,
   Sea)
Cedarfield (Colbert's
   Ferry)
Cedar Mills
Chambersville (Pottsboro)
Cherry Mound (Dugans-
   ville, Garlock)
Choctaw (Dugan's
   Chapel)
Clayton

Coffee's Station (Preston)
Colbert's Ferry (Cedar-
   field)
COLLINSVILLE (Spring-
   ville, Toadsuck)
Colville (Preston)
Cooks Springs (Ellsworth,
   Woodlake)
Cotton Mill Spur
Crossroads (Elmont)
Cutler (Weno)
Day (Bug Tussle, Hunter,
   Ober, Range Creek)
DENISON [Denison City]
   (Red River City)
Deaver (Hagerman,
   Steedman)
Dixie (Theodore)
DORCHESTER (Voelkle)
Dugan's Chapel (Choctaw)
Dugansville [Dugan's
   Store] (Cherry Mound)
Dudley Place (Gage)
Ellsworth (Cooks Springs,
   Woodlake)
Elmont (Crossroads, Fair
   Home, Pattie)
Elmview
Ethel
Fair Home (Elmont)
Farmington (Ferguson's)
Ferguson (Rock Creek)
Ferguson's (Farmington)
Fink (Georgetown)
Gage (Dudley Place, Plain
   View)
Garlock (Cherry Mound)
Georgetown (Fink)
Gordonville
Gospel Ridge (Bells)
Gover
Grayco
GUNTER
Hackberry Grove (Howe)
Hagerman (Deaver,
   Steedman)
Hanger
Highway
Hilton
HOWE (Hackberry Grove,
   Summit)
Hunter (Day)
Ida (King's Point)
Indian Grove (White
   Mound)
Jameson
Jaques Spur
Joe
Kendall
Kentucky Town (Ann Eliza)
Key (Carpenter's Bluff,
   Sea)
King's Point (Ida)
KNOLLWOOD
Lickskillet (Pilot Grove)
Lincoln Park (Ossaba)
Little Mineral (Woodbor-
   ough, Woodbury)
Locust (Morton)
Lower Station (Preston)
Luella (Lyon)
Lyon (Luella)
Macomb

Martin Springs
Midway Center
Mills
Mormon Grove (Sperry)
Morton (Locust)
Norton (Terrace)
Oak Grove
Oak Ridge
Ober (Day)
Ossaba (Lincoln Park)
Pattie (Elmont)
Penland
Pilot Grove (Allen's Grove,
   Lickskillet)
Pink Hill (Washburn)
Plain View (Gage)
POTTSBORO (Chambers-
   ville)
Preston (Colville, Coffee's
   Station, Lower Station,
   Washita)
Randall
Range Creek (Day)
Ray
Reavesville [Reevesville]
Red Branch
Red River
Red River City
Red River City (Denison)
Reddam
Reevesville [Reavesville]
Rock Creek (Ferguson)
SADLER (Talley)
Sandusky
Sea (Carpenters Bluff,
   Key)
SHERMAN
Sherwood Shores
Smith Oaks
South Gale
SOUTHMAYD
Sperry (Mormon Grove)
Springville (Collinsville)
Standard
Steedman (Deaver, Hager-
   man)
Summit (Howe)
Sunbeam
Talley (Sadler)
Terrace (Norton)
Theodore (Dixie)
TIOGA
Toadsuck (Collinsville)
Todd
TOM BEAN
Tribune (Bain)
Valley
VAN ALSTYNE
Voelkle (Dorchester)
Warner Junction
Washburn (Pink Hill)
Washita (Preston)
Waterloo
Weno (Cutler)
White Mound (Indian
   Grove)
White Rock
White's Colony (Whites-
   boro)
WHITESBORO[gh]
   (White's Colony)
WHITEWRIGHT
Woodborough (Little Min-

eral)
Woodbury (Little Mineral)
Woodlake (Cooks
  Springs, Ellsworth)
Yakima

Gregg Co.
Bodie
Calhoun
Camp Switch
Camps
CLARKSVILLE CITY
Crews Church (Swamp
  City)
Danville
EASTON
Elderville (Lakeport)
Footes
Forest Lake
Fredonia
GLADEWATER
Greggton
Hog Eye
Hughey
Judson
KILGORE
LAKEPORT (Elderville)
Liberty City
LONGVIEW
Melrose
Omega
Peatown
Rolling Meadows
Sabine
Seven Pines
Shell Camp
Spring Hill
Swamp City (Crews
  Church)
Teneryville
WARREN CITY
WHITE OAK

Grimes Co.
Adkins' Store (Davisville)
Aid
Alta Mira (Anderson)
ANDERSON (Alta Mira,
  Fanthorp's)
Apolonia (Lowery, Tickle-
  foot)
Bay (Fairview 1)
Becker
Bedi (Plaster)
Bedias
Betts
Carlos (Gibbons Creek)
Cawthon (Mesa)
Chaille
Cottage Home (Plaster)
Cotton
Courtney
Cross
Darby
Davisville (Adkins' Store)
Dolph (Fairview 1)
Erwin (Fuqua [Prairie,
  Store])
Fairview 1(Bay, Dolph,
  Key)
Fairview 2 (Iola)
Fanthorp's (Anderson)
Fuqua [Prairie, Store]
  (Erwin)

Gibbons Creek (Carlos)
Giesinger (Star)
Grimes Prairie
Grimes Switch
Grimesville
Groce's Retreat
Hadley's Prairie (Roans
  Prairie)
Hanrahan
Harmony
High Point (Jones Store)
Hollandale (Navasota)
Iola (Fairview 2)
Jones Store (High Point)
Keith (Martin['s] Prairie)
Kellum's Springs (White
  Sulphur Springs)
Key (Fairview 1)
Klondike (Mesa)
Lake Grove
Larimer
Levin
Lowery (Apolonia)
Lynn Grove
Manila (Singleton)
Martin['s] Prairie (Keith)
McCormack
McDaniel
McGuffin's
Mesa (Cawthon, Klondike)
Mount Pleasant
NAVASOTA (Hollandale,
  Nolanville)
Neason (Shiro)
Nolanville (Navasota)
Northwood (Ulmer)
Oakland Church (Roans
  Prairie)
Pankey
Piedmont [Springs]
Pilgrim Point
Plantersville
Plaster[ville] (Bedi,
  Cottage Home)
Polk
Prairie Plains
Red Star
Retreat
Richards
Roans Prairie [Roan's],
  (Hadley's Prairie, Oak-
  land Church,
  Steadmanville)
Rusk
Saint Holland
Saint Mary
Salem
Shiro (Neason)
Singleton (Manila)
Star (Giesinger)
Steadmanville (Roans
  Prairie)
Stoneham
Sulphur Springs
Ticklefoot (Apolonia)
TODD MISSION [Todd]
Ulmer (Northwood)
Wallace Prairie (White
  Hall)
White Hall (Wallace
  Prairie)
White Sulphur Springs
  (Kellum's Springs)

Woodswitch
Yarboro[ugh]

Guadalupe Co.
Acona (Mill Creek,
  Ramage)
Appling (Burl)
Barbarosa
Barrowdale
Beck's Store (Cameo)
Behring Store
Bernhardsville (Clear
  Spring)
Blumberg (McQueeney)
Blumberg Spur
Bonita
Brenner (Cameo)
Burl (Appling)
Cameo (Beck's Store,
  Brenner)
Camp Willow
Cardova
CIBOLO   (Cibolo Valley,
  Fromme's Store,
  Sartor)
Cibolo Valley (Cibolo)
Clear Spring (Bernhards-
  ville)
Clemens (Zuehl)
Cutoff (Schertz)
Dietz (Frankfort)
Divide (Zorn)
Dugger
Elmer
Elm Grove Camp
Faust (Junior)
Frankfort (Dietz)
Frier (McCellan's, Valley,
  Weir's)
Fromme's Store (Cibolo)
Galle
Gander Slue
Geronimo (Navarro)
Graeb
Grover (York Creek)
Guadalupe
Hickory Forrest
Hilda
Hillsboro
Hoover
Ilka
Jakes Colony
Junior (Faust)
Kingsbury
Lake Dunlap
Lake Placid
Laubach
Ligonville
Los Nogales (Seguin)
Lowell
Lowesville (Olmos)
MARION
McCellan's (Valley)
McQueeney (Blumberg)
Meadow Lake
Mill Creek (Acona,
  Ramage)
Navarro (Geronimo)
NEW BERLIN
Nixon
Nolte
Northcliff
O'Daniel (Sandy Elm)

Olmos [Olmus] (Lowes-
  ville)
Orchard
Parkview Estates
Perryman's Crossing
  (Zuehl)
Ramage (Acona, Mill
  Creek)
Redwood
Sandy Elm (O'Daniel)
Santa Clara
Sartor (Cibolo)
Scenic Hills
SCHERTZ (Cutoff, The
  Valley)
School (Zuehl)
Schumansville
SEGUIN (Los Nogales,
  Walnut Springs)
SELMA
Southridge Estates
Springs Hill
Staples [Staples' Store]
Sullivan [Siding]
Sweet Home
The Valley (Schertz)
Timm's Store (Zorn)
Treasure Island
Valley (Frier, McCellan's,
  Weir's)
Wade (Williams Store)
Walnut Springs (Seguin)
Weinert
Weir's (Frier, McCellan's,
  Valley)
Williams' Store (Wade)
York Creek [Valley]
  (Grover)
Zion Hill
Zippville
Zorn (Divide, Timm's
  Store)
Zuehl (Clemens, Perry-
  man's Crossing, School)

Hale Co.
ABERNATHY
Alley
Barton [Bartonsite]
Bebe
Boone
Central Plains (Seth Ward)
Clisbee
Copenhagen (Lakeview,
  Norfleet)
Cotton Center
Crawfish (Speedwell)
Cresco (Edmonson)
Edenville
EDMONSON (Cresco,
  Running Water, Wads-
  worth)
Ellen
Epworth (Hale Center)
Freeport (Seth Ward)
Finney
Furguson
HALE CENTER (Epworth,
  Hale City)
Hale City (Hale Center)
Halfway
Happy Union
Kennebunk

Lakeview (Copenhagen, Norfleet)
Mayfield
New Epworth
Norfleet (Copenhagen, Lakeview)
PETERSBURG
PLAINVIEW
Prairieview
Progress
Quarterway
Reinkin
Running Water (Edmonson)
Seth Ward (Central Plains, Freeport)
Snyder
Speedwell (Crawfish)
Strip
Underwood
Wadsworth (Edmonson)
Wasson
Wright

Hall Co.
Brice
Cone's Ranch (Ephraim)
Cone Springs (Ephraim)
Deep Lake (Shoe-Bar Ranch)
Deep Lake (Way)
Dothan
Eli (Elite, Twin Buttes)
Elite (Eli)
Elmore (Felix)
Ephraim (Cone's Ranch, Cone Springs)
ESTELLINE
Felix (Elmore)
Gazelle (Red River)
Gipaw
Greasy Neck (Parnell)
Hulver (Nebo, Red River Valley)
LAKEVIEW
Lesley
Locus (Plaska)
Lodge (Plaska)
MEMPHIS (Pope)
Nebo (Hulver)
Newlin
Ostella (Turkey)
Parnell (Greasy Neck)
Plaska (Locus, Lodge)
Pope (Memphis)
Poperanch (Webster's)
Red River (Gazelle)
Red River Valley (Hulver)
Rothwell (Tell)
Salisbury
Settlement
Shoe-Bar Ranch (Deep Lake)
South Brice
Tampico
Tell (Rothwell)
TURKEY [Turkey Roost] (Ostella)
Twin Buttes (Eli)
Way (Deep Lake)
Webster's (Poperanch)
Weatherly

Hamilton Co.

Agee (Lee)
Aleman (Piggtown, Pleasant Point)
Beulah (Shive)
Blue Ridge
Bristow (Vista)
Busyton
Carlton
Delta (Lancing)
EVANT
Evergreen
Fairy (Martins Gap)
Gentrys Mill [Gentry]
Germantown (Knox)
Gooch's Mill Shop (Ohio)
Gum Branch
HAMILTON (Hampton)
Hampton (Hamilton)
HICO
Honey Creek
Indian Gap
Jonesboro
Knox (Germantown)
Lancing (Delta)
Lanham
Lee (Agee)
Liberty
Littleville
Martins Gap (Fairy)
McGirk
Midway
Montvale
Mount (Vista)
Neill's Creek
Ohio (Gooch's Mill Shop)
Olin (Ridenhower)
Ondee
Pecan Wells
Piggtown (Aleman)
Pleasant Point (Aleman)
Pottsville
Rail (Rockett)
Ridenhower (Olin)
Rockett (Rail)
Rose (Strobel)
Schoolerville
Shive (Beulah)
Snowsville
Strobel (Rose)
Twin Mountain
Vista (Bristow, Mount)
West Point
Whitesboro (Whiteway)
Whiteway (Whitesboro)

Hansford Co.
Appleton
Bernstein
Buran (Lucern)
Chester (Hansford)
Cooper (Gruver)
Farwell
GRUVER (Cooper)
Hansford (Chester)
Hitchland
Kirksey
Lakeside (Record)
Lucern (Buran)
McKibben
Morse
Murlock
Oslo
Palo Duro Creek (Zulu)

Phillips Camp
Record (Lakeside)
Selmer (Spearman)
SPEARMAN (Selmer)
Wardville (Waverlan)
Waverlan (Wardville)
Zulu (Palo Duro Creek)

Hardeman Co.
Acme
Agatite
Batson (Elder)
Bertie (Hazel)
Bibles (Hooley Anne, Riley)
Carnes
Cement
CHILLICOTHE
Damsite
Elba
Elder (Batson)
Evans
Goodlett (Gypsum)
Groesbeck (Kirkland)
Gypsum (Goodlett)
Hazel (Bertie)
Herg
Hooleyan [Hooley Anne], (Bibles, Riley)
Kirkland (Groesbeck)
Lazare
Lubbock (Quanah)
Medicine Mound
North Groesbeck
Pauline
Punkin Center
QUANAH (Lubbock)
Riley (Bibles, Hooley Anne)
Stroud
Wheatland
Williams

Hardin Co.
Ariola (Chance, Hooks Switch, Sharon, Thurman)
Batson [Batson's Prairie], (Otto)
Bragg
Bud Conner
Caney Head
Carroll (Nona)
Chance (Ariola)
Chanceville (Rosedale)
Collier (Pinoak)
Concord
Dearborn
Dies
Evans (Pinoak)
Fletcher
Fresenius
Friendship (Saratoga)
GRAYBURG
Gusher
Hardin (Old Hardin)
Hathaway
Hebert (Lillard)
Hester
Honey Island (Matile)
Hooks Switch (Ariola)
Jasmine (Rosedale)
Kirby Town

KOUNTZE
Lelavale
Lillard (Hebert)
Loeb
Long Station (Village Mills)
LUMBERTON
Matile (Honey Island)
McShane
Mount Holland
New Sour Lake (Saratoga)
Neyland (Village Mills)
Noble (Plank)
Nona (Carroll)
Old Hardin (Hardin)
Olive (Sunset)
Otto (Batson)
Paulineville [Paulinasville]
Pinewood Estates
Pinoak (Collier, Evans)
Plank (Noble)
Pleasant Grove
Providence Hill
Reeves
Rosedale (Chanceville, Jasmine)
ROSE HILL ACRES
Saratoga (Friendship, New Sour Lake)
Seth
Sharon (Aliola)
SILSBEE
SOUR LAKE [Spring]
Sunset (Olive)
Strain
Thicket (Williams)
Thurman (Ariola)
Tryon
Village Creek
Village Mills ([Village Creek], Long Station, Neyland)
Votaw
West Nona
Williams (Thicket)
Woodrow

Harris Co.
Addicks (Bear Creek, Groschkeville, Laticia)
Airline
Aldine (Colby)
Alief (Dairy)
Almeda
Armco
Ashford (Satsuma)
Avonak
Bammel
Barker
Barrett
Baurs (Cleo)
Bayland
BAYTOWN (Goose Creek, Pelly)
Bay View (Morgan's Point)
Bear Creek (Addicks)
Beaumont Place
BELLAIRE
Bender
Big Cypress
Billpark
Bordersville
Boudreaux Estates
Brandenburg

Bratton
BUNKER HILL VILLAGE
Brighton (Deepwater)
Brunner
Busco
Cane Island (Katy)
Casey
Cedar Bayou
Cedar Bluff
Chalmers
Champions
Channel (Houston Termi-
  nals)
Channelview
Clear Lake City
Cleo (Baurs)
Clopper's (Morgan's Point)
Cloverleaf
Coady
Colby (Aldine)
Cring
Croft's Mills (Spring Creek)
Crosby
Cypress[-Fairbanks]
  (Cypress Top)
Cypress Grove
Cypress Top (Cypress)
Dairy (Alief)
Dawes
Deco
Deepwater (Brighton,
  Syracuse)
DEER PARK
Dixico
Donnybrook Place
Dumont (South Houston)
Dyersdale
East Houston
Edclauder
Eden (Hamblin's)
Eldon
Elena
EL LAGO
Ellendale (Genoa)
Etta (Slayton)
Eureka Mills
Eyle
Fairbanks (Gum Island)
Fauna
Fern
Fondren
Fortune
Four Corners
GALENA PARK
Garden Oaks
Gardentown (Webster)
Garth
Genoa (Ellendale, Sunset
  Station)
Gentry
Gish
Golden Acres
Goose Creek (Baytown)
Greens Bayou (Penn City)
Groschkeville (Addicks)
Gum Island (Fairbanks)
Habermacher
Hamblin's (Eden)
Hardy
Harmaston
Harrisburg[h]
Heacker
HEDWIG VILLAGE

Hennessey
Highlands
Hillendahl
HILSHIRE VILLAGE
Hockley
Houmont Park
Houseville
HOUSTON
Houston Heights
Houston Terminals
  (Channel)
Howellville
Hudson
Huffman
Hufsmith
HUMBLE
Humble Camp
Hunter's (Morgan's Point)
HUNTERS CREEK VIL-
  LAGE
Ida (Spring Creek)
JACINTO CITY
Jacintoport
Jeannetta
JERSEY VILLAGE
Jetero
Joyce
Junker's Cove (Middle
  Bayou)
KATY (Cane Island)
Kingwood
Kinwood
Kirkwood
Klein
Kohrville
Korville (Pilotville)
Lakeside
Lakewood
LA PORTE
Laticia (Addicks)
Laura
Lenora
Lincoln City
Lois
Lomax
Londonderry
Lord
Lotus
Louetta (Mooney)
Lynchburg[h] [Lynch's
  Ferry]
Mabry
Magnolia Gardens
Mantu
McDonough
McNair
Mechanicsville
Medio
Melendy
Middle Bayou (Junker's
  Cove)
MISSOURI CITY
Mooney (Louetta)
Moonshine Hill
MORGAN'S POINT (Bay
  View, Clopper's,
  Hunter's, New Washing-
  ton, Orange Grove,
  Rightor's)
Mount Houston
Mykawa
Myrtle [Turf] (Rose Hill)
NASSAU BAY

New Washington (Mor-
  gan's Point)
North Houston (Scoville)
Oak Forest
Oakley
Olcott
Old Spanish Trail Acres
Orange Grove (Morgan's
  Point)
Orr
PASADENA
Peck (Tomball)
Pelly (Baytown)
Penn City (Greens Bayou)
Penn's (San Jacinto)
Pierce [Peirce] Junction
Pilotville (Korville)
Pine Grove
PINEY POINT VILLAGE
Prairie Anna
Quality
Red Bluff
Ridlon
Rightor's (Morgan's Point)
River Terrace
Rose Hill (Myrtle Turf)
Rosewood Hill
Rosslyn (White Oak)
San Jacinto
San Jacinto (Penn's)
Satsuma (Ashford, Thomp-
  son Switch)
Scoville (North Houston)
SEABROOK
Sellers
Settlers Village
Sharpstown
Sheldon
SHOREACRES
Spil[l]man's Island
Sinco
Slayton (Etta)
SOUTH HOUSTON
  (Dumont)
SOUTHSIDE PLACE
Spence
Spring
Spring Branch
Spring Creek (Croft's
  Mills, Ida)
SPRING VALLEY
Stella
Stewart Heights
Stone Creek
Strang
Streets
Stuebner
Sunset Heights
Sunset Station (Genoa)
Syracuse (Deepwater)
TAYLOR LAKE VILLAGE
Thompson
Thompson Switch
  (Satsuma)
Thompsonville
TOMBALL (Peck)
Victor
Vollmer
WALLER
WEBSTER [Websterville]
  (Gardentown)
West Junction
West Park

WEST UNIVERSITY
  PLACE
Westfield
Whit
White Oak (Rosslyn)
Willow
Wooster

Harrison Co.
Baldwin
Blocker
Canaan
Carterville
Cave Springs
Concord
Crossroads
Darco
Eight Mile Creek
Elysian Fields
Estes
Fitzpatrick
Five Notch
Fox
Friendship
Gallalia
Gill
Grange Hall
Grove Controls
Gum Springs
HALLSVILLE
Harleton
Jonesville
Karnack
Lansing
Latex
Leigh
Lemo
LONGVIEW
Lotta
Macedonia
Macon
MARSHALL
Marshall Northeast
Morton
NESBITT
Noonday
Pirkey
Pleasant Hill
Port Caddo
Pumps
Quincy
Rosborough Springs
Sabine Farms
Saint John
Saint Mary
SCOTTSVILLE
Scratch Eye
Shoe String
Smyrna
Tallys
Texla
UNCERTAIN
Walkers Mill
WASKOM
Woodall
Woodlawn

Hartley Co.
Bravo
CHANNING
DALHART
Dalmoor
Duncan
Exit

Exumrs
Hartley
Middle Water
Rehm
Romero
Twist
Wagner
Wilcors

HASKELL Co.
Ample (Routon, Varina)
Carney (O'Brien)
Cliff
HASKELL (Rice Springs)
Irby
Jack (Mid)
Josselet
Jud40
Leavitt
Marcy
McConnell, ars
Mid (Jack)
Mount Zora (Vontress)
Nabors
O'BRIEN (Carney)
Paint Creek (Tacitus)
Pinkerton
Rice Springs (Haskell)
ROCHESTER
Routon (Ample)
RULE
Sagerton [Sager]
STAMFORD
Tacitus (Paint Creek)
Varina (Ample, Routon)
Vontress (Mount Zora)
WEINERT

Hays Co.
BEAR CREEK
Barton Creek (Fitzhugh)
Blanco
Best
BUDA (Dupree)
Cannonville
Capt's Mill
Cedar Valley
Centerpoint
Centex
Chapparal Park
Driftwood (Liberty Hill)
DRIPPING SPRINGS
Dupree (Buda)
Fairview
Fitzhugh (Barton Creek)
Georgia Colony (String-town)
Goforth (Prairie Hill)
Good (Olive, West Point, Yell)
Grover (Hugo)
HAYS
Hays City
Henly [Henly Ranch]
Huaca (Jacob's Well)
Hugo (Grover, Purgatory [Springs])
Jacob's Well (Huaca)
Johnson's Institute
Kushla
KYLE
Liberty Hill (Driftwood)
Manchac
Millseat

Monkeyville
MOUNTAIN CITY
Mount Gainor [Mount Gaynor]
Mount Sharp
New Home
NIEDERWALD
Olive (Good)
Oral
Prairie Hill (Goforth)
Purgatory [Springs] (Hugo)
Rooster Springs
SAN MARCOS
Santa Cruz
Science Hall
Sid
Stringtown (Georgia Colony)
UHLAND
West Point (Good)
Wimberley
WOODCREEK
Yell (Good)
Yell Settlement

Hemphill Co.
Boggy Station (Springer Ranch)
CANADIAN
Cann
Cataline
Clear Creek (Stickley)
Drefoos
Gageby [Valley]
Gem [City]
Glazier
Grangerville
Hopkins
Isaacs
Mendota
Oak Hill (Seven Oaks)
Seven Oaks (Oak Hill)
Springer Ranch (Boggy Station)
Stickley (Clear Creek)
Washita
Zybach

Henderson Co.
Aberdeen
Acker's Ferry (Uneva)
Acme
Aley (Flat Foot)
Alfred
Alvin (Athens)
Ash
ATHENS (Alvin)
Baxter
BERRYVILLE
Bethel
BROWNSBORO[ugh] (Normandy)
Buffalo (Uneva)
Bute (Curry, Lewis)
CANEY CITY
Catfish
Centreville
CHANDLER (Stillwater)
COFFEE CITY
Cottage
Crescent Heights (Midway)
Cross Roads
Curry (Bute)
Dauphin (Frances)

De Graffenreid (Nell)
ENCHANTED OAKS
EUSTACE (Jolo, Lena, Moseley)
Fincastle
Flat Foot (Aley)
Fox (Perley)
Frances (Dauphin)
Garry (Ham)
Gerome
Goshen
Gossett Switch (Ham)
Greeson (Post Oak)
GUN BARREL CITY
Ham (Garry, Gossett Switch, Pauline)
Hudsonville (Leagueville)
Jolo (Eustace)
Kenelm
Kodal
Larue
Leagueville (Lutes, Hudsonville)
Lena (Eustace)
Lewis (Bute)
Lindsey (Murchison)
LOG CABIN
Loper
Lutes (Leagueville)
MABANK
MALAKOFF
Mallard Prairie (Payne Springs)
Mance (Shadeville)
Mankin
Merv (Powell Mills)
Midway (Crescent Heights)
Modoc
MOORE STATION
Moseley (Eustace)
MURCHISON (Lindsey)
Naught (Stockard)
Nell (De Graffenreid)
Neosho
New York
Normandy (Brownsboro)
Opelika (Wanda)
Pauline (Ham)
PAYNE['s] SPRINGS (Mallard Prairie)
Perley (Fox)
Pickens
Pine Grove
Pleasant Oaks
Pleasant Ridge
Post Oak (Greeson)
Powell Mills (Merv)
POYNOR [Poyner]
Rockville (Stump)
Ruth Springs
Science Hall
Scottsville
SEVEN POINTS
Shackelford
Shadeville (Mance)
Shady Oaks
Smitty
STAR HARBOR
Stewart (Tool)
Stillwater (Chandler)
Stockard (Naught)
Stump (Rockville)
Ten Mile

Tince
Tindel
Tolosa
TOOL (Stewart)
TRINIDAD (Trinity Switch)
Trinity Switch (Trinidad)
Uneva (Acker's Ferry, Buffalo)
Wanda (Opelika)
Wildcat
Yale Seminary

Hidalgo Co.
Abram-Perezville (Ojo de Agua)
ALAMO (Ebenezer, Forum, Swallow)
Alsonia
ALTON (Oblate)
Asadores Ranch (Runn)
Bates
Beatriz (East Donna, Hooks)
Bleakley
Booner
California Store (Red Gate)
Campo Alto
Cantu
Carlota
Ceniza
Cenizal
Chapin (Edinburg)
Chihuahua
Cipres (Sanramon, Santarita)
Citrus City
Closner (Peñitas)
Conway (Mission)
Cuevitas
Delfina (Esperanza Ranch, Laguna Seca Ranch, Vela)
Diaz (Mercedes)
DONNA
East Donna (Beatriz)
Ebenezer (Alamo)
EDCOUCH
EDINBURG (Chapin)
Edinburgh (Hidalgo)
El Gato
El Sal de Rey
El Sauz
ELSA
Esperanza Ranch (Delfina)
Faysville
Filigonio (Hargill)
Forum (Alamo)
GRANJENO
Guadalupe Ranch (Timothy)
Hargill (Filigonio)
Hauser
Havana (Peñitas)
Heidelberg
HIDALGO (Edinburgh, La Habitacion, Rancho San Luis, San Luisito)
Hidalgo Park (Las Mapas)
Hooks (Beatriz)
Jara China
Kane
Ken

Kodol
La Blanca
Laguna Seca Ranch
    (Delfina)
La Habitacion (Hidalgo)
La Homa
LA JOYA
Lake James
La Lomita (Mission)
Las Mapas-Hidalgo Park
Las Milpas
LA VILLA
Lindsay Gardens
Linn
Llano Grande
Lonsboro (Mercedes)
Lopezville
Los Ebanos
Lull
Madero (Mission)
McALLEN
McColl
McCook
MERCEDES (Diaz, Lons-
    boro)
Mercier
Merito
Mila Doce
MISSION (Conway, La
    Lomita, Madero)
Monte Alto
Monte C[h]risto
Monte Cristo
North Alamo
Oblate (Alton)
Ojo de Agua (Abram)
PALMHURST
PALMVIEW
Panchita
PEÑITAS (Closner,
    Havana)
Perezville (Abram-Perez-
    ville)
PHARR
Prajedis (San Jose)
PROGRESO (Toluca)
PROGRESO LAKES
Puerto Rico
Ramona
Rancho San Luis (Hidalgo)
Red Gate (California Store,
    Solino)
Reedyville (Relampago)
Relampago (Reedyville,
    Rudyville)
Rincon
Rogerslacy
Rudyville (Relampago)
Runn [Run] (Asadores
    Ranch)
Samfordyce
San Carlos
San Jose (Prajedis)
SAN JUAN
San Luisito (Hidalgo)
San Manuel
Sanramon (Cipres)
Sanramon (Timothy)
Santarita (Cipres)
Savage
Scissors
Sharyland
Solino (Red Gate)

Spaulding
Stockholm
Stone
Sullivan City
Swallow (Alamo)
Tabasco
Thayer
Tierra Blanca
Timothy [Timo] (Guada-
    lupe Ranch, Sanramon)
Toluca (Progreso)
Tom Gill
Val Verde
Vela (Delfina)
Villa Nueva
Waite
WESLACO

Hill Co.
ABBOTT
AQUILLA (Mud Town, Pat-
    ton's Mill)
Ash Creek (Halfway)
Bat (Matson)
Bell Springs (Massey)
Bethlehem
Birome
Blanton
BLUM
Bonanza
Brandon (Jackson, White
    Rock)
Brazlime
Brigman (Pollard)
Brushy Knob (Derden)
Burdette
BYNUM
Calera (Prairie Valley)
CARL'S CORNER
Carr's (Liberty Grove)
Cedar Creek Park
Chatt
Cochran (Penelope)
COVINGTON
Coxville
Crimea
Culp (White's Wells)
Derden (Brushy Knob,
    Yaterville)
Eufaula
Fair View
Farmers' Point (Hanover)
Files Valley [Files]
Fort Graham (Robertson)
Fraser
Gist (Huron)
Greenwade's Mills
    (Towash)
Halfway (Ash Creek)
Hammels Branch (Story)
Hanover (Farmers' Point)
Heckler (Lakenon)
Heritage (Lakenon)
HILLSBORO[ouh]
HUBBARD [City]
    (McLainsborough,
    Slap Out)
Huron (Gist, Neal)
Irene
ITASCA
Iverson (Sanford, Sevier)
Jackson (Brandon)
Jessie (Quillin's Store)

Kerby (Neugent)
Lakenon (Heckler, Heri-
    tage)
Lee (Tyson)
Liberty Grove (Carr's)
Lingo (Prairie Valley)
Lovelace
MALONE
Martin
Massey (Bell Springs)
Matson (Bat)
Mayfield
McLainsborough (Hub-
    bard)
Menlow
MERTENS
Midway
Monterey
MOUNT CALM
Mountain Springs
Mud Town (Aquilla)
Mulkey
Neal (Huron)
Neugent (Kerby)
Oak Springs
Oak Valley
Old Towash
Osceola
Patton's Mill (Aquilla)
PENELOPE (Cochran,
    Zeevee)
Peoria
Pollard (Brigman)
Prairie Valley (Calera, Lin-
    go, Tittle, Valley Springs)
Quillin's Store (Jessie)
Retreat
Rienzi
Robertson (Fort Graham)
Sanford (Iverson)
Sevier (Iverson)
Shale
Slap Out (Hubbard)
Stanley
Story (Hammels Branch)
Tittle (Prairie Valley)
Towash (Greenwade's
    Mills)
Tyson (Lee)
Union Bluff
Valley Springs (Prairie
    Valley)
Vaughan
Walling
White Rock (Brandon)
White's Wells (Culp)
WHITNEY
Woodbury
Yaterville (Brushy Knob,
    Derden)
Yates
Zeevee (Penelope)

Hockley Co.
ANTON
Arnett
Balch
Busterville
Clauene
Coble
Dean
Fairview
Farm Home

LEVELLAND
Lockettville
Oklahoma Flat
Opdyke
OPDYKE WEST
Pep
Pettit
ROPESVILLE
Roundup
SMYER
SUNDOWN
Whitharral

Hood Co.
Acton (Camanche
    [Comanche] Peak)
Add-Ran
Arrowhead Shores
Ball Knob [Bald Knob]
Barnardville (Fort Spunky)
Brushy
Centre [Center] Mill
Chapin
Camanche Peak (Acton)
Colvin (Neri)
Comanche Cove
Comanche Harbor
Cresson
DeCordova
Fairview
Fort Spunky (Barnardville)
Goather's (Paluxy)
GRANBURY
Haley's Mill (Paluxy)
Haynesburgh
Hill City
Himmons (Paluxy)
Jabco
Jones (Mambrino)
Indian Harbor Estates
Kristenstad
Laguna Tres Estates
LIPAN
Mambrino (Jones)
Neri (Colvin)
Oak Hill
Oak Trail Shores
Paluxy (Goather's, Haley's
    Mill, Himmons, Pull
    Tight)
Panter [Branch]
Pecan Plantation
Pull Tight (Paluxy)
Rock Harbor
Rolling Hills Shores
Sky Harbor
Slocum
Spanish Trail
Squaw Creek
Squaw Creek Station
    (Tolar)
Sulphur Springs
Thorp [Thorp's] Spring
TOLAR (Squaw Creek
    Station)
Waples

Hopkins Co.
Addran (Corinth, Ewing)
Arbala (Clifton's Prairie)
Askew (Bethel)
Bacchus (Como)
Barker Springs (Shirley)
Beckham

Bethel (Askew)
Birthrigt (Lone Star)
Black Jack Grove (Cumby)
Black Oak
Bonanza (Cold Hill, Fowler's Store)
Booneville (Dike)
Branom
Brashear (Mahoney)
Bright Star (Sulphur Springs)
Brinker
Carroll's Prairie (Como)
Carrollton (Como)
Chapman Arms (Tira)
Chappell (Tira)
Clifton's Prairie (Arbala)
Cold Hill (Bonanza)
COMO (Bacchus, Carroll's Prairie, Carrollton)
Corinth (Addran)
Cornersville (Grotto, Leta)
Crisp (Posey)
Crossroads
CUMBY (Black Jack Grove, Theodocia)
Daisy
Dennis Chapel (Tira)
Dike (Booneville, Rhodes)
Dillon
Divide
East Caney
Emblem (Soon-over)
Evans Point
Ewing (Addran)
Fabius (Irvin)
Fairyland (Peerless)
Flora
Fowler's Store (Bonanza)
Frazer (Shirley)
Gafford
Gay's Mill (Peerless)
Glade Creek
Gold Dollar
Gold Hill
Good Neighbor
Greenpond
Greenview
Greenwood (Penn)
Grotto (Cornersville)
Hager
Hatchetville
Hill Dale (Peerless)
Hulsey (Tige)
Igie
Irvin (Fabius)
Jacksonville (Pickton)
Lake Fork
Leta (Cornersville)
Liberty
Line
Lone Star (Birthright)
Liberty
Lynch
Mahoney (Brashear)
Mahoney (Whiteoak)
Martin Springs
Miller Grove
Mount Pisgah (Pine Forest)
Nelta
New Birthright
North Hopkins

Oakdale
Oak Grove
Old Tarrant
Patmos
Peerless (Fairyland, Gay's Mill, Hill Dale)
Penn (Greenwood)
Pickton (Jacksonville)
Pine Forest (Mount Pisgah)
Pleasant Grove
Pleasant Hill
Posey (Crisp, Reuben)
Post Oak Grove
Reilly Springs
Retina
Reuben (Posey)
Rhodes (Dike)
Ridgeway
Ruff
Saltillo (Twin Groceries)
Seymore
Sherley (Shirley)
Shirley (Barker Springs, Frazer, Sherley)
Six Mile (Whiteoak)
Soon-over (Emblem)
Sulphur Bluff
SULPHUR SPRINGS (Bright Star)
Tarrant
Tazewell
Tenrag
Theodocia (Cumby)
Thermo
Tige (Hulsey)
TIRA (Chapman Arms, Chappell, Dennis Chapel)
Topp
Twin Groceries (Saltillo)
Union
Valparaiso
Valton
Weaver
Weir
Weirville
Whiteoak (Mahoney, Six Mile)
White Oak
White Oak Junction
Winterfield
Wolfpen
Woodland
Yesner

Houston Co.
Abe
Alabama (Wiggins)
Alma (Tadmor)
Alum Wells (Belott)
Antioch (Prairie)
Arbor [Grove] (Pleasant Grove)
Ash (Chandler)
Ashby
Augusta (Boston)
Austonio (Creek, Georgia Camp, Pearville)
Baker's Mill (Holly)
Bass (Waneta)
Belott (Alum Wells)
Bennett's (Fort Bennett)
Berea

Bird (Center Hill)
Boston (Augusta)
Bradley (Plain)
Broxson (Whitesville)
Burrantown
Byrd (Center Hill)
Calhoun's Ferry
Camel (Udston)
Center Grove
Center Hill (Bird, Byrd)
Chandler (Ash)
Coltharp
Cooper
Creath
Creath (Hickory Creek)
Creek (Austonio)
Creswell [Criswell]
CROCKETT
Cut (Paso Station)
Dalys
Daniel (Oak Hill, Vilas)
Dixon-Hopewell
Dodson[ville]
Doxie (Tesla)
Druso (Mayfield)
Edmond (New Prospect)
Eliza
Elkhart (Halls Bluff)
Fife (Hagerville)
Fodice
Fort Bennett (Bennett's)
Georgia Camp (Austonio)
Germany
Glencoe
GRAPELAND (Grapevine)
Grapevine (Grapeland)
Hagerville (Fife)
Hailesburgh (Hailville)
Hailville (Hailesburgh, Mustang Prairie)
Halls Bluff (Elkhart)
Hancock (James)
Hickory Creek (Creath, Kyleville)
High Prairie (Volga)
Holly (Baker's Mill)
Hopewell
James (Hancock)
Joe (Waneta)
Julian
KENNARD
Kent[s Hill, Store] (Reynard)
Kyleville (Hickory Creek)
LATEXO (Oldham, Stark's Switch)
Lewis' (Masters')
Liberty Hill
Lone Pine
Longstreet
LOVELADY
Lundy (Selvin)
Luray
Mapleton
Masters' (Lewis')
Mayfield (Druso)
Mound City
Mount Vernon
Murchison's Prairie (Percilla)
Mustang Prairie (Hailville)
Naches
Neche

New Prospect (Edmond)
Oak Hill (Daniel)
Old Glover
Oldham (Latexo)
Oriole
Parker's Mills
Paso Station (Cut)
Pearsons Chapel (Post Oak)
Pearville (Austonio)
Pennington
Percilla (Murchison's Prairie, San Pedro)
Pettit's
Pine Branch (Udston)
Plain (Bradley)
Pleasant Grove (Arbor)
Porter Springs
Post Oak (Pearsons Chapel)
Prairie (Antioch)
Randolph
Ratcliff [Ratcliff's Mills]
Refuge
Reynard (Kent['s Hill, Store])
Roadville
Robbins Ferry
San Pedro (Percilla)
Sand Ridge
Sea
Selvin (Lundy)
Shady Grove
Sheridan
Shiloh
Smith Grove
Stark
Stark's Switch (Latexo)
Sorghumville
Stubblefield
Stumpville
Sullivan's Bluff (Tesla)
Sunshine
Tadmor (Alma)
Telegraph Mills (Udston)
Tesla (Doxie, Sullivan's Bluff)
Time (Vistula)
Udston (Camel, Pine Branch, Telegraph Mills)
Vilas (Daniel)
Vistula (Time)
Volga (High Prairie)
Waneta (Bass, Joe)
Webb (Wiggins)
Weches
Weldon
Wheeler Springs
Whitesville (Broxson)
Wigfall
Wiggins (Alabama, Webb)
Wooters

Howard Co.
Auto (Light, Walker)
BIG SPRING
Bisco
Chalkton [Chalk Lease, Chalk Store] (Otis Chalk)
COAHOMA (Minterville)
Earl
Elbow
Fairview
FORSAN

Knott
Light (Auto)
Lomax
Luther *(Nall)*
Midway
Minterville (Coahoma)
Morita
Morris *(Willow Creek)*
Nall (Luther)
Otis Chalk *(Chalkton)*
Ross City
Sand Springs
Soash
South Haven
Vealmoor
Vincent *(Vinson)*
Vinson (Vincent)
Wakefield
Walker (Auto)
Willow Creek *(Morris)*

Hudspeth Co.
Ables
Ables Springs
Acala
Acme (Allamoore)
Allamoore *(Acme, Carrizo)*
Arispie (La Valley)
Birchville *(Smith's Ranch)*
Bola
Camp Rice (Fort Hancock)
Carrizo (Allamoore)
Cornudas
Crusher
Dalberg
DELL CITY
Eagle Flat
Esperanza
Etholen
Finlay, ars
Fort Hancock *(Camp Rice, Fort Rice)*
Fort Rice (Fort Hancock)
Fort Quitman
Grayton
Gypsum
Hardwick
Harris
Hot Wells
Iser
Lasca
La Valley *(Arispie)*
Madden
Mallie
McNary *(Nulo)*
Mica
Nulo (McNary)
Salt Flat
Sierra Blanca
Small
Smith's Ranch *(Birchville)*
Stevenson
Taza
Torbert
Torcer
Villa

Hunt Co.
Aberfoyle
Allah
Alliance *(Harrell, Lone Cottonwood, Stinson)*
Ardis *(Neyland)*
Ashland (Commerce)

Ashville
Bean Creek
Benson
Big Four (Theta)
Bissell (Fox)
Black Cat (Lilly)
Bradburn *(Celeste)*
Bruceton
Brumley's Mill (Timber Creek)
Burrow
Byzone
Caddo Camp
CADDO MILLS *[Caddo]*
Caddo Villa
CAMPBELL *(Oliverea, Tom Campell)*
Cash *(Sylvia)*
CELESTE *(Bradburn)*
Center Point
Clair (Humphrey)
Clinton *(Haney)*
COMMERCE *(Ashland, Cowhill)*
Concord
Cowhill (Commerce)
Culberson
Decorah (Harlow)
Dent
Devenport *(Neola)*
Dewey *(Dulaney)*
Dickson (Dixon)
Dixon *(Dickson)*
Donelton
Dulaney *(Dewey)*
Dyer *(Lester)*
Elm Creek
Fairlie *(Hinckley)*
Fergus
Floyd *(Foster Station, Oliverea)*
Foster Station (Floyd)
Fox *(Bissell, Wells' Gin)*
Graham Prairie *(Hunt)*
Granby
Green's Point
GREENVILLE
Half Way *(Raney)*
Haney (Clinton)
Harlow *(Decorah)*
Harrell *(Alliance, Stinson)*
HAWK COVE
Hawley *(Theta)*
Hendricks
Hetty
Hickory Creek
Hickory Hollow
Hillcrest
Hillville (Wieland)
Hinckley (Fairlie)
Hogeye
Holiness *[University] (Peniel)*
Hooker
Hoover's Gin (Scatter Branch)
Humboldt
Humphrey *(Clair)*
Hunt *(Graham Prairie)*
Jacobia *(Jacob's Prairie)*
Jacob's Prairie (Jacobia)
Jardin
Jot-Em-Down

Kellogg
Kenser
Kingston *(Whynot)*
Kitsee Ridge
Lane
Lester *(Dyer)*
Lilly *(Black Cat)*
Lone Cottonwood *(Alliance)*
LONE OAK
Meadowview
Melton
Merit[t]
Mexico
Middle Caddo
Mina
Mineral Heights
Mohegan
Muddig
Nay *(Neola)*
Neola *(Devenport, Nay)*
Neyland *(Ardis)*
NEYLANDVILLE
Oliverea *(Campbell)*
Oliverea *(Floyd)*
Orion *(Wagner)*
Orleans *(Van Sickle)*
Paynes Store
Peniel *(Holiness)*
Pleasant Valley
Prairie Hill *(Wynton)*
Prairie Valley *(Sodom)*
QUINLAN
Raney *(Half Way)*
Rich
Roberts
Sabine Lake
Scatter Branch *(Hoover's Gin)*
Shiloh
Sikes
Simtrott
Sodom *(Prairie Valley)*
South Sulphur
Spencer *(Tony)*
Stinson *(Alliance, Harrell)*
Stringtown
Sylvia *(Cash)*
Theta *(Big Four, Hawley)*
Tidwell
Tidwell Creek *(White Rock)*
Timber Creek *(Brumley's Mill)*
Tom Campbell *(Campbell)*
Tony *(Spencer)*
Turkey Creek
Union Valley
Van Sickle *(Orleans)*
Wagner *(Orion)*
Wells' Gin *(Fox)*
WEST TAWAKONI
Whitehead
White Rock *(Tidwell Creek)*
Whynot *(Kingston)*
Wieland *(Hillville)*
WOLFE CITY *(Wolf's Mill)*
Wolf's Mill *(Wolf[e] City)*
Wynton *(Prairie Hill)*
Yancy
Yowell

Hutchinson Co.
Adobe
Adobe Walls
Alhambra
Alpha *(Parksdale)*
Big Creek *(Horace)*
BORGER
Brack *(Salome)*
Bugbee *[Heights]*
Bunavista
Corner *(Jeffry)*
Dial
Double Diamond Estates
Electric City
FRITCH
Gewhitt
Glenn *(Peacevale)*
Granada
Granada *(Isom)*
Gulf Dial
Harmony *(Lieb)*
Horace *(Big Creek)*
Ideal
Ingerton *(Oil City)*
Isom *(Granada)*
Jeffry *(Corner)*
Lieb *(Harmony)*
Mayfield *(Parksdale)*
Oil City *(Ingerton)*
Pantex
Parksdale *(Alpha, Mayfield)*
Peacevale *(Glenn)*
Phillips *(Whittenburg)*
Plemons
Pringle
Salome *(Brack)*
SANFORD
Signal Hill
Spring Creek
STINNETT
Texroy
Whittenburg *(Phillips)*
Windom

Irion Co.
Arden
Barnhart
Camp Charlotte
Irion City
MERTZON
Sherwood

Jack Co.
Adieu *(Bartons Chapel)*
Antelope *[Antelope Prairie]*
Arctic *(Grove, Pleasant Valley)*
Avis *(Dar Corner, Draper)*
Bartons Chapel *(Adieu, Keechi)*
Berwick *(Jeannette)*
Bob Town
Brummets Ranch *(Groveland)*
BRYSON
Burton Springs *(Veto)*
Cloyd *(Finis)*
Como *(Ovid)*
Cottonwood *(Mount Hecla)*
Coxton *(Gibtown)*
Cundiff *(Howard Valley)*
Dar Corner *(Avis)*
De Gress

Dick (Marmaduke)
Dillingham Prairie (Perrin)
Draper (Avis)
Echo (Handy)
Elkhorn
Field Senate
Finis (Cloyd, Marshall's Store)
Friendship
Gertrude[s]
Gibtown (Coxton, New Hope City)
Greathouse (Stewarton)
Grove (Arctic)
Groveland (Brummets Ranch)
Guthrie
Haley
Haley Springs (Joplin)
Handy (Echo)
Hensley
Hogeye
Howard Valley (Cundiff)
JACKSBORO[ugh] (Lost Creek, Mesquiteville)
Jackson's Gin (Squaw)
Jeannette (Berwick)
Jermyn
Joplin (Haley Springs)
Keechi (Bartons Chapel)
Kuchton (Long Hollow)
Little Lost Valley (Mount Hecla)
Long Hollow (Kuchton)
Lost Creek (Jacksboro)
Lunarville
Marmaduke (Dick)
Marshall's Store (Finis)
Maryetta
Mesquiteville (Jacksboro)
Mount Hecla (Cottonwood, Little Lost Valley)
New Hope City (Gibtown)
Newport, Clay-Jack
New Vineyard (Vineyard)
Oakland
Ovid (Como, Ruby, Union Point)
Paulina (Ross Valley)
Perrin (Dillingham Prairie)
Pleasant Valley (Arctic)
Postoak
Ross Valley (Paulina)
Ruby (Ovid)
Salt Hill
Sebree (Vineyard)
Senate
Squaw [Mountain] (Jackson's Gin)
Stewarton (Greathouse)
Truce
Union Point (Ovid)
Veto (Burton Springs)
Vineyard (New Vineyard, Sebree)
Vineyard (Wizard Wells)
Web City
Westbrook
Wilson Station
Wizard Wells (Vineyard)

Jackson Co.
Bacontown

Bennview (La Salle)
Benwest (La Salle)
Benzine (Devil's Drag, Kerr's, La Baca, Lavacca, Stapp's, Morales de Lavaca)
Big Motte (Edna)
Bonham's Store (Navidad)
Buhler (Caranchua, McDowell, Rose)
Carancahua (Cheeseburg, Lewis' Wharf)
Caranchua (Buhler)
Cheeseburg (Carancahua)
Cordele
Cordull
Crossroads
Devil's Drag (Benzine)
Dixie
EDNA [Ednaville] (Big Motte, Macaroni Station)
El Toro
Francitas
GANADO (Mustang Settlement)
Gandy
Kerr's (Benzine)
La Baca (Benzine)
LaSalle (Bennview, Benwest)
Lavacca (Benzine)
LA WARD
Lewis' Wharf (Carancahua)
Lolita
Macaroni Station (Edna)
Manson
Matilda
McDowell (Buhler)
McFarland (Mustang Settlement)
Menefee's (Texana)
Minnie (Navidad)
Morales
Morales De Lavaca (Benzine)
Mustang Settlement (Granado)
Navidad
Navidad (Bonham's Store, Minnie)
Red Bluff
Rose (McDowell)
Santa Anna (Texana)
Stapp's (La Baca)
Stonewall
Swan Lake
Texana (Menefee's, Santa Anna)
Vanderbilt
Weedhaven
White Hall
Wood Port

Jasper Co.
Aldridge
Applegate
Barclay (Kyles Quarry)
Beans [Place]
Beech [Beach] Grove (Curtis)
Beech Grove (Duncan)
Bell's Ferry

Bessmay
Bevilport
Bevil Settlement (Jasper)
Big Creek (Erin)
Blox
Bon Ami (Leeton)
BROWNDELL
Buna (Carrolla)
Bunker Hill
Byerly's Gin (Curtis)
Cairo [Springs]
Call Junction
Carrolla (Buna)
Chambersburgh
Clear Creek (Howell)
Cogniac (Roy)
Collins
Cross (Horger)
Curtis (Beech [Beach] Grove, Byerly's Gin)
Dryburg (Harrisburg)
Duncan (Beech Grove)
Ebenezer
Eclipse
Erin (Evadale)
Erin (Big Creek, Faircloth)
Evadale (Erin, Ford's Bluff, Jasper Mills, Richardson's [Bluff])
Faircloth (Erin)
Ferguson
Floy (Ford's Mill)
Forbes
Ford's Bluff (Evadale)
Ford's Mill (Floy)
Friendship
Gilmerville (Remlig)
Gist (Slade's Camp)
Graham
Grand [Grant's] Bluff (Weiss Bluff)
Grange (Holly Springs)
Harrisburg (Dryburg)
Haywood (Shoup)
Holly Springs (Grange)
Holmes'
Horger (Cross)
Horton
Howell (Clear Creek)
JASPER (Bevil Settlement)
Jasper Mills (Evadale)
Keithton Switch
Kenerly
KIRBYVILLE
Kyles Quarry (Barclay)
La Verte
Leeton (Bon Ami)
Lewis Ferry (Morris Ferry)
Magnolia Springs (Pinetucky)
Meritt's
Morris Ferry (Lewis Ferry)
Mount Jordan
Mount Union
New Blox
Newtonville (Roganville)
Pace's Ferry
Parkers
Pinetucky (Magnolia Springs)
Peach Tree
Proserpina (Westbrook)

Remlig (Gilmerville)
Richardson's [Bluff] (Evadale)
Robertson
Roganville (Newtonville)
Roy (Cogniac)
Sam Rayburn
Science Hall
Shoup (Haywood)
Slade's Camp (Gist)
Spring Hill
Temco
Temple Springs
Tram
Turpentine
Union
Walnut Run
Weiss Bluff (Grand Bluff)
Wenasco
Westbrook (Proserpina)
West Bevilport
Woodlawn
Wright's
Zavalla
Zeirath
Zion Hill

Jeff Davis Co.
Casey
Chihuahua (Fort Davis)
Chispa
El Alamo de San Juan (Fort Davis)
Fort Davis (Chihuahua, El Alamo de San Juan, Limpia Cañon, Painted Comanche Camp)
Huelster (San Solomon)
Legard's Ranch (Musquis)
Limpia
Limpia Cañon (Fort Davis)
Madera Springs
Musquis (Legard's Ranch)
Painted Comanche Camp (Fort Davis)
Povenir
Rubio
San Solomon (Huelster)
VALENTINE
Wendell

Jefferson Co.
Amelbulk
Amelia (Cornstreet, Elizabeth)
Atreco
Aurora (Port Arthur)
BEAUMONT (Beaumont Neches, Tevis Bluff)
Beaumont Neches (Beaumont)
Beaux Art Gardens
BEVIL OAKS
Boyt
Brooks
Broussard's Store (LaBelle)
Bunch
Buttfield (Nome)
Central Gardens
Chaison
Cheek
CHINA (Nashland, Turnertown)

China Grove
Concord
Cornstreet (Amelia)
Delphine
Dowling
Elizabeth (Amelia)
El Vista
Elwood (Voth)
Evora
Fannett (Taylor's Bayou)
Frankston (Voth)
Funston (Obal)
Galloway
Garner's
Gilburg
Gladys (Guffey)
Grenada (Obal)
Griffing Park
Grigsby [Bluff] (Smiths Bluff)
GROVES (Pecan Grove)
Guffey (Gladys [City])
Hamshire (Paul Wheeler)
Hayes
Hebert
Hebron (Rosedale)
Helbig
Higgins
Keith Lake
LaBelle (Broussard's Store, Lower Taylor Bayou)
Lakeview
Lower Taylor Bayou (LaBelle)
Magpetco
Meeker
Morey
Nashland (China)
NEDERLAND
New Bethel
NOME (Buttfield, Sour Lake)
Obal (Funston, Grenada)
Odelia
Paul Wheeler (Hamshire)
Pear Ridge
Pecan Grove (Groves)
Pine Island
Port Acres
PORT ARTHUR (Aurora)
PORT NECHES
Rosedale (Hebron)
Sabine
Sabine Pass [Sabine City]
Smiths Bluff (Grigsby, Smyth's Bluff)
Smyth's Bluff (Smiths Bluff)
Sour Lake (Nome)
Spindletop
Steeltown
Sun
Taylor's Bayou (Fannett)
Tevis Bluff (Beaumont)
Turnertown (China)
Viterbo
Voth (Elwood, Frankston)
Walden
West Port Arthur
Westbury [Westberry]
Williams
Wolf Point
Woodruff

Zummo

Jim Hogg Co.
Agua Nueva
Altavista (Jones' Ranch)
Baldaras
Colorado (Guerra)
Cuevitas
El Sordo
Guerra (Colorado)
Hebbronville (Peña Station)
Humble Colorado Camp
Jones' Ranch (Altavista)
Old San Antonio
Peña Station (Hebbronville)
Petroleum
Ramirez (Ramirito)
Ramirito (Ramirez, San Pedro)
Randado
Salado
San Pedro (Ramirito)
Thompsonville

Jim Wells Co.
Alfred (Driscoll)
ALICE (Bandana, Kleberg)
Armagosa
Bandana (Alice)
Ben Bolt
Bentonville
Camada Ranch (Springfield)
Casa Blanca (Wade's City)
Collins
Driscoll (Alfred)
El Carro
El Par
El Tacalote
Ella
Eva (Palito Blanco)
Galvez
Kleberg (Alice)
Knolle Nueces
La Gloria
Los Machos
Mae
Mary
Midway
Modern
ORANGE GROVE
Palito Blanco (Eva)
Penitas
PERNITAS POINT
PREMONT
Rancho Alegre
Rancho de la Parita
Sandia
SAN DIEGO
Seeligson
Springfield (Camada Ranch)
Torian
Wade's City (Casa Blanca)

Johnson Co.
ALVARADO
Antioch (Heugh)
Arum (Egypt)
Auburn
Bailey's (Buchanan)
Barnesville

Beulah (Mustang Creek)
Billingsley (Bono)
Bishop
Bono (Billingsley)
Bradley
BRIAROAKS
Bruce
Buchanan (Bailey's)
Buel (Meredith)
Bullard (Donald)
BURLESON
Caddo Grove
Caddo Peak (Joshua)
Caleb
Camp Creek (Freeland)
Camp Henderson (Cleburne)
Clark (Parker)
CLEBURNE (Camp Henderson)
Clinton (Joshua)
Concord
Cresson
CROSS TIMBER
Cuba
Dancl
Donald (Bullard, Ham's Creek)
Egan
Egypt (Arum)
Ellis
Elm Grove (Keene)
Equestria (Lone Willow)
Falls
Freeland (Camp Creek, Lavada)
Goatneck (Greenway)
GODLEY
Gossip (Venus)
GRANDVIEW
Greenway (Goatneck, Watters)
Ham's Creek (Donald)
Happy Hill
Heugh (Antioch)
Hines
Hogan Acres
JOSHUA (Caddo Peak, Clinton)
Keeler
KEENE (Elm Grove)
Laura
Lavada (Freeland)
Liberty Chapel
Lillian
Lone Willow (Equestria)
MANSFIELD
Marystown [Marysville]
Meredith (Buel)
Midway (Venus)
Mustang Creek (Beulah)
Nathan (Parker)
Nolans River [Nolan's River]
O'Hair
Orr (Parker)
Parker (Clark, Nathan, Orr)
Pleasant Point
Ponetta
Quicksand
Republic
Retta
RIO VISTA

Rock Creek
Sand Flat
Stovall
Stubblefield (Westbrook)
Sullivan
VENUS (Gossip, Midway)
Virgile
Wardville
Watters (Greenway)
Westbrook (Stubblefield)
Wooded Hills

Jones Co.
Abbie
ANSON (Jones City)
Avo (Spring Creek Community)
Avoca
Banner (Neinda)
Bonita (Tuxedo)
Boyds Chapel
Bush
California (Lenore)
Centerline
Corinth
Dean (Sinclair)
Dee (Duley)
Delk (McCamant)
Duley (Dee)
East Stamford
Eaton (Truby)
Ericksdahl
Essie (Rosson)
Fort [Phantom Hill]
Funston (Grow)
Gist (Noodle)
Golan
Green Valley (Nugent)
Grow (Funston)
HAMLIN
HAWLEY (Iota, Zelo)
Hodges (Lockett, Midway)
Iota (Hawley)
Jones City (Anson)
Lockett (Hodges)
Lenore (California)
Linksville
Longorio (Truby)
LUEDERS
Lystra
McCamant (Delk)
Midway (Hodges)
Mont Truby (Truby)
Nabors
Neinda (Banner, Willard)
New Hope
Newmanville
Newsom [City] (Truby)
Noodle (Gist)
North Abilene
Nugent (Green Valley)
Onion
Pastura
Pleasant Valley
Radium
Rising Sun
Rosson (Essie)
Sandersville
Sinclair (Dean)
Spring Creek Community (Avo)
STAMFORD
Stith
Truby (Eaton, Longorio,

Zanzenburg (Center Point)

Kimble Co.
Buck Hollow
Cleo
JUNCTION
Kimbleville
London
New Knoxville
Noxville
Roosevelt
Segovia
Teacup
Telegraph
Yates [Crossing]

King Co.
Bala (Grow)
Copper City (Grace)
Dumont
Finney
Gibson (Lynn)
Grace (Copper City)
Grow (Bala, Ila)
Guthrie
Ila (Grow)
Lynn (Gibson)
Malta
South Camp

Kinney Co.
Amanda (Buckner, Olds)
Anacacho
BRACKETTVILLE (Fort
    Clark, Fort Riley)
Buckner (Amanda)
Dolores
Fehlis
Fort Clark (Brackettville)
Fort Clark Springs
Fort Riley (Brackettville)
Hillcoat (Hutchison's
    Ranch)
Howerton's Ranch (Tula-
    rosa)
Hutchison's Ranch (Hill-
    coat)
Jones City (Macie)
Las Moras
Macie (Jones City)
Odlaw
Olds (Amanda)
Pavo
Pinto
Ramal
Sotol (Tularosa)
SPOFFORD
Standart
Tularosa (Howerton's
    Ranch, Sotol, West
    Nueces, Whistler)
West Nueces (Tularosa)
Whistler (Tularosa)
Woodward

Kleberg Co.
Caesar
King Ranch Headquarters
KINGSVILLE
Kingsville Naval Air Stn.
Loyola Beach
Ricardo
Riviera
Riviera Beach
Santa Gertrudes

Knox Co.
BENJAMIN (Cousinville)
China Lake (Truscott)
Comal (Goree)
Cousinville (Benjamin)
Coyote (Gilliland)
Gilliland (Coyote)
GOREE (Comal, Riley
    Springs)
Hefner
Kasoga (Laura)
KNOX CITY (Orient)
Laura (Kasoga)
Maud (Munday)
MUNDAY (Maud)
Orient (Knox City)
Rhineland
Riley Springs (Goree)
Truscott (China Lake)
Vera (White Flat)
White Flat (Vera)

Lamar Co.
Ambia (Martin)
Amherst
Arthur City
Atlas (Pool)
Baird (Biardstown)
Ballard's
Belk (Round Prairie)
Betner
Biardstown [Biard] (Baird)
BLOSSOM [Blossom Prai-
    rie]
Bluebird (Luther)
Boggy
Box
Broadway
Brodie
Brookston
Bunker Hill
Byrdtown
Camp Maxey
Cathron's Store (Tiger-
    town)
Caviness
Centre Spring (Chicota)
Chicota (Centre Spring)
Clardy (Jennings, Niland)
Cleere
Compass (Mound Prairie)
Cothrans Store
Cotton Plant
Coursey (Wayne)
Cox (Frisco)
Coxburgh (Sumner)
Cox's (Sumner)
Craig's (Slate Shoals)
Cunningham
Da Honey
Davis (Reno)
Deeville (Deport)
DEPORT (Deeville)
Diamond City (Direct)
Direct (Diamond City)
Dixie
Dowlin (Petty)
East Direct
Emberson
Ettra (Wayne)
Faught
Faulkner

Finch (Postoak)
Forest Chapel
Forest Hill
Fort Shelton (Shelton's)
Forward
Franklin (Fulton, U.S.
    Factory)
Frean (Slate Shoals)
Frisco (Cox)
Fulton (Franklin)
Gadsden (Gadston)
Gadston (Gadsden)
Gantt (Postoak)
Garretts Bluff (Garretts)
Georgia [Georgiaville]
    (May, Need, Oakland)
Gibson
Givens
Globe
Glory (Ratliff's Store)
Grove (New Pleasant
    Grove)
Haman's
Harmon (Noble)
Harrellton
Haynes (Razor)
High
Hinckley
Hoover
Hopewell
Howland
Inglewood
Jennings
Jennings (Clardy)
Johnnie
Lafayette
Lamar Court House (Shel-
    ton's)
Lenoir (Powderly)
Lone Spring (Noble)
Lone Star
Lookout Station (Petty)
Lowman
Luther (Bluebird)
Martin (Ambia)
Martin (Ozark)
Marvin
Maxey (Wilhite)
May (Georgia)
Mayer
Medill (Spring Hill, Tinnin)
Midcity
Miller's
Milton (Minton)
Minter (Parker's Voting
    Box)
Minton (Milton)
Mound Prairie (Compass)
Mount Vernon
Need (Georgia)
New Pleasant Grove
    (Grove)
Niland (Clardy)
Noble (Lone Spring)
Noble (Harmon)
Novice
Nowell (Roy)
Oakland (Georgia)
Odd's Creek
Ozark (Martin)
Paddock
PARIS (Pinhook)
Parker's Voting Box

(Minter)
Parkerton
Pattonville
Perkins
Petty (Dowlin, Lookout
    [Station])
Pine Creek
Pinhook (Paris)
Pleasant Grove
Pool (Atlas)
Postoak (Finch, Gantt)
Powderly (Lenoir)
Prairie Mount (Roxton)
Price's Store
Ragland
Ragtown
Ralph
Ratliff's Store (Glory)
Razor (Haynes)
RENO (Davis)
Rockford
Round Prairie
ROXTON (Prairie Mount)
Roy (Nowell)
Rucker's Bridge
Scott
Shelton's (Fort Shelton,
    Lamar Court House)
Shiloh Academy
Shockeys Prairie
Slabtown
Slate Shoals (Craig's,
    Frean)
Spring Hill (Medill)
Starkesville
State Bank (Tinnin's)
Sumner (Cox's, Coxburgh)
SUN VALLEY
Sylvan
Taylor Town
Tigertown (Cathron's
    Store)
Tinnin (Medill)
Tinnin's (State Bank)
TOCO
Tolette [Tollette]
Tollett's Prairie (Williams')
Trout
Unity
U.S. Factory (Franklin)
Viewpoint
Wales (West Paris)
Wayne (Coursey, Ettra)
West Paris (Wales)
Wilhite (Maxey)
Williams'
Wrightsville

Lamb Co.
AMHERST
Bainer
Beck
Circle
Cofferville
Corry
EARTH (Fairlawn, Tulsa)
Fairlawn (Earth)
Fieldton
Friendship
Hart Camp
Janes (Sudan)
LITTLEFIELD
Lums Chapel
OLTON

Pleasant Valley
Spade
SPRINGLAKE
SUDAN *(Janes)*
Tulsa (Earth)
Yellow House

Lampasas Co.
Ada *(School Creek)*
Adamsville
Alverde
Antelope Gap
Atherton *(Sims Creek)*
Bula *(Rescue)*
Burleson (Lampasas)
Chadwick *(Senterfitt)*
Falls Creek
Gilliamsville (Izoro)
Grundyville
Higgins Gap (Izoro)
Izoro *(Gilliamsville, Higgins Gap)*
KEMPNER
LAMPASAS *[Lampasas Springs]* (Burleson)
Lightfoot *(Walk)*
LOMETA *(Montvale)*
Lucile *(Mace)*
Lynchs Creek
Mace *(Lucile)*
McAnnelly's Bend
McCreaville
Moline *(Slayden)*
Montvale *(Lometa)*
Nix
Nutsford
Ogle[s]
Radio Junction
Rescue *(Bula)*
Round Mountain *(Taylors Creek)*
Rumley
Salt Creek
School Creek *(Ada)*
Senterfitt
Senterfitt *(Chadwick)*
Sims Creek *(Atherton)*
Slaughtersville
Slayden *(Moline)*
Taylors Creek *(Round Mountain)*
Townsen Mills
Walk *(Lightfoot)*

La Salle Co.
Ancaster (Encinal)
Artesia *(Pactific, Twohig)*
Artesia Wells *(Bart)*
Atlee
Bart *(Artesia Wells)*
Bolton Switch *(Harriss Valley)*
Buckley['s Ranch]
Burks
Cibolo Station (Millett)
Cochina *(Iuka)*
COTULLA *(La Salle)*
Dull['s] Ranch] *(Nettaville)*
ENCINAL
Farmington
Fort Ewell *(Gaujoco)*
Fowlerton
Gardendale
Gaujoco *(Fort Ewell)*

Happle
Harriss Valley *(Bolton Switch)*
Iuka *(Cochina)*
La Salle *(Cotulla)*
Los Angeles
Machos (Encinal)
McCarty
Millett *(Cibolo Station)*
Nettaville *(Dull)*
Nopal *(Peru)*
Pacific *(Artesia)*
Peru *(Nopal)*
Souz Creek
Twohig *(Artesia)*
Tuna
Vesper
Waugh's Rancho
Woodward

Lavaca Co.
Allis School *(Old Moulton)*
Antioch *(Koerth)*
Baurs
Bearden
Bila Hora
Bovine
Boxville
Branon
Breslau
Brushy Settlement (Yoakum)
Brushyville
Buchell's Store *(Hope)*
Conroy
Creole *(Garner)*
Ezzell *(Green Grove)*
Fabien *(Worthing)*
Gandy[bend]
Garner *(Creole)*
Glecker *(Lilla)*
Goldenrod *(Krajina)*
Good Hope
Green Grove (Ezzell)
Hackberry
Halfmoon *(Shiner)*
HALLETTSVILLE *[Hallett's]*, (Hidesville, Ives')
Hidesville (Hallettsville)
Henkhaus
Hope *(Buchell's Store)*
Ives' (Hallettsville)
Karney (Koerth)
Kinkler *(Mixon)*
Koerth['s Mill, Store] (Antioch,Karney,Yellow Bank)
Komensky
Krajina *(Goldenrod)*
Lilla *(Glecker)*
Midway
Miller's Farm *(Seclusion)*
Mixon *(Kinkler)*
Monserate
Mont
Moravia
MOULTON *(Topeka Junction)*
Moulton Institute *(Old Moulton)*
Mount Olive
Mustang
Novohrad
Oakland *(Prairie Point)*

Oakwood
Old Moulton *(Allis School, Moulton Institute)*
Orsack *(Worthing)*
Prairie Point *(Oakland)*
Petersburg[h]
Post Oak Grove
Rocky Mills
Seclusion *(Miller's Farm)*
Shiloh
SHINER *(Halfmoon)*
Smoothing Iron
Speakeville (Speaks)
Speaks *(Speakeville)*
Star
Sublime
Sweet Home
Tommie
Topeka Junction (Moulton)
Velehrad
Vienna
Vsetin
Vysehrad
Wellersburgh
Wied
Williamsburg[h]
Witting *[Wittinghouse]*
Worthing *(Fabien, Orsack)*
Yellow Bank (Koerth)
YOAKUM *(Brushy Settlement)*

Lee Co.
Adina *(Cain)*
Antioch
Blue *[Blue Branch]* *(Ruthven's Gin)*
Bluff Creek *(Fedor)*
Brown's Mills *(Yegua)*
Cain *(Adina)*
Celynda
Colvin['s Gin] *(Clark)*
Clark *(Colvin)*
Darden Springs
Dime Box
Doddville *(Nunnsville)*
Doak Springs
Evergreen *(Lincoln)*
Fedor *(Bluff Creek, Moab, West Yegua)*
GIDDINGS
Gleam *(Knobbs Springs)*
Grassyville
Hawthorn
Hicks *(Niles)*
Hills *(Hillspur)*
Hillspur *(Hills)*
Hranice
Knobbs Springs *(Gleam, New Anhalt, The Knobbs)*
Kruse
Ledbetter
Leo
LEXINGTON *(String Prairie)*
Lincoln *(Evergreen, Rose, Smada)*
Loebau
Low Pin Oak *(Serbin)*
Manheim
Moab *(Fedor)*
Mosquito Prairie

New Anhalt *(Knobbs Springs)*
New Serbin *(Northrup)*
Niles *(Hicks)*
Northrup *(New Serbin)*
Nunnsville *(Doddville)*
Old Dime Box
Old Evergreen
Post Oak
Prospect
Rocky
Rose *(Lincoln)*
Ruthven's Gin *(Blue)*
Sand Fly
Schkade
Serbin *(Low Pin Oak)*
Smada (Lincoln)
String Prairie *(Lexington)*
Sweet Home
Tanglewood
The Knobbs *(Knobbs Springs)*
West Yegua *(Fedor)*
Yegua *(Brown's Mills)*
Yegua

Leon Co.
Bear Grass
Beavens
Birch Creek
Boggy *[Mills]*
Bowery *(Malvern)*
Bowling
Britt
Brunson
BUFFALO *(Cane Branch)*
Cairo
Caldwell's Store
Canary
Cane Branch *(Buffalo)*
Carver
Centerview
CENTERVILLE *[Centreville]*
Clapp's Creek
Concord *(Frankville)*
Connor *(Flynn)*
Copeland *(Snow)*
Corinth
Crescent Lake *(Homewood)*
Cullinan
Davisville
Dean
Dety
Dickey
Durst's
Eagle Valley
Egypt
Ephesus
Eunice *(Morrison's Chapel)*
Eva
Evansville
Fay *(Keechi)*
Flo *(Kidd's Mills, Oden['s], Roebuck)*
Flynn *(Connor, Leon)*
Fort Boggy
Frankville *(Concord)*
Friendship
Glover
Guys Store
Hardin's *[Harden's]* Store

(Malvern)
Haskins Mill (Oneta)
Hilltop Lakes
Homewood (Crescent
   Lake)
Hopewell (Normangee)
Hogg (Oneta)
Hunts Store
Independent
JEWETT
Keechi [Keechie] (Fay)
Kidd's Mills (Flo)
Leon (Flynn)
LEONA
Leona Mills
Little Flock
Long Hollow
Lookout
Malvern (Bowery, Hardin's
   Store, Melvern, Rein-
   hardt's Store)
Margie
MARQUEZ
Melvern (Malvern)
Middleton
Moody's Cross Roads
Morrison's Chapel (Eunice)
Navarro [Crossing] (Tax)
Newby
New Salem
Nineveh
NORMANGEE (Hopewell)
Nubbin Ridge
OAKWOOD (Wolf Hollow)
Oden['s] (Flo)
Old Bowling
Old Midway
Oneta (Haskins Mill, Hogg)
Peeler
Pine Top
Pleasant Ridge
Pleasant Springs
Poor (Wealthy)
Quito
Raymond
Red Branch
Redland
Reinhardt's Store
   (Malvern)
Rich Row
Riley's
Ringgold
Robbins
Roebuck (Flo)
Rogers Prairie
Running Creek (Wealthy)
Russell [Russell's Mill]
Saint Paul
Sand Flat
Sardis
Shiloh
Siam
Snow (Copeland)
Sparksville (Vanetia)
Spillers Store
Sweet Oak
Tax (Navarro [Crossing])
Timesville
Toccoa
Van
Vanetia (Sparksville)
Venetia
Wealthy (Poor, Running

Creek)
Wolf Hollow (Oakwood)
Zelda

Liberty Co.
Africa (Keahey)
AMES
Arion
Atascosito (Liberty)
Audrey
Bendetsen
Big Creek
Big Ridge
Big Thicket
Brick (Vidette)
Carter's Station (Devers)
Cedar Bayou
Cedar Station (Jarvis)
Clark (Fields)
CLEVELAND
Concord
DAISETTA (Dorne, Wilda)
Davis Hill
Daystown (Dayton)
DAYTON (Daystown, West
   Liberty)
DAYTON LAKES
DEVERS [Woods]
   (Carter's Station)
Dewdrop
Dewey (Miriam)
Dolen (Maxson)
Dorne (Daisetta)
Drake (Morard)
Eastgate
Enterprise Farm (Kirkham)
Esperson
Excelsior (Minora)
Felicia
Fields (Clark)
Finley (Lakeland)
Fostoria
Fouts (Halladay)
Fox (Meriam, Pelican)
Fullerton
Fuqua (Klumco, Menard)
Gladstell
Glenn
Grady
Grand Cane (Ironwood)
Green's
Halladay (Fouts)
HARDIN (Walter)
Hightower (Lamb)
Hoop and Holler
Hull
Ironwood (Grand Cane)
Jarvis (Cedar Station)
Joentz
Keahey (Africa)
KENEFICK
Keno
Kevin
Kirkham (Enterprise Farm)
Klumco (Fuqua)
Lake Charlotte
Lakeland (Finley)
Lamb (Hightower)
LIBERTY (Atascosito)
Lyric
Macedonia
Marysee
Maxson (Dolen)
Menard (Fuqua)

Meriam (Fox, Pelican)
Milvid
Minora (Excelsior)
Miriam (Dewey)
Morard (Drake, Riceland)
Moss Bluff (Salvation)
Moss Hill (New Hope,
   Perryman)
New Hope (Moss Hill)
NORTH CLEVELAND
Oakdale
Old River Lake
Old Snake River
Pedeco
Pelican (Fox, Meriam)
Pen Oak
Perryman (Moss Hill)
Pickett (South Liberty)
PLUM GROVE
Rayburn
Raywood
Riceland (Morard)
River (Romayor)
Romayor (River)
Rye
Salvation (Moss Bluff)
Sandune
Seaman
Sheeks
Simmons Bottom
Sines
Snuff Ridge
South Liberty (Pickett)
Stilson
Tarkington['s] Prairie
Trinity River Spur
Turtle Bayou
Vern (Vidette)
Vidette (Brick, Vern)
Walter (Hardin)
West Liberty (Dayton)
Wilda (Daisetta)
Williams
Wise

Limestone Co.
Alon (Lost Prairie)
Armour (Coolidge)
Bear Grass
Ben Hur
Beulah
Big Hill
Billington
Box Church
Buffalo Mop
Buffalo Mott (Odds)
Calina [Callina] (Wood Val-
   ley)
Canaan (Dump)
Cedar Island (Island)
Center
Central Institute (Hickory
   Grove)
Ceyola (Coker, Mitchell's
   Valley)
Coal
Coit
Coker (Ceyola)
Condor (Munger)
COOLIDGE [Cooledge]
   (Armour, Doyle, Sandy
   Creek)
Datura (Oliver)
Darwin (Hancock)

Davis Prairie
Delia (Elmo, Popp)
Dooley
Doyle (Major, Roberta,
   Shady Grove)
Doyle (Coolidge)
Dump (Canaan)
Dyer (Prairie Hill)
Echols
Elm Grove (Kirk)
Elmo (Delia)
Eutaw (Kosse)
Fair Oaks
Fallon
Farrar (Littleglade, Tiger
   Prairie)
Felix
Forest Glade
Fort Parker
Fort Parker State Park
Frosa
GROESBECK [Groes-
   beeck]
Gude
Hancock['s] (Darwin)
Harmony
Hickory Creek
Hickory Grove (Central
   Institute)
Holden
Horn Hill [Horn] (Mount
   Vernon)
Iron Clad (Louisville)
Island (Cedar Island)
Kirk (Elm Grove)
KOSSE (Eutaw)
La Salle
Lavender (Marx, Wilson)
Limestone
Link (Yarbroville)
Littleglade (Farrar)
Lo (Shiloh)
Locus (Odds)
Lost Prairie (Alon)
Lost Prairie (Personville)
Louis (Roda)
Louisville (Iron Clad)
Luther (Shiloh)
Major (Doyle)
Marx (Lavender)
McDaniel
MEXIA
Midway
Mitchell's Valley (Ceyola)
Mount Calm
Mount Vernon (Horn)
Munger (Condor)
Mustang
New Home
New Hope
Nus [Ranch]
Old Springfield
Odds (Buffalo Mott, Locus)
Old Union
Oletha (Pottersville)
Oliver (Datura)
Parker's Point (Stroud's)
Personville (Lost Prairie)
Pleasant Grove
Point Enterprise
Popp (Delia)
Pottersville (Oletha)
Prairie Grove (Varela)

Prairie Hill *(Dyer)*
Roberta (Doyle)
Roda *(Louis)*
Red Hill
Sandy
Sandy Creek (Coolidge)
Shady Grove (Doyle)
Shiloh *(Lo, Luther)*
Springfield
Steel's Creek *(Tidwell)*
Storrs[ville]
Stroud's *(Parker's Point)*
TEHUACANA *(Tewockony Springs)*
Tewockony Springs (Tehuacana)
Thelma
THORNTON
Tidwell *(Steel's Creek)*
Tiger Prairie (Farrar)
Tucker's Mills
Varela *(Prairie Grove)*
Victoria
Watt
Wilson (Lavender)
Woodland
Wood Valley (Calina)
Yarbroville *(Link)*

Lipscomb Co.
Barton Corners
BOOKER
Buchanan (Mable)
Coburn
DARROUZETT *(Longwood, Lourwood)*
FOLLETT
Gaylord *(Nailton)*
HIGGINS
Kiowa *(Plains)*
Lipscomb
Longwood (Darrouzett)
Lourwood (Darrouzett)
Mable (Buchanan)
Magoun
Mammoth
Mitchell
Morton *(Royal)*
Nailton *(Gaylord)*
Plains (Kiowa)
Royal *(Morton, Second Creek)*
Second Creek (Royal)
Shadeland
Sherlock
Stillwater
Timm[s] City
Valley Park

Live Oak Co.
Annarose (Kentuck)
Argenta *(Ego*
Barlow's Ferry (Dinero)
Caron (Karon)
Clegg
Cornelia (Neelie)
Cuba (Mahala)
Dinero *(Barlow's Ferry)*
Echo *(The Point)*
Ego *(Argenta)*
Esseville
Fant City (Suniland)
Fort Merrill
Fox Nation (Gussettville)

GEORGE WEST
Gussettville *(Fox Nation)*
Hamiltonburg (Three Rivers)
Ike
Karon *(Caron, Votaw)*
Kentuck *(Annarose)*
Lagarto *(Roughtown)*
Lapara
La Posta *(Ramirena)*
Mahala *(Cuba)*
Mikeska
Neelie *(Cornelia)*
Nell
Oakville *(Puente Piedra)*
PERNITAS POINT
Puente Piedra (Oakville)
Ramirena *(La Posta)*
Ray Point
Roughtown (Lagarto)
Simmons
Suniland *(Fant City)*
Swinney Switch
The Point *(Echo)*
THREE RIVERS *(Hamiltonburg)*
Votaw (Karon)
Whitsett

Llano Co.
Almon *(Esbon)*
Babyhead
Barber *(Republic)*
Bennett (Prairie Mountain)
Bessemer
Bettina
Beverly
Blue Lake Estates
Bluffton *(Forman's, Stonewall)*
Bristow *(Esbon)*
Buchanan Dam *(Hamilton Dam)*
Buchanan Lake Village
Bugscuffle (Valley Spring)
Buzzard Roost *(Pack Saddle)*
Byfield's Store *(Click)*
Castell
Cat Town *(Oxford)*
Cedar Point
Click *(Byfield's Store, Lone Star, Sandy Valley)*
Crestwood
Deer Haven
Doke
Esbon *(Almon, Bristow, Simpson's Bend, Slayden)*
Field Creek
Forman's *(Bluffton)*
Gainesville
Golden Beach
Graceland
Graphite
Hamilton Dam (Buchanan Dam)
Hickory *(Prairie Mountain)*
Hobart
Hondo
Honey Creek *(Pack Saddle)*

Hoovers Valley
Horseshoe Bay
Indian Hills
Kingsland *(Kingsville)*
Kingsville (Kingsland)
Lakeside Heights
Legion
Lehmberg
Leroy *(Republic)*
LLANO
Lone Grove
Lone Star *(Click)*
Long Mountain
Nob Hill
Oak Ridge
Ocie *(Prairie Mountain)*
Oxford *(Cat Town)*
Pack Saddle *(Buzzard Roost, Honey Creek)*
Palo *(Republic)*
Phillips Ranch (Valley Spring)
Prairie Mountain *(Bennett, Hickory, Ocie, Putnam, Starkes)*
Putnam (Prairie Mountain)
Republic *(Barber, Leroy, Palo)*
Royal Oaks
Sandy
Sandy Harbor
Sandy Mountain
Sandy Valley *(Click)*
San Fernando *(Valley Spring)*
Simpson's Bend
Sixmile
Slayden *(Esbon)*
Starkes (Prairie Mountain)
Stolz
Stonewall (Bluffton)
SUNRISE BEACH
Tow *[Tow Valley]*
Valley Spring *(Bugscuffle, Phillips Ranch, San Fernando, Whistleville)*
Whistleville (Valley Spring)

Loving Co.
Hayflat
Juanita (Mentone)
Mentone *(Juanita, Porterville)*
Mentone (Ramsey)
Porterville (Mentone)
Ramsey (Mentone)
Woody

Lubbock Co.
ABERNATHY
Acuff
Afton (Shallowater)
Barton
Becton *(Bledsoe, Moody Store)*
Bledsoe (Becton)
Block Twenty (Slide)
Broadview
BUFFALO SPRINGS
Caldwell
Canyon
County Line
Estacado
Grovesville (Ophir)

Heckville
Hurlwood
IDALOU
Kitalou
Liberty
LUBBOCK *(Monterrey, Singer's Store)*
McClung
Midway
Monroe (New Deal)
Monterrey (Lubbock)
Moody Store (Becton)
NEW DEAL *(Monroe)*
Ophir (Grovesville, Twin Ranch & Farm)
Otta
Pacita (Shallowater)
Posey
RANSOM CANYON
Reese Village
Roosevelt
Ripley *(Shallowater)*
SHALLOWATER *(Afton, Pacita, Ripley)*
Singer's Store (Lubbock)
SLATON
Slide *(Block Twenty)*
Tech
Twin Ranch & Farm (Ophir)
Union
West Carisle
WOLFFORTH
Woodrow

Lynn Co.
Draw
Gordon
Grassland
Lakeview
Morgan
NEW HOME
New Lynn
New Moore
O'DONNELL
Petty
Redwine
Skeen
TAHOKA
Wayside
Wells
West Point
WILSON

Madison Co.
Antioch
Canary
Concord
Connor
Cottonwood
Cross Roads
Elwood
George
Hollis
Hopewell
Island
Jozye
Laceola
MADISONVILLE
Mecca
MIDWAY
Mitchells
Neal
NORMANGEE
North Zulch

Shiloh
Trinidad
Willow Hole
Zulch

Marion Co.
Alleys Mill (Nash's
Foundry, Texas Iron
Works)
Amicus (The Rock)
Berea
Big Oaks
Brooks Store (Una)
Comet (Hart)
Copeland Creek
Crestwood
Epperson (Hoodville)
Erambert's Mill (Rambert)
Four Mile Branch (Kelly-
ville)
French (Ragley)
Garrett's Store (Sidney)
Gay Assembly
Gethsemane
Grady
Grant (Orr's)
Gray
Hall
Hart (Comet)
Hartzo (Simmons)
Hoodville (Epperson)
Jackson
JEFFERSON
Johnson Creek
Kellyville [Kelleysville]
(Four Mile Branch)
Lakeview
Lassater [Lasater [Station]
(Pyland)
Lockett (Myrtle)
Lodi (Monterey Station)
Lodwick
Lumber (Wathen)
Mims [Store]
Mims Chapel
Monterey [Old, Point
Monterey]
Monterey Station (Lodi)
Myrtle (Lockett)
Nash's Foundry (Alley's
Mills, Texas Iron Works)
Orrs [Orrville]
Pleasure Point
Port Monterey
Pyland (Lassater)
Ragley (French)
Rambert (Erambert's Mill)
Rock Island
Sarber
Sidney (Garrett's Store)
Simmons (Hartzo)
Smithland
Smithland (Smith's Land-
ing)
Smith's Landing (Smith-
land)
Stalls
Sunview
Texas Iron Works (Alley
Mills, Nash's Foundry)
The Rock (Amicus)
Una (Brooks Store)
Vivian

Warlock
Wathen (Lumber)
Watts
Wayside
Whatley
Whiteoak

Martin Co.
ACKERLY
Baden
Brown
Brownlee
Courtney
Dix
Flower Grove
Lenorah (Plainview,
Willingham Store)
Loyola
Marienfeld (Stanton)
Merrick
Plainview (Lenorah)
South Plains (Tarzan)
STANTON (Marienfeld)
Tarzan (South Plains)
Tex-Harvey
Three Leagues
Walcott
Willingham Store (Leno-
rah)

Mason Co.
Adullam (Wagram)
Air (Camp Air)
Art (Plehweville, [Upper]
Willow Creek)
Barton Springs (Fredonia)
Beaver Creek (Hilda)
Blucher (Granda)
Blue Mountain
Blue Stretch (Wagram)
Bluff Creek (Erna)
Bluff Creek (Streeter)
Camp Air (Air)
Capitola (Jenkins Ranch,
Ten Mile)
Cold Spring (Loyal Valley)
Deer Creek (Fredonia)
Deerton (Fredonia)
Erna (Bluff Creek, India-
napolis, Long Mount)
Flemingville (Fly Gap)
Fly Gap (Flemingville)
Fort Mason (Mason)
Fredonia (Barton Springs,
Deer Creek, Deerton)
Funston (Grit)
Granda (Blucher)
Grit (Funston, Hey)
Grossville
Hedwigs Hill
Hersfeld
Hey (Grit)
Hilda (Beaver Creek)
Holt
Honey Creek (Streeter)
Indianapolis (Erna)
Jenkins Ranch (Capitola)
Katemcy
Koocksville
Long Mount (Erna)
Long Mountian
Loyal Valley (Cold Spring)
MASON (Fort Mason)
Plehweville (Art)

Pontotoc
Ranch Branch
Streeter (Bluff Creek,
Honey Creek)
Ten Mile (Capitola)
Wagram (Adullam, Blue
Stretch)
Willow Creek (Art)

Matagorda Co.
Allenhurst
Ashby
Ashwood
Austin
BAY CITY
Blessing
Buckeye
Camp Hulen
Caney
Cedar Lake
Cedar Lane
Chalmers
Chinquapin
Citrus Grove
Clemville
Collegeport
Demings Bridge
Elmaton
Gainesmore
Gulf
Gulf Hill
Hawkinsville
Kenner
Live Oak Bend
Markham
Matagorda
Midfield
McCroskey
PALACIOS
Pheasant
Pledger
Podo
Poole Pens
Prairie Center
Rugeley
Rymers
Sargent
Selkirk Island
Simpsonville
Sugar Valley
Tin Top
Van Vleck
Wadsworth

Maverick Co.
Crain (Fresnito, Pecosa)
Darling
Dolchburg
EAGLE PASS (Fort Dun-
can)
El Indio
Fort Duncan (Eagle Pass)
Fresnito (Crain, Pecosa)
Guerrero
Indio [Ranch] (Precidio)
La Gloria (Seco Mines)
Lamar
Lehmann's Ranch (Nor-
mandy)
Muela
Normandy (Lehmann's
Ranch, Quemado,
Upson)
Olmos

Paloma
Pecosa (Crain, Fresnito)
Quemado (Quemado
Spur)
Quemado (Normandy)
Quemado Spur (Que-
mado)
Seco Mines
Upson (Normandy)

McCulloch Co.
BRADY
Broadmoor
Brown Town (Stacy)
Calf Creek (Deland,
Tucker)
Camp San Saba
Cowboy (Deep Creek)
Crewville (Rochelle)
Crothers (Rochelle)
Deep Creek (Cowboy)
Deland (Calf Creek)
Doole (Gansel)
Dugout (Milburn)
East Sweden
Fife (Finlay, Mark)
Finlay (Fife)
Gansel (Doole)
Gaultville (Placid)
Lohn [Valley]
Marco
Mark (Fife)
McCulloch
MELVIN
Mercury
Milburn (Dugout)
New Sweden
Niblock
Nine
Pear Valley (Saddle
Creek)
Placid (Gaultville)
Pueblo (Waldrip)
Rochelle (Crewville,
Crothers)
Saddle Creek (Pear Valley)
Salt Gap
Satuit
Selman
Spillers Rancho
Stacy (Brown Town)
Tucker (Calf Creek)
Voca
Waldrip (Pueblo)
West Sweden
Whiteland

McLennan Co.
Acomb (Corbett)
Amanda (Wayside)
Amonda (Wayside)
Artesia
Asa
Atco
Avon Park
Axtell
Baggett
Banks
Battle [Institute]
BELLMEAD
Beverly
BEVERLY HILLS
Bishop (Ely)
Blackland

Blue Bluff
Bluebonnet
Bold Springs (West)
Bosqueville
Bowling Green
BRUCEVILLE (Cow
  Bayou, Masterville)
Castle Heights
Cato (Wayside)
Chase (Farmer)
China Spring
Coke (Comanche Springs)
Comanche Springs (Coke)
Corbett (Acomb)
Cordova (Stone Wall)
Cottonwood
Cow Bayou (Bruceville)
CRAWFORD
Crush
Downs
Downsville (Price)
Duraglas
East Waco
Eddy (Marvin)
Elk
Elm Mott (Geneva Station,
  Union Grove)
Elrod (Montero)
Erath (Union Hill)
Ely (Bishop)
Farmer (Chase)
Farr (Walker's Store)
Farwell Heights (North
  Waco)
Freedom
Fryar
Garrett's Mills (Patrick)
Geneva Station (Elm Mott)
Gerald
GHOLSON (Sardis)
Gilbert
Gilpin
GOLINDA [Golindo]
Greer
Hague (Robinson)
HALLSBURG
Harris Creek
Harrison
Hermoson (North Waco)
HEWITT
Highland
Hillside
Hoen
Hog Creek
Hurstland
Jackson
Jaynes (Olive Branch)
Jewell
LACY-LAKEVIEW
Lake Creek
Lakeview
Leland
Leroy
LEROY
Levi
Line Creek
LORENA
Lusk (Spring Valley)
MART (Willow Springs)
Marvin (Eddy)
Masterville (Bruceville)
McGREGOR [Springs]
Middle Bosque

Middle Bosque (Mount
  Olivet)
Montero (Elrod)
MOODY
Mount Olivet (Middle
  Bosque)
Nalley['s Store]
Neale
Nichol[a]sville
Northcrest
North Waco (Farwell
  Heights, Hermoson)
Norwood
Oaklake
Oak Grove (Rosenthal)
Oak Valley
Ocaw
Ocee
Olive Branch (Jaynes)
Patrick (Garrett's Mills)
Patton
Perry
Prairie Chapel
Price (Downsville)
Prospect (Riesel)
Richie (Stanford)
Ritchie
RIESEL (Prospect,
  Roddy)
ROBINSON (Hague)
Rock Creek
Roddy (Riesel)
Rogers Hill
Rosenthal (Oak Grove)
ROSS
Ruby (Waldo)
Ryan
St. Martinville (Tours)
Sardis (Gholson)
Searsville
Sheid
Smead
South Bosque
Speegleville
Spring Valley (Lusk)
Stanford (Richie)
Stark Grove
Stone Wall (Cordova)
Teka
Texand
Tokio
Tonk Creek (Waldo)
Tours (St. Martinville)
Tradinghouse Creek
Union Grove (Elm Mott)
Union Hill (Erath)
Valley View
WACO [Village]
Waldo (Ruby, Tonk Creek)
Walker's Store (Farr)
Wardlaw
Wayside (Amonda,
  Amanda, Cato)
Vernal (Webb)
Webb (Vernal)
WEST (Bold Springs)
West Waco
Willow Grove
Willow Springs (Mart)
Windsor
WOODWAY

McMullen Co.
Calliham

Cross
Crowther
Franklin Settlement
Frio
Loma Alta
Prince
Tilden
Zella

Medina Co.
Arundel
Bader
Baldwin (Dunlay)
Biry[ville] (Briar Branch)
Black Creek
Breckenridge
Briar Branch (Biry)
CASTROVILLE
Chicon (Chico South)
Chico South (Chicon)
Clifden (Gallagher's
  Ranch)
Cliff
Coal Mine
DEVINE
D'Hanis
Dunlay (Baldwin, Enter-
  prise [Station], Harper,
  Murray, Summit)
Elstone
Enterprise [Station] (Dun-
  lay)
Fernando (La Coste)
Flint Hill
Francisco (San Francisco)
Gallagher's Ranch
  (Clifden)
Grit
Haby (Riomedina)
Harper (Dunlay)
HONDO [City]
LA COSTE (Fernando)
LYTLE [Station]
Maverick
Medina Lake (Mico)
Medmill
Mico (Medina Lake)
Moss (Yancey)
Murphy
Murray (Dunlay)
NATALIA
New Fountain (Soldiers
  Camp)
Noonan
Pearson
Quihi
Riomedina (Haby, San
  Geronimo)
San Francisco (Francisco)
San Geronimo (Riome-
  dina)
Seco
Siesta Dara
Soldiers' Camp (New
  Fountain)
Summit (Dunlay)
Upper Hondo
Upper Quihi
Vandenburg
Verdina
Yancey (Moss)
Zig Zag

Menard Co.

Algereta
Callan
Camp San Saba (Fort
  McKavett)
Embrey
Erna (Indianapolis)
Fort McKavett (Camp San
  Saba)
Hext (Marengo)
Indianapolis (Erna)
Marengo (Hext)
MENARD [Menardville]
Saline
Scalp Creek
Speckville

Midland Co.
Carson (Warfield)
Cotton Flat
Germania (Lagonda, Paul)
Greenwood
Lakeview (Midkiff)
Lagonda (Germania)
Longview (Midkiff)
Midkiff (Lakeview, Long-
  view)
MIDLAND (Midway)
Midway (Midland)
Paul (Germania)
Pegasus
Slaughter
Spraberry
Terminal [Midland Air Ter-
  minal]
Warden (Warfield)
Warfield (Carson, Warden)

Milam Co.
Ad Hall
Allen's Mills (Belmena)
Allenville (Belmena)
Arcadia (Hoyte)
Bailey's Store (Baileyville)
Baileyville (Bailey's Store,
  Smithland)
Bailie
Barron (Collier)
Batte (Mortimer)
Belmena (Allenville,
  Allen's Mills, Terry, Wil-
  low Springs)
Ben Arnold [Benarnold]
Big Lump
Black
Black Land (Bryant['s]
  Station)
Bowers
Brackenville (Port Sullivan)
Branchville
Briary (Teresita, White)
Briquette (Hord)
Bryant['s] Station (Black
  Land)
BUCKHOLTS
Burlington (Irish Settle-
  ment, Waterford)
CAMERON
Clarkson (Viola)
Clymore
Collier (Barron)
Cone
Cone's Switch (Hoyte)
Conoley
Cox (Hanover)

Cross Roads
Crush (Walter)
Davilla
Davis Gin (Sharp)
Detmold
Dudeville (San Gabriel)
Eagle (Holliman)
Elevation
Elm Ridge
Everett (Thorndale)
Fletcher
Forest Grove
Friendship
Gardner (Watson Branch)
Gause
Gay Hill
Handy
Hanover (Cox)
Hill Top
Holliman (Eagle)
Hord (Briquette)
Hoyte (Arcadia, Cone's Switch)
International
Irish Settlement (Burlington)
Jones Prairie
Kolbs (San Anders)
Leachville (Oak Mott)
Liberty
Liberty Hill
Lilac
Little River
Lonepine
Lucas (Minerva)
Mada
Magill (Marlow)
Marak[sville]
Marjorie
Marlow (Magill)
Marvel Wells
Maysfield (Old Graball)
Milam (Milano)
MILANO (Milam)
Millerton
Minerva (Lucas)
Mortimer (Batte)
Nashville [Nashville-on-the-Brazos, New Nashville]
New Clarkson
Nile (Rome, Watson)
North Elm
Oak Mott (Leachville)
Old Graball (Maysfield)
Oxford [City]
Pettibone
Pleasant Hill
Poet
Port Sullivan (Brackenville)
Praesel
Quinif
ROCKDALE
Rome (Nile, Watson)
Salem
Salty
San Anders
San Anders (Kolbs)
San Andres
Sandow
San Gabriel (Dudeville)
Sauer
Sharp (Davis Gin)

Shields Gin (Tracy)
Silver City
Sipe Springs
Smithland (Baileyville)
Splawn
Stalty
Teresita (Briary)
Terry (Belmena)
THORNDALE (Everett)
Todd
Tracy (Shields Gin)
Val Verde
Viola (Clarkson)
Walter (Crush)
Waterford (Burlington)
Watson (Nile, Rome)
Watson Branch (Gardner)
White (Briary)
Willow Springs (Belmena)
Witcher
Wokaty
Woodal Farm
Yarrellton [Yaralton]

Mills Co.
Antelope Gap (Minor)
Big Valley [Bigvalley]
Bowlder
Bozar
Buffalo (Ebony)
Caradan (Lookout)
Castor
Clements
Center City (Hughes' Store)
Cold Springs (Ridge)
Coy
Democrat
Duren (Pompey)
Ebony (Buffalo, Percy)
GOLDTHWAITE
Gorey
Hanna Valley (Regency)
Hannaville (Regency)
Hero (Payne)
Hughes' Store (Center City)
Hydesport
Jones [Mill, Valley] (Ratler)
Lookout (Caradan)
Los Dinero (Scallorn)
Meyer City (Priddy)
Minor (Antelope Gap)
Mount Olive
MULLIN (The Switch)
Payne [Gap] (Hero)
Percy (Ebony)
Pleasant Grove (Sneed)
Pompey (Duren)
Priddy (Meyer City)
Ratler (Jones)
Regency (Hannaville, Hanna Valley)
Ridge (Cold Springs)
Scallorn (Los Dinero)
Simms (Sneed)
Sneed (Pleasant Grove, Simms)
Star [Mountain]
The Switch (Mullin)
Villa
Williams Ranch

Mitchell Co.

Armenderez (Buford)
Belen (Buford)
Buford (Armenderez, Belen, Center Point)
Car[r] (New Hope)
Center Point (Buford)
COLORADO CITY [Colorado]
Cuthbert (Visco)
Dome
Herbert (Spade)
H.S. Ranch (Hyman)
Hyman (H.S. Ranch)
Iatan (Satan's Flat, Spring Valley, Vista)
Kane (Winston)
Latan
Link
LORAINE
New Hope (Car)
Rodet
Satan's Flat (Iatan)
Spade (Herbert)
Spring Valley (Iatan)
Teville
Valley View
Visco (Cuthbert)
Vista (Iatan)
Vliets
WESTBROOK
Winston (Kane)

Montague Co.
Adora [City] (Queen Peak)
Alp (Res)
Amo (Gladys)
Bear Hill
Belcherville [Belcher]
Bonita
BOWIE
Burlington (Spanish Fort)
Capps Corner
Celeste
Coth
Denton Creek (Tilton)
Denver
Dewey
Dorsey (Gorgona, Lake Valley)
Duxbury (Virginia Mills)
Dry Valley
Dye [Mound]
Eagle Point (Pearson)
Elser
Ferguson
Forestburg[h] (Forest Hill, Hagler's Store, Horn Hill)
Forest Hill (Forestburg)
Fruitland (Plano, Woodswitch)
Gladys (Amo)
Gorgona (Dorsey, Lake Valley)
Hagler's Store (Forestburg)
Hardy (Willa Walla)
Harp['s Store] (New Harp)
Harrisonia (Ringgold)
Head of Elm (St. Jo)
Horn Hill (Forestburg)
Huddleston
Hynds City
Illinois Bend (Waidville)
Jacksonville (Sunset)

Joe (St. Jo)
Key West
Lake Valley (Dorsey, Gorgona)
Lamb's Mill (Salona)
Lelan (Stephen's Gin)
Lost
Lucky (Todd, Williams Ranch)
Mallard
Mary (Tage)
McCollum
McDonald
Montague
New Harp (Harp['s Store])
NOCONA
Norwood
Oliver (Zim)
Parmley
Pearson (Eagle Point)
Plano (Fruitland)
Queen[s] Peak (Adora, Victoria Peak)
Redbud
Red River Station (Salt Creek)
Res (Alp)
Riley (Stoneburg)
Ringgold (Harrisonia)
Rip
Rowland
ST. JO (Head of Elm, Joe)
Salt Creek (Red River Station)
Salona (Lamb's Mill, Spat)
Ship
Smithton (Sunset)
Spanish Fort (Burlington)
Spat (Salona)
Spencer
Stephen's Gin (Lelan)
Stoneburg (Riley)
SUNSET (Jacksonville, Smithton)
Tage (Mary)
Tilton (Denton Creek)
Todd (Lucky, Williams Ranch)
Uz
Victoria Peak (Queen Peak)
Virginia Mills (Duxbury)
Waidville (Illinois Bend)
Willa Walla (Hardy)
Williams Ranch (Lucky, Todd)
Woodswitch (Fruitland)
Zim (Oliver)
Zinnia

Montgomery Co.
25 Mile Post (Porter)
Ada (Esperanza)
Alethia
Allendale
Arnold (Leonidas)
Arnold Mills
Beach
Bell (Bobville)
Bennette['s Mills] (Security)
Blueberry Hill
Bobbin (Bobville)

Bobville (Bobbin, Bell,
  Shannon)
Boy
Brantley (Honea)
Bristow (Copeland)
Brook Forest
Browder (Highland)
Bruin (Leslieville)
Buck Hills
Callie (Magnolia)
Caney Station (New
  Caney)
CHATEAU WOODS
Clinesburg (Fostoria)
Coletown
Collins Mill (Honea)
CONROE [Conroe's
  Switch]
Copeland (Bristow, Ryals)
Coxey (Splendora)
Cox's Switch (Splendora)
Crossroads
Cudlip Switch (Hazel)
CUT AND SHOOT
Dacus (Hopewell)
Danville (Lenley's)
Decker Prairie
Dobbin
Edison
Egypt
Egypt (Tamina)
Enchanted Forest
Entre (Porter)
Esperanza (Ada)
Fostoria (Clinesburg)
Four Corners
Gary
Grand Lake
Grangerland
Groceville
Grover (Magnolia)
Guyler
Hackney's Mill (New
  Caney)
Haltom's
Hartley
Hazel (Cudlip Switch)
Heron (Maggie)
Highland (Browder)
Honea (Brantley, Collins
  Mill, Sans Souci)
Hopewell (Dacus)
Hunters Retreat (Pine-
  hurst)
Jackson
Johnson
Karen (Sammons)
Keefer
Keenan
Keisler
Laird
Lakeland
Lenley's (Danville)
Leonidas (Arnold)
Leslieville (Bruin)
Lone Oak
Longstreet
Maggie (Heron, Progress)
Magnolia (Callie)
MAGNOLIA (Grover, Mel-
  ton, Mink[s Prairie],
  Prismoid)
McRae

Meadowbrook
Medley
Melton (Magnolia)
Melvin
Midline
Midway
Milvid (Timber)
Mink (Magnolia)
Minnocks (Wilmoth)
MONTGOMERY
Mosley
Mosswood
Mostyn
Mount Zion
New Caney (Caney Sta-
  tion, Hackney's Mill, Phil-
  lips, Robinson,
  Roweville)
OAK RIDGE NORTH
Oklahoma
Osborne
PANORAMA
PATTON VILLAGE
Pauli
Peel Junction
Phillips (New Caney)
Pinehurst (Hunters
  Retreat)
Pinery
Piney Point
Pittsville
Pocahontas (Security)
Porter [Porter's] ville, Mill]
  (Entre, 25 Mile Post)
Porter Heights
Prairie Home (Tillis Prairie)
Presswood
Prismoid
Prismoid (Magnolia)
Progress (Maggie)
Rayford
Riverbrook
River Plantation
Riverwood
Robinson (New Caney)
ROMAN FOREST
Roweville (New Caney)
Ryals (Copeland)
Sammons (Karen)
Sandy Hills
Sans Souci (Honea)
Security (Bennette, Poca-
  hontas, Sumatra)
Shannon['s] (Bobville)
SHENANDOAH
Silver City
Sleepy Hollow
SPLENDORA (Coxey,
  Cox's Switch)
Spring Forest
Spring Woods
STAGECOACH
Sumatra (Security)
Tamina (Egypt)
Teddy
Texas National
Tharp
The Woodlands
Tillis Prairie (Prairie Home)
Timber (Milvid, Vidor)
Ventura
Vicksburg
Vidor (Timber)

Virgie
Walden
Ware's Settlement
Waukegan
Wigginsville
Wilburton
WILLIS
Wilmoth (Minnocks)
WOODBRANCH
Wood Creek
Woodhaven
Wood Hollow
Woodlawn
WOODLOCH
Youens
Zither

Moore Co.
Altman (Sunray)
Aqua (Bennie)
Bautista
Belle Plain (Burden)
Bennie (Aqua)
Beulah (Sunray)
Bryden
Burden (Belle Plain)
CACTUS
Capps
DUMAS
Etter
Excel
Festus
Flo (Inman)
Four Way
Inman (Flo)
Machovec
Masterson
Mission (Ouida)
Ouida (Mission)
Quarton
Sheerin
SUNRAY (Altman, Beulah,
  Thomas)
Thomas (Sunray)
Trumble

Morris Co.
Belden (Naples)
Bond
Cason (Snow Hill)
Center Vine
DAINGERFIELD
Elliott's Mill (Omaha)
Gavett (Omaha)
Gillis
Iron Bluff (Lone Star)
Jenkins (Lilley)
Laman
Lilley (Jenkins)
LONE STAR (Iron Bluff)
Morristown (Omaha)
Mount Mitchell
NAPLES (Belden, Station
  Belden)
Oak Grove
OMAHA (Elliott's Mill,
  Gavett, Morris[town])
Oneal
Ore
Pewitt
Rocky Branch
Snow Hill (Cason)
Station Belden (Naples)
Veals

Vineyard
Westside
Wheatville

Motley Co.
Ballard (Matador)
Bitter Lake (Northfield)
Bundy
Dutchman (Roaring
  Springs)
Flomot (Gilpin)
Folley [Follie]
Gilpin (Flomot)
Humbra (Russellville)
Lyman
MacBain
MATADOR (Ballard)
Northfield (Bitter Lake)
Pitts (Whitestar)
ROARING SPRINGS
  (Dutchman)
Russellville (Humbra)
Summit
Tee Pee City [Teepee City]
Whiteflat
Whitestar (Pitts)
Whitestone

Nacogdoches Co.
Alazan
Aldridge's (Mount Sterling)
APPLEBY
Arthur (Stoker)
Attoyac (Black Jack)
Black Jack (Attoyac)
Bristow (Stoker)
Caro
Central Heights
Cherino (Chireno)
CHIRENO (Cherino,
  Flournoy's)
Clevenger (Tubbes)
Climax
Chinita (Smyrna)
Crossroads (Nat)
Cross Roads (Swift)
Cruseville [Cruse's Store]
  (Lera, Thrash)
CUSHING
Decoy (Fern)
Dextra
Dorr Junction
Douglass
Eden
Etoile (Fisher)
Fern (Decoy)
Fisher (Etoile)
Flournoy's (Chireno)
Freeman's Store (Libby)
Fritze
GARRISON
Goodman's Crossing
  (Mount Sterling)
Greenwood (Wonders)
Hampton
Hardeman's
Harmony
Harrington (La Nana)
Hayward
Henning
Hoya
Johnston Store
King's Store (Woden)
Kingtown

Laceyville
Lakeland
La Nana (Harrington)
Leggs Store
Lera (Cruseville, Thrash)
Libby (Freeman's Store)
Lilbert
Lilly Grove
Linn Flat
Looneyville
Lowery (Smyrna)
Lucknow
Mahl
Martinsville *[Martin['s Mill, City]*
Mayotown *[Mayo]* (Sterne)
McClures
Melrose
Mount Huling (Mount Sterling)
Mount Sterling (Aldridge's, Goodman's Crossing, Mount Huling)
Nacalina
NACOGDOCHES
Nat (Crossroads, Old Philadelphia)
Needmore
New Camp
Nivac
Oak Flat
Oak Ridge
Old Philadelphia (Nat)
Oval (Woden)
Pisgah
Pleasant Hill
Poe
Redfield
River Fork (Smyrna)
Sacul
Shirley Creek
Simpson's
Smyrna (Chinata, Lowery, River Fork)
Sterne (Mayotown)
Stoker (Arthur, Bristow)
Swift (Cross Roads)
Thrash (Cruseville, Lera)
Thors
Toliver
Trawick
Tubbes (Clevenger)
Upshaw
Venice (Wonders)
Woden (Oval, King's Store)
Wonders (Greenwood, Venice)

Navarro Co.
Alliance Hall
ANGUS
Antioch
Arbor
Baizett (Bazette)
BARRY (Sloan)
Bazette (Baizett)
Belle Point (Purdon)
Belt's Store (Ellis)
Birdston
Black Hills (Ryan)
BLOOMING GROVE (Gradyville)

Board
Bragg (Roane)
Bray (Corbet)
Bright (Talbot)
Brown Chapel
Brushie Prairie
Burney's Bridge (Rodney)
Cade Chapel *[Cade]*
Campbell
Carl
Center Point (Currie)
Chatfield
Cheneyboro
Chesnutt (Frost)
Cody (Tupelo)
Conner
Cook's Schoolhouse (Corbet)
Corbet (Bray, Cook's Schoolhouse, Waters *[Station]*)
Corinth (Mann)
CORSICANA
Cross Roads (Grimes' Gin)
Cryer Creek (Wilson)
Currie (Center Point, Rabbit Hill)
DAWSON (Spring Hill)
Dover
Drane
Dresden (Melton's)
Eldorado Center
Ellis (Belt's Store)
Elm Flat
Elm Hill (Milred)
EMHOUSE (Lyford)
Emmett (Grover)
EUREKA
Forks of the Creek (Pelham)
French
FROST
Frost (Chesnutt)
Frost (Re)
Gable
Germany (Roane)
GOODLOW
Goodnight
Gradyville (Blooming Grove)
Grimes' Gin (Cross Roads)
Grover (Emmet)
Hardys Chapel
Hester (School Land)
Hopewell (Navarro)
Irvine (Milred)
Jester (Switch)
Johnson's Gin (Kelm)
Kelat (Pelham)
Kelm (Johnson's Gin, Prairie Home, Tinkle)
KERENS
Key
Kingwillow
Locust Grove
Locket (Tupelo)
Lone Oak
Lyford (Emhouse)
Mann (Corinth)
McAllister
MILDRED
Melton's (Dresden)
Milred (Elm Hill, Irvine)

Montfort (Muskete)
Moreland
Muskete (Montfort)
MUSTANG
NAVARRO (Hopewell)
Navarro Mills
Nestorville
OAK VALLEY
Pansy (Union Flat, Wilmerding)
Park Community
Payne (Rodney)
Pelham (Forks of the Creek, Kelat)
Petty's Chapel
Pickett
Pinkston (Sloan)
Pisgah
Porters Bluff (Taos)
Post Oak
Post Oak School (Roane)
POWELL
Prairie Home (Kelm)
Pryor (Retreat)
Purdon (Belle Point)
Pursley
Rabbit Hill (Currie)
Raleigh (Sue)
Re (Frost)
RETREAT (Pryor)
RICE
RICHLAND
Richland Crossing
Roane (Germany, Post Oak School)
Rodney *[Calm]* (Burney's Bridge, Payne)
Round House
Round Prairie
Rural Shade
Rush Creek
Rushing
Ryan (Black Hills)
Samaria
School Land (Hester)
Silver City
Sloan (Barry)
Sloan (Pinkston)
Spring Hill
Spring Hill (Dawson)
Stansell
STREETMAN
Sue (Raleigh)
Switch (Jester)
Talbot (Bright)
Taos (Porters Bluff)
Timothy
Tinkle (Kelm)
Tupelo (Cody, Locket)
Union Flat (Pansy)
Union High
Valley Farms
Wadeville
Wainwright
Waters Station (Corbet)
Wilmerding (Pansy)
Wilson (Cryer Creek)
Winkler
Woods
Younger

Newton Co.
Adsul

Allardale (Jacks)
Allarton (Jacks)
Autryville
Belgrade (Biloxi)
Bencini
Biloxi (Lawhon's Mills)
Biloxi (Belgrade)
Bleakwood (Cavins Mill, Cotland, Frisco Junction)
Bon Wier
Buckhorn
Bull Run
Burkeville (Newton *[Court House]*)
Call
Caney Creek (Lees Mill)
Cavins Mill (Bleakwood)
Clark's Store (Rainbow)
Cochran's Retreat
Colville (Toledo)
Conn (Salem)
Cotland (Bleakwood)
Cow Creek (Farrsville)
Cow Creek (Salem)
Cypress Crossings (Princeton)
Delma (Snell's)
Deweyville (Possum Bluff)
Farrsville (Cow Creek)
Fawil
Frisco Junction (Bleakwood)
Grange (Holly Springs)
Happiness (Princeton)
Harrells
Hartburg
Hiawatha (Jacks)
Holly Springs (Grange)
Howards
Hughes
Idalia
Indian Hill
Indian Lake
Jacks (Allardale, Allarton, Hiawatha, New Columbia)
Jamestown (Westbrook Mill)
Kerrdale (Spears Chapel)
Klondike (Trotti)
Larch (Tulip)
Laurel
Laurel Hill (Little Cow Creek)
Lawhon's Mills (Biloxi)
Lees Mill (Caney Creek, Livonia)
Liberty
Lillie
Little Cow Creek (Laurel Hill)
Liveoak
Livonia (Lees Mill)
Logtown
Mattox *[Mill]*
Mayflower (Surveyville, The Survey)
Midway
New Columbia (Jacks)
NEWTON
Newton *[Court House]* (Burkeville)
Nibletts Bluff

Oak Grove (Wightman)
Oakhill (Salem)
Old Salem (Salem)
Pine Grove
Possum Bluff (Deweyville)
Princeton (Cypress Crossings, Happiness)
Pulltype
Quicksand
Rainbow (Clark's Store)
River Bend
Ruliff
Sabine Sands
Salem (Conn, Cow Creek, Oakhill, Old Salem)
Salem
Sand Jack
Sand Pit
Scrappin Valley
Shankleville
Singletary Sites
Snell's [Store] (Delma)
Spears Chapel (Kerrdale)
Stringtown
Surveyville (Mayflower)
The Survey (Mayflower)
Todd
Toledo (Colville)
Toledo Village
Trotti (Klondike)
Trout Creek
Tulip (Larch)
Weeks Settlement
Westbrook Mill (Jamestown)
Wiergate
Wightman (Oak Grove)
Wihan
Woodmyer

Nolan Co.
BLACKWELL (James)
Blue Goose (Sweetwater)
Centerview (Maryneal)
Champion
Cottonwood
Crutcher
Decker (Rex)
Dinsmore (Zuniga)
Dora
Edleona
Fain (Zuniga)
Fish Creek (Hylton)
Grimes
Handy (Zuniga)
Happy Land
Herndon
Hillsdale Pit
Hylton (Fish Creek)
James (Blackwell)
Janus
Katula (Roscoe)
Maryneal (Centerview)
Neely (Wastella)
Nolan
Olga (Rex)
Pete
Pyramid
Rex (Decker)
Rex (Olga)
ROSCOE (Katula, Vista)
Shaufler
Sowell

Stamper
SWEETWATER (Blue Goose)
Tesco
Vista (Roscoe)
Wastella (Neely)
Zuniga (Dinsmore, Fain, Handy)

Nueces Co.
AGUA DULCE
Alfred (Noma)
Annaville
Arlington Heights
Banquete
Banquete (Nueces[town])
BISHOP (Julia)
Bluntzer (Santa Margarita)
Brighton (Flour Bluff)
Calallen (Calvin City)
Chapman Ranch (Pottsville)
Chemcel
Clarkwood (Woodland Park)
Calvin City (Calallen)
Coldris (Driscoll)
Concordia
CORPUS CHRISTI
Corpus Christi NAS
DRISCOLL (Coldris)
Five Points
Flour Bluff
Flour Bluff (Brighton)
Gardendale
Highway Village
Juan Saenz
Julia (Bishop)
Knolle
La Rosa
Leona Schroder
Lon Hill
McNorton
Midway
Mustang Island (Port Aransas)
Noma (Alfred)
North Pole
North San Pedro
Nueces[town] (Banquete, The Motts, Villa Nueva)
Oyster Point (Rincon)
Palo Alto
Peary Place
PETRONILA
Pottsville (Chapman Ranch)
PORT ARANSAS (Mustang Island, Ropesville, Star, Tarpon)
Rabb
Rincon (Oyster Point)
ROBSTOWN
Ropesville (Port Aransas)
San Juan
San Pedro
Santa Margarita (Bluntzer)
Skunk Hill
South San Pedro
Star (Port Aransas)
Sunshine
Tarpon (Port Aransas)
The Motts (Nueces[town])

Tulosa
Villa Nueva (Nueces[town])
Viola
Violet
West Oso
Woodland Park (Clarkwood)

Ochiltree Co.
Alfalfa (Wolf Creek)
Barcee (Jines)
BOOKER
Buler
Burnside (Waka)
Cora (Taz)
Cresswell (Pioneer)
Farnsworth (Nogal, Olds, Rogers[town])
Gilaloo
Grogan
Halfway House (Notla)
Hope (Waka)
Huntoon
Jines [Springs] (Barcee)
Lord
McHall (Perryton)
Nogal (Farnsworth)
Notla (Halfway House)
Ochiltree
Olds (Farnsworth)
Pauline
PERRYTON (McHall)
Pioneer (Cresswell)
Rogers[town] (Farnsworth)
Taz (Cora)
Twichell
Waka (Burnside, Hope, Wawaka)
Wawaka (Waka)
Wolf Creek (Alfalfa)

Oldham Co.
ADRIAN
Alamositas
Atascosa (Tascosa)
Boise
Boot Hill
Boston Ranch (Hayes)
Boys' Ranch ([Old] Tascosa)
Cheyenne (Magenta)
Everett
Gruhlkey
Hayes ([Boston, Victoria] Ranch)
Jude
Landergin
Lathrop
Magenta (Cheyenne)
Murdo
Old Tascosa (Boys' Ranch)
Ontario
Rock Lake
Tascosa (Atascosa)
Trygillo
VEGA
Victoria Ranch (Hayes)
Wildorado

Orange Co.
Adams Bayou (Orange)
Adrian (Muskegon)
Alexander Spur (Oilla)
Bancroft

Bobsher
BRIDGE CITY
Brownwood-Oakland
Bruce (Texla)
Bunn's Bluff
Cannett
Connell (Duncan's Woods)
Cove City
Cow Bayou (Oilla)
Doty
Duncan's Woods (Connell)
East Beaumont (Worbaino)
East Jefferson (Orange)
Echo
Forest Heights
Francis
Gilmer
Grand Bluff (Orange)
Gratis
Green's Bluff (Orange)
Huntley (Orange)
Kilowatt
Korf
Lakeview
Lemonville
Little Cypress
Madison (Orange)
Mauriceville
Mulford
Muskegon (Adrian)
Oilla (Alexander Spur, Cow Bayou, Terry)
Oneida
ORANGE (Adams Bayou, East Jefferson, Grand Bluff, Green's Bluff, Huntley, Madison, Strong's Bluff)
Orangefield
Pattillos
Pearl (Terry)
Peveto
PINE FOREST
PINEHURST
ROSE CITY
Schneider (Vidor)
Spooner
Strong's Bluff (Orange)
Terry [Station] (Pearl, Walles' Store)
Terry (Oilla)
Texla (Bruce)
Tulane
VIDOR (Schneider)
Walles' Store (Terry)
WEST ORANGE
Williamson Settlement
Woodridge
Worbaino (East Beaumont)

Palo Pinto Co.
Angoria (Brazos)
Anita (Salesville)
Barber Mountain (Hitson's Crossing)
Beth (Posideon)
Beulah (Ioni)
Birmingham
Black Springs (Oran)
Brad (Cedar Knob, Oxford)
Brazos (Angoria)
Calgando (Santo)
Cedar Knob (Brad)

Christian (Russell's Store)
Coalville (Gordon Coal
  Mines, Hoxie)
Cokelan (Graford)
Cove
Cresco (Santo)
Dodson Prairie
Ednaville (Mineral Wells)
Everton (Strawn)
Ewen (Randal's Store)
Folger
Golconda (Palo Pinto)
GORDON
Gordon Coal Mines
  (Coalville)
Gordon Junction
GRAFORD (Cokelan)
Grand Ranche (Santo)
Hampton
Hitson's Crossing (Barber
  Mountain)
Housh (Lyra)
Hoxie (Coalville)
Ioni (Beulah)
Jerehart
Lanham (Randal's Store)
Lone Camp
Loving's Valley (Salesville)
Lyra (Housh)
McCain Point
Metcalf Gap
MINERAL WELLS (Edna-
  ville, Willow Pond)
MINGUS (Thurber Junc-
  tion)
Natalie
New Salem
Oran (Black Springs)
Oxford (Brad)
Palo Pinto (Golconda)
Peadenville
Pickwick (Westerville)
Pleasant Valley (Salesville)
Pollard [Crossing]
Posideon (Beth)
Randal's Store (Ewen,
  Lanham)
River Bend
Russell's Store (Christian)
Salesville [Sale's Store
  ] (Anita, Loving's Valley,
  Pleasant Valley)
Santo (Calgando, Cresco,
  Grand Ranche, Sparta)
Sparta (Santo)
STRAWN (Everton)
Sturdivant
Thurber Junction (Mingus)
Trion
Walnut Creek
Westerville (Pickwick)
Willow Pond (Mineral
  Wells)

Panola Co.
Adams Store
Adams[ville] (Haywood)
Ajax (Tacoma)
Anacostia
Antioch
Arleston (Sunny Point)
Bacon (Biggs)
BECKVILLE (Vilas,

Yancey)
Bell Fountain (Kinlock)
Bethany (Vernon)
Big Cut (Haysland)
Biggs (Bacon, Crocketts-
  ville, Duke)
Booker (Logan)
Boren
Breckenridge Springs
  (Midyett)
Brewster's Bluff (Grand
  Bluff)
Bristow's Ferry
Brooks
Broome
Brushy (Dotson)
Burns Mill (Dargan)
Buncombe
Bunkum
Cariker (Clayton)
CARTHAGE
Centennial (Harmony)
Center Point
Clayton (Cariker)
Cozart (Ragley)
Crockettsville (Biggs)
Daniels
Dargan (Burns Mill, Fur-
  man, Lineville)
Davis (Parry's)
Deadwood (Linus)
DeBerry (Evergreen)
Delray (Walton)
Dixie (Dotson)
Dotson (Brushy, Dixie,
  Freeman, Thurman,
  Walnut Hill)
Duke (Biggs)
Evergreen (DeBerry)
Fair Play
Fork Point
Freeman (Dotson)
Front
Furman (Dargan)
Furrh
Galloway
GARY (Murvaul, Zuber)
Golden Vale
Gourdneck
Grand Bluff (Brewster's
  Bluff)
Greensborough (Kinlock)
Grover (Midyett)
Halls Store
Harmony (Centennial)
Harris Chapel
Haysland (Big Cut, Hays
  Station)
Hays Station (Haysland)
Haywood (Adams)
Hickey (Towers)
Hickey's Store (Lowery)
Holland Quarters
Holmes (Sandy Hook)
Horton
Hudson (Ragley)
Hull's Store (Woods)
Ingleside
Jones'
Jumbo (Scott)
Kinlock (Bell Fountain,
  Greensborough, Mount
  Mourne)

Latex (Panola)
Lineville (Dargan)
Linus (Deadwood)
Logan (Booker, McNeece)
Long Branch
Lowry (Hickey's Store)
Mahon
Martin Lake Junction
Marville
McCoy
McMillans
McNeece (Logan)
Midyett (Breckenridge
  Springs, Grover)
Miller's (Murvaul)
Mount Bethel (Thomas)
Mount Mourne (Kinlock)
Murray
Murvaul (Miller's, Ritter)
Murvaul (Gary)
Odesco (Panola)
Old Center
Page (Snap)
Panola (Odesco)
Panola (Latex)
Parry's (Davis)
Pulaski
Ragley (Cozart, Hudson)
Reed's Settlement
Riderville
Ritter (Murvaul)
River Hill
Sandy Hook (Holmes)
Scott (Jumbo)
Shady Grove
Sharon
Shed (Win Town)
Snap (Page)
Stone's Mill
Sugar Hill
Sunny Point (Arleston)
Sweeten
Tacoma (Ajax)
TATUM
Timmons'
Thomas (Mount Bethel)
Thurman (Dotson)
Towers (Hickey)
Vernon (Bethany)
Vilas (Beckville)
Walnut Hill (Dotson)
Walton (Delray)
Watsonville (Wayside)
Wayside (Watsonville,
  Wells)
Wells (Wayside)
Win Town (Shed)
Woods (Hull's Store)
Yancey (Beckville)
Zuber (Gary)

Parker Co.
Adell (Cream, Dry Creek,
  Fondren's Store)
Advance (Glen)
Agnes (Barnard's Store)
Agricola
ALEDO (McConnellsville,
  Parker['s Station])
ANNETTA
ANNETTA NORTH
ANNETTA SOUTH
Authon (Copper Hill, Dry

Creek)
AZLE
Baker
Balch
Ballew [Springs]
Barnard's Store (Agnes)
Bear Creek
Bennett (Lakota)
Bluff City (Dennis)
Brannon's Store (Sam)
Briar
Brock (Olive Branch)
Brock Junction
Buckner
Carter[sville]
Charity (Mercy)
Clear Fork (Dicey)
Clovis
COOL
Copper Hill (Anthon)
Cougar (Rayville)
Cream (Adell)
Cream Level [or Liel],
  (Veal's Station)
Deacon
Delphine
Dennis (Bluff City)
Dicey (Clear Fork, Nebo,
  Power)
Dry Creek (Authon)
Dry Creek (Adell)
Eagle Rock (Eagleville)
Eagleville (Eagle Rock,
  Woodville)
Fondren's Store (Adell)
Fox (Lambert)
Franco
Fremont (Peaster)
Gamma
Garner
Gilliland (McKinley)
Glen (Advance)
Grindstone
Half-Way House (Whitt)
Highland Addition
Hiner (Wade's Chapel)
HUDSON OAKS
Iona
Knob
Kyle's Station (Mary's
  Creek)
La Junta
Lakota (Bennett)
Lambert (Fox)
Lemley
Littleton's Springs (Spring-
  town)
Littletonville (Springtown)
Lotta (Morgan Springs)
Mary's Creek (Kyle's
  Station)
Maud (Wallace)
McConnellsville (Aledo)
McFarland
McKinley (Gilliland)
McIntosh
Mercy (Charity)
MILLSAP
Morgan Springs (Lotta)
Nebo (Dicey)
Newburg
Old Milsap
Olive Branch (Brock)

Parker['s Station] (Aledo)
Parker's Shop (Reno)
Parsons (Woodstock)
Peaster[ville] (Fremont)
Poolville
Power (Dicey)
Pugh
Ray School (Toto)
Rayville (Cougar)
RENO (Parker's Shop,
  Rogersville)
Rhea
Roberts (Steele Gin)
Rock Creek
Rogersville (Reno)
Roy (Sam)
Sabathany
Sam (Brannon's Store,
  Roy)
SANCTUARY
Slover (Tyro)
Spencer (Worley)
SPRINGTOWN (Littleton's
  Springs, Littletonville)
Steele Gin (Roberts)
Tin Top
Toto (Ray School)
Tyro (Slover)
Veals Station (Cream
  Level)
Wade's Chapel (Hiner)
Walker
Wallace (Maud)
WEATHERFORD
Weland
Western Lake
Wheatland
Whitt (Half-Way House)
WILLOW PARK
Woodstock (Parsons)
Woodville (Eagleville)
Worley (Spencer)

Parmer Co.
Black
BOVINA (Bull Town)
Bull Town (Bovina)
Clays Corner
FARWELL
Frio (Friona)
FRIONA (Frio)
Hub
Lariat
Lazbuddie
Oklahoma Lane
Parmerton
Rhea
Texico
Wilsey

Pecos Co.
Abell City
Adams (Bakersfield)
Bakersfield (Adams)
Bakersfield Valley
Baldridge
Belding
Borrillo
Buenavista
Camp Stockton (Fort
  Stockton)
Carmel
Chancellor
Comanche Springs (Fort

Stockton)
Coyanosa
Fort Gall (Fort Stockton)
FORT STOCKTON (Camp
  Stockton, Comanche
  Springs, Fort Gall)
Girvin (Granada)
Granada (Girvin)
Hodgins
Hovey
Imperial (Redlands)
IRAAN
Levin (Rutherford)
Longfellow
Nations
Owego
Pecos Springs (Sheffield)
Phenix
Red Barn
Redlands (Imperial)
Rutherford (Levin)
Santa Lucia
Sheffield (Pecos Springs)
Tessie
Zimerman

Polk Co.
Ace (Coshatte Bluff,
  Geneva, Hirams', Smith-
  field)
Acol
Alabama-Coushatta
Indian Reservation
Asia
Baker (Bowers)
Baldwin (Lamont)
Barnes (Hassett)
Barnum
Bear Creek (Hortense)
Benford (Silver Hill)
Bering (Valda)
Big Sandy (Dallardsville)
Big Spring (Midway)
Blanchard (West Tempe)
Bluewater (Dowden)
Blue Water (Knight)
Bluff Creek (Soda)
Bold Springs (Nettie,
  Marsh)
Bowers (Baker, Clevilas)
Bracewell
Bridges
Buck (Stanley)
Caleta (Colita)
Camden
Camp Providence (Provi-
  dence)
Camp Ruby (Carter, Char-
  ity, Lucky, Old Hope)
Camp Seale
Canary (Long Bridge)
Carmona
Carter (Camp Ruby)
Charity (Camp Ruby)
Clevilas (Bowers)
Colita (Caleta, Louisiana
  Settlement)
Corrie (Deaton)
CORRIGAN [Corrigon]
Coshatte Bluff (Ace)
Dallardsville [Dollardsville]
  (Big Sandy)
Darden

Deason (Tibbie, Mulvey)
Deaton (Corrie, Kern)
Dock
Dowden (Bluewater)
Drews Landing [Drew's
  Corners] (Marianna)
Easom [Easom Hill]
  (Wakefield)
East Tempe
Elbert
Emmit (Midway)
Erie (Soda)
Fant['s Mill] (Wakefield)
Free
Freeman (New Williard)
Geneva (Ace)
Glade (Hatton, India)
GOODRICH
Grace Hill
Green's [Greenville]
  (Moscow)
Guelph
Hackneyville (Phoenix)
Halifax
Hammock
Hanner
Hassett (Barnes)
Hatton (Glade)
Henry County Settlement
Hightown
Hirams' [Hiroms'] (Ace)
Holly Grove
Hortense (Bear Creek)
Hutto's Grove (Indian
  Spring)
Ilah
India (Glade)
Indian Spring (Hutto's
  Grove, Jones Prairie,
  Shady Grove)
Indian Springs
Israel
Jack Camp
Jones Prairie (Indian
  Spring)
Kern (Deaton)
Kiam
Kickapoo (Pershing)
Knight (Blue Water,
  Menard)
Lamont (Baldwin)
Laurelia
Leggett (Red Horse)
Lily Island
LIVINGSTON (Springfield)
Long Bridge (Canary)
Long King
Louisiana Settlement (Col-
  ita)
Lucky (Camp Ruby)
Mack
Marianna [Marienne]
  (Drews Landing)
Market
Marr (Midway)
Marsh (Bold Springs)
Marston (Norma)
Marstonville
Menard['s Chapel] (Knight)
Menard's Mills
Midway (Big Spring,
  Emmit, Marr, Morgan-
  ville, Pinckney, Trot,

Wood's Creek)
Moore Hill
Morganville (Midway)
Moscow (Green's)
Mount Rose
Mulvey (Deason)
Nettie (Bold Springs)
New Camp Ruby
New Hope
New Willard (Freeman)
Norma (Marston)
Oakdale
Oak Shade
Old Hope (Camp Ruby)
Ollie (Rice)
ONALASKA
Patonia
Pershing (Kickapoo)
Petersville (Potomac)
Phoenix (Hackneyville)
Pinckney (Midway)
Pluck (Stryker)
Potomac (Petersville)
Providence (Camp Provi-
  dence)
Providence Camp
Red Horse
Rhoden
Rice (Ollie)
Schwab City
Segno
SEVEN OAKS
Shady Grove (Indian
  Spring)
Silver Hill (Benford)
Smithfield (Ace)
Soda (Bluff Creek, Erie)
Springfield (Livingston)
Stanley (Buck)
Stryker (Pluck)
Stubblefield's (Swartwout)
Swartwout (Stubblefield's)
Temple Junction
Thicket
Tibbie (Deason)
Tin Top
Tobacco Patch
Trot (Midway)
Valda (Bering)
Wakefield (Easom, Fant['s
  Mill], Wheeler's Switch)
Washington Mills
West Tempe (Blanchard)
Wheeler's Switch (Wake-
  field)
Wood's Creek (Midway)

Potter Co.
Ady
AMARILLO (Oneida)
Aqua
BISHOP HILLS
Boden
Bushland [Bush]
Chunky
Cliffside
Excel
Folsom
Gentry
Gluck
James
Julliard
Marsh

Masterson
Mayer
Nagiller (Noble)
Noble (Nagiller)
North Heights
Oneida (Amarillo)
Pleasant Valley
Puente
Pullman
Rolling Hills
St. Francis
Soncy
Tascosa Hills
Walnut Hills
Wheeler

Presidio Co.
Adobes
Alamito (Dysart)
Aragon
Brite [Ranch]
Buena Suerte (Los Fresnos)
Candelaria (Gallina)
Casa Piedra
Chinati
Daniel (Porvenir)
Dysart (Alamito)
Gallina (Candelaria)
Haciendito
Indio
Los Fresnos (Buena Suerte)
MARFA
Nopal
Ochoa
Paisano
Perdiz
Plata
Polaris (Porvenir)
Porvenir (Daniel, Polaris)
PRESIDIO (Spencer's Ranch)
Polvo (Redford)
Pulvo (Redford)
Quebec
Redford (Polvo, Pulvo)
Rindosa
Ruidosa
Ryan
Shafter
Spencer's Ranch (Presidio)
Tinaja
Zulime

Rains Co.
ALBA
Bois d'Arc
Bright Star
Bruton
Clearning
Colony
County Line
Daugherty (Dougherty)
Dougherty (Daugherty)
Dunbar
EAST TAWAKONI
Elm
EMORY
Flats
Freedom
Giner
Ginger

Grit
Hermits Cove
Hogansville
Hooker Ridge
Hookers
Lynch
Pilgrim Rest
POINT
Poole
Prospect
Rains
Richland
Rocky Point
Sand Flat
Smyrna
Wattsville
Willow Springs
Woosley

Randall Co.
AMARILLO
CANYON [City]
Ceta
Cita
Cleta
Dee (Ingram)
Handville
Haney
Heyser (Price)
Highland
Holton
Ingram (Dee)
LAKE TANGLEWOOD
Mesa (Portsmouth)
Mescalero Park
Ogg
PALISADES
Plemons
Portsmouth (Mesa)
Price (Heyser)
Ralls
Ralph
TIMBERCREEK CANYON
Umbarger
Zita

Reagan Co.
Best
BIG LAKE
High Lonesome (Stiles)
Isaac
Reaganview (Seven D)
Rita Santa
Santa Rita
Seven D (Reaganview)
Stiles (High Lonesome)
Texon
Witco

Real Co.
Auld (Buck Den)
Big Paint
Buck Den (Auld, Shackelford Ranch)
Bull Head (Vance)
CAMP WOOD
Exile
Floral
Frio Water Hole
LEAKEY
Lula
Prade Ranch
Rio Frio (The Ditch)
Shackelford Ranch (Buck

Den)
The Ditch (Rio Frio)
Vance (Bull Head)

Red River Co.
Acworth (Bason)
Addielou (Hudson)
Aikin [Aiken] Grove
Albion (Parks Bluff)
Almond Grove (English)
ANNONA (Oakland, Walker Station)
AVERY (Douglass, Isaca)
Bagwell
Bason (Acworth)
Batesville
Bennett (Detroit)
Birmingham (Nicks)
Blakeney (Hamburg)
BOGATA (Maple Springs)
Bowden (Midway)
Boxelder
Bryarly (Mound City, Rowland, Walnut Grove)
Calvin
Caton[ville]
Ceries (Home, Reed)
Cherry
Choctaw
Clair
CLARKSVILLE
Cold Springs (Kiomatia)
Cravens [Mill]
Cuthand (Enterprise, Garvinsville)
Davenport (Jonesboro[ugh])
DETROIT (Bennett, Starkesville)
Dilworth
Dimple
Douglass (Avery)
Elkhorn
Emmett (Vandalia)
English (Almond Grove)
Enterprise (Cuthand)
Etta (Mena)
Flintham's Tan Yard
Four
Fryar
Fulbright (Possum Trot)
Garvinsville (Cuthand)
Gear's Tanyard (Milton)
Gertie
Grantville (Rugby)
Greenwood
Halesboro[ugh] (Wrightsville)
Hamburg (Blakeney)
Harris Ferry (River View)
Harts Bluff
Harvey's Mill (Vessey)
Hokah (Opah)
Home (Ceries)
Hooks' Ferry (Towson)
Hopewell (Ira, Mulberry)
Hortonville
Hudson (Addielou)
Hudson (Kiomatia)
Ima
Ira (Hopewell)
Isaca (Avery)
Johntown

Jonesboro[ugh] (Davenport)
Kanawha
Kiomache (Kiomatia)
Kiomatia (Cold Springs, Hudson, Kiomache, Pecan Point, Scrap)
La Grange (Madras)
Leila
Lelia
Lydia
Mabry (Martin, Rear)
Madras (La Grange)
Manchester (Taylor)
Maple
Maple Springs (Bogata)
Martin (Mabry)
McCoy
McCulloch (Rogers Ferry)
Mena (Etta)
Merret (Vessey)
Midway (Bowden)
Mill Creek (Pinchem)
Milton (Gear's Tanyard)
Mobberly
Mollie
Monterey
Mosely
Mound City (Bryarly)
Mulberry (Hopewell)
Nicks (Birmingham)
Negley
Oakland (Annona)
Opah (Hokah)
Otis
Parks Bluff (Albion)
Pecan Point (Kiomatia)
Pecan Point (Schraeder, Watson)
Petersburg (Peter's Prairie)
Peter's Prairie (Petersburg)
Pinchem (Mill Creek)
Pine Bluff (Pine Hills)
Pine Branch
Pine Creek
Pine Hills (Pine Bluff)
Possum Trot (Fulbright)
Prairie View (Rugby)
Readsville (Vandalia)
Rear (Mabry)
Reed (Ceries)
Reeds Settlement
River Crest
River View (Harris Ferry)
Robbinsville
Rogers Ferry (McCulloch)
Rosalie (Wayland)
Rowland (Bryarly)
Rugby (Grantville, Prairie View)
Savannah [Springs]
Schraeder (Pecan Point, Watson)
Scrap (Kiomatia)
Shadowland
Shawnee
Sherry
Silver City
Spencer
Stanley
Starkesville (Detroit)
Stephensborough
Swanntown

Swanville
Taylor (Manchester)
Tomaha
Towson (Hooks' Ferry)
Vandalia (*Emmett, Reads-
ville*)
Vessey (*Harvey's Mill, Mer-
ret, Vesey*)
Walker Station (Annona)
Walnut Grove (Bryarly)
Ward's
Watson (*Pecan Point,
Schraeder*)
Wayland (Rosalie)
White Rock
Woodland
Wrightsville (*Hales-
boro[ugh]*)

Reeves Co.
Angeles
Arno
BALMORHEA
Brogado
Collier Spur
Gozar
Hermosa
Hoban
Locker Spur
Mann
Masons
Orla
Patrole
PECOS
Permian
Red Bluff
Riverton
Robinson Arms Landing
San Martine
Saragosa
TOYAH
Toyahvale
Valley Farm
Verhalen
Worsham

Refugio Co.
AUSTWELL
BAYSIDE
Bonnie View
Campbell's Retreat (*La
Villa De Los Jacallas*)
Copano
Carnell
Church (Woodsboro)
Crescent Village (*Hynes-
ville*)
Dubois
Greta
Humble Camp
Hynesville (*Crescent
Village*)
Inari
La Villa De Los Jacallas
(*Campbell's Retreat*)
Maudlowe
Port Preston
Redlew (Vidauri)
REFUGIO [*Mission*] (*Wax-
ford*)
Ryanville
Saint Mary[s of Aransas]
Tegaco
Tivoli

Vidauri (Redlew)
Warbonnet
Waxford (Refugio)
WOODSBORO (Church)

Roberts Co.
Codman (Presto, Red
Deer)
Couch (Walstad)
Gardner
Hargrave (Parsell's Ranch)
Lora
MIAMI
Oran (Parnell)
Parnell (Oran)
Parsell's Ranch (Hargrave)
Peacevale
Presto (Codman)
Red Deer (Codman)
Walstad['s Ranch] (Couch)
Wayside

Robertson Co.
Acorn (Easterly)
Astin
Bald Prairie
Barton
Beck Prairie (Nesbitt)
Benchley (*Staggers
Point*)
Black Bridge
Black Jack
Boone Prairie
Box Quarter
BREMOND
Brown Springs (Hearne)
Bufkin
CALVERT
Calvert Junction
Camp Creek Lake
Carley
Cross Roads (Seale)
Dunn's
Durant
Easterly (*Acorn, Kirk-
patrickville, Morganlea*)
Eaton
Elliott (*Harland, Una*)
Engelwood
Eutaw
FRANKLIN (*Morgan, Old
Franklin, Volney*)
Glass
Goodland
Hammond
Harland (Elliott)
Hayes
Heads Prairie (Headsville)
Headsville (*Heads Prairie*)
HEARNE (*Brown
Springs*)
Hogg
Holly Springs (Ridge)
Kellogg's (Wheelock)
Kirkpatrickville (Easterly)
Lake [Station]
Lansdale
Little Brazos (*Rowe's
Store*)
Maguire
Marvin
McKnight (Sutton)
Morgan (Franklin)
Morganlea (Easterly)

Mumford
Navasota [Navasotto]
Nesbitt (*Beck Prairie,
Winn*)
New Baden
Nicholas
Old Franklin (Franklin)
Owensville
Petteway
Phillipsburgh
Post Oak
Ridge (*Holly Springs*)
Round Prairie
Rowe's Store (*Little Bra-
zos*)
Rufinch
Salter
Seale (*Cross Roads,
Shaw*)
Seger
Shaw (Seale)
Staggers Point (*Bench-
ley*)
Sterling
Suman
Sutton['s Station]
(*McKnight*)
Tatsie
Tidwell Prairie
Tinnen's
Una (Elliott)
Valley Junction
Volney (Franklin)
Watts
Winn (Nesbitt)
Wheelock (*Kellogg's*)
White Rock
Whites
Willow Creek (Woodland)
Wood
Woodland (Willow Creek)
Wootan [Wooten] Wells

Rockwall Co.
Barnes City
Blackland
Chisholm (McLendon-
-Chisholm)
Clark
FATE
HEATH
McLENDON-CHISHOLM
MOBILE CITY
Mount Zion
Munson
ROCKWALL
ROWLETT
ROYSE CITY
Valley View

Runnels Co.
BALLINGER (*Hutchings
City, Toombs*)
Baronsville (Rowena)
Benoit (*Norwood*)
Bethel
Blanton
Bolf (Rowena)
Brookshier
Content (*Hale's Store,
Tokeen*)
County Line (Drasco)
Crews
Draco (Drasco)

Drasco (*County Line,
Draco*)
Guest's Station (Walthall)
Hale's Store (Content)
Hatchel
Hutchings City (Ballinger)
La Vierne (Pony)
Marie
Maverick
Mazeland
McKandles' Store (*Win-
gate*)
MILES [*Station*]
Milliken (Vale)
New Hope (Pumphrey)
Norton
Norwood (Benoit)
Olfen
Oxien
Plate's Store (Winters)
Pony (La Vierne)
Pumphrey (*New Hope*)
Rowena (*Baronsville, Bolf*)
Runnels [*City*]
Tokeen (Content)
Toombs (Ballinger)
Truitt
Vale (Milliken)
Valley View
Walthall (Guest's Station)
Wilmeth
Wingate (*McKandles
Store*)
WINTERS (*Plate's Store*)

Rusk Co.
Abner (Oak Ridge)
Alma
Anadarco (Gourdneck)
Anadarko [Anadarco]
Arlam
Barlow (Hendricks)
Barnhart (Ector)
Belleview
Blackjack (Stewart)
Blossom Hill (Chapman)
Brachfield (Murva[u]l)
Bradshaw
Bryce (*Eulalie, Liles,
Wragg's Hill*)
Bunker Hill
Burns Siding (Crim)
Caison's (*Williams Settle-
ment*)
Caledonia
Calhoun
Camden (Wallings Ferry)
Carlisle (Price)
Centre (Joinerville)
Chalk Hill (*Chalkville,
Pepper*)
Chalkville (Chalk Hill)
Chapman (*Blossom Hill*)
Church Hill
Clark (Craig)
Compton
Concord
Cotton Plant
Craig (*Clark, Irwin's
Chapel, Tate*)
Crim (*Burns Siding,
Farmers Institute*)
Crims Chapel
Cross Roads

Cyril (Joinerville)
Dealey (Flanagan)
Dewey (Pone)
Dirgin
EASTON
Ector (Barnhart)
Enon (Pylas)
Eulalie (Bryce)
Fairview
Farmers Institute (Crim)
Flanagan (Dealey)
Flanagan's Mills
Freeneytown
Friar
Fussell
Gage's
Gaston (Tasso)
Gibsontown (Henderson)
Glenfawn
Golden Drain (Vannoy's)
Goodsprings [Good Springs] (Scooba)
Gould
Gourdneck (Anadarco)
Griffin Store (Jacinto)
Hanson's
Harmony Hill (Nip and Tuck)
Harris Chapel (McFaddens Store)
HENDERSON (Gibsontown)
Hendricks (Barlow)
Iron Mountain
Irwin
Irwin's Chapel (Craig)
Jacinto (Griffin Store, Kinney)
Jacobs
Joinerville (Centre, Cyril, Miller [Schoolhouse])
June (Rhodes)
Kinney (Jacinto)
KILGORE
Laird Hill (Pistol Hill)
Laneville
Lawsonville
Leverett's Chapel
Liberty
Liberty Hill (Oak Hill)
Liles (Bryce)
Locklin (Rook, Sand Hill[s])
Locust Grove
London (Norfolk)
Lyle
March
Mayflower
McFaddens Store (Harris Chapel)
McKnight
McNulty (San Cosme)
Miller [Schoolhouse] (Joinerville)
Millville (Oak Hill)
Mims
Minden
Monroe
Motley (Oak Hill)
MOUNT ENTERPRISE (Mulberry Grove)
Mulberry Grove
Murval [Murvaul] (Brachfield)

New Carlisle (Price)
New Danville
New Hope
NEW LONDON
New Prospect
New Salem
Nip and Tuck (Harmony Hill)
Norfolk (London)
Oak Flats
Oak Hill (Liberty Hill, Millville, Motley, Walling's Mills
Oak Ridge (Abner)
Old Minden
Orr (Rhodes)
OVERTON (Summer Grove)
Pepper (Chalk Hill)
Pinehill (Rake Pocket)
Pitner Junction
Pistol Hill (Laird Hill)
Pleasant Grove (Sardis)
Poindexter
Price ([New] Carlisle [Carlysle], Reagan)
Pirtle
Pone (Dewey, Short Pone)
Pylas (Enon)
Rabbit Creek
Rake Pocket (Pinehill)
Reagan (Price)
Redbuck
Reeds
REKLAW
Rhodes (June, Orr, Wood)
Rook (Locklin)
San Cosme (McNulty)
Sand Hill[s] (Locklin)
Sand Mountain (Scott's)
Sardis (Pleasant Grove)
Scott's (Sand Mountain)
Scooba (Goodsprings)
Selman City
Sexton City
Shawnee Town
Shiloh
Shire
Short Pone (Pone)
Smyrna
Spivey (Wiggins)
Stevens
Stewart (Black Jack)
Sulphur Springs
Summer Grove (Overton)
Tasso (Gaston)
Tate (Craig)
TATUM
Trukton
Turnertown
Vannoy's (Golden Drain)
Valley Grove
Walker's
Wallings Ferry (Camden)
Walling's Mills (Oak Hill)
Welch [Springs]
Wherry['s]
Wiggins (Spivey)
Williams Settlement (Caison's)
Wood (Rhodes)
Wooten's
Wragg's Hill (Bryce)

Zion Grove

Sabine Co.
Akin (Bear Creek)
Alford
Bayou (Oakdale)
Bear Creek (Akin)
Bear Creek (Brookeland)
Bennett (Time)
BRONSON
Brookeland (Bear Creek, Norvell's, Weed Station)
Connville (Gravel Hill)
East Mayfield
Fairdale
Fairmount
Fontella
Gaines Ferry
Geneva (Jim Town)
Gravel Hill (Connville)
HEMPHILL
Hickory Ridge
Hornbeck (Pineland)
Isla
Jim Town (Geneva)
John Adams' Mill (Pineland)
La Merle [Lamerle]
Longwood
Magasco
Magnolia Mills (Talltimber)
McElroy
McMahan Chapel
Milam (Red Mound)
Nolia (Talltimber)
Norvell's (Brookeland)
Oakdale (Bayou)
Old Sabinetown
Pendleton (Red Mount)
PINELAND (Hornbeck, John Adams' Mill)
Plainview
Red Mound (Milam)
Red Mount (Gaines Ferry, Pendleton, Sabine)
Roland (Vesta)
Rosevine
Sabine (Red Mount)
Sabinetown
Sexton
Spring Hill
Strickland Crossing
Talltimber (Magnolia Mills, Nolia)
Tebo
Time (Bennett)
Vesta (Roland)
Watsonville
Weed Station
White's
Yellowpine

San Augustine Co.
Altonia (Ransom, Saint Helena)
Ashton (Benina)
Attoyac [Attoyaque] (Price's Hill, Stedham's)
Ayish Bayou (Kendrick's)
Bannister
Bland Lake
Benina (Ashton, Borens Mills, Wade Mill)

Borens Mills (Benina)
Blandlake (Stop)
Blue Spring (Gay)
BROADDUS
Brooke (Dwire)
Caddell
Calcote
Calgary
Camp Worth
Chinquapin
Conville
Creech (Cupp)
Cupp (Creech)
Denning
Dogwood Grove (Macune)
Dwire (Brooke)
Eva (Gay)
Evie (Gay)
Fords Corner
Gay (Eva, Evie, Blue Spring)
Goodwin
Halltown
Ironosa
Kendrick's (Ayish Bayou)
Lake View (White City)
Lenor (Zana)
Logville
Long Leaf
Macune (Dogwood Grove, Sharpville)
Massie
Millerton
Neely
New Hope
Palo Gacho (Pollygacho, Sneedville)
Pink
Pollyga[t]cho (Palo Gacho, Sneedville)
Price's Hill (Attoyac)
Ransom (Altonia)
Rebecca
Saint Helena (Altonia)
SAN AUGUSTINE
Sharpville (Macune)
Sneedville (Palo Gacho, Pollygacho)
Stedham's (Attoyac)
Steep Creek
Stop (Blandlake)
Sturgis (White City)
Swannville
Townsend
Union
Veach
Venable
Wade Mill (Benina)
Wellswood
White City (Lake View, Sturgis)
White Rock
Zana (Lenor)

San Jacinto Co.
Big Creek
Byspot (Teddy)
Camilla
Carolina
Chinquapin (Kelly Store, Poplar, Teddy, Turkey Creek)
Clermont

COLDSPRING
Coonskin
Darby Hill
Davisville
Dayton (Randolphsville)
Dixie (Mercy)
Dolive (Gasca, Raven Hill)
Drury (Mill Creek)
Embryfield (Staley)
Evergreen
Everitt (Magnolia)
Fireman's Hill
Gasca (Dolive)
Geneva
Kelly Store (Chinquapin)
Lake Tejas
Lake Water Wheel
Lincoln
Magnolia *(Everitt)*
Maynard *(Rockyville)*
McGee's
Mercy (Dixie)
Mill Creek (Drury)
Milledge
Mount Hope (Velpo)
Napier
Newport
OAKHURST *(Snowtown)*
Old Waverly
Palmer's
Palmetto
Patricks Ferry
POINTBLANK
Poplar (Chinquapin)
Pumpkin
Quail Creek
Randolphsville (Dayton)
Rankin's
Raven Hill (Dolive)
Rettig (San Jacinto, Walch)
Riverbottom
Rockyville (Maynard)
Rose Hill
San Jacinto (Rettig)
SHEPHERD
Snowtown (Oakhurst)
Spring Hill
Staley *(Embryfield)*
Stephens Creek
Teddy (Byspot)
Teddy (Chinquapin)
Turkey Creek (Chinquapin)
Urbana
Velpo (Mount Hope)
Walch (Rettig)
Waterwood
Waverly
Westcott
Willow Springs
Wonderland Forest

San Patricio Co.
Alguna
Angelita
Aransas Harbor (Aransas Pass)
ARANSAS PASS *(Aransas Harbor)*
Baylor
Cage
Caliche
Chiltipin
Cove (Ingleside-on-the-Bay)

Edroy
Ewelder
GREGORY
Harbor City
Hubert
INGLESIDE *(Loma, McCampbell Switch, Palomas, Peak)*
INGLESIDE-ON-THE-BAY *(Cove, Ingleside Park, Inwood)*
Ingleside Park (Ingleside-on-the-Bay)
Inwood (Ingleside-on-the-Bay)
Kaleta
Lafruta [La Fruita]
LAKE CITY
LAKESIDE
Loma (Ingleside)
MATHIS
McCampbell Switch (Ingleside)
Mesquital (Taft)
Mesquite Acres Island
Midway
Millsville
ODEM
Palomas (Ingleside)
Peak (Ingleside)
Point Loma
PORTLAND
Rachal (Rosita)
Ramirena (Sharpsburg)
Redfish
Rosita (Rachal, White Point)
St. Paul
SAN PATRICIO
Sharpsburg[h] (Ramirena)
SINTON
Sodville
TAFT *(Mesquital)*
Taft Southwest
Vahlsing
Walters
West St. Paul
West Sinton
White Point (Rosita)

San Saba Co.
Algerita [Algereta]
Apex (Cold Creek, Potter's Ranche, Ripley)
Bend *(Eagle, McAnelly's Bend, Schleicher's Bend)*
Bennett (Chappel)
Bethel (Lone Hand, Velma)
Bomar (Spring Creek)
Bowser
Bowser Bend
Chappel *(Bennett)*
Cherokee
China Creek
Cold Creek (Apex)
Eagle (Bend)
Elm Grove
Hall [Valley]
Harkeyville
High Valley
Holland Hill (Maxwelton)
Holt
Keeney's [Ranch] (Tyro)

Knob (Locker)
Locker (Knob, Mount Pleasant)
Lone Hand (Bethel)
Maxwelton (Holland Hill)
McAnelly's Bend (Bend)
McMillan
Mount Pleasant (Locker)
Pecan Grove
Potter's Ranche (Apex)
Red Bluff
Richards (Self)
RICHLAND SPRINGS
Ripley (Apex)
Rock Shoals (Sloan)
Rough Creek
SAN SABA
Schleicher's Bend (Bend)
Self (Richards)
Skeeterville
Sloan (Rock Shoals)
Spring Creek *(Bomar)*
Tyro (Keeney's [Ranch])
Velma (Bethel)
Wallace Creek

Schleicher Co.
Adams
Akers (Rudd)
Bailey Ranch
Elder (Kaffir)
ELDORADO *(Wallick)*
Gwynn
Jackson & Ake Ranch (Rudd)
Kaffir (Elder)
Lamesa (Stone Ranch)
Hulldale
Mayer (Middle Valley)
Middle Valley (Mayer)
Rudd (Akers, Jackson & Ake Ranch)
Ryburn (Thorpe)
Stone Ranch (Lamesa)
Thorpe (Ryburn)
Tierra Alta
Verand (Vermont Ranch)
Vermont Ranch (Verand)
Wallick (Eldorado)

Scurry Co.
Afra (Camp Springs)
Arah (Dannie, Dock, Sears)
Biddle
Bison (Knapp)
Bookout (Dermott)
Bowers (Pyron)
Brand
Britt (Dermott)
Camp Springs *(Afra, Ida, Sand Rock Springs)*
China Grove
Cottonwood Flat
Dannie (Arah)
Dark (Flap Top)
Day (Fluvanna)
Dermott (Bookout, Britt)
Dock (Arah)
Dunn
Ennis
Flap Top (Dark)
Fluvanna (Day, Light)
Foch (Hermleigh)

Franklin Center
Fullerville
Hermleigh (Foch, Wheat)
Hidetown (Synder)
Highland (Maize)
Hud[d]
Ida (Camp Springs)
Inadale
Ira
Kane (Winston)
Knapp (Bison)
Light (Fluvanna)
Link
Lloyd Mountain
Maize (Highland, Rye)
Midway
Plainview
Pyron (Bowers)
Rye (Maize)
Sand Rock Springs (Camp Springs)
Sears (Arah)
Sharon
SNYDER *(Hidetown)*
Union
Wheat (Hermleigh)
Winston (Kane)

Shackelford Co.
Acampo
ALBANY
Battle Creek
Berryhill
Budmatthews
Chimney
Fort Griffin
Hicks (Moran)
Hulltown (Moran)
Ibex
MORAN *(Hicks, Hulltown)*
Newcomb
Pen
Penrose
Rising Sun
Sedwick (Vesta)
Taos
Vesta (Sedwick)

Shelby Co.
Aiken (Aken, Biggs)
Aken (Aiken)
Alexanders Store
Alfred (Wylma)
Antioch
Arcadia (Burtonsville, Toomey)
Ashton['s]
Barnes Store (Silas)
Battle Ridge (Silas)
Bear Bayou (Silas)
Beech[wood]
Bermuda (Sunny Slope)
Biggs (Aiken)
Blair
Bobo (Meldrum)
Brady
Brittain (Dolce)
Brooklyn
Buck Snort (Buena Vista)
Buena Vista (Buck Snort)
Burtonsville (Arcadia)
Campti
Carroll's Store (Thurman)
Cedar Yard

CENTER
Choat (Mount Hermon)
Choice
Clay's Mound
Cleon (Clio)
Clio (Cleon)
Cora (Hurstown)
Courtland
Dacha
Dreka (Gilford, Grover, Payne)
Dolce (Brittain)
Duff
Eagle Mills (Sholar, Spivey)
East Hamilton (Hamilton, Milton)
Fineza (Morgan's Store)
Flat Fork
Folsom
Gagne
Gallagher
Gilford (Dreka)
Goober Hill
Graham's Mills
Grover (Dreka)
Grigsby
Halbert (Hurstown)
Halfway (Prater)
Hamilton['s] (East Hamilton)
Hanson Mill (Sarat)
Haslam
Hawthorne
Hermon (Mount Hermon)
Hilliard's (Straw's)
Hot (Killen)
Huber (Otho, Pleasant Grove)
Hurst (Hurstown)
Hurstown (Cora, Halbert, Hurst, Jakin, Mount Olive, Rather)
HUXLEY (Roosterville)
Isbelle (Short)
Jackson
Jakin (Hurstown)
James
Jericho
JOAQUIN
Jordans Store
Koonce (Mount Hermon)
Killen (Hot)
Lamar
Lato (Pounds Mill)
Lemit (Truit's Store)
Linwood (Meldrum)
McClelland
Meldrum (Bobo, Linwood)
Milton (East Hamilton)
Morgan's Store (Fineza)
Mott Springs
Mount Hermon (Choat, Hermon, Koonce, Word)
Mount Olive (Hurstown)
Myricks [Ferry]
Nashville (Shelbyville)
Neuville
New Harmony
North Jericho
Oak Hill (Rex)
Otho (Huber)
Patroon

Pauls Store
Paxton (Spivey)
Payne (Dreka)
Pleasant Grove (Huber)
Pounds Mill (Lato)
Powell (Short)
Prater (Halfway)
Rainsville
Ralph
Ramsey (Royal)
Rather (Hurstown)
Rex (Oak Hill)
Rite-Care
Roosterville (Huxley)
Royal (Ramsey)
Rue
Sarat (Hanson Mill)
Sardis (Willaluce)
Saxet
Shelbyville (Nashville)
Shelton's Store
Sholar (Eagle Mills, Spivey)
Short (Isbelle, Powell)
Silas (Barnes Store, Battle Ridge, Bear Bayou)
Simpson's
Spivey (Eagle Mills, Sholar)
Spivey (Paxton)
South Jericho
Stack
Stockman (Wallace Mill, Wilson Springs)
Straw's (Hilliard's)
Strong
Sunny Slope (Bermuda)
TENAHA
Tennessee
Thurman (Carroll's Store)
TIMPSON
Todd's [Mill]
Tomday (Willow Grove)
Tomday (Wylma)
Toomey (Arcadia)
Truit's Store (Lemit)
Wallace Mill (Stockman)
Waterman
Webb
Willaluce (Sardis)
Willow Grove (Tomday)
White Cottage
Wilson Springs (Stockman)
Word (Mount Hermon)
Wylma (Alfred, Tomday)

Sherman Co.
Bradley
Coldwater
Cordaro
Edmund (Stratford)
Frisco (Stratford)
Ideal
Lautz
Mallett
Ruby
Satren
Spurlock
Stevens
STRATFORD (Edmund, Frisco)
Tata (Velma)

TEXHOMA
Velma (Tata)

Smith Co.
Aberdeen (Wallisburgh)
Akron
Amigo Station (Lumpkin)
Antioch
Arab
ARP (Jarvis [Switch], Strawberry)
Bascom (Talo)
Bass' [Mill] (Findit)
Bean's Saline (Neches Saline)
Bellwood
Belzora (Florence, Patton's Port)
Berrien (Jamestown)
Blackjack
Bostick
Brooks' Saline (Neches Saline)
Browning
BULLARD
Camp Ford
Canton (Omen)
Carroll (Grady)
Chapel Hill
Cherokee Hill
Cobb
Clopton (Omen)
Copeland
Coplen (Shady)
Crockett's Bluff
Deanville
Debard's
Dogwood City
Douglas
Dowco
Duncan (Lock)
Dutch (Schley)
Eads
Elkton
Elkton
Emerald Bay
Esparanza
Etna
Findit (Bass)
Flint
Flora
Florence (Belzora)
Friendship
Fruit (Pine Springs)
Galena (Snuff City)
Galilee
Garden Valley
Gardner's Saline (Neches Saline)
Gibbs
Glen (Sand Hill)
Goodson
Grady (Carroll)
Greenbrier
Gresham
Gum Spring
Gumwood
Hewsville
Hickory Grove
Hide-A-Way Lake
Highland
Hopewell (Swan)
Indian Creek

Jamestown
Jamestown [Jimtown] (Berrien)
Jarvis [Switch] (Arp)
Joy
Kirk (Red Springs)
Knollwood
Lee Spring
LINDALE (Lindsey, Lyndale)
Lindsey (Lindale)
Lyndale (Lindale)
Lock (Duncan)
Loftin
Lumpkin (Amigo Station)
Magnet
Malcom (Yancy)
Midway
Moss (Red Springs)
Mount Carmel
Mount Sylvan
Mud Creek
Nebo
Neches Saline ([Bean's, Brooks', Gardner's] Saline)
NEW CHAPEL HILL
New Harmony
New Hope
NOONDAY
Ogburn
Old Canton (Omen)
Oldenburg
Omen (Canton, Clopton, Old Canton, Roundhill, Troup)
OVERTON
Owentown
Patton's Port (Belzora)
Pine Springs (Fruit)
Randall
Red Springs (Kirk, Moss, Utica)
Rice
Roundhill (Omen)
Salem
Sand Flat
Sand Hill (Glen)
Schley (Dutch)
Seven Leagues
Shady (Coplen)
Shady Grove
Silver Pines
Sinclair City
Snuff City (Galena)
Spring Branch
Starr's Mill
Starrville
Strawberry (Arp)
Summer Grove
Swan[n] (Hopewell)
Swinneytown
Talo (Bascom)
Teaselville
Thackwell
Thedford
Tilecrete
Troup (Omen)
TROUP [Troupe] (Zavala)
TYLER
Utica (Red Springs)
Wallisburgh (Aberdeen)
Walnut Grove

Warwick
Weakley
WHITEHOUSE
Willingham
WINONA
Wood Springs
Wright City
Yancy (Malcom)
Youngsboro
Zavala (Troup)
Zeno

Somervell Co.
Barnard's Mill (Glen Rose)
Chalk Mountain
Cottonwood
George's Creek
Glass
GLEN ROSE (Barnard's
   Mill)
Hargrove (Hucal)
Hopewell
Hucal (Hargrove)
Johnson[ville] (Nemo)
Lanham Mill
Nemo (Johnson[ville])
Porter (Rainbow)
Rainbow (Porter)
Rock Creek
Ward Branch

Starr Co.
Alto Bonito
Arkansas City
Chapena
Cuevitas
Delmita (Zaragoza)
Dreamland (Santa Cruz)
El Acha (Fronton)
El Arroyo
El Centro
El Sauz
Escobares
Falcon Heights
Falcon Village
Fort Ringgold
Fronton (El Acha)
Garceño
Garcias
Garcias Ranch (Roma)
Garciasville (La Casita-
   Garciasville)
Grulla, (see La Grulla)
Kelsay
La Casita-Garciasville
La Copita (Robberson)
La Gloria
LA GRULLA
La Reforma
Las Escobas
Los Barreras
Los Saenz
Olmos
Rancho Davis (Rio
   Grande City)
Ratcliff
Rincon
Rio Grande City
   [Riogrande] (Rancho
   Davis)
Robberson (La Copita)
ROMA-Los Saenz (Gar-
   cias Ranch)
Rosita

Salineno
San Carlos
San Domingo
San Isidro
San Juanito Ranch
   (Santa Elena)
San Roman (Viboras)
Santa Anna
Santa Catarina
Santa Cruz (Dreamland)
Santa Elena (San Juanito
   Ranch)
Starrco
Sun Oil Camp
Viboras (San Roman
   Ranch)
Villareales
Zaragosa (Delmita)

Stephens Co.
Algoma (Caddo)
Bear Branch Mills (Lewalt)
Bivouac (Bray, Randal's
   Store)
Bray (Bivouac)
BRECKENRIDGE (Pick-
   etville)
Breckwalker
Burkett (Eolian)
Caddo (Algoma)
Carroll
Carter
Cobb (Gentry)
Cotton Plant (Necessity)
Crystal Falls
Duff Prairie (South Prairie)
Edward[s Gin] (Necessity)
Eolian (Burkett, Rock Hill)
Eureka
Fambrough
Finley Point (Ivan)
Fleetwood [Park]
Frankell
Gentry (Cobb)
Gilking
Gudger
Gunsight
Harpersville
Hight
Hilo
Ivan (Finley Point)
Jimkurn
Ketch
La Casa
Leeray (Ray Lee)
Lewalt (Bear Branch Mills)
Maxbury
McGuire
Morg
Moses
Necessity (Cotton Plant,
   Edward[s Gin])
Orland
Parks Camp [Parks]
Pickettville (Breckenridge)
Plateau
Randal's Store (Bivouac)
Ray Lee (Leeray)
Ringling Junction
Rock Hill (Eolian)
Satterfield (Wiles)
Sebrick
South Hanlon

South Prairie (Duff Prairie)
Trigg
Wards
Wayland
Wiles (Satterfield)
Zelma

Sterling Co.
Bliss (County Line)
Broome
Cavan (Lynnell)
County Line (Bliss)
Cummins
Drennan (Preloch)
Earnest (Pearson's
   Ranch)
Eudor (Sterling)
Foster
Gibbs (Montvale)
Iolanthe (Lone Mill,
   Relda)
Lone Mill (Iolanthe)
Lynnell (Cavan)
Montvale (Gibbs, St. Elmo,
   Zareda)
Moon Chapel
Nanhattie
Pearson's Ranch (Ear-
   nest)
Preloch (Drennan, Tom)
Relda (Iolanthe)
Rice Ranch (Sterling)
St. Elmo (Montvale)
Sterling (Eudor, Rice
   Ranch)
STERLING CITY
Tom (Preloch)
Zareda (Montvale)

Stonewall Co.
Alluvia (Peacock)
Antioch (Oriana)
ASPERMONT (Rhom-
   berg, Sunflower Flat)
Brandenburg (Old Glory)
Crotan (Victoria)
Dolman
Dorras (Neff)
Double Mountain (Jack-
   son, Waldrop's Gin)
Flat Top
Gatling
Geneview
Golden Pond
Graydale (Peacock)
Grayflat (Lingo)
Guest
Hooker (Tell)
Jackson (Double Moun-
   tain)
Johnson's Chapel
Lingo (Grayflat)
Mattie
Neff (Dorras)
Neva
New Brandenberg (Old
   Glory)
Old Glory ([New] Branden-
   berg, Brandenburg)
Oriana (Antioch)
Orient
Peacock (Alluvia, Gray-
   dale)
Peek (Uno)

Rath City
Rayner
Rhomberg (Aspermont)
Sandlin
Shinnery Lake
Sunflower Flat (Asper-
   mont)
Swenson
Tell (Hooker, Wilford)
Uno (Peek)
Victoria (Crotan)
Waldrop's Gin (Double
   Mountain)
Wilford (Tell)

Sutton Co.
Camp Allison
Owenville
SONORA

Swisher Co.
Adair
Arby
Auburn
Bagley (Twist)
Beverly (Olga)
Center Plains
Claytonville
Community
Dreka
Eunice
Fanchon (Pearl, Union
   Hall)
HAPPY (Happy Hollow,
   Liner)
Happy Hollow (Happy)
Henry (Tulia)
Jackson (Kress)
Kaffir
KRESS (Jackson,
   Wright)
Lakeview
Liner (Happy)
Madison (Mitchell)
McKenzie
Mitchell (Madison)
Nisbet (Zenith)
Olga (Beverly)
Pearl (Fanchon)
Price (Whitfield)
Taggart
TULIA (Henry)
Twist (Bagley)
Union Hall (Fanchon)
Vigo Park [Vigo] (79088)
Whitfield (Price)
Wright (Kress)
Wynne
Zenith (Nisbet)

Tarrant Co.
ARLINGTON (Hayter)
Arlington Downs
Ashland
Atchison's Point
Athol (Keller)
Avondale
Arwine (Hurst)
AZLE (Fowler's Store,
   O'Bar, Shell Rock)
Bear Creek (McAfee, Rob-
   inson's Mills)
BEDFORD (Bobo's)
BENBROOK (Miranda,

Wilton)
Bethel (Bransford)
Birds
Bird[s]ville
Bisbee
BLUE MOUND
Bobo's (Bedford)
Boss
Bowman's Springs (Webb)
Brambleton (Dodson, Lantier)
Bransford['s Store]
(Bethel, Pleasant Run,
Red Rock)
Briar
Britton
Brooklyn Heights (Rushing)
Burr (Jellico)
Candon (Tarrant)
Calef
Carswell Base
Center Point
Clear Fork (Eureka)
COLLEYVILLE
CROWLEY
Dalworth
DALWORTHINGTON
GARDENS
Dido (Gilmore)
Dido (Saginaw)
Dodson (Brambleton)
Double Springs (Keller)
Dove (Lonesome Dove)
Dunnville (Grapevine)
Eagle Mountain
East Fort Worth
(Manchester Mills)
Eden (Enon)
Ederville (Seltser)
EDGECLIFF
Edna (Enon)
Ed Pit
Edgecliff
Enon (Eden, Edna, Jenkins' Store)
Estelle
Estill's Station
EULESS
Eureka (Clear Fork)
EVERMAN (Oak Grove)
Ferguson
FOREST HILL
FORT WORTH
Fossil (Wataga)
Fowler's Store (Azle)
Gertie (Moro, Mountain
Creek)
Gilmore (Dido)
Glade
GRAND PRAIRIE
GRAPEVINE [Grape Vine
Prairie], (Dunnville)
Haines
HALTOM CITY
Handley
Hart Spur
HASLET
Hawkinsville
Hayter (Arlington)
Hicks
Hodge [Junction]
HURST (Arwine, Ormel)

Hurst (Randol)
Indian Creek
Jamestown
Jellico (Burr)
Jenkins' Store
Johnsons Station
KELLER (Athol, Double
Springs)
KENNEDALE
Kirkwood
Kyley (Saginaw)
LAKESIDE
Lakeview
LAKE WORTH
Lantier (Brambleton)
Linberg
Lonesome Dove (Dove)
Lytle
Manchester Mills (East
Fort Worth)
MANSFIELD
Mara
Mary's Creek
Marine (North Fort Worth)
May
McAfee (Bear Creek)
Minter[s] (Muriel)
Miranda (Benbrook)
Moro (Gertie, Mountain
Creek)
Mountain Creek (Gertie,
Moro)
Muriel (Minter)
Niles City
North Forth Worth
(Marine)
NORTH RICHLAND HILLS
Norton's Grove
Oak Grove
Oak Grove (Everman)
Oak Knoll
Oaks
O'Bar (Azle)
Old Union
Orme
Ormel (Hurst)
Ossey
PANTEGO
Peden (Roy)
PELICAN BAY
Plascido
Pleasant Run (Bransford)
Plover
Polytechnic
Pontiac (Saginaw)
Primrose
Randol['s Mill] (Hurst)
Red Rock (Bransford)
Rendon
Retta
RICHLAND HILLS
RIVER OAKS
Robinson's Mills (Bear
Creek)
Roy (Peden)
Rushing (Brooklyn
Heights, Stove Foundry)
SAGINAW (Dido, Kyley,
Pontiac)
SANSOM PARK
Seltser (Ederville)
Seminary Hill
Shell Rock (Azle)

Smithfield
SOUTHLAKE
Stove Foundry (Rushing)
Sublett
Sylvania
Tadlock
Tannahill
Tarrant (Candon)
Tate Springs
Wataga (Fossil)
WATAUGA
Watsonville
Webb (Bowman's
Springs)
WESTLAKE
Westland
WESTOVER HILLS
WESTWORTH VILLAGE
Wheatland
WHITE SETTLEMENT
Wilton (Benbrook)
Winscott

Taylor Co.
ABILENE (Elm Creek)
Audra (Bradshaw)
Bagdad
Bald Eagle (Ovalo)
Blair
Borders [Chapel, Hill]
(Caps)
Bowman
Bradshaw (Audra, Funston, Lent)
Brewer's Station
BUFFALO GAP
Camp Barkley
Caps (Borders [Chapel,
Hill])
Caps Sides (View)
Coats
Corners (Hamby)
Delphi (Nubia)
Dubwright
Dyess Air Force Base
Elm Creek (Abilene)
Elmdale
Fairview (Iberis)
Funston (Bradshaw)
Guion (Lemons Gap)
Hamby (Corners)
Happy Valley
Hash Knife (Simpson's
Ranch)
Hattie (Inkum)
Hines (Tye)
Hunter's Store
Iberis (Fairview, Kincaid,
Ola)
IMPACT
Inkum (Hattie)
Kincaid (Iberis)
Lanius
LAWN (Ned, Oak Lawn)
Lemons Gap (Guion)
Lent (Bradshaw)
Lytle (Onward)
Lytle Cove (Potosi)
MERKEL (Windmill
Town)
Moro [Mount Moro] (Oil
Spring)
Ned (Lawn)

North Park
Nubia (Delphi)
Oak Lawn (Lawn)
Oil Spring (Moro)
Ola (Iberis)
Onward (Lytle)
Ovalo (Bald Eagle)
Piel
Pollard (Potosi)
Potosi (Lytle Cove, Pollard)
Rogers
Sambo (Vance)
Shep
Simpson's Ranch (Hash
Knife)
Stanley
Tebo (Tye)
The Flat (Tuscola)
TRENT
TUSCOLA (The Flat)
TYE (Hines, Tebo)
Vance (Sambo)
View [City] (Caps Sides)
Windmill Town (Merkel)
Wylie

Terrell Co.
Chandler (Stover)
Chevo (Stover)
Drum (Mayers Spring)
Dryden (Thurst[on])
Emerson
Fedora
Free (Tarver)
Gas Plant
Gavilan
Independence
Lozier, ars
Malvado
Mayers Spring (Drum)
Mofeta
Oak Grove (Stover)
Sanderson (Strawbridge)
Shaw
Strawbridge (Sanderson)
Stover (Chandler, Chevo,
Oak Grove)
Thurst[on] (Dryden)
Traver (Free)
Watkins

Terry Co.
BROWNFIELD
Copeland's Store
(Meadow)
Earl
Foster
Gomez
Harris
Johnson
Lahey
Mason's Ranch (Siam)
MEADOW (Copeland's
Store, Primrose)
Needmore
Primrose (Meadow)
Schooler's Store (Siam)
Siam (Mason's Ranch,
Schooler's Store)
Tokio
Union
WELLMAN

Throckmorton Co.
Camp Cooper
Elbert
Lusk
Masters
Spring Creek
THROCKMORTON
WOODSON

Titus Co.
Adora (Farmers Academy)
Argo (*Early Grove*)
Asander (*Lone Star*)
Barrett (Winfield)
Bethesda (Centenary)
Black (*Cora, Hewitt, Home*)
Blalock (Maple Spring)
Blodgett
Bly (*Cox*)
Bridges Chapel (*Stonewall*)
Buchanan (*Snow Hill*)
Carr (Winfield)
Centenary (Bethesda, Hutchingsville)
Center Grove
Clay Hill (*Cookville*)
Cookville (*Clay Hill*)
Coopers Chapel
Cora (Black)
Cottage Hill (*Tuscaloosa*)
Cox (Bly)
Crawford (*Gilpin*)
Crescent
Culberson
Dorsey
Early Grove (Argo)
Eickhoff
Eunice (Gilpin)
Farmers Academy *(Adora)*
Gilpin (*Crawford, Eunice, Oak Grove*)
Gladewater
Goolesboro (Talco)
Gouldsborough (Talco)
Green Hill
Hanks (*Titus*)
Hastings (Maple Spring)
Hewitt (Black)
Home (Black)
Hutchingsville (Centenary)
Lone Star (Asander)
Maple Spring *[Maple]* (Blalock, Hastings)
Maple Springs (Wilkinson)
Midway
MILLER'S COVE
Monticello
MOUNT PLEASANT
Nodena
Oak Grove (Gilpin)
Presley
Ripley
Roeder
Running Spring
Snow Hill (Buchanan)
Stonewall (Bridges Chapel)
Sugar Hill (Wilkinson)
TALCO (*Goolesboro, Gouldsborough*)
Titus (Hanks)

Tuscaloosa (*Cottage Hill*)
Union Bridge
Welsh
White Oak
Wilkinson (*Maple Springs, Sugar Hill*)
WINFIELD (*Carr, Barrett*)

Tom Green Co.
Argenta (*Yandell*)
Ben Ficklen
Bohemia
Broncho
Byrne
Carlsbad (*Hughes*)
Christoval (*Delong, South Concho*)
Clarksville
Concho (San Angelo)
Delong (Christoval)
Edge Hill (Manestee)
Fisherville (Mereta)
Fort Concho
Goodfellow Air Force Base
Grape Creek
Harriet[t]
Hughes (Carlsbad)
Kiesling
Klattenhoff
Knickerbocker
Lake Gardens
Lipan (Mereta)
Lipan (Wall)
MacGrath (Tankersly)
Manestee (Edge Hill, Watters)
Mayes' Store (Water Valley)
Mayesville (Water Valley)
Mereta (Fisherville, Lipan)
Midway
Mogul
Mullin (Veribest)
Orient
Pecan Creek
Pulliam
Rethaville (Water Valley)
SAN ANGELO [San Angela] (Concho)
Sanatorium
South Concho (Christoval)
Stella (Yandell)
Tankersley (MacGrath)
Vancourt
Veribest (Mullin)
Wall (Lipan)
Water Valley (Mayes' Store, Mayesville, Rethaville)
Watters (Manestee)
Wooland
Yandell (Argenta, Stella)

Travis Co.
Abercrombie
Algeria (Evelyn)
Anderson Mill [Anderson's Mills]
Apache Shores
AUSTIN (Waterloo)
BEE CAVE[s]
Bitting (Littig)

Bluff Springs
BRIARCLIFF
Buaas (Hamilton Pool)
Buffalo Gap
Butter Krust
Cameron Flatt (Flatt)
Carl (*Minerva, Pleasant Valley, Willow Spring*)
Carlson
Case's [Mills] (Rogers Hill)
Cedar Valley
Cele (*Richland*)
Centerville
Charles
Circleville
Clover
Colberg
Colton
Comanche
Comanche Pass
Cottonwood (Kimbro)
Coxville
CREEDMOOR (*Willow [Prairie, Springs]*)
Cross Creek (Nameless)
Currie (Tate)
Daffan (*Hill, Muckymuck, Swinson*)
Decker
Del Valle
Delwau
Dessau
Dodd City (Volente)
Doxey
Driskill (Elroy)
Dunlap (*Huntersville*)
Dunlay (Hornsby Bend)
Dutch Waterhole (Elroy)
Duval
Eanes
Eck (Teck)
Elroy (*Driskill, Dutch Waterhole, Hume*)
Ernest (Hamilton Pool)
Evelyn (*Algeria, Storey's Store*)
Fair Hill
Fairview (Nameless)
Fiskville
Flatt (Cameron Flatt)
Flintrock [Hill]
Ford Oaks
Fort Colorado (John)
Fort Prairie (John)
Four Points (Hickmuntown)
Fromme
Garfield (*Haynie's Chapel, Oswego, Wallace*)
Gilesburg
Gilleland Creek
Grassdale (Manor)
Gregg (Manor)
Hamburg
Hamilton Pool (Buaas, Ernest)
Haynie Flat
Haynie's Chapel (Garfield)
Hickmuntown (Four Points)
Hickory Grove
Hill (Daffan)
Hogeye
Hornsby Bend

[Hornsby's] (Dunlay)
Hudson Bend
Hume (Elroy)
Huntersville (Dunlap)
Imperial Valley
Jehoy (Jonestown)
John [Grove's Store] (Fort [Colorado, Prairie])
Johnstown
Jonestown (Jehoy)
JONESTOWN
Kimbro (Cottonwood)
Kincheonville
Knight's Ranch (New Sweden)
LAGO VISTA
LAKEWAY
Lakewood
Littig (Bitting)
Live Oak Springs (Oak Hill)
Lost Creek
Lund (Pleasant Hill)
Maha
Manchaca (*Manchac [House]*)
Manchac [House] (Manchaca)
Manda (Willow)
MANOR (*Grassdale, Gregg, Wheeler's Store*)
Marshall Ford [Dam]
Maxey (Mud)
McNeil
Merrilltown
Milby
Minerva (Carl)
Montopolis
Moore's Crossing
Mountain View
Mount Juliet (Red Store)
Mouth of Pedernales
Muckymuck (Daffan)
Mud (Maxey)
MUSTANG RIDGE
Nameless (*Cross Creek, Fairview*)
New Sweden [New Sweeden] (Knight's Ranch)
Oak Hill (*Live Oak Springs, Oatmanville, Shiloh*)
Oak Park
Oatmanville (Oak Hill)
Ogarita
Old Ferry
Onion Creek
Oswego (Garfield)
Parson's Seminary
Penfield
Perdenales [Pedernales]
Pershing
PFLUGERVILLE
Pilot Knob
Pleasant Hill
Pleasant Hill (Lund)
Pleasant Valley (Carl)
Point Venture
Red Store (Mount Juliet)
Richland (Cele)
Rogers Hill (Case's [Mills])

ROLLINGWOOD
Round Mountain
Saint Elmo (Tumey's
Store)
SAN LEANNA
Scenic Brook
Shiloh (Oak Hill)
Skellyville
Smithwick's (Webberville)
Smoot
Sneed
Spicewood Springs
Spring Valley
Sprinkle
Storey's Store (Evelyn)
Summerville (Watters)
SUNSET VALLEY
Swinson (Daffan)
Tanglewood Forest
Tate (Currie)
Teck (Eck)
Three Points
Travis Peak
Tumey's Store (Saint
Elmo)
Turnersville
Vinson
VILLAGE OF THE HILLS
Volente (Dodd City)
Wallace (Garfield)
Walnut Station
Waterloo (Austin)
Waters Park
Watters (Summerville)
Watters Park
Webber's Prairie (Webber-
ville)
Webberville (Smithwick's,
Webber's Prairie)
Wells Branch
WEST LAKE HILLS
West Oaks
Wheeler's Store (Manor)
Willow (Manda)
Willow Prairie (Creed-
moor)
Willow Spring (Carl)
Willow Springs (Creed-
moor)
Windemere

Trinity Co.
Alabama (Helmic)
Alabama (Nathan)
Alabama Creek
Apple Springs (May Apple
Springs)
Apple Springs (Helmic)
Barnes Switch
Baucis (Pagoda)
Beasley's Store (Nogalus
Prairie)
Bissell (Glendale)
Bold Springs (Vaughan's
Mill)
Buck (Iris)
Carlisle
Center Point
Centerville
Centerville (Helmic)
Centralia
Chapman (Chita)
China Grove (Nogalus

Prairie)
Chita (Chapman)
Colita
Crecy (Deaton)
Crete (East Prairie, Wire)
Deaton (Crecy)
Dunbar (Nigton)
East Prairie (Crete)
Escom Hill (Wheeler's Hill)
Flat Prairie
Friday
Fritzvann
Flat Prairie
Friday
Friendship
Glendale (Bissell)
GROVETON
Helmic (Alabama, Apple
Springs, Centerville)
Iris (Buck)
Jason (Woodlake)
Josserand [Josservand]
Kay
Kayser's Prairie (Trinity)
Lacy
Lake
Luce
Massie (Nigton)
May Apple Springs (Apple
Springs)
McGinty
Nathan (Alabama)
Nigton (Dunbar, Massie)
Nogalus Prairie [Nogallis
Prairie, Nogalus] (Beas-
ley's Store, China Grove)
North Cedar
Pagoda (Baucis)
Pegoda
Pennington (Tyler's Prairie)
Piney Point
Red Branch
Saron
Saunders (Sumpter)
Sebastopol
Sequoyah
South Groveton
Sulphur Springs
Sumpter (Saunders)
Sylvester
Trevat [Trevathan]
TRINITY (Kayser's Prairie)
Tyler's Prairie (Pennington)
Vair
Vaughan's Mill (Bold
Springs)
Westville
Wheeler's Hill (Esom Hill)
Willard (Woodlake)
Wire (Crete)
Woodlake (Jason, Willard)

Tyler Co.
Acol
Aleck
Allisonville
Alsobrooks (Leah)
Barclay's
Beech Creek
Belt's (Boon's Ferry)
Bendy's Landing (Smith's
Ferry)
Bethany (Billum's Creek)
Billum's Creek (Bethany)

Boons Ferry (Belt's)
Carroll Switch (Doucette)
Cherokee (Dies)
CHESTER
Cima
COLMESNEIL (Ogden)
Dam B - Dogwood Station
Dies (Cherokee, Laird)
Dock
Dogwood
Doucette (Carroll Switch)
Emille[e] (Ratcliff's, Wolf
Creek)
Fleming Station (Hampton)
Fort Lindsey (Sadell)
Fort Teran
Fred (Josie)
Grimes [Bluff]
Hampton (Fleming Station)
Haralson Lakes
Hicksbaugh (Hicksville)
Hicksville (Hicksbaugh)
Hillister (Hollister)
Hollister (Hillister)
Hollomon (Vida)
Hooker's
Hyatt
Josie (Fred)
Laird (Dies)
Leah (Alsobrooks, Spring
Creek [Mills], Vera)
Milton
Mitchell Hill
Mobile
Mount Hope
Natches (Town Bluff)
Ogden (Colmesneil)
Oldham
Pamplin's Creek
Peach Tree Village (Plum
Tree Village)
Pedigo
Pineville
Pinyville
Plum Tree Village (Peach
Tree Village)
Ratcliff's (Emille)
River Acres
Rockingham (Rockland)
Rockland (Rockingham)
Sadell (Fort Lindsey)
Seneca (Vida)
Smith[s] Ferry (Bendy's
Landing)
Spring Creek [Mills] (Leah)
Spurger[ville]
Steeles Grove
Summit
Town Bluff (Natches)
Vida (Hollomon, Seneca)
Vera (Leah)
Warren
Wilson's
Wolf Creek (Emille)
WOODVILLE

Upshur Co.
Ashland
Bethlehem [Old Bethlehem]
Bettie
BIG SANDY
Boxwood
Brumley

Calloway
Cedar Springs
Center Point
Coffeeville
Concord
Cox
Delrose
Diana [New, Old Diana]
EAST MOUNTAIN
Elam Springs
Enoch
Enon
Ewell
Fazenda
Friendship
GILMER
GLADEWATER
Glenwood
Graceton
Grice
Indian Rock
James
Kelsey
LaFayette
Latch
Lone Mountain
Midway
Mings Chapel
Neals
New Diana (Diana)
New Mountain
Old Diana (Diana)
ORE CITY
Pattonfield
Piedmont
Pleasant Grove
Pritchett
Red Rock
Rhonesboro
Rosewood
Sand Hill
Seven Pines
Shady Grove
Simpsonville
Smith
Snow Hill
Soules Chapel
Stamps
Thomas
Toddville
UNION GROVE
Valley View
Wallace Chapel
WARREN CITY
West Mountain
Wilkins

Upton Co.
Crossett
McCAMEY
Midkiff
RANKIN
Upland

Uvalde Co.
Aldine
Blewett (Carbonville)
Boonesboro[ugh]
Bowles
Carbonville (Blewett)
Chatfield (Knippa)
Cline (Turkey Creek, Wal-
lace)
Concan

Keeran)
Thrasher
VICTORIA *(Cypress Grove, Guadalupe Victoria)*
Wood Hi
Woodport

Walker Co.
Ague *(Falba)*
Arlo *(Kenneth)*
Angle *(Phelps)*
Arizona
Auburn
Barado *(Kelley's)*
Bath *(Booth, Holloways Store, Possum Walk, Union Hill)*
Boone
Booth *(Bath)*
Boswell
Carmel *(Waverly)*
Carolina *(Home)*
Cecil *(Farris Store, Felton, Yam)*
Cincinnati *(New Cincinnati)*
Country Campus
Crabbs Prairie
Danville
Dido
Dodge *[Station]*
Ebenezer *(Loma)*
Ebenezer *(Randalia)*
Elmina *(Oliphint, Walker)*
Eunice *(Falba)*
Falba *(Ague, Eunice)*
Falls
Farris Store *(Cecil)*
Felton *(Cecil)*
Flox *(Macedonia, Mustang Prairie)*
Four Notch
Galilee
Gladstone *(Hopkins Store)*
Goshen *(Hutcheson)*
Hawthorne *(Wilbourn)*
Hegar
Hines *(Yero)*
Holloways Store *(Bath)*
Home *(Carolina)*
Hopkins Store *(Gladstone)*
HUNTSVILLE
Hutcheson *(Goshen)*
Jordan *(Sion)*
Kelley's *(Barado)*
Kelow *(Sion)*
Kenneth *(Arlo)*
Kittrell*['s Cut-Off]*
Largacinta
Loma *(Ebenezer)*
Macedonia *(Flox)*
McAdams *[Store]*
McKenzie
Mossy Grove
Mustang Prairie *(Flox)*
New Cincinnati *(Cincinnati)*
Newport
NEW WAVERLY
Old Carolina
Old Waverly *(Waverly)*
Oliphint *(Elmina)*
Patella
Phelps

Phelps *(Angle)*
Pine Hill
Pine Prairie
Pinedale
Pine Valley
Possum Walk *(Bath)*
Randalia *(Ebenezer)*
RIVERSIDE
San Jacinto
Shepherds Valley
Sion *(Jordan, Kelow)*
Sky Lakes
Snowball
Star
Townley
Tuscaloosa *(Wyser's Bluff)*
Union Hill *(Bath)*
Walker *(Elmina)*
Waverly *(Carmel, Old Waverly)*
Werners Bluff
Wesley Grove
Wilbourn *(Hawthorne)*
Wyser[']s Bluff *(Tuscaloosa)*
Yam *(Cecil)*
Yero *(Hines)*

Waller Co.
Arnold's
Bell Bottom
Bracy Island
Bracy's Ferry
Bradville *(Joseph)*
BROOKSHIRE *(Kellner)*
Bush's Store *(Fenella)*
Cardiff
Cedar Creek
Clemons
Cody *(Fetzer)*
Enos
Fenella *(Bush's Store)*
Fetzer *(Cody)*
Fields Store
Gladish
Harmon
Harvester *(Spring Creek, Unit)*
Hegar*['s Store]*
HEMPSTEAD
Holik
Howth *[Station]*
Iron Creek *(Jewell, Phosopolis, Waller's Store)*
Jewell *(Iron Creek)*
Johnsue
Joseph *(Bradville)*
KATY
Kellner *(Brookshire)*
Leslie *(Pittsville Switch)*
Liendo *(Monaville)*
Macedonia
Mill Creek
Monaville *(Liendo)*
Patterson*['s Station])* *(Pattison)*
PATTISON *(Patterson['s Station])*
Perryman's
Phosopolis *(Iron Creek)*
Pine Grove
PINE ISLAND

Pittsville Switch *(Leslie)*
PRAIRIE VIEW
Rock Island
Rogersville
Rolling Hills
Second Corinth
Spring Creek *(Harvester)*
Sunnyside
WALLER
Waller's Store *(Iron Creek)*
Whitfield's
Unit *(Harvester)*

Ward Co.
Allentown *(Royalty)*
Aroya *(Wickett)*
BARSTOW
GRANDFALLS *(Great Falls)*
Great Falls *(Grandfalls)*
Gulf Camp
Manoah
MONAHANS *[Monahan[s Well] (Trueheart)*
Ozarking
PYOTE
Quito
Royalty *(Allentown)*
Sand Hills
THORNTONVILLE
Trueheart *(Monahans)*
WICKETT *(Aroya)*

Washington Co.
Alcorn *(Klump)*
Allcorn's
Armstrong *(Odell)*
Berlin *(Pesch)*
BRENHAM
Brown College
BURTON
Buster's *(Mount Vernon)*
Carter's Prairie *(Flatprairie)*
Cedar Creek *(Chappell Hill)*
Cedar Spring *(Whitesides)*
Chappell Hill *[Chapel Hill] (Cedar Creek)*
Coles' *[Settlement]* *(Independence)*
Day
Earlywine
Felder
Flatprairie *(Carter's Prairie)*
Frieden
Gay Hill
Gnarled Oaks
Graball
Gray Hill
Greenvine *(Vine Green)*
Independence *(Coles')*
Jacksonville
Jerrys Quarters
Kiel *(Rehburg)*
Klump *(Alcorn)*
Krug's Store *(Pleasant Hill)*
La Bahia *(Matejowsky)*
La Bahia *(Washington)*
Landes
Latium
Longpoint *[Long Point]*

Lott *(McCraven)*
Matejowsky *(La Bahia)*
McCraven *(Lott, Whiting's Farm)*
Mill Creek
Montville
Mount Vernon *(Buster's)*
Muellersville
Mustang
Oak Grove
Odell *(Armstrong)*
Old Gay Hill
Pesch *(Berlin)*
Phillipsburg*[h]* *(Phillips Station)*
Phillips Station *(Phillipsburg)*
Pleasant Hill *(Krug's Store)*
Prairie Hill
Quarry
Rehburg *(Kiel)*
Rock Island
Samuel
Sandy Hill
Sauney Stand
Stone *(Watson)*
Tigertown
Trouble *(Winedale)*
Truebsal *(Winedale)*
Turkey Creek
Union *[Hill]*
Vine Green *(Greenvine)*
Vine Grove
Walnut Grove
Warren
Washington*[-on-the-Brazos] (La Bahia)*
Watson *(Stone)*
Wesley
Whitesides *(Cedar Spring)*
Whiting's Farm *(McCraven)*
Whitman*[s]*
Wiedeville
Winedale *(Trouble, Truebsal)*
William Penn
Wren
Zion*[sville]*

Webb Co.
Aguilares
Benavides Hill
Bermuda *(Nye)*
Bruni*[ville]*
Bullseye
Cactus
Callaghan
Callahan *(Shea)*
Cannel *(Darwin)*
Carbon *(Gilliam)*
Century City
Cone
Corvey
Darwin *(Cannel)*
Del Mar Hills
Dellwood
Dodd
Dolores *(San Jose)*
EL CENIZO
Farias
Feliz *(Joyce)*
Fort McIntosh

Paso Real
Porfirio
Port Mansfield (Redfish Bay)
RAYMONDVILLE
Redfish Bay (Port Mansfield)
SAN PERLITA
Santa Margarita
Santa Monica
Sebastian
Willamar
Yturria

Williamson Co.

Allison (Conel)
Anderson Mill
Andersonville (Round Rock)
Andice (Stapp)
Bagdad
BARTLETT
Beaukiss
Behrnville
Berry's Creek (Jackson's Gin)
Beyersville
Block House
Blue Hill (Rices Crossing)
Boone
Brizendine Mills (Gabriel Mills)
Brooksville (Florence)
Bruegerhoff (Cedar Park)
Burkland
Burleson's Springs (Hopewell)
Brushy
Brushy Creek (Round Rock)
Brushy Creek
Buttercup (Dodd's Store)
CEDAR PARK (Bruegerhoff, Running Brushy)
Center Star (Gower)
Chapman City
Circleville
Concordia (Walburg)
Conel (Allison)
Corn Hill
Coupland
Cross Roads (Gravis)
Cross Roads (Lawrence Chapel)
Dodd's Store (Buttercup)
Draco (Rock House)
Elm Grove (Laneport)
Eureka Mills (Jonah)
Evans
Everett (Thorndale)
Excelsior Mill (Weir)
Feld
FLORENCE (Brooksville)
Frame Switch
Friendship
Gabriel Mills (Brizendine Mills, Mather Mills)
Gabriel River
Gano (Wilder's Gin, Willton)
GEORGETOWN
Gower (Center Star, Morgan)

GRANGER
Gravis (Cross Roads, Wyattsville)
Grover
Grove Ranch (Laneport)
Hare (Prairie Lea)
Hochkirk (Noack)
Hopewell (Burleson's Springs)
Hoxie
Huff
HUTTO
Jackson's Gin (Berry's Creek)
Jarrell
Jollyville
Jonah (Eureka Mills, Parks, Water Valley)
Keliehor
Kellerville
Kerr
Laneport (Elm Grove, Grove Ranch)
Lawrence Chapel (Cross Roads)
LEANDER
Leubner
LIBERTY HILL
Mather Mills (Gabriel Mills)
Monodale
Montadale
Morgan (Gower)
Mozo
Naizerville (Neusser)
Neusser (Naizerville)
New Bern
New Corn Hill
Noack (Hochkirk)
Norman
Old Round Rock (Round Rock)
Parks (Jonah)
Peyton
Pond Spring[s] (Rutledge)
Ponton (Tucumcari)
Post Oak Island
Prairie Lea (Hare)
Rattan
Rices Crossing (Blue Hill, Tompkins Store)
Rock House (Draco)
ROUND ROCK (Andersonville, Brushy Creek, Old Round Rock)
Running Brushy (Cedar Park)
Rutledge (Pond Spring)
Sandoval (Streichville, Turkey Creek)
San Gabriel
Saul's Mills
Schwertner
Serenada
Shiloh
Siloam
Small
Somerset (Waterloo)
South Gabriel
Stapp (Andice)
Stiles Ranch (Thrall)
Streichville (Sandoval)
Structure

Sweet Farms
TAYLOR[sville]
Theon
THORNDALE (Everett)
THRALL (Stiles Ranch)
Tidwell
Tompkins Store (Rice's Crossing)
Tonkawa Springs
Towns' Mill (Weir)
Townsville (Weir)
Tucumcari (Ponton)
Turkey Creek (Sandoval)
Type
Valley View
Walburg (Concordia)
Walkerton
Walsh
Waterloo (Somerset)
Water Valley (Jonah)
WEIR (Excelsior Mill, Towns' Mill, Townsville)
White Stone
Whitetail
Wilder's Gin (Gano)
Wild Plum Valley
Willton (Gano)
Wilson Springs
Wyattsville (Gravis)

Wilson Co.

Albuquerque
Alum
Calaveras
Canada Verde
Carpenter
Denhawken
DeWees
Fairview
FLORESVILLE
Graytown
Kicaster
Kosciusko
Labatt
LA VERNIA
Lodi
Loire
NIXON
Nocke[r]nut
Old Sutherland
Pandora
POTH
Saspamco
STOCKDALE
Sunnyside
Sutherland Springs
Three Oaks
Tower Lake
Union

Winkler Co.

Chesterfield (Theodore)
Cheyenne
Duval
Hayflat
Joiel
KERMIT
Theodore (Chesterfield)
Tulsa (Winkler City)
Magwalt
Norman
Pog
Vesrue
WINK

Winkler City (Tulsa)

Wise Co.

Allison
ALVORD (Nina)
Anneville
Audubon
AURORA
Bald Knob
Balsora (Wild Horse Prairie)
Bishop's Hill (Decatur)
Blewett
Boonsville
BOYD (Parkhurst)
Boyd's Mill
Briar
BRIDGEPORT
Brumlow
Cactus Hill
Catlett's Creek
CHICO
Cottondale
Cowen
Crafton
Cuba
Dan
DECATUR (Bishop's Hill, Howell's Store, Taylorsville)
Dovie
Draco (Tyler Springs)
Eldorado (Paradise)
FAIRVIEW
Foster (Owl)
Garvin (West Eden)
Gentry (Muse)
Gertrude
Greenwood
Gum (Scruggs)
Hanna (Liberty Point, Maud)
Herman
Hickory Plains (Slidell)
Hippie Ridge
Howell's Store (Decatur)
Huff Valley (Newark)
Jeffries (Prairie Point)
Jimned
Keeter (Kuter)
Kingsville (Pickett)
Kuter (Keeter)
Lake
LAKE BRIDGEPORT
Liberty Point (Hanna)
Maud (Hanna)
Mina
Modeville
Muse (Gentry)
NEWARK (Huff Valley, Odessa, Ragtown, Sueville)
Nickleville
Nina (Alvord)
Odessa (Newark)
Opal
Owl (Foster)
PARADISE [Prairie] (Eldorado)
Parkhurst (Boyd)
Park Springs (Prindle)
Paschall
Pecan Acres

Pella
Perch Hill
Pickett (Kingsville)
Plainview (Slidell)
Prairie Point (Jeffries)
Prairie Point (Rhome)
Prindle (Park Springs)
Ragtown (Newark)
Rex
RHOME *(Prairie Point)*
Rickels
RUNAWAY BAY
Scruggs *(Gum)*
Slidell *(Hickory Plains, Plainview)*
Sueville (Newark)
Sunset
Sycamore
Taylorsville (Decatur)
Triplett
Tyler Springs (Draco)
West Eden (Garvin)
West Fork
White City
Wild Horse Prairie (Balsora)
Willow Point

Wood Co.
ALBA *(Simpkins Prairie)*
Andrews (Oak Grove)
Angler
Ben
Big Dollar
Bruton (Tippett's Crossing)
Burlton (Redland)
Calloway's Gin *(Smilax)*
Cartwright
Chalybeate
Chapman (Hoyt)
Chilton
Coke
Concord (Smilax)
Crow *(Graham)*
Crystal Springs
Debbie
Drusilla (Philadelphia)
Dupree (Hainesville)
Eagle *(Mooresville)*
East Point
Elberta (Peach)
Evana *(Scroggins)*
Falcon (Merrimac)
Forest Hill
Fouke
Golden
Graham (Crow)
Hainesville *(Dupree)*
HAWKINS *[Store]*
Hoard
Holly Spring[s] (Little Hope)

Hoyt (Chapman)
Hurley
Jarvis
Jim Hogg (Merrimac)
Kirkwood (Ogburn)
Lake Fork
Lake Fork
Little Hope (*Holly Spring, Phillips Store, Speer*)
Lottie (Mapes)
Low (Mikado)
Mapes (Lottie)
Merrimac *(Falcon, Jim Hogg)*
Mikado (Low)
Milo (Stout)
MINEOLA *(Sodom)*
Mooresville (Eagle)
Mutt and Jeff
Musgrove
New Hope
Oak Grove *(Andrews)*
Ogburn *(Kirkwood)*
Parryville (Perryville)
Peach (Elberta)
Peron
Perryville (*Parryville*)
Philadelphia (Drusilla)
Phillips Store (Little Hope)
Pine Mills *(Reedsville)*
Pineview
Pleasant Grove
Prospect Hill (Webster)
QUITMAN
Redland (Burlton)
Reedsville (Pine Mills)
Richards Store (Stout)
Richardsville
Rock Hill
Sand Spring[s]
Scroggins (Evana)
Sharon
Simpkins Prairie (Alba)
Smilax *(Calloway's Gin, Concord)*
Sodom (Mineola)
Speer (Little Hope)
Stagner
Stormville
Stout *(Milo, Richards Store)*
Tippett's Crossing (Bruton)
Webster (Prospect Hill)
Weimer
West Mineola
WINNSBORO*[ugh]*
YANTIS *[Mill]*

Yoakum Co.
Aldie (Ivanhoe)

Allred
Bennett
Bronco
DENVER CITY *(Wasson)*
Glenpark
Ivanhoe (Aldie)
PLAINS
Pleasant Hill
Sligo
Wasson (Denver City)

Young Co.
Arkansas (South Bend)
Belknap (Fort Belknap)
Bitter Creek
Brazos Agency
Brush (Farmer)
Bullock
Bunger *(Caseyville, Lin)*
Carbondale
Caseyville (Bunger)
Cottonwood Springs
Crossland (Crozier)
Crozier (Crossland)
Dearmore
Donnell's Mill (Eliasville)
Drummond
Eliasville *(Donnell's Mill)*
Farmer (Brush)
Fish Creek (Morgan)
Fort Belknap (Belknap)
Fort Murray (Murray)
GRAHAM
Grimshaw (Oil City)
Herron City
Highland (Proffitt)
Indian Mound (Plaxco)
Jean *(Rogatton, Salt Creek)*
Lacy
Lin (Bunger)
Lisle
Loving
Manle (Markley)
Markley *(Manle, Plum Grove, Thurman)*
McMannis' Store (South Bend)
Morgan (Fish Creek)
Murray *(Fort Murray, Prairie View)*
NEWCASTLE *(Van Camp)*
Oil City (Grimshaw)
OLNEY
Orth
Padgett
Plaxco *(Indian Mound, Rocky Mound)*
Plum Grove (Markley)
Prairie View (Murray)

Proffitt*['s Valley] (Highland)*
Rocky Mound (Plaxco)
Rogatton (Jean)
Salt Creek (Jean)
Sewell
South Bend *(Arkansas, McMannis' Store)*
Swain
Tonk (Valley Grove)
Thurman (Markley)
True
Valley Grove (Tonk)
Van Camp (Newcastle)

Zapata Co.
Bellville (Zapata)
Bustamante *(Comitas)*
Carrizo (Zapata)
Chihuahua Farm
Clareno
Comitas (Bustamante)
Cuellar Store (Escobas)
Escobas *(Cuellar Store, Laguna de Escobas)*
Falcon *(Ramireno)*
Garcias (La Presa)
Guadalupe (Lopeno)
Laguna de Escobas (Escobas)
La Presa (Garcias)
Lopeno *[Lopena] (Guadalupe)*
Ramireno
Ramireno (Falcon)
San Bartolo (Zapata)
San Jose de Lopeno
San Pedro
San Ygnacio
Zapata *(Bellville, Carrizo, San Bartolo)*

Zavala Co.
Batesville *[Bates Switch]*
Cinonia (New California)
Cometa
Crain
CRYSTAL CITY
Edison
Frances (Indio)
Indio (Frances)
Jackson
La Pryor
Loma Vista *[Luma Vista]*
Muela
New California (Cinonia)
Palo Blanco
Pulliam
Regna
River
Washer
Zavalla

www.TexasAlmanac.com
for links to even more Texas
information that's current, official and reliable

Constitution of Texas

The complete official text of the Constitution of Texas, including the original document, which was adopted on Feb. 15, 1876, plus all amendments approved since that time, is available on the State of Texas Web page at this address: **www.capitol.state.tx.us/txconst/toc.html**. An index at that site points you to the Article and Section of the Constitution that deals with a particular subject.

For election information — upcoming elections, amendment or other election votes, and voter registration information — on the Web: **www.sos.state.tx.us/function/elec1/**

Amendment of the Texas Constitution requires a two-thirds favorable vote by both the Texas House of Representatives and the Texas Senate, followed by a majority vote of approval by voters in a statewide election.

Prior to 1973, amendments to the constitution could not be submitted by a special session of the Legislature. But the constitution was amended in 1972 to allow submission of amendments if the special session was opened to the subject by the governor.

Constitutional amendments are not subject to a gubernatorial veto. Once submitted, voters have the final decision on whether to change the constitution as proposed.

The following table lists the total number of amendments submitted to voters by the Texas Legislature and shows the year in which the Legislature approved them for submission to voters; e.g., the Seventieth Legislature in 1987 approved 28 bills proposing amendments to be submitted to voters — 25 in 1987 and three in 1988.

Year	No.	Year	No.	Year	No.
1879	1	1925	4	1969	16
1881	2	1927	8	1971	18
1883	5	1929	7	1973	9
1887	6	1931	9	1975	12
1889	2	1933	12	1977	15
1891	5	1935	13	1978	1
1893	2	1937	7	1979	12
1895	2	1939	4	1981	10
1897	5	1941	5	1982	3
1899	1	1943	3	1983	19
1901	1	1945	8	1985	17
1903	3	1947	9	1986	1
1905	3	1949	10	1987	28
1907	9	1951	7	1989	21
1909	4	1953	11	1990	1
1911	5	1955	9	1991	15
1913	7	1957	12	1993	18
1915	7	1959	4	1995	14
1917	3	1961	14	1997	15
1919	13	1963	7	1999	17
1921	5	1965	27		
1923	2	1967	20		

Amendments, 1997

The following amendment was submitted to the voters by the 75th Legislature on **Aug. 9, 1997**, just after this section of the Almanac went to press:

HJR 4 — Increasing the amount of the school property tax residence homestead exemption and providing for the continuation and reduction of the school tax limitation on the homesteads of certain persons. Passed: 693,522 in favor; 45,619 against.

The following 14 amendments were submitted to the voters by the 75th Legislature on **Nov. 4, 1997**:

HJR 8 — Extending the full faith and credit of the state to support the Texas tomorrow fund. Passed: 811,873 in favor; 314,516 against.

HJR 31 — Permitting an encumbrance against homestead property for certain extensions of equity credit. Passed: 698,870 in favor; 474,443 against.

HJR 55 — Relating to a deadline for supreme court action on a motion for rehearing. Passed: 858,513 in favor; 253,254 against.

HJR 59 — Limiting debt payable from the general revenue fund. Passed: 742,798 in favor; 350,317 against.

HJR 83 — Allowing the legislature to prescribe the qualifications of constables. Passed: 869,156 in favor; 244,472 against.

HJR 96 — Authorizing the legislature to authorize an ad valorem tax of five cents for each $100 of taxable property in rural fire prevention districts in Harris County. Passed: 558,400 in favor; 492,666 against.

HJR 104 — Eliminating duplicate numbering in and certain obsolete provisions of the Texas Constitution. Passed: 865,397 in favor; 232,350 against.

SJR 17 — Creating the Texas Water Development Fund II; authorizing the Texas Water Development Board to administer the fund and issue bonds relating to it; and regarding repayment of Texas agricultural water conservation bonds. Passed: 707,498 in favor; 398,795 against.

SJR 19 — Relating to the place at which the Supreme Court of Texas sits to transact business. Passed: 665,617 in favor; 458,791 against.

SJR 33 — Relating to the purposes for which money in the compensation to victims of crime fund and the compensation to victims of crime auxiliary fund may be used. Passed: 763,646 in favor; 345,563 against.

SJR 36 — Allowing a municipal court judge to hold more than one civil office of emolument at the same time. Failed: 423,793 in favor; 731,044 against

SJR 39 — Allowing the Texas growth fund to continue to invest in businesses without requiring those businesses to disclose investments in South Africa or Namibia. Failed: 562,535 in favor; 564,070 against.

SJR 43 — Providing for limitations on increases in the appraised value of residence homesteads for ad valorem taxation and for the transfer to a different residence homestead of the school property tax freeze on residence homesteads of the elderly and their spouses. Passed: 852,031 in favor; 273,957 against.

SJR 45 — Authorizing the legislature to permit a taxing unit to grant an exemption or other relief from ad valorem taxes on property on which a water conservation initiative has been implemented. Passed: 681,060 in favor; 420,923 against.

Amendments, 1999

The following 17 amendments were submitted to the voters by the 76th Legislature in an election on **Nov. 2, 1999:**

HJR 4 — Authorizing the exemption from ad valorem taxation of property owned by institutions engaged primarily in public charitable functions.

HJR 16 — Authorizing garnishment of wages for the enforcement of court-ordered spousal maintenance.

HJR29 — Authorizing the legislature to provide that certain state boards, commissions or other agencies shall be governed by a board composed of an odd number of three or more members.

HJR36 — Permitting spouses to agree to convert separate property to community property.

HJR44 — Revising the provisions for filling of a vacancy in the office of governor or lieutenant governor.

HJR58 — Relating to the investment of the permanent university fund and to distributions from that fund to the available university fund

HJR62 — Eliminating duplicative, executed, obsolete, archaic and ineffective constitutional provisions.

HJR69 — Permitting a political subdivision to purchase property and casualty insurance from certain mutual insurance companies.

HJR71 — Providing for the number of precincts that certain counties must create for justices of the peace and constables.

HJR74 — Providing that the commissioner of health and human services serves at the pleasure of the governor.

HJR95 — Providing that the adjutant general serves at the pleasure of the governor.

SJR10 — Authorizing the legislature to create a judicial compensation commission.

SJR12 — Relating to the making of advances under and payment of a reverse mortgage.

SJR16 — Providing for the issuance of $400 million in general-obligation bonds to finance educational loans to students.

SJR21 — Authorizing the legislature to exempt from ad valorem taxation leased motor vehicles not held primarily for the production of income.

SJR22 — Increasing the maximum size of an urban homestead to 10 acres, prescribing permissible uses of urban homesteads and preventing the overburdening of a homestead.

SJR26 — Relating to compensation for state employees serving as members of local governing boards. ☆

Declaration of Independence of the Republic of Texas

The Declaration of Independence of the Republic of Texas was adopted in general convention at Washington-on-the-Brazos, March 2, 1836.

Richard Ellis, president of the convention, appointed a committee of five to write the declaration for submission to the convention. However, there is much evidence that George C. Childress, one of the members, wrote the document with little or no help from the other members. Childress is therefore generally accepted as the author.

The text of the declaration is followed by the names of the signers of the document. The names are presented here as the signers actually signed the document. Our thanks to the staff of the Texas State Archives for furnishing a photocopy of the signatures.

UNANIMOUS

DECLARATION OF INDEPENDENCE,

BY THE

DELEGATES OF THE PEOPLE OF TEXAS,

IN GENERAL CONVENTION,

AT THE TOWN OF WASHINGTON,

ON THE SECOND DAY OF MARCH, 1836.

When a government has ceased to protect the lives, liberty and property of the people from whom its legitimate powers are derived, and for the advancement of whose happiness it was instituted; and so far from being a guarantee for the enjoyment of those inestimable and inalienable rights, becomes an instrument in the hands of evil rulers for their oppression; when the Federal Republican Constitution of their country, which they have sworn to support, no longer has a substantial existence, and the whole nature of their government has been forcibly changed without their consent, from a restricted federative republic, composed of sovereign states, to a consolidated central military despotism, in which every interest is disregarded but that of the army and the priesthood — both the eternal enemies of civil liberty, and the ever-ready minions of power, and the usual instruments of tyrants; When long after the spirit of the Constitution has departed, moderation is at length, so far lost, by those in power that even the semblance of freedom is removed, and the forms, themselves, of the constitution discontinued; and so far from their petitions and remonstrances being regarded, the agents who bear them are thrown into dungeons; and mercenary armies sent forth to force a new government upon them at the point of the bayonet. When in consequence of such acts of malfeasance and abdication, on the part of the government, anar-

chy prevails, and civil society is dissolved into its original elements: In such a crisis, the first law of nature, the right of self-preservation — the inherent and inalienable right of the people to appeal to first principles and take their political affairs into their own hands in extreme cases — enjoins it as a right towards themselves and a sacred obligation to their posterity, to abolish such government and create another in its stead, calculated to rescue them from impending dangers, and to secure their future welfare and happiness.

Nations, as well as individuals, are amenable for their acts to the public opinion of mankind. A statement of a part of our grievances is, therefore, submitted to an impartial world, in justification of the hazardous but unavoidable step now taken of severing our political connection with the Mexican people, and assuming an independent attitude among the nations of the earth.

The Mexican government, by its colonization laws, invited and induced the Anglo-American population of Texas to colonize its wilderness under the pledged faith of a written constitution, that they should continue to enjoy that constitutional liberty and republican government to which they had been habituated in the land of their birth, the United States of America. In this expectation they have been cruelly disappointed, inasmuch as the Mexican nation has acquiesced in the late changes made in the government by General Antonio Lopez de Santa Anna, who, having overturned the constitution of his country, now offers us the cruel alternative either to abandon our homes, acquired by so many privations, or submit to the most intolerable of all tyranny, the combined despotism of the sword and the priesthood.

It has sacrificed our welfare to the state of Coahuila, by which our interests have been continually depressed, through a jealous and partial course of legislation carried on at a far distant seat of government, by a hostile majority, in an unknown tongue; and this too, notwithstanding we have petitioned in the humblest terms, for the establishment of a separate state government, and have, in accordance with the provisions of the national constitution, presented the general Congress, a republican constitution which was without just cause contemptuously rejected.

It incarcerated in a dungeon, for a long time, one of our citizens, for no other cause but a zealous endeavor to procure the acceptance of our constitution and the establishment of a state government.

It has failed and refused to secure on a firm basis, the right of trial by jury; that palladium of civil liberty, and only safe guarantee for the life, liberty, and property of the citizen.

It has failed to establish any public system of education, although possessed of almost boundless resources (the public domain) and, although, it is an axiom, in political science, that unless a people are educated and enlightened it is idle to expect the continuance of civil liberty, or the capacity for self-government.

It has suffered the military commandants stationed among us to exercise arbitrary acts of oppression and tyranny; thus trampling upon the most sacred rights of the citizen and rendering the military superior to the civil power.

It has dissolved by force of arms, the state Congress of Coahuila and Texas, and obliged our representatives to fly for their lives from the seat of government; thus depriving us of the fundamental political right of representation.

It has demanded the surrender of a number of our citizens, and ordered military detachments to seize and carry them into the Interior for trial; in contempt of the civil authorities, and in defiance of the laws and constitution.

It has made piratical attacks upon our commerce; by commissioning foreign desperadoes, and authorizing them to seize our vessels, and convey the property of our citizens to far distant ports of confiscation.

It denies us the right of worshipping the Almighty according to the dictates of our own consciences, by the support of a national religion calculated to promote the temporal interests of its human functionaries rather than the glory of the true and living God.

It has demanded us to deliver up our arms; which are essential to our defense, the rightful property of freemen, and formidable only to tyrannical governments.

It has invaded our country, both by sea and by land, with intent to lay waste our territory and drive us from our homes; and has now a large mercenary army advancing to carry on against us a war of extermination.

It has, through its emissaries, incited the merciless savage, with the tomahawk and scalping knife, to massacre the inhabitants of our defenseless frontiers.

It hath been, during the whole time of our connection with it, the contemptible sport and victim of successive military revolutions and hath continually exhibited every characteristic of a weak, corrupt and tyrannical government.

These, and other grievances, were patiently borne by the people of Texas until they reached that point at which forbearance ceases to be a virtue. We then took up arms in defense of the national constitution. We appealed to our Mexican brethren for assistance. Our appeal has been made in vain. Though months have elapsed, no sympathetic response has yet been heard from the Interior. We are, therefore, forced to the melancholy conclusion that the Mexican people have acquiesced in the destruction of their liberty, and the substitution therefor of a military government — that they are unfit to be free and incapable of self-government.

The necessity of self-preservation, therefore, now decrees our eternal political separation.

We, therefore, the delegates, with plenary powers, of the people of Texas, in solemn convention assembled, appealing to a candid world for the necessities of our condition, do hereby resolve and DECLARE that our political connection with the Mexican nation has forever ended; and that the people of Texas do now constitute a FREE, SOVEREIGN and INDEPENDENT RE-PUBLIC, and are fully invested with all the rights and attributes which properly belong to the independent nations; and, conscious of the rectitude of our intentions, we fearlessly and confidently commit the issue to the decision of the Supreme Arbiter of the destinies of nations.

RICHARD ELLIS, president of the convention and Delegate from Red River.

Charles B Stewart

Thos Barnett
John S.D. Byrom

Fran^{co} Ruiz
J. Antonio Navarro
Jesse B. Badgett
Wm D. Lacey
William Menefee
Jno Fisher
Mathew Caldwell
William Mottley
Lorenzo de Zavala
Stephen H. Everitt
Geo W Smyth

Elijah Stapp
Claiborne West

W^m B Scates
M.B. Menard
A.B. Hardin
J.W. Bunton
Thos J. Gasley
R. M. Coleman
Sterling C. Robertson
Benj Briggs Goodrich
G.W. Barnett
James G. Swisher
Jesse Grimes
S. Rhoads Fisher
John W. Moore
John W. Bower
Saml A Maverick from Bejar
Sam P. Carson
A. Briscoe
J.B. Woods

Jas Collinsworth
Edwin Waller
Asa Brigham
Geo. C. Childress
Bailey Hardeman
Rob. Potter
Thomas Jefferson Rusk
Chas. S. Taylor
John S. Roberts

Robert Hamilton
Collin McKinney
Albert H Latimer
James Power

Sam Houston
David Thomas

Edwd Conrad
Martin Parmer
Edwin O. LeGrand
Stephen W. Blount
Ja^s Gaines
Wm Clark, Jr
Sydney O. Penington
Wm Carrol Crawford
Jno Turner

Test. H.S. Kimble, Secretary

Republicans Sweep Statewide Offices

By Carolyn Barta

The era of Democratic domination ended in Texas as the state approached the end of the century. Boosted by a watershed election in 1998, Republicans became the dominant power in state government.

Republican candidates, led by Gov. George W. Bush, won the 14 statewide elections on the 1998 ballot, giving the GOP ownership of all 29 offices elected by statewide vote.

Tony Garza is the first Hispanic Republican to be elected to statewide office; Susan Combs is the first woman to hold the post of agriculture commissioner; and Michael L. Williams is the first black to serve on the Railroad Commission (left to right). Dallas Morning News file photos.

The GOP sweep left Texas Democrats at their lowest ebb this century, though the long-powerful party continued to hold a majority of county offices, congressional and Texas House seats.

But not since the post-Civil War period of Reconstruction had Democrats been shut out of the state's top elected offices. To boot, Texas was one of only four where the GOP controlled all statewide elected offices.

In Texas, that includes six executive posts, three Railroad Commissioners, 18 judges on the Texas Supreme Court and Court of Criminal Appeals, and two U.S. senators.

Gov. Bush's 2-to-1 landslide victory over Garry Mauro, veteran land commissioner, made him the first governor to win consecutive elections since Texas switched to four-year terms in 1974.

The eldest son of former President George Bush carried all but 14 of the state's 254 counties, racking up a 69 percent win, the largest margin of victory for a gubernatorial candidate since John Connally won his last term in 1966.

Rick Perry became the first Republican in more than 100 years to be elected lieutenant governor, to preside over a State Senate controlled by his party — though by a scant majority of 16 to 15.

If the governor should fail to finish his term, the lieutenant governor would replace him.

The lieutenant governor's race pitted rising stars from both parties, with Perry defeating John Sharp, the state's highly regarded comptroller and former state senator. Once a Democrat, Perry had served in the Texas House, where he switched parties, and then as agriculture commissioner.

The GOP also won additional courthouse seats, giving Republicans the reins of power in 48 of the state's 254 counties. After the election, one in five offices in county courthouses — long regarded as the Democrats' domain — was held by a Republican. The GOP claimed 1,098 of an estimated 5,000 county offices.

The Texas House remained the last Democratic bastion of power in Austin. Democrats maintained a 78-72 advantage in the House, and Speaker Pete Laney, a Panhandle cotton farmer elected by fellow House members to his post, became state government's highest-ranking Democrat.

Gov. Bush called it a historic election that opened "the doors of the Republican Party to new faces, new voices." Exit polls indicated he far surpassed his goal of winning more than 40 percent of the Hispanic vote — a record for a GOP statewide candidate in Texas.

In a state with a mushrooming Hispanic population, he avoided harsh rhetoric over such issues as immigration and bilingual education.

Democrats complained that they got "Bushwhacked," attributing their losses to Gov. Bush's popularity.

"This election was a mandate for one man, not for the Republican Party," said State Democratic Chairwoman Molly Beth Malcolm.

Gov. Bush's first term had been marked by extraordinary cooperation between Republicans and Democrats in the Capitol. The governor's bipartisan approach earned him the endorsement of outgoing Democratic Lt. Gov. Bob Bullock.

Gov. Bush said voters responded to his "compassionate conservative" message, which emphasized opportunity and personal responsibility. And a robust economy guaranteed additional state revenues, enabling Bush to put forward a legislative agenda of tax cuts and more spending for education.

Mauro, the Democrat, had served four terms as land commissioner and was a longtime friend of President Clinton and first lady Hillary Rodham Clinton. The Clintons and Vice President Al Gore headlined more than a dozen campaign and fund-raising events for Mauro in Texas and Washington. Even so, he was outspent 4-to-1.

Each of the state's four offices headed by a single elected official — attorney general, comptroller, land commissioner and agriculture commissioner — got a new chief in the 1998 election.

The Democrat who came closest to winning a statewide office was Paul Hobby who, like Gov. Bush, had a name well known to Texans. His father was longtime lieutenant governor Bill Hobby and his grandfather, William P. Hobby, a former governor.

Hobby was narrowly defeated in a race for comptroller by Carole Keeton Rylander, a Texas Railroad Commissioner and former mayor of Austin. Rylander became the first woman to serve as comptroller. Hobby was making his first run for office.

The 1998 elections resulted in three other "firsts" in state government involving a woman, a black and a Hispanic Republican.

Vassar-educated Susan Combs was elected to a position that had never been occupied by a woman, agriculture commissioner. Owner-operator of the 70,000 acre Combs Ranch in the Big Bend country, 400 miles from her home in Austin, Combs also had a law degree and experience in the Texas Legislature.

Supporters hoped Combs would help bridge the widening chasm between rural and urban interests in a state that, while the second most populous, maintained strong agricultural traditions. She easily defeated L.P. (Pete) Patterson, agriculture committee chairman of the Texas House.

Shortly after his re-election, Gov. Bush appointed attorney Michael L. Williams, a former federal prosecutor, to fill the last two years of Rylander's term on the Railroad Commission. Williams was the first black to serve on the 107-year-old board, which regulates the oil and gas industry, and the only African-American to hold a statewide office.

Tony Garza became the first Hispanic Republican to win a statewide election after serving in the appointive office of secretary of state. He defeated Joe B. Henderson for a seat on the Texas Railroad Commission. Hispanics who won previous statewide elections were Democrats.

Another Hispanic Republican, Al Gonzales, was appointed to the State Supreme Court by Gov. Bush to fill an unexpired term.

In other elections, Democrat Jim Mattox, who cast himself as the "people's lawyer," was foiled in his attorney general comeback attempt. Mattox, who had been the state's lawyer in the 1980s, was defeated by former Texas Supreme Court Justice John Cornyn.

And Houston businessman David Dewhurst defeated State Rep. Richard Raymond for land commissioner.

Two weeks before the election, polls showed Mattox ahead in his race and Hobby and Patterson in dead heats with their Republican opponents. Analysts said the better-funded Republicans were helped across the finish line by money poured into advertising in the final days and Gov. Bush's appeal at the top of the GOP ticket.

Mattox warned dispirited Democrats that their fortunes could get worse, with colleagues facing the redistricting process after the 2000 census without a single Democratic state official to fight for districts favorable to Democrats. As a result, the party could lose its edge in both the Texas House and Congress.

State government also said goodbye to the Democrats' ranking officeholder and a forceful Capitol personality when Lt. Gov. Bob Bullock retired after four decades in politics. Beginning his career in 1957 as a state legislator, he put his stamp on public policy as secretary of state, comptroller and for eight years as lieutenant governor. Bullock, who was best-known for his traditional closing remark, "God Bless Texas," died in 1999. ☆

Carolyn Barta is a staff writer of The Dallas Morning News.

1998 Extraordinary Political Year for Texans

The 1998 political year will be remembered as an extraordinary time.

Nationally, a president was impeached by the U.S. House but survived a Senate trial that could have expelled him from office. And a Texan was catapulted into the national scene as a likely presidential contender.

Polls showed Texas Gov. George W. Bush to be the frontrunner throughout 1998 without his ever setting foot on the national stage.

His landslide gubernatorial re-election, bipartisan approach in Texas and demonstrated ability to broaden the party's appeal by attracting traditionally Democratic voters, including Hispanics, bolstered his presidential credentials.

Gov. Bush promised not to become actively involved in a national race until after the 1999 legislative session. But there was little question that he hoped the national party would adopt his compassionate conservative message to soften the GOP image as the party of impeachment and to increase its mainstream appeal.

On a personal level, Gov. Bush achieved sweet revenge against former Gov. Ann Richards when he helped level the Democratic ticket in Texas. The tart-tongued Ms. Richards had called him "shrub" in the 1994 gubernatorial campaign, as in: What do you call the son of a Bush?

Rarely has Texas seen as strong coattails as Gov. Bush had in the 1998 election. Most candidates, Republican or Democrat, ran as friends of Bush in the Year of Bush. Some Democrats even used his picture in their campaign commercials.

Meanwhile, Texas had other players on the national stage.

U.S. Rep. Dick Armey, R-Irving, won a third term as House majority leader but had to fight off two challengers who claimed to have better communications skills than the blunt-speaking Texan. Armey kept his job largely on his ability to set an agenda and manage legislation on the floor.

U.S. Rep. Tom DeLay, R-Sugar Land, was re-elected to be majority whip, the party's chief vote-counter and third-highest leadership position in the House GOP. DeLay led the effort to block a vote to censure the president instead of impeaching him in the House.

Gov. George W. Bush announces his campaign for the presidency in Des Moines, Iowa, in June 1999 AFP/Dallas Morning News file.

After four years as chairman of the Democratic Congressional Campaign Committee, Rep. Martin Frost, D-Dallas, was elected by his party as Democratic caucus chairman. Frost became the first Jewish member elected to a leadership position by House Democrats.

Party members credited Frost with raising record amounts of money and helping Democrats regain seats in midterm elections.

Two Democrats crossed over and voted to impeach President Clinton. Rep. Charles Stenholm, D-Abilene, and Rep. Ralph Hall, D-Rockwall, were among five Democrats in the House who voted for impeachment.

Meanwhile, Rep. Sheila Jackson Lee, D-Houston, was an outspoken advocate for the president on the

House Judiciary Committee.

All 13 Republican House members from Texas voted to bring articles of impeachment against President Clinton for perjury and obstruction of justice resulting from a sex scandal.

In the Senate trial, which failed to muster the two-thirds majority to remove the president from office, Sens. Phil Gramm and Kay Bailey Hutchison, Texas Republicans, voted for the articles of impeachment.

While Democrats maintained their 17-13 majority in the Texas congressional delegation in 1998, they lost delegation dean Henry B. Gonzalez, who retired for health and family reasons after 37 years as a congressman.

Called "Henry B.," the legendary Gonzalez was the first Hispanic elected to Congress from Texas. A colorful figure and voice for the less fortunate, he was known as a trailblazer for civil rights and economic justice. Gonzalez is credited with helping repeal the poll tax in Texas, bringing the World's Fair to San Antonio in 1968, and boosting the political fortunes of a young John F. Kennedy.

The second-most senior member of the House, he was succeeded in his San Antonio district by his son, Charlie Gonzalez.

Rep. Bill Archer, R-Houston, who was first elected to Congress in 1970, became the most senior Texan in Congress. And Frost, first elected in 1978, became the senior Texas Democrat upon Gonzalez's retirement. — *Carolyn Barta.*

General Election, 1998

Below are the voting returns of the general election held November 3, 1998, for all statewide races, and for contested congressional, state senate, courts of appeals and state board of education races. These are official returns as canvassed by the State Canvassing Board. Abbreviations used are (Dem.) Democrat, (Rep.) Republican, (Lib.) Libertarian and (Ind.) Independent.

Governor
George W. Bush (Rep.) 2,550,831
Garry Mauro (Dem.) 1,165,592
Lester R. (Les) Turlington Jr.(Lib.) 20,711
Susan Lee Solar (Write-in) 954
 Total Vote 3,738,078

Lieutenant Governor
Rick Perry (Rep.). 1,858,837
John Sharp (Dem.) 1,790,106
Anthony Garcia (Lib.). .65,150
 Total Vote 3,714,093

Attorney General
John Cornyn (Rep.). 2,002,794
Jim Mattox (Dem.). 1,631,045
Mike Angwin (Lib.). 57,604
 Total Vote 3,691,443

Comptroller of Public Accounts
Carole Keeton Rylander (Rep.) 1,821,231
Paul Hobby (Dem.) 1,801,008
Alex Monchak (Lib.). .53,536
 Total Vote 3,675,775

Commissioner of the General Land Office
David Dewhurst (Rep.) 2,072,604
Richard Raymond (Dem.) 1,438,378
J. Manuel (Monte) Montez (Lib.) 98,321
 Total Vote 3,609,303

Commissioner of Agriculture
Susan Combs (Rep.). 2,021,385
L.P. (Pete) Patterson (Dem.) 1,511,045
Jimmy T. LaBaume (Lib.) 54,669
Michael J. Yarbrough (Write-in) 3,628
 Total Vote 3,590,727

Railroad Commissioner
Tony Garza (Rep.) 2,051,253
Joe B. Henderson (Dem.) 1,464,278
Jim Spurlock (Lib.). 87,999
 Total Vote 3,603,530

Justice, Supreme Court, Place 1
Craig T. Enoch (Rep.). 2,049,640
Mike Westergren (Dem.) 1,473,220
 Total Vote 3,522,860

Justice, Supreme Court, Place 2
Harriet O'Neill (Rep.) 1,891,339
Rose Spector (Dem.). 1,642,334
 Total Vote 3,533,673

Justice, Supreme Court, Place 3
Greg Abbott (Rep.) 2,104,828
David Van Os (Dem.). 1,396,924
 Total Vote 3,501,752

Justice, Supreme Court, Place 4
Deborah Hankinson (Rep.). 1,995,811
Jerry Scarbrough (Dem.) 1,511,539
 Total Vote 3,507,350

Judge, Court of Criminal Appeals, Place 1
Mike Keasler (Rep.) 1,889,069
Charles F. (Charlie) Baird (Dem.) 1,611,538
 Total Vote 3,500,607

Judge, Court of Criminal Appeals, Place 2
Cheryl Johnson (Rep.) .2,013,959
Winston Cochran (Dem.) 1,471,200
 Total Vote 3,485,159

Judge, Court of Criminal Appeals, Place 3
Lawrence (Larry) Meyers (Rep.). 2,189,508
Larry S. Perry (Lib.). 495,691
 Total Vote 2,685,199

U.S. HOUSE OF REPRESENTATIVES
District 1
Dennis Boerner (Rep.) 55,191
Max Sandlin (Dem.) 80,788
 Total Vote 135,979

District 2
Brian Babin (Rep.) 56,891
Jim Turner (Dem.). 81,556
Wendell Drye (Lib.). 1,142
 Total Vote 139,589

District 3
Sam Johnson (Rep.). 106,690
Ken Ashby (Lib.) 10,288
 Total Vote 116,978

District 4
Jim Lohmeyer (Rep.) 58,954
Ralph Hall (Dem.) 82,989
Jim Simon (Lib.). 2,137
 Total Vote 144,080

District 5
Pete Sessions (Rep.) 61,714
Victor M. Morales (Dem.) 48,073
Michael D. Needleman (Lib.). 880
 Total Vote 110,667

District 6
Joe Barton (Rep.). 112,957
Ben B. Boothe (Dem.). 40,112
Richard A. Bandlow (Lib.). 1,817
 Total Vote 154,886

District 7
Bill Archer (Rep.) 111,010
Drew Parks (Lib.) 7,889
John Skone-Palmer (W-I) 47
 Total Vote 118,946

District 8

Kevin Brady (Rep.)	123,372
Don L. Richards (Lib.)	9,576
Total Vote	132,948

District 9

Tom Cottar (Rep.)	49,107
Nick Lampson (Dem.)	86,055
Total Vote	135,162

District 10

Lloyd Doggett (Dem.)	116,127
Vincent J. May (Lib.)	20,155
Total Vote	136,282

District 11

Chet Edwards (Dem.)	71,142
Vince Hanke (Lib.)	15,161
Total Vote	86,303

District 12

Kay Granger (Rep.)	66,740
Tom Hall (Dem.)	39,084
Paul Barthel (Lib.)	1,917
Total Vote	107,741

District 13

Mac Thornberry (Rep.)	81,141
Mark Harmon (Dem.)	37,027
Georganne Baker Payne (Lib.)	1,298
Total Vote	119,466

District 14

Ron Paul (Rep.)	84,459
Loy Sneary (Dem.)	68,014
Cynthia Newman	390
Total Vote	152,863

District 15

Tom Haughey (Rep.)	34,221
Ruben Hinojosa (Dem.)	47,957
Total Vote	82,178

District 16

Silvestre Reyes (Dem.)	67,486
Stu Nance (Lib.)	5,329
Lorenzo Morales (Ind.)	3,952
Total Vote	76,767

District 17

Rudy Izzard (Rep.)	63,700
Charlie Stenholm (Dem.)	75,367
Gordon Mobley (Lib.)	1,618
Total Vote	140,685

District 18

Sheila Jackson Lee (Dem.)	82,091
James Galvan (Lib.)	9,176
Total Vote	91,267

District 19

Larry Combest (Rep.)	108,266
Sidney Blankenship (Dem.)	21,162
Total Vote	129,428

District 20

James Walker (Rep.)	28,347
Charlie Gonzalez (Dem.)	50,356
Alejandro (Alex) DePena (Lib.)	1,010
Total Vote	79,713

District 21

Lamar Smith (Rep.)	165,047
Jeffrey Charles Blunt (Lib.)	15,561
Total Vote	180,608

District 22

Tom DeLay (Rep.)	87,840
Hill Kemp (Dem.)	45,386
Steve Grupe (Lib.)	1,494
Total Vote	134,720

District 23

Henry Bonilla (Rep.)	73,177
Charlie Urbina Jones (Dem.)	40,281
William A. (Bill) Stallknecht (Lib.)	1,262
Total Vote	114,720

District 24

Shawn Terry (Rep.)	40,105
Martin Frost (Dem.)	56,321

David A. Stover (Lib.)	736
George Arias (Ind.)	830
Total Vote	97,992

District 25

John M. Sanchez (Rep.)	41,848
Ken Bentsen (Dem.)	58,591
Eric Atkisson (Lib.)	830
Total Vote	101,269

District 26

Dick Armey (Rep.)	120,332
Joe Turner (Lib.)	16,182
Total Vote	136,514

District 27

Erol A. Stone (Rep.)	34,284
Solomon P. Ortiz (Dem.)	61,638
Mark G. Pretz (Lib.)	1,476
Total Vote	97,398

District 28

Ciro D. Rodriguez (Rep.)	71,849
Edward Elmer (Lib.)	7,504
Total Vote	79,353

District 29

Gene Green (Dem.)	44,179
James P. Chudleigh (Lib.)	1,439
Lea Sherman (Ind.)	2,013
Total Vote	47,631

District 30

Carrie Kelleher (Rep.)	21,338
Eddie Bernice Johnson (Dem.)	57,603
Barbara L. Robinson (Lib.)	811
Total Vote	79,752

STATE SENATE
District 4

Michael Galloway (Rep.)	62,237
David Bernsen (Dem.)	76,540
Total Vote	138,777

District 5

Steve Ogden (Rep.)	77,227
Mary M. Moore (Dem.)	61,508
Total Vote	138,735

District 11

Mike Jackson (Rep.)	63,492
Edward Wesley (Dem.)	47,696
Total Vote	111,188

District 17

J.E. (Buster) Brown (Rep.)	96,846
Ronnie Ellen Harrison (Dem.)	40,331
Total Vote	137,117

District 18

Reese Turner (Rep.)	58,195
Ken Armbrister (Dem.)	85,291
Total Vote	143,486

District 20

Joe Gardner (Rep.)	41,338
Carlos F. Truan (Dem.)	57,298
Total Vote	98,636

District 30

Tom Haywood (Rep.)	82,996
Greg Underwood (Dem.)	49,483
Total Vote	132,479

COURTS OF APPEALS
Chief Justice, Third District

Lee Yeakel (Rep.)	176,192
Marilyn Aboussie (Dem.)	193,138
Total Vote	369,330

Justice, First District

Davie L. Wilson (Rep.)	400,796
George Ellis (Dem.)	324,581
Total Vote	725,377

Justice, Third District

David Puryear (Rep.)	178,694
Jan Patterson (Dem.)	186,915
Total Vote	365,609

Justice, Fourth District, Place 2
Karen Angelini (Rep.)............................193,882
Jim Branton (Dem.)..............................163,289
Total Vote 357,171

Justice, Eighth District
Jerry Woodard (Rep.) 72,315
Susan Larsen (Dem.)............................83,797
Total Vote 156,112

Justice, Ninth District
Ralph Harrison (Rep.) 88,598
Don Burgess (Dem.) 107,319
Total Vote 195,917

Justice, Tenth District
Tom Gray (Rep.)....................................80,557
Katherine Logue O'Herren (Dem.)............77,815
Total Vote 158,372

Justice, Eleventh District
Terry McCall (Rep.) 54,374
Randy Wilson (Dem.)............................41,927
Total Vote 96,301

Justice, Fourteenth District, Place 1
Don Wittig (Rep.)..................................419,912
Geoffrey (Jeff) Hutson (Dem.) 306,420

Total Vote.....................726,332

STATE BOARD OF EDUCATION
District 1
Donna Ballard (Rep.) 71,424
Rene Nunez (Dem.) 106,623
Total Vote......................178,047

District 2
Shirley Persons Pigott (Rep.) 78,393
Mary Helen Berlanga (Dem.) 104,778
Total Vote......................183,171

District 8
Grace Shore (Rep.)..............................153,336
Charlotte H. Coffelt (Dem.) 109,385
Total Vote......................262,721

District 9
Don McLeroy (Rep.) 145,556
Mary Delk (Dem.) 119,149
Total Vote......................264,705

District 14
Richard Watson (Rep.) 149,921
Allan Butcher (Dem.)...........................115,055
Total Vote......................264,976

1998 General Election Results by County

Below are the official results by county. Listed are the two candidates who received the most votes for governor, lieutenant governor and attorney general. The total number of voters who cast ballots, 3,738,078, was 32.39 percent of those registered to vote. The voting age population was 14,088,872. The statewide turnout in the gubernatorial election of 1994 was 50.87 percent. *Source: Texas Secretary of State.*

County	Registered Voters October 98	Governor BUSH (Rep.)	Governor MAURO (Dem.)	Turnout Percent	Lt. Governor PERRY (Rep.)	Lt. Governor SHARP (Dem.)	Attorney General CORNYN (Rep.)	Attorney General MATTOX (Dem.)
Anderson	26,140	6,762	2,927	37.23	4,824	4,724	4,844	4,687
Andrews	7,601	2,082	455	33.67	1,457	1,013	1,408	1,079
Angelina	49,655	10,880	6,437	35.04	7,381	9,746	8,413	8,612
Aransas	12,953	4,292	1,449	44.59	2,900	2,697	2,996	2,559
Archer	6,086	2,018	653	44.03	1,488	1,163	1,223	1,378
Armstrong	1,527	683	102	51.60	517	249	504	238
Atascosa	21,079	4,252	1,777	28.82	2,675	3,164	3,263	2,589
Austin	14,115	5,157	1,321	46.05	3,608	2,774	3,855	2,477
Bailey	3,661	1,454	356	49.54	957	778	828	868
Bandera	9,940	3,583	649	42.98	2,796	1,379	3,094	1,012
Bastrop	28,688	7,638	4,040	41.09	4,971	6,564	5,259	6,129
Baylor	3,140	839	428	40.47	535	717	493	713
Bee	17,196	4,593	2,952	44.05	2,949	4,311	2,871	4,436
Bell	130,969	24,244	8,815	25.36	17,610	14,790	18,727	13,343
Bexar	818,370	147,136	78,801	27.74	101,714	118,811	124,923	95,920
Blanco	5,318	2,104	485	49.17	1,389	1,183	1,586	892
Borden	461	218	42	56.83	158	95	125	120
Bosque	9,818	3,263	1,192	45.53	2,151	2,242	2,502	1,867
Bowie	53,723	11,250	6,770	33.60	8,102	9,699	7,829	9,956
Brazoria	135,443	34,285	11,163	33.75	24,915	19,395	27,039	17,047
Brazos	76,095	19,522	6,544	34.47	15,372	10,408	14,924	10,618
Brewster	5,660	1,371	836	39.75	974	1,168	900	1,221
Briscoe	1,331	459	172	47.55	277	335	255	346
Brooks	6,657	489	1,097	23.82	208	1,323	214	1,353
Brown	22,302	6,851	1,976	39.71	4,891	3,846	4,987	3,711
Burleson	9,563	2,778	1,467	44.55	1,884	2,294	1,771	2,379
Burnet	19,381	6,656	2,277	46.38	4,750	4,107	5,060	3,714
Caldwell	18,175	3,604	1,997	31.02	2,249	3,255	2,545	2,940
Calhoun	12,806	3,154	1,378	35.53	1,181	3,290	1,950	2,442
Callahan	8,699	2,703	750	39.83	1,989	1,433	1,947	1,438
Cameron	137,673	19,747	13,357	24.18	12,626	19,374	12,672	19,609
Camp	6,384	1,734	1,285	47.41	1,165	1,821	1,198	1,741
Carson	4,639	1,969	444	52.31	1,389	956	1,387	922

Lt. governor's election

☐ **Perry**
▨ **Sharp**

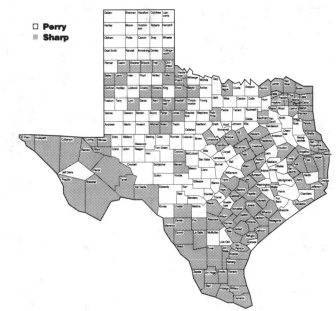

The race for lieutenant governor was one of the closest. It pitted rising stars from both parties, with Republican Rick Perry defeating Democrat John Sharp.

In the governor's race, GOP incumbent George W. Bush won more votes than Democrat Garry Mauro in all of Texas' 254 counties except 14.

County	Registered Voters October 98	Governor BUSH (Rep.)	Governor MAURO (Dem.)	Turnout Percent	Lt. Governor PERRY (Rep.)	Lt. Governor SHARP (Dem.)	Attorney General CORNYN (Rep.)	Attorney General MATTOX (Dem.)
Cass	19,106	3,951	2,663	34.70	2,608	3,926	2,542	3,950
Castro	4,817	1,440	562	41.72	958	963	815	1,086
Chambers	16,070	3,921	1,400	33.25	2,837	2,388	2,929	2,232
Cherokee	25,834	6,715	2,867	37.22	4,934	4,544	4,698	4,720
Childress	4,108	1,032	404	35.02	648	761	701	692
Clay	7,123	2,149	785	41.33	1,506	1,485	1,291	1,654
Cochran	2,356	846	265	47.28	480	525	370	602
Coke	2,549	953	261	47.90	639	554	564	594
Coleman	6,820	2,115	662	40.83	1,386	1,358	1,237	1,423
Collin	263,573	71,066	12,544	31.90	59,020	23,548	62,968	18,864
Collingsworth	2,402	694	343	43.29	485	539	481	517
Colorado	11,558	4,235	1,345	48.45	2,612	2,846	2,756	2,620
Comal	50,975	15,304	3,132	36.40	11,593	6,656	13,477	4,534
Comanche	8,392	2,630	1,225	46.11	1,757	2,036	1,781	1,983
Concho	1,861	701	214	49.32	405	479	400	468
Cooke	22,259	7,550	1,757	41.98	5,630	3,513	6,032	3,004
Coryell	32,633	5,754	1,787	23.26	3,886	3,564	4,055	3,334
Cottle	1,602	410	243	41.07	254	375	220	386
Crane	2,884	931	236	40.60	595	498	516	569
Crockett	2,763	1,026	386	51.35	627	603	488	817
Crosby	4,214	1,041	466	35.85	608	838	543	895
Culberson	2,196	230	226	20.90	136	284	137	282
Dallam	2,712	706	130	30.89	510	324	515	273
Dallas	1,146,673	221,055	118,938	29.81	175,394	160,820	195,137	139,585
Dawson	8,658	2,262	576	32.90	1,554	1,067	1,448	1,241
Deaf Smith	10,136	2,761	646	33.73	2,036	1,243	2,098	1,254
Delta	3,153	400	854	39.89	617	691	602	671
Denton	246,655	54,129	13,454	27.62	44,155	22,476	47,592	18,403
DeWitt	12,285	3,431	806	34.64	1,709	2,433	2,432	1,606
Dickens	1,640	419	260	41.58	253	412	192	456
Dimmit	8,582	595	1,016	18.84	361	1,171	429	1,139
Donley	2,576	1,191	264	56.48	862	560	850	533
Duval	10,447	825	2,906	35.84	427	3,203	415	3,257
Eastland	10,934	3,753	1,247	45.95	2,676	2,244	2,614	2,256
Ector	67,675	15,132	5,811	31.19	11,504	9,056	11,377	9,082

County	Registered Voters	Governor		Turnout	Lt. Governor		Attorney General	
	October 98	BUSH (Rep.)	MAURO (Dem.)	Percent	PERRY (Rep.)	SHARP (Dem.)	CORNYN (Rep.)	MATTOX (Dem.)
Edwards	1,546	650	200	55.23	402	343	350	368
Ellis	62,621	15,527	4,929	32.82	11,957	8,238	13,343	6,781
El Paso	332,020	46,035	45,378	27.72	30,571	56,315	28,101	60,781
Erath	18,392	5,399	1,905	39.86	3,735	3,466	4,270	2,862
Falls	9,754	2,119	1,334	35.60	1,286	2,109	1,432	1,910
Fannin	16,952	3,967	2,366	37.52	2,962	3,288	2,938	3,237
Fayette	13,180	5,144	1,590	51.25	3,135	3,554	3,490	3,065
Fisher	2,928	789	632	48.63	477	915	381	988
Floyd	4,970	1,142	248	28.02	803	563	889	757
Foard	1,149	206	205	36.11	122	284	112	281
Fort Bend	175,820	43,225	16,094	33.86	32,478	26,262	35,644	22,752
Franklin	5,507	1,911	750	48.59	1,287	1,344	1,267	1,318
Freestone	10,177	3,131	1,509	45.80	2,123	2,445	2,356	2,187
Frio	9,607	1,270	1,001	23.80	772	1,427	966	1,232
Gaines	6,768	2,127	487	38.82	1,352	1,186	1,114	1,430
Galveston	168,481	33,986	20,435	32.49	23,958	29,642	27,169	26,224
Garza	3,002	818	255	35.87	549	498	526	492
Gillespie	13,196	5,690	784	49.40	4,485	1,964	5,016	1,368
Glasscock	773	476	42	67.01	372	136	314	158
Goliad	4,580	1,432	568	43.93	669	1,285	995	939
Gonzales	11,668	3,468	1,090	39.23	2,115	2,294	2,300	2,045
Gray	15,804	5,365	990	40.42	4,314	1,972	4,307	1,974
Grayson	68,355	16,682	6,868	34.59	12,890	10,349	13,171	9,857
Gregg	76,785	18,168	6,146	31.77	13,476	10,639	14,961	9,090
Grimes	11,243	2,760	1,273	36.13	1,991	1,987	1,974	1,979
Guadalupe	51,709	12,663	3,273	31.03	9,276	6,419	10,631	4,892
Hale	20,256	5,819	1,312	35.37	3,815	3,075	3,478	3,491
Hall	2,585	604	317	35.70	364	536	397	501
Hamilton	5,139	1,950	714	52.15	1,273	1,357	1,414	1,181
Hansford	3,279	1,517	148	50.83	1,141	459	1,068	492
Hardeman	2,918	781	409	40.91	469	722	425	736
Hardin	33,048	8,239	3,392	35.32	5,738	5,719	5,137	6,272
Harris	1,755,809	350,309	183,045	30.55	265,426	257,642	288,137	233,442
Harrison	41,141	9,511	4,988	35.36	6,226	8,103	6,296	7,941
Hartley	2,819	1,083	231	46.78	776	524	828	460
Haskell	4,469	1,357	802	48.48	994	1,168	701	1,367
Hays	56,107	14,054	5,819	35.77	9,473	9,875	10,443	8,931
Hemphill	2,332	859	151	43.52	660	340	662	308
Henderson	43,370	10,909	4,663	36.06	7,746	7,683	8,988	6,319
Hidalgo	223,729	25,325	22,305	21.37	16,502	29,352	16,329	28,468
Hill	17,577	4,624	1,953	37.57	3,095	3,433	3,705	2,756
Hockley	13,949	4,048	869	35.40	2,500	2,288	2,371	2,422
Hood	26,161	8,428	2,530	42.03	6,663	4,182	7,307	3,464
Hopkins	18,424	5,223	2,432	41.67	3,574	3,991	3,787	3,637
Houston	14,615	3,812	2,082	40.48	2,762	3,058	2,555	3,251
Howard	18,957	5,513	1,938	39.47	4,021	3,260	3,724	3,506
Hudspeth	1,672	348	197	33.01	226	288	219	335
Hunt	43,699	10,759	3,834	33.59	7,812	6,566	8,888	5,325
Hutchinson	17,612	4,702	1,074	32.93	3,738	1,990	3,806	1,911
Irion	1,300	445	84	40.92	302	210	262	239
Jack	4,921	1,330	547	38.26	931	926	954	873
Jackson	8,918	2,494	737	36.33	1,085	2,104	1,623	1,436
Jasper	20,548	4,737	2,655	36.09	3,107	4,186	3,031	4,270
Jeff Davis	1,514	410	160	38.30	327	233	303	238
Jefferson	166,645	31,647	29,767	36.98	21,204	39,233	20,678	39,604
Jim Hogg	4,054	524	873	34.53	213	1,098	205	1,136
Jim Wells	26,608	2,957	3,887	25.78	1,935	4,736	1,930	4,853
Johnson	65,891	16,598	5,823	34.19	12,351	9,724	14,018	7,909
Jones	10,133	3,164	1,257	43.75	2,036	2,330	1,832	2,461
Karnes	8,338	2,155	935	37.20	1,157	1,805	1,529	1,456
Kaufman	40,060	9,656	3,934	34.08	6,576	6,661	7,894	5,360
Kendall	14,683	5,485	872	43.56	4,241	2,033	4,860	1,318
Kenedy	346	69	61	37.57	37	88	45	79

County	Registered Voters October 98	Governor BUSH (Rep.)	MAURO (Dem.)	Turnout Percent	Lt. Governor PERRY (Rep.)	SHARP (Dem.)	Attorney General CORNYN (Rep.)	MATTOX (Dem.)
Kent	852	290	128	49.41	172	235	118	267
Kerr	30,168	10,857	2,120	43.36	8,489	4,331	9,594	3,123
Kimble	2,792	938	227	41.90	639	486	642	464
King	228	131	37	73.68	101	55	56	82
Kinney	2,442	654	224	36.11	441	393	493	334
Kleberg	19,477	3,373	2,698	31.35	1,991	3,881	1,987	3,972
Knox	2,996	831	431	42.22	600	650	403	807
Lamar	30,453	7,112	3,493	34.94	5,195	5,268	5,121	5,232
Lamb	8,910	2,816	764	40.26	1,703	1,726	1,547	1,824
Lampasas	9,384	3,376	860	45.53	2,296	1,869	2,322	1,833
LaSalle	4,111	503	699	29.38	326	830	365	798
Lavaca	12,479	4,021	1,393	43.63	2,022	3,353	2,664	2,570
Lee	8,246	2,758	1,101	46.93	1,828	1,965	1,849	1,882
Leon	10,440	2,877	1,104	38.23	2,102	1,823	1,983	1,917
Liberty	39,323	8,802	3,866	32.39	5,970	6,554	6,059	6,309
Limestone	12,970	2,777	1,828	35.58	1,842	2,725	2,060	2,472
Lipscomb	1,986	856	168	51.76	618	372	595	373
Live Oak	7,174	1,848	582	34.17	1,321	1,074	1,384	970
Llano	11,703	5,029	1,456	55.71	3,751	2,692	4,041	2,310
Loving	158	82	22	68.35	47	49	42	55
Lubbock	147,535	40,564	8,900	33.73	29,420	18,684	28,880	19,462
Lynn	4,169	1,201	322	36.67	678	800	672	769
Madison	6,686	1,886	812	40.56	1,390	1,271	1,220	1,412
Marion	8,041	1,464	1,067	31.53	812	1,651	932	1,551
Martin	2,742	809	182	36.28	565	379	525	401
Mason	2,542	997	266	50.31	731	536	759	491
Matagorda	22,866	6,373	2,689	39.85	3,538	5,248	4,312	4,493
Maverick	20,623	2,252	2,566	23.49	991	3,163	975	3,414
McCulloch	5,552	1,554	569	38.34	1,076	983	979	1,030
McLennan	122,683	27,512	12,616	32.82	18,169	21,572	20,759	18,803
McMullen	718	258	41	41.92	196	93	195	84
Medina	20,322	5,619	1,647	36.01	3,901	3,209	4,562	2,515
Menard	1,751	555	253	46.48	374	402	337	430
Midland	69,824	21,650	3,757	36.64	17,770	7,351	18,280	6,692
Milam	14,514	3,417	2,159	38.65	2,068	3,463	2,251	3,219
Mills	2,837	1,221	414	57.87	805	784	754	778
Mitchell	5,226	1,221	547	34.02	782	950	686	1,030
Montague	12,281	3,462	1,409	39.89	2,327	2,491	2,324	2,426
Montgomery	159,571	43,488	8,384	32.67	35,835	15,556	37,712	13,301
Moore	9,888	3,021	534	36.23	2,240	1,252	2,228	1,263
Morris	9,613	1,982	1,882	40.29	1,119	2,649	1,181	2,595
Motley	1,002	393	97	49.40	283	196	243	202
Nacogdoches	36,307	8,835	3,661	34.58	6,277	6,018	6,622	5,502
Navarro	24,994	6,344	3,280	38.66	4,198	5,284	4,956	4,540
Newton	9,509	1,509	1,470	31.43	953	1,996	922	2,018
Nolan	10,653	2,684	1,133	36.12	1,681	2,074	1,468	2,245
Nueces	197,622	38,165	24,290	31.76	25,117	35,342	25,136	35,641
Ochiltree	5,052	1,793	160	38.81	1,408	510	1,496	400
Oldham	1,532	464	85	35.90	357	181	348	181
Orange	54,828	12,386	7,592	36.61	8,406	11,323	7,382	12,302
Palo Pinto	17,024	3,654	1,815	32.33	2,676	2,717	3,001	2,382
Panola	15,057	4,133	1,915	40.31	2,839	3,139	2,706	3,264
Parker	51,863	15,081	4,540	38.03	11,513	7,863	12,899	6,299
Parmer	4,637	1,708	270	42.70	1,219	707	1,256	691
Pecos	8,372	2,254	885	37.98	1,417	1,634	1,272	1,815
Polk	33,028	6,723	3,354	30.67	4,859	5,099	5,158	4,700
Potter	55,523	12,590	3,988	30.04	9,774	6,555	10,457	5,912
Presidio	3,841	530	806	35.01	305	931	257	1,001
Rains	5,172	1,401	663	40.08	935	1,098	1,098	901
Randall	70,779	22,644	3,733	37.43	18,414	7,826	19,892	6,208
Reagan	1,980	515	97	30.90	349	237	336	255
Real	2,451	1,085	213	53.73	730	450	684	450
Red River	8,756	1,996	1,368	38.60	1,290	1,966	1,229	2,013

County	Registered Voters	Governor		Turnout	Lt. Governor		Attorney General	
	October 98	BUSH (Rep.)	MAURO (Dem.)	Percent	PERRY (Rep.)	SHARP (Dem.)	CORNYN (Rep.)	MATTOX (Dem.)
Reeves	7,808	1,288	1,366	34.24	759	1,736	711	1,833
Refugio	5,813	1,558	867	41.85	771	1,574	810	1,527
Roberts	831	367	34	48.37	289	105	274	119
Robertson	10,564	2,085	1,893	37.78	1,437	2,494	1,397	2,521
Rockwall	24,897	7,677	1,326	36.34	6,123	2,764	6,886	1,940
Runnels	7,209	2,315	637	41.15	1,552	1,344	1,401	1,415
Rusk	28,955	6,816	2,398	31.97	5,032	4,094	5,239	3,878
Sabine	8,017	2,103	1,183	41.23	1,344	1,869	1,318	1,899
San Augustine	6,597	1,178	850	30.87	723	1,295	819	1,186
San Jacinto	13,424	3,203	1,688	36.70	2,335	2,491	2,386	2,436
San Patricio	40,159	6,922	3,462	26.00	4,692	5,437	4,750	5,377
San Saba	3,391	1,018	297	39.16	649	632	635	647
Schleicher	1,863	720	195	49.49	472	371	387	469
Scurry	11,386	3,315	755	35.93	2,141	1,845	1,940	2,016
Shackelford	2,457	861	177	42.32	604	418	549	433
Shelby	15,416	4,028	1,731	37.48	2,806	2,895	2,420	3,216
Sherman	1,655	749	118	52.38	553	293	554	289
Smith	95,541	27,579	8,840	38.80	22,631	13,503	24,165	11,833
Somervell	4,685	1,531	502	43.62	1,014	935	1,106	801
Starr	24,049	2,811	4,760	31.72	1,073	5,817	757	6,206
Stephens	5,851	1,649	504	36.95	1,247	890	1,224	895
Sterling	1,068	527	95	58.42	357	221	279	282
Stonewall	1,270	394	259	51.57	262	379	202	422
Sutton	2,501	652	158	32.54	456	331	400	362
Swisher	5,061	1,276	682	38.74	817	1,120	749	1,168
Tarrant	814,547	178,068	77,310	31.53	141,033	111,008	156,451	94,502
Taylor	78,957	23,646	5,489	37.06	18,079	10,655	17,466	11,124
Terrell	860	180	117	35.11	128	160	98	184
Terry	7,938	1,945	522	31.15	1,218	1,183	1,235	1,164
Throckmorton	1,253	454	166	49.80	338	265	267	322
Titus	14,604	3,999	2,073	41.65	2,466	3,542	2,485	3,514
Tom Green	63,409	18,171	4,920	36.57	13,123	9,536	13,238	9,408
Travis	499,696	105,544	66,872	34.96	71,378	99,598	81,113	88,348
Trinity	11,332	2,655	1,883	40.22	1,756	2,706	1,707	2,759
Tyler	12,956	3,054	1,839	37.90	2,019	2,821	1,949	2,867
Upshur	21,594	5,589	2,627	38.24	3,727	4,416	3,892	4,195
Upton	2,401	528	180	29.57	382	324	324	373
Uvalde	16,335	3,785	1,784	34.30	2,424	2,883	2,707	2,680
Val Verde	22,494	4,199	3,083	32.55	2,675	4,157	2,801	4,256
Van Zandt	30,266	9,125	3,140	40.65	6,429	5,645	7,327	4,663
Victoria	53,008	15,344	4,313	37.24	5,526	13,884	10,181	8,379
Walker	29,041	7,411	2,779	35.25	5,384	4,677	5,499	4,515
Waller	18,539	4,411	2,711	39.04	3,028	4,013	3,220	3,794
Ward	7,138	2,009	851	40.59	1,176	1,529	1,056	1,653
Washington	18,420	6,329	1,684	43.63	4,640	3,321	4,796	3,085
Webb	79,392	7,805	8,163	20.19	2,967	12,157	3,195	12,357
Wharton	22,009	6,583	2,416	41.03	3,709	5,127	4,685	4,119
Wheeler	3,651	1,420	344	48.42	1,021	699	945	718
Wichita	80,434	20,298	7,739	35.07	14,756	12,615	12,898	14,418
Wilbarger	8,819	2,442	773	36.58	1,690	1,460	1,447	1,653
Willacy	10,585	1,267	1,028	21.83	670	1,544	722	1,478
Williamson	136,466	42,075	11,724	39.73	30,832	22,331	32,596	19,940
Wilson	18,699	5,662	2,488	43.78	3,532	4,322	4,156	3,698
Winkler	4,612	1,052	361	31.04	635	733	602	776
Wise	26,573	6,899	2,518	35.63	4,887	4,414	5,599	3,590
Wood	19,813	7,229	2,324	48.42	5,481	3,963	5,735	3,671
Yoakum	4,332	1,514	326	42.72	952	803	809	943
Young	12,174	3,694	1,333	41.44	2,808	2,155	2,621	2,258
Zapata	6,500	731	851	24.44	330	1,158	293	1,206
Zavala	8,580	1,041	2,227	38.24	491	2,496	515	2,552
Statewide	11,538,235	2,550,821	1,165,592	32.39	1,858,837	1,790,106	2,002,794	1,631,045

Political Party Organizations

Democratic State Executive Committee

Chair, Molly Beth Malcolm, 919 Congress, Ste. 600, Austin 78701; **Vice Chair**, Carl Davis, 1423 Hawthorne No. 11, Houston 77006; **Vice Chair for Financial Affairs**, Clara Caldwell, 4414 Akard, Houston 77047; **Secretary**, Walter Hinojosa, 7801 Lowdes Dr., Austin 78745; **Treasurer**, Mary Almendarez, 608 Joyce St., Houston 77009; **Co-parliamentarians**, Ed Cogburn, 5002 Doliver, Houston 77056, and Frank Thompson, 6937 Peyton, Houston 77028. **Office Address:** 919 Congress, Ste. 600, Austin 78701, (512) 478-9800; **www.txdemocrats.org**.

National Committee Members: Carol Alvarado, Houston; Billie Carr, Houston; Al Edwards, Houston; Hazel Falke-Obey, Austin; Liz Lara-Carreno, Houston; William Leo, La Joya; Mike Lopez, Donna; K. T. McLeaish, Odessa; Ed Miller, Texarkana; Robert Slagle, Sherman; Oscar Soliz, Corpus Christi; Rosa Walker, Austin.

District — Member and Hometown

1. Patsy Johnson, Sulphur Springs; Leonard Rockwell, Mount Pleasant.
2. Martha Williams, Terrell; Ken Molberg, Dallas.
3. Kathleen Hawkins, Buna; Dennis Teal, Livingston.
4. Mary Kirkwood, Beaumont; John Baker, Bridge City.
5. Eddie Truitt, Wortham; Neely Lewis, Bryan.
6. Earlene Sullivan, Houston; Frumencio Reyes, Houston.
7. Linda Fischer, Spring; Bill Scruggs, Spring.
8. Peggy Wildman, Dallas; Barry Sprouse, Irving.
9. Lisa Payne, Dallas; Ron Spurlock, Lewisville.
10. Harriet Irby, Pantego; Donald Winters, Fort Worth.
11. Ceole Speight, Pasadena; Sam Munn, La Marque.
12. Gwen Marlin, Fort Worth; Grover Swift, Fort Worth.
13. Mary Seymore, Houston; Rodney Griffin, Missouri City.
14. Cecilia Crossley, Austin; Rolando Pina, Austin.
15. Etta Crockett, Houston; Keith King, Houston.
16. Theresa Daniel, Dallas; Shannon Bailey, Dallas.
17. Pat McGuire Strong, Houston; Douglas Peterson, Houston.
18. Donna Cole, Victoria; Marion Garcia, Thompsons.
19. Jo Ann McCall, San Antonio; Ben Alexander, San Antonio.
20. Susie Luna-Saldana, Corpus Christi; John Bell, Corpus Christi.
21. Minnie Dora Bunn Haynes, Laredo; Howard C. Berger, Floresville.
22. June Tucker Hicks, Carbon; Jesse Sapp, Waco.
23. Ruth Wyrick, Dallas; Roberto Alonzo, Dallas.
24. Avaloy Lanning, Brownwood; Wayne Bachus, Belton.
25. Barbara Mayo, Cedar Park; Steve Burch, San Antonio.
26. Diana Ortega, San Antonio; Darby Riley, San Antonio.
27. Graciela Sanchez, Weslaco; Mike Vega, San Benito.
28. Linda De Leon, Lubbock; Clayton Condra, Lubbock.
29. Blanche Darley, El Paso; Bob Neill, El Paso.
30. Dorthy Wise, Wichita Falls; Calvin Gambill, Seymour.
31. Linda Lowrey, Plains; George Dowlen, Amarillo.

Texas Democratic Women: Pres., Nettie Ruth Bratton, RR 2 Box 368, Kingsland 78639; Vice Pres., Mae Jackson, Waco.

Coalition of Black Democrats: Bernice G. Conley, 3034 S. Beckley, Dallas 75224; Gene O. Collins, Odessa.

Non-Urban Caucus: Chair, Anna Marie Hornsby, 3017 Newport, Texarkana 75503; Vice Chair, Michael Whitehurst, Kyle.

Tejano Democrats: Norma Chavez, El Paso; Bill Callejo, Dallas.

Young Democrats: Pres., Marisa Schouten, Austin; Vice Pres., T.G. Caraway, Lubbock.

County Chair Association: Pres., Ted Lewis, 1245 Dallas Dr., Denton 76205; Vice Pres., Lennie C. Simms, Wellington.

Republican State Executive Committee

Office Address: 211 E. 7th, Ste. 620, Austin 78701; www.texasgop.org. **Chairman,** Susan Weddington, 217 Halbert Dr., San Antonio 78213; **Vice Chairman,** David Barton, P.O. Box 397, Aledo 76008; **Secretary,** Mrs. Loyce McCarter, 150 Black Jack Rd., La Vernia 78121; **Treasurer,** Gina Parker, 3300 West Waco Dr., Waco 76710; **Associate General Counsel,** Cynthia Diaz, 8122 Datapoint Ste. 900, San Antonio 78229; **Parliamentarian,** Chris Maska, 4i601 Balcones Woods Dr. Austin 78759.

National Committeeman, Tim Lambert, P.O. Box 6621, Lubbock 79493; **National Committeewoman,** Cathy McConn, 654 Ramblewood Rd., Houston 77079-6905.

District — Member and Hometown

1. Glenn Canfield Jr., Longview; Claudia Rocha, Mount Pleasant.
2. Jeff Fisher, Canton; Connie Reese, Canton.
3. Marcia Daughtrey, Jacksonville; B.L. Dockens, Livingston.
4. Mary Jane Avery, Beaumont; David LaBrot, Kingwood.
5. R. Jean Killgore, College Station; Barnie O. Henderson Jr., Cameron.
6. Larry Bowles, Houston; Carmen Castillo, Houston.
7. Tina Johns Benkiser, Houston; Thomas M. Moon, Houston.
8. Kay C. Copeland, Dallas; Wayne Tucker, Plano.
9. Fred Kinney, Coppell; Shirley Spellerberg, Corinth.
10. Melba McDow, Arlington; John F. Mauldin, Arlington.
11. Sheryl Berg, Houston; Kenneth Clark, League City.
12. Michele A. Quinones, Haltom City; James A. Borchert, Fort Worth.
13. Betty Lou Martin, Houston; Ronald C. Meinke, Houston.
14. Kirk Overbey, Austin; Devora Kristen Griggs, Pflugerville.
15. Martha S. Greenlaw, Houston; Louis Butch Davis, Houston.
16. Denise McNamara, Dallas; Bruce Bishop, Mesquite.
17. Terese A. Raia, Sugar Land; Timothy J. Turner, Bellaire.
18. Robert K. Long, Bastrop; Myrna Patterson McLeroy, Gonzales.
19. Cindi Geeslin, San Antonio; Randy Hurt, Fort Stockton.

20. Richard L. Bowers, Corpus Christi; Patsy Sparkman, Corpus Christi.

21. Roy Casanova, San Antonio; Mrs Loyce McCarter, La Vernia.

22. Beverly S. Parks, Hico; Sam Walls, Cleburne.

23. Lawrence J. Phillips, Desoto; Suzette F. Hestilow, Grand Prairie.

24. Nancy Boston, Temple; David L. Kithil, Marble Falls.

25. Carol Everett, Austin; Allan E. Parker, San Antonio.

26. Shirley O. Thompson, San Antonio; Gene Ryder, San Antonio.

27. Debbie Moutsos, South Padre Island; Tom Wingate, McAllen.

28. Dwain Fox, Big Spring; Mrs. Skeet Workman, Ropesville.

29. Elaine Hawkins, El Paso; Roger O'Dell, El Paso.

30. Patricia C. Peale, Lake Kiowa; Frank Alvarez, Sherman.

31. Rick C. Davis Jr., Midland; Sue Hershey, Amarillo.

Texas Primary Elections, 1998

Below are the official returns for contested races only in the Republican and Democratic Party primaries held March 10, 1998. Included are statewide races and selected district races. The runoffs were held on April 14.

Democratic Primary

Attorney General
Gene Kelly	87,097
Jim Mattox	444,746
Morris L. Overstreet	122,311
Total Vote	654,154

Commissioner of Agriculture
Ernesto L. De Leon	238,791
L.P. (Pete) Patterson	353,889
Total Vote	592,680

Railroad Commissioner
Gary Dugger	206,641
Joe B. Henderson	353,171
Total Vote	559,812

Prop. 1 - Texans under HMOs to choose doctors
Yes	637,026
No	27,506
Total Vote	664,532

Prop. 2 - Prohibit sales tax on food and medicine
Yes	578,654
No	85,438
Total Vote	664,092

Prop. 3 - Recruit and retain teachers
Yes	590,119
No	56,194
Total Vote	646,313

U.S. HOUSE OF REPRESENTATIVES
District 5
William A. Foster III	7,968
Victor M. Morales	17,907
Total Vote	25,875

District 13
Mark Harmon	17,162
Ed True	8,051
Total Vote	25,213

District 14
Margaret Dunn	11,056
Roger M. Elliott	3,912
Tom Reed	12,123
Loy Sneary	18,149
Total Vote	45,240

District 20
Maria Antonietta Berriozabal	4,809
Armando Falcon	1,572
Richard Garcia	344
Charlie Gonzalez	9,482
Christine Hernandez	2,731
Walter Martinez	2,109
Steve Walker	529
Total Vote	21,576

District 23
Charlie Urbina Jones	20,686
Allen Rindfuss	5,334
Joseph P. (Joe) Sullivan	19,961
Total Vote	45,981

District 28
Lauro A. Bustamante	4,763
Oscar H. Flores	4,207
Ciro D. Rodriguez	28,201
Total Vote	37,171

COURTS OF APPEALS
Justice, Third District
Jan Patterson	41,522
Bob Roller	14,251
Total Vote	55,773

STATE BOARD OF EDUCATION
District 2
Mary Helen Berlanga	47,630
Simon O. Calvillo	9,250
Jose E. Esparza	17,114
Total Vote	73,994

Democratic Runoff

U.S. Representative, Dist. 14
Tom Reed	14,307
Loy Sneary	15,727
Total Vote	30,034

U.S. Representative, Dist. 20
Maria Antonietta Berriozabal	8,189
Charlie Gonzalez	13,439
Total Vote	21,628

U.S. Representative, Dist. 23
Charlie Urbina Jones	9,172
Joseph P. (Joe) Sullivan	8,236
Total Vote	17,408

Republican Primary

Governor
George W. Bush	576,528
R.C. Crawford	20,311
Total Vote	596,839

Attorney General
John Cornyn	176,269
Tom Pauken	162,180
Barry Williamson	208,345
Total Vote	546,794

Commissioner of the General Land Office
David Dewhurst	265,363
Don Loucks	36,706
Jerry Patterson	216,250
Total Vote	518,319

Commissioner of Agriculture
Susan Combs	388,583
Hamp Hodges	129,445
Total Vote	518,028

Railroad Commissioner
Tony Garza	292,318
Steve Stockman	257,747
Total Vote	550,065

Justice, Supreme Court, Place 2

Harriet O'Neill	313,533
Candace G. Tyson	174,951
Total Vote	488,484

Justice, Supreme Court, Place 4

Deborah Hankinson	291,053
Steve Smith	198,797
Total Vote	489,850

Judge, Court of Criminal Appeals, Place 1

David Barron	70,450
Vicki Isaacks	104,648
Mike Keasler	164,142
Lloyd W. Oliver	53,931
David A. Schulman	62,444
Total Vote	455,615

Judge, Court of Criminal Appeals, Place 2

Murff F. Bledsoe	45,360
Harvey Hudson	111,104
Cheryl Johnson	117,201
Jeffrey Brian Keck	31,600
Forrest Lumpkin	34,893
John C. Moncure	21,110
William Harrison Ray	31,676
Jerry E. Smith	47,379
Total Vote	440,323

Judge, Court of Criminal Appeals, Place 3

Herb Hancock	186,017
Lawrence (Larry) Meyers	248,972
Total Vote	434,989

U.S. HOUSE OF REPRESENTATIVES
District 4

Ray Hall	6,258
Douglas Jones	1,457
Jim Lohmeyer	19,205
Geoffrey Fielding Walsh	975
Total Vote	27,895

District 6

Joe Barton	21,480
Greg Mullanax	7,965
Total Vote	29,445

District 7

Bill Archer	28,625
Gene Hsiao	961
Total Vote	29,586

District 8

Kevin Brady	34,841
André Dean	4,452
Total Vote	39,293

District 9

Don Beagle	1,944
Tom Cottar	5,451
Onzelo Markum	2,048
Adonn Slone	2,617
Total Vote	12,060

District 13

Richard Amon	1,345
Mac Thornberry	19,827
Total Vote	21,172

District 20

John Shull	3,384
James Walker	5,729
Total Vote	9,113

District 24

Stan C. Penn	2,715
Shawn Terry	6,723
Total Vote	9,438

District 25

Bill Brock	2,362
Beverley Clark	5,027
John M. Sanchez	6,673
Total Vote	14,062

STATE SENATE
District 4

Michael Galloway	9,834
Bill Leigh	8,400
Total Vote	18,234

COURTS OF APPEALS
Justice, Third District

David Puryear	33,909
Lee Yeakel	13,426
Total Vote	47,335

Justice, Tenth District

Tom Gray	13,738
Bill Vannatta	7,155
Total Vote	20,893

Justice, Eleventh District

Terry McCall	11,035
Robert Pelton	2,139
Kollin Shadle	3,557
Total Vote	16,731

Justice, Twelfth District

Charles Holcomb	13,262
Jim Worthen	14,684
Total Vote	27,946

STATE BOARD OF EDUCATION
District 1

Donna Ballard	12,962
Mary Helen Cantú	4,836
Total Vote	17,798

District 9

Lee Burch	13,279
Don McLeroy	19,944
Total Vote	33,223

District 15

Nancy Neal	32,318
Judy Strickland	33,351
Total Vote	65,669

Republican Runoff

Attorney General

John Cornyn	135,130
Barry Williamson	98,218
Total Vote	233,348

Judge, Court of Criminal Appeals, Place 1

Vicki Isaacks	77,575
Mike Keasler	130,764
Total Vote	208,339

Judge, Court of Criminal Appeals, Place 2

Harvey Hudson	100,818
Cheryl Johnson	104,773
Total Vote	205,591

U.S. Representative, Dist. 9

Tom Cottar	2,646
Adonn Slone	2,057
Total Vote	4,703

U.S. Representative, Dist. 25

Beverley Clark	3,953
John M. Sanchez	6,057
Total Vote	10,010

Constitutional Amendment Elections

Held Aug. 9, 1997
Prop. 1 - Increasing residence homestead exemption

In Favor	693,522
Against	45,619
Total Vote	739,141

Held Nov. 4, 1997
Prop. 1 - Municipal court judges to hold more than one office

In Favor	423,793
Against	731,044
Total Vote	1,154,837

Prop. 2 - Limit increases in residence homesteads for ad valorem tax

In Favor	852,031
Against	273,957
Total Vote	1,125,988

Prop. 3 - Granting exemption on property for water conservation initiative

In Favor	681,060

Against. 420,923
   Total Vote 1,101,983

**Prop. 4 - Eliminate duplicate numbering
in Constitution**
In Favor 865,397
Against. 232,350
   Total Vote 1,097,747

Prop. 5 - Supreme Court to sit anywhere in Texas
In Favor 665,617
Against. 458,791
   Total Vote 1,124,408

**Prop. 6 - Allow Texas Growth Fund to continue
to invest without disclosure**
In Favor 562,535
Against. 564,070
   Total Vote 1,126,605

**Prop. 7 - Texas Water Development to transfer bonds
for water supply, etc.**
In Favor 707,498
Against. 398,795
   Total Vote 1,106,293

**Prop. 8 - Expand types of liens
for home equity loans**
In Favor 698,870
Against. 474,443
   Total Vote 1,173,313

**Prop. 9 - Authorize ad valorem tax rate in rural
fire prevention districts**

In Favor 558,400
Against. 492,666
   Total Vote 1,051,066

**Prop. 10 - Compensation to victims of crime fund
and crime auxiliary fund**
In Favor 763.646
Against. 345,563
   Total Vote 1,109,209

**Prop. 11 - Limiting amount of state debt payable
from general revenue fund**
In Favor 742,798
Against. 350,317
   Total Vote 1,093,155

**Prop. 12 - Deadline for Supreme Court on motion
for rehearing**
In Favor 858,513
Against. 253,254
   Total Vote 1,111,767

**Prop. 13 - Establish Texas tomorrow fund
as protected trust fund**
In Favor 811,873
Against. 314,516
   Total Vote 1,126,389

**Prop. 14 - Legislature to prescribe qualifications
of constables**
In Favor 869,156
Against. 244,472
   Total Vote 1,113,628

Elections of Texas Governors, 1845-1994

Following are the results of elections of governors since Texas became a state in 1845. Party primaries, as well as general elections, are included whenever possible, although Republican totals are not available for some elections. Prior to 1857, most candidates ran independently. Party designations are in parentheses; an explanation of abbreviations is at the end of the list.

1845
J.P. Henderson 7,853
J.B. Miller. 1,673
Scattering 52
   Total vote.   9,578

1847
George T. Wood. 7,154
J. B. Miller 5,106
N. H. Darnell 1,276
J. J. Robinson 379
Scattering 852
   Total vote 14,767

1849
P. H. Bell 10,319
George T. Wood. 8,764
John T. Mills. 2,632
   Total vote 21,715

1851
P. H. Bell 13,595
M. T. Johnson. 5,262
John A. Greer 4,061
B. H. Epperson 2,971
T. J. Chambers. 2,320
Scattering 100
   Total vote 28,309

1853
E. M. Pease 13,091
W. B. Ochiltree. 9,178
George T. Wood. 5,983
L. D. Evans 4,677
T. J. Chambers. 2,449
John Dancy 315
   Total vote 35,693

1855

E. M. Pease 26,336
D. C. Dickson 18,968
M. T. Johnson 809
George T. Wood 226
   Total vote. 46,339

1857
H. R. Runnels (Dem.) . . . 32,552
Sam Houston 28,628
   Total vote. 61,180

1859
*Sam Houston 36,227
H. R. Runnels (Dem.) . . . 27,500
Scattering. 61
   Total vote. 63,788
*Ran as independent but received support of Know-Nothing Party.
Edward Clark succeeded Sam Houston on March 16, 1861, shortly after Texas seceded.

1861
F. R. Lubbock 21,854
Edward Clark 21,730
T. J. Chambers 13,759
   Total vote. 57,343

1863
Pendleton Murrah. 17,511
T. J. Chambers 12,455
Scattering. 1,070
   Total vote. 31,036

A. J. Hamilton was named governor under Reconstruction administration June 17, 1865.

1866
J. W. Throckmorton. 49,277
E. M. Pease 12,168

   Total vote 61,445
E. M. Pease was appointed governor July 30, 1867.

1869
E. J. Davis. 39,901
A. J. Hamilton 39,092
Hamilton Stuart. 380
   Total vote 79,373

1873
Richard Coke (Dem.) . . . 85,549
E. J. Davis (Rep.) 42,633
   Total vote 128,182

1876
Richard Coke (Dem.) . . 150,581
William Chambers(Rep.) . 47,719
   Total vote 198,300
Lt. Gov. R. B. Hubbard succeeded Dec. 1, 1876, when Coke became U.S. Senator.

1878
O. M. Roberts (Dem.) . . 158,933
W. H. Hamman (Greenback) 55,002
A. B. Norton (Rep.) 23,402
Scattering 99
   Total vote 237,436

1880
O. M. Roberts (Dem.) . . 166,101
E. J. Davis (Rep.) 64,382
W. H. Hamman (Greenback) 33,721
   Total vote 264,204

1882
John Ireland (Dem.) . . . 150,809

G. W. Jones (Green-back)	102,501
J. B. Robertson (I.Dem.)	334
Total vote	253,644

1884

John Ireland (Dem.)	212,234
Geo. W. Jones(Green-back)	88,450
A. B. Norton (Rep.)	25,557
Total vote	326,241

1886

L. S. Ross (Dem.)	228,776
A. M. Cochran (Rep.) . . .	65,236
E. L. Dohoney (Prohi.) . .	19,186
Scattering	102
Total vote	313,300

1888

L. S. Ross (Dem.)	250,338
Marion Martin (Ind.Fus.).	98,447
Total vote	348,785

1890

J. S. Hogg (Dem.)	262,432
W. Flanagan (Rep.)	77,742
E. C. Heath (Prohi.)	2,235
Total vote	342,409

1892

J. S. Hogg (Dem.)	190,486
George Clark (Dem.) . . .	133,395
T. L. Nugent (Peo.)	108,483
A. J. Houston (Ref.Rep.).	1,322
D. M. Prendergast (Prohi.)	1,605
Scattering	176
Total vote	435,467

1894

C. A. Culberson (Dem.) .	207,167
T. L. Nugent (Peo.)	152,731
W. K. Makemson (Rep.) .	54,520
J. B. Schmitz (L.W.Rep.).	5,036
J. M. Dunn (Prohi.)	2,196
Scattering	1,076
Total vote	422,726

1896

C. A. Culberson (Dem.)	298,528
J. C. Kearby (Peo.)	238,692
Randolph Clark (Prohi.)	1,876
Scattering	682
Total vote	539,778

1898

J. D. Sayers (Dem.)	291,548
Barnett Gibbs (Peo.) . . .	114,955
R. P. Bailey (Prohi.)	2,437
G. H. Royall (Soc. Lab.) .	552
Scattering	62
Total vote	409,554

1900

J. D. Sayers (Dem.)	303,586
R. E. Hanney (Rep.)	112,864
T. J. McMinn (Peo.)	26,864
G. H. Royall (Soc. Lab.) .	155
Scattering	6,155
Total vote	449,624

1902

S. W. T. Lanham (Dem.) .	219,076
George W. Burkett (Rep.)	65,706
J. M. Mallett (Peo.)	12,387
G. W. Carroll (Prohi.) . . .	8,708
Scattering	3,273
Total vote	309,150

1904

S. W. T. Lanham (Dem.) .	206,160
J. G. Lowden (Rep.)	56,865
Pat B. Clark (Peo.)	9,301
W. D. Jackson (Prohi.). . .	4,509
Frank Leitner (Soc. Lab.)	552
W. H. Mills (Soc. Dem.)..	2,487
Total vote	279,874

1906

The popular vote in the state's first primary in the Democratic party was as follows:

Thomas M. Campbell . . .	90,345
M. M. Brooks.	70,064
O. B. Colquitt.	68,529
Charles K. Bell	65,168
Total vote	294,106

General Election

T. M. Campbell (Dem.) . .	148,264
C. A. Gray (Rep.)	23,711
J. W. Pearson (Prohi.) . . .	5,252
G. C. Edwards (Soc.) . . .	2,958
A. S. Dowler (Soc. Lab.).	260
A. W. Atcheson (Reor. Rep.)	5,395
Total vote	185,840

1908
Democratic Primary

T. M. Campbell	202,608
R. R. Williams	117,459
Total vote	320,067

General Election

T. M. Campbell (Dem.) . .	218,956
J. N. Simpson (Rep.)	73,305
J. C. Rhodes (Soc.)	8,100
W. B. Cook (Soc. Lab.) . .	234
E. C. Heath (Prohi.)	148
Total vote	300,743

1910
Democratic Primary

O. B. Colquitt.	146,526
William Poindexter	79,711
R. V. Davidson.	53,187
Cone Johnson	76,050
J. Marion Jones	1,906
Total vote	357,380

General Election

O. B. Colquitt (Dem.)	174,596
J. O. Terrell (Rep.)	26,191
Redding Andrews (Soc.).	11,538
A. J. Houston (Prohi.) . . .	6,052
Carl Schmidt (Soc. Lab.).	426
Total vote	218,803

1912
Democratic Primary

O. B. Colquitt.	218,812
William F. Ramsey	177,183
Total vote	395,995

General Election

O. B. Colquitt (Dem.)	234,352
Ed Lasater (Prog.)	15,794
C. W. Johnson (Rep.) . . .	23,089
A. J. Houston (Prohi.) . . .	2,356
Redding Andrews (Soc.).	25,258
K. E. Choate (Soc. Lab.).	308
Total vote	301,157

1914
Democratic Primary

James E. Ferguson.	237,062
Thomas H. Ball	191,558

Total vote	428,620

General Election

J. E. Ferguson (Dem.) . .	176,599
F. M. Etheridge (Prog.). .	1,794
John W. Philp (Rep.) . . .	11,411
E. Meitzen (Soc.)	24,977
Total vote	214,781

1916
Democratic Primary

James E. Ferguson	240,561
Charles H. Morris.	174,611
H. C. Marshall	6,731
Total vote	421,903

General Election

J. E. Ferguson (Dem.) . .	296,667
R. B. Creager (Rep.) . . .	49,118
E. Meitzen (Soc.)	14,580
H. W. Lewis (Prohi.)	3,200
Total vote	363,565

In 1917 Ferguson was removed from office and succeeded by Hobby.

1918
Democratic Primary

W. P. Hobby	461,479
James E. Ferguson	217,012
Total vote	678,491

General Election

W. P. Hobby (Dem.)	148,982
Chas. A. Boynton (Rep.).	26,713
Wm. D. Simpson (Soc.) .	1,660
Total vote	177,355

1920

In 1918 the primary election law had been amended, requiring a majority for nomination. The **first double primary in the governor's race** was in 1920.

1st Democratic Primary

Pat M. Neff.	149,818
Robert E. Thomason . . .	99,002
Joseph W. Bailey	152,340
Ben F. Looney	48,640
Total vote	449,800

2nd Democratic Primary

Pat M. Neff.	264,075
Joseph W. Bailey	184,702
Total vote	448,777

General Election

Pat M. Neff (Dem.).	289,188
J. G. Culberson (Rep.) . .	90,217
H. Capers (B. T. Rep.) . .	26,091
T. H. McGregor (Amer.) .	69,380
L. L. Rhodes (Soc.)	6,796
Scattering	59
Total vote	481,731

1922
Democratic Primary

Pat M. Neff.	318,000
W. W. King	18,368
Fred S. Rogers	195,941
Harry T. Warner	57,671
Total vote	589,926

General Election

Pat M. Neff (Dem.)	334,199
W. H. Atwell (Rep.)	73,329
Total vote	407,528

1924
1st Democratic Primary

Felix D. Robertson	193,508
George W. Dixon	4,035

W. E. Pope	17,136
Joe Burkett	21,720
Miriam A. Ferguson	146,424
Lynch Davidson	141,208
V. A. Collins	24,864
T. W. Davidson	125,011
Thomas D. Barton	29,217
Total vote	703,123

2nd Democratic Primary

Miriam A. Ferguson	413,751
Felix D. Robertson	316,019
Total vote	729,770

General Election

Miriam A. Ferguson (Dem.)	422,558
George C. Butte (Rep.)	294,970
Total vote	717,528

1926
1st Democratic Primary

Lynch Davidson	122,449
Miriam A. Ferguson	283,482
Kate M. Johnston	1,029
Dan Moody	409,732
Edith E. Wilmans	1,580
O. F. Zimmerman	2,962
Total vote	821,234

2nd Democratic Primary

Miriam A. Ferguson	270,595
Dan Moody	495,723
Total vote	766,318

Republican Primary
(Party's first statewide.)

H. H. Haines	11,215
E. P. Scott	4,074
Total vote	15,289

General Election

Dan Moody (Dem.)	233,068
H. H. Haines (Rep.)	31,531
M. A. Smith (Soc.)	908
Total vote	265,507

1928
Democratic Party

Wm. E. Hawkins	32,076
Dan Moody	442,080
Louis J. Wardlaw	245,508
Edith E. Wilmans	18,237
Total vote	737,901

General Election,

Dan Moody (Dem.)	582,972
W. H. Holmes (Rep.)	120,504
T. Stedman (Com.)	109
L. L. Rhodes (Soc.)	738
Scattering	2,683
Total vote	707,006

1930
1st Democratic Primary

Miriam A. Ferguson	242,959
Thomas B. Love	87,068
Paul Loven	2,724
Earle B. Mayfield	54,459
Barry Miller	54,652
C. C. Moody	4,382
Frank Putnam	2,365
Clint C. Small	138,934
Ross S. Sterling	170,754
James Young	73,385
C. E. Walker	1,760
Total vote	833,442

2nd Democratic Primary

Ross S. Sterling	473,371
Miriam A. Ferguson	384,402

Total vote	857,773

Republican Primary

George C. Butte	5,001
H. E. Exum	2,773
John F. Grant	1,800
John P. Gaines	203
Total vote	9,777

General Election

Ross S. Sterling (Dem.)	252,738
Wm. E. Talbot (Rep.)	62,224
Total vote	314,962

1932
1st Democratic Primary

Roger Q. Evans	3,974
Miriam A. Ferguson	402,238
C. A. Frakes	2,338
J. Ed Glenn	2,089
Tom F. Hunter	220,391
Frank Putnam	2,962
Ross S. Sterling	296,383
M. H. Wolfe	32,241
George W. Armstrong	5,312
Total vote	967,928

2nd Democratic Primary

Ross S. Sterling	473,846
Miriam A. Ferguson	477,644
Total Vote	951,490

General Election

M.A. Ferguson (Dem.)	528,986
Orville Bullington (Rep.)	317,807
George C. Edwards (Soc.)	1,866
George W. Armstrong (Jacksonian Dem.)	706
Otho L. Heitt (Liberty)	101
Philip L. Howe (Com.)	72
Total vote	849,538

1934
1st Democratic Primary

C. C. McDonald	206,007
James V. Allred	297,656
Clint C. Small	124,206
Tom F. Hunter	241,339
Edgar Witt	62,208
Edward K. Russell	4,408
Maury Hughes	58,187
Total vote	994,011

2nd Democratic Primary

James V. Allred	497,808
Tom F. Hunter	457,785
Total vote	995,593

Republican Primary

D. E. Waggoner	13,043

General Election

James V. Allred (Dem.)	421,422
D. E. Wagonner (Rep.)	13,534
George C. Edwards (Soc.)	1,877
Enoch Hardaway (Com.)	244
Total vote	437,077

1936
Democratic Primary

James V. Allred	553,219
P. Pierce Brooks	33,391
F. W. Fischer	145,877
Tom F. Hunter	239,460
Roy Sanderford	81,170
Total vote	1,053,117

General Election

James V. Allred (Dem.)	782,083

C. O. Harris (Rep.)	58,842
Carl Brannin (Soc.)	962
Homer Brooks (Com.)	283
Total vote	842,170

1938
Democratic Primary

W. Lee O'Daniel	573,166
Ernest O. Thompson	231,630
William McCraw	152,278
Tom F. Hunter	117,634
S. T. Brogdon	892
Joseph King	773
Clarence E. Farmer	3,869
P. D. Renfro	8,127
Karl A. Crowley	19,153
Clarence R. Miller	667
James A. Ferguson	3,800
Thomas Self	1,405
Marvin P. McCoy	1,491
Total vote	1,114,885

General Election

W. Lee O'Daniel (Dem.)	473,526
Alexander Boynton (Rep.)	10,940
Earl E. Miller (Soc.)	398
Homer Brooks (Com.)	424
Total vote	485,288

1940
Democratic Primary

W. Lee O'Daniel	645,646
Ernest O. Thompson	256,923
Harry Hines	119,121
Miriam A. Ferguson	100,578
Jerry Sadler	61,396
Arlon B. "Cyclone" Davis Jr.	3,625
R. P. Condron	2,001
Total vote	1,189,290

General Election

W. Lee O'Daniel (Dem.)	1,019,338
George C. Hopkins (Rep.)	59,885
Ben H. Lauderdale (Com.)	202
Scattering	113
Total vote	1,079,538

1942
Democratic Primary

Hal H. Collins	272,469
Alex M. Ferguson	8,370
Gene S. Porter	4,933
Charles L. Somerville	4,853
Coke R. Stevenson	651,218
Hope Wheeler	9,373
Total vote	951,216

General Election

Coke R. Stevenson (Dem.)	280,735
C. K. McDowell (Rep.)	9,204
Total vote	289,939

1944
Democratic Primary

Coke R. Stevenson	696,586
Martin Jones	21,379
W. J. Minton	8,537
Alex M. Ferguson	12,649
Minnie F. Cunningham	48,039
Gene S. Porter	15,243
Edward L. Carey	4,633
William F. Grimes	9,443
Herbert E. Mills	6,640
Write-in votes	311
Total vote	823,460

General Election

Coke R. Stevenson (Dem.)	1,007,826
B. J. Peasley (Rep.)	100,287
Total vote	1,108,113

1946
1st Democratic Primary

Floyd Brinkley	4,249
William V. Brown	3,902
A. J. Burks	4,881
Chas. B. Hutchison	4,616
Beauford Jester	443,804
Walter Scott McNutt	4,353
Caso March	20,529
W. J. Minton	2,398
Homer P. Rainey	291,282
Jerry Sadler	103,120
Grover Sellers	162,431
C. R. Shaw	9,764
John Lee Smith	102,941
Reese Turner	4,914
Total vote	1,163,184

2nd Democratic Primary

Beauford H. Jester	701,018
Homer P. Rainey	335,654
Total vote	1,056,672

General Election

Beauford Jester (Dem.)	345,513
Eugene Nolte Jr. (Rep.)	33,231
Total vote	378,744

1948
Democratic Primary

Beauford H. Jester	642,025
Sumpter W. Stockton	21,243
Roger Q. Evans	279,602
Charles B. Hutchison	24,441
Holmes A. May	20,538
Caso March	187,658
W. J. Minton	13,659
Denver S. Whiteley	16,090
Write-in votes	1
Total vote	1,205,257

General Election

Beauford H. Jester (Dem.)	1,024,160
Alvin H. Lane (Rep.)	177,399
Gerald Overholt (Prohi.)	3,554
Herman Wright (Prog.)	3,747
Total vote	1,208,860

1950
Democratic Primary

Allan Shivers	829,730
Caso March	195,997
Charles B. Hutchison	16,048
Gene S. Porter	14,728
J. M. Wren	14,138
Benita Louise Marek Lawrence	9,542
Wellington Abbey	6,381
Total vote	1,086,564

General Election

Allan Shivers (Dem.)	355,010
Ralph W. Currie (Rep.)	39,737
Total vote	374,747

1952
Democratic Primary

Allan Shivers'	883,861
Ralph W. Yarborough	488,345
Allene M. Trayler	34,186
Total vote	1,356,392

General Election

*Allan Shivers (Dem.)	1,375,547
*Allan Shivers (Rep.)	468,319
Total vote	1,843,866

*Ran on both tickets.

1954
1st Democratic Primary

Allan Shivers	668,913
Ralph W. Yarborough	645,994
J. J. Holmes	19,591
Arlon B. "Cyclone" Davis	16,254
Total vote	1,350,752

2nd Democratic Primary

Allan Shivers	775,088
Ralph W. Yarborough	683,132
Total vote	1,458,220

General Election

Allan Shivers (Dem.)	569,533
Tod R. Adams (Rep.)	66,154
Other	1,205
Total vote	636,892

1956
1st Democratic Primary

Price Daniel	628,914
J. Evetts Haley	88,772
J. J. Holmes	10,165
W. Lee O'Daniel	347,757
Reuben Senterfitt	37,774
Ralph Yarborough	463,416
Write-in	72
Total vote	1,576,870

2nd Democratic Primary

Price Daniel	698,001
Ralph Yarborough	694,830
Total vote	1,392,831

General Election

Price Daniel (Dem.)	1,350,736
William R. Bryant (Rep.)	261,283
W. Lee O'Daniel (Write-in)	110,234
Other	1,838
Total vote	1,724,091

1958
Democratic Primary

Price Daniel	799,107
Henry B. Gonzalez	246,969
Joe A. Irwin	33,643
W. Lee O'Daniel	238,767
Write-in	6
Total vote	1,317,492

General Election

Price Daniel (Dem.)	695,779
Edwin S. Mayer (Rep.)	94,086
Total vote	789,865

1960
Democratic Primary

Jack Cox	619,834
Price Daniel	908,992
Write-in	8
Total vote	1,528,834

General Election

Price Daniel (Dem.)	1,627,698
Wm. M. Steger (Rep.)	609,808
Total vote	2,237,506

1962
1st Democratic Primary

John Connally	431,498
Price Daniel	248,524
Marshall Formby	139,094
Edwin A. Walker	138,387
Will Wilson	171,617

Don Yarborough	317,986
Write-in	9
Total vote	1,447,115

2nd Democratic Primary

John Connally	565,174
Don Yarborough	538,924
Total vote	1,104,098

Republican Primary

Jack Cox	99,170
Roy Whittenburg	16,136
Total vote	115,306

General Election

John Connally (Dem.)	847,038
Jack Cox (Rep.)	715,025
Jack Carswell (Con.)	7,135
Total vote	1,569,198

1964
Democratic Primary

John Connally	1,125,884
Don Yarborough	471,411
M. T. Banks	22,047
Johnnie Mae Hackworthe	10,955
Total vote	1,630,297

Republican Primary

Jack Crichton	128,146

General Election

John Connally (Dem.)	1,877,793
Jack Crichton (Rep.)	661,675
John C. Williams (Con.)	5,257
Write-in	28
Total vote	2,544,753

1966
Democratic Primary

John Connally	932,641
Stanley C. Woods	291,651
Johnnie Mae Hackworthe	31,105
Write-in votes	3
Total vote	1,255,400

Republican Primary

T. E. Kennerly	49,568

General Election

John Connally (Dem.)	1,037,517
T. E. Kennerly (Rep.)	368,025
Tommye Gillespie (Con.)	10,454
Bard Logan (Conserv.)	9,810
Write-ins	55
Total vote	1,425,861

1968
1st Democratic Primary

Preston Smith	386,875
Pat O'Daniel	47,912
John Hill	154,908
Waggoner Carr	257,543
Eugene Locke	218,118
Dolph Briscoe	225,686
Edward L. Whittenburg	22,957
Don Yarborough	421,607
Alfonso Veloz	9,562
Johnnie Mae Hackworthe	5,484
Total vote	1,750,652

2nd Democratic Primary

Preston Smith	767,490
Don Yarborough	621,226
Total vote	1,388,716

Republican Primary

Paul Eggers	65,501
John Trice	28,849

Wallace Sisk	10,415
Total vote	104,765

General Election
Preston Smith (Dem.)	1,662,019
Paul Eggers (Rep.)	1,254,333
Total vote	2,916,352

1970
Democratic Primary
Preston Smith	1,011,300

Republican Primary
Paul Eggers	101,875
Roger Martin	7,146
Total vote	109,021

General Election
Preston Smith (Dem.)	1,232,506
Paul Eggers (Rep.)	1,073,831
Other	428
Total vote	2,306,765

1972
1st Democratic Primary
Ben Barnes	392,356
Dolph Briscoe	963,397
Frances Farenthold	612,051
Robert E. Looney	10,225
William H. Posey	13,727
Preston Smith	190,709
Gordon F. Wills	10,438
Total vote	2,192,903

2nd Democratic Primary
Dolph Briscoe	1,095,168
Frances Farenthold	884,594
Total vote	1,979,762

1st Republican Primary
Albert Fay	24,329
Henry C. Grover	37,118
John A. Hall Sr.	8,018
J. A. Jenkins	4,864
Tom McElroy	19,559
David Reagan	20,119
Total vote	114,007

2nd Republican Primary
Albert Fay	19,166
Henry C. Grover	37,842
Total vote	57,008

General Election
Dolph Briscoe (Dem.)	1,633,493
Henry C. Grover (Rep.)	1,533,986
Ramsey Muniz (Raza)	214,118
Deborah Leonard (Soc.)	24,103
Other	3,891
Total vote	3,409,501

1974
Democratic Primary
Dolph Briscoe	1,025,632
Frances Farenthold	437,287
W. H. Posey	31,498
Steve S. Alexander	26,889
Total vote	1,521,306

Republican Primary
Jim Granberry	53,617
Odell McBrayer	15,484
Total vote	69,101

General Election
Dolph Briscoe (Dem.)	1,016,334
Jim Granberry (Rep.)	514,725
Ramsey Muniz (Raza)	93,295
Sherry Smith (Soc.)	8,171
S. W. McDonnell (Am.)	22,208
Other	251

Total vote	1,654,984

1978
Democratic Primary
Donald R. Beagle	14,791
Dolph Briscoe	753,309
John Hill	932,345
Ray Allen Mayo	20,249
Preston Smith	92,202
Total vote	1,812,896

Republican Primary
William P. Clements Jr.	115,345
Ray Hutchison	38,268
Clarence Thompson	4,790
Total vote	158,403

General Election
John Hill (Dem.)	1,166,919
Bill Clements (Rep.}	1,183,828
Mario C. Compean (Raza)	14,213
Sara Jean Johnston (Soc.)	4,624
Other	115
Total vote	2,369,699

1982
Democratic Primary
David L. Young	25,386
Bob Armstrong	262,189
Mark White	592,658
Donald R. Beagle	15,649
Ray Allen Mayo	20,088
*Buddy Temple	402,693
Total vote	1,318,663

*Temple declined to participate in runoff; White declared winner of race.

Republican Primary
William P. Clements Jr.	246,120
Duke Embs	19,731
Total vote	265,851

General Election
Mark White (Dem.)	1,697,870
William P. Clements Jr. (Rep.)	1,465,937
David Hutzelman (Ind.)	19,143
Bob Poteet (Con.)	8,065
Other	76
Total vote	3,191,091

1986
Democratic Primary
Sheila Bilyeu	39,370
Andrew C. Briscoe III	248,850
A. Don Crowder	120,999
Bobby Locke	58,936
Ron Slover	38,861
Mark White	589,536
Total vote	1,096,552

Republican Primary
William P. Clements Jr	318,808
Kent Hance	108,238
Tom Loeffler	117,673
Total vote	544,719

Following are the **vote totals as canvassed by the Republican Party:**
William P. Clements Jr.	318,938
Kent Hance	108,583
Tom Loeffler	118,224
Total vote	545,745

General Election
Mark White (Dem.)	1,584,515
William P. Clements Jr.(Rep.)	1,813,779
Theresa Doyle (Lib.)	42,496

Other	670
Total vote	3,441,460

1990
1st Democratic Primary
Stanley Adams	16,118
Theresa Hearn-Haynes	31,395
Earl Holmes	17,904
Jim Mattox	546,103
Ray Rachal	9,388
Ann W. Richards	580,191
Mark White	288,161
Total vote	1,487,280

2nd Democratic Primary
Jim Mattox	481,739
Ann W. Richards	640,995
Total vote	1,122,734

Republican Primary
Ed Cude	1,077
Kent Hance	132,142
Tom Luce	115,835
W. N. Otwell	2,310
Royce X. Owens	1,392
Jack Rains	82,461
Clayton Williams	520,014
Total vote	855,231

General Election
Clayton Williams (Rep.)	1,826,431
Ann W. Richards (Dem.)	1,925,670
Jeff Daiell (Lib.)	129,128
Write-Ins (19)	11,517
Total vote	3,892,746

1994
1st Democratic Primary
Gary Espinosa	230,337
Ann W. Richards	806,607
Total vote	1,036,944

1st Republican Primary
George W. Bush	520,130
Ray Hollis	37,210
Total vote	557,340

General Election
Ann W. Richards (Dem.)	2,016,928
George W. Bush (Rep.)	2,350,994
Keary Ehlers (Lib.)	28,320
Total vote	4,396,242

Abbreviations used are:
(Dem.) Democrat,
(Rep.) Republican,
(Lib.) Libertarian,
(Ind.) Independent,
(I. Dem.) Independent Democrat,
(Prohi.) Prohibitionist,
(Ind. Fus.) Independent Fusion,
(Peo.) People's (Populist),
(Ref. Rep.) Reformed Republican,
(L.W. Rep.) Lily White Republican,
(Soc. Lab.) Socialist-Labor,
(Reor. Rep.) Reorganized Republican,
(Soc.) Socialist,
(Prog.) Progressive,
(B.T. Rep.) Black and Tan Republican,
(Amer.) American,
(Com.) Communist,
(Con.) Constitution,
(Conserv.) Conservative,
(Raz.) La Raza Unida.

State Government

Texas state government is divided into executive, legislative and judicial branches under the Texas Constitution adopted in 1876. The chief executive is the Governor, whose term is for 4 years. Other elected state officials with executive responsibilities include the Lieutenant Governor, Attorney General, Comptroller of Public Accounts, Commissioner of the General Land Office and Commissioner of Agriculture. The terms of those officials are also 4 years. The Secretary of State is appointed by the Governor.

Except for making numerous appointments and calling special sessions of the Legislature, the Governor's powers are limited in comparison with those in most states.

Current state executives and their addresses, phone numbers and proposed salaries for the 2000-2001 biennium (the salaries were subject to review at press time in summer, 1999):

Governor: George W. Bush
P.O. Box 12428, Austin 78711
512-463-2000; www.governor.state.tx.us
$115,345

Lt. Governor: Rick Perry
P.O. Box 12068, Austin 78711
512-463-0001; www.senate.state.tx.us
For salary, see note* below.

Attorney General: John Cornyn
P.O. Box 12548, Austin 78711
512-463-2100; www.oag.state.tx.us
$92,217

Comptroller of Public Accounts: Carole Keeton Rylander
PO Box 13528, Austin 78774
512-463-4000; www.cpa.state.tx.us
$92,217

Land Commissioner: David Dewhurst
1700 N. Congress, Austin 78701
512-463-5256; www.glo.state.tx.us
$92,217

Commissioner of Agriculture: Susan Combs
P.O. Box 12847, Austin 78711
512-463-7664; www.agr.state.tx.us
$92,217

Secretary of State: Elton Bomer
P.O. Box 12887, Austin 78711
512-463-5770; www.sos.state.tx.us
$76,966

Salary of Lt. Gov. is same as a Senator when serving as Pres. of Senate; same as Gov. when serving as Gov.

Ombudsman Office (Citizens' Advocate): Part of the Governor's office, the Ombudsman Office receives citizens's comments and complaints over the toll-free assistance hotline and passes them to government officials and refers citizens to sources of help.
Citizens' Assistance Hotline: 1-800-843-5789.

Texas Legislature

The Texas Legislature has **181 members: 31 in the Senate and 150 in the House of Representatives.** Regular sessions convene on the second Tuesday of January in odd-numbered years, but the governor may call special sessions. Article III of the Texas Constitution deals with the legislative branch. On the Web: **www.capitol.state.tx.us**.
The following lists are of members of the 76th Legislature, which convened on Jan. 12, 1999.

State Senate

Thirty-one members of the State Senate are elected to **four-year, overlapping terms. Salary:** The salary of all members of the Legislature, both Senators and Representatives, is $7,200 per year and $119 per diem during legislative sessions; mileage allowance at same rate provided by law for state employees. The per diem payment applies during each regular and special session of the Legislature.

Senatorial Districts include one or more whole counties and some counties have more than one Senator.

The **address of Senators** is Texas Senate, P.O. Box 12068, Austin 78711-2068; phone 512-463-0001; Fax: 512-463-0326. On the Web: www.senate.state.tx.us.

President of the Senate is Lt. Gov. Rick Perry; **President Pro Tempore — Interim**, Rodney Ellis (D-Houston); **Secretary of the Senate**, Betty King; **Sergeant-at-Arms**, Carleton Turner.

Texas State Senators
Dist., Name, Party-Hometown; Year Current Term Ends; Occupation.

1. Bill Ratliff, R-Mt. Pleasant; 2003; consulting engineer.
2. David Cain, D-Dallas; 2001; attorney.
3. Drew Nixon, R-Carthage; 2001; CPA, securities/insurance agency.
4. David Bernsen, D-Beaumont; Jan. 2003; attorney.
5. Steve Ogden, R-Bryan; 2003; oil and gas producer.
6. Mario Gallegos Jr., D-Galena Park; 2003; ret. fire capt.
7. Jon Lindsay, R-Houston; 2001; business consultant.
8. Florence Shapiro, R-Plano; 2001; businesswoman.
9. Jane Nelson, R-Flower Mound; 2001; businesswoman.
10. Chris Harris, R-Arlington; 2001; attorney.
11. Mike Jackson, R-La Porte; 2003; businessman.
12. Mike Moncrief, D-Fort Worth; 2001; businessman.
13. Rodney Ellis, D-Houston; 2003; director, securities firm/attorney.
14. Gonzalo Barrientos, D-Austin; 2001; advertising/public relations.
15. John Whitmire, D-Houston; 2001; attorney.
16. John J. Carona, R-Dallas; 2003; company pres.
17. J. E. "Buster" Brown, R-Lake Jackson; 2003; attorney.
18. Kenneth Armbrister, D-Victoria; 2003; businessman.
19. Frank L. Madla, D-San Antonio; 2003; real estate, insurance.
20. Carlos F. Truan, D-Corpus Christi (**Dean of the Senate**); 2003; insurance.
21. Judith Zaffirini, D-Laredo; 2001; communications specialist.
22. David Sibley, R-Waco; 2003; attorney.
23. Royce West, D-Dallas; 2003; attorney.
24. Troy Fraser, R-Horseshoe Bay; 2001; businessman.
25. Jeff Wentworth, R-San Antonio; 2001; attorney, realtor.
26. Gregory Luna, D-San Antonio; 2001; attorney.
27. Eddie Lucio Jr., D-Brownsville; 2001; advertising.
28. Robert L. Duncan, R-Lubbock; 2003; attorney.
29. Eliot Shapleigh, D-El Paso; 2001; attorney.
30. Tom Haywood, R-Wichita Falls; 2003; businessman.
31. Teel Bivins, R-Amarillo; 2003; businessman, cattleman.

House of Representatives

This is a list of the 150 members of the House of Representatives in the 76th Legislature. They were elected for two-year terms from the districts shown below. Representatives and senators receive the same salary (see State Senate). The **address of all Representatives** is House of Representatives, P.O. Box 2910, Austin, 78768; phone: 512-463-3000; Fax: 512-463-5896. On the Web: www.house.state.tx.us/

Speaker: James E. "Pete" Laney (D-Hale Center). **Speaker Pro Tempore**, D.R. "Tom" Uher (D-Bay City). **Chief Clerk**, Sharon Carter. **Sergeant-at-Arms**, Rod Welsh.

Members of Texas House of Representatives

District, Member, Party-Hometown, Occupation

1. Barry B. Telford, D-DeKalb, businessman.
2. Tom Ramsay, D-Mount Vernon; real estate, rancher.
3. Mark Homer, D-Paris; restaurant owner.
4. Betty Brown, R-Greenville; homemaker, rancher.
5. Bob Glaze, D-Gilmer; chiropractor, rancher.
6. Leo Berman, R-Tyler; retired military officer.
7. Tommy Merritt, R-Longview; businessman.
8. Paul Sadler, D-Henderson; attorney.
9. Wayne Christian, R-Center; investment advisor.
10. Jim Pitts, R-Waxahachie; attorney.
11. Todd Staples, R-Palestine; real-estate appraiser.
12. Clyde H. Alexander, D-Athens; rancher, businessman.
13. Charles Jones, R-Rockdale; rancher.
14. Fred Brown, R-Bryan; car dealer.
15. Thomas "Tommy" Williams, R-The Woodlands; CPA/financial services.
16. Ruben Hope, R-Conroe; attorney.
17. Jim McReynolds, D-Lufkin; petroleum landman.
18. Dan Ellis, D-Huntsville; business administrator.
19. Ron Lewis, D-Mauriceville; insurance, real estate.
20. Zeb Zbranek, D-Liberty; attorney.
21. Allan Ritter, D-Nederland; lumber-company president.
22. Joe Deshotel, D-Beaumont; attorney, contractor.
23. Patricia Gray, D-Galveston; attorney.
24. Craig Eiland, D-Dickinson; attorney.
25. Dennis Bonnen, R-Angleton; insurance.
26. Charlie Howard, R-Sugar Land; real-estate developer.
27. Dora Olivo, D-Stafford; attorney.
28. Robert "Robby" Cook, D-Eagle Lake; farmer.
29. D.R. "Tom" Uher, D-Bay City; attorney.
30. Geanie Morrison, R-Victoria; homemaker.
31. Judy Hawley, D-Portland; teacher.
32. Gene Seaman, R-Corpus Christi; insurance, real estate.
33. Vilma Luna, D-Corpus Christi; attorney.
34. Jaime Capelo, D-Corpus Christi; attorney.
35. Irma Rangel, D-Kingsville; attorney.
36. Kino Flores, D-Mission; businessman.
37. Rene Oliveira, D-Brownsville; attorney.
38. Jim Solis, D-Harlingen; attorney.
39. Miguel D. "Mike" Wise, D-Weslaco; attorney.
40. Juan Hinojosa, D-McAllen; attorney.
41. Roberto Gutierrez, D-McAllen; petroleum-products distributor.
42. Henry Cuellar, D-Laredo; attorney, customs broker.
43. Tracy King, D-Uvalde; hearing-aid specialist.
44. Ignacio Salinas Jr., D-Alice; teacher.
45. Edmund Kuempel, R-Seguin; salesman.
46. Rick Green, R-Dripping Springs; attorney/businessman.
47. Terry Keel, R-Austin; attorney.
48. Sherri Greenberg, D-Austin; public-finance specialist.
49. Elliott Naishtat, D-Austin; attorney.
50. Dawnna Dukes, D-Austin; business consultant.
51. Glen Maxey, D-Austin; data manager.
52. Mike Krusee, R-Taylor; small-business owner.
53. Harvey Hilderbran, R-Kerrville; businessman.
54. Suzanna Gratia Hupp, R-Lampasas; chiropractor, horse breeder.
55. Dianne Delisi, R-Temple; self-employed.
56. Kip Averitt, R-Waco; manufacturing.
57. Jim Dunnam, D-Waco; attorney.
58. Arlene Wohlgemuth, R-Burleson; flight instructor.
59. David Lengefeld, D-Hamilton; insurance agent.
60. Jim Keffer, R-Eastland; sales.
61. Phil King, R-Weatherford; attorney.
62. Ron Clark, R-Sherman, attorney.
63. Mary Denny, R-Denton; businesswoman/rancher.
64. Ronny Crownover, R-Lewisville; veterinarian.
65. Burt Solomons, R-Carrollton; attorney.
66. Brian McCall, R-Plano; insurance executive.
67. Jerry Madden, R-Plano; insurance.
68. Rick Hardcastle, D-Vernon; rancher, businessman.
69. David Farabee, D-Wichita Falls; insurance agent.
70. David Counts, D-Knox City; real estate.
71. Bob Hunter, R-Abilene; university administrator.
72. Robert A. Junell, D-San Angelo; attorney.
73. Bob Turner, D-Coleman; farmer, rancher.
74. Pete Gallego, D-Alpine; attorney.
75. Manny Najera, D-El Paso; NA.
76. Norma Chavez, D-El Paso; businesswoman.
77. Paul Moreno, D-El Paso; attorney.
78. Pat Haggerty, R-El Paso; real-estate broker.
79. Joseph Pickett, D-El Paso; real-estate broker.
80. Gary Walker, R-Plains; water conservation/landfill consultant.
81. George "Buddy" West, R-Odessa; safety engineer.
82. Tom Craddick, R-Midland; sales representative.
83. Delwin Jones, R-Lubbock; businessman, farmer.
84. Carl Isett, R-Lubbock; accountant.
85. James E. "Pete" Laney, D-Hale Center; farmer.
86. John Smithee, R-Amarillo; attorney.
87. David Swinford, R-Amarillo; agribusiness.
88. Warren Chisum, R-Pampa; oil & gas producer.
89. Sue Palmer, R-Fort Worth; petroleum distributor.
90. Lon Burnam, D-Fort Worth; consultant.
91. Bill Carter, R-Fort Worth; insurance agent.
92. Todd Smith, R-Bedford; attorney.
93. Toby Goodman, R-Arlington; attorney.
94. Kent Grusendorf, R-Arlington; pres., mfg. co.
95. Glenn Lewis, D-Fort Worth; attorney.
96. Kim Brimer, R-Arlington; Insurance.
97. Anna Mowery, R-Fort Worth; state representative.
98. Vicki Truitt, R-Keller; health-care consultant.
99. Ken Marchant, R-Carrollton; investor.
100. Terri Hodge, D-Dallas; retired.
101. Elvira Reyna, R-Mesquite; state representative.
102. Tony Goolsby, R-Dallas; insurance.
103. Steven Wolens, D-Dallas; attorney.
104. Domingo Garcia, D-Dallas; attorney.
105. Dale Tillery, D-Dallas; attorney.
106. Ray Allen, R-Grand Prairie; businessman.
107. Harryette Ehrhardt, D-Dallas; teacher.
108. Kenn George, R-Dallas; printing, real estate.
109. Helen Giddings, D-DeSoto; small-business owner.
110. Jesse Jones, D-Dallas; professor.
111. Yvonne Davis, D-Dallas; small-business owner.
112. Fred Hill, R-Richardson; NA.
113. Joe Driver, R-Garland; insurance agent.
114. Will Hartnett, R-Irving; attorney.
115. Leticia Van de Putte, D-San Antonio; pharmacist.
116. Leo Alvarado Jr., D-San Antonio; attorney.
117. John Longoria, D-San Antonio; attorney.
118. Carlos Uresti, D-San Antonio; attorney.
119. Robert Puente, D-San Antonio; attorney.
120. Ruth J. McClendon, D-San Antonio; company pres.
121. Bill Siebert, R-San Antonio; businessman.
122. John Shields, R-San Antonio; attorney.
123. Frank Corte, R-San Antonio; businessman.
124. Juan Solis, D-San Antonio; marketing director.
125. Arthur "Art" Reyna Jr., D-San Antonio; attorney.
126. Peggy Hamric, R-Houston; small-business owner.
127. Joe Crabb, R-Kingwood; minister, attorney.
128. Fred Bosse, D-Houston; attorney.
129. John Davis, R-Houston; roofing contractor.
130. John Culberson, R-Houston; attorney.
131. Ron Wilson, D-Houston; attorney.
132. Scott Hochberg, D-Houston; software developer.
133. Joe Nixon, R-Houston; attorney.
134. Kyle Janek, R-Houston; physician.
135. Gary Elkins, R-Houston; businessman, consultant.
136. Beverly Woolley, R-Houston; small-business owner.
137. Debra Danburg, D-Houston; attorney.
138. Ken Yarbrough, D-Houston; executive director.
139. Sylvester Turner, D-Houston; attorney.
140. Kevin Bailey, D-Houston; political consultant.
141. Senfronia Thompson, D-Houston; attorney.
142. Harold Dutton Jr., D-Houston; attorney.
143. Joe E. Moreno, D-El Paso; NA.
144. Robert Talton, R-Pasadena; attorney.
145. Rick Noriega, D-Houston; businessman.
146. Al Edwards, D-Houston; real estate.
147. Garnet Coleman, D-Houston; loan consultant.
148. Jessica Farrar, D-Houston; architect intern.
149. Talmadge Heflin, R-Houston; businessman.
150. Paul Hilbert, R-Houston; attorney. ☆

State Judiciary

The judiciary of the state consists of nine members of the State Supreme Court; nine members of the Court of Criminal Appeals; 80 of the Courts of Appeals; 396 of the State District Courts, including 10 Criminal District Courts; 453 County Courts; 838 Justice of the Peace Courts; and 1,224 Municipal Courts.

In addition to its system of formal courts, the State of Texas has established 15 **Alternative Dispute Resolution Centers**. The centers help ease the caseload of Texas courts by using mediation, arbitration, negotiation and moderated settlement conferences to handle disputes without resorting to more costly, time-consuming court actions. Centers are located in Amarillo, Austin, Beaumont, Conroe, Corpus Christi, Dallas, El Paso, Fort Worth, Houston, Lewisville, Lubbock, McKinney, Richmond, San Angelo and San Antonio. For the fiscal year ending Aug. 31, 1998, the mediation sections of the centers had closed 19,813 cases and had 2,406 cases still pending.

(The list of U.S. district courts in Texas can be found in the federal government section of this edition.)

State Higher Courts

The state's higher courts are listed below with corrections to **July 1, 1999**. Notations in parentheses indicate dates of expiration of terms of office. Judges of the Supreme Court, Court of Criminal Appeals and Courts of Appeals are elected to 6-year, overlapping terms. District Court judges are elected to 4-year terms.

The salaries for judges as of Sept. 1, 1998, were as follows: Chief Justice of the Supreme Court and the Presiding Judge of the Court of Criminal Appeals: each $115,000; Justices, $113,000; Chief Justices of the Courts of Appeals, $107,850; justices, $107,350 from the state. A supplemental amount may be paid by counties, not to exceed $15,000 per year, and total salary must be at least $1,000 less than that received by Supreme Court justices. District Court judges receive $101,700 from the state, plus supplemental pay from various subdivisions. Their total salary must be $1,000 less than that received by justices of the Court of Appeals in which the district court is located.

Below is given information on only the Supreme Court, Court of Criminal Appeals and Courts of Appeals. The information was furnished by each court as of April 1999. Names of county court judges are given by counties on pages 479-482. Names of District Court Judges are given by District number on pages 441-442. To get the District numbers of the District Court(s) in a particular county, look on pages 439-440.

Supreme Court

Chief Justice, Thomas R. Phillips (12-31-02). **Justices:** Alberto R. Gonzales (12-31-00); Greg Abbott (12-31-04); Nathan L. Hecht (12-31-00); Deborah G. Hankinson (12-31-02); James A. Baker (12-31-02); Craig Enoch (12-31-04); Harriet O'Neill (12-31-04); and Priscilla R. Owen (12-31-00). **Clerk of Court,** John T. Adams. Location of court, Austin. Web: **www.supreme.courts.state.tx.us**.

Court of Criminal Appeals

Presiding Judge, Michael J. McCormick (12-31-00). **Judges:** Lawrence E. Meyers (12-31-05); Stephen W. Mansfield (12-31-00); Sharon Keller (12-31-00); Tom Price (12-31-02); Sue Holland (12-31-02); Paul Womack (12-31-02); Cheryl Johnson (12-31-05); and Mike Keasler (12-31-05). **State's Attorney,** Matthew Paul. **Clerk of Court,** Troy C. Bennett Jr. Location of court, Austin. Web: **www.cca.courts.state.tx.us**.

Courts of Appeals

These courts have jurisdiction within their respective supreme judicial districts. A constitutional amendment approved in 1978 raised the number of associate justices for Courts of Appeals where needed. Judges are elected from the district for 6-year terms. Another amendment adopted in 1980 changed the name of the old Courts of Civil Appeals to the Courts of Appeals and changed the jurisdiction of the courts.

First District—*Houston. Chief Justice, Michael H. Schneider (12-31-04). **Justices:** Murry B. Cohen (12-31-00); Margaret G. Mirabal (12-31-02); Adele Hedges (12-31-00); Michol O'Connor (12-31-00); Davie L. Wilson (12-31-04); Eric Andell (12-31-00); Tim G. Taft (12-31-00); Sam Nuchia (12-31-00). **Clerk of court,** Margie Thompson. Counties in the First District: Austin, Brazoria, Brazos, Burleson, Chambers, Colorado, Fort Bend, Galveston, Grimes, Harris, Trinity, Walker, Waller, Washington.

Second District—Fort Worth: Chief Justice, John Cayce (12-31-00). **Justices:** Dixon W. Holman (12-31-02); Sam J. Day (12-31-00); Terrie Livingston (12-31-00); Lee Ann Dauphinot (12-31-00); David Richards (12-31-00); and William H. Brigham (12-31-04). **Clerk of court,** Stephanie Lavake. Counties in Second District: Archer, Clay, Cooke, Denton, Hood, Jack, Montague, Parker, Tarrant, Wichita, Wise, Young.

Third District—Austin: Chief Justice, Marilyn Aboussie (12-31-02). **Justices:** J. Woodfin Jones (12-31-00); Mack Kidd (12-31-00); Bea Ann Smith (12-31-00); Lee Yeakel (12-31-00); and Jan Patterson (12-31-04). **Clerk of court,** Diane O'Neal. Counties in the Third District: Bastrop, Bell, Blanco, Burnet, Caldwell, Coke, Comal, Concho, Fayette, Hays, Irion, Lampasas, Lee, Llano, McCulloch, Milam, Mills, Runnels, San Saba, Schleicher, Sterling, Tom Green, Travis, Williamson.

Fourth District—San Antonio: Chief Justice, Phil Hardberger (12-31-00). **Justices:** Catherine M. Stone (12-31-00); Tom Rickhoff (12-31-04); Alma L. Lopez (12-31-00); Paul W. Green (12-31-00); Sarah B. Duncan (12-31-00); and Karen Angelini (12-31-00). **Clerk of court,** Herb Schaefer. Counties in the Fourth District: Atascosa, Bandera, Bexar, Brooks, Dimmit, Duval, Edwards, Frio, Gillespie, Guadalupe, Jim Hogg, Jim Wells, Karnes, Kendall, Kerr, Kimble, Kinney, La Salle, McMullen, Mason, Maverick, Medina, Menard, Real, Starr, Sutton, Uvalde, Val Verde, Webb, Wilson, Zapata, Zavala.

Fifth District—Dallas: Chief Justice, Linda Thomas (12-31-00). **Justices:** Sue Lagarde (12-31-00); Mark Whittington (12-31-02); Ed Kinkeade (12-31-00); John Ovard (12-31-00); Joseph B. Morris (12-31-00); Frances Maloney (12-31-02); Ron Chapman (12-31-04); Tom James (12-31-00); Carolyn Wright (12-31-02); David Bridges (12-31-02); Jim Moseley (12-31-00); John Roach (12-31-00); and Michael O'Neill (12-31-04). **Clerk of Court,** Lisa Rombok. Counties in the Fifth District: Collin, Dallas, Grayson, Hunt, Kaufman, Rockwall, Van Zandt.

Sixth District—Texarkana: Chief Justice, William J. Cornelius (12-31-00). **Justices:** Donald R. Ross (12-31-00) and Ben Z. Grant (12-31-02). **Clerk of court,** Tibby Hopkin. Counties in the Sixth District: Bowie, Camp, Cass, Delta, Fannin, Franklin, Gregg, Harrison, Hopkins, Hunt, Lamar, Marion, Morris, Panola, Red River, Rusk, Titus, Upshur, Wood.

Seventh District—Amarillo: Chief Justice, John T. Boyd (12-31-00). **Justices:** Brian Quinn (12-31-00); Don H. Reavis (12-31-00); and Phil Johnson (12-31-04). **Clerk of court,** Peggy Culp. Counties in the Seventh District: Armstrong, Bailey, Briscoe, Carson, Castro, Childress, Cochran, Collingsworth, Cottle, Crosby, Dallam, Deaf Smith, Dickens, Donley, Floyd, Foard, Garza, Gray, Hale, Hall, Hansford, Hardeman, Hartley, Hemphill, Hockley, Hutchinson, Kent, King, Lamb, Lipscomb, Lubbock, Lynn, Moore,

Motley, Ochiltree, Oldham, Parmer, Potter, Randall, Roberts, Sherman, Swisher, Terry, Wheeler, Wilbarger, Yoakum.

Eighth District—El Paso: Chief Justice, Richard Barajas (12-31-02). **Justices:** Susan Larsen (12-31-04); Ann Crawford McClure (12-31-00; and David W. Chew (12-31-00). **Clerk of court,** Denise Pacheco. Counties in the Eighth District: Andrews, Brewster, Crane, Crockett, Culberson, Ector, El Paso, Gaines, Glasscock, Hudspeth, Jeff Davis, Loving, Martin, Midland, Pecos, Presidio, Reagan, Reeves, Terrell, Upton, Ward, Winkler.

Ninth District—Beaumont: Chief Justice, Ronald L. Walker (12-31-02). **Justices:** Don Burgess (12-31-04) and Earl B. Stover (12-31-00). **Clerk of court,** Carol Anne Flores. Counties in the Ninth District: Angelina, Hardin, Jasper, Jefferson, Liberty, Montgomery, Newton, Orange, Polk, San Jacinto, Tyler.

Tenth District—Waco: Chief Justice, Rex Davis (12-31-00). **Justices:** Tom Gray (12-31-04) and Bill Vance (12-31-02). **Clerk of court,** Sharri Roessler. Counties in the Tenth District: Bosque, Brazos, Coryell, Ellis, Falls, Freestone, Hamilton, Hill, Johnson, Leon, Limestone, McLennan, Madison, Navarro, Robertson, Somervell.

Eleventh District—Eastland: Chief Justice, William G. Arnot (12-31-00). **Justices:** Terry McCall (12-31-04) and Jim R. Wright (12-31-02). **Clerk of court,** Sherry Williamson. Counties in the Eleventh District: Baylor, Borden, Brown, Callahan, Coleman, Comanche, Dawson, Eastland, Erath, Fisher, Haskell, Howard, Jones, Knox, Mitchell, Nolan, Palo Pinto, Scurry, Shackelford, Stephens, Stonewall, Taylor, Throckmorton.

Twelfth District—Tyler: Chief Justice, Tom B. Ramey Jr. (12-31-02). **Justices:** Roby Hadden (12-31-00) and Jim Worthen (12-31-04). **Clerk of court,** Cathy S. Lusk. Counties in the Twelfth District: Anderson, Cherokee, Gregg, Henderson, Hopkins, Houston, Kaufman, Nacogdoches, Panola, Rains, Rusk, Sabine, San Augustine, Shelby, Smith, Upshir, Van Zandt, Wood.

Thirteenth District—Corpus Christi: Chief Justice, Robert J. Seerden (12-31-00). **Justices:** J. Bonner Dorsey (12-31-02); Federico G. Hinojosa Jr. (12-31-00); Linda Reyna Yañez (12-31-04); Melchor Chavez (12-31-00); and Nelda V. Rodriguez (12-31-00). **Clerk of court,** Cathy Wilborn. Counties in the Thirteenth District: Aransas, Bee, Calhoun, Cameron, DeWitt, Goliad, Gonzales, Hidalgo, Jackson, Kenedy, Kleberg, Lavaca, Live Oak, Matagorda, Nueces, Refugio, San Patricio, Victoria, Wharton, Willacy.

Fourteenth District—Houston†: Chief Justice, Paul C. Murphy (12-31-02). **Justices:** Leslie Brock Yates (12-31-04); Maurice Amidei (12-31-00); John S. Anderson (12-31-00); J. Harvey Hudson (12-31-00); Wanda McKee Fowler (12-31-00); Kem Thompson Frost (12-31-02); Richard H. Edelman (12-31-00); and Don Wittig (12-31-00). **Clerk of court,** Mary Jane Gay. Counties in the Fourteenth District: Austin, Brazoria, Brazos, Burleson, Chambers, Colorado, Fort Bend, Galveston, Grimes, Harris, Trinity, Walker, Waller, Washington.

*The location of the First Court of Appeals was changed from Galveston to Houston by the 55th Legislature, with the provision that all cases originated in Galveston County be tried in that city and with the further provision that any case may, at the discretion of the court, be tried in either city.

†Because of the heavy workload of the Houston area Court of Appeals, the 60th Legislature, in 1967, provided for the establishment of a Fourteenth Appeals Court at Houston.

Administrative Judicial Districts of Texas

There are nine administrative judicial districts in the state for administrative purposes. An active or retired dis-

trict judge or an active or retired appellate judge with judicial experience in a district court serves as the Presiding Judge upon appointment by the Governor. They receive extra compensation of $5,000 paid by counties in the respective administrative districts.

The Presiding Judge convenes an annual conference of the judges in the administrative district to consult on the state of business in the courts. This conference is empowered to adopt rules for the administration of cases in the district. The Presiding Judge may assign active or retired district judges residing within the administrative district to any of the district courts within the administrative district. The Presiding Judge of one administrative district may request the Presiding Judge of another administrative district to assign a judge from that district to sit in a district court located in the administrative district of the Presiding Judge making the request.

The Chief Justice of the Supreme Court of Texas convenes an annual conference of the nine Presiding Judges to determine the need for assignment of judges and to promote the uniform administration of the assignment of judges. The Chief Justice is empowered to assign judges of one administrative district for service in another whenever such assignments are necessary for the prompt and efficient administration of justice.

First District — Pat McDowell, Dallas: Anderson, Bowie, Camp, Cass, Cherokee, Collin, Dallas, Delta, Ellis, Fannin, Franklin, Grayson, Gregg, Harrison, Henderson, Hopkins, Houston, Hunt, Kaufman, Lamar, Marion, Morris, Nacogdoches, Panola, Rains, Red River, Rockwall, Rusk, Shelby, Smith, Titus, Upshur, Van Zandt and Wood.

Second District — Olen Underwood, Conroe: Angelina, Bastrop, Brazoria, Brazos, Burleson, Chambers, Fort Bend, Freestone, Galveston, Grimes, Hardin, Harris, Jasper, Jefferson, Lee, Leon, Liberty, Limestone, Madison, Matagorda, Montgomery, Newton, Orange, Polk, Robertson, Sabine, San Augustine, San Jacinto, Trinity, Tyler, Walker, Waller, Washington and Wharton.

Third District — B. B. Schraub, Seguin: Austin, Bell, Blanco, Bosque, Burnet, Caldwell, Colorado, Comal, Comanche, Coryell, Falls, Fayette, Gonzales, Guadalupe, Hamilton, Hays, Hill, Johnson, Lampasas, Lavaca, Llano, McLennan, Mason, Milam, Navarro, San Saba, Somervell, Travis and Williamson.

Fourth District — David Peeples, San Antonio: Aransas, Atascosa, Bee, Bexar, Calhoun, DeWitt, Dimmit, Frio, Goliad, Jackson, Karnes, LaSalle, Live Oak, Maverick, McMullen, Refugio, San Patricio, Victoria, Webb, Wilson, Zapata and Zavala.

Fifth District — Darrell Hester, Brownsville: Brooks, Cameron, Duval, Hidalgo, Jim Hogg, Jim Wells, Kenedy, Kleberg, Nueces, Starr and Willacy.

Sixth District — Stephen B. Ables, Kerrville: Bandera, Brewster, Crockett, Culberson, Edwards, El Paso, Gillespie, Hudspeth, Jeff Davis, Kendall, Kerr, Kimble, Kinney, Medina, Pecos, Presidio, Reagan, Real, Sutton, Terrell, Upton, Uvalde and Val Verde.

Seventh District — Dean Rucker, Midland: Andrews, Borden, Brown, Callahan, Coke, Coleman, Concho, Crane, Dawson, Ector, Fisher, Gaines, Garza, Glasscock, Haskell, Howard, Irion, Jones, Kent, Loving, Lynn, McCulloch, Martin, Menard, Midland, Mills, Mitchell, Nolan, Reeves, Runnels, Schleicher, Scurry, Shackelford, Sterling, Stonewall, Taylor, Throckmorton, Tom Green, Ward and Winkler.

Eighth — Jeff Walker, Fort Worth: Archer, Clay, Cooke, Denton, Eastland, Erath, Hood, Jack, Montague, Palo Pinto, Parker, Stephens, Tarrant, Wichita, Wise and Young.

Ninth — Ray D. Anderson, Lubbock: Armstrong, Bailey, Baylor, Briscoe, Carson, Castro, Childress, Cochran, Collingsworth, Cottle, Crosby, Dallam, Deaf Smith, Dickens, Donley, Floyd, Foard, Gray, Hale, Hall, Hansford,

Hardeman, Hartley, Hemphill, Hockley, Hutchinson, King,   Oldham, Parmer, Potter, Randall, Roberts, Sherman,
Knox, Lamb, Lipscomb, Lubbock, Moore, Motley, Ochiltree,   Swisher, Terry, Wheeler, Wilbarger and Yoakum. ☆

Texas Courts by County, 1999

Below are listed the state district court or courts, court of appeals district, administrative judicial district and U.S. judicial district for each county in Texas as of April 1999. For the names of the district court judges, see table by district number on pages 441-442. For the names of other judges, see listing on pages 437-438.

County	State Dist. Court(s)	Ct. of App'ls Dist.	Adm. Jud. Dist.	U.S. Jud. Dist.
Anderson	3, 87, 349, 369	12	1	E-Tyler
Andrews	109	8	7	W-Mid.-Od.
Angelina	159, 217	9	2	E-Lufkin
Aransas	36, 156, 343	13	4	S-C.Christi
Archer	97	2	8	N-W. Falls
Armstrong	47	7	9	N-Amarilllo
Atascosa	81, 218	4	4	W-San Ant.
Austin	155	1, 14	3	S-Houston
Bailey	287	7	9	N-Lubbock
Bandera	216	4	6	W-San Ant.
Bastrop	21, 335	3	2	W-Austin
Baylor	50	11	9	N-W. Falls
Bee	36, 156, 343	13	4	S-C.Christi
Bell	27, 146, 169, 264	3	3	W-Waco
Bexar	37, 45, 57, 73, 131, 144, 150, 166, 175, 186, 187, 224, 225, 226, 227, 285, 288, 289, 290	4	4	W-San Ant.
Blanco	33	3	3	W-Austin
Borden	132	11	7	N-Lubbock
Bosque	220	10	3	W-Waco
Bowie	5, 102, 202	6	1	E-Texark.
Brazoria	23, 149, 239, 300	1, 14	2	S-Galves.
Brazos	85, 272, 361	1, 10, 14	2	S-Houston
Brewster	394	8	6	W-Pecos
Briscoe	110	7	9	N-Amarilllo
Brooks	79	4	5	S-C.Christi
Brown	35	11	7	N-S. Ang.
Burleson	21, 335	1, 14	2	W-Austin
Burnet	33	3	3	W-Austin
Caldwell	22, 207, 274	3	3	W-Austin
Calhoun	24, 135, 267	13	4	S-Victoria
Callahan	42	11	7	N-Abilene
Cameron	103, 107, 138, 197, 357	13	5	S-Brownsville
Camp	76, 276	6	1	E-Marshall
Carson	100	7	9	N-Amarilllo
Cass	5	6	1	E-Marshall
Castro	64, 242	7	9	N-Amarilllo
Chambers	253, 344	1, 14	2	S-Galves.
Cherokee	2, 369	12	1	E-Tyler
Childress	100	7	9	N-Amarilllo
Clay	97	2	8	N-W. Falls
Cochran	286	7	9	N-Lubbock
Coke	51	3	7	N-S. Ang.
Coleman	42	11	7	N-S. Ang.
Collin	199, 219, 296, 366, 380	5	1	E-Sherman
Collingsworth	100	7	9	N-Amarilllo
Colorado	25, 2nd 25	1, 14	3	S-Houston
Comal	22, 207, 274	3	3	W-San Ant.
Comanche	220	11	3	N-Ft. Worth
Concho	119, 198	3	7	N-S. Ang.
Cooke	235	2	8	E-Sherman
Coryell	52	10	3	W-Waco
Cottle	50	7	9	N-W. Falls
Crane	109	8	7	W-Mid.-Od.
Crockett	112	8	6	N-S. Ang.
Crosby	72	7	9	N-Lubbock
Culberson	205, 394	8	6	W-Pecos
Dallam	69	7	9	N-Amarilllo
Dallas	14, 44, 68, 95, 101, 116, 134, 160, 162, 191, 192, 193, 194,195, 203, 204, 254, 255, 256, 265, 282, 283, 291, , 292, 298, 301, 302, 303, 304, 305, 330, 363, Cr.1, Cr2, Cr.3, Cr.4, Cr.1	5	1	N-Dallas
Dawson	106	11	7	N-Lubbock
Deaf Smith	222	7	9	N-Amarilllo
Delta	8, 62	6	1	E-Paris
Denton	16, 158, 211, 362, 367	2	8	E-Sherman
DeWitt	24, 135, 267	13	4	S-Victoria
Dickens	110	7	9	N-Lubbock
Dimmit	293, 365	4	4	W-San Ant.
Donley	100	7	9	N-Amarilllo
Duval	229	4	5	S-C.Christi
Eastland	91	11	8	N-Abilene
Ector	70, 161, 244, 358	8	7	W-Mid.-Od.
Edwards	63	4	6	W-Del Rio
Ellis	40, 378	10	1	N-Dallas
El Paso	34, 41, 65, 120, 168, 171, 205, 210, 243, 327, 346, 383, 384	8	6	W-El Paso
Erath	266	11	8	N-Ft. Worth
Falls	82	10	3	W-Waco
Fannin	6, 336	6	1	E-Paris
Fayette	155	3	3	S-Houston
Fisher	32	11	7	N-Abilene
Floyd	110	7	9	N-Lubbock
Foard	46	7	9	N-W. Falls
Fort Bend	240, 268, 328	1, 14	2	S-Houston
Franklin	8, 62	6	1	E-Texark.
Freestone	77, 87	10	2	W-Waco
Frio	81, 218	4	4	W-San Ant.
Gaines	106	8	7	N-Lubbock
Galveston	10, 56, 122, 212, 306	1, 14	2	S-Galves.
Garza	106	7	7	N-Lubbock
Gillespie	216	4	6	W-Austin
Glasscock	118	8	7	N-S. Ang.
Goliad	24, 135, 267	13	4	S-Victoria
Gonzales	25, 2nd 25	13	3	W-San Ant.
Gray	31, 223	7	9	N-Amarilllo
Grayson	15, 59, 336	5	1	E-Sherman
Gregg	124, 188, 307	6, 12	1	E-Tyler
Grimes	12, 278	1, 14	2	S-Houston
Guadalupe	25, 2nd 25, 274	4	3	W-San Ant.
Hale	64, 242	7	9	N-Lubbock
Hall	100	7	9	N-Amarilllo
Hamilton	220	10	3	W-Waco
Hansford	84	7	9	N-Amarilllo
Hardeman	46	7	9	N-W. Falls
Hardin	88, 356	9	2	E-B'mont.
Harris	11, 55, 61, 80, 113, 125, 127, 129, 133, 151, 152, 157, 164, 165, 174, 176, 177, 178, 179, 180, 182, 183, 184, 185, 189, 190, 208, 209, 215, 228, 230, 232, 234, 245, 246, 247, 248, 257, 262, 263, 269, 270, 280, 281, 295, 308, 309, 310, 311, 312, 313, 314, 315, 333, 334, 337, 338, 339, 351	1, 14	2	S-Houston
Harrison	71	6	1	E-Marshall
Hartley	69	7	9	N-Amarilllo
Haskell	39	11	7	N-Abilene
Hays	22, 207, 274	3	3	W-Austin
Hemphill	31	7	9	N-Amarilllo
Henderson	3, 173, 392	12	1	E-Tyler
Hidalgo	92, 93, 139, 206, 275, 332, 370	13	5	S-McAllen
Hill	66	10	3	W-Waco
Hockley	286	7	9	N-Lubbock
Hood	355	2	8	N-Ft. Worth

County	State Dist. Court(s)	Ct. of App'ls Dist.	Adm. Jud. Dist.	U.S. Jud. Dist.
Hopkins	8, 62	6, 12	1	E-Paris
Houston	3, 349	12	1	E-Lufkin
Howard	118	11	7	N-Abilene
Hudspeth	205, 394	8	6	W-Pecos
Hunt	196, 354	5, 6	1	N-Dallas
Hutchinson	84, 316	7	9	N-Amarillo
Irion	51	3	7	N-S. Ang.
Jack	271	2	8	N-Ft. Worth
Jackson	24, 135, 267	13	4	S-Victoria
Jasper	1, 1A	9	2	E-B'mont.
Jeff Davis	394	8	6	W-Pecos
Jefferson	58, 60, 136, 172, 252, 279, 317, Cr.	9	2	E-B'mont.
Jim Hogg	229	4	5	S-Laredo
Jim Wells	79	4	5	S-C.Christi
Johnson	18, 249	10	3	N-Dallas
Jones	259	11	7	N-Abilene
Karnes	81, 218	4	4	W-San Ant.
Kaufman	86	5, 12	1	N-Dallas
Kendall	216	4	6	W-San Ant.
Kenedy	105	13	5	S-C.Christi
Kent	39	7	7	N-Lubbock
Kerr	198, 216	4	6	W-San Ant.
Kimble	198	4	6	W-Austin
King	50	7	9	N-W. Falls
Kinney	63	4	6	W-Del Rio
Kleberg	105	13	5	S-C.Christi
Knox	50	11	9	N-W. Falls
Lamar	6, 62	6	1	E-Paris
Lamb	154	7	9	N-Lubbock
Lampasas	27	3	3	W-Austin
La Salle	81, 218	4	4	S-Laredo
Lavaca	25, 2nd 25	13	3	S-Victoria
Lee	21, 335	3	2	W-Austin
Leon	12, 87, 278	10	2	W-Waco
Liberty	75, 253	9	2	E-B'mont.
Limestone	77, 87	10	2	W-Waco
Lipscomb	31	7	9	N-Amarillo
Live Oak	36, 156, 343	13	4	S-C.Christi
Llano	33	3	3	W-Austin
Loving	143	8	7	W-Pecos
Lubbock	72, 99, 137, 140, 237, 364	7	9	N-Lubbock
Lynn	106	7	7	N-Lubbock
Madison	12, 278	10	2	S-Houston
Marion	115, 276	6	1	E-Marshall
Martin	118	8	7	W-Mid.-Od.
Mason	33	4	3	W-Austin
Matagorda	23, 130	13	2	S-Galves.
Maverick	293, 365	4	4	W-Del Rio
McCulloch	198	3	7	W-Austin
McLennan	19, 54, 74, 170	10	3	W-Waco
McMullen	36, 156, 343	4	4	S-Laredo
Medina	38	4	6	W-San Ant.
Menard	198	4	7	N-S. Ang.
Midland	142, 238, 318, 385	8	7	W-Mid.-Od.
Milam	20	3	3	W-Waco
Mills	35	3	7	N-S. Ang.
Mitchell	32	11	7	N-Abilene
Montague	97	2	8	N-W. Falls
Montgomery	9, 221, 284, 359, 410	9	2	S-Houston
Moore	69	7	9	N-Amarillo
Morris	76, 276	6	1	E-Marshall
Motley	110	7	9	N-Lubbock
Nacogdoches	145	12	1	E-Lufkin
Navarro	13	10	3	N-Dallas
Newton	1, 1A	9	2	E-B'mont.
Nolan	32	11	7	N-Abilene
Nueces	28, 94, 105, 117, 148, 214, 319, 347	13	5	S-C.Christi
Ochiltree	84	7	9	N-Amarillo
Oldham	222	7	9	N-Amarillo
Orange	128, 163, 260	9	2	E-B'mont.
Palo Pinto	29	11	8	N-Ft. Worth
Panola	123	6, 12	1	E-Tyler
Parker	43	2	8	N-Ft. Worth
Parmer	287	7	9	N-Amarillo
Pecos	83, 112	8	6	W-Pecos
Polk	258, 411	9	2	E-Lufkin
Potter	47, 108, 181, 251, 320	7	9	N-Amarillo
Presidio	394	8	6	W-Pecos
Rains	8, 354	12	1	E-Tyler
Randall	47, 181, 251	7	9	N-Amarillo
Reagan	83, 112	8	6	N-S. Ang.
Real	38	4	6	W-San Ant.
Red River	6, 102	6	1	E-Paris
Reeves	143	8	7	W-Pecos
Refugio	24, 135, 267	13	4	S-Victoria
Roberts	31	7	9	N-Amarillo
Robertson	82	10	2	W-Waco
Rockwall	382	5	1	N-Dallas
Runnels	119	3	7	N-S. Ang.
Rusk	4	6, 12	1	E-Tyler
Sabine	1, 273	12	2	E-Lufkin
San Augustine	1, 273	12	2	E-Lufkin
San Jacinto	258, 411	9	2	S-Houston
San Patricio	36, 156, 343	13	4	S-C.Christi
San Saba	33	3	3	W-Austin
Schleicher	51	3	7	N-S. Ang.
Scurry	132	11	7	N-Lubbock
Shackelford	259	11	7	N-Abilene
Shelby	123, 273	12	1	E-Lufkin
Sherman	69	7	9	N-Amarillo
Smith	7, 114, 241, 321	12	1	E-Tyler
Somervell	18, 249	10	3	W-Waco
Starr	229, 381	4	5	S-McAllen
Stephens	90	11	8	N-Abilene
Sterling	51	3	7	N-S. Ang.
Stonewall	39	11	7	N-Abilene
Sutton	112	4	6	N-S. Ang.
Swisher	64, 242	7	9	N-Amarillo
Tarrant	17, 48, 67, 96, 141, 153, 213, 231, 233, 236, 297, 322, 323, 324, 325, 342, 348, 352, 360, 371, 372, Cr.1, Cr.2, Cr.3, Cr.4	2	8	N-Ft. Worth
Taylor	42, 104, 326, 350	11	7	N-Abilene
Terrell	63	8	6	W-Del Rio
Terry	121	7	9	N-Lubbock
Throckmorton	39	11	7	N-Abilene
Titus	76, 276	6	1	E-Texark.
Tom Green	51, 119, 340	3	7	N-S. Ang.
Travis	53, 98, 126, 147, 167, 200, 201, 250, 261, 299, 331, 345, 353	3	3	W-Austin
Trinity	258, 411	1, 14	2	E-Lufkin
Tyler	1A, 88	9	2	E-Lufkin
Upshur	115	6, 12	1	E-Marshall
Upton	83, 112	8	6	W-Mid.-Od.
Uvalde	38	4	6	W-Del Rio
Val Verde	63	4	6	W-Del Rio
Van Zandt	294	5, 12	1	E-Tyler
Victoria	24, 135, 267, 377	13	4	S-Victoria
Walker	12, 278	1, 14	2	S-Houston
Waller	9, 155	1, 14	2	S-Houston
Ward	143	8	7	W-Pecos
Washington	21, 335	1, 14	2	W-Austin
Webb	49, 111, 341	4	4	S-Laredo
Wharton	23, 329	13	2	S-Houston
Wheeler	31	7	9	N-Amarillo
Wichita	30, 78, 89	2	8	N-W. Falls
Wilbarger	46	7	9	N-W. Falls
Willacy	103, 107, 138, 197, 357	13	5	S-Brownsville
Williamson	26, 277, 368	3	3	W-Austin
Wilson	81, 218	4	4	W-San Ant.
Winkler	109	8	7	W-Pecos
Wise	271	2	8	N-Ft. Worth
Wood	114, 294	6, 12	1	E-Tyler
Yoakum	121	7	9	N-Lubbock
Young	90	2	8	N-W. Falls
Zapata	49	4	4	S-Laredo
Zavala	293, 365	4	4	W-Del Rio

District Judges in Texas, 1999

Below are the names of all district judges, as of April 1999, in Texas listed in district court order. To determine which judges have jurisdiction in specific counties, refer to the table on pages 439-440.

Source: Texas Judicial System Directory 1999, Office of Court Administration.

Court	Judge	Court	Judge	Court	Judge
1	Joe Bob Golden	63	George M. Thurmond	128	Patrick A. Clark
1A	Monte D. Lawlis	64	Jack R. Miller	129	Patrick W. Mizell
2	John Robert Adamson	65	Alfredo Chavez	130	Joseph Ann Ottis
3	James N. Parsons III	66	F.B. (Bob) McGregor Jr.	131	John D. Gabriel Jr.
4	J. Clay Gossett	67	Jon Barton	132	Ernie B. Armstrong
5	Jack Carter	68	Gary Hall	133	Lamar McCorkle
6	Jim D. Lovett	69	Ron Enns	134	Anne Ashby
7	Louis B. Gohmert Jr.	70	Jay Gibson	135	K. Stephen Williams
8	Robert Newsom	71	Bonnie Leggat	136	Milton Gunn Shuffield
9	Frederick E. Edwards	72	J. Blair Cherry Jr.	137	Cecil G. Puryear
10	David E. Garner	73	Andy Mireles	138	Robert Garza
11	Mark Davidson	74	Alan M. Mayfield	139	Leticia Hinojosa
12	William Lee McAdams	75	J.C. "Zeke" Zbranek	140	Jim Bob Darnell
13	John Howard Jackson	76	Jimmy L. White	141	Paul Wendell Enlow
14	John McClellan Marshall	77	Horace Dickson Black Jr.	142	George David Gilles
15	James Fry	78	John Keith Nelson	143	Bob Parks
16	John Narsutis	79	Terry A. Canales	144	Mark Luitjen
17	Fred W. Davis	80	Scott Reiter Link	145	Jack Pierce
18	John Edward Neill	81	Olin B. Strauss	146	Jack Richard Morris
19	Ralph T. Strother	82	Robert M. Stem	147	Wilford Flowers
20	Charles E. Lance	83	Alex R. Gonzalez	148	Rose Vela
21	John L. Placke	84	William D. (Bill) Smith	149	Robert May
22	Charles R. Ramsay	85	J.D. Langley	150	Janet P. Littlejohn
23	Ben Hardin	86	Glen M. Ashworth	151	Caroline E. Baker
24	Joseph P. Kelly	87	Sam Bill Bournias	152	Harvey G. Brown Jr.
25	Dwight E. Peschel	88	Earl Stover III	153	Ken C. Curry
2nd 25	Gus J. Strauss	89	Juanita Pavlick	154	Felix Klein
26	Billy Ray Stubblefield	90	Stephen O. Crawford	155	Dan R. Beck
27	Joe Carroll	91	Steven R. Herod	156	Joel B. Johnson
28	Nanette Hasette	92	Edward G. Aparicio	157	David M. Medina
29	David Cleveland	93	Fernando Mancias	158	Phillip Vick
30	Robert P. Brotherton	94	Jack E. Hunter	159	Gerald Alton Goodwin
31	Steven R. Emmert	95	Sally L. Montgomery	160	David C. Godbey
32	Weldon Kirk	96	Jeff Walker	161	Tryon D. Lewis
33	Guilford L. "Gil" Jones	97	Roger E. Towery	162	Bill Rhea
34	William E. Moody	98	W. Jeanne Meurer	163	David A. Dunn
35	Stephen Ellis	99	Mackey K. Hancock	164	Mary K. (Katie) Kennedy
36	Ronald M. Yeager	100	David M. McCoy	165	Elizabeth Ray
37	David Berchelmann Jr.	101	Jay Patterson	166	Martha B. Tanner
38	Mickey Ray Pennington	102	John F. Miller Jr.	167	Mike F. Lynch
39	Charles L. Chapman	103	Menton Murray Jr.	168	Guadalupe Rivera
40	Gene Knize	104	Billy John Edwards	169	Oliver Kelley
41	Mary Anne Bramblett	105	J. Manuel Banales	170	Joe N. Johnson
42	John Wilson Weeks	106	George H. Hansard	171	Bonnie Rangel
43	James O. Mullin	107	Benjamin Euresti Jr.	172	Donald J. Floyd
44	Margaret Keliher	108	Abe Lopez	173	Jack H. Holland
45	Carol R. Haberman	109	James L. Rex	174	George H. Godwin
46	Tom Neely	110	John R. Hollums	175	Mary R. Roman
47	David Gleason	111	Raul Vasquez	176	James Brian Rains
48	Robert (Bob) McCoy	112	Brock Jones Jr.	177	Carol G. Davies
49	Manuel R. Flores	113	Patricia Hancock	178	William T. Harmon
50	David Wayne Hajek	114	Cynthia Stevens Kent	179	Mike Wilkinson
51	Barbara L. Walther	115	Lauren L. Parish	180	Debbie Mantooth-Stricklin
52	Philip H. Zeigler	116	Martin Richter	181	Samuel C. Kiser
53	Mary Pearl Williams	117	Robert Blackmon	182	Jeannie S. Barr
54	George H. Allen	118	Robert H. Moore III	183	Joan Huffman
55	Sherry Radack	119	John E. Sutton	184	Jan Krocker
56	Norma Venso	120	Robert Dinsmoor	185	Susan Brown
57	Patrick J. Boone	121	Kelly Glen Moore	186	Sam Katz
58	James William Mehaffy Jr.	122	Frank T. Carmona	187	Raymond C. Angelini
59	Rayburn M. (Rim) Nall Jr.	123	Guy W. Griffin	188	David Brabham
60	James Gary Sanderson	124	Alvin G. Khoury	189	Jeff Work
61	John Donovan	125	John A. Coselli	190	John Phillip Devine
62	Jim Noble Thompson	126	Ernest C. Garcia	191	Catarina Haynes
		127	Sharolyn P. Wood		

Court	Judge	Court	Judge	Court	Judge
192	Merrill L. Hartman	261	Lora J. Livingston	330	Theo Bedard
193	David Evans	262	Mike Anderson	331	Robert A. Perkins
194	Harold Entz	263	Jim Wallace	332	Mario E. Ramirez Jr.
195	John Nelms	264	Martha J. Trudo	333	Joseph "Tad" Halbach Jr.
196	Joe M. Leonard	265	Keith Dean	334	Jesse W. Wainwright
197	Migdalia Lopez	266	Donald R. Jones	335	H.R. Towslee
198	Emil Karl Prohl	267	Whayland W. Kilgore	336	Ray Felty Grisham
199	Robert T. Dry Jr.	268	Brady G. Elliott	337	Jim Barr
200	Paul R. Davis Jr.	269	John T. Wooldridge	338	Elsa Alcala
201	Suzanne Covington	270	Brent Gamble	339	Caprice Cosper
202	Bill Peek	271	John H. Fostel	340	Dick Alcala
203	Lana Rolf McDaniel	272	John M. Delaney	341	Elma Teresa Salinas Ender
204	Mark Nancarrow	273	John W. Mitchell	342	Bob McGrath
205	Kathleen H. Olivares	274	Gary L. Steel	343	Alonzo "Al" T. Rodriguez
206	Rose Guerra Reyna	275	Juan R. Partida	344	Carroll E. Wilborn Jr.
207	Jack Hollis Robison	276	William R. (Bill) Porter	345	F. Scott McCown
208	Denise Collins	277	John R. Carter	346	Jose J. Baca
209	Michael Thomas McSpadden	278	Jerry A. Sandel	347	Joaquin Villarreal III
210	Sam M. Paxson	279	Tom Mulvaney	348	Dana M. Womack
211	Lawrence Dee Shipman	280	Tony Lindsay	349	Jerry L. Calhoon
212	Susan Criss	281	Jane Nenninger Bland	350	Jesse Aaron Holloway
213	Robert K. Gill	282	Karen J. Greene	351	Mark Kent Ellis
214	Mike Westergren	283	Molly Meredith Francis	352	Bonnie Sudderth
215	Dwight Eugene Jefferson	284	Olen Underwood	353	Margaret A. Cooper
216	Stephen B. Ables	285	Michael Peden	354	Richard (Rick) Beacom
217	David V. Wilson	286	Andy Kupper	355	Ralph Walton
218	Stella H. Saxon	287	Gordon Houston Green	356	Britton Edward Plunk
219	Curt B. Henderson	288	Frank Montalvo	357	Rogelio (Roy)Valdez
220	James Edward Morgan	289	Carmen Kelsey	358	Bill McCoy
221	Suzanne Stovall	290	Sharon MacRae	359	James H. (Jim) Keeshan
222	David Wesley Gulley	291	Gerry Meier	360	V. Sue Koenig
223	Lee Waters	292	Henry Wade Jr.	361	Steve Smith
224	David Peeples	293	Cynthia L. Muniz	362	David C. White
225	John J. Specia Jr.	294	Tommy W. Wallace	363	Faith Johnson
226	Sid L. Harle	295	Tracy E. Christopher	364	Bradley S. Underwood
227	Philip A. Kazen Jr.	296	Betty Ann Caton	365	Amado Abascal III
228	Ted Poe	297	Everett Young	366	Nathan E. White Jr.
229	Alex W. Gabert	298	Adolph Canales	367	Lee Gabriel
230	Belinda Hill	299	Jon Neil Wisser	368	Burt Carnes
231	Randy Catterton	300	Kenneth Randall	369	Bascom W. Bentley III
232	Mary Lou Keel	301	Susan Amanda Rankin	370	Noe Gonzalez
233	William Wren Harris	302	Frances A. Harris	371	James R. Wilson
234	Scott A. Brister	303	Richard Johnson	372	Scott Wisch
235	Jerry W. Woodlock	304	Harold C. "Hal" Gaither	377	Robert C. Cheshire
236	Thomas Wilson Lowe III	305	Cheryl Lee Shannon	378	Roy A. Scoggins Jr.
237	Sam Medina	306	Susan Baker Olsen	380	Charles F. Sandoval
238	John Hyde	307	Robin D. Sage	381	John A. Pope III
239	J. Ray Gayle III	308	Georgia Dempster	382	Sue Pirtle
240	Thomas R. Culver III	309	John D. Montgomery	383	Reed Leverton
241	Diane V. DeVasto	310	Lisa Ann Millard	384	Patrick Garcia
242	Edward L. Self	311	Doug Warne	385	Willie Bryan DuBose
243	David C. Guaderrama	312	James Douglas Squier	392	Carter W. Tarrance
244	Gary L. Watkins	313	Pat Shelton	394	Kenneth D. DeHart
245	Annette Galik	314	Mary M. Craft	410	K. Michael Mayes
246	Donald Gene Ritter	315	(Earl) Kent Ellis	411	Robert Hill Trapp
247	Bonnie Crane Hellums	316	John La Grone		
248	Joan Campbell	317	Larry Thorne		**Criminal District Courts**
249	D. Wayne Bridewell	318	Dean Rucker		
250	John K. Dietz	319	Martha Huerta		
251	Pat Pirtle	320	Don Emerson	Dallas 1	Janice Warder
252	Leonard Giblin Jr.	321	Carole Clark	Dallas 2	Edwin V. King
253	Chap Cain	322	Frank Sullivan	Dallas 3	Robert Francis
254	Dee Miller	323	Jean Hudson Boyd	Dallas 4	John Coleman Creuzot
255	Craig Fowler	324	Brian A. Carper	Dallas 5	Manny D. Alvarez
256	Brenda Garrett Green	325	Judith G. Wells	Jefferson	Charles Dana Carver
257	Linda Motheral	326	Aleta Hacker	Tarrant 1	Sharen Wilson
258	Elizabeth E. Coker	327	Philip R. Martinez	Tarrant 2	Wayne Francis Salvant
259	Quay Parker	328	Tom Stansbury	Tarrant 3	Don Leonard
260	Buddie J. Hahn	329	Daniel R. Sklar	Tarrant 4	Joe Drago III

State Agencies

On the following pages is information about several of the many state agencies. The agencies themselves supplied this information to the Texas Almanac. The Web address for more information about state agencies, boards and commissions is: **www.texas.gov/agency/agencies.html**.

Department of Human Services

Source: Texas Department of Human Services

The **Texas Department of Human Services (DHS)**, administers state and federal programs that provide financial, health and social services to three main categories of clients: low-income families with children, the elderly or disabled, and victims of family violence. The department's headquarters are in Austin, but its services are provided through 10 administrative regions and more than 400 local offices serving all 254 Texas counties. Determining client eligibility for programs and services is a primary agency function; most direct client services are provided by local service providers that contract with the agency.

Texas Works

Texas Works is the agency's welfare-to-work program, emphasizing personal responsibility in helping clients identify resources that can assist them in achieving economic self-sufficiency.

• The **Temporary Assistance for Needy Families** (TANF) program provides basic financial assistance for needy children and the parents or caretakers with whom they live. As a condition of eligibility, caretakers must sign and abide by a personal-responsibility agreement. Time limits for benefits have been set by both state and federal welfare-reform legislation. A typical TANF family of three (caretaker and two children) can receive a maximum monthly grant of $188. In fiscal year 1998, an average 474,755 children and caretakers received TANF assistnce each month, compared to 600,128 per month in 1997.

• The **Food Stamp program** is an entirely federally funded program that assists low-income families, the elderly and single adults to obtain a nutritionally adequate diet. Those eligible for food stamps include households receiving TANF or federal Supplemental Security Income benefits and non-public asstance households having incomes below 130 percent of the poverty level.

Food stamp and TANF benefits are delivered through the Electronic Benefit Transfer system, through which clients access benefits at 13,000 retail locations statewide with Lone Star debit cards. In fiscal year 1998, an average of 1.7 million Texans per month received food-stamp benefits totaling $1.4 billion for the year.

• DHS determines eligibility for **Medicaid**, which provides access to vital health-care services. The TANF-related Medicaid program provides medical coverage to TANF recipients and other income-eligible families, women and children who do not receive TANF cash assistance. Transitional Medicaid is available for up to 18 months for recipients who lose TANF cash assistance because of job earnings.

Long-Term Care Services

The DHS provides assistance to Medicaid-eligible clients who are elderly or disabled in community-based programs or nursing facilities. The **Nursing Facility** program pays for nursing-home care for Medicaid recipients who have a documented medical condition requiring the skills of a licensed nurse on a regular basis. **Community Care** programs are designed to avoid prematurely placing elderly or disabled individuals in nursing homes or other facilities by providing services including assistance with personal care, home-delivered meals, emergency response, client-managed attendant services, grants for architectural modifications or major-equipment purchases, adult day-activity and health services, supervised residential-care services, adult foster care and respite care.

The **Long-Term Care Regulatory** (LTC-R) program licenses and certifies nursing homes and intermediate-care facilities for persons with mental retardation. Adult day-care facilities and personal-care homes also are licensed. LTC-R staff investigates complaints and allegations of abuse, neglect and noncompliance.

Other Programs

The **Family Violence** program educates the public about domestic violence and offers emergency shelter and support services to victims and their children. The program is administered through contracts with family-violence service providers

The **Disaster Assistance program** processes grant applications for victims of presidentially declared disasters, such as tornados, floods and hurricanes. Victims are eligible for assistance from this state-administered federal program if they do not have insurance and cannot qualify for low-interest loans from the Small Business Administration.

The entirely federally funded **Refugee Resettlement program** provides cash, health care and social services to eligible refugees to help them become self-sufficient as soon as possible after arriving in the United States.

Eight **Special Nutrition** programs, completely funded by the U.S. Dept. of Agriculture, provide meals to eligible recipients, including elderly or functionally impaired adults and to children and low-income individuals and families.

On the Web: **www.dhs.state.tx.us**. ☆

Costs of Services

Costs of most services are shared by the state and federal governments. Expenditures for fiscal year 1998 are as follows (does not include the value of food stamps ($1.4 bilion) and food distributed by DHS):

Family self-sufficiency services . .	$835,597,207
Family violence services	14,272,292
Long-term care services	2,436,988,117
Support services (includes administrative costs).	91,001,947
Total	$3,377,859,563

www.TexasAlmanac.com
for links to even more Texas
information that's current, official and reliable

The General Land Office

Source: General Land Office of Texas

History of the General Land Office

(Please note that a more comprehensive history of the General Land Office can be found in the 1998-1999 Texas Almanac. On the Web: www.glo.state.tx.us)

The Texas General Land Office is one of the oldest governmental entities in the state, dating back to the Republic of Texas. The first General Land Office was established in the constitution of the Republic of Texas in 1836, and the first Texas Congress enacted the provision into law in 1837. The General Land Office was established to oversee the distribution of public lands, to register titles (called patents) on land grants, and to maintain records.

In the early years of statehood, Texas established the precedent of using its vast public domain for public benefit. The first use was to sell or trade off land to eliminate the huge debt remaining from the War for Independence and early years of the Republic.

Texas also gave away land for internal improvements, including railroads, homesteads, veterans grants, capitol construction and for settlement of boundary disputes.

The public domain was closed in 1898 when the Texas Supreme Court declared that there was no more vacant and unappropriated land in Texas. Only some small tracts were left, and in 1900, all remaining unappropriated land was set aside by the Texas legislature for the benefit of the public schools.

Today 20.3 million acres are considered to be in the public domain. This includes almost 4 million acres of submerged coastal lands, which are bays, inlets and the area from the Texas shoreline to the three-marine-league line (10.36 miles) in the Gulf of Mexico. (For a more thorough discussion of the Texas Tidelands controversy see the 1972-1973 Texas Almanac.) In addition, more than one million acres are estimated to make up the state's riverbeds and vacant areas. The University of Texas System holds title to 2,109,000 fee acres, and other state agencies or special schools hold title to approximately 2 million acres. Texas owns mineral rights alone in approximately 7.5 million acres covered under the Relinquishment Act, the Free Royalty Act and the various sales acts, and has outright ownership to approximately 784,264 upland acres, mostly west of the Pecos. Texas has liens on 1.5 million acres of land in the active accounts of the Veterans Land Board and another 1.7 million acres of excess land that are not calculated into any category.

The General Land Office handles leases and revenue accounting on all lands dedicated to the Permanent School Fund and on land owned by various state agencies.

Commissioner of the General Land Office is David Dewhurst.

Veterans Programs

Veterans Land Program

In 1946, the Legislature created a bond program to aid veterans in purchasing farm land. Up to $1.5 billion in bonding authority has been authorized over the years in a series of constitutional amendments; as of March 30, 1999, more than $1.31 billion of the bonds had been sold to fund loans.

Loans cannot exceed $40,000, and tracts purchased through the program must be at least five acres. To date, more than 115,109 veterans have participated in the land program, purchasing more than 4.8 million acres of land.

Veterans Housing Assistance Program

The 68th Legislature created the Veterans Housing Assistance Program, which also is funded through bond proceeds. Over the years, the people of Texas have passed constitutional amendments authorizing the selling of $2 billion in bonds to finance this program. To date,

$1.385 billion in bonds have been sold to fund housing loans.

Eligible veterans may borrow up to $45,000 toward the purchase of a home; the balance of the purchase price is financed through private-sector lending institutions. When the low-interest veterans loan is combined with private-sector interest rates, monthly payments are significantly reduced. Since the program began operation in January 1984, more than 39,000 veterans have received housing loans.

Veterans Home Improvement Program

In 1986, the Veterans Land Board implemented the Veterans Home Improvement Program, which is funded through the Veterans Housing Assistance Program. This program allows Texas veterans to borrow up to $25,000 to make substantial home repairs and improvements.

To date, more than 3,000 veterans have received home improvement loans. More than $45 million has been loaned since the program's inception.

All three programs are administered by the **Texas Veterans Land Board**, which is chaired by the Commissioner of the General Land Office. The bonded debt for the programs and all administrative costs are completely financed by the veterans who use the programs; there is no cost to Texas taxpayers. Eligible veterans may participate in each of the three veterans programs once.

Details about the programs may be obtained from the Texas Veterans Land Board by calling toll free 1-800-252-VETS.

Texas State Veterans Homes

In 1997, the 75th Texas Legislature approved legislation authorizing the Texas Veterans Land Board to construct and operate Texas State Veterans Homes under a cost-sharing program with the U.S. Department of Veterans Affairs (DVA) and to issue revenue bonds to obtain the state's necessary share. The homes will provide affordable, quality, long-term care for Texas' aging veteran population. The state provides the land and 35 percent of construction costs; the DVA provides 65 percent of construction costs. Four 160-bed homes will be built. At press time in mid-1999, the homes in Temple and Floresville were scheduled to open in late 1999, while the Big Spring and Bonham homes were scheduled to open in the spring of 2000. ☆

Distribution of the Public Lands of Texas

Purpose	Acres
Settlers	68,027,108
Spain and Mexico	24,583,923
Spanish and Mexican Grants south of the Nueces River, recognized by Act of Feb. 10, 1852	3,741,241
Headrights	30,360,002
Republic colonies	4,494,806
Pre-emption land	4,847,136
Military	9,874,262
Bounty	5,354,250
Battle donations	1,162,240
Veterans donations	1,377,920
Confederate	1,979,852
Improvements	37,155,714
Road	27,716
Navigation	4,261,760
Irrigation	584,000
Ships	17,000
Manufacturing	111,360
Railroads	32,153,878
Education	52,329,168
University, public school and eleemosynary institutions	52,329,168
Total of distributed lands	**167,386,252**

Texas Natural Resource Conservation Commission

Created in 1993, the Texas Natural Resource Conservation Commission (TNRCC), is one of the most comprehensive state environmental agencies in the nation. The agency strives to protect the state's human and natural resources in a manner consistent with sustainable economic development. The goals are clean air, clean water and the safe management of waste, with an emphasis on pollution prevention.

The TNRCC works to reduce the release of pollutants and contaminants, ensuring that waste is properly managed and safely disposed of, and expediting the cleanup of contaminated sites. The agency also manages the state's water resources and enforces compliance with state and federal clean air and water laws. The agency oversees such wide-ranging areas as water runoff from agricultural lands, ozone pollution in highly congested urban areas, leakage from petroleum-storage tanks and water quality in the estuaries of Corpus Christi and Galveston bays.

The executive director of the agency is Jeffrey A. Saitas. The agency can be contacted at: P.O. Box 13087, Austin   78711-3087;   phone   512-239-1000;   Web: www.tnrcc.state.tx.us. The 24-hour emergency spill reporting hotline is 1-800-832-8224. ☆

Texas Department of Economic Development

The Texas Department of Economic Development is the state's major economic development agency. Its mission is to create a positive business climate that attracts new companies, promotes Texas as a travel destination and trains today's work force for tomorrow's high-skill jobs. It disseminates information on international trade, worker-training incentives, tourism and other business matters. The department's three program divisions are:

• The **Trade and Investment Division** oversees initiatives airmed at retaining and expanding the state's existing business and industrial base while marketing Texas nationally and internationally as an ideal spot for locating or expanding a company. This division supports businesses in the areas of business services, corporate expansion and recruitment, international business and through the State of Texas Mexico Office.

• The **Tourism Division** promotes Texas as the premier travel destination to the domestic and international travel market. The division works with convention and visitor bureaus, chambers of commerce, travel-related organizations and associations to promote Texas in all tourism marketing arenas.

• The **Information and Planning Division** includes the areas of communcations, governmental relations, state and federal relations, strategic planning, and serving as an economic information clearinghouse. This division endeavors to ensure that governmental resources are available to the state's small businesses, rural communities and defense-dependent communities.

The agency can be contacted at P.O. Box 12728, Austin 78711-2728; phone 512-936-0100; fax 512-936-0303; Web: **www.tded.state.tx.us**. ☆

Texas Youth Commission

Source: Texas Youth Commission

The following institutions are under the direction of the **Texas Youth Commission,** the agency that administers the juvenile corrections system of the state. The date of founding of each facility, the superintendent's name and the average daily population are included. In the case of newly constructed schools, where the daily population at press time was far below eventual population, the capacity of the facility is included.

Brownwood State School — Brownwood; 1970; Dan Humeniuk; 322. **Brownwood Girls Unit** — Brownwood; 1970; Dan Humeniuk; 143. **Corsicana State Home and School** — Corsicana; 1897; Chester Clay Jr.; 153. **Crockett State School** — Crockett; 1947; Rey Gomez; 249. **Evins Regional Juvenile Center** — Edinburg; 1990; Butch Held; 230. **Gainesville State School** — Gainesville; 1915; Dr. Theodore Shorten; 353. **Giddings State Home and School** — Giddings; 1972; Stan DeGerolami; 383.

Also, **J.W. Hamilton Jr. State School** — Bryan; 1997;

Delbert Price; 417. **Jefferson County State School** — Beaumont; 1995; Marie Murdoch; 317. **Marlin Orientation and Assessment Unit** — Marlin; 1995; (Vacancy); 47. **McLennan County State Juvenile Correctional Facility** - Mart; Nov. 1999; John Hopkins; (352 capacity). **San Saba State School** — San Saba; 1996; Lydia Barnard; 362. **Texas Youth Commission Bootcamp** — Sheffield; 1995; Al Elizondo (commandant); 58. **Victory Field Correctional Academy** — Vernon; 1997; (Vacancy); 161. **West Texas State School** — Pyote; 1966; Lemuel "Chip" Harrison; 243.

In addition, the commission operates nine **half-way houses,** each of which has an average daily population of between 18 and 24 youth. These are located in Austin, Corpus Christi, Dallas, El Paso, Fort Worth, Harlingen, McAllen, Roanoke and San Antonio.

Steve Robinson is executive director of the commission.

On the Web: **www.tyc.state.tx.us** ☆

Texas Department of Criminal Justice

On the Web: **www.tdcj.state.tx.us**

The Texas Department of Criminal Justice, formed by the Texas Legislature in 1989, is composed of 11 divisions. Those most in the public view are:

• The **Institutional Division**, which manages the Department's prisons (more details below).

• The **Parole Division** is responsible for processing

offenders for release on parole or mandatory supervision and the subsequent provision of supervision and rehabilitative services for reintegration into the community. In fiscal year 1998, 80,000 adult offenders were under parole or mandatory supervision. More than 29,000 offenders were processed for release from prison and other facilities.

• The **State Jail Division** was established in 1993 to

provide community-oriented rehabilitation for property and drug offenders. As of July 15, 1999, there were 17 state jails with a total capacity of 24,261, located in *Austin, *Bartlett, Beaumont, Bonham, *Dallas, Dayton, Edinburg, El Paso, Gatesville, *Henderson, Houston, Humble, Hutchins, *Jacksboro, Plainview, *Raymondville and San Antonio. Those marked with an asterisk (*) are operated by private companies. In February 1996, the State Jail Division assumed administrative management of the Substance Abuse Felony Punishment facilities. As of July 15, 1999, there were SAFP facilities in Breckenridge, Brownwood, Burnet, Dayton, Hondo, Plainview, San Diego and Winnsboro, with a total capacity of 4,072.

• The **Community Justice Assistance Division**, provides supervision and oversight of the community supervision and corrections departments that work directly with probationers. As of July 1999, about 250,000 felony probationers and 189,000 misdemeanor probationers were under community supervision.

The remaining seven divisions are primarily internal in scope: Programs and Services, Health Services, Victim Services, Public Information Office, General Counsel, Executive and Financial Services.

The **Texas Board of Criminal Justice** guides the administration and operation of the department in the areas of policy, planning and budget. For a list of members, see Boards and Commissions list following this article. Allan B. Polunsky has been board chairman since March 1995. TDCJ executive director is Wayne Scott.

Institutional Division

The Institutional Division is responsible for the confinement of adult felony offenders who are sentenced to prison (juvenile offenders are under the jurisdiction of the Texas Youth Commission). The division's headquarters are in Huntsville, with Gary Johnson as director.

The Institutional Division currently consists of 72 major facilities: 58 prisons and 14 transfer facilities, as well as one boot camp, four medical facilities, three psychiatric facilities and two work camps. The **total number of inmates** on hand at the end of fiscal year 1998 was 146,269. This population compares with 18,151 on Aug. 31, 1975.

The **Agriculture Division** operates and manages 145,337 acres located in 46 counties, employing more than 300 full-time employees and using 5,800 inmates each year in operations on 50 prison units. They operate packing plants, cotton gins and feed mills as well as raising crops and tending livestock.

Texas Correctional Industries operates 43 factories or plants at 35 prison units. These industries utilizing inmate labor produce goods and services for the TDCJ and other tax-supported agencies and governmental entities. Product categories include automobile repairs and products, textile and leather products and metal and wood products. During fiscal 1998, these industries employed 6,880 inmates and generated sales of more than $72 million.

These enterprises help keep the daily costs per inmate to $38.71. This compares with $44.40 in 1995.

In 1969, an **independent school** (Windham School District) was created to offer education in grades 1-12 and special education leading to a GED or high-school diploma. Participation is mandatory for those who cannot read at the sixth-grade level. Participation is voluntary for those deemed literate but who have less than a high-school diploma. In fiscal 1997-98, more than 75,000 inmates participated in the WSD's programs; 4,290 GED certificates, 7,458 career and technology education certificates and vocational certificates were awarded.

Cooperative programs in **higher education** are offered on several units at nearby junior colleges, leading to associate degrees. Four-year and graduate degrees can be earned from cooperating senior colleges and universities. In the 1997-98 school year, 341 associate degrees, 33 baccalaureate degrees and 6 master's degrees were conferred on inmates. Also, 1,809 inmates earned junior

Inmate Profile

Age/Sex/Ethnicity

94 % are male	47 % are black
Average age: 33	28 % are white
	25 % are Hispanic

Sentences/Length of Time Served

Average sentence: 23 years
Average part of sentence served: 25%
More than 50% of inmates have been in prison before.

Education

Average IQ: 92
More than 60% don't have a high school diploma.
Average education achievement score: 7th grade

college vocational credit certificates.

Rehabilitative programs are also available in the fields of physiological and psychiatric health care, varied recreational programs, legal services, religious activities, inmate self-help groups, work-release programs, job placement services, pre-release programs and support programs in conjunction with other state agencies.

Prison Units

The town listed is the nearest one to the facility, although the unit may actually be in another county. For instance, the Middleton transfer unit is in Jones County, but the nearest city is Abilene, which is in Taylor County. Units marked by an asterisk (*) are operated by private companies.

Allred, Iowa Park, Wichita Co.; **Beto I**, Tennessee Colony, Anderson Co.; *Bridgeport, Bridgeport, Wise Co.; **Briscoe**, Dilley, Frio Co.; **Central**, Sugar Land, Fort Bend Co.; **Clemens**, Brazoria, Brazoria Co.; **Clements**, Amarillo, Potter Co.; *Cleveland, Cleveland, Liberty Co.; **Coffield**, Tennessee Colony, Anderson Co.; **Connally**, Kenedy, Karnes Co.; **Dalhart**, Dalhart, Dallam Co.; **Daniel**, Snyder, Scurry Co.; **Darrington**, Rosharon, Brazoria Co.; **Diagnostic**, Huntsville, Walker Co.; *Diboll, Diboll, Angelina Co.; **Eastham**, Lovelady, Houston Co.; **Ellis**, Huntsville, Walker Co.; **Estelle & Estelle High Security**, Huntsville, Walker Co.; **Ferguson**, Midway, Madison Co.; **Gatesville**, Gatesville, Coryell County (Women's Unit); **Goree**, Huntsville, Walker Co.; **High-tower**, Dayton, Liberty Co.; **Hilltop**, Gatesville, Coryell Co.; **Hobby**, Marlin, Falls Co.; **Hodge**, Rusk, Cherokee Co.; **Hospital Galveston**, Galveston, Galveston Co.; **Hughes**, Gatesville, Coryell Co.; **Huntsville**, Huntsville, Walker Co.; **Jester I, II, III and IV**, Richmond, Fort Bend Co.; **Jordan**, Pampa, Gray Co.; *Kyle, Kyle, Hays Co.; **Lewis**, Woodville, Tyler Co.; *Lockhart, Lockhart, Caldwell Co.; **Luther**, Navasota, Grimes Co.; **Lynaugh**, Fort Stockton, Pecos Co.; **McConnell**, Beeville, Bee Co.; **Michael**, Tennessee Colony, Anderson Co.; **Montford**, Lubbock, Lubbock Co.; *B. Moore, Overton, Smith Co.; **Mountain View**, Gatesville, Coryell Co.; **Murray**, Gatesville, Coryell Co.; **Neal**, Amarillo, Potter Co.; **Pack**, Navasota, Grimes Co.; **Powledge**, Palestine, Anderson Co.; **Ramsey I, II and III**, Rosharon, Brazoria Co.; **Retrieve**, Angleton, Brazoria Co.; **Roach**, Childress, Childress Co.; **Robertson**, Abilene, Taylor Co.; **Skyview**, at Rusk State Hospital, Cherokee Co.; **Smith**; Lamesa, Dawson Co.; **Stevenson**, Cureo, DeWitt Co.; **Stiles**, Beaumont, Jefferson Co.; **Telford**, New Boston, Bowie Co.; **Terrell**, Livingston, Polk Co.; **Texas City**, Texas City, Galveston Co.; **Torres**, Hondo, Medina Co.; *Venus, Venus, Johnson Co.; **Wallace**, Colorado City, Mitchell Co.; **West Texas**, Lubbock, Lubbock Co.; **Wynne**, Huntsville, Walker Co.

Transfer Units

Cotulla, Cotulla, LaSalle Co.; **Duncan**, Diboll, Angelina Co.; **Fort Stockton**, Fort Stockton, Pecos Co.; **Garza East & West**, Beeville, Bee Co.; **Goodman**, Jasper, Jasper Co.; **Gurney**, Tennessee Colony, Anderson Co.; **Holliday**, Huntsville, Walker Co.; Jefferson Co.; **Middleton**, Abilene, Jones Co.; **C. Moore**, Bonham, Fannin Co.; **Rudd**, Brownfield, Terry Co.; **Segovia**, Edinburg, Hidalgo Co.; **Tulia**, Tulia, Swisher Co.; **Ware**, Colorado City, Mitchell Co. An additional seven contract transfer facilities are used by TDCJ.

Parole-ISF: Pampa, Pampa, Gray Co. ☆

Texas State Boards and Commissions

Following is a list of appointees to state boards and commissions, as well as names of other state officials, revised to July 1, 1999. Information includes, where available, (1) date of creation of agency; (2) whether the position is elective or appointive; (3) length of term; (4) number of members; (5) names of appointees, their hometowns and the dates of the terminations of their terms. In some instances the dates of expiration of terms have already passed; in such cases, no new appointment had been made by press time, and the official is continuing to fill the position until a successor can be named. Most positions marked "apptv." are appointed by the Governor. Where otherwise, appointing authority is given. Most advisory boards are not listed. Salaries for commissioners and administrators are those that were authorized by the appropriations bill passed by the 76th Legislature for the 2000-01 biennium; at press time, the salaries had not yet received final approval.

Accountancy, Texas State Board of Public - (1945 with 2-year terms; reorganized 1959 as 9-member board with 6-yr. overlapping terms; number of members increased to 12 in 1979; increased to 15 in 1989); per diem and expenses; 15 members: Billy M. Atkinson Jr., Sugar Land (1/31/05); Nita J. Clyde, Dallas (1/31/99); K. Michael Conaway, Midland (1/31/01); Jerry A. Davis, Houston (1/31/01); Kimberly Dryden, Amarillo (1/31/05); April L. Eyeington, College Station (1/31/05); Edwardo B. Franco, Irving (1/31/05); Gwen B. Gilbert, Dallas (1/31/03); Rebecca Beard Junker, Richmond (1/31/03); Robert C. Mann, Fort Worth (1/31/05); Jimmie L. Mason, Lubbock (1/31/01); Reagan S. McCoy, San Antonio (1/31/03); Lou Miller, San Antonio (1/31/01); Janet F. Parnell, Canadian (1/31/01); Barbara J. Thomas, Houston (1/31/03); I. Lee Wilson, Rockwall (1/31/97). Exec. Dir., William Treacy ($62,000), 333 Guadalupe, Suite 3-900, Austin 78701-3900.

Acupuncture Examiners, Texas State Board of - (1993); apptv.; 6 yrs.; per diem; 9 members: Rebecca Atchley, Lubbock (1/31/03); Lawrence Woon-Chung Chan, Amarillo (1/31/01); Cheng Ming Chang, San Antonio (1/31/01); Everett G. Heinze Jr., Austin (1/31/03); Shen Ping Liang, Houston (1/31/99); Dee Ann Newbold, Austin (1/31/05); Jacquelyn Diane Pearson, Plano (1/31/03); Claire H. Smith, Dallas (1/31/05); Annette M. Zaharoff, San Antonio (1/31/01).

Ad Valorem Tax Rate, Board to Calculate the - (1907); ex officio; term in other office; 3 members: Governor, State Comptroller of Public Accounts and State Treasurer.

Adjutant General - (1836 by Republic of Texas; present office established 1905); apptv.: Brig. Gen. Daniel James III (2/1/01) ($63,431, plus house and utilities), PO Box 5218, Austin 78763.

Adjutant General - Assistant for Air: Col. Michael B. Smith, PO Box 5218, Austin 78763.

Adjutant General - Assistant for Army: Brig. Gen. Wayne D. Marty, PO Box 5218, Austin 78763.

Administrative Judicial Districts of Texas, Presiding Judges - (Apptv. by Governor); serve terms concurrent with term as District Judge, subject to reappointment if re-elected to bench. No extra compensation. For names of judges, see Administrative Judicial Districts in index.

Aerospace Commission, Texas - (1987; re-established in 1989); apptv.; 6-yr.; 9 members: Gale E. Burkett, League City (2/1/05); Michael J. Butchko, Austin (2/1/05); David W. Carr, Austin (2/1/95); J. Jan Collmer, Dallas (2/1/05); R. Walter Cunningham, Houston (2/1/03); Anne H. McNamara, Dallas (2/1/01); Bryon D. Sehlke, Austin (2/1/03); T.C. Selman II, Lake Jackson (2/1/01); Norma H. Webb, Midland (2/1/03). Exec. Dir., Tom Moser ($75,000), PO Box 12088, Austin 78711-2088.

Aging, Texas Board on - (1965 as Governor's Committee on Aging; name changed in 1981 to present form; due to go out of existence 9-1-97 unless continued operation needed); apptv.; 6-yr.; expenses; 9 apptv. members: Nancy S. Bohman, San Antonio (2/1/99); Jack Burton, Cleburne (2/1/01); Miriam Ann Burton, Montgomery (2/1/03); Elena B. Gonzalez, Edinburg (2/1/99); Thomas E. Oliver, Baytown (2/1/03); Jan Patterson, Dallas (2/1/01); Dan Roberts, Fort Worth (2/1/99); William Toler Shaner, Midland (2/1/03); Holly H. Williamson, Houston (2/1/01). Exec. Dir., Mary Sapp ($65,000), PO Box 12786, Austin 78711.

Agricultural Finance Authority, Texas - (1987); expenses; 2-yr.; 6 members: Gina Davis, Spearman (1/1/00); Darwin D. DeWees, San Angelo (1/1/01); Sydney M. Golden, Lake Jackson (1/1/00); Robert Hensley Henry, Vernon (1/1/01); Susan Kennedy, Nacogdoches (1/1/01); Renato Ramirez, Zapata (1/1/01); Jane Anne Stinnett, Lubbock (1/1/00).

Agricultural Resources Protection Authority - (1989 with 9 members; changed to 15 members, 1995); 2-yr.; expenses; 15 members: 9 ex officio: Dir., Texas Agricultural Experiment Station; Dean, College of Agricultural Sciences of Texas Tech University; Dean, University of Texas School of Public Health, Houston; Dir. of Environmental Epidemiology at Texas Department of Health; Chief of Groundwater Conservation section, Texas Natural Resource Conservation Commission; Dir. of Institute for International Agribusiness Studies, Prairie View A&M; Commissioner of Agriculture; Exec. Dir., Texas Structural

Pest Control Board; Exec. Dir., State Soil and Water Conservation Board; 6 apptd. by Gov.: Craig Estes, Wichita Falls (2/1/97); L.C. Harrison, Wichita Falls (2/1/97); Gary Johnson, Dalhart (2/1/99); David K. Langford, San Antonio (2/1/97); David M. Nix, Lamesa (2/1/97); Julian H. Treviño, San Antonio (2/1/97).

Aircraft Pooling Board, State - (1979); apptv.; 6-yr.; 5 members — 2 ex officio: representative of State Auditor's Office and representative of General Services Commission; 3 apptv. — one by Gov., one by Speaker and one by Lt. Gov. Gov.'s appointee: Scott E. Rozzell, Houston (1/31/01). Exec. Dir., Bob DuLaney ($62,000), 4900 Old Manor Road, Austin 78723.

Alcohol and Drug Abuse, Texas Commission on - (1953 as Texas Commission on Alcoholism; name changed and membership increased to 9 in 1986; members reduced to 6 and term reduced to 2-yr. in 1995); apptv.; 2-yr.; per diem and expenses; 6 members: Rolland C. Allen, Corpus Christi (2/1/03); Beverly Barron, Odessa (2/1/01); Lisa F. Dickson, Dallas (2/1/05); James C. Oberwetter, Dallas (2/1/01); Dorothy C. Pettigrew, League City (2/1/03); Robert A. Valadez, San Antonio (2/1/05). Exec. Dir., Terry Faye Bleier ($90,000), PO Box 80529, Austin 78708-0529.

Alcoholic Beverage Commission, Texas - (1935 as Liquor Control Board; name changed 1970); apptv.; 6-yr; per diem and expenses; administrator apptd. by commission; 3 members: Martha S. Dickie, Austin (11/15/99); Allan Shivers Jr., Austin (11/15/01); John T. Steen Jr., San Antonio (11/15/03). Admin., Doyne Bailey ($83,991), 5806 Mesa Dr., Austin 78731.

Alzheimer's Disease and Related Disorders, Texas Council on - (1987); 2-yr.; expenses; 17 members: 5 agency heads or their designees: Depts. of Aging, Health, Human Services, Mental Health and Mental Retardation and the Long-Term Care Coordinating Council for the Elderly; plus four apptd. by Lt. Gov.; 4 apptd. by Speaker; 4 apptd. by Gov. as follows: Nancy J. Armour, Dallas (8/31/03); Johnnie B. Elliott, Brownwood (8/31/01); Ellen A. MacDonald, Houston (8/31/03); Margaret Pace Sykes, Fort Worth (8/31/01).

Angelina and Neches River Authority, Board of Directors - (1935 as Sabine-Neches Conservation Dist.; reorganized 1950 and name changed to Neches River Conservation Dist.; changed to present name in 1977); apptv.; expenses; 6-yr.; 9 members: Janelle C. Ashley, Nacogdoches (9/5/99); Margie C. Benge, Jacksonville (9/5/97); Susan W. Heckmann, Tyler (9/5/01); Henry H. Holubec Jr., Lufkin (9/5/99); Stewart M. Kenderdine, Palestine (9/5/01); Paul H. (Pete) Smith, Nacogdoches (9/5/97); Roy L. Stark, Palestine (9/5/99); Jack C. Sweeny, Diboll (9/5/01); Herman Wright, Jasper (9/5/97). Gen. Mgr., Gary L. Neighbors, PO Box 387, Lufkin 75902-0387.

Animal Health Commission, Texas - (1893 as Texas Livestock Sanitary Commission; name changed in 1959, membership increased to 9 in 1973; raised to 12 in 1983); apptv.; per diem and expenses; 6-yr.; 12 members: Quincy Barnes, San Antonio (9/6/03); Don Berend, Windthorst (9/6/01); Brad Bouma, El Paso (9/6/99); Tommy Bozka, Shiner (9/6/01); R.A. (Rob) Brown Jr., Throckmorton (9/6/01); Tevis Herd, Midland (9/6/01); Ernesto A. Morales, Devine (9/6/99); Dick Sherron, Beaumont (9/6/03); Marsha Stein, Snook (9/6/99); Joe W. Templeton, College Station (9/6/01); Richard C. Traylor, Carrizo Springs (9/6/03); Richard W. Winters, Brady (9/6/99). Exec. Dir., Terry Beals, DVM ($72,500), PO Box 12966, Austin 78711-2966.

Appraiser Licensing and Certification Board, Texas - (1991); 2-yr.; apptd.; per diem on duty; 9 members: Exec. Sec. of Veterans' Land Board and 8 apptees: Ben E. Barnett, Dallas (1/31/00); Jacqueline G. Humphrey, Amarillo (1/31/00); Eduardo A. Lopez, Corpus Christi (1/31/01); L.W. (Wayne) Mayo, Richardson (1/31/01); Debra S. Runyan, San Antonio (1/31/00); Robert A. "Pete" Seale Jr., Houston (1/31/01); James M. Synatzske, Stephenville (1/31/01); Angelina Velarde-White, El Paso (1/31/00). Commissioner, Renil C. Linér, PO Box 12188, Austin 78711-2188.

Architectural Examiners, Texas Board of - (1937 as 3-member board; raised to 6 members in 1951; increased to 9 in 1977); apptv.; 6-yr.; per diem and expenses; 9 members:

Maricela R. Barr, Austin (1/31/99); Mary Ann Bryan, Houston (1/31/99); Mary French Cable, Sulphur Springs (1/31/99); Paula C. Day, Fort Worth (1/31/01); Steven Ellinger, Abilene (1/31/03); John Only Greer, Bryan (1/31/01); Chao Chiung Lee, Bellaire (1/31/03); Dorothy Virginia Roberts, Austin (1/31/03); Cleveland Turner III, Amarillo (1/31/01). Exec. Dir., Cathy L. Hendricks, ($60,000), PO Box 12337, Austin 78711-2337.

Arts, Texas Commission on the - (1965 as Texas Fine Arts Commission; name changed to Texas Commission on the Arts and Humanities and membership increased to 18 in 1971; name changed to present form in 1979); apptv.; 6-yr.; expenses; 18 members: Malouf Abraham Jr., Canadian (8/31/01); Doris Alexander, Amarillo (8/31/01); Sue Schrier Bancroft, Argyle (8/31/03); Tony L. Chauveaux, Beaumont (8/31/03); David R. Durham, Abilene (8/31/99); Celso Gonzalez-Falla, Corpus Christi (8/31/03); Anne Lamkin Kinder, Houston (8/31/01); Nelda S. Lee, Odessa (8/31/99); Mary Anne McCloud, Eastland (8/31/01); Joan McGuire Mellard, San Antonio (8/31/99); Alyn Brown Morton, El Paso (8/31/01); Idell G. Rabin, Dallas (8/31/99); C.A. "Tony" Sherman, Missouri City (8/31/03); Kathleen B. Stevens, Fort Worth (8/31/03); Frances Annette Strake, Houston (8/31/93); Catherine B. Taylor, Midland (8/31/03); Jay M. Vogelson, Dallas (8/31/99); Constance M. Ware, Marshall (8/31/01); Gilberto Zepeda Jr., San Juan (8/31/99). Exec. Dir., John Paul Batiste ($62,000), PO Box 13406, Austin 78711-3406.

Athletic Trainers, Advisory Board of - (1971 as Texas Board of Athletic Trainers; name changed and membership increased to 6 in 1975); expenses; 6-yr.; 6 members: Kaye Cosby, San Antonio (1/31/99); John W. Harvey, Houston (1/31/03); Michael D. Saly, Conroe (1/31/01); Natalie Steadman, Lubbock (1/31/03); Michael K. Stephens, Austin (1/31/01); Paul T. Zeek, Nederland (1/31/99). Program Dir., Kathy Craft, Texas Dept. of Health, 1100 W. 49th, Austin 78756-3183.

Attorney, State Prosecuting - apptv.: Matthew Paul ($82,209), PO Box 12405, Austin 78711.

Auditor, State - (1929); apptv. by Legislative Audit Committee, a joint Senate-House committee; 2-yr.: Lawrence F. Alwin, PO Box 12067, Austin 78711-2067.

Banking Commissioner, State - (1923); apptv. by State Finance Commission; 2-yr.: Catherine A. Ghiglieri ($105,000), 2601 N. Lamar Blvd., Austin 78705 (See also Finance Commission of Texas).

Bar of Texas, State - (1939 as administrative arm of Supreme Court); 30 members elected by membership; 3-yr. terms; expenses paid from dues collected from membership. President, president-elect, vice president and immediate past president serve as ex officio members. Exec. Dir., Antonio Alvarado, PO Box 12487, Austin 78711.

Barber Examiners, State Board of - (1929 as 3-member board; membership increased in 1975); apptv.; 6-yr.; per diem and expenses; 6 members: William "Kirk" Kuykendall, Austin (1/31/05); H. Wayne Moore, Garland (1/31/03); Ernest W. Pack Sr., Waco (1/31/01); Hoye D. Tibbets, Grandview (1/31/99); Janice E. Wiggins, Kingsland (1/31/03); Charles Williams, San Antonio (1/31/01). Exec. Dir., Will K. Brown ($45,000), 333 Guadalupe, Ste. 2-110, Austin 78701.

Battleship Texas Advisory Board - (1983; superseded Battleship Texas Commission; apptv.; 6-yr.; 9 members: Charles A. Alcorn, Houston (2/1/01); Carol G. Calvert, Waxahachie (2/1/01); Carter Casteel, New Braunfels (2/1/97); Blaine G. Corman, Crosby (2/1/97); Gen. Hugh W. Hardy, Houston (2/1/99); Joshua Hill Sr., Houston (2/1/99); Jerry D. Neel, Friendswood (2/1/99); Thomas J. Perich, Sugar Land (2/1/01); Quinton Rogers, Marshall (2/1/97). Office Address: 3527 Battleground Rd., LaPorte 77571.

Blind and Severely Disabled Persons, Committee on Purchases of Products of - (See **Disabilities, Texas Council on Purchasing** from People with)

Blind and Visually Impaired, Governing Board of Texas School for the - (1979); apptv.; 6-yr.; expenses; 9 members: Mary G. Behnke, Orange (1/31/97); Anita Bonanno, Houston (1/31/01); Michael David Connolly, Nacogdoches (1/31/01); Roseanna Davidson, Lubbock (1/31/99); Kerry L. Goodwin, Dallas (1/31/99); Edward F. Guerro, Austin (1/31/97); Gloria Smith, Lufkin (1/31/97); Mary Sue Staples, Fort Worth (1/31/99); Frankie D. Swift, Miles (1/31/01). Exec. Dir. ($84,000), 1100 W. 45th, Austin 78756.

Blind, Texas Commission for the - (1931 as 6-member State Commission for the Blind; raised to 9 members in 1979; name changed in 1985); apptv.; 6-yr.; expenses; 9 members: James L. Caldwell, Austin (2/1/01); C. Robert Keeney Jr., Houston (2/1/01); W. Frank Mullican Jr., Lubbock (2/1/01); Joseph Muniz, Harlingen (2/1/05); Mary K. Norman (2/1/05); Don W. Oates, Nacogdoches (2/1/03); Robert K. Peters, Tyler (2/1/05); Beverly A. Stiles, Freer (2/1/03); John M. Turner, Dallas (2/1/03). Exec. Dir., Terrell I. Murphy ($70,000), PO Box

12866, Austin 78711.

Board of (Note: In most instances, state boards are alphabetized under key word, as **Accountancy, Texas State Board of Public.**)

Brazos River Authority, Board of Directors - (1929 as Brazos River Conservation and Reclamation Dist.; name changed to present form in 1953); apptv.; 6-yr; expenses; 21 members: Mary E. Ainslie, Sugar Land (2/1/03); Robert Bates Arnot, Breckenridge (2/1/03); Deborah H. Bell, Abilene (2/1/01); Lynn Elliott, Navasota (2/1/01); Jack Farrar, Hico (2/1/01); Ramiro A. Galindo, Bryan (2/1/01); Rodolfo Garcia, Alvin (2/1/03); Shirley M. Herring, Brenham (2/1/03); Joe B. Hinton, Crawford (2/1/05); Andrew Jackson, Missouri City (2/1/05); Celeste L. Kotter, Marlin (2/1/05); Ernest M. Koy, Bellville (2/1/03); Robert B. Lane, Clifton (2/1/05); J. Rodney Lee, Waco (2/1/03); Linda Kay Lyle, Plainview (2/1/01); Steve D. Pena, Round Rock (2/1/05); M. Lance Phillips, Mexia (2/1/05); Nancy N. Rabb, Round Rock (2/1/03); Ruth Schiermeyer, Lubbock (2/1/01); Janet Kay Sparks, Cleburne (2/1/05); Judith Vernon, Evant (2/1/01). Gen. Mgr., Gary Gwyn, P. O. Box 7555, Waco 76714-7555.

Canadian River Compact Commissioner - (1951); apptv.; salary and expenses; (function is to negotiate with other states respecting waters of the Canadian): Roger S. Cox, Amarillo (12/31/03) ($10,767).

Cancer Council, Texas - (1985); 6-yr.; 16 members: 1 State Senator; 1 State Representative; Chmn., Board of Health; Chmn., Board of Human Services; 12 apptd: Joseph Switz Bailes, Dallas (2/1/00); Karen Bonner, Corpus Christi (2/1/04); Grover L. Bynum Jr., Austin (2/1/96); Audrey Jane Castro, San Antonio (2/1/04); Clare Buie Chaney, Dallas (2/1/02); James D. Dannenbaum, Houston (2/1/96); Karen Hausinkveld, Arlington (2/1/96); C. Stratton Hill Jr., Houston (2/1/00); William C. Levin, Galveston (2/1/96); Donald C. Spencer, Austin (2/1/00); Courtney Townsend Jr., Galveston (2/1/98); J. Taylor Wharton, Houston (2/1/98). Exec. Dir., Emily F. Untermeyer ($57,691), PO Box 12097, Austin 78711.

Central Colorado River Authority (See **Colorado River Authority, Central.**)

Chemist, State - (1911); ex officio, indefinite term: George W. Latimer, P. O. Box 3160, College Station 77841-3160.

Childhood Intervention, Interagency Council on Early - (1981); apptv.; 2-yr.; expenses; 9 members: one apptd. by exec. dir. of Texas Education Agency, 8 apptd. by Gov.: Claudette W. Bryant, Dallas (2/1/99); Timothy James Flannery, Seabrook (2/1/01); Bess Althaus Graham, Austin (2/1/99); Tanya Huerta, San Antonio (2/1/99); Connie L. Hughes, Idalou (2/1/01); Susan C. Mengden-Ellis, San Antonio (2/1/03); Patrick J. Oliver III, Webster (2/1/01); Dimas Vasquez Jr., El Paso (2/1/03). Exec. Dir., Mary Elder ($68,000), 1100 W. 49th, Austin 78756.

Children's Trust Fund of Texas Council - (1985; became independent agency in 1991); apptv., 6-yr; 9 members: Patricia Aguayo, El Paso (9/1/01); Randy Burton, Spring (9/1/99); Thelma Sanders Clardy, DeSoto (9/1/99); Anne C. Crews, Dallas (9/1/01); Kathleen R. Ehlinger, Raymondville (9/1/03); Ann D. Louden, Fort Worth (9/1/03); Sylvia Martinez-Flores, Lubbock (9/1/99); Juan M. Parra, San Antonio (9/1/01); Sederick E. Susberry, Houston (9/1/03). Exec. Dir., Janie D. Fields ($53,914), 8929 Shoal Creek Blvd., #200, Austin 78757-6854.

Chiropractic Examiners, Texas Board of - (1949); apptv.; 6-yr.; expenses; 9 members: Cheryl Belinda Barber, Houston (2/1/03); Robert L. Coburn, Sweeny (2/1/05); Serge P. Francois, Irving (2/1/05); Richard L. Gillespie, San Marcos (2/1/03); Hubert Pickett Jr., Abilene (8/3/99); Oliver R. Smith Jr., El Paso (2/1/01); Dora Innes Valverde, Mission (2/1/01); Cynthia Sue Vaughn, Austin (2/1/03); John C. Weddle, Rockwall (2/1/01). Exec. Dir., Gary K. Cain ($52,000), 333 Guadalupe, Ste. 3-825, Austin 78701.

Coastal Water Authority, Board of Directors - (1967 as Coastal Industrial Water Authority, Board of Directors of; name changed in 1985); 7 members — 4 apptd. by mayor of Houston with advice and consent of governing body of Houston; 3 apptd. by Gov.; per diem and expenses; 2-yr.; Gov's. apptees: Buster E. French, Dayton (4/1/00); Darryl L. King, Houston (4/1/01); Gary R. Nelson, Baytown (4/1/01). Exec. Dir., Ralph T. Rundle, 1200 Smith St., Ste. 2260, Houston 77002.

College Opportunity Act Committee - (1989); 6-yr.; 9 members: 6 ex officio: Commissioner, General Land Office; Exec. Admin., Texas Water Development Board; Comptroller; State Treasurer; Exec. Dir., Bond Review Board; Commissioner of Higher Education. 3 apptd.: Laura Haley Bley, Fort Worth (2/1/03); Barbara J. Dugas-Patterson, Houston (2/1/97); Joe Munoz, San Angelo (2/1/01).

Colorado River Authority, Central, Board of Directors - (1935); apptv.; 6-yr.; per diem on duty; 9 members: Herman B. Cassaday, Talpa (2/1/97); Robert J. Cheaney II, Santa Ana (2/

1/93); Thelbert Elkins, Coleman (2/1/97); Jimmie S. Hobbs, Coleman (2/1/97); Ann Miller Hargett, Coleman (2/1/01); Clifford L. Horn, Talpa (2/1/93); Nicholas J. Knox, Burkett (2/1/93); Nan Knox Markland, Burkett (2/1/01); Ronald W. Owens, Coleman (2/1/01). Operations Mgr., Laneal Maedgen, PO Box 964, Coleman 76834.

Colorado River Authority, Lower, Board of Directors - (1934 as 9-member board; membership increased in 1951 and 1975); apptv.; 6-yr.; per diem on duty; 15 members: Pamela R. Akins, Marble Falls (2/1/03); Ann E. Jones, Brownwood (2/1/03); Patricia Kirk, San Saba (2/1/03); David L. Kithil, Marble Falls (2/1/05); Hilda C. Kroll, Johnson City (2/1/01); F. Scott LaGrone, Georgetown (2/1/05); Robert W. Lambert, Horseshoe Bay (2/1/05); Gale Lincke, La Grange (2/1/03); John H. Matthews, Eagle Lake (2/1/05); Arthur J. Milberger, Bay City (2/1/03); Charles Patrick Oles Jr., Austin (2/1/01); E. Peter Pincoffs, Austin (2/1/99); Steve D. Rivers, Bastrop (2/1/99); Louis Romero Jr., Kerrville (2/1/01); Rosemary Ann Rust, Wharton (2/1/05). Gen. Mgr., Mark Rose, P. O. Box 220, Austin 78767-0220.

Colorado River Authority, Upper, Board of Directors - (1935 as 9-member board; reorganized in 1965); apptv.; 6-yr.; per diem and expenses; indefinite number of members: Ray Alderman, Winters (2/1/01); Jack H. Brewer, Robert Lee (2/1/03); Fred R. Campbell, Paint Rock (2/1/03); C. Skeete Foster, Sterling City (2/1/99); Ruby N. Gutierrez, San Angelo (2/1/99); Ralph E. Hoelscher, Miles (2/1/01); Hope W. Huffman, San Angelo (2/1/03); Jeffie Roberts, Robert Lee (2/1/99); Dorris Sonnenberg, Bronte (2/1/01). Ellen Groth, Admin. Asst., PO Box 1482, San Angelo 76902-1482.

Commissioner of (See keyword, as **Agriculture, Commissioner of.)**

Concho River Water and Soil Conservation Authority, Lower - (1939); 6-yr.; 9 members: Leroy Paul Beach, Millersview (2/1/93); Howard E. Loveless, Eden (2/1/99); Billy J. Mikeska, Eola (2/1/99); Eugene R. Rogers, Eden (2/1/97); Benjamin O. Sims, Paint Rock (2/1/97); Edwin T. Tickle, Eden (2/1/01); T.E. Wells, Paint Rock (2/1/01); Harvey P. Williams, Eola (2/1/01). Office Address: Rt. 1, PO Box 4, Paint Rock 76866.

Conservatorship Board, State - (1979); apptv.; expenses; 6-yr.; 3 members: Carolyn Gallagher Austin (2/1/01); Byron Tunnell, Bullard (2/1/97); J. Michael Weiss, Lubbock (2/1/99).

Consumer Credit Commissioner - Leslie L. Pettijohn ($90,000), 2601 N. Lamar, Austin 78705-4207.

Cosmetology Commission, Texas - (1935 as 3-member State Board of Hairdressers and Cosmetologists; name changed and membership increased to 6 apptv. and one ex officio in 1971); apptv.; per diem and expenses; 6-yr.; apptv. members: Comer J. Cottrell Jr., Dallas (12/31/01); Robin D. Crump, Temple (12/31/99); Virginia G. Dillman, Dallas (12/31/99); William (B.J.) Joseph, Harlingen (12/31/03); Heliana L. Kiessling, Friendswood (12/31/03); Clare Taylor, Corsicana (12/31/03). Exec. Dir., Delores L. Alspaugh ($46,338), PO Box 26700, Austin 78755-0700.

Counselors, Texas State Board of Examiners of Professional - (1981); apptv.; 6-yr.; expenses; 9 members: Ana C. Bergh, Edinburg (2/1/05); Judy Broussard, Levelland (2/1/01); Joseph D. Dameron, Denton (2/1/01); J. Lee Jagers, Richardson (2/1/01); Gay T. McAlister, Longview (2/1/01); Suzanne Moore, San Antonio (2/1/03); Anthony P. Picchioni, Grapevine (2/1/99); Judy Powell, The Woodlands (2/1/05); Gene Ryder, San Antonio (2/1/01). Exec. Sec., John L. Luther, 1100 W. 49th, Austin 78756-3183.

Court Reporters Certification Board - (1977 as 9-member Texas Reporters Committee; name changed to present form and membership increased to 12 in 1983); apptv. by State Supreme Court; 6-yr.; expenses Exec. Secy., Peg Liedtke ($40,000), 205 W. 14th St., Ste. 101, Austin 78701.

Credit Union Commission - (1949 as 3-member Credit Union Advisory Commission; name changed and membership increased to 6 in 1969; increased to 9 in 1981); apptv.; 6-yr.; expenses; 9 members: Garold R. Base, Plano (2/15/01); Floyd W. Burnside Jr., San Antonio (2/15/05); Cynthia Cabaza, Weslaco (2/15/03); Richard Allen Glasco Jr., Austin (2/15/03); Fran V. Hawkins, Robstown (2/15/05); Robert S. Hayes, Amarillo (2/15/01); Karen A. Jacks, Longview (2/15/05); Carlos Puente, Fort Worth (2/15/05); J. Howell Thomas, Baytown (2/15/03); . Commissioner, Harold E. Feeney ($90,000), 914 E. Anderson Ln., Austin 78752-1699.

Crime Stoppers Advisory Council - (1981); apptv.; 2-yr.; 5 members (all terms expire 9/1/99): Vernon V. Cook, Waco; Janice C. Gillen, Rosenberg; Juan F. Jorge, Tomball; Lennie C. Sims, Wellington.

Criminal Justice, Texas Board of - (1989: assumed duties of former Texas Board of Corrections and Adult Probation Commission; also oversees Board of Pardons and Paroles Division); apptd; 6-yr.; expenses; 9 members: Patricia A. Day, Dallas (2/1/03); Lawrence G. Francis, El Paso (2/1/99); John David Franz, Hidalgo (2/1/01); Gilberto Hinojosa, Corpus Christi (2/1/99); Alfred C. Moran, Arlington (2/1/03); Allan B. Polunsky, San Antonio (2/1/01); Alfred M. "Mac" Stringfellow, San Antonio (2/1/03); Carol S. Vance, Houston (2/1/99); Carole S. Young, Dallas (2/1/01). Exec. Dir, Dept. of Criminal Justice: Wayne Scott ($150,000), PO Box 13084, Austin 78711. (512) 463-9988.

Criminal Justice Policy Council - (1983); all terms at pleasure of appointor; 11 members: 3 ex officio — Gov., Lt. Gov., Speaker; 2 apptd. by Lt. Gov.; 2 apptd. by Speaker; 4 apptd. by Gov. Gov's apptees: Col. James B. Adams, Austin; John Holmes, Houston; D.L. "Sonny" Keesee, Lubbock; Susan D. Reed, San Antonio. Exec. Dir., Tony Fabelo ($90,000), 205 W. 14th St., Ste. 701, Austin 78701.

Deaf and Hearing Impaired, Governing Board of the Texas School for the - (1979); 6-yr.; expenses; 9 members: Beatrice M. Burke, Big Spring (1/31/01); Johnelle M. Cortner, Houston (1/31/97); Aulby Lawrence (Larry) Gillett, San Angelo (1/31/01); Nancy Ellen Munger, Kyle (1/31/95); Nanci Pagoda-Ciccone, Dallas (1/31/99); Robert E. Parrish, Dallas (1/31/99); Mary Lynch VanManen, Sugar Land (1/31/97); Polly Piercy Walton, Beaumont (1/31/97). Exec. Dir., Marvin B. Sallop ($84,000), P. O. Box 3538, Austin 78764.

Deaf and Hard of Hearing, Texas Commission for the - (1971 as 6-member board; membership raised to 9 in 1979); apptv.; 6-yr.; expenses; 9 members: Douglas L. Bush, Houston (1/31/03); Larry M. Correu, San Antonio (1/31/99); Delores Erlandson, Big Spring (1/31/99); Jean Hale Matney, Fort worth (1/31/01); Timothy B. Rarus, Austin (1/31/01); Robin E. Riccardi, Shallowater (1/31/03); Linda Phillips Thune, Austin (1/31/99); Benna Timperlake, Corpus Christi (1/31/03); Eva Davie Williams, El Lago (1/31/01). Exec. Dir., David W. Myers ($64,200), P. O. Box 12904, Austin 78711.

Dental Examiners, State Board of - (1919 as 6-member board; increased to 9 members in 1971; increased to 12 in 1981; increased to 15 in 1991; sunsetted in 1994; reconstituted with 18 members in 1995); appt.; 6-yr.; per diem while on duty; 18 members: Patricia Blackwell, Midland (2/1/01); Tammy R. Fisher, Bedford (2/1/01); Karen F. Hembry, Dallas (2/1/05); Cornelius O. Henry, Tyler (2/1/03); J. Kevin Irons, Austin (2/1/05); Amy Landess Juba, Amarillo (2/1/03); James W. Kenedy, Sugar Land (2/1/03); H. Grant Lappin, Houston (2/1/01); Martha Manley Malik, Victoria (2/1/05); Michael Nogueira, Rancho Viejo (2/1/01); David O. Olson, Bridge City (2/1/01); Michael D. Plunk, Dallas (2/1/03); Ronald G. Smith, Lubbock (2/1/01); Kent T. Starr, Waco (2/1/05); Nathaniel George Tippit Jr., Houston (2/1/05); Marcia Waugh, El Paso (2/1/03); Gail Wilks, Longview (2/1/03); Joe D. Zayas, Rancho Viejo (2/1/01). Exec. Dir., Douglas A. Beran ($61,500), 333 Guadalupe, Ste. 3-800, Austin 78701.

Depository Board, State - (1905); 3 ex officio, term in other office: State Treasurer, Banking Commissioner, Comptroller; one apptd. by Gov. for 2-yr. term: (Vacancy). Office Address: PO Box 12608, Austin 78711.

Developmental Disabilities, Texas Planning Council for - (1971); apptv.; 6-yr.; 27 members — 8 ex offico: Representatives from Dept. of Mental Health and Mental Retardation, Rehabilitation Commission, Dept. of Health, Dept. of Human Services, Texas Dept. on Aging, Texas Education Agency, Texas Commission for the Blind, Texas Commission for the Deaf; 19 apptv. members: David Lee Benson, Houston (2/1/99); Joe Colunga III, Brownsville (2/1/97); Shenikwa Cox, Dallas (2/1/97); Gary D. Day, Austin (2/1/01); Mary M. Durheim, McAllen (2/1/99); Debbie B. Francis, Dallas (2/1/93); Raul Garza Jr., San Benito (2/1/99); Genevieve T. Hearon, Austin (2/1/97); J. Robert Hester Jr., Arlington (2/1/01); Jerijean Houchins, Austin (2/1/01); Theda N. Hoyt, Cypress (2/1/01); Barbara G. Loera, Austin (2/1/97); Federico Marquez, El Paso (2/1/97); Rebecca P. Ratliff, Coppell (2/1/01); Jan Reimann Newsom, Dallas (2/1/01); Margaret Robinson, Amarillo (2/1/97); Hector Saenz, San Antonio (2/1/97); Charley L. Tiggs, Lubbock (2/1/99); Linda Vancil, Ballinger (2/1/01). Exec. Dir., Roger A. Webb, 4900 N. Lamar, Austin 78751.

Diabetes Council, Texas - (1983; with 5 ex officio and 6 public members serving 2-yr. terms; changed in 1987 to 3 ex officio and 8 public members; changed to present configuration in 1991; term length changed from 4 to 6 years eff. 1997); 6-yr.; 17 members — 5 ex officio; 12 apptv. public members as follows: Maria C. Alen, McAllen (2/1/01); Belinda Bazan-Lara, San Antonio (2/1/01); Gene Bell, Lubbock (2/1/03); John Stuart Fitts, Dallas (2/1/01); Victor Hugo González, McAllen (2/1/03); Judith L. Haley, Houston (2/1/05); Jan B. Hamilton, Plainview (2/1/03); Richard S. Hayley, Corpus Christi (2/1/05); Lawrence B. Harkless, San Antonio (2/1/01); T. Ray McCann, Mount Pleasant (2/1/01); Mike Thompson Jr., Austin (2/1/05); Rosa M.

Valenzuela, El Paso (2/1/03). Address: Texas Dept. of Health, 1100 W. 49th, Austin 78756.

Dietitians, Texas State Board of Examiners of - (1983); apptv.; 6-yr.; per diem and expenses: 9 members: Elizabeth S. Blakely, San Angelo (9/1/03); Lucille DiDomenico, Arlington (9/1/99); Lucinda M. Flores, Brownsville (9/1/03); Ethelind S. Gibson, Nacogdoches (9/1/01); Patricia Mayers Krug, Converse (9/1/01); Margarette Leggitt Harden, Lubbock (9/1/99); Helen P. O'Reilly, Plano (9/1/99); Amy W. Scott, Spring (9/1/03); Dorothy M. Shafer, Fredericksburg (9/1/01). Texas Dept. of Health, 1100 W. 49th, Austin 78756.

Disabilities, Governor's Committee on People with - (1991); 16 members: 4 ex officio: Chmn., TEC; Commissioner, Texas Rehabilitation Comm.; Dir., Texas Commission for the Blind; member, Texas Comm. for the Deaf; 12 members apptd. by Governor serve 2-year terms: Mary Ann Board, Houston (2/1/99); James Laurence Caldwell, Austin (2/1/00); Victoria Christman, Dallas (2/1/99); Douglas F. Grady Jr., Fort Worth (2/1/00); Peter Grojean, San Antonio (2/1/00); Roland Guzman, Corpus Christi (2/1/01); Thomas P. Justis, Fort Worth (2/1/99); Kym I. King, Houston (2/1/00); Debbie H. Morrill, Austin (2/1/99); James G. Olson, Houston (2/1/99); Shirley Ann Pacetti, Houston (2/1/00); Judy Castle Scott, Dallas (2/1/00). Exec. Dir., Pat Pound, 4900 N. Lamar, Austin 78751-2613.

Disabilities, Texas Council on Purchasing from People with - (1979 as 10-member Committee on Purchases of Products and Services of Blind and Severely Disabled Persons; name changed and members reduced to 9 in 1995); apptd.; expenses; 6-yr.; 9 members: Byron E. Johnson, El Paso (1/31/01); John W. Luna, Euless (1/31/03); Eugene F. Matthews, Denton (1/31/99); Gwendolyn C. Morrison, Fort Worth (1/31/99); Margaret Pfluger, San Angelo (1/31/99); Robert A. Swerdlow, Beaumont (1/31/01); Bobbie F. Templeton, Driftwood (1/31/03); Arnold Thorner, Houston (1/31/01); Pat Wilson, Longview (1/31/03).

Economic Development, Governing Board of the Texas Department of - (1987 as Texas Dept. of Commerce Policy Bd.; present name 1997); apptv.;6-yr.; exp.; 9 members: Tucker S. Bridwell, Abilene (2/1/01); Javier Garza, Laredo (2/1/01); Patricia Z. Holland-Branch, El Paso (2/1/01); Limas Jefferson, Seabrook (2/1/05); Mark Langdale, Dallas (2/1/03); George T. Richardson Jr., Littlefield (2/1/03); Rance G. Sweeten, McAllen (2/1/03); Marion Szurek, San Angelo (2/1/05); Martha J. Wong, Houston (2/1/05). Exec. Dir., Rick Thrasher ($112,352), PO Box 12728, Austin 78711-2728.

Education, Board of Control for Southern Regional - (1969); apptv.; 4-yr.; 5 members: Gov. ex officio, 4 apptd.: Teel Bivins, Austin (6/30/01); Kent Grusendorf, Austin (6/30/00); Rene Nuñez, Austin (6/30/98); Carol J. Spencer, Dallas (6/30/99). Mark E. Musick, Pres., Southern Regional Education Board, 592 10th St. N.W., Atlanta, GA 30318-5790.

Education, Commissioner of - (1866 as Superintendent of Public Instruction; 1949 changed to present name by Gilmer-Aiken Law); apptv. by State Board of Education; 4-yr.: Dr. Michael A. (Mike) Moses ($156,014) (See also Education, State Board of).

Education, State Board of - (1866; re-created 1928 and re-formed by Gilmer-Aikin Act in 1949 to consist of 21 elective members from districts co-extensive with 21 congressional districts at that time; membership increased to 24 with congressional redistricting in 1971, effective 1973; membership increased to 27 with congressional redistricting in 1981, effective 1983; reorganized by special legislative session as 15-member apptv. board in 1984 to become elective board again in 1988; expenses; 4-yr.; 15 members (numerals before names indicate district numbers): (1) Rene Nuñez, El Paso (1/1/99); (2) Mary Helen Berlanga, Corpus Christi (1/1/99); (3) Joe J. Bernal, San Antonio (1/1/01); (4) Dr. Alma A. Allen, Houston (1/1/01); (5) Robert H. Offutt, San Antonio (1/1/01); (6) Chase Untermeyer, Houston (1/1/01); (7) David Brandley, Beaumont (1/1/01); (8) Grace Rose Shore, Longview (1/1/99); (9) Randy Stevenson, Tyler (1/1/99); (10) Will D. Davis, Austin (1/1/97); (11) Diane Patrick, Arlington (1/1/97); (12) Geraldine "Tincy" Miller, Dallas (1/1/01); (13) Rosie Collins Sorrells, Dallas (1/1/99); (14) Richard Watson, Gorman (1/1/99); (15) Monte Hasie, Lubbock (1/1/99). Commissioner of Education, Dr. Michael (Mike) A. Moses, Texas Education Agency, 1701 N. Congress Ave., Austin 78701-1494 (see also Education, Commissioner of).

Educator Certification, State Board for - (1995); apptv.; 6-yr.; expenses; 15 members: 3 non-voting - rep. of Comm. of Education; rep of Comm. of Higher Education; 1 dean of a college of education apptd. by Gov.; 12 voting members apptd. by Gov.: Kenneth R. Craycraft, Huntsville (2/1/05); Annette T. Griffin, Carrollton (2/1/05); James D. Harris, Lubbock (2/1/03); Arthur (Art) Lacy, McKinney (2/1/03); James E. Nelson, Odessa (2/1/01); Edward (Ed) Nash Patton Jr., Abilene (2/1/

01); Cynthia Tassos Phillips, Austin (2/1/01); James B. (Jim) Price, Cooper (2/1/03); Mary E. Resendez, San Antonio (2/1/01); Xavier Rodriguez, San Antonio (2/1/05); Antonio Sanchez, Mission (2/1/05); Mary Margaret Rucker, Nassau Bay (2/1/03); Keith Sockwell, Plano (2/1/03). Exec. Dir., Pamela B. Tackett ($75,000), 1001 Trinity, Austin 78701-2603.

Egg Marketing Advisory Board - (1957); apptv.; 6-yr.; 11 members — 2 ex officio: Commissioner of Agriculture is chairman; one apptd. by head of Poultry Science Dept., Texas A&M University; 9 apptv.: Leroy Baeza, Fort Davis (9/27/01); Larry J. Berend, Wichita Falls (9/27/97); Gilbert A. Burton, Lufkin (9/27/97); Jack Wilson Evans Jr., Dallas (9/27/93); Charles Jeffrey Hardin, La Grange (9/27/01); Kervin E. Jacob, Houston (9/27/97); James M. (Mike) Robinson, San Antonio (9/27/99); Elias (Alex) Rodgers, Eden (9/27/99); Terry C. Wright, Gilmer (9/27/01). Address: Dept. of Agriculture, PO Box 12847, Austin 78711.

Election Commission, State - (1973); 9 members, ex officio and apptv. as indicated: Chmn. of Democratic State Executive Committee; Chmn. of Republican State Executive Committee; Chief Justice of Supreme Court; Presiding Judge, Court of Criminal Appeals; 2 persons to be named, one a justice of the Court of Appeals apptd. by Chief Justice of Supreme Court, one a District Judge apptd. by presiding judge of Court of Criminal Appeals; 2 county chairmen, one each from Democratic and Republican parties, named by the parties; Secretary of State.

Emancipation Juneteenth Cultural and Historical Commission, Texas - (1997); expenses; 6 yr.; 11 members: 5 ex officio, nonvoting - 2 apptd. by Lt. Gov., 2 apptd. by Speaker of House, and exec. dir. of Texas Historical Comm.; 6 apptd by Gov.: Maceo Crenshaw Dailey Jr., El Paso (2/1/03); Byron E. Miller, San Antonio (2/1/03); Eddie Price Richardson, Lubbock (2/1/99); Stella Roland, Austin (2/1/99); Willard Stimpson, Dallas (2/1/01); Lynda J. Tarr, Houston (2/1/01).

Emergency Communications, Advisory Commission on State - (1985); expenses; 17 members: 5 ex offico: exec. directors of Texas Advisory Commission on Intergovernmental Relations, Depts. of Health, Public Safety, Criminal Justice Policy Council and the major association representing regional planning commissions; 12 public members (6 yr.): 8 apptd. by Gov., 2 by Lt. Gov., 2 by Speaker: Glenda Burdick, Rockport (9/1/03); Jimmy Burson, Silverton (9/1/01); David Cain, Dallas (9/1/01); Ernest J. Carey, Kingwood (9/1/03); Bill Carter, Fort Worth (9/1/01); Patrick A. Craven, Austin (9/1/99); Eloy A. DeLao Jr., San Antonio (9/1/01); Ron Harris, McKinney (9/1/99); Terry Keel, Austin (9/1/01); Bill Munn, Dallas (9/1/99); David M. Sibley, Austin (9/1/03); Wayne Whiteaker, Littlefield (9/1/99). Exec. Dir., James D. Goerke ($69,638), 333 Guadalupe St., Ste. 2-212, Austin 78701.

Employment Commission, Texas - (See **Workforce Commission, Texas**)

Engineers, State Board of Registration for Professional - (1937 as 6-member board; membership increased to 9 in 1981); apptv.; per diem and expenses; 6-yr.; 9 members: Brenda A. Bradley, Houston (9/26/03); E.D. Dorchester, Midland (9/26/01); Edmundo R. Gonzalez Jr., Brownsville (9/26/01); Jose I. Guerra, Austin (9/26/99); Joe Paul Jones, Fort Worth (9/26/03); Hubert Oxford III, Beaumont (9/26/99); Danny R. Perkins, Houston (9/26/01); C.H. (Herb) Treat, San Antonio (9/26/99); Kathleen C. Walker, El Paso (9/26/03). Exec. Dir., John R. Speed ($75,000), 1917 S. IH-35, Austin 78741.

Ethics Commission, Texas - (1991); apptd.; 4-yr.; 8 members: 2 apptd. by Speaker, 2 apptd. by Lt. Gov, 4 apptd. by Gov.: John E. Clark, San Antonio (11/19/99); Ernestine Glossbrenner, Alice (11/19/01); Jerome W. Johnson, Amarillo (11/19/99); Norman Lyons, Fort Worth (11/19/99); Louis E. Sturns, Fort Worth (11/19/01). Exec. Dir., Tom Harrison ($93,000), 201 E. 14th St., 10th Fl., Austin 78701.

Evergreen Underground Water Conservation District - (1965); 2-year; 5 members — 4 elected: 2 each from Wilson and Atascosa counties; one apptd. by Gov.: Amond Douglas Brownlow, Floresville (2/1/03).

Family Practice Residency Advisory Committee - (1977); 3-yr.; expenses; 12 members apptv. as follows: one practicing physician apptd. by Texas Osteopathic Medical Assn.; 2 apptd. by Assn. of Directors of Family Practice Training Programs; one apptd. by Texas Medical Assn.; 2 administrators of hospitals apptd. by Texas Hospital Assn.; president, Texas Academy of Family Physicians; and 3 public members apptd. by the Gov., as follows: Tamara J. Cowen Brownsville (8/29/97); Dr. Jack L. Eidson, Weatherford (8/29/93); Judith A. Youngs, Dallas (8/29/95).

Finance Commission, State - (1923 as Banking Commission; reorganized as Finance Commission in 1943 with 9 members; membership increased to 12 in 1983; changed back to 9 members in 1989); apptv.; 6-yr.; per diem and traveling expenses; 9 members: Jeff Austin Jr., Jacksonville (2/1/00); Steven C. Hastings, Southlake (2/1/00); Wilburn D. Hilton Jr., Greenville (2/1/02); Deborah H. Kovacevich, Jewett (2/1/04); Marlene Martin, San Antonio (2/1/02); Manuel J. Mehos, Houston (2/1/02); Victor (Buddy) Puente Jr., Pantego (2/1/04); John Snider, Center (2/1/00); Robert V. Wingo, El Paso (2/1/04). Banking Commissioner, Catherine A. Ghiglieri ($97,072), 2601 N. Lamar, Austin 78705, appointee of Finance Commission. (See also Banking Commissioner, State.)

Fire Ant Advisory Board - (1987); apptv.; expenses; 6-yr.; 9 members: 3 ex officio: Commissioner of Agriculture, exec. dir. of Parks and Wildlife Dept., engineer-director of Texas Department of Transportation; 6 apptd. — 2 by Commissioner of Agriculture, 4 apptd. by Gov.: Stanley Carter Haddock, Dallas (1/1/99); Juan D. Nichols, Quitman (1/1/97); Wayne R. Snodgrass, Nassau Bay (1/1/95); Davis Whitehurst Jr., Longview (1/1/99).

Fire Fighters' Pension Commissioner - (1937); apptv.; 2-yr.: Morris E. Sandefer Jr., Lumberton (7/1/99) ($45,000), PO Box 12577, Austin 78711.

Fire Fighters' Relief and Retirement Fund - (1977); apptv.; expenses; 6-yr.; 9 members: Jennifer S. Armstrong, Mansfield (9/1/99); Robert Barrett, Seminole (9/1/99); Donald A. Eernisse, Alvin (9/1/97); Weir Labatt, San Antonio (9/1/01); Paul V. Loeffler, Alpine (9/1/01); Glenn D. Neutzler, Brenham (9/1/97); Joe Rice, Canyon (9/1/01); Frank Torres, Raymondville (9/1/99); Thomas N. Tourtellotte, Driftwood (9/1/97). Commissioner, Helen L. Campbell, PO Box 12577, Austin 78711.

Fire Protection, Texas Commission on - (1991; formed by consolidation of Fire Dept. Emergency Board and Commission on Fire Protection Personnel Standards and Education); apptv.; 6-yrs.; expenses; 12 members: David Abernathy Pittsburg (2/1/01); Juan J. Adame, Corpus Christi (2/1/01); Pat Barrett, Bryan (2/1/03); Marvin G. Dawson, Brownfield (2/1/01); Michael D. Jolly, Georgetown (2/1/05); Alonzo Lopez Jr., Kingsville (2/1/05); Robert H. Price, Grapevine (2/1/01); Gilbert Robinson, Galveston (2/1/03); Ricardo Saldaña, Mission (2/1/05); Kelley Stalder, Parker (2/1/03); Peggy Trahan, South Padre Island (2/1/03); Carl D. Wren, Manchaca (2/1/05). Exec. Dir., Gary L. Warren Sr. ($72,000), PO Box 2286, Austin 78768.

Food and Fibers Commission, Texas - (1941 as Cotton Research Committee; name changed in 1971 to Natural Fibers and Food Protein Committee; changed to commission in 1975; changed to present name 1989); 4 members are presidents and chancellor of four major universities (Pres., Texas Woman's University, Denton; Pres., Texas Tech University, Lubbock; Chancellor, Texas A&M University System, College Station; Pres., University of Texas at Austin serving indefinite terms; and one ex officio member who is director of administrative office in Dallas, apptd. to 2-year term: Exec. Dir., Steve Verett ($60,833), 17360 Coit Rd., Dallas 75252.

Funeral Service Commission, Texas - (1903 as State Board of Embalming; 1935 as State Board of Funeral Directors and Embalmers; 1953 as 6-member board; membership increased to 9 in 1979; name changed to present form in 1987); apptv.; per diem and expenses; 6-yr.; 9 members: Evelyn S. Collins, Texarkana (1/31/99); Kenneth Jerry Hughes, Nacogdoches (1/31/99); Patricia Gail Keegan, Rockwall (1/31/01); John Q. Taylor King, Austin (1/31/03); Roy H. Kiser, Plainview (1/31/03); Charles Richard McNeil, Fort Worth (1/31/01); Leo T. Metcalf III, Conroe (1/31/01); Martha J. Rhymes, White Oak (1/31/03); Jim C. Wright, Wheeler (1/31/05). Exec. Dir., Eliza May ($43,680), 510 S. Congress, Ste. 206, Austin 78704-1716.

General Services Commission - (1919 as Board of Control; name changed to State Purchasing and General Services Commission in 1979; changed to present form and increased to 6 commissioners in 1991); apptv.; 6-yr.; expenses; 6 members: James A. Cox Jr., Austin (1/31/05); Tomas Cardenas Jr., El Paso (1/31/05); Dionicio Vidal (Sonny) Flores, Houston (1/31/01); Alphonso Jackson, Dallas (1/31/01); Barbara N. Rusling, China Spring (1/31/03); Gene Shull, Tyler (1/31/03). Exec. Dir., John Pouland ($81,100), PO Box 13047, Austin 78711-3047.

Growth Fund Board of Trustees, Texas - (1988); apptd.; 6-yr.; 9 members — one member from and elected by membership of each of the following: Board of Regents, University of Texas System; Board of Regents, Texas A&M University System; Board of Trustees, Teacher Retirement System; Board of Trustees, Employees Retirement System; State Board of Education; 4 public members apptd. by Gov.: J. Michael Bell Sr., Fredericksburg (2/1/99); H. Scott Caven, Houston (2/1/99); Timothy P. Roth, El Paso (2/1/03); Catherine S. Woodruff, Houston (2/1/03).

Guadalupe River Authority, Upper - (1939); apptv.; 6-yr.; 9 members: Jerry Ahrens, Kerrville (2/1/05); Joseph David Armistead Sr., Center Point (2/1/03); Marsha E. Copeland, Kerrville (2/1/01); T. Beck Gipson, Kerrville (2/1/01); George Grif-

fin, Hunt (2/1/03); Peggy J. Henderson, Kerrville (2/1/03); George G. MacDonald Jr., Kerrville (2/1/01); Janet F. Robinson, Kerrville (2/1/05); Calvin Ray Weinheimer, Kerrville (2/1/05). Gen. Mgr., Jim T. Brown, 125 Lehman Dr., # 100, Kerrville 78028.

Guadalupe-Blanco River Authority - (1935); apptv.; per diem and expenses on duty; 6-yr.; 9 members: William A. Blackwell, Cuero (2/1/01); Anne Cooper, San Marcos (2/1/01); Kathleen A. Devine, New Braunfels (2/1/05); Pamela M. Hodges, Boerne (2/1/03); Catherine R. McHaney, Victoria (2/1/97); Frederick S. Schlather, Cibolo (2/1/03); John P. Schneider Jr., Lockhart (2/1/05); Ashley H. Turberville, Nixon (2/1/01); Stephen F. Wilson, Port Lavaca (1/2/05). Gen. Mgr., W.E. West Jr., 933 E. Court St., Seguin 78155.

Gulf Coast Waste Disposal Authority - (1969); apptv.; 2-yr.; per diem and expenses on duty; 9 members: 3 apptv. by Gov., 3 by County Commissioners Courts of counties in district, 3 by Municipalities Waste Disposal Councils of counties in district. Gov's. apptees: Louis S. Dell'Olio Jr., Galveston (8/31/00); Rafael Ortega, Houston (8/31/99); Shirley U. Seale, Anahuac (8/31/00). Gen. Mgr., Dick Brown, 910 Bay Area Blvd., Houston 77058.

Gulf States Marine Fisheries Commission - (1949); apptv.; 3-yr.; 3 members — 2 ex officio: exec. dir., Texas Parks & Wildlife Dept.; one member of House; one apptd. by Gov.: L. Don Perkins, Houston (3/17/02). Exec. Dir., Larry B. Simpson, PO Box 726, Ocean Springs, MS 30564.

Health, Commissioner of - (1879 as State Health Officer; 1955 changed to Commissioner of Health; 1975 changed to Director, Texas Department of Health Resources; 1977 changed to Commissioner, Texas Department of Health; apptv.; 2-yr.: Dr. William "Reyn" Archer ($148,683), 1100 W. 49th, Austin 78756.

Health, Texas Board of - (1903 as State Board of Health; superseded similar department created in 1891; name changed in 1975 to Texas Board of Health Resources and membership increased to 18; name changed in 1977 to present form; membership decreased to 6); apptv.; per diem and expenses on duty; 6-yr.; 6 members: Kent M. Adams, Beaumont (2/1/03); Mario R. Anzaldua, Mission (2/1/03); Mary E. Ceverha, Dallas (2/1/01); Beverly Harris Robinson, Windcrest (2/1/05); Margo Sneller Scholin, Houston (2/1/05); Walter D. Wilkerson Jr., Conroe (2/1/01). Commissioner of Health, Dr. William "Reyn" Archer ($148,683), 1100 W. 49th, Austin 78756.

Health and Human Services, Commissioner of - (1991); apptd.; 2-yr.; one commissioner: Don Allen Gilbert ($157,500), (2/1/01). 4900 N. Lamar Blvd., Austin 78731.

Health Benefits Purchasing Cooperative, Texas, Board of Trustees - (1993); 6-yr.; apptd.; expenses; 6 members: Maria E. Crowley, Dallas (2/1/95); Matrice Ellis-Kirk, Dallas (2/1/95); Cappy R. McGarr, Dallas (2/1/99); Joseph F. Phillips, Mission (2/1/99); Marvin L. Ragsdale, Georgetown (2/1/97); Philip Patrick Sun, Missouri City (2/1/97).

Health Care Information Council, Texas - (1995); expenses; 18 members: 3 nonvoting ex officio state agency members (commissioner of public health, commissioner of health and human services, commissioner of insurance); 15 apptd. to 6-yr. terms: Jack Gerhardt Blaz, Dallas (9/1/01); David Cortez, San Antonio (9/1/99); George H. Crowling Jr., Dallas (9/1/03); Bobby S. De Rossett, Flint (9/1/03); Arthur Garson, Houston (9/1/97); Woody F. Gilliland, Abilene (9/1/03); Robert W. Gracy, Fort Worth (9/1/03); Jacinto Pablo Juarez, Laredo (9/1/99); Gail Dowdy Neas, Houston (9/1/99); Susan M. Nelson, Plano (9/1/01); Imogen S. Papadopoulos, Houston (9/1/01); Robert E. Schorlemer, San Antonio (9/1/99); Laura P. Stevens, Plano (9/1/99); Nelda P. Wray, Houston (9/1/01).

Health Care Reimbursement Alternatives, Texas Commission on - (1987); term at pleasure of Gov.; apptd.; expenses; 18 members — 4 representatives and 3 public members apptd. by Speaker; 4 senators and 3 public members apptd. by Lt. Gov.; 3 public members and chairman apptd. by Gov.; Gov's apptees: Joel T. Allison, Corpus Christi; Lynda Calcote, Abilene; William P. Daves Jr., Dallas; Carol Carlson Dean, Lakeside City.

Healthcare System Board of Directors, Statewide Rural - (1997); 18 members (6 representatives of care providers; 12 apptd. by Gov.); 6 yr.; Gov's apptees.: Dana W. Cooley, Snyder (2/1/01); Harold R. High, Cuero (2/1/03); Ralph H. Meriwether, Alpine (2/1/03); Thomas E. Mueller, La Grange (2/1/03); Pervaiz Rahman, Gainesville (2/1/99); Doris L. Reding, Littlefield (2/1/03); Joyce A. Roberts, Mount Vernon (2/1/01); Lucille H. Rochs, Fredericksburg (2/1/99); Joe Tom Terrell, Jacksonville (2/1/99); Pablo C. Teveni, Stanton (2/1/01); B.R. (Skipper) Wallace, Lampasas (2/1/01); Hugh H. Wilson Jr., Hale Center (2/1/99).

Health Coordinating Council, Statewide - (1975); apptv.; 2-yr.; membership decreased from 21 to 15 in 1993; number increased to 17 in 1997; apptv., as follows: Annabel Barker, Big Spring (8/31/95); Joan Wood Biggerstaff, Plano (8/31/97); Nick U. Curry, Fort Worth (8/31/95); Dana S. Fitzsimmons, Houston (8/31/97); Barbara Ann Gonzalez, Alice (8/31/99); John P. Howe III, San Antonio (8/31/97); Man-Ja C. Lee, Little Elm (8/31/99); Linda C. Lopez, San Antonio (8/31/95); Adena W. Loston, Houston (8/1/01); Polly L. McFadden, El Paso (8/31/99); Betty Fox McLemore, Longview (8/31/99); Shirley McManigal, Lubbock (8/31/99); Therese Ruffing, Austin (8/31/95); Betty J. Shinn, Nacogdoches (8/31/97); deSaussure M. Treviño, Pharr (8/31/95); David A. Valdez, San Antonio (8/1/01); Francisco J. Velazquez, San Antonio (8/31/97). Exec. Dir., A. Spires, Texas Dept. of Health, 1100 W. 49th, Austin 78756-3199.

Healthy Kids Corporation, Texas, Board of Directors - (1997); all terms expire 9/1/99: J. Coalter Baker, Austin; Rene Daniel Pena, El Paso; Gwyn Shea, Irving; Dorothy (Dot) Nelson Snyder, Waco; Kenneth D. Wells, Houston.

Hearing Instruments, State Committee of Examiners in the Fitting and Dispensing of - (1969); apptv.; 6-yr.; expenses; 9 members: Larry W. Farris, Universal City (12/31/99); Robert M. Komorn, Houston (12/31/01); Carlos T. Oliveira, Laredo (12/31/01); Andrew Peña, El Paso (12/31/99); Jane W. Porter, Irving (12/31/97); Michael L. Shobe, Lubbock (12/31/03); Ursula Singleton, La Joya (12/31/01); Eve-Anne D. Wall, San Angelo (12/31/03); John Westmoreland, Waco (12/31/03). Exec. Dir., Bobby D. Schmidt ($55,000), 4800 N. Lamar, Ste. 150, Austin 78756.

Higher Education Coordinating Board, Texas - (1953 as temporary board; 1955 as permanent 15-member Texas Commission on Higher Education; increased to 18 members in 1965; name changed to present form in 1987); apptv.; 6-yr.; expenses; 18 members: William C. Atkinson, Bryan (8/31/01); Martin Basaldúa, Kingwood (8/31/03); Dolores H. Carruth, Irving (8/31/01); Joaquin G. Cigarroa Jr., Laredo (8/31/99); Kevin Paul Eltife, Tyler (8/31/03); Robert I. Fernandez, Fort Worth (8/31/01); Douglas Sloan Harlan, San Antonio (8/31/03); Jodie L. Jiles, Houston (8/31/01); Joseph R. Krier, San Antonio (8/31/99); Steve Late, Odessa (8/31/01); Adair Wakefield Margo, El Paso (8/31/03); Wendy Marsh, Amarillo (8/31/99); Janie S. McGarr, Dallas (8/31/99); Tom C. Nichols, Lubbock (8/31/99); Leonard Rauch, Houston (8/31/01); Robert W. Shepard, Harlingen (8/31/03); Carlos Villa, El Paso (8/31/99); Pamela P. Willeford, Austin (8/31/03). Commissioner of Higher Education, Dr. Don W. Brown ($125,106), PO Box 12788, Austin 78711.

Higher Education Tuition Board, Prepaid - (1995); apptv.; expenses; 6-yr.; 7 members: State Comptroller, 2 apptd. by Lt. Gov., 2 apptd. by Gov. Gov's apptees: Michael D. Gollob, Tyler (2/1/03); Beth Miller Weakley, San Antonio (2/1/05.

Historical Commission, Texas - (1953); apptv.; expenses; 6-yr.; 18 members: Jean Ann Ables-Flatt, Terrell (2/1/05); Bruce T. Aiken, Brownsville (2/1/01); Jane Cook Barnhill, Brenham (2/1/01); Gail Loving Barnes, Odessa (2/1/05); J.P. Bryan, Houston (2/1/03); Diane D. Bumpas, Dallas (2/1/05); Shirley W. Caldwell, Albany (2/1/01); Chris John Carson, San Antonio (2/1/03); T.R. Fehrenbach, San Antonio (2/1/01); Frank Gorman Jr., El Paso (2/1/01); Eileen Johnson, Lubbock (2/1/03); Mamie L. McKnight, Dallas (2/1/05); Carl R. McQueary, Salado (2/1/03); Susan Mead, Dallas (2/1/01); John L. Nau III, Houston (2/1/05); Juan F. Sandoval, El Paso (2/1/05); Linda A. Valdez, San Antonio (2/1/03); Clinton P. White, Wharton (2/1/03). Exec. Dir., F. Lawerence Oaks, PO Box 12276, Austin 78711 ($77,500).

Historical Records Advisory Board, Texas - (1976); apptv.; 3-yr.; 9 members: State Archivist, 6 apptd. by by director and librarian of Texas State Library and Archives Comm.; two members apptd. by Gov. Public members: Eloise L. Burges, Mason (2/1/00); Martha Doty Freeman, Austin (2/1/99). State Historical Records Coordinator, Chris LaPlante (2/1/01), State Library, PO Box 12927, Austin 78711.

Housing and Community Affairs, Board of Texas Dept. of - (1979 as Texas Housing Agency; merged with Department of Community Affairs and name changed in 1991); apptv.; expenses; 6-yr.; 9 members: Donald R. Bethel, Lamesa (1/31/01); Margie Lee Bingham, Houston (1/31/01); Robert O. Brewer, San Angelo (1/31/01); C. Kent Conine, Dallas (1/31/03); James A. Daross, El Paso (1/31/03); Florita Bell Griffin, College Station (1/31/03); Michael E. Jones, Tyler (1/31/05); Lydia R. Saenz, Carrizo Springs (1/31/05); Marsha L. Williams, Dallas (1/31/05). Exec. Dir., Daisy A. Stiner ($112,352), 507 Sabine, Austin 78701.

Housing Corporation Board of Directors, Texas State Affordable - (1997); 6 members: 2 ex officio, four apptd. by Gov. with term at Gov's pleasure: Jeffrey S. Baloutine, Houston; Donald S. Currie, Rancho Viejo; Dawn Enoch Moore, Dallas; Jerry Romero, El Paso.

Human Rights, State Commission on - (1983); apptv.; 6-yr.; expenses; 6 members: Laura Ayoub Keith, El Paso (9/24/01); David J. Manning, Fort Worth (9/24/03); Rev. Ransom

Howard, Port Arthur (9/24/99); Lynn Ellen Rubinett, Austin (9/24/99); Richard A. Solo, Dallas (9/24/97); Charles W. Taylor Jr., Houston (9/24/01). Exec. Dir., William M. Hale ($56,959), P. O. Box 13493, Austin 78711.

Human Services, Texas Board of - (1941 as State Board of Public Welfare; name changed to present form in 1985); apptv.; 6-yr.; per diem and expenses; 6 members: David Herndon, Austin (1/20/01); Bill Jones, Houston (1/20/03); Anchi H. Ku, Dallas (1/20/99); Elizabeth Darling Seale, San Antonio (1/20/03); Carlela K. Vogel, Fort Worth (1/20/99); Carole A. Woodard, Galveston (1/20/01). Commissioner, Burton F. Raiford ($150,000), PO Box 149030, Austin 78714-9030.

Humanities, Texas Council for the - Kathleen Ford Bay, Austin (12/31/99); Linden Heck Howell, Portland (12/31/98); Randolph D. Hurt Jr., Fort Stockton, (12/31/99); Wright L. Lassiter Jr., Dallas (12/31/99); J. Landon Short, Houston (12/31/98). Exec. Dir., Richard T. Hull, 3809 S. 2nd St., Ste. A100, Austin 78704-7095.

Incentive and Productivity Commission, Texas - (1987 as Productivity and Bonus Commission and Employee Incentive Commission; commissions merged and name changed to present form in 1989); 9 members — 6 state officials (term on commission is term in other office): Gov.; Lt. Gov.; Comptroller; State Treasurer; Administrator, Texas Workforce Comm.; Chmn., Texas Higher Education Coordinating Bd.; 3 apptd. by Gov.: Janice E. Collins, San Antonio (2/1/01); John Mitchell Moore, Stephenville (2/1/01); Sherry L. Phelps, Bartonville (2/1/98). Exec. Dir., Ed Bloom ($49,500), PO Box 12482, Austin 78711.

Information Resources, Department of - (1981 as Automated Information and Telecommunications Council; name changed in 1990); 6-yr.; expenses; 3 members recommended by Speaker of House, 3 by Lt. Gov.; 3 by Gov.: 9 members: Walter A. Bradley III, Dallas (2/1/01); Jim C. Brunjes, Lubbock (2/1/99); Mario J. Gonzalez, Austin (2/1/03); Carole S. Greisdorf, Plano (2/1/03); Rolf R. Haberecht, Dallas (2/1/03); Scott Hochberg, Houston (2/1/99); Robert Junell, Austin (2/1/03); Harry H. Richardson, San Antonio (2/1/01); Jennifer Stamper, Dallas (2/1/01). Exec. Dir., Carolyn Purcell ($100,000), PO Box 13564, Austin 78711.

Insurance, Commissioner of - José O. Montemayor (2/1/01); ($157,500), PO Box 149104, Austin 78714.

International Trade Commission - (1991); apptv.; 6-yr.; 6 members: Robert W. Hsueh, Dallas (2/1/01); José E. Martinez, San Antonio (2/1/99); Robert B. Reeves, Center (2/1/01); Phillip S. Shinoda, Dallas (2/1/97); Patricia J. Smothers, San Antonio (2/1/99). Dir., J. David Bamberger (member), San Antonio (2/1/97), c/o Texas Dept. of Commerce.

Interstate Mining Compact Commission - Melvin Hodgkiss, Austin. Exec. Dir.: Gregory Conrad, 459B Carlisle Drv., Herndon, VA 22070.

Interstate Oil and Gas Compact Commission, Texas Rep. - (1935); ex officio or apptv., according to Gov's. choice; per diem and expenses. (Approximately 150 other appointees serve on various committees.) Official representatives for Texas: Antonio O. Garza Jr., Charles R. Matthews, Michael L. Williams. Exec. Dir., Christine Hansen, PO Box 53127, Oklahoma City, OK 73152.

Interstate Parole Compact Administrator - (1951); apptv.: Knox Fitzpatrick, Dallas.

Jail Standards, Texas Commission on - (1975); apptv.; 6-yr.; expenses; 9 members: Terry G. Box, McKinney (1/31/03); Marc Cisneros, Premont (1/31/03); Larry T. Craig, Tyler (1/31/01); C.O. Hadnot, Hillister (1/31/99); J.D. Johnson, Fort Worth (1/31/99); Carmella Jones, Claude (1/31/03); Patrick O. Keel, Austin (1/31/01); Manuel Rivera, El Paso (1/31/99); Marcia Saunders, Lake Kiowa (1/31/01). Exec. Dir., Jack E. Crump ($61,000), PO Box 12985, Austin 78711.

Judicial Conduct, State Commission on - (1965 as 9-member Judicial Qualifications Commission; name changed in 1977 to present form and membership raised to 11); expenses; 6-yr.; 11 members: 5 apptd. by Supreme Court; 2 apptd. by State Bar; 4 apptd. by Gov. as follows: Jean Birmingham, Marshall (11/19/99); Carol Jean MacLean, Cleburne (11/19/97); L. Scott Mann, Lubbock (11/19/01); Rosa Walker, Austin (11/19/97). Exec. Dir., Robert C. Flowers ($90,000), PO Box 12265, Austin 78711.

Judicial Council, Texas - (1929 as Texas Civil Judicial Council; name changed in 1975); ex officio terms vary; apptv.; 6-yr. terms; expenses; 19 members, increased to 22 in 1997: 16 ex officio and 6 apptd. from general public. Public members: James Boswell, Plano (6/30/03); James R. Brickman, Dallas (6/30/01); Joseph Alan Callier, Kingwood (6/30/03); Kathleen Cardone, El Paso (6/30/01); Diego J. Peña, San Antonio (6/30/99); Sharon Warfield Wilkes, Austin (6/30/99). Exec. Dir., Jerry Benedict, PO Box 12066, Austin 78711.

Judicial Districts Board - (1985); 12 ex officio members (term in other office); one apptv. (4 yrs.); ex officio: Chief Justice of Texas Supreme Court; Presiding Judge, Court of Criminal Appeals; Presiding Judge of each of 9 Administrative Judicial Districts; pres. of Texas Judicial Council.

Judicial Districts of Texas, Admin., Presiding Judges of - (See Administrative Judicial Districts, Presiding Judges).

Juvenile Probation Commission, Texas - (1981); apptv.; 6-yr.; expenses; 9 members — 3 judges of District Courts and 6 private citizens: Robert P. Brotherton, Wichita Falls (8/31/01); Michael E. Cantrell, Garland (6/30/04); Judge Mary Craft, Houston (6/30/04); Raul Garcia, San Angelo (8/31/99); Keith H. Kuttler, College Station (8/31/01); Betsy Lake, Houston (8/31/99); William E. "Bill" Miller, Lubbock (6/30/04); Byron K. Reed, Plano (8/31/01); Robert Tejeda, San Antonio (8/31/99). Exec. Dir., Vicki Spriggs ($85,000), PO Box 13547, Austin 78711.

Lamar University System, Board of Regents - (abolished Sept. 1995 upon the transfer of Lamar University System to the Texas State University System).

Land Board, School - (1939); one ex officio (term in other office); 2 apptd. — one by Atty. Gen. and one by Gov. for 2-yr. term; per diem and expenses; ex officio member: Comm. of General Land Office; Gov's. apptee: C. Louis Renaud, Midland (8/29/97).

Land Surveying, Texas Board of Professional - (1979); formed from consolidation of membership of Board of Examiners of Licensed Land Surveyors, est. 1977, and State Board of Registration for Public Surveyors, est. 1955); apptv.; 6-yr.; 10 members — Commissioner of General Land Office serving by statute; 3 members of general public, 2 licensed land surveyors, 4 registered public surveyors, as follows: Jerry M. Goodson, Lampasas (1/31/01); Betty H. Little, Amarillo (1/31/03); James Noble Johnson, Austin (1/31/99); Paul P. Kwan, Houston (1/31/99); A.W. Osborn, Tyler (1/31/01); Robert Pounds, El Paso (1/31/03); Andrew L. Sikes, Houston (1/31/99); Joan White, Brownsville (1/31/03); Raul Wong Jr., Dallas (1/31/01). Exec. Dir., Sandy Smith ($47,000), 7701 N. Lamar, Ste. 400, Austin 78752.

Lands, Board for Lease of University - (1929 as 3-member board; membership increased to 4 in 1985); ex officio; term in other office; 4 members: Commissioner of General Land Office, 2 members of Board of Regents of University of Texas, 1 member Board of Regents of Texas A&M University.

Lavaca-Navidad River Authority, Board of Directors - (1954 as 7-member Jackson County Flood Control District; reorganized as 9-member board in 1959; name changed to present form in 1969); apptv.; 6-yr.; per diem and expenses; 9 members: Sandra R. Green, LaWard (5/1/01); Harry Lee Hafernick, Edna (5/1/97); Charles M. Hasdorff, Ganado (5/1/01); J.B. Housson, Ganado (5/1/97); Theresa McCaig, Ganado (5/1/97); Michael W. Menefee, Edna (5/1/01); Callaway S. Vance, Edna (5/1/99); Robert J. Whitworth, Edna (5/1/99). Gen. Mgr., Jack C. Nelson, PO Box 429, Edna 77957.

Law Enforcement Officer Standards & Education, Comm. on - (1965); expenses; 14 members — 5 ex officio: Atty. Gen., Directory of Public Safety, Commissioner of Education, Exec. Dir. of Governor's Office Criminal Justice Division, and Commissioner of Higher Education; 9 apptv. members: Claudia A. Bretz, Odessa (8/30/01); Ray Hunt, Houston (8/30/03); Frances A. Kaiser, Kerrville (8/30/01); Onzelo Markum III, League City (8/30/01); H. L. O'Neal, Lubbock (8/30/99); Benigno G. Reyna, Brownsville (8/30/03); Joe A. Stivers, Huntsville (8/30/99); Sally Werst, Fort Worth (8/30/99); Charles W. "Chuck" Williams, Marshall (8/30/03). Exec. Dir., D.C. Jim Dozier ($76,000), 6330 E. Hwy. 290, Ste. 200, Austin 78723.

Law Examiners, Board of - Nine attorneys apptd. by Supreme Court biennially for 2-year terms expiring September 30 of odd-numbered years. Compensation set by Supreme Court not to exceed $20,000 per annum. Exec. Dir., Rachael Martin, PO Box 13486, Austin 78711.

Law Library Board, State - (1971); ex officio; expenses; 3 members: Chief Justice Supreme Court, Presiding Judge Court of Criminal Appeals and Atty. General. Dir., Kay Schlueter ($58,000), PO Box 12367, Austin 78711.

Legislative Budget Board - (1949); 10 members; 6 ex officio members: Lt. Gov.; Speaker of House; Chmn., Senate Finance Comm.; Chmn., Senate State Affairs Comm.; Chmn., House Appropriations Comm.; Chmn., House Ways and Means Comm.; plus 4 other members of Legislature. Director, John Keel, PO Box 12666, Austin 78711-2666.

Legislative Council, Texas - (1949); 17 ex officio members — 4 senators named by Lt. Gov.; 9 representatives named by Speaker; Chmn., House Administration Committee; Chmn., Senate Administration Committee; Lt. Gov.; and Speaker. Exec. Dir., Robert I. Kelly, PO Box 12128, Austin 78711.

Legislative Redistricting Board - (1948); 5 ex officio members; term in other office: Lt. Gov., Speaker of House, Atty. Gen., Comptroller and Commissioner of General Land Office.

Librarian, State - (Originally est. in 1839; present office est. 1909); apptv., indefinite term: Robert S. Martin ($65,000), PO Box 12927, Austin 78711.

Library and Archives Commission, Texas State - (1909 as 5-member Library and State Historical Commission; number of members increased to 6 in 1953; name changed to present form in 1979); apptv.; per diem and expenses on duty; 6-yr.; 6 members: Carolyn P. Armstrong, San Antonio (9/28/01); Kenneth R. Carr, El Paso (9/28/03); Patrick Heath, Boerne (9/28/99); Sandy Melton, Dallas (9/28/01); Sandra J. Pickett, Liberty (9/28/03); Marvin Rich, Houston (9/28/99). Dir. and Librarian Robert S. Martin ($85,000), PO Box 12927, Austin 78711.

Library, State Legislative Reference - (1909); indefinite term; Director: Sally Reynolds. Box 12488, Austin 78711.

Licensing and Regulation, Texas Commission on - (1989); apptv.; 6-yr.; expenses; 6 members: Mickey Christakos, Allen (2/1/03); William Fowler, Valley Spring (2/1/01); Elliott B. McConnell, Rockport (2/1/03); Gina Parker, Waco (2/1/01); Patricia P. Stout, San Antonio (2/1/05); Leo R. Vasquez III, Houston (2/1/05). Exec. Dir., Rachelle A. Martin ($70,000), PO Box 12157, Austin 78711.

Lottery Commission, Texas - (1993); 6-yrs.; apptv.; expenses; 3 members: C. Thomas Clowe Jr., Waco (2/1/05); Harriet Ellan Miers, Dallas (2/1/01); Anthony J. Sadberry, Cypress (2/1/97). Exec. Dir., Linda Cloud ($110,000), PO Box 16630, Austin 78761-6630.

Lower Colorado River Authority - (See Colorado River Authority, Lower).

Marriage & Family Therapists, Texas State Board of Examiners of - (1991); apptd.; 6 yrs.; per diem and transportation expenses; 9 members: Joe Ann Clack, Missouri City (2/1/03); Ellen Harrison, El Paso (2/1/01); Waymon Ray Hinson, Abilene (2/1/01); Marvarene Oliver, Corpus Christi (2/1/03); George P. Pulliam, Dickinson (2/1/01); Carl S. Strain, San Angelo (2/1/03); William H. Watson, Lubbock (2/1/05); Jackie M. Weimer, Plano (2/1/05). Exec. Dir., Bobby D. Schmidt, Dept. of Health, 1100 W. 49th St., Austin 78756-3183.

Medical Examiners District Review Committee: Dist. 1 - (1977); apptv.; 6-hr.; expenses; 20 members — five from each of 4 districts: Jerome L. Armbruster, Pearland (1/15/94); A. David Axelrad, Houston (1/15/00); Robert J. Bacon Sr., Houston (1/15/98); Herman L. Koester, Dickinson (1/15/02); Thomas A. Reiser, Houston (1/15/00). **Dist. 2:** David Baucom, Sulphur Springs (1/15/00); H. Jane Chihal, Carrollton (1/15/02); Allan N. Shulkin, Dallas (1/15/00); B.R. Sienbenlist, Jonesville (1/15/98); Rodney M. Wiseman, Tyler (1/15/00). **Dist. 3:** Robert C. Henderson, Amarillo (1/15/02); Thomas L. Marvelli, Fort Worth (1/15/00); ; Nalin H. Tolia, Odessa (1/15/98)Robert Allan Watson, Fort Worth (1/15/00); Irvin E. Zeitler Jr., San Angelo (1/15/00). **Dist. 4:** Manuel G. Guajardo, Brownsville (1/15/02); Larry Hufford, San Antonio (1/15/00); Julian Gomez III, McAllen (1/15/00); Gladys C. Keene, Laredo (1/15/98); Ann L. Nolen, La Grange (1/15/00).

Medical Examiners, Texas State Board of - (1907 as 12-member board, membership raised to 15 in 1981, raised to 18 in 1993); apptv.; 6-yr.; per diem on duty; 18 members: Lee S. Anderson, Fort Worth (4/13/03); Penny Angelo, Midland (4/13/01); Carlos Campos, New Braunfels (4/13/99); Peter Chang, Houston (4/13/03); William H. Fleming III, Houston (4/13/01); Edward S. Hicks Sr., Corpus Christi (4/13/03); Thomas D. Kirksey, Austin (4/13/01); Paul G. Meyer, Lubbock (4/13/01); Eddie J. Miles Jr., San Antonio (4/13/01); Charles W. Monday Jr., Huntsville (4/13/99); Connie Navar-Clark, El Paso (4/13/99); William A. Pollan, Ballinger (4/13/99); Larry Price, Temple (4/13/03); Vernon L. Ryan, San Angelo (4/13/01); Ann Forehand Sibley, Garland (4/13/99); R. Russell Thomas Jr., Eagle Lake (4/13/99); Janet Tornelli-Mitchell, Dallas (4/13/03); Jenat T. Turner, Austin (4/13/03). Exec. Dir., Bruce A. Levy ($85,000), PO Box 149134, Austin 78714-9134.

Medical Physicists, Texas Board of Licensure for Professional - (1991); apptv.; 6-yrs.; 9 members: Ralph Blumhardt, San Antonio (2/1/01); Stewart C. Bushong, Houston (2/1/99); Louis H. Deiterman, Temple (2/1/99); Shannon Cox, Austin (2/1/03); Kumar Krishen, Seabrook (2/1/05); Adrian LeBlanc, Houston (2/1/01); Louis Levy, San Antonio (2/1/03); Isabel Menendez, Portland (2/1/03); Paul Murphy, Houston (2/1/01).

Mental Health and Mental Retardation, Texas Board of - (1965, superseded Board of Texas State Hospitals and Special Schools); apptv.; 6-yr.; per diem and expenses; 9 members: Kenneth Z. Altshuler, Dallas (1/31/05); Rodolfo Arredondo Jr., Lubbock (1/31/01); Sharon Swift Butterworth, El Paso (1/31/05); Charles M. Cooper, Dallas (1/31/01); Virginia Eernisse, Alvin (1/31/97); Harriet M. Helmle, San Antonio (1/31/03); William A. Lawson, Houston (1/31/97); James I. Perkins, Rusk (1/31/01); Lynda K. Scott, The Woodlands (1/31/05). Commissioner of MHMR Don A. Gilbert, PO Box 12668, Austin 78711-2668 ($140,000).

Midwestern State University, Board of Regents - (1959); apptv.; 6-yr.; 9 members: Mac Cannedy Jr., Wichita Falls (2/25/00); Margaret F. Darden, Dallas (2/25/98); Barbara Jean Dorman, Plainview (2/25/02); Ervin Garnett, Fort Worth (2/25/98); Elizabeth A. Gifford, Amarillo (2/25/02); Arnold W. Oliver, Wichita Falls (2/25/02); Edward L. Watson, Dallas (2/25/00); Robert G. West, Fort Worth (2/25/98); Kathryn Anne Yeager, Wichita Falls (2/25/00). Pres., Dr. Louis J. Rodriguez, 3400 Taft, Wichita Falls 76308.

Military Facilities Commission, Texas - (1935 as 3-member National Guard Armory Board; reorganized as 6-member board in 1981; name changed 1997); 6-yr.; 6 members: Darrel Baker, Austin (4/30/01); Lillian Dunlap, San Antonio (4/30/99); Constance Linbeck, Houston (4/30/03); Federico Lopez III, Harlingen (4/30/99); Gary McClure, San Angelo (4/30/03); Michael G. White, El Paso (4/30/01). Exec. Dir., Jerry D. Malcolm ($57,000), PO Box 5426, Austin 78763.

Military Planning Commission, Texas Strategic - (1997); 3 yrs.; exp.; 11 members: 2 ex officio (chairs of House and Senate committees having to do with military matters) and 9 apptv. Apptd. members: Chino Chapa, Dallas (2/1/01); Lewis E. Curtis III, Fair Oaks Ranch (2/1/00); Charles de Wetter, El Paso (2/1/02); Tom Gann, Lufkin (2/1/00); Charles Hines, Prairie View (2/1/01); Fred Hughes, Abilene (2/1/01); S. Loyd Neal Jr., Corpus Christi (2/1/00); Horace G. Taylor, Belton (2/1/02); Robert E. Tokerud, Irving (2/1/02).

Motor Vehicle Board, Texas Department of Transportation - (1971 as 6-member board; membership increased to 9 in 1979; reduced to 6 in 1987; made division of Texas Dept. of Transportation, name changed to present form and membership increased to 9 in 1992; decreased to 6); apptv.; 6-yr.; per diem and expenses; members: Robert C. Barnes, Odessa (1/31/03); D. Diane Dillard, Houston (1/31/03); Patricia F. Harless, Spring (1/31/01); Robena E. Jackson, Austin (1/31/05); N. Scott Jones, Cleburne (1/31/01); Manuel Marrufo, El Paso (1/31/01); Kevin D. Pagan, McAllen (1/31/05); Joe W. Park, Dallas (1/31/05); Jimmy C. Payton, Euless (1/31/03). Division Dir. Brett Bray, PO Box 2293, Austin 78768.

Municipal Retirement System (See Retirement System, Municipal, Board of Trustees).

National Guard Armory Board, Texas - (see Military Facilities Commission, Texas).

National Research Laboratory Commission, Texas - (1986); apptv.; expenses; 6-yr.; 9 members: J. Fred Bucy, Dallas (2/1/01); G.W. Ceverha, Dallas (2/1/01); Charles R. Delgado, Galveston (2/1/99); Peter Flawn, Austin (2/1/97); Rolf R. Haberecht, Dallas (2/1/01); Jerome Johnson, Amarillo (2/1/97); N.B. Jordan, Waxahachie (2/1/99); Thomas D. Williams, Dallas (2/1/99). Exec. Dir., Edward C. Bingler, 2275 N. Highway 77, #100, Waxahachie 75165.

Natural Resource Conservation Commission, Texas - (1913 as State Board of Water Engineers; name changed in 1962 to Texas Water Commission; reorganized and name again changed in 1965 to Water Rights Commission; reorganized and name changed back to Texas Water Commission in 1977 to perform judicial function for the Texas Dept. of Water Resources; changed to present form Sept. 1, 1993); apptv.; 6-yr.; 3 members full-time at $97,000-$99,500: John M. Baker Jr., Temple (8/31/01); Robert J. Huston (8/31/03); R.B. (Ralph) Marquez, Texas City (8/31/99). Exec. Dir., Jeffrey Saitas ($120,000), PO Box 13087, Austin 78711.

Neches River Municipal Water Authority, Upper - (Est. 1953 as 9-member board; membership changed to 3 in 1959); apptv.; 6-yr.; 3 members: Joe Crutcher, Palestine (2/1/01); Jesse D. Hickman, Palestine (2/1/03); Cathy Stark, Palestine (2/1/99). Gen. Mgr., T.G. Mallory, PO Box 1965, Palestine 75802.

Neches Valley Authority, Lower - (1933); apptv.; per diem and expenses on duty; 6-yr.; 9 members: R.C. Aldrich, Nome (7/28/01); Lonnie Arrington, Beaumont (7/28/01); Gaylyn Cooper, Beaumont (7/28/99); Lois B. Henderson, Warren (7/28/03); Patricia M. Neild, Beaumont (7/28/03); M. Arnold Pierce, Sour Lake (7/28/99); John W. Robinson, Silsbee (7/28/03); Thomas A. Thomas, Port Arthur (7/28/99). Gen. Mgr. A. T. Hebert Jr., PO Box 3464, Beaumont 77704.

North Texas Tollway Authority Board of Directors - (1997); apptv.; per diem and expenses; 2-yr.; 7 members: commissioners courts of Collin, Dallas, Denton and Tarrant counties each appt. one member; Gov. appts 3. Gov.'s. apptees.: Donald B. Dillard, Dallas (9/1/99); Jere W. Thompson Jr., Dallas (9/1/98); Marilyn Kay Walls, Cleburne (9/1/99).

Nueces River Authority Board of Directors - (1953 as Nueces River Conservation and Reclamation District; name changed in 1971); apptv.; 6-yr.; per diem and expenses; 21 members: W. Scott Bledsoe III, Oakville (2/1/01); Margaret

Bowman, San Antonio (2/1/99); Ernestine Carson, Barksdale (2/1/01); William I. Dillard, Uvalde (2/1/01); James F. Dodson, Robstown (2/1/01); George A. Finley III, Corpus Christi (2/1/99); Ariel A. Garcia, Corpus Christi (2/1/01); Hazel R. Graff, Hondo (2/1/01); Susan C. Griffith, Uvalde (2/1/99); John William Howell, Portland (2/1/03); Kay Lynn Jasik, Poteet (2/1/01); Leslie L.W. Kinsel, Cotulla (2/1/03); Beth Reavis Knolle, Sandia (2/1/99); August Linnartz Jr., Carrizo Springs (2/1/03); Susan A. Lynch, Rio Frio (2/1/99); Patty Puig Mueller, Corpus Christi (2/1/01); Mary Melissa Ramos, Floresville (2/1/99); Thomas M. Reding Jr., Portland (2/1/03); Patricia H. Sugarek, Skidmore (2/1/99); Patricia Keane Sutton, Camp Wood (2/1/03); Lawrence H. Warburton Jr., Alice (2/1/03). Exec. Dir., Con Mims, PO Box 349, Uvalde 78802-0349.

Nurse Examiners, State Board of - (1909 as 6-member board; reorganized and membership increased to 9 in 1981); apptv.; per diem and expenses; 6-yr.; 9 members: Nancy Boston, Temple (1/31/01); Mary Letrice Brown, Dallas (1/31/01); John Fonteno Jr., Houston (1/31/03); Roselyn Holloway, Lubbock (1/31/99); Marcelo Laijas Jr., Floresville (1/31/99); Kenneth W. Lowrance, Clifton (1/31/01); Thalia H. Munoz, Roma (1/31/03); Elizabeth C. Poster, Arlington (1/31/03); Doris Price-Nealy, Beaumont (1/31/99). Exec. Dir., Katherine A. Thomas ($62,000), 333 Guadalupe, Suite 3-460, Austin 78701.

Nurse Examiners, State Board of Vocational - (1951 as 8-member board; membership increased to 12 in 1981; later increased to 15); apptv.; 6-yr.; 15 members: Janette L. Bowers, Alpine (9/6/03); Ginger M. Brenner, Sugar Land (9/6/01); Lillian K. Brown, San Angelo (9/6/01); Susie Belle Cheney, Pittsburg (9/6/99); Elmer G. Ellis, Tyler (9/6/03); Melody Hart, Andrews (9/6/99); Geneva Harvey, Clifton (9/6/03); Carla Sue McCroan, Royse City (9/6/99); Cathy Parrott, Gatesville (9/6/03); Vangie Perez, Needville (9/6/99); Kathleen Gleeson Powell, North Richland Hills (9/6/01); William H. Rice, Austin (9/6/03); Maria Olivia Rivas, Brownsville (9/6/99); Frank D. Sandoval Jr., San Antonio (9/6/01); Betty E. Sims, Victoria (9/6/01). Exec. Dir., Mary M. Strange ($58,000), 333 Guadalupe St., Ste. 3-400, Austin 78701.

Nursing Facility Administrators, Texas Board of - (Abolished effective Sept. 1997; responsibilities transferred to the Texas Department of Human Services.)

Occupational Therapy Examiners, Texas Board of - (1983); apptv.; 6-yr.; per diem and expenses; 6 members: Esperanza J. Brattin, McAllen (2/1/97); Benny O. McGehee, El Paso (2/1/97); Gwendolyn L.R. Parker, Odessa (2/1/01); Jean E. Polichino, Houston (2/1/05); Charles Paul R. Turco Sr., Beaumont (2/1/01); Jo Ann Wofford, Fort Worth (2/1/05). Exec. Dir., John Maline, 333 Guadalupe St., Ste. 2-510, Austin 78701.

Offenders with Mental Impairments, Texas Council on - (1987); apptv.; expenses; 6-yr.; 27 members: 18 heads of agencies or their designees: Texas Dept. of Criminal Justice, Texas Dept. of MHMR, Board of Pardons and Paroles, Texas Adult Probation Commission, Texas Juvenile Probation Commission, Texas Youth Commission, Texas Rehabilitation Commission, Texas Education Agency, Criminal Justice Policy Council, Mental Health Assn. in Texas, Texas Commission on Alcohol and Drug Abuse, Commission on Law Enforcement Officer Standards and Education, Texas Council of Community MHMR Centers, Commission on Jail Standards, Texas Planning Council for Developmental Disabilities, Texas Assn. for Retarded Citizens, Texas Alliance for the Mentally Ill, and Parent Assn. for the Retarded of Texas; 9 apptd. by Gov. as follows: Michael R. Arambula, San Antonio (2/1/99); Dollie Brathwaite, Houston (2/1/99); James H. Cromwell, Rusk (2/1/01); Carl Hays, Dallas (2/1/01); Corinne Ann Mason, Richardson (2/1/01); Melissa L. Mojica, Laredo (2/1/03); Carol A. Oeller, Houston (2/1/99); Susan A. Stone, Rosanky (2/1/03); Sharon Wilson, Fort Worth (2/1/03). Exec. Dir., Dee Kifowit, 8610 Shoal Creek Blvd., Austin 78757.

Old San Antonio Road Preservation Commission - (1989); term at pleasure of governor; 9 members: 4 representatives of state agencies: Texas Dept. of Transportation, Texas Historical Commission, Parks and Wildlife, Texas Dept. of Commerce (Tourism Div.); 5 at large recommended by Texas Historical Commission and apptd. by Gov.: Dr. Archie P. McDonald, Nacogdoches; Gen. John R. McGiffert, San Antonio; Ingrid B. Morris, Hemphill; Nan Olsen, Bastrop; Rose T. Treviño, Laredo.

Optometry Board, Texas - (1921 as 6-member State Board of Examiners in Optometry; name changed to present form in 1981 and membership increased to 9); apptv.; per diem; 6-yr.; 9 members: Ann A. Bradford, Midland (1/31/05); Carolyn R. Carman-Merrifield, Arlington (1/31/01); Joe W. DeLoach, Garland (1/31/05); Kevin D. DeWolfe, Austin (1/31/01); Judy M. Eidson, San Antonio (1/31/01); B.J. Garner, Houston (1/31/03); Katherine M. Gear, Mineral Wells (1/31/03); Donald R. Glenz,

Houston (1/31/03); Mark A. Latta, Amarillo (1/31/05); Donnya Elle Stephens, Nacogdoches (1/31/99). Exec. Dir., Lois Ewald ($52,000), 333 Guadalupe St., Ste. 2-420, Austin 78701.

Orthotics and Prosthetics, Texas Board of - (1998); apptv.; compensation and travel expenses; 6-yr.; 6 members: Scott Atha, Pflugerville (2/1/03); Wanda Furgason, Brownwood (2/1/05); Kenneth Hart, Kilgore (2/1/01); Thomas Lunsford, The Woodlands (2/1/01); Stanley Thomas, San Antonio (2/1/03); Lupe M. Young, San Antonio (2/1/05).

Pardons and Paroles Division, Board of - (1893 as Board of Pardon Advisers; changed in 1936 to Board of Pardons and Paroles with 3 members; membership increased to 6 in 1983; made a division of the Texas Department of Criminal Justice and membership increased to 18 in 1990); apptv.; 6-yr.; 18 members: Lynn F. Brown, Carrollton (2/1/03); Paddy Lann Burwell, Westhoff (2/1/05); Lafayette Collins, Round Rock (2/1/05); Linda Garcia, La Porte (2/1/05); Gerald L. Garrett, Gatesville (2/1/01); Juanita Maria Gonzalez, Round Rock (2/1/03); James Paul Kiel Jr., Tyler (2/1/05); Daniel Ray Lang, Houston (2/1/01); Thomas W. Moss, Amarillo (2/1/01); Rissie L. Owens, Huntsville (2/1/03); Filiberto (Bert) Reyna, Waco (2/1/05); Victor Rodriguez, San Antonio (2/1/01); Brendolyn Rogers-Gardner, Duncanville (2/1/01); Alvin A. Shaw, San Antonio (2/1/03); Charles A. Shipman, Wichita Falls (2/1/03); Lucinda "Cindy" Simons, Hereford (2/1/05); Cynthia S. Tauss, League City (2/1/01); Sandie Walker, Bryan (2/1/03).

Pardons and Paroles Policy Board, Board of - (1997); apptv.; 6 members, apptd. from membership of Board of Pardons and Paroles; 6-yr. term concurrent with term on Board of Pardons and Paroles. 6 members: Linda Garcia, La Porte (2/1/05); Gerald L. Garrett, Gatesville (2/1/01); James Paul Kiel Jr., Tyler (2/1/05); Rissie Owens, Huntsville (2/1/03); Victor Rodriguez, San Antonio (2/1/01); Alvin A. Shaw, San Antonio (2/1/03).

Parks and Wildlife Commission, Texas - (1963 as 3-member board; membership increased to 6 in 1971; increased to 9 in 1983); apptv.; expenses; 6-yr.; 9 members: Ernest Angelo Jr., Midland (2/1/03); John Avila Jr., Fort Worth (2/1/03); Lee M. Bass, Fort Worth (2/1/01); Carol E. Dinkins, Houston (2/1/03); Richard W. Heath, Dallas (2/1/01); Alvin L. Henry, Houston (2/1/05); Katharine A. Idsal, Dallas (2/1/05); Nolan Ryan, Alvin (2/1/01); Mark E. Watson Jr., San Antonio (2/1/05). Exec. Dir., Andrew S. Sansom ($115,000), 4200 Smith School Rd., Austin 78744.

Pecos River Compact Commissioner - (1942); apptv.; 6-yr.; expenses: Julian W. Thrasher Jr., Monahans (1/23/05). ($32,247).

Pension Boards - For old age, blind and dependent children's assistance, see Human Services, State Board of. For retirement pay to state and municipal employees and teachers, see proper category under Retirement.

Pension Review Board, State - (1979); apptv.; 6-yr.; 9 members — one senator apptd. by Lt. Gov., one representative apptd. by Speaker, 7 apptd. by Gov. as follows: Rafael A. Cantu, Houston (1/31/01); Craig S. Goralski Sr., Houston (1/31/03); Ronald L. Haneberg, Rockwall (1/31/01); William Mahomes Jr., Dallas (1/31/03); Frederick E. Rowe Jr., Dallas (1/31/03); Shari Ovalline Shivers, Austin (1/31/03); Jeanie Rabke Wyatt, San Antonio (1/31/01). Exec. Dir., Rita Horwitz ($52,000), PO Box 13498, Austin 78711.

Perfusionists, Texas State Board of Examiners of - (1993); apptv.; per diem; 6-yr.; 9 members: Vincent Conti, Galveston (2/1/01); H.B. Bell, Dallas (2/1/01); Debra Sue Douglass, Grapevine (2/1/03); Gaye Jackson, Houston (2/1/05); M. Adam Mahmood, El Paso (2/1/03); Steve A. Raskin, Richmond (2/1/03); Thomas A. Rawles, Plano (2/1/05); Thomas Kurt Wilkes, Lubbock (2/1/05); Jose Ybarra, San Antonio (2/1/01).

Pest Control Board, Texas Structural - (1971 as 7-member board, membership raised to 9 in 1979); apptv.; 6-yr.; expenses; 9 members — 3 ex officio: Commissioner of Agriculture; Commissioner of Health; and head of Entomology Dept., Texas A&M University; 6 apptv. members: Jo-Christy Brown, Austin (2/1/01); Charles G. Coyle, Fresno (2/1/99); Madeline K. Gamble, Dallas (2/1/05); Gary L. Gillen, Rosenberg (2/1/01); Les Hoyt, Amarillo (2/1/03); Jay D. Stone, Lubbock (2/1/03). Exec. Dir., Benny M. Mathis ($59,553), 1106 Clayton Ln., Ste. 100 LW, Austin 78723-1066.

Pharmacy, State Board of - (1907 as 6-member board; membership increased to 9 in 1981); apptv.; 6-yr.; 9 members: Gilbert P. Acuna, Kingsville (8/31/99); Kim A. Caldwell, Plano (8/31/03); Wiki Erickson, Waco (8/31/03); Doyle E. High, Haskell (8/31/01); Susan H. Jacobson, El Paso (8/31/99); Wayne McConnell, Houston (8/31/01); Oren M. Peacock Jr., Sachse (8/31/99); Bill C. Pittman, Austin (8/31/01); Donna B. Rogers, San Antonio (8/31/03). Exec. Dir., Gay Dodson ($70,000), 333 Guadalupe St., Ste. 3-600, Austin 78701.

Physical Therapy Examiners, Texas State Board of - (1971); apptv.; 6-yr.; expenses; 9 members: Harvey D. Aikman, Mission (1/31/03); Mark G. Cowart, Odessa (1/31/03); Mary R. Daulong, Houston (1/31/01); Sylvia A. DAvila, San Antonio (1/31/05); Cynthia Fisher, El Paso (1/31/03); Holly R. Hall, Sherman (1/31/05); Michael Grady Hines, Tyler (1/31/05); Mary Thompson, Celina (1/31/05); Susan K. Tripplehorn, Pampa (1/31/01). Coordinator Gerard Swain, 333 Guadalupe St., Ste. 3-510, Austin 78701.

Physician Assistant Examiners, Texas State Board of - (1995); apptv.; 6-yr.; per diem; 9 members: Pamela W. Baker, Corpus Christi (2/1/05); Abigail Barrera, San Antonio (2/1/03); Michael Belgard, Center (2/1/03); G. Al Bendeck, Lubbock (2/1/05); Stephen D. Benold, Georgetown (2/1/05); Jerry K. Clements, Dallas (2/1/01); Dwight M. Deter, El Paso (2/1/01); Glenn S. Forbes, Fort Worth (2/1/03); Tony Gene Hedges, Littlefield (2/1/01).

Plumbing Examiners, State Board of - (1947 as 6-member board; membership increased to 9 in 1981); apptv.; expenses; 6-yr.; 9 members: Walter L. Borgfeld Jr., Lufkin (9/5/03); José L. Cárdenas, Euless (9/5/01); Greg Contreras, Duncanville (9/5/99); Lawrence Lemon Jr., Slaton (9/5/03); Nelda Martínez, Corpus Christi (9/5/01); Terry Wayne Moore, Sachse (9/5/03); DeWitt Morrow Jr., Houston (9/5/99); Fernando Rico Jr., El Paso (9/5/99); Joe Rocha Jr., Blanco (9/5/01). Admin., Doretta A. Conrad ($62,000), 929 E. 41st, Austin 78751.

Podiatric Medical Examiners, State Board of - (1923 as 6-member State Board of Chiropody Examiners; name changed to State Board of Podiatry Examiners in 1967; made 9-member board in 1981; name changed to present form in 1997); apptv.; 6-yr.; expenses; 9 members: Teresa Barrios-Ogden, San Antonio (7/10/01); Katherine M. Boyd, Georgetown (7/10/99); C. Stanley Churchill Jr., Carrollton (7/10/01); Donald Wayne Falknor, Sugar Land (7/10/03); Alex L. Garcia Jr., Corpus Christi (7/10/01); Preston Goforth, Temple (7/10/99); Jim D. Lummus, San Angelo (7/10/03); Paul H. Schwarzentraub, Lubbock (7/10/99); Barbara G. Young, Bellaire (7/10/03). Exec. Dir., Allen M. Hymans ($52,000), 333 Guadalupe St., Ste. 2-320, Austin 78701.

Polygraph Examiners Board - (1965); apptv.; 6-yr.; 6 members: Elizabeth Perez Bellegarde, El Paso (6/18/01); Michael C. Gougler, Austin (6/18/99); Edward L. Hendrickson, Katy (6/18/99); Robert J. Kruckemeyer, Spring (6/18/03); Horacio Ortiz, Corpus Christi (6/18/01); Antonio V. Suarez-Barrio, Killeen (6/18/97); William K. Teigen, Dallas (6/18/03). Exec. Officer, Frank DeTucci ($35,000), PO Box 4087, Austin 78773.

Preservation Board, State - (1983); 2-yr.; 7 members — 4 ex officio: Gov., Lt. Gov., Speaker and Architect of Capitol; 3 apptv.: one apptd. by Gov., one senator apptd. by Lt. Gov. and one representative apptd. by Speaker. Gov's. apptee: Dealey D. Herndon, Austin (2/1/97). Exec. Dir., Richard L. Crawford ($80,000), PO Box 13286, Austin 78711.

Prison Board, Texas - (See Criminal Justice, Texas Dept. of).

Prison Industry Oversight Authority, Private Sector - (1997); six-yr.; expenses; apptd; 9 members: George Fedo, Wichita Falls (2/1/99); Kathy C. Flanagan, Houston (2/1/01); Albert Gonzalez, Dallas (2/1/01); Charles D. "Mickey" Harr, Brownwood (2/1/99); Raymond G. Henderson, Austin (2/1/01); Thomas Ann Hines, Plano (2/1/03); Kelley Renee Siegler, Houston (2/1/03); Carl Casey Spencer, Huntsville (2/1/01); Steven L. Varga, San Antonio (2/1/03).

Private Investigators and Private Security Agencies, Board of - (1969); apptv.; expenses; 6-yr.; 8 members — 2 ex officio: Dir., Dept. of Public Safety and Atty. Gen.; 6 apptd. members: Jim G. Bray Jr., Plano (1/31/03); George B. Craig, Corpus Christi (1/31/03); Joel K. Glenn, Colleyville (1/31/99); Ben C. Nix, Arlington (1/31/99); Jess Ann Thomason, Midland (1/31/01); Matthew Washington, Missouri City (1/31/01). Exec. Dir., Jay Kimbrough ($75,000), PO Box 13509, Austin 78711.

Produce Recovery Fund Board - (1977 as 3-member board; membership increased to 6 in 1981); apptv.; expenses; 6-yr.; 6 members — 2 each from commission merchants, general public and producer representatives. Steven Dexter Jones, Lubbock (1/31/01); Robert B. Lyons, Amarillo (1/31/03); Ly H. Nguyen, Lake Jackson (1/31/03); Joyce Cook Obst, Alamo (1/31/03); David Wayne Smith, Hart (1/31/99); Byron Edward White, Arlington (1/31/01). Admin., Margaret Alvarez, PO Box 12847, Austin 78711.

Protective and Regulatory Services, Board of - (1992); apptv.; 6-yr.; 6 members: Jon M. Bradley, Dallas (2/1/01); Maurine Dickey, Dallas (2/1/01); Richard S. Hoffman, Brownsville (2/1/03); Naomi W. Lede, Huntsville (2/1/05); Catherine C. Mosbacher, Houston (2/1/03); Edward L. Wagner, Harker Heights (2/1/05). Exec. Dir., James R. Hine ($115,000), PO Box 149030, Austin 78714-9030.

Psychologists, Texas Board of Examiners of - (1969 as 6-member board; membership increased to 9 in 1981); apptv.; 6-yr.; per diem and expenses; 9 members: Barry E. Dewlen, San Antonio (10/31/01); Don Goldston, Denton (10/31/99); Jane Halebian, Dallas (10/31/99); Betty Holmes Ray, Abilene (10/31/03); M. David Rudd, Belton (10/31/03); Denise Shade, Dallas (10/31/99); Nelda Smith, Longview (10/31/01); Brian H. Stagner, College Station (10/31/03); Emily G. Sutter, Friendswood (10/31/01). Exec. Dir., Sherry L. Lee ($52,000), 333 Guadalupe St., Ste. 2-450, Austin 78701.

Public Accountancy, State Board of - (See Accountancy, State Board of Public).

Public Finance Authority, Texas - (1984, assumed duties of Texas Building Authority); apptv.; per diem and expenses; 6-yr.; membership increased from 3 to 6 in 1991: Daniel H. Branch, Dallas (2/1/01); Helen Huey, Houston (2/1/05); John C. Kerr, San Antonio (2/1/01); Cynthia L. Meyer, San Antonio (2/1/03); H.L. Bert Mijares Jr., El Paso (2/1/05); Daniel T. Serna, Arlington (2/1/03). Exec. Dir., Kimberly K. Edwards ($90,000), 300 W. 15th St., Ste. 411, Austin 78701.

Public Safety Commission - (1935); apptv.; expenses; 6-yr.; 3 members: James B. Francis Jr., Dallas (12/31/99); Robert B. Holt, Midland (12/31/01); M. Colleen McHugh, Corpus Christi (12/31/03). Dir. of Texas Dept. of Public Safety, Dudley M. Thomas ($102,000), PO Box 4087, Austin 78773-0001.

Public Utility Commission - (1975); apptv.; 6-yr., 3 members at $97,000-$99,500: Brett A. Perlman, Houston (9/1/03); Judy W. Walsh, Fair Oaks Ranch (9/1/99); Presiding Officer Patrick Henry Wood III, Austin (9/1/01). Exec. Dir., W. Lane Sanford ($85,000), PO Box 13326, Austin 78711-3326.

Racing Commission, Texas - (1986); 6-yr.; per diem and expenses; 8 members — 2 ex officio: Chmn. of Public Safety Commission and Comptroller; 6 apptv.: Larry Jay Christopher, Crockett (2/1/01); David C. Garza, Brownsville (2/1/03); Lukin T. Gilliland Jr., San Antonio (2/1/99); Terri Lacy, Houston (2/1/03); Deorsey E. McGruder Jr., Dallas (l2/1/99); James L. Schulze, Conroe (2/1/01). Exec. Dir., Paula C. Flowerday ($77,760), PO Box 12080, Austin 78711.

Radiation Advisory Board - (1961 as 9-member board, membership increased to 18 in 1981); apptv.; 6-yr.; expenses; 18 members: Jimmy L. Barker, Granbury (4/16/01); Susan E. Best, Dallas (4/16/03); Thomas M. Burnette, Plano (4/16/01); Donald S. Butler, Colleyville (4/16/01); Earl P. Erdmann, Midland (4/16/01); Michael S. Ford, Amarillo (4/16/03); David N. Henkes, San Antonio (4/16/99); Walter Kim Howard, Longview (4/16/03); Glen Keith King, Houston (4/16/99); Dale Edward Klein, Austin (4/16/03); Jack S. Krohmer, Georgetown (4/16/99); Justin P. LeVasseur, Wichita Falls (4/16/01); Odis R. Mack, Katy (4/16/01); Troy Marceleno, Dauncanville (4/16/03); Bruce A. Matson, Houston (4/16/03); Connie Rogers, Driftwood (4/16/99); William R. Underdown Jr., George West (4/16/99); Philip M. Wentworth, Plano (4/16/99).

Radioactive Waste Disposal Authority, Texas Low-Level - (1981); apptv.; 6-yr.; expenses; 6 members: Claudia A. Ball, Comstock (2/1/03); James L. Carroll, El Paso (2/1/03); William L. Fisher, Austin (2/1/99); Milton J. Guiberteau, Houston (2/1/01); Macario Marquez, Sierra Blanca (2/1/99); John E. Simek, Bryan (2/1/01). Gen. Mgr., Douglas E. Bell ($79,440), 7701 N. Lamar Blvd., Ste. 300, Austin 78752.

Railroad Commission of Texas - (1891); elective; 6-yr.; 3 members, $92,217 each: Tony Garza (1/1/04); Michael L. Williams (1/1/02); Charles R. Matthews (1/1/00). Dir., Kathy Pyka ($88,408), PO Box 12967, Austin 78711.

Real Estate Commission, Texas - (1949 as 6-member board; membership increased to 9 in 1979); apptv.; per diem and expenses; 6-yr.; 9 members: C. Michael Brodie, Richardson (1/31/03); Jay Brummett, Austin (1/31/01); Pete Cantu Sr., Helotes (1/31/99); Christine T. Folmer, El Paso (1/31/01); Maria Gonzalez-Gil, San Antonio (1/31/03); Mitchell Katine, Houston (1/31/99); Hazel W. Lewis, Arlington (1/31/99); Deanna Mayfield, San Angelo (1/31/01); Kay Sutton, Midland (1/31/03). Admin., Wayne Thorburn ($70,000), PO Box 12188, Austin 78711.

Real Estate Research Advisory Committee - (1971); apptv.; 6-yr.; 10 members — one ex officio: representative of Texas Real Estate Commission; 9 apptv. members: Joe Adame, Corpus Christi (1/31/03); Carlos Madrid Jr., San Antonio (1/31/01); Catherine Miller, Arlington (1/31/03); Celia Ross Goode-Haddock, College Station (1/31/99); Marjory Kay Moore, Big Spring (1/31/99); Angela S. Myres, Houston (1/31/01); Jerry L. Schaffner, Lubbock (1/31/03); John P. Schneider Jr., Austin (1/31/99); Gloria Van Zandt, Arlington (1/31/01). Dir., James Christian, Texas A&M, College Station 77843-2115.

Red River Authority, Board of Directors - (1959); apptv.; 6-yr.; per diem and expenses; 9 members: George W. Arrington, Canadian (8/11/01); Carol Carlson, Lakeside City (8/11/03); William K. Daniel, Wichita Falls (8/11/03); Paul F.

Engler, Amarillo (8/11/99); James P. Fallon, Sherman (8/11/99); Betty P. Peveto, Gainesville (8/11/01); Edna M. Shepherd, Texarkana (8/11/99); Cliff A. Skiles Jr., Hereford (8/11/03); W.F. Smith Jr., Quanah (8/11/01). Gen. Mgr., Ronald J. Glenn, 520 Hamilton Bldg., Wichita Falls 76301.

Red River Compact Commissioner - (1949); apptv.; 4-yr.; (Function of commissioner is to negotiate with other states respecting waters of the Red.): Lowell Cable, Sulphur Springs (2/1/99); ($24,225).

Redistricting Board, Legislative - (See Legislative Redistricting Board).

Rehabilitation Commission, Texas - (1969); apptv.; expenses; 6-yr.; 6 members: Matthew T. Doyle, Texas City (8/31/99); Jerry Kane, Corpus Christi (8/31/99); Diane M. Novy, Sugar Land (8/31/97); Beverly Stribling, San Angelo (8/31/03); A. Kent Waldrep Jr., Plano (8/31/01); Ray A. Wilkerson, Austin (8/31/01). Commissioner, Vernon M. Arrell ($95,000), 4900 N. Lamar Blvd., Austin 78751-2316.

Retirement System, Municipal, Board of Trustees - (1947); apptv.; 6-yr.; expenses; 6 members: Kathleen Gunn Buehner, Mansfield (2/1/01); Patricia Hernandez, Plainview (2/1/05); Victoria Lee H. LaFollett, Longview (2/1/03); Rick Menchaca, Midland (2/1/01); Isaac Duane Turner, McKinney (2/1/05); Charles E. Windwehen, Victoria (2/1/03). Exec. Dir., Gary W. Anderson, PO Box 149153, Austin 78714-9153.

Retirement System of Texas, Employees - (1949); apptv.; 6-yr.; 6 members — one apptd. by Gov., one by Chief Justice of State Supreme Court and one by Speaker; 3 are employee members of the system serving 6-yr. overlapping terms: Pamela A. Carley, Austin (8/31/97); Carolyn Gallagher, Austin (8/31/00); Milton Hixson, Austin (8/31/98); Frank J. Smith, Austin (8/31/99); Byron Tunnell, Austin (8/31/96); Janice R. Zitleman, Austin (8/31/01). Exec. Dir., Sheila W. Beckett ($123,000), PO Box 13207, Austin 78711-3207.

Retirement System, Teacher - (1937 as 6-member board; membership increased to 9 in 1973); expenses; 6-yr.; 9 members — 2 apptd. by State Board of Education, 3 apptd. by Gov. and 4 TRS members apptd. by Gov. after being nominated by popular ballot of members of the retirement system: James P. Cummings, San Angelo (8/31/01); H. Barham Fulmer II, Lindale (8/31/03); Brenda L. Jackson, Dallas (8/31/03); Cecilia M. Moreno, Laredo (8/31/03); James H. Simms, Amarillo (8/31/01); Kathryn S. Stream, Denton (8/31/99); Wendell Whittenburg, Sweetwater (8/31/01); Lee R. Williamson, Wichita Falls (8/31/99); Kneeland Youngblood, Dallas (8/31/99). Exec. Dir., Charles Dunlap, 1000 Red River, Austin 78701.

Retirement System, Texas County and District - (1967); apptv.; 6-yr.; 9 members: Giles W. Dalby, Post (12/31/97); Maxine Darst, Terrell (12/31/99); Martha Gustavsen, Conroe (12/31/99); Kathy Hynson, Rosenberg (12/31/95); Steve Radack, Houston (12/31/95); Kathy Reeves, Midland (12/31/03); Sam D. Seale, Port Lavaca (12/31/99); Bill W. Wallis, Tyler (12/31/95); John Willy, Angleton (12/31/03). Dir., Terry Horton, 400 W. 14th, Austin 78701-1688.

Rio Grande Compact Commissioner of Texas - (1929); apptv.; 6-yr.: Joe G. Hanson, El Paso (6/9/01). Box 1917, El Paso 79950-1917 ($41,195).

Runnels County Water Authority, Board of Directors - (1955); apptv.; 6-yr.; 9 members: Pamela Bauerlein, Ballinger (2/1/97); James D. Condra, Talpa (2/1/95); Dalton E. Crockett, Ballinger (2/1/97); L. Aubrey Faubion Jr., Ballinger (2/1/97); Leon Frerich, Norton (2/1/93); Marvin W. Gerhart, Winters (2/1/95); Werner Harsch, Miles (2/1/93); Elliott J. Kemp, Ballinger (2/1/93); Kenneth H. Slimp, Winters (2/1/95).

Rural Healthcare System Board of Directors, Statewide - (see **Healthcare**)

Sabine River Authority, Board of Directors - (1949); apptv.; per diem and expenses; 6-yr.; 9 members: Walta Pippen Cooke, Carthage (7/6/99); Sammy Dean Dance (7/6/01); Karen C. Hampton, Tyler (7/6/01); Joyce Plummer Hugman, Gladewater (7/6/03); Margin Stovall Latham, Sulphur Springs (7/6/01); Richard A. Linkenauger, Greenville (7/6/03); Ruben S. Martin III, Longview (7/6/03); Jerry Stallworth, Marshall (7/6/99); Clarence Earl Williams Jr., Orange (7/6/99). Exec. Vice Pres. & Gen. Mgr., Sam F. Collins, PO Box 579, Orange 77630.

Sabine River Compact Commission - (1953); apptv.; 6-yr.; $8,487 each; 5 members — one member and chmn. apptd. by President of United States without a vote; 2 from Texas and 2 from Louisiana. Texas members: Frank Edward Parker, Center (7/12/01); Danny Choate, Orange (7/12/98). Box 579, Orange 77630. ($8,487).

San Antonio River Authority - apptv., 6 yr., 12 members: Ruben Expronceda, San Antonio (1/31/01); Roger V. Gary, San Antonio (1/31/99); Leo J. Gleinser, Goliad (1/31/03); Truett Hunt, Kenedy (1/31/01); Alois "Al" D. Kollodziej Jr., Poth (1/16/99); Martha C. McNeel, San Antonio (1/31/01); R.H. Ramsey

Jr., Goliad (1/31/01); Louis E. Rowe, San Antonio (1/31/03); H.B. Ruckman III, Karnes City (1/31/03); Nancy Steves, San Antonio (1/31/99); J.C. Turner, Floresville (1/31/03); Otis L. Walker, Goliad (1/31/97); Thomas G. Weaver, San Antonio (1/31/03). Gen. Mgr., Gregory E. Rothe, 100 E. Guenther St., San Antonio 78283-0027.

San Jacinto Historical Advisory Board - (1907 as San Jacinto State Park Commission; changed to San Jacinto Battleground Commission and changed again in 1965 to present name; apptv.; 6-yr.; 5 members — 2 ex officio: Dir., Parks Div., Parks and Wildlife Dept. and pres. of San Jacinto Museum of History Assn.; 3 apptd. by Gov.: Mary C. Burke, Houston (9/1/97); Joel Moore Nash, Bellaire (9/1/95); Frank Calhoun, Houston (9/1/99). Parks Section, Parks and Wildlife Dept., 4200 Smith School Rd., Austin 78744.

San Jacinto River Authority, Board of Directors - (1937); apptv.; expenses while on duty; 6-yr.; 6 members: Henry T. Brooks, Conroe (10/16/99); John H. Choate, Humble (10/16/97); James T. Edmonds, Houston (10/16/99); David L. Mendez, Houston (10/16/97); R. Gary Montgomery, The Woodlands (10/16/95); Walter D. Wilkerson Jr., Conroe (10/16/95). Gen. Mgr., James R. Adams, PO Box 329, Conroe 77305.

Savings and Loan Commissioner - Apptv. by State Finance Commission: James L. Pledger ($92,676), PO Box 1089, Austin 78767.

School Land Board - (See Land Board, School).

Securities Board, State - (Est. 1957, the outgrowth of several amendments to the Texas Securities Act, originally passed 1913); act is administered by the Securities Commissioner, who is appointed by the board members; expenses; 6-yr.; 3 members: Kenneth W. Anderson Jr., Dallas (1/20/05); Nicholas C. Taylor, Midland (1/20/01); José Adan Treviño, Bellaire (1/21/03). Securities Commissioner, Denise Voigt Crawford ($90,000), PO Box 13167, Austin 78711-3167.

Seed and Plant Board, State - (1959); apptv.; 2-yr.; 6 members: A. James Allison, Tulia (10/6/99); Dick L. Auld, Lubbock (10/6/99); Joe M. Crane, Bay City (10/6/00); Charles Leamons, Brenham (10/6/00); Katherine Cave Patrick, Bishop (10/6/00); W. David Worrall, Vernon (10/6/99). Exec. Secy., Charles A. Leamons, Texas Dept. of Agriculture, PO Box 12847, Austin 78711.

Sex Offender Treatment, Council on - (1997); apptv.; 6-yr.; expenses; 6 members: Liles Arnold, Plano (2/1/03); Kristy M. Carr, Austin (2/1/05); Richard N. Mack, Lubbock (2/1/05); David Swinson Jr., Hewitt (2/1/01). Exec. Dir., Eliza May ($39,816), PO Box 12546, Austin 78711.

Skill Standards Board, Texas - (1995); 11 members serving terms at pleasure of Gov.; expenses; members: Gary Forrest Blagg, Grapevine; Michael L. Brown, Waxahachie; Les T. Csorba, Houston; Ramon H. Dovalina, Laredo; Roger E. Elliott, Sulphur Springs; Beth Ann Graham, Hallsville; Denise Laman, Plano; Edward "Ted" Lloyd O'Rourke, Galveston; Wayne J. Oswald, Freeport; Billie Conley Pickard, Raymondville; Dick Weinhold, Bedford.

Social Worker Examiners, Texas State Board of - (1993); apptd.; 6-yr.; per diem and travel expenses; 9 members: Ramiro Cabrera, Corpus Christi (2/1/99); Cathy Clancy, Houston (2/1/97); Deborah Hammond, Austin (2/1/01); Jeannie M. Heller, College Station (2/1/03); Marlene LaRoe, Houston (2/1/99); Sgt. Willie McGee, Plainview (2/1/01); Shonna Lynette Olford, Longview (2/1/97); Sylvia S. Ramirez, Portland (2/1/97); Hoye D. Tibbets, Grandview (2/1/97); Gerrianne Waring, El Paso (2/1/01).

Soil and Water Conservation Board, Texas State - (1939); elected by members of individual districts; 2 yrs.; 5 members. Exec. Dir., Robert G. Buckley ($62,400), PO Box 658, Temple 76503.

Speech-Language Pathology and Audiology, State Board of Examiners for - (1983); apptv.; 6-yr.; per diem and expenses; 9 members: John K. Ashby, Abilene (8/31/99); Elsa Cardenas-Hagan, Olmito (8/31/01); Judy A. Chambers, Crosby (8/31/03); George E. Cire, Victoria (8/31/01); Deloris Johnson, Houston (8/31/99); Harvey Komet, San Antonio (8/31/01); Teri Mata-Pistokache, Edinburg (8/31/99); Lee Reeves, Plano (8/31/03); R. Eric Reynolds, Southlake (8/31/03). Exec. Secy., Dorothy Cawthon, 1100 W. 49th, Austin 78756-3183.

Stephen F. Austin State University, Board of Regents - (1969); apptv.; expenses; 6-yr.; 9 members: Ron Adkison, Henderson (1/31/99); Richard A. Brookshire, Lufkin (1/31/01); Penny H. Butler, Houston (1/31/03); Michael W. Enoch, Mont Belvieu (1/31/03); Pattye Greer, Nacogdoches (1/31/01); Simon Lynn Montes, Lufkin (1/31/99); Jimmy W. Murphy, Houston (1/31/01); Susan Scheumack Roberds, Dallas (1/31/03); Murray Shaw, Austin (1/31/99). Pres., Dr. Dan Angel, PO Box 6078, SFA Sta., Nacogdoches 75962.

Student Loan Corporation, Texas Guaranteed - (1979); 6-yr.; 11-members — one ex officio; Comptroller of Public Accounts; one apptd. by Commissioner of Higher Education and one apptd. by Chmn. of Coordinating Board; 8 apptd. by Gov. as follows: Ruben E. Esquivel, DeSoto (1/31/03); Jennifer Jen'Nan Ghazal, Wichita Falls (1/31/99); Jorja L. Kimball, Kingsville (1/31/99); Jerry Don Miller, Canyon (1/31/99); Albert Myres, Houston (1/31/03); Jane Phipps, San Antonio (1/31/99); Alan V. Rash, El Paso (1/31/01); W. Bruce Robinson, Corsicana (1/31/03); Brent Thompson, Tyler (1/31/01); Charley V. Wootan, College Station (1/31/01). Pres., Milton G. Wright, PO Box 201725, Austin 78720.

Sulphur River Basin Authority, Board of Directors - (1985); apptd.; 6-yr.; per diem and expenses; 6 members: John McCool Howison, Bogata (2/1/99); Mike Huddleston, Wake Village (2/1/03); Charles L. Lowry, Mt. Vernon (2/1/03); Patsy R. McClain, Sulphur Springs (2/1/01); Maxine J. Nanze, Atlanta (2/1/99); Robert L. Parker, Paris (2/1/01).

Sunset Advisory Commission - (1977); 10 members: 4 members of House of Representatives, 4 members of Senate, one public member apptd. by Speaker, one public member apptd. by Lt. Gov.; 4-yr.; expenses. Public members: Robert Lanier, Houston; Bill Jeter, Houston. Dir., Joey Longley, PO Box 13066, Austin 78711.

Tax Board, State - (1905); ex officio; term in other office; no compensation; 3 members: Comptroller, Secretary of State and State Treasurer.

Tax Professional Examiners, Board of - (1977 as Board of Tax Assessor Examiners; name changed to present form 1983); apptv.; expenses; 6-yr.; 6 members: Michael A. Amezquita, Harlingen (3/1/05); Carol Autry, Amarillo (3/1/01); Wayne R. Hawkins, Texarkana (3/1/01); Deborah M. Hunt, Austin (3/1/05); Linda D. Jaynes, Plainview (3/1/03); Foy Mitchell Jr., Plano (3/1/03). Exec. Dir., David E. Montoya ($52,000), 333 Guadalupe, Ste. 2-520 Austin 78701-3942.

Teacher Retirement System - (See Retirement System, Teacher).

Texas A&M University System - Board of Regents - (1875); apptv.; 6-yr.; expenses; 9 members: Robert H. Allen, Houston (2/1/01); Anne L. Armstrong, Armstrong (2/1/03); Dionel E. Aviles, Houston (2/1/03); Frederick Donald McClure, Dallas (2/1/01); Erle Allen Nye, Dallas (2/1/03); Donald E. Powell, Amarillo (2/1/01); Lionel Sosa, San Antonio (2/1/05); R.H. (Steve) Stevens Jr., Houston (2/1/05); Susan Rudd Wynn, Benbrook (2/1/05). Chancellor, Barry B. Thompson, College Station 77843-1123.

Texas Southern University, Board of Regents - (1947); expenses; 6-yr.; 9 members: Albert C. Black Jr., Rowlett (2/1/01); Enos M. Cabell Jr., Missouri City (2/1/01); Thomas H. Friedberg, Sugar Land (2/1/03); Regina Giovannini, Houston (2/1/05); Willard L. Jackson Jr., Houston (2/1/05); Lori H. Moon, Cedar Hill (2/1/05); Gene A. Moore Sr., Houston (2/1/01); Carroll W. Phillips, Houston (2/1/95); A. Martin Wickliff Jr., Houston (2/1/03); Fred S. Zeidman, Houston (2/1/03). Pres., James M. Douglas, 3100 Cleburne, Houston 77004.

Texas State Technical College, Board of Regents - (1960 as Board of the Texas State Technical Institute; changed to present name, 1991); apptv.; expenses; 6-yr.; 9 members: Edward B. Adams Sr., Austin (8/31/97); De la Garza, C. "Connie", Harlingen (8/31/01); Jere M. Lawrence, Sweetwater (8/31/01); Nat Lopez, Harlingen (8/31/99); Charles D. Olson, Waco (8/31/99); Jerilyn Kyker Pfeifer, Abilene (8/31/01); Gerald D. Phariss, Garland (8/31/97); Tom L. Ragland, Waco (8/31/99); Thomas L. Whaley Sr., Marshall (8/31/01). Chancellor, Dr. Bill Segura, TSTC System, Waco 76705.

Texas State University System, Board of Regents - (1911 as Board of Regents of State Teachers Colleges; name changed in 1965 to Board of Regents of State Senior Colleges; changed to present form in 1975); apptv.; per diem and expenses; 6-yr.; 9 members: Patricia Diaz Dennis, San Antonio (2/1/05); Dionicio (Don) Flores, El Paso (2/1/05); John Philip Hageman, Round Rock (2/1/03); James A. "Jimmy" Hayley, Texas City (2/1/05); Thomas M. Moeller, Beaumont (2/1/01); Nancy R. Neal, Lubbock (2/1/03); Floyd Nickerson, Abilene (2/1/03); Pollyanna A. Stephens, San Angelo (2/1/01); Macedonio Villarreal, Sugar Land (2/1/01). Chancellor, Lamar G. Urbanovsky, 505 Sam Houston Bldg., Austin 78701.

Texas Tech University, Board of Regents - (1923); apptv.; expenses; 6-yr.; 9 members: Carin Marcy Barth, Houston (1/31/05); E.R. (Dick) Brooks, Dallas (1/31/05); J. Robert Brown, El Paso (1/31/01); Patsy W. Martin, Austin (1/31/97); Brian C. Newby, Austin (1/31/05); John C. Sims, Lubbock (1/31/97); James E. Sowell, Dallas (1/31/01); Elizabeth (Cissy) Ward, Houston (1/31/97); Alan B. White, Lubbock (1/31/01). Chancellor, Donald Haragan, PO Box 4039, Lubbock 79409.

Texas Woman's University Board of Regents - (1901); apptv.; expenses; 6-yr.; 9 members: Jerry L. Brownlee, Cleburne (2/1/05); Kay Williams Goodman, Sanger (2/1/01); Carlos R. Hamilton Jr., Houston (2/1/01); Richard D. Hayes, Denton (2/1/01); Linda R. Hughes, Dallas (2/1/05); Marie Chapman Martch, Belton (2/1/03); Douglas Bert Myers, Plano (2/1/03); Cynthia Shepard Perry, Houston (2/1/03); Delia M. Reyes, Dallas (2/1/05). Interim Pres., Dr. Beverley Byers-Pevitts, PO Box 23925, TWU Sta., Denton 76204-1925.

Texas-Mexico Authority Advisory Board - (1991); apptd.; 6-yr.; 6 members: Santiago F. Cantu, Austin (2/1/97); Marjorie C. Kastman, Lubbock (2/1/95); Mark Langdale, Dallas (2/1/01); William R. Leo, La Joya (2/1/99); William S. Tilney, El Paso (2/1/97).

Transportation Commission, Texas - (1917 as State Highway Commission; merged with Mass Transportation Commission and name changed to State Board of Highways and Public Transportation in 1975; merged with Texas Dept. of Aviation and Texas Motor Vehicle Commission and name changed to present form in 1991; apptv.; 6-yr.; ($15,914); 3 members: John W. Johnson, Houston (2/1/05); David M. Laney, Dallas (2/1/01); Robert Lee Nichols, Jacksonville (2/1/03). Exec. Dir., William G. Burnett, P.E. ($145,000), 125 E. 11th St., Austin 78701-2483.

Trinity River Authority, Board of Directors - (1955); apptv.; per diem and expenses; 6-yr.; 24 directors — 3 from Tarrant County, 4 from Dallas County, 2 from area-at-large and one each from 15 other districts: Judi Jones Benestante, Coldspring (3/15/99); Leslie C. Browne, Arlington (3/15/03); Anton B. Brucks, Dallas (3/15/97); Patricia A. Clapp, Dallas (3/15/01); Hector Escamilla Jr., Carrollton (3/15/03); Horace Perry Flatt, Terrell (3/15/99); Benny L. Fogleman, Livingston (3/15/03); Jane M. Fouty, Corsicana (3/15/03); Valerie Freeman, Dallas (3/15/01); Edward Eugene Hargett, Crockett (3/15/03); Michael P. Heiskell, Arlington (3/15/99); William H. Hodges, Huntsville (3/15/01); Jo Ann Jenkins, Waxahachie (3/15/99); John W. Jenkins, Hankamer (3/15/03); William M. Key, Athens (3/15/01); A. Dawn Knight, Madisonville (3/15/99); Maurice L. Locke, Liberty (3/15/01); James W. Porter, Dallas (3/15/99); H. Gene Reynolds Jr., Fairfield (3/15/01); Wanda W. Stovall, Fort Worth (3/15/01); Douglas Lee Sumrall, Palestine (3/15/01); F.L. Thompson, Leona (3/15/99); Jack C. Vaughn Jr., Dallas (3/15/03); Walter C. White, Trinity (3/15/99). Gen. Mgr., Danny F. Vance, PO Box 60, Arlington 76004-0060.

Tuition Board, Prepaid Higher Education - (1996); 6-yr.; 7 members: Comptroller; 4 apptd. by Lt. Gov.; 2 apptd. by Gov.

Tuition Scholarship Foundation Board, Texas Prepaid - (1996); indeterminate terms; 5 members: Comptroller; one apptd. by gov.; 3 apptd. jointly by Comptroller and gov's apptee. Gov's apptee: George H. McShan, Harlingen.

Turnpike Authority, Texas - (1953 as 9-member board; increased to 12 members in 1971; reorganized as part of Texas Dept. of Transportation 1997, and membership decreased to 7: one ex officio and 6 apptd.); 6 members: Samuel E. Barshop, San Antonio (2/15/05); Glenn Jarvis, McAllen (2/15/03); Alan L. Johnson, Harlingen (2/15/05); Mary Q. Kelly, San Antonio (2/15/01); Pete Winstead, Austin (2/15/03); Manuel Zuniga, Austin (2/15/01).

Underground Facility Notification Corporation, Texas - (1997); apptv.; no compensation; 3-yr.; 12 members: Ralph Edward Alonzo, San Antonio (8/31/00); Tony Boyd, DeSoto (8/31/01); Sheila Wilkes Brown, Austin (8/31/01); E. Leon Carter, Plano (8/31/99); Janet W. Holland, Mineral Wells (8/31/01); David Hooper, Portland (8/31/01); Lois W. Kolkhorst, Brenham (8/31/00); Steve F. Landon, Bedford (8/31/99); Howard T. Pebley Jr., McAllen (8/31/00); E. Ashley Smith, Houston (8/31/00); Nancy Lou Sullivan, Colorado City (8/31/99); José L. Valenciano, Lubbock (8/31/99).

Uniform State Laws, Commission on - (1941 as 5-member Commissioners to the National Conference on Uniform State Laws; name changed to present form; membership increased to 6 and term of office raised to 6 years in 1977); apptv.; 6-yr.; 6 members: Patrick C. Guillot, Dallas (9/30/94); Peter K. Munson, Denison (9/30/02); David Peeples, San Antonio (9/30/98); Marilyn E. Phelan, Lubbock (9/30/98); Rodney W. Satterwhite, Midland (9/30/02); Harry L. Tindall, Houston (9/30/02).

University of Houston, Board of Regents - (1963); apptv.; expenses; 6-yr.; 9 members: Eduardo Aguirre Jr., Houston (8/31/01); Zinetta A. Burney, Houston (8/31/97); Philip J. Carroll, Houston (8/31/99); Elyse Lanier, Houston (8/31/97); Charles E. McMahen, Houston (8/31/01); Wilhelmina R. Morian, Houston (8/31/97); John M. O'Quinn, Houston (8/31/99); Gary L. Rosenthal, Houston (8/31/01); Kay Kerr Walker, Victoria (8/31/99). Chancellor/President Arthur K. Smith, 4800 Calhoun,

Houston 77004.

University of North Texas Board of Regents - (1949); apptv.; 6-yr.; expenses; 9 members: Roy Gene Evans, Dallas (5/22/99); Jerry S. Farrington, Dallas (5/22/99); Joe Kirven, Dallas (5/22/01); Lucille G. Murchison, Dallas (5/22/99); George W. Pepper, Fort Worth (5/22/03); Burle Pettit, Lubbock (5/22/01); John Robert "Bobby" Ray, Plano (5/22/01); Gayle W. Strange, Aubrey (5/22/03); Martha Fuller Turner, Houston (5/22/03). Chancellor, Dr. Alfred F. Hurley, PO Box 13737, Denton 76203-3737.

University of Texas System, Board of Regents - (1881); apptv.; expenses; 6-yr.; 9 members: Linnet F. Deily, Houston (2/1/01); Donald L. Evans, Midland (2/1/01); Woody L. Hunt, Austin (2/1/05); Thomas G. Loeffler, San Antonio (2/1/01); Charles Miller, Houston (2/1/05); Patrick C. Oxford, Houston (2/1/03); A.W. Riter Jr., Tyler (2/1/03); Raul R. Romero, Houston (2/1/05); A.R. (Tony) Sanchez, Laredo (2/1/03). Chancellor, William H. Cunningham, PO Box N, University Sta., Austin 78713-7328.

Veterans Commission, Texas - (1927 as Veterans State Service Office; reorganized as Veterans Affairs Commission in 1947 with 5 members; membership increased to 6 in 1981; name changed to present form in 1985); apptv.; 6-yr.; per diem while on duty and expenses; 6 members: John A. Brieden III, Brenham (12/31/03); James Stewart Duncan, Austin (12/31/03); Herbert W. Odell, Fort Worth (12/31/99); Patsy L. Palmquist, Devine (12/31/99); Brig. Gen. Sue Ilen Turner (Ret.), San Antonio (12/31/01); Alexander Vernon, Killeen (12/31/01). Exec. Dir., James E. Nier ($68,000), PO Box 12277, Austin 78711.

Veterans Land Board - (Est. 1949 as 3-member ex officio board; reorganized 1956); 4-yr.; per diem and expenses; 3 members: one ex officio: Comm. of General Land Office; 2 apptd.: Lt. Gen. Neal "Tom" Jaco (Ret.), San Antonio (12/29/00); Darryl Ladd Pattillo, Austin (12/29/02). Exec. Sec., David Gloier (member), 1700 N. Congress Ave., Ste. 836, Austin 78701-1496.

Veterinary Medical Examiners, Texas State Board of - (1911; revised 1953; made 9-member board in 1981); apptv.; expenses on duty; 6-yr.; 9 members: Martin E. Garcia II, Raymondville (8/26/03); Howard Head, Littlefield (8/26/01); Robert I. Hughes, Center (8/26/99); D. Carter King, Roanoke (8/26/01); J. Lynn Lawhon, Abilene (8/26/03); Sharon O. Matthews, Albany (8/26/99); Michael J. McCulloch, Odessa (8/26/99); Jean McFaddin, Beaumont (8/26/01); Mary Rebecca Terry (Becky), Alpine (8/26/03). Exec. Dir., Ron Allen ($60,000), 333 Guadalupe St., Ste. 2-330, Austin 78701-3998.

Water Development Board, Texas - (1957; legislative function for the Texas Dept. of Water Resources, 1977); apptv.; per diem and expenses; 6-yr.; 6 members: Elaine M. Barron, El Paso (12/31/99); Noe Fernandez, McAllen (12/31/01); Charles L. Geren, Fort Worth (12/31/99); Jack Hunt, Houston (12/31/03); Wales H. Madden Jr., Amarillo (12/31/03); William B. Madden, Dallas (12/31/01). Exec. Admin., Craig D. Pedersen ($100,000), PO Box 13231, Austin 78711.

Workers' Compensation Commission, Texas - (1991); 6-yr.; apptv; expenses; 6 members: Jack Abla, Kilgore (2/1/01); Kenneth Lee Moore, Houston (2/1/05); Rebecca F. Olivares, San Antonio (2/1/03); Richard F. Reynolds, Austin (2/1/01); Joel B. (Burt) Terrill, San Angelo (2/1/03); Lonnie Watson, Cleburne (2/1/05). Exec. Dir., Leonard W. Riley Jr. ($95,000), 4000 S. IH-35, Austin 78704-1287.

Workers' Compensation Insurance Fund Board, Texas - (1991); expenses; 6-yr.; 9 members: Ernesto Ancira Jr., San Antonio (2/1/99); Patricia A. (Pat) Crawford, El Paso (2/1/99); Pat O'Neal, Dallas (2/1/01); Brenda Pejovich, Dallas (2/1/03); James D. Ross, Midland (2/1/01); Tommy G. Salome, Crawford (2/1/01); George Wesch Jr., Lake Hills (2/1/99); Charles Hugh Whiteside, Kilgore (2/1/03); Martin H. Young Jr., The Woodlands (2/1/01).

Workforce Commission, Texas - (1936 as Texas Employment Commission; name changed 1995); apptv.; $97,000-$99,500; 6-yr.; 3 members: Ron Lehman, Austin (2/1/03); Terrence P. O'Mahoney, Dallas (2/1/05); Diane D. Rath, San Antonio (2/1/01). Exec. Dir., Mike Sheridan ($125,000), 101 E. 15th St., Ste. 618 Austin 78778-0001.

Youth Commission, Texas - (1949 as 9-member board; reorganized 1957 and again in 1975); 6-yr.; per diem on duty; 6 apptv. members: Pete C. Alfaro, Baytown (8/31/01); Charles R. Henry, Pampa (8/31/03); Leonard E. Lawrence, San Antonio (8/31/03); John W. Odam Jr., Houston (8/31/99); Edna L. Tamayo, Harlingen (8/31/99); Lisa S. Teschner, Dallas (8/31/01). Exec. Dir., Steve Robinson ($110,000), PO Box 4260, Austin 78765. ☆

State Government Income and Expenditures

Taxes are the state government's primary source of income. On this and the following pages are summaries of state income and expenditures, tax collections, tax revenue by type of tax, a summary of the state budget for the 2000-01 biennium, Texas Lottery income and expenditures and the amount of federal payments to state agencies.

State Revenues by Source and Expenditures by Function
Amounts (in Millions) and Percent of Total

Revenues by Source	1998	%	1997	%	1996	%	1995	%	1994	%
Tax Collections	$22,634	50.9	$21,188	49.7	$19,763	48.8	$18,859	48.8	$18,106	49.3
Federal Income	12,632	28.4	12,128	28.4	11,658	28.8	11,408	29.5	10,552	28.7
Licenses, Fees, Permits, Fines, Penalties	4,113	9.2	3,866	9.1	3,841	9.5	3,768	9.7	3,151	8.6
Interest & Other Investment Income	1,565	3.5	1,860	4.4	2,076	5.1	1,715	4.4	1,697	4.6
Land Income	340	0.8	294	0.7	223	0.6	201	0.5	220	0.6
Sales of Goods & Services	256	0.6	237	0.5	198	0.5	173	0.5	141	0.4
Contributions to Employee Benefits	93	0.2	89	0.2	95	0.2	122	0.3	115	0.3
Settlements of Claims	10	0.0	6	0.0	15	0.1	6	0.0	12	0.1
Net Lottery Proceeds	1,650	3.7	1,857	4.4	1,718	4.2	1,662	4.3	1,586	4.3
Other Revenues	1,205	2.7	1,124	2.6	902	2.2	769	2.0	1,126	3.1
Total Net Revenues	**$44,497**	**100**	**$42,649**	**100**	**$40,488**	**100**	**$38,682**	**100**	**$36,707**	**100**

Expenditures by Function										
General Government - Total	$1,587	3.7	$1,490	3.6	$1,442	3.6	$1,473	3.7	$1,400	3.9
Executive	1,371	3.2	1,283	3.1	1,257	3.2	1,298	3.3	1,238	3.5
Legislative	91	0.2	97	0.2	81	0.2	83	0.2	72	0.2
Judicial	124	0.3	111	0.3	104	0.2	92	0.2	89	0.2
Education	16,607	38.4	15,317	36.9	14,779	37.3	14,510	36.9	13,416	37.6
Employee Benefits	1,767	4.1	1,712	4.1	1,785	4.5	1,732	4.4	1,618	4.5
Health and Human Services	14,700	34.0	15,026	36.2	13,593	34.3	13,540	34.4	12,005	33.7
Public Safety and Corrections	2,671	6.2	2,445	5.9	2,292	5.8	2,260	5.7	1,938	5.4
Transportation	3,292	7.6	3,021	7.3	3,364	8.5	2,741	7.0	2,726	7.7
Natural Resources and Recreational Services	733	1.7	712	1.7	666	1.7	953	2.4	589	1.7
Lottery Winnings Paid	388	0.9	430	1.0	381	1.0	454	1.2	429	1.2
Regulatory Agencies	184	0.4	174	0.4	171	0.4	166	0.4	169	0.5
Debt Service — Interest	529	1.2	553	1.3	526	1.3	463	1.2	348	1.0
Capital Outlay	767	1.8	580	1.4	671	1.7	1,045	2.7	999	2.8
Total Net Expenditures	**$43,224**	**100**	**$41,460**	**100**	**$39,669**	**100**	**$39,337**	**100**	**$35,638**	**100**

Amounts rounded.
Source: State of Texas 1998 Annual Cash Report, Vol. One, Summary of Financial Information for the year ended August 31, 1998, Comptroller of Public Accounts' Office.

State Tax Collections, 1987-1998

Fiscal Year‡	State Tax Collections	Resident Population	Per Capita Tax Collections	Taxes as % of Personal Income
1987	$10,266,162,781	16,615,360	$617.87	†4.4
1988	12,364,618,924	16,669,153	741.77	†5.0
1989	12,905,940,817	†16,795,955	768.40	†4.8
1990	13,632,640,459	†17,020,489	†800.95	†4.7
1991	14,922,113,980	†17,319,166	†861.60	†4.8
1992	15,848,915,148	†17,641,580	†898.38	†4.8
1993	17,010,737,258	†17,989,926	†945.57	4.9
1994	18,105,950,592	†18,340,852	†987.19	†4.9
1995	18,858,790,042	†18,693,032	†1,008.87	4.8
1996	19,762,504,349	†19,046,150	†1,037.61	†4.7
1997	21,187,868,235	*19,395,244	*1,092.43	†4.7
1998	22,634,019,737	*19,747,837	*1,146.15	*4.7

‡ Fiscal years end August 31.
* Estimated
† Revised
Sources: Texas Comptroller of Public Accounts, Annual Financial Reports of various years. Population and personal income figures, 1987 to 1996: U.S. Dept. of Commerce (Bureau of the Census and Bureau of Economic Analysis). Data for 1997 and 1998 include partial estimates by the Texas Comptroller of Public Accounts.

Tax Revenues, 1997, 1998

Below are listed the major taxes and the amounts each contributed to the state in fiscal years 1997 and 1998.

Type of Tax	FY 1998	FY 1997
Sales	$12,459,386,685	$11,340,069,309
Oil Production	303,795,247	429,149,036
Natural Gas Prod.	574,584,435	712,223,305
Motor Fuels	2,506,070,912	2,383,041,029
Motor Veh. Sales/Rnt*	2,276,721,555	2,050,102,516
Franchise	1,937,752,118	1,796,605,454
Cigarette/Tobacco	560,923,078	654,769,113
Alcoholic Bev.	456,036,596	431,651,428
Insurance Occupation	747,195,661	705,833,462
Utility	241,739,624	258,020,196
Inheritance	326,820,325	207,588,651
Hotel/Motel	207,179,101	185,606,055
Other Taxes**	35,814,403	33,208,683
Totals	**$22,634,019,740**	**$21,187,868,237**

*Includes tax on manufactured housing sales and taxes on interstate motor carriers.

State Government Budget Summary, 2000-01 Biennium

Source: Legislative Budget Board

Article (Govt. Division)	2000-01 Budget (all funds) (in millions)
Art. I, General Government	$ 2,525.6
Art. II, Health and Human Services	27,436.8
Art. III, Education	44,542.4
Art. IV, The Judiciary	360.0
Art. V, Public Safety & Criminal Justice	7,600.0
Art. VI, Natural Resources	1,863.4
Art. VII, Business & Economic Dev.	12,012.7
Art. VIII, Regulatory	468.9
Art. IX, General Provisions	614.6
Art. X, The Legislature	264.7
Art. XII, Tobacco Settlement Receipts	458.1
Total	**$ 98,147.2**

House Bill 1 passed by the 76th Legislature (and adjusted for other legislation and Governor's vetoes) provides for $98.1 billion in appropriations from all fund sources for state government operations for the 2000-01 biennium. This amount represents an increase of $9.6 billion, or 10.9 percent, from the 1998-99 biennial level. The appropriations for the 2000-01 biennium include $458.1 million in receipts collected from the 1998 Comprehensive Tobacco Settlement. In addition to the appropriations contained in House BIll 1, the 2000-01 biennial budget shown here reflects appropriations made pursuant to Senate Bill 4 and Senate Bill 928. Text of these bills may be obtained on the Texas Legislature's Internet site: **www.capitol.state.tx.us/**. ☆

Texas Lottery

Source: Texas Lottery Commission

The State Lottery Act was passed by the Legislature in July 1991. The constitutional amendment necessary to approve the lottery was passed in an election on Nov. 5, 1991, by a vote of 1,326,154 to 728,994. The first ticket was purchased on May 29, 1992.

Executive Director of the Texas Lottery is Linda Cloud.

Who Plays the Lottery?

The executive director of the Texas Lottery is required to conduct a biennial demographic survey of lottery players in order to determine the income, age, sex, race, education and frequency of participation of players. The information below is from the survey conducted for the Texas Lottery Commission by the Office of Survey Research of The University of Texas at Austin, College of Communication, in Oct. and Nov. 1998. A total of 1,720 interviews were completed with Texans 18 years of age and older. The margin of error for a sample of 1,720 is approximately plus or minus 2.4 percent.

The percentage of Texans who report purchasing at least one Texas Lottery ticket in the 12 months preceding the survey was 68 percent. Sixty-one percent reported playing Lotto, while 42 percent played scratch games and 22 percent played the daily Pick 3 game. Cash 5 was played by 25 percent, and 21 percent played Texas Million.

Age: Seventy-six percent of Texans between ages 46 and 55 played the lottery, followed by 72 percent of those 36 to 45; 71 percent of those 56 to 65; 70 percent of those 26 to 35; 58 percent of those 18 to 25; and 50 percent of Texans 66 and older.

Educational Level: Texans with some college were more likely to play the lottery (74%) than those with a high-school education (69%), college graduates (65%) or those with less than a high-school education (57%).

Income Level: Seventy-five percent of Texans making

Texas Lottery Financial Data

Start-up to August 31, 1998

Period	Value of Prizes Won (millions)	Cost of Product (millions)	Retailer Comm-issions (millions)	Admin-istration (millions)	To General Rev. Fund* (millions)
Start-up through FY 1993	$1,250	$151	$122	$23	$657
FY 1994	1,529	152	138	21	928
FY 1995	1,689	169	152	27	1,015
FY 1996	1,951	195	172	28	1,098
FY 1997	2,152	206	187	36	1,183
FY 1998	1,648	167	155	37	1,098

* All figures accrued.

between $30,000 and $49,999 per year played lottery games, as did 72 percent who made $50,000 or more; 70 percent who made between $20,000 and $29,999; 67 percent who made between $10,000 and $19,999; and 64 percent who made less than $10,000.

Ethnic Background: Seventy-three percent of Hispanic Texans play lottery games, as do 67 percent of Anglos, 65 percent of blacks and 68 percent of other ethnic groups.

Sex: Approximately 71 percent of men and 64 percent of women play lottery games.

Geography: Of the Texas Lottery's 10 sales districts, the one with the largest percentage of lottery players is Victoria (74%), followed by McAllen (73%), San Antonio (72%), Irving (69%), Abilene (68%), Houston and Austin (67%), El Paso (66%), Lubbock (63%) and Tyler (59%). ☆

Federal Revenue by State Agency

Source: Comptroller of Public Accounts, Annual Cash Report for the Year Ended August 31, 1998, Vol. One.

State Agency	1998	1997	1996	1995
Texas Health and Human Services Commission	$6,347,330,161	$6,403,094,272	$6,530,574	$692,694
Texas Department of Health	457,417,299	417,643,982	4,449,526,194	4,633,661,477
Department of Human Services	929,056,755	834,497,759	2,582,342,240	2,557,890,909
Texas Education Agency	1,790,451,074	1,629,880,091	1,624,804,412	1,486,163,829
Texas Department of Transportation	1,155,163,077	1,109,653,179	1,219,992,730	1,023,390,309
Texas Workforce Commission*	679,322,015	561,541,277	327,895,021	165,214,706
Department of Protective and Regulatory Services	157,779,632	132,300,556	211,567,471	204,678,631
Texas Rehabilitation Commission	236,523,760	209,913,129	191,143,413	201,608,287
Texas Department of Housing and Community Affairs	191,818,948	180,264,620	153,291,317	136,032,090
All Other Agencies	686,958,473	649,088,480	890,588,948	988,775,125
Total All Agencies	**$12,631,821,194**	12,127,877,345	$11,657,682,320	$11,408,108,057

* The 1995 numbers represent federal funds of the Texas Employment Commission. Effective June 1996, all of the functions of the TEC were transferred to the Texas Workforce Commission; the 1996-1998 numbers include federal funds of both TEC and TWC.

Texas' Chief Governmental Officials

On this and following pages are lists of the principal administrative officials who have served the Republic and State of Texas with dates of their tenures of office. In a few instances there are disputes as to the exact dates of tenures. Dates listed here are those that appear the most authentic.

★ ★ ★ ★ ★ ★ ★

Governors and Presidents

*Spanish Royal Governors

Domingo Terán de los Rios	1691-1692
Gregorio de Salinas Varona	1692-1697
Francisco Cuerbo y Valdéz	1698-1702
Mathías de Aguirre	1703-1705
Martín de Alarcón	1705-1708
Simon Padilla y Córdova	1708-1712
Pedro Fermin de Echevers y Subisa	1712-1714
Juan Valdéz	1714-1716
Martín de Alarcón	1716-1719
Joseph de Azlor, Marqués de San Miguel de Aguayo	1719-1722
Fernando Pérez de Almazan	1722-1727
Melchor de Media Villa y Azcona	1727-1730
Juan Antonio Bustillos y Ceballos	1730-1734
Manuel de Sandoval	1734-1736
Carlos Benites Franquis de Lugo	1736-1737
Prudencio de Orobio y Basterra	1737-1741
Tomás Felipe Wintuisen	1741-1743
Justo Boneo y Morales	1743-1744
Francisco García Larios	1744-1748
Pedro del Barrio Junco y Espriella	1748-1751
Jacinto de Barrios y Jauregui	1751-1759
Angel Martos y Navarrete	1759-1766
Hugo Oconór	1767-1770
Baron de Ripperda	1770-1778
Domingo Cabello	1778-1786
Bernardo Bonavia	1786-1786
Rafael Martínez Pacheco	1787-1788

The office of Governor was ordered suppressed and the province put under a presidial captain for a period in ... 1788-1789

Manuel Muñoz	1790-1798
José Irigoyen	1798-1800
Juan Bautista de Elguezábal	1800-1805
Antonio Cordero y Bustamante	1805-1810
Juan Bautista Casas	1811-1811
Manuel María de Salcedo	1811-1813
Cristóbal Domínguez	1814-1817
Ignacio Pérez	1817-1817
Manuel Pardo	1817-1817
Antonio Martínez	1817-1822

Some authorities would include Texas under administrations of several earlier Spanish Governors. The late Dr. C. E. Castañeda, Latin-American librarian of The University of Texas and authority on the history of Texas and the Southwest, would include the following four: Francisco de Garay, 1523-26; Pánfilo de Narváez, 1526-28; Nuño de Guzmán, 1528-30; Hernando de Soto, 1538-43.

Governors Under Mexican Rule

The first two Governors under Mexican rule, Trespalacios and García, were of Texas only as Texas was then constituted. Beginning with Gonzáles, 1824, the Governors were for the joint State of Coahuila y Texas.

José Felix Trespalacios	1822-1823
Luciano García	1823-1824
Rafael Gonzáles	1824-1826
Victor Blanco	1826-1827
José María Viesca	1827-1830
Ramón Eca y Músquiz	1830-1831
José María Letona	1831-1832
Ramón Eca y Músquiz	1832-1832
Juan Martín de Veramendi	1832-1833
Juan José de Vidáurri y Villasenor	1833-1834

Juan José Elguezábal	1834-1835
José María Cantú	1835-1835
Agustin M. Viesca	1835-1835
Marciel Borrego	1835-1835
Ramón Eca y Músquiz	1835-1835

Provisional Colonial Governor, Before Independence

Henry Smith (Impeached) ... 1835

James W. Robinson served as acting Governor just prior to March 2, 1836, after Smith was impeached.

Presidents of the Republic of Texas

David G. Burnet *(provisional President)*	Mar. 16, 1836-Oct. 22, 1836
Sam Houston	Oct. 22, 1836-Dec. 10, 1838
Mirabeau B. Lamar	Dec. 10, 1838-Dec. 13, 1841
Sam Houston	Dec. 13, 1841-Dec. 9, 1844
Anson Jones	Dec. 9, 1844-Feb. 19, 1846

Governors Since Annexation

J. Pinckney Henderson ... Feb. 19, 1846-Dec. 21, 1847

(Albert C. Horton served as acting Governor while Henderson was away in the Mexican War.)

George T. Wood	Dec. 21, 1847-Dec. 21, 1849
Peter Hansbrough Bell	Dec. 21, 1849-Nov. 23, 1853
J. W. Henderson	Nov. 23, 1853-Dec. 21, 1853
Elisha M. Pease	Dec. 21, 1853-Dec. 21, 1857
Hardin R. Runnels	Dec. 21, 1857-Dec. 21, 1859
Sam Houston *(resigned because of state's secession from the Union)*	Dec. 21, 1859-Mar. 16, 1861
Edward Clark	Mar. 16, 1861-Nov. 7, 1861
Francis R. Lubbock *(resigned to enter Confederate Army)*	Nov. 7, 1861-Nov. 5, 1863
Pendleton Murrah *(administration terminated by fall of Confederacy)*	Nov. 5, 1863-June 17, 1865

Fletcher S. Stockdale *(Lt. Gov. performed some duties of office on Murrah's departure, but is sometimes included in list of Governors. Hamilton's appointment was for immediate succession, as shown by the dates.)*

Andrew J. Hamilton *(Provisional, appointed by President Johnson)*	June 17, 1865-Aug. 9, 1866
James W. Throckmorton	Aug. 9, 1866-Aug. 8, 1867
Elisha M. Pease *(appointed July 30, 1867, under martial law)*	Aug. 8, 1867-Sept. 30, 1869

Interregnum

Pease resigned and vacated office Sept. 30, 1869; no successor was named until Jan. 8, 1870. Some historians extend Pease's term until Jan. 8, 1870, but in reality Texas was without a head of its civil government from Sept. 30, 1869, until Jan. 8, 1870.

Edmund J. Davis *(appointed provisional Governor after being elected)*	Jan. 8, 1870-Jan. 15, 1874
Richard Coke *(resigned to enter United States Senate)*	Jan. 15, 1874-Dec. 1, 1876
Richard B. Hubbard	Dec. 1, 1876-Jan. 21, 1879
Oran M. Roberts	Jan. 21, 1879-Jan. 16, 1883
John Ireland	Jan. 16, 1883-Jan. 18, 1887
Lawrence Sullivan Ross	Jan. 18, 1887-Jan. 20, 1891
James Stephen Hogg	Jan. 20, 1891-Jan. 15, 1895
Charles A. Culberson	Jan. 15, 1895-Jan. 17, 1899
Joseph D. Sayers	Jan. 17, 1899-Jan. 20, 1903
S. W. T. Lanham	Jan. 20, 1903-Jan. 15, 1907
Thos. Mitchell Campbell	Jan. 15, 1907-Jan. 17, 1911
Oscar Branch Colquitt	Jan. 17, 1911-Jan. 19, 1915
James E. Ferguson *(impeached)*	Jan. 19, 1915-Aug. 25, 1917
William Pettus Hobby	Aug. 25, 1917-Jan. 18, 1921

Pat Morris Neff.................. Jan. 18, 1921-Jan. 20, 1925
Miriam A. Ferguson .... Jan. 20, 1925-Jan. 17, 1927
Dan Moody .... Jan. 17, 1927-Jan. 20, 1931
Ross S. Sterling................. Jan. 20, 1931-Jan. 17, 1933
Miriam A. Ferguson .... Jan. 17, 1933-Jan. 15, 1935
James V. Allred .... Jan. 15, 1935-Jan. 17, 1939
W. Lee O'Daniel (*resigned to enter United States Senate*) ....Jan. 17, 1939-Aug. 4, 1941
Coke R. Stevenson ....Aug. 4, 1941-Jan. 21, 1947
Beauford H. Jester................Jan. 21, 1947-July 11, 1949
Allan Shivers (*Lt. Governor succeeded on death of Governor Jester. Elected in 1950 and re-elected in 1952 and 1954*) ....July 11, 1949-Jan. 15, 1957
Price Daniel........................ Jan. 15, 1957-Jan. 15, 1963
John Connally..................... Jan. 15, 1963-Jan. 21, 1969
Preston Smith .... Jan. 21, 1969-Jan. 16, 1973
**Dolph Briscoe................... Jan. 16, 1973-Jan. 16, 1979
William P. Clements .... Jan. 16, 1979-Jan. 18, 1983
Mark White .... Jan. 18, 1983-Jan. 20, 1987
William P. Clements .... Jan. 20, 1987-Jan. 15, 1991
Ann W. Richards .... Jan. 15, 1991-Jan. 17, 1995
George W. Bush ....Jan. 17, 1995 to Present

**Effective in 1975, term of office was raised to 4 years, according to a constitutional amendment approved by Texas voters in 1972. See introduction to State Government chapter in this edition for other state officials whose terms were raised to four years.

★ ★ ★ ★ ★ ★ ★

Vice Presidents and Lieutenant Governors

Vice Presidents of Republic

	Date Elected
Lorenzo de Zavala (*provisional Vice President*)	
Mirabeau B. Lamar	Sept. 5, 1836
David G. Burnet	Sept. 3, 1838
Edward Burleson	Sept. 6, 1841
Kenneth L. Anderson	Sept. 2, 1844

Lieutenant Governors

Albert C. Horton...1846-1847
John A. Greer..1847-1851
J. W. Henderson...Aug. 4, 1851
D. C. Dickson...1853-1855
H. R. Runnels...Aug. 6, 1855
F. R. Lubbock..Aug. 4, 1857
Edward Clark...Aug. 1, 1859
John M. Crockett..1861-1863
Fletcher S. Stockdale.......................................1863-1866
George W. Jones 1866
(*Jones was removed by General Sheridan.*)
J. W. Flanagan 1869
(*Flanagan was appointed U.S. Senator and was never inaugurated as Lt. Gov.*)
R. B. Hubbard..1873-1876
J. D. Sayers...1878-1880
L. J. Storey..1880-1882
Marion Martin..1882-1884
Barnett Gibbs..1884-1886
T. B. Wheeler...1886-1890
George C. Pendleton..1890-1892
M. M. Crane ....Jan. 17, 1893-Jan. 25, 1895
George T. Jester...1895-1898
J. N. Browning...1898-1902
George D. Neal...1902-1906
A. B. Davidson...1906-1912
Will H. Mayes...1912-1914
William Pettus Hobby...1914-1917
W. A. Johnson (*served Hobby's unexpired term and until* .... January, 1920)
Lynch Davidson...1920-1922
T. W. Davidson..1922-1924
Barry Miller..1924-1931
Edgar E. Witt..1931-1935
Walter Woodul...1935-1939
Coke R. Stevenson...1939-1941

John Lee Smith 1943-Jan. 21, 1947
Allan Shivers .... Jan. 21, 1947-July 11, 1949
(*Shivers succeeded to the governorship on death of Governor Beauford H. Jester.*)
Ben Ramsey 1951-Sept. 18, 1961
(*Ben Ramsey resigned to become a member of the State Railroad Commission.*)
Preston Smith 1963-1969
Ben Barnes 1969-1973
William P. Hobby Jr..1973-1991
Robert D. Bullock 1991-1999
Rick Perry...1999- Present

★ ★ ★ ★ ★ ★ ★

Secretaries of State
Republic of Texas

Raines Yearbook for Texas, 1901, gives the following record of Secretaries of State during the era of the Republic of Texas:

Under David G. Burnet — Samuel P. Carson, James Collingsworth and W. H. Jack.

Under Sam Houston (first term) — Stephen F. Austin, 1836. J. Pinckney Henderson and Dr. Robert A. Irion, 1837-38.

Under Mirabeau B. Lamar — Bernard Bee appointed Dec. 16, 1838; James Webb appointed Feb. 6, 1839; D. G. Burnet appointed Acting Secretary of State, May 31, 1839; N. Amory appointed Acting Secretary of State, July 23, 1839; D. G. Burnet appointed Acting Secretary of State, Aug. 5, 1839; Abner S. Lipscomb appointed Secretary of State, Jan. 31, 1840, and resigned Jan. 22, 1841; Joseph Waples appointed Acting Secretary of State, Jan. 23, 1841, and served until Feb. 8, 1841; James S. Mayfield appointed Feb. 8, 1841; Joseph Waples appointed April 30, 1841, and served until May 25, 1841; Samuel A. Roberts appointed May 25, 1841; reappointed Sept. 7, 1841.

Under Sam Houston (second term) — E. Lawrence Stickney, Acting Secretary of State until Anson Jones appointed Dec. 13, 1841. Jones served as Secretary of State throughout this term except during the summer and part of this term of 1842, when Joseph Waples filled the position as Acting Secretary of State.

Under Anson Jones — Ebenezer Allen served from Dec. 10, 1844, until Feb. 5, 1845, when Ashbel Smith became Secretary of State. Allen was again named Acting Secretary of State, March 31, 1845, and later named Secretary of State.

State Secretaries of State

Charles Mariner .... Feb. 20, 1846-May 4, 1846
David G. Burnet....................May 4, 1846-Jan. 1, 1848
Washington D. Miller ....Jan. 1, 1848-Jan. 2, 1850
James Webb .... Jan. 2, 1850-Nov. 14, 1851
Thomas H. Duval ....Nov. 14, 1851-Dec. 22, 1853
Edward Clark .... Dec. 22, 1853-Dec., 1857
T. S. Anderson .... Dec. 1857-Dec. 27, 1859
E. W. Cave ....Dec. 27, 1859-Mar. 16, 1861
Bird Holland ....Mar. 16, 1861-Nov., 1861
Charles West......................... Nov., 1861-Sept., 1862
Robert J. Townes..................Sept., 1862-May 2, 1865
Charles R. Pryor....................May 2, 1865-Aug., 1865
James H. Bell ....Aug., 1865-Aug., 1866
John A. Green ....Aug., 1866-Aug., 1867
D. W. C. Phillips ....Aug., 1867-Jan., 1870
J. P. Newcomb ....Jan. 1, 1870-Jan. 17, 1874
George Clark.......................Jan. 17, 1874-Jan. 27, 1874
A. W. DeBerry ....Jan. 27, 1874-Dec. 1, 1876
Isham G. Searcy ....Dec. 1, 1876-Jan. 23, 1879
J. D. Templeton ....Jan. 23, 1879-Jan. 22, 1881
T. H. Bowman ....Jan. 22, 1881-Jan. 18, 1883
J. W. Baines.......................Jan. 18, 1883-Jan. 21, 1887
John M. Moore ....Jan. 21, 1887-Jan. 22, 1891
George W. Smith ....Jan. 22, 1891-Jan. 17, 1895
Allison Mayfield ....Jan. 17, 1895-Jan. 5, 1897
J. W. Madden........................Jan. 5, 1897-Jan. 18, 1899
D. H. Hardy.........................Jan. 18, 1899-Jan. 19, 1901

John G. Tod	Jan. 19, 1901-Jan., 1903
J. R. Curl	Jan., 1903-April, 1905
O. K. Shannon	April, 1905-Jan., 1907
L. T. Dashiel	Jan., 1907-Feb., 1908
W. R. Davie	Feb., 1908-Jan., 1909
W. B. Townsend	Jan., 1909-Jan., 1911
C. C. McDonald	Jan., 1911-Dec., 1912
J. T. Bowman	Dec., 1912-Jan., 1913
John L. Wortham	Jan., 1913-June, 1913
F. C. Weinert	June, 1913-Nov., 1914
D. A. Gregg	Nov., 1914-Jan., 1915
John G. McKay	Jan., 1915-Dec., 1916
C. J. Bartlett	Dec., 1916-Nov., 1917
George F. Howard	Nov., 1917-Nov., 1920
C. D. Mims	Nov., 1920-Jan., 1921
S. L. Staples	Jan., 1921-Aug., 1924
J. D. Strickland	Sept., 1924-Jan. 1, 1925
Henry Hutchings	Jan. 1, 1925-Jan. 20, 1925
Mrs. Emma G. Meharg	Jan. 20, 1925-Jan., 1927
Mrs. Jane Y. McCallum	Jan., 1927-Jan., 1933
W. W. Heath	Jan., 1933-Jan., 1935
Gerald C. Mann	Jan., 1935-Aug. 31, 1935
R. B. Stanford	Aug. 31, 1935-Aug. 25, 1936
B. P. Matocha	Aug. 25, 1936-Jan. 18, 1937
Edward Clark	Jan. 18, 1937-Jan., 1939
Tom L. Beauchamp	Jan., 1939-Oct., 1939
M. O. Flowers	Oct. 26, 1939-Feb. 25, 1941
William J. Lawson	Feb. 25, 1941-Jan., 1943
Sidney Latham	Jan., 1943-Feb., 1945
Claude Isbell	Feb., 1945-Jan., 1947
Paul H. Brown	Jan., 1947-Jan. 19, 1949
Ben Ramsey	Jan. 19, 1949-Feb. 9, 1950
John Ben Shepperd	Feb. 9, 1950-April 30, 1952
Jack Ross	April 30, 1952-Jan. 9, 1953
Howard A. Carney	Jan. 9, 1953-Apr. 30, 1954
C. E. Fulgham	May 1, 1954-Feb. 15, 1955
Al Muldrow	Feb. 16, 1955-Nov. 1, 1955
Tom Reavley	Nov. 1, 1955-Jan. 16, 1957
Zollie Steakley	Jan. 16, 1957-Jan. 2, 1962
P. Frank Lake	Jan. 2, 1962-Jan. 15, 1963
Crawford C. Martin	Jan. 15, 1963-March 12, 1966
John L. Hill	March 12, 1966-Jan. 22, 1968
Roy Barrera	March 7, 1968-Jan. 23, 1969
Martin Dies Jr.	Jan. 23, 1969-Sept. 1, 1971
Robert D. (Bob) Bullock	Sept. 1, 1971-Jan. 2, 1973
V. Larry Teaver Jr.	Jan. 2, 1973-Jan. 19, 1973
Mark W. White Jr.	Jan. 19, 1973-Oct. 27,1977
Steven C. Oaks	Oct. 27, 1977-Jan. 16, 1979
George W. Strake Jr.	Jan. 16, 1979-Oct. 6, 1981
David A. Dean	Oct. 22, 1981-Jan. 18, 1983
John Fainter	Jan. 18, 1983-July 31, 1984
Myra A. McDaniel	Sept. 6, 1984-Jan. 26, 1987
Jack Rains	Jan. 26, 1987-June 15, 1989
George Bayoud Jr.	June 19, 1989-Jan. 15, 1991
John Hannah Jr.	Jan. 17, 1991-March 11, 1994
Ronald Kirk	April 4, 1994 to Jan. 17, 1995
Antonio O. "Tony" Garza Jr.	Jan. 18, 1995 to Nov. 24, 1997
Alberto R. Gonzales	Dec. 2, 1997 to Feb. 9, 1999
Elton Bomer	Feb. 9, 1999 to Present

★ ★ ★ ★ ★ ★ ★

Attorneys General

Of the Republic

David Thomas and Peter W. Grayson	Mar. 2-Oct. 22, 1836
J. Pinckney Henderson, Peter W. Grayson, John Birdsall, A. S. Thurston	1836-1838
J. C. Watrous	Dec., 1838-June 1, 1840
Joseph Webb and F. A. Morris	1840-1841
George W. Terrell, Ebenezer Allen	1841-1844
Ebenezer Allen	1844-1846

*Of the State

Volney E. Howard	Feb. 21, 1846-May 7, 1846
John W. Harris	May 7, 1846-Oct. 31, 1849

Henry P. Brewster	Oct. 31, 1849-Jan. 15, 1850
A. J. Hamilton	Jan. 15, 1850-Aug. 5, 1850
Ebenezer Allen	Aug. 5, 1850-Aug. 2, 1852
Thomas J. Jennings	Aug. 2, 1852-Aug. 4, 1856
James Willie	Aug. 4, 1856-Aug. 2, 1858
Malcolm D. Graham	Aug. 2, 1858-Aug. 6, 1860
George M. Flournoy	Aug. 6, 1860-Jan. 15, 1862
N. G. Shelley	Feb. 3, 1862-Aug. 1, 1864
B. E. Tarver	Aug. 1, 1864-Dec. 11, 1865
Wm. Alexander	Dec. 11, 1865-June 25, 1866
W. M. Walton	June 25, 1866-Aug. 27, 1867
Wm. Alexander	Aug. 27, 1867-Nov. 5, 1867
Ezekiel B. Turner	Nov. 5, 1867-July 11, 1870
Wm. Alexander	July 11, 1870-Jan. 27, 1874
George Clark	Jan. 27, 1874-Apr. 25, 1876
H. H. Boone	Apr. 25, 1876-Nov. 5, 1878
George McCormick	Nov. 5, 1878-Nov. 2, 1880
J. H. McLeary	Nov. 2, 1880-Nov. 7, 1882
John D. Templeton	Nov. 7, 1882-Nov. 2, 1886
James S. Hogg	Nov. 2, 1886-Nov. 4, 1890
C. A. Culberson	Nov. 4, 1890-Nov. 6, 1894
M. M. Crane	Nov. 6, 1894-Nov. 8, 1898
Thomas S. Smith	Nov. 8, 1898-Mar. 15,1901
C. K. Bell	Mar. 20, 1901-Jan., 1904
R. V. Davidson	Jan., 1904-Dec. 31, 1909
Jewel P. Lightfoot	Jan. 1, 1910-Aug. 31, 1912
James D. Walthall	Sept. 1, 1912-Jan. 1, 1913
B. F. Looney	Jan. 1, 1913-Jan., 1919
C. M. Cureton	Jan., 1919-Dec., 1921
W. A. Keeling	Dec., 1921-Jan., 1925
Dan Moody	Jan., 1925-Jan., 1927
Claude Pollard	Jan., 1927-Sept., 1929
R. L. Bobbitt (Apptd.)	Sept., 1929-Jan., 1931
James V. Allred	Jan., 1931-Jan., 1935
William McCraw	Jan., 1935-Jan., 1939
Gerald C. Mann (resigned)	Jan., 1939-Jan., 1944
Grover Sellers	Jan., 1944-Jan., 1947
Price Daniel	Jan., 1947-Jan., 1953
John Ben Shepperd	Jan., 1953-Jan. 1, 1957
Will Wilson	Jan. 1, 1957-Jan. 15, 1963
Waggoner Carr	Jan. 15, 1963-Jan. 1, 1967
Crawford C. Martin	Jan. 1, 1967-Dec. 29, 1972
John Hill	Jan. 1, 1973-Jan. 16, 1979
Mark White	Jan. 16, 1979 to Jan. 18, 1983
Jim Mattox	Jan. 18, 1983 to Jan. 15, 1991
Dan Morales	Jan. 15, 1991 to Jan. 13, 1999
John Cornyn	Jan. 13, 1999-Present

*The first few Attorneys General held office by appointment of the Governor. The office was made elective in 1850 by constitutional amendment and Ebenezer Allen was the first elected Attorney General.

★ ★ ★ ★ ★ ★ ★

Treasurers

Of the Republic

Asa Brigham	1838-1840
James W. Simmons	1840-1841
Asa Brigham	1841-1844
Moses Johnson	1844-1846

Of the State

James H. Raymond	Feb. 24, 1846-Aug. 2, 1858
*C. H. Randolph	Aug. 2, 1858-June, 1865
*Samuel Harris	Oct. 2, 1865-June 25, 1866
W. M. Royston	June 25, 1866-Sept. 1, 1867
John Y. Allen	Sept. 1, 1867-Jan., 1869
†George W. Honey	Jan., 1869-Jan., 1874
†B. Graham (short term)	beginning May 27, 1872
A. J. Dorn	Jan., 1874-Jan., 1879
F. R. Lubbock	Jan., 1879-Jan., 1891
W. B. Wortham	Jan., 1891-Jan., 1899
John W. Robbins	Jan., 1899-Jan., 1907
Sam Sparks	Jan., 1907-Jan., 1912
J. M. Edwards	Jan., 1912-Jan., 1919
John W. Baker	Jan., 1919-Jan., 1921
G. N. Holton	July, 1921-Nov. 21, 1921
C. V. Terrell	Nov. 21, 1921-Aug. 15, 1924

S. L. Staples	Aug. 16, 1924-Jan. 15, 1925	H. C. Hudson	Jan. 17, 1836-Oct. 22, 1836
W. Gregory Hatcher	Jan. 16, 1925-Jan. 1, 1931	E. M. Pease	June, 1837-Dec., 1837
Charley Lockhart	Jan. 1, 1931-Oct. 25, 1941	F. R. Lubbock	Dec., 1837-Jan., 1839
Jesse James	Oct. 25, 1941-Sept. 29, 1977	Jas. W. Simmons	Jan. 15, 1839-Sept. 30, 1840
Warren G. Harding	Oct. 7, 1977-Jan. 3, 1983	Jas. B. Shaw	Sept. 30, 1840-Dec. 24, 1841
Ann Richards	Jan. 3, 1983- Jan. 2, 1991	F. R. Lubbock	Dec. 24, 1841-Jan. 1, 1842
Kay Bailey Hutchison	Jan. 2, 1991 to June 1993	Jas. B. Shaw	Jan. 1, 1842-Jan. 1, 1846
‡Martha Whitehead	June 1993 to Aug. 1996		

*Randolph fled to Mexico upon collapse of Confederacy. No exact date is available for his departure from office or for Harris' succession to the post. It is believed Harris took office Oct. 2, 1865.

†Honey was removed from office for a short period in 1872 and B. Graham served in his place.

‡ The office of Treasurer was eliminated by Constitutional amendment in an election Nov. 7, 1995, effective the last day of August 1996.

★ ★ ★ ★ ★ ★ ★

Railroad Commission of Texas

(After the first three names in the following list, each commissioner's name is followed by a surname in parentheses. The name in parentheses is the name of the commissioner whom that commissioner succeeded.)

John H. Reagan	June 10, 1891-Jan. 20, 1903
L. L. Foster	June 10, 1891-April 30, 1895
W. P. McLean	June 10, 1891-Nov. 20, 1894
L. J. Storey (McLean)	Nov. 21, 1894-Mar. 28,1909
N. A. Stedman (Foster)	May 1, 1895-Jan. 4, 1897
Allison Mayfield (Stedman)	Jan. 5, 1897-Jan. 23, 1923
O. B. Colquitt (Reagan)	Jan. 21, 1903-Jan. 17, 1911
William D. Williams (Storey)	April 28, 1909-Oct. 1, 1916
John L. Wortham (Colquitt)	Jan. 21, 1911-Jan. 1, 1913
Earle B. Mayfield (Wortham)	Jan. 2, 1913-March 1, 1923
Charles Hurdleston (Williams)	Oct. 10, 1916-Dec. 31, 1918
Clarence Gilmore (Hurdleston)	Jan. 1, 1919-Jan. 1, 1929
N. A. Nabors (A. Mayfield)	March 1, 1923-Jan. 18, 1925
William Splawn (E. Mayfield)	March 1, 1923-Aug. 1, 1924
C. V. Terrell (Splawn)	Aug. 15, 1924-Jan. 1, 1939
Lon A. Smith (Nabors)	Jan. 29, 1925-Jan. 1, 1941
Pat M. Neff (Gilmore)	Jan. 1, 1929-Jan. 1, 1933
Ernest O. Thompson (Neff)	Jan. 1, 1933-Jan. 8, 1965
G. A. (Jerry) Sadler (Terrell)	Jan. 1, 1939-Jan. 1, 1943
Olin Culberson (Smith)	Jan. 1, 1941-June 22, 1961
Beauford Jester (Sadler)	Jan. 1, 1943-Jan. 21, 1947
William J. Murray Jr. (Jester)	Jan. 21, 1947-Apr. 10, 1963
Ben Ramsey (Culberson)	Sept. 18, 1961-Dec. 31, 1976
Jim C. Langdon (Murray)	May 28, 1963-Dec. 31, 1977
Byron Tunnell (Thompson)	Jan. 11, 1965-Sept. 15, 1973
Mack Wallace (Tunnell)	Sept. 18, 1973-Sept. 22, 1987
Jon Newton (Ramsey)	Jan. 10, 1977-Jan. 4, 1979
John H. Poerner (Langdon)	Jan. 2, 1978-Jan. 1, 1981
James E. (Jim) Nugent (Newton)	Jan. 4, 1979-Jan. 3, 1995
Buddy Temple (Poerner)	Jan. 2, 1981-March 2, 1986
Clark Jobe (Temple)	March 3, 1986-Jan. 5, 1987
John Sharp (Jobe)	Jan. 6, 1987-Jan. 2, 1991
Kent Hance (Wallace)	Sept. 23, 1987-Jan. 2, 1991
*Robert Krueger (Hance)	Jan. 3, 1991-Jan. 22, 1993
Lena Guerrero (Sharp)	Jan. 23, 1991-Sept. 25, 1992
James Wallace (Guerrero)	Oct. 2, 1992-Jan. 4, 1993
Barry Williamson (Wallace)	Jan. 5, 1993-Jan. 4, 1999
Mary Scott Nabers (Krueger)	Jan. 9, 1993-Dec. 9, 1994
Carole K. Rylander (Nabers)	Dec. 10, 1994-Jan. 4, 1999
Charles Matthews (Nugent)	Jan. 3, 1995-Present
Michael L. Williams (Rylander)	Jan. 4, 1999-Present
Antonio (Tony) Garza (Williamson)	Jan. 4, 1999-Present

* Robert Krueger resigned when Gov. Ann Richards appointed him interim U.S. Senator on the resignation of Sen. Lloyd Bentsen.

★ ★ ★ ★ ★ ★ ★

Comptroller of Public Accounts

Of the Republic

John H. Money	Dec. 30, 1835-Jan. 17, 1836

Of the State

Jas. B. Shaw	Feb. 24, 1846-Aug. 2, 1858
Clement R. Johns	Aug. 2, 1858-Aug. 1, 1864
Willis L. Robards	Aug. 1, 1864-Oct. 12, 1865
Albert H. Latimer	Oct. 12, 1865-Mar. 27, 1866
Robert H. Taylor	Mar. 27, 1866-June 25, 1866
Willis L. Robards	June 25, 1866-Aug. 27, 1867
Morgan C. Hamilton	Aug. 27, 1867-Jan. 8, 1870
A. Bledsoe	Jan. 8, 1870-Jan. 20, 1874
Stephen H. Darden	Jan. 20, 1974-Nov. 2, 1880
W. M. Brown	Nov. 2, 1880-Jan. 16, 1883
W. J. Swain	Jan. 16, 1883-Jan. 18, 1887
John D. McCall	Jan. 18, 1887-Jan. 15, 1895
R. W. Finley	Jan. 15, 1895-Jan. 15, 1901
R. M. Love	Jan. 15, 1901-Jan., 1903
J. W. Stephen	Jan., 1903-Jan., 1911
W. P. Lane	Jan., 1911-Jan., 1915
H. B. Terrell	Jan., 1915-Jan., 1920
M. L. Wiginton	Jan., 1920-Jan., 1921
Lon A. Smith	Jan., 1921-Jan., 1925
S. H. Terrell	Jan., 1925-Jan., 1931
Geo. H. Sheppard	Jan., 1931-Jan. 17, 1949
Robert S. Calvert	Jan. 17, 1949-Jan., 1975
Robert D. (Bob) Bullock	Jan., 1975-Jan. 3, 1991
John Sharp	Jan. 3, 1991 to Jan. 2, 1999
Carole Keeton Rylander	Jan. 2, 1999 to Present

★ ★ ★ ★ ★ ★ ★

U.S. Senators from Texas

U.S. Senators were selected by the legislatures of the states until the U.S. Constitution was amended in 1913 to require popular elections. In Texas, the first senator chosen by the voters in a general election was Charles A. Culberson in 1916. Because of political pressures, however, the rules of the Democratic Party of Texas were changed in 1904 to require that all candidates for office stand before voters in the primary. Consequently, Texas' senators faced voters in 1906, 1910 and 1912 before the U.S. Constitution was changed.

Following is the succession of Texas representatives in the United States Senate since the annexation of Texas to the Union in 1845:

Houston Succession

Sam Houston	Feb. 21, 1846-Mar. 4, 1859
John Hemphill	Mar. 4, 1859-July 11, 1861

Louis T. Wigfall and W. S. Oldham took their seats in the Confederate Senate, Nov. 16, 1861, and served until the Confederacy collapsed. After that event, the State Legislature on Aug. 21, 1866, elected David G. Burnet and Oran M. Roberts to the United States Senate, anticipating immediate readmission to the Union, but they were not allowed to take their seats.

†Morgan C. Hamilton	Feb. 22, 1870-Mar. 3, 1877
Richard Coke	Mar. 4, 1877-Mar. 3, 1895
Horace Chilton	Mar. 3, 1895-Mar. 3, 1901
Joseph W. Bailey	Mar. 3, 1901-Jan. 8, 1913
Rienzi Melville Johnston	Jan. 8, 1913-Feb. 3, 1913
‡Morris Sheppard (died)	Feb. 13, 1913-Apr. 9, 1941
Andrew J. Houston	June 2-26, 1941
W. Lee O'Daniel	Aug. 4, 1941-Jan. 3, 1949
Lyndon B. Johnson	Jan. 3, 1949-Jan. 20, 1961
William A. Blakley	Jan. 20, 1961-June 15, 1961
†John G. Tower	June 15, 1961-Jan. 21, 1985
†Phil Gramm	Jan. 21, 1985-Present

Rusk Succession

Thomas J. Rusk (died)	Feb 21, 1846-July 29, 1857
J. Pinckney Henderson (died)	Nov. 9, 1857-June 4, 1858
Matthias Ward (appointed interim)	Sept. 29, 1858-Dec. 5, 1859

Louis T. Wigfall .... Dec. 5, 1859-March 23, 1861

Succession was broken by the expulsion of Texas Senators following secession of Texas from Union. See note above under "Houston Succession" on Louis T. Wigfall, W. S. Oldham, Burnet and Roberts.

†James W. Flanagan .... Feb. 22, 1870-Mar. 3, 1875
Samuel B. Maxey.................... Mar. 3, 1875-Mar. 3, 1887
John H. Reagan *(resigned)* ... Mar. 3, 1887-June 10, 1891
Horace Chilton *(filled vacancy on
  appointment)* ....Dec. 7, 1891-Mar. 30,1892
Roger Q. Mills .... Mar. 30, 1892-Mar. 3, 1899
‡Charles A. Culberson .... Mar. 3, 1899-Mar. 4, 1923
Earle B. Mayfield.................... Mar. 4, 1923-Mar. 4, 1929
Tom Connally .... Mar. 4, 1929-Jan. 3, 1953
Price Daniel.........................Jan. 3, 1953-Jan. 15, 1957
William A. Blakley .... Jan. 15. 1957-Apr. 27, 1957
Ralph W. Yarborough .... Apr. 27, 1957-Jan. 12, 1971
§Lloyd Bentsen.................... Jan. 12, 1971-Jan. 20, 1993
Robert Krueger.................... Jan. 20, 1993-June 14, 1993
†Kay Bailey Hutchison..................June 14, 1993-Present

† *Republican members*
‡ *First election to U.S. Senate held in 1916. Prior to that time, senators were appointed by the Legislature.*
§ *Resigned from Senate when appointed U.S. Secretary of Treasury by Pres. Bill Clinton.*

★ ★ ★ ★ ★ ★ ★

Commissioners of the General Land Office

For the Republic

John P. Borden ....Aug. 23, 1837-Dec. 12, 1840
H. W. Raglin ....Dec. 12, 1840-Jan. 4, 1841
*Thomas William Ward ....Jan. 4, 1841-Mar. 20, 1848

For the State

George W. Smyth.................... Mar. 20, 1848-Aug. 4, 1851
Stephen Crosby..................... Aug. 4, 1851-Mar. 1, 1858
Francis M. White..................... Mar. 1, 1858-Mar. 1, 1862
Stephen Crosby..................... Mar. 1, 1862-Sept. 1, 1865
Francis M. White.....................Sept. 1, 1865-Aug. 7, 1866
Stephen Crosby.....................Aug. 7, 1866-Aug. 27, 1867
Joseph Spence..................... Aug. 27, 1867-Jan. 19, 1870
Jacob Kuechler.....................Jan. 19, 1870-Jan. 20, 1874
J. J. Groos............................Jan. 20, 1874-June 15, 1878
W. C. Walsh......................... July 30, 1878, Jan. 10, 1887
R. M. Hall ....Jan. 10, 1887-Jan. 16, 1891
W. L. McGaughey .... Jan. 16, 1891-Jan. 26, 1895
A. J. Baker ....Jan. 26, 1895-Jan. 16, 1899
George W. Finger ....Jan. 16, 1899-May 4, 1899
Charles Rogan ....May 11, 1899-Jan. 10, 1903
John J. Terrell......................Jan. 10, 1903-Jan. 11, 1909
J. T. Robison ....Jan, 1909-Sept. 11, 1929
J. H. Walker ....Sept. 11, 1929-Jan., 1937
William H. McDonald ....Jan, 1937-Jan., 1939
Bascom Giles.........................Jan., 1939-Jan. 5, 1955
J. Earl Rudder.......................Jan. 5, 1955-Feb. 1, 1958
Bill Allcorn..............................Feb. 1, 1958-Jan. 1, 1961
Jerry Sadler ....Jan. 1, 1961-Jan. 1, 1971
Bob Armstrong ....Jan. 1, 1971-Jan. 1, 1983
Garry Mauro ....Jan. 1, 1983-Jan. 7, 1999
David Dewhurst .... Jan. 7, 1999-Present
Part of term after annexation.

★ ★ ★ ★ ★ ★ ★

Speaker of the Texas House

The Speaker of the Texas House of Representatives is the presiding officer of the lower chamber of the State Legislature. The official is elected at the beginning of each regular session by a vote of the members of the House.

Speaker, Residence	Year Elected	Legislature
William E. Crump, Bellville	1846	1st
William H. Bourland, Paris	1846	1st

James W. Henderson, Houston	1847	2nd
Charles G. Keenan, Huntsville	1849	3rd
David C. Dickson, Anderson	1851	4th
Hardin R. Runnels, Boston	1853	5th
Hamilton P. Bee, Laredo	1855	6th
William S. Taylor, Larissa	1857	7th
Matt F. Locke, Lafayette	1858	7th
Marion DeKalb Taylor, Jefferson	1859	8th
Constantine W. Buckley, Richmond	1861	9th
Nicholas H. Darnell, Dallas	1861	9th
Constantine W. Buckley, Richmond	1863	9th
Marion DeKalb Taylor, Jefferson	1863	10th
Nathaniel M. Burford, Dallas	1866	11th
Ira H. Evans, Corpus Christi	1870	12th
William H. Sinclair, Galveston	1871	12th
Marion DeKalb Taylor, Jefferson	1873	13th
Guy M. Bryan, Galveston	1874	14th
Thomas R. Bonner, Tyler	1876	15th
John H. Cochran, Dallas	1879	16th
George R. Reeves, Pottsboro	1881	17th
Charles R. Gibson, Waxahachie	1883	18th
Lafayette L. Foster, Groesbeck	1885	19th
George C. Pendleton, Belton	1887	20th
Frank P. Alexander, Greenville	1889	21st
Robert T. Milner, Henderson	1891	22nd
John H. Cochran, Dallas	1893	23rd
Thomas Slater Smith, Hillsboro	1895	24th
L. Travis Dashiell, Jewett	1897	25th
J. S. Sherrill, Greenville	1899	26th
Robert E. Prince, Corsicana	1901	27th
Pat M. Neff, Waco	1903	28th
Francis W. Seabury, Rio Grande City	1905	29th
Thomas B. Love, Lancaster	1907	30th
Austin M. Kennedy, Waco	1909	31st
John W. Marshall, Whitesboro	1909	31st
Sam Rayburn, Bonham	1911	32nd
Chester H. Terrell, San Antonio	1913	33rd
John W. Woods, Rotan	1915	34th
Franklin O. Fuller, Coldspring	1917	35th
R. Ewing Thomason, El Paso	1919	36th
Charles G. Thomas, Lewisville	1921	37th
Richard E. Seagler, Palestine	1923	38th
Lee Satterwhite, Amarillo	1925	39th
Robert L. Bobbitt, Laredo	1927	40th
W. S. Barron, Bryan	1929	41st
Fred H. Minor, Denton	1931	42nd
Coke R. Stevenson, Junction	1933	43rd
"	1935	44th
Robert W. Calvert, Hillsboro	1937	45th
R. Emmett Morse, Houston	1939	46th
Homer L. Leonard, McAllen	1941	47th
Price Daniel, Liberty	1943	48th
Claud H. Gilmer, Rocksprings	1945	49th
William O. Reed, Dallas	1947	50th
Durwood Manford, Smiley	1949	51st
Reuben Senterfitt, San Saba	1951	52nd
"	1953	53rd
Jim T. Lindsey, Texarkana	1955	54th
Waggoner Carr, Lubbock	1957	55th
"	1959	56th
James A. Turman, Gober	1961	57th
Byron M. Tunnell, Tyler	1963	58th
Ben Barnes, DeLeon	1965	59th
"	1967	60th
Gus F. Mutscher, Brenham	1969	61st
"	1971	62nd
Rayford Price, Palestine	1972	62nd
Price Daniel Jr., Liberty	1973	63rd
Bill Clayton, Springlake	1975	64th
"	1977	65th
"	1979	66th
"	1981	67th
Gibson D. Lewis, Fort Worth	1983	68th
"	1985	69th
"	1987	70th
"	1989	71st
"	1991	72nd
James M. (Pete) Laney, Hale Center	1993	73rd
"	1995	74th
"	1997	75th
"	1999	76th

★ ★ ★ ★ ★ ★ ★

Chief Justice of the Supreme Court

Republic of Texas

James Collinsworth	Dec. 16, 1836-July 23, 1838
John Birdsall	Nov. 19-Dec. 12, 1838
Thomas J. Rusk	Dec. 12, 1838-Dec. 5, 1840
John Hemphill	Dec. 5, 1840-Dec. 29, 1845

Under the Constitutions of 1845 and 1861

John Hemphill	Mar. 2, 1846-Oct. 10, 1858
Royall T. Wheeler	Oct. 11, 1858-April 1864
Oran M. Roberts	Nov. 1, 1864-June 30, 1866

Under the Constitution of 1866
(Presidential Reconstruction)

*George F. Moore	Aug. 16, 1866-Sept. 10, 1867

*Removed under Congressional Reconstruction by military authorities who appointed members of the next court.

Under the Constitution of 1866
(Congressional Reconstruction)

Amos Morrill	Sept. 10, 1867-July 5, 1870

Under the Constitution of 1869

Lemuel D. Evans	July 5, 1870-Aug. 31, 1873
Wesley Ogden	Aug. 31, 1873-Jan. 29, 1874
Oran M. Roberts	Jan. 29, 1874-Apr. 18, 1876

Under the Constitution of 1876

Oran M. Roberts	Apr. 18, 1876-Oct. 1, 1878
George F. Moore	Nov. 5, 1878-Nov. 1, 1881
Robert S. Gould	Nov. 1, 1881-Dec. 23, 1882
Asa H. Willie	Dec. 23, 1882-Mar. 3, 1888
John W. Stayton	Mar. 3, 1888-July 5, 1894
Reuben R. Gaines	July 10, 1894-Jan. 5, 1911
Thomas J. Brown	Jan. 7, 1911-May 26, 1915
Nelson Phillips	June 1, 1915-Nov. 16, 1921
C. M. Cureton	Dec. 2, 1921-Apr. 8, 1940
†Hortense Sparks Ward	Jan. 8, 1925-May 23, 1925
W. F. Moore	Apr. 17, 1940-Jan. 1, 1941
James P. Alexander	Jan. 1, 1941-Jan. 1, 1948
J. E. Hickman	Jan. 5, 1948-Jan. 3, 1961
Robert W. Calvert	Jan. 3, 1961-Oct. 4, 1972
Joe R. Greenhill	Oct. 4, 1972-Oct. 25, 1982
Jack Pope	Nov. 29, 1982-Jan. 5, 1985
John L. Hill Jr.	Jan. 5, 1985-Jan. 4, 1988
Thomas R. Phillips	Jan. 4, 1988-Present

†Mrs. Ward served as Chief Justice of a special Supreme Court to hear one case in 1925.

Presiding Judges, Court of Appeals (1876-1891) and Court of Criminal Appeals (1891-Present)

Mat D. Ector	May 6, 1876-Oct. 29, 1879
John P. White	Nov. 9, 1879-Apr. 26, 1892
James M. Hurt	May 4, 1892-Dec. 31, 1898
W. L. Davidson	Jan. 2, 1899-June 27, 1913
A. C. Prendergast	June 27, 1913-Dec. 31, 1916
W. L. Davidson	Jan. 1, 1917-Jan. 25, 1921
Wright C. Morrow	Feb. 8, 1921-Oct. 16, 1939
Frank Lee Hawkins	Oct. 16, 1939-Jan. 2, 1951
Harry N. Graves	Jan. 2, 1951-Dec. 31, 1954
W. A. Morrison	Jan. 1, 1955-Jan. 2, 1961
Kenneth K. Woodley	Jan. 3, 1961-Jan. 4, 1965
W. T. McDonald	Jan. 4, 1965-June 25, 1966
W. A. Morrison	June 25, 1966-Jan. 1, 1967
Kenneth K. Woodley	Jan. 1, 1967-Jan. 1, 1971
John F. Onion Jr.	Jan. 1, 1971-Jan. 1, 1989
Michael J. McCormick	Jan. 1, 1989-Present

★ ★ ★ ★ ★ ★ ★

Administrators of Public Education

Superintendents of Public Instruction

Pryor Lea	Nov. 10, 1866-Sept. 12, 1867

Edwin M. Wheelock	Sept. 12, 1867-May 6, 1871
Jacob C. DeGress	May 6, 1871-Jan. 20, 1874
O. H. Hollingsworth	Jan. 20, 1874-May 6, 1884
B. M. Baker	May 6, 1884-Jan. 18, 1887
O. H. Cooper	Jan 18, 1887-Sept. 1, 1890
H. C. Pritchett	Sept. 1, 1890-Sept. 15, 1891
J. M. Carlisle	Sept. 15, 1891-Jan. 10, 1899
J. S. Kendall	Jan. 10, 1899-July 2, 1901
Arthur Lefevre	July 2, 1901-Jan. 12, 1905
R. B. Cousins	Jan. 12, 1905-Jan. 1, 1910
F. M. Bralley	Jan. 1, 1910-Sept. 1, 1913
W. F. Doughty	Sept. 1, 1913-Jan. 1, 1919
Annie Webb Blanton	Jan. 1, 1919-Jan. 16, 1923
S. M. N. Marrs	Jan. 16, 1923-April 28, 1932
C. N. Shaver	April 28, 1932-Oct. 1, 1932
L. W. Rogers	Oct. 1, 1932-Jan. 16, 1933
L. A. Woods	Jan. 16, 1933-*1951

State Commissioner of Education

J. W. Edgar	May 31, 1951-June 30, 1974
Marlin L. Brockette	July 1, 1974-Sept. 1, 1979
Alton O. Bowen	Sept. 1, 1979-June 1, 1981
Raymon Bynum	June 1, 1981-Oct. 31, 1984
W. N. Kirby	April 13, 1985-July 1, 1991
Lionel R. Meno	July 1, 1991-March 1, 1995
Michael A. Moses	March 9, 1995-Present

*The office of State Superintendent of Public Instruction was abolished by the Gilmer-Aikin act of 1949 and the office of Commissioner of Education created, appointed by a new State Board of Education elected by the people.

First Ladies of Texas

Martha Evans Gindratt Wood	1847-49
†Bell Administration	1849-53
Lucadia Christiana Niles Pease	1853-57; 1867-69
‡Runnels Administration	1857-59
Margaret Moffette Lea Houston	1859-61
Martha Evans Clark	1861
Adele Barron Lubbock	1861-63
Susie Ellen Taylor Murrah	1863-65
Mary Jane Bowen Hamilton	1865-66
Annie Rattan Throckmorton	1866-67
Ann Elizabeth Britton Davis	1870-74
Mary Home Coke	1874-76
Janie Roberts Hubbard	1876-79
Frances Wickliff Edwards Roberts	1879-83
Anne Maria Penn Ireland	1883-87
Elizabeth Dorothy Tinsley Ross	1887-91
Sarah Stinson Hogg	1891-95
Sally Harrison Culberson	1895-99
Orlene Walton Sayers	1899-1903
Sarah Beona Meng Lanham	1903-07
Fannie Brunner Campbell	1907-11
Alice Fuller Murrell Colquitt	1911-15
§Miriam A. Wallace Ferguson	1915-17
Willie Cooper Hobby	1917-21
Myrtle Mainer Neff	1921-25
Mildred Paxton Moody	1927-31
Maud Gage Sterling	1931-33
Jo Betsy Miller Allred	1935-39
Merle Estella Butcher O'Daniel	1939-41
**Fay Wright Stevenson	1941-42
**Edith Will Scott Stevenson	1942-46
Mabel Buchanan Jester	1946-49
Marialice Shary Shivers	1949-57
Jean Houston Baldwin Daniel	1957-63
Idanell Brill Connally	1963-69
Ima Mae Smith	1969-73
Betty Jane Slaughter Briscoe	1973-79
Rita Crocker Bass Clements	1979-83
Linda Gale Thompson White	1983-87
Rita Crocker Bass Clements	1987-91
Laura Welch Bush	1995-Present

†Gov. Peter Hansbrough Bell was not married while in office.
‡Gov. Hardin R. Runnels never married.
**Mrs. Coke R. (Fay Wright) Stevenson, the governor's wife, died in the Governor's Mansion Jan. 3, 1942. His mother, Edith Stevenson, served as Mistress of the Mansion thereafter. ☆

Local Governments

Texas has **254 counties**, a number which has not changed since 1931 when Loving County was organized. Loving had a population of 107 in the 1990 U.S. Census Bureau count, compared with 164 in 1970 and its peak of 285 in 1940. It is the **least-populous county** in Texas. In contrast, Harris County has **the most residents** in Texas, with a population in 1990 of 2,818,199.

Counties range in area from Rockwall's 148.6 square miles to the 6,193.1 square miles in Brewster, which is equal to the combined area of the states of Connecticut and Rhode Island.

The Texas Constitution makes a county a legal subdivision of the state. Each county has a **commissioners court**. It consists of four commissioners, each elected from a commissioner's precinct, and a county judge elected from the entire county. In smaller counties, the county judge retains judicial responsibilities in probate and insanity cases. For names of county and district officials, see tables on pages 479-489.

Eleven hundred and ninety-four **incorporated Texas municipalities** range in size from 24 residents to Houston's 1,700,672 in the 1998 population estimate by the State Data Center. More than 80 percent of the state's population lives in cities and towns meeting the U.S. Bureau of the Census definition of urban areas.

Texas had **298 municipalities with more than 5,000 population** in the 1990 U.S. census. Under law, these cities may adopt their own charters by a majority vote. Cities of less than 5,000 may be chartered only under the general law. Some of these cities now show fewer than 5,000 residents, because population has declined since they adopted their home-rule charters. **Home-rule cities are marked in this list by a single-dagger symbol (†) before the name.** ☆

Mayors and City Managers of Texas Cities

The list below was compiled from questionnaires sent out immediately after the municipal elections in May 1997. Included is the name of each city's mayor, as well as the name of the city manager, city administrator, city coordinator or other managing executive of munipalities having that form of government.

An asterisk (*) before the city name indicates that the Almanac received no response to the questionnaire and that the information on city officials is from the most recent information available to us from unofficial sources.

Abbott.................... Robert L. Tufts
  City Admin., Harry Frank Holland
Abernathy.................... Carl Johnson
  City Mgr., Frank Russell
†Abilene.................... Grady Barr
  City Mgr., Roy L. McDaniel
*Ackerly....................Jimmie L. Schuelke
†Addison....................R. Scott Wheeler
  City Mgr., Ron Whitehead
Adrian .... Larry Loveless
Agua Dulce .... Carl Vajdos
*†Alamo .... Rodolfo "Rudy" Villarreal
  City Mgr., James Pliska
†Alamo Heights (6116 Broadway, San
  Antonio 78209-4599)..... Robert Biechlin
  City Admin., Susan Rash
Alba .... Orvin Carroll
  City Mgr., Lindy McCarty
*Albany....................Harold Cox
Aledo.................... Robert A. Lewis
  City Admin., J.E. Fickett
†Alice .... Fidel R. Rul Jr.
  City Mgr., Gonzalo Chapa Jr.
†Allen....................Steve Terrell
  City Mgr., Peter Vargas
Alma (RR 1 Box 109, Ennis 75119-
  9753) .... Don Keilers
†Alpine.................... Paul R. Weyerts
  City Mgr., Doug Lively
Alto....................Sandra H. Wallace
  City Admin., Terri M. Grogan
*Alton (PO Box 9004, Mission 78572-
  9004)....................Salvador Vela
  City Mgr., Israel Sagredo
Alvarado.................... Jay Tidwell
†Alvin....................Troy Lewis
  City Mgr., Paul A. Hofmann
Alvord.................... Michael McKinney
  City Coord., Ricky Tow
†Amarillo.................... Kel Seliger
  City Mgr., John Q. Ward
Ames....................John White
Amherst ....George Thompson
*Anahuac ....Ottmar Schimek
  City Mgr., (Vacancy)
*Anderson ....John S. Freeman
†Andrews....................Greg Sweeney
  City Mgr., Len L. Wilson
*†Angleton ....Gerald Roberts
  City Admin., Ruth Hertel
Angus (6008 S. I-45 West,
  Corsicana 75110)....... Kathy McKissack
Anna ....Ron Ferguson
Annetta (PO Box 191, Aledo
  76008-0191)....................Bruce Moore
*Annetta North (PO Box 262,
  Aledo 76008)..........Edward K. Hensley

Annetta South (PO Box 61, Aledo
  76008)....................Kenneth E. Sanders
Annona....................George H. English
†Anson....................E.M. Spraberry
  City Mgr., Tex Middlebrook
Anthony....................Art Franco
*Anton....................Garland Cooper
  City Mgr., Larry G. Conkin
Appleby (RR 10, Box 5186, Nacog-
  doches 75961-9810).....N. F. Burt
*Aquilla....................Rebecca Montgomery
†Aransas Pass....................Karen Gayle
  City Mgr., Rick Ewaniszyk
*Archer City....................Max C. Wood Sr.
  City Mgr., L. B. Boren Jr.
Arcola....................Alvin Gipson
*Argyle....................Yvonne A. Jenkins
†Arlington....................Elzie Odom
  City Mgr., Chuck Kiefer
Arp....................Vernon L. Bedair
Asherton....................Sam Galvan Jr.
Aspermont....................P. C. Carr
  City Admin., Roger Parker
†Athens....................Jerry G. King
  City Admin., Pam J. Burton
*†Atlanta....................Kay Phillips
  City Mgr., Buddy Drake
Aubrey....................Jason L. Pierce
Aurora (PO Box 558, Rhome 76078-
  0558) .... Owen J.Landers
†Austin .... Kirk Watson
  City Mgr., Jesus Garza
†Austwell....................Dwight Mutschler
Avery .... Erby Stinson
Avinger .... Larry J. Skinner
†Azle .... R. Leck Heflin
  City Mgr., Jim Walker
Bailey....................J.R. Stephens
Bailey's Prairie (PO Box 71,
  Angleton 77516) ........J.S. McKinney Jr.
Baird....................Jon Hardwick
*Balch Springs....................David Haas
  City Mgr., Angie Warner
Balcones Heights (123 Altgelt Ave., San
  Antonio 78201) ....Lucille Wohlfarth
  City Admin., Roy L. Miller
†Ballinger .... Grant Lee
  City Mgr., Tommy New
Balmorhea....................Ismael Rodriguez
*Bandera....................Robert W. Cowan
  City Mgr., Don Reddout
Bangs....................C.B. Alexander
†Bardwell....................Michael Anthony
Barry....................John Wade Braly
*Barstow....................Salvador Villalobos
Bartlett....................Bruce Swope
Bartonville....................Lee Lazarus

Bastrop .... Tom Scott
  City Mgr., Randall E. Holly
*Bay City....................Charles Martinez Jr.
*Bayou Vista (2929 Highway 6, Ste 100,
  Hitchcock 77563-2723).....Joe R. Mims
Bayside.................... Timothy Delaney
†Baytown.................... Pete C. Alfaro
  City Mgr., Monte Mercer
Bayview (RR 3 Box 19A, Los Fresnos
  78566-9713) ..... Robert E. Middleton Jr.
Beach City (12723 Tri City Beach Rd.,
  Baytown 77520)....James E. Standridge
Bear Creek, Village of (6705 W.
  Hwy 290, #502-244, Austin
  78735).................... Kathryn Rosenbluth
*Beasley....................James Isbell
†Beaumont....................David W. Moore
  City Mgr., Stephen J. Bonczek
*Beckville .... Thomas R. Adams
†Bedford....................R.D. "Rick" Hurt
  City Mgr., Susan Thorpe
Bee Cave (13333 W. Highway 71,
  Austin 78738-3104)............Gene Butler
  City Mgr., James Fisher
*†Beeville ....Kenneth Chesshir
  City Mgr., Ford Patton
†Bellaire ....Charles J. Jacobus
  City Mgr., John L. Pape
Bellevue....................James Broussard
  City Mgr., Jay Anderson
*†Bellmead (3015 Bellmead Dr.,
  Waco 76705-3097) ....Robert Hawkins
  City Mgr., S.G. Radcliffe
Bells....................A.L. "Son"Isom
*Bellville .... Jim Bishop
  City Admin., Marcus Johnston
†Belton .... Bill Holmes
  City Mgr., Jeff Holberg
*Benavides ....Cynthia Oliveira
†Benbrook (PO Box 26569, Fort
  Worth 76126-6569)..............F.T. Hebert
  City Mgr., Cary Conklin
Benjamin .... Mike Sheedy
  City Mgr., Ron White
Berryville (PO Box 908, Frankston
  75763-0908) .... James Colvin
Bertram .... Robert Ricketson
*Bethel (Rt. 2, Box 109K, Whitewright
  75491-9712) .... Larry Schone
Beverly Hills (3418 Memorial Dr.,
  Waco 76711-1514) ...... Henry W. Wright
Bevil Oaks (7390 Sweetgum Rd.,
  Beaumont 77713-8422)....John Hignett
Big Lake .... Frank Sandel
Big Sandy .... David P. Smith
*†Big Spring ....Tim Blackshear
  City Admin., Thomas Ferguson

*Big Wells........................ Jorge Escobedo
*Bishop .... Wesley Rogers
Bishop Hills (1 Lancaster Rd.,
   Amarillo 79214-5711) .. Larry J. Johnson
Blackwell .... Ronald Harris
Blanco .... Louann Hayes
Blanket ....John H. Jones
Bloomburg................E.M. "Dickey" Davis
Blooming Grove .... Boyd Bryant
Blossom .... Ronnie Westbrook
   City Mgr., Tony Chance
Blue Mound (301 Blue Mound Rd.,
   Fort Worth 76131-1030) .. James Boyles
Blue Ridge .... Frances M. Slater
Blum............................... Craig Thompson
†Boerne .... Patrick Heath
   City Mgr., Ronald C. Bowman
Bogata ....Michael R. Garretson
†Bonham .... Bryan Peeler
   City Mgr., Jim Stiff
Bonney.......................Elmer Cannon Jr.
Booker .... James Roberts
   City Mgr., Lois J. Sheets
†Borger .... Judy Flanders
   City Mgr., David Willard
Bovina .... Galen Hromas
†Bowie ....Matthew C. Winters
   City Mgr., James Cantwell
*Boyd ....Steve Cotter
Brackettville............. Carmen M. Berlanga
   City Mgr., David G. Luna
†Brady...............................Clarence Friar
   City Mgr., Gary Broz
Brazoria.............................. W.V. James
   City Mgr., Pee Wee Drake
†Breckenridge............. Virgil E. Moore Jr.
   City Mgr., Gary G. Ernest
Bremond .... Ricky Swick
†Brenham .... Walter C. Schwartz
   City Mgr., C.J. Webster
Briarcliff (HCO 1, Box 24, Spice-
   wood 78669)................... V.E. McDaniel
*Briaroaks (PO Box 816, Burleson
   76097) ....Alan Myers
†Bridge City ....John P. Dubose
   City Mgr., Jeff Ellington
Bridgeport ....Wm. Ray Cook Jr.
Broaddus ....Billie Faye Sanders
Bronte .... Martin Lee
Brookshire...................... Keith A. Woods
Brookside Village .... George D. Carter
*Browndell (PO Box 430, Brooke-
   land 75931) ....Erma Garrett
†Brownfield ....Bradford L. Moore
   City Mgr., Eldon Jobe
Brownsboro..................Johnny B. Godwin
Brownsville.............Blanca Sanchez Vela
   City Mgr., Carlos Rubenstein
†Brownwood ....Bert V. Massey II
   City Mgr., Gary Butts
Bruceville-Eddy (143 Wilcox Dr.,
   #A, Eddy 76524-2587) .... Rick Eaton
†Bryan .... Lonnie Stabler
   City Mgr., Michael A. Conduff
Bryson ....Kennith Boland
*Buckholts ....Gwen Hauk
Buda .... Keith W. Thornsberry
   City Admin., W. Grey White
Buffalo .... Byron Ryder
*Buffalo Gap...........................John Brolls
Buffalo Springs (RR 10, Box 500,
   Lubbock 79404-9745) ..... W.B. McMillan
Bullard..................................B.J. Langford
Bulverde .... Bob Barton
   City Admin., Bob Hieronymus
Bunker Hill Village (11977 Memorial
   Dr., Houston 77024-
   6231) ....William H. Marshall
†Burkburnett ....Bill Vincent
   City Mgr., Mike Slye
Burke (RR 3, Box 315, Diboll
   75941-9714) .........................J.L. Bell
†Burleson .... Byron F. Black
   City Mgr., Kay Godbey
Burnet ....Howard Benton
   City Mgr., Johnny Sartain
Burton .... Peggy Sue Wilford
Byers................................W.A. Landrum
*Bynum ....Jerry Hooker

Cactus ....Cosme Venzor
   City Mgr., Darrel R. Read
Caddo Mills................................ Ed Locker
Caldwell...................... Bernard E. Rychlik
   City Admin., William L. Broaddus
Callisburg (59 Campbell St., Whites-
   boro 76273-4700) ...... Donald Robinson
Calvert................................... Bert Dunken
†Cameron................... James E. Lafferty
   City Mgr., Lanny C. French
Campbell .... Barbara LaMoore
Camp Wood...............James D. Blakeney
*Canadian.......................... Jim Pollard
   City Mgr., Dean Looper
*Caney City (15241 Barron Rd.,
   Malakoff 75148-4337) .... Joe Barron
Canton...............................Don Hackney
   City Mgr., Johnny Mallory
†Canyon .... Lois Rice
   City Mgr., Glen Metcalf
Carbon..............................Dale Walker
Carl's Corner (RR 3, Box 500, Hills-
   boro 76645-9402) ...... Carl W. Cornelius
Carmine.......................... Barney A. Eilers
†Carrizo Springs .... Gordon Baehre
   City Mgr., Mario A. Martinez
†Carrollton.................Milburn R. Gravley
   City Mgr., Gary W. Jackson
†Carthage ....Carson C. Joines
   City Mgr., Charles Thomas
*Castle Hills (6915 West Ave., San
   Antonio 78213-1822) ...... Martin Rubin
   City Mgr., David R. McLaughlin
*Castroville .... Dwight Green
   Interim City Admin., Donna L. Schueling
†Cedar Hill............................ Rob Franke
   City Mgr., Greg Vick
*†Cedar Park................ George A. Denny
   City Mgr., Don Birkner
Celeste .... Pat Jones
Celina .... Olen R. Long
   City Admin., Larry Bartlett
†Center....................... John D. Windham
   City Mgr., H. Frank Simpson
Center Point .... Mary Shults
Centerville ....Billy Walters
Chandler........................ Winston Reagan
Channing .... Ethel Hunnicutt
*Charlotte .... Mark T. Wilson
Chester ....Bobby Moore
*Chico............................... Nobie Tucker
†Childress ....Pat Y. Steed
   City Mgr., Jerry Cummins
Chillicothe .... Wallace Clay
China ....William T. Sanders
China Grove (2456 FM 1516, San
   Antonio 78263-5028) ..... John H. Vrzalik
*Chireno ............................G.V. Layton
   City Mgr., Joanna Johnson
*Christine.................. Walter W. Stevens
Cibolo .... Sam Bauder
   City Mgr., Ken Roberts
†Cisco .... Ronnie Ledbetter
   City Mgr., Michael Moore
Clarendon ....Leonard Selvidge
   City Admin., Janice Barbee
*Clarksville .... Wilson M. Hill
   City Mgr., Wayne Dial
*Clarksville City (PO Box 1209,
   Gladewater 75647) ...........H.E. Griffin
   City Mgr., B.F. Silvertooth Jr.
Claude .... Leon G. James
Clear Lake Shores...............Gary Moore
†Cleburne............. Thomas C. Hazlewood
   City Mgr., Joel Victory
†Cleveland..............................Joe B. Ivy
   City Mgr., Deck Shaver Jr.
Clifton .... Truman O. Blum
   City Admin., Chad Nehring
Clint .... G. Michael Goodwin
†Clute .... Jerry Adkins
   City Mgr., Barbara Hester
Clyde .... Jim Paylor
   City Admin., Lee Roy George
Coahoma...............................Bill Read
Cockrell Hill (4125 W. Clarendon Dr.,
   Dallas 75211-4919) .. Charles P. Slayton
   City Mgr., Rosa A. Rios
*Coffee City (PO Box 716, Frankston

75763) ....Michael Warren
Coldspring ....John Benestante
†Coleman .... Woodrow J. Maddox
   City Mgr., Randy Whiteman
†College Station ....Lynn McIlhaney
   City Mgr., George Noe
*†Colleyville .... Richard Newton
   City Mgr., C. Robert Stripling
Collinsville................. Wayne McCorkle
Colmesneil .... Jackie Brown
†Colorado City ....Jim Baum
   City Mgr., Stephen K. Shutt
Columbus .... Paul Frnka
   City Mgr., John H. Brasher
Comanche ....Jimmie Warren
   City Admin., Bill Flannery
Combes .... Silvestre "Silver" Garcia
   City Admin., Lonnie Bearden
*Combine (123 Davis Road, Seago-
   ville 75159-0231)......... Charles Stringer
†Commerce .... John R. Sands
   City Mgr., Roger McKinney
*Como.......................Margaret Anderson
†Conroe .... Carter Moore
   City Admin., Craig Lonon
†Converse........................... Craig Martin
   City Mgr., Samuel Hughes
*Cool (150 So. FM 113, Millsap
   76066-2100)............ Marsha McDonald
Coolidge............................. Bobby Jacobs
Cooper ....Richard C. Huie
†Coppell.......................Candy Sheehan
   City Mgr., Jim Witt
*†Copperas Cove............... J.A. Darossett
   City Mgr., Richard Torres
Copper Canyon (400 Woodland Dr.,
   Lewisville 75077)..........Chuck Wainscott
Corinth (2003 S. Corinth St.,
   Denton 76205) .... Shirley Spellerberg
   City Mgr., Richard H. Huckaby
†Corpus Christi........... Samuel L. Neal Jr.
   City Mgr., David Garcia
Corral City (14007 Corral City Dr.,
   Argyle 76226)............James E. Draper
Corrigan .... Robert R. "Bobby" Smiley
   City Mgr., B.K. Johnson
†Corsicana............................ Wilson Griffin
   City Mgr., Truitt Gilbreath
*Cottonwood (PO Box 293,
   Scurry 75158) .... Stephen Struck
*Cottonwood Shores (3915
   Cottonwood Dr., Marble Falls
   78654-9427) ....Dale Pickens
*Cotulla .... Pablo Gonzales
*Cove .... Carl Crowder
Covington........................Patti Estes
Crandall .... Gordon S. Black
   City Mgr., Judy Bell
*Crane............................. Terry L. Schul
   City Admin., Bill Sanders
Cranfills Gap .... Wade Lee
Crawford ....Robert L. Campbell
*Creedmoor .... Robert Wilhite
*†Crockett ....Bill Holcomb
Crosbyton .... Jacky Dewbre
   City Mgr., Nathan Davis
Cross Plains........................ Ray Purvis
   City Mgr., Debbie Gosnell
Cross Roads (11700 Hwy. 380 E.,
   Aubrey 76227-8246)......... Doug Daffron
*Cross Timber (PO Box 2042,
   Burleson 76097)......Wava McCullough
Crowell............................Robert Kincaid
*Crowley ....Chuck Rutherford
   City Admin., Jay Singleton
†Crystal City...................Frank Moreno Jr.
   City Mgr., Ramon de la Fuente Jr.
*†Cuero................... Michael Thamm
   City Mgr., Corlis Riedesel
*Cumby ....LaVerne Battle
*Cuney.........................Ethylene King
Cushing........................ Ben G. Baldwin
Cut and Shoot (PO Box 7364,
   Conroe 77306)........ Lang Thompson
†Daingerfield............. Lou Irvin Slaughter
   City Mgr., Kevin Carruth
*Daisetta ....Jimmy May
†Dalhart ....Gene Rahll
   City Mgr., Greg Duggan

†Dallas ....Ronald Kirk
City Mgr., Ted Benavides
*Dalworthington Gardens (2600
Roosevelt Dr., Arlington 76016-
5809) .... Albert A. Taub
City Admin., J. Gregory Shugart
Danbury ....Kenneth W. Walters Jr.
Darrouzett .... Bob Forgey
City Mgr., Terry Howard
*Dawson.......................... Yvonne Woods
†Dayton............... Guy L. "Larry" Harris
City Mgr., Robert Ewart
Dayton Lakes (PO Box 1476,
Dayton 77535).........Leavy Darby Lowe
*Dean (RR 5, Box 516, Wichita
Falls 76031-9597)........ Steve L. Sicking
Decatur..............................Bobby Wilson
City Mgr., Brett Shannon
*†Deer Park ....Jimmy Burke
City Mgr., Ron Crabtree
De Kalb .... Paul G. Meadows
†De Leon .... Norma Jo Locke
Dell City .... Bill Williams
*†Del Rio .... Roberto Chavira
City Mgr., Beth Eby
†Denison .... Bill Lindsay
City Mgr., Larry Cruise
†Denton ....Jack Miller
City Mgr., Mike Jez
†Denver City ....Sidney C. Reinert
City Mgr., Stan David
Deport .... Charles W. Foster
†DeSoto ....Richard Rozier
City Mgr., Jim Baugh
Detroit .... Margaret Missildine
*Devers ................................R.B. Evans
Devine.............................. Steve A. Lopez
City Admin., Linda L. Gunn
Diboll .... James P. Simms
City Mgr., Lanny Parish
Dickens .... Bob Porter
†Dickinson .... K.R. Hufstetler
City Admin., Don Taylor
*Dilley ....Mary Ann Obregon
†Dimmitt............................Wayne Collins
City Mgr., Don Sheffy
*Dodd City .... Jackie Lackey
*Dodson ............................H.M. Riddle
*Domino .... Frank Propps
†Donna ....Lonnie Flores
City Mgr., Carlos Verena
Dorchester .... Alice F. Stewart
Double Oak .... Bill Wilkinson
*Douglassville ....Douglass B. Heath
Dripping Springs .... Wayne E. Smith
City Mgr., Rick Coneway
*Driscoll............................ Tony Arredondo
Dublin ....James A. Seigars
City Mgr., Corrin J. McGrath
*†Dumas .... Rowdy Rhoades
City Mgr., Ron Bottoms
†Duncanville .... Glenn Repp
City Mgr., Larry Shaw
Eagle Lake .... Michael Cooper
City Mgr., Ronald Holland
†Eagle Pass................. José A. Aranda Jr.
City Mgr., Felix M. Cerna
Early..............................James Lewis
City Mgr., Ken Thomas
Earth ....R. R. Daniel Jr.
†Eastland ....Dale Squiers
City Mgr., Paul Catoe
East Mountain (RR 1, Box 500,
Gilmer 75644).........Edith Wilson Beisch
Easton.......................... Willis Sammons
*East Tawakoni (700 Briggs Blvd.,
Lone Oak 75453).......Bobbie J. Harman
Ector .... Kenneth Abbott
Edcouch .... Ramiro Silva
City Admin., Eloy Z. González
Eden .... Thomas F. Kelso
Edgecliff Village (1605 Edgecliff Rd.,
Edgecliff 76134-1198) ...... Ed Lucas
Edgewood...................H. Leon Slaughter
City Mgr., Donna Seale
†Edinburg..............................Joe Ochoa
City Mgr., John R. Milford
Edmonson..........................Don Ketchum
†Edna ....Joe D. Hermes

City Mgr., Gerald G. Decker
Edom (RR 1, Box 512, Browns-
boro 75756-9602) . Mary Hornsby Scott
*†El Campo .... Kenneth G. Martin
City Mgr., Terry K. Roberts
*El Cenizo (507 Cadena, Laredo
78046-7947) .... San Juana E. Gomez
Eldorado .... John Nikolauk
†Electra .... LaJune Lewis
City Admin.., Kandi Waterstreet
†Elgin ....Eric W. Carlson
City Mgr., Jim D. Dunaway
Elkhart ....Garth Moran
El Lago .... Michael J. O'Brien
*Elmendorf....................Mary Jane Nunez
†El Paso .... Carlos M. Ramirez
†Elsa .... Gregorio "Greg" Madrigal
City Mgr., Leonardo Camarillo
*Emhouse (3825 Joe Johnson Dr.,
Corsicana 75110-0891) Harold Clemens
Emory........................... Rubye McKeown
Enchanted Oaks (PO Box 5019, Gun
Barrel City 75147-5000).....Olena Boner
Encinal.............. María Elena Rodriguez
City Admin., Rosa Rodriguez
†Ennis .... Bill Lewis
City Mgr., Steve Howerton
Estelline .... Bob Willoughby
†Euless....................... Mary Lib Saleh
City Mgr., Joe Hennig
Eureka (1305 FM 2859, Corsicana
75110-0754) ....Barney Thomas
Eustace.............................Troy L. Allen
Evant ....Alma "Fritz" Green
†Everman......................Cathey Thurston
City Mgr., Earl Keaton
Fairchilds (8713 Fairchilds Rd.,
Richmond 77469-8804) ...Robert Myska
Fairfield........................ Patricia M. Wood
City Admin., Mike Boxley
Fair Oaks Ranch .... E.L. Gaubatz
City Mgr., Roy Thomas
Fairview (500 S. Highway 5,
McKinney 75069).............. Don Phillips
City Mgr., Scott Albert
Fairview (PO Box 855, Rhome
76078-0855) ....John Christian Sr.
Falfurrias .... J. Michael Guerra
Falls City............................ Vi Malone
†Farmers Branch....................Bob Phelps
City Mgr., Richard L. Escalante
Farmersville .... George Crump
City Mgr., Alan Hein
Farwell ....Jimmie Mace
Fate .... Gerry Boren
*Fayetteville .... Ronald Pfughaupt
City Mgr., Sylvester Schmitt Jr.
Ferris .... Jimmie Birdwell
Flatonia................................ Lori Berger
City Mgr., Robert Wood
Florence .... Lee Roy Knauth
Floresville ....Raymond M. Ramirez
City Mgr., Gary Pelech
†Flower Mound.....................Lori L. DeLuca
City Mgr., Van James
*Floydada .... Hulon Carthel
City Mgr., Gary Brown
*Follett ....Lynn Blau
City Mgr., Robert Williamson
†Forest Hill (6800 Forest Hill Dr.,
Fort Worth 76140-1299) .. Billy T. Wilson
City Mgr., David Vestal
†Forney .... Weldon L. Bowen
City Mgr., Jim McConnell
*Forsan.........................Johnny Sherman
Fort Stockton ....Howard McKissack
City Mgr., Jesse "Chuy" Garcia
†Fort Worth .... Kenneth Barr
City Mgr., Robert Terrell
*Franklin .... Charles Ellison
Frankston.......................... James Gouger
City Admin., Jean Jennings
†Fredericksburg.......... Linda Langerhans
City Mgr., Gary Neffendorf
†Freeport.................James A. Barnett Jr.
City Mgr., Ken Maltby
Freer ....Arnoldo Cantu
†Friendswood ....Harold L. Whitaker
City Mgr., Ronald E. Cox

*Friona .... Clarence Monroe
City Mgr., Paula Wilson
†Frisco .... Kathleen A. Seei
City Mgr., George Purefoy
Fritch................................Darrell Neal
Frost..................................Ken Reed
Fruitvale .... Bea Whisenhunt
Fulshear.......................... Carl G. Utley
Fulton............................ Leslie Cole Sr.
City Admin., Linda J. Burgess
†Gainesville .... Kenneth Kaden
City Mgr., Mike Land
†Galena Park........... R.P. "Bobby" Barrett
City Admin., John L. Cooper
*Gallatin .... Bobby Wellborn
†Galveston................ Roger "Bo" Quiroga
City Mgr., Steven J. LeBlanc
Ganado ....Russell J. Johnson
Garden Ridge .... Jay F. Feibelman
City Admin., Mike Castro
†Garland ....Jim Spence
City Mgr., Jeff Muzzy
Garrett (208 N. Ferris St., Ennis
75119-8338) .... Jami Rogers
Garrison .... Darrell Lunsford Jr.
Gary.............................. Jean L. Heaton
†Gatesville............ James E. (Jamie) Erwin
City Mgr., Bob Stevens
†Georgetown .... MaryEllen Kersch
City Mgr., Bob Hart
†George West............August E. Caron Jr.
City Mgr., Terri Garza
*Gholson (1277 Wesley Chapel Rd.,
Waco 76705-5957).....Howard T. Sexton
†Giddings............................ Paul R. Kipp
City Mgr., D.E. Sosa
†Gilmer ....Everett Dean
City Mgr., Scott Thompson
*†Gladewater .... Curtis E. Bright
City Mgr., Sharon G. Johnson
Glen Rose ....Connie Kirk
City Mgr., Jeff Mackey
*†Glenn Heights................Stephen Pape
City Mgr., Sheyi Ipaye
Godley .... Larry A. Richeson
Goldsmith...................... William Edwards
Goldthwaite .... Richard H. Poss
City Mgr., Dale Allen
Goliad .... Buddy Zavesky
City Admin., Jayne Hoff
*Golinda (7021 Golinda Drive,
Lorena 76655-4334)... Ennis Degrate Jr.
†Gonzales.............................Bobby O'Neal
City Mgr., E.T. Gibson
*Goodlow (PO Box 248, Kerens
75141) .... Willie H. Washington
Goodrich......................... Mark H. Ryman
Gordon .... David Johnson
Goree.............................. George Cotton
†Gorman .... Jack Simpson
Graford...........Alice Sain, Mayor Pro Tem
†Graham ....Douglas A. Stroud
City Mgr., Larry M. Fields
†Granbury......................David Southern
City Mgr., Robert Brockman
Grandfalls ....James Everett
City Admin., Joy Chew
†Grand Prairie ....Charles England
City Mgr., Tom Hart
*Grand Saline ....J. Ray Rucker
City Mgr., Sam Beeler
Grandview......................Louise Hudson
Granger.............................. Dollie Hajda
Granite Shoals .... Pat Crochet
Granjeno (6603 S. FM 494, Mission
78572-1501)....................Rafael Garza
City Admin., Alfonso Chapa Jr.
*Grapeland............................ Dick Bridges
*Grapevine .... William D. Tate
City Mgr., Roger Nelson
*Grayburg (RR 9, Box 1034, Sour
Lake 77659-0023) .... J.W. Floyd
*Grays Prairie (12294 S. FM 148,
Scurry 75158-3769) ........C.W. Johnson
†Greenville......................Sue Ann Harting
City Mgr., Ed Thatcher
Gregory........................Luis Galvan
Grey Forest (18502 Scenic Loop Rd.,
Helotes 78023-3210)...... Edwin L. Faust

Groesbeck.....................Jim Longbotham
Groom ....Joe Homer
†Groves ....Billy L. Job
    City Mgr., Davis Brinson
Groveton ....Paul E. Snyder
Gruver...................................Mark K. Irwin
    City Mgr., A. J. Ratliff
†Gun Barrel City .... Joe Agnes
    City Mgr., Tom Donaldson
*Gunter ....James H. Donohoe
Gustine ....Ken Huey
*Hackberry (119 Maxwell Rd. , Ste.
    B-7, Frisco 75034)....... Chester Thomas
*Hale Center ....Gordon Russell
Hallettsville................. Warren Grindeland
    City Admin., Tom Donnelly
Hallsburg (1693 Wilbanks Dr.,
    Waco 76705) ....Margie N. Wilbanks
Hallsville..........................T. Bynum Hatley
†Haltom City ....Nancy Watkins
    City Mgr., Bill Eisen
Hamilton.................................Ray Sparks
    City Admin., Bill Funderburk
Hamlin...................................Earl Gregory
Happy...................................R.N. McDonald
*Hardin.....................Douglas C. Tinkle Jr.
*†Harker Heights...................Mary Gauer
    City Mgr., Steve Carpenter
†Harlingen .... C. Connie de la Garza
    City Mgr., Natalie Flores Prim
Hart ....Marguerite McLain
Haskell ....Ken Lane
    City Admin., Sam Watson
Haslet................................ Gary D. Hulsey
Hawk Cove (1704 Hortense St.,
    Quinlan 75474-3949).......... Ava Havens
Hawkins ...............................W.C. Maynard
*Hawley .... Don Tatum
Hays (PO Box 1285, Buda
    78610) .... (Vacancy)
†Hearne ....Ruben Gomez
    City Mgr., Kenneth W. Pryor
Heath ....Chris Cuny
    City Admin., Dennis Watson
Hebron (RR 2, Box 184, Carrollton
    75010) .... Joe Fred Everett
Hedley..Janie Hill
Hedwig Village (955 Piney Point Rd.,
    Houston 77024-2797).......Sue V. Speck
Helotes...........................Steven F. Hodges
    City Admin., Vicki Graham
*Hemphill ....Robert Hamilton
    City Mgr., Frank Coday
Hempstead ....Herbert L. Johnson
    City Admin., James Vines
†Henderson ....Wallace Read
    City Mgr., Kenneth Taylor
Henrietta ....Rick Langford
    City Mgr., Joe Pence
*†Hereford..... Robert D. "Bob" Josserand
    City Mgr., Chester Nolen
†Hewitt.............................Bob Griffin Sr.
    City Mgr., Dennis H. Woodard
*Hickory Creek (PO Box 453,
    Lake Dallas 75065) .... John Malloy
Hico.....................................Jesse Jones
*†Hidalgo...............John David Franz
    City Mgr., Joe Vera III
Higgins.............................Linda Nicholson
    City Mgr., Randy Immel
Highland Haven ....John Josefy
†Highland Park (4700 Drexel Dr.,
    Dallas 75205) ....Gifford Touchstone
    City Admin., L.A. Patterson
†Highland Village .... Austin Adams
    City Mgr., William F. Lundberg Jr.
*Hill Country Village (116 Aspen Ln.,
    San Antonio 78232-4302) .... Bill Ford
    City Mgr., Terry Lively
Hillcrest Village (PO Box 1172,
    Alvin 77512) ......................C.W. Vowell
†Hillsboro ....Henry Moore
    Acting City Mgr., Lauralee Vallon
Hilshire Village (1003 Wirt Rd., Ste.
    103, Houston 77055). Steven Tacconelly
*†Hitchcock...................Leon Evans Sr.
Holiday Lakes (RR 4, Box 747,
    Angleton 77515-8412)...........M.A. Berg
Holland..............................Harold Rohde

Holliday.................................Cody West
Hollywood Park ....Gary W. Mercer
Hondo....................................Jim Barden
    City Mgr., David Chavez
Honey Grove .... Maquestia J. Johnson
    City Admin., (Vacancy)
Hooks ....Michael W. Babb
†Horizon City............. Thomas "Tom" Ruiz
†Houston ....Lee P. Brown
Howardwick (HC 2 Box 2230,
    Clarendon 79226) ....Margaret Pettit
Howe ....Ray Bledsoe
    City Admin., Ray Houston
Hubbard.................................. Bill Eitel
    City Admin., O.G. (Sonny) Minze
Hudson (201 Mount Carmel Rd.,
    Lufkin 75904-8661)...... Robert M. Smith
    City Admin., John T. Long
Hudson Oaks (150 N. Oakridge Dr.,
    Weatherford 76087)....... Gene L. Voyles
    City Admin., Roger M. Elliott
Hughes Springs................. Reba Simpson
    City Mgr., George Fite
†Humble ....Wilson Archer
    City Mgr., James P. Baker
Hunters Creek Village (1 Hunters Creek
    Pl., Houston 77024) ......Jack W. Howeth
Huntington ....Lamar Tinsley
    City Admin., Robert Walker
†Huntsville.........................William B. Green
    City Mgr., Gene Pipes
†Hurst.....................................Bill Souder
    City Mgr., W. Allan Weegar
Hutchins .... Mary L. Washington
Hutto .... Glen Pierce
    City Admin., Mel Yantis
Huxley (RR 1, Box 1410,
    Shelbyville 75973-9735) ...Larry Vaughn
Idalou...............................Mike Mauldin
    City Mgr., Russell Hamilton
Impact (PO Box 3116, Abilene
    79604-3116) .... Dallas Perkins
Indian Lake (62 S. Aztec Cove Dr.,
    Los Fresnos 78566)..... James C. Collum
Industry ....Alan W. Kuehn
†Ingleside ..............................C.H. Lewis
    City Mgr., Marilyn Hall
Ingleside on the Bay (PO Box 8,
    Ingleside 78362-1301) ... Alfred Robbins
*Ingram.......................Monroe Schlabach
Iowa Colony (12003 County Road 65,
    Rosharon 77583-5719)....... Robert Wall
Iowa Park......................Timothy W. Hunter
    City Admin., Michael C. Price
*Iraan .... Randy Peterson
Iredell.............................. A. D. Woody Jr.
†Irving ....Joe Putnam
    City Mgr., Stephen McCullough
*Italy .... Dennis Crecelius Jr.
    City Admin., Lyall Kirton
Itasca.................................... Les Alley
*†Jacinto City ....David Gongre
    City Mgr., Joann Griggs
Jacksboro .... Jerry Craft
    City Mgr., Michael Webb
†Jacksonville .... Thomas C. Dement
    City Mgr., Jim Anderson
Jamaica Beach (PO Box 5264,
    Galveston 77554) .... Kenneth R. Dennis
    City Admin., Dennis McDuffie
†Jasper.......................................R.C. Horn
    City Mgr., Kerry Lacy
Jayton .... Travis R. (Ray) Smith
Jefferson........................... Ned Fratangelo
†Jersey Village (16501 Jersey Dr.,
    Houston 77040) ... Stephen C. Schneider
    City Mgr., R. Dale Brown
Jewett................................James L. Winn
Joaquin...............................Steve Hughes
Johnson City................................Joe Ginn
Jolly (RR 2, Box 305, Wichita Falls
    76301-9514) ....Carroll Vicars
Jones Creek (7207 Stephen F. Austin
    Rd., Freeport 77541) .... Kevin Pitts
    City Admin., Linda Shepard
Jonestown .... Sam Billings
    City Admin., Ray Litton
Josephine ....Richard Murray
†Joshua...................... Kenneth Bransom

    City Mgr., Terry Smith
*Jourdanton .... Bob Orr
    City Mgr., Roy D. Underwood
Junction ....Jamie Roy Jacoby
Justin ....Jon Beck
Karnes City ....Don Tymrak
    City Admin., David Carrothers
†Katy.............................. M.H. Schmidt Jr.
    City Admin., Johnny Nelson
†Kaufman...........................James Y. Wynne
    City Mgr., Joseph S. Portugal
*Keene .... Gary Heinrich
    City Mgr., Rick Voorhies
†Keller.............................David C. Phillips
    City Mgr., Lyle H. Dresher
Kemah ....Richard A. Diehl
Kemp ....Vidal Jones
    City Mgr., Stephone Taylor
Kempner ....Roger Fancher
Kendleton ....Carolyn Jones
Kenedy............................Randy C. Jurgajtis
    City Admin., Ben R. Shelton
Kenefick (RR 5, Box 525A,
    Dayton 77535)............. Barry D. Bowling
Kennard ....Bill L. Thomas
    City Admin., Glenn Westbrook
†Kennedale.......................Mark S. Wright
    City Mgr., Ted Rowe
Kerens .... Tim Crawford
†Kermit ....Ted Westmoreland
    City Mgr., Wayne Reynolds
*†Kerrville .... Ben R. Low
    City Mgr., Glenn D. Brown
†Kilgore ....Joe T. Parker
    City Mgr., Ron Stephens
†Killeen .... Fred Latham
    City Mgr., David Blackburn
*†Kingsville ...... Filemon "Phil" Esquivel Jr.
    City Mgr., Carlos E. Lerma
*†Kirby ....Johnny Duffek Jr.
    City Mgr., Cindy Fox
*Kirbyville .... Fred Herron
    City Supvr., Roy G. Stark
*Kirvin .....................J.W. "Billy" Walthall
Knollwood (100 Collins St.,
    Sherman 75092) .... Richard Roelke
Knox City ....Tommie Reynolds
    City Mgr., Danny Parker
Kosse .... W. Robert O'Neal
*Kountze .... W.H. Hicks Dunlap
    City Mgr., Joe Blair
Kress...................................Louise Kirk
    City Admin., Kenny Hughes
Krugerville (100 Kruger Rd.,
    Aubrey 76227-9532)..Janice Baughman
Krum .... Floyd Watson
Kyle .... James L. Adkins
    City Admin., Stephen Harrison
*La Coste .... Andy Keller
    City Admin., Ken Roberts
†Lacy-Lakeview (PO Box 154549,
    Waco 76715) .... Dennis Cogliati
    City Mgr., Michael Nicoletti
Ladonia .... Leon Hurse
†La Feria...........................Carlos Cantu
    City Mgr., Sunny K. Philip
*Lago Vista........................ Glen Hartman
    City Admin., Kelvin Knauf
†La Grange.........................David R. Noak
    City Mgr., Shawn Raborn
*La Grulla (PO Box 197, Grulla
    78548-0197)............Helen S. Gonzalez
Laguna Vista (122 Fernandez St.,
    Port Isabel 78578)........Hap Fairhart
*La Joya.............................Rodolfo Farias
    City Admin., Oscar Cuellar Jr.
Lake Bridgeport (RR 2, Box 244F,
    Bridgeport 76426) ...Jeanita VanDerLee
Lake City (PO Box 177, Mathis
    78368) .... Harold B. McCown
*Lake Dallas.................Rodney Courtney
    City Mgr., Stewart Fairburn
†Lake Jackson ....Jim Martin
    City Mgr., William P. Yenne
Lakeport (PO Box 7728, Longview
    75607-7728).....................Ricky Shelton
*Lakeside (129 Lakewood Dr.,
    Mathis 78368) .... James M. Thomas
Lakeside (9830 Confederate Park Rd.,

Fort Worth 76108) ..... Raymond E. Beck
City Admin., William F. Mohr
Lakeside City (PO Box 4287,
Wichita Falls 76308) .... Dave Schmitt
City Admin., Don Sheppard
Lake Tanglewood (RR 8, Box 35-15,
Amarillo 79118-9430) .... Robert Karrh
Lakeview .... Kelly Clark
†Lakeway .... Charles Edwards
City Mgr., Dave Benson
*Lakewood Village .... Brian Refoy
†Lake Worth .... Walter Bowen
City Mgr., Mark Todd
†La Marque .... Pete W. Rygaard
City Mgr., Carol McLemore
†Lamesa .... Mike C. Tyler
†Lampasas .... Jack Calvert
City Mgr., Mike Talbot
†Lancaster .... Martha Wallace
City Mgr., Anthony (Biff) Johnson
†La Porte .... Norman Malone
City Mgr., Robert T. Herrera
†Laredo .... Elizabeth G. Flores
City Mgr., Florencio Peña
*Latexo .... Billie Jo Bennett
La Vernia .... Charles R. Malloy
La Villa .... Carlos Perez
City Mgr., Luciano Ozuna
Lavon .... Chris Wess
*La Ward .... Tillman M. Hunt Sr.
Lawn .... Johnny B. Hudson
*†League City .....A.T. "Tommy" Frankovich
City Admin., Nicholas J. Finan
†Leander .... Charles Eaton
City Mgr., Jake Krauskopf
*Leary (RR 5, Box 435, Texarkana
75501-9434) .... Donald McGonigal
Lefors .... J.W. Franks
Leona .... Travis Oden
Leonard .... Stan Barker
City Admin., George Henderson
Leon Valley .... Marcy Meffert
City Mgr., Hank Brummett
Leroy .... David Williams
†Levelland .... Hugh Lynn Bradley
City Mgr., Gregory M. Ingham
†Lewisville .... Bobbie J. Mitchell
City Mgr., Claude King
Lexington ....Robert Lee Willrich Sr.
†Liberty .... Bruce E. Halstead
City Mgr., Norman W. Dykes
Liberty Hill .... Nathan Wetzel
*Lincoln Park (110 Parker Pkwy.,
Aubrey 76227) .... Loretta Ray
City Mgr., Nat Parker III
Lindale .... Bobby McClenny
City Admin., Owen Scott
*Linden .... Marvin W. Kelly Sr.
Lindsay .... Robert P. Waltersheid
Lipan .... Alford Spencer
Little Elm .... Jim Pelley
†Littlefield .... Shirley Mann
City Mgr., Marty Mangum
Little River-Academy (PO Box 521,
Little River 76554) .... Ronnie White
†Live Oak .... Paula Stakes
City Mgr., Joseph W. Painter
*Liverpool .... Allan F. Moore
Livingston .... Ben R. Ogletree Jr.
City Mgr., Sam Gordon
Llano .... Terry Hutto
City Mgr., Philip Cook
†Lockhart .... Ray Sanders
City Mgr., (Vacancy)
*Lockney .... Gary D. Marr
*Log Cabin .... Robert L. Ford
Lometa .... Troy Duncan
*Lone Oak .... Harold Slemmons
Lone Star .... Patricia A. Wommack
†Longview .... David L. McWhorter
City Mgr., Rickey C. Childers
Loraine .... Catarino G. Martinez Jr.
Lorena .... Stacy Garvin
Lorenzo .... Lester C. Bownds
City Mgr., James Norris
Los Fresnos .... Roberto Cepeda
City Admin., (Vacancy)
Los Indios .... Diamantina Bennett

Los Ybáñez (1919 CR M, Box 52A,
Lamesa 79331) .... Mary A. Ybáñez
City Coord., Erica Hernández
Lott .... Jimmy Tobias
Lovelady .... Michael R. Broxson
Lowry Crossing (1405 S. Bridgefarmer
Rd., McKinney 75069) .... Tom Dillard
†Lubbock .... Windy Sitton
City Mgr., Bob Cass
Lucas (151 Country Club Rd., Allen
75002-7641) .... Andrea Calve
City Admin., (Vacancy)
Lueders .... Russell Mullins
†Lufkin .... Louis A. Bronaugh
City Mgr., C.G. Maclin
*†Luling .... J.B. Nickells
Interim City Mgr., Reuben Kimball
Lumberton .... Bill Nelson
City Admin., Norman P. Reynolds
Lyford .... Rodolfo S. Saldaña
Lytle .... Horace Fincher
Mabank .... Larry Teague
City Admin., Louann Confer
Madisonville .... Kirby H. Woehst
City Mgr., Jim White
Magnolia .... John W. Bramlett
City Coord., James Goudeau
*Malakoff .... Pat Isaacson
City Admin., (Vacancy)
Malone .... Elvis D. Lander
*Manor .... Joe Sanchez Jr.
†Mansfield .... David R. Harry
City Mgr., Clayton W. Chandler
Manvel .... Joel "J.C." Dean
City Mgr., Wayne Sabo
†Marble Falls .... Griff Morris
City Mgr., Michael Stoldt
Marfa .... C.M. "Fritz" Kahl
Marietta .... Gledus Wellborn
Marion .... Glenn A. Hild
†Marlin .... Harry Kenny
City Mgr., Arthur Douglas
Marquez .... Kenneth Clary
†Marshall .... Audrey Kariel
City Mgr., Tony N. Williams
Marshall Creek (PO Box 1070,
Roanoke 76262) .... Greg Dawsey
City Admin., James L. McDuffie
Mart .... G.E. Middleton
City Admin., Jim Stafford
Martindale .... Maebeth Bagley
Mason .... O. Lee Graham
City Admin., Mark Hahn
*Matador .... Gary Lancaster
Mathis .... Manuel Torres
City Admin., Manuel Lara
Maud .... Edward M. Holley
*Maypearl .... David Evans
*†McAllen .... Leo Montalvo
City Mgr., Mike R. Perez
McCamey .... Jimmy L. McClure
City Coord., Lou Ann Watson
*†McGregor .... Felix A. Morris
City Mgr., Bill Dake
†McKinney .... Don Dozier
City Mgr., Isaac Turner
*McLean .... Charles McClendon
McLendon-Chisholm (1248 S. St. Hwy.
205, Rockwall 75087) Michael D. Donegan
Meadow .... Dale Wylie
Meadowlakes .... Emory Bellard Jr.
Meadows Place .... Jim McDonald
Megargel .... Danny Fails
City Admin., Gneta Mahan
Melissa .... W.E. "Buck" Weatherby III
City Admin., Susan Bradley
Melvin .... James Ivy
Memphis .... Gilbert D. Srygley
*Menard .... Max E. Hooten
City Admin., James Cannon
*†Mercedes .... Miguel Castillo Jr.
City Mgr., Ernesto S. Silva
*Meridian .... Mervin Spitzer
*Merkel .... Earnest Reynolds
City Mgr., Robert Harris
Mertens .... Linda Maples
*Mertzon .... Patsy Kahlig
†Mesquite .... Mike Anderson
City Mgr., Ted Barron

†Mexia .... William G. McCullough
City Mgr., Lambert Little
Miami .... Gene Hodges
†Midland .... Robert E. Burns
City Mgr., Mike McGregor
†Midlothian .... David K. Setzer
Midway .... Patrick H. Wakefield
*Milano .... James Hartley
*Mildred (5417 FM 637, Corsicana
75110) .... Kelly Fitzgerald
Miles .... Everett Dodson
Milford .... Chris Vernon
Miller's Cove (RR 3, Box 470, Mt.
Pleasant 75455) .... Courtney Marshall
*Millican .... (Vacancy)
Millsap .... Julia Dinda-Weston
Mineola .... Gordon E. Tiner
City Mgr., Dion Miller
†Mineral Wells .... Earl Medlin
City Mgr., Lance Howerton
*Mingus .... Robert Bearden
*†Mission .... Norberto Salinas
City Mgr., Pat Townsend Jr.
*Missouri City .... Allen Owen
City Mgr., James Thurmond
Mobeetie .... Dennis Hilburn
*Mobile City (824 Lilac Ln.,
Rockwall 75087) .... Wanda Cooper
†Monahans .... David B. Cutbirth
City Mgr., David Mills
Mont Belvieu .... Bob Lee
City Admin., Douglass Maurer
*Montgomery .... William Cummings
*Moody .... Mike Alton
City Admin., Charleen Dowell
*Moore Station (RR 1, Box 133,
Larue 75770-9725) .... Arthur Earl
*Moran .... Marvin Kays
Morgan .... C. Pat Murphy Sr.
Morgan's Point (PO Box 839,
La Porte 77572) .... Russel Applebe
City Admin., David A. Paulissen
Morgan's Point Resort (8 Morgan's Point
Blvd., Belton 76513) .... Donna Hartman
City Mgr., Stacy Hitchman
Morton .... Ronnie D. Wallace
City Mgr., Suzanne Bilbrey
Moulton .... Harry E. Meyer
City Admin., Michael J. Slobojan
Mountain City (PO Box 1494, Buda
78610-1494) .... Kenneth B. Hiscoe
Mount Calm .... Gail Souders
Mount Enterprise .... Mark Jackson
†Mount Pleasant .... Jerry Boatner
City Mgr., Paul L. Parker
Mount Vernon .... H.H. Miller
City Admin., Eddie G. Turner
Muenster .... Henry Weinzapfel
City Admin., Stephen D. Broyles
†Muleshoe .... Robert Montgomery
City Mgr., Rick Hanna
Mullin .... A. R. Whisenhunt
Munday .... Gary Tidwell
City Mgr., John Weeks
Murchison .... Gayle Haynes
*Murphy .... Roy W. Bentle
*Mustang (PO Box 325, Corsicana
75151-0325) .... Glenn Albritton
Mustang Ridge (12800 Hwy. 183 S.,
Buda 78610-9407) .... Alfred Vallejo II
†Nacogdoches .... Richard D. Johnson
City Mgr., J.C. Hughes Jr.
Naples .... Willie J. Palmore
Nash .... David H. Slaton
City Admin., Elizabeth Lea
*†Nassau Bay (1800 NASA Rd. 1,
Houston 77058) .... Donald C. Matter
Interim City Mgr., David Quick
Natalia .... Ruberta C. Vera
Navarro (PO Box 7502, Corsicana
75110) .... Yvonne Capehart
†Navasota .... Tony Maddox
City Mgr., Eugene Daniel
Nazareth .... Ralph Brockman
†Nederland .... Homer E. Nagel
City Mgr., André Wimer
*Needville .... Kermit Blezinger
Nesbitt (RR 5, Box 88, Marshall
75670) .... James R. Watson

Nevada......................... Richard Caldwell
Newark............................. H.B. Malone
New Berlin (9180 FM 775, La
Vernia 78121)............Freddie Frederick
New Boston.....................Johnny Branson
†New Braunfels................Stone Williams
City Mgr., Mike Shands
Newcastle .... Darlton Dyer
*New Chapel Hill (14039 County Rd.
220, Tyler 75707)............ J. T. Pinkerton
New Deal .... Harry Ford
New Home .... Don Sharp
*New Hope (PO Box 562, McKinney
75070) .... Johnny Hamm
New London .... M.V. Hudson
New Summerfield................ Dan Stallings
City Mgr., Hilda McLeod
Newton.................................. David Hines
City Admin., Donnie Meek
New Waverly .... Dan Underwood
*Neylandville (General Delivery,
Greenville 75401)........ Lois K. Callagan
Niederwald .... Rickie Adkins
Nixon................................Collie L. Murray
City Mgr., John D. Byrd
Nocona ....Gene E. Fitzgerald
City Mgr., Joe Gambill
Nolanville .... Juanita K. "Nita" Sims
Nome ....David Studdert
Noonday (PO Box 6425, Tyler
75711) ....Bennie H. Smith
Nordheim .... Gilbert Pargmann
Normangee .... Doug Kyle
*North Cleveland (PO Box 1266,
Cleveland 77327) .... Woodrow Squier
Northlake (PO Box 729, Justin
76247) ....Michael J. Savoie
†North Richland Hills ....Charles Scoma
City Mgr., Larry J. Cunningham
*Novice.................................Don Poe
Oak Grove (PO Box 309, Kaufman
75142).................................J.W. Riddle
Oakhurst .... Frank G. AuBuchon
Oak Leaf .... Walter Adams
Oak Point .... Eileen Turner
City Admin., Bruce Crutchfield
*Oak Ridge (RR 3, Box 325 #27,
Gainesville 76240)..............Karen Price
Oak Ridge (PO Box 539, Kaufman
75142) ....Roy W. Perkins
Oak Ridge North (27326 Robinson Rd.,
Ste 115, Conroe 77385) ..... Joe Michels
City Admin., Paul Mendes
Oak Valley (PO Box 2193, Corsicana
75151-2193) .... Vicki Thomas
*Oakwood .... Dorothy Bell
O'Brien .... Charlene Brothers
Odem .... Jessie Rodriguez Sr.
†Odessa .... Mike Atkins
City Mgr., Jerry S. McGuire
*O'Donnell................... James E. Williams
Oglesby .... Kenneth Goodwin
*Old River-Winfree (PO Box 1169,
Mont Belvieu 77580) ....Joe Landry
Olmos Park (119 W. El Prado Dr., San
Antonio 78212) .... Gerald Z. Dubinski
City Mgr., (Vacancy)
†Olney................................ Phil Jeske II
City Admin., Jack R. Northrup
*Olton ....Mike Foskey
City Mgr., Marvin Tillman
*Omaha.................................D.D. Tuck
Onalaska ....Jeanne Ann Byrd
*Opdyke West (PO Box 1179,
Levelland 79336) .... Wayne Riggins
†Orange .... Essie L. Bellfield
City Mgr., Charles W. Pinto
Orange Grove .... Truett Thomas
City Admin., Perry R. Young
Orchard........................Eugene L. Demny
*Ore City .... Angela Edwards
*Overton.......................... Norma Hunter
Ovilla..................................Cindy Jones
City Admin., Scott Campbell
Oyster Creek (3210 FM 523,
Freeport 77541)....Richard D. Merriman
Paducah ....Bill Holley
*Paint Rock .... Paul Thorpe
Palacios .... Bob McMahan

City Admin., Charles Winfield
†Palestine..........................R.E. McKelvey
City Mgr., Curtis Snow
*Palisades (RR 7, Box 19-16,
Amarillo 79118).............. Randy Hooker
*Palmer..................... Henry M. Rhoades
City Mgr., Scott L. Albert
*Palmhurst (4501 N. Stewart Rd.,
Mission 78572) .... Elton L. Key
Palm Valley (1313 Stuart Place Rd.,
Harlingen 78552) ....Charles E. Burd
Palmview (RR 11, Box 1000,
Mission 78572) ....Jorge G. García
City Mgr., Jesse Lerma
*†Pampa.......................Robert Neslage
City Mgr., Robert Eskridge
*Panhandle........................ Les McNeill
City Mgr., Chris Coffman
Panorama (98 Hiwon Dr., Conroe
77304-1123) .... Howard L. Kravetz
Pantego ....Pat Richardson
City Mgr., Larry Smith
Paradise .... E.E. "Sonny" Read Jr.
†Paris .... Charles H. Neeley
City Mgr., Michael E. Malone
Parker (5700 E. Parker Rd., Allen 75002-
6799)........................David Hammel
City Admin., Betty McMenamy
*†Pasadena.......................Johnny Isbell
Pattison ....Linda Mladenka
Patton Village (16940 Main St.,
Splendora 77372) ....Cecil Ray White
Payne Springs (PO Box 1710,
Mabank 75147)................. J.D. Meredith
†Pearland ....Tom Reid
City Mgr., Glen Erwin
*†Pearsall .... Victor Vinton
City Mgr., R. Timothy Gump
*Pecan Gap .... Warner Cheney
Pecan Hill (PO Box 443, Red Oak
75154)................... Clinton A. Bittick Jr.
†Pecos .... Dot Stafford
City Mgr., Kenneth Neal
*Pelican Bay (1300 Pelican Cir.,
Azle 76020)................. Billy W. Heaton
City Admin., Robert de Saglio
*Penelope .... George Myers
Peñitas .... Servando Ramírez
City Admin., Efren Garza
*Pernitas Point (HCR 1, Box 1440,
Sandia 78383) .... Dorothy Keetch
Perryton .... David Hale
City Mgr., David Landis
*Petersburg...........................Jim Fox
City Mgr., Cullen J. Davis
Petrolia ............................G.W. Linton
Petronila (RR 3, Box 317, Robstown
78380-9611) ....William J. Ordner
*†Pflugerville .... Doyle Bridgefarmer
City Mgr., Steve Jones
†Pharr................................Ricardo Medina
City Mgr., Benito Lopez
Pilot Point .... Allen Groff
City Admin., Carolyn Boerner
Pine Forest (PO Box 1004, Vidor
77670-1004) .... William G. Elliott
City Admin., Peggy Richard
Pinehurst (3640 Mockingbird St.,
Orange 77630)........J.L. "Pete" Runnels
City Admin., C.R. Nash
Pine Island (RR 3, Box 86A,
Hempstead 77445) .... Debra Ferris
*Pineland.................John O. Booker Jr.
Piney Point Village (7721 San Felipe, Ste.
100, Houston 77063) ..C. Jim Stewart III
Pittsburg .... D. H. Abernathy
City Mgr., Ned Muse
Plains.............................. T. J. Miller
City Admin., David Brunson
†Plainview .... Lloyd C. Woods
City Mgr., James P. Jeffers
†Plano .... John Longstreet
City Mgr., Thomas H. Muehlenbeck
Pleak (5809 Pleak Rd., Richmond
77469)........................ Willie Poncik
Pleasant Valley (4006 Highway 287 E,
Iowa Park 76367)......Raymond Haynes
City Mgr., Jeff Watts
*†Pleasanton .... John Purcell

City Mgr., Larry Pippin
*Plum Grove (PO Box 1358,
Splendora 77372)...............T.W. Garrett
Point.........................Raymond O. Clifton
Point Blank (PO Box 474,
Pointblank 77364) ....Lillian Bratton
Point Comfort.................... Pam Lambden
*Ponder ....Charles Dollar
†Port Aransas .... Glenn Martin
City Mgr., Tommy M. Brooks
†Port Arthur ....Oscar G. Ortiz
City Mgr., Steve Fitzgibbons
†Port Isabel............... Patrick H. Marchan
City Mgr., Roberto J. García
†Portland .... A.R. (Dick) Moser
City Mgr., Michael Tanner
†Port Lavaca .... Tiney Browning
City Mgr., Thomas J. Blazek
†Port Neches .... Frances Monk
City Mgr., A.R. Kimler
*Post ....Jim Jackson
City Mgr., Rick L. Hanna
Post Oak Bend (1175 CR 278,
Kaufman 75142).......... Wayne Rebholz
City Coord., James A. Ball
*Poteet .... Diana M. Martinez
Poth................................Richard Pollok
*Pottsboro ....Steve Atkins
City Mgr., Lisa McCasland
*Powell .... Dennis Bancroft
*Poynor .... Dannie Smith
Prairie View........ Raymond E. Carreathers
Premont .... Norma Tullos
Presidio...................... Alcee Tavarez
City Admin., Michael Kovacs
Primera ....José J. Ramírez
Princeton ....Kathy Davis
Progreso .... Arturo Valdez
Dir., Ponciano Garcia
Progreso Lakes (PO Box 760,
Progreso 78579) .... Karen Evans
Prosper .... Stephen O. Coffman
City Admin., Shirley Jackson
Putnam .... Roy Petty
*Pyote ....Randy Earnest
†Quanah ....Ann Sparkman
Queen City.....................Bobby Bowman
*Quinlan ....Lois Cagle
City Admin., James M. Fletcher
Quintana .... Debbie Alongis
*Quitaque .... Wilburn Leeper
City Mgr., Clyde Dudley
Quitman ....Larry W. Robertson
Ralls........................... David A. Prewitt
City Admin., Mary Helen Jamerson
Rancho Viejo...................... B.D. Cummins
†Ranger .... Ken Parrack
†Rangerville (RR 4, Box 77, San
Benito 78586)............... Wayne Halbert
Rankin............. Cora Gaynelle McFadden
Ransom Canyon ....Leon Whetzel
†Ravenna ....Lyndon Hale
†Raymondville ....Joe M. Sosa
City Mgr., Eleazar García Jr.
Red Lick (PO Box 870, Nash
75569).................... Michael Peek
†Red Oak......................Dennis R. Brown
City Mgr., Ken Pfeifer
Redwater ....James B. Stokes
Refugio ....Ray Jaso
Reklaw ....Gilbert Stafford
Reno (165 Bybee St., Reno
75462)............................Sue Carico
City Admin., Shannon Barrentine
Reno (174 W. Reno Rd., Azle
76020)........................ Loyd L. Bailey
*Retreat (125 Ingham Rd.,
Corsicana 75110)......... Betty Carpenter
*Rhome .... Nell Fernandez
Rice..............................Roger A. Wear
†Richardson .... Gary A. Slagel
City Mgr., Bill Keffler
Richland.........................Dolores Baldwin
†Richland Hills (3200 Diana Dr.,
Fort Worth 76118)............. C.F. Kelley
City Mgr., James W. Quin
*Richland Springs .... Dale McKinnerney
*Richmond .... Hilmar G. Moore
City Mgr., R. Gilmore

Richwood .... Peggy Gartman
Riesel .... Keith Koester
Rio Bravo (1419 Centeno Lane,
   Laredo 78046) .... Feliciano Garcia Jr.
   City Admin., Jorge Luis Benavides
Rio Grande City .... Baldemar Garza
   City Admin., José A. Escamilla
*Rio Hondo .... Marcello Benavidez
   City Mgr., Jose Luis Lopez
Rio Vista .... Sam Bigham
Rising Star .... James Cook
†River Oaks (4900 River Oaks Blvd,
   Fort Worth 76114) .... Jack Adkison
   City Admin., Joy Williams
Riverside .... Randell L. Vincent
Roanoke .... Randy Corn
   City Mgr., Jimmy Stathatos
*Roaring Springs .... Joe Thacker
   City Mgr., Robert Osborn
Robert Lee .... Garland Davis
*Robinson .... Gene Hendon
*†Robstown .... Rafaela Lerma
*Roby .... Lance Green
   City Mgr., Claude A. Day
*Rochester .... Rod Townsend
   City Mgr., Danny Bass
†Rockdale .... Wallace Jones
   City Mgr., Sue Foster
†Rockport .... Glenda Burdick
   City Mgr., V. Lee Maness
†Rocksprings .... Charles Carson III
   City Mgr., Jeff Yeaman
†Rockwall .... Scott Self
   City Mgr., Julie Couch
*Rocky Mound (PO Box 795,
   Pittsburg 75686) .... Noble T. Smith
   City Mgr., Mary L. Smith
Rogers .... Billy Ray Crow
Rollingwood (403 Nixon Dr., Austin
   78746) .... Thom Farrell
   City Admin., Ryan Kelley
Roma .... Fernando PeÒa
   City Admin., Rogelio Salinas
*Roman Forest (2430 Roman Forest
   Blvd., New Caney 77357)... Sam Jones
Ropesville .... Vic Marrett
*Roscoe .... Tom Griffith
   City Mgr., Jerry Watts
Rosebud .... Ernestine Hill-Warren
   City Mgr., Ed Cole
Rose City (370 S. Rose City Dr.,
   Vidor 77662) .... Ruth Dubuisson
Rose Hill Acres (PO Box 8285,
   Lumberton 77711) .... Steve Barnett
Rosenberg .... Joe M. Gurecky
   City Mgr., Jeff D. Braun
*Ross .... Jim Jaska
*Rosser .... Albert Davis
Rotan .... Jerry A. Marshall
   City Admin., Harold Sanders
Round Mountain .... Alvin Gutierrez
†Round Rock .... Robert Stluka
   City Mgr., Robert L. Bennett Jr.
*Round Top .... Dave Nagel
†Rowlett .... H.K. "Buddy" Wall
   City Mgr., Mike Gibson
Roxton .... Luther Smith
Royse City .... Paul Fisk
   City Admin., Connie Goodwin
Rule .... Malcolm Herttenberger
Runaway Bay (101 Runaway Bay Dr.,
   Bridgeport 76426) ...... Barbara J. Blake
   City Coord., David Wilson
Runge .... Jack Roberson
*†Rusk .... Emmett Whitehead
   City Mgr., Mary Daly
Sabinal .... George Lee Moore
*†Sachse .... Hugh N. Cairns
   City Mgr., (Vacancy)
Sadler .... Thomas Filip
†Saginaw .... Monte Nichols
   City Mgr., Pat Moffatt
*St. Hedwig (PO Box 40, Saint
   Hedwig 78152) .... Albert Strzelcyzk
Saint Jo .... Tom Weger
St. Paul (2505 Butschers Block,
   Wylie 75098) .... Joyce Pockrus
*†San Angelo .... Johnny Fender
   City Mgr., Thomas L. Adams

*†San Antonio .... Howard W. Peak
   City Mgr., Alexander E. Briseno
San Augustine .... Gertrude Lane
   City Mgr., Duke Lyons
†San Benito .... Ricardo Morado
   City Mgr., Gabriel Gonzalez
Sanctuary (PO Box 125, Azle
   76098) .... Tony Gilliland
*San Diego .... Alfredo E. Cardenas
   City Mgr., Jose H. Jimenez
*San Elizario .... Raul Diaz
San Felipe .... Mark Miller
*Sanford .... James M. Gallentine
Sanger .... Tommy Kincaid
   City Admin., Jack L. Smith
†San Juan .... Roberto F. Loredo
   City Mgr., Jorge A. Arcuate
San Leanna (PO Box 1107,
   Manchaca 78652) .... John Linton
†San Marcos .... Billy G. Moore
   City Mgr., Larry D. Gilley
San Patricio (RR 2, Box 45, Mathis
   78368) .... Lonnie Glasscock III
*San Perlita .... Oscar de Luna
San Saba .... Marcus D. Amthor
   City Mgr., Joe Ragsdale
*Sansom Park (5500 Buchanan St.,
   Fort Worth 76114) .... David Henson
Santa Anna .... Karen Morris
   City Mgr., Douglas Watson
†Santa Fe .... Robert Cheek
   City Mgr., Joe Dickson
Santa Rosa .... Ruben Ochoa Jr.
   City Admin., Javier Mendez
Savoy .... Clete Stogsdill
†Schertz .... Harold D. Baldwin
   City Mgr., Kerry R. Sweatt
Schulenburg .... Connie Koopmann
   City Admin., Ronald Brossman
Scotland .... Grady Schenk Sr.
Scottsville .... John P. Verhalen Sr.
†Seabrook .... Robert (Bob) Robinson
   City Mgr., Ron Wicker
Seadrift .... Mark Daniel
†Seagoville .... Calvin Travers
   City Mgr., Philip Kloster
Seagraves .... Patrick L. McAdoo
†Sealy .... Betty Reinbeck
   City Mgr., Gary E. Stone
†Seguin .... Mark Stautzenberger
   City Mgr., Jack Ham
Selma .... Harold Friesenhahn
   City Admin., Margie Lubianski
†Seminole .... Bill Prince
   City Mgr., Tommy Phillips
*Seven Oaks (PO Box 540, Leggett
   77350) .... Gloria K. English
Seven Points .... Don Allsup
Seymour .... Benny Archer
   City Admin., James (Jim) Novak
Shady Shores (PO Box 362, Lake
   Dallas 75065) .... Olive Stephens
Shallowater .... Moe Dozier
Shamrock .... F.C. Hilburn Jr.
   City Mgr., Johnny W. Rhodes
Shavano Park (99 Saddletree Rd.,
   San Antonio 78231) ...... Thomas Peyton
   City Mgr., Michael Cernich
Shenandoah (29811 Interstate 45,
   Spring 77381) .... David J. Vetter Jr.
   City Admin., Paul Frederikson
Shepherd .... Wilbur L. Bridges
†Sherman .... Tom Osburn
   City Mgr., Jim Andrews
Shiner .... Arthur T. Ward
Shoreacres .... Wayne Gamble
†Silsbee .... Dean T. Robinson
   City Mgr., William Lewis
Silverton .... John Bowman
   City Admin., Jerry Patton
Simonton .... Jim Gammill
†Sinton .... Fernando Hernandez Jr.
   City Mgr., Jackie Knox Jr.
*Skellytown .... Ralph Tice
   City Mgr., Becky Ulmer
*†Slaton .... Don Kendrick
   City Mgr., Mitch Grant
Smiley .... Donald Janicek
Smithville .... Renee D. Blaschke

   City Mgr., Bob Miller
Smyer .... Mary Beth Sims
Snook .... Roland Junek
†Snyder .... Dayton Robertson
   City Mgr., John W. Gayle
Socorro .... Raymundo Rodriguez
Somerset .... Paul G. Cuellar
Somerville .... Donald L. Strickland
   City Admin., Lloyd A. Behm
Sonora .... JoAnn Hernandez
   City Mgr., Raymond Brent Gesch
*Sour Lake .... Bruce Robinson
   City Mgr., Kyle J. Jung
South Houston .... Albert Hernandez
†Southlake .... Rick Stacy
   City Mgr., Curtis E. Hawk
Southmayd .... Billy Kerr
*South Mountain (RR 2, Box 298A,
   Gatesville 76528) .... Billy Mayhew
*South Padre Island Edmund K. Cyganiewicz
   City Mgr., Raymond H. Kendall
Southside Place (6309 Edloe St.,
   Houston 77005) ...... Richard Rothfelder
   City Superintendent, Seth M. Young
Spearman .... Burl Buchanan
   City Mgr., Robert Patrick
Splendora .... Wayne Carley
*Spofford .... J. B. Hernden
Springlake .... Ben Royston
Springtown .... Robert Wilson
   City Admin., Bill Herrington
Spring Valley (1025 Campbell Rd.,
   Houston 77055) ...... Louise T. Richman
   City Admin., Richard R. Rockenbaugh
Spur .... Gene Roberson
Stafford .... Leonard Scarcella
Stagecoach (PO Box 364, Tomball
   77377) .... Mic Macmanus
†Stamford .... Louis E. Johnson
   City Mgr., Ken Roberson
Stanton .... Lester Baker
   City Mgr., Danny Fryar
Star Harbor (PO Box 949, Malakoff
   75148-0949) .... Grady L. Phillips
*†Stephenville .... John Moser
   City Admin., Don Davis
Sterling City .... Don Griffin
*Stinnett .... Anna Bishop
   City Mgr., James Stroud
Stockdale .... Tony Malik
   City Mgr., Carl Lambeck
*Stratford .... David Brown
   City Admin., Richard L. Walton
*Strawn .... Paul L. Stephen II
Streetman .... James M. Compton
Sudan .... Freddie Maxwell
†Sugar Land .... Dean A. Hrbacek
   City Mgr., David E. Neeley
*Sullivan City .... Gumaro Flores
   City Mgr., Robert Montes
*†Sulphur Springs .... Mike Miesse
   City Mgr., Marc Maxwell
Sundown .... Ronnie Popejoy
   City Mgr., Brad Stafford
Sunnyvale .... Jim Wade
   City Admin., Larry Graves
*Sunray .... Dow Brewer
   City Mgr., Greg Smith
Sunrise Beach Village (124 Sunrise Dr.,
   Sunrise Beach 78643) Dolores M. Smith
*Sunset .... R.J. Whitson
Sunset Valley (2 Lone Oak Trail,
   Austin 78745) .... Terry Cowan
   City Admin., Jayme Foley
*Sun Valley (RR 2, Box 800, Paris
   75462) .... Maria J. Wagnon
*Surfside Beach (1304 Monument Dr.,
   Freeport 77541) .... Larry Davison
Sweeny .... Larry G. Piper
   City Admin., Tim Moss
*†Sweetwater .... Jay Lawrence
   City Mgr., David Maddox
Taft .... Jerry L. King
   City Mgr., Mike Rhea
Tahoka .... Mike Mensch
   City Mgr., Jerry W. Webster
Talco .... K.M. (Mike) Sloan
Tatum .... Bob Harris
†Taylor .... Calvin T. Janak Sr.

City Mgr., Frank Salvato
Taylor Lake Village .... Einar Goerland
*Teague ....Earnest G. Pack
City Admin., David N. Moss
Tehuacana .... E.B. Trotter
†Temple .... Keifer Marshall Jr.
City Mgr., Mark S. Watson
Tenaha .... George N. Bowers
†Terrell .... Henry C. Madgwick Sr.
City Mgr., Gordon C. Pierce
*†Terrell Hills (5100 N. New Braunfels,
San Antonio 78209)Barbara B. Christian
City Mgr., Cal D. Johnson
†Texarkana ....James W. Bramlett
City Mgr., George Shackleford
†Texas City ....Charles T. Doyle
Dir., Mgmt. Svcs., Douglas M. Hoover
*Texhoma .... Garland Dahl
Texline .... James L. Bohls
City Mgr., Kelly Trujillo
*†The Colony .... Mary Blair Watts
City Mgr., Lanny S. Lambert
Thompsons ....G. W. Longserre
Thorndale....................Gerald Niemtschk
City Mgr., Keith Kiesling
Thornton ....James Jackson
City Admin., Michelle Nance
*Thorntonville (2414 W. 2nd St.,
Monahans 79756) .... Jim Clay Harkey
Thrall .... James Dvorak
*Three Rivers ....Jimmie M. Dewberry
City Admin., M.R. Forehand
Throckmorton......................John Kunkel
Tiki Island, Village of (802 Tiki Dr.,
Galveston 77554) ....Charles Everts
Timbercreek Canyon (RR 7, Box 4-5,
Amarillo 79118) .... Paul Siebenthal
City Admin., Lynda Barksdale
Timpson .... Douglas McDonald
Tioga................................ Stanley Kemp
*Tira (RR 7, Box 220, Sulphur
Springs 75482) ....Coy O. Vicars
Toco (2103 Chestnut Dr., Brookston
75421) .... John Jason Waller
*Todd Mission (390 N. Millcreek Dr.,
Plantersville 77363)...... George Coulam
Tolar .... Gayle S. Meyer
City Admin., Dana Kutej
†Tomball ...............H.G. "Hap" Harrington
City Mgr., Warren Driver
Tom Bean.............................. Bill Garner
Tool (RR 6, Box 843, Kemp
75143) .... Fran Sonka
Toyah .... Paul Budlong
Trent................................James Wallis
Trenton ....Randy Bartlett
Trinidad .............................J.C. Airheart
City Admin., Nelda Cartlidge
Trinity ....Lyle Stubbs
Trophy Club .... Marshall Engelbeck
City Mgr., Donna Welsh
Troup................................. Wiley V. Davis
City Admin., Jyl Moose
Troy .... Ernest Thompson
†Tulia .... John C. Emmitt
City Mgr., Bryan Easum
Turkey .... Suzie Johnson
City Mgr., Jerry Landry
Tuscola..............................Robert Philpot
Tye .... Gayland Childers
City Admin., Susie Quinn
†Tyler .... Kevin Eltife
City Mgr., Pinkney Butler
Uhland .... Dan T. Sorrells
*Uncertain ....Bill Mauthe
*Union Grove (RR 2, Box 196FF,
Gladewater 75647).. Randy Lee Simcox
†Universal City............ Wesley D. Becken
City Mgr., Gene Thorpe
†University Park (3800 University Blvd.,
Dallas 75205-1711) ....Harold Peek
City Mgr., Bob Livingston
†Uvalde................................Gus Neutze
Valentine .... Jesús Calderon
Valley Mills .... Howard Hillin
Valley View................John E. Fortenberry
Van...................................E.L. "Hut" Raulston
*Van Alstyne .... Teddie Ann Salmon
City Admin., Wayne E. Cummings

Van Horn .... Okey D. Lucas
City Admin., Rebecca L. Brewster
Vega .... Mark J. Groneman
Venus................................ James A. Flatt
City Mgr., John Daniel
†Vernon ....Kelly Couch
City Mgr., Jim Murray
†Victoria .... Gary Middleton
City Mgr., Denny Arnold
†Vidor................................. Joe Hopkins
City Mgr., Dan Graves
Village of the Hills (7 Chardon Ct.,
Austin 78738).......... George W. Sawyer
*Vinton (436 Vinton Rd., Anthony
79821)......................Samuel Monrreal
†Waco .... Michael D. Morrison
City Mgr., Kathy Rice
Waelder .... Roy Tovar
Wake Village .... Michael Huddleston
City Admin., Bob Long
Waller .... Danny Marburger
Wallis ....Tony I. Salazar Jr.
Walnut Springs ....David L. Keller
Warren City (3004 George Richey
Rd., Gladewater 75647)... John Shearer
Waskom............................ Jesse Moore
†Watauga ....Hector Garcia
City Mgr., Dale Cheatham
†Waxahachie......................Chuck Beatty
City Mgr., Robert Sokoll
†Weatherford ....Tom McLaughlin
City Mgr., (Vacancy)
†Webster .... Floyd H. Myers
City Mgr., Roger Carlisle
Weimar ....Bennie Kosler
City Mgr., Vince Slominski
Weinert ....Wade Raynes
*Weir............................. Mervin Walker
*Wellington ....Gary Brewer
City Mgr., Jon Sessions
Wellman .... Marty Lindsey
Wells ....William Bailey
†Weslaco .... Gene A. Braught
City Mgr., Francisco Castellanos
*West ....Russell D. Willsey
*Westbrook .... J. L. Rees
West Columbia ....David E. Foster
City Mgr., Roger L. Mumby
Westlake (3 Village Cr., Ste. 207,
Roanoke 76262) ....Scott Bradley
City Mgr., (Vacancy)
West Lake Hills............ Dwight Thompson
City Admin., Daniel E. Sowada
†Westminster ....Kenneth L. Haines
Weston .... Kay Hodges
†West Orange (2700 Austin Ave.,
Orange 77630)........ Roy C. McDonald
*Westover Hills (5824 Merrymount, Fort
Worth 76107)..........Earle A. Shields Jr.
City Mgr., B.J. Tuttleton
West Tawakoni (1533 E. Highway 276,
Quinlan 75474) ....Don Tanoos
City Admin., Dick Gillespie
†West University Place (3800 University
Blvd., Houston 77005) .... Linda Lewis
City Mgr., Sherman Yehl
*Westworth Village (311 Burton Hill Rd.,

Fort Worth 76114) ....Raymond L. Landy
†Wharton .... Joel D. Williams
City Mgr., Andres Garza Jr.
*Wheeler .... Wanda Herd
*White Deer...........................R.T. Laurie
Whiteface .... Mack Ashmore
City Admin., Syd Albus
†Whitehouse......................Dale E. Moran
City Mgr., Ronny Fite
*White Oak............................ Tim Vaughn
City Mgr., Ralph J. Weaver
Whitesboro .... Alfred C. Miller
City Mgr., Allen Barnes
†White Settlement..............James Herring
Whitewright .... Bill Goodson
Whitney ....Harold Lehmann
†Wichita Falls ....Kathryn A. Yeager
City Mgr., James P. Berzina
Wickett ....Harold Ferguson
Willis................................ Ruth Castleschouldt
City Admin., Michael C. Arthur
Willow Park (101 Stagecoach Trail,
Weatherford 76087)............. Les Cooley
City Admin., C. Guy Natale
Wills Point ................B.H. (Bill) Estes
City Mgr., Butch Girdley
Wilmer............................. Eugene Lowe
Wilson .... Jackie Bishop
Windcrest .... Don Myles
Windom ....Bill Roberts
Windthorst.............. Sue C. Steinberger
City Mgr., Donald Frerich
Winfield .... Mark Rigney
Wink ....Martin Garcia
Winnsboro ....Dayne Redding
City Admin., Jim Blanchard
Winona.........................Carl W. Granberry
Winters.................... Dawson McGuffin
City Mgr., Aref Hassan
Wixon Valley (PO Box 105, Kurten
77862) ....Charles P. Tanner
*Wolfe City ....Benny Richards Sr.
Wolfforth .... Glen Rasberry
City Admin., Frankie Pittman
*Woodbranch Village (PO Box 804,
New Caney 77357)....... Gerald Shirtz
Woodcreek (PO Box 1570, Wimberley
78676) ....Kenneth E. Jacobs
Woodloch (PO Box 1379, Conroe
77305) ....Diane L. Lincoln
Woodsboro................. Joseph Hernández
*Woodson .... Bobby Mathiews
Woodville ....Larry A. Phillips
City Mgr., Donald Shaw
†Woodway (PO Box 20937, Waco
76702) .... Donald "Don" J. Baker
City Mgr., Mark McDaniel
Wortham .... Marles L. Pace
†Wylie ....John Mondy
City Mgr., Mike Collins
Yantis .... Hershel Harris
†Yoakum ....M. W. Harbus Jr.
City Mgr., A.J. Veselka
Yorktown .... George Klein
City Admin., Milton Ledwig
Zavalla .... Hulon Miller

Texas Main Street Program

To encourage Texas cities to rehabilitate and reuse existing historic buildings, the Texas Historical Commission established the Texas Main Street Program in 1981. Each year, several towns, or neighborhoods within large cities, are designated Main Street cities. Each designated city/neighborhood hires a Main Street manager to coordinate its project. The Texas Main Street Program office provides architectural-design assistance, as well as supervision for the Main Street manager.

Following is a list of the Texas Main Street cities/neighborhoods that were designated between 1995 and 1999. An asterisk before the name denotes a city no longer active in the program. Self-initiated cities are listed last.

1995: Alpine, Bonham, Clifton, Kerrville and Rusk, plus Irving's commercial district. **1996:** *Duncanville, Fairfield, La Grange, Olton, Quanah. **1997:** Bowie, Breckenridge, Celina, Ferris, Weslaco. **1998:** Electra, Gilmer, Levelland, Monahans, Nacogdoches, Garland, Port Arthur, San Antonio-MidTown on Blanco. **1999:** Gatesville, Gladewater, Shiner, Taylor, Whitewright.

Self-initiated cities for 1999 include Cooper, San Benito, Amarillo and West Columbia. ☆

Regional Councils of Government

The concept of regional planning and cooperation, fostered by enabling legislation in 1965, has spread across Texas since organization of the **North Central Texas Council of Governments** in 1966.

Regional councils are voluntary associations of local governments that deal with problems and planning needs that cross the boundaries of individual local governments or that require regional attention. These concerns may include criminal justice, emergency communications, job-training programs, solid-waste management, transportation needs, and water-quality management. The councils make recommendations to member governments and may assist in implementing the plans.

The **Texas Association of Regional Councils** is at 508 W. 12th, Austin 78701; 512-478-4715; Fax: 512-463-1880. Financing is provided by the local governments, the state and the federal government.

A list of the **24 regional councils**, the **counties served** and the **executive director** as of July 1, 1999, follows:

Alamo Area Council of Governments: Counties — Atascosa, Bandera, Bexar, Comal, Frio, Gillespie, Guadalupe, Karnes, Kendall, Kerr, Medina and Wilson. Al J. Notzon III, 118 Broadway, Ste. 400, San Antonio 78205-1999.

Ark-Tex Council of Governments: Bowie, Cass, Delta, Franklin, Hopkins, Lamar, Morris, Red River, Titus, and Miller County, Ark. James C. Fisher, PO Box 5307, Texarkana, Texas 75505-5307.

Brazos Valley Council of Governments: Brazos, Burleson, Grimes, Leon, Madison, Robertson and Washington. Tom Wilkinson Jr., PO Box 4128, Bryan 77805-4128.

Capital Area Planning Council: Bastrop, Blanco, Burnet, Caldwell, Fayette, Hays, Lee, Llano, Travis and Williamson. Betty Voights, 2512 S. IH 35, Ste. 204, Austin 78704.

Central Texas Council of Governments: Bell, Coryell, Hamilton, Lampasas, Milam, Mills and San Saba. A.C. Johnson, PO Box 729, Belton 76513-0729.

Coastal Bend Council of Governments: Aransas, Bee, Brooks, Duval, Jim Wells, Kenedy, Kleberg, Live Oak, McMullen, Nueces, Refugio and San Patricio. John P. Buckner, PO Box 9909, Corpus Christi 78469-9909.

Concho Valley Council of Governments: Coke, Concho, Crockett, Irion, Kimble, Mason, McCulloch, Menard, Reagan, Schleicher, Sterling, Sutton and Tom Green. Robert R. Weaver, Box 60050, San Angelo 76906-0050.

Deep East Texas Council of Governments: Angelina, Houston, Jasper, Nacogdoches, Newton, Polk, Sabine, San Augustine, San Jacinto, Shelby, Trinity and Tyler. Walter G. Diggles, 274 E. Lamar, Jasper 75951.

East Texas Council of Governments: Anderson, Camp, Cherokee, Gregg, Harrison, Henderson, Marion, Panola, Rains, Rusk, Smith, Upshur, Van Zandt and Wood. Glynn Knight, 3800 Stone Rd., Kilgore 75662.

Golden Crescent Regional Planning Commission: Calhoun, DeWitt, Goliad, Gonzales, Jackson, Lavaca and Victoria. Patrick J. Kennedy, PO Box 2028, Victoria 77902-2028.

Heart of Texas Council of Governments: Bosque, Falls, Freestone, Hill, Limestone and McLennan. Leon A. Wilhite, 300 Franklin Ave., Waco 76701-2244.

Houston-Galveston Area Council: Austin, Brazoria, Chambers, Colorado, Fort Bend, Galveston, Harris, Liberty, Matagorda, Montgomery, Walker, Waller and Wharton. Jack Steele, PO Box 22777, Houston 77227-2777.

Lower Rio Grande Valley Development Council: Cameron, Hidalgo and Willacy. Kenneth N. Jones Jr., 311 N. 15th, McAllen 78501-4705.

Middle Rio Grande Development Council: Dimmit, Edwards, Kinney, La Salle, Maverick, Real, Uvalde, Val Verde and Zavala. Leodoro Martinez Jr., PO Box 1199, Carrizo Springs 78834-1199.

Nortex Regional Planning Commission: Archer, Baylor, Clay, Cottle, Foard, Hardeman, Jack, Montague, Wichita, Wilbarger and Young. Dennis Wilde, PO Box 5144, Wichita Falls 76307-5144.

North Central Texas Council of Governments: Collin, Dallas, Denton, Ellis, Erath, Hood, Hunt, Johnson, Kaufman, Navarro, Palo Pinto, Parker, Rockwall, Somervell, Tarrant and Wise. R. Michael Eastland, PO Box 5888, Arlington 76005-5888.

Panhandle Regional Planning Commission: Armstrong, Briscoe, Carson, Castro, Childress, Collingsworth, Dallam, Deaf Smith, Donley, Gray, Hall, Hansford, Hartley, Hemphill, Hutchinson, Lipscomb, Moore, Ochiltree, Oldham, Parmer, Potter, Randall, Roberts, Sherman, Swisher and Wheeler. Gary Pitner, PO Box 9257, Amarillo 79105-9257.

Permian Basin Regional Planning Commission: Andrews, Borden, Crane, Dawson, Ector, Gaines, Glasscock, Howard, Loving, Martin, Midland, Pecos, Reeves, Terrell, Upton, Ward and Winkler. Ernie Crawford, PO Box 60660, Midland 79711-0660.

Rio Grande Council of Governments: Brewster, Culberson, El Paso, Hudspeth, Jeff Davis, Presidio and Doña Ana Co., New Mexico. Justin R. Ormsby, 1100 N. Stanton, Ste. 610, El Paso 79902.

South East Texas Regional Planning Commission: Hardin, Jefferson and Orange. Don Kelly, PO Box 1387, Nederland 77627-1387.

South Plains Association of Governments: Bailey, Cochran, Crosby, Dickens, Floyd, Garza, Hale, Hockley, King, Lamb, Lubbock, Lynn, Motley, Terry and Yoakum. Jerry D. Casstevens, PO Box 3730, Lubbock 79452-3730.

South Texas Development Council: Jim Hogg, Starr, Webb and Zapata. Amando Garza, PO Box 2187, Laredo 78044-2187.

Texoma Council of Governments: Cooke, Fannin and Grayson. Frances Pelley, 3201 Texoma Pkwy., Ste. 200, Sherman 75090-1974.

West Central Texas Council of Governments: Brown, Callahan, Coleman, Comanche, Eastland, Fisher, Haskell, Jones, Kent, Knox, Mitchell, Nolan, Runnels, Scurry, Shackelford, Stephens, Stonewall, Taylor and Throckmorton. Brad Helbert, Box 3195, Abilene 79601. ☆

County Tax Appraisers

The following list of Chief Appraisers for Texas counties was furnished by the State Property Tax Division of the State Comptroller's office. It includes the mailing address for each appraiser and is current to March 30, 1999.

Anderson—Carson Wages, PO Box 279, Palestine 75802
Andrews—Mickey Green, 600 N. Main, Andrews 79714
Angelina—Keith Kraemer, PO Box 2357, Lufkin 75902
Aransas—Jad Smith, 601 S. Church, Rockport 78382
Archer—Edward H. Trigg III, PO Box 1141, Archer City 76351
Armstrong—Ron Patterson, Drawer 835, Claude 79019
Atascosa—Curtis Stewart, PO Box 139, Poteet 78065
Austin—Glen Whitehead, 906 E. Amelia St., Bellville 77418
Bailey—Kaye Elliott, 302 Main St., Muleshoe 79347
Bandera—P. H. Coates IV, PO Box 1119, Bandera 78003
Bastrop—Dana Ripley, Drawer 578, Bastrop 78602
Baylor—Ronnie Hargrove, 411 W. Idaho, Seymour 76380
Bee—Blaine Luthringer, PO Box 1262, Beeville 78104
Bell—Carl Moore, PO Box 390, Belton 76513
Bexar—John Gaines, PO Box 830248, San Antonio 78283
Blanco—Ms. Hollis Boatright, PO Box 338, Johnson City 78636
Borden—Royal D. Lewis, PO Box 298, Gail 79738
Bosque—F. Janice Henry, PO Box 393, Meridian 76665
Bowie—Wayne Hawkins, PO Box 6527, Texarkana 75505

Brazoria—Cheryl Evans, 500 N. Chenango, Angleton 77515
Brazos—Gerald L. Winn, 1673 Briarcrest Dr., #A-101, Bryan 77802
Brewster—Jerry Ratcliff, PO Box 1231, Alpine 79831
Briscoe—Carlye Fleming, PO Box 728, Silverton 79257
Brooks—Humberto Rivera, Drawer A, Falfurrias 78355
Brown—Doran E. Lemke, 403 Fisk, Brownwood 76801
Burleson—Elizabeth Boyd, PO Box 1000, Caldwell 77836
Burnet—Stan Hemphill, PO Box 908, Burnet 78611
Caldwell—Russell Sanders, PO Box 59, Lockhart 78644
Calhoun—Andrew J. Hahn, PO Box 48, Port Lavaca 77979
Callahan—Rodney Lewallen, PO Box 806, Baird 79504
Cameron—Mike Amezquita, PO Box 1010, San Benito 78586
Camp—Vaudeane Bennett, PO Box 739, Pittsburg 75686
Carson—Donita Davis, PO Box 970, Panhandle 79068
Cass—Ann Lummus, 502 N. Main St., Linden 75563
Castro—Jerry Heller, 204 S.E. 3rd (Rear), Dimmitt 79027
Chambers—Michael Fregia, PO Box 1520, Anahuac 77514
Cherokee—Sid R. Danner, PO Box 494, Rusk 75785

Childress—Anita Manley, PO Box 13, Childress 79201
Clay—A. G. Reis, 101 E. Omega, Henrietta 76365
Cochran—H. Loy Kern, 109 S.E. 1st, Morton 79346
Coke—Patsy N. Dunn, PO Box 2, Robert Lee 76945
Coleman—Bill W. Jones, PO Box 914, Coleman 76834
Collin—Jimmie Honea, 2404 Ave. K, Plano 75074
Collingsworth—Ann Wauer, 800 W. Ave., Rm. 104, Wellington 79095
Colorado—William T. Youens Jr., PO Box 10, Columbus 78934
Comal—Lynn E. Rodgers, PO Box 311222, New Braunfels 78131
Comanche—Rhonda Woods, PO Box 6, Comanche 76442
Concho—Eugene Dillard, PO Box 68, Paint Rock 76866
Cooke—Doug Smithson, 200 W. California, Gainesville 76240
Coryell—Darrell Lisenbe, PO Box 142, Gatesville 76528
Cottle—Rue Young, PO Box 459, Paducah 79248
Crane—Peggy Dickson, 511 W. 8th, Crane 79731
Crockett—W. Tom Stokes, Drawer H, Ozona 76943
Crosby—Darla Doss, PO Box 479, Crosbyton 79322
Culberson—Sally Carrasco, PO Box 550, Van Horn 79855
Dallam—Huie V. Stanley, PO Box 592, Dalhart 79022
Dallas—Foy Mitchell Jr., 2949 N. Stemmons Fwy., Dallas 75247
Dawson—Tom Anderson, PO Box 797, Lamesa 79331
Deaf Smith—Danny Jones, PO Box 2298, Hereford 79045
Delta—Toyce Phillips, PO Box 47, Cooper 75432
Denton—Joe Rogers, PO Box 2816, Denton 76202
DeWitt—John Haliburton, PO Box 4, Cuero 77954
Dickens—Dexter Clay, PO Box 119, Dickens 79229
Dimmit—Ricardo Martinez, 402 N. 7th, Carrizo Springs 78834
Donley—Paula Lowrie, PO Box 1220, Clarendon 79226
Duval—Ernesto Molina Jr., PO Box 809, San Diego 78384
Eastland—Steve Thomas, PO Box 914, Eastland 76448
Ector—James Goodwin, 1301 E. 8th, Odessa 79761
Edwards—Wiley Rudasill, PO Box 858, Rocksprings 78880
Ellis—Kathy Rodrigue, PO Box 878, Waxahachie 75165
El Paso—Cora Viescas, 5801 Trowbridge, El Paso 79925
Erath—Jerry Lee, PO Box 94, Stephenville 76401
Falls—Joyce Collier, Drawer 430, Marlin 76661
Fannin—Carrol Garrison, RR 4, Box 366, Bonham 75418
Fayette—Kathleen Giovannini, PO Box 836, La Grange 78945
Fisher—Betty Mize, PO Box 516, Roby 79543
Floyd—Sheila Faulkenberry, PO Box 249, Floydada 79235
Foard—Jo Ann Vecera, PO Box 419, Crowell 79227
Fort Bend—Gene Brewer, 2801 B.F. Terry Blvd., Rosenberg 77471
Franklin—Mike McKibben, PO Box 720, Mount Vernon 75457
Freestone—Bud Black, 218 N. Mount, Fairfield 75840
Frio—Irma Gonzalez, PO Box 1129, Pearsall 78061
Gaines—Betty Caudle, PO Box 490, Seminole 79360
Galveston—Ken Wright, PO Box 3647, Texas City 77592
Garza—Billie Windham, Drawer F, Post 79356
Gillespie—Bob Drury, PO Box 429, Fredericksburg 78624
Glasscock—Royce Pruit, PO Box 89, Garden City 79739
Goliad—E. J. Bammert, PO Box 34, Goliad 77963
Gonzales—Glenda Strackbein, PO Box 867, Gonzales 78629
Gray—W. Pat Bagley, PO Box 836, Pampa 79066
Grayson—Larry Ward, 205 N. Travis, Sherman 75090
Gregg—Marvin Hahn, 1333 Harrison Rd., Longview 75604
Grimes—Bill Sullivan, PO Box 489, Anderson 77830
Guadalupe—Pat Fox, 3000 N. Austin, Seguin 78155
Hale—Linda Jaynes, PO Box 29, Plainview 79073
Hall—Paullette Lipscomb, 721 Robertson, Memphis 79245
Hamilton—Doyle Roberts, 119 E. Henry, Hamilton 76531
Hansford—Alice Peddy, PO Box 519, Spearman 79081
Hardeman—Twila Butler, PO Box 388, Quanah 79252
Hardin—Amador Reyna, PO Box 670, Kountze 77625
Harris—Jim Robinson, PO Box 920975, Houston 77292
Harrison—David Whitmire, PO Box 818, Marshall 75671
Hartley—Donna Bryant, PO Box 405, Hartley 79044
Haskell—Kenny Watson, PO Box 467, Haskell 79521
Hays—Pete Islas, 21001 N. IH-35, Kyle 78640
Hemphill—William D. Lanier, PO Box 65, Canadian 79014
Henderson—Bill Jackson, PO Box 430, Athens 75751
Hidalgo—Daniel Boone, PO Box 632, Pharr 78577
Hill—Shirley Holub, PO Box 416, Hillsboro 76645
Hockley—Nick Williams, PO Box 1090, Levelland 79336
Hood—Jeff Law, PO Box 819, Granbury 76048
Hopkins—William Sherman, 109 College St., Sulphur Springs 75482
Houston—Kathryn Keith, PO Box 112, Crockett 75835
Howard—Keith Toomire, PO Box 1151, Big Spring 79721
Hudspeth—Zedoch L. Pridgeon, Box 429, Sierra Blanca 79851
Hunt—Mildred Compton, PO Box 1339, Greenville 75403
Hutchinson—George Nies, PO Box 5065, Borger 79008
Irion—Frances Grice, PO Box 980, Mertzon 76941
Jack—Gary Zeitler, PO Box 958, Jacksboro 76458
Jackson—Tommy Watson, 411 N. Wells, Rm. 109, Edna 77957
Jasper—David Luther, PO Box 1300, Jasper 75951
Jeff Davis—Zedoch L. Pridgeon, PO Box 373, Fort Davis 79734

Jefferson—Roland Bieber, PO Box 21337, Beaumont 77720
Jim Hogg—Arnoldo Gonzalez, PO Box 459, Hebbronville 78361
Jim Wells—Sidney Vela, PO Box 607, Alice 78333
Johnson—Don Gilmore, 109 N. Main, Cleburne 76031
Jones—Susan Holloway, PO Box 348, Anson 79501
Karnes—Oscar Caballero, 915 S. Panna Maria, Karnes City 78118
Kaufman—Jackie Self, PO Box 819, Kaufman 75142
Kendall—Leta Schlinke, PO Box 788, Boerne 78006
Kenedy—Clyde Hamilton Jr., PO Box 705, Bastrop 78602
Kent—Garth Gregory, PO Box 68, Jayton 79528
Kerr—David Oehler, PO Box 1885, Kerrville 78029
Kimble—Elaine Chaney, PO Box 307, Junction 76849
King—Sandy Burkett, PO Box 117, Guthrie 79236
Kinney—Joyce Fuentes, PO Box 1377, Brackettville 78832
Kleberg—Tina Flores, PO Box 1027, Kingsville 78364
Knox—Stanton Brown, PO Box 47, Benjamin 79505
Lamar—Cathy Jackson, PO Box 400, Paris 75461
Lamb—Vaughn McKee, PO Box 950, Littlefield 79339
Lampasas—Glenda Jackson (acting), Box 175, Lampasas 76550
La Salle—Joe R. Lozano, Drawer O, Cotulla 78014
Lavaca—Diane Munson, PO Box 386, Hallettsville 77964
Lee—Roy Holcomb, 218 E. Richmond, Giddings 78942
Leon—Jeff Beshears, PO Box 536, Centerville 75833
Liberty—Alan Conner, PO Box 10016, Liberty 77575
Limestone—Karen Wietzikoski, Drawer 831, Groesbeck 76642
Lipscomb—Jerry Reynolds, PO Box 128, Darrouzett 79024
Live Oak—Robert Dirks, PO Box MM, George West 78022
Llano—Gary Eldridge, 103 E. Sandstone, Llano 78643
Loving—J. W. Busby, PO Box 352, Mentone 79754
Lubbock—Dave Kimbrough, PO Box 10542, Lubbock 79408
Lynn—Marquita Scott, PO Box 789, Tahoka 79373
Madison—Larry Krumnow, PO Box 1328, Madisonville 77864
Marion—Brenda Vail, PO Box 690, Jefferson 75657
Martin—Delbert Dickinson, PO Box 1349, Stanton 79782
Mason—Deborah Geistweidt, Drawer 1119, Mason 76856
Matagorda—Vince Maloney, PO Box 179, Bay City 77404
Maverick—Victor Perry, PO Box 2628, Eagle Pass 78853
McCulloch—Orlando Rubio, 104 N. College, Brady 76825
McLennan—Charles Gauer, PO Box 2297, Waco 76703
McMullen—Jesse Bryan, PO Box 38, Tilden 78072
Medina—James Garcia, 1410 Ave. K, Hondo 78861
Menard—Judy Cavnar, PO Box 1058, Menard 76859
Midland—Ron Stegall, PO Box 908002, Midland 79708
Milam—Patricia Moraw, PO Box 769, Cameron 76520
Mills—Keryn McMahan, PO Box 565, Goldthwaite 76844
Mitchell—Kaye Cornutt, PO Box 358, Colorado City 79512
Montague—June Deaton, PO Box 121, Montague 76251
Montgomery—Jimmy Foreman, PO Box 2233, Conroe 77305
Moore—Joyce Cearley, PO Box 717, Dumas 79029
Morris—Rhonda Hall, PO Box 563, Daingerfield 75638
Motley—Brenda Osborn, PO Box 779, Matador 79244
Nacogdoches—Gary Woods, 216 W. Hospital, Nacogdoches 75961
Navarro—Bill Worthen, PO Box 3118, Corsicana 75151
Newton—Margie Herrin, Drawer X, Newton 75966
Nolan—Patricia Davis, PO Box 1256, Sweetwater 79556
Nueces—George Moff, 201 N. Chaparral, Corpus Christi 78401
Ochiltree—Terry Symons, 825 S. Main, #100, Perryton 79070
Oldham—Jen Carter, Drawer 310, Vega 79092
Orange—Ms. Pat Sanderson, PO Box 457, Orange 77630
Palo Pinto—Carol Holmes, PO Box 250, Palo Pinto 76484
Panola—Louis Wall, 2 Ball Park Rd., Carthage 75633
Parker—Larry Hammonds, 118 W. Columbia, Weatherford 76086
Parmer—Ron Proctor, PO Box 56, Bovina 79009
Pecos—Ann Stapp, PO Box 237, Fort Stockton 79735
Polk—Clyde Arrendell, 312 N. Washington, Livingston 77351
Potter—Jim Childers, PO Box 7190, Amarillo 79114
Presidio—Irma Salgado, PO Box 879, Marfa 79843
Rains—Linda Norell, PO Box 70, Emory 75440
Randall—Jim Childers, PO Box 7190, Amarillo 79114
Reagan—Byron Bitner, PO Box 8, Big Lake 76932
Real—Amelia Stayton, PO Box 158, Leakey 78873
Red River—Jan Raulston, PO Box 461, Clarksville 75426
Reeves—Carol King Markham, PO Box 1229, Pecos 79772
Refugio—Bettye Kret, PO Box 156, Refugio 78377
Roberts—Carol Johnson, PO Box 458, Miami 79059
Robertson—Dan Brewer, PO Box 998, Franklin 77856
Rockwall—Ray Helm, 841 Justin Rd., Rockwall 75087
Runnels—Tylene Gamble, PO Box 524, Ballinger 76821
Rusk—Terry Decker, PO Box 7, Henderson 75653
Sabine—Jim Nethery, PO Box 137, Hemphill 75948
San Augustine—Jamie Doherty, 122 N. Harrison, San Augustine 75972
San Jacinto—Mac Ridley, PO Box 1170, Coldspring 77331
San Patricio—Kathryn Vermillion, PO Box 938, Sinton 78387
San Saba—Henry J. Warren, 423 E. Wallace, San Saba 76877
Schleicher—Ray Ballew, PO Box 936, Eldorado 76936

Scurry—Larry Crook, 2612 College Ave., Snyder 79549
Shackelford—Bruce Bailey, PO Box 565, Albany 76430
Shelby—Robert Pigg, 724 Shelbyville St., Center 75935
Sherman—Teresa Edmond, PO Box 239, Stratford 79084
Smith—Michael Barnett, 245 South S.E. Loop 323, Tyler 75702
Somervell—Jim Yeats, 112 Allen Dr., Glen Rose 76043
Starr—Humberto Saenz Jr., PO Box 137, Rio Grande City 78582
Stephens—Troy Sloan, PO Box 351, Breckenridge 76424
Sterling—Linda Low, PO Box 28, Sterling City 76951
Stonewall—Ozella E. Warner, PO Box 308, Aspermont 79502
Sutton—Rex Ann Friess, 300 E. Oak, Sonora 76950
Swisher—Rose Lee Powell, PO Box 8, Tulia 79088
Tarrant—John Marshall, 2500 Handley-Ederville Rd., Fort Worth 76118
Taylor—Richard Petree, PO Box 1800, Abilene 79604
Terrell—Blain Chriesman, PO Box 747, Sanderson 79848
Terry—Ronny Burran, PO Box 426, Brownfield 79316
Throckmorton—Linda Carrington, Box 788, Throckmorton 76483
Titus—Katrina Perry, PO Box 528, Mount Pleasant 75456
Tom Green—Elvin Field, PO Box 3307, San Angelo 76902
Travis—Art Cory, PO Box 149012, Austin 78714
Trinity—Allen McKinley, PO Box 950, Groveton 75845
Tyler—Travis Chalmers, Drawer 9, Woodville 75979
Upshur—Louise Stracener, PO Box 280, Gilmer 75644

Upton—Sheri Stephens, PO Box 1110, McCamey 79752
Uvalde—Rufino H. Lozano, 209 N. High, Uvalde 78801
Val Verde—Buster Vernor, PO Box 1059, Del Rio 78841
Van Zandt—Chris Becker, PO Box 926, Canton 75103
Victoria—Terry Turner, 1611 E. North, Victoria 77901
Walker—Grover Cook, PO Box 1798, Huntsville 77342
Waller—David Piwonka, PO Box 159, Katy 77492
Ward—Arlice Wittie, PO Box 905, Monahans 79756
Washington—Charles Gaskamp, PO Box 681, Brenham 77834
Webb—Sergio Delgado, PO Box 719, Laredo 78042
Wharton—Larry Holub, PO Box 1068, Wharton 77488
Wheeler—Larry Schoenhals, PO Box 1200, Wheeler 79096
Wichita—Lanier Wilson, PO Box 5172, Wichita Falls 76307
Wilbarger—Doyle Graham, PO Box 1519, Vernon 76384
Willacy—Augustin Colchado, Rt. 2, Box 256, Raymondville 78580
Williamson—Bill Carroll, PO Box 1120, Georgetown 78627
Wilson—Carlton R. Pape, Box 849, Floresville 78114
Winkler—Helen Oldham, PO Box 1219, Kermit 79745
Wise—Mickey Hand, 206 S. State, Decatur 76234
Wood—Lois McKibben, PO Box 518, Quitman 75783
Yoakum—Saundra Stephens, PO Box 748, Plains 79355
Young—Pat Butler, PO Box 337, Graham 76450
Zapata—Rosalva Guerra, PO Box 2315, Zapata 78076
Zavala—Alberto Mireles, 323 W. Zavala, Crystal City 78839 ☆

Wet-Dry Counties

COUNTIES:
Wet/Dry
as to alcohol

■ Wet
▨ Wine/Beer
▧ Parts wet
▨ Beer only
☐ Dry

When approved in local-option elections in "wet" precincts of counties, sale of **liquor by the drink** is permitted in Texas. This resulted from adoption of an amendment to the Texas Constitution in 1970 and subsequent legislation, followed by local-option elections. This amendment marked the first time in 50 years that the sale of liquor by the drink was legal in Texas.

The list below shows the wet-or-dry status of counties in Texas as of Aug 31, 1997. A dagger (†) indicates counties in which the sale of mixed beverages is legal in all or part of the county (97). An asterisk (*) indicates counties wholly wet (37). All others are dry in part (79).

Counties in Which Distilled Spirits Are Legal (185): Anderson, †*Aransas, Archer, Atascosa, †*Austin, †Bandera, †*Bastrop, †*Bee, †Bell, †*Bexar, †Blanco, †Bosque, †Brazoria, †*Brazos, †*Brewster, Brooks, Brown, Burleson, †Burnet, †Calhoun, Callahan, †*Cameron, †Camp, Carson, Cass, Castro, Chambers, Childress, Clay, Coleman, Collin, †*Colorado, †*Comal, Comanche, Cooke, Coryell, Crane, *Crockett, *Culberson, Dallam, †Dallas, †Dawson, Deaf Smith, †Denton, †DeWitt, Dickens, †Dimmit, †Donley, †Duval, Eastland, †Ector, Edwards, Ellis, †*El Paso, †Falls, Fannin, Fayette, †*Fort Bend, †Frio, †Galveston, †Garza, †Gillespie, †Goliad, Gonzales, Gray, Grayson, Gregg, †Grimes, †Guadalupe, Hall, Hamilton, Hardin, †Harris, Harrison, Haskell, †Hays, †Henderson, †*Hidalgo, †Hill, †Hockley, Hood, †Howard, †*Hudspeth, Hunt, Hutchinson, Jack, †Jackson, †Jasper, Jeff Davis.

Also †Jefferson, †*Jim Hogg, †Jim Wells, *Karnes, Kaufman, †*Kendall, Kenedy, †Kerr, Kimble, King, †*Kinney, †Kleberg, †Lamar, Lampasas, †La Salle, †Lavaca, †Lee, Leon, Liberty, Lipscomb, Live Oak, †Llano, †*Loving, †Lubbock, Marion, †Matagorda, †Maverick, †McCulloch, †McLennan, †Medina, Menard, †Midland, Milam, Mills, Mitchell, Montague, †Montgomery, †*Moore, Nacogdoches, †Navarro, Newton, Nolan, †Nueces.

Also, †Orange, Palo Pinto, Parker, Pecos, †Polk, †Potter, †*Presidio, Rains, †Randall, *Reagan, Red River, †Reeves, Refugio, Robertson, †Rockwall, Runnels, San Augustine, San Jacinto, †San Patricio, San Saba, †Schleicher, Shackelford, Shelby, †*Starr, Stonewall, †*Sutton, †Tarrant, †Taylor, *Terrell, †Titus, †Tom Green, †*Travis, *Trinity, Upshur, *Upton, Uvalde, †Val Verde, †Victoria,

†Walker, †Waller, Ward, †*Washington, †*Webb, †Wharton, †Wichita, Wilbarger, †Willacy, †Williamson, †*Wilson, *Winkler, Young, †*Zapata, †Zavala.

Counties in Which Only 4 Percent Beer Is Legal (11): Baylor, Caldwell, Cherokee, Concho, Hartley, Irion, Mason, McMullen, Oldham, Sabine, Stephens.

Counties in Which 14 Percent or Less Alcoholic Beverages Are Legal (5): Glasscock, Johnson, Limestone, Somervell, Wise.

Counties Wholly Dry (53): Andrews, Angelina, Armstrong, Bailey, Borden, Bowie, Briscoe, Cochran, Coke, Collingsworth, Cottle, Crosby, Delta, Erath, Fisher, Floyd, Foard, Franklin, Freestone, Gaines, Hale, Hansford, Hardeman, Hemphill, Hopkins, Houston, Jones, Kent, Knox, Lamb, Lynn, Madison, Martin, Morris, Motley, Ochiltree, Panola, Parmer, Real, Roberts, Rusk, Scurry, Sherman, Smith, Sterling, Swisher, Terry, Throckmorton, Tyler, Van Zandt, Wheeler, Wood, Yoakum. ☆

County Courts

Below are listed county courts, including county courts at law, probate courts, juvenile/domestic relations courts, criminal courts and criminal courts of appeals as reported by the county clerks as of April 1999. Other courts with jurisdiction in each county can be found in the list on pages 439-440. Other county and district officials can be found on pages 479-489.

Anderson County Court at Law: J. Christopher Kolstad.

Angelina County Courts at Law: No. 1, Lisa G. Burkhalter; No. 2, Holly K. Perkins-Meyers.

Austin County Court at Law: Gladys M. Oakley.

Bastrop County Court at Law: M. Benton Eskew.

Bell County Courts at Law: No. 1, Edward S. Johnson; No. 2, H. John Barina Jr.; No. 3, Gerald M. Brown.

Bexar County Courts at Law: No. 1, Alfonso E. Alonso Jr.; No. 2, Paul Canales; No. 3, S. (Shay) Gebhardt; No. 4, Sarah Garrahan Moulder; No. 5, Timothy F. Johnson; No. 6, M'Liss Christian; No. 7, Bill C. White; No. 8, Karen Crouch; No. 9, Wayne A. Christian II. **County Probate Courts:** No. 1, Polly Jackson Spencer; No. 2, Sandee B. Marion.

Brazoria County Courts at Law: No. 1, Jerri Lee Mills; No. 2, Patrick Edward Sebesta; No. 3, James A. Blackstock.

Brazos County Courts at Law: No. 1, Randy Michel; No. 2, Richard W.B. Davis.

Caldwell County Court at Law: Edward L. Jarrett.

Calhoun County Court at Law: Alex R. Hernandez.

Cameron County Courts at Law: No. 1, Janet Leal; No. 2, Elia Cornejo-Lopez; No. 3, Daniel T. Robles.

Cherokee County Court at Law: A. LeRue Dixon III

Collin County Courts at Law: No. 1, Weldon Copeland; No. 2, Jerry Lewis; No. 3, John O'Keefe Barry; No. 4, Mark Rusch.

Comal County Court at Law: Brenda Borchers Freeman.

Coryell County Court at Law: Susan R. Stephens.

Dallas County Courts at Law: No. 1, David R. Gibson; No. 2, Carlos Lopez; No. 3, Robert C. Jenevein; No. 4, W. Bruce Woody; No. 5, Charles Stokes. **County Criminal Courts:** No. 1, Danny Clancy; No. 2, Jim Pruitt; No. 3, Dan Wyde; No. 4, Ralph Taite; No. 5, Tom Fuller; No. 6, Phil Barker; No. 7, Elizabeth H. Crowder; No. 8, Vickers L. Cunningham Sr.; No. 9, Keith Anderson; No. 10, David Finn. **County Probate Courts:** No. 1, Nikki DeShazo; No. 2, Robert E. Price; No. 3, Joe Hilton Loving Jr. **County Criminal Courts of Appeals:** No. 1, Kristin Wade; No. 2, Lynn Burson.

Denton County Courts at Law: No. 1, Darlene Whitten. **County Criminal Courts:** No. 1, Jim E. Crouch; No. 2, Virgil Vahlenkamp; No. 3, David Garcia; No. 4, Joe Bridges. **Probate Court:** Don R. Windle.

Ector County Courts at Law: No. 1, James Arnette Bobo; No. 2, Mark D. Owens.

Ellis County Court at Law: Bob Carroll.

El Paso County Courts at Law: No. 1, Ricardo Herrera; No. 2, Julie Gonzalez; No. 3, Javier Alvarez; No. 4, Alejandro Gonzalez; No. 5, Herbert Cooper; No. 6, M. Sue Kurita; No. 7, Peter S. Peca Jr. **County Probate Court:** Max D. Higgs. **Domestic Relations/Juvenile Court:** Phil Martinez.

Erath County Court at Law: Ernest Bart McDougal.

Fort Bend County Courts at Law: No. 1, Larry D. Wagenbach; No. 2, Walter S. McMeans; No. 3, Susan G. Lowery.

Galveston County Courts at Law: No. 1, Mary Nell Crapitto; No. 2, C.G. (Trey) Dibrell III; **County Probate Court:** Gladys B. Burwell.

Grayson County Courts at Law: No. 1, Donald L. Jarvis; No. 2, Carol M. Siebman.

Gregg County Court at Law: Rebecca Lynn Simpson.

Guadalupe County Court at Law: Linda Z. Jones.

Harris County Courts at Law: No. 1, Eugene Chambers; No. 2, Gary Michael Block; No. 3, Lynn Bradshaw-Hull; No. 4, Cynthia Marie Crowe. **County Criminal Courts at Law:** No. 1, Reagan Helm; No. 2, Michael Peters; No. 3, Donald Wayne Jackson; No. 4, James E. Anderson; No. 5, Janice Law; No. 6, Larry Standley; No. 7, Pam Derbyshire; No. 8, Neel Richardson; No. 9, Analia H. Wilkerson; No. 10, Sherman A. Ross; No. 11, Diane Bull; No. 12, Jo Robin Brown; No. 13, Mark Atkinson; No. 14, Michael R. Fields; No. 15, Jean Spradling Hughes. **County Probate Courts:** No. 1, Russell Parker Austin; No. 2, Mike Wood; No. 3, Rory R. Olsen; No. 4, William C. McCulloch.

Harrison County Court at Law: Jim Ammerman II.

Hays County Courts at Law: No. 1, Howard S. Warner II; No. 2, Linda Ann Rodriguez.

Henderson County Court at Law: D. Matt Livingston.

Hidalgo County Courts at Law: No. 1, Rodolfo (Rudy) Delgado; No. 2, G. Jaime Garza; No. 3, Homero Garza; No. 4, Federico (Fred) Garza.

Hopkins County Court at Law: Amy Smith.

Houston County Court at Law: Sarah Tunnell Clark.

Hunt County Court at Law: Steve H. Shipp.

Jefferson County Courts at Law: No. 1, Alfred S. Gerson; No. 2, Harold Plessala; No. 3, John Paul Davis.

Johnson County Courts at Law: No. 1, Robert B. Mayfield III; No. 2, William Roy Anderson Jr.

Kaufman County Court at Law: Joe Michael Parnell.

Kerr County Court at Law: Spencer W. Brown.

Kleberg County Court at Law: Martin J. Chiuminatto Jr.

Lamar County Court at Law: Deane Loughmiller

Liberty County Court at Law: Don Taylor.

Lubbock County Courts at Law: No. 1, Susan Scolaro; No. 2, Drue Farmer; No. 3, Paula Davis Lanehart.

McLennan County Courts at Law: No. 1, David L. Hodges; No. 2, Michael Brandon Gassaway

Medina County Court at Law: Watt Murrah.

Midland County Courts at Law: No. 1, Al Walvoord Jr.; No. 2, Marvin Lee Moore.

Montgomery County Courts at Law: No. 1, Dennis Watson; No. 2, Jerry Winfree; No. 3, E. Mason Martin II.

Moore County Court at Law: Delwin T. McGee.

Nacogdoches County Court at Law: J. Jack Yarbrough.

Nolan County Court at Law: Glen N. Harrison.

Nueces County Courts at Law: No. 1, Robert J. Vargas; No. 2, Hector de Peña Jr.; No. 3, Marisela Saldaña; No. 4, James Klager.

Orange County Court at Law: Michael W. Shuff.

Panola County Court at Law: Terry D. Bailey.

Parker County Court at Law: Graham Quisenberry.

Polk County Court at Law: Stephen Phillips.

Potter County Courts at Law: No. 1, W. F. (Corky) Roberts; No. 2, Pamela Cook Sirmon.

Randall County Court at Law: John J. Thorpe.

Reeves County Court at Law: Lee S. Green.

Rusk County Court at Law: Darrell Hyatt.

San Patricio County Court at Law: Michael Everett Welborn.

Smith County Courts at Law: No. 1, Thomas A. Dunn; No. 2, Randall Lee Rogers; No. 3, Floyd T. Gertz.

Starr County Court at Law: Jesús M. Alvarez.

Tarrant County Courts at Law: No. 1, R. Brent Keis; No. 2, Steve Wallace; No. 3, Vincent G. Sprinkle. **County Criminal Courts at Law:** No. 1, Sherry Hill; No. 2, Michael Mitchell; No. 3, Billy D. Mills; No. 4, Wallace Bowman; No. 5, Jamie Cummings; No. 6, Molly Jones; No. 7, Cheril Hardy; No. 8, Daryl Coffee; No. 9, Brent Carr; No. 10, Phil Sorrels. **Probate Courts:** No. 1, Steve M. King; No. 2, Patrick W. Ferchill.

Taylor County Courts at Law: No. 1, Jack R. Grant; No. 2, Barbara B. Rollins.

Tom Green County Court at Law: No. 1, David B. Read; No. 2, Penny Ann Roberts.

Travis County Courts at Law: No. 1, J. David Phillips; No. 2, Orlinda L. Naranjo; No. 3, David Fischer Crain; No. 5, Wilfred R. Aguilar; No. 6, Jan Breland; No. 7, Brenda P. Kennedy. **Probate Court:** Guy Herman.

Val Verde County Court at Law: Sergio J. Gonzalez.

Victoria County Courts at Law: No. 1, Laura A. Weiser; No. 2, Juan Velasquez II.

Walker County Court at Law: Barbara Wade Hale.

Waller County Court at Law: June Jackson.

Washington County Court at Law: Matthew A. Reue.

Webb County Courts at Law: No. 1, Alvino (Ben) Morales; No. 2, Jesús Garza.

Wichita County Courts at Law: No. 1, Jim Hogan; No. 2, Tom H. Bacus.

Williamson County Courts at Law: No. 1, Kevin D. Henderson; No. 2, Robert (Skip) Morse.

Wise County Court at Law: Melton D. Cude. ☆

Source: Texas Judicial System Directory, 1999, Office of Court Administration.

Texas County and District Officials — Table No. 1

County Seats, County Judges, County Clerks, County Attorneys, County Treasurers, Tax Assessors-Collectors and Sheriffs.

See Table No. 2 on pages following this table for District Clerks, District Attorneys and County Commissioners. Judges in county courts at law, as well as probate courts, county criminal courts and county criminal courts of appeal, can be found on page 478. The officials listed here are elected by popular vote. Names preceded by an asterisk (*) were not furnished to us by the county clerk; the name here is from most recent unofficial sources available to us.

County	County Seat	County Judge	County Clerk	County Attorney	County Treasurer	Assessor-Collector	Sheriff
Anderson	Palestine	Carey G. McKinney	Lena Smith	Douglas E. Lowe	Sharon Peterson	Connie Rose	John E. Hobson
Andrews	Andrews	Gary W. Gaston	F. Wm. Hoermann	Katrina Jackson	Office abolished 11-5-85.	Royce Underwood	Wayne Farmer
Angelina	Lufkin	Joe Berry	JoAnn Chastain	Ed Jones	JoAnn Denby	Bill Shanklin	Kent Henson
Aransas	Rockport	William Adams	Peggy L. Friebele	James L. Anderson	Marvine D. Wix	Jeri D. Cox	David L. Petrusaitis
Archer	Archer City	Paul O. Wylie Jr.	Jane Ham	R.B. Morris	Vicky Lear	Teresa Martin	Melvin Brown
Armstrong	Claude	Hugh Reed	Joe Reck		Ray C. Minkley	Ronald Patterson	Carmella Jones
Atascosa	Jourdanton	Deborah Herber	Laquita Hayden	R. Thomas Franklin	Lisa Royal	Barbara Schorsch	Tommy Williams
Austin	Bellville	Carolyn Bilski	Carrie Gregor		Betty Krueger	Joyce Kokemor	Dwayne Burger
Bailey	Muleshoe	Marilyn Cox	Sherri Harrison	Carrissa A. Cleavinger	Donna Kirk	Kathleen Hayes	Coy Plott
Bandera	Bandera	Richard A. Evans	Bernice Bates	Kerry Schneider	Kay Welch	Jean Stevens	James MacMillan
Bastrop	Bastrop	Ronnie McDonald	Shirley Wilhelm		Bobbie Gilmore	Barbara Brinkmeyer	Richard Hernandez
Baylor	Seymour	Robin Smajstrla	Doris Rushing	Lee Price Fermon	Melinda Kinnibrugh	Janette Holub	Luke Griffin
Bee	Beeville	José Luis Aliseda	Julia V. Torres	Michael J. Knight	Office abolished 11-2-82.	Andrea W. Gibbud	Robert L. Horn
Bell	Belton	Jon H. Burrows	Vada Sutton	Rick Miller	Charles E. Jones	Janelle Burson	Dan Smith
Bexar	San Antonio	Cyndi Taylor Krier	Gerry C. Rickhoff		Office abolished 11-6-84.	Sylvia S. Romo	Ralph Lopez
Blanco	Johnson City	George E. Byars Jr.	Dorothy Uecker	Dean C. Myane	Robin Hildebrandt	Hollis Boatright	William R. "Bill" Elsbury
Borden	Gail	Van Lee York	Joyce Herridge		Kenneth P. Bennett	Royale D. Lewis	Royale D. Lewis
Bosque	Meridian	Bobby Conrad	Brigitte Bronstad	Patricia Ferguson	Randy Pullin	Denise Wallace	Tim Gage
Bowie	Boston	James M. Carlow	Velma Moore		Pansy Baird	Toni Barron	Mary Choate
Brazoria	Angleton	John Willy	Joyce Hudman		Barbara S. Lorraine	Ray M. Cornett	E. J. "Joe" King
Brazos	Bryan	Al Jones	Mary Ann Ward	Jim Kuboviak	Kay Hamilton	Gerald "Buddy" Winn	Chris Kirk
Brewster	Alpine	Val C. Beard	Berta R. Martinez	Steve Houston	Hortencia L. Ramos	Jerry Ratcliff	Steve Whitley
Briscoe	Silverton	Ted Kingery	Bena Hester	William P. Smith	Mary Jo Brannon	Betty Stephens	Max Whitworth
Brooks	Falfurrias	Homer Mora	Pepe Garza	David T. Garcia	Gilberto Vela	Balde Lozano	Balde Lozano
Brown	Brownwood	E. Ray West III	Margaret Wood		Judy Stirman	Linda Lewis-Parker	Glen Smith
Burleson	Caldwell	Bob Doonan	Anna L. Schielack	Joseph J. Skrivanek III	Beth Andrews Bills	Sandra Faust	Thomas E. Barber
Burnet	Burnet	Martin McLean	Janet Parker	Robert Klaeger	Donna K. Klaeger	Sherri Frazier	Joe Pollock
Caldwell	Lockhart	H.T. Wright	Nina S. Sells		Amelia G. Rizzuto	Mary Smith	Mike Bading
Calhoun	Port Lavaca	Arlene N. Marshall	Marlene Paul		Sharron Marek	Annette Baker	B.B. Browning
Callahan	Baird	Roger Corn	Jeanie Bohannon	Allen Wright	Dianne Alexander	Bun Barry	Eddie Curtis
Cameron	Brownsville	Gilberto Hinojosa	Joe G. Rivera	Douglas C. Wright	Eddie A. Gonzalez	Tony Yzaguirre Jr.	Omar Lucio
Camp	Pittsburg	Preston Combest	Elaine Young	James W. Wallace	Pam Nelson	Brenda Irby	Alan McCandless
Carson	Panhandle	Lewis Powers	Sonya Millican	Scott Sherwood	Jeannie Cunningham	Barbara Cosper	Loren Brand
Cass	Linden	Charles L. McMichael	Jannis Mitchell		Martha Sheridan	Bobbie Derrick	Paul Boone
Castro	Dimmitt	Irene Miller	Joyce M. Thomas	Jerry Matthews	Janice Shelton	Billy Hackleman	C. D. Fitzgearld
Chambers	Anahuac	Jimmy Sylvia	Norma (Beanie) Rowland	Charles Brack	Carren Sparks	Margie J. Henry	Phil Burkhalter
Cherokee	Rusk	Harry G. Tilley	Laverne Lusk	Robert R. McNatt	Diann Norton	Linda Beard	James Campbell
Childress	Childress	Gene Currie	Zona Prince	Greg Buckley	Elizabeth Kitchens	Juanell Halford	Kevin Overstreet
Clay	Henrietta	Kenneth Liggett	Kay Hutchison	Eddy Atkins	Sue Sims Brock	Linda Overstreet	Paul Bevering
Cochran	Morton	James St. Clair	Rita Tyson	J. C. Adams Jr.	Jean Abbe	Betty J. Akin	Wallace Stalcup
Coke	Robert Lee	Jackie Walker	Mary Grim	Lane Arthur	Phelan Wrinkle	D. Kristeen Roe	Rick Styles
Coleman	Coleman	Sherrill Radsdale	JoAnn Hale	Joe Dan LeMay	Kay LeMay	Donna Seymore	Wade Turner
Collin	McKinney	Ron Harris	Helen Starnes		Office abolished 11-5-85.	Kenneth Maun	Terry Box
Collingsworth	Wellington	Jim Forrester	Jackie Johnson	Charles W. Darter	Yvonne Brewer	Rosemary Throne	Dale Tarver
Colorado	Columbus	Al G. Jamison	Darlene Hayek	John (Julian) Moore	Joyce Stancik	Mary Jane Poenitzsch	R.H. "Curley" Wied
Comal	New Braunfels	Danny Scheel	Joy Streater		Bart Bartholomew	Gloria Clennan	Bob Holder
Comanche	Comanche	James R. Arthur	Betty Conway	Charles B. Williams	Billy Ruth Rust	Gay Horton	Billy J. Works

County	County Seat	County Judge	County Clerk	County Attorney	County Treasurer	Assessor-Collector	Sheriff
Concho	Paint Rock	Allen Amos	Barbara K. Hoffman	Bill Campbell	Lisa J. Jost	William J. Fiveash	William J. Fiveash
Cooke	Gainesville	Belvin R. Harris	Evelyn Walterscheid	Tanya Davis	Judy Hunter	Billy Jean Knight	Mike Compton
Coryell	Gatesville	John Hull	Barbara Simpson	Edwin Powell Jr.	Donna Medford	Barbara McKamie	Gerald Kitchens
Cottle	Paducah	John D. Shaver	Beckey J. Tucker	John H. Richards	Atha Prater	Rue Young	Roy LeHew
Crane	Crane	Charles Blue	Judy Crawford	James McDonald	Gayla Phillips	Becky Gonzales	Danny Simmons
Crockett	Ozona	Jeffrey Sutton	Debbi Puckett-Moore	William S. Mason	Burl Myers	Tommy Stokes	Shane Fenton
Crosby	Crosbyton	Kenneth Witt	Betty J. Pierce	C. Michael Ward	Debra Riley	Anna Rodriguez	Lavoice "Red" Riley
Culberson	Van Horn	John Conoly	Linda McDonald	Stephen L. Mitchell	Norma Hernandez	Amalia "Molly" Hernandez	Glenn A. Humphries
Dallam	Dalhart	David D. Field	LuAnn Taylor	Greg Oelke	Wes Ritchey	Patricia Radford	E. H. Little
Dallas	Dallas	Lee Jackson	Earl Bullock		Bill Melton	David Childs	Jim Bowles
Dawson	Lamesa	Charles C. Arthur	Gloria Vera	Steven B. Payson	Gene DeFee	Diane Hogg	J. Terry Brown
Deaf Smith	Hereford	Tom Simons	David Ruland		Nan Rogers	Margaret del Toro	Joe C. Brown Jr.
Delta	Cooper	Hugh C. Whitney	Martha Jo Loder	Frank D. Moore	Glynana Herin	Dawn Curtis	Benny Fisher
Denton	Denton	Jeff Moseley	Cynthia Mitchell		Cindy Yeatts Brown	Mary Horn	Weldon Lucas
DeWitt	Cuero	Ben E. Prause	Elva Petersen	Raymond H. Reese	Peggy Ledbetter	Susie Dreyer	Cliff G. Foulds Jr.
Dickens	Dickens	Woodie McArthur Jr.	Winona Humphreys	Robert Heald	Druline Rape	Dexter Clay	Kenneth Brendle
Dimmit	Carrizo Springs	Charles D. Johnson	Mario Zuvia Garcia	James B. Davis	Elisa G. Duran	Esther Z. Perez	Candido R. DeAnda Jr.
Donley	Clarendon	Jack Hall	Fay Vargas	Stuart Messer (pro tem)	Rebecca Jackson	Wilma Lindley	William J. Thompson
Duval	San Diego	Edmundo B. Garcia Jr.	Oscar Garcia Jr.	José Ramón Falcon	Daniel S. Lopez Jr.	Zaragosa Gutierrez III	Santiago Barrera Jr.
Eastland	Eastland	Brad Stephenson	Cathy Jentho		Marti Heyser	Sandra Cagle	Wayne Bradford
Ector	Odessa	Jerry D. Caddel	Barbara Bedford	Tracey Bright	Carolyn Sue Bowen	Lea Taylor	Reggie Yearwood
Edwards	Rocksprings	Nick Gallegos	Sarah McNealy	Allen Ray Moody	Lupe S. Enriquez	Wiley Rudasill	Don G. Letsinger
Ellis	Waxahachie	Al Cornelius	Cindy Polley	Joe Grubbs	Mark Price	John Bridges	Ray Stewart
El Paso	El Paso	Dolores Brions	Hector Enriquez Jr.	José Rodriguez	Office abolished 1-1-86.	Victor Flores	Leo Samaniego
Erath	Stephenville	Tab Thompson	Gwinda Jones	William H. Oxford	Donna Kelley	Jennifer Schlicke Carey	Tommy Bryant
Falls	Marlin	Michael W. Meyer	Frances Braswell	Thomas Sehon	Sue Ryan	Kate Vande Veegaete	John Trousdale
Fannin	Bonham	Derrell Hall	Margaret Gilbert	James S. Moss	Florence Keahey	Earlene Wix	Talmage Moore
Fayette	La Grange	Edward F. Janecka	Carolyn Kubos Roberts	John W. Wied	Office abolished 11-3-87.	Carol Johnson	Rick Vandel
Fisher	Roby	Marshal Bennett	Melody Gordon	Robie Robinson	Marty Williamson	Betty Mize	Gene Pack
Floyd	Floydada	William D. Hardin	Marilyn Holcomb	Daryl R. Halencak	Mary Shurbet	Penny Golightly	Royce Gilmore
Foard	Crowell	Charles B. Bell	Sherry Weatherred	Ben W. "Bud" Childers	Esther Kajs	Jo Ann Vecera	Bobby Bond
Fort Bend	Richmond	James C. Adolphus	Dianne Wilson	Dan K. Parchman	Kathy Hynson	Marsha P. Gaines	Milton Wright
Franklin	Mount Vernon	A. Wayne Foster	Barbara Keith Campbell	Robert W. "Bob" Gage	Marla M. Carrell	Marjorie Jaggers	Charles J. (Chuck) White
Freestone	Fairfield	Linda K. Grant	Mary Lynn White	James W. Smith Jr.	Kay Carol Barger	Carolyn Varley	James R. Sessions Jr.
Frio	Pearsall	Carlos A. Garcia	Gloria Leal Cubriel	Sterling Harmon	Anna L. Hernandez	Ysabela C. Peña	Carl Burris
Gaines	Seminole	Judy Ray	Pat Lacy	Harvey Bazaman	Linda Clark	Susan Jones	Jon Key
Galveston	Galveston	James D. Yarbrough	Patricia Ritchie	Leslie C. Acker	Gerald A. Burks	Charles "Chuck" Wilson	Joe Max Taylor
Garza	Post	Giles W. Dalby	Sonny Gossett	Jay Weinheimer	Ruth Ann Young	Jeanette Hodges	Kenneth Ratke
Gillespie	Fredericksburg	Mark Stroeher	Debbie Wahl	Hardy Wilkerson	Laura Lundquist	Leola Brodbeck	Milton E. Jung
Glasscock	Garden City	Wilburn E. Bednar	Rebecca Batla	Brenda J. Heinold	Alan Dierschke	Royce Pruit	Royce Pruitt
Goliad	Goliad	Steven G. Paulsgrove	Gail M. Turley	Robert B. Scheske	Debbie Bego	Anna Lopez	J. K. McMahan
Gonzales	Gonzales	David Bird	Lee Riedel	Todd Alvey	Marie Scoggins	Norma Jean DuBose	D. J. Brzozowski
Gray	Pampa	Richard Peet	Susan Winborne	Robert I. Jarvis	Scott Hahn	Sammie Morris	Don Copeland
Grayson	Sherman	Horace Groff	Sara Jackson		Virginia Hughes	John Ramsey	J. Keith Gary
Gregg	Longview	Mickey Smith	Laurie Woloszyn	Joe Falco Jr.	Office abolished 1-1-88.	Kirk Shields	Bobby Weaver
Grimes	Anderson	Ira E. Haynie	David Pasket	Robert Covington	Phillis Allen	Connie Perry	Don Sowell
Guadalupe	Seguin	James E. Sagebiel	Lizzie M. Lorenz	Chris Prentice	Larry M. Jones	Tavie Murphy	Melvin Harborth
Hale	Plainview	Bill Hollars	Diane Williams	John M. Deaver II	Evelyn Carroll	Kemp Hinch	David Mull
Hall	Memphis	Kenneth Dale	Raye Bailey	Thomas E. White	Marion Bownds	Pat Floyd	Jarrett L. Wilde
Hamilton	Hamilton	Charles Garrett	Debbie Rudolph	John L. Hutchison	Karen S. Tyson	Cynthia Roberts	Randy Murphree
Hansford	Spearman	Jim D. Brown	Kim V. Vera	Stanley Watson	Wanda Wagner	Helen Dry	R. L. McFarlin Jr.
Hardeman	Quanah	K. D. McNabb	Judy Cokendolpher	David Sheffield	Mary Ann Naylor	Darlene Gamble	Randy Akers
Hardin	Kountze	Billy Caraway	Dee Hatton		Eddie Doggett	Shirley Stephens	Ed J. Cain

County	County Seat	County Judge	County Clerk	County Attorney	County Treasurer	Assessor-Collector	Sheriff
Harris	Houston	Robert A. Eckels	Beverly B. Kaufman	Michael P. Fleming	Jack Cato	Paul Bettencourt	Tommy Thomas
Harrison	Marshall	Rodney Gilstrap	Martha Dieste	Rick Berry	Jamie Noland	Betty Wright	Bob Greene
Hartley	Channing	Ronnie Gordon	Diane Thompson	William A. Cunningham	Dinkie Parman	John E. Williams	John E. Williams
Haskell	Haskell	David Davis	Rhonda Moeller	L. W. (Bill) Jones	Willie Faye Tidrow	Bobbye Collins	Johnny Mills
Hays	San Marcos	James Powers	Lee Carlisle		Michele Tuttle	Luanne Caraway	Don Montague
Hemphill	Canadian	Bob Gober	Charles M. Cole	Charles Kessie	Claudette Hand	Gladene Swires	Dean Butcher
Henderson	Athens	Tommy G. Smith	Gwen Moffeit	Nolan B. Wickel Jr.	Carolyn Herrington	Milburn Chaney	Howard B. Alfred
Hidalgo	Edinburg	José Eloy Pulido	J.D. Salinas		Norma G. Garcia	Armando Barrera	Enrique Escalon
Hill	Hillsboro	Kenneth Davis	Ruth Pelham	Mark F. Pratt	John Spangler III	T. J. Davis	Brent Button
Hockley	Levelland	Larry D. Sprowls	Mary K. Walker	J. M. "Pat" Phelan	Jo Beth Parks	Christy Clevenger	Donald Caddell
Hood	Granbury	Linda Steen	Sally Oubre	R. Kelton Conner	Peggy Moreno	Sandy Tidwell	Allen Hardin
Hopkins	Sulphur Springs	Cletis Millsap	Debbie Shirley	ValInda Hathcox	Betty Bassham	Jo Ruth Hodge	Charles "Butch" Adams
Houston	Crockett	R.C. "Chris" von Doenhoff	Bridget Lamb	Donna Gordon	Dianne Rhone	Joan Lucas	Jimbo Rains
Howard	Big Spring	Ben Lockhart	Donna Wright	Mike Thomas	Bonnie Franklin	Kathy Sayles	W.B. (Bill) Jennings
Hudspeth	Sierra Blanca	James Peace	Patricia Bramblett	Tom Chellis	Dora Ramirez	Kay Scarbrough	Jerry Kresta
Hunt	Greenville	Joe Bobbitt	Linda Brooks	Peter Morgan	Delores Shelton	Joyce Barrow	Don Anderson
Hutchinson	Stinnett	Jack L. Worsham	Carol Ann Herbst	Michael Milner	Kathy Sargent	Mary Lou Henderson	Michael Blackmon
Irion	Mertzon	Sid Mabry	Reba Criner	James F. Ridge Jr.	Linda Pierce	Joyce Gray	Jimmy Martin
Jack	Jacksboro	Mitchell G. Davenport	Shelly Clayton	Michael Mask	Floyd Easter	Sarah Pruit	Danny Nash
Jackson	Edna	Harrison Stafford II	Kenneth. McElveen		Marcell Maresh Jr.	Donna Atzenhoffer	Kelly R. Janica
Jasper	Jasper	Joe Folk	Debbie Newman		Mary Jane Hancock	Robert C. Pace Jr.	Billy E. Rowles
Jeff Davis	Fort Davis	Peggy Robertson	Sue Blackley	Joseph James	Geen Parrott	Steve Bailey	Steve Bailey
Jefferson	Beaumont	Carl R. Griffith Jr.	Sandy Walker	Tom Maness	Linda. Robinson	Miriam Johnson	Mitch Woods
Jim Hogg	Hebbronville	Agapito "Cuate" Molina Jr.	Pamela L. Benavides	Richard R. Gonzales	Linda Jo G. Soliz	Marina Vasquez	Gilberto Ybañez
Jim Wells	Alice	L. Arnoldo Saenz	Ruben Sandoval	Jesusa Sanchez-Vera	Becky Dominguez	Lucila Reynolds	Oscar Lopez
Johnson	Cleburne	Roger Harmon	Curtis H. Douglas	Bill Moore	Barbara Robinson-Cole	Ed Carroll	Bob L. Alford
Jones	Anson	Brad Rowland	Margaret Jones	Chad Cowan	Irene Hudson	Tom Isbell	Robby Wedeking
Karnes	Karnes City	Alfred Pawelek	Elizabeth Swize	Rubert Busselman	Sandra Garza	Phillis Pawelek	Bobby Mutz
Kaufman	Kaufman	Wayne Gent	Crissy Gann		Ginger Chambless	Donna Sprague	Robert Harris
Kendall	Boerne	James W. (Bill) Gooden	Darlene Herrin	Pamela K. McKay	Barbara J. Schwope	James A. Hudson	Henry B. Hodge
Kenedy	Sarita	J. A. Garcia Jr.	Barbara B. Turcotte	Roy C. Turcotte	John W. Turcotte	Eleuteria S. Gonzalez	Rafael M. Cuellar Jr.
Kent	Jayton	Tommy Stanaland	Rena Jones	Howard Freemyer	Linda McCurry	Charles Alderman	Charles Alderman
Kerr	Kerrville	Frederick L. Henneke	Jannett Pieper	David Motley	Barbara Nemec	Paula Rector	Frances A. Kaiser
Kimble	Junction	Delbert R. Roberts	Elaine Carpenter	Max Fischer	Sheila D'Spain	Mike Chapman	Mike Chapman
King	Guthrie	Carolyn McLaury	Linda Lewis	Bobby D. Burnett, pro tem	Suzann Adams	Sadie Mote	Terry Lambeth
Kinney	Brackettville	Herbert Senne	Dora Elia Sandoval	Tully Shahan	Janis J. Floyd	Martha P. Hooten	L.K. Burgess
Kleberg	Kingsville	Allen M. May	Sam D. Deanda	Delma Rios	Rachel S. Alaniz	Melissa A. Treviño	Antonio "Tony" Gonzalez
Knox	Benjamin	David N. Perdue	Ronnie Verhalen	Bobby Burnett	Penny Goodwin	Stanton Brown	Dean W. Homstad
Lamar	Paris	Chuck Superville	Kathy Marlowe	Kerye Ashmore	Latricia Miller	Peggy Noble	Billy Joe McCoy
Lamb	Littlefield	Danny Byers	Bill Johnson		Janice B. Wells	Linda G. Charlton	Jerry Collins
Lampasas	Lampasas	Virgil E. (Ed) Lilley	Connie Hartmann	Larry W. Allison	Jean Rainwater	Glenda Henderson	Gordon Morris
La Salle	Cotulla	Jimmy P. Patterson	Peggy Murray	Rene R. Barrientos	Joel Rodriguez Jr.	Elida A. Linares	Luis Rene Benavidez
Lavaca	Hallettsville	Charles J. Rother	Henry J. Sitka	James W. Carr	Lois Henry	Margaret M. Kallus	Robert E. Wurm
Lee	Giddings	Robert B. Lee	Carol Dismukes	Ted Weems	Joyce Mitschke	Virginia Jackson	Joe Goodson
Leon	Centerville	Donald Gene Douget	Carla Neyland McEachern	Tom Holleman	Audrey Grimes	Louise Wilson	Larry Watson
Liberty	Liberty	Lloyd "Tookie" Kirkham	Delia Sellers	A.J. Hartfel	Winn Skidmore	Mark McClelland	O.J. Stewart
Limestone	Groesbeck	Elenor F. Holmes	Sue Lown	Don Cantrell	Angela Roach	Barbara Rader	Doyle Coslin
Lipscomb	Lipscomb	Willis V. Smith	Terri Parker	Randy M. Phillips	Pat Wyatt	Ann Word	James Robertson
Live Oak	George West	Jim Huff	Mildred James	J.R. "Rob" Schneider Jr.	Violet Person	Larry R. Busby	Larry R. Busby
Llano	Llano	J.P. Dodgen	Bette Sue Hoy	Cheryll Mabray	Diana Cummings	Anna Henderson	Nathan Garrett
Loving	Mentone	Donald C. Creager	Beverly Hanson		Ann Blair	Richard Putnam	Richard Putnam
Lubbock	Lubbock	Thomas V. Head	Ann Davidson		Connie Hopping Nicholson	Stephen P. Watt	David Gutierrez
Lynn	Tahoka	J. F. Brandon	Susan Tipton	James Napper	Janet Porterfield	Sherry Pearce	Dennis "Jake" Diggs

County	County Seat	County Judge	County Clerk	County Attorney	County Treasurer	Assessor-Collector	Sheriff
Madison	Madisonville	Cecil N. Neely	Joyce M. Coleman	Jim Finstrom	Judy Weathers	Judy Nickerson	Dan Douget
Marion	Jefferson	Gene Terry	Clairece Ford	James L. McGilvray	Dorothy Whatley	Mary Alice Biggs	Eugene Telfetter
Martin	Stanton	Charles T. Blocker	Susie Hull	Rob Hofmann	H.D. Howard	Kathy Hull	Mike Welling
Mason	Mason	Bill Goad	Beatrice Langehennig	Jill Cornelius	Polly McMillan	Melvin James Metzger	Melvin James Metzger
Matagorda	Bay City	Greg B. Westmoreland	Gail Denn	Ernest G. Mireles	Suzanne Kucera	Bill Wiginton	James D. Mitchell
Maverick	Eagle Pass	Rogelio (Rocky) Escobedo	Sara Montemayor	Manuel Reyes Jr.	Manuel Reyes Jr.	Esteban Luna	Salvador Rios
McCulloch	Brady	Randy Young	Tina A. Smith	Steve Wadsworth	Donna Robinett	Deena G. Moore	Clyde "Earl" Howell
McLennan	Waco	Jim Lewis	J.A. (Andy) Harwell		Bill Helton	A.F. (Buddy) Skeen	Jack Harwell
McMullen	Tilden	Linda Lee Henry	Nell Hodgin		Donald Haynes Jr.	Mary E. Edwards	W. I. "Tito" Potts
Medina	Hondo	David F. Montgomery	Anna Van De Walle	Ralph J. Bernsen	Rita L. Moos	Loraine Neuman	Wesley Scott
Menard	Menard	Tim Childers	Elsie Maserang	Ben Neel	Robert Bean	Brent Bratton	Bruce Hough
Midland	Midland	Bill Morrow	Shauna Brown	Russell Malm	Julie Fry	Kathy Reeves	Gary Painter
Milam	Cameron	Frank R. Summers Jr.	La Verne Soefje	Hollis C. Lewis Jr.	Jeanie Schlemmer	Frances R. Price	Charles L. West
Mills	Goldthwaite	Randy Wright	Beulah L. Roberts	Tommy M. Adams	Patsy E. Miller	Darwin Odom	Darwin Odom
Mitchell	Colorado City	Ray Mayo	Debby Carlock	Mark Piland	Ann Hallmark	Faye Lee	Patrick Toombs
Montague	Montague	James O. Kittrell	Gayle Edwards	Jeb McNew	Patty Fenoglio	Lindy Ritchie	Chris Hamilton
Montgomery	Conroe	Alan B. Sadler	Mark Turnbull	Frank Bass	Martha Gustavsen	J. R. Moore	Guy Williams
Moore	Dumas	Kari Campbell	Rhonnie Mayer	Rayford A. Ratliff	Pam Cox	Joy Robertson	H.T. "Ted" Montgomery
Morris	Daingerfield	J.C. Jennings	Vicki Camp	Richard Townsend	Nita Beth Traylor	Jerry Chambliss	C.R. "Ricky" Blackburn
Motley	Matador	Laverna M. Price	Lucretia Campbell	Tempie Hutton-Angley	Joe E. Campbell	Elaine Hart	Jim Meador
Nacogdoches	Nacogdoches	Sue Kennedy	Carol Wilson	Bryan Davis	Kay Watkins	Janie Weatherly	Joe Evans
Navarro	Corsicana	James P. Bagnall	Brenda Hodge	Patrick Batchelor	Joe Graves	Peggy Blackwell-Moore	Leslie Cotten
Newton	Newton	Truman Dougharty	Mary Cobb	Atmar W. Davis Jr.	Bettie Hall Cobb	Beatrice Westbrook	Wayne Powell
Nolan	Sweetwater	Tim Fambrough	Elsie Pierce	Lisa Peterson	Gayle Biggerstaff	Fonda Holman	Donnie Rannefeld
Nueces	Corpus Christi	Richard M. Borchard	Ernest M. Briones	Carl Lewis	Office abolished 11-3-87.	Ramiro R. Canales	Larry Olivarez Sr.
Ochiltree	Perryton	Kenneth Donahue	Jane Hammerbeck	Bruce Roberson	Ginger Hays	Helen Bates	Joe Hataway
Oldham	Vega	Donnie Allred	Becky Groneman	Don Davis	Charlotte Cook	Cynthia Artho	David Medlin
Orange	Orange	Carl K. Thibodeaux	Karen Jo Vance	John D. Kimbrough	Vergie Moreland	Linda Gunstream	Mike White
Palo Pinto	Palo Pinto	Mickey D. West	Bobbie Smith	Phil Garrett	Mary M. Motley	Max Wheeler	Larry L. Watson
Panola	Carthage	John Cordray	Sue Grafton		Gloria Portman	Jean Whiteside	Jack Ellett
Parker	Weatherford	Mark Riley	Jeane Brunson	Glen Wilson	Jim Thorp	Marjorie King	Jay Brown
Parmer	Farwell	Bonnie J. Clayton	Colleen Stover	Charles F. Aycock	Anne G. Norton	Doris Herington	Walter Yerger
Pecos	Fort Stockton	Delmon Hodges	Judy Deerfield	Kriste Burnett	Barry McCallister	Santa Acosta	Bruce Wilson
Polk	Livingston	John Thompson	Barbara Middleton	Sonya Letson	Nola Reneau	Bid Smith	Billy Ray Nelson
Potter	Amarillo	Arthur Ware	Sue Daniel	Teresa Todd	Judy Messer	L. R. "Bob" Roberts	Jimmy Don Boydston
Presidio	Marfa	Jake Brisbin Jr.	Brenda M. Silva	L.M. Braziel	Mario S. Rivera	Norma Arroyo	Danny Dominguez
Rains	Emory	Robert Sisk	Mary Sheppard		Teresa Northcutt	Richard Wilson	Richard Wilson
Randall	Canyon	Ted Wood	Sue Wicker Bartolino	J. Russell Ash	Geneva Bagwell	Carol Autrey	Harold Hooks
Reagan	Big Lake	Mike Elkins	Terri Pullig	Patricia Foster	Nancy Ratliff	Sue Turner	Efrain Gonzales
Real	Leakey	W.B. "Sonny" Sansom	Bella A. Rubio	Jack Herrington	Kathy Brooks	Donna Brice	James Brice
Red River	Clarksville	L. D. Williamson	Lorie Moose	Walter M. Holcombe	Kathy Cheyne	Leslie Nix	Robert L. Edrington
Reeves	Pecos	Jimmy B. Galindo	Dianne O. Florez		Linda Clark	Elfida Zuniga	Arnulfo "Andy" Gomez
Refugio	Refugio	Roger C. Fagan	Janelle Morgan	Robert P. McGuill	Betty Greebon	Veronica Rocha	Jim Hodges
Roberts	Miami	Vernon H. Cook	Donna L. Goodman	Richard J. Roach	Billie Lansford	Carol S. Billingsley	Bill Britton
Robertson	Franklin	Billy Lee Stellbauer	Kathryn N. Brimhall	John C. Paschall	Jacqueline Vann	Charlene Bush	Gerald Yezak
Rockwall	Rockwall	Bill Bell	Paulette Burks		Sheree Jones	Kathryn Feldpausch	Jacques I. Kiere
Runnels	Ballinger	Marilyn Egan	Elesa Ocker	John W. McGregor	Margarette Smith	Robin Burgess	William A. "Bill" Baird
Rusk	Henderson	Sandra Hodges	Frank Hudson	Kyle Freeman	Nora Rousseau	Matt Johnson	James Stroud
Sabine	Hemphill	Jack Leath	Janice McDaniel	Steve Hollis, pro-tem	Tricia Jacks	Tammy Reeves	Thomas R. Philips
San Augustine	San Augustine	Curt Goetz	Diana Kovar	Michael J. Adams	Carol W. Vaughn	Deborah K. Woods	John M. Cartwright
San Jacinto	Coldspring	Joe Adams	Charlene Vann		Charlene Everitt	Barbara Shelly	Lacy Rogers
San Patricio	Sinton	Josephine W. Miller	Dottie Maley	David Akin	Judy Burr	Thelma Kelley	Leroy Moody
San Saba	San Saba	Harlen Barker	Kim Wells	David M. Williams	Gayla Hawkins	John Benner	John Benner

County	County Seat	County Judge	County Clerk	County Attorney	County Treasurer	Assessor-Collector	Sheriff
Schleicher	Eldorado	Johnny F. Griffin	Peggy Williams	Marian Overstreet	Karen Henderson	Lou Ann Turner	David Doran
Scurry	Snyder	Ricky Fritz	Joan Bunch	Michael W. Hartman	Charlie Bell	Rona Sikes	Darren Jackson
Shackelford	Albany	Ross Montgomery	Cheri Hawkins	Colton P. Johnson	Sherry Enloe	Larry V. Bonner	Larry V. Bonner
Shelby	Center	Floyd A. Watson	Peaches Conway	Gary Rholes	Carolyn Bush Golden	Janie Graves	Carl Shofner
Sherman	Stratford	W. C. Fesler	M.L. Albert	Kim Allen	Linda Keener	Valerie McAlister	Jack Hale
Smith	Tyler	Larry Craig	Judy Carnes		Joyce Woodward Smith	Kay M. Smith	J. B. Smith
Somervell	Glen Rose	Walter Maynard	Lovella Williams	Ronald Hankins	Vicki Crisp	Dorothy Keller	Mac Yocham
Starr	Rio Grande City	Eloy Vera	Omar J. Garza	Romero Molina	David D. Porras	Carmen A. Peña	Reymundo Guerra
Stephens	Breckenridge	Gary L. Fuller	Helen Haddock	Gary Trammel	Nancy Clary	Terry S. Sullivan	James Reeves
Sterling	Sterling City	Robert L. Browne	Diane A. Haar	Robert Herring	Wanda Foster	Joy Manning	Don Howard
Stonewall	Aspermont	Bobby F. McGough	Betty L. Smith	Norman Arnett	Linda Messick	Joyce McNutt	Bill Mullen
Sutton	Sonora	Carla Garner	Bobbie Smith	David Wallace	Joyce Chalk	Peggy Sharp	W. W. (Bill) Webster
Swisher	Tulia	Harold Keeter	Brenda Hudson	J. Michael Criswell	Lanelle Dovel	Virginia Thornton	Larry P. Stewart
Tarrant	Fort Worth	Tom Vandergriff	Suzanne Henderson		Office abolished 4-2-83.	June Garrison	David Williams
Taylor	Abilene	Lee Hamilton	Janice Lyons	Marsha Monroe	Lesa Crosswhite	Lavena Cheek	Jack Dieken
Terrell	Sanderson	Dudley Harrison	Martha Allen		Lynda Helmers	Blain Chriesman	Y. E. Duarte
Terry	Brownfield	Douglas Ryburn	Ann Willis	G. Dwayne Pruitt	Bobbye Jo Floyd	Redelle Cox	Jerry Johnson
Throckmorton	Throckmorton	Trey Carrington	Melanie Jones	Cheryl Taylor	Brenda Rankin	Greg Dunlap	Greg Dunlap
Titus	Mt. Pleasant	Danny Pat Crooks	Sherry Jo Mars	Tim Taylor	Cynthia "Sandy" Agan	June Roach	Ricky Poole
Tom Green	San Angelo	Michael D. Brown	Judith Hawkins	Tom Goff	Dianna Spieker	Cindy Jetton	Dan Gray
Travis	Austin	Sam Biscoe	Dana DeBeauvoir	Ken Oden	Dolores Ortega Carter	Nelda Wells Spears	Margo Frasier
Trinity	Groveton	Mark Evans	Diane McCrory	Joe Warner Bell	Jo Bitner Bartee	Kathy McCarty	Brent Phillips
Tyler	Woodville	Jerome P. Owens Jr.	Donece Gregory		Tina Bump	Sandra Harrison Crittenden	Gary Hennigan
Upshur	Gilmer	Charles L. Still	Rex A. Shaw		Myra Evans	Michael L. Smith	R. D. (Buck) Cross
Upton	Rankin	Vikki Bradley	Phyllis Stephens	Roy L. Scott	Nancy P. Poage	Dan W. Brown	Dan W. Brown
Uvalde	Uvalde	William R. Mitchell	Lucille C. Hutcherson	Pete Nieto	Joni Deorsam	Margarita Del Toro	Beaumont Watkins
Val Verde	Del Rio	Manuel (Mike) L. Fernandez	Maria Elena Cardenas	Ana Markowski Smith	Morris Taylor	Wayne H. Hyde	A. D'Wayne Jernigan
Van Zandt	Canton	Richard Lawrence	Elizabeth Everitt	Leslie Dixon	Judy Peoples	Joyce Fugate	Billy Dean
Victoria	Victoria	Helen R. Walker	Val D. Huvar		Cathy Bailey	Rena Scherer	Mike Ratcliff
Walker	Huntsville	Charles H. Wagamon	James D. Patton		Barbara McGilberry	Allan D. Rushing	Victor Graham
Waller	Hempstead	Glenn Taylor	Cheryl Peters		Susan Winfree	Ellen C. Shelburne	Randy Smith
Ward	Monahans	Sam G. Massey	Natrell Cain	Kevin D. Acker	Nell Berry	Dolores Fine	Ben Keele
Washington	Brenham	Dorothy Morgan	Beth A. Rothermel	Renee Ann Mueller	Norman Draehn	Candy Arth	J. W. Jankowski
Webb	Laredo	Mercurio Martinez Jr.	Henry Flores	Homero Ramirez	Billy Hall	Patricia Barrera	Juan Garza
Wharton	Wharton	Lawrence E. Naiser	Sandra K. Sanders	Karen Meinardus	Gus Wessels	Pat Kubala	Jess Howell
Wheeler	Wheeler	Jerry Dan Hefley	Margaret Dorman	Bobbie Carol Hill	Amy McCasland	Lewis Scott Porter	Jimmy Adams
Wichita	Wichita Falls	Woodrow Gossom Jr.	Lloyd M. Lueck		Marsha Watson	Lu Murdock	Thomas Callahan
Wilbarger	Vernon	Gary Streit	Frances McGee	Mike Baskerville	Joann Carter	JoAnn Bourland	David Quisenberry
Willacy	Raymondville	Simon Salinas	Terry Flores	Juan Angel Guerra	Arturo "Tuttie" Gomez	LaQuita Garza	Larry Spence
Williamson	Georgetown	John Doerfler	Nancy E. Rister	Eugene Taylor	Vivian Wood	Deborah Hunt	Ed Richards
Wilson	Floresville	Marvin Quinney	Eva S. Martinez	Russell H. Wilson	Carolyn Orth	Anna D. Gonzales	Joe D. Tackitt Jr.
Winkler	Kermit	Bonnie Leck	Shethelia Reed	Thomas Cameron	Dawn McLennan	Patti Franks	Robert L. Roberts Jr.
Wise	Decatur	L. B. McDonald	Sherry Parker	Todd Durden	Katherine Canova	Pat Younger	Phil Ryan
Wood	Quitman	W.J. Alexander	Brenda Taylor		June Robinson	Fred Morrow	Bill Skinner
Yoakum	Plains	Dallas Brewer	Deborah L. Rushing		Toni Jones	Wanda Smith	Jim Rice
Young	Graham	Ken Andrews	Shirley Choate	Boyd L. Richie	Charlotte Farmer	Tim Moreland	Carey W. Pettus
Zapata	Zapata	David Morales	Consuelo R. Villarreal	Jose A. Lopez	Alejandro R. Ramirez	Rosalva D. Guerra	Sigifredo Gonzalez Jr.
Zavala	Crystal City	Pablo Avila	Oralia G. Trevino	Joe W. Taylor	Susie Perez	Florinda Perez	Eusevio Salinas Jr.

Texas County and District Officials — Table No. 2

District Clerks, District Attorneys and County Commissioners

See Table No. 1 on preceding pages for County Seats, County Judges, County Clerks, County Attorneys, County Treasurers, Tax Assessors-Collectors and Sheriffs.

County	District Clerk	District Attorney*	Comm. Precinct 1	Comm. Precinct 2	Comm. Precinct 3	Comm. Precinct 4
Anderson	Maxine Barnette	Douglas E. Lowe	Joe W. Chaffin	Rodney A. Howard	T. L. Beard	Randy Watkins
Andrews	Cynthia Collinsworth	Katrina Jackson	Barney Fowler	Jerry Tochterman	Jerry McPherson	Paul Williams
Angelina	Jimmie F. Robinson	Clyde Herrington	Clayton Carroll Richardson	Kenneth Timmons	Jim Risinger	Delbert Jones
Aransas	Bobbie Rogers	Tom Bridges	Oscar Piña	Rudy Nava	Glenn Guillory	Larry Barnebey
Archer	Jane Ham	Tim Cole	Richard Shelley	James Wolf	Ben Buerger	D. W. Stone
Armstrong	Joe Reck	Rebecca King	Dee Adudell	Mike Ollinger	Foster Parker	C. M. Bryand Jr.
Atascosa	Jerome Brite	Lynn Ellison	Tommy Shearrer	Armand Martinez	Freddie Ogden	Weldon Cude
Austin	Marie Myers	Travis J. Koehn	Harlan Schroeder	Wilbert Frank Jr.	James (Bubba) Duke	Royce Burger
Bailey	Elaine Parker	Johnny Actkinson	Butch Vandiver	C. E. Grant	Joey Kindle	Jerry Damron
Bandera	Tammy Kneuper	E. Bruce Curry	Ronald Basinger	James Mormando Jr.	Ralph Chancy	Nancy J. Thompson
Bastrop	La Nelle Hibbs	Charles Penick	Johnny Sanders	Charles McKeown	G. L. Hanna	Lee Dildy
Baylor	Doris Rushing	Bill Neal	Don Matus	Jackie Brown	Jerry Pruitt	Eric Hostas
Bee	Sandra Clark	George P. Morrill	Adam V. Gonzales	Susan C. Stasny	Toribio "Toby" Ortiz	Walter E. "Butch" Smith
Bell	Shelia Faye Norman	Arthur C. Eads	Richard Cortese	Tim Brown	Leroy Schiller	John R. Stephenson
Bexar	Reagan Greer	Susan Reed	Robert Tejeda	Paul Elizondo	Lyle Larson	Tommy Adkisson
Blanco	Dorothy Uecker	Sam Oatman	Dorsey L. Smith	Victor Tellez	Robert A. Mauck	Paul Granberg
Borden	Joyce Herridge	Dana Cooley	Doug Isaacs	Larry D. Smith	Vernon Wolf	Hurston Lemons Jr.
Bosque	Sandra Woosley	B.J. Shepherd	Rick Kelley	Durwood Koonsman	Gary Arnold	James Burch
Bowie	Billy Fox	Bobby Lockhart	Jack Stone	John Addington	Dale Barrett	Carl Teel
Brazoria	Jerry Deere	Jeri Yenne	David Head	James D. "Jim" Clawson	Jack Harris	L.L. "Larry" Stanley
Brazos	Mark Hamlin	Bill Turner	Carey Cauley	Bill Thornton	Randy Sims	Tony Jones
Brewster	Jo Ann Salgado	Albert Valadez	Asa "Cookie" Stone	J.W. "Red" Pattillo	Emilio Salmon	Matilde "Wacky" Pallanez
Briscoe	Bena Hester	Becky McPherson	Terry Grimland	Danny Maynard	L. B. Garvin Jr.	Gary Weaks
Brooks	Noe Guerra Jr.	Joe Frank Garza	Gloria Garza	Ramon Navarro Jr.	Raul Ramirez	Salvador Gonzalez
Brown	Jan Brown	Lee Haney	Steve Adams	Adron Beck	Richard Gist	Vernon Moore
Burleson	Doris H. Brewer	Charles J. Sebesta Jr.	Frank L. Kristof	Don L. Groce	W. J. Stracener	John B. Landolt Jr.
Burnet	Kathy Barrow	Sam Oatman	James Holbrook	Buddy Feild	George DeSpain	James Oakley
Caldwell	Emma Jean Schulle	Charles R. Kimbrough	Morris Alexander	Charles Bullock	Ronnie Duesterheft	Joe Ivan Roland
Calhoun	Pamela Martin Hargrove	Dan W. Heard	Leroy Belk	Michael Balajka	H. Floyd	Kenneth W. Finster
Callahan	Sharon Owens	Allen Wright	Harold Hicks	Bryan Farmer	Tommy Holland	Charlie Grider
Cameron	Aurora De La Garza	Yolanda de Leon	Pedro "Pete" Benavides	Carlos H. Cascos	James R. Matz	Natividad "Tivie" Valencia
Camp	Doloria Bradshaw	Charles C. Bailey	Jack Efurd	Larry Mitcham	Hervy Hiner	Bobby Barrett
Carson	Sonya Millican	Randall Sims	Mike Britten	Kenneth Ware	Jerry Strawn	Kevin Howell
Cass	Becky Wilbanks	Randal Lee	Taylor Duncan	Larne Lancaster	Robert Buzbee	Freddie Tyson
Castro	Joyce M. Thomas	Jerry Matthews	Newlon Rowland	Clyde Damron	W.A. Baldridge	Dan Schmucker
Chambers	R. B. Scherer Jr.	Mike Little	Mark Huddleston	Judy Edmonds	W.E. "Buddy" Irby	Bill Wallace
Cherokee	Marlys Mason	James Cromwell	E. R. (Bob) Gregg	Kevin Pierce	F. E. Hassell	Billy J. McCutcheon
Childress	Zona Prince	Randall Sims	David Hill	Dan Imhof	Lyall Foster	Jack Burrus
Clay	Dan Slagle	Tim Cole	R.L. "Lindy" Choate	Harlan Hicks	Wilson Scaling	Brice Jackson
Cochran	Rita Tyson	Gary Goff	Gerald Ramsey	J.B. Allen	Stacey Dunn	Jimmy Mullinax
Coke	Mary Grim	Stephen Lupton	Paul Burns	Wayne McCutchen	Pat Percifull	Davis Rawlings
Coleman	Jo Dean Chapman	Ross Jones	Jim Porter	Billy Don McCrary	John K. Puckett	Alan Davis
Collin	Hannah Kunkle	Tom O'Connell	Phyllis Cole	Jerry Hoagland	Joe Jaynes	Jack Hatchell

County	District Clerk	District Attorney*	Comm. Precinct 1	Comm. Precinct 2	Comm. Precinct 3	Comm. Precinct 4
Collingsworth	Jackie Johnson	Randall Sims	Glen Taylor	Zeb Roberson	Joe Tipton	Pat Glenn
Colorado	Harvey Vornsand		Richard Seifert	Herbert (Herbie) E. Helmcamp	Tommy Hahn	Darrell D. Gertson
Comal	Margaret L. Herbrich	Dib Waldrip	Jack Dawson	Jay P. Millikin	Christina Zamora	Moe Schwab
Comanche	LaNell Williams	B.J. Shepherd	Garry Steele	Chris Biggs	Bobby Schuman	Clyde Brinson
Concho	Barbara K. Hoffman	Stephen H. Smith (119th); Ronald L. Sutton (198th)	R.M. Kingston	Ralph Willberg	Frankie Wojtek	Aaron B. Browning Jr.
Cooke	Pat Payne	Janelle Haverkamp	Phil Young	Bill V. Cox	Jerry Lewis	Virgil J. Hess
Coryell	Janice May	Riley Simpson	Jack Wall	Cliff Price	Hiram Davidson	Kyle Pruitt
Cottle	Beckey J. Tucker	Bill Neal	Paul Whitener	Hazel Biddy	Manuel Cruz Jr.	D.N. Gregory Jr.
Crane	Judy Crawford	Jim L. Rex	Gordon Hooper	Scott McMeans	Ellis Lane	Weldon McCutchen
Crockett	Debbi Puckett-Moore	Ori White	Frank Tambunga	Pleas Childress III	Freddie Nicks	Rudy Martinez
Crosby	Karla Isbell	C. Michael Ward	Gary Jordan	William "Bill" Odom	Larry Wampler	James Boydstun
Culberson	Linda McDonald	Jaime Esparza	Cornelio Garibay	Manuel "Manny" Molinar	John Jones	Israel "Rale" Navarrette
Dallam	LuAnn Taylor	Barry Blackwell	Bob Sheets	Oscar Przilas	Don Bowers	Carl French
Dallas	Jim Hamlin	Bill Hill	Jim Jackson	Mike Cantrell	John Wiley Price	Kenneth Mayfield
Dawson	Carolyn Turner	Ricky B. Smith	Delmar Moore	Bill Meares	Troy Howard	Guy Kinnison
Deaf Smith	Jean Schumacher	Roland Saul	Wayne W. Betzen	Sammy Gonzales Sr.	Troy Don Moore	Johnny Latham
Delta	Martha Jo Loder	Frank Long	C. D. (Mickey) Goforth	David Max Moody	James Campbell	Ted Carrington
Denton	Sheri Adelstein	Bruce Isaacks	Jeff Krueger	Sandy Jacobs	Scott Armey	Jim Carter
DeWitt	Tabeth Ruschhaupt	Michael Sheppard	Wallace Beck	Joe L. Machalec	John Oliver	Alfred Rangnow
Dickens	Winona Humphreys	Becky B. McPherson	Don Condron	Billy George Drennan	Doc Edwards	Duane "Slim" Durham
Dimmit	Alicia Lopez-Martinez	Roberto Serna	Larry Speer	Johnny Gloria	Oscar Alvarado	Rodrigo Jaime
Donley	Fay Vargas	Randall Sims	Randy White	Don Hall	Andy Wheatly	Bob Trout
Duval	Richard M. Barton	Heriberto Silva	Alejo C. Garcia	Rene M. Perez	Nestor Garza Jr.	Gilberto Uribe Jr.
Eastland	Bill Miears	Mike Siebert	Ken Lyerla	Calvin Ainsworth	L. T. Owen	Reggie Pittman
Ector	Jackie Sue Barnes	John Smith	Freddie Gardner	Greg Simmons	Tom Todd	Wilmer Ray
Edwards	Sarah McNealy	Thomas F. Lee	Robert Pena	Kenneth D. Sorrells	James E. Epperson Jr.	Chisholm Erwin Parks
Ellis	Billie Fuller	Joe Grubbs	Hallie Joe Robinson	Jerry Holland	Charles Waller	Ron Brown
El Paso	Edie Rubalcaba	Jaime Esparza	Charles Hooten	Carlos Aguilar	Miguel Teran	Daniel R. Haggerty
Erath	Thomas Pack	John Terrill	Jerry Martin	Don Stone	Douglas Eberhart	Randy Lowe
Falls	Larry Hoelscher	Thomas Sehon	Milton A. Albright	Roger Schneider	Tony Lynn Hoelscher	James Phillips
Fannin	Rochelle Turner	James S. Moss	Jerry Jenkins	Randy Davis	Dewayne Strickland	Pat Hilliard
Fayette	Virginia Wied	John W. Wied	Lawrence Adamcik	Gary Weishuhn	Wilbert L. Gross	Tom Muras
Fisher	Bettie Hargrove	Mark Edwards	Charlie Meek	Billy Henderson	Perry Thomson	Gene Terry
Floyd	Barbara Edwards	Becky McPherson	Ray Nell Bearden	Leonard Gilroy	George Taylor	Jon Jones
Foard	Sherry Weatherred	Dan Mike Bird	Rick Hammonds	Johnny Urquizo	Larry Wright	Edward Crosby
Fort Bend	Glory Hopkins	John Healey	R. L. "Bud" O'Shieles	Grady Prestage	Andy Meyers	James Patterson
Franklin	Barbara Keith Campbell	J. Frank Long	Jearl Cooper	Bobby R. Elbert	Deryl Carr	Charles Davis
Freestone	Janet Haydon Chappell	Robert W. Gage	Luke Ward Sr.	W. R. McSwane	Stanley Gregory	Johnny B. Massey
Frio	Ramona B. Rodriguez	Lynn Allison	Jesus "Chuy" Salinas	Jack D. Shanklin	Adolfo Alvarez	Jose "Pepe" Flores
Gaines	Virginia Stewart	George Hansard	Robert Wood	Terry Jeffries	Ray Garrett	Charlie Lopez
Galveston	Evelyn Wells Robison	Michael J. Guarino II	Eddie Barr	Eddie Janek	Wayne Johnson III	Ken Clark
Garza	Sonny Gossett	Ricky Smith	Lee Norman	Mason McClellan	John Valdez	Mike Sanchez
Gillespie	Barbara Meyer	Bruce Curry	Dayton E. Weidenfeller	William A. Roeder	James J. Knopp	Eldon Ray Feller
Glasscock	Rebecca Batla	Robert H. Moore III	Jimmy Strube	Mark Halfmann	Hugh Schafer	Michael Hoch
Goliad	Gail M. Turley	Michael Sheppard	Tony Garcia	Jerry Rodriguez	Louis Fromme Jr.	W. Wayne Key
Gonzales	Patricia Heinemeyer	W.C. Kirkendall	Kenneth O. "Dell" Whiddon	James "Jim" Kelso	David Kuntschik	Otis "Bud" Wuest
Gray	Gaye Hondrich	John Mann	Joe Wheeley	Jim Greene	Gerald Wright	James Hefley

County	District Clerk	District Attorney*	Comm. Precinct 1	Comm. Precinct 2	Comm. Precinct 3	Comm. Precinct 4
Grayson	Cyndi Mathis Spencer	Robert T. Jarvis	Douglas Walker	Johnnie "Butch" McCraw	Carol Shea	C.E. "Gene" Short
Gregg	Ruby Cooper	Bill Jennings	Charles Davis	Darryl Primo	David McBride	Danny Craig
Grimes	Wayne Rucker	Tuck Moody McLain	Doug Morris	Frank Glass	Zac Falkenbury	Marcus H. Mallard
Guadalupe	James Behrendt	W. C. Kirkendall	Shirley Hester	Cesareo Guadarrama III	Jim Wolverton	Wyatt L. Kunde
Hale	Anna Evans	Terry McEachern	Earle McDonough	Mario Martinez	Roy Borchardt	Benny Cantwell
Hall	Raye Bailey	Randall C. Sims	Larry Don Maddox	Terry D. Lindsey	Buddy, Logsdon	Ray Whitaker
Hamilton	Leoma Larance	B.J. Shepherd	Jim Boatwright	Mike Lewis	Jon Bonner	Marion Streigler
Hansford	Kim V. Vera	Clay Ballman	Butch Reed	Joe T. Venneman	Kent Guthrie	Danny Henson
Hardeman	Judy Cokendolpher	Dan Mike Bird	Charles McSpadden	Rodger Tabor	Charles Taylor	Van D. Foster
Hardin	Vicki Johnson	Charles Roach	Bob Burgess	James McGallion	Ken Pelt	Bobby Q. Franklin
Harris	Charles Bacarisse	John B. Holmes Jr.	El Franco Lee	Jim Fonteno	Steve Radack	Jerry Eversole
Harrison	Sherry Griffis	Rick Berry	James Mooney	Charles Bennett	Glen Hobbs	Jerry Armstrong
Hartley	Diane Thompson	Barry E. Blackwell	David Vincent	Andy Michael	James Yoder	R.B. Reynolds
Haskell	Penny Young	John Fouts	Billy Wayne Hester	Tiffen Mayfield	Kenny Thompson	C.A. (Bud) Turnbow
Hays	Cecelia Adair	Michael S. Wenk	Debbie Gonzales-Ingalsbe	H.S. "Susie" Carter	William "Bill" Burnett	Russ G. Molenaar Sr.
Hemphill	Charles M. Cole	John Mann	Joe Schaef	Ed Culver	John Ramp	Lynard Schafer
Henderson	Betty Ramsey	Donna Bennett	Bill Faulk	Wade McKinney	Cleburn Shavor	Jerry West
Hidalgo	Pauline G. Gonzalez	Rene Guerra	Sylvia Handy	Tito Palacios	Juan Rosel	Oscar Garza
Hill	Charlotte Barr	Dan Dent	J.K. Lane	Kenneth Reid	Mildred Brustrom	John Erwin
Hockley	Dennis Price	Gary Goff	Jack Ayers	El Lea Hensley	J. R. Stanley	Billy Thetford
Hood	Tonna Trumble	Richard Hattox	Robert (Bob) Anderson	Cliff Moody	Ron Cullers	Al Bulloch
Hopkins	Patricia Dorner	Frank Long	Beth Wisenbaker	H. W. Halcomb	Don Patterson	Calvin Prince
Houston	Pam Pugh	Cindy Garner	George "Buzzy" Bush	Willie E. Kitchen	Burtis Wooten	Billy Ray Duren
Howard	Glenda Brasel	Hardy Wilkerson	Emma Puga Brown	Jerry D. Kilgore	W. B. (Bill) Crooker	Gary N. Simer
Hudspeth	Patricia Bramblett	Jaime Esparza	Wayne West	Curtis Carr	Jim Kiehne	Larry Brewton
Hunt	Ann Prince	Duncan Thomas	Kenneth Thornton	Ralph Green	Jim Walker	Allen Martin
Hutchinson	Joan Carder	Clay Ballman	R. D. Cornelison	J. C. Berry	S.T. Isbell Jr.	John E. Bayless
Irion	Reba Criner	Steve Lupton	E. Wayne Smith	O.K. Wolfenbarger	John Nanny	Barbara Searcy
Jack	Lelia Vene Cozart	Barry Green	Lewis Kirk	Jerry Adams	James Cozart	Milton Pruitt
Jackson	Sharon Whittley	Robert E. Bell	Miller Rutledge	Erwin Skalicky	Priscilla Hurta	Larry Deyton
Jasper	Linda Ryall	Guy James Gray	Edgar W. Lewis	Rod Barger	James E. Smith	Mack Rose
Jeff Davis	Sue Blackey	Albert Valadez	Bill Cotton	Joe Dominguez	Billie Weston	William Gearhart
Jefferson	John S. Appleman	Tom Maness	Jimmie P. Cokinos	Mark L. Domingue	Waymon D. Hallmark	Edward C. Moore
Jim Hogg	Pamela L. Benavides	Heriberto Silva	Francisco X. Escobedo	Oscar O. Gonzalez	Ricardo E. Alaniz	Ruben Rodriguez
Jim Wells	R. David Guerrero	Joe Frank Garza	Zenaida Sanchez	C. L. Cornelius	Oswald "Wally" Alanis	Javier N. Garcia
Johnson	David Lloyd	Dale Hanna	R. C. McFall	Ron Harmon	Mark Carpenter	Troy Thompson
Jones	Nona Carter	Gary Brown	James Clawson	Mike Polk	J.L. Wylie	Steve Lollar
Karnes	Patricia Brysch	Lynn Ellison	Darrel Blaschke	Jeffrey Wiatrek	Juan Martinez	Isidro D. Rossett Jr.
Kaufman	Sandra Featherston	Louis Conradt Jr.	Rhea Fox	Ken Leonard	Ivan Johnson	Jerry Brewer
Kendall	Shirley R. Stehling	E. Bruce Curry	John C. Kight	L.M. Holman	Darrel L. Lux	Duane DuBose
Kenedy	Barbara B. Turcotte	Carlos Valdez	Leonard May	Roberto Salazar Jr.	Tobin Armstrong	Gus Puente
Kent	Rena Jones	John Fouts	Bob Hamilton	Don Long	Mike Owen	Don Trammel
Kerr	Linda Uecker	Ron Sutton (198th) Bruce Curry (216th)	Buster Baldwin	William H. Williams	Jonathan Letz	Larry Griffin
Kimble	Elaine Carpenter	Ronald Sutton	Ray Jacoby	Ilee Simon	George Wright	Victor Herbst
King	Linda Lewis	Bill Neal	Stephen Brady	Sam Fulton	Bob Tidmore	Darwood Marshall
Kinney	Dora Elia Sandoval	Tom F. Lee	Freddie Frerich	Joe Montalvo	Joe Williams	Pat Melancon
Kleberg	Martha I. Soliz	Carlos Valdez	David Rosse	Norma Nelda Alvarez	Dewey Hubert	Romeo Lomas

County	District Clerk	District Attorney*	Comm. Precinct 1	Comm. Precinct 2	Comm. Precinct 3	Comm. Precinct 4
Knox	Ronnie Verhalen	Bill Neal	Weldon Skiles	Jerry Parker	Jimmy Urbanczyk	Johnny Birkenfeld
Lamar	Marvin A. Patterson	Kerye Ashmore	Mike Blackburn	Carl Steffey	Rodney Pollard	Jackie Wheeler
Lamb	Celia Knox Kuykendall	Mark Yarbrough	Willie G. Green	Thurman Lewis	Emil Macha	Jimmy Young
Lampasas	Terri Cox	Larry Allison	Robert L. Vincent Jr.	Jerry H. Skiles	Travis Herring	Mary N. Casbeer
La Salle	Peggy Murray	Lynn Ellison	Raymond A. Landrum Jr.	Roberto F. Aldaco	Arcenio A. Garcia	Carlos B. Gonzalez
Lavaca	Calvin J. Albrecht	W. C. "Bud" Kirkendall	Maxie Brocker	Edwin Gaertner	Daniel Peters	Glen Blundell
Lee	Adeline Melcher	Ted Weems	Maurice Pitts Jr.	Douglas Hartfield	O. B. Johnson	Thomas Kovar
Leon	Gloria McCarty	Ray Montgomery	Joey Sullivan	F. G. (Bubba) Lipsey	Jim Miles	Burel Biddle
Liberty	Joy Kay McManus	Michael Little	Harry Hylton	Lee Groce	Melvin Hunt	Toby Wilburn
Limestone	Peggy Murray Hill	Don Cantrell	Keith Eaves	Billy Waldrop	G. Z. Stone	Don Ford
Lipscomb	Terri Parker	John Mann	Garner Schoenhals	Mark Cates	Marvin Born	Lewis Deeds
Live Oak	Lois Shannon	George P. Morrill II	J.J. Houdmann	Hilbert Kopplin	Jimmy Strause	Emilio Garza
Llano	Debbie Honig	Sam Oatman	Bill Kinney	Keith Faulkner	Duane Stueven	Leon Tucker
Loving	Beverly Hanson	Randy Reynolds	Harlan Hopper	Joe R. Renteria	Skeet Jones	Royce Creager
Lubbock	Jean Anne Stratton	William C. (Bill) Sowder	Kenny Maines	James Kitten	Gilbert Flores	Gary Schwantz
Lynn	Sandra Laws	Ricky B. Smith	Don Morton	Michael Braddock	Sandra Kizer	J.T. Miller
Madison	Joyce Batson	William (Bill) Bennett	Reed Reynolds	Don Farris	David Callaham	J.R. Andrus
Marion	Janie McCay	Jim Finstrom	R. M. Blevins	T. W. Smith	Eugene Robinson	Charles Treadwell
Martin	Susie Hull	Hardy L. Wilkerson	Doyle Hale	Homer Henson	Eldon Welch	Wade Turner
Mason	Beatrice Langehennig	Sam Oatman	Rolly Lumpkins	John D. Fleming	Drew Tallent	Billy Kothmann
Matagorda	Becky Denn	Steven E. Reis	Mike Pruett	George Deshotels	Leonard Lamar	Percy Carroll
Maverick	Diamantina Treviño	Roberto Serna	Johnny Martinez	Edward Sandoval	David Saucedo	Cesar Flores
McCulloch	Mackye Johnson	Ron Sutton	Joe Johnson	Jackie Behrens	Kenneth Adams	Jerry Tedder
McLennan	Joe Johnson	John Segrest	Wendall Crunk Sr.	Lester Gibson	Joe Mashek	Ray Meadows
McMullen	Nell Hodgin	George P. Morrill II	Asa Farrer	Rodney Swaim	Paul Koonce	Maximo Quintanilla Jr.
Medina	M. Eva Soto	Mickey Pennington	Royce R. Hartmann	Stanley Keller Jr.	Enrique G. Santos	Kelly Carroll
Menard	Elsie Maserang	Ronald Sutton	Rudy Gonzales	March Compton	Bart Wilkinson	Donald Kothmann
Midland	Vivian Wood	Al Schorre	Henry Goulet	Mike Bradford	Louisa Valencia	Randy Prude
Milam	Betty R. Robertson	Hollis C. Lewis Jr.	V. W. Hauk	Troy C. Mode	C. Dale Jaecks	Burke Bauerschlag
Mills	Beulah L. Roberts	Lee Haney	Joe Karnes	Carroll Bunting	Dale Henry	James Miller
Mitchell	Sharon Hammond	Mark Edwards	Edward B. Roach	Carl Guelker	Wyndell B. Inman	Billy H. Preston
Montague	Condell Lowrie	Tim Cole	Jon A. Kernek	Jerry Clement	Tommy L. Sparks	Tommie Sappington
Montgomery	Barbara Adamick	Mike McDougal	Mike Meador	Malcolm Purvis	Ed Chance	Ed Rinehart
Moore	Diane Hoefling	Barry E. Blackwell	A. Gordon Clark	Louis Dubuque	Keith Christie	Lynn Cartrite
Morris	Welton Walker	Richard Townsend	Coy L. Roney	Dearl Quarles	James Settles	Gary Camp
Motley	Lucretia Campbell	Beckey McPherson	John M. Russell	Donnie L. Turner	Franklin Jameson	J. N. Fletcher
Nacogdoches	Shelby Solomon	Tim James	Jimmy Daniels	Norman Henderson	Alvin Stanaland	Tom Strickland
Navarro	Marilyn Greer	Patrick Batchelor	Betty Armstrong	Billy McManus	William Baldwin	David Garrett
Newton	Abbie Nell Stark	Atmar W. Davis Jr.	Weldon Wilkinson	Thomas Gill	Melton Jarrell	Robert F. Green
Nolan	Vera Holloman	Mark Edwards	Edsel Bankhead	Leslie Bond	Tommy White	Tony Lara
Nueces	Oscar Soliz	Carlos Valdez	Frank Schwing	David Noyola	Oscar O. Ortiz	Joe McComb
Ochiltree	Shawn Bogard	Bruce Roberson	Jack Kile	Tom O'Dell	James. Clark	Larry Hardy
Oldham	Becky Groneman	Don Davis	Quincy Taylor	Donnie Knox	Roger Morris	Grady Skaggs
Orange	Vickie Edgerly	John D. Kimbrough	James D. Stringer	Sue Bearden	Don E. Cole	Bill Harland
Palo Pinto	Helen Slemmons	Jerry Ray	David Lee	Robert Murray	George Nowak	Earnest Pechacek
Panola	Sandra King	Danny Buck Davidson	Ronnie LaGrone	Doug Cotton	Joe Harris	Jimmy Davis
Parker	Elvera Johnson	Don Schnebly	Danny Choate	Mack Dobbs	Charlie Horton	Gary Plugge

County	District Clerk	District Attorney*	Comm. Precinct 1	Comm. Precinct 2	Comm. Precinct 3	Comm. Precinct 4
Parmer	Sandra Warren	Johnny Actkinson	John Tannahill	Thomas D. Ware	Jerry Davis	Raymond McGehee
Pecos	Janice Stockburger	Albert Valadez (83rd) Ori T. White (112th)	Gregg McKenzie	Tony Villarreal	Linda Webb	Paul Valenzuela
Polk	Nell Lowe	John Holleman	B. E. "Slim" Speights	Bobby Smith	James J. "Buddy" Purvis	R. R. "Dick" Hubert
Potter	Cindy Groomer	Rebecca King	John Stradley	Manuel Perez Villasenor	Strick Watkins	Iris Sanders Lawrence
Presidio	Brenda M. Silva	Albert Valadez	Felipe Angel Cordero	Eloy Aranda	Jaime Ramirez	Danny Watts
Rains	Mary Sheppard	Frank Long	Virgil McEnturff	William Potts	Gary Bishop	Rayford Briggs
Randall	Jo Carter	James Farren	Brian Barrett	Gene Parker	George Huskey	Craig Gualtiere
Reagan	Terri Pullig	Albert Valadez (83rd) Ori T. White (112th)	Jim O'Bryan	Michael Fisher	Bill Schneemann	Thomas Strube
Real	Bella A. Rubio	Tony Hackebeil	Allen Moffett	Wade Reagor	Castulo San Miguel	Joe W. Connell Sr.
Red River	Clara Gaddis	Jack Herrington	Ricky Daniels	Ronnie James	Elmer Caton	Mark Megason
Reeves	Juana Jaquez	Randall W. Reynolds	Felipe Arredondo	David Castillo	Herman S. Tarin	Gilberto "Hivi" M. Rayos
Refugio	Ruby Garcia	Michael A. Sheppard	Val Ortega	Janis M. Gillespie	James Henry	Richard Martinez
Roberts	Donna L. Goodman	John Mann	William H. Clark	Ken Gill	Kelly Flowers	James F. Duvall Jr.
Robertson	Cornelia A. Starkey	John C. Paschall	John Anderson	Jim Davis	Michael Byer	Marie Abraham
Rockwall	Kay McDaniel	Ray Sumrow	Jerry Wimpee	Dale Troutt	Bruce Beaty	Ernest Smith
Runnels	Loretta Michalewicz	Stephen F. Smith	Skipper Wheeless	Keith Collom	James T. Self	Richard W. (Ricky) Strube
Rusk	Linda Smith	Kyle Freeman	Bill Hale	Harold Kuykendall	Dan Cates	Kimble Harris
Sabine	Tanya Walker	Charles Mitchell	Keith Clark	Lynn Smith	Doyle Dickerson	Robert Gene Nethery
San Augustine	Jean Steptoe	Charles Mitchell	Tommy Hunter	Edward Wilson	Joey Holloway	Bill T. Langford
San Jacinto	Marilyn Nettles	Scott E. Rosekrans	Norman J. Street	Bruce Thomas	Thomas L. Bonds	Will Copeland
San Patricio	Patricia Norton	Tom Bridges	Nina Treviño	Fred Nardini	Pedro G. Rodriguez	Gordon Porter
San Saba	Kim Wells	Sam Oatman	Roger Crockett	Rickey Lusty	Wayland Perry	Roger McGehee
Schleicher	Peggy Williams	Stephen F. Lupton	Johnny G. Mayo Jr.	Bill Clark	Steve Minor	Ross Whitten
Scurry	Trina Rodgers	Dana Cooley	Ralph Trevey	Roy Idom	Howard Limmer	Chloanne Lindsey
Shackelford	Cheri Hawkins	Gary M. Brown	James Tabor	R. P. Mitchell	Jimmy T. Brooks	Stan West
Shelby	Marsha Singletary	Karren S. Price	Donnie Borders	Tony Denby	Spencer Hamilton	Larry Moreland
Sherman	M. L. Albert	Barry E. Blackwell	Wayne Cummings	Wood Craig	David Hass	Tommy Asher
Smith	Becky Dempsey	Jack Skeen	Sharon Emmert	Gus Ramirez	Derrell Cooper	Andrew R. Melontree
Somervell	Lovella Williams	Dale Hanna	Larry Hulsey	Foy Edwards	Randy Whitworth	Helen Kerwin
Starr	Juan Erasmo Saenz	Heriberto Silva	José Maria Alvarez	Raul Peña Jr.	Eloy Garza	Abel N. Gonzalez
Stephens	Shirley Parker	Steve Bristow	Jerry Toland	D. C. "Button" Sikes	Ozell Devenport	Carter Fore
Sterling	Diane A. Haar	Stephen Lupton	Billy Joe Blair	Russell Noletubby	Patsy Bynum	Skeete Foster
Stonewall	Betty L. Smith	John Fouts	Mike Hill	Pat Cumbie	Larry Dickerson	Gary Myers
Sutton	Bobbie Smith	Ori T. White	Mike Villanueva	John Wade	Bill Keel	Belia Castaneda
Swisher	Brenda Hudson	Terry McEachern	Lloyd Rahlfs	Joe Bob Thompson	Billy Settle	Tim Reed
Tarrant	Tom Wilder	Tim Curry	Dionne Bagsby	Marti VanRavenswaay	Glen Whitley	J. D. Johnson
Taylor	JoAnn Lackey	James Eidson	Jack Turner	Nowlin Cox	Stan Egger	Chuck Statler
Terrell	Martha Allen	Thomas F. Lee	Thelma Calzada	Santiago Flores	Lloyd Goldwire	Hudson Kerr
Terry	Paige Lindsey	G. Dwayne Pruitt	Earl J. Brown	Dale Andrews	Don Robertson	John Franks
Throckmorton	Melanie Jones	John Fouts	Doyle Wells	John Jones	Carlton Sullivan	George Seedig
Titus	Bobby LaPrade	Charles Bailey	Mike Price	Mike Fields	Billy Jack Thompson	Thomas Hockaday
Tom Green	Sheri Woodfin	Stephen R. Lupton (51st) Stephen Smith (119th)	Clayton Friend	Karl Bookter	Jodie Weeks	Richard Easingwood
Travis	Amalia Rodriguez-Mendoza	Ken Oden	Ron Davis	Karen Sonleitner	Todd Baxter	Margaret Gomez
Trinity	Cheryl Cartwright	Joe L. Price	Grover Worsham	Bill Burton	Cecil Webb	Travis Forrest
Tyler	Patricia Brown	Joe R. Smith	Maxie Riley	James T. (Rusty) Hughes	Joe Marshall	Henry Earl Sawyer Sr.

County	District Clerk	District Attorney*	Comm. Precinct 1	Comm. Precinct 2	Comm. Precinct 3	Comm. Precinct 4
Upshur	Frankie Hamberlin	Tim Cone	Gaddis Lindsey	Tommie L. Stanley	Rick Jackson	Russell Green Jr.
Upton	Phyllis Stephens	Albert G. Valadez (83rd) Ori White (112th)	Mack McKenzie	Tommy Owens	Willie Martinez	Leon Patrick
Uvalde	Lydia Steele	Anton E. (Tony) Hackebeil	Randy Scheide	Gilbert Torres	Jerry Bates	Jesse R. Moreno
Val Verde	Martha Germany	Thomas F. Lee	Frank Coronado	Rogelio (Roy) H. Musquiz	John M. Cody	Jesus E. (Cheo) Ortiz
Van Zandt	Nancy Young	Leslie Dixon	O. D. Hazel	John Durgan	Jimmy Don Wilson	Jim Wise
Victoria	Mary Elizabeth Jimenez	M.P. (Dexter) Eaves	Chris Rivera	Jerry Nobles	John Hammack	Wayne D. Dierlam
Walker	Bernice Coleman	David P. Weeks	B.J. Gaines	Robert E. Autery	James C. "Buddy" Reynolds	Tim Paulsel
Waller	Patricia Spadachene	Sherry Robinson	Leroy Singleton Sr.	John Isom	Frank D. Jackson	Louis Canales
Ward	Jo Ann Roark	Randy Reynolds	Julian Florez	Kathy Fausett	Larry Hunt	Rick McCurdy
Washington	Vicki Lehmann	Charles Sebesta	David Simpson	Robert Mikeska	Alfred Boeker Jr.	Joy Fuchs
Webb	Manuel Gutierrez	Joe Rubio	Jorge de la Garza	Judith Gutierrez	Rick Reyes	Mike Urdiales
Wharton	Evelyn Kramr	Josh McCown	Mickey Reynolds	Chris King	Phillip Miller	Jimmy Kainer
Wheeler	Sherri Jones	Steven R. Emmert	Kenneth Childress	Tom Puryear	Hubert Moore	Boyd Hiltbrunner
Wichita	Dorsey Trapp	Barry L. Macha	Joe Miller	Nadene "Pat" Norriss	Gordon Griffith	William Presson
Wilbarger	Wilda Byers	Dan Mike Bird	John Milner	Freddie Streit	Glen Turner	Lenville Morris
Willacy	Santiago "Chago" Fonseca	Juan Angel Guerra	Israel Tamez	Noe T. Loya	Alfred Serrato Jr.	Jose Isac "Joe" Jimenez
Williamson	Bonnie Wolbrueck	Ken Anderson	Michael Heiligenstein	Greg Boatright	David Hays	Frankie Limmer
Wilson	Shirley Polasek	Lynn Ellison	Roger Lopez	John P. Olenick	Robert "Bobby" H. Lynn	Wayne H. Stroud
Winkler	Sherry Terry	Michael L. Fostel	Tommy R. Smith	Robbie Wolf	Randy Neal	Jose G. Dominguez
Wise	Lawana Snider	Barry Green	Jerry Flusche	James A. Hubbard	Farley Bridges	L. Paul Wood
Wood	Novis Wisdom	Marcus D. (Mark) Taylor	Glenn Bevill	Kenneth Wilson	Roger Pace	Jerry Galloway
Yoakum	Vickie Blundell	Richard Clark	Woody Lindsey	J.R. Slentz	Jim Barron	Jack Cobb
Young	Carolyn Collins	Stephen E. Bristow	Duane Downey	John C. Bullock	R.L. Spivey	David Yoder
Zapata	Consuelo R. Villarreal	José A. Rubio Jr.	Jose Luis Flores	Angel Garza	Adolfo Gonzalez Jr.	Norberto Garza
Zavala	Frankie G. Mancha	Robert Serna	Jesús Vasquez	Josie Espinoza	Pilo Vasquez	Rosa Quijano

* If more than one District Attorney is listed for a county, the district court number is noted in parentheses after each attorney's name. If no District Attorney is listed, the County Attorney, whose name can be found in Table No. 1, assumes the duties of that office.

Texans in Congress

Besides the two members of the U.S. Senate allocated to each state, Texas is allocated 30 members in the U.S. House of Representatives. The term of office for members of the House is two years; the terms of all members will expire on Jan. 1, 2001. Senators serve six-year terms. Sen. Kay Bailey Hutchison's will end in 2001. Sen. Phil Gramm's term will end in 2003.

Addresses and phone numbers of the lawmakers' Washington and district offices are below, as well as the committees on which they serve. Washington **zip codes** are **20515** for members of the House and **20510** for senators. The telephone **area code** for Washington is **202**. On the Internet, the House members can be reached through **www.house.gov/**. Members of Congress receive a salary of $136,700.

U.S. Senate

GRAMM, Phil. Republican (Home: College Station); Washington Office: 370 RSOB, Washington, D.C. 20510-4302; (202) 224-2934, Fax 228-2856. Website, www.senate.gov/~gramm; e-mail, administrator@gramm.senate.gov.
Texas Offices: 222 E. Van Buren Ste. 404, **Harlingen** 78550, (512) 423-6118; 712 Main Ste. 1704, **Houston** 77002, (713) 718-4000; 1205 Texas Ave. Ste. 1205, **Lubbock** 79401, (806) 743-7533; 2323 Bryan Ste. 2150, **Dallas** 75201, (214) 767-3000; 310 N. Mesa Ste. 1004, **El Paso** 79901, (915) 534-6897; 100 E. Ferguson Ste. 1004, **Tyler** 75702, (903) 593-0902; 402 E. Ramsey Rd. Ste. 200, **San Antonio** 78216, (210) 366-9494. **Committees**: the Budget; Finance; Banking, Housing and Urban Affairs.

HUTCHISON, Kay Bailey. Republican (Home: Dallas); Washington Office: 284 RSOB, Washington, D.C. 20510-4304; (202) 224-5922, Fax 224-0776. Website, www.senate.gov/~hutchison; e-mail, senator@hutchison.senate.gov.
Texas Offices: 961 Federal Bldg., 300 E. 8th St., **Austin** 78701, (512) 482-5834; 500 Chestnut St. Ste. 1570, **Abilene** 79602, (915) 676-2937; 10440 N. Central Expy. Ste. 1160, **Dallas** 75231, (214) 361-3500; 1919 Smith St. Ste 800, **Houston** 77002, (713) 653-3456; 8023 Vantage Dr. Ste. 460, **San Antonio** 78230, (210) 340-2885. **Committees**: Commerce, Science and Transportation; Appropriations; Rules and Administration.

U.S. House of Representatives

ARCHER, Bill, R-Houston, District 7; Washington Office: 1236 LHOB; (202) 225-2571, Fax 225-4381; **District Office**: 10000 Memorial Dr., Suite 620, Houston 77024-3490, (713) 682-8828. **Committees**: Ways and Means (chairman); Joint Committee on Taxation (chairman).

ARMEY, Richard, R-Irving, District 26; Washington Office: 301 CHOB; (202) 225-7772, Fax 225-7614; **District Office**: 9901 E. Valley Ranch Parkway, Suite 3050, Irving 75063, (972) 556-2500. **House Majority Leader**.

BARTON, Joe, R-Ennis, District 6; Washington Office: 2264 RHOB; (202) 225-2002. Fax 225-3052; **District Offices**: 4521 S. Hulen, Ste. 210, Fort Worth 76109, (817) 543-1000; 303 West Knox, Suite 201, Ennis 75119-3942, (817) 543-1000; 805 Washington Dr. Ste. F, Arlington 76011, (817) 543-1000. **Committees**: Commerce, Science.

BENTSEN, Ken, D-Houston, District 25; Washington Office: 326 CHOB; (202) 225-7508, Fax 225-2947; **District Offices**: 6575 West Loop South Ste. 496, Bellaire 77401, (713) 667-3554; 1001 E. Southmore Ste. 810, Pasadena 77502-1296, (713) 473-4334, Fax 475-8887; 1300 Rollingbrook Ste. 517, Baytown 77521, (281) 837-8225. **Committees**: Banking and Financial Services, Budget.

BONILLA, Henry, R-San Antonio, District 23; Washington Office: 1427 LHOB; (202) 225-4511, Fax 225-2237; **District Offices**: 11120 Wurzbach Ste. 300, San Antonio 78230, (210) 697-9055; 1300 Matamoros Ste. 113B, Laredo 78040, (956) 726-4682; 111 E. Broadway Ste. 101, Del Rio 78840, (830) 774-6547; 4400 N. Big Spring Ste. 211, Midland 79705, (915) 686-8833. **Committee**: Appropriations.

BRADY, Kevin, R-The Woodlands, District 8; Washington Office: 1531 LHOB; (202) 225-4901. 111 East University Ste. 216, College Station 77840, (409) 846-6068, Fax (409) 260-2916; 616 FM 1960 West Ste. 315, Houston 77090 (281) 895-8892; 200 River Pointe Ste. 304, Conroe 77304, (409) 441-5700, Fax (409) 441-5757. **Committees**: International Relations, Resources, Science.

COMBEST, Larry, R-Lubbock, District 19; Washington Office: 1026 LHOB; (202) 225-4005, Fax (202) 225-9615; **District Office**: 5809 S. Western, No. 205, Amarillo 79110, (806) 353-3945; 1205 Texas Avenue, Room 810, Lubbock, 79401, (806) 763-1611; 3800 East 42nd, No. 205, Odessa 79762, (915) 550-0743. **Committees**: Agriculture (chairman), Small Business.

DeLAY, Tom, R-Sugar Land, District 22; Washington Office: 341 CHOB; (202) 225-5951, Fax 225-5117; **District Office:** 10707 Corporate Dr. Ste. 118, Stafford 77477, (281) 240-3700. House Majority Whip. **Committee**: Appropriations.

DOGGETT, Lloyd, D-Austin, District 10; Washington Office: 328 CHOB; (202) 225-4865, Fax 225-3073; **District Office**: 300 8th St. No. 763, Austin 78701, (512) 916-5921. **Committees**: Ways and Means.

EDWARDS, Chet, D-Waco, District 11; Washington Office: 2459 RHOB; (202) 225-6105, Fax 225-0350; **District Offices**: 116 South East, Belton 76513, (254) 933-2904; 701 Clay Ave. Ste. 200, Waco 76706, (254) 752-9600, Fax 752-7769. **Committee**: Appropriations.

FROST, Martin, D-Dallas, District 24; Washington Office: 2256 RHOB; (202) 225-3605, Fax 225-4951; **District Offices:** 400 South Zang Ste.506, Dallas 75208, (214) 948-3401; 3020 S.E. Loop 820, Fort Worth 76140, (817) 293-9231; 100 N. Main Ste. 534, Corsicana (903) 874-0760. **Committee**: Rules.

GONZALEZ, Charlie A., D-San-Antonio, District 20; Washington Office: 327 CHOB; (202) 225-3236, Fax 225-1915; **District Office**: 124-B Federal Building, 727 East Durango, San Antonio 78206, (210) 472-6199. **Committees**: Banking and Financial Services, Small Business.

GRANGER, Kay, R-Fort Worth, District 12; Washington Office: 435 CHOB; (202) 225-5071; **District Office**: 1600 W. Seventh Ste. 740, Fort Worth 76102, (817) 338-0909, Fax 335-5852. **Committee**: Appropriations.

GREEN, Gene, D-Houston, District 29; Washington Office: 2429 RHOB; (202) 225-1688, Fax 225-9903; **District Office**: 256 N. Sam Houston Pkwy. E. Ste. 29, Houston 77060, (281) 999-5879; 11811 I-10 East Ste. 430, Houston 77029, (713) 330-0761. **Committee**: Commerce.

HALL, Ralph M., D-Rockwall, District 4; Washington Office: 2221 RHOB; (202) 225-6673, Fax (202) 225-3332; **District Office**: 104 N. San Jacinto, 119 Federal Building, Rockwall 75087, (972) 771-9118; 101 E. Pecan, Sherman 75090, (903) 892-1112; 211 W. Ferguson Ste. 211, Tyler 75702, (903) 597-3729. **Committees**: Commerce, Science.

HINOJOSA, Rubén, D-Mercedes, District 15; Washington Office: 1032 LHOB; (202) 225-2531, Fax 225-5688; **District Office**: 311 N. 15 St., McAllen 78501, (210) 682-5545; 107 S. St. Mary's St., Beeville 78102, (512) 358-8407. **Committee**: Education and the Workforce, Small Business.

JOHNSON, Eddie Bernice, D-Dallas, District 30; Washington Office: 1123 LHOB; (202) 225-8885, Fax 226-1477; **District Office**: 2501 Cedar Springs Ste. 350, Dallas 75201, (214) 922-8885; 1634B W. Irving Blvd., Irving 75061, (972) 253-8885. **Committees**: Science, Transportation and Infrastructure.

JOHNSON, Sam, R-Dallas, District 3; Washington Office: 1030 LHOB; (202) 225-4201, Fax 225-1485; **District Office**: 801 E. Campbell Rd., Ste. 425, Richardson 75081, (972) 470-0892, Fax 470-9973. **Committees**: Education and the Workforce, Ways and Means.

LAMPSON, Nick, D-Beaumont, District 9; Washington Office: 417 CHOB; (202) 225-6565. District Office; 601 Rosenberg Ste. 216, Galveston, 77550, (409) 762-5877, Fax 763-4133. **Committees**: Science, Transportation and Infrastructure.

LEE, Sheila Jackson, D-Houston, District 18; Washington Office: 410 CHOB; (202) 225-3816, Fax 225-3317; **District Offices**: 1919 Smith St., No. 1180, Houston 77002, (713) 655-0050, Fax 655-1612; 6719 W. Montgomery Rd, Rm. 204, Houston 77091 (713) 691-4882; 420 W. 19th St., Houston 77008, (713) 861-4070. **Committees**: Judiciary, Science.

ORTIZ, Solomon P., D-Corpus Christi, District 27; Washington Office: 2136 RHOB; (202) 225-7742, Fax 226-1134; **District Offices**: 3649 Leopard Ste. 510, Corpus Christi 78408, (512) 883-5868; 3505 Boca Chica Blvd. Ste. 200, Brownsville 78521, (956) 541-1242. **Committees**: Armed Services, Resources.

PAUL, Ron, R-Surfside, District 14, Washington Office: 203 CHOB; (202) 225-2831; **District Offices**: 200 W. Second Ste. 210, Freeport, (409) 230-0000; 312

S. Main, Victoria 77901, (512) 576-1231; 301 Guadalupe Ste. 105, San Marcos 78665, (512) 396-1400. **Committees**: Banking and Financial Services, Education and the Workforce.

REYES, Silvestre, D-El Paso, District 16; Washington Office: 514 CHOB; (202) 225-4831, Fax 225-2016; **District Office**: 310 N. Mesa Ste. 400, El Paso 79901, (915) 534-4400. **Committees**: Armed Services, Veterans' Affairs.

RODRIGUEZ, Ciro D., D-San Antonio, District 28; Washington Office: 323 CHOB; (202) 225-1640, Fax 225-1641; **District Offices**: 1313 SE Military Hwy. Ste. 115, San Antonio 78214, (210) 924-7383; 202 E. St. Joseph Ste. 5, San Diego 78384, (512) 279-3097; 301 Lincoln, Roma 78584, (956) 847-1111. **Committees**: Armed Services, Veterans' Affairs.

SANDLIN, Max, D-Marshall, District 1; Washington Office: 214 CHOB; (202) 225-3035; **District Offices**: 1300 E. Pinecrest Ste. 30, Marshall 75670, (903) 938-8386, Fax 935-5772; 7000 James Bowie Dr., New Boston 75570, (903) 628-5594, Fax 628-3155; 320 Church St. Rm. 132, Sulphur Springs 75482, (903) 885-8682, Fax 885-2976. **Committees**: Banking and Financial Services, Transportation and Infrastructure.

SESSIONS, Pete, R-Dallas, District 5; Washington Office: 1318 LHOB; (202) 225-2231, Fax 225-5878. **District Offices**: 10675 E. Northwest Hwy. Ste. 1685, Dallas 75238, (214) 349-9996 or 1-800-967-6554, Fax 349-0738; 100 E. Corsicana St. Ste.208, Athens 75751, (903) 675-8288, Fax 675-8351. **Committees**: Rules, Banking and Financial Services (on leave).

SMITH, Lamar S., R-San Antonio, District 21; Washington Office: 2231 RHOB; (202) 225-4236, Fax 225-8628; **District Offices**: 1100 NE Loop 410 Ste. 640, San Antonio 78209, .(210) 821-5024; 4305 N. Garfield Ste. 228B, Midland 79705, (915) 653-5232; 33 E. Twohig Ste. 302, San Angelo 76903, (915) 653-3971; 1006 Junction Highway, Kerrville 78028, (210) 895-1414; 221 E. Main, Ste. 318, Round Rock 78664, (512) 218-4221. **Committees**: Standards of Official Conduct (chairman), Science, Judiciary.

STENHOLM, Charles W., D-Stamford, District 17, Washington Office: 1211 LHOB; (202) 225-6605, Fax 225-2234; **District Offices**: 903 E. Hamilton, P. O. Box 1237, Stamford 79553, (915) 773-3623, Fax 773-2833; 241 Pine Ste. 4A, Abilene 79601, (915) 673-7221, Fax 676-9547; 33 E. Twohig Ave., No. 318, San Angelo 76903, (915) 655-7994. **Committee**: Agriculture.

THORNBERRY, William M. (Mac), R-Clarendon, District 13; Washington Office: 131 CHOB; (202) 225-3706, Fax 225-3486; **District Offices**: 724 Polk Ste. 400, Amarillo 79101, (806) 371-8844; and 4245 Kemp Ste. 315, Wichita Falls 76308, (940) 692-1700. **Committees**: Armed Services, Budget, Resources.

TURNER, Jim, D-Crockett, District 2; Washington Office: 208 CHOB; (202) 225-2401, Fax 225-5955; **District Office**: 605 E. Goliad Ste. 102, Crockett 75835, (409) 544-8414; 701 N. First Rm. 201, Lufkin 75901, (409) 637-1700; 420 W. Green Ave., Orange 77630, (409) 883-4990. **Committees**: Armed Services, Government Reform. ☆

Medals of Freedom Honor Three Texans

The nation's highest civilian honor, the Medal of Freedom, was awarded to three Texans in 1998.

James Farmer, civil rights leader; Mario G. Obledo, voting rights activist; and Justin Dart Jr, an advocate for the disabled, received the honor from President Bill Clinton at the White House in January 1998.

James L. Farmer Jr. was born on Jan. 12, 1920, in Marshall, where his father was teaching at Wiley College. His father later taught at Huston College in Austin (now Huston-Tillotson College). The senior Farmer is evidently the first black man in Texas to have a Ph.D. James Jr.'s mother was Pearl Marion Houston Farmer.

James Farmer Jr. was a founder the Congress of Racial Equality (CORE) in 1942 and was an organizer of the Freedom Rides through the Deep South in 1961. Mr. Farmer said in a 1997 interview that he would like

James L. Farmer Jr.

to be known for those accomplishments and that he "attempted to bring Gandhian techniques of nonviolence to the struggle for racial equality in this country."

At the age of 14, Mr. Farmer entered Wiley, a Methodist college, as a freshman and in 1941 graduated from what was then called the School of Theology at Howard University in Washington, D.C.

He went to work for a pacifist organization in Chicago called the Fellowship of Reconciliation before leaving the group to start CORE.

In 1942, Mr. Farmer led the first sit-in of the U.S. civil rights struggle at a coffee shop near the University of Chicago.

He was an assistant secretary in the Department of Health, Education and Welfare at the beginning of the Nixon administration but resigned in his second year.

He returned to his alma mater in Marshall in March 1998 to unveil a historical marker honoring his father. Mr. Farmer died July 9, 1999, in Fredericksburg, Va.

Mario G. Obledo was born in San Antonio in 1932, one of 12 children orphaned at an early age. His parents had come to the United States from Mexico in 1915.

After graduating from Fox Tech High School in San Antonio, Mr. Obledo enrolled in the University of Texas in Austin. Naval service during the Korean War interrupted his education. He returned to UT-Austin and received a bachelor's degree in pharmacy in 1957.

While working as a pharmacist in San Antonio, he earned a law degree from St. Mary's University.

In 1964 Mr. Obledo ran unsuccessfully for the Texas Legislature. He then joined the Texas attorney general's office as an assistant attorney general.

Mr. Obledo helped form the Mexican American Legal Defense and Educational Fund (MALDEF) in 1968 and served as its first president.

He left MALDEF in 1973 and went into private law practice in California. Gov. Jerry Brown appointed him California's secretary of health and welfare in 1975, a

Mario Obledo receives the medal from President Clinton. The Dallas Morning News file photos.

position he held until 1983.

Mr. Oblado has been a teaching fellow at Harvard Law School and served as national president of the League of United Latin American Citizens. He currently resides in Sacramento, Calif.,

Justin Dart Jr. served in five different presidential appointments in the area of disablity policy and is credited with securing passage in 1990 of the Americans With Disabilities Act.

He was born in 1930 in Chicago. His maternal grandfather had started the Walgreen drugstores. In 1948 Justin was stricken with polio, and, as one biographer put it, he emerged "humbled" by his new status as a wheelchair-user in a land of conformity."

He enrolled in the University of Houston, earning a bachelor's degree in history and education in 1953 and a master's in history in 1954. During his years at the U of H he taught required history courses, formed an organization for racial desegregation on the campus and co-founded the liberal Harris County Democrats.

Justin Dart Jr.

He then attended the University of Texas School of Law and was in the honor fraternity but left before graduation.

In the early 1960s, he returned to the family business (Walgreens-Rexall-Tupperware) to run Japan Tupperware. However, a study tour of South Vietnam where he observed the poor conditions of orphans caused him in 1966 to leave the business world to dedicate himself to political organizing and lobbying on behalf of the disabled. Today, Mr. Dart resides in Washington.

The three Texans were among 15 persons honored in 1998. Others included Elliot Richardson, who served in four different U.S. cabinet positions; philanthropist David Rockefeller; Albert Shanker, teacher union leader, and Admiral Elmo Zumwalt Jr., former chief of naval operations.

The Medal of Freedom was established in 1945 by President Harry Truman. Other Texans who have received the honor include Barbara Jordan, Dr. Michael DeBakey, Lady Bird Johnson, Willie Velásquez and J. Frank Dobie. ☆

Federal Courts in Texas

Source: The following list of U.S. district courts was compiled from reports of the clerks of the individual courts.

U.S. District Courts

Texas is divided into four federal judicial districts, each of which comprises several divisions. Appeal from all Texas federal courts is to the **Fifth Circuit Court of Appeals,** New Orleans. U.S. district judges are appointed for life and receive a salary of $136,700 annually.

Northern Texas District

District Judges — Chief Judge, Jerry Buchmeyer, Dallas. **Senior Judges:** Barefoot Sanders, Dallas; David O. Belew Jr. and Eldon B. Mahon, Fort Worth; Halbert O. Woodard, Lubbock. **Judges:** Mary Lou Robinson, Amarillo; A. Joe Fish, Sidney A. Fitzwater, Jorge A. Solis, Joe Kendall, Robert B. Maloney and Sam A. Lindsay, Dallas; Sam R. Cummings, Lubbock. **Clerk of District Court:** Nancy Doherty, Dallas. **U.S. Attorney:** Paul Coggins, Dallas. **U.S. Marshal:** W.D. Bransom, Dallas. Court is in continuous session in each division of the Northern Texas District. Following are the different divisions of the Northern District and the counties in each division:

Dallas Division

Dallas, Ellis, Hunt, Johnson, Kaufman, Navarro and Rockwall. **Magistrates:** William F. Sanderson Jr., Jane Jackson, Jeff Kaplan and Paul Stickney, Dallas.

Fort Worth Division

Comanche, Erath, Hood, Jack, Palo Pinto, Parker, Tarrant and Wise. **Magistrate:** Charles Bleil, Fort Worth. **Deputy-in-charge:** Pam Murphy.

Amarillo Division

Armstrong, Briscoe, Carson, Castro, Childress, Collingsworth, Dallam, Deaf Smith, Donley, Gray, Hall, Hansford, Hartley, Hemphill, Hutchinson, Lipscomb, Moore, Ochiltree, Oldham, Parmer, Potter, Randall, Roberts, Sherman, Swisher and Wheeler. **Magistrate:** Clinton E. Averitte, Amarillo. **Deputy-in-charge:** Lynn Sherman.

Abilene Division

Callahan, Eastland, Fisher, Haskell, Howard, Jones, Mitchell, Nolan, Shackelford, Stephens, Stonewall, Taylor and Throckmorton. **Magistrate:** Billy W. Boone, Abilene. **Deputy-in-charge:** Marsha Elliott.

San Angelo Division

Brown, Coke, Coleman, Concho, Crockett, Glasscock, Irion, Menard, Mills, Reagan, Runnels, Schleicher, Sterling, Sutton and Tom Green. Magistrate: Philip R. Lane, San Angelo. **Deputy-in-charge:** Ann Light.

Wichita Falls Division

Archer, Baylor, Clay, Cottle, Foard, Hardeman, King, Knox, Montague, Wichita, Wilbarger and Young. **Magistrate:** R. Kerry Roach, Wichita Falls. **Deputy Clerk:** Allison Terry.

Lubbock Division

Bailey, Borden, Cochran, Crosby, Dawson, Dickens, Floyd, Gaines, Garza, Hale, Hockley, Kent, Lamb, Lubbock, Lynn, Motley, Scurry, Terry and Yoakum. **U.S. District Judge:** Sam R. Cummings, Lubbock. **Magistrate:** J. Q. Warnick Jr., Lubbock. **Deputy-in-charge:** Kristy Weinheimer.

Western Texas District

District Judges — Chief Judge, Harry Lee Hud-

speth, El Paso. **Senior Judges:** D. W. Suttle, San Antonio; Lucius D. Bunton III, Midland; William Wayne Justice, Austin. **Judges:** Edward C. Prado, H. F. Garcia, Orlando Garcia and Fred Biery, San Antonio; W. Royal Furgeson Jr. and David Briones, El Paso; James R. Nowlin and Sam Sparks, Austin; Walter S. Smith Jr., Waco. **Clerk of District Court:** William G. Putnicki, San Antonio. **Chief Deputy Clerk:** Michael J. Simon. **U.S. Attorney:** J. William (Bill) Blagg, San Antonio. **U.S. Marshal:** Jack Dean, San Antonio. Following are the different divisions of the Western District, and the counties in each division.

San Antonio Division

Atascosa, Bandera, Bexar, Comal, Dimmit, Frio, Gonzales, Guadalupe, Karnes, Kendall, Kerr, Medina, Real and Wilson. **Magistrates:** Pamela A. Mathy, John W. Primomo and Nancy Stein Nowak, San Antonio. **Bankruptcy Judges:** Leif M. Clark and Ronald B. King, San Antonio. **Clerk of Bankruptcy Court:** Larry Bick, San Antonio.

Austin Division

Bastrop, Blanco, Burleson, Burnet, Caldwell, Gillespie, Hays, Kimble, Lampasas, Lee, Llano, Mason, McCulloch, San Saba, Travis, Washington and Williamson. **Magistrates:** Alan D. Albright and Stephen H. Capelle, Austin. **Bankruptcy Judges:** Chief, Larry E. Kelly, and Frank P. Monroe. **District Court Deputy-in-charge:** Vacant. **Bankruptcy Court Deputy-in-charge:** Tina Warren.

El Paso Division

El Paso County only. **Magistrates:** Michael S. McDonald and Richard P. Mesa, El Paso. **Bankruptcy Judge:** Leif M. Clark, San Antonio. **District Court Deputy-in-charge:** Richard Delgado. **Bankruptcy Court Deputy-in-charge:** Mary Croy.

Waco Division

Bell, Bosque, Coryell, Falls, Freestone, Hamilton, Hill, Leon, Limestone, McLennan, Milam, Robertson and Somervell. **Magistrate:** Dennis Green, Waco. **Bankruptcy Judge:** Larry E. Kelly, Austin. **Deputy-in-charge:** Mark G. Borchardt.

Del Rio Division

Edwards, Kinney, Maverick, Terrell, Uvalde, Val Verde and Zavala. **Magistrates:** Durwood Edwards and Alia Ludlum, Del Rio. **Bankruptcy Judge:** Ronald B. King, San Antonio. **Deputy-in-charge:** Camille Cadena.

Pecos Division

Brewster, Culberson, Hudspeth, Jeff Davis, Loving, Pecos, Presidio, Reeves, Ward and Winkler. **Magistrate:** Katherine H. Baker, Pecos. **Bankruptcy Judge:** Ronald B. King, San Antonio. **Deputy-in-charge:** Karen J. White.

Midland-Odessa Division

Andrews, Crane, Ector, Martin, Midland and Upton. Court for the Midland-Odessa Division is held at Midland, but may, at the discretion of the court, be held in Odessa. **Magistrate:** L. Stuart Platt, Midland. **Bankruptcy Judge:** Ronald B. King, San Antonio. **District Court Deputy-in-charge:** John D. Neil, Midland. **Bankruptcy Court Deputy-in-charge:** Christy L. Carouth.

Eastern Texas District

District Judges — Chief Judge, Richard A. Schell, Beaumont. **Judges:** Joe J. Fisher, Thad Heartfield and Howell Cobb, Beaumont; William M. Steger, John Hannah Jr.; Paul N. Brown, Sherman; David J. Folsom, Texarkana. **Clerk of District Court:** David J. Maland, Tyler. **U.S. Attorney:** J. Michael Bradford, Beaumont. **U.S. Marshal:** Norris Batiste, Beaumont. **Chief U.S. Probation Officer:** Kenneth LaBorde, Beaumont. **Judges in Bankruptcy:** William Parker, Tyler, and Donald R. Sharp, Beaumont. **Federal Public Defender:** G. Patrtick Black, Tyler. Following are the divisions of the Eastern District and the counties in each division:

Tyler Division

Anderson, Cherokee, Gregg, Henderson, Panola, Rains, Rusk, Smith, Van Zandt and Wood. **Magistrates:** Henry W. McKee, Tyler, and Judith Guthrie, Tyler. **Chief Deputy:** Jeanne Henderson.

Beaumont Division

Hardin, Jasper, Jefferson, Liberty, Newton, Orange. **Magistrates:** Earl Hines and J. Michael Bradford, Beaumont. **Chief Deputy:** Kelly Gavagan.

Marshall Division

Camp, Cass, Harrison, Marion, Morris, Upshur. **Deputy-in-charge:** Peggy Anderson.

Sherman Division

Collin, Cooke, Denton and Grayson. **Magistrate:** Roger Sanders. **Deputy-in-charge:** Sandra Southerland.

Texarkana Division

Bowie, Franklin and Titus. **Magistrate:** Charles Attaway. **Deputy-in-charge:** Sue Jordan.

Paris Division

Delta, Fannin, Hopkins, Lamar and Red River.

Lufkin Division

Angelina, Houston, Nacogdoches, Polk, Sabine, San Augustine, Shelby, Trinity, Tyler.

Southern Texas District

District Judges — Chief Judge, George P. Kazen, Laredo. **Judges:** Nancy F. Atlas, Kenneth M. Hoyt, Sim Lake, Lynn N. Hughes, David Hittner, John D. Rainey, Melinda Harmon, Vanessa D. Gilmore, Ewing Werlein Jr. and Lee H. Rosenthal, Houston; Hayden W. Head Jr. and Janis Graham Jack, Corpus Christi; Samuel B. Kent, Galveston; Filemon B. Vela and Hilda G. Tagle, Brownsville; Ricardo H. Hinojosa, McAllen. **Clerk of Court:** Michael N. Milby, Houston. **U. S. Attorney:** Mervyn M. Mosbacker Jr., Brownsville. **U.S. Marshal:** Hiram Art Contreras, Houston. **Bankruptcy Judges:** Chief, Richard S. Schmidt, Corpus Christi; Manuel D. Leal, Letitia Z. Clark, William R. Greendyke, Karen K. Brown and Wesley W. Steen, Houston. Following are the different divisions of the Southern District and the counties in each division:

Houston Division

Austin, Brazos, Colorado, Fayette, Fort Bend, Grimes, Harris, Madison, Montgomery, San Jacinto, Walker, Waller and Wharton. **Magistrates:** Calvin Botley, Frances H. Stacy, Nancy Johnson, Marcia A. Crone and Mary Milloy. **Clerk:** Michael N. Milby.

Brownsville Division

Cameron and Willacy. **Magistrate:** John Wm. Black. **Deputy-in-charge:** Juan Barbosa.

Corpus Christi Division

Aransas, Bee, Brooks, Duval, Jim Wells, Kenedy, Kleberg, Live Oak, Nueces and San Patricio. **Magistrate:** B. Janice Ellington and Jane Cooper-Hill. **Deputy-in-charge:** Monica Seaman. **Bankruptcy Court Deputy-in-charge:** Joyce Bjork.

Galveston Division

Brazoria, Chambers, Galveston and Matagorda. **Magistrate:** John R. Froeschner. **Deputy-in-charge:** Marrianne Gore.

Laredo Division

Jim Hogg, La Salle, McMullen, Webb and Zapata. **Magistrate:** Marcel C. Notzon. **Deputy-in-charge:** Rosie Rodriguez.

Victoria Division

Calhoun, DeWitt, Goliad, Jackson, Lavaca, Refugio and Victoria. **Deputy-in-charge:** Maxine Gammon.

McAllen Division

Hidalgo and Starr. **Magistrate:** Peter E. Ormsby and Dorina Ramos. **Deputies-in-charge:** Eddie Leandro and Sylvia Martinez. ☆

U.S. Tax Collections in Texas

Source: *Internal Revenue Service*

Fiscal Year	Individual Income and Employment Taxes	Corporation Income Taxes	Estate Taxes	Gift Taxes	Excise Taxes	Total U.S. Taxes Collected in Texas
1997	$ 90,222,786,000	$ 13,875,653,000	$ 933,616,000	$ 159,111,000	$ 12,185,271,000	$ 117,376,440,000
1996	76,863,689,000	12,393,992,000	733,282,000	158,237,000	10,418,847,000	101,079,028,000
1995	69,706,333,000	10,677,881,000	869,528,000	152,683,000	11,135,857,000	92,342,282,000
1994	63,916,496,000	9,698,069,000	624,354,000	347,900,000	9,528,449,000	84,086,676,000
1993	59,962,756,000	7,211,968,000	618,469,000	111,896,000	7,552,247,000	75,457,335,000
1992	57,367,765,000	6,338,621,000	598,918,000	121,164,000	7,558,642,000	71,985,109,000
1991	55,520,001,000	8,761,621,000	588,298,000	87,739,000	6,647,312,000	71,604,791,000
1990	52,795,489,000	6,983,762,000	521,811,000	196,003,000	5,694,006,000	66,191,071,000
1989	50,855,904,000	8,675,006,000	458,106,000	96,699,000	5,766,594,000	66,052,309,000
1988	45,080,428,000	6,058,172,000	444,349,000	39,137,000	5,957,085,000	57,579,171,000
1987	43,165,241,000	4,124,164,000	443,947,000	27,342,000	3,908,826,000	51,669,519,000
1986	44,090,929,000	4,808,703,000	493,405,000	35,355,000	4,169,857,000	53,598,248,000
1985	41,497,114,000	5,637,148,000	528,106,000	41,560,000	6,058,110,000	53,762,038,000
1984	37,416,203,000	4,750,079,000	494,431,000	19,844,000	5,553,491,000	48,234,047,000
1983	36,072,975,000	6,574,940,000	624,559,000	6,789,000	6,880,102,000	50,159,365,000
1982	31,692,219,000	7,526,687,000	526,420,000	31,473,000	8,623,799,000	48,400,598,000
1981	25,707,514,000	7,232,486,000	453,830,000	23,722,000	4,122,538,000	37,540,089,000

Federal Funds to Texas by County, 1998

Texas received **$92,018,564,673** in 1998 from the federal government. Below, the distribution of funds is shown by county. The first figure represents total **direct expenditures to the county** for fiscal year 1998. The second and third figures are that part of the total that went directly for individuals, either in **retirement** payments, such as Social Security, or **other direct** payments, principally Medicare. *For a more complete explanation, see end of chart.

Source: Consolidated Federal Funds Report 1998, U.S. Commerce Dept.

COUNTY	TOTAL	For INDIVIDUALS	
		Retirement	Other direct
Anderson	$ 202,712,245	$ 95,512,460	$ 54,029,374
Andrews	44,111,777	22,071,652	11,097,395
Angelina	299,996,866	149,226,549	81,486,646
Aransas	93,407,340	53,160,493	21,065,075
Archer	42,945,248	25,536,294	5,467,018
Armstrong	12,063,546	4,505,478	2,005,160
Atascosa	117,936,563	56,659,431	27,239,960
Austin	259,665,432	42,478,707	22,959,837
Bailey	34,343,413	11,509,699	7,316,238
Bandera	66,160,869	43,809,882	9,497,125
Bastrop	165,224,917	89,220,224	33,657,950
Baylor	26,792,147	12,551,972	6,879,917
Bee	106,815,194	45,264,197	32,502,119
Bell	2,555,229,653	473,907,491	184,535,425
Bexar	8,424,484,708	3,027,082,464	1,186,421,359
Blanco	57,551,727	39,120,843	12,585,879
Borden	2,466,360	474,220	414,057
Bosque	73,007,706	44,498,036	18,666,212
Bowie	550,806,402	230,691,527	98,312,315
Brazoria	592,361,690	299,327,247	137,402,666
Brazos	483,506,859	149,397,969	85,181,041
Brewster	42,665,328	17,241,014	8,376,214
Briscoe	15,784,573	4,202,048	5,821,677
Brooks	40,417,995	13,773,132	11,546,868
Brown	167,527,398	85,150,172	49,868,163
Burleson	61,860,326	34,762,033	14,720,611
Burnet	114,892,909	73,968,831	25,080,162
Caldwell	104,453,315	52,998,206	27,409,949
Calhoun	70,912,043	33,747,289	15,242,254
Callahan	50,384,348	28,691,747	13,175,565
Cameron	1,204,171,129	386,482,804	283,124,779
Camp	50,212,731	27,944,326	14,795,420
Carson	32,240,638	12,144,948	6,294,998
Cass	143,727,589	77,026,751	38,206,344
Castro	38,846,725	10,413,010	7,136,220
Chambers	81,378,875	25,339,059	19,085,375
Cherokee	159,737,750	77,523,803	50,447,951
Childress	32,514,601	14,572,485	7,508,233
Clay	35,760,690	19,929,008	8,349,426
Cochran	22,574,182	6,889,499	4,112,395
Coke	15,786,100	8,840,026	3,641,247
Coleman	59,541,926	26,952,438	18,855,078
Collin	876,229,076	332,135,565	126,197,142
Collingsworth	21,740,190	7,711,961	4,990,436
Colorado	92,522,604	41,617,733	22,244,074
Comal	320,578,938	179,720,745	52,805,546
Comanche	64,955,998	31,428,246	20,509,618
Concho	15,377,863	6,162,174	4,049,126
Cooke	122,146,014	65,815,116	35,862,596
Coryell	196,786,488	124,274,524	28,393,491
Cottle	13,762,619	4,981,445	2,630,688
Crane	12,445,175	6,145,478	4,077,924
Crockett	13,987,835	6,417,744	2,409,769
Crosby	40,026,024	12,128,836	12,192,153

COUNTY	TOTAL	For INDIVIDUALS	
		Retirement	Other direct
Culberson	$ 11,590,556	$ 3,608,553	$ 2,968,946
Dallam	37,433,693	14,521,552	8,049,828
Dallas	8,643,465,582	2,665,215,900	1,510,268,573
Dawson	80,763,245	25,120,616	23,828,746
Deaf Smith	82,957,429	25,580,680	17,965,763
Delta	26,473,112	11,637,224	7,242,338
Denton	975,729,508	297,447,177	133,655,339
DeWitt	83,362,537	37,109,374	23,908,262
Dickens	19,858,498	6,289,936	6,746,806
Dimmit	48,174,566	14,068,586	11,661,180
Donley	19,496,008	9,906,116	5,201,741
Duval	63,895,474	21,415,129	21,150,904
Eastland	97,001,483	49,105,285	28,473,634
Ector	403,087,941	182,668,333	114,833,031
Edwards	12,592,899	3,653,333	5,714,607
Ellis	270,955,938	147,889,484	76,520,791
El Paso	3,070,076,372	1,062,044,892	516,595,052
Erath	122,880,609	58,340,179	31,054,388
Falls	86,726,629	40,119,722	19,209,793
Fannin	146,737,447	67,836,112	33,338,740
Fayette	91,657,575	50,943,522	26,667,210
Fisher	26,075,878	10,258,988	6,145,831
Floyd	45,169,956	13,689,475	10,876,256
Foard	12,352,930	4,404,930	2,489,992
Fort Bend	467,894,212	230,388,300	89,541,561
Franklin	32,418,298	16,791,883	11,224,409
Freestone	58,818,776	34,904,995	13,710,110
Frio	53,120,059	19,613,290	14,646,711
Gaines	54,811,842	16,166,512	12,400,700
Galveston	981,191,722	404,186,604	234,141,960
Garza	22,119,183	8,370,681	6,828,934
Gillespie	91,347,766	58,231,586	20,618,356
Glasscock	5,182,598	1,014,380	501,103
Goliad	27,116,078	12,781,724	7,314,076
Gonzales	77,340,518	38,646,535	18,983,049
Gray	110,996,514	52,121,141	34,687,210
Grayson	426,883,719	242,292,828	107,704,787
Gregg	438,056,987	238,150,329	118,434,162
Grimes	71,761,573	35,783,254	19,566,957
Guadalupe	275,345,501	175,686,159	51,050,940
Hale	149,225,664	58,193,742	40,612,155
Hall	23,686,817	9,035,800	5,899,724
Hamilton	41,252,322	20,413,518	14,026,142
Hansford	26,362,313	9,586,543	4,197,044
Hardeman	27,164,803	12,468,956	6,823,361
Hardin	155,808,744	82,981,977	46,555,278
Harris	14,375,097,117	3,571,281,182	2,246,289,899
Harrison	211,381,074	104,128,166	56,656,523
Hartley	15,046,063	1,841,387	772,590
Haskell	36,845,482	16,358,862	9,210,701
Hays	242,247,605	114,727,207	45,913,953
Hemphill	14,577,036	5,449,431	3,208,247
Henderson	238,538,853	122,126,797	62,991,927
Hidalgo	1,724,631,414	528,158,261	444,160,565
Hill	167,859,553	71,781,363	35,733,740
Hockley	101,469,098	34,884,654	24,921,408

COUNTY	TOTAL	For INDIVIDUALS		COUNTY	TOTAL	For INDIVIDUALS	
		Retirement	Other direct			Retirement	Other direct
Hood	$ 158,493,303	$ 107,135,203	$ 31,860,667	Nacogdoches	220,016,731	98,568,947	63,987,003
Hopkins	125,775,381	60,763,856	31,684,210	Navarro	163,247,119	87,410,305	43,600,835
Houston	102,669,313	51,170,889	28,604,181	Newton	56,796,950	26,364,357	14,403,518
Howard	206,368,753	74,818,551	44,902,510	Nolan	80,585,124	35,892,755	19,996,695
Hudspeth	12,293,826	3,628,835	2,144,239	Nueces	1,760,147,056	554,887,619	291,327,142
Hunt	431,895,302	140,003,721	72,788,642	Ochiltree	33,282,598	13,182,297	5,308,838
Hutchinson	89,087,775	50,931,336	22,025,200	Oldham	10,200,161	4,028,687	1,691,837
Irion	5,379,445	3,146,081	1,352,616	Orange	327,310,187	154,698,394	100,292,725
Jack	27,020,425	14,459,490	7,607,176	Palo Pinto	112,233,581	59,834,554	27,794,698
Jackson	73,415,088	25,178,145	17,094,168	Panola	81,119,374	42,423,444	24,606,924
Jasper	150,553,142	70,620,913	46,932,904	Parker	231,589,859	140,224,882	50,488,724
Jeff Davis	7,676,425	4,486,299	1,524,407	Parmer	42,817,105	14,157,533	6,641,373
Jefferson	1,238,479,982	477,970,736	349,719,441	Pecos	46,925,526	19,074,693	10,915,579
Jim Hogg	25,833,466	8,387,980	8,378,304	Polk	262,857,450	167,355,908	55,250,881
Jim Wells	165,672,141	65,078,479	50,341,179	Potter	968,105,832	320,608,423	126,720,719
Johnson	349,150,924	204,290,011	88,670,471	Presidio	34,471,997	12,367,194	5,589,458
Jones	73,810,645	34,449,826	20,332,217	Rains	28,757,951	16,908,059	7,001,587
Karnes	58,072,437	25,857,907	16,586,592	Randall	101,479,830	43,139,206	32,475,864
Kaufman	278,908,019	154,051,221	80,800,586	Reagan	10,265,915	4,400,315	2,005,319
Kendall	96,852,450	70,480,028	16,406,693	Real	14,888,918	9,109,403	3,466,074
Kenedy	1,067,492	428,570	259,546	Red River	73,739,806	36,476,450	19,231,361
Kent	7,285,130	2,232,196	1,036,067	Reeves	54,416,173	19,587,139	11,634,671
Kerr	243,354,887	153,443,533	47,249,090	Refugio	43,617,294	17,142,684	10,317,822
Kimble	17,611,543	9,887,753	4,452,955	Roberts	4,431,107	1,619,210	802,234
King	3,323,366	346,939	156,401	Robertson	71,244,325	34,020,316	17,456,800
Kinney	19,337,142	11,036,208	3,671,945	Rockwall	76,233,707	46,551,840	17,107,161
Kleberg	169,117,581	50,101,261	34,667,212	Runnels	54,588,412	27,700,277	12,864,989
Knox	27,045,917	10,242,320	6,778,799	Rusk	158,155,537	79,001,047	40,327,682
Lamar	206,298,495	100,740,642	52,157,777	Sabine	66,546,855	38,947,831	18,378,732
Lamb	81,437,412	27,991,963	19,103,445	S. Augustine	41,716,974	21,764,444	11,865,291
Lampasas	85,108,861	52,613,157	20,896,549	San Jacinto	66,912,245	35,410,594	18,723,347
La Salle	30,509,251	8,821,055	5,923,005	San Patricio	366,514,584	106,980,124	62,938,606
Lavaca	91,276,641	50,367,792	27,615,969	San Saba	31,873,013	12,846,571	8,545,790
Lee	40,937,682	23,624,265	10,105,330	Schleicher	10,685,117	5,147,091	2,699,138
Leon	72,582,321	41,457,600	20,477,787	Scurry	66,937,230	31,713,658	16.902,527
Liberty	251,517,467	107,935,665	78,009,918	Shackelford	13,972,054	7,836,664	3,360,320
Limestone	87,087,730	47,527,642	22,113,320	Shelby	111,896,038	52,920,045	31,562,543
Lipscomb	15,027,036	6,069,824	2,941,709	Sherman	18,779,514	4,939,975	2,359,030
Live Oak	70,434,289	15,903,881	10,455,148	Smith	680,261,003	335,583,724	159,340,123
Llano	83,692,701	57,521,359	19,801,681	Somervell	18,351,036	9,719,795	5,299,068
Loving	401,992	213,672	7,991	Starr	162,388,515	40,463,103	40,491,755
Lubbock	938,624,023	379,829,313	255,855,144	Stephens	38,604,270	19,312,004	12,224,207
Lynn	38,992,125	11,289,337	7,756,630	Sterling	3,614,958	1,744,656	1,033,041
Madison	39,562,192	19,966,270	9,099,918	Stonewall	10,218,970	4,490,788	2,292,823
Marion	46,586,138	23,406,163	12,341,710	Sutton	12,960,977	5,522,129	2,777,205
Martin	25,208,958	6,901,575	4,436,977	Swisher	45,934,292	15,771,277	8,887,948
Mason	16,638,156	9,379,461	4,353,632	Tarrant	6,259,982,376	1,918,035,654	877,768,352
Matagorda	164,839,739	62,431,363	32,311,564	Taylor	727,361,315	268,915,955	107,260,248
Maverick	165,715,231	50,837,080	42,786,082	Terrell	5,304,069	2,894,251	1,109,600
McCulloch	41,023,735	19,928,714	12,044,260	Terry	62,291,785	22,094,987	16,277,433
McLennan	1,008,071,839	427,230,410	173,254,112	Throckmorton	8,592,487	4,349,038	2,276,319
McMullen	2,523,139	1,406,321	504,209	Titus	104,435,581	46,518,505	26,504,861
Medina	121,827,404	67,412,446	26,617,135	Tom Green	463,377,528	216,380,265	81,613,172
Menard	11,620,595	6,112,490	3,686,346	Travis	4,643,853,554	1,010,208,003	392,262,281
Midland	347,809,571	167,443,524	83,084,089	Trinity	66,348,332	35,638,849	21,538,286
Milam	93,508,376	53,017,221	20,130,022	Tyler	83,855,096	46,259,857	24,687,999
Mills	22,003,667	11,680,388	7,036,782	Upshur	129,450,060	72,547,521	34,265,630
Mitchell	43,342,047	18,822,849	9,878,080	Upton	12,502,873	6,028,946	3,835,938
Montague	86,571,698	50,586,887	23,004,819	Uvalde	98,390,643	40,154,562	25,248,261
Montgomery	686,195,431	333,259,541	182,944,611	Val Verde	254,794,648	75,350,235	28,492,007
Moore	60,497,698	25,440,723	10,217,789	Van Zandt	175,202,514	96,314,867	50,437,483
Morris	63,531,851	36,309,575	17,066,967	Victoria	289,185,376	131,947,130	73,797,531
Motley	9,095,002	3,437,526	2,241,542	Walker	144,916,569	72,634,439	37,726,816

COUNTY	TOTAL	For INDIVIDUALS		COUNTY	TOTAL	For INDIVIDUALS	
		Retirement	Other direct			Retirement	Other direct
Waller	$ 98,838,131	$ 35,543,267	$ 27,542,689	Williamson	594,721,614	251,893,946	73,844,974
Ward	39,849,609	20,509,954	10,254,186	Wilson	83,001,303	49,376,633	17,696,528
Washington	112,558,450	59,192,157	26,865,812	Winkler	28,303,794	14,157,944	9,139,667
Webb	618,864,051	162,197,061	133,362,890	Wise	115,782,058	67,007,936	26,994,710
Wharton	172,836,845	70,711,952	43,640,884	Wood	158,803,176	95,246,780	41,513,061
Wheeler	44,948,159	13,292,392	9,775,102	Yoakum	27,441,574	10,937,656	5,881,905
Wichita	815,557,985	315,122,656	115,106,455	Young	79,603,348	42,571,580	22,657,836
Wilbarger	73,207,260	31,860,855	19,403,432	Zapata	38,173,521	13,410,574	14,127,692
Willacy	75,859,243	21,978,352	19,348,912	Zavala	46,026,442	14,573,796	12,160,524

*Total federal government expenditures include: grants, salaries and wages (Postal Service, Dept. of Defense, etc.), procurement contract awards, direct payments for individuals, and other direct payments other than for individuals, such as some agriculture programs.

Retirement and disability programs include federal employee retirement and disability benefits, Social Security payments of all type, and veterans benefit payments.

Other direct payments for individuals include Medicare, excess earned income tax credits, Food Stamps, unemployment compensation benefit payments and lower income housing assistance.

Source: Consolidated Federal Funds Report, Fiscal Year 1998, U.S. Department of Commerce, Bureau of the Census.

Major Military Installations

Below are listed the major military installations in Texas in 1999. Data are taken from U.S. Defense Department sources.

U.S. ARMY

Fort Bliss
Location: Northeast El Paso.
Address: Fort Bliss, Texas 79916-0058
Main phone number: (915) 568-2121
Personnel: 12,214 active-duty; 6,347 civilians.
Major units: Army Air Defense Artillery Center and School; Army Sergeants Major Academy; 11th Air Defense Artillery Brigade; 31st Air Defense Artillery Brigade; 6th Air Defense Artillery Brigade.

Fort Hood
Location: In Killeen.
Address: Fort Hood, Texas 76544-5066
Main phone number: (817) 287-1110
Personnel: 43,995 active-duty; 8,909 civilians.
Major units: III Armored Corps; 1st Cavalry Div.; 4th Infantry Div.; 3rd Armored Cavalry Reg.; 13th Corps Support Command; 3rd Signal Brigade; 89th Military Police Brigade; 504th Military Intelligence Brigade; 3rd Air Support Operations Group, 3rd Personnel Group; 13th Finance Group; 21st CAV Brigade (Air Combat); Dental Activity and Medical Support Activity; Test and Experimentation Command.

Fort Sam Houston
Location: In San Antonio.
Address: Fort Sam Houston, Texas 78234-5000
Main phone number: (210) 221-1211
Personnel: 6,920 active-duty; 25,938 civilians.
Major units: U.S. Army Garrison; U.S. 5th Army; Army Medical Command; Army Medical Dept. Center and School; Brooke Army Medical Center.

Red River Army Depot
Location: 18 miles west of Texarkana
Address: Red River Army Depot, Texarkana 75507
Main phone number: (903) 334-2141
Personnel: 12 active-duty; 2,822 civilians.
Major unit: U.S. Army Tank-automotive and Armaments Command.

U.S. AIR FORCE

Brooks Air Force Base
Location: In San Antonio.
Address: Brooks AFB, Texas 78235-5304
Main phone number: (210) 536-1110
Personnel: 2,174 active-duty; 2,300 civilians.
Major units: Headquarters, Human Systems Center; Air Force School of Aerospace Medicine; Armstrong Laboratory; Air Force Center for Environmental Excellence.

Dyess AFB
Location: On west side of Abilene.
Address: Dyess AFB, Texas 79607-1960
Main phone number: (915) 696-0212
Personnel: 4,800 active-duty; 490 civilians.
Major units: 7th Bomb Wing (Air Combat Command); 317th Airlift Group.

Goodfellow AFB
Location: On south side of San Angelo.
Address: Goodfellow AFB, San Angelo, Texas 76908-5000
Main phone number: (915) 654-3217
Personnel: 3,300 active-duty; 750 civilians.
Major units: 17th Training Wing; Trains all Air Force members entering the Intelligence career fields.

Kelly AFB
Location: Five miles southwest of San Antonio.
Address: Kelly AFB, Texas 78241-5842
Main phone number: (210) 925-1110
Personnel: 5,350 active-duty, 4,300 Guard and Reserve; 14,600 civilians.
Major units: San Antonio Air Logistic Center; Headquarters, Air Intelligency Agency; 76th Air Base Wing; HQ Air Force News Agency, 433rd Airlift Wing-Reserve; 149th Airlift Wing (Texas Air National Guard).

Lackland AFB
Location: Eight miles southwest of San Antonio.
Address: Lackland AFB, Texas 78236-5110
Main phone number: (210) 671-1110

Personnel: 7,600 active-duty, approximately 9,600 active duty-students; 4,200 civilians.

Major units: 37th Training Wing; Defense Language Institute English Language Center, Inter-American Air Forces Academy; 59th Medical Wing-Wilford Hall Medical Center.

Laughlin AFB

Location: Six miles east of Del Rio.

Address: Laughlin AFB, Texas 78843-5000

Main phone number: (830) 298-3511

Personnel: 1,300 active-duty; 950 civilians.

Major units: 47th Flying Training Wing.

Randolph AFB

Location: Within San Antonio city limits.

Address: Randolph AFB, Texas 78150-4562

Main phone number: (210) 652-1110

Personnel: 5,200 active-duty; 5,900 civilians.

Major units: Headquarters, Air Education Training Command; Air Force Personnel Center; Headquarters, 19th Air Force; 12th Flying Training Wing.

Sheppard AFB

Location: Four miles north of Wichita Falls.

Address: Sheppard AFB, Texas 76311-2943

Main phone number: (940) 676-2511

Personnel: 5,300 active-duty; 2,400 civilians.

Major units: 82nd Training Wing; 80th Flying Training Wing.

U.S. NAVY

Corpus Christi Naval Air Station

Location: 10 miles southeast of Corpus Christi in the Flour Bluff area.

Address: NAS Corpus Christi, 11001 D St., Corpus Christi 78419-5021

Main phone number: (361) 961-2372

Personnel: 2,159 active-duty; 1,241 civilians.

Major units: Headquarters, Naval Air Training Command; Training Air Wing 4; Commander of Mine Warfare Command; Coast Guard Air Group; Corpus Christi Army Depot.

Naval Air Station-Joint Reserve Base (Carswell Field)

Location: westside Fort Worth.

Address: NAS-JRB, 1215 Depot Ave., Fort Worth 76127-5000.

Main phone number: (817) 782-5000

Personnel: 3,021 active-duty; 662 civilians.

Major units: Fighter Squadron 201, Marine Air Group 41; 14th Marines; Fleet Support Squadron 59; Army Reserve; Coast Guard Reserve; and Texas Air Guard.

Ingleside Naval Station

Location: In Ingleside.

Address: 1455 Ticonderoga Rd., #W123, Ingleside 78362-5001

Main phone number: (361) 776-4200.

Personnel: 4,703 active-duty; 235 civilians.

Major units: Mine Countermeasures Groups 1, 2, and 3; Shore Intermediate Maintenance Activity; 12 mine countermeasures ships.

Kingsville Naval Air Station

Location: In Kingsville.

Address: NAS Kingsville, Texas 78363-5000

Main phone number: (351) 595-6136

Personnel: 753 active-duty; 511 civilians.

Major units: Naval Auxiliary Landing Field Orange Grove; Squadrons: VT-21, VT-22; Training Air Wing II; and McMullen Target Range, Escondido Ranch.

TEXAS GUARD

Camp Mabry

Location: 2210 W. 35th St. in Austin. Just west of MoPac.

Address: Box 5218, Austin, Texas 78763

Main phone number: (512) 465-5001

Web site: www.agd.state.tx.us

Personnel: Various offices employ 800.

State Adjutant General's office: Brigadier General Daniel James III.

Major units: Texas National Guard Academy; the U.S. Property and Fiscal Office; the Texas National Guard Armory Board; the Headquarters Armory of the 49th Armored Division. **Texas Military Forces Museum,** open Wednesday-Sunday, 10 a.m. - 4 p.m.

Tracing its history to early frontier days, the Texas Guard is organized into three separate entities: The Texas Army National Guard, the Texas Air National Guard and the Texas State Guard.

When not in active federal service, Camp Mabry, in northwest Austin, is the main storage maintenance and administrative headquarters for the Texas Guard.

Camp Mabry was established in the early 1890s as a summer encampment of the Texas Volunteer Guard, a forerunner of the Texas National Guard. The name, Camp Mabry, honors Woodford Haywood Mabry, adjutant general of Texas from 1891-98.

The Texas State Guard, an all-volunteer backup force, was originally created by the Texas Legislature in 1941. It became an active element of the state military forces in 1965 with a mission of reinforcing the National Guard in state emergencies, and of replacing National Guard units called into federal service. The Texas State Guard, which has a membership of approximately 1450 personnel, also participates in local emergencies.

When the Guard was reorganized following World War II, the Texas Air National Guard was added. Texas Air National Guard units serve as augmentation units to major Air Force commands, including the Air Defense Command, the tactical Air Command and the Strategic Air Command. Approximately 3,600 men and women make up the Air Guard in 50 units.

The Army National Guard is available for either national or state emergencies and has been used extensively during hurricanes, tornadoes and floods. There are more than 189 units located in 99 cities in Texas, with a total Army Guard membership of 17,245.

The governor of Texas is commander-in-chief of the Texas National and State Guards. This command function is exercised through an adjutant general appointed by the governor and approved by both federal and state legislative authority.

The adjutant general is the active administrative head of the Texas Guard, and head of the Adjutant General's Department, a state agency, working in conjunction with the National Guard Bureau, a federal agency.

When called into active federal service, National Guard units come within the chain of command of the Army and Air Force units. ☆

Crime in Texas, 1998

Source: Texas Department of Public Safety, Austin

The number of violent crimes reported in Texas decreased in 1998 for the second year in a row. Crime volume was down by 5.2 percent in 1998 compared with 1997. Of the seven index crimes, only murder showed an increase (1.1 percent) from 1997. The total estimated number of index crimes reported for 1998 was 1,009,868.

The crime rate is tabulated on seven major offenses designated by the Federal Bureau of Investigation as Index Crimes. These seven categories include four violent offenses (murder, rape, robbery and aggravated assault) and three nonviolent crimes (burglary, theft and motor-vehicle theft.) In Texas, these figures are collected by the Texas Department of Public Safety and are provided to the FBI. Every Texas county reported at least one major crime in 1998.

Except for the slight increase in the number of murders, violent crime in general was down 4.7 percent from 1997. The violent crime rate was 564.7 in 1998 compared to 602.3 the year before, a decrease of 6.2 percent.

Nonviolent crimes decreased 6.8 percent from 1997 to 1998. The value of property stolen during the commission of index crimes in 1998 was more than $1.4 billion. The value of stolen property recovered by Texas law-enforcement agencies in 1998 was more than $573 million.

In 1998, reported arson offenses totaled 8,457, down 3.7 percent from 8,786 reported in 1997. Property damage from arson was more than $112 million in 1998. ☆

Texas Crime History 1975-1998

Year	Murder	Rape	Robbery	Aggra-vated Assault	Burglary	Theft	Motor Vehicle Theft	Rate Per 100,000 Population
1975	1,639	3,430	20,076	22,658	203,821	362,665	47,386	5,407.2
1976	1,519	3,666	17,352	21,885	193,208	400,767	43,871	5,464.4
1977	1,705	4,338	19,552	26,714	205,672	383,451	51,018	5,397.1
1978	1,853	4,927	21,395	28,475	209,770	398,923	57,821	5,556.8
1979	2,226	6,028	25,636	33,909	239,263	411,555	72,687	5,911.7
1980	2,389	6,694	29,532	39,251	262,332	450,209	79,032	6,135.7
1981	2,438	6,816	28,516	40,673	275,652	454,210	83,244	6,042.4
1982	2,463	6,814	33,603	45,221	285,757	501,312	87,090	6,297.5
1983	2,238	6,334	29,769	42,195	262,214	503,555	82,522	5,907.1
1984	2,091	7,340	28,537	42,764	266,032	529,469	87,781	6,029.2
1985	2,124	8,367	31,693	47,868	289,913	596,130	99,561	6,570.9
1986	2,255	8,605	40,018	59,002	341,560	664,832	119,095	7,408.2
1987	1,960	8,068	38,049	57,903	355,732	711,739	123,378	7,724.3
1988	2,021	8,122	39,307	60,084	362,099	739,784	134,271	8,019.6
1989	2,029	7,953	37,910	63,978	342,360	741,642	150,974	7,926.8
1990	2,388	8,746	44,316	73,860	314,346	730,926	154,387	7,823.7
1991	2,651	9,265	49,698	84,104	312,719	734,177	163,837	7,818.6
1992	2,240	9,368	44,582	86,067	268,864	689,515	145,039	7,055.1
1993	2,149	9,923	40,464	84,892	233,944	664,738	124,822	6,438.5
1994	2,023	9,101	37,639	81,079	214,698	624,048	110,772	5,873.1
1995	1,694	8,526	33,666	80,377	202,637	632,523	104,939	5,684.5
1996	1,476	8,374	32,796	80,572	204,335	659,397	104,928	5,708.3
1997	1,328	8,007	30,513	77,239	200,966	645,174	101,687	5,478.2
1998	1,343	7,914	28,672	73,648	194,872	606,805	96,614	5,110.7

Source: Texas Department of Public Safety, Austin, and the Federal Bureau of Investigation, Washington. Population figures used to determine crime rate per 100,000 population based on U.S. Bureau of Census. The population figure used in determining the crime rate for 1998 in Texas was 19,760,000.

Family Violence in Texas

Family violence is defined in the Texas Family Code as an act by a member of a family or household against another member that is intended to result in physical harm, bodily injury, assault or a threat that reasonably places the member in fear of imminent physical harm.

By definition, "family" includes individuals related by blood or affinity, marriage or former marriage, biological parents of the same child, foster children, foster parents and members or former members of the same household, including roommates.

In 1998, 187,412 offenders were involved in reported incidents of family violence against 191,324 victims. In 57.2 percent of the incidents, the relationship of victim to offender was marital: 26.6 percent of those victims were wives, and 17.4 percent were common-law wives.

Of the remaining offenses, 16.3 percent involved parents against children or children against parents. Other family/household relationships, such as grandparents, grandchildren, siblings, step-siblings, roommates or in-laws were involved in 27.3 percent.

There are six general categories of family violence:

assaults, homicides, kidnapping/abductions, robberies, forcible sex offenses and nonforcible sex offenses. Assaults accounted for 98 percent of all offenses in 1998.

In 1997, there were 181,773 incidents of family violence reported, committed by 192,419 offenders. There were 195,670 victims.

Investigation of reports of domestic violence can be hazardous to police officers. During 1998, 692 Texas law officers were assaulted while investigating such reports. ☆

Hate Crimes in Texas in 1998

Hate crimes, as defined by the Texas Hate Crimes Act, are crimes motivated by prejudice and hatred. Federal law defines them as those that manifest evidence of prejudice based on race, religion, sexual orientation, ethnicity or disability. The total number of reported Texas hate crime incidents in 1998 was 316, a decrease of 4.5 percent from 1997. The incidents involved 299 victims and 375 offenders.

Motivation of 58.5 percent of hate crimes in 1998 was race, 21.2 percent was sexual orientation, 10.9 percent was ethnicity or national origin, 8.2 percent was religious, and 0.9 percent was physical or mental disability. ☆

Crime Profile of Texas Counties, 1998

County	Agencies	Commissioned Personnel †	Murder	Rape	Robbery	Assault	Burglary	Larceny	Auto Theft	Total Index Crimes (see page 499 for definition)	*Crime Rate Per 100,000
Anderson	3	66	0	20	25	268	413	1,031	80	1,837	3,439.6
Andrews	2	25	0	3	1	13	71	259	15	362	2,530.8
Angelina	4	131	7	33	57	358	1,034	1,930	180	3,599	4,610.1
Aransas	3	53	1	10	4	43	286	763	56	1,163	5296.7
Archer	2	9	0	1	1	1	18	23	2	46	546.8
Armstrong	1	3	0	0	0	1	6	22	0	29	1,313.4
Atascosa	5	50	2	5	4	36	224	434	43	748	2,086.5
Austin	4	47	0	1	3	46	106	338	24	518	2,225.0
Bailey	2	11	1	5	0	6	32	131	6	181	2,606.6
Bandera	1	15	1	6	1	10	112	216	16	362	2,373.3
Bastrop	4	78	1	10	16	101	445	795	79	1,447	2,903.2
Baylor	2	10	0	1	0	10	18	91	2	122	2,881.4
Bee	2	38	0	6	7	60	275	512	28	888	3,113.9
Bell	9	394	19	109	238	678	2,466	7,158	676	11,344	5,020.1
Bexar	28	3,229	101	829	1,924	3,354	13,734	59,868	7,789	87,599	6,467.0
Blanco	3	15	1	0	0	7	40	51	4	103	1,233.7
Borden	1	2	0	0	0	1	5	7	0	13	1,710.5
Bosque	3	20	0	2	3	29	99	153	19	305	1,798.3
Bowie	6	152	5	35	88	273	893	2,283	227	3,804	4,472.5
Brazoria	16	435	2	61	85	416	1,520	4,325	426	6,835	2,983.0
Brazos	4	300	3	95	84	349	1,495	5,441	244	7,711	5,703.2
Brewster	3	26	0	5	1	16	57	125	12	216	2,350.9
Briscoe	1	2	1	0	0	4	10	18	0	33	1,637.7
Brooks	2	18	0	0	1	5	145	81	2	234	2,721.6
Brown	4	60	3	20	11	137	377	1,117	77	1,742	4,643.8
Burleson	3	28	0	8	5	31	141	229	13	427	2,733.3
Burnet	7	76	0	13	3	47	210	422	63	758	2,424.6
Caldwell	4	48	3	9	0	74	192	456	27	761	2,387.5
Calhoun	4	45	0	4	2	64	275	477	63	885	4,184.4
Callahan	3	14	1	2	1	11	27	55	3	100	767.6
Cameron	15	543	22	52	276	1,330	3,670	10,578	970	16,898	5,181.9
Camp	2	14	1	2	5	27	85	206	15	341	3,055.8
Carson	2	9	0	0	3	7	23	61	3	97	1,424.6
Cass	2	27	1	5	6	115	246	374	57	804	2,591.7
Castro	3	18	0	1	0	26	66	110	20	223	2,640.9
Chambers	2	29	0	10	6	21	121	391	46	595	2,486.0
Cherokee	6	67	5	22	25	158	420	793	81	1,504	3,463.0
Childress	2	12	0	2	3	21	36	122	10	194	2,501.3
Clay	1	10	0	0	1	10	41	142	15	209	1,975.6
Cochran	1	8	0	0	0	5	48	87	4	144	3,560.8
Coke	1	4	0	0	0	3	16	43	0	62	1,780.1
Coleman	3	17	0	0	1	20	110	156	9	296	3,036.5
Collin	11	564	4	92	149	954	2,371	8,558	573	12,701	3,467.3
Collingsworth	1	6	0	0	1	4	38	45	2	90	2,658.8
Colorado	4	36	2	12	2	79	174	377	24	670	3,491.0
Comal	2	120	1	38	41	99	482	2,360	121	3,142	4,373.1
Comanche	3	18	1	2	0	27	38	126	15	209	1,512.4
Concho	2	7	0	0	0	2	11	16	3	32	1,014.3
Cooke	2	56	0	2	9	29	219	588	50	897	2,674.9
Coryell	3	77	1	28	10	267	366	1,023	70	1,765	2,242.2
Cottle	1	1	0	0	2	1	4	15	0	22	1,106.1
Crane	2	14	0	1	0	4	29	77	2	113	2,439.6
Crockett	1	11	0	0	0	8	21	76	6	111	2,416.7
Crosby	1	6	2	0	1	9	13	45	1	71	947.0
Culberson	1	7	0	2	0	4	7	19	1	33	1,035.1
Dallam	2	15	0	2	0	26	45	145	15	233	2,686.8
Dallas	35	5,338	283	1,039	6,830	11,766	27,680	84,294	22,076	153,968	7,010.2
Dawson	2	24	2	1	2	89	65	232	17	408	2,713.3
Deaf Smith	2	42	2	1	4	106	120	368	23	624	3,156.5
Delta	1	9	0	0	0	5	10	45	2	62	1,234.3
Denton	16	539	5	92	112	437	1,662	7,387	552	10,247	3,549.0
DeWitt	3	24	1	11	3	36	122	243	16	432	2,443.6
Dickens	2	3	0	0	0	8	7	17	0	32	1,396.8
Dimmit	1	11	1	2	2	25	151	164	18	363	3,405.6
Donley	1	5	0	0	1	11	18	35	6	71	1,833.2
Duval	3	25	0	1	2	57	94	178	24	356	2,430.4
Eastland	4	29	0	4	3	37	112	331	21	508	2,798.6
Ector	4	280	3	20	99	818	1,248	4,761	307	7,256	5,723.0
Edwards	1	4	0	0	0	4	37	21	8	70	1,842.1

County	Agencies	Commissioned Personnel †	Murder	Rape	Robbery	Assault	Burglary	Larceny	Auto Theft	Total Index Crimes (see page 499 for definition)	*Crime Rate Per 100,000
Ellis	8	172	0	25	60	174	1,062	2,351	286	3,958	3,873.5
El Paso	8	1,310	20	301	851	3,595	3,223	27,868	2,875	38,733	5,431.2
Erath	4	66	2	15	2	39	113	551	19	741	2,330.8
Falls	3	22	0	6	24	79	233	289	26	657	3,641.9
Fannin	2	30	0	9	0	66	167	389	36	667	2,372.7
Fayette	3	26	0	4	0	25	58	165	3	255	1,188.9
Fisher	1	6	0	0	0	7	22	35	1	65	1,469.3
Floyd	3	14	0	0	2	4	56	79	9	150	1,796.6
Foard	1	3	0	0	0	1	16	2	6	25	1,424.5
Fort Bend	11	526	11	84	233	574	1,880	5,282	626	8,690	2,601.7
Franklin	1	8	0	0	3	11	50	79	9	152	1,691.5
Freestone	3	27	0	1	0	22	97	132	17	269	1,508.7
Frio	3	27	1	0	1	32	154	249	12	449	2,782.4
Gaines	3	20	0	3	0	25	49	165	7	249	1,634.7
Galveston	15	747	22	129	316	909	3,371	8,888	1,122	14,757	5,974.7
Garza	1	8	0	8	1	12	22	66	7	116	2,463.9
Gillespie	2	35	0	0	0	9	110	285	13	417	2,060.5
Glasscock	1	3	0	0	1	5	4	4	1	15	1,014.9
Goliad	1	11	0	0	0	6	18	23	0	47	682.3
Gonzales	2	26	0	9	7	83	135	223	9	466	2,609.3
Gray	2	42	0	15	13	163	236	746	48	1,221	5,064.1
Grayson	7	179	11	28	57	216	1,012	3,253	223	4,800	4,650.4
Gregg	5	272	7	104	160	430	1,278	4,526	564	7,069	5,887.1
Grimes	2	35	3	4	6	75	310	433	31	862	3,711.8
Guadalupe	3	111	2	19	26	126	654	1,905	112	2,844	3,588.6
Hale	4	67	1	6	25	72	327	839	35	1,305	3,431.7
Hall	2	6	1	1	4	5	32	36	5	84	2,230.5
Hamilton	2	13	0	0	0	12	46	82	7	147	1,900.7
Hansford	3	10	0	1	0	8	27	73	7	116	2,114.9
Hardeman	2	8	0	2	1	9	12	29	4	57	1,192.7
Hardin	5	59	0	14	5	72	258	568	71	988	2,008.0
Harris	36	9,333	322	1,096	9,186	16,386	33,814	94,223	26,627	181,654	5,670.5
Harrison	2	84	4	25	39	157	651	1,275	183	2,334	3,846.9
Hartley	1	4	0	0	0	0	7	7	0	14	466.7
Haskell	3	8	0	0	0	9	30	57	2	98	1,587.6
Hays	4	175	6	34	35	225	657	2,774	122	3,853	4,392.9
Hemphill	1	9	0	0	0	2	24	43	4	73	1,984.8
Henderson	8	88	3	25	14	152	718	1,265	130	2,307	3,369.9
Hidalgo	18	811	41	119	503	2,008	7,751	17,147	2,838	30,407	5,854.7
Hill	5	57	2	2	15	43	294	635	55	1,046	3,426.3
Hockley	4	35	0	10	0	126	86	436	30	688	2,828.0
Hood	2	40	4	2	1	47	235	693	39	1,021	2,774.2
Hopkins	2	51	0	3	7	87	257	361	38	753	2,426.0
Houston	3	28	1	4	3	39	76	288	9	420	1,888.1
Howard	2	58	2	16	13	92	482	1,000	67	1,672	5,051.4
Hudspeth	1	10	0	1	0	7	20	16	1	45	1,330.2
Hunt	8	124	7	41	82	307	1,080	2,230	215	3,962	5,623.5
Hutchinson	2	48	1	12	9	35	136	530	42	765	3,139.2
Irion	1	4	0	0	1	5	8	20	4	38	2,204.2
Jack	2	19	0	2	0	10	50	99	6	167	2,246.1
Jackson	2	21	2	3	3	6	54	153	12	233	1,678.4
Jasper	3	36	3	10	9	66	204	425	24	741	2,195.5
Jeff Davis	1	3	0	0	1	8	1	7	0	17	748.6
Jefferson	7	530	20	254	502	1,044	3,517	8,689	1,289	15,315	6,227.3
Jim Hogg	1	18	0	0	0	13	23	31	0	67	1,338.4
Jim Wells	4	65	3	13	20	227	535	1,226	114	2,138	5,387.6
Johnson	6	154	4	39	40	240	858	2,192	180	3,553	3,022.8
Jones	5	25	0	5	2	30	116	178	19	350	1,938.7
Karnes	2	13	0	4	2	21	41	49	3	120	944.4
Kaufman	5	98	5	22	38	191	588	1,409	241	2,494	3,842.6
Kendall	2	47	0	0	2	17	82	301	13	415	2,001.8
Kenedy	1	9	0	0	0	1	3	0	2	6	1,382.5
Kent	1	4	0	0	0	3	0	0	0	3	342.1
Kerr	3	79	1	10	10	41	235	875	39	1,211	2,795.0
Kimble	2	10	0	0	1	0	17	42	5	65	1,523.0
King	1	1	0	0	0	0	0	1	0	2	565.0
Kinney	1	5	0	0	0	0	1	1	2	4	113.1
Kleberg	3	81	2	17	10	120	356	1,341	79	1,925	6,267.3
Knox	3	7	0	1	0	17	43	58	4	123	2,808.2
Lamar	3	78	7	18	42	373	572	2,104	162	3,278	7,045.2
Lamb	4	26	0	4	1	35	102	208	3	353	2,338.7

County	Agencies	Commissioned Personnel †	Murder	Rape	Robbery	Assault	Burglary	Larceny	Auto Theft	Total Index Crimes (see page 499 for definition)	*Crime Rate Per 100,000
Lampasas	2	36	3	0	0	26	70	269	18	386	2,171.0
La Salle	1	10	0	1	0	30	66	37	22	156	2,585.8
Lavaca	3	23	0	4	2	9	95	227	15	352	1,652.3
Lee	3	23	0	11	3	52	59	124	12	261	1,735.8
Leon	1	12	0	0	4	57	104	103	21	289	1,967.5
Liberty	4	84	2	31	31	90	734	1,078	141	2,107	3,241.3
Limestone	3	38	1	3	11	115	232	507	37	906	4,232.3
Lipscomb	1	5	0	1	1	10	11	26	2	51	1,657.5
Live Oak	2	17	1	0	1	5	76	39	7	129	1,249.4
Llano	2	24	0	5	3	9	94	159	10	280	2,102.1
Loving	1	2	0	0	0	0	1	0	0	1	925.9
Lubbock	9	509	16	143	257	1,736	3,017	7,917	692	13,778	5,896.6
Lynn	3	12	0	5	1	8	37	83	5	139	2,074.6
Madison	2	15	3	2	1	27	100	149	21	303	2,498.1
Marion	2	14	1	4	3	54	142	208	33	445	4,102.1
Martin	2	8	0	0	0	0	21	33	4	58	1,123.6
Mason	1	4	0	0	0	1	0	0	1	2	53.9
Matagorda	4	98	1	11	31	199	449	1,082	64	1,837	4,767.0
Maverick	2	85	0	7	14	112	446	1,384	110	2,073	4,259.5
McCulloch	2	12	1	0	1	10	60	141	1	214	3,138
McLennan	17	473	14	148	304	940	2,652	7,842	1,139	13,039	7,568
McMullen	1	3	0	0	0	2	0	0	0	2	254
Medina	3	37	0	19	6	59	328	561	64	1,037	2,770.1
Menard	1	5	0	0	0	3	2	11	1	17	716.7
Midland	3	262	2	80	75	258	956	3,036	302	4,709	3,904.0
Milam	3	29	0	4	8	64	128	312	26	542	2,197.3
Mills	1	5	0	0	0	4	17	18	1	40	824.7
Mitchell	2	12	1	0	3	18	51	193	5	271	3,040.5
Montague	3	24	0	5	4	30	185	351	33	608	3,270.2
Montgomery	7	414	9	57	192	889	1,991	5,788	738	9,664	3,683.1
Moore	2	33	2	2	4	42	86	433	38	607	3,060.7
Morris	3	20	4	2	6	51	119	212	20	414	3,061.7
Motley	1	2	0	0	0	0	5	2	0	7	538.0
Nacogdoches	3	98	4	20	22	150	471	1,015	79	1,761	3,054.5
Navarro	2	98	3	27	22	57	532	1,279	112	2,032	4,832.5
Newton	1	20	3	0	2	18	83	50	14	170	1,159.9
Nolan	3	32	1	4	8	40	124	244	26	447	2,667.4
Nueces	6	645	18	166	359	1,677	4,155	15,764	1,399	23,538	7,293.7
Ochiltree	2	17	0	5	0	26	44	183	15	273	3,016.9
Oldham	1	5	0	0	0	3	5	20	1	29	1,285.5
Orange	7	145	3	36	84	341	1,055	2,136	276	3,931	4,568.5
Palo Pinto	2	49	1	6	8	87	180	634	52	968	3,712.8
Panola	2	38	3	7	3	63	146	294	16	532	2,304.2
Parker	4	105	2	38	9	66	435	1,089	140	1,779	2,269.9
Parmer	3	12	0	3	1	11	45	93	10	163	1,530.8
Pecos	2	28	0	6	4	29	107	374	14	534	3,243.6
Polk	4	64	3	15	19	62	322	570	54	1,045	2,166.4
Potter	4	422	13	66	245	975	2,011	9,488	742	13,540	7,339.4
Presidio	2	12	2	0	0	5	29	36	12	84	963.4
Rains	1	7	0	1	1	6	87	155	17	267	3,198.0
Randall	3	94	1	2	6	36	125	406	46	622	2,293.5
Reagan	1	6	0	4	0	15	16	33	2	70	1,628.7
Real	1	3	0	0	0	2	24	11	1	38	1,391.9
Red River	2	20	0	4	4	23	112	130	12	285	2,032.5
Reeves	2	32	0	2	1	27	76	243	21	370	2,450.2
Refugio	2	21	0	5	2	7	29	67	8	118	1,472.8
Roberts	1	3	0	0	0	0	3	6	0	9	896.4
Robertson	2	20	0	2	5	64	126	150	15	362	2,292.4
Rockwall	4	69	0	10	9	71	120	511	62	783	2,718.3
Runnels	3	17	0	1	1	16	55	134	9	216	1,854.7
Rusk	4	67	2	20	18	279	417	1,076	136	1,948	4,403.0
Sabine	2	10	0	3	1	29	111	113	6	263	2,449.0
San Augustine	2	11	0	0	2	13	56	94	5	170	2,043.5
San Jacinto	1	14	1	0	5	37	180	279	39	541	2,551.4
San Patricio	7	97	0	12	16	153	651	1,242	84	2,158	3,006.8
San Saba	2	8	0	0	0	7	36	71	5	119	1,822.4
Schleicher	1	4	0	0	0	1	9	40	2	52	1,679.0
Scurry	2	26	0	6	3	24	118	224	10	385	2,082.8
Shackelford	1	4	0	0	1	0	9	6	0	16	472.0
Shelby	2	27	0	5	7	67	191	297	48	615	2,670.9
Sherman	2	7	1	0	0	1	10	21	2	35	1,185.2

County	Agencies	Commissioned Personnel †	Murder	Rape	Robbery	Assault	Burglary	Larceny	Auto Theft	Total Index Crimes (see page 499 for definition)	*Crime Rate Per 100,000
Smith	10	276	15	119	127	609	1,944	5,709	570	9,093	5,367.9
Somervell	1	16	0	0	1	6	33	99	7	146	2,303.6
Starr	3	75	2	20	25	140	622	791	103	1,703	3,015.4
Stephens	2	15	0	0	1	6	90	127	5	229	2,275.0
Sterling	1	3	0	3	0	0	2	6	1	12	852.3
Stonewall	1	3	0	1	0	4	1	13	1	20	1,088.7
Sutton	2	10	0	0	0	13	18	109	1	141	3,126.4
Swisher	3	16	0	2	3	31	67	165	10	278	3,276.4
Tarrant	38	3,388	89	618	2,142	4,841	13,710	45,837	7,775	75,012	5,592.5
Taylor	5	261	5	57	130	386	1,359	3,787	225	5,949	4,776.1
Terrell	1	3	0	0	0	1	0	1	0	2	165.4
Terry	2	26	0	2	0	41	57	234	12	346	2,617.6
Throckmorton	1	2	0	0	0	1	12	10	2	25	1,443.4
Titus	2	45	3	4	15	174	266	745	70	1,277	4,976.2
Tom Green	4	223	5	61	31	312	807	4,073	183	5,472	5,244.2
Travis	12	1,788	36	259	1,160	2,122	8,035	30,050	3,292	44,954	6,373.4
Trinity	2	16	0	0	4	60	174	178	25	441	3,495.8
Tyler	2	29	0	5	3	35	165	131	9	348	1,702.6
Upshur	4	39	1	15	5	33	223	472	39	788	2,351.2
Upton	1	8	0	0	0	3	18	38	1	60	1,547.2
Uvalde	3	43	1	0	2	61	205	595	40	904	3,471.3
Val Verde	2	84	3	1	23	133	406	1,221	100	1,887	4,305.6
Van Zandt	6	70	2	7	8	93	302	619	110	1,141	2,610.5
Victoria	2	214	6	29	42	402	800	2,354	145	3,778	4,531.2
Walker	2	66	1	19	36	205	390	1,011	96	1,758	3,171.7
Waller	5	61	1	10	16	68	288	465	85	933	3,573.8
Ward	2	26	0	10	2	23	93	267	13	408	3,375.5
Washington	2	61	0	18	8	94	184	605	44	953	3,229.2
Webb	4	450	12	72	223	572	2,057	9,109	1,447	13,492	7,244.2
Wharton	3	86	9	27	52	153	543	1,134	86	2,004	4,910.7
Wheeler	2	8	0	0	3	8	23	31	2	67	1,241.4
Wichita	6	254	6	86	127	577	1,101	4,246	383	6,526	4,983.4
Wilbarger	2	28	0	17	10	41	261	302	29	660	4,592.6
Willacy	3	42	1	2	13	90	197	313	29	645	3,227.1
Williamson	11	364	3	60	48	291	956	2,809	192	4,359	2,037.4
Wilson	3	45	3	1	0	50	119	291	14	478	1,557.4
Winkler	3	21	1	1	0	13	45	95	12	167	2,044.1
Wise	3	50	2	18	7	64	164	508	35	798	1,852.1
Wood	5	54	3	12	1	110	257	498	50	931	2,622.9
Yoakum	2	18	0	1	0	16	31	121	5	174	2,095.4
Young	3	35	0	7	1	21	165	401	25	620	3,470.5
Zapata	1	30	0	0	1	13	72	128	13	227	1,982.2
Zavala	2	16	1	2	7	33	80	215	12	350	2,880.2

* County population figures used for calculation of crime rate are the State Data Center estimates for Jan. 1, 1996.
† The commissioned officers listed here are those employed by sheriffs' offices and police departments of municipalities, universities and colleges, transit systems, park departments and medical facilities. In addition, the Texas Department of Public Safety has 2,884 commissioned personnel stationed statewide.

Crime Rates by States, 1996

(Index Crimes per 100,000 population*)

1.	Washington, D.C.	11,897
2.	Florida	7,497
3.	Arizona	7,067
4.	Louisiana	6,839
5.	New Mexico	6,602
6.	Hawaii	6,585
7.	Georgia	6,310
8.	South Carolina	6,214
9.	Maryland	6,062
10.	Nevada	5,992
11.	Utah	5,986
12.	Oregon	5,997
13.	Washington	5,909
14.	**Texas**	**5,709**

(United States **5,079**

Source: Statistical Abstract of the United States, 1998.
*Based on Bureau of the Census estimated resident population as of July 1, 1996.

Czech food, music add to state's culture

In December 1849, Rev. Josef Arnost Bergmann left his Czech homeland to minister to German Protestants in Texas.

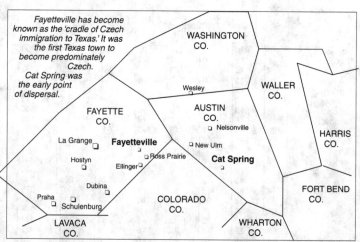

Fayetteville has become known as the 'cradle of Czech immigration to Texas.' It was the first Texas town to become predominately Czech.
Cat Spring was the early point of dispersal.

Pastor Bergmann and his family arrived in Galveston in 1850 and made their way to Cat Spring. There in Austin County he led the Easter service for the congregation that had hired him, and he soon wrote a letter praising Texas to the folks back home.

That letter, published in the *Moravské Noviny (Moravia News)*, suggested opportunity to the families struggling on the overcrowded farmlands of Central Europe. Also, it offered hope to merchants and craftsmen left frustrated after the failure of the 1848 social uprisings on the European continent. Among the reforms that had been sought in the Austrian Empire was more autonomy for ethnic groups like the Czechs. Bergmann's letter was the catalyst of opportunity that has earned him the designation of "father" of Czech immigration to Texas.

In late August 1851, 16 families from northeastern Bohemia left Hamburg, Germany, to begin an arduous 17-week voyage to the Texas coast. Those first Czech immigrants arrived in early 1852 and were followed in 1853 and 1854 by other Czech families. The immigrants continued to make Cat Spring their dispersal point before moving out to New Ulm and Nelsonville in Austin County and to neighboring Fayette County.

Although Protestants initiated the emigration to Texas, the majority of Czech immigrants — estimates range from 70 to 90 percent — were Catholics. Many of these families settled around Fayetteville, often referred to as the "cradle of Czech immigration" in Texas.

The first Catholic church to serve Czechs was built in 1855 just south of Fayetteville at Ross Prairie. The log chapel was replaced by a frame building in 1859, and in 1861 the church was moved closer to Ellinger (Live Oak Hill).

By 1856, there were Czechs at Dubina, Bluff (later renamed Hostyn), and Mulberry (now known as Praha, which is the Czech name for Prague). Because Fayetteville, Cat Spring and Ross Prairie had previously existed as German centers, various sources refer to Dubina or Hostyn as the first Czech settlement in Texas. The settlers of both places came over on the same ship. Catholic Czech Texans today honor St. Mary's Church (1865) in Praha as their "mother parish."

The first Czech Protestant service was held in 1855 near the present location of the Fayetteville Brethren Church. The Protestants were followers of a 15th-century reformist Bohemian priest, Jan Hus, and were known as Hussites in Europe, or the Brethren, as they called themselves.

These Czech Protestants eventually established in Texas a denomination called Unity of the Brethren. The first Brethren congregation was formed in 1864 in Vesely. The town, on the Austin and Washington county line, is known today as Wesley, and has an 1866 church that contains interior paintwork added by Pastor Bohuslav Lacjak in 1890.

Similiar paintwork, in a more elaborate style, was used in Catholic churches in the vicinity of Schulenburg. The churches, today called the "Painted Churches of Texas," have become a popular tourist pilgrimage.

By the Civil War there were about 700 Czechs in Texas, many with Unionist and abolitionist sentiments. However, some fought in the Confederate army, while others tried to remain neutral.

A second wave of Czech immigration in the 1870s and 1880s followed the war. These Czech settlers established themselves on the Coastal Prairie and the Blackland Prairie from Ellis County near Dallas in the north to Victoria County on the south. A third wave after 1900 moved eastward to Brazoria and Fort Bend counties near Houston.

Although there are Czechs throughout Texas and isolated Czech communities in South and West Texas today, the concentration of Czech settlements in a cluster of 15 counties gives a high profile to the culture and its traditions. Recent census figures show other ancestry groups in Texas have larger numbers. However, as a rule, they moved directly to urban areas and quickly assimilated into city life while Czechs maintain these identifiable places of cultural majority.

In the 1990 census, Texans who listed some Czech ancestry numbered 282,562. Other sources, including a statewide group called Texans of Czech Ancestry, say the numbers are closer to one million.

However, the impact on Texas culture is difficult to convey through numbers. Not until 1920, after the formation of Czechoslovakia, did the U.S. census or immigration services use a "Czech" designation. Often, "Austrian" might the listed in U.S. documents. One clue to the impact of Czechs on Texas might be seen in the census' 1920 figures for "Country of Birth of Foreign-Born Population." The three largest groups in Texas were: from Mexico, 69.2 percent; from Germany, 8.6 percent; from Czechoslovakia, 3.6 percent. Or in another tablulation, Czech "foreign white stock" (defined as those who spoke Czech at home) in 1940 was 62,680.

The two provinces of the Czech Republic are Bohemia, centered by the city of Prague, and Moravia, which lies to the east. The majority of Czech immigrants to Texas are Moravian, and the dialects spoken in Texas vary slightly from the Bohemian dialects spoken by most Czech-Americans.

Often 19th-century American accounts confuse the issue by calling certain Czech towns in Texas "Bohemian" when in fact the people were Moravian.

That the Czech language is still spoken in Texas is possibly a reaction to prohibitions by Austrian authorities on using the language. Early on, the new Czech-Texans established schools and newspapers to teach and maintain their language. Czech was being taught in the classroom in Cat Spring in 1855. The state's largest public college, the University of Texas at Austin, teaches Czech in the modern language department.

Today radio broadcasts in Czech can be heard in Central Texas. Also heard is the music that distinguishes the culture. The polkas and waltzes, and the musical instruments used, such as the accordian, so impacted the culture of Texas that the sounds crossed over into the

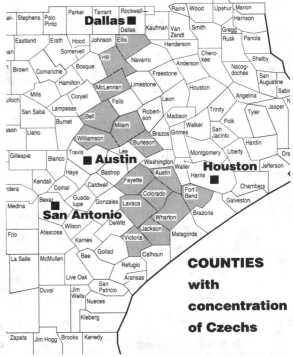

COUNTIES with concentration of Czechs

These 15 counties have high percentages of population with some Czech ancestry. Lavaca County (Hallettsville) is the largest with 50 percent. Fayette County (La Grange) is second with 35 percent, according to the 1990 U.S. census.

Mexican culture, becoming part of the *norteño* sound and blending into *conjunto* bands. It is a legacy that reaches into the *Tejano* music of today. These Spanish terms refer to music with elements of this style.

Numerous well-known Czech bands still play the dance halls and church bazaars throughout the state, and Ennis, one of the northernmost Czech towns, plays host to the National Polka Festival each May .

It is said that "wherever you find two Czechs you'll find three clubs." Thus, local lingo in Czech towns is a kind of "alphabet soup" of these groups. There will probably be an SPJST hall, a lodge known by the Czech initials for Slavonic Benevolent Order of the State of Texas It is a non-denominational fraternal group formed in 1897, initially to provide life insurance.

The KJT and KJZT are two other statewide organizations. The KJT, formed in 1888, stands for Katolicka Jednota Texaska, a Catholic men's group. The KJZT for women was formed in 1897, and the group today is known as the Catholic Family

The 1998 National Polka Festival in Ennis. Dallas Morning News file photo.

Fraternal of Texas - K.J.Z.T.

Another organization, the Sokol, is dedicated to the physical, mental, moral and cultural advancement of members through the use of gymnasiums. The idea begin in Prague in 1862 and the first such group in Texas was formed in Ennis in 1909. Others soon followed in Rowena, Guy, Crosby and Shiner and many other Czech communities. They survive in metropolitan areas and the north central Texas towns of West, as well as in Ennis.

The food of Czechs is literally the dessert of this ethnic group's story. Kolaches, a pastry with a filling, most often fruit, is well-known, and likely to be offered at any suburban doughnut shop in modern Texas. But, if absolute authenticity is required, the many Czech festivals and church bazaars throughout the state offer lots of samplings. Those include:

Festivals

Ammansville — annual Father's Day picnic in June.
Caldwell — Kolache Festival in September.
Damon — Sts. Cyril & Methodius bazaar in late September. (The saints were Greek blood brothers; missionaries to the Slavs in the 9th century).
Dubina — Sts. Cyril & Methodius festival, first Sunday in July.
East Bernard — Czech Kolache-Klobase Festival in June.
Ennis — National Polka Festival in May.
Flatonia — Czhilispiel in October.
Hallettsville — Kolache Fest in September; South Texas Polka and Sausage Fest in March.
High Hill — St. Mary's parish picnic on Labor Day Sunday.
Houston — Slavic Heritage Day in July.
Pasadena — Gulf Coast Czech Festival in late October.
Praha — Prazska Pout on Aug. 15; parish picnic close to Veterans Day.
Richmond-Rosenberg — Fort Bend County Czech Fest in May.
Schulenburg — St. John's parish festival, (southwest from town, 6 miles, FM 957) Independence Day.
Shiner — Bocktoberfest in October; church bazaar Labor Day Sunday. Shiner is the site of the Spoetzl Brewery whose beers are as much Czech as German.
West — Westfest on Labor Day weekend.

Museums and Associations

Austin — KJZT/Czech Family Fraternal of Texas headquarters.
Caldwell — Burleson County Czech Heritage Museum at chamber of commerce offices.
Fayetteville — Fayetteville Museum on square.
Missouri City — Czech Heritage Society of Texas.
Temple — SPJST headquarters; Czech Heritage Museum at

headquarters.
(Two groups, one in La Grange and another in Houston, are currently raising funds for construction of new museums of Czech-Texan heritage.)

Painted Churches (4)

Ammansville (St. John the Baptist)
Dubina (Sts. Cyril & Methodius)
High Hill (St. Mary's)
Praha (St. Mary's)
Other noted Czech churches: Granger (Sts. Cyril & Methodius), Shiner (Sts. Cyril & Methodius), Wesley (Brethren Church) 1864 congregation, 1866 building, 1890 interior.

Sources

"The Czech Texans," staff, University of Texas Institute of Texan Cultures, 1972.
"Czechs," by Clinton Machann, New Handbook of Texas, 1996.
"Through Fire and Flood," by James Talmadge Moore, Texas A&M Press, 1992.
Texas Highways, various:
   "Halls of Fame," by Larry D. Hodge, June 1998.
   "Room to Grow," by Richard Zelade, Sept. 1993.
   "Fayetteville," by Carol Barrington, Feb. 1998.
   "Shiner's Finest," by Jill L. Bates, Aug. 1991.
"Czech It Out," by Allan Turner, *Texas* (*Houston Chronicle* magazine), Aug. 31, 1997.
"The Churches of Fayette County," *The Dallas Morning News*, May 31. 1998.
"Czech Texans Take Steps to Preserve Heritage, Language," by Starita Smith, *Austin American-Statesman* (reprinted in *Houston Chronicle* July 7, 1996).
"Polka Party," by Nita Thurman, *The Dallas Morning News*, May 25, 1998.
Catholic Family Fraternal Journal, March/April 1998, CFF of Texas/KJZT, Austin.
"Texas' Presidential Corridor," by Carolyn Barta, *The Dallas Morning News*, July 5, 1998.
"Czechs in Fayette County," by Carolyn Meiners, unpublished. ☆

A basket of kolaches, a popular Czech dessert in Texas. The Dallas Morning News file photo.

Japanese changed landscape of Texas

The 15,172 Japanese-Texans counted in the U.S. census of 1990 represent less than one tenth of one percent of the state's population.

But through various fields, from architecture to agriculture, the physical and cultural landscape of Texas has been changed by their contributions.

Several metropolitan areas of the state have Japanese public gardens — some of them designed, planted and maintained by Japanese residents.

Stepping stones at the Japanese Garden in Fort Worth. Dallas Morning News file.

The famous "Sunken Gardens" of Brackenridge Park in San Antonio have been for generations of Texans a serene place to revive the spirit. And, in the state capital, the Japanese Garden in Zilker Park is visited by over 100,000 people each year. Isamu Taniguchi designed and built the Austin retreat in the late 1960s as a place of tranquillity for his fellow Texans.

Other Japanese have contributed in medicine, art and literature. Isamu Taniguchi's son, Alan Taniguchi, as one example, trained thousands of young architects in recent decades as dean of the School of Architecture at the University of Texas and director of Rice University's School of Architecture.

But, perhaps the most profound impact on the culture of the state has been the contribution made by Japanese agriculturists to the development of rice growing.

Rice has been cultivated in Texas from as early as 1853, and large-scale rice production was introduced from southern Louisiana into southeastern Texas in the 1880s. The rice seed used was from the rice first planted in the Carolinas in 1685.

Around 1900, the Houston Chamber of Commerce, with Japan's Consul General Sadatsuchi Uchida as intermediary, sought help in teaching Gulf coastal farmers new methods of rice-growing.

Consul General Uchida's interest was to develop more rice production for the crowded Japanese islands, with their growing population.

So, when Seito Saibara, a theology student in Connecticut, expressed an interest in staying in the United States, Uchida encouraged him to go to Texas.

In 1903, Seito Saibara and 30 other colonists from Japan arrived in Webster in southern Harris County. Rice seed was sent as a gift from the emperor, and within three years, area harvests almost doubled, from about 18 barrels an acre to 34 barrels an acre. Seito Saibara and his family, thus, have been credited with establishing the Gulf Coast rice industry.

Soon other families were arriving from Japan to engage in rice-growing. From 1903 through 1914 colonies were started in Port Lavaca (Calhoun County);

Fannett (Jefferson County) and Terry (Orange County); Mackay and El Campo (Wharton County); and Alvin (Brazoria County).

Japanese also settled in Mission, San Juan and San Benito in the Rio Grande Valley to grow vegetable and citrus crops. A second wave of Japanese arrived around 1920, many from California where they faced increasing anti-Japanese agitation. Most of these Japanese families settled in the lower Valley, as well.

Generally, the California families experienced less prejudice in Texas, perhaps because of the small numbers. However, the American Legion post in Harlingen warned Japanese newcomers to stay away, and in January 1921 a group of Japanese families from California was met by a hostile crowd and turned away from the Harlingen train station.

In April of 1921, the Texas legislature, in the wake of similiar legislation in California and other western states, passed a law restricting land ownership by Japanese. The legislation was blunted by the lobbying efforts of Saburo Arai, an entrepreneur in the Houston area community of Genoa. He led a newly-formed organization called the Japanese Association that successfully had the bill amended to exempt all Japanese already living in the state.

By 1940, there were 500 Japanese in Texas. With the attack on Pearl Harbor in December 1941 and war between Japan and the United States, hostility toward Japanese residents increased. Many Japanese men were questioned by federal authorities and some were detained, although only briefly.

In San Antonio, the Jingu family, who for two decades had maintained the Japanese Tea Garden, was evicted from the property and the site was renamed Chinese Tea Garden. In 1984, the city of San Antonio restored the original name.

After the initial fear of the first few months of World War II and some federal raids on homes, most Japanese in Texas were under a kind of house arrest in which they faced restriction on travel, on financial transactions and on group gatherings. "Suspicious items," were confiscated: items such as cameras, binoculars ("spyglasses") and guns.

Under a federal policy at the beginning of the war with Japan, several thousand Japanese where brought to Texas to internment camps at Kenedy and Crystal City in South Texas and Seagoville outside Dallas. Many were Japanese-Americans from the West Coast and others were Japanese alien residents of Latin American countries. In all, some 6,000 persons were involved, the majority of whom were Japanese, although some German families from Latin America were also housed in the camps.

After the war most of the internees left the state, but a few elected to stay, including Isamu Taniguchi who began farming in the Rio Grande Valley.

Also following the war, many Japanese taken from their California properties and placed in relocation centers throughout the United States chose not to return to the West Coast and moved to Texas. This new Japanese-Texas population of the 1950s moved into the booming cities, finding employment in business and working in the professions.

In the 1970s and 1980s, businesses from Japan placed employees in Texas cities. However, most of these residents are temporary residents and return to Japan.

In 1990, the census bureau reported more than two-thirds of Japanese-Texans lived in the metropolitan areas of Houston, San Antonio and Dallas-Fort Worth.

Gardens

Austin — Japanese Garden in Zilker Park near Barton Springs. Designed by Isamu Taniguchi in the 1960s.

Fort Worth — Japanese Garden in the Fort Worth Botanic Garden was built in the 1970s. The tea house and massive entrance gate were designed by Albert Komatsu, a well-known Fort Worth architect. The city stages festivals each spring and fall komo music, taiko drumming and calligraphy instructions.

Fredericksburg — Garden of Peace at the Admiral Nimitz Museum and Historical Center was constructed during 1976 at the boyhood home of the World War II hero. Designed in Japan, the traditional garden was built to honor Chester Nimitz and as a display of reconciliation between the United States and Japan.

Houston — Hermann Park's Japanese Garden was instituted in 1992 as a symbol of friendship between this country and Japan and was funded largely by the Japanese business community in Houston. The tea garden was designed by landscape architect Ken Nakajima and is the site of an annual Japan Festival each April.

Some early Japanese settlements and leaders

Webster (1903) — Harris County. Saibara family. Later others.
Port Lavaca (1903) — Calhoun County. Fujino.
Fannett (1906) — Jefferson County. Mayumi family.
El Campo (1906) — Wharton County. Arai.
Terry (1907) — Orange County. Kishi.
Mackay (1907) — Wharton County. Onishi family.
Alvin (1911) — Brazoria County. Arai.

Festival activities include origami (paper-folding) and other Japanese art forms.

San Antonio — The Japanese Tea Garden was built in a former rock quarry in 1917-18 with the assistance of Kimi Jingu. The Jingus maintained the garden and raised eight children while living on the site. Known as the Chinese Tea Garden or Sunken Gardens from the 1940s, it regained its original name in a rededication ceremony in October 1984. At that ceremony, a new gateway designed by Alan Taniguchi was added.

Sources
The Japanese Texans, by Thomas K. Walls, University of Texas Institute of Texan Cultures at San Antonio, 1987, 1996.
New Handbook of Texas, 1996. various:
"Japanese," by Edward J.M. Rhoads.
"Rice Culture," by Henry C. Dethloff.
"World War II Internment Camps," by Emily Brosveen.
"Wharton County," by Merle R. Hudgins.
"Harris County," by Margaret Swett Henson.
Building the Lone Star, by T. Lindsay Baker, Texas A&M University Press, 1986.
Texas Highways, "Back to Brackenridge Park," by Howard Peacock, June 1997.

Japanese internment camps in Texas

Crystal City — Zavala County. Had been federally-funded housing for migrant workers. Housed families, including Latin Americans of Japanese and German descent, and some Italians. Federal High School. Operated until 1947 when last Japanese-Peruvians left. Housed 4,000 at peak, two-thirds Japanese.

Seagoville — Dallas County. Had been federal reformatory for women built in 1940. Female internees, including language teachers from West Coast. Families from Latin America were housed in plywood huts which were added. Closed June 1945.

Kenedy — Karnes County. All-male. Had been Civilian Conservation Corps (CCC) camp. Nine large barracks. 200 one-room huts added, each housing 5 or 6. Closed September 1944.

Holidays, Anniversaries and Festivals, 2000 and 2001

Below are listed the principal federal and state government holidays, Christian, Jewish and Islamic holidays and festivals and special recognition days for 2000 and 2001. Technically, the United States does not observe national holidays. Each state has jurisdiction over its holidays, which are usually designated by its legislature. The list was compiled partially from *Astronomical Phenomena 2000* and *2001*, published by the U.S. Naval Observatory, and from the Texas Government Code. See the footnotes for explanations of the symbols.

2000

*§New Year's Day . . . . .Saturday, Jan. 1
Epiphany . . . . Thursday, Jan. 6
‡Sam Rayburn Day . . . . Thursday, Jan. 6
*§Martin Luther King's Birthday . . . . Monday, Jan. 17
†**Confederate Heroes Day. . . . . . . Wednesday, Jan. 19
*§∞Presidents' Day . . . . Monday, Feb. 21
†Texas Independence Day. . . . . Thursday, March 2
‡Sam Houston Day . . . . Thursday, March 2
‡Texas Flag Day. . . . . Thursday, March 2
Ash Wednesday . . . . .Wednesday, March 8
§§Islamic New Year . . . . Thursday, April 6
‡Former Prisoners of War Recognition Day Sunday, April 9
Palm Sunday . . . . Sunday, April 16
¶First Day of Passover (Pesach) . . . . . Thursday, April 20
§Good Friday . . . . Friday, April 21
†San Jacinto Day. . . . . Friday, April 21
Easter Day . . . . Sunday, April 23
Mother's Day . . . . .Sunday, May 14
Armed Forces Day . . . . Saturday, May 20
*§Memorial Day . . . . Monday, May 29
Ascension Day . . . . .Thursday, June 1
¶First Day of Shavuot (Feast of Weeks). . . Friday, June 9
Whit Sunday - Pentecost . . . . Sunday, June 11
Flag Day (U.S.). . . . . .Wednesday, June 14
Trinity Sunday. Sunday, June 18
Father's Day . . . . Sunday, June 18
†Emancipation Day in Texas (Juneteenth) Monday, June 19
*§Independence Day . . . . Tuesday, July 4
†Lyndon Baines Johnson Day . . . . Sunday, Aug. 27
*§Labor Day . . . . Monday, Sept. 4
¶First Day of Rosh Hashanah . . . . . . .Saturday, Sept. 30
¶Day of Atonement (Yom Kippur) . . . . . . Monday, Oct. 9
§‡Columbus Day . . . . Monday, Oct. 9
¶First Day of Sukkot (Tabernacles) . . . .Saturday, Oct. 14
Halloween . . . . Tuesday, Oct. 31
‡Father of Texas (Stephen F. Austin) Day . .Friday, Nov. 3
†General Election Day . . . . Tuesday, Nov. 7
*§Veterans Day . . . . Saturday, Nov. 11
*§††Thanksgiving Day. . . . . Thursday, Nov. 23
§§First Day of Ramadan . . . . Tuesday, Nov. 28
First Sunday in Advent. . . . . Sunday, Dec. 3
¶First Day of Hanukkah . . . . Friday, Dec. 22
*§Christmas Day . . . . Monday, Dec. 25

2001

*§New Year's Day. . . . . Monday, Jan. 1
Epiphany . . . . .Saturday, Jan. 6
‡Sam Rayburn Day . . . . .Saturday, Jan. 6
*§Martin Luther King's Birthday . . . . Monday, Jan. 15
†**Confederate Heroes Day . . . . Friday, Jan. 19
Inauguration Day . . . . .Saturday, Jan. 20
*§∞Presidents' Day . . . . Monday, Feb. 19
Ash Wednesday. . . . . Wednesday, Feb. 28
†Texas Independence Day . . . . Friday, March 2
‡Sam Houston Day . . . . Friday, March 2
‡Texas Flag Day . . . . Friday, March 2
§§Islamic New Year . . . . .Monday, March 26
Palm Sunday . . . . Sunday, April 8
¶First Day of Passover (Pesach) . . . . Sunday, April 8
‡Former Prisoners of War Recognition Day Monday, April 9
§Good Friday. Friday, April 13
Easter Day. . . . . Sunday, April 15
†San Jacinto Day. . . . . Saturday, April 21
Mother's Day .Sunday, May 13
Armed Forces Day. . . . . Saturday, May 19
Ascension Day. . . . . Thursday, May 24
*§Memorial Day . . . . Monday, May 28
¶First Day of Shavuot (Feast of Weeks) Monday, May 28
Whit Sunday - Pentecost . . . . Sunday, June 3
Trinity Sunday . . . . Sunday, June 10
Flag Day (U.S.) . . . . .Thursday, June 14
Father's Day. . . . . Sunday, June 17
†Emancipation Day in Texas (Juneteenth)Tuesday, June 19
*§Independence Day . . . . Wednesday, July 4
†Lyndon Baines Johnson Day . . . . Monday, Aug. 27
*§Labor Day . . . . .Monday, Sept. 3
¶First Day of Rosh Hashanah . . . . Tuesday, Sept. 18
¶Day of Atonement (Yom Kippur) . . . Thursday, Sept. 27
¶First Day of Sukkot (Tabernacles) . . . . . Tuesday, Oct. 2
§‡Columbus Day . . . . Monday, Oct. 8
Halloween . . . . Wednesday, Oct. 31
‡Father of Texas (Stephen F. Austin) DaySaturday, Nov. 3
*§Veterans Day . . . . Sunday, Nov. 11
§§First Day of Ramadan . . . . Saturday, Nov. 17
*§††Thanksgiving Day. . . . . Thursday, Nov. 22
First Sunday in Advent. . . . . Sunday, Dec. 2
¶First Day of Hanukkah . . . . Monday, Dec. 10
*§Christmas Day . . . . .Tuesday, Dec. 25

¶ §§ In these tables, the Jewish (¶) and Islamic (§§) dates, are tabular dates, which begin at sunset on the previous evening and end at sunset on the date listed above.

* National holidays observed by state employees.

† State holiday in Texas. For state employees, the Friday after Thanksgiving Day, December 24 and December 26 are also holidays; optional holidays are Rosh Hashanah, Yom Kippur or Good Friday.

‡ State Recognition Days, designated by the Texas Legislature. In addition, the legislature has designated the week of May 22-26 International Trade Awareness Week.

§ Federal legal public holidays.

** Confederate Heroes Day combines the birthdays of Robert E. Lee (Jan. 19) and Jefferson Davis (June 3).

∞ Presidents' Day combines the birthdays of George Washington (Feb. 15) and Abraham Lincoln (Feb. 12).

†† Between 1939 and 1957, Texas observed Thanksgiving Day on the last Thursday in November. As a result, in all Novembers having five Thursdays, Texas celebrated national Thanksgiving on the fourth Thursday and Texas Thanksgiving on the fifth Thursday. In 1957, Texas changed the state observance to coincide in all years with the national holiday. ☆

National Endowment for the Humanities Honors Texan

Source: National Endowment for the Humanities.

Rock musician Don Henley was among ten recipients of the 1997 National Humanties Medal.

The medal was inaugurated in 1997 to replace he Charles Frankel Prize, originated by the National Endowment for the Humanities in 1989. The award honors individuals who have made outstanding contributions to the public's understanding of history, literature, philosophy and other humanities disciplines.

The National Humanities Medal goes to up to 12 Americans selected annually for their achievements.

Mr. Henley was born in Gilmer and raised in Linden in East Texas. He attended Stephen F. Austin State University in Nacogdoches and the University of North Texas.

The national award was in recognition of his work to save the woods around Walden Pond in Massachusetts and as a major patron of the Thoreau Institute, the nation's premier center for Thoreau studies.

The former member of the Eagles rock group maintains homes in Dallas and at Caddo Lake.

The other 1997 recipients included: Martin E. Marty, Lutheran pastor and renowned scholar of U.S. religious history; author Studs Terkel; and philanthropist Paul Mellon.

The National Endowment for the Humanities is an independent federal agency created by Congress in 1965 to promote knowledge of human history and culture.

Don Henley

Past honorees include CBS correspondent Charles Kuralt and writer-journalist Richard Rodriguez.

Other Texans previously honored include journalist Bill Moyers; Latino scholar Arturo Madrid, who is on the board of directors of the A.H. Belo Corporation; Américo Paredes of San Antonio, and Louise Cowan of Dallas. ☆

Texas Institute of Letters Awards

Each year since 1939, the **Texas Institute of Letters** has honored outstanding works of literature and journalism that are either by Texans or about Texas subjects. Awards are for fiction, nonfiction, Southwest history, general information, magazine and newspaper journalism, children's books, poetry and book design. The awards for recent years are listed below:

Writer/Designer: Title

1998
C.W. Smith: *Understanding Women*
Susan Choi: *The Foreign Student*
William C. Davis: *Three Roads to the Alamo: The Lives and Fortunes of David Crockett, James Bowie, and*

William Barret Travis
Don Carleton: *A Breed So Rare: The Life of J.R. Parten, Liberal Texas Oil Man, 1896-1992*
B.H. Fairchild: "The Art of the Lathe"
Marian Schwartz: *The Ladies from St. Petersburg: Three Novellas*
James Hoggard: *Poems from Cuba: Alone Against the Sea*
Jane Roberts Wood: "My Mother Had a Maid"
Rick Bass: "Into the Fire"
Patrick Beach: "The Struggle for the Soul of Kreuz Market"
Bryan Woolley: "A Legend Runs Through It"
Pat Mora: *The Big Sky*
Lon Tinkle Award: Robert Flynn

1997
Lisa Sandlin: *A Message to the Nurse of Dreams*
Joseph Skibell: *A Blessing on the Moon*
Tara Holley with Joe Holley: *My Mother's Keeper: A Daughter's Memoir of Growing up in the Shadow of Schizophrenia*
John Miller Morris: *El Llano Estacado*
Bruce Bond: "Radiography"
Debbie Nathan and Willavaldo Delgadillo: *The Moon Will Forever Be a Distant Love*
Clifford Hudder: "Misplacement"
Skip Hollandsworth: "The Curse of Romeo and Juliet"
Michael Leahy: "Oswald: A Brother's Burden"
Jerry Herring: *Charles Schorre*
David Timmons: *The Wild and Vivid Land*
Naomi Shihab Nye: *Habibi*
Lon Tinkle Award: Rolando Hinojosa-Smith

Rolando Hinojosa-Smith

1996
Sandra Scofield: *A Chance to See Egypt*
Nolan Porterfield: *Last Cavalier: The Life and Times of John A Lomax*
Kathleen Cambor: *The Book of Mercy*
Rick Bass: *The Book of Yaak*
Isabel Nathaniel: "The Dominion of Light'"
Daniel Stern: "The Passion According to St. John by J.S. Bach"
Debbie Nathan: "The Death of Jane Roe"
Mike Tolson: "When Hope Dies"
D.J. Stout: *Heaven of Animals*
Thomas Taylor and Barbara Whitehead: *Trading in Santa Fe*
J.A. Benner: *Uncle Comanche*
Lon Tinkle Award: Cormac McCarthy

1995
Paul Scott Malone: *In an Arid Land: Thirteen Stories of Texas*
Mary Karr: *The Liars' Club: A Memoir*
Jewel Mogan: *Beyond Telling*
Ben Huseman: *Wild River, Timeless Canyon*
Paul Christensen: "Water"
Rick Bass: "The Fires Next Time'
Mike Tolson: "Race to the Future"
Dick Gerdes: *The Fourth World* (trans.)
Ellen McKie: *Codex Telleriano-Remensis*
Diane Stevens: *Liza's Blue Moon*
Lon Tinkle Award: William Humphrey ☆

Fine Arts Organizations Across State

The following information on the fine arts in Texas was prepared for the Texas Almanac *by the staff of the Texas Commission on the Arts.*

Culture in Texas, as in any market, is a mixture of activity generated by both the commercial and the non-profit sectors.

The commercial sector encompasses Texas-based profit-making businesses including commercial recording artists (such as the legendary Willie Nelson), nightclubs, record companies, private galleries, assorted boutiques that carry fine art collectibles and private dance and music halls. In addition, Texas is becoming an important media center, with Texas-based publications, television and film companies gaining national recognition.

Texas also has extensive cultural resources offered by nonprofit organizations that are engaged in charitable, educational and/or humanitarian activities.

The Texas Legislature has authorized six state agencies to administer cultural services and funds for the public good. The agencies, listed below, fall under the auspices of the Texas Legislature's State, Federal and International Relations Committee.

They are: **State Antiquities Committee**, Box 12276, Austin (78711); **Texas Commission on the Arts**, Box 13406, Austin (78711); **Texas Film Commission, the Governor's office**, Box 12428, Austin (78711); **Texas Historical Commission**, Box 12276, Austin (78711); **Texas State Library and Archives Commission**, Box 12927, Austin (78711); and the **State Preservation Board**, Box 13286, Austin (78711).

Although not a state agency, another organization that provides cultural services to the citizens of Texas is the **Texas Council for the Humanities**, 1604 Nueces, Austin 78701.

The Texas Commission on the Arts was established in 1965 to develop a receptive climate for the arts in Texas and to serve as a source of arts information to state government and Texas at large. The commission achieves these objectives by providing financial, informational and technical assistance.

The commission's assistance programs serve as a financial catalyst to assist individuals and organizations in opening doors to local resources. Its clientele includes theaters (professional, civic, children's, ethnic), media (radio, television, film, publications), festivals, music (folk, symphonic, chamber, choral, jazz, opera, and new music), visual arts (sculpture, crafts, photography, painting, environmental), dance (modern, ballet, folkloric), schools, presenters of cultural events, and service organizations.

In 1993, the Texas Legislature created the Texas Cultural Endowment Fund as a public/private funding source to enhance the performing, visual and literary arts and education. Goals of the Texas Cultural Endowment Fund are to: 1) create financial self-sufficiency for the Texas Commission on the Arts by providing a stable and predictable base of funding no longer dependent on tax-based legislative support; 2) enhance arts education, encourage economic development, and cultivate a

higher quality of life in communities throughout Texas; 3) demonstrate leadership by encouraging public and private partnerships, ensuring public access to the arts for all communities statewide; and 4) diversify revenue sources, and increase the state's capacity to introduce the arts to future generations, to build audiences, and to create supporters.

The Texas Commission on the Arts seeks support for the Texas Cultural Endowment Fund and is responsible for the management of the fund. The commission is also ultimately responsible for the distribution of the fund to artists, arts, cultural and educational projects and organizations throughout Texas. For more information about the services of the commission, call toll-free (800) 252-9415.

Some of Texas' major nonprofit arts institutions — orchestras, museums, dance companies, theaters and cultural centers — are listed below.

Addison — Addison Centre Theatre, Box 933, (75001).
Amarillo — Amarillo Symphony Orchestra, Box 2552 (79105); Lone Star Ballet, Box 1133 (79178).
Austin — Austin Symphony Orchestra, 1101 Red River (78701); Ballet Austin, 3002 Guadalupe (78705); Austin Art Museum - Laguna Gloria, Box 5568 (78763); Paramount Theatre for the Performing Arts, Box 1205 (78767).
Beaumont — Art Museum of Southeast Texas, 1111 9th St. (77702).
Corpus Christi — Art Museum of South Texas, 1902 N. Shoreline Dr. (78401); Corpus Christi Ballet, 5610 Everhart (78469).
Corsicana — Community Playhouse, Box 2224 (75110).
Dallas — Dallas Opera, 1925 Elm (75201); Dallas Museum of Art, 1717 N. Harwood (75201); Dallas Symphony Orchestra, Box 26207 (75226); Fort Worth Dallas Ballet (see Fort Worth); Dallas Theatre Center, 3636 Turtle Creek Blvd. (75219); Shakespeare Festival, 3630 Harry Hines (75210); Teatro Dallas, 2204 Commerce (75201); Theatre Three, 2800 Routh (75201).
El Paso — Museum Of Arts, 1211 Montana Ave. (79902); El Paso Symphony Orchestra, Box 180 (79942).
Fort Worth — Amon Carter Museum Of Western Art, Box 2365 (76101); Museum of Modern Art, 1309 Montgomery (76107); Fort Worth Dallas Ballet, 6845 Green Oaks Rd. (76116); Fort Worth Opera, 3505 W. Lancaster (76107); Fort Worth Symphony Orchestra, 4401 Trail Lake Dr. (76109); Kimbell Art Museum, Box 9440 (76107); Stage West, Box 2587 (76113); Van Cliburn Foundation, 2525 Ridgmar Blvd. (76116).
Houston — Alley Theatre, 615 Texas (77002); Contemporary Arts Museum, 5216 Montrose Blvd. (77006); Houston Ballet Foundation, Box 130487 (77219); Houston Grand Opera, 510 Preston, #500 (77002); Houston Museum of Fine Arts, Box 6826 (77265); Houston Symphony Orchestra, 615 Louisiana (77002); Texas Opera Theatre, 510 Preston, #440 (77002); Theatre Under the Stars, 4235 San Felipe (77027).
Midland/Odessa — Midland/Odessa Symphony and Chorale, Box 60658 (79711).
Round Top — James Dick Foundation for the Performing Arts, Box 89 (78954).
San Antonio — Carver Cultural Center, 226 N. Hackberry (78202); Guadalupe Cultural Arts Center, 1300 Guadalupe (78207); McNay Art Institute, Box 6069 (78209); San Antonio Art Institute, Box 6069 (78209); San Antonio Museum of Art, Box 2601 (78299-2601); San Antonio Symphony Orchestra, 109 Lexington Ave., Ste. 207 (78205); Southwest Craft Center, 300 Augusta (78205).

The **Texas Alliance for Education and the Arts**, 3530 Bee Caves Rd., Ste. 211, Austin 78746, promotes, develops and supports local arts agencies. Listed below are the some of the members as of mid-1999.

Abilene Cultural Affairs Council, 1101 N. First St. (79604).

Albany — The Old Jail Art Center, Rt. 1, Box 1 (76430).

Amarillo — Chamber Arts Committee, Box 9480 (79105).

Andrews Cultural Affairs Committee, 700 West Broadway (79714).

Arlington — Arts Arlington, 201 E. Abram Ste. 720 (76010).

Athens — Henderson County Arts Council, P.O. Box 2633 (75751).

Austin — Cultural Arts Division, City of Austin PARD, 1110 Barton Springs R. (78704).

Bastrop Assn. for the Arts, 807 Main (78602).

Bay City Cultural Assn., P.O. Box 419(77414).

Beaumont, Orange and Port Arthur — Southeast Texas Arts Council, Box 3925, Beaumont (77704).

Belton — Bell Fine Arts Assoc., P.O. Box 624 (76513).

Big Spring Cultural Affairs Council, Box 1391 (79720). West Texas Center for the Arts, Box 1810 (79720).

Borger — Magic Plains Arts Council, 601 W. 3rd (79007).

Bowie Alliance for Education & the Arts, 204 N. Mason (76230).

Breckenridge Fine Arts Center, Box 549 (76424).

Brenham — Arts Council of Washington County, 701 Milroy Dr. (77833).

Brownwood — Community Cultural Affairs Commission, P.O Box 880 (76804).

Buchanan Dam — Highland Lakes Art Council, Rt. 1 Box 118 (78605).

Canadian Arts Alliance, P.O. Box 698 (79014).

Carrizo Springs — Arts Council of Dimmit County, 412 Pena (78834).

Clifton — Bosque Co. Conservatory of Fine Arts, Box 373 (76634).

Coleman — Fine Arts League, Box 376 (76834).

College Station — Arts Council of Brazos Valley, 3501 Texas Ave. S. Ste. 105C (77840).

Columbus — Live Oak Art Center, 1014 Milam (78934).

Conroe — Montgomery County Performing Arts Society, Box 1714 (77305).

Corpus Christi — Municipal Arts Commission, PARD, Box 9277 (78401).

Corsicana — Navarro Council of the Arts, Box 2224 (75151).

Crockett — Piney Woods Fine Arts Assn., Box 1213 (75835).

Cuero — Oscar Scott Memorial Foundation, 203 E. Church (77954).

Dalhart Area Fine Arts Assn., 1022 Oak (79022).

Dallas — Event Services/Cultural Affairs, 1925 Elm, Ste. 500 (75201).

Del Rio Council for the Arts, 120 East Garfield (78840).

Denison Arts Council, P.O. Box 325 (75020).

Denton — Greater Denton Arts Council, 207 S. Bell (76201).

DeSoto Council of Cultural Arts, 624 Bentcreek Dr. (75115).

Devine Area Artist's Series Inc., R. 1 Box 89D (78016).

Dumas — Moore County Arts Assn., P.O. Box 74 (79029).

Duncanville Regional Arts Assn., Box 381014 (76138).

Eagle Pass — Arts Council of Eagle Pass, Box 2920 (78853).

El Paso — Arts Resources Department, City of El Paso, 2 Civic Center Plaza (79901).

Fort Worth — Arts Council of Fort Worth & Tarrant County, 505 Main Ste. 200 (76102).

Gainesville — Cooke County Arts Council, Box 194 (76241).

Garland Center for the Performing Arts, Box 469002 (75046).

Gilmer — Upshur County Arts Council, Box 433 (75644).

Grand Prairie Arts Council, Box 531613 (75053).

Harlingen Arts Council, Box 531105 (78553).

Hondo — Art League of Hondo, 3696 County Rd., (78861).

Houston — Cultural Arts Council of Houston, 3201 Allen Parkway (77019).

Huntsville Arts Commission, 1212 Ave. M (77340).

Ingram — Hill Country Arts Foundation, P.O. Box 1169 (78025).

Irving Arts Center, 3333 N. McArthur Ste. 300 (75062); Irving Cultural Affairs Council, same address.

Kerrville Arts & Culture Committee, 1700 Sidney Baker (78928).

Killeen Arts Commission, City of Killeen (76541).

Lake Jackson — Brazosport Center for Arts & Science, 400 College Dr. (77566).

Lakeway — Lake Travis Arts League, P.O. Box 340184 (78734).

Lampasas — Keystone Art Alliance, Box 1013 (76550).

Laredo Center for the Arts, 500 San Agustin (78040).

Lewisville — Greater Lewisville Arts Council, P.O. Box 294129 (75067).

Longview Arts & Culture Commission, P.O. Box 1133 (75606).

Lubbock Arts Alliance, Inc., 2109 Broadway (79401).

Lufkin Cultural Affairs Council, P.O. Box 1607 (75902).

Marble Falls — Highland Lakes Arts Guild, 318 Main (78654).

Marfa — Big Bend Arts Alliance, Alliance, 505 W. San Antonio (78654).

Marshall Regional Arts Council, Box C (75671).

Mesquite Arts Council, 1515 N. Galloway (75149).

Midland Arts Assembly, Box 3494 (79702).

Missouri City — Fort Bend Cultural Arts Council, E. Cartwright (77495).

Mount Vernon — Franklin County Arts Assoc., P.O. Box 1276 (75457).

Nassau Bay — Arts Alliance Center at Clear Lake, P.O. Box 580302 (77258).

New Braunfels — Greater New Braunfels Arts Council, Box 311171 (78131).

Odessa Cultural Council, Box 7195 (79760).

Pampa Fine Arts Assn., Box 818 (79065).

Paris Area Arts Alliance, P.O. Box 6085 (75461).

Pasadena — Recreational Supt., Pasadena PARD, 1104 Parkside (75502).

Pecos Arts Coalition, Box 2399 (79772).

Pittsburg/Camp County Arts Council, Box 72 (75686).

Plains — Yoakum County Art Assn., Box 38 (79355).

Plainview Cultural Council, 1900 W. Seventh (79702).

Plano — Art Center of Plano, Box 861011 (75086).

Point Aransas — Island Art Assoc., P.O. Box 1871 (78373).

Post — Caprock Cultural Assn., Box 37 (79356).

Richardson Arts Commission, Box 830309 (75083).

Rockport Center for the Arts, 902 Navigation Circle (78382).

Rockwall Cultural Arts Commission, 5446 Ranger Dr. (75032).

San Angelo Cultural Affairs Council, Box 2477 (76902).

San Antonio — City of San Antonio Arts and Cultural Affairs, P.O. Box 839966 (78205).

San Marcos — Performing Arts Assn., Box 651 (78666).

Schulenburg — Backstage Inc. Fine Arts Council, Box 66 (78956).

Seagoville Fine Arts Council, 2403 Seagoville Rd. (75159).

Sherman — Council for the Arts and Humanities, Box 1029 (75091).

Silsbee — Performing and Visual Arts Council, Rt. 1, Box 150 (77656).

Snyder — Cultural Affairs Council, P.O. Box 1072 (79551).

South Padre Island — Area Funds Foundation, Box 2326 (78597).

Stephenville — Cross Timbers Fine Arts Council, Box 1172 (76401).

Temple Cultural Activities Center, 3011 N. Third (76501).

Texarkana Regional Arts and Humanities Council Inc., Box 1171 (75504).

The Woodlands Art League, P.O. Box 7234 (77387).

Tomball — Regional Arts Center, Box 1321 (77377).

Uvalde Arts Council, 104 W. North (78801).

Vernon Council of the Arts, Box 222 (76384).

Victoria — Cultural Council of Victoria, Box 1758 (77902).

Waco — Greater Waco Council for the Arts, 400 Ivyi Ann Court (76712).

Waxahachie Arts Council, 311 Olive (75165).

Wichita Falls Arts Commission, 607 Tenth (76301).

Wimberley Institute of Cultures, Box 167 (78676). ☆

Film and Multimedia Work in Texas

Source: Texas Film Commission

The year 2000 marks Texas' 90th year as a center for film production. Besides such classics as **Giant, The Alamo** and the long-running television series **Dallas**, Texas has hosted more than 800 film and television projects.

Highlights from the past ten years include **Lonesome Dove, Austin City Limits, Rushmore, Varsity Blues, Hope Floats, All the Pretty Horses**, John Sayles' **Lone Star**, Chuck Norris' hit series **Walker, Texas Ranger** and the PBS series **Barney & Friends**.

Texas' wide diversity of locations give it a unique advantage in attracting filmmakers, who often use Texas locations to represent other places. **Arlington Road** filmed "Washington, D.C," in Houston, while **Courage Under Fire** found its "Washington, D.C." in Austin, and its "Kuwait" near El Paso. **Ace Ventura: When Nature Calls** spent five weeks in "Africa," near Hondo. Texas locations have doubled for Berlin, Manhattan, Iowa, Bolivia and many other worldwide locations.

But Texas' locations are only one of the reasons it has become one of the top spots in the nation for film production. Most states have only one major film center, but Texas has four: the Dallas/Fort Worth area, Austin, Houston and San Antonio, all of which offer labor pools of experienced film technicians and actors; local rental sources for cameras, lights and other specialized equipment. Another important incentive is Texas' sales tax exemption on equipment and materials used in film production.

The Texas Film Commission, a division of the Office of the Governor, is an economic development program devoted to maketing Texas to Hollywood. The film commission's free services include location research, employment referrals, and information on laws, weather, travel and other topics affecting filmmakers working in Texas.

The film commission's databases include more than 1,300 individuals and businesses serving every facet of the film industry, and working on every type of project: feature films; television movies, series and commercials; music videos; interactive entertainment; educational films; and corporate and marketing videos.

In 1998, total budgets on film and televison projects made in Texas topped $261 million. In 1997, the total was $212 million. The total for the past ten years has passed $1.9 billion.

Besides money spent directly on production, film dollars flow to hotels, location owners, car rental agencies, gas stations, lumberyards, dry cleaners, florists, fabric stores, utility providers, shippers, groceries, security services and office suppliers, among others. ☆

Major film projects in Texas by year

Year	Number	Gross Budgets
1985	27	$56,700,000
1986	27	102,100,000
1987	24	66,300,000
1988	24	93,900,000
1989	32	117,100,000
1990	31	42,100,000
1991	44	120,454,000
1992	28	143,207,800
1993	44	180,400,000
1994	41	191,500,000
1995	69	327,782,000
1996	65	277,161,000
1997	53	212,337,000
1998	42	$261,312,000

Source: Texas Film Commission

Texas Multimedia Program

Created as a division of the Texas Film Commission in 1993, the Texas Multimedia Program provides information on more than 1,400 Texas multimedia-related businesses and people.

Visitors to the web site can search for animators, Web designers, graphic artists, instructional designers, game developers, software developers, Internet Service Providers (ISPs), kiosk developers, asssociations, and other related industries by company name and region.

The program also publishes an online Guide to Texas Multimedia Education with information on more than 130 college programs.

Additional online resources include an events calendar, press list, and information on sales tax exemptions available for multimedia producers.

The Texas Multimedia Program can be reached at (512) 463-5842 or www.governor.state.tx.us/multimedia. ☆

Film Commissions

In addition to the offices listed below, many other Texas cities have employees who specialize in assisting filmmakers. The Texas Film Commission (**www.governor.state.tx.us/film**) can provide information on local contacts for most Texas cities and counties:

Texas Film Commission
1100 San Jacinto Ste. 3.410
Austin 78701
(512) 463-9200, Fax 463-4114
film@governor.state.tx.us

Amarillo Film Office
P.O. Box 9480
Amarillo 79105
(806) 374-1497, Fax 373-3909
(800) 692-1338
jutta@amarillo-cvb.org

Austin Film Office
201 E. 2nd St.
Austin 78701
(800) 926-2282 x4562
(512) 404-4562, Fax 404-4564
gbond@austintexas.org

Brownsville Area Film Commission
P.O. Box 4697
Brownsville 78523
(956) 546-3721, Fax 546-3972
(800) 626-2639
nreyna@brownsville.org

Dallas/Fort Worth Regional Film Commission
504 Business Parkway
Richardson 75081
(800) 234-5699 (outside Texas)
(972) 621-0400, Fax 912-0916
production@dfwfilm.com

El Paso Film Commission
1 Civic Center Plaza

El Paso 79901
(915) 534-0686, Fax 534-0686
(800) 351-6024
elpasotx@huntleigh.net

Houston Film Commission
801 Congress
Houston 77002
(713) 227-3100, Fax 227-6336
(800) 365-7575
www.houston-guide.com

Irving Texas Film Commission
6309 N. O'Connor Ste. 222
Irving 75039-3510
(972) 869-0303, Fax 869-4609
(800) 247-8464

San Antonio Film Commission
P.O. Box 2277
San Antonio 78298
(800) 447-3372 x730 or 777
(210) 207-6730, Fax 270-8782
filmsa@sanantonio.cvb.com

Public Libraries

The following information on Texas Public Libraries was furnished by Patty Davis of the Library Development Division of the Texas State Library and Archives Commission, Austin.

Public libraries continue to strive to meet the education and information needs of Texans by providing library services and materials in print, in audio-visual format, in programs, and in electronic format such as CD-ROM and the Internet.

A notable change in library legislation was the passage of a library districts act in 1997 that allowed the creation of library taxing districts. Voters have approved four library districts: Westbank, Salado, Wells Branch, and Benbrook.

Another notable piece of legislation was the expansion of grants from the Telecommunications Infrastructure Fund (TIF) to public libraries, making it possible for all public libraries to be connected to the Internet, and providing funds for hardware, software, and initial connectivity charges.

In 1997, the latest year for which data has been received, the public libraries in Texas served a population of 17,748,062, and answered 17,717,200 reference questions, both in person and via phone, Internet, and fax. 3,864,737 people attended programs at public libraries, including 2,486,492 children who attended library-sponsored programs such as story hours and summer reading programs.

From 1996 to 1997, local expenditures for library services increased. Total library income increased 7.18%; total expenditures increased 8.4%; and expenditures for library materials increased 10.35%.

Library services showed improvements in 1997. Circulation increased by 6.92%, a marked increase

from 1996. Also, three library service measures that have shown a decline since 1994 showed increases in 1997: library visits increased 8.54%; reference transactions increased 14.69%; and reference transactions per capita increased 9.89%.

The number of books and other materials checked out of Texas public libraries was 77,040,192, a total of 4.34 circulations per capita.

The challenges are varied. The costs for providing electronic and on-line sources, in addition to traditional services, are growing faster than library budgets. More than 1.3 million Texans are not served by a local library and there are three counties without any public library. Of the 522 public libraries reporting in 1997, 26 were unable to meet the minimum standards for accreditation by the Texas State Library and Archives Commission. In order to fill the growing education and information needs of Texans, there is a continuing need for funding, materials, and staff.

These and other statistics are available on the Library Development Division web page at: **www.tsl.state.tx.us/LD/info.htm**

The following table lists libraries with location, address and phone numbers.

Many of these libraries and branches are establishing web pages on the Internet. **Call the specific library for its web address,** or find a list of libraries with web addresses on the Library Development Division web page at: **www.tsl.state.tx.us/LD/PLS1997/index.html**

List of Principal Libraries

CITY	LIBRARY	ADDRESS	ZIP	AC	PHONE
Abernathy	Abernathy Public	P.O. Box 686	79311-0686	806	298-2546
Abilene	Abilene Public	202 Cedar Street	79601-5793	915	676-6328
Alamo	Lalo Arcaute Public	502 Duranta St.	78516	210	787-6160
Albany	Shackelford County	P.O. Box 445	76430-0445	915	762-2672
Aledo	East Parker County	P.O. Box 275	76008-0275	817	441-6545
Alice	Alice Public	401 East Third Street	78332-4798	512	664-9506
Allen	Allen Public	Two Allen Civic Plaza	75013-2559	972	727-0190
Alpine	Alpine Public	203 North 7th Street	79830-4693	915	837-2621
Alto	Stella Hill Memorial	Route 1 Box 724	75925-9791	409	858-4343
Alvarado	Alvarado Public	200 N. Spears	76009-3873	817	783-7323
Alvin	Alvin Branch	105 S. Gordon St.	77511-2332	281	388-4300
Alvord	Alvord Public	P.O. Box 323	76225-0323	817	427-2842
Amarillo	Amarillo Public	P.O. Box 2171	79189-2171	806	378-3050
Anahuac	Chambers County System	P.O. Box 520	77514-0520	409	267-8261
Andrews	Andrews County	208 NW 2nd Street	79714-6396	915	524-1432
Angleton	Brazoria County System	412 N. Front Street	77515-4428	409	849-5711
Anna	Anna Community	Rt 1 Box 280A	75003	214	924-2456
Anson	Anson Public	P.O. Box 528	79501-0528	915	823-2711
Aransas Pass	Ed & Hazel Richmond Public	110 North Lamont Street	78336-3698	512	758-2350
Archer City	Archer Public	P.O. Box 957	76351-0957	817	574-4954
Arlington	Arlington Public System	101 E. Abram Street	76010-1183	817	459-6901
Aspermont	Stonewall County	P.O. Box H	79502-0907	817	989-2730
Athens	Henderson County Murchison	121 South Prairieville St.	75751-2595	903	677-6350
Atlanta	Atlanta Public	101 West Hiram Street	75551-2509	903	796-2112
Aubrey	Aubrey Area	109 S. Main Street	76227-9164	817	365-9162
Austin	Austin Public	P.O. Box 2287	78768-2287	512	499-7300
Austin	Lake Travis Community	3322 Ranch Road 620 South	78734-6801	512	263-2885
Austin	Westbank Community	1309 Westbank Drive	78746-6565	512	327-3045
Azle	Azle Public	609 SE Parkway Street	76020-3654	817	444-7114
Baird	Callahan County	100 W. 4th, B-1	79504-5365	915	854-1718
Balch Springs	Balch Springs	4301 Pioneer Road	75180-4001	972	286-8856
Ballinger	Carnegie of Ballinger	204 8th Street	76821	915	365-3616
Bandera	Bandera County	P.O. Box 1568	78003-1568	210	796-4213

CITY	LIBRARY	ADDRESS	ZIP	AC	PHONE
Barksdale	Nueces Canyon Public	P.O. Box 58	78828-0058	210	234-3173
Barstow	Ward County Barstow	P.O. Box 74	79719-0074		
Bartlett	Teinert Memorial Public	Box 12	76511-0012	817	527-3208
Bastrop	Bastrop Public	P.O. Box 670	78602-0670	512	321-5441
Bay City	Bay City Public	1100 Seventh Street	77414-4915	409	245-6931
Baytown	Sterling Municipal	Mary Elizabeth Wilbanks Avenue	77520	281	427-7331
Beaumont	Jefferson County	2748 Viterbo Road - Box 7	77705-9554	409	727-2735
Beaumont	Beaumont Public System	P.O. Box 3827	77704-3827	409	838-6606
Bedford	Bedford Public	1805 L. Don Dodson Drive	76021-1897	817	952-2160
Beeville	Bee County Public	210 E. Corpus Christi Street	78102-4812	512	358-5541
Bellaire	Bellaire City	5111 Jessamine	77401-4498	713	662-8160
Bellville	Bellville Public	12 W. Palm Street	77418-1446	409	865-3731
Belton	Belton City	301 East First Avenue	76513-3168	817	933-5832
Benbrook	Benbrook Public	101-C Del Rio Street	76126-2557	817	249-6632
Bertram	Bertram Free	P.O. Box 243	78605-0243	512	355-2113
Big Lake	Reagan County	County Courthouse	76932	915	884-2854
Big Sandy	Holly Community	Route 1, Box 799	75755-9600	903	769-5142
Big Spring	Howard County	312 Scurry Street	79720-2559	915	264-2260
Blanco	Williams Memorial	P.O. Box 489	78606-0489	210	833-4280
Blessing	Blessing	P.O. Box 210	77419-0210	512	588-7717
Boerne	Kendall County System	210 N. Main Street	78006	210	249-3053
Bonham	Bonham Public	305 East 5th Street	75418-4002	903	583-3128
Booker	Booker School/Public	Drawer 288	79005-0288	806	658-9323
Borger	Hutchinson County	625 N. Weatherly Street	79007-3621	806	273-0126
Bowie	Bowie Public	315 W. Walnut Street	76230-4828	817	872-2681
Boyd	Boyd Public	733 East Rock Island Avenue	76023-3001	817	433-5580
Brackettville	Kinney County Public	P.O. Box 975	78832-0975	210	563-2884
Brady	F.M. (Buck) Richards Memorial	1106 South Blackburn Street	76825-6222	915	597-2617
Brazoria	Brazoria Branch	620 S. Brooks St.	77422-9022	409	798-2372
Breckenridge	Breckenridge	207 N. Breckenridge Avenue	76424-3503	817	559-5505
Brenham	Nancy Carol Roberts Memorial	100 West Academy Street	77833-3107	409	277-1271
Bridge City	Bridge City Public	101 Parkside Drive	77611-2442	409	735-4242
Bridgeport	Bridgeport Public	2159 Tenth Street	76426-2071	817	683-4412
Brookshire	Waller County Brookshire	P.O. Box 790	77423-0790	409	934-3516
Brownfield	Kendrick Memorial	301 West Tate	79316-4329	806	637-3848
Brownsville	Brownsville Public	2600 Central Blvd.	78520-8824	210	548-1055
Brownwood	Brownwood Public	600 Carnegie Boulevard	76801-7097	915	646-0155
Bryan	Bryan/College Station System	201 East 26th Street	77803-5389	409	361-3715
Buchanan Dam	Lakeshore Branch	Lakeshore Drive	78609	915	379-1174
Buda	Moreau Memorial	P.O. Box 608	78610-0608	512	295-5899
Buffalo	Buffalo Public	P.O. Drawer 1290	75831-1290	903	322-4146
Bullard	Bullard Community	P.O. Box 368	75757-0368	903	894-6125
Bulverde	Bulverde Public	P.O. Box 207	78163-0207	210	438-3666
Buna	Buna Public	P.O. Box 1571	77612-1571	409	994-5501
Burkburnett	Burkburnett	215 East 4th Street	76354-3446	817	569-2991
Burleson	Burleson Public	248 SW Johnson Avenue	76028-4765	817	295-6131
Burnet	Burnet County System	100 E. Washington Street	78611-3114	512	756-2328
Caldwell	Harrie P. Woodson Memorial	704 West Highway 21	77836-1198	409	567-4111
Cameron	Cameron Public	304 E. Third Street	76520-3350	817	697-2401
Camp Wood	Camp Wood Public	P.O. Box 108	78833-0108	210	597-3208
Canadian	Hemphill County	5th & Main Street	79014	806	323-5282
Canton	Van Zandt County	317 First Monday Lane	75103-1052	903	567-4276
Canyon	Canyon Public	301 16th Street	79015-2828	806	655-5015
Canyon Lake	Tye Preston Memorial	1321 Highway 2673	78133-5301	210	964-3744
Carrizo Springs	Dimmit County Public	200 N. 9th Street	78834-3704	210	876-5788
Carrollton	Carrollton Public	2001 Jackson Road	75006-1743	972	466-3360
Carthage	Sammy Brown	522 West College Street	75633-1408	903	693-6741
Castroville	Castroville Public	P.O. Box 532	78009-0532	210	538-2656
Cedar Hill	Zula B. Wylie	225 Cedar Street	75104-2655	972	291-7323
Cedar Park	Cedar Park Public	550 Discovery Blvd.	78613-2200	512	259-5353
Celina	Celina Community	P.O. Box 188	75009-0188	972	382-3750
Center	Fannie Brown Booth Memorial	619 Tenaha Street	75935-3535	409	598-5522
Centerville	Leon County	P.O. Box 567	75833-0567		
Chandler	Henderson County East	P.O. Box 301	75758-0301	903	849-4122
Charlotte	Charlotte Public	P.O. Box 757	78011-0757	210	277-1212
Chico	Chico Public	P.O. Box 707	76431-0707	817	644-2330
Childress	Childress Public	117 Avenue B, NE	79201-4509	817	937-8421
Cisco	Cisco Public	600 Avenue G	76437-3039	817	442-1020
Clarendon	G.B. Burton Memorial	Box 783	79226-0783	806	874-3641
Clarksville	Red River County Public	P.O. Box 508	75426-0508	903	427-3991
Claude	Claude Public	P.O. Box 109	79019-0109	806	226-7881
Cleburne	Cleburne Municipal	302 W. Henderson Street	76031-5494	817	645-0935
Cleveland	Austin Memorial	220 S. Bonham Street	77327-4591	281	592-3920

CITY	LIBRARY	ADDRESS	ZIP	AC	PHONE
Clifton	Nellie Pederson Civic	P.O. Box 231	76634	817	675-6495
Clint	Clint Public	P.O. Box 779	79836-0779	915	851-2344
Clute	Clute Branch	215 N. Shanks St.	77531-4122	409	265-4582
Clyde	Clyde Public	P.O. Box 679	79510-0679	915	893-5315
Cockrell Hill	Cockrell Hill Public	4125 West Clarendon Drive	75211-4919	214	330-9935
Coldspring	Coldspring Area Public	P.O. Box 1756	77331-1756	409	653-3104
Coleman	Coleman Public	402 Commercial Avenue	76834-4202	915	625-3043
College Station	College Station Public	2551 South Texas Ave., Ste E-1	77802-2330	409	764-3416
Colorado City	Mitchell County Public	340 Oak Street	79512-6214	915	728-3968
Columbus	Nesbitt Memorial	529 Washington Street	78934-2326	409	732-3392
Comanche	Comanche Public	P.O. Box 411	76442-0411	915	356-2122
Comfort	Comfort Public	P.O. Box 536	78013-0536	210	995-2398
Commerce	Commerce Public	P.O. Box 308	75429-0308	903	886-6858
Conroe	Montgomery County	P.O. Box 579	77305-0579	409	788-8377
Converse	Converse Area Public	502 Station Street	78109-1300	210	659-4160
Cooper	Delta County Public	300 W. Dallas Avenue	75432-1632	903	395-4575
Coppell	William T. Cozby Public	P.O. Box 478	75019-0478	972	304-3655
Copperas Cove	Copperas Cove Public	602 South Main Street	76522-2997	817	547-3826
Corpus Christi	Corpus Christi Public Libraries	805 Comanche Street	78401-2798	512	880-7070
Corpus Christi	Flour Bluff Branch	1456 Waldron Road	78418-4433	512	937-5222
Corrigan	Mickey Reily Public	604 South Mathews Street	75939-2645	409	398-4156
Corsicana	Corsicana Public	100 North 12th Street	75110-5205	903	654-4810
Cotulla	Alexander Memorial	201 South Center Street	78014-2255	210	879-2601
Crane	Crane County	701 South Alford Street	79731-2521	915	558-3142
Crockett	J.H. Wootters-Crockett Public	P.O. Box 1226	75835-1226	409	544-3089
Crosby	Crosby Branch	135 Hare Road	77532-8895	281	328-3535
Crosbyton	Crosby County	114 West Aspen Street	79322-2502	806	675-2673
Cross Plains	Cross Plains Public	P.O. Box 333	76443-0333	817	725-7722
Crowell	Foard County	P.O. Box 317	79227-0317	817	684-1250
Crowley	Crowley Public	Box 747	76036-0747	817	297-6707
Crystal City	Crystal City Memorial	101 E. Dimmit Street	78839-3505	210	374-3477
Cuero	Cuero Public	207 East Main Street	77954-3048	512	275-2864
Cushing	Cushing Community	P.O. Box 421	75760-0421	409	326-4608
Cypress	Northwest Branch	11355 Regency Green Drive	77429-4705	281	890-2665
Daingerfield	Daingerfield Public	207 Jefferson Street	75638-1713	903	645-2823
Dalhart	Dallam-Hartley County	420 Denrock Avenue	79022-2628	806	249-2761
Dallas	Dallas Public	1515 Young Street	75201-5499	214	670-1400
Dayton	Edmund E. & Nida Smith Jones	307 West Houston	77535-2537	409	258-7060
Decatur	Decatur Public	1700 Highway 51 South	76234-9292	817	627-5512
Deer Park	Deer Park Public	3009 Center Street	77536-5099	281	478-7208
Del Rio	Val Verde County	300 Spring Street	78840-5199	210	774-7595
Del Valle	Elroy Community	13512 F.M. 812	78617	512	243-1981
DeLeon	DeLeon Public	105 South Texas Street	76444-1862	817	893-2417
Dell City	Grace Grebing Public/School	P.O. Box 37	79837-0037	915	964-2468
Denison	Denison Public	300 West Gandy	75020-3153	903	465-1797
Denton	Denton Public	502 Oakland St.	76201-3102	817	566-8566
Denver City	Yoakum County/Cecil Bickley	P.O. Box 900	79323-0900	806	592-2754
DeSoto	DeSoto Public	211 E. Pleasant Run Rd., Suite C	75115-3939	972	230-9656
Devine	Driscoll Public	P.O. Box 619	78016-0619	210	663-2993
Diboll	TLL Temple Memorial	300 Park Street	75941-1633	409	829-5497
Dickinson	Mares Memorial	4324 Highway 3	77539-6801	281	534-3812
Dimmitt	Rhoads Memorial	103 SW 2nd	79027-2501	806	647-3532
Donna	Donna Public	301 South Main Street	78537-3288	210	464-2221
Dripping Springs	Dripping Springs Community	P.O. Box 279	78620-0279	512	858-7825
Dublin	Dublin Public	206 West Blackjack Street	76446-2204	817	445-4141
Dumas	Killgore Memorial	124 S. Bliss Avenue	79029-3804	806	935-4941
Duncanville	Duncanville Public	103 E. Wheatland Road	75116-4899	972	780-5050
Eagle Lake	Eula & David Wintermann	101 N. Walnut Avenue	77434-2326	409	234-5411
Eagle Pass	Eagle Pass Public	589 Main Street	78852	210	773-2516
Earth	Springlake-Earth Community	P.O. Box 259	79031-0259	806	257-3357
East Bernard	East Bernard Branch	P.O. Box 516	77435	409	335-6142
Eastland	Centennial Memorial	210 South Lamar Street	76448-2794	817	629-2281
Eden	Eden Public	P.O. Box 896	76837-0896	915	869-7761
Edinburg	Edinburg Public	401 East Cano	78539-4596	210	383-6246
Edna	Jackson County Memorial	411 North Wells Street	77957-2734	512	782-2162
El Campo	El Campo Branch	409 E. Hillje St.	77437-4503	409	543-2362
El Paso	El Paso Public	501 North Oregon Street	79901-1195	915	543-5413
El Paso	Ysleta Branch	9301 Alameda	79907-6803	915	858-0905
Eldorado	Schleicher County Public	P.O. Box 611	76936-0611	915	853-3767
Electra	Electra Public	401 North Waggoner Street	76360-2134	817	495-2208
Elgin	Elgin Public	404 N. Main Street	78621-2625	512	281-5678
Elsa	Elsa Public	P.O. Box 1447	78543-1447	210	262-3061
Emory	Rains County Public	P.O. Box 189	75440-0189	903	473-2221

CITY	LIBRARY	ADDRESS	ZIP	AC	PHONE
Ennis	Ennis Public	501 W. Ennis Avenue	75119-3803	972	875-5360
Euless	Euless Public	201 N. Ector Drive	76039-3595	817	685-1482
Everman	Everman Public	212 Race Street	76140-3297	817	551-0726
Fabens	El Paso County	P.O. Drawer 788	79838-0788	915	764-3635
Fairfield	Fairfield	350 W. Main Street	75840-3028	903	389-3574
Falfurrias	Ed Rachal Memorial	203 S. Henry Street	78355-4321	512	325-2144
Falls City	Falls City Public	P.O. Box 220	78113-0220	210	254-3361
Farmers Branch	Farmers Branch Manske Public	13613 Webb Chapel	75234-3799	972	247-2511
Farmersville	Charles J. Rike Memorial	P.O. Box 50	75442-0050	972	782-6681
Ferris	Ferris Public	514 S. Mable Street	75125-3028	972	544-3696
Flatonia	Flatonia Public	P.O. Box 656	78941-0656	512	865-3920
Florence	Florence Public	P.O. Box 430	76527-0430	817	793-2672
Floresville	Wilson County Public	One Lane	78114-2239	210	393-2886
Flower Mound	Flower Mound Public	2121 Cross Timbers Rd.	75028-2602	972	539-0120
Floydada	Floyd County	Floyd County Courthouse	79235-2749	806	983-4922
Forest Hill	Forest Hill Public	6619 Forest Hill Drive	76140-1260	817	483-9811
Forney	West Memorial	811 South Bois D'Arc	75126-	972	552-9555
Fort Davis	Jeff Davis County	Box 1054	79734-1054	915	426-3802
Fort Hancock	Ft.Hancock/Hudspeth Co. Public	P.O. Box 98	79839-0098	915	769-3868
Fort Stockton	Fort Stockton Public	500 North Water	79735-5634	915	336-3374
Fort Worth	Fort Worth Public	300 Taylor Street	76102-7333	817	871-7703
Franklin	Robertson County	P.O. Box 1027	77856-1027	409	828-4331
Frankston	Frankston Depot	P.O. Box 639	75763-0639	903	876-4463
Fredericksburg	Pioneer Memorial	115 West Main Street	78624-3751	210	997-6513
Freeport	Freeport Branch	410 Brazosport Blvd.	77541-	409	233-3622
Friendswood	Friendswood Public	416 S. Friendswood	77546-3906	281	482-7135
Friona	Friona Public	109 W. 7th Street	79035-2548	806	247-3200
Frisco	Frisco Public	8750 McKinney Road, Ste. 200	75034-3000	972	335-5510
Fritch	Hutchinson County Fritch	P.O. Box 430	79036-0430	806	857-3752
Gainesville	Cooke County	200 S. Weaver Street	76240-4790	817	665-2401
Galena Park	Galena Park Branch	100 Main Street	77547	713	674-2245
Galveston	Galveston County System	2310 Sealy Avenue	77550-2296	409	763-8854
Garland	Nicholson Memorial System	625 Austin Street	75040-6365	972	205-2543
Garwood	Veterans Memorial	P.O. Box 275	77442		
Gatesville	Gatesville Public	811 Main Street	76528-1432	817	865-5367
George West	Live Oak County	P.O. Box 698	78022-0698	512	449-1124
Georgetown	Georgetown Public	808 Martin Luther King Street	78626-5527	512	930-3551
Giddings	Rufus Young King	177 South Madison Street	78942-3317	409	542-2716
Gilmer	Upshur County	702 West Tyler Street	75644-2198	903	843-5001
Gladewater	Lee Public	P.O. Box 791	75647-0791	903	845-2640
Glen Rose	Somervell County	108 Allen Street	76043-4526	817	897-4582
Goldthwaite	Jennie Trent Dew	P.O. Box 101	76844-0101	915	648-2447
Goliad	Goliad County	P.O. Box 789	77963-0789	512	645-2291
Gonzales	Gonzales County System	P.O. Box 220	78629	210	672-6315
Gorman	Charlie Garrett Memorial	P.O. Box 219	76454-0219		
Graham	Graham	910 Cherry Street	76450-3547	817	549-0600
Granbury	Hood County Public	222 N. Travis Street	76048-2164	817	573-3569
Grand Prairie	Grand Prairie Memorial	901 Conover Drive	75051-1590	972	264-9536
Grand Saline	Grand Saline Public	201 E. Pacific Street	75140-1934	903	962-5516
Grandfalls	Ward County Grandfalls	P.O. Box 186	79742-0186	915	547-2861
Grapevine	Grapevine Public	1201 S. Main Street	76051-5545	817	481-0341
Greenville	W. Walworth Harrison Public	3716 Lee Street	75401-3999	903	457-2992
Groesbeck	Maffett Memorial	601 W. Yeagua Street	76642-1658	817	729-3667
Groom	Groom Branch	Box 308	79039-0308	806	248-7353
Groves	Groves Public	5600 West Washington Street	77619-3629	409	962-6281
Groveton	Groveton Public	P.O. Box 399	75845-0399	409	642-2483
Gruver	Gruver City	Box 701	79040-0701	806	733-2191
Guthrie	King County Public	Box 1	79236-0001	806	596-4385
Hale Center	Hale Center Public , Inc.	P.O. Box 214	79041-0214	806	839-2055
Hallettsville	Friench Simpson Memorial	P.O. Drawer 269	77964-0269	512	798-3243
Haltom City	Haltom City Public	P.O. Box 14277	76117-0277	817	831-6431
Hamilton	Hamilton Public	201 N. Pecan Street	76531-1925	817	386-3474
Harker Heights	Harker Heights Public	100 East Beeline Lane	76543-1262	817	699-5008
Harlingen	Harlingen Public	410 '76 Drive	78550	210	430-6650
Haskell	Haskell County	300 North Avenue E	79521-4924	817	864-2747
Hawkins	Allen Memorial Public	Drawer 329	75765-0329	903	769-2241
Hearne	Smith-Welch Memorial	114 W. 4th Street	77859-2506	409	279-5191
Hebbronville	Jim Hogg County Public	210 North Smith Avenue	78361-2899	512	527-3421
Hemphill	J.R. Huffman Public	P.O. Box 1036	75948-1036	409	787-4829
Hempstead	Waller County	2331 11th Street	77445-6799	409	826-8335
Henderson	Rusk County	106 East Main Street	75652-3117	903	657-8557
Henrietta	Edwards Public	P.O. Drawer 529	76365-0529	817	538-4791
Hereford	Deaf Smith County	211 East 4th Street	79045-5521	806	364-1206

CITY	LIBRARY	ADDRESS	ZIP	AC	PHONE
Hewitt	Hewitt Community	107 Hewitt Drive	76643	817	666-2442
Higgins	Higgins Public	P.O. Box 250	79046-0250	806	852-2214
Highland Park	Highland Park	4700 Drexel Drive	75205-3199	214	559-9400
Highlands	Stratford Branch	509 Stratford Street	77562-2547	281	426-3521
Hillsboro	Hillsboro City	118 South Waco Street	76645-7708	817	582-7385
Hitchcock	Genevieve Miller Hitchcock Pub.	8005 Barry Avenue	77563-3238	409	986-7814
Hondo	Hondo Public	1011 19th Street	78861-2431	210	426-5333
Honey Grove	Bertha Voyer Memorial	P.O. Box 47	75446-0047	903	378-2206
Hooks	Hooks Public	P.O. Box 1540	75561-1540	903	547-3365
Houston	Houston Public	500 McKinney Street	77002-2534	713	247-2700
Houston	Harris County Public	8080 El Rio Street	77054-4195	713	749-9000
Howe	Howe Community	Box 960	75059-0960	903	532-5519
Humble	Octavia Fields Branch	111 West Higgins Street	77338-4304	281	446-3377
Humble	Baldwin Boettcher Branch	22248 Aldine Westfield Road	77338-1080	281	821-1320
Huntsville	Huntsville Public	1216 14th Street	77340-4507	409	291-5472
Hurst	Hurst Public	901 Precinct Line Road	76053	817	788-7300
Hutchins	Hutchins-Atwell Public	P.O. Box 888	75141-0888	972	225-4711
Idalou	Idalou Public	P.O. Box 108	79329-0108	806	892-2114
Imperial	Imperial Public	P.O. Box 307	79743-0307	915	536-2236
Industry	West End	P.O. Box 179	78944-0179	409	357-4434
Ingleside	Ingleside Public	P.O. Drawer 400	78362-0400	512	776-2517
Iowa Park	Tom Burnett Memorial	400 West Alameda	76367-1616	817	592-4981
Iraan	Iraan Public	P.O. Box 638	79744-0638	915	639-2235
Irving	Irving Public	P.O. Box 152288	75015-2288	972	721-2639
Italy	S.M. Dunlap	Box A	76651	214	483-6481
Jacksboro	Gladys Johnson Ritchie Public	626 West College Street	76458-1655	817	567-2240
Jacksonville	Jacksonville Public	502 South Jackson Street	75766-2415	903	586-7664
Jasper	Jasper Public	175 East Water Street	75951-4438	409	384-3791
Jayton	Kent County	Box 28	79528-0028	806	237-3287
Jefferson	Jefferson Carnegie	301 W. Lafayette St.	75657	903	665-8911
Jewett	Jewett Public	P.O. Box 926	75846	903	626-4202
Johnson City	Johnson City	Box 332	78636-0332	210	868-4469
Jonestown	Jonestown Community	P.O. Box 5023	78645-0002	512	267-7511
Joshua	Joshua Community	909 S. Broadway	76058-	817	641-2285
Jourdanton	Jourdanton Community	1220 Simmons Avenue	78026-2896	210	769-3087
Junction	Kimble County	208 North 10th Street	76849	915	446-2342
Justin	Justin Community	P.O. Box 877	76247-0877	817	648-3649
Karnes City	Karnes City Public	302 S. Panna Maria Avenue	78118-3240	210	780-2539
Katy	Katy Branch	5702 Second Street	77493-2417	281	391-3509
Kaufman	Kaufman County	3790 S. Houston Street	75142-3714	972	932-6222
Keller	Keller Public	640 Johnson Road	76248-4136	817	431-3919
Kemp	Henderson County West	101 Causeway Beach	75143-9234	903	431-4185
Kendalia	Kendalia Public	P.O. Box 399	78027-0399	210	336-2002
Kenedy	Karnes County System	303 W. Main Street	78119-2795	210	583-3313
Kennedale	Kennedale	P.O. Box 213	76060-0213	817	478-7876
Kermit	Winkler County	307 South Poplar	79745-4300	915	586-3841
Kerrville	Butt-Holdsworth Memorial	505 Water Street	78028-5393	210	257-8422
Kilgore	Kilgore Public	301 N. Henderson Blvd.	75662-2799	903	984-1529
Killeen	Killeen Public	711 N. Gray Street	76541-4898	817	526-8379
Kingsland	Kingsland Branch	125 W. Polk St.	78639-5908	915	288-3170
Kingsville	Robert J. Kleberg Public	220 North 4th Street	78363-4410	512	592-6381
Kingwood	Kingwood Branch	4102 Rustic Woods Drive	77345-1350	281	360-6804
Kirbyville	Kirbyville Public	P.O. Box 567	75956-0567	409	423-4653
Kountze	Kountze Public	Drawer 39	77625-0039	409	246-2826
Krum	Krum Public	P.O. Box 780	76249-0780	817	482-3455
Kyle	Kyle Community	P.O. Box 366	78640-0366	512	268-7411
La Feria	Bailey H. Dunlap Memorial	Box 5804	78559-2580	210	797-1242
La Grange	Fayette Public	855 South Jefferson	78945-3230	409	968-3765
La Joya	La Joya Municipal	P.O. Box H	78560-	210	581-7002
La Marque	La Marque Public	1011 Bayou Road	77568-4195	409	938-9270
La Porte	La Porte Branch	526 San Jacinto	77571-5498	281	471-4022
La Vernia	La Vernia Branch	P.O. Box 667	78121-0667	210	779-2239
Lago Vista	Lago Vista Community	P.O. Box 4967	78645-0009	512	267-3868
Laguna Vista	Laguna Vista Public	122 Fernandez Street	78578	210	943-1793
Lake Dallas	Lake Cities	P.O. Box 775	75065-0775	817	497-3566
Lake Jackson	Lake Jackson Branch	250 Circle Way	77566-5203	409	297-1271
Lake Tanglewood	Lake Tanglewood Public	Rt. 8, Box 35-15	79118-9430	806	622-1242
Lake Worth	Mary Lou Reddick Public	3801 Adam Grubb Street	76135-3509	817	237-9681
Lamesa	Dawson County	P.O. Box 1264	79331-1264	806	872-6502
Lampasas	Lampasas Public	P.O. Box 308	76550-0308	512	556-3251
Lancaster	Lancaster Veterans Memorial	220 West Main Street	75146-3116	972	227-1080
Laredo	Laredo Public	1120 San Bernardo Ave.	78040-4489	210	722-2435
League City	Helen Hall	100 West Walker	77573-3899	281	338-4864

CITY	LIBRARY	ADDRESS	ZIP	AC	PHONE
Leakey	Real County Public	P.O. Box 108	78873-0108	210	232-5199
Leander	Leander Public	P.O. Box 410	78641-0410	512	259-5259
Leonard	Leonard Public	Box 264	75452-0264	903	587-2391
Levelland	Hockley County Memorial	Courthouse Box 8	79336-4594	806	894-6750
Lewisville	Lewisville Public	P.O. Box 299002	75029-9002	972	219-3570
Liberty	Liberty Municipal	1710 Sam Houston St.	77575-4796	409	336-8901
Lindale	Lindale	P.O. Box 1535	75771-1535	903	882-1900
Littlefield	Lamb County	232 Phelps Avenue	79339-3428	806	385-5223
Livingston	Murphy Memorial	601 West Church Street	77351-3199	409	327-4252
Llano	Llano County System	102 E. Haynie	78643-2072	915	247-5248
Lockhart	Dr. Eugene Clark	P.O. Box 209	78644-0209	512	398-3223
Lockney	Floyd County Branch	224 S. Main	79241	806	652-3561
Longview	Longview Public	222 West Cotton Street	75601-6348	903	237-1340
Lorenzo	Lorenzo	Box 426	79343-0426	806	634-5639
Los Fresnos	Ethel L. Whipple Memorial	402 W. Ocean Blvd.	78566-3650	210	233-5330
Louise	Louise Branch	P.O. Box 36	77455	409	646-2018
Lubbock	Lubbock City-County	1306 9th Street	79401-2798	806	767-2834
Lufkin	Kurth Memorial	101 N. Cotton Square	75901-2997	409	634-7617
Luling	Luling Public	215 S. Pecan Avenue	78648-2607	210	875-2813
Lumberton	Lumberton Public	P.O. Box 8733	77711-0733	409	755-7400
Lytle	Lytle Public	P.O. Box 841	78052-0841	210	772-3142
Mabank	Tri-County Resource Center	P.O. Box 1770	75147-1770	903	887-9622
Madisonville	Madison County	605 S. May Street	77864-2561	409	348-6118
Magnolia	Magnolia Branch	31350 Industrial Lane	77355-2603	281	259-8324
Malakoff	Red Waller Community	P.O. Box 1177	75148-1177	903	489-1818
Mansfield	Mansfield Public	110 South Main Street	76063-3101	817	473-4391
Manvel	Manvel Branch	7402 Masters Road	77578-4814	281	489-7596
Marathon	Marathon Public	P.O. Box 264	79842-0264		
Marble Falls	Marble Falls	801 4th Street	78654-5430	210	693-3023
Marfa	Marfa Public	P.O. Drawer U	79843-0609	915	729-4631
Marion	Marion Community	P.O. Box 619	78124-0619	210	914-4268
Marlin	Marlin Public	301 Winter Street	76661-2806	817	883-6602
Marshall	Marshall Public	300 S. Alamo Blvd.	75670-4273	903	935-4465
Mason	Mason County/Eckert Memorial	Drawer 780	76856-0780	915	347-5446
Matador	Motley County	Box 557	79244-0557	806	347-2717
Matagorda	Matagorda Branch	800 Fisher Street	77457	409	863-7925
Mathis	Mathis Public	103 Lamar Street	78368-2441	512	547-6201
Maud	Maud Public	P.O. Box 306	75567-0306	903	585-5255
McAllen	McAllen Memorial	601 North Main Street	78501-4666	210	682-4531
McAllen	Hidalgo County System	4305 North 10th St., Suite E	78504-3095	210	682-6397
McCamey	Upton County Public	Drawer L	79752-1112	915	652-8718
McGregor	McGinley Memorial	317 South Main Street	76657-1608	817	840-3732
McKinney	McKinney Memorial Public	220 North Kentucky Street	75069-3807	972	542-4461
McLean	Lovett Memorial	P.O. Box 8	79057-0008	806	779-2851
Melissa	Melissa Public	P.O. Box 325	75454-0325	972	837-4540
Memphis	Memphis Public	303 S. 8th	79245-3211	806	259-2062
Menard	Menard Public	P.O. Box 404	76859-0404	915	396-2717
Mercedes	Mercedes Memorial	434 S. Ohio	78570-3196	210	565-2371
Mertzon	Irion County	P.O. Box 766	76941-0766	915	835-2704
Mesquite	Mesquite Public	300 West Grubb Drive	75149-3492	972	216-6220
Mexia	Gibbs Memorial	305 East Rusk Street	76667-2398	817	562-3231
Miami	Roberts County	Box 143	79059-0143	806	868-3721
Midkiff	Midkiff Public	P.O. Box 160	79755-0160	915	535-2311
Midland	Midland County Public	301 W. Missouri Ave.	79701-5108	915	688-8991
Midlothian	A.H. Meadows	925 South Ninth Street	76065-3636	972	775-3417
Mineola	Mineola Memorial	301 North Pacific Street	75773-1799	903	569-2767
Mineral Wells	Boyce Ditto Public	2300 SE 7th Street	76067-5763	817	328-1383
Mirando City	Mirando City	P.O. Box 509	78369	512	586-4626
Mission	Speer Memorial	801 E. 12th Street	78572-4493	210	580-8750
Missouri City	Missouri City Branch	1530 Texas Parkway	77489-2101	281	499-4100
Monahans	Ward County	409 S. Dwight Street	79756-4609	915	943-3332
Mont Belvieu	West Chambers County Branch	P.O. Box 1289	77580-1289	281	576-2243
Montgomery	West Branch	51 Western Hills Plaza	77356	409	788-8314
Morton	Cochran County/Love Memorial	318 S. Main	79346-3006	806	266-5051
Mount Calm	Mount Calm Regional	P.O. Box 84	76673	817	993-2761
Mount Enterprise	Morrow Branch	P.O. Box 360	75681-0360	903	822-3532
Mount Pleasant	Mount Pleasant Public	213 N. Madison Ave.	75455-3944	903	572-2705
Mount Vernon	Franklin County	P.O. Box 579	75457-0579	903	537-4916
Muenster	Muenster Public	P.O. Drawer E	76252-0140	817	759-4291
Muleshoe	Muleshoe Area Public	322 W. 2nd Street	79347-3633	806	272-4707
Munday	City-County	Box 268	76371-0268	817	422-4877
Nacogdoches	Nacogdoches Public	206 E. Main St.	75961-5212	409	569-8281
Navasota	Navasota Public	1411 East Washington Avenue	77868-3240	409	825-6744

CITY	LIBRARY	ADDRESS	ZIP	AC	PHONE
Nederland	D. Bob Henson Memorial	1903 Atlanta Avenue	77627-5099	409	722-1255
Needville	Albert George Branch	9230 Gene Street	77461-8313	409	793-4270
New Boston	New Boston Public	127 N. Ellis Street	75570-2905	903	628-5414
New Braunfels	Dittlinger Memorial	373 Magazine Avenue	78130-5689	210	608-2150
New Caney	R.B. Tullis Branch	Route 2, Box 1035 K	77357-9045	281	354-6152
New Waverly	New Waverly Public	P.O. Box 843	77358-0843	409	344-2198
Newark	Newark Public	P.O. Box 1219	76071-1219	817	489-2224
Newton	Newton County Public	P.O. Box 657	75966-0657	409	379-8300
Nixon	Nixon Public	108 W. Third	78140	512	582-1913
Nocona	Nocona Public	10 Cooke Street	76255-2148	817	825-6373
North Richland Hills	North Richland Hills Public	6720 NE Loop 820	76180-7901	817	581-5700
Odem	Della Mae Baylor Public	P.O. Box 636	78370-0636	512	368-2831
Odessa	Ector County	321 W. 5th Street	79761-5066	915	332-0633
Olney	Olney Community/ Arts Center	Box 67	76374-0067	817	564-5513
Olton	Olton Branch	Box 675	79064-0675	806	285-7772
Orange	Orange Public	220 N. Fifth Street	77630-5796	409	883-1086
Orange Grove	Orange Grove School/Public	P.O. Box 534	78372-0534	512	384-2461
Overton	McMillan Memorial	302 South Street	75684-1818	903	834-6318
Ozona	Crockett County Public	Box 3030	76943-3030	915	392-3565
Paducah	Bicentennial City-County	Drawer AD	79248-1197	806	492-2006
Paint Rock	Harry Benge Crozier Memorial	P.O. Box 173	76866-0173		
Palacios	Palacios	326 Main Street	77465-5499	512	972-3234
Palestine	Palestine Public	1101 N. Cedar Street	75801-7697	903	729-4121
Pampa	Lovett Memorial	P.O. Box 342	79066-0342	806	669-5780
Panhandle	Carson County Public	Box 339	79068-0339	806	537-3742
Paris	Paris Public	326 South Main Street	75460-5825	903	785-8531
Pasadena	Pasadena Public	1201 Jeff Ginn Memorial Dr.	77506-4895	713	477-0276
Pearland	Pearland Branch	3523 Liberty Drive	77581	281	485-4876
Pearsall	Pearsall Public	200 East Trinity Street	78061-3351	210	334-9367
Pecos	Reeves County	505 S. Park Street	79772	915	445-5340
Perryton	Perry Memorial	22 SE 5th Avenue	79070-3112	806	435-5801
Petersburg	Petersburg Public	Box 65	79250-0065	806	667-3657
Pflugerville	Pflugerville Community	P.O. Box 307	78691-0307	512	251-9185
Pharr	Pharr Memorial	200 S. Athol Street	78577-4892	210	787-3966
Pilot Point	Pilot Point Community	P.O. Box 969	76258-0969	817	686-5004
Pineland	Arthur Temple Sr. Memorial	P.O. Box 296	75968-0296	409	584-2546
Pittsburg	Pittsburg-Camp County	613 Quitman Street	75686-9028	903	856-3302
Plains	Yoakum County	Box 419	79355-0419	806	456-8725
Plainview	Unger Memorial	825 Austin Street	79072-7235	806	296-1148
Plano	Plano Public System	P.O. Box 860356	75086-0356	972	964-4208
Pleasanton	Pleasanton Public	321 North Main Street	78064-3596	210	569-3622
Point Comfort	Point Comfort Branch	P.O. Box 382	77978-0382	512	987-2954
Port Aransas	Ellis Memorial	700 West Avenue A	78373-4128	512	749-4116
Port Arthur	Port Arthur Public	3601 Cultural Center Drive	77642-5799	409	985-8838
Port Isabel	Port Isabel Public	213 N. Yturria St.	78578-4602	210	943-1822
Port Lavaca	Calhoun County	200 W. Mahan Street	77979-3368	512	552-7323
Port Neches	Effie & Wilton Hebert Public	2025 Merriman Street	77651-3797	409	722-4554
Port O'Connor	Port O'Connor Branch	P.O. Box 424	77982-0424	512	983-4365
Portland	Bell/Whittington Public	2400 Memorial Parkway	78374-3208	512	643-6501
Post	Post Public	105 East Main St.	79356-3229	806	495-2149
Poteet	Poteet Public	P.O. Box 380	78065-0380	210	742-8917
Pottsboro	Pottsboro Area Public	P.O. Box 477	75076-0477	214	786-8274
Premont	Premont Public	P.O. Box 829	78375-0829	512	348-3815
Presidio	Presidio	P.O. Box K	79845-1231	915	229-3317
Quanah	Thompson-Sawyer Public	403 West Third Street	79252-3825	817	663-2654
Quemado	Quemado Public	P.O. Drawer 210	78877-0210	210	757-1313
Quinlan	Tawakoni Area Public	Rt. 1, Box 178-A11	75474-9759	903	447-3445
Quitaque	Caprock Public	P.O. Box 487	79255-0487	806	455-1225
Quitman	Quitman Public	P.O. Box 77	75783-0077	903	763-4191
Ralls	Ralls	Box 608	79357-0608	806	253-2755
Ranger	Ranger Community	P.O. Box 93	76470	817	647-3522
Rankin	Rankin Public	P.O. Box 6	79778-0006	915	693-2881
Raymondville	Reber Memorial	193 North Fourth Street	78580-1994	210	689-2930
Refugio	Refugio County Public	815 S. Commerce Street	78377-3107	512	526-2608
Rhome	Rhome Public	P.O. Box 57	76078-0057	817	636-2767
Richardson	Richardson Public	900 Civic Center Drive	75080-5298	972	238-4000
Richland Hills	Richland Hills Public	6724 Rena Drive	76118-6273	817	595-6630
Richmond	Fort Bend County Libraries	1001 Golfview Drive	77469-5199	281	342-4455
Rio Grande City	Starr County Public	600 N. Garza St.	78582-3538	210	487-4389
Rio Hondo	Rio Hondo Public	P.O. Box 740	78583-0740	210	748-3322
Rising Star	Rising Star Public	P.O. Box 303	76471-0303	817	643-6823
Roanoke	Roanoke Public	308 Walnut Street	76262-8635	817	491-2691
Robert Lee	Coke County	P.O. Box 637	76945-0637	915	453-2495

CITY	LIBRARY	ADDRESS	ZIP	AC	PHONE
Robstown	Nueces County	Nuces County Bldg.	78380	512	387-1032
Rockdale	Lucy Hill Patterson Memorial	201 Ackerman Street	76567-2901	512	446-3410
Rockport	Aransas County Public	701 East Mimosa St.	78382-4150	512	790-0153
Rocksprings	Edwards County Memorial	P.O. Box 262	78880-0262	210	683-6171
Rockwall	Rockwall County	105 S. First Street	75087-3649	972	771-2272
Ropesville	Ropes Branch	P.O. Box 96	79358-0096	806	562-3531
Rotan	Rotan Public	404 E. Snyder Ave.	79546-3820	915	735-3362
Round Rock	Round Rock Public	216 E. Main Ave.	78664-5245	512	218-7005
Rowlett	Rowlett Public	P.O. Box 1017	75030-1017	972	412-6161
Runge	Runge Public	P.O. Box 37	78151-0037	210	239-4192
Rusk	Singletary Memorial	207 E. 6th Street	75785-1103	903	683-5916
Sabinal	Sabinal Public	P.O. Box 61	78881-0061	210	988-2911
Sabine Pass	Sabine Pass Branch	5030 S. Gulfway Dr.	77655-	409	971-2944
Sachse	Sachse Public	3033 Sixth Street	75048-3118	972	530-8966
Saginaw	Saginaw Public	P.O. Drawer 79070	76179-0070	817	232-2100
Salado	Salado Public	P.O. Box 706	76571-0706	817	947-9191
San Angelo	Tom Green County System	113 West Beauregard Ave.	76903-5887	915	655-7321
San Antonio	San Antonio Public	600 Soledad St.	78205-1200	210	207-2500
San Augustine	San Augustine Public	413 E. Columbia Street	75972-2111	409	275-5367
San Benito	San Benito Public	101 West Rose Street	78586-5169	210	361-3860
San Diego	Duval County/San Diego Public	404 S. Mier St.	78384-	512	279-8201
San Juan	San Juan Public	506 S. Standard	78589	512	787-0943
San Marcos	San Marcos Public	625 E. Hopkins Street	78667-6313	512	393-8200
San Saba	Rylander Memorial	103 S. Live Oak St.	76877-4799	915	372-3079
Sanderson	Terrell County Public	P.O. Box 692	79848-0692	915	345-2294
Sanger	Sanger Public	P.O. Box 578	76266-0578	817	458-3257
Santa Anna	Santa Anna	Rt. 1 Box 299	76878-9520	915	348-3395
Santa Fe	Mae S. Bruce	P.O. Box 950	77510-0950	409	925-5540
Sargent	Sargent Branch	P.O. Box 4007	77404-4007	409	245-3032
Schertz	Schertz Public	608 Schertz Parkway	78154-1911	210	658-6011
Schulenburg	Schulenburg Public	700 Bohlmann Avenue	78956-1316	409	743-3345
Seabrook	Evelyn Meador Branch	2400 N. Meyer Rd.	77586-2964	281	474-9142
Seadrift	Seadrift Branch	P.O. Box 567	77983-0567	512	785-4241
Seagoville	Seagoville Public	702 N. Highway 175	75159-1799	972	287-7720
Seagraves	Gaines County Seagraves	P.O. Box 366	79359-0366	806	546-2480
Sealy	Virgil & Josephine Gordon	917 North Circle St.	77474-3333	409	885-7469
Seguin	Seguin-Guadalupe County Public	707 E. College Street	78155-3299	210	379-1531
Seminole	Gaines County	704 Hobbs Hwy.	79360-3402	915	758-4007
Seymour	Baylor County Free	101 South Washington Street	76380-2558	817	888-2662
Shamrock	Shamrock Public	415 East First Street	79079-2401	806	256-3921
Shepherd	Shepherd Public	P.O. Box 585	77371-0585	409	628-3515
Sheridan	Sheridan Memorial	Box 274	77475-0274		
Sherman	Sherman Public	421 N. Travis Street	75090-5975	903	892-7240
Shiner	Shiner Public	P.O. Box 1602	77984-1602	512	594-3044
Sierra Blanca	Sierra Blanca	P.O. Box 308	79851	915	369-2781
Silsbee	Silsbee Public	Santa Fe Park	77656-4000	409	385-4831
Silverton	Silverton Public	Box 69	79257-0069		
Simonton	Simonton/Fulshear Mini-Branch	P.O. Drawer A	77476-1001	281	533-9809
Sinton	Sinton Public	212 E. Sinton Street	78387-2655	512	364-4545
Skellytown	Skellytown Branch	Box 92	79080-0092	806	848-2551
Slaton	Slaton City	200 West Lynn St.	79364-4136	806	828-2008
Smiley	Stella Ellis Hart Public	P.O. Box 88	78159-0088	210	587-6101
Smithville	Smithville Public	101 NW Sixth Street	78957-1461	512	237-2707
Snyder	Scurry County	1916 23rd Street	79549-1910	915	573-5572
Sonora	Sutton County	212 S. Concho Ave.	76950-3729	915	387-2111
Sour Lake	Alma M. Carpenter Public	P.O. Box 536	77659-0536	409	287-3592
South Houston	South Houston Branch	607 Avenue A	77587-3659	713	941-2385
Spearman	Hansford County	122 Main Street	79081-2064	806	659-2231
Splendora	McCracken Public	P.O. Drawer 1937	77372-1937	713	689-0044
Spring	Cypress Creek Branch	6815 Cypresswood Drive	77379-7705	281	376-4610
Springtown	Springtown Public	P.O. Box 428	76082-0428	817	523-5862
Spur	Dickens County-Spur Public	P.O. Box 282	79370-0282	806	271-3714
Stafford	Mamie George Branch	320 Dulles Avenue	77477-4799	281	491-8086
Stamford	Stamford Carnegie	600 East McHarg Street	79553	915	773-2532
Stanton	Martin County	Box 1187	79782-1187	915	756-2472
Stephenville	Stephenville Public	174 North Columbia St.	76401-3421	817	965-5665
Sterling City	Sterling County Public	P.O. Box 1130	76951-1130	915	378-2212
Stinnett	Hutchinson County Stinnett	P.O. Box 478	79083-0478	806	878-4013
Stratford	Sherman County Public	P.O. Box 46	79084-0046	806	396-2200
Sugar Land	First Colony Branch	2121 Austin Parkway	77479-1219	281	265-4444
Sulphur Springs	Sulphur Springs Public	201 Davis St. N	75482-2636	903	885-4926
Sundown	Sundown Branch	Box 600	79372-0600	806	229-3131
Sunnyvale	Sunnyvale Public	402 Tower Place	75182-9278	972	226-4491

CITY	LIBRARY	ADDRESS	ZIP	AC	PHONE
Sunray	Britain Memorial	P.O. Box 180	79086-0180	806	948-5501
Sweeny	Sweeny Branch	205 W. Ashley Wilson Road	77480-1023	409	548-2567
Sweetwater	County-City	206 Elm Street	79556-4596	915	235-4978
Taft	Taft Public	P.O. Box 416	78390-0416	512	528-3512
Tahoka	City-County	Box 1018	79373-1018	806	998-4050
Tatum	Tatum Public	P.O. Box 1087	75691-1087	903	947-2211
Taylor	Taylor Public	721 Vance Street	76574-3266	512	352-3434
Teague	Teague Public	400 Main Street	75860-1641	817	739-3311
Temple	Temple Public	101 North Main Street	76501-7641	817	770-5556
Terrell	Terrell Public	301 N. Rockwall St.	75160-2618	972	551-6663
Texarkana	Texarkana Public	600 West Third Street	75501-5054	903	794-2149
Texas City	Moore Memorial Public	1701 9th Avenue North	77590-5496	409	643-5979
Texline	Texline Public	P.O. Box 356	79087-0356	806	362-4849
The Colony	The Colony Public	5151 N. Colony Blvd.	75056-1219	972	625-1900
The Woodlands	South Regional Branch	2101 Lake Robbins Dr.	77380-1152	281	298-9110
Three Rivers	Live Oak County Branch	P.O. Box 869	78071-0869	512	786-3037
Tivoli	Tivoli Public	Oleander Street	77990		
Tomball	Tomball Branch	701 James Street	77375-4506	281	351-7269
Trinity	Blanche K. Werner Public	P.O. Box 1168	75862-1168	409	594-2087
Troup	Troup Municipal	P.O. Box 721	75789-0721	903	842-3101
Tulia	Swisher County	127 SW 2nd Street	79088-2747	806	995-3447
Turkey	Turkey Public	Route 1, Johnson Avenue	79261-9801	806	423-1034
Tyler	Tyler Public	201 S. College Avenue	75702-7381	903	531-1317
Universal City	Universal City Public	100 Northview Drive	78148-4150	210	659-7048
Utopia	Utopia Memorial	P.O. Box 461	78884-0461	210	966-3448
Uvalde	El Progreso Memorial	129 West Nopal St.	78801-5284	210	278-2017
Valley Mills	Valley Mills Public	P.O. Box 914	76689-0025	817	932-6370
Van Alstyne	Van Alstyne Public	P.O. Box 629	75495-0629	903	482-5991
Van Horn	Van Horn City-County	Box 129	79855-0129	915	283-2855
Vega	Oldham County	P.O. Box 640	79092-0640	806	267-2635
Venus	Venus High School & Community	P.O. Box 364	76084-0364	972	366-8353
Vernon	Carnegie City-County	2810 Wilbarger Street	76384-4597	817	552-2462
Victoria	Victoria Public	302 N. Main	77901-6592	512	572-2704
Vidor	Vidor Public	440 East Bolivar St.	77662-5098	409	769-7148
Village Mills	Wildwood	P.O. Box 774	77663-0774	409	834-2261
Waco	Waco-McLennan County	1717 Austin Avenue	76701-1794	817	750-5941
Wadsworth	Wadsworth Branch	Wadsworth Community Building	77483	409	245-3447
Waelder	Waelder Public	P.O. Box 428	78959-0428	512	665-7331
Waller	Melanie Smith	P.O. Box 192	77484	409	372-3961
Wallis	Austin County System	P.O. Box 519	77485-0519	409	478-6813
Warrenton	Fayette County Bookmobile	P.O. Box 13	78961		
Watauga	Watauga Public	7109 Whitley Road	76148-2024	817	428-9412
Waxahachie	Nicholas P. Sims	515 W. Main	75165-3235	972	937-2671
Weatherford	Weatherford Public	1214 Charles Street	76086-5098	817	598-4150
Weimar	Weimar Public	#1 Jackson Square	78962-2019	409	725-6608
Wellington	Collingsworth Public	711 15th Street	79095-3605	806	447-2116
Wells	Rube Sessions Memorial	P.O. Box 120	75976-0120	409	867-4757
Weslaco	Weslaco Public	525 South Kansas Avenue	78596-6215	210	968-4533
West	West Public	P.O. Box 513	76691-0513	817	826-3070
West Columbia	West Columbia Branch	518 E. Brazos	77486-2944	409	345-3394
Wharton	Wharton County	1017 N. Alabama Road	77488-4299	409	532-8080
Wheeler	Wheeler Public	Box 676	79096-0676	806	826-5977
White Deer	White Deer Branch	Box 85	79097-0085	806	883-7121
White Settlement	White Settlement Public	8215 White Settlement Road	76108-1604	817	367-0166
Whitehouse	Whitehouse Community	107 Bascom Road	75791-3230	903	839-2949
Whitesboro	Whitesboro Public	308 West Main St.	76273-1639	903	564-5432
Whitewright	Whitewright Public	Box 128	75491-0128	903	364-2955
Whitney	Lake Whitney	P.O. Box 1669	76692-1669	817	694-4639
Wichita Falls	Kemp Public	1300 Lamar Street	76301-7096	817	761-8800
Willis	Meador Branch	709 W. Montgomery Street	77378-8682	409	856-4411
Wilmer	Gilliam Memorial Public	205 East Beltline Road	75172-1127	972	441-3713
Wimberley	Village Library	P.O. Box 1240	78676-1240	512	847-2188
Wink	Wink Branch	P.O. Box 457	79789-0457	915	527-3691
Winnie	Juanita Hargraves Mem. Branch	P.O. Box 597	77665-0597	409	296-8245
Winnsboro	Gilbreath Memorial	916 N. Main Street	75494-2120	903	342-6866
Winters	Winters Public	120 N. Main St.	79567-5108	915	754-4251
Wolfe City	Wolfe City Public	P.O. Box 109	75496-0109	903	496-7311
Wolfforth	City of Wolfforth	P.O. Box 36	79382-0036	806	866-9280
Woodville	Allan Shivers	302 N. Charlton St.	75979-4899	409	283-3709
Wylie	Rita & Truett Smith Public	800 Thomas Street	75098-3872	972	442-7566
Yoakum	Carl & Mary Welhausen	810 Front Street	77995-3058	512	293-5001
Yorktown	Yorktown Public	P.O. Box 308	78164-0308	512	564-3232
Zapata	Zapata County Public	Box 2806	78076-2806	210	765-5351

Southwest Research Institute Invents the Future

by Jennifer Files

All photos courtesy Southwest Research Institute.

At the foot of the hill country of south-central Texas, at the Southwest Research Institute, a thousand scientists try to solve a thousand problems every day.

They're working on behalf of the U.S government, American corporations and other clients from around the world. Since the San Antonio-based Institute was founded in 1947, its researchers have built instruments to measure particles in outer space, made cars run more efficiently and helped laundry detergents do a better job of cleaning clothes.

The Institute's history is a tale of post-World War II gumption and the space race, the energy crisis and corporate cutbacks. Through the years, it has shed some specialties and added others, soliciting private-sector customers when government spending declined, picking up jobs from overseas and building a $3.5 million internal-research program of projects designed eventually to generate corporate contracts. Its sprawling green campus west of downtown San Antonio has grown to encompass 2 million square feet of building space.

Fundamentally, however, the Institute's focus is still much as a second-generation oilman named Thomas Baker Slick Jr. imagined it: tackling tough scientific questions to help people understand more about the world.

"Any history of this place needs to say something about the pleasure and satisfaction of solving problems," said Charles T. Hare, director of emissions research, who, like many of his colleagues, has spent his working life at the Institute.

A short list of projects developed at Southwest with the potential to change consumers' lives:
• Fire-extinguishing garbage can liners;
• Germ-killing paint;
• Better cellular telephone systems;
• Work on a "smart" highway system capable of providing real-time traffic information;
• Liquid paper;
• Longer-lasting, safer tires;
• Air bags;
• Bar-code readers;
• Fire-proofing buildings and materials;
• Time-released medicine;
• Bright colors and fresh scents in detergents and cosmetics;
• Instant heating, cooling and lighting packages for comfort and emergency use;

• Polymers for better dental appliances; and
• Computer-based training systems for civilian police departments and military security forces.

California's Silicon Valley gets the lion's share of the credit for American innovation in the late 20th century. Southwest Research Institute could hardly be a more different place.

Its researchers aren't here for the stock options that make so many Silicon Valley computer programmers millionaires overnight. The non-profit Institute sharply limits employees' ability to build fortunes from the programs they work on. Research belongs to the client, and so do the profits the projects produce.

A few researchers leave to start competing, private-sector labs, but most stay. "Many of these achievements are not something that are going to be in the history book...but they can keep a scientist excited for his whole career," Hare said.

At any given time, the Institute's scientists work on about 1,000 projects for business or government customers.

Some past projects sound dated, such as the optimism that once surrounded nuclear-powered airplanes. Other internal research, such as a way of coating individual popcorn kernels so that they could be microwaved in whatever quantity a customer desired, never made it to market. (The popcorn looks like white gravel in its coating, and companies didn't think they could sell it.)

Tom Slick founded the Institute on property adjacent to his Essar Ranch, named for the first letters in the

An aerial view of the Southwest Research Institute's campus in southwest San Antonio.

SwRI founder Tom Slick

words "scientific research."

Slick, a Yale graduate, once considered becoming a scientist but instead chose to use his fortune to fund other researchers. The Institute was created Sept. 19, 1947, as a sister entity to his Foundation of Applied Research, now the Southwest Foundation for Biomedical Research, and Institute of Inventive Research, which was envisioned as a place where inventors could bring their ideas. The Institute for Inventive Research closed its doors in 1957.

Southwest's first offices were in the Cable House, a remodeled three-story, 18-room mansion that was once the winter home of railroad tycoon P.L. Cable.

Harold Vagtborg, president of Midwest Research Institute in Kansas City, Mo., became president of all three of Slick's research organizations in 1948.

Dozens of similar organizations, most associated with universities, had sprung up around the nation since World War II. Some built on the military research that helped the Allies win the war; others focused more sharply on regional concerns or individual sectors.

Southwest's mission? "The scope of its objectives is as broad as the immense industrial potentials of the Southwest itself," the Institute's first promotional brochure states. "Great factories and plants are contributing increasingly to the wealth produced by the Southwest's vast agricultural, forest, livestock, petroleum and other resources."

Southwest's first sizable contract, in 1948, was to help a Texas Gulf Coast chemical company treat its factory waste. Other early programs included automotive fuels and lubricants research, chemistry and chemical engineering, fire technology, radio direction finding, materials research, nondestructive evaluation and inspection, microencapsulation and services for the natural-gas industry.

"No problem or plan is too small or too large for consideration by the Institute," reads the brochure, illustrated with black-and-white photographs of scientists at work over microscopes and around conference-room tables.

From the outset, leaders linked the Institute's work with Texas' growing petroleum and agricultural sectors.

Southwest Research Institute at a glance

Founded: 1947
Employment: 2,500
President: J. Dan Bates
Location: San Antonio, with branch offices in Houston, Detroit and Washington, D.C.
Business: Nonprofit organization that conducts research for private industries and government agencies.

Evaluating and testing lubricants, computer simulation of pipeline-pumping systems and other energy-related projects provided a steady source of income that helped fill gaps when other research areas were forced to cut back.

In 1957, Southwest researchers began working on some of their own projects in an internal research program designed to eventually create applications corporate customers might fund.

By its 10th anniversary, the Institute employed more than 430, with revenue of more than $4.5 million.

Martin Goland, hired in 1955 to head Southwest's technical program, succeeded Vagtborg as Institute president in 1959. The move was a turning point for Southwest.

Goland, an aerospace engineer who had been director of engineering sciences at Midwest Research Institute, encouraged the Institute's scientists to take on increasingly ambitious projects, raising Southwest's profile.

"He raised the sights of people working here so they thought more broadly," said General Austin Betts, a consultant to the president and former senior vice president for operations at the Institute.

More frequently, projects involved integrating scientific disciplines, and the Institute began to break away from its early regional focus.

Enclosing substances in capsules designed to dissolve or break up under certain conditions was becoming one of Southwest's specialties — and one of the few research areas where it not only performed research and testing functions but also produced the end product.

Institute researchers began microencapsulation work within a few years after the Institute's founding. One project had patients with nerve damage wear socks treated with encapsulated dyes. The patients could tell whether their shoes fit by the way the color appeared on their feet.

About a dozen companies compete in microencapsulation, and many clients find it more feasible for Southwest to build the products.

Another high-profile research area at Southwest is fire technology. Institute researchers can test virtually everything in a building, ship, aircraft or automobile for their ability to resist fire.

Fires are ignited in a two-story building with cinder blocks on two sides, the materials to be tested on the others. Each test costs about $35,000, measuring factors including fire temperatures, flame spread and the time it takes a substance to burn. Computer testing is in the near future, and tests now gather information to develop computer models accurate enough to be accepted in industry standards.

After Congress passed the Clean Air Act of 1963, Institute researchers developed vehicle-emissions tests and control strategies that became part of federal rules.

New research areas in the Institute's second decade included communications and geoscience instrumentation and electromagnetic compatibility research — in

Harold Vagtborg   Martin Goland

addition to developing instrumentation, and later designing engines, for space flight.

Goland restructured the Institute's management in 1972, giving more authority to director-level employees. The move engendered a "fish-or-cut-bait" mentality, that led researchers to accept more responsibility for their projects and accelerated Southwest's growth in the years ahead, General Betts recalled.

The energy crisis of the 1970s was actually a boon to the Institute, creating a need — and needed funding — for programs to find alternative energy sources.

Institute researchers explored a range of possible energy supplies, including petroleum and natural gas, coal and lignite, nuclear energy, oil shale, tar sands, direct solar radiation, geothermal and geopressured formations, wind power, biomass-derived fuels and ocean thermal energy.

In 1974-1975, an impact sled test facility studied crash-restraint systems, including an "inflatable belt system" that "performed exceptionally well in a series of human-volunteer tests," according to an Institute report.

Southwest researchers also designed and built highway containment barriers and bridge rails. They developed a sulfur-based paving material that could substitute for asphalt, which is derived from petroleum.

Testing adds credibility and builds a steady base of customers, but the Institute limits that work to focus most heavily on research and development.

Southwest only occasionally builds final products for its clients. Exceptions have included the microencapsulation products and direction-finding equipment for ships.

By 1977, revenue topped $46 million, and the Institute employed nearly 1,500.

But when oil prices plummeted in the 1980s, many of the Institute's clients suddenly ran short of money to fund research. Financial results fell below projections, and some contracts dwindled.

The last decade of the 20th century has been a challenging time for the Institute.

In some cases, clients have pooled their resources to support joint projects. Southwest also beefed up its internal research program, taking on more of the burden of early-stage testing in the hope that clients would fund projects further on.

The institute gained some mega-contracts, including a program to monitor air quality on Johnston Atoll in the Pacific as the U.S. Army disposed of outdated chemical munitions. Institute scientists also were hired for a multiyear contract with the Nuclear Regulatory Commission center to help plan how to dispose of the nation's high-level nuclear waste.

With the end of the Cold War, the U.S. government sharply cut military-research budgets. Corporate cutbacks and layoffs added to the "tumultuous" R&D environment Goland described in the Institute's 1993-1994 annual report. Income fell 25 percent that year, causing Southwest to cut about three percent of its jobs.

Space exploration has become a major focus for the Institute.

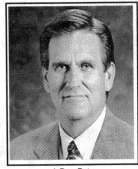

J. Dan Bates

"We're the guys who build cutting-edge instruments for measuring particles in space," said David T. Young, Institute Scientist in the Instrumentation and Space Sciences division.

The Cassini spacecraft, launched in Oct. 1997 for an 11-year mission to the Saturn system, carries two instruments built under Institute leadership that will study the chemical make-up of the system. Other missions carrying Southwest equipment have included Deep Space One, IMAGE and Rosetta.

In the last decade, the Institute's financial reports increasingly have discussed "acceptable" results, not fast growth. The Institute measures success by how much "good science and engineering" it develops and transfers to the public. New contracts continue to pour in. The fiscal 1998 figures show that the nonprofit Institute for the first time topped the $300 million mark in total revenues, up 12 percent from fiscal 1997. Net income was $7.6 million, little changed from the previous year.

After Goland's death in Oct. 1977, J. Dan Bates, formerly the Institute's executive vice president for finance, was named to succeed him.

"The work that we do is very competitive, and there are fewer dollars around to do what we do. It's more difficult to get research dollars today as compared with 20 years ago," said Bates. Corporate clients tend not to fund fundamental industry research, because such projects don't necessarily pay off.

He believed some new opportunities for Institute projects will come from Asian countries, despite the economic crunch in the late 1990s, because of the need for new technologies in the region. In the fall of 1998, for example, the Institute delivered to Chinese clients the design for a huge, 6,000-horsepower diesel locomotive engine.

Besides funding shortfalls, the Institute also is chasing a shortage of talented employees. One department that depends heavily on computer scientists was 70 people short in 1998, and the Institute competes not only with Silicon Valley start-ups but with giant Fortune 500 corporations.

"We're somewhere between a university and an industry," Bates said. "We fill an important niche for the country, and I think we will continue to do that."

Jennifer Files is a staff writer in the Business section of The Dallas Morning News.

Growth at Southwest Research Institute

Year	Revenue
1947	$0.1
1957	$4.5
1967	$13.6
1977	$46.9
1987	$149
1997	$270
1998	$304

Source: Southwest Research Institute

Nobel, World Food prizes to two scientists

Dr. Ferid Murad

Two Texans who are members of the National Academy of Sciences received international attention in 1997 and 1998 when they were given prestigious awards.

Ferid Murad received the Nobel Prize in medicine in 1998 for discovering that nitric oxide acts as a signal for the cardiovascular system. He is a pharmacologist at the University of Texas Health Science Center in Houston where he is chairman of the department of integrative biology, pharmacology and physiology.

Dr. Murad, whose father emigrated from Albania, was honored with his two colleagues in the research, Robert Furchgott and Louis Ignarro.

Perry L. Adkisson, another Texas member of the National Academy, was co-recipient along with Ray Smith of the 1997 World Food Prize. Dr. Adkisson, Chancellor Emeritus and Distinguished Professor Emeritus at Texas A&M University, and Smith were honored for developing an agriculture system of pest management that has cut insecticide use while increasing crop yields worldwide. The prize is presented by the World Food Prize Foundation. ☆

Texans in the National Academy of the Sciences

Source: National Academy of Sciences

The National Academy of Sciences is a private organization of scientists and engineers dedicated to the furtherance of science and its use for the general welfare.

Established by congressional acts of incorporation, which were signed by Abraham Lincoln in 1863, the science academy acts as official adviser to the federal government in matters of science or technology.

Election to membership in the Academy is one of the highest honors that can be accorded a U.S. scientist or engineer.

As of April 27, 1999, the total number of active members was 1,825. Fifty-one scientists affiliated with Texas institutions were full, voting members.

In addition, 313 scientists with citizenship outside the United States were nonvoting foreign associates.

In 1970, **D.H.R. Barton** from Texas A&M University, and, in 1997, **Johann Deisenhofer** of the University of Texas Southwestern Medical Center at Dallas, were elected as foreign associates.

In 1948, Karl Folkers of the University of Texas at Austin became the first Texan elected to the academy. Folkers, de Vaucouleurs and Starr are deceased.

Cecil H. Green of Texas Instruments Inc. was awarded a Public Welfare Medal in 1979. ☆

Academy Member	Affiliation*	Yr. Elected
Perry L. Adkisson	A&M	1979
Abram Amsel	UT-Austin	1992
Neal R. Amundson	U of H	1992
Charles J. Arntzen	A&M	1983
David H. Auston	Rice	1991
Allen J. Bard	UT-Austin	1982
Brian J.L. Berry	UT-Dallas	1975
Norman E. Borlaug	A&M	1968
Michael S. Brown	UTSWMC	1980
Karl W. Butzer	UT-Austin	1996
Luis A. Caffarelli	UT-Austin	1991
C. Thomas Caskey	Baylor Med.	1993
Joseph W. Chamberlain	Rice	1965
C.W. Chu	U of H	1989
F. Albert Cotton	A&M	1967
Robert F. Curl	Rice	1997
Gerard H. de Vaucouleurs	UT-Austin	1986
Bryce DeWitt	UT-Austin	1990
Ronald W. Estabrook	UTSWMC	1979
Karl Folkers	UT-Austin	1948
Marye Anne Fox	UT-Austin	1994
David L. Garbers	UTSWMC	1993
Quentin H. Gibson	Rice	1982
Alfred G. Gilman	UTSWMC	1985
Joseph L. Goldstein	UTSWMC	1980
William E. Gordon	Rice	1968
Verne E. Grant	UT-Austin	1968
Norman Hackerman	Welch	1971
A. James Hudspeth	UTSWMC	1991
James L. Kinsey	Rice	1991
Ernst Knobil	UTHSC-Houston	1986
Jay K. Kochi	U of H	1982
John L. Margrave	Rice	1974
S.M. McCann	UTSWMC	1983
Steven L. McKnight	UTSWMC	1992
Ferid Murad	UTHSC-Houston	1997
Jack Myers	UT-Austin	1975
Bert W. O'Malley	Baylor Med.	1992
Kenneth L. Pike	SIL	1985
Lester J. Reed	UT-Austin	1973
Richard E. Smalley	Rice	1990
Esmond E. Snell	UT-Austin	1955
Richard C. Starr	UT-Austin	1976
Max D. Summers	A&M	1989
Harry L. Swinney	UT-Austin	1992
John T. Tate	UT-Austin	1969
Karen K. Uhlenbeck	UT-Austin	1986
Jonathan W. Uhr	UTSWMC	1984
Roger H. Unger	UTSWMC	1986
Ellen S. Vitetta	UTSWMC	1994
Salih J. Wakil	Baylor Med.	1990
Steven Weinberg	UT-Austin	1972
D. Fred Wendorf	SMU	1987
Jean D. Wilson	UTSWMC	1983

Source: National Academy of Sciences

* A&M - Texas A&M University
UT-Austin - The University of Texas at Austin
U of H - University of Houston
UT-Dallas - The University of Texas at Dallas
UTSWMC - The University of Texas Southwestern Medical Center at Dallas
Baylor Med. - Baylor College of Medicine
Rice - Rice University
Welch - Robert A. Welch Foundation
UTHSC - Houston - The University of Texas Health Science Center at Houston
SIL - Summer Institute of Linguistics
SMU - Southern Methodist University

Death, Birth Rates Continue Trends in Texas Statistics

Heart disease and cancer remained the major causes of death in 1997, the latest year for which statistics are available from the Bureau of Vital Statistics, Texas Department of Health.

Heart disease claimed 43,553 victims, and cancer caused 32,144 deaths during the year.

Human Immunodeficiency Virus (HIV) dropped from among Texas' top killers, where it had been since 1990.

The death rate for the state in 1997 remained as in recent years at 7.4 percent per 1,000 estimated population. There were 142,569 deaths in Texas in 1997.

While the number of babies born to Texas' mothers continued to increase in 1997 (333,829), the state's birth rate remained steady in the last few years at 17.3 per 1,000 population. In 1961, that figure was 24.8.

Infant deaths also declined. The state's infant mortality rate fell to 6.4 per 1,000 births in 1997, an all-time low for the category. In 1961, that figure was 26.7.

Abortions, in decline from 1990-95, increased in 1996 to 91,619, but declined again in 1997 to 81,526. Abortions were induced in an estimated 18.2 percent of the state's pregnancies, down from 20 percent in 1995.

Health Care and Deaths in Texas Counties

County	Patient Care, 1997				Leading Causes of Death by County, 1997											Misc., 1997	
	Doctors	Nurses	Hospital Beds	Ambulances	Total Deaths	Heart Disease	Cancer	Cerebrovascular	Accidents	Pulmonary	Diabetes	Pneumonia	Suicides	Liver Disease	Septicemia	Pregnancy Rate*	Abortions
Statewide Total	27,817	141,129	NA	NA	142,569	43,553	32,144	10,137	7,150	6,696	4,753	4,614	2,137	2,024	1,493	92.3	81,526*
Anderson	66	426	247	5	569	152	142	35	31	22	15	22	14	6	5	87.7	110
Andrews	11	76	85	3	112	35	25	13	4	7	6	3	0	1	2	76.8	24
Angelina	72	618	369	10	751	225	171	86	40	44	14	34	6	7	6	87.4	94
Aransas	14	110	0	3	223	59	61	12	10	13	4	6	2	7	0	76.3	54
Archer	0	43	0	1	61	28	17	5	1	3	0	0	0	0	0	68.2	14
Armstrong	0	22	0	3	33	7	2	4	2	1	1	5	0	0	0	63.9	2
Atascosa	15	117	65	16	259	75	53	21	12	9	20	9	1	5	3	78.0	63
Austin	10	135	32	7	227	104	50	16	8	5	0	3	0	2	1	88.0	49
Bailey	4	27	31	3	65	20	9	5	4	1	1	3	2	0	0	89.4	9
Bandera	1	140	0	8	136	41	26	10	13	7	4	5	6	0	1	81.0	34
Bastrop	14	238	24	2	381	126	91	19	21	16	13	7	7	6	2	83.9	112
Baylor	2	39	49	2	64	21	11	7	1	7	3	7	1	1	0	68.8	4
Bee	22	102	69	5	243	74	45	27	6	6	20	5	1	4	4	84.1	74
Bell	463	1,988	997	19	1,459	543	335	63	92	51	33	47	23	14	6	127.3	936
Bexar	2,386	11,630	5,552	182	9,561	2,996	2,105	643	396	386	385	277	134	175	115	96.3	6,650
Blanco	2	47	0	5	91	26	22	7	4	6	6	5	3	0	0	80.2	7
Borden	0	2	0	3	2	0	1	0	0	0	0	1	0	0	0	41.1	2
Bosque	9	136	40	5	273	91	53	19	14	12	7	14	1	0	2	86.3	28
Bowie	201	877	858	20	890	273	170	70	35	39	31	44	17	12	15	66.8	79
Brazoria	142	1,690	364	30	1,509	472	406	88	70	75	54	32	24	11	12	83.0	479
Brazos	227	756	431	14	613	178	139	45	37	18	20	27	9	1	4	67.5	352
Brewster	4	56	50	8	85	17	18	7	11	4	2	4	4	1	1	57.7	26
Briscoe	0	9	0	4	28	12	7	0	1	1	0	2	1	0	1	74.3	3
Brooks	2	13	0	2	81	33	18	2	3	3	7	3	0	2	2	93.0	19
Brown	55	245	218	6	463	124	94	59	16	29	21	18	3	7	5	81.2	45
Burleson	4	47	37	3	163	58	39	11	13	5	6	8	1	1	0	84.1	27
Burnet	18	215	42	9	339	86	89	25	19	28	13	11	3	6	3	97.0	65
Caldwell	11	113	30	5	260	69	62	14	10	17	16	8	1	5	4	74.2	73
Calhoun	18	98	56	8	168	52	29	19	13	6	6	2	1	1	0	94.2	30
Callahan	1	110	0	4	127	51	30	6	7	6	9	3	1	0	1	70.3	12
Cameron	326	1,586	967	24	1,904	560	425	123	87	63	112	49	22	56	35	119.1	983
Camp	7	80	49	5	142	36	47	4	11	5	5	4	1	1	3	101.5	25
Carson	1	45	0	6	64	20	13	5	1	3	3	5	0	2	1	59.1	9
Cass	14	218	144	8	430	125	83	41	33	20	12	19	3	2	2	65.6	14
Castro	4	35	41	3	62	14	13	8	5	2	1	1	2	1	1	75.9	11
Chambers	4	81	79	8	152	49	38	11	12	4	1	2	5	2	3	76.9	37
Cherokee	56	263	197	4	514	164	110	58	29	26	10	18	8	3	4	91.1	68
Childress	10	41	60	3	108	38	30	5	3	8	1	1	2	1	0	88.1	4
Clay	3	46	32	0	104	39	16	7	6	7	6	2	1	1	0	67.3	19
Cochran	1	14	30	3	39	11	5	1	4	6	3	2	2	0	0	46.4	4
Coke	0	28	0	2	60	19	15	2	3	4	1	2	0	0	0	54.4	3
Coleman	4	47	46	2	175	60	27	20	7	14	4	6	1	0	3	82.9	13
Collin	416	3,339	753	19	1,451	403	373	112	101	75	21	47	32	11	8	83.6	1,103
Collingswth	4	15	25	3	51	24	11	3	0	1	0	1	2	0	1	64.7	1
Colorado	19	111	125	9	261	97	54	15	12	11	6	11	2	6	5	85.9	26
Comal	70	508	113	12	660	203	177	49	27	20	13	17	10	11	8	81.6	158
Comanche	9	76	65	6	192	78	42	3	5	9	2	5	3	2	1	87.2	14
Concho	2	26	20	3	55	14	7	4	2	8	1	5	2	2	2	58.4	3
Cooke	20	318	99	4	349	125	71	29	22	12	5	28	2	1	3	82.1	36
Coryell	18	295	55	8	313	89	77	9	17	19	7	7	9	4	1	64.0	163

Health Care and Deaths in Texas Counties

County	Patient Care, 1997				Leading Causes of Death by County, 1997											Misc., 1997	
	Doctors	Nurses	Hospital Beds	Ambulances	Total Deaths	Heart Disease	Cancer	Cerebrovascular	Accidents	Pulmonary	Diabetes	Pneumonia	Suicides	Liver Disease	Septicemia	Pregnancy Rate*	Abortions
Cottle	1	10	0	2	36	14	9	0	2	2	0	2	0	1	0	98.6	19
Crane	5	31	28	4	34	8	8	2	2	4	1	0	2	1	0	52.2	5
Crockett	2	19	0	5	33	13	9	0	1	2	2	1	0	0	0	98.4	11
Crosby	3	34	49	5	102	29	24	9	5	5	4	5	0	3	0	89.2	13
Culberson	1	13	25	1	18	6	6	0	3	3	0	0	0	0	0	48.4	4
Dallam	7	44	0	4	65	15	18	7	6	5	1	1	1	1	0	98.4	10
Dallas	4,233	15,072	7,863	241	13,390	3,957	3,102	994	690	569	381	391	241	181	134	101.4	12,914
Dawson	5	41	44	3	144	48	22	15	7	8	7	5	1	1	2	73.7	19
Deaf Smith	11	77	40	4	157	45	32	11	13	5	7	9	1	4	1	103.8	31
Delta	2	34	0	2	82	21	16	15	5	8	0	0	1	0	0	67.1	4
Denton	262	2,210	704	26	1,442	432	342	91	83	90	27	57	22	18	12	71.9	1,333
DeWitt	9	107	49	8	307	120	54	31	13	13	14	1	3	5	1	67.6	23
Dickens	0	10	0	3	45	10	5	2	2	7	2	2	1	2	0	70.4	5
Dimmit	8	26	49	2	88	26	26	7	3	1	3	5	1	1	2	88.0	12
Donley	1	21	0	3	63	20	17	4	2	3	2	0	0	0	1	86.4	7
Duval	2	26	0	5	122	47	19	5	3	9	5	5	2	1	2	94.7	75
Eastland	11	91	83	6	272	80	71	29	15	15	10	7	3	1	1	76.2	26
Ector	141	896	496	18	955	295	205	55	44	93	39	27	11	21	2	91.0	462
Edwards	1	9	0	3	23	9	9	0	1	1	0	1	1	0	0	43.8	2
Ellis	55	639	122	9	802	233	187	60	39	45	25	32	17	9	9	72.2	266
El Paso	694	3,695	2,062	52	3,765	991	826	218	216	164	206	109	44	102	45	96.5	2,143
Erath	29	206	98	5	298	99	49	24	12	17	4	10	6	0	1	77.4	107
Falls	7	71	44	6	261	78	50	16	10	11	8	32	2	3	6	82.1	32
Fannin	17	215	75	7	419	150	86	28	22	13	7	14	4	1	4	91.3	49
Fayette	24	102	60	5	294	107	46	29	14	8	10	18	2	0	7	79.9	28
Fisher	1	21	30	3	82	34	20	7	0	5	4	2	0	1	1	61.5	7
Floyd	4	27	27	4	74	22	15	16	1	2	0	1	1	0	1	83.7	6
Foard	0	7	0	2	22	7	1	1	1	0	1	1	1	0	0	79.6	7
Fort Bend	206	2,413	372	10	1,271	387	317	86	71	38	33	27	17	16	13	65.8	682
Franklin	7	60	49	0	103	23	28	9	3	5	7	8	0	4	0	67.6	7
Freestone	10	109	48	5	200	58	46	13	13	8	8	5	5	3	2	75.0	31
Frio	7	40	40	5	132	44	32	7	7	7	8	6	1	1	1	106.3	35
Gaines	5	40	49	6	108	33	21	17	7	9	2	0	1	2	0	82.6	21
Galveston	410	3,556	1,134	45	1,976	653	469	123	74	88	73	36	31	42	25	79.3	596
Garza	3	19	0	2	58	19	10	6	3	1	3	0	0	0	1	78.7	7
Gillespie	36	196	61	6	278	66	57	33	7	18	9	9	6	3	1	77.5	34
Glasscock	0	5	0	3	4	0	2	0	1	0	0	0	1	0	0	42.2	1
Goliad	2	36	0	3	77	29	14	2	6	2	5	1	2	0	1	58.2	4
Gonzales	7	69	110	5	191	56	46	9	9	13	11	5	1	3	1	78.2	31
Gray	27	149	107	4	290	95	54	13	18	22	9	14	5	2	1	76.1	18
Grayson	160	1,151	700	21	1,174	425	239	65	48	76	22	69	17	9	2	81.2	216
Gregg	205	1,056	573	25	1,131	344	238	88	55	63	33	47	9	12	17	79.6	122
Grimes	9	84	0	0	198	82	48	8	12	11	7	5	2	2	0	87.3	40
Guadalupe	42	438	94	19	639	190	154	51	33	26	28	17	14	5	16	71.3	172
Hale	38	167	140	11	288	86	63	20	13	18	10	7	3	4	2	96.4	54
Hall	3	15	42	5	66	27	12	9	3	3	3	2	0	0	0	103.1	6
Hamilton	6	70	49	3	139	56	28	7	3	9	2	6	6	0	1	103.7	9
Hansford	3	33	28	4	56	16	12	2	2	1	4	1	1	4	0	67.8	1
Hardeman	7	27	63	3	77	15	13	9	5	3	1	1	2	1	0	71.7	2
Hardin	17	359	69	22	443	141	98	32	33	23	15	23	4	5	5	75.7	69
Harris	6,024	23,407	15,104	433	18,944	5,505	4,420	1,383	933	732	619	492	323	334	230	104.9	22,562
Harrison	45	262	139	6	602	178	142	64	41	24	13	15	5	8	4	56.0	27
Hartley	0	2	28	2	22	7	4	0	2	2	0	2	0	1	0	100.7	8
Haskell	3	28	30	3	105	28	27	5	8	1	7	3	2	0	1	55.9	7
Hays	93	516	109	9	440	114	98	44	27	15	20	26	10	3	4	68.9	336
Hemphill	4	20	26	3	39	14	7	2	4	3	2	2	1	0	0	40.4	2
Henderson	38	394	115	0	835	267	217	58	40	56	20	23	10	8	9	86.8	131
Hidalgo	417	2,349	1,346	71	2,680	822	537	149	156	115	154	76	27	56	58	121.9	970
Hill	10	189	141	9	407	148	95	42	22	10	3	12	3	5	6	88.9	53
Hockley	13	148	78	6	212	74	49	21	8	8	10	3	4	4	0	70.5	53
Hood	31	295	56	6	440	129	109	41	18	33	16	13	8	5	3	66.7	70
Hopkins	19	157	100	5	413	126	95	47	23	20	8	13	3	3	3	77.3	61
Houston	13	132	93	2	342	109	79	21	15	17	5	12	4	2	3	75.7	25
Howard	43	320	150	8	398	144	73	25	12	26	13	16	5	3	7	84.9	57
Hudspeth	0	3	0	3	23	6	6	0	4	0	2	0	1	1	0	48.6	1
Hunt	54	295	178	0	761	268	144	58	49	29	22	26	14	12	4	79.1	167
Hutchinson	17	209	99	11	252	62	51	16	12	25	13	14	5	3	4	75.8	44

Health Care and Deaths in Texas Counties

County	Patient Care, 1997				Leading Causes of Death by County, 1997											Misc., 1997	
	Doctors	Nurses	Hospital Beds	Ambulances	Total Deaths	Heart Disease	Cancer	Cerebrovascular	Accidents	Pulmonary	Diabetes	Pneumonia	Suicides	Liver Disease	Septicemia	Pregnancy Rate*	Abortions
Irion	0	12	0	2	14	3	5	3	0	1	0	0	0	0	0	39.9	2
Jack	1	35	49	4	78	23	17	8	3	2	3	0	4	1	0	82.3	10
Jackson	7	69	35	7	160	71	24	10	10	7	4	3	2	0	0	84.8	18
Jasper	27	214	144	17	408	141	97	22	17	17	15	18	7	1	0	93.0	47
Jeff Davis	1	11	0	2	15	6	3	0	1	2	0	0	0	0	0	57.1	5
Jefferson	473	2,210	1,968	43	2,590	832	591	178	99	113	92	87	24	32	44	78.8	614
Jim Hogg	2	9	0	3	41	10	10	3	0	4	0	1	0	1	2	62.6	10
Jim Wells	24	152	131	8	317	114	62	19	20	13	6	10	3	1	2	91.0	86
Johnson	73	1,053	112	10	936	299	208	58	51	62	18	36	14	8	7	65.8	252
Jones	7	73	119	6	202	79	34	19	8	12	6	8	1	2	2	61.0	28
Karnes	4	49	43	2	179	57	25	19	6	9	10	2	1	2	1	70.8	15
Kaufman	67	612	221	0	553	159	120	36	34	29	16	30	6	7	6	67.9	146
Kendall	19	316	0	5	203	64	44	20	6	11	10	4	6	0	0	94.3	46
Kenedy	0	0	0	0	3	1	1	0	1	0	0	0	0	0	0	115.4	1
Kent	0	5	0	3	16	5	8	0	1	0	0	0	0	1	0	92.0	4
Kerr	85	434	200	5	579	151	142	27	20	47	20	24	0	11	5	81.7	86
Kimble	4	24	18	3	54	18	9	6	3	5	4	3	1	0	0	84.6	8
King	0	1	0	1	1	1	0	0	0	0	0	0	0	0	0	11.8	0
Kinney	1	10	0	2	40	14	11	2	2	1	0	2	0	3	0	76.6	5
Kleberg	28	122	100	5	222	81	44	13	14	4	9	6	0	4	5	84.9	123
Knox	2	27	28	4	62	18	14	7	1	1	2	3	0	0	2	67.2	10
Lamar	101	495	422	5	572	190	121	49	34	26	10	17	4	5	6	83.8	97
Lamb	7	80	75	11	165	66	27	12	11	4	2	9	2	2	0	92.2	10
Lampasas	4	96	0	0	189	69	52	4	10	5	7	0	4	2	0	104.9	37
La Salle	2	11	0	2	48	23	8	5	1	0	0	3	2	0	0	86.0	7
Lavaca	19	134	71	7	307	132	57	15	11	7	8	10	3	5	1	75.7	23
Lee	4	57	0	5	168	65	29	11	14	3	5	7	1	0	2	79.5	20
Leon	5	74	0	9	210	77	58	12	19	9	4	5	1	2	1	71.0	15
Liberty	39	255	150	15	614	191	141	32	42	40	24	19	7	8	15	91.2	85
Limestone	17	129	115	6	317	95	61	31	18	16	10	9	3	6	3	76.7	55
Lipscomb	1	14	0	8	37	17	6	0	1	5	0	0	0	1	1	70.7	0
Live Oak	3	18	0	3	120	37	33	5	5	8	3	5	4	1	1	73.4	33
Llano	13	98	30	6	246	69	67	11	9	16	5	13	4	2	1	96.8	16
Loving	0	0	0	0	0	0	0	0	0	0	0	0	0	0	0	90.9	2
Lubbock	563	2,881	1,845	41	1,835	563	373	136	76	88	56	65	23	26	21	81.2	842
Lynn	1	27	24	3	58	18	11	1	4	5	0	4	1	1	2	70.2	8
Madison	10	43	52	2	140	62	25	3	7	9	1	8	4	0	2	92.0	15
Marion	6	43	0	0	169	50	39	11	8	12	8	3	0	2	3	83.1	8
Martin	3	23	26	4	46	15	6	4	4	3	0	5	0	0	1	78.4	5
Mason	1	21	0	2	57	21	14	4	2	4	2	3	0	0	0	67.8	3
Matagorda	34	147	117	11	347	105	86	20	12	19	21	16	2	4	2	82.7	47
Maverick	25	137	77	3	250	72	53	12	15	5	18	8	2	8	3	110.9	53
McCulloch	6	41	49	3	127	50	21	12	3	9	3	7	2	4	1	81.2	11
McLennan	295	1,568	623	26	1,929	668	423	126	66	70	62	85	22	12	36	86.8	675
McMullen	0	2	0	1	9	5	1	2	0	0	0	0	0	0	0	90.3	2
Medina	12	174	34	7	312	89	73	20	17	10	12	11	3	8	3	95.5	80
Menard	0	11	0	0	35	12	5	8	1	1	0	2	0	1	0	68.7	2
Midland	152	896	482	24	821	254	197	44	40	50	24	42	15	8	7	74.9	315
Milam	9	90	91	4	295	95	66	25	12	15	5	16	1	3	2	86.5	46
Mills	2	43	0	2	74	22	13	4	4	3	5	1	3	0	0	90.1	7
Mitchell	7	38	39	3	116	40	21	5	6	7	3	7	1	2	0	72.4	13
Montague	12	136	94	8	308	97	66	34	16	12	11	20	1	2	2	90.8	25
Montgomery	183	853	621	51	1,716	533	418	98	124	97	42	26	36	23	11	83.8	421
Moore	9	87	60	5	139	40	33	4	14	8	3	3	3	1	0	108.7	25
Morris	5	103	0	2	162	44	34	12	6	13	8	12	0	1	0	82.3	24
Motley	1	7	0	2	25	7	6	7	0	0	1	0	0	0	0	108.1	2
Nacdoches	90	494	346	7	575	181	113	50	36	34	22	14	5	3	5	62.9	109
Navarro	46	303	168	1	507	149	119	45	40	19	13	19	5	4	2	81.4	81
Newton	4	42	0	2	130	50	24	10	9	7	2	5	1	0	1	69.7	20
Nolan	11	99	85	5	193	68	34	15	17	10	4	6	5	0	2	79.2	25
Nueces	601	2,780	1,748	47	2,418	684	526	159	85	125	124	95	37	47	22	97.9	1,567
Ochiltree	4	38	65	2	71	26	16	7	5	2	1	0	0	1	0	76.2	21
Oldham	0	14	0	3	19	6	4	0	3	2	0	0	1	0	1	65.8	4
Orange	42	650	239	7	802	275	184	61	46	50	25	22	15	9	10	73.0	133
Palo Pinto	23	144	99	12	342	105	86	33	12	27	10	11	4	3	3	82.5	45
Panola	10	123	91	0	236	57	62	23	21	9	6	3	0	1	3	61.1	8
Parker	36	585	97	6	580	182	150	38	25	41	21	11	7	5	3	58.0	161

Health Care and Deaths in Texas Counties

County	Patient Care, 1997				Leading Causes of Death by County, 1997											Misc., 1997	
	Doctors	Nurses	Hospital Beds	Ambulances	Total Deaths	Heart Disease	Cancer	Cerebrovascular	Accidents	Pulmonary	Diabetes	Pneumonia	Suicides	Liver Disease	Septicemia	Pregnancy Rate*	Abortions
Parmer	4	34	34	6	101	25	21	6	11	6	5	2	3	2	2	93.7	13
Pecos	9	51	51	9	110	31	31	6	8	5	3	2	3	0	0	72.0	28
Polk	12	182	45	1	472	187	100	20	25	19	9	15	5	6	4	87.3	28
Potter	383	2,307	1,122	21	1,169	311	237	73	55	94	42	41	27	18	10	99.8	343
Presidio	1	10	0	4	49	14	9	5	1	2	2	1	0	2	0	84.0	7
Rains	1	19	0	0	86	33	21	5	5	3	2	4	0	1	1	68.9	11
Randall	8	201	49	4	634	171	162	27	30	47	16	29	20	4	7	62.5	233
Reagan	2	8	14	2	33	3	11	5	3	1	0	1	2	0	0	69.7	4
Real	2	24	0	4	52	21	9	6	1	0	2	2	2	1	1	80.0	3
Red River	4	90	49	0	207	82	38	16	14	9	3	12	4	3	1	75.4	21
Reeves	7	28	62	8	118	38	36	5	7	7	1	6	1	4	1	69.8	22
Refugio	4	30	49	3	80	20	21	8	2	2	3	1	1	1	1	66.8	11
Roberts	0	2	0	2	9	2	2	0	0	2	0	0	1	0	0	24.4	2
Robertson	3	50	0	6	195	72	35	8	8	13	17	4	0	1	2	82.3	18
Rockwall	27	349	92	4	232	68	54	25	14	9	8	8	3	2	1	77.1	71
Runnels	7	101	55	7	150	40	38	10	4	10	4	7	1	0	0	86.9	9
Rusk	23	226	162	8	557	174	129	43	35	27	9	21	8	5	7	64.6	47
Sabine	3	52	36	3	157	65	32	12	13	10	4	3	3	0	2	71.5	3
S. Augustine	3	37	48	0	127	48	20	13	5	8	7	0	5	0	1	87.2	4
San Jacinto	2	49	0	3	191	60	53	10	14	7	3	3	2	4	1	68.9	20
SanPatricio	33	368	75	12	504	145	124	30	17	18	25	16	5	11	8	90.8	145
San Saba	1	23	0	3	83	25	16	7	6	6	2	8	2	1	0	64.1	6
Schleicher	3	23	16	2	34	11	10	1	3	1	2	3	0	0	0	62.1	3
Scurry	12	89	99	4	157	37	44	11	6	8	2	7	0	0	0	60.4	31
Shackelford	3	15	0	0	36	18	8	1	2	2	0	2	0	1	0	56.0	2
Shelby	10	94	54	10	348	115	79	27	19	24	9	5	5	5	1	88.9	9
Sherman	1	9	0	2	26	9	2	1	4	4	1	0	0	0	1	118.3	12
Smith	418	1,919	1,158	82	1,661	519	355	137	81	75	49	85	19	17	18	79.7	437
Somervell	4	38	16	4	62	18	11	7	5	4	1	0	1	0	0	74.9	12
Starr	10	70	44	3	232	62	49	9	16	8	15	6	2	11	6	106.3	56
Stephens	5	34	40	5	124	39	25	19	11	6	2	3	2	0	0	105.8	25
Sterling	0	3	0	2	12	4	3	1	0	0	1	0	0	0	0	65.5	2
Stonewall	0	10	25	1	27	13	4	3	1	1	0	0	0	0	0	60.8	2
Sutton	2	16	21	3	32	7	5	1	2	3	4	0	1	0	1	74.7	8
Swisher	3	36	30	4	80	20	15	10	2	9	3	1	2	0	1	90.0	14
Tarrant	2,061	10,071	4,523	89	8,917	2,719	1,967	706	394	470	271	262	157	116	86	80.7	6,640
Taylor	228	1,241	688	18	1,068	330	230	77	55	59	39	47	13	11	11	79.4	239
Terrell	1	2	0	2	13	1	6	1	1	0	0	0	0	1	2	76.6	9
Terry	8	43	71	3	119	36	21	8	4	10	5	2	2	1	1	78.3	19
Throckmortn	1	10	30	2	23	8	3	2	2	1	1	1	0	0	0	50.3	1
Titus	46	172	165	6	287	83	76	22	22	10	4	6	4	3	2	116.5	74
Tom Green	190	1,080	714	12	955	285	215	73	33	54	23	55	19	14	5	72.2	308
Travis	1,403	5,731	2,028	37	3,736	931	875	254	238	165	113	104	72	54	31	104.1	4,434
Trinity	2	64	30	5	184	67	43	8	10	7	5	6	3	4	3	85.7	13
Tyler	9	78	49	0	248	91	55	12	17	13	7	10	3	3	1	91.8	65
Upshur	8	208	0	9	405	113	90	27	20	29	7	23	11	4	6	68.9	25
Upton	6	20	36	4	21	12	3	0	3	0	1	0	0	0	0	63.1	3
Uvalde	21	103	62	9	239	69	65	12	11	9	9	8	3	1	5	92.4	60
Val Verde	24	172	93	6	272	96	67	13	12	9	13	6	0	5	3	110.8	92
Van Zandt	13	276	52	4	541	189	127	28	25	28	18	22	5	2	6	84.4	60
Victoria	172	789	705	15	663	209	167	52	41	29	16	15	10	8	4	81.4	144
Walker	54	245	144	27	447	132	102	28	18	10	10	16	10	8	4	60.6	101
Waller	4	81	0	7	237	82	42	15	13	6	13	10	4	1	4	83.9	81
Ward	10	62	49	6	112	31	23	5	7	13	1	7	0	3	0	69.7	24
Washington	35	158	60	4	336	117	70	20	13	12	15	33	0	2	2	69.3	54
Webb	150	727	433	16	905	259	187	67	38	9	52	44	8	20	13	145.2	688
Wharton	56	224	221	9	380	108	95	34	14	15	17	9	3	2	9	74.8	48
Wheeler	4	39	83	5	78	23	22	4	6	2	7	1	0	0	0	51.0	4
Wichita	216	1,161	631	12	1,196	364	284	96	37	81	42	22	18	21	8	77.6	357
Wilbarger	22	128	98	4	169	56	41	15	5	7	2	2	2	5	2	73.0	20
Willacy	10	43	0	4	116	33	20	14	3	8	7	4	1	2	2	102.7	40
Williamson	138	1,311	238	14	1,025	270	269	65	81	45	21	36	19	16	5	80.0	584
Wilson	5	184	44	7	237	69	52	22	17	8	5	14	4	4	2	69.9	49
Winkler	5	23	85	4	69	24	19	2	0	5	3	1	0	1	1	67.8	16
Wise	17	209	50	4	394	136	74	28	27	18	14	14	9	6	1	80.7	65
Wood	22	229	80	7	482	134	111	40	31	28	16	16	8	3	3	86.2	53
Yoakum	3	34	24	5	61	23	9	0	4	5	0	4	4	0	1	67.3	15

Health Care and Deaths in Texas Counties

County	Patient Care, 1997					Leading Causes of Death by County, 1997										Misc., 1997	
	Doctors	Nurses	Hospital Beds	Ambulances	Total Deaths	Heart Disease	Cancer	Cerebrovascular	Accidents	Pulmonary	Diabetes	Pneumonia	Suicides	Liver Disease	Septicemia	Pregnancy Rate*	Abortions
Young	11	120	92	7	261	80	60	17	6	18	5	24	2	3	2	79.5	27
Zapata	1	30	0	4	95	37	13	4	6	2	2	1	5	2	2	90.0	19
Zavala	3	15	0	3	91	26	18	6	2	4	6	3	2	6	1	82.1	18

Sources: Bureau of State Health Data and Policy Analysis, May 1997, and Texas Vital Statistics, 1997, of the Texas **Department of Health** (by county of residence).
Broader definition of patient care terms: Doctors - Direct Patient Care Physicians; Nurses - registered nurses; Hospital Beds - Acute Care Hospital Beds Licensed; Ambulances - permitted in county.
Broader definition of categories of death include: Heart - Diseases of the Heart; Cancer - Malignant Neoplasms; Cerebrovascular - Cerebrovascular diseases; Accidents - Accidents and adverse effects; Pulmonary - Chronic Obstructive Pulmonary Diseases & Allied Conditions; Diabetes - Diabetes Mellitus; Pneumonia - Pneumonia and Influenza (only 27 deaths from flu); Suicide - Suicide; Liver Disease - Liver Disease and Cirrhosis.
*Pregnancy Rate figured per 1,000 women age 15-44.
*Abortion total statewide includes abortions performed in Texas plus abortions obtained in other states by Texas residents.

Hospital Care in Texas

Source: Chiefly the Texas Hospital Association

As our population increases and technological advances continue, this field of essential services is greatly expanding in Texas. Houston, Dallas and other Texas cities are internationally known for their medical centers.

However, many small communities of the state have no hospital or access to professional medical care. As our population ages, access to health care becomes a greater concern for many Texans, as evidenced by the coverage of health-care issues in the Texas media.

Of the 533 hospitals in Texas in 1997, 407 were considered community hospitals. A community hospital is defined as either a nonfederal, short-term general hospital or a special hospital whose facilities and services are available to the public. A hospital may include a nursing-home type unit and still be classified as short term, provided the majority of its patients are admitted to units where the average length of stay is less than 30 days.

These 407 hospitals employed 244,408 full-time equivalent people (FTEs) with a payroll, including benefits, of more than $9.2 billion.

These community hospitals contained approximately 56,000 beds. One of every 12.4 community hospitals in the country is located in Texas.

The average length of stay was 5.3 days in 1997, compared to 6.8 days in 1975. This is almost one day less than the U.S. average of 6.1 days.

The average cost per admission in Texas was $5,961 or $1,124 per day. This was 4.8 percent less than the U.S. average of $6,261.

There were 2,125,619 admissions in Texas which accounted for 11,355,612 patient days.

There were 25,857,374 out-patient visits in 1997, of which 6,296,427 were emergency room visits.

Of the 3,742,191 births in U.S. hospitals in 1997, 320,542 were in Texas community hospitals.

Of the 244,408 FTEs working in community hospitals within Texas, there were 57,750 registered nurses, 14,495 licensed vocational nurses and 3,233 trainee FTEs. ☆

State Institutions for Mental Health Services

Source: Texas Department of Mental Health and Mental Retardation.

The mission of the Texas Department of Mental Health and Mental Retardation (TXMHMR) is to improve the quality and efficiency of public and private services for individuals with mental illness or retardation so they can increase their opportunities and abilities to lead lives of dignity and increased independence.

The agency administers state **hospitals** for persons with mental illness, state **schools** for persons with mental retardation, and state **centers** for persons with mental illness and/or mental retardation.

Since January 1996, 13 state-operated community service (SOCS) centers were formed by consolidating divisions formerly part of the state facilities. Now, the state central office oversees community MHMR servies. In 35 counties, a SOCS is the MHMR authority. Six of the orginal 13 centers either were combined with existing community MHMR centers or were transformed into new community MHMR centers. The remaining seven SOCS are scheduled to be part of the community MHMR center system by September 2001.

Individuals access the services through the authority for their county, which links people with appropriate service providers. Services range from 24-hour crisis care to supported housing and in-home assistance.

Additionally, TXMHMR contracts with 38 community MHMR centers to provide services. For areas not served by a community MHMR center, the SOCS or state center is the local MHA/MRA. Services are obtained through local MHAs/MRAs.

The mailing address for the TXMHMR central office is P.O. Box 12668, Austin 78711-2668; phone (512) 454-3761. The toll-free telephone number for Consumer Services/Rights Protection is 1-800-252-8154.

Information in the list following includes the city where the facility is located, the facility name, the year it was established and the name of the executive in charge.

The number of patients or individuals served for state hospitals and schools is the average daily census for Fiscal Year 1998, separated into mental health (MH) and mental retardation (MR) categories. The figures for state centers and community MHMR centers are the total number of individuals served during 1998.

During Fiscal Year 1998, a total of 175,085 persons received services from MHMR facilities: 149,033 received mental health services and 28,756 received mental retardation services.

Hospitals for Persons With Mental Illness

Austin State Hospital — Austin; 1857; Diane Faucher, superintendent; 256 patients.

Big Spring State Hospital — Big Spring; 1937; Ed Moughon, superintendent; 188 patients.

Kerrville State Hospital — Kerrville; 1950; Gloria P. Olsen, Ph.D., superintendent; 169 patients.

Rusk State Hospital — Rusk; 1919; Harold Parrish, superintendent; 342 patients.

San Antonio State Hospital — San Antonio; 1892; Robert C. Arizpe, superintendent; 356 patients.

Terrell State Hospital — Terrell; 1885; Beatrice Butler, superintendent; 325 patients.

Vernon State Hospital — Vernon; 1969; James E. Smith, superintendent; 345 patients.

Waco Center for Youth — Waco; 1979; Stephen Anfinson, superintendent; 77 patients.

Wichita Falls State Hospital — Wichita Falls; 1922; James E. Smith, superintendent; 314 patients.

Schools for Persons with Mental Retardation

Abilene State School — Abilene; 1901; Bill Waddill, superintendent; 607 individuals.

Austin State School — Austin; 1917; Robert Kifowit, superintendent; 439 individuals.

Brenham State School — Brenham; 1974; Gail Sharp, acting superintendent; 477 individuals.

Corpus Christi State School — Corpus Christi; 1970; Aurelio Valdez Jr., superintendent; 381 individuals.

Denton State School — Denton; 1960; Chris Adams, acting superintendent; 663 individuals.

Lubbock State School — Lubbock; 1969; Lonnie H. Willis, superintendent; 376 individuals.

Lufkin State School — Lufkin; 1962; Sandra Cain, M.S.W., superintendent; 451 individuals.

Mexia State School — Mexia; 1946; William H. Lowry, Ph. D., superintendent; 570 individuals.

Richmond State School — Richmond; 1968; Barbara Dawson, M.S., superintendent; 647 individuals.

San Angelo State School — Carlsbad; 1969; R. Allen Williams, superintendent; 314 individuals.

San Antonio State School — San Antonio; 1978; Dean Lasley, superintendent; 297 individuals.

State Centers

El Paso State Center — El Paso; 1974; John Mark Friedmann, director; 135 (MH); 135 (MR).

Rio Grande State Center — Harlingen; 1962; Sonia Hernandez-Keeble, M.S.W., director; 831 (MH); 107 (MR).

State-Operated Community Services

(The persons whose names appear in the list below are the executive directors of the centers, unless otherwise specified.)

Amarillo State Center — Amarillo; 1967; Richard Browder; 571 (MR).

Beaumont State Center — Beaumont; 1968; Gary Hidalgo; 791 (MR).

Camino Real SOCS — Lytle; 1996; Marcos Pena, director; 2,496 (MH); 428 (MR).

Central Gulf SOCS — Richmond; 1996; Jeff Enzinna; 229 (MH); 612 (MR).

Coastal Plain SOCS — Corpus Christi; 1996; Charles Sportsman; 2,316 (MH); 337 (MR).

Laredo State Center — Laredo; 1969; Yvonne Lopez, acting executive director; 1,555 (MH); 460 (MR).

The Lakes Regional SOCS — Terrell; 1996; Robert Evans, director; 2,221 (MH); 401 (MR).

Community Mental Health and Mental Retardation Centers

(The persons whose names appear in the list below are the executive directors of the centers, unless otherwise specified.)

Abilene — **Abilene Regional MHMR Center;** 1971; Don Teeler; 1,819 (MH); 313 (MR).

Amarillo — **Texas Panhandle Mental Health Authority;** 1968; Sanford Skelton; 2,966 (MH).

Austin — **Austin-Travis County MHMR Center;** 1967; David L. Evans; 5,977 (MH); 899 (MR).

Beaumont — **Life Resource;** 1967; N. Charles Harris, Ph.D.; 4,286 (MH).

Big Spring — **West Texas Centers for MHMR;** 1997; Shelley Smith, L.M.S.W.; 2,688 (MH); 346 (MR).

Brownwood — **Central Texas MHMR Center;** 1969; Ghasem Nahvipour; 1,081 (MH); 230 (MR).

Bryan-College Station — **MHMR Authority of Brazos Valley;** 1972; Jack Leon Bawcom; 1,721 (MH); 360 (MR).

Cleburne — **Johnson-Ellis-Navarro County MHMR Center;** 1985; Joseph P. Mirisciotti; 3,191 (MH); 230 (MR).

Conroe — **Tri-County MHMR Services;** 1983; Cynthia Sill; 2,619 (MH); 336 (MR).

Corpus Christi — **Nueces County MHMR Community Center;** 1970; Wallace E. Whitworth Jr.; 2,472 (MH); 487 (MR).

Dallas — **Dallas County MHMR Center;** 1967; Jim Blagg; 15,785 (MH); 2,015 (MR).

Denison — **MHMR Services of Texoma;** 1974; Anthony Mattox; 1,367 (MH); 209 (MR).

Denton — **Denton County MHMR Center;** 1987; Bill Drybread; 1,696 (MH); 352 (MR).

Edinburg — **Tropical Texas Center for MHMR;** 1967; Charles Justice, acting executve director; 5,362 (MH); 618 (MR).

El Paso — **Life Management Center;** 1968; Becky Ornelas, acting executive director; 5,641 (MH); 566 (MR).

Fort Worth — **Tarrant County MHMR Services;** 1969; Jim McDermott, Ph.D.; 10,018 (MH); 1,539 (MR).

Galveston — **Gulf Coast Center;** 1969; G. Michael Winburn; 2,876 (MH); 609 (MR).

Greenville — **Hunt County Family Services;** 1971; Rick Davis, Ph.D.; 1,111 (MH); 228 (MR).

Houston — **MHMR Authority of Harris County;** 1965; Steven Schnee, Ph.D.; 18,727 (MH); 3,529 (MR).

Jacksonville — **Anderson-Cherokee Community Enrichment Services;** 1995; John D. Gill; 1,533 (MH); 289 (MR).

Longview — **Sabine Valley Center;** 1970; Inman White; 3,432 (MH); 585 (MR).

Lubbock — **Lubbock Regional MHMR Center;** 1969; Danette Castle; 2,632 (MH); 830 (MR).

Lufkin — **Burke Center;** 1975; Susan Rushing; 2,927 (MH); 513 (MR).

McKinney — **Collin County MHMR Center;** 1986; Randy Routon, Ph.D.; 2,140 (MH); 352 (MR).

Midland/Odessa — **Permian Basin Community Centers for MHMR;** 1969; Larry Carroll; 1,653 (MH); 329 (MR).

Plainview — **Central Plains Center for MHMR and Substance Abuse;** 1969; Ron Trusler; 742 (MH); 206 (MR).

Round Rock — **Bluebonnet Trails Community MHMR Center;** 1997; Nancy Gettelfinger; 3,059 (MH); 612 (MR).

San Angelo — **MHMR Services for the Concho Valley;** 1969; Lynn Rutland, acting executive director; 1,112 (MH); 261 (MR).

San Antonio — **The Center for Health Care Services;** 1966; Robert von Rosenberg, acting executive director; 7,672 (MH); 1,811 (MR).

San Marcos — **Hill Country Community MHMR Center;** 1997; Janis Beck; 2,506 (MH); 648 (MR).

Stephenville — **Pecan Valley MHMR Region;** 1977; Theresa B. Mulloy, Ed.D.; 1,750 (MH); 183 (MR).

Temple — **Central Counties Center for MHMR Services;** 1967; Eldon Tietje; 2,424 (MH); 382 (MR).

Texarkana — **Northeast Texas MHMR Center;** 1974; Joe Bob Hall; 993 (MH); 160 (MR).

Tyler — **Andrews Center;** 1970; Richard DeSanto; 3,018 (MH); 605 (MR).

Victoria — **Gulf Bend MHMR Center;** 1970; Don Polzin; 1,846 (MH); 193 (MR).

Waco — **Heart of Texas Region MHMR Center;** 1969; Dean Maberry; 2,142 (MH); 361 (MR).

Wharton — **Riceland Regional Mental Health Authority;** 1988; Charlie Boone; 2,797 (MH).

Wichita Falls — **Helen Farabee Regional Centers;** 1969; Raymond Atkins; 1,291 (MH); 187 (MR). ☆

Public Schools

Source: Texas Education Agency (*www.tea.state.tx.us*)

Public school enrollment in Texas reached a peak of 3,900,488 in 1997-98, according to the **Texas Education Agency**. Enrollment in 1996-97 was 3,628,975.

The **seven largest districts** (listed in descending order by average daily attendance), are Houston, Dallas, Austin, Fort Worth, El Paso, San Antonio and Northside (Bexar Co.).

Texas has **three types of school districts**: independent, common and home-rule. Independent school districts are administered by a an elected, district-wide board of trustees and deal directly with Texas Education Agency. Common districts are supervised by elected county school superintendents and county trustees. Home-rule districts operate under a charter approved by the district's voters that must comply with graduation requirements, accountability, no-pass, no-play, federal law and court orders, compulsory attendance, pre-kindergarten, bilingual education, and information-reporting requirements; teacher certification and a few other basic matters. In 1999, there were six common districts and 1,056 independent districts. As of July 15, 1999, none of the state's school districts had sought home-rule status.

Brief History of Public Education

Public education was one of the primary goals of the early settlers of Texas, who listed the failure to provide education as one of their grievances in the **Texas Declaration of Independence** from Mexico.

As early as 1838, **President Mirabeau B. Lamar's** message to the Republic of Texas Congress advocated setting aside public domain for public schools. His interest caused him to be called the **"Father of Education in Texas."** In 1839 Congress designated three leagues of land to support public schools for each Texas county and 50 leagues for a state university. In 1840 each county was allocated one more league of land.

The Republic, however, did not establish a public school system or a university. The 1845 State Constitution advocated public education, instructing the Legislature to designate at least 10 percent of the tax revenue for schools. Further delay occurred until **Gov. Elisha M. Pease**, on Jan. 31, 1854, signed the bill setting up the **Texas public school system.**

The public school system was made possible by setting aside $2 million out of $10 million Texas received for relinquishing its claim to land to the north and west of its present boundaries in the Compromise of 1850.

During 1854, legislation provided for state apportionment of funds based upon an annual census and required railroads that were granted land to survey alternate sections to be set aside for public school financing. The **first school census** that year showed 65,463 students; state fund apportionment was 62¢ per student.

When adopted in 1876, the present Texas Constitution provided: "All funds, lands and other property heretofore set apart and appropriated for the support of public schools; all the alternate sections of land reserved by the state of grants heretofore made or that may hereafter be made to railroads, or other corporations, of any nature whatsoever; one half of the public domain of the state, and all sums of money that may come to the state from the sale of any portion of the same shall constitute a **perpetual public school fund.**"

Over 52 million acres of the Texas **public domain** were allotted for school purposes. (See table, **Distribution of the Public Lands of Texas** on page 413.)

The Constitution also provided for one-fourth of occupation taxes and a poll tax of one dollar for school support and made provisions for local taxation. No provision was made for direct ad valorem taxation for maintenance of an **available school fund**, but a maximum 20¢ state ad valorem school tax was adopted in 1883, and raised to 35¢ in connection with provision of **free textbooks** in the amendment of 1918.

In 1949, the **Gilmer-Aikin Laws** reorganized the state system of public schools by making sweeping changes in administration and financing. The Texas Education Agency, headed by the governor-appointed Commissioner of Education, administers the public school system. The policy-making body for public education is the 15-member State Board of Education, which is elected from separate districts for overlapping four-year terms. Current membership of the board may be found in the State Government section of this Almanac.

Recent Changes in Public Education

Members of the 68th Legislature passed a historic education-reform bill in the summer of 1984. House Bill 72 came in response to growing concern over deteriorating literacy in Texas' schoolchildren over two decades, reflected in Texas students' scores on standardized tests.

Provisions of HB 72 raised teachers' salaries, but tied those raises to teacher performance. It also introduced more stringent teacher certification and initiated competency testing for teachers.

Academic achievement was set as a priority in public education with stricter attendance rules, adoption of a **no-pass, no-play rule** prohibiting students who were failing courses from participating in sports and other extracurricular activities for a six-week period, and national norm-referenced testing through the grades to assure parents of individual schools' performance through a common frame of reference. No pass-no play now requires only a three-week suspension for failing a course grade, during which time the student can continue to practice, but not participate in competition.

The 74th Legislature passed the **Public Schools Reform Act of 1995**, which increased local control of public schools by limiting the Texas Education Agency to recommending and reporting on educational goals; granting, modifying and revoking campus charters; managing the permanent, foundation and available school funds; setting standards for graduation and curriculum; administering an accountability system; recommending educator appraisal and counselor evaluation instruments; and developing plans for special, bilingual, compensatory, gifted and talented, vocational and technology education.

High-school graduation requires passing either current exit-level TAAS (Texas Assessment of Academic Skills)

Enrollment and Expenditures per Student

School Year	Enrollment	Spending per student
1997-98	3,900,488	$5,597
1996-97	3,628,975	5,282
1995-96	3,740,260	5,358
1994-95	3,670,196	5,057
1993-94	3,601,839	4,898
1992-93	3,535,742	4,774
1991-92	3,460,378	4,452

Graduates and Dropouts

School Year	Graduates	Dropouts
1997-98	197,186	NA
1996-97	181,794	26,901
1995-96	171,844	29,207
1994-95	169,085	29,518
1993-94	163,191	40,211
1992-93	161,399	43,402
1991-92	158,242	53,420
1990-91	160,527	53,965

exams or end-of-course exams in algebra and English and biology or history.

The school accountability system rates school districts and campuses based on their performance on the Texas Assessment of Academic Skills (TAAS) test, dropout rates and attendance rates. The system requires schools to meet specific performance standards on the TAAS and dropout rates for the total student population, as well as for the four major Texas student groups (African American, Hispanic, white and economically disadvantaged). Ratings issued for school districts under the system are (from highest to lowest) exemplary, recognized, academically acceptable and academically unacceptable. Individual schools can receive ratings of exemplary, recognized, acceptable and low-performing.

A teacher may remove a disruptive student from class and, subject to review by a campus committee, veto the student's return to class. The district must provide alternative education for students removed from class. A student must be placed in alternative education for assault, selling drugs or alcohol, substance abuse or public lewdness. A student must be expelled and referred to the appropriate court for serious offenses, such as murder or aggravated assault.

Texas School Personnel, Salaries

Year/ Personnel Type	Personnel (Full-Time Equivalent)*	Average Total Salaries†
1996-97 Personnel	**476,877**	**$ 26,843**
Teachers	247,651	33,058
Campus Administrators	11,675	50,946
Central Administrators	4,207	60,484
Support Staff*	31,973	39.974
Total Professional	295,616	34,895
Educational Aides	42,886	12,094
Auxiliary Staff	138,574	14,209
1997-98 Personnel	**491,957**	**$ 27,940**
Teachers	254,558	34,133
Campus Administrators	12,287	52,247
Central Administrators	4,139	63,163
Support Staff*	33,670	40,962
Total Professional	304,654	36,015
Educational Aides	48,626	12,406
Auxiliary Staff	138,677	15,647

*Support staff includes supervisors, counselors, educational diagnosticians, librarians, nurses/physicians, therapists and psychologists.

†Supplements for non-teaching duties and career-ladder supplements are not included in this figure.

Charter Schools

Charter school legislation in Texas provides for three types of charter schools: the home-rule school district charter, the campus or campus-program charter and the open-enrollment charter.

As of June 1999, no districts had expressed official interest in home-rule charter status, because of its complex developmental procedures. Houston has developed a charter-school "district" of three elementaries and as many as 18 other campus and campus-program charters. Dallas, Nacogdoches and Spring Branch have also created campus-charter schools, and several other independent school districts are developing campus-charter models.

Open-enrollment charter schools are public, non-exclusive schools released from most of Texas education law and regulation in return for improved student success. Open enrollment means that the school can enroll students from anywhere; there are no geographical boundary restrictions. The State Board of Education (SBOE) reviews and evaluates each proposal. As of July 15, 1999, a total of 170 open-enrollment charter schools had been approved. Of those, one charter was returned by the sponsor and two schools have been closed by the TEA, leaving 167 approved charters. Of the charters approved, 90 schools are actually in operation as of the same date.

Beyond the state-wide accountability system, the TAAS testing program, PEIMS information system and accreditation process, each charter school develops its own level of student achievement beyond the state requirements. The charter schools are also evaluated by an outside, independent consortium established by the SBOE, consisting of the University of North Texas, the University of Houston, the University of Texas at Arlington, the Texas Center for Educational Research and the Texas Justice Foundation. The consortium makes a report to the SBOE each January. The charters also receive TEA site visits, budget analyses and technical assistance. Periodic progress reports are made to the SBOE. ☆

Permanent School Fund

The Texas public school system was established and the permanent fund set up by the Fifth Legislature, Jan. 31, 1854. .

Year	Total Investment Fund*	Total Income Earned by P.S.F.
1854	$ 2,000,000.00	...
1880	3,542,126.00	...
1900	9,102,872.75	$ 783,142.08
1910	16,752,406.93	1,970,526.52
1920	25,698,281.74	2,888,555.44
1930	38,718,106.35	2,769,547.05
1940	68,299,081.91	3,331,874.12
1950	161,179,979.24	3,985,973.60
1960	425,821,600.53	12,594,000.28
1970	842,217,721.05	34,762,955.32
1980	2,464,579,397.00	163,000,000.00
1985	5,095,802,979.00	417,080,383.00
1988	6,493,070,622.00	572,665,253.00
1989	6,873,610,771.00	614,786,823.00
1990	7,328,172,096.00	674,634,994.00
1991	10,227,777,535.00	661,744,804.00
1992	10,944,944,872.00	704,993,826.00
1993	11,822,465,497.00	714,021,754.00
1994	11,330,590,652.00	716,972,115.00
1995	12,273,168,900.00	737,008,244.00
1996	12,995,820,070.00	739,996,574.00
1997	15,496,646,496.00	692,678,412.00
1998	16,296,199,389.00	690,802,024.00

*For years before 1991, Includes cash — bonds at par and stocks at book value. For years beginning with 1991, includes cash, bonds and stocks at fair value.

PSF Apportionment, 1854-1998

The first apportionment by the state to public schools was for the school year 1854-55.
Source: Texas Education Agency

Years	Amount of P.S.F. Distributed to Schools
1854-55	$ 40,587
1880-81	679,317
1900-01	3,002,820
1910-11	5,931,287
1920-21	18,431,716
1930-31	27,342,473
1940-41	34,580,475
1950-51	93,996,600
1960-61	164,188,461
1970-71	287,159,758
1980-81	3,042,476
1985-86	807,680,617
1988-89	882,999,623
1989-90	917,608,395
1990-91	700,276,846
1991-92	739,200,044
1992-93	739,494,967
1993-94	737,677,545
1994-95	737,008,244
1995-96	739,996,574
1996-97	692,678,412
1997-98	690,802,024

A Short History of the University Interscholastic League

Our thanks to Bradley Wilson, former assistant academic director of University Interscholastic League, and Pat Wisdom, former UIL director of academic development, for their help in the preparation of this article.

Photos courtesy University Interscholastic League

The University Interscholastic League (UIL) is well-known to many of this century's Texas public-school students. UIL, which claims the title of the nation's largest and most comprehensive interscholastic organization, sponsors annual academic, fine arts and sports competitions among Texas high schools, junior highs and elementary schools.

Although UIL's best-known manifestation may be the Friday-night high-school football frenzy each fall, the organization began as a debating competition.

The UIL had its origins in 1904. Dr. Sidney E. Mezes, president of the University of Texas at that time, felt that the university was in danger of being considered elitist among much of Texas' population. He believed that an outreach program would give communities a connection to the University. The University's extension department, modeled on an extension department at a Wisconsin university, was launched in 1909 under the leadership of Harry Y. Benedict. Courses were taught by mail through the correspondence department. To encourage public knowledge of the issues of the day, the discussion and information department dispatched traveling libraries around the state. And the public welfare division issued bulletins on practical matters of the day, having to do with agricultural concerns, public schools and home economics.

However, Benedict believed that more should be done. John A. Lomax, UT registrar, investigated the outreach programs of several major universities in the Midwest and recommended that interscholastic competititions would be the most effective vehicle for reaching secondary-school students. In December 1910, the Texas High School Debating League was established with the cooperation of the Texas State Teachers Association with the objective of "the improvement of public speaking and debate among schools of Texas." Dr. E.D. Shurter of the UT department of public speaking was recruited to direct the new organization. The membership, restricted to schools affiliated with the University of Texas, was initially 28 schools.

The "Three-R Contestants" at the state meet in 1927.

The first state meet was held May 5-6, 1911, with 60 participants representing 10 debating teams. Only white males were allowed to compete; winners were awarded a debate scholarship to UT or $50 cash.

Coincidentally, the first invitational track meet sponsored by the UT Interscholastic Athletic Association, a separate organization,

Roy Bedichek, director of the UIL from 1922 to 1948.

was held the same weekend. The IAA would later merge with the Debating League to form the UIL.

In 1912, the debating league changed its name and its scope, becoming the Debating and Declamation League of Texas. Membership was expanded to include all schools in the state. That year, 128 schools joined, and by the following year, just under 400 schools were participating, with delegates divided into junior and senior divisions.

In 1913, the debating league and the athletic association agreed to merge, and Dr. Shurter became director of the new University Interscholastic League.

In the 1914-15 school year, girls were allowed to compete for the first time. They were limited to the country athletic and declamation events. Football, baseball and basketball were also added in 1914, but only at county and district levels, and a county spelling bee was added.

Events open to girls were expanded in 1915-16 to include senior declamation on the state level. Spelling became a state contest for both boys and girls, and an essay-writing contest was added.

By 1917, the UIL was the nation's largest interscholastic organization. That year, Roy Bedichek was hired as assistant director and director of athletics of the UIL. Bedichek, a native of Illinois who grew up in Eddy, Texas, was an intellectual, teacher, journalist and naturalist. Though he was director of athletics, Bedichek had no interest in sports. His goal was to use athletic competition, in conjunction with academic contests, to encourage superior performance in an atmosphere of mutual respect and sportsmanship. He held to the ideals of fair and honest competition exemplified by the ancient Greeks. Bedichek saw UIL competition as part of the students' overall educational experience, not as a means to bring glory to a school or town. He worked constantly to prevent athletic coaches from undermining these ideals with their "win at any cost" efforts, such as recruiting college athletes to play on high-school teams.

The Fort Worth High School team, shown with their coach, won the relay at the 1927 Class A state meet held in Fort Worth.

UIL officials regularly added and deleted contests in order to expand participation. They also refined and clarified the rules in an ongoing effort to keep the contests on an amateur basis and to encourage fair play and good sportsmanship.

In the debate competition in 1919, two girls defeated two boys. The following year, debate rules were changed so that boys debated boys and girls debated girls.

In 1922, Bedichek was named director of the UIL, a position he held until 1948. During his 26-year tenure as director, Bedichek shaped the UIL into its modern form, expanding its contests and refining its rules to bring it closer to the Greek ideal.

The one-act play contest was added in 1926, and a high-school press association was organized to serve as the focus of a journalism competition in the mid-1930s. The one-act play contest is now the largest high-school play-production contest in the world. More than 14,000 Texas high-school students participate annually in the competition, which culminates in a 40-production state meet spanning three days each spring.

Beginning with the 1946-47 school year, the UIL assumed responsibility for some state music competitions. Approximately 4,000 soloists and 7,000 ensemble members now participate annually. A marching-band contest is included.

Bedichek took a leave of absence to write in 1946, then retired as UIL director in 1948.

Rodney J. Kidd, athletic director from 1938 to 1948, served as acting director during Bedichek's leave, then assumed directorship when Bedichek retired. Kidd oversaw the reorganization of schools in 1947-48 into conferences so that schools competed against students from other schools close to their size. In 1947, the UIL set up three conferences: AA, A and B. The number expanded to five in 1948 (City, 2A, A, B and 2-year high school), returned to the original three categories in 1951, then expanded to six in 1952 (4A, 3A, 2A, A, B and 2-year).

Desegregation was probably the thorniest issue ever to confront the UIL. The UIL constitution limited membership to "public white schools." Black secondary schools participated in the Prairie View Interscholastic League through Prairie View State Normal and Industrial College (now Prairie View A&M University). Soon after the 1954 Supreme Court decision in

Brown vs. Board of Education, Topeka declared public-school segregation unconstitutional, officials of the UIL began moving slowly toward a desegregated UIL. The first tentative step by the UIL State Executive Committee, shortly after the *Brown vs. Board* decision, was a ruling that blacks attending recently desegregated schools could participate in UIL competitions. All-black schools were still unable to participate.

Not until 1965 was the word "white" stricken from the UIL constitution and membership was opened to all public schools. Since contests were scheduled two years in advance, black-school participation in football and basketball was delayed until the 1967-68 school year. Most black schools chose to remain in the PVIL until the 1969-70 school year.

Directors since Kidd have been Rhea Williams, 1969-1977; Bailey Marshall, 1977-1995; and William Farney, 1995 to present.

From the earliest years of the UIL, when girls were not allowed to participate in contests requiring "violent effort or great endurance," the number of athletic events available to girls slowly grew. During the 1960s and 1970s, it increased dramatically, and today it matches the number available to boys.

The number of academic competitions has increased, and changing technology has altered the nature of some of the older contests. Typewriting, for example, became keyboarding with the 1989-90 school year, then was changed to computer applications in 1994-95. Shorthand was dropped entirely after the 1990-91 school year. The slide rule contest of the 1940s had become, by the end of the 1970s, the calculator applications competition. Science and computer science are relatively new contests.

These days, a million and a half students from more than 1,150 high schools participate in UIL competitions each year: 22 literary and academic, five major music and 12 athletic contest areas. A complete list of contests offered today can be found in the table of winning schools for the years 1986-87 to 1998-99, which follows this article.

During the 1940s, Bedichek explored the possibility of establishing an association for awarding scholarships to UIL contestants, so that the brightest Texas students wouldn't leave the state to attend college. In 1959, the Texas Interscholastic League Foundation made its first scholarship awards. The program achieved a major goal in 1984, establishing an endowment of one million dollars. Today, more than $800,000 in scholarship funds are available annually. All state-meet academic participants who plan to attend accredited Texas colleges or universities are eligible to apply. In 1998-99, 534 students received UIL scholarships to 60 colleges.

In addition to high-school contests, UIL sponsors 14 academic competitions for elementary and junior-high students. More than 4,250 lower-grade Texas schools are UIL members. ☆

For Further Reading:

Educational Competition: The Story of the University Interscholastic League in Texas by Roy Bedichek; University of Texas Press, Austin, 1956.

A Brief History of the University Interscholastic League by Bobby Hawthorne, Director of Journalism, UIL, Austin, 1985.

University Interscholastic League Winning Schools for the School Years 1985-86 to 1998-99

Winners in the academic, music and the arts categories are listed first, then winners in sports categories. Sports winners in earlier years can be found in the 1986-1987 Texas Almanac. If years are missing in certain categories, that competition did not take place in those years. If there is a dash (—) in the box, there was no competition in that conference in that category for that year.

Academics

Year	Conference A	Conference AA	Conference AAA	Conference AAAA	Conference AAAAA
		Overall State Meet Academic Champions			
1990-91	San Isidro	Lytle	Vernon	Gregory-Portland	League City Clear Lake
1991-92	Lindsay	Ingram Tom Moore	Crane	Gregory-Portland	Lubbock
1992-93	Lindsay	Wimberley	Seminole	Austin Westlake	Klein
1993-94	Lindsay	Stamford	Seminole	Gregory-Portland	Fort Worth Dunbar
1994-95	Lindsay	Salado	Bridgeport	Gregory-Portland	Sugar Land Elkins
1995-96	Rule	Stinnett West Texas	Bridgeport	Austin LB Johnson	Sugar Land Elkins
1996-97	Rule	Stinnett West Texas	Bridgeport	Longview Pine Tree	College Station A&M C.
1997-98	Henrietta Midway	Lindsay	Bridgeport	Friendswood	Klein
1998-99	Valley View	Lindsay	Atlanta	Sulphur Springs	Klein
		Accounting			
1986-87	Menard	Florence	Dalhart	Monahans	Wichita Falls Rider
1987-88	Happy	Troup	Orangefield	Wichita Falls	Round Rock Westwood
1988-89	Abbott	Olney	Falfurrias	Port Neches-Groves	Converse Judson
1989-90	Jayton	Brackettville Brackett & Overton (tie)	Gonzales	Midlothian	Wichita Falls Rider
1990-91	Abbott	Rosebud-Lott	Orangefield	Stephenville	Duncanville
1991-92	Trenton	Cooper	Troy	Mineral Wells	Weslaco
1992-93	Trenton	Rosebud-Lott	Ferris	Livingston	Abilene
1993-94	Lazbuddie	Rosebud-Lott	Mont Belvieu Barbers Hill	Port Neches-Groves	Duncanville
1994-95	Lazbuddie	Idalou	Friona	Rockwall	Fort Worth Paschal
1995-96	Lazbuddie	Rosebud-Lott	Mont Belvieu Barbers Hill	Carthage	Humble Kingwood
1996-97	Era	Rosebud-Lott	Dalhart	Canyon Randall	Abilene
1997-98	Era	Stamford	Dalhart	Kaufman	Abilene
1998-99	Lazbuddie	Rosebud-Lott	Dalhart	Snyder	Abilene
		Accounting Team Event			
1992-93	Lazbuddie	Bangs	Cameron Yoe	Dayton	Abilene
1993-94	Lazbuddie	Rosebud-Lott	Mont Belvieu Barbers Hill	Sulphur Springs	Duncanville
1994-95	Lazbuddie	Rosebud-Lott	Mont Belvieu Barbers Hill	Rockwall	Duncanville
1995-96	Lazbuddie	Rosebud-Lott	Mount Vernon	Rockwall	Abilene
1996-97	Lazbuddie	Rosebud-Lott	Dalhart	Sherman	Duncanville
1997-98	Trenton	Rosebud-Lott	Dalhart	Snyder	Abilene
1998-99	Lazbuddie	Rosebud-Lott	Dalhart	Los Fresnos & Sherman (tie)	Abilene
		Calculator Applications			
1985-86	Windthorst & San Isidro (tie)	Plains, Seymour & Liberty Hill (3-way tie)	Spring Hill Longview	La Joya	Klein Oak
1986-87	Plains	Liberty Hill	Commerce	La Joya	Klein Oak
1987-88	Plains	Stamford	Commerce	Wichita Falls Hirschi	Klein Oak
1988-89	Plains	Stamford	Commerce	Wichita Falls Hirschi	San Antonio Roosevelt
1989-90	Plains & Westbrook (tie)	Van Horn	Bishop	Wichita Falls Hirschi	Lubbock
1990-91	San Isidro	Van Horn	Bandera	Carrizo Springs	Lubbock
1991-92	San Isidro	Stamford	Bandera	Azle	Lubbock
1992-93	San Isidro	Quanah	Bandera	Corpus Christi Flour Bluff	Odessa Permian
1993-94	Sterling City	Stamford	Bishop	Longview Pine Tree	Arlington Houston
1994-95	Rule	Hamilton	Bishop	Gregory-Portland	Wichita Falls Rider
1995-96	Rule	Stamford	Bridgeport	Gregory-Portland	Sugar Land Elkins
1996-97	Henrietta Midway	Plains	Bridgeport	Longview Pine Tree	Pharr-San Juan-Alamo
1997-98	Henrietta Midway	Stamford	Bridgeport	Azle	Pharr-San Juan-Alamo
1998-99	Valley View	Plains	Santa Rosa	Gregory-Portland	Klein
		Calculator Applications Team Event			
1988-89	Plains	Shallowater	Bishop	Port Neches-Groves	McAllen
1989-90	Plains	Shallowater	Bishop	Azle	Judson Converse
1990-91	Sterling City	Shallowater	Bandera	Carrizo Springs	Lubbock
1991-92	San Isidro	Stamford	Ingleside	Carrizo Springs	Lubbock
1992-93	Westbrook	Quanah	Carrizo Spring	Longview Pine Tree	McAllen
1993-94	Rule	Stamford	Carrizo Springs	Longview Pine Tree	Lubbock
1994-95	Rule	Stamford	Bridgeport	Gregory-Portland	Sugar Land Elkins
1995-96	Rule	Stamford	Bridgeport	Longview Pine Tree	Sugar Land Elkins
1996-97	Henrietta Midway	Plains	Bridgeport	Longview Pine Tree	Pharr-San Juan-Alamo
1997-98	Rule	Plains	Santa Rosa	Azle	Klein
1998-99	Valley View	Hamilton	Santa Rosa	Pharr-San Juan-Alamo	Klein

Year	Conference A	Conference AA	Conference AAA	Conference AAAA	Conference AAAAA
			Computer Science		
1996-97	Jayton	Geronimo Navarro	Clyde	Sulphur Springs	Houston Cypress Falls
1997-98	Rule	Hamilton	Jefferson	Bridge City	Fort Worth Dunbar
1998-99	Muenster	De Leon	Taylor	Fort Worth Dunbar	Garland
			Computer Science Team		
1990-91	—	—	—	Sweetwater	Houston Bellaire
1991-92	Brookeland	Lockney	La Vernia	Austin Westlake	Houston Langham Crk.
1992-93	Lazbuddie	Lockney	Lake Travis	Fort Stockton	Houston Langham Crk.
1993-94	Lazbuddie	Blanco	Queen City	Bridge City	Fort Worth Dunbar
1994-95	Lazbuddie	Blanco	Austin Lake Travis	Austin LB Johnson	Fort Worth Dunbar
1995-96	Rule	Stinnett West Texas	Teague	Stephenville	Fort Worth Dunbar
1996-97	Lazbuddie	Geronimo Navarro	Clyde	Whitehouse	Houston Cypress Falls
1997-98	Rule	Stinnett West Texas	Coldspring Jones	Sulphur Springs	Round Rock
1998-99	Muenster	Stockdale	Devine	Fort Worth Dunbar	Houston Langham Crk.
			Number Sense		
1985-86	Lenorah Grady & San Isidro (tie)	Earth Springlake & Quitman (tie)	Gladewater	Azle	Lubbock Monterey
1986-87	Plains	Springlake-Earth	Quitman	Azle	Klein Oak
1987-88	Meridian	Rosebud-Lott	Orangefield	Wichita Falls Hirschi	Klein Oak
1988-89	Moulton	Shallowater	Quitman	Wichita Falls Hirschi	Longview
1989-90	Plains	Shallowater	Bishop	Wichita Falls Hirschi	Longview, Lubbock & Mission (3-way tie)
1990-91	San Isidro	Ingram Tom Moore	Bandera	Azle	Mission
1991-92	San Isidro	Shallowater	Devine	Wichita Falls	Mission
1992-93	San Isidro	Stamford	Mont Belvieu Barbers Hill	Wichita Falls	Wichita Falls Rider
1993-94	Sterling City	Salado	Mont Belvieu Barbers Hill	Buda Hays	Wichita Falls Rider
1994-95	Wink	Salado	Bridgeport	Wichita Falls	Wichita Falls Rider
1995-96	Henrietta Midway	Salado	Bridgeport	Corpus Christi Flour Bluff	Sugar Land Elkins
1996-97	Henrietta Midway	Lockney	Port Isabel	Sweeny	Spring Westfield
1997-98	Henrietta Midway	Wellington	Bridgeport	Sweeny	Mission
1998-99	Valley View	De Leon	Sweeny	Edcouch-Elsa	Mission
			Team Number Sense		
1988-89	Plains	Shallowater	Quitman	Wichita Falls Hircshi	McAllen
1989-90	Plains	Shallowater	Orangefield	Wichita Falls Hirschi	Mission
1990-91	San Isidro	Quanah	Austin Lake Travis	Azle	Lubbock
1991-92	Sterling City	Shallowater	Devine	Wichita Falls	McAllen
1992-93	Sterling City	LIttle Elm	Crane	Wichita Falls	Lubbock
1993-94	Plains	Little Elm	Bridgeport	Buda Hays	Alvin
1994-95	Henrietta Midway	Salado	Bridgeport	Azle	Sugar Land Elkins
1995-96	Rule	Salado	Shallowater	Longview Pine Tree	Mission
1996-97	Henrietta Midway	Shallowater	Bridgeport	Longview Pine Tree	Spring Westfield
1997-98	Henrietta Midway	Plains	Santa Rosa	Longview Pine Tree	Mission
1998-99	Henrietta Midway	Salado	Santa Rosa	Sulphur Springs	Klein
			Current Issues & Events		
1990-91	Menard	Coleman	Altair Rice	Kerrville Tivy	Brownsville Pace
1991-92	San Isidro	Dublin	Crane	Jacksonville	Brownsville Pace
1992-93	Menard	McGregor	Texarkana Pleasant Grove	Longview Pine Tree	Grand Prairie
1993-94	Meadow	Sadler S&S	Gladwater Sabine	Beeville Jones	Grand Prairie
1994-95	Byers	Sadler S&S	Rusk	Friendswood	Fort Worth Dunbar
1995-96	Yantis	Sadler S&S	Teague	Friendswood	Round Rock
1996-97	Utopia	Sadler S&S	Teague	Friendswood	Austin Johnston
1997-98	Chillicothe	Valley View	Teague	Austin Johnson	Katy Taylor
1998-99	Chillicothe	Jourdanton	Atlanta	Fort Worth Dunbar	Round Rock
			Current Issues & Events Team		
1990-91	Menard	Coleman	La Grange	Burkburnett	Round Rock
1991-92	Lindsay	Woodsboro	Dalhart	Dallas Highland Park	Brownsville Pace
1992-93	Menard	Wimberley	Elgin	Jacksonville	Round Rock
1993-94	Lindsay	Sadler S&S Cons.	White Oak	McKinney	Bryan
1994-95	Apple Springs	Sadler S&S Cons.	Wimberley	Friendswood	Fort Worth Dunbar
1995-96	Lindsay	Sadler S&S	Teague	Friendswood	Laredo Alexander
1996-97	Texline	Sadler S&S	Teague	Friendswood	Edinburg North
1997-98	Rotan	Sadler S&S	Teague	Friendswood	Sugar Land Elkins
1998-99	Menard	Sadler S&S	Atlanta	Fort Worth Dunbar	Round Rock
			Typewriting		
1985-86	Gail Borden Co.	Johnson City Johnson	Mexia	Dayton	Katy Taylor
1986-87	Miles	Hardin	Falfurrias	Pampa	Austin Crockett
1987-88	Wink	Coleman	Madisonville	Snyder	Baytown Sterling
1988-89	Gunter	Tatum	Commerce	Dayton	Angleton
			Keyboarding		
1989-90	Darrouzett	Winters	Caldwell	Jacksonville	South Grand Prairie
1990-91	Robert Lee	Beckville	Denver City	Cedar Hill	Houston Northshore

Year	Conference A	Conference AA	Conference AAA	Conference AAAA	Conference AAAAA
1991-92	Beaumont Westbrook	Wellington	Perryton	Corpus Chri. Calallen	Alief Hastings
1992-93	Larue La Poyner	Gilmer Harmony	Perryton	Dayton	Temple
1993-94	Overton	Winters	Center	Dayton	San Benito

Computer Applications

Year	Conference A	Conference AA	Conference AAA	Conference AAAA	Conference AAAAA
1994-95	Menard	Van Alstyne	Cameron Yoe	Wichita Falls	Weslaco
1995-96	Era	Coahoma	Colorado City	Livingston	Duncanville
1996-97	Sulphur Bluff	Marion	Colorado City Colorado	Snyder	Duncanville
1997-98	Westbrook	Edgewood	Perryton	San Angelo Lake View	Lewisville Marcus
1998-99	Graford	Lindsay	Hamshire-Fannett	Brownwood	Weslaco

Shorthand

Year	Conference A	Conference AA	Conference AAA	Conference AAAA	Conference AAAAA
1985-86	Goldthwaite	Emory Rains	Sweeny	Dayton	Pearland
1986-87	Gail Borden Co.	Springlake-Earth	Hamshire-Fannett	Dayton	Brownsville Porter
1987-88	Roby	Brackettville	Mexia	Dayton	Arlington Houston
1988-89	Gail Borden Co.	Eustace	Colorado City Colorado	Dayton	Garland Lakevi'w Cen.
1989-90	Ropesville Ropes	Beckville	White Oak	Dayton	Pearland
1990-91	San Isidro	Lytle	Eustace	Mission Sharyland	El Paso Irvin

Literary Criticism

Year	Conference A	Conference AA	Conference AAA	Conference AAAA	Conference AAAAA
1987-88	Yantis	Blanco	Atlanta	Shertz Clemens	San Antonio Marshall
1988-89	Happy	Blanco	Bishop	College St'n A&M Co.	Corpus Christi Carroll
1989-90	Skidmore-Tynan	Blanco	Sealy	Schertz Clemens	Wichita Falls Rider
1990-91	Louise	Lytle	Dimmitt	Schertz Clemens	Sugar Land Kempner
1991-92	Anton	Clarendon	Burnet	Austin Travis	Odessa Permian
1992-93	Anton	Wheeler	Kaufman	League City Clear Br'k	McAllen
1993-94	Utopia	Lytle	Stafford	Longview Pine Tree	Weatherford
1994-95	Ben Wheeler M'rtin's Mill	Wallis Brazos	Alpine	Uvalde	San Antonio Clark
1995-96	Lindsay	Henrietta	Mont Belvieu Barbers Hill	Bridge City	North Garland
1996-97	Ben Wheeler M'rtin's Mill	Canadian	Lytle	Grapevine	Klein
1997-98	Ben Wheeler M'rtin's Mill	Buffalo	Mont Belvieu Barbers Hill	Stephenville	San Antonio Clark
1998-99	Wheeler	Van Alstyne	Atlanta	Friendswood	San Antonio Clark

Literary Criticism Team Event

Year	Conference A	Conference AA	Conference AAA	Conference AAAA	Conference AAAAA
1992-93	Anton	Wheeler	Stafford	Friendswood Cl'r Br'k	Odessa Permian
1993-94	Utopia	Krum	Atlanta	Longview Pine Tree	Grapevine
1994-95	Lindsay	Skidmore-Tynan	Stafford	Denison	Sugar Land Elkins
1995-96	Lindsay	Henrietta	Eastland	Bridge City	Plano East
1996-97	Wheeler	Lindsay	Henrietta	Grapevine	San Antonio Clark
1997-98	Ben Wheeler M'rtin's Mill	Salado	Atlanta	Bridge City	San Antonio Clark
1998-99	Wheeler	Idalou	Atlanta	Borger	Plano East

Ready Writing

Year	Conference A	Conference AA	Conference AAA	Conference AAAA	Conference AAAAA
1985-86	Knox City	Winters	Center	San Antonio Ala. H'ts	Burleson
1986-87	Ropesville Ropes	Seymour	Universal City Randolph	Dallas Hillcrest	Dallas Sunset
1987-88	Burton	Seymour	Palacios	Bridge City	Houston Washington
1988-89	High Island	Tahoka	Sealy	College St'n A&M Co.	Houston Memorial
1989-90	Chillicothe	Coleman	Frisco	Taylor	Austin Johnston
1990-91	Martinsville	China Spring	Decatur	Dickinson	San Antonio Churchill
1991-92	Port Aransas	Warren	Mont Belvieu Barbers Hill	Buda Hays	Houston Langham Cr'k
1992-93	Normangee	Woden	Crockett	Dallas Highland Park	San Antonio Clark
1993-94	Bremond	Olney	Austin Lake Travis	Dallas Highland Park	El Paso Burges
1994-95	Bremond	Weimar	Quitman	Austin McCallum	Dallas TAG Magnet
1995-96	Lindsay	Abernathy	White Oak	Friendswood Cl'r Br'k	Spring Westfield
1996-97	Mount Enterprise	Lexington	Atlanta	Grapevine Colleyville	Austin Johnston
1997-98	Meridian	Rosebud-Lott	Hamshire-Fannett	Palestine	Richardson Lake H'lnds
1998-99	Rocksprings	Port Aransas	Diboll	Port Neches Groves	Round Rock McNeil

Informative Speaking

Year	Conference A	Conference AA	Conference AAA	Conference AAAA	Conference AAAAA
1985-86	Ropesville Ropes	Hamilton	Premont	Georgetown	Lubbock Coronado
1986-87	Nazareth	Canadian	Mission Sharyland	Bay City	McAllen
1987-88	Grandfalls-Royalty	Ingram Tom Moore	Gatesville	Conroe Oak Ridge	McAllen
1988-89	Follett	Ingram Tom Moore	Vernon	Katy Taylor	Plano
1989-90	Austwell-Tivoli	Three Rivers	Premont	Conroe Oak Ridge	San Antonio Lee
1990-91	Menard	Lytle	Bishop	Hereford	Plano
1991-92	Austwell-Tivoli	Ingram Tom Moore	Bishop	Hereford	Humble
1992-93	Valley View	Premont	Bishop	Waco Midway	San Antonio MacArthur
1993-94	Overton	Premont	Ingram Moore	Friendswood	McAllen
1994-95	Lindsay	Honey Grove	Childress	Rosenburg Lamar C.	Klein
1995-96	Austwell-Tivoli	Karnes City	Childress	Buda Hays	Harlingen South
1996-97	Austwell-Tivoli	Stinnett West Texas	Denver City	Corpus Christi Cal'len	Carrollton N'man Smith
1997-98	Rankin	Rosebud-Lott	Denver City	Canyon Randall	Wichita Falls Rider
1998-99	Sulphur Springs North Hopkins	Olney	Brownfield	Paris North Lamar	Plano

Persuasive Speaking

Year	Conference A	Conference AA	Conference AAA	Conference AAAA	Conference AAAAA
1985-86	Wilson	Tahoka	Sonora	Waco Richfield	San Antonio Churchill
1986-87	Skidmore-Tynan	Shallowater	Kaufman	Mercedes	Conroe McCullough
1987-88	Ropesville Ropes	Seymour	Mission Sharyland	Buda Hays	Plano

Year	Conference A	Conference AA	Conference AAA	Conference AAAA	Conference AAAAA
1988-89	Robert Lee	Ozona	Muleshoe	Katy Taylor	Plano
1989-90	Ropesville Ropes	Early	Abilene Wylie	Snyder	El Paso Hanks
1990-91	Ropesville Ropes	Gainesville Callisburg	Zapata	Hereford	San Angelo Central
1991-92	Rocksprings	Ingram Tom Moore	Premont	Buda Hays	Amarillo Tascosa
1992-93	Meadow	Gainesville Callisburg	Ingram Tom Moore	Waco Midway	Amarillo Tascosa
1993-94	Meadow	Premont	Ingram Moore	Friendswood	San Antonio MacArthur
1994-95	Jayton	Stinnett West Texas	Diboll	Gregory-Portland	Klein
1995-96	Jayton	Premont	Bishop	New Braunfels	San Antonio Lee
1996-97	Blue Ridge	Karnes City	Bishop	Grapevine	San Antonio Lee
1997-98	Louise	Premont	Monahans	Buda Hays	Houston Cypress Cr'k
1998-99	Rocksprings	Holliday	Bishop	Friendswood	Midland Lee

Poetry Interpretation

Year	Conference A	Conference AA	Conference AAA	Conference AAAA	Conference AAAAA
1985-86	O'Donnell	Seymour	Vernon	Gregory-Portland	Alvin
1986-87	Barksdale Nueces Ca.	Canadian	Premont	Gregory-Portland	Austin Westlake
1987-88	Dell City	Hull-Daisetta	Sweeny	Snyder	League City Clear Lake
1988-89	Mertzon Irion Co.	Cotulla	Sonora	Gregory-Portland	El Paso Hanks
1989-90	Spur	Seagraves	Bishop	Snyder	El Paso Hanks
1990-91	Voss Panther Creek	Clifton	Bishop	Gregory-Portland	Houston Clear Lake
1991-92	O'Donnell	Bangs	Early	Gregory-Portland	El Paso Hanks
1992-93	Roscoe	Stinnett West Texas	Springtown	Austin Westlake	San Antonio Taft
1993-94	Lago Vista	Post	Mineola	Gregory-Portland	Denton
1994-95	Ben Wheeler M'rtin's Mill	Olney	Bishop	Texarkana Texas	San Angelo Central
1995-96	Rocksprings	Jewett Leon	Ingram Tom Moore	Gregory-Portland	San Angelo Central
1996-97	Channing	Idalou	Muleshoe	Schertz Clemens	Longview
1997-98	Channing	Kingsville Academy	Abilene Wylie	Gregory-Portland	Plano
1998-99	Menard	San Antonio Cole	Gladewater	Carthage	Rosenberg Terry

Prose Interpretation

Year	Conference A	Conference AA	Conference AAA	Conference AAAA	Conference AAAAA
1985-86	Wilson	Tatum	Red Oak	Gregory-Portland	Lubbock Coronado
1986-87	Wink	Colmesneil	Mineola	Mineral Wells	Kingwood
1987-88	Mertzon Irion Co.	Lexington	White Oak	Gregory-Portland	Mission
1988-89	Thorndale	Clifton	Bishop	Gregory-Portland	Killeen
1989-90	Vega	Big Lake Reagan Co.	Breckenridge	Gregory-Portland	Klein
1990-91	Paducah	Lexington	Liberty	Schertz Clemens	Spring Klein
1991-92	Vega	Marion	Van	Austin Westlake	Mission
1992-93	Rocksprings	Lytle	Seminole	Gregory-Portland	Spring Klein
1993-94	Rocksprings	Olney	Kaufman	Waco University	South Grand Prairie
1994-95	Rocksprings	Morton	Devine	Gregory-Portland	Lewisville
1995-96	Corsicana Mildred	Morton	Vernon	Freeport Brazosport	Pharr-San Juan-Alamo
1996-97	Rocksprings	Diana New Diana	Vernon	Corpus Christi Cal'len	San Antonio Madison
1997-98	Rocksprings	Kingsville Academy	Vernon	Grapevine	Austin Westlake
1998-99	Rocksprings	Kingsville Academy	Mineola	Denton Ryan	Houston Yates

Lincoln-Douglas Debate

Year	Conference A	Conference AA	Conference AAA	Conference AAAA	Conference AAAAA
1985-86	O'Donnell	Gladewater Union Grv	Vernon	Austin Westlake	El Paso Eastwood
1986-87	Roby	Junction	Mission Sharyland	Denison	San Antonio Madison
1987-88	Thorndale	Schulenburg	Cleveland Tarkington	Terrell	San Angelo Central
1988-89	Thorndale	Holliday	Muleshoe	Terrell	Conroe
1989-90	Thorndale	Early	Mission Sharyland	Terrell	Conroe
1990-91	Barksdale Nueces Ca.	Morton	Iowa Park	Crosby	Klein
1991-92	Lindsay	Elkhart	Bridgeport	Uvalde	Amarillo Tascosa
1992-93	Martins Mill	Ozona	Van	West Orange-Stark	San Angelo Central
1993-94	Star	Woodsboro	Needville	Friendswood	El Paso Hanks
1994-95	Lago Vista	Early	Bishop	Waco Midway	Houston Aldine
1995-96	Louise	Lytle	Llano	Rosenberg Lamar Con	McAllen Memorial
1996-97	Miami	Holliday	Warren	Wolfforth Frenship	San Antonio MacArthur
1997-98	Earth Springlake	Sunray	Muleshoe	Buda Hays	Duncanville
1998-99	Christoval	Crawford	Lytle	Austin Anderson	Amarillo

Team Debate

Year	Conference A	Conference AA	Conference AAA	Conference AAAA	Conference AAAAA
1985-86	Loop	Eldorado	Orangefield	Allen	San Antonio Churchill
1986-87	Austwell-Tivoli	Groveton	Marble Falls	Buda Hays	Carrollton Newm'n Smi.
1987-88	Thorndale	Vanderbilt Industrial	La Feria	Gregory-Portland	Houston Westbury
1988-89	Thorndale	Archer City	Mont Belvieu Barbers Hill	West Orange-Stark	Houston Westfield
1989-90	Thorndale	Karnes City	Mont Belvieu Barbers Hill	West Orange-Stark	San Antonio Lee

Cross Examination Team Debate

Year	Conference A	Conference AA	Conference AAA	Conference AAAA	Conference AAAAA
1990-91	Christoval	Karnes City	Vernon	Corpus Chri. Calallen	San Antonio Churchill
1991-92	Aspermont	Ingram Tom Moore	Crane	Buda Hays	San Antonio Clark
1992-93	Aspermont	Wall	Mont Belvieu Barbers Hill	Waco Midway	Katy Taylor
1993-94	Lindsay	Stratford	Sealy	Friendswood Cl'rbrook	Grapevine
1994-95	Lago Vista	Stinnett West Texas	Denver City	Hewitt Midway	Katy Taylor
1995-96	Lindsay	Karnes City	Denver City	Waco Midway	Katy Taylor
1996-97	Jayton	Wall	Denver City	Buda Hays	San Antonio Lee
1997-98	Christoval	Holliday	Denver City	Schertz Clemens	Spring

Year	Conference A	Conference AA	Conference AAA	Conference AAAA	Conference AAAAA
			Science		
1985-86	Lenorah Grady	Baird	Slaton	Austin Westlake	Arlington
1986-87	Lindsay	Liberty Hill	Slaton	Denison	Houston Stratford
1987-88	Lindsay	Clifton	Lampasas	Cedar Hill	Houston Stratford
1988-89	Plains	Redwater	Lampasas	Granbury	League City Clear Cr'k
1989-90	Avery	Redwater	Bishop	Kerrville Tivy	Houston Memorial
1990-91	Valley Mills	Springlake-Earth	Lampasas	Kerrville Tivy	Houston Clear Creek
1991-92	Valley Mills	Canadian	Troy	Carthage	Klein
1992-93	Lindsay	Wimberley	Seminole	Kingsville King	San Antonio Holmes
1993-94	Lindsay	Florence	Cuero	Kingsville King	San Antonio Holmes
1994-95	Rule	Troup	Waco Connally	Mesquite Poteet	Fort Worth Dunbar
1995-96	Rule	Franklin	Wimberley	Austin Johnson	Sugar Land Elkins
1996-97	Garden City	Canadian	Commerce	Austin Anderson	Humble
1997-98	Lenorah Grady	Sundown	Bridgeport	Austin Johnson	College Station A&M C.
1998-99	Lenorah Grady	Rogers & Jourdanton (tie)	Alvarado	Austin Johnson	Tyler Lee
			Science Team Event		
1990-91	Valley Mills	Canadian	Lampasas	Waco Midway	Lubbock
1991-92	Valley Mills	Canadian	Troy	Dallas Highland Park	Lubbock
1992-93	Lindsay	Wimberley	Seminole	Kingsville King	San Antonio Holmes
1993-94	Lindsay	Canadian	Cuero	Paris North Lamar	Fort Worth Dunbar
1994-95	Lindsay	Troup	Waco Connally	Paris North Lamar	Plano
1995-96	Rule	Canadian	Wimberley	Austin LB Johnson	Houston Bellaire
1996-97	Vega	Stinnett West Texas	Bridgeport	Waco Midway	Humble
1997-98	Moulton	Stinnett West Texas	Wimberley	Dallas Highland Park	Humble
1998-99	Lenorah Grady	Lindsay	Wimberley	Dallas Highland Park	Arlington Lamar
			Mathematics		
1992-93	San Isidro	Stamford	Bandera	Athens	Klein
1993-94	Wink	Stamford	Mont Belvieu Barbers Hill	College St'n A&M Co.	Klein
1994-95	Wink	Salado	Waco Connally	Austin LB Johnson	Plano
1995-96	Rule	Wellington	Bridgeport	Austin LB Johnson	Sugar Land Elkins
1996-97	Henrietta Midway	Wellington	Bridgeport	Weatherford	College Station A&M C.
1997-98	Henrietta Midway	Wellington	Bridgeport	Weatherford	College Station A&M C.
1998-99	Rule	Yorktown	Sweeny	Weatherford	College Station A&M C
			Mathematics Team Event		
1991-92	Crawford	Quanah	Ingleside	Katy Taylor	Lubbock
1992-93	Sterling City	Stamford	Carrizo Springs	Dallas Hillcrest	Klein
1993-94	Lindsay	Stamford	Carrizo Springs	College St'n A&M Co.	Lubbock
1994-95	Wink	Salado	Bridgeport	Austin LB Johnson	College Station A&M C.
1995-96	Rule	Salado	Bridgeport	Austin LB Johnson	College Station A&M C.
1996-97	Rule	Wellington	Bridgeport	Longview Pine Tree	College Station A&M C.
1997-98	Henrietta Midway	Wellington	Bridgeport	Longview Pine Tree	Klein
1998-99	Valley View	Salado	Santa Rosa	Longview Pine Tree	Mercedes Sci. Acad.
			Spelling		
1985-86	San Isidro	Harleton	White Oak	SW San Antonio	McKinney
1986-87	Barksdale Nueces Ca.	Hull-Daisetta	Kirbyville	Sulphur Springs	El Paso Eastwood
1987-88	Trent	Bruceville-Eddy	Brady	Lamesa	Del Rio & Wichita Falls (tie)
1988-89	Corsicana Mildred	Blanco	Lamesa	Sulphur Springs	Del Rio & Wichita Falls (tie)
1989-90	San Isidro & Corsicana Mildred (tie)	Wimberley	Devine	San Antonio Alamo Heights	Wichita Falls Rider
1990-91	Corsicana Mildred	DeLeon	Gonzales	Waco Midway	Brownsville Pace
1991-92	Lindsay	Pineland W. Sabine	Gonzales	Sulphur Springs	Brownsville Pace
			Spelling & Vocabulary		
1992-93	San Isidro	Eldorado	Atlanta	Sulphur Springs	Fort Worth Southwest
1993-94	Kopperl	Yorktown	Atlanta	Uvalde	Keller
1994-95	Jayton	Stockdale	Denver City	Livingston	Brownsville Pace
1995-96	Jayton	Abernathy	Mexia	Corsicana	Klein
1996-97	Bartlett	Schulenburg	Center	Orange Little Cypress	Fort Worth Paschal
1997-98	Valentine	Stockdale	Cuero	Friendswood	Leander
1998-99	Valley View	Schulenburg	Center	Friendswood	San Angelo Central
			Spelling & Vocabulary Team Event		
1992-93	San Isidro	East Bernard	Atlanta	Livingston	Mission
1993-94	San Isidro	China Spring	Atlanta	Sulphur Springs	Mission
1994-95	Bartlett	Yorktown	Denver City	Sulphur Springs	Plano East
1995-96	San Isidro	Stockdale	Atlanta	Sulphur Springs	Plano East
1996-97	Bartlett	Post	Henrietta	Liningston	Harlingen South
1997-98	Wink	Stockdale	Center	Friendswood	Arlington Lamar
1998-99	Wink	Post	Center	Hewitt Midway	Lufkin

Year	Conference A	Conference AA	Conference AAA	Conference AAAA	Conference AAAAA
Editorial Writing					
1985-86	Bruceville Eddy	Petersburg	Powderly North Lamar	Tomball	Houston Waltrip
1986-87	Port Aransas	Winona	Sonora	Edcouch-Elsa	Austin Lanier
1987-88	Windthorst	Pottsboro	Hardin-Jefferson	McKinney	Dallas Highland Park
1988-89	Fort Hancock	Iraan	Premont	Pleasanton	New Caney
1989-90	Gail Borden	Three Rivers	La Grange	Big Spring	El Paso Coronado
1990-91	Tilden McMullen Co.	Mart	San Antonio Cole	Austin Reagan	Houston Clear Lake
1991-92	Follett	Marion	Lampasas	Canyon Randall	San Antonio McCollum
1992-93	Booker	Olney	Montgomery	Buda Hays	Corpus Christi Carroll
1993-94	Tilden McMullen Co.	Karnes City	Hamshire-Fannett	Crosby	Tyler Lee
1994-95	Sanderson	Olney	Bowie	San Angelo Lake View	College Stat'n A&M Co.
1995-96	Tilden McMullen Co.	Olney	Kirbyville	Gregory-Portland	Edinburg North
1996-97	Farwell	Hasketll	Hamshire-Fannett	Dayton	Dallas Townview
1997-98	Price Carlisle	Florence	Decatur	Ft. Worth West. Hills	Dallas Townview
1998-99	Abbott	Sunray	Lytle	Kerrville Tivy	McKinney
Feature Writing					
1985-86	Groom	Austin Lake Travis	Castroville Medina Valley	Allen	Irving Nimitz
1986-87	Tornillo	Grandview	Crane	Gregory-Portland	Brownsville Porter
1987-88	Nazareth	Ozona	Mont Belvieu Barbers Hill	Henderson	Fort Worth Arling'n H'ts
1988-89	Rocksprings	Waskom	Texarkana Pleasant Grove	Sulphur Springs	Arlington
1989-90	Tenaha	Ganado	Bellville	Los Fresnos	San Antonio Clark
1990-91	Cushing	Forsan	Clint	Crosby	Houston Cypress-F'nks
1991-92	Groom	Bogata Rivercrest	Burnet	Austin Anderson	Copperas Cove
1992-93	Alvord	Stanton	Fredericksburg	Austin Westlake	Alief Hastings
1993-94	Paducah	Lytle	Burnet	Rockwall	Arlington
1994-95	Utopia	McGregor	Midland Greenwood	Port Lavaca Calhoun	El Paso Irvin
1995-96	Booker	Skidmore-Tynan	Dalhart	Whitehouse	College Station A&M C.
1996-97	Utopia	East Bernard	Atlanta	El Paso	El Paso Eastwood
1997-98	Perrin-Whitt	Mart	Pearsall	Friendswood Cl'r Br'k	San Antonio Clark
1998-99	Gordon	Aubrey	Hamshire-Fannett	Austin Johnston	Longview
Headline Writing					
1985-86	Windthorst	Palmer	Whitesboro	San Angelo Lake View	Longview
1986-87	Lindsay	Liberty Hill	Cameron Yoe	Borger	Harlingen
1987-88	Ropesville Ropes	White Deer	Cameron Yoe	Pleasanton	Beaumont West Brook
1988-89	Ropesville Ropes	Woodsboro	Mont Belvieu Barbers Hill	Cleburne	Laredo Martin
1989-90	Groom	Clarendon	Pearsall	West Orange-Stark	Houston Clear Lake
1990-91	Port Aransas	Overton	Odem	West Orange-Stark	Houston Clear Lake
1991-92	Moulton	Canadian	Ballinger	Mesquite Poteet	Corpus Christi Carroll
1992-93	Alvord	Sunray	Gatesville	Texarkana Texas	Alief Elsik
1993-94	Utopia	Sadler S&S Cons.	Dalhart	Brownwood	Houston Alief Elsik
1994-95	Tilden McMullen Co.	Clarendon	Fairfield	Magnolia	Corpus Christi Carroll
1995-96	Era	Ralls	China Spring	Round Rock McNeil	Duncanville
1996-97	Claude	Olney	China Spring	Coppell	Garland
1997-98	O'Donnell	La Villa	Lake Dallas	McKinney	Garland
1998-99	Overton	Yorktown	Waco Connally	Dallas Highland Park	El Paso Irvin
News Writing					
1985-86	Miles	Rains Emory	Crane	Jacksonville	Tyler Lee
1986-87	Moulton	Ozona	Hooks	Sulphur Springs	Bryan
1987-88	Blue Ridge	Hamilton	Sonora	Plugerville	Dallas Highland Park
1988-89	Granger	Stinnett West Texas	Hamshire-Fannett	Sn Angelo Lake View	Sugar Land Kempner
1989-90	Nazareth	Beckville	Quitman	Katy Taylor	Midland Lee
1990-91	Darrouzett	Quitman	Cuero	Lubbock Dunbar	Tyhler Lee
1991-92	Lindsay	Quitman	Texarkana Pleasant Grove	Buda Hays	DeSoto
1992-93	Utopia	Wall	Devine	Austin Westlake	Carrollton Turner
1993-94	Crawford	Wimberley	La Feria	Pampa	San Anton. Brack'ridge
1994-95	Byers	Waskom	Fairfield	Coppell	Garland
1995-96	Moulton	Canadian	Trinity	Fort Stockton	Humble Kingwood
1996-97	Nazareth	Plains	White Oak	Sour Lake Hardin-Jeff.	Austin
1997-98	Happy	Archer City	Atlanta	Grapevine	Tyler Lee
1998-99	Martinsville	Lindsay	Falfurrias	Tyler Chapel Hill	Sugar Land Kempner

Music and Theatre

Year	Conference A	Conference AA	Conference AAA	Conference AAAA	Conference AAAAA
One-Act Play					
1985-86	Port Aransas	Shallowater	Red Oak	Gregory-Portland	San Antonio MacArthur
1986-87	Port Aransas	Canadian	Mineola	Gregory-Portland	Klein
1987-88	Sabine Pass	Cooper	Mineola	Snyder	League City Clear Lake
1988-89	Port Aransas	Marion	Mineola	Gregory-Portland	Klein Oak
1989-90	Thorndale	Seagraves	Mineola	Gregory-Portland	Conroe McCullough
1990-91	Ropesville Ropes	Boys Ranch	Mineola	Katy Taylor	San Antonio MacArthur
1991-92	Trent	Seagraves	Cameron Yoe	Mineral Wells	Euless
1992-93	Munday	Wimberley	Sonora	Snyder	Klein
1993-94	Lindsay	Stinnett West Texas	Mineola	West Orange-Stark	San Angelo Central

Year	Conference A	Conference AA	Conference AAA	Conference AAAA	Conference AAAAA
1994-95	Rule	Yorktown	Mineola	Snyder	Hurst Bell
1995-96	Trent	Diana New Diana	Mont Belvieu Barbers Hill	Friendswood	Arlington Martin
1996-97	Overton	Stinnett West Texas	Bishop	Gregory-Portland	Plano
1997-98	Whiteface	Stinnett West Texas	Lake Dallas	La Marque	Arlington Martin
1998-99	Highland	New Diana	Barber's Hill	Bay City	San Antonio Madison
State Marching Band Contest					
1985-86	Asherton	Dripping Springs	Denver City	Georgetown	San Antonio MacArthur
1986-87	Nueces Canyon	Iraan	Denver City	Dickinson	Duncanville
1987-88	Sundown	Iraan	Pearsall	Allen	Houston Westfield
1988-89	Sundown	Olney	Denver City	Allen	Spring Westfield
1989-90	Sundown	Johnson City LBJ	Denver City	Dickinson	Spring Westfield
1990-91	Sudan	Iraan	Brownfield	Dickinson	Duncanville
1991-92	Plains	Iraan	—	Dickinson	—
1992-93	—	—	Brownfield	—	Spring
1993-94	Mertzon Irion Co.	Holliday	—	Dickinson	—
1994-95	—	—	Robinson	—	Spring
1995-96	Plains	Howe	—	Belton	—
1996-97	—	—	Robinson	—	Spring Westfield
1997-98	Jayton	Howe	—	Mesquite Poteet	—
1998-99	—	—	Hidalgo	—	Spring Westfield
Texas State Solo-Ensemble Contest Sweepstakes Winners					
1985-86	Iraan	Clint	Van	Georgetown	Duncanville
1986-87	Mertzon Irion Co.	Iraan	Crane	West Orange-Stark	Duncanville
1987-88	Wheeler	Salado	Crane	West Orange-Stark	Duncanville
1988-89	Laneville	Tatum	Denver City	West Orange-Stark	Duncanville
1989-90	Lazbuddie	Tatum	Crane	West Orange-Stark	Duncanville
1990-91	Laneville	Warren	Rockport-Fulton	West Orange-Stark	Duncanville
1991-92	Bronte, Forsan, Mertzon Irion (3-way tie)	Eldorado	Lubbock Cooper & Rockport-Fulton (tie)	Orange Little Cypress-Mauriceville	Duncanville
1992-93	Sudan	Stinnett West Texas	Sweeny	Austin Westlake	Duncanville
1993-94	Hico	Warren	Sweeny	Coppell	Duncanville
1994-95	Evadale	Stinnett West Texas	Sweeny	Coppell	Duncanville
1995-96	Munday	Early	Sweeny & Vernon (tie)	Coppell	Duncanville
1996-97	Whiteface	Early	Sabine	Coppell	Duncanville
1997-98	Ben Bolt	Canadian	Sabine	Coppell	Duncanville
1998-99	Whiteface	Harmony	Sabine	Coppell	Duncanville

Publications

	Yearbooks	Newspapers
1985-86	Irving	Duncanville
1986-87	North Mesquite	Austin Westlake
1987-88	Irving	Lubbock Monterey
1988-89	Irving	Duncanville
1989-90	Lubbock Monterey	San Antonio Marshall
1990-91	Austin Westlake	Duncanville
1991-92	Austin West Ridge Middle School; Duncanville; Deer Park; Wimberley; North Garland; Highland Park; Abilene; Texarkana Texas	Duncanville; San Antonio John Marshall; Houston Memorial; Follett; Austin Westlake; Austin SF Austin; Dallas Hillcrest
1992-93	Duncanville; Deer Park; Labay Junior High; Austin James Bowie; Stinnett West Texas; Highland Park; Abilene	Duncanville; South San Antonio, West Campus; San Antonio Marshall; Austin James Bowi; Austin Westlake; Houston Memorial
1993-94	Texarkana Pleasant Grove; Austin James Bowie; Stinnett West Texas; Highland Park; Texarkana Texas; Houston Cypress-Fairbanks	North Garland; Austin James Bowie; Dallas Hillcrest; Weatherford; Follett; El Paso Jefferson
1994-95	Austin Bowie; Texarkana Texas; Highland Park; Lockhart Jr. High; Abilene; Dallas Hillcrest; Stinnett West Texas	Austin James Bowie; Follett; Austin Westlake; Dallas Hillcrest; Duncanville; Austin Fulmore Middle School
1995-96	Duncanville; Austin Bowie; Amarillo Tascosa; Round Rock McNeil; LaVernia; Dallas Highland Park	Austin Westlake; Dallas Hillcrest; Austin Fulmore Middle School; Austin LBJ; Dallas Highland Park
1996-97	Duncanville; Amarillo Tascosa; El Paso Burges; San Antonio East Central; Texarkana Pleasant Grove; San Antonio McAuliffe MS	Duncanville; Dallas Hillcrest; Mansfield; The Woodlands McCullough Jr. High; Highland Park; Arlington
1997-98	Duncanville; San Antonio East Central; Dallas Hillcrest; Houston Bellaire	Duncanville; Dallas Hillcrest; The Woodlands McCullough Jr. High; Dallas Highland Park; Austin LBJ; Austin LC Anderson
1998-99	Houston Bellaire; Abilene; McKinney; Duncanville; San Antonio East Central; San Antonio McAuliffe MS	Austin Westlake; Duncanville; Austin Anderson; Dallas Hillcrest; The Woodlands; The Woodlands McCullough MS; Mansfield

Note: Before the 1991-92 school year, the UII named only one top yearbook and one top newspaper each year. Beginning with the 1991-92 school year, awards were presented to all yearbooks and newspapers judged to be worthy of the honors, which were divided into gold, silver and bronze categories. Only the gold-award winners are listed here for those years.

Athletics

Year	Conference A	Conference AA	Conference AAA	Conference AAAA	Conference AAAAA
			Baseball		
1985-86	Colmesneil	Riviera Kaufer	Pattonville Prairiland	Brenham	Houston Bellaire
1986-87	Burton	China Spring	San Augustine	Brenham	Abilene Cooper
1987-88	Apple Springs	Shelbyville	Sinton	Brenham	Abilene Cooper
1988-89	Maud	China Spring	Sinton	Paris	Sugar Land Dulles
1989-90	Colmesneil	Gilmer Harmony	Freer	Carthage	Duncanville
1990-91	Valley Mills	Van Horn	Falfurrias	Robstown	League City Clear Cr'k
1991-92	Valley Mills	Shiner	Queen City	Robstown	Freeport Brazoswood
1992-93	Flatonia	China Spring	Bellville	Mount Pleasant	Arlington Martin
1993-94	Gunter	East Bernard	Orange Grove	Belton	Houston Bellaire
1994-95	D'Hanis	East Bernard	Hallettsville	Coppell	Sugar Land Elkins
1995-96	Thorndale	Weimar	Crockett	Arlington Heights	Lubbock Monterey
1996-97	Fayetteville	Weimar	Hallettsville	Fort Worth Boswell	Round Rock
1997-98	Thrall	Gunter	Atlanta	Dallas Highland Park	Klein
1998-99	Collinsville	Cooper	West	Andrews	Houston Bellaire
			Basketball, Boys		
1985-86	Nazareth	Morton	Cleveland	Port Arthur Lincoln	Amarillo
1986-87	Paducah	Morton	Sweeny	Dallas Hillcrest	La Porte
1987-88	Paducah	Archer City	Sweeny	Port Arthur Lincoln	Houston Sam Houston
1988-89	Ladonia	Edgewood	San Antonio Cole	Port Arthur Lincoln	League City Clear Lake
1989-90	Santo	Ingram Moore	Navasota	Dallas Lincoln	Dallas Kimball
1990-91	Moulton	Abernathy	Sour Lake Hardin-Jeffers'n	Port Arthur Lincoln	Duncanville
1991-92	Laneville	Troup	Stafford	Dallas South Oak Cliff	Longview
1992-93	Laneville	Troup	Southlake Carroll	Dallas Lincoln	Fort Worth Dunbar
1993-94	Lipan	Krum	Ferris	Plainview	Sugar Land Willowr'dge
1994-95	Sudan	Larue LaPoyner	Clarksville	Port Arthur Lincoln	San Antonio E. Central
1995-96	Avinger	Krum	Sinton	Pampa	Dallas Kimball
1996-97	Wortham	Italy	Dallas Madison	San Antonio Fox Tech	Dallas Kimball
1997-98	Moulton	Krum	Clarksville	Houston Waltrip	Midland
1998-99	Moulton	Peaster	Mexia	Crowley	Duncanville
			Basketball, Girls		
1985-86	Snook	Abernathy	Sour Lake Hardin-Jeffers'n	Levelland	Victoria
1986-87	Sudan	Morton	Slaton	Levelland	Plainview
1987-88	Nazareth	Godley	Brownfield	Levelland	Duncanville
1988-89	Nazareth	Grapeland	Sour Lake Hardin-Jeffers'n	Levelland	Duncanville
1989-90	Nazareth	Tatum	Abilene Wylie	Corpus Christi Cal'llen	Duncanville
1990-91	Nazareth	Abernathy	Tulia	Levelland	Amarillo Tascosa
1991-92	Celeste	Panhandle	Canyon	Canyon Randall	San Marcos
1992-93	Celeste	Marion	Dimmitt	Austin Westlake	Amarillo
1993-94	Sudan	Tuscola Jim Ned	Dripping Springs	Waco Midway	Amarillo
1994-95	Sudan	Ozona	Bowie	Cleburne	Austin Westlake
1995-96	Nazareth	Ozona	Groesbeck	Canyon	Austin Westlake
1996-97	Whiteface	Poth	Mont Belvieu Barbers Hill	Levelland	Duncanville
1997-98	Karnack	Hamilton	Comanche	Canyon Randall	Alief Elsik
1998-99	Vega	Hughes Springs	Winnsboro	Dallas Lincoln	Mansfield
			Cross Country, Boys		
1985-86		Lockney	Midlothian	Brownsville Pace	Conroe McCullough
1986-87		Lockney	Yoakum	Midlothian	Conroe McCullough
1987-88		Eldorado	Boys Ranch	Canyon	Conroe McCullough
1988-89	Sundown	Boys Ranch	Corpus Christi W. Oso	Canyon Randall	Humble Kingwood
1989-90	Sundown	Boys Ranch	Corpus Christi W. Oso	Canyon Randall	Conroe McCullough
1990-91	Sabinal	Sundown	Corpus Christi W. Oso	Mesquite Poteet	Conroe McCullough
1991-92	Rocksprings	Boys Ranch	Gonzales	Mesquite Poteet	Houston MacArthur
1992-93	Utopia	Sundown	Gonzales	College Stn. A&M	Houston MacArthur
1993-94	Plains	Boys Ranch	Canyon	Mesquite Poteet	Humble Kingwood
1994-95	Priddy	Sundown	Fabens	Canyon	Humble Kingwood
1995-96	Priddy	Sundown	Santa Rosa	Canyon	Humble Kingwood
1996-97	Rocksprings	Boys Ranch	Yoakum	Uvalde	Humble Kingwood
1997-98	Medina	Dilley	Clint	El Paso	Humble Kingwood
1998-99	Rocksprings	Premont	Canton	Lockhart	Humble Kingwood
			Cross Country, Girls		
1985-86		Nazareth	Powderly North Lamar	Austin Westlake	League City Clear Lake
1986-87		Nazareth	Castroville Medina Valley	Powderly No. Lamar	El Paso Bowie
1987-88		Nazareth	Crystal City	Powderly Stone	Alief Elsik
1988-89	Munday	Spearman	Perryton	Dallas Highland Park	League City Clear Lake
1989-90	Munday	Marion	Canyon	Dallas Highland Park	Conroe McCullough
1990-91	Gruver	Abernathy	Canyon	Austin Westlake	Klein Oak
1991-92	Claude	La Villa	Canyon	Corpus Christi Cal'llen	Mission
1992-93	Booker	Hamilton	Canyon	Dallas Highland Park	Round Rock

Year	Conference A	Conference AA	Conference AAA	Conference AAAA	Conference AAAAA
1993-94	Sulphur Spr'gs N.Hop.	Hamilton	Canyon	New Braunfels	Grapevine
1994-95	Rocksprings	Hamilton	Sanford Fritch	New Braunfels	Humble Kingwood
1995-96	Rocksprings	Hamilton	Clint	New Braunfels	Humble Kingwood
1996-97	Rocksprings	Hamilton	Clint	Pampa	Flower Mound Marcus
1997-98	Rocksprings	Nacogdoches C'trl Hgt	Ingram Moore	Dallas Highland Park	Humble Kingwood
1998-99	Alvord	Crawford	Brownfield	Dallas Highland Park	Amarillo

Football

Year	6-man	A	AA	AAA	AAAA	AAAAA
1985-86	Jayton	Goldthwaite	Electra	Daingerfield	Sweetwater	Houston Yates
1986-87	Fort Hancock	Burkeville	Shiner	Jefferson	West Orange-Stark	Plano
1987-88	Lohn	Wheeler	Lorena	Cuero	West Orange-Stark	Plano
1988-89	Fort Hancock	White Deer	Corrigan-Camden	Southlake Carroll	Paris	Dallas Carter
1989-90	Fort Hancock	Thorndale	Groveton	Mexia	Tyler Chapel Hill	Odessa Permian
1990-91	Fort Hancock	Bartlett	Groveton	Vernon	Wilmer-Hutchins	Div. 1: Marshall / Div. 2: Houston Aldine
1991-92	Fort Hancock	Memphis	Schulenberg	Groesbeck	College Station A&M	Div. 1: Killeen / Div. 2: Odessa Permian
1992-93	Voss Panther Creek	Bartlett	Schulenburg	Southlake Carroll	Waxahachie	Div. 1: Converse Judson / Div. 2: Temple
1993-94	Voss Panther Creek	Sudan	Goldthwaite	Southlake Carroll	Stephenville	Div. 1: Converse Judson / Div. 2: Lewisville
1994-95	Amherst	Thorndale	Goldthwaite	Sealy	Stephenville	Div. 1: Plano / Div. 2: John Tyler
1995-96	Amherst	Thorndale	Celina	Sealy	La Marque	Div. 1:Converse Judson / Div. 2:San Ant. Roosevelt
1996-97	Gordon	Windthorst	Iraan	Sealy	Div. 1: Grapevine / Div. 2:La Marque	Div. 1:Lewisville / Div. 2:Austin Westlake
1997-98	Gail Borden	Granger	Stanton	Sealy	Div. 1: Texas City / Div. 2: La Marque	Div. 1:Katy / Div. 2:Flower Mound Marcus
1998-99	Trinidad	Tenaha	Div. 1: Omaha Pe'itt / Div. 2: Celina	Div. 1: Aledo / Div. 2: Newton	Div. 1: Grapevine / Div. 2: Stephenville	Div. 1: Duncanville / Div. 2: Midland Lee

Year	Conference A	Conference AA	Conference AAA	Conference AAAA	Conference AAAAA
			Golf, Boys		
1985-86	Salado	Stanton	Texarkana Pleasant Grove	Brownwood	Conroe
1986-87	Lago Vista	China Springs	Abilene Wylie	Andrews	Humble Kingwood
1987-88	Baird	China Spring	Mabank	Paris	Dallas Lake Highlands
1988-89	Baird	China Spring	Pleasant Grove	Dallas Highland Park	Plano
1989-90	Robert Lee	Weimar	Texarkana Pleasant Grove	Dallas Highland Park	Conroe
1990-91	Robert Lee	Weimar	Texarkana Pleasant Grove	Dallas Highland Park	Richardson Berkner
1991-92	Robert Lee	Olney	Abilene Wylie	Dallas Highland Park	El Paso Coronado
1992-93	Booker	Cisco	Graham	Dallas Highland Park	Conroe McCullough
1993-94	Baird	Quanah	Tulia	Austin Anderson	Plano
1994-95	Booker	Memphis	Lindale	Austin Anderson	El Paso Hanks
1995-96	Booker	Baird	Montgomery	Rockwall	Austin Westlake
1996-97	Meridian	Hamilton	Austin Lake Travis	Austin Anderson	San Antonio Churchill
1997-98	Shamrock	Hamilton	Mexia	Austin Anderson	San Antonio Churchill
1998-99	Sterling City	Hamilton	Sour Lake-Hardin-Jeffer.	Andrews	Austin Westlake
			Golf, Girls		
1985-86	Booker	Bullard	Canton	Snyder	Sugar Land Dulles
1986-87	Booker	Nocona	Alpine	Andrews	Sugar Land Dulles
1987-88	Booker	Nocona	Canton	Belton	Sugar Land Dulles
1988-89	Booker	Weimar	Gonzales	Andrews	Round Rock Westwood
1989-90	Booker	Boling	Yoakum	Andrews	Round Rock Westwood
1990-91	Booker	Bullard	Yoakum	Andrews	Round Rock Westwood
1991-92	Booker	Bullard	Yoakum	Andrews	Humble Kingwood
1992-93	Booker	China Spring	Yoakum	Bastrop	Midland Lee
1993-94	Robert Lee	China Spring	Graham	Bastrop	San Angelo Central
1994-95	Wheeler	Schulenburg	Yoakum	Bastrop	Humble Kingwood
1995-96	Wheeler	Post	Yoakum	Andrews	San Antonio Churchill
1996-97	Baird	Ozona	China Spring	Snyder	San Antonio Churchill-1
1997-98	Baird	Hamilton	China Spring - 1	Dallas Highland Park	San Antonio Churchill-1
1998-99	Baird	Hamilton	Lamesa	Dallas Highland Park	San Antonio Churchill
			Softball		
1992-93	—	—	—	—	Pasadena Dobie
1993-94	—	—	Mountt Vernon	—	Angleton
1994-95	—	—	Hawley	—	Pasadena Dobie
1995-96	—	Blooming Grove	Sweeny	Brenham	Pearland
1996-97	—	Hawley	Pollock Central	La Marque	Pasadena Dobie
1997-98	—	Coahoma	Kennedale	Waco Midway	Klein Oak
1998-99	—	Alto	Robinson	Magnolia	North Richland Hills

Soccer

Year	Girls	Boys
1985-86	Plano	Duncanville
1986-87	Duncanville	San Antonio Alamo Heights
1987-88	Plano	Klein Oak
1988-89	Plano	San Antonio Churchill
1989-90	Duncanville	Grapevine
1990-91	San Antonio Madison	Plano
1991-92	Arlington Martin	Plano
1992-93	San Antonio Madison	Plano
1993-94	Dallas Highland Park	New Braunfels
1994-95	Humble Kingwood	Plano
1995-96	Dallas Highland Park	El Paso Coronado
1996-97	Plano	Klein
1997-98	Arlington Martin	San Antonio Churchill
1998-99	4A:Colleyville Heritage 5A:Humble Kingwood	4A:Granbury 5A: Klein

Swimming & Diving

Year	Girls	Boys
1985-86	San Antonio Clark	Richardson Pearce
1986-87	Houston Cypress Creek	San Antonio Churchill
1987-88	Plano	San Antonio Churchill
1988-89	Conroe McCullough	San Antonio Churchill
1989-90	Conroe McCullough	Conroe McCullough & San Antonio Churchill (tie)
1990-91	Conroe McCullough	Plano
1991-92	Conroe McCullough	Plano
1992-93	Conroe McCullough	Humble Kingwood
1993-94	Humble Kingwood	Humble Kingwood
1994-95	Richardson Berkner	Houston Cypress Creek
1995-96	Austin Westlake	Conroe McCullough
1996-97	Austin Westlake	Conroe The Woodlands
1997-98	Plano	Conroe The Woodlands
1998-99	San Antonio Churchill	Conroe The Woodlands

Team Tennis

Year	AAAA	AAAAA
1985-86	Austin Westlake	San Antonio Churchill
1986-87	San Antonio Alamo Heights	San Antonio Churchill
1987-88	San Antonio Alamo Heights	Tyler Lee
1988-89	San Antonio Alamo Heights	Tyler Lee
1989-90	Dallas Highland Park	Klein
1990-91	Dallas Highland Park	El Paso Coronado
1991-92	Dallas Highland Park	Abilene
1992-93	Austin Westlake	Richardson Pearce
1993-94	San Antonio Alamo Heights	Abilene Cooper
1994-95	San Antonio Alamo Heights	Abilene Cooper
1995-96	San Antonio Alamo Heights	Abilene Cooper
1996-97	San Antonio Alamo Heights	Amarillo Tascosa
1997-98	Dallas Highland Park	Katy Taylor
1998-99	San Antonio Alamo Heights	Katy Taylor

Year	Conference A	Conference AA	Conference AAA	Conference AAAA	Conference AAAAA
Tennis, Boys Singles					
1985-86	Nueces Canyon	Mason	Marble Falls	Austin Westlake	Klein
1986-87	O'Donnell	Franklin	Austin Lake Travis	West Mesquite	Richardson
1987-88	Lohn	Anson	Hardin Jefferson	West Mesquite	Amarillo Tascosa
1988-89	Mertzon Irion Co.	Anson	Gladewater	Crowley	Texarkana
1989-90	Eden	Wall	Austin Lake Travis	Dallas Highland Park	Longview
1990-91	Nazareth	Wall	Marble Falls	Austin Westlake	El Paso Coronado
1991-92	Thorndale	Canadian	Hardin	Waco Midway	El Paso Coronado
1992-93	Nazareth	Shallowater	Canyon	Texarkana Texas	Tyler Lee
1993-94	Bruni	Shallowater	Clyde	San Antonio Al'mo Hts	Klein Forest
1994-95	Knippa	San Antonio Cole	Clyde	Corpus Christi Fl'r Bl'ff	Abilene Cooper
1995-96	Port Aransas	San Antonio Cole	Shallowater	Southlake Carroll	San Angelo Central
1996-97	Bruni	Clarendon	San Antonio Cole	Fort Worth Boswell	College St'n. A&M Con.
1997-98	Mertzon Irion Co.	Franklin	San Antonio Cole	Southlake Carroll	Houston Cypr'ss F'rbks
1998-99	Overton	Port Aransas	Vernon	Dallas Highland Park	Houston Cypr'ss F'rbks
Tennis, Boys Doubles					
1985-86	Nazareth	Mason	Marble Falls	San Antonio Al'mo H'hts	Corpus Christi King
1986-87	Nazareth	Mason	Pearsall	Waco Midway	Amarillo Tascosa
1987-88	Chilton	Mason	Gilmer	Corsicana	Corpus Christi King
1988-89	Eden	Franklin	Canyon	San Antonio Al'mo Hts	Midland
1989-90	Knippa	Mason	Austin Lake Travis	New Braunfels	Austin Westlake
1990-91	Knippa	Mason	Canyon	Texarkana	San Antonio Lee
1991-92	Memphis	Grand Saline	Port Isabel	Dallas Highland Park	Tyler Lee
1992-93	Paint Rock	Mason	Canyon	Dallas Highland Park	Richardson Pearce
1993-94	Nazareth	Mason	Canyon	Austin Westlake	Plano
1994-95	Priddy	Mason	Austin Lake Travis	San Antonio Al'mo Hts	Klein
1995-96	Bruni	Mason	Abilene Wylie	Dallas Highland Park	Sugar Land Clements
1996-97	Sabinal	Mason	Van	Dallas Highland Park	Sugar Land Clementsl
1997-98	Sabinal	Lexington	Liberty	Dallas Highland Park	San Antonio Churchill
1998-99	Mertzon Irion Co.	Mason	Vernon	Wichita Falls Rider	Amarillo Tascosa
Tennis, Girls Singles					
1985-86	Gail Borden Co.	Mason	Springtown	Athens	Corpus Christi King
1986-87	Baird	Mason	Springtown	Athens	Houston North Shore
1987-88	Baird	Rogers	Marble Falls	New Braunfels	Dallas Highland Park
1988-89	Nazareth	Mason	Aransas Pass	San Antonio Al'mo Hts	Houston Lamar
1989-90	Whitewright	Mason	Carrizo Springs	New Braunfels	Houston Bellaire
1990-91	Axtell	Aubrey	Cameron Yoe	Columbia W. Colum'a	Plano East
1991-92	Axtell	Malakoff Cross Roads	Cameron Yoe	Austin Anderson	Austin S.F. Austin
1992-93	Chillicothe	Malakoff Cross Roads	Cameron Yoe	Austin Westlake	El Paso Coronado

Year	Conference A	Conference AA	Conference AAA	Conference AAAA	Conference AAAAA
1993-94	Chillicothe	Malakoff Cross Roads	Cameron Yoe	Austin Westlake	Austin SF Austin
1994-95	Chillicothe	Malakoff Cross Roads	Royse City	F't Worth Arlingt'n H'ts	Austin Westlake
1995-96	Anton	Spearman	Breckenridge	New Braunfels	El Paso Franklin
1996-97	Menard	Eldorado	Texarkana Pleasant Grove	F't Worth Arlingt'n H'ts	El Paso Franklin
1997-98	Ben Bolt	Mason	Texarkana Pleasant Grove	Dallas Highland Park	El Paso Franklin
1998-99	Knippa	San Antonio Cole	Crandall	Dallas Highland Park	New Braunfels

Tennis, Girls Doubles

Year	Conference A	Conference AA	Conference AAA	Conference AAAA	Conference AAAAA
1985-86	Nazareth	Mason	Marble Falls	New Braunfels	Corpus Christi King
1986-87	Nazareth	Mason	Marble Falls	San Antonio Al'mo Hts	Lubbock Coronado
1987-88	Nueces Canyon	Mason	Falfurrias	San Angelo Lakeview	Sugar Land Dulles
1988-89	Nueces Canyon	Mason	Vernon	San Antonio Al'mo Hts	Klein Chester
1989-90	Gary	Mason	Vernon	Dallas Highland Park	Klein
1990-91	Fort Hancock	Mason	Canyon	Wichita Falls	Tyler Lee
1991-92	Nazareth	Spearman	Van	Katy Taylor	Amarillo Tascosa
1992-93	Hart	Mason	Groesbeck	Wichita Falls	Houston Stratford
1993-94	Fort Hancock	Mason	Fredericksburg	New Braunfels	Houston Memorial
1994-95	Sabinal	Mason	Wills Point	Texarkana Texas	Richardson Pearce
1995-96	Booker	Mason	Sweeny	New Braunfels	El Paso Franklin
1996-97	Rocksprings	Mason	Groesbeck	Grapevine Colleyville	El Paso Franklin
1997-98	Menard	Mason	Groesbeck	Dallas Highland Park	Round Rock Westwood
1998-99	Sabinal	Spearman	Groesbeck	Wichita Falls	Round Rock Westwood

Track & Field, Boys

Year	Conference A	Conference AA	Conference AAA	Conference AAAA	Conference AAAAA
1985-86	Gruver	Alto	Columbus	Lubbock Estacado	Galveston Ball
1986-87	Karnack	Refugio	Giddings	Dallas Lincoln	Galveston Ball
1987-88	Munday	Haskell	Cuero	Silsbee	Dallas South Oak Cliff
1988-89	Rotan	Corrigan-Camden	Atlanta	Dallas Hillcrest	Dallas South Oak Cliff
1989-90	Munday	Refugio	Crystal City	Bay City	Sugar Land Willowr'dge
1990-91	Munday	Celina	Marlin	Jasper	Killeen
1991-92	Calvert	Woodsboro	Sweeny	Austin Reagan	Odessa
1992-93	Chilton	Refugio	Waco Connally	San Angelo Lake View	Odessa Permian
1993-94	Sudan	Refugio	Tatum	La Marque	Beaumont West Brook
1994-95	Roscoe	Refugio	Daingerfield	Everman	Pflugerville
1995-96	Paducah	Alto	Tatum	Houston King	Dallas Kimball
1996-97	Paducah	Stamford	Atlanta	Jasper	Houston Langham Cr'k.
1997-98	Nueces Canyon	Holliday	Giddings	Houston Forest Brook	Fort Worth Wyatt
1998-99	Louise	Holliday	Hooks	Houston Forest Brook	Conroe Woodlands

Track & Field, Girls

Year	Conference A	Conference AA	Conference AAA	Conference AAAA	Conference AAAAA
1985-86	Cayuga	Hamlin	Refugio	Pampa	Houston Sterling
1986-87	Karnack	Refugio	Elgin	Brenham	Fort Worth Trimble Tech
1987-88	Munday	Refugio	Yoakum	Pampa	Dallas Carter
1988-89	Munday	Refugio	Bonham	Corsicana	Houston Sterling
1989-90	Munday	Weimar	Daingerfield	Del Valle	Houston Sterling
1990-91	Detroit & Munday (tie)	Albany	Columbus	Jasper	Fort Worth Dunbar
1991-92	Flatonia	Refugio	Fairfield	Dallas Madison	Galveston Ball
1992-93	Moulton	Schulenburg	Fairfield	Houston Forest Brook	Dallas Carter
1993-94	Cross Plains	Celina	Manor	Port Arthur Lincoln	Dallas Skyline
1994-95	Burkeville	Celina	Waco La Vega	Rosenberg Lamar C.	Dallas Carter
1995-96	Rocksprings	Alto	Groesbeck	New Braunfels	Dallas Skyline
1996-97	Rocksprings	Canadian	Dallas Madison	Dallas Lincoln	Houston Westbury
1997-98	Karnack	Woodsboro	Linden Kildare	Friendswood Cl'r Br'k	Houston Westbury
1998-99	Munday	San Augustine	Linden Kildare	Houston Forest Brook	Houston Westbury

Volleyball

Year	Conference A	Conference AA	Conference AAA	Conference AAAA	Conference AAAAA
1985-86	Flatonia	Plains	Refugio	Snyder	San Antonio Churchill
1986-87	Water Valley	Jewett Leon	Bellville	Lamesa	Houston Cypr'ss F'rbks
1987-88	Bronte	Jewett Leon	Devine	Pecos	Fort Worth Richland
1988-89	Plains	East Bernard	Devine	Dumas	Amarillo
1989-90	Plains	East Bernard	Kountze	Dumas	Houston Cypress Cr'k
1990-91	Plains	East Bernard	Bellville	Dumas	San Antonio Clark
1991-92	Bronte	Jewett Leon	Bellville	Austin Westlake	San Antonio Jay
1992-93	Windthorst	East Bernard	Needville	Red Oak	Austin
1993-94	Windthorst	East Bernard	Bellville	Austin Westlake	Houston Cypress Cr'k
1994-95	Windthorst	Freer	Dripping Springs	Friendswood	Amarillo
1995-96	Round Top-Carmine	Poth	Bellville	Red Oak	Duncanville
1996-97	Round Top-Carmine	Poth	Bellville	Hereford	Humble Kingwood
1997-98	Windthorst	Poth	Bellville	Hereford	Houston Cypress Cr'k
1998-99	Windthorst	Wallis Brazos	Caldwell	Dumas	Amarillo

Wrestling, Boys

1998-99	Weight Class 103: Dallas Highland Park; 112: Pilot Point Selz; 119: Dallas Highland Park; 125: El Paso Hanks; 130: Grapevine; 135: Amarillo Tascosa; 140: Canyon Randall; 152: Arlington Houston; 160: Amarillo Tascosa; 171: Plano East; 180: Amarillo Caprock: 189: San Antonio Roosevelt; 215: Dallas Highland Park; 275: Amarillo Tascosa.

Wrestling, Girls

1998-99	Weight Class 95: Amarillo Caprock; 102: Arlington Bowie; 110: Klein Oak; 119: Amarillo Caprock; 128: Arlington Houston; 138: Amarillo; 148: Amarillo Caprock; 165: Arlington Houston; 185: Waller; 215: Arlington.

Brief History of Higher Education in Texas

While there were earlier efforts toward higher education, the first permanent institutions established were church-supported schools: **Rutersville University**, established in 1840 by Methodist minister Martin Ruter in Fayette County, predecessor of **Southwestern University**, Georgetown, established in 1843; Baylor University, now at Waco, but established in 1845 at Independence, Washington County, by the Texas Union Baptist Association; and **Austin College**, now at Sherman, but founded in 1849 at Huntsville by the Brazos Presbytery of the Old School Presbyterian Church.

Other historic Texas schools of collegiate rank included: **Larissa College**, 1848, at Larissa, Cherokee County; **McKenzie College**, 1841, Clarksville; **Chappell Hill Male and Female Institute**, 1850, Chappell Hill; **Soule University**, 1855, Chappell Hill; **Johnson Institute**, 1852, Driftwood, Hays County; **Nacogdoches University**, 1845, Nacogdoches; **Salado College**, 1859, Salado, Bell County. **Add-Ran College**, established at Thorp Spring, Hood County, in 1873, was the predecessor of present **Texas Christian University**, Fort Worth.

Texas A&M and University of Texas

The **Agricultural and Mechanical College of Texas** (now **Texas A&M University**), authorized by the Legislature in 1871, opened its doors in 1876 to become the first publicly supported institution of higher education. In 1881, Texans established the **University of Texas** in Austin, with a medical branch in Galveston. The Austin institution opened Sept. 15, 1883, the Galveston school in 1891.

First College for Women

In 1901, the 27th Legislature established the **Girls Industrial College**, which began classes at its campus in Denton in 1903. A campaign to establish a state industrial college for women was led by the State Grange and Patrons of Husbandry. A bill was signed into law on April 6, 1901, creating the college. It was charged with a dual mission, which continues to guide the university today — to provide a liberal education and to prepare young women with a specialized education "for the practical industries of the age." In 1905 the name of the college was changed to the **College of Industrial Arts**; in 1934, it was changed to **Texas State College for Women**. Since 1957 the name of the institution, which is now the largest university principally for women in the United States, has been the **Texas Woman's University**.

Historic, Primarily Black Colleges

A number of Texas schools were established primarily for blacks, although collegiate racial integration is now complete in the state. The black-oriented institutions include state-supported **Prairie View A&M University** (originally established as **Alta Vista Agricultural College** in 1876), Prairie View; **Texas Southern University**, Houston; and privately supported **Huston-Tillotson College**, Austin; **Jarvis Christian College**, Hawkins; **Wiley College**, Marshall; **Paul Quinn College**, originally located in Waco, now in Dallas; and **Texas College**, Tyler. Predominantly black colleges that are important in the history of higher education in Texas, but that have ceased operations, include **Bishop College**, established in Marshall in 1881, then moved to Dallas; **Mary Allen College**, established in Crockett in 1886; and **Butler College**, originally named the **Texas Baptist Academy**, in 1905 in Tyler. ☆

Recent Developments in Texas Higher Education

Source: Texas Higher Education Coordinating Board.

State Appropriations

The $97.7 billion state budget approved by the 76th Texas Legislature for the 2000-2001 biennium included $12.4 billion for higher education — 12.7 percent of the total. This amount represents a 13.7 percent increase ($1.5 billion) in all-funds higher-education appropriations over the previous biennium.

The general-revenue portion of the all-funds state appropriation for the 2000-01 biennium totaled $55.1 billion, of which higher education received $8.5 billion — 15.4 percent of the total. This amount also represents a 13.5 percent increase ($1 billion) in funding for higher education.

Enrollment

Enrollment in Texas' public and independent colleges and universities in fall 1998 totaled 939,364 students, an increase of 4,853, or 0.13 percent, from fall 1997.

Enrollment in the 35 public universities increased by 1,993 students (0.5 percent). Nineteen public universities reported enrollment increases totaling a combined 6,379 students, while 16 reported a combined decrease of 4,386 students.

The state's public community-college districts reported fall 1998 enrollments totaling 412,684 students, down 947 students, or 0.23 percent, from fall 1997. Twenty-four of the 50 community-college districts reported enrollment increases totaling a combined 7,579 students, while 26 districts reported a combined decrease of 8,526 students.

The Texas State Technical College System, the state's public technical-college system, reported a fall 1998 enrollment of 8,724 students, an increase of 256 students (3.02 percent) over the previous fall.

Enrollments at the 38 independent, or private, senior colleges and universities in Texas increased to 102,489 students, up 3,559, or 3.6 percent, from the previous fall. The state's two independent junior colleges reported 673 students.

Public medical, dental, nursing and allied-health institutions of higher education reported enrollments totaling 15,374 students in fall 1998, up 41 students (0.27 percent) from fall 1997. Enrollment at independent, or private, health-related institutions totaled 1,174 students, down 12 students from the previous fall.

Effects of the Hopwood ruling

The 5th U.S. Circuit Court of Appeals ruled in Hopwood vs. Texas (1996) that the University of Texas at Austin School of Law could no longer consider race or ethnicity in admissions decisions. Subsequently, Texas Attorney General Dan Morales broadly interpreted that ruling to apply to admissions and financial-aid decisions at all Texas public higher-education institutions, thereby effectively eliminating the use of affirmative action to ensure access to higher education for the state's minorities.

As a result, the number of African-American and Hispanic first-time freshmen enrolled at the state's eight most selective undergraduate universities collectively decreased in fall 1997 before rebounding to an all-time high in fall 1998.

The state's public law schools reported the same general trend — decreases in African-American and Hispanic first-time enrollments in fall 1997, followed by increases in fall 1998. The number of African-American students did not fully recover to pre-Hopwood levels, but the number of Hispanics reached the highest levels ever.

At Texas medical schools, the number of African-American and Hispanic first-time students decreased in fall 1997. In fall 1998, their enrollments increased, but did not reach pre-Hopwood levels.

Admissions

To help ensure the full participation and full success of all Texans in higher education, the Legislature directed the Texas Higher Education Coordinating Board to develop and annually update a uniform strategy to identify, attract, retain and enroll students to reflect the population of the state. Higher-education institutions will implement the strategy and report annually to the Coordinating Board.

Health-related higher education

Funds received by the State of Texas as part of legal action against tobacco companies will be used to provide money for several health-related efforts. The Permanent Health Fund for Higher Education and Permanent Funds for Health-Related Institutions will benefit medical-research, health-education or treatment programs at the state's health-related higher-education institutions. The Permanent Fund for Higher Education Nursing, Allied Health, and Other Health-Related Programs will provide grants to public higher-education institutions that offer upper-level academic instruction and training in nursing, allied-health or other health-related education. The Permanent Fund for Minority Health Research and Education will provide grants to institutions that conduct research or educational programs addressing minority health issues or that form partnerships with minority organizations, colleges or universities to conduct research and educational programs addressing minority-health issues.

The 76th Legislature also established the Border Health Institute in El Paso, the Texas A&M University System Coastal Bend Health Education Center in Corpus Christi, and a University of Texas Health Science Center at San Antonio campus extension in Laredo.

The Texas Higher Education Coordinating Board was directed to review medical-training needs in the Texas-Mexico border region of Texas.

Financial Aid

The TEXAS (Toward EXcellence, Access, and Success) Grant Program, a new program to provide grants to Texas students who graduate from a public or accredited private Texas high school and enroll in a Texas public or independent higher-education institution, was established

by the 76th Texas Legislature in 1999. To be eligible, students must complete the college-preparatory curriculum in high school and meet financial-need requirements.

After the initial award, a student remains eligible for each semester in which he or she makes satisfactory academic progress toward an undergraduate degree or certificate. Supplementary conditional grants are available to junior- or senior-college students who are pursuing bachelor's degrees and teacher certification and who agree to teach in a geographic area or academic discipline with a critical shortage of teachers.

The 76th Texas Legislature also authorized, subject to voter approval in November 1999, the Texas Higher Education Coordinating Board to sell up to $400 million in state general-obligation bonds to provide money for financial-aid loans to Texas college students through the Hinson-Hazlewood College Student Loan Program.

In addition, the Legislature passed legislation allowing public higher-education institutions to match scholarships for Texas students who receive admissions and scholarship offers from out-of-state institutions.

New loan-repayment programs were established as incentives for encouraging students to pursue needed careers or work in needed areas of the state. These programs, which will repay student loans for eligible students, are for childcare workers and for dentists who practice in areas of the state that are underserved with dental care.

Tuition and fees

No general increase in tuition rates was approved for students enrolled in Texas public universities, but new legislation allows a university to reduce tuition for a student, within certain limits, as part of an institutional plan to increase graduation rates through positive incentives, such as encouraging students to increase their course load.

Another new law permits a public higher-education institution to waive a student fee if the student is not reasonably able to participate or use the activity, service or facility for which the fee is charged.

In addition, 13 bills authorizing institutions to adopt new fees or raise the levels of existing fees were passed.

To help universities construct new buildings and related facilities, the Legislature authorized $638 million in tuition revenue bonds to be issued by institutions. ☆

Universities and Colleges

Source: Texas Higher Education Coordinating Board and institutions. In some cases, dates of establishment differ from those given in the preceding discussion because schools use the date when authorization was given, rather than actual date of first classwork. For explanation of type of institution and other symbols, see notes at end of table.

Name of Institution; Location; (Type* - Ownership, if private sectarian institution); Date of Founding; President (unless otherwise noted)	Number in Faculty†	Fall Term 1998	Summer Session 1998	Extension or Continuing Ed.
		Enrollment		
Abilene Christian University—Abilene; (3 - Church of Christ); 1906 (as **Childers Classical Institute**; became **Abilene Christian College** by 1914; became university in 1976); Dr. Royce Money	303	4,643	1,898	260
ALAMO COMMUNITY COLLEGE DISTRICT (9) — Robert Ramsay, Chancellor				
Northwest Vista College — San Antonio; (7); 1995; Dr. Jacqueline Claunch	80	1,679	674	5
Palo Alto College—San Antonio; (7); 1985; Dr. Enrique Solis	400	6,572	3,472	690
St. Philip's College—San Antonio; (7); 1898; Dr. Charles A. Taylor	¶¶191	8,500	NA	5,000
San Antonio College—San Antonio; (7); 1925; Dr. Vern Loland	1,070	20,510	12,914	17,862
Alvin Community College—Alvin; (7); 1949; Dr. A. Rodney Allbright	250	3,435	3,325	1,004
Amarillo College—Amarillo; (7); 1929; Dr. Luther "Bud" Joyner	212	7,835	2,921	11,953
Amber University—Garland; (3); 1971; Dr. Douglas W. Warner	45	1,550	1,500	NA
Angelina College—Lufkin; (7); 1968; Dr. Larry Phillips	110	3,997	NA	12,004
Angelo State University—San Angelo (See **Texas State University System**)				
Arlington Baptist College—Arlington; (3 - Baptist); 1939 (as **Bible Baptist Seminary**; changed to present name in 1965); Dr. David Bryant	26	245	67	10
Austin College—Sherman; (3 - Presbyterian USA); 1849; Dr. Oscar C. Page	106	1,289	116	312
Austin Community College—Austin; (7); 1972; Dr. Richard Fonté	1,345	25,609	22,348	3,256

Name of Institution; Location; (Type* - Ownership, if private sectarian institution); Date of Founding; President (unless otherwise noted)	Number in Faculty†	Enrollment		Extension or Contin- uing Ed.
		Fall Term 1998	Summer Session 1998	
Austin Presbyterian Theological Seminary—Austin; Presbyterian; 3-yr; 1902 (successor to Austin School of Theology, est. 1884); Dr.Robert M. Shelton, President.	21	308	110	421
Baptist Missionary Association Theological Seminary—Jacksonville; Baptist Missionary, 3-yr.; 1955; Dr. Philip R. Bryan	12	52	17	11
Baylor College of Dentistry—(see Texas A&M University System)				
‡Baylor College of Medicine—Houston; (5 - Baptist until 1969); 1903 (Dallas; moved to Houston, 1943); Ralph D. Feigin, M.D.	—	1,162	—	—
Baylor University—Waco; (3 - So. Baptist); 1845 (at Independence; merged with Waco University in 1887 and moved to Waco); Dr. Robert B. Sloan Jr.	629	12,987	5,035	NA
Bee County College—Beeville (see Coastal Bend College)				
Blinn College—Brenham; (7); 1883 (as academy; jr. college, 1927); Dr. Donald E. Voelter . .	435	10,481	8,982	861
Brazosport College—Lake Jackson; (7); 1967; Dr. Millicent M. Valek	184	3,503	2,315	2,708
Brookhaven College—Farmers Branch (See Dallas County Community College District)				
Cedar Valley College—Lancaster (See Dallas County Community College District)				
Central Texas College—Killeen; (7); 1965; Dr. James R. Anderson.	1,412	8,362	9,717	2,509
Cisco Junior College—Cisco; (7); 1909 (as private institution; became state school in 1939); Dr. Roger C. Schustereit	68	2,638	§ 1,521	370
‡Clarendon College—Clarendon; (7); 1898 (as church school; became state school in 1927); Ray Hawkins (interim).	—	750	—	—
‡ Coastal Bend College—Beeville; (7); (1966 as Bee Co. College, name changed in 1999); Dr. Norman E. Wallace	—	2,730	—	—
College of the Mainland—Texas City; (7); 1967; Larry L. Stanley	350	3,308	2,596	6,894
College of St. Thomas More—Fort Worth; (**); (3-Roman Catholic); 1981 (as St. Thomas More Inst.; became college 1989; accredited as 2-year college 1994); Dr. James A. Patrick, Provost.	22	17	7	45
Collin County Community College—McKinney; (7); 1985; Dr. John H. Anthony	171	11,572	7,547	3,936
Concordia University—Austin; (3 - Mo. Lutheran); 1926 (as Concordia Lutheran College; name changed in 1995); Dr. David Zersen	92	744	118	NA
Cooke County College—Gainesville (See North Central Texas College)	85	4,150	1,600	3,500
Corpus Christi State University—(See Texas A&M University-Corpus Christi listing under Texas A&M University System)				
Dallas Baptist University—Dallas; (3 - Southern Baptist).; 1898 (as Decatur Baptist College; moved to Dallas and name changed in 1965); Dr. Gary Cook.	260	3,721	1,894	N
Dallas Christian College—Dallas; (3 - Christian); 1950; Dr. John Derry	35	280	NA	280
DALLAS COUNTY COMMUNITY COLLEGE DISTRICT (9) —J. William Wenrich, Chancellor				
Brookhaven College—Farmers Branch; (7); 1978; Dr. Alice W. Villadsen	660	7,607	4,362	3,413
Cedar Valley College—Lancaster; (7); 1977; Dr. Carol J. Spencer	95	2,700	1,665	1,222
Eastfield College—Mesquite; (7); 1970; Dr. Rodger A. Pool	†† 300	††8,200	††4,500	††3,500
El Centro College—Dallas; (7); 1966; Dr. Wright L. Lassiter Jr.	545	4,003	2,087	3,800
Mountain View College—Dallas; (7); 1970; Dr. Monique Amerman.	69	5,128	3,727	5,572
‡ North Lake College—Irving; (7); 1977; Dr. David England	—	5,882	—	—
Richland College—Dallas; (7); 1972; Dr. Stephen K. Mittelstet	400	12,110	§ 9,371	8,000
Dallas Theological Seminary—Dallas; private, graduate; 1924; Dr. Charles R. Swindoll . . .	90	1,602	875	168
Del Mar College—Corpus Christi; (7); 1935; Dr. Terry L. Dicianna	700+	††10,000	††6,000	††28,000
Eastfield College—Mesquite (See Dallas County Community College District)				
East Texas Baptist University—Marshall; (3 - Baptist); 1913 (as College of Marshall; became East Texas Baptist Coll., 1944; became university in 1984); Dr. Bob E. Riley . .	103	1,221	384	0
East Texas State University (see Texas A&M University-Commerce in Texas A&M System listing)				
East Texas State University at Texarkana (see Texas A&M University-Texarkana in Texas A&M System listing)				
El Centro College—Dallas (See Dallas County Community College District)				
El Paso Community College District—El Paso; (7); 1969; three campuses: Rio Grande, TransMountain and Valle Verde; Dr. William J. Campion	1,300	19,132	7,713	8,401
Episcopal Theological Seminary of the Southwest—Austin; Episcopal; Graduate-level; 1952; Very Rev. Durstan R. McDonald, Dean	26	118	NA	NA
Frank Phillips College—Borger; (7); 1948; Dr. William A. Griffin Jr.	¶¶ 28	1,142	563	††2,000
Galveston College—Galveston; (7); 1967; Dr. C.B. Rathburn	80	2,122	1,400	6,000
Grayson County College—Denison; (7); 1963; Dr. Alan Scheibmeir.	¶¶ 96	3,200	††1,500	††2,900
Hardin-Simmons University—Abilene; (3 - So. Baptist); 1891 (as Simmons College; changed to Simmons University, 1925; changed to present name, 1934); Dr. Lanny Hall	179	2,317	963	100
Hill College—Hillsboro; (7); 1923 (as Hillsboro Junior College; name changed, 1962); Dr. William R. Auvenshine.	67	2,422	1,115	431
Houston Baptist University—Houston; (3 - Baptist); 1960; Dr. E. D. Hodo	115	2,335	NA	NA
‡‡HOUSTON COMMUNITY COLLEGE SYSTEM—Houston; (9); 1971; **Dr. Ruth Burgos-Sasscer, Chancellor**	2,350	50,727	26,945	3,906
System consists of following colleges (president): Central College (Dr. Jack Daniels); College Without Walls (Dr. Margaret Forde); Northeast College (Dr. Margaret Forde); Northwest College (Dr. Zachary Hodges); Southeast College (Dr. Sylvia Ramos); Southwest College (Dr. Sue Cox).				
‡‡ Howard College—Big Spring; (7); 1945; (includes Southwest Collegiate Institute for the Deaf, Ron Brasel, Exec. Dir); Dr. Cheryl T. Sparks.	188	2,107	§ 908	2,615

Name of Institution; Location; (Type* - Ownership, if private sectarian institution); Date of Founding; President (unless otherwise noted)	Number in Faculty†	Enrollment		
		Fall Term 1998	Summer Session 1998	Extension or Continuing Ed.
Howard Payne University—Brownwood; (3 - Baptist); 1889; Dr. Rick R. Gregory	143	1,540	§ 508	180
Huston-Tillotson College—Austin; (3 - Methodist/Church of Christ); 1875 (**Tillotson College**, 1875, **Samuel Huston College**, 1876; merged 1952); Dr. Joseph T. McMillan Jr.	59	621	**	NA
International Bible College—San Antonio; (3); 1944; Rev. David W. Cook	21	75	NA	NA
Jacksonville College—Jacksonville; (8 - Missionary Baptist); 1899; Dr. Edwin Crank	27	363	102	16
Jarvis Christian College—Hawkins; (3); 1912; Dr. Sebetha Jenkins	48	505	NA	95
Kilgore College—Kilgore; (7); 1935; Dr. William M. Holda	144	4,154	§ 1,455	4,150
Lamar University and all branches (see **Texas State University System**)				
Laredo Community College—Laredo; (7); 1946; Dr. Ramon H. Dovalina	193	7,463	§ 4,351	1,262
LeTourneau University—Longview; (3); 1946 (as **LeTourneau Technical Institute**; became 4-yr. college in 1961); Dr. Alvin O. Austin	289	2,505	1,817	323
‡ Lee College—Baytown; (7); 1934; Dr. Jackson N. Sasser	—	5,906	—	—
Lon Morris College—Jacksonville; (8 - Methodist); 1854 (as **Danville Academy**; changed in 1873 to **Alexander Inst.**; present name, 1923); Dr. Clifford M. Lee	35	321	24	NA
‡ Lubbock Christian University—Lubbock; (3 - Church of Christ); 1957; Dr. L. Ken Jones	—	1,353	—	—
McLennan Community College—Waco; (7); 1965; Dr. Dennis Michaelis	250	5,700	3,400	3,500
McMurry University—Abilene; (3 - Methodist); 1923; Dr. Robert E. Shimp	¶¶ 73	1,366	725	NA
Midland College—Midland; (7); 1972; Dr. David E. Daniel	355	4,400	2,246	2,800
Midwestern State University—Wichita Falls; (2); 1922; Dr. Louis J. Rodriguez	227	5,694	2,313	NA
Mountain View College—Dallas (See **Dallas County Community College District**)				
Navarro College—Corsicana; (7); 1946; Dr. Richard Sanchez	226	3,500	1,600	1,200
North Central Texas College—Gainesville; 1924 (as **Gainesville Jr. College; Cooke County College**, 1960; present name, 1994); Dr. Ronnie Glasscock	242	4,041	1,597	431
Northeast Texas Community College—Mount Pleasant; (7); 1984; Dr. Charles B. Florio	120	2,045	1,360	635
‡‡NORTH HARRIS MONTGOMERY COMMUNITY COLLEGE DISTRICT (9)— John E. Pickelman, Chancellor. Includes these colleges, location (president): **Kingwood College**, Kingwood (Dr. Steve Head); **Montgomery College**, Conroe (Dr. Bill Law); **North Harris College**, Houston (Dr. Sanford Shugart); **Tomball College**, Tomball (Dr. Diane Troyer)	1,116	22,018	12,480	12,300
North Lake College—Irving (See **Dallas County Community College District**)				
Northwest Vista College (see **Alamo Community College District**)				
Northwood University—Cedar Hill; private; 1966; Dr. David E. Fry	36	1,295	NA	NA
Oblate School of Theology—San Antonio; Rom. Catholic, 4-yr.; 1903 (formerly **DeMazenod Scholasticate**); Rev. J. William Morell, O.M.I.	29	130	47	148
Odessa College—Odessa; (7); 1946; Dr. Vance E. Gipson	248	4,589	1,628	1,669
Our Lady of the Lake University of San Antonio—San Antonio; (3 - Catholic); 1895 (as acad. for girls; sr. college, 1911; university, in 1975); Sally Mahoney	259	3,689	§ 663	NA
Palo Alto College—San Antonio (See **Alamo Community College District**)				
Panola College—Carthage; (7); 1947 (as **Panola Junior College**; name changed, 1988); Dr. William F. Edmonson	¶¶ 57	1,510	§ 1,398	359
Paris Junior College—Paris; (7); 1924; Bobby R. Walters	305	3,103	1,084	3,647
Paul Quinn College—Dallas; (3); 1872 (in Waco; Dallas, 1990); Dr. Lee E. Monroe	43	741	0	130
Prairie View A&M University—Prairie View (See **Texas A&M University System**)				
Ranger College—Ranger; (7); 1926; Dr. Joe Mills	61	827	§ 705	60
Rice University (William Marsh)—Houston; (3); chartered 1891, opened 1912 (as **Rice Institute**; name changed in 1960); Dr. Malcolm Gillis	548	4,479	NA	4,111
Richland College—Dallas (See **Dallas County Community College District**)				
St. Edward's University—Austin; (3 - Roman Catholic); 1885; Dr. Robert Funk (interim)	246	3,422	1,410	NA
St. Mary's University of San Antonio—San Antonio; (3 - Catholic); 1852; Rev. John Moder	178	4,189	2,175	143
St. Philip's College—San Antonio (See **Alamo Community College District**)				
Sam Houston State University—Huntsville (See **Texas State University System**)				
San Antonio College—San Antonio (See **Alamo Community College District**)				
‡ SAN JACINTO COLLEGE DISTRICT (9) —Dr. Dr. James Horton, Chancellor. Includes these campuses, location (president): **Central**, Pasadena (Dr. Monte Blue); **North**, Houston (Dr. Edwin C. Lehr); **South**, Houston (Dr. Parker Williams)	—	19,374	—	—
Schreiner College—Kerrville; (3 - Presbyterian); 1923; Dr. J. Thompson Biggers	97	757	120	NA
South Plains College—Levelland; (7); 1957; Dr. Gary D. McDaniel	333	6,687	3,791	2,207
South Texas College of Law—Houston; private, 3-yr.; 1923; Frank T. Read, Dean and Pres.	59	1,200	530	NA
South Texas Community College—McAllen; (7); NA; Dr. Shirley A. Reed	444	9,460	6,897	1,161
‡ Southern Methodist University—Dallas; (3 - Methodist); 1911; Dr. R. Gerald Turner	—	10,038	—	—
Southwest Collegiate Institute for the Deaf — Big Spring (See **Howard College**)				
Southwestern Adventist University—Keene; (3 - Seventh-Day Adventist); 1893 (as **Keene Industrial Acad.**; named **Southwestern Jr. College** in 1916; changed to **Southwestern Union College** in 1963, then to **Southwestern Adventist College** in 1980; became university in 1996); Dr. Marvin Anderson	49	1,165	297	NA
Southwestern Assemblies of God University—Waxahachie; (3 - Assemblies of God); 1927 (in Enid, Okla., as **Southwestern Bible School**; moved to Fort Worth and merged with **South Central Bible Institute** in 1941; moved to Waxahachie as **Southwestern Bible Institute** in 1943; changed to **Southwestern Assemblies of God College**,1963; university since 1996); Dr. Delmer R. Guynes	58	1,622	NA	NA
Southwestern Baptist Theological Seminary—Fort Worth; Southern Baptist, 4-yr.; 1908; Dr. Kenneth S.Hemphill.	201	3,676	NA	514

Name of Institution; Location; (Type* - Ownership, if private sectarian institution); Date of Founding; President (unless otherwise noted)	Number in Faculty†	Enrollment		
		Fall Term 1998	Summer Session 1998	Extension or Continuing Ed.
Southwestern Christian College—Terrell; (3 - Church of Christ); 1948 (as Southern Bible Inst. in Fort Worth; moved to Terrell, changed name to present, 1950); Dr. Jack Evans Sr.	30	†† 200	30	NA
Southwestern University—Georgetown; (3 - Methodist); 1840 (Southwestern University was a merger of Rutersville (1840), Wesleyan (1846) and McKenzie (1841) colleges and Soule University (1855). First named Texas University; chartered under present name in 1875); Dr. Roy B. Shilling Jr.	150	1,255	539	NA
Southwest Texas Junior College—Uvalde; (7); 1946; Dr. Ismael Sosa	164	3,518	1,846	500
Southwest Texas State University—San Marcos (see Texas State University System)				
Stephen F. Austin State University—Nacogdoches; (2); 1921; Dr. Dan Angel	638	12,132	6,007	3,209
Sul Ross State University—Alpine (See Texas State University System)				
Sul Ross State University-Rio Grande College —Uvalde (See Texas State University System)				
Tarleton State University—Stephenville (See Texas A&M University System)				
Tarrant County College District—Fort Worth; (7); 1965 (as Tarrant County Junior College; name changed 1999); four campuses (location, campus president): Northeast (Hurst, Dr. Larry Darlage), Northwest (Fort Worth, Dr. Michael Saenz), South (Fort Worth, Dr. Ernest L. Thomas) and Southeast (Arlington, Dr. Judith J. Carrier); Dr. Leonardo de la Garza, Chancellor	1,170	25,570	7,251	10,520
Temple College—Temple; (7); 1926; Dr. Marc A. Nigliazzo	177	3,147	1,250	2,863
Texarkana College—Texarkana; (7); 1927; Dr. Carl M. Nelson	205	4,003	1,947	5,000
Texas A&I University—Kingsville (See Texas A&M University-Kingsville listing under Texas A&M University System)				
TEXAS A&M UNIVERSITY SYSTEM (1) —Dr. Howard D. Graves, Chancellor				
‡ Baylor College of Dentistry—Dallas; (5); 1905 (transferred to Texas A&M system 1995) Richard N. Buchanan	—	—	—	—
‡ Prairie View A&M University—Prairie View; (2); 1876 (as Alta Vista Agricultural College; changed to Prairie View State Normal Institute in 1879; later Prairie View Normal and Industrial College; in 1947 changed to Prairie View A&M College as branch of Texas A&M University System; present name since 1973); Dr. Charles A. Hines	—	5,995	—	—
Tarleton State University—Stephenville; (2); 1899 (as John Tarleton College; taken over by state in 1917 as John Tarleton Agricultural College; changed 1949 to Tarleton State College; present name since 1973); Dr. Dennis McCabe	359	6,333	2,944	NA
Tarleton State University Systems Center/Central Texas—Killeen; (3); 1973 (originally American Technological University; name changed to University of Central Texas, 1989; changed to present name in 1999); (Vacancy)	70	1,650	1,120	NA
Texas A&M International University-Laredo; (2); 1970 (as Laredo State University; name changed to present form 1993); Dr. J. Charles Jennett	155	3,001	§ 2,928	875
Texas A&M University—College Station; (2); 1876 (as Agricultural and Mechanical College of Texas; present name since 1963; includes College of Veterinary Medicine and College of Medicine at College Station); Dr. Ray M. Bowen	2,400	43,389	16,368	NA
Texas A&M University - Commerce—Commerce; (2); 1889 (as East Texas Normal College; renamed East Texas State Teachers College in 1923; "Teachers" dropped, 1957; university status conferred and named changed to East Texas State University, 1965; transferred to Texas A&M system 1995; includes ETSU Metroplex Commuter Facility, Mesquite); Dr. Keith D. McFarland	248	7,600	§ 6,054	2,936
Texas A&M University-Corpus Christi—Corpus Christi; (2); 1973 (as upper-level Corpus Christi State Univ.; present name since 1993; 4-year in 1994); Dr. Robert R. Furgason	¶ 278	6,335	§ 6,076	NA
Texas A&M University at Galveston—Galveston; (2); 1962 (as Texas Maritime Academy; changed to Moody College of Marine Sciences and Maritime Resources and became 4-yr. college in 1971); Dr. Michael Kemp, Vice President	100	1,250	500	400
Texas A&M University-Kingsville—Kingsville; (2); 1925 (as South Texas Teachers College; name changed to Texas College of Arts and Industries in 1929, to Texas A&I University in 1967; made part of Univ. of South Texas System in 1977; entered A&M system in 1993); Dr. Marc Cisneros	344	5,937	§ 6,241	NA
Texas A&M University - Texarkana—Texarkana; (2 - upper-level); 1971 (as East Texas State University at Texarkana, transferred to Texas A&M system and name changed, 1995); Dr. Stephen R. Hensley	32	1,153	631	NA
West Texas A&M University—Canyon; (2); 1910 (as West Texas State Normal College; became West Texas State Teachers College in 1923; West Texas State College, 1949; changed to West Texas State Univ., 1949; present name, 1993); Dr. Russell C. Long	363	6,348	§ 3,994	298
Texas Baptist Institute-Seminary—Henderson; (3 - Calvary Baptist); 1948; Dr. Ray O. Brooks	13	46	47	NA
Texas Christian University—Fort Worth; (3 - Disciples of Christ); 1873 (as Add- Ran College at Thorp Spring; name changed to Add-Ran Christian Univ. 1890; moved to Waco 1895; present name, 1902; moved to Fort Worth 1910); Dr. Michael R. Ferrari, Chancellor	550	7,395	2,360	120
Texas College—Tyler; (3 - C.M.E.); 1894; Dr. Haywood L. Strickland	40	292	NA	NA
Texas College of Osteopathic Medicine—Fort Worth (See University of North Texas Health Science Center at Fort Worth)				
Texas Lutheran University—Seguin; (3 - Lutheran); 1891 (in Brenham as Evangelical Lutheran College; moved to Seguin, 1912 and renamed Lutheran College of Seguin; renamed Texas Lutheran College, 1932; changed to university, 1996); Dr. Jon N. Moline	152	416	NA	NA
Texas Southern University—Houston; (2); 1926 (as Houston Colored Junior Coll.; upper level added, name changed to Houston College for Negroes in mid-1930s; became Texas State University for Negroes, 1947; present name, 1951); Priscilla Slade (acting)	115	1,520	350	2,000
	300	7,000	2,200	NA

Name of Institution; Location; (Type* - Ownership, if private sectarian institution); Date of Founding; President (unless otherwise noted)	Number in Faculty†	Enrollment		
		Fall Term 1998	Summer Session 1998	Extension or Continuing Ed.
Texas Southmost College—Brownsville (see The University of Texas at Brownsville under University of Texas System listing)				
‡‡TEXAS STATE TECHNICAL COLLEGE SYSTEM (6) — Bill Segura, Chancellor	623	8,727	6,388	1,628
Includes these colleges, locations (campus president): Texas State Technical College-Harlingen (Dr. Gilbert Leal);Texas State Technical College-Sweetwater (Homer Taylor, interim campus president);Texas State Technical College- Waco (established as James Connally Technical Institute; name changed in 1969), (Dr. Fred Williams) (The system also includes extension centers in Abilene, Breckenridge, Brownwood and Marshall.)				
TEXAS STATE UNIVERSITY SYSTEM (1)—Dr. Lamar G. Urbanovsky, Chancellor				
Angelo State University—San Angelo; (2); 1928; Dr. E. James Hindman	229	6,315	3,485	1,225
Lamar University—Beaumont; (2); 1923 (as South Park Junior Coll.; name changed to Lamar Coll., 1932; name changed to Lamar State Coll. of Technology, 1951; present name, 1971; transferred from Lamar Univ. System, 1995); Dr. William Johnson	423	8,241	5,115	79
Lamar University - Orange—Orange; (10); 1969 (transferred from Lamar University System, Sept. 1995); Dr. J. Michael Shahan	176	1,574	665	54
‡ Lamar University - Port Arthur—Port Arthur; (10); 1909 (as Port Arthur College; became part of Lamar Univ. in 1975; part of TSU system, 1995); Dr. W. Sam Monroe	—	2,401	—	—
Lamar University Institute of Technology—Beaumont; (10); (part of TSU system, 1995); Dr. Robert D. Krienke	135	2,056	NA	NA
Sam Houston State University—Huntsville; (2); 1879; Dr. Bobby K. Marks	525	12,205	8,662	1,765
Southwest Texas State University—San Marcos; (2); 1903 (as Southwest Texas Normal School; changed1918 to Southwest Texas State Normal College, in 1923 to Southwest Texas State Teachers College, in 1959 to Southwest Texas State College, and in 1969 to present form); Dr. Jerome H. Supple	946	21,504	8,358	468
Sul Ross State University—Alpine; (2); 1917 (as Sul Ross State Normal Coll.; changed to Sul Ross State Teachers Coll., 1923; to Sul Ross State Coll., 1949; present name since 1969); Dr. R. Vic Morgan	161	3,103	§ 6,222	NA
Sul Ross State University-Rio Grande College—Uvalde; (2 - upper-level); 1973 (name changed from Sul Ross State University, Uvalde Center 1995); Dr. Frank Abbott, Dean	31	856	657	NA
TEXAS TECH UNIVERSITY (1) —Dr. Donald Haragan, Chancellor				
Texas Tech University—Lubbock; (2); 1923 (as Texas Technological College; present name since 1969); Dr. Donald R. Haragan	1,745	24,158	9,049	2,400
Texas Tech University Health Sciences Center—Lubbock; (4); 1972; David Smith, M.D.	516	1,547	NA	NA
Texas Wesleyan University—Fort Worth; (3 - United Methodist); 1891 (as college; present name since 1989); Dr. Jake B. Schrum	320	3,086	1,652	NA
Texas Woman's University—Denton; (2); 1901 (as Coll. of Industrial Arts; name changed to Texas State Coll. for Women, 1934; present name, 1957); Dr. Beverley Byers-Pevitts (interim)	§§ 500	9,356	5,000	5,000
Trinity University—San Antonio; (3 - Presbyterian); 1869 (at Tehuacana; moved to Waxahachie, 1902; to San Antonio, 1942); Dr. John R. Brazil	218	2,571	352	NA
Trinity Valley Community College—Athens; also campus at Terrell; (7); 1946 (originally Henderson County Junior College); Dr. Ronald C. Baugh	121	4,623	3,059	1,737
Tyler Junior College—Tyler; (7); 1926; Dr. William R. Crowe	410	8,000	2,300	3,500
University of Central Texas—Killeen (see Texas A&M University System, Tarleton State University Systems Center/Central Texas)				
‡ University of Dallas—Irving; (3 - Catholic); 1956; Msgr. Milam J. Joseph	—	3,086	—	—
UNIVERSITY OF HOUSTON SYSTEM (1) — Arthur K. Smith, Chancellor				
‡ University of Houston—Houston; (2); 1927; Arthur K. Smith	—	32,296	—	—
University of Houston-Clear Lake—Houston; (2 - upper level and grad.); 1974; Dr. William A. Staples	424	6,806	3,939	1,000
University of Houston-Downtown—Houston; (2); 1948 (as South Texas College; became part of University of Houston in 1974) ; Dr. Max Castillo	453	8,325	3,573	697
University of Houston-Victoria—Victoria; (2 - upper-level); 1973; Dr. Karen S. Haynes	90	1,512	§ 1,480	739
University of the Incarnate Word—San Antonio; (3 - Catholic); 1881 (as Incarnate Word College; name changed 1996); Dr. Louis J. Agnese Jr.	333	3,583	939	681
University of Mary Hardin-Baylor—Belton; (3 - So. Baptist); 1845; Dr. Jerry G. Bawcom	104	2,479	1,115	NA
University of North Texas—Denton; (2); 1890 (as North Texas Normal College; name changed 1923 to North Texas State Teachers Coll.e; in 1949 to North Texas State Coll.; became university, 1961; present name since 1988); Dr. Alfred F. Hurley, Chancellor	1,851	25,514	§21,864	2,945
University of North Texas Health Science Center at Fort Worth—Fort Worth; (4);1966 (as private college; came under direction of North Texas State University in 1975; present name since 1993); Dr. David M. Richards	203	672	NA	NA
University of St. Thomas—Houston; (3); 1947; Fr. J. Michael Miller, CSB	215	2,696	1,576	NA
UNIVERSITY OF TEXAS SYSTEM (1) —William H. Cunningham, Chancellor (Retirement announced, effective August 2000)				
University of Texas at Arlington, The—Arlington; (2); 1895 (as Arlington Coll.; became state inst. in 1917 and renamed Grubbs Vocational Coll.; 1923 became North Texas Agricultural and Mechanical Coll.; became Arlington State Coll., 1949; present name since 1967); Dr. Robert E. Witt	1,215	18,662	§12,530	4,716

Name of Institution; Location; (Type* - Ownership, if private sectarian institution); Date of Founding; President (unless otherwise noted)	Number in Faculty†	Enrollment		
		Fall Term 1998	Summer Session 1998	Extension or Contin-uing Ed.
University of Texas at Austin, The—Austin; (2); 1883; Dr. Larry R. Faulkner	2,700	48,906	18,004	27,176
University of Texas at Brownsville, The (2 - upper-level) 1973 (as branch of Pan American Coll.; changed to Univ. of Texas-Pan American - Brownsville; present name, 1991) and Texas Southmost College (7); 1926 (as Brownsville Jr. Coll.; name changed, 1949) — Brownsville; Dr.Juliet V. Garcia.	235	8,144	§7,010	1,252
University of Texas at Dallas, The—Richardson; (2); 1961 (as Graduate Research Center of the Southwest; changed to Southwest Center for Advanced Studies in 1967; joined U.T. System and present name, 1969; full undergraduate program, 1975); Dr. Franklyn G. Jenifer.	463	9,517	5,340	NA
‡ University of Texas at El Paso, The—El Paso; (2); 1913 (as Texas Coll. of Mines and Metallurgy; changed to Texas Western Coll. of U.T., 1949; present name, 1967); Dr. Diana S. Natalicio	—	14,677	—	—
University of Texas-Pan American, The—Edinburg; (2); 1927 (as Edinburg Junior Coll.; changed to Pan American College and made 4-yr., 1952; became Pan American University in 1971; present name since 1991); Dr. Miguel A. Nevárez	530	12,373	§11,428	NA
‡ University of Texas of the Permian Basin, The—Odessa; (2); 1969 (as 2-yr. upper- level institution; expanded to 4-yr., Sept. 1991); Dr. Charles A. Sorber	—	2,214	—	—
University of Texas at San Antonio—San Antonio; (2); 1969; Dr.Ricardo Romo	858	18,397	8,734	NA
University of Texas at Tyler—Tyler; (2 - upper-level); 1971 (as Tyler State Coll.; became Texas Eastern University, 1975; joined U.T. System, 1979); Dr. Rodney H. Mabry	163	3.375	1,764	NA
UNIVERSITY OF TEXAS HEALTH SCIENCE CENTER AT HOUSTON (4) — Dr. M. David Low . . . . Established 1972; consists of following divisions (year of founding): Dental Branch (1905); Graduate School of Biomedical Sciences (1963); Medical School (1970); School of Allied Health Sciences (1973); School of Nursing (1972); School of Public Health (1967); Division of Continuing Education (1958).	¶ 993	3,140	3,140	NA
UNIVERSITY OF TEXAS HEALTH SCIENCE CENTER AT SAN ANTONIO (4) —Dr. John P. Howe III . . . . Established 1968; consists of following divisions (year of founding): Dental School (1970); Graduate School of Biomedical Sciences (1970); Health Science Center (1972); Medical School (1959 as South Texas Medical School of UT; present name, 1966); School of Allied Health Sciences (1976); School of Nursing (1969).	1,317	2,703	945	11,724
UNIVERSITY OF TEXAS MEDICAL BRANCH AT GALVESTON (4) — Dr. John D. Stobo . . . . Established 1891; consists of following divisions (year of founding): Graduate School of Biomedical Sciences (1952); Medical School (1891); School of Allied Health Sciences (1968); School of Nursing (1890).	2,362	1,987	NA	NA
UNIVERSITY OF TEXAS SOUTHWESTERN MEDICAL CENTER AT DALLAS (4) — Dr. Kern Wildenthal . . . . Established 1943 (as private institution; became Southwestern Medical Coll. of UT 1948; became UT Southwestern Medical School at Dallas, 1967; made part of UT Health Science Center at Dallas, 1972; consists of following divisions (year of founding): Graduate School of Biomedical Sciences (1947); School of Allied Health Sciences (1968); Southwestern Medical School (1943).	1,299	1,533	NA	NA
Vernon Regional Junior College—Vernon; (7); 1970; Dr. Wade Kirk	53	1,936	1,092	2,238
Victoria College, The —Victoria; (7); 1925; Dr. Jimmy Goodson	202	3,800	1,625	995
Wayland Baptist University—Plainview; (3 -Southern Baptist); 1910; Dr. Wallace Davis Jr..	84	4,395	6,576	NA
Weatherford College—Weatherford; (7); 1869 (as branch of Southwestern Univ.; 1922, became denominational junior college; became muni. jr. college, 1949); Dr. Don Huff. . . .	436	2,585	1,950	**
Western Texas College—Snyder; (7); 1969; Dr. Harry Krenek.	37	1,186	893	1,128
Wharton County Junior College—Wharton; (7); 1946; Dr. Frank Robert Vivelo.	115	4,213	1,662	1,226
‡Wiley College—Marshall; (3 - Methodist); 1873; Dr. Ronald L. Swain	—	659	—	—

*Type: (1) Public University System
     (2) Public University
     (3) Independent Senior College or University
     (4) Public Medical School or Health Science Center
     (5) Independent Medical or Dental School

(6) Public Technical College System
(7) Public Community College
(8) Independent Junior College
(9) Public Community College System
(10) Public Lower-Level Institution

† Unless otherwise noted, faculty count includes professors, associate professors, adjunct professors, instructors and tutors, both full and part-time, but does not include voluntary instructors.
‡ No reply received to questionnaire. Name of president and number of students enrolled in fall 1998 was obtained from the Texas Higher Education Coordinating Board Web site: www.thecb.state.tx.us.
§ Includes all students in two summer sessions.
¶ Full-time equivalents
** Information not supplied by institution.
†† Approximate count.
‡‡ Includes faculty and enrollment at all branches or divisions.
§§ Approximate count of full-time faculty only.
¶¶ Full-time faculty only.
NA - Not applicable

Belo Growing with Texas

Belo, a Dallas-based media concern, has a history parallel to that of Texas itself. Pioneered in 1842 as the one-page *Galveston News*, Belo has grown to become a leading diversified media company, encompassing newspaper publishing and network-affiliated television broadcasting op-erations across the country. The *Texas Almanac* is published by Belo's flagship newspaper, *The Dallas Morning News*.

The Early Days

Belo is the oldest continuously operating business in Texas. Founded by Samuel Bangs, a transplanted publisher from Boston, the company was in the publishing business three years before the Republic of Texas achieved statehood. Bangs sold the business within a year of its founding to Wilbur F. Cherry and Michael Cronican, and Cherry soon acquired sole ownership.

Another Massachusetts émigré, Willard Richardson, became editor of the paper a few years later. He campaigned editorially for annexation, fiscal responsibility and railroads. In 1857, Richardson conceived and founded the *Texas Almanac*, which he hoped would help attract settlers to the new state. Eight years later, he hired A.H. Belo, for whom the company was eventually named.

A.H. Belo, a former Confederate colonel from North Carolina, joined the company as bookkeeper. He was made a full partner in the growing company after only three months and carved out a new life for himself in the Southwest.

Nine years later, George Bannerman Dealey, a 15-year-old English emigrant, was hired as an office boy. Dealey, too, quickly moved up in the company. Working tirelessly, Dealey made his way from office boy to business manager and then to publisher of *The Dallas Morning News*. It was Dealey who chose the then-small settlement of Dallas as the site for a sister publication. Dealey and several other members of the *Galveston News*' staff relocated to Dallas, and the company prospered and grew.

Belo Was a Radio Broadcasting Pioneer

On June 26, 1922, Belo began operating a 50-watt radio station, WFAA-AM, which was the first network station in the state. The company sold its radio properties in 1987.

The Publishing Division

The Dallas Morning News began publication on Oct. 1, 1885, with a circulation of 5,000 subscribers. After being in operation only two months, *The Dallas Morning News* acquired its first competitor, the *Dallas Herald* (not to be confused with the *Dallas Times Herald* that closed in December 1991). Rather than compete with each other for subscribers, the two newspapers combined, keeping the name of *The Dallas Morning News*, but dating itself with the volume number of the former *Dallas Herald*.

In 1906, on the 21st anniversary of *The Dallas Morning News*, Dealey gave a speech that became the motto for the company: "Build The News upon the rock of truth and righteousness. Conduct it always upon the lines of fairness and integrity. Acknowledge the right of the people to get from the newspaper both sides of every important question." Today these words are carved in a three-story-high space above the entrance to *The Dallas Morning News*. The News building, a long-standing dream of Dealey's, was completed in 1949, three years after his death.

While Belo has become one of the nation's largest diversified media companies, *The Dallas Morning News* remains the flagship newspaper of the Company's publishing business.

On Dec. 26, 1995, Belo purchased *The Eagle*, a daily newspaper serving Bryan-College Station, and on Jan. 5, 1996, Belo acquired the *Messenger-Inquirer*, a daily newspaper in Owensboro, Ky.

On April 3, 1996, Belo launched the *Arlington Morning News* in Arlington, Texas. The newspaper was originally distributed Wednesday through Saturday, but it began daily publication in July 1996.

In 1997, Belo held a 38.45 percent interest in *The Press-Enterprise*, a daily newspaper serving Riverside County and the inland Southern California area. In July 1997, the Company purchased the remaining interest in The Press-Enterprise Company.

Through the acquisition of The Providence Journal Company on Feb. 28, 1997, Belo acquired *The Providence Journal*, the leading newspaper in Rhode Island and southeastern Massachusetts. Founded in 1829, *The Providence Journal* is America's oldest major daily newspaper of general circulation in continuous publication.

Belo acquired the assets of The Gleaner and Journal Publishing Company of Henderson, Ky., on March 31, 1997. Those assets included *The Gleaner*, a daily newspaper in Henderson, Ky.; seven weekly newspapers; printing operations; and an AM radio station.

On July 2, 1999, Belo acquired the Denton Publishing Company, whose assets include the *Denton Record-Chronicle*, a daily newspaper serving Denton County, and two free-distribution newspapers, the *Lewisville News* and *The Grapevine Sun*.

The Broadcast Division

Belo entered the television broadcasting business in 1950 with the acquisition of its flagship station, ABC affiliate WFAA-TV in Dallas/Fort Worth. In 1983, in the nation's largest broadcast acquisition to date, Belo acquired KHOU-TV (CBS) in Houston; KXTV (ABC), Sacramento/Stockton/Modesto, Calif.; WVEC-TV (ABC), Hampton/Norfolk, Va.; and KOTV (CBS), Tulsa, Okla. In June 1994, Belo acquired WWL-TV (CBS) in New Orleans, and in Sept. 1994, the company acquired KIRO-TV, Seattle/Tacoma, Wash.

On Feb. 28, 1997, Belo acquired The Providence Journal Company, the largest transaction to date in the Company's history. The acquisition included five NBC affiliates (KING-TV in Seattle/Tacoma, Wash.; KGW-TV, Portland, Ore.; WCNC-TV, Charlotte, N.C.; KHNL-TV, Honolulu, Hawaii; and KTVB-TV, Boise, Idaho); one ABC affiliate (WHAS-TV, Louisville, Ky.); one CBS affiliate (KREM-TV, Spokane, Wash.); two FOX affiliates (KASA-TV, Albuquerque/Santa Fe, and KMSB-TV, Tucson); and NorthWest Cable News (NWCN), Seattle/Tacoma. Belo also assumed the management of four television stations through local marketing agreements and became the managing general partner of The Television Food Network in New York, N.Y.

In connection with the acquisition of The Providence Journal Company, Belo agreed to exchange KIRO-TV for a station in another market to comply with Federal Communications Commission regulations, which prohibit a company from owning multiple television stations in a single market. The agreement resulted in Belo's June 2, 1997, acquisition of KMOV-TV (CBS) in St. Louis, Mo.

In early 1997, the Company opened its Capital Bureau in Washington, D.C., which houses Washington-based journalists representing the Company's 17 network-affiliated television stations as well as *The Dallas Morning News* and *The Providence Journal*.

With a strategy to focus on its two core businesses of television broadcasting and newspaper publishing, on Dec. 4, 1997, Belo exchanged its interest in the Television Food Network for KENS-TV (CBS) and KENS-AM in San Antonio.

On Feb.27, 1998, Belo's WFAA made television history by becoming the first VHF station in the country to transmit a digital signal on a permanent basis.

On Jan. 1, 1999, Belo launched Texas Cable News (TXCN), the first 24-hour regional cable news channel in Texas.

In May 1999, the Company formed Belo Online Inc. to pursue the development of online initiatives. Belo Enterprises was also formed to serve as a vehicle for the Company's investments in a variety of media businesses.

On June 1, 1999, Belo exchanged KXTV (ABC) in Sacramento/Stockton/Modesto for KVUE-TV (ABC) in Austin. This transaction increased Belo's reach to 67 percent of television households in Texas.

Today, Belo's Broadcast Division reaches 13.6 percent of all television households in the United States.

Officers and Directors

Officers of Belo are: Robert W. Decherd, chairman of the board, president and chief executive officer; Ward L. Huey Jr., vice chairman of the board, president/Broadcast Division; Burl Osborne president/Publishing Division, publisher, *The Dallas Morning News*; Michael J. McCarthy, executive vice president/general counsel; James M. Moroney, executive vice president, president, Belo Online Inc.; Dunia A. Shive, senior vice president/chief financial officer; Marian Spitzberg, secretary, vice president/deputy general counsel; Janice E. Bryant, vice president/controller; Harold F. Gaar Jr., vice president/financial and investor relations; Carey P. Hendrickson, vice president/strategic and financial planning; A. Jeff Lamb, vice president/administration; Brenda C. Maddox, vice president/treasurer; Jon Roe, vice president/information technology; Stephen E. Shelton, vice president/internal audit; Regina A. Sullivan, vice president/government and public affairs.

Members of Belo's board of directors are: John W. Bassett Jr.; Henry P. Becton Jr.; Judith L. Craven, M.D.; Robert W. Decherd; Roger A. Enrico; Stephen Hamblett; Dealey D. Herndon; Laurence E. Hirsch; Ward L. Huey Jr.; Arturo Madrid, Ph.D.; James M. Moroney Jr.; Burl Osborne; Hugh G. Robinson; William T. Solomon; and J. McDonald Williams.

Officers of Belo's Publishing Division include Burl Osborne, president; J. William Cox, senior vice president; and Dale Peskin, vice president/interactive media. Officers of *The Dallas Morning News* are Robert W. Mong Jr., president and general manager; Gilbert Bailon, vice president/executive editor; Stuart Wilk, managing editor; Rena Pederson, vice president/editorial page editor; Barry T. Peckham, executive vice president/operations; W. Richard Starks, senior vice president/sales and marketing; Fritzi G. Pikes, senior vice president/finance and administration; Sergio Salinas, vice president/advertising; Jeffrey A. Beckley, vice president/circulation; Susan Baker, vice president/finance; Nancy Barry, vice president/community services; Kate Rose Murphy, vice president/marketing; Ellen Silva Wilson, vice president/human resources; Ric Lutz, vice president/information technology; and Paul F. Webb, vice president/production.

Howard G. Sutton is publisher, president and chief executive officer of The Providence Journal Company. Officers of *The Providence Journal* are Joel P. Rawson, senior vice president and executive editor; Mark T. Ryan, senior vice president/legal and administration; Joel N. Stark, senior vice president/marketing and development; Robert A. Shadrick, senior vice president/operations; Robert B. Whitcomb, vice president editorial pages editor; Donald J. Ross, vice president/advertising; Carol Young, deputy executive editor; Michael J. Dooley, vice president/circulation; and Sandra J. Radcliffe, vice president/financial.

Officers of *The Press-Enterprise* include Marcia McQuern, president, editor and publisher. Officers of the *Messenger-Inquirer* include T. Edward Riney, publisher; Robert H. Ashley, editor; Dan Heckel, editorial page editor; and Laura Skillman, region editor. Officers of *The Eagle* include Donnis G. Baggett, publisher and editor; Joe Michael Feist, managing editor; and Robert C. Borden, opinions editor. Officers of the *Arlington Morning News* include Gary Jacobson, publisher and editor; Lawrence Young, managing editor; and June De Rousse, advertising director. Officers of *The Gleaner* include Steve Austin, publisher; Tony Maddox, general manager; Ron Jenkins, editor; and David Dixon, managing editor. Officers of the *Denton Record-Chronicle* include Bill Patterson, publisher and chief executive officer; Fred Patterson, publisher emeritus; and Jim Flansburg, executive editor.

Officers of Belo's Broadcast Division include Ward L. Huey Jr., president; Jack Sander, president/Television Group; H. Martin Haag Jr., senior vice president/news; Lee R. Salzberger, senior vice president/Television Group; Glenn C. Wright, senior vice president/Television Group; and Cathleen A. Creany, senior vice president/Television Group; Robert Turner, vice president/engineering services; J. William Mosley, vice president/controller; Flory Bramnick, vice president/interactive media; Sherri Brennen, vice president/management development. Officers of Belo's television stations are Kathy Clements-Hill, president and general manager, WFAA-TV; Peter Diaz, president and general manager, KHOU-TV; Dennis Williamson, president and general manager, KING-TV; Allan Cohen, president and general manager, KMOV-TV;

Ronald S. Longinotti, vice president and general manager, KGW-TV; Richard J. Keilty, president and general manager, WCNC-TV; Robert G. McGann, vice president and general manager, KENS-TV; Mario A. Hewitt, vice president and general manager, WVEC-TV; Jimmie Phillips, vice president and general manager, WWL-TV; Kenneth L. Middleton, president and general manager, WHAS-TV; Erick Steffens, president and general manager, KASA-TV; Albert (Bud) Brown, vice president and general manager, KOTV; Patti C. Smith, vice president and general manager, KVUE-TV; John L. Fink, president and general manager, KHNL-TV; Barry C. Barth, president and general manager, KREM-TV; Diane E. Frisch, vice president and general manager, KMSB-TV; Douglas Armstrong, president and general manager, KTVB-TV; and R. Paul Fry, vice president and general manager, KONG-TV.

David M. Cassidy is the broadcast bureau chief and Carl P. Leubsdorf is the publishing bureau chief for Belo's Capital Bureau; Craig E. Marrs is president and general manager of NorthWest Cable News; and Donald F. (Skip) Cass Jr., is vice president and general manager of Texas Cable News.

Robert W. Decherd

Robert W. Decherd has worked for Belo or its principal newspaper subsidiary, *The Dallas Morning News*, since his graduation from Harvard College in 1973.

Decherd graduated cum laude from Harvard, where he was president of the *Harvard Crimson*, recipient of an Honorary Freshman Scholarship, winner of the David McCord Award for literary contributions and class orator for the Class of 1973. Decherd began his career with Belo in a management-training program at *The Dallas Morning News*. Following three years in that program, Decherd was appointed assistant to the executive editor of *The Dallas Morning News*. In 1978, he became the company's first corporate staff executive. Beginning in 1991, Decherd served successively as vice president, executive vice president, chief operating officer and president of the Company.

In addition to his executive role, Decherd is Belo's largest shareholder. He was elected to the Company's board of directors in 1976, and he also serves as a director of Kimberly-Clark Corporation.

Decherd is a past president of the Dallas Society of Professional Journalists and the Freedom of Information Foundation of Texas Inc. He has served as a director and member of the executive committee of the Newspaper Association of America (NAA) and chaired NAA's Public Policy Committee. He has served on committees of the American Newspaper Publishers Association, the Southern Newspaper Publishers Association and as a director of the Newspaper Advertising Bureau.

In civic affairs, Decherd is a past president of several organizations, including the Dallas Symphony Association and St. Mark's School of Texas. As chairman of fund-raising campaigns for institutions ranging from St. Mark's to the YWCA to Paul Quinn College, Decherd has raised more than $100 million. He has been particularly active in public planning policy initiatives and in organizations that promote racial understanding and cooperation, such as the Tomás Rivera Policy Institute and the Dallas Together Forum.

Decherd has received a variety of industry and civic awards over the past two decades, including a citation of honor from the American Institute of Architects (1981), American Newspaper Executive of the Year (1985), the James Madison Award from the Freedom of Information Foundation of Texas Inc. (1989), the Henry Cohn Humanitarian Award from the Anti-Defamation League (1991), the Distinguished Alumnus Award from St. Mark's School of Texas (1998), and The Media Institute's Freedom of Speech Award (1998). In 1995, he became the youngest inductee ever to the Texas Business Hall of Fame.

Decherd is a great-grandson of George Bannerman Dealey, who founded *The Dallas Morning News* in 1885 and guided it until his death in 1946. Decherd's grandmother, Fannie Dealey Decherd, was G. B. Dealey's daughter. His father, H. Ben Decherd, served as Belo's chairman from 1968 until his death in 1972.

Ward L. Huey Jr.

Ward L. Huey Jr. has worked for Belo and played a role in

the Company's broadcast operations since 1960.

A 1960 graduate of Southern Methodist University, Huey worked as a copywriter and an account executive for Glenn Advertising in Dallas before joining Belo as part of WFAA-TV's production department. In 1961, Huey became the sales service manager, and over the next 10 years he served in a variety of sales and marketing positions at WFAA, including account executive, regional sales manager and general sales manager. He was also director of sales for Belo television stations

Huey was promoted to station manager of WFAA in 1972 and became a vice president in 1973. In 1975, he was named vice president and general manager of Belo's broadcast properties. He was elected a director of Belo in 1982 and vice chairman of the board in 1987. Huey was named president of Belo's Broadcast Division in 1987 and also serves on Belo's six-member Management Committee. In addition to his primary executive responsibilities, Huey is a trustee of the A.H. Belo Corporation Foundation.

Currently, Huey serves on the board of the Maximum Service Television Association and the Television Operators Caucus. He is a past chairman of both the ABC Television Affiliates Board of Governors and the Television Operators Caucus Board of Directors, and he has served on the board of the Television Bureau of Advertising.

In civic affairs, Huey serves as a trustee of Southern Methodist University and is on the boards of SMU's Meadows School of the Arts and the Maguire Center for Ethics and Public Responsibility. He is a trustee of both the Dallas Foundation and the State Fair of Texas, where he serves on the executive committee. He is a past president of the Salesmanship Club of Dallas and has served as a trustee of Children's Medical Foundation of Texas. He has also served on the boards of the Association of Broadcast Executives of Texas, the Dallas Advertising League, the SMU Alumni Association and Goodwill Industries of Texas.

In 1998 he was honored as a Distinguished Alumnus of Highland Park High School in Dallas.

Burl Osborne

Burl Osborne joined Belo in 1980 following a 20-year career with The Associated Press.

In 1960, Osborne graduated from Marshall University in Huntington, W. Va., with a degree in journalism. He earned a master's degree in business administration from Long Island University in 1984 and is a graduate of the Harvard Business School Advanced Management Program.

Osborne joined The Dallas Morning News as executive editor in 1980. In 1981, he became vice president and executive editor, and was promoted to senior vice president and editor in 1983. He was named president and editor in 1985 and became publisher in 1986. Osborne was elected a director of Belo in 1987 and was named president of Belo's Publishing Division in November 1995. He also serves on Belo's six-member Management Committee. In addition to Osborne's primary executive responsibilities, he is chairman of the A. H. Belo Corporation Foundation.

Osborne has served as a member and co-chairman of the Pulitzer Prize Board, president of the American Society of Newspaper Editors, chairman of the Foundation for American Communications, chairman of the American Press Institute, president and chairman of the Texas Daily Newspaper Association, trustee of the Southern Newspaper Publishers Association Foundation and chairman of the Presstime Advisory Committee of the Newspaper Association of America.

Currently, Osborne is a member of the executive committee of the board of The Associated Press and serves on the boards of the Newspaper Association of America, the Southern Newspaper Publishers Association and the World Association of Newspapers. He is also a trustee of Paul Quinn College and serves on the Advisory Committee for the Nieman Foundation at Harvard University.

Osborne received the National Press Foundation George David Beveridge Jr. Award for Editor of the Year in 1992, and he was awarded the Pat Taggart Texas Newspaper Leader of the Year Award in 1993.

James M. Moroney Jr.

James M. Moroney Jr., a grandson of George Bannerman Dealey, is the son of the late James M. Moroney and the late Maidie Dealey Moroney. He was born in Dallas, attended Highland Park High School and St. John's Military Academy in Delafield, Wis. He graduated from the University of Texas in Austin in 1943. During summer vacations, he worked part-time at radio and television stations WFAA and The Dallas Morning News.

During World War II, he entered the U.S. Navy, rising to the rank of lieutenant (jg). He was released from active duty in 1946.

Moroney joined The News as a reporter, served as an advertising salesman and worked in the promotion and circulation departments before becoming assistant to the business manager in 1950. He also spent a year at the radio and television stations.

In 1951 he was appointed assistant treasurer of the A. H. Belo Corporation and in 1952 was elected to the board of directors. He became treasurer in 1955, was promoted to vice president and treasurer in 1960 and was made executive vice president in 1970. In addition, Moroney was named president and chief executive officer of Belo Broadcasting Corporation and in 1974 became chairman of that corporation, a subsidiary of the A. H. Belo Corporation.

In 1980 Moroney was elected president and chief executive officer of The Dallas Morning News and president and chief operating officer of A. H. Belo Corporation. He was promoted to the position of president and chief executive officer of Belo in January 1983. In April 1984 he was elected to the additional position of chairman of the board. In January 1985 he relinquished the title of president.

Moroney retired from Belo on December 31, 1986, but retained his role as a director of the corporation, serving as chairman of the executive committee. He holds the record for the longest tenure on Belo's board, having been elected a director in 1952.

John W. Bassett Jr.

John W. Bassett Jr. was elected a director of Belo in 1979.

In 1960, Bassett graduated from Stanford University with a degree in economics. He graduated with honors from The University of Texas School of Law in 1964 having served as associate editor of The Texas Law Review. Following his graduation, he passed the Texas and New Mexico Bar examinations and practiced law in Roswell.

In 1966, Bassett was selected as a White House Fellow and served a year in Washington, D.C., as a special assistant to the Attorney General of the United States. He then returned to Roswell to practice law with the firm of Atwood, Malone, Mann & Turner, P.A., of which he was a shareholder-partner from 1967-1995. In October 1995, he formed a law firm known as Bassett & Copple, LLP. Through his law firm, Bassett represents numerous large corporations and educational and governmental entities.

A native of Roswell, Bassett is a former member of the Board of Education for the State of New Mexico. He is a Rotarian and a member of several boards of directors of local charitable institutions in Roswell.

Henry P. Becton Jr.

Henry P. Becton Jr., was elected a director of Belo in 1997, after having served as a director of The Providence Journal Company since 1990.

Since 1984, Becton has been president and general manager of WGBH Educational Foundation, which he joined as a producer in 1970. As president, Becton is responsible for Channels 2 and 44 in Boston, Channel 57 in Springfield and WGBH-FM in Boston, in addition to WGBH's national programming, educational publishing and access technology activities. Under Becton's direction, WGBH has received every major award for broadcasting excellence, including National and International Emmy Awards, the George Foster Peabody Award, the George Polk Award and the duPont-Columbia School of Journalism Award.

Becton has served on various public-broadcasting policy committees, is a member of the PBS board of directors and a founding director of the independent production company that produces the American Playhouse and P.O.V. series.

He is an overseer of the Boston Museum of Fine Arts, a member of the board of visitors of the Dimock Community Health Center, a member of the dean's council of Harvard University's Graduate School of Education and a trustee of several

Scudder Mutual Funds.

Judith L. Craven, M.D., M.P.H.

Judith L. Craven was elected a director of Belo in 1992.

Craven holds a bachelor of science degree from Bowling Green University, a doctor of medicine from Baylor College of Medicine and a master of public health from The University of Texas School of Public Health.

A Houston resident, Craven has served as president of the United Way of the Texas Gulf Coast, the fifth-largest United Way in the country in terms of dollars raised, since July 1992. Prior to 1992, Craven served nine years as dean of the School of Allied Health Sciences at The University of Texas Health Science Center at Houston, and five years concurrently as vice president of multicultural affairs for The University of Texas Health Science Center.

Dr. Craven has held many offices and served on many local, state and national committees and boards, including the Board of Directors of the Federal Reserve Bank of Dallas, Houston Branch; the Houston Committee for Private Sector Initiatives; the Rotary Club of Houston; and the Philosophical Society of Texas. She has chaired the State Board of Health Hospital Data Advisory Committee. She has received numerous awards and honors, including Women on the Move, YWCA Outstanding Women Award, Outstanding Young Women of America, NAACP Award and induction into the Texas Women's Hall of Fame.

Roger A. Enrico

Roger A. Enrico was elected a director of Belo in 1995.

A native of Minnesota, Enrico is a graduate of Babson College with a bachelor's degree in finance and holds an honorary doctorate of law from Babson.

Enrico is chairman of the board and chief executive officer of PepsiCo Inc. He has played a major role in PepsiCo's development since joining the corporation in 1971.

Enrico assumed his position as chief executive officer April 1, 1996. He was appointed vice chairman in 1994. Since the end of 1994, he has served as chairman and chief executive officer of PepsiCo Worldwide Restaurants. From 1991 to 1993, Enrico served in PepsiCo's snack food business first as chairman and chief executive officer of Frito-Lay, the corporation's U.S. snack-food business, then as chairman and chief executive officer of PepsiCo Worldwide Foods, the corporation's worldwide snack-food business. He was elected to the PepsiCo board of directors in 1987.

He serves on the boards of directors of Dayton Hudson Corporation, the Prudential Insurance Company of America, Lincoln Center for the Performing Arts, the American Film Institute and the National Center for Public Policy and Higher Education. He is a member of the Babson College Corporation and the executive board of the Dallas Symphony Association, and he is a director of the United Negro College Fund.

Stephen Hamblett

Stephen Hamblett was elected a director of Belo in 1997.

Hamblett joined The Providence Journal in 1957 after his graduation from Harvard College. In 1969 he was named assistant vice president/administration and in 1974 became vice president/marketing. He was named vice president/marketing and corporate development in 1979 and served in that capacity until 1983, when he was named executive vice president and assistant publisher of the company. In April 1985, Hamblett was named president and chief executive officer. In September, 1987, he was named chairman of the board, chief executive officer and publisher of The Providence Journal Company. In April 1999 he retired as CEO and publisher but retained the position of chairman of the board.

Hamblett is a member of the board of directors of the Associated Press, the American Press Institute, the Inter American Press Association and the Smithsonian National Board. In Rhode Island, Hamblett serves on the boards of the Providence Performing Arts Center, the Rhode Island School of Design and the Bank Boston Rhode Island State Board. He serves on the advisory board of the University of Rhode Island Marine Programs and Graduate School of Oceanography. He is a trustee of Save the Bay and the Providence Foundation.

Dealey D. Herndon

Dealey D. Herndon was elected a director of Belo in 1986.

A Dallas native, Herndon is a great-granddaughter of George Bannerman Dealey and the daughter of the late H. Ben Decherd and Isabelle Thomason Decherd. She is an honors graduate of The Hockaday School and the University of Texas at Austin.

Herndon is currently president of Herndon, Stauch & Associates, a Texas project and construction management firm in Austin, Texas. Prior to opening her firm, Herndon had overall responsibility for the Capitol Preservation and Extension Project, which she directed from 1988 to its completion in 1995. She also served as administrator of Friends of the Governor's Mansion from 1983 to 1984.

Prior to 1991, Herndon served as a community volunteer in a wide range of projects in Dallas and Austin, with a primary focus on historic preservation, finance and fund-raising. She served as president of the Seton Medical Center Development Board, the Austin History Center Association and Friends of the Governor's Mansion, and as treasurer of several organizations. She served as one of the six members of the State Preservation Board from 1987 to 1991 and was reappointed by Governor Bush in 1995. Herndon is the immediate past chair of the board of St. Edward's University and is a board member of the Capitol Area United Way, Just for the Kids, Friends of the Governor's Mansion, and the National Trust for Historic Preservation. She serves on the three-member Museum Advisory Committee directing the development of the Texas State History Museum, serves on the University of Texas School of Architecture Advisory Council and is a member of the Austin Area Research Organization.

Laurence E. Hirsch

Laurence E. Hirsch was elected a director of Belo in 1999.

Hirsch was elected chairman of the board of Centex Corporation in July 1991. Hirsch has been chief executive officer of Centex Corporation since July 1988. He joined the company as president, chief operating officer and a member of the board of directors in 1985. He also serves as chairman of the executive committee of Centex Construction Products Inc., a public company in which Centex owns a 61 percent interest.

Prior to joining Centex, Hirsch was president, CEO and a director of Southdown Inc. in Houston. An attorney, he previously had been a partner in the Houston-based law firm of Bracewell & Patterson. Hirsch, a native of New York City, received a B.S. in economics from The Wharton School at the University of Pennsylvania and a J.D. from the Villanova University School of Law in Villanova, Pa.

Currently, Hirsch serves as an advisory director of Heidelberger Zement A.G. and is a trustee of BlackRock Asset Investors. He is a member of the undergraduate executive board of The Wharton School and serves on the board of consultors of Villanova Law School. He also serves on the board of directors of Methodist Hospitals of Dallas and is an honorary director of Senior Citizens of Greater Dallas Inc.

Arturo Madrid, Ph.D.

Dr. Arturo Madrid was elected a director of Belo in 1994.

Since 1993, Madrid has been the Norine R. and T. Frank Murchison Distinguished Professor of the Humanities at Trinity University in San Antonio. A native of New Mexico and a leading scholar in Latino history and culture, Madrid served as the founding president of the Tomás Rivera Center for Policy Studies, the nation's first institute for policy studies on Latino issues, from 1984 to 1993. In addition to holding academic and administrative appointments at Dartmouth College; the University of California, San Diego; and the University of Minnesota, he has also served as director of the Fund for the Improvement of Post-Secondary Education, U.S. Department of Education and of the Ford Foundation's Graduate Fellowships for Mexican-Americans Program.

In 1996, Madrid was awarded the Charles Frankel Prize, the highest honor bestowed by the National Endowment for the Humanities. The Frankel Prize recognizes outstanding contributions to the public's understanding of history, literature, philosophy and other humanities disciplines.

Over the past two decades, Madrid has served on the boards of some of the country's most prominent organizations, including The College Board, the Association for the Advancement of Higher Education and the Council for Basic Education, the Center for Early Adolescence, the National Board for Professional Teaching Standards and the National Civic League. Madrid holds honorary doctorates from New

England College, Mt. Holyoke College and The California State University, Hayward. He is an elected fellow of the Council on Foreign Relations, the nation's premier foreign-policy association, and the National Academy for Public Administration, which honors persons with distinguished records in public administration.

Hugh G. Robinson

Hugh G. Robinson was elected a director of Belo in 1989. Robinson graduated from the U.S. Military Academy, West Point, in 1954. He earned a master's degree in civil engineering from Massachusetts Institute of Technology in 1959, and he holds an honorary doctor of laws degree from Williams College.

He entered the U.S. Army following his graduation from West Point and served until his retirement in 1983 with the rank of major general.

He is currently chairman and CEO of The Tetra Group, a construction management firm. For more than five years prior to that, Robinson was president of Cityplace Development Corporation, a real estate development subsidiary of The Southland Corporation, and vice president of The Southland Corporation.

Robinson received numerous military awards, including the Distinguished Service Medal. He is a former member of the board of directors of the Federal Reserve Bank of Dallas, and he is currently a member of the boards of directors of TXU; Circuit City Stores Inc.; Guarantee Federal Bank; the Better Business Bureau; Dallas Youth Services Corps; and the LBJ Foundation.

William T. Solomon

William T. Solomon was elected a director of Belo in 1983.

Solomon holds a civil engineering degree from Southern Methodist University and an M.B.A. from Harvard Graduate School of Business, where he was a Baker Scholar, in 1967.

Solomon is chairman and CEO of Austin Industries Inc., a Dallas general construction firm. Solomon joined the company full-time in 1967 and was named president in 1970.

A 1996 inductee into the Texas Business Hall of Fame, Solomon serves on the boards of the Dallas Citizens Council, the Hoblitzelle Foundation, Southern Methodist University and the Southwestern Medical Foundation. Among the many civic organizations that he has chaired are the Dallas Citizens Council, the Dallas Together Forum, the Greater Dallas Chamber, SMU's School of Engineering and Applied Science and Northaven United Methodist Church.

J. McDonald Williams

Don Williams was elected a director of Belo in 1985.

Williams graduated from Abilene Christian University in 1963 and from George Washington University Law School in 1966, both with honors.

He practiced law in Dallas seven years until he joined the Trammell Crow Company in May 1973. He entered the firm as the partner responsible for overseas development and was named managing partner in 1977, president and CEO in 1990 and chairman in August 1994.

He also serves on the boards of Mitchell Energy & Development Corporation, Pepperdine University, Abilene Christian University and George Washington University. Williams is a member of the boards of the Dallas Foundation and Dallas Together Forum. He was honored with the 1998 Linz Award, Dallas's oldest and most prestigious civic prize. ☆

Texas Newspapers, Radio and Television Stations

In the list of print and broadcast media below, frequency of publication of newspapers is indicated after the names by the following codes: (D), daily; (S), semiweekly; (TW), triweekly; (BW), biweekly; (SM), semimonthly; (M), monthly; all others are weeklies. The radio and television stations are those with valid operating licenses as of the dates noted at the end of the list. Not included are those with only construction permits or with applications pending. Sources: Newspapers: 1999 Texas Newspaper Directory, Texas Press Association; Broadcast media: Broadcasting and Cable Yearbook 1999; R.R. Bowker, New Providence, N.J., 1999.

Abernathy — Newspaper: Weekly Review.
Abilene — Newspaper: Reporter-News (D). **Radio-AM:** KGMM, 1280 khz; KYYD, 1340; KBBA, 1470; KMPC, 1560. **Radio-FM:** KGNZ, 88.1 MHz; KACU, 89.7; KULL, 92.5; KORQ, 100.7; KEAN, 105.1; KFQX, 106.3; KEYJ, 107.9. **TV:** KRBC-Ch. 9; KTAB-Ch. 32.
Alamo — Radio-FM: KJAV, 104.9 MHz.
Alamo Heights — Radio-AM: KDRY, 1100 khz.
Albany — Newspaper: News.
Aledo — Newspaper: Community News.
Alice — Newspaper: Echo-News (D). **Radio-AM:** KOPY, 1070 khz. **Radio-FM:** KOPY, 92.1 MHz; KNDA, 102.9.
Allen — Newspaper: American (S).
Alpine — Newspaper: Avalanche. **Radio-AM:** KVLF, 1240 khz. **Radio-FM:** KALP, 92.7 MHz.
Alvarado — Newspapers: Post; Star Bulletin.
Alvin — Newspaper: Sun. **Radio-AM:** KTEK, 1110 khz. **Radio-FM:** KACC, 89.7 MHz. **TV:** KHSH-Ch. 67.
Alvord — Newspaper: Gazette.
Amarillo — Newspapers: Globe-News (D); Southwest Stockman. **Radio-AM:** KGNC, 710 khz; KIXZ, 940; KTNZ, 1010; KZIP, 1310; KDJW, 1360; KPUR, 1440. **Radio-FM:** KART, 88.3 MHz; KLMN, 89.1; KACV, 89.9; KYFA, 91.9; KQIZ, 93.1; KBUY, 94.1; KMML, 96.9; KGNC, 97.9; KNSY, 98.7; KBZD, 99.7; KGNC, 97.9; KPQZ, 100.9; KATP, 101.9; KRGN, 103.1; KAEZ, 105.7. **TV:** KACV-Ch. 2; KAMR-Ch. 4; KVII-Ch. 7; KFDA-Ch. 10; KCIT-Ch. 14.
Amherst — Newspaper: Press (SM).
Anahuac — Newspaper: The Progress.
Andrews — Newspaper: Andrews County News (S). **Radio-AM:** KACT, 1360 khz. **Radio-FM:** KACT, 105.5 MHz.
Angleton — Newspaper: Times (S).
Anson — Newspaper: Western Observer. **Radio-FM:** KKHR, 98.1 MHz.
Aransas Pass — Newspaper: Progress.
Archer City — Newspaper: Archer County News.
Arlington — Newspaper: Morning News (D). **Radio-FM:** KWRD, 94.9 MHz. **TV:** KTXA-Ch. 21; KPXD-Ch. 68.
Aspermont — Newspaper: Stonewall County Courier.
Athens — Newspaper: Daily Review (D). **Radio-AM:** KLVQ,

1410 khz.
Atlanta — Newspaper: Citizens Journal (S). **Radio-AM:** KALT, 1610 khz. **Radio-FM:** KPYN, 100.1 MHz.
Austin — Newspapers: American-Statesman (D); Austin Business Journal; Lake Travis View; Texas Observer (BW); Texas Weekly; Westlake Picayune. **Radio-AM:** KLBJ, 590 khz; KVET, 1300; KFON, 1490. **Radio-FM:** KAZI, 88.7 MHz; KMFA, 89.5; KUT, 90.5; KVRX, 91.7; KLBJ, 93.7; KKMJ, 95.5; KVET, 98.1; KASE, 100.7; KPEZ, 102.3. **TV:** KTBC-Ch. 7; KLRU-Ch. 18; KVUE-Ch. 24; KXAN-Ch. 36; KEYE-Ch. 42; KNVA-Ch. 54.
Azle — Newspaper: News.
Baird — Newspapers: Banner; Callahan County Star.
Balch Springs — Newspaper: Suburban Tribune. **Radio-AM:** KSKY, 660 khz.
Ballinger — Newspaper: Ledger. **Radio-AM:** KRUN, 1400 khz. **Radio-FM:** KCSE, 103.1 MHz.
Bandera — Newspapers: Bulletin; Review. **Radio-FM:** KEEP, 98.3 MHz.
Bartlett — Newspaper: Tribune-Progress.
Bastrop — Newspaper: Advertiser (S) **Radio-FM:** KGSR, 107.1 MHz.
Bay City — Newspaper: Daily Tribune (D). **Radio-FM:** KXGJ, 101.7 MHz; KMKS, 102.5.
Baytown — Newspaper: Sun (D). **Radio-AM:** KWWJ, 1360 khz. **TV:** KVVV-Ch. 57.
Beaumont — Newspaper: Enterprise (D). **Radio-AM:** KLVI, 560 khz; KZZB, 990; KRCM, 1380; KAYD, 1450. **Radio-FM:** KTXB, 89.7 MHz; KVLU, 91.3; KQXY, 94.1; KYKR, 95.1; KAYD, 97.5; KTCX, 102.5; KXTJ, 107.9. **TV:** KFDM-Ch. 6; KBMT-Ch. 12; KITU-Ch. 34.
Beeville — Newspaper: Bee-Picayune (S). **Radio-AM:** KIBL, 1490 khz. **Radio-FM:** KYTX, 97.9 MHz; KTKO, 105.7.
Bellaire — Radio-AM: KILE, 1560 khz.
Bells — Radio - FM: KMKT, 93.1 MHz.
Bellville — Newspaper: Times. **Radio-AM:** KNUZ, 1090 khz.
Belton — Newspaper: Journal. **Radio-AM:** KTON, 940 khz. **Radio-FM:** KOOC, 106.3 MHz. **TV:** KNCT-Ch. 46.
Big Lake — Newspaper: Wildcat.
Big Sandy — Newspaper: Big Sandy-Hawkins Journal.

Radio-FM: KBAU, 90.7 MHz.
Big Spring — Newspaper: Herald (D). **Radio-AM:** KBYG, 1400; KBST, 1490. **Radio-FM:** KBTS, 94.3 MHz; KBST, 95.9. **TV:** KWAB-Ch. 4.
Bishop — Radio-FM: KFLZ, 106.9 MHz.
Blanco — Newspaper: Blanco County News.
Bloomington — Radio-FM: KLUB, 106.9 MHz.
Blossom — Newspaper: Times.
Boerne — Newspapers: Hill Country Recorder; Star (S). **Radio-AM:** KBRN, 1500 kHz. **Radio-FM:** KFYZ, 93.3 MHz.
Bogata — Newspaper: News.
Bonham — Newspaper: Daily Favorite (D). **Radio-AM:** KFYN, 1420 kHz. **Radio-FM:** KFYZ, 98.3 MHz.
Booker — Newspaper: News.
Borger — Newspaper: News-Herald (D). **Radio-AM:** KQTY, 1490 kHz. **Radio-FM:** KAVO, 91.5 MHz; KQFX, 104.3.
Bovina — Newspaper: Blade.
Bowie — Newspaper: News (S). **Radio-AM:** KRJT, 1410 kHz. **Radio-FM:** KRJT, 100.7 Mhz.
Brackettville — Newspaper: Brackett News.
Brady — Newspapers: Herald; Standard. **Radio-AM:** KNEL, 1490 kHz. **Radio-FM:** KNEL, 95.3 MHz.
Breckenridge — Newspaper: American (S). **Radio-AM:** KROO, 1430 kHz. **Radio-FM:** KLXK, 93.5 MHz.
Bremond — Newspaper: Press.
Brenham — Newspaper: Banner-Press (D). **Radio-AM:** KWHI, 1280 kHz. **Radio-FM:** KULF, 94.1 Mhz; KTTX, 106.1.
Bridgeport — Newspaper: Index. **Radio-FM:** KBOC, 98.3 MHz.
Brookshire — Newspaper: Times Tribune.
Brownfield — Newspaper: News (S). **Radio-AM:** KKUB, 1300 kHz. **Radio-FM:** KLZK, 104.3 MHz.
Brownsboro — Newspaper: Brownsboro and Chandler Statesman.
Brownsville — Newspaper: Herald (D). **Radio-AM:** KBOR, 1600 kHz. **Radio-FM:** KBNR, 88.3 MHz; KKPS, 99.5; KTEX, 100.3. **TV:** KVEO-Ch. 23.
Brownwood — Newspaper: Bulletin (D). **Radio-AM:** KXYL, 1240 kHz; KBWD, 1380. **Radio-FM:** KBUB, 90.3 MHz; KHPU, 91.7; KPSM, 99.3; KOXE, 101.5; KXYL, 104.1.
Bryan — Newspaper: Bryan-College Station Eagle (D). **Radio-AM:** KTAM, 1240 kHz; KAGC, 1510. **Radio-FM:** KXBK, 93.1 MHz; KORA, 98.3 MHz; KBMA, 99.5; KKYS, 104.7. **TV:** KBTX-Ch. 3; KYLE-Ch. 28.
Buda — Newspaper: Free Press.
Buffalo — Newspaper: Press.
Bullard — Newspaper: Bulletin Weekly News.
Buna — Newspaper: Beacon.
Burkburnett — Newspaper: Informer Star. **Radio-FM:** KYYI, 104.7 MHz.
Burleson — Newspaper: Star (S).
Burnet — Newspapers: Bulletin; Citizens Gazette. **Radio-AM:** KHLB, 1340 kHz. **Radio-FM:** KBLK, 92.5 MHz; KHLB, 106.9.
Caldwell — Newspaper: Burleson County Citizen-Tribune.
Callisburg — Radio-FM: KPFC, 91.9 MHz.
Calvert — Newspaper: Tribune.
Cameron — Newspaper: Herald. **Radio-AM:** KMIL, 1330 kHz. **Radio-FM:** KHLR, 103.9 MHz.
Canadian — Newspaper: Record.
Canton — Newspapers: Herald; Van Zandt News. **Radio-AM:** KVCI, 1510 kHz.
Canyon — Newspaper: News (S). **Radio-AM:** KZRK, 1550 kHz. **Radio-FM:** KWTS, 91.1 MHz; KPUR, 107.1; KZRK, 107.9.
Canyon Lake — Newspaper: Times Guardian and Comal County Chronicle.
Carrizo Springs — Newspaper: Javelin. **Radio-AM:** KBEN, 1450 kHz. **Radio-FM:** KCZO, 92.1 MHz.
Carthage — Newspaper: Panola Watchman (S). **Radio-AM:** KGAS, 1590 kHz. **Radio-FM:** KTUX, 98.9 MHz; KGAS, 104.3.
Castroville — Newspaper: News Bulletin.
Cedar Hill — Newspapers: Sentinel; Today.
Celina — Newspaper: Record.
Center — Newspapers: Light & Champion (S); Shelby Countian. **Radio-AM:** KDET, 930 kHz. **Radio-FM:** KDET, 102.3 MHz.
Centerville — Newspaper: News.
Chico — Newspaper: Texan.
Childress — Newspaper: Index (TW). **Radio-AM:** KCTX, 1510 kHz. **Radio-FM:** KSRW, 96.1 MHz.
Chillicothe — Newspaper: Valley News.
Cisco — Newspaper: Press (S).
Clarendon — Newspaper: Enterprise.
Clarksville — Newspaper: Times. **Radio-AM:** KCAR, 1350 kHz. **Radio-FM:** KGAP, 98.5 HMz.

Claude — Newspaper: News. **Radio-FM:** KARX, 95.7 MHz.
Clear Lake — Newspaper: Citizen.
Cleburne — Newspaper: Times-Review (D). **Radio-AM:** KCLE, 1120 kHz.
Cleveland — Newspaper: Advocate. **Radio-FM:** KKTL, 97.1 MHz.
Clifton — Newspaper: Record (S). **Radio-FM:** KWOW, 103.3 MHz.
Clute — Newspaper: The Facts (D).
Clyde — Newspaper: Journal.
Cockrell Hill — Radio-AM: KRVA, 1600 kHz.
Coleman — Newspaper: Chronicle & Democrat-Voice (S). **Radio-AM:** KSTA, 1000 kHz. **Radio-FM:** KSTA, 107.1 MHz.
College Station — Newspaper: Battalion (D). **Radio-AM:** WTAW, 1150 kHz. **Radio-FM:** KEOS, 89.1 MHz; KAMU, 90.9; KTSR, 92.1. **TV:** KAMU-Ch. 15.
Colleyville — Newspaper: News & Times.
Colorado City — Newspaper: Record. **Radio-AM:** KVMC, 1320 kHz. **Radio-FM:** KAUM, 106.3 MHz.
Columbus — Newspapers: Banner Press; Colorado County Citizen. **Radio-FM:** KULM, 98.3 MHz.
Comanche — Newspaper: Chief. **Radio-AM:** KCOM, 1550 kHz.
Comfort — Newspaper: News. **Radio-FM:** KRNH, 95.1 MHz.
Commerce — Newspaper: Journal (S) **Radio-FM:** KETR, 88.9 MHz; KEMM, 103.3.
Conroe — Newspaper: Courier (D). **Radio-AM:** KJOJ, 880 kHz; KCHC, 1140. **Radio-FM:** KKHT, 106.9 MHz. **TV:** KPXB-Ch. 49.
Cooper — Newspaper: Review.
Coppell — Newspaper: Citizens' Advocate.
Copperas Cove — Newspaper: Leader Press. **Radio-FM:** KOOV, 103.1 MHz.
Corpus Christi — Newspapers: Caller-Times (D); Coastal Bend Legal & Business News (D); Flour Bluff Sun; South Texas Catholic (BW). **Radio-AM:** KCTA, 1030 kHz; KCCT, 1150; KSIX, 1230; KRYS, 1360; KUNO, 1400; KEYS, 1440. **Radio-FM:** KFGG, 88.7 MHz; KEDT, 90.3; KBNJ, 91.7; KMXR, 93.9; KBSO, 94.7; KZFM, 95.5; KLTG, 96.5; KRYS, 99.1.**TV:** KIII-Ch. 3; KRIS-Ch. 6; KZTV-Ch. 10; KEDT-Ch. 16; KORO-Ch. 28.
Corrigan — Newspaper: Times.
Corsicana — Newspaper: Daily Sun (D). **Radio-AM:** KAND, 1340 kHz. **Radio-FM:** KDXX, 107.9 MHz.
Crane — Newspaper: News. **Radio-AM:** KXOI, 810 kHz. **Radio FM:** KKKK, 101.3 MHz.
Creedmoor — Radio AM: KQQA, 1530 kHz.
Crockett — Newspaper: Houston Co. Courier (S). **Radio-AM:** KIVY, 1290 kHz. **Radio-FM:** KIVY, 92.7 MHz; KBHT, 93.5.
Crosbyton — Newspaper: Crosby County News & Chronicle.
Cross Plains — Newspaper: Review.
Crowell — Newspaper: Foard County News.
Crowley — Newspaper: Star Review.
Crystal Beach — Radio FM: KSTB, 101.5 MHz.
Crystal City — Newspaper: Zavala County Sentinel. **Radio-FM:** KHER, 94.3 MHz.
Cuero — Newspaper: Record. **Radio-AM:** KTXC, 1600 kHz. **Radio-FM:** KVCQ, 97.7 MHz.
Cypress — Newspaper: KYND, 1520 kHz.
Daingerfield — Newspaper: Bee. **Radio-AM:** KEGG, 1560 kHz. **Radio-FM:** KKLK, 106.9 MHz.
Dalhart — Newspaper: Daily Texan (D). **Radio-AM:** KXIT, 1240 kHz. **Radio-FM:** KXIT, 95.9 MHz.
Dallas — Newspapers: The Dallas Morning News (D); Business Journal; Daily Commercial Record (D); Oak Cliff Tribune; Park Cities News; Park Cities People; Texas Jewish Post; White Rocker. **Radio-AM:** KLIF, 570 kHz; KGGR, 1040; KRLD, 1080; KLUV, 1190; KTCK, 1310; KDXX, 1480. **Radio-FM:** KNON, 89.3 HMz; KERA, 90.1; KCBI, 90.9; KVTT, 91.7; KZPS, 92.5; KRSM, 93.3; KBFB, 97.9; KLUV, 98.7; KRBV, 100.3; WRR, 101.1; KDMX, 102.9; KKDA, 104.5; KYNG, 105.3. **TV:** KDFW-Ch. 4; WFAA-Ch. 8; WFAA-DT-Ch. 9; KERA-Ch. 13; KDFI-Ch. 27; KDAF-Ch. 33; KXTX-Ch. 39; KDTX-Ch. 58.
Decatur — Newspaper: Wise County Messenger (S). **Radio-FM:** KRNB, 105.7 MHz. **TV:** KMPX-Ch. 29.
Deer Park — Newspaper: Progress.
De Kalb — Newspaper: News (S).
De Leon — Newspapers: Free Press; Monitor.
Dell City — Newspaper: Hudspeth County Herald.
Del Mar Hills — Radio-AM: KVOZ, 890 kHz.
Del Rio — Newspaper: News-Herald (D). **Radio-AM:** KDLK, 1230 kHz; KWMC, 1490. **Radio-FM:** KDLK, 94.3 MHz; KTDR, 96.3. **TV:** KTRG-Ch. 10.
Del Valle — Radio-AM: KIXL, 970 kHz.
Denison — Radio-AM: KKLF, 950 kHz. **Radio-FM:** KIKM, 101.7 MHz.

Denton — **Newspaper:** Record-Chronicle (D). **Radio-AM:** KTNO, 1440 kHz. **Radio-FM:** KNTU, 88.1 MHz; KHCK, 99.1; KHKS, 106.1. **TV:** KDTN-Ch. 2.
Denver City — **Newspaper:** Press (S).
Deport — **Newspaper:** Times.
DeSoto — **Newspapers:** Best Southwest Focus (S); Today.
Detroit — **Newspaper:** Weekly.
Devine — **Newspaper:** News. **Radio-FM:** KSJL, 92.1 MHz.
Diboll — **Newspaper:** Free Press. **Radio-AM:** KSML, 1260 kHz. **Radio-FM:** KSJL, 92.5 MHz; KAFX, 95.5.
Dimmitt — **Newspaper:** Castro County News. **Radio-AM:** KDHN, 1470 kHz. **Radio-FM:** KNNK, 100.5 MHz.
Dripping Springs — **Newspaper:** News-Dispatch.
Dublin — **Newspaper:** Citizen. **Radio-FM:** KSTV, 93.1 MHz.
Dumas — **Newspaper:** Moore County News-Press (S). **Radio-AM:** KDDD, 800 kHz. **Radio-FM:** KMRE, 95.3 MHz.
Duncanville — **Newspaper:** Today.
Eagle Lake — **Newspaper:** Headlight.
Eagle Pass — **Newspapers:** News Gram; News-Guide (S). **Radio-AM:** KEPS, 1270 kHz. **Radio-FM:** KEPI, 88.7 MHz; KEPX, 89.5; KINL, 92.7. **TV:** KVAW-Ch. 16.
East Bernard — **Newspaper:** Tribune.
Eastland — **Newspaper:** Telegram (S). **Radio-AM:** KEAS, 1590 kHz. **Radio-FM:** KVMX, 96.7 MHz; KEAS, 97.7.
Eden — **Newspaper:** Echo.
Edgewood — **Newspaper:** Enterprise.
Edinburg — **Newspaper:** Daily Review (D). **Radio-AM:** KURV, 710 kHz. **Radio-FM:** KOIR, 88.5 MHz; KBFM, 104.1; KVLY, 107.9.
Edna — **Newspaper:** Jackson County Herald-Tribune. **Radio-AM:** KTMR, 1130 kHz. **Radio-FM:** KGUL, 96.1 MHz.
El Campo — **Newspaper:** Leader-News (S). **Radio-AM:** KULP, 1390 kHz. **Radio-FM:** KIOX, 96.9 MHz.
Eldorado — **Newspaper:** Success.
Electra — **Newspaper:** Star-News.
Elgin — **Newspaper:** Courier. **Radio-AM:** KELG, 1440 kHz. **Radio-FM:** KKLB, 92.5 MHz.
El Paso — **Newspapers:** Times (D). **Radio-AM:** KROD, 600 kHz; KHEY, 690; KAMA, 750; KBNA, 920; KFNA, 1060; KSVE, 1150; KVIV, 1340; KTSM, 1380; KELP, 1590. **Radio-FM:** KTEP, 88.5 MHz; KXCR; 89.5; KVER, 91.1; KOFX, 92.3; KSII, 93.1; KINT, 93.9; KATH, 94.7; KLAQ, 95.5; KHEY, 96.3; KBNA, 97.5; KTSM, 99.9; KPRR, 102.1. **TV:** KDBC-Ch. 4; KVIA-Ch. 7; KTSM-Ch. 9; KCOS-Ch. 13; KFOX-Ch. 14; KINT-Ch. 26; KSCE-Ch. 38; KKWB-Ch. 65.
Emory — **Newspaper:** Rains County Leader.
Ennis — **Newspapers:** Daily News (D); The Press.
Everman — **Newspaper:** Times.
Fabens — **Radio-FM:** KPAS, 103.1 MHz.
Fairfield — **Newspaper:** Recorder. **Radio-FM:** KNES, 99.1 MHz.
Falfurrias — **Newspaper:** Facts. **Radio-AM:** KLDS, 1260 kHz. **Radio-FM:** KPSO, 106.3 MHz.
Farmersville — **Newspaper:** Times. **Radio-AM:** KTUB, 990 kHz. **Radio-FM:** KXEZ, 92.1 MHz.
Farwell — **Newspaper:** State Line Tribune. **Radio-FM:** KIJN, 1060 kHz. **Radio-FM:** KIJN, 92.3 MHz; KICA, 98.3.
Ferris — **Newspaper:** Ellis County Press. **Radio-AM:** KDFT, 540 kHz.
Flatonia — **Newspaper:** Argus.
Floresville — **Newspapers:** Chronicle-Journal; Wilson County News. **Radio-FM:** KWCB, 89.7 MHz; KLEY, 94.1.
Flower Mound — **Newspaper:** FlowerPlex PipeLine.
Floydada — **Newspaper:** Floyd County Hesperian-Beacon. **Radio-AM:** KFLP, 900 kHz. **Radio-FM:** KFLL, 95.3 MHz.
Follett — **Newspaper:** The Golden Spread.
Forney — **Newspaper:** Messenger.
Fort Davis — **Newspaper:** Jeff Davis Co. Mountain Dispatch.
Fort Stockton — **Newspaper:** Pioneer. **Radio-AM:** KFST, 860 kHz. **Radio-FM:** KFST, 94.3 MHz.
Fort Worth — **Newspapers:** Business Press; Commercial Recorder (D); Star-Telegram (D); Northwest Tarrant Co. Times-Record; Weekly Livestock Reporter. **Radio-AM:** WBAP, 820 kHz; KFJZ, 870; KHVN, 970; KESS, 1270; KAHZ, 1360; KZMP, 1540. **Radio-FM:** KTCU, 88.7 MHz; KLTY, 94.1; KSCS, 96.3; KEGL, 97.1; KPLX, 99.5; KTXQ, 102.1; KOAI, 107.5. **TV:** KXAS-Ch. 5; KTVT-Ch. 11; KFWD-Ch. 52.
Franklin — **Newspapers:** Advocate; News Weekly. **Radio FM:** KZTR, 101.9 MHz.
Frankston — **Newspaper:** Citizen.
Fredericksburg — **Newspaper:** Standard/Radio Post. **Radio-AM:** KNAF, 910 kHz.
Freeport — **Radio-AM:** KBRZ, 1460 kHz. **Radio-FM:** KJOJ, 103.3 MHz.
Freer — **Newspaper:** Press. **Radio-FM:** KBRA, 95.9 MHz.
Friendswood — **Newspapers:** Journal; Reporter News.

Friona — **Newspaper:** Star. **Radio FM:** KGRW, 94.7 MHz.
Frisco — **Newspaper:** Enterprise.
Fritch — **Newspaper:** Eagle Press.
Gail — **Newspaper:** Borden Star.
Gainesville — **Newspaper:** Register (D). **Radio-AM:** KGAF, 1580 kHz. **Radio-FM:** KDGE, 94.5 MHz.
Galveston — **Newspaper:** Galveston Co. Daily News (D). **Radio-AM:** KHCB, 1400 kHz; KGBC, 1540. **Radio-FM:** KLTO, 104.9 MHz; KQQK, 106.5. **TV:** KLTJ-Ch. 22; KTMD-Ch. 48.
Ganado — **Radio-AM:** KZAM, 104.7 MHz.
Garland — **Newspaper:** News (S). **Radio-AM:** KPBC, 770 kHz. **TV:** KUVN-Ch. 23.
Garrison — **Newspaper:** In the News.
Gatesville — **Newspaper:** Messenger and Star (S). **Radio-FM:** KRYL, 98.3 MHz.
Georgetown — **Newspapers:** Sunday Sun; Williamson County Sun. **Radio-FM:** KHFI, 96.7 MHz; KAHK, 107.7.
Giddings — **Newspaper:** Times & News. **Radio-FM:** KROX, 101.5 MHz.
Gilmer — **Newspaper:** Mirror (S). **Radio-AM:** KBNB, 1060 kHz. **Radio-FM:** KFRO, 95.3 MHz.
Gladewater — **Newspaper:** Mirror. **Radio-AM:** KEES, 1430 kHz.
Glen Rose — **Newspaper:** Reporter. **Radio-FM:** KTFW, 92.1 MHz.
Goldthwaite — **Newspaper:** Eagle.
Goliad — **Newspaper:** Texan Express. **Radio FM:** KHMC, 95.9 MHz.
Gonzales — **Newspaper:** Inquirer (S). **Radio-AM:** KCTI, 1450 kHz. **Radio-FM:** KCTI, 106.3 MHz.
Gorman — **Newspaper:** Progress.
Graham — **Newspaper:** Leader (S). **Radio-AM:** KSWA, 1330 kHz. **Radio-FM:** KWKQ, 107.1 MHz.
Granbury — **Newspaper:** Hood County News (S). **Radio-AM:** KPAR, 1420 kHz. **Radio-FM:** KDXT, 106.7 MHz.
Grand Prairie — **Newspaper:** News (S). **Radio-AM:** KKDA, 730 kHz.
Grand Saline — **Newspaper:** Sun.
Grandview — **Newspaper:** Tribune.
Granger — **Newspaper:** News.
Grapeland — **Newspaper:** Messenger.
Greenville — **Newspaper:** Herald-Banner (D). **Radio-AM:** KGVL, 1400 kHz. **Radio-FM:** KIKT, 93.5 MHz. **TV:** KTAQ-Ch. 47.
Greenwood — **Newspaper:** Ranger.
Groesbeck — **Newspaper:** Journal.
Groom — **Newspaper:** Groom/McLean News.
Groves — **Radio-FM:** KTFA, 92.5 MHz.
Groveton — **Newspaper:** News.
Gun Barrel City — **Newspaper:** Cedar Creek Pilot (S).
Hale Center — **Newspaper:** American.
Hallettsville — **Newspaper:** Tribune-Herald. **Radio-AM:** KHLT, 1520 kHz. **Radio-FM:** KTXM, 99.9 MHz.
Hallsville — **Newspaper:** Herald.
Haltom City — **Radio FM:** KKZN, 93.3 MHz.
Hamilton — **Newspaper:** Herald-News. **Radio-AM:** KCLW, 900 kHz.
Hamlin — **Newspaper:** Herald. **Radio-FM:** KCDD, 103.7 MHz.
Harker Heights — **Radio-FM:** KYUL, 105.5 MHz.
Harlingen — **Newspaper:** Valley Morning Star (D). **Radio-AM:** KGBT, 1530 kHz. **Radio-FM:** KMBH, 88.9 MHz; KFRQ, 94.5; KIWW, 96.1. **TV:** KGBT-Ch. 4; KLUJ-Ch. 44; KMBH-Ch. 60.
Harper — **Newspaper:** Herald.
Hart — **Newspaper:** Beat.
Haskell — **Newspaper:** Free Press. **Radio-FM:** KVRP, 95.5 MHz.
Hearne — **Newspaper:** Democrat. **Radio-FM:** KVJM, 94.3 MHz.
Hebbronville — **Newspapers:** Jim Hogg Co. Enterprise; View.
Helotes — **Radio-FM:** KONO, 101.1 MHz.
Hemphill — **Newspaper:** Sabine County Reporter. **Radio-AM:** KPBL, 1240 kHz.
Hempstead — **Newspaper:** Waller County News-Citizen.
Henderson — **Newspaper:** Daily News (D). **Radio-AM:** KWRD, 1470 kHz. **Radio-FM:** KDVE, 99.9 MHz.
Henrietta — **Newspaper:** Clay County Leader.
Hereford — **Newspaper:** Brand (D). **Radio-AM:** KPAN, 860 kHz. **Radio-FM:** KPAN, 106.3 MHz.
Hico — **Newspaper:** News Review.
Highland Park — **Radio-AM:** KDMM, 1150 kHz. **Radio-FM:** KVIL, 103.7 MHz.
Highlands — **Newspaper:** Star/Crosby Courier.
Hillsboro — **Newspaper:** Reporter (S). **Radio-AM:** KHBR, 1560 kHz. **Radio-FM:** KBRQ, 102.5 MHz.
Hondo — **Newspaper:** Anvil Herald. **Radio-AM:** KCWM, 1460

kHz. **Radio-FM:** KRBH, 98.5 MHz.
Honey Grove — **Newspaper:** Signal-Citizen.
Hooks — **Radio-FM:** KPWW, 95.9 MHz.
Hornsby — **Radio FM:** KOOP, 91.7 MHz.
Houston — **Newspapers:** Business Journal; Chronicle (D); Daily Court Review (D); Forward Times; Informer and Texas Freeman; Jewish Herald-Voice; Post (D); Texas Catholic Herald (SM). **Radio-AM:** KILT, 610 kHz; KBME, 720; KTRH, 740; KKBQ, 790; KEYH, 850; KPRC, 950; KLAT, 1010; KENR, 1070; KQUE, 1230; KXYZ, 1320; KCOH, 1430; KYOK, 1590. **Radio-FM:** KUHF, 88.7 MHz; KPFT, 90.1; KTSU, 90.9; KTRU, 91.7; KKRW, 93.7; KLDE, 94.5; KIKK, 95.7; KHMX, 96.5; KBXX, 97.9; KODA, 99.1; KILT, 100.3; KLOL, 101.1; KMJQ, 102.1; KLTN, 102.9; KRBE, 104.1; KHCB, 105.7. **TV:** KPRC-Ch. 2; KUHT-Ch. 8; KHOU-Ch. 11; KTRK-Ch. 13; KETH-CH. 14; KTXH-Ch. 20; KRIV-Ch. 26; KHOU-DT-Ch 31; KHTV-Ch. 39; KZJL-Ch. 61.
Howe — **Newspaper:** Texoma Enterprise. **Radio-FM:** KHYI, 95.3 MHz.
Hubbard — **Newspaper:** City News.
Humble — **Radio-AM:** KGOL, 1180 kHz. **Radio-FM:** KSBJ, 89.3 MHz.
Huntington — **Radio-FM:** KYBI, 101.9 MHz.
Huntsville — **Newspaper:** Item (D).**Radio-AM:** KHCH, 1400 kHz; KSAM, 1490. **Radio-FM:** KAXF, 88.3 MHz; KSHU, 90.5; KUST, 99.7; KSAM, 101.7.
Hutto — **Radio-FM:** KQQQ, 92.1 MHz.
Idalou — **Newspaper:** Beacon. **Radio-FM:** KRBL, 105.7 MHz.
Ingleside — **Newspaper:** Index. **Radio FM:** KCCG, 107.3 MHz.
Ingram — **Radio-FM:** KTXI, 90.1 MHz.
Iowa Park — **Newspaper:** Leader.
Iraan — **Newspaper:** News.
Irving — **Newspaper:** News (S).**TV:** KHSX-Ch. 49.
Italy — **Newspaper:** News-Herald.
Jacksboro — **Newspapers:** Gazette-News; Jack County Herald. **Radio-FM:** KJKB, 101.7 MHz.
Jacksonville — **Newspaper:** Daily Progress (D). **Radio-AM:** KEBE, 1400 kHz. **Radio-FM:** KBJS, 90.3 MHz; KLJT, 102.3; KOOI, 106.5. **TV:** KETK-Ch. 56.
Jasper — **Newspaper:** News/Boy. **Radio-AM:** KTXJ, 1350 kHz. **Radio-FM:** KWYX, 102.7 MHz; KJAS, 107.3.
Jefferson — **Newspaper:** Jimplecute. **Radio-FM:** KJTX, 104.5 MHz.
Jewett — **Newspaper:** Messenger.
Johnson City — **Newspaper:** Record-Courier. **Radio-FM:** KFAN, 107.9 MHz.
Joshua — **Newspaper:** Star Tribune.
Junction — **Newspaper:** Eagle. **Radio-AM:** KMBL, 1450 kHz. **Radio-FM:** KOOK, 93.5 MHz.
Karnes City — **Newspaper:** The Countywide. **Radio-AM:** KAML, 990 kHz.
Katy — **Newspaper:** Times (S).**TV:** KNWS-Ch. 51.
Kaufman — **Newspaper:** Herald.
Keene — **Newspaper:** Star Reporter. **Radio-FM:** KJCR; 88.3 MHz.
Kenedy — **Radio-AM:** KAML, 990 kHz. **Radio-FM:** KTNR, 92.1 MHz.
Kennedale — **Newspaper:** News.
Kerens — **Newspaper:** Tribune.
Kermit — **Newspaper:** Winkler County News. **Radio-AM:** KERB, 600 kHz. **Radio-FM:** KERB, 106.3 MHz.
Kerrville — **Newspapers:** Daily Times (D); Mountain Sun. **Radio-AM:** KERV, 1230 kHz. **Radio-FM:** KKER, 91.1 MHz; KITE, 92.3; KRVL, 94.3. **TV:** KRRT-Ch. 35.
Kilgore — **Newspaper:** News Herald (D). **Radio-AM:** KKTX, 1240 kHz. **Radio-FM:** KTPB, 88.7 Mhz; KKTX, 96.1.
Killeen — **Newspaper:** Daily Herald (D). **Radio-AM:** KRMY, 1050 kHz. **Radio-FM:** KNCT, 91.3 MHz; KIIZ, 92.3; KLNC, 93.3. **TV:** KAKW-Ch. 62.
Kingsville — **Newspaper:** Record and Bishop News (S). **Radio-AM:** KINE, 1330 kHz. **Radio-FM:** KTAI, 91.1 MHz; KKBA, 92.7; KFTX, 97.5.
Kirbyville — **Newspaper:** East Texas Banner.
Knox City — **Newspaper:** Knox County News.
Kress — **Newspaper:** Chronicle.
La Grange — **Newspaper:** Fayette County Record (S). **Radio-AM:** KVLG, 1570 kHz. **Radio-FM:** KBUK, 104.9 MHz.
Lake Dallas — **Newspaper:** Lake Cities Sun. **TV:** KLDT-Ch. 55.
Lake Jackson — **Newspaper:** Brazorian News. **Radio-FM:** KYBJ, 91.1 MHz; KTBZ, 107.5.
Lamesa — **Newspaper:** Press Reporter (S). **Radio-AM:** KPET, 690 kHz. **Radio-FM:** KIOL, 104.7 MHz.
Lampasas — **Newspaper:** Dispatch Record (S). **Radio-AM:** KCYL, 1450 kHz. **Radio-FM:** KJFK, 98.9 MHz.
Lancaster — **Newspaper:** Today.

La Porte — **Newspaper:** Bayshore Sun (S).
Laredo — **Newspaper:** Morning Times (D). **Radio-AM:** KLAR, 1300 kHz; KLNT, 1490. **Radio-FM:** KHOY, 88.1 MHz; KBNL, 89.9; KJBZ, 92.7; KOYE, 94.9; KRRG, 98.1; KNEX, 106.1. **TV:** KGNS-Ch. 8; KVTV-Ch. 13; KLDO-Ch. 27.
La Vernia — **Newspaper:** News.
Leakey — **Newspaper:** Real American. **Radio-FM:** KBLT, 104.3 MHz.
Leonard — **Newspaper:** Graphic.
Levelland — **Newspaper:** Hockley County News-Press (S). **Radio-AM:** KLVT, 1230 kHz. **Radio-FM:** KLVT, 105.5 MHz.
Liberty — **Newspaper:** Vindicator (S). **Radio-FM:** KSHN, 99.9 MHz.
Lindale — **Newspapers:** News and Times.
Linden — **Newspaper:** Cass County Sun.
Little Elm — **Newspaper:** Journal.
Littlefield — **Newspaper:** Lamb County Leader-News (S). **Radio-AM:** KZZN, 1490 kHz.
Livingston — **Newspaper:** Polk County Enterprise (S). **Radio-AM:** KETX, 1140 kHz. **Radio-FM:** KETX, 92.3 MHz.
Llano — **Newspaper:** News. **Radio-FM:** KBAE, 104.7 MHz. **TV:** KXAM-Ch. 14.
Lockhart — **Newspaper:** Post-Register. **Radio-AM:** KFIT, 1060 kHz.
Lometa — **Radio-FM:** KACQ, 101.9 MHz.
Longview — **Newspaper:** News-Journal (D). **Radio-AM:** KFRO, 1370 kHz. **Radio-FM:** KYKX, 105.7 MHz. **TV:** KFXK-Ch. 51.
Lorenzo — **Newspaper:** Examiner. **Radio-FM:** KKCL, 98.1 MHz.
Los Ybañez — **Radio-FM:** KYMI, 98.5 Mhz.
Lubbock — **Newspaper:** Avalanche-Journal (D). **Radio-AM:** KRFE, 580 kHz; KFYO, 790; KXTQ, 950; KKAM, 1340; KLFB, 1420; KBZO, 1460; KDAV, 1590. **Radio-FM:** KTXT, 88.1 MHz; KOHM, 89.1; KAMY, 90.1; KYFT, 90.9; KXTQ, 93.7; KFMX, 94.5; KLLL, 96.3; KCRM, 99.5; KONE, 101.1; KZII, 102.5; KEJS, 106.5. **TV:** KTXT-Ch. 5; KCBD-Ch. 11; KLBK-Ch. 13; KAMC-Ch. 28; KJTV- Ch. 34.
Lufkin — **Newspaper:** Daily News (D). **Radio-AM:** KRBA, 1340 kHz. **Radio-FM:** KLDN, 88.9 MHz; KSWP, 90.9; KUEZ, 99.3; KYKS, 105.1. **TV:** KTRE-Ch. 9.
Luling — **Newspaper:** Newsboy and Signal. **Radio-FM:** KAMX, 94.7 MHz.
Lytle — **Newspaper:** Medina Valley Times. **Radio-FM:** KXPZ, 91.3 MHz.
Mabank — **Newspaper:** Monitor (S).
Madisonville — **Newspaper:** Meteor. **Radio-AM:** KMVL, 1220 kHz. **Radio-FM:** KAGG, 96.1 MHz; KMVL, 100.5.
Malakoff — **Newspaper:** News. **Radio-FM:** KCKL, 95.9 MHz.
Mansfield — **Newspaper:** News-Mirror (S).
Marble Falls — **Newspapers:** Highlander (S); River Cities Tribune.
Marfa — **Newspaper:** Big Bend Sentinel.
Marion — **Radio-AM:** KBIB, 1000 kHz.
Marlin — **Newspaper:** Democrat. **Radio-FM:** KEYR, 92.9 MHz.
Marshall — **Newspaper:** News Messenger (D). **Radio-AM:** KCUL, 1410 kHz; KMHT, 1450. **Radio-FM:** KBWC, 91.1 MHz; KCUL, 92.3; KZEY, 103.9.
Mart — **Newspaper:** Texan.
Mason — **Newspaper:** Mason County News.
Matador — **Newspaper:** Motley County Tribune.
Mathis — **Newspaper:** News.
McAllen — **Newspapers:** Monitor (D). **Radio-AM:** KRIO, 910 kHz. **Radio-FM:** KHID, 88.1 MHz; KVMV, 96.9; KGBT, 98.5. **TV:** KNVO-Ch. 48.
McCamey — **Newspaper:** News.
McGregor — **Newspaper:** Mirror and Crawford Sun.
McKinney — **Newspaper:** Courier-Gazette (D). **Radio-FM:** KZDF, 106.9 MHz.
Memphis — **Newspaper:** Democrat. **Radio-FM:** KLSR, 105.3 MHz.
Menard — **Newspaper:** News and Messenger.
Mercedes — **Newspaper:** Enterprise. **Radio-FM:** KTJN, 106.3 MHz.
Meridian — **Newspaper:** Bosque County News.
Merkel — **Newspaper:** Mail. **Radio-AM:** KMXO, 1500 kHz. **Radio-FM:** KHXS, 102.7 MHz.
Mesquite — **Radio-FM:** KEOM, 88.5 MHz.
Mexia — **Newspaper:** Daily News (D). **Radio-AM:** KRQX, 1590 kHz. **Radio-FM:** KYCX, 104.9 MHz.
Miami — **Newspaper:** Chief.
Midland — **Newspaper:** Reporter-Telegram (D). **Radio-AM:** KCRS, 550 kHz; KWEL, 1070; KJBC, 1150; KMND, 1510. **Radio-FM:** KNFM, 92.3 MHz; KBAT, 93.3; KQRX, 95.1; KCRS, 103.3; KCHX, 106.7. **TV:** KMID-Ch. 2.
Midlothian — **Newspapers:** Mirror; Today.

Miles — Newspaper: Messenger.
Mineola — Newspaper: Monitor. **Radio-FM:** KMOO, 99.9 MHz.
Mineral Wells — Newspaper: Index (D). **Radio-AM:** KJSA, 1140 kHz. **Radio-FM:** KYXS, 95.9 MHz.
Mirando City — Radio-FM: KBDR, 100.5 MHz.
Mission — Newspaper: Progress-Times. **Radio-AM:** KIRT, 1580 kHz. **Radio-FM:** KTJX, 105.5 MHz.
Monahans — Newspaper: News. **Radio-AM:** KLBO, 1330 kHz. **Radio-FM:** KGEE, 99.9 MHz; KCDQ, 102.1.
Moody — Newspaper: Courier.
Morton — Newspaper: Tribune.
Moulton — Newspaper: Eagle.
Mount Pleasant — Newspaper: Daily Tribune (D). **Radio-AM:** KIMP, 960 kHz. **Radio-FM:** KPXI, 100.7 MHz.
Mount Vernon — Newspaper: Optic-Herald.
Muenster — Newspaper: Enterprise. **Radio-FM:** KXGM, 106.5 MHz.
Muleshoe — Newspapers: Bailey Co. Journal; Journal. **Radio-AM:** KMUL, 1380 kHz. **Radio-FM:** KMUL, 103.1 MHz.
Munday — Newspaper: Courier.
Nacogdoches — Newspaper: Daily Sentinel (D). **Radio-AM:** KSFA, 860 kHz; KEEE, 1230. **Radio-FM:** KSAU, 90.1 MHz; KJCS, 103.3; KTBQ, 107.7. **TV:** KLSB-Ch. 19.
Naples — Newspaper: Monitor.
Navasota — Newspaper: Examiner. **Radio-AM:** KWBC, 1550 kHz. **Radio-FM:** KMBV, 92.5 MHz.
Nederland — Radio-AM: KQHN, 1510 kHz.
Needville — Newspaper: Gulf Coast Tribune.
New Boston — Newspaper: Bowie County Citizens Tribune (S). **Radio-AM:** KNBO, 1530 kHz. **Radio-FM:** KEWL, 95.1 MHz; KZRB, 103.5.
New Braunfels — Newspaper: Herald-Zeitung (D). **Radio-AM:** KGNB, 1420 kHz. **Radio-FM:** KNBT, 92.1 MHz.
Newton — Newspaper: Newton County News.
New Ulm — Newspaper: Enterprise.
Nixon — Newspaper: Cow Country Courier.
Nocona — Newspaper: News.
Nolanville — Radio FM: KLFX, 107.3 MHz.
Normangee — Newspaper: Star.
Odem — Newspaper: Odem-Edroy Times. **Radio-FM:** KLHB, 98.3 MHz.
Odessa — Newspaper: American (D). **Radio-AM:** KENT, 920 kHz; KOZA, 1230; KRIL, 1410. **Radio-FM:** KENT, 90.5 MHz; KOCV, 91.3; KMRK, 96.1; KMCM, 96.9; KODM, 97.9; KLVW, 99.1; KQLM, 107.9. **TV:** KOSA-Ch. 7; KWES-Ch. 9; KPEJ-Ch. 24; KOCV-Ch. 36; KMLM-Ch. 42.
O'Donnell — Newspaper: Index-Press.
Olney — Newspaper: Enterprise.
Olton — Newspaper: Enterprise.
Orange — Newspaper: Leader (D). **Radio-AM:** KOGT, 1600 kHz. **Radio-FM:** KKMY, 104.5 MHz; KIOC, 106.1.
Overton — Newspaper: Press.
Ozona — Newspaper: Stockman. **Radio-FM:** KYXX, 94.3 MHz.
Paducah — Newspaper: Post.
Paint Rock — Newspaper: Concho Herald.
Palacios — Newspaper: Beacon. **Radio-FM:** KKOS, 99.7 MHz.
Palestine — Newspaper: Herald Press (D). **Radio-AM:** KNET, 1450 kHz. **Radio-FM:** KLIS, 96.7 MHz; KYYK, 98.3.
Pampa — Newspaper: News (D). **Radio-AM:** KGRO, 1230 kHz. **Radio-FM:** KOMX, 100.3 MHz.
Panhandle — Newspaper: Herald.
Paris — Newspaper: News (D). **Radio-AM:** KGDD, 1250 kHz; KPLT, 1490. **Radio-FM:** KOYN, 93.9 MHz; KBUS, 101.9; KPLT, 107.7.
Pasadena — Newspaper: Citizen (D). **Radio-AM:** KIKK, 650 kHz; KLVL, 1480. **Radio-FM:** KFTG, 88.1 MHz; KKBQ, 92.9.
Pearland — Newspapers: Journal; Reporter News.
Pearsall — Newspaper: Frio-Nueces Current. **Radio-AM:** KVWG, 1280 kHz. **Radio-FM:** KVWG, 95.3 MHz.
Pecos — Newspaper: Enterprise (D). **Radio-AM:** KIUN, 1400 kHz. **Radio-FM:** KPTX, 98.3 MHz.
Perryton — Newspaper: Herald (S). **Radio-AM:** KEYE, 1400 kHz. **Radio-FM:** KEYE, 95.9 MHz.
Petersburg — Newspaper: Post.
Pflugerville — Newspaper: Pflag.
Pharr — Newspaper: Pharr/San Juan/Alamo Advance News Journal. **Radio-AM:** KVJY, 840 kHz.
Pilot Point — Newspaper: Post-Signal. **Radio-FM:** KTCY, 104.9 MHz.
Pittsburg — Newspaper: Gazette. **Radio-FM:** KXAL, 103.1 MHz.
Plains — Radio-FM: KPHS, 90.3 MHz.
Plainview — Newspaper: Daily Herald (D). **Radio-AM:** KKYN,

1090 kHz; KVOP, 1400. **Radio-FM:** KWLD, 91.5 MHz; KVOP, 97.3; KKYN, 103.9.
Plano — Newspaper: Star Courier (D). **Radio AM:** KAAM, 620 kHz.
Pleasanton — Newspaper: Express. **Radio-AM:** KBOP, 1380 kHz. **Radio-FM:** KBUC, 98.3 MHz.
Port Aransas — Newspaper: South Jetty.
Port Arthur — Newspaper: News (D). **Radio-AM:** KALO, 1250 kHz; KOLE, 1340. **Radio-FM:** KOVE, 93.9 MHz; KHYS, 98.5. **TV:** KJAC-Ch. 4.
Port Isabel — Newspaper: Port Isabel/South Padre Press (S). **Radio-FM:** KVPA, 101.1 MHz.
Portland — Newspaper: News. **Radio-FM:** KRAD, 105.5 MHz.
Port Lavaca — Newspaper: Wave (S). **Radio-FM:** KPLV, 93.3 MHz.
Port Neches — Radio-AM: KUHD, 1150 kHz.
Post — Newspaper: Dispatch. **Radio-AM:** KPOS, 1370 kHz. **Radio-FM:** KOFR, 107.3 MHz.
Pottsboro — Newspaper: Press.
Prairie View — Radio-FM: KPVU, 91.3 MHz.
Premont — Radio-FM: KMFM, 104.9 MHz.
Presidio — Newspaper: The International.
Princeton — Newspaper: Herald.
Quanah — Newspaper: Tribune-Chief (S). **Radio-AM:** KVDL, 1150 kHz. **Radio-FM:** KIXC, 100.9 MHz.
Quinlan — Newspaper: Tawakoni News.
Quitaque — Newspaper: Valley Tribune.
Quitman — Newspaper: Wood County Democrat.
Ralls — Radio-AM: KCLR, 1530 kHz.
Ranger — Newspaper: Times (S).
Rankin — Newspaper: News.
Raymondville — Newspaper: Chronicle/Willacy County News. **Radio-AM:** KSOX, 1240 kHz. **Radio-FM:** KSOX, 102.1 MHz; KBIC, 105.7.
Red Oak — Newspapers: Ellis County Chronicle (S).
Refugio — Newspaper: County Advantage Press. **Radio-FM:** KTKY, 106.1 MHz.
Richardson — Newspaper: News (S).
Richmond: see **Rosenberg.**
Riesel — Newspaper: Rustler.
Rio Grande City — Newspaper: Rio Grande Herald. **Radio-FM:** KCTM, 103.1 MHz.
Rising Star — Newspaper: Rising Star.
Robert Lee — Newspaper: Observer/Enterprise.
Robstown — Newspaper: Nueces County Record-Star. **Radio-AM:** KGLF, 1510 kHz. **Radio-FM:** KLUX, 89.5 MHz; KSAB, 99.9; KMIQ, 105.1.
Rochester — Newspaper: Twin Cities News.
Rockdale — Newspaper: Reporter and Messenger. **Radio-FM:** KRXT, 98.5 MHz.
Rockport — Newspapers: Herald; Pilot (S). **Radio-FM:** KBTE, 102.3 MHz.
Rocksprings — Newspaper: Texas Mohair Weekly.
Rockwall — Newspapers: Chronicle; Texas Success (S).
Rollingwood — Radio-AM: KJCE, 1370 kHz.
Roma — Newspaper: South Texas Reporter. **Radio-FM:** KBMI, 97.7 MHz.
Rosebud — Newspaper: News.
Rosenberg — Newspaper: Herald-Coaster (D). **Radio-AM:** KRTX, 980 kHz. **Radio-FM:** KOVA, 104.9 Mhz. **TV:** KXLN-Ch. 45.
Rotan — Newspaper: Advance-Star-Record.
Round Rock — Newspaper: Leader (S). **Radio-FM:** KNLE, 88.1 MHz.
Rowena — Newspaper: Press.
Rowlett — Newspaper: Lakeshore Times.
Royse City — Newspaper: News.
Rusk — Newspaper: Cherokeean/Herald. **Radio-AM:** KTLU, 1580 kHz. **Radio-FM:** KWRW, 97.7 MHz.
Saint Jo — Newspaper: Tribune.
San Angelo — Newspaper: Standard-Times (D). **Radio-AM:** KGKL, 960 kHz; KKSA, 1260; KCRN, 1340. **Radio-FM:** KUTX, 90.1 MHz; KDCD, 92.9; KDCD, 92.9; KCRN, 93.9; KIXY, 94.7; KGKL, 97.5; KELI, 98.7; KYZZ, 100.1; KWFR, 101.9; KSJT, 107.5. **TV:** KACB-Ch. 3; KIDY-Ch. 6; KLST-Ch. 8.
San Antonio — Newspapers: Business Journal; Commercial Recorder (D); Express-News (D); North San Antonio Times; Today's Catholic (BW). **Radio-AM:** KTSA, 550 kHz; KSLR, 630; KKYX, 680; KTKR, 760; KONO, 860; KFIT EXP STN, 1060; KENS, 1160; WOAI, 1200; KZDC, 1250; KPOZ, 1310; KCOR, 1350; KCHL, 1480; KEDA, 1540. **Radio-FM:** KPAC, 88.3 MHz; KSTX, 89.1; KSYM, 90.1; KYFS, 90.9; KRTU, 91.7; KROM, 92.9; KXXM, 96.1; KAJA, 97.3; KISS, 99.5; KCYY, 100.3; KQXT, 101.9; KTFM, 102.7; KZEP, 104.5; KXTN, 107.5. **TV:** KMOL-Ch. 4; KENS-Ch. 5; KLRN-Ch. 9;

KSAT-Ch. 12; KHCE-Ch. 23; KABB-Ch. 29; KWEX-Ch. 41; KVDA-Ch. 60.

San Augustine — Newspaper: Tribune. **Radio-FM:** KCOT, 92.5 MHz.

San Benito — Newspaper: News (S).

Sanderson — Newspaper: Times.

San Diego — Newspaper: Duval County Picture. **Radio-FM:** KUKA, 105.9 MHz.

Sanger — Newspaper: Courier. Radio-FM: KXZN, 104.1 MHz.

San Juan — Radio-AM: KUBR, 1210 kHz.

San Marcos — Newspaper: Daily Record (D). **Radio-AM:** KUOL, 1470 kHz. **Radio-FM:** KTSW, 89.9 MHz; KEYI, 103.5.

San Saba — Newspaper: News & Star. **Radio-AM:** KBAL, 1410 kHz.

Santa Anna — Newspaper: News.

Schulenburg — Newspaper: Sticker.

Seabrook — Radio-FM: KRTS, 92.1 MHz.

Seadrift — Radio-FM: KMAT, 105.1 MHz.

Seagoville — Newspaper: Suburbia News.

Seagraves — Newspaper: Gaines County News.

Sealy — Newspaper: News (S).

Seguin — Newspaper: Gazette-Enterprise (D). **Radio-AM:** KWED, 1580 kHz. **Radio-FM:** KSMG, 105.3 MHz.

Seminole — Newspaper: Sentinel (S). **Radio-AM:** KIKZ, 1250 kHz. **Radio-FM:** KSEM, 106.3 MHz.

Seymour — Newspaper: Baylor County Banner. **Radio-AM:** KSEY, 1230 kHz. **Radio-FM:** KSEY, 94.3 MHz.

Shamrock — Newspaper: Irish Star-News; Texan. **Radio-FM:** KRMN, 92.7 MHz.

Shepherd — Newspaper: San Jacinto News-Times.

Sherman — Newspaper: Herald Democrat (D). **Radio-AM:** KXEB, 910 kHz; KJIM, 1500. **Radio-FM:** KNKI, 96.7 MHz; KIXL, 104.1. **TV:** KXII-Ch. 12.

Shiner — Newspaper: Gazette.

Silsbee — Newspaper: Bee. **Radio-AM:** KKAS, 1300 kHz. **Radio-FM:** KWDX, 101.7 MHz.

Silverton — Newspaper: Briscoe County News.

Sinton — Newspaper: San Patricio Co. News. **Radio-AM:** KDAE, 1590 kHz. **Radio-FM:** KNCN, 101.3 MHz; KOUL, 103.7.

Slaton — Newspaper: Slatonite. **Radio-FM:** KJAK, 92.7 MHz.

Smithville — Newspaper: Times.

Snyder — Newspaper: Daily News (D). **Radio-AM:** KSNY, 1450 kHz. **Radio-FM:** KSNY, 101.5 MHz. **TV:** KPCB-Ch. 17.

Somerset — Radio-AM: KSJL, 810 kHz.

Sonora — Newspaper: Devil's River News. **Radio-AM:** KHOS, 980 kHz. **Radio-FM:** KHOS, 92.1 MHz.

South Padre Island — Radio-FM: KESO, 92.7 MHz; KZSP, 95.3.

Spearman — Newspaper: Hansford County Reporter-Statesman. **Radio-FM:** KRDF, 98.3 MHz.

Springtown — Newspaper: Epigraph. **Radio-FM:** KMQX, 89.1 MHz.

Spur — Newspaper: Texas Spur.

Stamford — Newspaper: American. **Radio-AM:** KVRP, 1400 kHz.

Stanton — Newspaper: Martin County Messenger. **Radio-FM:** KKJW, 105.9 MHz.

Stephenville — Newspaper: Empire-Tribune (D). **Radio-AM:** KSTV, 1510 kHz. **Radio-FM:** KCUB, 98.3 MHz.

Sterling City — Newspaper: News-Record. **Radio-FM:** KKCN, 96.5 MHz.

Stinnett — Newspaper: Post

Stratford — Newspaper: Star.

Strawn — Newspaper: Quad City Messenger.

Sudan — Newspaper: Beacon-News.

Sugar Land — Newspaper: Fort Bend Mirror.

Sulphur Springs — Newspaper: News-Telegram (D). **Radio-AM:** KSST, 1230 kHz. **Radio-FM:** KDXE, 95.9 MHz.

Sweetwater — Newspaper: Reporter (D). **Radio-AM:** KXOX, 1240 kHz. **Radio-FM:** KXOX, 96.7 MHz. **TV:** KTXS-Ch. 12.

Taft — Newspaper: Tribune.

Tahoka — Newspaper: Lynn County News. **Radio-FM:** KMMX, 100.3 MHz.

Talco — Newspaper: Times.

Tatum — Newspaper: Trammel Trace Tribune.

Taylor — Newspaper: Daily Press (D). **Radio-AM:** KTAE, 1260 kHz. **Radio FM:** KQBT, 104.3 MHz.

Teague — Newspaper: Chronicle.

Temple — Newspaper: Daily Telegram (D). **Radio-AM:** KTEM, 1400 kHz. **Radio-FM:** KLTD, 101.7 MHz. **TV:** KCEN-Ch. 6.

Terrell — Newspaper: Tribune (D). **Radio-AM:** KPYK, 1570 kHz. **Radio-FM:** KZDL, 107.1 MHz.

Terrell Hills — Radio-AM: KLUP, 930 kHz. **Radio-FM:** KCJZ,

106.7 MHz.

Texarkana — Newspaper: Gazette (D). **Radio-AM:** KCMC, 740 kHz; KTFS, 940; KOWS, 1400. **Radio-FM:** KTXK, 91.5 MHz; KTAL, 98.1; KKYR, 102.5. **TV:** KTAL-Ch. 6.

Texas City — Newspaper: Sun (D). **Radio-AM:** KYST, 920 kHz.

Thorndale — Newspaper: Champion.

Three Rivers — Newspaper: Progress.

Throckmorton — Newspaper: Tribune.

Timpson — Newspaper: Timpson & Tenaha News.

Tomball — Radio-AM: KSEV, 700 kHz.

Trenton — Newspaper: Tribune.

Trinity — Newspaper: Standard.

Tulia — Newspapers: Herald; Sentinel. **Radio-AM:** KTUE, 1260 kHz. **Radio-FM:** KJMX, 104.9 Mhz.

Tuscola — Newspaper: Journal.

Tye — Radio-FM: KBCY, 99.7 MHz.

Tyler — Newspapers: Morning Telegraph (D); Catholic East Texas (BW). **Radio-AM:** KTBB, 600 kHz; KZEY, 690; KGLD, 1330; KYZS, 1490. **Radio-FM:** KVNE, 89.5 MHz; KGLY, 91.3; KDOK, 92.1; KTYL, 93.1; KNUE, 101.5; KKUS, 104.1. **TV:** KLTV-Ch. 7.

Universal City — Radio-AM: KSAH, 720 kHz.

Uvalde — Newspaper: Leader-News (S). **Radio-AM:** KVOU, 1400 kHz. **Radio-FM:** KBNU, 93.7 MHz; KUVA, 102.3; KYUF, 104.9.

Valley Mills — Newspaper: Progress.

Van Alstyne — Newspaper: Leader.

Van Horn — Newspaper: Advocate.

Vega — Newspaper: Enterprise.

Vernon — Newspaper: Daily Record (D). **Radio-AM:** KVWC, 1490 kHz. **Radio-FM:** KVWC, 102.3 MHz.

Victoria — Newspaper: Advocate (D). **Radio-AM:** KAMG, 1340 kHz; KNAL, 1410. **Radio-FM:** KXBJ, 89.3 MHz; KVRT, 90.7; KVLT, 92.3; KVIC, 95.1; KTXN, 98.7; KEPG, 100.9; KIXS, 107.9. **TV:** KVCT-Ch. 19; KAVU-Ch. 25.

Vidor — Newspaper: Vidorian.

Waco — Newspapers: Citizen (S); Tribune-Herald (D). **Radio-AM:** KBBW, 1010; KWTX, 1230 kHz; KKTK, 1460; KRZI, 1580. **Radio-FM:** KBCT, 94.5 MHz; KCKR, 95.5; KWTX, 97.5; WACO, 99.9; KWBU, 107.1. **TV:** KWTX-Ch. 10; KXXV-Ch. 25; KCTF-Ch. 34; KWKT-Ch. 44.

Wallis — Newspaper: News-Review.

Waskom — Newspaper: Review.

Waxahachie — Newspaper: Daily Light (D). **Radio-AM:** KBEC, 1390 kHz.

Weatherford — Newspapers: Democrat (D). **Radio-AM:** KZEE, 1220 kHz. **Radio-FM:** KYQX, 89.5 MHz.

Weimar — Newspaper: Mercury.

Wellington — Newspaper: Leader.

Weslaco — Radio-AM: KRGE, 1290 kHz. **TV:** KRGV-Ch. 5.

West — Newspaper: News.

West Lake Hills — Radio-AM: KTXZ, 1560 kHz.

Wharton — Newspaper: Journal-Spectator (S). **Radio-AM:** KANI, 1500 kHz.

Wheeler — Newspapers: Area News; Times. **Radio-FM:** KPDR, 90.5 MHz.

White Deer — Newspaper: News.

Whitehouse — Newspaper: Tri County Leader. **Radio-FM:** KISX, 107.3 MHz.

White Oak — Newspaper: Independent.

Whitesboro — Newspaper: News-Record.

Whitewright — Newspaper: Sun.

Whitney — Newspapers: Lake Whitney View (M).

Wichita Falls — Newspaper: Times-Record-News (D). **Radio-AM:** KWFS, 1290 kHz. **Radio-FM:** KMOC, 89.5 MHz; KTEO, 90.5; KNIN, 92.9; KLUR, 99.9; KQXC, 102.5; KWFS, 103.3; KTLT, 106.3. **TV:** KFDX-Ch. 3; KAUZ-Ch. 6; KJTL-Ch. 18.

Willis — Radio FM: KVST, 103.7 MHz.

Wills Point — Newspapers: Chronicle; Van Zandt News.

Wimberley — Newspaper: View.

Winfield — Radio-FM: KALK, 97.7 MHz.

Winnie — Newspaper: Hometown Press. **Radio FM:** KRTX, 100.7 MHz.

Winnsboro — Newspapers: News; Tribune. **Radio-FM:** KWNS, 104.7 MHz.

Winters — Newspaper: Enterprise.

Wolfe City — Newspaper: Mirror.

Woodville — Newspaper: Tyler County Booster. **Radio-AM:** KVLL, 1490 kHz. **Radio-FM:** KVLL, 94.7 MHz.

Wylie — Newspaper: News.

Yoakum — Newspaper: Herald-Times. **Radio-FM:** KYKM, 92.5 MHz.

Yorktown — Newspapers: News-View.

Zapata — Newspapers: Zapata County News. ☆

Agriculture in Texas

Source: Texas Agricultural Extension Service.

Agribusiness, the combined phases of food and fiber production, processing, transporting and marketing, is a leading Texas industry. Most of the following discussion is devoted to the phase of production on farms and ranches.

Information was provided by Agricultural Extension Service specialists, Texas Agricultural Statistics Service, U.S. Department of Agriculture and U.S. Department of Commerce. It was coordinated by Carl G. Anderson, Extension Marketing Economist, Texas A&M University. All references are to Texas unless otherwise specified.

Agriculture is one of the most important industries in Texas. Many businesses, financial institutions, and individuals are involved in providing supplies, credit, and services to farmers and ranchers and in processing and marketing agricultural commodities.

Including all its agribusiness phases, agriculture added about $40 billion in 1998 to the economic activity of the state. The estimated value of farm assets in Texas — the land, buildings, livestock, machinery, crops, inventory on farms, household goods and farm financial assets — totaled approximately $93 billion at the beginning of 1998.

Receipts from farm and ranch marketings in 1998 were estimated at $13.2 billion, compared with $13.5 billion in 1997.

With the increasing demand for food and fiber throughout the world, and because of the importance of agricultural exports to this nation's trade balance, agriculture in Texas is destined to play an even greater role in the future.

The number and nature of farms have changed over time. The number of farms in Texas has decreased from 418,000 in 1940 to 226,000 in 1998 with an average size of 582 acres. Average value per farm of all farm assets, including land and buildings, has increased from $20,100 in 1950 to $345,100 in 1998. The number of small farms is increasing, but they are operated by part-time farmers.

Mechanization of farming continues as new and larger machines replace manpower. Even though machinery price tags are high relative to times past, machines are technologically advanced and efficient. Tractors, mechanical harvesters and numerous cropping machines have virtually eliminated menial tasks that for many years were traditional to farming.

Revolutionary agricultural chemicals have appeared along with improved plants and animals and methods of handling them. Many of the natural hazards of farming and ranching were reduced by better use of weather information, machinery and other improvements; but rising costs, labor availability and high energy costs have added to concerns of farmers and ranchers.

Changes in Texas agriculture in the last 50 years include:
• Farmers and ranchers are keeping more detailed records.
• Choice or inputs/practices are more restricted.
• Precision agriculture is taking on new dimensions through the use of satellites, computers and other high-tech tools, helping producers manage such factors as seed, fertilizers, pesticides and water.
• Farms have become fewer, larger, specialized and much more expensive to own and operate, but far more productive.
• Irrigation has become more important in crop production.
• Production areas for crops and livestock have shifted, as in the concentration of cotton on the High Plains and livestock increases in Central and Eastern Texas.
• Pest- and disease-control methods have greatly improved. Herbicides are relied upon for weed control.
• Ranchers and farmers are better educated and informed, more science- and business-oriented.
• Feedlot finishing, commercial broiler production, artificial insemination, improved pastures and brush control,

Balance Sheet of Texas Farms and Ranches
Jan. 1, 1988-1997

Table below shows the financial status of Texas farms and ranches as of Jan. 1 of the years 1988-97.
(All amounts given in millions of dollars.)

Item	1988	1989	1990	1991	1992	1993	1994	1995	1996	§ 1997
ASSETS:										
Physical Assets:										
Real estate	$68,467	$58,853	$58,970	$57,239	$58,503	$60,071	$62,382	$63,459	$68,330	$74,024
Non-real estate:										
*Livestock and poultry	7,514	7,929	8,570	8,343	8,983	8,986	8,703	6,417	6,403	7,948
†Machinery and motor vehicles	5,437	5,411	5,556	5,546	5,491	5,694	5,820	5,923	6,069	6,026
‡Crops stored on and off farms	794	841	579	601	623	548	641	741	839	905
Purchased Inputs	317	222	133	110	170	151	194	124	159	186
Financial assets:	5,121	2,746	2,992	3,211	3,516	3,897	3,900	3,998	3,968	3,918
Total Assets.	****91,131**	**76,003**	**76,801**	**75,050**	**77,286**	**79,348**	**81,641**	**80,661**	**85,767**	**93,007**
LIABILITIES:										
††Real estate debt	5,143	4,560	4,637	4,621	4,538	4,495	4,523	4,679	4,870	5,256
‡‡Non-real estate debt:										
Excluding CCC loans	5,576	5,104	4,876	5,059	4,828	5,210	5,386	5,469	5,601	5,884
Total Liabilities	**10,718**	**9,663**	**9,513**	**9,680**	**9,366**	**9,704**	**9,909**	**10,149**	**10,472**	**11,140**
Owners' equities	80,412	66,339	67,288	65,370	67,920	69,643	71,732	70,512	75,296	81,867
TOTAL CLAIMS	**$91,131**	**$76,003**	**$76,801**	**$75,050**	**$77,286**	**$79,348**	**$81,651**	**80,661$**	**85,767$**	**93,007$**

*Excludes horses, mules and broilers.
†Includes only farm share value for trucks and autos.
‡All non-CCC crops held on farms plus value above loan rate for crops held under CCC.
§Preliminary.
**In 1988 only, total includes $3,482 million in household equipment and furnishings, categories not reported in subsequent years.
††Includes CCC storage and drying facilities loans.
‡‡Includes debt owed to institutional lender and to noninstitutional or miscellaneous lender. Excludes nonrecourse CCC loans secured by crops owned by farmers. These crops are included as assets in this balance sheet.

Source: "Economic Indicators of the Farm Sector: State Financial Summary 1985," USDA, ERS, January 1987, p.229.; 1988, 1989, 1991, 1993, p. 136 (including operator households). Farm Business Economics Report, Aug. 1996; Farm Business Sheet, April 1997.

reduced feed requirements and other changes have greatly increased livestock- and poultry-production efficiency. Biotechnology and genetic engineering promise new breakthroughs in reaching even higher levels of productivity.

• Horticultural plant and nursery businesses have expanded.

• Improved wildlife management has increased deer, turkey and other wildlife populations.

• Cooperation among farmers in marketing, promotion and other fields has increased.

• Agricultural producers have become increasingly dependent on off-the-farm services to supply production inputs such as feeds, chemicals, credit and other essentials.

Agribusiness

Texas farmers and ranchers have developed considerable dependence upon agribusiness. With many producers specializing in the production of certain crops and livestock, they look beyond the farm and ranch for supplies and services. On the input side, they rely on suppliers of production needs and services and, on the output side, they need assemblers, processors and distributors. The impact of production agriculture and related businesses on the Texas economy is about $40 billion annually.

Since 1940, the proportion of Texans whose livelihood is linked to agriculture has changed greatly. In 1940, about 23 percent were producers on farms and ranches, and about 17 percent were suppliers or were engaged in assembly, processing and distribution of agricultural products. The agribusiness alignment in 1998 was less than 2 percent on farms and ranches, with about 17 percent of the labor force providing production or marketing supplies and services and retailing food and fiber products.

Cash Receipts

Farm and ranch cash receipts in 1997 totaled $13.471 billion. With estimates of $648.6 million for government payments, $850 million of noncash income, and $1.053 billion of other farm-related income included, realized gross farm income totaled $16.560 billion. With farm production expenses of $12.967 billion, net farm income totaled $3.593 billion. The value of inventory adjustment was $427.5 million.

Farm and Ranch Assets

Farm and ranch assets totaled $93.0 billion in 1997. This was up from the 1996 level of $85.8 billion. Value of real estate increased almost 8 percent to $74 billion. Liabilities totaled $11.1 billion, up slightly from $10.5 billion in 1996.

Percent of Income From Products

Livestock and livestock products accounted for 60.8 percent of the $13.5 billion cash receipts from farm marketings in 1997 with the remaining 39.2 percent from crops. Receipts from livestock have trended up largely because of increased feeding operations and reduced crop acreage associated with farm programs and low prices. However, these relationships change because of variations in commodity prices and volume of marketings.

Meat animals (cattle, hogs and sheep) accounted for 42.2 percent of total cash receipts received by Texas farmers and ranchers in 1997. Most of these receipts were from cattle and calf sales. Dairy products made up 5.6 percent of receipts, poultry

and eggs 8.1 percent, and miscellaneous livestock 1.7 percent.

Cotton accounted for 11.2 percent of total receipts, feed crops 9.5 percent, food grains 3.8 percent, vegetables 2.4 percent, greenhouse/nursery products 7.7 percent, oil crops 1.8 percent, fruits and nuts 0.7 percent, and other crops 8.0 percent.

Texas' Rank Among States

Measured by cash receipts for farm and ranch marketings, Texas ranked second in 1997. California ranked first and Iowa third.

Texas normally leads all other states in numbers of farms and ranches and farm and ranch land, cattle slaughtered, cattle on feed, calf births, sheep and lambs slaughtered, goats, cash receipts from livestock marketings, cattle and calves, beef cows, sheep and lambs, wool production, mohair production, and exports of lard and tallow. The state also usually leads in production of cotton.

Texas' Agricultural Exports

The value of Texas' share of agricultural exports in fiscal year 1997 was $3.054 billion, compared to $3.477 billion in 1996. Cotton accounted for $564.2 million of the exports; feed grains and products, $329.5 million; wheat and products, $143.0 million; rice, $109.7 million; fats, oil and greases, $77.4 million; cottonseed and products, $27.6 million; hides and skins, $258.2 million; live animals and meat, excluding chickens, $654.9 million; fruits, $43.2 million; peanuts and products, $51.6 million; soybeans and products, $27.3 million; vegetables, $49.5 million; poultry and products, $140.3 million; dairy products, $23.5 million; and miscellaneous other products, $544.8 million.

Texas 1997 Crop Production

*Rank Among States	Crop	Planted Acres (000)	Harvested Acres (000)	Yield Per Acre	Production (000)
1	Upland Cotton	5,500.00	5,150.00	494.00	5,300 bales
1	All Cotton	5,532.00	5,182.00	496.00	5,355 bales
1	All Other Hay	—	4,300.00	2.40	10,320 tns
1	All Hay	—	4,400.00	2.45	10,790 tns
2	Sorghum for Grain	3,300.00	3,150.00	59.00	185,850 bu
2	Amer.-Pima Cotton	32.00	32.00	825.00	55 bales
2	Peanuts for Nuts	319.00	312.00	2,600.00	811,200 lbs
2	Blackeye (peas) Beans	12.00	11.20	1,000.00	112 cwt.
2	Pecans	—	—	—	70,000 lbs
3	Sunflower Sd., non-oil	65.00	63.00	900.00	56,700 lbs
3	Mid & Navel Oranges	—	7.50	173.00	1,300 bxs
3	All Oranges	—	8.70	163.00	1,420 bxs
3	All Grapefruit	—	20.40	260.00	5,300 bxs
3	Summer Potatoes	8.50	7.70	245.00	1,887 cwt
4	Winter Wheat	6,300.00	4,100.00	29.00	118,900 bu
4	All Rice	260.00	259.00	5,500.00	14,240 cwt
4	Sorghum for Silage	—	30.00	14.00	420 tons
4	Sugar Cane for Sugar	—	29.50	29.00	856 tons
4	Sugar Cane for Seed	—	2.00	23.00	46 tons
4	All Sugar Cane	—	31.50	28.60	902 tons
4	Valencia Oranges	—	1.20	100.00	120 boxes
5	Spring Potatoes	8.30	8.00	195.00	1,560 cwt
5	Sweet Potatoes	6.30	5.80	160.00	928 cwt
6	All Wheat	6,300.00	4,100.00	29.00	118,900 bu
6	All Sunflowers	88.00	85.00	926.00	78,700 lbs
7	Sunflower Seed, Oil	23.00	22.00	1,000.00	22,000 lbs
9	Oats	550.00	110.00	52.00	5,720 bu
9	Freestone Peaches	—	—	—	20,000 lbs
11	Sugar Beets	16.50	15.00	19.50	293 tons
12	Rye	130.00	10.00	33.00	330 bu
12	Corn for Grain	2,000.00	1,800.00	138.00	248,400 bu
12	Other Dry Edible Beans	1.50	1.40	1,000.00	14 cwt
14	Pinto Beans	1.50	1.40	1,210.00	17 cwt
15	All Potatoes	16.80	15.70	220.00	3,447 cwt
16	All Dry Edible Beans	15.00	14.00	1,020.00	143 cwt
20	Corn for Silage	—	60.00	23.50	1,410 tons
23	Soybeans for Beans	420.00	400.00	28.00	11,200 bu
26	Barley	10.00	5.00	47.00	235 bu
28	Alfalfa Hay	—	100.00	4.70	470 tons

*Based on production. *Source: U.S. and Texas Departments of Agriculture.*

Hunting

The management of wildlife as an economic enterprise through leasing for hunting makes a significant contribution to the economy of many counties. Hunting-lease income to farmers and ranchers in 1998 was estimated at $254 million. The demand for hunting opportunities is growing, while the land capable of producing huntable wildlife is decreasing. As a result, farmers and ranchers are placing more emphasis on wildlife management practices to help meet requests for hunting leases.

Irrigation

Texas farmers irrigate approximately 6 million acres of land (third in the nation behind California and Nebraska). Although some irrigation is practiced in nearly every county of the state, about 60 percent of the total irrigated acreage is on the High Plains of Texas. Other concentrated areas of irrigation are the Gulf Coast rice producing area, the Lower Rio Grande Valley, the Winter Garden district of South Texas, the Trans-Pecos area of West Texas, and the peanut-producing area in North Central Texas centered around Erath, Eastland and Comanche counties. Sprinkler irrigation was used on about 63 percent of the total irrigated acreage, with surface irrigation methods, primarily furrow and surge methods, being used on the remaining irrigated area.

Drip, or trickle, irrigation is primarily used on tree crops such as citrus, pecans, avocados, peaches and apples, or for irrigating vegetables under plastic mulch. Some drip irrigation of cotton and forages is being practiced in West Texas. The use of drip irrigation is increasing, with the present area estimated to be 104,000 acres.

Approximately 81 percent of the state's irrigated acreage is supplied with well water; surface water sources supply the remainder. Declining groundwater levels in several of the major aquifers is a serious problem. As the water level declines, well yields decrease and pumping costs increase.

Although only about 30 percent of the state's total harvested cropland acreage is irrigated, the value of crop production from irrigated acreage is 50 to 60 percent of the total value of all crop production. The percentage of total crop production that comes from irrigated lands varies from year to year, depending primarily upon the amount of rainfall received. In good rainfall years, the proportion of irrigated production to total production is somewhat less. However, in years of below-average rainfall, the percentage of the total production coming from irrigated lands increases. Thus, irrigation enables Texas farmers to produce a more dependable supply of food and fiber products without total dependence upon natural rainfall.

I. Principal Crops

In most recent years the value of crop production in Texas is less than half of the total value of the state's agricultural output. Cash receipts from farm sales of crops are reduced somewhat because some grain and roughage is fed to livestock on farms where produced.

Receipts from all Texas crops totaled $5.3 billion in 1997 and $5.1 billion in 1996.

Cotton, corn and grain sorghum account for a large part of the total crop receipts. In 1997, cotton contributed about 26.2 percent of the crop total; corn, 12.4 percent; sorghum grain, 8.5 percent; and wheat, 6.8 percent. Hay, vegetables, rice, cottonseed, peanuts and soybeans are other important cash crops.

Cotton

Cotton has been a major crop in Texas for more than a century. Since 1880, Texas has led all states in cotton production in most years, and today the annual Texas cotton harvest amounts to approximately a fourth of total production in the United States. The annual cotton crop has averaged 4.45 million bales since 1986.

Total value of upland and pima lint cotton produced in Texas in 1998 was $997.6 million. Cottonseed value in 1998 was $184.7 million, making the total value of the Texas crop around $1.182 billion.

Upland cotton was harvested from 3.3 million acres in 1998 and American-Pima from 32,000 acres, for a total of 3.382 million acres. Yield for upland cotton in 1998 was 509 pounds per acre, with American-Pima yielding 750 pounds per acre. Cotton acreage harvested in 1997 totaled 5.232 million, with a yield of 474 pounds per acre for upland cotton and 815 pounds per acre for American-Pima. Total cotton production was 3.550 million bales in 1998 and 5.194 million in 1997. Counties leading in production of upland cotton in 1997 included Gaines, Lubbock, Hale, Lynn, Terry and Lamb.

Cotton is the raw material for processing operations at gins, oil mills, compresses and a small number of textile mills in Texas. Less than 10 percent of the raw cotton is processed within the state.

Cotton in Texas is machine harvested. Growers in the 1994-95 season used stripper harvesters to gather 85 percent of the crop and spindle pickers to harvest the remaining 15 percent. Field storage of harvested seed cotton is gaining in popularity as gins decline in number. In 1994-95, 91 percent of the cotton was ginned from modules and 9 percent from trailers.

Much of the Texas cotton crop is exported; Japan, South Korea and Mexico are major buyers. With the development of open-end spinning and the improved strength of cotton, more utilization of cotton by mills within the state may develop. Unlike the conventional ring-spinning

*Realized Gross Income and Net Income from Farming, Texas, 1960-1997

Year	**Realized Gross Farm Income	Farm Production Expenses	Net Change In Farm Inventories	***Total Net Farm Income	***Total Net Income Per Farm
	— Million Dollars —				Dollars
1960	2,547.0	1,751.5	43.2	838.7	3,396.0
1970	4,026.5	3,232.5	106.8	900.8	4,249.0
1980	9,611.4	9,154.6	- 542.5	456.8	2,330.6
1981	11,545.7	9,643.1	699.9	1,902.6	9,756.9
1982	11,404.5	10,016.2	- 127.8	1,388.3	7,156.2
1983	11,318.1	9,796.5	- 590.7	1,521.6	7,843.3
1984	11,692.6	10,285.7	186.1	1,406.9	7,252.1
1985	11,375.3	9,882.4	- 9.0	1,492.9	7,775.5
1986	10,450.1	9,341.3	- 349.0	1,108.8	5,835.8
1987	12,296.6	10,185.0	563.2	2,111.5	11,231.4
1988	12,842.8	10,816.8	- 128.4	2,026.0	10,552.1
1989	12,843.1	10,703.7	- 798.6	2,139.4	11,027.8
1990	14,463.2	11,412.4	361.7	3,050.8	15,565.3
1991	14,393.4	11,551.4	150.0	2,842.0	14,426.4
1992	14,392.5	10,994.9	464.1	3,397.6	17,159.6
1993	15,758.5	11,612.1	197.0	4,146.4	20,732.0
1994	15,411.6	11,604.4	107.7	3,806.8	19,034.0
1995	15,603.2	12,886.6	243.6	2,743.6	13,582.0
1996	15,253.2	12,554.6	- 287.5	2,698.6	13,164.0
1997	16,560.0	12,966.9	427.5	3,593.1	17,527.0

*Details for items may not add to totals because of rounding. Series revised, September, 1981.
**Cash receipts from farm marketings, government payments, value of home consumption and gross rental value of farm dwellings.
***Farm income of farm operators.
§Starting in 1977, farms with production of $1,000 or more used to figure income.
Source: "Economic Indicators of the Farm Sector, State Financial Summary, 1985," 1987," 1989," 1993, USDA/ERS; "Farm Business Economics Report", Aug. 1996; "Texas Agricultural Statistics Service, 1997," Sept. 1998.

method, open-end spinning techniques can efficiently produce high-quality yarn from relatively strong, short staple cotton with fine mature fiber.

The state's major cotton-producing areas are tied together by an electronic marketing system. This system is a computer network that links producers through terminals that are usually located at gins to a relatively large number of buyers. The network provides farmers with a centralized market that allows many sellers and buyers to trade with each other on a regular basis.

The first high-volume instrument cotton-classing office in the nation opened at Lamesa in 1980.

Grain Sorghum

Grain sorghum in 1998 ranked fifth in dollar value. Much of the grain is exported, as well as being used in livestock and poultry feed throughout the state.

Total production of grain sorghum in 1998 was 59,248,000 hundredweight (cwt), with a 2,576 per acre yield. With an average price of $3.93 per cwt., the total value reached almost $233 million. In 1997, 3.15 million acres of grain sorghum were harvested, yielding an average of 3,304 pounds per acre for a total production of 104.1 million cwt. It was valued at $4.18 per cwt., for a total value of $434.9 million.

Although grown to some extent in all counties where crops are important, the largest concentrations are in the High Plains, Rolling Plains, Blackland Prairie, Coastal Bend and Lower Rio Grande Valley areas. Counties leading in production in 1997 were Nueces, San Patricio, Willacy, Cameron, Wharton and Hidalgo.

Development of high-yielding hybrids resistant to diseases and insect damage continues. A leader in this research, J. Roy Quinby, is principle author of a history of

Export Shares of Commodities

Commodity*	1994	1995	1996	1997	1997 % of U.S. Total
Rice	85.9	125.7	106.4	109.7	11.41
Cotton	736.8	786.2	666.4	564.2	23.11
Fats, Oils & Greases	75.0	123.8	99.6	77.4	14.79
Hides & Skins	218.8	273.1	247.7	258.2	15.25
Meats other than Poultry	620.8	722.3	745.5	654.9	13.38
Feed Grains	372.7	357.6	523.0	329.5	3.90
Poultry Products	85.0	111.0	137.0	140.3	4.95
Fruits	36.2	39.4	47.8	43.2	1.26
Vegetables	36.8	51.4	46.2	49.5	1.21
Wheat & Flour	178.0	144.6	218.2	143.0	3.30
Soybeans	11.7	20.1	21.8	27.3	0.30
Cottonseed & Prod.	40.2	42.4	28.1	27.6	25.00
Peanuts	35.6	49.8	46.5	51.6	18.82
Tree Nuts	8.4	9.8	14.9	8.9	0.70
Dairy Products	27.2	26.8	21.4	23.5	2.71
†All Other	472.2	494.6	509.5	544.8	7.41
TOTAL	3,041.3	3,378.6	3,477.0	3,053.6	5.32

Totals may not add because of rounding.
*Commodity and related preparations.
† Mainly confectionary, nursery and greenhouse, essential oils, sunflower seed oil, beverages, and other miscellaneous animal and vegetable products.
Source: *Foreign Agricultural Trade of the United States*.

grain sorghums which appeared in the 1972-73 edition of the *Texas Almanac*.

Rice

Rice, which is grown in about 20 counties on the Coastal Prairie of Texas, ranked third in value among Texas crops for a number of years. However, in recent years, cotton, grain sorghum, wheat, corn, peanuts and hay have outranked rice.

Farms are highly mechanized, producing rice through irrigation and using airplanes for much of the planting, fertilizing, and application of insecticides and herbicides.

Texas farmers grow long- and medium-grain rice only. The Texas rice industry, which has grown from 110 acres in 1850 to 642,000 acres in 1954, has been marked by significant yield increases and improved varieties. Record production was in 1981, with 27.2 million cwt. harvested. Highest yield was 6,250 pounds per acre in 1986.

Several different types of rice-milling procedures are in use today. The simplest and oldest method produces a product known as regular milled white rice, the most prevalent on the market today.

During this process, rice grains are subjected to additional cleaning to remove chaff, dust and foreign seed, and then husks are removed from the grains. This results in a product which is the whole, unpolished grain of rice with only the outer hull and a small amount of bran removed. This product is called brown rice and is sometimes sold without further treatment other than grading. It has a delightful, nutlike flavor and a slightly chewy texture.

When additional layers of the bran are removed, the rice becomes white in color and begins to appear as it is usually sold at retail level. The removal of the bran layer from the grain is performed in a number of steps using two or three types of machines. After the bran is removed, the product is ready for classification as to size. Rice is more valuable if the grains are not broken. In many cases, additional vitamins are added to the grains to produce what is called "enriched rice."

Another process may be used in rice milling to produce a product called parboiled rice. In this process, the rice is subjected to a combination of steam and pressure prior to the time it is milled. This process gelatinizes the

Value of Cotton and Cottonseed

Crop Year	Upland Cotton Production (Bales)	Upland Cotton Value	Cottonseed Production (Tons)	Cottonseed Value
	(All Figures In Thousands)			
1900	3,438	$157,306	1,531	$20,898
1910	3,047	210,260	1,356	31,050
1920	4,345	376,080	1,934	41,350
1930	4,037	194,080	1,798	40,820
1940	3,234	162,140	1,318	31,852
1950	2,946	574,689	1,232	111,989
1960	4,346	612,224	1,821	75,207
1970	3,191	314,913	1,242	68,310
*1980	3,320	1,091,616	1,361	161,959
1981	5,645	1,259,964	2,438	207,230
1982	2,700	664,848	1,122	90,882
1983	2,380	677,443	1,002	162,324
1984	3,680	927,360	1,563	157,863
1985	3,910	968,429	1,634	102,156
1986	2,535	560,945	1,053	82,118
1987	4,635	1,325,981	1,915	157,971
1988	5,215	1,291,651	2,131	238,672
1989	2,870	812,784	1,189	141,491
1990	4,965	1,506,182	1,943	225,388
1991	4,710	1,211,789	1,903	134,162
1992	3,265	769,495	1,346	145,368
1993	5,095	1,308,396	2,147	255,493
1994	4,915	1,642,003	2,111	215,322
1995	4,460	1,597,037	1,828	201,080
1996	4,345	1,368,154	1,784	230,136
1997	5,140	1,482,787	1,983	226,062
1998	3,500	976,080	1,410	184,710

*Beginning in 1971, the basis for cotton prices was changed from 500-pound gross weight to 480-pound net weight bale. To compute comparable prices for previous years, multiply price times 1.04167.
Source: "Texas Agricultural Facts," Annual Summary, Feb., 1999, and "Texas Ag Statistics," Texas Agricultural Statistics Service, Austin, various years.

starch in the grain, the treatment aiding in the retention of much of the natural vitamin and mineral content. After cooking, parboiled rice tends to be fluffy, more separate, and plump.

Still another type of rice is precooked rice, which is actually milled rice that has been cooked after milling, then dehydrated. Precooked rice requires a minimum of preparation time since it needs merely to have the moisture restored to it.

Rice production in 1998 totaled 15.8 million cwt. from 283,000 harvested acres, with a yield of 5,600 pounds per acre. The crop value totaled $145 million. Rice production was 14.2 million cwt. in 1997 on 259,000 harvested acres, yielding 5,500 pounds per acre. Total value in 1997 was $155.2 million. Counties leading in production in 1997 included Wharton, Colorado, Matagorda, Jefferson, Brazoria and Jackson.

Wheat

Wheat for grain is one of the state's most valuable cash crops. In 1998, wheat was exceeded in value by cotton, hay and corn. Wheat pastures also provide winter forage for cattle.

Texas' wheat production totaled 136.5 million bushels in 1998; yield averaged 35 bushels per acre. Planted acreage totaled 6.1 million acres; 3.9 million acres were harvested. With an average price of $2.70 per bushel, the 1998 wheat value totaled $368.6 million. In 1997, Texas wheat growers planted 6.3 million acres and harvested 4.1 million acres. The yield was 29.0 bushels per acre for 1997 with total production of 118.9 million bushels at $3.25 per bushel valued at $386.4 million.

Leading wheat-producing counties, based on production in 1997, were Dallam, Deaf Smith, Hansford, Ochiltree, Castro and Sherman. The leading counties, based on acreage planted in 1997, were Hansford, Deaf Smith, Knox, Swisher, Jones and Dallam.

Wheat was first grown commercially in Texas near Sherman about 1833. The acreage expanded greatly in North Central Texas after 1850 because of rapid settlement of the state and introduction of the well-adapted Mediterranean strain of wheat. A major family flour industry was developed in the Fort Worth/Dallas/Sherman area between 1875 and 1900. Now, around half of the state acreage is planted on the High Plains and about a third of this is irrigated. Most wheat grown in Texas is of the hard red winter class. The development of improved disease-resistant varieties and the use of wheat for winter pasture has increased wheat acreage in Central and South Texas.

Most wheat harvested for grain is used in some phase of the milling industry. The better-quality hard red winter wheat is used to make commercial bakery flour. Soft red winter wheat is used in family flours. By-products of milled wheat are used for feed.

Corn

Interest in corn production throughout the state has increased since the 1970s as yields improved with new varieties. Once the principal grain crop, corn acreage declined as plantings of grain sorghum increased. Only 500,000 acres were harvested annually until the mid-1970s when new hybrids were developed.

Harvested acreage was 1.9 million in 1998 and 1.8 million in 1997. Yields for the corresponding years were 100 and 138 bushels per acre, respectively. Most of the acreage and yield increase has occurred in Central and South Texas.

In 1998, corn ranked third in value among the state's crops. It was valued at $434.8 million in 1998 and $661.7 million in 1997. Corn is largely used for livestock feed, but is also used in food products.

The leading counties in production for 1997 were Dallam, Castro, Hartley, Moore and Parmer.

Rye

Rye is grown mainly on the Northern and Southern High Plains, the Northern Low Plains, Cross Timbers, Blackland and East Texas areas. Minor acreages are seeded in South Central Texas, the Edwards Plateau and the Upper Coast. Rye is grown primarily as a cover crop and for grazing during the fall, winter and early spring.

Rye production in 1998 totaled 400,000 bushels valued at $1.6 million. Of the 120,000 acres planted, 20,000 were harvested, yielding an average of 20 bushels per acre. In 1997, 10,000 of the 130,000 acres planted were harvested, with an average yield per acre of 33 bushels. Value of production for the 330,000 bushels was $1.3 million.

Oats

Oats are grown extensively in Texas for winter pasture, hay, silage and greenchop feeding, and some acreage is harvested for grain.

Of the 660,000 acres planted to oats in 1998, 130,000 acres were harvested. The average yield was 53.0 bushels per acre. Production totaled 6.9 million bushels with a value of $9.6 million. In 1997, 550,000 acres were planted; 130,000 acres were harvested, with an average yield of 52 bushels per acre, for a total of 6.8 million bushels. Average price per bushel was $2.36 for total production value of $16.0 million.

Leading oat grain-producing counties in 1997 were Medina, Uvalde, Hamilton, Gillespie and McLennan.

Barley

Texas barley acreage and production falls far below that of wheat and oats. In 1998, barley was harvested from 5,000 of the 10,000 acres planted. Production totaled 215,000 bushels and was valued at $441,000, with a yield of 43.0 bushels per acre. In 1997, farmers harvested 5,000 of the 10,000 acres planted to barley. Yields averaged 47.0 bushels per acre for total production of 235,000 bushels. Value of production was $541,000 with an average price of $2.30 per bushel.

Sugar Beets

Sugar beets have been grown on a commercial scale in Texas since 1964 when the first beet-sugar factory was built by Holly Sugar Company in Hereford. In 1998, numbers were not reported for sugar beets.

Sugar-beet production in 1997 totaled 270,000 tons from 15,000 harvested acres, a yield of 18.0 tons per acre.

Sugar Cane

Sugar cane is grown from seed cane planted in late summer or fall. It is harvested 12 months later and milled to produce raw sugar and molasses. Raw sugar requires additional refining before it is in final form and can be offered to consumers.

The sugarcane grinding mill operated at Santa Rosa, Cameron County, is considered one of the most modern mills in the United States. Texas sugar cane-producing counties are Hidalgo, Cameron and Willacy.

At a yield of 30 tons per acre, sugar-cane production in 1998 totaled 975,000 tons from 32,500 harvested acres. In 1997, 29,800 acres were harvested for total production of 902,000 tons valued at $23.1 million, or $25.60 per ton. The yield was 30.3 tons per acre.

Hay, Silage, and Other Forage Crops

A large proportion of Texas' agricultural land is devoted to forage-crop production. This acreage provides essentially the total feed requirements for most of the state's large domestic livestock population, as well as those of game animals.

Approximately 80 million acres of native rangeland, which are primarily in the western half of Texas, provide grazing for beef cattle, sheep, goats, horses and game animals. An additional 20 million acres are devoted to introducing forage species. Of this total, approximately 16 million acres are planted to improved perennial grasses and legumes and are harvested by grazing animals. The average annual acreage of crops grown for hay, silage and other forms of machine-harvested forage is close to 4 million acres, with an estimated value in excess of $600 million.

Hay accounts for a large amount of this production, with some corn and sorghum silage being produced. The most important hay crops are annual and perennial grasses and alfalfa. Production in 1998 totaled 6.9 million tons of hay from 4 million harvested acres at a yield of 1.7 tons per acre. Value of hay was $565.6 million, or $91 per ton. In 1997, 11 million tons of hay were produced from 4.4 million harvested acres at a yield of 2.47 tons per acre. The value in 1997 was $715.9 million, or $72 per ton.

Alfalfa hay production in 1998 totaled 630,000 tons with 140,000 acres harvested with a yield of 4.5 tons per acre. At a value of $150 per ton, total value was $94.5 million. In 1997, 635,000 tons of alfalfa were harvested from 135,000 acres at a yield of 4.7 tons per acre. Value was $86.4 million, or $136 per ton.

An additional sizable acreage of annual forage crops such as sudan and millet is grazed, as well as much of the small-grain acreage. Alfalfa, sweet corn, vetch, arrowleaf clover, grasses and other forage plants also provide income as seed crops.

Peanuts

Peanuts are grown on more than 300,000 acres in Texas. Well over half of the crop is irrigated. Texas ranked second nationally in production of peanuts in 1998. Among Texas crops, peanuts rank about sixth in value.

Until 1973, essentially all of the Texas acreage was planted to the Spanish type, which matured earlier and exhibited better drought tolerance than other types. The Spanish variety is also preferred for some uses due to its distinctive flavor. The Florunner variety, a runner market type, is now planted on a large part of the acreage where soil moisture is favorable. The variety is later maturing but better yielding than Spanish varieties under good growing conditions. Florunner peanuts have high enough quality to compete with the Spanish variety in most products.

In 1998, peanut production totaled 900.5 million pounds from 345,000 harvested acres, yielding 2,610 pounds per acre. At 23.2¢ per pound, value of the crop was estimated at $208.9 million. In 1997, peanut production amounted to 822.2 million pounds from 320,000 acres planted and 315,000 harvested. Average yield of 2,610 pounds per acre and average price of 24.3¢ per pound combined for a 1997 value of $199.8 million.

Leading counties in peanut production in 1997 included Gaines, Terry, Dawson, Frio, Collingsworth and Yoakum.

Soybeans

Production is largely in the areas of the Upper Coast, irrigated High Plains, and Red River Valley of Northeast Texas. Soybeans are adapted to the same general soil climate conditions as corn, cotton or grain sorghum, provided moisture, disease and insects are not limiting factors. The major counties in soybean production in 1997 were Liberty, Lamar, Wharton, Fannin, Red River, and Hale.

In low-rainfall areas, yields have been too low or inconsistent for profitable dryland production. Soybeans' need for moisture in late summer limits its potential in the Blacklands and Rolling Plains, while cotton root rot is a serious problem in the Blacklands. Limited moisture at critical growth stages may occasionally prevent economical yields, even in high-rainfall areas of Northeast Texas and the Coast Prairie.

Because of day-length sensitivity, soybeans should be planted in Texas during the long days of May and June for optimum yields. Varieties planted during this period usually begin to bloom and set fruit during the hot, usually dry months of July and August. When moisture is insufficient during this period, yields are drastically reduced. The risk of dryland soybean production in the Coast Prairie and Northeast Texas is considerably less when compared to other dryland areas, because moisture is available more often during the critical fruiting period.

The 1998 soybean crop totaled 5.9 million bushels and was valued at $28.5 million, or $4.80 per bushel. Of the 440,000 acres planted, 270,000 were harvested, with an average yield of 22 bushels per acre. In 1997, the soybean crop averaged 28 bushels per acre from 400,000 acres harvested. Total production of 11.2 million bushels was valued at $70.9 million, or $6.33 per bushel.

Sunflowers

Sunflowers constitute one of the most important annual oilseed crops in the world. The cultivated types, which are thought to be descendants of the common wild sunflower native to Texas, have been successfully grown in several countries including Russia, Argentina, Romania, Bulgaria, Uruguay, Western Canada and portions of the northern United States. Extensive trial plantings conducted in the Cotton Belt states since 1968 showed sunflowers have considerable potential as an oilseed crop in much of this area, including Texas. Sunflowers exhibit good cold and drought tolerance, are adapted to a wide range of soil and climate conditions, and tolerate higher levels of hail, wind and sand abrasion than other crops normally grown in the state.

In 1998, sunflower production totaled 29.7 million pounds and was harvested from 44,000 acres at a yield of 675 pounds per acre. With an average price of $14 per cwt., the crop was valued at $4.3 million. In 1997, 85,000 of the 88,000 acres planted to sunflowers were harvested, with an average yield of 926 pounds per acre. Total production of 78.7 million pounds was valued at $10.8 million, or $13.70 per pound. The leading counties in production in 1997 were Cochran, Bailey, Lamb, Lubbock and Hockley.

Reasons for growing sunflowers include the need for an additional cash crop with low water and nutrient requirements, the development of sunflower hybrids, and interest by food processors in Texas sunflower oil, which has a high oleic-acid content. Commercial users have found many advantages in this high-oleic oil, including excellent cooking stability, particularly for use as a deep-frying medium for potato chips, corn chips and similar products.

Sunflower meal is a high-quality, toxin-free protein source that can be included in rations for swine, poultry and ruminants. The hulls constitute a source of roughage that can also be included in livestock feed.

Flaxseed

Earliest flax planting was at Victoria in 1900. Since the first planting, Texas flax acreage has fluctuated depending on market, winterkill, and drought. Flax acreage has dropped in recent years and estimates were discontinued in 1980.

Forest Products

For information on Texas forest products, refer to the section titled "Texas Forest Resources."

Horticultural Specialty Crops

Production of horticulture specialty crops in Texas has increased as long-distance hauling rates have risen. This increase is noted especially in the production of container-grown bedding plants, foliage plants, sod and woody landscape plants.

Plant-rental services have become a multimillion-dollar business. This service provides plants and maintains them in office buildings, shopping malls, public buildings and even in some homes for a fee. Using plants to create interior landscapes is popular with people of all ages, from older people in retirement homes to students in dormitory rooms.

Cash receipts from horticultural specialty crops in Texas were estimated to be around $1.12 billion in 1998.

II. Truck Crops

Some market vegetables are produced in almost all Texas counties, but most of the commercial crop comes from about 200 counties. Hidalgo County is the leading Texas county in vegetable acres harvested, followed by Starr and Cameron counties. Other leading producing counties are: Frio, Uvalde, Duval, Webb, Hale and Zavala.

Texas is one of the five leading states in the production of fresh market vegetables. Nationally, in 1998, Texas ranked fifth in harvested acreage, exceeded by California, Florida, Arizona and Georgia. Texas ranked fourth in production and in value of fresh-market vegetables, exceeded by California, Florida and Arizona. Texas had 4.9 percent of the harvested acreage, 4.5 percent of the production and 4.2 percent of the value of fresh-market vegetables produced. Texas ranked first in the production of spinach for processing. Onions were the number one cash crop, with watermelons second. Other vegetables leading in value of production usually are cantaloupes, cabbage, Irish potatoes, bell peppers and carrots.

In 1998, total vegetable production of 21.9 million cwt. was valued at $366 million from 114,400 acres harvested. In 1997, Texas growers harvested commercial vegetable crops valued at $251.6 million from 115,900 acres with a production of 21.1 million cwt.

Onions

Onion production in 1998 totaled 4 million cwt. from 15,400 harvested acres and was valued at $90.2 million, at a yield of 264 cwt. per acre. In 1997, 3.1 million cwt. of onions were harvested from 13,800 acres and valued at $50.2 million at a yield of 228 cwt. per acre.

Carrots

Carrot production in 1998 totaled 980,000 cwt. from 4,000 harvested acres at a yield of 245 cwt. per acre. Production was valued at $20.1 million . In 1997, carrots were harvested from 2,400 acres with a value of $6.9 million . At a yield of 165 cwt. per acre, 1997 production was 396,000 cwt. The winter carrot production from South Texas accounts for about three-fourths of total winter-season production.

All Potatoes

In 1998, potatoes were harvested from 18,500 acres with production of 4.9 million cwt. valued at $45.5 million at a yield of 263 cwt. per acre. Potatoes were harvested from 17,200 acres with production of 4.5 million cwt. valued at $47.7 million in 1997, yielding 262 cwt. per acre.

Cantaloupes - Honeydews

Cantaloupe production in 1998 totaled 2.1 million cwt. from 10,000 harvested acres and was valued at $6.7 million at a yield of 210 cwt. per acre. In 1997, cantaloupes were harvested from 9,700 acres for total production of 1.4 million cwt. valued at $27.2 million, yielding 140 cwt. per acre.

Honeydew production totaled 437,000 cwt. and was valued at $16.7 million at a yield of 190 cwt. per acre in 1998. In 1997, 420,000 cwt. of honeydew melons were harvested from 2,000 acres for total value of $9.5 million, yielding 210 cwt. per acre.

Cabbage

In 1998, 8,500 acres were harvested and yielded total production of 3.4 million cwt. which was valued at $69.4 million. Yield was 400 cwt. per acre. In 1997, 8,500 acres of cabbage were

harvested, yielding total production of 2.9 million cwt., or 340 cwt. per acre, valued at $33.8 million.

Cauliflower

Estimates for cauliflower were discontinued in 1998. Production of cauliflower in 1997 was 63,000 cwt. on 700 acres at a value of $1.4 million. Yield equaled 90 cwt. per acre.

Broccoli

Broccoli production in 1998 totaled 83,000 cwt. from 1,000 harvested acres for a value of $2.2 million with a yield of 83 cwt. per acre. In 1997, at a yield of 66 cwt. per acre, broccoli production totaled 53,000 cwt. from 800 harvested acres, and valued at $1.8 million. Broccoli is primarily a South Texas crop.

Watermelons

Watermelon production in 1998 was 6.5 million cwt. from 38,400 acres with a value of $35.6 million, yielding 170 cwt. per acre. In 1997, at a yield of 170 cwt. per acre, 7.4 million cwt. of watermelons were harvested from 43,400 acres and valued at $58.4 million.

Tomatoes

Commercial tomatoes are marketed throughout the year from Texas partly as a result of recent increases in greenhouse production during the winter.

In 1998, 1,400 harvested acres of tomatoes at a yield of 100 cwt. per acre produced 140,000 cwt. of tomatoes with a value of $5.3 million. In 1997, 1,300 acres of tomatoes were harvested, producing 260,000 cwt. at a yield of 200 cwt. per acre for a value of $8.8 million.

Bell Peppers

Bell pepper production in 1998 was 180,000 cwt. from 1,500 harvested acres was valued at $6.5 million with a yield of 120 cwt. per acre. In 1997, bell peppers were harvested from 1,600 acres and valued at $9.7 million. At a yield of 175 cwt. per acre, 280,000 cwt. were produced.

Sweet Potatoes

In 1998, 210,000 cwt. sweet potatoes were harvested from 6,000 acres for a value of $4.7 million at a yield of 35 cwt. per acre. Sweet potatoes in 1997 produced 899,000 cwt. from 5,800 harvested acres with a value of $14.6 million. Yield was 155 cwt. per acre.

Spinach

Spinach production is primarily concentrated in the Winter Garden area of South Texas.

The 1998 production value of spinach was estimated at $8.9 million. Production of 225,000 cwt. was harvested

Texas 1997 Vegetable Production

*Rank Among States	Crop	Planted Acres (000)	Harvested Acres (000)	Yield Per Acre	Production (000)
1	Spinach, processed	5.00	4.70	9.50	45 tons
3	Broccoli, dual	1.30	1.30	67.00	87 cwts
3	Carrots, processed	4.80	4.20	20.00	84 tons
3	Celery, dual	0.90	0.90	590.00	531 cwts
3	Cantaloupes, fresh	12.50	9.70	140.00	1,358 cwts
3	Honeydew, fresh	3.30	2.00	210.00	420 cwts
3	Spinach, fresh	3.10	2.40	65.00	156 cwts
4	Cucumbers, processed	11.50	10.10	6.50	66 tons
4	Watermelons, fresh	42.00	37.50	170.00	6,375 cwts
4	Bell Peppers, dual	5.40	5.10	175.00	893 cwts
5	Cabbage, fresh	9.30	8.50	340.00	2,890 cwts
5	Cauliflower, dual	0.70	0.70	90.0	63 cwts
7	Carrots, fresh	3.70	3.50	165.00	578 cwts
9	Cucumbers, fresh	1.80	1.70	170.00	289 cwts
9	Onions, all fresh	16.30	11.80	222.00	2,623 cwts
9	Tomatoes, fresh	3.40	3.20	200.00	640 cwts
20	Sweet Corn, fresh	3.80	2.70	50.00	135 cwts

*Based on production.

Source: U.S. and Texas Departments of Agriculture.

from 2,500 acres with a yield of 90 cwt. per acre. In 1997, 2,400 acres were harvested with a value of $5.5 million. At a yield of 65 cwt. per acre, production was 156,000 cwt.

Cucumbers

In 1998, 1,500 acres of cucumbers were harvested. Production totaled 113,000 cwt. and was valued at $2.7 million. The 1998 yield was 75 cwt. per acre. In 1997, 1,700 acres of cucumbers were harvested with a value of $4.2 million. Production was 289,000 cwt. with a yield of 170 cwt. per acre.

Sweet Corn

In 1998, 432,000 cwt. of sweet corn was harvested from 4,800 acres. Value of production was estimated at $8.4 million with a yield of 90 cwt. per acre. In 1997, 250,000 cwt. sweet corn was produced from 5,000 harvested acres at a yield of 50 cwt. per acre and valued at $3.7 million.

Vegetables for Processing

In 1998, 2.9 million cwt. of cucumbers, snap beans, tomatoes and spinach for processing were harvested from

Cash Receipts for Commodities, 1993-1997

Commodity *	1993	1994	1995	1996	1997	% of 1997
	(All values in thousands of dollars)					
All Commodities:	$12,730,745	$12,932,250	$13,101,131	$12,959,924	$13,460,836	100.00
Livestock and products	8,211,274	8,112,253	8,450,603	7,820,737	8,183,935	60.80
Crops, Fruits and others	4,519,471	4,819,997	4,646,497	5,139,187	5,287,031	39.28
Livestock and products:						
Cattle and calves	6,188,563	5,882,207	6,295,596	5,395,427	5,849,076	43.45
Milk.	780,710	830,800	791,570	920,798	787,339	5.85
Broilers.	608,700	659,453	646,316	726,264	774,595	5.75
Eggs.	202,541	198,147	216,691	290,646	267,904	1.99
Hogs	89,367	76,838	79,448	92,378	104,723	0.78
Sheep and lambs.	68,032	63,917	64,082	74,500	66,214	0.49
Mohair	11,197	30,602	20,940	14,606	14,556	0.11
Wool.	11,050	15,582	15,488	8,316	11,607	0.09
† Other Livestock	215,114	354,707	320,472	297,802	307,921	2.29
Crops:						
Cotton lint.	1,414,351	1,645,296	1,177,366	1,544,729	1,385,689	10.29
Corn.	447,698	610,281	700,160	607,044	657,716	4.89
Sorghum grain	391,514	334,084	384,977	473,238	450,156	3.34
Wheat	334,258	225,344	283,661	326,983	362,366	2.69
Hay.	130,016	133,340	120,186	189,587	230,095	1.71
Cottonseed	207,659	191,843	180,355	199,011	196,358	1.46
Peanuts	162,852	172,587	154,980	170,872	193,205	1.44
Rice	79,481	173,231	137,011	192,555	168,126	1.25
Soybeans.	26,210	26,454	38,438	46,739	58,854	0.44
Watermelons	50,400	60,060	67,165	48,136	50,490	0.38
Onions	90,306	64,813	83,821	50,930	41,539	0.31
Cabbage	46,851	30,666	54,570	40,330	33,813	0.25
Peppers, Green	23,200	29,753	30,215	22,604	30,898	0.23
Cantaloupes.	37,306	52,348	54,659	47,124	27,160	0.20
Sugar cane for sugar	37,126	40,544	36,282	25,551	23,001	0.17
Potatoes.	30,433	34,293	26,464	33,653	22,931	0.17
Tomatoes, fresh	4,810	4,277	8,064	7,722	21,760	0.16
Cucumbers	14,296	19,938	15,105	12,236	18,503	0.14
Sweet potatoes	17,074	11,558	8,569	10,354	16,729	0.12
Carrots	13,718	12,839	18,303	18,904	16,551	0.12
Spinach	11,428	10,608	11,572	9,803	9,697	0.07
Sugar beets	25,513	18,290	12,812	7,865	9,523	0.07
Honeydew melons	17,888	14,760	21,156	12,352	9,492	0.07
Sunflowers	5,122	3,777	4,545	4,721	8,041	0.06
Celery	12,463	6,916	8,280	4,745	6,744	0.05
Oats	7,438	6,251	3,262	4,364	3,925	0.03
Broccoli	4,067	4,281	7,600	2,270	2,892	0.02
Beans, Dry.	8,529	6,494	3,478	2,827	2,308	0.02
Corn, sweet	3,150	1,555	2,720	1,120	1,998	0.01
Cauliflower.	905	1,933	1,382	1,404	1,429	0.01
Rye.	734	1,028	861	615	934	0.01
Barley.	584	534	466	908	403	0.00
†† Other crops	71,602	75,002	93,891	90,213	82,679	0.61
Fruits and Nuts						
Pecans	48,000	48,800	68,110	29,000	58,370	0.43
Grapefruit	17,835	13,486	19,461	21,777	14,841	0.11
Oranges.	4,904	3,151	8,541	7,823	3,332	0.02
Peaches	8,136	5,811	6,480	3,848	5,600	0.04
§§ Other fruits and nuts	4,614	2,771	2,560	7,679	5,927	0.04
Other Farm Income:						
Greenhouse/nursery	707,000	721,000	792,000	857,551	1,042,826	7.75

Commodities are listed in order of importance for 1996 by crop items and by livestock items.
† Includes milkfat, turkey eggs, equine, goats, goat milk and other poultry and livestock.
†† Miscellaneous vegetables, field crops.
§§ Miscellaneous fruits and nuts.
Source: 1997 Texas Agricultural Statistics, USDA/Texas Agricultural Statistics Service, Sept. 1998; ERS/USDA, November 1998.

22,600 acres and valued at $30 million. In 1997, 22,000 acres were harvested and valued at $26.1 million with a production of 3.8 million cwt.

III. Fruits and Nuts

Texas is noted for producing a wide variety of fruits. The pecan is the only commercial nut crop in the state. The pecan is native to most of the state's river valleys and is the Texas state tree. Citrus is produced in the three southernmost counties in the Lower Rio Grande Valley. Production has continued to increase since the severe freeze several years ago, and some new orchards have been planted. Peaches represent the next most important Texas fruit crop, and there is a considerable amount of interest in growing apples.

Citrus

Prior to the 1989 freeze, Texas ranked with Florida, California and Arizona as leading states in the production of citrus. Most of the Texas production is in Cameron, Hidalgo and Willacy counties of the Lower Rio Grande Valley. In 1997-98, grapefruit production was estimated at 4.8 million boxes with a yield of 208 boxes per acre. At $4.70 per box, value of production was $22.6 million. Grapefruit production in 1996-97 was 5.3 million boxes at $4.17 per box for a total value of $22.3 million. Yield was 260 boxes per acre in 1996-97.

Production of oranges in 1997-98 was 1.5 million boxes with a yield of 161 boxes per acre. At $3.88 per box, total value was $5.9 million. In 1996-97, production was 1.4 million boxes at $5.33 per box for a total value of $7.6 million. Yield was 163 boxes per acre.

Peaches

Primary production areas are East Texas, the Hill Country and the Western Cross Timbers. Production varies substantially depending on weather conditions. Recently, peach production has spread to South and West Texas. Low-chilling varieties for early marketings are being grown in Atascosa, Frio, Webb, Karnes and Duval counties.

The Texas peach crop totaled 19 million pounds in 1998 for a value of $9.9 million or 52¢ per pound and a yield of 2,820 pounds per acre. In 1997, production was 16 million pounds with a yield of 2,500 per acre. Value of production was $5.6 million at 35¢ per pound.

The demand for high-quality Texas peaches greatly exceeds the supply. Texas ranked seventh nationally in peach production in 1998. Leading Texas counties in production are Gillespie, Parker, Montague, Comanche, Limestone and Eastland.

Apples

Small acreages of apples, usually marketed within the state, are grown primarily in Montague and Gillespie counties. Other counties that produce apples include: Callahan, Collingsworth, Clay, Cass, Donley, Eastland, Hudspeth, Jeff Davis, Lampasas, Parker, San Saba and Young. The crop is harvested and marketed from July to October.

A large number of apple trees have been planted in the Hill Country, most of them new varieties of Red and Golden Delicious types on semi-dwarfing rootstocks. Trees are established in high-density plantings of 100 to 200 trees per acre. Most of the apples are sold at roadside stands or in nearby markets.

Pears

Well adapted for home and small-orchard production, the pear is not commercially significant in Texas. Usually the fruit goes for home consumption or to nearby markets. Comanche, Parker, Lampasas, Cooke, McCulloch and Eastland counties lead in trees.

Apricots

Not a commercial crop, apricots are grown chiefly in Comanche, Denton, Wilbarger, Parker and Collingsworth counties. Other counties reporting apricots include Martin, Clay, Young, Lampasas, Gillespie, Anderson, Erath, Wichita and Eastland.

Plums

Plum production is scattered over a wide area of the state, with heaviest production in East and Central Texas. Most of the production goes to nearby markets or to processors. The leading counties in production are Smith, Gillespie and Knox.

Blackberries

Smith County is a blackberry center ,with the Tyler-Lindale area having processed the crop since 1890. Other counties with blackberry acreage include Wood, Van Zandt and Henderson. The Brazos blackberry is grown as a local market or "pick-your-own" fruit in many sections of the state. Dewberries grow wild in Central and East Texas and are gathered for home use and local sale in May and June.

Strawberries

Atascosa County is the leading commercial area, although strawberries are grown for local markets in Wood, Van Zandt and Smith counties in East Texas. The most concentrated production occurs in the Poteet area below San Antonio.

Avocados

Avocados grow on a small acreage in the Lower Rio Grande Valley. Interest in this crop is increasing and production is expected to expand. Lulu is the principal variety.

Pecans

The pecan, the state tree, is one of the most widely distributed trees in Texas. It is native to more than 150 counties and is grown commercially in 30 other counties. The pecan is also widely used as a dual-purpose yard tree. Commercial plantings of pecans have accelerated in Central and West Texas. Many of these new orchards are being irrigated, principally with trickle-irrigation systems. The development and use of the new USDA pecan varieties have helped to increase quality and yields.

In 1998, pecan production totaled only 35 million pounds because of drought and was valued at $52.8 million or $1.51 per pound. In 1997, 90 million pounds were produced. Total value was estimated at $58.4 million as price averaged 65¢ per pound.

Nationally, Texas ranked second behind Georgia in pecan production in 1998. Leading Texas counties in pecan production are Hood, El Paso, Pecos, San Saba, Mills, Comanche, Wharton and Gonzales.

IV. Livestock and Their Products

Livestock and their products usually account for about 60 percent of the agricultural cash receipts in Texas. The state ranks first nationally in all cattle, beef cattle, cattle on feed, sheep and lambs, wool, goats and mohair.

Meat animals normally account for about 80 percent of total cash receipts from marketings of livestock and their products. Sales of livestock and products in 1997 totaled $8.184 billion, up from $7.821 billion in 1996.

Cattle dominate livestock production in Texas, contributing more than 70 percent of cash receipts from livestock and products each year. The Jan. 1, 1999, inventory of all cattle and calves in Texas totaled 14 million head, valued at $7 billion, compared to 14.5 million as of Jan. 1, 1998, valued at $7.830 billion.

On Jan. 1, 1999, the sheep and lamb inventory stood at 1.4 million head, valued at $95.9 million, compared with 1.5 million head as of Jan. 1, 1998, valued at $122.4 million. Sheep and lambs numbered 3.2 million on Jan. 1, 1973, down from a high of 10.8 million in 1943. Sheep and lamb production fell from 148.3 million pounds in 1973 to 71.6 million pounds on Jan. 1, 1999. Wool production

Cattle on a ranch near Llano huddle under an oak tree for shade from the noon sun. Dallas Morning News *file photo.*

ceding paragraph, auctions sold 131,000 hogs and 1.3 million sheep and lambs in 1997. This compared with 168,000 hogs and 1.6 sheep and lambs in 1996.

During 1998, the Commission reported 1.6 million cattle and calves shipped from Texas to other states and 2.7 million shipped in, compared with 1.6 million shipped out and 3.3 million shipped in during 1997. (Figures exclude cattle shipped directly to slaughter, where no health certificates are required.)

During 1998, 514,370 sheep and lambs were shipped out of the state and 78,144 were shipped in, compared with 424,225 shipped out and 94,468 shipped in during 1997.

Feedlot fattening of livestock, mainly cattle, is a major industry in Texas. Annual fed cattle marketings totaled 5.8 million for 1,000-and-more feedlot capacity (head) in 1997. Texas lots marketed a total of 5.5 million (including under-1,000 feedlot capacity) of grain-fed cattle in 1996. In recent years, more cattle have been fed in Texas than in any other state in the United States.

During 1997, there were 147 feedlots in Texas with capacity of 1,000 animals or more, compared with 150 in 1996.

Federally-inspected slaughter plants in Texas numbered 46 in 1998, compared with 41 in 1997. In 1998, the

decreased from 26.4 million pounds valued at $23.2 million in 1973 to 9.2 million pounds valued at $5.8 million in 1998. Production was 10,950,000 pounds in 1997 valued at $11.6 million. The price of wool per pound was 88¢ in 1973, $1.06 in 1997, and 63¢ in 1998.

Lamb prices averaged $73.30 per cwt. as of Jan. 1, 1999, $90.50 per cwt. in 1998, and $87.80 per cwt. in 1997. The average value per head of sheep was $37.10 per cwt. as of Jan. 1, 1999, $44.71 in 1998, and $34.20 in 1997.

Mohair production in Texas has dropped from a 1965 high of 31.6 million pounds to 4.7 million pounds in 1998. Production was valued at $12 million or $2.59 per pound. In 1997, production was 6.4 million pounds valued at $14.6 million or $2.28 per pound. Mohair production in 1996 was 7.5 million pounds valued at $14.6 million, or $1.95 per pound.

Beef Cattle

Raising beef cattle is the most extensive agricultural operation in Texas. In 1997, 43.4 percent of total cash receipts from farm and ranch marketings — $5.8 million of $13.5 million — came from cattle and calves, compared with $5.4 million of $13 million in 1996 (41.6 percent) and $6.3 million of $13.1 million in 1995 (48.1 percent). The next leading commodity is cotton.

Nearly all of the 254 counties in Texas derive more revenue from cattle than from any other agricultural commodity, and those that don't usually rank cattle second in importance.

Within the boundaries of Texas are 14.2 percent of all the cattle in the United States, as are 16.5 percent of the beef breeding cows and 13.6 percent of the calf crop, as of Jan. 1, 1999, inventory.

The number of all cattle in Texas on Jan. 1, 1999, totaled 14 million, compared with 14.5 million on Jan. 1, 1998.

Calves born on Texas farms and ranches in 1998 totaled 5.3 million, compared with 5.2 million in 1997.

Sale of cattle and calves at approximately 140 livestock auctions inspected by Texas Animal Health Commission totaled 5.6 million head in 1997 and 6.4 million head in 1996. The number of cattle and calves shipped into Texas totaled 2.7 million head in 1998 and 3.3 million head in 1997.

Livestock Industries

A large portion of Texas livestock is sold through local auction markets. In 1997, 140 livestock auctions were reported by the Texas Animal Health Commission. In addition to the sales of cattle and calves mentioned in the pre-

Texas Cattle Marketed, 1965-1998 by Size of Feedlot

	Feedlot Capacity (head)						
Year	Under 1,000	1,000- 1,999	2,000- 3,999	4,000- 7,999	8,000- 15,999	16,000 & Over	Total
	Cattle Marketed — 1,000 head —						
1965	104	108	205	324	107	246	1,094
1970	98	53	112	281	727	1,867	3,138
1975	50	22	51	134	485	2,325	3,067
1976	60	33	62	170	583	3,039	3,947
1977	146	22	38	206	604	3,211	4,277
1978	80	20	50	242	697	3,826	4,915
1979	54	19	46	227	556	3,543	4,445
1980	51	18	47	226	533	3,285	4,160
1981	50	20	50	220	510	3,110	3,960
1982	55	20	60	210	540	3,190	4,075
1983	100	20	80	130	490	3,580	4,400
1984	60	20	180	150	540	4,140	5,090
1985	70	10	20	170	620	4,140	5,030
1986	90	10	40	180	550	4,390	5,260
1987	90	20	35	170	625	4,375	5,255
1988	30	15	35	185	650	4,120	5,035
1989	40	15	40	165	675	3,810	4,745
1990	35	24	56	180	605	3,940	4,840
1991	35	25	45	225	500	4,250	5,080
1992	50	10	25	140	505	4,065	4,795
1993	30	20	70	160	640	4,370	5,290
1994	14	13	55	173	725	4,680	5,660
1995	12	24	43	166	630	4,665	5,540
1996	NA	17	43	180	460	4,800	5,500
1997	NA	17	48	250	485	5,000	5,800
1998	NA	10	20	140	420	5,470	6,060

Number of feedlots with 1,000 head or more capacity is number of lots operating any time during the year. Number under 1,000 head capacity and total number of all feedlots is number at end of year.
Source: "Texas Agricultural Facts, 1997," Texas Agricultural Statistics Service, Sept. 1998. Numbers for 1986-1992, "1993 Texas Livestock Statistics," Bulletin 252, August 1994. "Cattle on Feed" annual summary, USDA/NASS, Feb. 1999.

number of livestock slaughtered in Texas totaled 6.7 million cattle,174,700 hogs and 37,500 calves. This compared with 6.6 million cattle,181,100 hogs and 32,700 calves in 1997.

Feeding of cattle in commercial feedlots is a major economic development that has stimulated the establishment and expansion of beef-slaughtering plants. Most of this development is in the Panhandle-Plains area of Northwest Texas, which accounts for about 79 percent of the cattle fed in the state in 1997.

Feedlots with capacities of 1,000 head or more accounted for more than 99 percent of the cattle fed in Texas in 1997. Total feedlot marketings represented about 25 percent of total U.S. fed cattle marketings in 1997. Large amounts of capital are required for feedlot operations, which has forced many lots to become custom-feeding facilities.

Feedlots are concentrated on the High Plains largely because of extensive supplies of sorghum and other feed. Beef breeding herds have increased most in East Texas, where grazing is abundant.

Dairying

Ninety-five percent of the state's dairy industry is located east of the line from Wichita Falls to Brownwood to San Antonio to Corpus Christi. As of Jan. 1, 1998, leading counties in milk production are Erath, Hopkins, Comanche, Hudspeth, Archer and Johnson, which, combined, produce 55.5 percent of the milk in the state. Erath produces more than 24 percent of the total.

All milk sold by Texas dairy farmers is marketed under the terms of Federal Marketing Orders. Most Texas dairymen are members of one of four marketing cooperatives. Associated Milk Producers, Inc., is the largest, representing the majority of the state's producers.

Texas dairy farmers received an average price for milk of $15.70 per hundred pounds in 1998 and $13.70 in 1997. A total of 5.583 billion pounds of milk was sold to

plants and dealers in 1998, bringing in cash receipts from milk to dairy farmers of $876.5 million. This compared with 5.747 billion pounds sold in 1997, which brought in $787.3 million in cash receipts..

The annual average number of milk cows in Texas was 340,000 head as of Jan. 1, 1999, compared with 370,000 head as of Jan. 1, 1998. Average production per cow in the state has increased steadily over the past several decades. The average production per cow in 1998 was 15,923 pounds. Milk per cow in 1997 was 15,259 pounds. Total milk production in Texas was 5.605 billion pounds in 1998 and 5.768 billion pounds in 1997.

There were 3,200 operations reporting milk cows in Texas in 1998, down slightly from 1997, when 3,500 operations reported milk cows.

Dairy Manufacturing

The major dairy products manufactured in Texas include condensed, evaporated and dry milk, creamery butter and cheese. However, production data are not available because of the small number of plants producing these products.

Frozen Desserts

Production of frozen desserts in Texas totaled 120 million gallons in 1998 and 116.1 million gallons in 1997. Ice cream production in Texas in 1998 amounted to 59.2 million gallons, compared to 53.4 million in 1997. Ice cream mix production in 1998 amounted to 33.4 million gallons and 30.8 million in 1997. Milk-sherbert mix in Texas totaled 1.3 million gallons in 1998 and 1.3 million gallons in 1997. Milk-sherbet production in 1998 totaled 2.1 mil-

Hog Production, 1960-1998

Year	Production (1,000 Pounds)	Avg. Market Wt. (Pounds)	Avg. Price Per Cwt. (Dollars)	Gross Income (1,000 Dollars)
1960	288,844	228	$14.70	$44,634
1970	385,502	241	22.50	75,288
1980	315,827	259	35.90	111,700
1981	264,693	256	41.70	121,054
1982	205,656	256	49.60	112,726
1983	209,621	256	45.20	95,343
1984	189,620	262	45.50	95,657
1985	168,950	266	43.40	72,512
1986	176,660	269	47.30	82,885
1987	216,834	NA	50.60	103,983
1988	236,658	NA	41.30	100,029
1989	224,229	NA	39.90	93,178
1990	196,225	NA	48.20	92,222
1991	207,023	NA	45.10	97,398
1992	217,554	NA	36.40	79,436
1993	221,130	NA	39.90	90,561
1994	224,397	NA	35.10	78,394
1995	221,323	NA	35.50	81,509
1996	203,761	NA	45.90	93,526
1997	224,131	NA	47.40	106,238
1998	270,977	NA	30.70	83,190

Source: "1985 Texas Livestock, Dairy and Poultry Statistics," USDA, Bulletin 235, June 1986, pp. 32, 46; 1991 "Texas Livestock Statistics"; USDA, "Meat Animals - Prod., Dips., & Income," April 1998 and 1999; "1993 Texas Livestock Statistics," Bulletin 252, Texas Agricultural Statistics Service, August 1994. "Texas Agricultural Facts,1997," Sept. 1998.

Angora Goats and Mohair, 1900-1999

Year	Goats		Mohair	
	*Number	Farm Value	Production (lbs)	Value
1900	627,333	$923,777	961,328	$267,864
1910	1,135,000	2,514,000	1,998,000	468,000
1920	1,753,000	9,967,000	6,786,000	1,816,000
1930	2,965,000	14,528,000	14,800,000	4,995,000
1940	3,300,000	10,560,000	18,250,000	9,308,000
1950	2,295,000	13,082,000	12,643,000	9,735,000
1960	3,339,000	29,383,000	23,750,000	21,375,000
1970	2,572,000	19,033,000	17,985,000	7,032,000
1980	1,400,000	64,400,000	8,800,000	30,800,000
1981	1,380,000	53,130,000	10,100,000	35,350,000
1982	1,410,000	57,810,000	10,000,000	25,500,000
1983	1,420,000	53,250,000	10,600,000	42,930,000
1984	1,450,000	82,215,000	10,600,000	48,160,000
1985	1,590,000	76,797,000	13,300,000	45,885,000
1986	1,770,000	70,977,000	16,000,000	40,160,000
1987	1,780,000	82,592,000	16,200,000	42,606,000
1988	1,800,000	108,180,000	15,400,000	29,876,000
1989	1,850,000	100,270,000	15,400,000	24,794,000
1990	1,900,000	93,100,000	14,500,000	13,775,000
1991	1,830,000	73,200,000	14,800,000	19,388,000
1992	2,000,000	84,000,000	14,200,000	12,354,000
1993	1,960,000	84,280,000	13,490,000	11,197,000
1994	1,960,000	74,480,000	11,680,000	30,602,000
1995	1,850,000	81,400,000	11,319,000	20,940,000
1996	1,900,000	89,300,000	7,490,000	14,606,000
1997	1,650,000	70,950,000	6,384,000	14,556,000
1998	1,400,000	71,400,000	4,650,000	12,044,000
1999	1,350,000	71,550,000	NA	NA

*Goat number includes all goats, not just Angora goats.
NA = not available.
Source: "1985 Texas Livestock, Dairy and Poultry Statistics," USDA Bulletin 235, June 1986, p. 25. "Texas Agricultural Facts," Crop and Livestock Reporting Service, various years; "1993 Texas Livestock Statistics," Texas Agricultural Statistics Service, Bulletin 252, August 1994. "Texas Agricultural Statistics, 1997," Sept. 1998.*

lion gallons, compared with 1997 milk-sherbet production of 2 million gallons.

Swine

Texas had 640,000 head of swine on hand, Dec. 1, 1998 — 1 percent of the U.S. swine herd. Swine producers in the state usually produce about one-fifth of the pork consumed by the state's population, or about 1.2 million head marketed annually. Although the number of farms producing hogs has steadily decreased, the size of production units has increased substantially.

In 1998, 1.2 million head of hogs were marketed in Texas, producing 271 million pounds of pork valued at $30.70 per 100 pounds, or $83.2 million. In 1997, 827,000 head of hogs were marketed, producing 224.1 million pounds of pork valued at $106.2 million, or $47.40 per 100 pounds.

Goats and Mohair

Goats in Texas numbered 1.4 million on Jan. 1, 1999, compared with 1.4 million on Jan. 1, 1998. They had a value of $71.6 million or $53 per head in 1999 and $71.4 million or $51 per head in 1998.

The goat herd largely consists of Angora goats for mohair production. Angora goats totaled 550,000 as of Jan. 1, 1999, and 750,000 as of 1998. Spanish goats and others numbered 800,000 as of Jan. 1, 1999, and 650,000 as of 1998.

Mohair production during 1998 totaled 4.7 million pounds, compared with 6.4 million in 1997. Average price per pound in 1998 was $2.59 from 620,000 goats clipped for a total value of $12 million. In 1997, producers received $2.28 per pound from 840,000 goats clipped for a total value of $14.6 million.

Nearly half of the world's mohair and 92 percent of the U.S. clip are produced in Texas. The leading Texas counties in Angora goats are Edwards, Val Verde, Sutton, Uvalde, Kinney, Tom Green, Mills, Gillespie, Crockett and Terrell.

Sheep and Wool

The sheep herd continues to decline. Sheep and lambs in Texas numbered 1.4 million head on Jan.1, 1999, down from 1.5 million as of 1998. All sheep were valued at $95.9 million or $71 per head on Jan. 1, 1999, compared with $122.4 million or $80 per head as of Jan. 1, 1998.

Breeding ewes one year old and over numbered 880,000 as of Jan. 1, 1999, and 880,000 as of 1998. Replacement lambs under one year old totaled 130,000 head as of Jan. 1, 1999, and 200,000 as of 1998. Sheep operations in Texas were estimated at 7,000 as of Jan. 1, 1999, and 7,100 as of 1998.

Texas wool production in 1998 was 9.2 million pounds from 1.3 million sheep. Value totaled $5.8 million or 63¢ per pound. This compared with 11 million pounds of wool from 1.5 million sheep valued at $11.6 million or $1.06 per pound in 1997.

Most sheep in Texas are concentrated in the Edwards Plateau area of West Central Texas and nearby counties. As of Jan. 1, 1998, the 10 leading counties are Tom Green, Crockett, Val Verde, Pecos, Concho, Gillespie, Sterling, Menard, Schleicher and Coke. Sheep production is largely dual purpose, for both wool and lamb production.

San Angelo long has been the largest sheep and wool market in the nation and the center for wool and mohair warehouses, scouring plants and slaughterhouses.

Horses

Nationally, Texas ranks as one of the leading states in horse numbers and is the headquarters for many national horse organizations. The largest single-breed registry in America, the American Quarter Horse Association, has its headquarters in Amarillo. The National Cutting Horse Association and the American Paint Horse Association are both located in Fort Worth. In addition to these national associations, Texas also has active state associations that include Palominos, Arabians, Thoroughbreds, Appaloosa and Ponies.

Horses are still used to support the state's giant beef cattle and sheep industries. However, the largest horse numbers within the state are near urban and suburban areas where they are mostly used for recreational activities. State participation activities consist of horse shows, trail rides, play days, rodeos, polo and horse racing. Residential subdivisions have been developed within the state to provide facilities for urban and suburban horse owners.

Poultry and Eggs

Poultry and eggs annually contribute about 7 percent to the average yearly cash receipts of Texas farmers. In 1997, Texas ranked 6th among the states in broilers produced, 7th in eggs produced and 7th in hens.

In 1998, cash receipts to Texas producers from the production of poultry and eggs totaled $1.098 billion. This compares with $1.044 billion in 1997.

Gross income from eggs was $253.6 million in 1998, compared with $267.9 million in 1997. Eggs produced in 1998 totaled 4.26 billion, compared with 4.19 billion in 1997. The average price per dozen in 1998 was 71.5¢, compared with 76.8¢ in 1997.

Broiler production in 1998 totaled 480 million birds, compared with 455.1 million in 1997. Value of production from broilers totaled $842.4 million in 1998 and $774.6 million in 1997. Price per pound averaged 39.0¢ in 1998 and 37.0¢ in 1997. ☆

Texas Sheep and Wool Production, 1850-1999

Year	Sheep		Wool	
	*Number	Value	Production (lbs)	Value
1850	100,530	N A	131,917	N A
1860	753,363	N A	1,493,363	N A
1870	1,223,000	$2,079,000	N A	N A
1880	6,024,000	12,048,000	N A	N A
1890	4,752,000	7,128,000	N A	N A
1900	2,416,000	4,590,000	9,630,000	N A
1910	1,909,000	5,536,000	8,943,000	$1,699,170
1920	3,360,000	33,600,000	22,813,000	5,019,000
1930	6,304,000	44,758,000	48,262,000	10,135,000
1940	10,069,000	49,413,000	79,900,000	23,171,000
1950	6,756,000	103,877,000	51,480,000	32,947,000
1960	5,938,000	85,801,000	51,980,000	21,832,000
1970	3,708,000	73,602,000	30,784,000	11,082,000
1980	2,400,000	138,000,000	18,300,000	17,751,000
1981	2,360,000	116,820,000	20,500,000	24,600,000
1982	2,400,000	100,800,000	19,300,000	16,212,000
1983	2,225,000	86,775,000	18,600,000	15,438,000
1984	1,970,000	76,830,000	17,500,000	16,100,000
1985	1,930,000	110,975,000	16,200,000	13,284,000
1986	1,850,000	107,300,000	16,400,000	13,284,000
1987	2,050,000	133,250,000	16,400,000	19,844,000
1988	2,040,000	155,040,000	18,200,000	35,854,000
1989	1,870,000	133,445,000	18,000,000	27,180,000
1990	2,090,000	133,760,000	17,400,000	19,662,000
1991	2,000,000	108,000,000	16,700,000	13,861,000
1992	2,140,000	111,280,000	17,600,000	16,896,000
1993	2,040,000	118,320,000	17,000,000	11,050,000
1994	1,895,000	106,120,000	14,840,000	15,582,000
1995	1,700,000	100,300,000	13,468,000	15,488,000
1996	1,650,000	108,900,000	9,900,000	8,316,000
1997	1,400,000	100,800,000	10,950,000	11,607,000
1998	1,530,000	122,400,000	9,230,000	5,815,000
1999	1,350,000	95,850,000	NA	NA

*Number given here represents all sheep on farms as of Jan. 1; number clipped will vary because of spring and fall clipping.
NA = not available.
Source: "1985 Texas Livestock, Dairy and Poultry Statistics," USDA Bulletin 235, June 1986, pp. 24-25. "Texas Agricultural Facts," Annual Summary, Crop and Livestock Reporting Service, various years; "1993 Texas Livestock Statistics," Texas Agricultural Statistics Service, Bulletin 252, August 1994; "Texas Agricultural Statistics, 1997," Sept. 1998.

Texas Economy: Employment Growth and Low Inflation

Source: State of Texas Annual Cash Report 1998, Comptroller of Public Accounts

The Texas economy broke historical records on the upside during fiscal 1998. Mostly, the state's growth was grounded in real demand, unlike the speculative booms which have often accompanied a strong Texas economy in the past. In fiscal 1998, the state enjoyed a rather unusual situation of synchronous high employment growth and low inflation.

Although fiscal 1998 saw many economic measures reaching their best levels since the 1960s or 1970s, other factors suffered. Agriculture was beaten down by the second major drought in three years, and the state's oil industry, which was beaten down by worldwide overproduction, struggled with the lowest average prices for a fiscal year since 1979.

Most of the economic milestones of fiscal 1998 were positive. The statewide level of housing starts reached its highest annual point since fiscal 1985. Housing permits for fiscal 1998 exceeded those of fiscal 1997 by a striking 21 percent. Texas inflation, which averaged an annual rate of 1.4 percent during the fiscal year, took its smallest bite out of Texas pocketbooks since its one-year recessionary level in fiscal 1986, and the lowest sustained level since 1962. Mortgage rates dropped to their lowest point since the 1960s. The Texas unemployment rate worked its way down to the best level (at 4.9 percent during the fiscal year) seen since fiscal 1980. Meanwhile, annual personal income advanced at the fastest annual rate in eight years, and the state's number of help-wanted ads exceeded its all-time record in fiscal 1998.

Some Things Have Not Changed

As it has every year of the 1990s, Texas' rate of job growth again exceeded the nation's rate in fiscal 1998. For the sixth straight year, the Texas economy added more than 200,000 jobs, this time closing the year with 268,000 more jobs than it had at the beginning. This translated into an annual growth rate of 3.1 percent, compared to 2.5 percent nationwide. As fiscal 1998 closed, Texas ranked ninth among the 50 states in the rate of employment growth, and second in the total number of jobs added.

If Texas were still an independent nation, it would be the eleventh largest economy in the world, as measured by gross national product data from the *1998 World Bank Atlas*. In addition to generating more jobs, the Texas economy generated a higher standard of living for the average Texan in fiscal 1998.

Recent data reveal that the state's per capita gross state product now exceeds the nation's per capita gross domestic product by over one percent. Year-over-year personal income growth outpaced inflation and outgrew that of all but three states. Per capita income growth in Texas was up 8 percent during the first half of the fiscal year, while inflation in the state skimmed off only 1.4

percent from this nominal growth.

The biggest economic story for both Texas and the nation is fiscal 1998 was record-breaking consumer confidence, 43 points above its 100 baseline in July, according to a Conference Board survey. The Conference Board tracks regional consumer confidence — the level of optimism about the present and future economy — for subnational regions. Texas comprises two-thirds of the population in the West South Central region, which joined the nation in reaching the highest levels of consumer confidence since the survey began in 1981.

Even more than in most years, however, the Texas economic story varied widely from one industry to another.

Mining: The Flame Subsides Again

The mining sector (about 95 percent oil and gas) saw its best year of employment growth in fiscal 1997 since the end of an energy boom in 1982, but the sector was unable to sustain its gains in 1998. Overproduction in the Middle East pushed oil prices below $12 a barrel in fiscal 1998, and average price for the year was only about $14.50 (compared to over $20 in fiscal 1997). A lively natural gas market was not sufficient to counterbalance weakness in the oil prices, and there was virtually no net change in Texas mining jobs for the year, starting and ending the year at 167,000 jobs statewide.

Mortgage Rates Spur Residential Construction

Texas' residential housing starts were at their highest level since the speculative building boom in the early to mid-1980s. Housing permits reached about 144,000 for the fiscal year, taking advantage of low mortgage rates, high consumer confidence and strong income growth, to eclipse the 118,700 in fiscal 1997. The growth in apartment construction and multi-family housing starts exceeded that of single-family starts.

Although mortgage rates are causing a surge in housing starts nationwide, the surge is, not surprisingly, more definite in Texas. Texas accounted for 9.3 percent of the new houses constructed nationwide, despite the state having a 7.3 percent share of the national population. This share of the nation's housing starts has been rising every year since 1988, when the state had only 3.4 percent of the nation's total.

Nonresidential construction increased about 17 percent, to reach nearly 120 million square feet in fiscal 1998. The peak was 167 million in 1985, with the intervening low of 58.6 million in 1989. Increased international trade is boosting the need for warehouse and corporate space, particularly in Houston, while the growth of communications, high technology manufacturing, and recreational tourism are spurring commercial construction, particularly around Dallas, Austin and San Antonio.

Non-building construction, such as that of roads and bridges, now stands at about $4.9 billion annually, with

6.5 percent average annual increases over the past five years.

One result of all this activity has been stellar growth rates in construction employment. During fiscal 1998, the number of Texas construction jobs increased by 5.8 percent, from 457,700 to 484,400.

Manufacturing is High Tech

Texas manufacturing is increasingly comprised of high technology firms, which have been instrumental in boosting Texas' manufacturing employment from seventh among the states a decade ago to second in 1998. One-fourth of Texas' total manufacturing employment is directly in computers or electronic employment, accounting for over 7 percent of the nation's manufacturing employment in electronics and computers, and up from a 5.7 percent share in 1988. Another 21 percent of the state's manufacturing is in oil/gas related manufacturing, such as petrochemicals, petroleum refining and the manufacturing of oil and gas rigs, instrumentation and other equipment.

Toward the end of fiscal 1998, the Asian recession began to slow the rapid rise of Texas exports, which have quadrupled in value since 1986. Still, export value advanced at a double-digit rate during the year. Electronic products and computers make up nearly 45 percent of the state's total exports, followed by petrochemicals and transportation equipment, which account for another 25 percent of the total.

Texas exports of computers and electronics totaled $36.5 billion in 1997 and now accounts for over 15 percent of total U.S. exports of computers and electronics. Despite the cycles, exports are expected to underlie much of the growth in future Texas manufacturing.

Statewide employment in electronics, computers and other electrical and non-electrical machinery manufacturing has risen over 30 percent in only 5 years, from 215,700 at the end of fiscal 1993 to 281,200 at the end of fiscal 1998.

The state's high technology manufacturing has planted the seeds of its own growth, because Texas now has a high-technology infrastructure, readily available suppliers and a skilled, available labor force.

Despite job gains in manufacturing, the real story underlying the increasing importance of Texas manufacturing is in the growth of production. Because of improving productivity per worker, particularly with the aid of improving computer technology and robotics, the state's production of manufactured goods is growing faster than is indicated by employment alone. The gross state product in Texas manufacturing reached $100 billion in fiscal 1998, after growing an average 9.2 percent per year over the last five years.

Service-Producing Industries Top Sector

Service-producing industries are adding jobs at a faster rate than the goods-producing sectors and accounted for over 84 percent of total Texas jobs growth during fiscal 1998. Employment growth rates in the broad service-producing sectors are likely to remain around 2.5 to 3 percent annually in 1999 and 2000.

Transportation, Communications, Utilities

Employment growth in transportation, communication and public utilities, at 4.8 percent during fiscal year, ranked first among the nation's 50 states in the rate of increase during fiscal 1998. A growing market of new technology — including cellular telephones, pagers and modems used for online and Internet usage — sparked a recent boom in communications equipment and services. Three-fourths of the state's communications employment is related to telephone services, with most of the remainder being in cable and satellite services, radio and television.

Texas' communications companies added 11,700 jobs, for an unusually high growth rate of 9.4 percent. This contrasts with the 1983 to 1993 period, when there was no net growth in Texas' communications employment. With the spurt in growth of on-line computer applications and cellular telephones, communications employment in Texas has grown by 48 percent in the five years since the end of fiscal 1993.

The transportation services sector was not as hot as communications, but still has barreled along with the addition of 14,600 jobs during the fiscal year, for an increase of 4.5 percent. Employment growth over the previous ten years had been averaging close to 4 percent annually. Trucking and courier services have been the strongest subcomponents, due largely to the rapid growth of exports to Mexico and a strong national economy. Air transportation services have increased by 4,300 of these jobs, or 4.1 percent during the year.

Fiscal 1998 was the seventh straight year of declining employment for the Texas public utilities industry, where losses of 11,000 jobs since fiscal 1991 have left the industry with only 70,500 employees, equal to its 1980 employment level. Fifteen years ago, public utilities employed 13 of every 1,000 Texans, while today this proportion is 8 in 1,000.

Trade Grows with the Overall Economy

The growth of the trade sector, more than other industries, is driven by the overall growth of the Texas economy and retail sales. Over the last 25 years, trade growth matched overall employment growth (and tracked it closely) at just over 3 percent annually. Likewise, trade growth mirrored state employment growth during most of fiscal 1998, but began to slow in the last few months, to end the year with an employment increase of 2.3 percent.

Wholesale trade, which accounts for less than one-fourth of all trade jobs, added 13,100, for a 2.6 percent increase. Retail trade, drawing from particularly strong growth in restaurants and the sale of building materials, added 37,000 jobs, for a 2.4 percent increase. Reflecting a nationwide pattern, food stores lost 2 percent of their net jobs and apparel retailers suffered a more pronounced 4 percent loss (-3,000).

During the first half of fiscal 1998, total retail sales in Texas advanced by 4.8 percent, while inflation advanced only about 1.3 percent.

Finance, Insurance and Real Estate

Since 1995, the finance, insurance and real estate industry has been consolidating, but a healthy lending market and growing fee income, have sparked hiring in depository institutions. Although Texas banks and savings institutions lost over 20,000 jobs from 1988 to 1995, about 6,000 jobs have been added back since. Real estate and other finance hustled in response to a strong housing market and an even stronger stock market through most of the fiscal year, until it cooled. Insurance, too, enjoyed stability, owing in part to rapid personal income growth, which allowed consumers to purchase more insurable items and provided more disposable income to pay insurance premiums.

Texas banks, thrifts and credit unions added 3,900 jobs during fiscal 1998, for a growth rate of 3.3 percent. This represents the fastest rate of growth since the early 1980s. Real estate and other finance added 10,700 jobs (5.4 percent), taking advantage of mortgage rates which dropped to their lowest level since the 1960s. The slowest growing part of the sector was insurance, which still boosted its number of Texas jobs by 2.7 percent, with a net gain of 4,100 jobs.

Services in Action

Texas services employment advanced 4.7 percent in fiscal 1998. Although growing at a slower rate than construction and transportation/utilities, services continued to be the largest generator of new jobs in Texas. Services accounted for 112,100 new jobs during fiscal 1998, or 42 percent of all the nonfarm jobs added. Services employment in Texas has increased by 54 percent since the beginning of fiscal 1990, from 1.64 million to over 2.5 million at the end of fiscal 1998.

Business services typically grows in tandem with the overall economy, only faster. During fiscal 1998, business services added nearly 50,000 jobs statewide, for a formidable 8.3 percent increase, with particularly rapid growth in personnel services, adjustment and collection services, credit reporting services, direct mail advertising, building maintenance services and a variety of computer-related programming and design services. Personnel supply services, a subset of business and repair services, was the fastest growing sub-segment of the economy, with a net 26,200 jobs added in this sector during fiscal 1998, for a 12.6 percent increase. Much of this was due to the out-sourcing of activities previously done in-house by manufacturing and other large firms. Business, repair and engineering services now account for 11 percent of all nonfarm jobs, compared with 7.7 percent ten years ago.

Partly in response to an aging population, health services has grown from 6 percent of the state's total nonfarm employment ten years ago to almost 8 percent today. In fiscal 1998, health services added 29,200 (4.3 percent). Other services include a wide range of professional and personal services, including legal services, hotels, amusement parks and movies, landscape services, membership organizations, social services and housekeeping services. Combined, the "Other Services" category added 18,300 new jobs, for an increase of 2.2 percent.

Government Shrinking as Proportion

Recent trends toward decentralizing and localizing government have been clearly reflected in the number of government jobs in Texas. In fiscal 1998, local government grew, while the federal government continued to lose jobs. During the year, the federal civilian government sector in Texas lost 1,700 jobs, for a decline of -0.9 percent. This continues a long-term trend of downsizing, as the civilian federal government sector has been losing jobs every year since 1990, and staffing in

military government sector has declined in all but one year since 1985. The civilian federal government sector accounted for a post-World War peak of 50 out of every 1,000 nonfarm Texas jobs in 1967. This fell to 44 in 1970, to 29 by 1980, and to 21 in 1998.

State government (including public higher education) employed 37 of every 1,000 Texans in 1970, and rose to a recent high of 40 by 1993, before dropping back to 37 per 1,000 total employees in 1998. State government added 3,000 jobs in fiscal 1998, with 2,000 of those in state colleges and universities.

The only government sector where job growth approached that of the overall economy was in local government. During fiscal 1998, local government increased by 24,800 jobs, or 2.7 percent. Increased staffing in local school districts, where growth was 3.8 percent, has allowed the relatively brisk growth in this sub-sector. Local government employment outside of schools, on the other hand, grew by less than one percent. Total local government jobs, including those in school districts, rose from 101 of every 1,000 Texas jobs in 1970 to a recent peak of 118 in 1994, before falling back below 112 in 1998.

Cities in Review

Employment growth in the **Austin-San Marcos** metropolitan statistical area (MSA, including Bastrop, Caldwell, Hays, Travis and Williamson counties) continues to cool for the third consecutive year. While still adding 22,600 jobs, to record a 3.9 percent increase from 573,000 in August 1997 to 595,600 in August 1998, this rate of increase was lower than the rate of 6.5 percent posted between 1994 and 1995.

Employment increased in all sectors of the local economy, with major increases occurring in services (8,300 jobs), trade (6,100), construction (3,600), transportation, public utilities and communications (1,300), manufacturing (1,800) and government (1,300). In August 1998, the unemployment rate in Texas' capital city and the surrounding areas was 2.9 percent, 0.4 percentage points lower than a year ago.

Together, the services and trade sectors accounted for half of the area's total employment. Providing 171,900 jobs, the services sector — the area's largest employment sector — increased 5.1 percent, while the trade sector exhibited a 5 percent increase over the past year, employing 128,000. Between August 1997 and August 1998, the services and trade sectors accounted for two of every three new jobs in the metro area.

Construction jobs increased at 9.7 percent per year between 1994 and 1998, almost twice the area's average annual job growth rate of 5.1 percent. Between August 1997 and August 1998, construction employment increased 12.1 percent to 33,400 jobs, the highest total ever recorded in the MSA.

Contributing to construction employment were office, hospital and residential construction projects. Five construction and renovation projects for state and local government, totaling $52 million, were started in 1998.

Finally, residential construction surged 26 percent in the first seven months of 1998, compared to the same period in 1997. More than 5,050 single-family residential building permits were issued between January and July 1998, up from 4,017 permits issued during the same period in 1997.

A source of the area's economic strength has been production of computer chips, personal computers and associated hardware. Seven of the area's ten largest employers make semiconductors, personal computers or machinery to build semiconductors.

Employment growth in the government sector — one of the historical cornerstones of the city's workforce — remained virtually stable, adding 1,300 jobs, a one percent growth rate. Government employment in August 1998 totaled 133,100 and accounts for 22 percent of the area's employment base.

The **Dallas** metro area (Collin, Dallas, Denton, Ellis, Henderson, Hunt, Kaufman and Rockwall counties) experienced another year of remarkable growth, creating 76,000 new jobs and bringing total nonagricultural employment to 1,847,000.

Leading the way in employment gains was the services sector, which now accounts for 575,200 jobs, or 31 percent of total employment. Medical services account for one-fifth of the services sector. Business services, particularly those related to computer services, grew by half during the year. Substantial growth was also noted in the legal services sector.

The second largest employment sector, wholesale and retail trade, added 11,400 jobs from August 1997 to

August 1998 for a total of 443,000. Wholesale and retail trade now accounts for 24 percent of total employment.

Manufacturing employment in Dallas continues to reflect the steady expansion in manufacturing activity seen statewide, particularly in the electronic and electronic equipment sector. About 5,000 manufacturing jobs were added, increasing employment from 246,000 in August 1997 to 251,000 in August 1998.

The residential real estate market was particularly active, due in part to the planned construction of several senior housing projects and the overall attractiveness of the Dallas metro area as a retirement center. As of early 1998, a less than two-month supply of new homes remained unsold, indicating a tight market.

Stiff international competition for lower-skilled manufacturing jobs continues to slow employment growth in **El Paso**. Although employment increased 2.5 percent from 243,500 in August 1997 to 251,000 in August 1998, manufacturing employment declined by 2,400 during this time. During the past year, El Paso's unemployment rate fell slightly to 10.5 percent from 11.6 percent.

Most job growth occurred in services and trade, adding 4,550 workers and accounting for about three-fourths of the new jobs. Retail trade employment grew

Texas Gross State Product, 1989-1998, By Industry (in millions)

Industry	1989	1990	1991	1992	1993	1994	1995	1996	1997	1998*
Agriculture	$ 5,317	$ 6,682	$ 6,804	$ 7,140	$ 7,679	$ 7,838	$ 7,325	$ 7,327	$ 7,379	$ 5,937
%change	-1.3	25.7	1.8	4.9	7.5	2.1	-6.5	0.0	0.7	-19.5
Mining	30,994	40,199	37,884	34,629	36,364	32,845	34,965	41,278	46,500	47,207
%change	-2.1	29.7	-5.8	-8.6	5.0	-9.7	6.5	18.1	12.7	1.5
Construction	13,712	14,821	15,615	17,012	18,069	20,284	22,113	24,138	25,728	27,454
%change	2.9	8.1	5.4	8.9	6.2	12.3	9.0	9.2	6.6	6.7
Manufacturing	61,045	64,702	61,357	61,950	66,601	77,313	84,350	89,725	97,202	103,707
%change	6.1	6.0	-5.2	1.0	7.5	16.1	9.1	6.4	8.3	6.7
Transportation and Utilities	36,903	37,928	42,571	45,264	49,335	52,850	55,450	58,436	64,629	70,557
%change	8.3	2.8	12.2	6.3	9.0	7.1	4.9	5.4	10.6	9.2
Wholesale and Retail Trade	56,706	59,568	64,845	68,050	72,207	79,353	82,638	88,192	95,233	102,977
%change	5.4	5.0	8.9	4.9	6.1	9.9	4.1	6.7	8.0	8.1
Finance, Insurance and Real Estate	50,194	53,177	57,196	62,009	66,071	68,842	73,869	79,020	85,062	85,713
%change	14.1	5.9	7.6	8.4	6.6	4.2	7.3	7.0	7.6	0.8
Services	57,681	64,970	69,365	75,644	80,221	85,849	91,699	99,282	109,727	119,546
%change	10.6	12.6	6.8	9.1	6.1	7.0	6.8	8.3	10.5	8.9
Local, State and Federal Government	44,037	46,849	49,443	52,823	56,438	58,924	61,798	64,431	66,126	69,310
%change	6.2	6.4	5.5	6.8	6.8	4.4	4.9	4.3	2.6	4.8
TOTAL	$ 356,589	$ 388,896	$ 405,080	$ 424,521	$ 452,985	$ 484,098	$ 514,207	$ 551,829	$ 597,586	$ 632,408
%change	6.9	9.1	4.2	4.8	6.7	6.9	6.2	7.3	8.3	5.8
Total (in 1992 $)	$ 392,380	$ 404,058	$ 412,899	$ 424,520	$ 438,914	$ 465,528	$ 486,085	$ 502,903	$ 534,431	$ 559,853
% change	2.4	3.0	2.2	2.8	3.4	6.1	4.4	3.5	6.3	4.8

*1998 numbers are estimated from incomplete data.

Source: U.S. Bureau of Economic Analysis and Texas Comptroller of Public Accounts. The Bureau revised historical data contained in this table due to changes in methodology, inflation factors, price indicators and revisions to interim census figures. Texas 1998 Comprehensive Annual Financial Report.

despite some ongoing softness in retail sales attributable to the lower value of the peso. Retail sales for calendar 1997 dropped by $68 million from 1996's record high of about $5 billion.

El Paso is an important city for retail trade for far West Texas and northern Mexico, serving approximately 2.4 million inhabitants in the El Paso-Juarez area. Wholesale and retail trade employs roughly one-fourth of the workforce. The devaluation of the peso had a negative impact on the trade sector, but the slow return of some Mexican shoppers, combined with growth in the local economy, led to wholesale and retail trade employment increasing by 1,200 jobs to stand at 59,000 jobs in August 1998 — the highest trade employment level yet.

Government jobs continue to provide a measure of economic stability through two of the area's largest employers — the University of Texas-El Paso and the Army's Fort Bliss.

In the manufacturing sector, employment declined in the last year due to layoffs in the apparel industry. But a total of ten new manufacturers are locating in El Paso. These manufacturers will add approximately 1,700 new jobs and invest more than $61 million in the area.

Employment in the **Fort Worth-Arlington** metro area (made up of Hood, Johnson, Parker and Tarrant counties) increased by 26,200 jobs or by 3 percent from August 1997 to August 1998, reaching 732,600. More than 70 percent of this job growth was concentrated in the wholesale and retail trade and service sectors, underscoring Fort Worth's growing role as a regional trade and service center.

Wholesale and retail trade employment increased by 8,800 jobs or 5 percent to total 187,900 jobs. Employment in the services sector increased by 7,300 jobs. The amusement and recreational services sector, which includes entertainment facilities at Arlington, is the third largest component of the service sector.

The booming construction sector added 1,900 jobs. Residential construction is at a peak with hundreds of new apartment units being built.

The transportation, communication and public utilities sector and the finance, insurance and real estate sector continued to grow in the Fort Worth-Arlington area. Adding 5,000 jobs, these two sectors now account for 14 percent of total employment. The demand for international transportation services is fueling growth in this sector.

The **Houston** metro area (made up of Chambers, Fort Bend, Harris, Liberty, Montgomery and Waller counties) continues to show strong local job growth. August 1998 employment was up 4.2 percent from August 1997 to 1,977,800 jobs and unemployment is down to 4.1 percent.

Manufacturing employment grew by 6,100 jobs to total 215,600 in August 1998. In oil and gas exploration, the decline in domestic drilling activity continued, resulting in fewer rigs at work and growing natural gas storage levels. Rigs totaled 112 in the Gulf of Mexico as of Sept. 11, 1998, down from 126 in 1997.

Construction and retail trade jobs have held strong, making up for the slow employment growth in other industries. Wholesale and retail trade employs more than 600,000 workers, 22.9 percent of the total Houston area employment.

Combined commercial and residential construction continues to rise, creating a great deal of local expansion. The value of commercial construction was over $150 million — up over 30 percent from the previous year. New residential building permits totaled 1,401 in June 1998, a 27.6 percent increase from 1997. These permits represent an additional $114 million in new residential value. This growth has helped construction employment gain 7,964 jobs, 6.2 percent more than a year earlier.

The **San Antonio** metro area (including Bexar, Comal, Guadalupe and Wilson counties) has grown significantly.

The region's nonagricultural employment base gained 26,000 jobs to reach 691,000. Unemployment dropped slightly from 4.3 percent in August 1997 to 3.8 percent in August 1998, which remained below the state's 1998 average of about 5 percent.

According to a study conducted by the Weitzman Group in San Antonio, tourism has become one of the Alamo city's most important industries, supporting about 56,600 jobs. The Alamo and the Riverwalk are the top tourist attractions in the state. Each year over 7 million visitors bring $3 billion into the city's economy, half of which comes from convention attendees. The downtown convention center is in its third expansion/renovation, almost doubling the size of the exhibition hall. And, privatization of Kelly Air Force Base after its purchase by the City of San Antonio has spurred interest by several companies.

San Antonio has had a significant role in international trade. About one-third of the out-of-state companies that relocated to San Antonio in the past four years have had some link to NAFTA and the Mexican market. By mid-1998, Texas had experienced a 23 percent increase in exports to Mexico.

Manufacturing employment in the San Antonio area increased slightly from 50,200 workers in August 1997 to 50,500 in August 1998.

The construction employment sector, which displayed the highest percentage increase from 1997, has added 2,400 jobs to San Antonio for a total of 37,000 in August 1998. The 1998 office building completions totaled 1,577,400 squre feet, 62 percent of which was owner-occupied and 38 percent was in multi-tenant buildings. Another 1,274,800 square feet in retail building completions was scheduled by the end of 1998. Residential building permits totaled 6,250 for the 12 months ending in July 1997, then increased to 7,480 in July 1998.

Trade and services remain the backbone of San Antonio's economy. Trade sector employment makes up about 24 percent of the San Antonio's employment base and increased by 4,900 jobs last year to 166,000 in August 1998. Also, San Antonio's outer expressway, Loop 1604, is gaining retail importance with large grocery centers opening there.

Services employment, San Antonio's largest sector, accounting for 32 percent of total employment, grew from 210,200 in August 1997 to 224,000 in August 1998, a 6 percent increase. ☆

Employment in Texas by Industry

Source: Texas Workforce Commission. Additional information available at web site: www.twc.state.tx.us.

Employment in Texas increased to 9,131,500 in April 1999, up from 8,881,900 in April 1998.

The following table shows Texas Workforce Commission estimates of the nonagricultural labor force by industry for April 1998 and 1999. The final column shows the change in the number employed.

(in thousands)

Industry	1999	1998	Chng.
GOODS PRODUCING	1,769.2	1,758.4	10.8
Mining	154.3	167.5	-13.2
Oil & Gas Extraction	145.9	158.9	-13.0
Construction	519.4	487.3	32.1
Special Trade	303.6	280.2	23.4
Manufacturing	1,095.5	1,103.6	-8.1
Durable Goods	672.1	671.6	0.5
Lumber & Wood Products	47.8	45.9	1.9
Logging Camps, Sawmills, Planing Mills	7.5	7.5	0.0
Furniture & Fixtures	19.7	18.8	0.9
Stone, Clay & Glass Products	44.0	42.4	1.6
Concrete, Gypsum & Plaster - Prod.	21.8	20.2	1.6
Primary Metal Industries	29.7	31.5	-1.8
Fabricated Metal Industries	103.8	103.3	0.5
Fabr. Structural Metal Prod.	55.3	53.6	1.7
Industrial Machinery & Equipment	149.3	151.9	-2.6
Oil & Gas Field Machinery	29.5	33.1	-3.6
Electronic & Other Electrical Equipment	130.5	132.4	-1.9
Transportation Equipment	85.3	83.0	2.3
Aircraft & Parts	45.1	45.5	-0.4
Instruments & Related Products	40.8	41.8	-1.0
Misc. Manufacturing Industries	21.2	20.6	0.6
Non-Durable Goods	423.4	432.0	-8.6
Food & Kindred Products	95.5	97.8	-2.3
Meat Products	34.2	34.3	-0.1
Dairy Products	5.0	5.1	-0.1
Bakery Products	9.2	9.1	0.1
Malt Beverages	2.1	2.3	-0.2
Textile Mill Products	3.9	3.9	0.0
Apparel & Other Finished Textile Prod.	47.8	53.2	-5.4
Paper & Allied Products	28.8	29.7	-0.9
Printing & Publishing	75.8	75.9	-0.1
Newspapers, Periodicals, Books, Misc.	33.8	34.0	-0.2
Chemicals & Allied Products	84.2	83.8	0.4
Petroleum & Coal Products	24.9	26.0	-1.1
Petroleum Refining	21.1	22.2	-1.1
Rubber & Misc. Plastic Prod.	56.2	55.0	1.2
Leather & Leather Products	6.3	6.7	-0.4
SERVICE PRODUCING	7,362.3	7,123.5	238.8
Transportation & Public Utilities	557.9	533.7	24.2
Railroad Transportation	17.4	17.1	0.3
Transportation by Air	115.1	107.9	7.2
Communications	135.6	128.3	7.3
Electric, Gas & Sanitary Services	69.8	69.9	-0.1
Electric Services	30.8	30.9	-0.1
Gas Production & Distribution	23.2	23.5	-0.3
Trade	2,127.9	2,087.7	40.2
Wholesale Trade	530.0	514.8	15.2
Retail Trade	1,597.9	1,572.9	25.0
Building & Garden Supplies	65.3	62.8	2.5
General Merchandise	200.8	201.2	-0.4
Department Stores	180.9	180.3	0.6
Food Stores	244.9	246.0	-1.1
Automotive Dealers & Service Stations	166.0	163.6	2.4
Apparel & Accessory Stores	77.1	78.2	-1.1
Eating & Dining Places	601.8	583.2	18.6
Misc. Retail Trade	169.0	168.0	1.0
Finance, Insurance, Real Estate	510.9	489.8	21.1
Depository Insts.	128.4	124.7	3.7
Insurance Carriers	103.3	100.7	2.6
Insurance Agents	58.5	57.0	1.5
Real Estate	118.9	114.3	4.6
Services	2,604.5	2,490.9	113.6
Hotels & Other Lodging Places	94.0	91.5	2.5
Personal Services	90.4	92.3	-1.9
Business Services	671.3	625.4	45.9
Personnel Supply	235.3	216.5	18.8
Auto Repair Services	87.6	84.9	2.7
Misc. Repair Services	33.7	33.0	0.7
Amusement, including Motion Pictures	123.2	117.3	5.9
Health Services	694.5	679.0	15.5
Educational Services	110.7	106.0	4.7
Engineering & Mgmt Services	245.1	227.0	18.1
Total Government	1,561.1	1,521.4	39.7
Federal Government	187.2	185.1	2.1
State Government	325.8	326.5	-0.7
Local Government	1,048.1	1,009.8	38.3

Average Hours and Earnings

The following table shows the average weekly earnings, weekly hours worked and hourly wage in Texas for selected industries in 1999. Figures are provided by the Texas Workforce Commission and the U. S. Bureau of Labor Statistics.

Industry	Earnings	Hours	Wage
GOODS PRODUCING			
Mining, Oil & Gas Extraction	$ 738.15	43.6	$ 16.93
Manufacturing	529.81	43.4	12.21
Durable Goods	525.80	44.0	11.95
Lumber & Wood Products	425.39	43.9	9.69
Fabricated Metal Products	535.50	45.0	11.90
Industrial Machinery	539.21	44.6	12.09
Oil Field Machinery	649.12	47.8	13.58
Electronic Equipment	507.53	42.4	11.97
Transportation Equipment	663.38	43.5	15.25
Non-Durable Goods	537.61	42.6	12.67
Food & Kindred Products	413.34	42.7	9.68
Meat Products	393.31	48.2	8.16
Malt Beverages	1,052.09	47.2	22.29
Apparel & Other Textiles	297.23	37.2	7.99
Printing & Publishing	499.79	41.0	12.19
Chemicals & Allied Products	849.23	45.1	18.83
Petroleum & Coal Products	805.58	39.9	20.19
Petroleum Refining	851.24	39.3	21.66
Rubber & Misc. Plastics	489.75	45.9	10.67
SERVICE PRODUCING			
Transport., Communications	$ 666.83	42.5	$ 15.47
Electric, Gas & Sanitary	647.34	43.3	14.95
Trade	$ 306.53	32.3	$ 9.49
Wholesale	519.10	39.9	13.01
Drugs, Proprietaries	676.49	40.9	16.54
Farm-Produce Raw Matrls	261.27	30.1	8.68
Retail	242.40	30.0	8.08
Building & Garden Supply	357.40	37.9	9.43
Gen. Merchandise	264.23	32.5	8.13
Department Stores	268.95	32.6	8.25
Food Stores	250.59	31.6	7.93
Grocery Stores	250.89	31.4	7.99
Automotive Dealers	420.37	37.3	11.27
Apparel & Accessory	206.42	28.2	7.32
Eating & Drinking	155.65	25.6	6.08
Finance, Depository Insts.	392.92	37.6	10.45
Selected Metro Areas			
DALLAS			
Manufacturing	$ 533.75	42.7	$ 12.50
Durable Goods	557.92	44.0	12.68
Non-Durable Goods	488.84	40.3	12.13
FORT WORTH-ARLINGTON			
Manufacturing	575.46	43.3	13.09
Durable Goods	610.40	43.6	14.00
Non-Durable	510.08	42.9	11.89
HOUSTON			
Manufacturing	635.19	44.7	14.21
Durable Goods	545.40	45.0	12.12
Non-Durable	782.34	44.2	17.70
SAN ANTONIO			
Manufacturing	416.79	42.1	9.90
Durable Goods	445.88	43.5	10.25
Non-Durable Goods	384.89	40.6	9.48

Construction Industry

Contract awards for construction in 1998 totaled $4,951,275,224. Although the number of contracts stayed near 3,000, dollar value was considerably lower than the record volume of 1993: $5,394,342,718, as shown in the Comparision of Years table below. Another table shows the approved Texas construction for 1999. These data were compiled by editors of **Texas Contractor** from official sources.

Comparison of Construction Awards by Years, 1953-1998

Source: Texas Contractor

Year	Total Awards	Year	Total Awards	Year	Total Awards
1998	$4,951,275,224	1983	4,074,910,947	1967	1,316,872,998
1997	5,088,017,435	1982	3,453,784,388	1966	1,421,312,029
1996	4,383,336,574	1981	3,700,112,809	1965	1,254,638,051
1995	4,771,332,413	1980	3,543,117,615	1964	1,351,656,302
1994	4,396,199,988	1979	3,353,243,234	1963	1,154,624,634
1993	5,394,342,718	1978	2,684,743,190	1962	1,132,607,006
1992	4,747,666,912	1977	2,270,788,842	1961	988,848,239
1991	3,926,799,801	1976	1,966,553,804	1960	1,047,943,630
1990	3,922,781,630	1975	1,737,036,682	1959	1,122,290,957
1989	4,176,355,929	1974	2,396,488,520	1958	1,142,138,674
1988	3,562,336,666	1973	1,926,778,365	1957	1,164,240,546
1987	4,607,051,270	1972	1,650,897,233	1956	1,220,831,984
1986	4,636,310,266	1971	1,751,331,262	1955	949,213,349
1985	4,806,998,065	1970	1,458,708,492	1954	861,623,224
1984	3,424,721,025	1969	1,477,125,397	1953	1,180,320,174
		1968	1,363,629,304		

Approved Texas Construction, 1999

The following is a recapitulation of all approved Texas construction. The data were compiled by the editors of **Texas Contractor** from official sources.

Federal:

General Services Administration	$6,000,000
Federal Aviation Administration	93,500,000
Veterans Administration	17,500,000
NASA	2,300,000
Department of Defense	168,276,000
Rural Utilities Service	23,500,000
U.S. Department of Agriculture	101,500,000
Natual Res. Conserv. Service	4,000,000
Federal Highway Administration	1,393,682,927
Total Federal	**$1,810,358,927**

State:

Texas Dept. of Transportation	$2,099,923,927
State Agencies	379,508,967
State Colleges and Universities	503,080,188
Total State	**$2,982,513,082**

Water Projects:

Corps of Engineers	$69,944,000
Bureau of Reclamation	4,300,000
River Authorities	370,000,000
State Revolving Fund (SRF)	332,500,000
Drinking Water SRF	64,817,000
Total Water Projects	**$841,551,000**

Cities:

Schools, Colleges	$329,379,401
Streets, Bridges	352,884,056
Waterworks, Sewers	638,659,331
Apartments, Residences	1,180,443,825
Commercial	1,326,153,901
City Buildings	223,160,136
Total Cities	**$4,050,680,650**

Counties:

New Roads-County Funds	$53,706,557
Road Maintenance	192,206,889
Machinery Purchases	84,281,226
County Buildings	247,128,039
Miscellaneous	3,931,239
Total Counties	**$581,253,950**
Grand Total	**$10,266,357,609**

Analysis of Awards

The following table analyzes and classifies awards in Texas for the year 1998, as compared with 1997, as reported by **Texas Contractor**.

Category	1998		1997	
	No.	Amount	No.	Amount
Engineering Awards	1,756	$2,661,458,928	2,122	$2,858,774,646
Non-Residential Awards	1,187	2,289,816,296	1,012	2,229,242,789
Total	**2,943**	**$4,951,275,224**	**3,134**	**$5,088,017,435**

ENGINEERING AWARDS

Type of Project	1998		1997	
	No.	Amount	No.	Amount
Highways, Streets, Airports	1,160	$2,098,406,579	1,546	$2,351,057,329
Waterworks, Sewers, etc.	527	537,065,293	523	477,653,201
Irrigation, Drainage, etc.	69	25,987,056	53	30,064,116
Misc.	0	0	0	0
Total	**1,756**	**$2,661,458,928**	**2,122**	**$2,858,774,646**

NON-RESIDENTIAL CONSTRUCTION AWARDS

Type of Project	1998		1997	
	No.	Amount	No.	Amount
Educational Bldgs	357	$1,009,873,149	255	$1,013,806,254
Churches, Theaters, etc.	29	27,089,156	30	28,808,698
Hospitals, Hotels, Motels	64	120,743,977	55	45,457,768
Public Bldgs	362	786,933,428	280	668,094,179
Commercial/Industrial	375	345,176,586	392	473,075,890
Misc.	0	0	0	0
Total	**1,187**	**$2,289,816,296**	**1,012**	**$2,229,242,789**

Personal Income and Per Capita Personal Income by County

Source: Bureau of Economic Analysis, U.S. Department of Commerce.

Area	Total Income ($ mil)	% change 96 / 97	1997 Per Capita Income	Rank
United States	$ 6,770,650	5.7	$ 25,288	
Metropolitian	5,747,454	5.8	26,840	
Nonmetro	1,023,196	4.7	19,089	
Texas	$ 459,585	8.1	$ 23,707	
Metropolitian	404,858	8.2	24,776	
Nonmetro	54,727	7.0	17,972	
Anderson	$ 823	7.2	$ 15,731	213
Andrews	243	6.6	17,468	170
Angelina	1,511	5.4	19,719	93
Aransas	439	8.1	19,511	100
Archer	155	5.4	18,732	121
Armstrong	43	22.9	19,462	103
Atascosa	549	9.1	15,530	215
Austin	508	7.2	22,111	45
Bailey	142	2.9	20,973	62
Bandera	312	10.2	20,844	69
Bastrop	905	12.0	18,530	131
Baylor	78	2.6	18,683	124
Bee	420	8.2	15,007	226
Bell	4,373	5.8	19,714	94
Bexar	29,891	6.5	22,505	39
Blanco	172	11.0	20,952	65
Borden	11	57.1	14,509	230
Bosque	316	7.5	18,951	111
Bowie	1,781	5.6	21,254	57
Brazoria	4,787	6.1	21,285	55
Brazos	2,384	8.9	17,963	147
Brewster	159	12.0	17,571	165
Briscoe	39	0.0	20,069	82
Brooks	106	8.2	12,592	237
Brown	651	6.4	17,696	161
Burleson	264	9.1	17,125	183
Burnet	612	7.9	19,877	87
Caldwell	515	10.0	16,262	201
Calhoun	367	1.9	17,799	155
Callahan	220	7.8	17,265	179
Cameron	4,095	6.4	12,857	236
Camp	245	7.0	22,342	42
Carson	139	0.7	20,816	71
Cass	557	6.5	18,172	139
Castro	215	- 6.5	25,949	13
Chambers	479	6.4	20,589	75
Cherokee	808	6.7	18,851	115
Childress	116	6.4	15,255	223
Clay	188	7.4	17,973	146
Cochran	84	7.7	21,259	56
Coke	61	7.0	17,917	150
Coleman	170	10.4	17,587	164

Area	Total Income ($ mil)	% change 96 / 97	1997 Per Capita Income	Rank
Collin	13,453	16.5	33,540	2
Collingsworth	59	1.7	17,743	158
Colorado	390	5.4	20,551	77
Comal	1,782	11.9	25,293	18
Comanche	260	7.4	19,172	107
Concho	47	11.9	15,352	218
Cooke	656	8.6	19,979	85
Coryell	975	3.7	12,565	238
Cottle	36	16.1	18,137	140
Crane	74	2.8	16,436	199
Crockett	73	9.0	16,001	206
Crosby	127	5.8	17,272	178
Culberson	37	8.8	11,899	245
Dallam	217	14.2	33,990	1
Dallas	65,205	7.8	32,270	4
Dawson	274	9.6	18,553	129
Deaf Smith	429	6.7	22,261	43
Delta	98	11.4	19,778	91
Denton	9,309	11.4	25,521	15
De Witt	372	7.8	18,933	113
Dickens	42	5.0	18,651	125
Dimmit	117	9.3	11,230	247
Donley	63	1.6	16,616	194
Duval	169	10.5	12,446	239
Eastland	316	8.6	17,686	162
Ector	2,300	8.4	18,611	127
Edwards	40	11.1	11,183	248
Ellis	2,195	10.2	21,882	47
El Paso	10,504	6.2	15,216	224
Erath	590	4.6	18,907	114
Falls	279	6.5	15,522	216
Fannin	501	5.3	18,230	138
Fayette	462	6.5	21,859	48
Fisher	89	25.4	20,609	74
Floyd	186	- 3.1	22,659	37
Foard	32	- 5.9	18,689	123
Fort Bend	7,877	8.8	24,571	21
Franklin	171	9.6	17,918	149
Freestone	285	6.7	16,247	203
Frio	180	7.8	11,426	246
Gaines	236	8.3	15,973	207
Galveston	5,514	4.6	22,737	35
Garza	89	7.2	18,948	112
Gillespie	430	8.9	21,640	52
Glasscock	25	78.6	17,766	157
Goliad	105	9.4	15,339	219
Gonzales	342	7.5	19,511	100
Gray	550	6.2	23,266	30
Grayson	2,135	5.9	21,006	61
Gregg	2,663	6.5	23,575	28

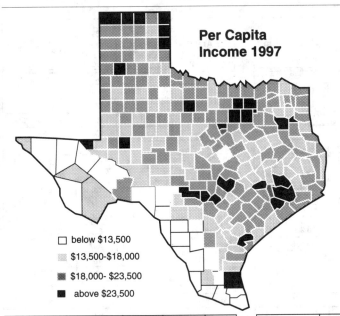

Per Capita Income 1997

Statewide average: $ 23,707

Per capita income in the 254 counties based on information from the Bureau of Economic Analysis, U.S. Department of Commerce.

The higher per capita incomes are clustered in four areas;
— around Houston
— and Dallas-Fort Worth,
— the agricultural counties in the northernmost Panhandle
— and the Hill Country area between Austin and San Antonio.

The counties of lower per capita incomes are along the Rio Grande in West and South Texas.

☐ below $13,500
▒ $13,500-$18,000
▓ $18,000- $23,500
■ above $23,500

Area	Total Income ($ mil)	% change 96 / 97	1997 Per Capita Income	Rank	Area	Total Income ($ mil)	% change 96 / 97	1997 Per Capita Income	Rank
Grimes	349	7.7	15,325	220	Jefferson	5,399	6.3	22,350	41
Guadalupe	1,520	8.6	19,573	97	Jim Hogg	87	10.1	17,829	154
Hale	711	- 1.8	19,499	102	Jim Wells	648	7.8	16,301	200
Hall	65	4.8	17,544	168	Johnson	2,254	8.8	19,763	92
Hamilton	159	6.0	20,824	70	Jones	284	8.0	15,198	225
Hansford	160	24.0	29,950	9	Karnes	212	9.3	16,997	186
Hardeman	93	10.7	19,992	84	Kaufman	1,335	9.3	20,905	66
Hardin	943	9.9	19,518	99	Kendall	575	11.2	28,237	10
Harris	95,228	8.7	30,192	8	Kenedy	11	22.2	25,348	17
Harrison	1,077	6.0	18,083	142	Kent	15	7.1	17,535	169
Hartley	116	12.6	22,585	38	Kerr	1,051	6.7	24,758	19
Haskell	119	9.2	19,406	104	Kimble	77	10.0	18,448	134
Hays	1,695	12.6	19,846	89	King	5	66.7	13,377	233
Hemphill	96	12.9	26,546	12	Kinney	37	5.7	11,056	249
Henderson	1,249	9.2	18,532	130	Kleberg	496	4.6	16,445	198
Hidalgo	6,058	7.0	12,005	243	Knox	74	1.4	17,136	182
Hill	535	8.5	17,791	156	Lamar	953	7.2	20,877	67
Hockley	426	3.1	17,896	151	Lamb	300	- 3.8	20,283	80
Hood	915	10.9	25,403	16	Lampasas	277	8.6	15,859	211
Hopkins	566	5.6	18,698	122	La Salle	72	10.8	12,125	241
Houston	415	9.2	19,051	110	Lavaca	386	8.1	20,576	76
Howard	641	7.4	19,782	90	Lee	265	10.0	17,983	144
Hudspeth	31	6.9	9,655	250	Leon	266	10.4	18,471	133
Hunt	1,360	9.1	19,625	96	Liberty	1,111	5.4	17,358	173
Hutchinson	495	2.7	20,676	72	Limestone	374	5.9	17,858	152
Irion	32	10.3	18,554	128	Lipscomb	74	10.4	24,454	22
Jack	123	7.9	16,777	190	Live Oak	176	9.3	17,423	172
Jackson	290	3.2	21,181	59	Llano	277	7.4	21,018	60
Jasper	643	8.2	19,324	106	Loving	3	0.0	32,305	3
Jeff Davis	36	16.1	16,019	205	Lubbock	5,082	4.7	22,032	46

Area	Total Income ($ mil)	% change 96 / 97	1997 Per Capita Income	Rank
Lynn	131	12.0	19,933	86
Madison	202	12.8	16,961	187
Marion	162	3.2	15.277	222
Martin	89	32.8	17,719	160
Mason	58	9.4	15,936	209
Matagorda	672	4.7	17,740	159
Maverick	437	6.3	9,327	252
McCulloch	151	7.1	17,212	180
McLennan	4,139	5.7	20,446	78
McMullen	18	- 14.3	22,846	34
Medina	610	10.1	16,607	195
Menard	40	5.3	16,930	189
Midland	3,588	10.6	30,439	6
Milam	422	10.5	17,460	171
Mills	83	9.2	17,563	167
Mitchell	136	14.3	14,146	231
Montague	344	7.2	18,771	120
Montgomery	6,268	9.6	24,272	23
Moore	419	10.6	21,709	51
Morris	250	8.7	18,804	119
Motley	22	0.0	17,197	181
Nacogdoches	1,018	5.2	17,957	148
Navarro	786	6.8	19,101	108
Newton	211	8.2	14,652	229
Nolan	289	8.2	17,571	165
Nueces	6,543	5.2	20,673	73
Ochiltree	200	3.1	22,719	36
Oldham	49	22.5	21,771	49
Orange	1,692	7.8	19,997	83
Palo Pinto	472	7.0	18,478	132
Panola	398	6.1	17,287	175
Parker	1,698	11.5	21,584	54
Parmer	230	3.1	22,257	44
Pecos	199	7.0	12,286	240
Polk	785	8.7	16,496	197
Potter	2,283	5.2	20,966	64
Presidio	78	8.3	9,391	251
Rains	122	8.9	14,792	228
Randall	2,293	5.5	23,249	31
Reagan	63	10.5	14,977	227
Real	44	7.3	16,548	196
Red River	235	6.8	17,059	184
Reeves	197	11.3	13,450	232
Refugio	189	8.0	23,950	24
Roberts	16	14.3	16,262	201
Robertson	259	8.4	16,718	193
Rockwall	1,085	11.7	30,418	7
Runnels	209	7.7	18,267	137
Rusk	857	6.6	18,811	118
Sabine	194	6.6	18,360	136
San Augustine	138	7.0	17,012	185

Area	Total Income ($ mil)	% change 96 / 97	1997 Per Capita Income	Rank
San Jacinto	331	8.9	15,888	210
San Patricio	1,096	7.7	15,729	214
San Saba	108	12.5	18,836	117
Schleicher	49	16.7	16,093	204
Scurry	339	10.4	18,635	126
Shackelford	76	10.1	22,997	33
Shelby	441	6.0	19,546	98
Sherman	90	9.8	30,863	5
Smith	3,943	7.0	23,696	25
Somervell	139	13.0	22,352	40
Starr	411	4.8	7,550	254
Stephens	180	6.5	18,084	141
Sterling	21	16.7	15,319	221
Stonewall	32	6.7	17,981	145
Sutton	77	10.0	17,343	174
Swisher	175	1.7	20,873	68
Tarrant	34,235	7.9	25,818	14
Taylor	2,566	5.9	21,202	58
Terrell	22	0.0	18,414	135
Terry	255	- 7.9	19,635	95
Throckmorton	41	5.1	23,663	27
Titus	512	7.1	20,379	79
Tom Green	2,146	5.9	20,968	63
Travis	19,136	9.5	27,610	11
Trinity	211	7.7	16,937	188
Tyler	316	6.4	15,783	212
Upshur	634	7.6	17,848	153
Upton	65	3.2	17,285	176
Uvalde	407	8.0	15,973	207
Val Verde	556	5.5	12,942	235
Van Zandt	776	8.7	18,021	143
Victoria	1,888	5.3	23,036	32
Walker	837	9.3	15,387	217
Waller	512	7.6	19,101	108
Ward	197	5.3	16,761	192
Washington	683	7.4	23,678	26
Webb	2,357	9.2	12,999	234
Wharton	809	4.4	20,194	81
Wheeler	132	- 2.9	24,756	20
Wichita	2,790	5.5	21,632	53
Wilbarger	281	6.0	19,851	88
Willacy	233	4.5	11,945	244
Williamson	4,943	14.2	23,453	29
Wilson	523	13.2	17,284	177
Winkler	132	7.3	16,777	190
Wise	820	11.7	19,329	105
Wood	602	6.2	17,625	163
Yoakum	151	3.4	18,837	116
Young	382	7.3	21,734	50
Zapata	134	4.7	12,007	242
Zavala	105	7.1	8,855	253

Insurance in Texas

Source: 1998 Annual Report, Texas Department of Insurance

The **Texas Department of Insurance** reported that on Aug. 31, 1998, there were **2,726** firms licensed to handle insurance business in Texas, including **828** Texas firms and **1,896** out-of-state companies.

Annual premium income of firms operating in Texas caused Dallas and some other cities to rank among the nation's major insurance centers.

The former **Robertson Law**, enacted in 1907 and repealed in 1963, encouraged the establishment of many Texas insurance firms.

It required life insurance companies operating in the state to invest in Texas three-fourths of all reserves held for payment of policies written in the state.

Many out-of-state firms withdrew from Texas. Later many companies re-entered Texas and the law was liberalized and then repealed.

Until 1993, the State Board of Insurance administered legislation relating to the insurance business. This agency was established in 1957, following discovery of irregularities in some firms.

It succeeded two previous regulatory groups, established in 1913 and changed in 1927.

Under terms of sunset legislation passed by the 73rd Legislature in the spring of 1993, most of the board's authority transferred on Sept. 1, 1993, to the **Commissioner of Insurance** appointed by the governor for a two-year term in each odd-numbered year and confirmed by the Texas Senate.

The new law permitted the board to continue its authority over the area of rates, policy forms and related matters until Aug. 31, 1994. On Nov. 18, 1993, however, the board voted unanimously to turn over full authority to the commissioner as of Dec. 16, 1993.

Companies in Texas

The following table shows the number and kinds of insurance companies licensed in Texas on Aug. 31, 1998:

Type of Insurance	Texas	Out-of-State	Total
Stock Life	158	572	730
Mutual Life	2	67	69
Stipulated Premium Life	46	0	46
Non-profit Life	0	1	1
Stock Fire	1	3	4
Stock Fire and Casualty	104	650	754
Mutual Fire and Casualty	8	58	66
Stock Casualty	12	100	112
Mexican Casualty	0	8	8
Lloyds	63	0	63
Reciprocal Exchanges	10	16	26
Fraternal Benefit Societies	10	26	36
Titles	4	19	23
Non-profit Legal Services	2	0	2
Health Maintenance	70	3	73
Risk Retention Groups	1	0	1
Multiple Employers Welfare Arrang.	5	3	8
Joint Underwriting Associations	0	7	7
Third Party Administrators	244	363	607
Continuing Care Retirement Communities	17	2	19
Total	757	1,898	2,655
Statewide Mutual Assessment	1	0	1
Local Mutual Aid Associations	9	0	9
Burial Associations	2	0	2
Exempt Associations	12	0	12
Non-profit Hospital Service	3	0	3
County Mutual Fire	24	0	24
Farm Mutual Fire	20	0	20
Total	71		71
Grand Total	828	1,898	2,726

Top Homeowner Insurers, 1997

Company	% of market
1. State Farm Lloyds	29.81
2. Allstate Texas Lloyds	10.28
3. Farmers Insurance Exchange	8.69
4. Fire Insurance Exchange	6.70
5. United Services Automobile Assoc.	4.41
6. Allstate Insurance Company	2.96
7. State Farm Fire & Casualty Co.	2.58

Premium Income and Losses Paid, 1997

(Texas business only)	Texas Companies	Out-of-State Companies
Legal Reserve Life Insurance Companies		
Life premiums	$ 742,144,082	$ 5,438,167,452
Claims & benefits paid	1,272,270,368	9,267,973,077
Accident & health premiums	3,831,927,923	5,245,460,689
Accident & health loss paid	3,561,345,661	3,859,353,571
Mutual Fire & Casualty Companies		
Premiums	$ 383,360,998	$ 3,114,467,805
Losses	240,131,285	1,979,724,574
Lloyds Insurance		
Premiums	$ 2,186,773,958	...
Losses	881,589,253	...
Reciprocal Insurance Companies		
Premiums	$ 614,780,395	$ 526,984,150
Losses	326,200,810	253,509,066
Fraternal Benefit Societies		
No. Life Certificates issued	17,187	31,137
Amount issued 1997	$ 444,193,412	$ 1,727,596,408
Considerations from members:		
Life	46,813,541	168,693,715
Accident & Health	2,229,761	18,100,623
Benefits paid to members:		
Life	27,323,891	112,509,991
Accident & Health	1,430,388	10,569,950
Amount of insurance in force	2,772,826,221	13,316,983,297
Title Guaranty Companies		
Premiums	$ 269,835,285	$ 418,273,794
Paid Losses	2,268,684	9,621,286
Stock Fire, Stock Casualty, and Stock Fire & Casualty Companies		
Premiums	$ 1,973,161,154	$ 7,295,292,613
Losses	1,185,625,414	4,284,536,825

Deposits and Assets of Insured Commercial Banks by County

Source: Federal Reserve Bank of Dallas as of Dec. 31, 1998

(in thousands of dollars)

COUNTY	Banks	Deposits	Assets
Anderson	3	$ 187,462	$ 211,212
Andrews	2	86,017	93,779
Angelina	2	273,378	298,146
Archer	1	26,614	29,444
Armstrong	1	38,713	41,608
Atascosa	3	133,121	156,825
Austin	5	431,948	487,543
Bailey	2	151,821	166,187
Bandera	1	18,226	20,443
Bastrop	4	315,871	357,306
Baylor	2	56,254	63,103
Bee	3	239,969	266,599
Bell	9	1,021,003	1,176,407
Bexar	12	15,880,898	18,615,313
Blanco	3	140,324	155,791
Bosque	3	138,025	154,328
Bowie	4	1,128,604	1,398,520
Brazoria	9	802,778	913,078
Brazos	1	207,197	232,123
Brewster	1	65,712	76,638
Briscoe	2	42,535	49,798
Brooks	2	55,249	67,163
Brown	2	218,080	243,652
Burleson	3	176,178	197,616
Burnet	3	178,853	207,728
Caldwell	3	167,460	187,152
Calhoun	2	133,355	155,079
Callahan	3	162,294	181,121
Cameron	6	1,717,462	2,017,753
Camp	1	106,777	127,533
Carson	1	12,688	14,583
Cass	4	167,974	186,367
Castro	1	181,388	199,685
Chambers	3	110,817	134,612
Cherokee	3	206,571	233,913
Childress	2	57,532	65,416
Clay	1	37,984	42,511
Coke	2	58,632	69,209
Coleman	3	111,642	125,697
Collin	9	884,983	983,499
Collingsworth	2	122,026	132,111
Colorado	4	256,429	308,281
Comanche	2	140,863	161,816
Concho	2	42,153	47,765
Cooke	3	348,798	392,699
Coryell	4	344,772	383,589
Cottle	1	33,243	38,672
Crockett	2	162,101	186,651
Crosby	3	92,199	104,237
Culberson	1	18,458	22,209
Dallam	2	57,588	62,334
Dallas	50	31,575,417	41,482,977
Dawson	2	254,086	288,738
Deaf Smith	1	74,802	82,995
Delta	3	49,150	56,108
Denton	9	1,300,216	1,625,400
De Witt	2	154,657	179,738
Dickens	1	24,562	26,805
Dimmit	1	22,198	24,087

COUNTY	Banks	Deposits	Assets
Donley	1	32,666	38,865
Duval	2	64,790	72,826
Eastland	2	79,369	93,488
Ector	2	200,599	235,020
Edwards	1	29,113	33,562
Ellis	6	348,329	383,108
El Paso	5	1,769,505	2,040,136
Erath	4	251,873	275,153
Falls	1	24,470	28,120
Fannin	5	195,398	229,860
Fayette	7	388,237	459,147
Fisher	1	36,155	40,514
Floyd	2	135,884	154,488
Foard	1	21,147	23,262
Fort Bend	4	406,325	462,475
Franklin	2	98,508	117,114
Freestone	2	81,915	91,294
Frio	2	147,353	223,219
Gaines	2	111,940	121,266
Galveston	10	1,094,732	1,229,568
Gillespie	2	339,593	388,609
Goliad	1	29,020	31,934
Gonzales	3	150,232	164,445
Gray	2	92,003	104,214
Grayson	8	900,429	982,202
Gregg	7	909,656	1,029,193
Grimes	3	132,403	149,323
Guadalupe	4	397,182	470,984
Hale	3	263,002	288,811
Hall	2	58,721	65,437
Hamilton	2	46,926	51,874
Hansford	3	137,584	160,420
Hardeman	3	80,894	90,507
Harris	57	34,980,958	44,781,063
Harrison	4	471,590	521,311
Haskell	4	124,267	136,553
Hemphill	2	75,797	85,837
Henderson	5	601,933	675,351
Hidalgo	11	2,854,309	3,167,395
Hill	4	123,113	146,699
Hockley	3	120,577	129,908
Hood	5	535,500	591,238
Hopkins	3	485,835	527,145
Houston	5	179,305	202,735
Howard	2	192,427	218,965
Hudspeth	1	11,733	13,590
Hunt	4	152,206	181,805
Hutchinson	1	33,868	39,072
Irion	1	85,433	97,788
Jack	2	129,909	141,940
Jackson	1	42,150	45,147
Jasper	2	246,798	273,944
Jeff Davis	1	29,681	31,686
Jefferson	2	554,852	611,566
Jim Hogg	2	76,537	92,396
Jim Wells	2	153,026	170,245
Johnson	6	530,379	589,828
Jones	2	86,480	102,061
Karnes	3	131,879	147,273
Kaufman	3	699,829	752,725
Kent	1	9,759	10,757

COUNTIES
Total
Bank Assets

No independent banks were reported in eighteen counties: Aransas, Borden, Cochran, Comal, Crane, Garza, Glasscock, Hardin, Hartley, Hays, Kendall, Kenedy, King, Kinney, Loving, Oldham, Randall and Willacy.

- ■ $10 bil +
- ▓ $1 bil +
- ▒ $500 mil +
- ▨ $250 mil +

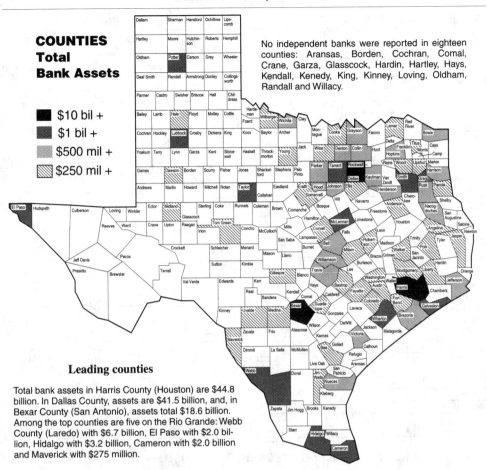

Leading counties

Total bank assets in Harris County (Houston) are $44.8 billion. In Dallas County, assets are $41.5 billion, and, in Bexar County (San Antonio) assets total $18.6 billion. Among the top counties are five on the Rio Grande: Webb County (Laredo) with $6.7 billion, El Paso with $2.0 billion, Hidalgo with $3.2 billion, Cameron with $2.0 billion and Maverick with $275 million.

COUNTY	Banks	Deposits	Assets
Kerr	1	$ 29,408	$ 33,486
Kimble	2	53,297	60,626
Kleberg	2	185,121	201,007
Knox	2	62,460	69,044
Lamar	4	321,427	371,726
Lamb	4	116,487	130,084
Lampasas	1	83,474	96,039
La Salle	1	28,802	32,039
Lavaca	3	205,633	240,321
Lee	2	78,401	92,464
Leon	4	114,784	137,510
Liberty	5	286,353	331,949
Limestone	4	164,124	182,120
Lipscomb	1	27,784	31,946
Live Oak	2	110,144	129,829
Llano	3	192,060	218,833
Lubbock	11	2,738,094	3,156,206
Lynn	3	112,827	129,556
Madison	2	153,111	169,682
Marion	1	30,152	34,604
Martin	1	38,038	46,309
Mason	2	48,716	59,525
Matagorda	2	53,679	60,341
Maverick	1	250,649	275,631
McCulloch	2	117,133	132,410

COUNTY	Banks	Deposits	Assets
McLennan	12	$ 1,086,231	$ 1,211,303
McMullen	1	36,733	40,732
Medina	7	269,141	298,258
Menard	2	30,671	35,756
Midland	3	283,168	320,775
Milam	4	352,870	414,892
Mills	1	104,062	115,808
Mitchell	2	83,736	95,168
Montague	2	203,986	232,460
Montgomery	1	110,518	121,414
Moore	1	91,476	100,420
Morris	3	116,155	127,295
Motley	1	9,532	10,485
Nacogdoches	2	506,489	560,247
Navarro	5	189,846	216,490
Newton	1	87,989	96,230
Nolan	3	199,797	219,965
Nueces	6	627,124	700,352
Ochiltree	1	47,839	54,423
Orange	2	95,024	104,851
Palo pinto	4	168,467	190,587
Panola	3	263,066	316,407
Parker	3	812,668	922,182
Parmer	2	139,018	164,189
Pecos	3	112,807	129,850

COUNTY	Banks	Deposits	Assets	COUNTY	Banks	Deposits	Assets
Polk	3	$ 362,836	$ 414,351	Terrell	1	$ 14,696	$ 15,999
Potter	4	1,505,067	1,892,316	Terry	1	112,009	129,029
Presidio	2	48,122	57,137	Throckmorton	1	19,684	21,993
Rains	1	52,728	58,114	Titus	2	291,647	326,094
Reagan	1	33,479	36,273	Tom Green	3	375,355	447,060
Real	1	24,619	27,387	Travis	4	314,691	365,751
Red River	1	17,040	18,922	Trinity	3	76,518	85,651
Reeves	2	143,545	163,270	Tyler	2	99,317	110,468
Refugio	2	75,650	92,094	Upshur	4	300,987	348,931
Roberts	1	25,195	27,906	Upton	2	81,941	88,983
Robertson	3	224,619	263,282	Uvalde	2	305,021	356,029
Rockwall	1	30,734	33,710	Val Verde	1	112,984	123,309
Runnels	4	101,339	114,391	Van Zandt	6	217,694	249,232
Rusk	4	507,486	570,704	Victoria	2	542,042	634,264
Sabine	2	130,054	143,858	Walker	2	243,093	267,870
San Augustine	1	42,895	50,365	Waller	1	40,238	44,858
San Jacinto	2	52,407	57,404	Ward	2	99,010	111,083
San Patrico	2	79,963	91,531	Washington	4	232,740	270,869
San Saba	1	34,777	41,639	Webb	6	4,890,445	6,677,735
Schleicher	1	33,605	39,280	Wharton	6	997,770	1,103,963
Scurry	2	169,563	191,769	Wheeler	2	43,304	47,651
Shackelford	1	146,595	170,118	Wichita	6	531,228	590,925
Shelby	3	178,026	202,582	Wilbarger	3	297,365	348,587
Sherman	1	113,392	129,092	Williamson	12	733,182	820,906
Smith	7	1,006,698	1,616,788	Wilson	2	136,231	151,319
Somervell	1	33,724	37,072	Winkler	2	62,468	72,691
Starr	1	41,605	50,085	Wise	3	396,013	425,270
Stephens	1	51,410	58,122	Wood	5	301,923	343,277
Sterling	1	26,362	33,066	Yoakum	2	16,792	19,708
Stonewall	1	23,838	32,930	Young	5	245,050	276,988
Sutton	1	76,860	83,229	Zapata	2	168,460	202,424
Swisher	2	99,519	110,789	Zavala	1	34,411	43,601
Tarrant	25	2,116,144	2,359,729				
Taylor	4	939,118	1,031,990	**Total 1998**	**797**	**$ 146,496,084**	**$ 179,475,792**

Texas Bank Resources and Deposits—1905-1998

Source: **Federal Reserve Bank of Dallas. (Thousands of Dollars)**

Date	National Banks			State Banks			Combined Total		
	No. Banks	Total Resources	Deposits	No. Banks	Total Resources	Deposits	No. Banks	Total Resources	Deposits
Sept. 30, 1905	440	$ 189,484	$ 101,285	29	$ 4,341	$ 2,213	469	$ 193,825	$ 103,498
Oct. 31, 1906	483	221,574	116,331	136	19,322	13,585	619	240,896	129,916
Dec. 3, 1907	521	261,724	141,803	309	34,734	20,478	830	296,458	162,281
Nov. 27, 1908	535	243,240	115,843	340	40,981	27,014	875	284,221	142,857
Dec. 31, 1909	523	273,473	139,024	515	72,947	51,472	1,038	346,420	190,496
Nov. 10, 1910	516	293,245	145,249	621	88,103	59,766	1,137	381,348	205,015
Dec. 5, 1911	513	313,685	156,083	688	98,814	63,708	1,201	412,499	219,791
Nov. 26, 1912	515	352,796	179,736	744	138,856	101,258	1,259	491,652	280,994
Oct. 21, 1913	517	359,732	183,623	832	151,620	101,081	1,349	511,352	284,704
Dec. 31, 1914	533	377,516	216,953	849	129,053	73,965	1,382	506,569	290,648
Dec. 31, 1915	534	418,094	273,509	831	149,773	101,483	1,365	567,867	374,992
Dec. 27, 1916	530	567,809	430,302	836	206,396	160,416	1,366	774,205	590,718
Dec. 31, 1917	539	679,316	531,066	874	268,382	215,906	1,413	947,698	746,972
Dec. 31, 1918	543	631,978	431,612	884	259,881	191,500	1,427	891,859	623,112
Dec. 31, 1919	552	965,855	777,942	948	405,130	336,018	1,500	1,370,985	1,113,960
Dec. 29, 1920	556	780,246	564,135	1,031	391,127	280,429	1,587	1,171,373	844,564
Dec. 31, 1921	551	691,087	501,493	1,004	334,907	237,848	1,555	1,025,994	739,341
Dec. 29, 1922	557	823,254	634,408	970	338,693	262,478	1,527	1,161,947	896,886
Sept. 14, 1923	569	860,173	648,954	950	376,775	306,372	1,519	1,236,948	955,326
Dec. 31, 1924	572	999,981	820,676	933	391,040	322,392	1,505	1,391,021	1,143,068
Dec. 31, 1925	656	1,020,124	832,425	834	336,966	268,586	1,490	1,357,090	1,101,011
Dec. 31, 1926	656	1,020,113	820,778	782	290,554	228,741	1,438	1,310,667	1,049,519
Dec. 31, 1927	643	1,134,595	938,129	748	328,574	267,559	1,391	1,463,168	1,205,688
Dec. 31, 1928	632	1,230,469	1,017,168	713	334,870	276,875	1,345	1,565,339	1,294,043
Dec. 31, 1929	609	1,124,369	897,538	699	332,534	264,013	1,308	1,456,903	1,161,551
Dec. 31, 1930	560	1,028,420	826,723	655	299,012	231,909	1,215	1,327,432	1,058,632

Date	National Banks			State Banks			Combined Total		
	No. Banks	Total Resources	Deposits	No. Banks	Total Resources	Deposits	No. Banks	Total Resources	Deposits
Dec. 31, 1931	508	865,910	677,307	594	235,681	172,806	1,102	1,101,591	850,113
Dec. 31, 1932	483	822,857	625,586	540	208,142	148,070	1,023	1,030,999	773,653
Dec. 30, 1933	445	900,810	733,810	489	185,476	132,389	934	1,086,286	866,199
Dec. 31, 1934	456	1,063,453	892,264	460	197,969	148,333	916	1,261,422	1,040,597
Dec. 31, 1935	454	1,145,488	1,099,172	442	205,729	162,926	896	1,351,217	1,172,098
June 30, 1936	456	1,192,845	1,054,284	426	228,877	169,652	882	1,421,722	1,223,936
Dec. 31, 1937	453	1,343,076	1,194,463	415	217,355	177,514	868	1,560,431	1,371,977
Sept. 28, 1938	449	1,359,719	1,206,882	406	217,944	170,286	855	1,577,663	1,377,168
Dec. 31, 1939	445	1,565,108	1,409,821	395	235,467	201,620	840	1,800,575	1,611,441
Dec. 31, 1940	446	1,695,662	1,534,702	393	227,866	179,027	839	1,923,528	1,713,729
Dec. 31, 1941	444	1,975,022	1,805,773	391	312,861	269,505	835	2,287,883	2,075,278
Dec. 31, 1942	439	2,696,768	2,525,299	391	417,058	353,109	830	3,113,826	2,878,408
Dec. 31, 1943	439	3,281,853	3,099,964	391	574,463	536,327	830	3,856,316	3,636,291
Dec. 31, 1944	436	4,092,473	3,891,999	398	780,910	738,779	834	4,873,383	4,630,778
Dec. 31, 1945	434	5,166,434	4,934,773	409	998,355	952,258	843	6,164,789	5,887,031
Dec. 31, 1946	434	4,883,558	4,609,538	418	1,019,369	964,938	852	5,902,927	5,574,476
Dec. 31, 1947	437	5,334,309	5,039,963	436	1,149,887	1,087,347	873	6,484,196	6,127,310
Dec. 31, 1948	437	5,507,823	5,191,334	444	1,208,884	1,137,259	881	6,716,707	6,328,593
Dec. 31, 1949	440	5,797,407	5,454,118	446	1,283,139	1,203,244	886	7,080,546	6,657,362
Dec. 31, 1950	442	6,467,275	6,076,006	449	1,427,680	1,338,540	891	7,894,955	7,414,546
Dec. 31, 1951	443	6,951,836	6,501,307	453	1,571,823	1,473,569	896	8,523,659	7,974,876
Dec. 31, 1952	444	7,388,030	6,882,623	457	1,742,270	1,631,757	901	9,130,300	8,514,380
Dec. 31, 1953	443	7,751,667	7,211,162	460	1,813,034	1,696,297	903	9,564,701	8,907,459
Dec. 31, 1954	441	8,295,686	7,698,690	465	1,981,483	1,851,724	906	10,277,169	9,550,414
Dec. 31, 1955	446	8,640,239	7,983,681	472	2,087,066	1,941,706	918	10,727,305	9,925,387
Dec. 31, 1956	452	8,986,456	8,241,159	480	2,231,497	2,067,927	932	11,217,953	10,309,086
Dec. 31, 1957	457	8,975,321	8,170,271	486	2,349,935	2,169,898	943	11,325,256	10,340,169
Dec. 31, 1958	458	9,887,737	9,049,580	499	2,662,270	2,449,474	957	12,550,007	11,499,054
Dec. 31, 1959	466	10,011,949	9,033,495	511	2,813,006	2,581,404	977	12,824,955	11,614,899
Dec. 31, 1960	468	10,520,690	9,560,668	532	2,997,609	2,735,726	1,000	13,518,299	12,296,394
Dec. 30, 1961	473	11,466,767	10,426,812	538	3,297,588	3,009,499	1,011	14,764,355	13,436,311
Dec. 28, 1962	486	12,070,803	10,712,253	551	3,646,404	3,307,714	1,037	15,717,207	14,019,967
Dec. 30, 1963	519	12,682,674	11,193,194	570	4,021,033	3,637,559	1,089	16,703,707	14,830,753
Dec. 31, 1964	539	14,015,957	12,539,142	581	4,495,074	4,099,543	1,120	18,511,031	16,638,685
Dec. 31, 1965	545	14,944,319	13,315,367	585	4,966,947	4,530,675	1,130	19,911,266	17,846,042
Dec. 31, 1966	546	15,647,346	13,864,727	591	5,332,385	4,859,906	1,137	20,979,731	18,724,633
Dec. 31, 1967	542	17,201,752	15,253,496	597	6,112,900	5,574,735	1,139	23,314,652	20,828,231
Dec. 31, 1968	535	19,395,045	16,963,003	609	7,107,310	6,489,357	1,144	26,502,355	23,452,360
Dec. 31, 1969	529	19,937,396	16,687,720	637	7,931,966	7,069,822	1,166	27,869,362	23,757,542
Dec. 31, 1970	530	22,087,890	18,384,922	653	8,907,039	7,958,133	1,183	30,994,929	26,343,055
Dec. 31, 1971	530	25,137,269	20,820,519	677	10,273,200	9,179,451	1,207	35,410,469	29,999,970
Dec. 31, 1972	538	29,106,654	23,892,660	700	12,101,749	10,804,827	1,238	41,208,403	34,697,487
Dec. 31, 1973	550	32,791,219	26,156,659	716	14,092,134	12,417,693	1,266	46,883,353	38,574,352
Dec. 31, 1974	569	35,079,218	28,772,284	744	15,654,983	13,758,147	1,313	50,734,201	42,530,431
Dec. 31, 1975	584	39,138,322	31,631,199	752	17,740,669	15,650,933	1,336	56,878,991	47,282,132
Dec. 31, 1976	596	43,534,570	35,164,285	761	19,846,695	17,835,078	1,357	63,381,265	52,999,363
Dec. 31, 1977	604	49,091,503	39,828,475	773	22,668,498	20,447,012	1,377	71,760,001	60,275,487
Dec. 31,1978	609	56,489,274	44,749,491	786	25,987,616	23,190,869	1,395	82,476,890	67,940,360
Dec. 31,1979	615	65,190,891	50,754,782	807	30,408,232	26,975,854	1,422	95,599,123	77,730,636
Dec. 31,1980	641	75,540,334	58,378,669	825	35,186,113	31,055,648	1,466	110,726,447	89,434,317
Dec. 31, 1981	694	91,811,510	68,750,678	829	42,071,043	36,611,555	1,523	133,882,553	105,362,233
Dec. 31, 1982	758	104,580,333	78,424,478	841	48,336,463	41,940,277	1,599	152,916,796	120,364,755
Dec. 31, 1983	880	126,914,841	98,104,893	848	55,008,329	47,653,797	1,728	181,923,170	145,758,690
Dec. 31, 1984	999	137,565,365	105,862,656	855	60,361,504	52,855,584	1,854	197,926,869	158,718,240
Dec. 31, 1985	1,058	144,674,908	111,903,178	878	64,349,869	56,392,634	1,936	209,024,777	168,295,812
Dec. 31, 1986	1,077	141,397,037	106,973,189	895	65,989,944	57,739,091	1,972	207,386,981	164,712,280
Dec. 31, 1987	953	135,690,678	103,930,262	812	54,361,514	47,283,855	1,765	190,052,192	151,214,117
Dec. 31, 1988	802	130,310,243	106,740,461	690	40,791,310	36,655,253	1,492	171,101,553	143,395,714
Dec. 31, 1989	687	133,163,016	104,091,836	626	40,893,848	36,652,675	1,313	174,056,864	140,744,511
Dec. 31, 1990	605	125,808,263	103,573,445	578	45,021,304	40,116,662	1,183	170,829,567	143,690,107
Dec. 31, 1991	579	123,022,314	106,153,441	546	46,279,752	41,315,420	1,125	169,302,066	147,468,861
Dec. 31, 1992	562	135,507,244	112,468,203	529	40,088,963	35,767,858	1,091	175,596,207	148,236,061
Dec. 31, 1993	502	139,409,250	111,993,205	510	44,566,815	39,190,373	1,012	183,976,065	151,183,578
Dec. 31, 1994	481	140,374,540	111,881,041	502	47,769,694	41,522,943	983	188,144,234	153,403,984
Dec. 31, 1995	456	152,750,093	112,557,468	479	49,967,946	42,728,454	935	202,718,039	155,285,922
Dec. 31, 1996	432	152,299,695	122,242,990	445	52,868,263	45,970,674	877	205,167,958	168,213,664
Dec. 31, 1997	417	180,252,942	145,588,677	421	54,845,186	46,202,808	838	235,098,128	191,791485
Dec. 31, 1998	402	$ 128,609,813	$ 106,704,893	395	$ 50,966,996	$ 42,277,367	797	$179,576,809	$148,982,260

Leading Commercial Banks Ranked by Deposits

Source: Federal Reserve Bank of Dallas, Dec. 31, 1998

Abbreviations: Bk-Bank; St-State; NB-National Bank; B&TC-Bank and Trust Company; NA-National Association

(Thousands of Dollars)

Rank	Name, Location	Deposits
1	Bank One Tx NA, Dallas	$ 19,118,446
2	Chase Bk Tx NA, Houston	18,857,883
3	Norwest Bk Tx NA, San Antonio	8,070,268
4	Frost NB, San Antonio	5,774,534
5	Wells Fargo Bk Tx NA, Houston	5,304,263
6	Bank America Tx NA, Dallas	4,484,435
7	Comerica Bk-Texas, Dallas	2,832,840
8	International Bk of Commerce, Laredo	2,759,226
9	Southwest Bk of Texas NA, Houston	1,734,108
10	Laredo NB, Laredo	1,623,482
11	Texas St Bk, McAllen	1,568,418
12	Sterling Bk, Houston	1,187,921
13	Prime Bk, Houston	966,796
14	Norwest Bk El Paso NA, El Paso	960,786
15	First St Bk of Tx, Denton	945,990
16	Amarillo NB, Amarillo	918,023
17	American St Bk, Lubbock	883,532
18	Broadway NB, San Antonio	849,389
19	Plains NB, Lubbock	802,301
20	Hibernia NB, Texarkana	752,217
21	Mercantile Bk NA, Brownsville	676,021
22	American NB Tx, Terrell	633,736
23	American Bk of Tx, Sherman	587,392
24	Texas Bk, Weatherford	569,588
25	First NB, Abiline	544,810
26	Merchants Bk, Houston	524,120
27	Southside Bk, Tyler	521,378
28	North Dallas B&TC, Dallas	517,712
29	Legacy Bk ofTx, Plano	514,925
30	Metrobank NA, Houston	491,620
31	First B&TC, Groves	473,366
32	First Victoria NB, Victoria	472,145
33	Woodforest NB, Houston	466,801
34	Northern Tr Bk of Tx NA, Dallas	429,414
35	First Valley Bk, Harlingen	417,211
36	First Prosperity Bk, El Campo	401,348
37	Bank Texas NA, Dallas	398,061
38	Riverway Bk, Houston	371,710
39	First NB, Edinburg	365,608
40	First Bk SW NA, Amarillo	350,439
41	Citizens NB, Henderson	346,541
42	Bank of the West, El Paso	346,345
43	International Bk of Cmrc, Brownsville	345,942
44	Klein Bk, Klein	339,907
45	Longview B&TC, Longview	339,002
46	Citizens NB of Texas, Bellaire	331,541
47	Inwood NB, Dallas	329,928
48	Inter NB, McAllen	328,257
49	Heritage Bk, Wharton	324,310
50	Texas First NB, Houston	321,635
51	American Bk NA, Corpus Christi	318,174
52	First NB, Temple	318,116
53	Jefferson St Bk, San Antonio	302,178
54	Moody NB, Galveston	300,452
55	Security St B&TC, Fredericksburg	290,522
56	First SVC Bk, Marshall	289,593
57	Alliance Bk, Sulphur Springs	285,571
58	First St Bk, Uvalde	280,638
59	Summit Community Bk NA, Ft. Worth	279,045

Rank	Name, Location	Deposits
60	First NB, Decatur	272,324
61	Commercial Bk, Nacogdoches	270,912
62	Citizens B&TC of Baytown Tx, Baytown	269,729
63	First Bk Katy NA, Katy	265,003
64	BankTexas NA, Houston	264,425
65	Hartland Bk NA, Austin	261,397
66	San Angelo NB, San Angelo	254,891
67	Bayshore NB, La Porte	253,345
68	NBC Bk NA, Eagle Pass	250,649
69	Camino Real Bk NA, San Antonio	248,400
70	First St Bk NA, Abilene	246,181
71	First NB of South Texas, San Antonio	243,564
72	Guaranty Bk, Mount Pleasant	242,383
73	American Bk Commerce, Wolfforth	240,699
74	Fredonia St Bk, Nacogdoches	235,577
75	Central NB, Waco	232,514
76	First St Bk, Athens	224,056
77	Southern NB of Texas, Sugar Land	223,966
78	First NB Tx, Killeen	222,897
79	TIB Independent Bankersbank, Irving	221,783
80	Lubbock NB, Lubbock	221,639
81	National Bk, Gatesville	219,371
82	Lone Star NB, Pharr	211,841
83	First St Bk, Rio Vista	210,720
84	First NB, Bryan	207,197
85	Community Bk, Granbury	207,085
86	American Bk, Houston	206,570
87	First NB Amarillo, Amarillo	205,853
88	Midland Amer Bk, Midland	204,009
89	Harlingen NB, Harlingen	203,723
90	South Texas NB, Laredo	203,702
91	Citizens 1st Bk, Tyler	203,596
92	Montwood NB, El Paso	203,453
93	First NB, Athens	199,926
94	Citizens Bk, Kilgore	196,337
95	Hale County St Bk, Plainvew	189,609
96	Omnibank NA, Houston	188,952
97	First St B&TC, Carthage	188,441
98	First St Bk, Temple	187,965
99	Summit NB, Fort Worth	186,356
100	Texas Gulf Bk NA, Freeport	186,263
101	Provident Bk, Dallas	185,461
102	Southwest Bk, Fort Worth	183,605
103	First NB Bowie, Bowie	182,856
104	First United Bk, Dimmitt	181,388
105	City Bk, Lubbock	179,362
106	First NB, Granbury	179,192
107	Western NB, Odessa	178,358
108	Swiss Ave St Bk, Dallas	175,550
109	Bank of Commerce, Fort Worth	173,823
110	First NB, Huntsville	171,025
111	State NB W Texas, Lubbock	169,330
112	First B&TC East Texas, Diboll	167,589
113	State B&T, Seguin	166,478
114	First NB, Livingston	166,338
115	Firstbank, Texarkana	165,951
116	Austin Bk NA, Longview	165,857
117	Liberty NB, Paris	165,731
118	First St Bk, Gainesville	165,663
119	Security NB, San Antonio	165,069
120	Main Bk NA, Dallas	163,503

Texas State Banks

Consolidated Statement, Foreign and Domestic Offices, as of Dec. 31, 1998
Source: Federal Reserve Bank of Dallas

Number of Banks	395

(All figures in thousand dollars)

Assets

Cash and due from banks:	
Non-interest-bearing balances and currency and coin	$ 2,531,931
Interest-bearing balances	453,015
Held-to-maturity securities	5,007,036
Available-for sale securities	12,627,511
Federal funds sold and securities purchased under agreement to resell	3,163,182
Loans and lease financing receivables:	
Loans and leases, net of unearned income:	25,298,272
Less: allowance for loan and lease losses	352,299
Less: allocated transfer risk reserve	0
Loans and leases, net	24,945,973
Assets held in trading accounts	1,145
Premises and fixed assets	1,056,089
Other real estate owned	50,652
Investments in unconsolidated subsidiaries and associated companies	3,525
Customers liability on acceptances outstanding	369
Intangible assets	302,171
Other assets	824,399
Total Assets	**$ 50,966,996**

Liabilities

Deposits:	
In domestic offices	$ 42,277,367
Non-interest-bearing	8,860,686
Interest-bearing	33,416,682
In foreign offices, edge & agreement subsidiaries & IBF's	-
Non-interest-bearing	-
Interest-bearing	-
Federal funds purchased and securities sold under agreements to repurchase	1,499,669
Demand notes issued to the U.S. Treasury	261,674
Trading Liabilities	0
Other borrowed money	
with remaining maturity one year or less	1,271,223
with remaining maturity one to three years	94,611
with remaining maturity more than three years	593,797
Banks' liability on acceptances executed and outstanding	369
Notes and debentures subordinated to deposits	50,200
Other liabilities	382,453
Total Liabilities	**$ 46,431,345**

Equity Capital

Perpetual preferred stock	4,187
Common stock	456,093
Surplus (exclude surplus related to preferred stock)	2,138,839
Undivided profits and capital reserves	1,873,532
Less: Net unrealized gains (losses) on available-for-sale securities	63,000
Cumulative foreign currency translation adjustments	
Total Equity Capital	**$ 4,535,651**
Total liabilities, limited-life preferred stock and equity capital	**$ 50,966,996**

Texas National Banks

Consolidated Statement, Foreign and Domestic Offices, as of Dec. 31, 1998
Source: Federal Reserve Bank of Dallas

Number of Banks	402

(All figures in thousand dollars)

Assets

Cash and due from banks:	
Non-interest-bearing balances and currency and coin	$ 9,832,830
Interest-bearing balances	4,011,131
Held-to-maturity securities	4,231,036
Available-for-sale securities	29,784,578
Federal funds sold and securities purchased under agreement to resell	5,373,339
Loans and lease financing receivables:	
Loans and leases, net of unearned income	70,086,686
Less: allowance for loan and lease losses	944,352
Less: allocated transfer risk reserve	0
Loans and leases, net	69,142,334
Assets held in trading accounts	189,490
Premises and fixed assets	2,351,600
Other real estate owned	59,046
Investments in unconsolidated subsidiaries and associated companies	8,536
Customers liability on acceptances outstanding	54,802
Intangible assets	1,439,645
Other assets	2,131,446
Total Assets	**$ 128,609,813**

Liabilities

Deposits:	
In domestic offices	104,218,717
Non-interest-bearing	30,097,780
Interest-bearing	74,120,937
In foreign offices, edge & agreement subsidiaries & IBF's	2,486,176
Non-interest-bearing	0
Interest-bearing	2,486,176
Federal funds purchased and securities sold under agreement to repurchase	5,667,784
Demand notes issued to the U.S. Treasury	309,259
Trading Liabilities	100,546
Other borrowed money:	
with remaining maturity one year or less	948,587
with remaining maturity one to three years	25,478
with remaining maturity more than three years	274,296
Banks' liability on acceptances executed and outstanding	54,802
Notes and debentures subordinated to deposits	1,338,384
Other liabilities	2,475,631
Total Liabilities	**$ 117,899,661**

Equity Capital

Perpetual preferred stock	10,205
Common stock	1,500,455
Surplus (exclude surplus related to preferred stock)	5,546,203
Undivided profits and capital reserves	3,490,574
Less: Net unrealized loss on marketable equity securities	162,717
Cumulative foreign currency translation adjustments	0
Total Equity Capital	**10,710,152**
Total liabilities, limited preferred stock and equity capital	**$ 128,609,813**

Texas Credit Unions

There are **778** credit unions in Texas, and 5,924,401 credit union members..

In **1998** at mid-year, share (savings) accounts stood at $24.28 billion, and loans amounted to $17.68 billion.

Nationally, there are 11,531 credit unions representing more than $381 billion in assets.

Credit unions are chartered at federal and state levels. The **National Credit Union Administration** (NCUA) is the regulatory agency for the federal chartered credit unions in Texas. The **Texas Credit Union Department**, Austin, is the regulatory agency for the state-chartered credit unions.

The **Texas Credit Union League** has been the state association for federal and state chartered credit unions since October 1934. The league's address is 4455 LBJ Freeway Ste. 909, Farmers Branch 75244-5998.

They also can be reached at (972) 980-5418, Fax 980-5479 or (800) 442-5762 x5418. Their website address is www.tcul.org. ☆

Source: Texas Credit Union League.

Savings Institutions

The state savings bank charter was approved by the Legislature in 1993 and the first state savings bank in Texas was chartered in January 1994. Savings banks have existed for many years, primarily in the Northeast and, in fact, are among the oldest types of financial-institution charters in the country. Savings banks operate similarly to savings and loans associations in that they are housing-oriented lenders.

Under federal law a state savings bank is categorized as a commercial bank and not a thrift. Therefore savings-bank information is also reported with state and national-bank information.

Texas Savings Banks

Year	No. Assn./Banks	Total Assets	*Mortgage Loans	†Cash	†Investment Securities	Savings Capital	FHLB Advances and other Borrowed Money	‡Net Worth
					Thousands of Dollars			
Dec. 31, 1998	23	$ 12,843,828	$ 7,806,738	$193,992		$ 7,299,636	$ 4,477,546	$1,067,977
Dec. 31, 1997	17	7,952,703	6,125,467	892,556		5,608,429	1,615,311	745,515
Dec. 31, 1996	15	7,872,238	6,227,811	856,970		5,329,919	1,930,378	611,941
Dec. 31, 1995	13	7,348,647	5,644,591	1,106,557	...	4,603,026	2,225,793	519,827
Dec. 31, 1994	8	6,347,505	2,825,012	3,139,573	...	3,227,886	2,628,847	352,363

Texas Savings and Loan Associations

Year	No. Assn./Banks	Total Assets	*Mortgage Loans	†Cash	†Investment Securities	Savings Capital	FHLB Advances and other Borrowed Money	‡Net Worth
Dec. 31, 1998	30	$ 40,021,239	$ 35,419,110	$5,236,596		$21,693,469	$ 15,224,654	$ 3,101,795
Dec. 31, 1997	32	40,284,148	33,451,365	4,556,626		21,854,620	15,190,014	3,089,458
Dec. 31, 1996	37	54,427,896	27,514,639	5,112,995	...	28,053,292	20,210,616	4,345,257
Dec. 31, 1995	45	52,292,519	27,509,933	5,971,364	...	28,635,799	15,837,632	3,827,249
Dec. 31, 1994	50	50,014,102	24,148,760	6,790,416	...	29,394,433	15,973,056	3,447,110
Dec. 31, 1993	62	42,983,595	14,784,215	10,769,889	...	25,503,656	13,356,018	2,968,840
Dec. 31, 1992	64	47,565,516	14,137,191	14,527,573	...	33,299,278	10,490,144	2,917,881
Dec. 31, 1991	80	53,500,091	15,417,895	11,422,071	...	41,985,117	8,189,800	2,257,329
Dec. 31, 1990§	131	72,041,456	27,475,664	20,569,770	...	56,994,387	17,738,041	-4,566,656
Conservatorship	51	14,952,402	6,397,466	2,188,820	...	16,581,525	4,304,033	-6,637,882
Privately Owned	80	57,089,054	21,078,198	18,380,950	...	40,412,862	13,434,008	2,071,226
Dec. 31, 1989§	196	90,606,100	37,793,043	21,218,130	...	70,823,464	27,158,238	-9,356,209
Conservatorship	81	22,159,752	11,793,445	2,605,080	...	25,381,494	7,103,657	-10,866,213
Privately Owned	115	68,446,348	25,999,598	18,613,050	...	45,441,970	20,054,581	1,510,004
Dec. 31, 1988	204	110,499,276	50,920,006	26,181,917	...	83,950,314	28,381,573	-4,088,355
Dec. 31, 1987	279	99,613,666	56,884,564	12,559,154	...	85,324,796	19,235,506	-6,677,338
Dec. 31, 1986	281	96,919,775	61,489,463	9,989,918	...	80,429,758	14,528,311	109,807
Dec. 31, 1985	273	91,798,890	60,866,666	10,426,464	...	72,806,067	13,194,147	3,903,611
Dec. 31, 1984	273	77,544,202	45,859,408	10,424,113	...	61,943,815	10,984,467	2,938,044
Dec. 31, 1983	273	56,684,508	36,243,290	6,678,808	...	46,224,429	6,317,947	2,386,551
Dec. 31, 1982	288	42,505,924	28,539,378	4,713,742	...	34,526,483	5,168,343	1,631,139
Dec. 31, 1981	311	38,343,703	30,013,805	3,294,327	...	30,075,258	4,846,153	1,493,795
Dec. 31, 1980	318	34,954,129	27,717,383	3,066,791	...	28,439,210	3,187,638	1,711,201
Dec. 31, 1979	310	31,280,006	25,238,483	2,512,797	...	25,197,598	2,969,838	1,640,049
Dec. 31, 1978	318	27,933,526	22,830,872	142,721	$ 1,876,882	22,848,519	2,251,631	1,444,607
Dec. 31, 1977	328	24,186,338	19,765,901	154,027	1,579,440	19,994,347	1,515,045	1,235,096
Dec. 31, 1976	316	19,921,694	16,096,166	196,790	1,344,623	16,908,949	949,231	1,044,611
Dec. 31, 1975	303	16,540,181	13,367,569	167,385	1,000,095	13,876,780	919,404	914,502
Dec. 31, 1974	295	13,944,524	11,452,013	117,097	806,302	11,510,259	1,038,386	834,892
Dec. 31, 1973	288	12,629,928	10,361,847	126,106	795,989	10,483,113	740,725	763,618
Dec. 31, 1972	278	10,914,627	8,919,007	155,901	841,904	9,249,305	459,019	678,086
Dec. 31, 1971	272	9,112,590	7,481,751	140,552	670,622	7,647,906	458,152	589,077
Dec. 31, 1970	271	7,706,639	6,450,730	122,420	509,482	6,335,582	559,953	531,733
Dec. 31, 1969	270	7,055,949	5,998,172	105,604	391,175	5,894,398	473,066	487,308
Dec. 31, 1968	267	6,601,846	5,556,617	131,440	415,958	5,712,331	287,588	429,087
Dec. 31, 1967	268	6,156,108	5,149,689	194,684	359,443	5,402,575	218,569	390,508
Dec. 31, 1966	268	5,693,908	4,816,505	190,820	280,927	4,898,223	331,694	361,697
Dec. 31, 1965	267	5,351,064	4,534,073	228,994	230,628	4,631,999	286,497	333,948
Dec. 31, 1964	262	4,797,085	4,071,044	208,083	218,993	4,145,085	266,242	296,444
Dec. 31, 1963	256	4,192,188	3,517,676	208,698	201,724	3,591,951	257,426	259,169
Dec. 31, 1962	248	3,533,209	2,960,182	173,343	180,192	3,049,144	185,476	230,920
Dec. 31, 1961	240	2,990,527	2,472,648	146,710	183,116	2,647,906	74,762	193,579
Dec. 31, 1960	233	2,508,872	2,083,066	110,028	157,154	2,238,080	48,834	166,927

* Beginning in 1982, net of loans in process.
† Beginning in 1979, cash and investment securities data combined.
‡ Net worth includes permanent stock and paid-in surplus general reserves, surplus and undivided profits.
§ In 1989 and 1990, the Office of Thrift Supervision, U.S. Department of the Treasury, separated data on savings and loans (thrifts) into two categories: those under the supervision of the Office of Thrift Supervision (Conservatorship Thrifts) and those still under private management (Privately Owned).

Details in the table above were supplied by the Dallas District of the Office of Thrift Supervision of the U.S. Department of the Treasury and the Texas Savings and Loan Department.

International Trade a Major Target

Since its days as an independent republic, Texas has attracted attention from foreign countries. With a gross state product larger than many nations in the world, the state is an attractive trading partner.

As the world economy further embraces that of the United States and Texas, channels of communications between nations become more important.

In 1857, the Texas Almanac reported that 17 foreign consuls and commercial agents from 16 countries were in Texas. All but three lived in Galveston. The others were in Indianola and Brownsville. Among nations represented were France, Great Britain, Mexico, Prussia, Switzerland, Uruguay, Austria and the Netherlands.

As the world economy of the 21st century develops, the Texas Department of Economic Development keeps private businesses informed about the possibilities in foreign trade. Through the Office of International Business, the state provides basic and advanced export counseling; distributes leads for trade and matches foreign needs with producers in Texas; and displays the state's wares at overseas trade shows and promotional events.

Information on services provided can be obtained by from the Office of International Business, P.O. Box 12728, Austin 78711. (512) 936-9249. Internet: Intrade@tded.state.tx.us or www.tded.state.tx.us/trade.

Foreign Trade Zones in Texas

Foreign-trade-zone status endows a domestic site with certain customs privileges, causing it to be considered to be outside customs territory and therefore available for activities that might otherwise be carried on overseas. Operated as public utilities for qualified corporations, the zones are established under grants of authority from the Foreign Trade Zones board, which is chaired by the U.S. Secretary of Commerce.

Zone facilities are available for operations involving storage, repacking, inspection, exhibition, assembly, manufacturing and other processing. A foreign-trade zone is especially suitable for export processing or manufacturing operations when foreign components or materials with a high U.S. duty are needed to make the end product competitive in markets abroad.

Additional information on the zones is available from each zone manager; from U.S. customs offices; from the executive secretary of the Foreign Trade Zones Board, Dept. of Commerce, Washington, D.C., or from the nearest Dept. of Commerce district office.

Source: The International Trade Reporter, *copyright 1979 by the* Bureau of National Affairs, Inc., Washington, D.C.

Source: U.S. Department of Commerce

There are 28 Foreign Trade Zones in Texas as of Jan. 8, 1999.

McAllen, FTZ No. 12
McAllen Economic Develop. Corp.
6401 South 33rd Street
McAllen 78501

Galveston, FTZ No. 36
Port of Galveston
P.O. Box 328
Galveston 77553

Dallas/Ft. Worth, FTZ No. 39
D/FW International Airport Board
P.O. Drawer 619428
D/FW Airport 75261-9428

Brownsville, FTZ No. 62
Brownsville Navigation District
1000 Foust Road
Brownsville 78521

El Paso, FTZ No. 68
City of El Paso
5B Butterfield Trail Blvd.
El Paso 79906-4945

San Antonio, FTZ No. 80
City of San Antonio
P.O. Box 839966
San Antonio 78283-3966

Harris County, FTZ No. 84
Port of Houston Authority
111 East Loop North
Houston 77029

Laredo, FTZ No. 94
Laredo International Airport
4719 Maher Avenue, Bldg. 132
Laredo 78041

Starr County, FTZ No. 95

Starr County Industrial Foundation
P.O. 502
Rio Grande City 78582

Eagle Pass, FTZ No. 96
Maverick County Development Corp.
P.O. Box 3693
Eagle Pass 78853

Del Rio, FTZ No. 97
City of Del Rio
114 West Martin Street
Del Rio 78841

Ellis County, FTZ No. 113
Trade Zone Operations Inc.
1500 N. Service Road, Highway 67
P.O. Box 788
Midlothian 76065

Beaumont, FTZ No. 115
Port Arthur, FTZ No. 116
Orange, FTZ No. 117
FTZ of Southeast Texas Inc.
2748 Viterbo Rd., Box 9
Beaumont 77705

Corpus Christi, FTZ 122
Port of Corpus Christi Authority
P.O. Box 1541
Corpus Christi 78403

Freeport, FTZ No. 149
Brazos River Harbor Navigation Dist.
Box 615
Freeport 77541

El Paso, FTZ No. 150
Westport Economic Dev. Corp.
4401 N. Mesa, Ste. 201
El Paso 79982

Calhoun/Victoria Counties FTZ No. 155
Calhoun-Victoria FTZ Inc.
P.O. Drawer 397
Point Comfort 77978

Weslaco, FTZ No. 156
City of Weslaco
500 South Kansas
Weslaco 78596

Midland, FTZ No. 165
City of Midland
c/o Midland International Airport
P.O. Box 60305
Midland 79711

Dallas/Fort Worth, FTZ No. 168
FTZ Operating Company of Texas
P.O. Box 742916
Dallas 75374-2916

Liberty County, FTZ No. 171
Liberty Co. E. D. Corp.
P.O. Box 857
Liberty 77575

Presidio, FTZ No. 178
Presidio E.D.C.
P.O. Box 1414
Presidio 79845

Austin, FTZ No. 183
FTZ of Central Texas Inc.
P.O. Box 742916
Dallas 75374-2916

Fort Worth, FTZ No. 196
Alliance Corridor Inc.
2421 Westport Pkwy Ste. 200
Fort Worth 76177

Texas City, FTZ No. 199
Texas City F.T.Z. Corp.
P.O. Box 2608
Texas City 77592

Gregg County, FTZ 234
Gregg County Airport
Rt. 3, Hwy. 322
Longview 75603

Foreign and Domestic Commerce Through Major Ports

Data in table below represent receipts and shipments for only the **13 major** Texas ports in **1997**. Total receipts and shipments for these ports amounted to **422,592,000** tons. Note that "0" means tonnage reported was less than 500 tons, a "-" indicates no tonnage was reported.
Source: U.S. Army Corps of Engineers

(All figures in short tons)

| Port | Total | Foreign | | Domestic | | | | Local |
| | | Imports | Exports | Coastwise | | Internal | | |
				Receipts	Shipments	Receipts	Shipments	
Sabine Pass	725,000	-	-	58,000	-	588,000	78,000	-
Orange	691,000	-	-	-	-	553,000	137,000	-
Beaumont	48,665,000	28,234,000	5,393,000	489,000	2,849,000	4,826,000	6,151,000	724,000
Port Arthur	37,318,000	26,927,000	2,782,000	45,000	814,000	2,602,000	4,051,000	77,000
Houston	165,456,000	72,641,000	30,206,000	2,808,000	9,170,000	21,941,000	15,814,000	13,076,000
Texas City	56,646,000	35,061,000	2,370,000	217,000	4,731,000	5,404,000	7,430,000	434,000
Galveston	10,126,000	3,184,000	2,922,000	137,000	1,918,000	1,596,000	361,000	8,000
Freeport	26,281,000	19,172,000	1,967,000	71,000	638,000	1,700,000	2,649,000	81,000
Corpus Christi	86,806,000	54,215,000	8,004,000	457,000	8,874,000	3,780,000	9,271,000	2,205,000
Port Isabel	88,000	-	-	-	-	88,000	-	-
Brownsville	2,284,000	662,000	229,000	-	22,000	1,177,000	194,000	-
Port Aransas (Harbor Island)	44,000	-	-	-	-	-	-	-
Port Mansfield	8,000	-	-	-	-	-	-	-

Tonnage Handled by Ports, 1990-1997

Source: Corps of Engineers, U.S. Army
Table below gives consolidated tonnage handled by ports. All figures are in short tons (2,000 lbs.).

Ports	1997	1996	1995	1994	1993	1992	1991	1990
Brownsville	2,284,000	2,401,000	2,656,000	3,396,000	1,734,526	1,594,222	1,610,295	1,371,606
Port Isabel	88,000	114,000	129,000	206,000	239,370	234,401	247,455	269,174
Corpus Christi	86,806,000	80,436,000	70,218,000	76,060,000	58,408,549	58,678,726	56,973,650	60,165,497
Freeport	26,281,000	24,571,000	19,662,000	17,450,000	14,024,604	14,952,599	15,665,993	14,526,096
Galveston	10,126,000	11,641,000	10,465,000	10,257,000	9,755,324	12,317,599	10,858,221	9,619,891
Houston	165,456,000	148,183,000	135,231,000	143,663,000	141,476,979	137,663,612	131,513,521	126,177,627
Texas City	56,646,000	56,394,000	50,403,000	44,351,000	53,652,781	43,104,101	43,289,659	48,052,157
Sabine	725,000	135,000	231,000	296,000	393,547	418,927	499,817	631,157
Port Arthur	37,318,000	37,158,000	49,800,000	45,586,000	38,326,902	33,525,819	29,835,115	30,680,942
Beaumont	48,665,000	35,705,000	20,937,000	21,201,000	25,409,757	22,701,500	22,383,039	26,728,664
Orange	691,000	616,000	693,000	686,000	579,062	552,504	849,307	709,940
Port Lavaca	-	-	-	-	5,892,656	5,899,832	6,266,244	6,097,107
Anahuac	-	0	-	-	0	0	0	0
Moss Bluff	-	-	-	-	0	0	0	0
Channel to Liberty	-	39,000	-	-	0	2,800	20,987	0
Double Bayou	0	0	-	0	0	240	0	0
Cedar Bayou	435,000	404,000	473,000	321,000	349,680	302,824	217,692	219,206
Colorado River	570,000	622,000	576,000	639,000	536,811	505,198	577,379	476,300
Sweeny	-	-	-	-	718,118	684,274	477,370	534,406
Palacios	-	0	-	-	0	0	0	0
Dickinson	669,000	625,000	657,000	556,000	423,368	449,336	532,184	555,523
Aransas Pass	91,000	39,000	181,000	45,000	25,226	13,398	16,851	169,020
Port Mansfield	8,000	8,000	20,000	10,000	3,781	2,657	120	102
Harlingen	-	-	-	-	898,132	786,994	795,305	764,577
Channel to Victoria	5,000,000	4,351,000	4,624,000	4,567,000	3,937,400	4,265,228	3,407,884	3,740,374
Chocolate Byu.	3,983,000	3,845,000	3,480,000	3,757,000	3,715,107	3,343,072	3,469,030	3,462,762
Johnsons Bayou	313,000	939,000	585,000	613,000	515,957	567,298	596,247	715,917
Rockport	1	1	-	3,000	0	0	0	643,563
Clear Creek	-	-	-	-	5,000	66	0	0
Other Ports	0	0	0	0	0	0	0	0
TOTAL	NA	NA	371,021,000	373,668,000	361,017,695	390,567,161	330,103,365	335,311,608

Foreign Consulates in Texas

In the list below, these abbreviations appear after the city: (CG) Consulate General; (C) Consulate; (VC) Vice Consulate. The letter "H" before the designation indicates honorary status. Compiled from "Foreign Consular Offices in the United States," U.S. Dept. of State, Fall/Winter 1997, and recent Internet sources. Note: Possible changes in telephone area codes.

Albania: Houston (HC); 10738 Villa Lea, 77071. (713) 790-1341.
Argentina: Houston (CG); 1990 S. Post Oak Rd., Ste. 770, 77056. (713) 871-8935.
Austria: Houston (HCG); 1717 Bissonet St. Suite 306. (713) 723-9979.
Barbados: Houston (HC); 25226 Sandi Lane, Katy, 77494. (281) 392-9794.
Belgium: Houston (HCG); 2929 Allen Pkwy., Ste. 2222, 77019. (713) 529-0775.
 Dallas (HC); 8350 N. Central Expy., Ste. 2000, 75206. (214) 987-4391.
 San Antonio (HC); 105 S. St. Mary's St., No. 2115, 78205. (210) 271-8820.
Belize: Dallas (HC); 1315 19th St., Ste. 2A, Plano, 75074. (972) 579-0070.
 Houston (HC); 7101 Breen, 77086. (713) 999-4484.
Bolivia: Houston (HCG); 1880 Dairy Ashford, Ste. 691, 77077. (713) 497-4068.
 Dallas (HC); 611 Singleton,75212. (214)571-6131.
Botswana: Houston (HC); 4615 Post Oak Pl., Ste. 104, 77027. (713) 622-1900.
Brazil: Houston (CG); 1700 W. Loop S., Ste. 1450, 77027. (713) 961-3063.
Cameroon: Houston (HC); 2711 Weslayan, 77027. (713) 499-3502.
Canada: Dallas (CG); 750 N. Saint Paul, Ste. 1700, 75201. (214) 922-9806.
Chile: Houston (CG):1360 Post Oak Blvd., Ste. 2330, 77056; (713) 621-5853.
 Dallas (HC); 3500 Oak Lawn, Apt. 200, 75219-4343. (214) 528-2731.
China: Houston (CG); 3417 Montrose, 77006. (713) 524-0780.
Colombia: Houston (CG); 2990 Richmond Ave., Ste. 544, 77098; (713) 527-8919.
Costa Rica: Houston (CG); 2901 Wilcrest, Ste. 275, 77042. (713) 266-0484.
 San Antonio (CG); 6836 San Pedro, Ste. 206-B, 78216. (210) 308-8623.
 Austin (C); 1730 E. Oltorf, Unit 320, 78741. (512) 445-0023.
Cyprus: Houston (HCG); 320 S. 66th St., 77011. (713) 928-2264.
Czech Republic: Dallas (HC); 3239 Oradell Lane, 75220. (214) 350-6871.
 Houston (HC); 4544 Post Oak Pl., Ste. 378, 77027. (713) 629-6963.
Denmark: Corpus Christi (HC); 22 Townhouse Lane (P.O. Box 4585), 78408. (512) 991-3012.
 Dallas (HC); 3200 Trammell Crow Center, 2001 Ross Ave., 75201. (214) 863-4221.
 Houston (HC); 5 Post Oak Park, Ste. 2370, 77027. (713) 622-9018.
Dominican Republic: Houston (C); 3300 S. Gessner, Ste. 113, 77024. (713) 467-4372.
 Dallas (HC); 12127 Ridgelake Dr., 75218. (214) 341-3250.
 El Paso (HC); 67977 Granero Dr., 79912.
Ecuador: Houston (CG); 4200 Westheimer, Ste. 218, 77027. (713) 622-1787.
Egypt: Houston (CG); 3 Post Oak Central, 1990 Post Oak Blvd., Ste. 2180, 77056. (713) 961-4915.
El Salvador: Dallas (CG); 1555 W. Mockingbird Lane, Ste. 216, 75235.
 Houston (CG); 6420 Hillcroft, Ste. 100, 77081.

(713) 270-6239.
Finland: Dallas (HC); 1445 Ross Ave., Ste. 3200, 75202. (214) 855-4715.
 Houston (HC); 2190 North Loop W., Ste. 410, 77018. (713) 680-2727.
France: Houston (CG); 2777 Allen Pkwy., Ste. 650, 77019. (713) 528-2181. **Trade Commission:** 5847 San Felipe, Ste. 1600, 77056. (713) 266-7595.
 Austin (HC); 2300 Interfirst Tower, Ste. 976, 78701. (512) 480-5605.
 Dallas (HC); 750 N. St. Paul, Ste. 220, 75201. (214) 855-5495.
 San Antonio (HC); Route 1, 78109. Box 229, 78109. (210) 659-3101.
Gambia: Houston (HC); 3040 Post Oak Blvd., Ste. 700, 77056. (281) 633-3500.
Germany: Houston (CG); 1330 Post Oak Blvd., Ste. 1850, 77056. (713) 627-7770.
 Corpus Christi (HC); 5440 Old Brownsville Rd., 78469. (512) 289-2416.
 Dallas (HC); 5580 Peterson Lane, Ste. 150, 75240. (214) 239-0788.
 San Antonio (HC); 1500 Alamo Bldg., 105 S. St. Mary's St., 78205. (210) 224-4455.
Ghana: Houston (HC); 3434 Locke Lane, 77027. (713) 960-8806.
Greece: Houston (CG); Cigna Tower, 1360 Post Oak Blvd., Ste. 2480, 77056. (713) 840-7522.
Guatemala: Houston (CG); 3600 S. Gessner Rd., Ste 200, 77063. (713) 953-9531.
 San Antonio (HC); 4840 Whirlwind, 78217.
Guyana: Houston (HC); 1810 Woodland Park Dr., 77077. (713) 497-4466.
Haiti: Houston (HC); 3535 Sage Rd., 77027.
Honduras: Houston (CG); 4151 Southwest Fwy., Ste. 700, 77027. (713) 622-4572.
Hungary: Houston (HC); Transco Tower, 2800 Post Oak Blvd., 77056. (713) 529-2727.
Iceland: Dallas (HC); 3205 Seaside, Irving, 75062. (972) 699-5417.
 Houston (HC); 2348 W. Settler's Way, The Woodlands, 77380. (713) 367-2777.
India: Houston (CG); 1990 Post Oak Blvd., Ste 600, 77056. (713) 626-2148.
Indonesia: Houston (CG); 10900 Richmond Ave., 77042.
Ireland: Houston (HC); 1331 Lamar St., Ste. 600, 77010, (713) 654-8115.
Israel: Houston (CG); Weslayan Tower, 24 Greenway Plz., Ste. 1500, 77046. (713) 627-3780.
Italy: Houston (CG); 1300 Post Oak Blvd., Ste. 660, 77056. (713) 850-7520.
 Dallas (HVC); 6255 W. Northwest Hwy., Apt. 304, 75225. (214) 368-4113.
Jamaica: Houston (HC); 7737 Southwest Fwy., Suite 580, 77074. (713) 541-3333.
Japan: Houston (CG);1000 Louisiana, Ste. 5300, 77002. (713) 652-2977.
 Dallas (HCG); 300 Crescent Ct., Ste. 200, 75201.
Jordan: Houston (HC); 723 Main St., Ste. 408, 77002. (713) 224-2911.
Korea: Houston (CG); 1990 Post Oak Blvd., Ste. 1250, 77056. (713) 961-0186.
 Dallas (HC); 13111 N. Central Expy., 75243. (214) 454-1112.
Lesotho: Austin (HC); 7400 Valburn Dr., 78731.
Liberia: Houston (HCG); 3300 S. Gessner, 77063.

Luxembourg: Fort Worth/Dallas (HC); 301 Commerce St., Ste 600, Fort Worth, 76102. (817) 878-8000.
Madagascar: Houston (HC); 18010 Widcombe Dr., 77084. (713) 550-2559.
Malta: Houston (HCG); 654 N. Belt E., Ste. 400, 77060. (713) 428-7800.
Dallas (HC); 500 N. akard St., Ste 4170, 75201. (214) 777-5210.
Mexico: Austin (CG); Littlefield Bldg., 200 E. 6th St., Ste. 200, 78701.
Brownsville (C); 724 E. Elizabeth 78520. (210) 542-4431.
Corpus Christi (C); 800 N. Shoreline, Ste. 410, 78401.
Dallas (CG); 8855 Stemmons Fwy, 75247. (214) 522-9740.
Del Rio (C); 300 East Losoya, 78840. (210) 775-2352.
Eagle Pass (C); 140 Adams St., 78852. (210) 773-9255.
El Paso (CG); 910 E. San Antonio St., 79901. (915) 533-3644.
Fort Worth (HC); 1 N. Commerce St., 76102. (817) 870-2270.
Houston (CG); 3015 Richmond Ave., Ste. 100, 77098. (713) 524-2300. **Tourism Office:** 2707 N. Loop, Ste. 450, 77008.
Laredo (C); 1612 Farragut St., 78040. (210) 723-6369.
McAllen (C); 600 S. Broadway, 78501. (210) 686-0243.
Midland (C); 511 W. Ohio St., Ste. 121, 79701.
San Antonio (CG); 127 Navarro St., 78205. (210) 227-9145. **Commercial Affairs Office**: 1100 NW Loop 410, Ste. 754, 78213.
Monaco: Dallas (HC); 4700 St. Johns Dr., 75205. (214) 521-1058.
Mongolia: Houston (HCAgent); 1221 Lamar, Ste. 1201, 77010. (713)759-1922.
Morocco: Houston (HC); 5555 Del Monte, No. 2405, 77056. (713) 963-9110.

Top Exporting Areas, 1997

Metropolitan areas	Value of exports (in billions)
1. New York	$29.083
2. San Jose, Calif.	29.057
3. Seattle-Bellevue-Everett	29.006
4. Detroit	25.967
5. Los Angeles-Long Beach	23.210
6. Chicago	23.210
7. **Houston**	**18.596**
8. Miami	12.692
9. Minneapolis-St. Paul	12.007
10. Phoenix-Mesa	11.108
15. **Dallas**	**8.646**
21. **El Paso**	**5.834**
35. **Laredo**	**3.959**
40. **Austin-San Marcos**	**3.355**
43. **Fort Worth-Arlington**	**3.046**
47. **Brownsville-Harlingen-San Benito**	**2.697**
Source: U.S. Department of Commerce	

Netherlands: Houston (CG); 2200 Post Oak Blvd., Ste. 610, 77056. (713) 622-8000.
New Zealand: Houston (HC); 2248 Robinhood St., 77005. (281) 366-5497.
Nicaragua: Houston (CG); 6300 Hillcroft, Ste. 312, 77081. (713) 272-9628.
Norway: Houston (CG); 2777 Allen Parkway, 77019. (713) 521-2900.
Dallas (HC); 4605 Live Oak St., 75204. (214) 826-5231.
Panama: Houston (CG); 24 Greenway Plaza, Ste. 1307, 77046. (713) 622-4451.
Peru: Houston (CG); 5847 San Felipe Ave., Ste. 1481, 77056. (713) 781-5000.
San Antonio (HC); 28055 Ruffian Drive., 78006.
Portugal: Houston (HC); 700 Louisiana, Ste. 4800, 77002. (713) 759-1188.
Qatar: Houston (CG); 4265 San Felipe St., Ste. 1100, 77027. (713) 968-9840.
Saint Kitts/Nevis: Dallas (HC); 6336 Greenville Ave., 75206.
Saint Lucia: Dallas (HC); Dallas City Hall, 1500 Marilla, 75201. (214) 670-3319.
Saudi Arabia: Houston (CG); 5718 Westheimer, Ste. 1500, 77057. (713) 785-5577.
Senegal: Houston (HCG); 3602 S. McGregor, 77021. (713) 748-5016.
Slovenia: Houston (HC); 2925 Briarpark, 7 Floor, 77042. (713) 430-7350.
Spain: Houston (CG); 1800 Bering Dr., Ste. 660, 77057. (713) 783-6200.
Dallas (HC); 5499 Glen Lakes Dr., Ste. 209, 75231. (214) 373-1200.
El Paso (HC); 420 Golden Springs Dr., 79912. (915) 534-0677.
San Antonio (HC); 8350 Delphian, 78148.
Sweden: Houston (HCG); 2401 Fountainview Dr., Ste 510, 77057. (713) 953-1417.
Dallas: (HC); 1341 W. Mockingbird Lane, Ste. 500, 75225; (214) 630-9112.
Switzerland: Houston (CG); 1000 Louisiana, Ste. 5670, 77002. (713) 650-0000.
Dallas (HC); 2651 N. Harwood, Ste. 455, 75201. (214) 965-1025.
Syria: Houston (HCG); 5433 Westheimer Rd., Ste. 1020, 77056. (713) 622-8860.
Thailand: Houston (HCG); 600 Travis St., Ste. 2800, 77002. (713) 229-8733.
Dallas (HCG); 1717 Main St., Ste. 4100, 75201.
El Paso (HCG); 4401 N. Mesa, Ste. 204, 79902. (915) 533-5757.
Turkey: Houston (CG); 1990 Post Oak Central, 77056. (713) 622-5849.
United Kingdom: Houston (CG); 1000 Louisiana St., Ste. 1900, 77002. (713) 659-6270.
Dallas (C); 2911 Turtle Creek, Ste. 940, 75219. (214) 637-3600.
Venezuela : Houston (CG); 2700 S. Post Oak Blvd., Ste. 1500, 77056. (713) 961-5141. ☆

Texas Transportation System

Texas is a leader among the states in a number of transportation indicators, including total road and street mileage, total railroad mileage and total number of airports. Texas ranks second behind California in motor-vehicle registrations and in number of general-aviation aircraft.

The Texas transportation system includes 296,000 miles of streets, highways and Interstate roads, more than 10,000 miles of **railroad line**, approximately 1,600 **airport facilities** and 12 deep-draft coastal **ports,** 15 shallow-draft ports, and two ferryboat operations. Texans operate almost 16 million motor vehicles and about 24,000 aircraft.

The transportation industry is a major employer in Texas. Texas Workforce Commission indicates that transportation employs some 350,000 Texans. The largest group, 135,000, is employed in trucking and warehousing. Air transportation involves 113,000 workers and water transportation 17,000.

The largest state agency involved, the **Texas Department of Transportation**, is responsible for highway construction and maintenance, motor vehicle titles and registration, general aviation, public transportation, commercial trucking, automobile dealer licensing and the state's official Tourist Welcome Centers. The **Railroad Commission** has intrastate authority over railroad safety, truck lines, buses and pipelines.

Interstate Highways in Texas

Vehicles, Highway Miles, Construction, Maintenance, 1998

The following mileage, maintenance and construction figures refer only to roads that are maintained by the state: Interstates, U.S. highways, state highways, farm-to-market roads and some loops around urban areas. Not included are city- or county-maintained streets and roads. A lane mile is one lane for one mile; i.e., one mile of four-lane highway equals four lane miles. Source: Texas Dept. of Transportation.

County	Vehicles Registered	Lane Miles of Highways	Vehicle Miles Driven Daily	County Maintenance Expenditures	State Construction Expenditures	Vehicle Registration Fees	County Net Receipts	State Net Receipts
Anderson	40,063	959	1,100,646	$5,086,028	$2,285,005	$2,283,246	$963,280	$1319966
Andrews	12,519	540	415,576	1,323,252	641,105	721,290	426,202	295,088
Angelina	71,413	915	1,957,654	4,507,058	13,889,968	4,385,622	1,456,669	2,928,953
Aransas	17,976	183	340,316	1,090,211	451,239	909,679	429,433	480,247
Archer	9,671	524	332,366	2,127,339	1,650,855	495,984	382,215	113,769
Armstrong	2,452	372	283,220	1,582,497	38,821	142,308	140,735	1,573
Atascosa	26,199	1,010	1,122,954	3,559,031	5,420,745	1,476,338	724,099	752,239
Austin	25,267	607	964,028	1,552,099	534,990	1,553,582	757,755	795,827
Bailey	6,014	473	188,728	1,018,941	519,754	389,189	352,018	37,171
Bandera	16,146	393	305,816	1,551,124	718,161	851,608	574,021	277,587
Bastrop	45,677	776	1,357,784	2,718,601	2,841,642	2,621,049	1,258,804	1,362,245
Baylor	4,993	437	174,774	2,239,990	3,136,495	310,413	284,818	25,595
Bee	19,120	640	550,521	1,588,551	1,120,214	1,117,646	648,090	469,556
Bell	183,126	1,431	4,618,063	7,051,809	14,866,051	10,804,463	3,661,404	7,143,059
Bexar	1,027,704	2,976	20,287,992	21,104,050	119,077,936	63,705,825	19,252,129	44,453,696
Blanco	8,788	451	370,383	1,040,605	1,495,081	540,545	385,070	155,476
Borden	924	344	52,409	1,356,868	0	36,509	36,072	437.05
Bosque	16,520	695	457,977	2,434,153	247,525	905,282	581,469	323,814
Bowie	78,407	1,157	2,471,281	7,111,280	24,190,676	4,515,021	1,673,728	2,841,293
Brazoria	201,803	1,179	3,664,643	8,734,664	31,137,917	10,744,118	2,772,656	7,971,462
Brazos	97,486	785	2,133,433	8,152,336	11,721,242	5,913,799	2,211,513	3,702,286
Brewster	7,488	587	224,016	3,998,055	2,099,941	403,580	294,836	108,744
Briscoe	2,010	328	52,139	1,162,774	317,175	116,454	114,816	1,638
Brooks	5,138	276	425,372	1,630,710	299,910	277,871	214,607	63,264
Brown	36,449	752	695,767	2,736,196	5,169,566	1,981,024	856,371	1,124,654
Burleson	15,687	517	573,353	1,782,839	2,411,726	935,263	575,292	359,970
Burnet	33,331	793	899,696	1,430,142	1,568,111	1,885,474	864,915	1,020,559
Caldwell	23,002	602	683,229	2,020,660	2,416,342	1,327,677	663,122	664,555
Calhoun	18,026	382	426,742	1,682,257	1,553,829	933,679	441,760	491,920
Callahan	14,745	744	798,426	2,347,606	1,347,266	834,808	600,690	234,118
Cameron	186,436	1,532	4,001,554	8,089,696	29,162,466	11,113,784	3,246,978	7,866,806

County	Vehicles Registered	Lane Miles of Highways	Vehicle Miles Driven Daily	County Maintenance Expenditures	State Construction Expenditures	Vehicle Registration Fees	County Net Receipts	State Net Receipts
Camp	11,299	271	260,876	720,097	695,044	859,804	467,440	392,364
Carson	6,428	776	707,015	2,328,266	233,868	348,559	314,137	34,422
Cass	28,967	974	966,216	4,924,564	9,682,326	1,659,639	813,048	846,591
Castro	7,546	529	255,399	1,459,926	26,624	530,371	427,392	102,978
Chambers	26,046	700	1,701,923	2,644,864	4,986,316	1,520,613	671,538	849,075
Cherokee	37,068	1,115	1,098,408	4,135,422	12,151,983	2,165,561	962,457	1,203,104
Childress	6,107	477	296,771	1,786,037	3,798,628	334,613	323,992	10,621
Clay	11,255	794	740,358	2,176,920	5,254,359	621,570	505,253	116,317
Cochran	3,303	470	93,168	927,130	4,196,476	180,720	178,517	2,203
Coke	4,457	357	170,124	646,250	62,987	230,400	226,696	3,704
Coleman	9,912	750	317,090	2,637,749	345,000	525,882	444,137	81,745
Collin	357,794	1,290	4,473,308	5,814,066	75,772,240	21,396,292	6,992,914	14,403,378
Collingsworth	3,252	445	86,502	1,460,390	13,457	175,982	173,221	2,761
Colorado	20,831	762	1,299,344	2,213,068	369,872	1,297,058	664,631	632,427
Comal	72,020	604	2,068,179	2,319,195	12,192,289	4,451,459	1,605,788	2,845,670
Comanche	14,380	734	417,466	2,202,659	720,603	815,426	577,775	237,651
Concho	2,923	432	218,324	1,783,604	2,556,410	145,152	142,869	2,283
Cooke	33,498	842	1,096,798	3,150,006	6,577,702	1,938,354	889,230	1,049,123
Coryell	39,108	682	894,518	3,361,132	3,041,376	2,150,179	961,684	1,188,495
Cottle	1,849	391	76,683	1,774,592	2,308,952	97,288	95,765	1,523
Crane	5,239	319	179,329	597,196	5,465,859	357,342	253,883	103,460
Crockett	4,113	782	433,100	1,569,955	1,380,468	210,995	208,149	2,846
Crosby	6,006	569	189,269	1,425,872	638,850	338,721	318,270	20,451
Culberson	2,159	744	568,820	2,799,559	672,859	113,540	112,077	1,464
Dallam	5,647	603	342,240	1,596,949	677,115	401,356	344,715	56,641
Dallas	1,707,342	2,926	29,936,868	26,926,302	207,650,122	110,596,097	34,856,955	75,739,142
Dawson	11,749	710	357,684	1,212,387	3,442,809	774,738	540,451	234,287
Deaf Smith	16,883	601	332,121	2,349,256	4,410,505	1,219,875	649,891	569,984
Delta	5,254	342	171,046	1,964,747	1,716,286	261,357	237,398	23,960
Denton	308,407	1,252	6,008,066	7,597,856	44,174,306	18,087,565	5,560,269	12,527,296
De Witt	16,819	641	426,153	2,080,116	6,945,649	937,317	604,188	333,129
Dickens	2,605	460	93,934	1,669,452	1,991,713	113,938	112,466	1,473
Dimmit	6,920	504	251,724	4,414,246	4,528,584	413,348	344,223	69,125
Donley	3,575	455	399,367	3,192,897	4,706,979	199,983	196,843	3,141
Duval	9,026	630	409,578	1,871,123	775,231	573,879	431,917	141,962
Eastland	19,085	1,025	966,184	2,865,977	5,913,765	1,140,251	639,249	501,002
Ector	111,369	927	1,410,248	3,733,004	2,478,279	7,254,064	2,430,358	4,823,706
Edwards	2,151	500	73,051	1,157,993	2,045,366	111,172	109,529	1,642
Ellis	101,587	1,451	3,029,803	10,240,013	20,458,833	24,514,910	7,170,659	17,344,251
El Paso	412,981	1,482	7,610,749	11,133,771	85,239,681	6,354,345	1,833,334	4,521,011
Erath	29,059	783	863,207	3,375,070	8,250,881	1,674,939	797,616	877,323
Falls	13,462	706	567,560	4,119,196	262,498	747,189	545,787	201,402
Fannin	29,431	944	662,864	4,984,458	14,402,608	1,605,089	837,301	767,789
Fayette	24,383	988	1,194,540	2,611,148	1,605,365	1,433,312	734,358	698,953
Fisher	4,277	553	142,464	1,923,340	27,396	220,201	216,777	3,424
Floyd	8,094	668	186,668	2,262,953	812,240	480,937	421,910	59,027
Foard	1,556	299	58,546	711,354	14,039	90,530	89,223	1,307
Fort Bend	238,069	1,009	4,071,721	5,909,823	49,979,180	14,093,249	4,577,693	9,515,556
Franklin	8,263	340	366,688	1,437,108	5,546,986	428,854	333,884	94,970
Freestone	17,098	822	1,126,575	3,235,225	5,552,499	915,782	644,507	271,275
Frio	9,935	758	733,875	2,476,897	2,983,154	630,430	481,963	148,468
Gaines	12,321	668	431,351	3,221,231	461,057	743,826	410,201	333,625
Galveston	198,389	984	3,949,964	5,483,375	25,325,372	11,326,796	3,447,654	7,879,142
Garza	4,145	460	335,174	852,931	8,841,023	232,318	217,673	14,645
Gillespie	20,669	703	555,784	2,175,218	194,034	1,171,361	684,800	486,561
Glasscock	2,146	274	157,585	762,968	921,928	124,374	123,360	1,014
Goliad	6,110	500	267,639	1,561,477	1,019,081	277,432	265,217	12,215
Gonzales	16,650	886	857,764	2,998,844	2,374,828	919,491	522,963	396,528
Gray	25,019	770	608,009	3,344,204	5,357,537	1,259,568	536,809	722,758
Grayson	102,583	1,183	2,499,358	6,235,683	17,049,093	5,948,416	2,104,467	3,843,949
Gregg	115,540	749	2,339,714	4,165,759	15,518,665	7,417,053	2,590,720	4,826,333
Grimes	19,602	610	644,100	5,651,520	5,513,734	1,098,812	653,290	445,522
Guadalupe	70,780	912	2,080,060	5,543,539	6,975,453	4,123,116	1,522,181	2,600,935
Hale	29,587	1,054	719,508	2,465,114	3,811,222	1,780,086	824,803	955,283
Hall	3,102	458	180,980	1,271,843	1,117,787	178,650	176,076	2,574
Hamilton	8,293	575	274,842	2,720,353	4,187,653	469,877	403,435	66,443
Hansford	6,315	523	135,348	1,529,573	669,151	408,446	363,553	44,893
Hardeman	4,477	466	270,909	1,647,680	517,130	252,429	248,649	3,781
Hardin	46,252	537	1,202,216	2,105,113	6,006,326	2,654,162	1,187,201	1,466,961
Harris	2,535,046	4,199	44,018,208	38,646,116	311,858,159	162,053,776	52,558,302	109,495,474
Harrison	52,985	1,166	2,118,752	4,196,326	7,521,671	3,072,242	1,154,253	1,917,989
Hartley	5,061	508	315,104	1,588,938	4,956,524	359,833	305,326	54,507
Haskell	7,090	646	202,476	2,075,303	175,413	403,468	378,233	25,235
Hays	69,015	634	2,548,345	3,985,024	6,653,001	4,025,694	1,524,561	2,501,133
Hemphill	4,627	384	128,989	2,052,350	4,184,992	277,463	247,337	30,126
Henderson	67,891	933	1,473,564	5,494,759	12,922,594	3,775,049	1,286,133	2,488,917

County	Vehicles Registered	Lane Miles of Highways	Vehicle Miles Driven Daily	County Maintenance Expenditures	State Construction Expenditures	Vehicle Registration Fees	County Net Receipts	State Net Receipts
Hildago	286,615	1,908	6,259,148	8,300,524	63,281,991	17,905,832	5,256,664	12,649,168
Hill	31,000	1,085	1,765,812	5,254,772	7,043,294	1,730,136	873,352	856,784
Hockley	20,566	750	529,615	1,811,748	935,633	1,242,695	578,584	664,111
Hood	40,864	375	741,800	1,668,364	1,554,943	2,297,077	995,213	1,301,864
Hopkins	32,059	955	1,231,863	3,873,782	3,233,172	2,078,716	933,801	1,144,915
Houston	19,651	841	563,178	2,432,944	2,607,454	1,144,209	650,659	493,550
Howard	28,069	841	774,213	3,460,134	5,474,039	1,705,080	809,199	895,880
Hudspeth	2,431	818	970,258	3,653,081	1,138,173	111,335	109,925	1,410
Hunt	68,681	1,279	2,080,562	6,502,444	14,826,615	3,399,297	1,066,675	2,332,622
Hutchinson	28,644	475	360,189	1,109,169	7,925,742	1,643,126	661,347	981,780
Irion	2,185	247	94,904	705,571	2,236,887	133,554	131,840	1,714
Jack	8,092	575	276,256	2,468,864	437,226	489,910	404,706	85,204
Jackson	13,686	636	736,387	3,046,870	5,193,693	753,048	533,993	219,055
Jasper	35,187	682	1,176,032	2,863,838	11,791,213	1,914,307	777,336	1,136,971
Jeff Davis	2,224	470	170,535	1,207,691	834,750	136,516	118,303	18,213
Jefferson	203,654	1,007	4,388,516	6,436,779	33,592,570	12,300,484	3,955,034	8,345,449
Jim Hogg	3,994	288	133,325	772,974	2,937,462	250,824	206,159	44,665
Jim Wells	29,419	633	895,170	2,324,076	16,117,756	1,945,681	792,182	1,153,498
Johnson	107,540	910	2,205,953	3,440,024	16,585,710	6,127,279	2,025,276	4,102,003
Jones	16,125	980	479,059	3,887,975	1,886,263	923,567	635,686	287,882
Karnes	10,140	692	334,262	2,228,361	49,327	568,989	464,264	104,726
Kaufman	62,842	1,191	2,883,721	5,902,175	9,479,449	3,441,837	1,339,142	2,102,695
Kendall	30,341	443	674,343	2,100,660	2,425,050	1,750,563	960,578	789,985
Kenedy	520	187	406,720	1,804,313	12,316	30,385	30,034	351
Kent	1,542	326	54,146	1,543,941	1,719,600	72,489	71,615	874
Kerr	41,728	702	926,657	3,133,560	4,247,509	2,372,144	1,021,475	1,350,670
Kimble	4,962	687	399,790	1,190,312	859,153	243,504	230,072	13,432
King	431	199	66,816	516,732	2,518,134	28,075	27,855	220
Kinney	2,642	407	169,094	1,114,352	145,804	144,258	130,009	14,249
Kleberg	22,275	363	569,018	1,124,526	500,408	1,330,063	622,133	707,931
Knox	3,748	434	127,438	1,512,722	2,455,827	234,387	231,172	3,216
Lamar	45,476	991	1,096,689	5,586,248	20,852,797	2,699,956	1,089,775	1,610,181
Lamb	13,209	809	439,657	2,282,695	3,376,267	786,053	557,071	228,981
Lampasas	16,586	476	393,015	2,011,690	6,983,397	937,601	646,237	291,364
La Salle	3,632	648	473,285	3,775,543	5,552,340	217,680	209,981	7,699
Lavaca	20,529	639	446,152	2,464,371	4,459,445	1,224,068	651,441	572,627
Lee	16,149	514	527,042	2,043,387	5,405,881	1,029,089	562,755	466,334
Leon	14,709	837	1,051,269	3,965,762	1,666,726	818,147	549,138	269,010
Liberty	55,776	805	1,659,513	3,975,623	11,507,632	3,461,785	1,227,019	2,234,767
Limestone	19,726	769	575,113	3,045,225	3,041,467	1,015,031	563,727	451,304
Lipscomb	3,235	447	73,737	1,368,667	14,995	247,059	244,469	2,590
Live Oak	10,347	947	1,036,445	3,583,225	935,501	588,667	494,368	94,298
Llano	17,196	498	389,065	1,224,794	42,289	967,593	611,943	355,650
Loving	253	67	14,010	154,735	0	12,059	11,966	93
Lubbock	198,501	1,640	2,933,233	4,930,986	34,033,934	12,239,243	4,245,149	7,994,094
Lynn	5,967	708	304,095	1,463,460	553,327	350,190	336,156	14,035
Madison	12,153	569	669,915	4,321,591	1,598,873	678,479	548,752	129,728
Marion	9,150	318	311,775	2,077,023	2,215,236	478,873	398,867	80,006
Martin	5,420	572	325,760	1,333,783	179,260	298,958	295,380	3,577
Mason	3,827	416	138,730	1,208,016	13,371	195,606	192,948	2,657
Matagorda	31,635	681	739,201	4,457,204	2,358,724	1,824,751	835,794	988,957
Maverick	22,470	447	515,394	1,589,168	7,480,198	1,464,406	587,204	877,272
McCulloch	9,203	608	260,579	2,238,509	1,257,246	496,021	412,216	83,804
McLennan	169,259	1,593	4,514,006	6,867,720	16,352,348	11,386,825	3,252,667	8,134,158
McMullen	1,929	317	105,981	1,433,399	1,059,695	185,770	165,588	20,182
Medina	32,893	727	951,338	4,319,059	10,328,068	1,756,688	804,426	952,262
Menard	2,659	346	114,542	628,369	2,081	139,501	136,079	3,422
Midland	110,922	935	1,655,601	2,962,621	6,677,478	7,164,026	2,335,176	4,828,850
Milam	22,214	685	690,416	3,929,918	3,687,162	1,251,943	663,392	588,551
Mills	6,048	441	219,584	1,604,372	851,013	306,376	301,902	4,474
Mitchell	6,744	662	432,439	3,245,924	613,114	339,013	313,769	25,244
Montague	19,696	853	640,173	3,051,088	723,683	1,126,547	641,341	485,207
Montgomery	233,078	1,092	5,467,373	6,123,693	21,988,680	13,844,970	4,374,892	9,470,078
Moore	17,467	467	429,048	1,517,217	7,011,515	1,181,225	604,395	576,830
Morris	13,118	357	448,289	1,320,766	5,294,911	764,707	461,590	303,117
Motley	1,540	331	61,557	1,662,206	44,859	81,604	80,291	1,313
Nacagdoches	46,094	910	1,581,334	3,144,753	8,591,490	2,677,167	1,128,025	1,549,143
Navarro	38,356	1,154	1,544,788	5,899,909	10,680,071	2,203,299	991,201	1,212,098
Newton	11,939	547	459,684	2,590,540	3,417,742	604,318	457,740	146,578
Nolan	14,555	689	698,954	3,139,273	7,989,765	868,844	584,621	284,223
Nueces	238,785	1,372	4,627,912	6,316,792	22,338,404	14,437,101	4,651,305	9,785,722
Ochiltree	9,990	428	206,389	1,457,230	2,679,976	695,900	525,976	169,924
Oldham	2,214	462	686,473	1,312,643	3,956,214	141,146	139,203	1,943
Orange	73,422	576	2,158,283	4,146,744	13,757,760	4,088,353	1,393,509	2,694,845
Palo Pinto	27,049	829	781,292	2,940,752	1,618,343	1,580,799	765,148	815,650

County	Vehicles Registered	Lane Miles of Highways	Vehicle Miles Driven Daily	County Maintenance Expenditures	State Construction Expenditures	Vehicle Registration Fees	County Net Receipts	State Net Receipts
Panola	22,528	750	912,822	2,654,173	8,058,793	1,096,815	475,575	621,240
Parker	87,850	855	2,178,383	3,760,026	9,023,079	4,941,463	1,845,098	3,096,365
Parmer	8,993	539	338,007	1,256,603	692,012	582,702	473,157	109,545
Pecos	12,630	1,661	873,343	4,795,861	4,085,925	652,695	398,908	253,786
Polk	45,446	839	1,607,707	2,884,480	13,178,622	2,982,087	1,065,882	1,916,205
Potter	97,341	879	2,252,915	5,344,753	17,907,631	5,875,372	2,207,105	3,668,267
Presidio	5,325	546	165,564	1,454,020	1,569,955	309,121	251,022	58,099
Rains	9,090	270	240,469	843,123	2,401,115	457,386	351,412	105,975
Randall	95,701	879	1,017,480	3,495,368	738,808	5,845,300	2,043,977	3,801,323
Reagan	3,664	320	114,207	740,672	0	246,080	215,383	30,697
Real	2,952	297	71,247	1,187,131	822,514	153,795	151,263	2,533
Red River	13,223	748	400,935	4,611,824	17,104,239	689,857	537,207	152,650
Reeves	9,039	1,175	684,376	2,708,547	3,233,979	485,331	409,054	76,277
Refugio	6,840	464	595,591	2,171,720	2,996,911	418,079	322,917	95,161
Roberts	1,116	241	72,690	792,897	206,855	54,544	53,852	692
Robertson	13,707	625	561,165	3,518,589	4,588,631	704,363	503,044	201,319
Rockwall	35,483	317	1,037,803	3,394,071	8,153,884	2,266,667	737,691	1,528,975
Runnels	12,213	735	327,147	5,461,125	272,924	745,744	543,794	201,950
Rusk	40,148	1,152	1,158,823	5,675,081	699,259	2,348,308	911,769	1,436,539
Sabine	10,002	472	297,974	2,852,484	2,673,525	594,988	473,779	121,209
San Augustine	8,054	525	294,349	1,721,031	2,748,959	488,196	420,317	67,880
San Jacinto	18,094	506	655,005	2,134,921	1,785,551	993,404	487,346	506,058
San Patricio	50,467	895	1,617,120	2,975,572	24,077,019	2,987,064	1,167,707	1,819,358
San Saba	6,728	427	148,061	1,258,328	1,155,758	380,911	371,003	9,908
Schleicher	3,465	362	123,470	627,213	5,949	182,989	180,629	2,360
Scurry	18,003	676	496,317	1,936,629	2,442,390	1,200,934	669,685	531,250
Shackelford	3,682	353	151,192	2,600,243	3,878,077	221,201	217,599	3,602
Shelby	21,441	858	855,687	2,683,480	5,779,079	1,530,021	740,933	789,088
Sherman	3,169	429	215,325	1,443,523	212,532	192,720	190,181	2,539
Smith	161,844	1,499	3,990,516	10,396,832	25,248,063	9,460,897	3,274,258	6,186,639
Somervell	6,264	184	175,327	1,157,673	233,003	293,082	210,642	82,440
Starr	24,998	463	825,248	1,410,337	10,959,489	1,477,068	720,598	756,471
Stephens	9,857	559	221,312	1,889,291	589,821	557,294	445,013	112,281
Sterling	1,672	240	156,137	508,185	4,135,780	72,404	69,673	2,732
Stonewall	2,216	329	91,836	1,189,466	2,028,583	138,055	136,710	1,345
Sutton	5,961	592	385,392	1,135,104	8,825,531	372,156	257,289	114,868
Swisher	7,068	808	342,977	1,507,171	1,297,018	424,560	385,252	39,308
Tarrant	1,159,748	2,821	22,843,076	24,521,364	126,379,818	70,161,732	21,475,911	48,685,821
Taylor	112,898	1,157	1,883,997	5,008,477	7,986,852	6,875,744	2,446,452	4,429,292
Terrell	1,103	352	79,223	794,885	662,059	54,849	54,031	818
Terry	12,800	631	394,420	1,282,404	2,416,888	895,311	570,847	324,464
Throckmorton	1,959	341	74,483	1,416,120	257,085	99,658	98,271	1,386
Titus	26,161	540	902,359	3,203,228	6,005,305	1,463,996	771,875	692,121
Tom Green	93,924	949	1,266,866	4,520,097	17,360,629	5,587,444	1,984,762	3,602,682
Travis	551,021	1,585	12,039,237	11,882,778	71,380,063	36,451,480	12,318,391	24,133,088
Trinity	12,136	429	335,310	1,425,282	2,490,965	649,701	424,891	224,810
Tyler	18,006	510	539,038	2,295,985	1,222,756	941,655	523,494	418,161
Upshur	31,922	744	863,563	3,372,451	8,408,045	1,669,472	745,572	923,899
Upton	3,415	388	142,624	761,907	308,218	188,221	161,177	27,044
Uvalde	19,913	719	585,046	3,040,754	1,042,708	1,276,640	620,253	656,386
Val Verde	33,471	675	434,694	1,655,549	7,844,651	1,924,866	835,061	1,089,804
Van Zandt	48,721	1,158	1,790,675	4,578,372	5,899,163	2,616,223	1,084,281	1,531,942
Victoria	76,168	716	1,622,761	3,218,794	17,270,930	4,237,987	1,327,717	2,910,270
Walker	36,995	783	1,589,125	5,577,106	4,927,101	2,207,560	1,005,695	1,201,863
Waller	34,974	550	1,144,708	4,649,165	3,537,553	2,037,231	1,404,170	633,061
Ward	10,897	672	472,369	1,740,120	711,491	628,056	391,918	236,138
Washington	30,133	627	835,576	3,521,478	8,642,414	1,919,225	841,393	1,077,832
Webb	93,734	925	1,908,402	3,614,000	24,689,772	6,915,215	1,922,499	4,992,716
Wharton	37,769	883	1,334,424	3,140,243	1,444,002	2,429,025	961,606	1,467,419
Wheeler	5,730	670	508,403	2,323,695	14,357,169	297,018	293,095	3,923
Wichita	112,174	1,063	1,766,288	4,216,961	12,618,428	6,097,866	1,737,169	4,360,696
Wilbarger	13,932	723	519,323	1,785,052	1,096,221	778,332	583,194	195,138
Willacy	12,167	478	393,656	2,581,021	2,285,509	724,066	512,960	211,105
Williamson	183,117	1,412	4,562,052	7,386,537	17,673,035	10,801,786	3,461,490	7,340,296
Wilson	25,545	739	648,178	2,902,457	669,151	1,383,921	719,318	664,602
Winkler	7,080	295	152,453	1,008,129	739,784	422,597	329,722	92,875
Wise	50,839	841	1,666,846	3,006,537	8,570,125	3,238,596	1,311,092	1,927,504
Wood	38,412	892	739,140	3,928,676	4,009,909	1,920,604	725,239	1,195,365
Yoakum	8,414	427	203,403	1,181,755	129,773	562,018	438,186	123,832
Young	20,297	711	342,479	2,614,375	330,061	1,259,417	658,416	601,002
Zapata	6,684	250	372,203	2,075,343	2,765,940	377,128	267,986	109,141
Zavala	6,216	556	239,617	2,080,910	561,957	360,313	284,132	76,181
State Totals	16,150,654	184,576	366,792,959	$842,097,369	$2,443,949,031	$985,512,576	$358,555,031	$626,957,545

Motor Vehicle Accidents, Losses

Year	No. Killed	†No. Injured	No. Fatal	Accidents by Kinds † No. Injury	† No. Non-Injury	† Total	‡ Vehicle Miles Traveled *Number	Deaths per 100 million miles	Economic Loss
1960	2,254	127,980	1,842	71,100	239,300	312,242	46,352,734,855	4.9	$ 350,022,500
1961	2,314	132,570	1,899	73,650	248,600	324,149	47,937,315,761	4.8	356,112,000
1962	2,421	144,943	2,002	80,524	277,680	360,206	49,882,977,516	4.9	387,843,000
1963	2,729	161,543	2,251	89,746	307,920	399,917	52,324,589,656	5.2	432,715,000
1964	3,006	182,081	2,486	101,156	351,120	454,762	55,677,488,273	5.4	486,846,000
1965	3,028	186,062	2,460	103,368	365,160	470,988	*52,163,239,027	5.8	498,087,000
1966	3,406	208,310	2,784	115,728	406,460	524,972	55,260,849,798	6.2	557,414,000
1967	3,367	205,308	2,778	114,060	768,430	885,268	58,123,603,943	5.8	793,094,000
1968	3,481	216,972	2,902	120,540	816,830	940,272	62,794,494,339	5.5	836,802,000
1969	3,551	223,000	2,913	124,000	850,000	976,913	67,742,000,000	5.2	955,300,000
1970	3,560	223,000	2,965	124,000	886,000	1,012,965	‡ 68,031,000,000	5.2	1,042,200,000
1971	3,594	224,000	2,993	124,000	890,000	1,016,993	70,709,000,000	5.1	1,045,000,000
1972	3,688	128,158	3,099	83,607	346,292	432,998	76,690,000,000	4.8	1,035,000,000
1973	3,692	132,635	3,074	87,631	373,521	464,226	80,615,000,000	4.6	1,035,000,000
1974	3,046	123,611	2,626	83,341	348,227	434,194	78,290,000,000	3.9	1,095,000,000
1975	3,429	138,962	2,945	92,510	373,141	468,596	84,575,000,000	4.1	1,440,000,000
1976	3,230	145,282	2,780	96,348	380,075	479,203	91,279,000,000	3.5	1,485,000,000
1977	3,698	161,635	3,230	106,923	393,848	504,001	96,998,000,000	3.8	1,960,000,000
1978	¶ 3,980	178,228	3,468	117,998	**304,830	**426,296	102,624,000,000	3.9	2,430,000,000
1979	4,229	184,550	3,685	122,793	322,336	448,814	101,909,000,000	4.1	2,580,000,000
1980	4,424	185,964	3,863	123,577	305,500	432,940	103,255,000,000	4.3	3,010,000,000
1981	4,701	206,196	4,137	136,396	317,484	458,017	111,036,000,000	4.2	3,430,000,000
1982	4,271	204,666	3,752	135,859	312,159	451,770	†† 124,910,000,000	3.4	3,375,000,000
1983	3,823	208,157	¶ 3,328	137,695	302,876	443,899	129,309,000,000	3.0	3,440,000,000
1984	3,913	220,720	3,466	145,543	293,285	442,294	137,280,000,000	2.9	§ 3,795,000,000
1985	3,682	231,009	3,270	151,657	300,531	452,188	143,500,000,000	2.6	3,755,000,000
1986	3,568	234,120	3,121	154,514	298,079	452,593	150,474,000,000	2.4	3,782,000,000
1987	3,261	226,895	2,881	146,913	246,175	395,969	151,221,000,000	2.2	3,913,000,000
1988	3,395	238,845	3,004	152,004	237,703	392,711	152,819,000,000	2.2	4,515,000,000
1989	3,361	243,030	2,926	153,356	233,967	390,249	159,679,000,000	2.1	4,873,000,000
1990	3,243	262,576	2,882	162,424	216,140	381,446	163,103,000,000	2.0	4,994,000,000
1991	3,079	263,430	2,690	161,470	207,288	371,448	162,780,000,000	1.9	5,604,000,000
1992	3,057	282,025	2,690	170,513	209,152	382,355	162,769,000,000	1.9	6,725,000,000
1993	3,037	298,891	2,690	178,194	209,533	390,417	167,988,000,000	1.8	§ 11,784,000,000
1994	3,142	326,837	2,710	192,014	219,890	414,614	172,976,000,000	1.8	12,505,000,000
1995	3,172	334,259	2,790	196,093	152,190	351,073	183,103,000,000	1.7	§ 13,005,000,000
1996	3,738	350,397	3,247	204,635	90,261	298,143	187,064,000,000	2.0	7,766,000,000
1997	3,508	347,881	3,079	205,595	97,315	305,989	194,665,000,000	1.8	$ 7,662,000,000

*Vehicle miles traveled since 1964 were estimated on the basis of new data furnished by U.S. Bureau of Public Roads through National Safety Council.

† In August 1967, amended estimating formula received from National Safety Council. Starting with 1972, actual reported injuries are listed rather than estimates.

‡ Vehicle miles traveled estimated by Texas Highway Department starting with 1970. Method of calculation varies from that used for prior years.

§ Economic loss formula changed. Beginning in July 1995, only property damage accidents having at least one vehicle towed due to damages is tabulated.

¶ Change in counting fatalities. In 1978, counted when injury results in death within 90 days of accident. In 1983, counted when injury results in death within 30 days.

**Total accidents and non-injury accidents for 1978 and after cannot be compared with years prior to 1978 due to changes in reporting laws.

†† Method of calculating vehicle miles traveled revised for 1982 by the Texas Department of Transportation. The 1981 mileage has been adjusted for comparison purposes.

Source: Analysis Section, Accident Records Bureau of the **Texas Department of Public Safety**, Austin.

Drivers' Licenses Issued

The following report from the Texas Department of Public Safety shows the number of drivers' licenses issued during the fiscal year and total drivers records on file at the end of each fiscal year.

Year ending Aug. 31:	*Licenses Issued during year	Total drivers records on file
1998	4,852,046	14,717,414
1997	4,996,774	14,408,399
1996	4,876,793	14,103,325
1995	4,373,019	13,785,992
1994	4,459,076	13,293,255
1993	4,484,179	13,293,255
1992	4,411,473	13,140,171

Year ending Aug. 31:	*Licenses Issued during year	Total drivers records on file
1991	3,998,300	13,011,502
1990	4,205,385	11,738,602
1989	4,397,140	11,672,696
1988	4,130,447	11,641,984
1987	3,886,622	11,550,219
1986	4,325,742	11,436,780
1985	4,677,788	11,241,367
1984	4,498,902	11,009,567
1983	4,090,602	10,805,539
1982	4,281,652	10,463,962
1981	3,818,303	9,909,721
1980	3,699,543	9,551,683
1979	3,616,754	9,189,198

Year ending Aug. 31:	*Licenses Issued during year	Total drivers records on file
1978	3,529,926	8,805,604
1977	3,418,606	8,420,678
1976	3,233,610	8,127,188
1975	2,980,024	7,806,703
1974	2,887,456	7,588,372
1973	2,807,828	7,334,913
1972	2,573,010	7,098,425
1971	2,418,170	6,768,319
1970	2,321,416	6,420,602
1969	3,403,122	6,035,944
1968	3,603,082	5,849,126
1967	3,516,794	5,772,852

*Includes renewals during year.

Amtrak Passengers On/Off at Texas Stations, 1990-1998

City	1998	1997	1996	1995	1994	1993	1992	1991	1990
Alpine	1,868	2,054	2,284	2,503	2,746	2,873	2,312	1,718	1,754
Austin	10,245	9,287	10,112	10,449	13,211	20,290	19,633	22,795	18,913
Beaumont	2,070	2,333	2,483	2,578	2,362	2,671	2,945	3,026	3,677
Cleburne	545	654	616	669	859	1,865	2,350	2,845	3,579
College Stat.-Bryan	—	—	—	—	4,287	10,603	10,687	10,582	8,370
Corsicana	—	—	—	—	889	1,985	2,110	2,141	2,380
Dallas	22,955	23,586	23,301	36,673	46,139	74,680	69,062	76,695	64,350
Del Rio	1,031	1,306	1,207	1,383	1,444	1,245	1,122	1,136	1,235
El Paso	12,388	11,126	14,977	17,729	22,099	22,193	19,300	18,591	19,676
Fort Worth	9,402	10,600	9,643	10,064	12,577	21,773	22,607	23,926	23,623
Hearne	—	—	—	—	289	374			
Houston	15,633	20,844	21,453	32,186	35,274	50,332	48,440	55,297	47,514
Longview	12,377	17,359	18,297	7,442	7,556	11,429	10,426	11,431	9,519
Marshall	2,346	2,633	3,274	4,147	4,870	7,985	8,389	8,349	6,901
McGregor	1,310	1,491	1,301	1,278	1,692	3,203	2,670	3,202	3,099
Mineola	1,473	1,787	1,312	—	—	—	—	—	—
San Antonio	46,838	44,091	32,202	33,443	38,839	51,730	46,217	48,667	43,186
Sanderson	190	223	—	—	365	313	297	380	413
San Marcos	757	754	793	869	1,264	2,067	1,805	2,541	2,211
Taylor	859	1,201	1,351	1,439	1,617	3,317	3,214	4,596	4,626
Temple	5,487	3,126	2,738	2,985	4,033	8,155	6,994	7,478	7,495
Texarkana	—	—	—	—	5,843	8,334	—	—	—
Totals	147,774	135,695	147,944	170,183	208,255	307,417	280,620	305,396	272,521

Source: Amtrak (National Railroad Passenger Corporation) 1999.

Statistical History of Railroad Operation in Texas, 1891-1998

The table below shows development and trends of railroad line operations, freight tonnage, operating revenues and expenses in Texas since the Railroad Commission's first report in 1891.

Year	Average Miles Operated Including Trackage Rights	Tons Revenue Freight	Railway Operating Revenues	Railway Operating Expenses	Operating Ratio	Net Revenue From Railway Operations (before interest, taxes)	Amounts per mile operated			Freight Revenue Per Ton Mile
							Freight Revenue	Passenger Revenue	Net From Operations	
1998	11,383	277,630,918	$ 1,908,143,000	$ 1,867,220,000	106.13	$ 40,930,000	$ 151,837.00	...	$ -3,156.00	$.0212
1997	11,409	272,040,046	2,312,791,000	1,816,636,000	103.48	496,155,000	168,774.00	...	10,345.00	.0219
1996	12,282	304,172,611	2,431,840,000	1,884,316,000	78.22	67,641,300	187,870.00	...	12,857.00	.0031
1995	10,804	298,544,547	2,355,731,000	1,928,125,000	78.30	427,606,000	206,809.00	...	33,267.00	.0245
1994	10,543	296,607,281	2,313,085,000	1,741,625,620	83.35	571,459,380	201,497.00	...	47,908.00	.0243
1993	10,430	283,533,150	2,265,753,000	1,793,032,000	80.93	472,721,000	201,524.00	...	39,667.00	.0260
1992	10,522	270,172,326	2,213,517,000	1,786,709,000	87.60	426,808,000	188,872.00	...	30,633.00	.0276
1991	11,396	262,484,463	2,110,479,000	1,886,405,000	89.40	223,975,000	162,630.00	...	8,700.00	.0260
1990	11,541	253,778,285	2,061,579,000	1,709,369,000	89.00	352,210,000	161,178.00	...	22,984.00	.0270
1989	12,225	265,583,737	2,098,829,000	1,801,451,000	89.30	297,378,000	157,927.00	...	22,547.00	.0270
1988	12,337	315,073,199	2,111,522,843	1,678,802,000	82.90	415,169,412	143,882.00	...	23,999.00	.0270
1985	12,860	217,096,477	2,026,001,000	1,713,245,620	83.90	312,755,380	148,040.00	...	26,816.00	.0300
1980	13,075	268,445,039	2,064,108,000	1,761,650,000	85.34	304,742,000	151,918.00	...	23,310.00	.0268
1975	14,717	230,120,781	1,073,029,254	792,786,773	73.88	280,242,481	69,982.79	...	19,042.09	.0196
1970	14,683	211,069,076	655,638,834	504,146,691	76.89	151,492,143	42,245.42	$ 170.71	10,317.52	.0134
1965	15,214	181,553,163	502,191,485	380,412,080	75.75	121,779,405	29,754.73	605.40	8,004.43	.0118
1960	15,445	149,360,161	438,531,081	347,353,628	79.21	91,177,453	26,149.41	937.69	5,903.36	.0121
1955	16,151	166,742,660	450,865,455	341,963,345	75.85	108,902,110	24,482.83	1,085.84	6,742.75	.0134
1950	16,296	155,970,914	420,864,968	310,731,697	73.83	210,133,271	22,021.66	1,366.76	6,758.30	.0132
1945	16,376	159,795,571	390,672,459	263,883,854	67.54	126,788,605	17,635.26	4,370.32	7,742.36	.0102
1940	17,057	69,107,695	144,124,269	110,626,057	76.76	33,498,212	7,028.74	944.72	1,963.85	.0106
1935	17,296	61,452,202	117,611,146	93,681,088	79.65	23,930,058	5,579.27	802.07	1,383.58	.0112
1930	17,569	88,942,552	204,371,667	152,169,952	74.46	52,201,715	9,557.06	1,739.55	2,971.24	.0123
1925	16,647	90,338,397	227,252,064	169,382,692	74.54	57,869,372	10,653.42	2,673.33	3,476.36	.0142
1920	16,383	77,803,926	235,353,895	234,718,643	99.73	635,252	9,714.47	4,291.77	38.77	.0139
1915	16,294	54,354,684	107,414,011	85,900,985	79.97	21,513,026	4,504.81	1,809.82	1,320.29	.0100
1910	14,339	47,084,828	94,731,430	72,524,020	76.56	22,207,410	4,601.92	1,981.27	1,548.72	.0103
1905	11,671	30,653,070	68,145,132	52,411,748	76.91	15,733,384	4,044.80	1,493.65	1,348.12	.0108
1900	9,971	22,380,607	47,062,868	35,626,922	75.70	11,435,946	3,537.81	1,106.78	1,167.98	.0096
1895	9,354	15,591,262	39,387,869	28,864,994	73.28	10,522,875	3,159.04	984.73	1,124.98	.0130
1891	8,719	10,944,195	35,666,498	28,762,836	80.64	6,903,662	2,956.58	1,081.59	791.83	.0146

Aviation in Texas

Source: Texas Transportation Institute

Air transportation is a vital and vigorous part of the Texas economy, and Texans are major users of air transportation. The state's airport system ranks as one of the busiest and largest in the nation. The state's 46,285 active pilots represent 7.9 percent of the nation's pilots.

The State of Texas has long been committed to providing air transportation to the public. In 1945, the Texas Aeronautics Commission (TAC) was created and directed by the Legislature to encourage, foster and assist in the development of aeronautics within the state, and to encourage the establishment of airports and air navigational facilities.

The Commission's first annual report of Dec. 31, 1946, stated that Texas had 592 designated aiports and 7,756 civilian aircraft.

The commitment to providing air transportation was strengthened on Oct. 18, 1989, when the TAC became the Texas Department of Aviation (TDA). This commitment was further strengthened on Sept. 1, 1991, when the Texas Department of Transportation (TxDOT) was created and the TDA became the Aviation Division within the department.

In 1997, Texas' commercial service airports with scheduled passenger service enplaned more than 60.3 million passengers; scheduled carriers served 27 Texas airports in 24 Texas cities; and more than 91 percent of the state's population lived within 50 miles of an airport with scheduled air passenger service.

Dallas/Fort Worth International, Dallas Love Field, Houston George Bush Intercontinental and Houston's William P. Hobby together accounted for 81 percent of these enplanements.

Texas leads the nation in the number of landing facilities with more than 1,600, followed by California with approximately 1,000.

One of TxDOT's goals is to develop a statewide system of airports that will provide adequate air access to the population and economic centers of the state and will rank as one of the finest in the United States.

In the Texas Aeronautical System Plan, TxDOT has identified 301 airports that are needed to meet the forecast aviation demand and to maximize access by aircraft to the state's population, business and agricultural and mineral resource centers. Of these 301 airports, 27 are commercial service airports, 23 are reliever airports, 56 are transport airports, 127 are general utility airports

Passenger Enplanements by Airport

Source: Quarterly Aviation Activity Report, Texas Department of Transportation, Division of Aviation

City	1995	1997
Abilene	69,555	52,864
Amarillo	454,536	450,432
Austin-Mueller	2,658,039	2,948,701
Beaumont-Jefferson	108,520	112,456
Brownsville/S. Padre	—	81,439
Brownwood	2,015	—
College Station	85,331	93,331
Corpus Christi	511,841	471,914
DFW Intl.	27,013,761	28,152,220
Dallas Love Field	3,355,238	3,413,519
El Paso	1,835,162	1,634,578
Harlingen	489,082	461,619
Houston Intercont.	10,165,671	13,212,686
Houston Hobby	4,111,175	3,949,236
Houston Ellington	NA	50,503
Killeen	59,126	84,963
Laredo	59,948	67,664
Longview	33,761	26,779
Lubbock	602,680	592,101
McAllen	313,082	313,506
Midland	566,904	527,760
San Angelo	52,674	41,404
San Antonio	3,058,274	3,343,818
Temple	15,976	—
Texarkana	45,242	36,367
Tyler	78,524	69,639
Victoria	19,517	21,656
Waco	55,824	58,742
Wichita Falls	59,275	53,942
Total	**57,751,285**	**60,329,687**

and 68 are basic utility airports.

Commercial service airports provide scheduled passenger service. The reliever airports provide alternative landing facilities in the metropolitan areas separate from the commercial service airports and, together with the transport airports, provide access for business and executive turbine-powered aircraft.

The general and basic utility airports provide access

Airline Markets: Leading U.S. Routes, 1997

Rank, Route	Passengers
1. New York to-from Los Angeles	3.73 million
2. NY to-from Miami	3.09 million
3. NY to-from Chicago	2.98 million
4. NY to-from Boston	2.69 million
5. Honolulu to-from Maui	2.62 million
6. NY to-from San Francisco	2.61 million
7. NY to-from Orlando	2.45 million
8. NY to-from Washington	2.40 million
9. **Dallas/Fort Worth to-from Houston**	2.22 million
10. LA to-from Las Vegas	2.11 million

Air Transport Assoc. of America

Aircraft Departures, 1996

Rank, State	Takeoffs
1. **Texas**	887,547
2. California	825,095
3. Florida	506,156
4. Illinois	474,345
5. Georgia	369,105
6. New York	335,887
7. Pennsylvania	335,723
8. Ohio	314,615
9. Missouri	311,225
10. Colorado	258,735

FAA Statistical Handbook 1998

for single- and multi-engine piston-powered aircraft to smaller communities throughout the state.

TxDOT is charged by the legislature with planning, programming and implementing improvement projects at approximately 274 general aviation airports. In carrying out these responsibilities, TxDOT channels the Airport Improvement Program (AIP) funds provided by the Federal Aviation Administration for all general aviation airports in Texas.

Since 1993, TxDOT has participated in the FAA's state block grant demonstration program. Under this program, TxDOT assumes most of the FAA's responsibility for the administration of the AIP funds for general aviation airports.

The Aviation Facilities Development Program (AFDP) oversees planning and research, assists with engineering and technical services and provides financial assistance through state grants and loans to public bodies operating airports for the purpose of establishing, constructing, reconstructing, enlarging or repairing airports, airstrips or navigational facilities.

The 76th Legislature appropriated funds to TxDOT, which subsequently allocated a portion of those funds to the Aviation Division. TxDOT allocated approximately $15 million annually for the 2000-2001 biennium to the Aviation Division in order to help implement and administer the AFDP.

The Aeronautical Services and Informational Section provides specialized training programs, aeronautical publications and safety information to individuals and groups throughout the state who are involved or interested in aviation.

Scheduled passenger traffic (air carriers and commuters) experienced strong growth from 1995 to 1997. The growth has mainly been in the larger cities, Dallas, Houston, San Antonio and Austin all recorded increases in passenger enplanements.

According to FAA data, Texas leads the nation in aircraft departures and ranks second after California in passengers enplaned by scheduled air carriers.

Top Ten Texas Cities — 1997

Source: Quarterly Aviation Activity Report, Texas Dept. of Transportation, Division of Aviation.

City Rank	Enplaned Passengers	Percent Total	Operations Performed	Percent Total
1. Dallas-Fort Worth	31,565,739	52	1,163,053	23
2. Houston	17,212,425	29	778,336	15
3. San Antonio	3,343,818	6	257,053	5
4. Austin	2,948,701	5	201,107	4
5. El Paso	1,634,578	3	137,018	3
6. Lubbock	592,101	1	88,011	2
7. Midland-Odessa	527,760	0.8	83,696	2
8. Corpus Christi	471,914	0.8	123,684	2
9. Harlingen	461,619	0.8	63,969	1
10. Amarillo	450,432	0.8	73,369	1

Air Traffic History

Source: FAA

Airline passenger traffic enplaned in Texas by scheduled certificated carriers.

Year	Passengers
1957	2,808,558
1967	7,983,634
1977	15,871,147
1978	18,241,029
1979	21,546,794
1980	25,303,214
1981	27,449,480
1982	29,541,788
1983	30,853,297
1984	35,130,762
1985	38,913,027
1986	39,957,392
1987	41,493,225
1988	42,655,971
1989	45,348,326
1990	46,435,641
1991	45,825,027
1992	48,869,034
1993	50,594,658
1994	55,633,180
1995	57,751,285
1996	60,344,460
1997	60,329,687

According to aviation industry officials, the state of general aviation is strong. For the third consecutive year, the industry has set new records for billings. In 1998, total billings reached $5.9 billion, which was up 25.7 percent from 1997. For the fourth consecutive year, total aircraft shipments increased in 1998, with total shipments increasing 41.5 percent over 1997.

These increases are in both piston- and turbine-powered aircraft. In 1998, piston-engine shipments increased 55.7 percent over the previous year, with 58.7 percent and 22.5 percent increases for single-engine and multi-engine aircraft respectively. Turbine-engine aircraft shipments increased 17.5 percent in 1998 over 1997, with 14.8 percent and 19.3 percent increases in turboprop and turbofan aircraft respectively.

General aviation remains a dominant force in aviation and it is expected that it will continue to play a very large role. The average general aviation aircraft fleet is expected to increase by one percent per year over the next decade. Increases are expected in all categories including single-engine piston, multi-engine piston, turbine-powered and rotorcraft aircraft. Continued demand in both the new and used markets, an array of new product developments, and heavy backlogs in the supply chain all point to a bright outlook for general aviation. Business aviation continues to lead the way as a strong national economy and fractional ownership programs stimulate demand. ☆

Nonfuel Mineral Production and Value, 1996, 1997 and 1998

Source: U.S. Dept. of the Interior, Bureau of Mines (Production measured by mine shipments, sales or marketable production, including consumption by producer.)

Mineral	1996		1997		1998*	
	Production	Value (add 000)	Production	Value (add 000)	Production	Value (add 000)
Cement:						
Masonry (thous. metric tons).	216	$20,300	203	$18,900	207	$19,900
Portland (thous. metric tons)	8,240	532,000	8,280	576,000	8,580	610,000
††Clays:						
Ball (thous. metric tons).	101	**	**	**	**	**
Common (thous. metric tons)	2,290	15,000	2,150	13,600	2,200	13,800
Kaolin (thous. metric tons).	28	**	35	7,600	**	**
Gemstones	†	511	†	11	†	11
Gypsum (thous. metric tons)	2,240	12,100	2,260	15,700	2,250	16,300
Lime (thous. metric tons)	1,360	87,100	1,470	91,500	1,520	91,900
Salt (thous. metric tons)	9,700	88,900	9,780	91,000	9,700	89,800
Sand and gravel:						
Construction (thous. metric tons)	61,300	278,000	60,100	284,000	67,500	328,000
Industrial (thous. metric tons)	1,420	38,200	1,830	48,800	1,870	55,500
Stone:						
Crushed (thous. metric tons)	86,500	341,000	81,200	347,000	93,000	465,000
Dimension (metric tons).	86,600	21,100	35,300	11,300	35,000	11,200
Talc and pyrophyllite (metric tons)	225,000	5,100	274,000	6,760	**	**
‡Combined value	. . .	293,000	. . .	281,000	. . .	223,000
‡‡Total Texas Values.	. . .	$1,730,000	. . .	$1,790,000	. . .	$1,920,000

*Estimated and preliminary. † Not available.
**Data withheld to avoid disclosing proprietary data; value included with "Combined value."
‡Includes value of clays [bentonite (1997-98), fuller's earth], greensand marl, helium, magnesium compounds, magnesium metal, sodium sulfate (natural), sulfur (Frasch), and values indicated by symbol **.
††Excludes certain clays; kind and value included in "Combined value."
‡‡Data do not add to total shown because of independent rounding.

Nonpetroleum Minerals

The nonpetroleum minerals that occur in Texas constitute a long list. Some are currently mined; some may have a potential for future development; some are minor occurrences only. Although overshadowed by the petroleum, natural gas and natural gas liquids that are produced in the state, many of the nonpetroleum minerals are, nonetheless, important to the economy. In 1998, they were valued at an estimated $1.92 billion. Texas is annually **among the nation's leading states in value of non-petroleum mineral production**. In 1995, **Texas ranked sixth nationally** in total mineral output.

The **Bureau of Economic Geology**, which functions as the state geological survey of Texas, revised the following information about nonpetroleum minerals for this edition of the Texas Almanac. Publications of the bureau, on file in many libraries, contain more detailed information. Among the items available are a map, "Mineral Resources of Texas," showing locations of resource access of many nonpetroleum minerals, and a computer-generated list of Texas nonpetroleum mineral producers.

A catalog of Bureau publications is also available free on request from the Bureau Publications Sales, University Station, Box X, Austin, TX 78713-7508; (512) 471-7144.

Texas' nonpetroleum minerals are as follows:

ALUMINUM — No aluminum ores are mined in Texas, but three Texas plants process aluminum materials in one or more ways. Plants in San Patricio and Calhoun counties produce **aluminum oxide (alumina)** from imported raw ore **(bauxite)**, and a plant in Milam County reduces the oxide to aluminum.

ASBESTOS — Small occurrences of amphibole-type asbestos have been found in the state. In West Texas, **richterite**, a white, long-fibered amphibole, is associated with some of the **talc deposits** northwest of **Allamoore** in Hudspeth County. Another type, **tremolite**, has been found in the **Llano Uplift** of Central Texas where it is associated with **serpentinite** in eastern Gillespie and western Blanco County. No asbestos is mined in Texas.

ASPHALT (Native) — Asphalt-bearing Cretaceous lime-

stones crop out in Burnet, Kinney, Pecos, Reeves, Uvalde and other counties. The most significant deposit is in southwestern Uvalde County where asphalt occurs naturally in the pore spaces of the Anacacho Limestone. The material is quarried and used extensively as **road-paving material**. Asphalt-bearing sandstones occur in Anderson, Angelina, Cooke, Jasper, Maverick, Montague, Nacogdoches, Uvalde, Zavala and other counties.

BARITE — Deposits of a heavy, nonmetallic mineral, barite (barium sulphate), have been found in many localities, including Baylor, Brown, Brewster, Culberson, Gillespie, Howard, Hudspeth, Jeff Davis, Kinney, Llano, Live Oak, Taylor, Val Verde and Webb counties. During the 1960s, there was small, intermittent production in the **Seven Heart Gap** area of the **Apache Mountains** in Culberson County, where barite was mined from open pits. Most of the deposits are known to be relatively small, but the Webb County deposit has not been evaluated. Grinding plants, which prepare barite mined outside of Texas for use chiefly as a **weighting agent** in well-drilling muds and as a **filler**, are located in Brownsville, Corpus Christi, El Paso, Galena Park, Galveston, and Houston.

BASALT (TRAP ROCK) — Masses of basalt — a hard, dark-colored, fine-grained igneous rock — crop out in Kinney, Travis, Uvalde and several other counties along the **Balcones Fault Zone**, and also in the Trans-Pecos area of West Texas. Basalt is quarried near Knippa in Uvalde County for use as **road-building material, railroad ballast and other aggregate.**

BENTONITE (see **CLAYS**).

BERYLLIUM — Occurrences of beryllium minerals at several Trans-Pecos localities have been recognized for several years. Evaluation and development of a beryllium prospect near **Sierra Blanca** in Hudspeth County, a portion of which is on state-owned land, is now underway. **Behoite** and other beryllium minerals are associated with **fluorspar** at this site.

BRINE (see also **SALT, SODIUM SULPHATE**) — Many wells in Texas produce brine by solution mining of subsurface salt deposits, mostly in West Texas counties such as Andrews, Crane, Ector, Loving, Midland, Pecos, Reeves, Ward and others. These wells in the Permian Basin dissolve salt from the **Salado Formation,** an enormous salt deposit that extends in the subsurface from north of the Big Bend northward to Kansas, has an east-west width of 150 to 200 miles, and may have several hundred feet of net salt thickness. The majority of the brine is used in the **petroleum industry,** but it also is used in **water softening, the chemical industry** and other uses. Three Gulf Coast counties, Fort Bend, Duval and Jefferson, have brine stations that produce from **salt domes.**

BUILDING STONE (DIMENSION STONE) — Granite and **limestone** currently are quarried for use as dimension stone. The granite quarries are located in Burnet, Gillespie, Llano and Mason counties; the limestone quarries are in Shackelford and Williamson counties. Past production of limestone for use as dimension stone has been reported in Burnet, Gillespie, Jones, Tarrant, Travis and several other counties. There has also been production of **sandstone** in various counties for use as dimension stone.

CEMENT MATERIALS — Cement is currently manufactured at 13 plants in Bexar, Comal, Dallas, Ector, Ellis, Hays, McLennan, Nolan, and Potter counties. Many of these plants utilize Cretaceous limestones and shales or clays as raw materials for the cement. On the Texas High Plains, a cement plant near Amarillo uses impure **caliche** as the chief raw material. **Iron oxide,** also a constituent of cement, is available from the iron ore deposits of East Texas and from smelter slag. **Gypsum,** added to the cement as a retarder, is found chiefly in North Central Texas, Central Texas and the Trans-Pecos area.

CHROMIUM — Chromite-bearing rock has been found in several small deposits around the margin of the Coal Creek **serpentinite** mass in northeastern Gillespie County and northwestern Blanco County. Exploration has not revealed significant deposits.

CLAYS — Texas has an abundance and variety of ceramic and non-ceramic clays and is one of the country's leading producers of clay products.

Almost any kind of clay, ranging from common clay used to make ordinary brick and tile to clays suitable for manufacture of specialty whitewares, can be used for ceramic purposes. **Fire clay** suitable for use as **refractories** occurs chiefly in East and North Central Texas; **ball clay,** a high-quality plastic ceramic clay, is found locally in East Texas.

Ceramic clay suitable for quality structural clay products such as **structural building brick, paving brick and drain tile** is especially abundant in East and North Central Texas. Common clay suitable for use in the manufacture of cement and ordinary brick is found in most counties of the state. Many of the Texas clays will expand or bloat upon rapid firing and are suitable for the manufacture of lightweight aggregate, which is used mainly in concrete blocks and highway surfacing.

Nonceramic clays are utilized without firing. They are used primarily as **bleaching and adsorbent clays, fillers, coaters, additives, bonding clays, drilling muds, catalysts** and potentially as sources of alumina. Most of the nonceramic clays in Texas are **bentonites and fuller's earth.** These occur extensively in the Coastal Plain and locally in the High Plains and Big Bend areas. **Kaolin clays** in parts of East Texas are potential sources of such nonceramic products as **paper coaters and fillers, rubber fillers and drilling agents.** Relatively high in alumina, these clays also are a potential source of metallic aluminum.

COAL (see also LIGNITE) — **Bituminous coal,** which occurs in North Central, South and West Texas, was a significant energy source in Texas prior to the large-scale development of oil and gas. During the period from 1895 to 1943, Texas mines produced more than 25 million tons of coal. The mines were inactive for many years, but the renewed interest in coal as a major energy source prompted a revaluation of Texas' coal deposits. In the late 1970s, bituminous coal production resumed in the state on a limited scale when mines were opened in Coleman, Erath and Webb counties.

Much of the state's bituminous coal occurs in North Central Texas. Deposits are found there in Pennsylvanian rocks within a large area that includes Coleman, Eastland, Erath, Jack, McCulloch, Montague, Palo Pinto, Parker, Throckmorton, Wise, Young and other counties. Before the general availability of oil and gas, underground coal mines near **Thurber, Bridgeport, Newcastle, Strawn** and other points annually produced significant coal tonnages. Preliminary evaluations indicate substantial amounts of coal may remain in the North Central Texas area. The coal seams there are generally no more than 30 inches thick and are commonly covered by well-consolidated overburden. Ash and sulphur content are high. Beginning in 1979, two bituminous coal mine operations in North Central Texas — one in southern Coleman County and one in northwestern Erath County — produced coal to be used as fuel by the cement industry. Neither mine is currently operating.

In South Texas, bituminous coal occurs in the Eagle Pass district of Maverick County, and bituminous **cannel coal** is present in the **Santo Tomas district** of Webb County. The Eagle Pass area was a leading coal-producing district in Texas during the late 1800s and early 1900s. The bituminous coal in that area, which occurs in the Upper Cretaceous Olmos Formation, has a high ash content and a moderate moisture and sulfur content. According to reports, Maverick County coal beds range from four to seven feet thick.

The **cannel coals** of western Webb County occur near the Rio Grande in middle Eocene strata. They were mined for more than 50 years and used primarily as a boiler fuel. Mining ceased from 1939 until 1978, when a surface mine was opened 30 miles northwest of Laredo to produce cannel coal for use as fuel in the cement industry and for export. An additional mine has since been opened in that county. Tests show that the coals of the Webb County Santo Tomas district have a high hydrogen content and yield significant amounts of gas and oil when distilled. They also have a high sulfur content. A potential use might be as a source of various petrochemical products.

Coal deposits in the Trans-Pecos country of West Texas include those in the Cretaceous rocks of the Terlingua area of Brewster County, the Eagle Spring area of Hudspeth County and the **San Carlos** area of Presidio County. The coal deposits in these areas are believed to have relatively little potential for development as a fuel. They have been sold in the past as a soil amendment (see **LEONARDITE**).

COPPER — Copper minerals have been found in the **Trans-Pecos** area of West Texas, in the **Llano Uplift** area of Central Texas and in redbed deposits of North Texas. No copper has been mined in Texas during recent years, and the total copper produced in the state has been relatively small. Past attempts to mine the North Texas and Llano Uplift copper deposits resulted in small shipments, but practically all the copper production in the state has been from the **Van Horn-Allamoore** district of Culberson and Hudspeth Counties in the Trans-Pecos area. Chief output was from the **Hazel copper-silver mine** of Culberson County that yielded over 1 million pounds of copper during 1891-1947. Copper ores and concentrates from outside of Texas are processed at **smelters** in El Paso and Amarillo.

CRUSHED STONE — Texas is among the leading states in the production of crushed stone. Most production consists of **limestone**; other kinds of crushed stone produced in the state include **basalt (trap rock), dolomite, granite, marble, rhyolite, sandstone** and **serpentinite.** Large tonnages of crushed stone are used as **aggregate** in concrete, as **road material** and in the manufacture of cement and lime. Some is used as **riprap, terrazzo, roofing chips, filter material, fillers** and for other purposes.

DIATOMITE (DIATOMACEOUS EARTH) — Diatomite is a very lightweight siliceous material consisting of the remains of microscopic aquatic plants (diatoms). It is used chiefly as a **filter and filler**; other uses are for **thermal insulation,** as an **abrasive,** as an **insecticide carrier** and as a **lightweight aggregate,** and for other purposes. The diatomite was deposited in shallow fresh-water lakes that were present in the High Plains during portions of the Pliocene and Pleistocene epochs. Deposits have been found in Armstrong, Crosby, Dickens, Ector, Hartley and Lamb counties. No diatomite is mined in Texas.

DOLOMITE ROCK — Dolomite rock, which consists largely of the mineral dolomite (calcium-magnesium carbonate), commonly is associated with limestone in Texas. Areas in which dolomite rock occurs include Central Texas, the Callahan Divide and parts of the Edwards Plateau, High Plains and West Texas. Some of the principal deposits of dolomite rock are found in Bell, Brown, Burnet, Comanche, Edwards, El Paso, Gillespie, Lampasas, Mills, Nolan, Taylor and Williamson counties. Dolomite rock can be used as crushed stone (although much of Texas dolomite is soft and not a good aggregate material), in the manufacture of lime and as a source of **magnesium.**

FELDSPAR — Large crystals and crystal fragments of feldspar minerals occur in the Precambrian pegmatite rocks that crop out in the **Llano Uplift** area of Central Texas — including Blanco, Burnet, Gillespie, Llano and Mason counties — and in the **Van Horn area** of Culberson and Hudspeth Counties in West Texas. Feldspar has been mined in Llano County for use as **roofing granules** and as a **ceramic material,** but is not currently mined anywhere within the state.

FLUORSPAR — The mineral fluorite (calcium fluoride), which is known commercially as fluorspar, occurs in both Central and West Texas. In Central Texas, the deposits that have been found in Burnet, Gillespie and Mason counties are not considered adequate to sustain mining operations. In West Texas, deposits have been found in Brewster, El Paso, Hudspeth, Jeff Davis and Presidio counties. Fluorspar has been mined in the **Christmas Mountains** of Brewster County and processed in Marathon. Former West Texas mining activity in the **Eagle Mountains** district of Hudspeth County resulted in the production of approximately 15,000 short tons of fluorspar during the peak years of 1942-1950. No production has been reported in Hudspeth County since that period. Imported fluorspar is processed in Brownsville, Eagle Pass, El Paso and Houston. Fluorspar is used in the **steel, chemical, aluminum, magnesium, ceramics and glass industries** and for various other purposes.

FULLER'S EARTH (see CLAY).

GOLD — No major deposits of gold are known in Texas. Small amounts have been found in the **Llano Uplift** region of Central Texas and in West Texas; minor occurrences have been reported on the **Edwards Plateau** and the **Gulf Coastal Plain** of Texas. Nearly all of the gold produced in the state came as a by-product of silver and lead mining at **Presidio mine,** near **Shafter,** in Presidio County. Additional small quantities were produced as a by-product of copper mining in Culberson County and from residual soils developed from gold-bearing quartz stringers in metamorphic rocks in Llano County. No gold mining has been reported in Texas since 1952. Total **gold production** in the state, 1889-1952, amounted to more than 8,419 troy ounces according to U.S. Bureau of Mines figures. Most of the production — at least 73 percent and probably more — came from the Presidio mine.

GRANITE — Granites in shades of red and gray and related intrusive igneous rocks occur in the **Llano Uplift** of Central Texas and in the **Trans-Pecos** country of West Texas. Deposits are found in Blanco, Brewster, Burnet, El Paso, Gillespie, Hudspeth, Llano, McCulloch, Mason, Presidio and other counties. Quarries in Burnet, Gillespie, Llano and Mason counties produce Precambrian granite for a variety of uses as **dimension stone and crushed stone.**

GRAPHITE — Graphite, a soft, dark-gray mineral, is a form of very high-grade carbon. It occurs in Precambrian schist rocks of the **Llano Uplift** of Central Texas, notably in Burnet and Llano counties. Crystalline-flake graphite ore formerly was mined from open pits in the **Clear Creek area** of western Burnet County and processed at a plant near the mine. The mill now occasionally grinds imported material. Uses of natural crystalline graphite are **refractories, steel production, pencil leads, lubricants, foundry facings and crucibles** and for other purposes.

GRINDING PEBBLES (ABRASIVE STONES) — Flint pebbles, suitable for use in **tube-mill grinding,** are found in the **Gulf Coastal Plain** where they occur in gravel deposits along rivers and in upland areas. Grinding pebbles are produced from **Frio River terrace** deposits near the McMullen-Live Oak county line, but the area is now part of the Choke Canyon Reservoir area.

GYPSUM — Gypsum is widely distributed in Texas.

Chief deposits are bedded gypsum in the area east of the **High Plains,** in the **Trans-Pecos** country and in **Central Texas.** It also occurs in **salt-dome caprocks** of the Gulf Coast. The massive, granular variety known as rock gypsum is the kind most commonly used by industry. Other varieties include **alabaster, satin spar and selenite.**

Gypsum is one of the important industrial minerals in Texas. Bedded gypsum is produced from surface mines in Culberson, Fisher, Gillespie, Hardeman, Hudspeth, Kimble, Nolan and Stonewall counties. Gypsum was formerly mined at **Gyp Hill salt dome** in Brooks County and at **Hockley salt dome** in Harris County. Most of the gypsum is calcined and used in the manufacture of **gypsum wallboard, plaster, joint compounds** and other construction products. Crude gypsum is used chiefly as a **retarder in portland cement** and as a **soil conditioner.**

HELIUM — Texas is a leading producer of this very light, non-flammable, chemically inert gas. Helium is extracted from natural gas of the **Panhandle area** at the **U.S. Bureau of Mines Exell plant** near Masterson in Moore County and at two privately owned plants in Moore and Hansford counties. As a conservation measure, the Bureau of Mines injects the helium that is not sold when the gas is produced into the **Cliffside gas field** near Amarillo for storage. Helium is used in **cryogenics, welding, pressurizing and purging, leak detection, synthetic breathing mixtures** and for other purposes.

IRON — Iron oxide (**limonite, goethite and hematite**) and **iron carbonate (siderite)** deposits occur widely in East Texas, notably in Cass, Cherokee, Marion and Morris counties, and also in Anderson, Camp, Harrison, Henderson, Nacogdoches, Smith, Upshur and other counties. **Magnetite (magnetic, black iron oxide)** occurs in Central Texas, including a deposit at **Iron Mountain** in Llano County. Hematite occurs in the **Trans-Pecos** area and in the **Llano Uplift** of Central Texas. The extensive deposits of **glauconite** (a complex silicate containing iron) that occur in East Texas and the hematitic and goethitic Cambrian sandstone that crops out in the northwestern Llano Uplift region are potential sources of low-grade iron ore.

Limonite and other East Texas iron ores are mined from open pits in Cherokee and Henderson counties for use in the preparation of **portland cement,** as a **weighting agent in well-drilling fluids,** as an **animal feed supplement** and for other purposes. East Texas iron ores also were mined in the past for use in the iron-steel industry.

KAOLIN (see CLAY).

LEAD AND ZINC — The lead mineral **galena (lead sulfide)** commonly is associated with zinc and silver. It formerly was produced as a by-product of West Texas silver mining, chiefly from the **Presidio mine at Shafter** in Presidio County, although lesser amounts were obtained at several other mines and prospects. Deposits of galena also are known to occur in Blanco, Brewster, Burnet, Gillespie and Hudspeth counties.

Zinc, primarily from the mineral **sphalerite (zinc sulphide),** was produced chiefly from the **Bonanza** and **Alice Ray** mines in the **Quitman Mountains** of Hudspeth County. In addition, small production was reported from several other areas, including the **Chinati** and **Montezuma mines** of Presidio County and the **Buck Prospect** in the **Apache Mountains** of Culberson County. Zinc mineralization also occurs in association with the lead deposits in Cambrian rocks of Central Texas.

LEONARDITE — Deposits of weathered (oxidized) low-Btu value bituminous coals, generally referred to as "leonardite," occur in Brewster County. The name leonardite is used for a mixture of chemical compounds that is high in humic acids. In the past, material from these deposits was sold as **soil conditioner.** Other uses of leonardite include **modification of viscosity of drill fluids and as sorbants in water-treatment.**

LIGHTWEIGHT AGGREGATE (see CLAY, DIATO-MITE, PERLITE, VERMICULITE).

LIGNITE — Lignite, a low-rank coal, is found in belts of Tertiary Eocene strata that extend across the Texas Gulf Coastal Plain from the Rio Grande in South Texas to the Arkansas and Louisiana borders in East Texas. The largest resources and best grades (approximately 6,500 BTU/pound) of lignite occur in the Wilcox Group of strata north of the Colorado River in East and Central Texas.

The near-surface lignite resources, occurring at depths of less than 200 feet in seams of three feet or thicker, are estimated at 23 billion short tons. **Recoverable reserves of strippable lignite** — those that can be economically mined under current conditions of price and technology — are estimated to be 9 billion to 11 billion short tons.

Additional lignite resources of the Texas Gulf Coastal Plain occur as deep-basin deposits. Deep-basin resources, those that occur at depths of 200 to 2,000 feet in seams of five feet or thicker, are comparable in magnitude to near-surface resources. The deep-basin lignites are a potential energy resource that conceivably could be utilized by *in situ* (in place) recovery methods such as underground gasification.

As with bituminous coal, lignite production was significant prior to the general availability of oil and gas. Remnants of old underground mines are common throughout the area of lignite occurrence. Large reserves of strippable lignite have again attracted the attention of energy suppliers, and Texas is now the nation's **6th leading producer of coal**, 99 percent of it lignite. Eleven large strip mines are now producing lignite that is burned for **mine-mouth electric-power generation**, and additional mines are planned. One of the currently operating mines is located in Milam County, where part of the electric power is used for **alumina reduction**. Other mines are in Atascosa, Bastrop, Freestone, Grimes, Harrison, Limestone, Rusk, Panola, Titus and Hopkins counties, where the electricity generated supplies municipal, domestic and industrial needs. Another Harrison County strip mine produces lignite that is used to make **activated carbon**.

LIME MATERIAL — Limestones, which are abundant in some areas of Texas, are heated to produce lime (calcium oxide) at a number of plants in the state. High-magnesium limestone and dolomite are used to prepare lime at a plant in Burnet County. Other lime plants are located in Bexar, Bosque, Comal, Hill, Johnson and Travis counties. Lime production captive to the kiln's operator occurs in several Texas counties. Lime is used in **soil stabilization, water purification, paper and pulp manufacture, metallurgy, sugar refining, agriculture, construction, removal of sulfur from stack gases** and for many other purposes.

LIMESTONE (see also **BUILDING STONE**) — Texas is one of the nation's leading producers of limestone, which is quarried in more than 60 counties. Limestone occurs in nearly all areas of the state with the exception of most of the Gulf Coastal Plain and High Plains. Although some of the limestone is quarried for use as **dimension stone**, most of the output is crushed for uses such as **bulk building materials (crushed stone, road base, concrete aggregate), chemical raw materials, fillers or extenders, lime and portland cement raw materials, agricultural limestone and removal of sulfur from stack gases**.

MAGNESITE — Small deposits of magnesite (natural magnesium carbonate) have been found in Precambrian rocks in Llano and Mason counties of Central Texas. At one time there was small-scale mining of magnesite in the area; some of the material was used as **agricultural stone** and as **terrazzo chips**. Magnesite also can be calcined to form **magnesia**, which is used in **metallurgical furnace refractories** and other products.

MAGNESIUM — On the Texas Gulf Coast in Brazoria County, magnesium chloride is **extracted from sea water** at a plant in Freeport and used to produce **magnesium compounds and magnesium metal**. During World War II, high-magnesium Ellenburger dolomite rock from Burnet County was used as magnesium ore at a plant near Austin.

MANGANESE — Deposits of manganese minerals, such as **braunite, hollandite and pyrolusite**, have been found in several areas, including Jeff Davis, Llano, Mason, Presidio and Val Verde counties. Known deposits are not large. Small shipments have been made from Jeff Davis, Mason and Val Verde counties, but no manganese mining has been reported in Texas since 1954.

MARBLE — Metamorphic and sedimentary marbles suitable for **monument and building stone** are found in the **Llano Uplift** and nearby areas of Central Texas and the **Trans-Pecos** area of West Texas. Gray, white, black, greenish black, light green, brown and cream-colored marbles occur in Central Texas in Burnet, Gillespie, Llano and Mason counties. West Texas metamorphic marbles include the bluish-white and the black marbles found southwest of Alpine in Brewster County and the white marble from **Marble Canyon** north of Van Horn in Culberson County. Marble can be used as **dimension stone**, **terrazzo and roofing aggregate** and for other purposes.

MERCURY (QUICKSILVER) — Mercury minerals, chiefly **cinnabar**, occur in the **Terlingua district** and nearby districts of southern Brewster and southeastern Presidio counties. Mining began there about 1894, and from 1905 to 1935, Texas was one of the nation's leading producers of quicksilver. Following World War II, a sharp drop in demand and price, along with depletion of developed ore reserves, caused abandonment of all the Texas mercury mines.

With a rise in the price, sporadic mining took place between 1951-1960. In 1965, when the price of mercury moved to a record high, renewed interest in the Texas mercury districts resulted in the reopening of several mines and the discovery of new ore reserves. By April 1972, however, the price had declined and the mines have reported no production since 1973.

MICA — Large crystals of flexible, transparent mica minerals in igneous pegmatite rocks and mica flakes in metamorphic schist rocks are found in the **Llano area** of Central Texas and the **Van Horn area** of West Texas. Most Central Texas deposits do not meet specifications for sheet mica, and although several attempts have been made to produce West Texas sheet mica in Culberson and Hudspeth counties, sustained production has not been achieved. A mica quarry operated for a short time in the early 1980s in the Van Horn Mountains of Culberson and Hudspeth counties to mine mica schist for use as an **additive in rotary drilling fluids**.

MOLYBDENUM — Small occurrences of molybdenite have been found in Burnet and Llano counties, and **wulfenite**, another molybdenum mineral, has been noted in rocks in the **Quitman Mountains** of Hudspeth County. Molybdenum minerals also occur at **Cave Peak** north of Van Horn in Culberson County, in the **Altuda Mountain area** of northwestern Brewster County and in association with uranium ores of the Gulf Coastal Plain.

PEAT — This spongy organic substance forms in bogs from plant remains. It has been found in the **Gulf Coastal Plain** in several localities including Gonzales, Guadalupe, Lee, Milam, Polk and San Jacinto counties. There has been intermittent, small-scale production of some of the peat for use as a **soil conditioner**.

PERLITE — Perlite, a glassy igneous rock, expands to a lightweight, porous mass when heated. It can be used as a **lightweight aggregate, filter aid, horticultural aggregate** and for other purposes. Perlite occurs in Presidio County, where it has been mined in the **Pinto Canyon area** north of the **Chinati Mountains**. No perlite is currently mined in Texas, but perlite mined outside of Texas is expanded at plants in Bexar, Dallas, El Paso, Guadalupe, Harris and Nolan counties.

PHOSPHATE — Rock phosphate is present in Paleozoic rocks in several areas of Brewster and Presidio counties in West Texas and in Central Texas, but the known deposits are not large. In Northeast Texas, sedimentary rock phosphate occurs in thin conglomeratic lenses in Upper Cretaceous and Tertiary rock units; possibly some of these low-grade phosphorites could be processed on a small scale for local use as a **fertilizer**. Imported phosphate rock is processed at a plant in Brownsville.

POTASH — The potassium mineral **polyhalite** is widely distributed in the subsurface Permian Basin of West Texas and has been found in many wells in that area. During 1927-1931, the federal government drilled a series of potash-test wells in Crane, Crockett, Ector, Glasscock, Loving, Reagan, Upton and Winkler counties. In addition to polyhalite, which was found in all of the counties, these wells revealed the presence of the potassium minerals **carnallite and sylvite** in Loving County and carnallite in Winkler County. The known Texas potash deposits are not as rich as those in the New Mexico portion of the Permian Basin and have not been developed.

PUMICITE (VOLCANIC ASH) — Deposits of volcanic ash occur in Brazos, Fayette, Gonzales, Karnes, Polk, Starr and other counties of the Texas Coastal Plain. Deposits also have been found in the Trans-Pecos area, High Plains and in several counties east of the High Plains. Volcanic ash is used to prepare **pozzolan cement, cleansing and scouring compounds and soaps and sweeping compounds**; as a **carrier for insecticides**, and for other purposes. It has been mined in Dickens, Lynn, Scurry, Starr and other counties.

QUICKSILVER (see **MERCURY**).

RARE-EARTH ELEMENTS AND METALS — The term, "rare-earth elements," is commonly applied to elements of the **lanthanide** group (atomic numbers 57 through 71) plus **yttrium**. Yttrium, atomic number 39 and not a member of the lanthanide group, is included as a rare-earth element because it has similar properties to members of that group and usually occurs in nature with them. The metals **thorium and scandium** are sometimes termed "rare metals" because their occurence is often associated with the rare-earth elements.

The majority of rare-earth elements are consumed as **catalysts** in petroleum cracking and other chemical industries. Rare earths are widely used in the **glass industry for tableware, specialty glasses, optics and fiber optics**. Cerium oxide has growing use as a **polishing compound** for glass, gem stones, cathode-ray tube faceplates, and other polishing. Rare earths are alloyed with various metals to produce materials used in the **aeronautic, space and electronics** industries. Addition of rare-earth elements may improve resistance to metal fatigue at high temperatures, reduce potential for corrosion, and selectively increase conductivity and magnetism of the metal.

Various members of this group, including **thorium**, have anomalous concentrations in the **rhyolitic and related igneous rocks** of the **Quitman Mountains** and the **Sierra Blanca area** of Trans-Pecos.

SALT (SODIUM CHLORIDE) (see also **BRINES**) — Salt resources of Texas are virtually inexhaustible. Enormous deposits occur in the subsurface **Permian Basin** of West Texas and in the **salt domes of the Gulf Coastal Plain**. Salt also is found in the alkali **playa lakes** of the High Plains, the **alkali flats or salt lakes in the Salt Basin** of Culberson and Hudspeth counties and along some of the bays and lagoons of the South Texas **Gulf Coast**.

Texas is one of the leading salt-producing states. **Rock salt** is obtained from underground mines in **salt domes at Grand Saline** in Van Zandt County. Approximately one-third of the salt produced in the state is from rock salt; most of the salt is produced by solution mining as brines from wells drilled into the underground salt deposits.

SAND, INDUSTRIAL — Sands used for special purposes, due to **high silica content** or to unique physical properties, command higher prices than common sand. Industrial sands in Texas occur mainly in the **Central Gulf Coastal Plain** and in **North Central Texas**. They include **abrasive, blast, chemical, engine, filtration, foundry, glass, hydraulic-fracturing (propant), molding and pottery sands**. Recent production of industrial sands has been from Atascosa, Colorado, Hardin, Harris, Liberty, Limestone, McCulloch, Newton, Smith, Somervell and Upshur counties.

SAND AND GRAVEL (CONSTRUCTION) — Sand and gravel are among the most extensively utilized resources in Texas. Principal occurrence is along the major streams and in stream terraces. Sand and gravel are important **bulk construction materials, used as railroad ballast, base materials** and for other purposes.

SANDSTONE — Sandstones of a variety of colors and textures are widely distributed in a number of geologic formations in Texas. Some of the sandstones have been quarried for use as **dimension stone** in El Paso, Parker, Terrell, Ward and other counties. **Crushed sandstone** is produced in Freestone, Gaines, Jasper, McMullen, Motley and other counties for use as **road-building material, terrazzo stone and aggregate**.

SERPENTINITE — Several masses of serpentinite, which formed from the alteration of basic igneous rocks, are associated with other Precambrian metamorphic rocks of the **Llano Uplift**. The largest deposit is the **Coal Creek serpentinite mass** in northern Blanco and Gillespie counties from which **terrazzo chips** have been produced. Other deposits are present in Gillespie and Llano counties. (The features that are associated with surface and subsurface Cretaceous rocks in several counties in or near the **Balcones Fault Zone** and that

are commonly known as **"serpentine plugs"** are not serpentine at all, but are altered igneous volcanic necks and pipes and mounds of altered volcanic ash — **palagonite** — that accumulated around the former **submarine volcanic pipes**.)

SHELL — Oyster shells and other shells in shallow coastal waters and in deposits along the **Texas Gulf Coast** have been produced in the past chiefly by dredging. They were used to a limited extent as raw material in the **manufacture of cement, as concrete aggregate and road base**, and for other purposes. No shell has been produced in Texas since 1981.

SILVER — During the period 1885-1952, the production of silver in Texas, as reported by the U.S. Bureau of Mines, totaled about **33 million troy ounces**. For about 70 years, silver was the most consistently produced metal in Texas, although always in moderate quantities. All of the production came from the **Trans-Pecos country** of West Texas, where the silver was mined in Brewster County (**Altuda Mountain**), Culberson and Hudspeth counties (**Van Horn Mountains and Van Horn-Allamoore district**), Hudspeth County (**Quitman Mountains and Eagle Mountains**) and Presidio County (**Chinati Mountains area, Loma Plata mine and Shafter district**).

Chief producer was the **Presidio mine in the Shafter district**, which began operations in the late 1800s, and, through September 1942, produced more than 30 million ounces of silver — more than 92 percent of Texas' total silver production. Water in the lower mine levels, lean ores and low price of silver resulted in the closing of the mine in 1942. Another important silver producer was the **Hazel copper-silver mine** in the Van Horn-Allamoore **district** in Culberson County, which accounted for more than 2 million ounces.

An increase in the price of silver in the late 1970s stimulated prospecting for new reserves, and exploration began near the old **Presidio mine**, near the old **Plata Verde mine** in the Van Horn Mountains district, at the **Bonanza mine** in the **Quitman Mountains** district and at the old **Hazel mine**. A decline in the price of silver in the early 1980s, however, resulted in reduction of exploration and mine development in the region. There is no current exploration in these areas.

SOAPSTONE (see **TALC AND SOAPSTONE**).

SODIUM SULFATE (SALT CAKE) — Sodium sulfate minerals occur in salt beds and brines of the alkali **playa lakes** of the High Plains in West Texas. In some lakes, the sodium sulfate minerals are present in deposits a few feet beneath the lakebeds. Sodium sulfate also is found in underground brines in the Permian Basin. Current production is from brines and dry salt beds at alkali lakes in Gaines and Terry counties. Past production was reported in Lynn and Ward counties. Sodium sulfate is used chiefly by the **detergent and paper and pulp industries**. Other uses are in the **preparation of glass and other products**.

STONE (see **BUILDING STONE** and **CRUSHED STONE**).

STRONTIUM — Deposits of the mineral **celestite (strontium sulfate)** have been found in a number of places, including localities in Brown, Coke, Comanche, Fisher, Lampasas, Mills, Nolan, Real, Taylor, Travis and Williamson counties. Most of the occurrences are very minor, and no strontium is currently produced in the state.

SULFUR — Texas is **one of the world's principal sulfur-producing areas**. The sulfur is mined from deposits of native sulfur, and it is extracted from sour (sulfur-bearing) natural gas and petroleum. **Recovered sulfur** is a growing industry and accounted for approximately 60 percent of all 1987 sulfur production in the United States, but only approximately 40 percent of Texas production. Native sulfur is found in large deposits in the caprock of some of the **salt domes** along the Texas Gulf Coast and in some of the surface and subsurface Permian strata of West Texas, notably in Culberson and Pecos counties.

Native sulfur obtained from the underground deposits is known as **Frasch sulfur**, so-called because of Herman Frasch, the chemist who devised the method of drilling wells into the deposits, melting the sulfur with superheated water and forcing the molten sulfur to the surface. Most of the production now goes to the users in molten form.

Frasch sulfur is produced from only one Gulf Coast salt dome in Wharton County and from West Texas underground

Permian strata in Culberson County. Operations at several Gulf Coast domes have been closed in recent years. During the 1940s, acidic sulfur earth was produced in the **Rustler Springs district** in Culberson County for use as a **fertilizer and soil conditioner.** Sulfur is recovered from sour natural gas and petroleum at plants in numerous Texas counties.

Sulfur is used in the preparation of **fertilizers and organic and inorganic chemicals, in petroleum refining** and for many other purposes.

TALC AND SOAPSTONE — Deposits of talc are found in the Precambrian metamorphic rocks of the **Allamoore area** of eastern Hudspeth and western Culberson counties. Soapstone, containing talc, occurs in the Precambrian metamorphic rocks of the **Llano Uplift** area, notably in Blanco, Gillespie and Llano counties. Current production is from surface mines in the **Allamoore area.** Talc is used in **ceramic, roofing, paint, paper, plastic, synthetic rubber** and other products.

TIN — Tin minerals have been found in El Paso and Mason counties. Small quantities were produced during the early 1900s in the Franklin Mountains north of El Paso. **Cassiterite (tin dioxide)** occurrences in Mason County are believed to be very minor. The **only tin smelter in the United States,** built at **Texas City** by the federal government during World War II and later sold to a private company, processes tin concentrates from ores mined outside of Texas, tin residues and secondary tin-bearing materials.

TITANIUM — The titanium mineral **rutile** has been found in small amounts at the **Mueller prospect** in Jeff Davis County. Another titanium mineral, **ilmenite,** occurs in sandstones in Burleson, Fayette, Lee, Starr and several other counties. Deposits that would be considered commercial under present conditions have not been found.

TRAP ROCK (see **BASALT**).

TUNGSTEN — The tungsten mineral **scheelite** has been found in small deposits in Gillespie and Llano counties and in the **Quitman Mountains** in Hudspeth County. Small deposits of other tungsten minerals have been prospected in the **Cave Peak area** north of Van Horn in Culberson County.

URANIUM — Uranium deposits were discovered in the **Texas Coastal Plain** in 1954 when abnormal radioactivity was detected in the Karnes County area. A number of uranium deposits have since been discovered within a belt of strata extending more than 250 miles from the middle Coastal Plain southwestward to the Rio Grande.

Various uranium minerals also have been found in other areas of Texas, including the **Trans-Pecos,** the **Llano Uplift** and the **High Plains.** With the exception of small shipments from the High Plains during the 1950s, all the uranium production in Texas has been from the Coastal Plain. Uranium has been obtained from surface mines extending from northern Live Oak County, southeastern Atascosa County, across northern Karnes County and into southern Gonzales County.

All mines are now reclaimed. All current uranium production is by **in-situ leaching,** brought to the surface through wells, and stripped from the solution at several Coastal Plain recovery operations. Decreased demand and price of uranium since 1980 has brought a sharp decline in operations in Texas.

VERMICULITE — Vermiculite, a mica-like mineral that expands when heated, occurs in Burnet, Gillespie, Llano, Mason and other counties in the **Llano region.** It has been produced at a surface mine in Llano County. Vermiculite, mined outside of Texas, is exfoliated (expanded) at plants in Dallas, Houston and San Antonio. Exfoliated vermiculite is used for **lightweight concrete aggregate, horticulture, insulation** and other purposes.

VOLCANIC ASH (see **PUMICITE**).

ZEOLITES — The zeolite minerals **clinoptilolite** and **analcime** occur in Tertiary lavas and tuffs in Brewster, Jeff Davis and Presidio counties, in West Texas. Clinoptilolite also is found associated with Tertiary tuffs in the southern Texas Coastal Plain, including deposits in Karnes, McMullen and Webb counties, and currently is produced in McMullen County. Zeolites, sometimes called **"molecular sieves,"** can be used in **ion-exchange processes to reduce pollution,** as a catalyst in **oil cracking,** in obtaining **high-purity oxygen and nitrogen** from air, in **water purification** and for many other purposes.

ZINC (see **LEAD AND ZINC**). ☆

Oil & Gas Drilling 1982-1998

Source: Texas Railroad Commission

Year	Rotary rigs active*		Permits†	Wells completed		Wells drilled**
	Texas	U.S.		Oil	Gas	
1982	994	3,117	41,224	16,296	6,273	27,648
1983	796	2,232	45,550	15,941	5,027	26,882
1984	850	2,428	37,507	18,716	5,489	30,898
1985	680	1,980	30,878	16,543	4,605	27,124
1986	313	964	15,894	10,373	3,304	18,707
1987	293	1,090	15,297	7,327	2,542	13,121
1988	280	936	13,493	6,441	2,665	12,261
1989	264	871	12,756	4,914	2,760	10,054
1990	348	1,009	14,033	5,593	2,894	11,231
1991	315	860	12,494	6,025	2,755	11,295
1992	251	721	12,089	5,031	2,537	9,498
1993	264	754	11,612	4,646	3,295	9,969
1994	274	775	11,030	3,962	3,553	9,299
1995	251	723	11,244	4,334	3,778	9,785
1996	283	779	12,669	4,061	4,060	9,747
1997	358	945	13,933	4,482	4,594	10,778
1998	303	827	9,385	4,509	4,907	11,057

*Source: Baker Hughes Inc.
†Totals shown for 1988 and after are number of drilling permits issued; data for previous years was total drilling applications received.
**Wells drilled are oil and gas well completions and dry holes drilled.

Major Oil Fields of Texas

Some of the Texas fields with signifcant production history are in the following list, which gives the name of the field, county and discovery date.

Data furnished by the **Oil and Gas Journal.**

Panhandle, Carson-Collingsworth-Gray-Hutchinson-Moore-Potter-Wheeler, 1910; **Thompson** (all fields), Fort Bend, 1921; **Howard-Glasscock,** Howard, 1925; **Iatan East,** Howard, 1926; **Yates,** Pecos, 1926; **Waddell,** Crane, 1927; **Van,** Van Zandt, 1929; **Ward Estes North,** Ward, 1929; **Cowden North,** Ector, 1930; **East Texas,** Gregg-Rusk, 1930; **Sand Hills,** Crane, 1930; **Conroe,** Montgomery, 1931; **Tom O'Connor,** Refugio, 1931; **Cowden South,** Ector, 1932; **Greta** (all fields), Refugio, 1933; **Tomball,** Harris, 1933; **Means** (all fields), Andrews-Gaines, 1934; **Anahuac,** Chambers, 1935; **Goldsmith** (all fields), Ector, 1935; **Hastings,** Brazoria, 1935; **Magnet Withers** (all fields), Wharton, 1936; **Seminole** (all fields), Gaines, 1936; **Talco,** Titus-Franklin, 1936; **Webster,** Harris, 1936; **Jordan,** Crane-Ector, 1937; **Slaughter,** Cochran, 1937; **Wasson** (all fields), Gaines, 1937; **Dune,** Crane, 1938; **West Ranch,** Jackson, 1938; **Keystone,** Winkler, 1939; **Diamond M,** Scurry, 1940; **Hawkins,** Wood, 1940; **Fullerton** (all fields), Andrews, 1941; **McElroy,** Crane, 1941; **Oyster Bayou,** Chambers, 1941; **Welch,** Dawson, 1941; **Quitman** (all fields), Wood, 1942; **Anton-Irish,** Hale, 1944; **TXL** (all fields), Ector, 1944; **Block 31,** Crane, 1945; **Levelland,** Cochran-Hockley, 1945; **Midland Farms** (all fields), Andrews; 1945; **Andector,** Ector, 1946; **Dollarhide,** Andrews, 1947; **Kelly-Snyder,** Scurry, 1948; **Cogdell Area,** Scurry, 1949; **Prentice,** Yoakum, 1950; **Salt Creek,** Kent, 1950; **Spraberry Trend,** Glasscock-Midland, 1952; **Lake Pasture,** Refugio, 1953; **Neches,** Anderson-Cherokee, 1953; **Fairway,** Anderson-Henderson, 1960; **Giddings,** Lee-Fayette-Burleson, 1971. ☆

A History of Fuel Minerals in Texas

Oil and natural gas are the most valuable minerals produced in Texas, contributing 23 percent of the oil production and 29 percent of the gas production in the United States in 1997.

Oil and gas have been produced from most areas of Texas and from rocks of all geologic eras except the Precambrian.

All of the major sedimentary basins of Texas have produced some oil or gas.

The well-known Permian Basin of West Texas has yielded large quantities of oil since 1921. It is an area of considerable promise for future production as well.

Although large quantities of petroleum have been produced from rocks of Permian age, production in the area also occurs from older Paleozoic rocks.

Production from rocks of Paleozoic age occurs primarily from North Central Texas westward to New Mexico and southwestward to the Rio Grande, but there is also significant Paleozoic production in North Texas in Tarrant, Grayson and Cooke counties.

Mesozoic rocks are the primary hydrocarbon reservoirs of the East Texas Basin and the area south and east of the Balcones Fault Zone. Cenozoic sandstones are the main reservoirs along the Gulf Coast and offshore state waters.

Coal and lignite occur in rocks of Pennsylvanian, Cretaceous and Tertiary ages. Coal was produced in Texas from about 1850 to the 1940s, when petroleum became the common fuel.

Significant production of coal did not resume until the mid-1970s. Most of the pre-1940 production was **bituminous coal** from North Central Texas, an area near Eagle Pass and an area near Laredo.

North Central Texas production was from Pennsylvanian rocks. Thurber, Newcastle and Bridgeport all had viable coal industries in the early 1900s.

As early as 1850, soldiers from Fort Duncan near Eagle Pass are reported to have mined coal from the Cretaceous rocks.

Commercial mining of coal from Eocene rocks near Laredo began in 1881. In addition to the commercial mining, small amounts of coal occurring in the Trans-

Pecos were used to roast the ore in mercury mining districts in the Big Bend.

Small amounts of "brown coal" or **lignite** have been produced throughout the history of the state. It was mined by many early settlers for family and small industry use. It was also used to generate "coal gas" or "producer gas" for Texas cities around the turn of the century.

Today, Texas ranks fifth nationally in coal production, and lignite accounts for most of this. Almost all of the lignite is consumed by mine-mouth electrical generating plants.

Petroleum Production and Income in Texas

Year	Crude Oil & Condensate			Natural Gas		
	Production (thousand bbls.)	Value (add 000)	Average Price Per Barrel	Production (MCF)	Value (add 000)	Average Price (Cents Per MCF)
1915	24,943	$ 13,027	$ 0 .52	13,324	$ 2,594	19.5
1925	144,648	262,270	1.81	134,872	7,040	5.2
1935	392,666	367,820	0.94	642,366	13,233	2.1
1945	754,710	914,410	1.21	1,711,401	44,839	2.6
1955	1,053,297	2,989,330	2.84	4,730,798	378,464	8.0
1965	1,000,749	2,962,119	2.96	6,636,555	858,396	12.9
1966	1,057,706	3,141,387	2.97	6,953,790	903,993	13.0
1967	1,119,962	3,375,565	3.01	7,188,900	948,935	13.2
1968	1,133,380	3,450,707	3.04	7,495,414	1,011,881	13.5
1969	1,151,775	3,696,328	3.21	7,853,199	1,075,888	13.7
1970	1,249,697	4,104,005	3.28	8,357,716	1,203,511	14.4
1971	1,222,926	4,261,775	3.48	8,550,705	1,376,664	16.1
1972	1,301,685	4,536,077	3.48	8,657,840	1,419,886	16.4
1973	1,294,671	5,157,623	3.98	8,513,850	1,735,221	20.4
1974	1,262,126	8,773,003	6.95	8,170,798	2,541,118	31.1
1975	1,221,929	9,336,570	7.64	7,485,764	3,885,112	51.9
1976	1,189,523	10,217,702	8.59	7,191,859	5,163,755	71.8
1977	1,137,880	9,986,002	8.78	7,051,027	6,367,077	90.3
1978	1,074,050	9,980,333	9.29	6,548,184	6,515,443	99.5
1979	1,018,094	12,715,994	12.49	7,174,623	8,509,103	118.6
1980	977,436	21,259,233	21.75	7,115,889	10,673,834	150.0
1981	945,132	32,692,116	34.59	7,050,207	12,598,712	178.7
1982	923,868	29,074,126	31.47	6,497,678	13,567,151	208.8
1983	876,205	22,947,814	26.19	5,643,183	14,672,275	260.0
1984	874,079	25,138,520	28.76	5,864,224	13,487,715	230.0
1985	860,300	23,159,286	26.92	5,805,098	12,665,114	218.0
1986	813,620	11,976,488	14.72	5,663,491	8,778,410	155.0
1987	754,213	13,221,345	17.53	5,516,224	7,612,389	138.0
1988	727,928	10,729,660	14.74	5,702,643	7,983,700	140.0
1989	679,575	12,123,624	17.84	5,595,190	8,113,026	145.0
1990	672,081	15,047,902	22.39	5,520,915	8,281,372	150.0
1991	672,810	12,836,080	19.05	5,509,990	7,713,986	140.0
1992	642,059	11,820,306	18.41	5,436,408	8,643,888	159.0
1993	572,600	9,288,800	16.22	4,062,500	7,365,800	181.0
1994	533,900	7,977,500	14.94	3,842,500	6,220,300	162.0
1995	503,200	8,177,700	16.25	3,690,000	5,305,200	143.0
1996	478,100	9,560,800	20.00	3,458,100	6,945,000	200.0
1997	464,900	$ 8,516,800	$ 18.32	3,672,300	$ 8,134,200	222.0

Sources: Texas Railroad Commission, Texas Mid-Continent Oil & Gas Association and, beginning in 1979, data are from Department of Energy and Texas State Comptroller of Public Accounts. Data for 1993-97 are from the state comptroller. DOE figures do not include gas that is vented or flared or used for pressure maintenance and repressuring, but do include non-hydrocarbon gases.

Approximately 20 percent of the electricity generated in the state in 1998 was from plants fired by Texas lignite.

Uranium occurs in several widely separated Texas localities, but production has been limited to the Cenozoic sandstones along the coastal plains of south-central Texas, roughly from Karnes County southwest to Webb County.

The surface mines, active from 1959 to the late-1980s, have largely been abandoned and reclaimed, and production today is all from in-situ leaching.

This requires the injection of a leaching fluid into the uranium-bearing strata, reaction of the fluid with the uranium ore and return of the fluid to the surface for stripping of the uranium. The fluid is then re-used.

Crude Oil

Indians found oil seeping from the soils of Texas long before the first Europeans arrived. They told explorers that the fluid had medicinal values. The first record of Europeans using crude oil, however, was the caulking of boats in 1543 by survivors of the **DeSoto expedition** near Sabine Pass.

Melrose, in Nacogdoches County, was the site in 1866 of the **first drilled well to produce oil** in Texas. The driller was **Lyne T. Barret** (whose name has been spelled several ways by historians). Barret used an auger, fastened to a pipe and rotated by a cogwheel driven by a steam engine — a basic principle of rotary drilling that has been used since, although with much improvement.

In 1867 **Amory (Emory) Starr** and **Peyton F. Edwards** brought in a well at **Oil Springs,** in the same area.

Other wells followed and **Nacogdoches County** was the site of Texas' **first commercial oil field, pipeline and effort to refine crude.** Several thousand barrels of oil were produced there during these years.

Other oil was found in crudely dug wells in Texas, principally in Bexar County, in the latter years of the 19th century.

But it was not until June 9, 1894, that Texas had a **major discovery**. This occurred in the drilling of a water well for the City of Corsicana. Oil caused that well to be abandoned, but a company formed in 1895 drilled several producing wells.

The first well-equipped refinery in Texas was built, and this plant usually is called the state's **first refinery,** despite the earlier effort at Nacogdoches. Discovery of the **Powell Field** near Corsicana followed in 1900.

Spindletop, 1901

Jan. 10, 1901, is the most famous date in Texas petroleum history. This is the date that the great gusher erupted in the oil well being drilled at **Spindletop,** near Beaumont, by a mining engineer, **Capt. A. F. Lucas.** Thousands of barrels of oil flowed before the well could be capped. This was the **first salt dome oil discovery**.

It created a sensation throughout the world, and encouraged exploration and drilling in Texas that has continued since.

Texas oil production increased from 836,039 barrels in 1900 to 4,393,658 in 1901; and in 1902 Spindletop alone produced 17,421,000 barrels, or 94 percent of the state's production. Prices dropped to 3c a barrel, an all-time low.

A water-well drilling outfit on the W. T. Waggoner Ranch in Wichita County hit oil, bringing in the **Electra Field** in 1911.

In 1917, came the discovery of the **Ranger Field** in Eastland County. The **Burkburnett Field** in Wichita County was discovered in 1919.

Oil discoveries brought a short era of swindling with oil stock promotion and selling on a nationwide scale. It ended after a series of trials in a federal court.

The **Mexia Field** in Limestone County was discovered in 1920, and the **second Powell Field** in Navarro County in 1924.

Another great area opened in 1921 with discovery of oil in the **Panhandle,** a field which developed rapidly with sensational oil and gas discoveries in Hutchinson and contiguous counties and the booming of **Borger.**

The **Luling Field** was opened in 1922 and 1925 saw the comeback of Spindletop with a production larger than that of the original field. Other fields opened in this period included **Big Lake**, 1923; **Wortham**, 1924-25 and **Yates**, 1926.

In 1925 **Howard County** was opened for production. **Winkler** in West Texas and **Raccoon Bend**, Austin County, were opened in 1927. **Sugar Land** was the most important Texas oil development in 1928.

The **Darst Creek Field** was opened in 1929. In the same year, new records of productive sand thickness were set for the industry at **Van**, Van Zandt County. **Pettus** was another contribution of 1929 in Bee County.

East Texas Field

The **East Texas field**, biggest of them all, was discovered near Turnertown and Joinerville, Rusk County, by veteran wildcatter **C. M. (Dad) Joiner,** in October 1930.

The success of this well — drilled on land condemned many times by geologists of the major companies — was followed by the biggest leasing campaign in history. The field soon was extended to Kilgore, Longview and northward. The East Texas field brought overproduction and a rapid sinking of the price. Private attempts were made to prorate production, but without much success.

On Aug. 17, 1931, **Gov. Ross S. Sterling** ordered the National Guard into the field, which he placed under **martial law.** This drastic action was taken after the **Texas Railroad Commission** had been enjoined from enforcing production restrictions.

After the complete shutdown, the Texas Legislature enacted legal **proration,** the system of regulation still utilized.

The most significant subsequent oil discoveries in Texas were those in **West Texas**, following a discovery well in Scurry County, Nov. 21, 1948, and later major developments in that region. Many of the leading Texas counties in minerals value are in that section. ☆

Texas Oil Production History

The table shows the year of oil or gas discovery in each county, oil production in 1997 and 1998 and total oil production from date of discovery to Jan. 1, 1999. The 21 counties omitted have not produced oil.

The table has been compiled by the Texas Almanac from information provided in past years by the Texas Mid-Continent Oil & Gas Assoc. Since 1970, production figures have been compiled from records of the Railroad Commission of Texas. In prior years, U.S. Bureau of Mines and State Comptroller reports were the basis of these compilations. The figures in the final column are cumulative of all previously published figures. The change in sources, due to different techniques, may create some discrepancies in year-to-year comparisons among counties.

County	Year of Discovery	Production in Barrels* 1997	Production in Barrels* 1998	Total Production to Jan. 1, 1999
Anderson	1929	1,252,551	1,170,716	293,850,539
Andrews	1930	30,554,718	29,150,250	2,630,145,041
Angelina	1936	259,494	53,754	797,908
Aransas	1936	556,046	498,106	83,166,847
Archer	1911	1,871,818	1,606,961	486,161,473
Atascosa	1917	744,816	729,652	145,577,936
Austin	1915	363,264	359,849	112,785,462
Bandera	1995	1,491	731	8,318
Bastrop	1913	221,191	253,538	15,674,177
Baylor	1924	215,822	173,695	57,153,718
Bee	1930	523,928	563,635	104,037,215
Bell	1980	0	0	446
Bexar	1889	229,842	191,318	34,988,043
Borden	1949	4,776,580	5,066,881	377,940,979
Bowie	1944	308,396	270,472	5,357,356
Brazoria	1902	3,343,275	3,006,014	1,255,091,452
Brazos	1942	3,120,420	2,540,597	122,791,782
Brewster	1969	0	0	56
Briscoe	1982	0	0	3,554
Brooks	1936	760,550	890,202	160,722,772
Brown	1917	200,076	165,120	52,543,010
Burleson	1938	6,269,560	4,787,630	172,291,001
Caldwell	1922	970,032	861,178	275,967,644
Calhoun	1935	889,228	752,755	100,577,038
Callahan	1923	475,035	383,747	84,416,584
Cameron	1944	2,786	2,679	456,825
Camp	1940	372,603	584,046	26,444,514
Carson	1921	533,511	456,284	177,616,167
Cass	1935	679,799	551,156	111,626,245
Chambers	1916	1,921,913	1,968,147	897,717,798
Cherokee	1926	438,268	344,451	68,950,340
Childress	1961	13,351	12,063	1,417,830
Clay	1902	1,245,898	983,714	198,929,204
Cochran	1936	5,628,330	5,200,700	477,260,249
Coke	1942	1,249,565	1,152,102	219,196,619
Coleman	1902	392,487	392,845	92,698,115
Collin	1963	0	0	53,000
Collingsworth	1936	3,598	4,542	1,220,810
Colorado	1932	1,065,363	774,694	37,805,667
Comanche	1918	11,139	8,652	5,893,842
Concho	1940	992,503	929,846	20,992,073
Cooke	1926	2,066,040	1,816,321	378,561,674
Coryell	1964	0	0	1,100
Cottle	1955	98,373	86,070	4,014,755
Crane	1926	14,332,295	13,935,363	1,677,109,459
Crockett	1925	3,515,146	3,174,370	340,627,757
Crosby	1955	896,198	830,837	20,309,088
Culberson	1953	180,907	149,547	24,021,008
Dallas	1986	0	0	231
Dawson	1937	6,860,078	6,640,016	345,931,573
Delta	1984	0	0	64,058
Denton	1937	13,363	13,505	3,464,506
DeWitt	1930	343,199	289,282	64,877,972

County	Year of Discovery	Production in Barrels* 1997	Production in Barrels* 1998	Total Production to Jan. 1, 1999
Dickens	1953	809,199	870,404	10,211,188
Dimmit	1943	972,698	909,927	101,580,691
Duval	1905	1,902,874	1,794,433	576,900,802
Eastland	1917	467,037	422,930	154,438,672
Ector	1926	26,719,864	25,281,639	2,963,409,438
Edwards	1946	13,357	14,166	481,854
Ellis	1953	3,710	2,710	832,968
Erath	1917	10,113	4,777	2,065,401
Falls	1937	6,802	5,158	882,278
Fannin	1980	0	0	13,281
Fayette	1943	5,572,704	4,568,131	134,116,866
Fisher	1928	1,290,181	1,147,673	243,075,951
Floyd	1952	2,063	1,966	146,500
Foard	1929	203,236	291,520	23,103,609
Fort Bend	1919	3,362,602	2,856,930	672,362,435
Franklin	1936	641,076	617,669	174,009,863
Freestone	1916	268,968	287,748	43,316,093
Frio	1934	1,267,732	1,053,775	141,544,427
Gaines	1936	36,976,256	36,016,018	1,981,612,048
Galveston	1922	1,079,313	1,738,372	440,841,433
Garza	1926	6,261,102	5,994,632	304,085,450
Glasscock	1925	6,576,946	6,363,309	237,300,089
Goliad	1930	630,798	688,713	78,456,271
Gonzales	1902	696,677	711,473	41,224,092
Gray	1925	2,407,843	2,224,091	662,209,850
Grayson	1930	1,725,231	1,953,304	246,750,089
Gregg	1931	16,112,519	12,943,293	3,256,062,659
Grimes	1952	1,259,358	648,851	16,427,209
Guadalupe	1922	1,096,597	1,333,390	197,810,975
Hale	1946	1,043,336	1,531,538	157,174,001
Hamilton	1938	1,625	796	143,929
Hansford	1937	347,245	293,561	37,845,549
Hardeman	1944	2,582,972	2,571,237	69,061,708
Hardin	1893	1,486,919	1,441,795	426,206,616
Harris	1905	4,033,596	3,724,162	1,359,711,152
Harrison	1928	990,694	965,913	83,694,475
Hartley	1937	377,983	373,451	5,434,339
Haskell	1929	828,194	741,019	113,546,183
Hays	1956	0	0	296
Hemphill	1955	445,195	415,248	32,959,840
Henderson	1934	1,637,416	1,512,062	170,971,806
Hidalgo	1934	3,644,374	4,384,121	87,832,243
Hill	1949	1,716	923	70,733
Hockley	1937	25,546,518	25,663,717	1,498,459,235
Hood	1958	3,612	2,760	110,184
Hopkins	1936	449,345	393,874	87,344,327
Houston	1934	868,055	1,008,485	51,797,743
Howard	1925	8,973,514	8,109,511	769,303,925
Hunt	1942	7,059	4,523	2,024,233
Hutchinson	1923	1,702,192	1,401,397	524,288,695
Irion	1928	2,713,291	2,583,927	90,788,983
Jack	1923	1,213,174	1,121,518	198,655,642
Jackson	1934	1,776,966	1,824,419	673,667,844
Jasper	1928	1,290,642	1,000,744	30,758,605

County	Year of Discovery	Production in Barrels* 1997	1998	Total Production to Jan. 1, 1999
Jeff Davis	1980	0	0	20,866
Jefferson	1901	4,255,634	2,924,711	521,935,379
Jim Hogg	1922	302,063	267,796	109,542,513
Jim Wells	1933	408,886	360,574	461,146,578
Johnson	1962	0	0	194,000
Jones	1926	1,071,175	978,386	215,676,248
Karnes	1930	450,746	458,142	106,059,259
Kaufman	1948	116,803	111,450	24,176,462
Kenedy	1947	661,564	720,176	36,384,063
Kent	1946	10,500,020	9,405,802	529,341,298
Kerr	1982	2,269	1,504	77,155
Kimble	1939	930	665	94,416
King	1943	3,628,326	3,001,482	160,371,420
Kinney	1960	0	0	402
Kleberg	1926	545,048	401,190	331,309,879
Knox	1946	373,392	351,085	60,172,048
Lamb	1945	601,465	595,784	31,900,402
Lampasas	1985	0	0	111
La Salle	1940	351,583	262,458	25,953,887
Lavaca	1941	588,594	603,064	26,926,596
Lee	1939	3,534,695	2,911,884	122,328,056
Leon	1936	1,470,312	1,259,698	56,578,383
Liberty	1905	1,946,877	1,916,958	514,390,186
Limestone	1920	256,060	227,147	118,335,303
Lipscomb	1956	788,272	731,961	56,732,451
Live Oak	1931	964,272	870,576	79,713,263
Llano	1978	0	0	647
Loving	1925	1,517,053	1,539,669	102,924,565
Lubbock	1941	1,842,346	1,777,164	58,406,695
Lynn	1950	237,382	239,252	17,799,354
Madison	1946	1,150,219	856,513	30,129,877
Marion	1910	242,650	270,447	54,360,192
Martin	1945	5,667,041	5,395,888	279,390,928
Matagorda	1904	865,244	1,582,932	270,376,139
Maverick	1929	943,902	842,500	45,321,989
McCulloch	1938	125,883	90,125	1,133,966
McLennan	1902	1,333	1,383	326,438
McMullen	1919	1,876,473	1,725,369	96,058,440
Medina	1901	111,577	104,160	10,235,225
Menard	1941	108,223	124,514	6,537,540
Midland	1945	13,225,765	13,729,842	549,051,543
Milam	1921	1,155,875	1,182,848	16,134,275
Mills	1982	0	0	28,122
Mitchell	1920	3,383,945	3,213,181	207,174,514
Montague	1924	1,530,708	1,511,053	281,550,855
Montgomery	1931	1,926,630	1,854,638	767,731,297
Moore	1936	429,159	382,737	28,171,492
Motley	1957	92,634	89,273	10,625,769
Nacogdoches	1866	51,035	42,790	3,270,492
Navarro	1895	334,357	311,869	216,256,612
Newton	1937	1,376,642	957,675	58,556,780
Nolan	1939	2,156,276	1,916,411	188,069,649
Nueces	1930	1,410,257	1,153,675	552,881,791
Ochiltree	1951	1,168,647	1,035,034	154,540,666
Oldham	1957	134,850	96,793	13,253,111
Orange	1913	2,141,175	1,602,102	151,143,056
Palo Pinto	1902	526,351	631,950	21,407,534
Panola	1917	2,176,547	2,348,285	79,988,846
Parker	1942	16,371	17,550	2,805,458
Parmer	1963	0	0	144,000
Pecos	1926	23,343,542	21,397,317	1,684,427,273
Polk	1930	4,007,096	3,142,127	113,667,546
Potter	1925	251,805	230,885	8,636,162
Presidio	1980	341	1,660	3,874
Rains	1955	0	0	148,886
Reagan	1923	7,387,291	7,040,029	471,727,671
Red River	1951	836,150	671,463	5,891,703
Reeves	1939	877,881	831,703	73,150,352
Refugio	1928	4,796,329	4,326,623	1,293,400,178
Roberts	1945	616,978	470,276	44,100,170
Robertson	1944	5,327,134	3,897,342	14,938,820
Runnels	1927	852,540	729,337	143,593,984
Rusk	1930	4,388,045	4,146,842	1,808,913,997
Sabine	1981	224,863	126,270	4,708,736
San Augustine	1947	200,441	81,283	2,328,494
San Jacinto	1940	294,196	295,299	24,479,211
San Patricio	1930	1,029,376	1,063,004	478,897,275
San Saba	1982	0	0	32,362
Schleicher	1937	619,815	587,087	84,625,480
Scurry	1923	6,835,262	6,570,926	1,976,642,765
Shackelford	1910	1,305,150	1,239,402	176,548,592
Shelby	1917	51,731	65,118	2,192,822
Sherman	1938	291,765	238,315	8,268,687
Smith	1931	1,772,647	1,616,000	256,267,038
Somervell	1978	0	0	119
Starr	1929	1,650,513	1,789,878	279,049,300
Stephens	1916	3,827,390	3,543,259	322,207,555
Sterling	1947	1,543,709	1,383,927	81,454,712
Stonewall	1938	2,486,812	2,087,489	253,281,813
Sutton	1948	85,020	90,957	7,230,960
Swisher	1981	0	0	6
Tarrant	1969	2	48	103
Taylor	1929	1,084,516	881,647	140,615,190
Terrell	1952	796,519	723,434	6,619,661
Terry	1940	5,446,484	4,992,162	410,233,283
Throckmorton	1924	1,649,277	1,650,948	213,578,054
Titus	1936	707,242	607,123	208,104,817
Tom Green	1940	773,605	661,738	89,134,132
Travis	1934	3,417	7,092	738,468
Trinity	1946	37,839	29,493	598,119
Tyler	1937	509,722	392,620	37,944,733
Upshur	1931	910,372	789,681	283,152,422
Upton	1925	11,217,533	10,248,494	769,750,101
Uvalde	1950	0	0	1,814
Val Verde	1935	2,997	2,101	127,153
Van Zandt	1929	1,963,851	2,505,380	541,022,966
Victoria	1931	962,110	952,918	247,129,060
Walker	1934	7,589	17,106	464,002
Waller	1934	87,395	170,079	20,159,847
Ward	1928	7,203,777	7,649,059	724,464,321
Washington	1915	745,606	588,214	27,058,727
Webb	1921	2,437,344	2,696,415	149,361,223
Wharton	1925	2,608,604	2,506,923	326,614,400
Wheeler	1921	693,858	755,109	97,161,625
Wichita	1910	3,088,994	2,914,209	814,336,830
Wilbarger	1915	910,806	858,076	259,649,680
Willacy	1936	725,345	690,886	109,728,428
Williamson	1915	11,332	10,602	9,489,382
Wilson	1941	595,317	568,007	46,538,223
Winkler	1926	5,417,789	5,034,149	1,048,118,964
Wise	1942	778,304	740,662	95,743,058
Wood	1941	6,413,952	6,374,644	1,164,344,772
Yoakum	1936	30,166,705	29,398,194	1,909,016,695
Young	1917	2,012,163	1,874,909	299,317,239
Zapata	1919	361,726	358,286	45,740,780
Zavala	1937	530,111	390,086	43,734,247

*Total includes condensate production.

State totals: (1997), 527,621,886; (1998), 496,290,093.
Source: Railroad Commission, 1997-98 production reports.

Receipts by Texas from Tidelands

The Republic of Texas had proclaimed its Gulf boundaries as three marine leagues, recognized by international law as traditional national boundaries. These boundaries were never seriously questioned when Texas joined the Union in 1845.

But, in 1930 a congressional resolution authorized the U.S. Attorney General to file suit to establish offshore lands as properties of the federal government.

Congress returned the disputed lands to Texas in 1953, and the U.S. Supreme Court confirmed Texas' ownership in 1960.

In 1978, the federal government also granted states a "fair and equitable" share of the revenues from offshore oil and gas leases within three miles of the states' outermost boundary. The states did not receive any such revenue until April 1986.

The following table shows receipts from tidelands in the Gulf of Mexico by the Texas General Land Office to Aug. 31, 1998. It does not include revenue from bays and other submerged area owned by Texas. *Source: General Land Office*

From	To	Total	Bonus	Rental	Royalty	Lease
6-09-1922	9-28-1945	$ 924,363.81	$ 814,055.70	$ 61,973.75	$ 48,334.36	...
9-29-1945	6-23-1947	296,400.30	272,700.00	7,680.00	16,020.30	...
6-24-1947	6-05-1950	7,695,552.22	7,231,755.48	377,355.00	86,441.74	...
6-06-1950	5-22-1953	55,095.04	—	9,176.00	45,919.04	...
5-23-1953	6-30-1958	54,264,553.11	49,788,639.03	3,852,726.98	623,187.10	...
7-01-1958	8-31-1959	771,064.75	—	143,857.00	627,207.75	...
9-01-1959	8-31-1960	983,335.32	257,900.00	98,226.00	627,209.32	...
9-01-1960	8-31-1961	3,890,800.15	3,228,639.51	68,578.00	593,582.64	...
9-01-1961	8-31-1962	1,121,925.09	297,129.88	127,105.00	697,690.21	...
9-01-1962	8-31-1963	3,575,888.64	2,617,057.14	177,174.91	781,656.59	...
9-01-1963	8-31-1964	3,656,236.75	2,435,244.36	525,315.00	695,677.39	...
9-01-1964	8-31-1965	54,654,576.96	53,114,943.63	755,050.12	784,583.21	...
9-01-1965	8-31-1966	22,148,825.44	18,223,357.84	3,163,475.00	761,992.60	...
9-01-1966	8-31-1967	8,469,680.86	3,641,414.96	3,711,092.65	1,117,173.25	...
9-01-1967	8-31-1968	6,305,851.00	1,251,852.50	2,683,732.50	2,370,266.00	...
9-01-1968	8-31-1969	6,372,268.28	1,838,118.33	1,491,592.50	3,042,557.45	...
9-01-1969	8-31-1970	10,311,030.48	5,994,666.32	618,362.50	3,698,001.66	...
9-01-1970	8-31-1971	9,969,629.17	4,326,120.11	726,294.15	4,917,214.91	...
9-01-1971	8-31-1972	7,558,327.21	1,360,212.64	963,367.60	5,234,746.97	...
9-01-1972	8-31-1973	9,267,975.68	3,701,737.30	920,121.60	4,646,116.78	...
9-01-1973	8-31-1974	41,717,670.04	32,981,619.28	1,065,516.60	7,670,534.16	...
9-01-1974	8-31-1975	27,321,536.62	5,319,762.85	2,935,295.60	19,066,478.17	...
9-01-1975	8-31-1976	38,747,074.09	6,197,853.00	3,222,535.84	29,326,685.25	...
9-01-1976	8-31-1977	84,196,228.27	41,343,114.81	2,404,988.80	40,448,124.66	...
9-01-1977	8-31-1978	118,266,812.05	49,807,750.45	4,775,509.92	63,683,551.68	...
9-01-1978	8-31-1979	100,410,268.68	34,578,340.94	7,318,748.40	58,513,179.34	...
9-01-1979	8-31-1980	200,263,803.03	34,733,270.02	10,293,153.80	155,237,379.21	...
9-01-1980	8-31-1981	219,126,876.54	37,467,196.97	13,100,484.25	168,559,195.32	...
9-01-1981	8-31-1982	250,824,581.69	27,529,516.33	14,214,478.97	209,080,586.39	...
9-01-1982	8-31-1983	165,197,734.83	10,180,696.40	12,007,476.70	143,009,561.73	...
9-01-1983	8-31-1984	152,755,934.29	32,864,122.19	8,573,996.87	111,317,815.23	...
9-01-1984	8-31-1985	140,568,090.79	32,650,127.75	6,837,603.70	101,073,959.34	...
9-01-1985	8-31-1986	516,503,771.05	6,365,426.23	4,241,892.75	78,289,592.27	$ 427,606,859.83
9-01-1986	8-31-1987	60,066,571.05	4,186,561.63	1,933,752.50	44,691,907.22	9,254,349.70
9-01-1987	8-31-1988	56,875,069.22	14,195,274.28	1,817,058.90	28,068,202.53	12,794,533.51
9-01-1988	8-31-1989	61,793,380.04	12,995,892.74	1,290,984.37	35,160,568.40	12,345,934.53
9-01-1989	8-31-1990	68,701,751.51	7,708,449.54	1,289,849.87	40,331,537.06	19,371,915.04
9-01-1990	8-31-1991	90,885,856.99	3,791,832.77	1,345,711.07	70,023,601.01	15,724,712.14
9-01-1991	8-31-1992	51,154,511.34	4,450,850.00	1,123,585.54	26,776,191.35	18,803,884.45
9-01-1992	8-31-1993	60,287,712.60	3,394,230.00	904,359.58	34,853,679.68	21,135,443.34
9-01-1993	8-31-1994	57,825,043.59	3,570,657.60	694,029.30	32,244,987.95	21,315,368.74
9-01-1994	8-31-1995	62,143,227.78	8,824,722.93	674,479.79	34,691,023.35	17,951,001.71
9-01-1995	8-31-1996	68,166,645.51	13,919,246.80	1,102,591.39	32,681,315.73	20,463,491.59
9-01-1996	8-31-1997	90,614,935.93	22,007,378.46	1,319,614.78	41,605,792.50	25,682,150.19
9-01-1997	8-31-1998	104,016,006.75	36,946,312.49	2,070,802.90	38,760,320.91	26,238,570.45
Total		$ 3,100,718,074.57	$ 648,405,751.19	$ 127,042,758.45	$ 1,576,581,349.71	$ 648,688,215.22
Inside three-mile line		$ 429,964,911.88	$ 153,892,717.76	$ 34,264,220.71	$ 241,807,973.41	0
Between three-mile line and three marine-league line		$ 2,019,239,581.89	$ 491,860,949.04	$ 92,605,256.55	$ 1,434,773,376.30	0
Outside three marine-league line		$ 651,513,580.80	$ 2,652,084.39	$ 173,281.19	0	$ 648,688,215.22

Oil and Gas Production by County 1998

IN 1998 in Texas, the total natural gas production was 4,803,638,408 MCF and total crude oil production was 457,499,130 BBL. Total condensate was 38,790,963 BBL. Total casinghead was 968,441,421 MCF.

Source: Texas Railroad Commission.
BBL refers to barrels and MCF to thousand cubic feet.

County	Gas Well Gas MCF	Conden- sate BBL	Crude Oil BBL	Casinghead MCF
Anderson	8,328,551	109,707	1,061,009	3,301,306
Andrews	2,951,544	8,039	29,142,211	36,776,108
Angelina	625,392	1,996	51,758	171,334
Aransas	8,867,044	280,246	217,860	805,476
Archer	15,470	47	1,606,914	480,269
Atascosa	16,244,139	46,289	683,363	276,671
Austin	12,739,553	28,262	331,587	532,801
Bandera	0	0	731	0
Bastrop	588,174	7,029	246,509	562,556
Baylor	0	0	173,695	161
Bee	18,697,354	95,410	468,225	398,000
Bexar	220	0	191,318	1,087
Borden	0	0	5,066,881	4,068,045
Bowie	52,482	5,444	265,028	71,647
Brazoria	45,836,440	576,013	2,430,001	1,554,030
Brazos	15,885,097	348,562	2,192,035	7,457,537
Brooks	41,791,870	628,495	261,707	538,765
Brown	1,620,839	2,006	163,114	431,087
Burleson	4,877,268	93,811	4,693,749	21,047,352
Caldwell	26,264	225	860,953	683,201
Calhoun	12,594,428	111,021	641,734	653,600
Callahan	954,903	2,219	381,528	615,820
Cameron	1,317,565	1,579	1,100	1,036
Camp	846,278	16	584,030	34,929
Carson	30,748,929	12	456,272	3,371,819
Cass	14,235,549	53,107	498,049	546,120
Chambers	58,787,071	657,766	1,310,381	4,884,325
Cherokee	15,584,025	54,338	290,113	477,234
Chldress	0	0	12,063	240
Clay	693,816	12,622	971,092	695,089
Cochran	486,844	1,936	5,198,764	4,155,093
Coke	1,327,104	4,050	1,148,052	3,999,113
Coleman	1,498,572	5,821	387,024	1,073,887
Collingswth	1,824,636	0	4,542	52,278
Colorado	30,819,882	306,094	468,600	1,723,913
Comanche	751,077	889	7,763	135,887
Concho	1,372,669	10,096	919,750	2,666,948
Cooke	75,522	137	1,816,184	551,773
Cottle	4,516,345	41,144	44,926	78,626
Crane	17,964,329	56,193	13,879,170	79,713,642
Crockett	140,395,122	268,035	2,906,335	5,962,788
Crosby	0	0	830,837	84,904
Culberson	214,073	0	149,547	159,107
Dallam	7,877	0	0	0
Dallas	46,661	0	0	0
Dawson	0	0	6,640,016	5,989,767
Denton	9,814,446	2,534	10,971	76
DeWitt	16,631,288	155,167	134,115	214,190
Dickens	0	0	870,404	14,431
Dimmit	1,177,907	5,264	904,663	1,693,791

County	Gas Well Gas MCF	Conden- sate BBL	Crude Oil BBL	Casinghead MCF
Donley	33,462	0	0	0
Duval	61,605,612	314,151	1,480,282	826,700
Eastland	5,029,440	47,397	375,533	1,440,452
Ector	31,480,029	11,646	25,269,993	29,859,876
Edwards	28,368,204	6,709	7,457	22
Ellis	0	0	2,710	24
Erath	3,287,813	1,352	3,425	18,939
Falls	14,003	0	5,158	137
Fayette	36,332,240	1,347,773	3,220,358	24,458,162
Fisher	108,598	951	1,146,722	1,485,856
Floyd	0	0	1,966	0
Foard	304,420	0	291,520	15,120
Fort Bend	27,838,123	443,137	2,413,793	1,338,036
Franklin	7,886,617	166,382	451,287	143,554
Freestone	69,463,059	182,932	104,816	75,730
Frio	748,869	184	1,053,591	789,058
Gaines	2,344,769	4,265	36,011,753	51,617,765
Galveston	21,894,064	849,332	889,040	1,279,687
Garza	0	0	5,994,632	1,256,664
Glasscock	1,587,689	21,962	6,341,347	17,277,127
Goliad	35,699,362	264,398	424,315	978,994
Gonzales	1,312,546	11,392	700,081	334,761
Gray	14,271,117	4,759	2,219,332	5,186,954
Grayson	2,826,399	15,592	1,937,712	5,094,735
Gregg	51,902,986	297,811	12,645,482	5,895,684
Grimes	62,017,293	507,916	140,935	792,750
Guadalupe	0	0	1,333,390	260,852
Hale	0	0	1,531,538	27,973
Hamilton	48,127	0	796	0
Hansford	28,065,269	27,034	266,527	942,536
Hardeman	0	0	2,571,237	974,564
Hardin	4,527,112	142,467	1,299,328	1,323,584
Harris	51,209,203	619,383	3,104,779	34,720,633
Harrison	54,704,456	360,104	605,809	2,058,978
Hartley	3,768,168	0	373,451	23
Haskell	19,084	426	740,593	383,349
Hemphill	81,099,352	276,608	138,640	2,663,261
Henderson	20,227,737	63,501	1,448,561	12,085,844
Hidalgo	285,945,177	4,296,392	87,729	187,707
Hill	0	0	923	12
Hockley	177,274	2,654	25,661,063	42,269,818
Hood	1,741,355	2,760	0	0
Hopkins	1,430,584	10,131	383,743	252,303
Houston	3,941,838	56,523	951,962	672,176
Howard	1,078,070	3,708	8,105,803	6,721,083
Hunt	0	0	4,523	1,411
Hutchinson	14,217,298	10,111	1,391,286	9,240,977
Irion	4,270,144	29,467	2,554,460	15,054,661
Jack	12,271,835	70,155	1,051,363	5,080,527
Jackson	19,970,397	379,683	1,444,736	2,265,746
Jasper	16,643,537	619,907	380,837	2,462,657
Jefferson	43,363,760	1,799,103	1,125,608	1,495,981
Jim Hogg	22,425,574	126,247	141,549	514,015

County	Gas Well Gas MCF	Condensate BBL	Crude Oil BBL	Casinghead MCF
Jim Wells	17,008,729	75,479	285,095	1,165,485
Johnson	19,250	0	0	0
Jones	148,723	747	977,639	693,715
Karnes	9,305,936	113,241	344,901	823,067
Kaufman	0	0	111,450	27,401
Kenedy	54,096,061	381,757	338,419	303,442
Kent	0	0	9,405,802	11,301,880
Kerr	0	0	1,504	0
Kimble	45,558	0	665	1,215
King	2,330,434	10,255	2,991,227	319,124
Kleberg	24,878,794	123,177	278,013	738,822
Knox	0	0	351,085	12,199
Lamb	0	0	595,784	32,648
La Salle	8,544,366	50,250	212,208	437,579
Lavaca	71,453,407	358,168	244,896	610,195
Lee	4,406,461	77,554	2,834,330	18,048,707
Leon	43,208,026	78,704	1,180,994	1,528,876
Liberty	6,927,326	180,198	1,736,760	1,411,731
Limestone	52,572,890	106,700	120,447	1,743
Lipscomb	45,744,627	196,122	535,839	4,178,637
Live Oak	27,527,801	372,844	497,732	772,897
Loving	18,563,458	4,951	1,534,718	3,303,512
Lubbock	0	0	1,777,164	52,004
Lynn	0	0	239,252	83,793
McCulloch	66,656	0	90,125	87,757
McLennan	0	0	1,383	87
McMullen	37,722,925	509,070	1,216,299	4,769,027
Madison	4,659,252	52,474	804,039	906,037
Marion	4,617,712	81,946	188,501	190,790
Martin	80,600	881	5,395,007	12,365,535
Matagorda	65,541,223	1,000,291	582,641	1,050,779
Maverick	5,268,596	47,829	794,671	267,517
Medina	0	0	104,160	504
Menard	356,627	0	124,514	37,825
Midland	44,909,690	1,443,342	12,286,500	37,681,345
Milam	33,695	176	1,182,672	620,814
Mitchell	0	0	3,213,181	715,238
Montague	697,343	4,666	1,506,387	1,672,643
Montgomery	68,960,114	693,318	1,161,320	3,368,533
Moore	60,173,217	1,966	380,771	3,776,943
Motley	0	0	89,273	3,039
Nacogdches	27,483,466	33,158	9,632	138,607
Navarro	563,095	5,414	306,455	48,031
Newton	6,823,081	426,855	530,820	1,566,607
Nolan	625,125	2,649	1,913,762	2,694,482
Nueces	34,415,415	331,036	822,639	1,489,885
Ochiltree	27,815,498	110,323	924,711	4,101,038
Oldham	454,958	0	96,793	16,849
Orange	13,915,499	761,132	840,970	1,140,043
Palo Pinto	14,332,590	40,060	591,890	2,607,053
Panola	260,181,939	1,633,715	714,570	5,908,518
Parker	7,870,521	11,412	6,138	45,788
Pecos	203,538,027	159,644	21,237,673	51,400,999
Polk	52,613,339	2,536,317	605,810	796,945
Potter	28,754,074	81	230,804	559,689
Presidio	0	0	1,660	0
Rains	8,978,441	0	0	0
Reagan	8,812,482	245,589	6,794,440	29,335,287

County	Gas Well Gas MCF	Condensate BBL	Crude Oil BBL	Casinghead MCF
Red River	0	0	671,463	20,555
Reeves	29,974,380	32,183	799,520	2,134,079
Refugio	19,743,213	32,684	4,293,939	18,981,658
Roberts	26,780,111	161,793	308,483	2,982,354
Robertson	29,048,995	789	3,896,553	1,567,759
Runnels	726,836	5,993	723,344	1,448,438
Rusk	77,721,713	323,834	3,823,008	2,562,901
Sabine	399,218	47,590	78,680	491,634
S.Augustine	8,712	0	81,283	701,576
San Jacinto	6,368,889	268,216	27,083	52,984
San Patricio	14,910,658	285,579	777,425	1,971,373
Schleicher	11,183,145	53,858	533,229	1,497,626
Scurry	0	0	6,570,926	25,780,358
Shackelford	2,998,390	14,850	1,224,552	2,177,200
Shelby	8,451,156	27,836	37,282	37,114
Sherman	27,794,481	7,657	230,658	346,568
Smith	8,102,406	71,410	1,544,590	2,693,279
Somervell	20,423	0	0	0
Starr	142,410,105	1,260,874	529,004	1,561,872
Stephens	7,909,464	27,588	3,515,671	3,037,319
Sterling	12,127,319	109,815	1,274,112	17,182,235
Stonewall	0	0	2,087,489	693,386
Sutton	58,654,446	70,685	20,272	27,456
Tarrant	561,156	48	0	0
Taylor	65,091	443	881,204	601,858
Terrell	75,834,229	694,630	28,804	619,079
Terry	492,693	0	4,992,162	2,259,985
Throckmrton	414,265	3,515	1,647,433	2,134,834
Titus	635,454	15,391	591,732	5,446
Tom Green	844,662	6,383	655,355	3,940,564
Travis	0	0	7,092	12
Trinity	169,038	5,341	24,152	355,378
Tyler	2,115,725	37,442	355,178	601,622
Upshur	61,543,721	607,053	182,628	37,278
Upton	26,610,224	322,219	9,926,275	30,001,889
Uvalde	14,915	0	0	0
Val Verde	16,788,451	1,511	590	0
Van Zandt	10,121,214	26,344	2,479,036	3,312,829
Victoria	16,525,369	88,886	864,032	864,010
Walker	977,943	12,522	4,584	24,160
Waller	9,284,727	1,160	168,919	9,182
Ward	40,700,837	116,276	7,532,783	16,853,045
Washington	74,495,011	147,034	441,180	2,796,273
Webb	336,821,051	2,427,124	269,291	261,376
Wharton	50,805,741	935,697	1,571,226	1,462,739
Wheeler	44,533,697	264,001	491,108	1,075,773
Wichita	0	0	2,914,209	223,028
Wilbarger	6,885	0	858,076	69,629
Willacy	47,215,375	24,895	665,991	598,147
Williamson	25,777	0	10,602	78
Wilson	55,925	758	567,249	66,493
Winkler	35,925,639	84,069	4,950,080	15,161,116
Wise	65,217,639	154,905	585,757	7,594,415
Wood	12,557,052	41,243	6,333,401	2,968,868
Yoakum	0	0	29,398,194	77,924,295
Young	2,044,213	15,334	1,859,575	2,460,070
Zapata	323,151,942	307,067	51,219	66,683
Zavala	3,284,956	4,921	385,165	383,800

Public Utilities: Telecommunications Face Changes

By Jennifer Files

The end of the 1990s brought major changes to Texas' telecommunications industry, one of the fastest-growing sectors of the state's economy. Giant corporations joined forces in multi-billion-dollar mergers while the Legislature debated new laws that would allow the state's telephone companies to compete more freely and at the same time would protect customers.

Telecommunications companies employ more than 100,000 Texans. Several of the world's largest telecom equipment manufacturers base their U.S. operations in the Dallas area. SBC Communications Inc., which owns Southwestern Bell, calls San Antonio home. And in 1998, GTE Corp. moved its main office from Stamford, Conn., to Irving, where it already employed approximately 12,000 workers at its telephone operations headquarters.

GTE's move appears to be a short-term relocation. The company accepted a $52 billion merger deal that would make it part of Bell Atlantic, the local telephone company for much of the northeastern United States. If regulators approve the merger, the combined company would be based in New York, where Bell Atlantic is now headquartered. SBC has its own merger under consideration, the acquisition of Chicago-based Ameritech Corp., which was valued at $62 billion.

The deal, which faces a difficult approval process, would make SBC the local phone company to about one-third of U.S. phone lines and the dominant local phone company in 20 of the nation's largest 50 cities. It would be SBC's third acquisition since the federal Telecommunications Act of 1996 opened the door for competition in the nation's local telephone markets.

SBC is also seeking permission to sell long-distance services in Texas. State regulators were set to give their approval in summer of 1999, paving the way for federal approval and for Southwestern Bell to begin selling long-distance service to its Texas customers by 2000. And in another acquisition that will affect millions of Texas customers, AT&T purchased Tele-Communications Inc, parent company of TCI Cable. AT&T plans to offer telephone service over TCI cable lines, in addition to high-speed Internet access and cable television.

For most of the telecommunications industry's history, business and the government believed a telephone system would operate most efficiently if only one company provided the service. This philosophy created AT&T, the phone system's "Ma Bell" and — after the government decided that control over the vast majority of U.S. local and long-distance telephone traffic was too much power — the break-off "Baby Bells," which include Southwestern Bell.

Southwestern Bell sells local phone service to three out of four Texas telephone customers, including nearly all of the state's urban residents. The company operates 9.3 million of Texas' 12.3 million access lines.

GTE Corp., provides local phone service to about 17 percent of Texans, mainly in suburbs or rural markets. GTE has 2.1 million access lines.

Nearly 60 other companies provide residential local telephone service in Texas. Most have fewer than 5,000 access lines, but together they cover 40 percent of the state's land. The largest of these providers include Central Telephone of Texas, with 204,214 lines; United Telephone Company of Texas, with 149,501 lines; and Lufkin-Conroe Telephone Exchange, with 97,925 lines.

As technology has improved, telecommunications businesses are chasing opportunities to sell to customers outside their traditional service areas.

Companies saw deregulation as a way to sell a variety of new services to their existing customers.

The Texas Public Utility Regulatory Act of 1995, effective Sept. 1995, proposed to open the state's phone markets to competition. Big long-distance companies would have had to build their own local phone networks, however, and they complained that would be prohibitively expensive.

The federal Telecommunications Act of 1996, signed by President Clinton in 1996, set different terms for competition.

It ordered AT&T's former local phone divisions to open their local phone territories to competition before they could sell long-distance services there.

One exception: GTE, which was never part of the AT&T system and doesn't dominate large sectors of the U.S. telephone market, was allowed to begin selling long-distance service immediately. GTE's lucrative head start over its Baby Bell competitors allowed it to reach one million long-distance customers within about one year after the law passed.

For many customers, competition has been slow in coming. Major local and long-distance companies have argued in private negotiations, arbitration hearings and courtrooms over how to structure the financial deals. Once deals are reached, technical problems, including how to transfer customers to a new company, cause further delays in true local phone competition.

The Legislature changed the law again in 1999, giving Southwestern Bell more freedom to compete while cutting the access charges it collects from long-distance companies for using its local phone network. New competitors, including Dallas-based Allegiance Telecom, charged that the new rules could make it even more difficult to compete, as Southwestern Bell gained flexibility in how it prices and sells its services.

Other new laws from the 1999 Legislature are intended to protect consumers, with measures including allowing customers who don't pay their long-distance bills to keep their local phone service. New laws also impose more strict penalties against companies that cheat customers by "slamming" — switching their phone company without permission — or "cramming" — adding unauthorized charges to their bills.

Improved technology has driven change and heightened competition in other telecommunications services sectors, including wireless telephone and paging services, cable and the Internet. Until the 1990s, pagers and wireless phones were niche services for doctors, stockbrokers or real estate agents. Computer modems were so slow that words crawled across the screens, and the few dial-up databases that existed required complex codes for finding information that most consumers didn't bother to learn.

Families either had cable or they didn't; the monopoly companies had no competition.

Today's pagers can transmit headline news, stock

quotes or voice messages. Cell phones have shrunk, with better call quality. Modems are speedier, and, with the Internet and online services such as America Online and CompuServe, the information that customers can find via computer turned immensely more interesting. And new digital satellite service has become the fastest-growing consumer product in history, challenging an entrenched cable sector to improve service or lose customers.

Like more traditional phone companies, many of the businesses that sell new telecommunications services picked Texas for their home. Dallas and Plano are home to so many large paging operations that North Texas has been dubbed the "Paging Prairie."

But from a financial perspective, the industry continues to struggle. Old strategies of gaining market share fail to reap profits, and customers have been slow to take up new services such as voice messaging via pager or two-way paging, which lets users send messages back and forth.

Competition is also increasing in the wireless telephone industry, as the the federal goverment auctioned off new licenses to broadcast phone signals.

Older companies provide cellular phone service, either through analog systems, which transmit speech through the air in waves, or through updated digital systems, which send the signals in groups of zeros and ones. Newer wireless providers sell a new kind of system called Personal Communications Services. PCS, a digital system, offers clearer voice quality and less static, though calls can still be disconnected suddenly when signals get too weak.

Higher demand for new products has been a boon to equipment makers, concentrated in Richardson's Telecom Corridor. The suburban-Dallas area includes the U.S. headquarters for some of the world's biggest telecommunications manufacturers.

So many smaller companies have sprouted up to sell technology or services to these telecommunications giants that businesses complain of a shortage of workers. A 1996 report by the North Texas Commission said the sector, combined with other communications and information industry business, is the third-largest industry in the Dallas-Fort Worth area, behind health

Telephone Access Lines

City	1994	1997	1999
Abilene	64,625	66,862	79,489
Amarillo	107,078	110,871	130,225
Arlington	128,143	134,176	162,873
Austin (Metro)	526,434	550,237	807,056
Bay City	12,758	14,300	15,204
Beaumont	71,920	75,041	89,271
Brownsville-Harlingen	90,733	94,428	113,092
Cleburne	21,409	22,476	26,821
Corpus Christi (Metro)	147,532	153,022	178,987
Corsicana	14,431	14,854	17,660
Dallas (Metro)	1,149,379	1,226,721	1,438,447
El Paso	274,209	271,756	325,140
Fort Worth	553,600	586,208	868,946
Galveston	38,267	39,043	43,217
Greenville	15,568	16,051	18,370
Houston	1,746,992	1,802,024	2,347,677
Laredo	65,342	68,512	85,948
Longview	59,036	61,407	74,362
Lubbock	131,305	137,106	159,903
McAllen-Edinburg	74,585	81,367	99,243
McKinney	19,672	22,853	34,063
Midland	70,739	72,361	81,443
Mineral Wells	9,244	9,468	10,699
Odessa	62,447	64,526	71,060
Paris	20,974	21,664	25,246
Port Arthur	33,276	33,438	36,326
San Antonio (Metro)	689,409	725,910	912,345
Temple	32,064	34,196	38,360
Texas City	15,951	16,249	19,648
Tyler	70,530	74,030	88,291
Vernon	6,906	6,997	7,840
Victoria	39,627	40,864	39,010
Waco	103,414	105,798	127,978
Wichita Falls	58,119	60,041	68,791

Source: Southwestern Bell

care and the convention/tourism industry. The companies spent $22.9 billion and paid wages and salaries of $6.2 billion. ☆

Jennifer Files is a staff writer of The Dallas Morning News.

Gas Utilities

Source: Gas Services Division, Texas Railroad Commission

Approximately **200** investor-owned gas companies in Texas are classified as gas utilities and come under the regulatory jurisdiction of the Texas Railroad Commission. Approximately **133** of these companies reported gas operating revenue of **$5.2** billion in 1997, with operating expenses of **$5** billion.

In 1997, fixed investment for distribution facilities in Texas was **$1.6** billion and for transmission facilities, **$3.5** billion. Investment in Texas plants in service totaled **$7.06** billion. There were **35** investor-owned and **86** municipally owned distribution systems in operation in 1997 serving **1,050** Texas cities.

The **eight** largest distribution systems — six private and two municipal — served **97** percent of all residential customers. In 1997, there were approximately **3.5** million residential customers, **307,797** small commercial and industrial users, **493** large industrial customers

and **13,400** other gas-utility customers. The breakdown of distribution sales to these customers was: **62** Mcf (thousand cubic feet) per residential customer, **489** Mcf per commercial customer, **149,315** Mcf per industrial customer and **1,311** Mcf for customers in the "other" category. Distribution sales amounted to **217.5** billion cubic feet in 1997. In addition to industrial sales made by distribution companies, transmission companies reported pipeline-to-industry sales of **1.1** trillion cubic feet and revenue from these sales of **$2.9** billion.

In 1997, the average annual residential gas bill in the United States was **$601**. The average annual bill in Texas for the same year was **$370**, up **$17** from the previous year. The State of Texas collected **$5.6** million in gas-utility taxes from gas utilities in fiscal year 1998.

Texas had a total of **120,833** miles of natural-gas pipelines in operation in 1997, including **7,911** miles of field and gathering lines, **36,143** miles of transmission lines and **76,779** miles of distribution lines. ☆

Electricity Utilities in Texas

By Dianne Solis

In Texas, ten investor-owned electricity utilities serve 8.6 million customers under the regulatory jurisdiction of the Texas Public Utility Commission.

Collectively, the utilities reported revenue of about $20 billion in 1998. The industry, however, is dominated by two powerhouses: Dallas-based TXU Corp. (formerly Texas Utilities Co.) and Houston-based Reliant Energy Inc. (formerly Houston Industries Inc.). Together, the duo supply electricity to nearly half the Texas market.

TXU serves 2.6 million customers through its electricity unit TU Electric; Reliant Energy serves 1.6 million customers through its electricity unit Houston Lighting and Power.

Other investor-owned electricity utilities serving Texans are Dallas-based Central & South West Corp., El Paso Electric Co. and New Orleans-based Entergy Corp. The five utilities have more than 70 percent of the state's market.

Thanks to the extreme Texas heat . . . the average residential bill for a Texan is an annual $1,063

Thanks to the extreme Texas heat and the need to consume more electricity to run air-conditioners, the average residential electricity bill for a Texan is an annual $1,063.12, compared with an annual $858.84 for the nation. Texas annual bills are the nation's fourth-largest.

But the average kilowatt hour that a Texas residential customer paid in 1999 was 7.77 cents, according to the Washington-based Edison Electric Institute. The average kilowatt hour for a residential customer in the nation was 8.93 cents. When the averages include muncipality-run utilities and cooperatives, average rates fall lower. Texans paid 7.61 per kilowatt hour, while the nation paid 8.36.

And that 7.77 cents is an important point. Complex deregulation legislation for the Lone Star state was passed in May 1999 that, theoretically, is designed to bust the monopoly power of the electricity utilities in their retail sales.

The 1999 legislation essentially freezes electricity rates until Jan. 1, 2002, when competition begins. Rates would fall 6 percent and remain there until 2005 -- or until the large electricity companies lose 40 percent of their customers.

To persuade companies to open their markets and to compete in other areas, the legislation provides for fines for large corporations that don't eventually lose 40 percent of their customers — unless they take on customers outside their traditional markets.

Texas lawmakers want new competitors to win customers by selling at lower prices than those the established companies charge.

Consumer advocates, however, argue that residential customers may be better off in the regulated markets of yesteryear.

The federal government has proposed deregulating retail electricity sales in the $250 billion national market by Jan. 1, 2003.

Many electricity utilities already own natural gas utilities or transmission-pipeline companies, as well. That will make it possible in the future for companies such as TXU and Reliant Energy to bundle services under one customer bill.

Earlier deregulation in the wholesale selling and generation side of the electricity industry has brought many non-utility newcomers to the power scene.

Among them have been Houston-based Enron Corp., which has transformed itself from a natural-gas pipeline firm into a global natural gas, electricity and water services giant.

Its trading unit arranges large power sales and uses futures contracts for electricity and other financial agreements to protect commercial and industrial customers from price swings.

Deregulation has also unshackled the geographic boundaries for many investor-owned utilities. TXU, for example, now has electricity customers from Australia to Great Britain, Mexico to the Czech Republic.

It has also changed the products that utility holding companies offer from only electricity to electricity, natural gas, water and even telecommunications.

During 1998, the Texas electricity market had a net system capacity of 65,071 megawatts and during peak demand used 61,698 megawatts.

In 1998, investor-owned utilities owned 71 percent of the capacity; municipality-owned utilities owned 12 percent; river authorities owned 3 percent; electricity co-operatives owned 2 percent; and non-utility generators owned the other 12 percent. ☆

Dianne Solis is a staff writer of The Dallas Morning News.

Electric Cooperatives

Source: The Texas Electric Cooperatives (www.texas-ec.org/coop/coop.html).

Electric cooperatives are nonprofit, consumer-owned utilities providing electric service primarily in rural areas. Rates and services are regulated by the Public Utility Commission of Texas.

They were organized in the 1930s and 1940s when investor-owned utilities neglected or refused to serve farms and rural communities.

By mid-1999, there were **73** electric-distribution cooperatives and **11** generation and transmission cooperatives (G&Ts) — which are owned by local distribution cooperatives — serving nearly **3** million member-customers in **244** of the 254 counties in Texas.

Three of the G&Ts generate power while the others represent their member distribution systems in wholesale power supply arrangements.

The systems operate more than **260,000** miles of line with an average density of fewer than **5** meters per mile of line.

The distribution systems and G&Ts employ more than 5,500 persons. ☆

Texas Pronunciation Guide

Texas' rich cultural diversity is reflected nowhere better than in the names of places. Standard pronunciation is used in many cases, but purely colloquial pronunciation often is used, too.

In the late 1940s, George Mitchel Stokes, a graduate student at Baylor University, developed a list of pronunciations of 2,300 place names across the state.

Stokes earned his doctorate and eventually served as director of the speech division in the Communications Studies Department at Baylor University. He retired in 1983.

In the following list based on Stokes longer list, pronunciation is by respelling and diacritical marking. Respelling is employed as follows: "ah" as in the exclarnation, ah, or the "o" in tot; "ee" as in meet; "oo" as in moot; "yoo" as in use; "ow" as in cow; "oi" as in oil; "uh" as in mud.

Note that ah, uh and the apostrophe(') are used for varying degrees of neutral vowel sounds, the apostrophe being used where the vowel is barely sounded. Diacritical markings are used as follows: bāle, băd, lĕt, rīse, rĭll, ōak, brōōd, fŏŏt.

The stressed syllable is capitalized. Secondary stress is indicated by an underline as in Atascosa—ăt uhs KŌ suh.

A

Abilene—ĂB uh leen
Acala—uh KĀ luh
Ackerly—ĂK er lĭ
Acton—ĂK t'n
Acuff—Ā kuhf
Addielou—ă dĭ LŌŌ
Afton—ĀF t'n
Agua Dulce—ah wuh DŌŌL sĭ
Agua Nueva—ah wuh nyōō Ā vuh
Alamo—ĂL uh mō
Alanreed—ĂL uhn reed
Albany—AWL buh nĭ
Aledo—uh LEE dō
Algoa—ăl GŌ uh
Alief—Ā leef
Alpine—ĂL pīn
Altair—awl TĂR
Alta Loma—ăl tuh LŌ muh
Alto—ĂL tō
Altoga—ăl TŌ guh
Alvarado—ăl vuh RĀ dō
Alvord—ĂL vord
Amarillo—ăm uh RĬL ŏ
Ammannsville—ĂM 'nz vĭl
Anahuac—ĂN uh wăk
Andice—ĂN dĭs
Angelina—ăn juh LEE nuh
Angleton—ĂNG g'l t'n
Annona—ă NŌ nuh
Anton—ĂNT n
Aquilla—uh KWĬL uh
Aransas—uh RĂN zuhs
Aransas Pass—uh răn zuhs PĂS
Arbala—ahr BĀ luh
Arcadia—ahr KĀ dĭ uh
Arcola—ahr KŌ luh
Argo—AHR gō
Argyle—ahr GĬL
Arlington—AHR lĭng t'n
Arneckeville—AHR nĭ kĭ vĭl
Arnett—AHR nĭt
Artesia Wells—ahr tee zh' WĔLZ
Aspermont—ĂS per mahnt
Atascosa—ăt uhs KŌ suh
Attoyac—AT uh yăk
Austin—AWS t'n
Austonio—aws TŌ nĭ ŏ
Austwell—AWS wĕl

Avalon—ĂV uhl n
Avinger—Ă vĭn jer
Avoca—uh VŌ kuh
Axtell—ĂKS t'l
Azle—Ā z'l

B

Ballinger—BĂL ĭn jer
Balmorhea—băl muh RĀ
Bandera—băn DĔR uh
Banquete—băn KĔ tĭ
Barclay—BAHRK lĭ
Bassett—BĂ sĭt
Bastrop—BĂS trahp
Beaukiss—bō KĬS
Beaumont—BŌ mahnt
Bebe—bee bee
Beckville—BĔK v'l
Becton—BĔK t'n
Bedias—BEE dĭs
Beeville—BEE vĭl
Belcherville—BĔL cher vĭl
Belton—BĔL t'n
Benarnold—bĕn AHR n'ld
Benavides—bĕn uh VEE d's
Ben Hur—bĕn HER
Berclair—ber KLĂR
Bertram—BERT r'm
Bessmay—bĕs MĀ
Bettie—BĔT ĭ
Bexar—BA är
Beyersville—BĪRZ vĭl
Biardstown—BĂRDZ t'n
Birome—bĭ RŌM
Blanco—BLĂNG kō
Blewett—BLŌŌ ĭt
Bluffton—BLUHF t'n
Boerne—BER nĭ
Bogata—buh GŌ duh
Boling—BŌL ĭng
Bolivar—BAH lĭ ver
Bomarton—BŌ mer t'n
Bonita—bō NEE tuh
Bonney—BAH nĭ
Bon Wier—bahn WEER
Borden—BAWRD n
Borger—BŌR ger
Bosque—BAHS kĭ
Boston—BAWS t'n

Bovina—bō VEE nuh
Bowie—BŌŌ Ĭ
Brachfield—BRĂCH feeld
Bracken—BRĀ kĭn
Brackettville—BRĂ kĭt vĭl
Brashear—bruh SHĬR
Brazoria—bruh ZŌ rĭ uh
Brazos—BRĂZ uhs
Bremond—bree MAHND
Brenham—BRĔ n'm
Brewster—BRŌŌ ster
Britton—BRĬT n
Broaddus—BRAW d's
Bronte—brahnt
Browndel—brown DĔL
Bruceville—BRŌŌS v'l
Brundage—BRUHN dĭj
Bruni—BRŌŌ nĭ
Bryarly—BRĬ er lĭ
Buchanan Dam—buhk hăn uhn DĂM
Buda—BYŌŌ duh
Buena Vista—bwa nuh VEES tuh
Bula—BYŌŌ luh
Bulverde—bŏŏl VER dĭ
Buna—BYŌŌ nuh
Burkburnett—berk ber NET
Burkett—BER kĭt
Burkeville—BERK vĭl
Burleson—BER luh s'n
Burnet—BER nĕt
Bustamante—buhs tuh MAHN tĭ

C

Caddo Mills—kă dō MĬLZ
Calallen—kăl ĂL ĭn
Calaveras—kăl uh VĔR's
Calliham—KĂL uh hăm
Callisburg—KĂ lĭs berg
Cameron—KĂM uh r'n
Canadian—kuh NĀ dĭ uhn
Candelaria—kăn duh LĔ rĭ uh
Canton—KĂNT n
Canyon—KĂN y'n
Caplen—KĂP lĭn
Caradan—KĂR uh dăn
Carlisle—KAHR lĭl
Carlsbad—KAHR uhlz bad
Carlton—KAHR uhl t'n
Carmine—kahr MEEN

Carmona—kahr MŌ nuh
Caro—KAH rō
Carrizo Springs—kuh ree zuh
     SPRĬNGZ
Carrollton—KĂR 'l t'n
Carson—KAHR s'n
Carthage—KAHR thĭj
Cason—KĀ s'n
Castell—kăs TĔL
Castro—KĂS trō
Castroville—KĂS tro vĭl
Catarina—kăt uh REE nuh
Caviness—KĀ vĭ nĕs
Cayuga—kā YŌŌ guh
Cedar Bayou—see der BĪ ō
Cee Vee—see VEE
Celeste—suh LĔST
Celina—suh LĬ nuh
Centralia—sĕn TRĂL yuh
Charco—CHAHR kō
Charleston—CHAHR uhls t'n
Charlotte—SHAHR l't
Chatfield—CHĂT feeld
Cheapside—CHEEP sīd
Cherokee—CHĔR uh kee
Chico—CHEE kō
Chicota—chĭ KŌ tuh
Childress—CHĬL drĕs
Chillicothe—chĭl ĭ KAH thĭ
Chilton—CHĬL t'n
Chireno—sh' REE nō
Chisholm—CHĬZ uhm
Chita—CHEE tuh
Chocolate Bayou—chah kuh lĭt BĪ ō
Chriesman—KRĬS m'n
Christine—krĭs TEEN
Christoval—krĭs TŌ v'l
Cibolo—SEE bō lō
Cisco—SĬS kō
Cistern—SĬS tern
Clairemont—KLĂR mahnt
Clairette—klăr ĭ ĔT
Clarendon—KLĂR ĭn d'n
Clareville—KLĂR vĭl
Cleburne—KLEE bern
Clemville—KLĔM vĭl
Cleveland—KLEEV l'nd
Clodine—klaw DEEN
Coahoma—kuh HŌ muh
Cockrell Hill—kahk ruhl HĬL
College Station—kah lĭj STĀ sh'n
Collin—KAH lĭn
Collingsworth—KAH lĭnz werth
Collinsville—KAH lĭnz vĭl
Colmesneil—KŌL m's neel
Colorado—kahl uh RAH dō
Colorado City—kah luh ră duh SĬT ĭ
Columbus—kuh LUHM b's
Comal—KŌ măl
Comanche—kuh MĂN chĭ
Combes—kōmz
Commerce—KAH mers
Como—KŌ mō
Concan—KAHN kăn
Concepcion—kuhn sep sĭ ŌN
Concho—KAHN chō
Conlen—KAHN lĭn
Conroe—KAHN rō
Cooper—KŌŌ per

Copeville—KŌP v'l
Coppell—kuhp PĔL or kuh PĔL
Copperas Cove—kahp ruhs KŌV
Corbett—KAWR bĭt
Cordele—kawr DĔL
Corinth—KAH rĭnth
Corley—KAWR lĭ
Corpus Christi—kawr p's KRĬS tĭ
Corrigan—KAWR uh g'n
Corsicana—kawr sĭ KĂN uh
Coryell—kō rĭ ĔL
Cottle—KAH t'l
Cotulla—kuh TŌŌ luh
Coupland—KŌP l'n
Courtney—KŌRT nĭ
Covington—KUHV ĭng t'n
Crafton—KRĂF t'n
Crandall—KRĂN d'l
Cranfills Gap—krăn f'lz GĂP
Creedmore—KREED mōr
Cresson—KRĔ s'n
Crockett—KRAH kĭt
Crowell—KRŌ uhl
Crowley—KROW li
Cuero—KWĔR o
Culberson—KUHL ber s'n
Cumby—KUHM bĭ
Cuney—KYŌŌ nĭ
Cunningham—KUHN ĭng hăm
Currie—KER rĭ
Cuthand—KUHT hănd
Cyclone—SĪ klōn
Cypress—SĪ prĕs

D

Dabney—DĂB nĭ
Dacosta—duh KAHS tuh
Dacus—DĂ k's
Daingerfield—DĀN jer feeld
Daisetta—dā ZĔT uh
Dalby Springs—dĂl bĭ SPRĬNGZ
Dalhart—DĂL hahrt
Dallam—DĂL uhm
Dallas—DĂ luhs
Damon—DĂ m'n
Danbury—DĂN bĕrĭ
Danciger—DĂN sĭ ger
Danevang—DĂN uh văng
Darrouzett—dăr uh ZĔT
Davilla—duh VĬL uh
Dayton—DĀT n
Deaf Smith—dĕf SMĬTH
Deanville—DEEN vĭl
De Berry—duh BĔ rĭ
Decatur—dee KĀT er
De Kalb—dĭ KĂB
De Leon—da lee AHN
Del Rio—dĕl REE o
Delta—DĔL tuh
Del Valle—dĕl VĂ lĭ
Delwin—DĔl wĭn
Denhawken—DĬN haw kĭn
Denison—DĔN uh s'n
Denton—DĔNT n
Deport—dĭ PŌRT
Desdemona—dĕz dĭ MŌ nuh
DeSoto—dĭ SŌ tuh
Detroit—dee TROIT
Devers—DĔ vers

Devine—duh VĬN
DeWitt—dĭ WĬT
Dexter—DĔKS ter
D'Hanis—duh HĂ nĭs
Dialville—DĪ uhl vil
Diboll—DĪ bawl
Dike—dīk
Dilley—DĬL i
Dilworth—DĬL werth
Dimmit—DĬM ĭt
Dinero—dĭ NĔ rō
Direct—duh RĔKT
Dobbin—DAH bĭn
Dobrowolski—dah bruh WAHL skĭ
Donie—DŌ nĭ
Doole—DOO lĭ
Dorchester—dawr CHĔS ter
Doucette—DŌŌ sĕt
Dougherty—DAHR tĭ
Douglass—DUHG l's
Dozier—DŌ zher
Dryden—DRĪD n
Dublin—DUHB lĭn
Duffau—DUHF ō
Dumas—DŌŌ m's
Dumont—DYŌŌ mahnt
Dundee—DUHN dĭ
Durango—duh RĂNG go
Duval—DŌŌ vawl

E

East Bernard—eest ber NAHRD
Easterly—EES ter lĭ
Eastland—EEST l'nd
Ector—ĔK ter
Edcouch—ĕd KOWCH
Eddy—E di
Edom—EE d'm
Edroy—ĔD roi
Egan—EE g'n
Egypt—EE juhpt
Elbert—ĔL bert
El Campo—ĕl KĂM pō
Eldorado—ĕl duh RĂ duh
Electra—ĭ LĔK truh
Elgin—ĔL jĭn
Eliasville—ee LĬ uhs vĭl
El Indio—ĕl ĬN dĭ ō
Elkhart—ĔLK hahrt
Ellinger—ĔL ĭn jer
Elliott—ĔL ĭ 't
Ellis—ĔL uhs
Elmendorf—ĔLM 'n dawrf
Elm Mott—ĕl MAHT
Elmo—ĔL mō
Eloise—ĔL o eez
El Paso—ĕl PĂS ō
Elysian Fields—uh lee zh'n FEELDZ
Encinal—ĕn suh NAHL
Encino—ĕn SEE nō
Enloe—ĔN lō
Ennis—ĔN ĭs
Enochs—EE nuhks
Eola—ee Ō luh
Era—EE ruh
Erath—EE răth
Esperanza—ĕs per RĂN zuh
Estelline—ĔS tuh leen
Etoile—ĭ TOIL

Etter—ĔT er
Eula—YŌŌ luh
Euless—YŌŌ lis
Eureka—yōō REE kuh
Eustace—YŌŌS t's
Evadale—EE vuh dāl
Evant—EE vănt
Everman—Ĕ ver m'n

F

Fabens—FĀ b'nz
Fairlie—FĀR lee
Falfurrias—făl FYŌŌ rĭ uhs
Fannett—fă NĔT
Fannin—FĂN ĭn
Farrar—FĂR uh
Farwell—FAHR w'l
Fashing—FĂ shĭng
Fayette—fă ĔT
Fayetteville—FĀ uht vĭl
Fentress—FĔN trĭs
Ferris—FĔR ĭs
Fieldton—FEEL t'n
Fife—fīf
Fisher—FĬSH er
Fischer—fĭ sher
Flatonia—flă TŌN yuh
Flomot—FLŌ maht
Florence—FLAH ruhns
Floresville—FLŌRZ vil
Florey—FLŌ ri
Floydada—floi DĀ duh
Fluvanna—flōō VĂN uh
Foard City—fōrd SĬT ĭ
Fodice—FŌ dĭs
Follett—fah LĔT
Fordtran—fōrd TRĂN
Forney—FAWR nĭ
Forsan—FŌR săn
Fort Chadbourne—fōrt CHĂD bern
Fort Worth—fōrt WERTH
Fowlerton—FOW ler t'n
Francitas—frăn SEE t's
Fredericksburg—FRĔD er rĭks berg
Fredonia—free DŌN yuh
Freer—FREE er
Frelsburg—FRĔLZ berg
Fresno—FRĔZ nō
Frio—FREE ō
Friona—free O nuh
Fritch—frĭch
Frydek—FRĬ dĕk
Fulshear—FUHL sher

G

Gail—gāl
Gainesville—GĀNZ vuhl
Galena Park—guh lee nuh PAHRK
Gallatin—GĂL uh t'n
Galveston—GĂL vĕs t'n
Ganado—guh NĀ dō
Garceno—gahr SĂ nō
Garciasville—gahr SEE uhs vĭl
Garland—GAHR l'nd
Garza—GAHR zuh
Gause—gawz
Geneva—juh NEE vuh
Geronimo—juh RAH nĭ mō
Giddings—GĬD ĭngz

Gillespie—guh LĔS pĭ
Gillett—juh LĔT
Gilliland—GĬL ĭ l'nd
Gilmer—GĬL mer
Girard—juh RAHRD
Girvin—GER vĭn
Gladewater—GLĂD wah ter
Glasscock—GLĂS kahk
Glazier—GLĀ zher
Glenfawn—glĕn FAWN
Glen Flora—glĕn FLŌ ruh
Glidden—GLĬD n
Gober—GŌ ber
Godley—GAHD lĭ
Goldthwaite—GŌLTH wāt
Goliad—GŌ lĭ ăd
Golindo—gō LĬN duh
Gonzales—guhn ZAH l's
Goodland—GŌŌD l'n
Goodlett—GŌŌD lĕt
Goree—GŌ ree
Gouldbusk—GŌŌLD buhsk
Granbury—GRĂN bĕ rĭ
Grand Saline—grăn suh LEEN
Granger—GRĂN jer
Greenville—GREEN v'l
Groesbeck—GRŌZ bĕk
Groveton—GRŌV t'n
Gruene—green
Grulla—GRŌŌL yuh
Gruver—GRŌŌ ver
Guadalupe—gwah duh LŌŌ pĭ
Guerra—GWĔ ruh
Gunter—GUHN ter
Gustine—GUHS teen
Guthrie—GUHTH rĭ

H

Hagansport—HĀ gĭnz pōrt
Hallettsville—HĂL ĕts vĭl
Hamon—HĂ m'n
Hamshire—HĂM sher
Handley—HĂND lĭ
Hankamer—HĂN kăm er
Hardeman—HAHR duh m'n
Hardin—HAHRD n
Hargill—HAHR gĭl
Harleton—HAHR uhl t'n
Harlingen—HAHR lĭn juhn
Harrold—HĂR 'ld
Haslam—HĂZ I'm
Haslet—HĂS lĕt
Hasse—HĂ sĭ
Hatchell—HĂ ch'l
Hawkins—HAW kĭnz
Hawley—HAW lĭ
Hearne—hern
Heath—heeth
Hebbronville—HĔB r'n vĭl
Hebron—HEE br'n
Hedley—HĔD lĭ
Heidenheimer—HĬD n hīmer
Helena—HĔL uh nuh
Helotes—hĕl Ō tĭs
Hemphill—HĔMP hĭl
Hempstead—HĔM stĕd
Hereford—HER ferd
Hermleigh—HER muh lee
Hewitt—HYŌŌ ĭt

Hico—HĬ kō
Hidalgo—hĭ DĂL gō
Hillister—HĬL ĭs ter
Hindes—hĭndz
Hitchland—HĬCH l'nd
Hochheim—HŌ hīm
Hondo—HAHN dō
Houston—HYŌŌS t'n or YŌŌS t'n
Howland—HOW l'nd
Huckabay—HUHK uh bĭ
Hudspeth—HUHD sp'th
Humble—HUHM b'l
Hungerford—HUHNG ger ferd
Huntsville—HUHNTS v'l
Hutchins—HUH chĭnz
Hutchinson—HUH chĭn s'n
Hutto—HUH tō
Hye—hī
Hylton—HĬL t'n

I

Iago—ī Ā gō
Idalou—Ī duh lōō
Inadale—Ī nuh dāl
Inez—ī NĔZ
Ingram—ĬNG gr'm
Iola—ī Ō luh
Ira—Ī ruh
Iraan—ī ruh ĂN
Iredell—Ī ruh dĕl
Ireland—Ī rĭ l'nd
Irene—ī REEN
Irion—ĬR i uhn
Ironton—ĬRN t'n
Irving—ER vĭng
Italy—ĬT uh lĭ
Itasca—ī TĂS kuh
Ivan—Ī v'n
Ivanhoe—Ī v'n hō

J

Jardin—JAHRD n
Jarrell—JĂR uhl
Jayton—JĀT n
Jeddo—JĔ dō
Jericho—JĔ rĭ kō
Jermyn—JER m'n
Jewett—JŌŌ ĭt
Jiba—HEE buh
Joaquin—waw KEEN
Joinerville—JOI ner vĭl
Jonah—JŌ nuh
Jourdanton—JERD n t'n
Juliff—JŌŌ lĭf
Juno—JŌŌ nō
Justin—JUHS tĭn

K

Kalgary—KĂL gĕ rĭ
Kamay—KĀ ĭm ā
Kanawha—KAHN uh wah
Karnack—KAHR năk
Katemcy—kuh TĔM sĭ
Kaufman—KAWF m'n
Keechi—KEE chĭ
Keene—keen
Kellerville—KĔL er vĭl
Kemah—KEE muh
Kendalia—kĕn DĀL yuh

Kennard—kuh NAHRD
Kennedale—KĚN uh dāl
Kerens—KER 'nz
Kilgore—KĬL gōr
Killeen—kuh LEEN
Kleberg—KLĀ berg
Klondike—KLAHN dīk
Knickerbocker—NĬK uh <u>bah</u> ker
Knippa—kuh NĬP uh
Kosciusko—kuh SHŌŌS kō
Kosse—KAH sĭ
Kountze—kōōntz
Kress—kres
Krum—kruhm
Kurten—KER t'n
Kyle—kīl

L

La Blanca—lah BLAHN kuh
La Coste—luh KAWST
Ladonia—luh DŌN yuh
LaFayette—lah fī ĚT
Laferia—luh FĚ rĭ uh
Lagarto—luh GAHR tō
La Gloria—lah GLŌ rĭ uh
La Grange—luh GRĀNJ
Laguna—luh GŌŌ nuh
La Joya—luh HŌ yuh
Lamarque—luh MAHRK
Lamasco—luh MĂS kō
Lamesa—luh MEE suh
Lamkin—LĂM kĭn
Lampasas—lăm PĂ s's
Lancaster—LĂNG k's ter
La Paloma—<u>lah</u> puh LŌ muh
La Porte—luh PŌRT
La Pryor—luh PRĪ er
Laredo—luh RĀ dō
Lariat—LĂ ri uht
La Rue—luh RŌŌ
LaSalle—luh SĂL
Lasara—luh SĚ ruh
Lassater—LĂ sĭ ter
Latexo—luh TĚKS ō
Lavaca—luh VĂ kuh
La Vernia—luh VER nĭ uh
La Villa—lah VĬL uh
Lavon—luh VAHN
La Ward—luh WAWRD
Leakey—LĀ kĭ
Leander—lee ĂN der
Leary—LĬ er ĭ
Lefors—lĭ FŌRZ
Leggett—LĚ gĭt
Lela—LEE luh
Lelia Lake—<u>leel</u> yuh LĀK
Lenorah—lĕ NŌ ruh
Leon—lee AHN
Leona—<u>lee</u> Ō nuh
Leon Springs—lee ahn SPRĬNGZ
Leroy—LEE roi
Levelland—LĚ v'l lănd
Levita—luh VĬ tuh
Lewisville—LŌŌ ĭs vĭl
Lexington—LĚKS ĭng t'n
Lillian—LĬL yuhn
Lindale—LĬN dāl
Linden—LĬN d'n
Lindenau—lĭn duh NOW

Lindsay—LĬN zĭ
Lingleville—LĬNG g'l vĭl
Lipan—lĭ PĂN
Lipscomb—LĬPS k'm
Lissie—LĬ sĭ
Liverpool—LĬ ver pōōl
Livingston—LĬV ĭngz t'n
Llano—LĂ nō
Locker—LAH ker
Lockett—LAH kĭt
Lockhart—LAHK hahrt
Lockney—LAHK nĭ
Lodi—LŌ dī
Lohn—lahn
Lolita—lō LEE tuh
Loma Alto—<u>lō</u> muh ĂL tō
Lometa—lō MEE tuh
Long Mott—lawng MAHT
Lopeno—lō PEE nō
Loraine—lō RĀN
Lorena—lō REE nuh
Los Angeles—laws AN juh l's
Los Ebanos—lōs ĚB uh nōs
Los Fresnos—lōs FRĚZ nōs
Los Indios—lōs ĬN dĭ ōs
Losoya—luh SAW yuh
Lott—laht
Lovelady—LUHV lā dĭ
Lubbock—LUH buhk
Lueders—LŌŌ derz
Luella—lōō ĚL uh
Lufkin—LUHF kĭn
Luling—LŌŌ lĭng
Lund—luhnd
Lutie—LŌŌ tĭ
Lyford—LĬ ferd
Lyons—LĬ 'nz
Lytton Springs—lĬt n SPRĬNGZ

M

Mabank—MĀ băngk
Macune—muh KŌŌN
Magnolia—măg NŌL yuh
Malakoff—MĂL uh kawf
Malone—muh LŌN
Malta—MAWL tuh
Manchaca—MĂN shăk
Manchester—MĂN chĕs ter
Manheim—MĂN hīm
Mankins—MĂN kĭnz
Manor—MĀ ner
Mansfield—MĂNZ feeld
Manvel—MĂN v'l
Marathon—MĂR uh th'n
Marfa—MAHR fuh
Markham—MAHR k'm
Marlin—MAHR lĭn
Marquez—mahr KĀ
Maryneal—mā rĭ NEEL
Marysville—MĀ rĭz vĭl
Matador—MĂT uh dōr
Matagorda—măt uh GAWR duh
Mathis—MĀ thĭs
Mauriceville—maw REES vĭl
Maverick—MĂV rĭk
Maxey—MĂKS ĭ
Maxwell—MĂKS w'l
Maydell—MĀ dĕl
Maypearl—<u>mā</u> PERL

McCamey—muh KĀ mĭ
McCaulley—muh KAW lĭ
McCulloch—muh KUH luhk
McKinney—muh KĬN ĭ
McLean—muh KLĂN
McLennan—muhk LĚN uhn
McLeod—măk LOWD
McMahan—măk MĂN
McQueeney—muh KWEE nĭ
Medill—mĕ DĬL
Medina—muh DEE nuh
Megargel—muh GAHR g'l
Melissa—muh LĬS uh
Melrose—MĚL rōz
Memphis—MĚM fĭs
Menard—muh NAHRD
Mendoza—mĕn DŌ zuh
Mentone—mĕn TON
Mercedes—<u>mer</u> SĀ deez
Mereta—muh RĚT uh
Meridian—muh RĬ dĭ uhn
Merkel—MER k'l
Mertens—<u>mer</u> TĚNZ
Mertzon—MERTS n
Mesquite—muhs KEET
Mexia—muh HĀ uh
Meyersville—MĪRZ vĭl
Miami—mĭ ĂM ĭ
Mico—MEE kō
Midland—MĬD l'nd
Midlothian—<u>mĭd</u> LŌ thĭ n
Milam—MĪ l'm
Milano—mĭ LĂ nō
Mildred—MĬL drĕd
Millett—MĬL ĭt
Millheim—MĬL hīm
Millican—MĬL uh kuhn
Millsap—MĬL săp
Minden—MĬN d'n
Mineola—mĭn ĭ Ō luh
Mineral Wells—mĭn er uhl WĚLZ
Minerva—mĭ NER vuh
Mingus—MĬNG guhs
Minter—MĬNT er
Mirando City—mĭ răn duh SĬT ĭ
Missouri City—muh zŏŏr uh SĬT ĭ
Mobeetie—mō BEE tĭ
Moline—mō LEEN
Monahans—MAH nuh hănz
Monaville—MŌ nuh vĭl
Montague—mahn TĀG
Montalba—mahnt ĂL buh
Mont Belvieu—mahnt BĚL vyōō
Montell—mahn TĚL
Montgomery—<u>mahnt</u> GUHM er ĭ
Monthalia—mahn THĂL yuh
Morales—muh RAH lĕs
Moran—mō RĂN
Moscow—MAHS kow
Mosheim—MŌ shīm
Motley—MAHT lĭ
Moulton—MŌL t'n
Mount Selman—mownt SĚL m'n
Mount Sylvan—mownt SĬL v'n
Muenster—MYŌŌNS ter
Muldoon—muhl DŌŌN
Muleshoe—MYŌŌL shōō
Munday—MUHN dĭ
Murchison—MER kuh s'n

Mykawa—mĭ KAH wuh
Myra—MĬ ruh
Myrtle Springs—<u>mert</u> I SPRĬNGZ

N

Nacogdoches—<u>năk</u> uh DŌ chĭs
Nada—NĀ duh
Natalia—nuh TĂL yuh
Navarro—nuh VĂ rō
Navasota—năv uh SŌ tuh
Nazareth—NĂZ uh r'th
Neches—NĀ chĭs
Nederland—NEE der l'nd
Needville—NEED vĭl
Nelsonville—NĔL s'n vĭl
Neuville—NYŌŌ v'l
Nevada—nuh VĂ duh
Newark—NŌŌ erk
New Baden—nyōō BĀD n
New Braunfels—nyōō BROWN fĕlz
Newsome—NYŌŌ s'm
Newton—NYŌŌT n
New Ulm—nyōō UHLM
Nimrod—NĬM rahd
Nineveh—NĬN uh vuh
Nocona—nō KŌ nuh
Nopal—NŌ păl
Nordheim—NAWRD hīm
Normandy—NAWR m'n dĭ
Normangee—NAWR m'n <u>jee</u>
Normanna—nawr MĂN uh
Northrup—NAWR thr'p
North Zulch—nawrth ZŌŌLCH
Novice—NAH vĭs
Nueces—nyōō Ā sĭs
Nugent—NYŌŌ j'nt

O

Oakalla—ō KĂL uh
Ochiltree—AH k'l tree
Odessa—ō DĔS uh
Oenaville—ō EEN uh v'l
Oglesby—Ō g'lz bĭ
Oilton—OIL t'n
Oklaunion—<u>ōk</u> luh YŌŌN y'n
Oldham—ŌL d'm
Olivia—<u>ō</u> LĬV ĭ uh
Olmito—awl MEE tuh
Olmos Park—ahl m's PAHRK
Olney—AHL ni
Olton—ŌL t'n
Omaha—Ō muh haw
Onalaska—<u>uhn</u> uh LĂS kuh
Oplin—AHP lĭn
Osceola—ō sĭ Ō luh
Otey—Ō tĭ
Otis Chalk—<u>ō</u> tĭs CHAWLK
Ottine—ah TEEN
Ovalo—ō VĂL uh
Ozona—ō ZŌ nuh

P

Paducah—puh DYŌŌ kuh
Palacios—puh LĂ sh's
Palestine—PAL uhs <u>teen</u>
Palito Blanco—p' <u>lee</u> to BLAHNG kō
Palo Pinto—<u>pă</u> lō PĬN tō
Paluxy—puh LUHK sĭ
Pampa—PĂM puh

Pandora—păn DŌR uh
Panna Maria—<u>păn</u> uh muh REE uh
Papalote—pah puh LŌ tĭ
Pasadena—<u>păs</u> uh DEE nuh
Patricia—puh TRĬ shuh
Patroon—puh TRŌŌN
Pawnee—paw NEE
Pearland—PĂR lănd
Pearsall—PEER sawl
Peaster—PEES ter
Pecan Gap—pĭ kahn GAP
Pecos—PĀ k's
Penelope—puh NĔL uh pĭ
Penitas—puh NEE t's
Penwell—PĬN wĕl
Peoria—pee Ō rĭ uh
Percilla—per SĬL uh
Perrin—PĔR ĭn
Petrolia—puh TRŌL yuh
Petteway—PĔT uh wā
Pflugerville—FLŌŌ ger vĭl
Pharr—fahr
Phelps—fĕlps
Pidcoke—PĬD kōk
Piedmont—PEED mahnt
Placedo—PLĂS ĭ dō
Placid—PLĂ sĭd
Plano—PLĂ nō
Plantersville—PLĂN terz vĭl
Plaska—PLĂS kuh
Plateau—plă TŌ
Pollock—PAHL uhk
Ponder—PAHN der
Ponta—pahn TĂ
Pontotoc—PAHNT uh tahk
Port Aransas—pōrt uh RĂN zuhs
Port Bolivar—<u>pōrt</u> BAH lĭ ver
Port Isabel—pōrt ĬZ uh bĕl
Port Lavaca—<u>pōrt</u> luh VĂ kuh
Port Neches—pōrt NĀ chĭs
Posey—PŌ zĭ
Poteet—pō TEET
Poth—pōth
Potosi—puh TŌ sĭ
Poynor—POI ner
Prairie Lea—prĕr ĭ LEE
Prairieville—PRĔR ĭ vĭl
Premont—PREE mahnt
Presidio—pruh SĬ dĭ ō
Priddy—PRĬ dĭ
Primera—<u>pree</u> MĔ ruh
Pritchett—PRĬ chĭt
Progreso—prō GRĔ sō
Purdon—PERD n
Purley—PER lĭ
Purmela—per MEE luh
Putnam—PUHT n'm
Pyote—PĪ ōt

Q

Quanah—KWAH nuh
Quemado—kuh MAH dō
Quihi—KWEE <u>hee</u>
Quintana—kwĭn TAH nuh
Quitaque—KĬT uh kwa
Quitman—KWĬT m'n

R

Ravenna—rĭ VĔN uh

Reagan—RĀ g'n
Real—REE awl
Realitos—<u>ree</u> uh LEE t's
Refugio—rĕ FYŌŌ rĭ ō
Reilly Springs—<u>rĭ</u> lĭ SPRĬNGZ
Reklaw—RĔK law
Rhineland—RĪN l'nd
Rhome—rōm
Rhonesboro—RŌNZ buh ruh
Ricardo—rĭ KAHR dō
Riesel—REE s'l
Ringgold—RĬNG gōld
Rio Frio—<u>ree</u> ō FREE ō
Rio Grande City—ree ō grahn dĭ SĬT ĭ
Rio Hondo—<u>ree</u> ō HAHN dō
Riomedina—<u>ree</u> ō muh DEE nuh
Rios—REE ōs
Rio Vista—<u>ree</u> ō VĬS tuh
Riviera—ruh VĪR uh
Roane—rōn
Roanoke—RŌN ōk
Roans Prairie—rōnz PRĔR ĭ
Roby—RŌ bĭ
Rochelle—rō SHĔL
Rochester—RAH chĕs ter
Rockwall—rahk WAWL
Roganville—RŌ g'n vĭl
Roma—RŌ muh
Romayor—rō MĀ er
Roosevelt—RŌŌ suh v'lt
Rosanky—rō ZĂNG kĭ
Roscoe—RAHS kō
Rosenberg—RŌZ n berg
Rosenthal—RŌZ uhn thawl
Rosharon—rō SHĔ r'n
Rosita—rō SEE tuh
Rosser—RAW ser
Roswell—RAHZ w'l
Rotan—rō TĂN
Rowena—rō EE nuh
Rowlett—ROW lĭt
Royse City—roi SĬT ĭ
Royston—ROIS t'n
Ruidosa—<u>ree</u> uh DŌ suh
Runge—RUHNG ĭ
Rutersville—RŌŌ ter vĭl

S

Sabinal—SĂB uh năl
Sabine—suh BEEN
Sabine Pass—suh <u>been</u> PĂS
Sabinetown—suh <u>been</u> TOWN
Sachse—SĂK sĭ
Sacul—SĂ k'l
Sadler—SĂD ler
Sagerton—SĂ ger t'n
Salado—suh LĂ dō
Salesville—SĂLZ vĭl
Salineno—suh LEEN yō
Salmon—SĂL m'n
Saltillo—săl TĬL ō
Samfordyce—săm FOR dis
Samnorwood—săm NAWR wŏŏd
San Angelo—<u>săn</u> ĂN juh lō
San Antonio—<u>săn</u> ăn TŌ nĭ ō
San Augustine—<u>săn</u> AW g's teen
San Benito—săn buh NEE tuh
Sanderson—SĂN der s'n
Sandia—săn DEE uh

San Diego—săn dĭ Ā gō
San Felipe—săn fuh LEEP
San Gabriel—săn GĂ brĭ uhl
San Jacinto—săn juh SĬN tuh
San Juan—săn WAHN
San Marcos—săn MAHR k's
San Patricio—săn puh TRĬSH ĭ ō
San Perlita—săn per LEE tuh
San Saba—săn SĂ buh
Santa Anna—săn tuh ĂN uh
Santa Elena—săn tuh LEE nuh
Santa Maria—săn tuh muh REE uh
Santa Rosa—săn tuh RŌ suh
Santo—SĂN tō
San Ygnacio—săn ĭg NAH sĭ ō
Saragosa—sĕ ruh GŌ suh
Saratoga—sĕ ruh TŌ guh
Sargent—SAHR juhnt
Sarita—suh REE tuh
Saspamco—suh SPĂM kō
Savoy—suh VOI
Schattel—SHĂT uhl
Schertz—sherts
Schleicher—SHLĪ ker
Schroeder—SHRĀ der
Schulenburg—SHŌŌ lĭn berg
Schwertner—SWERT ner
Scyene—sĭ EEN
Segno—SĔG nō
Segovia—sĭ GŌ vĭ uh
Seguin—sĭ GEEN
Seminole—SĔM uh nōl
Seymour—SEE mōr
Shackelford—SHĂK uhl ferd
Shafter—SHĂF ter
Shiro—SHĬ rō
Shive—shĭv
Sierra Blanca—sĭer ruh BLĂNG kuh
Siloam—suh LŌM
Silsbee—SĬLZ bĭ
Sinton—SĬNT n
Sipe Springs—SEEP sprĭngz
Sivells Bend—sĭ v'lz BĔND
Skidmore—SKĬD mōr
Slaton—SLĀT n
Slayden—SLĀD n
Slidell—slĭ DĔL
Slocum—SLŌ k'm
Smiley—SMĬ lĭ
Somervell—SUH mer vĕl
Somerville—SUH mer vĭl
Sonora—suh NŌ ruh
South Bosque—sowth BAHS kĭ
Southmayd—sowth MĀD
Sparenberg—SPĂR ĭn berg
Splendora—splĕn DŌ ruh
Spofford—SPAH ferd
Spurger—SPER ger
Stowell—STO w'l
Study Butte—styōō dĭ BYŌŌT
Sublime—s'b LĬM
Sudan—SŌŌ dăn
Sweeny—SWEE nĭ

T

Tahoka—tuh HŌ kuh
Talco—TĂL kō
Talpa—TĂL puh
Tarrant—TAR uhnt

Tarzan—TAHR z'n
Tascosa—tăs KŌ suh
Tavener—TĂV uh ner
Tehuacana—tuh WAW kuh nuh
Telferner—TĔLF ner
Tenaha—TĔN uh haw
Terlingua—TER lĭng guh
Texarkana—tĕks ahr KĂN uh
Texhoma—tĕks Ō muh
Texline—TĔKS lĭn
Texon—tĕks AHN
Thalia—THĂL yuh
Thorp Spring—thawrp SPRING
Thrall—thrawl
Tioga—tĭ Ō guh
Titus—TĬT uhs
Tivoli—tĭ VŌ luh
Tokio—TŌ kĭ ō
Tolar—TŌ ler
Tolbert—TAHL bert
Tolosa—tuh LŌ suh
Tomball—TAHM bawl
Tornillo—tawr NEE yō
Tow—tow
Toyah—TOI yuh
Toyahvale—TOI yuh văl
Trawick—TRĀ wĭk
Travis—TRĂ vĭs
Trickham—TRĬK uhm
Trinidad—TRĬN uh dăd
Troup—trōōp
Truby—TRŌŌ bĭ
Trumbull—TRUHM b'l
Truscott—TRUHS k't
Tuleta—tōō LEE tuh
Tulia—TŌŌL yuh
Tulsita—tuhl SEE tuh
Tundra—TUHN druh
Tunis—TŌŌ nĭs
Turlington—TER lĭng t'n
Turney—TER nĭ
Tuscola—tuhs KŌ luh
Tuxedo—TUHKS ĭ dō
Twitty—TWĬ tĭ
Tye—tĭ
Tynan—TĬ nuhn

U

Uhland—YŌŌ l'nd
Umbarger—UHM bahr ger
Urbana—er BĂ nuh
Utley—YŌŌT lĭ
Utopia—yōō TŌ pĭ uh
Uvalde—yōō VĂL dĭ

V

Valdasta—văl DĂS tuh
Valentine—VĂL uhn tīn
Valera—vuh LĬ ruh
Van Alstyne—văn AWLZ teen
Van Vleck—văn VLĔK
Van Zandt—văn ZĂNT
Vashti—VĂSH tĭ
Vega—VĂ guh
Velasco—vuh LĂS kō
Veribest—VĔR ĭ bĕst
Vernon—VER n'n
Vickery—VĬK er ĭ
Victoria—vĭk TŌ rĭ uh

Vidor—VĪ der
Vienna—vee ĔN uh
Vinegarone—vĭn er guh RŌN
Voca—VŌ kuh
Von Ormy—vahn AHR mĭ
Votaw—VŌ taw

W

Waco—WĂ kō
Waelder—WĔL der
Waka—WAH kuh
Waldeck—WAWL dĕk
Warda—WAWR duh
Waring—WĂR ĭng
Waskom—WAHS k'm
Wastella—wahs TĔL uh
Watauga—wuh TAW guh
Waxahachie—wawks uh HĂ chĭ
Weatherford—WĔ ther ferd
Webberville—WĔ ber vĭl
Weches—WEE chĭz
Weesatche—WEE săch
Weimar—WĬ mer
Weinert—WĬ nert
Weir—weer
Weldon—WĔL d'n
Weser—WEE zer
Weslaco—WĔS luh kō
Westhoff—WĔS tawf
Westphalia—wĕst FĂL yuh
Wharton—HWAWRT n
Wheelock—HWEE lahk
Whitharral—HWĬT hăr uhl
Whitsett—HWĬT sĭt
Whitson—HWĬT s'n
Whitt—hwĭt
Whon—hwahn
Wichita Falls—
wĭch ĭ taw FAWLZ
Wickett—WĬ kĭt
Wiergate—WEER găt
Wilbarger—WĬL bahr ger
Wildorado—wĭl duh RĂ dō
Willacy—WĬL uh sĭ
Winchester—WĬN ches ter
Windom—WĬN d'm
Windthorst—WĬN thr'st
Wingate—WĬN găt
Winnie—WĬ nĭ
Winnsboro—WĬNZ buh ruh
Winona—wĭ NŌ nuh
Woden—WŌD n
Wolfforth—WŌŌL forth
Woodbine—WŌŌD bīn
Woodland—WŌŌD l'nd
Wortham—WERTH uhm
Wrightsboro—RĪTS buh ruh
Wylie—WĬ lĭ

Y

Yantis—YĂN tĭs
Yoakum—YŌ k'm
Ysleta—ĭs LĔT uh

Z

Zapata—zuh PAH tuh
Zavalla—zuh VĂL uh
Zephyr—ZĔF er
Zuehl—ZEE uhl ☆

Obituaries July 1997-July 1999

Adkisson, Jack (Fritz Von Erich), 68; patriarch of wrestling's famous and tragic Von Erich family; in Lake Dallas, Sept. 10, 1997.

Atwell, Ben "Jumbo," 82; Democratic legislator 1951-75 from Dallas who wrote several tax bills during the 1960s that drew opposition from business interests; in Austin, June 29, 1998.

Autry, Gene, 91; the singing cowboy born in Tioga; besides his movie and television work, he was a sports team owner, broadcast tycoon and philanthropist; in Los Angeles, Oct. 2, 1998.

Barshop, Philip, 61; founded the La Quinta hotel chain with his brother; in San Antonio, Nov. 20, 1998.

Bass, Harry W. Jr., 71; oil executive who headed the Harry Bass Foundation, established by his father, which supported Dallas museums and charities; in Dallas, April 4, 1998.

Baxter, Norman E., 79; illustrator best known for his drawings of city skylines used as covers for the Southwestern Bell Yellow Pages for more than ten years; in Houston, Aug. 19, 1998.

Benavidez, Roy P., 63; retired Army master sergeant who received the Medal of Honor for his actions in the Vietnam War; in San Antonio, Nov. 29, 1998.

Bernal, Eloy, 61; Tejano star described as one of the great *bajo sexto* (12-string guitar) players and well-known Spanish gospel singers; in a wreck near Corpus Christi, April 22, 1998.

Blocker, John R., 76; Houston oilman and former Texas A&M University regent, contributor to Aggie causes; in Houston, Jan. 1, 1999.

Bode, Mary Jane, 71; a former state representative and longtime Texas newswoman; in Barrington, Ill., while visiting her daughter, Sept. 23, 1998.

Bradley, Tom, 80; former mayor of Los Angeles was born in Calvert; in Los Angeles, Sept. 29, 1998.

Bullock, Bob, 69; former Democratic lieutenant governor who crafted state policy for four decades; in Austin, June 18, 1999.

Bustin, John, 70; covered Austin entertainment for more than 50 years, 24 of those with the *Austin American-Statesman*; in Austin, April 8, 1998.

Butler, Joe Kelly, 87; Houston oilman, former chairman of the Texas State Board of Education and the Texas Board of Mental Health and Mental Retardation; in Houston, Sept. 19, 1998.

Byrd, James Jr., 49; victim whose brutal killing generated national attention as a racially-motivated act; in Jasper, June 7, 1998.

Cantu, Camilo, 90; accordion legend inducted into the Conjunto Hall of Fame in 1987; in Austin, March 3, 1998.

Chapa, Alfonso, 68; retired 4th Court of Appeals chief justice; in San Antonio, Aug. 28, 1998.

Cox, Murray, 86; farm reporter whose programs were broadcast from Dallas for more than 30 years; in Houston, March 28, 1999.

Dealey, Rev. Walter Allen Jr., 83; grandson of *Dallas Morning News* founder George Bannerman Dealey, an executive at the newspaper who became a Presbyterian minister; in Terrell, March 1999.

Decherd, Isabelle Thomason, 81; daughter of prominent Texas politician Robert Ewing Thomason, wife of former chairman of A.H. Belo Corp. H. Ben Decherd, and mother of Dealey Decherd Herndon and Robert W. Decherd, Belo directors; in Austin, Oct. 10, 1998.

De Menil, Dominique, 89; heiress to the Schlumberger oil field service company fortune; world famous art collector, philanthropist and advocate for human rights; in Houston, Dec, 31, 1997.

Denver, John, 53; singer graduated from Arlington Heights High School, Fort Worth; attended Texas Tech University; songs "Rocky Mountain High" and "Take Me Home, Country Roads"; in a plane crash off California, Oct. 12, 1997.

East, Alice Kleberg, 104; last surviving grandchild of Capt. Richard King, founder of the King Ranch; in Hebbronville, Sept, 6, 1997.

Edington, Andrew, 84; president emeritus of Schreiner College who headed the institute from 1950 until his retirement in 1971; in Kerrville, April 9, 1998

Ewell, Yvonne A., 71; educator and Dallas school trustee beginning in 1987; in Dallas, April 27, 1998.

Farah, William, 78; longtime head of the El Paso-based Farah garment manufacturing company founded by his parents; in El Paso, March 9, 1998.

Farmer, James L. Jr., 79; Marshall native was among the leaders of the civil rights movement of the 1950s and '60s as co-founder of the Congress of Racial Equality; in Fredericksburg, Va., July 9, 1999.

Flato, Paul, 98; Shiner native whose jewelry stores in New York and Beverly Hills served celebrity clients; in the 1970s he established a store in Mexico City, returning to Texas in 1990; in Fort Worth, July 17, 1999.

Folkers, Karl, 91; University of Texas professor who pioneered in vitamin research; first Texan named to the National Academy of Sciences in 1948; Dec. 9, 1997.

Fountaine, Fred, 73; chief cook at Louie Mueller's Barbecue in Taylor for 32 years; in Taylor, June 13, 1998.

Friedman, Bayard, 71; former Fort Worth mayor, founding member of the DFW airport board and former chairman of the Texas Christian University board of trustees; in Fort Worth, Oct. 3, 1998.

Goland, Martin, 78; steered Southwest Research Institute into an internationally renowned organization; in San Antonio, Oct. 29, 1997.

Gorham, Dean, 84; helped establish Texas' municipal retirement system and served as director for 32 years; in Austin, June 19, 1999.

Gottlieb, Dick, 73; popular Houston broadcaster, former city council member and mayoral candidate; in Houston, Aug. 29, 1997.

Harrington, Sybil, 89; philanthropist from Amarillo, benefactor to many civic projects in the Texas Panhandle; in Phoenix. Ariz., Sept. 17, 1998.

Harte, Janet, 75; philanthropist who championed human rights and environmental protection; in Corpus Christi, Feb. 23, 1999.

Holtz, Mark, 51; broadcaster, "voice of the Texas Rangers" for 17 seasons; from leukemia and bone marrow disease; in Dallas, Sept. 7, 1997.

Humphrey, William, 73; Clarksville native wrote best-selling *Home from the Hill* and twelve other books; in Hudson, N.Y., Aug. 20, 1997.

Jackson, Grace "Pete," 93; founder of Ranchman's Cafe in Ponder whose down-home cooking brought visitors from around the world; in Denton, June 12, 1998.

Jimenez, Raul Sr., 66; built the Jimenez Food Products empire; another legacy is the Thanksgiving dinners he hosted each year for thousands poor people; in San Antonio, Oct. 26, 1998.

Keeton, W. Page, 89; dean of the University of Texas School of Law from 1949-74 credited with helping develop it into one of top such institutions; in Austin, Jan. 10, 1999.

Kilgore, Joe M., 80; member of Congress from South Texas for 1954-64 and adviser to Lyndon Johnson; in Austin, Feb. 10, 1999.

Knox, Buddy, 65; rockabilly singer and songwriter of the 1950s who wrote "Party Doll"; born in Happy; in Bremerton, Wash., Feb. 14, 1999.

Kubiak, Dan, 60; Democratic legislator who served eleven terms in the Texas House beginning in 1969; in Rockdale, August 1998.

Lich, Glen Ernst, 49; former history professor at Baylor University and Schreiner College, wrote *The Ger-*

man *Texans* in 1981; slain at his ranch near Kerrville, Oct. 15, 1997.

Lieberman, Harry (Larry Kane), 62; Houston broadcaster who hosted a teen dance show in the 1950s and '60s; in Houston, Jan. 26, 1998.

Luby, Robert M., 88; founded the Luby's Cafeteria chain in San Antonio in 1947; in Colorado Springs, Colo., Aug. 13, 1998.

Luedecke, Alvin R., 87; retired Air Force general who headed the Atomic Energy Commission for six years and served as Texas A&M University president in 1970; in San Antonio, Aug. 9, 1998.

Lyle, Eldon W., 89; known nationally as the "Tyler rose doctor," made major contributions to rose research; in Tyler, Dec. 28, 1997.

Machado, Mike, 74; spent 41 years presiding over San Antonio municipal and state district courts; in San Antonio, July 29, 1998.

Marr, Dave, 63; Houston golfer who went on to become a PGA champion and popular TV broadcaster; in Houston, Oct. 5, 1997.

Martin, J.C. "Pepe," 85; longtime South Texas civic leader who served six terms as mayor of Laredo; in San Antonio hospital, Nov. 11, 1998.

Martin, Lecil Travis (Boxcar Willie), 67; mechanic from Mansfield and Arlington who found fame as country music entertainer; in Branson, Mo., April 12, 1999.

Matthews, Wilbur Lee, 95; noted lawyer described by the *San Antonio Express-News* as "one of the most influential men in San Antonio from the 1950s through the 1970s"; in San Antonio, March 17, 1998.

Michener, James, A., 90; Pulitzer Prize-winning author of such epic novels as *Texas* and *Hawaii* who taught at and eventually endowed the University of Texas; in Austin, Oct. 16, 1997.

Milford, Dale, 71; Dallas broadcaster and three-term Democratic member of Congress in the 1970s; in Howe, Dec. 26, 1997.

Miller, Vassar, 74; twice named poet laureate of Texas and a Pulitzer Prize nominee; in Houston, Oct. 31, 1998.

Moore, William T., 81; former state senator credited with leading the fight to get women admitted to Texas A&M University; in Bryan, May 27, 1999.

Moorman, Lewis J. Jr., 80; past chairman of the Southwest Foundation for Biomedical Research and trustee of the related institute; in San Antonio, Nov. 28, 1997.

Murphy, Charles A., 79; considered founder of Texas Southern University who as legislator from 1947-55 co-wrote the bill establishing it;

in Houston, March 23, 1998.

Naranjo, Ruben, 53; conjunto superstar, singer and accordionist known for his slow, danceable style; of heart failure, in Alice, Oct. 12, 1998.

North, Phillip R., 79; Former executive editor of the *Fort Worth Star-Telegram* who became chairman of the Tandy Corp.; in Fort Worth, April 12, 1998. His wife, **Janice Harris North,** 77, active in charity work, died July 26, 1998, in Fort Worth.

Oliphant, Rev. T.G., 83; pastored four West Texas churches over half a century and founded the NAACP in Taylor County; in Abilene, June 20, 1998.

Osteen, John, 77; founding pastor of one of Houston's largest churches and a popular television evangelist; in Houston, Jan. 23, 1999.

Paredes, Américo, 83; writer, folklorist and one of the founders and first director of the University of Texas Mexican American Studies program; in Austin, May 5, 1999.

Phelps, John C., 96; longtime Dallas civil rights leader; insurance man who fought for parks and recreation centers; in Dallas, May 16, 1999.

Pitzer, Kenneth S., 83; renowned chemist who served as president of Rice University (1961-69); in Berkeley, Calif., Dec. 26, 1997.

Ramsey, Buck, 59; one-time cowboy who became nationally acclaimed poet and musician; in Amarillo, Jan. 3, 1998.

Rogers, Julie, 83; Beaumont philanthropist who supported causes ranging from the arts to medicine; in Beaumont, Feb. 12, 1998.

Rogers, Ralph, 87; Dallas businessman instrumental in creating the Public Broadcasting System and reviving Parkland hospital and the Dallas Symphony; in Dallas, Nov. 4, 1997.

Schepps, George, 98; sports enthusiast and member of prominent Dallas business family, founded Texas Baseball Hall of Fame; Jan. 14, 1998.

Shepard, Alan, 74; one of the original Mercury 7 astronauts, he was the first American thrust into space on May 5, 1961; Houston-area business executive for many years; in Monterey, Calif., July 21, 1998. His wife, **Louise,** 76, died Aug. 25, 1998, in California.

Smith, Carl S., 89; served 51 years as Harris County's tax assessor and collector; in Houston, July 28, 1998.

Spelce, Fannie Lou, 89; called "the Grandma Moses of Texas," former nurse who after retiring at 64 gained notoriety as a folk artist; in Austin, April 11, 1998.

Stillwell, Hallie Crawford, 99; Big

Bend pioneer who became one of the region's most prominent and notable figures; in Alpine; Aug. 18, 1997.

Strauss, Annette, 74; the first woman to be elected mayor of Dallas (1987-91), arts patron and advertising executive; in Dallas, Dec. 14, 1998.

Taniguchi, Alan, 75; dean of the School or Architecture at the University of Texas from 1967-1972 when he left to head the architecture school at Rice University until 1978; in Austin, Jan. 14, 1998.

Tenayaca, Emma, 82; labor organizer, human rights activist and educator; in San Antonio, July 23, 1999.

Thomason, William, 85; longtime rancher, entrepreneur and attorney; on Gen. Douglas MacArthur's staff in World War II; in Bryan, June 20, 1999.

Tillman, Harrel Gordon Sr., 73; an actor on stage and in movies in the 1940s; appointed Houston's first black municipal court judge in 1964; in Houston, June 19, 1998.

Toomey, Anna, 99; retired staff artist for *The Dallas Morning News* who drew in 1941 the county maps still used in the *Texas Almanac*; in Dallas, Feb. 11, 1998.

Tucker, Karla Faye, 38; her execution for the pickax slayings of two persons became an international news event; in Huntsville, Feb. 3, 1998.

Vandergriff, Charles (Mrs. W.T.), 94; matriarch of leading Arlington family and philanthropist; in Arlington, Dec. 18, 1997.

Walker, Doak, 71; Heisman Trophy winner who propelled Southern Methodist University football into the national spotlight in the 1940s; in Steamboat Springs, Colo., Sept. 27, 1998.

Walls, B. Carmage, 90; newspaper entrepeneur who ended racial discrimination practices in his Southern papers; in Houston, Nov. 22, 1998.

Warnock, Barton H., 87; Trans-Pecos icon and leading authority on the botany of the Big Bend and the Chihuahuan Desert; in Alpine, June 9, 1998.

Welch, June Rayfield, 70; former chairman of the history department at the University of Dallas who was widely known for his Texas history radio shows; in Dallas, Sept. 2, 1998.

White, Richard C., 74; Democratic member of Congress 1965-1983 from West Texas; in El Paso, Feb. 18, 1998.

Zientek, Marion P., 57; longtime editor of the *Texas Catholic Herald* (1971-97) which rearched a circulation of 185,000 during his tenure; of a heart attack, in Houston, March 1, 1999. ☆

Advertisers' Index

General Index

For CITIES and TOWNS towns not listed in the index, see complete list of towns on pages 289-356.

For CITIES and TOWNS towns not listed in the index, see complete list of towns on pages 289-356.

For CITIES and TOWNS towns not listed in the index, see complete list of towns on pages 289-356.

For CITIES and TOWNS towns not listed in the index, see complete list of towns on pages 289-356.

For CITIES and TOWNS towns not listed in the index, see complete list of towns on pages 289-356.

For CITIES and TOWNS towns not listed in the index, see complete list of towns on pages 289-356.

For CITIES and TOWNS towns not listed in the index, see complete list of towns on pages 289-356.

For CITIES and TOWNS towns not listed in the index, see complete list of towns on pages 289-356.

For CITIES and TOWNS towns not listed in the index, see complete list of towns on pages 289-356.

For CITIES and TOWNS towns not listed in the index, see complete list of towns on pages 289-356.

For CITIES and TOWNS towns not listed in the index, see complete list of towns on pages 289-356.

For CITIES and TOWNS towns not listed in the index, see complete list of towns on pages 289-356.

For CITIES and TOWNS towns not listed in the index, see complete list of towns on pages 289-356.